UNDERSTANDING INTELLECTUAL PROPERTY LAW

by

DONALD S. CHISUM

and

MICHAEL A. JACOBS

LEGAL TEXT SERIES

Matthew Bender

 Times Mirror
Books

All Rights Reserved
Printed in United States of America
Library of Congress Catalogue Number: 91-076654
ISBN: 0-8205-0549-8

1996 Reprint

Also published in a version for the professional market as World
Intellectual Property Guidebook: United States

MATTHEW BENDER & CO., INC.
EDITORIAL OFFICES
11 PENN PLAZA, NEW YORK, NY 10001-2006 (212) 967-7707
2101 WEBSTER ST., OAKLAND, CA 94612-3027 (510) 446-7100

TABLE OF CONTENTS

Chapter 1

INTRODUCTION

Chapter 2

PATENTS

Chapter 3

TRADE SECRETS LAW

Chapter 4

COPYRIGHTS

Chapter 5

TRADEMARKS

Chapter 6

OTHER INTELLECTUAL PROPERTY RIGHTS

CONTRIBUTORS

JONATHAN BAND: Jonathan Band received an A.B. from Harvard (1982) and a J.D. from Yale (1985). He is a partner in Morrison & Foerster's Washington, D.C. office.

DONALD S. CHISUM: Donald Chisum received an A.B. (1966) and LL.B. (1968) from Stanford University, and clerked for Judge Shirley Hufstedler of the United States Court of Appeals for the Ninth Circuit. He is Of Counsel to Morrison & Foerster, specializing in intellectual property and patent law matters. Mr. Chisum is author of the multiple volume reference text, *Patents: A Treatise on the Law of Patentability, Validity & Infringement,* first published by Matthew Bender in 1978 and regularly revised thereafter. From 1969 through 1990, he was on the faculty of the University of Washington School of Law, Seattle, Washington. His professional activities include service on the Board of Directors of the American Intellectual Property Law Association and lectures at the Judicial Conference of the United States Court of Appeals for the Federal Circuit. In 1989, he received the Jefferson Medal Award from the New Jersey Patent Law Association for meritorious and outstanding contributions in support of the United States Constitutional provision for patents and copyrights.

LAURIE S. HANE: Laurie Hane received a B.A. from Knox College (1981) and a J.D. from Northwestern University (1984), and clerked for Judge Robert Peckham, of the United States District Court, Northern District of California. She is a partner in Morrison & Foerster's San Francisco office.

MICHAEL A. JACOBS: Michael Jacobs received a B.A. from Stanford University (1977) and a J.D. from Yale Law School (1983), and served in the United States Foreign Service, holding assignments in Kingston, Jamaica, and Washington, D.C. He is a partner in Morrison & Foerster's San Francisco office and co-heads the firm's Intellectual Property Group. Mr. Jacobs is currently chairman of the computer program copyright protection subcommittee of the American Bar Association's Patent, Trademark and Copyright Section.

GRANT L. KIM: Grant Kim received a B.A. from Pomona College (1978) and a J.D. from Hastings College of Law (1984), clerked for the office of Staff Attorneys of the United States Court of Appeals for the Ninth Circuit, and served in the Peace Corps in the Republic of Korea. He is an associate in Morrison & Foerster's San Francisco office.

KIM J. LANDSMAN: Kim Landsman received an A.B. from Vassar College, a M.A. from Oxford University and a J.D. from Yale Law School (1979), and clerked for Judge Arlin Adams of the United States Court of Appeals for the Third Circuit. He is a partner in Morrison & Foerster's New York office.

NEAL A. STENDER: Neal Stender received a B.A. from the University of California, Berkeley (1982) and a J.D. from Stanford University (1989). He is an associate in Morrison & Foerster's San Francisco office.

(Matthew Bender & Co., Inc.)　　　　　　　　　　　　　　　　　　　　　　　　　　　　　　　　　　(Pub.886)

PREFACE

Donald Chisum began work on this basic intellectual property text in 1987. Mr. Chisum became of counsel to Morrison & Foerster in 1990, and the firm's Intellectual Property Group brought the project to fruition. Mr. Chisum wrote the major chapters on patent, copyright, and trademark law, and sections on design protection, plant protection, unfair competition and misappropriation. Michael Jacobs, San Francisco, the Group's co-chairman, wrote the trade secrets chapter with Neal Stender's substantial assistance. Mr. Jacobs also reviewed portions of the copyright chapter. Kim Landsman, New York, wrote the false advertising and trademark remedies sections. Mr. Landsman also reviewed portions of the trademark chapter. Jonathan Band, Washington, D.C., wrote the publicity rights section. Laurie Hane, San Francisco, wrote the copyright remedies and idea submission sections. Grant Kim, San Francisco, wrote the semiconductorship protection section.

Mr. Chisum's academic background and Morrison & Foerster's spirit of inquiry, professionalism, and extensive intellectual property practice combined to make this book possible. The authors collected the relevant statutes, regulations, and court decisions and describe intellectual property law's evolution up to mid-1991 as accurately and objectively as possible. The book does not present personal views or the position of Morrison & Foerster or its clients on any particular point of law. Nor does it predict the law's future course. United States law has always been in flux; it is a process not a structure. Like a river crossing a plain, it will meander, but when and to where no one can say with certainty; environmental changes may affect the way the river changes. In no area is this more true than with intellectual property.

Mr. Chisum acknowledges West Publishing Company's assistance in providing him access to "WESTLAW" to prepare this book. Having written a multi-volume treatise on patent law the old-fashioned way with dusty books, 3" x 5" cards, and an IBM Selectric typewriter, he appreciates the speed, thoroughness and accuracy of data searching, quotation fetching, and word processing.

Barbara Nielsen, Mr. Chisum's editorial assistant, edited the entire text and verified its citations and quotations. She encouraged us to write directly.[, clearly, and without excessive verbiage.] To the extent our style falls short of that goal, it is not for want of effort by Ms. Nielsen.

Donald S. Chisum
Michael A. Jacobs
Morrison & Foerster

San Francisco
October 4, 1991

CHAPTER 1

INTRODUCTION

---

§ 1A Law and Human Creativity

Intellectual property law is concerned with fostering human creativity without unduly restricting dissemination of its fruits. It concerns the full spectrum of human creativity: literature, the visual arts, music, drama, compilations of useful information, computer programs, biotechnology, electronics, mechanics, chemistry, product design, new plant varieties, semiconductor circuitry design, human identity features, and trade identity symbols.

Intellectual property law is a growing industry in the United States and around the world. Increased interest in copyrights, patents, trademarks and related areas stems in part from an accumulation of major legal and economic events during the 1970s and 1980s, including enactment of the long-awaited Copyright Revision Act of 1976; the energy crisis and erosion of the United States' economic position among the developed countries, which focused renewed attention on the patent system, the traditional means of providing economic stimulation for research, development and investment;[1] the coming into force of two new international patent conventions—the Patent Cooperation Treaty and the European Patent Convention; the opening of the People's Republic of China and other new markets with resulting questions concerning the protection of trademarks and other industrial property rights; developing countries' demands for changes in the Paris Convention and for adoption of a code of conduct governing developed countries' companies' licensing and transfer of technology; the creation in the United States of the Court of Appeals for the Federal Circuit, with exclusive appellate jurisdiction over patent matters; negotiations on international patent law harmonization under the World Intellectual Property Organization's auspices; trilateral discussions among the United States, Japan, and European Patent Offices; General Agreement on Tariffs and Trade (GATT) focus on the trade-related aspects of intellectual property ("TRIPS"); and United States adoption of "intent-to-use" trademark procedures and implementation of the Berne copyright convention.

---

[1] At no time in history has there been greater public expectation that the science and technology community will devise solutions to dietary, health, environmental, and other problems. It is to this community that the public and public officials look for the prevention or cure of heart disease, cancer and AIDS, for better biodegradable materials, for more efficient energy use, etc.

This clamor for new technology comes at a time when there is public resistance to higher taxes, which are necessary to support high levels of government spending on research and development. Universities and private firms must rely increasingly on private financing for both basic and applied research, which may be unavailable without the prospect of financial return to which patents can contribute.

(Matthew Bender & Co., Inc.)

Even apart from these dramatic events, heightened interest in intellectual property is not surprising. Today more than ever before, the products of the mind—aesthetic, technological, and organizational—are humankind's most valuable assets.

"Intellectual" property may be a pretentious concept but is gaining common currency. It is the internationally recognized concept covering copyright and related matters and what is called "industrial property." The "World Intellectual Property Organization" ("WIPO"), a United Nations agency based in Geneva, administers international treaties in this area. The subcategory "industrial property," which includes patents, trademarks, designs, and unfair competition, is memorialized in the first major international treaty in this area—the Paris Convention of 1883 for the Protection of Industrial Property.

Intellectual "property" begs a major policy question concerning the role of law in fostering creativity: should there be property rights in creations such as ideas and the expression of ideas? To the extent there is a property interest in intellectual creations, it is an intangible interest that must be carefully distinguished from property in tangible materials that either make the creation possible or that the creation makes possible.[2] Copyright law explicitly states the distinction between intellectual property and tangible things: "Ownership of a copyright is distinct from ownership of any material object in which the work is embodied."[3]

§ 1B Intellectual Property Rights: An Overview

Intellectual property rights include utility patents, trade secrets, copyrights, trademarks, design patents, plant patents, plant variety protection, semiconductor mask work protection, false advertising remedies, misappropriation, and publicity rights.[1]

An intellectual property right's basic elements are: (1) the subject matter it covers; (2) the substantive requirements for obtaining it; (3) the method of obtaining it; (4) its content; and (5) its duration.

---

[2] See Moore v. University of California, 51 Cal. 3d 120, 271 Cal. Rptr. 146, 793 P.2d 479, 15 U.S.P.Q.2d 1753 (1990). In Moore, plaintiff alleged that the defendants took cell samples from his body and, without his knowledge or consent, used them to create biotechnological inventions, including a novel cell line, for which they obtained a patent and valuable commercial rights. The court held that plaintiff's complaint stated a cause of action for breach of the physician's disclosure obligations but not for conversion of any property interest plaintiff could claim in his cells or genetic materials or the patent.

"[T]he subject matter of the . . . patent—the patented cell line and the products derived from it—cannot be Moore's property. This is because the patented cell line is both factually and legally distinct from the cells taken from Moore's body. Federal law permits the patenting of organisms that represent the product of 'human ingenuity,' but not naturally occurring organisms. . . . Human cell lines are patentable because '[l]ong-term adaptation and growth of human tissues and cells in culture is difficult—often considered an art . . .' and the probability of success is low. . . . It is this inventive effort that patent law rewards, not the discovery of naturally occurring raw materials." 51 Cal. 3d at 141-42, 271 Cal. Rptr. at 159-60, 15 U.S.P.Q.2d at 1763-64.

[3] 17 U.S.C. § 202.

[1] See Chapter 6.

[1] Patents

The Patent Act defines potentially patentable subject matter as any "new and useful process, machine, manufacture, or composition of matter,"[2] which includes mechanical, chemical and electrical structures and processes. It includes the two most important technologies of our era—digital computing and biotechnology. An invention is patentable only if it meets three requirements—utility, novelty and unobviousness over the prior art.[3]

An inventor may obtain a patent only by filing a timely application with the United States Patent and Trademark Office ("PTO"), a federal government agency.[4] The application must describe the invention and present at least one precise verbal claim. The PTO will issue a patent if, after a search of the prior art and an examination, it determines that the claim or claims define a patentable invention. Patent procurement is expensive and procedurally complex.

A patent confers the right to exclude others from making, using, or selling in the United States the product or process claimed by the patent.[5] A patent owner may sue not only persons who directly infringe by making, selling or using the invention without authority but also persons who indirectly infringe by selling especially designed components of patented processes and combinations or by inducing others to infringe. Unlike a copyright, a patent covers independent development of the patented subject matter. A patent's exclusive rights last for 17 years from the date the PTO issues it.

[2] Trade Secrets

Trade secrets rights may extend to virtually any concrete information, including formulae, data compilations, programs, devices, processes, and customer lists.[6] Information is a trade secret only if it is secret in the sense that it derives "economic value . . . from not being generally known to, and not being readily ascertainable by proper means by, other persons" and it "is the subject of efforts that are reasonable under the circumstances to maintain secrecy."[7]

Unlike patents, copyrights, and trademarks, there are no formalities required to obtain trade secrets rights. The owner of a trade secret may prevent its unauthorized use or disclosure by a person who acquired it by improper means or through a confidential relationship. Trade secrets rights last for as long as the trade secret's owner prevents the information from becoming common knowledge.

[3] Copyright

The Copyright Act includes works of authorship embodied in a tangible medium of expression.[8] It encompasses a wide variety of idea expression modes—traditional

---

[2] 35 U.S.C. § 101.

[3] *See* § 2C.

[4] *See* § 2D.

[5] *See* §§ 2E and 2F.

[6] *See* Chapter 3.

[7] Uniform Trade Secrets Act § 1(4).

[8] *See* § 4C.

(literature, drama, music, and visual art) and contemporary (sound recordings, video games, and computer programs). A work must be original, that is, the author's own creation rather than one copied from another. There is no requirement that it be particularly new or strikingly different from prior creations.

Copyright arises automatically at the moment an author, or one acting with his or her authority, fixes a work in a tangible medium of expression. A copyright notice requirement applied to copies distributed to the public before March 1, 1989. Under the Berne Convention Implementation Act of 1988, there is no notice requirement as to copies distributed to the public after March 1, 1989. A mandatory copies deposit requirement applies if copies of a work are publicly distributed in the United States; the owner of the copyright or of the exclusive right of publication must deposit two copies of the best edition of the work with the Register of Copyrights for the use of the Library of Congress. The owner of the copyright in a work or of any exclusive right in a work may register his or her copyright interest by filing an application with the Copyright Office. Registration is optional, but an owner must register prior to filing suit for infringement. Under the Berne Convention Implementation Act, the owner of a non-United States "Berne Convention" work is exempted from the necessity of registering prior to filing suit.

Copyright confers specific exclusive rights. As its name implies, the primary right is against another *copying* or distributing copies of the protected work without permission. Copyright also includes rights relating to derivative work preparation and *public performance* or display of work, which are of critical importance to musical and dramatic works.

Copyright protects only the expression of ideas. It confers no rights over ideas themselves. Nor does copyright protect against independent creation of similar works. To establish that an accused work infringes the copyright on a protected work, the copyright owner must prove that the accused work was copied from the protected work and that the accused work is substantially similar in expression to the protected work.

There are a number of limitations on the exclusive rights of copyrights; the most important is the fair use doctrine.

A copyright lasts for the author's life plus 50 years after the author's death. For "works for hire," the copyright term is 75 years. Before 1978, the term was 28 years plus a renewal period of 28 more years. The 1976 Act adjusts the copyright term for pre-1978 published and unpublished works but does not revive copyrights on works in the public domain.

[4] Trademarks

Any word, symbol or device a manufacturer or merchant adopts and uses to identify his goods and distinguish them from those of others may serve as a trademark.[9] The Lanham Act, the federal trademark registration statute, provides for the registration of service marks, certification marks, and collective marks, as well as trademarks.

---

[9] *See* § 5D.

A protectable mark must distinguish the origin of the goods or services to which it relates. It must be neither descriptive of the qualities or origin of the goods or services nor confusingly similar to marks used by others. The mark adopted need not be new or original.

A manufacturer or merchant establishes trademark rights in a mark by using the mark on goods in commerce. After acquiring mark ownership by use, the owner can sue for infringement under state trademark and unfair competition law and Lanham Act Section 43(a). A mark owner may file an application to register the mark under either state or federal law. Registration offers procedural and remedial advantages. Under the 1988 Trademark Revision Act, persons may file applications to register a mark based on a good faith "intent to use" it, but they must use the mark to obtain registration.

Ownership of a mark confers the right to exclude others from using any mark that creates a likelihood of confusion as to the origin or sponsorship of goods or services. A mark remains protectable for as long as it is used and retains its distinctiveness.

[5] Other Intellectual Property Rights

Beyond the major intellectual property rights, utility patents, trade secrets, copyright, and trademarks, there are other intellectual property rights pertaining to particular conduct, situations or subject matter, including design patents,[10] plant patents and plant variety protection,[11] and semiconductor chip protection,[12] false advertising,[13] misappropriation,[14] and publicity rights.[15]

§ 1C Policy

Significant human mental creations share three characteristics: (1) humans produce them either rarely or with great time, effort, and expense; (2) others can duplicate them without an equivalent expenditure of time, effort, and expense; and (3) others' uses of them do not physically interfere with the first creator's use.

The major intellectual property law policy issues arise from these three characteristics. Two sets of opposing concepts encapsule these issues: (1) incentive versus competition, and (2) property versus monopoly. Incentive and competition clash on a utilitarian battleground; property and monopoly on a moral one.

Here is a flavor of the utilitarian battle. Incentive's champions ask: Will people have an incentive to create if others can copy the results without authority and without paying compensation? And even if they will create, will anyone invest in the initial production and distribution if such copying is likely to arise?[1] The answers to these

---

[10] See § 6B.

[11] See § 6C.

[12] See § 6D.

[13] See § 6E.

[14] See § 6F.

[15] See § 6G.

[1] Incentives champions may also argue that granting exclusive intellectual property rights not only provides an incentive for the first creator but also an incentive for others to produce new, different and superior competing creations.

questions are not always clear. Economists refer to the copying problem as the "free rider" effect. Competition's champions respond that a major premise of United States public policy is that consumers benefit from free competition among producers. The effect is more efficient resource distribution and lower prices. Price approaches the full marginal cost of production. Granting exclusive rights to a creation is wasteful and anticompetitive because the marginal cost of using such an intangible is zero. There is little doubt, for example, that copyright leads to higher book prices.

The moral battle closely tracks the utilitarian one. Persons who are more persuaded by incentive arguments argue that exclusive intellectual property rights are indeed property, not monopoly.[2] Giving exclusive rights to an author or inventor is no more a monopoly or anticompetitive than other species of real or personal property. Persons who are more persuaded by the competition arguments argue that intellectual property rights are indeed "monopolies," though they may be tolerated for policy reasons.[3]

But the moral battle has independent content. Some persons are unimpressed by arguments concerning competition and economic efficiency. There is a natural rights school of thought, which favors recognizing the rights of authors and inventors regardless of the economic effects. Recognizing author or inventor control is a matter of human and moral right. This school has had more influence in Europe and other

---

[2] *E.g.*, Panduit Corp. v. Stahlin Bros. Fibre Works, Inc., 575 F.2d 1152, 1158 n.5, 197 U.S.P.Q. 726 (6th Cir. 1978) (Markey: "The right to exclude others from free use of an invention protected by a valid patent does not differ from the right to exclude others from free use of one's automobile, crops, or other items of personal property. Every human right, including that in an invention, is subject to challenge under appropriate circumstances. That one human property right may be challenged by trespass, another by theft, and another by infringement, does not affect the fundamental indicium of all 'property,' i.e., the right to exclude others.").

Compare Roberts v. Sears, Roebuck & Co., 723 F.2d 1324, 1345, 221 U.S.P.Q. 504, 522 (7th Cir. 1983) (Posner, dissenting: "Since new knowledge is a social good, it might seem that no limits should be placed on the scope or duration of patent protection. The problem is that patent protection has a dark side, to which the term 'patent monopoly' is a clue. A patent enables its owner to monopolize the production of the things in which the patented idea is embodied. To deny that patent protection has this effect, . . . is—with all due respect—to bury one's head in the sand.").

[3] When reading court opinions, one should be alert to the terminology the judge uses. If limited or legal "monopoly" appears frequently, it is likely that the court will give a narrow interpretation to the patent or copyright. If "intellectual property" is used, it is likely that the court will give a broader interpretation. *See, e.g.,* Sony Corp. v. Universal City Studios, Inc., 464 U.S. 417 (1984) (extending fair use doctrine to home taping of copyrighted movies for time-shifting):

"The *monopoly privileges* that Congress may authorize are neither unlimited nor primarily designed to provide a special private benefit. Rather, the limited grant is a means by which an important public purpose may be achieved. It is intended to motivate the creative activity of authors and inventors by the provision of a special reward, and to allow the public access to the products of their genius after the limited period of exclusive control has expired.

"As the text of the Constitution makes plain, it is Congress that has been assigned the task of defining the scope of the *limited monopoly* that should be granted to authors or to inventors in order to give the public appropriate access to their work product." 464 U.S. at 429 (Emphasis added).

countries than in the United States, but one encounters reflections on natural rights in United States intellectual property jurisprudence.

§ 1D   Intellectual Property and the Constitution

United States intellectual property law policy intertwines with the constitutional federal system, which distributes legislative power between the federal government and state governments and restricts state and federal legislative power.

United States Constitution Article I gives Congress, the federal legislative body, several powers. Two are directly relevant to intellectual property: the power to regulate interstate and foreign commerce, and the power to enact patent and copyright laws. The latter, article I, section 8, clause 8, provides that Congress shall have the power:

> "To promote the Progress of Science and useful Arts, by securing for limited Times to Authors and Inventors the exclusive Right to their respective Writings and Discoveries."

The patent-copyright clause is unusual among the Article I legislative powers because it not only confers regulatory power over a subject area (writings and discoveries) but specifies both the power's purpose (to promote science and the useful arts) and the means for achieving it (exclusive rights for limited times).

The Constitution's most direct and obvious impact on intellectual property law policy is in granting Congress power to create the patent and copyright systems, a power Congress has exercised continuously since 1790. Serious and difficult questions arise on the constitution's role in intellectual property policy beyond this enabling function. Does the constitution restrict Congress' power to define legislatively the scope and conditions of patent and copyright protection? Does the patent-copyright clause limit Congress' power to protect intellectual property through use of the interstate commerce clause? To what extent does the patent-copyright clause imply exclusion or limitation of state laws' ability to provide intellectual property protection? Do other constitutional provisions, such as the First Amendment free speech and press guarantee, limit state and federal intellectual property laws?

[1]   Constitutional Restriction of Congress' Patent and Copyright Powers

Unquestionably, Congress cannot exercise its article I, section 8, clause 8 patent-copyright power to protect subject matter that does not constitute a "writing" or a "discovery" in the constitutional sense. Nor, presumably, could it use the clause to protect writings and discoveries for more than a "limited time."[1] *The*

---

[1] The copyright term is extraordinarily long—the author's life plus 50 years. See § 4E[1]. At the time the Constitution was adopted, the prevailing copyright model, that of Britain, provided a much shorter term, 28 years. See § 4D[1][a]. Can so long a term be deemed a "limited Time" in the constitutional sense? Is a useful measuring stick of a "limited Time" that it be short enough that a significant number of adults living when a work is created will survive long enough to see the work's copyright expire?

Trade-mark Cases,[2] holding that Congress cannot use the clause to provide trademark protection because a trademark is neither a writing nor a discovery, is the only instance in which the Supreme Court invalidated a congressional intellectual property statute. In *Burrows-Giles Lithographic*,[3] the Court held that a photograph was a "writing" in the constitutional sense and thus that Congress did not exceed its clause powers by extending copyright to photography.

Whether the clause restricts Congress's power to define the patentability and copyrightability requirements of novelty and originality is less clear. The clause does not explicitly refer to standards, but they may be implicit in the statement of purpose ("To promote Science and the Useful Arts") and in the concept of an "author" and "inventor." In *Graham*,[4] the Supreme Court confirmed that the clause does impose a minimum patentability standard that restricts Congress' power to authorize patents.

> "The Congress in the exercise of the patent power may not overreach the restraints imposed by the stated constitutional purpose. Nor may it enlarge the patent monopoly without regard to the innovation, advancement or social benefit gained thereby. Moreover, Congress may not authorize the issuance of patents whose effects are to remove existent knowledge from the public domain, or to restrict free access to materials already available. Innovation, advancement, and things which add to the sum of useful knowledge are inherent requisites in a patent system which by constitutional command must 'promote the Progress of . . . useful Arts.' This is the *standard* expressed in the Constitution and it may not be ignored."[5]

The court held that the Section 103 nonobviousness requirement fulfilled the constitutional minimum.

Similarly, in *Feist*,[6] the Court, in holding that a white page telephone directory was not sufficiently original to be copyrightable, stressed that the clause imposes a minimum creativity standard for copyrights.

> "Originality is a constitutional requirement. The source of Congress' power to enact copyright laws is Article I, § 8, cl. 8, of the Constitution, which authorizes Congress to 'secur[e] for limited Times to Authors . . . the exclusive Right to their respective Writings.' In two decisions from the late 19th Century—*The Trade-Mark Cases* . . . and *Burrow-Giles Lithographic Co. v. Sarony* . . . —this Court defined the crucial terms 'authors' and 'writings.' In so doing, the Court made it unmistakably clear that these terms presuppose a degree of originality."[7]

---

[2] The Trade-Mark Cases, 100 U.S. 82 (1879), discussed at § 5B.

[3] Burrow-Giles Lithographic Co. v. Sarony, 111 U.S. 53 (1884), discussed at § 4B.

[4] Graham v. John Deere Co., 383 U.S. 1, 148 U.S.P.Q. 459 (1966), discussed at §§ 2B[6] and 2C[4][a].

[5] 383 U.S. at 5-6 (Emphasis in original.)

[6] Feist Publications, Inc. v. Rural Telephone Service Company, Inc., 111 S. Ct. 1282, 18 U.S.P.Q.2d 1275 (1991).

[7] 111 S. Ct. at 1288, 18 U.S.P.Q.2d at 1278.

The Court's discussion was, arguably, gratuitous in that the current Copyright Act explicitly requires copyrightable works of authorship, including compilations, to be original.[8]

[2] Commerce Clause Regulation of Intellectual Property

An unresolved question is whether Congress may use other Article I powers, especially the power to regulate interstate and foreign commerce, to provide intellectual property protection for types of subject matter or periods of duration beyond what the clause authorizes or for subject matter within the patent-copyright clause (writings and discoveries) that does not meet the clause's minimum novelty and creativity standards.

That Congress may provide protection for at least some types of subject matter beyond the clause is confirmed by the assumed constitutionality of the Lanham Act, which relies on the commerce clause power to provide trademark and unfair competition protection.[9]

Whether Congress may undermine the clause's novelty and creativity standards has no definitive answer. In the Plant Variety Protection Act[10] and the Semiconductor Chip Protection Act,[11] Congress expressly relied on both the patent-copyright clause and the commerce clause. Both statutes protect subject matter that most likely falls within the clause's concept of an inventor's discovery and yet impose eligibility standards less strict than patent law's nonobviousness condition.

[3] Preemption

Whether and to what extent federal intellectual property policy, expressed in the patent-copyright clause or in the patent and copyright statutes, preempts state laws is the subject of a series of Supreme Court decisions and of Copyright Act Section 301[12] and cases interpreting it.

The preemption cases give insight into intellectual property law's nature and purpose. To determine preemption, courts must balance the policies underlying the federal intellectual property systems, primarily patent and copyright law, with those underlying a spectrum of state rights. This forces them to identify and articulate what those policies are.

The Supreme Court's intellectual property preemption decisions can be segregated into two lines. The first deals with federal policy's impact on state unfair competition and trade secret laws; the second deals with its impact on state contract law. In each instance, the Court began in the 1960s with a strong preemptive posture, giving state law little permissible scope, and later moved to a more balanced position that accommodates federal and state policy.

---

[8] See § 4C[5].

[9] See § 5D[1][d].

Cf. San Francisco Arts & Athletics, Inc. v. United States Olympic Committee, 483 U.S. 522, 3 U.S.P.Q.2d 1145 (1987), discussed at § 1D[4].

[10] See § 6C.

[11] See § 6D.

[12] 17 U.S.C. § 301.

Section 301 represents Congress' partial attempt to define the parameters of federal preemption of state laws touching on intellectual property.

[a] Unfair Competition—Copying Publicly Disclosed Subject Matter

[i] *Product Simulation:* Sears-Compco. In *Sears*[13] and *Compco*,[14] the Supreme Court held that federal policy preempted any state unfair competition law that purported to prevent the copying of an article that patent or copyright law does not protect. *Sears* and *Compco* dealt with product designs that were subject matter eligible for federal design protection but that did not meet patent novelty and unobviousness standards. Indeed, the plaintiffs had obtained design patents for the designs, but the lower courts held the patents invalid.

The Court's opinions are tantalizingly vague as to whether the preempting federal intellectual property policy stems from the Constitution's patent-copyright clause or rather from Congress' occupation of the area by enacting patent and copyright legislation pursuant to the clause. *Sears* suggested a statutory occupation theory.

> "[T]he patent system is one in which uniform federal standards are carefully used to promote invention while at the same time preserving free competition. Obviously a State could not consistently with the Supremacy Clause of the Constitution, extend the life of a patent beyond its expiration date or give a patent on an article which lacked the level of invention required for federal patents. To do either would run counter to the policy of Congress of granting patents only to true inventions, and then only for a limited time. Just as a State cannot encroach upon the federal patent laws directly, it cannot, under some other law, such as that forbidding unfair competition, give protection of a kind that clashes with the objectives of the federal patent laws."[15]

Compco hinted that the preemptive policy lay in the constitution as well as the federal patent statutes.

> "To forbid copying would interfere with the federal policy, *found in Art. I, § 8, cl. 8, of the Constitution* and in the implementing federal statutes, of allowing free access to copy whatever the federal patent and copyright law leave in the public domain."[16]

The preempting policy's source is important because, if it is the clause itself, then preemption would extend to subject areas not covered by Congressional legislation and without regard to congressional intent. Nine years later, in *Goldstein,*[17] the Court confined the preemption doctrine to congressional occupation.

[ii] *Record Piracy:* Goldstein. In *Goldstein,*[18] the Court upheld the constitutionality of state laws that barred copying of pre-1972 sound recordings, which fell within the constitutional concept of an author's "writing" but which were not included

---

[13] Sears, Roebuck & Co. v. Stiffel. Co., 376 U.S. 225, 140 U.S.P.Q. 524 (1964).

[14] Compco Corp. v. Day-Brite Lighting, Inc., 376 U.S. 234, 140 U.S.P.Q. 528 (1964).

[15] 376 U.S. at 230-31.

[16] 376 U.S. at 237 (Emphasis added).

[17] Goldstein v. California, 412 U.S. 546, 178 U.S.P.Q. 129 (1973), discussed below.

[18] Goldstein v. California, 412 U.S. 546, 178 U.S.P.Q. 129 (1973).

in federal statutory copyright.[19] Petitioners were convicted under a California statute making it a criminal offense to "pirate" recordings produced by others. They challenged the statute as inconsistent with the patent-copyright clause and the federal statutes enacted thereunder.

The Court addressed two preemption issues. The first was whether the patent-copyright clause of its own weight made "writings" protection a federal matter forbidden to the states. It discerned no "such . . . unyielding national interest as to require an inference that state power to grant copyrights has been relinquished to exclusive federal control."[20]

> "Although the Copyright Clause . . . recognizes the potential benefits of a national system, it does not indicate that all writings are of national interest or that state legislation is, in all cases, unnecessary or precluded. The patents granted by the States in the 18th century show, to the contrary, a willingness on the part of the States to promote those portions of science and the arts which were of local importance. Whatever the diversity of people's backgrounds, origins, and interests, and whatever the variety of business and industry in the 13 Colonies, the range of diversity is obviously far greater today in a country of 210 million people in 50 States. In view of that enormous diversity, it is unlikely that all citizens in all parts of the country place the same importance on works relating to all subjects. . . . [T]he subject matter to which the Copyright Clause is addressed may thus be of purely local importance and not worthy of national attention or protection. . . . "[21]

State intellectual property protection would not entail such inevitable and severe conflicts among states as to compel the conclusion that "state power has been relinquished to the exclusive jurisdiction of Congress."[22] Nor would concurrent congressional and state exercise of copyright power "necessarily and inevitably lead to

---

[19] See § 4C[1][g].

[20] 412 U.S. at 558.

[21] 412 U.S. at 556-58.

[22] 412 U.S. at 558. The Court noted:

"[A] copyright granted by a particular State has effect only within its boundaries. If one State grants such protection, the interests of States which do not are not prejudiced since their citizens remain free to copy within their borders those works which may be protected elsewhere. The interests of a State which grants copyright protection may, however, be adversely affected by other States that do not; individuals who wish to purchase a copy of a work protected in their own State will be able to buy unauthorized copies in other States where no protection exists. . . . Obviously when some States do not grant copyright protection—and most do not—that circumstance reduces the economic value of a state copyright, but it will hardly render the copyright worthless. The situation is no different from that which may arise in regard to other state monopolies, such as a state lottery, or a food concession in a limited enclosure like a state park; in each case, citizens may escape the effect of one State's monopoly by making purchases in another area or another State. " 412 U.S. at 558-559.

difficulty."[23] Finally, state copyright protection of *indefinite* duration did not contravene the patent-copyright clause's "limited Times" concept.[24]

The second preemption issue was "whether the challenged state statute is void under the Supremacy Clause," which depends on whether in the particular case the state law standards are "an obstacle to the accomplishment and execution of the full purposes and objectives of Congress."[25] The Court found no specific congressional intent to exempt recordings from state control. Congress's 1909 Copyright Act extended composers' rights to reproduction of their works in records but did not grant rights in recordings themselves. There was no evidence Congress intended recordings "to be free of state control." In 1909, means for easy mechanical reproduction of recordings did not exist.[26]

Sears and *Compco* do not support an argument that "Congress so occupied the field of copyright protection as to pre-empt all comparable state action."

> "In those cases, the question was whether a State could, under principles of a state unfair competition law, preclude the copying of mechanical configurations which did not possess the qualities required for the granting of a federal design or mechanical patent.

> . . .

---

[23] "At any time Congress determines that a particular category of 'writing' is worthy of national protection and the incidental expenses of federal administration, federal copyright protection may be authorized. Where the need for free and unrestricted distribution of a writing is thought to be required by the national interest, the Copyright Clause and the Commerce Clause would allow Congress to eschew all protection. In such cases, a conflict would develop if a State attempted to protect that which Congress intended to be free from restraint or to free that which Congress had protected. However, where Congress determines that neither federal protection nor freedom from restraint is required by the national interest, it is at liberty to stay its hand entirely. . . . Since state protection would not then conflict with federal action, total relinquishment of the States' power to grant copyright protection cannot be inferred." 412 U.S. at 559.

[24] "Section 8 enumerates those powers which have been granted to Congress; whatever limitations have been appended to such powers can only be understood as a limit on congressional, and not state, action. Moreover, it is not clear that the dangers to which this limitation was addressed apply with equal force to both the Federal Government and the States. When Congress grants an exclusive right or monopoly, its effects are pervasive; no citizen or State may escape its reach. As we have noted, however, the exclusive right granted by a State is confined to its borders. Consequently, even when the right is unlimited in duration, any tendency to inhibit further progress in science or the arts is narrowly circumscribed." 412 U.S. at 560-61.

[25] 412 U.S. at 561 (quoting Hines v. Davidowitz, 312 U.S. 52 (1941)).

[26] 412 U.S. at 566.

The Court considered but rejected the possibility that the state anti record-piracy statute interfered with composers' 1909 Act Section 1(e) right to receive compulsory license royalties for "similar use" recordings of their works. Subsequent lower court decisions dismiss this discussion, which assumes that the Section 1(e) compulsory license applies to pirated records and tapes, as dictum and hold that the license does not apply, *e.g.,* Jondora Music Publishing Co. v. Melody Recordings, Inc., 506 F.2d 392, 184 U.S.P.Q. 326 (6th Cir. 1974), *cert. denied,* 421 U.S. 1012, 186 U.S.P.Q. 73 (1975), holdings that the 1976 Act confirms. 17 U.S.C. § 115(a)(1).

"In regard to mechanical configurations, Congress had balanced the need to encourage innovation and originality of invention against the need to insure competition in the sale of identical or substantially identical products. The standards established for granting federal patent protection to machines thus indicated not only which articles in this particular category Congress wished to protect, but which configurations it wished to remain free. The application of state law in these cases to prevent the copying of articles which did not meet the requirements for federal protection disturbed the careful balance which Congress had drawn and thereby necessarily gave way under the Supremacy Clause of the Constitution. No comparable conflict between state law and federal law arises in the case of recordings of musical performances. In regard to this category of 'Writings,' Congress has drawn no balance; rather, it has left the area unattended, and no reason exists why the State should not be free to act."[27]

Two groups of Justices dissented; both found *Sears-Compco* controlling.[28]

[iii] *Trade Secrets: Kewanee. Kewanee*[29] began as a typical trade secret case. Plaintiff, an employer, charged that defendants, former employees and their new company, were improperly using the employer's trade secret technology (a process for growing synthetic crystals) which plaintiff revealed to the former employees in a confidential relationship and pursuant to an employment contract forbidding unauthorized disclosure.[30] Applying Ohio trade secrets law, the district court enjoined the defendants from disclosure or use of 20 of plaintiff's 40 asserted trade secrets until such time as the trade secrets had otherwise generally become available to the public, or had been obtained by defendants from sources having the legal right to convey the information.

---

[27] 412 U.S. 569-70.

[28] Justice Douglas, joined by Justices Brennan and Blackmun, pinned the state power ouster on the constitution: "*Sears* and *Compco* make clear that the federal policy expressed in Art I, § 8, cl. 8, is to have 'national uniformity in patent and copyright laws,'. . ." 412 U.S. at 573. He cited Judge Learned Hand's dissent in Capital Records, Inc. v. Mercury Records Corp., 221 F.2d 657, which argued that state variation in what is protected against copyright together with practical difficulties in preventing importation from nonprotecting states into protecting states was "exactly the kind of evil at which the [patent-copyright]clause is directed." Justice Marshall, also joined by Justices Brennan and Blackmun, pinned the ouster on presumed Congressional intent. He noted that "because of the realities of the legislative process, it is generally difficult to infer from a failure to act any affirmative conclusions." *Sears-Compco* adopted a different approach for patents and copyrights. "In view of the importance of not imposing unnecessary restraints on competition, the Court adopted in those cases a rule of construction that, unless the failure to provide patent or copyright protection for some class of works could clearly be shown to reflect a judgment that state regulation was permitted, the silence of Congress would be taken to reflect a judgment that free competition should prevail." 412 U.S. at 577-78. The record piracy business "is not an attractive one." "[P]ersons . . . capitalize on the talents of others without needing to assess independently the prospect of public acceptance of a performance. But the same might be said of persons who copy 'mechanical configurations.' Such people do provide low-cost reproductions that may well benefit the public." 412 U.S. at 579.

[29] Kewanee Oil Co. v. Bicron Corp., 416 U.S. 470, 181 U.S.P.Q. 673 (1974).

[30] For a discussion of trade secret law, see Chapter 3.

(Matthew Bender & Co., Inc.)

The court of appeals held that state law could not confer monopoly protection for processes that were potentially patentable subject matter but that would be barred from patenting because they had been in commercial use for more than one year.[31] The holding seemed radical, but certain language and reasoning in the Supreme Court's *Lear* decision[32] had suggested that patent policy constrained enforcement of state trade secret obligations.

The Supreme Court held that "Ohio's law of trade secrets is not pre-empted by the patent laws of the United States." Just as states are not absolutely forbidden from encouraging and protecting constitutionally copyrightable "writings," as *Goldstein* had held, so they are not forbidden from exercising regulatory power over constitutionally patentable "discoveries." The Court went on to consider whether the patent laws preempt state trade secret law because of a "clash" of "objectives." Patent law's objective is to promote progress of the useful arts by offering a limited period exclusion right to inventors in exchange for a full disclosure of the invention.[33] Trade secret law's objectives are the "maintenance of standards of commercial ethics and the encouragement of invention."

Trade secret law protects subject matter not eligible for patent protection, such as customer lists.[34] As in *Goldstein*, Congress has struck no balance between protection and competition for such subject matter, and there is no reason state law should not be free to act. State trade secret protection will not cause persons to avoid the patent system and its strict public disclosure requirements.

For "those items, which are proper subjects for consideration for a patent," there is no clash between trade secret law and the patent policies of encouraging invention

---

[31] Commercial use, even in secret, of an invention for more than one year before applying for a patent constitutes a bar to patenting. 35 U.S.C. § 102(b). *See* § 2C[5][b][iii].

[32] Lear, Inc. v. Adkins, 395 U.S. 653, 162 U.S.P.Q. 1 (1969), discussed at § 1D[3][b][ii].

[33] "The patent laws promote ['the Progress of Science and useful Arts'] by offering a right of exclusion for a limited period as an incentive to inventors to risk the often enormous costs in terms of time, research, and development. The productive effort thereby fostered will have a positive effect on society through the introduction of new products and processes of manufacture into the economy, and the emanations by way of increased employment and better lives for our citizens. In return for the right of exclusion— . . . the patent laws impose upon the inventor a requirement of disclosure. To insure adequate and full disclosure so that upon the expiration of the 17-year period 'the knowledge of the invention enures to the people, who are thus enabled without restriction to practice it and profit by its use,' . . . the patent laws require . . . that the patent application shall include a full and clear description of the invention and 'of the manner and process of making and using it' so that any person skilled in the art may make and use the invention. 35 U.S.C. § 112. When a patent is granted and the information contained in it is circulated to the general public and those especially skilled in the trade, such additions to the general store of knowledge are of such importance to the public weal that the Federal Government is willing to pay the high price of 17 years of exclusive use for its disclosure, which disclosure, it is assumed, will stimulate ideas and the eventual development of further significant advances in the art. The Court has also articulated another policy of the patent law: that which is in the public domain cannot be removed therefrom by action of the States." 416 U.S. at 480-81.

[34] *See* § 3C[1][b][iv].

and of assuring that subject matter in the public domain remains there. Trade secret law furthers the same policies. "The more difficult objective of the patent law to reconcile with trade secret law is that of disclosure. . . . " The Court adopted the Second Circuit's *Painton* [35] analysis, which distinguishes three categories:

> " '(1) the trade secret believed by its owner to constitute a validly patentable invention; (2) the trade secret known to its owner not to be so patentable; and (3) the trade secret whose valid patentability is considered dubious.' " [36]

For the second category, inventions known to be not patentable, the patent disclosure policy would gain little by abolishing trade secret protection because the PTO would reject any application filed seeking a patent and an abandoned application does not become publicly accessible. [37] Trade secret protection for this category "will have a decidedly beneficial effect on society," encouraging minor innovations, sparing companies the expense of extraordinary self-help measures to preserve their innovations' secrecy, [38] and facilitating licensing. [39] States have an interest in deterring industrial espionage and "the inevitable cost to the basic decency of society when one firm steals from another."

For the third category, the Court found that "[e]liminating trade secret law for the doubtfully patentable invention is . . . likely to have deleterious effects on society and patent policy which we cannot say are balanced out by the speculative gain which

---

[35] Painton & Co. v. Bourns, Inc., 442 F.2d 216, 169 U.S.P.Q. 528 (2d Cir. 1971).

[36] 416 U.S. at 484.

[37] *See* § 2D[1][c].

[38] "Even if trade secret protection against the faithless employee were abolished, inventive and exploitive effort in the area of patentable subject matter that did not meet the standards of patentability would continue, although at a reduced level. Alternatively with the effort that remained, however, would come an increase in the amount of self-help that innovative companies would employ. Knowledge would be widely dispersed among the employees of those still active in research. Security precautions necessarily would be increased, and salaries and fringe benefits of those few officers or employees who had to know the whole of the secret invention would be fixed in an amount thought sufficient to assure their loyalty. . . . Smaller companies would be placed at a distinct economic disadvantage, since the costs of this kind of self-help could be great, and the cost to the public of the use of this invention would be increased. The innovative entrepreneur with limited resources would tend to confine his research efforts to himself and those few he felt he could trust without the ultimate assurance of legal protection against breaches of confidence. As a result, organized scientific and technological research could become fragmented, and society, as a whole, would suffer." 416 U.S. at 485-86.

[39] "The holder of a trade secret would not likely share his secret with a manufacturer who cannot be placed under binding legal obligation to pay a license fee or to protect the secret. The result would be to hoard rather than disseminate knowledge. . . . Instead, then, of licensing others to use his invention and making the most efficient use of existing manufacturing and marketing structures within the industry, the trade secret holder would tend either to limit his utilization of the invention, thereby depriving the public of the maximum benefit of its use, or engage in the time-consuming and economically wasteful enterprise of constructing duplicative manufacturing and marketing mechanisms for the exploitation of the invention. The detrimental misallocation of resources and economic waste that would thus take place if trade secret protection were abolished with respect to employees or licensees cannot be justified by reference to any policy that the federal patent law seeks to advance." 416 U.S. at 486-87.

might result from the encouragement of some inventors with doubtfully patentable inventions which deserve patent protection to come forward and apply for patents."[40]

For the first category, clearly patentable inventions, "the federal interest in disclosure is at its peak."[41] The Court found "no reasonable risk of deterrence from patent application by those who can reasonably expect to be granted patents exists."[42] Patent protection is attractively stronger than trade secret protection.[43] "Nor does society face much risk that scientific or technological progress will be impeded from the rare inventor with a patentable invention who chooses trade secret protection over patent protection."[44] Someone else may invent the same thing, a prospect made more likely if the first inventor makes commercial use of his invention.[45]

---

[40] "The risk of eventual patent invalidity by the courts and the costs associated with that risk may well impel some with a good-faith doubt as to patentability not to take the trouble to seek to obtain and defend patent protection for their discoveries, regardless of the existence of trade secret protection. Trade secret protection would assist those inventors in the more efficient exploitation of their discoveries and not conflict with the patent law. In most cases of genuine doubt as to patent validity the potential rewards of patent protection are so far superior to those accruing to holders of trade secrets, that the holders of such inventions will seek patent protection, ignoring the trade secret route. For those inventors 'on the line' as to whether to seek patent protection, the abolition of trade secret protection might encourage some to apply for a patent who otherwise would not have done so. For some of those so encouraged, no patent will be granted . . .

". . . [T]hose who might be encouraged to file for patents by the absence of trade secret law will include inventors possessing the chaff as well as the wheat. Some of the chaff— the nonpatentable discoveries—will be thrown out by the Patent Office, but in the meantime society will have been deprived of use of those discoveries through trade secret-protected licensing. Some of the chaff may not be thrown out. This Court has noted the difference between the standards used by the Patent Office and the courts to determine patentability. *Graham v. John Deere Co.* . . . In *Lear, Inc. v. Adkins*, . . . the Court thought that an invalid patent was so serious a threat to the free use of ideas already in the public domain that the Court permitted licensees of the patent holder to challenge the validity of the patent. Better had the invalid patent never issued. More of those patents would likely issue if trade secret law were abolished." 416 U.S. at 487-89.

[41] 416 U.S. at 489.

[42] *Id.*

[43] "While trade secret law does not forbid the discovery of the trade secret by fair and honest means, *e.g.*, independent creation or reverse engineering, patent law operates 'against the world,' forbidding any use of the invention for whatever purpose for a significant length of time. The holder of a trade secret also takes a substantial risk that the secret will be passed on to his competitors, by theft or by breach of a confidential relationship, in a manner not easily susceptible of discovery or proof. . . . Where patent law acts as a barrier, trade secret law functions relatively as a sieve." 416 U.S. at 490.

[44] 416 U.S. at 490.

[45] "The ripeness-of-time concept of invention, developed from the study of the many independent multiple discoveries in history, predicts that if a particular individual had not made a particular discovery others would have, and in probably a relatively short period of time. If something is to be discovered at all very likely it will be discovered by more than one person. Singletons and Multiples in Science (1961), in R. Merton, The Sociology of Science 343 (1973); J. Cole & S. Cole, Social Stratification in Science 12—13, 229—230 (1973); Ogburn & Thomas, Are Inventions Inevitable?, 37 Pol.Sci.Q. 83 (1922). . . . Even were an inventor

The Court rejected "partial preemption," which would refuse trade secret protection to patentable inventions, because it could "create serious problems for state courts in the administration of state trade secret law."[46]

Perhaps sensing that the above analysis is strained—as it is, because it is common knowledge that inventors and companies do commonly forego patent protection on at least some otherwise patentable inventions when trade secrets are a less costly option—the Court cited Congress' acquiescence in the long history 0f patent-trade secret coexistence.[47]

[iv] *Plug Molding:* Bonito Boats. In *Bonito Boats*,[48] the Court confirmed *Sears-Compco*'s basic thrust, holding that federal patent policy preempted a Florida statute prohibiting the direct molding reproduction of vessel hulls.

---

to keep his discovery completely to himself, something that neither the patent nor trade secret laws forbid, there is a high probability that it will be soon independently developed. If the invention, though still a trade secret, is put into public use, the competition is alerted to the existence of the inventor's solution to the problem and may be encouraged to make an extra effort to independently find the solution thus known to be possible. The inventor faces pressures not only from private industry, but from the skilled scientists who work in our universities and our other great publicly supported centers of learning and research." 416 U.S. at 490-91.

Perhaps unwittingly, the Court's assertion questions the basis of the patent system.

[46] "As a preliminary matter in trade secret actions, state courts would be obliged to distinguish between what a reasonable inventor would and would not correctly consider to be clearly patentable, with the holder of the trade secret arguing that the invention was not patentable and the misappropriator of the trade secret arguing its undoubted novelty, utility, and nonobviousness. Federal courts have a difficult enough time trying to determine whether an invention, narrowed by the patent application procedure . . . and fixed in the specifications which describe the invention for which the patent has been granted, is patentable. . . . Although state courts in some circumstances must join federal courts in judging whether an issued patent is valid, . . . it would be undesirable to impose the almost impossible burden on state courts to determine the patentability—in fact and in the mind of a reasonable inventor—of a discovery which has not been patented and remains entirely uncircumscribed by expert analysis in the administrative process." 416 U.S. at 492.

[47] "Trade secret law and patent law have co-existed in this country for over one hundred years. . . . Congress, by its silence over these many years, has seen the wisdom of allowing the States to enforce trade secret protection. Until Congress takes affirmative action to the contrary, States should be free to grant protection to trade secrets." 416 U.S. at 493.

In concurring, Justice Marshall stressed coexistence.

"I have no doubt that the existence of trade secret protection provides in some instances a substantial disincentive to entrance into the patent system, and thus deprives society of the benefits of public disclosure of the invention which it is the policy of the patent laws to encourage.

". . . State trade secret laws and the federal patent laws have co-existed for many, many years. During this time, Congress has repeatedly demonstrated its full awareness of the existence of the trade secret system, without any indication of disapproval. Indeed, Congress has in a number of instances given explicit federal protection to trade secret information provided to federal agencies. See, e.g., 5 U.S.C. § 552(b)(4); 18 U.S.C. § 1905." 416 U.S. at 494.

[48] Bonito Boats, Inc. v. Thunder Craft Boats, Inc., 489 U.S. 141, 9 U.S.P.Q.2d 1847 (1989).

"At the heart of *Sears* and *Compco* is the conclusion that the efficient operation of the federal patent system depends upon substantially free trade in publicly known, unpatented design and utilitarian conceptions. . . . While . . . our decisions since *Sears* have taken a decidedly less rigid view of the scope of federal pre-emption under the patent laws, . . . the *Sears* Court correctly concluded that the States may not offer patent-like protection to intellectual creations which would otherwise remain unprotected as a matter of federal law. Both the novelty and the nonobviousness requirements of federal patent law are grounded in the notion that concepts within the public grasp, or those so obvious that they readily could be, are the tools of creation available to all. They provide the baseline of free competition upon which the patent system's incentive to creative effort depends. A state law that substantially interferes with the enjoyment of an unpatented utilitarian or design conception which has been freely disclosed by its author to the public at large impermissibly contravenes the ultimate goal of public disclosure and use which is the centerpiece of federal patent policy. Moreover, through the creation of patent-like rights, the States could essentially redirect inventive efforts away from the careful criteria of patentability developed by Congress over the last 200 years."[49]

The state direct molding statute "does not operate to prohibit 'unfair competition' in the usual sense that the term is understood."[50] *Kewanee*,[51] which upheld state trade secret law against a federal patent policy preemption challenge, is distinguishable. Unlike trade secret law, the Florida statute impinged upon the right to copy and innovate through reverse engineering of a publicly-circulated product. Of no consequence is the fact that the statute "does not remove all means of reproduction and sale."

"In essence, the Florida law prohibits the entire public from engaging in a form of reverse engineering of a product in the public domain. This is clearly one of the rights vested in the federal patent holder, but has never been a part of state protection under the law of unfair competition or trade secrets. . . . The duplication of boat hulls and their component parts may be an essential part of innovation in the field of aquadynamic design. Variations as to size and combination of various elements may lead to significant advances in the

---

[49] 489 U.S. at 156-57, 9 U.S.P.Q.2d at 1854.

[50] "The law of unfair competition has its roots in the common-law tort of deceit: its general concern is with protecting *consumers* from confusion as to source. While that concern may result in the creation of 'quasi-property rights' in communicative symbols, the focus is on the protection of consumers, not the protection of producers as an incentive to product innovation.

"With some notable exceptions, including the interpretation of the Illinois law of unfair competition at issue in *Sears* and *Compco*, . . . the common-law tort of unfair competition has been limited to protection against copying of nonfunctional aspects of consumer products which have acquired secondary meaning such that they operate as a designation of source. . . . The 'protection' granted a particular design under the law of unfair competition is thus limited to one context where consumer confusion is likely to result; the design 'idea' itself may be freely exploited in all other contexts." 489 U.S. at 157-58, 9 U.S.P.Q.2d at 1854-55.

[51] Kewanee Oil Co. v. Bicron Corp., 416 U.S. 470, 181 U.S.P.Q. 673 (1974), discussed at § 1D[3][a][iii].

field. Reverse engineering of chemical and mechanical articles in the public domain often leads to significant advances in technology. If Florida may prohibit this particular method of study and recomposition of an unpatented article, we fail to see the principle that would prohibit a State from banning the use of chromatography in the reconstitution of unpatented chemical compounds, or the use of robotics in the duplication of machinery in the public domain.

"[T]he competitive reality of reverse engineering may act as a spur to the inventor, creating an incentive to develop inventions which meet the rigorous requirements of patentability.

"The Florida statute substantially reduces this competitive incentive, thus eroding the general rule of free competition upon which the attractiveness of the federal patent bargain depends. The protections of state trade secret law are most effective at the developmental stage, before a product has been marketed and threat of reverse engineering becomes real. During this period, patentability will often be an uncertain prospect, and to a certain extent, the protection offered by trade secret law may 'dovetail' with the incentives created by the federal patent monopoly. . . . In contrast, under the Florida scheme, the would-be inventor is aware from the outset of his efforts that rights against the public are available regardless of his ability to satisfy the rigorous standards of patentability. Indeed, it appears that even the most mundane and obvious changes in the design of a boat hull will trigger the protections of the statute." [52]

"[A]llowing the States to create patent-like rights in various products in public circulation would lead to administrative problems of no small dimension.

"The federal patent scheme provides a basis for the public to ascertain the status of the intellectual property embodied in any article in general circulation.

. . .

"The Florida scheme blurs this clear federal demarcation between public and private property. One of the fundamental purposes behind the Patent and Copyright Clauses of the Constitution was to promote national uniformity in the realm of intellectual property. . . . Given the inherently ephemeral nature of property in ideas, and the great power such property has to cause harm to the competitive policies which underlay the federal patent laws, the demarcation of broad zones of public and private right is 'the type of regulation that demands a uniform national rule.' . . . Absent such a federal rule, each State could afford patent-like protection to particularly favored home industries, effectively insulating them from competition from outside the State." [53]

The Court carefully distinguished and confirmed its prior decisions, including *Goldstein*,[54] which recognize state power to "promote originality and creativity" in

---

[52] 489 U.S. at 160-61, 9 U.S.P.Q.2d at 1856.

[53] 489 U.S. at 161-63, 9 U.S.P.Q.2d at 1856-57.

[54] Goldstein v. California, 412 U.S. 546, 178 U.S.P.Q. 129 (1973), discussed at § 1D[3][a][ii].

areas untouched by federal patent and copyright policy and to provide protection against unfair competition and trade secret misappropriation. Lanham Act Section 43(a) provides an affirmative Congressional indication "that both the law of unfair competition and trade secret protection are consistent with the balance struck by the patent laws."[55]

[b] **Contracts and Confidential Relationships.** Federal intellectual property law operates to create rights, including patents, copyrights, and trademarks, and to bestow them with property status. Federal law prescribes conditions of initial ownership and transfer formalities.[56] Otherwise, state property and contract laws govern ownership, transfer, and contract rights relating to federal intellectual property.[57]

Having ceded control over contract and ownership matters to the states, federal intellectual property law intrudes back into state law to preempt rules and doctrines that undermine its policies on incentives, disclosure obligations, and competition. The misuse doctrine is an example: a patent or copyright owner's exercise of state-based contract rights, such as imposing restrictive license conditions, can constitute misuse, causing the courts to withhold enforcement of the patent or copyright.[58] Federal policy may also preclude enforcement of state law-based contracts pertaining to actual or potential intellectual property rights.[59]

[i] *Post-Patent Expiration Royalties:* Brulotte. In *Brulotte,*[60] plaintiff sold defendants its patented hop-picking machines for a flat sum and issued a license for their use, which required a minimum per-season royalty ($500) or $33.33 1/3 per 200 pounds of dried hops, whichever is greater. The licenses listed 12 patents but only seven covered the machines. All seven patents expired on or before 1957, but the license continued beyond that date. Defendants refused to make royalty payments accruing before and after the patents' expiration. The Washington state courts granted plaintiff judgment. The Supreme Court reversed the judgment "insofar as it allows royalties to be collected which accrued after the last of the patents incorporated into the machines had expired."[61]

> "A patent empowers the owner to exact royalties as high as he can negotiate with the leverage of that monopoly. But to use that leverage to project those royalty payments beyond the life of the patent is analogous to an effort to enlarge the monopoly of the patent by [tying] the sale or use of the patented article to the purchase or use of unpatented ones."[62]

---

[55] 489 U.S. at 166, 9 U.S.P.Q.2d at 1858. For a discussion of Lanham Act Section 43(a) trade dress protection, see § 5C[2][c][iv].

[56] *See* §§ 2G and 4G.

[57] *E.g.,* Farmland Irrigation Co., Inc. v. Dopplmaier, 48 Cal. 2d 208, 308 P.2d 732, 113 U.S.P.Q. 88 (1957).

[58] *See* §§ 2F[4][c] and 4F[4][c].

[59] Lear, Inc. v. Adkins, 395 U.S. 653, 162 U.S.P.Q. 1 (1969); Brulotte v. Thys Co., 379 U.S. 29, 143 U.S.P.Q. 264 (1964). Compare Aronson v. Quick Point Pencil Co., 440 U.S. 257, 201 U.S. 1 (1979).

[60] Brulotte v. Thys Co., 379 U.S. 29, 143 U.S.P.Q. 264 (1964).

[61] 379 U.S. at 30.

[62] 379 U.S. at 33.

The Court refused to construe the license agreement as a form of installment plan for paying the machines' purchase price. The licenses stated that the payments were for use of the machines, post-expiration payments were the same as pre-expiration, and licenses prohibited the machines' removal from the county in which they were used.

> "Those restrictions are apt and pertinent to protection of the patent monopoly; and their applicability to the post-expiration period is a telltale sign that the licensor was using the licenses to project its monopoly beyond the patent period. They forcefully negate the suggestion that we have here a bare arrangement for a sale or a lease at an undetermined price based on use. The sale or lease of unpatented machines on long-term payments based on a deferred purchase price or on use would present wholly different considerations. Those arrangements seldom rise to the level of a federal question. But patents are in the federal domain; and . . . a projection of the patent monopoly after the patent expires is not enforceable. The present licenses draw no line between the term of the patent and the post-expiration period. The same provisions as respects both use and royalties are applicable to each. The contracts are, therefore, on their face a bald attempt to exact the same terms and conditions for the period after the patents have expired as they do for the monopoly period. We are, therefore, unable to conjecture what the bargaining position of the parties might have been and what resultant arrangement might have emerged had the provision for post-expiration royalties been divorced from the patent and nowise subject to its leverage.

> "In light of those considerations, we conclude that a patentee's use of a royalty agreement that projects beyond the expiration date of the patent is unlawful per se. If that device were available to patentees, the free market visualized for the post- expiration period would be subject to monopoly influences that have no proper place there."[63]

In *Brulotte*, the Court initially refers to the licensees' "defense" as "misuse of the patents through extension of the license agreements beyond the expiration date of the patents,"[64] but neither the facts nor the holding evoke the usual misuse doctrine, which restricts a patent's enforceability. The plaintiff was suing on its contract, not the patent. If the post-expiration royalty clause constituted misuse, the remedy would be withholding enforcement of *all* of plaintiff's rights—even for the royalty payments due before expiration. *Brulotte*'s holding must be viewed as applying federal patent policy to restrict state contract law. The Court does not precisely identify the policy, but it does refer to the impropriety of state law being used as "leverage" to extend a patent's restraining force beyond its statutory scope and interfere with the patent policy of free use and competition in items not subject to patent protection.

[*ii*] *Licensee Estoppel to Contest Validity—Liability for Unpaid Royalties:* Lear. In *Lear*,[65] the Court more explicitly articulated and applied federal patent policy to

---

[63] 379 U.S. at 32-33.

[64] 379 U.S. at 30.

[65] Lear, Inc. v. Adkins, 395 U.S. 653, 162 U.S.P.Q. 1 (1969).

restrict state contract law. *Lear* is significant in the history of United States intellectual property law history because it is the last of a series of Supreme Court decisions exhibiting a fundamental skepticism toward the patent examination system and the role of patents.[66]

Lear hired Adkins to solve a gyroscope problem. The parties agreed that all "new ideas, discoveries, and inventions" became Adkins' property and that Adkins would grant Lear a license "on a mutually satisfactory royalty basis." Adkins found a solution, which he disclosed to Lear, and applied for a patent. On September 15, 1955, after lengthy negotiations, Lear and Adkins approved a use-royalty contract, which included the following provision on possible Patent Office rejection of Adkin's application or invalidation of an issued patent.

> "[If] the U.S. Patent Office refuses to issue a patent on the substantial claims [contained in Adkins' original patent application] or if such a patent so issued is subsequently held invalid, then in any of such events Lear at its option shall have the right forthwith to terminate the specific license so affected or to terminate this entire Agreement. . . . "[67]

Adkins did not obtain a patent until 1960. According to the Court, he began with an "ambitious claim" to his "entire method." "The Patent Office rejected this initial claim, as well as two subsequent amendments, which progressively narrowed the scope of the invention sought to be protected. Finally, Adkins narrowed his claim drastically to assert only that the design of the apparatus used to achieve gyroscope accuracy was novel. . . . In response, the Office issued its 1960 patent, granting a 17-year monopoly on this more modest claim."[68]

---

[66] Other notable decisions in the 1960s and 1970s were Sakraida v. Ag Pro, Inc., 425 U.S. 273, 189 U.S.P.Q. 449 (1976); Gottschalk v. Benson, 409 U.S. 63, 175 U.S.P.Q. 673 (1972); Brenner v. Manson, 383 U.S. 519, 148 U.S.P.Q. 689 (1966).

By 1980, the Court's attitude toward patents and intellectual property became more balanced. *See* § 2B[6].

[67] 395 U.S. at 657.

[68] 395 U.S. at 659.

The Court's opinion implicitly criticized the slow pace and inefficient nature of Patent Office prosecution:

> "The regulations do not require the Office to make a final judgment on an invention's patentability on the basis of the inventor's original application. While it sometimes happens that a patent is granted at this early stage, it is far more common for the Office to find that although certain of the applicant's claims may be patentable, certain others have been fully anticipated by the earlier developments in the art. In such a situation, the Patent Office does not attempt to separate the wheat from the chaff on its own initiative. Instead, it rejects the application, giving the inventor the right to make an amendment which narrows his claim to cover only those aspects of the invention which are truly novel. It often happens, however, that even after an application is amended, the Patent Office finds that some of the remaining claims are unpatentable. When this occurs, the agency again issues a rejection which is subject to further amendment. And so the process of rejection and amendment continues until the Patent Office Examiner either grants a patent or concludes that none of the inventor's claims could possibly be patentable, at which time a final rejection is entered on the Office's records. Thus, when Adkins made his original application in 1954, it took the average inventor more than three years before

During the lengthy prosecution, Lear decided that Adkins would not obtain effective patent protection, relying on a prior art patent it believed fully anticipated his discovery.[69] In 1957, it terminated royalty payments on gyroscopes made at its Michigan plant; two years later, it terminated payments on its California plant gyroscopes.

In 1960, Adkins sued Lear for breach of contract in a California state court, contending that both the Michigan and California gyroscopes used his patented invention, and that Lear's failure to pay royalties breached the 1955 contract and quasi-contractual obligations. Adkins also asserted a tort claim for trade secret misappropriation, but, when the trial judge required Adkins to choose between his contract and tort theories, he chose the former.

The trial judge held that Lear was estopped from contesting the licensed patent's validity and granted Adkins' directed verdict motion that the license covered the California gyroscopes, awarding $16,351.93. Lear contended that it developed its Michigan gyroscopes "independently of Adkins' ideas." After full trial, the jury rendered an $888,122.56 verdict on the Michigan gyroscopes. The trial court granted Lear's motion for judgment notwithstanding the verdict on the ground that "Adkins' invention had been completely anticipated by the prior art." Both sides appealed. The district court of appeals held that Lear properly terminated its license, that Adkins must sue in federal court for patent infringement for post-termination damages, and that Lear must pay pre-termination contract royalties regardless of the patent's validity. Both sides appealed again. Reinstating the jury's verdict, the California Supreme Court held that Lear did not properly terminate the license, the license was still in force, and licensee estoppel barred Lear from challenging the patent: "one of the oldest doctrines in the field of patent law establishes that so long as a licensee is operating under a license agreement he is estopped to deny the validity of his licensor's patent in a suit for royalties under the agreement. The theory underlying this doctrine is that a licensee should not be permitted to enjoy the benefit afforded by the agreement while simultaneously urging that the patent which forms the basis of the agreement is void."[70]

The United States Supreme Court noted that the California courts' interpretation of the licensing agreement "is solely a matter of state law" and the only issue before it was those courts' "reliance upon the doctrine of estoppel to bar Lear from proving that Adkins' ideas were dedicated to the common welfare by federal law."[71] Before the California courts, Lear did not ask for complete repudiation of licensee estoppel but urged "an exception . . . so sweeping as to undermine the doctrine's vitality completely." Lear argued "on the basis of federal as well as state cases, that a licensee may escape the impact of estoppel simply by announcing that it has repudiated the licensing agreement, regardless of the contract's terms." The Supreme

---

he obtained a final administrative decision on the patentability of his ideas, with the Patent Office acting on the average application from two to four times." 395 U.S. at 658-59. For a discussion of PTO patent examination, see § 2D[1].

[69] For a discussion of patent law's novelty requirement, see § 2C[3].

[70] Adkins v. Lear, Inc., 67 Cal. 2d 882, 891, 64 Cal. Rptr. 545, 549, 435 P.2d 321, 325—26 (1967), rev'd, 395 U.S. 653 (1969).

[71] 395 U.S. at 661-62.

Court, therefore, rejected Adkins' argument that Lear did not preserve the federal question of the licensee estoppel doctrine's continuing validity.

In considering estoppel, it was "not writing on a clean slate" because Supreme Court and lower court licensee estoppel cases date back to the mid-19th century. These cases started with a general rule of estoppel and then eroded it with exceptions. Licensee estoppel's uncertain status "is a product of judicial efforts to accommodate the competing demands of the common law of contracts and the federal law of patents. On the one hand, the law of contracts forbids a purchaser to repudiate his promises simply because he later becomes dissatisfied with the bargain he has made. . . . On the other hand, federal law requires that all ideas in general circulation be dedicated to the common good unless they are protected by a valid patent."[72] The search for "an intermediate position which somehow would remain responsive to the radically different concerns of the two different worlds of contract and patent . . . has been a failure."[73] Rather than renew the search, the Court decided to reconsider the arguments for and against estoppel.

The Court began with the simpler, typical situation in which a patentee and manufacturer negotiate a license after a patent issues. Here, "the technical requirements of contract doctrine must give way before the demands of the public interest":[74] if licensees, who are "often . . . the only individuals with enough economic incentive to challenge the patentability of an inventor's discovery," "are muzzled," that is, cannot challenge the licensed patent, "the public may continually be required to pay tribute to would-be monopolists without need or justification."[75]

Analyzed as a contract matter, a patent license offers the licensee only two benefits.

> "Since the Patent Office makes an inventor's ideas public when it issues its grant of a limited monopoly, a potential licensee has access to the inventor's ideas even if he does not enter into an agreement with the patent owner. Consequently, a manufacturer gains only two benefits if he chooses to enter a licensing agreement after the patent has issued. First, by accepting a license and paying royalties for a time, the licensee may have avoided the necessity of defending an expensive infringement action during the period when he may be least able to afford one. Second, the existence of an unchallenged patent may deter others from attempting to compete with the licensee. . . . [Of course, the value of this second benefit may depend upon whether the licensee has obtained exclusive or nonexclusive rights to the use of the patent. Even in the case of nonexclusive licenses, however, competition is limited to the extent that the royalty charged by the patentee serves as a barrier to entry]."[76]

These two benefits constitute sufficient consideration to support a contract under "ordinary . . . principles . . . regardless of the validity of the underlying patent," but, tested "by the standard of good-faith commercial dealing," this "simple contract

---

[72] 395 U.S. at 667.
[73] 395 U.S. at 668.
[74] 395 U.S. at 670.
[75] 395 U.S. at 670.
[76] 395 U.S. at 669 and n.16.

approach entirely ignores the position of the licensor who is seeking to invoke the court's assistance on his behalf."[77] The licensor's "equities . . . do not weigh very heavily when they are balanced against the important public interest in permitting full and free competition in the use of ideas which are in reality a part of the public domain."[78]

> "Consider, for example, the equities of the licensor who has obtained his patent through a fraud on the Patent Office. It is difficult to perceive why good faith requires that courts should permit him to recover royalties despite his licensee's attempts to show that the patent is invalid.

> "Even in the more typical cases, not involving conscious wrongdoing, the licensor's equities are far from compelling. A patent, in the last analysis, simply represents a legal conclusion reached by the Patent Office. Moreover, the legal conclusion is predicated on factors as to which reasonable men can differ widely. Yet the Patent Office is often obliged to reach its decision in an ex parte proceeding, without the aid of the arguments which could be advanced by parties interested in proving patent invalidity. Consequently, it does not seem to us to be unfair to require a patentee to defend the Patent Office's judgment when his licensee places the question in issue, especially since the licensor's case is buttressed by the presumption of validity which attaches to his patent. Thus, although licensee estoppel may be consistent with the letter of contractual doctrine, we cannot say that it is compelled by the spirit of contract law, which seeks to balance the claims of promisor and promisee in accord with the requirements of good faith."[79]

The Court concluded that "the technical requirements of contract doctrine must give way before the demands of the public interest in the typical situation involving the negotiation of a license after a patent has issued."[80]

The case presented "a far more complicated estoppel problem than the one which arises in the most common licensing context" because the license predated the patent's issue by four years and the licensee Lear obtained the additional benefit of early access to Adkins' ideas: "At the core of this case . . . is the difficult question whether federal patent policy bars a State from enforcing a contract regulating access to an unpatented secret idea."[81]

The Court could not accept patentee Adkins' "extreme position" that because Lear obtained privileged access to his ideas, it should pay royalties for the periods before and after the patent's issue without regard to validity. That position "would permit inventors to negotiate all important licenses during the lengthy period while their applications were still pending at the Patent Office, thereby disabling entirely all those who have the strongest incentive to show that a patent is worthless. While the equities supporting Adkins' position are somewhat more appealing than those

---

77 395 U.S. at 669.
78 395 U.S. at 670.
79 395 U.S. at 669-70.
80 395 U.S. at 670-71.
81 395 U.S. at 672.

supporting the typical licensor, we cannot say that there is enough of a difference to justify such a substantial impairment of overriding federal policy."[82]

A less extreme position would allow the licensee to challenge the patent but "comply with its contract and continue to pay royalties until its claim is finally vindicated in the courts." The Court found that the "parties' contract . . . is no more controlling on this issue than is the State's doctrine of estoppel, which is also rooted in contract principles." If the licensee were liable for litigation period royalties, the patentee would have an incentive to engage in delay tactics.

> "The decisive question is whether overriding federal policies would be significantly frustrated if licensees could be required to continue to pay royalties during the time they are challenging patent validity in the courts.

> "It seems to us that such a requirement would be inconsistent with the aims of federal patent policy. Enforcing this contractual provision would give the licensor an additional economic incentive to devise every conceivable dilatory tactic in an effort to postpone the day of final judicial reckoning. We can perceive no reason to encourage dilatory court tactics in this way. Moreover, the cost of prosecuting slow-moving trial proceedings and defending an inevitable appeal might well deter many licensees from attempting to prove patent invalidity in the courts. The deterrent effect would be particularly severe in the many scientific fields in which invention is proceeding at a rapid rate. In these areas, a patent may well become obsolete long before its 17-year term has expired. If a licensee has reason to believe that he will replace a patented idea with a new one in the near future, he will have little incentive to initiate lengthy court proceedings, unless he is freed from liability at least from the time he refuses to pay the contractual royalties. Lastly, enforcing this contractual provision would undermine the strong federal policy favoring the full and free use of ideas in the public domain."[83]

For these reasons, the Court held that the licensee "must be permitted to avoid the payment of all royalties accruing after [the] patent issued if [it] can prove patent invalidity."[84]

The final and "much more difficult" question was the licensee's liability for royalties accruing before the patent issued, which "squarely raises the question whether, and to what extent, the States may protect the owners of unpatented inventions who are willing to disclose their ideas to manufacturers only upon payment of royalties." Because it lacked the California courts' views on the enforceability of this obligation once the estoppel doctrine is removed, the Court did not decide the issue. The Court hinted that its estoppel decision might "revolutionize" state law on inventors' contract rights.

---

[82] 395 U.S. at 672-73.

[83] 395 U.S. at 673-74.

[84] The Court refused to confine its new licensee estoppel rule to contracts concluded after its decision. The estoppel rule had been so eroded by exceptions that patent owners could not have confidently relied on it. "Moreover, the public's interest in the elimination of specious patents would be significantly prejudiced if the retroactive effect of [its] decision were limited in any way." 395 U.S. at 674.

"Our decision today will, of course, require the state courts to reconsider the theoretical basis of their decisions enforcing the contractual rights of inventors and it is impossible to predict the extent to which this reevaluation may revolutionize the law of any particular State in this regard. Consequently, we have concluded, after much consideration, that even though an important question of federal law underlies this phase of the controversy, we should not now attempt to define in even a limited way the extent, if any, to which the States may properly act to enforce the contractual rights of inventors of unpatented secret ideas. Given the difficulty and importance of this task, it should be undertaken only after the state courts have, after fully focused inquiry, determined the extent to which they will respect the contractual rights of such inventors in the future. Indeed, on remand, the California courts may well reconcile the competing demands of patent and contract law in a way which would not warrant further review in this Court."[85]

Lear's final passage was a source of great concern for it cast into doubt state law contract and tort obligations pertaining to the disclosure of ideas and trade secrets in confidence. *Kewanee*[86] and *Aronson*[87] dispelled most of these concerns.

[iii] *License Royalty Obligations on Unpatented, Publicly-Disclosed Products:* Aronson. In *Aronson*,[88] Aronson filed a patent application on a new form of keyholder in October 1955. She negotiated a contract with Quick Point, which was embodied in two documents. The first provided that Quick Point would pay a $750 advance and agreed to pay a 5% royalty in return for the exclusive right to make and sell keyholders "of the type shown" in Aronson's patent application. Aronson could rescind the contract if Quick Point did not sell a million keyholders by the end of 1957. Quick Point could cancel the agreement whenever "the volume of sales does not meet our expectations." The document said nothing further about duration. The second document stated that if Aronson's patent application was "not allowed within five (5) years, Quick Point Pencil Co. [would] pay . . . two and one half percent (2 1/2%) of sales . . . so long as you [Quick Point] continue to sell same."[89]

In 1961, the PTO finally rejected Aronson's application. Quick Point reduced its payments to the lower royalty figure but continued paying for 14 years. By 1975, Quick Point's sales were being eroded by competitors that copied the design. Quick Point commenced an action, seeking a declaratory judgment that its state contract law royalty obligation was unenforceable because of federal patent policy. The district court held the contract enforceable. The court of appeals reversed, holding that

---

[85] 395 U.S. at 675.

[86] Kewanee Oil Co. v. Bicron Corp., 416 U.S. 470, 181 U.S.P.Q. 673 (1974), discussed at § 1D[3][a][iii].

[87] Aronson v. Quick Point Pencil Co., 440 U.S. 257, 201 U.S.P.Q. 1 (1979).

[88] *Id.*

[89] 440 U.S. at 259.

In a letter concerning Aronson's husband's plans to market a different keyholder, Quick Point argued that the license covered what was disclosed in Aronson's patent application, not what was specifically claimed, and acknowledged that it would be obligated to pay a royalty even if no patent issued.

Lear meant that the contract became unenforceable once Aronson failed to obtain a patent. A continuing royalty obligation was contrary to federal policy favoring free use of public domain ideas. If Aronson had obtained a patent, *Brulotte* would have required termination of royalty obligations when the patent expired.

The Supreme Court reversed. "[T]he parties contracted with full awareness of both the pendency of a patent application and the possibility that a patent might not issue."[90] "Commercial agreements traditionally are the domain of state law. State law is not displaced merely because the contract relates to intellectual property which may or may not be patentable; the states are free to regulate the use of such intellectual property in any manner not inconsistent with federal law."[91] Enforcement of the Quick Point-Aronson agreement "is not inconsistent" with the federal patent system's purposes of fostering invention, promoting invention disclosure "to stimulate further innovation and to permit the public to practice the invention once the patent expires," and assuring that "ideas in the public domain remain there for the free use of the public."

> "Permitting inventors to make enforceable agreements licensing the use of their inventions in return for royalties provides an additional incentive to invention. Similarly, encouraging [them] to make arrangements for the manufacture of [their inventions] furthers the federal policy of disclosure of inventions; these simple devices display the novel idea which they embody wherever they are seen.
>
> . . .
>
> ". . . Enforcement of the agreement does not withdraw any idea from the public domain. The design . . . was not in the public domain before [the licensee] obtained its license . . .
>
> "Requiring [the licensee] to bear the burden of royalties for the use of the design is no more inconsistent with federal patent law than any of the other costs involved in being the first to introduce a new product to the market, such as outlays for research and development, and marketing and promotional expenses."[92]

The Court distinguished *Lear* and *Brulotte*.

> "[*Lear*] held that a person licensed to use a patent may challenge the validity of the patent, and that a licensee who establishes that the patent is invalid need not pay the royalties accrued under the licensing agreement subsequent to the issuance of the patent. Both holdings relied on the desirability of encouraging licensees to challenge the validity of patents, to further the strong federal policy that only inventions which meet the rigorous requirements of patentability shall be withdrawn from the public domain. . . . Accordingly, neither the holding nor the rationale of *Lear* controls when no patent has issued, and no ideas have been withdrawn from public use.

---

[90] 440 U.S. at 261.
[91] 440 U.S. at 262.
[92] 440 U.S. at 262-63.

"[*Brulotte*] held that the obligation to pay royalties in return for the use of a patented device may not extend beyond the life of the patent. The principle underlying that holding was simply that the monopoly granted under a patent cannot lawfully be used to 'negotiate with the leverage of that monopoly.' . . . Here the reduced royalty which is challenged, far from being negotiated 'with the leverage' of a patent, rested on the contingency that no patent would issue within five years.

"No doubt a pending patent application gives the applicant some additional bargaining power for purposes of negotiating a royalty agreement. The pending application allows the inventor to hold out the hope of an exclusive right to exploit the idea, as well as the threat that the other party will be prevented from using the idea for 17 years. However, the amount of leverage arising from a patent application depends on how likely the parties consider it to be that a valid patent will issue. Here, where no patent ever issued, the record is entirely clear that the parties assigned a substantial likelihood to that contingency, since they specifically provided for a reduced royalty in the event no patent issued within five years.

"This case does not require us to draw the line between what constitutes abuse of a pending application and what does not. It is clear that whatever role the pending application played in the negotiation of the 5% royalty, it played no part in the contract to pay the 2 1/2% royalty indefinitely."[93]

Kewanee was persuasive authority because "[e]nforcement of this royalty agreement is even less offensive to federal patent policies than state law protecting trade secrets."

"The most commonly accepted definition of trade secrets is restricted to confidential information which is not disclosed in the normal process of exploitation. . . . Accordingly, the exploitation of trade secrets under state law may not satisfy the federal policy in favor of disclosure, whereas disclosure is inescapable in exploiting a device like the Aronson keyholder.

"Enforcement of these contractual obligations, freely undertaken in arm's-length negotiation and with no fixed reliance on a patent or a probable patent grant, will

'encourage invention in areas where patent law does not reach, and will prompt the independent innovator to proceed with the discovery and exploitation of his invention. Competition is fostered and the public is not deprived of the use of valuable, if not quite patentable, invention.' (Footnote omitted.) 416 U.S., at 485.

"The device which is the subject of this contract ceased to have any secrecy as soon as it was first marketed, yet when the contract was negotiated the inventiveness and novelty were sufficiently apparent to induce an experienced novelty manufacturer to agree to pay for the opportunity to be first in the market. Federal patent law is not a barrier to such a contract."[94]

---

[93] 440 U.S. at 264–65.
[94] 440 U.S. at 266.

By distinguishing rather than overruling *Lear* and *Brulotte*, *Aronson* suggests that a licensing contract will be limited to a patent's validity and duration if there is a "fixed reliance on a patent or a probable patent grant" or a pending application provides the "leverage" for the contract.

[c] **Copyright Act Preemption.** The 1976 Copyright Act's Section 301 preempts state legal and equitable remedies that are "equivalent to any of the exclusive rights within the general scope of copyright"[95] and "come within the subject matter of copyright."[96]

The Semiconductor Chip Protection Act contains a preemption section similar to Section 301.[97]

Section 301 is a statutory basis for preemption.[98] It does not supersede constitutional preemption standards, such as those *Bonito Boats* applies.[99]

Section 301 imposes a two-part preemption test: "First, [the subject matter] 'must come within the "subject matter of copyright" as defined in Sections 102 and 103 of the Copyright Act. Second, the rights granted under state law must be "equivalent to any of the exclusive rights within the general scope of copyright as specified by Section 106 [of the Copyright Act]." ' "[100]

---

[95] Section 106 lists five exclusive rights: copy reproduction, derivative work preparation, copy distribution, public performance, and public display. 17 U.S.C. § 106. *See* § 4E.

[96] Section 102 defines copyrightable subject matter as "original works of authorship fixed in any tangible medium of expression." 17 U.S.C. § 102. For a discussion of copyrightable subject matter, see § 4C[1].

[97] 17 U.S.C. § 912(c).

[98] Section 301 provides:

"(a) On and after January 1, 1978, all legal or equitable rights that are equivalent to any of the exclusive rights within the general scope of copyright as specified by section 106 in works of authorship that are fixed in a tangible medium of expression and come within the subject matter of copyright as specified by sections 102 and 103, whether created before or after that date and whether published or unpublished, are governed exclusively by this title. Thereafter, no person is entitled to any such right or equivalent right in any such work under the common law or statutes of any State.

"(b) Nothing in this title annuls or limits any rights or remedies under the common law or statutes of any State with respect to—

(1) subject matter that does not come within the subject matter of copyright as specified by sections 102 and 103, including works of authorship not fixed in any tangible medium of expression; or

(2) any cause of action arising from undertakings commenced before January 1, 1978; or

(3) activities violating legal or equitable rights that are not equivalent to any of the exclusive rights within the general scope of copyright as specified by section 106.

. . .

"(d) Nothing in this title annuls or limits any rights or remedies under any other Federal statute." 17 U.S.C. § 301.

[99] *See* § 1D[3][a][iv].

[100] Del Madera Properties v. Rhodes & Gardner, Inc., 820 F.2d 973, 3 U.S.P.Q.2d 1283, 1285 (9th Cir. 1987).

[i] *Subject Matter.* The Section 106 copyrightable subject matter test part is the easier of the two parts. In most instances, it will be clear whether the subject matter that plaintiff contends was copied, used, or otherwise misappropriated is a work of authorship fixed in a tangible medium of expression.[101]

In *Del Madera Properties,*[102] Del Madera acquired land in Tiburon, California, and hired an engineer, architect, and consultant to prepare a master plan showing the proposed lot, road, and open space placement. Del Madera submitted the plan to the Town of Tiburon in April 1980. In April 1981, Tiburon approved the plan; in August 1981, it approved a "Tentative Map" based on the plan. Del Madera defaulted on notes securing the property. After foreclosure, the new owner, Balfour, hired the same consultant and developed the property according to the "Tentative Map." Del Madera sued the new owner, the consultant and others, asserting unfair competition and unjust enrichment claims based on the defendants' misappropriation of the "Tentative Map," supporting documents, time and effort spent in creating the map and supporting documents, and time and effort spent seeking the plan's approval. The Ninth Circuit held that Section 301 preempted all Del Madera's claims except that for misappropriation of the time and effort to secure Tiburon's approval of the plan. The map and the supporting documents were copyrightable subject matter as pictorial and literary works.[103]

> "Effort expended to create the Tentative Map and supporting documents is effort expended to create tangible works of authorship. As such, this effort is within the scope of copyright protection. *See Mayer v. Josiah Wedgwood & Sons, Ltd.,* 601 F. Supp. 1523, 1535 (S.D.N.Y.1985) (misappropriation of author's talent and effort in creating a work 'is precisely the type of misconduct the copyright laws are designed to guard against'). Effort expended to obtain subdivision approval, however, is not effort expended to create a tangible work of authorship. As such, it is not copyrightable subject matter, and it is not subject to preemption under the Copyright Act."[104]

The subject matter analysis is only into whether the work is the type of literary, musical, dramatic, pictorial, graphic, sculptural, audiovisual or sound recording work

---

[101] *E.g.,* Mayer v. Josiah Wedgwood & Sons, Ltd., 601 F. Supp. 1523, 225 U.S.P.Q. 776 (S.D. N.Y. 1985) (snowflake design for Christmas plate; the design was a pictorial work potentially subject to copyright protection).

For a questionable decision, see Baltimore Orioles, Inc. v. Major League Baseball Players Association, 805 F.2d 663, 231 U.S.P.Q. 673, 681 (7th Cir. 1986), *cert. denied,* 480 U.S. 941 (1987) (publicity right claim for broadcast of baseball players' performances: the players' performances were copyrightable subject matter because the telecast videotaping fixed them in a tangible expression medium: "[O]nce a performance is reduced to tangible form, there is no distinction between the performance and the recording of the performance for the purpose of preemption under § 301(a)."). For criticism, see P. Goldstein, Copyright § 15.22.1.1 (1989) ("the court erred in its evident assumption that the broadcast's fixation constituted fixation of the players' [individual] performances.").

[102] Del Madera Properties v. Rhodes & Gardner, Inc., 820 F.2d 973, 3 U.S.P.Q.2d 1283 (9th Cir. 1987).

[103] *See* § 4C[1].

[104] 820 F.2d at 976-77, 3 U.S.P.Q.2d at 1285.

that Copyright Act Section 102 makes potentially eligible for protection. A work meets the subject matter test part even though it is not in fact copyrighted because of failure to meet formalities[105] or because it contains insufficient creativity to meet copyright law's originality requirement.[106]

A difficult question concerns "ideas" or "facts" that copyright law does not protect.[107] Some decisions indicate that Section 301's subject matter test part is not met if the claimant only charges misappropriation of the work's ideas—even though the misappropriated ideas are contained in a work that is a potentially copyrightable expression of ideas.[108] Assuming these decisions' correctness, the

---

[105] Mayer v. Josiah Wedgwood & Sons, Ltd., 601 F. Supp. 1523, 1532, 225 U.S.P.Q. 776 (S.D. N.Y. 1985).

[106] *E.g.*, Baltimore Orioles, Inc. v. Major League Baseball Players Association, 805 F.2d 663, 676, 231 U.S.P.Q. 673, 682 (7th Cir. 1986), *cert. denied*, 480 U.S. 941 (1987) ("Congress contemplated that '[a]s long as a work fits within one of the general subject matter categories of section 102 and 103, . . . [section 301(a)] prevents the States from protecting it even if it fails to achieve Federal copyright because it is too minimal or lacking in originality to qualify.' House Report at 131 . . . [Footnote: The reason that § 301(a) preempts rights claimed in works that lack sufficient creativity to be copyrightable is to prevent the states from granting protection to works which Congress has concluded should be in the public domain.] Hence, § 301(a) preempts all equivalent state-law rights claimed in any work within the subject matter of copyright whether or not the work embodies any creativity. Regardless of the creativity of the Players' performances, the works in which they assert rights are copyrightable works which come within the scope of § 301(a) because of the creative contributions of the individuals responsible for recording the Players' performances. Therefore, the Players' rights of publicity in their performances are preempted if they are equivalent to any of the bundle of rights encompassed in a copyright.").

[107] *See* § 4C[1][d].

[108] United States Trotting Association v. Chicago Downs Association, Inc., 665 F.2d 781 (7th Cir. 1981) (no Section 301 preemption in claim by plaintiff, a national harness racing association, that defendants, who operate race tracks, misappropriated plaintiff's racing horse registration and eligibility certificates by using such certificates to conduct racing without complying with plaintiff's regulations); Mayer v. Josiah Wedgwood & Sons, Ltd., 601 F. Supp. 1523, 1532 n.16, 225 U.S.P.Q. 776, 781 n.16 (S.D. N.Y. 1985) ("Federal copyright law does not protect ideas, 17 U.S.C. § 102(b). Rather, it protects only the author's particular expression of those ideas. . . . Thus, state laws that protect ideas, as distinct from their expression, are without the subject matter of copyright and therefore not preempted under § 301."); Rand McNally & Co. v. Fleet Management Systems, Inc., 591 F. Supp. 726, 739, 221 U.S.P.Q. 827, 838 (N.D. Ill. 1983) (compilation of distance information that claimant distributes and which is filed with a federal agency as part of tariff schedules: claimant asserted misappropriation in "use, as opposed to the reproduction, of the factual data." "[A] print-out of one particular distance (as opposed to a print-out of the entire compilation) would not be within the subject matter of the [Copyright Act], as it is a fact not a part of a compilation. . . . A question remains whether a state-created protection of such a fact would violate the first amendment. The court does not now address this issue, as the parties have not framed their discussion in these terms . . . The court finds now only that as use of the reproduced data bank may be outside of the subject matter test of § 301(a), it is outside of the scope of the preemption doctrine." Claimant also asserted copying of "the procedures, processes, and systems for calculating mileage data. As these procedures are expressly excluded from copyright protection, § 102(b), they fail the subject matter test of § 301(a) and are not preempted."); Wer-

claimant faces considerable difficulty showing a state law basis for unauthorized use of an idea in a publicly disclosed product or document if there is no contractual restraint or breach of confidentiality.[109] Further, Section 301 aside, constitutional supremacy standards may operate to preempt a state remedy against copying unpatented ideas.[110]

[ii] *Equivalent Right.* The Section 102 equivalent right test part is more difficult. Determining when a state-based right is "equivalent" to a federal copyright exclusive right has proven to be a difficult task, and case results cannot always be

---

lin v. Reader's Digest Association, Inc., 528 F. Supp. 451, 467, 213 U.S.P.Q. 1041 (S.D. N.Y. 1981) (plaintiff submitted an article to defendant; defendant had another person write an article based on plaintiff's idea; "To the extent it was an article, it enjoyed federal copyright protection; to the extent it was an idea, it enjoyed no federal copyright protection but limited state law protection.").

Cf. Stillman v. Leo Burnett Co., Inc., 720 F. Supp. 1353, 1362, 13 U.S.P.Q.2d 1203, 1211 (N.D. Ill. 1989) (Section 301 does not preempt plaintiff's claim that defendants took his idea for a "silent" television commercial, created a different commercial based on the same idea, and implicitly misrepresented to the public that they were the source of the idea; "an important consideration in copyright preemption inquiries is whether the state law serves the same goals as the copyright laws. . . . The copyright laws serve to protect [plaintiff's] to reap the benefits of the particular expression he employed in creating [his] silent commercial. The state laws, by contrast, will protect [plaintiff's] right to prevent others from fraudulently taking credit for, and presumably benefiting in the future from [plaintiff's] ability to develop novel ideas. The copyright laws do not prohibit the copying of ideas, but when a copier misrepresents that he is the creator, nothing in the copyright laws prohibits the states from providing a remedy.").

Compare Harper & Row Publishers, Inc. v. Nation Enterprises, 723 F.2d 195, 199-200, 220 U.S.P.Q. 321, 325-26 (2d Cir. 1983), *rev'd on other grounds*, 471 U.S. 539 (1985) (for Section 301 preemption purposes, copyrightable subject matter embraces literary works, such as former President Ford's memoirs, even though the memoirs "may consist of uncopyrightable material," such as United States government works or other persons' expressions: "Were this not so, states would be free to expand the perimeters of copyright protection to their own liking, on the theory that preemption would be no bar to state protection of material not meeting federal statutory standards."); Nash v. CBS, Inc., 704 F. Supp. 823, 832, 10 U.S.P.Q.2d 1026, 1033 (N.D. Ill. 1989), *aff'd*, 899 F.2d 1537, 14 U.S.P.Q.2d 1755 (7th Cir. 1990) ("Nash misses the point when he argues that, because Counts II and III seek, in part, recovery for the appropriation of facts, ideas, research, and other uncopyrightable material, they escape preemption. The critical point is that Nash's books are materials within the subject matter of copyright. State law claims do not avoid preemption simply because they are based upon the improper use of uncopyrightable material contained in works properly subject to copyright.").

[109] *Cf.* Mayer v. Josiah Wedgwood & Sons, Ltd., 601 F. Supp. 1523, 1532 n.16, 225 U.S.P.Q. 776, 781 n.16 (S.D. N.Y. 1985) ("Mayer is seeking to protect her right to use her snowflake design from appropriation by JWS Ltd. She does not—indeed, realistically no one can—claim rights in the *idea* of using snowflake designs on Christmas items. . . . Here, by contrast, Mayer is complaining of use by JWS Ltd. of her design itself, not the idea of using a snowflake design for Christmas items.")

For a discussion of trade secret law, see Chapter 3. For a discussion of misappropriation, see § 6F.

[110] *See* § 1D[3][a].

reconciled. The label the claimant uses is not determinative of whether the asserted right is equivalent to a copyright exclusive right.[111]

During Congress's consideration of the 1976 Copyright Act, Section 301(b)(3) initially contained a listing of non-preempted state legal and equitable rights. Controversy over inclusion of "misappropriation" led Congress to delete the entire list.[112] Because of confusion as to the deletion's purpose, courts give this legislative history little weight.[113]

Courts apply an "extra element" test.[114] The asserted state-based right must entail an "extra element" "which changes the nature of the action so that it is *qualitatively* different from a copyright infringement claim." "Elements such as awareness or intent, which alter the action's scope but not its nature, will not save it from preemption under § 301."[115]

---

[111] *E.g.*, Crow v. Wainwright, 720 F.2d 1224, 1226 (11th Cir. 1983), *cert. denied*, 469 U.S. 819 (1984) (Section 301 preempts a state criminal law punishing dealing in "stolen property" arising from sale of pirated tapes of copyrighted sound recordings; "Despite the name given the offense, the elements essential to establish a violation of the Florida statute in this case correspond almost exactly to those of the tort of copyright infringement."); Editorial Photocolor Archives, Inc. v. Granger Collection, 61 N.Y.2d 517, 474 N.Y.S.2d 964, 967, 463 N.E.2d 365, 368 (1984) ("Plaintiffs' only claims for 'unfair competition' relate to defendant's violation of plaintiffs' alleged reproduction rights in the transparencies. That plaintiffs have chosen to enforce such rights to reproduce, display, sell, lease or license for reproduction, the transparencies in the form of causes of action for unfair competition, interference with contractual relations, or violation of section 368-d of the General Business Law (which may require additional elements not necessary to secure copyright protection) does not make the underlying rights sought to be enforced any less equivalent to copyright, or remove plaintiffs' claims from the Federal preemptive scheme.").

[112] For a discussion of this controversy, see § 6F[4].

[113] *E.g.*, Baltimore Orioles, Inc. v. Major League Baseball Players Association, 805 F.2d 663, 677 n.25, 231 U.S.P.Q. 673, 682 n.25 (7th Cir. 1986), *cert. denied*, 480 U.S. 941 (1987) ("Because the House's debate concerning the effect of the amendment is ambiguous, if not contradictory, and because the Senate concurred without discussion in the House's version of § 301, almost any interpretation of the concept of equivalent rights can be inferred from the legislative history. Therefore, in determining whether a particular right is equivalent to a copyright, we place little weight on the deletion of the list of nonequivalent rights.").

[114] *E.g.*, Harper & Row Publishers, Inc. v. Nation Enterprises, 723 F.2d 195, 199-200, 220 U.S.P.Q. 321, 326 (2d Cir. 1983), *rev'd on other grounds*, 471 U.S. 539 (1985) ("When a right defined by state law may be abridged by an act which, in and of itself, would infringe one of the exclusive rights, the state law in question must be deemed preempted. . . . Conversely, when a state law violation is predicated upon an act incorporating elements beyond mere reproduction or the like, the rights involved are not equivalent and preemption will not occur.").

[115] Mayer v. Josiah Wedgwood & Sons, Ltd., 601 F. Supp. 1523, 1535, 225 U.S.P.Q. 776, 784 (S.D. N.Y. 1985).

See also Del Madera Properties v. Rhodes & Gardner, Inc., 820 F.2d 973, 977, 3 U.S.P.Q.2d 1283, 1285 (9th Cir. 1987) ("[t]o survive preemption, the state cause of action must protect rights which are qualitatively different from the copyright rights. . . . The state claim must have an 'extra element' which changes the nature of the action."); Harper & Row Publishers, Inc. v. Nation Enterprises, 723 F.2d 195, 201, 220 U.S.P.Q. 321, 327 (2d Cir. 1983), *rev'd on other grounds*, 471 U.S. 539 (1985) (the "additional elements of awareness and inten-

(1) *Misappropriation—Conversion*. Courts view claims that in essence allege unauthorized copying and distribution of the claimant's work as equivalent to copyright exclusive rights—whether described as "misappropriation," "unfair competition," "conversion," or "interference with contract or business relations."[116]

In *Harper & Row*,[117] the major copyright fair use case, issues arose as to Section 301's preemptive effect on state law conversion and contract interference claims. Former president Gerald Ford granted publishers Harper & Row and Reader's Digest rights to his memoirs. The publishers licensed *Time* magazine to publish pre-publication excerpts. In late 1979, an "unidentified person" brought a copy of the Ford manuscript to *Nation* magazine's editor, Victor Navasky. Navasky read the manuscript, prepared an article paraphrasing and quoting portions of it, and returned the copy to its source. He published the article in *Nation*. *Time* cancelled its excerpt arrangement

---

tional interference" are "not part of a copyright infringement claim" but merely go "to the scope of the right;" they do not "establish qualitatively different conduct on the part of the infringing party, nor a fundamental nonequivalence between the state and federal rights implicated."); Crow v. Wainwright, 720 F.2d 1224, 1226 (11th Cir. 1983), *cert. denied*, 469 U.S. 819 (1984) ("The state criminal statute differs only in that it requires the prosecution to establish scienter, which is not an element of an infringement claim, on the part of the defendant. This distinction alone does not render the elements of the crime different in a meaningful way. . . . Section 506 of the Copyright Act, which sets forth criminal penalties for copyright infringement, also requires the prosecution to prove scienter as an element of the case. . . . The additional element of scienter traditionally necessary to establish a criminal case merely narrows the applicability of the statute. The prohibited act—wrongfully distributing a copyrighted work—remains the same"); Nash v. CBS, Inc., 704 F. Supp. 823, 833, 10 U.S.P.Q.2d 1026, 1034 (N.D. Ill. 1989), *aff'd*, 899 F.2d 1537, 14 U.S.P.Q.2d 1755 (1990) ("the elements of 'scienter,' 'intent,' and 'commercial immorality' required for state law actions for wrongful appropriation are not sufficiently 'different in kind' to preclude preemption").

[116] *E.g.*, Xerox Corp. v. Apple Computer, Inc., 734 F. Supp. 1542, 1550, n.25, 14 U.S.P.Q.2d 1512, 1519 n.25 (N.D. Cal. 1990) ("State law claims of unfair competition based on misappropriation of copyrighted material are preempted by the Copyright Act."); Patsy Aiken Designs, Inc. v. Baby Togs, Inc., 701 F. Supp. 108, 111 (E.D. N.C. 1988) (Section 301 preempts claim for misappropriation of designs on children's clothing; "Federal courts have repeatedly held that state law claims for 'misappropriation' or 'unfair trade practices,' seeking protection against copying, are preempted by the Copyright Act of 1976, 17 U.S.C. § 301. . . . Plaintiff's allegation that defendants' copying caused consumer confusion is not sufficient to support a state law claim for copying. Claims of unfair competition based only on the sale of copies, and no other act, do not contain this extra element, and are, therefore, preempted. . . . Supreme Court holdings . . . also make it clear that federal law preempts state law claims based on confusion caused by a federally protected act of copying."); Galerie Furstenberg v. Coffaro, 697 F. Supp. 1282, 1291, 9 U.S.P.Q.2d 1201, 1206 (S.D. N.Y. 1988) (Section 301 preempts claim that defendants, by selling forged Salvador Dali art works, misappropriate plaintiff's business as an exclusive vendor of Dali drawings and etchings; "Even if [the misappropriation claim] is based upon the New York state law of unfair competition which "requires unfairness and an unjustifiable attempt to profit from another's expenditure of time, labor and talent,' rather than the 'misappropriation form of unfair competition,' it is still preempted under the federal copyright law. 1 Nimmer, § 1.01[B], 1-21.").

[117] Harper & Row Publishers, Inc. v. Nation Enterprises, 723 F.2d 195, 199-200 (2d Cir. 1983), *rev'd on other grounds*, 471 U.S. 539 (1985).

because *Nation* had "scooped" Ford's new revelations concerning former president Richard Nixon's resignation and pardon. The publishers sued *Nation* for copyright infringement and added state law conversion and tortious interference with contractual rights claims. The trial judge dismissed the state law claims upon motion, finding them preempted by Section 301.[118] The Second Circuit affirmed. The publishers' "conversion claim," based on the *Nation* article's authorized publication, is "coextensive with an exclusive right already safeguarded by the Act—namely, control over reproduction and derivative use of copyrighted material."[119] Based solely on *Nation's* temporary possession of the physical papers, the claim would not be preempted[120] but lacks merit as a matter of state law.[121] Their tortious interference claim, based on *Nation's* interference with their opportunity to benefit from pre-book publication serialization rights, is not qualitatively different from the copyright's exclusive derivative work preparation right:[122] "In both cases, it is the act of unauthorized publication which causes the violation. The enjoyment of benefits from derivative use is so intimately bound up with the right itself that it could not possibly be deemed a separate element."[123]

In *Mayer*,[124] plaintiff, an artist, made snowflake designs. In 1979, she contributed a design to the United Nations Children's Fund (UNICEF) for use on a Christmas

---

[118] Harper & Row, Publishers, Inc. v. Nation Enterprises, 501 F. Supp. 848, 212 U.S.P.Q. 274 (S.D. N.Y. 1980), *aff'd*, 723 F.2d 195, 220 U.S.P.Q. 321 (2d Cir. 1983), *rev'd on other grounds*, 471 U.S. 539 (1985).

[119] 703 F.2d at 200, 220 U.S.P.Q. at 326. Accord: Ehat v. Tanner, 780 F.2d 876, 878, 228 U.S.P.Q. 679, 680 (10th Cir. 1985), *cert. denied*, 479 U.S. 820 (1986) (defendants published material that had been surreptitiously copied from plaintiff's scholarly work product, which included quotations from historical documents; that the defendants " 'bodily appropriated the work product of plaintiff' and derived a profit from their misappropriation" does not distinguish the claim from one of copyright infringement; the plaintiff "did not allege a state law claim of conversion to recover for the physical deprivation of his notes. Instead, he sought to recover for damage flowing from their reproduction and distribution.").

[120] *Accord:* Oddo v. Ries, 743 F.2d 630, 635, 222 U.S.P.Q. 799, 802 (9th Cir. 1984) (Section 301 does not preempt claim for "conversion of the papers comprising [plaintiff's] manuscript": "Conversion of tangible property involves actions different from those proscribed by the copyright laws, and thus is not preempted."); Ronald Litoff, Ltd. v. American Express Co., 621 F. Supp. 981, 986, 228 U.S.P.Q. 739, 742 (S.D. N.Y. 1985) ("Insofar as plaintiffs allege a tort involving personal, tangible property, their claim is not preempted. . . . Insofar as plaintiffs allege a claim involving intellectual property, assuming such a claim for conversion exists, their claim is equivalent to a copyright claim and is preempted.").

[121] "Conversion, as thus described, is a tort involving acts—possession and control of chattels—which are qualitatively different from those proscribed by copyright law, and which therefore are not subject to preemption. Cross-appellants have failed, however, to state a conversion claim. Conversion requires not merely temporary interference with property rights, but the exercise of unauthorized dominion and control to the complete exclusion of the rightful possessor. . . . Merely removing one of a number of copies of a manuscript (with or without permission) for a short time, copying parts of it, and returning it undamaged, constitutes far too insubstantial an interference with property rights to demonstrate conversion." 723 F.2d at 201, 220 U.S.P.Q. at 326-27.

[122] For a discussion of the derivative work preparation right, see § 4E[3][b].

[123] 723 F.2d at 201, 220 U.S.P.Q. at 327.

[124] Mayer v. Josiah Wedgwood & Sons, Ltd., 601F. Supp. 1523, 225 U.S.P.Q. 776 (S.D. N.Y. 1985).

card. The card, as published, contained no copyright notice. Plaintiff's agent submitted a proposal to defendant Wedgwood for possible use of the design on a Christmas plate. Wedgwood did not accept the proposal. In 1982, Wedgewood issued a snowflake plate. Plaintiff sued Wedgwood stating two state law claims, conversion of her design, and unfair competition. The court held that Section 301 preempted the claims.[125] The key issue was whether "actions for conversion and the misappropriation branch of unfair competition protect rights that are 'equivalent' to those protected by federal copyright law." Plaintiff's "conversion" claim was not directed to vindication of her right to the physical print that was given to Wedgwood but rather to "the deprivation of the rights flowing from the labor and expertise which she embodied in the snowflake."[126] Her "misappropriation" claims evoked the expansive New York misappropriation action that includes a broad category of " 'commercial immorality' . . . it protects against a defendant's competing use of a valuable product or idea created by the plaintiff through investment of time, effort, money and expertise."[127]

> "The conversion claim fails on its own terms. Count I of the complaint alleges that Mayer 'possessed the right to use, sell, assign or reproduce [the] design' . . . and that JWS Ltd. 'wrongfully converted plaintiff's snowflake design to its own use and benefit by reproducing said design on a 1982 Wedgwood Christmas ornament'. . . . Thus, the rights asserted are clearly the same as those protected by § 106 of the copyright law, and the act constituting the alleged violation of plaintiff's rights corresponds exactly to the act necessary for a copyright infringement. . . . Thus, even assuming that plaintiff may assert a claim for conversion of an intangible property right under New York law . . . that claim is preempted here.

> "As for misappropriation, Mayer asserts that there is in fact an extra element that will save the action from preemption—commercial immorality. But it is hard to see how this is an extra element. In this case, the alleged misappropriation of Mayer's time, talent and effort is by the reproduction of the product of her time, talent and effort, i.e. the snowflake design. . . . That

---

[125] The court held that Section 301 applies to causes of action arising after January 1, 1978, even though the work in question was created before that date.

[126] 601 F. Supp. at 1533, 225 U.S.P.Q. at 782.

Compare National Presto Industries, Inc. v. Hamilton Beach, Inc., 18 U.S.P.Q.2d 1993, 2006 (N.D. Ill. 1990) (distinguishing *Harper & Row* and *Mayer* and finding no preemption of state "conversion" claim based on allegations that defendant obtained a stolen "pilot production unit" of plaintiff's product, which it used to making a competing product; defendant argued that "that in reality [the conversion claim] represents two distinct causes of action, one for common law conversion and another for copying of the product and its packaging and use manual" and that Section 301 preempts the second part; "The preemption analysis has two prongs: first, the product must be copyrightable, and this is not disputed; second, the state law rights must be the equivalent of those conferred by § 106 of the Act. . . . The second prong is the sticking point here. . . . In Illinois, an essential element of the tort of conversion is that 'there . . . be an unauthorized assumption of the right to possession or ownership.' . . . In the Copyright Act, there is no requirement of exclusive control . . . ").

[127] 601 F. Supp. at 1533, 225 U.S.P.Q. at 783.

For a discussion of New York misappropriation doctrine, see § 6F[3].

is precisely the type of misconduct the copyright laws are designed to guard against. To call such conduct immoral adds nothing. 'Commercial immorality' appears to be merely a judgmental label attached to odious business conduct, not an extra element.

"If, however, it is an extra element, it is not the type that would save the action from preemption. It is an extra element in the same sense that awareness and intent are: it alters the *scope* of the action but not its nature. That is, it would permit the action to go forward when the infringing conduct is immoral, but not when it is not immoral. The basic act which constitutes the infringement of plaintiff's rights, however, is the same as that of copyright. The claimed use rights are identical as well. Thus, the cause of action asserted here is not qualitatively different from one for copyright infringement, and accordingly it is preempted."[128]

(2) Misrepresentation, Deception and Unfair Competition. Courts view unfair competition claims requiring proof of misrepresentation or deception or a likelihood of consumer confusion as not equivalent to copyright exclusive rights.[129]

(3) Contract, Trade Secret and Fraud Claims. Courts view contract, trade secret, breach of fiduciary duty, and fraud claims as not equivalent to copyright exclusive rights.[130]

---

[128] 601 F. Supp. at 1535-36, 225 U.S.P.Q. at 784.

[129] Donald Frederick Evans & Associates, Inc., 785 F.2d 897, 229 U.S.P.Q. 321 (11th Cir. 1986); Warner Bros. Inc. v. American Broadcasting Companies, Inc., 720 F.2d 231, 247, 222 U.S.P.Q. 101, 114 (2d Cir. 1983) ("to the extent that plaintiffs are relying on state unfair competition law to allege a tort of 'passing off,' they are not asserting rights equivalent to those protected by copyright and therefore do not encounter preemption."); Nash v. CBS, Inc., 704 F. Supp. 823, 10 U.S.P.Q.2d 1026 (N.D. Ill. 1989), aff'd, 899 F.2d 1537, 14 U.S.P.Q.2d 1755 (7th Cir. 1990) (Section 301 does not preempt state unfair competition law directed at preventing consumer confusion through "reverse passing off," that is, defendant distributing as his own goods or services copied from plaintiff).

[130] *E.g.,* Valente-Kritzer Video v. Pinckney, 881 F.2d 772, 776, 11 U.S.P.Q.2d 1727, 1730 (9th Cir. 1989), *cert. denied,* 110 S. Ct. 879 (1990) ("two district courts have held that common law fraud is not preempted by § 301 because the element of misrepresentation is present. *See Tracy v. Skate Key, Inc.,* 697 F. Supp. 748, 751 (S.D.N.Y.1988); *Brignoli v. Balch Hardy & Scheinman, Inc.,* 645 F. Supp. 1201, 1205 (S.D.N.Y.1986). This conclusion appears to be consistent with congressional intent. See H.R.Rep. No. 94-1476, 94th Cong., 2d Sess. 132 . . . ('[T]he general laws of defamation and fraud, would remain unaffected as long as the causes of action contain elements . . . that are different in kind from copyright infringement.')"); Oddo v. Ries, 743 F.2d 630, 635, 222 U.S.P.Q. 799, 802 (9th Cir. 1984) (Section 301 does not preempt claim for breach of fiduciary arising from plaintiff's and defendant's relation as partners: "Because a partner's duty to his co-partner is quite different from the interests protected by copyright, this cause of action is also not preempted."); Brignoli v. Balch Hardy & Scheinman, Inc., 645 F. Supp. 1201, 1205-06 (S.D. N.Y. 1986) (plaintiff created computer programs "incorporating liquid secondary option market formulas for use in options account management;" plaintiff and defendant agreed that defendant would rent the programs to its clients and pay plaintiff 30% of the proceeds; plaintiff sued defendant alleging various claims, including breach of oral and written agreements and false representations concerning the payments he received, and sought relief against defendant's continued use of the

Merely placing an "implied contract" or "fiduciary duty" label on an improper copying or use claim will not destroy its equivalence to a copyright infringement claim. For example, in *Del Madera*,[131] discussed above, the court held that Del Maderas' fiduciary duty and implied contract claims were copyright equivalents. The consultant's alleged breach of fiduciary duty in using documents and information developed in her relationship with Del Madera to assist the subsequent owner "does not add any 'extra element' which changes the nature of the action" because it "is constructed upon the premise that the documents and information" belonged to Del Madera. "Del Madera's ownership of this material, and the alleged misappropriation

programs; "A claim that a defendant made unauthorized use of copyrightable material falls squarely within § 301 and thus is pre-empted. . . . Nevertheless, plaintiff's claims allege more than unauthorized use. Claims One, Two, Four, and Five are essentially breach of contract claims that involve an element beyond unauthorized reproduction and use—a promise to pay plaintiff for use of his product. . . . The Fourth Claim is one for fraud, involving the extra element of misrepresentation. . . . Although that part of Brignoli's second claim which alleges 'willful unauthorized use of plaintiff's property' might seem to come within § 301, Brignoli's allegations that the programs are trade secrets makes this claim 'qualitatively different' from a copyright claim. To succeed on a trade secret claim, a plaintiff must demonstrate that '(1) it possessed a trade secret, and (2) defendant is using that trade secret in breach of an agreement, confidence, or duty, or as a result of discovery by improper means.' "; "the Sixth Claim alleges a breach of an agreement of confidentiality or duty of confidentiality. Such a claim is not equivalent to a copyright claim. . . . The Seventh Claim survives as a 'palming off' claim, . . . and as such is not pre-empted."); Smith v. Weinstein, 578 F. Supp. 1297, 1307, 222 U.S.P.Q. 381 (S.D. N.Y. 1984), *aff'd*, 38 F.2d 419 (2d Cir. 1984) (table) (Section 301 does not preempt a quasi-contract claim based on submission of ideas: "Plaintiff cannot merely rephrase the same claim citing contract law and thereby obtain relief equivalent to that which he has failed to obtain under copyright law. . . . But plaintiff also claims that Weinstein agreed, expressly or implicitly, to pay him for the value of his ideas if she decided to use them. A party may by contract agree to pay for ideas, even though such ideas could not be protected by copyright law. Rights under such an agreement are qualitatively different from copyright claims, and their recognition creates no monopoly in the ideas involved. Similarly, plaintiff's breach of confidence claim is nonequivalent to the rights one can acquire under copyright law; rather it rests on an obligation not to disclose to third parties ideas revealed in confidence, which obligation is judicially imposed only upon a party that accepts the relationship, and thus results in no monopoly. In short, these claims, narrowly read, focus on the relationship between individual parties and make actionable breaches of agreements between parties, or breaches of the trust they place in each other because of the nature of their relationship."). *Compare* Valente-Kritzer Video v. Pinckney, 881 F.2d 772, 11 U.S.P.Q.2d 1727 (9th Cir. 1989), *cert. denied*, 110 S. Ct. 879 (1990) (action for breach of oral agreement to transfer rights to make a videocassette version of plaintiff's book is preempted because the Copyright Act requires copyright transfers to be in writing; plaintiff's contention that the oral agreement can be severed into two parts, one to transfer, and one to pay a "finder's fee," the latter being enforceable, must be rejected because "the agreement between the parties embodied only one exchange and one agreement.;" claim for "tortious breach of contract" is preempted for the same reason); Videotronics, Inc. v. Bend Electronics, 564 F. Supp. 1471, 223 U.S.P.Q. 296 (D. Nev. 1983) (federal copyright policy preempts plaintiff's trade secret and misappropriation claims based on defendant's copying of the videogame computer program).

[131] Del Madera Properties v. Rhodes & Gardner, Inc., 820 F.2d 973, 3 U.S.P.Q.2d 1283 (9th Cir. 1987).

by the defendants, are part and parcel of the copyright claim."[132] Del Madera based its unjust enrichment claim on the defendants' violation of an implied promise derived from the parties' relation not to use the Tentative Map and supporting documents, but "an implied promise not to use or copy materials within the subject matter of copyright is equivalent to the protection provided by section 106 of the Copyright Act."[133]

(4) Publicity Rights. Many personal identity aspects, such as name and likeness, are not works of authorship eligible for copyright protection and therefore Section 301 does not preempt the protection afforded by publicity rights.[134] When an aspect, such as a person's distinctive performance, is a work and is sufficiently fixed in a tangible medium of expression, Section 301's rights equivalency requirement must be applied.

In *Baltimore Orioles,*[135] the Seventh Circuit held that Section 301 preempted major league baseball players' claim that television broadcast of their game performances violated their state law publicity rights. The players' asserted publicity rights in broadcasts of their performances were rights equivalent to the copyright right of public performance, which includes broadcasting.[136] The players argued that "their rights of publicity in their performances are not equivalent to the rights contained in a copyright because rights of publicity and copyrights serve different interests."

[132] 820 F.2d at 977, 3 U.S.P.Q.2d at 1286.

[133] *Id.*

[134] *See* § 6G[4][c][ii].

[135] Baltimore Orioles, Inc. v. Major League Baseball Players Association, 805 F.2d 663, 231 U.S.P.Q. 673 (7th Cir. 1986), *cert. denied,* 480 U.S. 941 (1987). *See also* Brode v. Tax Management, Inc., 14 U.S.P.Q.2d 1195 (N.D. Ill. 1990) (Section 301 preempts plaintiff's publicity right claim based on unauthorized reproduction and distribution of his copyrighted work).

Compare Factors Etc., Inc. v. Pro-Arts, Inc., 496 F. Supp. 1090, 1100, 208 U.S.P.Q. 529 (S.D. N.Y. 1980), *rev'd on other grounds,* 652 F.2d 278, 211 U.S.P.Q. 1 (2d Cir.1981), *cert. denied,* 456 U.S. 927 (1982) (concerning Elvis Presley memorabilia; "the exploitation of a celebrity's name and image during his lifetime creates a 'separate intangible property right.' . . . This right is not 'equivalent' to a copyright, and in [an] action for its infringement requires elements distinct from a copyright violation suit. . . . In light of the Congressional intent reflected in the legislative history of the 1976 Act, Supreme Court decisions discussing the interplay between state-created rights and federal copyright or patent law and the distinctions between the right of publicity and copyright, this Court concludes that the plaintiffs' right of publicity is neither contrary to nor preempted by federal law. This right covers an 'area unattended' by federal law and is not equivalent to the general scope of copyright law. The plaintiffs' prior right to exploit the Presley name and image cannot be defeated by the defendants' attempt to copyright individual items. Nor is the defendants' allegation that the photograph was in the public domain an adequate defense to the plaintiffs' infringement action. The right of exploitation had previously been established and exercised and could not be thwarted by the use of a published photograph. The right of publicity . . . would be severely undermined if it could be so easily circumvented by using a photograph or representation allegedly copyrighted or within the public domain.").

For other discussions of *Baltimore Orioles,* see §§ 1D[3][c][i] and 6G[4][c][ii].

[136] *See* § 4E[4].

"In their view, the purpose of federal copyright law is to secure a benefit to the public, but the purpose of state statutory or common law concerning rights of publicity is to protect individual pecuniary interests. We disagree.

"The purpose of federal copyright protection is to benefit the public by encouraging works in which it is interested. To induce individuals to undertake the personal sacrifices necessary to create such works, federal copyright law extends to the authors of such works a limited monopoly to reap the rewards of their endeavors. . . . Contrary to the Players' contention, the interest underlying the recognition of the right of publicity also is the promotion of performances that appeal to the public. The reason that state law protects individual pecuniary interests is to provide an incentive to performers to invest the time and resources required to develop such performances. In *Zacchini* . . . the Supreme Court recognized that the interest behind federal copyright protection is the advancement of the public welfare through the encouragement of individual effort by personal gain, . . . and that a state's interest in affording a cause of action for violation of the right to publicity 'is closely analogous to the goals of patent and copyright law.' . . . Because the right of publicity does not differ in kind from copyright, the Players' rights of publicity in their performances cannot escape preemption." [137]

The court disagreed with other court decisions that broadly state that Section 301(a) does not preempt publicity rights because the latter are derived from privacy interests. [138]

---

[137] 805 F.2d at 677-79, 231 U.S.P.Q. at 683.

For discussions of *Zacchini*, see §§ 1D[4] and 6G[4][b].

[138] "The Players cite to four opinions to support their assertion that § 301(a) does not preempt the right of publicity. See *Factors Etc., Inc. v. Pro Arts, Inc.*, 652 F.2d 278, 289 (2d Cir.1981) (Mansfield, J., dissenting), *cert. denied*, 456 U.S. 927, 102 S. Ct. 1937, 72 L. Ed. 2d 422 (1982); *Bi-Rite Enterprises, Inc. v. Button Master*, 555 F. Supp. 1188, 1201 (S.D.N.Y.1983); *Apigram Publishing Co. v. Factors Etc., Inc.*, No. C 78-525, slip op. (N.D.Ohio July 30, 1980) (available on LEXIS); *Lugosi v. Universal Pictures*, 25 Cal. 3d 813, 850, 603 P.2d 425, 448, 160 Cal. Rptr. 323, 346 (1979) (Bird, C.J., dissenting). Each opinion is premised upon an erroneous analysis of preemption. The *Factors* dissent, the *Bi-Rite* court, and the *Lugosi* dissent assert without discussion that the right of publicity is not preempted because the work that it protects—a public figure's persona—cannot be fixed in a tangible medium of expression. We disagree. Because a performance is fixed in tangible form when it is recorded, a right of publicity in a performance that has been reduced to tangible form is subject to preemption.

"The *Apigram* court stated without extended discussion or citation to authority that the right of publicity is not preempted because it requires additional elements other than the reproduction, performance, distribution or display of a copyrighted work. We disagree. Congress intended that '[t]he evolving common law rights of "privacy," "publicity," and trade secrets and the general law of defamation and fraud, would remain unaffected [by § 301(a)] so long as the causes of action contain elements such as an invasion of privacy or a breach of trust or confidentiality, that are different in kind from copyright infringement.' House Report at 132 . . . (emphasis added). Thus, a right is equivalent to a copyright if (1) it is infringed by the mere act of reproduction, performance, distribution, or display, or (2) it requires additional elements to make out a cause of action, but the additional elements do not differ in kind from those necessary for copyright infringement. . . . Contrary to the belief of the *Apigram*

(5) *Artists' and Authors' Moral Rights.* State laws provide artists and authors with rights of attribution, integrity, and resale royalties in their works.[139] These are comparable to the "moral rights" of authors recognized in Europe and the Berne copyright convention. Courts view these rights as not preempted because they involved extra elements.[140] In 1990, Congress enacted the Visual Artists Rights Act, which contains a preemption provision.[141]

In *Morseburg*,[142] the Ninth Circuit held that the 1909 Copyright Act and constitutional preemption principles did not preempt California's Resale Royalties Act,[143] which required sellers of fine art works to pay a 5% royalty to the artist.[144]

---

court, the right of publicity does not require an invasion of personal privacy to make out a cause of action. It is true that the rights of publicity and of privacy evolved from similar origins; however, whereas the right of privacy protects against intrusions on seclusion, public disclosure of private facts, and casting an individual in a false light in the public eye, the right of publicity protects against the unauthorized exploitation of names, likenesses, personalities, and performances that have acquired value for the very reason that they are known to the public. . . . Because the right of publicity does not require a qualitatively different additional element, it is equivalent to a copyright and is preempted to the extent that it is claimed in a tangible work within the subject matter of copyright." 805 F.2d at 678 n.26, 231 U.S.P.Q. 683-84 n.26.

[139] *See* § 4E[6].

[140] Morseburg v. Balyon, 621 F.2d 972, 207 U.S.P.Q. 183 (9th Cir. 1980), *cert. denied*, 449 U.S. 983, 208 U.S.P.Q. 464 (1980); Wojnarowicz v. American Family Association, 745 F. Supp. 130, 17 U.S.P.Q.2d 1337 (S.D. N.Y. 1990).

Compare Peckarsky v. American Broadcasting Company, Inc., 603 F. Supp. 688, 695-96 (D. D.C. 1984) (Section 301 preempts plaintiff's claim that defendant's used his copyrighted article in newscasts without attributing authorship to him: "The rights to control the use or reproduction of copyrighted work are explicitly protected by section 106 of the Copyright Act. . . . Although section 106 does not explicitly protect the right of attribution of authorship, assertion of such a claim in an otherwise pre-empted common law action will not save the common law claim from pre-emption.").

[141] 17 U.S.C. § 301(f)(1).

See § 4E[6].

[142] Morseburg v. Balyon, 621 F.2d 972, 207 U.S.P.Q. 183 (9th Cir. 1980), *cert. denied*, 449 U.S. 983, 208 U.S.P.Q. 464 (1980).

[143] The court described the California statute's origins.

"[I]t is frequently the case that ['works of fine art'] are not copyrighted and that the sales proceeds realized by the artist upon its first sale are significantly less than the prices at which it subsequently changes hands. . . . There are several explanations for both circumstances. The failure to utilize copyright protection has its source in, among other things, ignorance, a distaste for legal details, weak bargaining power, and the desire to avoid defacing the work with a copyright symbol. . . . An increase in the price of an artist's works after they have left his hands may be the result of greater recognition of the artist, an increase in the overall demand for art works, inflation, unpredictable shifts in fashion and taste, or some combination of the above. The California Act functions under these conditions. It is an American version of what the French call the droit de suite, an art proceeds right. . . . It provides by force of state law a conditional economic interest of a limited duration in the proceeds of sales other than the initial one. Similar rights perhaps could be obtained by contract. . . . Opinions differ as to whether the existence of such an interest, without regard to its source, will increase the incentives to produce available to the young and not well known artist. . . . Some argue that only a few artists

It noted that "[w]ith respect to preemption the Supreme Court's emphasis varies from time to time."[145] The basic doctrinal notions are "the extent to which the federal law has 'occupied the field' and the presence of 'conflict' between the federal and state law."[146] The emphasis placed on these notions varies not only with the Supreme Court's "cyclical" attitude toward preemption but also with "the area of the law in which the issues arises." In the area of intellectual property, *Goldstein* reflects a lenient attitude toward state law and policy. The California Act does not conflict with the 1909 Copyright Act's exclusive right to "vend" copyrighted works, including works of art.

> "[T]he 1909 Copyright Act has not occupied the area with which we are concerned and that the California Act is not in conflict with it. A resale royalty is not provided by the 1909 Act; no hostility toward such a royalty is expressed by the Act; and, on the facts before us, the obligation to pay a resale royalty does not impermissibly restrict resales by the owners of works of fine art. The teaching of *Goldstein* is not limited to situations in which the matter regulated by state law is not covered by the 1909 Act. *Kewanee Oil Co. v. Bicron Corp.* . . . The crucial inquiry is not whether state law reaches matters also subject to federal regulation, but whether the two laws function harmoniously rather than discordantly. We find no discord in this instance."[147]

In *Wojnarowicz*,[148] the court held that Section 301 did not preempt an artist's claim based on the New York Artists' Authorship Rights Act that the defendant reproduced and distributed "mutilated" versions of his works in a pamphlet. The court distinguished *Tracy*[149] and *Ronald Litoff*,[150] which "involved the preemption of a

---

will benefit, as appears to have been the French experience, while others believe such an interest prevents exploitation of the artist's creativity." 621 F.2d at 975–76.

[144] Section 301 did not apply because the 1976 Act became effective after the sales in question. Though applying only the 1909 Act and constitutional preemption principles, the court noted that "[i]t is unavoidable that certain of our reasons will be weighed and measured to determine their applicability to the 1976 Act." 621 F.2d at 975.

[145] "At times the preemption doctrine has been applied with nationalistic fervor while during other periods with generous tolerance of state involvement in areas already to some extent the subject of national concern." 621 F.2d at 976.

[146] "The nature of the Court's emphasis at a particular time is revealed by whether 'occupation of the field' and 'conflict' are easily found to exist or not. 'Occupation' can require no more than the existence of a federal law generally applicable to a significant portion of the area in question to no less than an express statement demonstrating an intention to occupy the area duly enacted by Congress. 'Conflict,' likewise, can require no more than a mechanical demonstration of potential conflict between federal and state law to no less than a showing of substantial frustration of an important purpose of the federal law by the challenged state law. When the emphasis is to protect and strengthen national power 'occupation' and 'conflict' are easily found while not so easily found when the emphasis is to promote federalism." 621 F.2d at 976.

[147] 621 F.2d at 978.

[148] Wojnarowicz v. American Family Association, 745 F. Supp. 130, 17 U.S.P.Q.2d 1337 (S.D. N.Y. 1990), discussed at § 4E[6].

[149] Tracy v. Skate Key, Inc., 697 F. Supp. 748 (S.D. N.Y. 1988).

[150] Ronald Litoff, Ltd. v. American Express Co., 621 F. Supp. 981 (S.D. N.Y. 1985).

section of the N.Y. Arts and Cultural Affairs Law concerning only the right of reproduction, a property right expressly granted in, and thus preempted by the Copyright Act." "Neither case concerned a claim that defendant had mutilated an artwork, attributed it to the plaintiff and damaged his reputation."[151]

> "Although the rights to reproduce and to produce derivative work are protected by the Copyright Act, section 14.03 of the New York Artists' Authorship Rights Act as amended is indeed qualitatively different than federal copyright law in both its aim and its elements. The state Act endeavors to protect an artist's reputation from the attribution to him of altered, defaced, mutilated or modified works of art. . . . Moreover, a claim under this statute requires proof of elements not required to prove copyright infringement, namely (a) the artwork must be altered, defaced, mutilated or modified; (b) the altered, defaced, mutilated or modified artwork must be attributed to the artist, or displayed in such circumstances as to be reasonably understood to be his work; and (c) this attribution must be reasonably likely to damage the artist's reputation. . . . While both plaintiff's state law and copyright claims are based upon the same cropped reproductions contained in the AFA pamphlet, they are qualitatively different and hence there is no preemption."[152]

[4] Other Constitutional Restraints on State and Federal Intellectual Property Laws

Because intellectual property laws both provide incentives for and restrict the public expression of ideas, it is not surprising that rights claimants and accused infringers have on occasion challenged particular applications of those laws as contrary to the Constitution's first amendment free speech-free press guarantees. Courts reject most challenges because intellectual property laws contain limiting doctrines that prevent impingement upon first amendment values.[153]

In *Harper & Row,*[154] the Supreme Court saw no need for a "public figure" exception to copyright: "In view of the First Amendment protections already embodied in the Copyright Act's distinction between copyrightable expression and uncopyrightable facts and ideas, and the latitude for scholarship and comment traditionally afforded by fair use, we see no warrant for expanding the doctrine of fair use to create what amounts to a public figure exception to copyright."[155]

---

[151] 745 F. Supp. at 135 n.1, 17 U.S.P.Q.2d at 1341 n.1.

[152] 745 F. Supp. at 135-36, 17 U.S.P.Q.2d at 1341.

[153] *See, e.g.,* § 4F[3][d] (copyright fair use doctrine); § 5F[1][d][ii] (trademark parody).

[154] Harper & Row, Publishers, Inc. v. Nation Enterprises, 471 U.S. 539, 556, 225 U.S.P.Q. 1073, 1079 (1985), discussed at § 4F[3][a][ii] (copyright's idea and expression dichotomy " 'strike[s] a definitional balance between the First Amendment and the Copyright Act by permitting free communication of facts while still protecting an author's expression.' ").

[155] 471 U.S. at 560, 225 U.S.P.Q. at 1080-81.

See also Zacchini v. Scripps-Howard Broadcasting Co., 433 U.S. 562, 577 n.13, 205 U.S.P.Q. 741 (1977) ("We note that Federal District Courts have rejected First Amendment challenges to the federal copyright law on the ground that 'no restraint (has been) placed on the use of an idea or concept.' *United States v. Bodin,* 375 F. Supp. 1265, 1267 (W.D. Okla. 1974). *See also Walt Disney Productions v. Air Pirates,* 345 F. Supp. 108, 115-116 (N.D.Cal.1972)

In *Zacchini*,[156] the Court held that the first amendment was no defense to a state publicity right damage claim for unauthorized television news broadcast of a performer's entire 15-second "human cannonball" act. It distinguished cases limiting state law defamation recovery.

> "None of [the defamation cases] involve an alleged appropriation by the press of a right of publicity existing under state law. . . . [Those cases] involved the reporting of events; in none of them was there an attempt to broadcast or publish an entire act for which the performer ordinarily gets paid. . . . [P]etitioner's state-law right of publicity would not serve to prevent respondent from reporting the newsworthy facts about petitioner's act. . . . Wherever the line in particular situations is to be drawn between media reports that are protected and those that are not, we are quite sure that the First and Fourteenth Amendments do not immunize the media when they broadcast a performer's entire act without his consent. The Constitution no more prevents a State from requiring respondent to compensate petitioner for broadcasting his act on television than it would privilege respondent to film and broadcast a copyrighted dramatic work without liability to the copyright owner."[157]

In *Mitchell*,[158] the Fifth Circuit noted that "Congress in not enacting an obscenity exception to copyrightability avoids substantial practical difficulties and delicate First Amendment issues."

First amendment problems occasionally arise when claimants seek to expand state or federal intellectual property rights beyond their traditional limits. For example, in *L.L. Bean*,[159] the First Circuit relied in part on free expression concerns to deny state anti-dilution protection against noncommercial trademark parody.

(Text continued on page 1–48)

(citing Nimmer, *Does Copyright Abridge The First Amendment Guarantees of Free Speech and Press?*, 17 UCLA Rev. 1180 (1970), who argues that copyright law does not abridge the First Amendment because it does not restrain the communication of ideas or concepts); *Robert Stigwood Group Ltd. v. O'Reilly*, 346 F. Supp. 376 (Conn.1972) (also relying on Nimmer, *supra*).").

[156] Zacchini v. Scripps-Howard Broadcasting Co., 433 U.S. 562, 578, 205 U.S.P.Q. 741 (1977), discussed at § 6G[4][b].

[157] 433 U.S. at 574–75.

[158] Mitchell Brothers Film Group v. Cinema Adult Theater, 604 F.2d 852, 203 U.S.P.Q. 1041 (5th Cir. 1979), *cert. denied, sub nom.*, Bora v. Mitchell Brothers Film Group, 445 U.S. 917 (1980).

Compare In re McGinley, 660 F.2d 481, 211 U.S.P.Q. 668 (CCPA 1981) (first amendment does not guarantee a right to register an immoral or scandalous mark even though the subject matter of the mark is not obscene under first amendment standards).

[159] L.L. Bean, Inc. v. Drake Publishers, Inc., 811 F.2d 26, 1 U.S.P.Q.2d 1753 (1st Cir. 1987), *appeal dismissed, cert. denied*, 483 U.S. 1013 (1987). *Compare* Dallas Cowboys Cheerleaders, Inc. v. Pussycat Cinema, Ltd., 604 F.2d 200 (2d Cir. 1979).

In Silverman v. CBS Inc., 870 F.2d 40, 9 U.S.P.Q.2d 1778 (2d Cir. 1989), the court held that the owner of trademark rights in the "Amos and Andy" characters, which formed the basis of popular radio broadcast shows from 1928 to 1955, legally abandoned those rights by ceasing to use the marks for 21 years "in response to complaints by civil rights organizations, including the NAACP, that the programs were demeaning to Blacks." For a discussion

(Text continued on page 1–48)

of trademark abandonment, see § 5D[3][a][iii]. CBS refused grant Silverman a license to produce a Broadway show based on the characters. The court relied in part on first amendment free expression concerns.

"An adjudication of trademark rights often involves a balancing of competing interests. . . . In weighing the competing interests and reaching our conclusion concerning abandonment, we are influenced in part by the context in which this dispute arises—one in which the allegedly infringing use is in connection with a work of artistic expression. Just as First Amendment values inform application of the idea/expression dichotomy in copyright law, . . . in similar fashion such values have some bearing upon the extent of protection accorded a trademark proprietor against use of the mark in works of artistic expression. Ordinarily, the use of a trademark to identify a commodity or a business 'is a form of commercial speech and nothing more.' . . . Requiring a commercial speaker to choose words and labels that do not confuse or deceive protects the public and does not impair expression. . . . *cf.* Vidal Sassoon, Inc. v. Bristol- Myers Co., 661 F.2d 272, 276 n. 8 (2d Cir. 1981) (First Amendment concerns do not justify alteration of normal standard of preliminary injunctive relief on Lanham Act claim involving shampoo advertisements). In the area of artistic speech, however, enforcement of trademark rights carries a risk of inhibiting free expression, . . . not only in the case at hand but in other situations where authors might contemplate use of trademarks in connection with works of artistic expression. . . . From the standpoint of the proprietor of a mark in a work of artistic expression, there is also an interest in expression, along with the traditional trademark interest in avoiding public confusion as to source. Trademark law can contribute to a favorable climate for expression by complementing the economic incentive that copyright law provides to create and disseminate artistic works . . . In this case, however, the expression interest on CBS's side is markedly diminished by its decision to withhold dissemination of the works with which its marks are associated. The interest of CBS, and the public, in avoiding public confusion, an interest obviously entitled to weight in every trademark case, is also somewhat diminished in the context of this case. This interest is not as weighty as in a case involving a non-artistic product whose trademark is associated with high quality or other consumer benefits. Though Silverman undoubtedly hopes that some of his audience will be drawn from those who favorably recall the Amos 'n Andy' programs, we doubt if many who attend Broadway musicals are motivated to purchase tickets because of a belief that the musical is produced by the same entity responsible for the movie, book, or radio or television series on which it is based. That is not to say that the musical is in a sufficiently distinct line of commerce to preclude all protection; the holder of a mark associated with a television series would normally be entitled to 'bridge the gap' and secure some protection against an infringing use of the mark in connection with a Broadway musical. It is to say, however, that most theater-goers have sufficient awareness that the quality of a musical depends so heavily on a combination of circumstances, including script, score, lyrics, cast, and direction, that they are not likely to be significantly influenced in their ticket-purchasing decision by an erroneous belief that the musical emanated from the same production source as the underlying work. The point must not be overstated. Trademark protection is not lost simply because the allegedly infringing use is in connection with a work of artistic expression. But in determining the outer limits of trademark protection—here, concerning the concept of abandonment—the balance of risks just noted is relevant and in some cases may tip the scales against trademark protection." 870 F.2d at 47–49.

Two Supreme Court decisions involve First Amendment challenges to state and federal laws defining what may constitute intellectual property. In *Rogers*,[160] the Court upheld a state law withholding a traditional form of intellectual property right, trademark protection, from a particular kind of business. In *San Francisco Arts and Athletics*,[161] it upheld a federal law extending protection beyond traditional limits by granting rights in a work without regard to likelihood of confusion of origin or endorsement. In *Rogers*, the plaintiff challenged a Texas law that prohibited optometrists from doing business under a tradename. The Court noted that a tradename enjoys little First Amendment protection because it is a "commercial speech that has no intrinsic meaning." Use of tradenames can create opportunities to deceive the public that a state may wish to prevent.[162] An *established* trade name may become a valuable property interest,[163] but "a property interest in a means of communication does not enlarge or diminish the First Amendment protection of that communication."

---

[160] Friedman v. Rogers, 440 U.S. 1 (1979).

[161] San Francisco Arts & Athletics, Inc. v. United States Olympic Committee, 483 U.S. 522, 3 U.S.P.Q.2d 1145 (1987).

[162] "A trade name conveys no information about the price and nature of the services offered by an optometrist until it acquires meaning over a period of time by associations formed in the minds of the public between the name and some standard of price or quality. . . . Because these ill-defined associations of trade names with price and quality information can be manipulated by the users of trade names, there is a significant possibility that trade names will be used to mislead the public.

"The possibilities for deception are numerous. The trade name of an optometrical practice can remain unchanged despite changes in the staff of optometrists upon whose skill and care and [*sic*: the] public depends when it patronizes the practice. Thus, the public may be attracted by a trade name that reflects the reputation of an optometrist no longer associated with the practice. A trade name frees an optometrist from dependence on his personal reputation to attract clients, and even allows him to assume a new trade name if negligence or misconduct casts a shadow over the old one. By using different trade names at shops under his common ownership, an optometrist can give the public the false impression of competition among the shops. The use of a trade name also facilitates the advertising essential to large-scale commercial practices with numerous branch offices, conduct the State rationally may wish to discourage while not prohibiting commercial optometrical practice altogether." 440 U.S. at 12–13.

[163] "A trade name that has acquired such associations to the extent of establishing a secondary meaning becomes a valuable property of the business, protected from appropriation by others. The value as a business asset of a trade name with secondary meaning has been recognized in the limitations imposed on the Federal Trade Commission's remedial powers under § 5 of the Federal Trade Commission Act, 15 U.S.C. § 45, which prohibits 'unfair methods of competition.' Because of the property value of trade names, the Court held in *FTC. v. Royal Milling Co.*, 288 U.S. 212, 217-218 (1933), and *Jacob Siegel Co. v. FTC* 327 U.S. 608, 611-613 (1946), that before prohibiting the use of a trade name under § 5, the F.T.C. must determine that the deceptive or misleading use of the name cannot be remedied by any means short of its proscription. But a property interest in a means of communication does not enlarge or diminish the First Amendment protection of that communication. Accordingly, there is no First Amendment rule, comparable to the limitation on § 5, requiring a State to allow deceptive or misleading commercial speech whenever the publication of additional information can clarify or offset the effects of the spurious communication." 440 U.S. at 13 n.11.

The plaintiffs did not assert that their property interests had been taken.

San Francisco Arts and Athletics concerned the Amateur Sports Act of 1978,[164] which authorizes the United States Olympic Committee ("USOC") to prohibit certain commercial and promotional uses of the word "Olympic."

---

[164] 36 U.S.C. §§ 371–396. The Act's Section 110 provides:

"(a) Without the consent of the [USOC], any person who uses for the purpose of trade, to induce the sale of any goods or services, or to promote any theatrical exhibition, athletic performance, or competition—

"(1) the symbol of the International Olympic Committee, consisting of 5 interlocking rings;

"(2) the emblem of the [USOC], consisting of an escutcheon having a blue chief and vertically extending red and white bars on the base with 5 interlocking rings displayed on the chief;

"(3) any trademark, trade name, sign, symbol, or insignia falsely representing association with, or authorization by, the International Olympic Committee or the [USOC]; or

"(4) the words 'Olympic', 'Olympiad', 'Citius Altius Fortius', or any combination or simulation thereof tending to cause confusion, to cause mistake, to deceive, or to falsely suggest a connection with the [USOC] or any Olympic activity;

"shall be subject to suit in a civil action by the [USOC] for the remedies provided in the Act of July 5, 1946 (60 Stat. 427; popularly known as the Trademark Act of 1946 [Lanham Act]) [15 U.S.C. § 1051 *et seq.*]. However, any person who actually used the emblem in subsection (a)(2) of this section, or the words, or any combination thereof, in subsection (a)(4) of this section for any lawful purpose prior to September 21, 1950, shall not be prohibited by this section from continuing such lawful use for the same purpose and for the same goods or services. In addition, any person who actually used, or whose assignor actually used, any other trademark, trade name, sign, symbol, or insignia described in subsections (a)(3) and (4) of this section for any lawful purpose prior to September 21, 1950 shall not be prohibited by this section from continuing such lawful use for the same purpose and for the same goods or services.

"(b) The [USOC] may authorize contributors and suppliers of goods or services to use the trade name of the [USOC] as well as any trademark, symbol, insignia, or emblem of the International Olympic Committee or of the [USOC] in advertising that the contributions, goods, or services were donated, supplied, or furnished to or for the use of, approved, selected, or used by the [USOC] or United States Olympic or Pan-American team or team members.

"(c) The [USOC] shall have exclusive right to use the name United States Olympic Committee'; the symbol described in subsection (a)(1) of this section; the emblem described in subsection (a)(2) of this section; and the words 'Olympic', 'Olympiad', 'Citius Altius Fortius' or any combination thereof subject to the preexisting rights described in subsection (a) of this section." 36 U.S.C. § 380.

The Court noted that "[t]his grant by statute of exclusive use of distinctive words and symbols by Congress is not unique."

"Violation of some of these statutes may result in criminal penalties. *See, e.g.,* 18 U.S.C. § 705 (veterans' organizations); § 706 (American National Red Cross); § 707 (4-H Club); § 711 ("Smokey Bear"); § 711a ("Woodsy Owl"). *See also* Federal Trade Comm'n v. A.P.W. Paper Co., Inc., 328 U.S. 193 (1946) (reviewing application of Red Cross statute). Others, like the USOC statute, provide for civil enforcement. *See, e.g.,* 36 U.S.C. § 18c (Daughters of the American Revolution); § 27 (Boy Scouts); § 36 (Girl Scouts); § 1086 (Little League Baseball); § 3305 (American National Theater and Academy)." 483 U.S. at 532 n.8.

Formed in 1981, San Francisco Arts & Athletics, Inc. ("SFAA") planned and promoted the "Gay Olympic Games," the inaugural games to be held in San Francisco in August 1982. The lower courts granted the USOC a permanent injunction prohibiting SFAA from using "Olympic." They held that (1) the Act granted the USOC exclusive use of the word "Olympic" without requiring the USOC to prove that an unauthorized use was confusing in the trademark law sense,[165] (2) SFAA's contention that the USOC enforced its rights in a discriminatory manner need not be reached because the USOC is not a state actor bound by the Constitution's due process and equal protection constraints, and (3) USOC's "property right[s] [in the word 'Olympic' and its associated symbols and slogans] can be protected without violating the First Amendment."[166]

A sharply divided Supreme Court affirmed. The majority, in an opinion by Justice Powell, held that "the language and legislative history of § 110 indicate clearly that Congress intended to grant the USOC exclusive use of the word 'Olympic' without regard to whether use of the word tends to cause confusion, and that § 110 does not incorporate defenses available under the Lanham Act."[167] It rejected SFAA's arguments that (1) "Olympic" is a generic word that cannot gain trademark protection, and the First Amendment prohibits Congress from granting a trademark in a generic word, (2) "the First Amendment prohibits Congress from granting exclusive use of a word absent a requirement that the authorized user prove that an unauthorized use is likely to cause confusion", and (3) "USOC's enforcement of [its statutory] right is discriminatory in violation of the Fifth Amendment."

First, the majority recognized that "words are not always fungible, and that the suppression of particular words 'run[s] a substantial risk of suppressing ideas in the process'," but this recognition "always has been balanced against the principle that when a word acquires value 'as the result of organization and the expenditure of labor, skill, and money' by an entity, that entity constitutionally may obtain a limited property right in the word."[168] Congress did not "simply [pluck] a generic word out of the English vocabulary and [grant] its exclusive use to the USOC." Congress could reasonably conclude that the word's commercial and promotional value was the product of the USOC's time, effort and expense.[169]

---

[165] For a discussion of trademark law's likelihood of confusion standard, see § 5F.

[166] International Olympic Committee v. San Francisco Arts & Athletics, 781 F.2d 733, 737, 228 U.S.P.Q. 585, 587 (9th Cir. 1986).

[167] 483 U.S. at 530, 3 U.S.P.Q.2d at 1149.

[168] 483 U.S. at 532, 3 U.S.P.Q.2d at 1150.

The Court cited International News Service v. Associated Press, 248 U.S. 215, 239 (1918), the controversial misappropriation decision, discussed at § 6F[1].

[169] "The USOC, together with respondent International Olympic Committee (IOC), have used the word 'Olympic' at least since 1896, when the modern Olympic Games began. . . . Baron Pierre de Coubertin of France, acting pursuant to a government commission, then proposed the revival of the ancient Olympic Games to promote international understanding. . . . Coubertin sought to identify the 'spirit' of the ancient Olympic Games that had been corrupted by the influence of money and politics.

"Coubertin . . . formed the IOC, that has established elaborate rules and procedures for the conduct of the modern Olympics. . . . In addition, these rules direct every national committee to protect the use of the Olympic flag, symbol, flame, and motto from unauthorized

"Congress reasonably could find that since 1896, the word 'Olympic' has acquired what in trademark law is known as a secondary meaning—it 'has become distinctive of [the USOC's] goods in commerce.' Lanham Act, § 2(f), 15 U.S.C. § 1052(f). . . . The right to adopt and use such a word 'to distinguish the goods or property [of] the person whose mark it is, to the exclusion of use by all other persons, has been long recognized.' Trade-Mark Cases, . . . 100 U.S. (10 Otto), at 92. Because Congress reasonably could conclude that the USOC has distinguished the word 'Olympic' through its own efforts, Congress' decision to grant the USOC a limited property right in the word 'Olympic' falls within the scope of trademark law protections, and thus certainly within constitutional bounds." [170]

Therefore, "[t]here is no need in this case to decide whether Congress ever could grant a private entity exclusive use of a generic word." [171]

Second, the majority concluded that "Congress also acted reasonably when it concluded that the USOC should not be required to prove that an unauthorized use of the word 'Olympic' is likely to confuse the public." Most of the prohibited uses are to promote sales of goods, services and events and therefore commercial speech, which receives only limited First Amendment protection. The Act might apply to noncommercial political speech, but any "restrictions on expressive speech properly are characterized as incidental to the primary congressional purpose of encouraging and rewarding the USOC's activities." [172]

"The appropriate inquiry is . . . whether the incidental restrictions on First Amendment freedoms are greater than necessary to further a substantial governmental interest.

"One reason for Congress to grant the USOC exclusive control of the word 'Olympic', as with other trademarks, is to ensure that the USOC receives the benefit of its own efforts so that the USOC will have an incentive to continue to produce a 'quality product,' that, in turn, benefits the public. . . . But in the special circumstance of the USOC, Congress has a broader public interest in promoting, through the activities of the USOC, the participation of amateur athletes from the United States in 'the great four-yearly sport festival, the Olympic Games.' . . . Section 110 directly advances these governmental interests by supplying the USOC with the means to raise money to support the Olympics and encourages the USOC's activities by ensuring that it will receive the benefits of its efforts.

"The restrictions of § 110 are not broader than Congress reasonably could have determined to be necessary to further these interests. Section 110 primarily

---

use. . . . Under the IOC Charter, the USOC is the national olympic committee for the United States with the sole authority to represent the United States at the Olympic Games. . . . Pursuant to this authority, the USOC has used the Olympic words and symbols extensively in this country to fulfill its object under the Olympic Charter of 'ensur[ing] the development and safeguarding of the Olympic Movement and sport.'" 483 U.S. at 533-34, 3 U.S.P.Q.2d at 1150.

[170] 483 U.S. at 534-35, 3 U.S.P.Q.2d at 1151.

[171] 483 U.S. at 532, 3 U.S.P.Q.2d at 1150.

[172] 483 U.S. at 536, 3 U.S.P.Q.2d at 1150-51.

applies to all uses of the word 'Olympic' to induce the sale of goods or services. Although the Lanham Act protects only against confusing uses, Congress' judgment respecting a certain word is not so limited. Congress reasonably could conclude that most commercial uses of the Olympic words and symbols are likely to be confusing. It also could determine that unauthorized uses, even if not confusing, nevertheless may harm the USOC by lessening the distinctiveness and thus the commercial value of the marks. See Schechter, The Rational Basis of Trademark Protection, 40 Harv. L. Rev. 813, 825 (1927) (one injury to a trademark owner may be 'the gradual whittling away or dispersion of the identity and hold upon the public mind of the mark or name' by nonconfusing uses).

"In this case, the SFAA sought to sell T-shirts, buttons, bumper stickers and other items, all emblazoned with the title 'Gay Olympic Games.' The possibility for confusion as to sponsorship is obvious. Moreover, it is clear that the SFAA sought to exploit the 'commercial magnetism' . . . of the word given value by the USOC. There is no question that this unauthorized use could undercut the USOC's efforts to use, and sell the right to use, the word in the future, since much of the word's value comes from its limited use. . . . Even though this protection may exceed the traditional rights of a trademark owner in certain circumstances, the application of the Act to this commercial speech is not broader than necessary to protect the legitimate congressional interest and therefore does not violate the First Amendment."[173]

Finally, SFAA's contention that the USOC's enforcement of its right is discriminatory in violation of the Fifth Amendment lacks merit because USOC is not a government actor subject to constitutional equal protection obligations. The majority noted that "the SFAA's claim of discriminatory enforcement is far from compelling."[174]

---

[173] 483 U.S. at 537-40, 3 U.S.P.Q.2d at 1152-53.

[174] "As of 1982 when this suit began, the USOC had brought 22 oppositions to trademark applications and one petition to cancel. . . . For example, the USOC successfully prohibited registration of the mark 'Golden Age Olympics.' . . . The USOC also litigated numerous suits prior to bringing this action, prohibiting use of the Olympic words and symbols by such entities as the National Amateur Sports Foundation, . . . a shoe company, . . . the International Federation of Body Builders, . . . and a bus company . . . Since 1982, the USOC has brought a number of additional suits against various companies and the March of Dimes Birth Defects Foundation. . . . The USOC has authorized the use of the word 'Olympic' to organizations that sponsor athletic competitions and events for handicapped persons ('Special Olympics') and for youth ('Junior Olympics' and 'Explorer Olympics'). . . . Both of these uses directly relate to a purpose of the USOC established by its charter. . . . The USOC has not consented to any other uses of the word in connection with athletic competitions or events.

"The USOC necessarily has discretion as to when and against whom it files opposition to trademark applications, and when and against whom it institutes suits. The record before us strongly indicates that the USOC has acted strictly in accord with its charter and that there has been no actionable discrimination." 483 U.S. at 542-43 n.22, 3 U.S.P.Q.2d at 1154 n.22.

PATENTS

---

§ 2A Introduction

Patent law protects new, unobvious, and useful inventions, such as machines, devices, chemical compositions, and manufacturing processes.

To obtain a patent grant, an inventor must file, in a timely fashion, an application with the United States Patent and Trademark Office ("PTO"). The application must include a specification describing and precisely claiming the invention. The PTO assigns each application to an examiner with technical training in the pertinent technology who conducts a search of the prior art and determines whether the applicant's invention complies with the legal requirements of patentability: novelty, utility, nonobviousness, enabling disclosure, and clear claiming. If the examiner reaches a favorable decision, he or she allows the claims. In due course, the PTO issues a patent. The patent is a printed publication and includes (1) the complete specification as filed by the inventor, with any amendments made during examination, and (2) a cover sheet giving data on the patent, such as the patent number, the issue date, the application filing date, the inventor, prior art publications and patents cited during the examination. Patents are important sources of technical information.

A patent confers the right to exclude others from making, using, or selling the claimed invention in the United States for a term of 17 years from the issue date.

A patent owner may file a civil suit for infringement against anyone who, without authority, makes, uses or sells the patented invention.

Patents have the attributes of personal property and may be assigned or licensed.

§ 2B   Historical Development

[1]   Constitutional Enablement: The 1790 and 1793 Acts

The United States Constitution empowered Congress to establish a national patent system: it provides that Congress shall have the power "To promote the progress of science and useful arts, by securing for limited times to authors and inventors the exclusive right to their respective writings and discoveries."[1] The clause intermixes copyright and patent concepts. The patent concepts are "useful arts," "inventors" and "discoveries."

In 1790, Congress enacted the first patent statute.[2] It authorized patents for "any useful art, manufacture, engine, machine, or device, or any improvement therein not before known or used," provided a designated group of executive officers (the Secretary of State, the Secretary of War, and the Attorney General) determined that the invention was "sufficiently useful and important."

Three years later, Congress replaced the 1790 Act.[3] The 1793 Act omitted the importance determination and authorized patents for "any useful art, machine,

---

[1] Article I, § 8, cl. 8.

In *Graham,* the Supreme Court discussed the origins and effect of the patent clause.

> "The clause is both a grant of power and a limitation. This qualified authority, unlike the power often exercised in the sixteenth and seventeenth centuries by the English Crown, is limited to the promotion of advances in the 'useful arts.' It was written against the backdrop of the practices—eventually curtailed by the Statute of Monopolies—of the Crown in granting monopolies to court favorites in goods or businesses which had long before been enjoyed by the public. . . . The Congress in the exercise of the patent power may not overreach the restraints imposed by the stated constitutional purpose."

Graham v. John Deere Co., 383 U.S. 1, 5-6, 148 U.S.P.Q. 459 (1966).

During the debate on adoption of the Constitution, James Madison, later President of the United States, in Federal Paper No. 43, commented on the Patent-Copyright Clause as follows:

> "The utility of this power will scarcely be questioned. The copyright of authors has been solemnly adjudged, in Great Britain, to be a right of common law. The right to useful inventions seems with equal reason to belong to the inventors. The public good fully coincides in both cases with the claims of individuals. The States cannot separately make effectual provision for either of the cases, and most of them have anticipated the decision of this point, by laws passed at the instance of Congress."

[2] Act of Apr. 10, 1790, ch. 7, 1 Stat. 109.

Early United States patent law drew heavily on English patent law, which, in turn, derived from the 1623 Statute of Monopolies, 21 Jac. 1, c. 3. The 1623 Act sought to dismantle royal monopoly grants but contained an important exception, which allowed 14 year grants of "letters patents" for "new manufactures."

[3] In *Graham,* the Court noted the involvement of Thomas Jefferson, later President of the United States, in the first two patent statutes: "Thomas Jefferson, who as Secretary of

manufacture, or composition of matter, or any new and useful improvement [thereon], not known or used before the application. . . . "

The 1790 and 1793 patent statutes, and court decisions interpreting them, introduced fundamental concepts that remain features of United States patent law.

One example is the 1793 Act's four category approach to the definition of patentable subject matter; the four categories are still in force.[4]

Another example is invalidity defenses. The 1790 and 1793 statutes authorized a patent owner to sue for infringement but allowed the accused infringer to defend by alleging and proving the patented invention lacked novelty or was insufficiently disclosed in the inventor's specification.[5] These defenses are still important features of the United States patent system.

Yet another example is the distinction between *lack of novelty*, meaning discovery by others before the inventor's invention, and *loss of right*, meaning public use or sale by the inventor before applying for a patent. In *Pennock*,[6] the inventors, Pennock and Sellers, devised a new method of making hose in 1811. They authorized Jenkins to make and sell 13,000 feet of hose using the method. In 1818, the inventors applied for and obtained a patent. The Court affirmed a jury verdict that the patent was invalid because the invention was, in the meaning of 1793 Act Section 6, "known or used before the application." The Court conceded that Section 6 could not be interpreted literally; necessarily, at least the inventor would "know" of the invention before he or she could apply for a patent thereon. For policy reasons, the Court interpreted "known or used" as including public or commercial use by the inventor.

State was a member of the group, was its moving spirit . . . He was not only an administrator of the patent system under the 1790 Act, but was also the author of the 1793 Patent Act." Graham v. John Deere Co., 383 U.S. 1, 7, 148 U.S.P.Q. 459 (1966).

[4] The term "art" meant process or method. In 1952, Congress replaced "art" with "process" in the four-category definition but emphasized that "The term 'process' means process, art, or method." 35 U.S.C. § 101.

[5] Section 6 of the 1793 Act provided the following defenses:

(1) "[T]he specification, filed by the plaintiff, does not contain the whole truth relative to his discovery, or . . . contains more than is necessary to produce the described effect, which concealment or addition shall fully appear to have been made, for the purpose of deceiving the public;"

(2) "[T]he thing, thus secured by patent, was not originally discovered by the patentee, but had been in use, or had been described in some public work anterior to the supposed discovery of the patentee, or that he had surreptitiously obtained a patent for the discovery of another person."

As to the first defense, the Supreme Court held that, despite the language on "deceiving the public," a patent issuing on a defective specification was invalid without regard to the inventor's intent or purpose. Grant v. Raymond, 31 U.S. (6 Pet.) 218, 247-48 (1832) (the statute "requires, as preliminary to a patent, a correct specification and description of the thing discovered. This is necessary in order to give the public, after the privilege shall expire, the advantage for which the privilege is allowed, and is the foundation of the power to issue the patent.").

[6] Pennock v. Dialogue, 27 U.S. (2 Pet.) 1 (1829).

"[T]he true meaning must be, not known or used by the public, before the application. And, thus construed, there is much reason for the limitation thus imposed by the Act. . . . If an inventor should be permitted to hold back from the knowledge of the public the secrets of his invention; if he should for a long period of years retain the monopoly, and make, and sell his invention publicly, and thus gather the whole profits of it, relying upon his superior skill and knowledge of the structure, and then, and then only, when the danger of competition should force him to secure the exclusive right, . . . it would materially retard the progress of science and the useful arts, and give a premium to those who should be least prompt to communicate their discoveries." [7]

This policy orientation remains to this day a feature of the law of public use and sale. [8]

[2] The 1836 and 1870 Acts

In 1836, Congress enacted a major revision of the patent laws. [9] The 1836 Act created a Patent Office and a system of examination of patent applications for compliance with the requirement of novelty over the prior art. [10] It introduced a statutory requirement of clear claiming. [11] It codified the *Pennock* doctrine by

---

[7] 27 U.S. at 19.

[8] *E.g.,* Envirotech Corp. v. Westech Engineering Inc., 904 F.2d 1571, 1574, 15 U.S.P.Q. 1230, 1232 (Fed. Cir. 1990) ("the policies or purposes underlying the on sale bar, in effect, define it").

[9] The Act was approved on Independence Day, the 4th of July.

[10] A Senate Report accompanying the Act cited four "evils" in the existing system of issuing patents "without any examination into the merit or novelty of the invention."

"1. A considerable portion of all the patents granted are worthless and void, as conflicting with, and infringing upon one another, or upon, public rights not subject to patent privileges; arising either from a want of due attention to the specifications of claim, or from the ignorance of the patentees of the state of the arts and manufactures, and of the inventions made in other countries, and even in our own.

"2. The country becomes flooded with patent monopolies, embarrassing to bona fide patentees, whose rights are thus invaded on all sides; and not less embarrassing to the community generally, in the use of even the most common machinery and long-known improvements in the arts and common manufactures of the country.

"3. Out of this interference and collision of patents and privileges, a great number of lawsuits arise, which are daily increasing in an alarming degree, onerous to the courts, ruinous to the parties, and injurious to society.

"4. It opens the door to frauds, which have already become extensive and serious. . . . [I]t is not uncommon for persons to copy patented machines in the model-room; and having made some slight immaterial alterations, they apply in the next room for patents. . . . [T]hey go forth on a retailing expedition, selling out their patent rights . . . to those who have no means at hand of detecting the imposition . . . This speculation in patent rights has become a regular business, and several hundred thousand dollars, it is estimated, are paid annually for void patents, many of which are thus fraudulently obtained."

Senate Report Accompanying Senate Bill No 239, 24th Cong., 1st Sess. (April 28, 1836).

[11] Act of July 4, 1836, ch. 357, § 6, 5 Stat. 117. The Supreme Court had already interpreted the 1793 Act as requiring the inventor in his patent specification to "distinguish" his invention as well as provide an enabling disclosure. Evans v. Eaton, 20 U.S. (7 Wheat.) 356 (1822).

providing that an inventor's discovery be "not, at the time of his application for a patent, *in public use or on sale,* with his consent or allowance."[12]

In 1839, Congress amended the public use and on sale provision to add a two-year grace period; henceforth, public use or on sale activity was fatal only if it dated more than two years before the inventor applied for a patent. The grace period remains a feature of United States patent law, though Congress shorted the period to one year in 1939.

In the mid-19th century, the Supreme Court, in reviewing patent infringement judgments, established fundamental patent law concepts. *Hotchkiss*[13] established the obviousness standard of patentability; a literally new device was not patentable if it would have been obvious to a person of ordinary skill in the art. *Gayler*[14] interpreted the "known or used" novelty standard as requiring knowledge or use accessible to the public. *Winans*[15] established the doctrine of equivalents; a device that did not respond literally to the language of the patent claim would nevertheless infringe if it obtained the same result in the same way as the patented invention. *O'Reilly*[16] established the principle of undue patent claim breadth; an inventor of one means of achieving a useful result can claim only that means, not all possible means of achieving the result. *Godfrey*[17] established the concept of a continuing application; a second patent application could obtain the benefit of the filing date of a prior application disclosing the same invention. *Seymour*[18] established the enablement standard for prior art publications; a publication would anticipate a later patent claim only if it provided sufficient information to enable one skilled in the art to make and use the invention. *City of Elizabeth*[19] established the experimental use doctrine; use otherwise public was excused if it was for experimentation, to "bring the invention to perfection," rather than for profit.

In 1870, Congress replaced the 1836 Act with a new codification. For the most part, the 1870 Act retained the 1836 Act's provisions and requirements.[20] In 1897,

---

[12] Act of July 4, 1836, ch. 357, § 6, 5 Stat. 117.

The requirement that public use or sale be with the inventor's "consent or allowance" was later eliminated so that any public use or on sale activity would constitute a bar. Scholars dispute whether the consent or allowance provision was eliminated by the 1839 Act or the 1870 Act. *See* D. Chisum, Patents § 6.02[1][b][iii]. *Cf.* Andrews v. Hovey (The Driven Well Cases), 123 U.S. 267 (1887). The issue is not without contemporary significance. It remains unclear whether and to what extent Congress intended that the standards of public use and on sale activity should be the same for the inventor-patentee and others.

[13] Hotchkiss v. Greenwood, 52 U.S. (11 How.) 248 (1850).

[14] Gayler v. Wilder, 51 U.S. (10 How.) 477 (1850).

[15] Winans v. Denmead, 56 U.S. (15 How.) 330 (1853).

[16] O'Reilly v. Morse, 56 U.S. (15 How.) 62 (1854).

[17] Godfrey v. Eames, 68 U.S. (1 Wall.) 317 (1864).

[18] Seymour v. Osborne, 78 U.S. (11 Wall.) 516 (1870).

[19] City of Elizabeth v. American Nicholson Pavement Co., 97 U.S. (7 Otto.) 126 (1877).

[20] The 1870 Act's sections were renumbered as part of the 1874 "Revised Statutes" codification. For example, Section 61 of the 1870 Act, which was based on Section 6 of the 1836 Act, became Section 4920 of the Revised Statutes. Reported court decisions construing pre-1952 Act statutes cite the appropriate Revised Statutes section number.

Congress made two changes in the statutory bar provision, adding patenting and description in a printed publication to the public use and on sale bars as loss of right events, and specifying that public use or on sale activity must be "in this country" to be a bar.[21]

[3]　The First Invention Concept

The United States patent system stands alone in the world in determining priority among competing inventors by reference to who was the "first to invent."

The 1790 and 1793 statutes did not explicitly establish a first-to-invent priority rule but did require a patentee to be "the first and true inventor." The 1836 Act established a procedure for resolving "the question of priority of right of invention." 1836 Act Section 15 introduced the diligence concept by providing that an inventor's patent was invalid if it was for an invention "invented or discovered by another, who was using reasonable diligence in adapting and perfecting the same."[22] The courts read Section 15 to mean that one who was the first to reduce an invention to practice would lose priority to another who was the first to "invent" in the sense of conceiving the invention, provided that the latter exercised diligence in the reduction to practice.[23]

The 1870 Act created within the Patent Office the position of "examiner in charge of interference," beginning a tradition of separating priority determinations from patentability determinations that continued until a 1984 statute merged the "Board of Appeals" and the "Board of Patent Interferences."

From about 1890 to about 1910, lower court decisions established the basic rules on priority of invention, including definitions of the key concepts: conception, reduction to practice, and diligence. Landmarks included *Mergenthaler*,[24] defining conception; *Mason*,[25] holding that a first inventor loses priority by abandoning, suppressing or concealing the invention after reduction to practice; *Automatic Weighing Machine*,[26] holding that the filing of a patent specification adequately disclosing the invention is constructive reduction to practice; and *Sydeman*,[27] summarizing a long series of decisions on what constitutes an actual reduction to practice. The rules thus established have enjoyed remarkable longevity. In 1952, Congress codified them in Section 102(g). The only significant new invention priority rule since 1910 is that recognized in *Paulik*:[28] one losing the benefit of an actual reduction to practice by abandonment, suppression or concealment may establish priority by reference to resumption of activity on the invention.

---

[21] This codified the Supreme Court's ruling in Gandy v. Main Belting Co., 143 U.S. 587 (1891).

[22] Act of July 4, 1836, ch. 357, § 15, 117.

[23] Dietz v. Wade, 7 F. Cas. 684 (No. 3903) (C.C.D.C. 1859); Reed v. Cutter, 20 F. Cas. 435 (No. 11,645) (C.C.D. Mass. 1841).

[24] Mergenthaler v. Scuder, 11 App. D.C. 264 (1897).

[25] Mason v. Hepburn, 13 App. D.C. 86 (1898).

[26] Automatic Weighing Machine Co. v. Pneumatic Scale Corp., 166 F. 288 (1st Cir. 1909).

[27] Sydeman v. Thomas, 32 App. D.C. 362 (1909).

[28] Paulik v. Rizkalla, 796 F.2d 456, 230 U.S.P.Q. 434 (Fed. Cir. 1986).

[4] Shifting Supreme Court Attitudes Toward Patents

[a] **Patents Under Fire: 1880–1892.** In the late 19th century, the volume of patent cases reaching the Supreme Court increased markedly.[29] The Court's decisions began to decry abuses of the patent system. In *Atlantic Works,*[30] Justice Bradley complained that "It was never the object of [the patent] laws to grant a monopoly for every trifling device, every shadow of a shade of an idea, which would naturally and spontaneously occur to any skilled mechanic or operator in the ordinary progress of manufactures." The Court held many patents invalid for "want of invention," a phrase that came to encapsulate the *Hotchkiss* obviousness concept.[31]

[b] **Patents in Favor: 1892–1930.** Beginning in 1892, the tide turned from hostility to receptiveness.[32] The turn was attributable in part to improved economic conditions[33] and in part to the enactment of the Evarts Act, which created regional courts of appeal and relieved the Supreme Court of the burden of reviewing appeals in all patent infringement suits.[34]

Until about 1930, the Supreme Court upheld the validity of many patents, emphasizing the importance of inference evidence, such as the commercial success of the invention after its introduction into the marketplace,[35] and warning against the use of "hindsight" in determining obviousness.[36]

The Court continued to develop doctrinal refinements. In *Mast, Foos,*[37] it confirmed that the *Hotchkiss* mechanic of ordinary skill in the art should be conclusively presumed to have knowledge of all the prior art, such as patents and publications, even prior art that was obscure or not known to actual ordinary workmen. In *Milburn,*[38] the Court held that the full text of patent specifications were prior

---

[29] *See* D. Chisum, Patents § 5.02.

[30] Atlantic Works v. Brady, 107 U.S. (17 Otto) 192 (1883).

[31] *E.g.,* McClain v. Ortmayer, 141 U.S. 419 (1891); Hollister v. Benedict & Burnham Mfg. Co., 113 U.S. 59 (1885).

[32] In that year, the Supreme Court upheld the patent on barbed wire even though numerous other inventors had devised similar solutions: "In the law of patents it is the last step that wins." Washburn & Moen Mfg. Co. v. Beat 'Em All Barbed-Wire Co., 143 U.S. 275, 283 (1892).

[33] *See* Mayers, *The United States Patent System in Historical Perspective,* 3 Pat., Trademark & Copyright J. of Research & Educ. 33 (1959).

[34] Act of March 3, 1891, ch. 517, 26 Stat. 826.

[35] *E.g.,* Minerals Separation, Ltd. v. Hyde, 242 U.S. 261 (1916).

[36] *E.g.,* Diamond Rubber Co. v. Consolidated Rubber Tire Co., 220 U.S. 428, 435-36 (1911) ("Knowledge after the event is always easy, and problems once solved present no difficulties, indeed, may be represented as never having had any, and expert witnesses may be brought forward to show that the new thing which seemed to have eluded the search of the world was always ready at hand and easy to be seen by a merely skillful attention. But the law has other tests of the invention than subtle conjectures of what might have been seen and yet was not. It regards a change as evidence of novelty, the acceptance and utility of change as further evidence, even as demonstration. . . . Nor does it detract from its merit that it is the result of experiment and not the instant and perfect product of inventive power.").

[37] Mast, Foos & Co. v. Stover Manufacturing Co., 177 U.S. 485 (1900).

[38] Alexander Milburn v. Davis-Bournonville Co., 270 U.S. 390 (1926).

art as of their Patent Office filing date, rather than their issue date, even though patent application disclosures became publicly available only upon issue and printing. The theory was the Patent Office's delay in examining and issuing a patent on a senior-filed application should not affect the patentability of an invention in a junior-filed application.

[c] **Patents under Renewed Fire: 1930–1950.** Beginning in 1930, the Supreme Court reverted to pre-1892 anti-patent attitudes, reflected in several lines of decisions. First, the Court expanded the patent misuse doctrine, which rendered a patent unenforceable if the patent owner extended the scope of the patent through tying agreements and other improper practices.[39] The misuse line culminated in *Mercoid*,[40] which severely curtailed remedies against contributory patent infringement by sale of specially adapted components.

Second, the Court enforced stringent requirements as to patent claim clarity and breadth.[41] *Halliburton*[42] invalidated the common practice of defining invention elements in terms of "means" for performing a specified "function."

Third, and most important, the Court raised the "invention" patentability standard. In *Cuno Engineering*,[43] Justice Douglas stated, somewhat hyperbolically, that a new device, to be patentable, "must reveal the flash of creative genius." In *Great Atlantic & Pacific Tea*,[44] the Court decreed that a combination of old mechanical elements was patentable only if it showed "unusual or surprising consequences" and cautioned that courts should "scrutinize combination patent claims with a care proportioned to the difficulty and improbability of finding invention in an assembly of old elements." The Court's anti-patent bias was so pronounced that Justice Jackson would complain, in dissent, that the only valid patents were those the Court had not been able to get its hands on.[45]

---

[39] *E.g.,* Carbice Corp. v. American Patents Development Corp., 283 U.S. 27 (1931).

[40] Mercoid Corp. v. Mid-Continent Inv. Co., 320 U.S. 661, 60 U.S.P.Q. 21 (1944).

[41] *E.g.,* General Electric Co. v. Wabash Appliance Co., 304 U.S. 364 (1938).

[42] Halliburton Oil Well Cementing Co. v. Walker, 329 U.S. 1, 71 U.S.P.Q. 1 (1946).

[43] Cuno Engineering Corp. v. Automatic Devices Corp., 314 U.S. 84, 51 U.S.P.Q. 272 (1941).

[44] Great Atlantic & Pacific Tea Co. v. Supermarket Equipment Co., 340 U.S. 147, 87 U.S.P.Q. 303 (1950).

The patent in question was a "cashier's counter equipped with a three-sided frame, or rack, with no top or bottom, which, when pushed or pulled, will move groceries deposited within it by a customer to the checking clerk and leave them there when it is pushed back to repeat the operation." Under the Court's view, each element of the invention was old: store counters were old, and three-sided racks to push and pull goods were old. 340 U.S. at 149.

[45] Jungersen v. Ostby & Barton Co., 335 U.S. 560, 80 U.S.P.Q. 32 (1949) (dissenting opinion). Justice Jackson noted:

> "It would not be difficult to cite many instances of patents that have been granted, improperly I think, and without adequate tests of invention by the Patent Office. But I doubt that the remedy for such Patent Office passion for granting patents is an equally strong passion in this Court for striking them down so that the only patent that is valid is one which this Court has not been able to get its hands on."

335 U.S. at 571.

The Supreme Court's anti-patent bias in the 1930's and 1940's was not total. In *Transparent-Wrap*,[46] the Court refused to hold per se illegal or unenforceable "grant back" clauses in patent licenses, which required the licensee to grant back to the licensor rights in the licensee's improvement inventions. In *Graver Tank*,[47] the Court confirmed the continuing vitality of the doctrine of equivalents.

[5] The 1952 Act

In 1952, Congress passed a new patent act, United States Code Title 35, which is still in effect. To a large extent, the 1952 Act rearranged existing statutory provisions and stated in statutory form matters previously recognized only in court decisions and Patent Office practice[48] but did make several specific changes and additions.[49]

Some 1952 Act provisions were in response to the 1930-1950 Supreme Court anti-patent decisions: (1) a paragraph in Section 112 overturned *Halliburton* and confirmed use of "means-plus-function" claim limitations; (2) a sentence in Section 103 disapproved of *Cuno Engineering*'s "flash of creative genius" test by providing that "Patentability shall not be negatived by the manner in which the invention was made;" and (3) a section defining infringement, inducement of infringement, and contributory infringement, Section 271, part (d) of which overturned *Mercoid*.

Perhaps most significantly, Congress for the first time included a statutory provision on nonobviousness, Section 103. Whether Congress intended to repudiate the Supreme Court's stringent "invention" decisions leading up to *Great Atlantic & Pacific Tea* or merely to codify existing standards was a matter of dispute among the lower courts and commentators.[50]

[6] The 1966 *Graham* Trilogy and Beyond

The Supreme Court did not reach the issue of the proper interpretation of Section 103 until 1966, when the Court granted certiorari in three patent cases. In *Graham*,[51] the Court pointedly confirmed that Section 103 *codified* the judicially developed

---

[46] Transparent Wrap Mach. Corp. v. Stokes & Smith Co., 329 U.S. 637, 72 U.S.P.Q. 148 (1947).

[47] Graver Tank & Mfg. Co. v. Linde Air Products Co., 339 U.S. 605, 85 U.S.P.Q. 328 (1950).

[48] An example is Section 120 on continuation applications. 35 U.S.C. § 120.

[49] Some changes restricted prior patenting practices that were perceived as having been subject to abuse. For example, Section 251 put a two-year limit on the filing of reissue applications to broaden the scope of patent claims. Section 253 ended the prior practice of disclaiming a portion of a patent claim. Section 253 did introduce the concept of terminal disclaimers, which the courts thereafter used to mold the law of double patenting.

[50] *See, e.g.*, Reiner v. I. Leon Co., 285 F.2d 501, 503, 128 U.S.P.Q. 25 (2d Cir. 1960), *cert. denied*, 366 U.S. 929 (1961)(Judge Learned Hand: "There can be no doubt that the Act of 1952 meant to change the slow but steady drift of judicial decision that had been hostile to patents. . . . "); Hawley Prods. Co. v. U.S. Trunk Co., 259 F.2d 69, 118 U.S.P.Q. 424 (1st Cir. 1958) (mere codification); Beckett, *Judicial Construction of the Patent Act of 1952—Codification v. Substantive Change*, 37 J. Pat. Off. Soc'y 467 (1955).

[51] Graham v. John Deere Co., 383 U.S. 1, 148 U.S.P.Q. 459 (1966); United States v. Adams, 383 U.S. 39, 148 U.S.P.Q. 479 (1966).

nonobviousness requirement.[52] Congress did focus inquiry on objective obviousness and, in effect, directed abandonment of "invention," which the courts had previously used to encapsulate the obviousness standard. "Invention" had led to conceptual confusion. But, according to the Court, Section 103 did not, and constitutionally could not, "lower" or fundamentally alter the patentability standard. On the merits, the Court held two of three patents invalid; it held a third patent valid, emphasizing that the invention, a battery that provided strong current with the addition of a water electrolyte, was met with initial skepticism by experts but later was used extensively by the United States government.

In two decisions dealing with "combination" patents,[53] the Supreme Court held patents invalid, using language suggesting continued vitality of special "invention" tests. Neither decision had significant impact on subsequent lower court decisions. *Graham* remains the commonly-cited Supreme Court decision on the nonobviousness patentability requirement.

In 1960's and 1970's, Supreme Court decisions introduced doctrinal refinements. In *Manson*,[54] the Court interpreted the utility patentability condition as requiring an inventor to discover a substantial minimal utility for an invention, including new chemical compounds. In *Benson*,[55] the Court decreed that mathematical algorithms were unpatentable, launching two decades of confusion on what types of computation inventions were proper subjects for patents.

The 1980's saw a upward surge in the role and importance of the patent system. In *Chakrabarty*,[56] the Supreme Court held that genetically-altered living microorganisms are patentable subject matter. The *Chakrabarty* decision spurred new interest in patents, particularly in the nascent biotechnology industry. In *Dawson*,[57] the Court applied Section 271(d) to hold that the owner of a patent claiming a process of using a certain chemical compound was not guilty of patent misuse by selling the compound and refusing to issue licenses to competing manufacturers of the compound because the compound was a "nonstaple," that is, was not suited for commercial use other than in the patented process.

In the 1980's, Congress enacted important patent legislation. In 1982, it created a Court of Appeals for the Federal Circuit with exclusive appellate jurisdiction over

---

[52] The Court noted that "while the clear language of Section 103 places emphasis on an inquiry into obviousness, the general level of innovation necessary to sustain patentability remains the same," 383 U.S. at 4, that "the section was intended merely as a codification of judicial precedents embracing the *Hotchkiss* condition, with congressional directions that inquiries into the obviousness of the subject matter sought to be patented are a prerequisite to patentability," 383 U.S. at 17, and that "[t]he standard has remained invariable in this Court," 383 U.S. at 19.

[53] Sakraida v. Ag Pro, Inc., 425 U.S. 273, 189 U.S.P.Q. 449 (1976); Anderson's-Black Rock, Inc. v. Pavement Salvage Co., 396 U.S. 57, 163 U.S.P.Q. 673 (1969).

[54] Brenner v. Manson, 383 U.S. 519, 148 U.S.P.Q. 689 (1966).

[55] Gottschalk v. Benson, 409 U.S. 63, 175 U.S.P.Q. 673 (1972).

[56] Diamond v. Chakrabarty, 447 U.S. 303, 206 U.S.P.Q. 193 (1980).

[57] Dawson Chem. Co. v. Rohm & Haas Co., 448 U.S. 176, 206 U.S.P.Q. 385 (1980).

cases that arise in whole or in part under the patent laws.[58] Today, the Federal Circuit's patent-related decisions guide the practical administration of the patent system in the Patent and Trademark Office, in district court patent litigation, and in International Trade Commission proceedings pertaining to patents.[59]

In the Patent Law Amendments Act of 1984, Congress adopted amendments to Sections 103, 116 and 120, which changed "a complex body of case law which discourages communication among members of research teams"[60] and made exportation of components of a patented combination an act of infringement.[61] The same year, it enacted the Drug Price Competition and Patent Term Restoration Act, providing for extension of the terms of certain patents on drug and other products that had been subject to regulatory review by the Food and Drug Administration.[62] In 1988, it enacted the Patent Misuse Reform Act, restricting application of the misuse doctrine to certain patent licensing and sales practices.[63] The same year, it enacted the Process Patent Amendments Act, extending to process patent owners the right to exclude unauthorized importation of unpatented products made abroad by use of the patented process.[64]

§ 2C Patentability

Patent law establishes four basic conditions an invention must meet to qualify for patent protection. The invention must be (1) in a statutory subject matter category, (2) useful, (3) novel in relation to the prior art, and (4) not obvious from the prior art to a person of ordinary skill in the art at the time the invention was made. An inventor can secure a patent by promptly filing a suitably drafted patent application.[1]

The inventor defines his or her invention in claims, precise verbal expressions included at the end of the specification that is filed with the application. The claimed invention is typically broader and more abstract than the examples the inventor discloses or puts into commercial practice. Claim drafting and interpretation are critical to patentability problem resolution.

---

[58] Federal Courts Improvement Act of 1982, P.L. 97-164, 96 Stat. 25 (April 2, 1982). The Act merged two existing courts, the Court of Customs and Patent Appeals, which had five judges, and the Court of Claims, which had seven judges. The Federal Circuit came into existence on October 1, 1982.

[59] For analysis of the Federal Circuit's patent-related decisions, see D. Chisum, Patent Law Digest: Abstracts of Federal Circuit Decisions 1982-90, Case Tables, and Selected Statutes and Rules (1991).

[60] Patent Law Amendments Act of 1984, P.L. 98-622, § 104, 98 Stat. 3383.

[61] 35 U.S.C. § 271(f).

[62] P.L. 98-417, Title II, 98 Stat. 1585.

[63] Patent Misuse Reform Act of 1988, P.L. 100-73, 102 Stat. 4674. The Act added two subsections to 35 U.S.C. Section 271(d).

[64] Omnibus Trade and Competitiveness Act of 1988, P.L. 100-418, Title IX, Subtitle A, 102 Stat. 1563.

[1] See § 2D.

[1] Patentable Subject Matter

The patent statutes provide for utility,[2] design,[3] and plant[4] patents. Utility patents are the most common and cover new and useful inventions, such as measurement instruments, medical devices, chemical compounds, and processes for making fabrics. Design patents cover new and ornamental designs of useful articles, such as furniture, containers, toys, and shoes.[5] Plant patents cover new and distinct plant varieties, such as flowering plants and fruit trees.[6]

[a] **General Definitions.** Section 101 defines what is eligible for a utility patent: "Whoever invents or discovers any new and useful *process, machine, manufacture, or composition of matter,* or any new and useful improvement thereof, may obtain a patent therefor . . . [7] "Process" is further defined as "process, art or method" and includes "a new use of a known process, machine, manufacture, composition of matter, or material."[8]

The four utility patent categories—process, machine, manufacture, and composition of matter—first appeared in 1793.[9] The only category change was in the 1952 Act, which substituted "process" for "art."[10] The courts interpret the old categories to include developing new technologies such as electronics, computers and biotechnology.

Processes are methods and procedures (roughly speaking: how to do something). Court decisions variously define process,[11] but no one definition is accepted as the comprehensive exclusive and inclusive test of process patent eligibility.[12] The most

---

[2] 35 U.S.C. § 101.

[3] 35 U.S.C. § 171.

[4] 35 U.S.C. § 161.

[5] Design protection is discussed in § 6B.

[6] Plant protection is discussed in § 6C.

[7] 35 U.S.C. § 101 (emphasis added).

[8] 35 U.S.C. § 100(b).

[9] Act of Feb. 21, 1793, ch. 11, § 1, 1 Stat. 319.

[10] This alteration was solely for clarity. *See* Reviser's Note, 35 U.S.C. § 112, H.R. Rep. No. 1923, 82d Cong., 2d Sess. (1952) ("The word 'art' in the corresponding section of the existing statute has a different meaning than the same word as used in other places in the statute; it has been interpreted by the courts as being practically synonymous with process or method. 'Process' has been used as its meaning is more readily grasped than 'art' as interpreted, and the definition in section 100(b) makes it clear that process or method' is meant.").

[11] Cochrane v. Deener, 94 U.S. (4 Otto.) 780 (1877) ("A process is a mode of treatment of certain materials to produce a given result. It is an act, or a series of acts, performed upon the subject-matter to be transformed and reduced to a different state or thing."); *In re* Durden, 763 F.2d 1406, 1410, 226 U.S.P.Q. 359, 362 (Fed. Cir. 1985) ("A process . . . is a manipulation according to an algorithm . . . doing something to or with something according to a schema.").

[12] *See* § 2C[1][f][ii](3)(dd). *Cf.* Gottschalk v. Benson, 409 U.S. 63, 70, 175 U.S.P.Q. 673 (1972) ("We do not hold that no process patent could ever qualify if it did not meet the requirements of our prior precedents.").

In re Tarczy-Hornoch, 397 F.2d 856, 158 U.S.P.Q. 141 (CCPA 1968), traced the development of the patentable process definition and rejected the old rule that the "mere function of a machine" could not be patented as a process.

troublesome areas are computing methods and mathematical algorithms.[13] A method for making high-strength polymer fabric[14] and a method for controlling weeds near rice plants by applying a specific chemical compound are examples of process inventions.[15] The first is a method of *making* something; the second is a method of *using* something.[16]

The product categories, "machine," "manufacture," and "composition of matter," are structural (roughly speaking: things). The courts give the categories broad definitions. A "composition of matter" includes a new molecule.[17] A "manufacture" is "anything under the sun that is made by man,"[18] a residual category sweeping up

---

Tarczy-Hornoch upheld a patent claim for a method of counting electrical pulses at extremely high repetition rates that exceeded the capacity of available single counting apparatus. The court reasoned that the inventor was entitled to claim this method even though the inventor disclosed and separately claimed a new counting apparatus that inherently carried out the method. It stated:

> "[T]he basic rationale of the patent system demands the upholding of properly drawn claims for new, useful, and unobvious processes, regardless of whether the inventor has invented one, two, or more machines to carry them out. . . . The essential difficulty is in the fact that, although at the time of application only one apparatus may be known which is capable of carrying out the process, others may become available later. In which case, of course, the inventor may be cheated of his invention."

397 F.2d at 867, 868.

[13] *See* § 2C[1][f].

[14] *See* claim 13 from U.S. Patent No. 3,767,756:

> "A method comprising extruding a spinning dope from an orifice through a layer of gas and into an aqueous bath at a temperature of under 50°C, said dope comprising a polyamide and a solvent of sulfuric acid of at least 98% concentration at a concentration of at least 40 grams of said polyamide per 100 ml. of solvent, said polymide having an inherent viscosity of at least 3.0 and being poly(p-phenylene terephthalamide)."

The court held this claim valid and infringed in Akzo N.V. v. U.S. Int'l Trade Comm'n, 808 F.2d 1471, 1478 n.10, 1USPQ2d 1241, 1245 n.10 (Fed. Cir. 1986), *cert. denied*, 482 U.S. 909 (1987). The fabric made by the method is sold under the Du Pont trademark "KEVLAR."

[15] *See* claim 1 of U.S. Patent 3,816,092:

> "A method for selectively inhibiting growth of undesirable plants in an area containing growing undesirable plants in an established crop, which comprises applying to said area 3,4-dichloropropionanilide at a rate of application which inhibits growth of said undesirable plants and which does not adversely affect the growth of said established crop."

The court held this claim unenforceable because of inequitable conduct in the procurement of the patent in Rohm & Haas Co. v. Crystal Chem. Co., 722 F.2d 1556, 220 USPQ 289 (Fed. Cir. 1983), *cert. denied*, 469 U.S. 851 (1984). Propanil itself was not patentable to the inventor who discovered its herbicidal properties because it had already been invented.

[16] *See* § 2C[4][e][iv].

[17] Schering Corp. v. Gilbert, 153 F.2d 428, 68 U.S.P.Q. 84 (2d Cir. 1946). *See also* Diamond v. Chakrabarty, 447 U.S. 303, 308, 206 U.S.P.Q. 193 (1980) (" 'composition of matter' has been construed consistent with its common usage to include all compositions of two or more substances and . . . all composite articles, whether they be the results of chemical union, or of mechanical mixture, or whether they be gases, fluids, powders, or solids.' ").

[18] H.R. Rep. No. 1923, 82d Cong., 2d Sess. (1952), cited in Diamond v. Chakrabarty, 447 U.S. 303, 206 U.S.P.Q. 193 (1980).

all inventions not included in the other categories. A soft-contact lens with a laser-etched marking,[19] and an instant camera are examples of product inventions.[20]

A technological advance is often defined in terms of several categories. Inventors seek and obtain claims to processes and compositions, manufactures or machines in a single or related patents.[21] For example, an inventor who devises a new method of stretching polytetra-flourethyline tape to produce a product impermeable to water but not to water vapor could claim (1) the stretching method (a process); (2) apparatus for carrying out the stretching method (a machine); and (3) products resulting from the method (a manufacture or composition of matter).[22]

---

[19] See claim 1 from U.S. Patent 4,194,814:

"An ophthalmic lens adapted to be placed in direct contact with eye tissue formed of a transparent cross-linked polymer material, said lens being characterized by identifying indicia engraved in a surface thereof by subjecting said lens to a beam of radiation emerging from a laser having an intensity and wavelength at least sufficient to sublimate said polymer and form depressions in said lens surface to a depth less than the thickness of said lens, said lens having a smooth surface of unsublimated polymer material surrounding said depressions and by varying in a predetermining manner the point at which said laser beam impinges upon said lens surfaces to engrave said identifying indicia in said lens surface."

The court reviewed this claim in Bausch & Lomb, Inc. v. Barnes-Hind/Hydrocurve, Inc., 796 F.2d 443, 445, 230 U.S.P.Q. 416, 417 (Fed. Cir. 1986).

[20] See claim 8 from U.S. 3,753,211:

"A self-developing camera comprising:

"means for receiving a film unit;

"a housing member having film unit exit means;

"means for exposing said film unit;

"means for distributing a processing fluid across the exposed portion of said film unit response to said film unit's being progressively advanced therepast, said exit means being positioned with respect to said fluid distributing means so that, in the course of advancing said film unit after exposure thereof past said fluid distributing means and thence through said exit means, a first fluid treated section of said exposed film unit is accessible exteriorly of said camera and thus exposed to ambient light while a second section of said exposed film unit extends on the opposite side of said fluid distributing means from said exit means being yet untreated with said fluid, with another section of said exposed film being disposed intermediate said fluid distributing means and said exit means, said exit means being disposed out of the path said exposed film would normally follow as it emerged from said fluid distributing means; and

"means for deflecting said exposed film unit from the path it would normally follow as it initially emerged from said fluid distributing means and guiding it towards said exit means."

The court held this claim valid and infringed in Polaroid Corp. v. Eastman Kodak Co., 789 F.2d 1556, 229 U.S.P.Q. 561 (Fed. Cir. 1986), cert. denied, 479 U.S. 850 (1986). Successful enforcement of this and several other patents covering Polaroid's SX-70 instant camera caused Kodak to withdraw from the instant photography field.

[21] Reference to the process for making it is another way to define an article. See § 2D[3][d][vi].

[22] The example is from W.L. Gore & Associates, Inc. v. Garlock, Inc., 721 F.2d 1540, 220 U.S.P.Q. 303 (Fed. Cir. 1983), cert. denied, 469 U.S. 851 (1984), upholding the "Goretex" fabric patent.

A patent or application need not, and typically does not, identify the category of patentable subject matter to which the claimed invention belongs.

[b] **Exclusions and Exceptions.** The only statutory exclusion from Section 101's broad patentable subject matter categories relates to inventions useful *solely* to utilize special nuclear material or atomic energy in an atomic weapon.[23]

[c] **New Uses of Old Products.** A process includes "a new use of a known process machine, manufacture, composition of matter, or material."[24] Inventors who discover a new use of a known material, for example, an existing chemical compound's previously unknown therapeutic quality, cannot claim the old product because only *new* inventions are patentable,[25] but patent law encourages the search for new uses of existing materials by authorizing method-of-use claims.[26]

A method-of-use claim cannot cover a newly discovered characteristic or advantage of an old product or process if that characteristic or advantage is inherent in the existing use of the product or process.[27]

---

[23] 42 U.S.C. § 2181(a). *See, In re* Brueckner, 623 F.2d 184, 206 U.S.P.Q. 415 (CCPA 1980).

[24] 35 U.S.C. § 101(b). *See generally* D. Chisum, Patents § 1.02[8].

[25] Cochrane v. Badische Anilin & Soda Fabrik, 111 U.S. 293 (1884); Titanium Metals Corp. v. Banner, 778 F.2d 775, 227 U.S.P.Q. 773 (Fed. Cir. 1985).
This novelty bar is avoided if the inventor can define the claimed product in a way that distinguishes it from the old product. *E.g., In re* Bergstrom, 427 F.2d 1394, 1402-03, 166 USPQ 256 (CCPA 1970) (claim to prostaglandin extract; "by definition, pure materials necessarily differ from less pure or impure materials and, if the latter are the only ones existing and available as a standard of reference . . . perforce the 'pure' materials are 'new' with respect to them"). A similar result is reached as to "products of nature." *See* § 2C[1][d].

[26] *Cf.* Dawson Chem. Co. v. Rohm & Haas Co., 448 U.S. 176, 221-22, 206 U.S.P.Q. 385 (1980) ("[T]he characteristics of practical chemical research are such that this form of patent protection is particularly important to inventors in that field. The number of chemicals either known to scientists or disclosed by existing research is vast. It grows constantly, as those engaging in 'pure' research publish their discoveries. The number of these chemicals that have known uses of commercial or social value, in contrast, is small. Development of new uses for existing chemicals is thus a major component of practical chemical research. It is extraordinarily expensive. It may take years of unsuccessful testing before a chemical having a desired property is identified, and it may take several years of further testing before a proper and safe method for using that chemical is developed.").

[27] *E.g., In re* King, 801 F.2d 1324, 1326, 231 U.S.P.Q. 136, 138 (Fed. Cir. 1986) ("the discovery of a new use for an old structure based on unknown properties of the structure [may be] patentable to the discoverer as a process," but, "[u]nder the principles of inherency," a claim is anticipated "if a structure in the prior art necessarily functions in accordance with the limitations of a process or method claim . . ."); *In re* May, 574 F.2d 1082, 197 U.S.P.Q. 601 (CCPA 1978) (the discovery that a known analgesic compound had the property of nonaddictiveness will not support a patent claiming the method of effecting "nonaddictive" analgesia by use of a certain generic class of compounds because the prior art showed use of a species compound within that generic class to effect analgesia).
Cf. In re Dillon, 919 F.2d 688, 16 U.S.P.Q.2d 1897 (Fed. Cir. 1990) (*en banc*), discussed at § 2C[4][c][iii].

[d] **Biotechnology: Products of Nature—Living Organisms.** A naturally occurring product cannot be patented even if its existence was unknown,[28] but the discoverer may claim it in a purified, isolated, or altered form.[29]

Patents claiming *processes* using living organisms have been allowed in the United States since the 1970's.[30] In 1980, the Supreme Court held that genetically-altered living organisms are patentable as "manufactures" or "compositions of matter." The utility patent statute contains no provision excluding patent protection for such living organisms, and the Court refused to infer one.

The Supreme Court's 1980 *Chakrabarty* decision,[31] a landmark in biotechnology patent law history, involved using bacteria to degrade oil. Chakrabarty and an associate discovered that certain plasmids in bacteria control their ability to degrade oil components. Chakrabarty later discovered a process for transferring the plasmids in stable form from four bacteria to a single bacterium, which itself had no capacity for degrading oil. The PTO allowed claims to the process but rejected claims for the genetically-altered bacterium. The Supreme Court reversed, reasoning that (1) the bacterium was not a product of nature because a human made it, (2) no patent statute excluded living things, and (3) the plant patent acts were directed to other problems[32] and did not represent a Congressional determination not to allow patents on

---

[28] Diamond v. Chakrabarty, 447 U.S. 303, 309, 206 U.S.P.Q. 193 (1980) ("a new mineral discovered in the earth or a new plant found in the wild is not patentable subject matter"); General Elec. v. De Forest, 28 F.2d 614 (3d Cir. 1928); *Ex parte* Latimer, 1889 Comm'n Dec. 13 (1889); *Ex parte* Grayson, 51 U.S.P.Q. 413 (Pat. Off. Bd. App. 1941) (shrimp with head and digestive organs removed).

Cf. Funk Bros. Seed Co. v. Kalo Inoculant Co., 333 U.S. 126, 76 USPQ 280 (1948), discussed at § 2C[1][f][ii](2).; American Fruit Growers v. Brogdex co., 283 U.S. 1, 8 U.S.P.Q. 131 (1931). *Compare* Merck v. Olin Mathieson Chemical Corp., 253 F.2d 156, 116 U.S.P.Q. 484 (4th Cir. 1958).

[29] *E.g.,* Scripps Clinic & Research Foundation v. Genentech, Inc., 927 F.2d 1565, 18 U.S.P.Q.2d 1001 (Fed. Cir. 1991) (patent relating to the human protein, pure Factor VIII:C, the blood clotting factor: Claim 24: "A human VIII:C preparation having a potency in the range of 134 to 1172 units per ml. and being substantially free of VIII:RP."); Amgen, Inc. v. Chugai Pharmaceutical Co., 927 F.2d 1200, 18 U.S.P.Q.2d 1016 (Fed. Cir. 1991) (two patents relating to human erythropoietin (EPO), a 165 amino acid protein that stimulates red blood cell production; U.S. Patent 4,703,008, Claim 2, to "A purified and isolated DNA sequence consisting essentially of a DNA sequence encoding human erythropoietin;" U.S. Patent 4,677,195, Claim 1, to "Homogeneous erythropoietin characterized by a molecular weight of about 34,000 daltons on SDS PAGE, movement as a single peak on reverse phase high performance liquid chromatography and a specific activity of at least 160,000 IU per absorbance unit at 280 nanometers"); In re Kratz, 592 F.2d 1169, 201 U.S.P.Q. 71 (CCPA 1979); In re Bergy, 563 F.2d 1031, 1036, 195 U.S.P.Q. 344 (CCPA 1977), *remanded sub nom.* Parker v. Bergy, 438 U.S. 902, 198 U.S.P.Q. 257 (1978), *on remand,* 596 F.2d 952, 201 U.S.P.Q. 352 (CCPA 1979) (a biologically-pure strain of a microorganism found in a soil sample is not a product of nature).

[30] *See, e.g., In re* Mancy, 499 F.2d 1289, 182 U.S.P.Q. 303 (CCPA 1974).

[31] Diamond v. Chakrabarty, 447 U.S. 303, 206 U.S.P.Q. 193 (1980).

[32] *See* § 6C.

non-plant living things. Congress, not the judiciary, should weigh genetic-engineering and life form patenting policy implications.[33]

The Board of Patent Appeals and Interferences applied *Chakrabarty* to confirm the patentability of plants and animals. In *Hibberd*,[34] it held that a corn plant, corn seed and corn tissue culture were proper subjects for a utility patent even though the plant and the seed might also be protectable under the Plant Patent Act or the Plant Variety Protection Act. In *Allen*,[35] the Board held that a genetically altered oyster was a proper subject for a utility patent.

In 1988, the PTO issued the first patent claiming a multicellular animal, a genetically-altered mouse.[36]

A patent application that claims biological material has special problems in complying with the enabling disclosure requirement.[37]

[e] Systems—Methods of Treatment of Humans and Animals—Presentations of Information. Early case law and Patent Office practice developed three vague limitations on patentable subject matter: (1) business systems, (2) printed matter, and (3) methods of treatment of humans and animals.[38] All three limitations lack firm footing in statutory language or well-reasoned, extrastatutory policy, and are, therefore, of questionable contemporary vitality.

A 1908 Second Circuit decision stated that a "system of transacting business disconnected from the means for carrying out the system" is not patentable subject matter[39]

---

[33] "The grant or denial of patents on micro-organisms is not likely to put an end to genetic research or to its attendant risks . . . . Whether respondent's claims are patentable may determine whether research efforts are accelerated by the hope of reward or slowed by want of incentives, but that is all. What is more important is that we are without competence to entertain these arguments . . . The choice we are urged to make is a matter of high policy for resolution within the legislative process after the kind of investigation, examination, and study that legislative bodies can provide and courts cannot." 447 U.S. at 317.

[34] *Ex parte* Hibberd, 227 U.S.P.Q. 443 (PTO Bd. Pat. App. & Int'f 1985).

[35] *Ex parte* Allen, 2 U.S.P.Q.2d 1425 (PTO Bd. Pat. App. & Int'f 1987), *aff'd*, 846 F.2d 877 (Fed. Cir. 1988) (unpublished).

In *Allen*, the applicants developed a method for producing polyploid Pacific oysters of the species *Crassostrea gigas*. Sterile oysters do not devote significant portions of their body weight to reproduction, thereby remaining edible year round. Natural oysters are considered inedible during the Summer breeding season—the non-"R" months. The examiner allowed the applicants' method claims but rejected their product-by-process claims as being directed to "living entities" and therefore beyond Section 101. The Board reversed the Section 101 rejection, relying upon *Chakrabarty* and *Hibberd* but affirmed a Section 103 obviousness rejection.

[36] The patent, No. 4,736,866, issued on April 12, 1988 to Harvard University as assignee of Professors Phillip Leder and Timothy Stewart, claims "a transgenic non-human mammal" the cells of which are altered to contain a recombinant activated oncogene. The preferred embodiment is a rodent in the form of a mouse. The patent stresses the utility of the claimed mice for cancer research and testing.

[37] *See* § 2D[3][a][vi].

[38] *See generally* D. Chisum, Patents §§ 1.02[4], 1.03[3], [5].

[39] Hotel Security Checking Co. v. Lorraine Co., 160 F. 467 (2d Cir. 1908) (holding unpatentable a method for maintaining restaurant records so as to prevent frauds by waiters).

but offered no precise reason for the exclusion. There have been few recent cases on business systems.[40] Two decisions, apparently recognizing the excludability of business systems "as such," hold that a business or accounting system implemented on a computer is patentable subject matter.[41]

Early court decisions held that an invention consisting of the arrangement of information on a substrate, however new and useful, is not patentable subject matter unless the invention calls for a new relationship between the information and the substrate.[42] The limitation was closely related to that on business systems because most attempts to patent "printed matter" involved information arrangements designed to implement a business system.[43] The decisions give no reason for excluding printed matter independent of a desire not to subvert the business system exclusion. Recent decisions question the printed matter limitation's scope without directly repudiating it.[44]

Two instructive "printed matter" cases deal with information matter on a medium for direct machine interaction. In each instance, the claimed subject matter was found not excludable.[45]

---

[40] Patents regularly issue claiming what might be characterized as business or other informational organizing systems. *See, e.g.,* U.S. Patent No. 4,483,680, Nov. 20, 1984 ("genealogical information recording and arrangement method and apparatus"); U.S. Patent No. 4,464,122, Aug. 7, 1984 ("health potential summary and incentive system").

[41] *In re* Johnston, 502 F.2d 765 (CCPA 1974), *rev'd, on other grounds sub nom.* Dann v. Johnston, 425 U.S. 219 (1976); Paine, Webber, Jackson & Curtis, Inc. v. Merrill Lynch, Pierce, Fenner & Smith, 564 F. Supp. 1358, 218 U.S.P.Q. 212 (D. Del. 1983).

[42] *E.g., In re* Russell, 48 F.2d 668 (CCPA 1931) (directories with surnames indexed in a certain manner are not patentable); United States Credit System Co. v. American Credit Indemnity Co., 59 F. 139 (2d Cir. 1893) (business forms with appropriate headings are not patentable).

[43] *See* Note, *Patentability of Printed Matter: Critique and Proposal,* 18 Geo. Wash. L. Rev. 475, 476 (1950) ("The origin of the printed-matter doctrine is found in the long-standing rule that abstractions, mental theories or business methods are not patentable subject matter.").

[44] *In re* Gulack, 703 F.2d 1381, 217 U.S.P.Q. 401 (Fed. Cir. 1983); *In re* Miller, 418 F.2d 1392, 164 U.S.P.Q. 46 (CCPA 1969).

[45] *In re* Jones, 373 F.2d 1007, 153 U.S.P.Q. 77 (CCPA 1967); *Ex parte* Carver, 227 U.S.P.Q. 465 (PTO Bd. Pat. App. & Int'f 1985).

Jones concerned a certain analog-to-digital encoder in which light passes through a rotating disc with a pattern of transparent areas onto a photocell and related reading means for converting the light into digital signals. The disc code pattern is of great importance. Jones' contribution was solely in the pattern or informational content on the disc (the "software"). The disc ("hardware") was otherwise the same as the prior art. The court held Jones' claims to suitably patterned discs were patentable subject matter not subject to the printed matter exclusion. (Claims to the *method* (*i.e.* process) of encoding analog information into digital values utilizing the new disc pattern had already been allowed by the PTO.)

> "Certainly there is no 'printing' . . . in the form of words or other symbols intended to convey intelligence to a reader nor in the form of rulings as on a business form. The user of the disc is not supposed to contemplate it as he would a mathematical table, weighing scale chart, or the like in order to derive some information. The disc is devised, made and used as a component part of a machine utilizing optics and electronics to perform functions. . . . We think it is error to confuse the lines of a patent drawing, which may have the appearance of 'printed matter,' with functional elements of a mechanism which

Early court and Patent Office decisions indicated that therapeutic treatment methods were not patentable.[46] The Patent Office has changed position and indicated that medical methods are patentable if they meet the process definition and the conditions of utility, novelty and nonobviousness.[47]

[f] **Computer Software: Algorithms and Mathematical Inventions.** Whether computing methods are patentable is the subject of much controversy, in the United States and elsewhere.[48]

Neither a mathematical formula nor an algorithm for making mathematical computations or conversions can be patented *as such.*[49] Nor can processes involving "mental steps," that is, human thought or calculation, be patented if the steps require subjective or aesthetic human judgment.[50] Systems using mathematical formulae or mental systems can be patented as processes, and a process is not precluded from eligibility for patent protection merely because one step is use of a suitably

---

in use actuate other mechanisms or electrical circuits or devices intended to be illustrated by the drawing."

373 F.2d at 1013.

Carver concerned a stereophonic recording pattern. When played on a stereo player in a defined human hearing environment, the recording generated compensating signals such that the recorded left channel included signals that substantially cancelled certain sound patterns received at a left ear location from the right speaker. Correspondingly, the recording generated signals to cancel out sounds received at the right ear location from the left speaker. The PTO Board of Appeals held that the claims could not be rejected as for nonstatutory "recorded" or "printed matter" even though, again, the only difference between the claimed product and prior art recordings was in the recorded sound pattern (the software).

Some patent applicants rely on these cases to draft computer program patent claims, for example, a claim to "A computer storage disk containing a program" etc.

[46] *Ex parte* Brinkerhoff, 24 Comm'n MS Decision 349, 27 J. Pat. Off. Soc'y 797 (1883) (method of treating "piles" not patentable). *Cf.* Morton v. New York Eye Infirmary, 17 F. Cas. 879 (No. 9865) (S.D. N.Y. 1862).

Morton has historic interest. Jackson and Morton were surgical pioneers, the first to discover that ether gas would produce both sleep and insensitivity to pain, a discovery that greatly alleviated surgical pain. Prior to their discovery, it was known that inhaled ether caused intoxication but not that it caused pain insensitivity. The two obtained a patent claiming the performance of surgery "combining therewith the application of ether" as described in the patent specification. The court lauded the inventors for their discovery but held the method nonpatentable. The rationale for the decision was unclear. The court stated that a "new force or principle" must be "embodied and set to work" and can only be patented "in combination with the means by which . . . it operates." As to the combination with such means, "[n]either the natural functions of an animal upon which or through which it may be designed to operate, nor any of the useful purposes to which it may be applied can form any essential parts of the combination." 17 F.Cas. at 884.

[47] *Ex parte* Scherer, 103 U.S.P.Q. 107 (Pat. Off. Bd. App. 1954).

[48] *See generally* D. Chisum, Patents § 1.03[6].

For a comparative study, see H. Hanneman, The Patentability of Computer Software (1985).

[49] Parker v. Flook, 437 U.S. 584, 198 U.S.P.Q. 193 (1978); Gottschalk v. Benson, 409 U.S. 63, 175 U.S.P.Q. 673 (1972).

[50] *See, In re* Musgrave, 431 F.2d 882, 167 U.S.P.Q. 280 (CCPA 1970).

programmed digital computer.[51] Today, it is common for patents to issue claiming computer software structures and computing methods.[52]

[i]   *Abstract Ideas—Mental Steps.* Current law on mathematical algorithm and computer software patentability can be adequately understood only by considering two lines of cases, one on principles and abstract ideas and the other on "mental steps."

As to principles and abstract ideas, Supreme Court and lower court decisions back to the mid-19th century contained language to the effect that "a principle, in the abstract, is a fundamental truth . . . [which] cannot be patented."[53] These cases did

---

[51] Diamond v. Diehr, 450 U.S. 175, 209 U.S.P.Q. 1 (1981).

[52] Most prominent is a patent (No. 4,744,028), issued on May 10, 1988, to American Telephone and Telegraph Company, A T & T Bell Laboratories, as assignee of Dr. Narendra Karmarkar, that claims a "method and apparatus for optimizing resource allocations" based on Dr. Karmarkar's formulation of a new and more efficient algorithm for attacking linear programming models, such as the problem of determining the optimum routing of long-haul telephone traffic through the national telephone network, which involves a large number of possible linkages, all with associated costs and constraints. What is most unusual about the patent is the last paragraph. Instead of boilerplate language about the specification giving only illustrative examples and the ability of persons of ordinary skill in the art to perceive alternative embodiments that will fall within the invention as defined by the claims, the paragraph states, in part:

> "[T]he claims of this invention relate only to the application of this novel method to arrangements that determine the optimum allocation of resources in real world technological and industrial systems . . . All other uses of the new method, such as computation research, algorithm research, or linear algebra research activities, form no part of the present invention. Similarly, use of the new method in non-technological or non-industrial systems likewise form no part of the present intention."

For other examples of computer software related patents, see the following United States patents:

No. 4,555,775: "dynamic generation and overlaying of graphic windows for multiple active program storage areas"

No. 4,499,553: "locating digital coded words which are both acceptable misspellings and acceptable inflections of digital coded query words"

No. 4,509,119: "method for managing a buffer pool referenced by batch and interactive processes"

No. 4,507,752: "in-place index compression"

No. 4,517,658: "picture information filing system for permanently storing portions of previously permanently stored data logically combining the portions"

No. 4,502,128: "translation between natural languages"

No. 4,497,039: "joint operation processing system in relational model"

No. 4,468,728: "data structure and search method for a data base management system".

No.4,441,163: "dynamic send queue modification system"

No. 4,309,756: "method of automatically evaluating source language logic condition sets and of compiling machine executable instructions directly therefrom"

No. 4,197,590: "method for dynamically viewing image elements stored in a random access memory array."

[53] *E.g.,* Le Roy v. Tatham, 55 U.S. (14 How.) 156, 14 L. Ed. 367 (1852); Wyeth v. Stone, 30 F. Cas. 723 (No. 18,107) (C.C.D. Mass. 1840).

not explain clearly the distinction between a "principle," which could not be patented, and a "process," which could be patented without reference to specific hardware.[54] These cases can be explained in terms of more specific propositions, such as:

(1)   an inventor who discovers one means for achieving a useful result cannot claim all means for achieving that result;[55]

(2)   an inventor who merely shows how a known product or process operates cannot obtain a patent;[56]

(3)   the discoverer of a good business "idea" cannot obtain a patent unless he or she also develops a nonobvious product or process to carry it out.[57]

In *Wyeth*, the patentee invented a new machine for cutting ice and stated in his patent "It is claimed, as new, to cut ice of a uniform size, by means of an apparatus worked by any other power than human." Justice Story held this broad claim invalid.

[54] *See* Tilghman v. Proctor, 102 U.S. 707, 26 L. Ed. 279 (1880).

[55] *See* Dolbear v. American Bell Telephone Co., 126 U.S. 1 (1888); O'Reilly v. Morse, 56 U.S. 1, 15 How. 62 (1854).

In *O'Reilly*, the Supreme Court upheld several claims of Morse's telegraph patent but held invalid for undue breadth the following claim:

"Eighth. I do not propose to limit myself to the specific machinery or parts of machinery described in the foregoing specification and claims; the essence of my invention being the use of the motive power of the electric or galvanic current, which I call electro-magnetism, however developed, for making or printing intelligible characters, letters or signs, at any distances, being a new application of that power of which I claim to be the first inventor or discoverer." 56U.S. (15 How.) at 84-85.

Today, the PTO would not allow a claim in such loose language.

In *Dolbear* (the Telephone Case), the Court upheld the following claim in Morse's patent.

"The method of, and apparatus for, transmitting vocal or other sounds telegraphically, as herein described by causing electrical undulations, similar in form to the vibrations of the air accompanying the said vocal or other sounds, substantially as set forth." 126 U.S. at 53.

The claim was broad—but not quite so broad as to cover any means for transmitting sound telegraphically. The claim was limited by the concept of producing undulations in telegraphic (electrical) signals that were analogous to sound vibrations. That was what Alexander Graham Bell discovered, and the Court upheld his patent—even as applied to a telephone system that used a different electric mechanism (variable resistance) than he disclosed (electro-magnetic).

This problem is best analyzed as one of claim breadth: an inventor is entitled to claim only such means as he or she has invented and disclosed in the patent specification. The scope of the claim must be commensurate with the scope of the "enabling" disclosure. *See* § 2D[3][a][i].

Legal trivia buffs may be interested to know that the Telephone Case consumes the entire volume 126 of United States Reports.

[56] *E.g., In re* King, 801 F.2d 1324, 1325, 231 U.S.P.Q. 136 (Fed. Cir. 1986).

[57] *E.g.,* Rubber-Tip Pencil Co. v. Howard, 87 U.S. (20 Wall.) 498 (1874).

Rubber-Tip Pencil has been cited for the proposition that "An idea of itself is not patentable." In fact, the case simply held that a patent on attaching a rubber eraser to a pencil was invalid for obviousness. The phrase—"An idea of itself is not patentable"—was meant to say that a "good idea" for a product (good from a business or marketing point of view) did not meet the nonobviousness standard if the product itself was an obvious modification of the prior art from a technical point of view. The full language in context was as follows:

The "mental steps" cases dealt with attempts to patent processes involving mathematical calculations and other "thinking steps." The leading case upholding the mental steps doctrine was *Abrams*,[58] which implicitly approved three "rules" the inventor's counsel suggested: (1) if a claimed method consists wholly of "mental" steps, then the subject matter is not patentable; (2) if a claimed method consists of both physical steps and mental steps, and the novel element lies in the mental steps, then the subject matter is not patentable; and (3) if a claimed method consists of both physical steps and mental steps, and the novel element lies in the physical steps, then the subject matter is patentable. In *Abrams*, the court disallowed a claim for an improved petroleum prospecting seismic data analysis method because the alleged novelty was in the last two steps, which involved data calculation and interpretation.

In the computer age processes involving "mental steps" are no longer necessarily performed by humans but can be performed by programmed digital computers. Relying in part on the mental steps doctrine, the Patent Office would not allow patents on "software" or computer programming inventions.[59] But, in a three-year period beginning in 1969, the Court of Customs and Patent Appeals, in reviewing Office actions rejecting software patent applications, dismantled the mental steps doctrine.[60]

"Everybody knew, when the patent was applied for, that if a solid substance was inserted into a cavity in a piece of rubber smaller than itself, the rubber would cling to it. The small opening in the piece of rubber, not limited in form or shape, was not patentable; neither was the elasticity of the rubber. What, therefore, is left for this patentee but the idea that if a pencil is inserted into a cavity in a piece of rubber smaller than itself the rubber will attach itself to the pencil, and when so attached become convenient for use as an eraser?

"An idea of itself is not patentable, but a new device by which it may be made practically useful is. The idea of this patentee was a good one, but his device to give it effect, though useful, was not new."

87 U.S. at 507.

The language in context cannot be construed as saying that *no* ideas, including technical ideas, can be patented. Every patent covers one or more technical "ideas." The scope of a patent is determined by one or more claims. Claims list elements, which establish that scope. All claims (with the possible exception of so-called "fingerprint" claims involving chemical compounds and microorganisms) cover a variety of embodiments that may differ significantly from each other. To use a simple example, a patent might claim "A drinking composition consisting of a non-toxic fluid, a nontoxic dye, and sugar." This claim would cover both (1) an embodiment with water, red dye, and dextrose sugar, and (2) an embodiment with alcohol, blue dye, and sucrose sugar. A patent may claim a generic class of products only if it has sufficient supporting disclosure.

Whether a generic class of products or processes is an "idea" depends, of course, on one's definition of an "idea."

[58] *In re* Abrams, 188 F.2d 165 (CCPA 1951).

[59] *See* Bender, *Computer Programs: Should They Be Patentable?*, 68 Colum. L. Rev. 241, 255-256 (1968).

[60] The sequence of decisions was *In re* Prater, 415 F.2d 1378, 159 U.S.P.Q. 583 (CCPA 1968), *on rehearing*, 415 F.2d 1393, 162 U.S.P.Q. 641 (CCPA 1969); *In re* Bernhart, 417 F.2d 1395, 163 U.S.P.Q. 611 (CCPA 1969); *In re* Mahoney, 421 F.2d 742, 164 U.S.P.Q. 572 (CCPA 1970); and *In re* Musgrave, 431 F.2d 882, 167 U.S.P.Q. 280 (CCPA 1970).

Since these decisions, "mental steps" objections to patents or patent applications are rarely raised. *See* Alco Standard Corp. v. Tennessee Valley Authority, 808 F.2d 1490, 1496, 1

The culminating decision, *Musgrave*,[61] involving a seismic prospecting method, noted that the mental steps doctrine was a case law creation not founded on statutory language. *Abrams* "rules" 2 and 3 were "logically unsound" because "the identical process cannot be first within and later without the categories of statutory subject matter," depending on the state of the prior art. Prior art considerations relate only to the separate statutory requirements of novelty and nonobviousness, not to the statutory definition of a process. Rule 1's soundness "would depend on how one interprets 'purely mental.' "

> "If so construed as to encompass only steps incapable of being performed by a machine or apparatus, it might lead to a correct result. . . . If the expression 'purely mental' is construed . . . so as to encompass steps performable by apparatus, as well as mentally, then the Rule is unsound. . . ."[62]

The court noted that nothing in the statutory definition of a process required that all of the steps of a process be physical acts. It concluded:

> "We cannot agree . . . that these claims (all the steps of which can be carried out by the disclosed apparatus) are directed to non-statutory processes merely because some or all the steps therein can also be carried out in or with the aid of the human mind or because it may be necessary for one performing the processes to think. All that is necessary, in our view, to make a sequence of operational steps a statutory process' within 35 U.S.C. § 101 is that it be in the technological arts so as to be in consonance with the Constitutional purpose to promote the progress of useful arts.' Const. Art. 1, sec. 8.

> "Of course to obtain a valid patent the claim must also comply with all the other provisions of the statute, including definiteness under 35 U.S.C. § 112. A

U.S.P.Q.2d 1337, 1341 (Fed. Cir. 1986), *cert. dismissed*, 483 U.S. 1052 (1987) ("The inclusion in a patent of a process that may be performed by a person, but that also is capable of being performed by a machine, is not fatal to patentability.").

[61] *In re* Musgrave, 431 F.2d 882, 167 U.S.P.Q. 280 (1970).

The groundwork for the opinion and result in *Musgrave* was laid in *In re* Prater, 415 F.2d 1378, 159 U.S.P.Q. 583 (CCPA 1968), *on rehearing*, 415 F.2d 1393, 162 U.S.P.Q. 641 (CCPA 1969). *Prater* involved a claimed means of analyzing spectrographic data that was based on the applicants' discovery of a certain mathematical relationship. In theory, the method could be carried out by a human using pencil and paper. In practice, the necessary computations were so large that the method could only be usefully utilized on a computer. In the initial opinion, Judge Smith systematically and convincingly demolished the mental steps doctrine and concluded that "patent protection for a process disclosed as being a sequence or combination of steps, capable of performance without human intervention and directed to an industrial technology—a 'useful art' within the intendment of the Constitution—is not precluded by the mere fact that the process could alternatively be carried out by mental steps." 415 F.2d at 1389. The court granted rehearing, and seemingly accepted Judge Smith's analysis of the mental steps doctrine, but held the method claims failed to meet Section 112 disclosure and clear claiming requirements because they covered *human* as well as *machine* implementation. The court approved claims to a special purpose analog computer for carrying out the described analysis.

A human interest aspect of *Prater* is that Judge Arthur M. Smith, an intellectual leader on the CCPA, died the day the first *Prater* opinion was handed down (November 20, 1968).

[62] 431 F.2d at 889-90.

(Matthew Bender & Co., Inc.)

step requiring the exercise of subjective judgment without restriction might be objectionable as rendering a claim indefinite, but this would provide no statutory basis for a rejection under 35 U.S.C. § 101."[63]

[ii] *Supreme Court Intervention: Benson.* The two lines of cases—abstract ideas and mental steps—came together in the Supreme Court's *Benson*[64] ruling that an algorithm for converting binary-coded decimals into binary numerals could not be patented because it was an abstract idea or natural principle. Many interpreted *Benson* as severely limiting computer software method patentability.

(1) *The BCD-to-Binary Conversion Algorithm.* The applicants, Gary Benson and Arthur Tabbot, filed a patent application claiming a method of converting "binary coded decimals" to pure binary numbers. A binary coded decimal (BCD) is an intermediate step between decimal numerals and binary numerals. BCD numerals involve substituting for the decimal numerals (0-9) their individual binary equivalents. A decimal "21" is converted to "10 01" in BCD and from there to "10101" in binary.

Benson focused on two claims—claim 8 for the method carried out on a piece of hardware (a reentrant shift register)[65] and claim 13 for a "data processing method" with no reference to hardware.[66] A person can carry out the claim 13 method using

---

[63] 431 F.2d at 893.

[64] Gottschalk v. Benson, 409 U.S. 63, 155 U.S.P.Q. 673 (1972). For an extensive critique of the *Benson* opinion, see Chisum, *The Patentability of Algorithms*, 47 U. Pitt. L. Rev. 959 (1986).

[65] Claim 8 reads as follows:
"The method of converting signals from binary coded decimal form into binary which comprises the steps of
    (1)   storing the binary coded decimal signals in a reentrant shift register,
    (2)   shifting the signals to the right by at least three places, until there is a binary '1' in the second position of said register,
    (3)   masking out said binary '1' in said second position of said register,
    (4)   adding a binary '1' to the first position of said register,
    (5)   shifting the signals to the left by two positions,
    (6)   adding a '1' to said first position, and
    (7)   shifting the signals to the right by at least three positions in preparation for a succeeding binary '1' in the second position of said register."

[66] Claim 13 reads as follows:
"A data processing method for converting binary coded decimal number representations into binary number representations comprising the steps of

"(1) testing each binary digit position 'i,' beginning with the least significant binary digit position of the most significant decimal digit representation for a binary '0' or a binary '1;'

"(2) if a binary '0' is detected, repeating step (1) for the next least significant binary digit position of said most significant decimal digit representation;

"(3) if a binary '1' is detected, adding a binary '1' at the (i + 1)th and (i + 3)th least significant binary digit positions of the next lesser significant decimal digit representation, and repeating step (1) for the next least significant binary digit position of said most significant decimal digit representation;

"(4) upon exhausting the binary digit positions of said most significant decimal digit representation, repeating steps (1) through (3) for the next lesser significant decimal digit representation as modified by the previous execution of steps (1) through (3); and

pencil and paper by following the specified steps. Using the method—even with pencil and paper—is "mechanical" (i.e. machine-like),[67] and requires no "thinking" or judgment other than concentration on carefully following the instructions.

(2)   *The Definition of an Algorithm.* What is an "algorithm?"[68] Mathematics and computer science literature offers definitions of an algorithm that differ in wording

---

"(5) repeating steps (1) through (4) until the second least significant decimal representation has been so processed."

[67] An example of carrying out the Benson-Tabbot is given in Chisum, Patents § 1.03[6][c] at n. 57:

"The number 125 is converted into BCD as 0001 0010 0101. The following steps are then followed:

"1. Start with the group of symbols farthest to the left (called 'the most significant decimal digit representation'). This is 0001.

"2. Within the group selected (0001), start with the number farthest to the right (called 'the least significant binary digit position'). This is a '1' (0001).

"3. The number in the position determined in step 2 is now 'tested.' If it is a '0,' then nothing is done and the testing moves on to the number to the left. If it is a '1' (which it is), then something must be added to the group of symbols to the right of the group in question (called the 'next lesser significant decimal digit representation'). The group to the right is 0010. What is added is a binary '1' to the second and fourth numbers from the right. Adding is done in binary means so that $1 + 0 = 1$ and $1 + 1 = 10$. Thus the addition is to the 2d and 4th positions [(0010)] because the test position (called 'i') in this instance was one, and under the method the addition to the group to the right is to the i + 1 and i + 3 positions. [The result is that the group to the right is changed to 1100—which is 0010 + 1010).]

"4. The testing continues, moving to the left within the group of symbols (i.e. to i + 1, then to i + 2, etc.). When the testing finds a '0,' no addition is made. The result is that no more additions are made as to 0001 since it contains only one '1.'

"5. The testing now moves to the group of symbols to the right (as modified by the prior additions). (In the claim, this is called "the next lesser significant decimal digit representation as modified" by the prior testing.) That group is now '1100.' Each of the number positions is again tested, moving from right to left. An addition must be made as to the 3d position (which has a '1'). A '1' is added to the 4th and 6th (i.e., i + 1 and i + 3, with i = 3) positions of the group to the right. The group to the right is 0101, and addition yields 101101. Another addition must be made as to the 4th position. A '1' is added to the 5th and 7th positions of 101101. This yields 1111101.

"6. The testing always stops after exhausting the group of symbols that is second from the right ('the second least significant decimal digit representation'). Thus, the resulting representation is 1111101. It will be seen that this is in fact 125 in binary numerals."

[68] As to the origin of the term "algorithm," see Knuth, 1 The Art of Computer Programming: Fundamental Algorithms 1 (2d ed. 1973):

"The word did not appear in *Webster's New World Dictionary* as late as 1957; we find only the older form 'algorism' with its ancient meaning, i.e. the process of doing arithmetic using Arabic numerals. In the middle ages, abacists computed on the abacus and algorists computed by algorism. Following the middle ages, the origin of this word was in doubt. . . . Finally, historians of mathematics found the true origin of the word algorism: it comes from the name of a famous Persian textbook author, Abu Ja far

but are for the most part consistent. Some authors describe an algorithm informally, such as "a recipe or specific set of rules or directions for performing a task"[69] or "a set of formal directions for obtaining the required solution."[70] Others offer more formal definitions, such as the following:

> "A *method of solution for problem P on device M* is a description in a language comprehensible to M of discrete steps performable by *M* and an ordering of these steps, such that given proper data, if *M* performs the prescribed steps in the prescribed order, a solution to the problem P. will result, if one exists. A method of solution will be called a *semi-algorithm* for *P* on *M* if the solution to *P* (if one exists) appears after the performance of finitely many steps. A semi-algorithm will be called an *algorithm* if, in addition, whenever the problem has no solution the method enables the device to determine this after a finite number of steps and halt."[71]

One author differentiates algorithms from other problem solving methods (such as "recipe, process, method, technique, procedure, routine") by listing five "important features" of an algorithm:

> "1) Finiteness. An algorithm must always terminate after a finite number of steps . . . .

> "2) Definiteness. Each step of an algorithm must be precisely defined; the actions to be carried out must be rigorously and unambiguously specified for each case . . . .

> "3) Input. An algorithm has zero or more inputs, i.e., quantities which are given to it initially before the algorithm begins. These inputs are taken from specified sets of objects . . . .

> "4) Output. An algorithm has one or more outputs, i.e. quantities which have a specified relation to the inputs . . . .

> "5) Effectiveness. An algorithm is also generally expected to be *effective*. This means that all of the operations to be performed in the algorithm must be sufficiently basic that they can in principle be done exactly and in a finite length of time by a man using pencil and paper."[72]

Mohammed ibn Mûsâ al-Khowârizmî (c 825) . . . Khowârizm is today the small Soviet city of Khiva. . . .

"Gradually the form and meaning of 'algorism' became corrupted; as explained by the Oxford English Dictionary, the word was 'erroneously refashioned' by 'learned confusion' with the word *arithmetic*."

[69] Machtey & Young, An Introduction to the General Theory of Algorithms 1 (1978).

[70] Aiserman, Gusey, Rozonoer, Smirnova & Tal, Logic, Automata, and Algorithms 305 (1971).

[71] Korfhage, Logic and Algorithms with Applications to the Computer and Information Sciences 89 (1966). The author makes it clear that a "device" can include a human being.

[72] Knuth, 1 The Art of Computer Programming: Fundamental Algorithms 4-6 (2d ed. 1973). By the reference to pencil and paper, this author seems to assume that an algorithm is primarily for information or number processing. Such is not necessarily the case. *See* n. 76 *infra*.

Another work lists three "empirical properties" that have been found to be present "in all algorithms constructed so far."

Many algorithms have another feature—recursiveness: one or more steps entail going back and repeating prior steps.[73]

Benson discussed the meaning of algorithm in the course of describing the Benson-Tabbot method.

> "A procedure for solving a given type of mathematical problem is known as an 'algorithm.' The procedures set forth in the present claims are of that kind; that is to say, they are a generalized formulation for programs to solve mathematical problems of converting one form of numerical representation to another. From the generic formulation, programs may be developed as specific applications."[74]

The Court erred both in implying that algorithms relate only to mathematical problems and in characterizing the Benson method as directed to "mathematical" problems. Algorithms may solve problems of a mathematical nature[75] but may also solve nonmathematical problems.[76]

> "(a) *Determinacy.* The procedure is specified so clearly and precisely that there is no room for arbitrary interpretation. A procedure of this kind can be communicated to another person by a finite number of instructions. The operations described by these instructions do not depend on the whim of the operator and constitute a determinate process which is completely independent of the person carrying it out.
>
> "(b) *Generality.* An algorithm is applicable to more than just one specific problem: it is used for solving a class of problems, with the procedural instructions valid for any particular set of initial data . . . .
>
> "(c) *Efficacy.* This property, sometimes called the *directionality* of an algorithm, means that application of an algorithmic procedure to any problem of a given kind will lead to a "stop" instruction in a finite number of steps, at which point one must be able to find the required solution."

Aiserman, Gusev, Rozonoer, Smirnova, & Tal, Logic, Automata, and Algorithms 308-09 (1971).

[73] For a discussion of the theoretical associations of recursiveness with algorithms, see Machtey & Young, An Introduction to the General Theory of Algorithms 2 (1978): "[A]ll evidence indicates that the class of partial recursive functions is exactly the class of effectively computable functions; that is, that the partial recursive functions are exactly the functions which can be computed by finite procedures, algorithms, or computer programs."

[74] 409 U.S. at 65.

[75] Perhaps the most famous is the algorithm derived from Euclid for finding the greatest common divisor of two positive integers a and b. One text relates the algorithm as follows:

"1. Compare a and b ($a = b$, or a $<$ b, or a $>$ b). Go on to 2.

"2. If $a = b$ then either is the greatest common divisor. Stop the computation. If $a =/ b$ go on to 3.

"3. Subtract the smaller from the larger number and write down the subtrahend and the remainder. Go to the next instruction.

"4. Assign symbol a to the subtrahend, and symbol b to the remainder. Return to direction 1.

"The procedure is repeated until $a = b$. Then the computation is stopped."

Aiserman, Gusev, Rozonoer, Smirnova, & Tal, Logic, Automata and Algorithms 306 (1971).

[76] *See* Wirth, *Data Structures and Algorithms*, 251 Sci. Am. (No. 3) 65 (1984):

"The first algorithms were invented to solve numerical problems such as multiplying numbers, finding the greatest common divisor, calculating trigonometric functions, and

A conversion of decimal numbers to binary-coded numbers to binary numbers is only loosely a "mathematical" problem.[77] It is a translation problem—comparable to converting temperature values from Fahrenheit to Celsius. The algorithm involves some arithmetic steps, such as adding in binary form, but the problem solved is not a mathematical one, such as finding the greatest common divisor of two numbers or a trigonometric function.

The Court's imprecision in characterizing an algorithm makes its algorithm exclusionary rule's scope uncertain.[78]

(3) *Clearing the Confusion in the* Benson *Opinion.* Benson held that the two Benson and Tabbot claims did not constitute proper subject matter for a patent (no matter how useful or new the claimed invention may have been).[79] The opinion offers thirteen paragraphs of reasoning, consisting primarily of recitations from Supreme Court decisions dating back to the mid-19th century. None of the reasoning adequately supports a *per se* rule excluding algorithm patents.

(aa) *Ideas and Phenomena of Nature.* In *Benson*, the Court cited prior Supreme Court cases, which it interprets as relating to "idea" and "phenomenon of nature" patentability.

---

so on. Today non-numerical algorithms are of equal importance; they have been devised for tasks such as finding the smallest element in a sequence, searching for a given word in a text, scheduling events, and sorting data into some specified order."
(Note the author's use of the patent art word "invented.")
"The literature gives some simple examples of nonmathematical algorithms, such as the following:
"Suppose . . . that one must traverse a simple maze without loops. This is easily accomplished by choosing to follow a specific direction.
"1. Whenever a branching of the maze is encountered, choose the right-most branch.
"2. Whenever a dead-end is encountered, turn around, and continue."
Korfhage, Logic and Algorithms with Applications to the Computer and Information Sciences 91 (1966). *See also* Note, *The Policy Implications of Granting Patent Protection to Computer Software: An Economic Analysis*, 37 Vand. L. Rev. 147, 153 (1984) (giving an algorithm for a "safe procedure for lifting a cup of coffee off a saucer").

[77] The Court erred in indicating the algorithm could be used to solve "problems" (plural). It would be more accurate to say that the algorithm could be used to write more efficient programs that in turn could be used to solve all sorts of problems—mathematical and non-mathematical.

[78] *See, e.g., In re* Toma, 575 F.2d 872, 197 U.S.P.Q. 852 (CCPA 1978) (method for "translation between source and target natural languages using a programmable digital computer" did not involve a "mathematical algorithm" in the *Benson* sense); *In re* Freeman, 573 F.2d 1237, 197 U.S.P.Q. 464 (CCPA 1978) (computer-based control system for typesetting alphanumeric information (including mathematical symbols) is not an algorithm in the *Benson* sense even though the applicant himself characterized his invention as a "local positioning algorithm;" the claimed method contained "no mathematical calculations, equations, or formulae").

[79] It could well be that the Benson-Tabbot method should not have been patented because it failed to meet the statutory novelty and nonobviousness standards, 35 U.S.C. §§ 102, 103, but, to determine patentability under those standards, one must uncover and consider the pertinent prior art. By ruling that the methods were not for patentable subject matter, the Court short-circuited any such consideration.

MacKay Radio & Telegraph [80] involved a patent claiming a radio antennae in which a mathematical formula defined the antenna wires' angle, wire length, and the propagated radio wave length. The formula was an empirical one derived from another formula devised by someone else thirty years before the invention. The Court held the patent applicable only to antennae of wire lengths that were exact multiples of half wave lengths. The patentee's attempt to extend the patent to other wave lengths to show infringement would render the patent invalid. [81]

Benson quotes one sentence from *MacKay Radio*: "While a scientific truth, or the mathematical expression of it, is not patentable invention, a novel and useful structure created with the aid of knowledge of scientific truth may be." This statement related not to patentable subject matter, which was not an issue in the case, but to what constitutes a "patentable invention," the short-hand phrase used before the 1952 Patent Act for the nonobviousness requirement. [82] The statement is certainly acceptable because any statement, such as a mathematical formula, that *describes* natural relations is not a "new" process or product.

Benson quotes passages from *Rubber-Tip Pencil*, [83] discussed above, and *LeRoy*, [84] another ancient case, which held that the practical application of a newly-discovered principle could be patented but only in the form of a product or process that was itself new. The inventor discovered a property of lead—that it would form a perfect bond if poured under defined pressure and temperature conditions. The inventor obtained a patent claiming standard pipe-making machinery "when used to form pipe of metal, under heat and pressure," etc. The Court held the patent invalid. The patentee's principal problem was in the language of the claim—it was for machinery that was already known in the art. [85]

After quoting the above cases, *Benson* offered a dogmatic statement: "Phenomena of nature, though just discovered, mental processes, and abstract intellectual concepts are not patentable, as they are the basic tools of scientific and technological work." This statement makes three assertions—two explicit and one implicit. The explicit assertions are that (1) natural phenomena, mental processes, and abstract intellectual concepts are to be lumped together as unpatentable subject matter, and (2) the reason for such unpatentability is that all are "basic tools" of technological work. The implicit assertion is that an algorithm is a phenomenon of nature, mental process or abstract intellectual concept.

None of the assertions is true. First, an algorithm is neither a phenomenon of nature nor an abstract concept. The Benson-Tabbot algorithm is a human construction. One cannot perceive an algorithm in nature. The algorithm does not describe natural

---

[80] MacKay Radio & Telegraph Co. v. Radio Corp. of America, 306 U.S. 86, 37 U.S.P.Q. 471 (1939).

[81] *See* § 2F[2][b][viii].

[82] *See* § 2B[4].

[83] Rubber Tip Pencil Co. v. Howard, 87 U.S. (20 cWall.) 498 (1874). *See* § 2C[1][f][i].

[84] Leroy v. Tatham, 55 U.S. (14 How.) 156 (1852).

[85] It remains the law today that one cannot obtain a patent claiming an old product by discovering a previously unknown use or advantageous property of that product. *See* § 2C[1][c], [3][c].

phenomena or relationships and indeed does not describe anything other than a series of operations to be performed by a machine or human being. It is certainly not analogous to the formulae at issue in *MacKay Radio*, which did describe relationships relating to radio wave phenomenon. Neither is the algorithm fairly described as an "abstract intellectual" concept (such as "all persons are created equal" or "for every action there is an equal and opposite reaction"). Algorithms are by definition highly specific rather than abstract and prescriptive rather than descriptive.

Second, there is no basis for lumping together phenomena of nature and abstract concepts with "mental steps." A process consisting partially or wholly of "mental steps" does not exist in nature and can be quite specific. The Court's reference to "mental processes" is terse. Arguably, the Benson-Tabbot algorithm in claim 13 (but not in the machine claim 8) did involve "mental processes" if the claim is construed to cover human and not just machine implementation. The Court did not cite the long line of lower court cases on the mental steps doctrine.[86] Did it intend by the use of two words to resurrect the *Abrams* rules?

Third, the unpatentability of "phenomena of nature" is not self-evident.[87] The primary pre-*Benson* phenomena of nature Supreme Court decision is *Funk Bros. Seed.*[88] Various bacteria of the genus Rhizobium enable leguminous plants to fix nitrogen. A major problem was that different species of the genus were effective for different plants. Bacterial inoculant manufacturers sold single specie inoculants because the different species produced an inhibitory effect on each other. The inventor discovered that certain strains of certain species were noninhibitive to each other. This discovery enabled the production of a mixed culture, eliminating the need to select and use a variety of inoculants. The patent contained claims to (1) the process (or method) of making mixed cultures, and (2) the product consisting of mixed cultures. *Funk Bros. Seed* concerned only the product claims. The Court held the claims invalid, reasoning that (1) the property of non-inhibition was a natural phenomenon that could not be patented, and (2) given that phenomenon, the making of a mixed culture "fell short of invention" (*i.e.* was obvious)—it was no more than convenient packaging.

Funk Bros. Seed's reasoning has serious analytical shortcomings,[89] exposed in Justice Frankfurther's concurring opinion. Whatever the shortcomings, *Funk Bros. Seed* did concern a discovered natural phenomenon and a patent claim so broadly worded as to cover any inoculant that took advantage of that phenomenon.[90] The

---

[86] *See* § 2C[1][f][i].

[87] *See* § 2C[1][d].

[88] Funk Bros. Seed Co. v. Kalo Inoculant Co., 333 U.S. 127 (1948).

[89] The primary shortcoming is using the inventor's discovery of the phenomenon as prior art against him in assessing the patentability of a new product or process the discovered phenomenon makes possible. The phenomenon's unpatentability does not dictate that it be deemed prior art when, in fact, the prior art literature does not disclose it.

[90] Claim 4 reads:

"An inoculant for leguminous plants comprising a plurality of selected mutually non-inhibitive strains of different species of bacteria of the genus Rhizobium, said strains being unaffected by each other in respect to their ability to fix nitrogen in the leguminous plant for which they are specific."

333 U.S. at 127 n.1.

claim flaw, if there was one, was undue breadth, the patentee claimed more than he had invented and disclosed.[91]

Finally, the *Benson* "basic tools" rationale, *i.e.* that phenomena of nature, mental processes, and abstract intellectual concepts should not be patentable because they "are the basic tools of scientific and technology work," is only superficially attractive. The "basic tools" of research are matters in the body of accumulated human knowledge on science and technology. No process or structure within that body of knowledge can be patented, not because it does not qualify as patentable subject matter, but simply because it is not new and nonobvious. Patents are regularly allowed for processes and structures that have primary and even sole utility in research, including chemical processes, electrical apparatus, and optical instruments. A microscope is a "basic tool" for scientific work, but no one would assert that a new and nonobvious microscope improvement is inherently unpatentable.

(bb)   Abstract and Sweeping Scope—Unknown End Uses. Benson relies on the algorithm's alleged abstract nature and the sweeping scope of its potential use as grounds for finding it unpatentable *per se.*

> "Here the 'process' claim is so abstract and sweeping as to cover both known and unknown uses of the BCD to pure binary conversion. The end use may (1) vary from the operation of a train to verification of drivers' licenses to researching the law books for precedents and (2) be performed through any existing machinery or future-devised machinery or without any apparatus."[92]

---

[91] Undue breadth violates the statutory enabling disclosure requirement. 35 U.S.C. § 112. *See* § 2D[3][a]. *See generally* 2 Chisum, Patents § 7.03[7][b].

In concurring, Justice Frankfurter noted that the accused infringer used noninhibitive strains differing from those the patent owner discovered.

> "[The patent owner] appears to claim that since he was the originator of the idea that there might be mutually compatible strains and had practically demonstrated that some such strains exist, everyone else is forbidden to use a combination of strains whether they are or are not identical with the combinations that [the patent owner] selected and packaged together.

> "[Allowance of such a claim] would require, for instance in the field of alloys, that if one discovered a particular mixture of metals, which when alloyed had some particular desirable properties, he could patent not merely this particular mixture but the idea of alloying metals for this purpose, and thus exclude everyone else from contriving some other combination of metals which, when alloyed, had the same desirable properties. In patenting an alloy, I assume that both the qualities of the product and its specific composition would need to be specified.

333 U.S. at 133-34.

In dissenting, Justice Burton disagreed with Justice Frankfurter's overbreadth argument.

> "[I]t may be that a combination of strains of bacterial species, which strains are distinguished from one another and recognized in practice solely by their observed effects, can be definable reasonably only in terms of those effects. . . . There is no suggestion as to how it would be reasonably possible to describe the patented product more completely . . . . Bacteriologists, skilled in the applicable art, will not have difficulty in selecting the non-inhibitive strains by employing such standard and recognized laboratory tests as are described in the application for this patent." 333 U.S. at 137.

[92] 409 U.S. at 68.

As to "uses," the algorithm as claimed may be limited to *direct* uses, most likely primarily for creating programs for a particular type of machine—a digital computer. Even if the potential direct uses are vast and not fully known at the time the patent is applied for, it is unclear why this should matter. An inventor must find one specific practical utility for a new product or process,[93] but, once patentability is established, the patent covers all uses of the claimed invention—including ones not conceived by the inventor,[94] a common situation with chemical compounds and materials.

The Court focused on *end* uses. Why should it matter that a computer made more efficient by use of a better algorithm in its programming has a vast array of uses? To use an analogy, a new ignition system may have direct use primarily in automobiles, trains, and planes, which, in turn, have a vast number of uses. A method's usability on "any existing . . . or future-devised machinery or without any apparatus" is a reason for allowing, not denying, process claims.[95]

(cc) *Undue Breadth. Benson* recites the holdings and language from two famous 19th Century cases upholding the validity of the basic telegraph and the telephone patents.[96] These two cases stand for polar propositions on claim breadth. On the one hand, an inventor of one means of achieving a useful result cannot claim *all* possible means for achieving that result.[97] That would violate a basic tenet of the patent system—that an inventor may claim exclusive rights only over such means as he or she has invented and disclosed in the patent specification. On the other hand, an inventor should not be restricted to the particular preferred embodiment disclosed in that specification.[98] The inventor should be allowed to claim the invented "means" with an appropriate degree of generality.

Resolving the tension between these polar propositions is a difficult task,[99] but

---

[93] *See* § 2C[2].

[94] *See, e.g.,* B.G. Corp. v. Walter Kidde & Co., 79 F.2d 20, 22, 26 U.S.P.Q. 288, 290 (2d Cir. 1935) (Judge Learned Hand):

> "It is true that [the inventor of the patented improved spark plug] did not foresee the particular adaptability of his plug to the airplane; indeed we may assume that he did not even know the special needs of its engine. Nevertheless he did not shoot in the dark; he laid down with perfect certainty what he wished to accomplish and how; it was to conduct away the heat by his choice of metal for the 'shank,' to resist its loss by the metal in the 'head,' to use a metal for the 'point' which would stand up. The unsuspected value of this flexibility of heat control contributes to establish his discovery as an invention; he is not charged with a prophetic understanding of the entire field of its usefulness."

Cf. Ziegler v. Phillips Petroleum, 483 F.2d 858, 177 U.S.P.Q. 481 (5th Cir. 1973).

[95] *See* Cochrane v. Deener, 94 U.S. 780 (1877) ("That a process may be patentable, irrespective of the particular form of the instrumentalities used, cannot be disputed."). *See* § 2C[1][a].

[96] Dolbear v. American Bell Telephone Co., 126 U.S. 1 (1888); O'Reilly v. Morse, 56 U.S. 1, 15 How. 62 (1854). *See* § 2C[1][f][i].

[97] *See* §§ 2D[3][a][i] and 2D[3][d][vii].

[98] *See, e.g.,* Smith v. Snow, 294 U.S. 1, 11 (1935) (the patent laws require a patentee to disclose the best mode contemplated for carrying out the invention, but "he is not confined to that particular mode of use since the claims of the patent, not its specifications, measure the invention").

[99] *See* §§ 2D[3][a][i] and 2F[2][b][vii].

Benson and Tabbot's algorithm is an easy case: the claim is extraordinarily specific.[100] The telegraph and telephone cases would have been on point if, for example, Benson and Tabbot had claimed "A method of converting BCD numerals to binary numerals comprising use of an algorithm, said algorithm consisting of a limited number of discrete testing and adding steps."

(dd) A Process Definition—or Not? Benson cites prior Supreme Court decisions concerning chemical and mechanical processes. For example, Corning[101] listed several examples of a process, such as tanning, dyeing, and smelting ore, which Benson found significant in that chemical and raw material processes "are . . . sufficiently definite to confine the patent monopoly within rather definite bounds."

Cochrane,[102] which upheld a patent on refining flour, contains two sentences that can be interpreted as a process definition:

> "A process is a mode of treatment of certain materials to produce a given result. It is an act or a series of acts, performed upon the subject-matter to be transformed and reduced to a different state or thing."[103]

Relying on Cochrane, Benson states: "Transformation and reduction of an article 'to a different state or thing' is the clue to the patentability of a process claim that does not include particular machines."

What is meant by "the clue?" Is state or thing transformation a part of the definition of a patentable process—or not? Later, the Court leaves the definition issue indeterminate.

> "It is argued that a process patent must either be tied to a particular machine or apparatus or must operate to change articles or materials to a different state or thing.' We do not hold that no process patent could ever qualify if it did not meet the requirements of our prior precedents."[104]

(ee) Some Disclaimers. Benson emphasized what it does not hold or intend.

> "It is said that the decision precludes a patent for any program servicing a computer. We do not so hold. It is said that we have before us a program for a digital computer but extend our holding to programs for analog computers. We have, however, made clear from the start that we deal with a program only for digital computers. It is said we freeze process patents to old technologies, leaving no room for the revelations of the new, onrushing technology. Such is not our purpose."[105]

---

[100] It is certainly *clear*. It is hard to believe that there could be difficulty in determining whether there is infringement, *e.g.*, whether some person had without authority used the algorithm in a commercial computer program. The algorithm would be evident to a skilled programmer examining the source code of the program.

[101] Corning v. Burden, 56 U.S. (15 How.) 252 (1853).

[102] Cochrane v. Deener, 94 U.S. 780 (1877).

[103] 94 U.S. at 788.

The *Cochrane* court probably did not intend the statement to be a comprehensive process definition. Implicitly, "a process is" means "a process includes at least" or "includes things such as," not "a process is limited to."

[104] 409 U.S. at 71.

[105] 409 U.S. at 71.

The reference to a "program" for digital computers in the disclaimer is puzzling. Earlier in the opinion, the Court recognized that it was dealing with an algorithm as a "generic formulation" for programs, not with actual programs.

(ff) *The Nutshell. Benson* offered a one paragraph "nutshell" of "what we come down to."

> "It is conceded that one may not patent an idea. But in practical effect that would be the result if the formula for converting BCD numerals to pure binary numerals were patented in this case. The mathematical formula involved here has no substantial practical application except in connection with a digital computer, which means that if the judgment below is affirmed, the patent would wholly pre-empt the mathematical formula and in practical effect would be a patent on the algorithm itself."[106]

The "nutshell" demonstrates confusion as to nature of the subject matter at issue. The applicants were openly attempting to patent "the algorithm itself." The Court's task was to explain why the applicants were not entitled to the patent. "Mathematical formula," used here for the first time in the opinion does not accurately characterize the Benson-Tabbot method. A "formula" denotes a description of structure or ingredients (as in a chemical formula for ethyl alcohol, which is C_2H_5OH), not a prescription for action (as in an algorithm).

The Court does not say who "conceded" that one may not patent an "idea." "Wholly preempting" some class of product or process for a limited number of years is exactly how the patent system operates, and has operated for more than 200 years.

(gg) *Policy and the Prerogatives of Congress. Benson* conceded that "[i]t may be that the patent laws should be extended to cover these programs" but concludes that such extension is a policy matter that must be left to Congress. Whether the patent law would have to be "extended" to encompass algorithms begs the question whether the existing patent statutes, fairly interpreted, already cover algorithms.[107]

The Court quoted the 1966 Presidential Commission on the Patent System recommendation against extending patent protection to computer programs.

> "The Patent Office now cannot examine applications for programs because of a lack of a classification technique and the requisite search files. Even if these were available, reliable searches would not be feasible or economic because of the tremendous volume of prior art being generated. Without this search, the patenting of programs would be tantamount to mere registration and the presumption of validity would be all but nonexistent.

> "It is noted that the creation of programs has undergone substantial and satisfactory growth in the absence of patent protection and that copyright protection for programs is presently available."[108]

---

[106] 409 U.S. at 71–72.

[107] *See* Diamond v. Chakrabarty, 447 U.S. 303, 206 U.S.P.Q. 193 (1980), discussed at § 2C[1][d].

[108] "To Promote the Progress of . . . Useful Arts," Report of the President's Commission on the Patent System 13 (1966).

The Commission made a number of recommendations on reforming the patent system, all of which Congress ignored. The reference to Patent Office incompetency is hardly persuasive.[109] The implication is that the Office may choose not to accept patent applications in a new area of technology. Unless early applicants immediately and successfully bring court challenges to the Office's policy, the policy becomes self-justifying. Its refusal to examine results in an absence of trained examiners and a void of suitably classified prior art available to search and examine later applications in the technology. That void provides a later justification for not overturning the refusal to examine applications in the technology.

As to the difficulty of "reliable searches," PTO examiner searches are never fully reliable in any field of technology. Examiners primarily search documentary prior art, primarily English language sources such as prior U.S. patents, but all publications and matters in public use in the United States are also prior art.[110] If most prior art relating to computer technology is in nonpatent literature, examiners can be directed by Office policy to search such sources.[111] The problem of prior art that is obscure and not found by examiner searches is partially cured by the trend to impose on patent applicants an increased duty of full disclosure of known prior art.[112]

The Commission's assertion in 1966 of a satisfactory rate of software creation predates the development of a substantial independent software industry. In the 1950's and 1960's, computer vendors created software and sold it as part of bundled hardware-software systems. Today, companies develop and market software as a separate commodity.

[iii]   In Benson's *Wake*: Flook, and Diehr. Two Supreme Court decisions followed *Benson*, one expanding the algorithm unpatentability doctrine, the other contracting it. *Flook*[113] involved a method for updating an "alarm limit" value on a variable (such as temperature) in a catalytic chemical hydrocarbon conversion process.[114] The

---

[109] See Bender, *Computer Programs: Should They Be Patentable?*, 68 Colum. L. Rev. 241, 251-252 (1968).

[110] See § 2C[5].

[111] That nonpatent art is being cited and searched today can be verified by examining recent software patents. For example, in U.S. Patent No. 4,555,775, the "references cited" portion lists:

"The Smalltalk-80 System" by Xerox Learning Research Group, Byte Publications, Inc., vol. 6, No. 8, Aug. 1981, pp. 36-47.

"The Smalltalk Graphics Kernel" by D.H.H. Ingalls, Byte Publications, Inc., vol. 6, No. 8, Aug. 1981, pp. 168-194.

"The Smalltalk Environment" by L. Tesler, Byte Publications, Inc., vol. 6, No. 8, Aug. 1981, pp. 90-147.

[112] See § 2D[2].

[113] Parker v. Flook, 437 U.S. 584, 198 U.S.P.Q. 193 (1978).

[114] Claim 1 of Flook's application provided as follows:

"A method for updating the value of at least one alarm limit on at least one process variable involved in a process comprising the catalytic chemical conversion of hydrocarbons wherein said alarm limit has a current value of

$$Bo + K$$

wherein Bo is the current alarm base and K is a predetermined alarm offset which comprises:

Court treated the claimed subject matter as a method, one step of which was an "algorithm or mathematical formula" and the other steps of which were "conventional post-solution applications" of the formula.[115] The Court reasoned that (1) the applicant's only "novel" contribution to the prior art was the algorithm or mathematical formula, (2) because that algorithm or mathematical formula was, under *Benson*, not patentable subject matter, it must be treated as though it were "prior art," *i.e.* "as if the principle or mathematical formula were well known," even if it was not well known and the applicant was the first to formulate it;[116] and (3) the claim was not for patentable subject matter because the added "post-solution" activity was conventional. The applicant argued unsuccessfully that his claim did not "preempt the mathematical formula" because it was limited to a field of use, hydrocarbon catalytic conversion. The Court responded that the same was true in *Benson* in which "there was a specific end use contemplated for the algorithm—utilization of the algorithm in computer programming."[117]

Diehr[118] involved a method for heat curing synthetic rubber in a mold. With such molding, it is necessary to avoid both undercure (cooking too short, if you will) and overcure (cooking too long). The proper cure time was calculated according to Svante Arrhenius' formula, which took into account variables such as temperature, the composition being molded, and the mold's geometry.[119] A problem with applying the formula was that the temperature within the mold did not remain constant. It cooled to a varying extent during opening and then heated back up gradually after closing.

"(1) Determining the present value of said process variable, said present value being defined as PVL;

"(2) Determining a new alarm base B1, using the following equation:
$$B_1 = Bo(1.0 - F) + PVL(F)$$
where F is a predetermined number greater than zero and less than 1.0;

"(3) Determining an updated alarm limit which is defined as $B_1 + K$; and thereafter

"(4) Adjusting said alarm limit to said updated alarm limit value." 437 U.S. at 596-97.

[115] In fact, there was very little in the claim specifying "post-solution" activity (i.e. activity after use of the equation). The only such activity was the determination of an updated alarm limit (step 4). The more significant activity was "pre-solution"—that is, determining the present value of the process variable. That involved physical activity (temperature measurement, etc.), unlike the post-solution step, which was simply addition of two numbers.

[116] In fact, the "formula" probably *was* well known in the abstract because it is a simple equation for doing a weighted average alteration of one variable when another variable changes.

[117] 437 U.S. at 590, n.11.

[118] Diamond v. Diehr, 450 U.S. 175, 209 USPQ 1 (1981).

[119] The court gave the following description of the formula.

"The equation can be expressed as follows:
$$\ln v = CZ + x$$
wherein ln v is the natural logarithm of v, the total required cure time; C is the activation constant, a unique figure for each batch of each compound being molded, determined in accordance with rheometer measurements of each batch; Z is the temperature in the mold; and $\times$ is a constant dependent on the geometry of the particular mold in the press. A rheometer is an instrument to measure flow of viscous substances."

450 U.S. at 178, n.2.

Applicants James Diehr and Theodore Lutton claimed an improvement in rubber molding using the Arrhenius formula to calculate cure time. The method entailed, in addition to standard molding steps, (1) constantly determining temperature inside the mold, (2) repetitively calculating (i.e. updating) the cure time, (3) comparing the calculated proper cure time with the actual elapsed molding time, (4) opening the press when the two times were equal, and (5) removing the molded rubber product. The applicants stated their claims in different ways. One was to a "method of operating a rubber-molding press" "with the aid of digital computer." This claim specified that the computer should monitor the process, do the calculations, and "open the press automatically when [the] comparison indicates equivalence [of the total required cure time and the elapsed time]." Another claim was to the method in general terms. (As a practical matter, the continuous recalculation required by the method probably could not be performed except by some sort of computing device.)

In *Diehr*, the Court held the claim was for a typical industrial process—molding rubber products—and as such was subject matter eligible for patent protection if the other patentability requirements were met. Incorporation of computer use to improve the process did not make the process unpatentable subject matter. The Court retreated from *Flook's* direction that an unpatentable algorithm be considered as though it were prior art and stressed that whether a method falls within the Section 101 patentable subject matter categories is distinct from the question whether one or all of the elements of the method are novel or original with the inventor. The court did not overrule *Flook* and confirmed that "A mathematical formula as such is not accorded the protection of our patent laws" and that "insignificant post-solution activity will not transform an unpatentable principle into a patentable process."[120]

[iv] *The 1982 CCPA Decisions: The Two-Inquiry Test. Diehr*, which involved a typical industrial process, did not expressly approve patenting methods of computing or configuring a digital computer, but it was a catalyst for change. Four 1982 Court of Customs and Patent Appeals decisions approved patents on new and unobvious methods of computation unless the patent claim was for a *mathematical* algorithm *in the abstract.*[121] The CCPA articulated and refined a test that posed two inquiries. First, did the patent claim recite, directly or indirectly, a mathematical algorithm, formula, or "mental step?" (If not, then the claim was statutory subject matter; if so, the second inquiry must be reached.) Second, did the claim involve *application* of the algorithm, etc. to specific physical elements or process steps (something more than a field-of-use limitation or the addition of "non-essential post-solution activity?") (If so, the claim was for statutory subject matter; if not, the claim was not for statutory subject matter).

Abele[122] illustrates the difficulties encountered in applying the two-inquiry test. The applicant claimed an improvement in computed tomography ("CT scanning") image processing. CT scanning provides an image of a transverse slice of a human

---

[120] 450 U.S. at 191-192.

[121] *In re* Meyer, 688 F.2d 789, 215 U.S.P.Q. 193 (CCPA 1982); *In re* Pardo, 684 F.2d 912, 214 U.S.P.Q. 673 (CCPA 1982); *In re* Abele, 684 F.2d 902, 214 U.S.P.Q. 682 (CCPA 1982); *In re* Taner, 681 F.2d 787, 214 U.S.P.Q. 678 (CCPA 1982).

[122] *In re* Abele, 684 F.2d 902, 214 USPQ 682 (CCPA 1982).

organs, such as the liver or brain, by (1) rotating an X-ray source and detection means around the organ's perimeter (more or less radiation being detected depending on the type of tissue the radiation passes through); (2) mathematically interpreting the data, which requires use of a computer because numerous simultaneous equations must be solved); and (3) displaying the interpretation (e.g. on a television screen) for diagnosis. The image blurs out undesired regions and artifacts (such as the "shadow" of a bone). To reduce the amount of X-radiation necessary and the amount of data the computer must calculate, the applicants devised a means for taking a CT scan with a narrower beamed X-ray. The narrower beam provided less data and did not blur out artifacts. The applicants solved this problem and obtained a satisfactory image by employing certain calculations on the data (specifically, a calculation defined as a "Gaussian weighting function").

Of particular interest is the court's treatment of two method claims.

> "5. A method of displaying data in a field comprising the steps of calculating the difference between the local value of the data as a data point in the field and the average value of the data in a region of the field which surrounds said point for each point in said field, and displaying the value of said difference as a signed gray scale at a point in a picture which corresponds to said data point."

> "6. The method of claim 5 wherein said data is X-ray attenuation data produced in a two dimensional field by a computed tomography scanner."[123]

The court held both claims met the first inquiry because the "calculating" step "presents a mathematical formula or a sequence of mathematical operations."[124] Turning to the second inquiry, the court distinguished the two. Claim 5 was directed solely to "the mathematical algorithm" portion of the applicants' invention. Because it simply took data, computed, and produced a numerical result (or its equivalent in the form of a gray-scale picture), it was not patentable subject matter. Claim 6 was not directed solely to the algorithm because it required the antecedent step of acquiring data in a two dimensional field from a CT scanner. In upholding claim 6, the court did not rely on the "post-solution" step of displaying the data as a picture (which made the information more useful to a physician than mere numbers). In other words, the court said that the process would have been statutory even had the final step been solely number generation. The claimed process was tied to a "physical" or nonmathematical process—CT scanning. With the mathematical calculating step taken away, one was still left with a conventional CT scanning process of obtaining and displaying data.

[v] *The 1989 Federal Circuit Decisions:* Grams *and* Iwahashi. Two 1989 Federal Circuit decisions demonstrate the difficulty of applying *Benson* and the two-inquiry step test of mathematical algorithm patentability.

---

[123] 684 F.2d at 908.

[124] *Compare In re* Pardo, 684 F.2d 912, 916, 214 U.S.P.Q. 673 (CCPA 1982) (a method "for controlling the internal operations of a computer to govern the manner in which programs are executed" does not constitute a *mathematical* algorithm).

In *Grams*,[125] the Federal Circuit held that the PTO did not err in rejecting the applicants' claims to a clinical data analysis program as being directed to nonstatutory subject matter because the claims "in essence claim . . . a mathematical algorithm."

The invention disclosed in the applicants' specification "provides a method of testing a complex system to determine whether the system condition is normal or abnormal and, if it is abnormal, to determine the cause of the abnormality." Application claim 1 is a method of diagnosing an individual based on laboratory test data.[126]

The court noted that "intuitively" the applicants' diagnostic method is a "process" even without the "physical" data gathering step in limitation [a] but, conceded that because of *Benson*, "mathematical algorithms join the list of non-patentable subject matter not within the scope of section 101, including methods of doing business, naturally occurring phenomenon, and laws of nature." *Benson* remains the law despite the "liberal view" of Section 101 taken in *Chakrabarty*[127] and *Diehr*.[128]

The court viewed the claim as combining a physical step [a] with an algorithm (steps [b] to [e]) consisting of analyzing the data to ascertain an abnormality.[129] Determining

---

[125] *In re* Grams, 888 F.2d 835, 12 U.S.P.Q.2d 1824 (Fed. Cir. 1989).

[126] Claim 1 provides (with bracketed letters added by the court):

"A method of diagnosing an abnormal condition in an individual the individual being characterized by a plurality of correlated parameters of a set of such parameters that is representative of the individual's condition the parameters comprising data resulting from a plurality of clinical laboratory tests which measure the levels of chemical and biological constituents of the individual [sic] and each parameter having a reference range of values, the method comprising

[a] performing said plurality of clinical laboratory tests on the individual to measure the values of the set of parameters;

[b] producing from the set of measured parameter values and the reference ranges of values a first quantity representative of the condition of the individual;

[c] comparing the first quantity to a first predetermined value to determine whether the individual's condition is abnormal;

[d] upon determining from said comparing that the individual's condition is abnormal, successively testing a plurality of different combinations of the constituents of the individual by eliminating parameters from the set to form subsets corresponding to said combinations, producing for each subset a second quantity, and comparing said second quantity with a second predetermined value to detect a non-significant deviation from a normal condition;

[e] identifying as a result of said testing a complementary subset of parameters corresponding to a combination of constituents responsible for the abnormal condition, said complementary subset comprising the parameters eliminated from the set so as to produce a subset having said non-significant deviation from a normal condition." 888 F.2d at 836, 12 U.S.P.Q.2d at 1825.

[127] Diamond v. Chakrabarty, 447 U.S. 303, 206 U.S.P.Q. 193 (1980), discussed at § 2C[1][d].

[128] Diamond v. Diehr, 450 U.S. 175, 209 U.S.P.Q. 1 (1981).

[129] The applicants admitted that the claim includes a mathematical algorithm. The court noted that "[i]t is of no moment that the algorithm is not expressed in terms of a mathematical formula. Words used in a claim operating on data to solve a problem can serve the same purpose as a formula." 836 F.2d at 837 n.1, 12 U.S.P.Q.2d at 1826 n.1.

The court failed to note that an "algorithm" is not the same as a formula. A formula may constitute one step of an algorithm. *See* Chisum, *The Patentability of Algorithms*, 47 U.

when a claim that combines physical steps with an algorithm is eligible for patent protection is a difficult task. The two-inquiry *Walter* test[130] is not exclusive: "[T]hough satisfaction of the Walter test necessarily depicts statutory subject matter, failure to meet that test does not necessarily doom the claim." The court quoted language from *Abele*[131] interpreting the *Walter* test ("if the claim would be 'otherwise statutory' . . . albeit inoperative or less useful without the algorithm, the claim likewise presents statutory subject matter when the algorithm is included"), but declined to read *Abele's* "otherwise statutory" language as establishing a separate test:

> "We do not read the . . . sentence . . . as declaring patentable any claim that is statutory without the algorithm. We read it consistently with the previous sentence, and with *Walter*, as requiring (to meet the *Walter* test) not only that the physical steps in the claim (without the algorithm) constitute a statutory process but, also, that the algorithm operates on a claimed physical step."[132]

Rather, "[i]n all instances, this critical question must be answered: 'What did applicants invent?' " That determination is not based "solely on words appearing in the claims" but on a "careful interpretation of each claim in light of its supporting disclosure." In other parts of the opinion, the court phrased the inquiry as into whether "the claim in essence covers only the algorithm."

The court viewed the difficult analysis as "facilitated somewhat if, as here, the only physical step involves merely gathering data for the algorithm." After citing and quoting prior decisions dealing with antecedent data or value gathering steps,[133] the court cautioned:

> "Whether section 101 precludes patentability in every case where the physical step of obtaining data for the algorithm is the only other significant element in mathematical algorithm-claiming claims is a question we need not answer. Analysis in that area depends on the claims and the circumstances of each case."[134]

The applicants were "in essence, claiming the mathematical algorithm," especially because the inventor's specification did not "bulge with disclosure" on the physical step [a], that is, performing clinical tests on individuals to obtain data.[135]

In *Grams*, the court rejected applicant's argument that *Abele* dictated a reversal. In *Abele*, "the production and detection steps were not viewed as merely antecedent

---

Pitt. L. Rev. 959, 974-76, 994 (1986); Gemignani, *Should Algorithms Be Patentable?* 22 Jurimetrics J. 326, 332 n.129 (1982).

[130] *In re* Walter, 618 F.2d 758, 205 U.S.P.Q. 397 (CCPA 1980).

[131] *In re* Abele, 684 F.2d 902, 214 U.S.P.Q. 682 (CCPA 1982).

[132] 888 F.2d at 839 n.4, 12 U.S.P.Q.2d at 1827 n.4.

[133] *In re* Sarker, 588 F.2d 1330, 200 U.S.P.Q. 132 (CCPA 1978), *In re* Richman, 563 F.2d 1026, 195 U.S.P.Q. 340 (CCPA 1977); *In re* Christensen, 478 F.2d 1392, 178 U.S.P.Q. 35 (CCPA 1973).

[134] 888 F.2d at 840, 12 U.S.P.Q.2d at 1828.

[135] The specification stated that "The [computer] program was written to analyze the results of up to eighteen clinical laboratory tests produced by a standard chemical analyzer that measures the levels of the chemical biological components listed. . . . " and that "The invention is applicable to any complex system, whether it be electrical, mechanical, chemical or biological, or combinations thereof." 888 F.2d at 840, 12 U.S.P.Q.2d at 1828.

steps to obtain values to solve the algorithm." Rather, "the algorithm served to improve the CAT-scan process." As to applicant's claims, "because algorithm steps [b]-[e] do not operate to change any aspect of the physical process of step [a], the claim does not satisfy the *Walter* guideline. Though this by itself is not dispositive . . . patentability here is precluded by the fact that physical step [a] merely provides data for the algorithm." Applicants' claims were similar to those rejected in *Meyer*.[136]

The applicants appealed another rejected claim that required use of a programmed computer: "[A]pplicants have not persuaded us that performing the method of claim 1 with a computer requires a different result."

In *Iwahashi*,[137] the Federal Circuit held that the PTO erred in rejecting the applicants' claim to a voice recognition coefficient calculation apparatus. The PTO incorrectly found that the claim "is merely a mathematical algorithm." The claim language, which used means-plus-function terminology, was a machine or manufacture even though it embodied a mathematical formula.

The invention disclosed in the specification "relates to an auto-correlation unit for use in pattern (e.g. voice) recognition to obtain auto-correlation coefficients as for stored signal samples." Prior art auto-correlation coefficient calculation used a formula that required a multiplication step, which requires expensive multipliers and complicated circuitry. The inventors eliminated the multiplier, obtaining the desired coefficient's approximate value by squaring the sum of two equation factors and calculating the coefficient according to a stated formula. They set forth a block diagram of electronic circuitry embodying the invention.

The sole claim provides (with bracketed letters added by the court):

"[a] An auto-correlation unit for providing auto-correlation coefficients for use as feature parameters in pattern recognition for n.pieces of sampled input values X_n (n = 0 to N − 1), said unit comprising:

"[b] means for extracting n.pieces of sample input values X_n from a series of sample values in an input pattern expressed with an accuracy of optional multi-bits;

"[c] means for calculating the sum of the sample values X_n and $X_{n - r}$ (t = O − P, P < = N);

"[d] a read only memory associated with said means for calculating;

"[e] means for feeding to said read only memory the sum of the sampled input values as an address signal;

"[f] means for storing in said read only memory the squared value of each sum, $(X_n + X_{n - r})^2$;

"[g] means for fetching and outputting the squared values of each such sum of the sample input values from said read only memory when said memory is addressed by the sum of the sample input values; and

---

[136] *In re Meyer*, 688 F.2d 789, 215 U.S.P.Q. 193 (CCPA 1982).
[137] *In re Iwahashi*, 888 F.2d 1370, 12 U.S.P.Q.2d 1908 (Fed Cir. 1989).

"[h] means responsive to the output $(X_n + X_{n-r})^2$ of said read only memory for providing an auto-correlation coefficient for use as a feature parameter according to the following formula:

$$\frac{\sum\limits_{n=0}^{N-1} (X_n + X_{n-r})^2}{2 . \sum\limits_{n=0}^{N-1} X_n^2} - 1$$[138]

CCPA cases after *Benson* establish the *Freeman-Walter* two-inquiry test and "take the mystery out of the term ['algorithm']."

"[E]very step-by-step process, be it electronic or chemical or mechanical, involves an algorithm in the broad sense of the term. Since § 101 expressly includes processes as a category of inventions which may be patented and § 100(b) further defines the word 'process' as meaning process, art or method, and includes a new use of a known 'process, machine, manufacture, composition of matter, or material,' it follows that it is no ground for holding a claim is directed to nonstatutory subject matter to say it includes or is directed to an algorithm. This is why proscription against patenting has been limited to *mathematical* algorithms and abstract *mathematical* formulae which, like the laws of nature, are not patentable subject matter."[139]

The court emphasized the importance of claim language.

"The above-listed line of CCPA cases held some claims statutory and other claims nonstatutory, depending entirely on what they said. We have to do the same here. Appellants cautiously admit that their claim at least indirectly, recites an algorithm in 'some manner,' and thus meets the first part of the *Freeman-Walker* test, but argue strenuously and convincingly that it does not meet the second part of the test, relying, inter alia, on the following statement in *Walter* . . . :

'Once a mathematical algorithm has been found, the claim as a *whole* must be further analyzed. If it appears that the mathematical algorithm is implemented in a specific manner to define structural relationships between the physical elements of the claim (in apparatus claims) or to refine or limit claim steps (in process claims), the claim being otherwise statutory; the claim passes muster under § 101.'

. . . [A]ppellants . . . characterize what they claim as apparatus with specific structural limitations. . . . [W]e . . . agree. . . . The claim as a whole certainly defines apparatus in the form of a combination of interrelated means and we cannot discern any logical reason why it should not be deemed statutory subject matter as either a machine or a manufacture as specified in § 101. The fact that the apparatus operates according to an algorithm does not make it nonstatutory."[140]

---

[138] 888 F.2d at 1373, 12 U.S.P.Q.2d at 1910.
[139] 888 F.2d at 1374, 12 U.S.P.Q.2d at 1910.
[140] 888 F.2d at 1374-75, 12 U.S.P.Q.2d at 1911.

The court disagreed with the PTO solicitor's argument that the means-plus-function limitations in the claim cover every means for performing the function and therefore the claim should be regarded as a method claim. "Means" limitations are subject to Section 112's construction rule, that is, they only cover the corresponding structure, material or acts in the specification and equivalents[141]

[2]   Utility—Industrial Application—Immoral Creations

The utility requirement derives from the word "useful" in Section 101.[142]

The patent laws impose three related utility conditions: (1) a claimed product or process must in fact be useful;[143] (2) a person must have discovered the invention's utility to achieve a reduction to practice for the purposes of invention priority;[144] and (3) the inventor's patent specification must disclose how to use the claimed invention.[145]

An invention need only be operable and capable of satisfying some function of benefit to humanity.[146] It need not be more useful than prior art devices or processes[147] though superiority is relevant to other patentability standards such as nonobviousness.[148]

Examples of inventions lacking utility include those that (1) conflict with known scientific principles, for example, a perpetual motion machine,[149] (2) require means

---

[141] See §§ 2D[3][d][vii] and 2F[1][d].

[142] See generally D. Chisum, Patents § 4.01 et seq.

[143] 35 U.S.C. § 101.

[144] Brenner v. Manson, 383 U.S. 519, 148 U.S.P.Q. 689 (1966). See § 2D[6][a].

[145] 35 U.S.C. § 112. See § 2D[3][a].

[146] E.g., United States Steel Corp. v. Phillips Petroleum Co., 865 F.2d 1247, 9 U.S.P.Q.2d 1461 (Fed. Cir. 1989) (a 1953 parent application, which led, after a series of continuing applications, to issue of a patent claiming crystalline polypropylene, was not defective for inadequate disclosure of specific utility even though the polymer disclosed in the 1953 application was of such low molecular weight and intrinsic viscosity as to be of little commercial value); Du Pont de Nemours & Co. v. Berkley & Co., 620 F.2d 1247, 205 U.S.P.Q. 1 (8th Cir. 1980).

Only potential usefulness is required. Cf., Ex parte McKay, 200 U.S.P.Q. 324 (PTO Bd. App. 1975) (claims for processes for "obtaining oxygen from extraterrestrial materials:" "The recited method is . . . useful, although practical considerations would dictate against its commercial exploitation on earth. The latter, however, is not a standard by which the statutory requirement of utility is to be measured.").

[147] In re Ratti, 270 F.2d 810, 123 U.S.P.Q. 349 (CCPA 1959).

This interpretation of utility traces back to Justice Joseph Story's opinions. E.g., Bedford v. Hunt, 3 F. Cas. 37 (No. 1217) (C.C.D.Mass. 1817) ("The law . . . does not look to the degree of utility; it simply requires, that [the invention] shall be capable of use, and that the use is such as sound morals and policy do not discountenance or prohibit.").

[148] See § 2C[4][c].

[149] E.g., In re Ferens, 417 F.2d 1072, 163 U.S.P.Q. 609 (CCPA 1969). See also Newman v. Quigg, 877 F.2d 1575, 11 U.S.P.Q.2d 1340 (Fed. Cir. 1989) ("Energy Generation System Having Higher Energy Output Than Input"); Fregeau v. Mossinghoff, 776 F.2d 1034, 227 U.S.P.Q. 848 (Fed. Cir. 1985) (method for enhancing the flavor of a beverage by passing it through a magnetic field).

for accomplishing an unattainable result,[150] or (3) are inevitably unreasonably dangerous.[151]

Older cases indicated that utility was lacking if the invention was "frivolous or injurious to the well-being, good policy, or sound morals of society."[152] Today, the trend is to restrict this subjective public policy approach to utility.[153]

To establish a chemical compound's utility, the inventor must show a specific practical use for the compound exists or would be obvious.[154]

In *Manson*,[155] the inventor Manson filed an application claiming a new process for making a known steroid compound. Another inventor had already obtained a patent on the process, and Manson sought to establish that he was the first inventor.[156] Manson filed an affidavit with the Patent Office alleging that he had used the process to synthesize the compound prior to the filing date of the other inventor. The Supreme Court held this affidavit insufficient to show a *prima facie* invention date. Manson had not alleged either that he had discovered practical utility for the compound or that such utility was obvious to persons of ordinary skill in the art. It is not sufficient that the compound produced by the process was "the subject of serious scientific investigation." A process to produce a compound may be patented only if the compound has substantial utility.[157]

---

[150] Raytheon Co. v. Roper Corp., 724 F.2d 951, 220 U.S.P.Q. 592 (Fed. Cir. 1983), *cert. denied*, 469 U.S. 835, 225 U.S.P.Q. 232 (1984).

[151] Twentieth Century Motor Car v. Holcomb Co., 220 F. 669 (2d Cir. 1915).

[152] Lowell v. Lewis, 15 F. Cas. 1018 (No. 8568) (C.C.D. Mass. 1817).

The courts invalidated patents on devices whose sole purpose was gambling or committing frauds. *E.g.*, Meyer v. Buckley Mfg., 15 F. Supp. 640, 31 U.S.P.Q. 58 (N.D. Ill. 1936); Richard v. Du Bon, 103 F. 868 (2d Cir. 1900) (process for making cheap cigar wrapper tobacco leaf resemble leaf from choice locations). Courts refused to invalidate patents on devices merely capable of illegal or immoral uses. *E.g.*, Chicago Patent Corp. v. Genco, 124 F.2d 725, 52 U.S.P.Q. 3 (7th Cir. 1941) (pinball machine). *Cf.*, Naylor v. Alsop Process, 168 F. 911 (8th Cir. 1909) (upholding patent on flour bleaching process even though the process removed nutrients and could be used to make poor quality flour resemble better quality flour).

Fuller v. Berger, 120 F. 274 (7th Cir. 1903), distinguished two possible "immorality" defenses. One is that the patented invention lacked utility, a defense sustained only if the device was "incapable of serving any beneficial end." A second is that the patent owner was commercially practicing the invention for immoral purposes. The latter should not be grounds for denying a remedy against an infringer: "[I]f the defendant can do no more than show that the complainant has committed some legal or moral offense, which affects the defendant only as it does the public at large, the court must grant the equitable remedy and leave the punishment of the offender to other forums." 120 F. at 278.

For a discussion of the misuse defense, see § 2F[4][c].

[153] *Ex parte* Murphy, 200 U.S.P.Q. 801 (PTO Bd. App. 1977) (gambling device: "while some may consider gambling to be injurious to the public morals and the good order of society, we cannot find any basis in 35 U.S.C. 101 or related sections which justify a conclusion that inventions which are useful only for gambling ipso facto are void of patentable utility.").

[154] Brenner v. Manson, 383 U.S. 519, 148 U.S.P.Q. 689 (1966); *In re* Joly, 376 F.2d 906, 153 U.S.P.Q. 45 (CCPA 1967).

[155] 383 U.S. 519, 148 U.S.P.Q. 689 (1966).

[156] *See* § 2D[5][h][ii].

[157] *See also In re* Kirk, 376 F.2d 936, 153 U.S.P.Q. 48 (CCPA 1967). *Kirk* held a chemical intermediate used to produce compounds not useful if those compounds have no specific utility

Manson requires that practical utility for a claimed chemical compound be disclosed in a patent specification, or be obvious in view of the specification disclosures to be a constructive reduction to practice[158] and establish an effective filing date.[159]

A patent application that asserts no utility as to humans can meet the practical utility requirement by demonstrating specific effects on laboratory animals, for example, inhibiting tumors in rats, or preventing pregnancy in rabbits,[160] or by demonstrating pharmacological activity *in vitro*, the first important step in screening to identify compounds active *in vivo*, with possible human therapeutic application.[161]

A patent applicant need not establish a chemical compound's safety or effectiveness for human pharmaceutical use if the application does not assert human utility.[162] If the applicant does assert human utility, he must supply supporting evidence.[163] The evidence need only be convincing to a person of ordinary skill in the art; clinical or *in vivo* tests are not always required.[164] A pharmaceutical product or process need only be reasonably safe to meet the utility requirement.[165] The product or process need not meet regulatory commercial marketing requirements.[166]

Only one objective stated in the inventor's specification need be achieved to satisfy the utility requirement.[167] An application disclosing several distinct utilities, one adequately supported and others not adequately supported, meets the requirement, but the PTO may require deletion of nontenable utility assertions.[168]

[3] Novelty

To qualify for a patent, an invention must meet the novelty requirement.[169]

A "single source" anticipation rule applies to lack of novelty determinations. Anticipation exists only if all the elements of the claimed invention are present in a product

---

[158] For a discussion of constructive reduction to practice, see § 2D[5][d].

[159] Yasuko Kawai v. Metlesics, 480 F.2d 880, 178 U.S.P.Q. 158 (CCPA 1973); *In re* Joly, 376 F.2d 906, 153 U.S.P.Q. 45 (CCPA 1967).
For a discussion of utility disclosures in applications relying on a priority application filing date from another country, see § 2H[2][c].

[160] Nelson v. Bowler, 626 F.2d 853, 206 U.S.P.Q. 881 (CCPA 1980).

[161] Cross v. Iizuka, 753 F.2d 1040, 224 U.S.P.Q. 739 (Fed. Cir. 1985) (assertion that a compound inhibited an enzyme in human or bovine platelet microsomes is sufficient).

[162] *In re* Krimmel, 292 F.2d 948, 130 U.S.P.Q. 215 (CCPA 1961).

[163] *In re* Novak, 306 F.2d 924, 134 U.S.P.Q. 335 (CCPA 1962).

[164] *In re* Langer, 503 F.2d 1380, 183 U.S.P.Q. 288 (CCPA 1974); *In re* Irons, 340 F.2d 974, 144 U.S.P.Q. 153 (CCPA 1965).

[165] *In re* Sichert, 566 F.2d 1154, 196 U.S.P.Q. 209 (CCPA 1977).

[166] *In re* Anthony, 414 F.2d 1383, 162 U.S.P.Q. 594 (CCPA 1969).

[167] Standard Oil Co. v. Montedison, S.p.A., 664 F.2d 356, 212 U.S.P.Q. 327 (3d Cir. 1981).

[168] *In re* Gottlieb, 328 F.2d 1016, 140 U.S.P.Q. 665 (CCPA 1964). *See also In re* Hozumi, 226 U.S.P.Q. 353, 354 (Comm'r Pat. & Tm. 1985) ("it is appropriate for the Office to require removal of wildly speculative statements if the integrity of a patent as a technical disclosure document is to be maintained and if the Office can avoid misleading the public. It is the policy of the Office . . . to require cancellation of such speculative statements which do not contribute to the technical content of the disclosure.").

[169] 35 U.S.C. §§ 101, 102. *See generally* D. Chisum, Patents § 3.01 *et seq.*

or process disclosed, expressly or inherently, in a single prior art reference.[170] References may be combined only to determine the separate nonobviousness patentability requirement.[171]

The single source rule does not preclude use of multiple references to interpret a single reference or to show that a single reference disclosing the entire invention is "enabling."[172] A reference that discloses a claimed chemical compound but no method of making it does not anticipate if one of ordinary skill in the art could not make the compound.[173] The single reference will anticipate if other references make obvious a suitable method of making the compound.[174]

In *Scripps Clinic & Research Foundation,*[175] the Federal Circuit held that the district court erred in granting summary judgment that the patent's claims were invalid for anticipation.

> "Invalidity for anticipation requires that all of the elements and limitations of the claim are found within a single prior art reference. . . . There must be no difference between the claimed invention and the reference disclosure, as viewed by a person of ordinary skill in the field of the invention.

> "It is sometimes appropriate to consider extrinsic evidence to explain the disclosure of a reference. Such factual elaboration is necessarily of limited scope and probative value, for a finding of anticipation requires that all aspects of the claimed invention were already described in a single reference: a finding that is not supportable if it is necessary to prove facts beyond those disclosed in the reference in order to meet the claim limitations. The role of extrinsic evidence is to educate the decision-maker to what the reference meant to persons of ordinary skill in the field of the invention, not to fill gaps in the reference. . . . If it is necessary to reach beyond the boundaries of a single reference to provide missing disclosure of the claimed invention, the proper ground is not § 102 anticipation, but § 103 obviousness."[176]

In *Scripps,* the patent claimed purified, high specific activity human Factor VIII:C, the blood clotting factor. The inventors developed a method of purifying and concentrating Factor VIII:C using monoclonal antibodies specific to protein, Factor VIII:RP, to which Factor VIII:C is bound. The original patent contained process and product-by-process claims. The patentee applied for and obtained a reissue patent

---

[170] RCA Corp. v. Applied Digital Data Sys., Inc., 730 F.2d 1440, 221 U.S.P.Q. 385 (Fed. Cir. 1984), *cert. dismissed sub nom.* Hazeltine Corp. v. RCA Corp., 468 U.S. 1228 (1984).

[171] *See* § 2C[4][e][i].

[172] *E.g., In re* Donohue, 766 F.2d 531, 226 U.S.P.Q. 619 (Fed. Cir. 1985) (when a single publication discloses, expressly or inherently, a product (such as a chemical compound) containing all of the limitations of the claim, the claim is anticipated even though additional references must be relied upon to show that one of ordinary skill in the art could have made the disclosed product).

[173] *In re* Brown, 329 F.2d 1006, 141 U.S.P.Q. 245 (CCPA 1964).

[174] *In re* Samour, 571 F.2d 559, 197 U.S.P.Q. 1 (CCPA 1978).

[175] Scripps Clinic & Research Foundation v. Genentech, Inc., 927 F.2d 1565, 18 U.S.P.Q.2d 1001 (Fed. Cir. 1991).

[176] 927 F.2d at 1576, 1577, 18 U.S.P.Q.2d at 1010.

with additional claims to human VIII:C preparations of minimum high purity and activity levels. Three product claims provided:

> Claim 4: "A human VIII:C preparation having a potency in the range of 134 to 1172 units per ml. and being substantially free of VIII:RP."

> Claim 26: "A human VIII:C preparation of claim 24, wherein the ratio of VIII:C to VIII:RP is greater than 100,000 times the ratio in plasma."

> Claim 27: "A human VIII:C preparation of claim 24, wherein said VIII:C is isolated from VIII:C/VIII:RP and 90-100 percent of the VIII:RP has been removed."

The accused infringer asserted anticipation by a 1979 dissertation by Robert B. Harris entitled "Isolation and Characterization of Low Molecular Weight, Non-Aggregated Antihemophilic Factor from Fresh Human Plasma." The parties filed three successive declarations by Dr. Harris, each explaining his dissertation. In the first, Harris said he isolated "a low molecular weight antihemophilic factor." In the second, he said the factor was "not a naturally occurring substance and of low specific activity. . . . " In the third, he said he obtained "a human VIII:C preparation having a potency of 193 units/ml and being substantially free of VIII:RP, the ratio of VIII:C to VIII:RP being greater than 100,000 times the ratio in plasma."

> "To the extent that apparent inconsistencies among the three Harris declarations raise questions of credibility and weight, whether of witness or of interpretation of scientific data, they were improperly resolved on summary judgment. . . . Trial by document is an inadequate substitute for trial with witnesses, who are subject to examination and cross-examination in the presence of the decision-maker." [177]

[a] **The Infringement Test.** Novelty determination compares a single prior art reference and the patent claim. The lack of novelty (anticipation) test is the same as that for literal infringement. [178] If an item disclosed in a reference would have infringed

---

[177] 927 F.2d at 1578, 18 U.S.P.Q.2d at 1011.

[178] *See* Lewmar Marine, Inc. v. Barient, Inc., 827 F.2d 744, 3 U.S.P.Q.2d 1766 (Fed. Cir. 1987).

In *Lewmar Marine*, the Federal Circuit indicated that, in view of the restrictive usage of "anticipation" under the current patent act (enacted in 1952), which requires the presence in a single prior art disclosure of each and every element of a claimed invention, the "classic" test of anticipation—"that which infringes if later in time will anticipate if earlier than the patent"—must be modified to "That which would *literally* infringe if later in time anticipates if earlier than the date of invention." That which would infringe only under the doctrine of equivalents if later will not anticipate if earlier.

Even under the *Lewmar* modification of the "classic" anticipation test, the basic symmetry between infringement and patentability is maintained insofar as the relationship between the claimed subject matter and a *single* item is concerned. If that item would infringe under the doctrine of equivalents, it would most likely also render the claimed subject matter obvious when considered in relation to the rest of the prior art. Of course, this is a hypothetical inquiry because it is a fundamental rule that the doctrine of equivalents will not be extended to cover the teachings of the prior art. *See* § 2F[2][b][viii].

had it occurred after the patent issued, then it will anticipate when it comes before the inventor's invention date.[179]

[b] **Genus and Species; Combination and Element.** That a claim to a generic invention, for example, a class of chemical compounds, is anticipated by a prior art species falling within the claimed genus or class[180] follows from the infringement test of anticipation because a species later in time would infringe a claim to the genus. A claim to an element or subcombination is anticipated by the prior art disclosure of a combination that includes that element or combination.

A claim to a species is not anticipated by prior disclosure of a genus or class including that species unless disclosure actually names or clearly points to the claimed species.[181] The claimed species might exhibit unexpected properties differentiating it from the class or genus to which it belongs and renders it patentable over the generic disclosure.[182] A claim to a combination is not anticipated by the prior art disclosure of an element or subcombination.

[c] **Accidental, Unintended and Speculative Anticipations.** A product or process that appears or is inherent in a prior art reference anticipates a claim to that product or process even though the prior art product or process was used for a different purpose, in a different setting, or without recognition of valuable properties.[183]

Neither the accidental, unappreciated occurrence of a product or process in the prior art,[184] nor the speculative listing of a product (such as a chemical compound) as part of a large number of possible occurrences is an anticipation.[185]

---

[179] Lindemann Maschinenfabrik GMBH v. American Hoist & Derrick Co., 730 F.2d 1452, 221 U.S.P.Q. 481 (Fed. Cir. 1984); SSIH Equip. S.A. v. United States Int'l Trade Comm'n, 718 F.2d 365, 218 U.S.P.Q. 678 (Fed. Cir. 1983).

[180] Chester v. Miller, 906 F.2d 1574, 15 U.S.P.Q.2d 1333 (Fed. Cir. 1990); In re Slayter, 276 F.2d 408, 125 U.S.P.Q. 345 (CCPA 1960). See also In re Gosteli, 872 F.2d 1008, 1010, 10 U.S.P.Q.2d 1614, 1616 (Fed. Cir. 1989) ("Section 102(e) bars the issuance of a patent if its generic claims are anticipated by prior art disclosing individual chemical species."); Titanium Metals Corp. v. Banner, 778 F.2d 775, 227 U.S.P.Q. 773 (Fed. Cir. 1985) (when, as by a recitation of ranges, a claim covers several compositions, the claim is anticipated if one of the compositions is in the prior art).

[181] In re Schaumann, 572 F.2d 312, 197 U.S.P.Q. 5 (CCPA 1978).

[182] In re Ornitz, 376 F.2d 330, 153 U.S.P.Q. 454 (CCPA 1967).

[183] E.g., Verdegaal Brothers, Inc. v. Union Oil Co. of California, 814 F.2d 628, 2 U.S.P.Q.2d 1051 (Fed. Cir. 1987) (a claim to a process is anticipated by a prior art reference that discloses all of the limitations of that claim even though the reference does not expressly disclose the "inventive concept" or desirable property discovered by the patentee; it suffices that the prior art process inherently possessed that property); W.L. Gore & Associates, Inc. v. Garlock, Inc., 721 F.2d 1540, 220 U.S.P.Q. 303 (Fed. Cir. 1983), cert. denied, 469 U.S. 851 (1984); In re Bird, 344 F.2d 979, 154 U.S.P.Q. 418 (CCPA 1965).

[184] In re Marshall, 578 F.2d 301, 198 U.S.P.Q. 344 (CCPA 1978).

[185] In re Wiggins, 488 F.2d 538, 179 U.S.P.Q. 421 (CCPA 1973). Compare In re Sivaramakrishnan, 673 F.2d 1383, 213 U.S.P.Q. 441 (CCPA 1982) (naming of relatively small group of possible combinable ingredients is not mere speculation).

[4] Nonobviousness—Inventive Step

To qualify for a patent, subject matter claimed as an invention must meet the nonobviousness requirement. No valid patent may issue if the differences between the claimed subject matter and the prior art are such that the subject matter as a whole would have been obvious at the time the invention was made to a person having ordinary skill in the art to which the subject matter pertains.[186]

The nonobviousness requirement means that not all new and useful inventions qualify for patent protection. Most countries require something more than novelty to establish patentability. Europe and Japan use the concept "inventive step", but the legal test is basically the same—would the invention have been viewed, as of the relevant date, as obvious by a person of ordinary skill in the art in view of the prior art?

In the United States, courts originally developed the obviousness requirement when passing on the validity of patents in infringement suits.[187] In 1952, Congress included it in Section 103 of the patent statutes.[188] Nonobviousness is the most important

---

[186] *See generally* D. Chisum, Patents § 5.01 *et seq.*

[187] *See* § 2B.

[188] 35 U.S.C. Section 103 provides as follows:

"Conditions for patentability; non-obvious subject matter

A patent may not be obtained though the invention is not identically disclosed or described as set forth in section 102 of this title, if the differences between the subject matter sought to be patented and the prior art are such that the subject matter as a whole would have been obvious at the time the invention was made to a person having ordinary skill in the art to which said subject matter pertains. Patentability shall not be negatived by the manner in which the invention was made. Subject matter developed by another person, which qualifies as prior art only under subsection (f) or (g) of section 102 of this title, shall not preclude patentability under this section where the subject matter and the claimed invention were, at the time the invention was made, owned by the same person or subject to an obligation of assignment to the same person."

Section 103 breaks down into components. First, it address inventions that are "not identically disclosed or described as set forth in section 102 of this title." Section 102 sets forth conditions of novelty. For example, it bars a patent if the "invention" was described in a printed publication before the inventor's date of invention or more than one year before the inventor applied for a patent.

Second, Section 103 focuses on "the differences between the subject matter sought to be patented and the prior art." The phrase "subject matter sought to be patented" clearly refers to the inventor's claim, in a pending application or an issued patent. The "prior art" is not defined but, presumptively and subject to possible exceptions, refers to the novelty and statutory bar provisions of Section 102.

Third, it refers to the subject matter sought to be patented, that is, the claimed subject matter, "as a whole." This clearly means that a claimed invention should not be evaluated in parts. Court decisions and commentators read the "as a whole" directive expansively. For example, in chemical cases, the subject matter of a patent claim to a structural chemical compound is said to include the "properties" of the compound.

Fourth, it links patentability of the claimed whole subject matter to whether "it would have been obvious."

Fifth, it makes the relevant time period of obviousness "the time the invention was made." This "first-to-invent" concept meshes substantially, though perhaps not completely, with the Section 102 definition of "prior art."

patentability requirement[189] and the most difficult to apply. In practice, the most critical factors are: (1) the inventor's claim scope, and (2) the pertinent prior art's content. An invention may meet the requirement if it is narrowly defined but not if broadly defined.[190] Similarly, an invention may meet the requirement if the pertinent prior art is constricted but may not if expanded.[191]

[a] **General Test—*Graham v. Deere*—Level of Skill in the Art.** *Graham*, the leading Supreme Court decision on nonobviousness,[192] directed the lower courts and the Patent Office to apply the following test:

> "While the ultimate question of patent validity is one of law, . . . the § 103 condition, which is but one of three conditions, each of which must be satisfied, lends itself to several basic factual inquiries. Under § 103, the scope and content of the prior art are to be determined; differences between the prior art and the claims at issue are to be ascertained; and the level of ordinary skill in the pertinent art resolved. Against this background, the obviousness or nonobviousness of the subject matter is determined. Such secondary considerations as commercial success, long felt but unsolved needs, failure of others, etc., might be utilized to give light to the circumstances surrounding the origin of the subject matter sought to be patented. As indicia of obviousness or nonobviousness, these inquiries may have relevancy.

> "This is not to say, however, that there will not be difficulties in applying the nonobviousness test. What is obvious is not a question upon which there is likely to be uniformity of thought in every given factual context. The difficulties, however, are comparable to those encountered daily by the courts in such frames of reference as negligence and scienter, and should be amenable to a case-by-case development. We believe that strict observance of the

---

Sixth, it pinpoints a "person of ordinary skill" as the human actor to whom the invention must be obvious. The cases confirm what is perhaps obvious, to wit, that a person of ordinary skill is neither a highly sophisticated expert nor a layman without knowledge or skill of the technology.

Finally, it selects the ordinarily-skilled person from "the art to which said subject matter pertains."

[189] The utility requirement may be met by demonstrating only a minimal beneficial use. *See* § 2C[2]. The novelty requirement may be met by carefully confining the claim language so that it does not read on the disclosures of any single prior art reference. *See* § 2C[3]. The nonobviousness requirement is more fundamental and is supported by the patent system's constitutional purpose of promoting the progress of the useful arts. Graham v. John Deere Co., 383 U.S. 1, 148 U.S.P.Q. 459 (1966).

[190] Claim interpretation for patentability and infringement determination are discussed at § 2F.

[191] What constitutes the pertinent art is discussed at § 2C[4][6]. What items constitute sources of prior art (prior publications, matter in public use, etc.) is discussed at § 2C[5].

[192] Graham v. John Deere Co. 383 U.S. 1, 17-18, 148 U.S.P.Q. 459, 467 (1966). *Graham* involved two patent infringement suits. The Court held both patents invalid for obviousness. In a third suit decided the same date, the Court held a patent on a battery valid. United States v. Adams, 383 U.S. 39, 148 U.S.P.Q. 479 (1966).

requirements laid down here will result in that uniformity and definiteness which Congress called for in the 1952 Act."[193]

This passage is usually referred to as the "*Graham* test " or "*Graham* factors", and, for the most part, merely restates the language of Section 103. One factor not in Section 103 is the *level* of "ordinary skill in the art." *Graham* offered no analysis of this factor: in finding two patents invalid for obviousness, the Court made scant reference to the level of skill in the art. In subsequent lower court decisions, the level of skill finding rarely plays a major role in obviousness determinations.[194]

---

[193] 383 U.S. at 17-18.

In *Graham*, the Court stressed that the Patent and Trademark Office examiners should apply the same standard of obviousness in passing on the allowability of patent applications.

> "We have observed a notorious difference between the standards applied by the Patent Office and by the courts. While many reasons can be adduced to explain the discrepancy, one may well be the free rein often exercised by Examiners in their use of the concept of 'invention.' In this connection, we note that the Patent Office is confronted with a most difficult task. Almost 100,000 applications for patents are filed each year. Of these, about 50,000 are granted and the backlog now runs well over 200,000. This is itself a compelling reason for the Commissioner to strictly adhere to the 1952 Act as interpreted here. This would, we believe, not only expedite disposition but bring about a closer concurrence between administrative and judicial precedent." 383 U.S. at 18-19.

[194] *E.g.,* Kloster Speedsteel AB v. Crucible Inc., 793 F.2d 1565, 230 U.S.P.Q. 81 (Fed. Cir. 1986), *on rehearing,* 231 U.S.P.Q. 160 (Fed. Cir. 1986), *cert. denied,* 479 U.S. 1034 (1987). In *Kloster Speedsteel,* the Federal Circuit found no error in the district court's failure to make an express finding as to the level of skill in the art and its reliance on a finding that no one at "any level of skill" regarded the patented combination as theoretically possible.

> "The primary value in the requirement that level of skill be found lies in its tendency to focus the mind of the decisionmaker away from what would presently be obvious to that decisionmaker and toward what would, when the invention was made, have been obvious . . . 'to one of ordinary skill in the art.¢

> "This court has noted instances in which a particular level of skill finding did not improperly influence the ultimate conclusion under § 103. One such instance involved a determination that an invention would have been obvious to one of the lowest level of skill, i.e., that of a layman. . . . Another involved a determination that an invention would have been *nonobvious* to those of *extraordinary* skill, i.e., other inventors in the art." 793 F.2d at 1574, 230 U.S.P.Q. at 86.

Compare Custom Accessories, Inc. v. Jeffrey-Allan Industries, Inc., 807 F.2d 955, 962-63 U.S.P.Q.2d 1196, 1201 (Fed. Cir. 1986) (obviousness is determined by reference to a person of ordinary skill in the art, "not to the judge, or to a layman, or to those skilled in remote arts, or to geniuses in the art."

"The person of ordinary skill is a hypothetical person who is presumed to be aware of all the pertinent prior art. The actual inventor's skill is not determinative. Factors that may be considered in determining level of skill include: type of problems encountered in art; prior art solutions to those problems; rapidity with which innovations are made; sophistication of the technology; and educational level of active workers in the field. Not all such factors may be present in every case, and one or more of them may predominate." Failure to make a specific finding on the level of skill is not alone grounds for reversal of a district court finding of obviousness, but such failure may be "evidence that Graham was not in fact applied.").

In *Graham*, the Supreme Court granted certiorari in three patent suits, two from the Eighth Circuit, and one from the Court of Claims, to resolve an apparent split among the circuits on the proper legal test of obviousness for "combination" inventions. The Eighth Circuit found the Graham plow patent invalid because it did not "bring about a significantly new or different result, and would have been obvious to a person having ordinary skill in the art." The Eighth Circuit declined to follow two Fifth Circuit decisions upholding the Graham patent[195] on the ground that the Fifth Circuit applied too lenient a test: an improvement combination is patentable if "it produces an old result in a cheaper and otherwise more advantageous way."

The Supreme Court held neither the "significantly new or different result" test nor the "old result in cheaper and otherwise more advantageous way" test proper. The patents should be examined in terms of obviousness to one skilled in the art, not in terms of the results achieved by the invention.[196] The Court was not content with simply correcting the lower courts' standard of obviousness and remanding the cases; instead, it went on to analyze the three patents' validity, upholding Adam's battery patent but invalidating Graham's plow patent and Scoggin's insecticide container overcap patent.

The Court's analysis of the Graham patent is most instructive. The basic problem to which the Graham patent was addressed was how to construct a chisel plow that would not break upon striking obstructions in rocky soils.

> "Chisel plows . . . were developed for plowing in areas where the ground is relatively free from rocks or stones. Originally, the shanks were rigidly attached to the plow frames. When such plows were used in the rocky, glacial soils of some of the Northern States, they were found to have serious defects. As the chisels hit buried rock, a vibratory motion was set up and tremendous forces were transmitted to the shank near its connection to the frame. The shanks would break."[197]

Graham obtained two patents on vibrating plows.[198] The first, No. 2,493,811 ("811"), issued on January 10, 1950, claimed a spring clamp arrangement and was described in a prior Fifth Circuit case as follows:

---

[195] Graham v. Cockshutt Farm Equip., Inc., 256 F.2d 358, 117 U.S.P.Q. 439 (5th Cir. 1958) (valid but not infringed because combination patent in crowded art does not have wide application); Jeoffroy Mfg. Inc. v. Graham, 219 F.2d 511, 104 U.S.P.Q. 211 (5th Cir. 1955), *cert. denied*, 350 U.S. 826 (1955) (valid and infringed).

[196] It is doubtful that the Court meant to say "results," *i.e.*, performance characteristics, are irrelevant to the obviousness determination. The role of results, advantages, and performance characteristics is discussed at § 2C[4][c]. In context, the Court meant that "new results" was not the exclusive test of patentability, a common sense proposition. *Cf.* Jones v. Hardy, 727 F.2d 1524, 1530, 220 U.S.P.Q. 1021, 1026 (Fed. Cir. 1984) ("treating the advantage as the invention disregards the statutory requirement that the invention be viewed 'as a whole,' ignores the problem—recognition element, and injects an improper 'obvious to try' consideration.").

[197] 383 U.S. at 21.

[198] Graham had also obtained a patent on a device for clamping plow shanks to the frame, No. 2,464,255, issued March 15, 1949, which the Fifth Circuit held invalid in 1953. Graham v. Jeoffroy Mfg. Co., 206 F.2d 769, 98 U.S.P.Q. 421 (5th Cir. 1953).

"The patented device may be more particularly described as exhibiting a bracket, secured to the lower flange of the H-beam of a plow frame, with a fulcrum plate pivoted to the bracket and the forward end of the ground tool shank resiliently and frictionally held between. The front end of the shank has an opening through which a rod or bolt extends, and a coil spring around the rod is seated on the upper part of the bracket and held in place by a washer and nut. When a rearward and upward force is exerted on the ground working tool during operation, the forward end of the tool shank moves downward against the tension of the coil spring and rocks, or pivots, with the fulcrum plate of the clamp mechanism so as to enable the tool to pass over an obstruction, as well as to add further resiliency to the natural resiliency of the shank."[199]

The Fifth Circuit held the '811 patent valid and infringed in 1953.[200] The device patented in '811 was not entirely satisfactory however.

"In practice, the '811 patent arrangement permitted the shank to wobble or fishtail because it was not rigidly fixed to the hinge plate; moreover, as the hinge plate was below the shank, the latter caused wear on the upper plate, a member difficult to repair or replace."

To solve these difficulties, Graham devised and patented an improvement on the '811 patent that issued as patent No. 2,627,798 on February 10, 1953 (hereafter '798).

The question before the Court in *Graham* was '798's validity. The major change from '811 was reversing the position of the plow's shank plow and hinge plate. In '798, the shank was *below* the hinge plate, which shifted the point of wear from the bottom of the fixed upper plate to the top of the stirrup on the hinge plate, an advantage because "the rubbing [against the heel of the upper plate] was eliminated and the wear point was changed to the hinge plate, a member more easily removed or replaced for repair." The patent owner also argued that the reversal had another advantage: the shank could flex away from the hinge plate.

The Supreme Court held the '798 invention obvious in light of only two references: Graham's own '811 patent and an unpatented spring clamp sold by Glencoe Manufacturing, a device neither cited nor considered by the Patent Office when it passed on Graham's application.

The Glencoe spring clamp shank was above the hinge plate, as in prior art '811 patent but not in '798, the patent in question, but it passed through a stirrup and therefore had the same "wear and repair" advantage as '798. In the Court's view, the '798 device was a simple and obvious variation of Glencoe and achieved the same result.

---

[199] Jeoffroy Mfg. Inc. v. Graham, 206 F.2d 772, 773-74, 98 U.S.P.Q. 424 (5th Cir. 1953), *cert. denied*, 347 U.S. 920 (1954).

[200] Jeoffroy Mfg. v. Graham, 206 F.2d 772, 98 U.S.P.Q. 424 (5th Cir. 1953), *cert. denied*, 347 U.S. 920 (1954). In a later case, the Fifth Circuit held that '811 was not infringed by a device in which the plate and shank were reversed (*i.e.*, with shank below instead of on top of the hinged lower plate). Jeoffroy Mfg. Co. v. Graham, 219 F.2d 511, 513-17, 104 U.S.P.Q. 221 (5th Cir.), *cert. denied*, 350 U.S. 826 (1955).

> "[T]he stirrup in Glencoe serves exactly the same function as the heel of the hinge plate in '798. The mere shifting of the wear point to the heel of the '798 hinge plate from the stirrup of Glencoe—itself a part of the hinge plate—presents *no operative mechanical distinctions, much less nonobvious differences.*" (Emphasis added.)

The patent owner stressed that the positioning of the shank below the hinge plate in '798 permitted "flex" between the heel of the hinge plate and the bolted end of the shank, something not achieved by Glencoe. The Court rejected this argument on three grounds. First, anyone who wished to achieve such extra flex would naturally be led to Graham's arrangement.

> "If free-flexing, as petitioners now argue, is the crucial difference above the prior art, then it appears evident that the desired result would be obtainable by not boxing the shank within the confines of the hinge. . . . The only other effective place available in the arrangement was to attach it below the hinge plate and run it through a stirrup or bracket that would not disturb its flexing qualities. Certainly a person having ordinary skill in the prior art, given the fact that the flex in the shank could be utilized more effectively if allowed to run the entire length of the shank, would immediately see that the thing to do was what Graham did, i.e. invert the shank and the hinge plate."

Second, the "flex" argument was in reality a mere "afterthought," not stressed as an advantage in the specification or before the Patent Office. Finally, the evidence indicated that "the flexing advantages flowing from the '798 arrangement are not, in fact, a significant feature in the patent."

Curiously, the Court, after rejecting the Eighth Circuit's "new result" test for mechanical combination patents and stressing the need for a factual inquiry into obviousness, struck down the Graham patent primarily because it was a combination and performed no substantial new function. The Court made only conclusory statements about what would have been obvious to a person of ordinary skill in the pertinent art.

The patent owner in *Graham* relied on two alleged new and unexpected performance characteristics (advantages or properties) of the claimed structure—better "wear and repair" and "extra flex." The Court dismissed the "wear and repair" advantage because the Glencoe reference, not considered by the Patent Office, achieved the same advantage—though in another way. The Court dismissed the "extra flex" advantage for two reasons. First, it was not disclosed in the specification or prosecution history. Second, the Court opined that a person of ordinary skill in the art would "immediately see" that the claimed invention (reversing the positions of the hinge and shank) was the way to achieve the asserted advantage. The Court did not discuss whether it was obvious to one with ordinary skill in the pertinent art that extra flex was desirable or whether such an inquiry was appropriate under Section 103.[201]

[b] **Nonanalogous Art.** Patent law's nonobviousness requirement compares a patent claim's subject matter as a whole with the "prior art."[202] Prior art includes all

---

[201] *Compare* Eibel Process Corp. v. Minnesota & Ontario Paper Co., 261 U.S. 45 (1923) (invention can consist in the discovery of the source of a problem even though the solution to the problem involves a slight and simple change).

[202] For a discussion of prior art sources, see § 2C[5].

pertinent items, no matter how old or obscure and regardless of whether or not persons actually working in the field knew of the items.[203]

Prior art for obviousness does not include items in nonanalogous fields.[204] Arts are analogous if one seeking to solve a problem in one art would likely look for a solution in the other art.[205] It is not proper to use the inventor's specification teachings to determine whether prior art items are analogous.[206]

In *Deminski*,[207] the Federal Circuit applied a two-step test for determining whether a prior art reference is nonanalogous: (1) Is the reference "within the field of the inventor's endeavor?" and (2) If not, is the reference "reasonably pertinent to the particular problem with which the inventor was involved." The claimed invention and reference patents are within the same field of endeavor if they have essentially the same function and structure, for example, pumps and compressors, each of the double-acting piston type.

The "art" to which an invention pertains is defined in terms of the problem to be solved rather than in terms of the specific field in which the invention will be used.[208] For example, providing a proper fastener for a beehive is in the field of mechanics pertaining to fasteners, not beekeeping.[209] It matters not that beekeepers may have little knowledge of mechanics.

Courts give the PTO's classification system relatively little weight in determining whether a reference is within the same or an analogous art.[210]

---

[203] Merit Mfg. Co. v. Hero Mfg. Co., 185 F.2d 350, 87 U.S.P.Q. 289 (2d Cir. 1950). It has sometimes been said that the "inventor is presumed to know all the prior art," but this presumption has been rejected as a fiction; the person for determining obviousness is not the inventor but an imaginary person who is deemed to have access to all of the references in the public domain. Kimberly-Clark Corp. v. Johnson & Johnson, 745 F.2d 1437, 223 U.S.P.Q. 603 (Fed. Cir. 1984).

[204] *In re* Wood, 599 F.2d 1032, 202 U.S.P.Q. 171 (CCPA 1979). *See also* King Instrument Corp. v. Otari Corp., 767 F.2d 853, 226 U.S.P.Q. 402 (Fed. Cir. 1985) (as to a patent for loading magnetic tape into closed cassettes, a prior patent on splicing photographic textual film in the printing industry was not within the patentee's field of endeavor).
See generally D. Chisum, Patents § 5.03[1].

[205] *In re* Shapleigh, 248 F.2d 96, 115 U.S.P.Q. 129 (CCPA 1957).
For example, prior art on freezing fish carcasses to a platform for slicing was held to be analogous to an invention on holding workpieces such as gem stones to a work station. International Glass Co. v. United States, 408 F.2d 395, 404-05, 159 U.S.P.Q. 434 (Ct. Cl. 1969). On the other hand, prior art on tire puncture sealing was held to be not analogous to an invention on identification tags for animals' ears. *Ex parte* Murphy, 217 U.S.P.Q. 479 (PTO Bd. App. 1976).

[206] *In re* Wanderham, 378 F.2d 981, 154 U.S.P.Q. 20 (CCPA 1967).

[207] *In re* Deminski, 796 F.2d 436, 230 U.S.P.Q. 313 (Fed. Cir. 1986).

[208] *E.g.*, Orthopedic Equip. Co. v. United States, 702 F.2d 1005, 217 U.S.P.Q. 193 (Fed. Cir. 1983).

[209] *In re* Grout, 377 F.2d 1019, 153 USPQ 742 (CCPA 1967).

[210] *In re* Mlot-Fijalkowski, 676 F.2d 666, 213 U.S.P.Q. 713 (CCPA 1982). *Compare In re* Deminski, 796 F.2d 436, 442 n.3, 230 U.S.P.Q. 313, 315 n.3 (Fed. Cir. 1986) (a cross reference in the official PTO search notes is some evidence of analogy, particularly when "nearly identical classifications of the application and references . . . are the result of the close similarity in structure and function of the invention and the prior art.").

[c] **Comparative Utility—New and Unexpected Properties, the Inventor's Purpose, Problem and Solution**

[i]   *Testing Evidence.* Comparative utility is pertinent to the obviousness issue. The fact that the claimed invention achieves superior results compared to the closest prior art product or process tends to show it was not obvious. Inventors commonly rely on tests results comparing the claimed invention and the closest prior art to show nonobviousness of their inventions. What is the "closest" prior art depends on the circumstances.[211] The closest art may not be the commercial standard in the field.[212]

[ii] *Rationale for Giving Weight to Performance Differences—"Invention as a Whole".* Court decisions on the obviousness requirement focus on two kinds of differences between the claimed invention and the prior art.

> "The first is the differences between the claims and the prior art purely in terms of structure or methodology. For product claims, how does the claimed product differ in physical structure from the products in the prior art? For process claims, how does the claimed process differ in terms of operative steps from the processes in the prior art? 'Differences' in this sense are ascertained by interpretation of the teachings of the prior art and of the claims of the patent or application.

> "The second is the differences between the claims and the prior art in terms of functions and advantages (comparative utility). What functions, advantages and results does the claimed product or process have that the prior art products or processes do not in fact have?"[213]

The labels for the first type of difference—"structural" or "methodological"— are reasonably descriptive, though "physical" differences is more so. The label for the second type of difference—"properties"—is potentially ambiguous. "Performance" differences is clearer. The word "property" can be used to refer to physical characteristics, performance characteristics, or both. Also, one may use "properties" as an indirect means of describing physical differences.

The novelty patentability condition depends solely on *physical* differences between the claimed invention and prior art disclosures. An inventor cannot claim an old product or method even though he or she may discover heretofore unknown performance characteristics.[214]

---

211 *In re* Merchant, 575 F.2d 865, 197 U.S.P.Q. 785 (CCPA 1978).

212 *In re* Wright, 569 F.2d 1124, 193 U.S.P.Q. 332 (CCPA 1976).

213 D. Chisum, Patents § 5.03[5][a].

214 A good illustration is *In re* Spada, 911 F.2d 705, 15 U.S.P.Q.2d 1655 (Fed. Cir. 1990). In *Spada*, the applicants disclosed and claimed pressure sensitive adhesive compositions comprising a water-based latex containing a copolymer made from specified classes and proportions of monomers. A prior art reference, Smith, showed water-based latexes containing polymers made from classes and proportions of monomers that overlap those of the applicants. However, Smith discloses properties, such as hardness and abrasion resistance, that differ from those of the applicants.

The court held that the PTO properly rejected as *prima facie* unpatentable for lack of novelty the applicants' claims to a class of compositions that read on a prior art reference's disclosed compositions. That the applicants discovered and disclosed properties different from

Why does the nonobviousness condition focus on both physical and performance differences? If patents issue only for physically new things and methods, should not the focus be solely on the physical differences? One explanation:

> "[O]ne type of factual evidence often relied upon to refute the apparent obviousness of a claimed product or process which is structurally similar to matter in the prior art concerns comparative utility—i.e., evidence that the claimed product or process unexpectedly exhibits functions, properties, and advantages not possessed by the prior art. . . . *The relevance of such evidence is in part direct and in part inferential. It is direct in the sense that the new function is part of the inventive concept,* the 'subject matter as a whole,' which must be obvious under Section 103. . . . *The relevance is inferential in the sense that the prior art's failure to reveal the claimed invention despite its advantageous qualities tends to confirm that it was unexpected and unobvious.* It would be contrary to normal economic incentives for obvious, advantageous subject matter to remain dormant."[215]

The two rationales for giving weight to performance characteristics are distinct. Inference focuses on the issue of whether a physical thing or method that is literally new but similar to prior art things or methods would in fact have been obvious to a person skilled in the art. "Subject matter as a whole" is substantive, postulating the performance characteristics as part of the invention. If those characteristics are unexpected (not obvious), then the invention is not expected. Whether patent law policy supports the second rationale is unclear.

[iii] *New and Unexpected Properties—The Inventor's Purpose.* What is the role of properties of an invention in determining obviousness when the invention has new or unexpected properties compared to the prior art but also shares common properties with the prior art? What is the role of properties when the inventor discovers an unexpected property in a literally new product or process that is physically similar

---

or even mutually exclusive of those disclosed by the reference does not show novelty: "When the claimed compositions are not novel, they are not rendered patentable by recitation of properties, whether or not these properties are shown or suggested by the prior art." The PTO reasonably put the burden on applicants to show that their claimed products differed from those of the reference.

The PTO properly inferred that "the polymerization . . . of identical monomers, employing the same or similar polymerization techniques, would produce polymers having the identical composition. Products of identical chemical composition can not have mutually exclusive properties."

> "[W]hen the PTO shows sound basis for believing that the products of the applicant and the prior art are the same, the applicant has the burden of showing that they are not.
>
> ". . . While an inventor is not required to understand how or why an invention works, . . . the PTO was correct in view of the apparent identity of the compositions, in requiring [applicants] to distinguish [their] compositions from those of [the prior art reference]." 911 F.2d at 708-10, 15 U.S.P.Q.2d at 1658.

[215] D. Chisum, Intellectual Property: Copyright, Patent and Trademark 7-103, 104 (1980) (Emphasis added.)

to an old product or process that, unknown to the prior art, also possesses the unexpected property? Considerable controversy surrounds these questions.[216]

The question is most often discussed in connection with chemical inventions,[217] but it arises with all types of inventions. An example is *Wright*, decided by a Federal Circuit panel but later disapproved by the court *en banc* in *Dillon*.[218] *Wright*[219] involved an appeal from a PTO rejection of the appellant/applicant's claims to a carpenter's level with a barrel-shaped vial that contained a bubble, the vial having a core member disposed within the bore, the core serving the purpose of increasing the range of pitch-measurement capability.[220]

The PTO rejected the claim as obvious based on two prior art references. The first, Vaida U.S. Patent No. 3,871,109, showed levels with barrel-shaped vials, which were limited in their pitch-measuring capability because of the limited amount of curvature that can be formed in the molded vial shape. The second, Bishop U.S. Patent No. 771,801, showed a core pin in a cylindrical (non-barrel-shaped) vial, the core pin's purpose being to increase the visibility of the bubble. The PTO reasoned that, because the prior art suggested combining Bishop's core membered cylindrical vial with Vaida's barrel vial to increase visibility, the claimed subject matter would have been obvious even though the prior art contained no suggestion of the increased range advantage: "if it is obvious to combine the teachings of prior art references for any purpose, they may be combined in order to defeat patentability of the applicant's admittedly new structure" and "it is irrelevant that [the claimed] structure

---

216 *See In re* Dillon, 919 F.2d 688, 16 U.S.P.Q.2d 1897 (Fed. Cir. 1990), discussed below.
217 *See* § 2C[4][e][iii].
218 *See In re* Dillon, 919 F.2d 688, 16 U.S.P.Q.2d 1897 (Fed. Cir. 1990), discussed below.
219 *In re* Wright, 848 F.2d 1216, 6 U.S.P.Q.2d 1959 (Fed. Cir. 1988).
220 Application claim 1 provided:

"1. A level vial comprising a body having a bore formed with a barrel shaped portion having opposed ends and wherein the barrel curvature is defined by a first radius of curvature,

the barrel shaped portion of the bore having a cross-sectional dimension generally decreasing from the center thereof in axially opposed directions towards the ends thereof,

an axially elongated core member disposed within the bore and between the opposed ends thereof in coaxial relationship with the barrel shaped portion of the body and having a maximum cross-sectional dimension and having a second radius of curvature exceeding that of the first radius of curvature of the barrel shaped bore portion,

a quantity of fluid disposed within the bore and being insufficient to fill the bore and to provide a bubble therein having a dimension sufficient to simultaneously contact the surfaces of the barrel shaped bore portion and the core member,

means for hermetically sealing the bore to contain the fluid and to maintain the bubble therein,

the vial body having a transparent portion and indicator means associated therewith to permit visual bubble observation and for indicating preselected positions of the bubble in the vial and

wherein the surfaces of the barrel shaped bore portion and the core member coact with the bubble to produce gradual bubble movement axially within the barrel shaped bore portion without abrupt bubble acceleration and while providing a wide range of visually observable angular measures." 848 F.2d at 1217, 6 U.S.P.Q.2d at 1960.

was for a purpose, and has properties, that are neither obtainable from the prior art structures, nor suggested in the prior art."

A Federal Circuit panel reversed, holding that the references did not show a *prima facie* case of obviousness.

> "We repeat the mandate of 35 U.S.C. § 103: it is the invention as a whole that must be considered in obviousness determinations. The invention as a whole embraces the structure, its properties, and the problem it solves.
>
> "The determination of whether a novel structure is or is not 'obvious' requires cognizance of the properties of that structure and the problem which it solves, viewed in light of the teachings of the prior art.
>
> "Thus the question is whether what the inventor did would have been obvious to one of ordinary skill in the art attempting to solve the problem upon which the inventor was working.
>
> "The problem upon which Wright was working was improving the pitch-measuring capability of the level, not the visibility of the bubble. The PTO, having conceded that Wright's structure was unobvious for his intended purpose, erred in holding that this was not relevant. The problem solved by the invention is always relevant. The entirety of a claimed invention, including the combination viewed as a whole, the elements thereof, and the properties and purpose of the invention, must be considered.
>
> . . .
>
> "The PTO position that the claimed structure is prima facie obvious is not supported by the cited references. No reference shows or suggests the properties and results of Wright's claimed structure, or suggests the claimed combination as a solution to the problem of increasing pitch measurement capacity. *It is not pertinent whether Wright's new structure also has the prior art attribute of increased visibility of the bubble, for that is not his invention.*" (Emphasis added.)[221]

Wright postulates that the inventor's purpose, the "problem" he or she was seeking to solve, is relevant to obviousness and discounts the fact the invented structure

---

[221] 848 F.2d at 1219-20, 6 U.S.P.Q.2d at 1961-62. The PTO relied on a statement in *In re Wiseman*: "If the claimed subject matter would have been obvious from the references, it is immaterial that the references do not state the problem or advantages ascribed thereto by applicant." *In re* Wiseman, 596 F.2d 1019, 201 U.S.P.Q. 658 (CCPA 1979). The Federal Circuit was unpersuaded:

> ". . . *Wiseman* does not support the generalization that the Board attributes to it. In *Wiseman* the prior art reference showed a similar problem and suggested a similar solution to that of the applicant. Specifically, the prior art showed a disc brake having grooves for the purpose of venting dust generated during use; the applicant showed a disc brake having grooves for the purpose of venting steam generated during use. The applicant asserted no results or properties that were not fairly suggested by the prior art. The court's discussion in *Wiseman* must be viewed in context, and as with all section 103 decisions, judgment must be brought to bear based on the facts of each case." 848 F.2d at 1220, 6 U.S.P.Q.2d at 1962.

contains the performance characteristic that one would have expected from combining the primary and secondary references. There are problems with crediting an inventor's "purpose." For example, would the same structure be unpatentable if the inventor's purpose was to improve the visibility of the bubble?

One can conclude that Wright's invention was not obvious in light of the prior art without considering the inventor's subjective "purpose." If the newer Vaida reference (use barrel-shaped vial) had been available for a period of time, no one apparently responded to the possibility of combining the older Bishop reference (insert a core for visibility) with Vaida, for *any* purpose (visibility or greater range).

With an objective approach to obviousness, that is, one that does not consider the inventor's "purpose" and focuses on whether the prior art provided motivation to combine the teachings of multiple references for *any* purpose, it makes sense to consider the *importance* of an expected performance characteristic. If it is relatively unimportant and there is little dissatisfaction with the prior art means that achieve it, then one skilled in the art would not be motivated to make the combination. For example, if Bishop's core pin structure is "no big deal" in terms of improved visibility, then skilled artisans would be little inclined to include the core pin in future carpenter improvements, such as a barrel-shaped vial.

On the other hand, if the expected performance characteristic is important, then the invention should be considered obvious, and one skilled in the art had ample motivation to produce the invention. To allow a patent on the invention simply because the inventor discovered an additional advantage would remove subject matter from the public domain contrary to the constitutional purposes of the patent system. In *Eli Lilly*,[222] the patent claimed a method for increasing the feed utilization efficiency of ruminant animals, such as cattle, by administering a specified chemical compound (X537A or "lasalocid").[223] The primary prior art reference (Berger) disclosed that the same compound could cure a disease (coccidiosis) in fowl while causing such fowl to gain weight and that animals raised commercially for food and subject to coccidiosis are "poultry . . . , sheep, *cattle*, swine, etc."[224] The reference did not disclose or give

---

[222] *In re* Eli Lilly & Co., 902 F.2d 943, 14 U.S.P.Q.2d 1741 (Fed. Cir. 1990).

[223] Claim 1 provides:

"1. A method of increasing the efficiency of feed utilization of ruminant animals having a developed rumen function which comprises the oral administration to such animals of a propionate-increasing amount of an antibiotic chosen from the group consisting of X537A and its physiologically acceptable esters and salts." 902 F.2d at 944, 14 U.S.P.Q.2d at 1742.

[224] (Emphasis added.) The "Berger" reference actually consisted of several related United States and foreign patents. All the patents contained the following disclosure:

"The active ingredient when orally administered to coccidiosis susceptible domestic fowl, particularly turkeys and chickens, as a component of feed, effectively controls the disease by either preventing it or curing it after it occurs. Furthermore, the treated fowl either maintain their weight or actually gain weight when compared to controls. Thus, the compositions of this invention not only control coccidiosis, but also, aid in improving the efficiency of conversion of feed to weight gains." *Id.*

Berger's Southern Rhodesian patent included the following as claim 23: "A composition aiding in improving the efficiency of conversion of feed to weight gains in animals raised commercially for food purposes comprising . . . antibiotic X-537A and pharmaceutically acceptable salts thereof." *Id.*

data on administering the compound to healthy cattle. The PTO rejected the claim, finding that the reference rendered the patent claims *prima facie* obvious.

To rebut the *prima facie* case of obviousness, the patentee presented experimental data that mature cattle having a developed rumen function experienced a higher percentage weight gain due to X537A compared to calves, which have undeveloped rumen functions.[225] The patentee also presented expert opinion evidence. The experts opined that the Berger reference gave no data on the effects of X537A in any animal except chickens and did not state that the compound should be fed to healthy cattle or even healthy chickens. The experts viewed the reference as simply teaching that chickens relieved of the stress of the disease would gain weight.

The court affirmed the rejection, holding that the patentee failed to show that "a significant aspect of his claimed invention is unexpected in light of the prior art." The reference's "general teaching" that the compound could be used for improving weight gain in animals "was not shown to be incorrect."

> "The [reference] disclosure does not merely invite experimentation, for [it] states that this specific product has the specific property of aiding weight gain in animals, naming cattle and sheep. . . . Although we recognize and give weight to the unpredictability of biological properties, in [this] case the prior art teaches the claimed use with specificity."[226]

Before the Federal Circuit, both the patentee and the PTO relied on case precedents to support their respective positions of nonobviousness and obviousness. The patentee relied upon *Yates*,[227] *Orfeo*,[228] and *Chupp*.[229] the PTO relied upon *Nolan*.[230]

---

[225] An intervenor in the Federal Circuit appeal, Hoffman-La Roche, Inc., challenged the patentee's interpretation of its data, arguing that "Lilly's unweaned calves, even without treatment with X537A, were such highly efficient utilizers of their liquid feed that Lilly's comparisons are not probative of unexpected results with cattle." 902 F.2d at 946, 14 U.S.P.Q.2d at 1744.

[226] 902 F.2d at 946, 14 U.S.P.Q.2d at 1744.

[227] *In re* Yates, 663 F.2d 1054, 211 U.S.P.Q. 1149 (CCPA 1981).

[228] *In re* Orfeo, 440 F.2d 439, 169 U.S.P.Q. 487 (CCPA 1971).

[229] *In re* Chupp, 816 F.2d 643, 2 U.S.P.Q.2d 1437 (Fed. Cir. 1987).

Chupp is an interesting decision on the required scope of a showing of unexpected properties of a product, such as a chemical compound, found to be *prima facie* obvious in view of a prior art product. The applicants claimed a novel chemical compound useful as a herbicide. *See* § 2C[4][c]. The PTO found the compound *prima facie* obvious in view of a structurally similar prior art compound known to be useful as a herbicide. The applicant submitted testing evidence showing that the claimed compound gave superior results as to two weeds and two crops (corn and soybeans). The data showed that "the claimed compound was at best a run-of-the-mill performer in crops other than corn and soybeans." The court held the showing of unexpected results sufficient.

> "Under the . . . doctrine [of *In re* Papesch, 315 F.2d 381, 137 U.S.P.Q. 43 (CCPA 1963)], evidence of unobvious or unexpected advantageous properties may rebut a *prima facie* case of obviousness based on structural similarities. . . . Such evidence may include data showing that a compound is unexpectedly superior in a property it shares with prior art compounds.

. . .

The court held *Nolan* the most apt precedent.[231] *Nolan* held an improvement in gaseous discharge devices unpatentable "because although unexpected results were shown in some features, the results were not unexpected in the most significant feature."

> "Unlike *Yates*, [the inventor] is not claiming a narrow improvement limited to details not shown in the prior art. Unlike *Chupp*, [the inventor] has not shown unexpected superiority over the property taught in the prior art. Unlike *Orfeo*, [the inventor] has not shown that his claimed use with ruminants achieves unexpected results compared with the prior art disclosure of the same use with the same animals. Like *Nolan*, [the inventor] has not shown that a significant aspect of his claimed invention is unexpected in light of the prior art."[232]

In *Dillon*,[233] the Federal Circuit in banc decided *Wright* was wrong.

> "In particular, the statement that a *prima facie* obviousness rejection is not supported if no reference shows or suggests the newly-discovered properties and results of a claimed structure is not the law. Properties must be considered in the overall evaluation of obviousness, and the lack of any disclosure of useful properties for a prior art compound may indicate a lack of motivation to make

---

> ". . . *Papesch* held that a compound can be patented on the basis of its properties; it did not hold that those properties must produce superior results in every environment in which the compound may be used. To be patentable, a compound need not excel over prior art compounds in all common properties.
>
> . . .
>
> ". . . There is no set number of crops on which superiority must be shown, and the expectation that persons would want to use the compound to produce inferior results [on crops other than corn and soybeans] (or would want to fight lawsuits over such uses) is false." 816 F.2d at 646-647, 2 U.S.P.Q.2d at 1439-40.

How relevant is *Chupp* to the *Wright-Eli Lilly-Dillon* problem of combinations that might be obvious for one purpose but not for another? The claimed compound was, it can be argued, an obvious "run-of-the-mill" herbicide for crops other than corn and soybeans. If it is and would be expected to be an ordinary performer for crops, one can say there is no motivation for a person skilled in the art to produce it—for any purpose. Hence the *prima facie* obvious compound is not obvious in fact. But isn't that true even if the compound did not yield unexpected results on certain crops?

[230] *In re* Nolan, 553 F.2d 1261, 193 U.S.P.Q. 641 (CCPA 1977).

[231] The Federal Circuit summarized *Nolan* as follows:

> "In *Nolan* the applicant claimed the use of a specific ionizable noble gas composition as an improvement in a gaseous discharge display/memory device. Although the prior art showed the use of similar noble gas compositions in gaseous discharge devices, the applicant argued that his specific composition had unexpected performance benefits in memory devices. The court found that the most significant of Nolan's alleged performance benefits followed from the known ionization potential of the gas, and thus was taught in and expected from the prior art, whereas only some less significant benefits were shown to be unexpected from the prior art. The court held that the evidence of obviousness outweighed the evidence of unobviousness." 902 F.2d at 947, 14 U.S.P.Q.2d at 1745.

[232] 902 F.2d at 948, 14 U.S.P.Q.2d at 1746.

[233] *In re* Dillon, 919 F.2d 688, 16 U.S.P.Q.2d 1897 (Fed. Cir. 1990) (*en banc*).

related compounds, thereby precluding a *prima facie* case, but it is not correct that similarity of structure and a suggestion of *the activity of an applicant's compounds* in the prior art are necessary before a *prima facie* case is established." [234]

In *Dillon*, the court held that the PTO did not err in rejecting applicant Dillon's claims to hydrocarbon fuel/*tetra*-orthoester compositions and related methods of use, which exhibit the unexpected property of reducing particulate emissions (soot) during fuel combustion, as *prima facie* obvious in view of the teachings of primary and secondary prior art references that hydrocarbon fuel/*tri*-orthoester compositions scavenge water in the fuel and that tetra-orthoester is equivalent to *tri*-orthoester in scavenging water in hydraulic (nonhydrocarbon) fluids.

The claims at issue were to compositions comprising a hydrocarbon fuel and tetra-orthoesters and to a method of using the compositions. [235] The Board of Patent Appeals and Interferences held the claims unpatentable for obviousness in view of certain primary and secondary references. The primary reference showed hydrocarbon fuel compositions containing *tri*-orthoesters used for a different purpose, "dewatering" the fuels. These references did not suggest use of *tetra*-orthoesters. The secondary reference described both tri-orthoesters and tetra-orthoesters for use as water scavengers in hydraulic (nonhydrocarbon) fluids. The Board reasoned that (1) the secondary reference showed the equivalence of tetra-orthoesters and tri-orthoesters, creating *prima facie* obviousness, which prevented the claims from being patentable unless Dillon showed some unexpected superiority of her claimed tetra-orthoester compositions and methods as compared with tri-orthoester fuel compositions and methods; and (2) Dillon made no such showing; indeed, the data in Dillon's own patent specification showed that both tri- and tetra-orthoesters are effective in reducing particulate omissions. [236]

---

[234] 919 F.2d at 693, 16 U.S.P.Q.2d at 1901 (Emphasis in original.)

[235] The broadest composition claim, application claim 2, provided: "A composition comprising: a hydrocarbon fuel; and a sufficient amount of at least one orthoester *so as to reduce the particulate emissions from the combustion of the hydrocarbon fuel*, wherein the orthoester is of the formula: [formula omitted] . . . ." (Emphasis added.)

The broadest method claim, application claim 24, provided: "A method of reducing the particulate emissions from the combustion of a hydrocarbon fuel comprising combusting a mixture of the hydrocarbon fuel and *a sufficient amount* of at least one orthoester *so as to reduce the particulate emissions*, wherein the orthoester is of the formula: [formula omitted]. . . . " (Emphasis added.)

[236] The Federal Circuit held that the Board did not improperly use the inventor's own specification teaching of equivalency against her in determining obviousness.

> "While we caution against [the] practice [of using an inventor's own showing of equivalence against her], it is clear to us that references by the PTO to the comparative data in the patent application were not employed as evidence of equivalence between the tri- and tetra- orthoesters; the PTO was simply pointing out that the applicant did not or apparently could not make a showing of superiority for the claimed tetra-ester compositions over the prior art tri-ester compositions." 919 F.2d at 694, 16 U.S.P.Q.2d at 1902-03.

See §§ 2C[5][a] and 2C[5][g].

In affirming, the Federal Circuit noted that the claimed compositions "are not structurally or physically distinguishable from the prior art compositions by virtue of the recitation of their newly-discovered use." The "sufficient amount" recitation "is not a distinguishing limitation of the claims, unless that amount is different from the prior art and critical to the use of the claimed composition. . . . That is not the case here." "The amount of [tetra-orthoester] recited in the dependent claims can be from 0.05-49%, a very broad range; a preferred range is .05-9%, compared with a percentage in Sweeney[, the primary reference,] approximately equimolar to the amounts of water in the fuel which the ester is intended to remove (.01-5%)."

The structural similarity between applicant's claimed compositions and methods and the prior art created a presumption of obviousness. The court stressed that, in determining whether prior art creates *prima facie* obviousness, the art need not have provided "a suggestion . . . or expectation . . . that the claimed [invention] will have the same or a similar utility *as one newly discovered by applicant*."

> "This court, in reconsidering this case *in banc*, reaffirms that structural similarity between claimed and prior art subject matter, proved by combining references or otherwise, where the prior art gives reason or motivation to make the claimed compositions, creates a *prima facie* case of obviousness, and that the burden (and opportunity) then falls on an applicant to rebut that *prima facie* case. Such rebuttal or argument can consist of a comparison of test data showing that the claimed compositions possess unexpectedly improved properties or properties that the prior art does not have . . . , that the prior art is so deficient that there is no motivation to make what might otherwise appear to be obvious changes . . . , or any other argument or presentation of evidence that is pertinent. . . . [A]ll evidence of the properties of the claimed compositions and the prior art must be considered in determining the ultimate question of patentability, but . . . the discovery that a claimed composition possesses a property not disclosed for the prior art subject matter, does not by itself defeat a *prima facie* case."[237]

[iv] *Undisclosed Advantages and Properties.* A difficult problem arises when the result or advantage later relied upon to show nonobviousness is not disclosed in the specification.[238] The question is not free from doubt,[239] but the general rule is that an applicant or patentee may rely on an undisclosed advantage if it is inherent when the invention is used as disclosed in the specification[240] but not if it relates to a distinct utility not disclosed in the specification.[241] The inventor may use a continuation-in-part application, or possibly reissue, to add the utility or advantage to the specification without thereby losing the benefit of the original application's filing date.[242]

---

[237] 919 F.2d at 692-93, 16 U.S.P.Q.2d at 1901.

[238] *See* §§ 2D[1][d] and 2D[3][a][v].

[239] *See* Chisum, *"Afterthoughts" and Undisclosed Advantages as Evidence of Patentability: From Salt Dredges to Polystyrenes,* 57 J. Pat. Off. Soc'y 437 (1975). *See generally* D. Chisum, Patents § 5.03[5].

[240] *In re* Khelghatian, 364 F.2d 870, 150 U.S.P.Q. 661 (CCPA 1966).

[241] *In re* Davies, 475 F.2d 667, 177 U.S.P.Q. 381 (CCPA 1973).

[242] *See* § 2D[4][b][ii]. *Cf.* Carter-Wallace, Inc. v. Otte, 474 F.2d 529, 176 U.S.P.Q. 2, 452 (2d Cir. 1972), *cert. denied,* 412 U.S. 929, 178 U.S.P.Q. 65 (1973).

[v] *Claim Scope.* A showing of unexpected advantage must be commensurate in scope with the claim in question to be persuasive of nonobviousness.[243]

[d] **"Objective Evidence:" Long-Felt Need, Commercial Success, Copying, and Other Matters.** Nontechnical considerations, for example, commercial success and satisfaction of long-felt need, are relevant to an obviousness determination.[244] Economic and motivational factors provide a basis for making an inference about the ultimate issue of nonobviousness and guard against use of hindsight.

At one time, courts viewed nontechnical considerations as relevant only when the technical issue was "close,"[245] but today the Federal Circuit views them as always relevant in court suits concerning validity[246] and in PTO examination.[247]

[i] *Long-Felt Need—Failure of Others.* If (1) for a number of years an industry suffers a problem and efforts to solve it are unsuccessful, and (2) the invention solves that problem, then it can be inferred that the solution was not obvious to persons of ordinary skill in the art.[248] Long-felt need and failure of others will not be as persuasive if the need and failures were before the appearance of significant prior art.[249]

---

[243] *E.g., In re* Kulling, 897 F.2d 1147, 14 U.S.P.Q.2d 1056 (Fed. Cir. 1990); *In re* Lindner, 457 F.2d 506, 508, 173 U.S.P.Q. 356 (CCPA 1972) ("Here only one mixture of ingredients was tested. . . . The claims, however, are much broader in scope, covering mixtures of numerous compounds, and . . . there is no 'adequate basis for reasonably concluding that the greater number and variety of compositions included by the claims would behave in the same manner as the [single] tested composition.' "). *Compare In re* Chupp, 816 F.2d 643, 2 U.S.P.Q.2d 1437 (Fed. Cir. 1987), discussed at § 2C[4][c][iii].

In *Kulling,* the applicant's claims pertained to a process for the treatment of certain sulfuric acid solutions. The claims specified certain wash volumes at two steps of the process. The applicant argued that the claims were patentable despite prior art suggesting the combined process steps because "only minimal amounts of chromium and vanadium are extracted . . . when the wash volumes are limited as set forth in claim 1." The court held that the PTO properly rejected this argument because "the rejected claims read on a process for treating solutions which contain neither chromium nor vanadium," and there was no evidence either must be present in the specified sulfuric acid solution.

See generally D. Chisum, Patents § 5.06[1][b].

[244] *See generally* D. Chisum, Patents § 5.05.

[245] *E.g.,* Medical Laboratory Automation, Inc. v. Labcon, Inc., 670 F.2d 671, 213 U.S.P.Q. 537 (7th Cir. 1981).

[246] Stratoflex, Inc. v. Aeroquip Corp., 713 F.2d 1530, 218 U.S.P.Q. 871 (Fed. Cir. 1983).

Such evidence is not conclusive. *E.g.,* Merck & Co., Inc. v. Biocraft Laboratories, Inc., 874 F.2d 804, 809, 10 U.S.P.Q.2d 1843, 1848 (Fed. Cir. 1989) ("Commercial success is an indication of nonobviousness that must be considered in a patentability analysis, . . . but in the circumstances of this case, where it is the only such indication, it is insufficient to render [the patentee's] claimed invention nonobvious.").

[247] *In re* Sernaker, 702 F.2d 989, 217 U.S.P.Q. 1 (Fed. Cir. 1983).

[248] *E.g.,* Under Sea Industries, Inc. v. Dacor Corp., 833 F.2d 1551, 4 U.S.P.Q.2d 1772 (Fed. Cir. 1987); Reeves Instrument Corp. v. Beckman Instruments, Inc., 444 F.2d 263, 170 U.S.P.Q. 74 (9th Cir. 1971), *cert. denied,* 404 U.S. 951, 171 U.S.P.Q. 641 (1971).

[249] Graham v. John Deere Co., 383 U.S. 1, 148 U.S.P.Q. 459 (1966).

[*ii*]   *Commercial Success.* If a product that embodies the invention supplants prior art products and is a great commercial success, then it can be inferred that the invention was not obvious because otherwise persons lured by the prospect of success would have developed the invention sooner.[250] Commercial success both in the United States and in other countries is relevant under this theory.[251]

There must be a nexus between the commercial success and the claimed invention to prove nonobviousness.[252] The product success must flow from the functions and advantages disclosed or inherent in the patent specification.[253] Success attributable to other features in the product,[254] extensive advertising, or dominant market position is not persuasive.[255]

---

[250] *E.g.,* Akzo N.V. v. U.S. Int'l Trade Comm'n, 808 F.2d 1471, 1 U.S.P.Q.2d 1241 (Fed. Cir. 1986), *cert. denied,* 482 U.S. (1987); Hybritech Inc. v. Monoclonal Antibodies, Inc., 802 F.2d 1367, 231 U.S.P.Q. 81 (Fed. Cir. 1986), *cert. denied,* 480 U.S. 947 (1987); Simmons Fastener Corp. v. Illinois Tool Works, Inc., 739 F.2d 1573, 222 U.S.P.Q. 744 (Fed. Cir. 1984), *cert. denied,* 471 U.S. 1065 (1985).

As to the discoverability of third-party sales data, see American Standard, Inc. v. Pfizer Inc., 828 F.2d 734, 3 U.S.P.Q.2d 1817 (Fed. Cir. 1987). In *American Standard,* the Federal Circuit held that the district court did not err in limiting discovery of the confidential sales data of a third party, which was sought by a patent owner to establish commercial success of the claimed invention: "Although evidence of sales of different infringing articles showing commercial success of the claimed invention cannot be cumulative . . . , one seeking discovery of confidential sales information must nevertheless establish that it is reasonably necessary for a fair opportunity to develop and prepare the case for trial." 828 F.2d at 742, 3 U.S.P.Q.2d at 1822.

[251] Lindemann Maschinenfabrik GMBH v. American Hoist & Derrick Co., 730 F.2d 1452, 221 U.S.P.Q. 481 (Fed. Cir. 1984).

[252] Kansas Jack, Inc. v. Kuhn, 719 F.2d 1144, 219 U.S.P.Q. 857 (Fed. Cir. 1983).

[253] *In re* Vamco Machine & Tool, Inc., 752 F.2d 1564, 224 U.S.P.Q. 617 (Fed. Cir. 1985).

[254] *E.g.,* Sjolund v. Musland, 847 F.2d 1573, 6 U.S.P.Q.2d 2020 (Fed. Cir. 1988).

In *Sjolund,* the court reversed a jury verdict finding the patent in suit valid and for a nonobvious invention. The evidence pertaining to satisfaction of a long-felt need and to commercial success was insufficient to support the verdict. The patentee's device solved the problems encountered in the prior art, but, because the configuration of that device was not part of the *claimed* invention, "the advantages ascribed [to that configuration] are irrelevant in terms of the obviousness analysis."

> "Commercial success is relevant only if it flows from the merits of the *claimed* invention. . . . [A]ll the evidence was to the effect that its commercial popularity was due to . . . a feature not claimed. Thus, the jury was not entitled to draw the inference that the success of [the device] was due to the merits of the claimed invention. . . . Nor could the jury, from the bare evidence of units sold and gross receipts, draw the inference that the popularity of the [device] was due to the merits of the invention." 847 F.2d at 1582, 6 U.S.P.Q.2d at 2028.

[255] Pentec, Inc. v. Graphic Controls Corp., 776 F.2d 309, 227 U.S.P.Q. 766 (Fed. Cir. 1985); Cable Electric Products, Inc. v. Genmark, Inc., 770 F.2d 1015, 226 U.S.P.Q. 881 (Fed. Cir. 1985); Schwinn Bicycle Co.v. Goodyear Tire & Rubber Co., 444 F.2d 295, 168 U.S.P.Q. 258 (9th Cir. 1970); *In re* Caveney, 386 F.2d 917, 155 U.S.P.Q. 681 (CCPA 1967).

Compare Diversitech Corp. v. Century Steps, Inc., 850 F.2d 675, 7 U.S.P.Q.2d 1315 (Fed. Cir. 1988). In *Diversitech,* the Federal Circuit held that the district court erred in finding

In *Demaco Corp.*,[256] the Federal Circuit held that the district court erred by requiring the patentee to prove commercial success was *not* due to factors such as advertising, technical service to licensees, or the licensing of other products. The patentee only bears the burden of establishing a *prima facie* case of nexus between commercial success and the merits of the patented invention. A patentee meets this burden by showing that a thing (product or process) is commercially successful and is the invention disclosed and claimed in the patent. The court noted: "When the thing that is commercially successful is not coextensive with the patented invention—for example, if the patented invention is only a component of a commercially successful machine or process—the patentee must show prima facie a legally sufficient relationship between that which is patented and that which is sold."[257] This may consist of evidence that the patentee and its competitors consistently used the patented feature while varying other features or of evidence that the patented feature yields comparative advantages. "When the patentee has presented a prima facie case of nexus, the burden of coming forward with evidence in rebuttal shifts to the challenger. . . . It is thus the task of the challenger to adduce evidence to show that the commercial success was due to extraneous factors other than the patented invention, such as advertising, superior workmanship, etc."[258]

[iii]   *Licensing and Acquiescence by Competitors.* If major commercial competitors accept licenses under the patent, then it can be inferred that the invention was not obvious because otherwise those competitors would have challenged the patent's validity.[259] Licensing is not as persuasive if the royalty rates are low; competitors may simply have accepted the license to avoid litigation expenses.[260]

[iv]   *Copying and Laudatory Statements by the Infringer.* If the person challenging a patent's validity on grounds of obviousness deliberately copied the patented invention,[261] then it can be inferred that the invention was not obvious because otherwise the challenger would have either independently developed a product or copied prior

---

that the requisite nexus between the commercial success of the patentee's pad and the merits of the patented invention had not been established. There was no finding or evidence "of extraneous factors such as advertising or superior workmanship to rebut the patentee's evidence of substantial commercial sales, and sales growth, of the patented pad." The patentee established a *prima facie* case of the requisite nexus, which was not rebutted by the accused infringer. 850 F.2d at 679, 7 U.S.P.Q.2d at 1318.

[256] Demaco Corp. v. F. Von Langsdorff Licensing Ltd., 851 F.2d 1387, 7 U.S.P.Q.2d 1222 (Fed. Cir. 1988), *cert. denied*, 488 U.S. 956 (1988).

[257] 851 F.2d at 1392, 7 U.S.P.Q.2d at 1226.

[258] 851 F.2d at 1393, 7 U.S.P.Q.2d at 1226-27.

[259] Eibel Process Co. v. Minnesota & Ontario Paper Co., 261 U.S. 45 (1923).

[260] EWP Corp. v. Reliance Universal, Inc., 755 F.2d 898, 225 U.S.P.Q. 20 (Fed. Cir. 1985), *cert. denied*, 474 U.S. 843 (1985); Phillips Elec. & Pharmaceutical Indus. Corp. v. Thermal & Elec. Indus., Inc., 450 F.2d 1164, 171 U.S.P.Q. 641 (3d Cir. 1971).

[261] A person charged with patent infringement may defend on the ground that the patent claims are invalid for obviousness. *See* § 2F[4][a].

art products.[262] Weight may also be given to the infringer's praise of the invention.[263]

[v] *Near Simultaneous Invention.* If others develop solutions similar to the claimed invention at about the same time, then it can be inferred that the invention was obvious to persons of ordinary skill in the art.[264] Near simultaneous inventions can have inferential force even if they are not technically prior art.[265]

[e] **Other Guidelines.** No official rules set forth the nonobviousness requirement's application to particular types of inventions, but court decisions identify guidelines that are of assistance both in general and in specific situations.

[i] *Prior Art Suggestions—Obvious to Try.* The primary technical focus in assessing obviousness is on whether the prior art references collectively teach, expressly or implicitly, that various disclosed features may be combined in the manner of the claimed invention.[266] An invention may be obvious in view of a combination of

---

262 *E.g.,* Fromson v. Western Litho Plate & Supply Co., 853 F.2d 1568, 1571 n.4, 7 U.S.P.Q.2d 1606, 1609 n.4 (Fed. Cir. 1988) ("[I]n attributing sales to various factors, the [district] court overlooked [the accused infringer's] election to sell not its [prior art product] but the infringing [product] to the newspaper market, and the efforts of numerous companies in protesting reissue, efforts unlikely in relation to an unsuccessful invention or one for which noninfringing substitutes were readily available."); Vandenberg v. Dairy Equipment Co., 740 F.2d 1560, 224 U.S.P.Q. 195 (Fed. Cir. 1984).

Compare Cable Electric Products, Inc. v. Genmark, Inc., 770 F.2d 1015, 1028, 226 U.S.P.Q. 881, 888 (Fed. Cir. 1985) ("[M]ore than the mere fact of copying by an accused infringer is needed to make that action significant to a determination of the obviousness issue"; copying may be attributable to a general lack of concern for patent property or to contempt for the patentee's ability to enforce the specific patent).

263 Deere & Co. v. International Harvester Co., 658 F.2d 1137, 211 U.S.P.Q. 11 (7th Cir. 1981) *cert. denied,* 454 U.S. 969 (1981). *Compare* Medtronic, Inc. v. Cardiac Pacemakers, Inc., 721 F.2d 1563, 220 U.S.P.Q. 97 (Fed. Cir. 1983).

264 Concrete Appliance Co. v. Gomery, 269 U.S. 177, 46 S. Ct. 42, 70 L. Ed. 222 (1925); *In re* Merck & Co., Inc., 800 F.2d 1091, 231 U.S.P.Q. 375 (Fed. Cir. 1986) (evidence that four other groups of inventors independently and contemporaneously discovered the antidepressant properties of a certain chemical compound based on a knowledge of investigative techniques, including a theory (bioisosterism) as to the effect of chemical structural changes on biological properties, is evidence of the level of skill in the art at the time of the claimed invention (a method of using the compound as an antidepressant)).

265 Newell Companies, Inc. v. Kenney Manufacturing Co., 864 F.2d 757, 9 U.S.P.Q.2d 1417 (Fed. Cir. 1988), *cert. denied,* 110 S. Ct. 62 (1989) (though an internal memorandum may not be "technically 'prior art' . . .," it is admissible to show that persons of ordinary skill in the art suggested solutions to the problem similar to that claimed in the patent). *Compare* Hybritech Inc. v. Monoclonal Antibodies, Inc., 802 F.2d 1367, 231 U.S.P.Q. 81 (Fed. Cir. 1986), *cert. denied,* 480 U.S. 947 (1987); Environmental Designs, Ltd. v. Union Oil Co. of Calif., 713 F.2d 693, 218 U.S.P.Q. 865 (Fed. Cir. 1983), *cert. denied,* 464 U.S. 1043 (1984); E.I. Du Pont de Nemours & Co. v. Berkley & Co., 620 F.2d 1247, 205 U.S.P.Q. 1 (8th Cir. 1980) (near simultaneous invention is merely one of many indicia of obviousness).

266 *In re* Dow Chemical Co., 837 F.2d 469, 473, 5 U.S.P.Q.2d 1529, 1531-32 (Fed. Cir. 1988) ("The consistent criterion for determination of obviousness is whether the prior art would have suggested to one of ordinary skill in the art that this process should be carried out and would have a reasonable likelihood of success, viewed in the light of the prior art. . . . Both the

references even though the references' features cannot be physically substituted or combined to create the invention.[267] Furthermore, "[o]bviousness does not require absolute predictability; only a reasonable expectation that the beneficial result will be achieved is necessary to show obviousness."[268]

An "obvious to try" approach to the prior art to determine obviousness is improper.[269] Consider the following example:

> 1. Inventor A seeks a solution to a problem and decides that the solution might consist of a combination of ingredient X with a second ingredient having the general characteristics of Y.

> 2. The prior art lists 150 possible Y ingredients with defined characteristics but does not disclose any specific information as to how they may be combined with ingredient X to solve the problem confronting the inventor.

> 3. Inventor A discovers that Y(85) when combined with X achieves unexpected results in solving the problem.

The inventor's claim to the combination of X and Y(85) may not be rejected as obvious simply on the ground that it would have been obvious to try all of the 150 possibilities. There must be something in the prior art suggesting that Y(85) would achieve the desired result when combined with X.

In *O'Farrell*,[270] the court held a genetic engineering process (a method for producing a predetermined protein in a stable form in a transformed host species of bacteria) obvious in view of the applicants' own prior publication, which disclosed a method for translating a ribosomal RNA polypeptide chain by splicing a gene

---

suggestion and the expectation of success must be founded in the prior art, not in the applicant's disclosure. . . . In determining whether such a suggestion can fairly be gleaned from the prior art, the full field of the invention must be considered for the person of ordinary skill is charged with knowledge of the entire body of technological literature, including that which might lead away from the claimed invention."); *In re* Gordon, 733 F.2d 900, 221 U.S.P.Q. 1125 (Fed. Cir. 1984); *In re* Sernaker, 702 F.2d 989, 217 U.S.P.Q. 1 (Fed. Cir. 1983).

For a case example of an implicit prior art suggestion that established obviousness, see *In re* Kulling, 897 F.2d 1147, 14 U.S.P.Q.2d 1056 (Fed. Cir. 1990), in which the applicant's claims relating to a process for the treatment of certain sulfuric acid solutions were rejected as obvious in view of a primary reference and several secondary references. The primary reference showed the overall combination of process steps but showed neither (a) the specific use of "feed liquor" in a washing step nor (b) the numerical quantities of wash liquors. The secondary references indicated that a portion of the feed solution could be used in a wash. The precise amount of wash liquor "is a matter of routine optimization to one of ordinary skill in the art" because it involves a balancing of several "normal considerations." The Federal Circuit held that the PTO did not err in "finding that the secondary references, despite their relation to other specific but analogous chemical processes, provide an ample suggestion to bridge any factual 'shortcoming' of" the primary reference.

[267] Orthopedic Equipment Co., Inc. v. United States, 702 F.2d 1005, 217 U.S.P.Q. 193 (Fed. Cir. 1983).

[268] *In re* Merck & Co., Inc., 800 F.2d 1091, 231 U.S.P.Q. 375 (Fed. Cir. 1986).

[269] *In re* Goodwin, 576 F.2d 375, 198 U.S.P.Q. 1 (CCPA 1978). *See generally* D. Chisum, Patents § 5.04[1].

[270] *In re* O'Farrell, 853 F.2d 894, 7 U.S.P.Q.2d 1673 (Fed. Cir. 1988).

encoding for such RNA into bacteria and suggested that "it would be *interesting*" to examine the expression of a gene encoding for a normally translated protein (rather than ribosomal RNA). The publication rendered the claimed method obvious even though it was not certain that genes coding for proteins could be expressed as readthrough translation into the protein. The claim's rejection was not contrary to prior case law emphasizing that " 'obvious to try' is not the standard under § 103."

> "[T]he meaning of this maxim is sometimes lost. Any invention that would in fact have been obvious under § 103 would also have been, in a sense, obvious to try. The question is: when is an invention that was obvious to try nevertheless nonobvious?
>
> "The admonition that 'obvious to try' is not the standard under § 103 has been directed mainly at two kinds of error. In some cases, what would have been 'obvious to try' would have been to vary all parameters or try each of numerous possible choices until one possibly arrived at a successful result, where the prior art gave either no indication of which parameters were critical or no direction as to which of many possible choices is likely to be successful. . . . In others, what was 'obvious to try' was to explore a new technology or general approach that seemed to be a promising field of experimentation, where the prior art gave only general guidance as to the particular form of the claimed invention or how to achieve it." [271]

In *Amgen*,[272] the court found plaintiff's patent claims to a purified and isolated DNA sequence encoding human erythropoietin ("EPO"), and to host cells transformed with the sequence, nonobvious because there was no reasonable expectation of success in cloning the EPO gene using either the inventor's unique gene probing strategy (two fully-degenerate sets of probes to screen a human genomic library), nor the infringer's alternative suggested strategy (using the already known monkey EPO gene as a probe). Trial testimony supported the district court's conclusion that there was no reasonable expectation of success using the inventor's strategy. A witness from a biotechnology company stated he could not say whether his scientists would have succeeded in isolating the EPO gene if they had had the materials available to the inventor. A professor estimated that there would have been no more than a fifty percent chance of success. No one had successfully screened a genomic library using fully-degenerate probes of as high redundancy as the inventor's probes.

> "While the idea of using the monkey gene to probe for a homologous human gene may have been obvious to try, the realization of that idea would not have been obvious. There were many pitfalls. Hindsight is not a justifiable basis

---

271 853 F.2d at 903, 7 U.S.P.Q.2d at 1680.

See also In re Eli Lilly & Co., 902 F.2d 943, 945, 14 U.S.P.Q.2d 1741, 1743 (Fed. Cir. 1990) ("An 'obvious-to-try' situation exists when a general disclosure may pique the scientist's curiosity, such that further investigation might be done as a result of the disclosure, but the disclosure itself does not contain a sufficient teaching of how to obtain the desired result, or that the claimed result would be obtained if certain directions were pursued.").

272 Amgen, Inc. v. Chugai Pharmaceutical Co., Ltd., 927 F.2d 1200, 18 U.S.P.Q.2d 1016 (Fed. Cir. 1991).

on which to find that ultimate achievement of a long sought and difficult scientific goal was obvious."[273]

[ii] *Combination Inventions.* The patentability of combinations of mechanical elements individually well known in the art was formerly determined by special, strict tests.[274] More recent decisions hold that there are no special tests for combination inventions.[275]

[iii] *Chemical Compounds and Intermediates.* A novel and nonobvious chemical compound may be patented. Many new chemical compounds are structurally similar to known compounds and are considered "structurally obvious." A "structurally obvious" compound may nevertheless be patented if it has unexpected properties not possessed by the known compounds.[276]

Determining the patentability of a chemical compound is a two-step process. First, is the claimed compound structurally similar enough to prior art compounds to show *prima face* obviousness? The level of similarity is not precise.[277] A claimed compound may be part of a homologous series with the prior art compound but not necessarily *prima facie* obvious.[278] A compound disclosed in the prior art will not create *prima facie* obviousness if the prior art discloses no specific utility for the compound.[279]

---

[273] 927 F.2d at 1209, 18 U.S.P.Q.2d at 1023.

[274] *E.g.,* Sakraida v. Ag Pro, Inc., 425 U.S. 273, 189 U.S.P.Q. 449 (1976) (combination of old elements must achieve "synergism"); Anderson's Black Rock, Inc. v. Pavement Salvage, 396 U.S. 57, 163 U.S.P.Q. 673 (1969); Great Atlantic & Pacific Tea Co. v. Supermarket Equipment Corp., 340 U.S. 147, 87 U.S.P.Q. 303 (1950). *See* § 2B[4][c].

[275] *E.g.,* Raytheon Co. v. Roper Corp., 724 F.2d 951, 220 U.S.P.Q. 592 (Fed. Cir. 1983), *cert. denied,* 465 U.S. 835 (1984).

[276] *In re* Papesch, 315 F.2d 381, 137 U.S.P.Q. 43 (CCPA 1963). *See generally* D. Chisum, Patents § 5.04[6].

[277] *E.g., In re* Grabiak, 769 F.2d 729, 731, 226 U.S.P.Q. 870, 872 (Fed. Cir. 1985) ("[G]eneralization should be avoided insofar as specific chemical structures are alleged to be *prima facie* obvious one from the other;" there can be a *prima facie* case of obviousness even in an area as unpredictable as the biological properties of chemical compounds, but such a case must be based on support in the prior art for the structural change necessary to get from the prior art compound to the claimed compound).

[278] *In re* Mills, 281 F.2d 218, 126 U.S.P.Q. 513 (CCPA 1960).

[279] *In re* Stemniski, 444 F.2d 581, 170 U.S.P.Q. 343 (CCPA 1971). *See also In re* Lalu, 747 F.2d 703, 223 U.S.P.Q. 1257 (Fed. Cir. 1984) (there is no *prima facie* obviousness when a prior art reference disclosed that a compound homologous to the claimed compound was useful only as an intermediate to produce other compounds with utilities differing from those of the claimed compound.).

Compare In re Dillon, 919 F.2d 688, 16 U.S.P.Q.2d 1897 (Fed. Cir. 1990) (en banc) (applicant did not "show that the prior art compositions and use were so lacking in significance that there was no motivation for others to make obvious variants.;" "There was no attempt to argue the relative importance of the claimed compositions compared with the prior art.;" *Stemniski* "rather than destroying the established practice of rejecting closely-related compounds as *prima facie* obvious, qualified it by holding that a presumption is not created when the reference compound is so lacking in any utility that there is no motivation to make close relatives.").

Second, does the *prima facie* obvious claimed compound exhibit new and unexpected properties when compared with the closest prior art compounds?[280] Significantly greater effectiveness is equivalent to a new property.[281] A chemical compound's ability to operate as an intermediate to produce another compound (end product) that exhibits unexpected superior properties (compared to prior art end products) may rebut *prima facie* obviousness.[282]

If the claimed compound has an unexpected property not possessed by the closest prior art compound but shares a common property with the prior art compound, *prima facie* obviousness will be rebutted only if the unexpected property is much more significant than shared property.[283]

If an inventor discovers a significant unexpected property of a compound that cannot be claimed as such because it is old or obvious, he may obtain a patent claiming a new method of using the compound.[284]

[iv] *Process—Methods of Making and Using.* If an applicant formulates claims to both products and processes, the requirements of novelty and nonobviousness must be applied independently to each such claim.[285]

In *Durden*,[286] the Federal Circuit held that a claim to a process of making a chemical compound from a starting material is not necessarily nonobvious even though both the starting material and the resulting compound are nonobvious and patentable.

---

280 *In re Johnson*, 747 F.2d 1456, 223 U.S.P.Q. 1260 (Fed. Cir. 1984). *See also In re Dillon*, 919 F.2d 688, 692-93, 16 U.S.P.Q.2d 1897, 1901 (Fed. Cir. 1990) (en banc) ("[R]ebuttal [of a case of *prima facie* obviousness based on structural similarity] can consist of a comparison of test data showing that the claimed compositions possess unexpectedly improved properties or properties that the prior art does not have (*In re Albrecht*, 514 F.2d 1389, 1396, 185 U.S.P.Q. 585, 590 (CCPA 1975); *Murch*, 464 F.2d at 1056, 175 U.S.P.Q. at 92), that the prior art is so deficient that there is no motivation to make what might otherwise appear to be obvious changes (*Albrecht*, 514 F.2d at 1396, 185 U.S.P.Q. at 590; *In re Stemniski*, 444 F.2d 581, 170 U.S.P.Q. 343 (CCPA 1971); *In re Ruschig*, 343 F.2d 965, 145 U.S.P.Q. 274 (CCPA 1965)), or any other argument or presentation of evidence that is pertinent.").

281 *In re Lunsford*, 357 F.2d 380, 148 U.S.P.Q. 716 (CCPA 1966).

282 *In re Magerlein*, 602 F.2d 366, 202 U.S.P.Q. 473 (CCPA 1979).

283 *In re May*, 574 F.2d 1082, 197 U.S.P.Q. 601 (CCPA 1978). *Cf. In re Dillon*, 919 F.2d 688, 698, 16 U.S.P.Q.2d 1897, 1905 (Fed. Cir. 1990) (en banc), discussed above ("The dissent mentions positions advanced by the Commissioner, including citing the *In re Mod*, 408 F.2d 1055, 161 U.S.P.Q. 281 (CCPA 1969) and *In re de Montmollin*, 344 F.2d 976, 145 U.S.P.Q. 416 (CCPA 1965) decisions. We do not, however, in today's decision necessarily adopt any positions of the Commissioner other than those stated in our opinion and note that neither *Mod* nor *de Montmollin* dealt with the requirements of a *prima facie* case. They concerned the question whether the existence of a new property for claimed compounds in addition to a property common to both the claimed and related prior art compounds rendered the claimed compounds unobvious. We are not faced with that question today."). *See* § 2C[4][c][iii].

284 *See, e.g., In re Shetty*, 566 F.2d 81, 195 U.S.P.Q. 753 (CCPA 1977).

285 Providence Rubber Co. v. Goodyear, 76 U.S. (9 Wall.) 788 (1870). *See generally* D. Chisum, Patents § 5.04[8].

286 *In re Durden*, 763 F.2d 1406, 226 U.S.P.Q. 359 (Fed. Cir. 1985). *Compare In re Kuehl*, 475 F.2d 658, 177 U.S.P.Q. 250 (CCPA 1973).

In *Pleuddemann*,[287] it held that *Durden* did not apply to method-of-use claims. In *Pleuddemann*, an inventor filed an application relating to organosilane coupling agents useful for fiberglass-filled unsaturated polyesters. The inventor disclosed the structural formula for a class of organosilane reaction products (coupling agents). When the coupling agents are used to bind polyester resins to fiberglass fillers, a product with improved mechanical properties, including moisture resistance, results. Known prior art resins and fillers are used. The inventor included three groups of claims:

(1) the new organosilanes class;

(2) methods of (A) bonding polymerizable material to mineral fillers and (B) priming a surface to improve its bonding to certain organic resins, both by use of the new organosilanes class; and

(3) new articles of manufacture produced by using the new class and methods.[288]

In response to an examiner restriction requirement, the inventor elected the first group of claims, coupling agents. The PTO allowed those claims, and the inventor obtained a patent. The inventor filed a divisional application, asserting the bonding and priming method claims. The bonding claim provided, *inter alia*:

> "A process for bonding a polymerizable material to a mineral filler comprising: (a) mixing an organosilane with a polymerizable material . . . and a filler having hydroxyl functionality thereon . . . and (b) polymerizing the material . . . wherein said organosilane is represented by [a formula defining the new organosilanes class]."[289]

The priming claim provided, *inter alia*:

> "A method for priming a surface having hydroxyl functionality . . . comprising wetting the surface with a solution of an organosilane and then drying said surface, wherein said organosilane is represented by [a formula defining the new organosilane class]."[290]

The PTO rejected the claims, reasoning that a prior art reference taught the same bonding and priming steps using different silane coupling agents, and relying primarily on *Durden*.[291]

The Federal Circuit reversed, holding the PTO erred in rejecting the claims based on method-of-making cases, such as *Durden*, and in failing to apply method-of-use cases such as *Kuehl*.[292] The flaw in the PTO rejection is that it presumes that the inventor's new group of compounds, which is an essential limitation of the claims, is prior art.[293]

---

287 *In re* Pleuddemann, 910 F.2d 823, 15 USPQ2d 1738 (Fed. Cir. 1990).

288 910 F.2d at 824–25, 15 U.S.P.Q.2d at 1739.

289 910 F.2d at 824–25, 15 U.S.P.Q.2d at 1739.

290 910 F.2d at 824–25, 15 U.S.P.Q.2d at 1739.

291 The PTO also cited *In re* Kanter, 399 F.2d 249, 158 U.S.P.Q. 331 (CCPA 1968), and *In re* Neugebauer, 330 F.2d 353, 141 U.S.P.Q. 205 (CCPA 1964).

292 *In re* Kuehl, 475 F.2d 658, 177 U.S.P.Q. 250 (CCPA 1973).

293 *In re* Pleuddemann, 910 F.2d 823, 828, 15 U.S.P.Q.2d 1738, 1742 (Fed. Cir. 1990) ("[The] § 103 obviousness of [the bonding and priming claims] depends on the obviousness of us-

> "When a new and useful compound or group of compounds is invented or discovered having a *particular* use it is often the case that what is really a single invention may be viewed legally as having three or more different aspects permitting it to be claimed in different ways, for example: (1) the compounds themselves; (2) the method or process of making the compounds[;] and (3) the method or process of *using* the compounds for their intended purpose." [294]

There is "a real difference between a process of making and a process of using and the cases dealing with one involve different problems from the cases dealing with the other."

> " 'From the standpoint of patent law, a compound and all of its properties are inseparable; they are one and the same thing.' *In re Papesch*, 315 F.2d 381, 391, 137 U.S.P.Q. 43, 51 (CCPA 1963). It is the properties of appellant's compounds as bonding/priming agents for certain polymers and fillers or support surfaces that give them their utility. . . . [T]he compounds and their use are but different aspects of, or ways of looking at, the same invention and consequently that invention is capable of being claimed both as new compounds or as a new method or process of bonding/priming. . . . [A] process or method of making the compounds is a quite different thing; they may have been made by a process which was new or old, obvious or nonobvious." [295]

The court distinguished *Durden*.[296]

The *Durden* rule has implications for the territorial scope of United States patents. A patent claiming novel and nonobvious starting materials, such as genetically-altered cell cultures useful in making natural proteins, may not be effective against use of the starting materials abroad to produce an unpatented product, such as the protein, for importation into the United States.[297] Therefore, it is important to obtain *process* claims, such as to the method of *using* the cell cultures to *make* the protein.[298]

---

ing appellant's new compounds, which constitute the essential limitation of the claims, in light of the prior art. That being so, the board's hindsight comparison of the functioning of the new compounds with the functioning of the compounds of the prior art was legal error. It uses appellant's specification teaching as though it were prior art in order to make claims to methods of bonding/priming using his admittedly novel compounds appear to be obvious.").

294 910 F.2d at 825-26, 15 U.S.P.Q.2d 1740 (Emphasis in original.)

295 910 F.2d at 827, 15 U.S.P.Q.2d at 1741.

296 *Id.*

> "[It] was a case involving only the patentability of a process of making a novel insecticide and the single claim on appeal was held to be directed to obvious subject matter in view of a prior art patent disclosing a very similar process using similar reactants notwithstanding the facts that there were unobvious starting materials used and unobvious products obtained. We are not here concerned with a process of making bonding/priming agents but with the agents themselves in which the bonding/priming properties are inherent, for which reason we do not find *Durden* a controlling precedent as did the examiner and the board."

297 *See* Amgen Inc. v. U.S. Int'l Trade Comm'n, 902 F.2d 1532, 1538, 14 U.S.P.Q.2d 1734, 1739 (Fed. Cir. 1990).

298 For a discussion of the Process Patents Amendments Act, and of Tariff Act Section 337, which cover, under some circumstances, use abroad of a process patented in the United States, see § 2E[2][b][iii].

Neither *Durden* nor the *Pleuddemann* distinction between making methods and using methods make (or use common) sense in terms of logic or policy. How can a method of making a novel and nonobvious product be obvious if the method, as claimed, is limited to methods that begin with or result in something that is not obvious? By definition, the scope of the claim is confined to nonobvious subject matter. Saying that such a method is obvious in view of the prior art is infected by the fallacy condemned in *Pleudemann*: it assumes that the inventor's own discovery (the product) is prior art. Further, the difference between a method of making and a method of use is often only verbal. In *Pleudemann*, the bonding and priming claims could be viewed either as methods of using nonobvious coupling agents (to make fiberglass-filled polyesters) or methods of making fiberglass-filled polyesters (by use of unobvious coupling agents).

In *Dillon*,[299] discussed above, which involved soot reduction hydrocarbon fuel/tetra-orthoester compositions, the Federal Circuit declined to rule separately on the patentability of applicant's claims to methods of using the novel compositions apart from the patentability of her claims to the *compositions* themselves because applicant did not separately argue the patentability of her method claims. It noted that "We make no judgment as to the patentability of claims that Dillon might have made and properly argued to a method directed to the novel aspects of her invention, except to question the lack of logic in a claim to a method of reducing particulate emissions by combusting." It also commented on the PTO's citation of *Durden* "for the proposition that even 'substitution of an unobvious starting material into an old process does not necessarily result in an unobvious process.' "

> "The PTO has . . . applied *Durden* regularly to claims to processes of making and processes of using, on the ground that the type of step involved in the claimed process is not novel.

> ". . . [W]e do not regard *Durden* as authority to reject as obvious every method claim reading on an old *type of process*, such as mixing, reacting, reducing, etc. The materials used in a claimed process as well as the result obtained therefrom, must be considered along with the specific nature of the process, and the fact that new or old, obvious or nonobvious, materials are used or result from the process are only factors to be considered, rather than conclusive indicators of the obviousness or nonobviousness of a claimed process. When any applicant properly presents and argues suitable method claims, they should be examined in light of all these relevant factors, free from any presumed controlling effect of *Durden*. *Durden* did not hold that all methods involving old process steps are obvious; the court in that case concluded that the particularly claimed process was obvious; it refused to adopt an unvarying rule that the fact that nonobvious starting materials and nonobvious products are involved *ipso facto* makes the process nonobvious. Such an invariant rule always leading to the opposite conclusion is also not the law. Thus, we reject the Commissioner's argument that we affirm the rejection of the method claims under the precedent of *Durden*."[300]

---

[299] *In re* Dillon, 919 F.2d 688, 16 U.S.P.Q.2d 1897 (Fed. Cir. 1990) (en banc). *See* § 2C[4][c][iii].

[300] 919 F.2d at 695, 16 U.S.P.Q.2d at 1903.

[5] Prior Art

"Prior art" is a term of art in patent law. Patent law rules refer to the content of the prior art, to what is novel in relation to the prior art, to what a document suggested to a person of ordinary skill in the art and to what would have been obvious to that person.

The patent statutes do not expressly define prior art for obviousness. Section 103 on nonobviousness refers to the "prior art,"[301] and, in an amendment added in 1984, excludes specific subject matter from the prior art.[302] Section 112 on disclosure refers to the "art . . . to which [the invention] pertains."[303] Section 102 on novelty and loss of right does not use the term "prior art" but lists seven conditions (subsections (a) through (g)) that preclude the grant of a patent on an invention.[304]

Four of Section 102's conditions unquestionably define what is "prior art:" (1) Section 102(a), the primary novelty-defeating provision dealing with patents and

---

[301] The obviousness section, Section 103, refers to Section 102 by excluding from patentability an invention that would have been obvious in view of the "prior art" even though that invention is not "identically disclosed or described as set forth in section 102." The problem with reading this as a straightforward incorporation of Section 102 as a definition of prior art is that some of the subsections of 102 do not deal with disclosures or descriptions. For example, subsection (c) deals with abandonment of an invention.

[302] 35 U.S.C. § 103.

[303] 35 U.S.C. § 112.

[304] 35 U.S.C. Section 102 provides as follows:

"Conditions for patentability; novelty and loss of right to patent.

A person shall be entitled to a patent unless-

(a) the invention was known or used by others in this country, or patented or described in a printed publication in this or a foreign country, before the invention thereof by the applicant for patent, or

(b) the invention was patented or described in a printed publication in this or a foreign country or in public use or on sale in this country, more than one year prior to the date of the application for patent in the United States, or

(c) he has abandoned the invention, or

(d) the invention was first patented or caused to be patented, or was the subject of an inventor's certificate, by the applicant or his legal representatives or assigns in a foreign country prior to the date of the application for patent in this country on an application for patent or inventor's certificate filed more than twelve months before the filing of the application in the United States, or

(e) the invention was described in a patent granted on an application for patent by another filed in the United States before the invention thereof by the applicant for patent, or on an international application by another who has fulfilled the requirements of paragraphs (1), (2), and (4) of section 371(c) of this title before the invention thereof by the applicant for patent, or

(f) he did not himself invent the subject matter sought to be patented, or

(g) before the applicant's invention thereof the invention was made in this country by another who had not abandoned, suppressed, or concealed it. In determining priority of invention there shall be considered not only the respective dates of conception and reduction to practice of the invention, but also the reasonable diligence of one who was first to conceive and last to reduce to practice, from a time prior to conception by the other."

publications anywhere and matter "known or used" by others in the United States; (2) Section 102(b), the "loss of right" or "statutory bar" provision dealing with patents and publications anywhere and matter "on sale" or "in public use" in the United States by the inventor or anyone else more than the one-year "grace period" prior to the inventor's filing of a patent application;[305] (3) Section 102(e), the provision on senior-filed patents by persons other than the inventor; and (4) Section 102(g), the provision on prior inventions in the United States by other persons.[306]

Prior art for determining obviousness includes at least the following:

1. A printed publication or patent anywhere:

(a)   by another if dated before the inventor's invention date, or

(b)   by the inventor if dated more than one year before the date the inventor applies for a patent.

2. Anything in public use or on sale in the United States by the inventor or anyone else if dated more than one year before the date the inventor applies for a patent.[307]

3. Anything in secret commercial use by the inventor if dated more than one year before the date the inventor applies for a patent.

4. Anything "known or used" in a publicly accessible form in the United States by another if dated before the inventor's invention date.

5. Anything described in a United States patent, regardless of when it issues, by another if the application for that patent was filed in the United States before the inventor's invention date.

6. Anything invented in the United States by another if dated before the inventor's invention date.

A useful approach to "prior art" is to view it as having limits in four dimensions—(1) *source* (printed publication, patent, device in public use or on sale, device or process in secret use, unabandoned invention), (2) *place* (in the United States or in another country), (3) *time* (before the inventor's invention date or after that date but more than one year before the inventor's patent application filing date, and (4) *person* (the inventor or one other than the inventor).[308] An item is prior art only

---

[305] The similarity in wording between subsections 102(a) and 102(b) is a constant source of confusion in patent law. Section 102(a) is a *novelty* provision—determining whether subject matter is new as of the inventor's invention date in view of prior art of others. Section 102(b) is a *loss of right* provision, which contemplates that the right to a patent on an invention that was patentable as of the date of invention is lost when the inventor delays too long in filing a patent application. Different policy considerations support the two subsections.

[306] Whether other subsections, such as Section 102(f), constitute prior art is not well settled. *See* § 2C[5][e][ii].

[307] Public use or on sale activity may be excused by the experimental use doctrine. *See* § 2C[5][b][v].

[308] *See* Chisum, *Sources of Prior Art in Patent Law*, 52 Wash. L. Rev. 1 (1976); Chisum, *Foreign Activity: Its Effect on Patentability Under United States Law*, 11 Int'l Rev. Indus. Prop. & Cr. L. 26 (1980).

if it falls within the limits in all four dimensions. For example, the following item falls within all the limits and therefore qualifies as prior art.

Source:	Printed publication
Place:	China
Time:	A day before invention date but less than one year prior to the patent application date
Person:	X, a person other than the inventor

A change in one dimension may disqualify the item as prior art. If it is a device in public use but not a printed publication (change in source), it is not prior art. If it is by the inventor (change in person), rather than X, it is not prior art. But a change in another dimension may restore the item's status as prior art. If it is a device in public use rather than a printed publication but is in the United States (change in place), it is prior art. If it is a printed publication and by the inventor but is more than one year prior to the patent application filing date (change in time), it is prior art.

Why is prior art so complex? The answer lies primarily in history and inertia. The statutory language in Section 102 traces to patent statutes enacted in 1836, 1839, 1870 and 1897. These old statutes adopted distinctions, such as those between acts "in this country" and acts in "a foreign country," that made sense at the time but are now obsolete.[309] The 1952 Patent Act adopted and supplemented these old concepts. In 1966, a Presidential Commission recommended revision of the prior art provisions,[310] but Congress took no action on those recommendations. More recently, the United States joined multinational discussions of possible "harmonization" of the patent laws of major countries, which would necessarily bring major changes in the definition of prior art.

[a] **Documentary Sources: Patents and Publications.** Sections 102(a) and 102(b) list patents and descriptions in printed publications as patent-defeating events. Under Section 102(a), anything "patented" or "described in a printed publication" is prior art if it occurred before the inventor's invention date and is by one other than the inventor. Under Section 102(b), anything that is "patented" or "described in a printed publication" is prior art if it occurred more than one year before the inventor filed an application to obtain a patent on the invention and is by either the inventor or by anyone else.[311]

---

[309] *See* Chisum, *Foreign Activity: Its Effect on Patentability Under United States Law*, 11 Int'l Rev. Indus. Prop. & Cr. L. 26 (1980).

[310] President's Commission on the Patent System, *"To Promote the Progress of . . . Useful Arts" In an Age of Exploding Technology* (1966).

[311] To illustrate with an example, assume that inventor I invents a widget on June 1, 1986 and applies for a patent on January 1, 1987. The following publications are prior art: (1) by person J on May 31, 1986 (Section 102(a)—prior to the invention date), and (2) by inventor I on December 31, 1986 (Section 102(b)—by inventor but more than one year prior

[i] *Publications.* Any document reproduced and distributed anywhere in the world in a form accessible to the public is a "printed publication."[312]

A document need not be set in type and reproduced in the traditional way to be "printed."[313] For example, a patent application microfilmed and deposited at five sub-offices of the Australian Patent Office is a printed publication.[314]

Conference papers[315] and advertising circulars[316] are printed publications. Internal corporate documents[317] and documents circulated to a small group under a pledge of confidentiality[318] are not publications.

A single copy of a document deposited in a library is a printed publication if it is indexed and available to the public.[319]

---

to application filing). The following publications are not prior art: (1) by person J on July 1, 1986 (after date of invention but within one year of the application filing), and (2) by inventor I on January 2, 1986 (before invention date but by inventor and less than one year before application filing date).

[312] *See generally* D. Chisum, Patents § 3.04.

[313] Philips Elec. & Pharmaceutical Industries Corp. v. Thermal & Elec. Industries, Inc., 450 F.2d 1164, 171 U.S.P.Q. 641 (3d Cir. 1971).

[314] *In re* Wyer, 655 F.2d 221, 210 U.S.P.Q. 790 (CCPA 1981).

[315] Massachusetts Institute of Technology v. AB Fortia, 774 F.2d 1104, 227 U.S.P.Q. 428 (Fed. Cir. 1985) (a paper delivered at a conference in another country constitutes a "printed publication" when (1) prior to the conference, the author gave a copy of the paper to the head of the conference, (2) from 50 to 500 persons working in the pertinent art attended the conference, and (3) copies of the paper were distributed on request, without restrictions, to as many as six persons); Deep Welding, Inc. v. Sciaky Bros. Inc., 417 F.2d 1227, 163 U.S.P.Q. 144 (7th Cir. 1969), *cert. denied,* 397 U.S. 1037, 165 U.S.P.Q. 290 (1970).

[316] Jockmus v. Leviton, 28 F.2d 812 (2d Cir. 1928). *See also* Garrett Corp. v. United States, 422 F.2d 874, 877-78, 164 U.S.P.Q. 521 (Ct. Cl. 1970), *cert. denied,* 400 U.S. 951, 167 U.S.P.Q. 705 (1970).

[317] *In re* Kratz, 592 F.2d 1169, 201 U.S.P.Q. 71 (CCPA 1979).

[318] General Tire & Rubber Co. v. Firestone Tire & Rubber Co., 349 F. Supp. 345, 353, 174 U.S.P.Q. 438 (N.D. Ohio 1972), *aff'd,* 489 F.2d 1105, 180 U.S.P.Q. 98 (6th Cir. 1973), *cert. denied,* 417 U.S. 932, 182 U.S.P.Q. 1 (1974).

See also Northern Telecom, Inc. v. Datapoint Corp., 908 F.2d 931, 15 U.S.P.Q.2d 1321 (Fed. Cir. 1990), *cert. denied,* 111 S. Ct. 296 (1990); Preemption Devices, Inc. v. Minnesota Mining &Mfg. Co., 732 F.2d 903, 221 U.S.P.Q. 841 (Fed. Cir. 1984). In *Preemption Devices,* the court held that distribution of six copies of a brochure to a single person for use in obtaining financing was not a publication. In *Northern Telecom,* the court held that four reports on a complex military system, which were distributed to approximately 50 persons or organizations involved in a project, were not shown to be so accessible to the public as to be publications.

[319] *In re* Bayer, 568 F.2d 1357, 196 U.S.P.Q. 670 (CCPA 1978). *See also In re* Hall, 781 F.2d 897, 228 U.S.P.Q. 453 (Fed. Cir. 1986). In *Hall,* the Federal Circuit held that a doctoral thesis deposited in a library in Germany prior to the critical date of one year prior to the applicant's filing date was a printed publication as of the deposit date. The library director's affidavit described its regular procedures for indexing, cataloging and shelving theses. Failure to establish an exact public accessibility date is not important because, under the described procedures, the thesis would have been accessible approximately two and one-half months prior to the critical date. "The statutory phrase 'printed publication' has been interpreted to

A document is effective as a publication on the date when it first reaches members of the public or becomes accessible to the public.[320]

A publication's description anticipates, that is, completely defeats the novelty of a later invention, only if it is "enabling," that is, sufficient to teach a person of ordinary skill in the art how to make and use what is described.[321] A publication that is not enabling or that discloses an inoperative product or process does not anticipate but is part of the "prior art" for determining nonobviousness.[322]

---

give effect to ongoing advances in the technologies of data storage, retrieval and dissemination." 781 F.2d 898, 228 U.S.P.Q. at 455.

Compare In re Cronyn, 890 F.2d 1158, 1160-61, 13 U.S.P.Q.2d 1070, 1072-73 (Fed. Cir. 1989). In *Cronyn*, the Federal Circuit held that an undergraduate thesis deposited in a college library open to the public but neither cataloged nor indexed is not a printed publication because it is not accessible to the public. The three theses in question were written by Reed College students. The college's chemistry department lists chemistry theses on approximately 450 cards contained in a shoebox. Both the listing and the actual theses are available for public examination. "The decision whether a particular reference is a printed publication 'must be approached on a case-by-case basis.' "

[320] Constant v. Advanced Micro-Devices, Inc., 848 F.2d 1560, 1568-69, 7 U.S.P.Q.2d 1057, 1062-63 (Fed. Cir. 1988), *cert. denied*, 488 U.S. 892 (1988) ("The statutory phrase 'printed publication' has been interpreted to mean that before the critical date the reference must have been sufficiently accessible to the public interested in the art; dissemination and public accessibility are the keys to the legal determination whether a prior art reference was 'published.' . . . Evidence of routine business practice can be sufficient to prove that a reference was made accessible before a critical date. . . . Accessibility goes to the issue of whether interested members of the relevant public could obtain the information if they wanted to. If accessibility is proved, there is no requirement to show that particular members of the public actually received the information.").

[321] *E.g.*, Reading & Bates Construction Co. v. Baker Energy Resources Corp., 748 F.2d 645, 223 U.S.P.Q. 1168 (Fed. Cir. 1984). In *Reading*, the court held that a one-page promotional brochure boasting of the results of a process is insufficient to constitute an enabling disclosure. *Cf.* Constant v. Advanced Micro-Devices, Inc., 848 F.2d 1560, 1569, 7 U.S.P.Q.2d 1057, 1063 (Fed. Cir. 1988) ("A printed publication must . . . be enabling."). In *Constant*, the court rejected the patentee's argument that a prior art publication was not enabling because it failed to set forth a specific computer program because the patentee's specification also failed to set forth such a program: "The disclosure [in the reference] is at least at the same level of technical detail as the disclosure in the . . . patent. If disclosure of a computer program is essential for an anticipating reference, then the disclosure in the . . . patent would fail to satisfy the enablement requirement of 35 U.S.C. Section 112. . . . " 848 F.2d at 1569, 7 U.S.P.Q.2d at 1063.

[322] Beckman Instruments, Inc. v. LK.B. Produkter AB, 892 F.2d 1547, 13 U.S.P.Q.2d 1301 (Fed. Cir. 1989); Paperless Accounting, Inc. v. Bay Area Rapid Transit Sys., 804 F.2d 659, 231 U.S.P.Q. 649 (Fed. Cir. 1986), *cert. denied*, 480 U.S. 933 (1987); EWP Corp. v. Reliance Universal, Inc., 755 F.2d 898, 907, 225 U.S.P.Q. 20, 25 (Fed. Cir. 1985), *cert. denied*, 474 U.S. 843 (1985) ("A reference must be considered for everything it *teaches* by way of technology and is not limited to the particular *invention* it is describing and attempting to protect.").

In *Beckman*, the court held that the jury was properly instructed that "References relied upon to support a rejection for obviousness must provide an enabling disclosure. That is to say, they must place the claimed invention in the possession of the public" because "[i]n order to render a claimed apparatus or method obvious, the prior art must enable one skilled in

[ii] *Patents.* In the United States and most other countries, utility patents are printed for distribution and are, therefore, printed publications under Section 102(a). The question of what is "patented" arises with government protection grants that are not published on grant or are effective on a date earlier than publication.[323] Utility models, for example, a German *Gebrauchsmuster,*[324] and design registrations, for example, a German *Geschmacksmuster,*[325] are "patents."

The date exclusive rights vest in the patentee and can be enforced by an infringement suit is the patent date.[326] That date is no sooner than the date the contents of the document become publicly available.[327]

[b] Nondocumentary Sources: Public Use, On Sale, and Secret Commercial Exploitation

[i] *Known or Used by Others.* Section 102(a) bars a patent if the invention was, before the applicant's invention date, known or used by another in the United States.[328] "Known or used" means knowledge or use accessible to the public.[329] If someone uses a process or machine in a nonsecret manner to produce articles for commercial purposes, the use is accessible to the public.[330] Secret and private use are not sufficient.[331] An "abandoned experiment" is not prior art under Section 102(a).[332]

---

the art to make and use the apparatus or method." On the other hand, a patent expert's testimony that "a piece of prior art that doesn't work is not prior art" "was clearly a misstatement of the law." "Even if a reference discloses an inoperative device, it is prior art for all that it teaches." 892 F.2d at 1550-51, 13 U.S.P.Q.2d at 1304.

[323] Whether something has been patented is often important under the foreign patenting bar provision, 35 U.S.C. § 102(d), discussed at § 2C[5][b][vii].

[324] Bendix Corp. v. Balax, Inc., 421 F.2d 809, 164 U.S.P.Q. 485 (7th Cir. 1970), *cert. denied*, 399 U.S. 911, 166 U.S.P.Q. 65 (1970).

[325] *In re* Talbott, 443 F.2d 1397, 170 U.S.P.Q. 281 (CCPA 1971).

[326] *In re* Monks, 588 F.2d 308, 200 U.S.P.Q. 129 (CCPA 1978). In *Monks*, the court held, as to a patent under then existing British law, patenting occurred on the later "sealing" date, not the earlier publication date. Though a patentee could collect damages from the date of publication, an infringement suit could not be filed until the date of sealing.

See also Ex parte Fujishiro, 199 U.S.P.Q. 36 (PTO Bd. App. 1977). In *Fujishiro*, the Board held that first publication of an application for a Japanese utility model 18 months after filing does not constitute patenting because such publication only grants the right to demand compensation in the form of a royalty, which right is enforceable only after later action.

[327] *In re* Ekenstam, 256 F.2d 321, 118 U.S.P.Q. 349 (CCPA 1958).

[328] *See generally* D. Chisum, Patents § 3.05.

[329] Carella v. Starlight Archery, 804 F.2d 135, 231 U.S.P.Q. 644, 1 U.S.P.Q. 1209 (Fed. Cir. 1986); Connecticut Valley Enterprises, Inc. v. United States, 348 F.2d 949, 146 U.S.P.Q. 404 (Ct. Cl. 1965).

[330] W.L. Gore & Associates, Inc. v. Garlock, Inc., 721 F.2d 1540, 220 U.S.P.Q. 303 (Fed. Cir. 1983), *cert. denied*, 469 U.S. 851 (1984).

[331] Gillman v. Stern, 114 F.2d 28, 46 U.S.P.Q. 430 (2d Cir. 1940), *cert. denied*, 311 U.S. 718, 48 U.S.P.Q. 713 (1940); Kimball Int'l, Inc. v. Allen Organ Co., 212 U.S.P.Q. 584 (S.D. Ind. 1981).

[332] Lyon v. Bausch & Lomb Optical Co., 224 F.2d 530, 106 U.S.P.Q. 240 (2d Cir. 1955) *cert. denied*, 350 U.S. 911, 107 U.S.P.Q. 362 (1955).

Something may be "known" in the United States even though it is not reduced to practice. For example, something is known when it is described in an unpublished document available to the public.[333]

[ii] *Statutory Bars.* Section 102(b) bars a patent if the invention was (1) described in a printed publication in any country; (2) patented in any country; (3) on sale in the United States; or (4) in public use in the United States, more than one year prior to the effective filing date of the patent application disclosing the invention,. These four events are referred to as "statutory bars."[334]

Section 102(b) is similar to Section 102(a) but differs in two important respects. First, the events often are by the inventor or his or her assignee. For example, a publication of an inventor's own corresponding patent application in another country is a statutory bar if the publication is more than one year before the effective United States filing date. If the inventor files a continuation-in-part application in the United States with new matter that is not entitled to an earlier parent filing date, the foreign published counterpart of the parent application is a bar with respect to claims dependent on the new matter.[335]

Second, Section 102(b) relates to the date one year before the patent application's filing, commonly called the "critical date." The period from the critical date to the filing date is, in a sense, a grace period. An inventor has up to one year to file a patent application after a public disclosure or commercial use of the invention. In this respect, United States patent law differs from the laws of many other countries, which treat any public disclosure before the filing date as prior art.

The statutory bars create prior art for obviousness purposes.[336]

Two bars—patents and printed publications—are the same as for Section 102(a).[337] The following subsections discuss the "public use" and "on sale" bars in Section 102(b) and the judicially-created "experimental use" exception.

[iii] *Public Use in the United States.* Any nonsecret, nonexperimental use of the invention in the United States prior to the critical date is a public use bar.

In *Egbert*,[338] the Supreme Court held that a device could be in "public use" even though in ordinary use it was hidden from view. In 1855, one Barnes made a novel corset steel and gave it to his friend, Ms. Egbert. Ms. Egbert wore the steels for a considerable period, placing them in new corsets as the old ones wore out. Thereafter, Ms. Egbert and Mr. Barnes "intermarried." In 1863, Barnes had his wife cut open a corset and display the steels to another person. Barnes obtained a patent in 1866. The Court held the patent invalid because of public use more than one year prior to Barnes' patent application: "The inventor slept on his rights for eleven years."[339]

---

[333] *In re* Borst, 345 F.2d 851, 145 U.S.P.Q. 554 (CCPA 1965), *cert. denied*, Borst v. Brenner, 382 U.S. 973, 148 U.S.P.Q. 771 (1966).

[334] *See generally* D. Chisum, Patents § 6.02.

[335] *E.g., In re* Ruscetta, 255 F.2d 687, 118 U.S.P.Q. 101 (CCPA 1958). *See generally* D. Chisum, Patents § 6.02[9].

[336] *E.g., In re* Kaslow, 707 F.2d 1366, 217 U.S.P.Q. 1089 (Fed. Cir. 1983).

[337] *See* § 2C[5][a].

[338] Egbert v. Lippmann, 104 U.S. (14 Otto) 333 (1881).

[339] 104 U.S. (14 Otto) at 337.

"[T]o constitute the public use of a patent it is not necessary that more than one of the patented articles should be publicly used. . . . [O]ne well defined case of public use is just as effectual to annul the patent as many.

. . .

"[W]hether the use of an invention is public or private, does not necessarily depend upon the number of persons to whom it is known. If an inventor, having made his device, gives or sells it to another, to be used by the donee or vendee, without limitation or restriction, or injunction to secrecy, and it is so used, such is public, within the meaning of the statute, even though the use and knowledge of the use may be confined to one person.

"[S]ome inventions are by their very character only capable of being used where they cannot be seen or observed by the public eye. An invention may consist of a lever or spring, hidden in the running gear of a watch. . . . Nevertheless, if its inventor sells a machine of which his invention forms a part, and allows it to be used without restriction of any kind, the use is a public view.[340]

Private noncommercial use by the inventor is not public use,[341] but nonsecret use by a person who improperly obtained the idea from the inventor is.[342]

Secret use of a machine or process to make a product sold commercially is not public use if by someone other than the inventor[343] but is if by the inventor (or the inventor's employer or assignee).[344] Policy considerations govern the inventor secret commercial

---

[340] 104 U.S. (14 Otto.) at 336.

[341] Bergstrom v. Sears, Roebuck & Co., 457 F. Supp. 213, 199 U.S.P.Q. 269 (D. Minn. 1978), aff'd, 599 F.2d 62, 203 U.S.P.Q. 121 (8th Cir. 1979). See also Moleculon Research Corp. v. CBS, Inc., 793 F.2d 1261, 229 U.S.P.Q. 805 (Fed. Cir. 1986), cert. denied, 479 U.S. 1030 (1986) (the inventor's display of a wood model of his invention (a cube puzzle) to colleagues and friends is not "public" use even though there was no mention of an obligation of secrecy; based on personal relationships and the surrounding circumstances, the inventor retained control over the puzzle's use and the distribution of information concerning it).

[342] Lorenz v. Colgate-Palmolive-Peet Co., 167 F.2d 423, 77 U.S.P.Q. 138 (3d Cir. 1948).

[343] W.L. Gore & Associates, Inc. v. Garlock, Inc., 721 F.2d 1540, 220 U.S.P.Q. 303 (Fed. Cir. 1983), cert. denied, 469 U.S. 851 (1984).

Compare J.A. LaPorte, Inc. v. Norfolk Dredging Co., 787 F.2d 1577, 229 U.S.P.Q. 435 (Fed. Cir. 1986), cert. denied, 479 U.S. 884 (1986). In J.A. LaPorte, the Federal Circuit held that the sale of an embodiment of the invention prior to the critical date by a person other than the inventor creates an "on sale" bar to a patent on that invention. There is no requirement that the claimed invention be publicly disclosed with the sale by such a third party. Such a sale is not like the situation in which a third party secretly uses a process invention developed independently by another to sell unpatented products made by the process. Here, the invention was discoverable from the device that was sold. "[T]he question is not whether the sale, even a third party sale, 'discloses' the invention at the time of the sale, but whether the sale relates to a device that embodies the invention." 787 F.2d at 1583, 229 U.S.P.Q. at 439.

[344] Kinzenbaw v. Deere & Co., 741 F.2d 383, 222 U.S.P.Q. 929 (Fed. Cir. 1984), cert. denied, 470 U.S. 1004 (1985); Metallizing Engineering Co. v. Kenyon Bearing & Auto Parts Co., 153 F.2d 516, 68 U.S.P.Q. 54 (2d Cir. 1946), cert. denied, 328 U.S. 840, 69 U.S.P.Q. 631 (1946).

use rule; it is unfair for an inventor to use the invention for commercial profit for more than a year and thereafter apply for a patent because such activity delays commencement of the limited term of patent protection.[345]

Use outside the United States is not a public use bar, but extended use by the inventor before applying for a patent may constitute an abandonment of the invention.[346]

[iv] *On Sale in the United States.* Any sale or offer to sell an embodiment of the invention in the United States prior to the critical date is an "on sale" bar.[347] An actual sale is not required. For example, a bid for a government or private contract may create a bar even if the bid is not accepted.[348] An offer must be definite.[349]

Numerous recent Federal Circuit decisions construe the "on sale" bar. The court applies a policy-oriented, "totality of circumstances" approach.

> "Whether an invention is on sale is a question of law, and no single finding or conclusion is a *sine qua non* to its resolution. . . . The totality of the circumstances approach [to application of the on sale bar] is necessary because 'the policies or purposes underlying the on sale bar, in effect, define it.' . . . These policies include discouraging removal of inventions from the public domain that the public reasonably has come to believe are freely available; favoring the prompt and widespread disclosure of inventions; allowing the inventor a reasonable amount of time following sales activity to determine the potential economic value of a patent; and prohibiting the inventor from commercially exploiting his invention beyond the statutorily prescribed time."[350]

---

[345] *See* § 2B[2].

[346] *See* § 2C[5][b][vi].

[347] Milliken Research Corp. v. Dan River, Inc., 739 F.2d 587, 222 U.S.P.Q. 571 (Fed. Cir. 1984); General Elec. Co. v. United States, 654 F.2d 55, 211 U.S.P.Q. 867 (Ct. Cl. 1981). In *Milliken*, the court held that fabric samples sent out to customers before the critical date were "on sale."

[348] UMC Electronics v. United States, 816 F.2d 647, 2 U.S.P.Q.2d 1465 (Fed. Cir. 1987), *cert. denied*, 484 U.S. 1025 (1988).

[349] RCA Corp v. Data General Corp., 887 F.2d 1056, 1062, 12 U.S.P.Q.2d 1449, 1454 (Fed Cir. 1989) ("where there is no sale, a definite offer to sell is an essential requirement of the on-sale bar. . . . The requirement of a *definite* offer excludes merely indefinite or nebulous discussion about a possible sale. While this requirement may be met by a patentee's commercial activity which does not rise to the level of a formal 'offer' under contract law principles, . . . a definite offer in the contract sense clearly meets this requirement. . . . An offer to conduct experimental work may be as firm and definite, in the contract sense, as an offer to sell a product. However, such an offer may not constitute a bar because of policy considerations which allow an inventor to engage in experimentation to develop his invention. . . . On the other hand, a definite offer is not made *indefinite* because it concerns experimental work.").

[350] Envirotech Corp. v. Westech Engineering Inc., 904 F.2d 1571, 1574, 15 U.S.P.Q.2d 1230, 1232 (Fed. Cir. 1990).

The Federal Circuit's decisions draw fine distinctions. For example, in *RCA Corp.*,[351] it noted that an offer need not disclose details of the invention; on the other hand, in *Envirotech*,[352] it held no "on sale" event arises when the inventors make a bid to supply a prior art design with a "subjective, uncommunicated, and ultimate intention" to seek permission to substitute their invention for the bid design.

An offer to supply an item before the claimed invention has been established as functional is not an "on sale" bar,[353] but an "on sale" bar may arise even though there are no commercially marketable products on hand[354] and there has been no testing of the invention under actual use conditions.[355] In *UMC Electronics*,[356] the Federal Circuit held that a device need not necessarily be reduced to practice to be "on sale."

An offer to sell to a distributor may be a bar.[357] The offer to sell must be to a separate entity, but a bar may still arise even if the offeror and offeree are under partial common corporate ownership.[358]

The offer to sell must be of an embodiment of the invention. An offer to license or sell patent rights to an invention (rather than embodiments) will not necessarily cause a bar.[359] A sale of embodiments of an invention incidental to a corporate merger or reorganization is not a bar.[360]

In *Buildex*,[361] the Federal Circuit noted that it had "never recognized a 'joint development' exception to the 'on sale' bar:" "We have deliberately resisted rigid

---

[351] RCA Corp v. Data General Corp., 887 F.2d 1056, 1060, 12 U.S.P.Q.2d 1449, 1452 (Fed Cir. 1989) ("[M]erely offering to sell a product by way of an advertisement or invoice may be evidence of a definite offer for sale or a sale of a claimed invention even though *no* details are disclosed. That the offered product is in fact the claimed invention may be established by any relevant evidence, such as memoranda, drawings, correspondence, and testimony of witnesses.").

[352] Envirotech Corp. v. Westech Engineering Inc., 904 F.2d 1571, 15 U.S.P.Q.2d 1230 (Fed. Cir. 1990).

[353] Shatterproof Glass Corp. v. Libbey-Owens Ford Co., 758 F.2d 613, 225 U.S.P.Q. 634 (Fed. Cir. 1985), *cert. denied*, 474 U.S. 976 (1985).

[354] Barmag Barmer Maschinenfabrik AG v. Murata Mach., Ltd., 731 F.2d 831, 221 U.S.P.Q. 561 (Fed. Cir. 1984).

[355] Western Marine Electronics, Inc. v. Furuno Electric Co., 764 F.2d 840, 226 U.S.P.Q. 334 (Fed. Cir. 1985).

[356] UMC Electronics v. United States, 816 F.2d 647, 2 U.S.P.Q.2d 1465 (Fed. Cir. 1987), *cert. denied*, 484 U.S. 1025 (1988).

[357] In re Caveney, 761 F.2d 671, 226 U.S.P.Q. 1 (Fed. Cir. 1985).

[358] *Id.*

[359] Moleculon Research Corp. v. CBS, Inc., 793 F.2d 1261, 229 U.S.P.Q. 805 (Fed. Cir. 1986), *cert. denied*, 479 U.S. 1030 (1987) (an oral agreement by the inventor to assign patent rights to his employer does not evoke the "on sale" bar); Scott Paper Co. v. Moore Business Forms, Inc., 594 F. Supp. 1051, 1075, 224 U.S.P.Q. 11, 29 (D. Del. 1984).

[360] Micro-Magnetic Industries, Inc. v. Advance Automatic Sales Co., 488 F.2d 771, 180 U.S.P.Q. 118 (9th Cir. 1973).

[361] Buildex Inc. v. Kason Industries, Inc., 849 F.2d 1461, 7 U.S.P.Q.2d 1325 (Fed. Cir. 1988). In *Buildex*, at the request of a major customer, the patentee designed a certain hinge structure. Prior to the critical date, the patentee showed the customer a working model of the hinge and

formulas and per se exceptions in applying § 102(b), instead considering the totality of the circumstances in each case."[362]

An offer to sell or a sale is "in this country" if (1) the seller is located in the United States and there is significant activity in the United States in preparation for the sale,[363] or (2) the buyer is located in the United States and receives an offer from a seller in another country.[364]

[v] *Experimental Use Exception.* A public use or sale is not a statutory bar if the inventor's primary purpose is to conduct experiments on the nature and utility of the invention. This experimental use exception is not stated in the patent statutes but is recognized by the courts on policy grounds.[365]

In *City of Elizabeth*,[366] the Supreme Court confronted the following fact pattern: The inventor Nicholson conceived a new form of wooden road pavement. In 1848, he laid down 75 feet of the pavement on a toll road open to the public but owned by Nicholson's company. The road was used continuously until 1854, when Nicholson applied for a patent. Nicholson constructed the road to test its durability under the stress of heavily loaded wagons, constant use, and general weather conditions. The toll collector testified that Nicholson regularly inspected the road. The Court held that such experimental use to test the invention's qualities was not a "public use" within the meaning of the statute even though it was a use in public.

As the fact pattern in *City of Elizabeth* illustrates, the privilege of experimentation does not end when the invention is proven to be minimally workable; it continues while the inventor determines whether the invention is superior to prior art devices.[367]

---

gave a quotation that included a quantity and price. The patentee agreed to file a patent application on the hinge and to sell the hinge exclusively to the customer. The customer agreed to pay for certain tooling expenses. The court held that the exclusive selling arrangement between the patentee and its customer did not excuse the patentee's commercialization prior to the one year grace period. The patentee's goal was to make a profit. The policy behind Section 102(b) of not removing inventions from the public that the public has justifiably come to believe are freely available is implicated even though the invention was to be used exclusively by the customer. "The 'public' is not limited to ultimate users of the product, but includes manufacturers such as [the patentee's customer]." 849 F.2d at 1465, 7 U.S.P.Q.2d at 1329.

[362] 849 F.2d at 1465, 7 U.S.P.Q.2d at 1328.

[363] Robbins Co. v. Lawrence Mfg. Co., 482 F.2d 426, 434, 178 U.S.P.Q. 577 (9th Cir. 1973).

[364] *In re* Caveney, 761 F.2d 671, 226 U.S.P.Q. 1 (Fed. Cir. 1985).

[365] The experimental use exception, which relates to the effect of the inventor's activity on the right to obtain a patent, should be distinguished from the experimental purpose exception, which relates to liability for patent infringement. *See* § 2F[4][d].

[366] City of Elizabeth v. American Nicholson Pavement Co., 97 U.S. 126 (1878).

[367] Cali v. Eastern Airlines, Inc., 442 F.2d 65, 169 U.S.P.Q. 753 (2d Cir. 1971). *Compare* RCA Corp v. Data General Corp., 887 F.2d 1056, 1061, 12 U.S.P.Q.2d 1449, 1453 (Fed Cir. 1989) ("under our precedent, experimental use, which means perfecting or completing an invention to the point of determining that it will work for its intended purpose, ends with an actual reduction to practice.").

The experimental use exception applies only if there is genuine experimentation directed to the features of the invention that are the subject of the patent claim.[368] It does not apply to "market testing" to determine customer preferences.[369] Testing to obtain government approval to market a product is not necessarily "experimental" in a patent law sense.[370]

In *T.P. Laboratories, Inc.*,[371] the Federal Circuit listed the following factors to be considered in determining whether a given usage was experimental:

(1)   the length of the test period in relation to tests of similar devices;

(2)   whether payment is made for the device;

(3)   whether the user agreed to secret use;

(4)   whether progress records were kept;

(5)   whether persons other than the inventor conduct the asserted experiments.[372]

---

[368] Western Marine Electronics, Inc. v. Furuno Electric Co., 764 F.2d 840, 226 U.S.P.Q. 334 (Fed. Cir. 1985). *See also* RCA Corp v. Data General Corp., 887 F.2d 1056, 12 U.S.P.Q.2d 1449 (Fed. Cir. 1989) (the experimental use doctrine does not excuse the inventor's offer, before the critical date, of the invention, which had already been reduced to practice, merely because the offer was of a system with additional components or was an offer to do developmental work).

[369] *In re* Smith, 714 F.2d 1127, 218 U.S.P.Q. 976 (Fed. Cir. 1983). *See also In re* Mann, 861 F.2d 1581, 1582, 8 U.S.P.Q.2d 2030, 2031 (Fed. Cir. 1988). In *Mann*, the Federal Circuit held that display of a design for a wrought iron table at a trade show is a public use and is not subject to the experimental use exception: "Obtaining the reactions of people to a design . . . whether or not they like it. . . . is not 'experimentation'. . . . "

Compare Grain Processing Corp. v. American Maize-Products Corp., 840 F.2d 902, 906, 5 U.S.P.Q.2d 1788, 1792 (Fed. Cir. 1988). In *Grain Processing*, the patentee's shipping of samples of the later patented product (a starch hydrolysate) to a few food manufacturers was not a public use. It was an "industry custom" to submit samples of proposed products to food manufacturers for determination of the product's utility. This testing was necessary because such products may interact adversely with other food ingredients in the manufacturers' products. The testing period "was short, very small quantities of the samples were shipped, and they were free of charge."

[370] Pennwalt Corp. v. Akzona, Inc., 740 F.2d 1573, 222 U.S.P.Q. 833 (Fed. Cir. 1984).

[371] T.P. Laboratories, Inc. v. Professional Positioners, Inc., 724 F.2d 965, 220 U.S.P.Q. 577 (Fed. Cir. 1984), *cert. denied*, 469 U.S. 826, 224 U.S.P.Q. 616 (1984).

[372] *See also* U.S. Environmental Products Inc. v. Westall, 911 F.2d 713, 15 U.S.P.Q.2d 1898 (Fed. Cir. 1990).

In *U.S. Environmental Products*, the patent related to a sludge dewatering system. In 1976, the inventors filed an application claiming a *single* filter plate system. The PTO rejected the claim. On August 2, 1978, the inventors filed a continuation-in-part application claiming a *multiple* layer filter plate. In 1986, a patent issued on that application. In September 1976, the inventor's assignee signed an agreement with the City of Sunrise, Florida, to install a sludge dewatering system. The system became operational in January, 1977. Sunrise personnel controlled the system's operation.

The Federal Circuit held that the district court correctly found the patent invalid because of an "on sale" bar. A facility using the invention, which the patentee installed for a customer prior to the critical date, was for a commercial purpose rather than experimental use. The district court "chose appropriate factors . . . for determining experimental use, *i.e.*, that there was

In *Hamilton*,[373] the court emphasized the importance of inventor control over the alleged experimentation.

Objective evidence of experimentation is more persuasive than protestations of subjective intent,[374] but there is no *per se* rule that testimony of experimental use must be disregarded when it conflicts with the contemporaneous documentary evidence.[375]

The experimental use exception does not apply to the disclosures in a printed publication or patent.[376]

[*vi*] *Abandonment.* Section 102(c) bars a patent if the inventor "has abandoned the invention." Abandonment occurs when the inventor, by word or deed, intentionally relinquishes the right to obtain a patent.[377] Abandonment is rarely invoked as a basis for rejecting or invalidating patent claims.[378]

---

no sale of the invention within the meaning of the statute," including "lack of record-keeping, . . . lack of control by the inventor . . . , lack of secrecy obligations on the part of the user, . . . and the existence of promotional activities. . . . " That the patentee did not make a profit on the city installation but was only reimbursed for its costs "is not necessarily persuasive. A patent owner may have created an on-sale bar despite *losing* money on a sale." That the patentee and the buyer "understood that the technology was experimental" is not necessarily determinative: "The subjective belief of inventors or customers . . . must be weighed against objective evidence which indicates otherwise." 911 F.2d at 717, 15 U.S.P.Q.2d at 1901-02.

[373] *In re* Hamilton, 882 F.2d 1576, 11 U.S.P.Q.2d 1890 (Fed. Cir. 1989).

[374] *E.g.,* Harrington Manufacturing Co. v. Powell Manufacturing Co., 815 F.2d 1478, 2 U.S.P.Q.2d 1364 (Fed. Cir. 1986).

In *Harrington Manufacturing*, the Federal Circuit held that the district court properly granted partial summary judgment that a machine incorporating a claim of the patent in suit was in "public use" by virtue of its demonstration to a trade journalist. The journalist was under no promise of secrecy. The inventor's subjective intent as to the purpose of the demonstration (i.e. whether it was experimental) did not create a material factual issue because "an inventor's subjective intent is immaterial when objective evidence points otherwise." 815 F.2d at 1481 n.3, 2 U.S.P.Q.2d at 1366 n.3.

[375] Moxness Products, Inc. v. Xomed, Inc., 891 F.2d 890, 13 U.S.P.Q.2d 1169 (Fed. Cir. 1989).

In *Moxness*, the Federal Circuit held that the district court erred in granting judgment *n.o.v.* that the patent was invalid because of the "on sale" and "public use" bars but did not abuse its discretion in granting a new trial on public use and sale because, *inter alia*, the inventor's testimony that pre-critical date activities were for developmental purposes could not be reconciled with the documentary evidence. Prior to the critical date (that is, one year before the patent application's filing date), a company sent the assignee of the patent a letter relating to devices covered by the patent. The inventor and the assignee's president testified that the letter was a "request" "for developmental" purposes, not an "order." Neither the letter nor the related correspondence mentioned developmental purposes. 891 F.2d at 892, 13 U.S.P.Q.2d at 1171.

[376] Pickering v. Holman, 459 F.2d 403, 173 U.S.P.Q. 583 (9th Cir. 1972).

[377] Westinghouse Electric & Mfg. Co. v. Saranac Lake Electric Co., 108 F. 221 (N.D. N.Y. 1901).

[378] At one time, the Patent and Trademark Office followed a policy that an applicant for a patent "dedicated" or abandoned to the public subject matter disclosed but not

Mere delay in applying for a patent is not abandonment,[379] but abandonment may be inferred from an extended period of unexcused delay.[380]

Section 102(c) abandonment must be carefully distinguished from two other types of abandonment: (1) abandonment of a patent application, and (2) abandonment, suppression and concealment. As to the former, an inventor may file and then abandon a patent application without necessarily thereby abandoning rights in the invention.[381] The inventor may reapply if no other event creates a bar.[382] As to the latter, an inventor's delay in applying for a patent after a reduction to practice may be "abandonment, suppression and concealment" under Section 102(g), which will preclude the inventor from relying on the reduction to practice as the invention date for purposes of determining priority over a rival inventor.[383] The same delay would not necessarily justify a finding of abandonment of the invention and the inventor could have applied for and obtained a patent had a second inventor not appeared.

[vii] *Foreign Patenting.* Section 102(d) bars a patent if the inventor obtains a patent or inventor's certificate in a foreign country and does not promptly apply for a patent in the United States.[384] The bar applies only if three conditions are met: (1) the inventor (or his legal representatives or assigns) applies for a patent on the invention in another country on the invention; (2) the inventor fails to apply for a patent on the invention in the United States within twelve months; and (3) a patent in the other country issues before the application is filed in the United States.

What is a "patent" and the patenting date are discussed in connection with Section 102(a).[385] Section 102(d) may require precise determination of when a foreign application has been "filed" and whether the patent is "on" a particular invention. A foreign patent application will not be treated as an effective filing unless it adequately discloses the invention for which a patent is later sought in the United States under United States disclosure standards.[386]

---

claimed in a patent specification if, on the date a patent issued, no continuation application had been filed claiming that subject matter. This policy was overturned in *In re* Gibbs, 437 F.2d 486, 168 U.S.P.Q. 578 (CCPA 1971).

[379] Bates v. Coe, 98 U.S. 31 (1878); Paulik v. Rizkalla, 760 F.2d 1270, 226 U.S.P.Q. 224 (Fed. Cir. 1985); Moore v. United States, 194 U.S.P.Q. 423 (Ct. Cl. Trial Div. 1977).

Delay in filing a patent application may preclude a patent if one of the statutory bar events of Section 102(b) has occurred more than one year prior to the application date.

[380] *E.g.*, Levinson v. Nordskog Co., 301 F. Supp. 589, 163 U.S.P.Q. 52 (C.D. Cal. 1969).

[381] An applicant may abandon an application either expressly or by failing to file a timely response to an office action. *See* § 2D[1].

[382] Foster v. Magnetic Heating Corp., 297 F. Supp. 512, 518, 160 U.S.P.Q. 246 (S.D. N.Y. 1968), *aff'd*, 410 F.2d 12, 161 U.S.P.Q. 133 (2d Cir. 1969), *cert. denied*, 396 U.S. 829, 163 U.S.P.Q. 704 (1969).

[383] *See* § 2D[5][g].

[384] *See generally* D. Chisum, Patents § 6.04.

[385] *See* § 2C[5][a][ii].

[386] American Stainless Steel Co. v. Rustless Iron Corp., 2 F. Supp. 742, 17 U.S.P.Q. 17 (D. Md. 1933), *aff'd*, 71 F.2d 404, 22 U.S.P.Q. 114 (4th Cir. 1934).

See § 2H[2][c].

A Section 102(d) bar can be avoided if an inventor applies for a U.S. patent within one year of an effective foreign filing, which is desirable to take advantage of the Section 119 Paris Convention priority right.[387]

[c] **Grace Period: Pre-Filing Date Disclosures.** Most countries define the time dimension of prior art by reference to the patent application filing date rather than the invention date, as does the United States.[388] They provide a "grace period" for specific types of pre-filing date public disclosures by the inventor. Japan and certain other countries provide limited grace periods. European patent laws provide virtually no grace period.

United States patent statutes do not use the phrase "grace period," but Section 102(b) in effect provides a twelve-month grace period that excludes all publications disclosing the inventor's work and any publications of other person's work *if* the inventor shows an invention date before the publication. A public disclosure by or on behalf of the inventor more than twelve months before his or her filing date will not be prior art unless it qualifies as a printed publication, a public use in the United States or placing the invention "on sale" in the United States.

[d] **Senior-Filed Patents.** Section 102(e), a complicated rule that codifies *Milburn*,[389] bars an inventor from obtaining a patent for anything (except the inventor's own work [390]) disclosed in a United States patent granted to another ("the prior applicant") based on an application filed in the United States before the subsequent applicant's invention date.[391] Stated otherwise, everything disclosed in one inventor's United States patent with an effective United States filing date before a second applicant's invention date is prior art in determining novelty and nonobviousness of the second applicant's claimed invention—unless the disclosure is the second applicant's own work.

Section 102(e) does not apply to patents and applications by the same inventor because it refers to patents issued to "another." If a company or person owns different inventors' applications, Section 102(e)'s prior art effect may be avoided by careful planning.[392]

---

[387] *See* § 2H[2].

[388] The invention date is incorporated in the three novelty-defeating provisions, 102(a), 102(e), and 102(g).

[389] Alexander Milburn Co. v. Davis-Bournonville Co., 270 U.S. 390 (1926). *Milburn* adopts the whole contents approach to prior filed patent applications by others and applies that approach to both the novelty and "inventive step" requirements. This contrasts with the law of many other countries, which apply the whole contents approach to the determination of novelty but not inventive step.

[390] *See* § 2C[5][f].

[391] *See generally* D. Chisum, Patents § 3.07.

[392] If related applications are filed on the same date, Section 102(e) will not apply upon issue of any patents.

If related applications are filed on different dates, the applications may be combined into one continuation-in-part (CIP) application. This is made possible by a 1984 amendment. *See* § 2D[4][b][v]. The application may then issue as a single patent. If the combined inventions are viewed as separate and distinct, a restriction requirement may be entered, requiring the filing

[i]   *The Milburn Doctrine.* In *Milburn*,[393] the following fact pattern came before the Supreme Court:

1.   On January 31, 1911, Clifford applied for a patent. The application *disclosed* (but did not *claim*) item X.

2.   On March 4, 1911, Whitford applied for a patent claiming X.

3.   On February 6, 1912, a patent issued to Clifford.

4.   On March 4, 1912, a patent issued to Whitford.

The issue was whether Clifford's disclosure of X was prior art as to Whitford's patent claiming X. Because pending U.S. applications are held in secrecy, as of March 4, 1911 (Whitford's filing date and presumptive invention date), Clifford's disclosure was neither a publication nor a patent and was not available to the public.[394] Because Clifford did not *claim* X,[395] the doctrine that claimed subject matter is "constructively" reduced to practice and a prior invention did not apply.[396] Nevertheless, the Supreme Court held that Clifford's disclosure of X was prior art and rendered invalid Whitford's patent claiming X. Patent Office delays in examining and issuing patents should not impact substantive patent rights. If the Patent Office had promptly issued a patent to Clifford, the patent, as a publication, would have anticipated Whitford's claim to X.

In 1952, Congress codified the *Milburn* doctrine as Section 102(e).[397] In 1965, the Supreme Court held that Section 102(e) and the *Milburn* doctrine apply to the determination of prior art for nonobviousness as well as for novelty.[398] Consequently, everything disclosed in a United States patent is prior art as of its effective *filing* date in the United States Patent and Trademark Office.

An inventor may eliminate a United States patent as prior art by showing an invention date prior to the patent's filing date, even if the invention date is many years

---

of separate divisional applications. *See* § 2D[1][b]. If one application issues as a patent, it cannot be used as a "reference" against a related divisional application. *See* § 2D[1][b][iii] and 2D[4][a][vi].

If none of the above precautions are taken as to a senior-filed, commonly-owned application by a different inventorship entity, issue of a patent on the senior application will create Section 102(e) prior art. *See, e.g., In re* Bartfeld, 925 F.2d 1450, 17 U.S.P.Q.2d 1885 (Fed. Cir. 1991) (a "Section 102(e)/103 rejection," which uses as prior art for obviousness purposes an earlier-filed patent's disclosures against a later-filed, different inventive entity application or patent's claims, cannot be overcome by a terminal disclaimer; the Section 103 prior art disqualifier, added by a 1984 amendment, does not apply to Section 102(e)).

[393] Alexander Milburn Co. v. Davis-Bournonville Co., 270 U.S. 390 (1926).

[394] *See* § 2D[1][c].

[395] For that reason, no interference to determine priority of invention between Clifford and Whitford could be declared. *See* § 2D[5][h].

[396] *See* § 2D[5][d].

[397] 35 U.S.C. § 102(e): "A person shall be entitled to a patent unless— . . . (e) the invention was described in a patent granted on an application for patent *by another filed in the United States before the invention thereof by the applicant for patent, or on an international application by another who has fulfilled the requirements of paragraphs (1), (2), and (4) of section 371(c) of this title* before the invention thereof by the applicant for patent." (The italicized language was added later to implement the Patent Cooperation Treaty.)

[398] Hazeltine Research, Inc. v. Brenner, 382 U.S. 252, 147 U.S.P.Q. 429 (1965).

before the inventor's filing date.[399] "Swearing behind" a reference patent is not possible if the reference patent claims the same invention as the applicant or patentee because only an interference proceeding may resolve an invention priority issue.[400]

[ii] *Foreign Priority Applications.* A United States patent's filing date, for determining its prior art effect, is its actual United States filing date. A United States patent is not effective as a reference as of its foreign priority filing date.[401] In *Hilmer,*[402] the fact pattern was as follows:

1. On January 24, 1957, Habicht filed in Switzerland.

2. On July 31, 1957, Hilmer filed in Germany.

3. On January 23, 1958, Habicht filed in United States.

4. On July 25, 1958, Hilmer filed in United States.

5. A United States patent issued to Habicht.

The issue was whether the Habicht United States patent's disclosures were prior art as to Hilmer's claimed invention. Under the Paris Convention priority right and Section 119,[403] Hilmer was entitled to the German filing date as the invention date, but the court held that the Habicht patent was effective as a reference only as of its actual United States filing date, after Hilmer's effective priority filing date. Section 119, which provides that a foreign priority filing shall have the "same effect" as a filing in the United States, is only a patent-protecting, not a patent-defeating provision.

International attention has focused on whether *Hilmer* is a violation of Paris Convention Article 4B, which provides that a subsequent filing within the twelve month priority period "shall not be invalidated by reason of any acts accomplished in the interval, in particular, another filing. . . . " This Article relates to invention priority when two parties claim a patent on the same invention. *Hilmer* recognizes the right of the applicant with the earliest priority filing date to prevail in any contest over invention priority. In *Hilmer,* the person claiming patent rights (Hilmer) was accorded his priority filing date not only for the purpose of priority of invention but also for the purpose of determining what is prior art. An argument that *Hilmer* violates Article 4B assumes that the Article not only guarantees a priority applicant the right to a patent but also the right to be free of patent protection on related developments by subsequent applicants, that is, assures senior applicants, such as Habicht, that no subsequent filer can obtain a patent claiming anything disclosed in the senior-filed application.

---

[399] *See* § 2C[5][f]. A statutory bar (such as a U.S. or other patent that *issued* more than one year before the applicant/patentee's filing date) cannot be eliminated as a reference regardless of how early the date of invention of the applicant/patentee. *See* § 2C[5][c].

[400] *In re* Eickmeyer, 602 F.2d 974, 202 U.S.P.Q. 655 (CCPA 1979). *See* § 2D[5].

[401] An international application under the Patent Cooperation Treaty designating the United States is prior art as of the date certain formalities are complied with. *See* § 2H[3].

[402] *In re* Hilmer 359 F.2d 859, 149 U.S.P.Q. 480 (CCPA 1966).

[403] *See* § 2H[2][f].

Some of the unfortunate effects of *Hilmer* can be ameliorated by aspects of interference practice, such as by broadly defining the interference count, and by applying interference estoppel and the doctrine of lost counts.[404]

[iii] *Continuation Applications.* A United States patent's filing date for determining its prior art effect is the filing date of a prior United States application if at least one claim in the patent is entitled to the benefit of the prior application under Section 120.[405]

Consider the following example:

1. A files a parent application disclosing X.

2. A files a continuation-in-part ("CIP") application disclosing X and Y.

3. A files a continuation application claiming X and Y.

4. A obtains a patent claiming Y.

A's Y patent, which issued on the third application is entitled to the benefit of the second application filing date (assuming the conditions of Section 120 are met) but not the first application filing date because that application does not disclose element Y. Therefore, the patent will be effective as a reference for its disclosure of X only as of the second application filing date—even though the disclosure of X was carried forward from the first application to the patent.[406]

[iv] *Issuance—Abandoned Patent Applications—Statutory Invention Registrations.* A United States patent application's disclosures become effective as prior art as of its filing date only if the application *issues* as a patent containing those disclosures.

A patent application that is abandoned is not prior art as such.[407] A citation to a prior abandoned patent application in a later issued patent does not make that abandoned application prior art as of its filing date,[408] but such citation will make the abandoned application available to the public and evidence of public knowledge under Section 102(a) as of the issue date of the later patent.[409]

A 1985 statutory procedure provides for a "statutory invention registration" ("SIR") as an alternative to a patent.[410] A patent applicant may waive the right to

---

[404] *Cf. In re* Zletz, 893 F.2d 319, 13 U.S.P.Q.2d 1320 (Fed. Cir. 1989); *In re* Kroekel, 803 F.2d 705, 231 U.S.P.Q. 640 (Fed. Cir. 1986). *Compare In re* McKellin, 529 F.2d 1324, 188 U.S.P.Q. 428 (CCPA 1976). *See* § 2D[5][h][vi].

[405] *In re* Wertheim, 646 F.2d 527, 209 U.S.P.Q. 554 (CCPA 1981); *In re* Klesper, 397 F.2d 882, 158 U.S.P.Q. 256 (CCPA 1968).

Section 120 and continuation and continuation-in-part applications are discussed at § 2D[4][b].

[406] *In re* Wertheim, 646 F.2d 527, 209 U.S.P.Q. 554 (CCPA 1981).

[407] Brown v. Guild (The Corn-Planter Patent), 90 U.S. (23 Wall.) 181, 210-11 (1874).

As to the ways in which a patent application may become abandoned, see § 2D[1] and § 2D[4][b][iv].

An abandoned patent application is not a constructive reduction to practice of the invention by the applicant. *See* § 2D[5][d].

[408] *In re* Lund, 376 F.2d 982, 153 U.S.P.Q. 625 (CCPA 1967).

[409] 37 CFR § 1.14(b).

[410] 35 U.S.C. § 157. *See* 37 C.F.R. § 1.297.

receive a patent and request a SIR. The PTO may issue a SIR if it finds that the application complies with Section 112 disclosure requirements.[411] The SIR does not protect the claimed invention from unauthorized use[412] but is a way of making the application's disclosures prior art against other persons' subsequently filed applications because the SIR's disclosures are effective as prior art as of its effective United States filing date.[413]

[e] Prior Invention and Derivation

[i] *Prior Invention—Section 102(g).* Section 102(g) bars a patent if "before the applicant's invention thereof the invention was made in this country by another who had not abandoned, suppressed, or concealed it." Whether this subsection creates prior art has been a point of much controversy.[414]

First invention arises in priority disputes, such as in an interference in the Patent and Trademark Office.[415] For example, if A and B each apply for a patent on the same invention, the person who first invented the subject matter in the United States will prevail (unless that person derived the idea from the other party).

First invention also arises in patentability disputes. Consider the following example:

1. A reduces invention X to practice in the United States.

2. B applies for a patent on Y.

3. A applies for a patent on X.

4. A obtains a patent on X.

Section 102(e) will not apply because B has a filing date before A's filing date. Court decisions hold that A's invention of X may nevertheless be prior art against B's application on Y if it is prior invention made in the United States.[416] *Clemens*[417] suggested that such will be true only if B has actual knowledge of A's invention of X, but this suggestion was criticized in a subsequent decision, *Kimberly-Clark*.[418] In *E.I. du Pont*,[419] the Federal Circuit confirmed that "prior invention" is prior art

---

[411] See § 2D[3]. The application is not examined for compliance with the novelty or nonobviousness requirements.

[412] 35 U.S.C. § 157.
Concurrently with obtaining a SIR, the applicant may file a continuation-in-part application in order to obtain patent protection. *See* § 2D[4][b]. The disclosures and claims of the SIR will not be prior art or be used to establish a double patenting rejection against a claim in such an application, provided the later claim is not for the same subject matter that is claimed in the SIR. 37 C.F.R. Sec. 1.106(e). *See* § 2D[4][a][ii].

[413] If the patent application contents are simply published, the contents are effective as prior art only as of the publication date.

[414] 35 U.S.C. § 102(g). *See generally* D. Chisum, Patents § 5.03[3][c].

[415] *See* § 2D[5].

[416] *In re* Bass, 474 F.2d 1276, 177 U.S.P.Q. 178 (CCPA 1973); Sutter Products Co. v. Pettibone Mulliken Corp., 428 F.2d 639, 166 U.S.P.Q. 100 (7th Cir. 1970).

[417] *In re* Clemens, 622 F.2d 1029, 206 U.S.P.Q. 289 (CCPA 1980).

[418] Kimberly-Clark Corp. v. Johnson & Johnson, 745 F.2d 1437, 223 U.S.P.Q. 603 (Fed. Cir. 1984).

[419] E.I. du Pont de Nemours & Co. v. Phillips Petroleum Co., 849 F.2d 1430, 7 U.S.P.Q.2d 1129 (Fed. Cir. 1988), *cert. denied*, 488 U.S. 986 (1988).

for Section 103 obviousness purposes and that there is no requirement that Section 102(g) prior work of another be personally known to the applicant/patentee or be known to the art: "*Kimberly-Clark* distinguished as dictum the *Clemens* requirement of applicant's personal knowledge because '[Section] 102(g) contains no personal knowledge requirement.' " The court noted that "the requirement of proving no abandonment, suppression, or concealment does mollify somewhat the 'secret' nature of [Section] 102(g) prior art."

> "Because work is 'secret' does not necessarily mean that it has been 'abandoned, suppressed or 'concealed.' The latter determination depends on the overall facts of each case. For example, the filing of a United States patent application . . . maintains the secrecy of work, but is a factor cutting against abandonment, suppression or concealment."[420]

A 1984 amendment to Section 103, the statutory provision on nonobviousness, provides that "subject matter developed by another person, which qualifies as prior art only under subsection . . . (g) of section 102 . . . shall not preclude patentability under this section where the subject matter and the claimed invention were, at the time the invention was made, owned by the same person or subject to an obligation of assignment to the same person."[421] Under this amendment, in the above example, A's invention of X will not be prior art, which can be combined with another reference for purposes of determining obviousness, as to B's invention of Y if A and B, at the time of B's invention of Y, owe a legal obligation to assign any patent rights on inventions to a single person (such as their mutual employer).[422] The invention of A may still be used to show a complete anticipation of B's claimed invention under Section 102 because the 1984 Amendment only deals with prior art for purposes of Section 103 obviousness.

[ii]   *Derivation—Section 102(f)*. Section 102(f), which bars a patent if the applicant "did not himself invent the subject matter sought to be patented,"[423] enforces the originality requirement. A person may not obtain a patent on an invention derived from some other person or source.

The derivation issues frequently arise in invention priority disputes, such as in a PTO interference.[424] For example, if A and B separately apply for a patent on the same invention, A may contend that B derived a complete conception of the invention from A.[425] If A proves his contention, he prevails in the interference.

---

[420] 849 F.2d at 1437 n.5, 7 U.S.P.Q.2d at 1134 n.5.

[421] The amendment adds a new sentence to Section 103. The amendment, effective November 8, 1984, applies to pending applications and patents issued prior to its effective date, but persons who engaged in activity in reasonable reliance on the invalidity of a patent that would have been invalid but for the amendment may have vested rights to continue such activity. Also, the amendment does not affect cases pending in court on the effective date. P.L. 98-622, § 106.

[422] 37 C.F.R. 1.106(d). The same provision is made as to prior art under Section 102(f). See § 2C[5][e][ii]. As to patent right ownership of inventions created in an employment relationship, see § 2G[1].

[423] See generally D. Chisum, Patents §§ 5.03[3][f], 10.04[4].

[424] See § 2D[5].

[425] See Applegate v. Scherer, 332 F.2d 571, 573 n.1, 141 U.S.P.Q. 796, 798 n.1 (CCPA 1964).

The matter is not free from doubt, but it seems that if an inventor derives a specific item of information (but not the whole invention) from another, then the derived information is prior art.[426]

A 1984 amendment to Section 103 (the statutory provision on nonobviousness) provides that "subject matter developed by another person, which qualifies as prior art only under subsection (f) . . . of section 102 . . . shall not preclude patentability under this section where the subject matter and the claimed invention were, at the time the invention was made, owned by the same person or subject to an obligation of assignment to the same person." Under this provision, information that passes from A to B will not be prior art, which can be combined with another reference for purposes of determining obviousness, as to B's attempt to obtain a patent if A and B, at the time of B's invention, owe a legal obligation to assign any patent rights on inventions to a single person (such as their mutual employer).[427] Information from A may still be used to show a complete anticipation of B's claimed invention under Section 102 because the 1984 Amendment only deals with prior art for purposes of obviousness under Section 103.

[f] **Invention Date.** Prior art must, of course, be "prior." The three novelty provisions—Sections 102(a), 102(e), and 102(g)—refer expressly to the applicant's invention date.

The applicant's invention date is presumptively the filing date of a patent application adequately disclosing the invention. Pre-filing date references, for example, publications, patents, or items known or used in the United States, may be eliminated as prior art in three ways.

First, the applicant may establish an invention date before the reference.[428] An invention date is determined according to the same rules that apply in determining invention priority in an interference between rival inventors.[429]

---

[426] *See* 37 C.F.R. § 106(d).

[427] 37 C.F.R. 1.106(d). The same provision is made as to the prior art effect of prior invention under Section 102(g).

As to patent right ownership of inventions created in an employment relationship, *see* § 2G[1].

[428] During the course of an examination of a patent application, an examiner may reject a claim in view of a particular reference. *See* § 2D[1]. The applicant may eliminate that reference by filing a verified statement of facts establishing a date of invention prior to the reference. 37 C.F.R. § 1.131. Such a statement is commonly referred to as a "Rule 131 Affidavit."

A Rule 131 affidavit may be used to avoid a disclosure in a U.S. patent with a prior filing date only if that prior patent does not claim the same invention as the applicant. If the applicant and the reference patent claim substantially the same invention, then a Rule 131 affidavit is improper and the appropriate procedure is an interference to resolve the issue of priority of invention between the application and the prior patent. *See* § 2D[5]. *In re* Eickmeyer, 602 F.2d 974, 202 U.S.P.Q. 655 (CCPA 1979).

[429] *In re* Mulder, 716 F.2d 1542, 219 U.S.P.Q. 189 (Fed. Cir. 1983); *In re* Suska, 589 F.2d 527, 200 U.S.P.Q. 497 (CCPA 1979).

An invention date is established by showing a conception and reduction to practice in the United States. The rules on determining a date of invention are discussed at § 2D[5][a].

Second, the applicant may establish that the disclosures of the reference derive from his own work.[430] Consider the following example.

1.   A's publication discloses the combination of $X+Y+Z$.

2.   Inventor B seeks a patent on element X.

Inventor B may eliminate the publication disclosure of X by showing that A derived element X from B and element X was B's own creation.[431]

Third, the applicant may establish that he had, before the date of the reference, invented either as much of the subject matter of the claimed invention as is disclosed in the reference[432] or enough to make the reference disclosure obvious to a person of ordinary skill in the art.[433] This showing of partial invention possession suffices only if the subject matter is part of the claimed invention (as for example a species chemical compound falling within a claim to a generic class of chemical compounds).[434]

The above rules on avoiding a reference relate only to the three novelty provisions (Section 102(a), (e), and (g)). A reference that is a Section 102(b) statutory bar cannot be eliminated as a reference by showing a prior invention date.[435]

[g]   **Inventive Entities.** The three novelty provisions (Sections 102(a), 102(e), and 102(g)) refer, expressly or by implication, to acts and disclosures "by another," that is, by some person other than the inventor of the patent claim's subject matter.

A separate inventive entities theory governs whether a reference is "by another." Under this theory, the sole work by one person or the joint work of a group of persons is "by another" as to later work by a different person or group of persons even though one or more persons may be members of both entities.[436] For example, a patent by A, and a publication disclosing the joint work of A, B and C are regarded as by inventive entities differing from later work by A and B jointly, B and C jointly, and B alone.[437]

---

[430] *In re* DeBaun, 687 F.2d 459, 214 U.S.P.Q. 933 (CCPA 1982); *In re* Katz, 687 F.2d 450, 215 U.S.P.Q. 14 (CCPA 1982).

An inventor's own prior work and disclosures are not prior art against his later attempt to obtain a patent unless such work or disclosures are Section 102(b) statutory bars. *See* § 2C[5][b][ii].

[431] *In re* Mathews, 408 F.2d 1393, 161 U.S.P.Q. 276 (CCPA 1969); *In re* Facius, 408 F.2d 1396, 161 U.S.P.Q. 294 (CCPA 1969).

[432] *In re* Moore, 444 F.2d 572, 170 U.S.P.Q. 260 (CCPA 1971); *In re* Stempel, 241 F.2d 755, 113 U.S.P.Q. 77 (CCPA 1957).

[433] *In re* Rainer, 390 F.2d 771, 773, 159 U.S.P.Q. 334 (CCPA 1968).

[434] *In re* Tanczyn, 347 F.2d 830, 146 U.S.P.Q. 298 (CCPA 1965).

[435] 37 C.F.R. Sec. 1.131. *See In re* Foster, 343 F.2d 980, 145 U.S.P.Q. 166 (CCPA 1965).

[436] *In re* Land, 368 F.2d 866, 151 U.S.P.Q. 621 (CCPA 1966). *But cf.* Shields v. Halliburton Co., 667 F.2d 1232, 216 U.S.P.Q. 1066 (5th Cir. 1982).

[437] In the example, depending on the facts, the successive work by A, $A+B+C$, A and $B+C$ may be so closely connected in nature and result as to be a single joint invention. General Motors Corp. v. Toyota Motor Co., 667 F.2d 504, 212 U.S.P.Q. 659 (6th Cir. 1981), *cert. denied*, 456 U.S. 937, 215 U.S.P.Q. 95 (1982). *See* § 2D[3][e][i].

§ 2D   The Patenting Process

To obtain a patent, an inventor must file an application fully disclosing his invention in the Patent and Trademark Office (PTO). The PTO examines the application and, if the invention meets all patentability conditions, grants a patent.

[1]   Patent Application Filing and Prosecution: An Overview

Patent application drafting is an important and complex undertaking. The drafter must understand the technology surrounding an invention and describe the invention accurately and completely. The specification and drawings filed with the application must fully disclose the invention.[1] They are printed and distributed as part of the issued patent. The patent system's primary purpose is that information so disclosed benefit the public by promoting the progress of the useful arts.[2]

A PTO examiner can reject any or all claims. The inventor may respond by amending the claims or offering evidence supporting their patentability. The examiner reexamines the claims in light of the applicant's response. Applicant-PTO examiner dialogue is referred to as "prosecution."

Prosecution involves the following:

(1)   The applicant (or someone on his or her behalf) files an application with the PTO.[3]

(2)   The PTO classifies the subject matter and forwards the application to the appropriate examining group.[4]

(3)   Applications are assigned to an individual examiner in order of filing,[5] unless the examination is expedited by a petition to make the application special.[6]

If each inventive entity is under an obligation to assign patent rights to a single person (e.g. a common employer), the separate developments are not prior art under Sections 102(f) or (g) for obviousness purposes. *See* § 2C[5][e]. Developments by separate inventive entities will still constitute prior art under Sections 102(f) and (g) for novelty purposes and are prior art under Sections 102(a) and 102(e) for both novelty and obviousness purposes. *See* § 2C[5][d].

[1] *See* §§ 2D[3][a] and [c]. Section 112, *first* paragraph's disclosure requirements differ from Section 112, *second* paragraph's claim definiteness requirements. *In re* Borkowski, 422 F.2d 904, 164 U.S.P.Q. 642 (CCPA 1970); *In re* Wakefield, 422 F.2d 897, 903, 164 U.S.P.Q. 636 (CCPA 1970). *See* § 2D[3][d].

[2] U.S. Const. art. I, § 8, cl. 8; Kewanee Oil Co. v. Bicron Corp., 416 U.S. 470, 181 U.S.P.Q. 673 (1974).

[3] The filing date is when PTO actually receives the specification (including at least one claim) and drawings (if necessary). 37 C.F.R. § 1.53(b). The filing date is the mailing date if the applicant uses "Express Mail." 37 C.F.R. § 1.10.

[4] 37 C.F.R. § 1.101.

[5] 37 C.F.R. § 1.110. No action may be taken on Patent Cooperation Treaty international applications before 21 months from the priority date unless a request has been filed under 35 U.S.C. § 371(f).

[6] 37 C.F.R. § 1.102.

(4) The examiner reviews the application and the prior art and, if the application claims more than one independent and distinct invention, enters a restriction requirement.[7]

(5) If the examiner enters a restriction requirement, the applicant may traverse the requirement but must, at the same time, provisionally elect one invention for further prosecution.[8]

(6) The examiner searches the prior art, examines the application for compliance with patentability conditions, and enters an "office action" that:

   (a) cites the best prior art references uncovered in the search;[9]

   (b) indicates allowance or rejection as to each claim;[10]

   (c) cites each rejection's statutory basis (e.g., 35 U.S.C. Section 101, 102, 103 or 112) with pertinent prior art and comments;[11]

   (d) sets a time period for response.

(7) After the first action, the applicant may request an interview—by telephone or in person—to discuss the action.[12]

(8) Within the response period (or an extension thereof),[13] the applicant

---

[7] If the plural inventions' distinctiveness and independence are clear, restriction may be required *before* any action on the merits or may be required as part of the first action on the merits. 37 C.F.R. § 1.142(a).
See § 2D[1][b].

[8] 37 C.F.R. § 1.143.

[9] 37 C.F.R. § 1.106(b).

[10] To properly reject a claim as unpatentable on grounds such as obviousness or nonenablement, the examiner must establish a *prima facie* case based on the prior art and the evidence. *In re* Warner, 379 F.2d 1011, 1016-17, 154 U.S.P.Q. 173, 177-78 (CCPA 1967), *cert. denied*, 389 U.S. 1057 (1968); *In re* Marzocchi, 439 F.2d 220, 169 U.S.P.Q. 367 (CCPA 1971). In *Marzocchi*, the court held that the specification must be taken as enabling unless there is reason to doubt the veracity of the statements therein.
An examiner may establish *prima facie* obviousness by citing prior art references that closely resemble the claimed invention or disclose severally the parts of the claimed invention. *See* § 2C[4][c][iii]. If the applicant presents rebuttal evidence in response, the *prima facie* case disappears and the examiner must reconsider *all* the evidence. *In re* Piasecki, 745 F.2d 1468, 223 U.S.P.Q. 785 (Fed. Cir. 1984). In resolving factual disputes, the examiner bears the burden of proof by a preponderance of the evidence.

[11] 37 C.F.R. § 1.106.

[12] 37 C.F.R. § 1.133. PTO rules require all business to be conducted in writing and no attention can be paid to oral promises, stipulations, or understandings. 37 C.F.R. § 1.2. *See* Rite-Hite Corp. v. Kelley Company, Inc., 819 F.2d 1120, 2 U.S.P.Q.2d 1915 (Fed. Cir. 1987); Litton Sys., Inc. v. Whirlpool Corp., 728 F.2d 1423, 221 U.S.P.Q. 97 (Fed. Cir. 1984).

[13] The statutory response period is six months, but the PTO may, and habitually does, set a shorter period, typically three months. An applicant may file a response after the set period, but before the expiration of statutory period, by paying a special fee.
If the PTO receives no response within the statutory period, the application is abandoned, but applicant may revive it within a 12 month period by showing the abandonment was unintentional, 37 C.F.R. § 1.137(b), or at any time by a showing the abandonment was unavoidable. 37 C.F.R. § 1.137(a). *See also* Morganroth v. Quigg, 885 F.2d 843, 12 U.S.P.Q.2d 1125 (Fed Cir. 1989).

prepares and files a response,[14] which may contain one or more of the following:

    (a)   amendment or cancellation of claims, or submission of new claims;[15]

    (b)   amendment to the specification's descriptive portion or to the drawings;[16]

    (c)   arguments why the original or amended claims are patentable in view of the cited prior art;[17]

    (d)   Rule 131 affidavit showing an invention date before the effective date of any prior art reference cited that is not a statutory bar;[18] or

    (e)   Rule 132 affidavit presenting factual evidence supporting patentability, for example, long-felt need, commercial success, expert opinion, and data from tests comparing the claimed invention with the closest prior art product or process.[19]

(9)   The examiner reexamines the case and enters another action allowing or rejecting claims.[20]

(10)   The action and response steps ((6)-(9)) continue until the examiner either:

    (a)   determines that the remaining claims are allowable, or

    (b)   enters a "Final Action" rejecting one or more claims.[21]

(11)   If the examiner allows claims, he sends a notice closing prosecution, which eliminates the right to make amendments as of right.[22]

(12)   Later, the PTO sends the applicant an allowance notice, which sets an issue fee payment time period.[23]

(13)   After receipt of the allowance notice,[24] the applicant may:

---

[14] 37 C.F.R. § 1.111. The response must be a genuine effort to advance the case to final action. A general allegation that the claims define a patentable invention will not suffice.

[15] 37 C.F.R. § 1.119.

[16] 37 C.F.R. § 1.118. The "new matter" prohibition restricts the right to make specification amendments. See § 2D[1][d].

[17] A response to an examiner action may create a prosecution history estoppel. See § 2F[2][c].

[18] 37 C.F.R. § 1.131. See § 2C[5][f]. An affidavit alleging a pre-filing invention date must set forth specific facts. In re Harry, 333 F.2d 920, 142 U.S.P.Q. 164 (CCPA 1964).

[19] 37 C.F.R. § 1.132. See §§ 2C[4][c] and [d].

Commercial success evidence is most commonly introduced in patent infringement suits, but may be submitted to support a pending application as well. In re Sernaker, 702 F.2d 989, 217 U.S.P.Q. 1 (Fed. Cir. 1983).

[20] 37 C.F.R. § 1.112.

[21] 37 C.F.R. § 1.113. Current PTO practice is to make a second action final.

[22] Ex parte Quayle, 1935 C.D. 11, 453 O.G. 213 (Comm'r Pat. 1935). The examiner will enter claim amendments after final action only if they put the claims in better form for an appeal, or, if the amendments touch on the merits, on a showing of good reasons why they are necessary and were not earlier presented. 37 C.F.R. § 1.116(b).

[23] 35 U.S.C. § 151; 37 C.F.R. § 1.311.

[24] An applicant does not have an absolute right to make amendments after the allowance notice. 37 C.F.R. § 1.312.

(a) pay the issue fee, after which the PTO issues a patent;[25] or

(b) abandon the application by not paying the issue fee,[26] and, if desired, file a continuation or continuation-in-part application.[27]

(14) If the examiner finally rejects any claim (10(b)), the applicant may:

(a) cancel rejected claims so a patent can issue on allowed claims;[28]

(b) appeal to the Board of Patent Appeals and Interferences;[29] or

(c) abandon the application, expressly or by failure to make a response,[30] and, if desired, file a continuation or continuation-in-part application.[31]

(15) In an appeal (14(b), the applicant may file a brief[32] and request an oral hearing before the Board.[33]

(16) The examiner will file an answer to the applicant's brief;[34] the applicant may file a reply brief to any new points in the examiner's answer or to any new grounds for rejection.[35]

(17) The Board affirms or reverses the rejections and may enter new rejections.[36]

(18) If the Board reverses all rejections, it remands the case to the examiner to carry into effect its decision.[37]

(19) If the Board affirms all rejections or enters new rejections, the applicant may:

---

[25] 37 C.F.R. § 1.314.

[26] 37 C.F.R. § 1.316. An applicant may revive an application abandoned for failure to pay the issue fee by showing that the failure was unintentional or unavoidable, just as with abandonment for failure to respond to an office action.

[27] See § 2D[4][b].

[28] 37 C.F.R. § 1.113. The applicant may take such action and also file a continuation-in-part application in order to pursue other claims. See § 2D[4][b].

[29] 37 C.F.R. § 1.191. Appeal may be taken after any of the claims have been twice rejected, even if the rejection is not made final, by filing a notice identifying the rejected claims and paying a fee.

[30] 37 C.F.R. § 1.138.

[31] See § 2D[4][b].

[32] 37 C.F.R. § 1.192.

[33] 37 C.F.R. § 1.194.

[34] 37 C.F.R. § 1.193(a).
The examiner may alter his position and allow the appealed claims after considering the applicant's appeal brief.

[35] 37 C.F.R. § 1.193(b).

[36] 37 C.F.R. § 1.196. The Board passes only on appealed rejected claims, but if it knows of grounds for rejecting an allowed claim, it may recommend rejection. 37 C.F.R. § 1.196(d).
The Board may enter a new ground for rejection. 37 C.F.R. § 1.196(b).

[37] 37 C.F.R. § 1.197-198.

    (a)   file an appeal to the Court of Appeals for the Federal Circuit or file a civil action in the District Court for the District of Columbia,[38] or

    (b)   abandon the application, expressly or by failure to file an appeal or civil action, and, if desired, file a continuation or continuation-in-part application.

  (20)   If the Court of Appeals or the District Court affirms the claim rejections,[39] the applicant may:

    (a)   abandon the application (expressly or by failure to file an appeal or civil action),[40] and

    (b)   file a continuation or continuation-in-part application.[41]

    [a] Fee Structure. Various fees are payable to the PTO as part of the patenting process.[42] Currently, "small entities" receive a 50 percent discount on certain fees.[43]

    [i] Types. There are seven types of fees: filing,[44] application processing,[45] patent issue,[46] document supply,[47] maintenance,[48] reexamination,[49] and miscellaneous fees

---

[38] 35 U.S.C. §§ 141, 145. These two ways of seeking judicial review, appeal and civil action, differ substantially. An appeal to the Federal Circuit is based on the PTO record and new evidence may not be presented. The Federal Circuit reviews PTO fact findings under a "clearly erroneous" standard. *In re* Andersen, 743 F.2d 1578, 223 U.S.P.Q. 378 (Fed. Cir. 1984), *cert. denied sub nom.* Estate of Krem v. Comm'r of Patents & Trademarks, 471 U.S. 1015 (1985). It freely reviews legal conclusions, such as obviousness. *In re* McCarthy, 763 F.2d 411, 226 U.S.P.Q. 99 (Fed. Cir. 1985).

In a civil action, the district court holds a trial on any disputed issue of fact, and the applicant may present further evidence supporting patentability, including expert testimony. The whole PTO record developed is considered along with any testimony. Zenith Radio Corp. v. Ladd, 310 F.2d 859, 863, 135 U.S.P.Q. 216, 219 (D.C. Cir. 1962). The applicant or the PTO may appeal the district court's decision to the Federal Circuit.

[39] The decisions of the Court of Appeals for the Federal Circuit may be reviewed by the United States Supreme Court by a petition for a writ of certiorari. The Supreme Court rarely grants such petitions.

[40] *See* Morganroth v. Quigg, 885 F.2d 843, 12 U.S.P.Q.2d 1125 (Fed Cir. 1989) (the PTO correctly held that it has no authority to revive a patent application abandoned, allegedly unintentionally, because the applicant failed to file a timely appeal of a district court decision affirming the PTO's rejection of applicant's application).

[41] *See* § 2D[4][b].

[42] 35 U.S.C. § 41. The patent fee structure was substantially revised in 1980 and 1982. Fees were raised, and maintenance fees were adopted for the first time. The objective of the changes is to make the PTO substantially fee-supported insofar as patent prosecution activities are concerned.

A separate set of fees applies to international applications under the Patent Cooperation Treaty. 37 C.F.R. § 1.445. *See* § 2H[3].

[43] *See* § 2D[1][a][vi].

[44] 37 C.F.R. § 1.16.

[45] 37 C.F.R. § 1.17.

[46] 37 C.F.R. § 1.18.

[47] 37 C.F.R. § 1.19.

[48] 37 C.F.R. § 1.20.

[49] 37 C.F.R. § 1.20(c), 1.26(c).

and charges.[50] The filing, prosecution, maintenance, and reexamination fees are of significant interest.

[ii]   *Filing Fees.* An applicant must pay the basic filing fee for a utility patent application[51] with additional amounts if the claims exceed a certain number or the claims are in multiple dependent format.[52] Design,[53] plant[54] and reissue[55] applications have separate fees. A surcharge is due if the basic filing fee, or oath or declaration are submitted after the filing date.[56]

[iii]   *Prosecution Fees.* Obtaining automatic examiner action response time extensions,[57] reviving an application abandoned for failure to respond or pay the issue fee,[58] and filing an appeal to the Board of Patent Appeals and Interferences require fees.[59]

[iv]   *Maintenance Fees.* A patent lapses 4 years, 8 years, or 12 years after issue if maintenance fees are not timely paid.[60] The fees are due six months before the lapse date;[61] if the fees are paid during the six month grace period, a surcharge is due.[62] If a patent lapses for maintenance fee nonpayment, the patentee may pay the fee and revive the patent upon a satisfactory showing that the delay was "unavoidable."[63]

[v]   *Reexamination Fees.* Filing a petition to reexamine a patent requires a substantial fee,[64] a major portion of which is refunded if a reexamination is not ordered.[65]

[vi]   *Small Entities.* Small entities receive a 50% discount on some fees to alleviate the impact on individual inventors, small businesses, and nonprofit institutions of recent fee increases.[66]

The discount applies to: (a) individual inventors;[67] (b) small businesses;[68] and (c)

---

[50] 37 C.F.R. § 1.21.

[51] 37 C.F.R. § 1.16(a).

[52] 37 C.F.R. § 1.16(b)-(d).

[53] 37 C.F.R. § 1.16(f).

[54] 37 C.F.R. § 1.16(g).

[55] 37 C.F.R. § 1.16(h).

[56] 37 C.F.R. § 1.16(e).

[57] 37 C.F.R. § 1.17(a)-(d).

[58] 37 C.F.R. § 1.17(l)-(m).

[59] 37 C.F.R. § 1.17(e)-(g).

[60] 35 U.S.C. § 41(b). Maintenance fees apply only to patents applied for on or after December 12, 1980. They do not apply to design or plant patents.

[61] 37 C.F.R. § 1.362-363, 1.20(e)-(j).

[62] 37 C.F.R. § 1.20(k), (l).

[63] 35 U.S.C. § 41(c)(1); 37 C.F.R. § 1.378. Persons who engage in infringing activity during the lapse period have intervening rights comparable to those with reissue patents. *See* § 2D[6][b][v].

[64] 37 C.F.R. § 1.20(c). *See* § 2D[6][a].

[65] 37 C.F.R. § 1.26(c).

[66] Public Law 97-247, § 1. Currently, the PTO is reassessing what fees should be eligible for a small entity discount.

[67] 37 C.F.R. §§ 1.9(c), 1.27(b).

[68] 37 C.F.R. §§ 1.9(d), 1.27(c). To be a small business, the company and its affiliates must not have more than 500 employees.

nonprofit institutions and universities.[69] These entities must not have transferred, licensed, or agreed to transfer or license any right in the patent to anyone other than another eligible small entity. Government agencies are not eligible for the discount, but entities outside the United States are eligible if they meet the stated criteria.

A verified statement establishes small entity status.[70] An applicant who establishes small entity status at the time of filing but loses such status thereafter, for example, by making a transfer of rights, must inform PTO when paying issue and maintenance fees.[71]

[b] **Unity of Invention—Restriction.** If an inventor claims two or more independent and distinct inventions in one application, the PTO examiner may require restriction to one of the inventions.[72]

Restriction's purpose is to preserve the integrity of the PTO fee and classification systems.

[i] *Independent and Distinct Inventions.* "Independent and distinct" inventions do not form a single general inventive concept.[73] In chemical cases and cases involving joinder of claims to a product, process of making the product, and a process of using the product, the determination whether there are single or multiple inventive concepts can be particularly complex.

An inventor may include separate claims to a reasonable number of species if there is an allowable generic claim.[74]

An examiner may not direct restriction to a single claim, such as a generic claim to chemical compounds defined by one or more Markush groups,[75] but may reject a Markush claim on the merits for improper grouping.[76]

[ii] *Restriction and Election.* If the examiner requires restriction,[77] the applicant must elect one of the independent and distinct inventions,[78] and only claims reading

---

[69] 37 C.F.R. §§ 1.9(e), 1.27(d).

[70] 37 C.F.R. § 1.27(a).

[71] 37 C.F.R. § 1.28(b).

[72] 35 U.S.C. § 121.

[73] 37 C.F.R. § 1.141(a).

[74] 37 C.F.R. § 1.146. If the generic claim that links the species is not allowed, the applicant may only obtain claims readable on the species.

[75] *In re* Weber, 580 F.2d 455, 198 U.S.P.Q. 328 (CCPA 1978). *See* § 2D[3][d][v].

[76] *In re* Harnisch, 631 F.2d 716, 206 U.S.P.Q. 300 (CCPA 1980).

[77] The restriction and election requirement may be made before examination on the merits and usually will be made by a telephone call to the applicant's attorney or agent.

[78] The applicant may request reconsideration by the examiner of the requirement but must still make a provisional election. 37 C.F.R. § 1.143. A restriction requirement is not a rejection on the merits and cannot be appealed to the Board of Patent Appeals and Interferences. 35 U.S.C. § 121; 37 C.F.R. § 1.144.

on the elected invention will be examined.[79] An examiner's restriction requirement cannot be appealed but is subject to review by petition to the Commissioner.[80]

If the examiner does *not* require restriction and a patent issues, the patent's validity may not later be challenged for misjoinder of independent inventions.[81]

[*iii*] *Divisional Applications.* The applicant may pursue patent protection for the non-elected inventions by filing divisional applications,[82] which are entitled to the filing date of the application ("parent") from which they divide.[83] Failure to file a timely divisional application is not an "error" correctable by reissue.[84]

A patent issuing on a parent application may not be used as a "reference" against the claims in a divisional application if two conditions are met: (1) the filing of the divisional application is in response to an actual restriction requirement[85] and (2) the claims in the divisional application maintain the line of division between the

---

[79] The test of what a claim "reads on" is the same as the test for infringement of the claim. *See* § 2E[2][a].

[80] *See In re* Watkinson, 900 F.2d 230, 233, 14 U.S.P.Q.2d 1407, 1409 (Fed. Cir. 1990) ("[N]either this court nor the board has jurisdiction in this proceeding to review the merits of a requirement for restriction under section 121, as a restriction requirement is a matter within the discretion of the examiner and is not tantamount to a rejection of claims.").

[81] 35 U.S.C. § 121.

[82] 35 U.S.C. § 121. There is a procedure for filing divisional applications without an inventor's oath or declaration.

[83] The divisional application may involve a different grouping of inventors than is named in the parent application. *See* § 2D[4][b][v].

[84] *See In re* Watkinson, 900 F.2d 230, 14 U.S.P.Q.2d 1407 (Fed. Cir. 1990). In *Watkinson,* the appellant's original patent application related to compositions for and methods of inhibiting the growth of timber fungus. The PTO examiner imposed a restriction requirement, requiring the applicant to elect one of two groups of claimed inventions: (i) claims drawn to a composition, and method of use thereof, having at least two components, and (ii) claims drawn to a method of using a composition having only one component. The applicant elected the first group, canceled the claim to the nonelected group, and reserved the right to file a divisional application containing claims to the nonelected group. The patent issued on November 6, 1984. The applicant filed a reissue application on January 9, 1986, adding claims to the nonelected invention. She alleged that her acquiescence in the restriction requirement was an error correctable by reissue because the restriction requirement had, in fact, been improper and that her failure to traverse the requirement was due to her patent agent's mistaken belief that the invention of the nonelected claim was unpatentable. The court held the reissue attempt inappropriate whether or not the examiner's restriction requirement was correct: "Upon compliance with the relevant PTO regulations, [the applicant] could have received from the examiner and the Commissioner [consideration of the merits of the restriction requirement in the original application] . . . However, after acquiescing in the restriction requirement, cancelling the non-elected claim and allowing the . . . patent to issue, [the inventor] has lost her opportunity to challenge the propriety of the restriction requirement." 900 F.2d at 230, 14 U.S.P.Q.2d at 1410.

[85] There is no protection from such use as a reference if the applicant voluntarily files a divisional application, *In re* Ockert, 245 F.2d 467, 468-69, 114 U.S.P.Q. 330, 322 (CCPA 1957), or if the PTO withdraws the restriction requirement, *In re* Ziegler, 443 F.2d 1211, 170 U.S.P.Q. 129 (CCPA 1971).

inventions stated in the restriction requirement.[86] Section 121's third sentence, less than a model of clear drafting, provides:

> "A patent issuing on an application with respect to which a requirement for restriction under this section has been made, or on an application filed as a result of such a requirement, shall not be used as a reference either in the Patent and Trademark Office or in the courts against a divisional application or against the original application or any patent issued on either of them, if the divisional application is filed before the issuance of the patent on the other application."[87]

Section 121's prohibition against use as a "reference" has long been controversial.[88] It precludes using a patent's claimed subject matter in determining a divisional application's claims.[89] It may also protect the second patent from a double patenting invalidation,[90] but only if the claims in the second patent are "consonant" with the restriction requirement.

In *Gerber Garment Technology*,[91] the Federal Circuit, confronting a first impression issue, held that Section 121's third sentence does not absolutely protect from double patenting invalidity a patent issuing on a divisional or continuing application filed as a result of an examiner restriction requirement. The Section 121 shield from use of a first patent as a "reference" applies only when a second patent's claims are consonant with the claims not elected by the inventor in response to the restriction requirement.

> "Compliance with a restriction requirement means the claims in a divisional application must be consonant with those not elected under that requirement. Noncompliance with the consonance requirement is normally detected by the PTO examiner. . . . Examiners' compliance with MPEP § 804.01 [,which provides that Section 121's double patenting protection does not apply where the claims are not consonant with, i.e., 'have been changed in material respects

---

[86] Lerner v. Ladd, 216 F. Supp. 81, 84, 136 U.S.P.Q. 624, 626 (D.D.C. 1962).

[87] 35 U.S.C. § 121.

[88] *Cf. In re* Ziegler, 443 F.2d 1211, 170 U.S.P.Q. 129 (CCPA 1971).

[89] Illinois Tool Works. Inc. v. Foster Grant Co., 395 F. Supp. 234, 256, 181 U.S.P.Q. 553, 569 (N.D. Ill. 1974), *cert. denied*, 431 U.S. 929, 194 U.S.P.Q. 576 (1977).

[90] *Cf.* Studiengesellschaft Kohle mbH v. Northern Petrochemical Co., 784 F.2d 351, 228 U.S.P.Q. 837 (Fed. Cir. 1983), *cert. dismissed*, 478 U.S. 1028 (1983). In *Studiengesellschaft*, the court reversed the district court's double patenting invalidation of a second-issued patent because the accused infringer offered no evidence of obviousness. The first patent, issued 1963, claimed a catalyst composition. The second patent, issued 1978, claimed a process of polymerizing ethylene using that catalyst. The court suggested that, in any event, a double patenting invalidation would be improper because the claims were divided into separate patents as a result of a PTO examiner restriction requirement. In such a situation, Section 121 protects against use of the first patent "as a reference" against the second patent. The "appallingly long" delay in issuance of the second patent was attributable to an intervening interference and not any violation of PTO rules or inequitable delay by the applicant/patentee.

[91] Gerber Garment Technology, Inc. v. Lectra Systems, Inc., 916 F.2d 683, 16 U.S.P.Q.2d 1436 (Fed. Cir. 1990).

from' the claims subject to the restriction requirement,] may account for the absence of court decisions on the precise fact pattern before us. . . ."[92]

The court rejected Gerber's argument that Section 121's third sentence is a "clear, unambiguous, and absolute prohibition against any use of the patent issued on the parent application." Gerber "reads that sentence in isolation." The "applicable rule of statutory interpretation . . . requires that the third sentence be read in the context of the entire statutory provision."

"Section 121 provides for restriction when 'independent and distinct inventions' are claimed in one application. The prohibition against use of a parent application 'as a reference' against a divisional application applies only to the divisional applications that are 'filed as a result of a restriction requirement. Plain common sense dictates that a divisional application filed as a result of a restriction requirement may not contain claims drawn to the invention set forth in the claims elected and prosecuted to patent in the parent application.

"It is true that the disclosure in the patent containing the elected claims cannot be used as a 'reference' on which to reject a claim in a divisional application under 35 U.S.C. § 103, for that disclosure is the applicant's and is not in the 'prior art.' That is not to say, however, that the elected claims may not be looked to in assessing compliance with the prohibition against claiming the same invention in two patents."

"Consonance requires that the line of demarcation between the 'independent and distinct inventions' that prompted the restriction requirement be maintained. Though the claims may be amended, they must not be so amended as to bring them back over the line imposed in the restriction requirement. Where that line is crossed the prohibition of the third sentence of Section 121 does not apply."[93]

In *Gerber*, the Federal Circuit affirmed the district court's determination that the second patent's claims had been so amended during prosecution as to render them not consonant with the examiner's original restriction requirement.[94]

---

[92] 916 F.2d at 685-86, 16 U.S.P.Q.2d at 1438.

[93] 916 F.2d at 687, 688, 16 U.S.P.Q.2d at 1440.

[94] Gerber's patents relate to automated fabric cutting, including "use of a vacuum to hold a stack of multiple layers of fabric on a penetrable surface while a vertically reciprocating cutting blade cuts the fabric." 916 F.2d at 684, 16 U.S.P.Q.2d at 1437.

On May 5, 1969, Gerber filed an original patent application. The PTO examiner imposed a restriction requirement between (1) a cutting apparatus (application claims 1-11 and 16-28), and (2) a work holding means (claims 12-15). Gerber elected the first invention, a cutting apparatus. On February 17, 1970, the '492 patent issued to Gerber. On February 2, 1970, Gerber filed a continuation-in-part application directed to the second invention, "work holding means." During four years of prosecution, Gerber amended and substituted claims. On February 5, 1974, the '154 patent issued to Gerber.

The second ('154) patent's claims 15 and 16 are not consonant with the restriction requirement. Claims 15 and 16 are to an apparatus for holding an object and have a preamble reciting "a machine having . . . a cutting blade" as well as the limitations of certain "support means," "a panel of . . . sheet material," and "means for producing a vacuum." The preamble, which recites a "cutting blade," is a claim limitation, "not merely an aspect of the claim

[c] **Confidentiality.** The PTO holds applications in confidence until a patent has issued[95] and releases information on a pending application as of right only to the applicant, the assignee of record, or an attorney or agent of record.[96] Confidentiality extends to abandoned applications.[97] The PTO grants public access to abandoned applications referred to by serial number in United States patents.[98] It may grant access to a patent application under special circumstances.[99]

The confidentiality policy directly impacts only the PTO because, upon a proper showing, a court will order a patent application's disclosure if it is relevant to litigation.[100]

Japan's and Europe's patent systems publish applications 18 months after their effective filing date and provide the applicant a right of reasonable compensation as to unauthorized use of the invention defined by the published claims, provided a patent eventually issues on the application. This practice dilutes the confidentiality of U.S. applications if, as is increasingly common, the U.S. applicant files, or has previously filed, in another country a patent application corresponding to the U.S. application. For example, U.S. company A may wish to know what areas of technology its U.S. competitors, company B and company C, are currently working on. It cannot obtain copies of those companies' pending U.S. applications from the PTO but can obtain published versions filed in Japan and the European Patent Office, which will indicate a priority claim based on a U.S. prior application. The U.S. and corresponding published foreign applications's disclosures are most likely the same, though the claims that eventually issue in the U.S. may differ significantly from those in the non-U.S. applications.

[d] **Amendments.** After filing an application with the PTO, an applicant may amend the specification, claims or drawings, but only within the severe constraints

---

environment." "When it made the cutting blade a limitation of claims 15 and 16 Gerber crossed back over the line of demarcation between the 'cutting apparatus' claims and 'work holding means' claims drawn by the examiner in the restriction requirement." That Gerber added the "cutting blade" language to the preamble "at the examiner's 'insistence' to 'better define [the work holding means] over the prior art' is to no avail: "An applicant is at liberty to resist any such suggestion . . . and if the claim was improper in the divisional application, the applicant's acceptance of that claim cannot be excused on the ground that 'the examiner made me do it.'" 916 F.2d at 688, 16 U.S.P.Q.2d at 1441.

[95] 35 U.S.C. § 122. *See generally* D. Chisum, Patents § 11.02[4]. Public access is granted to all reissue applications because a reissue application relates to a published patent and cannot add new matter. *See* § 2D[6][b].

The "freedom of information" laws do not apply to pending or abandoned patent applications or PTO decisions relating thereto. Irons & Sears v. Dann, 606 F.2d 1215, 202 U.S.P.Q. 798 (D.C. Cir. 1979), *cert. denied,* 444 U.S. 1075, 204 U.S.P.Q. 1060 (1980); Lee Pharmaceuticals v. Kreps, 577 F.2d 610, 198 U.S.P.Q. 601 (9th Cir. 1978), *cert. denied,* 439 U.S. 1073, 200 U.S.P.Q. 832 (1979).

[96] 37 C.F.R. § 1.14(a).

[97] 37 C.F.R. § 1.14(b).

[98] 37 C.F.R. § 1.14.

[99] 35 U.S.C. § 122.

[100] James B. Clow & Sons, Inc. v. United States Pipe & Foundry Co., 313 F.2d 46, 51, 136 U.S.P.Q. 397 (5th Cir. 1963).

of the rule barring "new matter" additions to pending patent applications.[101] New matter is a technical patent law term that cannot be precisely defined.[102] The new matter prohibition severely restricts the right to add to or alter the specification[103] and forces use of continuation-in-part applications to introduce new information into a filed patent specification.[104]

Amendments may clarify the original disclosure[105] or conform originally-filed specification, claims and drawings to each other.[106]

The new matter bar applies to reissue applications.[107]

Claim amendments and additions are not "new matter" and are permissible if, but only if, they are supported by the original specification disclosures.[108]

Some courts applied a "late claiming" doctrine to preclude claim amendments covering products in public use or on sale more than one year before the amendment.[109] Courts now repudiate late claiming: the sole test is whether the specification adequately supports the added or amended claims.[110]

In *Kingsdown*,[111] the Federal Circuit noted:

> "[T]here is nothing improper, illegal or inequitable in filing a patent application for the purpose of obtaining a right to exclude a known competitor's product from the market; nor is it in any manner improper to amend or insert claims intended to cover a competitor's product the applicant's attorney has learned about during the prosecution of a patent application. Any such amendment or insertion must comply with all statutes and regulations, of course, but, if it does, its genesis in the marketplace is simply irrelevant and cannot of itself evidence deceitful intent."[112]

---

[101] 35 U.S.C. § 132. *See generally* D. Chisum, Patents § 11.04.

[102] *In re* Oda, 443 F.2d 1200, 1203, 170 U.S.P.Q. 268, 270 (CCPA 1971).

[103] *But see In re* Lundak, 773 F.2d 1216, 227 U.S.P.Q. 90 (Fed. Cir. 1985) (the new matter bar is not violated when an applicant (1) deposits a cell line with a recognized depository five days after filing the application, and (2) amends the specification to add depository data (including an accession number)).

[104] *See* § 2D[4][b].

[105] *In re* Oda, 443 F.2d 1200, 170 U.S.P.Q. 268 (CCPA 1971); *In re* Wright, 343 F.2d 761, 767, 145 U.S.P.Q. 182, 188 (CCPA 1965).

[106] *In re* Heinle, 342 F.2d 1001, 1007, 145 U.S.P.Q. 131, 136 (CCPA 1965).

[107] *See* § 2D[6][b].

[108] *In re* Rasmussen, 650 F.2d 1212, 211 U.S.P.Q. 323 (CCPA 1981).

All claims must meet the enablement requirement. *See* § 2D[3][a]. Claims added after the original filing date must also meet the description requirement. *See* § 2D[3][b].

[109] Kahn v. Dynamics Corp. of America, 367 F. Supp. 63, 180 U.S.P.Q. 247 (S.D.N.Y. 1973), *aff'd*, 508 F.2d 939, 184 U.S.P.Q. 260 (2d Cir. 1975), *cert. denied*, 421 U.S. 930, 185 U.S.P.Q. 505 (1975).

[110] Westphal v. Fawzi, 666 F.2d 575, 212 U.S.P.Q. 321 (CCPA 1981).

[111] Kingsdown Medical Consultants, Ltd. v. Hollister Inc., 863 F.2d 867, 9 U.S.P.Q.2d 1384 (Fed. Cir. 1988), *cert. denied*, 490 U.S. 1067 (1988), *order vacated*, 866 F.2d 1398, 9 U.S.P.Q.2d 1831 (1989).

[112] 863 F.2d at 874, 9 U.S.P.Q.2d at 1390.

[2] Duty of Candor—Inequitable Conduct.

Patent applicants have a duty to disclose to the PTO information of which they are aware that is material to the examination and to refrain from misrepresenting facts.[113] Violation of this candor duty may be "inequitable conduct"[114] that renders the patent's claims unenforceable.[115]

[a] Historical Development. Before 1900, case law focused on Government efforts to cancel allegedly fraudulently procured patents.[116]

Four post-1900 Supreme Court decisions are of interest. In *Keystone Driller,*[117] the Court held several patents unenforceable in an infringement suit because the patent owner, in a prior suit involving one of the patents, participated in corrupting a witness who had knowledge of public use activity that invalidated the patent. In *Hazel-Atlas,*[118] it held that fabrication of a journal article lauding an invention to induce the Patent Office to issue, and a court to uphold, a patent was such fraud as to warrant vacation of an otherwise final patent infringement judgment. In *Precision Instrument,*[119] it held that the plaintiff in an infringement suit was barred, under the equitable "unclean hands" doctrine, from enforcing two patents it obtained without disclosing to the Patent Office its knowledge of perjury in an interference proceeding. In *Walker Process Equip.,*[120] it held that fraudulent patent procurement could support affirmative recovery of damages under the antitrust laws—but only if the antitrust claimant could show that the illegal patent caused monopolization of the relevant market and the patentee was guilty of more than an "honest mistake" ("technical fraud") in misrepresenting facts to the Patent Office.

Fraudulent patent procurement has always been unquestionably improper. *Keystone Driller* and *Precision Instruments* established fraudulent procurement as a defense to a patent infringement charge. Less certain was whether inventors and their

---

113 37 C.F.R. § 1.56. *See generally* D. Chisum, Patents §§ 11.03[4], 19.03. For discussion of copyright registration inequitable conduct, see § 4F[4][b].

The oath or declaration submitted with a patent application must contain an acknowledgement of the duty of disclosure.

114 J.P. Stevens & Co., Inc. v. Lex Tex, Ltd., 747 F.2d 1553, 223 U.S.P.Q. 1089 (Fed. Cir. 1984), *cert. denied,* 474 U.S. 822 (1985).

The constitutional jury trial right does not apply to the inequitable conduct defense, which "is derived from the doctrine of unclean hands and is purely equitable in nature." Gardco Manufacturing, Inc. v. Herst Lighting Co., 820 F.2d 1209, 1212, 2 U.S.P.Q.2d 2015, 2018 (Fed. Cir. 1987). *See also* Kingsdown Medical Consultants, Ltd. v. Hollister Inc., 863 F.2d 867, 9 U.S.P.Q.2d 1384 (Fed. Cir. 1988), *cert. denied,* 109 S. Ct. 2068 (1988), *order vacated,* 866 F.2d 1398, 9 U.S.P.Q.2d 1831 (1989).

115 *See* § 2F[4][b].

116 United States v. American Bell Tel. Co., 167 U.S. 224 (1897); United States v. American Bell Tel. Co., 128 U.S. 315 (1888); Mowry v. Whitney, 81 U.S. (14 Wall.) 434 (1871).

117 Keystone Driller Co. v. General Excavator Co., 290 U.S. 240 (1933).

118 Hazel-Atlas Glass Co. v. Hartford Empire Co., 322 U.S. 238, 61 U.S.P.Q. 241 (1944).

119 Precision Instrument Mfg. Co. v. Automotive Maintenance Mach. Co., 324 U.S. 806, 65 U.S.P.Q. 133 (1945).

120 Walker Process Equip. Inc. v. Food Mach. & Chem. Corp., 382 U.S. 172, 147 U.S.P.Q. 404 (1965).

representatives had an affirmative duty to disclose material information, such as prior art references. Through the 1950's, a belief commonly held among practitioners was that the Patent Office was obliged in law to, and would, search for and consider prior art references. In *Standard Electric Time*,[121] Judge Wyzanski dismissed the Government's suit to cancel a patent on the ground that the inventor failed to disclose to the Patent Office prior art references that did not anticipate the invention but that, allegedly, were "of such relevance that they should be cited in the specification."

> "Of course, a putative inventor must disclose any printed publication which he either knows or believes describes the very invention claimed. . . . More than this, if he knows of a printed publication which plainly describes his claimed invention, or comes so close thereto that every reasonable man would say the invention claimed was not original but had been anticipated, then regardless of his personal view that he is the original inventor, he will not be excused for his failure to disclose his knowledge. But *the applicant has no duty to cite every publication of which he knows, or which he has used, merely because the publication is one likely to be referred to by a vigilant examiner* in the Patent Office . . . "[122]

In the late 1960's and early 1970's, court decisions expanded the candor duty beyond the *Standard Elec. Time* anticipation standard. In *Beckman Instruments*,[123] the Fifth Circuit articulated an affirmative disclosure duty:

> "The Patent Office does not have full research facilities of its own, and it has never been intended by Congress that it should. In examining patents, the Office relies heavily upon the prior art references that are cited to it by applicants. It is therefore evident that our patent system could not function successfully if applicants were allowed to approach the Patent Office as an arm's length adversary."[124]

Patent Office Rule 56 provided for "striking" a patent application in connection with which any fraud had been committed. In *Norton*,[125] the Court of Customs and Patent Appeals held that Rule 56 "fraud" included the expanded candor duty recognized in infringement suit court decisions.

---

[121] United States v. Standard Elec. Time Co., 155 F. Supp. 949, 116 U.S.P.Q. 14 (D. Mass. 1979), *appeal dismissed,* 254 F.2d 598, 116 U.S.P.Q. 422 (1st Cir. 1958).

[122] 155 F. Supp. at 952-53 (Emphasis added.)

[123] Beckman Instruments, Inc. v. Chemtronics, Inc., 439 F.2d 1369, 165 U.S.P.Q. 355 (5th Cir. 1970). *See also* Monolith Portland Midwest Co. v. Kaiser Aluminum & Chemical Corp., 407 F.2d 288, 295, 160 U.S.P.Q. 577 (9th Cir. 1969) (failure to disclose known possible public use bar: "Whatever theory [the patentee] may have had in mind about the legal effect of the . . . uses, it failed to disclose openly and fully the facts to the Patent Office."); American Cyanamid Co. v. F.T.C., 363 F.2d 757, 150 U.S.P.Q. 135 (6th Cir. 1966), *cert. denied sub. nom.* Pfizer v. FTC, 394 U.S. 920 (1969) (possible inequitable conduct in procurement of tetracycline "wonder drug" patent).

[124] 428 F.2d at 564-65.

See also Jaskiewicz v. Mossinghoff, 822 F.2d 1053, 1058, 3 U.S.P.Q.2d 1294, 1299 (Fed. Cir. 1987) ("[T]he P.T.O. is under severe limitations as to time and manpower, and it is incumbent upon attorneys and agents who prosecute patent applications to follow the procedural rules of the P.T.O.").

[125] Norton v. Curtiss, 433 F.2d 779, 167 U.S.P.Q. 532 (CCPA 1970).

In 1977, the PTO amended Rule 56, incorporating an express "duty of candor." Some subsequent court decisions read Rule 56 as "codifying" existing disclosure duties,[126] but others candidly recognized that it encapsulated a trend significantly expanding patent applicants' disclosure obligations.[127] In *Digital Equipment*,[128] the First Circuit upheld Rule 56's procedural aspects, including the PTO's authority to strike reissue applications for inequitable conduct,[129] but remanded the PTO's striking of the application in question because of its failure to set forth a basis reasonably supporting its fraud finding.

In 1982, the PTO made inequitable conduct a ground for *rejection*, which could be appealed, rather than *striking*, which could be reviewed only by petition[130] and directed that inequitable conduct questions not be decided by regular examiners but rather be directed, after the patentability examination was completed, to a group of examiners with legal training assigned to the Assistant Commissioner for Patents.

In 1988, in the wake of *Harita*,[131] which emphasized an intent-to-deceive culpability standard for PTO inequitable conduct findings, the PTO announced that it would no longer examine applications for candor duty compliance, leaving it to the courts, which are better equipped to deal with problems of proving intent. In 1989, the PTO proposed to replace Rule 56 with a new Rule 57.[132]

[b] Disclosure Standard—Materiality. Candor duty compliance problems may arise with respect to:

(1) public use and on sale activity by the inventor and his assignee that may constitute a statutory bar;[133]

---

[126] *In re* Jerabek, 789 F.2d 886, 890 n.10, 229 U.S.P.Q. 530, 553 n.10 (Fed. Cir. 1986) ("the present PTO standard . . . codifies the PTO policy on fraud and inequitable conduct"); True Temper Corp. v. CF & I Corp., 601 F.2d 495, 504 n.9, 202 U.S.P.Q. 412 (10th Cir. 1979) ("The amended rule merely represented a codification of existing case law on the obligation of applicants to disclose pertinent information or prior art, or face possible invalidation of the patent once issued.").

[127] *In re* Harita, 847 F.2d 801, 808, 6 U.S.P.Q.2d 1930, 1935 (Fed. Cir. 1988) (amended Rule 56 "inaugurated a whole new way of life in the prosecution of patent applications. The rule begins with a recital of 'A duty of candor and good faith toward the' PTO which has effectively made applicants, their associates, and attorneys partners with the PTO examining corps in producing for PTO consideration the prior art which is needed to operate a reasonably effective examination system.").

[128] Digital Equip. Corp. v. Diamond, 653 F.2d 701, 210 U.S.P.Q. 521 (1st Cir. 1981).

[129] For a discussion of reissue, see § 2D[6][b].

[130] 47 Fed. Reg. 21756 (May 20, 1982).

[131] *In re* Harita, 847 F.2d 801, 6 U.S.P.Q.2d 1930 (Fed. Cir. 1988).

[132] PTO, "Notice of Proposed Rule: Duty of Disclosure and Practitioner Misconduct," 54 Fed. Reg. 11334 (March 17, 1989).

[133] *E.g.*, Argus Chemical Corp. v. Fibre Glass-Evercoat Co., Inc., 759 F.2d 10, 225 U.S.P.Q. 1100 (Fed. Cir. 1985), *cert. denied*, 474 U.S. 903 (1985). *Compare* Reactive Metals & Alloys Corp. v. ESM, Inc., 769 F.2d 1578, 226 U.S.P.Q. 821 (Fed. Cir. 1985). *See* § 2C[5][b][iii] and [iv].

(2) prior art references of which the examiner may not be aware that are more pertinent than those the examiner considered;[134]

(3) testing and other data submitted in support of patentability;[135]

(4) affidavits establishing a pre-filing invention date;[136]

(5) intentional failure to disclose in the patent specification the best mode for carrying out the invention;[137] and

(6) other acts or representations.[138]

The disclosure duty extends to material information and prior art. Court decisions identify at least three materiality tests: objective "but for," subjective "but for," and relevance to patentability. Federal Circuit decisions adopt the Rule 56 variant of the last test:[139] an item is material if there is substantial likelihood that a reasonable examiner would consider it important in deciding whether to allow the application to issue as a patent.[140] Prior art or other information may be relevant even though it does not render an applicant's claim unpatentable as anticipated or obvious.[141]

---

[134] *E.g.,* J.P. Stevens & Co. Inc. v. Lex Tex, Ltd., 747 F.2d 1553, 223 U.S.P.Q. 1089 (Fed. Cir. 1984), *cert. denied,* 474 U.S. 822 (1985).

[135] Rohm & Hass Co. v. Crystal Chem. Co., 722 F.2d 1556, 220 U.S.P.Q. 289 (Fed. Cir. 1983), *later proceeding,* 736 F.2d 688, 222 U.S.P.Q. 97 (Fed. Cir. 1984), *cert. denied,* 469 U.S. 851 (1984). *See* §§ 2C[4][c] and [d]. An affidavit offering test data constitutes a representation by the applicant that the showing is a fair and accurate representation of the closest prior art of which he is aware. Norton v. Curtis, 433 F.2d 779, 167 U.S.P.Q. 532 (CCPA 1970).

[136] Timely Prod. Corp. v. Arron, 523 F.2d 288, 187 U.S.P.Q. 257 (2d Cir. 1975).

[137] Consolidated Aluminum Corp. v. Foseco International Ltd., 910 F.2d 804, 15 U.S.P.Q.2d 1481 (Fed. Cir. 1990).

[138] *Cf.* Burlington Industries, Inc. v. Dayco Corp., 849 F.2d 1418, 7 U.S.P.Q.2d 1158 (Fed. Cir. 1988) (statements concerning nature of invention).

[139] 37 C.F.R. § 1.56(a).

[140] *E.g.,* J.P. Stevens & Co. Inc. v. Lex Tex, Ltd., 747 F.2d 1553, 1559, 223 U.S.P.Q. 1089, 1092 (Fed. Cir. 1984), *cert. denied,* 474 U.S. 822 (1984) (Rule 56 "is the appropriate starting point because it is the broadest and because it most closely aligns with how one ought to conduct business with the PTO.").

A higher materiality standard may apply when a claimant asserts an unfair competition or antitrust laws damage claim. *E.g.,* Litton Industrial Products, Inc. v. Solid State Systems Corp., 755 F.2d 158, 225 U.S.P.Q. 34 (Fed. Cir. 1985).

The inquiry is not into whether the *actual* examiner of the patent considered the information important. *See* Western Electric Co. v. Piezo Technology, Inc., 860 F.2d 428, 8 U.S.P.Q.2d 1853 (Fed. Cir. 1988) (upholding PTO policy restricting depositions of examiners as to their thought processes during examination).

[141] Merck & Co., Inc. v. Danbury Pharmacal, Inc., 873 F.2d 1418, 1421, 10 U.S.P.Q.2d 1682, 1686 (Fed. Cir. 1989) ("To be material, a misrepresentation need not be relied on by the examiner in deciding to allow the patent. The matter misrepresented need only be within a reasonable examiner's realm of consideration."); Gardco Manufacturing, Inc. v. Herst Lighting Co., 820 F.2d 1209, 2 U.S.P.Q.2d 2015 (Fed. Cir. 1987).

Information is not material if it is cumulative to other material considered by the PTO examiner.[142] When can it be assumed that the examiner actually "considered" information? Often, the examiner of the application leading to the patent in question has been exposed to the uncited prior art or information in question, for example, when the examiner previously cited or examined an undisclosed patent. *Driscoll*[143] and *J.P. Stevens*[144] emphasized that one could not presume examiner knowledge when a reference is in a searched class.[145] *Pacific Furniture*[146] emphasized the undisclosed prior art design in question had been the subject of an application copending with the application for the patent in question.[147] *Gardco*[148] rejected the

---

[142] *E.g.*, Halliburton Co. v. Schlumberger Technology Corp., 925 F.2d 1435, 1440-41, 17 U.S.P.Q.2d 1834, 1839-40 (Fed. Cir. 1991) ("[A] patentee has no obligation to disclose an otherwise material reference if the reference is cumulative or less material than those already before the examiner. . . . When weighing whether uncited prior art is more material than that before the examiner, a trial court considers similarities and differences between prior art and the claims of the patent. In making this determination, the trial court must consider portions of prior art references which teach away from the claimed invention."); Specialty Composites v. Cabot Corp., 845 F.2d 981, 992, 6 U.S.P.Q.2d 1601, 1609 (Fed. Cir. 1988) ("Failure to cite nonmaterial, cumulative references is not inequitable conduct.").

[143] Driscoll v. Cebalo, 731 F.2d 878, 221 U.S.P.Q. 745 (Fed. Cir. 1984).

In *Driscoll*, a failure to cite a known anticipatory prior art reference constituted inequitable conduct even though (a) a new attorney for the inventor had amended the claim to avoid the reference disclosure prior to action by the examiner, and (b) the prosecution of the party's application was suspended pending an interference prior to allowance of the claims affected by the withheld reference. The inventor's interference opponent uncovered the facts concerning the withholding of the reference and the amendment to the claims.

[144] J.P. Stevens & Co., Inc. v. Lex Tex, Ltd., 747 F.2d 1553, 223 U.S.P.Q. 1089 (Fed. Cir. 1984), *cert. denied*, 474 U.S. 822 (1985).

[145] *See also* FMC Corp. v. Hennessy Industries, Inc., 836 F.2d 521, 5 U.S.P.Q.2d 1272 (Fed. Cir. 1987).

Hennessy Industries held that the district court erred in finding no inequitable conduct based on failure to cite information solely on the basis of "prosecution history evidence that the examiner searched the class and subclass that contained the omitted information." The examiner's "indication of a generalized search would not of itself relieve [the applicants and their representatives] from the duty of candor." The argument by the assignee of the patent that the examiner was fully cognizant of the nondisclosed items because he had cited them during the examination of a prior patent "must fail because [the assignee] had no relation whatever to the prosecution [of that prior patent, which] issued long before the . . . application [for the patent in question] was filed." "The duty of candor requires 'more than an assumption that the examiner will recall something from a previous application.' " 836 F.2d at 526-27, 5 U.S.P.Q.2d at 1276.

[146] Pacific Furniture Mfg. Co. v. Preview Furniture Corp., 800 F.2d 1111, 231 U.S.P.Q. 67 (Fed. Cir. 1986).

[147] *See also* Allen Organ Co. v. Kimball International, Inc., 839 F.2d 1556, 5 U.S.P.Q.2d 1769 (Fed. Cir. 1988), *cert. denied*, 488 U.S. 850 (1988); FMC Corp. v. Hennessy Industries, Inc., 836 F.2d 521, 526, 5 U.S.P.Q.2d 1272, 1276 (Fed. Cir. 1987) (as to the alleged failure to cite a certain prior art device during the prosecution of one of the patents in suit, the threshold level of intent was not met, given that the assignee disclosed that device in another of its applications "that was pending before the same examiner at the very same time.").

[148] Gardco Manufacturing, Inc. v. Herst Lighting Co., 820 F.2d 1209, 2 U.S.P.Q. 2015 (Fed. Cir. 1987).

patentee's copendency argument by noting that the "copending application was not prior art" while "earlier exhibition, sale and use of the undisclosed [devices] was."

Arguments, opinions, and actions on matters the examiner can independently verify in the prosecution file are unlikely to amount to material misrepresentation,[149] but inequitable conduct may arise if an applicant knowingly takes advantage of examiner error.[150]

[c] **Culpability.** Prior to creation of the Federal Circuit, the regional Courts of Appeal and the Court of Customs and Patent Appeals required a showing of culpability as well as materiality to sustain an inequitable conduct charge.[151] Sufficient culpability could lie in gross negligence;[152] subjective good faith did not necessarily prevent a finding of inequitable conduct.[153]

---

[149] *E.g.,* Akzo N.V. v. U.S. Int'l Trade Comm'n, 808 F.2d 1471, 1482, 1 U.S.P.Q.2d 1241, 1247 (Fed. Cir. 1986) ("The mere fact that [the applicant] attempted to distinguish the [claimed] process from the prior art does not constitute a material omission or misrepresentation. The examiner was free to reach his own conclusion regarding the [claimed] process based on the art in front of him."); Environmental Designs, Ltd. v. Union Oil Co. of California, 713 F.2d 693, 698, 218 U.S.P.Q. 865, 870 (Fed. Cir. 1983), *cert. denied,* 464 U.S. 1043 (1984) ("Fraud cannot consist of a failure to duplicate what is in the file wrapper.").

[150] Kangaroos U.S.A., Inc. v. Caldor, Inc., 778 F.2d 1571, 1576, 228 U.S.P.Q. 32, 35 (Fed. Cir. 1985) ("There is no reprieve from the duty of square dealing and full disclosure that rests on the patent practitioner in dealings with the PTO. . . . [T]his duty is not done by one who knowingly takes advantage of an error by the PTO.").

Compare Northern Telecom, Inc. v. Datapoint Corp., 908 F.2d 931, 938, 15 U.S.P.Q.2d 1321, 1327 (Fed. Cir. 1990), *cert. denied,* 111 S. Ct. 296 (1990) ("Although lapse on the part of an examiner does not exculpate an applicant whose acts are intentionally deceptive, . . . any doubt as to whether the examiner lapsed in his duty does not increase the burden on the applicant. Nor does the applicant's obligation of candor replace the examiner's duty to examine the claims."); Kingsdown Medical Consultants, Ltd. v. Hollister Inc., 863 F.2d 867, 874 n.8, 9 U.S.P.Q.2d 1384, 1390 n.8 (Fed. Cir. 1988), *cert. denied,* 109 S. Ct. 2068 (1989), *order vacated,* 866 F.2d 1398, 9 U.S.P.Q.2d 1831 (1989) ("[We do not] suggest that the presumed compliance of the examiner with his duty to examine the claims in a continuation would relieve an applicant of its duty to avoid mistakes in describing a submitted claim as corresponding to an allowed version of an earlier claim in the parent application. . . . [A]n examiner has a right to expect candor from counsel. [The district court's] indication that examiners 'must' rely on counsel's candor would be applicable . . . only when the examiner does not have the involved documents or information before him, as the examiner did here. Blind reliance on presumed candor would render examination unnecessary, and nothing in the statute or Manual of Patent Examining Procedure would justify reliance on counsel's candor as a substitute for an examiner's duty to examine the claims.").

[151] *E.g.,* Parker v. Motorola, Inc., 524 F.2d 518, 188 U.S.P.Q. 225 (2d Cir. 1975), *cert. denied,* 425 U.S. 975, 190 U.S.P.Q. 172 (1976); Monolith Portland Midwest Co. v. Kaiser Aluminum & Co., 407 F.2d 288, 294, 160 U.S.P.Q. 577 (9th Cir. 1969).

[152] *E.g.,* International Tel. & Tel. Corp. v. Raychem Corp., 538 F.2d 453, 461, 191 U.S.P.Q. 1 (1st Cir. 1976), *cert. denied,* 429 U.S. 886, 191 U.S.P.Q. 409 (1976).

[153] *E.g.,* Norton v. Curtiss, 433 F.2d 779, 167 U.S.P.Q. 532 (CCPA 1970).

Some Federal Circuit panel decisions adopted gross negligence as a culpability threshold.[154] Other panel decisions required a finding of intent to mislead the PTO.[155] In *Kingsdown*,[156] all the active Federal Circuit judges ruled that a finding of gross negligence does not compel the necessary finding of intent to mislead the PTO:

> "Some of our opinions have suggested that a finding of gross negligence compels a finding of an intent to deceive. . . . Others have indicated that gross negligence alone does not mandate a finding of intent to deceive.
>
> " 'Gross negligence' has been used as a label for various patterns of conduct. It is definable, however, only in terms of a particular act or acts viewed in light of all the circumstances. We adopt the view that a finding that particular conduct amounts to 'gross negligence' does not of itself justify an inference of intent to deceive; the involved conduct, viewed in light of all the evidence, including evidence indicative of good faith, must indicate sufficient culpability to require a finding of intent to deceive."[157]

Later panel decisions require an express district court finding as to intent to mislead,[158] which stemmed the rising tide of the inequitable conduct defense.[159]

---

[154] *E.g.*, Specialty Composites v. Cabot Corp., 845 F.2d 981, 992, 6 U.S.P.Q.2d 1601, 1608 (Fed. Cir. 1988) ("proof of the requisite intent does not require evidence of deliberate scheming; in proper circumstances, gross negligence is sufficient."); J.P. Stevens & Co. v. Lex Tex. Ltd., 747 F.2d 1553, 223 U.S.P.Q. 1089 (Fed. Cir. 1984), *cert. denied*, 474 U.S. 822 (1985).

[155] FMC Corp. v. Hennessy Industries, Inc., 836 F.2d 521, 5 U.S.P.Q.2d 1272 (Fed. Cir. 1987); FMC Corp. v. Manitowoc Co., Inc., 835 F.2d 1411, 5 U.S.P.Q.2d 1112 (Fed. Cir. 1987).

In *Manitowoc Co.*, the court offered the following nutshell summary of the elements of an inequitable conduct defense:

> "To be guilty of inequitable conduct, one must have intended to act inequitably. Thus, one who alleges a 'failure to disclose' form of inequitable conduct must offer clear and convincing proof of: (1) prior art or information that is material; (2) knowledge chargeable to applicant of that prior art or information and of its materiality; and (3) failure of the applicant to disclose the art or information resulting from an intent to mislead the PTO. That proof may be rebutted by a showing that: (a) the prior art or information was not material (e.g., because it is less pertinent than or merely cumulative with prior art or information cited to or by the PTO); (b) if the prior art or information was material, a showing that the applicant did not know of that art or information; (c) if applicant did know of that art or information, a showing that applicant did not know of its materiality; (d) a showing that applicant's failure to disclose art or information did not result from an intent to mislead the PTO." 835 F.2d at 1415, 5 U.S.P.Q.2d at 1115.

[156] Kingsdown Medical Consultants, Ltd. v. Hollister Inc., 863 F.2d 867, 876, 9 U.S.P.Q.2d 1384, 1392 (Fed. Cir. 1988), *cert. denied*, 490 U.S. 1067 (1989), *order vacated*, 866 F.2d 1398, 9 U.S.P.Q.2d 1831 (1989).

[157] 863 F.2d at 876, 9 U.S.P.Q.2d at 1392.

[158] *E.g.*, Hoffman-La Roche Inc. v. Lemmon Co., 906 F.2d 684, 15 U.S.P.Q.2d 1363 (Fed. Cir. 1990); Hewlett-Packard Co. v. Bausch & Lomb Inc., 882 F.2d 1556, 11 U.S.P.Q.2d 1750 (Fed. Cir. 1989), discussed above. *Cf.* Halliburton Co. v. Schlumberger Technology Corp., 925 F.2d 1435, 1443, 17 U.S.P.Q.2d 1834, 1841 (Fed. Cir. 1991) (the district court's finding that the inventor's assignee and its representatives acted with intent to mislead the PTO in failing to disclose known prior art references is clearly erroneous; "[N]egligent conduct can support an inference of intent only when, 'viewed in light of all the evidence, including evidence indicative of good faith,' the conduct is culpable enough 'to require a finding of intent to deceive.' ").

The Federal Circuit continues to affirm district court inequitable conduct rulings adequately supported by materiality and culpability findings.[160]

[d] Information Disclosure Statements—Timely Disclosure. An applicant may submit to the PTO an "information disclosure statement" listing patents, publications, and other information relevant to patentability.[161] The statement is optional, but its submission is encouraged as a means of complying with the candor duty. An item's

---

In *Hewlett-Packard,* the court held that a conclusion of inequitable conduct cannot be supported without a finding of intent to mislead the PTO even though the district court "characterized [the patentee's] conduct as evidencing '[s]tudied ignorance' of the facts and 'reckless indifference' to the truth, and further noted the complete absence of evidence of good faith . . . "

> "Although the proof of gross negligence may be circumstantial evidence which gives rise to an inference of intent to mislead in some instances, the label 'gross negligence' covers too wide a range of culpable conduct to create such an inference in all cases. Thus, grossly negligent conduct may or may not compel an inference of an intent to mislead. Such an inference depends upon the totality of the circumstances, including the nature and level of culpability of the conduct and the absence or presence of affirmative evidence of good faith." 882 F.2d at 1562, 11 U.S.P.Q.2d at 1755.

The court noted that " '[S]tudied ignorance' of the facts, . . . a 'reckless indifference' to the truth, and . . . the complete absence of evidence of good faith" are "circumstances [the Federal Circuit has] held may give rise to an inference of wrongful intent. . . . " 882 F.2d at 1562, 11 U.S.P.Q.2d at 1755.

[159] In the late 1980's, Federal Circuit opinions decried the proliferation of inequitable conduct charges in patent litigation. *E.g.,* Burlington Industries, Inc. v. Dayco Corp., 849 F.2d 1418, 1422, 7 U.S.P.Q.2d 1158, 1161 (Fed. Cir. 1988):

> "[T]he habit of charging inequitable conduct in almost every major patent case has become an absolute plague. Reputable lawyers seem to feel compelled to make the charge against other reputable lawyers on the slenderest grounds, to represent their client's interests adequately, perhaps. They get anywhere with the accusation in but a small percentage of the cases, but such charges are not inconsequential on that account. They destroy the respect for one another's integrity. . . . A patent litigant should be made to feel, therefore, that an unsupported charge of 'inequitable conduct in the Patent Office' is a negative contribution to the rightful administration of justice."

See also Northern Telecom, Inc. v. Datapoint Corp., 908 F.2d 931, 939, 15 U.S.P.Q.2d 1321, 1327 (Fed. Cir. 1990), *cert. denied,* 111 S. Ct. 296 (1990) ("Intent to deceive should be determined in light of the realities of patent practice, and not as a matter of strict liability whatever the nature of the action before the PTO. . . . Given the ease with which a relatively routine act of patent prosecution can be portrayed as intended to mislead or deceive, clear and convincing evidence of conduct sufficient to support an inference of culpable intent is required.").

[160] *E.g.,* Fox Industries, Inc. v. Structural Preservation Systems, Inc., 922 F.2d 801, 804, 17 U.S.P.Q.2d 1579, 1581 (Fed. Cir. 1990) (the district court did not err in finding that the inventor and his patent attorney intended to mislead the PTO when they failed to disclose the inventor's prior art sales brochure, which contained disclosures that were more relevant than any other prior art reference cited during prosecution and which anticipated most of the patent's claims; "The record contains no evidence of good faith."); Merck & Co., Inc. v. Danbury Pharmacal, Inc., 873 F.2d 1418, 10 U.S.P.Q.2d 1682 (Fed. Cir. 1989).

[161] 37 C.F.R. § 1.97.

inclusion is not an admission that it is a pertinent prior art reference nor a representation that a prior art search has been made.[162] An information disclosure statement must concisely explain the listed item's relevance.[163] The applicant may update the statement to disclose later discovered items by submitting a supplemental statement or by incorporating them in other communications to the examiner.[164]

Court decisions do not clearly resolve whether an inventor is under a duty to disclose known material information early in the application's prosecution, for example, prior to PTO examination.[165] If there is a duty to make early disclosure, an applicant could, conceivably, breach the candor duty by failing to disclose information that the PTO examiner found during examination.[166]

---

[162] 37 C.F.R. § 1.97(b).

[163] 37 C.F.R. § 1.98(a). Copies of the cited items should be enclosed. If an item is in a language other than English, a translation should be provided if one is readily available to applicant. 37 C.F.R. § 1.98(b).

[164] 37 C.F.R. § 1.99.

[165] *Cf.* Andrew Corp. v. Gabriel Electronics, Inc., 847 F.2d 819, 823, 6 U.S.P.Q.2d 2010, 2014 (Fed. Cir. 1988), *cert. denied*, 488 U.S. 927 (1988) (a European patent application that was disclosed in a Rule 312 amendment (i.e., after the notice of allowance) was "reasonably timely disclosed and was not material to the prosecution of the . . . patent.").

[166] *E.g.*, A.B. Dick Co. v. Burroughs Corp., 798 F.2d 1392, 230 U.S.P.Q. 849 (Fed. Cir. 1986) (references not cited to an examiner were material when (1) claims in an application were allowed, (2) after a delay caused by an interference, the examiner rejected the claims after independently discovering those references, and (3) the claims were allowed after amendment).

Cf. Fox Industries, Inc. v. Structural Preservation Systems, Inc., 922 F.2d 801, 803-04, 17 U.S.P.Q.2d 1579, 1581 (Fed. Cir. 1990) (the patentee's argument that inequitable conduct "pertained only to rejected claims," which a patent attorney drafted and presented to the PTO without disclosing the inventor's prior art sales brochure used in drafting the specification, and not to the patent's claims, which were drafted by a second patent attorney who replaced the first, lacks merit; "The duty of candor extends throughout the patent's entire prosecution history. In determining inequitable conduct, a trial court may look beyond the final claims to their antecedents. . . . [A] breach of the duty of candor early in the prosecution may render unenforceable all claims which eventually issue from the same or a related application. [The first attorney] knew that the . . . brochure was material and withheld it from the PTO with intent to deceive.;" the attorney "had an obligation to disclose the brochure to the PTO notwithstanding the fact that none of the claims issued in the form in which he drafted them. A fortuitous rejection does not cure a breach of the duty of candor. Moreover, the brochure discloses the entirety of the structure set forth in most of the issued claims.").

Compare Scripps Clinic & Research Foundation v. Genentech, Inc., 927 F.2d 1565, 18 U.S.P.Q.2d 1001, 1018 (Fed. Cir. 1991) ("A reference that is material only to withdrawn claims can not be the basis of a holding of inequitable conduct.;" "When a reference has been considered by the examiner, it is not controlling how it came to the examiner's attention.;" "When a reference was before the examiner, whether through the examiner's search or the applicant's disclosure, it can not be deemed to have been withheld from the examiner."); Kimberly-Clark Corp. v. Johnson & Johnson, 745 F.2d 1437, 223 U.S.P.Q. 603 (Fed. Cir. 1984) (when an issued patent is attacked, inequitable conduct must be judged by reference to the claims of the patent, not to cancelled claims that had been rejected for reasons not involving the uncited prior art).

[e] **Persons Subject to Duty—Duty to Search—Imputed Knowledge.** The candor duty extends to the (1) inventor or inventors, (2) attorney or agent who prepares or prosecutes the application, and (3) any individual who is substantively involved in the application's preparation or prosecution and who is associated with the inventor, the assignee, or anyone to whom there is an obligation to assign the application.[167]

The candor duty extends to patent agents or attorneys in other countries who have primary responsibility for an application's prosecution and act through a corresponding United States attorney or agent.[168]

The candor duty generally extends only to information known by the inventor or his or her representative. There is no duty to search the prior art. In *Hennessy Industries Inc.,*[169] the court noted:

> "As a general rule, there is no duty to conduct a prior art search, and thus there is no duty to disclose art of which an applicant could have been aware. . . . However, one should not be able to cultivate ignorance, or disregard numerous warnings that material information or prior art may exist, merely to avoid actual knowledge of that information or prior art. When one does that, the 'should have known' factor becomes operative."[170]

It also noted "[o]ne attempting to prove inequitable conduct must prove by clear and convincing evidence that the conduct of the person *charged* was inequitable;" the fact that a party "alleges inequitable conduct against a great number of people does not diminish the burden of proof which it must meet as to each of them."[171]

[f] **Inequitable Conduct—Consequences.** In 1988, the PTO ended its practice of rejecting original or reissue patent applications because of inequitable conduct during prosecution, leaving to the courts the candor duty compliance determination task.[172]

Rohm & Haas[173] confirmed a patent applicant's ability to "cure" inequitable

---

[167] 37 C.F.R. § 1.56(a).

[168] Gemveto Jewelry Co., Inc. v. Lambert Bros., Inc., 542 F. Supp. 933, 216 U.S.P.Q. 976 (S.D. N.Y. 1982). In *Gemveto,* the court held that inequitable conduct occurred when an agent in another country withheld material information from the U.S. corresponding attorney and such information was never disclosed to the PTO examiner.

Compare In re Harita, 847 F.2d 801, 6 U.S.P.Q.2d 1930 (Fed. Cir. 1988).

[169] FMC Corp. v. Hennessy Industries Inc., 836 F.2d 521, 5 U.S.P.Q.2d 1272 (Fed. Cir. 1987).

[170] 836 F.2d at 526 n.6, 5 U.S.P.Q.2d at 1275 n.6.

[171] 836 F.2d at 525 n.5, 5 U.S.P.Q.2d at 1275 n.5

[172] In the pre-1988 period, it was the practice to reject a continuation or reissue application if inequitable conduct occurred in connection with an original or parent application. 37 C.F.R. § 1.56(d). *See* Digital Equip. Corp. v. Diamond, 653 F.2d 701, 210 U.S.P.Q. 521 (1st Cir. 1981). Also, inequitable conduct was a basis for awarding priority against a party to an interference (whether against an applicant or a patentee). Driscoll v. Cebalo, 731 F.2d 878, 221 U.S.P.Q. 745 (Fed. Cir. 1984); Langer v. Kaufman, 465 F.2d 915, 175 U.S.P.Q. 172 (CCPA 1972). The latter practice could be criticized on the ground that a first inventor's inequitable conduct, though justifying denial of patent protection to such an inventor, did not justify issuance of a patent to a later inventor.

[173] Rohm & Haas Co. v. Crystal Chem. Co., 722 F.2d 1556, 220 U.S.P.Q. 289 (Fed. Cir. 1983), *cert. denied,* 469 U.S. 851 (1984). *Compare* Hewlett-Packard Co. v. Bausch & Lomb

conduct discovered while an application is pending before the PTO. To effect a cure, the applicant must advise the PTO of the prior misrepresentation, disclose the facts, and establish the claimed subject matter's patentability.

Inequitable conduct renders all the patent's claims unenforceable, including claims dealing with subject matter not related to the misconduct.[174] In *Kingsdown,*[175] the Federal Circuit confirmed the "all claims" approach: "When a court has finally determined that inequitable conduct occurred in relation to one or more claims during prosecution of the patent application, the entire patent is rendered unenforceable."[176]

Inequitable conduct must be established by clear and convincing evidence.[177] The Federal Circuit adopts a "two step analysis" in determining whether inequitable conduct occurred in a patent's prosecution.[178] First, the court determines whether the misrepresentation or omission meets the materiality and intent thresholds. Second, the court balances the degrees of materiality and intent to determine whether there is inequitable conduct. The "ultimate question of whether inequitable conduct occurred is equitable in nature" and "committed to the discretion of the trial court" and "reviewed [on appeal] under an abuse of discretion standard."[179]

Inequitable conduct in procurement of one patent can render related patents unenforceable. In *Consolidated Aluminum,*[180] the Federal Circuit applied the

---

Inc., 882 F.2d 1556, 1563 n.7, 11 U.S.P.Q.2d 1750. 1756 n.7 (Fed. Cir. 1989) (dictum: "It is well settled that, in the . . . case of inequitable conduct during prosecution of the original application, reissue is not available to obtain new claims and thereby rehabilitate the patent.").

[174] J.P. Stevens & Co., Inc. v. Lex Tex, Ltd., 747 F.2d 1553, 223 U.S.P.Q. 1089 (Fed. Cir. 1984), *cert. denied,* 474 U.S. 822 (1985).

[175] Kingsdown Medical Consultants, Ltd. v. Hollister Inc., 863 F.2d 867, 9 U.S.P.Q.2d 1384 (Fed. Cir. 1988), *cert. denied,* 490 U.S. 1067 (1989), *order vacated,* 866 F.2d 1398, 9 U.S.P.Q.2d 1831 (1989).

[176] 863 F.2d at 877, 9 U.S.P.Q.2d at 1392. *See also* Hewlett-Packard Co. v. Bausch & Lomb Inc., 882 F.2d 1556, 11 U.S.P.Q.2d 1750 (Fed. Cir. 1989) (inequitable conduct committed during reissue proceedings renders the entire patent, including claims carried over from the original patent, unenforceable).

[177] *E.g.,* FMC Corp. v. Manitowoc Co., Inc., 835 F.2d 1411, 5 U.S.P.Q.2d 1112 (Fed. Cir. 1987).

[178] *E.g.,* Halliburton Co. v. Schlumberger Technology Corp., 925 F.2d 1435, 1439, 17 U.S.P.Q.2d 1834, 1838 (Fed. Cir. 1991) ("The doctrine of inequitable conduct requires a trial court to undertake a two-step analysis. The trial court must discern whether the withheld references satisfy a threshold level of materiality. The court must also determine whether the applicant's conduct satisfies a threshold showing of intent to mislead. Next, assuming satisfaction of the thresholds, the trial court must balance materiality and intent. . . . The more material the omission, the less culpable the intent required, and vice versa. . . . The trial court has discretion to determine inequitable conduct.").

[179] Kingsdown Medical Consultants, Ltd. v. Hollister Inc., 863 F.2d 867, 9 U.S.P.Q.2d 1384 (Fed. Cir. 1988), *cert. denied,* 109 S. Ct. 2068 (1989), *order vacated,* 866 F.2d 1398, 9 U.S.P.Q.2d 1831 (1989).

[180] Consolidated Aluminum Corp. v. Foseco International Ltd., 910 F.2d 804, 15 U.S.P.Q.2d 1481 (Fed. Cir. 1990).

Consolidated Aluminum involved three patents on the manufacture and use of ceramic foam filters for molten metal, particularly aluminum. The '917 patent, during the prosecution

Supreme Court's *Keystone Driller*[181] and *Precision Instrument*[182] "unclean hands" doctrine decisions. *Keystone Driller* held plaintiff's five patents, which covered "important, if not essential parts of the same machine," unenforceable because the plaintiff suppressed evidence of an invalidating public use to obtain relief on one patent in an earlier suit and used the result of that earlier suit to obtain relief in a subsequent suit to enforce that patent and the four other patents. *Precision Instrument* held plaintiff's three patents unenforceable because, during a PTO interference proceeding between an application it owned and an application owned by another, the plaintiff, after learning that the other party filed a false invention date statement, entered into a settlement agreement and obtained an assignment of the other party's application.

Inequitable conduct in connection with a patent's procurement may render an infringement suit "exceptional," justifying an award of attorney fees and expenses.[183]

If the inequitable conduct involves highly material information, is willfully committed, and results in the improper creation of a monopoly in a defined relevant market,

---

of which inequitable conduct occurred, named Pryor and Gray as inventors. It disclosed and claimed a method of filtering molten metal by pouring it through a ceramic foam filter. The filter's preparation involves, *inter alia*, impregnating an open cell flexible organic foam with an aqueous ceramic slurry. The assignee of the '971 patent, with the knowledge of the named inventors, did not disclose its preferred slurry, the CS1-B slurry, and, instead, disclosed a slurry that omitted certain critical ingredients. A different group of inventors, Yardwood, Dore and Preuss, developed the preferred CS1-B slurry. The assignee filed two applications, one leading to the '081 patent, and one leading to '363 patent. The preferred CS1-B slurry was disclosed in both applications. The '363 patent specifically claimed the preferred slurry. The '081 patent claimed a filter with specified air permeability and other properties. The '212 and '303 patents issued on applications that were continuations-in-part of the '081 application. In prosecuting the '081 patent application, the assignee overcame a rejection based on the '917 patent disclosure by arguing that key characteristics were obtained because of the manner of preparing the filter, which included details of the CS1-B slurry. The claims in the '212 and '303 patents contained a limitation derived from the CS1-B slurry. The Federal Circuit concluded: the patent owner's "concealment of the [best mode] CS1-B slurry from the '917 patent permeated the prosecution of the other patents-in-suit and renders them unenforceable." 910 F.2d at 812, 15 U.S.P.Q.2d at 1487.

[181] Keystone Driller Co. v. General Excavator Co., 290 U.S. 240, 245-46, 19 U.S.P.Q. 228, 230 (1933).

[182] Precision Instrument Mfg. Co. v. Automotive Maintenance Machinery Co., 324 U.S. 806, 815, 65 U.S.P.Q. 133, 138 (1945).

[183] *See* § 2655. *But cf.* Gardco Manufacturing, Inc. v. Herst Lighting Co., 820 F.2d 1209, 2 U.S.P.Q.2d 2015 (Fed. Cir. 1987) (the district court did not err in failing to award attorney fees to the accused infringer even though it found the patent unenforceable because of inequitable conduct: "[I]t has not been held that every case of proven inequitable conduct must result in an automatic attorney fee award, or that every instance of inequitable conduct mandates an evaluation of the case as 'exceptional'. After the district court determines that a case is exceptional, there remains in every case its freedom to exercise its discretion 'informed by the court's familiarity with the matter in litigation and the interest of justice.' ").

then a person injured by such misconduct may sue for damages under either the federal antitrust laws or state unfair competition laws.[184]

Inequitable conduct may lead to PTO disciplinary proceedings against a patent attorney or agent.[185]

[3] Application Contents—Disclosure and Claiming Requirements

A complete patent application has four parts: (1) a specification, including at least one claim; (2) drawings, if "necessary to the understanding of the subject matter sought to be patented;"[186] (3) an inventor's oath or declaration;[187] and (4) a

---

[184] Walker Process Equip., Inc. v. Food Mach. & Chem. Corp., 382 U.S. 172, 147 U.S.P.Q. 404 (1965); Hewlett-Packard Co. v. Bausch & Lomb Inc., 882 F.2d 1556, 1563, 11 U.S.P.Q.2d 1750, 1756 (Fed. Cir. 1989) ("When a party seeks to collect monetary damages from a patentee because of alleged violations of the antitrust laws, it is appropriate to require a higher degree of misconduct for that damage award than when a party asserts only a defense against an infringement claim."); FMC Corp. v. Manitowoc Co., Inc., 835 F.2d 1411, 1413 n.3, 1418 n.16, 5 U.S.P.Q.2d 1112, 1114 n.3, 1118 n.16 (Fed. Cir. 1987) (a *Walker Process* antitrust claim would require proof of fraud.;" "Mere procurement of a patent, whatever the conduct of the applicant in the procurement, cannot without more affect the welfare of the consumer and cannot in itself violate the antitrust laws."); Argus Chemical Corp. v. Fibre Glass-Evercoat Company, Inc., 812 F.2d 1381, 1 U.S.P.Q.2d 1971 (Fed. Cir. 1987); Litton Industrial Products, Inc. v. Solid State Systems Corp., 755 F.2d 158, 225 U.S.P.Q. 34 (Fed. Cir. 1985); American Hoist & Derrick Co. v. Sowa & Sons, Inc., 725 F.2d 1350, 220 U.S.P.Q. 763 (Fed. Cir. 1984), *cert. denied,* 469 U.S. 821, 224 U.S.P.Q. 520 (1984).

Willful inequitable conduct in procurement of a patent may also violate Section 5 of the Federal Trade Commission Act. 15 U.S.C. § 45(a)(1); American Cyanamid Co. v. F.T.C., 363 F.2d 757, 150 U.S.P.Q. 135 (6th Cir. 1966).

Even without inequitable conduct, filing, or threatened filing, of a patent infringement suit in bad faith and without a genuine belief in the possibility of success may be an antitrust violation. Handsgards, Inc. v. Ethicon, Inc., 743 F.2d 1282, 223 U.S.P.Q. 214 (9th Cir. 1984), *cert. denied,* 469 U.S. 1190 (1985).

[185] *E.g.,* Klein v. Peterson, 866 F.2d 412, 417, 9 U.S.P.Q.2d 1558, 1561 (Fed. Cir. 1989); Jaskiewicz v. Mossinghoff, 822 F.2d 1053, 3 U.S.P.Q.2d 1294 (Fed. Cir. 1987).

[186] 35 U.S.C. § 113; 37 C.F.R. § 1.81(a). If drawings are necessary, they must be submitted with the specification to establish a filing date. A drawing that illustrates the subject matter but is not necessary may be submitted after the filing date. A post-filing date drawing cannot overcome a enabling disclosure deficiency or be used to interpet the scope of any claim. 37 C.F.R. §§ 1.81(c), (d).

Mechanical and electrical inventions usually require drawings; chemical inventions usually do not because compounds and compositions can be described by accepted chemical nomenclature. PTO rules impose strict standards for drawings, 37 C.F.R. § 1.83-.84, which are usually prepared by a professional patent draftsman under the supervision of the patent attorney or agent of the inventor.

The drawings may be considered along with the specification in determining disclosure requirement compliance. *In re* Wolfensperger, 302 F.2d 950, 133 U.S.P.Q. 537 (CCPA 1962).

[187] The person or persons identified as the inventor or inventors in the application must execute an oath or declaration. 35 U.S.C. § 115. If the application is made by one other than the inventor, the oath or declaration is made by the applicant. 37 C.F.R. § 1.64.

An "oath" (or "affirmation") is a sworn statement made before a properly authorized officer. In the United States, such an officer may be a notary public authorized to administer oaths

filing fee.[188] To obtain a filing date,[189] the applicant must file the first two items with the PTO.[190] The last two items may be provided within a specified time period.[191]

The patent application must be in English or accompanied by a verified translation.[192]

under the laws of the various states. In another country, an oath may be made (1) before a United States diplomatic or consular officer, or (2) before any officer of the foreign country having an official seal and authorized to administer oaths, whose authority is certified by either a U.S. diplomatic or consular officer (or by "an apostille of the official designated by a foreign country which, by treaty or convention, accords like effect to apostilles of designated officials in the United States."). 37 C.F.R. § 1.66(a). With an oath taken in another country, the application papers must be suitably ribboned together. 37 C.F.R. § 1.66(b).

A "declaration" may be used in lieu of an oath if the declarant is warned in the declaration that any willful false statements are punishable by criminal prosecution and may jeopardize the validity of the application or patent. 35 U.S.C. § 25; 37 C.F.R. § 1.68.

In the oath or declaration, the inventor must state that he or she (1) has reviewed and understands the specification and claims; (2) believes that he or she is the original and first inventor of the claimed subject matter; and (3) acknowledges the duty to disclose information that is material to the examination of the application. The oath or declaration must state the applicant's citizenship. If the application makes a claim to priority based on an application previously filed in another country, the oath or declaration must also "identify the foreign application for patent or inventor's certificate on which priority is claimed, and any foreign application having a filing date before that of the application on which priority is claimed, by specifying the application number, country, day, month and year of its filing." 37 C.F.R. § 1.63(c).

If the claims are amended so as to cover subject matter originally described but not substantially embraced in the original claims or statement of invention, a supplemental oath or declaration may be required. 37 C.F.R. § 1.67. No supplemental oath or declaration is required if the amended claims merely clarify the invention for which a patent is sought. American Safety Table Co. v. Schreiber, 269 F.2d 255, 122 U.S.P.Q. 29, (2d Cir. 1959), cert. denied, 361 U.S. 915 (1959).

"New matter," disclosures not present in the description and claims of the specification or in the drawings, may not be added by amendment even if a supplemental oath or declaration is submitted. Steward v. American Lava Co., 215 U.S. 161 (1909).

[188] 35 U.S.C. § 111.

[189] An early filing date is important to avoid the possible statutory bars under 35 U.S.C. § 102(b) (see § 2C[5][b][ii]) and to take advantage of the right of priority based on an application previously filed in another country (see § 2H[2]). The first person to file is also the presumptive first inventor in an invention priority interference. See § 2D[5][a]. As to obtaining a U.S. filing date under the Patent Cooperation Treaty, see § 2H[3].

[190] 35 U.S.C. § 111; 37 C.F.R. § 1.53(b), (d).

[191] 37 C.F.R. § 1.53(d). Another fee is due if the last two items are submitted separately.

[192] 37 C.F.R. § 1.52(a). An application filing date may be obtained by submitting an application in a non-English language with the translation provided within a specified time period. 37 C.F.R. § 1.52(d).

The oath or declaration must be in a language the individual understands. 37 C.F.R. § 1.69(a).

Models, exhibits and specimens need not and generally should not be submitted with an application.[193]

Inventions involving microorganisms may require a culture deposit to comply with the enablement requirement.[194] The deposit is not with the PTO.

Listings or print-outs of computer programs necessary to carry out a claimed invention may appear in the specification's descriptive portion or as a drawing.[195] Lengthy listings may be submitted as a microfiche appendix that will be available to the public but will not be a part of the printed patent.[196]

The specification has two parts: (1) a portion describing the invention, and (2) the claims, which precisely define the scope of the exclusive rights a patent will confer.[197] The descriptive portion must comply with the disclosure requirements;[198] the claims must comply with the clarity requirements.[199]

The Patent Act imposes no rigid rules on specification format, but PTO rules prescribe a certain arrangement of subparts[200] and provide that the specification should "describe completely a specific embodiment of the process, machine, manufacture, composition of matter or improvement" and should "explain the mode of operation or principle whenever applicable."[201]

[a] **Enablement Requirement.** The specification and drawings must provide sufficient information about the invention so as "to enable any person skilled in the art to which it pertains, or with which it is most nearly connected, to make and use the same."[202]

---

[193] 37 C.F.R. § 1.91. *See In re* Breslow, 616 F.2d 516, 205 U.S.P.Q. 221 (CCPA 1980). The PTO may, rarely, require the applicant to furnish a specimen, etc. for inspection or experiment. 35 U.S.C. § 114; 37 C.F.R. § 1.92-.93.

[194] *See* § 2D[3][a][vi].

[195] 37 C.F.R. § 1.96.

[196] 37 C.F.R. § 1.96(b).

[197] 35 U.S.C. § 112.

[198] *See* §§ 2D[3][a], [b], and [c].

[199] *See* § 2D[3][d].

[200] 37 C.F.R. § 1.77. The prescribed elements are:

   (1) a title of the invention;

   (2) a cross-reference to any related applications;

   (3) a reference to any microfiche appendix (i.e. a lengthy computer program listing);

   (4) a brief summary of the invention;

   (5) a brief description of the drawings;

   (6) a detailed description making reference to the drawings by number;

   (7) the claims;

   (8) an abstract of the disclosure;

   (9) a signed oath or declaration; and

   (10) drawings.

[201] 37 C.F.R. § 1.71(b). The courts have held that the "specific embodiment" rule imposes no greater specificity requirement than is required by the Section 112 enablement and the best mode requirements, which are discussed at §§ 2D[3][a] and [c]. *In re* Gay, 309 F.2d 769, 135 U.S.P.Q. 311 (CCPA 1962).

[202] 35 U.S.C. § 112. *See generally* D. Chisum, Patents § 7.03.

[i] *Claim Scope—Undue Breadth—Unpredictable Technologies.* The patent claims define the "invention" for enablement purposes.

The amount of supporting disclosure depends on the patent claim's breadth [203] and the degree of predictability in the pertinent art (technological area). The broader the claim and the less predictable the art, the narrower must be the claim. For example, in *Fisher*,[204] the applicant discovered and disclosed a method of making a certain hormone with a potency ranging from 111 to 230 percent of a recognized standard. Prior art methods produced only about 50 percent of the standard. Though the applicant had a patentable invention, a claim to all such hormones with a potency in excess of 100 percent, which would cover hormones with a potency in excess of 230 percent, was rejected because the disclosures did not justify the claim's breadth given the unpredictability in the particular chemical art.

Fisher recognizes that disclosure of one or a limited number of embodiments is more likely to provide sufficient enabling support for a broader, more generic claim in "predictable" arts, such as mechanics or electronics, than "unpredictable" arts, such as chemistry or biotechnology.[205]

---

[203] *In re* Hyatt, 708 F.2d 712, 714, 218 U.S.P.Q. 195, 197 (Fed. Cir. 1983). In *Hyatt*, the court stated "the enabling disclosure of the specification [must] be commensurate in scope with the claim under consideration."

An amendment that *narrows* a claim's scope by adding a specific limitation may fail to find adequate support in the specification and thus violate either the enablement requirement or the description requirement. Therefore, under some circumstances, a broader claim may be supported while a narrower claim is not. *Cf.* DeGeorge v. Bernier, 768 F.2d 1318, 226 U.S.P.Q. 758 (Fed. Cir. 1985). In *DeGeorge*, the court construed a claim to electrical circuitry in a word processor as not including word processing features such as a printer and a data recording mechanism. Consequently, the specification was sufficiently enabling even though it made insufficient disclosure of such features.

[204] *In re* Fisher, 427 F.2d 833, 166 U.S.P.Q. 18 (CCPA 1970).

[205] For cases on enablement of biotechnology inventions, see Scripps Clinic & Research Foundation v. Genentech, Inc., 927 F.2d 1565, 18 U.S.P.Q.2d 1001 (Fed. Cir. 1991); Amgen, Inc. v. Chugai Pharmaceutical Co., Ltd., 927 F.2d 1200, 18 U.S.P.Q.2d 1016 (Fed. Cir. 1991), discussed below; Hormone Research Foundation, Inc. v. Genentech, Inc., 904 F.2d 1558, 15 U.S.P.Q.2d 1039 (Fed. Cir. 1990), *cert. dismissed*, 111 S.Ct. 1434 (1991); *In re* Wands, 858 F.2d 731, 8 U.S.P.Q.2d 1400 (Fed. Cir. 1988), discussed below; Ex parte Sizto, 9 U.S.P.Q.2d 2081, 2083 (PTO Bd. Pat. App. & Int'f 1988); *Ex parte* Hitzeman, 9 U.S.P.Q.2d 1821, 1823 (PTO Bd. Pat. App. & Int'f 1988).

In *Sizto*, the Board held not enabled a claim to an improved immunoassay method with a calibration surface employing a receptor that is capable of specific binding to a conjugate of a *catalyst* with a member of an immunological pair ("mip") but is incapable of binding to the catalyst or the mip apart from the conjugate. The specification disclosing a single example in which the *catalyst is an enzyme* is not enabling as to *catalysts generally* even though it incorporates by reference a patent disclosing a "wide variety" of non-enzymatic catalysts. The Board noted:

"[W]here the enzyme and non-enzyme catalysts are so divergent [and where the nature of the catalyst is critical to the claimed method because the claim is specific to cata-lyst-mip conjugates], it is not unreasonable to require a reasonable number of examples in support of the broad claim. While we agree with appellants' citation of the general rule to the effect that there need only be an enumeration of a sufficient number of members

Fisher does not establish a *per se* prohibition on broad claims in unpredictable technologies. In *Telectronics,*[206] the patent claimed a bone fractures healing stimulation system, which involved applying a constant current of "a selected value within a predetermined microampere range" so as to promote bone formation and avoid fibrous tissue formation. The patent specification disclosed how to practice the invention when stainless steel electrodes and a current range of 5-20 microamperes are used, but the claims were not limited to the specific metal/current combination. Nevertheless, the Federal Circuit upheld the patent specification as enabling. The time and cost of a dose response study that would be required to determine the appropriate current with other materials "may be taken into account," but did not, under the circumstances of the case, show that the experimentation necessary to practice the invention is excessive: "Since one embodiment is . . . disclosed in the specification, along with the general manner in which its current range was ascertained, . . . other permutations of the invention could be practiced by those skilled in the art without undue experimentation." The infringer argued that "the scope of the protection must bear a reasonable relationship to the scope of enablement," relying on *Fisher*[207] and *Bowen.*[208] The court disagreed, distinguishing those two cases.

> "*Fisher* and *Bowen* both involved chemical reactions, recognized by our predecessor court as having a high degree of unpredictability and therefore requiring an increased enablement disclosure. Yet in *Bowen* the board's non-enablement rejection was reversed where 'claims literally comprehend numerous polymers in addition to the one specifically described in appellant's specification' because no persuasive reason was given by the Patent Office why the specification does not realistically enable one skilled in the art to practice the invention as broadly as it is claimed."[209]

> of a diverse group, we also are persuaded that where, as here, there is unpredictability as to the characteristics of conjugates prepared from, e.g., metal complexes and electron transfer agents as compared to enzymes, the scope of enablement must be commensurate with the scope of the claims." 9 U.S.P.Q.2d at 2083.

In *Hitzeman,* the Board held that claims involving preparation of vectors or yeast transformations generally are not enabled by a specification that discloses the making of a vector replicable in *Saccharomyces cerivisae* because, *inter alia,* "the broad term 'yeast' used in the appealed claims includes a number of diverse fungi which are quite different, morphologically and biochemically, from *Saccharomyces cerivisae*":

> "[A] single embodiment may provide broad enablement in cases involving predictable factors, such as mechanical or electrical elements. In cases involving unpredictable factors, such as most chemical reactions and physiological activity, more is required. . . . Here, appellant's specification fails to provide those having ordinary skill in the art reasonable assurance, *as by* adequate representative examples, that vectors and yeast transformants falling within the scope of the appealed claims can be prepared and used." 9 U.S.P.Q.2d at 1823.

[206] United States v. Telectronics, Inc., 857 F.2d 778, 8 U.S.P.Q.2d 1217 (Fed Cir. 1988), *cert. denied,* 490 U.S. 1046 (1989).

[207] *In re* Fisher, 427 F.2d 833, 166 U.S.P.Q. 18 (CCPA 1970), discussed above.

[208] *In re* Bowen, 492 F.2d 859, 181 U.S.P.Q. 48 (CCPA 1974).

[209] 857 F.2d at 786, 8 U.S.P.Q.2d at 1224.

The only impediments to determining the appropriate current parameters for other electrode materials are the time and cost of dose response studies, which the district court found could be performed by persons skilled in the art. The infringer's device using different materials actually operated within the current parameters disclosed in the specification.

There is no rigid requirement as to the number of examples that must be provided in order to support a broad claim.[210] Evidence of tests conducted after the application filing may be submitted to verify the enabling quality of specification statements.[211]

A claim may be too broad if it covers a significant number of inoperative embodiments and one of ordinary skill in the art would have to experiment unreasonably to determine the operative embodiments. For example, a claim to a broad class of chemical compounds is improper if the applicant demonstrates only that a small number of the compounds within the class are operative for a stated utility and fails to provide assurance that substantially all of the compounds are useful.[212] On the other hand, a claim is not improper if one of ordinary skill in the art would be able to readily determine which embodiments are operable.[213]

In *Amgen*,[214] the Federal Circuit held that the district court properly held invalid for want of enablement the patentee's generic claims to all possible genetic sequences that have activity resembling that of the specific DNA sequence encoding for a protein the patentee discovered. The patent related to human erythropoietin (EPO), a 165 amino acid protein that stimulates red blood cell production. The inventor used a novel technique, screening a human genomic library with two fully-degenerate sets of probes, to isolate the EPO gene. It transformed mammalian host cells with the gene, enabling those cells to produce erythropoietin for harvesting and purification.

The patent contained both DNA isolate claims (*e.g.*, "purified and isolated DNA sequence consisting essentially of a DNA sequence encoding human erythropoietin") and transformed host cell claims (*e.g.* "procaryotic or eucaryotic host cell transformed or transfected with" the EPO DNA sequence). The court upheld these claims. The patent also contained generic claims "covering all possible DNA sequences that will encode any polypeptide having an amino acid sequence 'sufficiently duplicative' of EPO to possess the property of increasing production of red blood cells."[215] The

---

[210] *In re* Borkowski, 422 F.2d 904, 164 U.S.P.Q. 642 (CCPA 1970).

[211] *See In re* Marzocchi, 439 F.2d 220, 169 U.S.P.Q. 367 (CCPA 1971).

[212] *In re* Cavalitto, 282 F.2d 357, 127 U.S.P.Q. 202 (CCPA 1960).

[213] Atlas Powder Co. v. E.I. du Pont De Nemours & Co., 750 F.2d 1569, 224 U.S.P.Q. 409 (Fed. Cir. 1984). In *Atlas Powder,* the court held that a claim to a composition consisting of a combination of three elements was sufficiently supported even though the specification did not give specific amounts as to each element. A person of ordinary skill in the art would be able to select appropriate amounts to suit a particular situation.

[214] Amgen, Inc. v. Chugai Pharmaceutical Co., Ltd., 927 F.2d 1200, 18 U.S.P.Q.2d 1016 (Fed. Cir. 1991).

[215] Claim 7 is for "A purified and isolated DNA sequence consisting essentially of a DNA sequence encoding a polypeptide having an amino acid sequence sufficiently duplicative of that of erythropoietin to allow possession of the biological property of causing bone marrow cells

court noted that "[T]he number of claimed DNA encoding sequences that can produce an EPO-like product is potentially enormous:" "[O]ver 3,600 different EPO analogs can be made by substituting at only a single amino acid position, and over a million different analogs can be made by substituting three amino acids." The patentee's head EPO analog program person testified "he did not know whether the fifty to eighty EPO analogs [the patentee] had made 'had the biological property of causing bone marrow cells to increase production of reticulocytes and red blood cells, and to increase hemoglobin synthesis or iron uptake." In finding insufficient disclosure support for claim 7, the district court "relied in particular on the lack of predictability in the art . . . After five years of experimentation . . . '[the patentee] is still unable to specify which analogs have the biological properties set forth in claim 7.' "

"The essential question . . . is whether the scope of enablement of claim 7 is as broad as the scope of the claim. That some experimentation is necessary does not constitute a lack of enablement; the amount of experimentation, however, must not be unduly extensive.

". . . [T]he trial court arrived at the correct decision . . . for the wrong reason. By focusing on the biological properties of the EPO analogs, it failed to consider the enablement of the DNA sequence analogs, which are the subject of claim 7. . . . [I]t is not necessary that a patent applicant test all the embodiments of his invention . . . ; what is necessary is that he provide a disclosure sufficient to enable one skilled in the art to carry out the invention commensurate with the scope of his claims. For DNA sequences, that means disclosing how to make and use enough sequences to justify grant of the claims sought. [The patentee] has not done that here.

". . . [A] patent applicant is entitled to claim his invention generically, when he describes it sufficiently to meet the requirements of Section 112. . . . [D]espite extensive statements in the specification concerning all the analogs of the EPO gene that can be made, there is little enabling disclosure of particular analogs and how to make them. Details for preparing only a few EPO analog genes are disclosed. . . . This 'disclosure' might well justify a generic claim encompassing these and similar analogs, but it represents inadequate support for [the patentee's] desire to claim all EPO gene analogs.

. . .

"Considering the structural complexity of the EPO gene, the manifold possibilities for change in its structure, with attendant uncertainty as to what utility

---

to increase production of reticulocytes and red blood cells, and to increase hemoglobin synthesis or iron uptake."

The patent specification states "one may readily design and manufacture genes" differing from that for mature EPO "in terms of the identity or location of one or more residues":

"[T]he present invention . . . comprehend[s] all DNA sequences suitable for use in securing expression in a . . . host cell of a polypeptide . . . having at least a part of the primary structural conformation and one or more of the biological properties of erythropoietin, and selected from among: (a) the DNA sequences set out in FIGS. 5 and 6; (b) DNA sequences which hybridize to the DNA sequences defined in (a) or fragments thereof; and (c) DNA sequences which, but for the degeneracy of the genetic code, would hybridize to the DNA sequences defined in (a) and (b)." 927 F.2d at 1212-13, 18 U.S.P.Q.2d at 1026.

will be possessed by these analogs, . . . more is needed concerning identifying the various analogs that are within the scope of the claim, methods for making them, and structural requirements for producing compounds with EPO-like activity. It is not sufficient, having made the gene and handful of analogs whose activity has not been clearly ascertained, to claim all possible genetic sequences that have EPO-like activity."[216]

A claim so broad that it covers products or processes in the prior art is improper because of the novelty and nonobviousness requirements regardless of the disclosure's adequacy.[217]

[ii] *Person Skilled in the Art—Experimentation.* The specification and drawings must be enabling to a person of ordinary skill in the pertinent art but need not disclose what is well known in the art.[218] They must enable the *claimed* invention but need not be detailed "production documents."[219]

A specification disclosure that requires a person of ordinary skill in the art to make adjustments or experiment to make and use the claimed invention is enabling if the amount and kind of experimentation required is reasonable.[220] It is not enabling if

---

[216] 927 F.2d at 1213-14, 18 U.S.P.Q.2d at 1026.

[217] *See* §§ 2C[3] and [4].

[218] Lindemann Maschinenfabrik GMBH v. American Hoist & Derrick Co., 730 F.2d 1452, 221 U.S.P.Q.2d 481 (Fed. Cir. 1984), *appeal after remand,* 895 F.2d 1403, 13 U.S.P.Q.2d. 1871 (1990).
The applicant or patentee may cite publications, patents and other well-known items of prior art to show the patent specification's enabling quality. Items not well-known or readily accessible may not be relied upon to show enablement even when those same items are prior art for patentability. *In re* Howarth, 654 F.2d 103, 210 U.S.P.Q. 689 (CCPA 1981); *In re* Glass, 492 F.2d 1228, 190 U.S.P.Q. 422 (CCPA 1976). In *Howarth,* the court held that patent applications filed in several countries and laid open for public inspection should not be considered in determining enablement. In *Glass,* the court held that the disclosures of a United States patent cannot be relied upon as of its filing date in determining enablement because it is prior art as of its filing date but is not actually available to the public until its issue date. *See* § 2C[5][d].

[219] *E.g.,* Christianson v. Colt Industries Operating Corp., 822 F.2d 1544, 1562, 3 U.S.P.Q.2d 1241, 1254 (Fed. Cir. 1987), *vacated, and remanded with instructions to transfer appeal to Court of Appeals for the Seventh Circuit,* 486 U.S. 800, 7 U.S.P.Q. 1109 (1988), *on remand,* 870 F.2d 1292, 10 U.S.P.Q.2d 1352 (7th Cir. 1989) ("nothing in the patent law requires that a patentee must disclose data on how to mass-produce the invented product, in patents obtained on either individual parts of the product or on the entire product. . . . [T]he law has never required that a patentee who elects to manufacture its claimed invention must disclose in its patent the dimensions, tolerances, drawings, and other parameters of mass production not necessary to enable one skilled in the art to practice (as distinguished from mass-produce) the invention. Nor is it an objective of the patent system to supply, free of charge, production data and production drawings to competing manufacturers.").

[220] *E.g.,* Cross v. Iizuka, 753 F.2d 1040, 224 U.S.P.Q. 739 (Fed. Cir. 1985) (the enablement requirement's how-to-use aspect was met even though the specification did not disclose dosage levels for the claimed compounds because (1) the disclosed utility was pharmacological activity in an *in vitro* environment, rather than a therapeutic use, and (2) one skilled in the art could determine the dosage level without undue experimentation).

unreasonable experimentation is required.[221] For example, a specification is not enabling as to a claimed computer-directed machining process if it does not disclose a listing of a necessary computer program and it would take several man-years to write such a program.[222] How much experimentation is reasonable depends on the circumstances, including prevailing practices in the technological area. For example, in *Wands*,[223] the applicants claimed a hepatitis B surface antigen (HBsAg) immunoassay method by using high-affinity IgM antibodies ("binding affinity constant for . . . HBsAg determinants of at least 10^9 M $-$ [1].") The prior art discouraged use of IgM antibodies and favored IgG antibodies because of the former's sensitivity to reducing agents and tendency to self-aggregate and precipitate. Applicants found that IgM antibodies with a high affinity for HBsAg showed unexpectedly high sensitivity and specificity and deposited a specific hybridoma cell line that secretes IgM antibodies against HBsAg (the "1F8" cell line) in a recognized public

---

[221] *In re* Gardner, 427 F.2d 786, 166 U.S.P.Q. 138 (CCPA 1970). *Compare In re* Bundy, 642 F.2d 430, 209 U.S.P.Q. 48 (CCPA 1981).

[222] White Consolidated Indus., Inc. v. Vega Servo-Control, Inc., 713 F.2d 788, 218 U.S.P.Q. 961 (Fed. Cir. 1983). *See also* Allen Organ Co. v. Kimball International, Inc., 839 F.2d 1556, 5 U.S.P.Q.2d 1769 (Fed. Cir. 1988), *cert. denied*, 488 U.S. 850 (1988) (there was substantial evidence supporting the jury's verdict that the patent on a system for a digital electronic organ was invalid for want of enablement in view of testimony by the infringer's witnesses that they could not build a circuit from the details of the recognition logic block in a figure of the patent specification).

Compare Northern Telecom, Inc. v. Datapoint Corp., 908 F.2d 931, 15 U.S.P.Q.2d 1321 (Fed. Cir. 1990), *cert. denied*, 111 S. Ct. 296 (1990). In *Northern Telecom*, the Federal Circuit held that the district court erred in holding certain claims of the patent in suit invalid for lack of enablement. The patent specification failed to set forth a computer program for carrying out the claimed invention, but the great weight of the evidence indicated that "a programmer of reasonable skill could write a satisfactory program with ordinary effort."

> "When the challenged subject matter is a computer program that implements a claimed device or method, enablement is determined from the viewpoint of a skilled programmer using the knowledge and skill with which such a person is charged. The amount of disclosure that will enable practice of an invention that utilizes a computer program may vary according to the nature of the invention, the role of the program in carrying it out, and the complexity of the contemplated programming, all from the viewpoint of the skilled programmer. . . .

> "The claimed invention of the . . . patent [in suit] is not in the details of the program writing, but in the apparatus and method whose patentability is based on the claimed combination of components or steps. . . . The possible design of superior software, or whether each programmer would work out the details in the identical way, is not relevant in determining whether the inventor has complied with the enablement requirement. . . .

> ". . . Although there have been circumstances wherein production of the computer program was not routine, as in White Consol. Indus., Inc. v. Vega Servo-Control, Inc. . . . where the production of the program required one and one half to two person-years of work, such circumstances were not shown or suggested for the . . . invention [claimed in the patent]." 908 F.2d at 941, 15 U.S.P.Q.2d at 1329, 1330.

[223] *In re* Wands, 858 F.2d 731, 8 U.S.P.Q.2d 1400 (Fed. Cir. 1988). *Compare In re* Hata, 6 U.S.P.Q.2d 1652 (Bd. Pat. App. & Int'f 1987).

depository for the stated purpose of complying with the best mode requirement of 35 U.S.C. Section 112. Applicants presented claims to the specified hybridomas and to a generic class of antibodies and methods exhibiting the desired high affinity characteristic.[224] The PTO rejected the generic claims. The Federal Circuit reversed. The evidence indicated that those skilled in the monoclonal antibody art could, given the state of the art and applicants' written disclosures, produce and screen new hybridomas secreting other monoclonal antibodies falling within the generic class without undue experimentation.[225] Therefore, the applicants' claims did not have to be limited to the specific antibody secreted by the deposited hybridoma cell line.

---

[224] The broadest method claims provided:

"1. An immunoassay method utilizing an antibody to assay for a substance comprising hepatitis B-surface antigen (HBsAg) determinants which comprises the steps of:

contacting a test sample containing said substance comprising HBsAg determinants with said antibody; and

determining the presence of said substance in said sample;

wherein said antibody is a monoclonal high affinity IgM antibody having a binding affinity constant for said HBsAg determinants of at least 10^9 M $-$ 1." 858 F.2d at 734, 8 U.S.P.Q.2d at 1402.

Among the composition of matter claims were the following:

"19. Monoclonal high affinity IgM antibodies immunoreactive with HBsAg determinants, wherein said antibodies are coupled to an insoluble solid phase, and wherein the binding affinity constant of said antibodies for said HBsAg determinants is at least 10^9 M^{-1}.

"26. Monoclonal high affinity IgM antibodies immunoreactive with hepatitis B surface antigen." 858 F.2d at 741, 8 U.S.P.Q.2d at 1407.

[225] The court described the procedure for making specific antibodies as follows:

"The first step for making monoclonal antibodies is to immunize an animal [, such as a mouse, against a specific antigen, such as hepatitis B surface antigen]. . . . Next, the spleen, an organ rich in lymphocytes [, which are blood cells that, when exposed to a particular antigen, produce clones that secrete a particular antibody to the antigen, but that cannot survive for long outside of the body in cell culture,] is removed and lymphocytes are separated from the other spleen cells. The lymphocytes are mixed with myeloma cells [, which are cancerous cells that divide indefinitely in vitro,] and the mixture is treated to cause a few of the cells to fuse with each other [to form hybridomas, hybrid cells that contain genetic material from both the lymphocyte and the myeloma, that secrete the same antibody as the lymphocyte but acquire the ability of the myeloma to divide and grow.] Hybridoma cells that secrete the desired antibodies then must be isolated from the enormous number of other cells in the mixture. This is done through a series of screening procedures.

"The first [screening] step is to separate the hybridoma cells from unfused lymphocytes and myeloma cells. The cells are cultured in a medium in which all the lymphocytes and myeloma cells die, and only the hybridoma cells survive. The next step is to isolate and clone hybridomas that make antibodies that bind to the antigen of interest. Single hybridoma cells are placed in separate chambers and are allowed to grow and divide. After there are enough cells in the clone to produce sufficient quantities of antibody to analyze, the antibody is assayed to determine whether it binds to the antigen. . . . [B]y screening enough clones (often hundreds at a time), hybridomas may be found that secrete antibodies against the antigen of interest." 858 F.2d at 737-738, 8 U.S.P.Q.2d at 1404-1405.

In *Amgen*,[226] the Federal Circuit held that the district court erred by not invalidating for want of enablement a patentee's claim to a homogeneous protein of a minimum specific activity level. The evidence indicated that the patentee's disclosed purification process did not produce a protein with the claimed activity level.[227]

In *Wands,* the PTO relied on data supplied by the applicants on the hybridoma fusion and screening experiments that led to the making of the antibodies within the claims. The first four fusions were unsuccessful, failing to produce appropriate hybridomas. (The applicants attributed these failures to their lack of knowledge on cell fusion techniques.) The next six fusions produced hybridomas secreting antibodies specific for HBsAg, 143 of which were high binding antibodies that were likely to have the high affinity specified by the claims. The applicants selected nine hybridomas from two fusions for further screening, the remainder of the 143 hybridomas being saved by freezing. Of the nine selected hybridomas, four fell within the claim in question, three were IgG rather than IgM and two were not measured for affinity. The PTO contended that the failure to analyze the 134 other hybridomas established want of enablement because only 2.8% of the hybridomas were proven to fall within the claim and because the established antibodies came from only 2 of 10 fusions. The court discounted these contentions and credited the applicants' contentions that four of the nine hybridomas selected for screening fell within the claims, a respectable 44%, and that the remaining 134 unanalyzed, stored cell lines should not be written off as failures, especially because many of them showed high binding, an indication of probable high affinity. The court said:

> "The nature of monoclonal antibody technology is that it involves screening hybridomas to determine which ones secrete antibody with desired characteristics. Practitioners of this art are prepared to screen negative hybridomas in order to find one that makes the desired antibody. No evidence was presented by either party on how many hybridomas would be viewed by those in the art as requiring undue experimentation to screen. However, it seems unlikely that undue experimentation would be defined in terms of the number of hybridomas that were never screened. Furthermore, in the monoclonal antibody art it appears that an experiment' is not simply the screening of a single hybridoma, but is rather the entire attempt to make a monoclonal antibody against a particular antigen." 858 F.2d at 740, 8 U.S.P.Q.2d at 1407.

[226] Amgen, Inc. v. Chugai Pharmaceutical Co., Ltd., 927 F.2d 1200, 18 U.S.P.Q.2d 1016 (Fed. Cir. 1991).

[227] Erythropoietin (EPO) is a 165 amino acid protein that stimulates red blood cell production. Genetic Institute's patent disclosed a method of purifying human EPO using reverse phase high performance liquid chromatography (RP-HPLC) and claimed both the method and purified EPO of defined characteristics, including "a specific activity of at least 160,000 IU per absorbance unit at 280 nanometers." The claims' specific activity measurement is "expressed as a ratio of International Units (which measure the ability of EPO to cause formation of red blood cells) per absorbance unit (the amount of light absorbed by a sample of EPO measured by a spectrophotometer at a given wavelength), 280 nanometers, *i.e.,* IU/AU." The district court found that "in the absence of an express statement in the patent, the claims would be construed to refer to *in vivo* rather than *in vitro* specific activity."

The patentee "produced no evidence that it ever prepared EPO with a specific activity of at least 160,000 IU/AU *in vivo* using the disclosed methods." Rather, the inventor obtained the 160,000 figure by calculation. He subjected EPO to RP-HPLC, obtained a value of 83,000, and determined by chromatography that at least 50% of matter was something other than EPO. In a report to the Food and Drug Administration (FDA), the patentee stated it used RP-HPLC to purify EPO from natural urine sources (uEPO) and achieved a specific activity

[iii]   *Time Frame.* The specification and drawings must be enabling as of the application filing date. Prior art that becomes available after that date cannot be considered in determining sufficiency of disclosure.[228]

Post-filing date developments that enable previously unknown variations cannot be relied upon to establish nonenablement.[229] In *United States Steel*,[230] the Federal Circuit held that a specification, filed in 1953, which disclosed a crude "novel tacky and solid" polymer produced by a chromium oxide catalyst that was in fact crystalline polypropylene adequately supported a patent claim to crystalline polypropylene ("Normally solid polypropylene, consisting essentially of recurring propylene units, having a substantial crystalline polypropylene content") even though the disclosed polymer was of such low molecular weight and intrinsic viscosity as to be

---

of 109,000, based on *in vivo* bioassays. Other scientists used the inventor's purification method and obtained about 101,000 IU/AU.

The district court erred in relying on certain *in vitro* data as support for claims containing what was found to be an *in vivo* limitation. Also, the *in vitro* test on uEPO showed 173,640, and the accused infringer argued that the *in vivo* equivalent would be only 65%, less than 160,000.

The patent gave an example of purification of EPO purified from recombinant sources (rEPO), that is, by isolating the gene encoding the protein, inserting it into a host cell, replicating the cell, causing the cell to excrete the protein into a culture medium, and harvesting the protein. The rEPO example indicated that the inventor did not obtain purified rEPO. "Thus, the patent fails to enable purification of either rEPO or uEPO."

The Federal Circuit cautioned: "We do not hold that one must always prove that a disclosed process operates effectively to produce a claimed product."

[228] *In re* Glass, 492 F.2d 1228, 181 U.S.P.Q. 31 (CCPA 1974). In *Glass,* the court held that an applicant could not rely on four patents issuing after the filing date to show conditions necessary to produce claimed product.

[229] *In re* Hogan, 559 F.2d 595, 194 U.S.P.Q. 527 (CCPA 1977).

[230] United States Steel Corp. v. Phillips Petroleum Co., 865 F.2d 1247, 9 U.S.P.Q.2d 1461 (Fed. Cir. 1989).

See also Hormone Research Foundation, Inc. v. Genentech, Inc., 904 F.2d 1558, 1567-68, 15 U.S.P.Q.2d 1039, 1047 (Fed. Cir. 1990), *cert. dismissed,* 111 S.Ct. 1434 (1991). In *Hormone Research Foundation,* the district court granted summary judgment invalidating patent claims for lack of enabling disclosure. The patent contains product and process claims to a 190 amino acid sequence protein, similar but not identical to natural human growth hormone (HGH). The district court reasoned, *inter alia,* that "the solid phase peptide synthesis process disclosed in the [patent's] specification would not have been sufficient to produce materials as lengthy as the claimed . . . sequence or in a pure form and having the potency of natural HGH." The Federal Circuit reversed because the district court did not consider the *Hogan-United States Steel* principle: "Although . . . [the accused infringer] produced considerable evidence tending to show that the disclosed sequencing method could not have yielded . . . sequences as lengthy as that of [the specification's] Figure 2 (190 amino acids), other evidence . . . raises a genuine issue about this material fact.": "Merely because purer and more potent forms of the [disclosed] compound might be produced using later-discovered technology does not necessarily mean that the . . . specification did not provide sufficient enabling disclosures as of the filing date of the application. . . . It is unclear whether the high degree of potency and purity contemplated by the district court's analysis of enablement was influenced by the potency and purity obtainable through recombinant DNA methodology. . . . [I]t is unclear from the record before us whether that technology existed at the time the application was filed."

of little commercial value. The 1954 development of "Ziegler catalysts," which made high molecular weight and intrinsic viscosity polypropylene possible, did not make the 1953 specification nonenabling as of its filing date. "[I]n determining sufficiency of support it is the state of the art in 1953 and level of skill in the art at that time that is critical." The court noted that " 'overbreadth' . . . has . . . been discredited as a basis for determining sufficiency of a specification."

> "[A]dequacy of support is judged in relation to the scope of the claims . . . but . . . 'application sufficiency under § 112, first paragraph, must be judged as of the filing date.' "

> ". . . [S]upport need be found for only the claimed invention, in view of how one skilled in the art at [the time the application was filed] would construe the claims and would read its specification."[231]

[iv] *Incorporation by Reference.* A specification may incorporate by reference other sources such as issued patents, pending patent applications, publications and other documents in lieu of reciting them in full. Material necessary for enablement requirement compliance may not be incorporated by reference if the material is not publicly accessible.[232] PTO policy is that only U.S. patents or allowed U.S. patent applications may be incorporated by reference to supply information essential for enablement requirement compliance. Publications and foreign patents may be incorporated only as background or illustration of the state of the art.[233]

Material improperly incorporated by reference may in some circumstances be added to the specification by amendment.[234] It is best not to use incorporation by reference so heavily that the application is difficult to understand without continuous reference to that material.

[v] *Theories, Properties and Advantages.* New and unexpected properties and advantages of a claimed invention are often critical to establishing a new product's patentability if it closely resembles prior art products.[235] For policy reasons, it is desirable that the properties and advantages be disclosed in the specification,[236] but their disclosure is not necessary to comply with the enablement requirement, which relates to information on making and using the invention. Therefore, properties or

---

[231] 865 F.2d at 1251, 9 U.S.P.Q.2d at 1464-65.

[232] Quaker City Gear Works, Inc. v. Skil Corp., 747 F.2d 1446, 223 U.S.P.Q. 1161 (Fed. Cir. 1984), *cert. denied,* 471 U.S. 1136 (1985). In *Quaker City,* the court held that a German industrial standard that was not readily accessible to persons in the United States could not be incorporated by reference.

[233] U.S.P.T.O., Manual of Patent Examining Procedure § 608.01(p).

[234] *In re* Hawkins, 486 F.2d 569, 179 U.S.P.Q. 157 (CCPA 1973). *Compare In re* Hawkins, 486 F.2d 579, 179 U.S.P.Q. 167 (CCPA 1973).

To make an amendment adding material that is secret as of the filing date, the material must be specifically identifiable. *In re* Fouche, 439 F.2d 1237, 169 U.S.P.Q. 429 (CCPA 1971). In *Fouche,* the applicant filed one application that referred to an example in "our application No. .... " The applicant was allowed to amend to add the serial number and filing date of the other application since there was only one such application pending.

[235] *See* § 2C[4][c].

[236] *In re* Davies, 475 F.2d 667, 177 U.S.P.Q. 381 (CCPA 1973).

advantages may be added in a continuation-in-part application, or possibly in a reissue, without losing the original filing date.[237]

An inventor need not disclose or even understand how his invention works, as long as he makes adequate disclosure of how to make and use the invention.[238]

[vi] *Starting Material Availability—Deposit of Biological Material.* If a product or process cannot be made without access to special materials, machinery, or methods, the applicant must assure that the public has access to the materials, machinery, or methods when the patent issues.[239]

Starting material availability is a problem when the claimed product or process requires biological material, for example, a particular strain of microorganism or genetically-altered cells, because it may be impossible to adequately describe how to isolate that particular strain without extensive effort.[240] The applicant may comply

---

[237] Carter-Wallace, Inc. v. Otte, 474 F.2d 529, 176 U.S.P.Q. 2 (2d Cir. 1972), *cert. denied,* 412 U.S. 929, 178 U.S.P.Q. 65 (1973). See § 3D[2].

[238] *In re* Bowden 183 F.2d 115, 119, 86 U.S.P.Q. 419, 423 (CCPA 1950). *Compare* Newman v. Quigg, 877 F.2d 1575, 1581-82, 11 U.S.P.Q.2d 1340, 1345 (Fed. Cir. 1989), *cert. denied,* 110 S. Ct. 2173 (1990) ("While it is not a requirement of patentability that an inventor correctly set forth, or even know, how or why the invention works, . . . neither is the patent applicant relieved of the requirement of teaching how to achieve the claimed result, even if the theory of operation is not correctly explained or even understood.").

One cannot patent the discovery of the correct theory as to how a known product or process operates or achieves its functions. General Battery Corp. v. Gould, Inc., 545 F. Supp. 731, 215 U.S.P.Q. 1007 (D. Del. 1982).

[239] White Consolidated Indus., Inc. v. Vega Servo-Control, Inc., 713 F.2d 788, 218 U.S.P.Q. 961 (Fed. Cir. 1983); *In re* Ghiron, 442 F.2d 985, 991, 169 U.S.P.Q. 723, 727-28 (CCPA 1971). In *White,* the court held that a specification did not meet the enablement requirement when it failed to set forth a necessary computer program, which could be produced only by substantial effort. In *Ghiron,* the court held that a specification did not meet the enablement requirement as to a computer method when the method required modification of computer hardware and the applicant failed to show that a person of ordinary skill in the art would have known how to make such modifications.

[240] As to when a deposit is in fact required, see *Ex parte* Rinehart, 10 U.S.P.Q.2d 1719, 1720 (Bd. Pat. App. & Int'f 1989); *Ex parte* Goeddel, 5 U.S.P.Q.2d 1449 (Bd. Pat. App. & Int'f 1987). *See also* Amgen, Inc. v. Chugai Pharmaceutical Co., Ltd., 927 F.2d 1200, 18 U.S.P.Q.2d 1016 (Fed. Cir. 1991), discussed below (no best mode violation by failure to deposit cell cultures transformed with the patented DNA sequence).

In *Rinehart,* the Board held that a deposit of biological materials was unnecessary under the circumstances. The claimed process involved, *inter alia,* extracting "a suitable marine tunicate from the family Didemnidae with MeOH:toluene (3:1)." The Board noted that "the source of the marine organisms necessary for practice of the invention is described in detail in the specification by reference to specific locations in the sea. . . . The marine tunicate are a well known class of marine microorganisms having definitive characteristics. . . . [The applicant] has described the phylum, subphylum, class, order and suborder as well as where the organisms are located and how they can be obtained. The marine microorganisms are neither new nor unique but are commonly known and generally available to the public without any undue experimentation."

In *Amgen,* the court noted:

with the enablement requirement by depositing the biological material in a permanent culture collection depository and providing that, when the patent issues, the public has access to the material.[241]

In *Lundak*,[242] the court held that the applicant need not have made a deposit of biological material with an independent depository as of the patent application's effective filing date. A deposit in the inventor's own laboratory or in a colleague's laboratory satisfies the Section 112 "second function"—establishment of a *prima facie* invention date as of the filing date. A deposit with an independent depository after filing but before the patent issues satisfies Section 112 "first function"—complete public disclosure of invention. In 1990, the PTO adopted regulations pertaining to materials deposits for patent purposes.[243]

[b] **Description Requirement.** The specification must contain a written description of the invention. The description requirement's purposes are to assure that the applicant was in full possession of the claimed subject matter on the application filing date and to allow other inventors to develop and obtain patent protection for later improvements and subservient inventions that build on applicant's teachings.[244]

[i] *Original Claims.* The description requirement is relevant only if claims are added or amended after the original filing date.[245] Original claims constitute their

---

"For many years, it has been customary for patent applicants to place microorganism samples in a public depository when such a sample is necessary to carry out a claimed invention. . . . This practice arose out of the development of antibiotics, when microorganisms obtained from soil samples uniquely synthesized antibiotics which could not be readily prepared chemically or otherwise. . . . Such a deposit has been considered adequate to satisfy the *enablement* requirement of 35 U.S.C. § 112, when a written description alone would not place the invention in the hands of the public and physical possession of a unique biological material is required."

. . .

". . . When a biological sample required for the practice of an invention is obtained from nature, the invention may be incapable of being practiced without access to that organism. . . . [W]hen . . . the organism is created by insertion of genetic material into a cell obtained from generally available sources, then all that is required is a description of the best mode and an adequate description of the means of carrying out the invention, not deposit of the cells. If the cells can be prepared without undue experimentation from known materials, based on the description in the patent specification, a deposit is not required." 927 F.2d at 1210-11, 18 U.S.P.Q.2d at 1024-25.

241 *In re* Argoudelis, 434 F.2d 1390, 168 U.S.P.Q. 99 (CCPA 1970).

The depository may be outside the United States. Feldman v. Aunstrup, 517 F.2d 1351, 186 U.S.P.Q. 108 (CCPA 1975), *cert. denied*, 424 U.S. 912, 188 U.S.P.Q. 720 (1976).

The United States is a party to the Budapest Treaty on the International Recognition of the Deposit of Microorganisms for the Purposes of Patent Procedure.

242 *In re* Lundak, 773 F.2d 1216, 227 U.S.P.Q. 90 (Fed. Cir. 1985).

243 *See* 37 C.F.R. §§ 1.801.-.809.

244 Fields v. Conover, 443 F.2d 1386, 170 U.S.P.Q. 276 (CCPA 1971).

245 *In re* Smith, 481 F.2d 910, 914, 178 U.S.P.Q. 620, 623-624 (CCPA 1973):

"Satisfaction of the description requirement insures that subject matter presented in the form of a claim subsequent to the filing date of the application was sufficiently

own description.[246]

[ii] *Adequate Description Standard.* To comply with the description requirement, the specification must clearly convey to those of ordinary skill in the art that the applicant has invented the specific subject matter later claimed.[247] It is not necessary to describe the later claim's subject matter literally (*"in haec verba"*);[248] the claimed subject matter may be inherent in the specification's disclosure.[249]

> disclosed at the time of filing so that the *prima facie* date of invention can fairly be held to be the filing date of the application. This concept applies whether the case factually arises out of an assertion of entitlement to the filing date of a previously filed application under [Section] 120 . . . or arises in the interference context wherein the issue is support for a count in the specification of one or more of the parties . . . or arises in an *ex parte* case involving a single application, but where the claim at issue was filed subsequent to the filing of the application . . . Where the claim is an original claim, the underlying concept of insuring disclosure as of the filing date is satisfied, and the description requirement has likewise been held to be satisfied."

[246] *In re* Koller, 613 F.2d 819, 204 U.S.P.Q. 702 (C.C.P.A. 1980).

[247] *In re* Wertheim, 541 F.2d 257, 262, 191 U.S.P.Q. 90 (CCPA 1976).

[248] *In re* Lukach, 442 F.2d 967, 969, 169 U.S.P.Q. 795 (CCPA 1971). *See also In re* Wright, 866 F.2d 422, 9 U.S.P.Q.2d 1649 (Fed. Cir. 1989). In *Wright,* the Federal Circuit held that, as to a patent claim for a method of forming images that included the step of depositing a layer of photosensitive microcapsules in the form of a free-flowing powder, the addition by amendment of a limitation specifying that the powder be "distributed upon said support but *not permanently fixed thereto*" (emphasis added) did not violate Section 112's description requirement. The specification as filed did not include the exact phrase "not permanently fixed," but the original specification disclosure unequivocally taught the absence of permanently fixed microcapsules. For example, the specification's examples warned that it is important that the microcapsules not be distributed so as to change their position until the image is formed by rupturing, showing that the microcapsules are not permanently fixed.

> "When the scope of a claim has been changed by amendment in such a way as to justify an assertion that it is directed to a *different invention* than was the original claim, it is proper to inquire whether the newly claimed subject matter was *described* in the patent application when filed as the invention of the applicant. That is the essence of the so-called 'description requirement' of § 112, first paragraph, which opens with the words: 'The specification shall contain a written description of the invention. . . . ' The invention is, necessarily, the subject matter defined in the claim under consideration." 866 F.2d at 424, 9 U.S.P.Q.2d at 1651.

[249] *E.g.,* Kennecott Corp. v. Kyocera International, Inc., 835 F.2d 1419, 5 U.S.P.Q.2d 1194 (Fed. Cir. 1987), *cert. denied,* 486 U.S. 1008 (1988).

In *Kennecott,* the Federal Circuit held that patent claims, which issued on a continuation-in-part ("CIP") application, were entitled to the benefit of the filing date of a parent application and therefore avoided a potential "on sale" bar that occurred after the parent filing but more than one year prior to the CIP filing. The parent application disclosed and claimed a certain sintered ceramic body. The continuation-in-part application added a description of and photomicrographs showing the ceramic equiaxed microstructure. The patent claims contained the words "equiaxed microstructure," which were not present in the parent application. The accused infringer conceded that the examples in the parent application produced, without undue experimentation, a product having an equiaxed microstructure. The court held that this was in effect a concession that the equiaxed microstructure is inherent in the patent specification's disclosed structure. From this it followed that the addition to the descriptive

[iii] *Distinction Between Enablement and Description.* The description requirement is distinct from the enablement requirement.[250] A specification may contain sufficient information to enable a person of ordinary skill in the art to make and use a later claimed invention but fail to describe that invention.[251] For example, a specification may discuss only a single compound (X) and contain no language indicating that a broader invention is contemplated. The disclosure of X may enable a person of ordinary skill in the art to make and use compounds Y and Z. Nevertheless, the class consisting of X, Y, and Z has not been adequately described. A claim to the class of X-Y-Z added after the filing date would not be entitled to that date.[252]

[iv] *Broadening and Narrowing Claim Changes.* The description requirement applies to claims that broaden or narrow the the original claims.

The description requirement is not met if a claim is broadened to encompass subject matter not described in the original specification and drawings.[253] Not all broadening changes are prohibited. Such a change will be proper if the specification's tenor is

---

portion of the patent and to the claims of the reference to a "equiaxed microstructure" did not deprive the patent of the benefit of the parent filing date: "The disclosure in a subsequent patent application of an inherent property of a product does not deprive that product of the benefit of an earlier filing date. Nor does the inclusion of a description of that property in later-filed claims change this reasonable result." 835 F.2d at 1423, 5 U.S.P.Q. at 1198.

The court noted cases in the interference context holding that the burden on an applicant seeking to establish a constructive reduction to practice by disclosure in an application is to show that the "necessary and only reasonable construction to be given the disclosure by one skilled in the art is one which will lend clear support to" the limitation in question. This standard of inherency "is consistent with that of the other cases on the issue of compliance with section 112, first paragraph." "[T]he earlier and later applications need not use the identical words, if the earlier application shows the subject matter that is claimed in the later application, with adequate direction as to how to obtain it. . . . [A]n invention may be described in different ways and still be the same invention." 835 F.2d at 1422, 5 U.S.P.Q.2d at 1197.

For a discussion of continuation-in-part applications, see § 2D[4][b][i].

[250] *In re* Wilder, 736 F.2d 1516, 222 U.S.P.Q. 369 (Fed. Cir. 1984), *cert. denied,* Wilder v. Mossinghoff, 469 U.S. 1209 (1985); *In re* Barker, 559 F.2d 588, 194 U.S.P.Q. 470 (CCPA 1977), *cert. denied,* Barker v. Parker, 434 U.S. 1064, 197 U.S.P.Q. 271 (1978).

[251] *In re* DiLeone, 436 F.2d 1404, 168 U.S.P.Q. 592 (CCPA 1971).

[252] A continuation-in-part application may be filed adding material to the specification to support the claim to the class of A-B-C (see § 2D[4][b][i]) but that application would not be entitled to the benefit of the original application's filing date as to the X-Y-Z claim.

[253] *E.g.,* Chester v. Miller, 906 F.2d 1574, 15 U.S.P.Q.2d 1333 (Fed. Cir. 1990); *In re* Gosteli, 872 F.2d 1008, 10 U.S.P.Q.2d 1614 (Fed. Cir. 1989) (foreign priority application disclosing only a subgenus of chemical compounds did not provide a written description of an encompassing genus); *In re* Wertheim, 541 F.2d 257, 263-64, 191 U.S.P.Q. 90 (CCPA 1976).

In *Wertheim,* the court held that the description requirement was *prima facie* not complied with when (a) the specification described a certain range as 25-60% and gave specific examples of 36% and 50%, and (b) the claim was for a range of "at least 35%."

that the invention is a generic one[254] or is appropriately described in terms of functions and properties.[255]

The description requirement is not be met if a claim is narrowed by limitations not supported by the specification.[256]

The description requirement may not be met by a claim to a subgeneric class that falls between an originally claimed generic class and covers an originally disclosed species within that class,[257] but, in these situations, the description requirement is not applied hypertechnically.[258] If the applicant described a class of elements using a Markush group,[259] that may be taken as an adequate description of the combination with each or a limited number of the Markush group members.[260] Consider the following example:

1. Applicant A discloses and claims a product consisting of Z and a second element selected from the group consisting of S, T, U, V, W, X, and Y.

2. Applicant amends the application to add (a) a claim to a product consisting of Z and a second ingredient selected from the group consisting of W, X, and Y, and (b) a claim to a product consisting of Z and W.

The description requirement will likely be viewed as being complied with as to the new claims because a Markush group (particularly one with a small number of members) is taken as an implied statement of interchangeability.

[c] **Best Mode Requirement.** The specification must set forth the "best mode contemplated by the inventor of carrying out his invention."[261] The best mode requirement's purpose is to prevent inventors from obtaining patent protection while concealing from the public preferred embodiments of their inventions.[262]

Before the 1952 Patent Act's enactment, the patent statutes stated the enablement requirement in terms similar to the first part of Section 112 (1st Paragraph). They

---

[254] *In re* Peters, 723 F.2d 891, 221 U.S.P.Q. 952 (Fed. Cir. 1983); *In re* Smith, 481 F.2d 910, 178 U.S.P.Q. 620 (CCPA 1973).

[255] *In re* Smythe, 480 F.2d 1376, 178 U.S.P.Q. 279 (CCPA 1973). In *Smythe,* the specification and original claims described an element as "air or other gas which is inert to the liquid." The court found compliance with the description requirement as to amended claims describing the element as an "inert fluid." The description of the function and properties of the element made it clear that the applicants' invention would include use of any "inert fluid."

[256] *In re* Kaslow, 707 F.2d 1366, 217 U.S.P.Q. 1089 (Fed. Cir. 1983). In *Kaslow,* the court found noncompliance with the description requirement when the applicant sought to add as a limitation an "auditing step" that was not described in the specification. *Compare In re* Eickmeyer, 602 F.2d 974, 202 U.S.P.Q. 655 (CCPA 1979); *In re* Herschler, 591 F.2d 693, 200 U.S.P.Q. 711 (CCPA 1979).

[257] *In re* Smith, 458 F.2d 1389, 173 U.S.P.Q. 679 (CCPA 1972).

[258] *In re* Johnson, 558 F.2d 1008, 1019, 194 U.S.P.Q. 187 (CCPA 1977).

[259] Markush groups are discussed at § 2D[3][d][v].

[260] *In re* Driscoll, 562 F.2d 1245, 195 U.S.P.Q. 434 (CCPA 1977).

[261] 35 U.S.C. § 112. *See generally* D. Chisum, Patents § 7.05.

[262] *In re* Gay, 309 F.2d 769, 772, 135 U.S.P.Q. 311, 315 (CCPA 1962). *See also* Christianson v. Colt Industries Operating Corp., 870 F.2d 1292, 1302 n.8, 10 U.S.P.Q.2d 1352, 1360 n.8 (7th Cir. 1989), *cert. denied,* 110 S. Ct. 81 (1989) ("[T]he best mode requirement is intended to allow the public to compete fairly with the patentee following the expiration of the patents.").

also stated that "in case of a machine, he [the inventor] shall explain the principle thereof, and the best mode in which he has contemplated applying that principle, so as to distinguish it from other inventions." Another provision made it a defense to an infringement suit that "for the purpose of deceiving the public the description and specification filed by the patentee in the Patent Office was made to contain less than the whole truth relative to his invention."[263]

The 1952 Act broadened the "best mode" provision to cover all inventions. Legislative history is sparse; the Revisers' Notes indicate the broader provision derived not only from the "best mode" provision but also from the "whole truth" defense.

The best mode requirement differs from the enablement requirement; a patent specification may comply with the latter but not the former.

> "[C]ompliance with the best mode requirement focuses on a different matter than does compliance with the enablement requirement. Enablement looks to placing the subject matter of the claims generally in the possession of the public. If, however, the applicant develops specific instrumentalities or techniques which are recognized at the time of filing as the best way of carrying out the invention, then the best mode requirement imposes an obligation to disclose that information to the public as well."[264]

[i]   *Subjective Standard.* The "best mode" is the one the inventor considers best, not the best in fact.[265] The standard is subjective and focuses on whether the inventor failed to reveal an embodiment he knew of and preferred.[266] Consider the following example:

> 1. In a patent application, A discloses and claims a process that includes the steps of (1) adding a compound selected from a broad class, and (2) heating the compound to a temperature between 150 and 250 degrees.

> 2. Before filing the application, A discovers that the process works best when a particular compound in the class is used and the compound is heated to 240 degrees.

> 3. The application does not disclose the particular compound or temperature.

---

[263] Rev. Stat. 4920 (Emphasis added), *reproduced in* D. Chisum, Patents, App. 19-77.

[264] Spectra-Physics, Inc. v. Coherent, Inc., 827 F.2d 1524, 1532, 3 U.S.P.Q.2d 1737, 1742 (Fed. Cir. 1987), *cert. denied,* 484 U.S. 954 (1987).

Spectra-Physics concerned two patents relating to gas lasers, one on an improved laser discharge tube with copper cups attached by "brazing" to the inside wall of a ceramic tube, and one on a method of fabricating the tube with cups. The court held the patentee failed to comply with the best mode requirement by failing to set forth specific information as to the preferred method of brazing the copper cups to the ceramic tube (TiCuSil, copper silver eutectic with titanium—active metal brazing involving six stages). The six stage brazing cycle was not disclosed in either the patent or the prior art. The patents did comply with the *enablement* requirement because they disclosed other methods of brazing the cups to the tube.

[265] *E.g.,* Chemcast Corp. v. Arco Industries Corp., 913 F.2d 923, 926, 16 U.S.P.Q.2d 1033, 1035 (Fed. Cir. 1990) ("The best mode inquiry focuses on the inventor's state of mind as of the time he filed his application—a subjective, factual question.").

[266] *In re* Bundy, 642 F.2d 430, 209 U.S.P.Q. 48 (CCPA 1981).

The application does not comply with the best mode requirement because it fails to disclose the particular compound and temperature limitations preferred by the inventor.

An inventor, or his assignee, can subsequently adopt a commercial embodiment that differs from the one disclosed in the specification without necessarily violating the best mode requirement.[267]

The best mode requirement is not "subjective" in a culpability sense. The inventor need not have intended to conceal something from the public; the Federal Circuit has found no best mode violation when the inventor *did* intend to conceal something.[268]

Few decisions deal explicitly with whose intent controls. The cases recite the statutory requirement that it is the "inventors" contemplated best mode. For many patent law purposes, the patent rights owner, such as an inventor's employer who has taken those rights by assignment, is placed in the inventor's shoes, but there is no judicial suggestion that this is the case with the best mode requirement.

[ii]   *Mode Disclosure Adequacy.* A patent specification need not be as detailed as a "production specification."[269] If the specification discloses the best mode's general parameters, that will be sufficient if one with ordinary skill in the art can use that disclosure to make and use the invention.[270]

The PTO has a long standing rule that the patent specification shall "describe completely a specific embodiment of the process, machine, manufacture, composition

---

[267] Benger Laboratories, Ltd. v. R.K. Laros Co., 209 F. Supp. 639, 644-45, 135 U.S.P.Q. 11, 15 (E.D. Pa. 1962), *aff'd*, 317 F.2d 455, 137 U.S.P.Q. 693 (3d Cir. 1963), *cert. denied*, 375 U.S. 833, 139 U.S.P.Q. 566 (1963).

[268] Randomex, Inc. v. Scopus Corp., 849 F.2d 585, 7 U.S.P.Q.2d 1050 (Fed. Cir. 1988).

[269] Christianson v. Colt Industries Operating Corp., 822 F.2d 1544, 3 U.S.P.Q.2d 1241 (Fed. Cir. 1987), *vacated and remanded with instructions to transfer appeal to the Court of Appeals for the Seventh Circuit,* 486 U.S. 800, 7 U.S.P.Q.2d 1109 (1988), *on remand,* 870 F.2d 1292, 10 U.S.P.Q.2d 1352 (7th Cir. 1989), *cert. denied,* 110 S. Ct. 81 (1989).

In *Christianson,* the Federal Circuit and Seventh Circuit held that the patentee, in obtaining patents on rifle parts, did not violate the best mode requirement by failing to provide sufficient production information so as to enable persons to make parts interchangeable with the military procurement specifications for M-16 rifles. Therefore, its assertion of state law trade secret rights in M-16 production data was not contrary to federal patent law. The Federal Circuit stressed that the best mode requirement "has nothing to do with mass production or with sales to customers having particular requirements." Because the interchangeability with M-16 parts does not appear as a limitation in any claim of the patents in question, and the patents make no reference to the M-16 rifle, "the best mode for making and using and carrying out the *claimed inventions* does not entail or involve either the M-16 rifle or interchangeability." 822 F.2d at 1563, 3 U.S.P.Q.2d at 1255.

After the case was redirected by the Supreme Court to the Seventh Circuit for jurisdictional reasons, the Seventh Circuit reached the same conclusion as the Federal Circuit.

[270] *In re* Sherwood, 613 F.2d 809, 204 U.S.P.Q. 537 (CCPA 1980), *cert. denied,* Diamond v. Sherwood, 450 U.S. 994, 210 U.S.P.Q. 776 (1981).

Compare Spectra-Physics, Inc. v. Coherent, Inc., 827 F.2d 1524, 1536, 3 U.S.P.Q.2d 1737, 1745 (Fed. Cir. 1987) ("Even though there may be a general reference to the best mode, the quality of the disclosure may be so poor as to effectively result in concealment.").

of matter or improvement invented, and must explain the mode of operation or principle whenever applicable."[271] Does the best mode requirement, alone or in combination with PTO Rule 71(b), mean that an inventor must set forth a specific example even if no example or specific mode is in fact reduced to practice or conceived as of the filing date? In *Gay*,[272] the court said no. The application claimed a rice cooking container with a perforated bag filled with uncooked rice, the number and size of the perforations to be large enough to allow water and starch to pass but small enough to restrict pressure release. The PTO rejected the claims for failure to disclose a specific embodiment setting forth, *inter alia*, a bag with a specific number and size of perforations. The court reversed.

[*iii*] *Prior Art Reliance.* Early Federal Circuit cases confirmed that best mode disclosure sufficiency depended, in part, on the prior art.[273]

In *Dana Corp.*,[274] the court limited a patentee's ability to rely upon prior art disclosures to show compliance. The patent related to a valve stem seal composed of an elastomeric material. In a test report prepared prior to filing the patent application, the inventor indicated that seal designs were satisfactory or acceptable only when the elastomeric material (rubber) was subjected to a fluoride surface treatment. The patent specification did not disclose fluoride treatment even though it indicated that other types of surface coatings might be useful in some instances.

The patentee showed that fluoride treatment was disclosed and known in the prior art. The court dismissed the showing: "The best mode requirement is not satisfied by reference to the level of skill in the art, but entails a comparison of the facts known to the inventor regarding the invention at the time the application was filed and the disclosure in the specification."

In *Northern Telecom*,[275] the court held that the district court did not err in holding certain claims of the patent in suit invalid for best mode nondisclosure. The patent related to data batch processing, one aspect of which involved recording data on a magnetic tape cassette. The specification stated that cassettes "of the type which are almost universally available for audio purposes" were suitable. The assignee knew before the filing date that standard audio tape was not the best mode. It purchased cassettes of its own design that differed from standard cassettes in yield strength and magnetic characteristics. As to the assignee's argument that the higher quality cassettes were commercially available at the time of filing, the court stated:

---

[271] 37 C.F.R. § 1.72(b).

[272] *In re* Gay, 309 F.2d 769, 135 U.S.P.Q. 311 (CCPA 1962).

[273] W.L. Gore & Associates, Inc. v. Garlock, Inc., 721 F.2d 1540, 220 U.S.P.Q. 303 (Fed. Cir. 1983), *cert. denied*, 469 U.S. 851 (1984). *Cf.* Hybritech Inc. v. Monoclonal Antibodies, Inc., 802 F.2d 1367, 231 U.S.P.Q. 81 (Fed. Cir. 1986), *cert. denied*, 480 U.S. 947 (1987) (evidence that screening methods used to identify monoclonal antibodies with necessary characteristics (such as affinity, i.e., ability to bind with a particular antigen) is labor-intensive, time-consuming, and carried out by sophisticated persons does not show concealment of a best mode for screening or producing monoclonal antibodies).

[274] Dana Corp. v. IPC Limited Partnership, 860 F.2d 415, 8 U.S.P.Q.2d 1692 (Fed. Cir. 1988), *cert. denied*, 109 S. Ct. 2068 (1989).

[275] Northern Telecom, Inc. v. Datapoint Corp., 908 F.2d 931, 15 U.S.P.Q.2d 1321 (Fed. Cir. 1990), *cert. denied*, 111 S. Ct. 296 (1990).

"If so, it is this tape (or [the assignee's] own specifications) that had to be disclosed to satisfy the best mode requirement. . . . While [the assignee's] argument may be relevant to enablement, it does not establish the best mode 'contemplated by the inventor,' which is a subjective inquiry."[276]

In *Chemcast*,[277] the court clarified the *Dana* statement, stressing that the level of skill in the art is considered in determining the disclosure's "adequacy," as opposed to its necessity.

"The best mode inquiry focuses on the inventor's state of mind as of the time he filed his application—a subjective, factual question. But this focus is not exclusive. Our statements that 'there is no objective standard by which to judge the adequacy of a best mode disclosure,' and that 'only evidence of concealment (accidental or intentional) is to be considered,' . . . assumed that both the level of skill in the art and the scope of the claimed invention were additional, objective metes and bounds of a best mode disclosure.

"Of necessity, the disclosure required by section 112 is directed to those skilled in the art. . . . Therefore, one must consider the level of skill in the relevant art in determining whether a specification discloses the best mode. We have consistently recognized that whether a best mode disclosure is adequate, that is, whether the inventor concealed a better mode of practicing his invention than he disclosed, is a function of not only what the inventor knew but also how one skilled in the art would have understood his disclosure. . . . Thus, the level of skill in the art is a relevant and necessary consideration in assessing the adequacy of a best mode disclosure.

"The other objective limitation on the extent of the disclosure required to comply with the best mode requirement is, of course, the scope of the claimed invention.

"In short, a proper best mode analysis has two components. The first is whether, at the time the inventor filed his patent application, he knew of a mode of practicing his claimed invention that he considered to be better than any other. This part of the inquiry is wholly subjective, and resolves whether the inventor must disclose any facts in addition to those sufficient for enablement. If the inventor in fact contemplated such a preferred mode, the second part of the analysis compares what he knew with what he disclosed—is the disclosure adequate to enable one skilled in the art to practice the best mode or, in other words, has the inventor 'concealed' his preferred mode from the 'public'? Assessing the *adequacy* of the disclosure, as opposed to its *necessity*, is largely an objective inquiry that depends upon the scope of the claimed invention and the level of skill in the art."[278]

[iv] *"Burying" the Best Mode.* Must an inventor not only set forth the best mode but also state that it is preferred? In *Randomex*,[279] the Federal Circuit found

---

[276] 908 F.2d at 940, 15 U.S.P.Q.2d at 1328.

[277] Chemcast Corp. v. Arco Industries Corp., 913 F.2d 923, 16 U.S.P.Q.2d 1033 (Fed. Cir. 1990).

[278] 913 F.2d at 926, 16 U.S.P.Q.2d at 1035.

[279] Randomex, Inc. v. Scopus Corp., 849 F.2d 585, 7 U.S.P.Q.2d 1050 (Fed. Cir. 1988).

that, under the particular circumstances before it, the indiscriminate disclosure of the preferred mode along with other modes did not violate the best mode requirement. The patent claimed a portable mainframe computer magnetic disk pack cleaning apparatus. The patent did not specifically claim a cleaning fluid, but such a fluid is needed to practice the invention. The patent specification disclosed: "The cleaning solution employed should be of a type adequate to clean grease and oil from the disc surfaces, such as a 91 percent alcohol solution or a non-residue detergent solution such as Randomex Cleaner No. 50281." The first-mentioned fluid, a 91 percent alcohol solution, was inferior because it might cause an explosion. The court held that the indiscriminate disclosure by tradename of the patentee's proprietary cleaning fluid along with inferior fluids satisfied the best mode requirement because (i) the patent described the brand as a "non-residue detergent solution," (ii) commercial substitutes were readily available, and (iii) the accused infringer easily "reverse engineered" the patentee's cleaning fluid.[280] "Although a trade name alone may be inappropriate in a best mode disclosure when suitable substitutes are unavailable, . . . here, commercial substitutes were readily available in the prior art and the trade name is mere surplusage . . . " The patentee disclosed the content of the fluid as a "non-residue detergent solution," the same as used in the prior art.[281]

[v]   *Computer Programs.* Court decisions give a mixed message on whether a complete version, such as by source code, of a preferred computer program used in carrying out the invention must be disclosed. In *Sherwood,*[282] the court found no violation in the applicant's failure to disclose an existing computer program suitable for carrying out the claimed seismic prospecting method. The specification did describe the program's features. The applicant presented affidavit evidence that the specification would enable a skilled programmer to prepare a suitable program.

---

[280] The trial court held the patent invalid based on two jury responses to specific interrogatories—even though the jury found no best mode violation. The Federal Circuit interpreted the jury responses differently.

The jury's affirmative response to an interrogatory whether the patentee deliberately refrained from disclosing its cleaner formula, intending that users would be led to purchase its cleaner rather than to experiment themselves to find the best cleaner, was not controlling. Those of ordinary skill in the art are not "users." Anyone seeking to discover the best cleaner would ask those skilled in the cleaning fluid art. The interrogatory was directed to the issue of patent misuse rather than best mode compliance.

The jury's negative response to an interrogatory whether the disclosure was so inadequate that a person skilled in the art who did not use plaintiff's cleaner would have had to engage in undue experimentation to use the invention and find the best mode of such use was sufficient to support its finding of no best mode violation—even though the interrogatory was poorly framed and directed more to enablement than best mode.

[281] 849 F.2d at 589-90, 7 U.S.P.Q.2d at 1054.

Judge Mayer dissented:

"[N]ot only did [the patentee] fail to point out that the [tradename] solution was the best mode, he also disclosed solutions that he knew could be harmful and even dangerous. . . . [H]e buried his best mode in a list of less satisfactory ones. . . . [I]f there is a best mode known to the inventor he must say so; he cannot require the public to hunt for it."

[282] *In re* Sherwood, 613 F.2d 809, 204 U.S.P.Q. 537 (CCPA 1980), *cert. denied,* Diamond v. Sherwood, 450 U.S. 994, 210 U.S.P.Q. 776 (1981).

"In general, writing a computer program may be a task requiring the most sublime of the inventive faculty or it may be a task requiring only droning use of a clerical skill. The difference between the two extremes lies in the creation of mathematical methodology to bridge the gap between the information one starts with (the 'input') and the information that is desired (the 'output'). If these bridge-gapping tools are disclosed, there would seem to be no cogent reason to require disclosure of the menial tools known to all who practice this art." [283]

On the other hand, in *White Consolidated*,[284] the court held a patent on a computer control machine tool system invalid for noncompliance with the *enablement* requirement because the specification indicated that a computer language named "SPLIT" was used to carry out the invention and SPLIT was a company's trade secret. The district court also invalidated the patent for best mode noncompliance, but the appeals court did not rule on that issue.

In *Mendenhall*,[285] the patent claimed an interrupt circuit safety device-equipped surge bin asphalt weighing and dispensing method. The accused infringer argued that the patent was invalid for nondisclosure of a computer program used in the patentee's commercial embodiment. The district court found no best mode violation.

"The evidence indicated that the patent disclosed sufficient information that a person skilled in the art of industrial process controls could write a computer program to carry out the steps called for in the patent. . . . The patent simply discloses that the best mode for practicing the invention would be with a microprocessor control system which was 'within the skill of the art'— meaning, presumably, the art of designing computer programs for microprocessors not the art of engineering asphalt plants.

. . .

". . . [T]he patent . . . discloses the best method of its performance (i.e., —with a microprocessor) and gives sufficient information to enable others to practice the invention. The computer circuitry actually required to practice this 'best method' appears to have been well within the skill of the art at the time of the invention." [286]

The Federal Circuit affirmed in an unpublished opinion that cannot be cited as precedent.

[vi] *Biotechnology—Cell Cultures.* Best mode compliance problems arise with patents on biotechnology inventions, such as genetically-altered organisms, monoclonal antibodies, and purified and recombinantly-produced human proteins.

In *Amgen*,[287] the patent claimed purified and isolated DNA encoding for human

---

[283] 613 F.2d at 816.

[284] White Consolidated Indus., Inc. v. Vega Servo-Control, Inc., 713 F.2d 788, 218 U.S.P.Q. 961 (Fed. Cir. 1983).

[285] Mendenhall v. Astec Industries Inc., 14 U.S.P.Q.2d 1134 (E.D. Tenn. 1988), aff'd, 891 F.2d 299, 14 U.S.P.Q.2d 1140 (Fed. Cir. 1989) (unpublished opinion).

[286] 14 U.S.P.Q.2d at 1140.

[287] Amgen Inc. v. Chugai Pharmaceutical Co., Ltd., 13 U.S.P.Q.2d 1737, 1773 (D. Mass. 1989), aff'd in part, vacated in part, 927 F.2d 1200, 18 U.S.P.Q.2d 1016 (Fed. Cir. 1991).

erythropoietin (EPO). The inventor isolated the DNA by using certain gene cloning techniques, The isolated DNA's utility is to transfect host cells that can express recombinant EPO in quantities far exceeding what is available by purifying EPO from natural sources.

The first best mode issue arose because the specification disclosed many embodiments of the cloned EPO gene in various transfected eukaryotic and prokaryotic hosts cells, including, in example 10, Chinese hamster ovary (CHO) cells, but did not state that CHO cells were the preferred embodiment. The Magistrate noted that, although the patent owner "did not specify or deposit the preferred mode or embodiment, there is no clear and convincing evidence that one skilled in the art would not understand that CHO host cells as described in Example 10 were the best mode."

> "EPO is a glycosylated protein which cannot be expressed in a sialated form in prokaryotic cells, like E. Coli and yeast cells. . . . Moreover, there were recognized problems with using COS cells to express protein in light of their lack of stability.
>
> . . .
>
> ". . . While [the inventor] did not distinguish between cells amplified at 100 nM and 1 micromolar MTX so as to indicate which cell strain was the preferred best mode, the indiscriminate disclosure in this instance of the preferred best mode along with one other possible mode satisfies the best mode requirement."[288]

The second best mode issue arose because the inventor did not make a public deposit of its "best mode" cell line. Amgen and the inventor used a technique known as "gene amplification" to obtain a cell line with a high EPO expression level. Through selective antibiotic pressure on cells, gene amplification produces a unique homogenous cell line that has a high number of copies of the EPO gene and its companion antibiotic resistance gene. The Magistrate found no best mode violation even though Amgen and the inventor did not deposit their preferred amplified cell line.

> "[T]he court declines in the circumstances of this case to hold that the only way to meet the best mode requirement for a transfected host cell is to deposit, although . . . a deposit is 'cheap insurance' to ensure this best mode requirement has been met. . . . The testimony is clear that no scientist could ever duplicate exactly the best mode used by Amgen, but that those of ordinary skill in the art could produce mammalian host cell strains or lines with similar levels of production identified [in the patent specification]."[289]

The Federal Circuit affirmed, noting that a disclosure may be adequate even though it does not allow skilled workers to *exactly* duplicate the inventor's best mode.[290]

---

[288] 13 U.S.P.Q.2d at 1773.

[289] 13 U.S.P.Q.2d at 1774.

[290] *See also* Scripps Clinic & Research Foundation v. Genentech, Inc., 927 F.2d 1565, 18 U.S.P.Q.2d 1001 (Fed. Cir. 1991) (the district court erred in holding the patentee violated the best mode requirement by failing to make publicly accessible its antibody 2.2.9, used in carrying out the patent's claimed process for preparing a purified protein).

In *Scripps*, the accused infringer did not charge "concealment of special manipulations, or undisclosed techniques." Rather, its argument "is primarily that because of the laborious nature

That scientists are "unable to duplicate [the inventor's] genetically-heterogeneous best mode cell strain" is not dispositive. "[T]he issue is whether the disclosure is 'adequate,' not that an exact duplication is necessary. . . . What is required is an adequate disclosure of the best mode, not a guarantee that every aspect of the specification be precisely and universally reproducible."

[vii]   *Claimed Subject Matter: Relevance.* Court decisions state that the "best mode" is that of carrying out the "invention" defined by the claims.

A claim change can change what is the best mode of carrying out the invention. For example, in *DeGeorge*,[291] the court construed the claims so as to exclude a certain component as a limitation with the result that there was no obligation to disclose information on the preferred form of the component. In *Amgen*,[292] the court noted that "Absent inequitable conduct, a best mode defense only affects those claims covering subject matter the practice of which has not been disclosed in compliance with the best mode requirement."[293]

The decisions do not state a precise test for the relationship between the preferred mode and the claimed subject matter.

In *Randomex*,[294] the court gave the following hypothetical example:

> "[I]f one should invent a new and improved internal combustion engine, the best mode requirement would require a patentee to divulge the fuel on which it would run best. This patentee, however, would not be required to disclose the formula for refining gasoline or any other petroleum product. Every requirement is met if the patentee truthfully stated that the engine ran smoothly and powerfully on Brand X super-premium lead free 'or equal.' Making engines and refining petroleum are different arts, and the person skilled in the art of making engines would probably buy the suggested gasoline. But if the

of the process of screening monoclonal antibodies, the inventors should have voluntarily placed in a depository and made available to the public the antibody to Factor VIII:RP designated 2.2.9, which was the first effective antibody obtained by [the patentee's] screening, and was used . . . in carrying out the claimed invention." The patentee argued that "the procedures in the specification produce monoclonal antibodies having the characteristics set forth in the specification, that the process of obtaining these antibodies was fully disclosed, that the data in [the specification] are for the 2.2.9 antibody, and that the 2.2.9 antibody was not concealed."

> "There was no evidence . . . that the antibodies used by [the inventors] differed from those obtainable according to the process described in the specification. The laborious nature of this work was recognized in . . . *In re Wands*, 858 F.2d 731, 737-38, 8 U.S.P.Q.2d 1400, 1406-07 (Fed. Cir. 1988). In *Wands* this court, considering the question of enablement, declined to require the deposit of antibody samples that could be obtained by screening following the procedures in the specification. . . . 'There are numerous references demonstrating the ease with which high affinity monoclonal antibodies could be obtained to Factor VIII:R[P].' " 927 F.2d at 1579, 18 U.S.P.Q.2d at 1012.

[291] DeGeorge v. Bernier, 768 F.2d 1318, 226 U.S.P.Q. 758 (Fed. Cir. 1985).
[292] 927 F.2d 1200, 18 U.S.P.Q.2d 1016 (Fed. Cir. 1991).
[293] 927 F.2d at 1209 n.5, 18 U.S.P.Q.2d at 1023 n.5.
[294] Randomex, Inc. v. Scopus Corp., 849 F.2d 585, 7 U.S.P.Q.2d 1050 (Fed. Cir. 1988).

hypothetical maker or user of the engine did not want to use the Brand X super-premium, he would then explore the 'or equal' alternative of the patent disclosure." [295]

In *Chemcast*,[296] the Federal Circuit offered the following analysis:

"[An] objective limitation on the extent of the disclosure required to comply with the best mode requirement is, of course, the scope of the claimed invention. 'It is concealment of the best mode of practicing the *claimed invention* that section 112 ¶ 1 is designed to prohibit.' *Randomex,* 849 F.2d at 588, 7 U.S.P.Q.2d at 1053 . . . Thus, in *Randomex*, the inventor's deliberate concealment of his cleaning fluid formula did not violate the best mode requirement because his 'invention neither added nor claimed to add anything to the prior art respecting cleaning fluid.' . . . Similarly, in *Christianson*, the inventor's failure to disclose information that would have enabled the claimed rifle parts to be interchangeable with all M-16 rifle parts did not invalidate his patents because 'the best mode for making and using and carrying out the *claimed inventions* [did] not entail or involve either the M-16 rifle or interchangeability.' . . . Finally, in *DeGeorge* we reversed a finding that an inventor's nondisclosure of unclaimed circuitry with which his claimed circuitry interfaced violated the best mode requirement: 'Because the properly construed count does not include a word processor, failure to meet the best mode requirement here should not arise from an absence of information on the word processor.' " [297]

In *Chemcast*, the patent in suit claims "a sealing member in the form of a grommet or plug button that is designed to seal an opening in, for example, a sheet metal panel." [298] The claimed grommet, a "dual durometer grommet," is composed "either

---

[295] 849 F.2d at 590, 7 U.S.P.Q.2d at 1054.

[296] Chemcast Corp. v. Arco Industries Corp., 913 F.2d 923, 16 U.S.P.Q.2d 1033 (Fed. Cir. 1990).

[297] 913 F.2d at 927, 16 U.S.P.Q.2d 1036.

[298] The court noted that "Claim 6, the only claim in suit, depends from Claim 1." These claims provide:

"1. A grommet for sealing an opening in a panel, said grommet comprising

an annular base portion having a continuous circumferential and axial extending sealing band surface,

an annular locking portion having a continuous circumferential and axial extending ridge portion approximately the same diameter as said sealing band surface,

said sealing band surface constituting an axial extending continuation of said ridge portion, said locking portion and said base portion being in contact with each other and integrally bonded together,

said base portion comprising an elastomeric material and said locking portion being more rigid than said base portion,

whereby when the grommet is installed in a panel opening, the locking portion is inserted through the opening to a position on the opposite side of the panel from the base portion locking the grommet in place, and said sealing band surface forms a complete seal continuously around the entire inner periphery of the panel opening."

of two materials that differ in hardness or of a single material that varies in hardness." The different hardnesses are "measured with different durometers: Shore A for the softer base portion and Shore D for the harder locking portion." The claim required that the base portion have "a durometer hardness reading of less than 60 Shore A" and the locking portion have "a durometer hardness reading of more than 70 Shore A."

The patent specification did not disclose the type, hardness, or supplier of the material the inventors used to make the locking portion, a polyvinyl chloride plastisol with a hardness of 75 +/− Shore D from Reynosol Corporation (tradename: "R-4467").[299] The district court found a best mode violation. On appeal, the patentee argued that the district court failed "to focus, as required, on the claimed invention." The Federal Circuit found no merit in the argument:

> "[The patentee] first argues that, because the '879 patent does not claim any specific material for making the locking portion of the grommet, [the inventor's] failure to disclose the particular material that he thought worked the best does not violate the best mode requirement. This argument confuses best mode and enablement. A patent applicant must disclose the best mode of carrying out his claimed invention, not merely a mode of making and using what is claimed. A specification can be enabling yet fail to disclose an applicant's contemplated best mode. . . . Indeed, most of the cases in which we have said that the best mode requirement was violated addressed situations where an inventor failed to disclose non-claimed elements that were nevertheless necessary to practice the best mode of carrying out the claimed invention. *See, e.g., Dana, 860 F.2d at 419, 8 USPQ2d at 1695 (failure to disclose unclaimed fluoride surface treatment that was necessary for satisfactory performance of claimed seal violated best mode); Spectra-Physics, 827 F.2d at 1536, 3 USPQ2d at 1745* (failure to disclose specific braze cycle constituting preferred means of attachment violated best mode even though no particular attachment means claimed).

> "Moreover, [the patentee] is mistaken in its claim interpretation. While the critical limitation of Claim 6 is a hardness differential of 10 points on the Shore A scale between the grommet base and locking portions, and not a particular material type, *some* material meeting both this limitation and that of Claim 1, that 'said base portion compris[e] an elastomeric material and said

---

"6. The grommet as defined in claim 1 wherein the material forming said base portion has a durometer hardness reading of less than 60 Shore A and the material forming said locking portion has a durometer hardness reading of more than 70 Shore A." 913 F.2d at 924, 16 U.S.P.Q.2d at 1034.

[299] The specification disclosed the following:

"The annular locking portion [ ] of the sealing member [ ] is preferably comprised of a rigid castable material, such as a castable resinous material, either a thermoplastic or thermosetting resin, or any mixtures thereof, for example, polyurethane or polyvinyl chloride. The [locking] portion [ ] also should be made of a material that is sufficiently hard and rigid so that it cannot be radially compressed, such as when it is inserted in the opening [ ] in the panel [ ]. Materials having a durometer hardness reading of 70 Shore A or harder are suitable in this regard." Col. 4, lines 53-63. 913 F.2d at 929, 16 U.S.P.Q.2d at 1038.

locking portion be[ ] more rigid than said base portion,' is claimed. That the claim is broad is no reason to excuse noncompliance with the best mode requirement. Here, the information the applicant is accused of concealing is not merely necessary to practice the claimed invention, as in *Dana* fluoride surface treatment was 'necessary to satisfactory performance' of the claimed valve stem seal, 860 F.2d at 418; it also describes the preferred embodiment of a claimed element, as in *Spectra-Physics* the undisclosed braze cycle was the preferred 'means for attaching' and 'securing' claimed in the patents at issue." [300]

[*viii*]   *Trade Secrets.* The best mode requirement forces the inventor to disclose information he might otherwise preserve as a trade secret. Must an inventor disclose details of a contemplated best mode if they include trade secrets owned by another? In *Chemcast*,[301] the court stated that an inventor need not disclose what he or she does not know but that otherwise trade secrecy is no excuse for failure to set forth a contemplated best mode. The patentee's claimed invention required that a grommet's locking portion be of material of a specified hardness. The inventor preferred the material of a certain supplier ("R-4467" from Reynosol Corporation). The inventor's specification identified neither the supplier nor the trademark nor the material's characteristics.

> "That [the inventor's supplier] Reynosol considered the formulation of R-4467 a trade secret and that it offered the compound only to [the patentee] . . . do not bear on the state of [the inventor] Rubright's knowledge or the quality of his disclosure. First, it is undisputed that Rubright did not know either the precise formulation or method of manufacture of R-4467; he knew only that it was a rigid PVC plastisol composition denominated 'R-4467' by Reynosol. Whatever the scope of Reynosol's asserted trade secret, to the extent it includes information known by Rubright that he considered part of his preferred mode, section 112 requires that he divulge it. See *White Consol. Indus. v. Vega Servo-Control,* 713 F.2d 788, 791 (Fed.Cir.1983). Second, whether and to whom [the supplier] Reynosol chooses to sell its products cannot control the extent to which [the inventor] Rubright must disclose his best mode. Were this the law, inventors like Rubright could readily circumvent the best mode requirement by concluding sole-user agreements with the suppliers of their preferred materials." [302]

It also dismissed as irrelevant "the fact that [the inventor] developed his preferred mode with the requirements of a particular customer in mind."

> "[C]ompliance with section 112 does not turn on why or for whom an inventor develops his invention. An inventor need not disclose manufacturing data or the requirements of a particular customer *if* that information is not part of the best mode of practicing the claimed invention, see *Christianson,* . . . but the converse also is true. Whether characterizable as 'manufacturing

---

[300] 913 F.2d at 928, 16 U.S.P.Q.2d 1036.

[301] Chemcast Corp. v. Arco Industries Corp., 913 F.2d 923, 16 U.S.P.Q.2d 1033 (Fed. Cir. 1990).

[302] 913 F.2d at 930, 16 U.S.P.Q.2d 1038.

data,' 'customer requirements,' or even 'trade secrets,' information necessary to practice the best mode simply must be disclosed." [303]

[ix]   *Time Frame.* Case law confirms that the best mode is that contemplated as of the *filing date;* a patentee's use of a different mode in commercial embodiments does not establish a best mode violation.[304] The date-of-filing rule entails grave risk of an inadvertent violation when a patent application discloses one mode and the inventor, still working in the laboratory, develops a better mode a day or two before the application is filed.

Whether an applicant on filing a continuation or continuation- in-part application must "update" the best mode disclosure is an issue upon which there is a dearth of authority. The statutory basis for finding a duty to update would simply be that a continuation or CIP application is still an application with a specification and Section 112 states that the specification shall set forth the best mode. On the other hand, imposing the duty to update may be a considerable burden on applicants; if a new best mode has been generated since the filing date, the applicant could not file a "continuation" because the addition of the new mode would probably be viewed as "new matter" that would convert the application to a "continuation-in-part." [305]

---

[303] 913 F.2d at 930, 16 U.S.P.Q.2d 1038.

[304] Texas Instruments Inc. v. U.S. Int'l Trade Comm'n, 871 F.2d 1054, 1061, 10 U.S.P.Q.2d 1257, 1262 (Fed. Cir. 1989) (that the patent's assignee manufactured products containing a different or better form of product than that disclosed in the patent "is not pertinent to whether the specification disclosed" the best mode).

[305] In Johns-Manville Corp. v. Guardian Indus. Corp., 586 F. Supp. 1034, 221 U.S.P.Q. 319 (E.D. Mich. 1983), aff'd, 770 F.2d 178 (Fed. Cir. 1985) (unpublished opinion), the district court dealt with the issue of updating the best mode as follows:

> "There is no dispute that plaintiff disclosed the best mode of the invention in the original application, filed December 22, 1972. Defendants urge, however, that when plaintiff filed a subsequent continuation-in-part application, January 27, 1975, the inventors were obligated to also disclose refinements that had been developed in the interim. Defendants claim that J-M failed to disclose the heat shield combustion chamber, trade secret No. 6, and the alternating straight and vee jets on the air ring, trade secret No. 8, and that therefore the patent is invalid.
>
> . . .
>
> "The heat shield combustion chamber (trade secret No. 6) was first disclosed August 28, 1973, in a HERM status report by Don Simmers. . . . *Plaintiff would have been obligated to disclose this refinement if it were essential to the successful practice of the invention, and if it related to amendments to the continuation-in-part which were not present in the parent application.* Neither of those conditions obtains. None of the alterations made in J-M's CIP application was related to the heat shield disclosed in the original application. The same drawings were used throughout the application process. The disclosure and specifications which related to the heat shield were not changed during the application process and, therefore, were not a factor in the ultimate decision to grant the patent. Plaintiff, not being aware that the heat shield combustion chamber comprised the best mode of the invention on December 22, 1972, was under no obligation to disclose it on a continuation-in-part application. *See* Sylgab Wire & Steel Corp. v. Imoco Gatway Corp., 357 F. Supp. 657, 659, 178 U.S.P.Q. 22, 23 (N.D. Ill. 1973).

When an inventor or company files a patent application abroad and then, within a year, files a corresponding application in the United States, Section 119 provides a right of priority.[306] Generally, a "foreign priority" application must disclose the invention in the manner required by the U.S. patent disclosure statute, 35 U.S.C. Section 112,[307] which includes the best mode requirement. Thus, the foreign inventor or company must, to obtain U.S. priority benefits, set forth the "best mode" as of the filing abroad even though the laws of the country in question may not require such a disclosure. Must the best mode disclosure be updated upon filing in the United States? The district court decision in *Tyler Refrigeration Corp.*,[308] said no: Section 119 "provides that the effective date of the later filed U.S. . . . . application is entitled to the . . . filing date . . . in Japan. Thus, in determining the best mode under Section 112, it is the knowledge held at and before that date and not at some later date."

[x]   *Cure.* Is there a sound policy justification for denying entitlement to the filing date of a patent application that adequately discloses the invention and how to make and use it but fails to disclose the best mode? There are good arguments for nondenial when the original nondisclosure was without deceptive intent and the applicant adds the best mode as of the original filing date before the patent issues. The addition might be accomplished without violating the new matter prohibition by filing a continuation-in-part application. In other contexts, the courts distinguish between disclosures necessary to show full possession of the invention, which must be present on the filing date, and disclosures necessary to provide full information to the public.[309]

"The parties dispute when the HERM development team first concluded that the *best* mode of operating the air rings was the alternating straight and vee jets, which was disclosed by Simmers in a report dated April 23, 1975. . . . There is no credible, documented testimony . . . to support Faulkner's assertion that the vee jets were in use prior to January 27, 1975, or that they were known to be the best mode of operating the air ring at the time the continuation-in-part was filed.[Footnote 33]

["(Footnote 33) *Because the continuation made only minor technical and clerical changes to the claims and specifications, no obligation arose to update disclosures when it was filed* September 20, 1976. Sylgab, *supra*, at 658, 178 U.S.P.Q. at 23. Furthermore, because the continuation, like the continuation-in-part, met all of the requirements of 35 U.S.C. § 120, J-M remained entitled to the benefits of the earlier filing date." (Emphasis added.)] 586 F. Supp. at 1065-66, 221 U.S.P.Q. at 344-45 (Emphasis added.)

[306] *See* § 2H[2].

[307] Kawai v. Metlesics, 480 F.2d 880, 178 U.S.P.Q. 158 (CCPA 1973). *Kawai* did not deal with best mode disclosures but rather with the U.S. requirement that a minimum utility for an invention be disclosed, but states a general principle that foreign priority applications must comply with U.S. disclosure requirements.

[308] Tyler Refrigeration Corp. v. Kysor Industrial Corp., 601 F. Supp. 590, 605, 225 U.S.P.Q. 492, 504 (D. Del. 1985), *aff'd*, 777 F.2d 687, 227 U.S.P.Q. 845 (Fed. Cir. 1985).

[309] *E.g., In re* Lundak, 773 F.2d 1216, 227 U.S.P.Q. 90 (Fed. Cir. 1985) (deposit of disclosed microorganism may be after filing but before issue); *In re* Hawkins, 486 F.2d 569, 179 U.S.P.Q. 157 (CCPA 1973) (full text of material incorporated by reference); *In re* Davies, 475 F.2d 667, 177 U.S.P.Q. 381 (CCPA 1973) (unexpected properties that support the patentability of the claimed chemical compound).

The principal question regarding a continuation-in-part application that adds the best mode as of the parent application's filing date is whether the CIP will retain the benefit of that date. Section 120 provides that a continuing application is entitled to the benefit of the filing date of a prior application only if it is "for an *invention disclosed* [in the prior application] in the manner provided by the first paragraph of section 112."[310] Section 112 provides that the inventor must (a) "describe" "the invention" and how to make and use it, and (b) "set forth" the best mode, etc. Section 120 may apply to (a) but not (b).

[d] **Claims.** The specification filed as part of the application must "conclude with one or more claims particularly pointing out and distinctly claiming the subject matter which the applicant regards as his invention."[311]

Claims serve two functions. First, they measure the invention for determining patentability.[312] The utility, novelty, nonobviousness, and disclosure requirements' focus is on the invention defined by the claims.[313] Second, they measure the invention for determining infringement.[314] A patentee has no exclusive rights to subject matter disclosed in the specification or drawings but not covered by a claim.

The Patent Act imposes no rules on the format or terminology of claims, but the PTO imposes ordering and format requirements.[315] A claim is the object of a single sentence and contains a preamble and one or more "elements" or "limitations." "[T]he terms and phrases used in the claims must find clear support and an antecedent basis in the description so that the meaning of the terms in the claims may be ascertainable by reference to the description."[316]

[i] *Definiteness.* Claims must be definite enough to provide clear warning as to what constitutes infringement and to provide a clear measure of the invention in order to facilitate the patentability determination.[317]

A claim must reasonably apprise persons of ordinary skill in the art of the invention's scope.[318] A claim as precise as the subject matter permits complies with

---

[310] 35 U.S.C. § 120 (Emphasis added.) *See* § 2D[4][b][ii].

[311] 35 U.S.C. § 112 (2d paragraph).

[312] Jackson Jordan, Inc. v. Plasser American Corp., 747 F.2d 1567, 1578, 224 U.S.P.Q. 1, 9 (Fed. Cir. 1984) ("the *claims,* not particular embodiments, must be the focus of the obviousness inquiry.").

[313] *See generally* D. Chisum, Patents § 8.03.

[314] Sealed Air Corp. v. United States Int'l Trade Comm'n, 645 F.2d 976, 985, 209 U.S.P.Q. 469, 477 (CCPA 1981) ("it is axiomatic that the claims measure the invention, and courts may neither add to nor detract from a claim."). *See* § 2F.

[315] 37 C.F.R. § 1.75.

[316] 37 C.F.R. § 1.75(d)(1).
In drafting the specification and claims, the applicant need not use generally accepted terminology and may choose his or her own terms, so long as the meaning is clear. W.L. Gore & Associates, Inc. v. Garlock, Inc., 721 F.2d 1540, 1558, 220 U.S.P.Q. 303, 316 (Fed. Cir. 1983), *cert. denied,* 469 U.S. 851 (1983) ("a patent applicant may be his own lexicographer").

[317] United Carbon Co. v. Binney & Smith Co., 317 U.S. 228, 236, 55 U.S.P.Q. 381 (1942).

[318] Georgia-Pacific Corp. v. United States Plywood Corp., 258 F.2d 124, 134-38, 118 U.S.P.Q. 122, 130 (2d Cir. 1958), *cert. denied,* 358 U.S. 884, 119 U.S.P.Q. 501 (1958).

the definiteness requirement.[319]

In determining definiteness, a claim must not be read abstractly but rather in light of the prior art and the teachings of the specification and drawings.[320] The specification may render an apparently clear term indefinite or an apparently unclear term definite.[321]

A claim may include relation, degree, range and approximation terms if the specification provides sufficient guidance to allow a person of ordinary skill in the art to determine whether a particular product or process falls within the claim.[322]

---

[319] Shatterproof Glass Corp. v. Libbey-Owens Ford Co., 758 F.2d 613, 225 U.S.P.Q. 634 (Fed. Cir. 1985), cert. dismissed, 474 U.S. 976 (1985).

[320] In re Moore, 439 F.2d 1232, 1235, 169 U.S.P.Q. 236 (CCPA 1971). See § 4B[1].

Courts determine claim definiteness in view of the prior art as of the filing date and consider later issuing patents only insofar as they reflect the filing date state of the art. In re Voss, 557 F.2d 812, 819 n.15, 194 U.S.P.Q. 267, 272 n.15 (CCPA 1977). It is impermissible to rely on post-filing date developments and publications to show claim language uncertainty. W.L. Gore & Associates, Inc. v. Garlock, Inc., 721 F.2d 1540, 220 U.S.P.Q. 303 (Fed. Cir. 1983), cert. denied, 469 U.S. 851 (1984).

[321] In re Cohn, 438 F.2d 989, 169 U.S.P.Q. 95 (CCPA 1971).

[322] Seattle Box Co., Inc. v. Industrial Crating & Packing, Inc., 731 F.2d 818, 221 U.S.P.Q. 568 (Fed. Cir. 1984); Rosemount, Inc. v. Beckman Instruments, Inc., 727 F.2d 1540, 221 U.S.P.Q. 1 (Fed. Cir. 1984); W.L. Gore & Associates, Inc. v. Garlock, Inc., 721 F.2d 1540, 220 U.S.P.Q. 303, 316 (Fed. Cir. 1983), cert. denied, 469 U.S. 851 (1984); In re Marosi, 710 F.2d 799, 218 U.S.P.Q. 289 (Fed. Cir. 1983). Compare Amgen, Inc. v. Chugai Pharmaceutical Co., Ltd., 927 F.2d 1200, 18 U.S.P.Q.2d 1016 (Fed. Cir. 1991).

In Seattle Box, the court held the phrase "substantially equal" not impermissibly indefinite. In W.L. Gore, the court held the phrase "stretching . . . at a rate exceeding about 10% per second" not impermissibly indefinite. In Marosi, the court held the phrase "essentially free of alkali metal" not impermissibly indefinite.

In Amgen, the court held invalid for indefiniteness claims to a purified protein of "at least about" a numerically specific activity level. The patent disclosed a method of purifying human erythropoietin (EPO) using reverse phase high performance liquid chromatography (RP-HPLC). Several claims recite "a specific activity of at least 160,000 IU per absorbance unit at 280 nanometers." Claims 4 and 6 recite specific activity of "at least about 160,000." The inventor amended the claims' activity level from 120,000 to 160,000 after the examiner rejected the claims on a reference showing a 128,620 activity. The district court found that bioassays provided imprecise measurement such that "use of the term 'about' 160,000 IU/AU, coupled with the range of error already inherent in the specific activity limitation, served neither to distinguish the invention over the close prior art . . . nor to permit one to know what specific activity values below 160,000, if any, might constitute infringement." The inventor testified that "somewhere between 155[,000], might fit within that number." The patent owner's joint venture partner questioned whether the specific activity value of 138,000 IU/AU for its own EPO was within the claim coverage."

"A decision as to whether a claim is invalid under this provision requires a determination whether those skilled in the art would understand what is claimed. . . . [N]othing in the specification, prosecution history, or prior art provides any indication as to what range of specific activity is covered by the term 'about,' and . . . no expert testified as to definite meaning for the term in the context of the prior art. . . . When the meaning of claims is in doubt, especially when . . . there is close prior art, they are properly declared invalid. . . . [O]ur holding that the term 'about' renders indefinite claims 4 and 6 should

An interesting issue is whether a claim can be fatally indefinite under Section 112 because there are two plausible interpretations, both definite in scope. Courts often assume this is a problem of proper claim interpretation, not indefiniteness.[323]

[ii] *New Terminology.* The applicant need not use conventional terminology in claims even though use of variant or new terminology makes comparison of the claimed subject matter with the prior art more difficult.[324]

[iii] *Format: Preamble, Transition, Elements— Preambles as Claim Limitation.* Claims commonly have three parts: a preamble, a transition, and a body of limitations.

Consider the following claim:

> "A porous material consisting essentially of highly crystalline polytetra-fluoroethylene polymer, which material has a microstructure characterized by nodes interconnected by fibrils and has a matrix tensile strength in at least one direction above about 73,000 psi."[325]

---

not be understood as ruling out any and all uses of this term in patent claims. It may be acceptable in appropriate fact situations. . . . " 927 F.2d at 1218, 18 U.S.P.Q.2d at 1031.

[323] In Hoffman-LaRoche Inc. v. Burroughs Wellcome Co., 10 U.S.P.Q.2d 1602, 1607 (D. Md. 1989), the patent claimed "human leukocyte interferon as a *homogeneous* protein species." U.S. Patent No. 4,503,035. Two scientists postulated the existence of interferon in 1957, but efforts to purify and isolate interferon from its non-interferon contaminants by use of traditional purification methods failed. In the late 1970's, the inventors, two Hoffman-LaRoche scientists, Pestka and Rubinstein, used high performance liquid chromatography to obtain an alpha interferon preparation that was free of non-protein contaminants. They discovered, unexpectedly, that the interferon was separated into numerous homogeneous alpha interferon subtypes of species. Before allowing the claims, the PTO examiner instructed Hoffman-LaRoche to use the term "homogeneous" in conjunction with the term "species."

The accused infringer, Burroughs Wellcome, produced an unisolated mixture of pure interferon species. It moved for summary judgment that it did not infringe because the patent claims should be construed as limited to "a single isolated species of interferon or mixtures of once-isolated species." The patentee responded that the patent claims cover "homogeneous" interferon in the sense of the substance itself free from non-protein contaminants, whether it appears in a mixture of contaminant-free interferon or in a single-species purification. The district court denied this motion, finding disputed fact issues as to which of the two constructions was the proper one.

Alternatively, the accused infringer moved for summary judgment that the claim was ambiguous because of the two plausible but substantially different interpretations of the meaning of "homogeneous." Again, the court denied the motion: "The only argument here is a factual one— whether the '035 patent does or does not apply to mixed families of non-contaminated interferon. There is no possible issue of law that could resolve this question." 10 U.S.P.Q.2d at 1607.

[324] *In re* Fisher, 427 F.2d 833, 838, 166 U.S.P.Q. 18 (CCPA 1970).

If the PTO finds the claim resembles the prior art but uses different terminology, it may require the applicant to submit comparative evidence.

[325] This is claim 1 from U.S. Patent No. 4,187,390, held valid in W.L. Gore & Associates, Inc. v. Garlock, Inc., 721 F.2d 1540, 220 U.S.P.Q. 303 (Fed. Cir. 1983), *cert. denied,* 469 U.S. 851 (1984).

In this claim, the preamble is "a porous material," the transition is "consisting essentially of," and the remainder is the body of elements.[326]

Whether a preamble limits the claim's scope for patentability or infringement purposes is a frequently raised issue. A preamble that states an intended use or inherent property, the body of limitation being a complete definition of the product or process, is not a limitation.[327] A preamble that states the structure or steps necessary to give meaning to the claim and properly define the invention is a limitation.[328]

In *Corning Glass Works*,[329] the court stressed:

> "No litmus test can be given with respect to when the introductory words of a claim, the preamble, constitute a statement of purpose for a device or are, in themselves, additional structural limitations of a claim. To say that a preamble is a limitation if it gives 'meaning to the claim' may merely state the problem rather than lead one to the answer. The effect preamble language should be given can be resolved only on review of the entirety of the patent to gain an understanding of what the inventors actually invented and intended to encompass by the claim."[330]

The court interpreted a claim's preamble, "an optical waveguide," as a structural limitation rather than a statement of purpose.[331] Read in light of the

---

[326] The three-part structure can also be used to define an element in a claim, for example, "A book comprising a plurality of pages and a cover consisting of imprinted plastic."

[327] *In re* Pearson, 494 F.2d 1399, 1402-03, 181 U.S.P.Q. 641 (CCPA 1974); Marston v. J.C. Penney Co., 353 F.2d 976, 148 U.S.P.Q. 25 (4th Cir. 1965), *cert. denied*, 385 U.S. 974, 151 U.S.P.Q. 757 (1966); Western Broadcasting Co., Ltd. v. Capitol Records, Inc., 218 U.S.P.Q. 94 (N.D. Calif. 1981).

In *Marston,* the claim was to a "buoyant, flexible filler pad comprising a plurality of strip portions arranged in laterally disposed relation" etc. The defendant's product used the arrangement as chair webbing. The court held that the preamble reference to a buoyant pad was not a limitation and that the chair infringed the claim even though it was not buoyant.

[328] Perkin-Elmer Corp. v. Computervision Corp., 732 F.2d 888, 221 U.S.P.Q. 669 (Fed. Cir. 1984), *cert. denied*, 469 U.S. 857 (1984); Kropa v. Robie, 187 F.2d 150, 88 U.S.P.Q. 478 (CCPA 1951).

In *Kropa,* the claim was to an "abrasive article comprising abrasive grains and a hardened binder comprising the additive reaction product of a substantially neutral unsaturated monomeric material" etc. In an interference, Kropa asserted the benefit of the filing date of a prior application that disclosed the reaction product but did not disclose an "abrasive article" as such. The court held that the preamble reference to an abrasive article was a limitation because it called for a distinct relationship between the ingredients recited in the body of claims. Therefore, Kropa was not entitled to the benefit of the filing date of the prior application.

For a discussion of prior application reliance rights, see § 2D[4][b]. For a discussion of interferences, see § 2D[5].

[329] Corning Glass Works v. Sumitomo Electric U.S.A., 868 F.2d 1251, 9 U.S.P.Q.2d 1962 (Fed. Cir. 1989).

[330] 868 F.2d at 1257, 9 U.S.P.Q.2d at 1966.

[331] The claim at issue provides, in pertinent part: "An *optical waveguide* comprising (a) a cladding layer formed of [selected] material . . . , and (b) a core formed of fused silica to which a dopant material . . . has been added to a degree in excess of that of the cladding layer so that the index of refraction thereof is of a value greater than the index of refraction of said cladding layer. . . . " (Emphasis added.)

specification, an "optical waveguide" means the structural dimensions and refractive index differential are set by a complex equation so the claimed structure will function as an optical waveguide, that is, a medium for guiding the coherent light of a laser a distance suitable for optical communications. So limited, the claim was not anticipated by prior art references that did not show optical wave guides.[332]

There are three common transitions. The first, "comprising," creates an "open" claim in which the recited elements may be only part of the product or process.[333] A claim to a product "comprising W, X, and Y" covers products with elements W, X, and Y and additional elements (such as Z). The second, "consisting of,"creates a "closed" claim in which the product or process includes the recited elements and no others.[334] A claim to a product "consisting of W, X, and Y" does not cover a product with W, X, Y and Z. The third type uses the phrase "consisting essentially of" and covers products or processes that have additional elements but only if the added elements do not materially affect the basic and novel characteristics of the product defined in the balance of the claim.[335]

The body following the transition lists one or more limitations (sometimes referred to as "elements"),[336] which define the claimed product or process. The claim covers

---

[332] The court noted:

"To read the claim in light of the specification indiscriminately to cover all types of optical fibers would be divorced from reality. The invention is restricted to those fibers that work as waveguides as defined in the specification. . . . [T]he claim preamble in this instance does not merely state a purpose or intended use for the claimed structure. . . . Rather, those words do give 'life and meaning' and provide further positive limitations to the invention claimed. . . . [T]he core and cladding limitations . . . are not the only limitations of the claim. . . . The claim requires, in addition, the particular structural relationship defined in the specification for the core and cladding to function as an optical waveguide." 868 F.2d at 1257, 9 U.S.P.Q.2d at 1967.

[333] Reese v. Hurst, 661 F.2d 1222, 211 U.S.P.Q. 936 (CCPA 1981); Ex parte Schaefer, 171 U.S.P.Q. 110 (Pat. Off. Bd. App. 1970). Cf. Moleculon Research Corp. v. CBS, Inc., 793 F.2d 1261, 229 U.S.P.Q. 805 (Fed. Cir. 1986), cert. denied, 479 U.S. 1030 (1987) (when used in a transitional phrase, "comprising" is a term of art and means that the claim does not exclude additional, unrecited elements, but when used other than in a transition, "comprising" is subject to normal interpretative rules and may mean "having" rather than "having at least.").

[334] In re Certain Slide Fastener Stringers & Machines & Components Thereof for Producing Such Slide Fastener Stringers, 216 U.S.P.Q. 907 (U.S. Int'l Trade Comm'n 1981). See also Mannesmann Demag Corp. v. Engineered Metal Products Co., Inc., 793 F.2d 1279, 230 U.S.P.Q. 45 (Fed. Cir. 1986) (when the phrase "consisting of" appears in one claim limitation, rather than in the preamble, it closes only the limitation; the phrase does not prevent the claim as a whole from reading on devices with additional elements).

[335] Atlas Powder Co. v. E.I. du Pont De Nemours & Co., 750 F.2d 1569, 224 U.S.P.Q. 409 (Fed. Cir. 1984); In re Herz, 537 F.2d 549, 190 U.S.P.Q. 461 (CCPA 1976). See also Water Technologies Corp. v. Calco, Ltd., 850 F.2d 660, 7 U.S.P.Q.2d 1097 (Fed. Cir. 1988), cert. denied, 488 U.S. 968 (1988) (the phrase "consisting essentially of" does not exclude additional ingredients that do not materially affect the invention's characteristics).

[336] The Federal Circuit prefers "limitation." See Perkin-Elmer Corp. v. Westinghouse Electric Corp., 822 F.2d 1528, 3 U.S.P.Q.2d 1321 (Fed. Cir. 1987):

a product or process only if it contains all claim limitations.[337] A claim to a product "comprising W, X, and Y" does not literally cover a product with only W or with W and Z.[338]

[*iv*] *Jepson Claims.* A Jepson claim is to an improvement on an existing device, process or combination,[339] and includes (1) a preamble reciting conventional elements or steps, (2) a transition phrase such as "wherein the improvement comprises," and (3) the elements or steps the applicant considers to be new.

Jepson claims are not mandatory, but the PTO encourages their use "where the nature of the case admits."[340] Courts approve of and even favor Jepson claims because they separate old from new.[341] A Jepson claim is used when the novel elements relate to a very small part of an old product or process.

A Jepson claim preamble is a limitation, not a statement of intended use.[342]

If an inventor places an element in a Jepson preamble, he presumptively admits that the element is prior art[343] but may rebut the presumption.[344] No presumption arises if the preamble refers to matter in the inventor's prior patent.[345]

"References to 'elements' can be misleading. 'Elements' often is used to refer to structural parts of the accused device or of a device embodying the invention. 'Elements' is also used in the phrase '[a]n element of a claim' in 35 U.S.C. § 112 ¶ 6. An element of an embodiment of the invention may be set forth in the claim. . . . It is the *limitation* of a claim that counts in determining both validity and infringement, and a limitation may include descriptive terms . . . [C]larity is advanced when sufficient wording is employed to indicate when 'elements' is intended to mean a component of an accused device or of an embodiment of an invention and when it is intended to mean a feature set forth in or as a limitation in a claim." 822 F.2d at 1533 n.9, 3 U.S.P.Q.2d at 1325 n.9.

[337] The courts may extend a claim's scope of protection beyond its literal coverage by applying the doctrine of equivalents. *See* § 2F[2][b].

[338] Builders Concrete, Inc. v. Bremerton Concrete Products Co., 757 F.2d 255, 225 U.S.P.Q. 240 (Fed. Cir. 1985).

This rule applies to both patentability and infringement determinations. In the text example, products X and W + Z will neither anticipate the claim (if they are part of the prior art) nor be direct infringements (if they are made, sold, or used during the patent term without the patentee's authority). *See* § 2C[3][a].

Sale of a component part may be contributory infringement or inducement of infringement. *See* § 2E[2][c].

[339] "Jepson" claims are named for the Patent Office decision approving this format. *Ex parte* Jepson, 1917 Comm. Dec. 62, 243 O.G. 525 (Ass't Comm'r Pat. 1917).

[340] 37 C.F.R. § 1.75(e).

[341] Williams Mfg. Co. v. United Shoe Machinery Corp., 316 U.S. 364, 53 U.S.P.Q. 478 (1942); Blair v. Westinghouse House Elec. Corp., 291 F. Supp. 664, 160 U.S.P.Q. 155 (D.D.C. 1968), *aff'd*, Blair v. Dowd's, Inc., 438 F.2d 136, 167 U.S.P.Q. 18 (1970).

[342] Wells Mfg. Corp. v. Littelfuse, Inc., 547 F.2d 346, 192 U.S.P.Q. 256 (7th Cir. 1976). *See* § 2D[3][d][iii].

[343] *In re* Fout, 675 F.2d 297, 213 U.S.P.Q. 532 (CCPA 1982).

[344] *In re* Ehrreich, 590 F.2d 902, 200 U.S.P.Q. 504 (CCPA 1979).

[345] Reading & Bates Construction Co. v. Baker Energy Resources Corp., 748 F.2d 645, 650, 223 U.S.P.Q. 1168, 1172 (Fed. Cir. 1984).

[v] *Alternative Limitations—Markush Groups.* Early Patent Office rules prohibited alternative limitations on the ground that they were inherently ambiguous.[346] For example, a claim to "a compound consisting of A and B or C or D" was improper.

The alternative limitations ban was not a serious obstacle to claiming mechanical and electrical inventions because a suitable generic term was often available to cover the alternatives.[347] The ban was more significant with chemical inventions for which there was no suitable generic term.[348] To alleviate this problem, the Patent Office allowed use of an artificial group, referred to as a "Markush" group, in chemical applications.[349] Instead of "B or C or D", the applicant could use the form "selected from a group consisting of B and C and D."

The PTO no longer prohibits alternative limitations;[350] applicants may use "or" or a Markush group.

An applicant may use a Markush group subgeneric to a true generic class or use a plurality of Markush groups of diminishing scope.[351] For example, an applicant may state separate claims describing an element as (a) "fluids;" (b) "a fluid selected from the group consisting of water, oil, and alcohol;" and (c) "a fluid selected from the group consisting of oil and alcohol."

Markush and alternative groups may cause unity of invention problems.[352] For example, consider a claim to "A compound consisting of a first element selected from the group consisting of O, P, Q and R, a second element selected from the group consisting of S, T, U, and V and a third element selected from the group consisting of W, X, Y and Z." This claim has 64 permutations, which may vary from each other. An examiner may not impose a restriction requirement directed to a single claim, but may reject a claim for want of unity of invention if it groups independent and distinct inventions.[353]

---

[346] *Ex parte* McDougall, 18 O.G. 130, 1880 C.D. 147 (1880).

[347] Also, inventors can use "means-plus-function" limitations to describe their inventions in suitable generic terms. *See* §§ 2D[3][d][vii] and 2F[1][d].

[348] The applicant can use a separate claim for each of the elements in combination with the element A. In the text example, the applicant could include three claims: 1. A and B; 2. A and C; and 3. A and D. This significantly increases the claims and the fees.

[349] The group is named after the decision that approved of its use. *Ex parte* Markush, 1925 C.D. 126, 340 O.G. 839 (Comm'r Pat. 1924).

Prior to *Markush,* inventors claimed chemical structures in terms of one or more "R" groups defining optional substituents on a central nucleus. The technique was used to obtain appropriate generic claim coverage, not to avoid the Patent Office's alternative claim language prohibition.

[350] *See, e.g., Ex parte* Head, 214 U.S.P.Q. 551 (PTO Bd. App. 1981).

Two recent decisions refuse to condemn "optionally" as indefinite. *Ex parte* Cordova, 10 U.S.P.Q.2d 1949 (Bd. Pat. App. & Int'f 1988); *Ex parte* Wu, 10 U.S.P.Q.2d 2031 (Bd. Pat. App. & Int'f 1989).

[351] *In re* Schechter, 205 F.2d 185, 189, 98 U.S.P.Q. 144, 149 (CCPA 1953); *In re* Greider, 186 F.2d 718, 722, 88 U.S.P.Q. 384, 388 (CCPA 1951).

[352] *See* § 2D[1][b][i].

[353] *In re* Harnisch, 631 F.2d 716, 206 U.S.P.Q. 300 (CCPA 1980).

A Markush group is an implied representation that the group members are alternatively suitable for the invention's purpose,[354] but use of the group is not an admission on the state of the prior art.[355] For example, assume an applicant originally claims a compound selected from the group consisting of W, X, Y, and Z. If a specific compound of element Z is found in the prior art, the claim is not allowable. The applicant may amend the claim to narrow the group to W, X, and Y, and the applicant's own statement concerning the equivalency of Z and the other members of the group cannot be used to show obviousness.[356]

[vi] *Product-by-Process Claims.* A "product-by-process" claim defines a new product by reference to the process by which it is made. Product-by-process claims are proper if they meet the definiteness requirement.[357] The following is a product-by-process claim:

> "Shakes manufactured from a shake bolt by the process of making a plurality of cuts into and across the shake bolt to an extent to establish predetermined tip lengths, and splitting the weather end portions of the shakes from the bolt by starting the splits at the inner ends of the cuts and continuing the splits to the end of the bolt."[358]

Reference to a process defines a product-by-process claim's subject matter, but the claim is one for the product, not the process. If a product identical to that claimed is present in the prior art, then the claim is not allowable regardless of how the prior art product was made.[359] An accused product made by a different process will

---

[354] *In re* Driscoll, 562 F.2d 1245, 195 U.S.P.Q. 434 (CCPA 1977). *See* § 2D[3][b][iv].

[355] A person's own discoveries are not prior art in patentability determinations of that person's inventions. *See* §§ 2C[5][a] and [g].

[356] *In re* Ruff, 256 F.2d 590, 118 U.S.P.Q. 340 (CCPA 1958).

[357] *In re* Pilkington, 411 F.2d 1345, 162 U.S.P.Q. 145 (CCPA 1969); *In re* Steppan, 394 F.2d 1013, 156 U.S.P.Q. 143 (CCPA 1967).

Under prior practice, the Patent Office allowed product-by-process claims only if the product could not be defined in structural language. *See, e.g., In re* Brown, 29 F.2d 873, 874 (D.C. Cir. 1928). In favor of this restrictive rule is the fact that it is more difficult to determine what products are covered by a product-by-process claim: one must know how an article was or could be made. *See In re* Hughes, 496 F.2d 1216, 182 U.S.P.Q. 106 (CCPA 1974).

[358] This claim was approved in *In re* Hughes, 496 F.2d 1216, 1217, 182 U.S.P.Q. 106 (CCPA 1974).

[359] *In re* Thorpe, 777 F.2d 695, 227 U.S.P.Q. 964 (Fed. Cir. 1985) (even though product-by-process claims are limited and defined by the process, the determination of the patentability of such claims is based on the product itself; if the product in a product-by-process claim is the same as or obvious from a product of the prior art, the claim is unpatentable even though the prior art product was made by a different process); *In re* Hirao, 535 F.2d 67, 69 n.3, 190 U.S.P.Q. 15 (CCPA 1976); *In re* Brown, 459 F.2d 531, 535, 173 U.S.P.Q. 685 (CCPA 1972).

See also In re Marosi, 710 F.2d 799, 803, 218 U.S.P.Q. 289, 292-93 (Fed. Cir. 1983). In *Marosi,* the court stated that "Where a product-by-process claim is rejected over a prior art product that appears to be identical, although produced by a different process, the burden is upon the applicants to come forward with evidence establishing an unobvious difference between the claimed product and the prior art product." *See also In re* Fessman, 489 F.2d 742, 180 U.S.P.Q. 324 (CCPA 1974).

infringe the claim if it is structurally the same.[360]

In *Scripps Clinic & Research Foundation*,[361] the court confirmed that "the correct reading of product-by-process claims is that they are not limited to product prepared by the process set forth in the claims." The patent relates to a human protein, pure Factor VIII:C, the blood clotting factor, which is a small fraction of total blood plasma protein (1 of 350,000), making concentration and isolation difficult. Factor VIII:C exists in complex association with another protein, Factor VIII:RP, in a weight ratio of 1 (C) to 100 (RP). The inventors, Scripps scientists, developed a process for preparing highly purified and concentrated human or porcine Factor VIII:C. The process uses a monoclonal antibody specific for Factor VIII:RP. The patent contains process claims[362] and product-by process claims.[363]

The accused infringer produced Factor VIII:C by recombinant DNA technology, that is, by isolating the gene encoding the protein, inserting into a host cell, replicating the cell, causing the cell to excrete the protein into a culture medium, and purifying the protein from the medium using Factor VIII:C monoclonal antibodies. The Federal Circuit noted that the district court's remark that "the product-by-process claims would not be infringed unless the same process were practiced" "appears to diverge from our precedent."

> "[T]his precedent arose in the context of patent prosecution, not patent infringement. . . . In determining patentability we construe the product as not limited by the process stated in the claims. Since claims must be construed the same way for validity and for infringement, the correct reading of product-by- process claims is that they are not limited to product prepared by the process set forth in the claims."[364]

[vii] *Functionality—Means-Plus-Function Claims.* A claim may use functional language to partially define the subject matter of an invention if it meets three

---

[360] *E.g.*, Scripps Clinic & Research Foundation v. Genentech, Inc., 927 F.2d 1565, 18 U.S.P.Q.2d 1001 (Fed. Cir. 1991); *In re* Hirao, 535 F.2d 67, 69 n.3, 190 U.S.P.Q. 15 (CCPA 1976). Some older decisions adopt a contrary position. General Elec. Co. v. Wabash Appliance Corp., 304 U.S. 364, 373 (1938); *In re* Moeller, 117 F.2d 565, 568, 48 U.S.P.Q. 542 (CCPA 1941).

[361] Scripps Clinic & Research Foundation v. Genentech, Inc., 927 F.2d 1565, 18 U.S.P.Q.2d 1001 (Fed. Cir. 1991).

[362] For example, claim 1 is to:
"An improved method of preparing Factor VIII pro-coagulant activity protein comprising the steps of
"(a) adsorbing a VIII:C/VIII:RP complex from a plasma or commercial concentrate source onto particles bound to a monoclonal antibody specific to VIII:RP,
"(b) eluting the VIII:C,
"(c) adsorbing the VIII:C obtained in step (b) in another adsorption to concentrate and further purify same,
"(d) eluting the adsorbed VIII:C, and
"(e) recovering highly purified and concentrated VIII:C."

[363] For example, claim 13 is to "Highly purified and concentrated human or porcine VIII:C prepared in accordance with the method of claim 1."

[364] 927 F.2d at 1583, 18 U.S.P.Q.2d at 1016.

requirements: (1) definiteness;[365] (2) enablement (a claim for *all* means to achieve a desirable result fails to meet this requirement because the specification discloses only specified means of achieving such a result);[366] and (3) novelty- nonobviousness (if the claim covers products or processes found in the prior art, it is not allowable even if it recites a new use or intended function).[367]

Section 112's last paragraph provides that an element in a "combination" claim may be expressed as means for performing a specified function[368] and directs that "means" be construed to cover the corresponding structure, material or acts described in the specification and equivalents thereof.[369] A "combination" includes chemical compositions as well as mechanical combinations;[370] a "single means" claim is improper.[371]

---

[365] *In re* Swinehart, 439 F.2d 210, 169 U.S.P.Q. 226 (CCPA 1971).

An example of a claim using functional language is that approved in *Swinehart:*

"A new composition of matter, *transparent to infra-red rays* and resistant to thermal shock, the same being a solidified melt of two components present in proportion approximately eutectic, one of said components being BaF_2 and the other being CaF_2."

What set the composition of the claim apart from prior art compositions was the desirable function of being "transparent to infra-red rays."

Another example is a claim with the limitation "an inorganic salt that is capable of holding a mixture of [a] carbohydrate and protein in colloidal suspension in water." *See In re* Fuetterer, 319 F.2d 259, 138 U.S.P.Q. 217 (CCPA 1963).

[366] *E.g.,* Holland Furniture Co. v. Perkins Glue Co., 277 U.S. 245 (1928); *In re* Hyatt, 708 F.2d 712, 218 U.S.P.Q. 195 (Fed. Cir. 1983).

[367] *E.g., In re* King, 801 F.2d 1324, 231 U.S.P.Q. 136 (Fed. Cir. 1986); *In re* Pearson, 494 F.2d 1399, 1402-03, 181 U.S.P.Q. 641 (CCPA 1974). *See* §§ 2C[3][c] and 2C[3][c][ii].

[368] 35 U.S.C. § 112 (last paragraph).

This provision repudiates Halliburton Oil Well Cementing v. Walker, 329 U.S. 1 (1946), which was critical of means-plus-function phrases. *See* §§ 2B[4][c] and 2B[5]. *See also In re* Fuetterer, 319 F.2d 259, 138 U.S.P.Q. 217 (CCPA 1963).

[369] 35 U.S.C. § 112 (last paragraph). *See* § 2F[1][d]. *See generally* D. Chisum, Patents §§ 8.04[2], 18.03[5].

This inquiry into equivalents is more specific than that under the equitable doctrine of equivalents. *See* § 2F[2][b]. A means-plus-function clause equivalents inquiry is for the purpose of determining *literal* infringement. The focus is solely on whether the means in the accused device that performs the function stated in the claim is the same as or an equivalent of the corresponding structure described in the patentee's specification as performing that function. Palumbo v. Don-Joy Co., 762 F.2d 969, 226 U.S.P.Q. 5 (Fed. Cir. 1985); D.M.I., Inc. v. Deere & Co., 755 F.2d 1570, 225 U.S.P.Q. 236 (Fed. Cir. 1985).

See also RCA Corp. v. Applied Digital Data Sys., 730 F.2d 1440, 221 U.S.P.Q. 385 (Fed. Cir. 1984), *cert. dismissed,* 468 U.S. 1228 (1984). In RCA, the court held that, in determining novelty and anticipation, a means-plus-function format claim limitation cannot be met by a prior art reference element that performs a different function.

[370] *In re* Barr, 444 F.2d 588, 170 U.S.P.Q. 330 (CCPA 1971).

"Combination" covers processes because Section 112 refers to "steps" and "acts," which, logically, relate to process claims.

[371] O'Reilly v. Morse, 56 U.S. 62, 112 (1853); *In re* Hyatt, 708 F.2d 712, 218 U.S.P.Q. 195 (Fed. Cir. 1983). *Hyatt* disapproved of the following claim:

"A Fourier transform processor for generating Fourier transformed incremental output signals in response to incremental input signals, said Fourier transform processor

[viii] *Negative Limitations.* A claim may contain one or more negative limitations if the claim's meaning is clear. Older cases held that a negative limitation, such as "a metal other than copper" rendered a claim inherently indefinite or unduly broad.[372] More recent cases hold that negative limitations are proper if they define a clear alternative and the specification supports the claim breadth.[373]

[ix] *Multiple Claims—Dependent Claims.* A patent application may include more than one claim if the claims differ substantially and are not unduly multiplied.[374] The PTO may reject patent application claims for undue multiplication if the number of claims obscures the invention.[375]

An applicant includes claims of varying scope to effectively protect the disclosed invention. Satisfactory definition of the invention in a single claim is often impossible because of uncertainty about the prior art and future embodiments. An application may put claims in dependent form by referring back to another claim.[376] A dependent claim includes all the elements of the claims on which it depends.

Consider the following four claims.

1. A composition comprising a fluid and soap.

2. The composition of claim 1 wherein the fluid is water.

3. The composition of claim 2 further including a dye.

4. The composition recited in claim 1 or 2 wherein the soap is lye soap.

Claim 1 is an *independent* claim because it is self-contained and refers to no other claim. Claim 2 is a *dependent* claim that narrows claim 1's scope by narrowing one element. The claim 1 soap element is incorporated into claim 2. Claim 3 is a dependent claim that narrows claim 2's scope by adding an element (a dye). The claim 1 soap element and the claim 2 water element are incorporated into claim 3.[377] Claim 4 is a multiple dependent claim that alternatively incorporates claim 1 and claim 2's elements and narrows claim 1 and 2's soap element.

Because a dependent claim incorporates all the elements of the claims to which it refers, nothing can fall within a dependent claim without also falling within all of

---

comprising incremental means for incrementally generating the Fourier transformed incremental output signals in response to incremental input signals."
A single means claim necessarily violates the enablement requirement because it covers every conceivable means for achieving the stated result and the specification discloses only those means known to the inventor.

[372] *In re* Schechter, 205 F.2d 185, 98 U.S.P.Q. 144 (CCPA 1953).

[373] *In re* Duva, 387 F.2d 402, 408, 156 U.S.P.Q. 90 (CCPA 1967); *In re* Bankowski, 318 F.2d 778, 782-83, 138 U.S.P.Q. 75 (CCPA 1963).

[374] *Cf.* 37 C.F.R. § 1.75(b). Separate claims often differ minimally. *Cf.* Wahpeton Canvas Company, Inc. v. Frontier, Inc., 870 F.2d 1546, 1553 n.10, 10 U.S.P.Q.2d 1201, 1207 n.10 (Fed. Cir. 1989) ("Like many, if not most, dependent claims, most of those present here present minute structural details but were allowed because they contain all the limitations of allowed claims from which they depend.").

[375] *In re* Wakefield, 422 F.2d 897, 164 U.S.P.Q. 636, 165 U.S.P.Q. 612 (CCPA 1970).

[376] 35 U.S.C. § 112; 37 C.F.R. § 1.75(c).

[377] If claim 3 only referred to claim 1, it would not contain the water element of claim 2.

the claims on which it depends,[378] and usually a dependent claim is patentable if the claim on which it depends is patentable.[379]

Each claim in an issued patent is presumed valid. A dependent claim is presumed valid even though it is dependent upon an invalid claim.[380]

[e] **Inventor Identification—Joint Invention.** A patent application must be "made, or authorized to be made, by the inventor"[381] except in statutorily defined exceptional

---

[378] Teledyne McCormick Selph v. United States, 558 F.2d 1000, 195 U.S.P.Q. 261 (Ct. Cl. 1977). *See also* Wahpeton Canvas Company, Inc. v. Frontier, Inc., 870 F.2d 1546, 10 U.S.P.Q.2d 1201 (Fed. Cir. 1989). *Compare* Wilson Sporting Goods Co. v. David Geoffrey & Associates, 904 F.2d 677, 685, 14 U.S.P.Q.2d 1942, 1949 (Fed. Cir. 1990), *cert. denied*, 111 S.Ct. 537 (1990) (axiom that "dependent claims cannot be found infringed unless the claims from which they depend have been found to have been infringed" "is no doubt generally correct" but does not apply when the prior art restricts the scope of the doctrine of equivalents for the independent claim in a way that does not apply to a dependent claim).

In *Wahpeton*, the Federal Circuit lamented the patentee's assertion of numerous dependent claims in a jury trial and wondered why a patentee would, on appeal, seek reversal of a judgment of noninfringement of numerous *dependent* claims when a reversal of the judgment of noninfringement of the *independent* claim would give the patentee all the relief to which it is entitled, invalidity not being an issue.

"Because a reversal on appeal on one independent claim would give [the patentee] all it needs for victory, submission of the infringement issue on a plethora of dependent claims in [a JNOV] motion and appeal is difficult to understand. Infringement of an independent claim would result in the same damage award as would infringement of all claims dependent thereon and non-infringement of an independent claim carries with it non-infringement of all claims dependent thereon.

"If validity were in issue, dependent claims might serve a useful role, for a necessarily narrower dependent claim may be valid when the claim from which it depends is not." 870 F.2d at 1552 n.10, 10 U.S.P.Q.2d at 1207 n.10.

[379] *In re* Johnson, 589 F.2d 1070, 200 U.S.P.Q. 199 (CCPA 1978). *See also* Hartness International, Inc. v. Simplimatic Engineering Co., 819 F.2d 1100, 1108, 2 U.S.P.Q.2d 1826, 1831 (Fed. Cir. 1987) (the district court erred in holding a dependent claim invalid for lack of novelty; because the court had held the claim on which it depended not invalid for obviousness, "[a] *fortiori*, [the] dependent claim . . . was nonobvious (and novel) because it contained all the limitations of [the independent] claim . . . plus a further limitation.").

A dependent claim may add an element that lacks specification support and hence will fail to meet the description or enablement requirement even though a broader claim on which it depends is totally valid. *See* §§ 2D[3][a] and[b].

[380] 35 U.S.C. § 282. *See* § 2F[4][a][i].

A person challenging a patent's claims validity must submit evidence supporting an invalidity conclusion as to each challenged claim. Shelcore, Inc. v. Durham Indus., Inc., 745 F.2d 621, 624, 223 U.S.P.Q. 584, 586 (Fed. Cir. 1984). *Compare* N.V. Akzo v. E.I. du Pont de Nemours & Co., 810 F.2d 1148, 1 U.S.P.Q.2d 1704 (Fed. Cir. 1987) (the district court did not err in failing to address each claim separately; because each claim contained a 5% limitation found to be insufficient to distinguish the prior art, the basis for rejecting the broadest claim applied to all claims).

[381] 35 U.S.C. § 111; 37 C.F.R. § 1.41(a). If an inventor's authorization is questioned, then the applicant must show authorization. 37 C.F.R. § 41(d).

In an application containing multiple claims, not all the named inventors need be inventors of all the claims' subject matter. *See* § 2D[3][e][iv].

circumstances.[382] The inventor or inventors must apply even if they have assigned ownership rights to another, such as an inventor's employer.[383] The inventor must read and understand the application and sign a declaration or oath stating that he believes he is the first inventor. Even in the exceptional cases in which some one other than the inventor applies, the application must identify the actual inventor or inventors. Inventor identification may be corrected upon a satisfactory proof that an error was made without deceptive intent.[384]

[i]   *Sole and Joint Inventorship.* An invention may be sole or joint. When more than one person works on a project, who is an inventor depends on the quality of the contributions each makes to the claimed invention.[385]

[ii]   *Sole Invention.* A sole invention occurs when one person conceives of the essential features or elements that represent an advance over the prior art. A person remains a sole inventor if others posed a problem to be solved (rather than devised the solution),[386] made minor contributions or suggestions,[387] or participated in reducing the invention to practice by building and testing an embodiment.[388] One who conceives of a complete invention is a sole inventor even though another discovers its novelty or distinguishing features.[389]

---

[382] 35 U.S.C. §§ 117-118.

Section 117 allows a legal representative of the inventor to apply if the inventor is dead or legally incapacitated. *See* 37 C.F.R. § 1.43.

Section 118 allows a person other than the inventor (including a company) to apply if that person establishes a "sufficient proprietary interest" (*i.e.* ownership of the patent rights of the inventor) and either (1) the inventor cannot be reached or found after a diligent effort, or (2) the inventor refuses to sign. *See* 37 C.F.R. § § 1.42-.43. Similarly, in the case of a joint invention, one joint inventor may apply alone on behalf of the joint inventors if the other joint inventor cannot be found or refuses to join. 35 U.S.C. § 116; 37 C.F.R. § 47(a).

The ownership of patent rights is discussed at § 2F.

[383] 37 C.F.R. § 1.46. After the application is filed in the name of the inventor, further prosecution of the application may be carried on by the assignee of the whole interest to the exclusion of the inventor. 37 C.F.R. § 1.32.

[384] *See* § 2D[3][e][v].

[385] Inventorship rules differ from country to country. Person A may be the sole inventor of an invention in the United States but a joint inventor with person B in another country. A United States application must comply with United States inventorship standards—even when the application relies on a priority filing in another country. *See* § 2H[2][d].

[386] Garrett Corp. v. United States, 422 F.2d 874, 881, 164 U.S.P.Q. 521, 526 (Ct. Cl. 1970), *cert. denied,* 400 U.S. 951, 167 U.S.P.Q. 705 (1970).

[387] Shatterproof Glass Corp. v. Libbey-Owens Ford Co., 758 F.2d 613, 225 U.S.P.Q. 634 (Fed. Cir. 1985), *cert. dismissed,* 474 U.S. 976 (1985).

[388] Minerals Separation, Ltd. v. Hyde, 242 U.S. 261 (1916).

[389] MacMillan v. Moffett, 432 F.2d 1237, 1239, 167 U.S.P.Q. 550, 552 (CCPA 1970); *In re* Zenitz, 333 F.2d 924, 142 U.S.P.Q. 158 (1964). *Compare* General Tire & Rubber Co. v. Jefferson Chem. Co., 497 F.2d 1283, 182 U.S.P.Q. 70 (2d Cir. 1974), *cert. denied,* 419 U.S. 968, 186 U.S.P.Q. 513 (1974).

   In *MacMillan,* the court discussed the matter as follows:

   "We do not think that the conceiver must know the unexpected properties associated with the conceived invention . . . nor even that the conceived subject matter is new.

[iii]   *Joint Invention.* A joint invention occurs when two or more persons contribute to the invention conception.[390] People may be joint inventors "even though (1) they did not physically work together or at the same time, [or] (2) each did not make the same type or amount of contribution."[391]

In *General Motors,*[392] the Sixth Circuit held that a joint invention may occur when one person or a group of people makes an operable but imperfect embodiment of an invention and a second person or group makes an improved embodiment, all part of a research project.

[iv]   *Separate Claims.* A patent application may contain more than one claim, each claim varying in coverage.[393] Early cases stated that the inventor or inventors named in the application must be the correct inventive entity as to the subject matter of all the claims. For example, it was not proper for A and B to file an application with claim 1 covering X and claim 2 covering Y if A and B were the joint inventors of X but A was the sole inventor of Y.

A 1984 amendment provides that persons may apply for a patent jointly even though "each did not make a contribution to the subject matter of every claim of the patent."[394] In the example, A and B's application claiming X and Y is proper. In *Smithkline Diagnostics,*[395] the court held that the amendment codifies the better

---

These facts are of course relevant to patentability, but there is no requirement in the law that a conceiver be aware of the facts which render the conceived subject matter *patentable*. The 'appreciation' requirement is no more than a recognition requirement applied in cases wherein the invention is produced unintentionally."

[390] In Monsanto Co. v. Kamp, 269 F. Supp. 818, 154 U.S.P.Q. 259 (D.D.C. 1967), the court discussed joint invention:

"A joint invention is the product of collaboration of the inventive endeavors of two or more persons working toward the same end and producing an invention by their aggregate efforts. To constitute a joint invention, it is necessary that each of the inventors work on the same subject matter and make some contribution to the inventive thought and to the final result. Each needs to perform but a part of the task if an invention emerges from all of the steps taken together. It is not necessary that the entire inventive concept should occur to each of the joint inventors, or that the two should physically work on the project together. One may take a step at one time, the other an approach at different times. One may do more of the experimental work while the other makes suggestions from time to time. The fact that each of the inventors plays a different role and that the contribution of one may not be as great as that of another, does not detract from the fact that the invention is joint, if each makes some original contribution, though partial, to the final solution of the problem." 269 F. Supp. at 824.

The Congressional Report on the 1984 amendment to Section 116, which partially defines joint invention, cites *Monsanto.*

[391] 35 U.S.C. § 116. The quoted phrases were added to Section 116 by a 1984 amendment.

[392] General Motors Corp. v. Toyota Motor Co., 667 F.2d 504, 212 U.S.P.Q. 659 (6th Cir. 1981), cert. denied, 456 U.S. 937, 215 U.S.P.Q. 95 (1982).

[393] See § 2D[3][d][ix].

[394] 35 U.S.C. § 116.

[395] Smithkline Diagnostics, Inc. v. Helena Laboratories Corp., 859 F.2d 878, 8 U.S.P.Q.2d 1468 (Fed. Cir. 1988).

rule prevailing prior to its enactment and, therefore, applies to pending cases involving pre-1984 cases.

When multiple inventors are named, it is still necessary that each has made an inventive contribution to at least one claim.[396] The PTO may require the applicants to identify the inventive entity and invention date of each claim's subject matter.[397] Identification may be necessary because one claim's subject matter may be prior art in determining the another claim's patentability.[398]

Claim amendments or additions may change the inventive entities. In the example above, if the claim to X (by A and B) is cancelled, leaving only the claim to Y (by B), the application must be amended to delete A.[399] If a third claim for subject matter Z is added, and Z is a joint invention by A, B, and C, the application must be amended to add C.[400]

[v] *Inventorship Error Correction.* It is difficult to determine who is an inventor, and errors are often made in identifying inventors in patent applications. If the error was made without deceptive intention, the inventor identification may be corrected. For example, if a patent issues to A for X, and B is the correct sole inventor of X, it is possible to correct the patent and substitute B for A as the named inventor. Factual errors and judgment errors are correctable.[401]

Section 116 provides for correcting inventorship in pending patent applications.[402]

---

[396] 37 C.F.R. § 1.45(c).

[397] 37 C.F.R. § 1.110.

[398] 37 C.F.R. § 78(c). For a discussion of prior art, see §§ 2C[5] and 2C[5][g].

In the text example, the separately claimed subject matters X and Y are not prior art to each other for obviousness purposes under Section 102(f) or 102(g) if the inventive entities A-B and A were under a duty to assign the patent rights to a single entity (such as their employer). *See* §§ 2C[5][e] and [g]. Separately invented and claimed subject matters X and Y may be prior art to each other under Sections 102(f) or 102(g) if A and B worked for different companies that separately owned the patent rights, or under Section 102(a) if they have been published or patented anywhere or known or used in the United States. *See* § 2C[5][a].

Placing the subject matters of X and Y in one application rather than in separate applications eliminates the problem of one being prior art against the other under Section 102(e). *See* § 2C[5][d].

[399] 37 C.F.R. § 1.48(b). The amendment is by a petition, which must include a statement "identifying each named inventor who is being deleted and acknowledging that the inventor's invention is no longer being claimed in the application."

[400] 37 C.F.R. § 1.48(c).

[401] *In re* Schmidt, 293 F.2d 274, 130 U.S.P.Q. 404 (CCPA 1961).

[402] 35 U.S.C. § 116; 37 C.F.R. § 1.48.

The applicant must diligently seek correction after discovering the error. *See* Van Otteren v. Hafner, 278 F.2d 738, 126 U.S.P.Q. 151 (CCPA 1960). A correcting amendment must be accompanied by (1) a verified statement of facts by the originally named inventor or inventors; (2) an oath or declaration by the actual inventors; (3) consent of any assignee of the patent application; and (4) a fee. 37 C.F.R. § 1.48.

The statement of facts must be specific as to how and why the error occurred. Coleman v. Dines, 754 F.2d 353, 224 U.S.P.Q. 857 (Fed. Cir. 1985).

Because a statement and declaration of all concerned persons is required, it is not possible to use the PTO petition correction procedure when there is a dispute among those persons

Section 256 provides two methods for correcting inventorship in issued patents.[403] First, the parties and assignees may petition the PTO. Second, a court before whom an inventorship question is raised may order correction. With the latter method, correction may be possible even if there is a dispute among the parties.[404]

In *MCV Inc.*,[405] the Federal Circuit interpreted Section 256 as explicitly authorizing judicial resolution of co-inventorship contests.

> "Section 256 affords the opportunity to correct the patent . . . If the patentees and their assignees agree, correction can be had on application to the Commissioner. In the event consensus is not attained, however, the second paragraph of section 256 permits redress in federal court.

> "The statute prescribes only one prerequisite to judicial action: all parties must be given notice and an opportunity to be heard. If that is done, there is subject matter jurisdiction in the district court over a dispute raising solely a joint inventorship issue among contending co-inventors."[406]

In *MCV Inc.*, the court held plaintiff equitably estopped from asserting co-inventorship. Plaintiff's principal worked as a consultant with defendant's employees on new product development. When plaintiff suggested its principal be listed as a co-inventor on a patent application, defendant replied that company policy prohibited naming non-employees on its patents. Deciding that exclusive marketing rights were more important than patent rights, plaintiff's principal agreed to assist in preparing the application, and plaintiff did not question patent inventorship again until defendant and plaintiff's relations became acrimonious. "To the extent [plaintiff] would justify its delay because an earlier assertion might have jeopardized business dealings with [defendant], the excuse is insufficient." Whether failure to name plaintiff's principal as a co-inventor violated Section 116 is not relevant: "[W]here [plaintiff] knew [defendant] was seeking a patent, and knew what was being claimed, it was incumbent upon him timely, explicitly and tenaciously to apprise [defendant] of his purported inventorship so it could be maturely considered."

[4] Related Applications

[a] **Double Patenting.** The double patenting doctrine prohibits issue of more than one patent that claims the same or substantially the same invention to the same inventorship entity or to a common assignee of several inventorship entities.[407] The

---

as to who is the correct inventor. Competing inventors may file separate applications, resulting in an interference proceeding to determine who is the first and original inventor. In some circumstances, however, the Patent and Trademark Office may waive the requirement that all original inventors join in the statement of facts. *In re* Hardee, 223 U.S.P.Q. 1122 (Ass't Comm'r Pat. 1984).

[403] 35 U.S.C. § 256; 37 C.F.R. § 1.324.

[404] Iowa State University Research Foundation v. Sperry Rand Corp., 444 F.2d 406, 170 U.S.P.Q. 374 (4th Cir. 1971).

[405] MCV Inc. v. King-Seeley Thermos Co., 870 F.2d 1568, 10 U.S.P.Q.2d 1287 (Fed. Cir. 1989).

[406] 870 F.2d at 1570, 10 U.S.P.Q.2d at 1288.

[407] *See generally* D. Chisum, Patents § 9.02.

For a discussion of inventive entities, see § 2C[5][g].

doctrine's purposes are to prevent extension of the term of patent protection[408] and to protect potential accused infringers from multiple patent suits.

A terminal disclaimer in a second or subsequent patent eliminates a double patenting objection unless the two patents claim the same invention.

[i] *Claim Comparison.* Double patenting analysis compares the *claims* of two patents (or a patent and an application). Subject matter *disclosed* but not claimed in the first patent is not used in determining double patenting.[409] Consider the following example:

1. A files application M, disclosing X, Y and Z and claiming X.

2. A files application N, claiming Y.

3. A patent issues to A on application M, claiming X.

Double patenting prohibits a second patent on application N claiming Y if, but only if, Y is an obvious variation of X. The first patent's disclosure of Y and Z is not prior art in making this determination.

[ii] *Identical Inventions.* Double patenting absolutely prohibits issue of more than one patent claiming identical subject matter to the same inventorship entity or a common assignee of several inventorship entities. A terminal disclaimer cannot eliminate identity-type double patenting.[410]

If there is any conceivable product or process that would fall literally within one patent's claims without falling within the other patent's claims, the two patents do not claim the identical invention.[411] A claim language difference will not overcome identity-type double patenting if there is no scope change,[412] but there is no identity-type double patenting if the respective patents' claims have independent scope.[413]

---

[408] *See* § 2E[1].

[409] *E.g., In re* Kaplan, 789 F.2d 1574, 229 U.S.P.Q. 678 (Fed. Cir. 1986); Panduit Corp. v. Dennison Mfg. Co., 774 F.2d 1082, 227 U.S.P.Q. 337 (Fed. Cir. 1985), *remanded,* 475 U.S. 809, 229 U.S.P.Q. 478 (1986), *on remand,* 810 F.2d 1561, 1 U.S.P.Q.2d 1593 (Fed. Cir. 1987), *cert. denied,* 481 U.S. 1052 (1987) (double patenting involves a comparison of the claims of the multiple patents; a prior patent is not "prior art" as to a later patent by the same inventor).

The first patent's disclosures may be used to interpret its claims. *In re* Avery, 518 F.2d 1228, 186 U.S.P.Q. 161 (CCPA 1975).

The first patent's disclosures may be prior art on some ground other than double patenting. For example, if a patent issues more than one year before the effective filing date of the second patent, it is a statutory bar. *See* §§ 2C[5] and 2C[5][c].

[410] *See* § 2D[4][a][v].

[411] *In re* Avery, 518 F.2d 1228, 1232, 186 U.S.P.Q. 161, 164 (CCPA 1975).

For a discussion of literal infringement, see § 2E[2][a].

[412] *E.g., In re* Griswold, 365 F.2d 834, 150 U.S.P.Q. 804 (CCPA 1966).

[413] *In re* Deters, 515 F.2d 1152, 185 U.S.P.Q. 644 (CCPA 1975); *In re* Vogel, 422 F.2d 438, 441, 164 U.S.P.Q. 619, 621-22 (CCPA 1970).

In *Deters,* a claim that included an element of "at least one" surface was held not identical to a claim in which the element was for "a plurality" of surfaces because the former but not the latter literally read on a one-surface structure.

[iii] *Obvious Variation.* Double patenting conditionally prohibits issue of more than one patent claiming obvious modifications of the same subject matter to the same inventor or a common assignee of several inventors.[414] A terminal disclaimer eliminates obviousness-type double patenting.[415]

The test for obvious variation is the same as the nonobviousness patentability condition,[416] *i.e.*, whether the subject matter of the claim in the subsequent patent or application would have been obvious to a person of ordinary skill in the art in view of the prior art and the subject matter of the claim of the prior patent.[417] One claim may be an obvious variation of another claim even though the two claims are mutually exclusive in scope.[418]

[iv] *Design and Utility Patents.* Double patenting applies, in limited circumstances, to design and utility patents on related subject matter.

Design and utility patents cover conceptually distinct subject matter. A design patent claims an article's ornamental appearance;[419] a utility patent claims an article's functional aspects.[420] Separate design and utility patents may be obtained covering the same article. Design-utility double patenting exists only if (1) the claimed design is an obvious variation of the utility patent's claimed subject matter, *and* (2) the utility patent's claimed subject matter is an obvious variation of the claimed design.[421] There is no double patenting if the utility aspects do not flow inevitably from the design even if the design is obvious in view of the claimed utility aspects.

---

[414] *E.g.,* Hartness International, Inc. v. Simplimatic Engineering Co., 819 F.2d 1100, 2 U.S.P.Q.2d 1826 (Fed. Cir. 1987) (patent invalid for obviousness-type double patenting because it was "primarily a refinement" of the subject matter claimed in the inventor's prior patent).

[415] *See* § 2D[4][a][v].

[416] *In re* Vogel, 422 F.2d 438, 164 U.S.P.Q. 619 (CCPA 1970).
See § 2C[4].

[417] *E.g., In re* Kaplan, 789 F.2d 1574, 229 U.S.P.Q. 678 (Fed. Cir. 1986) (that a claim in a second patent or patent application "dominates" subject matter claimed in a first patent does not, by itself, give rise to double patenting; to establish "obviousness-type" double patenting as to an attempt to obtain a patent on a variation of an invention claimed in a prior patent, there must be some clear evidence to establish why the variation would have been obvious. The evidence must relate to material that qualifies as prior art.).

In *Kaplan,* the court reversed a double patenting rejection of a patent application claim by inventor A to an improvement in a process of making certain alkane diols and triols, the improvement comprising reacting certain elements in the presence of a "solvent mixture of tetraglyme and sulfolane." A prior patent to joint inventors A and B claimed the process of making alkane polyols (diols and triols) in the presence of an "organic solvent." An example in the prior patent showed a mixture of tetraglyme and sulfolane as the organic solvent, but that example was not prior art for determining obviousness-type double patenting. The example was the work of subsequent applicant A and was disclosed in the specification of the prior patent as part of the best mode of practicing the claimed invention.

[418] *In re* Conix, 405 F.2d 1315, 160 U.S.P.Q. 420 (CCPA 1969).

[419] *See* § 6B.

[420] *See* § 2C[1].

[421] Shelcore, Inc. v. Durham Industries, Inc., 745 F.2d 621, 223 U.S.P.Q. 584 (Fed. Cir. 1984); Carman Indus., Inc. v. Wahl, 724 F.2d 932, 220 U.S.P.Q. 481 (Fed. Cir. 1983).

[v] *Terminal Disclaimers.* An applicant or patentee may disclaim any "terminal part of the term" of a patent applied for or issued[422] to eliminate obviousness-type double patenting.[423]

The applicant or patentee disclaims the time period the second patent would otherwise be in force beyond expiration of the first patent and conditions the second patent's enforceability on its being owned by the first patent's owner.[424]

Consider the following example:

1. On January 10, 1980, A obtains a patent claiming X.

2. A seeks a patent claiming Y, an obvious modification of X.

3. A files a disclaimer that provides (a) the term of protection of any patent claim to Y shall terminate upon expiration of the patent on X (1997), and (b) the patent claim to Y shall be enforceable only during such period as the patent is commonly owned with the patent claiming X.

The disclaimer eliminates any grounds for a double patenting rejection.

A terminal disclaimer eliminates the evils double patenting seeks to prevent—*i.e.* extension of the patent term, and potential harassment of accused infringers by

---

[422] 35 U.S.C. § 253:

"Whenever, without any deceptive intention, a claim of a patent is invalid the remaining claims shall not thereby be rendered invalid. A patentee, whether of the whole or any sectional interest therein, may, on payment of the fee required by law, make disclaimer of any complete claim, stating therein the extent of his interest in such patent. Such disclaimer shall be in writing, and recorded in the Patent and Trademark Office; and it shall thereafter be considered as part of the original patent to the extent of the interest possessed by the disclaimant and by those claiming under him.

"*In like manner any patentee or applicant may disclaim or dedicate to the public the entire term, or any terminal part of the term, of the patent granted or to be granted.*" (Emphasis added.)

[423] *In re* Robeson, 331 F.2d 610, 141 U.S.P.Q. 485 (CCPA 1964).

[424] 37 C.F.R. § 1.321(b); *In re* Van Ornum, 686 F.2d 937, 214 U.S.P.Q. 761 (CCPA 1982). In *Van Ornum*, the first patent had been assigned to one company and the application in question had been assigned to another company. The applicant filed a terminal disclaimer that did not (and could not) tie ownership of the application to that of the patent. The court held that the disclaimer was ineffective.

In Merck & Co., Inc. v. United States Int'l Trade Comm'n, 774 F.2d 483, 227 U.S.P.Q. 779 (Fed. Cir. 1985), the court held that the U.S. International Trade Commission erred in holding that petitioner's '284 patent expired because of a terminal disclaimer common ownership provision, which stated that the patent should "expire immediately if it ceases to be commonly owned" with four other patents. The patents' owner, a Japanese company, originally assigned only the '284 patent to petitioner, but the petitioner should have the opportunity to show that the patent owner and petitioner's intent was to convey all rights necessary to enforce the '284 patent, which would include ownership of the other four patents. The petitioner paid substantial consideration for the patent to initiate a U.S. International Trade Commission export exclusion investigation. Whether the assignment conveyed the necessary rights was presumptively determinable according to Japanese law, which the assignment agreement stated should cover its construction.

multiple patent owners. Allowing a second patent benefits the public by providing disclosure of additional useful information on the first patent's invention.[425]

[vi] *Different Inventors' Commonly Assigned Applications.* Double patenting applies to related applications and patents by different inventorship entities owned by the same person or company,[426] but does not apply if the related applications are not commonly owned. In the latter situation, three courses of action are possible: the PTO will (a) declare an interference proceeding to resolve invention priority; (b) reject one application's claims because of the other patents' prior art effect; or (c) allow related patents.

Double patenting rejections apply in common ownership situations even if one inventorship entity's disclosure is not prior art as to a second inventorship entity's claims.

Consider the following example:

1. On January 3, 1991, A files an application in Japan claiming X.

2. On January 4, 1991, B files an application in Japan claiming X + Y.

3. On January 7, 1991, C files an application in Germany claiming X + Y + Z.

4. On January 2, 3, and 7, 1992, A, B, and C respectively file in the United States applications corresponding to their prior foreign filings.

5. Company J owns the A and B applications. Company G owns the C application.

6. The inventions X, X+Y, and X+Y+Z are distinct but unpatentably obvious in view of each other.

If A obtains a patent, the common assignee J must file a terminal disclaimer as to B's application. Company G need not file a disclaimer as to C's application because there is no common ownership with the A and B applications. Because of the *Hilmer* doctrine, the A and B patent disclosures will not constitute prior art as to C.[427] The PTO may seek to avoid issuing patents with closely related claims by declaring an interference between the A, B and C applications, using a generic "phantom" count

---

[425] *In re* Eckel, 393 F.2d 848, 157 U.S.P.Q. 415 (CCPA 1968); *In re* Jentoft, 392 F.2d 633, 641, 157 U.S.P.Q. 363, 370 (CCPA 1968).

Eckel and *Jentoft* note the advantages of allowing two patents on related inventions. The alternative for an inventor with a continuing research program is to file a continuation-in-part application adding improvements and abandon the parent application, thus delaying the invention's disclosure and the commencement of the parent claims' patent term.

See § 2D[4][b].

[426] From 1967 to 1984, the PTO did not apply double patenting rejections to applications and patents by different inventors owned by the same assignee. It changed this policy because of the 1984 Patent Law Amendments Act. The prior policy was disapproved in *In re* Longi, 759 F.2d 887, 893-94, 225 U.S.P.Q. 645, 649 (Fed. Cir. 1984), which held that obviousness-type double patenting rejections were appropriate as to applications and patents by different inventors owned by the same assignee.

[427] *See* § 2C[5][d][ii].

and designating various claims in A, B and C's applications as corresponding to the count.[428]

[b] **Continuation Applications—Improvements.** An application filed during the pendency of a prior application can gain the benefit of the prior application's filing date if it meets Section 120's four conditions: disclosure continuity, cross-referencing, copendency, and inventorship.[429] The benefit of an earlier application's filing date may serve to avoid prior art references or statutory bars [430] or establish invention priority in an interference.[431]

[i] *Types.* A continuation application carries forward identically a prior application's disclosure. It may be used to secure further examination if some or all claims are under final rejection and the applicant does not wish to pursue an appeal or wishes to add or amend claims.[432]

A continuation-in-part ("CIP") application repeats a substantial part of a prior application and adds new matter. A CIP may be used to add improvements developed after a prior application's filing date or to overcome insufficient disclosure problems.[433] A CIP application (or patent issuing thereon) may have two effective filing dates, one for originally disclosed material and one for new matter.[434] Claims dependent upon the new matter are entitled only to the later CIP filing date.[435]

---

[428] *See* § 2D[5][h][i].

[429] 35 U.S.C. § 120. *See generally* D. Chisum, Patents § 13.01 *et seq.*
Section 120 provides:

> "An application for patent for an invention disclosed in the manner provided by the first paragraph of section 112 of this title in an application previously filed in the United States, or as provided by section 363 of this title, which is filed by an inventor or inventors named in the previously filed application shall have the same effect, as to such invention, as though filed on the date of the prior application, if filed before the patenting or abandonment of or termination of proceedings on the first application or on an application similarly entitled to the benefit of the filing date of the first application and if it contains or is amended to contain a specific reference to the earlier filed application."

[430] *See* § 2C[5][b][ii].

[431] *See* § 2D[5].

[432] See §§ 2D[1] and 2D[1][d].

[433] *E.g.*, Paperless Accounting, Inc. v. Bay Area Rapid Transit Sys., 804 F.2d 659, 663, 231 U.S.P.Q. 649, 652 (Fed. Cir. 1986), *cert. denied*, 480 U.S. 933 (1987) ("Law and policy liberally authorize the filing of [CIP] applications for a number of reasons, whether to enlarge the disclosure to include new technological information, thereby providing the public with knowledge of recent developments or improvements; or to enable more extensive prosecution or improved draftsmanship of specification or claims; or to provide a vehicle for prosecution of non-elected claims.").

[434] Litton Sys., Inc. v. Whirlpool Corp., 728 F.2d 1423, 221 U.S.P.Q. 97 (Fed. Cir. 1984).

[435] *In re* Kyser, 588 F.2d 303, 200 U.S.P.Q. 211 (CCPA 1978); *In re* Scheiber, 587 F.2d 59, 199 U.S.P.Q. 782 (CCPA 1978).
In *Scheiber*, the parent application disclosed a particular compound (X). The CIP application added further disclosure necessary to support a claim to a generic class of compounds that included X. The CIP was not entitled to the parent application's filing date to avoid an intervening reference disclosing X.

(Matthew Bender & Co., Inc.)

When a continuation or CIP application is entitled to the benefit of a prior application, the latter is commonly referred to as a "parent" application. In a chain of applications, there may be a remote grandparent application, great grandparent, etc. In *Henriksen*,[436] the CCPA held there is no limit to the number of applications chained together provided Section 120's requirements are met.

A design patent application can gain a prior utility patent application's filing date if it meets Section 120's requirements.[437]

[ii] *Disclosure Continuity—Acquiescence.* To meet Section 120's disclosure continuity condition, an application must be for an invention disclosed in the prior application as required by Section 112, first paragraph.[438] The prior application's disclosure must support claims added or amended in a continuation or CIP application, "support" meaning compliance with the enablement, description, and, possibly, best mode requirements.[439]

If a prior application does not disclose a practical use for the claimed invention, a CIP application adding such use cannot gain the prior application's filing date.[440]

If a CIP's added disclosure makes explicit what was inherent in the parent application, and if a person of ordinary skill in the art would necessarily equate the added matter with the parent's disclosure, the CIP can retain the parent's filing date.[441]

If an inventor files a CIP adding new matter after a PTO examiner rejected parent application claims for insufficient disclosure, the acquiescence doctrine may bar the inventor from later arguing that the claims are in fact entitled to the benefit of the parent application filing date. For example, in *Pennwalt*,[442] the court held filing a

---

[436] *In re* Henriksen, 399 F.2d 253, 158 U.S.P.Q. 224 (CCPA 1968).

[437] Racing Strollers Inc. v. TRI Industries Inc., 878 F.2d 1418, 11 U.S.P.Q.2d 1300 (Fed. Cir. 1989).

[438] 35 U.S.C. § 120. The CIP or continuation's claims need not have been asserted in a prior application if the disclosures of the prior application adequately support those claims. Kangaroos U.S.A., Inc. v. Caldor, Inc., 778 F.2d 1571, 228 U.S.P.Q. 32 (Fed. Cir. 1985).

[439] *See* §§ 2D[3][a], [b], and [c]. As to whether the parent application's best mode disclosure must be updated when filing a continuation or CIP, see § 2D[3][c][ix].

[440] *In re* Hafner, 410 F.2d 1403, 161 U.S.P.Q. 783 (CCPA 1969). *See* § 2C[2].

If the parent discloses one utility, a CIP is entitled to the parent's filing date even though the CIP discloses a different utility, provided the two utilities are not factually inconsistent. *In re* Kirchner, 305 F.2d 897, 134 U.S.P.Q. 324 (CCPA 1962).

[441] Wagoner v. Barger, 463 F.2d 1377, 175 U.S.P.Q. 85 (CCPA 1972).

[442] Pennwalt Corp. v. Akzona, Inc., 740 F.2d 1573, 222 U.S.P.Q. 833 (Fed. Cir. 1984). *See also* Litton Sys., Inc. v. Whirlpool Corp., 728 F.2d 1423, 221 U.S.P.Q. 97 (Fed. Cir. 1984).

Compare Paperless Accounting, Inc. v. Bay Area Rapid Transit Sys., 804 F.2d 659, 231 U.S.P.Q. 649 (Fed. Cir. 1986), *cert. denied*, 480 U.S. 933 (1987); State Industries, Inc. v. A.O. Smith Corp., 751 F.2d 1226, 224 U.S.P.Q. 418 (Fed. Cir. 1985) (filing a CIP creates no presumption that the parent does not support the CIP claims when the CIP filing is not in response to a PTO rejection).

In *Paperless Accounting*, the court held the filing of a continuation-in-part application that added text to the parent application's specification was not a binding admission that the parent did not support the CIP claims when the examiner withdrew a previous Section 112 rejection

CIP after an examiner rejected claims as lacking support constituted *prima facie* acquiescence in the rejection and barred the patentee from later claiming the benefit of the parent application's filing date. The patentee offered no evidence to rebut the *prima facie* case, for example, by showing that the CIP was for the purpose of adding later improvements.

[*iii*] *Cross References.* To meet Section 102's cross reference condition, an application must contain, or be amended before issue to contain, "a specific reference to the earlier filed application."[443] The cross reference enables persons searching PTO records to determine a patent's effective filing date.[444]

The cross reference should include all immediate and remote applications the applicant wishes to rely on.[445] Consider the following example:

1. A files application M.

2. A files application N and abandons M.

3. A files application O and abandons N.

O should refer to M and N; N should refer to M.[446]

A reissue application may be used to add a cross-reference.[447]

[*iv*] *Copendency.* To meet Section 120's copendency condition, an application must be filed prior to abandonment, patenting, or termination of proceedings on the prior application.[448] For a chain of applications M, N, and O, N must be filed during the pendency of M, and O during the pendency of N.[449]

[*v*] *Inventorship.* To meet Section 120's inventorship condition, an application's claimed subject matter must be by an inventor named in the prior application.[450]

---

of the parent claims carried forward to the CIP. The applicant did not acquiesce in the examiner's initial Section 112 rejection in the parent prosecution because the rejection, not forming the basis of the final rejection, could not have been appealed. "[T]he mere filing of a continuation-in-part with additional matter or revised claims is not of itself an admission that the matter is 'new' or that the original application was legally insufficient to support the claims." 804 F.2d at 664, 231 U.S.P.Q. at 652.

[443] 35 U.S.C. § 120.

The reference should provide the following: (1) the prior application's serial number; (2) the prior application's filing date; and (3) the applications' relationship (e.g. continuation, continuation-in-part, divisional). 37 C.F.R. § 1.78(a).

[444] Sampson v. Ampex Corp., 463 F.2d 1042, 174 U.S.P.Q. 417 (2d Cir. 1972).

[445] Hovlid v. Asari, 305 F.2d 747, 134 U.S.P.Q. 162 (9th Cir. 1962).

[446] Clover Club Foods Co. v. Gottschalk, 178 U.S.P.Q. 505 (C.D. Calif. 1973).

[447] Sticker Industrial Supply Corp. v. Blaw-Knox Co., 321 F. Supp. 876, 167 U.S.P.Q. 442 (N.D. Ill. 1970).

[448] 35 U.S.C. § 120. Patenting is the issue date. Abandonment may occur by failure to prosecute, express statement, or failure to pay the issue fee. Termination of proceedings may occur upon final rejection of all claims in an application and exhaustion of any appeal right. *See* §§ 2D[1] and 2D[1][a][iii].

[449] Lemelson v. TRW, Inc., 760 F.2d 1254, 225 U.S.P.Q. 697 (Fed. Cir. 1985).

[450] 35 U.S.C. § 120; 37 C.F.R. § 1.78(a).

Before a 1984 amendment, a subsequent application's claims had to be by the same inventor or inventors as the prior application. Consider the following example:

1. A, B and C jointly file application M, disclosing X, Y and Z and claiming X.

2. A and B jointly file CIP application N, disclosing X, Y and Z and claiming Y.

3. A files CIP application O, disclosing X, Y, and Z and claiming Z.

Before 1984, the claims in applications N and O could not gain the benefit of M's filing date unless there was an error in the original inventorship entity designation.[451] After 1984, the N and O applications could gain the benefit of M's filing date provided that (1) the named inventors are in fact inventors of the subject matter claimed in that application and (2) there was adequate disclosure support for the claims in the prior application.

[5] Interferences—Priority—Invention Date.

An interference proceeding's purpose is to resolve the question of invention priority when more than one person seeks a patent claiming substantially the same invention.[452] Interferences are complex proceedings that use unique procedures.[453]

The following sections focus on the substantive rules for determining an invention date.[454] Interference practice and procedure are covered only briefly.[455]

[a] Priority Rules—First to Invent.

The following rules govern the determination of invention priority.

(1) Presumptively, the first inventor is the one who first reduces the invention to practice. Filing a patent application adequately disclosing the invention is a constructive reduction to practice,[456] so the invention date can not be later than the filing date (unless the application is later completely

---

[451] In re Schmidt, 293 F.2d 274, 130 U.S.P.Q. 404 (CCPA 1961).

[452] 35 U.S.C. § 135.

[453] The standard reference work on interference practice is Rivise & Caesar, Interference Law and Practice (1943).

Interference practice was substantially revised in 1985. Under prior law, a Board of Patent Interferences had jurisdiction over issues of priority of invention. That Board could decide only invention priority issues and disputed issues "ancillary" to priority. That Board could not decide patentability issues, which were considered to be within the expertise of the regular examiners. See, e.g., Case v. CPC International, Inc., 730 F.2d 745, 221 U.S.P.Q. 196 (Fed. Cir. 1984), cert. denied, 469 U.S. 872, 224 U.S.P.Q. 736 (1984). A 1984 statutory amendment merged the Board of Appeals and the Board of Patent Interferences into a new Board of Patent Appeals and Interferences with jurisdiction to decide both patentability and priority issues.

A set of new rules, effective for interferences declared on or after February 11, 1985, have been adopted by the PTO. 37 C.F.R. § 1.601-688.

[454] The same rules govern the determination of what constitutes prior art for patentability purposes. See § 2C[5][f].

[455] See § 2D[5][h].

[456] See § 2D[5][d].

abandoned). An actual reduction to practice occurs when a person makes and tests an embodiment of the invention.[457]

(2) The invention date is presumed to be the filing date,[458] but evidence can establish a pre-filing invention date.[459]

(3) The second person to reduce the invention to practice may prevail by showing (a) prior conception of the invention,[460] and (b) continuous diligent effort toward reduction to practice (actual or constructive) from a date just prior to conception of the invention by the first person.[461]

(4) The first inventor by virtue of an actual reduction to practice loses priority if he abandons, suppresses or conceals the invention after reduction to practice.[462]

(5) The inventor who abandons, suppresses or conceals his invention after reduction to practice but later resumes activity may rely on the date of resumption as the invention date.[463]

(6) An inventor cannot rely upon activity outside the United States to establish a date of conception or actual reduction to practice.[464]

(7) If a person derived his conception of an invention from another person, the latter is entitled to priority regardless who first reduced it to practice.[465]

---

[457] See § 2D[5][d].

[458] Bates v. Coe, 98 U.S. 31 (1878).

[459] See 37 C.F.R. § 1.657. The evidence production burden is met if the person introduces credible evidence to support facts showing a pre-filing invention date.

If there is an evidence conflict, the persuasion burden governs its resolution. The persuasion burden rests on the junior party (that is, the person with the later effective filing date). If the junior party filed his application before the senior party's patent issue date, the persuasion burden is preponderance of the evidence, the normal civil suit burden. Linkow v. Linkow, 517 F.2d 1370, 1373, 186 U.S.P.Q. 223 (CCPA 1975). If the junior party filed his application after the issue date, that is, after the applicant has access to the senior party's published patent specification, the burden is beyond a reasonable doubt. Wolter v. Belicka, 409 F.2d 255, 161 U.S.P.Q. 335 (CCPA 1969).

If there is a "tie," that is, more than one party shows entitlement to the same invention date, priority in an interference is awarded to the first party to file an application. Oka v. Youssefyeh, 849 F.2d 581, 584, 7 U.S.P.Q.2d 1169, 1172 (Fed. Cir. 1988) ("In the event of a tie, . . . priority must be awarded to the senior party;" the senior party filed on October 31; the junior party proved entitlement to a pre-filing invention date as of the "last week of October"; the last week of October means October 31, because "where testimony merely places the acts within a stated time period, the inventor has not established a date for his activities earlier than the last day of the period.").

[460] See § 2D[5][c].

[461] E.g., Brown v. Barton, 102 F.2d 193, 197, 41 U.S.P.Q. 99 (CCPA 1939). See § 2D[5][e].

[462] See § 2D[5][g].

[463] Paulik v. Rizkalla, 760 F.2d 1270, 226 U.S.P.Q. 224 (Fed. Cir. 1985).

[464] See § 2D[5][b].

[465] Applegate v. Sherer, 332 F.2d 571, 141 U.S.P.Q. 796 (CCPA 1964).

A party may prove derivation by evidence of events outside the United States. Hedgewick v. Akers, 497 F.2d 905, 182 U.S.P.Q. 167 (CCPA 1974).

[b]   Activity in Other Countries. An inventor may not establish an invention date by reference to knowledge, use of, or other activity with respect to the invention in an another country,[466] but may rely on a Paris Convention Section 119 priority right.[467]

Consider the following example:

1. In January 1985, A reduces an invention to practice in Japan.

2. In February 1985, B reduces the same invention to practice in the United States.

3. In March 1985, A files a patent application on the invention in Japan.

4. In April 1985, A files a corresponding application in the United States.

5. In May 1985, B files a patent application on the invention in the United States.

In an interference, B may establish a February 1985 invention date. A is limited to the March 1985 priority filing date. Therefore, B prevails even though A was the first to reduce to practice (in Japan) and filed in both Japan and the United States before B's filing.

A person who makes an invention in another country may establish an invention date by reference to the date the invention is introduced into the United States ("domestic introduction").[468] For example, sending a patent application to a United States representative is a conception.[469] Domestic introduction must be followed by diligence to a reduction to practice, for example, the filing of a patent application.[470]

---

[466] 35 U.S.C. § 104.

For a critique of this statute, see Chisum, *Foreign Activity: Its Effect on Patentability under United States Law*, 11 Int'l Rev. Indus. Prop. & Cr. L. 26 (1980).

[467] *See* § 2H[2].

[468] *E.g.*, Breuer v. DeMarinis, 558 F.2d 22, 194 U.S.P.Q. 308 (CCPA 1977).

In *Breuer*, a German company's employees invented a chemical compound and sent a sample and a record including an infra-red spectrum analysis to company employees in the United States. The court held the company could rely on the domestic introduction date and could use evidence of knowledge and practices in Germany to verify the fact of domestic introduction.

Compare Shurie v. Richmond, 699 F.2d 1156, 216 U.S.P.Q. 1042 (Fed. Cir. 1983) (as to a *process*, there was no reduction to practice in the United States when the process produced a product of known utility in Canada and then the *product* was imported into the United States for testing).

[469] *Ex parte* Hachiken, 223 U.S.P.Q. 879 (PTO Bd. App. 1984). *See* § 2D[5][c].

Compare In re Costello, 717 F.2d 1346, 1348, 1349, 219 U.S.P.Q. 389, 390-391 (Fed. Cir. 1983) (an applicant who reduces an invention to practice in a foreign country cannot establish an invention date in this country by reference to either (1) the filing date of a U.S. application that was abandoned, or (2) the date of coworkers' publication by disclosing his invention).

[470] *In re* Mulder, 716 F.2d 1542, 219 U.S.P.Q. 189 (Fed. Cir. 1983).

Mulder involved the following fact pattern:

1. On July 15, 1974, A mailed a preliminary version of a patent application to the United States.

2. On October 7, 1974, an article by B was published.

3. On October 9, 1974, A filed a patent application in the Netherlands.

Activity in a another country may establish that one person derived the invention from another.[471] In the example above, A might be able to show that B derived the invention from A in Japan rather than independently inventing it. If A establishes such derivation, then A prevails.

[c] **Conception.** Conception is the mental formulation and the disclosure of a complete idea for a product or process.[472] Conception must be complete enough to enable one of ordinary skill in the art to reduce the invention to practice without undue experimentation or the exercise of inventive skill.[473] A conception may be disclosed in a drawing, model, or even the inventor's testimony with corroborating witnesses.[474]

---

4. On August 6, 1975, A filed a corresponding patent application in the United States. The court held that A was entitled to the priority filing date (October 9, 1974) as a constructive reduction to practice and to the domestic introduction date (July 15, 1974) as a conception in the United States, but A was not entitled to the domestic introduction date (July 15, 1974) as an invention date for the purpose of eliminating the B article as a prior art reference. There was no evidence of diligence by A in the United States as to the two day period from October 7 to October 9, 1974 nor as to the whole period from July 15, 1974 to August 6, 1975.

[471] Hedgewick v. Akers, 497 F.2d 905, 182 U.S.P.Q. 167 (CCPA 1974).

[472] Gunter v. Stream, 573 F.2d 77, 197 U.S.P.Q. 482 (CCPA 1978).

A conception must be of the *means* for achieving the object of the invention. A mental formulation of a desirable result or a problem to be solved is not a conception. Morgan v. Hirsch, 728 F.2d 1449, 221 U.S.P.Q. 193 (Fed. Cir. 1984).

[473] Coleman v. Dines, 754 F.2d 353, 359, 224 U.S.P.Q. 857, 862 (Fed. Cir. 1985). *See also* Oka v. Youssefyeh, 849 F.2d 581, 583, 7 U.S.P.Q.2d 1169, 1171 (Fed. Cir. 1988) ("Conception requires (1) the idea of the structure of the chemical compound, and (2) possession of an operative method of making it. . . . When . . . a method of making a compound with conventional techniques is a matter of routine knowledge among those skilled in the art, a compound has been deemed to have been conceived when it was described . . . .").

Evidence of the ease or difficulty of the actual reduction of the invention to practice after the date of an alleged conception is persuasive (though not conclusive) of the completeness of that conception. Meitzner v. Corte, 410 F.2d 433, 437-38, 161 U.S.P.Q. 599, 603 (CCPA 1969).

[474] Draeger v. Bradley, 156 F.2d 64, 70 U.S.P.Q. 183 (CCPA 1946).

See also Hybritech Inc. v. Monoclonal Antibodies, Inc., 802 F.2d 1367, 231 U.S.P.Q. 81 (Fed. Cir. 1986), *cert. denied*, 480 U.S. 947 (1987). *Hybritech* involved a patent claiming a "sandwich assay" using monoclonal antibodies with a high antigen affinity ("at least about 10^8 liters/mole"). The court granted the patentee a prefiling invention date based on conception followed by diligence and reduction to practice, which permitted the patentee to eliminate four potential pre-filing date prior art references before the filing date. Conception was adequately shown even though (a) the inventors' notebooks did not expressly state the liters/mole limitation, and (b) certain notebook pages were not witnessed until later when a person more sensitive to patent matters joined the company. The court held the patentee's "claim of conception, generally, [to be] evidenced by the sometimes sparsely documented work of a start-up company whose first small advances evolved into the myriad activities of a mature company with efforts directed toward developing the claimed invention by first employing the Kohler and Milstein technology to produce the necessary monoclonal antibodies and using those antibodies in diagnostic sandwich assay kits." The testimony of the officials of the patentee indicated that "the screening procedures used. . . ensured that only monoclonal antibodies

An inventor must appreciate that a new structure exists.[475] For example, if a chemist experiments with reactions and produces a mixture of compounds without realizing that a new compound is present, there is no conception of the new compound.[476] The inventor need not appreciate the new or unexpected properties that make the structure patentable.

Some early decisions suggested that there can be no conception of an invention prior to testing and reduction to practice in arts (such as some areas of chemistry) that are unpredictable.[477] In such instances, there is "simultaneous conception and reduction to practice."[478] More recent decisions emphasize that there are no *per se* rules on this matter and that routine research and testing of a product to determine its operability or utility will not necessarily preclude a prior conception of the product and of its utility.[479]

In *Amgen*,[480] the court applied the simultaneous conception and reduction to practice doctrine to hold that prior invention of another[481] does not invalidate plaintiff's patent claims to a purified and isolated DNA sequence encoding human erythropoietin ("EPO"), and to host cells transformed with the sequence. Plaintiff Amgen's scientist, Dr. Fu-Kuen Lin, first reduced the invention to practice by cloning the gene. Defendant Genetic Institute's scientist, Dr. Fritsch, may have been the first to conceive the eventually successful strategy for cloning the EPO gene, *i.e.* screening a human genomic DNA library with two sets of fully-degenerate cDNA probes from different EPO gene regions, but, because of the "uncertainties of the method and lack of information concerning the amino acid sequence of the EPO protein. . . neither party had an adequate conception of the DNA sequence until reduction to practice had been achieved. . . ."

> "Conception requires both the idea of the invention's structure and posses-
> sion of an operative method of making it. . . . In some instances, an inventor
> is unable to establish a conception until he has reduced the invention to
> practice through a successful experiment. This situation results in a simulta-
> neous conception and reduction to practice."[482]

---

having at least 10^8 liters/mole would be used in assays." The court noted "Under a reasoned analysis and evaluation Hybritech, within a reasonable time [after the contemporaneous entry of facts on research] prudently had researchers other than those who performed the particular experiments witness the notebooks in response to [a new executive's] advice." 802 F.2d at 1376-77, 231 U.S.P.Q. 88-89.

[475] Knorr v. Pearson, 671 F.2d 1368, 213 U.S.P.Q. 196 (CCPA 1982).

[476] Heard v. Burton, 333 F.2d 239, 142 U.S.P.Q. 97 (CCPA 1964).

[477] Smith v. Bousquet, 111 F.2d 157, 45 U.S.P.Q. 347 (CCPA 1940).

[478] *See generally* D. Chisum, Patents § 10.04[5].

[479] Rey-Bellet v. Engelhardt, 493 F.2d 1380, 181 U.S.P.Q. 453 (CCPA 1974).

[480] Amgen, Inc. v. Chugai Pharmaceutical Co., Ltd., 927 F.2d 1200, 18 U.S.P.Q.2d 1016 (Fed. Cir. 1991).

[481] For a discussion of prior invention of another as prior art, see § 2C[5][e].

[482] 927 F.2d at 1206, 18 U.S.P.Q.2d at 1020-21. The EPO DNA sequence was unknown until plaintiff cloned it.

> "A gene is a chemical compound, albeit a complex one, and . . . conception of a
> chemical compound requires that the inventor be able to define it so as to distin-

[d] **Reduction to Practice.** There are two types of reduction to practice: constructive and actual.

Constructive reduction to practice occurs when an inventor files a patent application providing full invention disclosure.[483] An applicant need not have built or tested an embodiment of the invention before filing an application.[484] An application retains constructive reduction to practice status only if the applicant maintains prosecution continuity.[485] An abandoned patent application is not a constructive reduction to practice though it is evidence of a conception date.[486]

guish it from other materials, and to describe how to obtain it . . . . Conception does not occur unless one has a mental picture of the structure of the chemical, or is able to define it by its method of preparation, its physical or chemical properties, or whatever characteristics sufficiently distinguish it. It is not sufficient to define it solely by its principal biological property, *e.g.*, encoding human erythropoietin, because an alleged conception having no more specificity than that is simply a wish to know the identity of any material with that biological property. . . . [W]hen an inventor is unable to envision the detailed constitution of a gene so as to distinguish it from other materials, as well as a method of obtaining it, conception has not been achieved until reduction to practice has occurred, *i.e.*, until after the gene has been isolated.

"Fritsch had a goal of obtaining the isolated EPO gene, whatever its identity, and even had an idea of a possible method of obtaining it, but he did not conceive a purified and isolated DNA sequence encoding EPO and a viable method for obtaining it until after Lin."

Neither Fritsch nor Lin invented EPO or the EPO gene; the claimed invention is "the novel *purified and isolated* sequence which codes for EPO, and neither . . . knew the structure or physical characteristics of it and had a viable method of obtaining that subject matter until it was actually obtained and characterized." (Emphasis in original.) Defendant's argument that it had priority because Fritsch's two-probe strategy was found by the trial court to distinguish the invention over the prior art lacks merit. Fritsch's alleged conception was "mere speculation" and not "sufficiently specific that one skilled in the relevant art would succeed in cloning the EPO gene. . . . Clearly, he did not have that conception because he did not know the structure of EPO or the EPO gene. . . . As expert testimony from both sides indicated, success in cloning the EPO gene was not assured until the gene was in fact isolated and its sequence known." 927 F.2d at 1207, 18 U.S.P.Q.2d at 1021.

[483] Travis v. Baker, 137 F.2d 109, 111, 58 U.S.P.Q. 558, 560 (CCPA 1943).

For a discussion of disclosure requirements, see § § 2D[3][a], [b], and [c].

[484] Dolbear v. American Bell Tel. Co., 126 U.S. 1, 535-36 (1888).

An application filed in another country is a constructive reduction to practice if a corresponding United States application is entitled to the benefit of that filing date. *See* § 2H[2][f].

[485] Conover v. Downs, 35 F.2d 59, 3 U.S.P.Q. 58 (CCPA 1929).

In *Conover*, person A filed a patent application disclosing, but not claiming, a process X. The application issued as a patent, still with no claim to X. A then filed a second application claiming X and became involved in an interference with person B over priority of invention of X. The court held that the first application filing was evidence of A's conception but was not a constructive reduction to practice because the second application was filed after issuance of the patent and was not entitled to the benefit of the first application filing date.

[486] *In re* Costello, 717 F.2d 1346, 219 U.S.P.Q. 389 (Fed. Cir. 1983). An abandoned patent application's prior art status is discussed at § 2C[5][a].

Actual reduction to practice occurs when an inventor (or someone acting on the inventor's behalf[487]) builds an embodiment of the invention[488] and tests it to determine that it will be operable in its intended functional setting.[489] An embodiment must be tested under either actual working conditions or conditions that sufficiently simulate working conditions.[490] The testing need not establish commercial refinement or acceptability.[491]

Reduction to practice must demonstrate the invention's utility.[492]

[e] **Diligence.** To establish a prior invention date, a person who is first to conceive but last to reduce to practice must show continuous diligent effort toward reduction to practice from a date just prior to conception of the invention by another person.[493] The critical diligence period is from a date just before the conception by another party to first conceiver's later reduction to practice.

---

[487] The reduction to practice need not be by the inventor personally and may be carried out by co-employees or even suppliers or customers of the inventor's employer so long as such activity is on the behalf of the inventor. Litchfield v. Eigen, 535 F.2d 72, 190 U.S.P.Q. 113 (CCPA 1976); MacMillan v. Moffett, 432 F.2d 1237, 167 U.S.P.Q. 550 (CCPA 1970); Hogue v. Cowling, 101 F.2d 541, 549-50, 40 U.S.P.Q. 492, 499 (CCPA 1939).

[488] A patent claim defines "the invention." In an interference proceeding, a "count" defines the contested subject matter. See § 2D[5][h][i]. A party must demonstrate that the built and tested embodiment contained every limitation of the interference count. E.g., Newkirk v. Lulejian, 825 F.2d 1581, 3 U.S.P.Q.2d 1793 (Fed. Cir. 1987). In Newkirk, the appellant failed to show a reduction to practice falling within the interference count, which related to an electronic glassware conveyer delivery apparatus and which required, inter alia, a motor speed being varied by a stored program and "means for electronically altering said pushout robot rotational operation by changing said stored program." In the appellant's physical embodiment the program stored in a PROM was not altered as of the critical date (the other party's filing date).

[489] Kimberly-Clark Corp. v. Johnson & Johnson, 745 F.2d 1437, 1445, 223 U.S.P.Q. 603, 607 (Fed. Cir. 1984).

[490] Paivinen v. Sands, 339 F.2d 217, 144 U.S.P.Q. 1 (CCPA 1964).

[491] Shurie v. Richmond, 699 F.2d 1156, 1160, 216 U.S.P.Q. 1042 (Fed. Cir. 1983).

[492] See § 2C[2].

A sufficient showing of any utility will suffice unless the "count" that forms the basis of the interference is defined in terms of utility. As to the role of interference counts, see § 2D[5][h][i].

The utility relied upon to show an actual reduction to practice need not necessarily be that asserted in the patent specification. Engelhardt v. Judd, 369 F.2d 408, 411, 151 U.S.P.Q. 732, 734 (CCPA 1966).

Tests relied upon to show an actual reduction to practice must be measured in terms of the inventor's objective, Knapp v. Anderson, 477 F.2d 588, 590, 177 U.S.P.Q. 688, 690 (CCPA 1973), but the inventor need not have achieved his ultimate objective. Archer v. Papa, 265 F.2d 954, 121 U.S.P.Q. 413 (CCPA 1959). In Archer, the court held that tests showing usefulness of a compound as a cholecystographic agent in cats were sufficient even though the applicant's ultimate objective was usefulness in human beings.

[493] There is no diligence "race." One who is first to reduce to practice need not show diligence from a prior conception, whether it was before or after the date of conception of the other party. Steinberg v. Seitz, 517 F.2d 1359, 1364, 186 U.S.P.Q. 209, 212-13 (CCPA 1975).

Lack of diligence after an alleged actual reduction to practice is relevant only insofar as it provides an inference that no reduction to practice actually occurred or that the inventor had abandoned, suppressed, or concealed the invention. See §§ 2D[5][d] and [g].

Consider an example:

1. On January 1, 1982, A conceives of invention X but delays further work on X.

2. On January 1, 1984, A begins working toward a reduction to practice.

3. On February 1, 1984, B conceives and reduces X to practice.

4. On May 1, 1984, A reduces X to practice.

A is the first inventor if A shows diligent activity, or a recognized excuse for inactivity, for the entire period from just prior to February 1, 1984 until the May 1, 1984, reduction to practice.

A person must account for the entire critical period by showing either activity devoted to a reduction to practice or a recognized excuse for inactivity.[494] Any lapse in diligence during the critical period is fatal no matter how short the critical or lapse period.[495]

Activity must be directed to reducing the invention to practice, either building and testing an embodiment or preparing a patent application. Activity directed to commercial exploitation or to other inventions is not sufficient.[496]

Recognized excuses for inactivity include:

(a) the inventor's patent attorney's reasonably organized prior case work-load,[497]

(b) employment demands,[498]

(c) the need to develop a closely related invention to test the primary invention,[499] and

(d) the inventor's extreme and continuous poverty or illness.[500]

In *Bey*,[501] the court found sufficient attorney diligence. To show diligence in work toward constructive reduction to practice by filing a patent application on a conceived invention, the patent attorney to whom the inventor's disclosure is given need not drop all other cases. She need only show reasonable diligence in taking up the cases on her docket. If the cases are *unrelated*, the patent attorney must show

---

[494] Gould v. Schawlow, 363 F.2d 908, 150 U.S.P.Q. 634 (CCPA 1966).

[495] Wilson v. Sherts, 81 F.2d 755, 28 U.S.P.Q. 379 (CCPA 1936). *Cf. In re* Mulder, 716 F.2d 1542, 219 U.S.P.Q. 189 (Fed. Cir. 1983).

[496] *In re* Nelson, 420 F.2d 1079, 1080-81, 164 U.S.P.Q. 458, 459 (CCPA 1970); Fitzgerald v. Arbib, 268 F.2d 763, 766, 122 U.S.P.Q. 530, 532 (CCPA 1959).

[497] Bey v. Kollonitsch, 806 F.2d 1024, 231 U.S.P.Q. 967 (Fed. Cir. 1986); Rines v. Morgan, 250 F.2d 365, 369, 116 U.S.P.Q. 145 (CCPA 1957).

[498] Gould v. Schawlow, 363 F.2d 908, 919, 150 U.S.P.Q. 634 (CCPA 1966).

[499] Watkins v. Wakefield, 443 F.2d 1207, 170 U.S.P.Q. 274 (CCPA 1971). *Compare* Hudson v. Giuffrida, 328 F.2d 918, 140 U.S.P.Q. 569 (CCPA 1964).

[500] Wallace v. Scott, 15 App. D.C. 157 (1899).

Insufficient funds for an actual reduction to practice will not excuse a failure to seek a constructive reduction to practice by preparation and filing of a patent application. Preston v. White, 97 F.2d 160, 165, 37 U.S.P.Q. 802, 806-07 (CCPA 1938).

[501] Bey v. Kollonitsch, 806 F.2d 1024, 231 U.S.P.Q. 967 (Fed. Cir. 1986).

that the cases were taken up in chronological order. If the cases are *related*, the attorney need not make such a showing. Work on another related case will be credited toward reasonable diligence if the work on the related case contributes substantially to the ultimate preparation and filing of the involved application.[502]

Doubts about the invention's value or general failure to give it priority do not excuse inactivity.[503]

In *Griffith*,[504] a university delayed for months applying for a patent or working to reduce a professor's conceived invention to practice. As excuses, the university cited (a) its policy of requiring outside funding for projects, and (b) the professor's decision to delay work on the concept until a particular graduate student matriculated. Neither was sufficient. Courts "may consider the reasonable everyday problems and limitations encountered by an inventor," but the university's "excuses sound more in the nature of commercial development, not accepted as an excuse for delay, than the 'hardship' cases. . . . Delays in reduction to practice caused by an inventor's efforts to refine an invention to the most marketable and profitable form have not been accepted as sufficient excuses for inactivity."[505]

[f] **Corroboration.** The inventor's uncorroborated testimony does not establish conception, actual reduction to practice, and diligence.[506] Witnesses who are neither the inventor nor co-inventors, verified notebooks, and records can provide corroboration. A "rule of reason" applies to the corroboration requirement.[507] For example, in *Lacotte*,[508] the inventor's notebook kept as part of an organized and routinely

---

[502] The court noted "In priority determinations, the inventor should not be penalized because his attorney reasonably prepared the closely related applications together, thereby *expediting* the filing of the applications and the prompt disclosure to the public of the closely related inventions contained therein." 806 F.2d at 1029, 231 U.S.P.Q. at 970.

To gain the benefit of the "related case" doctrine, the inventor need not show that all of the cases were on the patent attorney's docket at the same time or were filed on the same date or that the cases " '*had* to be worked on as an integrated whole.' "

Bey held that the PTO Board erred in denying priority to the junior party in an interference for want of proof of diligence during the 41 day critical period (from the senior party's filing date to that of the junior party) when: (1) disclosures (which ultimately resulted in 22 patent applications) relating to irreversible enzyme inhibitors developed by a small group of researchers in France were assigned to a single experienced pharmaceutical patent attorney; (2) assignment to a single attorney was reasonable in order to reduce duplication of effort and travel and achieve an overall savings in time and expense; (3) there were substantial interrelationships among the applications in chemistry, structure, utility and inventorship; and (4) there was corroborated evidence that the attorney worked on the related applications almost every working day in the critical period.

[503] Powell v. Poupitch, 167 F.2d 514, 77 U.S.P.Q. 379 (CCPA 1948).

[504] Griffith v. Kanamaru, 816 F.2d 624, 2 U.S.P.Q.2d 1361 (Fed. Cir. 1987).

[505] 816 F.2d at 626, 628, 2 U.S.P.Q.2d at 1362, 1363.

[506] Coleman v. Dines, 754 F.2d 353, 224 U.S.P.Q. 857 (Fed. Cir. 1985); Reese v. Hurst, 661 F.2d 1222, 211 U.S.P.Q. 936 (CCPA 1981); Naber v. Cricchi, 567 F.2d 382, 196 U.S.P.Q. 294 (CCPA 1977), *cert. denied*, 439 U.S. 826, 200 U.S.P.Q. 64 (1978).

[507] Berry v. Webb, 412 F.2d 261, 162 U.S.P.Q. 170 (CCPA 1969).

[508] Lacotte v. Thomas, 758 F.2d 611, 225 U.S.P.Q. 633 (Fed. Cir. 1985).

practiced research program within a corporation and records of the use of related supplies by the inventor sufficiently corroborated an actual reduction to practice.

A notebook system in which researchers make regular entries on work in progress and a person capable of understanding but not actually involved in the work regularly witnesses the entries by dated signature is the best procedure for the verification of dates of conception and reduction to practice.

In Hahn,[509] the contested invention was an organic chemical compound, a solid crosslinkable homopolymer of a olefinic benzocyclobutene monomer. The inventors, who were the second to file, failed to provide sufficient corroborating evidence of their alleged reduction to practice prior to the date on which their rival filed an application. They submitted three affidavits. In one, a co-inventor stated that, prior to the rival's filing date, he prepared compounds, recorded the results on pages in his laboratory notebooks, and appended reduced photocopies of plots resulting from analyses of the compounds he prepared. He did not explain the plots' significance. In two "corroborating" affidavits, the inventor's co-employees stated that they "read" and "understood" the laboratory notebook pages but did not state that "the experiments described by [the co-inventor] were actually performed at all or on any particular date, explain[] the meaning of the analyses graphs, or state[] that they were what they purported to be." The court held the affidavits insufficient to corroborate reduction to practice because they "established only that those pages existed on a certain date; they did not independently corroborate the statements made on those pages."[510]

[g] **Abandonment, Suppression and Concealment.** A person who first conceives and reduces to practice an invention loses the right to rely on the reduction to practice date if he abandons, suppresses, or conceals the invention.[511]

A person is guilty of abandonment, suppression or concealment if (1) he makes an invention but delays filing a patent application for a long time, (2) a second person independently makes the same invention and promptly files for a patent, and (3) he is "spurred" back into action by knowledge of the second person's activity.[512]

---

[509] Hahn v. Wong, 892 F.2d 1028, 13 U.S.P.Q.2d 1313 (Fed. Cir. 1989).

[510] 892 F.2d at 1030-31, 13 U.S.P.Q.2d at 1315-16.

The court distinguished Berges v. Gottstein, 618 F.2d 771, 205 U.S.P.Q. 691 (CCPA 1980). There, the inventor submitted not only an affidavit and spectrographic analyses of the claimed compound but also "affidavits showing that he was a member of a highly organized research team involved in developing. . . the compound in question" and explaining "the routine procedure for identifying, preserving and testing new compounds. . . ." The court held that this created a "cohesive 'web of allegedly corroborative evidence.' " Unlike Berges, "facts independent of the inventor's own assertions were needed to interpret the graphs." 892 F.2d at 1032-34, 13 U.S.P.Q.2d at 1318.

[511] 35 U.S.C. § 102(g). This section codifies the abandonment, suppression, and concealment doctrine, which the leading decision, Mason v. Hepburn, 13 App. D.C. 86 (D.C. Cir. 1898), adopted for policy reasons.

[512] Engelhardt v. Judd, 369 F.2d 408, 151 U.S.P.Q. 732 (CCPA 1966).

Spurring evidence strongly supports, but is not essential to, an abandonment, suppression or concealment finding. Peeler v. Miller, 535 F.2d 647, 190 U.S.P.Q. 117 (CCPA 1976).

Long delay in filing a patent application creates an inference of abandonment, suppression, or concealment.[513] Making the invention available to the public, for example, by a public sales demonstration, may rebut the inference if the inventor files a patent application within the one-year Section 102(b) grace period.[514]

In *Lutzker*,[515] the court held a party's "deliberate policy not to disclose his invention to the public until he [was] ready to go into commercial production" to be "evidence of an intent to suppress or conceal the invention." The party's fifty-one month delay from reduction to practice to first public disclosure was "unreasonably long and sufficient to give rise to an inference of an intent to abandon, suppress, or conceal the invention." His efforts to "improve" the invention during the delay period were directed toward commercial refinement, none of which were reflected in the patent application. The invention was a device for making canapes, and the party's activities related to development of a recipe book and a "blister card."[516]

> "[W]hen there is an unreasonable delay between the actual reduction to practice and the filing of a patent application, there is a basis for inferring abandonment, suppression or concealment. . . . The inventor's activities during the delay period may excuse the delay (e.g., he may have worked during that period to improve or perfect the invention disclosed in the patent application).
>
> . . .
>
> ". . . When, however, the delay is caused by working on refinements and improvements which are not reflected in the final patent application, the delay will not be excused. . . . Further, when the activities which cause the delay go to commercialization of the invention, the delay will not be excused."[517]

A person who abandons, suppresses or conceals an invention but later resumes work before a second person's invention date may rely on the resumption date to show priority.[518] Consider the following example:

> 1. In November 1970, A reduces an invention to practice. A's company takes no immediate action to prepare a patent application.

---

[513] Shindelar v. Holdeman, 628 F.2d 1337, 207 U.S.P.Q. 112 (CCPA 1980), *cert. denied,* 451 U.S. 984, 210 U.S.P.Q. 776 (1981). *Compare* Piher, S.A. v. CTS Corp., 664 F.2d 122, 212 U.S.P.Q. 914 (7th Cir. 1981).

Evidence of the inventor's or his assignee's intention to manufacture the invention as circumstances warrant does not rebut the inference of abandonment, suppression or concealment arising from unreasonable delay. Young v. Dworkin, 489 F.2d 1277, 180 U.S.P.Q. 388 (CCPA 1974).

Evidence of commercial exploitation does not rebut the inference if the inventor intends to keep the invention secret indefinitely. Palmer v. Dudzik, 481 F.2d 1377, 178 U.S.P.Q. 608 (CCPA 1973).

[514] Correge v. Murphy, 705 F.2d 1326, 217 U.S.P.Q. 753 (Fed. Cir. 1983). The one-year grace period is discussed at § 2C[5][c].

[515] Lutzker v. Plet, 843 F.2d 1364, 6 U.S.P.Q.2d 1370 (Fed. Cir. 1988).

[516] 843 F.2d at 1368, 6 U.S.P.Q.2d at 1372.

[517] 843 F.2d at 1367, 6 U.S.P.Q.2d at 1371-72.

[518] Paulik v. Rizkalla, 760 F.2d 1270, 226 U.S.P.Q. 224 (Fed. Cir. 1985). *See also* Paulik v. Rizkalla, 796 F.2d 456, 230 U.S.P.Q. 434 (Fed. Cir. 1986).

2. In January 1975, A's patent agent begins diligent work to prepare a patent application.

3. In March 1975, B files an application on the invention.

4. In June 1975, A files an application.

A's long delay is abandonment, suppression or concealment that precludes A from relying on the 1970 reduction to practice, but A may rely on the January 1975 date as conception. If A shows due diligence to the June 1975 filing date, he is prior to B, assuming B's invention date is March 1975.

[h] **Interference Procedure.** The PTO declares an interference when two or more parties claim the same patentable invention.

A PTO interference has stages: (a) declaration of the interference; (b) a motion period; (c) preparation and filing of preliminary statements; (d) discovery; (e) a testimony period or periods; (f) a hearing; (g) judgment; and (h) court review.

[i] *Counts.* The PTO formulates one or more "counts," which define the interfering subject matter.[519] One or more claims in each application and patent correspond to the count, identically or substantially.[520] A count may be broader than any claims corresponding to it; this is known as a "phantom count."[521]

[ii] *Declaration—Suggestion of Interference—Copying Claims—Right to Make.* The PTO may declare an interference between two or more pending applications or between a patent or patents and at least one application.[522] It will not declare or

---

[519] *See* 37 C.F.R. § 1.601(f).

[520] A claim in an application must be patentable to the applicant. 37 C.F.R. §§ 1.603, 1.606.

[521] 37 C.F.R. § 1.603. See *In re* Kroekel, 803 F.2d 705, 709-10, 231 U.S.P.Q. 640, 643 (Fed. Cir. 1986) (" 'The purpose of the count is to determine what evidence is relevant to the issue of priority.' . . . The phantom count merely represents the inventive concept which may in some cases portray two mutually exclusive, but patentably indistinct, sets of claims."); Case v. CPC International, Inc., 730 F.2d 745, 221 U.S.P.Q. 196 (Fed. Cir. 1984), *cert. denied,* 224 U.S.P.Q. 736 (1984).

In Orikasa v. Oonishi, 10 U.S.P.Q.2d 1996 (Comm'r Pat. & Tm. 1989), Commissioner Quigg gave an illustration of a phantom count bridging a method of making a material and the material itself.

"[T]he count must be drawn to include, in the alternative, both the material and the method for making the material. For example, if the material is a copolymer of ethylene and styrene and the method is copolymerizing ethylene and styrene, then the count should read:

'A copolymer of ethylene and styrene

'or

'A method of making a copolymer of ethylene and styrene comprising copolymerizing ethylene and styrene.'

"All claims of both parties directed to either the copolymer or the method of making the copolymer may then be designated to correspond to the count. The important fact is that proof of priority with respect to an embodiment within the scope of the count will suffice to establish priority of the 'patentable' invention in question." 10 U.S.P.Q.2d at 2003.

[522] 37 C.F.R. § § 1.602-608.

continue an interference between applications or patents owned by the same person except for good cause shown.[523] A PTO decision not to declare an interference is not subject to judicial review.[524]

When two pending applications contain interfering subject matter, neither applicant may know of the conflict because pending applications are confidential. An examiner may suggest that an applicant present a claim "for the purpose of an interference with another application on a patent;" refusal to present the suggested claim "shall be taken without further action as a disclaimer by the applicant of the invention defined by the suggested claim."[525]

When an application and a patent contain interfering subject matter, the applicant may provoke an interference by copying a patent claim.[526] If the applicant's filing

---

The PTO has no jurisdiction over an interference that is between only issued patents. 35 U.S.C. § 135(a). A patent owner may file a reissue application to provoke an interference with another patent.

Alternatively, a court suit may be filed to resolve an interference between patents. 35 U.S.C. § 291. See Albert v. Kevex Corp., 729 F.2d 757, 221 U.S.P.Q. 202, on rehearing, 741 F.2d 396, 223 U.S.P.Q. 1 (Fed. Cir. 1984). See also Advance Transformer Co. v. Levinson, 837 F.2d 1081, 5 U.S.P.Q.2d 1600 (Fed. Cir. 1988). In Advance Transformer, the Federal Circuit found no error in the district court's refusal to declare an interference between two patents. Section 291 uses the words "interfering patents" rather than "interfering claims," but the patents' claims control the determination whether they are for the same invention and thus "interfering."

> "[I]nterfering patents are not patents that are or may be infringed by the same device; interfering patents are patents that claim the same subject matter.

> "It is . . . necessary . . . to compare claims, not disclosures, when comparing issued patents under section 291.

> . . .

> ". . . As a guide to determining whether the claimed subject matter is the same, the district court did not err in determining whether the claims cross-read' on the disclosure of the other's patent, and thus whether each patentee could have made, based on his own disclosure, the claims that were granted to the other."

837 F.2d at 1083-84, 5 U.S.P.Q.2d at 1602.

[523] 37 C.F.R. § 1.602(a). If one person owns an application by one inventor and a patent or application by another inventor, the owner may be required to state which inventor is first during the prosecution of the application. 37 C.F.R. § 1.78(c). As to whether the invention or disclosures by one inventor is prior art as to the other, see §§ 2C[5][d] and [e], and 2D[4][a].

[524] Ewing v. United States ex rel. The Fowler Can Co., 244 U.S. 1 (1917).

[525] 37 C.F.R. § 1.605(a).

[526] Section 135(b) imposes a one-year limit on patent claim copying. An applicant who wishes to provoke an interference with an issued patent must make a claim to substantially the same subject matter as the patent within one year of the patent's issue. 35 U.S.C. § 135(b). See In re Sasse, 629 F.2d 675, 207 U.S.P.Q. 107 (CCPA 1980).

See also Parks v. Fine, 773 F.2d 1577, 227 U.S.P.Q. 432 (Fed. Cir. 1985), opinion modified, 783 F.2d 1036, 228 U.S.P.Q. 677 (Fed. Cir. 1986) (an applicant who copies a patent's claim after the one-year limit must show that a limitation in the patent claim that was absent from the claims made by the applicant before the limit was either not material or was inherent in those claims in view of the specification; as to a limitation that a reaction conducted at 700 degrees be "in the absence of a catalyst," the applicant's pre-limit claims specified a temperature range of 600 to 1700 degrees but did not mention a catalyst; the applicant's

date is more than three months after the patent's filing date, the applicant must present affidavit evidence showing *prima facie* evidence of priority.[527] In *Hahn*,[528] the court approved dismissal of an applicant-patentee interference because of the applicants' failure to make a *prima facie* showing of invention (reduction to practice) prior to the patentee's filing date. The applicants provided insufficient corroboration of their alleged reduction to practice. The Board of Patent Appeals and Interferences properly refused to consider applicants' subsequently submitted additional evidence of corroboration because they failed to show "good cause" for failure to submit the evidence earlier.[529]

---

specification indicated that the desired reaction would take place below 600 degrees with use of a catalyst, but this did not justify reading the 600-1700 degree claims as inherently requiring that a catalyst *not* be used; at most it justified reading them as making use of a catalyst optional; that the limitation was material was verified by the fact that the patentee added it in response to a prior art rejection by the examiner.).

[527] 37 C.F.R. § 1.608(b).

See Hahn v. Wong, 892 F.2d 1028, 13 U.S.P.Q.2d 1313 (Fed. Cir. 1989):

> "Both the patent statute and the regulations of the Patent and Trademark Office authorize an interference between an application for a patent and an issued patent. . . . If the effective filing date of the application is more than three months after the effective filing date of the patent, . . . the applicant is required to file evidence demonstrating that the 'applicant is *prima facie* entitled to a judgment relative to the patentee,' and 'an explanation stating with particularity' why he 'is *prima facie* entitled to the judgment.'
>
> "When an application for an interference is filed, a primary examiner makes a preliminary determination 'whether a basis upon which the applicant would be entitled to a judgment relative to the patentee is alleged and, if a basis is alleged, an interference may be declared.'
>
> "If the primary examiner makes a preliminary determination that the application meets that requirement, the application is referred to an examiner-in-chief to determine whether an interference should go forward . . .. If the examiner-in-chief determines that a *prima facie* case for priority has been established, the interference proceeds. . . . If . . . the examiner-in-chief concludes that a *prima facie* case has not been shown, . . . the examiner-chief declares an interference but 'enter[s] an order stating the reasons for the opinion and directing the applicant . . . to show cause why summary judgment should not be entered against the applicant.' . . . If such an order to show cause issues, the applicant 'may file a response to the order and state any reasons why summary judgment should not be entered.' . . . [Rule 617(b)] states [that] 'Additional evidence shall not be presented by the applicant or considered by the Board unless the applicant shows good cause why any additional evidence was not initially presented with the evidence filed under § 1.608(b).' . . . A panel of the Board then determines whether (1) summary judgment should be entered against the applicant or (2) the interference should proceed." 892 F.2d at 1030, 13 U.S.P.Q.2d at 1315.

[528] Hahn v. Wong, 892 F.2d 1028, 13 U.S.P.Q.2d 1313 (Fed. Cir. 1989).

[529] In *Hahn*, the court held that the Board did not abuse its discretion in holding that the applicants failed to show "good cause," Rule 617(b), for failure to present at the time of their initial submission their additional evidence corroborating a reduction to practice. The new interference rules "imposed stricter standards governing the circumstances under which the Patent and Trademark Office would consider additional evidence submitted to support a proposed interference." The PTO's notice accompanying the new rules stated that "Under the

A person copying a patent claim has the burden of proving by clear and convincing evidence that he has the right to make the claim—that is, that the claim is supported by the filed application disclosure upon which he relies.[530] In *Martin*,[531] the court held that the party copying a claim bears both (a) the burden of going forward and presenting a *prima facie* case for support for the copied claim in its specification, and (b) the ultimate persuasion burden. "It is immaterial whether the copier has the senior or junior filing date."

> "In considering whether [a party] has the right to make the claim corresponding to the count for interference purposes, the only inquiry is whether [the copier's] disclosure contains, in accordance with the principles of section 112 paragraph 1, support for all material limitations of the claim as presented in [the other party's] patent."[532]

The copier of claims for interference purposes must show support in the copier's specification for every material limitation of the proposed count.

The copied claim is given the broadest reasonable construction,[533] making it easier for the copying party to carry its burden of proof. The specification of the patent from which the claim is copied is referred to only when there are inherent claim language ambiguities.[534]

'good cause' standard, ignorance by a party or counsel of the provisions of the rules or the substantive requirements of the law would not constitute good cause." 892 F.2d at 1034, 13 U.S.P.Q.2d at 1318-19.

Applicants asserted two grounds for their failure to include the additional evidence with their initial submission: (i) that their counsel did not appreciate the kind of corroboration required to demonstrate a *prima facie* case for a complete reduction to practice, and (ii) that their counsel did not fully appreciate the significance of certain reduced photocopies of plots generated from certain polymer analysis, for which no proper authentication was provided in the initial submission.

The court found both grounds insufficient because they "fell afoul of the [PTO's] warning that 'ignorance by a party or counsel of the provisions of the rules or the substantive requirements of the law would not constitute good cause.' . . . [T]he requirement of corroboration independent of the inventor's own statements was well established, even before the new rules. . . . [T]he new rules specifically require that '[a]ny printed publication or other document which is not self-authenticating shall be authenticated and discussed with particularity in an affidavit.' 37 C.F.R. § 1.608(b)." 892 F.2d at 1035, 13 U.S.P.Q.2d at 1319.

[530] Burson v. Carmichael, 731 F.2d 849, 221 U.S.P.Q. 664 (Fed. Cir. 1984).

To copy a claim, the applicant's specification disclosure must adequately support the full scope of that claim. Squires v. Corbett, 560 F.2d 424, 194 U.S.P.Q. 513 (CCPA 1977). *See* § 2D[3][a],[b], and [c].

[531] Martin v. Mayer, 823 F.2d 500, 3 U.S.P.Q.2d 1333 (Fed. Cir. 1987).

[532] 823 F.2d at 504-05, 3 U.S.P.Q.2d at 1336, 1337.

[533] *E.g*, DeGeorge v. Bernier, 768 F.2d 1318, 1321, 226 U.S.P.Q. 758, 760-61 (Fed. Cir. 1985) ("Interference counts are given the broadest reasonable interpretation possible, and resort to the specification is necessary only when there are ambiguities inherent in the claim language or obvious from arguments of counsel.").

[534] DeGeorge v. Bernier, 768 F.2d 1318, 226 U.S.P.Q. 758 (Fed. Cir. 1985); Woods v. Tsuchiya, 754 F.2d 1571, 225 U.S.P.Q. 11 (Fed. Cir. 1985), *cert. denied*, 474 U.S. 825 (1985).

[iii] *Preliminary Motions—Patentability—Interference-In-Fact—Benefit.* Interference parties may raise by preliminary motion issues other than the central issues of invention priority and derivation.[535] For example, a preliminary motion may dispute whether (a) an opponent's claim corresponding to the interference count is patentable;[536] (b) there is an "interference-in-fact;"[537] or (c) a claim in his or his opponent's application is entitled to a remote application's filing date.[538]

Under the "new" interference rules, adopted in 1985, the Board of Patent Appeals and Interferences has jurisdiction to consider the patentability of the parties' claims as well as invention priority. In *Perkins*,[539] the court held the Board may find priority in favor of a junior party-applicant and against a senior party-patentee even though it also finds the junior party applicant's claims unpatentable because of a Section 102(b) statutory bar. The PTO must make a threshold determination of patentability of claimed subject matter to any potential party before declaring an interference. Neither party was entitled to a patent.[540]

---

[535] 37 C.F.R. § 1.633.

[536] 37 C.F.R. § 1.633(a). For example, the mover may contend that the opponent's claim is not patentable because of a statutory bar dating more than one year prior to the opponent's filing date. *See* § 2C[5][b][ii].

Under the pre-1985 rules, "third party" inventorship (*i.e.* invention by someone other than the parties to the interference) was not "ancillary" to priority and would not be resolved by the Board of Interferences. *E.g.*, Morgan v. Hirsch, 728 F.2d 1449, 221 U.S.P.Q. 193 (Fed. Cir. 1984). Under new rules, third-party inventorship, along with any other issue relating to the patentability of a corresponding claim, may be raised by motion.

[537] 37 C.F.R. § 1.633(b). An "interference-in-fact" exists only if claims by the parties that correspond to the count define the same patentable invention. 37 C.F.R. § 1.601(j). A claim defines the same patentable invention as another claim if the former would be anticipated or obvious assuming that the latter constituted prior art. 37 C.F.R. § 1.601(n). If the claims are identical (as when a party has copied the claim of another party's patent), then no motion based on this ground may be asserted. 37 C.F.R. § 1.633(b)(2).

[538] 37 C.F.R. § 1.633(f), (g). *See* §§ 2D[4][b] and 2H[2]. *See also* Utter v. Hiraga, 845 F.2d 993, 998, 6 U.S.P.Q.2d 1709, 1713 (Fed. Cir. 1988) ("A party who. . . relies on an earlier-filed application under 35 U.S.C. §§ 119 or 120 has the burden to show that the foreign or parent application supports later-added claims under 35 U.S.C. § 112 ¶ 1, regardless of whether that party is the junior or senior party in an interference.").

The senior party has the earliest effective filing date. 37 C.F.R. § 1.601(m). All other parties are junior parties and bear the burden of persuasion on factual issues. A junior party may achieve senior status through a motion to obtain the benefit of the filing date of a prior application, such as a parent United States application or an application in another country.

If a party wishes to rely on the filing date of an earlier application not identified in the notice of declaration of interference, he must make a preliminary motion. 37 C.F.R. § 1.630.

[539] Perkins v. Kwon, 886 F.2d 325, 12 U.S.P.Q.2d 1308 (Fed. Cir. 1989).

[540] Perkins ("senior party-patentee") filed an application describing and claiming a "golf swing plane sensor" on September 16, 1982 and obtained a patent on June 26, 1984. Kwon ("junior party-applicant") filed a patent application on July 16, 1984. The PTO declared an interference between Perkins' patent and Kwon's application. The senior party-patentee moved for judgment under Rule 633(a) on the ground that junior party- applicant's claims were unpatentable because of senior party-patentee's publication, sale and public use of the invention at least as early as June 16, 1982.

[iv]   *Preliminary Statement—Testimony—Hearing—Appeal.* If a party intends to rely on a pre-filing invention date,[541] it must file a preliminary statement that identifies whom and where an invention was made or whether the invention was derived from the party by the opponent. Statements are sealed until preliminary motions are decided.[542]

Testimony concerning a pre-filing invention date is taken by deposition or affidavit.[543] A party who wishes to use a subpoena to take the testimony of an unwilling witness must obtain permission from the examiner-in-chief in charge of the interference.[544] A party may obtain production of documents and other material during the cross-examination of an opponent's witness in a deposition.[545] Additional discovery may be ordered by the examiner-in-chief.[546]

The Board holds a final hearing[547] and enters a decision resolving the issues.[548]

At senior party-patentee's request, the examiner deferred the patentability issue to final hearing, stating that testimony was necessary to establish the senior party-patentee's allegations. At final hearing, the Board ruled (i) junior party-applicant was the prior inventor, but (ii) the count was unpatentable to junior party-applicant because of senior party-patentee's sales two years prior to junior party-applicant's filing date.

Senior party-patentee argued that the Board should not have determined priority of invention so as to invalidate senior party-patentee's patent when it had held the count not patentable to junior party-applicant.

> "The determination that [junior party-applicant's] application contained patentable subject matter was made, in the first instance, *ex parte* before the interference was declared. That was the practice before the consolidation of [the Board of Appeals and the Board of Patent Interferences]. . . and continues to be the practice. . . . In this case, however, the reason for unpatentability of the subject matter. . . was not known to the examiner until it was raised by [the senior party-patentee's] motion after the interference was declared." 886 F.2d at 326, 12 U.S.P.Q.2d at 1309-10.

The grant of senior party-patentee's request that determination of the issue of patentability be delayed to final hearing is within the authority of Rules 633(a) and 640(b): "[I]ssues of patentability and priority that have been fully developed before the Board should be resolved by the Board." The legislative history of the statute consolidating the two boards "shows that Congress intended that if patentability is fairly placed at issue in the proceeding, it will be determined. . . . The public interest in the benefits of a patent system is best met by procedures that resolve administratively questions affecting patent validity that arise before the PTO." 886 F.2d at 328-29, 12 U.S.P.Q.2d at 1311.

[541] 37 C.F.R. § 1.629(c). Dates in the statement are binding on the party as the earliest provable dates for the stated events.

[542] 37 C.F.R. § 1.631(a).

[543] 37 C.F.R. § 1.672, 679. Testimony of a witness in another country may be authorized. 37 C.F.R. § 1.684.

[544] 37 C.F.R. § 1.672(c).

[545] 37 C.F.R. § 1.687(b).

[546] 37 C.F.R. § 1.687(c).

[547] The hearing is before a three-person panel.

[548] 37 C.F.R. § 1.658.

A problem with past interference proceedings was the time required to resolve priority. The PTO's goal under the 1985 interference rules is to proceed from declaration to final decision in no more than two years.

Judicial review of the decision is available either by a direct appeal to the Court of Appeals for the Federal Circuit[549] or by a civil action in a district court.[550]

[v] *Settlement—Arbitration.* Parties may settle an interference but must file with the PTO any agreement or understanding made in connection with a settlement.[551]

Parties may agree to arbitrate interference issues.[552] Arbitration is dispositive between the parties but does not bind the PTO as to any patentability issue.

[vi] *Estoppel—Lost Counts.* An interference judgment awards invention priority as to the specified count or counts and may estop a losing party from raising in *ex parte* prosecution or in another interference matters that could have been raised by motion in the interference.[553]

In *Kroekel*,[554] applicants lost an interference defined by a phantom count because the opposing party successfully showed a prior invention date. Later, applicants sought a claim that was generic to the lost phantom count, offering to prove that they invented the subject matter of that claim before the opposing party's date. Interference estoppel barred the applicants' claim. The applicants never attempted to broaden the interference count to conform to their later claim. The court noted "The doctrine of interference estoppel is directed to finality of an interference, at least with respect to all issues which *might have been* presented in the interference" and "Estoppel should be decided on the facts of each case with reference to principles of equity." It found no merit in applicants' argument that the other party's application would not have supported a generic claim and that therefore a motion in the interference to broaden the count to conform to the generic claim would have been futile. A phantom count might have been adopted even though it lacked support in one or both of the parties' applications.

Another problem with interferences was that, after priority resolution, further *ex parte* prosecution was required to resolve patentability issues. Under the 1985 rules, the Board resolves patentability and priority.

[549] 35 U.S.C. § 141. If a party appeals to the Federal Circuit, any adverse party to the interference may force the appealing party to dismiss the appeal and file a Section 146 civil action.

[550] 35 U.S.C. § 146.

[551] 35 U.S.C. § 135(c); 37 C.F.R. § 1.666. *See* CTS Corp. v. Piher Int'l Corp., 727 F.2d 1550, 221 U.S.P.Q. 11 (Fed. Cir. 1984), *cert. denied*, 469 U.S. 871 (1984).

[552] 35 U.S.C. § 135(d).

[553] The current PTO interference estoppel rule is Rule 658(c). Adopted in 1985 as part of a new set of interference rules, Rule 658(c) is a significant change from previous estoppel Rule 257. In adopting Rule 658(c), the PTO noted:

> "The definition of interference estoppel is designed to encourage parties in interference cases to settle as many issues as possible in one proceeding. Section 1.658(c) creates an estoppel both as to senior and junior parties unlike the present practice (37 CFR 1.257) which limits estoppel in some instances to junior parties. An estoppel would *not* apply with respect to any claims which correspond, or which properly could have corresponded to a count as to which the party was awarded a favorable judgment."

USPTO, Discussion Accompanying Adoption of New Interference Rules, 49 Fed. Reg. 48416 (Dec. 12, 1984), *reproduced* in D. Chisum, Patents App. 35. In its discussion, the PTO gives a series of examples of interference estoppel.

[554] *In re* Kroekel, 803 F.2d 705, 231 U.S.P.Q. 640 (Fed. Cir. 1986). *See also In re* Zletz, 893 F.2d 319, 13 U.S.P.Q.2d 1320 (Fed. Cir. 1989).

The "lost counts" doctrine is related to interference estoppel. Some decisions held that the count lost in an interference becomes, in effect, prior art that may be used to reject the losing party's subsequent attempt to obtain claims differing in scope from the lost count but not "patentably distinct." *McKellin* suggested that a lost count may not be "prior art" if it lacks a Section 102 basis.[555] In *Tytgat*,[556] the PTO frankly questioned *McKellin*'s wisdom on the ground it could lead to issuance of separate patents claiming essentially the same invention or to repeated interferences. The problem is alleviated by adoption of broadly-defined counts[557] and the application of interference estoppel.

[6] Post-Issuance Procedures

[a] **Reexamination and Protest.** The United States patent system provides no general procedures for opposition to a patent grant or cancellation of a patent by parties who are or would be damaged by the patent's issue. In contrast, the trademark registration system provides to a person who is or would be damaged by a mark's registration rights to oppose or to cancellation of a registration. Other countries' patent systems provide opposition or cancellation rights.

A person who believes the PTO erroneously issued a patent may, if sued for patent infringement, defend by asserting invalidity. A person may also file a suit for a declaratory judgment of invalidity. Neither remedy is available to a person not currently infringing the patent or making substantial preparations to do so.[558]

A person may protest patent issue,[559] but the protest right is limited in two ways. First, the PTO rule governing protests severely restricts the protestor's right to submit information or otherwise participate in examination proceedings.[560] Second, the confidentiality of pending applications keeps interested persons unaware of the application's existence. Protests are most commonly filed on reissue applications as to which the confidentiality policy does not apply.[561]

---

[555] *In re* McKellin, 529 F.2d 1324, 188 U.S.P.Q. 428 (CCPA 1978). *Cf. In re* Zletz, 893 F.2d 319, 13 U.S.P.Q.2d 1320 (Fed. Cir. 1989).

In *McKellin*, the applicant lost the prior interference only because the prevailing party's patent disclosure was entitled to the benefit of a foreign priority date under 35 U.S.C. § 119. The "lost count" did not fit within any of the Section 102 prior art categories. For example, it was not prior invention under Section 102(g) because it was not "in this country."*See* § 2C[5][d][ii].

[556] *Ex parte* Tytgat, 225 U.S.P.Q. 907 (PTO Bd. App. 1985), *rev'd,* — F.2d —— (Fed. Cir. xxx) (unpublished opinion).

[557] *Cf.* Orikasa v. Oonishi, 10 U.S.P.Q.2d 1996, 2000 n.10 (Comm'r Pat. & Tm. 1989) ("a count should be drawn broad enough to include all *patentable* subject matter falling within all claims designated to correspond to the count.").

[558] *Cf.* Syntex (U.S.A.) Inc. v. U.S. Patent & Trademark Office, 882 F.2d 1570, 1576, 11 U.S.P.Q.2d 1866, 1870 (Fed. Cir. 1989) ("[A] potential infringer may not sue the PTO seeking retraction of a patent issued to another by reason of its improper allowance by the PTO. A remedy must await confrontation with the patent owner.").

[559] *See generally* D. Chisum, Patents § 11.03[3][b].

[560] 37 C.F.R. § 1.291.

[561] *See* § 2D[1][c].

In 1980, Congress enacted a limited reexamination procedure.[562] Any person, including the patent owner or an accused patent infringer, may file a request for reexamination of the validity of any claim in a patent on the basis of cited prior art patents or printed publications.[563]

The PTO enters a reexamination order if it determines that cited art presents a new patentability question as to the claim.[564] A reexamination is conducted under the rules that apply to examination of original patent applications.[565]

---

[562] 35 U.S.C. §§ 301, 302. See generally D. Chisum, Patents § 11.07[4].

The reexamination statute applies to patents applied for or issued before 1980. See Patlex Corp. v. Mossinghoff, 758 F.2d 594, 225 U.S.P.Q. 243 (Fed. Cir. 1985), on rehearing, 771 F.2d 480, 226 U.S.P.Q. 985 (Fed. Cir. 1985) (rejecting constitutional attacks on the retroactivity of the reexamination statute).

[563] See Syntex (U.S.A.) Inc. v. U.S. Patent & Trademark Office, 882 F.2d 1570, 1573, 11 U.S.P.Q.2d 1866, 1868 (Fed. Cir. 1989) ("The category of third-party requesters is. . . open-ended and includes, for example, attorneys representing a principal whose identity is not disclosed to the PTO or patentee.").

Cf. Joy Manufacturing Co. v. National Mine Service Co., 810 F.2d 1127, 1130, 1 U.S.P.Q.2d 1627, 1629 (Fed. Cir. 1987) (a request for reexamination by a party to a settlement agreement did not breach the provision of the agreement that the party not file any "suit" in "court" contesting the validity of the patent; reexamination and civil litigation are "distinctly different proceedings.;" the relief sought by the other party—an injunction stopping the reexamination—would be unavailable because the decision of the Commissioner to institute reexamination "is not subject to review" and an injunction directed against the requesting party "would have no effect on reexamination since [the requestor] has no future role to play in that ex parte proceeding.").

As to a possible remedy against bad faith reexamination requests, see Ball Corp. v. Xidex Corp., 705 F. Supp. 1470, 1471, 9 U.S.P.Q.2d 1491, 1492 (D. Colo. 1988) (refusing to dismiss plaintiff's unfair competition claim alleging that the defendants, in filing a request for reexamination of plaintiff's patent, "perpetrated a fraud on the PTO by knowingly misrepresenting evidence on the commercial success and non-obviousness of [the invention described in the] patent, by withholding evidence on these issues which defendants had in their possession and by preventing [plaintiff] from submitting that evidence under the pretext of this court's protective order in prior litigation [in which plaintiff charged defendant with infringement of the patent].").

[564] 35 U.S.C. § 304. If no reexamination is ordered, a substantial portion of the reexamination request fee will be refunded. See § 2D[1][a][iv]. The decision not to order reexamination is nonappealable.

Cf. Patlex Corp. v. Mossinghoff, 771 F.2d 480, 226 U.S.P.Q. 985 (Fed. Cir. 1985) (a PTO rule barring any consideration of submissions by the patent owner in the determination of whether a new question of patentability exists which warrants reexamination violates neither the reexamination statute nor the constitutional demands of due process of law. The provision for a refund of a part of the reexamination fee does not unconstitutionally bias the decision by the PTO; a policy that "doubts" are to be resolved in favor of granting reexamination is void as contrary to the intent of Congress that patentees be protected from harassment by persons requesting reexamination.).

[565] 35 U.S.C. § 305.

Only the patent owner may actively participate in a reexamination or appeal an adverse decision.[566] A patentee may add or amend claims during a reexamination but may not enlarge the scope of any of the patent's claims.[567]

The statutory patent validity presumption does not apply during reexamination.[568] Examiners give the claims the broadest reasonable construction, as is the case with original and reissue examination.[569] The examination is limited to the patentability of the claims based on patents and printed publications.[570]

If a reexamined claim is found unpatentable, it will be cancelled; if it is found patentable, a certificate of confirmation will issue.[571] After confirmation, the validity presumption continues to apply.[572] The intervening rights doctrine applies to claims

---

[566] A person other than the patent owner is limited to (1) citing patents and printed publications and (2) filing a request for reexamination, explaining the pertinency of the cited art. If a reexamination is ordered at the request of a person other than the patent owner, and the patent owner files a statement in response to the order, the requester may file a reply statement. 35 U.S.C. § 304.

See Syntex (U.S.A.) Inc. v. U.S. Patent & Trademark Office, 882 F.2d 1570, 11 U.S.P.Q.2d 1866 (Fed. Cir. 1989). In *Syntex*, the Federal Circuit held that a nonpatentee reexamination requester's suit alleging that the PTO failed to comply with its rules in conducting reexamination of a patent must be dismissed for want of jurisdiction and lack of standing. *Cf. In re* Opprecht, 868 F.2d 1264, 10 U.S.P.Q.2d 1718 (Fed. Cir. 1989) (denying a party's motion to intervene or to file a brief *amicus curiae* in a patentee's appeal from an adverse decision on reexamination of a patent; the party did not file a reexamination request or participate before the PTO in the reexamination to the limited extent authorized by statute); Boeing Co. v. Commissioner of Patents and Trademarks, 853 F.2d 878, 7 U.S.P.Q.2d 1487 (Fed. Cir. 1988) (a reexamination requester who was allowed to participate as an intervenor in a patentee's 35 U.S.C. Section 145 suit to review the PTO's rejection of patent claims has no standing to appeal an order dismissing the suit without prejudice and remanding the matter to the PTO).

[567] 35 U.S.C. § 305.

[568] *In re* Etter, 756 F.2d 852, 225 U.S.P.Q. 1 (Fed. Cir. 1985), *cert. denied*, 474 U.S. 828 (1985).

[569] *In re* Yamamoto, 740 F.2d 1569, 222 U.S.P.Q. 934 (Fed. Cir. 1984). During an examination or reexamination an applicant may amend the claims to clarify their scope. In an infringement suit, claims are given a more restricted interpretation in order to sustain their validity. *See* § 2F[1][e].

[570] 37 C.F.R. § 1.552. Issues such as the public use bars or inequitable conduct are not considered. Disclosure requirement compliance is considered only as to new or amended claims.

[571] 35 U.S.C. § 307.

[572] *Cf.* Greenwood v. Hattori Seiko Co., Ltd., 900 F.2d 238, 14 U.S.P.Q.2d 1474 (Fed. Cir. 1990).

In *Greenwood*, the district court erred in holding the patent invalid because, in essence, it exercised inappropriate review of the PTO reexamination proceeding that confirmed the claim's patentability. During reexamination, the PTO examiner rejected all the patent's claim as unpatentable in view of prior art references. The applicant overcame the rejection by filing a Rule 131 affidavit showing an invention date before the references' effective dates. The PTO confirmed the patent claims. The district court held, in granting a motion for summary judgment of invalidity of the patent claims, that (a) the Rule 131 affidavit was insufficient because it made no showing of diligence connecting the alleged conception and reduction to practice, and (b) the PTO's initial unpatentability finding should be reinstated because the applicant made no attempt to undermine the PTO's original showing of unpatentability over the cited references.

amended during reexamination.[573]

A patent may be involved simultaneously in a PTO reexamination and district court patent infringement litigation. In *Ethicon*,[574] the court held that the PTO may not stay reexamination pending litigation over the patent's validity because the reexamination statute requires proceedings to be conducted with "special dispatch."[575] In dictum, the court commented on the effect of a court validity ruling on PTO reexamination.

> "To the extent MPEP § 2286 states that the PTO is bound by a court's decision upholding a patent's validity, it is incorrect. . . . The doctrine of collateral estoppel does not prevent the PTO from completing the reexamination [in the situation where a court determines that a patent is not invalid]. Courts do not find patents 'valid.'. . . only that the patent challenger did not carry the 'burden of establishing invalidity in the *particular case* before the court' under 35 U.S.C. § 282. . . . [I]f a court finds a patent invalid, and that decision is either upheld on appeal or not appealed, the PTO may discontinue its reexamination. . . .. Of course, in the end it is up to the court, not the PTO, to decide if the patentee had a 'full and fair chance' to litigate the validity of the patent. But it is admissible for the PTO to act on the standing judgment unless and until a court has said it does not have res judicata effect."[576]

[b] Reissue. A patentee may apply for a reissue patent to correct errors made without deceptive intent that cause the patent to be wholly or partly inoperative or invalid by reason of a defective specification or drawing, or by reason of the patentee claiming more or less than he has a right to claim.[577]

[i] Inoperativeness and Invalidity. Reissue applicants most commonly seek to alter the original patent's claims[578] but may also correct other deficiencies.[579] Reissue

---

The appeals court stated: "In an infringement suit before a district court, the invalidity of a patent under 35 U.S.C. § 103 must be decided on the basis of prior art adduced in the proceeding before the court. The issue cannot be decided merely by accepting or rejecting the adequacy of the positions taken by the patentee in order to obtain a Certificate of Reexamination for the patent. Once issued by the PTO, a patent is presumed valid and the burden of proving otherwise rests solely on the challenger." 900 F.2d at 240-41, 14 U.S.P.Q.2d at 1476.

[573] 35 U.S.C. § 307(b). *See* § 2D[6][b][v].

See Fortel Corp. v. Phone-Mate, Inc., 825 F.2d 1577, 1580-81, 3 U.S.P.Q.2d 1771, 1774 (Fed. Cir. 1987) (the reexamination statute incorporates both paragraphs of Section 252; any damage cause of action as to acts occurring before issue of a reexamination certificate is extinguished except as to patent claims confirmed without substantive change; the intervening rights doctrine, codified in the Section 252, second paragraph, has nothing to do with liability for acts occurring before the reexamination certificate date; "That [the independent claim in suit as amended in the reexamination] is substantively different from [the] original claim. . . is an inescapable conclusion upon a mere reading of those claims.;" the patentee admitted that the limitations inserted were "slightly broader" than the original limitations).

[574] Ethicon, Inc. v. Quigg, 849 F.2d 1422, 7 U.S.P.Q.2d 1152 (Fed. Cir. 1988).

[575] 35 U.S.C. § 305.

[576] 849 F.2d at 1429 n.3, 7 U.S.P.Q.2d at 1157 n.3.

[577] 35 U.S.C. § 251. *See generally* D. Chisum, Patents § 15.01 *et seq.*

[578] *See* § 2D[6][b][ii].

[579] *Compare In re* Keil, 808 F.2d 830, 1 U.S.P.Q.2d 1427 (Fed. Cir. 1987); *In re* Weiler, 790 F.2d 1576, 229 U.S.P.Q. 673 (Fed. Cir. 1986).

applications may (1) more precisely define the subject matter;[580] (2) cure claim indefiniteness;[581] (3) correct an obviously-correctable error in the specification;[582] (4) add a specific reference or priority claim to obtain benefit of a prior application's filing date;[583] and (5) correct inventor identification.[584]

From 1977 to 1982, the PTO allowed "no defect" reissue applications to secure patent reexamination in view of newly-discovered prior art. Often, the patent was the subject of a pending patent infringement suit. The patentee's litigation opponent participated in the reissue proceeding as a protestor. In *Dien*,[585] the court held

---

In *Keil*, the court held that an application for reissue of a patent, filed for the purpose of provoking an interference with another patent and alleging, essentially, that the PTO committed error by failing to declare an interference when the applications leading to the issuance of the two patents were copending, must be dismissed because no change in the specification or claims was sought. The application was "merely a request for an advisory opinion" and beyond an Article III court's jurisdiction.

In *Weiler*, the specification as originally filed stated claims to three types of subject matter: an assay method, an organic compound, and a protein compound. In response to a restriction requirement, the applicant elected the first type and obtained a patent thereon. The applicant failed to file a timely divisional application on the second and third types. The court found no "error" supporting the applicant's reissue application that sought to claim two other types of subject matter (a method of developing citrus fruit strains and an antibody) even though the specification provided disclosure support for those claims.

[580] *In re* Wadlinger, 496 F.2d 1200, 181 U.S.P.Q. 826 (CCPA 1974). In *Wadlinger*, the court upheld the use of reissue to insert a more precise "fingerprint" description of a chemical compound.

There must be some showing that the original claim is defective because the reissue statute does not authorize reissue to add claims of the same scope, using different language. *In re* Wittry, 489 F.2d 1299, 180 U.S.P.Q. 320 (CCPA 1974).

[581] *In re* Altenpohl, 500 F.2d 1151, 183 U.S.P.Q. 38 (CCPA 1974).

[582] *In re* Oda, 443 F.2d 1200, 170 U.S.P.Q. 268 (CCPA 1971). In *Oda*, the term "nitric acid" was mistranslated from Japanese to English as "nitrous acid." The error and its correction were obvious in the context because the specification stated a specific gravity of 1.45, which cannot apply to nitrous acid.

The new matter prohibition restricts reissue. 35 U.S.C. § 251. *See* § 2D[6][b].

[583] Brenner v. State of Israel, 400 F.2d 789, 158 U.S.P.Q. 584 (D.C. Cir. 1968). *See* §§ 2D[4][b][iii] and 2H[2][e].

A reissue application cannot cure failure to comply with the fundamental requirement that a subsequent application be filed during pendency of a prior application to be entitled to the latter's filing date. *In re* Watkinson, 900 F.2d 230, 231, 14 U.S.P.Q.2d 1407, 1409 (Fed. Cir. 1990) ("failure to file a divisional application [claiming a nonelected invention], regardless of the propriety of the underlying restriction requirement, is not an error correctable by reissue"); *In re* Orita, 550 F.2d 1277, 193 U.S.P.Q. 145 (CCPA 1977). *See* § 2D[1][b][iii].

[584] *Ex parte* Scudder, 169 U.S.P.Q. 814 (Pat. Off. Bd. App. 1971).

[585] *In re* Dien, 680 F.2d 151, 214 U.S.P.Q. 10 (CCPA 1982). *Dien* held that, if the claims were rejected as unpatentable and the applicant refused to amend the claim, the applicant could not appeal to the courts, which have jurisdiction only over actual controversies.

If the claims in the reissue application were determined to be *patentable*, they would be rejected because the PTO has no statutory authority to reissue a patent that is not defective. If the claims were determined to be *unpatentable*, they would also be rejected. In the latter case, the applicant could abandon the reissue application and retain the original patent.

these no defect reissues to be mere advisory proceedings. A unwilling patent owner could not be ordered to file a reissue.[586] In 1982, the PTO eliminated no defect reissues and curtailed the rights of protestors[587] to reduce the PTO's burdens[588] and to recognize the new, more limited, statutory reexamination procedure.[589]

[ii] *Claim Scope Alteration.* A patent claim may be so broad as to render it invalid in view of the prior art or so narrow as to fail to cover a product embodying the invention.[590] A reissue application may add a limitation that distinguishes the prior art[591] or eliminates an unnecessary limitation that distinguishes the product.[592]

In *Hewlett-Packard Co.*,[593] the court questioned, in dictum, whether a patentee could use reissue to obtain claims intermediate in scope as a precaution against the possibility that a broad claim would be held invalid and a narrow claim not infringed.[594] In *Scripps*,[595] it confirmed the propriety of adding claims when the inventor's attorney failed to claim the invention sufficiently broadly.

---

[586] Johnson & Johnson, Inc. v. Wallace A. Erickson & Co., 627 F.2d 57, 206 U.S.P.Q. 873 (7th Cir. 1980).

[587] *See* § 2D[6][a].

[588] *See* PPG Industries, Inc. v. Celanese Polymer Specialties Co., Inc., 840 F.2d 1565, 6 U.S.P.Q.2d 1010 (Fed. Cir. 1988).

[589] *See* § 2D[6][a]. A statutory reexamination is not the same in scope as an examination pursuant to a reissue. The former is confined to documentary prior art sources (patents and publications). The latter includes nondocumentary sources (such as matter in public use and on sale). *See* § 2C[5][b].

[590] *See* Hewlett-Packard Co. v. Bausch & Lomb Inc., 882 F.2d 1556, 1564-65, 11 U.S.P.Q.2d 1750, 1757 (Fed. Cir. 1989), *cert. denied*, 110 S. Ct. 1125 (1990) ("'[T]he expression 'less than he had a right to claim' generally refers to the scope of a claim. . . . [T]hat provision covers the situation where the claims in the patent are narrower than the prior art would have required the patentee to claim and the patentee seeks broader claims. Conversely, the alternative that the patentee claimed 'more . . . than he had a right to claim' comes into play where a claim is too broad in scope in view of the prior art or the specification and the patentee seeks narrower claims.").

[591] The amended claim must be supported by the original specification disclosure. Because of this, a narrowed claim may fail to comply with the description requirement. *See* § 2D[3][b][iv].

[592] *E.g., In re* Peters, 723 F.2d 891, 221 U.S.P.Q. 952 (Fed. Cir. 1983).

[593] Hewlett-Packard Co. v. Bausch & Lomb Inc., 882 F.2d 1556, 11 U.S.P.Q.2d 1750 (Fed. Cir. 1989).

[594] The court noted the patentee, in seeking reissue, did not assert that the patent claims were inoperative "by reason of the patentee claiming either too much or too little in scope but because he included, in a sense, *too few* claims."

> "Although neither 'more' nor 'less' in the sense of the scope of the claims, the practice of allowing reissue for the purpose of including narrower claims as a hedge against the possible invalidation of a broad claim has been tacitly approved, at least in dicta, in our precedent . . . . For purposes of this case, we will assume that that practice is in accordance with the remedial purpose of the statute, although [the patent owner] clearly did not allege an 'error' in the patent which meets the literal language of the statute. We need not decide here whether omission of narrow claims which more specifically cover a broadly claimed invention meets the first prong of the requirement for error . . . because [the patentee] clearly did not establish the second prong, namely, inadvertent error in conduct." 882 F.2d at 1565, 11 U.S.P.Q.2d at 1757-58.

A reissue application that seeks to broaden any claim must be filed within two years of the original patent's issue.[596] A claim is broader if it is in any respect broader than the claims of the original patent (even though it may be narrower in some respects). A claim is broader if any conceivable product or process would infringe a reissue claim but not an original claim.[597]

Reissue claims must be for an invention disclosed in the original patent specification.[598]

A reissue application may not recapture subject matter intentionally surrendered during the original prosecution.[599] The recapture rule depends on direct evidence of intent and on inferences of intent drawn from comparing the originally cancelled claim and the reissue claim.[600] Consider the following example:

1. Applicant A originally asserts a claim to $X+Y$.

2. After the examiner rejects the claim, A narrows the claim by adding element Z $(X+Y+Z)$.

The recapture rule may preclude a reissue claim to $X+Y$ or, perhaps, to X. It will not necessarily preclude a claim to $W+X+Y+Z$, which is narrower because it requires W, or to $W+Y+Z$, which is narrower because it requires W, and broader because it does not require X.

---

[595] Scripps Clinic & Research Foundation v. Genentech, Inc., 927 F.2d 1565, 18 U.S.P.Q.2d 1001 (Fed. Cir. 1991), discussed *infra*.

[596] 35 U.S.C. § 251 (last paragraph).

If the application is filed within the two year period, this requirement is satisfied even if broader claims are added by an amendment filed after the period. *In re* Doll, 419 F.2d 925, 164 U.S.P.Q. 218 (CCPA 1970).

If the reissue application seeks to enlarge the claims, it cannot be made by the assignee alone. *But cf. In re* Bennett, 766 F.2d 524, 226 U.S.P.Q. 413 (Fed. Cir. 1985) (an error by a patent assignee in filing a reissue application that seeks to enlarge patent claims within the two-year period allowed under 35 U.S.C. Section 251, but without the required declaration of the actual inventor, may be corrected by the filing of the declaration after the two year period).

[597] Tillotson, Ltd. v. Walbro Corp., 831 F.2d 1033, 4 U.S.P.Q.2d 1450 (Fed. Cir. 1987); *In re* Price, 302 F.2d 741, 133 U.S.P.Q. 527 (CCPA 1962).

Reissues that correct defects not related to claim scope do not broaden those claims and need not be filed within the two-year period. Fontijn v. Okamoto, 518 F.2d 610, 186 U.S.P.Q. 97 (CCPA 1975) (addition of cross-reference priority claims necessary to obtain benefit of a prior application filing date did not broaden the scope of the claims). *See* §§ 2D[4][b][iii] and 2H[2][e].

[598] *In re* Hounsfield, 699 F.2d 1320, 216 U.S.P.Q. 1045 (Fed. Cir. 1983) (rejecting statements in prior decisions that reissue claims must be for subject matter the applicant originally "intended" to claim; "intent to claim" is not a separate test for reissue).

[599] Ball Corp. v. United States, 729 F.2d 1429, 221 U.S.P.Q. 289 (Fed. Cir. 1984).

[600] *See, e.g.,* Whittaker Corp. v. UNR Industries, Inc., 911 F.2d 709, 15 U.S.P.Q.2d 1742 (Fed. Cir. 1990) (recapture rule does not invalidate a reissue claim because limitation makes it narrower in scope than a similar claim cancelled during original prosecution; the district court erred in construing the limitation added in reissue as merely making explicit what was implicit in a cancelled original claim).

[*iii*]   *Error.* A patentee may obtain reissue only if the patent's inoperativeness or invalidity resulted from an error committed without deceptive intent. A common error is the inventor's failure to adequately communicate the nature of his invention to his patent attorney or agent.[601] Error includes errors of law, judgment, or fact.[602] The error need not have been discovered by the patentee.[603]

In *Hewlett-Packard Co.,*[604] the Federal Circuit held that a patentee does not establish "error" sufficient to support reissue merely by showing a nonintentional failure to obtain claims narrower in scope than the patent claims: "a reissue applicant does not make a *prima facie* case of error in conduct merely by submitting a sworn statement which parrots the statutory language."[605]

The district court found:

(a)   The patent related to "X-Y plotters" in which chart paper moves under a marking pen. The inventor Yeiser obtained the patent in 1973. It contained 9 claims. Milton Roy Co. obtained the patent and produced commercial embodiments only briefly.

(b)   Later, Hewlett-Packard (HP) introduced a successful moving-paper X-Y plotter. Bausch & Lomb (B&L) bought the Yeiser patent to obtain leverage in license negotiations with HP.

(c)   B&L became concerned that claim 1, the patent's broadest claim, which arguably covered HP's plotter, might be too broad in relation to the prior art. B&L decided to file a reissue application to obtain narrower claims that would still read on HP's plotter.

(d)   B&L's reissue application carried forward the 9 original patent claims and added three new claims (10- 13). The reissue declaration stated that the patent was "partly or wholly inoperative. . . by reason of the patentee claiming less than he had a right to claim in that he had a right to claim [his invention] more specifically" and that the omission of the dependent claims arose "because of oversight and without deceptive intent"

---

[601] *Cf. In re* Wilder, 736 F.2d 1516, 1519, 222 U.S.P.Q. 369, 371-72 (Fed. Cir. 1984), *cert. denied,* Wilder v. Mossinghoff, 469 U.S. 1209 (1985); *In re* Richman, 424 F.2d 1388, 165 U.S.P.Q. 509 (CCPA 1970).

Compare In re Weiler, 790 F.2d 1576, 1579, 229 U.S.P.Q. 673, 675 (Fed. Cir. 1986) (although the reissue statute is remedial in nature and should be construed liberally, "not every event or circumstance that might be labeled 'error' is correctable by reissue.").

[602] Rohm & Haas Co. v. Roberts Chemicals, Inc., 245 F.2d 693, 113 U.S.P.Q. 423 (4th Cir. 1957); Moist Cold Refrigerator Co. v. Lou Johnson Co., 217 F.2d 39, 103 U.S.P.Q. 410 (9th Cir. 1954), *cert. denied,* 348 U.S. 952, 104 U.S.P.Q. 409 (1980). In *Rohm & Haas,* the court upheld a reissue that added a method of use claim because a statutory amendment after the original patent's issue made it clear that such claims were permissible. In *Moist Cold Refrigerator,* the court upheld a reissue that added a claim to clarify impermissibly vague functional language in the original patent claims.

[603] *In re* Richman, 424 F.2d 1388, 165 U.S.P.Q.509 (CCPA 1970).

[604] Hewlett-Packard Co. v. Bausch & Lomb Inc., 882 F.2d 1556, 11 U.S.P.Q.2d 1750 (Fed. Cir. 1989).

[605] 882 F.2d at 1565, 11 U.S.P.Q.2d at 1758.

on the part of the inventor or his attorney. A B&L vice president who knew nothing about the alleged error, either personally or based on others' investigations, signed the declaration.

(e)   The PTO examiner rejected the application because the reissue declaration did not specify an error.

(f)   B&L's outside patent attorney contacted Fleming, the attorney who prosecuted Yeiser's application. He drafted an affidavit for Fleming, which was submitted to the PTO. In the affidavit, Fleming averred that he had only limited contact with the inventor and received little substantive help during the prosecution from Yeiser or his assignee.

(g)   The PTO examiner indicated that the Fleming affidavit was "acceptable" for what it stated but that it failed to show "how and by whom the scope of the subject matter claimed was determined and why."

(h)   An in-house patent attorney for B&L took over the prosecution and prepared a second affidavit for Fleming in which Fleming averred he had been given a "crude model of the invention" to review on only one occasion for about two hours and that he determined the scope of the invention solely on that brief exposure.

(i)   The district court found that parts of the two Fleming affidavits were false. Fleming's time records indicated that he had frequent contact with the inventor during the preparation and prosecution of the application.

The Federal Circuit found no error in the district court's finding that the original reissue declaration was insufficient to establish "error" and, therefore, that the supplemental Fleming affidavit was necessary. "[T]he statutorily required 'error' of section 251 has two parts: . . . error in the patent, and. . . error in conduct." The court did not pass on whether there was an error in the patent [606] because the patentee "clearly did not establish the second prong, namely, inadvertent error in conduct."

"[A] reissue applicant does not make a *prima facie* case of error in conduct merely by submitting a sworn statement which parrots the statutory language.

"Were [the] theory [that, whenever it is apparent that narrower claims could have been obtained, error warranting reissue exists] correct, it is difficult to conceive of any extant patent for which a right of reissue would not exist, a view which this court has unequivocally and repeatedly rejected. . . .. [R]eissue is not intended to give the patentee simply a second chance to prosecute the patent application." [607]

In *Scripps*,[608] the Federal Circuit held that the district court erred as a matter of law in holding the patentee failed to show sufficient error when it sought reissue

---

[606] *Id.*

[607] 882 F.2d at 1565, 221 U.S.P.Q. at 1758.

[608] Scripps Clinic & Research Foundation v. Genentech, Inc., 927 F.2d 1565, 18 U.S.P.Q.2d 1001 (Fed. Cir. 1991).
The patent relates to a human protein, pure Factor VIII:C, the blood clotting factor. The inventors developed a method of purifying and concentrating Factor VIII:C using monoclonal antibodies specific to protein, Factor VIII:RP, to which Factor VIII:C is bound.

to add pure product claims to the original patent's process and product-by-process claims. The accused infringer did not contest that an error occurred or assert that the inventors' attorney's initial view that product claims were unavailable involved deceptive intention, but the district court interpreted the reissue statute, 35 U.S.C. Section 251, to require a showing that the error could not have been avoided.

"The law does not require that no competent attorney or alert inventor could have avoided the error sought to be corrected by reissue. Failure of the attorney to claim the invention sufficiently broadly is 'one of the most common sources of defects'. *In re Wilder*, 736 F.2d 1516, 222 U.S.P.Q. 369 (Fed. Cir. 1984), *cert. denied*, 469 U.S. 1209 (1985).

. . .

"Subjective intent is not determinative of whether the applicants erred in claiming less than they had a right to claim. . . . 'Intent to claim' is not the criterion for reissue, and has been well described as 'but judicial shorthand, signifying a means of measuring whether the statutorily required *error* is present.' *In re Weiler*, 790 F.2d 1576, 1581, 229 U.S.P.Q. 673, 676 (Fed. Cir. 1986) (emphasis in original). The statutory standard of reissuable error is objective, and does not require proof of subjective state of mind."[609]

[iv] *Oath or Declaration—Examination.* The patentee must file an oath or declaration with the reissue application setting forth facts showing sufficient reissue grounds, including the existence of a defect and how the error arose.[610] If the patentee fails to establish error, the claims added by reissue are invalid.[611]

The provisions governing original patent applications apply to reissue applications,[612] but an application may be made by and sworn to by the owner of the entire interest

---

The original patent contained process and product-by-process claims. The patentee applied for and obtained a reissue patent with additional claims to human VIII:C preparations of minimum high purity and activity levels. In their reissue declaration, the inventors stated they had always viewed the Factor VIII:C product as their invention, pointing to the specification's statement that the invention's object was to produce highly purified Factor VIII:C.

[609] 927 F.2d at 1575, 18 U.S.P.Q.2d at 1009.

[610] 37 CFR § 1.175(a). *See In re* Wilder, 736 F.2d 1516, 222 U.S.P.Q. 369 (Fed. Cir. 1984), *cert. denied*, Wilder v. Mossinghoff, 469 U.S. 1209 (1985); *In re* Keller, 642 F.2d 413, 427, 208 U.S.P.Q. 871, 883 (CCPA 1981).

See also Orthokinetics, Inc. v. Safety Travel Chairs, Inc., 806 F.2d 1565, 1577, 1 U.S.P.Q.2d 1081, 1089 (Fed. Cir. 1986) (a reissue oath stating that the inventor believed the original patent "to be wholly inoperative or invalid" because certain claims "are unpatentable over" a certain prior art reference is "not. . . a 'binding admission' of anticipation.;" the trial court erred in applying the claims of the original patent as prior art in determining the patentability of the reissue claims).

[611] Hewlett-Packard Co. v. Bausch & Lomb Inc., 882 F.2d 1556, 11 U.S.P.Q.2d 1750 (Fed. Cir. 1989).

[612] 35 U.S.C. § 251 (third paragraph).

Unlike original applications, reissue applications are not held in confidence. *See* § 2D[1][c]. Notice of a reissue filing is published in the PTO *Official Gazette*, and the public may inspect a reissue application. 37 C.F.R. § 1.11(b). This may allow the filing of a protest. *See* § 2D[6][a].

in the patent if the application does not seek to enlarge the original patent claims' scope.[613]

Because a reissue application is examined under the same procedures as an original patent application,[614] all claims must meet the novelty, nonobviousness, utility and adequate disclosure support patentability conditions.[615] The PTO's original allowance of the claims is not binding during reissue examination.[616]

[v] *Effect of Reissue—Intervening Rights.* The original patent is surrendered on reissue.[617] The reissue patent is effective as of its issue date and endures for the original patent's unexpired term.[618]

Damage claims for infringing acts before reissue are preserved only insofar as the claims of the original and reissue patents are identical.[619] An amended claim may be identical if the amendment clarifies but does not alter the the claim's scope.[620] A patentee should retain as many claims from the original patent as possible to preserve damage claims.

---

[613] 35 U.S.C. § 251 (third paragraph).

If an owner files an application that seeks a claim enlargement within the two year period but erroneously makes the application without an oath or declaration by the inventor, the error may be corrected even after the two year period. *In re* Bennett, 226 U.S.P.Q. 413 (Fed. Cir. 1985).

[614] 37 C.F.R. § 1.176. The PTO acts on reissue applications before other applications but in no case sooner than two months after announcement of the filing in the *Official Gazette*, which allows members of the public to submit pertinent information on the patent. *See* §§ 2D[1][a], 2D[1][c].

[615] Hewlett-Packard Co. v. Bausch & Lomb Inc., 882 F.2d 1556, 11 U.S.P.Q.2d 1750 (Fed. Cir. 1989) ("Reissue is essentially a reprosecution of all claims. For example, original claims which a patentee wants to maintain unchanged may nevertheless be rejected on any statutory ground.").

[616] *In re* Doyle, 482 F.2d 1385, 179 USPQ 227 (CCPA 1973), *cert. denied* , Doyle v. Commissioner of Patents, 416 U.S. 935, 181 USPQ 417 (1974).

[617] 35 U.S.C. § 252. The reissue patent is printed with brackets and italics indicating changes.

[618] 35 U.S.C. § 251.

[619] 35 U.S.C. § 252. *See* Fortel Corp. v. Phone-Mate, Inc., 825 F.2d 1577, 3 USPQ2d 1771 (Fed. Cir. 1987); Seattle Box Co., Inc. v. Industrial Crating & Packing, Inc., 731 F.2d 818, 829-30, 221 USPQ 568, 574-75 (Fed. Cir. 1984).

[620] *E.g.*, Tennant Co. v. Hako Minuteman, Inc., 878 F.2d 1413, 1417, 11 U.S.P.Q.2d 1303, 1306 (Fed. Cir. 1989) ("Claims amended during reexamination are entitled to the date of the original patent if they are without substantive change or are legally 'identical,' to the claims in the original patent. . . . If not 'identical,' the patentee has no right to recover infringement damages for periods prior to the date that the reexamination certificate issued."); Slimfold Manufacturing Co., Inc. v. Kinkead Industries, Inc., 810 F.2d 1113, 1 U.S.P.Q.2d 1563 (Fed. Cir. 1987).

In *Tennant Co.*, during reexamination (reexamined patents being subject to the same intervening rights provisions as reissued patents), the claim was amended to add the word "bottom" as follows: "hopper having a movable first *bottom* wall section, a main part that includes a second bottom wall section. . . ." The court noted that "The [patent] specification makes numerous references to a movable bottom wall. . . . Because a second cannot exist without a first, common sense dictates that the claimed first wall section is also a bottom wall section." 878 F.2d at 1417, 11 U.S.P.Q.2d at 1307.

A reissue patent affects the continued right of a person to use or sell a "specific thing" made prior to reissue only if the making, using, or selling of that thing infringes a "valid claim" in both the original and reissue patents.[621]

A court may provide for equitable intervening rights to allow for continued manufacture, use or sale of a product or process after reissue if a person, prior to reissue, made, purchased or used the product or process or made substantial preparation for such making, purchase or use.[622]

The validity presumption applies to reissued patents.[623] Statements and actions in reissue prosecution are relevant to claim interpretation, including claims carried forward from the original patent.[624]

[c] **Disclaimers.** A patent owner, or owner of any sectional interest therein, may file a disclaimer of any complete claim.[625] The disclaimer cancels the claim.[626] A patent owner may disclaim a claim if he discovers clear evidence that it is invalid. Failure to disclaim does not invalidate the patent's other claims but will prevent the

---

[621] 35 U.S.C. § 252; Southern Saw Service, Inc.v. Pittsburgh-Erie Saw Corp., 239 F.2d 339, 111 U.S.P.Q. 362 (5th Cir. 1956), *cert. denied,* 353 U.S. 964, 113 U.S.P.Q. 549 (1957).

[622] *E.g.,* Seattle Box Co., Inc. v. Industrial Crating & Packing, Inc., 756 F.2d 1574, 225 U.S.P.Q. 357 (Fed. Cir. 1985).

[623] *E.g.,* American Hoist & Derrick Co. v. Sowa & Sons, Inc., 725 F.2d 1350, 220 U.S.P.Q. 763 (Fed. Cir. 1984), *cert. denied,* 469 U.S. 821, 224 USQP 520 (1984) (a jury should be instructed that the PTO's upholding of claims in a reissue application, in the light of additional prior art discovered by the defendant, renders the defendant's unpatentability proof burden more difficult to sustain). *See also* Interconnect Planning Corp. v. Feil, 774 F.2d 1132, 227 U.S.P.Q. 543 (Fed. Cir. 1985) (when a patent is reissued with claims not substantially identical to original claims, the invention as a whole, as claimed, must be evaluated in terms of the nonobviousness requirement; the original claims, whether valid or invalid, are not prior art against the reissue claims; because the statutory validity presumption derives in part from recognition of the PTO examiners' technological expertise, and because a reissue examination focuses on the prior art references that occasioned the reissue, a court, in determining patent validity, should give due weight to the PTO's decision to reissue).

[624] Howes v. Medical Components, Inc., 814 F.2d 638, 645, 2 U.S.P.Q.2d 1271, 1275 (Fed. Cir. 1987) (in a suit for infringement of a claim in a reissue application that was identical to a claim in the original patent, "whether the suit is denominated as for infringement of the original claim or of the identical reissue claim, it is still necessary to look at the prosecution history of the reissue in order to construe the disputed claim."). *See also* E.I. du Pont de Nemours & Co. v. Phillips Petroleum Co., 849 F.2d 1430, 1439, 7 U.S.P.Q.2d 1129, 1136 (Fed. Cir. 1988), *cert. denied,* 488 U.S. 986 (1988) ("Statements made during reissue are relevant prosecution history when interpreting claims.").

[625] 35 U.S.C. § 253. *See generally* D. Chisum, Patents § 11.07[2].

[626] Refractarios Monterrey, S.A. v. Ferro Corp., 606 F.2d 966, 203 U.S.P.Q. 568 (CCPA 1979), *cert. denied,* 445 U.S. 943, 205 U.S.P.Q. 488 (1980).
The disclaimer does not affect the patent's other claims, including claims that might not be considered patentably distinct from the disclaimed claim. Allen Archery, Inc. v. Browning Mfg., 819 F.2d 1087, 2 U.S.P.Q.2d 1490 (Fed. Cir. 1987); Allen Archery, Inc. v. Jennings Compound Bow, Inc., 686 F.2d 780, 216 U.S.P.Q. 585 (9th Cir. 1982).

patent owner from recovering court costs in an infringement suit based on other claims in the patent.[627]

A terminal disclaimer may be used to overcome a double patenting problem.[628]

[d] **Correction Certificates.** The PTO may issue correction certificates for three types of errors: (1) a mistake in the patent arising from the fault of the Office;[629] (2) an applicant's clerical, typographical or minor mistake;[630] and (3) an inventorship designation error.[631] These corrections will not affect the patent's validity or enforceability.[632]

§ 2E Rights

A patent grants "to the patentee, his heirs or assigns, for the term of seventeen years, subject to the payment of [maintenance] fees . . . the right to exclude others from making, using, or selling the invention throughout the United States, and, if the invention is a process, . . . the right to exclude others from using or selling throughout the United States, or importing into the United States, products made by that process, referring to the specification for the particulars thereof."[1]

[1] Duration

A United States utility patent endures for seventeen years from its issue date.[2] Other major patent systems, for example, the European and the Japanese, measure the patent term from the application filing date, typically twenty years. Using the filing date rather than the issue date removes any incentive to prolong prosecution to delay patent term commencement.

---

[627] 35 U.S.C. § 288. Costs denial is the only sanction for failure to disclaim an invalid claim in a patent. Wycoff v. Motorola, Inc., 502 F. Supp. 77, 94, 209 U.S.P.Q. 115, 130 (N.D. Ill. 1980), *aff'd without opinion*, 688 F.2d 843 (7th Cir. 1982).

If an invalid claim was obtained with "deceptive intention," the disclaimer is ineffective, Kearney & Trecker Corp. v. Cincinnati Milacron, Inc., 562 F.2d 365, 195 U.S.P.Q. 402 (6th Cir. 1977), and all the claims of the patent are invalid. See § 2D[2][f].

[628] See § 2D[4][a].

[629] 35 U.S.C. § 254.

[630] 35 U.S.C. § 255. No "new matter" may be added. See § 2D[1][d].

[631] 35 U.S.C. § 256. See § 2D[3][e].

[632] Because no change of substance is involved, the intervening rights doctrine applicable to reissues and reexaminations does not apply. Eagle Iron Works v. McLanahan Corp., 429 F.2d 1375, 166 U.S.P.Q. 225 (3d Cir. 1970). See § 2D[6][f][v].

[1] 35 U.S.C. § 154.

Section 271(a) defines infringement and incorporates the three basic exclusive rights: "whoever without authority makes, uses or sells any patented invention, within the United States during the term of the patent therefor, infringes the patent." Section 271(g) makes comparable provision for unauthorized importation, sale and use of products of a patented process.

[2] 35 U.S.C. §§ 154, 271(a). *See generally* D. Chisum, Patents § 16.04. For design and plant patent duration, *see* §§ 6B and 6C.

A United States patent owner must pay maintenance fees at three intervals to prevent patent lapse.[3]

A patent is effective only after issue; acts of making, using, or selling prior to issue do not give rise to liability for direct infringement.[4] Trade secret law or an express or implied contract may give an inventor rights against unauthorized use of an invention before a patent issues.[5] Unauthorized use of a patented device after issue constitutes infringement even though the device was acquired prior to issue.[6]

A patent's effectiveness ceases at the end of its seventeen-year term.[7] One who makes or uses another's patented device before the patent expires infringes even if the device is not sold until after expiration.[8] A patent license royalty obligation may not be based on use of the patented invention after expiration of the patent.[9]

A 1984 statute provides for patent term extension, under limited circumstances, if the commercial marketing of a human drug product or a medical device, food additive, or color additive covered by a patent, or the making or use of which is covered

---

[3] See § 2D[1][a][iv]. See generally D. Chisum, Patents § 11.02[1][d][iv].

[4] Foster v. American Mach. & Foundry Co., 492 F.2d 1317, 1323, 182 U.S.P.Q. 1 (2d Cir. 1974), cert. denied, 419 U.S. 833, 183 U.S.P.Q. 321 (1974).

"Patent pending" is commonly used to give notice to potentially infringing manufacturers but has no specific legal effect. State Industries, Inc. v. A.O. Smith Corp., 751 F.2d 1226, 1236, 224 U.S.P.Q. 418, 425 (Fed. Cir. 1985).

Sales before patent issue may be contributory infringement if the seller knows that issue is imminent and that customers will resell or use the patented invention after issue. Procter & Gamble Co. v. Nabisco Brands, Inc., 604 F. Supp. 1485, 1490, 225 U.S.P.Q. 929, 931 (D. Del. 1985).

[5] Hoeltke v. C.M. Kemp Mfg. Co., 80 F.2d 912, 922-23, 26 U.S.P.Q. 114, 125-26, 28 U.S.P.Q. 176 (4th Cir. 1935), cert. denied, 298 U.S. 673 (1936).

Federal patent law does not preempt state trade secret and confidential idea licensing law. Aronson v. Quick Point Pencil Co., 440 U.S. 257, 201 U.S.P.Q. 1 (1979); Kewanee Oil Co. v. Bicron Corp., 416 U.S. 470, 181 U.S.P.Q. 673 (1974). See § 1D[3][a] and [b].

[6] Cohen v. United States, 487 F.2d 525, 179 U.S.P.Q. 859 (Ct. Cl. 1973). If the device was acquired with the consent of the patent owner, there is an implied license to continue use after issue. See generally D. Chisum, Patents § 16.04[3].

[7] Damages may be collected for infringing acts occurring during the term of a patent in a suit filed after patent expiration. Recovery is subject to the statutory limitation barring recovery of damages for infringing acts occurring more than six years prior to the filing of suit. See § 2F[4][f].

[8] Paper Converting Machine Co. v. Magna-Graphics Corp., 745 F.2d 11, 223 U.S.P.Q. 591 (Fed. Cir. 1984). See also Roche Prods., Inc. v. Bolar Pharmaceutical Co., 733 F.2d 858, 221 U.S.P.Q. 937 (Fed. Cir. 1984), cert. denied, 469 U.S. 856, 225 U.S.P.Q. 792 (1984).

Pre-expiration use solely for obtaining FDA approval to market a drug or medical device after expiration may be exempt under Section 271(e). See § 2F[4][d].

[9] Brulotte v. Thys Co., 379 U.S. 29, 143 U.S.P.Q. 264 (1964).

A license conveying trade secrets or know-how in addition to patent rights and providing for royalties beyond expiration of the patent is enforceable if it clearly allocates royalties between the patent and the trade secrets and know-how. Pitney-Bowes, Inc. v. Mestre, 517 F. Supp. 52, 211 U.S.P.Q. 681 (S.D. Fla. 1981), aff'd, 701 F.2d 1365, 218 U.S.P.Q. 987 (11th Cir. 1983), cert. denied, 464 U.S. 893 (1983). Cf. Boggild v. Kenner Prod., 776 F.2d 1315, 228 U.S.P.Q. 130 (6th Cir. 1985), cert. denied, 477 U.S. 908 (1986).

by a patent, has been delayed by a period of regulatory review.[10] In 1988, Congress provided for similar term extension for animal drug patents.[11] Congress has, on occasion, extended a particular patent's term by special legislation.

[2] Exclusive Rights

A patent's rights to exclude include making, using, and selling.[12] Direct infringement is unauthorized performance of any one of these acts, in the United States, during the patent's term.[13] Indirect infringement is unauthorized sale of a specially designed component for use in a patented combination or process (contributory infringement) or active inducement.

Recent amendments added three infringing acts: (1) exporting specially adapted components of patented combinations;[14] (2) filing an application for government approval to sell a drug claimed by a patent prior to the expiration of the patent;[15]

---

[10] 35 U.S.C. § 156. *See generally* D. Chisum, Patents § 16.04[5]. The extension provision was added in 1984.

An extension application must be made within 60 days of receipt of the regulatory agency's permission for commercial marketing or use.

Determination of the conditions for and amount of extension is extremely complex. *See* Glaxo Operations UK Ltd. v. Quigg, 894 F.2d 392, 13 U.S.P.Q.2d 1628 (Fed. Cir. 1990); Unimed, Inc. v. Quigg, 888 F.2d 826, 12 U.S.P.Q.2d 1644 (Fed Cir. 1989); Fisons plc v. Quigg, 876 F.2d 99, 10 U.S.P.Q.2d 1843 (Fed. Cir. 1989).

[11] Pub. L. 100-670, 102 Stat. 3971.

[12] 35 U.S.C. § 154.

[13] *See* 35 U.S.C. § 271.

[14] 35 U.S.C. § 271(f).

[15] 35 U.S.C. § 271(e)(2), (3). In Eli Lilly and Co. v. Medtronic, Inc., 110 S. Ct. 2683, 2692, 15 U.S.P.Q.2d 1121, 1129-30 (1990), the Supreme Court described the new Section 271(e)(2) infringement remedy, and its relationship to the Section 271(e)(1) exemption for regulatory testing, *see* § 2F[4][d], as follows.

"The function of [Sections 271(e)(2) and (4)] is to define a new (and somewhat artificial) act of infringement for a very limited and technical purpose that relates only to certain drug applications. As an additional means of eliminating the *de facto* extension at the end of the patent term in the case of drugs, and to enable new drugs to be marketed more cheaply and quickly, § 101 of the 1984 Act amended § 505 of the FDCA, . . . to authorize abbreviated new drug applications (ANDAs), which would substantially shorten the time and effort needed to obtain marketing approval. An ANDA may be filed for a generic drug that is the same as a so-called 'pioneer drug' previously approved, . . . or that differs from the pioneer drug in specified ways, ... The ANDA applicant can substitute bioequivalence data for the extensive animal and human studies of safety and effectiveness that must accompany a full new drug application . . . . In addition, § 103 of the 1984 Act amended § 505(b) of the FDCA, . . . to permit submission of a so-called paper new drug application (paper NDA), an application that relies on published literature to satisfy the requirement of animal and human studies demonstrating safety and effectiveness. . . Like ANDAs, paper NDAs permit an applicant seeking approval of a generic drug to avoid the costly and time-consuming studies required for a pioneer drug.

"These abbreviated drug-application provisions incorporated an important new mechanism designed to guard against infringement of patents relating to pioneer drugs. Pio-

and, most importantly, (3) importing unpatented products made abroad with processes covered by United States patents.[16]

A patent grants only the right to *exclude* others, not an affirmative right to make, use or sell an invention. The patent owner may be prevented from making, using or selling a product embodying the patented invention because another patent's claims dominate it[17] or government regulations restrain its marketing.[18] A person has no privilege to infringe another's patent simply because he has a patent covering the infringing product or process. Consider the following example:

> neer drug applicants are required to file with the FDA the number and expiration date of any patent which claims the drug that is the subject of the application, or a method of using such drug . . . . ANDAs and paper NDAs are required to contain one of four certifications with respect to each patent named in the pioneer drug application: (1) 'that such patent information has not been filed,' (2) 'that such patent has expired,' (3) 'the date on which such patent will expire,' or (4) 'that such patent is invalid or will not be infringed by the manufacture, use, or sale of the new drug for which the application is submitted.'
>
> "This certification is significant, in that it determines the date on which approval of an ANDA or paper NDA can be made effective, and hence the date on which commercial marketing may commence. If the applicant makes either the first or second certification, approval can be made effective immediately. . . . If the applicant makes the third certification, approval of the application can be made effective as of the date the patent expires. . . . If the applicant makes the fourth certification, however, the effective date must depend on the outcome of further events triggered by the Act. An applicant who makes the fourth certification is required to give notice to the holder of the patent alleged to be invalid or not infringed, stating that an application has been filed seeking approval to engage in the commercial manufacture, use, or sale of the drug before the expiration of the patent, and setting forth a detailed statement of the factual and legal basis for the applicant's opinion that the patent is not valid or will not be infringed . . . . Approval of an ANDA or paper NDA containing the fourth certification may become effective immediately only if the patent owner has not initiated a lawsuit for infringement within 45 days of receiving notice of the certification. If the owner brings such a suit, then approval may not be made effective until the court rules that the patent is not infringed or until the expiration of (in general) 30 months, whichever first occurs.
>
> "This scheme will not work, of course, if the holder of the patent pertaining to the pioneer drug is disabled from establishing in court that there has been an act of infringement. And that was precisely the disability that the new § 271(e)(1) imposed, with regard to use of his patented invention only for the purpose of obtaining premarketing approval. Thus, an act of infringement had to be created for these ANDA and paper NDA proceedings. That is what is achieved by § 271(e)(2)—the creation of a highly artificial act of infringement that consists of submitting an ANDA or a paper NDA containing the fourth type of certification that is in error as to whether commercial manufacture, use, or sale of the new drug (none of which, of course, has actually occurred) violates the relevant patent. Not only is the defined act of infringement artificial, so are the specified consequences, as set forth in paragraph (e)(4). Monetary damages are permitted only if there has been 'commercial manufacture, use, or sale.' 35 U.S.C. § 271(e)(4)(C). Quite obviously, the purpose of (e)(2) and (e)(4) is to enable the judicial adjudication upon which the ANDA and paper NDA schemes depend."

[16] *See* § 2E[2][b].

[17] *E.g.,* Atlas Powder Co. v. E.I. du Pont de Nemours, 750 F.2d 1569, 224 U.S.P.Q. 409 (Fed. Cir. 1984).

[18] *E.g.,* Patterson v. Kentucky, 97 U.S. (7 Otto.) 501 (1879).

1. A invents and obtains a patent on a combination of $X+Y+Z$.

2. B invents and obtains a patent on an improvement in the combination in which a particular type of Z is used (Z').

B may be unable to sell its combination $(X+Y+Z')$ because of A's patent, and A may be unable to sell the improvement, which falls within its patent, because of B's patent.

[a] **Basic Rights: Direct Infringement.** Unauthorized making, using and selling are distinct and independent acts of infringement.[19] Making without use or sale may infringe; for example, a person makes a machine for sale in another country or use after expiration of the patent.[20] Using without making or sale may infringe; for example, a person purchases and uses a machine.[21] Selling without making or using may infringe; for example, a person purchases and resells a patented product.[22]

"Making" includes manufacture of an operable assembly of a machine claimed in the patent.[23] In *Paper Converting Machine*,[24] a company infringed a patent on a machine during the term of the patent when it (1) manufactured all the parts of the machine, (2) tested the machine in various stages of partial assembly, and (3) shipped the parts to a customer who agreed to and did in fact delay assembling the machine until after the patent expired. The Federal Circuit distinguished *Deepsouth Packing*,[25] which found no infringement by manufacture and export of the parts of a patented combination machine, on the ground that (1) a lower court "must be cautious in extending five to four decisions by analogy," and (2) *Deepsouth Packing* "was intended to be narrowly construed as applicable only to the issue of the extraterritorial effect of the American patent law."

"Use" includes a sales demonstration,[26] but probably not mere possession or display.[27]

---

[19] Paper Converting Machine Co. v. Magna-Graphics Corp., 745 F.2d 11, 16, 223 U.S.P.Q. 591, 594 (Fed. Cir. 1984). The Patent Act does not further define these three concepts. *See generally* D. Chisum, Patents § 16.02.

[20] Underwood Typewriter Co. v. Elliott-Fisher Co., 156 F. 588 (S.D.N.Y. 1907); Ketchum Harvester Co. v. Johnson Harvester Co., 8 F. 586 (N.D.N.Y. 1881).

[21] Aro Mfg. Co. v. Convertible Top Replacement Co., 377 U.S. 476, 141 U.S.P.Q. 681 (1961); Roche Products, Inc. v. Bolar Pharmaceutical Co., Inc., 733 F.2d 858, 221 U.S.P.Q. 937 (Fed. Cir. 1984), *cert. denied*, 469 U.S. 856, 225 U.S.P.Q. 792 (1984).

[22] American Chem. Paint Co. v. Thompson Chem. Corp., 244 F.2d 64, 113 U.S.P.Q. 103 (9th Cir. 1957).

[23] Deepsouth Packing Co. v. Laitram Corp., 406 U.S. 518, 173 U.S.P.Q. 769 (1972). *See* § 2E[2][b][i].

[24] Paper Converting Machine Co. v. Magna-Graphics Corp., 745 F.2d 11, 223 U.S.P.Q. 591 (Fed. Cir. 1984). *See* § 2E[1].

[25] *See* § 2E[2][b][i].

[26] Grinnell Corp. v. American Monorail Co., 285 F. Supp. 219, 158 U.S.P.Q. 129 (D.S.C. 1967).

[27] Beidler v. Photostat Corp., 10 F. Supp. 628, 26 U.S.P.Q. 237 (W.D.N.Y. 19315) *aff'd*, 81 F.2d 1015 (2d Cir. 1936).

"Sale" includes passing title along with the right to immediate possession of a product.[28]

A person who performs a process's operative steps directly infringes a patent claiming the process. Having a supplier perform one of the process steps does not necessarily avoid direct infringement.[29]

Before the 1988 Process Patents Amendments Act, purchase or use of an unpatented product made by a patented process was not direct infringement.[30] After the 1988 Act, sale or use "within the United States [of] a product made by a process patented in the United States" is direct infringement.[31] The Act restricts the patent's remedy against retail sellers and noncommercial users.[32]

[b] **Territorial Scope: Importation and Exportation.** A patent's rights to exclude cover only activity within the United States.[33] Activity outside the United States may be contributory infringement or inducement of infringement if it causes unauthorized making, use or sale of the invention in the United States.[34]

---

[28] Ecodyne Corp. v. Croll-Reynolds Engineering Co., Inc., 491 F. Supp. 194, 206 U.S.P.Q. 601 (D. Conn. 1979).

[29] Shields v. Halliburton Co., 493 F. Supp. 1376, 1389, 207 U.S.P.Q. 304, 315-316 (W.D. La. 1980), aff'd, 667 F.2d 1232, 216 U.S.P.Q. 1066 (5th Cir. 1982). *Compare* University Patents, Inc. v. Questor Corp., 517 F. Supp. 676, 213 U.S.P.Q. 711 (D. Colo. 1981). *See generally* D. Chisum, Patents § 16.02[6].

For example, a patent may claim the process of making Z comprising using W to make intermediate product X and using X to make final product Z. If A, without the patentee's authority, purchases intermediate product X from a supplier who uses W to make X and A uses X to make Z, a court may conclude that A infringes the patented process.

[30] *Cf.* Koratron Co., Inc. v. Lion Uniform, Inc., 449 F.2d 337, 171 U.S.P.Q. 452 (9th Cir. 1971).

Sale of products that are used by others to carry out a patented process may constitute contributory infringement. *See* § 2E[2][c].

[31] 35 U.S.C. § 271(g). *See* § 2E[2][b].

[32] It provides: "In an action for infringement of a process patent, no remedy may be granted for infringement on account of the noncommercial use or retail sale of a product unless there is no adequate remedy under this title for infringement on account of the importation or other use or sale of that product." 35 U.S.C. § 271(g). *See* § 2E[2][b].

[33] 35 U.S.C. § § 154, 271(a). *See generally* D. Chisum, Patents § 16.05.

[34] *E.g.*, Honeywell, Inc. v. Metz Apparatewerke, 509 F.2d 1137, 1141, 184 U.S.P.Q. 387 (7th Cir. 1975).

Cf. Spindelfabrik Suessen-Schurr v. Schubert & Salzer Maschinenfabrik Aktiengesellschaft, 903 F.2d 1568, 14 U.S.P.Q.2d 1913 (Fed. Cir. 1990) (the district court did not err by enjoining an infringer who makes its machinery abroad from "engaging in any activity which in any way relates to the manufacture, sale, use, . . . or commercialization of any automated rotor spinning machines, *either in the United States or for use in the United States* . . ." or by requiring the infringer to notify the court and the patentee of proposed sales of modified devices. (Emphasis added).) In *Spindelfabrik*, the court rejected the infringer's argument that the "injunction impermissibly extends the reach of American patent law beyond the boundaries of the United States by applying its prohibitions to" machines made abroad: "The requirements . . . apply only to machines 'in the United States or for use in the United States,' . . . or which are 'destined for delivery to the United States'. . . . These provisions are a reasonable and permissible endeavor to prevent infringement in the United States and not a prohibited extra-

The United States includes the fifty states, territories and possessions (for example, Puerto Rico).[35] Use of a patented device aboard a vessel or space craft under a United States national's ownership and control is within the United States.[36] Use of a patented system with necessary components in both the United States and other countries is within the United States.[37]

[*i*] *Exportation.* Making an entire patented product in the United States may infringe even though the product is for export and use in another country.[38]

Until 1984, making and exporting the unassembled components of a patented combination did not infringe. In *Deepsouth,*[39] the patent was for a shrimp deveining machine. The defendant manufactured all the machine's parts and shipped them in separate boxes to customers in other countries. The Supreme Court found no infringement; the patent covered only the machine as a combination, and there was no "making" or sale of the combination in the United States.

A 1984 amendment establishes two acts of infringement, active inducement by export of components[40] and export of specially adapted components.[41] It

---

territorial application of American patent law. They were well within the district court's authority."

[35] 35 U.S.C. § 100(c).

[36] Gardiner v. Howe, 9 F. Cas. 1157 (C.C.D.Mass. 1865).

The rule extends to use aboard a United States controlled craft in outer space. *Ex parte* McKay, 200 U.S.P.Q. 324 (PTO Bd. App. 1975). *Cf.* Ocean Science & Eng'r, Inc. v. United States, 595 F.2d 572, 204 U.S.P.Q. 438 (Ct. Cl. 1979). In 1990, Congress enacted 35 U.S.C. Section 105, providing:

"(a) Any invention made, used or sold in outer space on a space object or component thereof under the jurisdiction or control of the United States shall be considered to be made, used or sold within the United States for the purposes of this title, except with respect to any space object or component thereof that is specifically identified and otherwise provided for by an international agreement to which the United States is a party, or with respect to any space object or component thereof that is carried on the registry of a foreign state in accordance with the Convention on the Registration of Objects Launched into Outer Space.

"(b) Any invention made, used or sold in outer space on a space object or component thereof that is carried on the registry of a foreign state in accordance with the Convention on Registration of Objects Launched into Outer Space, shall be considered to be made, used or sold within the United States for the purposes of this title if specifically so agreed in an international agreement between the United States and the state of registry."

[37] Decca, Ltd. v. United States, 544 F.2d 1070, 191 U.S.P.Q. 439 (Ct. Cl. 1976).

[38] Packard Instrument Co. v. Beckman Instruments, Inc., 346 F. Supp. 408, 175 U.S.P.Q. 282 (N.D. Ill. 1972).

[39] Deepsouth Packing Co. v. Laitram Corp., 406 U.S. 518, 173 U.S.P.Q. 769 (1972).

[40] 35 U.S.C. § 271(f)(1). *See generally* D. Chisum, Patents § 16.02[7]

Under this provision, a person commits infringement by, without authority, (1) supplying or causing to be supplied in or from the United States, (2) all or a substantial portion of the components of a patented invention, where such components are uncombined in whole or in part, (3) in such manner as to actively induce the combination of such components outside of the United States in a manner that would infringe the patent if such combination occurred within the United States.

This is similar to the provision on active inducement of infringement within the United States. *See* § 2E[2][c][iii].

overturned *Deepsouth* but went beyond it and made export of less than all components of a patented combination an infringement. The subsection does not appear to include export of components for use in a patented process or the act of purchasing a whole product in the United States and exporting it.[42]

[ii] *Importation.* Importing a patented product into the United States is not, alone, an infringement,[43] but any subsequent sale or use of the product may infringe.[44] Until 1988, it was not an infringement of a process or machine patent to import into the United States a product made abroad by the process or machine.[45] The 1988 Process Patent Amendments Act altered this rule as to processes, as discussed below.

Under Tariff Act 337, a patent owner may petition the United States International Trade Commission (ITC) for an order prohibiting importation of a product.[46] The exclusion remedy is available for patent infringement only "if an industry in the United States, relating to the articles protected by the patent. . . concerned, exists

---

[41] 35 U.S.C. § 271(f)(2). Under this provision, a person commits infringement by, without authority, (1) supplying or causing to be supplied in or from the United States, (2) any component of a patented invention that is especially made or especially adapted for use in the invention and not a staple article or commodity of commerce suitable for substantial noninfringing use, where such component is uncombined in whole or in part, (3) knowing that such component is so made or adapted, and (4) intending that such component will be combined outside of the United States in a manner that would infringe the patent if such combination occurred within the United States.

This is similar to the provision on contributory infringement within the United States. *See* § 2E[2][c][ii]. It differs in requiring the additional element that the seller "intended" that the component be combined, etc.

[42] Such purchase and export have previously been held not to constitute an infringement. Dowagiac Mfg. Co. v. Minnesota Moline Plow, Co., 235 U.S. 641 (1913). In such a situation, the patent owner has a potential remedy against the manufacturer in the United States who sold to the exporter if the manufacture occurred during the patent term.

[43] Ironically, the 1988 Process Patents Amendments Act makes unauthorized importation of a product, whether patented or unpatented, an act of infringement if the product is made abroad by a patented process. 35 U.S.C. § 271(g).

[44] Sale and use are independent acts of infringement. *See* § 2E[2][a].

Infringement occurs only if the activity is unauthorized. Under the first sale doctrine one who purchases a product from the patent owner or his licensee is authorized to use or resell the product. *See* § 2E[3]. As applied to an importation, one who purchases a product in another country from a person who owns the patent in both that country and the United States may import and resell the product in the United States, Holiday v. Mattheson, 24 F. 185 (S.D. N.Y. 1885), but if the patent in the United States is owned by (or the subject of an exclusive license to) one other than the owner of the patent in the other country, importation and sale may constitute an infringement. Griffin v. Keystone Mushroom Farm, Inc., 453 F. Supp. 1283, 199 U.S.P.Q. 428 (E.D. Pa. 1978); Sanofi, S.A. v. Med-Tech Veterinary Prod., Inc., 565 F. Supp. 931, 220 U.S.P.Q. 416 (D. N.J. 1983). *Cf.* Boesch v. Graff, 133 U.S. 697 (1890).

[45] *Cf.* Keplinger v. De Young, 23 U.S. (10 Wheat.) 358, 6 L. Ed. 341 (1825); *In re* Amtorg Trading Corp., 75 F.2d 826, 24 U.S.P.Q. 315 (C.C.P.A. 1935), *cert. denied,* Int'l Agri. Corp. v. Amtorg Trading Corp., 296 U.S. 576 (1935).

[46] 19 U.S.C. § 1337.

or is in the process of being established."[47] Section 337 offers patent owners procedural and remedial advantages. By statute, the ITC must complete its investigation within one year, or, in "complicated cases," within eighteen months.[48] Its remedies, an exclusion order or cease and desist order, are effective in preventing further importation. Because the ITC cannot award damages, a patent owner often sues for patent infringement in a district court in addition to seeking Section 337 relief.

In *Amgen*,[49] the Federal Circuit held Section 337's reference to "articles . . . made . . . by means of . . . a process covered by the claims of a . . . patent" precludes its application "to prohibit the importation of articles made abroad by a process in which a *product* claimed in a U.S. patent is used."[50]

---

[47] Before a 1988 amendment to Section 337, the provision required a specific finding of economic injury to an efficiently operated United States industry. The 1988 amendment eliminated the injury requirement for proceedings based on patents, registered trademarks, copyrights and protected mask works, but retained the domestic industry requirement. The 1988 amendment added the following definition of an "industry" in patent, trademark, copyright and mask work proceedings:

"[A]n industry in the United States shall be considered to exist if there is in the United States, with respect to the articles protected by the patent, copyright, trademark, or mask work concerned—

(A) significant investment in plant and equipment;

(B) significant employment of labor or capital; or

(C) substantial investment in its exploitation, including engineering, research and development, or licensing." 19 U.S.C. § 1337(a)(3).

[48] 19 U.S.C. § 1337(b).

[49] Amgen Inc. v. U.S. Int'l Trade Comm'n, 902 F.2d 1532, 14 U.S.P.Q.2d 1734 (Fed. Cir. 1990).

[50] In *Amgen*, the patent claim in question relates to cells genetically altered to produce a human hormone, erythropoietin ("EPO"). A representative claim is to "A procaryotic or eucaryotic host cell transformed or transfected with a DNA sequence according to claim 1, 2, or 3 in a manner allowing the host cell to express erythropoietin." Claim 2 is for a "purified and isolated DNA sequence consisting essentially of a DNA sequence encoding human erythropoietin." The inventors isolated the DNA sequence by using gene cloning techniques. The patent did not claim the product EPO. A company used transformed cells in Japan to produce EPO and imported the EPO into the United States. The patentee petitioned the International Trade Commission ("ITC") for an order excluding the respondent company's EPO from importation into the United States. The petitioner argued that the respondent's product was made by a "process covered by the claims" of its patent for two related reasons: (1) the cell claims, though appearing to be for products, not processes, were in fact unique hybrid process-product claims, covering the intracellular process of cell production of EPO; and (2) because a United States patent claiming a product confers the right to exclude others from using the product, the respondent's use abroad of the patented product would be an infringement if done in the United States; therefore, the product claim should be viewed as "covering" the process of using the patented product (the EPO gene cells) to make the imported product (EPO). The ITC dismissed the petition for want of subject matter jurisdiction, reasoning that the patentee's patent did not cover a process for making the imported product. The Federal Circuit agreed with the ITC's statute interpretation but directed that the matter be dismissed on the merits rather than for want of subject matter jurisdiction. The court rejected the petitioner's hybrid claim argument: "On their face, the host cell claims. . . are limited to just that: host

[*iii*]   *Process Patent Protection.* In the Process Patent Amendments Act of 1988,[51] Congress added to the bundle of rights of a patent the right, if the invention is a process, to exclude others from using or selling throughout the United States, or importing into the United States, products made by that process.[52]

Four facets of the new "process patent" statute warrant discussion.[53]

First, the product, which may be unpatented itself, must be "made by" a patented process. The connection between a patented process and product can vary from immediate (for example, a method of synthesizing a chemical compound and the compound itself) to remote (a method of air-conditioning a factory and the products manufactured in the factory). Congress eschewed the word "directly," used in other countries' patent laws to describe the relationship between product and process.[54]

---

cells." It interpreted Section 337(a)'s language "process covered" by a patent as meaning a process claimed in the patent. "[I]n normal parlance among patent lawyers, to whom patent statutes are directed, a patent 'covering' a process is a patent containing at least one claim defining a process." Nothing in the legislative histories of the 1940 enactment of the statute or its amendment in 1988 indicate a contrary Congressional intention.

[51] *See generally* D. Chisum, Patents § 16.02[6].

The Act was part of the Omnibus Trade and Competitiveness Act of 1988, P.L. 100-418 (Title IX, Subtitle A, Sections 9001-07), 102 Stat. 1563. The most relevant documents include a House Report, H.R. No. 100-60, 100th Cong., 1st Sess. (1987), a Senate Report, S. No. 100-83, 100th Cong., 1st Sess. (1987), and a Conference Report, Conference Report H.R. No. 100-576, 1085-90 (April 20, 1988). In the notes below, these three reports are abbreviated as "Senate Rep.," "House Rep." and "Conference Rep."

The Act went into effect six months after the date of enactment. (The President signed the bill on August 23, 1988.) The Act contains a "grandfather" provision:

> "The amendments made by this subtitle shall not abridge or affect the right of any person or any successor in business of such person to continue to use, sell, or import any specific product already in substantial and continuous sale or use by such person in the United States on January 1, 1988, or for which substantial preparation by such person for such sale or use was made before such date, to the extent equitable for the protection of commercial investments made or business commenced in the United States before such date. This subsection shall not apply to any person or any successor in business of such person using, selling, or importing a product produced by a patented process that is the subject of a process patent enforcement action commenced before January 1, 1987, before the International Trade Commission, that is pending or in which an order has been entered." P.L. 100-418, § 9006(b).

[52] The Act amended 35 U.S.C. Section 154 and added new Sections 271(g), 287(b), and 295.

[53] The sections added by the Act refer in several places to "process patent." In fact, a single United States patent commonly contains both claims to processes or methods and claims to products (that is, machines, compositions of matter or manufactures). In view of this universally-accepted practice, and the accepted rule that each claim of a patent is treated, in law, as though it were a separate patent, *see, e.g.,* 35 U.S.C. § 282, references in the legislation to "process patent" should be interpreted as meaning "patent claiming a process."

Problems remain as to when a particular patent in fact claims a process rather than a product. *See, e.g.,* Amgen Inc. v. U.S. Int'l Trade Comm'n, 902 F.2d 1532, 14 U.S.P.Q.2d 1734 (Fed. Cir. 1990).

[54] The Senate Report indicates:

Instead, it inserted a partial negative definition: "A product which is made by a patented process will . . . not be considered to be so made after—(1) it is materially changed by subsequent processes; or (2) it becomes a trivial and nonessential component of another product."[55] The Senate Report indicates that "the courts will have to assess the permutations of this issue of proximity to or distance from the process on a case-by-case basis."[56] The House,[57] Senate,[58] and Conference Reports[59] give

---

"[T]he Committee decided against including the word 'directly' in the statute out of concern that the word 'directly' might have been construed too broadly and possibly exempt too many products that have been altered in insignificant ways after manufacture by the patented process. These products ought to be treated as infringing under the bill. The Committee expects the courts to exercise careful judgement in distinguishing those products that are too far removed from the patented process, and those that have been changed only in insignificant ways. The Committee believes that the courts will be in a better position to settle such issues without the standard of 'directly' constraining their judgment." Senate. Rep. at 49.

[55] The House-passed version used the phrase "*minor or* nonessential component of another product." The Senate-passed version used "*trivial and* nonessential component of another product." The House acceded to the Senate version. The Senate and final version gives greater protection to process patents than the House version. Many components could be considered "minor" or "nonessential" but not "trivial and nonessential."

[56] Senate Rep. at 46.

[57] House Rep. at 13-14. The House Report "examples" are based on the "minor or nonessential" language, which differs from the "trivial and nonessential" language of the Senate bill and final legislation.

[58] Senate Report at 50-52. For example, the Senate Report gives an example from semiconductor technology.

"In the semiconductor industry, a manufacturer may have a process patent for forming a semiconductor structure in a semiconductor substrate. Subsequent processing to complete and finish the component does not materially change the semiconductor substrate in which the semiconductor structure formed. In addition, a court could determine that the cost of a semiconductor component was trivial in relation to the cost of the whole product, but if that same component is essential to the intended function of the whole product then it would be covered by this title."

[59] Conference Report at 1086-87. The Conference Report gives a single example involving biotechnology, which is example No. 4 from the Senate Report.

"In the biotechnology field it is well known that naturally occurring organisms contain within them particular genetic sequences composed of unique structural characteristics. The patented process may be for the process of preparing a DNA molecule comprising a specific genetic sequence. A foreign manufacturer uses the patented process to prepare the DNA molecule which is the product of the patented process. The foreign manufacturer inserts the DNA molecule into a plasmid or other vector and the plasmid or other vecot [sic: vector] containing the DNA molecule is, in turn [sic], inserted into a host organism; for example, a bacterium. The plasmid-containing host organism still containing the specific genetic sequence undergoes expression to produce the desired polypeptide. Even if a different organism was created by this biotech procedure, if it would not have been possible or commercially viable to make the different organism and product expressed therefrom but for the patented process, the product will be considered to have been made by the patented process."

specific "examples." The Senate Report also suggests a two-step approach to resolving the process-product connection problem.[60]

Second, Section 271(g) contains an "exhaustion of remedies" provision:

> "In an action for infringement of a process patent, no remedy may be granted for infringement on account of the noncommercial use or retail sale of a product unless there is no adequate remedy under this title for infringement on account of the importation or other use or sale of that product."[61]

A process patent owner can obtain "no remedy" against a noncommercial user or retail seller of an unpatented product made by a patented process if the process patent owner has an adequate remedy against others, such as the manufacturer or importer. In many situations, it is uncertain whether such a remedy exists. For example, it may be unclear whether a manufacturer in another country has sufficient contacts with a State or the United States to justify personal jurisdiction in an infringement suit.

Third, Section 295 provides a presumption as to when a product is made by a patented process to ease "the great difficulty a patentee may have in proving that the patented process was used in the manufacture of the product in question where the manufacturer is not subject to the service of process in the United States."[62]

---

[60] Senate Report at 50:

"1. A product will be considered made by the patented process regardless of any subsequent changes if it would not be possible or commercially viable to make that product but for the use of the patented process. In judging commercial viability, the courts shall use a flexible standard which is appropriate to the competitive circumstances.

"2. A product will be considered to have been made by a patented process if the additional processing steps which are not covered by the patent do not change the physical or chemical properties of the product in a manner which changes the basic utility of the product by the patented process. However, a change in the physical or chemical properties of a product, even though minor, may be 'material' if the change relates to a physical or chemical property which is an important feature of the product produced by the patented process. Usually, a change in the physical form of a product (e.g. the granules to powder, solid to liquid) or minor chemical conversion, (e.g., conversion to a salt, base, acid, hydrate, ester, or addition or removal of a protection group) would not be a 'material' change."

[61] 35 U.S.C. § 271(g). The House version extended the exhaustion-of-remedies requirement to those engaged in "use or retail sale." The Senate version restricted the requirement to those engaged in "*noncommercial* use or retail sale." The House acceded to the Senate version.

The Senate Report discusses "noncommercial" use as follows:

"The Committee intends the limitations on remedies against 'noncommercial users' to be for the protection of those purchasers who enjoy personal use and consumption of the product produced by the allegedly infringing process, such as the patient who consumes a drug product or a home gardener who sprays a pesticide. The Committee does not intend this protection to be enjoyed by a party who uses a product produced by an allegedly infringing process in the production of another product, or who otherwise engages in further manufacturing, processing, or other industrial or business use of the product, other than that which may fall under the provision of Sec. 287(b)(2)." Senate Rep. at 48.

[62] Senate Rep. at 57. The House Report notes:

Congress indicated the presumption "cannot be casually established."[63] To "minimize the risk of aggressive litigation intended to discourage firms from carrying competing products,"[64] the statute requires the court to find two conditions: "(1) a substantial likelihood exists that the product was made by the patented process," and (2) "the plaintiff has made a reasonable effort to determine the process actually used in the production of the product and was unable to so determine." The presumption's effect is "the burden of establishing that the product was not made by the process shall be on the party asserting that it was not so made." Neither the statute's language nor its legislative history indicate when the court should determine whether the two conditions are satisfied and evoke the presumption. Resolving the matter prior to trial gives the parties a clear advanced indication of their respective trial proof burdens.

Fourth, Section 287(b) provides for "modification of remedies," which gives innocent sellers and users a grace period to dispose of products in their possession or "in transit." The versions of this grace period passed by the House and the Senate versions differed significantly, and Section 287(b) represents a synthesis of the two.[65]

[c] **Contributory Infringement—Active Inducement**. A person may infringe a patent (1) by selling an unpatented component of a patented product or an unpatented material or apparatus for use in a patented process or (2) by actively inducing others to infringe a patent.[66]

[i] *Relation to Direct Infringement*. Contributory infringement and active infringement inducement must result in direct infringement.[67] In *Aro*,[68] the patent

---

"This presumption addresses a great difficulty a patentee may have in proving that the patented process was actually used in the manufacture of the product in question in those cases, where the manufacturer is not subject to discovery under the Federal Rules of Civil Procedure. For example, patent owners will frequently be unable to obtain information concerning the nature of the processes being practiced by foreign manufacturers. Shifting the presumption should create no substantial burden, as an accused infringer should be in a much better position to establish that the product was made by another method." House Rep. at 16.

[63] House Rep. at 16. The Senate Report notes: "Importers and subsequent purchasers may be unable to obtain the information needed to overcome such presumptions when the products in question were not made by patented processes. At a minimum, the existence of the presumption will require a party who uses, sells, or imports a product that might have been made by a patented process to exercise greater care in business dealings to avoid increased liability." Senate Rep. at 57.

[64] Senate Rep. at 57.

[65] *See generally* D. Chisum, Patents § 16.02[6].

[66] 35 U.S.C. § 271(b), (c). *See generally* D. Chisum, Patents § 17.01. *See also* Hewlett-Packard Co. v. Bausch & Lomb Inc., 909 F.2d 1464, 15 U.S.P.Q.2d 1525 (Fed. Cir. 1990) (discussing Section 271(b) and (c)'s origins).

If the component, material, or apparatus is separately claimed in a patent, its sale may be a direct infringement.

[67] *Cf.* Moleculon Research Corp. v. CBS, Inc., 793 F.2d 1261, 229 U.S.P.Q. 805 (Fed. Cir. 1986), *cert. denied*, 479 U.S. 1030 (1987) (inducement of infringement of a method claim of a patent may be established by circumstantial evidence that direct infringement occurs as a result of the accused infringer's acts).

[68] Aro Mfg. Co. v. Convertible Top Replacement Co., 365 U.S. 336, 128 U.S.P.Q. 354 (1961).

claimed an automobile convertible top mechanism with (a) mechanical parts, and (b) a cloth top. The defendant sold cloth tops to replace worn-out tops on General Motors cars, which were made and sold with a license. The Supreme Court held the owners of those cars had the right to "repair" their cars by replacing tops.[69] Because the owners did not commit direct infringement, the defendant did not commit contributory infringement. The defendant also sold cloth tops to replace worn-out tops on Ford cars, which were made and sold without a license. The Court held Ford car owners had no right to use their cars or to perpetuate use by replacing the tops.[70] Because the Ford owners committed direct infringement, the defendant committed contributory infringement.

[ii] *Contributory Infringement.* A person who sells a component may be liable for contributory infringement if (1) the component is a material part of the invention specially made or adapted for infringing use, (2) the component is not a staple article suitable for noninfringing use,[71] and (3) he knows of the patent and of the purchaser's intended use.[72]

Consider the following example:

1. A discovers that compound X has unexpected beneficial properties as a herbicide on rice plants.

2. Compound X was known in the prior art but had no known utility.

3. A obtains a patent claiming the method of using compound X as a herbicide.[73]

4. B knows of A's patent and without A's authority sells compound X to rice farmers, knowing that they will use it as a herbicide as claimed in the patent.[74]

---

[69] *See* § 2E[3].

[70] Aro Mfg. Co. v. Convertible Top Replacement, 377 U.S. 476, 141 U.S.P.Q. 681 (1964).

[71] For a component to be a staple or suitable for noninfringing use, it must have some substantial, as opposed to theoretical, noninfringing use. Fromberg, Inc. v. Thornhill, 315 F.2d 407, 137 U.S.P.Q. 84 (5th Cir. 1963); Johnson & Johnson v. W.L. Gore & Assoc., Inc., 436 F. Supp. 704, 195 U.S.P.Q. 487 (D. Del. 1977).

See also Hodosh v. Block Drug Co., 833 F.2d 1575, 4 U.S.P.Q.2d 1935 (Fed. Cir. 1987), *cert. denied*, 485 U.S. 1007 (1988) (in determining whether a product useful in carrying out a patented method is a "staple article of commerce," the proper focus is on the product that is actually sold, not on one ingredient of that product—even though use of that ingredient was critical to the patentability of the claimed invention).

Use of a component as a replacement or repair part on products originally sold with the permission of the patent owner may be a noninfringing use. *See* § 2E[3].

[72] Aro Mfg. Co. v. Convertible Top Replacement Co., 377 U.S. 476, 141 U.S.P.Q. 681 (1964). *Cf.* Trell v. Marlee Electronics Corp., 912 F.2d 1443, 16 U.S.P.Q.2d 1059 (Fed. Cir. 1990) (a court may not award contributory patent infringement damages for sales made prior to a contributory infringer's knowledge of the patent in question; the knowledge requirement is satisfied if the patent owner has sent a letter to the seller identifying the patent and the grounds for contributory infringement).

Knowledge is not an element of liability for direct infringement. *See* § 2F[3][b].

[73] Because the compound is known, A cannot obtain a patent claiming that compound *per se. See* § 2C[1][c].

[74] The example is based on the facts of Dawson Chem. Co. v. Rohm Haas Co., 448 U.S. 176, 206 U.S.P.Q. 385 (1980). In *Dawson*, the Supreme Court held that the patent owner

It is impractical for A to sue the direct infringers (the growers),[75] but A may sue B for contributory infringement because the compound X is not a staple commodity and has no substantial use other than in the patented process.

[iii] *Active Inducement.* A person commits active inducement if he actively and knowingly encourages or aids another person's infringement.[76] Inducement may include: (1) selling a component with instructions on how to make a patented combination or carry out a patented process;[77] (2) designing a patented product for construction by others;[78] (3) providing a warranty or other services connected with a patented product;[79] (4) repairing or servicing previously sold infringing systems,[80] and (5) licensing and controlling another's manufacture of an infringing product.[81]

In *Hewlett-Packard Co.,*[82] the accused infringer did not induce infringement by selling its division that made the infringing product and agreeing to indemnify the purchaser for patent infringement liability.[83]

---

did not commit patent misuse by refusing to license other manufacturers of the unpatented chemical X for use in connection with the patented process. For a discussion of misuse, *see* § 2F[4][c].

[75] There would be many growers and the potential damages recoverable from each might be too small to justify suits against the farmers. Class action law suits are provided for in the Federal Rules of Civil Procedure, but rarely permitted in patent litigation because of venue restrictions. *E.g.,* Tracor, Inc. v. Hewlett-Packard Co., 176 U.S.P.Q. 505 (N.D. Ill. 1973).

[76] *E.g.,* Hewlett-Packard Co. v. Bausch & Lomb Inc., 909 F.2d 1464, 15 U.S.P.Q.2d 1525 (Fed. Cir. 1990) ("[P]roof of actual intent to cause the acts which constitute the infringement is a necessary prerequisite to finding active inducement."); Water Technologies Corp. v. Calco, Ltd., 850 F.2d 660, 668, 7 U.S.P.Q.2d 1097 (Fed. Cir. 1988) ("[A]ppropriate relief against one inducing infringement may be the same as that against the direct infringer. . . . Although section 271(b) does not use the word 'knowing,' the case law and legislative history uniformly assert such a requirement. . . . While proof of intent is necessary, direct evidence is not required; rather, circumstantial evidence may suffice.").

[77] Honeywell, Inc. v. Metz Apparatewerke, 509 F.2d 1137, 184 U.S.P.Q. 387 (7th Cir. 1975).
There can be inducement under Section 271(b) even though the component has noninfringing uses and its sale does not constitute contributory infringement under Section 271(c).

[78] Baut v. Pethick Construction Co., 262 F. Supp. 350, 152 U.S.P.Q. 212 (M.D. Pa. 1966).

[79] C. Van der Lely N.V. v. F. lli Maschio S.n.c., 222 U.S.P.Q. 399 (S.D. Ohio 1984).

[80] *E.g.* Preemption Devices, Inc. v. Minnesota Mining & Mfg. Co., 803 F.2d 1170, 231 U.S.P.Q. 297 (Fed. Cir. 1986).

[81] E.g. Water Technologies Corp. v. Calco, Ltd., 850 F.2d 660, 7 U.S.P.Q.2d 1097 (Fed. Cir. 1988) (the district court did not err in finding one defendant liable as an active inducer of infringement when the defendant exerted control over the other defendant's manufacture of the infringing products, as owner of a trademark used by the latter on its product, and through license agreements).

[82] Hewlett-Packard Co. v. Bausch & Lomb Inc., 909 F.2d 1464, 15 U.S.P.Q.2d 1525 (Fed. Cir. 1990).

[83] In 1982 or 1983, Bausch & Lomb's Houston Instruments Division began selling a product later found to infringe Hewlett-Packard's patent rights. In 1985, Bausch & Lomb sold Houston Instruments to Ametek, Inc. for $43,000,000. Bausch & Lomb agreed to indemnify Ametek for liability for infringement of Hewlett-Packard's patent up to $4.6 million and to work with Ametek to develop a noninfringing product. The court found that Bausch & Lomb did not induce infringement subsequent to the 1985 sale because, *inter alia,* there was no proof of

[iv] *Corporations—Officers and Directors*. Corporations are liable for their employees' and agents' infringing acts under agency law principles.[84]

Corporate officers and directors may be personally liable for actively inducing the corporation's infringement.[85]

In Manville Sales,[86] the Federal Circuit held that the district court erred in holding two officers of a corporate infringer personally liable for direct infringement and active inducement of infringement. Paramount, a corporation, infringed Manville's patent on an iris arm lighting device. DiSimone, Paramount's corporate secretary, obtained a copy of a drawing of Manville's device and sent it to Butterworth, Paramount's president. Butterworth gave the drawing to a Paramount employee for use in designing the infringing product. The district court found DiSimone and Butterworth guilty of direct infringement and inducement of infringement.

For corporate officers to be personally liable for their corporation's acts of patent infringement, "there must be evidence to justify piercing the corporate veil."

Bausch & Lomb's intent to cause acts which constitute infringement. The sale transferred all of Houston Instrument's assets, including specific plans for making the infringing product and key personnel knowledgeable in its manufacture; however, the seller, Bausch & Lomb, had "no interest in nor control over what Amtek [the buyer] chose to do with the plans or the personnel." The agreement to try to design a noninfringing product "establishes, if anything, an intent . . . *not* to induce infringement. . . ." "The most troubling aspect of the agreement between B&L and Ametek is the indemnification clause."

> "Cases have held that an indemnification agreement will generally not establish an intent to induce infringement, but that such intent can be inferred when the primary purpose is to overcome the deterrent effect that the patent laws have on would-be infringers . . . . While overcoming the deterrent of the patent laws *might* have been the ultimate effect of the indemnification agreement in the present case, we cannot say that that was its purpose . . . . [W]hat B&L really wanted out of this agreement was the sale of Houston Instruments at the greatest possible price. Therefore B&L agreed that, if Ametek should wish to continue the manufacture and sale of [the product], B&L would bear the risk of those [products] ultimately being found to infringe the . . . patent. The indemnification agreement certainly facilitated the sale of Houston Instruments at the particular price at which it was sold, but we cannot agree that B&L used it to induce infringement by Ametek." 909 F.2d at 1470, 15 U.S.P.Q.2d at 1529-30.

[84] *E.g.* Westinghouse Elec. & Mfg. Co. v. Independent Wireless Co., 300 F. 748 (S.D.N.Y. 1924); Poppenhusen v. New York Gutta Percha Comb. Co., 19 F. Cas. 1059 (No. 11,283) (C.C.S.D.N.Y. 1858).

See generally D. Chisum, Patents § 16.06.

[85] *E.g.* Fromson v. Citiplate, Inc., 886 F.2d 1300, 12 U.S.P.Q.2d 1299 (Fed Cir. 1989) ("The cases are legion holding corporate officers and directors personally liable for 'participating in, inducing, and approving acts of patent infringement' by a corporation."); Orthokinetics, Inc. v. Safety Travel Chairs, Inc., 806 F.2d 1565, 1 U.S.P.Q.2d 1081 (Fed. Cir. 1986); Power Lift, Inc. v. Lang Tools, Inc., 774 F.2d 478, 227 U.S.P.Q. 435 (Fed. Cir. 1985). *Compare* Manville Sales Corp. v. Paramount Systems, Inc., 917 F.2d 544, 16 U.S.P.Q.2d 1587 (Fed. Cir. 1990).

[86] Manville Sales Corp. v. Paramount Systems, Inc., 917 F.2d 544, 16 U.S.P.Q.2d 1587 (Fed. Cir. 1990).

"Often a party asking a court to disregard the corporate existence will attempt to show that the corporation was merely the alter ego of its officers . . . . More generally, a court may exert its equitable powers and disregard the corporate entity if it decides that piercing the veil will prevent fraud, illegality, injustice, a contravention of public policy, or prevent the corporation from shielding someone from criminal liability. . . . The court, however, must 'start from the general rule that the corporate entity should be recognized and upheld, unless specific, unusual circumstances call for an exception.'

". . . Although these facts support the conclusion that the officers had knowledge of their acts, these acts were within the scope of their employment and thus were protected by the corporate veil."[87]

To hold the officers personally liable would be an abuse of equitable powers because the evidence shows the officers were not attempting to avoid liability under the protection of the corporate veil.

Under Section 271(b), "corporate officers who actively assist with their corporation's infringement may be personally liable for inducing infringement *regardless* of whether the circumstances are such that a court should disregard the corporate entity and pierce the corporate veil."

"The alleged infringer must be shown . . . to have *knowingly* induced infringement. . . . It must be established that the defendant possessed specific intent to encourage another's infringement and not merely that the defendant had knowledge of the acts alleged to constitute inducement. The plaintiff has the burden of showing that the alleged infringer's actions induced infringing acts *and* that he knew or should have known his actions would induce actual infringements."[88]

The two officers could not be guilty of inducement because they were not aware of the patent until suit was filed, and thereafter they acted in good faith belief, based on advice of counsel, that the corporation's product did not infringe.

A parent corporation's liability for its subsidiaries' patent infringement depends on the circumstances.[89]

[3] First Sale—Exhaustion—Repair and Reconstruction

The first authorized sale of a patented product exhausts the patent owner's exclusive rights.[90] The purchaser may thereafter use, repair and resell the product.

Consider the following example:

1. A obtains a patent claiming product X.

---

[87] 917 F.2d at 552-53, 16 U.S.P.Q.2d at 1593-94.

[88] 917 F.2d at 553, 16 U.S.P.Q.2d at 1594.

[89] *See, e.g.,* A. Stucki Co. v. Worthington Industries, Inc., 849 F.2d 593, 7 U.S.P.Q.2d 1066 (Fed. Cir. 1988).

[90] Keeler v. Standard Folding-Bed Co., 157 U.S. 659 (1895); Adams v. Burke, 84 U.S. (17 Wall.) 453 (1873). *See generally* D. Chisum, Patents § 16.03[2].

2. A grants B an exclusive license to make and sell X only in California.

3. C buys an X from A in New York, takes it to California and resells it to D for D's use.

Neither C's resale nor D's use of the product violates either A or B's rights because the patentee A's sale exhausted his exclusive patent rights.[91]

The first sale doctrine applies only to authorized sales. Sales beyond a limited license's scope are unauthorized.[92] In the above example, if B travels to New York and sells X to E, B's act is unauthorized and an infringement.[93] E's use would also be an infringement.[94]

An authorized purchaser's use right includes repair and replacement of worn-out parts necessary to continue use,[95] but the purchaser may not reconstruct a patented product from the parts of worn-out products.[96]

Numerous cases apply the repair-reconstruction distinction.[97] In *Everpure, Inc.*,[98]

---

[91] The rule is otherwise in the international situation in which patent rights in different countries are owned by or subject to exclusive rights of different persons. *See* § 2E[2][b][ii].

[92] General Talking Pictures Co. v. Western Elec. Co., 304 U.S. 175 (1938), *on rehearing*, 305 U.S. 124 (1938), *rehearing denied*, 305 U.S. 675 (1939).

Restrictions in patent licenses are subject to scrutiny under the antitrust laws and the patent misuse doctrine. *See* § 2F[4][c]. For example, a restriction on the price at which a purchaser may resell a product is improper. United States v. Univis Lens Co., 316 U.S. 241, 53 U.S.P.Q. 404 (1942). Similarly, most provisions that attempt to fix the price at which licensees may sell products covered by a patent are improper. *See, e.g.,* United States v. Line Material Co., 333 U.S. 287, 76 U.S.P.Q. 399 (1948).

[93] Security Materials Co. v. Mixermobile Co., 72 F. Supp. 450, 75 U.S.P.Q. 58 (S.D. Cal. 1947).

[94] *Cf.* General Talking Pictures Co. v. Western Elec. Co., 304 U.S. 175 (1938), *on rehearing*, 305 U.S. 124 (1938), *rehearing denied*, 305 U.S. 675 (1939); Chemagro Corp. v. Universal Chemical Co., 244 F. Supp. 486, 146 U.S.P.Q. 466 (E.D. Tex. 1965).

[95] Wilbur-Ellis Co. v. Kuther, 377 U.S. 422, 141 U.S.P.Q. 703 (1964); Aro Mfg. Co. v. Convertible Top Replacement Co., 365 U.S. 336, 128 U.S.P.Q. 354 (1961); General Elec. Co. v. United States, 572 F.2d 745, 778-86, 198 U.S.P.Q. 65, 93-100 (Ct. Cl. 1978).

For a discussion of *Aro, see* § 2E[2][c][i].

[96] American Cotton-Tie Co. v. Simmons, 106 U.S. (16 Otto.) 89 (1882); Hydril Co. v. Crossman Engineering, Inc., 152 U.S.P.Q. 171 (E.D. Tex. 1966).

[97] *E.g.* Dana Corp. v. American Precision Co., 827 F.2d 755, 3 U.S.P.Q.2d 1852 (Fed. Cir. 1987); Met-Coil Systems Corp. v. Korners Unlimited, Inc., 803 F.2d 684, 231 U.S.P.Q. 474 (Fed. Cir. 1986) (repair); Porter v. Farmers Supply Service, Inc., 790 F.2d 882, 229 U.S.P.Q. 814 (Fed. Cir. 1986) (replacement of an unpatented part that is subject to wear by a purchaser of a machine from the patentee is permissible "repair" rather than impermissible "reconstruction;" one who sells a part to purchasers without the authority of the patentee is not a contributory infringer; the legal distinction between "repair" and "reconstruction" is not affected by whether the element of a combination is an "essential" or "distinguishing" part of the claimed invention).

Compare Lummus Industries, Inc. v. D.M. & E Corp., 862 F.2d 267, 8 U.S.P.Q.2d 1983 (Fed. Cir. 1988) (reconstruction; "The law entitles the purchasers of a patented apparatus to repair and replace worn or broken parts, but replacement that amounts to a 'second creation of the patented entity' is not permissible.").

the court confronted a novel fact pattern. The patented invention was a combination of a head with a neck and a filter cartridge. Only the cartridges' filter wore out and needed replacement, but the patentee sold whole replacement cartridges. The defendant sold a different filter cartridge and supplied free of charge an adapter that enabled its customers to fit the cartridges to the plaintiff's head. The court found "repair" rather than "reconstruction" even though the part replaced, as a whole, was not worn out. The patentee's argument that use of the accused infringer's adapter constituted impermissible reconstruction because the adapter replaced an unworn part (the neck) of the patentee's cartridge and because the adapter changed the structure and operation of the combination was not convincing. The patentee was "hoist[ed] on its own petard" because it "made the business decision to sell disposable cartridges and to render its filter irreplaceable without replacement of the entire cartridge."

[4] Government Use

Government entities, including cities and counties,[99] and other countries' agencies and instrumentalities, may be sued for patent infringement.[100]

In *Chew*,[101] the Federal Circuit held that states are immune from federal court patent infringement suits. The *Atascadero*[102] rule provides that Congress may abrogate state immunity from federal court suit but must do so in unmistakably clear statutory language. The word "whoever" in the patent infringement statute, 35 U.S.C. Section 271(a), "is not the requisite unmistakable language of congressional intent necessary to abrogate Eleventh Amendment immunity." A patent owner's entitlement to a remedy in state court "is a question not before us."[103] Recently, Congress

---

In *Lummus*, the patent claimed an apparatus and method of cutting continuous filament textile fiber bundles into uniform, short lengths. The accused infringers sold cutter reels specially designed to fit into the patented apparatus. The jury found that the accused infringers committed contributory infringement because their customers' replacement of reels in the apparatus constituted impermissible reconstruction rather than permissible repair. The court affirmed a jury verdict of contributory infringement.

[98] Everpure, Inc. v. Cuno, Inc., 875 F.2d 300, 10 U.S.P.Q.2d 1855 (Fed. Cir. 1989), *cert. denied*, 110 S. Ct. 154 (1989).

[99] *E.g.* May v. County of Ralls, 31 F. 473 (E.D. Mo. 1887).

[100] *See generally* D. Chisum, Patents § 16.06[3]-[6].

Liability of foreign states and agencies and instrumentalities of foreign states is governed by the Foreign Sovereign Immunities Act of 1976. 28 U.S.C. § § 1330, 1602-1611.

[101] Chew v. California, 893 F.2d 331, 13 U.S.P.Q.2d 1393 (Fed. Cir. 1990), *cert. denied*, 111 S. Ct. 44 (1990).

[102] Atascadero State Hospital v. Scanlon, 473 U.S. 234 (1985).

[103] 893 F.2d at 336, 13 U.S.P.Q.2d at 1397. The court noted that "Congress has similarly not provided a forum for patent infringement suit against the United States in Title 35. Rather it has provided for a suit for compensation in the United States Claims Court . . . . Such a suit is based on principles related to the taking of property, namely a patent license, and subjects the United States to payment of appropriate compensation therefore, not to the liability or relief (such as treble damages) provided in the patent statute." 893 F.2d at 336, 13 U.S.P.Q.2d at 1397.

The court dismissed the concern, expressed by the Ninth Circuit in a copyright decision, BV Engineering v. University of California, 858 F.2d 1394, 8 U.S.P.Q.2d 1421 (9th Cir. 1988), *cert.*

did abrogate state immunity from *copyright* infringement liability.[104]

A United States Claims Court reasonable compensation suit is the exclusive remedy for any use or manufacture of a patented invention by or for the United States government.[105] This remedy includes private contractor or subcontractor use or manufacture that is authorized or consented to by the United States government.[106] Because the Claims Court remedy is exclusive, any district court infringement suit against a contractor for patent infringement based solely on sales or activity for the United States must be dismissed.[107]

---

denied, 489 U.S. 1090 (1989), and pressed by the appellant in *Chew*, that, because federal courts have exclusive jurisdiction over patent infringement suits, patent owners will suffer a taking of their property without just compensation. A claim that *Congress* violates the 5th Amendment proscription against the taking of property without just compensation by failing to abrogate the states' Eleventh Amendment immunity is properly addressed to the United States, not a state. Similarly, a patent infringement suit is not the appropriate legal remedy for vindicating a "takings" claim against a state.

> "While the *BV Engineering* court expressed concern about reaching a result that precluded any forum for bringing a copyright infringement action against a *state*, we think that this concern is misplaced to the extent it is premised on the assumption that, without a forum for an *infringement* suit, an owner of a patent or copyright has *no* legal recourse against a state. This decision. . . simply forecloses one avenue of recourse—the specific relief for infringement of patent rights otherwise provided by federal statute." 893 F.2d at 336 n.5, 13 U.S.P.Q.2d at 1397 n.5.

In the suit in question, the plaintiff filed a claim with a state agency but her claim was rejected. She had six months thereafter to file suit on her claim but did not pursue that course of action in state court.

[104] *See* 17 U.S.C. § 511.

[105] 28 U.S.C. § 1498(a). In a Claims Court suit against the United States, no injunctive relief may be granted. The theory of such a suit is that the government takes a license by eminent domain and is obliged to pay reasonable compensation. Leesona Corp. v. United States, 599 F.2d 958, 202 U.S.P.Q. 424 (Ct. Cl. 1979), *cert. denied*, 444 U.S. 991, 204 U.S.P.Q. 352 (1979). Therefore, the government cannot be assessed for multiple damages or attorneys fees because of willful infringement. *See* §§ 2F[5][c] and [e].

The defenses normally applicable in an infringement suit—including the defense of invalidity of the patent—apply in a Claims Court action.

The government cannot be held liable for contributory infringement or inducement of infringement. Decca, Ltd. v. United States, 640 F.2d 1156, 209 U.S.P.Q. 52 (Ct. Cl. 1980), *cert. denied*, 454 U.S. 819, 214 U.S.P.Q. 584 (1981).

[106] Typically, when the United States deals with a contractor, it secures an agreement under which the contractor indemnifies the government for any compensation required to be paid as the result of a Claims Court suit on a patent.

[107] *See, e.g.,* Trojan, Inc. v. Shat-R-Shield, Inc., 885 F.2d 854, 12 U.S.P.Q.2d 1132 (Fed. Cir. 1989) (a district court may not grant injunctive relief precluding a party from bidding on government contracts under which the party would supply products that have been held to infringe the opposing party's patent; "[A] supplier or potential supplier of an infringing product *for the government* is 'immune' from injunctive relief barring manufacture, sale, or bidding to supply such a product. . . . Section 1498(a) would be emasculated if a patent holder could enjoin bidding to supply infringing products. . . . [A] patent owner may not use its patent to cut the government off from sources of supply, either at the bid stage or during performance of a government contract."); W. L. Gore & Associates Inc. v. Garlock Inc., 842 F.2d 1275,

§ 2F Infringement

Infringement is the unauthorized invasion of a patent owner's exclusive rights,[1] as defined by the patent's claims. Determining infringement involves interpreting the claim language, assessing the nature of the accused infringer's acts, and applying the interpreted claims to those acts. Only *acts*, such as unauthorized making of a device, constitute infringement, but it is commonplace to say that a device "infringes" when discussing the relationship of an accused device to a patent claim.

An accused infringer may assert defenses to the infringement charge, for example, invalidity, unenforceability, laches, misuse, or experimental use.

Patent infringement remedies include preliminary and permanent injunctions, damages, interest, and, in some cases, attorney fees and multiple damages.

[1] Claim Language Interpretation

Claim interpretation is a critical and recurring problem for every patent system participant:[2] the inventor and his or her attorney in composing claim language that both adequately distinguishes the invention from the prior art and provides meaningful protection against misappropriation; the PTO in determining whether the claimed invention is patentable; potential and actual licensees or competitors of the patent owner in assessing the scope and validity of the patent; the courts in deciding whether to hold a patent claim invalid or infringed.

Ideally, patent claim language would be so clear and unambiguous that there could be no dispute as to its meaning, but experience shows this ideal cannot be achieved.

---

6 U.S.P.Q.2d 1277 (Fed. Cir. 1988) (the district court did not err in denying the infringer's request that the permanent injunction against infringement be modified to allow it to bid as a second tier subcontractor on a United States government supply contract because 28 U.S.C. Section 1498 of its own force is controlling and would make a Claims Court suit against the United States the exclusive remedy despite the apparently absolute injunction); TVI Energy Corp. v. Blane, 806 F.2d 1057, 1 U.S.P.Q.2d 1071 (Fed. Cir. 1986) (a person who is bidding for a Government contract and who demonstrates a product as part of a Government procurement procedure is immune under 28 U.S.C. Section 1498 from a district court suit for patent infringement; because the demonstration was required by the bidding procedure and the only purpose of such demonstration was to comply with such procedure, the use was "for the United States;" "Authorization and consent" was provided by the procurement procedures even though the Government did not issue an express "authorization and consent" letter; it is not necessary that the consent "absolutely require [the defendant] to infringe" a patent: "To limit the scope of § 1498 only to instances where the Government requires by specification that a supplier infringe another's patent would defeat the Congressional intent to allow the Government to procure whatever it wished regardless of possible patent infringement.;" it is unnecessary to decide whether the patentee has a cause of action under Section 1498 based on the demonstration); Ling-Temco-Vought, Inc. v. Kollsman Instrument Corp., 372 F.2d 263, 269-70, 152 U.S.P.Q. 446, 451-45211 (2d Cir. 1967).

The suit may continue if the accused infringer makes more than a *de minimis* number of sales to non-government customers. J. &G. Development Co. v. All-Tronics, Inc., 198 F. Supp. 392, 131 U.S.P.Q. 162 (E.D. N.Y. 1961).

1 Exclusive patent rights are discussed at § 2E.

2 *See generally* D. Chisum, Patents § 18.03.

Claims are written by people with imperfect expression skills and incomplete understanding of the invention, the prior art that determines its patentability, and the forms in which it may later be cast. The law requires that patent claims be clear enough to provide reasonable guidance to those whom the patent affects, but a patent system cannot operate fairly to achieve its purpose of encouraging innovation and disclosure of inventions if it has an unreasonably high standard of particularity in claim draftsmanship.

Human imperfection only partially explains claim language's failure to achieve clarity. The nature of language and the task the patent system assigns to written claims make absolute clarity impossible.

> "Claims cannot be clear and unambiguous on their face. A comparison must exist. The lucidity of a claim is determined in light of what ideas it is trying to convey. Only by knowing the idea, can one decide how much shadow encumbers the reality.

> "The very nature of words would make a clear and unambiguous claim a rare occurrence. . . . An invention exists most importantly as a tangible structure or a series of drawings. A verbal portrayal is usually an afterthought written to satisfy the requirements of patent law. This conversion of machine to words allows for unintended idea gaps which cannot be satisfactorily filled. Often the invention is novel and words do not exist to describe it. The dictionary does not always keep abreast of the inventor. It cannot. Things are not made for the sake of words, but words for things." [3]

Claim interpretation requires more than determining claim words' dictionary or technically-accepted meanings. [4] Meaning derives from the context in which patent claim language is used. The context includes the specification, other claims in the patent, and the record of the examination proceedings that led to the issuance of the patent ("prosecution history").

Bausch & Lomb [5] illustrates the "plain meaning" approach's inadequacy. The patent claimed a soft contact lens with a laser-etched positioning marking, the surface

---

[3] Autogiro Co. v. America v. United States, 384 F.2d 391, 396-97, 155 U.S.P.Q. 697 (Ct. Cl. 1967).

[4] Dictionary definitions are relevant but not conclusive. *E.g.*, Advanced Cardiovascular Systems, Inc. v. Scimed Life Systems, Inc., 887 F.2d 1070, 12 U.S.P.Q.2d 1539 (Fed. Cir. 1989) (the patent claim to balloon dilation catheters required that there be a balloon portion *"formed integral with"* the tube portion (emphasis added); the accused catheter had a separate balloon segment, which was glued to a tube segment; a disputed fact issue as to the meaning of "integral" arose, in part, because the patentee cited a dictionary definition of "integral" as including "essential to completeness" as well as "formed as a unit with another part," "composed of integral parts" and "lacking nothing essential."); Senmed, Inc. v. Richard-Allan Medical Industries, Inc., 888 F.2d 815, 12 U.S.P.Q.2d 1508 (Fed Cir. 1989).

[5] Bausch & Lomb, Inc. v. Barnes-Hind/Hydrocurve, Inc., 796 F.2d 443, 230 U.S.P.Q. 416 (Fed. Cir. 1986), *cert. denied*, 484 U.S. 823 (1987). *See also* Smithkline Diagnostics, Inc. v. Helena Laboratories Corp., 859 F.2d 878, 8 U.S.P.Q.2d 1468 (Fed. Cir. 1988). In *Smithkline Diagnostics*, the patent claimed a specimen test for detecting occult blood in fecal matter, reciting that the positive monitor contain a catalyst "that reacts to environmental conditions *similar* to hemoglobin" (Emphasis added.). Admitting that the "ordinary" meaning of "similar

surrounding the marking being "smooth." "Smooth" is a word that, in the abstract, has clear meaning. The accused infringer attempted to circumvent the claim by showing that its marking edges were not absolutely ridge-free, *i.e.*, not "smooth," when scrutinized with a scanning electron microscope (SEM). The court looked to extrinsic evidence, including the specification, other claims in the patent, and the prosecution history, which indicated that "smooth," in the patent's context, did not mean absolutely ridge-free under SEM scrutiny but smooth enough to serve the inventor's purpose, which was to avoid both irritation of the wearer's eyelid and a partial blurring of vision. Testimony indicated that a person of ordinary skill in the art would use an optical microscope, not an SEM, to gauge smoothness.

[a] **The Role of Interpretation "Rules" and "Canons."** Court decisions recite claim interpretation rules, such as "Words in a claim 'will be given their ordinary and accustomed meaning unless it appears that the inventor used them differently' "[6] and "Claims should be construed as they would be by those skilled in the art".[7] Specific rules have limited utility.

> "[I]n addition to the general rules of construction applicable to all written instruments, the courts over the years have formulated a great number of minor rules or canons of construction applicable to patents only. . . . Possibly the courts, as non-expert tribunals, felt inadequate to definitely and finally decide the question of the meaning of such a highly technical document as a patent . . . and hoped by formulating these minor rules to provide definite guides to meaning for themselves and others to follow in the future. If this was the hope it seems to us that it has not been realized but that on the contrary these numerous overlapping and sometimes conflicting canons of construction and the exceptions thereto shed only an illusion of light upon, and so only add confusion to the exceedingly difficult question of the meaning of a patent.
>
> . . .
>
> ". . . [W]e prefer to decide the question of the meaning of a patent, not by heavy reliance upon subsidiary canons of construction, but rather by resorting to broad general principles applicable to the construction of all similar written instruments.
>
> "The courts have said . . . that letters patent are contracts. This seems to us too broad a statement. If patents are contracts at all, surely they are contracts of a peculiar sort. But the fact remains that patents, like contracts, are bilateral instruments, and this common feature makes the rules of the construction of contracts applicable to them. Thus as we see it our problem is to determine first what a patentee intended to claim as his invention or discovery and second upon what invention or discovery the patent office intended to grant a temporary

---

to" excludes "identical," the court nevertheless construed "similar to hemoglobin" as including hemoglobin. *Compare* Hormone Research Foundation, Inc. v. Genentech, Inc., 904 F.2d 1558, 15 U.S.P.Q.2d 1039 (Fed. Cir. 1990), *cert. dismissed*, 111 S. Ct. 1434 (1991) (the specification and prosecution history establish that the term "corresponding" in the patent claims in question means "identical to" rather than similar).

[6] Envirotech Corp. v. Al George, Inc., 730 F.2d 753, 759, 221 U.S.P.Q. 473, 477 (Fed. Cir. 1984).

[7] Loctite Corp. v. Ultraseal Ltd., 781 F.2d 861, 867, 228 U.S.P.Q. 90, 93 (Fed. Cir. 1985).

monopoly. To make this determination we turn to the words of the patent, viewing them as objectively as we would view the words of any ordinary contract.

"The rule that the claim or claims of a patent measure the scope of the invention is . . . well established . . . and equally well established is the rule that claims are to be construed with reference to the specification and in the light of the drawings and the prior state of the same and analogous arts. That is, a claim in a patent, like a clause in a contract, is to be construed in connection with the other terms of the instrument of which it forms a part and the whole instrument is to be interpreted with reference to the circumstances surroundings its inception."[8]

[b] **Extrinsic Material Pertaining to Claim Interpretation.** To interpret a patent claim, one must consider, in addition to the claim's bare language, "extrinsic evidence," which includes the specification, other claims in the same patent, the prosecution history, and expert testimony.[9]

[i] *Specification—The Patentee as "Lexicographer."* The patent specification describes the invention and methods of making and using it, but the claims, not the specification, define the patent's scope for patentability and infringement. A patent's claims are not limited to the specification's best mode, preferred embodiment, specific objects, or illustrative examples,[10] and it is error to read limitations from the specification into the claims.[11] Conversely, a patent confers no rights over subject matter disclosed but not claimed.[12]

The specification is important in interpreting claim language. In *Standard Oil,*[13] the court stressed that the specification is the primary basis for construing the claims. The specification functions as a special dictionary, defining the claim's terms. Claim language may, on its face, be ambiguous enough to raise questions of invalidity for indefiniteness and yet, after the specification is considered, be quite clear.[14] The

---

[8] Doble Engineering Co. v. Leeds & Northrup Co., 134 F.2d 78, 84-85, 56 U.S.P.Q. 426 (1st Cir. 1943).

[9] *E.g.,* Moeller v. Ionetics, Inc., 794 F.2d 653, 229 U.S.P.Q. 992 (Fed. Cir. 1986).

[10] *E.g.,* Laitram Corp. v. Cambridge Wire Cloth Co., 863 F.2d 855, 865, 9 U.S.P.Q.2d 1289, 1299 (Fed. Cir. 1988), *cert. denied,* 490 U.S. 1068 (1989) ("References to a preferred embodiment, such as those often present in a specification, are not claim limitations.;" "[t]hat the inventor preferred and adopted commercially [one specific embodiment] . . . is not a basis for limiting [a claim] to [that embodiment]."); Specialty Composites v. Cabot Corp., 845 F.2d 981, 6 U.S.P.Q.2d 1601 (Fed. Cir. 1988); Rolls-Royce Ltd. v. GTE Valeron Corp., 800 F.2d 1101, 1108, 231 U.S.P.Q. 185, 190 (Fed. Cir. 1987) ("Reference to an object does not constitute in itself a limitation in the claims.").

[11] *E.g.,* Intervet America, Inc. v. Kee-Vet Laboratories, Inc., 887 F.2d 1050, 12 U.S.P.Q.2d 1474 (Fed Cir. 1989).

[12] *E.g.,* Environmental Instruments, Inc. v. Sutron Corp., 877 F.2d 1561, 1564, 11 U.S.P.Q.2d 1132, 1134 (Fed. Cir. 1989) ("[T]he disclosure of a patent is in the public domain save as the claims forbid. The claims alone delimit the right to exclude; only they may be infringed.").

[13] Standard Oil Co. v. American Cyanamid Co., 774 F.2d 448, 227 U.S.P.Q. 293 (Fed. Cir. 1985).

[14] *E.g., In re* Moore, 439 F.2d 1232, 1235-36, 169 U.S.P.Q. 236 (CCPA 1971).

converse is also possible: an apparently clear phrase may be rendered indefinite when considered in light of the specification.[15]

The line between using the specification to interpret the claims, which is mandatory, and reading limitations from the specification into the claims, which is prohibited, is fine.[16] In *E.I. du Pont de Nemours & Co.*,[17] the Federal Circuit held that the district court erred in incorporating two properties, environmental stress crack resistance and impact strength, from the specification into the claim to distinguish the claimed subject matter (a copolymer) from a prior art disclosure.

> "It is entirely proper to use the specification to interpret what the [p]atentee meant by a word or phrase in the claim. . . . But this is not to be confused with adding an extraneous limitation appearing in the specification, which is improper. By 'extraneous,' we mean a limitation read into a claim from the specification wholly apart from any need to interpret what the patentee meant by particular words or phrases in the claim."[18]

A venerable patent claim interpretation principle is that the inventor is "his own lexicographer," *i.e.*, may define his terms as he chooses, provided that he makes his meaning clear.[19] The inventor need not use conventional terminology. The definition privilege has limits: the inventor must use words in the same way in the

---

[15] *In re* Cohn, 438 F.2d 989, 169 U.S.P.Q. 95 (CCPA 1971) (phrase "opaque finish" used in inherently inconsistent ways in the specification). *See also In re* Merat, 519 F.2d 1390, 186 U.S.P.Q. 471 (CCPA 1975) (claim phrase "normal chickens" rendered indefinite by specification).

[16] *E.g.*, Corning Glass Works v. Sumitomo Electric U.S.A., 868 F.2d 1251, 1257, 9 U.S.P.Q.2d 1962, 1967 (Fed. Cir. 1989) ("a court may not redraft a claim for purposes of avoiding a defense of anticipation," and 'extraneous' limitations from the specification . . . [should not] be read into the claim wholly apart from any need to interpret what the patentee meant by particular *words or phrases in the claim*," but "[i]t is entirely proper to use the specification to interpret what the patentee meant by a word or phrase in the claim."); Sjolund v. Musland, 847 F.2d 1573, 1581, 6 U.S.P.Q.2d 2020, 2027 (Fed. Cir. 1988) ("[W]hile it is true that claims are to be interpreted *in light of* the specification and with a view to ascertaining the invention, it does not follow that limitations from the specification may be read into the claims. . . . ").

See also Datascope Corp. v. SMEC, Inc., 879 F.2d 820, 824, 11 U.S.P.Q.2d 1321, 1323 (Fed. Cir. 1989), *cert. denied*, 110 S. Ct. 729 (1990) (a patent claim specifying "support means" should not be limited to "solid objects" merely because the embodiments in the specification use rods and wires; "The claims . . . do not limit 'support means' to solid objects and the specification states in several places that illustrations are provided for purposes of 'example and not limitation.' . . . [There was] no evidence suggesting the propriety of anything other than a plain and ordinary reading of the claims.").

[17] E.I. du Pont de Nemours & Co. v. Phillips Petroleum Co., 849 F.2d 1430, 7 U.S.P.Q.2d 1129 (Fed. Cir. 1988), *cert. denied*, 488 U.S. 986, *on remand*, 711 F. Supp. 1205, 11 U.S.P.Q.2d 1081 (D. Del. 1989).

[18] 849 F.2d at 1433, 7 U.S.P.Q.2d at 1131.

[19] *E.g., In re* Castaing, 429 F.2d 461, 463, 166 U.S.P.Q. 550 (CCPA 1970) ("Whether the terms are conventional is not necessarily controlling. An applicant is ordinarily entitled to be his own lexicographer, so long as his meaning is clear. . . . ").

claims and the specification[20] and must not use terminology that is so confusing, inconsistent or incorrect as to render the claim language invalid for indefiniteness.[21]

An inventor's post-patenting testimony on a claim's meaning carries little weight, especially if it is inconsistent with the specification and prosecution history.[22] In *Senmed*,[23] the patent, which related to surgical staplers, claimed means to "constantly urge and advance" a "row of staples" to "place a forwardmost staple *on*" an anvil surface and "a staple driver . . . shiftable . . . between a. . . . position *closely adjacent* said forwardmost staple on said anvil surface and a lower position. . . ."[24] The accused staplers place the forwardmost staple slightly above the anvil surface, the gap being from 9- to 13- thousands of an inch. The inventor testified that "on" means "between the upper surface of the anvil, the coextensive anvil surface, and the lower limit of whatever abutting means is above it" and that, given "manufacturing tolerances," "one could not mass produce a stapler at reasonable costs without providing some gap between the stapler and the anvil." The court found that the specification,[25] other language in the claim,[26] and the prosecution history[27] pointed

---

[20] Fonar Corp. v. Johnson & Johnson, 821 F.2d 627, 3 U.S.P.Q.2d 1109 (Fed. Cir. 1987), *cert. denied*, 484 U.S. 1027 (1988).

Fonar is instructive on the importance of the specification and other claims. The patent claimed a cancer detecting method using nuclear magnetic resonance (NMR), including the limitations that (a) standard relaxation times for normal and cancerous tissue be measured and established, (b) those times for a patient's suspected tissue be measured, and (c) the two sets of values be compared. The court held that those limitations do not encompass a comparison involving the "experience and images carried in the minds of doctors" who use the accused machines, which display an image on a screen but do not require numerical computation of times. The word "standard" in patent claim 1 does not encompass images stored in a doctor's memory because the patent specification does not use "standard" in that sense. Other, non-asserted claims used "standard" in a manner consistent with the specification, referring to "reference tables" as comprising the standards.

[21] *E.g., Ex parte* Wolk, 225 U.S.P.Q. 225, 227 (PTO Bd. App. 1984) ("Appellant's specification contains inconsistent and confusing teachings. Thus the principle that a patent applicant may be his own lexicographer can not apply here. The definition of ash as 'noncatalytic' is wrong. Therefore the statement in the claims that reaction is 'in the absence of a catalyst' is inaccurate and indefinite."). *Cf.* Codex Corp. v. Milgo Electronics Corp., 717 F.2d 622, 219 U.S.P.Q. 499 (1st Cir. 1983), *cert. denied*, 466 U.S. 931 (1984).

[22] Even inventor testimony adverse to the patentee's interests is not binding. *E.g.,* Smithkline Diagnostics, Inc. v. Helena Laboratories Corp., 859 F.2d 878, 8 U.S.P.Q.2d 1468 (Fed. Cir. 1988). *Compare* Jonsson v. The Stanley Works, 903 F.2d 812, 819, 14 U.S.P.Q.2d 1863, 1869 (Fed. Cir. 1990) (in granting summary judgment of noninfringement, the district court did not err by relying, in part, on the inventor's deposition testimony on a patent claim term's meaning).

[23] Senmed, Inc. v. Richard-Allan Medical Industries, Inc., 888 F.2d 815, 12 U.S.P.Q.2d 1508 (Fed Cir. 1989).

[24] 888 F.2d at 816, 12 U.S.P.Q.2d at 1509 (Emphasis added).

[25] The specification "thrice describes the relationship of the forwardmost staple with the anvil surface:" "rests upon," "on" and "located upon."

[26] The claim includes a "closely adjacent" limitation as well as the disputed "on" limitation: "If [the inventor's] litigation-induced testimony that 'on' means 'juxtaposed' be accepted, two terms clearly intended to have different meanings in the claim's context . . . would mean the same thing."

to "on" meaning in physical contact. The inventor's contrary testimony is a "fatally weak reed on which to lean."

" 'On' is clearly neither a technical term nor a word of art having special meaning to those skilled in the art such that expert testimony is required for its interpretation. . . . Lawyers may create a 'dispute' about any word, but there is nothing ambiguous or linguistically obscure about 'on' as used in the present claim. Where as here 'on' was clearly given its ordinary meaning in the specification and prosecution history, [the inventor's] self-serving, *post-hoc* opinion testimony on the legal question of whether it should have a different meaning was of little if any significance. . . . Nothing of record indicates [the inventor] used 'on' differently until he got to court. Lastly, an inventor may not be heard to proffer an interpretation that would alter the undisputed public record (claim, specification, prosecution history) and treat the claim as a 'nose of wax.' "[28]

[ii] *Other Claims—Claim Differentiation.* In construing a patent claim, one must consider the patent's other claims. The claim differentiation doctrine embodies the common sense notion that a court should ordinarily not interpret one claim so as to make it identical to another. For example, in *Environmental Designs,*[29] the patent claimed a process for removing sulphur from a gas stream, one step being "separating condensed water from the hydrogenated gas stream." The accused infringer argued the claimed step means separation "prior to contact with an aqueous absorption solution" because the inventor argued during the prosecution of the patent that there was a "significant utility . . . in removing water . . . prior to contact with an aqueous absorption solution." The court refused to read a "prior to . . . " limitation into claim 1, noting claim 11 explicitly set forth that limitation and it would be "improper for courts to read into an independent claim a limitation explicitly set forth in another claim."

---

[27] The inventor's original claims required only that there be means for moving a row of staples "toward said anvil surface." The PTO examiner rejected the claim as unpatentable over the Fishbein reference, in which the forwardmost staple was above the anvil surface, the gap being of "some substantial length, depending upon the circumstances." (Testimony indicated that the Fishbein gap was "a little over half an inch.") The inventor's attorney amended the claim to its allowed form to distinguish Fishbein, arguing that the claimed invention is "markedly different" from Fishbein in that the "staple driver need only form the staple about the anvil surface, the driver not having to shift the staple to the anvil surface." Also, the amended claim "now calls for means . . . to place a forwardmost staple . . . *on the anvil surface*" and "indicates that the normal upper position of the staple driver is . . . *closely adjacent* to the forwardmost staple on the anvil surface." The attorney's remarks, which are binding on the inventor, show that he "knew perfectly well the difference between 'on' and 'closely adjacent' when he amended the claim to avoid the reference and obtain allowance of the claim." 888 F.2d at 820, 12 U.S.P.Q.2d at 1513.

[28] 888 F.2d at 819 n.8, 12 U.S.P.Q.2d at 1512 n.8.

[29] Environmental Designs Ltd. v. Union Oil Co. of California, 713 F.2d 693, 218 U.S.P.Q. 865, 871 (Fed. Cir. 1985), *cert. denied,* 464 U.S. 1043, 224 U.S.P.Q. 520 (1984). *See also* Marsh-McBirney, Inc. v. Montedoro-Whitney Corp., 882 F.2d 498, 11 U.S.P.Q.2d 1794 (Fed. Cir. 1989).

Some court opinions characterize claim differentiation as an absolute, immutable rule,[30] but, in fact, it is a guide to construction and may not be determinative in a particular case.[31] In *Autogiro*, the court stated "[c]laim differentiation is a guide, not a rigid rule. If a claim will bear only one interpretation, similarity will have to be tolerated."[32]

In *Moleculon Research*,[33] the patent related to a "cube puzzle." The court interpreted claim 3, which recited only rotation of cubes around a first axis and a second axis, as implicitly limited to structures that can also rotate around a third axis even though that interpretation rendered dependent claim 4, which specified rotation around a third axis, completely redundant.

In *Hormone Research Foundation*,[34] the patent related to human growth hormone (HGH). Independent method claim 1 was for a specified process for making a polypeptide chain in the sequence of "natural human pituitary growth hormone." Independent claim 18 was for a composition produced by the claim 1 method. Independent method claims 3 and 11 and composition claims 12, 17, 20 and 25 pertained to a sequence or structure "corresponding to" patent specification Figure 2, which set forth a 190 amino acid sequence. In the specification, the inventor asserted that Figure 2 was synonymous with natural human growth hormone. After filing his original and continuation-in-part patent applications, the inventor discovered that natural HGH differed from the Figure 2 sequence in certain respects. The court interpreted the phrase "sequence of natural human pituitary growth hormone" in

---

[30] D.M.I. v. Deere & Co., 755 F.2d 1570, 1574, 225 U.S.P.Q. 236, 239 (Fed. Cir. 1985) ("Where, as here, the limitation sought to be 'read into' a claim already appears in another claim, the rule is far more than 'general.' It is fixed. It is long and well established. It enjoys an immutable and universally applicable status comparatively rare among rules of law. Without it, the entire statutory and regulatory structure governing the drafting, submission, examination, allowance, and enforceability of claims would crumble."). The Federal Circuit's language is hyperbolic and dictum because it was commenting on the trial court's concession that "as a general rule a limitation cannot be read into a claim to avoid infringement."

[31] *E.g.*, Tandon Corp. v. U.S. Int'l Trade Comm'n, 831 F.2d 1017, 1028, 4 U.S.P.Q.2d 1283, 1292 (Fed. Cir. 1987) ("[T]he doctrine of claim differentiation does not allow unrestrained expansion of claims beyond the description of the invention on the specification, and explanations and representations made to the PTO in order to obtain allowance of the claims.;" "[t]here is presumed to be a difference in meaning and scope when different words or phrases are used in separate claims. To the extent that the absence of such difference in meaning and scope would make a claim superfluous, the doctrine of claim differentiation states the presumption that the difference between claims is significant. . . . At the same time, practice has long recognized that 'claims may be multiplied . . . to define the metes and bounds of the invention in a variety of different ways.' . . . Thus two claims which read differently can cover the same subject matter. . . . Whether or not claims differ from each other, one can not interpret a claim to be broader than what is contained in the specification and claims as filed.").

[32] Autogiro Co. of America v. United States, 384 F.2d 391, 404, 155 U.S.P.Q. 697 (Ct. Cl. 1967).

[33] Moleculon Research Corp. v. CBS, Inc., 793 F.2d 1261, 229 U.S.P.Q. 805 (Fed. Cir. 1986), *cert. denied*, 479 U.S. 1030 (1987).

[34] Hormone Research Foundation, Inc. v. Genentech, Inc., 904 F.2d 1558, 15 U.S.P.Q.2d 1039 (Fed. Cir. 1990), *cert. dismissed*, 111 S. Ct. 1434 (1991)

claims 1 and 18 as limited to a hormone having the Figure 2 structure. Claim differentiation did not dictate a different conclusion: "That doctrine, although well-established in our cases, cannot overshadow the express and contrary intentions of the patent draftsman. . . . It is not unusual that separate claims may define the invention using different terminology, especially where . . . independent claims are involved."[35]

Whether claim differentiation applies to claims in separate but closely related patents is unclear.[36]

[iii] *Prosecution History.* During prosecution, the inventor, through his patent attorney or agent, may, in response to PTO examiner actions, make arguments supporting patentability or amend the claims.

Prosecution arguments and amendments affect a patent's scope in two ways. First, the arguments and amendments are pertinent to interpretation.[37] Second, the arguments and amendments may create prosecution history estoppel, which restrains the doctrine of equivalents. The two effects are distinct. For example, a prosecution history event may lead to a narrow claim interpretation but not preclude resort to the doctrine of equivalents to find infringement.[38]

Cases illustrate prosecution history's relevance to claim interpretation. In *Standard Oil*,[39] the patent related to a catalytic process making acrylamide. The claim recited the use of selected "copper ions in solution." During reissue examination, the patentee, in response to an examiner rejection based on a reference showing a "Urushibara copper" catalyst, argued that the reference disclosed use of a "metallic copper" and that metallic copper catalysts were outside the claim's scope. The court held that the patentee's argument to the examiner precluded any claim interpretation that would

---

[35] 904 F.2d at 1567 n.15, 15 U.S.P.Q.2d at 1047 n.15.

[36] In Jonsson v. The Stanley Works, 903 F.2d 812, 14 U.S.P.Q.2d 1863 (Fed. Cir. 1990), the Federal Circuit held that a patent's prosecution history and specification dictated that a claim requiring "*means* for emitting a diverging beam of *diffuse* radiation" cover only systems with *multiple* radiation emitters that simultaneously operate to emit diffuse light even though a related patent explicitly claims a "*plurality*" of emitting elements that emit diffuse light.

[37] Graham v. John Deere Co., 383 U.S. 1, 33, 148 U.S.P.Q. 459 (1966) ("an invention is construed not only in the light of the claims, but also with reference to the file wrapper or prosecution history in the Patent Office . . . . Claims as allowed must be read and interpreted with reference to rejected ones and to the state of the prior art; and claims that have been narrowed in order to obtain the issuance of a patent by distinguishing the prior art cannot be sustained to cover that which was previously by limitation eliminated from the patent"); Howes v. Medical Components, Inc., 814 F.2d 638, 645, 2 U.S.P.Q.2d 1271, 1273, 1274-75 (Fed. Cir. 1987) ("during the prosecution of a patent, claim language may take on new meanings, possibly different from that which was originally intended").

[38] E.g., E.I. du Pont de Nemours & Co. v. Phillips Petroleum Co., 849 F.2d 1430, 1439, 7 U.S.P.Q.2d 1129, 1136 (Fed. Cir. 1988), cert. denied, 488 U.S. 986 (1988) ("[M]erely because certain prosecution history is used to define the claims more narrowly, there still may be—even in light of that same prosecution history—an appropriate range of equivalents under the doctrine of equivalents.").

[39] Standard Oil Co. v. American Cyanamid Co., 774 F.2d 448, 227 U.S.P.Q. 293 (Fed. Cir. 1985).

include metallic copper catalysts.[40] In *Loctite,*[41] two related patents used "anaerobic;" the court held that "anaerobic" had a different meaning in the two patents because certain arguments were made in the prosecution of one of the patents but not in the other.

Because prosecution history is important to claim interpretation, a person must obtain and study a patent's prosecution history to determine its scope and validity. In *Underwater Devices,*[42] the court noted that studying the prosecution history of the patent is a step "normally considered to be necessary and proper in preparing an opinion" on infringement or validity.

The impact of prosecution statements or actions on claim interpretation may lead to differences of opinion. For example, in *SRI International,*[43] a deeply-divided Federal Circuit, sitting in banc, held that the trial court erred in granting a summary noninfringement judgment based on prosecution history estoppel.

The weight of prosecution history in interpreting a claim is limited. In *Intervet America,*[44] the court emphasized "When it comes to the question of which should control, an erroneous remark by an attorney in the course of prosecution of an application or the claims of the patent as finally worded and issued by the Patent and Trademark Office as an official grant, we think the law allows for no choice. The claims themselves control."[45]

---

[40] After finding noninfringement based on this claim construction, the Federal Circuit went on to find the patent claim invalid for indefiniteness and obviousness. In a later case involving a patent on a closely-related process, the Federal Circuit confirmed a finding of validity, noting that "although the *Standard Oil* case and this one involve generally similar conversion processes . . . the claims, patents, and records in these cases are dissimilar and thus we are in no way bound by that prior decision." Dow Chemical Co. v. American Cyanamid Co., 816 F.2d 617, 618, 2 U.S.P.Q.2d 1350, 1351 (Fed. Cir. 1987), *cert. denied,* 484 U.S. 849 (1987).

[41] Loctite Corp. v. Ultraseal Ltd., 781 F.2d 861, 228 U.S.P.Q. 90 (Fed. Cir. 1985).

[42] Underwater Devices Inc. v. Morrison-Knudsen Co., 717 F.2d 1380, 219 U.S.P.Q. 569 (Fed. Cir. 1983).

[43] SRI International v. Matsushita Electric Corporation of America, 775 F.2d 1107, 227 U.S.P.Q. 577 (Fed. Cir. 1985) (in banc).

[44] Intervet America, Inc. v. Kee-Vet Laboratories, Inc., 887 F.2d 1050, 12 U.S.P.Q.2d 1474 (Fed Cir. 1989).

[45] In *Intervet America,* the patent related to live vaccines effective against Infectious Bursal Disease in poultry. Claim 1 recited a "vaccine effective . . . upon a single administration to birds . . . comprising a live Infectious Bursal Disease virus belonging to the strain deposited at the ATCC under No. VR-2041." Other claims, including claims 4, 5, and 7, referred to virus suspensions, virus compositions, and methods using the deposited virus. In response to a PTO examiner prior art rejection, the attorney amended claim 1's preamble to recite a "single administration" but did not similarly amend claims 4, 5, and 7. Yet, the attorney argued to the examiner that "the claims are restricted to a single vaccination scheme." The Federal Circuit reversed the district court's finding that all the claims were limited to a single administration: "[t]he claims must be dealt with on the basis of what they say, not remarks made by the attorney in discussion of a reference. . . ."

"There are, of course, situations in which what an attorney says or does during prosecution may be held against a patentee on the theory of estoppel. For example, when a patentee attempts to *expand* the literal meaning of a claim under the patent law

[iv] *Expert Testimony.* Parties to infringement suits may offer expert testimony on the pertinent technology and on patent procedure and claim interpretation.[46] Expert testimony on claim interpretation and the application of claim language to accused devices or methods is not mandatory in every case,[47] but, in some cases, a trial court may err if it fails to admit expert testimony on what a term in the claim means to a person of ordinary skill in the art.[48]

[c] **Claim Interpretation as a Question of "Law" or "Fact."** Whether claim interpretation is a question of "law" or "fact" is significant in patent validity and infringement disputes. Under United States judicial procedure, trial courts (such as district courts in infringement suits) and agencies (such as the Patent and Trademark Office and the U.S. International Trade Commission) resolve *fact* questions. An appeals court (such as the Federal Circuit) has limited power to overturn fact findings. Further, in an infringement suit, either party may request trial by a jury of citizens. The jury resolves fact questions, and the trial judge and the appeals court have only limited powers to overturn the jury's verdict.[49] If a dispute is a *fact* question, it can usually be resolved only after a full trial.

---

doctrine of equivalents and the prosecution history shows that the expanded scope would be inclusive of subject matter the attorney had represented to the examiner was *not* intended to be included in order to get the claim allowed, the patentee may be estopped to contend otherwise. . . . But that is not the situation here where the patentee was granted broad claims in spite of the statement by the attorney that he was amending them, though he never did so. The examiner was not misled or deceived. The erroneous remark was not the end of the prosecution. The examiner was fully aware of what claims he was allowing. . . . The presumption of validity . . . carries with it a presumption the examiner did his duty and knew what claims he was allowing. In any event, the claims as allowed are what we have to deal with and it is not for the courts to say that they contain limitations which are not in them." 887 F.2d at 1054, 12 U.S.P.Q.2d at 1477.

[46] *E.g.,* Snellman v. Ricoh Company, Ltd., 862 F.2d 283, 287, 8 U.S.P.Q.2d 1996, 2000 (Fed. Cir. 1988), *cert. denied,* 109 S. Ct. 3199 (1989) ("Although claim interpretation is a question of law, . . . expert testimony is admissible to explain the meaning of technical terms in the claims and to give an opinion on the ultimate question of infringement;" substantial evidence supported the jury's verdict of infringement in view of the specification language and the patentee's patent expert's testimony on the claim's interpretation).

[47] Moleculon Research Corp. v. CBS, Inc., 793 F.2d 1261, 229 U.S.P.Q. 805 (Fed. Cir. 1986), *cert. denied,* 479 U.S. 1030 (1987).

[48] Moeller v. Ionetics, Inc., 794 F.2d 653, 657, 229 U.S.P.Q. 992, 995 (Fed. Cir. 1986)(summary judgment was not appropriate because there was a dispute as to the meaning of a term ("electrode") in the patent claim, and expert testimony by persons skilled in the art would be helpful extrinsic evidence in interpreting the claim; although expert testimony is generally a matter of discretion with the trial judge, it was, under the circumstances of the case, an abuse of discretion not to allow such testimony; "In a patent case involving complex scientific principles, it is particularly helpful to see how those skilled in the art would interpret the claim."). *Compare* Howes v. Medical Components, Inc., 814 F.2d 638, 2 U.S.P.Q.2d 1271 (Fed. Cir. 1987) (expert testimony on the meaning of terms was not required because they were "not technical terms or terms of art").

[49] *See, e.g.,* Orthokinetics, Inc. v. Safety Travel Chairs, Inc., 806 F.2d 1565, 1 U.S.P.Q.2d 1081 (Fed. Cir. 1986).

In contrast, an appeals court may freely review a trial court or agency *law* question determination. In a jury trial, the trial judge instructs the jurors about law questions. Any dispute over a law question may be resolved prior to trial by a motion procedure ("summary judgment").

Early Supreme Court decisions treated claim interpretation as a question of law,[50] a position most likely based on the concept that a patent was an integrated document, like a contract, which could be read and interpreted without reference to extrinsic evidence.[51] Courts later abandoned that concept, and the prevailing view today is that it is necessary to consider extrinsic evidence, such as the prosecution history, which may involve factual matters or expert testimony. Nevertheless, the Federal Circuit follows the old position, repeatedly stating in its opinions that claim interpretation is a question of law.[52]

Despite the Federal Circuit's stated position that claim interpretation is a question of law, some of its decisions indicate that claim interpretation may necessitate the resolution of factual matters.[53] For example, in *Moeller,*[54] for example, it reversed a trial court's grant of a summary noninfringement judgment because there existed a dispute as to the meaning of the term "electrode" in the claim, and expert testimony as to how persons of ordinary skill in the art would interpret the term would have been helpful.[55]

The right to trial by jury does not apply to "equitable" issues, such as unenforceability because of breach of the duty of candor owed to the PTO. Gardco Manufacturing, Inc. v. Herst Lighting Co., 820 F.2d 1209, 2 U.S.P.Q.2d 2015 (Fed. Cir. 1987).

[50] *E.g.,* Bates v. Coe, 98 U.S. (8 Otto.) 31, 38-39 (1878) ("In construing patents, it is the province of the court to determine what the subject-matter is upon the whole face of the specification and the accompanying drawings.").

[51] *See* D. Chisum, Patents § 18.06[2].

[52] *E.g.,* Senmed, Inc. v. Richard-Allan Medical Industries, Inc., 888 F.2d 815, 818, 12 U.S.P.Q.2d 1508, 1511 (Fed. Cir. 1989) (the district court's judgment entered on a jury verdict of infringement must be reversed because, as a matter of law, the claims of the patent in suit cannot be interpreted so as to cover the accused infringer's product; "Construction of claim scope (claim interpretation). . . . is a question of law for decision by the trial judge on motion for JNOV and by this court on appeal."); George v. Honda Motor Co., Ltd., 802 F.2d 432, 434, 231 U.S.P.Q. 382, 383 (Fed. Cir. 1986) ("The determination of scope of the claims is a question of law, and dispute respecting that legal issue does not preclude summary judgment."); Ashland Oil, Inc. v. Delta Resins & Refractories, Inc., 776 F.2d 281, 227 U.S.P.Q. 657 (Fed. Cir. 1985), *cert. denied,* 475 U.S. 1017 (1986).

[53] *E.g.,* McGill, Inc. v. John Zink Co., 736 F.2d 666, 221 U.S.P.Q. 944 (Fed. Cir. 1984), *cert. denied,* 469 U.S. 1037 (1984) (if the meaning of a term of art is disputed in a jury trial and extrinsic evidence is needed to explain the meaning, the construction of the claims should be left to the jury; the jury cannot be directed as to the disputed meaning of the term of art).

[54] Moeller v. Ionetics, Inc., 794 F.2d 653, 229 U.S.P.Q. 992 (Fed. Cir. 1986).

[55] Moeller v. Ionetics, Inc., 794 F.2d 653, 229 U.S.P.Q. 992 (Fed. Cir. 1986). *See also* Advanced Cardiovascular Systems, Inc. v. Scimed Life Systems, Inc., 887 F.2d 1070, 12 U.S.P.Q.2d 1539 (Fed Cir. 1989) (the district court erred in granting summary judgment of noninfringement of the patent in suit because the meanings of patent claim terms were disputed and were not clear from the specification and the incomplete prosecution history in the record; expert testimony would be helpful in resolving the dispute); Howes v. Medical Components, Inc., 814 F.2d 638, 2 U.S.P.Q.2d 1271 (Fed. Cir. 1987).

In *Perini America, Inc.,* [56] a Federal Circuit panel attempted to clarify the confusion over claim interpretation as a question of law or fact.

"That a claim must be interpreted in a certain way is a conclusion of law . . . Like all legal conclusions, that conclusion rises out of and rests on a foundation built of established (undisputed or correctly found) facts. Interpretation of a claim, or of its scope, should not be assayed until that foundation is in place. If the meaning of terms in the claim, the specification, other claims, or prosecution history is disputed, that dispute must be resolved as a question of fact before interpretation can begin. Confusion may be caused by the circumstance in which resolution of the question on the meaning of a term or terms dictates the interpretation of the claim, but that is not unusual, legal conclusions being dictated by established facts and not the other way around, and does not change the nature of the meaning-of-terms inquiry from one of fact to one of law. With the meaning of terms in the claims, specification, etc. established, it may still be necessary to interpret the claim, with its now-defined terms, in light of the specification and prosecution history, with their now-defined terms. It is that interpretation based on established facts that constitutes a legal conclusion reviewable as a matter of law." [57]

In *Johnston,* [58] the court expressed reservations about the "unqualified, broad statement in *Perini*", which "would conflict with our . . . precedent . . . and, therefore could not be controlling."

"Where . . . no underlying fact issue must be resolved, claim interpretation is a question of law. Thus, a mere dispute over the meaning of a term does not itself create an issue of fact. This is true even where the meaning cannot be determined without resort to the specification, the prosecution history or other extrinsic evidence provided upon consideration of the entirety of such evidence the court concludes that there is no genuine underlying issue of material fact. . . .

". . . However, the [*Perini*] statement need merely be qualified to be in line with prior decisions. A disputed issue of fact may, of course, arise in connection with interpretation of a term in a claim if there is a genuine evidentiary conflict created by the underlying probative evidence pertinent to the claim's interpretation. . . . However, without such evidentiary conflict, claim interpretation may be resolved as an issue of law by the court on summary judgment taking into account the specification, prosecution history or other evidence. . . . Conflicting opinions on the meaning of a term which are merely conclusory do not create such evidentiary conflict. . . . In sum, any broad statement in our precedent which could be read to say that a disagreement over the meaning of a term in a claim *ipso facto* raises an issue of fact is not the law of this circuit and may not be invoked or relied on as precedent." [59]

---

[56] Perini America, Inc. v. Paper Converting Machine Co., 832 F.2d 581, 4 U.S.P.Q.2d 1621 (Fed. Cir. 1987).

[57] 832 F.2d at 584, 4 U.S.P.Q.2d at 1624.

[58] Johnston v. IVAC Corp., 885 F.2d 1574, 12 U.S.P.Q.2d 1382 (Fed. Cir. 1989).

[59] 885 F.2d at 1579-80, 12 U.S.P.Q.2d at 1385-86.

In *Johnston,* the court affirmed a summary noninfringement judgment because the patentee offered no evidence other than inventor's and his attorney's conclusory affidavits that the accused device, a thermometer with a probe having a separately formed ring to which a cover is *friction*-fitted, was equivalent to the patent claim, which specified that there be a "deformed" "integral" section of the probe to which a cover is *inscription*-fitted.

[d] **"Means-Plus-Function" Limitations.** Patent Act Section 112 prescribes a rule of claim interpretation for "means-plus-function" limitations:

> "An element in a claim for a combination may be expressed as a means or step for performing a specified function without the recital of structure, material, or acts in support thereof, and such claim shall be construed to cover the corresponding structure, material, or acts described in the specification and equivalents thereof."[60]

Federal Circuit decisions interpret and apply means-plus-function limitations, some in the PTO examination context,[61] others in patent validity determination,[62] but most in infringement determination.[63] In *Pennwalt,*[64] it emphasized that a means-plus-function limitation requires identity of function and equivalency of means.

> "[S]ection 112, paragraph 6, rules out the possibility that any and every means which performs the function specified in the claim *literally* satisfies that limitation. While encompassing equivalents of those disclosed in the specification, the provision, nevertheless, acts as a restriction on the literal satisfaction of a claim limitation. . . . If the required function is not performed *exactly*

---

[60] 35 U.S.C. § 112.

[61] *In re* Bond, 910 F.2d 831, 15 U.S.P.Q.2d 1566 (Fed. Cir. 1990) (the Section 112, last paragraph, means-plus-function limitation interpretation rule applies to claims under PTO examination). Cf. *In re* Queener, 796 F.2d 461, 230 U.S.P.Q. 438 (Fed. Cir. 1986).

[62] Polaroid Corp. v. Eastman Kodak Co., 789 F.2d 1556, 1570, 229 U.S.P.Q. 561, 572 (Fed. Cir. 1986), *cert. denied,* 479 U.S. 850 (1986) (prior art structures performing the recited function did not render the claimed subject matter obvious because the specification and statements in the prosecution history justified giving the means-plus-function element a narrow scope of equivalence); RCA Corp. v. Applied Digital Data Sys., 730 F.2d 1440, 221 U.S.P.Q. 385 (Fed. Cir. 1984), *cert. dismissed,* 468 U.S. 1228 (1984) (a claim element stated in a means-plus-function format cannot be met by an element in a prior art reference that performs a different function).

[63] *E.g.,* Perini America, Inc. v. Paper Converting Machine Co., 832 F.2d 581, 4 U.S.P.Q.2d 1621 (Fed. Cir. 1987); Data Line Corp. v. Micro Technologies, Inc., 813 F.2d 1196, 1 U.S.P.Q.2d 2052 (Fed. Cir. 1987); Texas Instruments, Inc. v. U.S. Int'l Trade Comm'n, 805 F.3d 1558, 231 U.S.P.Q. 833 (Fed. Cir. 1986), *rehearing denied,* 846 F.2d 1369, 6 U.S.P.Q.2d 1886, 7 U.S.P.Q.2d 1414 (Fed. Cir. 1988); Medtronic Inc. v. Intermedics, Inc., 799 F.2d 734, 230 U.S.P.Q. 641 (Fed. Cir. 1986), *cert. denied,* 479 U.S. 1033 (1987); King Instrument Corp. v. Otari Corp., 767 F.2d 853, 226 U.S.P.Q. 402 (Fed Cir. 1985), *cert. denied,* 475 U.S. 1016 (1986); Palumbo v. Don-Joy Co., 762 F.2d 969, 22 U.S.P.Q. 5 (Fed. Cir. 1985); D.M.I. Inc. v. Deere & Co., 755 F.2d 1570, 225 U.S.P.Q. 236 (Fed. Cir. 1985); Radio Steel & Mfg. Co. v. MTD Products, Inc., 731 F.2d 840, 221 U.S.P.Q. 657 (Fed. Cir. 1984), *cert. denied,* 469 U.S. 831 (1984).

[64] Pennwalt Corp. v. Durand-Wayland, Inc., 833 F.2d 931, 4 U.S.P.Q.2d 1737 (Fed. Cir. 1987) (in banc), *cert. denied,* 479 U.S. 1033 (1987).

in the accused device, it must be borne in mind that section 112, paragraph 6 equivalency is not involved. Section 112, paragraph 6, plays no role in determining whether an equivalent function is performed by the accused device under the doctrine of equivalents.

". . . To determine whether a claim limitation is met literally, where expressed as a means for performing a stated function, the court must compare the accused structure *with the disclosed structure*, and must find equivalent *structure* as well as *identity* of claimed *function* for that structure."[65]

Identity of function is a straightforward claim interpretation and application exercise. Equivalency of means is more complicated. One must first examine the patent specification to determine what structure, material or acts are described that correspond to the "means" recited in the claim. One then must compare the described structure, material or act with the structure, material, or act that performs the recited function in the accused device or method (or the prior art if the issue is patentability). The claim will cover that device or method if, upon comparison, the structure, material or act is equivalent to that disclosed in the specification of the patent, and if the other elements of the claim are also found in that device or method.

The Section 112 equivalents inquiry is not the same as the doctrine of equivalents. It determines a claim's *literal* scope[66] and is solely into whether the means in the accused device or method that performs the stated function is equivalent to the corresponding structure described in the specification as performing that function. In contrast, the doctrine of equivalents applies only when the claim, properly interpreted, does not cover an accused device or method. Equitable considerations guide application of the doctrine of equivalents. For example, a particularly important invention—a "pioneer"—receives a wider scope of equivalence than a narrow improvement. Equivalence is more likely if the accused infringer deliberately copies the patent's technology. These considerations do not apply to the focused Section 112 equivalency inquiry.[67]

In *Texas Instruments*,[68] a Federal Circuit panel adopted a whole subject matter approach to a claim containing a series of means-plus-function limitations. The patent disclosed the pioneering portable electronic calculator;[69] claim 1 contained three

---

[65] 833 F.2d at 934, 4 U.S.P.Q.2d at 1739. *See also* Johnston v. IVAC Corp., 885 F.2d 1574, 1580, 12 U.S.P.Q.2d 1382, 1386 (Fed Cir. 1989) ("'[S]ection 112 ¶ 6 does not . . . *expand* the scope of the claim. An element of a claim described as a means for performing a function, if read literally, would encompass *any* means for performing the function. . . . But section 112 ¶ 6 operates to *cut* back on the types of *means* which could literally satisfy the claim language. . . . [T]he section has no effect on the function specified—it does not extend the element to equivalent functions. . . . Properly understood section 112 ¶ 6 operates more like the reverse doctrine of equivalents than the doctrine of equivalents because it restricts the scope of the literal claim language.").

[66] D.M.I., Inc. v. Deere & Co., 755 F.2d 1570, 225 U.S.P.Q. 236 (Fed. Cir. 1985).

[67] Palumbo v. Don-Joy Co., 762 F.2d 969, 226 U.S.P.Q. 5 (Fed. Cir. 1985).

[68] Texas Instruments, Inc. v. U.S. Int'l Trade Comm'n, 805 F.2d 1558, 231 U.S.P.Q. 833 (Fed. Cir. 1986), *opinion on denial of rehearing*, 846 F.2d 1369, 6 U.S.P.Q.2d 1886 (Fed. Cir. 1988), *rehearing en banc denied*, 7 U.S.P.Q.2d 1414 (Fed. Cir. 1988).

[69] The court noted that the inventors' prototype calculator "was accepted for the permanent collection of the Smithsonian's Museum of History and Technology."

"means-plus-function" elements: (1) input means including a keyboard with a single set of number keys, (2) electronic memory, arithmetic and transfer means, and (3) display means.[70]

The patent owner petitioned the United States International Trade Commission to exclude certain pocket calculators made in other countries from importation on the ground that they infringed the patent. The accused pocket calculators unquestionably contained means that performed each of the three functions, but the means differed from the corresponding patent specification means and embodied subsequently developed, improved technology. For the input keyboard means, the accused devices used a scanning matrix encoder instead of the specification's conductive strips. For the arithmetic, memory and transfer means, they used metal oxide semiconductors instead of the specification's bipolar semiconductors. For the display means, they used a liquid crystal display instead of the specification's thermal printer.

The Administrative Law Judge ("ALJ"), in findings and conclusions which the Commission adopted, concluded that the claims as construed in light of the specification were not infringed literally or through the doctrine of equivalents because accused devices performed the three functions by means not equivalent to the specification means.

The court affirmed the noninfringement determination even though it agreed with the patent owner that "when each changed means is considered separately, as part of the overall device as described by the inventors, substantial evidence may not support the finding that the resultant device is not an infringement."[71] Section 112,

---

[70] Claim 1, U.S. Patent No. 3,819,921, provides:

"1. A miniature, portable, battery operated electronic calculator comprising:

a. input means including a keyboard for entering digits of numbers and arithmetic commands into said calculator and generating signals corresponding to said digits and said commands, the keyboard including only one set of decimal number keys for entering plural digits of decimal numbers in sequence and including a plurality of command keys;

b. electronic means responsive to said signals for performing arithmetic calculations on the numbers entered into the calculator and for generating control signals, said electronic means comprising an integrated semi-conductor circuit array located in substantially one plane, the area occupied by the integrated semiconductor array being no greater than that of the keyboard, said integrated semiconductor circuit array comprising:

i. memory means for storing digits of the numbers entered into the calculator,

ii. arithmetic means coupled to said memory means for adding, subtracting, multiplying and dividing said numbers and storing the resulting answers in the memory means, and

iii. means for selectively transferring numbers from the memory means through the arithmetic means and back to the memory means in a manner dependent upon the commands to effect the desired arithmetic operation;

c. means for providing a visual display coupled to said integrated semiconductor circuit array and responsive to said control signals for indicating said answer; and

d. the entire calculator including keyboard, electronic means, means for providing a visual display, and battery being contained within a 'pocket size' housing."

[71] It held there was no substantial evidence to support the ALJ's "determination of non-equivalence as to each claim clause considered separately" and the ALJ "interpreted the claims too narrowly when he, in effect, limited each means to the embodiment shown in the specification."

paragraph 6 "provides, and extensive judicial analysis has reinforced, that when the claimed invention is a novel combination of steps, all possible methods of carrying out each step of the combination are not required to be described in the specification," but "where all of the claimed functions are performed in the accused devices by subsequently developed or improved means, [it is not appropriate] to view each such change as if it were the only change from the disclosed embodiments of the invention. It is the entirety of the technology embodied in the accused devices that must be compared with the patent disclosure."[72] The court concluded that "[t]aken together, [the] accumulated differences distinguish the accused calculators from that contemplated in the . . . patent and transcend a fair range of equivalents of the . . . invention."[73]

The panel denied a request for rehearing, noting that its "subject matter as a whole" approach was distinct from the reverse doctrine of equivalents.[74]

> "It is a distortion of the accused devices to evaluate the equivalency of each changed means as if *all* the other functions are performed by the original means described in the . . . specification. To do so is to evaluate some theoretical device made up of all but one of the patentee's disclosed structures plus one new structure: a device that does not exist.

> "Each function in a claim is part of a combination, not a separate invention. In cases . . . in which all functions are performed but multiple means are changed, the equivalency of each changed means is appropriately determined in light of the other structural changes in the combination. As in all cases involving assertions of equivalency, wherein the patentee seeks to apply its claims to structures not disclosed by the patentee, the court is required to exercise judgment. In cases of complex inventions, the judgment must take account of situations where the components of the claimed combination are of varying importance or are changed to varying degrees. This is done by viewing the components in combination."[75]

[e] **Consistency: Interpretation During Examination, Infringement and Validity Proceedings.** A patent claim must be interpreted consistently in determining both validity and infringement.[76] If the inventor secures a narrow interpretation to sustain validity, he cannot show infringement by giving a broader interpretation. If the inventor secures a broad interpretation to show infringement, a court can invalidate the claim if, as interpreted, it reads on the prior art's disclosures.[77]

------

[72] 805 F.2d at 1569-70, 231 U.S.P.Q. at 839-40.

[73] 805 F.2d at 1570, 231 U.S.P.Q. at 841.

[74] *See* § 2F[2][b][vii].

[75] 846 F.2d at 1371, 6 U.S.P.Q.2d at 1888-89.

[76] *E.g.,* Kimberly-Clark Corp. v. Johnson & Johnson, 745 F.2d 1437, 1449, 223 U.S.P.Q. 603, 610 (Fed. Cir. 1984) (claims "must be construed in the identical way for both infringement and validity").

[77] Smith v. Hall, 301 U.S. 216 (1937).

A related problem is whether a narrow construction of a claim entered against a patent owner is binding in subsequent suits brought by the patent owner against other accused infringers. *See* Jackson Jordan, Inc. v. Plaser American Corp., 747 F.2d 1567, 224 U.S.P.Q. 1, 10

Consistent interpretation for validity and infringement is a serious problem in patent systems in which cancellation or invalidation proceedings are separate from infringement proceedings. This problem is not as serious in the United States because validity may be raised by an accused infringer as a defense. Problems do arise if validity or infringement must be re-tried because of legal error. In one case, the error directly affected only the infringement determination. Yet, because the infringement trial would be to a different jury panel, the court felt that it was necessary to retry validity as well.[78]

The claim interpretation consistency principle is subject to a major caveat. If a patent claim's validity is challenged, the claim will be construed narrowly, if reasonably possible, to sustain validity.[79] During PTO examination, a claim is given the "broadest reasonable construction." [80] In *Burlington Industries*,[81] the court discussed the reason for this rule:

> "Patent application claims are given their broadest reasonable interpretation during examination proceedings, for the simple reason that before a patent is granted the claims are readily amended as part of the examination process. . . . Claims may be amended for the purpose of distinguishing cited references, or in response to objections [as to definiteness or the adequacy of disclosure support] raised under section 112. Issues of judicial claim interpretation such as arise after patent issuance, for example, during infringement litigation, have no place in prosecution of pending claims before the PTO, when any ambiguity or excessive breadth may be corrected by merely changing the claim." [82]

(Fed. Cir. 1984); A.B. Dick Co. v. Burroughs Corp., 713 F.2d 700, 218 U.S.P.Q. 965 (Fed. Cir. 1983), *cert. denied*, 464 U.S. 1042 (1984) (judicial statements on claim scope have a collateral estoppel effect in a later suit only to the extent that the scope determination was essential to a final judgment on validity or infringement).

[78] Witco Chemical Corp. v. Peachtree Doors, Inc., 787 F.2d 1545, 1549, 229 U.S.P.Q. 188, 191 (Fed. Cir. 1986), *cert. dismissed*, 479 U.S. 877 (1986) ("In order to determine infringement, the scope of disputed claims must be construed in light of the patent's specification and prosecution history. Here the arguments against infringement are indistinguishably woven with the factual underpinnings of the validity and enforceability determinations. . . . Consequently, the entire judgment is vacated and the case remanded for a new trial."). *Compare* Perkin-Elmer Corp. v. Computervision Corp., 732 F.2d 888, 221 U.S.P.Q. 669 (Fed. Cir. 1984), *cert. denied*, 469 U.S. 857, 225 U.S.P.Q. 792 (1984) (no retrial of the validity issue is required after an appellate reversal of the noninfringement finding absent evidence that the appellate court in finding infringement interpreted the claims differently from the jury that found the patent valid).

[79] *E.g.*, ACS Hospital Sys., Inc. v. Montefiore Hospital, 732 F.2d 1572, 221 U.S.P.Q. 929 (Fed. Cir. 1984).

[80] *E.g., In re* Heck, 699 F.2d 1331, 216 U.S.P.Q. 1038 (Fed. Cir. 1983); *In re* Prater, 415 F.2d 1393, 1404–05, 162 U.S.P.Q. 541 (CCPA 1969).

[81] Burlington Industries, Inc. v. Quigg, 822 F.2d 1581, 3 U.S.P.Q.2d 1436 (Fed. Cir. 1987).

[82] 822 F.2d at 1583, 3 U.S.P.Q.2d at 1438.

See also In re Zletz, 893 F.2d 319, 321, 13 U.S.P.Q.2d 1320, 1322 (Fed. Cir. 1989) ("[D]uring patent prosecution when claims can be amended, ambiguities should be recognized, scope and breadth of language explored, and clarification imposed. . . . An essential purpose of patent examination is to fashion claims that are precise, clear, correct and unambiguous. Only in this way can uncertainties of claim scope be removed, as much as possible, during the administrative process.").

The "broadest reasonable interpretation" rule applies to patent reissue and reexamination,[83] which can cause a patent owner substantial hardship if the claim would have been held valid over the prior art under the normal interpretation standard but is considered unpatentable under the broadest interpretation standard. To save the rejected claim, the patentee must amend it. Any substantive amendment made during reissue or reexamination extinguishes the patentee's right to recover damages for infringement of that claim as to activity occurring prior to the reissue or reexamination confirmation.[84] Amendments that cure formal defects or clarify the claim do not extinguish the right,[85] but an amendment required to distinguish prior art is substantive.[86]

[2] Claim Application

A patent's claims measure its exclusive rights and, therefor, what constitutes infringement.[87]

To determine infringement, the patent claim's words must be interpreted[88] and applied to the accused product or process. If the claim covers the accused product or process in a clear, literal way, there is literal infringement.[89] If the claim does not literally cover the accused product or process but the accused product or process is substantially the same as the claimed product or process, there may be infringement under the doctrine of equivalents.[90]

---

[83] *In re* Yamamoto, 740 F.2d 1569, 222 U.S.P.Q. 934 (Fed. Cir. 1984). *See also In re* Queener, 796 F.2d 461, 230 U.S.P.Q. 438 (Fed. Cir. 1986).

For a discussion of reissue and reexamination, see §§ 2D[6][a] and [b].

[84] *See, e.g.,* Fortel Corp. v. Phone-Mate, Inc., 825 F.2d 1577, 3 U.S.P.Q.2d 1771 (Fed. Cir. 1987). A right to recover damages for infringement of a claim survives reissue or reexamination only if a claim in the reissued or reexamined patent is "identical" to a claim in the original patent.

[85] Slimfold Manufacturing Co., Inc. v. Kinkead Industries, Inc., 810 F.2d 1113, 1 U.S.P.Q.2d 1563 (Fed. Cir. 1987); Kaufman Company, Inc. v. Lantech, Inc., 807 F.2d 970, 1 U.S.P.Q.2d 1202 (Fed. Cir. 1986).

[86] For this reason, the PTO ruled that the broad construction rule should not apply to reexamination of expired patents. *See Ex parte* Papst-Motoren, 1 U.S.P.Q.2d 1655 (Bd. Pat. App. & Int'f 1986). The owner of an expired patent can potentially recover damages for infringing acts occurring before expiration. Amendments to the claims of an expired patent would serve no purpose other than to deprive the patent owner of a damage remedy.

[87] Section 271(a) defines infringement as the making, using or selling of the "patented invention" within the United States during the patent term without the patentee's authority. 35 U.S.C. § 271(a). The statute does not expressly state that "patented invention" is determined by reference to the claims, but this is a natural inference from the statutory requirement that the patent specification "conclude with one or more claims particularly pointing out and distinctly claiming the subject matter which the applicant regards as his invention." 35 U.S.C. § 112.

[88] *See* § 2F[1].

[89] *See* § 2F[2][a].

[90] *See* § 2F[2][b].

[a] **Literal Infringement.** Claims contain one or more limitations, sometimes referred to as "elements."[91] A claim reads on a product or process if that product or process has every element or limitation of the claim.[92]

[i] Omissions. Omission of any claim element avoids literal infringement.[93] Consider the following example:

1. The claim in the patent is for "a product comprising X, Y, and Z, said X consisting of U, V and W."

2. The accused product contains elements X, Y and Z but the X consists of T, U, and V.

There is no literal infringement because the specified type of element X is not in the accused product.

[ii] *Additions and Improvements.* Neither addition of elements not stated in the claim[94] nor improvement on a claimed element—even a patentable improvement—[95] avoids infringement. In the above example, an accused product will infringe if the claim contains the specified X, Y, and Z elements even though it may add an element W or involve an improvement on the element Y.

[b] **Doctrine of Equivalents.** Unauthorized purchase, sale or use of an accused product or process not literally within a claim may infringe under the doctrine of equivalents if the product or process performs substantially the same function in substantially the same way to obtain the same result as the claimed invention.

Courts recognize the importance of clear claiming[96] but are unwilling to confine

---

[91] See § 2D[3][d][iii].

[92] Builders Concrete, Inc. v. Bremerton Concrete Products Co., 757 F.2d 255, 257, 225 U.S.P.Q. 240, 241 (Fed. Cir. 1985).

[93] E.g., Lemelson v. United States, 752 F.2d 1538, 551, 224 U.S.P.Q. 526, 533 (Fed. Cir. 1985) ("each element of a claim is material and essential, and . . . in order for a court to find infringement, the patent owner must show the presence of every element or its substantial equivalent in the accused device").

The "all elements" rule also applies to the doctrine of equivalents. See § 2F[2][b].

[94] Uniroyal, Inc. v. Rudkin-Wiley Corp., 837 F.2d 1044, 5 U.S.P.Q.2d 1434 (Fed. Cir. 1988), cert. denied, 488 U.S. 825 (1988) ("Adding features to an accused device will not result in noninfringement if all the limitations in the claims, or equivalents thereof, are present in the accused device.").

The addition of an element may avoid literal infringement if the claim is drafted in a closed form. See § 2D[3][d][iii].

[95] Hoyt v. Horne, 145 U.S. 302 (1892); Studiengesellschaft Kohle, m.b.H. v. Dart Indus., Inc., 726 F.2d 724, 728, 220 U.S.P.Q. 841, 843 (Fed. Cir. 1984). See also Marsh-McBirney, Inc. v. Montedoro-Whitney Corp., 882 F.2d 498, 504, 11 U.S.P.Q.2d 1794, 1798 (Fed. Cir. 1989), cert. granted, judgment vacated, 111 S. Ct. 775 (1991) ("Advances subsequent to the patent may still infringe.").

But see Texas Instruments, Inc. v. U.S. Int'l Trade Comm'n, 805 F.2d 1558, 231 USPQ 833 (Fed. Cir. 1986), opinion on denial of rehearing, 846 F.2d 1369, 6 U.S.P.Q.2d 1886 (Fed. Cir. 1988), rehearing en banc denied, 7 U.S.P.Q.2d 1414 (Fed. Cir. 1988), discussed at § 2F[1][d].

[96] See, e.g., Merrill v. Yeomans, 94 U.S. (4 Otto) 568, 573-74 (1877) ("nothing can be more just and fair both to the patentee and to the public, than that the former should understand and correctly describe just what he has invented and for what he claims a patent.").

patentees to their claims' strict literal wording and may find infringement when an accused infringer adopts an equivalent structure. Extension of a patent's protective scope beyond literal claim language is known as the "doctrine of equivalents." According to Judge Learned Hand, the doctrine is an "anomaly."

> "[A]fter all aids to interpretation have been exhausted, and the scope of the claims has been enlarged as far as the words can be stretched, on proper occasions courts make them cover more than their meaning will bear. If they applied the law with inexorable rigidity, they would never do this, but would remit the patentee to his remedy of re-issue, and that is exactly what they frequently do. Not always, however, for at times they resort to the 'doctrine of equivalents' to temper unsparing logical and prevent an infringer from stealing the benefit of the invention. No doubt, this is, strictly speaking, an anomaly; but it is one which courts have frankly faced and accepted almost from the beginning." [97]

[i] *The Graver Tank Decision.* The Supreme Court first recognized the doctrine of equivalents in 1853;[98] its leading decision is *Graver Tank*.[99] The patent contained

---

[97] Royal Typewriter Co. v. Remington Rand, Inc., 168 F.2d 691 (2d Cir. 1948), *cert. denied*, 335 U.S. 825 (1948).

[98] Winans v. Denmead, 56 U.S. (15 How.) 330 (1853).

Winans' patent was a new coal carrying railroad car. Before Winans, coal cars had a rectangular floor plan. Winans perceived that the dispersion of the force of the coal in a rectangular car was uneven, requiring substantial reinforcement. He designed a conically-shaped car that evenly distributed the pressure and facilitated coal discharge through an aperture in the bottom. The shape enabled Winans to build cars with a larger load-car weight ratio. Winan's patent claimed:

> "What I claim as my invention, and desire to secure by letters patent, is making the body of a car for the transportation of coal, etc., in *the form of a frustrum of a cone*, substantially as herein described, whereby the force exerted by the weight of the load presses equally in all directions, and does not tend to change the form thereof, so that every part resists its equal proportion, and by which, also, the lower part is so reduced as to pass down within the truck frame and between the axles, to lower the center of gravity of the load without diminishing the capacity of the car as described." (Emphasis added.) 56 U.S. at 330.

Defendant's cars were "octagonal and pyramidal" in shape, rather than "cylindrical and conical," but achieved substantially all the advantages of Winans' car. Plaintiff and defendant were competitors, and defendant created its design after seeing plaintiff's cars. Despite these equities in plaintiff's favor, the trial judge instructed the jury that there could be no infringement because the defendant's car was rectilinear and the patent claim required a conical shape.

A sharply-divided Supreme Court reversed. For the majority, Justice Curtis relied on a presumption that the patentee claimed all that he was entitled to claim and noted that it would be unreasonable to apply the term "cone" literally.

> "It may safely be assumed, that neither the patentee nor any other constructor has made, or will make, a car exactly circular. . . . How near to a circle, then, must a car be, in order to infringe?. . . [I]t . . . must be so near to a true circle as substantially to embody the patentee's mode of operation, and thereby attain the same kind of result as was reached by his invention." 56 U.S. at 343.

Four justices dissented in an opinion by Chief Justice Taney.

> "The plaintiff confines his claim to the use of the conical form, and excludes from his specification any allusion to any other. He must have done so advisedly. He might

two sets of claims to electric welding flux. One set, which included the generic limitation "silicate," was held invalid. A second set, which included a more specific limitation "alkaline earth metal silicate," was held valid. The patent owner used *magnesium*, an alkaline earth metal silicate. Because the accused infringer used *manganese*, a silicate but not an alkaline earth metal silicate, the valid claims were not literally infringed. Nevertheless, the Supreme Court affirmed the trial court's finding of infringement under the doctrine of equivalents. Expert testimony indicated that manganese and magnesium serve the same purpose in fluxes. Prior art patents taught the use of manganese in welding fluxes. The accused infringer substituted manganese for magnesium without conducting independent research.

The court made the following points about the doctrine of equivalents:

1. It is based on the concept that "one may not practice a fraud on a patent." [100]

2. It operates not only in favor of pioneer inventions but also in favor of secondary inventions that produce new and useful results (though the area of equivalency may vary under the circumstances). [101]

3. It may be used against, as well as in favor of, a patentee in situations in which an accused device falls within the claim's literal words but performs the same or a similar function in a substantially different way. [102]

4. Equivalency is not determined by a formula but must be determined within the context of the patent, the prior art, and the particular circumstances of the case.

5. Complete identity for every purpose and in every respect is not required. [103]

---

have been unwilling to expose the validity of his patent, by the assertion of a right to any other. Can he abandon the ground of his patent, and ask now for the exclusive use of all cars which, by experiment, shall be found to yield the advantages which he anticipated for conical cars only?. . .

"The patentee is obliged, by law, to . . . particularly 'specify and point out' what he claims as his invention. . . . Nothing . . . will be more mischievous, more productive of oppressive and costly litigation, of exorbitant and unjust pretensions and vexatious demands, more injurious to labor, than a relaxation of these wise and salutary requisitions of the Act of Congress." 56 U.S. at 347.

[99] Graver Tank & Mfg. Co. v. Linde Air Products Co., 339 U.S. 605, 85 U.S.P.Q. 328 (1950).

[100] *Graver Tank's* statement that the doctrine's purpose is to prevent the practicing of "a fraud on a patent" is hardly precise or accurate. Many accused infringers have and should be found guilty of infringement under the doctrine of equivalents even though they believed in good faith that they had designed around the patented invention.

What then is the purpose of the doctrine? One can argue that it is to protect inventors from the misunderstandings and short-sightedness of their patent attorneys in drafting claims. Time and time again, patent claims contain word limitations that are unnecessary in view of the nature of the disclosed invention, the prior art, and the actions of the patent examiner. It is not a matter of negligence or incompetence on the part of claim drafters. Drafting appropriate claims is extremely difficult.

[101] *See* § 2F[2][b][v].

[102] *See* § 2F[2][b][vii].

[103] Substantial rather than exact identity is required. Perkin-Elmer Corp. v. Computervision Corp., 732 F.2d 888, 900, 221 U.S.P.Q. 669, 678 (Fed. Cir. 1984), *cert. denied*, 469 U.S. 857, 225 U.S.P.Q. 792 (1984).

6. Things that are equal to the same thing may not be equal to each other; things for most purposes different may sometimes be equivalent to each other.

7. Consideration must be given to the purpose for which an ingredient is used in a patent, the qualities it has when combined with other ingredients, and the function it is intended to perform.

8. An important factor is whether persons reasonably skilled in the art would have known of the interchangeability of an ingredient that was not included in the patent with one that was so included.[104]

9. Equivalency is a determination of fact and may be proved by expert testimony, documents, texts and treatises, and prior art disclosures.[105]

[ii] *Utility of the "Tri-Partite" Test.* The tri-partite test—whether a device or process falling outside a claim's literal scope "performs substantially the same function in substantially the same way to obtain the same result"— rarely provides a clear guide in determining infringement by equivalency. In *Claude Neon Light*,[106] Judge Learned Hand noted:

"Each case is inevitably a matter of degree, as so often happens, and other decisions have little or no value. The usual ritual, which is so often repeated and which has so little meaning, that the same result must follow by substantially the same means, does not help much in application; it is no more than a way of stating the problem."[107]

The primary reason the tri-partite test is not helpful is that it does not control the level of generality that may be used in characterizing the invention's "way," "result" or "function." Patentees in litigation characterize the way, function and result broadly to show similarity between the patented invention and the accused product; accused infringers characterize the way narrowly to show differences. The court rules for or against equivalency based on which characterization it accepts. In *Perkin-Elmer*,[108] the claimed invention combined a helical resonator with a EDL. A radio frequency (r-f) power source was connected to the helical coil at a point near the grounded end. Two limitations of the claim required a autotransformer-type "tap" coupling such that (a) the coupler was tuned to the frequency of the radio frequency (r-f) power source, and (b) the impedance of the lamp and the coupling means at the tap point substantially matched the impedance of the r-f power source. The accused device used a "loop" coupling in which the connecting point was not fixed for frequency tuning or impedance matching. The accused device created an "impedance mismatch," which was remedied by varying the length of an external cable and positioning an "iris capacitor."

---

[104] *See* § 2F[2][b][vi].

[105] *See* Martin v. Barber, 755 F.2d 1564, 225 U.S.P.Q. 233 (Fed. Cir. 1985).

[106] Claude Neon Lights, Inc. v. E. Machlett & Sons, 36 F.2d 574, 575-76, 3 U.S.P.Q. 220 (2d Cir. 1929), *cert. denied*, 281 U.S. 741 (1930).

[107] Judge Hand refers only to a two-part test — result and means. The case law does not clearly distinguish "way" from "function."

[108] Perkin-Elmer Corp. v. Westinghouse Electric Corp., 822 F.2d 1528, 3 U.S.P.Q.2d 1321 (Fed. Cir. 1987).

A Federal Circuit panel majority held that the accused device did not operate in substantially the same way as the claimed invention even though a prior art publication taught the interchangeability of tap and loop transformer coupling to transfer power to a helical resonator. For the majority, Judge Markey noted: "To be a 'substantial equivalent,' the element substituted in the accused device for the element set forth in the claim must not be such as would substantially change the way in which the function of the claimed invention is performed." He rejected the patentee's argument that the "invention and the accused devices all match impedance:" "That argument misses the mark, for it disregards the *way* impedance is matched in its claimed invention and the different way impedance is matched in the accused devices."[109] Judge Newman dissented, contending "the same transformer function is performed in a known interchangeable way with the same result."

The Federal Circuit continues to stress the tri-partite test. In *Lear Siegler, Inc.,*[110] it mandated a specific proof method; in a jury trial, the patentee must provide "particularized testimony and linking argument" as to application of the three-part *Graver Tank* test. At trial, particularly through cross-examination of the accused device designer, the patentee's counsel sought to establish that the accused device was "the same design" and "functioned the same" as the patentee's commercial device, which allegedly incorporated all the claim's features. In closing argument, counsel reminded the jurors of that testimony. The jury responded to a special verdict form by indicating that the patent was infringed, not literally, but under the doctrine of equivalents. The Federal Circuit overturned the jury verdict: ". . . [A] jury must be separately directed to the proof of each *Graver Tank* element . . . . The evidence and argument on the doctrine of equivalents cannot merely be subsumed in plaintiff's case of literal infringement."

[iii] *Comparison Standard—The "All Elements" Rule*—Pennwalt *and* Corning Glass. The Federal Circuit struggled with the problem of the relationship between claim limitations and an allegedly equivalent product or process. In *Pennwalt,*[111] the court, sitting *en banc*, emphasized there must be in an accused structure or process an equivalent of each claim limitation. In *Corning Glass,*[112] a panel explained there is no rigid formula for equivalency and *Pennwalt* requires that "An equivalent must be found for every limitation of the claim somewhere in an accused device, but not necessarily in a corresponding component."

Pennwalt and *Corning Glass* merit close scrutiny. In *Pennwalt*, the patent claimed an apparatus for sorting items such as fruit (apples or oranges). The apparatus conveyed the item across a weighing device and an optical scanner, which produced electric signals proportionate to the item's weight and color. "Comparison means"

---

[109] Emphasizing the word "way" does not make the court's standard of "way" equivalency any clearer.

[110] Lear Siegler, Inc. v. Sealy Mattress Company of Michigan, Inc., 873 F.2d 1422, 10 U.S.P.Q.2d 1767 (Fed. Cir. 1989).

[111] Pennwalt v. Durand-Wayland, Inc., 833 F.2d 931, 4 U.S.P.Q.2d 1737 (Fed. Cir. 1987), *cert. denied,* 485 U.S. 961, 1009 (1988).

[112] Corning Glass Works v. Sumitomo Electric U.S.A., 868 F.2d 1251, 9 U.S.P.Q.2d 1962 (Fed. Cir. 1989).

compared the weight and color signals with reference values. The apparatus combined the weight and color signals and sent an appropriate signal to discharge the item when it was over the container appropriate for its color and weight. The patent's claims contained limitations on "position indicating means." For example, claim 10 required a "first position indicating means . . . for generating a signal . . . for continuously indicating the position of an item to be sorted" while it is in transit between the color and weight detectors. It required a similar "second position indicating means" for generating a signal indicative of the position of the item after it passed through the two detectors.[113] The "first position indicating means" is "responsive to . . . [the] signal" from a "second comparison means" (*i.e.,* the means for comparing the signal generated from the item by the color sensor with reference values).

The patent's specification disclosed a "hard-wired network" that used shift registers responsive to clock pulses to indicate the positions. The accused device had no position indicating means that registered precisely the location of the item being sorted. Rather, it stored in a computer memory information corresponding to the color value and weight value of items with "queue pointers" to the memory location having data about an item.

In a split *en banc* decision, the court held that the district court did not commit clear error in finding that the accused device did not infringe under the doctrine of

---

[113] Claim 10 provides:

"An automatic sorting apparatus comprising

[1] electronic weighing means for generating a signal proportional to the weight of an item to be sorted,

[2] first reference signal means for providing a predetermined number of reference signals, the value of each signal being established according to a predetermined criteria,

[3] first comparison means for comparing the signal generated by said electronic weighing means to the reference signals provided by said first reference signals means,

[4] optical detection means for generating a signal proportional to the color of an item to be sorted,

[5] second reference signal means for providing a predetermined number of reference signals, the value of each signal being established according to predetermined criteria,

[6] second comparison means for comparing the signal generated by said optical detection means to the reference signals provided by said second reference signals means, and generating a signal therefrom,

[7] clock means for incrementally signaling changes in the position of the item to be sorted,

[8] *first position indicating means responsive to a signal from said clock means and said signal from said second comparison means for continuously indicating the position of an item to be sorted while the item is in transit between said optical detection means and said electronic weighing means,*

[9] *second position indicating means responsive to the signal from said clock means, the signal from said first comparison means and said first position indicating means for generating a signal continuously indicative of the position of an item to be sorted after said item has been weighed,* and

[10] discharge means responsive to the signal from said second position indicating means for discharging the item at a predetermined one of a plurality of sorting positions."
(Emphasis added; numerals added for clarity.)

equivalents. There are four opinions: Judge Bissel's majority opinion for seven judges, Judge Bennett's dissenting opinion for four judges, "Additional Views" by Judge Nies, who was in the majority group, and "Commentary" by Judge Newman, who was in the dissenting group.

The majority opinion stressed that the district court correctly relied on an element-by-element comparison to conclude that there was no infringement under the doctrine of equivalents. The claim limitations in "means-plus-function" format are met only if the identical function (literal infringement) or equivalent function (infringement by equivalency) is present: "[I]f . . . even a single function required by a claim or an equivalent function is not performed by [an accused device], . . . [a] finding of no infringement must be upheld." "[T]he invention was not a pioneer, but an improvement in a crowded art." The claims were broad with respect to the type of product sorted but were narrow as to how the sorter operated. The "continuously" "position indicating means" limitations were critical to patentability as evidenced by the fact that, during the patent's prosecution, the limitations were added to overcome rejections of the claim as unpatentable over the prior art.

The majority rejected the patent owner's argument that the accused device contained the equivalent of the positioning indicating means and that the accused infringer "merely changed the position of an operable element."

> "First, the claim requires that the 'position indicating means' must be responsive to certain specified signals. Thus, finding some combination of components in the accused device that might also be *labeled* a 'position indicating means' is a meaningless exercise when such combination is not responsive to the specified signal.

> "Second, the district court correctly rejected [the patent owner's] assertion that the memory component of [the accused device] which stores information as to weight and color of an item performed substantially the same functions as claimed for the position indicating means. The district court found that a memory function is not the same or substantially the same as the function of 'continuously indicating' where an item is physically located in a sorter. On this point the record is indisputable that before the words 'continuously indicating' were added as an additional limitation, the claim was unpatentable in view of *prior art* which, like the accused machines, stores the information with respect to sorting criteria in memories, but did not 'continuously' track the location."[114]

The majority commented on the patent owner's contention that the "accused devices differ only in substituting a computer for hard-wired circuitry." Conceding that if it were true, the patent owner would "have a stronger position for arguing that the accused devices infringe the claims," the majority noted:

> "[T]he facts here do not involve later-developed computer technology which should be deemed within the scope of the claims to avoid the pirating of an invention. On the contrary, the inventors could not obtain a patent with claims in which the functions were described more broadly. . . . [T]he memory

---

[114] 833 F.2d at 938, 4 U.S.P.Q.2d at 1742.

components of the [accused] sorter were not programmed to perform the same or an equivalent function of physically tracking the items to be sorted from the scanner to the scale or from the scale to its appropriate discharge point as required by the claims."[115]

In dissent, Judge Bennett contended that the majority's analysis requiring element-by-element equivalency was inconsistent with *Graver Tank*.[116] Neither the district court nor the majority had addressed the "real question . . . whether the queues and pointers [of the accused device] perform in substantially the same way the functions of the claimed position indicating means when the latter are interpreted in light of the specification:" "If, as under the district court's and the majority's analyses, the use of software and a computer or microprocessor to perform the function of hard-wired circuitry is enough to find that a device employing a microprocessor performs different functions and operations, then no device that employs computers or micro-processors could ever under the doctrine of equivalents infringe a prior patent on a device that employs hard-wired circuitry." The majority's treatment of the "responsive to" limitation was "the clearest illustration of the shortcomings of the majority's approach to the doctrine of equivalents."

"In the claimed invention, the color grade from the color head is compared to the reference values and converted into data form, which then is stored directly in the first position indicating means while the item is in transit to the weight scale. In the [accused] device, the color grade is stored directly and is not compared to the reference values until the item has reached the weight scale.

"The majority rejected as significantly flawed [the patent owner's] assertion that [the accused infringer's] mere change of the position of an operable element was not enough to avoid infringement under the doctrine of equivalents. However, the only apparent flaw noted by the majority is that the claim requires that the position indicating means be responsive to certain signals and that without being responsive to the specified signal, any other combination of elements cannot be deemed to contain an equivalent of the functional limitations describing the position indicating means. In my view, a comparison to the color reference values occurring in the [accused] device after the item

---

[115] 833 F.2d at 938-39, 4 U.S.P.Q.2d at 1742-43.

[116] He noted:

"To require a one-to-one correspondence creates a bright line rule easier to apply, but costly in terms of unfair results in exceptional cases. . . .

"The application of the doctrine of equivalents to 'the claimed invention as a whole' . . . is inherent in the policy expressed in *Graver Tank*. In order to determine equivalency in light of 'the purpose for which an ingredient is used in a patent' and 'the qualities it has when combined with the other ingredients' as mandated by the Supreme Court, it is indeed necessary to view the entire claim as a whole, and not merely to conduct an element by element comparison. It is only after such an analysis that the fact finder can determine in light of the entire claim and all of its limitations, whether the changes or substitutions made alter substantially the way that the accused device works when compared to the claimed invention as a whole." 833 F.2d at 947-48, 4 U.S.P.Q.2d at 1750.

reaches the weight scale is an equivalent function whether or not its first position indicating means is responsive to a signal from a comparison means, when the accused device is viewed in its entirety and compared to the claimed invention as a whole. To preclude the possibility of finding equivalent functions and therefore preclude finding infringement under the doctrine of equivalents simply because the accused device does not perform its functions in the same order as the claimed invention reduces the doctrine of equivalents, in practical effect, to nothing more than the test for literal infringement."[117]

Judge Nies reviewed Supreme Court and lower court precedent, concluding "[W]hen an element is entirely *missing*, that is, when the accused device does not contain either the exact element of the claim *or* its equivalent, there is no infringement."[118] She did concede that "One-to-one correspondence is not required. Elements may be combined in some instances to achieve an equivalent element."

Judge Newman reviewed at length the history of claim drafting and interpretation "to balance the historical record on which the majority bases its decision."

> "Determination of equivalency is not unlike determination of substantial similarity in copyright law or determination of nonobviousness in patent law. Such determinations require judicial wisdom, not a catalog of narrow rules.
>
> . . .
>
> "The vitality of the doctrine of equivalents has been tested and reaffirmed for a hundred years. At its best, it is a guardian of justice and an enemy of fraud. . . . [T]he doctrine depends for its implementation on judicial wisdom."[119]

Two comments are in order. First, the *Pennwalt* majority opinion leaves unresolved the status of *Hughes Aircraft*,[120] which was, prior to *Pennwalt*, widely understood as giving broad scope to the doctrine of equivalents and not mandating an all elements approach.[121] In *Hughes Aircraft*, the Federal Circuit reversed as erroneous

---

[117] 833 F.2d at 944, 4 U.S.P.Q.2d at 1747-48.

[118] 833 F.2d at 949, 4 U.S.P.Q.2d at 1752.

"Congress placed in the statute the requirement that the patent application 'conclude with one or more claims particularly pointing out and distinctly claiming the subject matter which the applicant regards as his invention.' . . . That requirement reflects the need for notice of what constitutes violation of a patentee's rights. . . . An infringement standard as vague as application of the 'invention as a whole,' which permits claim limitations to be read out of the claim, would nullify the statutory requirement and violate due process." 833 F.2d at 954, 4 U.S.P.Q.2d at 1755.

[119] 833 F.2d at 970, 974-75, 4 U.S.P.Q.2d at 1772.

[120] Hughes Aircraft Co. v. United States, 717 F.2d 1351, 219 U.S.P.Q. 473 (Fed. Cir. 1983).

[121] The other three opinions assumed *Hughes* was implicitly overruled, or limited. Judge Bennett stated it is clearly being overruled, by the majority, despite not even being mentioned in its opinion. Judge Newman protested that "Critical changes should not be made within a stonewall of silence." Judge Nies distinguished *Hughes Aircraft*:

"The coupling of the *Graver Tank* doctrine with the expression 'invention as a whole' first appears in *Hughes Aircraft* . . . The conclusion could reasonably be drawn therefrom that literal infringement requires element-by- element analysis and infringement under the

a district court finding of noninfringement, noting that "The failure to apply the doctrine of equivalents to the claimed invention as a whole, and the accompanying demand for 'obvious and exact' equivalents of two elements the presence of which would have effectively produced literal infringement, was error."[122]

Second, whether an accused structure completely "omits" a claim limitation or substitutes an equivalent is dependent on claim drafting considerations that should not bear on the basic equities of infringement by equivalence. Consider the following example.

Inventor A obtains a patent claiming a new floor tile configuration. Assume all prior floor tiles were round or oval. A's idea is square or diamond tiles, which have the advantage of fitting together more neatly, etc. Claim 1 is for "A floor tile comprising a regular four-sided polygon with each side of approximately equal length." Claim 2 is for: "A floor tile comprising (a) a first side, (b) a second side, a first end of said second side joined at a first end of said first side, (c) a third side, a first end of said third side joined at a second end of said first side, and (d) a fourth side joined at a second end of said second side and a second end of said third side, wherein each of said sides are of approximately equal length."

Both claims literally cover the same subject matter. Assume that a tile accused of infringement is an equilateral triangle. There is no literal infringement of either claim. Analysis of infringement by equivalents of Claim 1 would be the traditional one. The accused device substitutes a three-sided polygon for the claim limitation requiring a four-sided polygon. Is it equivalent? That depends on the specification disclosure, prior art, prosecution history and other factors. If the prior art truly showed only round and oval tiles, a conclusion of equivalents is conceivable. If *Pennwalt* means each claim limitation must find an equivalent in the accused device, the analysis of infringement by equivalents of Claim 2 is different. One could say that there is no equivalent of the function of one of the limitations—limitation (d) providing for a fourth side, which would end the inquiry.

Should the analysis differ depending on claim drafting style if each claim covers the same literal subject matter? In each case, the proper question should be: what inventive concept was disclosed? Would one of ordinary skill in the art immediately characterize the concept as the generic one of having regular, simple-shaped tiles that mesh? Or was it confined to the advantages of four-sided tiles?

---

doctrine of equivalents discards element-by-element analysis in favor of an 'invention as a whole' analysis. One difficulty of an expert in a legal field writing on a problem is the 'everyone-knows-that' syndrome. One must read the *Hughes* opinion in the light of the 'given' principle that, to establish infringement, each and every element of a claim, of course, must be satisfied in accordance with established precedent. The *Hughes* panel could not and did not depart from that precedent. The *Hughes* analysis was directed to the confusing concept of equivalency under the doctrine and the different concept of equivalency under section 112-6. When it spoke of the doctrine applying to the 'invention as a whole,' it was not *by implication* or *sub silentio* rejecting the All Elements Rule." 833 F.2d at 953, 4 U.S.P.Q.2d at 1754-55.

[122] 717 F.2d at 1364, 219 U.S.P.Q. at 483.

A response might be that *Pennwalt* does not dictate so simple an analysis of claim 2. One could argue that the "function" of the limitation (d)—a fourth side—was simply to close the regular, straight-sided shape, and that this function was distributed among other elements of the accused device, that is, among its three sides. But if this is how *Pennwalt* is to be applied, the "rule" on omission of claim limitations, which was so controversial among the judges of the Federal Circuit, becomes fair and valid but relatively insignificant because it does not really confine the scope of the doctrine of equivalents.

Corning Glass[123] suggests *Pennwalt* may be satisfied if an apparently omitted limitation's function is performed by other elements in the accused device.[124] The plaintiff's patent disclosed the first optical waveguide fiber with an attenuation of 20db/km, the transmission efficiency of copper wire. It showed a fiber with a pure fused silica cladding and a fused silica core containing approximately three percent by weight of titania and stressed the necessity of careful selection of the core diameter and core-cladding refraction index (R.I.) differential. The disclosed invention limits the transmitted light to preselected rays or "modes."

The patent claim recited a fiber with a cladding and a core, the core being "positively" doped so as to create a R.I. differential.[125] The defendants' optical waveguide fibers created a R.I. differential by "negatively" doping the cladding rather than positively doping the core.

At the time of filing the patent application, the inventor had experimented with dopants, such as titania, that increased the R.I. of fused silica. The specification discloses only positive dopants. The inventors did not know of specific dopants that would decrease the R.I. of fused silica, although it was known in the art that fluorine decreased the R.I. of certain multicomponent glasses. The defendants' fibers had the R.I. differential between core and cladding specified by the claim and the structural dimensions necessary for the preselection of modes of light waves, but a negative dopant, fluorine, altered the index of refraction of the fused silica of the cladding. Therefore, the claim limitation requiring a positive dopant in the core was not present literally in the accused device.

The Federal Circuit found unpersuasive the defendant's argument that the district court's finding of equivalency was clear error because "an element of a claim is entirely missing."

---

[123] Corning Glass Works v. Sumitomo Electric U.S.A., 868 F.2d 1251, 9 U.S.P.Q.2d 1962 (Fed. Cir. 1989).

[124] *See also* Sun Studs, Inc. v. ATA Equipment Leasing, Inc., 872 F.2d 978, 989, 10 U.S.P.Q.2d 1338, 1347 (Fed. Cir. 1989) ("One-to-one correspondence of components is not required, and elements or steps may be combined without *ipso facto* loss of equivalency.").

[125] "An optical waveguide comprising

(a) a cladding layer formed of a material selected from the group consisting of pure fused silica and fused silica to which a dopant material on at least an elemental basis has been added, and

(b) a core formed of fused silica to which a dopant material on at least an elemental basis has been added to a degree in excess of that of the cladding layer so that the index of refraction thereof is of a value greater than the index of refraction of said cladding layer, said core being formed of at least 85 percent by weight of fused silica and an effective amount up to 15 percent by weight of said dopant material."

> "The premise . . . known as the 'All Elements' rule . . . correctly states the law of this circuit adopted in banc in *Pennwalt*. . . . However, we do not agree that an 'element' of the claim is entirely 'missing' from the [accused] fibers.
>
> "[The defendant's analysis] illustrates the confusion sometimes encountered because of misunderstanding or misleading uses of the term 'element' in discussing claims. 'Element' may be used to mean a single limitation, but it has also been used to mean a series of limitations which, taken together, make up a component of the claimed invention. In the All Elements rule, 'element' is used in the sense of a *limitation* of a claim. . . . [The defendant's analysis] is faulty in that it would require equivalency in components. . . . However, the determination of equivalency is not subject to such a rigid formula. An equivalent must be found for every limitation of the claim somewhere in an accused device, but not necessarily in a corresponding component, although that is generally the case."[126]

[iv] *Importance of the Limitations—"Heart of the Invention."* Federal Circuit opinions oscillate on whether it is appropriate to consider the relative importance of claim limitations to the inventive concept, equivalency being more likely when the accused device embodies literally the "heart of the invention" and substitutes different elements for less important limitations. In *Atlas Powder,*[127] the court found no reversible error in the district court's consideration of the "heart of the invention" in determining equivalency, but in *Perkin-Elmer,*[128] a panel majority opined that such prior language was "dicta."

> "Though the doctrine of equivalents is designed to do equity, and to relieve an inventor from a semantic strait jacket when equity requires, it is not designed to permit wholesale redrafting of a claim to cover non-equivalent devices, *i.e.,* to permit a claim expansion that would encompass more than an insubstantial change."
>
> "We are aware of dicta that state consideration of the 'essence', 'gist', or 'heart' of the invention may be helpful in determining infringement under the doctrine of equivalents. . . . That dicta may not be read as implying that specific claim limitations can be ignored as insignificant or immaterial in determining infringement. It must be read as shorthand for the considerations set forth in *Graver Tank,* i.e., that the infringer should not appropriate the invention by making substitutions for those limitations, when the substitutions do not substantially change the function performed, or the way it is performed, by the invention."[129]

"Heart of the invention" is a vague concept that gives a trier of fact free rein to selectively characterize the patented invention, introducing excessive subjectivity

---

[126] 868 F.2d at 1259, 4 U.S.P.Q.2d at 1968.

[127] Atlas Powder Co. v. E.I. du Pont De Nemours & Co., 750 F.2d 1569, 224 U.S.P.Q. 409, 418 (Fed. Cir. 1984).

[128] Perkin-Elmer Corp. v. Westinghouse Electric Corp., 822 F.2d 1528, 3 U.S.P.Q.2d 1321 (Fed. Cir. 1987).

[129] 822 F.2d at 1532–1533 & n.8, 3 U.S.P.Q.2d at 1325 & n.8.

in validity determinations.[130] For that reason, the law rejects "heart of the invention" characterizations in favor a "subject matter as a whole" approach.[131] Because a patent claim must be interpreted consistently for validity and infringement, it follows that the "heart of the invention" approach should be rejected for infringement determinations via the doctrine of equivalents as well. But the proposition that each claim limitation, indeed each word in a claim, must be given equal importance in determining equivalents is untenable. For example, an implication of the doctrine of prosecution history estoppel is that some claim limitations must be more faithfully adhered to than others.[132] Once one departs from the claim's literal terms, by definition the claim can no longer provide the sole guide to the invention. The appropriate supplementary guide is the specification, which provides the full description of the inventor's contribution to the art.

The similarity between obviousness and equivalents breaks down. Any limitation that keeps a claim from reading on obvious subject matter should be given full effect, but in an equivalents situation, the claim is, by definition, unnecessarily underinclusive, that is, it could be broader and still avoid the prior art. The point of the doctrine is that the interest in reliance on express claim language should yield when it is obvious to a person of ordinary skill in the art that the disclosed invention extends beyond such claim language. It seems quite reasonable to permit a broader scope of equivalents for those limitations that would appear most clearly to be unnecessary.

[v]   *Range of Equivalents—Pioneer Patents.* The range of equivalents varies according to the importance of the claimed invention: a "pioneer" invention gains a broad range of equivalents, a substantial improvement a substantial range of equivalents,[133] a narrow improvement a limited range of equivalents.[134]

A pioneer invention achieves a function never before performed, is a wholly new product, or one of such novelty and importance that it marks a distinct step in the progress of the art.[135]

---

[130] Loctite Corp. v. Ultraseal Ltd., 781 F.2d 861, 228 U.S.P.Q. 562 (Fed. Cir. 1986).

[131] *See* § 2C[4][c].

[132] *See* § 2F[2][c].

[133] Eibel Process Co. v. Minnesota & Ontario Paper Co., 261 U.S. 45, 63 (1923); Hughes Aircraft Co. v. United States, 717 F.2d 1351, 219 U.S.P.Q. 473 (Fed. Cir. 1983).

[134] Kinzenbaw v. Deere & Co., 741 F.2d 383, 389, 222 U.S.P.Q. 929, 933 (Fed. Cir. 1984), *cert. denied,* 470 U.S. 1004 (1985).

[135] Boyden Power-Brake Co. v. Westinghouse, 170 U.S. 537, 569 (1898). *See also* Sun Studs, Inc. v. ATA Equipment Leasing, Inc., 872 F.2d 978, 987, 10 U.S.P.Q.2d 1338, 1346 (Fed. Cir. 1989) (the jury verdict finding infringement by equivalency is supported by substantial evidence, whether or not the patented invention "merits the encomium of 'pioneer.' The concept of the 'pioneer' arises from an ancient jurisprudence, reflecting judicial appreciation that a broad break-through invention merits a broader scope of equivalents than does a narrow improvement in a crowded technology. But the 'pioneer' is not a separate class of invention, carrying a unique body of law. The wide range of technological advance between pioneering breakthrough and modest improvement accommodates gradations in scope of equivalency. . . The place of a particular invention in this spectrum depends on all the circumstances. . . and is decided as a factual matter. . . "); Perkin-Elmer Corp. v. Westinghouse Electric Corp., 822 F.2d 1528,

The fact that an invention is a combination of mechanical elements does not affect the range of equivalents.[136]

[vi] *Later Developed Equivalents—Equivalency of Patented Improvements.* The fact that a person of ordinary skill in the art would have known of the equivalency at the time of the invention or the filing of the patent is a positive factor that suggests equivalency,[137] but equivalency may extend to elements or devices that are developed after the dates of invention and filing.[138]

In *Hughes Aircraft*,[139] the patent related to synchronous communications satellite attitude control. The claim specified that the satellite have means for receiving and directly executing control signals from an earth ground control station. Later developed satellites did not respond directly to ground control signals as required by the claims because they utilized on-board microprocessors to receive control signals and execute them after processing. The microprocessors were unknown at the time the application for the patent was filed. The court found infringement, stressing that an inventor is not required to predict all future developments that enable the practice of his invention in substantially the same way.[140]

1532, 3 U.S.P.Q.2d 1321, 1324 (Fed. Cir. 1987) ("A pioneer invention is entitled to a broad range of equivalents;" the claimed invention, a resonator coupler for an electrodeless discharge lamp (EDL) useful for chemical analysis by atomic absorption spectroscopy (AAS), was not a "pioneer" because prior art devices, including EDL's, were also devoted to provision of light for AAS and because the invention was described in the specification as an improvement; "That an improvement enjoys commercial success and has some industry impact, as many do, cannot compel a finding that an improvement falls within the pioneer category.").

[136] Amstar Corp. v. Envirotech Corp., 730 F.2d 1476, 221 U.S.P.Q. 649 (Fed. Cir. 1984), *cert. denied*, 469 U.S. 924, 224 U.S.P.Q. 616 (1984).

[137] Graver Tank & Mfg. Co. v. Linde Air Products Co., 339 U.S. 605, 85 U.S.P.Q. 328 (1950). *See also* Corning Glass Works v. Sumitomo Electric U.S.A., 868 F.2d 1251, 1261, 9 U.S.P.Q.2d 1962, 1969 (Fed. Cir. 1989) ("[T]he substitution of an ingredient known to be an equivalent to that required by the claim presents a classic example for a finding of infringement under the doctrine of equivalents.").

[138] Marsh-McBirney, Inc. v. Montedoro-Whitney Corp., 882 F.2d 498, 504, 11 U.S.P.Q.2d 1794, 1798 (Fed. Cir. 1989) ("Advances subsequent to the patent may still infringe."); Moleculon Research Corp. v. CBS, Inc., 872 F.2d 407, 409, 10 U.S.P.Q.2d 1390, 1392 (Fed. Cir. 1989) ("Although a 'partial variation in technique, an embellishment made possible by post-[patent] technology, does not allow the accused [method] to escape the "web of infringement," ' . . . under the facts of [the] case, that web does not extend to [the accused method]."); American Hospital Supply Corp. v. Travenol Laboratories, Inc., 745 F.2d 1, 9, 223 U.S.P.Q. 577, 583 (Fed. Cir. 1984).

Equivalency is determined as of the time infringement takes place. Atlas Powder Co. v. E.I. du Pont De Nemours & Co., 750 F.2d 1569, 1581, 224 U.S.P.Q. 409, 417 (Fed. Cir. 1984).

[139] Hughes Aircraft Co. v. United States, 717 F.2d 1351, 219 U.S.P.Q. 473 (Fed. Cir. 1983). Whether *Hughes Aircraft* survived *Pennwalt* is discussed at § 2F[2][b][iii].

[140] *Compare* American Hospital Supply Corp. v. Travenol Laboratories, Inc., 745 F.2d 1, 9, 223 U.S.P.Q. 577, 583 (Fed. Cir. 1984) (the accused product was not equivalent to the claimed product when (a) the claim contained several specific ingredient range limitations based on a certain theory, and (b) the accused product varied one such range in following later developments based on a competing theory).

A patented modification may be equivalent to a previously patented invention. In *Atlas Powder*,[141] the patent claimed a water resistant blasting agent with a "water-in-oil" emulsion. The accused infringer used a blasting agent in which an "oil-in-water" emulsion turned into water-in-oil when applied *in situ*. The court upheld a finding of equivalence even though the accused infringer had a patent on its improvement because the infringer's patent was not based on unexpected results,[142] which would have negated the "substantially the same result" equivalency requirement.

[vii] *Reverse Equivalents.* Equivalents may operate in reverse. An accused product apparently within a claim's literal language does not infringe if it is "so far changed in principle . . . that it performs the same or a similar function in a substantially different way."[143]

In *Leesona*,[144] the claim to a battery electrode structure required a "porous self-sustaining metal layer of uniform and controlled porosity." The specification disclosed a microporous layer with pores of about 1 to 50 microns in diameter, which functioned to control bubble pressure. The accused product had a conventional metal screen that could be characterized as a uniformly porous layer as described in the claim, but it had openings much larger than 50 microns and relieved bubble pressure only in an incidental, insignificant way. The court found no infringement.

In *United States Steel*,[145] the court rejected a reverse equivalency defense. The patent claimed crystalline polypropylene, and the specification gave a crude, low molecular weight example. The accused infringers sold high molecular weight polypropylenes made possible by later development of superior catalysts. The court reasoned that the "principle" of the claimed invention, as corroborated by the inventors' work before filing their 1953 patent application and by their application disclosures, "is the

---

[141] Atlas Powder Co. v. E.I. du Pont de Nemours & Co., 750 F.2d 1569, 1581, 224 U.S.P.Q. 409, 417 (Fed. Cir. 1984).

[142] Evidence of unexpected results may be the basis for the patentability of an invention that is *prima facie* obvious in view of the prior art. *See* § 2C[4][c].

[143] Graver Tank & Mfg. Co. v. Linde Air Products Co., 339 U.S. 605, 85 U.S.P.Q. 328 (1950). *Cf.* Texas Instruments, Inc. v. U.S. Int'l Trade Comm'n, 805 F.2d 1558, 231 U.S.P.Q. 833 (Fed. Cir. 1986) (on denial of rehearing):

> "[The] so-called 'reverse doctrine of equivalents'. . . might better be called a doctrine of non-equivalence. . . . Its invocation requires both that (1) there must be apparent literal infringement of the words of the claims; and (2) the accused device must be sufficiently different from that which is patented that despite the apparent literal infringement, the claims are interpreted to negate infringement.
>
> "The reverse doctrine of equivalents is invoked when claims are written more broadly than the disclosure warrants. The purpose of restricting the scope of such claims is not only to avoid a holding of infringement when a court deems it appropriate, but often is to preserve the validity of claims with respect to their original intended scope." 846 F.2d at 1371, 6 U.S.P.Q.2d at 1888.

[144] Leesona Corp. v. United States, 530 F.2d 896, 192 U.S.P.Q. 672 (Ct. Cl. 1976).

[145] United States Steel Corp. v. Phillips Petroleum Co., 865 F.2d 1247, 9 U.S.P.Q.2d 1461 (Fed. Cir. 1989).

production for the first time of crystalline polypropylene."[146] The infringers made no change in that principle; their polypropylene products, though of much higher molecular weight and viscosity than the polymer disclosed in the 1953 application, were crystalline.

[viii] *Limiting Effect of the Prior Art.* Numerous decisions hold that the range of equivalents cannot extend to encompass the prior art.[147]

In *Wilson Sporting Goods,*[148] Judge Rich staked out a new approach to prior art constraint of the doctrine of equivalents.[149]

---

[146] The court conceded that "The reverse doctrine of equivalents can in some cases be seen as conceptually and linguistically difficult to apply when the claim is drawn to chemical compounds or compositions. The doctrine speaks of performance of a 'function' in a substantially different 'way.' The district court here did not face that difficulty, having focused on the 'principle' of the contribution made by the inventor and found it unchanged in the accused product." 865 F.2d at 1253 n.9, 9 U.S.P.Q.2d at 1466 n.9.

[147] *E.g.,* Senmed, Inc. v. Richard-Allan Medical Industries, Inc., 888 F.2d 815, 821, 12 U.S.P.Q.2d 1508, 1513 (Fed. Cir. 1989) ("[L]imitations in a claim cannot be given a range of equivalents so wide as to cause the claim to encompass anything in the prior art."); Stewart-Warner Corp. v. City of Pontiac, 767 F.2d 1563, 226 U.S.P.Q. 676 (Fed. Cir. 1985). *Compare* Corning Glass Works v. Sumitomo Electric U.S.A., 868 F.2d 1251, 1261, 9 U.S.P.Q.2d 1962, 1969 (Fed. Cir. 1989) ("Nothing is taken from the 'public domain' when the issue of equivalency is directed to a limitation only, in contrast to the entirety of the claimed invention."); Ryco, Inc. v. Ag-Bag Corp., 857 F.2d 1418, 1426, 8 U.S.P.Q.2d 1323, 1330 (Fed. Cir. 1988) (the accused device "superficially resembles" that of a prior art device, but "[l]ooking closer,. . . it is apparent that the two are similar in name only and not in function.").

[148] Wilson Sporting Goods Co. v. David Geoffrey & Associates, 904 F.2d 677, 14 U.S.P.Q.2d 1942 (Fed. Cir. 1990), *cert. denied,* 111 S. Ct. 537 (1990).

[149] Judge Rich first noted that the doctrine of equivalents does not, properly speaking, expand claims.

"This court on occasion has characterized claims as being 'expanded' or 'broadened' under the doctrine of equivalents. . . .

"To say that the doctrine of equivalents extends or enlarges *the claims* is a contradiction in terms. The claims—i.e., the scope of patent protection *as defined by* the claims—remain the same and application of the doctrine *expands the right to exclude* to 'equivalents' of what is claimed.

"The doctrine of equivalents, by definition, involves going beyond any permissible interpretation of the claim language; i.e., it involves determining whether the accused product is 'equivalent' to what is described by the claim language." 904 F.2d at 683, 14 U.S.P.Q.2d at 1948. (Emphasis in original.)

He then addressed "an interesting question:"

"If the doctrine of equivalents does not involve expanding the claims, why should the *prior art* be a limitation on the range of permissible equivalents? It is *not* because we construe claims narrowly if necessary to sustain their validity . . . . [T]he doctrine of equivalents does not involve expansion of the *claims.* Nor is it because to hold otherwise would allow the patentee to preempt a product that was in the public domain prior to the invention. The accused products here, as in most infringement cases, were never 'in the public domain.' They were developed long after the invention and differ in several respects from the prior art." 904 F.2d at 684, 14 U.S.P.Q.2d at 1948. (Emphasis in original.)

"Whether prior art restricts the range of equivalents of what is literally claimed can be a difficult question to answer. To simplify analysis and bring the issue onto familiar turf, it may be helpful to conceptualize the limitation on the scope of equivalents by visualizing a *hypothetical* patent claim, sufficient in scope to *literally* cover the accused product. The pertinent question then becomes whether that hypothetical claim could have been allowed by the PTO over the prior art. If not, then it would be improper to permit the patentee to obtain that coverage in an infringement suit under the doctrine of equivalents. If the hypothetical claim could have been allowed, then *prior art* is not a bar to infringement under the doctrine of equivalents."

"Viewing the issue in this manner allows use of traditional patentability rules and permits a more precise analysis than determining whether an *accused product* (which has no claim limitations on which to focus) would have been obvious in view of the prior art. . . . In fact, the utility of this hypothetical broader claim may explain why 'expanded claim' phraseology, which we now abandon, had crept into our jurisprudence. . . . Finally, it reminds us that [the patentee] is seeking patent coverage beyond the limits considered by the PTO examiner."[150]

The patentee bears the burden of proving the patentability of the hypothetical claim literally covering the accused product or process.

"[T]he burden is on [the patentee] to prove that the range of equivalents which it seeks would not ensnare the prior art [products or processes]. The patent owner has always borne the burden of proving infringement, . . . and there is no logical reason why that burden should shift to the accused infringer simply because infringement in this context might require an inquiry into the patentability of a *hypothetical* claim. Any other approach would ignore the realities of what happens in the PTO and violate established patent law. Leaving this burden on [the patentee] does not, of course, in any way undermine the presumed validity of [the patentee's] actual patent claims."[151]

He offered an answer:

"The answer is that a patentee should not be able to obtain, under the doctrine of equivalents, coverage which he could not lawfully have obtained from the PTO by literal claims. The doctrine of equivalents exists to prevent a fraud on a patent, . . . *not* to give a patentee something which he could not lawfully have obtained from the PTO had he tried. Thus, since prior art always limits what an inventor could have claimed, it limits the range of permissible equivalents of a claim." 904 F.2d at 684, 14 U.S.P.Q.2d at 1948. (Emphasis in original.)

[150] 904 F.2d at 684-85, 14 U.S.P.Q.2d at 1498 (Emphasis in original.)
[151] 904 F.2d at 685, 14 U.S.P.Q.2d at 1948-49 (Emphasis in original.)

As to the standard of appellate review over the question of the limiting effect of prior art on the doctrine of equivalents, Judge Rich noted:

"This issue—whether an asserted range of equivalents would cover what is already in the public domain—is one of law, which we review *de novo*, . . . but we presume that the jury resolved underlying evidentiary conflicts in the [patentee's] favor [because of its verdict of infringement under the doctrine of equivalents]." 904 F.2d at 683, 14 U.S.P.Q.2d at 1948.

In *Wilson Sporting Goods*, the patent related to golf ball cover dimple configuration. The invention achieved a more symmetrical dimple distribution by dividing the ball into 80 imaginary spherical triangles by (1) dividing the ball into an icosahedron, which is 20 imaginary equilateral triangles, and (2) dividing each triangle by joining the midpoint of each side to form four smaller subtriangles (three "apical triangles", i.e., ones containing an apex or tip of the larger triangles, and one "central triangle"). The lines joining the 20 primary triangles' midpoints, which are the central triangles's sides, form six great circles around the sphere. The invention required that dimples be so placed on the ball that no dimple intersects a great circle.[152] The claimed dimple arrangement results in a ball with six axes of symmetry compared to prior balls, which had only one axis of symmetry.

Twenty-six dependent claims specify the number and location of dimples in the sub-triangles.

The prior art included Pugh's 1932 British patent and a Uniroyal golf ball sold in the 1970's and related Uniroyal patents. Pugh teaches, among other things, that a golf ball can be divided into any regular polyhedron, including a icosahedron, and that each of the 20 icosahedral triangles can be divided into smaller triangles. In one example, the larger triangles are divided into 16 sub-triangles, which are merely further divisions of four larger subtriangles. The Uniroyal ball is an icosahedral ball having six great circles with 30 or more dimples intersecting five of the great circles by about 12-15 thousandths of an inch.

The patent owner, Wilson, brought suit, alleging that four balls sold by Dunlop infringed the patent. At trial, the jury found that all four balls infringed under the doctrine of equivalents. The accused Dunlop balls had either 432 or 480 dimples. The accused balls' dimples were arranged in an icosahedral pattern having six great circles. The six great circles were not dimple-free as the claims literally required. The great circles intersected 60 dimples each of which is 0.06-0.08 of an inch in radius. The extent of intersection on the four balls was 0.0075, 0.0087, 0.004, and 0.004 respectively.

Applying its new hypothetical claim approach, the court concluded that the prior art precluded application of the doctrine of equivalents to the accused products. The independent claim, hypothetically amended to read literally on the accused infringer's balls, must permit 60 or fewer dimples (or, stated in terms of relative number of intersecting dimples to total dimples, up to 14% of total dimples) to intersect the great circles by at least 0.009 inch (13% of dimple radius). The prior art Uniroyal ball with 30 intersecting dimples (12% of total dimples) would literally meet the dimple number

---

[152] Claim 1, the patent's only independent claim, provides:

"A golf ball having a spherical surface with a plurality of dimples formed therein and six great circle paths which do not intersect any di[m]ples, the dimples being arranged by dividing the spherical surface into twenty spherical triangles corresponding to the faces of a regular icosahedron, each of the twenty triangles being sub-divided into four smaller triangles consisting of a central triangle and three apical triangles by connecting the midpoints [of the sides] of each of said twenty triangles along great circle paths, said dimples being arranged so that the dimples do not intersect the sides of any of the central triangles."

limitation (fewer than 60, or 14% of total dimples) and would approximate the dimple radius limitation (13% or less versus 17-21% in the prior art ball).

> "[T]hese differences are so slight and relatively minor that the hypothetical claim—which permits twice as many intersecting dimples, but with slightly smaller intersections—viewed as a whole would have been obvious in view of the [prior art] Uniroyal ball. As Dunlop puts it, there is simply 'no principled difference' between the hypothetical claim and the prior art Uniroyal ball. Accordingly, Wilson's claim 1 cannot be given a range of equivalents broad enough to encompass the accused Dunlop balls."[153]

[c] **Prosecution History Estoppel.** Prosecution history estoppel precludes claim scope expansion to resurrect subject matter surrendered to obtain a patent.[154] It prevents circumvention of PTO examination and appeal procedures.[155] If an applicant believes an examiner's claim rejection is erroneous, he should appeal the rejection rather than amend the claim or give it a narrow scope by argument and later, in an infringement suit, seek to expand the claim to its original scope by the doctrine of equivalents.

[i] *The Exhibit Supply Decision.* Early Supreme Court decisions show ambivalence about Patent Office activity's impact on patent claim interpretation and application.[156]

The leading modern Supreme Court decision is *Exhibit Supply*.[157] The plaintiff's patent claimed a pinball machine switch that closed an electric current when a ball hit a target. Claim 4 had three elements: a standard anchored in the table, a coil spring, and a conductor "embedded in the table." The patent's drawing illustrated a conductor

---

[153] 904 F.2d at 685, 14 U.S.P.Q.2d at 1949.

[154] The doctrine was originally known as "file wrapper estoppel." Decisions now refer to "prosecution history estoppel." Thomas & Betts Corp. v. Litton Sys., Inc., 720 F.2d 1572, 1579, 220 U.S.P.Q. 1, 6 (Fed. Cir. 1983).

[155] Musher Foundation, Inc. v. Alba Trading Co., 150 F.2d 885, 888, 66 U.S.P.Q. 183, 185-86 (2d Cir. 1945), *cert. denied*, 326 U.S. 770, 67 U.S.P.Q. 359 (1945).

[156] Shepard v. Carrigan, 116 U.S. 597-98 (1886) ("Where an applicant for a patent to cover a new combination is compelled by the rejection of his application by the Patent Office to narrow by the introduction of a new element, he cannot after the issue of the patent broaden his claim by dropping the element which he was compelled to include in order to secure his patent. . . . If an applicant, in order to get his patent, accepts one with a narrower claim than that contained in his original application he is bound by it. If dissatisfied with the decision rejecting his application, he should pursue his remedy by appeal."); Goodyear Dental Vulcanite Co. v. Davis, 102 U.S. (12 Otto) 222, 227 (1881) ("We do not mean to be understood as asserting that any correspondence between the applicant for a patent and the Commissioner of Patents can be allowed to enlarge, diminish, or vary the language of a patent afterwards issued. Undoubtedly a patent, like any other written instrument, is to be interpreted by its own terms. But when a patent bears on its face a particular construction, inasmuch as the specification and claim are in the words of the patentee, it is reasonable to hold that such a construction may be confirmed by what the patentee said when he was making his application. The understanding of a party to a contract has always been regarded as of some importance in its interpretation.").

[157] Exhibit Supply Co. v. Ace Patents Corp., 315 U.S. 126, 52 U.S.P.Q. 275 (1942).

in the form of a ring set in the table with its flange projecting slightly above the table surface. The leg pending from the coil spring contacted the conductor at a point near or below the table surface.

The infringement suit involved three types of accused devices, all similar to the patented switch except for the conductor's form and placement. The first type substituted for the ring conductor a nail driven into the table and surrounded by a ring attached to the end of a spring. When a ball struck the spring, contact was formed at a point above the table. The second and third types used a similar nail, but it was supported by a metal plate on the table top. A wire passed through a hole in the table. The accused infringer argued that none of the devices used a conductor element "embedded in the table."

The Supreme Court reviewed the Patent Office "file wrapper record." After the examiner rejected the applicant's original six claims, the applicant substituted a new set of claims, including claim 7 covering a conductor means "carried by the table." The examiner rejected claim 7 as insufficient to distinguish the applicant's device from the prior art and suggested a claim to the applicant's particular type of device— extension to the coil spring (the leg) to engage an annular conductor embedded in the table. The applicant resisted that language because the claim could be avoided by removing the leg from the spring and embedding it as a pin in the table. Instead, he amended the claim by substituting "embedded in the table" for "carried by the table" but did not confine the "means" for carrying the spring downward to a leg structure. This became patent claim 4.

The Court held the first type of accused device was within the patent. The accused infringer did not seriously dispute that the claim read on that type of device or contend that the pin was not literally "embedded in the table." Neither the dictionary definition of "embed" nor the patent specification and drawings of the patent supported the view that "embedded" meant "wholly between the upper and nether surfaces of the table." The background of the amendment adding the phrase "embedded" indicated no contrary conclusion. The examiner expressly agreed with the applicant's concern over a device with a pin arrangement extending above the table. The Court construed "embedded" as embracing "any conductor means solidly set or firmly fixed in the table, whether or not it protrudes above or below the surface."

On the other hand, the Court held the second and third types were outside the patent. The patent owner conceded that the conductor means were not literally "embedded in the table" but argued for application of the doctrine of equivalents. The accused infringer conceded that the devices were the mechanical equivalent of conductor means embedded in the table but argued for abolition of the doctrine of equivalents as contrary to the statutory clear claiming requirement. The Court declined to pass on the doctrine of equivalents,[158] holding it inapplicable where the patent owner was seeking to recover surrendered subject matter.

> "Whatever may be the appropriate scope and application of the doctrine of
> equivalents, where a claim is allowed without a restrictive amendment, it has

---

[158] Eight years after *Exhibit Supply*, the Supreme Court did uphold the continuing vitality of the doctrine of equivalents. Graver Tank & Mfg. Co. v. Linde Air Products Co., 339 U.S. 605, 85 U.S.P.Q. 328 (1950). *See* § 2F[2][b][i].

long been settled that recourse may not be had to that doctrine to recapture claims which the patentee has surrendered by amendment.

"Assuming that the patentee would have been entitled to equivalents embracing the accused devices had he originally claimed a 'conductor means embedded in the table,' a very different issue is presented when the applicant in order to meet objections in the Patent Office, based on references to the prior art, adopted the phrase as a substitute for the broader one 'carried by the table.' Had claim 7 been allowed in its original form it would have read upon all the accused devices since in all the conductor means complementary to the coil spring are 'carried by the table:' By striking that phrase from the claim and substituting for it 'embedded in the table' the applicant restricted his claim to those combinations in which the conductor means, though carried on the table, is also embedded in it. By the amendment he recognized and emphasized the difference between the two phrases and proclaimed his abandonment of all that is embraced in that difference. . . . The difference which he thus disclaimed must be regarded as material, and since the amendment operates as a disclaimer of the difference it must be strictly construed against him. . . . As the question is one of construction of the claim it is immaterial whether the examiner is right or wrong in rejecting the claim as filed. . . . It follows that what the patentee, by a strict construction of the claim, has disclaimed—conductors which are carried by the table but not embedded in it—cannot now be regained by recourse to the doctrine of equivalents, which at most operates by liberal construction, to secure to the inventor the full benefits, not disclaimed, of the claims allowed."[159]

[ii] *Acts Giving Rise to Prosecution History Estoppel.* The most common acts giving rise to an estoppel are amendments and cancellations in response to an examiner's prior art rejection in which the applicant narrows the scope of the claimed subject matter to secure a patent.

Prosecution history estoppel may arise even though the claim was not amended—for example, when a related claim is cancelled or amended in a way that gives meaning to terms in the claim in question.[160]

Estoppel may arise without any claim amendment—as when the applicant argues for a narrow construction of the claims to distinguish the prior art.[161]

---

[159] 315 U.S. at 136-37.

[160] Builders Concrete, Inc. v. Bremerton Concrete Products Co., 757 F.2d 255, 225 U.S.P.Q. 240 (Fed. Cir. 1985); Keith v. Charles E. Hires Co., 116 F.2d 46, 47 U.S.P.Q. 402 (2d Cir. 1940).

[161] Hughes Aircraft Co. v. United States, 717 F.2d 1351, 219 U.S.P.Q. 473 (Fed. Cir. 1983); Coleco Industries, Inc. v. U.S. Int'l Trade Comm'n, 573 F.2d 1247, 1257, 197 U.S.P.Q. 472, 479-80 (CCPA 1978).

Earlier decisions refused to afford the force of an estoppel to mere arguments. *E.g.*, Catalin Corp. v. Catalazuli Mfg. Co., 79 F.2d 593, 594, 27 U.S.P.Q. 371, 373 (2d Cir. 1935).

Decisions hold there is no estoppel if an amendment clarified the claim's meaning and was not made to distinguish prior art.[162] The reason is that the applicant did not surrender anything or circumvent PTO examination of a broad claim's substance in relation to the prior art. The clarity exception is fertile ground for dispute and litigation. Confronted with an amendment and apparent estoppel, a patent owner retorts that the amendment was "merely for clarity." In *Moeller*,[163] the patent claimed an electrode system for measuring the concentration of certain cations (such as potassium) in the presence of other cations. It entailed interposing a membrane bearing cation specific components between the cations and the sensing device. The claim specified that there be "means including an electrode body for supporting the membrane." At the prosecution's end, an examiner's amendment added the phrase "an electrode '*disposed within* said body' " In the accused device, the electrode protruded somewhat and thus was not altogether within the electrode body. The court held that this amendment did not, under the circumstances and in the context of a motion for summary judgment of noninfringement, preclude application of the doctrine of equivalents.[164] There was no indication that applicant or examiner intended the amendment to make the claim not read on a device such as that accused of infringement. The amendment's stated purpose was to "more particularly point out the invention."[165]

"Estoppel may arise from amendments to overcome non-art rejections directed to the claim breadth, for example, lack of enabling support in the specification."[166]

Estoppel may arise from amendments or arguments in proceedings other than the patent's original prosecution, for example, a reissue or reexamination.[167]

---

[162] *E.g.*, Hubbell v. United States, 179 U.S. 77, 80 (1900) (suggesting in dictum that little weight should be given to amendments or changes made solely for purposes of clarity: "It is quite true that, where the differences between the claim as made and as allowed consist of mere changes of expression, having substantially the same meaning, such changes, made to meet the views of the examiners, ought not to be permitted to defeat a meritorious claimant.").

[163] Moeller v. Ionetics, Inc., 794 F.2d 653, 229 U.S.P.Q. 992 (Fed. Cir. 1986).

[164] The court noted that "In both devices, it is the membrane and not the body that separates the electrode tip from the solution to be tested." 794 F.2d at 660, 229 U.S.P.Q. at 997.

[165] *Compare* Mannesmann Demag Corp. v. Engineered Metal Products Co., Inc., 793 F.2d 1279, 1284-85, 230 U.S.P.Q. 45, 48-49 (Fed. Cir. 1986) ("In cases where a patentee's amendments were not required in response to an examiner's rejection or critical to the allowance of the claims, no estoppel has been found . . . . Similarly, estoppel is not necessarily created by an amendment designed only to remove a § 112 indefiniteness rejection.;" however, under the circumstances, the claim limitation in question was added in response to an art rejection, i.e. "to clearly recite the significant, novel and non-obvious features of the invention;" an estoppel applies because the accused device "falls squarely within the claim scope that [the patentee] relinquished to overcome the cited references").

[166] Ellipse Corp. v. Ford Motor Co., 452 F.2d 163, 168, 171 U.S.P.Q. 513 (7th Cir. 1971), *cert. denied*, 406 U.S. 948, 173 U.S.P.Q. 705 (1972).

Cf. Pennwalt Corp. v. Akzona, Inc., 740 F.2d 1573, 222 U.S.P.Q. 833 (Fed. Cir. 1984). *Compare* Paperless Accounting, Inc. v. Bay Area Rapid Transit Sys., 804 F.2d 659, 231 U.S.P.Q. 649 (1986), *cert. denied*, 480 U.S. 933 (1987), discussed at § 2D[4][b][ii].

[167] *E.g.*, Howes v. Medical Components, Inc., 814 F.2d 638, 643, 645, 2 U.S.P.Q.2d 1271, 1273, 1274-75 (Fed. Cir. 1987).

[iii]   *Effect of Prosecution History Estoppel.* Prosecution history estoppel restrains the doctrine of equivalents. It is not pertinent to literal infringement,[168] but the prosecution history is an important claim language interpretation tool.[169]

Prosecution history estoppel does not completely bar application of the doctrine of equivalents.[170] Federal Circuit decisions oscillate between a hardline approach, refusing to "speculate" whether an amendment in response to a prior art rejection was necessary to distinguish the prior art, and a flexible approach, emphasizing the amendment's nature and purpose and the prior art.

Hughes[171] is an early flexible approach decision. The examiner rejected the claims to a satellite, relying on a prior art patent on a self-guiding satellite. The applicant amended the claims to specify that there be means on the satellite for receiving and

---

Cf. Caterpillar Tractor Co. v. Berco, S.p.A., 714 F.2d 1110, 1116, 219 U.S.P.Q. 185, 188 (Fed. Cir. 1983) ("Though no authority is cited for the proposition that instructions to foreign counsel and a representation to foreign patent offices should be considered, and the varying legal and procedural requirements for obtaining patent protection in foreign countries might render consideration of certain types of representations inappropriate, there is ample such authority in decisions of other courts and when such matters comprise relevant evidence they must be considered.").

Compare Water Technologies Corp. v. Calco, Ltd., 850 F.2d 660, 667, 7 U.S.P.Q.2d 1097, 1102 (Fed. Cir. 1988) (the accused infringer failed to offer a reason "why arguments made by a different attorney prosecuting *later* patent applications for a different inventor should be used to limit an earlier-issued patent . . . .").

[168] *E.g.,* Fromson v. Advance Offset Plate, Inc., 720 F.2d 1565, 1571, 219 U.S.P.Q. 1137, 1141 (Fed. Cir. 1983) ("If there be literal infringement. . . the doctrine of [prosecution history ('file wrapper') estoppel] is irrelevant."). *Compare* Standard Oil Co. v. American Cyanamid Co., 774 F.2d 448, 227 U.S.P.Q. 293 (Fed. Cir. 1985) (the prosecution history limits the interpretation of claims so as to exclude any interpretation that may have been disclaimed or disavowed during prosecution to obtain claim allowance.)

See also Keith v. Charles E. Hires Co., 116 F.2d 46, 48, 47 U.S.P.Q. 402 (2d Cir. 1940) (Learned Hand):

> "The 'estoppel' is itself important only as a bar to any resort to the doctrine of equivalents. Without that doctrine every claim is indeed entitled to be interpreted in the light of the specifications as a whole, and not to be read merely with a dictionary. But often even with the most sympathetic interpretation the claim cannot be made to cover an infringement which in fact steals the very heart of the invention; no matter how auspiciously construed, the language forbids. It is then that the doctrine of equivalents intervenes to disregard the theory that the claim measures the monopoly and ignores the claim in order to protect the real invention. . . . The 'estoppel' of the file-wrapper puts an end to the court's power to do this; the applicant has abandoned his privilege to resort to an equivalent of the differentia, which all infringements must therefore embody. He may still insist that his claim shall be generously interpreted, but his monopoly stops where interpretation stops."

[169] *See* § 2F[1][b][iii].

[170] Bayer Aktiengesellschaft v. Duphar International Research B.V., 738 F.2d 1237, 222 U.S.P.Q. 649 (Fed. Cir. 1984); Tektronix, Inc. v. United States, 445 F.2d 323, 328, 170 U.S.P.Q. 100 (Ct. Cl. 1971).

[171] Hughes Aircraft Co. v. United States, 717 F.2d 1351, 219 U.S.P.Q. 473 (Fed. Cir. 1983). *See* § 2F[2][b][vi].

directly executing control signals. Because the amendment was for distinguishing self-guiding satellites, it did not estop the patentee from expanding the direct execution control signal means to cover an equivalent means, microprocessor controlled signal execution, that was not part of a self-guiding satellite.

> "Amendment of claims is a common practice in prosecution of patent applications. No reason or warrant exists for limiting application of the doctrine of equivalents to those comparatively few claims allowed exactly as originally filed and never amended. Amendments may be of different types and may serve different functions. Depending on the nature and purpose of an amendment, it may have a limiting effect within a spectrum ranging from great to small to zero. The effect may or may not be fatal to application of a range of equivalents broad enough to encompass a particular accused product. It is not fatal to application of the doctrine itself."[172]

Two Federal Circuit panel decisions take a hardline approach. In *Kinzenbaw*,[173] the court found estoppel. The applicant narrowed his claims by adding two limitations in response to an examiner's prior art rejection. The patent owner argued that only one of the limitations was necessary to render the claims patentable over the examiner's cited art and therefore the other limitation should be expanded by equivalents to encompass the alleged infringer's device. The court disagreed:

> "The doctrine of equivalents is designed to protect inventors from unscrupulous copyists . . . and unanticipated equivalents. . . . The present case, in which Kinze [the alleged infringer] utilized a characteristic that the inventor specifically eliminated from his claim, is a far cry from either of those situations. . . . Kinze adopted the very element that Pust had eliminated for the stated purpose of avoiding the examiner's rejection and obtaining the patent."[174]

In *Prodyne Enterprises*,[175] the court refused to engage in a "speculative inquiry" into whether the claim limitation added by the applicant was necessary to overcome the prior art relied upon by the examiner.

In *LaBounty Manufacturing*,[176] the court reaffirmed the flexible approach, holding that the International Trade Commission Administrative Law Judge (ALJ) erred in restricting the patentee to the literal claim language and denying the assertion of infringement under the doctrine of equivalents. In looking at the prosecution history only to the extent of determining that the claim limitations not literally present in the accused device were added by amendment in response to a rejection based on prior art, and in refusing to analyze the prior art in detail, the ALJ misinterpreted Federal Circuit precedent, including *Prodyne Enterprises*.

---

[172] 717 F.2d at 1363, 219 U.S.P.Q. at 481.

[173] Kinzenbaw v. Deere & Co., 741 F.2d 383, 389, 222 U.S.P.Q. 929 (Fed. Cir. 1984), *cert. denied*, 470 U.S. 1004 (1985).

[174] 741 F.2d at 389, 222 U.S.P.Q. at 174.

[175] Prodyne Enterprises, Inc. v. Julie Pomerantz, Inc., 743 F.2d 1581, 223 U.S.P.Q. 477 (Fed. Cir. 1984).

[176] LaBounty Manufacturing, Inc. v. U.S. Int'l Trade Comm'n, 867 F.2d 1572, 9 U.S.P.Q.2d 1995 (Fed. Cir. 1989).

"Our precedent does not preclude an analysis of the prior art pertinent to a limitation which was added to overcome a rejection based on that art.

". . . *Prodyne* does not stand for the broad proposition that, if an amendment adds a limitation which distinguishes a feature of the invention from a prior art reference, no equivalent of that feature can be asserted and, thus, no analysis of the prior art disclosure is necessary or appropriate. In *Prodyne*, the patentee argued that an added limitation was 'unnecessary.'. . . [The patentee] does not so argue here. [The patentee] accepts the limitation but objects to the denial of any equivalents thereof. It seeks consideration of the prior art to show that it is not attempting to resurrect coverage for prior art structures which provide the basis for the accused device. The prior art disclosures, per [the patentee,] are markedly different from both the patented invention and [the accused device]."[177]

The debate on estoppel effect reflects the law's classic tension between microscopic fairness and macroscopic certainty. The flexible approach avoids unfair restriction of the patentee's rights. If patent rights are arbitrarily limited, the patent system's basic incentive functions are diluted. But fairness on a case-by-case basis means sacrifice of predictability, which is part of the rationale of prosecution history estoppel, indeed of any estoppel doctrine.[178] Hence one can foresee periodic re-emergence of the hardline approach, in deed if not in word.[179]

Two case examples show the fine distinctions courts draw in determining estoppel effect. In *Sun Studs*,[180] the patent ('968) related to a method for sawing logs to obtain maximum salable wood products. The method included placing a log in a carrier, scanning a log to determine its dimensions, using a computer to generate the largest parallelogram that would fit within the determined dimensions, and repositioning the log to align the center axis of the largest parallelogram with an index line of the sawing equipment. Application claim 1 defined the invention in broad terms;[181] it was generic as to shape—"preselected shape"—but required that it be the largest that would fit within the measured dimensions of the logs. Application claim 2, which

---

[177] 867 F.2d at 1575, 9 U.S.P.Q.2d at 1998-99.

[178] The flexible approach to prosecution history makes it more difficult to predict infringement under the doctrine of equivalents because one must analyze the prior art and what the inventor actually surrendered by cancelling or amending a claim in response to a rejection.

[179] *E.g.,* Senmed, Inc. v. Richard-Allan Medical Industries, Inc., 888 F.2d 815, 12 U.S.P.Q.2d 1508 (Fed. Cir. 1989).

[180] Sun Studs, Inc. v. ATA Equipment Leasing, Inc., 872 F.2d 978, 10 U.S.P.Q.2d 1338 (Fed. Cir. 1989).

[181] "In a method or [sic: of] processing a log the steps of

[1] positioning the log in a reference position,

[2] scanning the log to determine certain of its dimensions with respect to said reference position,

[3] computing in a data processing equipment the center axis of the largest surface of a *preselected shape* that can be superimposed within the measured dimensions, and

[4] repositioning the log with the center axis parallel to an index line of a log processing equipment."

(Emphasis added.)

became patent claim 1,[182] was narrower as to shape, requiring a "parallelogram," not just a "preselected shape."

The examiner rejected all applicant's claims on the ground that the invention would have been obvious from one reference (Ottosson), either alone, or when combined with another reference (Graham).[183] The applicant responded by cancelling the broad claim 1 "to narrow the issues." In "Remarks" accompanying the amendment, the applicant emphasized the "repositioning" limitation, which was in both the cancelled and the remaining claim, as the primary distinction between the claimed invention and the prior art, particularly the Ottosson reference.[184]

---

[182] "A method of processing a log to obtain the optimum amount of wood products of a selected grade therefrom, comprising the steps of

[1] positioning the log with respect to a reference location,

[2] scanning the log to determine certain of its dimensions with respect to the reference location,

[3] plotting in a data processing equipment at least one planar profile of the dimensions of the log, said profile being taken in a plane passing through the ends of the log,

[4] computing in a data processing equipment at least the center axis of *the widest parallelogram* that can be superimposed within the plotted profile of the log, and

[5] repositioning the log with the center axis parallel to an index line of a log processing equipment." (Emphasis added.)

[183] The applicant's own patent specification described the Ottosson reference as follows:

"The Ottosson system . . . includes means for examining an incoming log with a photocell array to determine the smallest diameter of the log, and uses this information to automatically set the saw array for dividing the log. In other words, in the Ottosson system, each log is sawed in accordance with a programmed cutting schedule determined by the measured minimum diameter of the log. This tends to reduce the wastage that occurs as a result of log taper, and can partially compensate for irregularities in the logs surface that result in noticeable reduction in the log diameter. However, the Ottosson system does not include means for repositioning a log after scanning. Consequently, a crooked log of a given diameter is processed in the same fashion as a straight log of the same diameter, with significant wastage resulting. Furthermore, unnecessary wastage results due to the other factors such as elliptical diameter and irregular surface depressions and extensions."

[184] The "Remarks" stated:

"[I]n the Ottosson system a log is sawed in accordance with a programmed cutting schedule determined by the measured minimum diameter of the log and, in particular Ottosson does not disclose or suggest any means for repositioning the log after it has been conveyed through a scanning device to better align or orient the log relative to the index line of the log processor (e.g., the saw array). In contradistinction, in applicant's apparatus and method, the log is first seized by a charger means and carried past the scanner and thereafter, following processing of the information from the scanner determinative of the profile dimensions of the log, the data processor (computer) provides output signals which result in a repositioning of the log as it is delivered to a subsequent carriage means which conveys the log through the processing equipment. . . . In this manner, . . . not only are the coordinates of the largest surface of preselected form (e.g., a parallelogram) that can be super-imposed within the measured dimensions of the log profile determined by the computer, but, through repositioning of the log prior to its processing,

The accused log scanning systems generated the widest trapezoid and then repositioned according to the center axes of the shape and the saw equipment.[185] These systems were not within the claim's literal terms because a trapezoid is not a "parallelogram"—though it would have fallen within rejected claim 1 because a trapezoid is, literally, a "preselected shape." The jury found infringement under the doctrine of equivalents. The trial judge overturned the verdict, relying on prosecution history estoppel. In reinstating the jury verdict of infringement by equivalents, the Federal Circuit panel noted that a reasonable jury could have found that "the accused and claimed systems perform in substantially the same way to obtain substantially the same result . . . whether step 4 is based on a parallelogram or trapezoid." Prosecution history estoppel did not apply. The inventor's argument for patentability over the prior art (Ottosson) focused on the repositioning step, which was in both the broad, cancelled claim and the allowed claims and did not stress geometric shape.

Sun Studs illustrates the flexible approach's strengths and weaknesses. On the merits, a fair result may have been reached; the added limitation was unnecessary to distinguish the prior art, but that result required a complex, case-by-case inquiry, the necessity for which promotes uncertainty.

Environmental Instruments[186] was a similar geometric shape case with an opposite result. The patent in suit related to devices for measuring fluid flow, particularly wind speed and direction, through "hot film" anemometry.[187] The claim requires that a

---

the central axis of such a surface can then be oriented relative to the index axis of the saw array or veneer lathe of the log processor.

". . . At best, a combination of Graham with Ottosson would suggest to one skilled in the art only that the initial retention of the log by the gripping members 10 should be along the natural center axis of the log, and this would not imply or suggest the further step of repositioning the log after scanning so as to align, not the center axis of the log, but rather the center axis of the largest parallelogram that can be superimposed within the log dimensions. In the not atypical case of a log having a substantial crook, the variation between the log axis, and the center axis of the parallelogram would be quite significant.

"Method claim 2 recites the aforementioned distinguishing characteristics of the disclosed system, namely, the step of repositioning the log after scanning so as to align the center axis of the widest parallelogram which can be superimposed within the log profile parallel to an index line of the log processing equipment. This is a significantly novel step in applicant's method which is not present in the prior art and accordingly renders the claim patentable."

[185] The accused system used trapezoids in their models in order to take log taper into account.

[186] Environmental Instruments, Inc. v. Sutron Corp., 877 F.2d 1561, 11 U.S.P.Q.2d 1132 (Fed. Cir. 1989).

[187] The court gives the following description of the technology:

"[T]he commercial version of the '819 invention comprises a pair of 'sensing elements:' two ceramic tubes filmed with platinum, arrayed side-by-side with their major axes parallel. An insulator between the elements closes the space between them, and the overall cross-sectional configuration of the sensor or probe is defined in the '819 claim to be a 'figure eight.'

"In operation, the two elements are connected in series. A feed-back-controlled heating current is passed through the elements to heat them to an elevated operating tempera-

sensor with two conductors have the "overall shape" of a "figure eight in cross section" and that each conductor be "exposed to ventilation over at least a majority of its surface." The accused sensors had an overall oval or "racetrack" shape, thereby escaping the claim's literal scope. During prosecution, the following occurred:

1. The applicant's original broadest claim specified that there be "a thermo insulating means operatively disposed between said electrical conductors over a majority of the length of the conductors." These claims "clearly read" on the accused sensors.

2. The examiner rejected the claim in view of the Hayakawa reference, which taught "tandem-type hot-wire velocity meter probes" with two wire members disposed at the ends of the insulating support member. It showed wires mounted along the side ends of the insulating support members.

3. The applicant amended the claims to provide as to shape: "the major shape of the sensor being defined by the conductors and not by the bridging means."[188] The purpose of the amendment was to distinguish Hayakawa, in which the insulating member defined the shape, the wires being small appendages on the ends of the member.

4. The examiner again rejected the claim based on Hayakawa. (Arguably, the examiner was in error; at least at first blush, the added limitation did seem to distinguish Hayakawa, in which the major shape of the sensor was defined by

---

ture, which corresponds to a constant total series resistance across the two elements. Since the elements are at a higher temperature than the surrounding fluid (air), there is a transfer of energy from the elements to the fluid in the form of heat. The energy needed to maintain the elements at the chosen operating temperature is measured as the total difference in potential across the two elements. This difference in potential is a function of, and may be translated into, wind speed. Wind direction may also be determined, simultaneously, by measuring the potential difference across each individual element and comparing the two differences in potential. The sensing element facing the fluid stream, or leading element, is stream-cooled to a greater degree than the sensing element at the trailing edge of the device. Thus, the difference in potential across the leading element will be different from the difference in potential across the trailing element. These two differences may be compared and the resulting value is indicative of direction flow, i.e., wind direction. It appears that a distinct advantage of the sensor configuration claimed in the '819 patent is its ability to measure wind direction more satisfactorily than previously known sensors. The claimed sensors have no moving parts and have their main use as cross-wind sensors in battle tank fire control systems."

[188] Subpart (c) of the claim, as once amended, read as follows:

"(c) a thermo insulating *bridging* means operatively disposed between, and *closing the gap between* [connecting] said electrical conductors over [a majority of] the length of the conductors, *thereby preventing connected flow around one conductor independent of the other conductor, the major shape of the sensor being defined by the conductors and not by the bridging means, with each conductor exposed to ventilation over at least a majority of its surface, and with the conductor pair cross section itself used to define the fluid dynamic cross section which is exposed to the fluid stream where the resulting local stagnation region caused by impinging flow at its point of separation against an electric conductor cross section, each conductor exhibiting a change in electrical resistivity as a function of temperature."*

the bridging means, not the conductors.) The examiner added a Section 112 indefiniteness rejection on the ground that "major shape" lacked an antecedent basis and was unclear.

5. The applicant amended the claims a second time to provide as to shape: "the overall shape of the sensor being figure eight in cross section." In accompanying remarks, the applicant argued that the figure eight shaped structure "is not taught or suggested by Hayakawa."

In affirming the district court's conclusion as to estoppel, the Federal Circuit noted:

> "[T]he reasons for the amendment were to overcome: (1) the § 102 rejection; (2) the § 103 rejection, and (3) the § 112 rejection. The first two reasons, the amendment itself, and the examiner's allowance of the claim, convince us that the figure eight limitations fall on the highly limiting end of the 'spectrum' of 'limiting effect.' See Hughes Aircraft Co. v. United States . . . . That a second, concurrent amendment was made, and that [the claim limitation added to distinguish the reference] made the claim more definite, do not alter our conclusion. On these facts, we think the district judge was right to limit [the patentee] to a reading of 'figure eight' that does not cover the accused sensor having the 'racetrack' or oval configuration."[189]

Environmental Instruments can reasonably be distinguished from *Sun Studs*. In each case, the applicant amended the claims by limiting them to a greater extent than was necessary to distinguish the prior art and the effect of the amendment was to eliminate literal coverage of the accused device. In *Environmental Instruments*, unlike *Sun Studs*, the examiner was persistent, entering two rejections, and the applicant stressed the importance of the added limitation in remarks accompanying the amendment. The cases teach that prosecution history estoppel is a tool judges use to achieve what they perceive to be a fair result, fairness being determined by a large set of factors and equities.

[3] Proof of Infringing Activity

[a] **Burden of Proof.** The patent owner must prove infringement by a preponderance of the evidence.[190] The burden of producing some evidence on a specific issue may be on the accused infringer. For example, if the accused infringer is a dealer reselling a product, he bears the burden of showing that the product was originally made or sold with the patent owner's authority.[191]

In *Andrew Corp.*,[192] the trial judge ruled against the patent owner because he could not understand the technical subject matter sufficiently to resolve the conflicting

---

[189] 877 F.2d at 1566, 11 U.S.P.Q.2d at 1136.

[190] Bene v. Jeantet, 129 U.S. 683 (1889); Wilson Sporting Goods Co. v. David Geoffrey & Associates, 904 F.2d 677, 685, 14 U.S.P.Q.2d 1942, 1949 (Fed. Cir. 1990), *cert. denied*, 111 S. Ct. 537 (1990) ("The patent owner has always borne the burden of proving infringement. . . . ").

[191] Sherman, Clay & Co. v. Searchlight Horn Co., 225 F. 497, 500 (9th Cir. 1915) ("the burden is upon the dealer to show that he or it is dealing with an article under license from the patentee, or in articles from which the patent monopoly has been released or removed.").

[192] Andrew Corp. v. Gabriel Electronics, Inc., 847 F.2d 819, 6 U.S.P.Q.2d 2010 (Fed. Cir. 1988), *cert. denied*, 488 U.S. 927 (1988).

testimony of the parties' experts on infringement. The Federal Circuit held that this use of the burden of proof was erroneous.

> "A true equipoise of evidence may indeed defeat the party with the burden of proof, . . . but there is no authority for holding evidence to be in equipoise for the sole reason that the court could not decide between conflicting experts. . . . Given the complexity of modern technology, it may well happen that qualified experts will appear on both sides, that their testimony will conflict, and that the testimony or the technology or both of them may be difficult to understand. However, to decline to decide the issue when conflicting evidence appears to be counterbalancing solely because the subject matter is technically complex, will defeat the party with the burden of proof without a fair hearing."[193]

[b]   **Intent.** An unauthorized act invading the patentee's exclusive rights is infringement even if committed without knowledge of the patent.[194] Knowledge and intent are relevant to determining liability for contributory infringement[195] and may affect the measure of damages.[196]

[c]   **Agency—Corporate Officers and Employees.** Under agency law principles, patent infringement liability extends to corporations and other organizations whose agents or employees commit acts of infringement.[197]

A corporate officer or director may be liable with his corporation for the corporation's infringing acts on either of two theories: active inducement of infringement and alter ego.[198]

[4]   Defenses

An accused infringer in a patent suit may rely on a number of defenses, including invalidity of the patent, inequitable conduct, misuse, and laches and estoppel.

[a]   **Invalidity—Challenges by Licensees.** A defense to a patent infringement charge is that the patent claims are invalid for failure to meet patentability standards.[199]

---

[193] 847 F.2d at 824, 6 U.S.P.Q.2d at 2015.

[194] Thurber Corp. v. Fairchild Motor Corp., 269 F.2d 841, 845, 849, 122 U.S.P.Q. 305, 311 (5th Cir. 1959).

[195] See § 2E[2][c].

[196] See § 2F[5][c].

[197] See, e.g., Westinghouse Elec. & Mfg. Co. v. Independent Wireless Tel. Co., 300 F. 748 (S.D. N.Y. 1924). In *Westinghouse*, the court granted an injunction against infringement even though the defendant company had purportedly forbidden its employees to install a circuit in a fashion that would infringe the patent. The evidence indicated that the employees were installing such circuits anyway. *Compare* Duplex Envelope Co. v. Denominational Envelope Co., 80 F.2d 179, 27 U.S.P.Q. 325 (4th Cir. 1935).

[198] See Manville Sales Corp. v. Paramount Systems, Inc., 917 F.2d 544, 16 U.S.P.Q.2d 1587 (Fed. Cir. 1990), discussed at § 2E[2][c][iv].

[199] E.g., Constant v. Advanced Micro-Devices, Inc., 848 F.2d 1560, 1564, 7 U.S.P.Q.2d 1057, 1058-59 (Fed. 1988), *cert. denied*, 488 U.S. 892 (1988) (the statutory provision that permits the federal courts to adjudicate a patent's validity, 35 U.S.C. Section 282, is not contrary to the Patent Clause of the Constitution, which states that Congress has the power to pro-

A patent claim may be invalid because of lack of novelty,[200] occurrence of a statutory bar,[201] obviousness,[202] or lack of adequate disclosure.[203]

[i] *Presumption of Validity.* A patent is presumed valid.[204] A validity challenger bears a clear and convincing evidence persuasion burden on disputed fact issues.[205] He also bears the initial evidence production burden on fact issues but may shift that burden to the patent owner by establishing a *prima facie* case of unpatentability.[206]

The presumption of validity remains in effect regardless of what evidence was before the examiner during prosecution of the application that became the patent.[207] If the challenger relies on more pertinent prior art references than those considered by the examiner, the challenger's burden of persuasion is more easily carried.[208] If the challenger relies on the same references as the examiner, the burden is less easily carried.[209]

The presumption of validity applies independently to each claim of a patent.[210]

[ii] *Standing to Challenge Validity—Licensees.* A person may challenge patent validity even though he is a licensee. In *Lear*,[211] a California state court held that

---

mote the useful arts by "securing" to inventors the exclusive rights to their discoveries; "securing" does not require that patents issued by the PTO be conclusively valid and unchallengeable; "Since the adoption of the first Patent Act in 1790, Congress has permitted judicial review of the validity of patents. The courts, the interpreters of the meaning of the Constitution, have consistently construed the Patent and Copyright Clause to permit judicial review of patents. . . . Public policy requires that only inventions which fully meet the statutory standards are entitled to patents. This policy is furthered when the validity of a patent, which was originally obtained in *ex parte* proceedings in the PTO, can be challenged in court. . . . Nowhere does the Constitution require that the determination of patent validity be vested solely in the PTO (or even that there be a PTO).").

200 *See* § 2C[3].

201 *See* § 2C[5][b][ii].

202 *See* § 2C[4].

203 *See* § § 2D[3][a], [b], and [c].

204 35 U.S.C. § 282.

205 Trans-World Mfg. Corp. v. Al Nyman & Sons, Inc., 750 F.2d 1552, 1560, 224 U.S.P.Q. 259, 263 (Fed. Cir. 1984); Railroad Dynamics, Inc. v. A. Stucki Co., 727 F.2d 1506, 1517, 220 U.S.P.Q. 929, 939 (Fed. Cir. 1984), *cert. denied*, 469 U.S. 871, 224 U.S.P.Q. 520 (1984).

206 For example, if a challenger makes a *prima facie* case of public use, the production burden on experimental use shifts to the patent owner. Hycor Corp. v. Schlueter Co., 740 F.2d 1529, 222 U.S.P.Q. 553 (Fed. Cir. 1984); TP Laboratories, Inc. v. Professional Positioners, Inc., 724 F.2d 965, 220 U.S.P.Q. 577 (Fed. Cir. 1984), *cert. denied*, 469 U.S. 826, 224 U.S.P.Q. 616 (1984). *See* § 2C[5][b][ii].

207 Stratoflex, Inc. v. Aeroquip Corp., 713 F.2d 1530, 1534, 218 U.S.P.Q. 871, 875-76 (Fed. Cir. 1983).

208 Aktiebolaget Karlstads Mekaniska Werkstad v. U.S. Int'l Trade Comm'n, 705 F.2d 1565, 217 U.S.P.Q. 865 (Fed. Cir. 1983).

209 Hughes Aircraft Co. v. United States, 717 F.2d 1351, 219 U.S.P.Q. 473 (Fed. Cir. 1983).

210 35 U.S.C. § 282; Preemption Devices, Inc. v. Minnesota Mining & Mfg. Co., 732 F.2d 903, 221 U.S.P.Q. 841 (Fed. Cir. 1984).

211 Lear, Inc. v. Adkins, 395 U.S. 653, 162 U.S.P.Q. 1 (1969), discussed at § 1D[3][b][ii].

a licensee could not, in a suit for enforcement of a patent license contract, contest the patent's validity. The United States Supreme Court reversed, overruling the licensee estoppel doctrine on policy grounds. Federal policy favoring the removal of invalid patents overrides contract law policy.

> "[T]he licensor's equities are far from compelling. A patent, in the last analysis, simply represents the legal conclusion reached by the Patent Office. Moreover, the legal conclusion is predicated on factors as to which reasonable men can differ widely. Yet the Patent Office is often obligated to reach its decision in an ex *parte* proceeding, without the aid of the arguments which could be advanced by parties interested in proving patent invalidity.
>
> . . .
>
> ". . . Licensees may often be the only individuals with enough economic incentive to challenge the patentability of an inventor's discovery. If they are muzzled the public may continually be required to pay tribute to would-be monopolists without need or justification." [212]

If a licensee successfully challenges validity, he may escape liability for unpaid royalties that have accrued since he first raised the challenge. [213]

---

[212] 395 U.S. at 670.

[213] *See, e.g.,* Rite-Nail Packaging Corp. v. Berryfast, Inc., 706 F.2d 933, 219 U.S.P.Q. 104 (9th Cir. 1983). A licensee must pay unpaid royalties that have accrued prior to the date the licensee challenges the validity of the patent.

Royalties already paid may not be recovered unless the licensee was defrauded into entering into the license. Transitron Electronic Corp. v. Hughes Aircraft Co., 649 F.2d 871, 210 U.S.P.Q. 161 (1st Cir. 1981).

> *Compare* Hemstreet v. Spiegel, Inc., 851 F.2d 348, 7 U.S.P.Q.2d 1502 (Fed. Cir. 1988). In *Hemstreet,* the court held a settlement order signed by the parties and the court, which provides for the payment of license royalties "notwithstanding that [the patent] may be held invalid and/or unenforceable in any other proceeding at a later date," is binding even though the patent in question is later found unenforceable because of inequitable conduct in its procurement and regardless of whether the order "adjudicated the validity and infringement" of the patent: "The law strongly favors settlement of litigation, and there is a compelling public interest and policy in upholding and enforcing settlement agreements voluntarily entered into." *Lear v. Adkins* "did not involve a settlement of litigation, but only the right of a patent licensee to challenge the validity of the licensed patent. The enforcement of settlement of litigation involves another public policy totally absent in *Lear*: the encouragement of settlement of litigation and the need to enforce such settlements in order to encourage the parties to enter into them."

See also RCA Corp v. Data General Corp., 887 F.2d 1056, 1064, 12 U.S.P.Q.2d 1449 (Fed. Cir. 1989) ("*Lear* simply does not address" the issue of entitlement to breach of contract damages where a licensee does not pay royalties; "*Lear abrogated* the doctrine of 'licensee estoppel' principles developed under state law, and also precluded the award of royalties to the licensor under the facts of *that case* from the date the patent issued if the patent were later held invalid. *Lear* does not in fact discuss a licensor's right to royalties where a license agreement was entered *after* a patent issued . . . Nor does it deal with a licensor's right to terminate or rescind a license agreement, or dictate what *must* be held a breach of contract, or what damages *must* be awarded for a breach, or under what circumstances, if any, a licensee can recover royalties paid. Those questions continue to be matters dependent on particular fact

Lear reflects judicial skepticism of PTO examination and the patent validity presumption. Subsequent lower court decisions decline to extend *Lear* beyond licensee estoppel. For example, in *Cordis I*,[214] the Federal Circuit held that *Lear* does not authorize a court to permit a licensee to deposit royalties due under a license into an escrow account during a lawsuit challenging a patent's validity. It also held that *Lear* does not authorize a preliminary injunction barring the licensor from cancelling a license for nonpayment of royalties in breach of the license. In *Cordis II*,[215] it held that the district court did not err in preliminarily enjoining the patentee from terminating a license agreement covering pacemaker endocardial leads. The licensee paid royalties on one form of lead ("tined") but not on another form ("finned"). After the patentee threatened to terminate the license unless the licensee paid royalties on the finned lead devices, the licensee filed a declaratory judgment suit. The district court found (1) the harm to the licensee if relief were not granted outweighed the injury to the patentee if it were, and (2) the licensee showed sufficient likelihood of success on the issues that finned lead devices do not infringe and that the patentee was guilty of laches or estoppel.

In *Diamond Scientific*,[216] the Federal Circuit applied assignor estoppel to bar an inventor and his new company from challenging the validity of a patent on his own invention, which he had assigned to the plaintiff, his previous employer.

[iii]   *Effect of Judgment.* A patent invalidity judgment extends only to the claims that were contested by an infringement charge or a declaratory judgment counterclaim.[217]

An *invalidity* judgment binds the patent owner in suits against other accused infringers unless "he did not have 'a fair opportunity procedurally, substantively, and evidentially to pursue his claim the first time.'"[218] A final judgment of invalidity is usually the equivalent of cancellation of the claim.

---

situations, contract provisions and state contract law, albeit they must be resolved in harmony with general principles discernible from *Lear*.").

[214] Cordis Corp. v. Medtronic, Inc., 780 F.2d 991, 228 U.S.P.Q. 189 (Fed. Cir. 1985), *cert. denied*, 476 U.S. 1115 (1986).

[215] Cordis Corp. v. Medtronic, Inc., 835 F.2d 859, 5 U.S.P.Q.2d 1118 (Fed. Cir. 1987).

[216] Diamond Scientific Co. v. Ambico, Inc., 848 F.2d 1220, 6 U.S.P.Q.2d 2028 (Fed. Cir. 1988), *cert. dismissed*, 487 U.S. 1265 (1988). *See also* Shamrock Technologies, Inc. v. Medical Sterilization, Inc., 903 F.2d 789, 14 U.S.P.Q.2d 1728 (Fed. Cir. 1990) (assignor estoppel precludes the accused infringers' invalidity and inequitable conduct defenses).

[217] Jervis B. Webb Co. v. Southern Sys., Inc., 742 F.2d 1388, 222 U.S.P.Q. 943 (Fed. Cir. 1984); Stearns v. Beckman Instruments, Inc., 737 F.2d 1565, 222 U.S.P.Q. 457 (Fed. Cir. 1984).

A finding of inequitable conduct renders all the patent's claims unenforceable. *See* § 2D[2][f].

[218] Blonder-Tongue Laboratories, Inc. v. University of Illinois Foundation, 402 U.S. 313, 332, 169 U.S.P.Q. 513 (1971). *See also* Dana Corp. v. NOK, Inc., 882 F.2d 505, 508, 11 U.S.P.Q.2d 1883, 1885 (Fed. Cir. 1989) (an appellate holding that a patent is invalid in a suit against one infringer collaterally estops the patent owner from asserting that the patent is valid in litigation against another infringer, even when the invalidity holding in the former suit occurs after the patent has been held valid and an appeal taken in the latter suit; a remand for a determination of whether the patentee was deprived of a full and fair opportunity to litigate the validity of its patent is unnecessary; even if the records in the prior and instant

A *validity* judgment does not bind accused infringers not in privity with the first accused infringer,[219] but the results of the first suit will carry some weight.[220]

[b] **Inequitable Conduct—Fraud.** Inequitable conduct or fraud during a patent's prosecution may render the patent unenforceable.[221]

[c] **Misuse.** If a patent owner commits misuse by improperly exploiting his patent,[222] the courts withhold any remedy for infringement or for breach of a license agreement.[223] If the patent owner abandons the improper practice and purges its harmful consequences, the courts restore his rights.[224] An accused infringer may assert the misuse defense even though he is not harmed by the improper practice.[225] The misuse defense "is an extension of the equitable doctrine 'of unclean hands' to the patent field,"[226] and deters improper "extension" of a patent's exclusivity. Critics

---

cases "differ materially, this alone will not defeat the application of collateral estoppel.;" "The party opposing a plea of estoppel must establish that it did not have a full and fair opportunity to litigate; it must demonstrate that 'without fault of his own the patentee was deprived of crucial evidence or witnesses in the first litigation.' . . . The most [the patentee] has asserted here is that it had evidence to rebut or counter the evidence on which invalidity was based but that this evidence was not presented by [the patentee] in the [prior] litigation. There is no indication that such evidence was then not in existence or was otherwise not available to [the patentee] through no fault of its own.").

An International Trade Commission invalidity decision may not have the same preclusive effect in later court suits. *See* Tandon Corp. v. U.S. Int'l Trade Comm'n, 831 F.2d 1017, 1019, 4 U.S.P.Q.2d 1283, 1285 (Fed. Cir. 1987) ("[T]he Commission's primary responsibility is to administer the trade laws, not the patent laws: [I]n patent-based cases, the Commission considers, for its own purposes under section 337, the status of imports with respect to the claims of U.S. patents. The Commission's findings neither purport to be, nor can they be, regarded as binding interpretations of the U.S. patent laws in particular factual contexts. Therefore, it seems clear that any disposition of a Commission action by a Federal Court should not have a res judicata or collateral estoppel effect in cases before such courts.' S.Rep. No. 1298, 93d Cong., 2d Sess. 196 . . ."). *See* § 2E[2][b][ii].

[219] *E.g.,* Allen Archery, Inc. v. Browning Manufacturing Co., 819 F.2d 1087, 1091, 2 U.S.P.Q.2d 1490, 1492-93 (Fed. Cir. 1987) ("The *Blonder-Tongue* rule . . . 'is of necessity a one-way street,' . . . and does not bar someone charged with infringement from challenging the validity of patent claims that were upheld in a prior infringement suit to which it was not a party."; as to the patentee's argument that a prior ruling of validity should be given "great weight," "[t]he statutory presumption of patent validity . . . is not augmented by an earlier adjudication of patent "validity." ").

[220] *E.g.,* Gillette Co. v. S.C. Johnson & Son, Inc., 919 F.2d 720, 723, 16 U.S.P.Q.2d 1923, 1926 (Fed. Cir. 1990) ("The fact that the validity of [the patent] claims [in suit] has previously been upheld in an earlier litigation is. . . to be given weight, though not *stare decisis* effect.").

[221] *See* § 2D[2][f].

[222] *See generally* D. Chisum, Patents § 19.04.

[223] B.B. Chem. Co. v. Ellis, 314 U.S. 495, 52 U.S.P.Q. 33 (1942); Morton Salt Co. v. G.S. Suppiger Co., 314 U.S. 488, 52 U.S.P.Q. 30 (1942).

[224] *E.g.,* Preformed Line Prod. Co. v. Fanner Mfg. Co., 328 F.2d 265, 278, 140 U.S.P.Q. 500 (6th Cir. 1964), *cert. denied,* 379 U.S. 846, 143 U.S.P.Q. 464 (1964).

[225] Morton Salt Co. v. G.S. Suppiger Co., 314 U.S. 488, 52 U.S.P.Q. 30 (1942).

[226] United States Gypsum v. National Gypsum, 352 U.S. 457, 465, 112 U.S.P.Q. 340 (1957).

question the misuse doctrine's soundness insofar as it prescribes practices that do not violate the antitrust laws.[227] Section 271(d), added by the 1952 Patent Act, limits misuse's constraining effect on the contributory infringement remedy.[228] A 1988 amendment to Section 271(d) further limited misuse.[229] Examples of misuse include price fixing[230] and patent license provisions tying the right to use a patented invention to purchase of unpatented supplies.[231]

A patent owner does not commit misuse by asserting exclusive control over an unpatented nonstaple component of the invention.[232]

[d] **Experimental or Personal Use.** Unauthorized making and using a patented process or product is not infringement if done solely for research or experimentation.[233] The research exception does not apply if the infringer conducts experiments to adapt the patented invention to his business.[234]

In *Roche*,[235] the patent covered a pharmaceutical drug. Near the end of the patent's term, the accused infringer obtained the drug outside the United States and used it in a limited testing program to obtain regulatory approval to market a generic version of the patented drug after the patent expired. The court held that the testing was an infringement not excused by the experimental purpose exception.[236]

A 1984 amendment partially abrogates *Roche* by providing that it is not infringement to make, use or sell a patented invention solely for uses reasonably related to

---

[227] *E.g.,* USM Corp. v. SPS Technologies, Inc., 694 F.2d 505, 216 U.S.P.Q. 959 (7th Cir. 1982).

[228] *See* 35 U.S.C. § 271(d). *See also* § 2E[2][c][ii].

[229] The 1988 Act provides that a patent owner is not guilty of misuse by reason of having:

"(4) refused to license or use any rights to the patent; or

"(5) conditioned the license of any rights to the patent or the sale of the patented product on the acquisition of a license to rights in another patent or purchase of a separate product, unless, in view of the circumstances, the patent owner has market power in the relevant market for the patent or patented product on which the license or sale is conditioned." 35 U.S.C. § 271(d).

[230] *E.g.,* United States Gypsum v. National Gypsum, 352 U.S. 457, 112 U.S.P.Q. 340 (1957).

[231] *E.g.,* Senza-Gel Corp. v. Seiffhart, 803 F.2d 661, 231 U.S.P.Q. 363 (Fed. Cir. 1986). In *Senza-Gel*, the court found misuse when (1) the patent owner indicated that it never licensed a process patent without also leasing a machine for carrying out the patented process, (2) a witness testified that his request to license the process without the machine was refused, and (3) the machine as leased was suitable for substantial non-infringing use and therefore a staple article of commerce.

[232] 35 U.S.C. § 271(d); Dawson Chem. Co. v. Rohm & Haas Co., 448 U.S. 176, 206 U.S.P.Q. 385 (1980). This allows the patent owner to suppress contributory infringement. *See* § 2E[2][c][ii].

[233] Chesterfield v. United States, 159 F. Supp. 371, 116 U.S.P.Q. 445 (Ct. Cl. 1958). *See generally* D. Chisum, Patents § 16.03[1].

[234] Roche Products, Inc. v. Bolar Pharmaceutical Co., 733 F.2d 858, 221 U.S.P.Q. 937 (Fed. Cir. 1984), *cert. denied,* 469 U.S. 856, 225 U.S.P.Q. 792 (1984); Pitcairn v. United States, 547 F.2d 1106, 192 U.S.P.Q. 612 (Ct. Cl. 1976), *cert. denied,* 434 U.S. 1051, 196 U.S.P.Q. 864 (1978).

[235] Roche Prod. Inc. v. Bolar Pharmaceutical Co., 733 F.2d 858, 221 U.S.P.Q. 937 (Fed. Cir. 1984), *cert. denied,* 469 U.S. 856, 225 U.S.P.Q. 792 (1984).

[236] The court also refused to imply a limitation from federal drug regulation policies.

the development and submission of information under a Federal law that regulates the manufacture, use or sale of drugs.[237] In *Eli Lilly*,[238] the Supreme Court held this exemption applies to medical devices as well as drugs.

[e] **Notice—Patent Marking.** A patent owner may place a mark consisting of the word "patented" or "pat." and the patent's number on patented products he or a licensee sells.[239] If the patent owner or his licensee fail to mark products, the patent owner may not recover damages for infringements that occur before giving the infringer notice.[240] This damage limitation is the only consequence of failure to mark.

If the patent is for a machine or a process, there is no duty to mark products made by the machine or process.[241]

Failure to mark does not limit the reasonable compensation that a patent owner may recover for United States government use.[242]

False and counterfeit patent markings are prohibited.[243]

[f] **Delay in Filing Suit: Laches and Estoppel.** There is no statute of limitations on patent infringement suits, but a patent owner may not recover damages for infringing acts committed more than six years before filing suit.[244]

Laches and estoppel may limit or bar relief against patent infringement.[245]

Laches applies if a patent owner unreasonably delays filing suit after he knows or should reasonably know of the infringement and the delay prejudices the infringer.[246]

---

[237] 35 U.S.C. § 271(e)(1). This amendment was part of the Drug Price Competition and Patent Term Restoration Act of 1984.

[238] Eli Lilly and Co. v. Medtronic, Inc., 110 S. Ct. 2683, 15 U.S.P.Q.2d 1121 (1990).

[239] 35 U.S.C. § 287. If a patent owner licenses others to make and sell the product, he must take reasonable steps to assure that the licensees mark the products. Butterfield v. Oculus Contact Lens Co., 332 F. Supp. 750, 171 U.S.P.Q. 527 (N.D. Ill. 1971).

[240] The patent owner must give the infringer actual notice. It is not sufficient that the infringer has knowledge of the patent from other sources. Lemelson v. Fisher Price Corp., 545 F. Supp. 973, 218 U.S.P.Q. 504 (S.D. N.Y. 1982).

Filing suit is notice. 35 U.S.C. § 287.

[241] Wine Railway Appliance Co. v. Enterprise Railway Equip. Co., 297 U.S. 387 (1936); Bandag, Inc. v. Gerrard Tire Co., 704 F.2d 1578, 1581, 217 U.S.P.Q. 977, 979 (Fed. Cir. 1983).

[242] Motorola, Inc. v. United States, 729 F.2d 765, 221 U.S.P.Q. 297 (Fed. Cir. 1984).

[243] 35 U.S.C. § 292. There is a possible fine of up to $500 for each offense.

[244] 35 U.S.C. § 286.

See Standard Oil Co. v. Nippon Shokubai Kagaku Kogyo Co., Ltd., 754 F.2d 345, 224 U.S.P.Q. 863 (Fed. Cir. 1985) (Section 286's six-year damage limitation for an alleged contributory infringement by sale of a catalyst useful in carrying out a patented process begins on the date the catalyst was sold, not the later date when the purchaser used the catalyst to practice the process.).

[245] *See generally* D. Chisum, Patents § 19.05.

[246] *E.g.*, Jamesbury Corp. v. Litton Industrial Products, Inc., 839 F.2d 1544, 5 U.S.P.Q.2d 1779 (Fed. Cir. 1988), *cert. denied*, 488 U.S. 828 (1988).

Compare Sun Studs, Inc. v. ATA Equipment Leasing, Inc., 872 F.2d 978, 10 U.S.P.Q.2d 1338 (Fed. Cir. 1989) (a jury verdict of laches cannot stand where there is no substantial evidence of prejudice to the infringer from the patentee's delay in filing suit).

If the delay is more than six years, courts presume unreasonableness and prejudice.[247] The patent owner may show an excuse for the delay, for example, pursuit of other litigation on the patent after giving the infringer notice of intent to sue.[248] Laches bars damages for infringing acts before filing suit but not an injunction or damages for post-filing acts.[249] Laches does not apply if the infringer was guilty of "egregious conduct," for example, willful, secret infringement or misrepresentations.[250]

Estoppel applies if a patent owner represents to an infringer, expressly or implicitly, that he will not enforce his patent against the infringer's business and the infringer relies on that representation.[251] A patent owner's silence does not create an estoppel,[252] but an estoppel may arise if (1) the patent owner threatens suit and then unreasonably delays filing suit, and (2) the infringer, relying on the owner's silence and inaction, continues and expands his business.[253]

[g] **Implied License—First Sale.** License is a defense to a patent infringement charge[254] because the definition of infringement includes absence of the patent owner's authority.

A license may be implied as well as express.[255] For example, if a process patent owner sells a machine that has no practical use except in carrying out the process, purchaser gains an implied license to use the process.[256] If the machine has other uses, the purchaser gains no implied license.[257] In *Met-Coil*,[258] the court identified

---

247 Leinoff v. Louis Milona & Sons, Inc., 726 F.2d 734, 220 U.S.P.Q. 845 (Fed. Cir. 1984).

248 *E.g.*, Meyers v. Brooks Shoe Inc., 912 F.2d 1459, 16 U.S.P.Q.2d 1055 (Fed. Cir. 1990); Jamesbury Corp. v. Litton Industrial Products, Inc., 839 F.2d 1544, 5 U.S.P.Q.2d 1779 (Fed. Cir. 1988), *cert. denied*, 488 U.S. 828 (1988); Hottel Corp. v. Seaman Corp., 833 F.2d 1570, 4 U.S.P.Q.2d 1939 (Fed. Cir. 1987) (because the patent owner failed to provide adequate notice of the patents and the nature of the other proceeding involving them, the "other litigation" exception did not apply).

249 *E.g.*, Olympia Werke Aktiengesellschaft v. General Elec. Co., 712 F.2d 74, 219 U.S.P.Q. 107 (4th Cir. 1983).

250 *E.g.*, Bott v. Four Star Corp., 807 F.2d 1567, 1 U.S.P.Q.2d 1210 (Fed. Cir. 1986). *Cf.* Fromson v. Western Litho Plate & Supply Co., 853 F.2d 1568, 7 U.S.P.Q.2d 1606 (Fed. Cir. 1988).

251 Jensen v. Western Irrigation & Mfg., Inc., 650 F.2d 165, 207 U.S.P.Q. 817 (9th Cir. 1980).

252 *E.g.*, Hottel Corp. v. Seaman Corp., 833 F.2d 1570, 4 U.S.P.Q.2d 1939 (Fed. Cir. 1987).

253 *Cf.* MCV, Inc. v. King-Seeley Thermos Co., 870 F.2d 1568, 10 U.S.P.Q.2d 1287 (Fed. Cir. 1989).

254 *E.g.*, Lisle Corp. v. Edwards, 777 F.2d 693, 227 U.S.P.Q. 894 (Fed. Cir. 1985).

255 Implied license is closely related to the first sale doctrine. *See* § 2E[3].

256 *E.g.*, Devices for Medicine, Inc. v. Boehl, 822 F.2d 1062, 1068, 3 U.S.P.Q.2d 1288, 1293-94 (Fed. Cir. 1987) (the law "implies a license to practice [the patentee's] claimed method [to the use of a product] to anyone who purchases one of [the patentee's] claimed [products].").

257 *E.g.*, Bandag, Inc. v. Al Bolser's Tire Stores, Inc., 750 F.2d 903, 223 U.S.P.Q. 982 (Fed. Cir. 1984).

258 Met-Coil Systems Corp. v. Korners Unlimited, Inc., 803 F.2d 684, 231 U.S.P.Q. 474 (Fed. Cir. 1986).

See also King Instrument Corp. v. Otari Corp., 814 F.2d 1560, 2 U.S.P.Q.2d 1201 (Fed. Cir. 1987) (an infringer's payment of a judgment for damages for sales of infringing devices provides full compensation to the patent owner; after such payment, the infringer receives an implied license as to those sales for the useful life of the devices and may provide to its customers spare parts needed for repairs of those devices).

"two requirements for the grant of an implied license by virtue of a sale of nonpatented equipment used to practice a patented invention: First, the equipment involved must have no noninfringing uses. . . . Second, the circumstances of the sale must 'plainly indicate that the grant of a license should be inferred.' " The patentee sold roll-forming machines its customers used to shape flanges on metal heating ducts. The patentee also sold specially shaped corner pieces to fit on the shaped flanges. The patentee sued the defendant, who sold corner pieces to plaintiff's customers, for contributory infringement, arguing that the corner pieces had no use other than carrying out its patented duct connection process. The court held that sale of the machines conferred on the buyer an implied license to the patented process because they had no other use. The patentee's written notices to customers warning against purchase of corner pieces from unlicensed sources were to no avail because they were *after* the sale of the machine: "The subsequent notices are not a part of the circumstances at the time of the sale, when the implied license would have arisen." Because the defendant sold corner pieces only to those with an implied license, it could not be a contributory infringer.[259]

[5] Remedies

A court may grant the following remedies for patent infringement: injunctions, monetary damages, interest, and attorney fees.[260]

[a] **Injunctions.** A court may grant an injunction to prevent patent infringement "in accordance with the principles of equity . . . on such terms as the court deems reasonable."[261] One who violates an injunction may be found in contempt and face severe sanctions.[262]

[i] *Preliminary Injunctions.* A preliminary injunction restrains an accused infringer during the lawsuit to prevent irreparable injury to the patent owner. The four traditional factors governing preliminary injunctions are likelihood of success on the merits, irreparable harm, balance of injury, and public interest.[263]

---

[259] 803 F.2d at 686, 231 U.S.P.Q. at 476.

[260] For imported products that infringe or are produced by a process covered by a United States patent, the patent owner may have an additional remedy in the United States International Trade Commission. *See* § 2E[2][b][ii].

[261] 35 U.S.C. § 283.

[262] *See* Spindelfabrik Suessen-Schurr v. Schubert & Salzer Maschinenfabrik Aktiengesellschaft, 903 F.2d 1568, 14 U.S.P.Q.2d 1913 (Fed. Cir. 1990); Graves v. Kemsco Group, Inc., 864 F.2d 754, 9 U.S.P.Q.2d 1404 (Fed. Cir. 1988); Eli Lilly and Co. v. Premo Pharmaceutical Laboratories, Inc., 843 F.2d 1378, 6 U.S.P.Q.2d 1367 (Fed. Cir. 1988); Amstar Corp. v. Envirotech Corp., 823 F.2d 1538, 3 U.S.P.Q.2d 1412 (Fed. Cir. 1987); Joy Manufacturing Co. v. National Mine Service Co., 810 F.2d 1127, 1 U.S.P.Q.2d 1627, 1628 n.2 (Fed. Cir. 1987); Preemption Devices, Inc. v. Minnesota Mining & Mfg. Co., 803 F.2d 1170, 231 U.S.P.Q. 297 (Fed. Cir. 1986); KSM Fastening Sys., Inc. v. H.A. Jones Co., Inc., 776 F.2d 1522, 227 U.S.P.Q. 676 (Fed. Cir. 1985); MAC Corporation of America v. Williams Patent Crusher & Pulveriser Co., 767 F.2d 882, 226 U.S.P.Q. 515 (Fed. Cir. 1985); Paper Converting Machine Co. v. Magna-Graphics Corp., 745 F.2d 11, 223 U.S.P.Q. 591 (Fed. Cir. 1984).

[263] *E.g.,* Chrysler Motors Corp. v. Auto Body Panels of Ohio Inc., 908 F.2d 951, 953, 15 U.S.P.Q.2d 1469, 1470 (Fed. Cir. 1990) ("no one factor, taken individually, is necessarily

Courts formerly granted preliminary injunctions in patent cases only when the patent owner established validity and infringement "beyond question."[264] The Federal Circuit rejected the "beyond question" rule and equated patent infringement preliminary injunction standards with those in other areas, such as copyright law, which require only a reasonable likelihood of success on the merits.[265]

In *Hybritech*,[266] the patentee showed a reasonable likelihood of success on validity even though the PTO declared an interference between the patent and a pending application in which the patentee was named a junior party in view of the other party's prior filing date.[267] The Federal Circuit's decision upholding the plaintiff's patent against another infringer[268] indicated that Hybritech would be able to show a pre-filing date of invention sufficiently early to establish priority in the interference: *"[I]n context of a motion for preliminary injunction against further infringement of a patent, the patent holder may use a prior adjudication of patent validity involving a different defendant as evidence supporting its burden of proving likelihood of success on the merits."*[269]

If the patent owner clearly shows validity and infringement, the court presumes irreparable injury,[270] but the accused infringer may rebut the presumption.[271]

---

dispositive. If a preliminary injunction is granted by the trial court, the weakness of the showing regarding one factor may be overborne by the strength of others. If the injunction is denied, the absence of an adequate showing with regard to any one factor may be sufficient, given the weight or lack of it assigned the other factors, to justify the denial."); Hybritech Inc. v. Abbott Laboratories, 849 F.2d 1446, 1451, 7 U.S.P.Q.2d 1191, 1195 (Fed. Cir. 1988) (the four factors guiding the issuance of preliminary injunctions "taken individually, are not dispositive; rather the district court must weigh and measure each factor against the other factors and against the form and magnitude of the relief requested.").

[264] *E.g.*, Rosenberg v. Groov-Pin Corp., 81 F.2d 46, 28 U.S.P.Q. 327 (2d Cir. 1936).

[265] H.H. Robertson, Co. v. United Steel Deck, Inc., 820 F.2d 384, 387, 2 U.S.P.Q.2d 1926, 1927 (Fed. Cir. 1987) ("The standards applied to the grant of a preliminary injunction are no more nor less stringent in patent cases than in other areas of the law.;" as to the concerns cited in the past to justify a "more severe" rule, such as the inherent unreliability of *ex parte* examination by the PTO, the existing standards "fairly applied, can accommodate any special circumstances that may arise."); Atlas Powder Co. v. Ireco Co., 773 F.2d 1230, 227 U.S.P.Q. 289 (Fed. Cir. 1985) (a patent owner seeking a preliminary injunction must make a "clear showing" of the validity and infringement of the patent but need not make a showing "beyond question.").

Compare Power Controls Corp. v. Hybrinetics, Inc., 806 F.2d 234, 240, 231 U.S.P.Q. 774 (Fed. Cir. 1986) (denying preliminary injunction against design patent infringement; the presumption of validity "is a permissible basis for supporting a preliminary injunction," but the accused infringer's strong showing of functionality "established that [the patent owner] had shown 'no reasonable likelihood of success on the issue of validity.' ").

[266] Hybritech Inc. v. Abbott Laboratories, 849 F.2d 1446, 7 U.S.P.Q.2d 1191 (Fed. Cir. 1988).

[267] For a discussion of interferences, *see* § 2D[5].

[268] Hybritech Inc. v. Monoclonal Antibodies, Inc., 802 F.2d 1367, 231 U.S.P.Q. 81 (Fed. Cir. 1986), *cert. denied*, 480 U.S. 947 (1987).

[269] 849 F.2d at 1452, 7 U.S.P.Q.2d at 1196 (Emphasis in original).

[270] Smith International, Inc. v. Hughes Tool Co., 718 F.2d 1573, 219 U.S.P.Q. 686 (Fed. Cir. 1983), *cert. denied*, 464 U.S. 996, 220 U.S.P.Q. 385 (1983).

The balance of hardship factor requires the court to weigh "[t]he magnitude of the threatened injury to the patent owner . . . in the light of the strength of the showing of likelihood of success on the merits, against the injury to the accused infringer if the preliminary decision is in error."[272]

"[I]n a patent infringement case, although there exists a public interest in protecting rights secured by valid patents, the focus of the district court's public interest analysis should be whether there exists some critical public interest that would be injured by the grant of preliminary relief."[273] In *Hybritech*,[274] the Federal Circuit held that the district court properly considered the public interest factor when it exempted the accused infringer's cancer and hepatitis test kits but otherwise rejected its arguments that the diagnostic community relied on its products, that a change of vendors was expensive and time consuming, and that supply shortages might result if the patentee had difficulty filling orders.

---

[271] *E.g.,* T. J. Smith and Nephew Ltd. v. Consolidated Medical Equipment, Inc., 821 F.2d 646, 3 U.S.P.Q.2d 1316 (Fed. Cir. 1987) (the patentee's argument that it was entitled to a presumption of irreparable harm was refuted by the record: (a) the absence of a showing of a likelihood of success on infringement precludes a presumption of irreparable harm; (b) "the presumption of validity on which it rests is procedural, not substantive, . . . and is not 'strengthened' by reissue;" (c) the district court held only that it could not conclude that the reissue patent in suit was clearly and convincingly shown to be invalid; (d) the patentee waited 15 months before seeking a preliminary injunction; (e) the patentee had licensed its patent to two licensees; and (f) the patentee's delay in seeking an injunction and its grant of licenses were "acts incompatible with the emphasis on the right to exclude that is the basis for the presumption [of irreparable harm] in a proper case."); Roper Corp. v. Litton Sys., Inc., 757 F.2d 1266, 225 U.S.P.Q. 345 (Fed. Cir. 1985) (no preliminary injunction should issue if neither the patent owner nor the accused infringer is currently making and selling a product covered by the patent).

Compare Hybritech Inc. v. Abbott Laboratories, 849 F.2d 1446, 1456-57, 7 U.S.P.Q.2d 1191, 1200 (Fed. Cir. 1988) (the district court properly relied on a wide range of factors in finding the existence of irreparable injury; "[B]ecause the principal value of a patent is its statutory right to exclude, the nature of the patent grant weighs against holding that monetary damages will always suffice to make the patentee whole.;" the patentee's delay in seeking a preliminary injunction while it was litigating its patent against another infringer did not preclude a finding of irreparable harm; the patentee established good cause for seeking relief against the other infringer first, "given its particular situation and financial resources.").

[272] H.H. Robertson, Co. v. United Steel Deck, Inc., 820 F.2d 384, 2 U.S.P.Q.2d 1926 (Fed. Cir. 1987). *Compare* Hybritech Inc. v. Abbott Laboratories, 849 F.2d 1446, 1458, 7 U.S.P.Q.2d 1191, 1201 (Fed. Cir. 1988) (it is not a prerequisite to awarding a preliminary injunction that a district court expressly find that the balance of hardships tips in favor of the movant. The district court found that "'neither party has a clear advantage.' ").

[273] Hybritech Inc. v. Abbott Laboratories, 849 F.2d 1446, 1458, 7 U.S.P.Q.2d 1191, 1201 (Fed. Cir. 1988).

[274] Hybritech Inc. v. Abbott Laboratories, 849 F.2d 1446, 7 U.S.P.Q.2d 1191 (Fed. Cir. 1988). *See also* Datascope Corp. v. Kontron Inc., 786 F.2d 398, 229 U.S.P.Q. 41 (Fed. Cir. 1986) (the trial court did not err in finding that the public interest would be harmed by grant of an injunction because the defendant's device (an intra-aortic balloon catheter) was preferred by some doctors over the patentee's device).

[*ii*] *Permanent Injunctions.* "It is the general rule that an injunction will issue when infringement has been adjudged, absent a sound reason for denying it."[275] No injunction may issue or continue after a patent expires.[276]

A court may stay an injunction pending appeal. In *Standard Havens Products*,[277] the Federal Circuit granted a stay because, *inter alia*, "without a stay [the appellant] is likely to suffer irreparable harm in the form of employee layoffs, immediate insolvency, and, possibly, extinction." The stay applicant showed a "substantial case" that it would prevail on invalidity and proposed that it be subject to financial restrictions and obligations pending the appeal. The court cautioned against mechanical application of *Windsurfing International's*[278] admonition that "One who elects to build a business on a product found to infringe cannot be heard to complain if an injunction against continuing infringement destroys the business so elected."

"In deciding whether to grant this motion, we must apply the four factors that always guide our discretion to issue a stay pending appeal: '(1) whether the stay applicant has made a strong showing that he is likely to succeed on the merits; (2) whether the applicant will be irreparably injured absent a stay; (3) whether issuance of the stay will substantially injure the other parties interested in the proceeding; and (4) where the public interest lies.' . . . Each

---

[275] Richardson v. Suzuki Motor Co., Ltd., 868 F.2d 1226, 1247, 9 U.S.P.Q.2d 1913, 1929 (Fed. Cir. 1989), *cert. denied*, 110 S. Ct. 154 (1989) (the district court erred in denying the plaintiff's motion for injunction after entering final judgment that the defendants sale of motorcycles infringed plaintiff's patent and trade secret rights: "Infringement having been established, it is contrary to the laws of property, of which the patent law partakes, to deny the patentee's right to exclude others from use of his property."); W.L. Gore & Associates Inc. v. Garlock Inc., 842 F.2d 1275, 1281-82, 6 U.S.P.Q.2d 1277, 1283 (Fed. Cir. 1988) ("The fact that the defendant has stopped infringing is generally not a reason for denying an injunction against future infringement unless the evidence is very persuasive that further infringement will not take place."); Windsurfing International, Inc. v. AMF Inc., 782 F.2d 995, 1003, 228 U.S.P.Q. 562, 568 (Fed. Cir. 1986), *cert. denied*, 477 U.S. 905 (1986) (grant or denial of an injunction is within the trial court's discretion, but "[t]he relative size of multiple infringers should not serve as a basis for enjoining continued infringement by some and not by others.;" that an injunction might put an infringer out of business cannot justify denial of an infringement).

Compare Roche Products, Inc. v. Bolar Pharmaceutical Co., 733 F.2d 858, 866-867, 221 U.S.P.Q. 937, 942-943 (Fed. Cir. 1984), *cert. denied*, 469 U.S. 856, 225 U.S.P.Q. 792 (1984).

Once a trial court decides to grant injunctive relief, that relief should be effective under the circumstances. Trans-World Mfg. Corp. v. Al Nyman & Sons, Inc., 750 F.2d 1552, 224 U.S.P.Q. 259 (Fed. Cir. 1984) (improper to grant an injunction against the *making* and *sale* of an invention when the infringer only *used* it). In *Trans-World*, the court noted that if a monetary award of damages is computed on the basis of an assumed license for the remaining term of the patent, no injunction against continued use is appropriate. *See also* Stickle v. Heublein, Inc., 716 F.2d 1550, 219 U.S.P.Q. 377 (Fed. Cir. 1983).

[276] *See* Clark v. Wooster, 119 U.S. 322 (1886). *See* § 2E[1].

[277] Standard Havens Products Inc. v. Gencor Industries Inc., 897 F.2d 511, 13 U.S.P.Q.2d 2029 (Fed. Cir. 1990).

[278] Windsurfing International, Inc. v. AMF, Inc., 782 F.2d 995, 1003 n.12, 228 U.S.P.Q. 562, 567 n.12 (Fed. Cir. 1986), *cert. denied*, 477 U.S. 905 (1986).

factor, however, need not be given equal weight. . . . Also, likelihood of success in the appeal is not a rigid concept.

"When harm to applicant is great enough, a court will not require 'a strong showing' that applicant is 'likely to succeed on the merits.' "[279]

[b] **Compensatory Damages.** Compensatory damages may include the patentee's lost profits, an established royalty, and a reasonable royalty. The patentee may not recover the infringer's actual illicit profits,[280] except in design patent infringement cases.[281]

A court may award lost profits when the patent owner, or an exclusive licensee, manufactures, uses or sells the patented invention.[282] In *Del Mar Avionics*,[283] the Federal Circuit held that the district court erred in granting a 5% royalty instead of lost profits or a higher royalty to the patentee, who was producing the patented item.

"Although the statute states that the damage award shall not be 'less than a reasonable royalty', 35 U.S.C. § 284, the purpose of this alternative is not to provide a simple accounting method, but to set a floor below which the courts are not authorized to go.

. . .

"The approach taken by the district court is suited to circumstances where there is an established royalty or licensing program, or if the patentee is not itself in the business, or if profits are too speculative to estimate."[284]

The patent owner must establish, to a reasonable probability, that, but for the infringement, he would have made greater sales, charged higher prices or incurred lower costs.[285] The court may infer "but for" causation if (1) the patented product

---

[279] 897 F.2d at 512-13, 13 U.S.P.Q.2d at 2029-30.

[280] *See* Water Technologies Corp. v. Calco, Ltd., 850 F.2d 660, 672, 7 U.S.P.Q.2d 1097, 1107 (Fed. Cir. 1988) ("[U]nlike copyright and trademark infringements, patent infringement carries no remedy of an accounting for an infringer's profits.").

A 1946 statute eliminated the equitable remedy of accounting for a patent infringer's profits. *See* D. Chisum, Patents § 20.02[4].

[281] *See* § 6B[4].

[282] An exclusive licensee, including a person who has an exclusive right to distribute in the United States without any right to manufacture, may recover lost profits. Weinar v. Rollform, Inc., 744 F.2d 797, 223 U.S.P.Q. 369 (Fed. Cir. 1984), *cert. denied*, 470 U.S. 1084 (1985). *See also* Kalman v. Berlyn Corp., 914 F.2d 1473, 16 U.S.P.Q.2d 1093 (Fed. Cir. 1990) (the district court erred in denying a patentee's motion to add as co-plaintiff a sole manufacturing licensee, of which the patentee was a 50% owner, and in limiting the patentee's damages to 50% of the licensee's lost profits).

[283] Del Mar Avionics, Inc. v. Quinton Instrument Co., 836 F.2d 1320, 5 U.S.P.Q.2d 1255 (Fed. Cir. 1987).

[284] 836 F.2d at 1326, 1328, 5 U.S.P.Q.2d at 1260, 1261.

[285] Dowagiac Mfg. Co. v. Minnesota Moline Plow Co., 235 U.S. 641 (1915); Railroad Dynamics, Inc. v. A. Stucki Co., 727 F.2d 1506, 220 U.S.P.Q. 929 (Fed. Cir. 1984), *cert. denied*, 469 U.S. 871, 224 U.S.P.Q. 520 (1984); Lam, Inc. v. Johns-Manville Corp., 718 F.2d 1056, 219 U.S.P.Q. 670 (Fed. Cir. 1983). In *Lam*, the court affirmed an award for profits lost due to retarded sales growth caused by the infringement.

was in demand, (2) no acceptable non-infringing alternative was available, and (3) the patentee or his licensees had the capacity to produce the demanded quantity.[286] A lost profits award is most appropriate when the patent owner and the infringer were the only two significant competitors in the market.[287] Courts use the incremental income method to measure lost profits,[288] and consider the infringer's actual profits in estimating the patent owner's lost profits.[289] A court may award lost profits for unpatented auxiliary components if the evidence shows that the

---

[286] Gyromat Corp. v. Champion Spark Plug Co., 735 F.2d 549, 222 U.S.P.Q. 4 (Fed. Cir. 1984); Panduit Corp. v. Stahlin Bros. Fibre Works, Inc., 575 F.2d 1152, 197 U.S.P.Q. 726 (6th Cir. 1978). *See also* Datascope Corp. v. SMEC, Inc., 879 F.2d 820, 11 U.S.P.Q.2d 1321 (Fed. Cir. 1989), *cert. denied*, 110 S. Ct. 729 (1990) (the district court committed clear error in finding that a certain device sold by a third party (Kontron) was an acceptable noninfringing alternative; it also erred in considering alleged customer preference for the infringer's product as relevant to the third element of the *Panduit* test—"the manufacturing/marketing *capability* of the patentee to meet the demand" for the patented product).

Compare Water Technologies Corp. v. Calco, Ltd., 850 F.2d 660, 7 U.S.P.Q.2d 1097 (Fed. Cir. 1988). In *Water Technologies*, the Federal Circuit overturned a lost profits award. Neither the patentee nor its exclusive licensee had the capacity to sell the infringing product over the entire time period.

"[A] lost profits award is appropriate only if [the patentee] proved that it would have made sales of its . . . product 'but for' [the defendants'] infringement, *i.e.*, that causation existed.

"While damages are to be proved, not presumed, a patent owner need not demonstrate causation with certainty. A reasonable probability that the patent owner would have made some or all of the sales is sufficient. . . . Where a patent owner maintains that it lost sales *equal in quantity* to the infringing sales, our precedent has approved generally the four-part test set forth in *Panduit Corp. v. Stahlin Brothers Fibre Works*, 575 F.2d 1152, 197 U.S.P.Q. 726 (6th Cir. 1978).

. . .

". . . The *Panduit* test in part (2) [absence of acceptable noninfringing substitutes] embodies the idea stated in other precedent that lost profits for all sales made by an infringer are easier to obtain where there are only two suppliers in the market, the infringer and the patent owner." 850 F.2d at 671-72, 7 U.S.P.Q.2d at 1106.

[287] Marsh-McBirney, Inc. v. Montedoro-Whitney Corp., 882 F.2d 498, 11 U.S.P.Q.2d 1794 (Fed. Cir. 1989), *cert. granted, judgment vacated*, 111 S. Ct. 775 (1991) (the district court did not err in awarding the patentee lost profits for infringement in view of the court's finding that the patentee and the infringer "operate in a unique sector of the domestic market," a "separate niche"); Lam, Inc. v. Johns-Manville Corp., 718 F.2d 1056, 219 U.S.P.Q. 670 (Fed. Cir. 1983).

[288] Paper Converting Machine Co. v. Magna-Graphics Corp., 745 F.2d 11, 223 U.S.P.Q. 591 (Fed. Cir. 1984). Under this approach, gross profit is reduced by the incremental costs of making that sale. Fixed costs are disregarded because the patent owner or exclusive licensee would have incurred those costs whether or not the additional sale was made.

[289] *See* Water Technologies Corp. v. Calco, Ltd., 850 F.2d 660, 673, 7 U.S.P.Q.2d 1097, 1107 (Fed. Cir. 1988), *cert. denied*, 488 U.S. 968 (1988) (the infringer's profits "are not, as such, a measure of the patent owner's damages," but may be "used for comparison purposes with the profit margin figure of the patent owner to determine the reasonableness of the latter figure."); Kori Corp. v. Wilco Marsh Buggies & Draglines, Inc., 761 F.2d 649, 225 U.S.P.Q. 985 (Fed. Cir. 1985).

patentee, or a hypothetical licensee, would anticipate selling the components along with the patented device.[290]

An established royalty is a royalty rate agreed to and paid by enough persons to indicate general acquiescence.[291] A court will adopt a market-established royalty as the best measure.[292] A single license or offer is usually not sufficient to establish a royalty.[293]

---

[290] *E.g.,* Beatrice Foods Co. v. New England Printing & Lithographing Co., 899 F.2d 1171, 1175, 14 U.S.P.Q.2d 1020, 1024 (Fed. Cir. 1990) ("The law does not bar the inclusion of convoyed sales" in an award of lost profits damages.); Del. Mar Avionics, Inc. v. Quinton Instrument Co., 836 F.2d 1320, 1327, 5 U.S.P.Q.2d 1255, 1261 (Fed. Cir. 1987) ("[I]n appropriate circumstances the patentee may prove the extent of its lost profits by the 'entire market value rule', . . . based on a showing that the patentee could reasonably anticipate the sale of the unpatented components together with the patented components."); Kori Corp. v. Wilco Marsh Buggies & Draglines, Inc., 761 F.2d 649, 225 U.S.P.Q. 985 (Fed. Cir. 1985), *cert. denied,* 474 U.S. 902 (1985) (recovery of profits lost on unpatented components is appropriate if the patentee (or his licensee) can normally anticipate selling such components together with the patented device); Paper Converting Machine Co. v. Magna-Graphics Corp., 745 F.2d 11, 223 U.S.P.Q. 591 (Fed. Cir. 1984) (lost profits may be awarded for auxiliary units that are not integral parts of the patented machine if, in all reasonable probability, the patent owner would have made the sales of those units which the infringer made).

Compare King Instrument Corp. v. Otari Corp., 767 F.2d 853, 226 U.S.P.Q. 402 (Fed. Cir. 1985), *cert. denied,* 485 U.S. 1016 (1986) (there was no evidence to support the award of profits on "spare parts" that were allegedly sold as part of a package with the original machine; the touchstone for including non-patented spare parts in a damage award is whether the patentee would normally anticipate the sale of the non-patented component together with the sale of the patented components).

A court may award damages for loss of sales of an unpatented product made by a patented process. Central Soya Co., Inc. v. Geo. A. Hormel & Co., 723 F.2d 1573, 220 U.S.P.Q. 490 (Fed. Cir. 1983).

[291] Rude v. Westcott, 130 U.S. 152, 165 (1889); Hanson v. Alpine Valley Ski Area, Inc., 718 F.2d 1075, 1078, 219 U.S.P.Q. 679, 682 (Fed. Cir. 1983); Deere & Co. v. International Harvester Co., 710 F.2d 1551, 218 U.S.P.Q. 481 (Fed. Cir. 1983).

The established royalty must be for rights under the patent that are commensurate with what the infringer has appropriated. A royalty that includes other rights or services will not suffice to set an established royalty. Bandag, Inc. v. Gerrard Tire Co., 704 F.2d 1578, 217 U.S.P.Q. 977 (Fed. Cir. 1983).

[292] Seymour v. McCormick, 57 U.S. (16 How.) 480 (1853); Nickson Industries, Inc. v. Rol Manufacturing Co., Ltd., 847 F.2d 795, 798, 6 U.S.P.Q.2d 1878, 1879-80 (Fed. Cir. 1988) ("Where an established royalty rate exists, it will usually be the best measure of what is a 'reasonable' royalty. . . . [A] higher figure may be awarded when the evidence clearly shows that widespread infringement made the established royalty artificially low.").

Compare Beatrice Foods Co. v. New England Printing & Lithographing Co., 899 F.2d 1171, 14 U.S.P.Q.2d 1020 (Fed. Cir. 1990) (the district court did not err in awarding the patentee's lost profits on the infringer's sales even though, at the time the patentee first gave notice of infringement, it offered the infringer a license at a modest royalty rate and has since offered and granted royalty-bearing licenses to others).

[293] Trell v. Marlee Electronics Corp., 912 F.2d 1443, 16 U.S.P.Q.2d 1059 (Fed. Cir. 1990); Railroad Dynamics, Inc. v. A. Stucki Co., 727 F.2d 1506, 220 U.S.P.Q. 929 (Fed. Cir. 1984).

A court must award "in no event less than a reasonable royalty."[294] A reasonable royalty is the amount a willing licensor and licensee would have agreed to had they negotiated a license the day infringement began.[295] The court considers numerous factors,[296] including:

(a)   the infringer's anticipated profits,[297]

---

[294] 35 U.S.C. § 284. *Compare* Lindemann Maschinenfabrik GmbH v. American Hoist & Derrick Co., 895 F.2d 1403, 1407, 13 U.S.P.Q.2d 1871, 1874-75 (Fed. Cir. 1990), *cert. denied*, 469 U.S. 871, 224 U.S.P.Q. 520 (1984) ("[T]he statute [35 U.S.C. Section 284] obviates the need to show the fact of damage when infringement is admitted or proven, but that does not mean that a patentee who puts on little or no satisfactory evidence of a reasonable royalty can successfully appeal on the ground that the amount awarded by the court is not 'reasonable' and therefore contravenes section 284.").

In setting the reasonable royalty, the court may consider the fact that the party using the invention is an infringer rather than an actual willing licensee. Stickle v. Heublein, Inc., 716 F.2d 1550, 1563, 219 U.S.P.Q. 377, 386 (Fed. Cir. 1983). *See also* Sun Studs, Inc. v. ATA Equipment Leasing, Inc., 872 F.2d 978, 10 U.S.P.Q.2d 1338 (Fed. Cir. 1989) ("compensation for infringement can take cognizance of the actual commercial consequences of the infringement, and that the hypothetical negotiators need not act as if there had been no infringement, no litigation, and no erosion of market position or patent value . . . ").

For a table of adjudicated reasonable royalty rates, *see* D. Chisum, Patents, § 20.03[3][d].

[295] Trans-World Mfg. Corp. v. Al Nyman & Sons, Inc., 750 F.2d 1552, 224 U.S.P.Q. 259 (Fed. Cir. 1984); Panduit Corp. v. Stahlin Bros. Fibre Works, 575 F.2d 1152, 197 U.S.P.Q. 726 (6th Cir. 1978).

The measuring date is the commencement of infringement, but post-commencement evidence may be relevant. *E.g.*, Studiengesellschaft Kohle, m.b.H. v. Dart Industries, Inc., 862 F.2d 1564, 1571, 9 U.S.P.Q.2d 1273, 1280 (Fed. Cir. 1988) (no rigid rule that "all post-infringement evidence is irrelevant to a reasonable royalty calculation.")

[296] Georgia-Pacific Corp. v. U.S. Plywood Corp., 318 F. Supp. 1116, 1120, 166 U.S.P.Q. 235, 238 (S.D. N.Y. 1970), *modified*, 446 F.2d 295, 170 U.S.P.Q. 369 (2d Cir. 1971), *cert. denied*, 404 U.S. 870, 171 U.S.P.Q. 322 (1971).

[297] TWM Manufacturing Co., Inc. v. Dura Corp., 789 F.2d 895, 229 U.S.P.Q. 525 (Fed. Cir. 1986), *cert. denied*, 479 U.S. 852 (1986) (the district court did not abuse its discretion in adopting the special master's findings that (1) relied on the infringer's management's memorandum projecting a 52.7% gross margin on infringing sales, and (2) used an "analytical approach" which subtracted the infringer's usual profit (6.56% to 12.5%) and overhead (10.7%) to reach a 30% royalty; the invention's immediate commercial success, its satisfaction of a long-felt need, and the absence of noninfringing alternatives that possessed "all of its beneficial characteristics" supported the high royalty rate); Trans-World Mfg. Corp. v. Al Nyman & Sons, Inc., 750 F.2d 1552, 224 U.S.P.Q. 259 (Fed. Cir. 1984).

Evidence of the infringer's *actual* profits from the infringement is admissible as probative of the profits that would have been anticipated. *Compare* Datascope Corp. v. SMEC, Inc., 879 F.2d 820, 11 U.S.P.Q.2d 1321 (Fed. Cir. 1989), *cert. denied*, 110 S. Ct. 729 (1990) (the district court did not err in selecting a 5% royalty even though the patentee and the infringer enjoyed large gross profit margins (71% for the infringer).

It is error to set the reasonable rate at a level that would have left the licensee with no anticipated profits or a profit less than the licensee would ordinarily make on its sales. Lindemann Maschinenfabrik GmbH v. American Hoist & Derrick Co., 895 F.2d 1403, 13 U.S.P.Q.2d 1871 (Fed. Cir. 1990); Hughes Tool Co. v. Dresser Industries, Inc., 816 F.2d 1549, 1558, 2 U.S.P.Q.2d 1396, 1404 (Fed. Cir. 1987), *cert. denied*, 484 U.S. 914 (1987) ("[A]

(b)   estimated cost savings,[298]

(c)   comparable licenses,[299]

(d)   typical industry licensing practices,[300]

(e)   noninfringing alternatives,[301] and

---

reasonable royalty must be fixed so as to leave the infringer a reasonable profit."); Tektronix, Inc. v. United States, 552 F.2d 343, 193 U.S.P.Q. 385 (Ct. Cl. 1977), *cert. denied sub nom.* Hickok Elec. Instrument Co. v. Tektronik, Inc., 439 U.S. 1048 (1978); Georgia-Pacific Corp. v. United States Plywood Corp., 446 F.2d 295, 170 U.S.P.Q. 369 (2d Cir. 1971), *cert. denied*, 404 U.S. 870, 171 U.S.P.Q. 322 (1971).

Compare Radio Steel & Mfg. Co. v. MTD Products, Inc., 788 F.2d 1554, 1557, 229 U.S.P.Q. 431, 433 (Fed. Cir. 1986) (10% royalty not unreasonable even though it may have exceeded the infringer's actual profits because "the determination of a reasonable royalty . . . is based not on the infringer's profit, but on the royalty to which a willing licensor and a willing licensee would have agreed at the time the infringement began.;" also, the infringer's products may have been utilized as loss-leaders).

[298] Hanson v. Alpine Valley Ski Area, Inc., 718 F.2d 1075, 219 U.S.P.Q. 679 (Fed. Cir. 1983).

[299] Rates in licenses the patent owner granted are probative of a reasonable royalty even when such rates do not qualify as an established royalty. Trio Process Corp. v. L. Goldstein's Sons, Inc., 533 F.2d 126, 189 U.S.P.Q. 561 (3d Cir. 1976). Rates in a license that confers rights other than to the patent are not probative of a reasonable royalty. *E.g.,* Trell v. Marlee Electronics Corp., 912 F.2d 1443, 16 U.S.P.Q.2d 1059 (Fed. Cir. 1990).

Actual rates are less probative when the patent owner is forced to lower the rates in the face of industry-wide infringement of the patent. *E.g.,* Fromson v. Western Litho Plate & Supply Co., 853 F.2d 1568, 1577 n.15, 7 U.S.P.Q.2d 1606, 1614 n.15 (Fed. Cir. 1988) ("In determining the true measure of a reasonable royalty, a court should not select a 'diminished royalty rate' a patentee may have been forced to accept by the disrepute of his patent and the open defiance of his rights.' "). *Compare* Studiengesellschaft Kohle, m.b.H. v. Dart Industries, Inc., 862 F.2d 1564, 9 U.S.P.Q.2d 1273 (Fed. Cir. 1988) (proper to consider settlement agreement with another infringer entered after patent held valid and infringed).

License offers are admissible as evidence of a reasonable royalty unless the offers are to settle existing or threatened litigation. Deere & Co. v. International Harvester Co., 710 F.2d 1551, 218 U.S.P.Q. 481 (Fed. Cir. 1983); Pitcairn v. United States, 547 F.2d 1106, 192 U.S.P.Q. 613 (Ct. Cl. 1976), *cert. denied*, 434 U.S. 1051, 196 U.S.P.Q. 864 (1978).

[300] *E.g.,* Stickle v. Heublein, Inc., 716 F.2d 1550, 219 U.S.P.Q. 377 (Fed. Cir. 1983). In *Stickle*, the court held that it was error to base a reasonable royalty on a percentage of the sale price of products produced by the infringing machine when there was no evidence that the particular industry accepted those types of licenses. Typical industry practice was to pay a sum per machine for a paid-up license.

[301] *E.g.,* State Industries, Inc. v. Mor-Flo Industries, Inc., 883 F.2d 1573, 1581, 12 U.S.P.Q.2d 1026, 1032 (Fed Cir. 1989), *cert. denied*, 110 S. Ct. 725 (1990) (as to the patentee's argument that the 3% royalty rate was too low and its rate of 8 to 10% was reasonable, "it was well within the district court's province to conclude . . . that potential licensees would have stayed with lesser alternatives promising some profit, rather than risk losing money by signing on at that high a rate.").

Compare TWM Manufacturing Co., Inc. v. Dura Corp., 789 F.2d 895, 229 U.S.P.Q. 525 (Fed. Cir. 1986), *cert. denied*, 479 U.S. 852 (1986) (argument that a lower rate was proper because of the existence of an alternative was undercut by evidence of (1) the infringer's failure to design independently its own device, (2) the infringer's election to infringe "despite having

    (f) benefits from sales of parts or related components.[302]

The court has discretion in selecting a damage computation method.[303] It may apply different damages measures to distinct infringing activities, for example, lost profits for some infringing sales and a reasonable royalty for others.[304] In *State Industries*,[305] the Federal Circuit affirmed a market share award; the patentee, which held 40% of the national market, received lost profits on 40% of the infringer's sales and a reasonable royalty on the balance.

The court may order an accounting to determine infringing sales volume.[306]

---

expended only minimal sums when notified of infringement;" (3) willful infringement; (4) failure of the infringer successfully to market alternative designs; (5) violation of an injunction against infringement, and (6) withdrawal from the business after enforcement of the injunction).

    Alternatives availability is determined as of the date infringement begins. Panduit Corp. v. Stahlin Bros. Fibre Works, 575 F.2d 1152, 197 U.S.P.Q. 726 (6th Cir. 1978).

[302] TWM Manufacturing Co., Inc. v. Dura Corp., 789 F.2d 895, 901, 229 U.S.P.Q. 525, 528 (Fed. Cir. 1986), *cert. denied*, 479 U.S. 852 (1986) (the special master did not err by including in the royalty base unpatented wheels and axles as well as the patented truck suspension: "Where a hypothetical licensee would have anticipated an increase in sales of collateral unpatented items because of the patented device, the patentee should be compensated accordingly."); Deere & Co. v. International Harvester Co., 710 F.2d 1551, 1559, 218 U.S.P.Q. 481, 487 (Fed. Cir. 1983).

[303] State Industries, Inc. v. Mor-Flo Industries, Inc., 883 F.2d 1573, 1576, 12 U.S.P.Q.2d 1026, 1028 (Fed. Cir. 1989), *cert. denied*, 110 S. Ct. 725 (1990) ("Deciding how much to award as damages is not an exact science, and the methodology of assessing and computing damages is committed to the sound discretion of the district court.").

[304] *E.g.*, Bio-Rad Laboratories, Inc. v. Nicolet Instrument Corp., 739 F.2d 604, 222 U.S.P.Q. 654 (Fed. Cir. 1984), *cert. denied*, 469 U.S. 1038 (1984).

[305] State Industries, Inc. v. Mor-Flo Industries, Inc., 883 F.2d 1573, 12 U.S.P.Q.2d 1026 (Fed. Cir. 1989), *cert. denied*, 110 S. Ct. 725 (1990).

[306] *See* Beatrice Foods Co. v. New England Printing & Lithographing Co., 899 F.2d 1171, 14 U.S.P.Q.2d 1020 (Fed. Cir. 1990) (rejecting infringer's contention that there was insufficient evidence to support the district court's finding as to infringing sales volume because the infringer previously destroyed records that identified what had been sold and in what quantity); Nickson Industries, Inc. v. Rol Manufacturing Co., Ltd., 847 F.2d 795, 799, 6 U.S.P.Q.2d 1878, 1880 (Fed. Cir. 1988) ("[W]here it is 'impossible to make a mathematical or approximate apportionment' between infringing and noninfringing items, the infringer must bear the burden of the entire risk.;" the district court did not err in finding that 59% of the infringer's sales were noninfringing; a document prepared by the infringer but introduced into evidence by the patentee provided a basis for making a reasonable approximation of noninfringing sales); Amstar Corp. v. Envirotech Corp., 823 F.2d 1538, 1545, 3 U.S.P.Q.2d 1412, 1417 (Fed. Cir. 1987) ("During an accounting, as during the liability trial, a patentee must prove infringement by a preponderance of the evidence. . . . [W]hether one is determining infringement at trial, in an accounting, or in a contempt proceeding, . . . it is a *claim* that is infringed and a *claimed* invention that is patented. Thus comparison with an adjudicated device cannot serve to encompass within the patent's exclusionary scope a device that does not in fact constitute an infringement of the claim, either literally or under the doctrine of equivalents.").

[c] **Multiple or Punitive Damages: Willful Infringement.** Section 284 provides that the court "may increase the damages up to three times the amount found or assessed."[307]

The court will not increase damages if the infringer acted in good faith, for example, without knowledge of the patent[308] or with a reasonable belief he did not infringe or the patent was invalid.[309]

The most common basis for increased damage awards is willful infringement.[310] In *Underwater Devices*[311] and *Central Soya Co.*,[312] the Federal Circuit confirmed that a person with actual notice of another's patent rights has an affirmative duty to exercise due care to determine whether his acts will be infringing, including the duty to seek and follow competent legal advice before beginning activity that may constitute patent infringement.

Courts consider the "totality of the circumstances" in determining willfulness.[313]

---

[307] 35 U.S.C. § 284. The "up to" language means that a court may award less than full trebling. *E.g.*, Del Mar Avionics, Inc. v. Quinton Instrument Co., 836 F.2d 1320, 5 U.S.P.Q.2d 1255 (Fed. Cir. 1987) (doubling).

[308] State Industries, Inc. v. A.O. Smith Corp., 751 F.2d 1226, 1235-36, 224 U.S.P.Q. 418, 424 (Fed. Cir. 1985).

[309] Paper Converting Machine Co. v. Magna-Graphics Corp., 745 F.2d 11, 20, 223 U.S.P.Q. 591, 597-98 (Fed. Cir. 1984).

[310] *E.g.*, Spindelfabrik Suessen-Schurr v. Schubert & Salzer Maschinenfabrik Aktiengesellschaft, 903 F.2d 1568, 14 U.S.P.Q.2d 1913 (Fed. Cir. 1990); Avia Group International, Inc. v. L.A. Gear California, Inc., 853 F.2d 1557, 7 U.S.P.Q.2d 1548 (Fed. Cir. 1988); Kaufman Company, Inc. v. Lantech, Inc., 807 F.2d 970, 1 U.S.P.Q.2d 1202 (Fed. Cir. 1986); Orthokinetics, Inc. v. Safety Travel Chairs, Inc., 806 F.2d 1565, 1 U.S.P.Q.2d 1081 (Fed. Cir. 1986); Rosemount, Inc. v. Beckman Instruments, Inc., 727 F.2d 1540, 221 U.S.P.Q. 1 (Fed. Cir. 1984); Leinoff v. Louis Milona & Sons, Inc., 726 F.2d 734, 220 U.S.P.Q. 845 (Fed. Cir. 1984).

Compare Modine Manufacturing Co. v. Allen Group, Inc., 917 F.2d 538, 543, 16 U.S.P.Q.2d 1622, 1625 (Fed. Cir. 1990) (the district court did not abuse its discretion by refusing to award increased damages even though the jury found willful infringement by clear and convincing evidence; "a finding of willful infringement merely *authorizes*, but does not *mandate*, an award of increased damages.").

[311] Underwater Devices, Inc. v. Morrison-Knudsen Co., Inc., 717 F.2d 1380, 1390, 219 U.S.P.Q. 569, 576-577 (Fed. Cir. 1983) (advice of counsel does not shield a company from a willful infringement finding when it commenced infringing activity with knowledge of a patent; an award of multiple damages is proper when (1) the company embarked on the activity prior to consulting counsel, (2) counsel was in-house and not a patent attorney, and (3) counsel initially ordered a patent search but only later obtained a file history).

[312] Central Soya Co., Inc. v. Geo. A. Hormel & Co., 723 F.2d 1573, 220 U.S.P.Q. 490 (Fed. Cir. 1983) (counsel's advice does not shield a company from a willful infringement finding when it recruited the patentee's key employee and commenced infringement with knowledge of the patent; a multiple damages award is proper when (1) counsel's advice of probable patent invalidity was based solely on file history prior art, and (2) the company took no steps for two years to verify that its operations fell within the parameters specified in counsel's noninfringement advice).

[313] *E.g.*, Bott v. Four Star Corp., 807 F.2d 1567, 1572, 1 U.S.P.Q.2d 1210, 1213 (Fed. Cir. 1986) ("In determining whether an infringer acted in bad faith as to merit an increase in

Acting on patent counsel's timely advice may shield an infringer from a willful infringement charge.[314] Absence of counsel's advice suggests[315] but does not mandate[316] a willfulness finding. In *Rite-Hite*,[317] the Federal Circuit held the district

---

damages awarded against him, the court will consider the totality of circumstances . . . including (1) whether the infringer deliberately copied the ideas or design of another; (2) whether the infringer, when he knew of the other's patent protection, investigated the scope of the patent and formed a good faith belief that it was invalid or that it was not infringed, and (3) the infringer's behavior as a party to the litigation.").

[314] *E.g.*, Kalman v. Berlyn Corp., 914 F.2d 1473, 1484, 16 U.S.P.Q.2d 1093, 1101 (Fed. Cir. 1990) (the district court did not commit clear error in finding no willful infringement; the infringer acted with counsel's advice and, after one product was found to infringe, it began to develop a noninfringing substitute; "In determining willfulness, it is . . . relevant to note whether the infringer acted in good faith during the litigation.").

Compare Datascope Corp. v. SMEC, Inc., 879 F.2d 820, 828, 11 U.S.P.Q.2d 1321, 1327 (Fed. Cir. 1989), *cert. denied*, 110 S. Ct. 729 (1990) (the district court committed clear error in failing to find willful infringement; as to the infringer's reliance on an opinion of counsel, "[t]hat opinion said nothing whatever about the validity of the . . . patent, and the opinion's reference to infringement is not only conclusory, but ignores entirely the question of infringement under the doctrine of equivalents. Further, an opinion on equivalents . . . would have been impossible, [the infringer's] attorneys having never ordered, let alone consulted, the [patent's] prosecution history before rendering their opinion.").

[315] *E.g.*, Ryco, Inc. v. Ag-Bag Corp., 857 F.2d 1418, 8 U.S.P.Q.2d 1323 (Fed. Cir. 1988); Avia Group International, Inc. v. L.A. Gear California, Inc., 853 F.2d 1557, 7 U.S.P.Q.2d 1548 (Fed. Cir. 1988).

[316] *E.g.*, Nickson Industries, Inc. v. Rol Manufacturing Co., Ltd., 847 F.2d 795, 6 U.S.P.Q.2d 1878 (Fed. Cir. 1988); Rolls-Royce Ltd. v. GTE Valeron Corp., 800 F.2d 1101, 231 U.S.P.Q. 185 (Fed. Cir. 1986).

See also Studiengesellschaft Kohle, m.b.H. v. Dart Industries, Inc., 862 F.2d 1564, 9 U.S.P.Q.2d 1273 (Fed. Cir. 1988). In *Studiengesellschaft Kohle*, the Federal Circuit held that the district court correctly reversed a special master's willfulness finding. The master discounted the infringer's reliance on counsel's noninfringement opinion because (a) the opinion was by "in-house" counsel; (b) the opinion consisted of "mere conclusionary statements without analytic backup;" (c) the opinion was based on conclusions "mostly irrelevant to infringement;" and (d) the infringer "deviated from its usual practice of getting opinions from competent counsel not employed by it." "[T]his court has not issued any edict requiring' a potential infringer to obtain advice of counsel. The affirmative duty is to exercise due care." In overturning the master's finding, the district court did not apply a "clean heart, empty head" standard. The infringer's management acted reasonably in electing to rely on its in-house attorney, a qualified patent attorney who had been monitoring the relevant field for three years. The attorney's opinion "although later shown to be incorrect, contained significant, scientifically based *objective* factors to justify [his] conclusion of no infringement." The opinion was contrasted to "those in other cases which lacked any appearance of competence, authoritativeness, or internal indicia of credibility."

Cf. Spindelfabrik Suessen-Schurr v. Schubert & Salzer Maschinenfabrik AG, 829 F.2d 1075, 1084 n.13, 4 U.S.P.Q.2d 1044, 1051 n.13 (Fed. Cir. 1987), *cert. denied*, 484 U.S. 1063 (1988) (finding willfulness; "in respect of willfulness, there cannot be hard and fast *per se* rules . . . Though it is an important consideration, not every failure to seek an opinion of competent counsel will mandate an ultimate finding of willfulness . . . Conversely, that an opinion of counsel was obtained does not 'always and alone' dictate a finding that the infringement was not willful.").

[317] Rite-Hite Corp. v. Kelley Company, Inc., 819 F.2d 1120, 2 U.S.P.Q.2d 1915 (Fed. Cir. 1987).

court did not commit clear error in finding no willful infringement even though the infringer did not introduce into evidence a counsel opinion letter and the infringer made its device through examination of the patentee's device. The copying of a certain feature was "not exact," and the infringer's intent to "design around" the patentee's claims "weighs on the side" of the conclusion of nonwillfulness.

> " 'Willfulness' in infringement, as in life, is not an all-or-nothing trait, but one of degree. It recognizes that infringement may range from unknowing, or accidental, to deliberate, or reckless, disregard of a patentee's legal rights. The role of a finding of 'willfulness' in the law of infringement is partly as a deterrent—an economic deterrent to the tort of infringement—and partly as a basis for making economically whole one who has been wronged, for example by assessment of attorney fees under 35 U.S.C. § 285.

> "The term 'willfulness' thus reflects a threshold of culpability in the act of infringement that, alone or with other considerations of the particular case, contributes to the court's assessment of the consequences of patent infringement. . . . Whether or not 'willfulness' is found, the court has authority to consider the degree of culpability of the tortfeasor."[318]

In *Gustafson*,[319] the Federal Circuit held that the district court erred in finding willful infringement of two patents when the infringer became aware of the patents only "as of" the date suit was filed on each. The infringer designed the infringing product to compete with the patentee's. It began manufacturing and selling its product before the second patent issued.

> "[A] party cannot be held liable 'for infringement', and thus not for 'willful' infringement, of a *nonexistent* patent, i.e., no damages are payable on products manufactured and sold before the patent issued. Whether an act is 'willful' is by definition a question of the actor's *intent*, the answer to which must be inferred from the circumstances. Hence a party cannot be found to have 'willfully' infringed a patent of which the party had no knowledge. Nor is there a universal rule that to avoid willfulness one must cease manufacture of a product immediately upon learning of a patent, or upon receipt of a patentee's charge of infringement, or upon the filing of suit. Exercising due care, . . . a party may continue to manufacture and may present what in good faith it believes to be a legitimate defense without risk of being found on that basis alone a willful infringer. That such a defense proves unsuccessful does not establish that infringement was willful.

> "In our patent system, patent applications are secret, and patentees are authorized to sue 'innocent' manufacturers immediately after their patents issue and without warning. To hold such patentees entitled to increased damages or attorney fees on the ground of willful infringement, however, would be to reward use of the patent system as a form of ambush."[320]

---

[318] 819 F.2d at 1125-26, 2 U.S.P.Q.2d at 1919.

[319] Gustafson, Inc. v. Intersystems Industrial Products, Inc., 897 F.2d 508, 13 U.S.P.Q.2d 1972 (Fed. Cir. 1990).

[320] 897 F.2d at 511, 13 U.S.P.Q.2d at 1975. *Compare* Pacific Furniture Mfg. Co. v. Preview Furniture Corp., 800 F.2d 1111, 1115 n.9, 231 U.S.P.Q. 67, 69 n.9 (Fed. Cir. 1986)

[d] **Interest.** Section 284 provides for a damage award "together with interest . . . as fixed by the court."[321] In *Devex*,[322] the Supreme Court held "prejudgment interest should ordinarily be awarded where necessary to afford the plaintiff full compensation for the infringement."

> "In the typical case an award of prejudgment interest is necessary to ensure that the patent owner is placed in as good a position as he would have been in had the infringer entered into a reasonable royalty agreement. An award of interest from the time that the royalty payments would have been received merely serves to make the patent owner whole, since his damages consist not only of the value of the royalty payments but also of the foregone use of the money between the time of infringement and the date of the judgment."[323]

In *Devex*, the Court recognized that a court may limit or deny prejudgment interest under special circumstances, such as when the patent owner causes undue delay in filing and prosecuting the infringement suit. Federal Circuit decisions emphasize prejudgment interest is the rule, not the exception,[324] and narrowly restrict the circumstances justifying interest denial.[325]

("The fact that [the infringers] may have started [their] infringement before the patents issued (or before [they] were aware of the patents) does not bar an award of increased damages or attorney fees."); Power Lift, Inc. v. Lang Tools, Inc., 774 F.2d 478, 482, 227 U.S.P.Q. 435, 438 (Fed. Cir. 1985) (willful infringement was properly found by the jury even though the infringement suit was filed just nine days after the patent issued; the infringer knew of the patent on the day of its issuance because he refused the patentee's offer of a license, stating that "before he would pay a nickel, he'd see [the patentee] in the courthouse."); Shiley, Inc. v. Bentley Laboratories, Inc., 794 F.2d 1561, 230 U.S.P.Q. 112 (Fed. Cir. 1986), *cert. denied*, 479 U.S. 1087 (1987) (that the infringer began to market its infringing product one month before issuance of the patents in question does not preclude as a matter of law a finding of willful infringement because willfulness is to be determined under the totality of the circumstances).

[321] 35 U.S.C. § 284.

[322] General Motors Corp. v. Devex Corp., 461 U.S. 648, 217 U.S.P.Q. 1185 (1983).

[323] 461 U.S. at 648-49.

[324] *E.g.*, Nickson Industries, Inc. v. Rol Manufacturing Co., Ltd., 847 F.2d 795, 800, 6 U.S.P.Q.2d 1878, 1881 (Fed. Cir. 1988) ("Generally, prejudgment interest should be awarded from the date of infringement to the date of judgment. . . . District courts have discretion to limit prejudgment interest where, for example, the patent owner has caused undue delay in the lawsuit, . . . but there must be justification bearing a relationship to the award.").

[325] Kalman v. Berlyn Corp., 914 F.2d 1473, 16 U.S.P.Q.2d 1093 (Fed. Cir. 1990) (not error to award interest even though the patentee delayed six years to file suit after it learned of the defendant's infringement; during the delay period, the patentee engaged in litigation against one of defendant's customers, and defendant controlled and financed the customer's defense of that litigation); Allen Archery, Inc. v. Browning Manufacturing Co., 898 F.2d 787, 14 U.S.P.Q.2d 1156 (Fed. Cir. 1990) (error to exclude from the interest period the time during which the present case for infringement was stayed pending the decision in another case involving the validity of the same patent); Richardson v. Suzuki Motor Co., Ltd., 868 F.2d 1226, 9 U.S.P.Q.2d 1913 (Fed. Cir. 1989), *cert. denied*, 110 S. Ct. 154 (1989) (error to deny interest on the damage awards for patent infringement and violation of trade secret rights); Hughes Tool Co. v. Dresser Industries, Inc., 816 F.2d 1549, 1558, 2 U.S.P.Q.2d 1396, 1404 (Fed. Cir. 1987), *cert. denied*, 484 U.S. 984 (1987) (the district court's withholding of prejudgment interest

The district court has discretion to set the interest rate and whether it should be simple or compound.[326] Most decisions award compound interest at a market rate.[327]

The court may not grant prejudgment interest on the increased portion of a damage award[328] but may award interest on an attorney fee award.[329]

[e] **Attorney Fees and Expenses.** Section 285 provides that "[t]he court in exceptional cases may award reasonable attorney fees to the prevailing party."[330] This is an exception to the general American law rule that prevailing litigants bear their own attorney fees.

If the patent owner prevails, the court may find the case exceptional because the infringement was willful[331] or the litigation was pursued in bad faith.[332]

---

for the period of time after the patent had been held invalid by another district court in a suit against another accused infringer and the reversal of that holding on appeal "was based on [a] misunderstanding that prejudgment interest can never be awarded in such a circumstance."); Radio Steel & Mfg. Co. v. MTD Products, Inc., 788 F.2d 1554, 1558, 229 U.S.P.Q. 431, 434 (Fed. Cir. 1986) (the patentee's failure to remove a patent notice from its products for one-and-one-half years after the patent expired is not a justification for the denial of prejudgment interest; a justification for denial "must have some relationship to the award of prejudgment interest.").

[326] E.g., Studiengesellschaft Kohle, m.b.H. v. Dart Industries, Inc., 862 F.2d 1564, 9 U.S.P.Q.2d 1273 (Fed. Cir. 1988) (the district court did not abuse its discretion in adopting the special master's award of quarterly-compounded, prime rate prejudgment interest; "the question of the rate at which . . . an award [of prejudgment interest] should be made is a matter left to the sound discretion of the trier of fact . . . "); Nickson Industries, Inc. v. Rol Manufacturing Co., Ltd., 847 F.2d 795, 6 U.S.P.Q.2d 1878 (Fed. Cir. 1988) (the patentee failed to show that the district court abused its discretion by awarding simple interest).

Compare Bio-Rad Laboratories, Inc. v. Nicolet Instrument Corp., 807 F.2d 964, 969, 1 U.S.P.Q.2d 1191, 1194 (Fed. Cir. 1986), cert. denied, 482 U.S. 915 (1987) (the district court erred in limiting prejudgment interest to the State judgment interest rate of 7% uncompounded; "The rate of prejudgment interest and whether it should be compounded or uncompounded are matters left largely to the discretion of the district court;" however, the district court must be guided by the purpose of prejudgment interest, which is to provide full compensation to the patent owner; the only evidence in the record suggested use of either the prime rate or the rate the patentee paid on its corporate borrowings during the period of infringement).

[327] E.g., Datascope Corp. v. SMEC, Inc., 879 F.2d 820, 829, 11 U.S.P.Q.2d 1321, 1327-28 (Fed. Cir. 1989), cert. denied, 110 S. Ct. 729 (1990) (the district court did not err in providing for annual rather than quarterly or monthly compounding; the district court was "entitled to credit [the] affidavit [of the president of the infringer] that [the infringer] would have been unable to comply with any requirement to report royalties more frequently than annually."); Studiengesellschaft Kohle, m.b.H. v. Dart Industries, Inc., 862 F.2d 1564, 9 U.S.P.Q.2d 1273 (Fed. Cir. 1988) (prime rate compounded quarterly); Lam, Inc. v. Johns-Manville Corp., 718 F.2d 1056, 219 U.S.P.Q. 670 (Fed. Cir. 1983) (average year-by-year prime rate; the patent owner, a small company, demonstrated that it had to borrow money at or above the prime rate in order to continue operations in the face of the defendant's infringement).

[328] Lam, Inc. v. Johns-Manville Corp., 718 F.2d 1056, 219 U.S.P.Q. 670 (Fed. Cir. 1983).

[329] Mathis v. Spears, 857 F.2d 749, 8 U.S.P.Q.2d 1551 (Fed. Cir. 1988).

[330] 35 U.S.C. § 285.

[331] E.g., Ryco, Inc. v. Ag-Bag Corp., 857 F.2d 1418, 8 U.S.P.Q.2d 1323 (Fed. Cir. 1988); Avia Group International, Inc. v. L.A. Gear California, Inc., 853 F.2d 1557, 1567, 7 U.S.P.Q.2d

If the accused infringer prevails, the court may find the case exceptional because of inequitable conduct in patent procurement[333] or bad faith litigation.[334]

1548, 1556 (Fed. Cir. 1988) ("Although an award of attorney fees, because discretionary, does not automatically follow from the willfulness of an infringement, . . . the willfulness of the infringement by the accused infringer may be a sufficient basis in a particular case for finding the case 'exceptional' for purposes of awarding attorney fees to the prevailing patent owner."); Spindelfabrik Suessen-Schurr v. Schubert & Salzer Maschinenfabrik AG, 829 F.2d 1075, 1085, 4 U.S.P.Q.2d 1044, 1051-52 (Fed. Cir. 1987), cert. denied, 484 U.S. 1063 (1988) ("Where a finding of willful and deliberate infringement and a collateral finding of exceptional circumstances are premised on the same basis, this court has found no abuse of discretion in awarding both increased damages and attorney fees.").

[332] See Beckman Instruments, Inc. v. LK.B. Produkter AB, 892 F.2d 1547, 1551-53, 13 U.S.P.Q.2d 1301, 1305-06 (Fed. Cir. 1989) (the district court did not commit clear error in finding the case "exceptional" because of the infringer's "strategy of vexatious activity" but abused its discretion by awarding the patentee its entire attorney fees in view of the finding that the infringer was not guilty of willful infringement and the infringer's success in showing invalidity and noninfringement of some of the claims in suit: "When infringement is found to be willful, the policy behind § 285 of discouraging infringement might justify imposing all of the patent owner's attorney fees on the infringer, even if the infringer prevailed as to some of the claims in suit. . . . [W]hen the sole basis for imposing attorney fees is 'gross injustice,' and one party prevails on some claims in issue while the other party prevails on other claims, this fact should be taken into account when determining the amount of fees under § 285.").

[333] E.g., A.B. Chance Co. v. RTE Corp., 854 F.2d 1307, 1312, 7 U.S.P.Q.2d 1881, 1885 (Fed. Cir. 1988) ("Inequitable conduct is a separate defense to patent infringement and, either alone or in conjunction with trial conduct, may constitute the basis for an award of attorney fees under 35 U.S.C. § 285.").

Compare J. P. Stevens Company, Inc. v. Lex Tex. Ltd., Inc., 822 F.2d 1047, 1052, 3 U.S.P.Q.2d 1235, 1238 (Fed. Cir. 1987) (the district court did not err in failing to award attorney fees to the accused infringer even though it had found the patent unenforceable because of inequitable conduct; neither 35 U.S.C. Section 285 nor case law "requires or contemplates that attorneys' fees be awarded to the alleged infringer in an inequitable conduct case 'absent compelling countervailing circumstances.'"); Gardco Manufacturing, Inc. v. Herst Lighting Co., 820 F.2d 1209, 2 U.S.P.Q.2d 2015 (Fed. Cir. 1987) ("[I]t has not been held that every case of proven inequitable conduct must result in an automatic attorney fee award, or that every instance of inequitable conduct mandates an evaluation of the case as 'exceptional.' After the district court determines that a case is exceptional, there remains in every case its freedom to exercise its discretion 'informed by the court's familiarity with the matter in litigation and the interest of justice.'").

[334] E.g., Eltech Systems Corp. v. PPG Industries, Inc., 903 F.2d 805, 811, 14 U.S.P.Q.2d 1965, 1970 (Fed. Cir. 1990) (the district court neither committed clear error in finding the case exceptional nor abused its discretion by awarding attorney fees against the patentee for filing and pursuing a groundless infringement suit; "Where . . . the patentee is manifestly unreasonable in assessing infringement, while continuing to assert infringement in court, an inference is proper of bad faith, whether grounded in or denominated wrongful intent, recklessness, or gross negligence."); Mathis v. Spears, 857 F.2d 749, 754, 8 U.S.P.Q.2d 1551, 1554 (Fed. Cir. 1988) ("The only deterrent to the . . . improper bringing of clearly unwarranted suits on obviously invalid or unenforceable patents is Section 285. No award under Section 285 can fully compensate a defendant subjected to bad faith litigation, e.g., for loss of executives' time and missed business opportunities . . . In determining the compensatory quantum of an award under Section 285 in such an egregious case, . . . courts should not be, and have not been,

The trial court has discretion whether to award fees[335] but cannot make an award without finding a sufficient basis for declaring the case exceptional.[336]

If a suit combines patent and nonpatent claims, Section 285 authorizes an award only for attorney services pertaining to the patent claims.[337] If, in a suit with multiple patents or claims, each party prevails to some extent, "the amount of fees awarded to the 'prevailing party' should bear some relation to the extent to which that party actually prevailed."[338]

§ 2G　Ownership and Transfer

Ownership rights in a patent vest initially in the inventor or inventors.[1] A patent has "the attributes of personal property,"[2] and a person may transfer ownership in a patent or patent application to another by written instrument.[3] A patent owner may grant exclusive or nonexclusive licenses.

---

limited to ordinary reimbursement of only those amounts paid by the injured party for purely legal services of lawyers, or precluded from ordinary reimbursement of legitimate expenses defendant was unfairly forced to pay.").

Compare Machinery Corp. of America v. Gullfiber AB, 774 F.2d 467, 227 U.S.P.Q. 368 (Fed. Cir. 1985) (the trial court erred in granting an award of attorney fees in a declaratory judgment suit against a patent owner solely on the ground that the patent owner sent an infringement warning notice to 162 potential customers of the plaintiff without first consulting patent counsel).

[335] *E.g.,* Modine Manufacturing Co. v. Allen Group, Inc., 917 F.2d 538, 543, 16 U.S.P.Q.2d 1622, 1626 (Fed. Cir. 1990) ("An express finding of willful infringement is a sufficient basis for classifying a case as 'exceptional,' and indeed, when a trial court denies attorney fees in spite of a finding of willful infringement, the court must explain why the case is *not* 'exceptional' " within the meaning of 35 U.S.C. Section 285; "Nevertheless, the decision whether or not to award fees is still committed to the discretion of the trial judge, and '[e]ven an exceptional case does not require in all circumstances the award of attorney fees.' "; the district court sufficiently "articulated the basis of [its] determination that this case, though exceptional' under section 285, does not justify an award of attorney fees.").

[336] *E.g.,* Advance Transformer Co. v. Levinson, 837 F.2d 1081, 5 U.S.P.Q.2d 1600 (Fed. Cir. 1988) (a finding of exceptional circumstances requires proof of actual wrongful intent or gross negligence).

[337] *E.g.,* Water Technologies Corp. v. Calco, Ltd., 850 F.2d 660, 7 U.S.P.Q.2d 1097 (Fed. Cir. 1988), *cert. denied,* 488 U.S. 968 (1988) (an award of the full amount of the patentee's fees cannot stand because the services fees were in part for a nonpatent claim of unfair competition).

[338] Beckman Instruments, Inc. v. LK.B. Produkter AB, 892 F.2d 1547, 1554, 13 U.S.P.Q.2d 1301, 1306-07 (Fed. Cir. 1989).

[1] Joint inventors acquire equal, undivided interests in a patent. Absent an agreement to the contrary, each joint owner may use or authorize others to use the subject matter claimed in the patent without accounting to the other owner or owners. 35 U.S.C.§ 262.

[2] 35 U.S.C. § 261.

[3] 35 U.S.C. § 261.

State contract, tort, and fiduciary laws govern most patent ownership, transfer and licensing questions. Farmland Irrigation Co., Inc. v. Dopplmaier, 48 Cal. 2d 208, 308 P.2d 732, 113 U.S.P.Q. 88 (1957). *See* D. Chisum, Patents § 22.03[4].

[1] Employee and Contractor Inventions

An employee owns the patent rights to his or her inventions conceived or reduced to practice during the course of employment,[4] with two important exceptions. First, an employee must assign patent rights to his employer if he was initially hired or later directed to solve a specific problem or to exercise inventive skill.[5] Second, an employee must assign patent rights if he signed an assignment contract.[6] Companies commonly use assignment contracts. An Executive Order controls the ownership by federal government employees of patent rights in their inventions.[7] A court may order a contractually obligated employee to assign and cooperate in the patent application process.[8] An employer or other person with a proprietary interest in the invention may file a patent application if the inventor refuses to do so.[9]

If an employee uses his employer's resources to conceive of or reduce to practice an invention, the employer acquires a "shop right," a nonexclusive, royalty-free, non-transferable license to make and use the invention.[10] A shop right is not an ownership interest because the employee as patentee retains all other rights, including licensing and filing infringement suits. A shop right continues even if the

---

[4] United States v. Dubilier Condenser Corp., 289 U.S. 178, 17 U.S.P.Q. 154 (1933).
See generally D. Chisum, Patents § 22.03.

[5] Standard Parts Co. v. Peck, 264 U.S. 52 (1924); National Development Co. v. Gray, 316 Mass. 240, 55 N.E.2d 783, 62 U.S.P.Q. 205 (1944).

[6] E.g., United Aircraft Products, Inc. v. Warrick, 79 Ohio App. 165, 72 N.E.2d 669, 73 U.S.P.Q. 128 (1945). Cf. Shamrock Technologies, Inc. v. Medical Sterilization, Inc., 903 F.2d 789, 794, 14 U.S.P.Q.2d 1728, 1733 (Fed. Cir. 1990) ("Employment, salary and bonuses are valid consideration for [an employee's] assignment [of patent rights in his or her work-related inventions] . . . ").
Such contract provisions vary in wording as they are privately prepared and negotiated documents.
Several state statutes restrict employee invention assignment agreements. See, e.g., Cal. Labor Code, § 2870-72; Wash. Rev. Code 49.44.140-.150; Minn. Stat. Ann. § 181.78; N.C. Gen. Stat. § 66.57.1-.2, which invalidate agreements requiring assignment of inventions made by the employee on his or her own time and do not relate to the employer's business or its actual or demonstrably anticipated research and development.

[7] See, e.g., Heinemann v. United States, 796 F.2d 451, 230 U.S.P.Q. 430 (Fed. Cir. 1986), cert. denied, 480 U.S. 930 (1987) (administrative determination of the ownership of patent rights in inventions by federal employees under Executive Order 10096 is subject to judicial review under the Administrative Procedure Act; such review is governed by the "arbitrary or capricious" standard; Order 10096 supercedes the common law standard of property rights that previously controlled, is not contrary to statute, and does not constitute a taking of property in violation of the Constitution's due process clause).

[8] E.g., Grove v. Grove Valve & Regulator Co., 4 Cal. App. 3d 299, 84 Cal. Rptr. 300 (1st Dist. 1970).

[9] 35 U.S.C. § 118. See also D. Chisum, Patents § 11.02[2].

[10] Wommack v. Durham Pecan Co., Inc., 715 F.2d 962, 219 U.S.P.Q. 1153 (5th Cir. 1983).
Shop right scope depends on the circumstances; it is not limited to the particular machines on which the invention had been used during the time of the inventor's employment. Tin Decorating Co. of Baltimore v. Metal Package Corp., 29 F.2d 1006 (S.D.N.Y. 1928), aff'd on other grounds, 37 F.2d 5, 4 U.S.P.Q. 253 (2d Cir. 1930), cert. denied, 281 U.S. 759 (1930).

inventor leaves the employment.[11] Shop rights usually arise in employment but may also arise in other relationships, for example, supplier and customer.[12]

[2] Ability to Sue Infringers

A patent owner or exclusive licensee may file a suit against an accused infringer.[13] An nonexclusive licensee may not sue for infringement.[14] A license is exclusive if the licensee receives exclusivity over a geographic area, a field of use, or a time period.[15] A license may be exclusive even if the patent owner has previously granted nonexclusive licenses or reserved the right to make, use or sell the invention himself.[16]

[11] Wiegand v. Dover Mfg. Co., 292 F. 255 (N.D. Ohio 1923).

[12] Francklyn v. Guilford Packing Co., 695 F.2d 1158, 1160-61, 217 U.S.P.Q. 317, 319 (9th Cir. 1983); Kurt H. Volk, Inc. v. Foundation for Christian Living, 534 F. Supp. 1059, 1083-84, 213 U.S.P.Q. 756, 778 (S.D. N.Y. 1982).

[13] D. Chisum, Patents § 21.03[2].

If there are joint owners of a patent (e.g., A owns 50% and B owns 50%), normally both should join in bringing any suit against an alleged infringer. See Willingham v. Lawton, 555 F.2d 1340, 194 U.S.P.Q. 249 (6th Cir. 1977); Catanzaro v. International Tel. & Tel. Corp., 378 F. Supp. 203, 183 U.S.P.Q. 273 (D. Del. 1974).

[14] Waterman v. Mackenzie, 138 U.S. 252 (1891); Life Time Doors, Inc. v. Walled Lake Door Co., 505 F.2d 1165, 184 U.S.P.Q. 1 (6th Cir. 1974). Cf. Kalman v. Berlyn Corp., 914 F.2d 1473, 1481, 16 U.S.P.Q.2d 1093, 1099 (Fed. Cir. 1990) ("It is well settled that a nonexclusive licensee of a patent has no standing to sue for infringement.").

In *Kalman*, the Federal Circuit held that the district court erred in denying a patentee's motion to add as co-plaintiff a sole manufacturing licensee, of which the patentee was a 50% owner, and in limiting the patentee's damages to 50% of the licensee's lost profits.

"[W]e do not give any licensee who joins the patentee standing to sue an infringer. When the sole licensee, however, has been shown to be directly damaged by an infringer in a two supplier market, and when the nexus between the sole licensee and the patentee is so clearly defined as here, the sole licensee must be recognized as the real party in interest. . . . [I]n determining that [the licensee] has standing to join as a co-plaintiff, we not only give effect to principles of equity, but also the Congressional mandate that, in patent actions, '[u]pon finding for the claimant the court shall award the claimant damages adequate to compensate for the infringement . . . ' 35 U.S.C. § 284 (1982)." 914 F.2d at 1481-82, 16 U.S.P.Q.2d at 1099-1100.

A nonexclusive licensee may extract a contractual commitment requiring the patent licensor to sue infringers. The licensor's failure to sue infringers is a breach of contract but is not grounds for allowing the licensee to sue. Philadelphia Brief Case Co. v. Specialty Leather Prod. Co., Inc., 145 F. Supp. 425, 430, 111 U.S.P.Q. 180, 183 (D. N.J. 1956), aff'd, 242 F.2d 511, 113 U.S.P.Q. 100 (3d Cir. 1957).

[15] Independent Wireless Telegraph Co. v. Radio Corp. of America, 269 U.S. 459 (1926); Weinar v. Rollform, Inc., 744 F.2d 797, 223 U.S.P.Q. 369 (Fed. Cir. 1984), cert. denied, 470 U.S. 1084 (1985); Pratt & Whitney v. United States, 153 F. Supp. 409, 411, 114 U.S.P.Q. 246, 248 (Ct. Cl. 1957).

[16] E.g., Western Elec. Co. v. Pacent Reproducer Corp., 42 F.2d 116, 119 (2d Cir. 1930), cert. denied, 282 U.S. 873 (1930). Cf. Weinar v. Rollform, Inc., 744 F.2d 797, 223 U.S.P.Q. 369 (Fed. Cir. 1984), cert. denied, 470 U.S. 1084 (1985) (one who is an exclusive distributor in the United States, but lacks authority to manufacture, may properly be awarded damages in an infringement suit).

If an exclusive licensee files a patent infringement suit, the patent owner/licensor is a necessary party and, if unwilling to join voluntarily, will be joined as an "involuntary plaintiff."[17]

[3] Compulsory Licenses

A patent owner has discretion to grant or refuse licenses.[18] Statutes provide for compulsory licensing of patents relating to inventions in certain areas.[19] In an antitrust case, a court may order compulsory patent licensing at reasonable royalty rates if patents are intimately associated with and contributed to anticompetitive conduct and licensing is necessary to restore competition in the relevant market.[20]

§ 2H International Aspects.

Inventors may apply for a United States patents regardless of citizenship or national origin. A person filing a patent application in another country may, under certain conditions, obtain a priority right when filing a corresponding United States application.

The United States is a party to the Patent Cooperation Treaty.

Any person making an invention in the United States must comply with the Invention Secrecy Act before applying for a patent in another country.

[1] Filing in Other Countries: National Security.

Any invention made in the United States[1] is subject to the Invention Secrecy Act.[2]

[a] **License Requirement.** A person may not file a patent application in another country on an invention made in the United States without (1) obtaining a license from the Commissioner of Patents and Trademarks, or (2) filing an application on the invention in the United States and waiting six months,[3] which allows PTO review of applications to determine whether national security concerns justify a secrecy order.[4]

Filing a patent application in the PTO is deemed an application for a license to file in other countries.[5] The PTO filing receipt sent to applicants indicates whether

---

[17] Independent Wireless Telegraph Co. v. Radio Corp. of America, 269 U.S. 459 (1926). See Rule 19 of the Federal Rules of Civil Procedure.

[18] *E.g.,* United States v. Studiengesellschaft Kohle, 670 F.2d 1122, 212 U.S.P.Q. 889 (D.C. Cir. 1981); SCM Corp. v. Xerox Corp., 645 F.2d 1195, 209 U.S.P.Q. 899 (2d Cir. 1981), *cert. denied,* 455 U.S. 1016, 215 U.S.P.Q. 96 (1982).

[19] *E.g.,* Clean Air Act, 42 U.S.C. 1875h 6; Atomic Energy Act, 42 U.S.C. § 2183(g).

[20] *See* United States v. Glaxo Group, Ltd., 410 U.S. 52, 176 U.S.P.Q. 289 (1973).

[1] An invention is made at the place where it is reduced to practice. Sealectro Corp. v. L.V.C. Indus., Inc., 271 F. Supp. 835, 153 U.S.P.Q. 610 (E.D. N.Y. 1967).

[2] 35 U.S.C. § 181-188. *See generally* D. Chisum, Patents § 1.06.

[3] 35 U.S.C. § 184.

[4] *See* § 2H[1][c].

[5] 37 C.F.R. § 5.12(a).

a license is granted.[6] If an inventor has not filed a United States application, or if he needs a license before return of the filing receipt, he may petition for a license.[7]

A licensing requirement violation results in rejection of a United States application.[8] The PTO may grant a retroactive license curing the violation.[9] Before 1988, the PTO could grant a license only if the violation was "inadvertent." The 1988 Patent Law Foreign Filing Amendments Act relaxes the standard to "error and without deceptive intention"[10] and provides that a violation will not invalidate an issued patent if the failure to procure the license was "through error and without deceptive intent."[11]

[b] **Amendments to Applications in Other Countries.** An amendment or alteration to an application in another country is a new application for which a license must be obtained.[12] A filing-receipt license allows amendments and additions to an application filed abroad if the subject matter's general nature is not changed.[13]

[c] **Secrecy Orders.** The Commissioner of Patents and Trademarks may issue a secrecy order as to the subject matter in a filed patent application if publication or disclosure would be detrimental to national security.[14] Such an order prohibits publication or disclosure of the subject matter and filing of an application in another country until the order is withdrawn or modified. A patent is withheld until the order is withdrawn. A person has a remedy for compensation for damages caused by the secrecy order.[15]

[2] Priority Based on Filing in Another Country.

A patent application filed in the United States within twelve months of the filing of a corresponding application for the same invention in another country may have the filing date benefit of the first application if certain conditions are met.[16]

---

[6] The grant may include not only a license to file, as required by 35 U.S.C. § 184, but also permission to export information for patent preparation purposes under various United States regulations that restrict the export of technology. 37 C.F.R. § 5.11.

[7] 37 C.F.R. § 5.13, 14.

[8] 35 U.S.C. § 185. Rejection applies to the entire patent application, not just those claims related to the subject matter as to which a license violation occurred. *In re* Gaertner, 604 F.2d 1348, 202 U.S.P.Q. 714 (CCPA 1979).

[9] 35 U.S.C. § 184. The license may be granted even after the patent has issued. Minnesota Mining & Mfg. Co. v. Norton Co., 366 F.2d 238, 151 U.S.P.Q. 1 (6th Cir. 1966), *cert. denied,* 385 U.S. 1005, 152 U.S.P.Q. 844 (1967).

[10] P.L. 100-418, Title IX, Subtitle B, Section 9101, 102 Stat. 1563.

[11] 35 U.S.C. § 185.

[12] *In re* Gaertner, 604 F.2d 1348, 202 U.S.P.Q. 714 (CCPA 1979). In *Gaertner*, the applicant filed an application in the United States for certain herbicidal compounds. Without obtaining a license, the applicant amended various corresponding applications in other countries to insert an additional specific example. The court held the addition was an unlicensed application in another country that required rejection of the United States application.

[13] 35 U.S.C. § 184; 37 C.F.R. § 5.15.

[14] 35 U.S.C. § 181.

[15] 35 U.S.C. § 183.

[16] 35 U.S.C. § 119. *See generally* D. Chisum, Patents § 14.01 *et seq.*

[a] **Eligibility.** The priority application must have been filed in a country that affords "similar privileges" to applications filed first in the United States,[17] which includes, but is not limited to, all Paris Convention member countries.

The priority application must have been for a "patent," which includes utility models, design registrations and, under certain circumstances, inventor's certificates.[18]

[b] **The Priority Period.** A United States application must be filed within twelve months of the earliest date of a regularly filed application for the same invention in another country.[19]

The first regularly filed application is one adequately disclosing the invention.[20] An earlier filed document lacking full disclosure does not start the twelve month period.[21]

[c] **Compliance with United States Disclosure Requirements.** The priority application must comply with United States disclosure requirements so as to support the claims in the subsequent United States application.[22] *Yasuko Kawai*[23] involved four appeals. Three were from PTO examiner rejections affirmed by the Board of Appeals, with the following fact pattern:

> 1. Inventor A filed a provisional specification in Great Britain that disclosed chemical compounds but failed to disclose a practical utility for the compounds as required by the *Manson* doctrine and the how-to-use aspect of the enablement requirement.[24]

> 2. Later, B and C published similar research that would render A's claims to the compounds unpatentable.

---

[17] 35 U.S.C.§ 119.

[18] American Infra-Red Radiant Co. v. Lambert Indus., Inc., 360 F.2d 977, 149 U.S.P.Q. 722 (8th Cir. 1966), *cert. denied*, 385 U.S. 920, 151 U.S.P.Q. 757 (1966); *Ex parte* Marinissen, 155 U.S.P.Q. 528 (PTO Bd. App. 1966).

An application for an inventor's certificate can provide a basis for a priority right only if the inventor had a choice between a patent and a certificate. 35 U.S.C. § 119; 37 C.F.R. § 1.55(b).

[19] 35 U.S.C. § 119. The priority period is six months for design patent applications. 35 U.S.C. § 172.

Under a 1961 amendment to Section 119, an applicant may rely on a second or later application filed in another country if all previous applications were abandoned before being laid open and are not the basis for any priority right.

The priority right is based only on the application filing in another country followed by timely filing in the United States. The priority application's subsequent fate in the country of filing is irrelevant; it does not matter that the priority application was abandoned or rejected. Wickman v. Vinco Corp., 288 F.2d 310, 129 U.S.P.Q. 43 (6th Cir. 1961). *Cf.* Stein Associates, Inc. v. Heat and Control, Inc., 748 F.2d 653, 657, 223 U.S.P.Q. 1277, 1280 (Fed. Cir. 1984).

[20] *See, e.g., Ex parte* Yamaguchi, 6 U.S.P.Q.2d 1805, 1807 (Bd. Pat. App. & Int'f 1987).

[21] *Cf. In re* Crouch, 129 F.2d 690, 54 U.S.P.Q. 316 (CCPA 1942).

[22] The enablement, description, and best mode disclosure requirements are discussed at § 2D[3].

[23] Yasuko Kawai v. Metlesics, 480 F.2d 880, 178 U.S.P.Q. 158 (CCPA 1973).

[24] The utility requirement is discussed at § 2C[2].

3. A filed a United States application within one year of the British filing. The United States application contained a utility disclosure.

Inventor A attempted to eliminate the intervening publications by relying on his British filing date as an invention date.

The remaining appeal was from a Board of Interferences award of priority of invention with the following fact pattern:

1. Inventor A filed an application in Japan disclosing a chemical compound and stating that such compound had "pharmacological effects on the central nervous system."

2. Inventor B filed an application in the United States disclosing the same invention.

3. A filed a corresponding application in the United States.

4. An interference is declared between A and B.

5. A sought the benefit of the prior application in Japan.

In all four appeals, the court held that applicant A was not entitled to the prior filing date. The priority application did not comply with United States disclosure requirements, including the requirement that a utility for a chemical compound be disclosed.[25] The priority applications were therefore not constructive reductions to practice of the subject matter later claimed in the corresponding United States applications.[26]

In *Gosteli*,[27] the Federal Circuit held that a priority application must fully support what is claimed to avoid a prior art reference dated after the priority filing date but before the U.S. filing date.[28] It is not sufficient that the priority application discloses as much of the claimed invention as is disclosed in the intervening reference.

---

[25] *Compare* Cross v. Izuka, 753 F.2d 1040, 224 U.S.P.Q. 739 (Fed. Cir. 1985). In *Cross*, the court emphasized that, in assessing whether a priority application adequately discloses a utility, due regard must be given to the fact that applications in other countries are typically arranged with a style and format differing from that of United States applications. Hence, it may be difficult to ascertain what the stated utility is. In United States applications, the "objectives" of the invention are set forth in a section on the "Summary of the Invention," and these objectives will be consonant with the disclosed utility.

[26] *See* § 2D[5][d].

[27] *In re* Gosteli, 872 F.2d 1008, 10 U.S.P.Q.2d 1614 (Fed. Cir. 1989).

[28] The court concluded that a 1965 Court of Customs and Patent Appeals (CCPA) decision, *In re* Ziegler, 347 F.2d 642, 146 U.S.P.Q. 76 (CCPA 1965), had been effectively overruled, *sub silentio* by later CCPA decisions.

It indicated the actual *holding* of *Ziegler* could be distinguished.

"*Ziegler* never mentions section 112 by name in its analysis of section 119 . . . . *Ziegler* did not examine section 112 compliance because the issue was not in dispute. The court stated that '[t]here is no question here that the [foreign priority] applications adequately support the broad claims, once the references have been antedated as to the narrow subject matter which they disclose.' . . . In other words, all claims in the United States application were properly supported, as required by section 112, ¶ 1, by Ziegler's foreign priority applications. Furthermore, both *Kawai* . . . and *Wertheim* . . . cite *Ziegler*; neither case recognizes a conflict nor an inconsistency." 872 F.2d at 1011, 10 U.S.P.Q.2d at 1617.

In *Gosteli*, the appellants claimed bicyclic thia-aza compounds. The claims in question were generic to a class of such compounds. The examiner rejected the claims as anticipated by a reference with an effective date prior to appellant's filing date. The reference disclosed two specific compounds falling within the appellant's claims. The appellant attempted to antedate the reference by claiming the benefit of its Luxembourg patent application's filing date. The foreign priority application disclosed a subgenus of the genus claimed in the U.S. application and specifically described the two species in the reference. The PTO denied the appellant the benefit of its priority filing date because the foreign application did not provide a written description of the "invention." The appellant attempted to swear behind the reference by filing a Rule 131 declaration,[29] which the PTO rejected because the declaration did not show completion of the invention "in this country."

The Federal Circuit affirmed the rejection.

> "Generally, an applicant may antedate prior art by relying on the benefit of a previously filed foreign application to establish an effective date earlier than that of the reference.
>
> . . .
>
> ". . . Section 119 provides that a foreign application shall have the same effect' as if it had been filed in the United States. . . . Accordingly, if the effective filing date of what is claimed in a United States application is at issue, to preserve symmetry of treatment between sections 120 and 119, the foreign priority application must be examined to ascertain if it supports, within the meaning of section 112, ¶ 1, what is claimed in the United States application.
>
> . . .
>
> ". . . An application relying on the benefit of an earlier filing date in the United States would receive the same treatment under 35 U.S.C. § 120."

[d] **Inventorship.** The priority application must be for an invention by the same inventorship entity as is named in the corresponding United States application.[30] A legal representative or assignee may file an application in the inventor's name.

[e] **Formal Requirements.** No priority claim need be made in the initially filed United States application, but the inventor oath or declaration must identify any prior application.[31] A priority claim must be filed, together with a certified copy of the

---

The court agreed that "there is inconsistent language" in *Ziegler*, and later CCPA decisions: "To the extent that *Ziegler's* language is inconsistent with that in [*Kawai v. Metlesics*, 480 F.2d 880, 178 U.S.P.Q. 158 (CCPA 1973)], [*In re Wertheim*, 541 F.2d 257, 191 U.S.P.Q. 90 (CCPA 1976)], and [*In re Scheiber*, 587 F.2d 59, 199 U.S.P.Q. 782 (CCPA 1978)], that inconsistency has already been *sub silentio* removed. The CCPA's later decisions control because that court always sat *en banc*." 872 F.2d at 1011, 10 U.S.P.Q.2d at 1617.

[29] 37 CFR § 1.131.

[30] Vogel v. Jones, 486 F.2d 1068, 1072, 179 U.S.P.Q. 425, 428 (CCPA 1973); Schmitt v. Babcock, 377 F.2d 994, 153 U.S.P.Q. 719 (CCPA 1967).

As to the proper applicant for a United States application, see § 2D[3][e]. The inventorship entity may be different as to different claims in the same application.

[31] 37 C.F.R. § 1.63(c). *See* § 2D[3].

priority application, no later than the date when the issue fee is paid.[32] An erroneously omitted priority claim may be added by reissue.[33]

[f] **Effect of Priority.** A priority application is entitled to the "same effect" as an application filed in the United States.[34]

The priority date is a constructive reduction to practice of the disclosed invention for determining priority in an interference.[35] The priority date is the date of invention for avoiding prior art references.

A priority filing date has no effect when the invention is, more than one year prior to the actual filing date in the United States, either patented or described in a printed publication or in public use or on sale in the United States.[36] Consider the following example:

1. On January 1, 1984, A offers invention X for sale in the United States.

2. On March 1, 1984, A files an application disclosing X in Japan.

3. On February 1, 1985, A files a corresponding application in the United States.

The sales offer (January 1, 1984) is a bar even though A is entitled to the March 1, 1984 priority date. Had A filed directly in the United States within one year of the offer, no bar would have arisen.

A United States patent issuing on an application entitled to a priority filing date is effective as prior art only as of the United States filing date, not the priority filing date.[37]

[3] Patent Cooperation Treaty

The Patent Cooperation Treaty (PCT) has been implemented in the United States.[38] The PCT does not alter substantive requirements of patentability in the United States[39] but does facilitate procedures for obtaining patents in various countries including the United States.

---

[32] 37 C.F.R. § 1.55(a).

[33] Fontijn v. Okamoto, 518 F.2d 610, 186 U.S.P.Q. 97 (CCPA 1975); Brenner v. State of Israel, 400 F.2d 789, 158 U.S.P.Q. 584 (D.C. Cir. 1968).

See § 2D[6][b][i].

[34] 35 U.S.C. § 119.

[35] Broos v. Barton, 142 F.2d 690, 61 U.S.P.Q. 447 (CCPA 1944). *Cf. In re* Mulder, 716 F.2d 1542, 219 U.S.P.Q. 189 (Fed. Cir. 1983). In *Broos*, the applicant was given the benefit of a priority filing date even though the invention was conceived in the United States. A filing in another country on an invention made in the United States must comply with the Invention Secrecy Act. *See* § 2H[1][a].

[36] 35 U.S.C. § 119.

[37] *See* § 2C[5][d][ii].

[38] 35 U.S.C. §§ 351-376; 37 C.F.R. § 1.401-482.

[39] Once an international application that designates the United States enters the "national stage," questions of substance (and, within the scope of the requirements of the PCT and its implementing regulations), procedure are determined under the standards applicable to regular national applications.

An international application may be filed in a PCT receiving office designating one or more countries in which patent protection is desired. A PCT application designating the United States establishes an effective filing date in the United States.[40]

---

[40] 35 U.S.C. § 363.

CHAPTER 3

TRADE SECRETS LAW

SYNOPSIS

§ 3A Introduction

Trade secrets law protects secret business information against unauthorized use or disclosure by one who obtained it through improper means or through a confidential relationship.

Originating in the early 19th century, trade secrets law has evolved to accommodate the changing nature of business secrets, competition, technology, and employment patterns. In recent years, accelerating technological change, increased spending on research and development, greater employee mobility and entrepreneurial activity, the internationalization of business competition, and the growing complexity of the task of integrating different technologies have heightened trade secrets law's significance.

Trade secrets law reflects economic policy judgments about how to encourage innovation, competition, and consumer welfare and ethical notions about proper business behavior. In the latter respect, trade secrets law is a subset of the general norms of morality and good faith that are also reflected in the torts of unfair competition and breach of confidence.

Defining "secret" and reconciling confidentiality obligations with policies favoring free competition and employee mobility are complexities that have led to well-developed trade secrets doctrine, but the underlying moral principles retain force and may lead to judicial intervention when fact patterns do not conform to trade secrets doctrine.[1] These decisions are difficult to reconcile with precedent, and economic policy judgments may be submerged, but they are best explained as reflecting courts' discomfort with the behavior in question from an ethical standpoint.

Courts base trade secrets doctrine on two distinct principles: (1) a property interest in secret business information; and (2) a duty to respect the confidentiality of information. In applying the property principle, courts examine whether particular information is sufficiently secret and valuable to be considered private property. In applying the duty principle, courts put primary emphasis on the circumstances under which an alleged misappropriator obtained the information and may impose a duty to avoid its use or disclosure if it was obtained through a confidential relationship or improper means—even if its secrecy has not been definitely established.

Some courts and commentators reject the concept of a property interest in a trade secret, usually citing *Du Pont*,[2] a 1917 Supreme Court case, which stated:

> ". . . The word 'property' as applied to . . . trade secrets is an unanalyzed expression of certain secondary consequences of the primary fact that the law makes some rudimentary requirements of good faith. Whether the plaintiffs have any valuable secret or not the defendant knows the facts, whatever they are, through a special confidence that he accepted. The property may be denied, but the confidence cannot be."[3]

This language is frequently misconstrued; as a recent Supreme Court decision put it, the opinion "did not deny the existence of a property interest," it only "deemed determination of the existence of that interest irrelevant to resolution of the case."[4] The concept of a property interest in trade secrets is in fact indispensable to the logic of trade secrets law. In *Ruckelshaus*,[5] the Supreme Court held trade secrets to be a property right protectable under the Constitution.

In some situations, a case outcome may depend on which principle the court emphasizes. For example, if information's secrecy is not clearly established but a defendant

---

[1] For a discussion of non-secret information protection, see § 3C[4].

[2] E.I. du Pont de Nemours & Co. v. Masland, 244 U.S. 1016 (1917).

[3] 244 U.S. at 1019.

[4] Ruckelshaus v. Monsanto Co., 467 U.S. 986, 1004 n.9 (1983).

[5] 467 U.S. at 1000–05. *See also* Thomas v. Union Carbide, 473 U.S. 568, 584 (1985).

acquired information through improper means, a court emphasizing the property principle would find no protectable trade secret; a court emphasizing the duty principle would penalize the defendant. Trade secrets law's equitable nature and ethical roots invite emphasis on the duty principle when a defendant's conduct offends the court's notions of fairness and morality.[6]

Courts emphasizing the property principle have developed an extensive body of precedents defining protectable trade secrets.[7] As for courts emphasizing the duty principle, some apply broad definitions of trade secrets; others accept narrower definitions but find duties of non-use and non-disclosure even if information does not qualify as a trade secret.[8] The divergent emphases lead to occasional lack of clarity and predictability in trade secrets law.

In addition to confusion about underlying principles, two other factors enhance the potential for inconsistent decisions in trade secrets cases. First, trade secrets law defines the secrecy underlying the property principle in relative terms.[9] Second, the duty principle relies on the blurry distinction between proper and improper behavior.[10]

Notwithstanding these ambiguities, it is clear in many fact-patterns which principle courts will emphasize and what results they will reach. In a case of theft or industrial espionage, the obvious misconduct may call for sanctions whether or not the information technically qualifies as protectable property. In contrast, where information is voluntarily disclosed to a party with merely an implied duty to maintain it in confidence, the absence of misconduct usually leads courts to require that the secrecy and value of the information be established as a prerequisite to restricting the recipient's use of it.

Trade secrets cases became less predictable in the 1980s and early 1990s, perhaps because the increased pace of technological change made it harder for reasonable people to agree about when asserted secrets differ from information widely known in an industry,[11] or perhaps because increased mobility and entrepreneurial activity by erstwhile employees have changed assumptions about employment relationships and the extent of one's duty to an employer. Whether these or other explanations are preferred, it is difficult to predict how courts will apply traditional trade secrets principles to situations in new high technology industries.

Because not all the fine lines can be clearly drawn, prudent businesspersons are usually advised to err on the side of caution in designing programs to protect trade secrets and avoid inadvertent or apparent misappropriation of others' trade secrets.[12]

---

[6] See § 3C[4].

[7] See § 3C[1].

[8] See § 3C[4].

[9] Today, secrecy must only be "relative," or the subject of efforts that are "reasonable under the circumstances." See § 3C[1][c].

[10] For a discussion of proper and improper means, see § 3D[7][b].

[11] See § 3C[1][c][vi].

[12] For a discussion of preventive programs, see § 3H.

[1] State Law v. Federal Law

Unlike patent, trademark and copyright laws, in which federal statutes played an early and increasingly dominant role, trade secrets remain a matter of state law. Each state is free to develop its own rules, as long as they do not conflict with federal intellectual property law policy, but states' laws are substantially similar because modern trade secrets law has been dominated by two major sources, the 1939 Restatement of Torts and the 1979 Uniform Trade Secrets Act.

[2] Trade Secrets Law's Relationship to Patent Law

Accused trade secret misappropriators argue that state law trade secret protection conflicts with, and should be preempted by, patent law because it diminishes the incentive for inventors to publicly disclose their inventions to obtain limited patent rights. In *Kewanee*,[13] the Supreme Court rejected this argument, noting that, although the United States Congress has the power to preempt state laws conflicting with federal patent and copyright laws, "Congress, by its silence over these many years, has seen the wisdom of allowing the States to enforce trade secret protection."[14] As a policy matter, federal patent law does not preempt state trade secrets laws because the latter (1) do not protect any matter once it has been pubicly disclosed (2) are weaker than patent law because they do not bar reverse engineering or independent development, and (3) protect non-economic interests such as privacy.

In holding that patent law does not preempt trade secret law, the Supreme Court relied on both the ethical and economic bases of trade secret doctrine:

> "Trade secret law and patent law have co-existed in this country for over one hundred years. Each has its particular role to play, and the operation of one does not take away from the need for the other. Trade secret law encourages the development and exploitation of those items of lesser or different invention than might be accorded protection under the patent laws, but which items still have an important part to play in the technological and scientific advancement of the Nation. Trade secret law promotes the sharing of knowledge, and the efficient operation of industry; it permits the individual inventor to reap the rewards of his labor by contracting with a company large enough to develop and exploit it."[15]

The Court painted a bleak picture of life without trade secrets law:

> "The holder of a trade secret would not likely share his secret with a manufacturer who cannot be placed under binding legal obligation to pay a license fee or to protect the secret. The result would be to hoard rather than disseminate knowledge."[16]

> "Instead, then, of licensing others to use his invention and making the most efficient use of existing manufacturing and marketing structures within the

---

[13] Kewanee Oil Co. v. Bicron Corp., 416 U.S. 470, 181 U.S.P.Q. 673 (1974).

[14] 416 U.S. at 493, 181 U.S.P.Q. at 682.

[15] 416 U.S. at 493, 181 U.S.P.Q. at 680.

[16] 416 U.S. at 486, citing Painton & Co. v. Bourns, Inc., 442 F.2d 216, 169 U.S.P.Q. 528 (2d Cir. 1971).

(Matthew Bender & Co., Inc.)

industry, the trade secret holder would tend either to limit his utilization of the invention, thereby depriving the public of the maximum benefit of its use, or engage in the time-consuming and economically wasteful enterprise of constructing duplicative manufacturing and marketing mechanisms for the exploitation of the invention."[17]

"In addition to the increased costs for protection from burglary, wiretapping, bribery, and the other means used to misappropriate trade secrets, there is the inevitable cost to the basic decency of society when one firm steals from another. A most fundamental human right, that of privacy, is threatened when industrial espionage is condoned or is made profitable."[18]

"Smaller companies would be placed at a distinct economic disadvantage, since the costs of this kind of self-help could be great, and the cost to the public of the use of this invention would be increased."[19]

In short, trade secret-patent coexistence is well-established, and the two are in harmony because they serve different economic and ethical functions.

§ 3B Historical Development

Originating in early 19th century England, trade secrets law was adopted and developed in the United States by common law court decisions, "restated" in 1939 and codified in many states beginning in 1979. Its basic principles have changed remarkably little.

[1] Early English Cases

The first United States trade secrets cases cited English equity court decisions. Equity was a body of principles administered without juries by the English Chancery. Instead of monetary damage awards available from law courts, equity courts issued decrees enjoining or compelling specified conduct. Equity courts acted when monetary damages were an inadequate remedy for the plaintiff. Judicial reform measures have merged courts of equity and law, but equitable principles and remedies live on in United States jurisprudence.

The early English cases, concerned mostly with secret medicine recipes, anticipated many of modern trade secrets law's doctrinal and practical issues, including the relationship between trade secrets and patents, the conceptual difficulty of defining a trade secret as "property," and the free competition-trade secret relationship.

As early as 1817 English courts acknowledged that an agreement to preserve a non-patented secret was binding. *Newberry*[1] considered a request to decree specific performance of a manufacturer-supplier's agreement to refrain from disclosing medicinal recipes and manufacturing techniques learned in confidence from an inventor-distributor. The court advised the plaintiff to seek damages in a law court, because

---

[17] 416 U.S. at 486–67.

[18] 416 U.S. at 487, 181 U.S.P.Q. at 680.

[19] 416 U.S. at 486, 181 U.S.P.Q. at 680.

[1] Newberry v. James, 2 MER. 446 (1817).

it considered issuance and enforcement of a specific performance injunction to be impossible without destroying the secret by requiring its disclosure to the court. *Williams*[2] upheld an injunction ordering a defendant-son-employee to return to the plaintiff-father-employer recipes and medicine that had been misused, together with profits from medicine that had been sold. Finding the alleged recipes' secrecy to be unproven (and difficult for a court to ascertain), the court declined to order non-disclosure, but stated that if an agreement of confidentiality were proven, a plaintiff's entitlement to a court order of specific performance would be "a question which would require great consideration."

Within a few years, English equity courts overcame their ambivalence toward protecting trade secrets and abandoned their assumption that confidentiality could not be ordered and enforced without disclosing and destroying the secrets. In *Yovat*,[3] a veterinary trainee surreptitiously copied medicine recipes and usage directions in violation of an understanding that his job training would be confined to more general knowledge. The court enjoined the trainee-defendant from using or disclosing the information, but, as was traditional in equity courts, accommodated non-parties' welfare by refusing to interrupt veterinary treatment already in progress.[4]

In *Bryson*,[5] the first reported case concerning secrets other than medicinal recipes, the court ordered the seller of a dyeing business to perform his contractual obligations of non-disclosure, non-use, and non-competition. The court accommodated non-party interests and the public policy against excessively broad non-competitive agreements by interpreting the non-competition covenant to be limited in duration and territory. This case was a forerunner of the later tendency for trade secrets claims to become entangled with questions of whether to enforce anti-competitive contractual provisions.[6]

In *Green*,[7] a mother disclosed a secret eye-ointment recipe to her eldest son for the benefit of his siblings, who later sued him for an accounting of his profits from the recipe. The court asserted that "[t]here can be no property" in a "substance so shadowy" as a "mere verbal secret,"[8] but, typical of later courts that would reject the concept of property in trade secrets, based its denial of relief primarily on other grounds: the defendant received the information under no express or implied obligations and may have given valuable consideration for it. By 1851, a court could survey and draw upon a wealth of authorities supporting injunctions against disclosure and use of an improperly acquired secret.

In *Morison*,[9] a case in which the defendant-partner acquired secret recipes of plaintiff-partners either surreptitiously or through a confidential disclosure for a limited purpose, the court noted that the doctrinal basis for these injunctions was disparate:

---

[2] Williams v. Williams, 3 MER. 157 (1817).

[3] Yovat v. Winyard, 1 JAC & W. 394 (1820).

[4] 1 JAC & W. at 395.

[5] Bryson v. Whitehead, 1 SIM & ST. 73 (1822).

[6] For a discussion of covenants not to compete, see § 3D[6][c].

[7] Green v. Folgham, 1 SIM & ST. 398 (1823).

[8] 1 SIM. & ST. at 403.

[9] Morison v. Moat, 9 HARE 241 (1851).

"Different grounds have indeed been assigned for the exercise of that jurisdiction. In some cases it has been referred to property, in others to contract, and in others, again, it has been treated as founded upon trust or confidence. . . ."[10]

Morison relied on *Green* and *Williams* for the propositions that an express or implied duty to preserve confidentiality may be enforced. Addressing the potential conflict between patent law and trade secret protection, the court rejected the defendant's argument that protecting trade secrets "would be to give the Plaintiffs a better right than that of a patentee."[11]

"[W]hat we have to deal with here is, not the right of the Plaintiffs against the world, but their right against the Defendant. It may well be that the Plaintiffs have no title against the world in general [as would be granted by a patent], and may yet have good title against this Defendant. . . ."[12]

[2] Early United States Cases

United States courts faced with confidential information misappropriation controversies looked to the early English cases for authority and sought to "do equity" in light of progressively more diverse factual situations and more complex industrial relationships and to elaborate the principles that underlay their decisions. They developed a body of judicial precedent constituting each state's common (i.e., nonstatutory) trade secrets law.[13]

Vickery,[14] the first reported United States trade secrets case, involved a dispute about the sale of a chocolate-making business that included secret manufacturing methods. The seller had initially promised to convey exclusive title to his secrets, and the buyer had used the seller's written promises to secure investor participation. The seller then refused to do more than communicate the secrets to the buyers with an express reservation of the right to communicate the same secrets to others. Citing *Bryson*, the Massachusetts court rejected the seller's argument that the obligation of non-disclosure was void as a trade restraint:

"The public are not prejudiced by the transfer of [the defendant's secret art] to the plaintiff . . . [because] it is of no consequence to the public whether the secret art be used by the plaintiff or by the defendant."[15]

In *Taylor,*[16] the parties manufactured and sold shoe-cutting equipment and accessories as business partners. Defendant, who "was wholly ignorant of the business," promised plaintiff, who was experienced and established in the business, not to disclose any business secrets. The court acknowledged the principle that "the public has no

---

[10] 9 HARE at 255.

[11] 9 HARE at 500.

[12] 9 HARE at 258–59.

[13] After 1979, many states codified their trade secrets law in statutes modeled after the Uniform Trade Secrets Act, which is discussed in § 3B[4], but the law's common law flavor remains intact.

[14] Vickery v. Welch, 36 Mass. 523 (1837).

[15] 36 Mass. at 527.

[16] Taylor v. Blanchard, 95 Am. Dec. 203, 95 Mass. 370 (1866).

right to" a businessman's trade secrets and that a contract for their exclusive use is not a restraint of trade but did not regard the information as a secret because "[a]lthough it was not generally known to the public, it was carried on in three different towns in the Commonwealth, by three different parties." [17]

In *Peabody*,[18] the court enforced a defendant-employee's agreement not to disclose secret inventions and adaptations of gunny cloth manufacturing machinery despite his argument that the information had lost its secrecy through disclosure to other workers. Emphasizing the time and money the plaintiff-employer hd expended to develop the information, and noting that the defendant had had greater access to the information than had other employees, the court held that "A secret of trade or manufacture does not lose its character by being confidentially disclosed to agents or servants, without whose assistance it could not be made of any value." [19]

In *Salomon*,[20] the court granted a preliminary injunction restraining two former employees from using the employer's secret methods in violation of an alleged oral non-disclosure agreement but permitted the former employees to disclose prices and suppliers and customers because that information was of a character that, in the absence of a proven contractual restriction, employees should be free to use after an employment relationship.[21]

In *Tabor*,[22] the court upheld an injunction restraining a trade secrets owner's competitor from using pump design drawings surreptitiously copied by a repairman. It held that a duty of confidentiality extends to parties who have no direct relationship with a trade secret owner, ignoring a dissent's assertion that because "[t]he cases cited to sustain the judgment arose out of the relation of master servant, or between partners," [23] confidentiality obligations should be limited to persons who have a relationship with the trade secrets owner. It held that misappropriation is not excused by the fact that defendants could have learned the secrets by combining study of plaintiff's product with additional experimentation. The information could "only be ascertained by a series of experiments, involving the expenditure of both time and money"; "because this discovery may be possible by fair means, it would not justify a discovery by unfair means." [24]

> ". . . Even if resort to the patterns of the plaintiff was more of a convenience than a necessity . . . the defendant had no right to obtain it by unfair means, or to use it after it was thus obtained." [25]

Other cases of historical significance include *Thum*(1897), *Stone* (1903), and *Pressed Steel* (1904). In *Thum*,[26] a sticky fly paper manufacturer persuaded the court to enjoin

---

[17] 95 Mass. at 374.

[18] Peabody v. Norfolk, 98 Mass. 452 (1868).

[19] 98 Mass. at 461.

[20] Salomon v. Hertz, 2 A. 379 (N.J. Eq. 1886).

[21] 2 A. at 381.

[22] Tabor v. Hoffman, 23 N.E. 12 (1889).

[23] 23 N.E. at 13.

[24] 23 N.E. at 13.

[25] 23 N.E. at 13.

[26] O. & W. Thum Co. v. Tloczynski, 114 Mich. 149, 72 N.W. 140 (1897).

a former employee from disclosing manufacturing processes or machinery designs despite the absence of a written non-disclosure (or employment) agreement.

In *Stone*,[27] a chemical manufacturer's former employee disclosed to his new employer secret methods of mixing and treating non-secret hair-removing compound ingredients. The court enjoined the employee from making further disclosures and enjoined the new employer from using the disclosed methods, having found that the new employer had known of the employee's confidentiality duty.

In *Pressed Steel*,[28] a railroad car manufacturer gave car design blueprints to prospective and actual customers to enable them to (1) verify that the design met their requirements, (2) verify that cars did not vary from the required specifications, and (3) order spare parts and make repairs. The blueprints were not labeled confidential but were circulated only to customer-railroad companies and receipts were required from every recipient. The court found a competitor's acquisition of blueprint copies from customers to be in violation of an implied customer agreement that the blueprints and the design information in them would be used only for limited purposes. It enjoined the defendant-competitor from using the copies and ordered them returned to the plaintiff.

The decisions discussed above were widely cited by courts in later cases; they were the most significant contributors to the body of precedent that was the primary authority for United States trade secrets law until the late 1930s.

[3] The Restatement

As part of the early 20th century United States movement to make state laws more uniform, prominent lawyers, judges and professors collected and synthesized opinions and underlying principles of particular areas of law into a series of "Restatements."[29] The 1939 Restatement of Torts included two sections on trade secrets.[30]

The Restatements were not binding. As one legal historian describes them,

> "The Restatements . . . were not designed to be (and were not) enacted as statutes by any legislature. The idea or the hope was that the Restatement formulations would exert a persuasive . . . force in purging the common law of eccentricities which might have arisen in particular jurisdictions and in promoting a soundly based uniformity throughout the country."[31]

The same historian points out the Restatements' persuasiveness was sometimes undermined by unresolved ambiguities about the Restatement project:

> "[W]ere the Restaters supposed to be 'codifying' the law as it was? In situations where conflicting rules had evolved, were they supposed always to

---

[27] Stone v. Goss, 65 N.J. Eq. 756, 55 A. 736 (1903).

[28] Pressed Steel Car Co. v. Standard Steel Car Co., 210 Pa. 464, 60 A. 4 (1904).

[29] Some legal historians characterize the Restatements as "the reaction of a conservative establishment, eager to preserve a threatened status quo." *E.g.*, G. Gilmore, The Ages of American Law, at 73.

[30] Restatement of Torts, §§ 757 and 758. A third section, 759, discussed protection for non-confidential information. *See* § 3C[4].

[31] G. Gilmore, The Ages of American Law 72 (1977).

choose the 'majority rule'? If a common law rule was felt to be unsatisfactory or unjust, were they at liberty to 'restate' a 'better rule' . . . ?"[32]

The Restatement's persuasiveness was adversely affected less in the area of trade secrets law because it adopted a core concept of "commercial morality" that was sufficiently elastic and circumstance-specific to permit the Restatement and the courts to rationalize doctrinally contradictory decisions. The Restatement's trade secret provisions used previous case law mainly as examples for broad generalizations. Most courts adopted the Restatement, but the few areas where the Restatement sought to simplify trade secrets law's rationale, it was not widely followed. For example, the Restatement rejected the premise that trade secrets law encourages invention, commenting that its protection "is not based on a policy of rewarding or otherwise encouraging the development of secret processes or devices. The protection is merely against breach of faith and reprehensible means of learning another's secret."[33]

This comment was consistent with the various Restatements' lack, as another legal historian has said, "of any notion that rules had social or economic consequences,"[34] but it failed to persuade the courts, which eventually came to consider commercial morality to be merely a means to the greater end of encouraging inventions and their most efficient exploitation.[35]

The Restatement's authors also sought to purge the property principle from trade secrets law, stating:

> "The suggestion that one has a right to exclude others from the use of his trade secret because he has a right of property in the idea has been frequently advanced and rejected."[36]

> "The theory that has prevailed is that the protection is afforded only by a general duty of good faith. . . ."[37]

In fact, the theory that has prevailed in the post-Restatement era is that a property right in a trade secret, although terminable by public disclosure, will be upheld against misappropriators and protected in a variety of contexts.[38]

On the whole, the Restatement led to a greater consistency of authority, language and, to a lesser extent, substantive doctrine among different states' trade secrets decisions. Substantial inconsistencies remained, however, in part because the Restatement emphasized general and subjective concepts such as "relative" secrecy[39] and "generally accepted standards of commercial morality and reasonable conduct,"[40] giving courts substantial room to differ on the application of its principles to various

---

[32] G. Gilmore, 73.

[33] Restatement § 757 comment b.

[34] L. Friedman, History of American Law 582 (1973).

[35] See, e.g., Kewanee Oil Co. v. Bicron Corp., 416 U.S. 470 (1974).

[36] Restatement § 757 Comment a.

[37] Restatement § 757 Comment a.

[38] For a discussion of the property principle, see § 3A.

[39] For a discussion of relative secrecy, see § 3C[1][c].

[40] For a discussion of improper means, see § 3D[7][b].

factual situations. The Restatement also suggested avenues outside trade secrets law for protecting non-secret information.[41]

A second Restatement of Torts, published in 1978, omitted trade secrets because trade secrets law had become "no more dependent on Tort law than it is on many other general fields of the law and upon broad statutory developments . . . ."[42]

[4] The Uniform Act

Further trade secrets law standardization was taken up by another legal reform movement, which sought to codify various areas of law by means of uniform acts designed to be adopted by individual states. The National Conference of Commissioners on Uniform State Law published the Uniform Trade Secrets Act (the "Uniform Act") in 1979 with the stated goals of unifying definitions of trade secrets and misappropriation and standardizing statutes of limitations.[43] By the end of 1990, the Uniform Act, with state to state modifications, had been adopted in 34 jurisdictions.[44]

Generally, the Uniform Act codified state court common law decisions, many of which followed the 1939 Restatement, but it also used post-Restatement experience to develop clearer guidelines on remedies.[45] By stating a goal of increased uniformity, it caused Uniform Act state courts to give greater attention to decisions of courts in other Uniform Act jurisdictions.

The Act's prefatory note stated:

> "[It] contains general concepts . . . [and substitutes] unitary definitions of trade secret and trade secret misappropriation, and a single statute of limitations for the various . . . theories of noncontractual liability utilized at common law [and] codifies the results of the better reasoned cases concerning [trade secrets] remedies."[46]

---

[41] For a discussion of non-secret information, see § 3C[4].

[42] Restatement of Torts, 2 Div. 9 at 1.

[43] Uniform Act, prefatory note.

[44] Alphabetically, the jurisdictions are: Alabama, Alaska, Arizona, California, Colorado, Connecticut, Delaware, District of Columbia, Florida, Hawaii, Idaho, Illinois, Indiana, Iowa, Kansas, Kentucky, Louisiana, Maine, Maryland, Minnesota, Montana, Nevada, New Hampshire, New Mexico, North Dakota, Oklahoma, Oregon, Rhode Island, South Dakota, Utah, Virginia, Washington, West Virginia, and Wisconsin.

The chronological order of state and District of Columbia adoption is as follows: Minnesota (1-1-1981), Kansas (7-1-1981), Louisiana (7-19-1981), Washington (1-1-1982), Indiana (2-25-1982), Delaware (4-15-1982), Connecticut (6-23-1983), North Dakota (7-1-1983), California (1-1-1985), Montana (1985: exact date is unclear), Oklahoma (1-1-1986), Wisconsin (4-25-1986), Colorado (7-1-1986), Rhode Island (7-1-1986), Virginia (7-1-1986), West Virginia (7-1-1986), Nevada (3-5-1987), Maine (5-22-1987), Alabama (8-12-1987), Illinois (1-1-88), Oregon (1-1-1988), South Dakota (7-1-1988), Alaska (8- 2-1988), Florida (10-1-1988), Idaho (1-1-1989), District of Columbia (3-16-1989), New Mexico (4-3-1989), Utah (5-1-1989), Hawaii (7-1-1989), Maryland (7-1-1989), New Hampshire (1-1-1990), Kentucky (4-6-1990), Arizona (4-11-1990), Iowa (4-27-1990).

[45] See § 3F.

[46] Uniform Act Prefatory Note.

(Matthew Bender & Co., Inc.)

The Uniform Act and the Restatement are largely consistent, but the Act differs on a few points where the Restatement was not widely followed. The Act dropped the Restatement requirement that a trade secret be "continuously used in one's business,"[47] and rejected the Restatement's conferral of absolute immunity on innocent purchasers for value.[48] The Act also defined misappropriation to include mere acquisition by improper means, dropping the traditional requirement of actual or threatened use or disclosure.[49]

Four Uniform Act Amendments published in 1985 clarified (1) injunctive relief requirements, (2) alternative measures of damages,[50] (3) the Act's lack of effect on contract-law remedies,[51] and (4) the Act's inapplicability to misappropriation that began before its effective date.[52]

Even in the thirty-four Uniform Act jurisdictions, Restatement-influenced judicial decisions pre-dating the Uniform Act-based statute usually retain interpretive value unless they are expressly contradicted by the statute.

§ 3C   Nature of Protection—Rights

[1]   Information That Qualifies as a Trade Secret

To qualify as a trade secret, information must be eligible for protection, be secret, and have commercial value.

[a]   **Definitions.** Trade secrets law traditionally emphasized application of equitable principles to specific facts rather than providing precise definitions. The Restatement stated that "[a]n exact definition of a trade secret is not possible,"[1] and contented itself with non-exclusive description and a list of factors to be considered. Uniform Act-based statutes created statutory definitions, but the definitions contain only "general concepts."[2] As one court stated, "[i]n the law of trade secrets, . . . examples may be more helpful than definition or attempted redefinition."[3]

The Restatement defines a trade secret as:

> "[A]ny formula, pattern, device or compilation of information which is used in one's business, and gives him an opportunity to obtain an advantage over competitors who do not know or use it . . . [if it is] a process or device for continuous use in the operation of the business [rather than] information as to a single or ephemeral events."[4]

---

[47] For a discussion of continuous use, see § 3C[1][b][v].

[48] For a discussion of innocent receipt, see § 3D[7][c].

[49] For a discussion of use or disclosure as an element of misappropriation, see § 3D[8].

[50] For a discussion of the amended provision, see § 3F[2][a][i].

[51] For a discussion of the amended provision, see § 3D[2].

[52] All quotations in this text are of the post-1985 language.

[1] Restatement Comment b.

[2] Uniform Act prefatory note.

[3] K & G Oil Tool & Serv. Co., Inc. v. G & G Fishing Tool Serv., 158 Tex. 594, 606, 314 S.W.2d 782, 790 (1958), cert. denied, 358 U.S. 898, reh'g denied, 359 U.S. 921 (1959).

[4] Restatement § 757 Comment b.

The Restatement lists the following six factors to "be considered in determining whether given information is one's trade secret."

"(1) the extent to which the information is known outside of his business;

(2) the extent to which it is known by employees and others involved in his business;

(3) the extent of measures taken by him to guard the secrecy of the information;

(4) the value of the information to him and to his competitors;

(5) the amount of effort or money expended by him in developing the information;

(6) the ease or difficulty with which the information could be properly acquired or duplicated by others."[5]

The Uniform Act defines a trade secret as:

"information, including a formula, pattern, compilation, program, device, method, technique, or process, that:

"(i) derives independent economic value, actual or potential, from not being generally known to, and not being readily ascertainable by proper means by, other persons who can obtain economic value from its disclosure or use, and

"(ii) is the subject of efforts that are reasonable under the circumstances to maintain secrecy."[6]

Individual state statutes may differ from the Uniform Act definitions and comments quoted below, where state legislatures adopted modified versions or adopted and retained pre-1985 language of the Act that has been subsequently amended by the Uniform Laws.[7]

[b] **Eligible Subject Matter.** Virtually any "concrete" information can be a trade secret. Non-technical information has long been eligible, as have combinations of otherwise unprotectable information. A few jurisdictions condition protection of customer lists on express contractual covenants. The Restatement "continuous use" requirement was never widely accepted and has been largely abandoned. The Uniform Act endorses the majority position protecting "negative" trade secrets.

One instance of dismissal due to ineligible subject matter occurred in *Lehman*,[8] in which a trade secret claim was made in connection with alleged misappropriation of information on company availability and attractiveness as a "takeover candidate". The court found that "availability information could never have been a trade secret [because the plaintiff] had no control over its disclosure," and that the plaintiff's

---

[5] Restatement § 757 Comment b.

[6] Uniform Act § 1(4).

[7] All quotes are from the amended 1985 version. The few pre-amendment differences are described in the accompanying footnotes. For an annotated version of the Uniform Act, with listings of state variations and clear indications of the pre- and post-amendment text, see Uniform Laws Annotated, Vol. 14, West Pub. Co., 1990.

[8] Lehman v. Dow Jones & Co., Inc., 783 F.2d 285, 299 (2d Cir. 1986).

opinion about a takeover candidate's attractiveness to a defendant "is simply not the kind of information that qualifies as a trade secret."

[i] *Concreteness.* The Restatement phrase "a process or device"[9] reflects a traditional requirement that a trade secret be more concrete than an idea, theory, possibility or emotion, and relatively specific in its intended implementation. The Uniform Act does not mention concreteness, thereby leaving courts free to apply or reject this traditional requirement as they see fit.

In *Lamson*,[10] the defendant, who sold a company and agreed to convey title to all of his "inventions," later received a patent. The buyer sued to obtain the patent, arguing that, when the deal was made, the invention must have existed and was covered by contract. The court held that a "vague mental conception" in existence at the time the contract was executed, which defendant had not reduced to practice or made into a model or drawing, was not an "invention" under the contract.[11]

In *Jones*,[12] the inventor of a fertilizer spreader orally disclosed his idea to a manufacturer who later disputed whether the information was concrete enough to be protectable. The court noted that trade secrets law does not require information to be in tangible or material form, found that the idea was for a specific device, as shown by the manufacturer's ability to construct the device within 24 hours of learning the details, and held that it was not a mere theory and was concrete enough for protection.[13]

In *Epstein*,[14] the court denied a claim based on confidential disclosure of an idea for a clothes-tag design because the verbally communicated idea, which the plaintiff acknowledged was just a "possibility," did not meet the requirement that "[t]he disclosure must be in sufficient detail and have such definiteness that there is no doubt as to what is disclosed."[15]

In *Vekamaf*,[16] a group of companies engaged in designing, manufacturing and marketing industrial equipment alleged misappropriation of eleven distinct trade secrets by a prospective customer to whom disclosures had been made in confidence. One asserted trade secret was an assurance, based on experience and experimentation, of the quality of the plaintiff's techniques for bending pipes. Finding no authority for protecting "an emotion" as a trade secret, the court stated that a trade secret must be something "of form and substance."[17]

> "It is difficult to see how an expression of confidence can in any way constitute a trade secret. It is nothing more than a representation of the superiority of

---

[9] Restatement § 757 Comment b.

[10] Lamson v. Martin, 159 Mass. 557, 35 N.E. 78 (Mass. 1893).

[11] 35 N.E. at 81.

[12] Jones v. Ulrich, 342 Ill. App. 16, 95 N.E.2d 113 (Ill. App. Ct. 1950).

[13] 95 N.E.2d at 120.

[14] Epstein v. Dennison Mfg. Co., 314 F. Supp. 116, 164 U.S.P.Q. 291 (S.D.N.Y. 1969).

[15] 314 F. Supp. at 126, 164 U.S.P.Q. 298-99.

[16] Vekamaf Holland B.V. v. Pipe Benders, Inc., 211 U.S.P.Q. 955 (D. Minn. 1981), *aff'd*, 696 F.2d 608, 217 U.S.P.Q. 32 (8th Cir. 1982).

[17] 211 U.S.P.Q. at 978.

a product comparable to those expounded by every manufacturer of a product offered for public sale. Certainly, plaintiffs did not intend to keep this confidence secret."[18]

[ii] *Nontechnical Information.* Trade secrets can protect nontechnical information including sales data,[19] marketing plans,[20] and bid price information,[21] as well as price codes, market studies, cost reports, and bookkeeping methods.

[iii] *Combinations.* Although not explicitly stated in the Restatement or the Uniform Act, the rule that trade secrets may include a combination of characteristics or components, each in the public domain, but which as a unified design affords a competitive advantage and is not publicly known, finds acceptance in case law.[22] For example, in the computer software industry, the "manner in which . . . generic utility programs interact" is protectable even if the component utility programs are not.[23]

[iv] *Customer Lists.* Customer lists are the subject of much litigation, yielding differing results. Courts often focus on the ease with which a particular list could be duplicated. Facts relevant to this determination include the industry's nature, the effort invested in compiling the list, the inclusion of information in addition to names and addresses, and the extent to which listed customers seek to make themselves known to plaintiff's competitors.

In *American Paper*[24] the court noted:

"[L]ists of customers who operate manufacturing concerns and who need shipping supplies to ship their products . . . may not be generally known to the public [but] they certainly would be known or readily ascertainable to other persons in the shipping business. The compilation process in this case is neither sophisticated nor difficult nor particularly time consuming."[25]

In *Courtesy*,[26] the court distinguished *American Paper's* facts because of the work effort that went into a list: "If a customer list is acquired by lengthy and expensive

---

[18] 211 U.S.P.Q. at 980.

[19] *See,e.g.,* American Standard Inc. v. Pfizer Inc., 828 F.2d 734, 3 U.S.P.Q.2d 1817 (Fed. Cir. 1987).

[20] *See, e.g.,* Clark v. Bunker, 453 F.2d 1006, 172 U.S.P.Q. 420 (9th Cir. 1972).

[21] *See, e.g.,* Sperry-Rand Corp. v. Electronic Concepts, Inc., 325 F. Supp. 1209, 170 U.S.P.Q. 410 (E.D. Va. 1970), *vacated on other grounds sub nom.* Sperry Rand v. A-T-O, Inc., 447 F.2d 1387, 171 U.S.P.Q. 775 (4th Cir. 1971), *cert. denied,* 405 U.S. 1017, 173 U.S.P.Q. 193 (1972).

[22] *See, e.g.,* Imperial Chem. Indus. Ltd. v. National Distillers and Chem. Corp., 342 F.2d 737, 144 U.S.P.Q. 695 (2d Cir. 1965).

[23] Integrated Cash Mgmt. Services, Inc. v. Digital Transactions, Inc., 920 F.2d 171, 17 U.S.P.Q.2d 1054 (2d Cir. 1990).

[24] American Paper & Packaging Products Inc. v. Kirgan, 183 Cal. App. 3d 1318, 228 Cal. Rptr. 713 (1986).

[25] 183 Cal. App. 3d at 1326, 228 Cal. Rptr. at 717.

[26] Courtesy Temporary Serv., Inc. v. Camacho, 222 Cal. App. 3d 1278, 272 Cal. Rptr. 352 (1990).

efforts which, from a negative viewpoint, indicate those entities that have not subscribed to plaintiff's services, it deserves protection as a 'trade secret'. . . ."[27]

In *SI Handling,*[28] the identity of key decisionmakers within General Motors was distinguished from a typical customer list because it "involves only one customer that is well-known in the industry and that . . . actively seeks to disseminate the information."[29]

A customer list is particularly likely to be protected if it contains not only names and addresses but also the "identity of the person to be contacted at each customer location, a detailed sales history revealing products purchased, quantities purchased, container sizes, prices paid, and frequency of purchases."[30]

Wisconsin courts are notable for refusing trade secrets protection to customer lists on public policy grounds but will enforce contractual covenants against customer list use.[31]

[v] *Continuous Use.* The Restatement requires that information be put to "continuous use" in business operations.[32] Many courts ignored or rejected this requirement when faced with information that had demonstrable business value even if plaintiff was not using it when the alleged breach occurred.[33] The Uniform Act endorses the business value view with a "broader definition" of trade secret that does not require continuous use.[34]

A rare modern example of protection denied in part for lack of continuous use occurred in *Lehman.*[35] The court refused to characterize information on the availability and attractiveness of companies as takeover candidates as a trade secret, cited the

---

[27] 222 Cal. App. 3d at 1287–88, 228 Cal. Rptr. at 357-58, citing Hollingsworth Solderless Terminal Co. v. Turley, 622 F.2d 1324 (9th Cir. 1980).

[28] SI Handling Systems, Inc. v. Heisley, 753 F.2d 1244, 225 U.S.P.Q. 441 (3d Cir. 1985).

[29] 753 F.2d at 1258, 225 U.S.P.Q. at 449. This distinction, and the true degree of G.M.'s active dissemination, is questionable in light of the lower court's finding that "[i]t was only after peeling through layer and layer of personnel and following many false leads that SI was finally able to reach the real decisionmakers as to its product." *Id.*

[30] NCH Corp. v. Broyles, 749 F.2d 247, 252 (5th Cir. 1985).

[31] *See, e.g.,* Corroon & Black-Rutters & Roberts, Inc. v. Hosch, 109 Wis. 2d 290, 325 N.W.2d 883, 887–88 (1982).

[32] Restatement Torts § 757, Comment (b): "It is not simply information as a single or ephemeral events in the conduct of the business, as, for example, the amount or other terms of a secret bid for a contract or the salary of certain employees, or the security investments made or contemplated, or the date fixed for the announcement of a new policy or for bringing out a new model or the like. A trade secret is a process or device for continuous use in the operation of the business."

[33] *See, e.g.,* Ferroline Corp. v. General Aniline & Film Corp., 207 F.2d 912, 99 U.S.P.Q. 240 (7th Cir. 1953), *cert. denied,* 347 U.S. 953, *reh'g denied,* 347 U.S. 979 (1954); Sikes v. McGraw-Edison Co., 665 F.2d 731, 213 U.S.P.Q. 983 (5th Cir. 1982), *cert. denied,* 458 U.S. 1108 (1982); and Sinclair v. Aquarius Electronics, Inc., 42 Cal. App. 3d 216, 116 Cal. Rptr. 654, 184 U.S.P.Q. 682 (1974).

[34] Uniform Act Comment to § 1.

[35] Lehman v. Dow Jones & Co., Inc., 783 F.2d 285 (2d Cir. 1986).

Restatement continuous use requirement, and distinguished information that was the "product" for sale from information "used in running [a] business."[36]

[vi] *Negative Information.* The Uniform Act definition of trade secret includes:

"information that has commercial value from a negative viewpoint[.] [F]or example the results of lengthy and expensive research which proves that a certain process will not work could be of great value to a competitor."[37]

In non-Uniform Act states, negative information protectability is not completely settled. Most decisions, recognizing the "competitive edge the competitor gains by avoiding the developer's blind alleys"[38] and the helpfulness of information demonstrating "what pitfall to avoid,"[39] uphold the protectability of experience showing which research avenues are not worth pursuing.[40] A few decisions distinguish negative know-how from affirmative manufacturing know-how,[41] question the protectability of negative know-how,[42] and exclude it from trade secret protection.[43]

The positive and negative information distinction is often "unintelligible."[44] As one court said, "every human process" results "from realizations of what not to do":

"the selection of one action at a given moment involves the rejection of every other conceivable one that might have been chosen . . . . Knowing what not to do often leads automatically to knowing what to do."[45]

[c] **Secrecy.** Under trade secrets law's property principle, secrecy is "the threshold issue in every case,"[46] but the secrecy's sufficiency is judged in light of the circumstances, including the industry's level of general knowledge, the information's ascertainability, the offensiveness of a misappropriator's conduct and anything else that affects a court's perception of a situation's equities. As discussed in the following

---

[36] 783 F.2d at 298.

[37] Uniform Act Comment to § 1.

[38] Johns-Manville Corp. v. Guardian Indus. Corp., 586 F. Supp. 1034, 1073, 221 U.S.P.Q. 319, 352 (E.D. Mich.1983), *modified,* 223 U.S.P.Q. 974 (E.D. Mich. 1984), citing Allis-Chalmers Mfg. Co. v. Continental Aviation & Eng. Corp., 255 F. Supp. 645, 151 U.S.P.Q. 25 (E.D. Mich. 1966).

[39] Syntex Opthalmics, Inc. v. Novicky, 214 U.S.P.Q. 272, 278 (N.D. Ill. 1982), *aff'd,* 701 F.2d 677, 219 U.S.P.Q. 962 (7th Cir. 1983).

[40] Gillette Company v. Williams, 360 F. Supp. 1171, 1173, 178 U.S.P.Q. 327, 328 (D. Conn. 1973).

[41] Megapulse, Inc. v. Lewis, 672 F.2d 959, 970 (D.C. Cir. 1982).

[42] Hurst v. Hughes Tool Co., 634 F.2d 895, 899, 209 U.S.P.Q. 284, 288 (5th Cir. 1981), *cert. denied,* 454 U.S. 829 (1981). *See also* Detachable Bit v. Timkin Roller Bearing Co., 133 F.2d 632, 635 (6th Cir. 1943).

[43] *E.g.,* Materials Development Corp. v. Atlantic Advanced Metals, Inc., 172 U.S.P.Q. 595, 606 (Mass. Super. Ct. 1971).

[44] Metallurgical Industries Inc. v. Fourtek, Inc., 790 F.2d 1195, 1203, 229 U.S.P.Q. 945, 950 (5th Cir. 1986).

[45] 790 F.2d at 1203, 229 U.S.P.Q. at 950.

[46] Microbiological Research Corp. v. Muna, 625 P.2d 690, 698, 214 U.S.P.Q. 567 (Utah 1981); *see also* Selection Research Inc. v. Murman, 230 Neb. 786, 433 N.W.2d 526, 10 U.S.P.Q.2d 1361, 1356 (1989).

sections, secrecy can be destroyed by insufficient precautions, by the marketing of a product that discloses the secret, by compliance with patent laws, or by disclosure in judicial proceedings or to government agencies. Any substantial efforts will usually be enough to avoid dismissal based solely on insufficient precautions, but lackadaisical efforts may affect a court's overall balancing of equities both in the initial liability determination and in any subsequent remedies determination.

In general, relative secrecy survives confidential disclosure on a "need to know" basis to employees, joint venturers, customers and suppliers.[47]

Secrecy questions involve three related issues: (1) the owner's precautions, (2) the level of general knowledge in an industry, and (3) the ascertainability of information from proper sources. These often intermingle, because ineffective precautions may permit information to become generally known in an industry, and the level of general knowledge is a crucial determinant of whether otherwise secret information is readily ascertainable.

[i]   *Definitions.* Neither the Restatement nor the Uniform Act define secrecy, trade secret law's central concept, but the courts discuss it at length.

The Restatement states that "matters of public knowledge or of general knowledge in an industry cannot be appropriated by one as his secret."[48]

The Uniform Act "does not require that information be generally known to the public for trade secret rights to be lost. If the principal persons who can obtain economic benefit from information are aware of it, there is no trade secret."[49]

The Act requires that efforts to maintain secrecy be "reasonable under the circumstances" in a characterization of, rather than a departure from, the previous Restatement-influenced common law. The Act's comment approvingly summarizes the common law requirements as follows:

> "[R]easonable efforts to maintain secrecy have been held to include advising employees of the existence of a trade secret, limiting access to a trade secret on 'need to know basis,' and controlling plant access. On the other hand, public disclosure of information through display, trade journal publications, advertising, or other carelessness can preclude protection."[50]

The courts do not require that extreme and unduly expensive procedures be taken to protect trade secrets against flagrant industrial espionage.[51]

A 1948 case illustrated the secrecy requirement by stating that trade secrets law is concerned with secrecy "in the legal and equitable sense. Was it secret in the sense that a disclosure by an employee would lessen its value? Was it a secret in the sense that third parties would be willing to pay for a breach of trust in order to ascertain its nature?"[52]

---

[47] See § 3H[1] for discussion of how trade secrets owners can seek to ensure that all disclosures are confidential.

[48] Restatement Comment (b).

[49] Uniform Act Comment to § 1.

[50] Uniform Act Comment to § 1.

[51] Uniform Act Comment to § 1.

[52] L.M. Rabinowitz & Co. v. Dasher, 82 N.Y.S.2d 431, 437 (1948).

[*ii*] *Application of Secrecy Requirement.* Precautions to preserve secrecy can be categorized as procedures for (1) *security*, to prevent intrusion by outsiders, and (2) *confidentiality*, to identify secret information to, and secure obligations of confidentiality from, insiders and business contacts.

Electro-Craft,[53] a Uniform Act case, illustrates the importance of circumstances in evaluating both procedures. The court forgave lax *security* where most plant entrances were unguarded and had no signs warning of limited access, a badge system was abandoned, documents were not in locked storage, and discarded drawings and plans were not destroyed, because there was little industrial espionage in the industry, but it declined to forgive plaintiff's lax *confidentiality* procedures where plaintiff "treated its information as if it were not secret."

> "None of its technical documents were marked 'Confidential', and drawings, dimensions and parts were sent to customers and vendors without special marking. Employee access to documents was not restricted. [The plaintiff] never issued a policy statement outlining what it considered to be secret. Many informal tours were given to vendors and customers without warnings as to confidential information. Further, two plants each had an 'open house' at which the public was invited to observe manufacturing processes."[54]

The court stated that the plaintiff's "efforts were especially inadequate because of the nonintuitive nature of [plaintiff's] claimed secrets here. The dimensions, etc., of [plaintiff's] motors are not trade secrets in as obvious a way as a 'secret formula' might be."[55]

Syntex[56] underlined the link between circumstances and courts' holdings on secrecy sufficiency, stating "where the security lapses were not the cause of the misappropriation, those lapses should not be the basis for denying protection."[57]

In *Dickerman,*[58] the court reached a similar result with respect to the sufficiency of confidentiality measures, holding that preliminary demonstrations of accounting and management software to potential customers who were not asked to sign confidentiality agreements did not destroy secrecy. The demonstrations did not reveal the program's entire menu, all its submenus or any user's guide or manual, and therefore did not permit the customers to understand the program's design and architecture.

In *Defiance,*[59] the court reached a contrary result, strictly applying the property principle to information inadvertently made accessible to a competitor. The plaintiff sold the defendant a computer without erasing secret information from the computer's memory. The filename or password needed to access the information was contained

---

[53] Electro-Craft Corp. v. Controlled Motion, 332 N.W.2d 890, 220 U.S.P.Q. 811 (Minn. 1983).

[54] 332 N.W.2d at 903, 220 U.S.P.Q. at 821.

[55] 332 N.W.2d at 902, 220 U.S.P.Q. at 820–21.

[56] Syntex-Opthalmics, Inc. v. Novicky, 214 U.S.P.Q. 272 (N.D. Ill. 1982), *aff'd sub nom.* Syntex Ophthalmics, Inc. v. Tsuetaki, 701 F.2d 677, 219 U.S.P.Q. 962 (7th Cir. 1983).

[57] 214 U.S.P.Q. at 277.

[58] Dickerman Associates v. Tiverton Bottled Gas, 594 F. Supp. 30, 33-34 (D. Mass. 1984).

[59] Defiance Button Mach. Co. v. C & C Metal Products, 759 F.2d 1053, 1063–64, 225 U.S.P.Q. 797, 804 (2d Cir. 1985), *cert. denied,* 474 U.S. 844 (1985).

in a book that was not subject to secrecy precautions. The defendant obtained the password from the plaintiff's former employee rather than from the unprotected book. The plaintiff was held to have forfeited protection of the information by failing to erase it.

In *Innovative Construction Systems*,[60] the court found a manufacturer's relatively loose secrecy procedures to be sufficient. That suppliers, job applicants and employees' friends had free access to the manufacturing area was not relevant to the secrecy of a formula, which was kept out of view in a notebook in the plant manager's office. Plaintiff's reliance on oral non-disclosure agreements from prospective buyers of the plaintiff's company was reasonable because this was standard industry practice.

In *Wheelabrator*,[61] the court held a steel shot cleaning abrasives manufacturer to a higher secrecy standard in the context of a claim against a former employee where the existence of a confidentiality obligation was a close question. Plaintiff's fence and guardposts protected the entire plant including non-secret facilities but provided no special security for facilities where allegedly secret processes were used for steel shot drying, heat treating, separation, screening and packaging. Plaintiff routinely admitted technically sophisticated customers and contractors to the plant subject to no express confidentiality notice or agreement and published a photograph of allegedly secret equipment. The court found insufficient secrecy.

One case found sufficient secrecy even though (1) a cut-away model of a ski disclosed its interior construction at a public conference (because the alleged misappropriator did not attend the conference), and (2) plaintiff gave tours of its factory (because no competitors were permitted to see the manufacturing procedure during the tours).[62] Another case found sufficient secrecy even though a computer manufacturer distributed thousands of circuitry drawings to customers, third party users, vendors and trainees. The drawings bore a restricted use legend prohibiting unauthorized reproduction and use.[63]

Three other courts that found insufficient secrecy emphasized the fact that (1) drawings were distributed without restrictive use legends,[64] (2) employees were not instructed as to the secrecy of technical information,[65] or (3) an allegedly secret design was embodied in a sample displayed for two months in one relatively small store.[66]

[iii] *Ascertainability from Products and Public Sources.* An alleged trade secret is readily ascertainable if, in light of the general knowledge in an industry, information available through proper means (e.g., examination of publicly available products, publicly circulated materials and public records) effectively reveals the purported trade secrets to any interested competitor without substantial research time or expense.

---

[60] *In re* Innovative Construction Systems, Inc., 793 F.2d 875, 230 U.S.P.Q. 94 (7th Cir. 1986).

[61] Wheelabrator Corporation v. Fogle, 317 F. Supp. 633, 167 U.S.P.Q. 72 (W.D. La. 1970), aff'd, 438 F.2d 1226, 168 U.S.P.Q. 679 (5th Cir. 1971).

[62] K-2 Ski Co. v. Head Ski Co., Inc., 506 F.2d 471, 183 U.S.P.Q. 724 (9th Cir. 1974).

[63] Data General Corp. v. Digital Computer Controls, Inc., 357 A.2d 105, 188 U.S.P.Q. 276 (Del. Cir. Ch. 1975).

[64] Midland-Ross Corp. v. Yokana, 293 F.2d 411, 413 (3d Cir. 1961).

[65] National Rejectors, Inc. v. Trieman, 152 U.S.P.Q. 120, 135 (Mo. S. Ct. 1966).

[66] Skoog v. McCray Refrigerator Co., 211 F.2d 254, 101 U.S.P.Q. 1 (7th Cir. 1954).

The Restatement requires that "except by the use of improper means, there would be difficulty in acquiring the information," and specifies that "[m]atters which are completely disclosed by the goods which one markets cannot be his secret."[67]

The Uniform Act Comment states that "Information is readily ascertainable if it is available in trade journals, reference books, or published materials. Often, the nature of a product lends itself to being readily copied as soon as it is available on the market."[68]

The product disclosure paradigm is a "simple device, widely circulated, the construction of which [is] ascertainable at a glance."[69]

There is no clear test for distinguishing readily ascertainable information from information ascertainable only with difficulty. One court stated that the time needed for reverse engineering is a factor in determining whether information is readily ascertainable;[70] another disagreed, citing the Uniform Act for the proposition that "the possibility of reverse engineering a trade secret . . . is not a factor in determining whether an item is a trade secret, but rather is a factor in deciding how long the injunctive relief should last."[71]

One court held:

> "[A plaintiff] cannot recover for appropriation of information which had been so completely disclosed to the public as to dispel the existence of a trade secret and thus to negate the confidential relationship which had been established . . . . [However] where the extent of disclosure is arguable, and where the information had not been clearly placed in the public domain . . . [the defendant should not be allowed] to avoid the consequences of the breach of confidence by piecing together in retrospect bits of information which had been disclosed in a variety of places and which as a combination were not clearly a matter of public knowledge."[72]

Information is often ascertainable from a product only if substantial time is invested examining the product. If many competitors ascertain the information or the information otherwise becomes widely known in the industry, courts reach a variety of holdings, but in recent years they tend to focus on a misappropriation's "head start" value and extend protection for a head start time period against a misappropriating defendant.[73]

If competitors have not ascertained the information, "[a]ny finding of discoverability must be reconciled with the fact of non-discovery."[74]

---

[67] Restatement § 757 Comment b.

[68] Uniform Act Comment to § 1.

[69] Smith v. Dravo Corp., 203 F.2d 369, 375, 97 U.S.P.Q. 98, 103 (7th Cir. 1953). *See also* Carver v. Harr, 132 N.J. Eq. 207, 27 A.2d 895 (1942).

[70] Electro-Craft Corp. v. Controlled Motion, 332 N.W.2d 890, 899, 220 U.S.P.Q. 811, 817 (Minn. 1983).

[71] Minuteman, Inc. v. Alexander, 147 Wis. 2d 842, 434 N.W.2d 773, 778–79 (1989), citing the Minnesota Uniform Act.

[72] Servo Corp. of America v. General Elec. Co., 393 F.2d 551, 555, 157 U.S.P.Q. 470, 473 (4th Cir. 1968).

[73] *See* §§ 3F[1][c] and 3F[2][a][ii].

[74] Zotos Intern., Inc. v. Young, 830 F.2d 350, 353, 4 U.S.P.Q.2d 1330, 1333 (D.C. Cir. 1987).

[iv] *Copyrighted Material.* Public distribution of copyrighted materials[75] causes any trade secrets disclosed therein to enter the public domain. One decision holds that a "limited publication"[76] for copyright purposes, if subject also to appropriate trade secret restrictions, is not inconsistent with retaining a work's secret character.[77]

[v] *Patented Material.* Issuance of a United States patent causes all information (whether claimed or merely disclosed) in the patent application to become a public record and enter the public domain even if the patent is subsequently declared invalid by a court. A technology rights owner can be left with neither patent nor trade secret protection if a patent is declared invalid.[78] Prior to issuance, United States patent applications are confidential, but patent applications in many countries become public records long before they are approved or rejected.[79]

Patent law requires that a patent specification claiming an invention disclose not only sufficient information to enable persons skilled in the art to make and use that invention but also the "best mode" the inventor contemplates, as of the patent application filing date, for carrying out the invention.[80] The "best mode" requirement restricts an owner's ability to seek a patent on some facets of an invention while retaining trade secrets rights over preferred embodiments or techniques.[81]

[vi] *Novelty v. General Knowledge in an Industry.* Courts sometimes characterize the distinction between a trade secret and information generally known within an industry as a "novelty" requirement.[82] Protectable information must differ from widely known information, and the difference must have commercial value: "Mere variations in general processes known in the field which embody no superior advances are not protected."[83] The Supreme Court, in summarizing trade secrets law requirements, stated: "some novelty will be required if merely because that which does not possess novelty is usually known; secrecy, in the context of trade secrets, thus implies at least minimal novelty."[84]

A defendant relying on the trade secret novelty requirement must show the generally known information to be virtually identical to the alleged trade secret because, as one

---

[75] See § 4D[1].

[76] The 1976 Copyright Act abolished the distinction between "limited" and "general" publications. See § 4D[1].
The Copyright Office allows registration of computer program and "secure test" works in a form that will not necessarily cause disclosure of the ideas expressed in the works. See § 4D[3].

[77] Technicon Medical Information Systems Corp. v. Green Bay Packaging, 687 F.2d 1032, 1039, 215 U.S.P.Q. 1001, 1007 (7th Cir. 1982), cert. denied, 459 U.S. 1106 (1983).

[78] The Uniform Act Prefatory Note cites this as a key reason for businesses to rely on trade secrets protection.

[79] See § 2D[1][c].

[80] See § 2D[3][c][viii].

[81] E.g., Chemcast Corp. v. Arco Indus. Corp., 913 F.2d 923, 16 U.S.P.Q.2d 1033 (Fed. Cir. 1990).

[82] See, e.g., Anaconda Co. v. Metric Tool & Die Co., 485 F. Supp. 410, 205 U.S.P.Q. 723 (E.D. Pa. 1980).

[83] Jostens Inc. v. National Computer Systems, 318 N.W.2d 691, 698, 214 U.S.P.Q. 918, 923 (Minn. 1982) (surveying and summing up variety of judicial comments on novelty requirements).

[84] Kewanee Oil Co. v. Bicron Corp., 416 U.S. 470, 476, 181 U.S.P.Q. 673, 676 (1974).

court said of a trade secret, it "may seem (and perhaps be) a simple idea, easily conceivable. But actual experience demonstrated that the idea was not so readily understood."[85]

In *SI Handling*,[86] the court declined to protect information on low-cost parts suppliers' identity and prices, finding that it was known outside the plaintiff's business by the suppliers themselves "who have every incentive, and every right, to disclose it to their customers," but did protect custom ball bearing and bearing lubrication, specifications ordered on a confidential basis from a bearing and lubrication supplier because the supplier's obligation of confidentiality prevented the specifications from being widely known except through breach of confidence.

[vii] *Disclosure to Government Agencies.* Government agencies collect information with potential trade secret status in connection with regulatory, purchasing and research activities. The agencies' practices differ, and most have regulations protecting trade secrets, but trade secrets submitted to the government continue to run a substantial risk of being disclosed to third parties.

Disclosure to a government agency that does not have a duty to maintain the information's confidentiality causes forfeiture of trade secret status.[87] Disclosure to an agency in confidence does not terminate trade secret protectability,[88] but an agency promise to keep the information confidential can be overridden. An agency subpoena may be denied enforcement if a court finds the agency unwilling or unable to prevent detrimental disclosure of subpoenaed trade secrets.[89]

The Freedom of Information Act (the "FOIA")[90] provides that each federal government executive branch agency shall promptly make available to any person upon request all records unless one or more exemptions apply.[91] An agency promise to a submitter that information will be kept confidential does not protect it from mandated FOIA disclosure.[92] If an FOIA exemption applies to the information, the agency is permitted, but not required,[93] to withhold it from a requestor.[94]

---

[85] Franke v. Wiltschek, 209 F.2d 493, 499, 99 U.S.P.Q. 431, 436 (2d Cir. 1953).

[86] SI Handling Systems, Inc. v. Heisley, 753 F.2d 1244, 1257, 225 U.S.P.Q. 441, 449 (3d Cir. 1985), aff'd, 772 F.2d 896 (3d Cir. 1985) (unpublished).

[87] *See* Thomas v. Union Carbide Agricultural Products Co., 473 U.S. 568, 584 (1985). *See also* Ruckelshaus v. Monsanto Co., 467 U.S. 986, 1005–08 (1983).

[88] *See, e.g.*, Boeing Co. v. Sierracin Corp., 108 Wash. 2d 38, 738 P.2d 665, 4 U.S.P.Q.2d 1417 (1987).

[89] Wearly v. FTC, 462 F. Supp. 589 (D.N.J. 1978), *vacated on other grounds*, 616 F.2d 662 (3d Cir. 1980), *cert. denied*, 449 U.S. 822 (1980). *See also* St. Michael's Convalescent v. State of Cal., 643 F.2d 1369 (9th Cir. 1981); South Fla. Growers Ass'n v. U.S. Dept. of Agr., 554 F. Supp. 633 (S.D. Fla. 1982).

[90] 5 U.S.C. § 552. This was enacted by Congress in 1966 to revise § 3 of the Administrative Procedures Act, with subsequent amendments in 1974 and 1976.

[91] Exemptions 3 and 4 are relevant to trade secrets.

[92] *See, e.g.*, AT&T Information Sys., Inc. v. Gen. Servs. Admin., 627 F. Supp. 1396 (D.D.C. 1986), *rev'd on other grounds*, 810 F.2d 1233 (D.C. Cir. 1987).

[93] The statutory language is not clear on this point, but the U.S. Supreme Court held that the exemptions are permissive. Chrysler Corp. v. Brown, 441 U.S. 281 (1979).

The Fifth Amendment protects trade secrets that are products of individuals' labor and invention as property; government agency disclosure of a person's trade secrets is a "taking" of that property if the person had a reasonable expectation that the trade secret submitted to the agency was to be kept confidential.[95]

[viii] *Laws Mandating Disclosure.* Laws or regulations sometimes mandate disclosure of someone else's trade secrets. A new and unsettled question involves securities law "disclose or abstain" rules that prohibit a party from trading a corporation's stock while possessing material inside information about the corporation.[96] If the inside information is a trade secret, a party caught between the securities law disclosure requirements and trade secrets law non-disclosure requirements can be forced to delay, or even abort, plans to buy stock.[97] The handful of district court decisions on this question have come to a variety of conclusions but have generally scrutinized the degree of competitive harm that would result from public disclosure of alleged trade secret information.[98] As in most trade secret cases, the decisions usually consider the particular situation's equities.[99]

[d] Commercial Value and Use

[i] *Value.* A "value" requirement is implicit in the Restatement's formulation of "advantage over competitors,"[100] but it is intermingled with the secrecy, novelty, concreteness, and continuous use requirements. Plaintiff's efforts to protect secrecy may show value.[101] The Uniform Act makes explicit, and puts more weight on, the value requirement.[102] It has been held that the Uniform Act requirement of "commercial value" excludes the purely "spiritual value" of scriptural materials for which no commercial value was asserted.[103]

---

[94] Withholding of trade secrets may be required by the Federal Trade Secrets Act, 18 U.S.C. § 1905. For an extensive discussion of the relation between the Trade Secrets Act and the FOIA, see CNA Financial Corp. v. Donovan, 265 U.S. App. D.C. 248, 830 F.2d 1132 (1987), *cert. denied,* 485 U.S. 977 (1988).

[95] Ruckelshaus v. Monsanto Co., 467 U.S. 986, 1000–04 (1983).

[96] *E.g.,* Rule 10(b), 15 U.S.C. § 78(b) and rule 14e–3, 17 C.F.R. 240, of the Securities and Exchange Act of 1934.

[97] *See, e.g.,* General Portland, Inc. v. LaFarge Coppee S.A., et al., Fed. Sec. L. Rep. (CCH) para. 99, 148 (N.D. Tx. 1981).

[98] *See, e.g.,* A. Copeland Enterprises, Inc. et al. v. Guste, Fed. Sec. L. Rep. (CCH) para. 95,001 (E.D. La. 1988).

[99] *See* Cendali & Juceam, *Enjoining a Tender Offer for Misuse of Confidential Information: Is it a Show-stopper or Can the Bidder Cure ?* The Journal of Proprietary Rights, Vol. 1, No. 12, Dec. 1989, and Vol. 2, No. 1, Jan. 1990.

[100] Restatement § 757 Comment b.

[101] *See* Rockwell Graphic Systems v. DEV Indus., 925 F.2d 174, 178-9, 17 U.S.P.Q.2d 1780, 1783–84 (7th Cir. 1991).

[102] For the Uniform Act definition of trade secrets, see § 3C[1][a].

[103] Religious Technology Center v. Wollersheim, 796 F.2d 1076, 1091 (9th Cir. 1986), *cert. denied,* 479 U.S. 1103 (1987). In a later appeal, the Ninth Circuit explained and limited its holding. Religious Tech. Ctr., Ch. of Scientology v. Scott, 869 F.2d 1306, 1309–10, 10 U.S.P.Q.2d 1379, 1381 (9th Cir. 1989).

[*ii*] *Cost of Development.* Expenditures of money and time to develop information are not required for trade secret protection—fortuitous discoveries are protectable, but courts sometimes refer to such expenditures as evidence of commercial value [104] and as an indicator of damages. [105] If an alleged trade secret is but marginally protectable, courts may be more lenient to defendants if a plaintiff spent little time, effort or expense to develop it. [106]

[2] Exclusive Rights

A trade secret's owner has the right to prevent its unauthorized use or disclosure by a person who acquired it through improper means. The owner has no rights against any person who acquires the purported secret through other means, "as, for example, by inspection or analysis of the commercial product embodying the secret, or by independent invention, or by [unrestricted] gift or purchase from the owner." [107]

[3] Duration and Termination

Trade secrets may be protected as long as the owner successfully prevents them from becoming widely known. [108] In contrast, patents last only seventeen years but offer broader protection. [109] If information becomes common knowledge, it ceases to be a trade secret. [110]

[4] Non-Secret Information Protection

Improper conduct may be actionable even when some trade secrets law definitional requirements are not satisfied. If a defendant's conduct offends the court, it may deemphasize the trade secrets law property principle and protect information that might not fully qualify as property. Some courts do this under the rubric of trade secrets law; others do it pursuant to the broader equitable principles from which trade secrets law evolved.

In rejecting the property principle and endorsing the duty principle, [111] the Restatement reflected the tendency to broaden the trade secrets concept where necessary to protect against breaches of confidence. The Restatement also provided

---

[104] *See, e.g.*, Metallurgical Indus. Inc. v. Fourtek, Inc., 790 F.2d 1195, 1201, 229 U.S.P.Q. 945, 949 (5th Cir. 1986); Cybertek Computer Prods., Inc. v. Whitefield, 203 U.S.P.Q. 1020, 1023 (Cal. Super. Ct. 1977).

[105] *See, e.g.*, Metallurgical Indus. Inc. v. Fourtek, Inc., 790 F.2d 1195, 1208, 229 U.S.P.Q. 945, 954 (5th Cir. 1986).

[106] *See, e.g.*, Arnold's Ice Cream Co. v. Carlson, 171 U.S.P.Q. 333 (E.D.N.Y. 1971).

[107] Restatement § 757 Comment a.

[108] *See, e.g.*, Restatement Comment (a) ("protection . . . not limited to a fixed number of years.").

[109] Patents cover unauthorized manufacture, use or sale of the claimed invention even if independently developed. *See* § 2F[3][b].

[110] Protection may continue for a "head start" or "lead time" period against a person who is found to have misappropriated it before it became common knowledge. *See* §§ 3F[1][c] and 3F[2][a][ii].

[111] For a discussion of the Restatement's rejection of the property principle, see § 3B[3].

an alternative, non-trade secrets avenue of protection, stating that "abuse of confidence or impropriety in learning the secret . . . may exist also where the information is not a trade secret and may be equally a basis for liability."[112]

In a separate section devoted to protection of "information about one's business whether or not it constitutes a trade secret,"[113] the Restatement provides as follows:

> "One who, for the purpose of advancing a rival business interest, procures by improper means information about another's business is liable to the other for the harm caused by his possession, disclosure or use of the information."[114]

Franke[115] concerned defendants' misappropriation of face towel designs, production methods and costs they learned by misrepresenting themselves as interested wholesale buyers with a 13-person sales force. The court found it doubtful whether the defendants ever intended to buy the plaintiff's product. Rejecting the defense that the information was publicly available in an expired patent, the court stated:

> "The essence of [this trade secret] action is . . . breach of faith. It matters not that defendants could have gained their knowledge [properly]. The fact is that they did not. Instead they gained it from plaintiffs via their confidential relationship, and in so doing incurred a duty not to use it to plaintiffs' detriment."[116]

In *Goldberg*,[117] a physician-inventor of heart pacemaker electrical leads demonstrated his invention to a manufacturer who, while continuing to express interest in collaboration, began a covert and successful parallel development effort. The manufacturer asserted that the inventor's British and West German patents made the asserted secrets public knowledge. The court held that the defendant-manufacturer "could not avoid its obligation of confidence due to the availability of lawful means of obtaining the concept when those means were not employed."[118]

In *Crocan*,[119] a supplier fraudulently gained a manufacturer's confidence to learn about tie-down strap design, materials, manufacturing processes, and packaging and marketing methods. The defendant could have easily developed all the information independently or by studying publicly available products, but it saved the time and expense of doing so. The court relied on the Restatement for the proposition that "improper means used to gain information is a separate basis of liability, regardless of whether the information constitutes a technical trade secret in the narrow sense of the word."[120]

In *Metallurgical Industries*,[121] one court suggested that non-secret information can be protected not only against improper means but also against breach of confidence.

---

[112] Restatement § 757 Comment b.

[113] Restatement § 759 Comment a.

[114] Restatement § 759.

[115] Franke v. Wiltschek, 209 F.2d 493, 99 U.S.P.Q. 431, (2d Cir. 1953).

[116] 209 F.2d at 495, 99 U.S.P.Q. at 433.

[117] Goldberg v. Medtronic, Inc., 686 F.2d 1219, 216 U.S.P.Q. 89 (7th Cir. 1982).

[118] 686 F.2d at 1225, 216 U.S.P.Q. at 93.

[119] Crocan Corp. v. Sheller-Globe Corp., 385 F. Supp. 251, 185 U.S.P.Q. 211 (N.D. Ill. 1974).

[120] 385 F. Supp. at 254, 185 U.S.P.Q. at 213.

[121] Metallurgical Indus. Inc. v. Fourtek, Inc., 790 F.2d 1195, 229 U.S.P.Q. 945 (5th Cir. 1986).

Phrasing the issue as one of whether a disclosure was limited in purpose, the court stated that secrecy "is not requisite; it is only a factor to consider. Whether a disclosure is limited is an issue the resolution of which depends on weighing many facts."[122]

In *National Starch*,[123] the court took a contrary position. Asked to decide the relevance of the defendant-former employee's defense that secret formulas and manufacturing processes allegedly disclosed by the plaintiff-employer in confidence were widely known in the industry, it held that "[t]here is no betrayal of confidence unless there is a secret to be imparted,"[124] implicitly emphasizing the property principle.

In *Electro-Craft*,[125] a Uniform Act case, the court reviewed an electric motor manufacturer's claim against a competing company established by former employees of misappropriation of moving coil motor dimensions, tolerances, manufacturing processes, and components. Emphasizing the plaintiff's extraordinarily lax secrecy maintenance efforts, the court denied relief, specifically rejected *Goldberg*,[126] and warned against the danger of "expanding [trade secrets law] into a catchall for industrial torts."[127]

Non-secret information is not within the Uniform Act's scope,[128] but whatever other remedies, Restatement-influenced or otherwise, that particular states have developed remain intact unless courts modify or displace them.

§ 3D   Trade Secret Misappropriation Litigation

A threshold practical issue in litigation is the danger of disclosure through the public records of judicial proceedings or in open court. The Restatement states:

> "In order to protect trade secrets against disclosure in the course of litigation, testimony involving such disclosure is generally taken by the court privately rather than in public and the record of such testimony is appropriately safeguarded against public disclosure."[1]

The Uniform Act provides that courts shall preserve secrecy by:

> "[G]ranting protective orders in connection with discovery proceedings, holding in-camera hearings, sealing the records of the action, and ordering any person involved in the litigation not to disclose an alleged trade secret without prior court approval."[2]

---

[122] 790 F.2d at 1200, 229 U.S.P.Q. at 948.

[123] National Starch Products, Inc., v. Polymer Indus., Inc., 79 N.Y.S.2d 357, 77 U.S.P.Q. 644 (N.Y. App. Div. 1948).

[124] 79 N.Y.S.2d at 361, 77 U.S.P.Q. at 646.

[125] Electro-Craft Corp. v. Controlled Motion, 332 N.W.2d 890, 220 U.S.P.Q. 811 (Minn. 1983).

[126] Goldberg v. Medtronic, Inc., 686 F.2d 1219, 216 U.S.P.Q. 89 (7th Cir. 1982).

[127] Electro-Craft Corp. v. Controlled Motion, 332 N.W. 2d 890, 897 (Minn. 1983).

[128] Uniform Act § 7.

[1] Restatement § 757 Comment f.

[2] Uniform Act § 5.

The accompanying Comment states that "a court must ensure that a respondent is provided sufficient information to present a defense and a trier of fact sufficient information to resolve the merits,"[3] and approvingly mentions that courts sometimes preserve secrecy by:

> "[R]estricting disclosures to a party's counsel and his or her assistants and by appointing a disinterested expert as a special master to hear secret information and report conclusions to the court."[4]

Federal and many state civil procedure rules explicitly balance a trade secret owner's interest in non-disclosure against the court's need for the information. Discovery rules require an inquiry into:

> "[W]hether the material sought is likely to be sufficiently useful to justify the burden imposed by the discovery request, [and] whether the information could be obtained through some less burdensome or less intrusive device, etc."[5]

Some states give judges discretion to exclude a party from *in camera* hearings that take evidence on whether, and what, trade secrets exist.[6]

[1] Definition of Misappropriation

The Restatement definition of conduct triggering liability and the Uniform Act definition of misappropriation are substantially identical, with one exception. The Restatement includes disclosure or use as an essential element. The Uniform Act provides that mere wrongful acquisition—without use or disclosure—can be a misappropriation.

The Restatement states:

> "One who discloses or uses another's trade secret, without a privilege to do so, is liable to the other if
>
> "(a) he discovered the secret by improper means, *or*
>
> "(b) his disclosure or use constitutes a breach of confidence reposed in him by the other in disclosing the secret to him, *or*
>
> "(c) he learned the secret from a third person with notice of the facts that it was a secret and that the third person discovered it by improper means or that the third person's disclosure of it was otherwise a breach of his duty to the other, *or*
>
> "(d) he learned the secret with notice of the facts that it was a secret and that its disclosure was made to him by mistake."[7]

The Uniform Act defines misappropriation as

---

[3] Uniform Act Comment to § 5.

[4] Uniform Act Comment to § 5.

[5] Advanced-Semiconductor v. Tau Laboratories, 229 U.S.P.Q. 222, 224 (N.D. Cal. 1986).

[6] *See, e.g.,* Air Products and Chemicals Inc. v. Johnson, 296 Pa. Super. 405, 442 A.2d 1114, 1128–29, 215 U.S.P.Q. 547, 559–60 (1982) (discussing Pennsylvania Rule of Civil Procedure 223).

[7] Restatement § 757 (emphasis added).

"(i) acquisition of a trade secret of another by a person who knows or has reason to know that the trade secret was acquired by improper means; *or*

"(ii) disclosure or use of a trade secret of another without express or implied consent by a person who

"(A) used improper means to acquire knowledge of the trade secret; *or*

"(B) at the time of the disclosure or use, knew or had reason to know that his knowledge of the trade secret was

"(I) derived from or through a person who had utilized improper means to acquire it;

"(II) acquired under circumstances giving rise to a duty to maintain its secrecy or limit its use; *or*

"(III) derived from or through a person who owed a duty to the person seeking relief to maintain its secrecy or limit its use; *or*

"(C) before a material change of his or her position, knew or had reason to know that it was a trade secret and that knowledge of it had been acquired by accident or mistake."[8]

[2] Theories of Law

The common law of trade secrets originated in tort, but alternative causes of action include breach of express or implied contract. The Restatement includes "breach of contract" in the "general duty of good faith" affording protection to trade secrets,[9] and the Uniform Act expressly leaves intact any contract claims. Thus, in both Uniform Act and non-Uniform Act states, plaintiffs typically plead various tort and contract causes of action.

[a] **Contract Law Theories.** The Uniform Act provides that it "displaces conflicting tort, restitutionary, and other law of [the enacting] State providing civil remedies for misappropriation of a trade secret"[10] but does not affect any contractual remedies, criminal remedies, or "other civil remedies that are not based upon misappropriation of a trade secret."[11] The Uniform Act Comment further explains that the Act:

"[A]pplies to a duty to protect competitively significant secret information that is imposed by law. It does not apply to a duty voluntarily assumed through an express or implied-in-fact contract . . . [or to] a duty imposed by law that is not dependent upon the existence of competitively significant secret information . . ."[12]

A trade secret owner may allege breach of contractual obligation against use or disclosure of the trade secret in a variety of situations. A confidentiality duty may

---

[8] Uniform Act § 1(2) (emphasis added).

[9] Restatement § 757 Comment a.

[10] Uniform Act § 9(a). The text of § 7 was modified as part of the 1985 Amendments discussed in § 3B[4].

[11] Uniform Act § 7(b).

[12] Uniform Act Comment § 7.

arise from express contractual provisions, implied-in-fact contract terms based on a court's interpretation of the parties' understanding, or implied-in-law contract terms based on public policy.

Implied-in-law contractual obligations frequently arise from employment or other confidential relationships.[13] Implied-in-fact contractual obligations arise when parties' conduct indicates that they intended confidentiality as a condition of disclosure.

Because contract law theories are based on confidentiality obligations that defendants actually or implicitly undertake voluntarily, the theories support broader definitions of protectable information[14] and tighter restrictions on defendants' activities.[15] Also, contract law can provide a basis for suits against the United States government.[16] On the other hand, an attempt to disclaim a confidential relationship is more likely to be upheld for purposes of contract law than for tort law.[17] Contract and tort theories also involve different rules for conflicts of law, statutes of limitations, and damages.

[b] Tort Law Theories. The tort of breach of confidence, the original basis for trade secrets law,[18] has always been the most broadly used theory in trade secrets actions. A tort law claim exists whether or not the same confidence creates implied or express contractual obligations.

[c] Conflicts of Laws. Because different states' laws may conflict, courts must decide which states' laws apply to a claim. States' conflicts of laws rules vary, and, in some states, may depend on whether an action is based on contract or tort.

Absent a contractual choice of law agreement, a court addressing potentially conflicting laws first applies the conflict of laws rules of the state in which it sits (the "forum state"). This entails (1) examining whether the rules are different for actions based, respectively, on contract and tort; (2) applying these rules to select the procedural and substantive laws applicable to each cause of action; (3) applying to each action the statute of limitations of the state whose procedural laws have been selected; and, if the statute has not run, (4) applying to each action the law of the state whose substantive laws have been selected.[19]

For substantive issues, the forum state's conflicts rules may require use of its own law or the law of the state where the wrong is alleged to have occurred. If the

---

[13] See discussion of employer-employee in § 3D[6][a][i](2) and other confidential relationships in § 3D[7][a].

[14] See discussion of protectable information in § 3C[1] and discussion of customer lists in Wisconsin etc. in § 3C[1][b][iv].

[15] See discussion of agreements not to compete in § 3D[6][c].

[16] The United States has waived its sovereign immunity for most contract claims but only for a restricted list of tort claims.

[17] See Burten v. Milton Bradley Co., 763 F.2d 461, 226 U.S.P.Q. 605 (1st Cir. 1985).

[18] For a discussion of early English cases, see § 3B[1].

[19] See, e.g., Rohm and Haas Co. v. Adco Chemical Co., 689 F.2d 424, 215 U.S.P.Q. 1081 (3d Cir. 1982); FMC Corp. v. Varco Int'l, Inc., 677 F.2d 500, 217 U.S.P.Q. 135 (5th Cir. 1982); Smith v. Dravo Corp., 203 F.2d 369, 97 U.S.P.Q. 98 (7th Cir. 1953); Goldberg v. Medtronic, Inc., 686 F.2d 1219, 216 U.S.P.Q. 89 (7th Cir. 1982); Lehman v. Dow Jones & Co., Inc., 606 F. Supp. 1152 (S.D.N.Y. 1985), aff'd, 783 F.2d 285 (2d Cir. 1986).

applicable state law on substantive questions is vague, federal courts hearing trade secrets cases resort to guessing its meaning,[20] and to analyzing the "general law."[21]

[i] *Contract Law Conflicts.* If a breach of contract claim is alleged, most states apply the law of the forum where a contract was entered into, but some look to the forum having the greatest number of contacts with the transaction, and some to the forum where performance occurs. California applies the law of the state whose interest would be "more impaired if its policy were subordinated to the policy of the other state."[22] Many courts will disregard a contractual governing law clause if substantive issues involve a public policy of a state that has materially greater interests in the transaction than those of the contractually stipulated state.[23]

[ii] *Tort Law Conflicts.* If a tort claim is alleged, most states apply the law of the forum where the injury occurred, but some apply the contracts-style contacts or relationship test the Restatement (Second) Conflict of Laws endorses.[24] The test factors are the place of the injury, the place where the conduct causing the injury occurred, the parties' domicile, and the place where the parties' relationship, if any, is centered.[25]

[iii] *Statutes of Limitations.* At common law, it is unsettled whether trade secrets misappropriation is a continuing wrong for statute of limitations purposes. This issue is significant because it dictates whether the period in which an action must be brought starts when the misappropriation begins, or whether the statute is tolled as long as the misappropriation continues.

In *Underwater*,[26] a federal court applying District of Columbia law noted that the Restatement protects against not only disclosure but also use of a trade secret and held that continuing wrongful use of a trade secret is a continuing tort.[27]

In *Monolith*,[28] a federal court applying California law attributed the *Underwater* holding to a property theory of trade secrets law, concluded that California law used a duty theory, and held that, under a duty theory, misappropriation is not a continuing wrong. Rather than protecting a property right which is damaged with

---

[20] Wheelabrator Corporation v. Fogle, 317 F. Supp. 633, 636, 167 U.S.P.Q. 72, 75 (W.D. La. 1970), aff'd, 438 F.2d 1226, 168 U.S.P.Q. 679 (5th Cir. 1971).

[21] Telex Corp. v. International Business Mach. Corp., 510 F.2d 894, 930, 184 U.S.P.Q. 521, 546 (10th Cir. 1975), cert. dismissed, 423 U.S. 802 (1975).

[22] Lehman v. Dow Jones & Co., Inc. 606 F. Supp. 1152, 1157 (S.D.N.Y. 1985), aff'd, 783 F.2d 285 (2d Cir. 1986).

[23] See, e.g., Barnes Group, Inc. v. C & C Products, Inc., 716 F.2d 1023, 1029 (4th Cir. 1983). See also Restatement (Second) of Conflict of Laws (1971) § 186.

[24] Restatement (Second) Conflict of Laws (1971), § 145.

[25] Restatement 2d Conflict of Laws (1971) § 145.

[26] Underwater Storage, Inc. v. United States Rubber Co., 371 F.2d 950, 151 U.S.P.Q. 90 (D.C. Cir. 1966), cert. denied, 386 U.S. 911, 152 U.S.P.Q. 844 (1967).

[27] 371 F.2d at 955, 151 U.S.P.Q. at 93. See also Anaconda Co. v. Metric Tool & Die Co., 485 F. Supp. 410, 205 U.S.P.Q. 723 (E.D. Pa. 1980).

[28] Monolith Portland Midwest Co. v. Kaiser Aluminum & Chemical Corp., 407 F.2d 288, 160 U.S.P.Q. 577 (9th Cir. 1969).

each adverse use, *Monolith* stated that trade secrets law protects only a confidential relationship, the fabric of which "once rent is not torn anew with each added use or disclosure . . ."[29] *Monolith* also stated that the limitation period's start should not be delayed until the plaintiff's discovery of the misappropriation because discovery was not an element of the cause of action.

The Uniform Act rejects the *Underwater* theory of a continuing wrong, adopts most of the *Monolith* court approach, but provides for a three-year limitation period that does not begin until the trade secrets owner knows or should know of the misappropriation.[30] Because wrongful acquisition constitutes misappropriation under the Uniform Act,[31] the limitation period begins when the owner knows or should know of any wrongful acquisition.[32]

[d] Related Non-Trade Secrets Claims. Factual situations underlying trade secret claims typically also give rise to a variety of other claims not based on trade secrets law. Misappropriated information may have been protected, or used together with other information protected by patent, copyright or trademark law. Trade secret misappropriation may also constitute a tort, such as unfair competition or interference with economic advantage, a breach of implied-in-law contract terms such as a covenant of good faith and fair dealing, or a theft of articles embodying the trade secret. Intentional misrepresentations about planned use or disclosure of a secret may constitute fraud.

[3] Evidence

Neither the Restatement nor the Uniform Act provide guidance on the evidentiary standard to be applied to various aspects of a trade secrets claim. Because direct evidence of use or disclosure is often unavailable, courts are receptive to circumstantial evidence:

> "Misappropriation and misuse can rarely be proved by convincing direct evidence. In most cases plaintiffs must construct a web of perhaps ambiguous circumstantial evidence . . ."[33]

In *Dickerman*,[34] an example of a court finding misappropriation based on circumstantial evidence, similarities between the defendants' and the plaintiffs' computer software program, the defendants' use of a confidential manual belonging to the plaintiffs and the speed with which the defendants assembled their competing program, made the conclusion "inescapable" that they copied substantial portions of the plaintiff's program.[35]

In *Imperial Chemical*,[36] the court, in deciding whether an alleged trade secret was

---

[29] 407 F.2d at 293, 160 U.S.P.Q. at 580.

[30] Uniform Act § 6.

[31] See definitions of misappropriation in § 3D[1].

[32] Ashton-Tate Corp. v. Ross, 916 F.2d 516, 16 U.S.P.Q.2d 1541 (9th Cir. 1990).

[33] Greenberg v. Croydon Plastics Co., Inc., 378 F. Supp. 806, 814, 182 U.S.P.Q. 673, 679 (E.D. Pa.), *modified*, 184 U.S.P.Q. 27 (E.D. Pa. 1974).

[34] Dickerman Associates v. Tiverton Bottled Gas, 594 F. Supp. 30 (D.Mass. 1984).

[35] 594 F. Supp. at 36.

[36] Imperial Chem. Indus. Ltd. v. National Distillers and Chem. Corp., 342 F.2d 737, 144 U.S.P.Q. 695 (2d Cir. 1965).

readily ascertainable from publicly available sources, attached evidentiary value to the fact that a company not a party to the suit was "paying about $6,000,000 for information it could [according to the defendants] easily get from a technical library."[37] In *SI Handling*,[38] that plaintiff's engineers only began using a procedure after a number of years of experience manufacturing the product was considered evidence that it was not known outside the plaintiff's business. In *Clark*,[39] the defendants' reliance on misappropriated plans for the sale of pre-paid funeral services was considered evidence of the difficulty of acquiring the information by proper means. In *Courtesy*,[40] the defendant's lack of any clients whose names were not in the plaintiff's customer list was considered evidence that the defendant used the list. In *Rockwell*,[41] the court decided that a plaintiff's efforts to protect information's secrecy was evidence a defendant could not have obtained it through proper means: "The greater the [plaintiff's] precautions . . . the lower the probability that [the defendant] obtained them properly . . ."[42]

[4] Proof Burdens

The trade secret owner has the burden of proving, by a preponderance of the evidence, the existence, ownership and misappropriation of a protectable trade secret.[43] With regard to misappropriation, although the trade secret owner formally has the burden of proof, courts respond to practical difficulties by inferring misappropriation if the owner proves access and similarity.[44]

[5] Proof Elements—Law and Fact Questions

In most Uniform Act states, a trade secret claim's formal elements are: (1) the claim subject qualifies as a statutory "trade secret";[45] *and* (2) the defendant's conduct constitutes statutory "misappropriation" of plaintiff's trade secrets.[46]

In both Uniform Act and non-Uniform Act states, the underlying factual elements are best understood and organized as follows:

---

[37] 342 F.2d at 744, 144 U.S.P.Q. at 700.

[38] SI Handling Sys., Inc. v. Heisley, 753 F.2d 1244, 1256, 225 U.S.P.Q. 441, 448 (3d Cir. 1985).

[39] Clark v. Bunker, 453 F.2d 1006, 1010, 172 U.S.P.Q. 420, 423 (9th Cir. 1972).

[40] Courtesy Temporary Serv., Inc. v. Camacho, 222 Cal. App. 3d 1278, 272 Cal. Rptr. 352 (1990).

[41] Rockwell Graphic Systems v. DEV Industries, 925 F.2d 174, 17 U.S.P.Q.2d 1780 (7th Cir. 1991).

[42] 925 F.2d at 179, 17 U.S.P.Q.2d at 1784.

[43] *See, e.g.*, Vekamaf Holland B.V. v. Pipe Benders, Inc., 211 U.S.P.Q. 955, 978 (D. Minn. 1981), *aff'd*, 696 F.2d 608, 217 U.S.P.Q. 32 (8th Cir. 1982); Greenberg v. Croydon Plastics Co., Inc., 378 F. Supp. 806, 811, 182 U.S.P.Q. 673, 677–78, *modified*, 184 U.S.P.Q. 27 (E.D. Pa. 1974); GTI Corporation v. Calhoon, 309 F. Supp. 762, 767, 165 U.S.P.Q. 621, 624 (S.D. Ohio 1969).

[44] *See, e.g.*, Aries Information Sys., Inc. v. Pacific Mgmt. Sys. Corp., 366 N.W.2d 366, 369, 226 U.S.P.Q. 440, 443 (Minn. Ct. App. 1985).

[45] For the Uniform Act definition of "trade secret," see § 3C[1][a].

[46] For the Uniform Act definition of "misappropriation," see § 3D[1].

(1) Specified information qualifies as a trade secret because it meets the applicable state trade secret law's secrecy and subject matter protection requirements.

(2) Plaintiff owns the trade secret because plaintiff (a) acquired exclusive knowledge of, or the exclusive right to use, the information through proper means *and* (b) subsequently made reasonable efforts to maintain its secrecy.

(3) Defendant possesses plaintiff's trade secret in the form of (a) information *or* (b) an embodiment of the information.

(4) Defendant has a duty to the plaintiff of non-use and/or non-disclosure, because the defendant knows, knew or should have known of plaintiff's rights in the trade secret, and defendant took possession of the trade secret (a) by means of an express or implied confidential relationship with the plaintiff, *or* (b) through improper means.

(5) Defendant has used or disclosed, or will use or disclose, the trade secret to the plaintiff's detriment, or (in Uniform Act states) acquired the trade secret through improper means.

Courts articulate these elements in a variety of ways, generally "without greatly affecting the concept."[47]

Most courts consider whether a trade secret existed and whether a breach of confidence occurred to be fact questions, to which a clearly erroneous appellate review standard applies. A minority view treats trade secret existence as a question of law,[48] or a "mixed question of law and fact,"[49] giving appellate courts a free hand to reconsider lower courts' determinations that a trade secret did or did not exist:

> "The first question is what, in fact, actually happened. The second question, whether those facts as a matter of law fulfill a particular legal standard, is a question of law."[50]

[6] Trade Secret Ownership—Employment

To establish ownership, plaintiff must show he or she learned the information through means that were proper and gave rise to no use restrictions. This most typically occurs through independent development, but a person may have ownership and standing to sue a misappropriator based on acquisition of information by gift, sale, license (if the license confers sufficient rights),[51] reverse engineering, or other lawful means. Most disputes are over a protectable trade secret's existence, but ownership is sometimes disputed, most frequently between an employer and employee or between joint venturers.

---

[47] Vekamaf Holland B.V. v. Pipe Benders, Inc., 211 U.S.P.Q. 955, 978 (D. Minn. 1981), aff'd, 696 F.2d 608, 217 U.S.P.Q. 32 (8th Cir. 1982).

[48] *See, e.g.,* Agriculture Labor Rel. Bd. v. Richard A. Glass Co., 175 Col. App. 3d 703, 713, 221 Cal. Rptr. 63, 68 (1985); Uribe v. Howie, 19 Cal. App. 3d 194, 207, 96 Cal. Rptr. 493, 500 (1971).

[49] Corroon & Black–Rutters & Roberts v. Hosch, 109 Wis. 290, 325 N.W.2d 883, 885 (1982).

[50] 325 N.W.2d at 885, citing Department of Revenue v. Exxon Corp., 281 N.W.2d 94 (1979).

[51] For a discussion of licensing, see § 3I.

Issues particular to the employer/employee context include the original source of the information (employer or employee), the nature of an employee's job and responsibilities, the scope of the employment relationship, and the time when information is developed.

As between an employee and an employer if there is no enforceable express agreement, common law implications and rules apply to (1) information protectability, (2) ownership, and (3) the existence of a confidentiality obligation. Protectability depends on whether information differs from the general knowledge, skill and experience which a typical employee gains from employment. Ownership depends on the original source of the information and the scope of the employment. An employee's duty of confidentiality depends on his or her position and responsibilities.

Express agreements can establish protectability, ownership and duties where they would not otherwise exist, but various public policies limit the enforceability of such agreements against employees.

[a] Common Law Implications

[i] *Information Protectability.* Every employee has the right to use and disclose all information that falls within the scope of the general knowledge, skill and experience that a typical employee gains from an employer during employment. This test corresponds closely to the "novelty" requirement,[52] and depends in large part on the state of "general knowledge" within an industry.

In *Rohm*,[53] a paint manufacturer sued a competitor for misappropriation of information disclosed in confidence to a former employee subsequently hired by the competitor. The employee's admission that he relied on memory rather than ability was held to be persuasive evidence that the information was not general knowledge, experience or skill.[54]

[ii] *Ownership.* Employers own any trade secrets they impart to employees and may claim ownership of an employee-developed trade secret. The key issue is the scope of the employment contract.[55]

Whether trade secret ownership resides in an employer or an employee depends upon (1) the nature of the work the employee was hired to perform; (2) the invention's relation to the employer's business; and (3) the extent to which the employee used the employer's resources in the invention's conception and development.[56] Ownership is heavily fact-dependent, and must be considered on a case-by-case basis. Other factors may be important in special situations. For instance, an employee-inventor who is a corporate officer or director may be required to assign rights to the company because of a fiduciary duty not to compete with the company.

---

[52] For a discussion of novelty and general knowledge, see § 3C[1][c][vi].

[53] Rohm and Haas Co. v. Adco Chem. Co., 689 F.2d 424, 215 U.S.P.Q. 1081 (3d Cir. 1982).

[54] 689 F.2d at 433, 215 U.S.P.Q. at 1087.

[55] Rules on employer-employee trade secret ownership resemble the rules on ownership of patent rights on employee inventions. *See* § 2G[1]. For a discussion of copyright ownership in the employment context, see § 4G[2].

[56] *See* Wexler v. Greenberg, 299 Pa. 569, 581, 160 A.2d 430, 435–37 (1960).

If an employee is hired to invent or develop particular information or assigned the duty of accomplishing a specific task, the employer is generally deemed to have an implied contractual and equitable right to require the employee to assign his or her rights to any resulting protectable information. At the other extreme, if an employee is not hired to use any inventive or creative skills, there is no implied agreement and the employer is not entitled to an assignment.

The middle ground, and harder question, involves an employee who is hired to pursue his or her inventive skills generally, but not to create anything in particular. In this case an employer may own rights to particular information if it was developed during working hours, it is in the scope of business of the employer and the employee-inventor was assigned tasks related to the creations.

In *Wexler*,[57] plaintiff, a sanitation and maintenance chemical manufacturer, sought to enjoin a former employee and a competing company of which the employee had become an officer from using or disclosing formulas and processes the employee developed during his employment with plaintiff. The employee was a skilled chemist whose work for the plaintiff had been limited to modifying competitors' formulas and had included no research, experimentation or invention. The court noted that the plaintiff provided no appreciable assistance or supervision beyond usual employee job expenses, found nothing that should have put the employee on notice that proprietary formula development was the employment relationship's purpose, and held that the formulas were part of the employee's technical knowledge and skill.[58]

In *Q-Co*,[59] the plaintiff, a computer software manufacturer, sued former employee programmers, who had no express confidentiality agreements, for misappropriation of software the former employees had developed for plaintiff. The court applied the following language to find that the plaintiff-employer had established a likelihood of successfully proving misappropriation:

> "When an individual is expressly employed to devote his time to the development of process and machinery and was to receive therefore [*sic*] a stated compensation, the resulting development is the property of him who engage [*sic*] the services and paid for them."[60]

If an employer does not own an employee's invention or idea, it may have a more limited "shop right" to use the invention if the employee used a sufficient amount of the employer's time, facilities, or materials.[61] A "shop right" is a non-exclusive, non-transferable, royalty-free license for the employer to use an employee's intellectual property.[62] It is an equitable right given to the employer because of the employee's use of the employer's time, facilities, or materials. If an employer is entitled to a shop right, the employer may manufacture, use and sell devices that embody the employee's creation before and after termination of the employment relationship. The employee

---

[57] Wexler v. Greenberg, 399 Pa. 569, 160 A.2d 430. (1960).

[58] 399 Pa. at 581, 160 A.2d at 436–37.

[59] Q-Co. Indus., Inc. v. Hoffman, 625 F. Supp. 608, 228 U.S.P.Q. 554 (S.D.N.Y. 1985).

[60] 625 F. Supp. at 617, 228 U.S.P.Q. at 560 (citations omitted).

[61] See U.S. v. Dubilier Condenser Corp., 289 U.S. 178 (1932).

[62] See § 2G[1].

also may use, manufacture and market the invention, or license the employer's competitors to do so.

[*iii*] *Employment as a Confidential Relationship.* An individual employee's position and responsibilities define the degree to which confidentiality obligations will be implied in the employment contract. At common law, a confidential relationship, and a corresponding duty not to use or disclose the employer's inventions or trade secrets, will generally be implied where employees were in a position to gain an intimate knowledge of the employer's business.[63]

[b] **Express Agreements.** Express agreements can establish employer trade secret ownership, and employee confidentiality duties, even in circumstances where they would not be created by implication, but information protectability is determined according to trade secret law principles and information characterized as a trade secret by agreement still may be held unprotectable by courts.

[*i*] *Ownership—Assignment Agreements.* Express agreements by which employees obligate themselves to assign intellectual property rights to their employer are generally enforceable, subject to traditional contract doctrines such as fraud, duress, mutual mistake, adhesion, and lack of consideration. A few states have passed statutes making such agreements unenforceable unless equipment, supplies, facilities or trade secret information of the employer are used or the idea relates directly to the business of the employer or its actual or anticipated research and development, or resulted from work performed for the employer.[64]

[*ii*] *Timing of Creation.* Employers have no implied (non-contractual) rights to valuable ideas conceived by an employee before or after the employment period. "Hold-over" clauses requiring assignment of post-employment ideas are strictly construed[65] and only enforceable if limited to reasonable times and to ideas based on the employer's proprietary information or other subject matter which the employee worked on or had knowledge of during his former employment.[66]

A hold-over clause is reasonable if it is (1) no greater than needed to protect the employer's legitimate interests; (2) not unduly harsh and oppressive to the employee; and (3) not injurious to the public.[67]

If a former employee reduces an idea to practice or commercialization quickly after employment termination, courts may infer that the idea was conceived during the employment.[68]

[*iii*] *Consideration.* Employee non-disclosure agreements must be supported by consideration. Courts often require that they be executed at the time of hiring or

---

[63] Zoecon Indus. v. American Stockman Tag Co., 713 F.2d 1174, 1178 (5th Cir. 1983).

[64] *See* § 2G[1].

[65] *See, e.g.,* Armorlite Lens Co. v. Campbell, 340 F. Supp. 273, 275, 173 U.S.P.Q. 470, 471 (S.D. Cal. 1972).

[66] Dorr-Oliver, Inc. v. United States, 432 F.2d 447, 452, 165 U.S.P.Q. 517, 520 (Ct. Cl. 1970).

[67] *See, e.g.,* GTI Corp. v. Calhoon, 309 F. Supp. 762, 773, 165 U.S.P.Q. 621, 628 (S.D. Ohio 1969) (five year holdover clause void).

[68] *E.g.,* Syntex Opthalmics, Inc. v. Tsuetaki, 701 F.2d 677, 219 U.S.P.Q. 962 (7th Cir. 1983).

promotion, but one court held an agreement enforceable where the subsequently executed written non-disclosure agreement memorialized a prior oral agreement.[69]

Another court surveyed the authorities on consideration for employee non-disclosure agreements: "Where no raises or promotions resulted, where other employees with similar access [to the employer's information] were not asked to sign, the mere continuation of employment for [plaintiffs] is not enough."[70]

[iv] *Protectability.* Employment agreements that define trade secrets are not conclusive, and courts make their own determinations of whether trade secrets exist.[71]

[c] Non-competition Agreements

Agreements not to compete, also known as restrictive covenants, are outside the scope of trade secrets law, but their enforcement is often sought in actions that also allege trade secret misappropriation, and trade secret protection is often put forth as the reason why such an agreement should be enforced.

Agreements not to compete are strictly construed and are unenforceable under most states' public policy unless they are reasonable under the circumstances. Common law tests for reasonableness include: (1) whether the restriction is ancillary to a legitimate business purpose or agreement; (2) whether there is a legitimate business interest to protect; (3) whether the restrictions are reasonable with respect to subject matter, time, and territory; and (4) whether there is adequate consideration.[72] Legitimate business purposes may include the sale or transfer of a business, creation of an employment contract,[73] or the protection of trade secrets.[74]

State laws differ on reasonableness standards and on what constitutes adequate consideration. Many states will enforce those terms of a restrictive covenant that are reasonable by reforming or deleting unenforceable terms. Courts sitting in a state that has a fundamental policy against restrictive covenants may decline to apply the law of another state that would violate policy.[75]

Reasonableness of geographical area depends on the facts, and many states will uphold broad geographical restrictions if justified by a business' multistate or international scope,[76] but the type and scope of activity restricted must not be overbroad.

---

[69] Cybertek Computer Prod., Inc. v. Whitfield, 203 U.S.P.Q. 1020, 1022 (Cal. Super. Ct. 1977).

[70] Jostens, Inc. v. National Computer Sys., 318 N.W.2d 691, 703, 214 U.S.P.Q. 918 (Minn. 1982).

[71] *See, e.g.,* American Paper & Packaging Prods. Inc. v. Kirgan, 183 Cal. App. 3d 1318, 1325, 228 Cal. Rptr. 713 (1986).

[72] *See, e.g.,* Jostens, Inc., v. National Computer Sys., Inc., 318 N.W.2d 691, 214 U.S.P.Q. 918 (Minn. 1982).

[73] *See* Modern Controls, Inc. v. Andreadakis, 578 F.2d 1264, 1267–68 (8th Cir. 1978).

[74] *See, e.g.,* Mixing Equip. Co. v. Philadelphia Gear, Inc., 436 F.2d 1308, 169 U.S.P.Q. 257 (3d Cir. 1971); Gillette Co. v. Williams, 360 F. Supp. 1171, 178 U.S.P.Q. 327 (D. Conn. 1973).

[75] *See, e.g.,* NCH Corp. v. Broyles, 749 F.2d 247, 250–51 (5th Cir. 1985).

[76] *See, e.g.,* Mixing Equip. Co. v. Philadelphia Gear, Inc., 436 F.2d 1308, 169 U.S.P.Q. 257 (3d Cir. 1971).

Business interests need not qualify as a trade secret to be protectable by restrictive covenants in most states, and might include customer relationships, specialized training of an employee, or even goodwill. The covenant may be given greater scope if it is protecting a trade secret.

[7] Duty

A trade secret claimant must prove that the accused misappropriator acquired the information from the claimant through a confidential relationship or improper means. If the claimant proves the accused had *access* to the information in either way, then many courts shift to the accused the burden of showing that the information was acquired from another source.[77]

[a] **Confidential Reception.** A confidential relationship may arise expressly by contract or implicitly from the parties' conduct or relationship. Persons subject to implied confidential obligations may include employees,[78] student-trainees,[79] independent contractors,[80] negotiators,[81] licensees,[82] customers,[83] suppliers,[84] and joint venturers.[85]

[b] **Improper and Proper Means.** Trade secrets law concerns the means by which access is gained to information, not the means by which the information is subsequently recorded and transported. A misappropriator's reliance on memory, as opposed to physical copies, is therefore not excused.[86] Surreptitious physical copying may still be significant in various ways, for example, by undermining an employee's argument that information was general knowledge and skill, or adding to the impression that a misappropriator acted willfully and maliciously, thus expanding the remedies available and generally affecting the balance of equities.

[i] *Improper Means.* The Restatement states that improper means are those "which fall below the generally accepted standards of commercial morality and reasonable conduct,"[87] including

> "[T]heft, trespass, bribing or otherwise inducing employees or others to reveal the information in breach of duty, fraudulent misrepresentations, threats of harm by unlawful conduct, wire tapping, procuring one's own employees or

---

[77] *See, e.g.,* Cybertek Computer Prods., Inc. v. Whitfield, 203 U.S.P.Q. 1020 (Cal. Super. Ct. 1977).

[78] *See* discussion in § 3D[6][a][i].

[79] *See, e.g.,* By-Buk Co. v. Printed Cellophane Tape Co., 163 Cal. App. 2d 157, 329 P.2d 147 (1958).

[80] *See, e.g.,* Jones v. Ulrich, 344 Ill. App. 16, 95 N.E.2d 113 (1950).

[81] *See, e.g.,* Schreyer v. Casco Products Corp., 190 F.2d 921 (2d Cir. 1951), *cert. denied,* 342 U.S. 913 (1952).

[82] *See* § 3I.

[83] *See, e.g.,* Pressed Steel Car Co. v. Standard Steel Car Co., 210 Pa. 464, 60 A. 4 (1904).

[84] *See, e.g.,* Williams v. Williams, 3 MER. 157 (1817).

[85] *See, e.g.,* Morison v. Moat, 9 HARE 241 (1851).

[86] *See, e.g.,* Cybertek Computer Prods., Inc. v. Whitfield, 203 U.S.P.Q. 1020, 1025 (Cal. Super. Ct. 1977).

[87] Restatement § 757 Comment f.

agents to become employees of the other for purposes of espionage, and so forth." [88]

The Uniform Act defines improper means to include

"[T]heft, bribery, misrepresentation, breach or inducement of a breach of a duty to maintain secrecy, or espionage through electronic or other means." [89]

[ii] *Proper Means.* The Uniform Act states that proper means include

"1. Discovery by independent invention;

"2. Discovery by 'reverse engineering';

"3. Discovery under a license from the owner of the trade secret;

"4. Observation of the item in public use or on public display;

"5. Obtaining the trade secret from published literature." [90]

[iii] *Otherwise Lawful Conduct.* The Restatement states that "means may be improper . . . even though they do not cause any other harm than that to the interest in the trade secret." [91] The Uniform Act states that "[i]mproper means could include otherwise lawful conduct which is improper under the circumstances." [92]

The Uniform Act comment endorses the leading case on this point, *DuPont*,[93] which found improper means when an airplane overflight was used to ascertain secret aspects of the layout of a competitor's plant under construction. The court held that "we need not require the discoverer of a trade secret to guard against the unanticipated, the undetectable, or the unpreventable methods of espionage now available." [94] Similar forms of competitive monitoring, as well as national intelligence gathering, are not uncommon, but in *Kewanee*,[95] the Supreme Court approvingly cited *Du Pont*, which continues to be good law and reliable authority.

[c] **Innocent Receipt.** A person who obtains another's secret through neither improper means nor a confidential relationship has no duty prior to receiving notice of the owner's rights in the secret. Innocent receipt may occur through mistake or actions of a third party's misappropriation. Even after receiving notice, remedies may be limited (Uniform Act) or liability nonexistent (Restatement) if the defendant has in good faith paid value for the secret or has otherwise detrimentally relied on the right to use or disclose the secret.

The Restatement's general rule on indirect receipt of information is:

"One who learns another's trade secret from a third person without notice that it is a secret and that the third person's disclosure is a breach of his duty

---

[88] Restatement § 759 Comment c, referenced by § 757 Comment f.

[89] Uniform Act § 1(1).

[90] Uniform Act Comment to § 1.

[91] Restatement Comment on Clause(a), § f.

[92] Uniform Act Comment to § 1.

[93] E.I. du Pont de Nemours & Co. v. Christopher, 431 F.2d 1012, 166 U.S.P.Q. 421 (5th Cir. 1970), *cert. denied*, 400 U.S. 1024, 168 U.S.P.Q. 385, *reh'g denied*, 401 U.S. 967 (1971).

[94] 431 F.2d at 1016, 166 U.S.P.Q. at 424.

[95] Kewanee Oil Co. v. Bicron Corp., 416 U.S. 470, 476, 181 U.S.P.Q. 673 (1974).

to the other, or who learns the secret through a mistake without notice of the secrecy and the mistake,

"(a) is not liable to the other for a disclosure or use of the secret prior to receipt of such notice, and

"(b) is liable to the other for a disclosure or use of the secret after the receipt of such notice, *unless prior thereto he has in good faith paid value for the secret or has so changed his position that to subject him to liability would be inequitable.*" [96]

In contrast to this Restatement language, which provides for no liability in good faith payment or reliance cases, the Uniform Act provides for a limited remedy: "an injunction conditioning future use upon payment of a reasonable royalty" to the trade secrets owner. [97]

The key factor is defendant's notice of the information's confidentiality. The Uniform Act does not define notice, but the Restatement discusses it at some length, stating that no particular form of notice is required.

"The question is simply whether in the circumstances B knows or should know that the information is A's trade secret and that its disclosure is made in confidence." [98]

The Uniform Act includes, within its definition of misappropriation, use or disclosure by a person who:

"[A]t the time of disclosure or use, knew or had reason to know that his knowledge of the trade secret was

"(I) derived from or through a person who had utilized improper means to acquire it;

"(II) acquired under circumstances giving rise to a duty to maintain its secrecy or limit its use;

"(III) derived from or through a person who owed a duty to the person seeking relief to maintain its secrecy or limit its use." [99]

so that

"[A] trade secret owner's notification to a good faith third party that the third party has knowledge of a trade secret as a result of misappropriation by another . . . suffices to make the third party a misappropriator thereafter." [100]

[8]　Defendant's Detrimental Use or Disclosure—Recipient Modification

It was traditionally not enough that a defendant be shown to possess the secret information. Damages normally required proof that the defendant used or disclosed

---

[96] Restatement, § 758 at 18 (emphasis added).

[97] *See* § 3F[1][d].

[98] Restatement § 757 Comment J.

[99] Uniform Act § 1(b).

[100] Uniform Act Comment to § 2.

the trade secrets to plaintiff's detriment;[101] injunctive relief was available upon proof that detrimental use or disclosure was imminent or inevitable.[102] Detrimental use includes the acceleration of product or process development.[103] The Uniform Act definition of misappropriation includes mere acquisition by improper means, without a further use or disclosure requirement.[104]

The Restatement states that:

> "[A recipient] may be liable even if he uses it with modifications or improvements upon it effected by his own efforts . . . . The liability is avoided only when the contribution by the other's secret is so slight that the actor's process can be said to be derived from other sources."[105]

The Uniform Act makes no special provision for a misappropriator's modifications aside from considering it as a factor in balancing harms in the determination of remedies.

Variation between the plaintiff's trade secrets and the information the defendant uses may be evidence that a defendant received or developed the information from a source other than plaintiff's trade secrets.[106]

§ 3E   Defenses

Most defenses in trade secret cases are a mirror image of misappropriation claim elements, including independent development, public domain/absence of secrecy, and reverse engineering. If all the claim elements are established, a defendant may still prevent recovery through the equitable defenses of unclean hands and laches.

[1]   Independent Development

A person who independently discovers or develops information identical to another's trade secrets without relying on confidentially received information or improper means incurs no duty under trade secrets law.[1] Independent development is a complete defense to a claim of trade secret misappropriation.

[2]   Absence of Secrecy—Public Domain

If a purported trade secret fails the Restatement test of "substantial secrecy," so that others have no "difficulty acquiring the information," the Uniform Act test of "reasonable efforts" in relation to "other persons who can obtain economic value"

---

[101] For a discussion of damages, see § 3F[2].

[102] For a discussion of injunctive relief, see § 3F[1].

[103] Engelhard Indus., Inc. v. Research Instrumental Corp., 324 F.2d 347, 353 (9th Cir. 1963), cert. denied, 377 U.S. 923, 141 U.S.P.Q. 949 (1964).

[104] For a discussion of definitions of misappropriation, see § 3D[1].

[105] Restatement § 757 Comment c. In such a case the actor is still subject to liability for harm caused by his disclosure or possession of the secret.

[106] See RTE Corp. v. Coatings, Inc., 84 Wis. 2d 105, 267 N.W.2d 226, 233–34 (1978).

[1] See §§ 3C[2] and 3D[7].

from the information, or has failed to meet other requirements for protection,[2] then it is in the public domain and is completely unprotectable under trade secrets law's property principle.[3]

[3] Reverse Engineering

Reverse engineering trade secrets from products obtained by proper means is a complete defense to a claim of trade secret misappropriation.[4] The Restatement lists "inspection or analysis of the commercial product embodying the secret" as an example of proper discovery means.[5] The Uniform Act Comment describes reverse engineering as

"[S]tarting with the known product and working backward to find the method by which it was developed. The acquisition of the known product must, of course, also be by a fair and honest means, such as purchase of the item on the open market for reverse engineering to be lawful."[6]

Defendants often assert that information "could have been" reverse engineered from a publicly available product and that no protectable trade secret exists.[7] This defense is rarely successful where nobody else has legitimately reverse-engineered the trade secret[8] Even where others have successfully reverse-engineered the product, the courts often give primacy to trade secrets law's duty principle and enjoin the defendant from reaping the fruits of improper conduct.[9]

[4] Privilege

The Restatement provides that liability only exists where use or disclosure is not privileged[10] by the general need to promote a public interest or by an individual's need to defend against an infringement charge.[11] The paradigm of privilege is where a witness is compelled by law to disclose trade secrets in testimony.[12] This testimonial privilege does not protect a defendant from breach of contract liability based on a voluntary disclosure, as an expert witness, in violation of a non-disclosure contract.[13]

---

[2] See discussion of requirements in § 3C[1].

[3] Any liability must be based either on the trade secrets law's duty principle or by reaching outside trade secrets law for broader equity principles. For a discussion of the duty and property principles, see § 3A.

[4] This is critical to the Supreme Court's *Kewanee* holding that federal patent law does not preempt trade secrets law. Bonito Boats, Inc. v. Thunder Craft Boats, Inc., 489 U.S. 141, 156, 9 U.S.P.Q.2d 1847, 1854 (1989), discussed at § 1D[3][a][iv].

[5] Restatement § 757 Comment a.

[6] Uniform Act Comment to § 1.

[7] *See, e.g.*, Electro-Craft Corp. v. Controlled Motion, 332 N.W.2d 890, 220 U.S.P.Q. 811 (Minn. 1983): Minuteman, Inc. v. Alexander, 147 Wis. 2d 842, 434 N.W.2d 773 (1989); Sheridan v. Mallinckrodt, Inc., 568 F. Supp. 1347, 223 U.S.P.Q. 441 (N.D.N.Y. 1983).

[8] For a discussion of ascertainability, see § 3C[1][c][iii].

[9] For a discussion of non-secret information, see § 3C[4].

[10] Restatement § 757.

[11] Restatement § 757 Comment d.

[12] Restatement § 757 Comment d.

[13] ITT Telecom Products Corp. v. Dooley, 214 Cal. App. 3d 307, 262 Cal. Rptr. 773 (1989).

[5] Equitable Defenses

[a] **Unclean Hands.** Under equity's morality-based principles, courts may deny relief to a claimant who has "unclean hands." Unclean hands in a trade secret claim includes willful and intentional deceit related to a claim or bad faith prosecution of a claim. In *Emery*,[14] the negligent signing of an untrue oath on a patent application could have constituted unclean hands in connection with a patent infringement claim but was not sufficiently egregious or related to the trade secret claim to prevent relief.[15]

[b] **Laches.** In *Anaconda*,[16] the court described the equitable laches defense in the usual way, as "inexcusable delay in instituting suit and prejudice resulting to the defendant from such delay," but said that "plaintiff may avoid or diminish the effect of laches by showing that defendant was a conscious wrongdoer." "Prejudice" to the defendant "must be more than the mere continued use of a misappropriated trade secret," but "the expansion of one's business and the expenditure of capital to undertake and activity" is sufficient. After balancing the defendant's "conscious wrongdoing [against the plaintiff's] seeming acquiescence,"[17] *Anaconda* denied a damage claim but granted a lead time injunction.

[c] **Reliance-Estoppel.** Reliance and estoppel may bar equitable relief. If a defendant changes position to his or her detriment in reasonable reliance on plaintiff's representation that no misappropriation claim will be made, the plaintiff is estopped from making a claim.

§ 3F Remedies

The Restatement states merely that a trade secret owner

> "[m]ay recover damages for past harm, or be granted an injunction against future harm by disclosure or adverse use, or be granted an accounting of the wrongdoer's profits, or have the physical things embodying the secret . . . surrendered by the wrongdoer for destruction [and] may have two or more of these remedies in the same action."[1]

The Uniform Act has a much more detailed discussion of remedies than the Restatement, because trade secrets remedies were an area of confusion and inconsistency in the Restatement period.

---

[14] A.H. Emery Company v. Marcan Products Corp., 389 F.2d 11, 156 U.S.P.Q. 529 (2d Cir.), *cert. denied*, 393 U.S. 835, 159 U.S.P.Q. 799 (1968).

[15] Ferroline Corp. v. General Aniline & Film Corp., 207 F.2d 912, 916, 99 U.S.P.Q. 240, 242 (7th Cir. 1953), *cert. denied*, 347 U.S. 953, *reh'g denied*, 347 U.S. 979 (1954).

[16] Anaconda Co. v. Metric Tool & Die Co., 485 F. Supp. 410, 205 U.S.P.Q. 723 (E.D. Pa. 1980).

For a discussion of the laches defense in patent and trademark infringement suits, see § 2F[4][f] and 5F[2][e].

[17] 485 F. Supp. at 429–30, 205 U.S.P.Q. at 740.

[1] Restatement § 757 Comment e.

[1] Injunctions

United States courts grant injunctive relief only when monetary damages are inadequate, but they traditionally issue injunctions in trade secret cases because trade secret rights can be destroyed by disclosure and the competitive advantage at stake may be immeasurable.

[a] Preliminary Injunctions. Injunctions to maintain the status quo between the parties during discovery and trial are common in trade secret cases.[2] Because public disclosure terminates trade secret protectability, "an imminent threat"[3] of disclosure[4] constitutes "irreparable injury,"[5] a prerequisite for a preliminary injunction.[6] Some courts will grant a preliminary injunction based on the inevitability of disclosure which would result from an employment relationship.[7] A preliminary injunction against disclosure or use need not set forth the trade secrets themselves, but must describe the restricted acts in "reasonable detail":[8]

> "There must be an imminent threat of the allegedly harmful disclosure. . . . [i]njunctions will not be issued merely to allay the fears and apprehensions or to soothe the anxieties of the parties. Nor will an injunction be issued 'to restrain one from doing what he is not attempting and does not intend to do.' "[9]

[b] Scope of Injunctions. Injunctions must generally be narrow, reaching only activities and information whose restriction is necessary to protect the threatened trade secrets. An injunction's scope must balance the need to cover derivations from the original trade secrets[10] with the need to permit the defendant to use any information that is not a trade secret.

In *American Can*,[11] an ink manufacturer sought to enjoin an ex-employee chemist from using secret formulas. The court reviewed the decisional law on injunction scope

---

[2] *See* Salomon v. Hertz, 2 A. 379 (N.J. Eq. 1886) (preliminary injunction granted for technical business information). *See also* Dekar Industries, Inc. v. Bissett-Berman Corp., 434 F.2d 1304, 168 U.S.P.Q. 71 (9th Cir. 1970), *cert. denied*, 402 U.S. 945, 169 U.S.P.Q. 528 (1971); National Chemshare Corp. of Missouri v. Schultz, 173 U.S.P.Q. 218 (D. Ind. 1972); Gillette Co. v. Williams, 360 F. Supp. 1171, 178 U.S.P.Q. 327 (D. Conn. 1973).

[3] Continental Group, Inc. v. Amoco Chem. Corp., 614 F.2d 351, 359 (3d Cir. 1980).

[4] *E.g.*, FMC Corp. v. Varco International, Inc., 677 F.2d 500, 503, 217 U.S.P.Q. 135, 138 (5th Cir. 1982) (a single trade secret).

[5] Fed. R. Civ. P. 65(b).

[6] Other prerequisites are a reasonable probability of eventual success on the merits, a balancing of hardships to the parties, and the public interest.

[7] Air Products and Chemicals, Inc. v. Johnson, 296 Pa. Super. 405, 442 A.2d 1114, 215 U.S.P.Q. 547, (1982); FMC Corp. v. Varco International, Inc., 677 F.2d 500, 217 U.S.P.Q. 135 (5th Cir. 1982). (*But see* Continental Group, Inc. v. Amoco Chem. Corp., 614 F.2d 351 (3d Cir. 1980)).

[8] Dekar Industries, Inc. v. Bissett-Berman Corp., 434 F.2d 1304, 1306, 168 U.S.P.Q. 71, 72 (9th Cir. 1970), *cert. denied*, 402 U.S. 945, 169 U.S.P.Q. 528 (1971).

[9] Continental Group, Inc. v. Amoco Chem. Corp., 614 F.2d 351, 358–59 (3d Cir. 1980).

[10] For a discussion of modifications, see § 3D[8].

[11] American Can Co. v. Mansukhani, 742 F.2d 314, 223 U.S.P.Q. 97 (7th Cir. 1984).

and decided to lift injunctions against selling inks compositionally similar to the plaintiff's formulas. Important factors in limiting the permissible scope of the injunctions were the narrow scope of plaintiff's trade secrets (similar formulas were widely known in the industry) and defendant's substantial experience and knowledge.

[c] Duration of Injunctions. Like trade secrets themselves, injunctions can theoretically last indefinitely, but questions about their duration and termination often arise because of the tendency for trade secrets, especially those that have been misappropriated, to lose their secrecy and protectability.

Post-Restatement common law cases split over whether injunctive relief should be available against a misappropriator if the secret became public after the misappropriation. The *"Shellmar* Rule"[12] called for injunctions whenever information was obtained by improper means; the *"Conmar* Rule"[13] prohibited injunctions when the misappropriated information was public. Decisions to follow one or the other rule often depended on the question of who (owner, misappropriator or third person) had caused the trade secret to become public. Some decisions narrowed the split by granting limited "lead time" injunctions, intended to eliminate any competitive advantage that might otherwise result from the misappropriation.[14] The Uniform Act adopted lead time injunctions, but common law states may still choose between divergent lines of authority.

Because the length of lead time gained may be indefinite, courts sometimes issue perpetual injunctions and permit the defendant to apply to the court to have the injunction lifted when the trade secrets cease to be secret.[15]

The Uniform Act states that an injunction should:

> "terminate when a former trade secret becomes either generally known to good faith competitors or generally knowable to them because of the lawful availability of products that can be reverse engineered to reveal a trade secret."[16]

> "If a misappropriator either has not taken advantage of lead time or good faith competitors already have caught up with a misappropriator at the time that a case is decided, future disclosure and use of a former trade secret by a misappropriator will not damage a trade secret owner and no injunctive restraint of future disclosure and use is appropriate."[17]

The Uniform Act also provides that:

> "In appropriate circumstances, affirmative acts to protect a trade secret may be compelled by court order."[18]

---

[12] *See* Shellmar Products Co. v. Allen-Qualley Co., 87 F.2d 104 (7th Cir. 1937).

[13] Conmar Products Corp. v. Universal Slide Fastener Co., 172 F.2d 150, 80 U.S.P.Q. 108 (2d Cir. 1949).

[14] *See, e.g.,* Schreyer v. Casco Products Corp., 190 F.2d 921 (2d Cir. 1951), *cert. denied,* 342 U.S. 913 (1952).

[15] *See, e.g.,* Boeing Co. v. Sierracin Corp., 108 Wash. 2d 38, 738 P.2d 665, 682 (1987).

[16] Uniform Act Comment to § 2.

[17] Uniform Act Comment to § 2.

[18] Uniform Act § 2(c).

An "affirmative act" order could include:

> "[m]andatory injunctions requiring that a misappropriator return the fruits of misappropriation to an aggrieved person, *e.g.*, the return of stolen blueprints or the surrender of surreptitious photographs or recordings."[19]

[d] **Royalty-Injunctions.** In case of a misappropriator's innocent reliance on the trade secrets, an overriding public interest, or other exceptional circumstances, the Uniform Act provides for an injunction conditioning trade secret use on payment of a reasonable royalty.

[2] Damages

[a] **Compensatory Damages.** Prerequisite to any damage recovery, misappropriated trade secrets must be not merely known but "used," which can mean not only embodiment in a product, but also acceleration of a product's development,[20] solicitation of sales and service contracts,[21] or any activity which unjustly enriches another party or causes economic detriment[22] to the trade secrets owner.[23]

[i] *Calculation of Damages.* The common law of trade secrets damage calculation has gone through various permutations. Prominent decisions have measured defendant's profits,[24] measured plaintiff's lost profits including certain fixed costs,[25] allowed recovery of both plaintiff's lost profits and defendant's profits,[26] and combined both measures to make plaintiff whole, taking care to prevent double recovery.[27] Some states allow recovery of the greater of the two measures, illicit profits and damages. The Uniform Act uses both measures to make the plaintiff whole but denies double recovery.[28] If the plaintiff meets the burden of proving the fact of damages, the burden shifts to the defendant to show that no part of its profits is attributable to the trade secret.[29] If the amount of damages is uncertain, a jury's estimate will

---

[19] Uniform Act Comment to § 2.

[20] Engelhard Indus., Inc. v. Research Instrumental Corp., 324 F.2d 347, 353 (9th Cir. 1963), *cert. denied*, 377 U.S. 923, 141 U.S.P.Q. 949 (1964).

[21] University Computing Co. v. Lykes-Youngstown Corp., 504 F.2d 518, 540-42, 183 U.S.P.Q. 705, 717–18 (5th Cir. 1974), *rehearing denied*, 505 F.2d 1304 (5th Cir. 1974) (unpublished).

[22] Or, presumably, detriment to the fundamental right of privacy, linked to trade secrets law by Kewanee Oil Co. v. Bicron Corp., 416 U.S. 470, 181 U.S.P.Q. 673 (1974).

[23] Von Brimer v. Whirlpool Corp., 367 F. Supp. 740, 743, 181 U.S.P.Q. 187, 188 (N.D. Cal. 1973), *modified*, 536 F.2d 838, 190 U.S.P.Q. 528 (8th Cir. 1976).

[24] International Industries v. Warren Petroleum Corp., 248 F.2d 696, 699, 115 U.S.P.Q. 104, 106, *reh'g denied*, 248 F.2d 696, 115 U.S.P.Q. 159 (3rd Cir. 1957), *cert. dismissed*, 355 U.S. 943 (1958).

[25] Sperry-Rand Corp. v. A-T-O, Inc., 447 F.2d 1387, 1392-94, 171 U.S.P.Q. 775, 778-79 (4th Cir. 1971), *cert. denied*, 405 U.S. 1017, 409 U.S. 892 (1972).

[26] Clark v. Bunker, 453 F.2d 1006, 1011, 172 U.S.P.Q. 420, 423–24 (9th Cir. 1972).

[27] Telex Corp. v. International Business Mach. Corp., 510 F.2d 894, 930–33, 184 U.S.P.Q. 521, 547–48 (10th Cir. 1975), *cert. dismissed*, 423 U.S. 802 (1975).

[28] Uniform Act § 3.

[29] Jet Spray Cooler, Inc. v. Crampton, 377 Mass. 159, 385 N.E.2d 1349, 1358 n.14, 203 U.S.P.Q. 363, 372 n.14 (1979).

receive great deference.[30] Evidence of the amount of damages can be evaluated at a special hearing,[31] by a special master,[32] or at a separate trial.[33]

The Uniform Act provides, as an alternative measure of damages, a reasonable royalty to be paid for the misappropriator's use or disclosure of the trade secret.[34]

[ii] *Effect of a Public Disclosure.* Under trade secrets law, damages are generally not recoverable for activities occurring after the misappropriated trade secret enters the public domain, but damages may be recoverable for any unjust enrichment caused by the misappropriator's wrongfully acquired head start in understanding and using the (former) trade secret.[35]

A Restatement provision that one may be liable for procuring by improper means any business information, whether or not a trade secret,[36] has been applied to award post-publication damages for formerly secret information,[37] and for information that had not qualified as a trade secret at the time it was improperly acquired.[38]

The Uniform Act allows monetary recovery only for the period during which information is protectable, plus the value of any lead-time advantage.

[b] **Punitive Damages.** Punitive damages are available for willful and wanton tortious acts. Courts have found malicious breach of trade secret contracts to be tortious breaches of a confidential relationship,[39] and have awarded punitive damages for "willful and malicious misappropriation."[40] The Uniform Act limits punitive damages to an amount not exceeding twice the compensatory damage award.[41]

---

[30] *In re* Innovative Const. Systems, Inc., 793 F.2d 875, 887–88, 230 U.S.P.Q. 94, 103–04 (7th Cir. 1985).

[31] *See, e.g.*, K-2 Ski Co. v. Head Ski Co., Inc., 506 F.2d 471, 183 U.S.P.Q. 724 (9th Cir. 1974).

[32] International Industries v. Warren Petroleum Corp., 248 F.2d 696, 115 U.S.P.Q. 104, 106, *reh'g denied*, 248 F.2d 696, 115 U.S.P.Q. 159 (3d Cir. 1957) *cert. dismissed*, 355 U.S. 943 (1958).

[33] Rohm & Haas Co. v. AZS Corp., 229 U.S.P.Q. 399 (N.D. Ga. 1986) (bifurcated for trial but not discovery).

[34] Uniform Act § 3(a). This line was added as part of the 1985 Amendments. For a discussion of the 1985 Amendments, see § 3B[4].

[35] Schreyer v. Casco Products Corp., 190 F.2d 921 (2d Cir. 1951), *cert. denied*, 342 U.S. 913 (1952); Engelhard Industries, Inc. v. Research Instrumental Corp., 324 F.2d 347, 353, 139 U.S.P.Q. 179, 184 (9th Cir. 1963), *cert. denied*, 377 U.S. 923 (1964); Molinaro v. Burnbaum, 201 U.S.P.Q. 83 (D. Mass. 1977), *damage accounting settled*, 201 U.S.P.Q. 150 (D. Mass. 1978).

[36] Restatement § 759 Comment (b). See discussion in § 3C[4].

[37] Crocan Corp. v. Sheller-Globe Corp., 385 F. Supp. 251, 255, 185 U.S.P.Q. 211, 213 (N.D. Ill. 1974).

[38] Nucor Corp. v. Tennessee Forging Steel Service, Inc., 476 F.2d 386, 177 U.S.P.Q. 353 (8th Cir. 1973).

[39] *See* Cherne Indus., Inc. v. Grounds & Associates, Inc., 278 N.W.2d 81, 205 U.S.P.Q. 854 (Minn. 1979); Crutcher-Rolfs-Cummings, Inc. v. Ballard, 540 S.W.2d 380, 388, 193 U.S.P.Q. 570 (Tex. Ct. App. 1976), *cert. denied*, 433 U.S. 910 (1977)

[40] *See, e.g.*, Boeing Co. v. Sierracin Corp., 108 Wash. 2d 38, 738 P.2d 665 (1987); Aries Information Systems, Inc. v. Pacific Management Systems Corp., 366 N.W.2d 366, 226 U.S.P.Q. 440 (Minn. Ct. App. 1985).

[41] Uniform Act § 3(b).

[3] Attorney Fees and Court Costs

Most states follow the "American Rule" that parties should generally pay their own attorneys' fees, but awards in trade secret cases are sometimes made, for example, in cases of blatantly "oppressive and bad faith conduct." [42]

The Uniform Act provides that reasonable attorney fees may be awarded to the prevailing party:

> "If (i) a claim of misappropriation is made in bad faith, (ii) a motion to terminate an injunction is made or resisted in bad faith, (iii) willful and malicious misappropriation exists . . . ." [43]

The accompanying Comment states that this remedy is available for its deterrent value and allows the judge to determine whether attorney's fees should be awarded even if the trial is to a jury. [44]

[4] Seizure of Embodiments

Where trade secret theft involves tangible embodiments of the secrets, state replevin statutes can be used to remove the embodiments from the control of the misappropriator and put them under the control of the owner or of a neutral third party. A trade secret violation may form the basis of a United States International Trade Commission exclusion or cease and desist order. [45]

§ 3G Criminal Penalties

Neither the Uniform Act nor the Restatement address criminal penalties for trade secret misappropriation. Criminal penalties for trade secret misappropriation may be available through (1) statutes specifically designed to cover trade secrets or (2) statutes generally covering property misappropriation. The former were enacted to overcome the actual and potential deficiencies of the latter, but the more general statutes reach more broadly if it is established that trade secrets are "property" within the meaning of the relevant statute.

§ 3H Preventive Programs

A trade secrets protection program is the best way to ensure that confidential information cannot reach one's competitors or the public except through improper means and that courts will recognize information's secret character and value. In many

---

[42] Sperry-Rand v. Electronic Concepts, Inc., 325 F. Supp. 1209, 1219, 170 U.S.P.Q. 410, 416 (E.D. Va. 1970), *vacated on other grounds, sub nom.* Sperry Rand v. A-T-O, Inc., 447 F.2d 1387, 171 U.S.P.Q. 775 (4th Cir. 1971), *cert. denied,* 405 U.S. 1017, 173 U.S.P.Q. 193 (1972).

[43] Uniform Act § 4.

[44] Uniform Act Comment to § 4.

[45] *See, e.g.,* Viscofan, S.A. v. U.S. Int'l Trade Comm'n, 787 F.2d 544, 229 U.S.P.Q. 118 (Fed. Cir. 1986). For a discussion of U.S.I.T.C. proceedings involving patents, see § 2E[2][b][ii].

industries, a program to document the information sources used may be equally important to insulate against allegations of misappropriating trade secrets.

[1] Measures to Protect One's Valuable Information

Trade secrets law protects only what the owner has made reasonable efforts to keep secret. This requirement includes both *security*, preventing outsider intrusion and access, and *confidentiality*, preventing insider disclosure or misappropriation. For organization and implementation purposes, information protection programs can be divided into five major categories: those (1) directed at the information itself, (2) for employees, (3) for visitors, (4) for marketing disclosures, and (5) with vendors, consultants, joint venturers, governmental agencies and the like.

Particular measures' expense may outweigh their usefulness. A cost-benefit analysis assists in selecting appropriate levels of protection and combinations of measures. A court assessing the reasonableness of efforts will make a similar analysis and will view the security program as evidence of the value the proprietor places on the confidential information.[1]

A "cost" factor is that precautions may undermine researchers' and other employees' efficiency and enthusiasm by restricting their informal exchanges with persons outside their own organization.

[a] **Information-Directed Procedures.** Information-directed procedures include identifying sensitive information, notifying all those who may have access to it, marking documents and other media with stamps or legends, denying access to people who do not need the information, securing computerized data with passwords, putting physical notices on terminals and electronic notices on computer files and locked storage of recorded and printed data, encoding secret information that is physically accessible, placing signs and locks at entry points to entire facilities and to specific locations, destroying discarded records (*e.g.*, computer print-outs), restricting access to copying machines, permanently erasing data from old computers being sold or discarded, dividing a process into steps and separating the various departments that work on the several steps, using unnamed or coded ingredients, destroying laboratory samples and trash on the premises, and using checkpoints, self-locking doors, alarms, closed circuit surveillance television, log-in procedures, watchmen, vaults, and shredding machines.

The utility of most of these measures is obvious, but a few merit additional discussion:

A book to log sensitive documents in and out enables the monitor to know at any time if any document is missing and to know who has copies of documents whenever they are not in the file.

Because copiers are often used to duplicate sensitive documents, a short notice on copiers can be posted to remind employees of the sensitive nature of documents and their lack of authority to use company information for personal or other purposes

---

[1] *See* Rockwell Graphic Systems v. DEV Indus., 925 F.2d 174, 17 U.S.P.Q.2d 1780 (7th Cir. 1991).

unrelated to their work. Management may also restrict the copier to business uses by requiring employees to obtain a copier card from a trusted employee. The trusted employee can also maintain a log book in which the copier user must insert a description of the document copied, the purpose of the copy, and the number of copies made. It is also advisable to keep copiers far away from confidential documents to make surreptitious copying more difficult.

A legend's value lies in notifying all employees, even those with whom the company has no specific confidentiality agreement, that a specific document is considered confidential. A drawback is that a court may limit the broad definition of proprietary information found in confidentiality agreements to those documents or information containing a legend. On the other hand, a broad definition of proprietary information, e.g., all information relating to the company, without any legends or a more specific definition may not give employees sufficient notice of what information to protect. The prudent course is to (i) use the legend on particularly sensitive information and (ii) include both a broad and a specific definition of proprietary information in the agreements used by the company.

[b]   **Employee-Directed Procedures.** Employee-directed procedures include signing confidentiality and non-disclosure agreements, giving notice of what information is particularly sensitive, conducting entry and exit interviews, restricting access to those employees who "need to know" specific information, and sending post employment letters.

The employer should require employees to execute agreements, which may be part of an employment contract, containing non-disclosure and confidentiality provisions, provisions for assignment of discoveries to the employer, and covenants not to solicit fellow employees to leave and not to solicit customers of former employers.[2] The employer should also consider using carefully crafted non-competition provisions.

When an employee resigns or is terminated, the employer should conduct an exit interview at which the employee is (1) reminded of the employee's obligation to transfer certain ideas and inventions to the company and to keep confidential any information learned and developed in the course of the employee's service to the company, (2) asked to return all materials and property of the company in the employee's possession, and (3) asked to complete and execute a termination certificate which identifies the trade secret information to which he or she had access and which contains non-disclosure provisions with respect to such trade secrets.

The employer should send the employee a letter reminding the employee of his or her obligations about a week or two after the employee has been terminated or resigns. A second letter addressed to the employee's new employer puts the new employer on notice of the employee's obligations to the former employer.

[c]   **Visitor-Directed Procedures.** Visitor-directed procedures include accompanying them, issuing admission badges, denying access to particularly sensitive areas, notifying employees that visitors are present, and requiring visitors to sign confidentiality agreements.

---

[2] For a discussion of ownership, obligations and enforceability of agreements between employers and employees, see § 3D[6][a].

[d]   **Marketing and Public Disclosure Procedures.** Disclosure procedures should include delegating review of all material to people well informed about the company's valuable information; restricting the level of detail and explanatory value of materials intended for general circulation, such as advertising, speeches and articles for publication; limiting the degree of disclosure, and including confidentiality provisions in materials intended for limited circulation such as customer handbooks, repair manuals, specifications, bids and proposals. Another technique is to include deliberate typographical or other errors in confidentially disclosed materials in order to make it easier to trace the source of misused information.

[e]   **Other Contractual and Regulatory Relationships.** Procedures for dealing with outsiders (*e.g.*, vendors, consultants, joint-venturers and governmental agencies) should include inserting non-disclosure provisions in all license agreements, franchise agreements and consulting agreements that relate to confidential information. The company should seek non-disclosure agreements at the beginning of any negotiations in which trade secrets may be disclosed. A trade secret owner may wish to keep vendors' and customers' identities secret and ask vendors to label sensitive goods with a code when shipping to the company.

[2]   Recipient's Measures to Avoid Inadvertent Misappropriation

Avoiding inadvertent, or apparent, misappropriation depends on using proper means of developing information and documenting that use. In some cases, "tainted" information must be segregated and a record kept to demonstrate that it was not used.

[a]   **Measures to Demonstrate Proper Means.** In industries where competitors routinely have access to each other's trade secrets, successful defense of trade secrets claims may depend on a defendant having taken measures to demonstrate the proper and non-confidential sources of information actually used and to actively avoid the inadvertent or apparent use of improper or confidential sources. Because trade secrets cases may depend on notions of business morality rather than legal technicalities, documentation policies are important in demonstrating a company's good faith and clean hands.

[b]   **Recipient's Identification of Unprotected Information.** Unprotected information is easy to define: Any information acquired other than through a confidential relationship or improper means. Unfortunately for the recipient of business information, it is often difficult to conclude with complete assurance that any particular information is unprotected, or "untainted." Helpful measures include entrance interviews to clarify any confidentiality obligations new employees may have to previous employers, and careful assessment of sources of information, followed by written guidelines to employees about what sources may or may not be used.

§ 3I   Licensing

Licensing is important to extracting economic value from trade secrets, serving as a basis for royalty payments to inventors from licensees who have the means to develop, manufacture or market the resulting products or as an alternative to the sale of products embodying easily copied or reverse engineered trade secrets.

[1] Characterization As a Sale

A licensing contract may include restrictions on use, disclosure and reverse engineering. Characterization of the transaction as a sale would render these restrictions unenforceable. This issue is particularly important in connection with high-value, easily copied or reverse-engineered trade secrets in computer hardware and software. Courts look to a transaction's substance, rather than its form, to decide whether a purported license is actually a sale.[1]

Courts may characterize a purported license as a sale when the license term exceeds the product's life, the license is not terminable except in case of reverse engineering, there is no negotiated, signed agreement, or the product is acquired from a retail sales outlet or by mail order.

[2] Duration of Royalties

Unlike patent licenses, which are enforceable only for the patent term and so long as the patent is not held invalid, licenses for trade secrets royalties may be enforceable in perpetuity.

In *Warner-Lambert*,[2] a licensee sought to discontinue royalty payments after several decades of using the formula for "Listerine" mouthwash. The court applied the clearly bargained for contract terms and enforced the perpetual royalty obligation, noting that the licensee had "obtained a head start in the field . . . of incalculable value through the years."[3]

In a "hybrid" license covering both patents and trade secrets, trade secrets royalties must be clearly distinguished from patent royalties to be enforceable after the patents expire. It must also be clear to the court that the trade secrets royalties were not negotiated as compensation for use of a patented invention.

In *Brulotte*,[4] the Supreme Court refused to enforce trade secrets royalties after the expiry of licensed patents because the royalties for each were not clearly distinguished. The court inferred that the provision for post-expiration royalties had been subject to the "leverage" (bargaining power) of the patent monopoly and held that those provisions were an unenforceable attempt to "project the [patent] monopoly beyond the patent period."[5]

---

[1] See, e.g., United States v. Wise, 550 F.2d 1180, 194 U.S.P.Q. 59 (9th Cir. 1977), cert. denied, 434 U.S. 929, 199 U.S.P.Q. 128, reh'g denied, 434 U.S. 977 (1977); Vault Corp. v. Quaid Software Ltd., 655 F. Supp. 750, 2 U.S.P.Q.2d 1407 (E.D. La. 1987), aff'd, 847 F.2d 255, 7 U.S.P.Q.2d 1281 (5th Cir. 1988).

[2] Warner-Lambert Pharm. Co. v. John J. Reynolds, Inc., 178 F. Supp. 655, 123 U.S.P.Q. 431 (S.D.N.Y. 1959), aff'd, 280 F.2d 197, 126 U.S.P.Q. 3 (2d Cir. 1960).

[3] 178 F. Supp. at 666, 123 U.S.P.Q. at 439.

[4] Brulotte v. Thys Co., 379 U.S. 29 (1964), reh'g denied, 379 U.S. 985 (1965) discussed at § 1D[3][b][i].

[5] 379 U.S. at 32.

In *Aronson*,[6] the Supreme Court refused to invalidate a license for perpetual trade secrets royalty payments, even though a patent application for the idea was later rejected, because the pending patent application had "played no part in the contract to pay the . . . royalty indefinitely."[7] The key facts supporting this conclusion were that the parties knew the patent might be rejected and that the licensee-manufacturer had clearly agreed to pay for "the opportunity to be the first in the market."[8]

In *Pitney-Bowes*,[9] the district court distinguished *Aronson* and held that a hybrid license terminated when the last underlying patent expired.

> "[T]here is no explicit language in the agreement differentiating between the two forms of protection underlying the royalty obligation and . . . there is no division or allocation of royalties vis-a-vis the two forms of protection underlying the royalty obligation."[10]

[3] Confidentiality and Post-Termination Clauses

Trade secrets licenses should include a confidentiality clause that specifies steps the licensee must take to protect confidentiality and to make the confidentiality requirements known to and binding on the licensee's employees, affiliates and consultants.

A post-termination clause may require that the licensee return all tangible embodiments of the licensor's confidential information and may extend secrecy requirements beyond termination of the license and beyond the entry of any trade secret into the public domain.[11]

---

[6] Aronson v. Quick Point Pencil Co., 440 U.S. 257, 201 U.S.P.Q. 1 (1979) discussed at § 1D[3][b][iii].

[7] 440 U.S. at 265, 201 U.S.P.Q. at 6.

[8] 440 U.S. at 266, 201 U.S.P.Q. at 6.

[9] Pitney-Bowes, Inc. v. Mestre, 517 F. Supp. 52, 211 U.S.P.Q. 681, (S.D. Fla. 1981), *modified*, 701 F.2d 1365, 218 U.S.P.Q. 987 (11th Cir. 1983).

[10] 517 F. Supp. at 63, 211 U.S.P.Q. at 690.

See also Meechan v. PPG Industries, Inc., 802 F.2d 881, 886, 231 U.S.P.Q. 400, 403 (7th Cir. 1986) ("Although . . . parties can contract for trade secret payments to extend beyond the life of a patent, there must be some provision that distinguishes between patent royalties and trade secret royalties."); Boggild v. Kenner Prodc., General Mills, 776 F.2d 1315, 1321, 228 U.S.P.Q. 130, 135 (6th Cir. 1985), *cert. denied*, 477 U.S. 908 (1986) ("the *Brulotte* rule of *per se* invalidity precludes enforcement of license provisions which were developed in anticipation of patent protection and which require royalty payments for use, sale or manufacture of a patented item beyond the life of the patent . . . . [O]nce the pending patent issues, enforcement of royalty provisions for other rights which conflict with and are indistinguishable from royalties for patent rights, is precluded . . . . The terms of the licensing agreement compel the conclusion that, at the time the parties executed the license, the plaintiffs exerted considerable leverage from the anticipated patents. In our view, the absence of a filed patent application is, under these circumstances, irrelevant to the analysis under *Brulotte* . . . . In the case at bar, the agreement calls for royalties on the sales of the patented [device] for a minimum of twenty-five years. As in *Brulotte*, the agreement contains neither provisions for reduction of royalties in the event valid patents never issued nor terms for reduction of post-expiration royalties.").

[11] For a discussion of perpetual enforceability of trade secret contract provisions, see § 3I[2].

CHAPTER 4

COPYRIGHT

(Pub.886)

§ 4A Introduction

Copyright law protects original works of authorship embodied in a tangible medium of expression. Copyrightable subject matter includes literature, music, drama, the visual arts, sound recordings, and computer programs. Copyright arises automatically when an author creates a work and subsists for the author's life plus 50 years after the author's death.

Copyright law confers exclusive rights to reproduce the work, to prepare derivative works based on the work, to distribute copies or phonorecords of the work, and to publicly perform or display the work. It protects only a work's expression of ideas, not ideas themselves, and confers no rights over independent creation and dissemination of similar works. A nonliteral paraphrase or modified work may infringe a copyright but only if it is substantially similar in expression to the copyrighted work.

> " 'The copyright law, like the patent statutes, makes reward to the owner a secondary consideration.' . . . However, it is 'intended definitely to grant valuable enforceable rights to authors, publishers, etc., without burdensome requirements; "to afford greater encouragement to the production of literary [or artistic] works of lasting benefit to the world.' . . .

> "The economic philosophy behind the clause empowering Congress to grant patents and copyrights is the conviction that encouragement of individual effort by personal gain is the best way to advance public welfare through the talents of authors and inventors in 'Science and useful Arts.' Sacrificial days devoted to such creative activities deserve rewards commensurate with the services rendered." [1]

§ 4B Historical Development

United States copyright law evolved through three major eras: (1) from adoption of the Constitution and the first copyright statute in 1790 to enactment of the 1909 Act; (2) the 1909 Act; and (3) the current Copyright Act of 1976.

The United States Constitution authorized Congress to enact copyright laws to secure for "authors" the exclusive rights in their "writings" for a limited time for the purpose of advancing the "Progress of Science." [1]

---

[1] Mazer v. Stein, 347 U.S. 201, 219 (1954).

[1] Article I, Section 8, Clause 8 provides that Congress shall have the power:

> "To promote the progress of science and useful arts, by securing for limited times to authors and inventors the exclusive right to their respective writings and discoveries."

Historical sources indicate that the Constitution's framers intended promotion of "science" to be copyright's province; promotion of "useful arts" pertained to patent protection. *See In re* Bergy, 596 F.2d 952, 201 U.S.P.Q. 352 (CCPA 1979), *aff'd sub nom.* Diamond v. Chakrabarty, 447 U.S. 303, 206 U.S.P.Q. 193 (1980).

In 1790, the first Congress enacted a statute that extended copyright protection to "maps, charts, and books." The subsequent "history of copyright law has been one of gradual expansion of the types of works accorded protection."[2]

The inclusion in early copyright statutes of types of works, such as maps and photographs, that are not "writings" in a literary sense raised constitutional issues. In *Burrow-Giles Lithographic Co.*,[3] the Supreme Court upheld the constitutionality of copyright on photographs of posed subjects. It broadly defined the constitutional terms "writings" and "authors."

> "An author in that sense is 'he to whom anything owes its origin; originator; maker; one who completes a work of science or literature.' . . . So, also, no one would now claim that the word writing in this clause of the Constitution, though the only word used as to subjects in regard to which authors are to be secured, is limited to the actual script of the author, and excludes books and all other printed matter. By writings in that clause is meant the literary productions of those authors, and Congress very properly has declared these to include *all forms of writing, printing, engraving, etching, &c., by which the ideas in the mind of the author are given visible expression.*"[4]

[2] H.R. Report No. 94–1476, 94th Cong., 2d Sess. 51 (1976).
The history up to enactment of the 1909 Act was reviewed by the Supreme Court in 1954 as follows:

> "In 1790, the First Congress conferred a copyright on 'authors of any map, chart, book or books already printed' . . . Later, designing, engraving and etching were included; . . . in 1831 musical composition; . . . dramatic compositions in 1856; . . . and photographs and negatives thereof in 1865. . . .
>
> "The Act of 1870 defined copyrightable subject matter as: '. . . any book, map, chart, dramatic or musical composition, engraving, cut, print, or photograph or negative thereof, or of a painting, drawing, chromo, *statue, statuary, and of models or designs intended to be perfected as works of the fine arts.*' (Emphasis supplied.) . . . The italicized part added three-dimensional works of art to what had been protected previously. . . ."

Mazer v. Stein, 347 U.S. 201, 100 U.S.P.Q. 325 (1954).
[3] Burrow-Giles Lithographic Co. v. Sarony, 111 U.S. 53 (1884). *Compare* Trade-Mark Cases, 100 U.S. 82, 94 (1879) (Article I patent-copyright clause does not authorize Congress to provide protection for trademarks because a trademark is not the writing of an author).
[4] 111 U.S. at 58.
The photograph in *Burrows-Giles* was a posed portrait of Oscar Wilde. The Court reasoned that, although photography was mechanical reproduction, the photographer exercised intellectual creativity in posing the subject and arranging his costume and accessories. The Court reserved the question whether a photographer who passively captured a scene and took no part in posing the subject could be considered the "author" of a "writing." Later cases upheld copyrights on unposed photographs. Pagano v. Chas. Beseler Co., 234 F. 693 (2d Cir. 1916) (street scene showing the Public Library on Fifth Avenue in New York); Time, Inc. v. Bernard Geis Associates, 293 F. Supp. 130 (S.D. N.Y. 1968) ("When President Kennedy was killed in Dallas on November 22, 1963, Abraham Zapruder, A Dallas dress manufacturer, was by sheer happenstance at the scene taking home movie pictures with his camera"; HELD: photographs are copyrightable subject matter).

In *Goldstein*,[5] the Supreme Court defined constitutional "writings" more broadly, eliminating reference to "visible" expressions: 'although the word writings' might be limited to script or printed material, it may be interpreted to include any physical rendering of the fruits of creative intellectual or aesthetic labor."

Early copyright statutes distinguished published and unpublished works. Common law copyright protected unpublished works indefinitely but ended upon publication. Publication was said to "divest" the author of those common law rights. To secure protection for a published work, the author must have taken the steps prescribed by the federal copyright statutes. Publication of a work in compliance with those formalities was said to "invest" the author with federal copyright but only for a limited period of years.

In 1909, Congress enacted a comprehensive new copyright law. Section 4 provided that "the works for which copyright may be secured under this Act shall include all the writings of an author." Because this language was identical to the Constitution, it could be argued that Congress had extended copyright protection to the full extent of the Constitution. However, it came to be recognized that the statutory definition of protectable writings was narrower than the constitutional definition and that there were types of works, such as sound recordings, that could constitutionally be included but were not.[6]

In 1976, Congress replaced the 1909 Act with a new copyright code, which went into effect on January 1, 1978.[7] The 1976 Act made two fundamental changes in copyright law. First, it extended federal statutory copyright protection to unpublished as well as published works, restricting state common law copyright protection to works not fixed in a tangible medium of expression. Second, it altered the copyright term to provide protection for the life of the author plus 50 years after the author's death. Congress has amended the 1976 Act several times, most notably by the 1988 Berne Convention Implementation Act.

§ 4C Copyrightability

There are three basic conditions of copyrightability: a work must be (1) within the constitutional and statutory definitions of a work of authorship, (2) fixed in a tangible medium of expression, and (3) original.

---

[5] Goldstein v. California, 412 U.S. 546, 178 U.S.P.Q. 129 (1973).

[6] Mazer v. Stein, 347 U.S. 201, 100 U.S.P.Q. 325 (1954) ("Some writers interpret this section as being co-extensive with the constitutional grant, . . . but the House Report, while inconclusive, indicates that it was 'declaratory of existing law' only .. . .").

[7] The process of revising the out-dated 1909 Act began in 1955. The Copyright Office published 35 monographs and submitted a report to Congress in 1961. A Revision Bill was introduced in Congress in 1964. The basic design of the Bill remained unchanged for the next twelve years, but enactment was delayed by controversy over provisions that affected particular industries, such as cable television.

[1] Copyrightable Subject Matter

Copyright protects the original *expression* of ideas, not ideas themselves. Copyrightable works include fiction and nonfictional verbal works, periodicals, dictionaries, directories, technical drawings, maps, paintings, prints, translations, sculptures, photographs, musical compositions, sound recordings, plays, motion pictures, cartoon characters, toys, dolls, fabric designs, choreography, pantomimes, video games, data bases, computer programs, and architectural drawings.

Computer programs [1] and useful article designs [2] present especially difficult problems in determining copyrightable subject matter.

[a] General Definition—Categories of Works—Choreography. Copyright Act Section 102(a) defines copyrightable subject matter: "Copyright protection subsists . . . in original works of authorship fixed in any tangible medium of expression . . . ." [3] and lists eight categories:

(1) literary works;

(2) musical works, including any accompanying words;

(3) dramatic works, including any accompanying music;

(4) pantomimes and choreographic works; [4]

(5) pictorial, graphic and sculptural works;

(6) motion pictures and other audiovisual works;

(7) sound recordings; and

(8) architectural works. [5]

The list is "illustrative and not limitative"; the seven categories "do not necessarily exhaust the scope of 'original works of authorship' . . . ." [6] A work may fall into more than one category.

Section 101 defines five of the eight categories: literary works; pictorial, graphic, and sculptural works; [7] sound recordings; [8] audiovisual works (with a further definition

---

[1] *See* § 4C[2].

[2] *See* § 4C[3].

[3] 17 U.S.C. § 102(a).

Congress adopted "original works of authorship" rather than the constitutional language "writings" of an "author," which 1909 Act Section 4 used, "to avoid exhausting the constitutional power of Congress to legislate in this field, and to eliminate the uncertainties arising from the latter phrase." *See* H.R. Rep. No. 94–1476, 94th Cong., 2d Sess. 51–52 (1976). Congress did "not intend either to freeze the scope of copyrightable subject matter at the present stage of communications technology or to allow unlimited expansion into areas completely outside the present congressional intent." *Id.* at 51. Further, "there are unquestionably . . . areas of existing subject matter that [the statutory language] does not propose to protect but that future Congresses may want to." *Id.* at 52.

See § 4B.

[4] *See* below at n.12.

[5] A 1990 amendment added the eighth category (architectural works). *See* § 4C[3][f].

[6] H.R. Rep. No. 94–1476, 94th Cong., 2d Sess 53 (1976).

[7] *See* § 4C[3].

[8] *See* § 4C[1][e].

of the subcategory of motion pictures); and architectural works.[9] The literary work definition is broad, encompassing "works . . . expressed in words, numbers or other verbal or numerical symbols or indicia, regardless of the nature of the material objects, such as books, periodicals, manuscripts, phonorecords, film, tapes, disks, or cards, in which they are embodied."[10] It includes not only fiction and nonfiction works but also such works as computer programs and data bases.[11]

A work's classification does not affect its copyrightability but may affect its exclusive rights. For example, some Section 110 limitations apply only to "nondramatic" literary or musical works.

The 1976 Act is the first United States copyright statute to include pantomimes and choreographic works.[12] In *Horgan*,[13] the Second Circuit held that still photographs of a ballet performance by the New York City Ballet Company infringed George Balanchine's copyrighted choreographic work, "The Nutcracker." The court discussed the history of dance protection.

> "Explicit federal copyright protection for choreography is a fairly recent development, and the scope of that protection is an uncharted area of the law. The 1976 Copyright Act . . . was the first federal copyright statute expressly to include 'choreographic works' . . . Choreography . . . could only be registered [under prior law] . . . as a species of 'dramatic composition.' Dance was protectible only if it told a story, developed or characterized an emotion, or otherwise conveyed a dramatic concept or idea. . . . The rights of a choreographer in his work were not clearly defined, in part because the means for reducing choreography to tangible form had become readily available only comparatively recently, . . . and in part because of resistance to the acceptance of abstract, non-literary dance as a worthy form of artistic expression. See also Comment, Moving to a New Beat: Copyright Protection for Choreographic Works, 24 U.C.L.A. L. Rev. 1287, 1288–94 (1977). [FN3: The cited Comment describes the Laban system of notation, and refers to the Benesh system; in addition, film and video tape are now available.]

> ". . . [T]he Copyright Office recommended . . . in 1961 that the law be amended to insure protection for 'abstract' as well as traditional dramatic ballet. . . . By including choreographic works . . . , the 1976 Act broadened the scope of its protection considerably.

> "The Act does not define choreography, and the legislative reports on the bill indicate only that 'social dance steps and simple routines' are not included. . . . The Compendium of Copyright Office Practices, Compendium II (1984) . . . defines choreographic works as follows:

---

[9] See § 4C[3][f].

[10] 17 U.S.C. § 101. *See also* H.R. Rep. No. 94–1476, 94th Cong., 2d Sess. 54 (1976) ("The term 'literary works' does not connote any criterion of literary merit or qualitative value: it includes catalogs, directories, and similar factual, reference, or instructional works and compilations of data.").

[11] See § 4C[2].

[12] *See generally* P. Goldstein, Copyright § 2.10 (1989).

[13] Horgan v. MacMillan, Inc., 789 F.2d 157, 160–61, 229 U.S.P.Q. 684, 686–87 (2d Cir. 1986).

'Choreography is the composition and arrangement of dance movements and patterns, and is usually intended to be accompanied by music. Dance is static and kinetic successions of bodily movement in certain rhythmic and spatial relationships. Choreographic works need not tell a story in order to be protected by copyright.'

"Section 450.01. Under 'Characteristics of choreographic works,' Compendium II states that

'Choreography represents a related series of dance movements and patterns organized into a coherent whole.'

"Section 450.03(a). 'Choreographic content' is described as follows:

'Social dance steps and simple routines are not copyrightable. . . . Thus, for example, the basic waltz step, the hustle step, and the second position of classical ballet are not copyrightable. However, this is not a restriction against the incorporation of social dance steps and simple routines, as such, in an otherwise registrable choreographic work. Social dance steps, folk dance steps, and individual ballet steps alike may be utilized as the choreographer's basic material in much the same way that words are the writer's basic material.' "

[b] **Compilations and Collections.** Compilations are copyrightable subject matter.[14] A compilation is "a work formed by the collection and assembling of preexisting materials or of data that are selected, coordinated, or arranged in such a way that the resulting work as a whole constitutes an original work of authorship."[15]

[i] *Data Compilations.* Facts and data are not copyrightable, but original compilations of them may be.[16] Compilations, such as directories, are

---

[14] 17 U.S.C. § 103(a). *See generally* P. Goldstein, Copyright §§ 2.14.2, 2.16.1 (1989).

[15] 17 U.S.C. § 101.

[16] *E.g.*, Harper House Inc. v. Thomas Nelson Inc., 889 F.2d 197, 204–05, 12 U.S.P.Q.2d 1779, 1786 (9th Cir. 1989) ("organizer" is copyrightable compilation of forms, calendars, maps, etc.; "A copyrightable compilation can consist mainly or entirely of uncopyrightable elements" but receive "only limited protection"); Educational Testing Services v. Katzman, 793 F.2d 533, 538–39, 230 U.S.P.Q. 156, 159–60 (3d Cir. 1986) (copyright protection extends to particular questions in a standardized test even though the test is registered as a compilation; "The fact that a registrant denominates the material as a compilation does not in itself signify that the constituent material is not also covered by the copyright. . . . Although compilations or 'collective' works may include uncopyrightable works, as well as previously copyrighted works, the fact that the registration was for compilations does not preclude protection for the material therein contributed by the author."); Apple Barrel Prods. v. Beard, 730 F.2d 384, 387–88, 222 U.S.P.Q. 956, 958 (5th Cir. 1984) (country music show, "The Country Kids Show," featuring children performers may be a copyrightable compilation of uncopyrightable elements, such as characters, sets, costumes, songs, and dances: "Copyright protection may extend to such a compilation, even if the material of which it is composed is not copyrightable itself or is already subject to a previous copyright"); Roth Greeting Cards v. United Card Co., 429 F.2d 1106, 1109, 166 U.S.P.Q. 291 (9th Cir. 1970) ("studio greeting cards;" "the textual matter of each card, considered as apart from its arrangement on the cards and its association with artistic representations, was not original to [plaintiff] and therefore not copyrightable.

copyrightable if they involve original authorship in the selection or arrangement of data. For example, in *Schroeder*,[17] the court upheld copyright in a listing of names and addresses of suppliers of seeds, plants, publications, and other items useful to gardeners. A directory's copyright protects against unauthorized copying of the collection, not the individual components unless those components involve original authorship. It does not prevent others from independently making a compilation of data on the same subject. A "second compiler" may use a first compiler's work to check for errors and omissions.[18]

In *Feist*,[19] the Supreme Court, holding a white page telephone directory compilation not copyrightable for want of originality,[20] noted that data compilations involve "the interaction of two well-established propositions," each of "impeccable pedigree." "The first is that facts are not copyrightable; the other, that compilations of facts generally are."[21]

> "There is an undeniable tension between these two propositions.
>
> "Many compilations consist of nothing but raw data—*i.e.*, wholly factual information not accompanied by any original written expression. On what basis may one claim a copyright in such a work? Common sense tells us that 100 uncopyrightable facts do not magically change their status when gathered together in one place. Yet copyright law seems to contemplate that compilations that consist exclusively of facts are potentially within its scope."[22]

The key to resolving the tension lies in understanding why facts are not copyrightable.

However, proper analysis of the problem requires that all elements of each card, including text, art work, and association between art work and text, be considered as a whole.").

See also Harper & Row, Publishers, Inc. v. Nation Enterprises, 471 U.S. 539, 547–48 (1985), discussed § 4F[3][a][ii] ("no author may copyright facts or ideas" but that "[c]reation of a nonfiction work, even a compilation of pure fact, entails originality. . . . [E]specially in the realm of factual narrative, the law is currently unsettled regarding the ways in which uncopyrightable elements combine with the author's original contributions to form protected expression.").

[17] Schroeder v. William Morrow & Co., 566 F.2d 3, 198 U.S.P.Q. 143 (7th Cir. 1977). *See also* Edwards & Deutsch Lithographing Co. v. Boorman, 15 F.2d 35 (7th Cir. 1926), *cert. denied*, 273 U.S. 738 (1926) (compilation of logarithms).

[18] *See* Rockford Map Publishers, Inc. v. Directory Service Company of Colorado, Inc., 768 F.2d 145, 226 U.S.P.Q. 1025 (7th Cir. 1985), *cert. denied*, 474 U.S. 1061 (1986).

In *Rockford*, the court cited two venerable decisions, Jewelers' Circular Pub. Co. v. Keystone Pub. Co., 274 F. 932, 935 (S.D.N.Y. 1921) (L. Hand, J.), *aff'd*, 281 F. 83 (2d Cir.), *cert. denied*, 259 U.S. 581 (1922) ("a second compiler may check back his independent work upon the original compilation"), and Kelly v. Morris, [1866] 1 Eq. 697, 701 (Wood, V.C.) ("A subsequent compiler is bound to set about doing for himself what the first compiler has done.").

[19] Feist Publications, Inc. v. Rural Telephone Service Company, Inc., 111 S. Ct. 1282, 18 U.S.P.Q.2d 1275 (1991).

[20] *See* § 4C[1][b][i](2).

[21] 111 S. Ct. at 1287, 18 U.S.P.Q.2d at 1277.

[22] 111 S. Ct. at 1287, 18 U.S.P.Q.2d at 1277–78.

"The *sine qua non* of copyright is originality. To qualify for copyright protection, a work must be original to the author. . . .[23]

. . . .

"It is this bedrock principle of copyright that mandates the law's seemingly disparate treatment of facts and factual compilations. 'No one may claim originality as to facts.' . . . This is because facts do not owe their origin to an act of authorship. The distinction is one between creation and discovery: the first person to find and report a particular fact has not created the fact; he or she has merely discovered its existence. . . .

"Factual compilations, on the other hand, may possess the requisite originality. The compilation author typically chooses which facts to include, in what order to place them, and how to arrange the collected data so that they may be used effectively by readers. These choices as to selection and arrangement, so long as they are made independently by the compiler and entail a minimal degree of creativity, are sufficiently original that Congress may protect such compilations through the copyright laws. . . . Thus, even a directory that contains absolutely no protectible written expression, only facts, meets the constitutional minimum for copyright protection if it features an original selection or arrangement. . . . This protection is subject to an important limitation. The mere fact that a work is copyrighted does not mean that every element of the work may be protected. Originality remains the sine qua non of copyright; accordingly, copyright protection may extend only to those components of a work that are original to the author. . . . Thus, if the compilation author clothes facts with an original collocation of words, he or she may be able to claim a copyright in this written expression. Others may copy the underlying facts from the publication, but not the precise words used to present them. . . . Where the compilation author adds no written expression but rather lets the facts speak for themselves, the expressive element is more elusive. The only conceivable expression is the manner in which the compiler has selected and arranged the facts. Thus, if the selection and arrangement are original, these elements of the work are eligible for copyright protection. . . . No matter how original the format, however, the facts themselves do not become original through association.

"This, then, resolves the doctrinal tension: Copyright treats facts and factual compilations in a wholly consistent manner. Facts, whether alone or as part of a compilation, are not original and therefore may not be copyrighted. A factual compilation is eligible for copyright if it features an original selection or arrangement of facts, but the copyright is limited to the particular selection or arrangement. In no event may copyright extend to the facts themselves."[24]

The most difficult problem with directories is defining what constitutes original authorship.

---

[23] *Id.*

[24] 111 S. Ct. at 1288–90, 18 U.S.P.Q.2d 1278–80.

(1) *Pre-Feist Lower Court Decisions.* Court decisions oscillate between two originality[25] standards for data and fact compilations.[26]

The "sweat of the brow" theory, which focused on the labor expended to make the compilation, originated in a 1922 decision upholding copyright in a catalog: "The man who goes through the streets of a town and puts down the names of each of the inhabitants, with their occupations and their street number, acquires material of which he is the author. He produces by his labor a meritorious composition, in which he may obtain a copyright, and thus obtain the exclusive right of multiplying copies of his work."[27] Even under the sweat of the brow theory, a minimum amount of selection, coordinating and arrangement of facts is required to make a compilation an original work of authorship.[28] Carrying the sweat of the brow theory to an extreme is a line of lower court decisions upholding copyright in white page telephone directories even though compilation of such directories involve virtually no judgment.[29] In *Feist*, the Supreme Court held a simple white page telephone directory

---

[25] *See* § 4C[5][c].

[26] *E.g.,* Dow Jones & Company, Inc. v. Board of Trade of the City of Chicago, 546 F. Supp. 113, 115, 217 U.S.P.Q. 901, 903-04 (S.D.N.Y. 1982) (Dow Jones lists of component stocks is a copyrightable compilation). In *Dow Jones*, Judge Carter noted:

> "The cases reveal two separate but interrelated justifications for granting copyright protection to compilations of factual materials. Some directories are considered original works because of the labor expended in their preparation. . . . Other compilations, however, are protected because the author exercised subjective judgment and selectivity in choosing items to list."

Judge Carter also noted an unresolved conflict between the line of cases holding compilations copyrightable and another line of cases holding mere listings of ingredients or contents uncopyrightable. *E.g.,* Kitchens of Sara Lee, Inc. v. Nifty Foods Corp., 266 F.2d 541, 121 U.S.P.Q. 359 (2d Cir. 1959).

[27] Jeweler's Circular Publishing Co. v. Keystone Publishing Co., 281 F. 83, 88 (2d Cir. 1922), *cert. denied,* 259 U.S. 581 (1922).

[28] For example, in Triangle Publications, Inc. v. New England Newspaper Pub. Co., 46 F. Supp. 198, 201 (D. Mass. 1942), the court suggested that the report of raw data on a single event, such as a horse race, will not suffice:

> "To constitute a copyrightable compilation, a compendium must ordinarily result from the labor of assembling, connecting and categorizing disparate facts which in nature occurred in isolation. A compilation, in short, is a synthesis. It is rare indeed that an analysis of any one actual occurrence could be regarded as a compilation. For an account of a single event to be subject to copyright, it must have individuality of expression or must reflect peculiar skill and judgment."

[29] *E.g.,* Hutchinson Telephone Co. v. Fronteer Directory Co., 770 F.2d 128, 131, 228 U.S.P.Q. 537, 539 (8th Cir. 1985) (telephone directory is copyrightable even though the copyright owner was required by state law to collect the information; "As to originality, where a telephone directory is assembled from data collected and constantly revised by the telephone company, courts consistently have held that such a directory is copyrightable. . . . [A] directory compiled by a telephone company from its internally maintained records may be said to be independently created."); Southern Bell Telephone & Telegraph Co. v. Associated Telephone Directory Publishers, 756 F.2d 801, 225 U.S.P.Q. 899 (11th Cir. 1985); Leon v. Pacific Tel. & Tel. Co., 91 F.2d 484 (9th Cir. 1937)(copyright on telephone directory listing phone subscribers with numbers alphabetically was valid and infringed by defendant's director, which re-organized the subscribers by street address).

uncopyrightable.[30]

The "judgment/creativity" theory focused on the quality of the labor and result, not the quantity of labor expended.[31] Decisions following this approach treat the directory cases as special and caution against extending broad copyright protection to facts and ideas discovered or formulated by arduous research.[32] In *Rockford Map Publishers*,[33] Judge Easterbrook noted: "The collector may change the form of information and so make it more accessible, or he may change the organization and so make the data more understandable. . . . In each case the copyright depended on the fact that the compiler made a contribution—a new arrangement or presentation of facts—and not on the amount of time the work consumed."

---

[30] *See* § 4C[1][b][i](2).

[31] *E.g.*, Financial Information Inc. v. Moody's Investors Services Inc., 808 F.2d 204, 207, 1 U.S.P.Q.2d 1279, 1281 (2d Cir. 1986), *cert. denied*, 484 U.S. 820 (1987) (copyright owner's recording on cards of basic facts concerning municipal bonds that have been called for redemption is not copyrightable; the accused infringer included information on called municipal bonds in its bi-weekly publication; "The researchers had five facts to fill in on each card—nothing more and nothing less.; [t]he statute . . . requires that copyrightability not be determined by the amount of effort the author expends, but rather by the nature of the final result. To grant copyright protection based merely on the 'sweat of the author's brow' would risk putting large areas of factual research material off limits and threaten the public's unrestrained access to information."); Eckes v. Card Prices Update, 736 F.2d 859, 222 U.S.P.Q. 762 (2d Cir. 1984) (division of 18,000 baseball cards into two categories, premium (5000 cards) and common, with prices, is copyrightable because the selection of the premium cards involved creativity).

[32] *E.g.*, Worth v. Selchow & Richter, 827 F.2d 569, 573, 4 U.S.P.Q.2d 1144, 1148 (9th Cir. 1987), *cert. denied*, 485 U.S. 977 (1988) (no copyright infringement when the defendants, originators of a "trivia" game took a substantial number of trivia facts from the plaintiff's copyrighted trivia encyclopedias; "to the extent that *Leon* suggests that research or labor is protectible, later cases have rejected that theory"); Miller v. Universal City Studios, Inc., 650 F.2d 1365, 1369-70, 212 U.S.P.Q. 345 (5th Cir. 1981) (holding legally erroneous a jury instruction that an author's research on factual matters is copyrightable; "It is difficult to adequately distinguish some of the directory cases, and particularly the language of the opinions. . . . A copyright in a directory, however, is properly viewed as resting on the originality of the selection and arrangement of the factual material, rather than on the industriousness of the efforts to develop the information. . . . Copyright protection does not extend to the facts themselves, and the mere use of the information contained in a directory without a substantial copying of the format does not constitute infringement. . . . In any event, it may be better to recognize the directory cases as being in a category by themselves rather than to attempt to bring their result and rationale to bear on nondirectory cases.").

The *Miller* statement that copyright in a directory is limited to the original selection and arrangement of the data does not adequately distinguish all of the directory cases. In *Leon*, the accused work arranged public domain information, the names and addresses of phone subscribers, in a different way, by street address rather than alphabetically by surname.

[33] Rockford Map Publishers, Inc. v. Directory Service Company of Colorado, Inc., 768 F.2d 145, 149, 226 U.S.P.Q. 1025, 1027 (7th Cir. 1985).

In *Rockford Map*, the court upheld the copyrightability of plaintiff's "plat maps" showing land and location, size, and ownership, prepared by tracing the topographical features of government aerial photographs, drawing lines showing townships and sections, and drawing ownership boundary lines based on information taken from land title records.

In *West Publishing*,[34] the Eighth Circuit held plaintiff's arrangement of court opinions into paginated volumes to be a copyrightable compilation and found infringement in defendant's use of plaintiff's page numbers in its "LEXIS" legal data base. Plaintiff conceded that the defendant could use an opinion's volume and first page number but challenged defendant's use of subsequent page numbers ("jump cites"). Rejecting defendant's argument that prior case law made case arrangements not copyrightable,[35] the court found the necessary minimum intellectual creativity in plaintiff's acts of (1) collecting and separating state and federal court opinions, (2) assigning the opinions to appropriate reporter series, (3) sorting some opinions by subject matter, and (4) assigning cases a volume and an arrangement within the volume (*e.g.*, grouping together opinions by circuit). The court also rejected defendant's contention that "all [the plaintiff] seeks to protect is numbers on pages."

> "If this is a correct characterization, [defendant] wins: two always comes after one, and no one can copyright the mere sequence of Arabic numbers. . . . [T]he specific goal of this suit is to protect some of [plaintiff's] page numbers, those occurring within the body of individual court opinions. But protection for the numbers is not sought for their own sake. It is sought, rather, because access to these particular numbers—the 'jump cites'—would give users of LEXIS a large part of what [plaintiff] has spent so much labor and industry in compiling, and would *pro tanto* reduce anyone's need to buy [plaintiff's] books. The key to this case, then, is not whether numbers are copyrightable, but whether the copyright on the books as a whole is infringed by the unauthorized appropriation of these particular numbers."[36]

(2)   *Feist*. In *Feist*,[37] the Supreme Court held that a white page telephone directory was not a copyrightable compilation because the "selection, coordination, and arrangement of [the copyright claimant's] white pages do not satisfy the minimum constitutional standards for copyright protection."[38]

Rural Telephone provides telephone service in several northeast Kansas communities under a state-granted monopoly franchise. Pursuant to a state law requirement,

---

[34] West Publishing Co. v. Mead Data Central, Inc., 799 F.2d 1219, 230 U.S.P.Q. 801 (8th Cir. 1986), *cert. denied*, 479 U.S. 1070 (1987).

[35] The prior cases included Callaghan v. Myers, 128 U.S. 617 (1888); Wheaton v. Peters, 33 U.S. (8 Pet.) 591, 8 L. Ed. 1055 (1834); and Banks Law Publishing Co. v. Lawyer's Co-Operative Publishing, 169 F. 386 (2d Cir. 1909), *appeal dismissed by stipulation*, 223 U.S. 738 (1911).

[36] 799 F.2d at 1227, 230 U.S.P.Q. at 805.

Compare Toro Co. v. R & R Products Co., 787 F.2d 1208, 1213, 229 U.S.P.Q. 282, 285–86 (8th Cir. 1986) (plaintiff's system of numbering parts for its lawn care machines was not copyrightable because plaintiff arbitrarily assigned numbers to parts: "There was no evidence that a particular series or configuration of numbers denoted a certain type or category of parts or that the numbers used encoded any kind of information at all. . . . This is not to say that all parts numbering systems are not copyrightable. A system that uses symbols in some sort of meaningful pattern, something by which one could distinguish effort or content, would be an original work.").

[37] Feist Publications, Inc. v. Rural Telephone Service Company, Inc., 111 S. Ct. 1282, 18 U.S.P.Q.2d 1275 (1991).

[38] 111 S. Ct. at 1296, 18 U.S.P.Q.2d at 1284.

it produces an annually updated "white page" telephone directory listing all subscribers in alphabetical order with city and phone number. It publishes the directory together with a "yellow page" section containing business advertisements. It distributes the directory free of charge, earning revenue by selling the advertisements.

Feist publishes white and yellow page telephone directories that cover geographic areas wider than those serviced by local telephone companies such as Rural. To assemble its northeast Kansas directory, Feist offered to pay for the right to use the white page listings of the 11 local telephone companies in the area. Only Rural Telephone refused, apparently hoping to lessen Feist's competition for yellow page advertising by making its white page directory less comprehensive and therefore less attractive.[39]

To complete its directory, Feist took 4,935 listings from Rural's directory and had employees verify the data and add street addresses. Notwithstanding these efforts and additions, Feist's directory reproduced identically 1309 of Rural's 46,878 listings, including four fictitious ones that Rural had inserted to detect copying. In Rural's copyright infringement suit against Feist, the Tenth Circuit affirmed the district court's grant of summary judgment of infringement.

The Supreme Court reversed in a unanimous opinion written by Justice O'Connor. It repudiated the "sweat of the brow" theory as contrary to the Court's decisions,[40] the 1976 Act's provisions, and copyright law's basic principles. The theory's "most glaring" flaw was "it extended copyright protection in a compilation beyond selection and arrangement—the compiler's original contributions—to the facts themselves. Under the doctrine, the only defense to infringement was independent creation." " 'Sweat of the brow' courts thereby eschewed the most fundamental axiom of copyright law— that no one may copyright facts or ideas."[41] The sweat of the brow doctrine cases "handed out proprietary interests in facts and declared that authors are absolutely precluded from saving time and effort by relying upon the facts contained in prior works."[42] Protection for research is available, if at all, only under an unfair competition, not a copyright theory.

The 1976 Act's provisions implicitly confirmed the "sweat of the brow" theory's inappropriateness.[43] Section 102(a) made originality an explicit requirement, and

---

[39] The Supreme Court noted that, in a decision subsequent to the one it was reviewing, the district court found that Rural's "refusal was motivated by an unlawful purpose 'to extend its monopoly in telephone service to a monopoly in yellow pages advertising.' " Rural Telephone Service Co. v. Feist Publications, Inc., 737 F. Supp. 610, 622 (Kan. 1990)." 111 S. Ct. at 1296, 18 U.S.P.Q.2d at 1277.

[40] The Court cited International News Service v. Associated Press, 248 U.S. 215 (1918), which applied an unfair competition misappropriation theory to bar the purloining of current news, and noted, incidentally, that copyright did not extend to facts in a news story. See § 6F[1].

[41] The "sweat of the brow" courts misinterpreted the 1909 Act's Section 5, which listed "directories, gazetteers, and other compilations" in the categories of copyrightable subject matter. Section 5 "was purely technical in nature," but it "led some courts to infer erroneously that directories and the like were copyrightable per se." 111 S. Ct. at 1291, 18 U.S.P.Q.2d at 1280.

[42] 111 S. Ct. at 1291, 18 U.S.P.Q.2d at 1281.

[43] The Act deletes the 1909 Act's specific mention of directories.

Section 102(b) excluded copyright protection of ideas, procedures, etc. Two 1976 Act provisions deal directly with compilations. The Section 101 Act definition "identifies three distinct elements and requires each to be met for a work to qualify as a copyrightable compilation: (1) the collection and assembly of pre-existing material, facts, or data; (2) the selection, coordination, or arrangement of those materials; and (3) the creation, by virtue of the particular selection, coordination, or arrangement, of an 'original' work of authorship." The first and third requirements are illuminating,[44] but the "key to the statutory definitions is the second requirement:"

> "It instructs courts that, in determining whether a fact-based work is an original work of authorship, they should focus on the manner in which the collected facts have been selected, coordinated, and arranged. This is a straightforward application of the originality requirement. Facts are never original, so the compilation author can claim originality, if at all, only in the way the facts are presented. To that end, the statute dictates that the principal focus should be on whether the selection, coordination, and arrangement are sufficiently original to merit protection.

> "Not every selection, coordination, or arrangement will pass muster. . . . [The statute] implies that some 'ways' will trigger copyright, but that others will not. . . . [T]he statute envisions that there will be some fact-based works in which the selection, coordination, and arrangement are not sufficiently original to trigger copyright protection.

> "[T]he originality requirement is not particularly stringent. A compiler may settle upon a selection or arrangement that others have used; novelty is not required. Originality requires only that the author make the selection or arrangement independently (i.e., without copying that selection or arrangement from another work), and that it display some minimal level of creativity. Presumably, the vast majority of compilations will pass this test, but not all will. There remains a narrow category of works in which the creative spark is utterly lacking or so trivial as to be virtually nonexistent."[45]

The second 1976 Act provision on compilations is Section 103, the point of which is that even copyrightable compilations receive only limited protection.

> "[C]opyright is not a tool by which a compilation author may keep others from using the facts or data he or she has collected. . . . Rather, the facts contained in existing works may be freely copied because copyright protects

---

[44] What makes the first significant is "it is not the *sole* requirement": "It is not enough for copyright purposes that an author collects and assembles facts." 111 S. Ct. at 1294, 18 U.S.P.Q.2d at 1282. The third requirement emphasizes, redundantly, the compilations are copyrightable only if they satisfy the originality requirement:

> "Although § 102 states plainly that the originality requirement applies to all works, the point was emphasized with regard to compilations to ensure that courts would not repeat the mistake of the 'sweat of the brow' courts by concluding that fact-based works are treated differently and measured by some other standard." 111 S. Ct. at 1294, 18 U.S.P.Q.2d at 1282.

[45] 111 S. Ct. at 1294, 18 U.S.P.Q.2d at 1283.

only the elements that owe their origin to the compiler—the selection, coordination, and arrangement of facts."[46]

Turning to the facts of the case before it, the Court acknowledged that Feist took "a substantial amount of factual information" from Rural's directory, at least 1309 subscribers' names, towns, and telephone numbers, but "[n]ot all copying . . . is *copyright* infringement." It concluded that "[t]he selection, coordination, and arrangement of Rural's white pages do not satisfy the minimum constitutional standards for *copyright* protection."

"Rural's selection of listings could not be more obvious: it publishes the most basic information—name, town, and telephone number—about each person who applies to it for telephone service. This is 'selection' of a sort, but it lacks the modicum of creativity necessary to transform mere selection into copyrightable expression. Rural expended sufficient effort to make the white pages directory useful, but insufficient creativity to make it original. We note in passing that the selection featured in Rural's white pages may also fail the originality requirement for another reason. Feist points out that Rural did not truly 'select' to publish the names and telephone numbers of its subscribers; rather, it was required to do so by the Kansas Corporation Commission as part of its monopoly franchise. . . . Accordingly, one could plausibly conclude that this selection was dictated by state law, not by Rural.

"Nor can Rural claim originality in its coordination and arrangement of facts. The white pages do nothing more than list Rural's subscribers in alphabetical order. This arrangement may, technically speaking, owe its origin to Rural; no one disputes that Rural undertook the task of alphabetizing the names itself. But there is nothing remotely creative about arranging names alphabetically in a white pages directory. It is an age-old practice, firmly rooted in tradition and so commonplace that it has come to be expected as a matter of course. . . . It is not only unoriginal, it is practically inevitable. This time-honored tradition does not possess the minimal creative spark required by the Copyright Act and the Constitution."[47]

[ii] *Collections.* Included within the definition of compilation is a "collective work:" "a work, such as a periodical issue, anthology, or encyclopedia, in which a number of contributions, constituting separate and independent works in themselves, are assembled into a collective whole."[48] For example, an assembly of public domain musical compositions or judicial opinions may be copyrightable as a collective work.[49] A collective work's copyright does not create or extend any exclusive right in the components themselves. The copyrighted "work" is the original selection or arrangement.

---

[46] 111 S. Ct. at 1295, 18 U.S.P.Q.2d at 1283.

[47] 111 S. Ct. at 1297, 18 U.S.P.Q.2d at 1285.

[48] 17 U.S.C. § 101.

[49] *See, e.g.,* Axelbank v. Rony, 277 F.2d 314 (9th Cir. 1960) (collection of public domain documentary film on Russian Revolution); Consolidated Music Publishers, Inc. v. Ashley Publications, Inc., 197 F. Supp. 17, 18 (S.D.N.Y. 1961) (collection of piano music ("Easy Classics to Moderns") with addition of "editorial matter such as marks of fingering, phrasing, expression etc.").

The Copyright Act addresses the special problems of copyright notice on collective works.[50]

[c] **Derivative Works.** A derivative work is "based upon one or more preexisting works, such as a translation, musical arrangement, dramatization, fictionalization, motion picture version, sound recording, art reproduction, abridgement, condensation, or any other form in which a work may be recast, transformed, or adapted."[51] Also, a "work consisting of editorial revisions, annotations, elaborations, or other modifications which, as a whole, represent an original work of authorship, is a 'derivative work.'"

A host of copyright issues surround derivative works: (1) does copyrightable subject matter include works based on prior works? (2) is the original work copyright owner's consent a prerequisite to the derivative work's copyrightability? (3) is matter taken from the original work covered by the derivative work's copyright? (4) how much change must the derivative work introduce to meet the originality condition?[52] (5) do the original work's copyright exclusive rights include the right to make or authorize the making of derivative works?[53] (6) does modification of a copy of the original work violate the original work copyright owner's right to authorize derivative works?[54] (7) does renewal or termination of transfers of the original work's copyright affect the derivative work copyright owner's right to continue to use the derivative work?[55] This subsection deals with the first three issues; the other issues are covered in subsequent sections.

Section 103's direction that derivative works are copyrightable subject matter[56] is probably unnecessary. A second work based on a prior work is copyrightable if, but only if, the second work meets the originality requirement.[57] The second

---

[50] *See* § 4D[2][b][iv].

[51] 17 U.S.C. § 101. *See generally* P. Goldstein, Copyright § 2.16.2 (1989).

[52] *See* § 4C[5][b].

[53] *See* § 4E[3][b].

[54] *See* § 4E[3][c][iii].

[55] *See* § 4G[4][c].

[56] 17 U.S.C. § 103(a).

[57] *E.g.,* Signo Trading International v. Gordon, 535 F. Supp. 362, 214 U.S.P.Q. 793 (N.D. Calif. 1981). In *Signo Trading International*, defendant, a manufacturer of hand-held electronic language translators, gave plaintiff a list of English words and phrases, such as "how are you." Plaintiff translated the words into Arabic counterparts, spelled phonetically using Roman letters. After termination of the business relationship between the parties, plaintiff sued defendant for infringement of its copyright in the translations and transliterations. The district court held that the translations and transliterations were not sufficiently original to constitute a copyrightable derivative work. It noted that "Although the English word list may be copyrightable, . . . it clearly is not copyrightable by Plaintiff because it was devised by Defendant." As to the translations, the court commented:

> "Translations of many things, such as literary works, are copyrightable to the extent that the translation involves originality. . . . It is not the translations of the individual words that makes these works copyrightable, it is rather the originality embodied in the translator's contributions, for example, conveying nuances and subtleties in the translated work as a whole. Such originality is lacking from Plaintiff's translations of the

work's creator must make more than a trivial change in first work. If the second work involves a creative change, it is copyrightable as an original work of authorship[58] and would undoubtedly be so regarded even if the Copyright Act made no reference to derivative works.[59]

The Copyright Act extends protection only to the "new matter" added by the creator of the derivative work. The derivative work copyright implies no exclusive right in the "preexisting material employed in the work" and "does not affect or enlarge the scope, duration, ownership, or subsistence of, any copyright protection in the preexisting material."[60]

The Act gives an original work copyright owner the exclusive right to make derivative works.[61] Section 103(b) ties the copyrightability of derivative works to the

---

single words and short phrases. Once it is determined what dialect is to be used, the translation of the word list, consisting primarily of single words, is a fairly mechanical process requiring little if any originality." 535 F. Supp. at 364, 214 U.S.P.Q. at 795.

As to the transliterations, the court commented:

"Plaintiff . . . argues that the transliterating of Arabic words, in particular the selection of various Roman letters and combinations of Roman letters to create a phonetic sound as close as possible to the Arabic word, embodies sufficient originality . . . The phonetic spelling of foreign words, using standard Roman letters, simply does not embody sufficient originality to be copyrightable. . . . Indeed, the transliterations are only effective to the extent that the pronunciations are obvious and do not involve originality." 535 F. Supp. at 364, 214 U.S.P.Q. at 795.

[58] See § 4C[5][b].

[59] 1909 Act Section 7 provided that "Compilations or abridgments, adaptations, arrangements, dramatizations, translations, or other versions of works in the public domain or of copyrighted works when produced with the consent of the proprietor of the copyright in such works, or works republished with new matter, shall be as new works subject to copyright. . . ."

In Rohauer v. Killiam Shows, Inc., 551 F.2d 484 (2d Cir. 1977), the Second Circuit reviewed the statutory history:

"The 1909 Copyright Act was the first in this country to provide explicit protection for derivative works, although § 5 of the 1891 Act had provided that 'new alterations, revisions, and additions' made to books of foreign authors could be copyrighted . . . ; § 4 of the 1865 Act provided that the 'books' subject to copyright under the 1831 Act included 'any second or subsequent edition which shall be published with any additions,' . . . ; and the 1856 Act made explicit the copyright protection of dramatic compositions, . . . although the right to dramatize an underlying work was not reserved to the author of the work until 1870 . . . Protection for derivative works was further provided under case law, which considered compilations, digests, and translations as among the works subject to copyright, see Gray v. Russell, 10 F. Cas. 1035 (No. 5,728) (C.C.D.Mass 1839)(Story, J.); Banks v. McDivitt, 2 F. Cas. 759 (No. 961) (C.C.S.D.N.Y. 1875); Shook v. Rankin, 21 F. Cas. 1335 (No. 12,804) (C.C.N.D.Ill. 1875)." 551 F.2d at 488, n.3.

[60] 17 U.S.C. § 103(b). Cf. Stewart v. Abend, 110 S. Ct. 1750, 1761, 14 U.S.P.Q.2d 1614, 1622 (1990), discussed at § 4G[4][c][i] ("The aspects of a derivative work added by the derivative author are that author's property, but the element drawn from the pre-existing work remains on grant from the owner of the pre-existing work.")

[61] See § 4E[3][b].

right to exclude others from making such works by providing that "protection for a work employing preexisting material in which copyright subsists does not extend to any part of the work in which such material has been used unlawfully."[62]

G. Ricordi & Co.,[63] illustrates original work, derivative work relationships. Puccini's opera "Madame Butterfly," copyrighted in 1914, was based on Belasco's 1909 play, which was based on Long's 1897 novel. The play was a derivative work of the novel, and the opera was a derivative work of both the play and the novel. Because each work was produced with permission, each was separately copyrightable, but the copyright extended only to the "new matter" added and conferred no right in the prior works.

In *G. Ricordi*, copyright in the "middle" derivative work, the play, expired when it was not renewed. The parties, who owned respectively the novel and opera rights, contested the right to make yet another derivative work—a motion picture based on the opera. The end result was that both parties' permission was necessary because the motion picture would necessarily reproduce elements of the novel as well as the opera. That the play had fallen into the public domain did not mean that persons were free to use the copyrighted portions of the novel and opera without permission.

[d] **Idea and Expression.** Section 102(b), which provides "In no case does copyright protection for an original work of authorship extend to any idea, procedure, process, system, method of operation, concept, principle, or discovery, regardless of the form in which it is described, explained, illustrated, or embodied in such work,"[64] codifies the established principle that copyright protects expressions, not ideas.[65]

[i] *Baker v. Selden.* In *Baker*,[66] the Supreme Court's enigmatic 1879 decision, Selden published a book that explained a new book-keeping system consisting of an explanatory essay and forms with ruled lines and headings for carrying out the

---

[62] 17 U.S.C. § 103(a). This carries forward 1909 Act Section 7, which provided that a derivative work shall be regarded as a copyrightable "new work" only if it is produced "with the consent of the proprietor of the copyright" in the original work unless that original work is in the public domain.

See also JBJ Fabrics, Inc. v. Brylane, Inc., 714 F. Supp. 107, 110, 12 U.S.P.Q.2d 1839, 1841 (S.D. N.Y. 1989) ("the fact that plaintiff did not receive either a formal assignment of the right to make derivative works or an exclusive license is not dispositive here. Section 103 of the Act . . . does no more than limit plaintiff's copyright protection to those aspects of its design which it has not unlawfully adopted, and, as the Second Circuit has held, unauthorized use is not equivalent to unlawful use. *See* Eden Toys Inc. v. Florelee Undergarment Co., 697 F.2d 27, 34 n.6 (2d Cir. 1982). If the Farkas painting is not itself the subject of copyright, or if plaintiff did indeed have informal authorization from Farkas to use the painting in its fabric design, such as a non-exclusive license, then it is not using the painting unlawfully and may not face any limits on the scope of its copyright protection.").

[63] G. Ricordi & Co. v. Paramount Pictures, Inc., 189 F.2d 469 (2d Cir.), *cert. denied*, 342 U.S. 849 (1951).

[64] 17 U.S.C. § 102(b). *See generally* P. Goldstein, Copyright § 2.3.1 (1989).

[65] Idea uncopyrightability influences the substantial similarity test of copyright infringement. *See* § 4F[2][a].

[66] Baker v. Selden, 101 U.S. 99 (1879).

system. Baker sold account books that used a "similar plan" as Selden but made "a different arrangement of the columns, and use[d] different headings." The copyright owner sued Baker for infringement. The Court found no infringement.

Baker puts forth three distinct propositions, each of which influenced subsequent copyright law development. The first proposition is that Baker copied only Selden's system, that is, "idea," not his expression of it, because Baker's and Selden's explanations and forms were different. Ideas receive protection, if at all, under the patent system.[67] Baker's copyright on a book explaining a system does not prevent another from explaining the same system.[68]

The second proposition is that a person may copy even the expression of the author "for the purpose of practical application" rather than for the purpose of "explanation."[69] This proposition later became critical to the scope of copyright protection in architectural works and computer programs.

The third proposition is that the bookkeeping forms were not copyrightable subject matter because they were not an author's "writings."[70] This proposition persists in the rule that mere forms for recording information are not copyrightable.

---

[67] For example, the Court stated: "To give to the author of the book an exclusive property in the art described therein, when no examination of its novelty has ever been officially made, would be a surprise and a fraud upon the public. That is the province of letters-patent, not of copyright." 101 U.S. at 102. Later, the Court commented: "Whether the art might or might not have been patented, is a question which is not before us. It was not patented, and is open and free to the use of the public." *Id.* at 104.

   For a discussion of printed matter and business system patentability, *see* § 2C[1][e].

[68] *See also* Brief English Systems, Inc. v. Owen, 48 F.2d 555, 556 (2d Cir. 1931) (book on short-hand system; "There is no literary merit in a mere system of condensing written words into less than the number of letters usually used to spell them out. Copyrightable material is found, if at all, in the explanation of how to do it. . . . [T]he way to obtain the exclusive property right to an art, as distinguished from a description of the art, is by letters patent and not by copyright.").

[69] The Court stated:

   "The very object of publishing a book on science or the useful arts is to communicate to the world the useful knowledge which it contains. But this object would be frustrated if the knowledge could not be used without incurring the guilt of piracy of the book. And where the art it teaches cannot be used without employing the methods and diagrams used to illustrate the book, or such as are similar to them, such methods and diagrams are to be considered as necessary incidents to the art, and given therewith to the public; not given for the purpose of publication in other works explanatory of the art, but for the purpose of practical application." 101 U.S. at 103.

Professor Nimmer criticized the *Baker* copying for use doctrine. M. Nimmer, Nimmer on Copyright § 2.18[C][2]. *But see* Feist Publications, Inc. v. Rural Telephone Service Company, Inc., 111 S. Ct. 1282, 1290, 18 U.S.P.Q.2d 1275, 1279 (1991) (quoting *Baker* and noting "the fact/expression dichotomy limits severely the scope of protection in fact-based works.").

[70] The Court cited an English case denying copyright protection for a cricket scoring sheet, Page v. Wisden (20 L.T.n.s. 435), and stated at the end of its opinion "blank account-books are not the subject of copyright." 101 U.S. at 107.

[*ii*] *Forms.* Cases hold that blank forms for recording information are copyrightable only if and to the extent that they also convey information.[71]

The blank form rule derives from *Baker.* In *Bibbero Systems,*[72] Judge Henderson noted that "Cases interpreting the 'blank-form' rule and its 'information conveyance' exception do not form a consistent line of reasoning" and fail to "yield a test that establishes when blank forms convey sufficient information to be copyrightable."

---

[71] For cases holding blank forms uncopyrightable, *see* M.M. Business Forms Corp. v. Uarco, Inc., 472 F.2d 1137, 176 U.S.P.Q. 456 (6th Cir. 1973) (television repair form with spaces for repairs and costs); Taylor Instruments Companies v. Fawley-Brost Co., 139 F.2d 98 (7th Cir. 1943), *cert. denied,* 321 U.S. 785 (1944) (ruled paper for use with a recording thermometer); Safeguard Business Systems, Inc. v. Reynolds and Reynolds Co., 14 U.S.P.Q.2d 1829 (E.D. Pa. 1990), *aff'd,* 919 F.2d 136 (3d Cir. 1990); Matthew Bender & Co. v. Kluwer Law Book Publishers Inc., 672 F. Supp. 107, 5 U.S.P.Q.2d 1363 (S.D. N.Y. 1987) (chart form for listing personal injury awards and settlements; plaintiff and defendant used the same form but the defendant made a different compilation of actual case data); Januz Marketing Communications, Inc. v. Doubleday & Co., Inc., 569 F. Supp. 76, 222 U.S.P.Q. 389 (S.D.N.Y. 1982)(time log chart).

For cases holding forms copyrightable as conveying information, *see* Edwin K. Williams & Co. v. Edwin K. Williams, 542 F.2d 1053, 1060-61, 191 U.S.P.Q. 563 (9th Cir. 1976), *cert. denied,* 433 U.S. 908, 195 U.S.P.Q. 93 (1977) ("[The book] contains several pages of instructions These instructions both precede and follow 31 pages of blank forms one page for each day of the month. The dealer fills in the day's transactions in the various boxes on the blank forms. Some of the instructions show the dealer how to fill in the forms . . . . Other instructions show the dealer how to operate his business . . . . All of this information is carefully explained in step-by-step procedures under such headings as 'What Successful Dealers Say' . . . . In our view, the instructions and the blank forms constituted an integrated work entitled to copyright protection."); Norton Printing Co. v. Augustine Hospital, 155 U.S.P.Q. 133 (N.D. Ill. 1967) (form for recording medical laboratory test results; "All business, medical, legal and other forms are . . . not per se excluded from copyright protection, but the determination turns on whether they actually convey information or whether they are merely to be used to record it. . . . This distinction has been strongly criticized . . . . It is argued that where originality and intellectual effort exist on the creation or design of forms, copyright protection should be available as it is to other 'writings,' such as commercial circus posters, mass-produced lamp bases, and cartoon figures.").

[72] Bibbero Systems Inc. v. Colwell Systems Inc., 731 F. Supp. 403, 404, 7 U.S.P.Q.2d 1174, 1175 (N.D. Calif. 1988), *aff'd,* 893 F.2d 1004, 13 U.S.P.Q.2d 1634 (9th Cir. 1990). *Bibbero* held uncopyrightable the plaintiff's "super bill." "The superbill is a one page form containing spaces on the top of the page for patient information, and a chart below containing lists of procedures and diagnoses to be performed by doctors. The form is designed so that a doctor may write in a fee for the services next to the applicable space, and check a box for the applicable diagnosis. The completed form is then sent to the patient's insurer."

Judge Henderson acknowledged that the form, by calling for certain categories of information, conveys information by stressing the importance or relevance of those categories. However, "[a]ll forms designed to record information call the recorder's attention to only certain categories of relevant information." If such highlighting constituted the conveyance of information, "[t]he blank form rule would cease to apply to a large number of cases." 731 F. Supp. at 405, 7 U.S.P.Q.2d at 1176.

In *Harcourt, Brace & World*,[73] the district court upheld the copyrightability of printed answer sheets for standardized tests designed to be corrected by optical scanning machines. The answer sheets embodied original expression.

> "[T]he area for originality of design is limited by the requirements of the optical scanning machine used. . . . However, within these confines the designer may structure the division of response positions across the page, may ask what information (name, age, date, etc.) the student should record on the face of the answer sheet, may devise the symbolic code indicating what question is being asked and what possible alternative answer slots may be selected, may insert any instruction explaining how to use the answer sheet in conjunction with an examination, may set forth examples illustrating such use, etc. . . . The creation of an answer sheet requires the skill, expertise and experience together with the personal judgment and analysis of the designer or author."[74]

The answer sheets also conveyed information. They guided students in recording their answers. Some answer sheets included text and examples.

[iii] *"Merger" of Idea and Expression.* In dealing with functional and fact works, such as contest rules, games, useful article designs,[75] video games, and computer software,[76] the courts postulate that, in rare instances, there may be so limited a number of ways of expressing an idea that the expression "merges" with the idea. They deny copyright protection to the merged expression because ideas are not copyrightable.

In *Morrissey*,[77] the germinal merger case, plaintiff secured copyright in rules for a simple sales promotion contest that used participants' social security numbers. Defendants launched a promotion using virtually identical rules.[78] The First Circuit found there was some, though not much, creativity in plaintiff's expression of the rules. Given the two rules' near identity, it could not "invoke the principle of a stringent standard for showing infringement . . . when the subject matter involved admits of little variation in form of expression." Yet it ruled for defendant because the "idea," that is, the contest, admitted of only a limited number of expressions.

> "When the uncopyrightable subject matter is very narrow, so that the 'topic necessarily requires,' . . . if not only one form of expression, at best only a limited number, to permit copyrighting would mean that a party or parties, by copyrighting a mere handful of forms, could exhaust all possibilities of future use of the substance. In such circumstances it does not seem accurate to say that any particular form of expression comes from the subject matter. However,

---

[73] Harcourt, Brace & World Inc. v. Graphic Controls Corp., 329 F. Supp. 517, 171 U.S.P.Q. 219 (S.D. N.Y. 1971).

[74] 329 F. Supp. at 523.

[75] *See* § 4C[3].

[76] *See* § 4C[2].

[77] Morrissey v. Procter & Gamble, 379 F.2d 675, 154 U.S.P.Q. 193 (1st Cir. 1967).

[78] For example, plaintiff's rule 1 began: "Entrants should print name, address and social security number on a boxtop, or a plain paper." Defendant's rule 1 began "Entrants should print name, address and Social Security number on a *Tide* boxtop, or *on* [a] plain paper." (additions in italics; omissions in brackets). 379 F.2d at 678.

it is necessary to say that the subject matter would be appropriated by permitting the copyrighting of its expression. We cannot recognize copyright as a game of chess in which the public can be checkmated.

". . . [The operation of this principle] need not await an attempt to copyright all possible forms. It cannot be only the last form of expression which is to be condemned, as completing defendant's exclusion from the substance. Rather, in these circumstances, we hold that copyright does not extend to the subject matter at all, and plaintiff cannot complain even if his particular expression was deliberately adopted."[79]

In *Herbert Rosenthal Jewelry*,[80] the Ninth Circuit applied merger to deny copyright protection to a jeweled bee pin.[81]

Accused infringers' merger arguments rarely prevail.[82] An exception is *Kern River*,[83]

---

[79] 379 F.2d at 678–79.

[80] Herbert Rosenthal Jewelry Corp. v. Kalpakian, 446 F.2d 738, 170 U.S.P.Q. 557 (9th Cir. 1971).

[81] The plaintiff's pin had 19 small white jewels on its back. Plaintiff claimed infringement by "defendants' entire line of a score or more jeweled bees in three sizes decorated with from nine to thirty jewels of various sizes, kinds, and colors." 446 F.2d at 740.

"What is basically at stake is the extent of the copyright owner's monopoly—from how large an area of activity did Congress intend to allow the copyright owner to exclude others? We think the production of jeweled bee pins is a larger private preserve than Congress intended to be set aside in the public market without a patent. A jeweled bee pin is therefore an 'idea' that defendants were free to copy. Plaintiff seems to agree, for it disavows any claim that defendants cannot manufacture and sell jeweled bee pins and concedes that only plaintiff's particular design or 'expression' of the jeweled bee pin 'idea' is protected under its copyright. The difficulty . . . is that on this record the 'idea' and its 'expression' appear to be indistinguishable. There is no greater similarity between the pins of plaintiff and defendants than is inevitable from the use of jewel-encrusted bee forms in both.

"When the 'idea' and its 'expression' are thus inseparable, copying the 'expression' will not be barred, since protecting the 'expression' in such circumstances would confer a monopoly of the 'idea' upon the copyright owner free of the conditions and limitations imposed by the patent law." 446 F.2d at 738.

The court's use of merger to invalidate the copyright was unnecessary. It could simply have dismissed the plaintiff's assertion that *all* jeweled bees infringed as an improper attempt to expand the scope of copyright protection on a particular original bee design to cover the idea, rather than just the expression. The court did avoid the need to determine which of defendants' bees were substantially similar in expression and which were not, an avoidance justified by the plaintiff's overreaching approach.

[82] *E.g.*, Concrete Machinery Co. v. Classic Lawn Ornaments Inc., 843 F.2d 600, 6 U.S.P.Q.2d 1357, 1361 (1st Cir. 1988) ("[A]s idea and expression merge, fewer and fewer aspects of a work embody a unique and creative expression of the idea; a copyright holder must then prove substantial similarity to those few aspects of the work that are expression not *required* by the idea"; no merger as to copyrighted lawn ornaments in the shape of animals, such as deer; "the various animal representations, while lifelike and allowing of fewer possibilities, are nonetheless somewhat stylized versions of these creatures in terms of posture and facial expression"); Educational Testing Services v. Katzman, 793 F.2d 533, 540, 230 U.S.P.Q. 156, 160 (3d Cir.

a suit between rivals seeking Federal Energy Regulatory Commission approval to build a pipeline. Plaintiff drew lines and mile markings for a proposed route on 1:250,000 and 1:24,000 scale United States Geological Survey maps after conducting field work along the proposed route. Defendant copied plaintiff's 1:24,000 scale maps to support its application. The appeals court held that the marked 1:24,000 maps were not copyrightable even though they met copyright law's originality requirement.

> "The idea of the proposed location of a prospective pipeline is not copyrightable. The 1:250,000 maps consisted of lines representing the proposed location of the pipeline drawn on maps sold to the general public. Such map markings are certainly the only effective way to convey the idea of the proposed location of a pipeline across 1,000 miles of terrain. To extend protection to the lines would be to grant [plaintiff] a monopoly of the idea for locating a proposed pipeline in the chosen corridor, a foreclosure of competition that Congress could not have intended to sanction through copyright law. . . .

> "The quad maps, drawn on a scale of 1:24,000, do not differ from the larger-scale maps to such a degree that copyright protection should attach. They also consist of lines representing the proposed location of a pipeline on standard reference, publicly available maps. Only the scale differs." [84]

Decisions on computer programs and screen displays find no idea-expression merger.[85] In *Lotus Development*,[86] Judge Keeton did find merger in some elements of

---

1986) (copyrighted standard achievement test; "We need not define the limits of the merger principle in this case. . . . ETS' questions do not represent the only means of expressing the ideas thereon. . . . Although ETS cannot appropriate concepts such as rules of punctuation, analogies, vocabulary or other fundamental elements of English composition, it can, using its own resources, devise questions designed to test these concepts and secure valid copyrights on these questions. Other persons, similarly resourceful, have ample latitude and opportunity to frame noninfringing questions testing the same subjects."); Toro Co. v. R & R Products Co., 787 F.2d 1208, 1212, 229 U.S.P.Q. 282, 285 (8th Cir. 1986) (parts numbering system is not copyrightable for want of originality but the merger doctrine does not apply; "we are convinced that appellant's parts numbering system does not fall within the small category of works to which merger applies. Under the copyright law doctrine of merger, a close cousin to the idea/expression dichotomy, copyright protection will be denied to even some *expressions* of ideas if the idea behind the expression is such that it can be expressed only in a very limited number of ways.").

Compare Matthew Bender & Co. v. Kluwer Law Book Publishers Inc., 5 U.S.P.Q.2d 1363, 1365 (S.D.N.Y. 1987) (chart form for presenting personal injury awards; "While in theory there are numerous ways to place this information in chart form, from a practical point of view the number of ways to organize this information in a useful and accessible manner is limited.").

[83] Kern River Gas Transmission Co. v. Coastal Corp., 899 F.2d 1458, 14 U.S.P.Q.2d 1898 (5th Cir.), *cert. denied,* 111 S. Ct. 374 (1990).

[84] 899 F.2d at 1464, 14 U.S.P.Q.2d at 1902–03.

[85] *See, e.g.,* Apple Computer, Inc. v. Franklin Computer Corp., 714 F.2d 1240, 219 U.S.P.Q. 113, 124 (3d Cir. 1983), *cert. dismissed,* 464 U.S. 1033 (1984) (referring to "the somewhat metaphysical issue of whether particular ideas and expressions have merged"); Digital Communications Associates, Inc. v. Softklone Distributing Corp., 659 F. Supp. 449, 460, 2 U.S.P.Q. 1385, 1392 (N.D. Ga. 1987) ("status screen" of a communications program; "It cannot be said that the idea of the status screen, i.e., using two symbol commands to change the operations

plaintiff's Lotus 1-2-3 computer program electronic spreadsheet user interface, including the "rotated 'L' screen display" and use of the slash keyboard key to invoke the menu command system, because decision-makers regard these "as either essential to every expression of an electronic spreadsheet, or at least 'obvious' if not essential." Most, if not all, spreadsheet programs use these elements. He found no merger in other elements, including Lotus 1-2-3's specific menu command system, because "the idea of a menu structure for an electronic spreadsheet . . . could be expressed in a great many if not literally unlimited number of ways . . . [T]he fact that some of these specific command terms are quite obvious or merge with the idea of such a particular command term does not preclude copyrightability for the command structure taken as a whole."[87]

The merger doctrine's usefulness for solving copyright protection scope problems is limited. It is more useful to confront directly the question whether sustaining a claim of infringement by a copyright owner will result in an exclusive right to the functional aspects of a design or procedure or to factual information.[88] The merger doctrine adds a layer of analysis without clarifying the difficult problems of what is "idea," not "expression," what is function, and, most importantly, what impact

---

of the computer program and reflecting that fact on a screen listing the computer program's parameters/commands with their operative values, could not have been expressed in a large variety of ways."); Broderbund Software, Inc. v. Unison World, Inc., 648 F. Supp. 1127, 1132, 231 U.S.P.Q. 700, 702 (N.D. Calif. 1986) (menu screens and sequencing of screens for creating and printing custom cards and banners; the existence of a third program that differs from the copyrighted and accused programs but performs the same functions "proves that there do exist other, quite different ways of expressing the ideas embodied" in the copyrighted program).

Compare Manufacturers Technologies Inc. v. Cams Inc., 706 F. Supp. 984, 995, 10 U.S.P.Q.2d 1321, 1327 (D. Conn. 1989) ("In the adoption of a uniform format and the placement of common components of screen pages within that format, the plaintiff has adopted conventions from a very narrow range of possibilities. The plaintiff's conventions are not subject to copyright protection.").

See generally § 4C[2].

[86] Lotus Development Corp. v. Paperback Software International, 740 F. Supp. 37, 15 U.S.P.Q.2d 1577 (D. Mass. 1990).

[87] 740 F. Supp. at 67, 15 U.S.P.Q.2d at 1597.

Judge Keeton described the spreadsheet menu command "idea" as including: "the overall structure, the order of commands in each menu line, the choice of letters, words, or 'symbolic tokens' to represent each command, the presentation of these symbolic tokens on the screen (i.e., first letter only, abbreviations, full words, full words with one or more letters capitalized or underlined), the type of menu system used (i.e., one-, two-, or three-line moving-cursor menus, pull-down menus, or command-driven interfaces), and the long prompts . . . ." 740 F. Supp. at 64, 15 U.S.P.Q. at 1599.

[88] Cf. Feist Publications, Inc. v. Rural Telephone Service Company, Inc., 111 S. Ct. 1282, 18 U.S.P.Q.2d 1275 (1991), discussed at § 4C[1][b][i](2); NEC Corp. v. Intel Corp., 10 U.S.P.Q.2d 1177, 1179 (N.D. Calif. 1989) ("as a matter of practicality, the issue of a limited number of ways to express an idea is relevant to infringement, but should not be the basis for denying the initial copyright. The Register of Copyrights will not know about the presence or absence of constraints that limit ways to express an idea. The burden of showing such constraints should be left to the alleged infringer.").

upholding of copyright has on the public interest in free competition, including competition by copying unpatented ideas.[89]

[iv] *"Scenes a faire."* Related to merger is *scenes a faire,* "incidents, characters or settings which are as a practical matter indispensable . . . in the treatment of a given topic."[90] The courts equate *scenes a faire* with ideas and accordingly refuse to extend copyright protection to them.[91]

In *Reyher,*[92] the Second Circuit found that defendant's story and television skit "The Most Beautiful Woman in the World" did not infringe plaintiff's copyrighted children's book "My Mother is The Most Beautiful Woman in the World."

> "Another helpful analytic concept is that of *scenes a faire,* sequences of events which necessarily follow from a common theme. Copyrights . . . do not protect thematic concepts or scenes which necessarily must follow from certain similar plot situations. . . . [B]oth works present the thematic concept that to a lost child, the familiar face of the mother is the most beautiful face, even though the mother is not, in fact beautiful to most. . . . The overlapping sequences of events concern the lost child finding his or her mother, albeit with some difficulty because of the description given. This similarity of events, however, may be considered *scenes a faire,* scenes which necessarily result from identical situations. . . . Thus, where a lost child is the protagonist, there is likely to be a reunion with parents. . . . More importantly, however, the two works differ in 'total feel.' "[93]

---

[89] *Cf.* Bonito Boats v. Thunder Craft Boats, Inc., 489 U.S. 141, 146, 150–51, 9 U.S.P.Q.2d 1847, 1852 (1989), discussed at § 1D[3][a][iv] ("From their inception, the federal patent laws have embodied a careful balance between the need to promote innovation and the recognition that imitation and refinement through imitation are both necessary to invention itself and the very lifeblood of a competitive economy. . . . The federal patent system . . . embodies a carefully crafted bargain for encouraging the creation and disclosure of new, useful, and nonobvious advances in technology and design in return for the exclusive right to practice the invention for a period of years. . . . The attractiveness of such a bargain, and its effectiveness in inducing creative effort and disclosure of the results of that effort, depend almost entirely on a backdrop of free competition in the exploitation of unpatented designs and innovations.").

[90] Atari, Inc. v. North American Philips Consumer Elecs. Corp., 672 F.2d 607, 616, 214 U.S.P.Q.2d 33 (7th Cir.), *cert. denied,* 459 U.S. 880 (1982) (video game; noting that the concept was developed in the context of literary works and has been applied to written game rules and the pictorial display of game boards).

[91] *See* Whelan Associates v. Jaslow Dental Laboratory, 797 F.2d 1222, 1236, 230 U.S.P.Q.2d 481, 491 (3d Cir. 1986), *cert. denied,* 479 U.S. 1031 (1987), discussed at § 4C[2][d][i] (computer program; "*Scenes a faire* are afforded no protection because the subject matter represented can be expressed in no other way than through the particular *scene a faire.* . . . This is merely a restatement of the hypothesis . . . . that the purpose or function of a work or literary device is part of that device's 'idea' (unprotectable portion). It follows that anything necessary to effecting that function is also, necessarily, part of the idea, too.").

[92] Reyher v. Children's Television Workshop, 533 F.2d 87, 190 U.S.P.Q. 387 (2d Cir.), *cert. denied,* 429 U.S. 980, 192 U.S.P.Q. 64 (1976).

[93] *See also* Landsberg v. Scrabble Crossword Game Players, Inc., 736 F.2d 485, 489, 221 U.S.P.Q. 1140 (9th Cir. 1984), *cert. denied,* 469 U.S. 1037 (1984) (books on Scrabble game strategy; "a second author does not infringe even if he reproduces verbatim the first au-

Scenes a faire may be a useful tool for determining copyright infringement, that is, whether an accused work is substantially similar in expression to a copyrighted work—it reflects the principle that copyright protection scope should vary with the protected work's degree of originality and distinctiveness[94] —but, as with merger, little is accomplished by categorizing *scenes a faire* as unprotectable expression.[95]

[v] *Short Phrases and Simple Shapes.* Short phrases and simple designs do not contain enough creative expression to be copyrightable works of authorship.[96] In

---

thor's expression, if that expression constitutes 'stock scenes or scenes that flow[ ] necessarily from common unprotectable ideas . . . because to hold otherwise would give the first author a monopoly on the commonplace ideas behind the scenes a faire' "); See v. Durang, 711 F.2d 141, 143, 219 U.S.P.Q. 771, 772 (9th Cir. 1983) (two plays, "Fear of Acting" and "The Actor's Nightmare"; the district court's "characterization of the doctrine as relating to unprotected '*ideas*' may have been technically inaccurate, but the court properly applied the doctrine to hold unprotectable forms of expression that were either stock scenes or scenes that flowed necessarily from common unprotectable ideas. 'Common' in this context means common to the works at issue, not necessarily . . . commonly found in other artistic works"); Hoehling v. Universal City Studios, Inc., 618 F.2d 972, 979, 205 U.S.P.Q. 681, 685 (2d Cir. 1980).

In *Hoehling*, the copyrighted and accused works dealt with the tragic destruction of the Hindenburg dirigible. In finding no infringement, the court discounted certain similarities relied upon by the copyright owner.

> "[The works] contain a scene in a German beer hall, in which the airship's crew engages in revelry prior to the voyage. Other claimed similarities concern common German greetings of the period, such as 'Heil Hitler,' or songs, such as the German national anthem. These elements, however are merely *scenes a faire* . . . . Because it is virtually impossible to write about a particular historical era or fictional theme without employing certain 'stock' or standard literary devices, we have held that *scenes a faire* are not copyrightable as a matter of law." 618 F.2d at 979, 205 U.S.P.Q. at 685.

[94] *See* § 4F[2][a][iv].

[95] *Cf.* Atari Games Corp. v. Oman, 888 F.2d 878, 886, 12 U.S.P.Q.2d 1791, 1797 (D.C. Cir. 1989) (remanding for clarification the Register of Copyright's refusal to register "break-out" video game and suggesting that *scenes a faire* restricts the scope of copyright protection, not copyrightability).

[96] *E.g.,* Alberto-Culver Co. v. Andrea Dumon, Inc., 466 F.2d 705, 175 U.S.P.Q. 194 (7th Cir. 1972) (label phrase "most personal sort of deodorant" is not copyrightable under 1909 Act). *See generally* P. Goldstein, Copyright § 2.7.3 (1989).

The Copyright Office's regulations contain two pertinent provisions:

> "The following are examples of works not subject to copyright . . . :
>
> (a) Words and short phrases such as names, titles, and slogans; familiar symbols or designs; mere variations of typographic ornamentation, lettering or coloring; mere listing of ingredients or contents; . . .
>
> (d) Works consisting entirely of information that is common property containing no original authorship, such as, for example: Standard calendars, height and weight charts, tape measures and rulers, schedules of sporting events, and lists or tables taken from public documents or other common sources."

37 C.F.R. § 202.1. *See also* Harper House Inc. v. Thomas Nelson Inc., 889 F.2d 197, 12 U.S.P.Q.2d 1779, 1785 (9th Cir. 1989) ("copyright protection does not extend to common property such as standard calendars and area code maps").

John Muller,[97] the Second Circuit held uncopyrightable a soccer team logo consisting of a design and script word "Arrows." "[T]he issue here is creativity, not originality."[98]

In *Applied Innovations,*[99] the court held that statements used in a psychological test, the Minnesota Multiphasic Personality Inventory (MMPI) are copyrightable. The statements are short, simple, declarative sentences, for example, "I am a good mixer," and "No one seems to understand me."

> "[The statements] are not merely fragmentary words and phrases within the meaning of 37 C.F.R. § 202.1(a). They are not names or titles or slogans.

> "[T]he test statements satisfy the minimal standard for original works of authorship. . . . *Rubin v. Boston Magazine Co.,* 645 F.2d 80, 83 (1st Cir. 1981) (particular questions about love and romance held copyrightable as original forms of expression); *cf. Educational Testing Service v. Katzman,* 793 F.2d 533, 539 (3d Cir. 1986) (questions in scholastic aptitude and achievement tests); *Association of American Medical Colleges v. Mikaelian,* 571 F. Supp. 144, 150 (E.D. Pa. 1983) (questions in medical school admission test), *aff'd without opinion,* 734 F.2d 3 (3d Cir. 1984); *National Conference of Bar Examiners v. Multistate Legal Studies, Inc.,* 495 F. Supp. 34, 36 (N.D. Ill. 1980) (questions in bar exam), *aff'd in part and rev'd in part,* 692 F.2d 478 (7th Cir. 1982), *cert. denied,* 464 U.S. 814 (1983)."[100]

[vi]   *Characters.* Whether copyright protects characters, graphical and literary, apart from the works in which they appear, is a thorny issue.[101]

Graphical characters, such as cartoon figures, are conceptually simpler than literary characters because of their specific, transferable characteristics. In *Walt Disney,*[102] the court found infringement in defendant's use of characters closely resembling cartoon characters appearing in plaintiff's copyrighted works, including Mickey and Minnie Mouse,[103] Donald Duck, the Big Bad Wolf, the Three Little Pigs, and Goofy.

Compare Atari Games Corp. v. Oman, 888 F.2d 878, 883, 12 U.S.P.Q.2d 1791, 1795 (D.C. Cir. 1989) ("simple shapes, when selected or combined in a distinctive manner indicating some ingenuity, have been accorded copyright protection both by the Register and in court," citing fabric design cases).

[97] John Muller & Co. v. New York Arrows Soccer Team, 802 F.2d 989, 231 U.S.P.Q.2d 319 (8th Cir. 1986). *See also* Magic Marketing, Inc. v. Mailing Services of Pittsburgh, Inc., 634 F. Supp. 769, 230 U.S.P.Q. 230 (W.D. Pa. 1986) (invalidating copyright on envelope with black stripe and words "PRIORITY MESSAGE: CONTENTS REQUIRE IMMEDIATE ATTENTION" and "TELEGRAM").

[98] 802 F.2d at 990, 231 U.S.P.Q. at 319.

[99] Applied Innovations Inc. v. University of Minnesota, 876 F.2d 626, 11 U.S.P.Q.2d 1041, 1049 (8th Cir. 1989).

[100] 876 F.2d at 635, 11 U.S.P.Q.2d at 1049–50. The infringers sold a computer program for scoring MMPI tests. One version of the program contained 38 of MMPI's 550 test statements.

[101] *See generally* P. Goldstein, Copyright §§ 2.7.2, 2.11.3 (1989).

[102] Walt Disney Productions v. Air Pirates, 581 F.2d 751, 199 U.S.P.Q. 769 (9th Cir. 1978).

[103] The court found it unnecessary to determine the precise relationship between Mr. Mouse and Ms. Mouse. *See* § 4F[3][d].

"In some instances Disney's copyrights cover a book and others an entire strip of several cartoon panels. The fact that its characters are not the separate subject of a copyright does not preclude their protection, however, because Section 3 of the [1909] Copyright Act provided that Disney's copyrights included protection for 'all the copyrightable component parts of the work copyrighted' . . . ."

"The essence of defendants' argument is that characters are never copyrightable and therefore cannot in any way constitute a copyrightable component part. That argument flies in the face of a series of cases dating back to 1914 that have held comic strip characters protectable under the old Copyright Act. *See Detective Comics, Inc. v. Bruns Publications Inc.,* 111 F.2d 432 (2d Cir. 1940); *Fleischer Studios v. Freundlich,* 73 F.2d 276 (2d Cir. 1934), *certiorari denied,* 294 U.S. 717, 55 S. Ct. 516, 79 L. Ed. 1250; *King Features Syndicate v. Fleischer,* 299 F. 533 (2d Cir. 1924); *Detective Comics, Inc. v. Fox Publications Inc.,* 46 F. Supp. 872 (S.D.N.Y. 1942); *Hill v. Whalen & Martell, Inc.,* 220 F. 359 (S.D.N.Y. 1914)."[104]

As to literary characters, in *Nichols,*[105] Judge Learned Hand suggested that a character could be so distinctly described and developed as to be protectable apart from a particular literary or dramatic sequence.

"[W]e do not doubt that two plays may correspond in plot closely enough for infringement. . . . Nor need we hold that the same may not be true as to the characters, quite independently of the 'plot' proper, though, as far as we know, such a case has never arisen. If Twelfth Night were copyrighted, it is quite possible that a second comer might so closely imitate Sir Toby Belch or Malvolio as to infringe, but it would not be enough that for one of his characters he cast a riotous knight who kept wassail to the discomfort of the household, or a vain and foppish steward who became amorous of his mistress. These would be no more than Shakespeare's 'ideas' in the play, as little capable of monopoly as Einstein's Doctrine of Relativity, or Darwin's theory of the Origin of the Species. It follows that the less developed the characters, the less they can be copyrighted; that is the penalty an author must bear for marking them too indistinctly."[106]

In *Warner Brothers ("Maltese Falcon"),*[107] Dashiell Hammett and his publisher assigned to Warner the motion picture and broadcasting rights to Hammett's classic detective novel "The Maltese Falcon," in which the central character is Sam Spade. Hammett used the Sam Spade character in subsequent books (sequels) and conferred motion picture rights therein to others. Warner sued for copyright infringement. The

---

[104] 581 F.2d at 754–55.

[105] Nichols v. Universal Pictures Corp., 45 F.2d 119 (2d Cir. 1930).

See also Filmvideo Releasing Corp. v. Hastings, 668 F.2d 91, 218 U.S.P.Q. 750 (2d Cir. 1981); Silverman v. CBS, Inc., 870 F.2d 40, 9 U.S.P.Q. 1178 (2d Cir. 1989), *cert. denied,* 109 S. Ct. 3219 (1989).

[106] 45 F.2d at 121.

[107] Warner Brothers, Inc. v. Columbia Broadcasting System, 216 F.2d 945 (9th Cir. 1954), *cert. denied,* 348 U.S. 971 (1955).

Ninth Circuit denied relief, relying primarily on its interpretation of the contract. It reasoned that the parties did not intend by the contract "to buy and sell the future use of the personalities in the writing." The court went on to consider "whether it was ever intended by the copyright statute that characters with their names should be under its protection." It restrictively interpreted the *Nichols* dictum:

> "It is conceivable that the character really constitutes the story being told, but if the character is only the chessman in the game of telling the story he is not within the area of the protection afforded by the copyright. . . . [E]ven if the Owners assigned their complete rights in the copyright to the *Falcon,* such assignment did not prevent the author from using the characters used therein, in other stories. The characters were vehicles for the story told, and the vehicles did not go with the sale of the story."[108]

Warner's result and reasoning were colored by the case's equities. It is one thing to bar a stranger from using an author's distinctively carved character. It is quite another to bar the creator from using his character in new works simply because the creator transferred the copyright in earlier works in which the character appears.

In *Warner Bros. ("Superman")*,[109] the Second Circuit found plaintiff's "Superman" character copyrightable but not infringed by defendant's "The Greatest American Hero."

> "When . . . the claim concerns infringement of a character, rather than a story, the idea-expression distinction has proved to be especially elusive. . . . Copyrightability of a literary character has on occasion been recognized . . . . However, there has been no doubt that copyright protection is available for characters portrayed in cartoons, even before *Nichols* . . . .
>
> . . . .
>
> ". . . Plaintiffs make no claim that the Hero pilot, subsequent episodes, or 'promos' infringed the story of any Superman works. Their contention is that the Hero character, Ralph Hinkley, is substantially similar to Superman . . . .
>
> "The total perception of the Hinkley character is not substantially similar to that of Superman. On the contrary, it is profoundly different. Superman

---

[108] 216 F.2d at 950.

[109] Warner Bros. Inc. v. American Broadcasting Companies, Inc., 720 F.2d 231, 222 U.S.P.Q. 101 (2d Cir. 1983). An earlier appeal affirmed denial of a preliminary injunction. Warner Bros. Inc. v. American Broadcasting Companies, Inc., 654 F.2d 204, 211 U.S.P.Q. 97 (2d Cir. 1981).

For another Superman case, see Detective Comics, Inc. v. Bruns Publications, Inc., 111 F.2d 432, 433-34 (2d Cir. 1940) ("the pictorial representations and verbal descriptions of 'Superman' " presented more than "a benevolent Hercules" and thus constituted "proper subjects of copyright," but the owners of the Superman copyrights are not "entitled to a monopoly of the mere character of a 'Superman' who is a blessing to mankind."; the defendant's "Wonderman" comic character infringed the plaintiff's copyrighted Superman works because the "only real difference between them is that 'Superman' wears a blue uniform and 'Wonderman' a red one."; defendants "used more than general types and ideas and . . . appropriated the pictorial and literary details embodied in the complainant's copyrights.").

looks and acts like a brave, proud hero, who has dedicated his life to combating the forces of evil. Hinkley looks and acts like a timid, reluctant hero, who accepts his missions grudgingly and prefers to get on with his normal life.

"However, we do not accept defendants' mode of analysis whereby every skill the two characters share is dismissed as an idea rather than a protected form of expression. That approach risks elimination of any copyright protection for a character, unless the allegedly infringing character looks and behaves exactly like the original. A character is an aggregation of the particular talents and traits his creator selected for him. That each one may be an idea does not diminish the expressive aspect of the combination. But just as similarity cannot be rejected by isolating as an idea each characteristic the characters have in common, it cannot be found when the total perception of all the ideas as expressed in each character is fundamentally different.

"An infringement claim would surely be within the range of reasonable jury fact issues if a character strongly resembled Superman but displayed some trait inconsistent with the traditional Superman image. If a second comer endowed his character with Superman's general appearance, demeanor, and skills, but portrayed him in the service of the underworld, a jury would have to make the factual determination whether the second character was Superman gone astray or a new addition to the superhero genre. In this case, however, a reasonable jury could not conclude that Hinkley is substantially similar to the Superman character with only a change of name. The overall perception of the way Hinkley looks and acts marks him as a different, non-infringing character who simply has some of the superhuman traits popularized by the Superman character and now widely shared within the superhero genre."[110]

In *Olson*,[111] the Ninth Circuit revisited the literary character protection question. Olson alleged that NBC's television series "The A-Team" infringed his copyrighted screenplay "Cargo." "Cargo" and "The A-Team" shared a common idea: "Both are group action-adventure series designed to show Vietnam veterans in a positive light," but "this idea, standing alone, is not protectable." There was "little similarity between

---

[110] 720 F.2d at 240, 243, 222 U.S.P.Q. at 108.

See also Walker v. Time Life Films, Inc., 784 F.2d 44, 228 U.S.P.Q. 505, 509 (2d Cir.), *cert. denied*, 476 U.S. 1159 (1986) ("As to Walker's claim that the film misappropriates characters from his book, we must consider the 'totality of [their] attributes and traits' as well as the extent to which the defendants' characters capture the 'total concept and feel' of figures in the book. . . . The characters of [the film] however, are quite different from those in the book. In the film, Murphy is an independent-minded, cynical, divorced patrolman contemptuous of authority, once demoted for insubordination. Murphy's romantic scenes reveal tenderness; his soul-searching over whether to denounce fellow officers reveal[s] both integrity and loyalty. By contrast, his boss, Captain Connolly, is a hard-driving disciplinarian eager to 'go by the book' and establish the rule of law in the South Bronx. Walker, the book's narrator, is a pragmatic, happily-married lieutenant who never disobeys an order or questions his superiors. In his life history, outlook, rank and marital status he bears little resemblance to any of the film's characters.")

[111] Olson v. National Broadcasting Co., Inc., 855 F.2d 1446, 1450–51, 8 U.S.P.Q.2d 1231, 1234–35 (9th Cir. 1988).

'The A-Team' and the 'Cargo' works in terms of overall plot, sequence, dialogue or setting." Infringement, if any, resided in substantial similarity of "series concept" and characters. Any "series concept" similarities "are common to the genre of action-adventure television series and movies and therefore do not demonstrate substantial similarity." Olson's substantial similarity claim "is supported most strongly by a comparison between the characters in 'Cargo' and those in 'The A-Team'," but Olson's characters were not protectable under either the *Warner* "story being told" test or the more liberal *Nichols* specific development test.

> "In what is arguably dicta, the [*Warner Bros.*] court . . . stated that 'if the character is only the chessman in the game of telling the story he is not within the area of the protection afforded by the copyright.'

> "We recognize that cases subsequent to *Warner Bros.* have allowed copyright protection for characters who are especially distinctive. For example, cartoon characters may be afforded copyright protection notwithstanding *Warner Bros.* . . . For similar reasons, copyright protection may be afforded to characters visually depicted in a television series or in a movie.

> "Even if the statements in *Warner Bros.* concerning the unprotectability of characters are considered to be dicta, the 'Cargo' characters are not protectable even under the more lenient standards adopted elsewhere.

> ". . . The 'Cargo' characters are depicted only by three- or four-line summaries in the 'Cargo' treatment and screenplay, plus whatever insight into their characters may be derived from their dialogue and action. Although such lightly sketched characters may be descriptive enough to sustain a finding of infringement where other . . . factors are also copied, 'Cargo' contained no descriptions which could be sufficient to afford copyright protection to a character taken alone."[112]

A problem with copyright protection for characters is that the characters may appear in a series of works, some copyrighted and some not, or may be changed in later works. In *Silverman*,[113] Silverman proposed to develop a musical play based on the famous "Amos 'n' Andy" characters. Charles Correll and Freeman Gosden created and portrayed the two characters in 1928. Radio programs broadcast from 1928 to 1948 are not subject to copyright. CBS holds copyrights in radio and television

---

[112] 855 F.2d at 1451–52, 8 U.S.P.Q.2d at 1235–36.

Compare Anderson v. Stallone, 11 U.S.P.Q.2d 1161, 1170 (C.D. Calif. 1989) ("Rocky" movie character is protectable under either the *Nichols* specific development test or the *Warner Bros.* "story being told" test) *with* Jones v. CBS Inc., 733 F. Supp. 748, 753, 15 U.S.P.Q.2d 1380, 1384 (S.D. N.Y. 1990) ("Sister Sadie," a "conjure lady" in plaintiff's "Peachtree Street" pilot script is not copyrightable so as to be infringed by two "voodoo" practitioners in defendant's "Frank's Place.": "Copyright law provides very limited protection to the characters presented in a creative work. Basic character types are not copyrightable. . . . [O]nly a uniquely developed character with some degree of novelty is copyrightable. . . . Sister Sadie is not one of those rare copyrightable characters, largely because she is too undeveloped in the pilot script . . . to be more than a stock character.").

[113] *See* Silverman v. CBS, 870 F.2d 40, 9 U.S.P.Q.2d 1778 (2d Cir.), *cert. denied,* 109 S. Ct. 3219 (1989).

broadcasts from 1948 to 1953 and sought to bar Silverman's use of the characters. The court held that only the further delineation of the characters after 1948 was protectable.

> "With respect to the 'Amos 'n Andy' characters, . . . we have no doubt that they were sufficiently delineated in the pre-1948 radio scripts to have been placed in the public domain. See *Nichols v. Universal Pictures* . . . .

> "Since only the increments of expression added by the films are protectable, Silverman would infringe only if he copies these protectable increments. It is, of course, likely that the visual portrayal of the characters added something beyond the delineation contained in the public domain radio scripts, but surely not every visual aspect is protected. For example, the fact the characters are visibly Black does not bar Silverman from placing Black 'Amos 'n Andy' characters in this musical, since the race of the characters was a feature fully delineated in the public domain scripts. Similarly, any other physical features adequately described in the pre-1948 radio scripts may be copied even though those characteristics are visually apparent in the television films or tapes."[114]

[e] **Sound Recordings.** Sound recordings are copyrightable subject matter.[115] The Copyright Act severely limits a sound recording copyright's exclusive rights: the reproduction right extends only to the duplication of the actual sounds fixed in the recording; the derivative right extends only to the rearranging, remixing or other altering of those actual sounds. A sound recording copyright includes no rights against others who independently fix sounds that imitate or simulate those in the copyrighted work. Unlike copyright in other types of works, it protects only against physical misappropriation.

The history of the legal protection against unauthorized reproduction of sound recordings is long and complex. When the 1909 Act was enacted, the recording industry was in its infancy. One year before that statute's passage, the Supreme Court decided *White-Smith Music Publishing Co.*[116] Plaintiffs, musical composition copyright owners, alleged that defendants infringed the copyrights by embodying the compositions on player piano rolls. The roll perforations caused player pianos to perform the musical composition. Under pre-1909 law, the defendants would be guilty of infringement only if they produced "copies" of the protected music works. The Court held that the piano rolls were parts of machines, not "copies." A "copy" was a written record, such as printed sheet music, that could be perceived by humans directly. A human could not "read" the perforations on the rolls, at least not without special expertise.

---

[114] 870 F.2d at 50, 9 U.S.P.Q.2d at 1785–86.

[115] 17 U.S.C. § 102(a)(7). *See generally* P. Goldstein, Copyright § 2.13 (1989).

"Sound recordings" are "works that result from the fixation of a series of musical, spoken, or other sounds, but not including the sounds accompanying a motion picture or other audiovisual work, regardless of the nature of the material objects, such as disks, tapes, or other phonorecords, in which they are embodied." 17 U.S.C. § 101.

[116] White-Smith Music Publishing Co. v. Apollo Co., 209 U.S. 1 (1908).

White-Smith's impact on the fixation requirement is discussed at § 4C[4][a].

In the 1909 Act, Congress guardedly responded to *White-Smith Music*. To protect composers' economic interests, it extended their works' copyrights to "any form of record" from which the musical composition could be reproduced but imposed a compulsory recording license.[117] Significantly, Congress did not address whether the recording itself was a copyrightable work and did not alter the *White-Smith Music* copy definition, which excluded recordings. Because under the 1909 Act copyright could only be secured in works as to which "copies" could be deposited with the Copyright Office, the 1909 Act necessarily excluded copyright protection for sound recordings.[118]

Early attempts to prevent unauthorized commercial copying of records and tapes focused on state remedies, first, common law remedies such as misappropriation and unfair competition,[119] and, later, criminal and civil statutes enacted by state legislatures. In time, the Supreme Court determined that federal constitutional copyright policy did not preempt state remedies.[120]

Faced with the need for a uniform national solution to the record and tape "piracy" problem made possible by sound reproduction technology, Congress in 1971 extended copyright protection to sound records on a provisional basis. The 1976 Act made the extension permanent[121] but only for sound recordings fixed on or after February 15, 1972. State law remedies continue to be important.[122]

The House Report on the 1976 Act discusses the interesting issue of who is the "author" of a sound recording.

> "The copyrightable elements in a sound recording will usually, though not always, involve 'authorship' both on the part of the performers whose performance is captured and on the part of the record producer responsible for setting up the recording session, capturing and electronically processing the sounds, and compiling and editing them to make the final sound recording. There may, however, be cases where the record producer's contribution is so minimal that the performance is the only copyrightable element in the work, and there may be cases (for example, recordings of birdcalls, sounds of racing cars, et cetera) where only the record producer's contribution is copyrightable."[123]

---

[117] See 17 U.S.C. § 115(a). See § 4E[7].

[118] See Capital Records v. Mercury Records Corp., 221 F.2d 657 (2d Cir. 1955).

[119] E.g., Mercury Record Prod., Inc. v. Economic Consultants, Inc., 64 Wis. 2d 163, 218 N.W.2d 705 (1974).

[120] Goldstein v. California, 412 U.S. 546 (1973). See § 1D[3][a][ii].

[121] See H.R. Rep. No. 94–1476, 94th Cong., 2d Sess. 55–56 (1976):

> "As a class of subject matter, sound recordings are clearly within the scope of the 'writings of an author' capable of protection under the Constitution, and the extension of limited statutory protection to them was too long delayed. Aside from cases in which sounds are fixed by some purely mechanical means without originality of any kind, the copyright protection that would prevent the reproduction and distribution of unauthorized phonorecords of sound recordings is clearly justified."

[122] See 17 U.S.C. § 301(c). See § 6F[5][a].

[123] H.R. Rep. No. 94–1476, 94th Cong., 2d Sess. 56 (1976).

[f] Exclusions—Immoral Works. The Copyright Act has no content-based exclusion but two authorship-based exclusions.[124] Section 104 relates to national origin.[125] Section 105 excludes copyright in "any work of the United States Government."[126]

Court decisions withhold copyright protection from judicial opinions, legislation, and administrative regulations[127] but decline to impose public policy limitations on copyright protection. For example, in *Mitchell Brothers*,[128] the court held that the copyrighted work's allegedly obscene character was no defense to an infringement charge.[129] In *Hutchinson Telephone*,[130] the court held that a telephone company

---

[124] *See generally* P. Goldstein, Copyright § 2.5 (1989).

[125] *See* § 4D[4].

[126] 17 U.S.C. § 105. A "work of the United States Government" is defined as "a work prepared by an officer or employee of the United States Government as part of that person's official duties." 17 U.S.C. § 101.

[127] As to judicial opinions, the Supreme Court noted in 1834 that "no reporter has or can have any copyright in the written opinions delivered by this Court, and . . . the judges thereof cannot confer on any reporter any such right." Wheaton v. Peters, 33 U.S. (8 Peters) 591, 668 (1834).

Abstracts and headnotes included with judicial opinions are copyrightable. The compilation and arrangement of judicial opinions may also be copyrightable. *See* § 4C[1][b][i].

As to legislation and administrative regulations, see Building Officials & Code Administrators International, Inc. v. Code Technology, Inc., 628 F.2d 730, 207 U.S.P.Q. 81 (1st Cir. 1980); Georgia v. Harrison Co., 548 F. Supp. 110 (N.D. Ga. 1982), *vacated by agreement*, 559 F. Supp. 37 (N.D. Ga. 1983).

In *Building Officials*, a private, nonprofit organization ("BOCA") developed and published a detailed model building code, claiming copyright therein. The Commonwealth of Massachusetts, under license from BOCA, adopted the BOCA Code, making only minor alterations. BOCA then published and distributed the code. The defendant Code Technology published its own version of the Massachusetts Building Code. The district court granted a preliminary injunction. The appeals court reversed, finding that BOCA's probability of success on the merits to be insufficient to justify such a preliminary injunction. After reviewing the cases on judicial opinions and legislation, which recognize "the very important and practical policy that citizens must have free access to the laws which govern them," the court concluded: "While we do not rule finally on the question, we cannot say with any confidence that the same policies applicable to statutes and judicial opinions may not apply equally to regulations of this nature."

[128] Mitchell Brothers Film Group v. Cinema Adult Theater, 604 F.2d 852, 203 U.S.P.Q. 1041 (5th Cir. 1979), *cert. denied sub nom.* Bora v. Mitchell Brothers Film Group, 445 U.S. 917 (1980).

[129] The court noted:

> "Congress has been hostile to content-based restrictions on copyrightability. In contrast Congress has placed explicit content-related restrictions in the current statutes governing the related areas of trademarks and patents. The Lanham Act prohibits registration of any trademark that 'consists of or comprises immoral, deceptive, or scandalous matter,' 15 U.S.C. § 1052(a), and inventions must be shown to be 'useful' before a patent is issued. See 35 U.S.C. § 101.

> . . .

> "Denying copyright protection to works adjudged obscene by the standards of one era would frequently result in lack of copyright protection (and thus lack of financial

could claim copyright in its white pages directory even though it is required to publish the directory as a condition of its state-sanctioned telephone monopoly: "Where Congress has enacted a clear and comprehensive statute pursuant to a broad constitutional grant of power, . . . it is not for the courts to undermine legislative intent by carving out exceptions that Congress did not choose to make."

[2] Computer Programs—Video Games

Computer programs are copyrightable subject matter.[131] Among contemporary copyright law's most difficult issues is determining the proper scope of protection for computer program "expression." Courts have held that copyright extends beyond a program's literal code and protects some facets of its structure, sequence, and organization, screen displays, and user interface.

[a] **Background.** In 1964, the Copyright Office began accepting computer programs for registration. The 1976 Copyright Act did not mention computer programs but defined "literary works" broadly.[132] The House Report affirmed that "the term 'literary works' includes computer data bases, and computer programs to the extent that they incorporate authorship in the programmer's expression of original ideas, as distinguished from the ideas themselves."[133]

---

incentive to create) for works that later generations might consider to be not only non-obscene but even of great literary merit.

"Further, Congress in not enacting an obscenity exception to copyrightability avoids substantial practical difficulties and delicate First Amendment issues." 604 F.2d at 855, 857, 858.

The court considered the constitutionality of extending copyright to obscene works, which, arguably, do not further the Constitutional purpose of promoting "science and the useful arts."

"[A]lthough Congress could require that each copyrighted work be shown to promote the useful arts (as it has with patents), it need not do so. . . . Congress could reasonably conclude that the best way to promote creativity is not to impose any governmental restrictions on the subject matter of copyrightable works. By making this choice Congress removes the chilling effect of governmental judgments on potential authors and avoids the strong possibility that governmental officials (including judges) will err in separating the useful from the non-useful." 604 F.2d at 860.

Finally, it rejected the defendants' reliance on the equitable doctrine of "unclean hands," which some courts have used to deny redress in infringement suits to holders of copyrights on immoral or obscene works: "Creating a defense of obscenity—in the name of unclean hands or through any other vehicle—adds a defense not authorized by Congress that may . . . actually frustrate the congressional purpose underlying an all-inclusive copyright statute." 604 F.2d at 861.

For a discussion of the registrability of "immoral" trademarks, see § 5C[2][d][i].

[130] Hutchinson Telephone Co. v. Fronteer Directory Co. of Minnesota, 770 F.2d 128, 228 U.S.P.Q. 537 (8th Cir. 1985). *But cf.* Feist Publications, Inc. v. Rural Telephone Service Company, Inc., 111 S. Ct. 1282, 18 U.S.P.Q.2d 1275 (1991), discussed at § 4C[1][b][i](2) (white page directories lack originality).

[131] *See generally* P. Goldstein, Copyright § 2.15.2 (1989).

[132] 17 U.S.C. § 101.

[133] H.R. Rep. No. 94–1476, 94th Cong., 2d Sess. 54 (1976).

In 1974, Congress created the Commission on New Technological Uses of Copyrighted Works ("CONTU") to study and report to Congress on several topics, including photocopying and computer uses of copyrighted works. In 1979, the Commission recommended that the copyright law be amended "to make it explicit that computer programs, to the extent that they embody an author's original creation, are proper subject matter of copyright."[134] It recommended two specific statutory changes—a definition of computer programs, and a limitation on exclusive rights "to ensure that rightful possessors of copies of computer programs may use and adapt these copies to their use."

In 1980, Congress followed CONTU's recommendation,[135] adding a definition—"A 'computer program' is a set of statements or instructions to be used directly or indirectly in a computer in order to bring about a certain result" and amending Section 117 to set forth adaptation and archival copying limitations.[136]

[b] **The Video Game Cases.** Early cases on computer program copyrightability and computer implementable works dealt with videogames,[137] which "can roughly be described as computers programmed to create on a television screen cartoons in which some of the action is controlled by the player."[138]

---

[134] National Commission on New Technological Uses of Copyrighted Works, Final Report 1 (1979). The members of the Commission differed in their views on the copyrightability of computer programs.

For a scholarly critique of CONTU's work on computer program copyrightability, see Samuelson, *CONTU Revisited: The Case Against Copyright Protection for Computer Programs in Machine-Readable Form*, 1984 Duke L. J. 663.

[135] Act of Dec. 12, 1980, Pub. L. No. 96-517, § 10, 94 Stat. 3015, 3028. *See* H.R. Rep. No. 1307, 96th Cong., 2d Sess. 23.

In assessing computer program copyrightability, the courts look to the CONTU Report. *E.g.*, Vault Corp. v. Quaid Software Ltd., 847 F.2d 255, 261, 7 U.S.P.Q.2d 1281, 1287 (5th Cir. 1988) ("The absence of an extensive legislative history and the fact that Congress enacted proposed section 117 with only one change have prompted courts to rely on the CONTU Report as an expression of legislative intent.").

Compare Whelan Associates, Inc. v. Jaslow Dental Laboratory, 797 F.2d 1222, 1242, 230 U.S.P.Q. 481, 495 (3d Cir. 1986), *cert. denied*, 479 U.S. 1031 (1987) ("the CONTU Report has force only insofar as it can be said to represent the will of Congress. There is no sense in which it represents the will of Congress with respect to provisions not amended in response to the Report."); Lotus Development Corp. v. Paperback Software International, 740 F. Supp. 37, 54, 15 U.S.P.Q.2d 1577, 1588 (D. Mass. 1990) ("CONTU, of course, was not an official voice of Congress, and its views are not, without more, attributable to Congress. Thus, courts must not treat the CONTU report as legislative history, in the ordinary sense, much less as an authoritative statement about manifested legislative intent . . . Congress, however, did not ignore CONTU. Indeed, . . . Congress adopted practically verbatim the Commission's proposed statutory changes with respect to computer programs. Thus, the expressed views of the Commission, to the extent not repudiated by Congress, may help to explain the context in which Congress acted, which in turn may support inferences about the meaning of any otherwise ambiguous passages in what Congress declared.").

[136] *See* § 4C[2][e].

[137] *See generally* P. Goldstein, Copyright § 2.12.2 (1989).

[138] Stern Electronics, Inc. v. Kaufman, 669 F.2d 852, 213 U.S.P.Q. 443 (2d Cir. 1982). *See also* Williams Electronics, Inc. v. Artic International, Inc., 685 F.2d 870, 871-72, 215 U.S.P.Q. 405, 406 (3d Cir. 1982):

In *Stern Electronics*,[139] the Second Circuit confirmed that a video game's sequence of sounds and images is copyrightable as an audiovisual work separate and apart from the computer program.[140] Limiting copyright to the program that generates the game would allow a copyist to write a new computer program "that would interact with the hardware components of a video game to produce on the screen the same images . . . accompanied by the same sounds" as the original work. The court rejected contentions that a videogame is not copyrightable because it is not fixed in a tangible medium of expression and is not original.

> "Both contentions arise from the fact that the sequence of some of the images appearing on the screen during each play of the game will vary depending upon the actions taken by the player.

> "If the content of the audiovisual display were not affected by the participation of the player, there would be no doubt that the display itself, and not merely the written computer program, would be eligible for copyright. The display satisfies the statutory definition of an original 'audiovisual work,' and the memory devices of the game satisfy the statutory requirement of a 'copy' in which the work is 'fixed.'

> ". . . [M]any aspects of the sights and the sequence of their appearance remain constant during each play of the game. . . . The repetitive sequence of a substantial portion of the sights and sounds of the game qualifies for copyright protection as an audiovisual work."[141]

"A video game machine consists of a cabinet containing inter alia, a cathode ray tube (CRT), a sound system, hand controls for the player, and electronic circuit boards. The electronic circuitry includes a microprocessor and memory devices, called ROMs (R ead O nly M emory), which are tiny computer 'chips' containing thousands of data locations which store the instructions and data of a computer program. The microprocessor executes the computer program to cause the game to operate."

See also United States v. Goss, 803 F.2d 638, 642 n.4, 231 U.S.P.Q. 730, 732 n.4 (11th Cir. 1986) (as to "what component or components of a video game constitutes the 'copy' in which the audiovisual work is fixed," the evidence indicated that the works were fixed in memory chips, not circuit boards).

[139] Stern Electronics, Inc. v. Kaufman, 669 F.2d 852, 213 U.S.P.Q. 443 (2d Cir. 1982).

[140] *See also* M. Kramer Manufacturing Co., Inc. v. Andrews, 783 F.2d 421, 435, 228 U.S.P.Q. 705, 714 (4th Cir. 1986) (finding infringement of plaintiff's copyrighted "HI-LO DOUBLE UP JOKER POKER" by defendant's poker games; "The district court . . . suggests that, 'video games' are never copyrightable and that for this reason the plaintiff's copyright which in effect covers a video game, is invalid. Strictly speaking the game, idea of the game itself, is not protected but the shape and characteristics of the cards and the 'shapes, sizes, colors, sequences, arrangements and sounds [that] provides something "new or additional over the idea" ' are protected.").

[141] 669 F.2d at 855-57, 213 U.S.P.Q. at 445-46. *Accord* Williams Electronics, Inc. v. Artic International, Inc., 685 F.2d 870, 215 U.S.P.Q. 405, 408 (3d Cir. 1982) ("Defendant . . . contends that the player's participation withdraws the game's audiovisual work from copyright eligibility because there is no set or fixed performance and the player becomes a co-author of what appears on the screen. . . . [T]here is always a repetitive sequence of a substantial portion of the sights and sounds of the game, and many aspects of the display remain constant from game to game regardless of how the player operates the controls. . . . Furthermore, there is no player participation in the attract mode which is displayed repetitively without change.").

The court cautioned that "[w]e need not decide at what point the repeating sequence of images would form too insubstantial a portion of an entire display to warrant a copyright, nor the somewhat related issue of whether a sequence of images . . . might contain so little in the way of particularized form of expression as to be only an abstract idea portrayed in noncopyrightable form."[142]

In *Williams Electronics*,[143] the Third Circuit reached the issues of the copyrightability and infringement of the computer program that generated a video game. The plaintiff registered the "play" mode and "attract" mode as audiovisual works; it separately registered the computer program that generated its game as a literary work.

Conceding that a computer program is copyrightable "as a literary text," defendant contended that copyright protection did not extend to ROM ("read only memory") chips, which it purchased and distributed, because ROMS "are utilitarian objects or machine parts." The court disagreed: the issue was not whether the ROM chip itself is protectable but rather whether the plaintiff can "protect its artistic expression in original works which have met the statutory fixation requirement through their embodiment in the ROM devices."[144]

The defendant also contended that "a distinction must be drawn between the 'source code' . . . and 'object code' " versions of a program: "Its theory is that a 'copy' must

---

[142] 213 U.S.P.Q. at 446.

[143] Williams Electronics, Inc. v. Artic International, Inc., 685 F.2d 870, 215 U.S.P.Q. 405 (3d Cir. 1982).

[144] The court disapproved a district court decision that a ROM is not a "copy." Data Cash Systems, Inc. v. JS&A Group, Inc., 480 F. Supp. 1063 (N.D. Ill. 1979), *aff'd on other grounds*, 628 F.2d 1038 (7th Cir. 1980).

The Supreme Court's 1909 *White-Smith* decision defined a "copy" in terms of human readability, which would exclude a ROM chip. The 1976 Act broadened the general definition to include material objects "from which the work can be perceived, reproduced, or otherwise communicated, either directly or with the aid of a machine or device." *Data Cash System* interpreted Section 117 of the Copyright Act of 1976 as preserving the *White-Smith* definition of a "copy" for works stored in computer accessible form. Section 117 of the Copyright Act of 1976, which became effective on January 1, 1978, provided, *inter alia*, that "this title does not afford to the owner of copyright in a work any greater or lesser rights with respect to the use of the work in conjunction with automatic systems capable of storing, processing, retrieving, or transferring information, or in conjunction with any similar device, machine or process, than those afforded to works under the law . . . in effect on December 31, 1977 . . . ." In 1980, Section 117 was replaced by a provision dealing with archival copying. *See* § 4C[2][e].

In *Tandy*, another district court disagreed with *Data Cash* and finding that "section 117, as it existed in the 1976 Act, was aimed at the problem of copyrighted material input into a computer, such as books, magazines, and even computer programs." Tandy Corp. v. Personal Micro Computers, Inc., 524 F. Supp. 171, 214 U.S.P.Q. 178 (N.D. Calif. 1979) (denying the defendant's motion to dismiss plaintiff's suit alleging infringement of its program providing an "input-out" routine for its "TRS-80" home computers; plaintiff alleged that the defendants copied the program and used it in their "PMC-80" computers.)

> "It was not intended to provide a loophole by which someone could duplicate a computer program fixed on a silicon chip. . . . Such a duplication of a chip is not the use of a copyrighted program 'in conjunction with' a computer; it is simply the copying of a chip. Moreover, any other interpretation would render the theoretical ability to copyright computer programs virtually meaningless." 524 F. Supp. at 175.

be intelligible to human beings and must be intended as medium of communication to human beings." The court disagreed: "Congress opted for an expansive interpretation of the terms 'fixation' and 'copy' which encompass technological advances such as those represented by the electronic devices in this case."[145]

[c] **Apple v. Franklin: Operating System Programs and Microcode.** In *Apple Computer*,[146] the Third Circuit confirmed computer program copyrightability, regardless of storage medium ("object code" on disks, ROM chips directly implementable on a computer, or human perceivable source code) and program nature (operating system or user application).[147]

Apple, the pioneering personal computer manufacturer, sold over 400,000 Apple II computers. Both Apple and independent developers provide computer programs ("software") that run on the Apple II. Franklin manufactured and sold the "ACE 100," designed to be "Apple II compatible" in the sense that it would run programs written for the Apple II. Apple sued Franklin, alleging copyright infringement of fourteen computer programs as well as patent infringement, unfair competition, and misappropriation. The parties characterized the fourteen programs as "operating system programs." "Application programs usually perform a specific task for the computer user, such as word processing, checkbook balancing, or playing a game. In contrast, operating system programs generally manage the internal functions of the computer or facilitate use of application programs."[148]

Apple moved for a preliminary injunction on the copyright claim. After a three-day hearing, the district court found that Franklin's programs were virtually identical to Apple's; variations "were minor, consisting merely of such things as deletion of reference to Apple or its copyright notice." Franklin's DOS program did add "16 bytes (out of 9000) that allowed use of upper and lower case.") Franklin admitted copying Apple's programs, contending it was not feasible to write a compatible operating system program without copying.

---

[145] 685 F.2d at 877, 215 U.S.P.Q. at 410.

[146] Apple Computer, Inc. v. Franklin Computer Corp., 714 F.2d 1240, 219 U.S.P.Q. 113 (3d Cir. 1983), *cert. dismissed*, 464 U.S. 1033 (1984).

[147] *Accord* Cable/Home Communication Corp. v. Network Productions Inc., 902 F.2d 829, 843, 15 U.S.P.Q.2d 1001, 1010 (11th Cir. 1990) ("We find persuasive . . . the reasoning of the Third Circuit in *Franklin*, analyzing not only the copyrightability of a program embedded on a ROM (Read Only Memory) or semi-conductor chip inserted into the circuitry of a computer, but also the copyright protection for a program communicating with the operating system of a computer as opposed to the user."); Apple Computer, Inc. v. Formula International, Inc., 725 F.2d 521, 525, 221 U.S.P.Q. 762, 765 (9th Cir. 1984) ("Apple introduced evidence that numerous methods exist for writing the programs involved here, and Formula does not contend to the contrary. . . . Thus, Apple seeks to copyright only its particular set of instructions, not the underlying computer process. . . . Formula provides absolutely no authority for its contention that the 'expression' required in order for a computer program to be eligible for copyright protection is expression that must be communicated to the computer user when the program is run on a computer. . . . The computer program when written embodies expression; never has the Copyright Act required that the expression be communicated to a particular audience.").

[148] 714 F.2d at 1243, 219 U.S.P.Q. at 116.

Despite the evidence of copying and substantial similarity, the district court denied a preliminary injunction.[149] To obtain such an injunction, the plaintiff must show, *inter alia*, a reasonable probability of success on the merits, irreparable injury, the improbability of harm to other interested persons, and consistency with the public interest. The district court found that there was "some doubt as to the copyrightability of the programs described in this litigation." It also found that Apple, a large company, was "better suited to withstand whatever injury it might sustain during litigation than is Franklin to withstand the effects of a preliminary injunction."

The Third Circuit reversed. It read the district court opinion as presenting four legal issues: "(1) whether copyright can exist in a computer program expressed in object code, (2) whether copyright can exist in a computer program embedded on a ROM, (3) whether copyright can exist in an operating system program, and (4) whether independent irreparable harm must be shown for a preliminary injunction in copyright infringement actions."[150]

[i] *Protectability of Programs in Object Code.* The court found authority for object code protectability in *Williams*, its video game decision. Also, the Copyright Act, as amended in 1980, defines a computer program as a set of instructions to be used "directly or indirectly" in a computer, and "only instructions expressed in object code can be used 'directly' by the computer." The district court's concern whether a computer program in object code can be classified as a "literary work" had no merit because prior court decisions define copyrightable literature broadly. For example, *Reiss* held copyrightable a code book of coined words designed for cable use.[151]

[ii] *Protectability of Programs on Machine-Readable "Chips."* *Williams* also resolved the second issue, holding that "the statutory requirement of 'fixation,' . . . is satisfied through the embodiment of the expression in the ROM devices."

[iii] *Protectability of Operating System Programs.* *Williams* did not resolve the third issue, the "heart of Franklin's position"—whether "computer operating system programs . . . are not the proper subject of copyright regardless of the language or medium in which they are fixed"—because *Williams* involved an "applications" program, a video game, not an operating system. In *Apple*, the Third Circuit upheld the copyrightability of computer program operating systems.

(1) *Operating Systems as Processes.* The court rejected Franklin's argument, based on *Baker* and Copyright Act Section 102(b), that an operating system is an

---

[149] Apple Computer, Inc. v. Franklin Computer Corp., 545 F. Supp. 812, 215 U.S.P.Q. 935 (E.D. Pa. 1982), *rev'd,* 714 F.2d 1240, 219 U.S.P.Q. 113 (3d Cir. 1983), *cert. denied,* 464 U.S. 1033 (1984).

[150] As to irreparable harm, the appeals court applied the rule that "a showing of a prima facie case of copyright infringement or reasonable likelihood of success on the merits raises a presumption of irreparable harm." 714 F.2d at 1254, 219 U.S.P.Q. at 125. *See* § 4F[5][a][i](2). Alternatively, Apple produced substantial evidence of irreparable harm in that Franklin's "wholesale copying" would jeopardize Apple's investment in the development of its programs. That the injunction might have a "devastating effect" on Franklin's business was not determinative; "If that were the correct standard, then a knowing infringer would be permitted to construct its business around its infringement."

[151] Reiss v. National Quotation Bureau, Inc., 276 F. 717 (S.D.N.Y. 1921).

uncopyrightable "process" or "system."[152] This argument was inconsistent with Franklin's concession that applications programs are copyrightable. A "literal construction" of *Baker*'s language on copying for use would support Franklin's position precluding copyrightability if the work is put to a utilitarian use, but the Supreme Court in *Mazer* rejected that interpretation.[153]

> "[T]he most convincing item leading us to reject Franklin's argument is that the statutory definition of a computer program as a set of instructions to be used in a computer in order to bring about a certain result, 17 U.S.C. § 101, makes no distinction between application programs and operating programs."[154]

(2) *Idea and Expression—Achieving Compatibility.* Alternatively, Franklin relied on the idea-expression dichotomy. The Third Circuit directed that the district court on remand make findings "as to whether some or all of Apple's operating programs represent the only means of expression of the idea underlying them." With an operating system program, the line between idea and expression "must be a pragmatic one, which also keeps in consideration 'the preservation of the balance between competition and protection reflected in the patent and copyright laws.' "[155] The focus is "on whether the idea is capable of various modes of expression."

> "If other programs can be written or created which perform the same function as Apple's operating system program, then that program is an expression of the idea and hence copyrightable. In essence, this inquiry is no different than that made to determine whether the expression and idea have merged, which has been stated to occur where there are no or few other ways of expressing a particular idea."[156]

In an enigmatic paragraph, the court commented on what is the "idea" or "function," suggesting but not clearly holding that "idea" or "function" does not include achievement of compatibility.

> "Franklin claims that whether or not the programs can be rewritten, there are a limited 'number of ways to arrange operating systems to enable a computer

---

[152] *See* § 4C[1][d].

[153] *Mazer* is discussed in § 4C[3]. The Third Circuit's suggestion that *Mazer* altered *Baker* as to copying for use is not accurate. *Mazer* involved an artistic work, a sculpture, embedded in a useful article, a lamp, *by the copyright owner*. The Supreme Court held that such intended commercial use did not constitute a misuse of the copyright in the artistic work. The *Baker* statement addresses copying for use of nonartistic ideas (or expressions thereof) *by a potential infringer*. *Baker* expressly cautioned that its observations as to copying for use "are not intended to apply to ornamental designs, or pictorial illustrations addressed to the taste." 101 U.S. at 103.

[154] 714 F.2d at 1252, 219 U.S.P.Q. at 123.

[155] 714 F.2d at 1253, 219 U.S.P.Q. at 124, quoting Herbert Rosenthal Jewelry Corp. v. Kaplakian, 446 F.2d 738, 742, 170 U.S.P.Q. 557, 559 (9th Cir. 1971).

In other areas, the courts draw the line between protectable elements and unprotectable elements pragmatically to balance the interests in competition and the preservation of intellectual property rights. *See, e.g.,* § 4C[3] (copyrightability of three-dimensional designs), and § 5C[2][c] (trademark rights in packaging and product configuration).

[156] 714 F.2d at 1253, 219 U.S.P.Q. at 124. For a discussion of idea-expression merger, see § 4C[1][d][iii].

to run the vast body of Apple-compatible software' . . . . This claim has no pertinence to either the idea/expression dichotomy or merger. The idea which may merge with the expression, thus making the copyright unavailable, is the idea which is the subject of the expression. The idea of one of the operating system programs is, for example, how to translate source code into object code. If other methods of expressing that idea are not foreclosed as a practical matter, then there is no merger. *Franklin may wish to achieve total compatibility with independently developed application programs written for the Apple II, but that is a commercial and competitive objective which does not enter into the somewhat metaphysical issue of whether particular ideas and expression have merged."*[157]

[iv]   *Microcode.* In *NEC,*[158] the district court extended *Apple* to "microcode,"[159] which "consists of a series of instructions that tell a microprocessor which of its thousands of transistors to actuate in order to perform the tasks directed by the macroinstruction set."[160] Microcode fits within Section 101's definition of a computer program.

Intel's 8086 and 8088 microprocessor microcode consisted of approximately 90 microroutines or microsequences. The court rejected NEC's argument that many of Intel's microsequences were uncopyrightable because they were short sequences, consisting of a few obvious steps dictated by functional considerations (the architecture of the microprocessor). Such may be true of several of the microsequences, but they are only small segments of the copyrighted microcode. Overall, Intel's microcode exceeds "the required modicum of originality."

It rejected NEC's argument that the microcode was an integral part of the computer itself and thus could not be a "set of statements to be used *in* a computer" within

---

[157] 714 F.2d at 1253, 219 U.S.P.Q. at 124. (Emphasis added.)

[158] NEC Corp. v. Intel Corp., 10 U.S.P.Q.2d 1177 (N.D. Calif. 1989). *See also* Allen-Myland Inc. v. International Business Machines Corp., 746 F. Supp. 520, 16 U.S.P.Q.2d 1817 (E.D. Pa. 1990).

[159] The lower court in *Apple v. Franklin* quoted a passage on microcode from T. Kidder, The Soul of a New Machine 97-101 (1981):

"At the level of the microcode, physical and abstract meet. The microcode controls the actual circuits. . . . Indeed, the physical machine responds only to microcode. It was microcode, at bottom, that caused [the computer] to translate [the division symbol] into microcode. In this sense, the computer chases its tail. . . . Writing microcode, however, is no simple task. The code is by definition intricate. To make the machine execute just one of its two hundred or three hundred basic instructions, the coder usually has to *plan the passage of hundreds of signals through hundreds of gates.* Limited storage space forces the coder to economize—to make one microinstruction accomplish more than one task, for example. At the same time, though, the coder must take care that one microinstruction does not foul up the performance of another."

Apple Computer, Inc. v. Franklin Computer Corp., 545 F. Supp. 812, 822 n.14, 215 U.S.P.Q. 935, 944 n.14 (E.D. Pa. 1982). The Third Circuit noted: "Apple introduced testimony that none of the works [at issue in that case] contain 'microcode.' " 714 F.2d at 1249 n.7, 219 U.S.P.Q. at 120 n.7.

[160] 10 U.S.P.Q.2d at 1178.

the meaning of the Section 101 definition of a computer program.[161] *Apple* held that the Copyright Act makes no distinctions among computer programs based on function.

Finally, it rejected NEC's argument that the idea and expression and merger doctrines precluded microcode copyrightability because hardware constraints severely limit the ways in which the ideas in microcode can be expressed. "[A]s a matter of practicality, the issue of the limited number of ways to express an idea is relevant to infringement, but should not be the basis for denying the initial copyright."[162]

[d] **Scope of Protection.** Most early computer software copyright cases involved either mechanical or near-literal copying of code. Later cases deal with allegations of infringement through nonliteral similarity or copying of a program's "look and feel," including its user interface.[163] These cases probe computer program copyright's limits. Theoretically, copying the functional aspects or the "ideas" of a computer program is not copyright infringement, and protection for functional features and ideas is available only under the patent system. Some courts depart from these principles and accord broad protection to computer programs.

[i] *Nonliteral Similarity of Coding—"Structure, Sequence and Organization."* In *Whelan*, [164] the Third Circuit held that computer program copyright protection

---

[161] *See also* NEC Corp. v. Intel Corp., 645 F. Supp. 590, 593, 1 U.S.P.Q.2d 1492, 1494 (N.D. Calif. 1986) ("Defendant's microprograms are a set of statements used, directly or indirectly to bring about the result of interpreting the INTEL 8086 instruction set. . . . Storage of microprograms in Read Only Memory (ROM) which is located in the control section of the computer does not render the microprogram part of the control of the computer. The control section of the computer executes instructions. A microprogram directs the control section to interpret or execute instructions. . . . The loading of an 8086 program into a ROM is accomplished in the same manner as would attend upon the loading of an application program into a ROM. . . . The control signals generated in a nonmicroprogrammed computer perform the same kind of tasks generated in a microprogrammed computer.").

[162] 10 U.S.P.Q.2d at 1179. The court also found noninfringement because Intel's copyrighted microcode and NEC's accused microcode were not substantially similar overall and similarities as to particular microsequences were attributable to hardware constraints. NEC had a license under Intel's patents covering aspects of the 8086 and 8088 chip architecture. The court noted:

> "Having granted to NEC a license to duplicate the hardware of its 8086/88 to the extent comprehended by the Intel patents, and having conceded at trial that NEC had a right to duplicate the hardware of the 8086/88 because it was not otherwise protected by Intel, Intel is in no position to challenge NEC's right to use the aspects of Intel's microcode that are mandated by such hardware." 10 U.S.P.Q.2d at 1188.

It concluded that "the expression of the ideas underlying the shorter, simpler microroutines . . . may be protected only against virtually identical copying." 10 U.S.P.Q.2d at 1189.

Alternatively, the court held that Intel had forfeited its copyrights by failure to comply with the Copyright Act's notice requirements. *See* § 4D[2].

[163] *See generally* P. Goldstein, Copyright § 2.15.3 (1989).

[164] Whelan Associates, Inc. v. Jaslow Dental Laboratory, Inc., 797 F.2d 1222, 230 U.S.P.Q. 481 (3d Cir. 1986).

extended beyond literal code to a program's structural aspects.[165] Whelan developed "Dentalab," a program for handling bookkeeping and administrative tasks of a dental prosthetics company. Dentalab was written in "EDL" (Event Driven Language) to run on an IBM Series One computer. Later, Jaslow developed "Dentcom PC," which performed essentially the same operations as Dentalab. Dentcom PC was written in BASIC to run on personal computers. Whelan sued for copyright infringement. The district court determined that Jaslow did not own an interest in the Whelan copyright even though Whelan wrote the program for Jaslow pursuant to contract, that Jaslow did not write his computer program independently, and that Jaslow's program was substantially similar to Whelan's copyrighted program. The sole issue on appeal was whether the district court erred in finding substantial similarity.

The Third Circuit affirmed. First, it related some "technological background." Creation of a computer program "often takes place in several steps": (1) "identifying the problem that the computer programmer is trying to solve"; (2) outlining "a solution," which "can take the form of a flowchart, which will break down the solution into a series of smaller units called 'subroutines' or 'modules,' each of which deals with elements of the larger problem";[166] (3) refining the program structure by deciding "what data is needed, where along the program's operations the data should be introduced, how the data should be inputted, and how it should be combined with other data";[167] and (4) coding the detailed design of the program, that is, writing source code in a program language, such as EDL or BASIC, and then translating the source code into object code by compilation, translation or assembly. "[T]he coding process is a comparatively small part of programming." The bulk of Whelan's time in writing Dentalab involved organizing the modules, subroutines, and data arrangements; coding consumed a comparatively small amount of time.

Second, it addressed the "appropriate test for substantial similarity in computer program cases." The "ordinary observer" test,[168] which was developed for fictional and artistic works and does not permit expert testimony on similarity, "is of doubtful

---

[165] The computer software copyright issue dealt with in *Whelan* has come to be known as that of the protectability of the "structure, sequence, and/or organization" of a program ("SSO"). The *Whelan* court stated that "We use the terms 'structure,' 'sequence,' and 'organization' interchangeably when referring to computer programs, we intend them to be synonymous. . . . " 797 F.2d at 1225 n.1, 230 U.S.P.Q. at 481, n.1.

[166] "A program's efficiency depends in large part on the arrangements of its modules and subroutines; although two programs could produce the same result, one might be more efficient because of different internal arrangements of modules and subroutines. Because efficiency is a prime concern in computer programs . . . the arrangement of modules and subroutines is a critical factor for any programmer." 797 F.2d at 1230, 230 U.S.P.Q. at 485.

[167] "The arrangement of data is accomplished by means of data files . . . and is affected by the details of the program's subroutines and modules, for different arrangements of subroutines and modules may require data in different forms. Once again, there are numerous ways the programmer can solve the data-organization problems she or he faces. Each solution may have particular characteristics—efficiencies or inefficiencies, conveniences or quirks—that differentiate it from other solutions and make the program more or less desirable." 797 F.2d at 1230, 230 U.S.P.Q. at 486.

[168] See § 4F[2][a][ii].

value in cases involving computer programs on account of the programs' complexity and unfamiliarity to most members of the public." [169]

Third, it considered "whether mere similarity in the overall structure of programs can be the basis for a copyright infringement."

> "By analogy to other literary works, it would . . . appear that the copyrights of computer programs can be infringed even absent copying of the literal elements of the program." [170]

Jaslow argued that the structure of a program is by definition its "idea," which cannot be protected by copyright. The court derived from the case law the following rule for distinguishing idea from expression in the context of computer programs:

> "[T]he purpose or function of a utilitarian work would be the work's idea, and everything that is not necessary to that purpose or function would be part of the expression of the idea." [171]

The court found support in *Baker*,[172] doctrines relating to *scenes a faire* and fact-intensive works,[173] economic considerations,[174] and jurisprudential concerns.[175] It

---

[169] 797 F.2d at 1230, 230 U.S.P.Q. at 486. Expert testimony has played a significant role in determining substantial similarity of expression in computer program copyright infringement actions. For example, in Pearl Systems Inc. v. Competition Electronics, Inc., 10 U.S.P.Q.2d 20 (S.D. Fla. 1988), the successful copyright owner used two experts. One was asked to write a suitable program to carry out the functions of the computing device (a programmed pistol shot timing device). The expert produced a program that differed from that of either the accused or the protected program. A second expert examined the source codes of all three versions.

By way of contrast, in NEC Corp. v. Intel Corp., 10 U.S.P.Q.2d 1177 (N.D. Calif. 1989), discussed in § 4C[2][c][iv], the accused infringer established the absence of infringement of plaintiff's copyrighted microcode for a microprocessor by (1) having an expert prepare a "Clean Room microcode," that is, one prepared with only the use of functional and hardware specifications, and (2) showing that the similarities between the Clean Room microcode and the accused microcode were at least as great as the similarities between the accused microcode and the copyrighted microcode. The court interpreted this as showing that the similarities between the protected and the accused programs flowed from hardware and functional constraints, not from copying protected expression.

[170] 797 F.2d at 1234, 230 U.S.P.Q. at 489.

[171] 797 F.2d at 1236, 230 U.S.P.Q. at 490.

[172] See § 4C[1][d][i].

[173] See § 4C[1][d][iv].

[174] Noting that "the more significant costs in computer programming are those attributable to developing the structure and logic of the program," the court asserted that its ruling "would provide the proper incentive for programmers by protecting their most valuable efforts, while not giving them a stranglehold over the development of new computer devices that accomplish the same end." 797 F.2d at 1237, 230 U.S.P.Q. at 491.

It considered and rejected the principal economic argument against extending protection beyond literal code: "that computer programs are so intricate . . . that they are almost impossible to copy except literally, and that anyone who attempts to copy the structure of a program without copying its literal elements must expend a tremendous amount of effort and creativity[, which should not be discouraged or penalized.]" In the court's view, "one can approximate a program and thereby gain a significant advantage over competitors even

disagreed with Jaslow's argument that the CONTU report supported limiting computer program copyright to a program's literal elements,[176] and disagreed with one commentator's assertion[177] that "progress in computer technology or technique is qualitatively different from progress in other areas of science or the arts," being more dependent upon the ability to use prior works as "stepping stones." "[T]he copyright law has always recognized and tried to accommodate the fact that all intellectual pioneers build on the work of their predecessors."[178]

The court found that "the purpose of the utilitarian Dentalab program was to aid in the business operations of a dental laboratory" and that "the structure of the program was not essential to that task: there are other programs on the market . . . that perform the same functions but have different structures and designs."[179]

---

though additional work is needed to complete the program." Further, "the fact that it will take a great deal of effort to copy a copyrighted work does not mean that the copier is not a copyright infringer." 797 F.2d at 1237, 230 U.S.P.Q. at 491.

[175] It noted a commentator's argument that "the concept of structure in computer program is too vague" but concluded: "[I]t is surely true that limiting copyright protection to computers' literal codes would be simpler and yield more definite answers than does our answer here. Ease of application is not, however, a sufficient counterweight to the considerations we have adduced. . . . " 797 F.2d at 1237–38, 230 U.S.P.Q. at 492.

[176] The court found that the CONTU Report did not unequivocally advocate a literal similarity standard. Further, it denied that CONTU was binding upon it as "a surrogate legislative history" of the 1980 Amendments, especially because "the only statutory provision relevant to this case is § 102(b), . . . in which no changes were made as a result of the CONTU Report." 797 F.2d at 1241, 230 U.S.P.Q. at 495.

[177] Note, *Copyright Infringement of Computer Programs: A Modification of the Substantial Similarity Test*, 68 Minn. L. Rev. 1264 (1984).

[178] 797 F.2d at 1238, 230 U.S.P.Q. at 492.

[179] *Id.*

The court agreed with SAS Institute, Inc. v. S & H Computer Systems, Inc., 605 F. Supp. 816, 225 U.S.P.Q. 916 (M.D. Tenn. 1985) (defendant adapted plaintiff's copyrighted statistical programs to run on a different computer system; "the copying proven at trial does not affect only the specific lines of code cited by [plaintiff's expert]. Rather, to the extent that it represents copying of the organization and structural details of [plaintiff's programs], such copying pervades the entire [accused] product.") and disagreed with Judge Higginbotham's "scholarly opinion" in Synercom Technology, Inc. v. University Computing Co., 462 F. Supp. 1003, 199 U.S.P.Q. 537 (N.D. Tex. 1978) (holding "input forms"—the configurations and collations of the information entered into a computer program—to be ideas, not expression, and hence unprotectable). *See* § 4C[2][d][i]. It answered Judge Higginbotham's "powerful rhetorical question—if sequencing and ordering [are] expression, what separable idea is being expressed?":

> "[T]he idea is the efficient organization of a dental laboratory. . . . Because there are a variety of program structures through which that idea can be expressed, the structure is not a necessary incident to the idea." 797 F.2d at 1240, 230 U.S.P.Q. at 494.

Whelan's broad definition of a work's purpose or function in terms of its single overall objective is much criticized. With the unprotectable "idea" so generally defined, lower level but functional program characteristics become protectable expression.

Cf. Lotus Development Corp. v. Paperback Software International, 740 F. Supp. 37, 15 U.S.P.Q.2d 1577 (D. Mass. 1990):

Finally, it rejected Jaslow's argument that its program is not substantially similar to Whelan's program, even assuming that the scope of computer program copyright protection is not limited to literal coding. It found no error in the trial court's evaluation of expert testimony on the two programs' file structure,[180] screen outputs[181] and subroutine similarity.[182]

Whelan's approach, which defines a program's "idea" abstractly in terms of its overall function and finds copyrightable expression in the original structure or

"The advocate of broad copyrightability . . . has an incentive to urge that the court conceive the 'idea' in a very generalized sense; then many different expressions of the idea would be possible, and protection might be claimed for the work. The advocate of freedom to copy—and of narrow copyrightability—has an incentive to urge that the court conceive the 'idea' in a very particularized sense; then only one or a few expressions of an idea defined in such particularized terms would be possible, and no copyright protection for those few expressions would be available because the idea and expression would merge completely, or nearly so. Such extreme positions would fail to assist the court in determining, for purposes of the first element, where properly to place the idea along the abstractions scale.

"There is risk for each advocate, however, in yielding too readily to these respective incentives. The argument of an advocate who presses too far in one or the other of these directions of generality or specificity in defining the idea will not only lose the argument advanced but also lose credibility for later advancing a more sensible alternative that proposes a less extreme but still favorable position along the scale. Upon reflection, then, advocates on both sides will be—or at least should be—encouraged to moderate their ultra-contentious and extreme positions in favor of more supportable propositions that will more sharply focus the issue for adjudication." 740 F. Supp. at 62, 15 U.S.P.Q.2d at 1594.

[180] Jaslow argued that file structures are irrelevant to copyright infringement because they are analogous to blank forms, which are not copyrightable, see § 4C[1][d][ii], but the court disagreed, citing cases upholding copyright in forms that "are sufficiently innovative that their arrangement of information is itself informative." 797 F.2d at 1242, 230 U.S.P.Q. at 496.

[181] The district court considered the two programs' screen output similarities to be probative of substantial similarity of the programs themselves. The accused infringer argued that screen outputs, though a result of a only a small portion of the programs, were vivid and easily understood and might be given disproportionate weight by the trier of fact. The Third Circuit held that screen output similarities had some, limited probative value and were not so prejudicial as to justify exclusion.

In *Whelan*, the copyright owner did not assert infringement of any separate copyright in its screen displays. Thus, the Third Circuit did *not* address copyright protection for screen displays and "user interfaces." *See* § 4C[2][d][ii].

[182] Whelan's expert testified as to the similarity of five subroutines. Jaslow argued that substantial similarity of the programs' *structures* cannot be established by a comparison of only a small fraction of the two works. The Third Circuit disagreed, noting that in copyright law generally "[t]here is no general requirement that most of each of two works be compared before a court can conclude that they are substantially similar:" "the court must make a qualitative, not quantitative, judgment about the character of the work as a whole and the importance of the substantially similar portions of the work." 797 F.2d at 1245, 230 U.S.P.Q. at 498.

sequencing of a program that achieves but is not dictated by that function, has not met with universal approval by other courts.[183]

In *Plains Cotton Cooperative,*[184] the Fifth Circuit affirmed denial of a preliminary injunction against distribution of "GEMS," a cotton price and supply information program for personal computers that emulated the functions of "TELCOT," a program for mainframe computers. The accused GEMS program was created by former employees of the plaintiff. The court noted testimony in the record (1) "that the similarity between the two programs exists on a level not protected by [plaintiff's] copyright;" and (2) "that a mainframe program . . . could be altered to run on a personal computer only with enormous changes so that rewriting the programs would be faster than modifying them." The court favored *Synercom Technology* over *Whelan*:

> "We decline to embrace *Whelan* for two reasons. First, the issue is presented to us on review of a denial of a motion for preliminary injunction. Thus, the record is only partially developed, and our review is one step removed from the actual merits of the case. Second, appellees presented evidence that many of the similarities between the GEMS and Telcot programs are dictated by the externalities of the cotton market. . . . The record supports the inference that market factors play a significant role in determining the sequence and organization of cotton marketing software, and we decline to hold that those patterns cannot constitute 'ideas' in a computer context."[185]

By "externalities of the cotton market," the court meant "standardized information," that is, the information that appears on the industry's "cotton recap" sheet: "the facts

---

[183] Some decisions follow Whelan in granting protection to computer program structure. *E.g.,* Pearl Systems Inc. v. Competition Electronics Inc., 8 U.S.P.Q.2d 1520 (S.D. Fla. 1988) (finding copyright infringement because defendant's "shot timer" for pistol shooting emulated plaintiff's "shot review" subroutine and "part time entry" subroutine; "A subroutine is basically a discrete part of a computer program with a readily identifiable task. . . . The part time entry subroutine was designed to provide a method for the user to set a part time. That is the idea. The shot review subroutine was designed to allow the user to review the shots he or she has fired and to learn of the time that elapsed between each shot. That is also an idea. The subroutines themselves are expressions of those ideas;" "[B]y protecting the rights of programmers to their developments, programmers will be encouraged to develop new modes of 'computer thinking,' knowing that their work product is safe from the vagaries of program copiers.").

See generally Manufacturers Technologies Inc. v. Cams Inc., 706 F. Supp. 984, 991 n.12, 10 U.S.P.Q.2d 1321, 1326 n.12 (D. Conn. 1989) ("To generalize broadly, courts examining this issue have fallen into two schools of thought. The first, favoring broad protection, has determined that the copyright in a computer program extends not only to the program's literal elements, the source and object code, but also to the 'structure, sequence, and organization' of the program which may include the screen displays. . . . The second school of thought favors withholding copyright protection for a program's user interface and/or structure, sequence and organization, classifying those program elements as uncopyrightable ideas or functional imperatives.").

[184] Plains Cotton Cooperative Association of Lubbock, Texas v. Goodpasture Computer Service Inc., 807 F.2d 1256, 1 U.S.P.Q.2d 1635 (5th Cir.), *cert. denied,* 484 U.S. 821 (1987).

[185] 807 F.2d at 1262, 1 U.S.P.Q.2d at 1640.

of this case fit squarely within *Synercom's* powerful analogy to the hypothetical development of gear stick patterns."[186]

In *Johnson Controls*,[187] the Ninth Circuit stated: "Whether the nonliteral components of a program, including the structure, sequence, organization and user interface, are protected depends on whether, on the particular facts of each case, the component in question qualifies as an expression of an idea, or an idea itself." It affirmed the district court's finding for preliminary injunction purposes that the structure, sequence, and organization of plaintiff's JC-5000S wastewater treatment plant control program was expression. The evidence showed that "there may be room for individualized expression in the accomplishment of common functions" and "some discretion and opportunity for creativity exist in the structure."

[ii] *Screen Displays—User Interfaces.* The video games cases recognized that computer program generated images and sounds, to the extent they embody original expression, are copyrightable as audiovisual works separate from the program itself.[188] One who copies the game by writing a different computer program infringes the audiovisual copyright.

Recognition of video game display copyright did not stretch copyright principles because game images and sounds are the kind of fanciful graphical and audio expressions that have always been protectable by copyright. Attempts to extend copyright to textual and graphical screen displays of other types of computer programs ran into several constraints of copyright law, including the bans on protection for ideas, or useful articles designs, processes and methods, and blank forms.

District court decisions uphold copyright claims on some aspects of screen displays and user interfaces. In *Broderbund Software*,[189] plaintiff's program "Print Shop" was a menu-driven program which ran on Apple personal computers and enabled users to create and print cards and banners. While negotiating with plaintiff for a license to make an IBM PC-compatible version of the program, the defendant had a programmer begin copying "Print Shop." After the negotiations broke down, defendant had the programmer complete the project. The programmer used various screen menus of Print Shop and adopted its "user interface" for picture editing to save time—even though he originally had another user interface in mind. When defendant released its "Printmaster," plaintiff sued for copyright infringement. The court found infringement. First, it found no idea-expression merger because a third-party program, "Sticky-Bear Printer," achieved the same functions with a different set and sequence of menu screens. Second, it found that "the structure, sequence, and layout of the audiovisual displays in 'Print Shop' were dictated primarily by artistic and aesthetic considerations, and not by utilitarian or mechanical ones." Third, applying the ordinary observer test of substantial similarity, rather than *Whelan's* "integrated" test involving expert testimony and analytical dissection, the court found infringement:

---

[186] *See* § 4C[2][d][iv].

[187] Johnson Controls Inc. v. Phoenix Control Systems Inc., 886 F.2d 1173, 1175, 12 U.S.P.Q.2d 1566, 1569 (9th Cir. 1989).

[188] *See* § 4C[2][b].

[189] Broderbund Software, Inc. v. Unison World, Inc., 648 F. Supp. 1127, 231 U.S.P.Q. 700 (N.D. Calif. 1986).

"The ordinary observer could hardly avoid being struck by the eerie resemblance between the screens of the two programs."[190]

In *Digital Communications,*[191] plaintiff's program "CROSSTALK XVI" was a personal computer modem communications system. Defendant developed a CROSS-TALK "clone," "MIRROR," after receiving legal counsel's advice that CROSS-TALK's source and object code were copyrightable but that use of similar or even identical screen displays would not be copyright infringement. In December of 1985, defendant began marketing its program. That same month, plaintiff, which had previously obtained copyright registrations on its programs and its user manual, filed an application to register its "status screen"[192] as a compilation of program terms.[193] After the Copyright Office issued the registrations, the plaintiff sued defendant for infringement of its copyrighted status screen. The court found infringement of the copyright on the screen display as a compilation of commands but not of the copyright on the underlying program. Preliminarily, it decided that "copyright protection of a computer program does not extend to screen displays generated by

---

[190] The court explained the similarities as follows:

"In general, the sequence of the screens and the choices presented, the layout of the screens, and the method of feedback to the user are all substantially similar. Specifically, the following similarities exist, *inter alia*: the structures of the 'Main Menu' screens; the 'staggered' layout of 3-2-3-2-3, totaling thirteen graphics; the 'tiled' layout of 5 × 7 in both programs; the second screen in the 'Custom Layout' function, in which the word 'place' is highlighted and the word 'remove' is inversely highlighted in both programs; the fact that the 'tiled' option disappears in both programs in the medium-size graphic mode; the use of only left and right arrow keys on both keyboards, despite the fact that the IBM-keyboard has up and down arrow capability; the offering in both programs of only three types of lines (solid, outline, and three-dimensional); and the fact that both programs require the user to create the front of the printed product before creating the inside of it." 648 F. Supp. at 1137, 231 U.S.P.Q. at 706.

[191] Digital Communications v. Softklone Distributing Corp., 659 F. Supp. 449, 2 U.S.P.Q.2d 1385 (N.D. Ga. 1987).

[192] The district court described the plaintiff's status screen as follows:

"The 'status screen' screen display . . . contains in its upper portion an arrangement and grouping of parameter/command terms under various descriptive headings. Next to each of the parameter/command terms are values, either numerical or verbal. The value of each parameter/command reflects the value at which the program is operating and is either selected by the user or by the computer program ('default settings'), e.g., the number 300 next to the 'SPeed' parameter/command indicates the byte or baud rate at which the computer program is communicating with other computers. Two letters of each parameter/command term are capitalized and highlighted. By typing those two letters, the user can effectuate that specific command.

"The lower portion of the status screen display, excluding the bottom line, called the 'window,' can display a wide variety of text including anything the user might wish to cause to appear there. Upon typing in a 'HElp' command, the user can call up into the 'window' a list of all the Crosstalk XVI parameter/command terms.

"The bottom line of the status screen is the 'command' line. On this line, the user can enter 'commands' or instructions to the computer to change the values at which it operates." 659 F. Supp. at 452–53, 2 U.S.P.Q.2d at 1385–86.

[193] For a discussion of compilations, see § 4C[1][b].

the program," disagreeing with *Broderbund*.[194] After rejecting the defendant's reliance on the idea-expression dichotomy[195] and the "blank forms" doctrine,[196] the court held that the status screen was copyrightable "to the extent of its arrangement and design of parameter/command terms."

> "The specific placement, arrangement and design of the parameter/command terms on the status screen is neither arbitrary nor predetermined but, rather, is the result of extensive original human authorship. While some of the choices

---

[194] It stated:

> "[S]creen displays generated by computer programs are not direct 'copies' or 'reproductions' of the literary or substantive content of the computer programs. This distinction results from the fact that the same screen can be created by a variety of separate and independent computer programs. It is somewhat illogical to conclude that a screen can be a 'copy' of many different programs. Therefore, it is this court's opinion that a computer program's copyright protection does not extend to the program's screen displays and that copying of a program's screen displays, without evidence of copying of the program's source code, object code, sequence, organization or structure, does not state a claim of infringement." 659 F. Supp. at 455–56, 2 U.S.P.Q.2d at 1388.

On the other hand, the court agreed that, under M. Kramer Mfg. Co. v. Andrews, 783 F.2d 421, 228 U.S.P.Q. 705 (4th Cir. 1986), a computer program is a copy of a screen display and a copyright on the latter protects the former. This "anomaly" is created by the "unusual nature of computers."

> "The distinction between programs and screen displays lies in the fact that if one has a fixed computer program, one can, with the aid of a computer, repeatedly produce the same screen display. Thus, a computer program is a copy of a screen display. The converse, however, is not true. If one has a fixed screen display, one cannot, even with the aid of a machine, repeatedly create the same program (source or object code) as many different programs can create the same screen display." 659 F. Supp. at 456, 2 U.S.P.Q.2d at 1389.

In a 1988 Policy Statement, the Copyright Office responded to this portion of *Softklone* by indicating that it would only accept a single registration application for a computer program, which would cover all copyrightable portions of the work, including screen displays. *See infra.*

[195] The court sorted out expression from idea in the status screen as follows:

> "Certain aspects . . . are clearly 'ideas' which any other party . . . [can] legally copy. The use of a screen to reflect the status of the program is an 'idea;' the use of a command driven program is an 'idea;' and the typing of two symbols to activate a specific command is an 'idea.' All of these elements relate to how the computer program receives commands or instructions from the user and how operationally the computer program reflects the results of those commands. Certain aspects of the status screen, however, are unrelated to how the computer program operates and are 'expression.' The arrangement of the parameter/command terms has no relation to how the computer operates. That is to say, the computer allows for any sequence in the entering of commands, e.g., first entering a 'SPeed' command and then entering a 'DAta' command has the same effect as first entering a 'DAta' command and then entering a 'SPeed' command. Likewise, the highlighting and capitalizing of two specific letters of the parameter/command terms listed on the status screen has no relation to how the status screen functions., i.e., the user need not type in two highlighted, capitalized symbols to effectuate a command." 659 F. Supp. at 460, 2 U.S.P.Q.2d at 1391.

See § 4C[1][d].

[196] *See* § 4C[1][d][ii].

of the two symbols to represent certain parameter/command terms may not be original, there was some limited evidence that other earlier programs had used the first two letters of a command term, other choices of symbols, are clearly original, e.g., 'RQ' for the 'request' command term (changed by the plaintiff to 'RQuest'). The status screen's arrangement and design of the command/parameter terms is fixed in the computer program. . . . The arrangement and design of the status screen is perceivable on the screen display."[197]

It then found infringement because the "Mirror status screen captures the 'total concept and feel' of the Crosstalk XVI status screen."[198]

In *Manufacturers Technologies*,[199] plaintiff's program "COSTIMATOR" enabled users to estimate the cost of machining a manufactured part. Defendants, who for a time were sales representatives for plaintiff, developed programs, "QUICKCOST" and "RAPIDCOST," which they promoted as "K-Mart" cost estimators rather than a "Cadillac" cost estimator (COSTIMATOR). The plaintiff registered separately (1) its computer program, (2) its user manual, which contained representations of screen displays from the program, and (3) a selection of screens (11 out of approximately 300 displays generated by the program), as compilations. The plaintiff sued defendants for copyright infringement. In an extensive opinion, the court found infringement as to some aspects of plaintiff's copyrights, including the sequence and flow of certain screens and the content of particular screens. The court found other aspects of plaintiff's screen displays to be uncopyrightable as either dictated by functional considerations or lacking originality.

In *Manufacturers Technology*, the court began by noting that the question whether "a copyright in a computer program extends to its screen displays has been the subject of some confusion and disagreement." It noted a recent change in Copyright Office policy, discussed below, stating that the Office would not thereafter grant separate registrations for computer programs and computer displays because a single copyright registration of a computer program extends copyright to both the program and the screen displays it generates. This change "calls into doubt the validity of the first part of . . . *Softklone*." The court opted for treating "the single registration of the computer program as accomplishing two interrelated yet distinct registrations: one of the program itself and one of the screen displays or user interface of that program, to the extent that each contains copyrightable subject matter."[200]

---

[197] 659 F. Supp. at 465, 2 U.S.P.Q.2d at 1395.

[198] The court noted:

"Placement of the plaintiff's status screen side-by-side with the defendants' clearly points up the substantial similarity between the two screen displays. While there is some difference between the two screens in their arrangement of the 'window' list of commands, the upper portion of the two screens are virtually identical, the single exception being the insertion of the name 'Mirror' in the place of the name 'Crosstalk' on the top line of the screen." 659 F. Supp. at 466, 2 U.S.P.Q.2d at 1396.

[199] Manufacturers Technologies Inc. v. Cams Inc., 706 F. Supp. 984, 10 U.S.P.Q.2d 1321 (D. Conn. 1989).

[200] 706 F. Supp. at 993, 10 U.S.P.Q.2d at 1327.

Treating the screen displays, individually and as an expressive "sequence and flow," as covered by the copyrighted computer program overcame the problem created by plaintiff's

The court distinguished the "external" and "internal" aspects of the copyrighted screen display compilations. As to the external aspects, that is, the "flow and sequencing" of screens, the court found infringement of copyrightable expression as to one sequence, the "creating-an-estimate" flow. The flow, which "drive[s] the user's thought processes through a number of manufacturing and engineering decisions," was not dictated solely by functional considerations, as evidenced by the testimony of both parties' experts to the effect that "cost-estimating is part science and part art" and that "the process of creating a cost-estimate is unique to the individual manually performing the estimate or the computer program and screen displays assisting in the same."

As to the internal aspects, that is, the individual screen displays, the court found that some but not all of the aspects of the individual screen displays were copyrightable and infringed. The copyrightable aspects were (1) the specific method used to identify and display the operation being utilized, the tooling, and the tooling material;[201] and (2) the "job identification" screen, which asks the user to input nine items of information about that job being performed, such not being necessarily incident to the function of identifying the job because, *inter alia*, "the fact of the redundancy [sic] in the first four items of identification listed."[202] The uncopyrightable aspects were (1) the screen display formatting style, as to which plaintiff "adopted conventions from a very narrow range of possibilities," (2) the "internal method of navigation" (e.g., use of space bar and backup key to move up and down a list of selections), as to which allowance of protection to plaintiff "would come dangerously close to allowing it to monopolize a significant portion of the easy-to-use internal navigational conventions for computers"); (3) the two-column alphabetical listing of 20 machine shop departments "because it is necessarily incident to the idea of listing the departments to which shop rates need to be assigned and because there is no original authorship in this unadorned two-column alphabetical listing;" (4) a screen displaying in four

---

submission of only a limited number of screen displays in its separate screen display compilation registration: "To hold only that the copyright of the screen display registration has been infringed is insufficient because that registration is limited only to the eleven screens submitted therewith and as such does not fully encompass, for example, the expression of the creating-an-estimate sequence." 706 F. Supp. at 1002, 10 U.S.P.Q.2d at 1335.

[201] As to this aspect of the screens, the court distinguished idea and expression as follows: "The idea of apprising the user of the status of one's efforts in cost-estimating a part is not copyrightable. Plaintiff's expression is not a necessary incident to this idea. That expression reflects selection as to what should be made part of the status report, arrangement of the terms therein, assignment of numbers to specific operations/departments and tools, and coordination in the manner of building on the status report as the user progresses through various steps." 706 F. Supp. at 996, 10 U.S.P.Q.2d at 1330.

[202] The court rejected the suggestion that the screen was uncopyrightable as a "blank form" for recording information. See § 4C[1][d][ii]. The screen "form" conveys information so as to be copyrightable expression because it (1) "suggests that identifying a job entails more than just naming the prospective purchaser . . . as is evidenced by the identification of a job number, part number, part name, and customer name" and (2) "suggests to the user . . . that certain attributes of the part to be manufactured need to be considered when identifying a particular job . . . because those attributes will affect the derivation of an estimate." 706 F. Supp. at 997, 10 U.S.P.Q.2d at 1331.

columns previously entered information and "a variety of calculations pertaining to the operations of tapping drilling and countersinking a specified number of holes" because it is necessarily incident to the idea and lacks original authorship.[203]

In *Telemarketing*,[204] the district court granted summary judgment that the "look and feel" of defendant's "Grandview" outlining program was not substantially similar in expression to plaintiff's "PC Outline" outlining program. Extracting a list of asserted similarities,[205] the court found that many of the similarities were either

---

[203] The court noted:

"The idea expressed in this display is the formatting and selection of cost-estimating data pertaining to calculations relating to specific tooling operations done in a specific department. The use of a columnar format and the use of both upper and lower case letters are not sufficient on their own to warrant copyright protection because they lack originality. . . . Nor is the listing of the items for which data is supplied subject to copyright because, in the language of the machining industry, speeds and feeds, machining times and costs, and data specific to the size, depth, and diameter of the hole is all closely related to and hence incident to the idea of displaying this data to the cost-estimator . . . that functional considerations play a significant role in determining what data is given to the user is corroborated [by another screen in the program] which also contains a list which is very similar . . . for a different operation in a different department." 706 F. Supp. at 998, 10 U.S.P.Q.2d at 1331.

[204] Telemarketing Resources v. Symantec Corp., 12 U.S.P.Q.2d 1991 (N.D. Calif. 1989).

[205] The similarities list was:

"a. Both present an opening menu labeled 'OPENING MENU.'

"b. Both opening menus are enclosed in a single line box and appear in contrasting color to the rest of the title screen.

"c. A reverse video cursor or 'highlighting bar' appears over the options on both menus. The user moves the highlighting bar with the cursor arrows and presses the enter key to select an option.

"d. In both programs, as an alternative to using the highlighting bar, the user can select any option by hitting the capitalized letter for that option.

"e. Both opening menus have the same four options, although Grandview adds three more.

"f. Both programs permit a new outline to be begun from the opening menu. The user must enter a filename for the new outline and the program then displays a main editing screen.

"g. Both programs permit the selection of an existing outline. The outline list is pulled down and the user selects an outline with the arrow and enter keys.

"h. Both editing screens have file, cursor location and window information across the top of the screen. Both use pull down menus, and display a list of the available menus on a 'menu bar' across the top of the screen. A help line is on the bottom of the screen. Both programs have a line around the screen. Plaintiffs also assert similarities in the color scheme of the programs.

"i. The main editing screens are used to edit and enter new data in both programs.

"j. A new outline element is entered by pressing the enter key while holding down the control key in both programs. The new element may be dragged around if no text is added.

"k. Pull down menus are selected by first pressing a 'menu attention' key. (In Grandview, the default menu attention key is the f10 key, in PC-Outline either the insert or '/' key is used as the menu attention key.)

"l. Once the menu attention key is pressed, the initial letter of each of the menus is highlighted. The word MENU is also displayed at the right end of the menu bar.

unprotectable ideas or were the subject of a license to the defendant.[206]

In *Lotus Development*,[207] the district court held plaintiff's Lotus 1-2-3 user interface consisting of a specific menu command system was copyrightable expression, not a useful article or idea. "To begin to get an understanding of the legally significant contrasts among an idea, non-copyrightable expressions of the idea, and a copyrightable expression," Judge Keeton reviewed four concepts: originality, functionality, obviousness,[208] and merger, concluding that "If . . . the expression of an idea has elements that go beyond all functional elements of the idea itself, and beyond the obvious, and if there are numerous other ways of expressing the non-copyrightable

"m. A menu is selected by either pressing the highlighted initial letter for the desired menu, or moving the cursor across the screen to the desired menu. The menu is displayed in reverse video in a pull down window.

"n. The form of the menu window is the same in both programs, inasmuch as it is surrounded by a single line border with a reverse video highlighting bar which is moved up and down with the arrow keys. A highlighted option is selected by pressing the enter key. Alternatively, a user can select an option by typing the appropriate code letter, usually the first letter of the option. The codes are displayed at the left of the menu as single, uppercase letters.

"o. In both programs, certain of the commands displayed on the pull down menus may be directly selected from the main editing screen through the use of special combinations of keys.

"p. Both programs offer nine pull down menus. Of those nine, four of the menu description words are identical, the other five are different, but the functions are the same or similar.

"q. Finally, plaintiffs note that 'virtually every function performed by PC-Outline is also performed by Grandview.' " 12 U.S.P.Q.2d at 1994-95.

[206] One feature was use of pull down menus. The court noted "Plaintiffs may not claim copyright protection of an idea and expression that is, if not standard, then commonplace in the computer software industry." 12 U.S.P.Q.2d at 1995. Also, "the pull down windows look different" and have different wording.

Another feature was choice of a blue background on the main editing screen.

"Defendant submitted declarations from an expert describing the functional role of the blue background 'relating to the physiology of the human eye, the characteristics of computer video displays and the connotations of the color blue for financial and corporate institutions.' The Rules of the Copyright Office also specifically exclude from copyright registration 'typographic ornamentation, lettering or coloring.' 37 C.F.R. § 202.1. Finally, the limited number of background colors for computer programs precludes copyright protection for such choices." 12 U.S.P.Q.2d at 1995-96.

[207] Lotus Development Corp. v. Paperback Software International, 740 F. Supp. 37, 15 U.S.P.Q.2d 1577 (D. Mass. 1990).

Lotus Development deals with issues of idea-expression merger, compatibility, and what is a "useful article." *See* §§ 4C[1][d][iii], 4C[2][d][iv], and 4C[3][d].

[208] "When a particular expression goes no farther than the obvious, it is inseparable from the idea itself. Protecting an expression of this limited kind would effectively amount to protection of the idea, a result inconsistent with the plain meaning of the statute." 740 F. Supp. at 58-59, 15 U.S.P.Q.2d at 1592.

Lotus's use of "obviousness," a familiar patent law concept, in a copyright context is novel, but is supported by the authorities denying copyright protection to short phrases and simple designs. *See* § 4C[1][d][v].

idea, then those elements of expression, if original and substantial, are copyrightable."[209] He distilled from principle and precedent a three-element copyrightability test:

"FIRST, in making the determination of 'copyrightability,' the decisionmaker must focus upon alternatives that counsel may suggest, or the court may conceive, *along the scale from the most generalized conception to the most particularized*, and choose some formulation—some conception or definition of the 'idea'— for the purpose of distinguishing between the idea and its expression.

"SECOND, the decisionmaker must focus upon whether an alleged expression of the idea is limited to elements essential to expression of *that* idea (or is one of only a few ways of expressing the idea) or instead includes identifiable elements of expression not essential to every expression of that idea.

"THIRD, having identified elements of expression not essential to every expression of the idea, the decisionmaker must focus on whether those elements are a substantial part of the allegedly copyrightable 'work.' "[210]

Applying the test's first element, a computer spreadsheet is both functional and obvious and therefore an unprotectable idea, but "[i]t does not follow . . . that every possible method of designing a metaphorical spreadsheet is obvious, or that no form of expressing the idea of the spreadsheet metaphor can possibly have such originality in pressing beyond the obvious as is required for copyrightability. . . ."[211] A two-line moving cursor menu is also functional and obvious and therefore an idea, but "it does not follow that every possible method of designing a menu system that includes a two-line moving cursor is uncopyrightable." Similarly, the rotated "L" spreadsheet display is an idea.

Applying the second element, the Lotus 1-2-3 user interface as a collection of specific commands and function "could be expressed in a great many if not literally unlimited number ways" and "is an original and nonobvious way of expressing a command structure."

Applying the third element, the Lotus 1-2-3 user interface is a substantial part of the copyrighted work because it is Lotus 1-2-3's "most unique element," the one that makes it so popular; defendant's effort to copy that element "is a testament to its popularity."

[iii] *Copyright Office Policy.* Computer software developers interpreted *Softklone* as mandating registration of screen displays separate from the program to assure copyright protection for the displays.[212]

Faced with "a large number of claims to register textual and pictorial screen displays separate from the program that generate them," the Copyright Office held hearings and, on June 3, 1988, issued a "Notice of Policy," confirming its existing general policy of "one registration per work" and indicating that it would "require that all copyrightable expression embodied in a computer program, including computer screen displays,

---

[209] 740 F. Supp. at 59, 15 U.S.P.Q.2d at 1592.
[210] 740 F. Supp. at 60–61, 15 U.S.P.Q.2d at 1593–94.
[211] 740 F. Supp. at 65, 15 U.S.P.Q.2d at 1597.
[212] For a discussion of Copyright Office registration, see § 4D[3][b].

and owned by the same claimant, be registered on a single application form"[213] as a textual work (Form TX), unless audiovisual authorship predominates, in which case it should be registered as a performing arts work (Form PA).

In requiring a single registration, the Office rejected arguments that computer program and screen displays involve substantially different types of authorship: "In creating copyright subject matter, it is common to merge several different types of authorship to form a single work." It also discounted the argument that separate registration of screen displays would enable users to better determine "the boundaries of the copyright claim." The increased clarity that separate registration would provide to users was offset by the advantages of single registration, including the desirability of providing "a clear, accurate, easily understandable" record, elimination of the danger of multiple infringement actions and multiple claims for statutory damages, and the reduction in filing fees to applicants and administrative burdens on the Office. The Office hoped its policy would assist the courts in determining the scope of computer software copyright protection.[214]

> "Judicial decisions do not yet lend clear guidance on the copyrightability of screen displays (other than videogame displays), apart from the computer program. . . .

> ". . . Ultimately . . . the courts determine the precise scope of protection.

> "The courts have not fully examined the implications of protection for screen displays except in the videogame context where standardization of user interface screens is not a significant public policy issue. The practices adopted today

---

[213] Copyright Office, *Notice of Registration Decision: Registration and Deposit of Computer Screen Displays*, 36 Pat. Trademark & Copyright J. (BNA) 152 (1988).

[214] In Manufacturers Technologies Inc. v. Cams Inc., 706 F. Supp. 984, 10 U.S.P.Q.2d 1321 (D. Conn. 1989), the court relied upon the Office's policy statement.

See also Lotus Development Corp. v. Paperback Software International, 740 F. Supp. 37, 15 U.S.P.Q.2d 1577 (D. Mass. 1990):

> "[I]t is appropriate to consider 'screen displays' in a broader sense that also includes the structure, sequence, and organization of the underlying program as manifested in the menus presented on the screen displays. I conclude that plaintiff's certificates of copyright registration in the 'entire work' of 1-2-3 are sufficient to extend copyright protection to the 'screen displays,' in this broader sense, of Lotus 1-2-3.

> . . .

> "Most computer programs, like 1-2-3, are registered on Form TX as nondramatic literary works. . . . Some computer programmers, however—notably authors of video games—have instead registered for copyright the screen displays created by the program. . . . This form of registration is particularly appropriate where the chief function, and the bulk of creative expression, of a particular computer program is the creation of a series of pictorial images on the computer screen as with video games.

> "Other authors of computer programs have applied for dual registrations for computer programs—one 'literary' registration to cover the code, and a separate 'audiovisual' registration to cover the screen displays. . . . This practice has since been rejected by the Copyright Office as duplicative.

> "In any event, when Lotus attempted to register separately the screen displays of 1-2-3 as an audiovisual work, the Copyright Office denied the registration." 740 F. Supp. at 80–81, 15 U.S.P.Q.2d at 1610–11.

by the Office should facilitate judicial consideration of the relationship between computer program code authorship and screen displays."

As to deposits, the Office indicated that its policy was unchanged;[215] a separate deposit of material showing screen displays was permissible but would be required only if an applicant refers to "screen displays" in the application form's "nature of authorship" space.

[iv] *Reverse Engineering and Compatibility.* As a whole, the scope of protection cases fail to give a clear and consistent answer to two fundamental questions about computer software copyright.

The first question is: Does party B infringe the copyright of party A in a computer program if B "reverse engineers" A's program,[216] either (1) directly by analyzing A's program and writing a new program that performs all of the functions of A's program,[217] or (2) indirectly by having one person or group of persons define the functional specifications of A's program, and giving only those specifications to another person or group of persons, who then write a new program meeting those specifications. A simple, traditional answer is that party B's program does not infringe because B only copied A's "ideas," which are not protectable. But it can be argued that B's program does infringe if it is otherwise substantially similar in expression to A's program. While an accused work does not infringe if it is created independently of the protected work,[218] B's program is, by hypothesis, not created without any knowledge of A's copyrighted program. B did use A's ideas to create a program that, in fact, is substantially similar in expression to A's program.[219]

---

[215] The Office stated: "In general, the first 25 pages or the equivalent and the last 25 pages or the equivalent of computer source code should deposited in seeking registration. 37 CFR § 202.20(c)(2)(vii)." For a discussion of the deposit requirement, see § 4D[3][a].

[216] For a discussion of "reverse engineering" in trade secret law, see §§ 3D[1], 3D[7][b], and 3E[3].

[217] *Cf.* E.F. Johnson Co. v. Uniden Corp. of America, 623 F. Supp. 1485, 1502, 228 U.S.P.Q. 891, 903 (D. Minn. 1985).

In *E.F. Johnson,* the court granted a preliminary injunction against defendant's sale of "logic trunked radio system" equipment, which was compatible with plaintiff's system, because defendant's equipment contained copies of plaintiff's computer program. Defendant used a "dumping" technique to copy plaintiff's software. In dictum, the court opined that "dumping" for analysis would not have been unlawful.

> "The mere fact that defendant's engineers dumped, flow charted, and analyzed plaintiff's code does not, in and of itself, establish pirating. As both parties' witnesses admitted, dumping and analyzing competitors' codes is a standard practice in the industry. Had Uniden contented itself with surveying the general outline of the EFJ program, thereafter converting the scheme into detailed code through its own imagination, creativity, and independent thought, a claim of infringement would not have arisen. . . . While defendant may have permissibly dumped, flow charted, and analyzed plaintiff's code, it could not permissibly copy it." 623 F. Supp. at 1502 n.17, 228 U.S.P.Q. at 903 n.17.

[218] Proof of "copying" in the derivation sense is necessary to establish infringement. *See* § 4F[1].

[219] In *NEC,* discussed at § 4C[2][c][iv], the accused infringer did not "reverse engineer" the accused program but did use a third program created by a "clean room" procedure to show that functional considerations dictated the accused and protected programs' similarities.

The second question is: to what extent is "compatibility" with existing software and hardware or user preferences a function or idea that cannot be protected under copyright law? As to software and hardware compatibility, *Apple* left the issue in a state of uncertainty, remanding the matter for a factual determination whether "Apple's operating programs represent the only means of expression of the idea underlying them," leaving unclear whether achieving some level of Apple software compatibility was an idea or expression.[220]

As to user preferences,[221] the *Synercom*[222] "gearshift pattern" hypothetical[223] suggested that an idea implementation might, when created, be arbitrary, expressive and not dictated by function, but become a standard demanded by users simply because they are familiar with it. *Plains Cotton* and *Manufacturers Technologies* suggested that screen displays and other aspects of computer software that are industry-standard are not protectable. On the other hand, decisions involving works other than computer software give little weight to the alleged expression's status as a standard.[224] In *Lotus Development*,[225] the defendants, in designing their "VP-Planner"

---

[220] *See* § 4C[2][c].

[221] For a discussion of consumer preference in the context of trade dress protection, see § 5C[2][c][v](6).

[222] Synercom Technology, Inc. v. University Computing Co., 462 F. Supp. 1003, 1013, 199 U.S.P.Q. 537, 546 (N.D. Tex. 1978).

[223] The gear stick pattern hypothetical is as follows:

"A hypothetical, oversimplified, may serve to illuminate the idea versus expression controversy. The familiar 'figure-H' pattern of an automobile stick is chosen arbitrarily by an auto manufacturer. Several different patterns may be imagined, some more convenient for the driver or easier to manufacture than others, but all representing possible configurations. The pattern chosen is arbitrary, but once chosen, it is the only pattern which will work in a particular model. The pattern . . . may be expressed in several different ways: by a prose description in a driver's manual, through a diagram, photograph, or driver training film, or otherwise. Each of these expressions may presumably be protected through copyright. But the copyright protects copying of the particular expressions of the pattern, and does not prohibit another manufacturer from marketing a car using the same pattern. Use of the same pattern might be socially desirable, as it would reduce the re-training of drivers." 462 F. Supp. at 1013, 199 U.S.P.Q. at 546.

[224] *E.g.*, Educational Testing Services v. Katzman, 793 F.2d 533, 230 U.S.P.Q. 156 (3d Cir. 1986) (finding infringement of standardized test questions).

In *ETS*, the defendant argued that "ETS's domination of the field of college testing" meant that "anyone who wishes to prepare students for ETS's exams must use questions that are 'methodologically similar to ETS's questions.' " The defendant relied on two district court cases, McGraw-Hill, Inc. v. Worth Publishers, Inc., 335 F. Supp. 415, 172 U.S.P.Q. 482 (S.D.N.Y. 1971) (relying, to find noninfringement of copyright in an economics text, upon the fact that Professor Samuelson's text "had become a model for succeeding tests [sic: texts]"); Kepner-Tregoe, Inc. v. Carabio, 203 U.S.P.Q. 124 (E.D. Mich. 1979) (copyright on teaching materials for "management training programs," which plaintiff dominated). As to these cases, the Third Circuit noted: "Neither case suggests that copying or appropriation of copyrighted material can be excused because the copyright registrant is 'dominant' in the field." 793 F.2d at 540, 230 U.S.P.Q. at 161.

[225] Lotus Development Corp. v. Paperback Software International, 740 F. Supp. 37, 15 U.S.P.Q.2d 1577 (D. Mass. 1990).

spreadsheet program, copied plaintiff's "Lotus 1-2-3" spreadsheet menu command user interface to assure that "macros" generated by plaintiff's customers would work in defendant's program. Judge Keeton ruled that copying plaintiff's user interface was not in fact necessary for macro compatibility because others, including plaintiff, provided macro conversion utilities.[226] He went on to dismiss compatibility:

"These points do not weigh significantly in the present decision, however, because even if VP-Planner otherwise would have been a commercial failure, and even if no other technological ways of achieving macro and menu compatibility existed, the desire to achieve 'compatibility' or 'standardization' cannot override the rights of authors to a limited monopoly in the expression embodied in their intellectual 'work.' "[227]

[e] **Archival and Adaptation Copying.** Section 117, enacted in 1980, sets forth the following limitation relating to the use of computer programs:

"Notwithstanding the provisions of section 106, it is not an infringement for the owner of a copy of a computer program to make or authorize the making of another copy or adaptation of that computer program provided:

(1) that such a new copy or adaptation is created as an essential step in the utilization of the computer program in conjunction with a machine and that it is used in no other manner, or

(2) that such new copy or adaptation is for archival purposes only and that all archival copies are destroyed in the event that continued possession of the computer program should cease to be rightful.

Any exact copies prepared in accordance with the provisions of this section may be leased, sold or otherwise transferred, along with the copy from which such

---

[226] See also E.F. Johnson Co. v. Uniden Corp. of America, 623 F. Supp. 1485, 1503, 228 U.S.P.Q. 891, 904 (D. Minn. 1985) ("the mere fact that defendant set out with the objective of creating an LTR-compatible radio does not, without more, excuse its copying of plaintiff's code. . . . [C]opying plaintiff's code was not the only and essential means of creating an LTR-compatible software program. Defendant was required to copy plaintiff's Barker word. . . . Virtually all other aspects of defendant's program could have been independently created, however, without violence to defendant's compatibility objective. Defendant has reproduced the expression, not merely the idea of plaintiff's copyrighted program.").

[227] 740 F. Supp. at 69, 15 U.S.P.Q.2d at 1600.

See also Allen-Myland Inc. v. International Business Machines Corp., 746 F. Supp. 520, 533, 16 U.S.P.Q.2d 1817, 1825 (E.D. Pa. 1990):

"Whether it would be economically feasible for AMI [the accused infringer] to write its own program to perform the 3090 processor controller functions without copying any of IBM's [copyrighted] 3090 microcode . . . is not relevant to the idea/expression distinction. Otherwise, a computer program so complex that vast expenditures of time and money would be required to develop a different program expressing the same idea would not be protected, even if innumerable different programs expressing that idea could be written, while a simpler program requiring less significant expenditures of time and money might be protected. So long as other expressions of the idea are possible, a particular expression of the idea can enjoy copyright protection, regardless of whether a copying party possesses the resources to write a different expression of the idea."

copies were prepared, only as part of the lease, sale, or other transfer of all rights in the program. Adaptations so prepared may be transferred only with the authorization of the copyright owner."[228]

Congress enacted the limitation on recommendation of CONTU. Because there is little legislative history on Section 117, the courts give weight to the CONTU Report's explanation of the limitation's purpose.[229]

Early district court decisions gave the Section 117 limitation a restrictive interpretation. In *JS&A*,[230] the court relied on the CONTU Report's reference to the risk of "mechanical or electrical failure" to hold the limitation inapplicable to programs stored on ROM chips. Because there was little or no risk of mechanical or electrical failure with ROM chips, there was no legitimate reason to make an archival ("backup") copy.[231] In *Micro-Sparc*,[232] another court held the limitation inapplicable to programs printed in source code in a magazine.[233]

---

[228] 17 U.S.C. § 117.

[229] *See* § 4C[2][a]. The Report provides, at pages 31–32:

"Because the placement of a work into a computer is the preparation of a copy, the law should provide that persons in rightful possession of copies of programs be able to use them freely without fear of exposure to copyright liability. Obviously, creators, lessors, licensors and vendors of copies of programs intend that they be used by their customers, so that rightful users would but rarely need a legal shield against potential copyright problems. It is easy to imagine, however, a situation in which the copyright owner might desire, for good reason or none at all, to force a lawful owner or possessor of a copy to stop using a particular program. One who rightfully possesses a copy of a program, therefore, should be provided with a legal right to copy it to that extent which will permit its use by that possessor. This would include the right to load it into a computer and to prepare archival copies of it to guard against destruction or damage by mechanical or electrical failure. But this permission would not extend to other copies of the program. Thus one could not, for example, make archival copies of a program and after sell some to another while retaining some for use. The sale of a copy of a program by a rightful possessor to another must be of all rights in the program, thus creating a new rightful possessor and destroying that status as regards the seller. This is in accord with the intent of that portion of the law which provides that owners of authorized copies of a copyrighted work may sell those copies without leave of the copyright proprietor."

[230] Atari, Inc. v. JS&A Group Inc., 597 F. Supp. 5 (N.D. Ill. 1983).

[231] The court noted:

"The dangers to ROMs presented by [defendant] are *physical* dangers not unlike the risk that a handwritten computer program will be shredded accidentally. Virtually every copy of a copyrighted work, be it a book, a phonograph record or a videotape, faces that kind of risk. Yet Congress did not enact a general rule that making back-up copies of copyrighted works would not infringe. Rather, according to the CONTU report, it limited its exception to computer program which are subject to 'destruction or damage by mechanical or electrical failure.' Some media must be especially susceptible to this danger. [Defendant] has simply offered no evidence that a ROM in a 2600-compatible video game cartridge is such a medium." 597 F. Supp. at 9–10.

[232] Micro-Sparc Inc. v. Amtype Corp., 592 F. Supp. 33, 223 U.S.P.Q. 1210 (D. Mass. 1984).

[233] In *Micro-Sparc*, the plaintiff published copyrighted computer programs for Apple personal computers in a monthly magazine. Readers of the magazine may type the programs into their

In *Vault Corp.*,[234] the Fifth Circuit refused to restrict Section 117's literal scope. Plaintiff Vault marketed a system ("PROLOK") for preventing unauthorized duplication of programs placed on ("floppy") diskettes by computer software companies. A PROLOK diskette contains a "fingerprint," a physical mark on the surface containing unique identifying information, and a Vault program, which interacts with the fingerprint to prevent a computer from operating a user program recorded on the PROLOK diskette unless the computer verifies that the original PROLOK diskette, as identified by the fingerprint, is in the computer's disk drive. "While a purchaser can copy a PROLOK protected user program onto another diskette, the computer will not read the program into its memory from the copy unless the original PROLOK diskette is also in one of the computer's disk drives."

Defendant Quaid sells a diskette called "COPYWRITE" that includes a "RAM-KEY" feature, which allows users to create a fully functional copy of a program on a PROLOCK diskette by copying a PROLOCK diskette's contents onto the COPYWRITE diskette. RAMKEY "interacts with Vault's program to make it appear to the computer that the CopyWrite diskette contains the 'fingerprint.' "

The plaintiff sued defendant for copyright infringement, asserting two distinct theories. The first theory, "direct copying," was that the defendant made an infringing copy of plaintiff's copyrighted program by loading it into a computer system to analyze its structure and design an antidote. The court held that defendant's use fell squarely within Section 117(1)'s provision on making a copy "as an essential step in the utilization of the computer program in conjunction with a machine." It rejected as without support in the statutory language plaintiff's argument that "this exception should be interpreted to permit only the copying of a computer program for the purpose of using it for *its intended purpose.*"[235]

The second theory, "contributory infringement," was that defendant committed contributory copyright infringement[236] by selling a product uniquely designed to

---

computers. Because typing a lengthy program is a time-consuming, tedious task, plaintiff offered the programs on disk for between $20 and $30 per disk. A program on a disk can be easily transferred to, stored, and utilized by the computer. Defendant offered a "typing service" to readers. For about $10, a reader can buy from defendant a disk with all the programs in an issue of plaintiff's magazine. Plaintiff sued defendant for copyright infringement. Defendant relied upon the Section 117 exemption, arguing that magazine readers, being lawful owners of the printed source code versions of the programs had a right to "make" or to "authorize the making" of another copy (by defendant). The court ruled that Section 117(1) was strictly limited to "inputting" a program into a computer, that is, loading the program into the computer's memory in the course of using the program. It ruled that Section 117(2), on "archival" copies, did not apply under the rationale of the *Atari* decision. The printed magazine versions of the program were not subject to the special kind of "mechanical or electrical" destruction cited by the CONTU Report.

[234] Vault Corp. v. Quaid Software Ltd., 847 F.2d 255, 7 U.S.P.Q.2d 1281 (5th Cir. 1988).

[235] 847 F.2d at 261, 7 U.S.P.Q.2d at 1287. (Emphasis in original.)

Compare Allen-Myland Inc. v. International Business Machines Corp., 746 F. Supp. 520, 536, 16 U.S.P.Q.2d 1817, 1825 (E.D. Pa. 1990) ("The *Vault* Court did not address the type of copying in which AMI has engaged, i.e. making copies on tape and on a hard disk to build a library of different versions of the program and to supply with a computer other than the one with which the program originally was supplied.").

[236] For a discussion of contributory infringement, see § 4F[3][a][i](1).

enable others (defendant's customers) to infringe copyrighted programs (those placed on PROLOK diskettes by plaintiff's customers). The court held that defendant was not guilty of contributory infringement because its product (CopyWrite) had a substantial noninfringing use, to wit, use by customers to make archival or backup copies of the copyright programs sold on PROLOK diskettes as permitted by Section 117(2). Because of the existence of such uses, it was not liable even though it had actual knowledge that others use its product to make unauthorized copies of copyrighted material.

In *Vault*, the plaintiff argued that making a complete functioning copy of programs sold on PROLOK diskettes was unnecessary to protect against erasure because a copy of an erased program could be copied back onto the original fingerprinted PROLOK diskette to recreate a functioning copy. The court refused to restrict Section 117(2) to copying necessary to guard against erasures.

> "Congress imposed no restriction upon the purpose or reason of the owner in making the archival copy; only the use made of that copy is restricted. . . . An owner of a program is entitled, under § 117(2), to make an archival copy of that program in order to guard against *all* types of risks, including physical and human mishap as well as mechanical and electrical failure." [237]

In *Foresight Resources*, [238] the district court construed Section 117's "authorize" "adaptation" right broadly. Pfortmiller modified his client Hall-Kimbrel's copy of Foresight Resources' copyrighted Drafix 1+ computer aided design (CAD) program by adding five files to produce the HK Digitizer. Hall-Kimbrell used the modified program "in-house" in its asbestos removal consulting business.

> "There is a dearth both of legislative history and case law interpreting the word 'adaptation.' . . . According to the Commission [on New Technological Uses of Copyrighted Works] report, '[t]he conversion of a program from one higher-level language to another to facilitate use would fall within this right [of adaptation], *as would the right to add features to the program that were not present at the time of rightful acquisition.* These rights would necessarily be more private in nature than the right to load a program by copying it and could only be exercised so long as they did not harm the interests of the copyright proprietor. Unlike the exact copies authorized as described above, this right of adaptation could not be conveyed to others along with the licensed or owned program without the express authorization of the owner of the copyright in the original work. Preparations of adaptations could not, of course, deprive the original proprietor of copyright in the underlying work. The adaptor could not vend the adapted program, under the proposed revision of the new law, nor could it be sold as the original without the author's permission. Again, it is likely that many transactions involving copies of programs are entered into with full awareness that users will modify their copies to suit their own needs, and this should be reflected in the law. The comparison of this practice to extensive marginal note-taking in a book is appropriate: note-taking is arguably the creation of a

---

[237] 847 F.2d at 267, 7 U.S.P.Q.2d at 1292.

[238] Foresight Resources Corp. v. Pfortmiller, 719 F. Supp. 1006, 13 U.S.P.Q.2d 1721 (D. Kan. 1989).

derivative work, but unless the note-taker tries to copy and vend that work, the copyright owner is unlikely to be very concerned. Should proprietors feel strongly that they do not want rightful possessors of copies of their programs to prepare such adaptations, they could, of course, make such desires a contractual matter.'

. . . .

". . . Construing § 117 to cover the enhancements defendant made to Hall-Kimbrell's copy of plaintiff's program, in these circumstances, would serve two important goals of the copyright laws. On the one hand, allowing sophisticated software users to enhance copies of copyrighted programs they have purchased eliminates the need to choose between either buying the latest version of a program or possibly infringing the program's owner's copyright. At the same time, allowing such enhancements to be used only in-house preserves the market for improvements made by the copyright holder.

"Like what constitutes an 'adaptation,' there is some question as to the nature of the 'authorization' that will suffice to bring an adaptation within the exception carved out by § 117. Again, scholarly commentary suggests that § 117 should not be restricted to prohibit owners from authorizing custom-made enhancements to their copies of copyrighted programs. . . . Stern, *Section 117 of the Copyright Act: Charter of Software Users' Rights or an Illusory Promise?*, 7 W. New Eng. L. Rev. 459, 468 (1985) (footnote omitted)."[239]

[3] Three-Dimensional Works

Copyright extends to "sculptural works," which include, under some circumstances, the ornamental designs of useful articles.[240] In 1990, Congress added architectural works to the copyrightable subject matter list.[241]

[a] *Mazer v. Stein*. In *Mazer*,[242] the germinal Supreme Court useful article ornamental design decision, plaintiffs created a human dancing figure statuette, copies of which they used as lamp bases. They registered the statuette as a "work of art" under the 1909 Copyright Act. Defendant copied the statuettes and sold them as lamp bases without plaintiffs' authorization. The plaintiffs sued for copyright infringement. The Supreme Court upheld the copyright's validity.

Defendants posed a single question: "Can statuettes be protected in the United States by copyright when the copyright applicant intended primarily to use the statuettes in the form of lamp bases to be made and sold in quantity and carried the intentions into effect?" The Court found that this accurately summarized the issue before it[243] and held that a creation, such as the traditional statuette in *Mazer*, did

---

[239] 719 F. Supp. at 1009–10, 7 U.S.P.Q.2d at 1723–24. (Emphasis in original.)

[240] 17 U.S.C. § 102(a)(5). *See generally* P. Goldstein, Copyright §§ 2.5.3, 2.11 (1989).

[241] *See* § 4C[3][f].

[242] Mazer v. Stein, 347 U.S. 201, 100 U.S.P.Q. 325 (1954).

[243] 347 U.S. at 204–05. The defendants' further statement that "Stripped down to its essentials, the question presented is: Can a lamp manufacturer copyright his lamp bases? . . . unjustifiably . . . broadens the controversy. The case requires an answer, not as to a manufacturer's right to register a lamp base but as to an artist's right to copyright a work of art intended to be reproduced for lamp bases." 347 U.S. at 205.

not lose its status as a copyrightable art work simply because the creator intended to embed the creation in a useful article.

The Court reviewed the successive copyright statutes; the 1909 Act's legislative history; and the Copyright Office's practice in registering three-dimensional objects. Because "[i]ndividual perception of the beautiful is too varied a power to permit a narrow or rigid concept of art," the Court approved the Copyright Office's regulation including as works of art, "works of artistic craftsmanship, in so far as their form but not their mechanical or utilitarian aspects are concerned, such as artistic jewelry, enamels, glassware, and tapestries, as well as all works belonging to the fine arts, such as paintings, drawings and sculpture."

The Court responded to the defendants' argument that Congress' enactment of the design patent law, which protects the ornamental design of articles of manufacture,[244] "should be interpreted as denying protection to artistic articles embodied or reproduced in manufactured articles." It declined to rule on the question of election, that is, whether obtaining one (copyright or patent) bars a grant of the other (patent or copyright) but rejected the proposition that "because a thing is patentable it may not be copyrighted."

> "Unlike a patent, a copyright gives no exclusive right to the art disclosed; protection is given only to the expression of the idea—not the idea itself. . . . The copyright protects originality rather than novelty or invention—conferring only 'the sole right of multiplying copies.' Absent copying there can be no infringement of copyright. . . . The dichotomy of protection for the aesthetic is not beauty and utility but art for the copyright and the invention of original and ornamental design for design patents. We find nothing in the copyright statute to support the argument that the intended use or use in industry of an article eligible for copyright bars or invalidates its registration."[245]

[b] Administrative and Legislative Response to Mazer. After *Mazer*, the Copyright Office amended its regulations, adding the separate identity, independent existence test for design copyrightability:

> "If the sole intrinsic function of an article is its utility, the fact that the article is unique and attractively shaped will not qualify it as a work of art. However, if the shape of a utilitarian article incorporates features, such as artistic sculpture, carving, or pictorial representation, which can be identified separately and are capable of existing independently as a work of art, such features will be eligible for registration."[246]

No specific *Mazer* language supports this test, but *Mazer's* facts illustrate its application. The dancing figure statuette lamp base was a feature that can be identified separately from the utilitarian article (the lamp) and is capable of existing independently as a work of art.

---

[244] *See* § 6B.

[245] 347 U.S. at 217–18.

[246] 37 C.F.R. § 202.10(c), quoted in Esquire, Inc. v. Ringer, 591 F.2d 796, 199 U.S.P.Q. 1 (D.C. Cir. 1978), *cert. denied*, 440 U.S. 908, 201 U.S.P.Q. 256 (1979). *Esquire* thoroughly reviews the administrative and legislative developments from *Mazer* to enactment of the 1976 Act.

In the 1976 Act, Congress adopted the Copyright Office's post-*Mazer* separate identity, independent existence test, listing "pictorial, graphic, and sculptural works" as one category of copyrightable subject matter, including in the category's definition "three-dimensional works of fine, graphic, and applied art," and providing:

> "[Three-dimensional works of fine, graphic, and applied art] shall include works of artistic craftsmanship insofar as their form but not their mechanical or utilitarian aspects are concerned; the design of a useful article, as defined in this section, shall be considered a pictorial, graphic, or sculptural work only if, and only to the extent that, such design incorporates pictorial, graphic, or sculptural *features* that can be *identified separately from, and are capable of existing independently of, the utilitarian aspects* of the article."[247]

The House Report expressed a desire "to draw as clear a line as possible between copyrightable works of applied art and uncopyrightable works of industrial design" but created confusion by mentioning the possibility of "conceptual" as well as physical separability.[248]

[c] Judicial Interpretation—"Conceptual" Separability. Court decisions struggle with the separate identity, independent existence test, especially with "conceptual" separability, which the House Report mentions but does not explain.[249]

In *Esquire, Inc.*,[250] the District of Columbia Circuit held an outdoor lighting fixture uncopyrightable. In *Norris Industries*[251] the Eleventh Circuit held automobile wire wheel covers uncopyrightable. In *Kieselstein-Cord*,[252] the Second Circuit held an abstract artistic belt buckle's design copyrightable because the design was conceptually separable from the buckle's utilitarian aspects. In *Carol Barnhart*,[253] it held four life-sized, anatomically correct human torso forms uncopyrightable. In *Brandir International*,[254] it held an ornamental "RIBBON Rack" bicycle rack uncopyrightable.

---

[247] 17 U.S.C. § 101 (Emphasis added.)

[248] "[A]lthough the shape of an industrial product may be aesthetically satisfying and valuable, the Committee's intention is not to offer it copyright protection under the bill. Unless the shape of an automobile, airplane, ladies' dress, food processor, television set, or any other industrial product contains some element that, physically *or conceptually*, can be identified as separable from the utilitarian aspects of that article, the design would not be copyrighted under the bill." H.R. Rep. No. 1476, 94th Cong., 2d Sess. 55. (Emphasis added.)

[249] Masquerade Novelty Inc. v. Unique Industries, Inc., 912 F.2d 663, 670, 15 U.S.P.Q.2d 1881, 1887 (3d Cir. 1990) ("Courts have twisted themselves into knots trying to create a test to effectively ascertain whether the artistic aspects of a useful article can be identified separately from and exist independently of the article's utilitarian function.").

[250] Esquire, Inc. v. Ringer, 591 F.2d 796, 199 U.S.P.Q. 1 (D.C. Cir. 1978), *cert. denied*, 440 U.S. 908, 201 U.S.P.Q. 256 (1979).

[251] Norris Indus., Inc. v. International Tel. & Tel. Corp., 696 F.2d 918, 217 U.S.P.Q. 226 (11th Cir.), *cert. denied*, 464 U.S. 818, 220 U.S.P.Q. 385 (1983).

[252] Kieselstein-Cord v. Accessories By Pearl, Inc., 632 F.2d 989, 208 U.S.P.Q. 1 (2d Cir. 1980).

[253] Carol Barnhart Inc. v. Economy Cover Corp., 773 F.2d 411, 228 U.S.P.Q. 385 (2d Cir. 1985). *Compare* Animal Fair, Inc. v. Amfexco Indus., Inc., 620 F. Supp. 175, 227 U.S.P.Q. 817 (D. Minn. 1985), *aff'd*, 794 F.2d 678 (8th Cir. 1986) (unpublished opinion).

[254] Brandir Int'l v. Cascade Pacific Lumber Co., 834 F.2d 1142, 5 U.S.P.Q.2d 1089 (2d Cir. 1987).

In *Brandir*, Judge Oakes for the majority, noted " '[c]onceptual separability' is . . . alive and well" in the Second Circuit, the problem being "determining exactly what it is and how it is to be applied." There are several possible tests of conceptual separability: (1) "whether the primary use is as a utilitarian article as opposed to an artistic work," (2) "whether the aesthetic aspects of the work can be said to be 'primary,' " and (3) "whether the article is marketable as art." None is satisfactory. The majority in *Carol Barnhart* rejected as too ethereal to be administrable the "temporal displacement" test, suggested by dissenting Judge Newman, which inquired whether "the article . . . stimulate[s] in the mind of the beholder a concept that is separate from the concept evoked by its utilitarian function."[255]

Judge Oakes adopted a legal scholar's suggested test:[256] "[I]f design elements reflect a merger of aesthetic and functional considerations, the artistic aspects of a work cannot be said to be conceptually separable from the utilitarian elements. Conversely, where design elements can be identified as reflecting the designer's artistic judgment exercised independently of functional influences, conceptual separability exists." This test would be easier to administer because the trier of fact determines, on the basis of "evidence relating to the design process and the nature of the work, . . . whether the aesthetic design elements are significantly influenced by functional considerations."[257]

Applying this test to the bicycle rack, Judge Oakes affirmed the finding of uncopyrightability because of the absence of conceptual separability. The creator made ribbon sculptures of tubing with no thought of their being used as bicycle racks. A friend suggested such use. The creator made a number of alterations in order "to accommodate and further" the utilitarian purpose.

> "While the RIBBON Rack may be worthy of admiration for its aesthetic qualities alone, it remains nonetheless the product of industrial design. Form and function are inextricably intertwined in the rack, its ultimate design being as much the result of utilitarian pressures as aesthetic choices."[258]

In *Brandir*, Judge Winter dissented:

> ". . . [T]he relevant question is whether the design of a useful article, however intertwined with the article's utilitarian aspects, causes an ordinary reasonable observer to perceive an aesthetic concept not related to the article's use. The answer to this question is clear in the instant case because any reasonable observer would easily view the Ribbon Rack as an ornamental sculpture.

> "My colleagues . . . allow too much to turn upon the process or sequence of design followed by the designer of the Ribbon Rack. . . . I cannot agree that copyright protection for the Ribbon Rack turns on whether [the designer] serendipitously chose the final design of the Ribbon Rack during his initial sculptural musings or whether the original design had to be slightly modified to accommodate bicycles. Copyright protection, which is intended to generate incentives for

---

[255] 834 F.2d at 1144, 5 U.S.P.Q.2d at 1091.
[256] *See* Denicola, *Applied Art and Industrial Design: A Suggested Approach to Copyright in Useful Articles*, 67 Minn. L. Rev. 707 (1983).
[257] 834 F.2d at 1145–46, 5 U.S.P.Q.2d at 1092.
[258] 834 F.2d at 1147, 5 U.S.P.Q.2d at 1094.

designers by according property rights in their creations, should not turn on purely fortuitous events. For that reason, the Copyright Act expressly states that the legal test is how the final article is perceived, not how it was developed through various stages."[259]

[d] "Useful Article." The restrictive separate identity, independent existence test only applies to a "useful article," one "having an intrinsic utilitarian function that is not merely to portray the appearance of the article or to convey information."[260]

In *Gay Toys,*[261] the Sixth Circuit held a toy airplane was not a "useful article," disagreeing with the district court's conclusion that "children need toys for growing up and that a 'toy airplane is useful and possesses utilitarian and functional characteristics in that it permits a child to dream and to let his or her imagination soar.' " A toy has no utilitarian function other than to portray the appearance of the article.

"To be sure, a toy airplane is to be played with and enjoyed, but a painting of an airplane, which is copyrightable, is to be looked at and enjoyed.

". . . The intention of Congress was to exclude from copyright protection industrial products such as automobiles, food processors, and television sets. . . . The function of toys is much more similar to that of works of art than it is to the 'intrinsic utilitarian function' of industrial products.

"Indeed under the district court's reasoning, virtually any 'pictorial, graphic, and sculptural work' would not be copyrightable as a 'useful article.' A painting of Lindbergh's Spirit of St. Louis invites the viewer 'to dream and to let his or her imagination soar,' and would not be copyrightable under the district court's approach. But the statute clearly intends to extend copyright protection to paintings."[262]

The 1976 Act may have broadened the class of "useful articles" by defining such as any article with "*an* intrinsic utilitarian function" (case law under the 1909 Act disallowing copyrightability only when the *sole* function of the article was utility),[263]

---

[259] 834 F.2d at 1152, 5 U.S.P.Q.2d at 1095–96.

[260] 17 U.S.C. § 101.

[261] Gay Toys, Inc. v. Buddy L Corp., 703 F.2d 970, 218 U.S.P.Q. 13 (6th Cir. 1983). *Compare* Norris Industries v. International Tel. & Tel. Corp., 696 F.2d 918, 922, 217 U.S.P.Q. 226 (11th Cir.), *cert. denied,* 464 U.S. 818, 220 U.S.P.Q. 385 (1983) (wire-spoke wheel covers for automobiles are useful articles; the creator "contends . . . that its wheel covers are ornamental articles, not useful, designed to beautify, embellish, and adorn the wheels of automobiles. The district court held that the wheel covers are utilitarian articles serving as hubcaps to protect lugnuts, brakes, wheels, and axles from damage and corrosion, as had been determined by the Register in rejecting the copyright application. . . . [W]e find no error in the district court's reliance on the Register's opinion that Norris' wheel covers are useful articles as that term is used in the Act.").

[262] 703 F.2d at 973, 218 U.S.P.Q. at 15.

[263] *See* Fabrica Inc. v. El Dorado Corp., 697 F.2d 890, 893, 217 U.S.P.Q. 698, 700 (9th Cir. 1983) (plaintiff's high-quality carpet display folder, covered with simulated white suede, with saddle stitching along the borders and brass tips at the corners, with a unique fold-out

but this did not alter the result: "toys do not have *an* intrinsic function other than the portrayal of the real item." The court rejected as irrelevant the fact that economic considerations, such as ease of shipment, dictated some aspects of the toy airplane design: "The designer's or manufacturer's selection of certain features for economical reasons has nothing to do with whether the article is, to the consumer, a 'useful article' under the statute."[264]

Court decisions treat garments as useful articles, which restricts clothing design copyrightability.[265] In *Whimsicality*,[266] the court found the plaintiff's copyright registration of costumes invalid because, in application to the Copyright Office, it misrepresented the works as "soft sculptures."[267]

---

book format featuring a full-page carpet sample on the inside left panel and small carpet samples on the inside right panel is a useful article: "The significant change from the prior law is that the courts need no longer determine whether an article's function is *solely* utilitarian. Now, if an article has *any* intrinsic utilitarian function, it can be denied copyright protection except to the extent that its artistic features can be identified separately and are capable of existing independently as a work of art.").

See also Harper House, Inc. v. Thomas Nelson, Inc., 889 F.2d 197, 12 U.S.P.Q.2d 1779 (9th Cir. 1989) (various features of plaintiff's "organizer" are useful articles, including special hinges, pockets to hold keys, coins, calculator, and graph paper).

[264] 703 F.2d at 974, 218 U.S.P.Q. at 16.

[265] Patterns for clothes are protectable against copying, but only if they convey images or information. *See* Beverly Hills Design Studio (N.Y.) Inc. v. Morris, 13 U.S.P.Q.2d 1889, 1895 (S.D. N.Y. 1989):

"Plaintiffs argue that these patterns are copyrightable drawings of utilitarian objects, the apparel, and are not useful articles themselves. They liken them to architectural plans, which are copyrightable, while the useful article depicted by those plans, the house, is not. . . .

"The analogy is off the mark. Architectural plans are copyrightable because they are 'technical drawings, diagrams, and models' under 17 U.S.C. § 101. . . . The architectural plans are not 'useful articles because the intrinsic function of an architectural plan is precisely to "convey information" as to the manner in which a building may be constructed.' . . . Here, the patterns are not 'technical drawings, diagrams, and models', nor do they either portray the appearance of the garments or convey information about them. They are simply used to cut fabric for the manufacture of garments. Because the patterns are intrinsically utilitarian and functional, they are not eligible for copyright protection."

[266] Whimsicality, Inc. v. Rubie's Costume Co., Inc., 891 F.2d 452, 13 U.S.P.Q.2d 1296 (2d Cir. 1989).

[267] *See* § 4F[4][b].

The court noted that plaintiff should "have acknowledged in its application that the articles in question were costumes, and have requested registration for only the features it claimed were separable." 891 F.2d at 455, 13 U.S.P.Q.2d at 1299. The court distinguished National Theme Productions, Inc. v. Jerry B. Beck Inc., 696 F. Supp. 1348 (S.D. Calif. 1988), in which the district court held that plaintiff's Halloween masquerade costumes, "Rabbit In Hat," "Tigress," "Magic Dragon," and "Pampered Pup," have an intrinsic utilitarian function and cannot be copyrighted as costumes, but the costumes have copyrightable features that can be identified separately and are capable of existing independently as a work of art.

In *National Theme Productions*, plaintiff obtained Copyright Office registration by depositing its packaging inserts, which served as labels for the costumes and contained a photograph of a model wearing the costume. Its registration stated: "Text, Graphics[,] Photographs, and

"We have long held that clothes, as useful articles, are not copyrightable. *Fashion Originators Guild v. FTC*, 114 F.2d 80, 84 (2d Cir. 1940) (L. Hand, J.), aff'd, 312 U.S. 457, 61 S. Ct. 703, 85 L. Ed. 949 (1941). . . . The Copyright Act of 1976 did not affect the prior law in this regard.

"While the pictorial, graphic and sculptural aspects of useful articles may be copyrightable if they are separable from the article, physically or conceptually, . . . clothes are particularly unlikely to meet that test—the very decorative eleme..ts that stand out being intrinsic to the decorative function of the clothing.

. . . .

". . . [C]ases about stuffed animals and toys [do not] lend support to the contention that costumes may be registered as soft sculpture. The word sculpture implies a relatively firm form representing a particular concept. The costumes in question have no such form. If hung from a hook or laid randomly on a flat surface, the particular animal or item depicted by the costume would be largely unidentifiable. The intended depiction is in fact recognizable only when the costume is worn by a person or is carefully laid out on a flat surface to reveal that depiction.

". . . At issue in [*Animal Fair, Inc. v. Amfesco Indus., Inc.*, 620 F. Supp. 175 (D. Minn. 1985), aff'd, mem., 794 F.2d 678 (8th Cir. 1986)], was a slipper in the shape of a bear's paw, which the court held to be copyrightable. Although slippers and costumes are similar in that they are wearable, we distinguish *Animal Fair* . . . [A] slipper, unlike a costume, has a relatively firm form which can be identified for copyright purposes."[268]

Whether an article is useful is a fact question. In *Poe*,[269] plaintiff Poe created "Aquatint No. 5." Poe's friend, Carla Weber, photographed a member of a rock band,

---

Original Artistic Expression of Accessory Items Shown in Photographs—No claim is made on designs of clothing, but in designs of artwork on clothing," or, in the case of Magic Dragon: "Photographs; graphics, compilation of terms; sculpture and artwork in masquerade costumes and accessory items shown in photographs; no claim is made on functional designs of clothing." 696 F. Supp. at 1352.

[268] 891 F.2d at 455–456, 13 U.S.P.Q.2d at 1299–1300.

Compare Masquerade Novelty Inc. v. Unique Industries, Inc., 912 F.2d 663, 15 U.S.P.Q.2d 1881 (3d Cir. 1990). In *Masquerade Novelty*, the court held that pig, elephant, and parrot "nose masks" allowing persons to masquerade in an animal's nose are not useful articles.

"That nose masks are meant to be worn by humans to evoke laughter does not distinguish them from clearly copyrightable works of art like paintings. When worn by a human being, a nose mask may evoke chuckles and guffaws from onlookers. When hung on a wall, a painting may evoke a myriad of human emotions, but we would not say that the painting is not copyrightable because its artistic elements could not be separated from the emotional effect its creator hoped it would have on persons viewing it. The utilitarian nature of an animal nose mask or a painting of the crucifixion of Jesus Christ inheres solely in its appearance, regardless of the fact that the nose mask's appearance is intended to evoke mirth and the painting's appearance a feeling of religious reverence." 912 F.2d at 663, 15 U.S.P.Q.2d at 1887.

Could a pig nose mask have at least one "intrinsic utilitarian function" other than portraying—to wit, concealing the appearance of an author's ugly nose?

[269] Poe v. Missing Persons, 745 F.2d 1238, 223 U.S.P.Q. 1297 (9th Cir. 1984).

Missing Persons, wearing "Aquatint No. 5." Later, without plaintiff's permission, defendant used the photograph on an album cover. Poe sued for copyright infringement. In his application to register his claim of copyright, Poe described Aquatint No. 5 as "a three dimensional work of art in primarily flexible clear-vinyl and covered rock media." The district court granted defendant's summary judgment motion on the ground that Aquatint No. 5 was a utilitarian article of clothing, a swimsuit, not a work of art, relying in part on plaintiff's deposition, which indicated that he was "an artist and fashion designer whose clothing styles are recognized in the fashion world" and that Aquatint No. 5 is "an artist's impression or rendering of an article of clothing." The appeals court reversed, finding disputed material fact issues, which precluded summary judgment. From its own visual examination, it was "unable to determine merely looking at Poe's creation whether a person wearing this object can move, walk, swim, sit, stand, or lie down without unwelcome or unintended exposure. It disagreed with defendant's contention that "there is no evidence which Poe could present that would be relevant to the question of usefulness."

> "We can identify relevant evidence which may be presented to the trier of fact in this matter: (1) expert evidence may be offered concerning the usefulness of the article and whether any apparent functional aspects can be separated from the artistic aspects . . . ; (2) evidence of Poe's intent in designing the article may be relevant in determining whether it has a utilitarian function . . . ; (3) testimony concerning the custom and usage within the art world and the clothing trade concerning such objects also may be relevant . . . ; and (4) the district court may also consider the admissibility of evidence as to Aquatint No. 5's marketability as a work of art." [270]

In *Lotus Development*,[271] the district court rejected defendant's argument that plaintiff's Lotus 1-2-3 computer program spreadsheet user interface is a useful article: "the mere fact that an intellectual work is useful or functional—be it a dictionary, directory, map, book of meaningless code words, or computer program—does not mean that none of the elements of the work can be copyrightable."

[e] Depictions of Useful Articles—Technical Drawings. Drawings, photographs, and other two-dimensional and three-dimensional expressions that visually depict three-dimensional objects are copyrightable.[272]

Whether the copyright in the depiction confers exclusive rights over the object depicted depends on the nature of the object. If the object is an uncopyrightable useful article, copyright in the depiction does not extend to reproduction of the object. If the object is a copyrightable art work, the copyright in the depiction does extend

---

[270] 745 F.2d at 1243, 223 U.S.P.Q. at 1301.

[271] Lotus Development Corp. v. Paperback Software International, 740 F. Supp. 37, 15 U.S.P.Q.2d 1577 (D. Mass. 1990).

See § 4C[2][d][ii].

[272] *See generally* P. Goldstein, Copyright § 2.5.3.2 (1989).

Section 101's definition of "pictorial, graphic, and sculptural works" includes "two-dimensional and three-dimensional works of fine, graphic, and applied art, photographs, prints and art reproductions, maps, globes, charts, diagrams, models, and technical drawings, including architectural plans." 17 U.S.C. § 101.

to the object.[273] For example, copyright in a photograph of a lamp does not extend to reproduction of the lamp (unless the lamp's design meets the separate identity, independent existence test), but copyright in a fanciful cartoon character does extend to a toy based on the character.

In the 1976 Act, Congress deliberately left open the question of the scope of protection for works depicting useful articles. Section 113(b) provides:

> "This title does not afford, to the owner of copyright in a work that portrays a useful article as such, any greater or lesser rights with respect to the making, distribution, or display of the useful article so portrayed than those afforded to such works under the law, whether title 17 or the common law or statutes of a State, in effect on December 31, 1977, as held applicable and construed by a court in an action brought under this title."[274]

In other words, Congress continued the law the courts had previously developed. Section 113(b) responds to a Register of Copyright report, which "stated, on the basis of judicial precedent, that 'copyright in a pictorial, graphic, or sculptural work, portraying a useful article as such, does not extend to the manufacture of the useful article itself'" but recommended that "'the distinctions drawn in this area by existing court decisions' not be altered by the statute" because of "the insuperable difficulty of finding 'any statutory formulation that would express the distinction satisfactorily.'"[275]

[f] Architectural Works. United States Berne Convention adherence[276] and the 1990 Architectural Works Copyright Protection Act significantly altered copyright protection for an architect's work product.

[i] Pre-1991 Law. Architectural work copyright protection under pre-1991 law breaks down into four issues. The first—whether architectural plans and models are copyrightable—is the easiest.[277] The 1976 Act's "pictorial, graphic, and sculptural work" category covers plans and models. The 1988 Berne Convention Implementation Act added an explicit reference to "technical drawings, including architectural plans."

The second issue—whether copying a plan for the purpose of building the structure is infringement—is more difficult. *Baker's* dictum indicated that copying a work explaining a system for "use," as opposed to copying for "explanation," was not infringement.[278] Subsequent case law refuses to apply the dictum to architectural designs.[279]

---

[273] King Features Syndicate v. Fleischer, 299 F. 533 (2d Cir. 1924).

[274] 17 U.S.C. § 113(b).

[275] H.R. Rep. No. 94-1476, 94th Cong., 2d Sess. 105 (1976).

[276] *See* § 4D[2][c].

[277] *See generally* P. Goldstein, Copyright § 2.15.1.2 (1989).

[278] *See* § 4C[1][d][i].

[279] Imperial Home Corp. v. Lamont, 458 F.2d 895, 899, 173 U.S.P.Q. 519 (5th Cir. 1972) ("nothing in Baker v. Selden prevents . . . a copyright [in architectural plans] from vesting the law's grant of an exclusive right to make copies of the copyrighted plans so as to instruct a would-be builder on how to proceed to construct the dwelling pictured"); Demetriades v. Kaufman, 680 F. Supp. 658, 665, 6 U.S.P.Q.2d 1737, 1742-43 (S.D.N.Y. 1988) ("the unauthorized reproduction of copyrighted architectural plans constitutes infringement").

The third issue—whether a building structure constructed according to copyrighted architectural plans is a "copy" of the plans—is part of the general problem of the scope of protection for copyrightable works that depict useful articles.[280] Cases hold that a copyright in architectural drawings gives no right to exclude others from constructing the depicted structure.[281] The copyright owner's rights to prevent copying plans provides substantial protection against unauthorized use of architectural designs. As a practical matter, it is difficult, if not impossible, to construct a building without making multiple copies of plans for the use of contractors, building inspectors, etc. In *Demetriades*,[282] plaintiff Demetriades, a developer specializing in luxury homes, built a $2 million house at 12A Cooper Road in Scarsdale, New York, using plans prepared by an architect. Defendant Kaufman contracted with another builder, the Gallo Brothers, for construction of a home at 24 Cooper Road, Scarsdale, the house to be of "substantially identical design" as the Demetriades house. The plaintiff obtained an assignment of the copyright from its architect and sued Kaufman and the Gallo Brothers for copyright infringement. Finding infringement, the court declined to "enjoin construction of the Kaufmann house based on alleged infringement of the . . . architectural plans" but prohibited further copying of the plans, prohibited reliance on any infringing copies, and impounded all infringing copies of the plans within defendants' control. The court recognized that "the effect of our ruling may be to shut down construction for a certain period of time, at least until new plans can be drawn up and submitted to the Scarsdale Architectural Review Board for consideration."[283]

The fourth issue—whether the design of a building or other structure can itself be considered a copyrightable work—is part of the general problem of the copyrightability of useful articles.[284] Generally, under pre-1991 law, buildings are not copyrightable, no matter how novel and ornamental, because buildings are useful articles and their ornamental features cannot be identified separately from, and are not capable of existing independently of, its utilitarian aspects.

In adhering to the Berne Convention in 1988, the United States assumed the obligation of providing adequate copyright protection for the subject matter entitled to protection under the Berne Convention, which includes architectural works. Congress amended the Section 101 definition of "pictorial, graphic and sculptural works"

A Sixth Circuit decision suggested that the *Baker* copying for use doctrine prevents an architectural plans copyright owner from prohibiting the unauthorized copying of drawings when the purpose of the copying is to use the drawings to construct a building. Scholz Homes, Inc. v. Maddox, 379 F.2d 84, 154 U.S.P.Q. 197 (6th Cir. 1967). Subsequent cases, including *Imperial Home* and *Demetriades*, distinguish and limit the *Scholz Homes* suggestion.

[280] See § 4C[3][e].

[281] Imperial Home Corp. v. Lamont, 458 F.2d 895, 898, 173 U.S.P.Q. 519 (5th Cir. 1972) ("no architect who copyrights his blueprints could thereby acquire a monopoly on the right to build a house with 2 × 4s or with a pitched roof or with a slab foundation or any other particular feature, no matter how unique"); Demetriades v. Kaufman, 680 F. Supp. 658, 6 U.S.P.Q.2d 1737 (S.D.N.Y. 1988).

[282] Demetriades v. Kaufman, 680 F. Supp. 658, 6 U.S.P.Q.2d 1737 (S.D.N.Y. 1988).

[283] 680 F. Supp. at 664, 666 n.13, 6 U.S.P.Q.2d at 1741, 1743 n.13.

[284] See § 4C[3].

by adding a reference to "architectural plans" but expressed its intent to codify existing law on the scope of protection for architectural plans and works.

[ii] *The 1990 Architectural Works Copyright Protection Act.* The 1990 Architectural Works Copyright Protection Act addresses the fourth issue discussed above, the copyrightability of a building. The Act is prospective, protecting only works created on or after the enactment date and works "unconstructed and embodied in unpublished plans or drawings" on the enactment date.[285]

The Act adds "architectural works" to Section 102(a)'s list of copyrightable work categories and defines architectural works as:

> "[T]he design of a building as embodied in any tangible medium of expression, including a building, architectural plans, or drawings. The work includes the overall form as well as the arrangement and composition of spaces and elements in the design, but does not include individual standard features."[286]

The definition contains several facets. First, it is limited to *building* designs and does not extend to three-dimensional structures not characterizable as buildings.[287] Second, the building design may be "fixed" in any tangible expression medium, not solely in an actual building.[288] Third, it includes "overall form" and "the arrangement

---

[285] P.L. 101–650, 104 Stat. 5089, 5133. "[T]he general definition in section 101 . . . will apply" in determining whether and when plans are published. H.R. Rep. No. 101–735, 101st Cong., 2d Sess. (1990). *See* § 4D[1][b].

[286] 17 U.S.C. § 101.

[287] During consideration of the 1990 Act, Congress deleted the phrase "or three dimensional structure."

"This phrase was included in H.R. 3990 to cover cases where architectural works [are] embodied in innovative structures that defy easy classification. Unfortunately, the phrase also could be interpreted as covering interstate highway bridges, cloverleafs, canals, dams, and pedestrian walkways. . . .

"The sole purpose of legislating at this time is to place the United States unequivocally in compliance with its Berne Convention obligations. Protection for bridge and related nonhabitable three-dimensional structures is not required by the Berne Convention. Accordingly, the question of copyright protection of these works can be deferred to another day. . . .

". . . Obviously, the term ['building'] encompassed habitable structures such as houses and office buildings. It also covers structures that are used, but not inhabited by human beings, such as churches, pergolas, gazebos, and garden pavilions." H.R. Rep. No. 101–735, 101st Cong., 2d Sess. (1990).

The House Committee recognized that "Monumental, nonfunctional works of architecture are currently protected under section 102(a)(5) of title 17 as sculptural works. These works are, nevertheless, architectural works, and as such, will not be protected exclusively under section 102(a)(8)." H.R. Rep. No. 101–735, 101st Cong., 2d Sess. (1990).

[288] The original version of the bill referred only to architectural works "as embodied" in buildings. Congress changed the language to alleviate concern that "a defendant with access to the plans or drawings could construct an identical building but escape liability so long as the plans or drawings were not copied." H.R. Rep. No. 101–735, 101st Cong., 2d Sess. (1990).

Despite the change, Congress intended to keep separate copyright in the architectural work and copyright in plans and drawings.

and composition of spaces and elements"[289] but excludes "individual standard features."[290]

The Act "incorporates the general standard of originality applicable to all other copyrightable subject matter."[291] The general infringement standard also applies.

> "The references in the definition of 'architectural work' to 'overall form,' and to the nonprotectibility of 'individual standard features' are not intended to indicate that a higher standard of similarity is required to prove infringement of an architectural work, or that the scope of protection of architectural works is limited to verbatim or near-verbatim copying. These definitional provisions are intended merely to give the courts some guidance regarding the nature of the protected matter. The extent of protection is to be made on an ad hoc basis."[292]

The Act disentangles architectural works from the separability test applicable to designs of other useful articles, but the legislative history indicates that the Copyright Office and courts should not "ignore functionality."

> "A two-step analysis is envisioned. First, an architectural work should be examined to determine whether there are original design elements present, including overall shape and interior architecture. If such design elements are present, a second step is reached to examine whether the design elements are functionally required. If the design elements are not functionally required, the work is protectible without regard to the physical or conceptual separability. . . . [T]he aesthetically pleasing overall shape of an architectural work could be protected. . . . "[293]

The Act adds Section 120 limiting the scope of exclusive rights in architectural works.

> "An individual creating an architectural work by depicting that work in plans or drawing will have two separate copyrights, one in the architectural work (section 102(a)(8)), the other in the plans or drawings (section 102(a)(5)). Either or both of these copyrights may be infringed and eligible separately for damages. In cases where it is found that both the architectural work and the plans have been infringed, courts or juries may reduce an award of damages as necessary to avoid double remuneration, but the basic concept of election of protection is important and must be preserved."

[289] "The phrase 'arrangement and composition of spaces and elements' recognizes that (1) creativity in architecture frequently takes the form of a selection, coordination, or arrangement of unprotectable elements into an original, protectable whole; (2) an architect may incorporate new, protectable design elements into otherwise standard, unprotectable building features; and (3) interior architecture may be protected." H.R. Rep. No. 101–735, 101st Cong., 2d Sess. (1990).

[290] "Consistent with other provisions of the Copyright Act [17 U.S.C. § 102(b)] and Copyright Office regulations [37 CFR 202.1], the definition makes clear that protection does not extend to individual standard features, such as common windows, doors and other staple building components. . . . The provision is not . . . intended to exclude from the copyright in the architectural work any individual features that reflect the architect's [sic] creativity." H.R. Rep. No. 101–735, 101st Cong., 2d Sess. (1990).

[291] H.R. Rep. No. 101–735, 101st Cong., 2d Sess. (1990).

[292] *Id.*

[293] H.R. Rep. No. 101–735, 101st Cong., 2d Sess. (1990).

"(a) *Pictorial Representations Permitted.*—The copyright in an architectural work that has been constructed does not include the right to prevent the making, distributing, or public display of pictures, paintings, photographs, or other pictorial representations of the work, if the building in which the work is embodied is located in or ordinarily visible from a public place.

"(b) *Alterations to and Destruction of Buildings.*—Notwithstanding the provisions of section 106A(2)(c), the owners of a building embodying an architectural work may, without the consent of the author or copyright owner of the architectural work, make or authorize the making of alterations to such building, and destroy or authorize the destruction of such building."[294]

Section 120(a) uses "do not interfere with the normal exploitation of architectural works."[295] Section 120(b) limits the exclusive derivative work preparation right in architectural works by allowing a building's owners to alter or destroy the building without the copyright owner's consent.[296]

[4] Fixation

To be copyrightable subject matter, a work of authorship must be fixed in a tangible medium of expression from which it can be perceived, reproduced, or otherwise communicated, either directly or with the aid of a machine.[297] The fixing must be under authority of the author[298] and sufficiently permanent to permit communication of the work for a period of more than transitory duration. The material object in which a work is fixed is either a copy or a phonorecord.

Unfixed works, such as lectures and live performances, may qualify for state common law copyright protection.[299]

---

[294] 17 U.S.C. § 120.

[295] H.R. Rep. No. 101–735, 101st Cong., 2d Sess. (1990). "Given the important public purpose served by these uses and the lack of harm to the copyright owner's market, the Committee chose to provide an exemption, rather than rely on the doctrine of fair use, which requires ad hoc determinations."

For a discussion of fair use, see § 4F[3].

[296] The provision limits the newly-enacted moral rights as well as traditional economic copyright rights. *See* § 4E[6].

[297] *See generally* P. Goldstein, Copyright § 2.4 (1989).

[298] In an infringement situation, the accused infringer may well have fixed the work but without the authority of the author, as might occur when a member of an audience records or transcribes a lecture.

[299] Copyright Act Section 301 preempts state law only as to works of authorship that are "fixed in a tangible medium of expression." 17 U.S.C. § 301(a).

For cases on state law protection of unfixed conversations, see Estate of Hemingway v. Random House, Inc., 23 N.Y.2d 341, 244 N.E.2d 250, 296 N.Y.S.2d 771, 160 U.S.P.Q. 561 (1969); Falwell v. Penthouse International, Ltd., 521 F. Supp. 1204, 215 U.S.P.Q. 975 (W.D. Va. 1981).

California provides protection by statute to "any original work of authorship that is not fixed in any tangible medium of expression . . . as against all persons except one who originally and independently creates the same or similar work." Cal. Civ. Code § 980(a)(1).

[a] **Background:** *White-Smith* v. *Apollo.* Pre-1976 copyright statutes did not expressly require fixation, but it was commonly assumed that a work could be copyrighted only if recorded in a permanent, tangible form. Professor Nimmer argued that fixation in a tangible form is a constitutional requirement stemming from Article I's concept of a writing.[300]

In *White-Smith Music Publishing,*[301] the Supreme Court fostered the idea that fixation must be in a form that allows a human to perceive the work directly and without the aid of a machine. Plaintiffs held copyrights on musical compositions. Defendants encoded performances of those compositions on player-piano rolls. The Court held the rolls were not "copies" of the work because humans could not readily read the musical work. It defined "copy" narrowly.

> "Various definitions have been given by the experts called in the case. The one which most commends itself . . . defines a copy of a musical composition to be 'a written or printed record of it in intelligible notation.' . . . [I]n a broad sense a mechanical instrument which reproduces a tune copies it; but this is a strained and artificial meaning. When the combination of musical sounds is reproduced to the ear it is the original tune as conceived by the author which is heard. These musical tones are not a copy which appeals to the eye. In no sense can musical sounds which reach us through the sense of hearing be said to be copies, as that term is generally understood, and as we believe it was intended to be understood in the statutes under consideration. A musical composition is an intellectual creation which first exists in the mind of the composer; he may play it for the first time upon an instrument. It is not susceptible of being copied until it has been put in a form which others can see and read. The statute has not provided for the protection of the intellectual conception apart from the thing produced, however meritorious such conception may be, but has provided for the making and filing of a tangible thing, against the publication and duplication of which it is the purpose of the statute to protect the composer.
>
> . . . .
>
> ". . . [W]hat is the perforated roll? . . . [E]ven those skilled in the making of these rolls are unable to read them as musical compositions, as those in staff notations are read by the performer. . . . [T]here is some testimony to the effect that great skill and patience might enable the operator to read this record as he could a piece of music written in staff notation. But the weight of the testimony is emphatically the other way, and they are not intended to be read as an ordinary piece of sheet music. . . .
>
> "These perforated rolls are parts of a machine which, when duly applied and properly operated in connection with the mechanism to which they are adapted, produce musical tones in harmonious combination. But we cannot think that they are copies within the meaning of the copyright act."[302]

---

[300] 1 Nimmer on Copyright § 1.08 (1978).

[301] White-Smith Music Publishing Co. v. Apollo Co., 209 U.S. 1 (1908). For the impact of *White-Smith* on the protectability of sound recordings, see § 4C[1][e].

[302] 209 U.S. at 17–18.

White-Smith dealt with copyright infringement, not the form in which a work must be fixed to qualify for copyright protection, but because the copyright statute in effect at that time required an author to deposit two "copies" of his work to secure protection, it followed that a copyrightable work must be fixed in a copy as defined by *White-Smith*.

In the 1909 Act, Congress did not alter the *White-Smith* definition of a copy though it did give composers recording rights.[303]

[b] **The 1976 Act.** In the 1976 Act, Congress retained the requirement that a work be permanently fixed by authority of the author but altered the *White-Smith* definition. The Act's definitions of fixation, copy, and phonorecord,[304] include objects from which the work can be perceived directly *or* with the aid of a machine.

[c] **Unfixed Works: Performances, Video Games, Characters.** Examples of unfixed works are impromptu performances and lectures.

Decisions consider whether a video game meets the fixation requirement insofar as it is treated as an audio-visual work distinct from the computer program that generates the game.[305] The game's sights and sounds vary as players operate it in the "play" mode. Most video games have, in addition to the "play" mode, an "attract"

---

[303] *See* §§ 4C[1][e] and 4E[7].

[304] 17 U.S.C. § 101:

> " 'Copies' are material objects, other than phonorecords, in which a work is fixed by any method now known or later developed, and from which the work can be perceived, reproduced, or otherwise communicated, either directly or with the aid of a machine or device. The term 'copies' includes the material object, other than a phonorecord, in which the work is first fixed."

> . . . .

> "A work is 'fixed' in a tangible medium of expression when its embodiment in a copy or phonorecord, by or under the authority of the author, is sufficiently permanent or stable to permit it to be perceived, reproduced, or otherwise communicated for a period of more than transitory duration. A work consisting of sounds, images, or both, that are being transmitted, is 'fixed' for purposes of this title if a fixation is being made simultaneously with its transmission.

> . . . .

> " 'Phonorecords' are material objects in which sounds, other than those accompanying a motion picture or other audiovisual work, are fixed by any method now known or later developed, and from which the sounds can be perceived, reproduced, or otherwise communicated, either directly or with the aid of a machine or device. The term 'phonorecords' includes the material object in which the sounds are first fixed."

Congress did not overrule *White-Smith's* narrow holding, which was that a piano roll, being a device that can, when operated with a machine, produce sounds, is not a "copy." Under the 1976 Act, a piano roll would be a "phonorecord" rather than a "copy." Most Copyright Act rights apply to both copies and phonorecords. *See, e.g.,* 17 U.S.C. § 106(1) (conferring the exclusive right to "reproduce the copyrighted work in copies *or phonorecords*" (emphasis added)).

[305] *See* § 4C[2][b]. The computer program itself is clearly fixed—usually in several tangible media of expression (paper print-outs of code, ROM chips and magnetic disks or diskettes).

mode (that is, one that runs repetitively to attract the attention of potential customer-players). The courts uniformly find sufficient permanency in the game's visual and aural characteristics, including its "attract" mode, to satisfy the fixation requirement.[306]

The fixation requirement may be an obstacle to copyright protection for a character or performance style.[307] In *Columbia Broadcasting*,[308] plaintiff created a character, "Paladin," who wore distinctive black Western clothing and passed out cards saying "Have Gun Will Travel" and containing a chess knight symbol. Plaintiff appeared at rodeos and horse shows, often staging a western gunfight. Some ten years later, defendant CBS produced a television series, "Have Gun Will Travel," with actor Richard Boone portraying a character remarkably similar to plaintiff's character. Plaintiff sued under a state law unfair competition theory, to wit, misappropriation of his character. Apparently, plaintiff had not taken steps to secure copyright protection for any portion of his character.[309] The defendant asserted a preemption defense, contending that plaintiff's character was a "writing of an author" in the constitutional sense and could be protected, if at all, only by federal copyright statutes. The First Circuit agreed that any state intellectual property law could not constitutionally apply because plaintiff's character was indeed a constitutional writing—though it was probably barred from statutory protection because of the fixation requirement.[310] It rejected the argument that "a character is not copyrightable."[311]

---

[306] *E.g.*, Williams Electronics, Inc. v. Artic International, Inc., 685 F.2d 870, 874, 215 U.S.P.Q. 405, 408 (3d Cir. 1982) ("Although there is player interaction with the machine during the play mode which causes the audiovisual presentation to change in some respects from one game to the next in response to the player's varying participation, there is always a repetitive sequence of a substantial portion of the sights and sounds of the game, and many aspects of the display remain constant from game to game regardless of how the player operates the controls. . . . Furthermore, there is no player participation in the attract mode which is displayed repetitively without change."); Midway Mfg. Co. v. Dirkschneider, 543 F. Supp. 466, 214 U.S.P.Q. 417 (D. Neb. 1981).

[307] *See* § 4C[1][d][vi].

[308] Columbia Broadcasting Sys., Inc. v. DeCosta, 377 F.2d 315 (1st Cir. 1967), *cert. denied*, 389 U.S. 1007, 156 U.S.P.Q. 719 (1967).

[309] The court indicated that at least the cards were copyrightable subject matter under then existing law, but plaintiff failed to place a copyright notice on the cards.

[310] The preemption theory upheld in *DeCosta*—that state law may not protect against copying any published work that is a "Writing" within the meaning of the United States constitution, even though the work falls outside the current statutory scope of copyright protection—is based on an interpretation of the *Sears-Compco* doctrine that was later revised by the Supreme Court in *Goldstein*. *See* § 1D[3][a][ii]. *DeCosta* remains as a provocative judicial consideration of the status of a character as a potentially copyrightable writing of an author.

[311] As to the *Warner Bros.* decision, discussed above, the court noted:

"[*Warner*] held that assignee of the copyright of the novel *The Maltese Falcon* could not prevent the author from using the character Sam Spade in a sequel. But that case is inapposite, because it held only (a) that the contract of assignment did not convey the exclusive right to use the characters in the novel, and (b) that the sequel, *The Kandy Tooth*, was not so similar as to infringe the copyright. That is far from saying that characters are inherently uncopyrightable." 377 F.2d at 320.

See § 4C[1][d][vi].

To the "more substantial argument" that a constitutional writing "should be limited to mean some identifiable, durable, material form" and that "plaintiff's creation, being a personal characterization, was not reduced and could not be reduced to such a form," the court responded:

> "First, while more precise limitations on —'writings' might be convenient in connection with a statutory scheme of registration and notice, we see no reason why Congress's power is so limited. Second, we cannot say that it would be impracticable to incorporate into the copyright system a procedure for registering 'characters' by filing pictorial and narrative description in an identifiable, durable, and material form." [312]

[d] **Live Broadcasts: Simultaneous Fixation and Transmission.** Section 101's definition of "fixed" addresses the problem of live works, that is, those created simultaneously with their performance or broadcast.[313] The definition requires that the fixation be permanent or stable, which excludes an unrecorded broadcast but provides that "A work consisting of sounds, images, or both, that are being transmitted, is 'fixed' for purposes of this title if a fixation of the work is being made simultaneously with its transmission." This provision covers virtually all radio and television broadcasts, which networks and stations record.

A broadcast may entail several layers of fixed and therefore copyrighted works. A live, simultaneously-recorded broadcast of a sporting or news event, such as a football game or press conference, involves only copyrightable authorship in the broadcast itself, the selection of camera angles, etc.[314] The event itself is not a

---

[312] 377 F.2d at 315.

[313] The House Report on the 1976 Act explains the effect of these provisions as follows.

"[The Act] seeks to resolve, through the definition of 'fixation' in section 101, the status of live broadcasts—sports, news coverage, live performances of music, etc.—that are reaching the public in unfixed form but that are simultaneously being recorded. When a football game is being covered by four television cameras, with a director guiding the activities of the four cameramen and choosing which of their electronic images are sent out to the public and in what order, there is little doubt that what the cameramen and the director are doing constitutes 'authorship.' The further question to be considered is whether there has been a fixation. If the images and sounds to be broadcast are first recorded (on a video tape, film, etc.) and then transmitted, the recorded work would be considered a 'motion picture' subject to statutory protection against unauthorized reproduction or re-transmission of the broadcast. If the program content is transmitted live to the public while being recorded at the same time, the case would be treated the same; the copyright owner would not be forced to rely on common law rather than statutory rights in proceeding against an infringing user of the live broadcast.

"Thus, assuming it is copyrightable—as a 'motion picture' or 'sound recording,' for example—the content of a live transmission should be regarded as fixed and should be accorded statutory protection if it is being recorded simultaneously with its transmission. On the other hand, the definition of 'fixation' would exclude from the concept purely evanescent or transient reproductions such as those projected briefly on a screen, shown electronically on a television or other cathode ray tube, or captured momentarily in the 'memory' of a computer." H.R. Rep. No. 94–1476, 94th Cong., 2d Sess. (1976).

[314] A live broadcast of sporting event is a copyrightable work of authorship. See Baltimore Orioles, Inc. v. Major League Baseball Players Ass'n, 805 F.2d 663, 231 U.S.P.Q. 673, 676

work of authorship, and no copyright in the broadcast would be infringed if another made a similar broadcast or description of the uncopyrightable event.[315] On the other hand, the live, simultaneously-recorded broadcast of an event that is itself a copyrightable work, such as an original dance, play, or comic routine, may give rise to both a copyrighted broadcast and a copyrighted choreographic, dramatic, or literary work (the recording of the performance being the fixation if one has not previously occurred).

[5] Originality.

To be eligible for copyright protection a work must be original, that is, the product of the author's own mind rather than a mere copy of an existing work. Original-ity carries no requirement of substantial ingenuity, aesthetic merit, or novelty.[316] An independently created work is original though identical to a prior work. A work that copies a prior work or records a natural object or scene is original to the extent that it introduces a substantial and creative variation to the work, object or scene.

Court decisions define the fundamental copyright requirement of originality.[317]

(7th Cir. 1986), *cert. denied*, 480 U.S. 941 (1987) ("The many decisions that must be made during the broadcast of a baseball game concerning camera angles, types of screens, and shot selection . . . supply the creativity required for the copyrightability of the telecasts.").

[315] *Cf.* Production Contractors, Inc. v. WGN Continental Broadcasting Co., 622 F. Supp. 1500, 228 U.S.P.Q. 604 (N.D. Ill. 1985). In *Production Contractors*, the plaintiff organized a Christmas parade to take place on public streets in Chicago. The parade included decorative floats, marching bands, novelty acts, and the "first appearance of the year by Santa Claus in Chicago." Plaintiff sold "exclusive" television rights to a network and its affiliated Chicago station. The defendant, another station, proposed to telecast the parade, using its own personnel and equipment. The court dismissed the plaintiff's suit for copyright infringement because a parade is not an original work of authorship and because defendant would not infringe any copyright in the broadcast.

Unauthorized photographing or broadcast of an event may violate rights other than those arising from the copyright laws.

[316] *Cf.* Feist Publications, Inc. v. Rural Telephone Service Company, Inc., 111 S. Ct. 1282, 1287, 18 U.S.P.Q.2d 1275, 1278 (1991) ("Original, as the term is used in copyright, means only that the work was independently created by the author (as opposed to copied from other works), and that it possesses at least some minimal degree of creativity. . . . To be sure, the requi-site level of creativity is extremely low; even a slight amount will suffice. . . . originality is not a stringent standard; it does not require that facts be presented in an innovative or surprising way"); Baltimore Orioles, Inc. v. Major League Baseball Players Ass'n, 805 F.2d 663, 668 n.6, 231 U.S.P.Q. 673, 675 n.6 (7th Cir. 1986), *cert. denied*, 480 U.S. 941 (1987) ("It is important to distinguish among three separate concepts—originality, creativity, and novelty. A work is original if it is the independent creation of its author. A work is creative if it embodies some modest amount of intellectual labor. A work is novel if it differs from existing works in some relevant respect. For a work to be copyrightable, it must be original and creative, but need not be novel.").

[317] *See* Feist Publications, Inc. v. Rural Telephone Service Company, Inc., 111 S. Ct. 1282, 18 U.S.P.Q.2d 1275 (1991), discussed at §§ 4C[1][b][i] and 4C[5][a].

For early court decisions establishing a low minimum standard of originality, see Gray v. Russell, 10 F. Cas. 1035 (No. 5728) (C.C. D. Mass. 1839) (accumulation and combination of annotations to accompany a public domain text on Latin grammar); Emerson v. Davis, 8 F.

In codifying copyright law in the 1976 Act, Congress purposely left the standard undefined.[318]

[a] Novelty and Independent Creation: Constitutional Standards of Originality. Copyright law imposes no novelty requirement. A later work may be copyrightable even though it is identical to a prior work, provided that the later work is original, that is, neither directly nor indirectly derived from the prior work. In a famous and often-quoted passage, Judge Learned Hand opined:

> "[I]t is plain beyond peradventure that anticipation as such cannot invalidate a copyright. Borrowed the work must indeed not be, for a plagiarist is not himself pro tanto an 'author,' but if by some magic a man who had never known it were to compose anew Keats's Ode on a Grecian Urn, he would be an 'author,' and, if he copyrighted it, others might not copy that poem, though they might of course copy Keats's . . . But though a copyright is for this reason less vulnerable than a patent, the owner's protection is more limited for just as he is no less an 'author' because others have preceded him, so another who follows him, is not a tort-feasor unless he pirates his work. . . . If the copyrighted work is therefore original, the public demesne is important only on the issue of infringement; that is, so far as it may break the force of the inference to be drawn from likenesses between the work and putative piracy. If the defendant has had access to other material which would have served him as well his disclaimer becomes more plausible."[319]

Cas. 615 (No. 4436) (C.C.D. Mass. 1845) (map created with cartographer's own skill may be copyrightable even though the resulting work product is nearly identical to prior maps).

[318] According to the House Committee Report on the 1976 Copyright Act, "the phrase 'original works of authorship' [in Section 102(a)], which is purposely left undefined, is intended to incorporate without change the standard of originality established by the courts under the present copyright statute. This standard does not include requirements of novelty, ingenuity, or aesthetic merit, and there is not intention to enlarge the standards of copyright protection to require them." H.R. Rep. No. 94–1476, 94th Cong., 2d Sess. 51 (1976).

[319] Sheldon v. Metro-Goldwyn Pictures Corp., 81 F.2d 49 (2d Cir. 1936), aff'd, 309 U.S. 390 (1940). One cannot but enjoy Judge Learned Hand's sparkling writing style; as a District Judge and later Circuit Judge, for a 50 year period, he wrote many opinions in the patent and copyright field. See Godula, *Judge Learned Hand and the Conception of Invention*, 9 IDEA 159 (1965); Note, *Judge Learned Hand and the Law of Patents and Copyrights*, 60 Harv. L. Rev. 394 (1947).

See also Feist Publications, Inc. v. Rural Telephone Service Company, Inc., 111 S. Ct. 1282, 1287-88, 18 U.S.P.Q.2d 1275, 1278 (1991) ("Originality does not signify novelty; a work may be original even though it closely resembles other works so long as the similarity is fortuitous, not the result of copying. To illustrate, assume that two poets, each ignorant of the other, compose identical poems. Neither work is novel, yet both are original and, hence, copyrightable."); Alfred Bell & Co., Ltd. v. Catalda Fine Arts, Inc., 191 F.2d 99, 102 (2d Cir. 1951) (noting the ambiguity of the word "original"; "It may mean startling, novel or unusual, a marked departure from the past. Obviously this is not what is meant when one speaks of 'the original package,' or the 'original bill,' or . . . an 'original' document; none of those things is highly unusual in creativeness. 'Original' in reference to a copyrighted work means that the particular work 'owes its origin' to the 'author.' . . . No large measure of novelty is necessary.").

Independent creation of a work identical to a previous work is not improbable when the expression in the work is relatively simple or is influenced by factual or functional considerations.[320] Independent creation of a complex, fanciful work, such as Keats's Ode, is not probable (and, undoubtedly, is cited by Judge Hand as a hypothetical only to illustrate the principle).

In Lee,[321] dissenting from the Supreme Court's denial of certiorari, Justice William O. Douglas suggested that the constitutional clause authorizing Congress to enact the copyright system may dictate a minimum novelty requirement. Plaintiff published a book on face lifting exercises. Defendant, a former employee of plaintiff, published a later book explaining the same system of exercises. According to Justice Douglas, the defendant used different language and yet was found guilty of copyright infringement by the lower courts.[322] His dissenting opinion can be interpreted as simply quarreling with the results in the particular case on the ground that the finding of infringement pushed copyright over the line from the protection of expression to the protection of ideas,[323] but, in the opinion, he challenged the constitutionality of the

---

[320] See, e.g., Fred Fisher, Inc. v. Dillingham, 298 F. 145 (S.D.N.Y. 1924). In Dillingham, Judge Hand held that a musical phrase, an "ostinato" or constantly repeated figure accompanying the melody in the copyrighted work, plaintiff's "Dardanella," was original and infringed by the accompaniment in the accused work, defendant's "Kalua," even though the exact same phrasing appeared in several prior published musical works. The defendant, at least unconsciously, copied plaintiff's work, which he had heard shortly before composing the accused work. Plaintiff was unaware of the prior musical compositions. Judge Hand noted that plaintiff's work was "original" "if by original one means that it was the spontaneous, unsuggested result of the author's imagination." He concluded that "originality is alone the test of validity."

   "Any subsequent person is, of course, free to use all works in the public domain as sources for his compositions. No later work, though original, can take that from him. But there is no reason in justice or law why he should not be compelled to resort to the earlier works themselves, or why he should be free to use the composition of another, who himself has not borrowed. If he claims the rights of the public, let him use them; he picks the brains of the copyright owner as much, whether his original composition be old or new. The defendant's concern lest the public should be shut off from the use of works in the public domain is therefore illusory; no one suggests it. That domain is open to all who tread it; not to those who invade the closes of others, however similar." 298 F. at 150.

[321] Lee v. Runge, 404 U.S. 887, 171 U.S.P.Q. 322 (1971). Justice Douglas' opinion is in no sense for the Supreme Court. His opinion stimulated scholarly discussion of copyright's originality standard but had little effect on the course of copyright law.

[322] See Runge v. Lee,, 441 F.2d 579 (9th Cir. 1971). Plaintiff's book presented a series of 16 exercises. Defendant's book presented the same 16 exercises, adding only one of her own. One might argue that what defendant took was plaintiff's compilation of exercises, compilations constituting copyrightable works in themselves. The finding for plaintiff was based on a jury verdict. The jury was instructed:

   "If you find that a subsequent writer used her own labors, skills or common sources of knowledge open to all men, and that the resemblances are accidental, or arise from the nature of the subject matter, this does not amount to a wrongful copying. . . . " 441 F.2d at 582.

The instruction is odd but seemed to say that the jury should not find infringement solely because the defendant copied the plaintiff's ideas.

[323] See § 4C[1][d].

traditional copyright originality concept and the absence of a novelty requirement. Quoting *Graham*,[324] the germinal 1966 Supreme Court patent case in which the Court stressed that Congress could not authorize the grant of patents that failed to meet a constitutional minimum novelty standard, Justice Douglas argued that the copyright and patent systems stem from the same constitutional clause and should be governed by the same economic philosophy and therefore should be bound by the same novelty standard.[325]

In *Feist*,[326] the Supreme Court confirmed that copyright originality "does not signify novelty" but emphasized that originality has a constitutional basis that requires a minimum degree of creativity.

> "Originality is a constitutional requirement. The source of Congress' power to enact copyright laws is Article I, § 8, cl. 8, of the Constitution, which authorizes Congress to 'secur[e] for limited Times to Authors . . . the exclusive Right to their respective Writings.' In two decisions from the late 19th Century—*The Trade-Mark Cases*, 100 U.S. 82 (1879); and *Burrow-Giles Lithographic Co. v. Sarony*, 111 U.S. 53 (1884)—this Court defined the crucial terms 'authors' and 'writings.' In so doing, the Court made it unmistakably clear that these terms presuppose a degree of originality.

> "In *The Trade-Mark Cases*, the Court addressed the constitutional scope of 'writings.' For a particular work to be classified 'under the head of writings of authors,' the Court determined, 'originality is required.' . . . The Court explained that originality requires independent creation plus a modicum of creativity: '[W]hile the word *writings* may be liberally construed, as it has been, to include original designs for engraving, prints, & c., it is only such as are

---

[324] Graham v. John Deere Co., 383 U.S. 1, 148 U.S.P.Q. 459 (1966), discussed at § 2B[6] and 2C[4][a].

[325] *Compare* Alfred Bell & Co., Ltd. v. Catalda Fine Arts, Inc., 191 F.2d 99, 100–102 (2d Cir. 1951), discussed at § 4C[5][b]:

> "Congressional power to authorize both patents and copyrights is contained in Article 1, Sec. 8 of the Constitution. . . . [P]ointing to the Supreme Court's . . . requirement that, to be valid, a patent must disclose a high degree of uniqueness, ingenuity and inventiveness, the defendants assert that the same requirement constitutionally governs copyrights. . . . But the very language of the Constitution differentiates (a) 'authors' and their 'writings' from (b) 'inventors' and their 'discoveries.' Those who penned the Constitution, . . . of course, knew the difference.

> ". . . [Under the] patent statute, enacted April 10, 1790, . . . the applicant for a patent was obliged to file a specification 'so particular' as 'to distinguish the invention or discovery from other things before known and used . . . ' . . . The Copyright Act, enacted May 31, 1790, . . . covered 'maps, charts, and books.'

> "Thus legislators peculiarly familiar with the purpose of the Constitutional grant, by statute, imposed far less exacting standards in the case of copyrights. They authorized the copyrighting of a mere map which, patently, calls for no considerable uniqueness. They exacted far more from an inventor.

> ". . . [N]othing in the Constitution commands that copyrighted matter be strikingly unique or novel."

[326] Feist Publications, Inc. v. Rural Telephone Service Company, Inc., 111 S. Ct. 1282, 18 U.S.P.Q.2d 1275 (1991), discussed at § 4C[1][b][i](2).

original, and are founded in the creative powers of the mind. The writings which are to be protected are *the fruits of intellectual labor*, embodied in the form of books, prints, engravings, and the like.' Ibid. (emphasis in original).

"In *Burrow-Giles*, the Court distilled the same requirement from the Constitution's use of the word 'authors.' The Court defined 'author,' in a constitutional sense, to mean 'he to whom anything owes its origin; originator; maker.' . . . As in *The Trade-Mark Cases*, the Court emphasized the creative component of originality. It described copyright as being limited to 'original intellectual conceptions of the author,' *ibid.*, and stressed the importance of requiring an author who accuses another of infringement to prove 'the existence of those facts of originality, of intellectual production, of thought, and conception.' . . .

"The originality requirement articulated in *The Trade-Mark Cases* and *Burrow-Giles* remains the touchstone of copyright protection today. See *Goldstein v. California*, 412 U.S. 546, 561–562 (1973). It is the very 'premise of copyright law.' *Miller v. Universal City Studios, Inc.*, 650 F.2d 1365, 1368 (CA5 1981)."[327]

[b] **Creativity—Substantial Variation.** A person who copies another work or reproduces an existing object produces an original work only if he or she makes a substantial and creative variation in the subject.[328] A vexing copyright law problem is determining what variations are sufficiently "creative." Should the focus be on the *quantity of difference* between the original and the new work, on the *quality of the effort* that went into the creation of the new work—or on both? Future cases will

---

[327] 111 S. Ct. at 1288, 18 U.S.P.Q.2d at 1278. For a discussion of *Burroughs-Giles*, see § 4B. For a discussion of the TradeMark Cases, see § 5B.

[328] One must distinguish (1) the degree of variation necessary to meet the originality requirement in a work which relies on a prior work from (2) the degree of variation necessary to exculpate an accused work from an infringement charge. *See* Puddu v. Buonamici Statuary, Inc., 450 F.2d 401, 402, 171 U.S.P.Q. 709 (2d Cir. 1971) ("The tests for eligibility for copyright and avoidance of infringement are not the same. Originality sufficient for copyright protection exists if the 'author' has introduced any element of novelty as contrasted with the material previously known to him. Introduction of a similar element by the copier of a copyrighted design will not avoid liability for infringement if 'the ordinary observer, unless he set out to detect the disparities, would be disposed to overlook them, and regard their aesthetic appeal as the same.' ").

See also Eden Toys, Inc. v. Florelee Undergarment Co., 697 F.2d 27, 34, 217 U.S.P.Q. 201, 206 (2d Cir. 1982) ("A work which makes non-trivial contributions to an existing one may be copyrighted as a derivative work and yet, because it retains the 'same aesthetic appeal' as the original work, render the holder liable for infringement of the original copyright if the derivative work were to be published without permission from the owner of the original copyright. An example is the second edition of a textbook, which is copyrightable even though it makes only minor revisions of or additions to the first edition. By its very nature a 'derivative work', which is copyrightable as such, borrows substantially from existing works, and is so defined. . . . Yet it is entitled to registration as a copyrighted work even though it would infringe the original copyrighted work if it were created without the permission of the owner of copyright in the underlying work.").

undoubtedly be influenced by *Feist,* [329] which, in the context of data compilations, rejected the "sweat of the brow" theory and confirmed creativity as a constitutional standard of copyrightability.

Courts eschew substantive standards of artistic or literary merit in determining originality. In *Bleistein,* [330] the works were advertisements, circus posters with portraits and figures of performers. The lower court held the works' copyrights invalid because the posters depicted actual persons and groups and lacked sufficient artistic merit.[331] The Supreme Court reversed. In a colorful opinion, Justice Holmes wrote:

> "[T]he plaintiff's case is not affected by the fact, if it be one, that the pictures represent actual groups—visible things. They seem from the testimony to have been composed from hints or description, not from sight of a performance. But even if they had been drawn from the life, that fact would not deprive them of protection. The opposite proposition would mean that a portrait by Velasquez or Whistler was common property because others might try their hand on the same face. Others are free to copy the original. They are not free to copy the copy. . . . The copy is the personal reaction of an individual upon nature. Personality always contains something unique. It expresses itself [singularly] even in handwriting, and a very modest grade of art has in it something irreducible, which is one man's alone. That something he may copyright unless there is a restriction in the words of the act.
>
> . . .
>
> "It would be a dangerous undertaking for persons trained only to the law to constitute themselves final judges of the worth of pictorial illustrations, outside of the narrowest and most obvious limits. At the one extreme some works of genius would be sure to miss appreciation. Their very novelty would make them repulsive until the public had learned the new language in which their author spoke. . . . At the other end, copyright would be denied to pictures which appealed to a public less educated than the judge. Yet if they command the interest of any public, they have a commercial value,—it would be bold to say that they have not an aesthetic and educational value,—and the taste of any public is not to be treated with contempt. It is an ultimate fact for the moment, whatever may be our hopes of a change."[332]

In *Alfred Bell & Co.,* [333] the Second Circuit articulated and applied a minimalist creativity standard to sustain the copyrightability of copied works. Plaintiff made

---

[329] Feist Publications, Inc. v. Rural Telephone Service Company, Inc., 111 S. Ct. 1282, 18 U.S.P.Q.2d 1275 (1991), discussed § 4C[1][a][i](2).

[330] Bleistein v. Donaldson Lithographing Co., 188 U.S. 239 (1903).

[331] The posters, which are reproduced in a number of copyright law case books, display artistry and probably have value today to poster art collectors.

[332] 188 U.S. at 249–50, 251–52. *Compare* Gracen v. The Bradford Exchange Ltd., 698 F.2d 300, 217 U.S.P.Q. 1294 (7th Cir. 1983), discussed below.

[333] Alfred Bell & Co. v. Catalda Fine Arts, 191 F.2d 99 (2d Cir. 1951). The facts of the case are reported at 74 F. Supp. 973 and 86 F. Supp. 399.

See generally P. Goldstein, Copyright § 2.11.4 (1989).

mezzotint engravings of old master paintings. The mezzotint engraving process's objective was to make as faithful a copy of the original as possible, in other words, to be as "unoriginal" as one can be, but the reproduction could never be perfect or consistent and inevitably introduced color and form changes. The individual engraver exercised skill and judgment in two stages—making the plate and coloring the plate to make proofs. The result was a very high quality reproduction.

The old master paintings that plaintiff reproduced were in the public domain, that is, not subject to copyright protection, but during wartime, from the late 1930s to the mid-1940s, United States citizens had limited or no access to the original paintings, many of which were in museums in enemy-controlled territory. The defendant made lithographic reproductions of plaintiff's mezzotints. No doubt, defendants were taking a free ride on plaintiff's efforts, but was it a copyright infringement? Defendant made the not insubstantial argument that the plaintiff's works were themselves slavish copies and therefore could not be considered original in a copyright sense. The district court found sufficient distinguishing variations between the mezzotint and the painting it reproduced and even among the multiple mezzotints of the same painting. Ironically, the variations were not intentional and, indeed, resulted not from the engraver's creativity but from the human inability to achieve perfection in the art. Based on these findings, the Second Circuit affirmed the mezzotints' copyrightability as, in the words of the 1909 Act, "reproductions of a work of art" and as "other versions of works in the public domain." Judge Jerome Frank relied on the finding that the mezzotints were not identical to the paintings they copied. He suggested that the reasons for the variations were irrelevant.

> "There is evidence that [the mezzotints] were not intended to, and did not, imitate the paintings they reproduced. But even if their substantial departures from the paintings were inadvertent, the copyrights would be valid. . . . A copyist's bad eyesight or defective musculature, or a shock caused by a clap of thunder, may yield sufficiently distinguishable variations. . . . Having hit upon such a variation unintentionally, the 'author' may adopt it as his and copyright it."[334]

Critical to upholding mezzotint copyrightability in *Alfred Bell* was that the engravers exercised individual skill and judgment in making their creations. The variations from the original, though perhaps an unintended by-product, nevertheless arose from human intellectual expression not dictated by mechanical or functional considerations.[335]

---

[334] 191 F.2d at 104–05.

Judge Frank evoked by analogy the patent law doctrine that "a patentable invention may stem from an accidental discovery." *See* § 2C[4][c][iii].

[335] *Cf.* Feist Publications, Inc. v. Rural Telephone Service Company, Inc., 111 S. Ct. 1282, 1296, 18 U.S.P.Q.2d 1275, 1284 (1991) ("the selection and arrangement of facts cannot be so mechanical or routine as to require no creativity whatsoever. The standard of originality is low, but it does exist").

Is exact reproduction copyrightable, assuming that the reproduction resulted from painstaking human creative effort? A case that almost, but not quite, presented that problem, is Alva Studios, Inc. v. Winninger, 177 F. Supp. 265 (S.D.N.Y. 1959), which upheld the copyrightability of an exact scale reduction to museum specifications of Rodin's statue, "Hand of God." *Cf.*

Cases after *Alfred Bell* do not consistently adhere to Judge Frank's suggestion that any "distinguishable variation" will render a copied work sufficiently original.[336] A leading case, again by the Second Circuit, is *L. Batlin & Sons*.[337] Snyder obtained

---

Gracen v. The Bradford Exchange Ltd., 698 F.2d 300, 304, 217 U.S.P.Q. 1294, 1298 (7th Cir. 1983), discussed below (noting that "A contemporary school of art known as 'Super Realism' attempts with some success to make paintings that are indistinguishable to the eye from color photographs.").

The problem is analogous to patent law's "product of nature" doctrine in patent law under which a person cannot patent an existing, natural product even though that person is the first to discover the product but may claim a patent right if the product is altered, refined or purified in a significant way. *See* § 2C[1][d].

[336] *See, e.g.,* Sherry Mfg. Co. v. Towel King of Florida, Inc., 753 F.2d 1565, 1569, 1568, 225 U.S.P.Q. 1005, 1008, 1007 (11th Cir. 1985) (beach and palm tree towel design based on prior public domain towel design lacked originality; most variations were "virtually unnoticeable upon a cursory comparison of the two towels;" such variations as are noticeable are too insubstantial "to reap the benefits normally afforded to works with more recognizable originality. . . . [E]specially . . . where the primary purpose of making the changes was to make the work copyrightable, and not to make it more aesthetically appealing; . . . [a]dmittedly, the difference between what constitutes sufficient originality and what amounts to a trivial, insubstantial variation, is a fine line indeed"); Durham Industries, Inc. v. Tomy Corp., 630 F.2d 905, 910, 208 U.S.P.Q. 10 (2d Cir. 1980) (plaintiff's toys, based on famous Disney characters, are such close copies of the characters as to lack "even a modest degree of originality;" the originality requirement cannot "be satisfied by the mere reproduction of a work of art in a different medium, or by the demonstration of some 'physical' as opposed to 'artistic' skill"); Secure Services Technology Inc. v. Time and Space Processing Inc., 722 F. Supp. 1354, 1363, 12 U.S.P.Q.2d 1617, 1624 (E.D. Va. 1989) (plaintiff SST's facsimile machine "handshake protocol" that implements an industry standard protocol ("CCITT T.30") is not original: "the form, timing, order and content of SST's handshake protocol are dictated largely by the requirements of the T.30 protocol. . . . [Plaintiff] could, within the T.30 protocol, vary specific bits within certain signals. The T.30 protocol restraints, however, sharply limit these variations. Thus, the protocol specifies which bit to vary, what the variation means, and when the variation can occur. . . . Such minor reordering or variance of binary signals does not rise to the level of copyrightable material. . . . [Plaintiff's] protocol does not contain sufficient choice and selection to qualify for copyright protection.").

Compare Eden Toys, Inc. v. Florelee Undergarment Co., 697 F.2d 27, 34–35, 217 U.S.P.Q. 201, 206 (2d Cir. 1982) (drawing of "Paddington Bear," based on prior copyrighted illustration, is sufficiently original; "The numerous changes made by Gibson—the changed proportions of the hat, the elimination of individualized fingers and toes, the overall smoothing of lines—combine to give the Eden/Gibson drawing a different, cleaner 'look' than the Ivor Wood sketch on which it is based."); Soptra Fabrics, Corp. v. Stafford Knitting Mills, Inc., 490 F.2d 1092, 1094, 180 U.S.P.Q. 545 (2d Cir. 1974) (textile design; "The embellishment or expansion of the original design in repeat, so as to broaden the design and thereby cover a bolt of cloth, together with beginning the pattern in a particular way so as to avoid showing an unsightly joint when the pattern is printed on textiles on a continual basis, constitutes modest but sufficient originality so as to support the copyright."); Doran v. Sunset House Distributing Corp., 197 F. Supp. 940, 944 (S.D. Cal. 1961), *aff'd,* 304 F.2d 251 (9th Cir. 1962) (life-size Santa Claus dummy; the traditional features of Santa are not original, but "the originality here lies in the form—three-dimensional—and the medium—plastic—which plaintiffs have used to express the idea of Santa Claus").

[337] L. Batlin & Son, Inc. v. Snyder, 536 F.2d 486, 191 U.S.P.Q. 588 (2d Cir.), *cert. denied,* 429 U.S. 87 (1976).

an antique cast metal iron "Uncle Sam" coin bank, had it reproduced in plastic by a Hong Kong firm, and began widescale reproduction and distribution. Snyder registered a claim of copyright to his reproduction of the bank. Batlin, a business rival, began importing a similar plastic bank. Snyder filed a notice with the United States Customs Service to exclude Batlin's banks from importation. Batlin sued to bar Snyder from maintaining the notice and enforcing the copyright on the ground the copyrighted work lacked sufficient originality. The court agreed, distinguishing *Alfred Bell* and the "Hands of God" decision,[338] and emphasizing that no artistic skill was involved in altering the antique Uncle Sam bank so as to make it suitable for reproduction by plastic molding.

> "[T]he reproduction must contain 'an original contribution not present in the underlying work of art' and be 'more than a mere copy.'
>
> . . . .
>
> "Nor can the requirement of originality be satisfied simply by the demonstration of 'physical skill' or 'special training' . . . A considerably *higher* degree of skill is required, true artistic skill, to make the reproduction copyrightable. . . . [I]t took [the copyright claimant's representative] '[a]bout a day and a half, two days work' to produce the plastic mold sculpture from the metal Uncle Sam bank. If there be a point in the copyright law pertaining to reproductions at which sheer artistic skill and effort can act as a substitute for the requirement of substantial variation, it was not reached here.
>
> . . . .
>
> "Absent a genuine difference between the underlying work of art and the copy of it for which protection is sought, the public interest in promoting progress in the arts . . . could hardly be served. To extend copyrightability to minuscule variations would simply put a weapon for harassment in the hands of mischievous copiers intent on appropriating and monopolizing public domain work."[339]

Batlin's concern for preventing "copiers" from "appropriating" public domain ignores Judge Hand's powerful opinion in *Dillingham*.[340] *Gracen*[341] expresses the same concern in the course of holding that plaintiff's portrait of Judy Garland (as "Dorothy" in the classic film, "Wizard of Oz," posed with her dog Toto), was not

---

[338] *Batlin* noted that "Originality was found by the district court [in the 'Hands of God' case] to consist primarily in the fact that '[i]t takes "an extremely skilled sculptor" many hours working directly in front of the original' to effectuate a scale reduction. . . . The court, indeed, found the exact replica to be so original, distinct, and creative as to constitute a work of art in itself. The complexity and exactitude there involved distinguishes that case amply from the one at bar." 536 F.2d at 491. It noted further that the copyright claimant's "plastic bank is neither in the category of exactitude required by [the 'Hands of God' case] nor in the category of substantial originality; it falls within . . . a copyright no-man's land." 536 F.2d at 492.

This passage emphasizes the quality of the creative effort rather than the quantity of the variation between the original and copied work.

[339] 536 F.2d at 491–92.

[340] Fred Fisher, Inc. v. Dillingham, 298 F. 145 (S.D.N.Y. 1924), discussed at § 4C[5][a].

[341] Gracen v. The Bradford Exchange Ltd., 698 F.2d 300, 217 U.S.P.Q. 1294 (7th Cir. 1983).

sufficiently original to support a copyright. Plaintiff's portrait was based on still photographs from the film. Judge Posner focused specifically on proof problems that would arise if copyright in a copied work were upheld: it would be difficult to determine whether the alleged copier copied the base work or the derivative work: "the purpose of the term ['original'] in copyright law is not to guide aesthetic judgments but to assure a sufficiently gross difference between the underlying and the derivative work to avoid entangling subsequent artists depicting the underlying work in copyright problems."[342] He distinguished representational art that closely reflects scenes from life or nature, as to which little or no variation from the scene depicted is required by the copyright originality standard.

> "We are speaking . . . only of the requirement of originality in derivative works. If a painter paints from life, no court is going to hold that his painting is not copyrightable because it is an exact photographic likeness. If that were the rule photographs could not be copyrighted, . . . but of course they can be. . . . The requirement of originality is significant chiefly in connection with derivative works, where if interpreted too liberally it would paradoxically inhibit rather than promote the creation of such works by giving the first creator a considerable power to interfere with the creation of subsequent derivative works from the same underlying work."[343]

Gracen is an aberrational deviation from copyright law's well-established originality standard. Plaintiff's work was an original painting that closely tracked but did not slavishly copy the photograph. It introduced more than a trivial variation to the underlying work and the variation resulted from artistic effort, not mere mechanical adaptation (as was the case in *Batlin*). Problems in proving copying, such as whether the accused infringer copied the copyrighted derivative work itself or the derivative work's source, are inherent in the copyright system. Accused infringers are protected, *inter alia*, by placing the burden of proving copying on the copyright owner and by removing any inference of copying based on the similarities between the copyrighted and the accused work once the accused infringer shows that those similarities could arise from a common source.[344]

---

[342] Judge Posner acknowledged that "judges can make fools of themselves pronouncing on aesthetic matters" but emphasized that "artistic originality is not the same thing as the legal concept of originality in the Copyright Act."

"Artistic originality indeed might inhere in a detail, a nuance, a shading too small to be apprehended by a judge.

"But especially as applied to derivative works, the concept of originality in copyright law has as one would expect a legal rather than aesthetic function—to prevent overlapping claims. . . . Suppose Artist A produces a reproduction of the Mona Lisa, a painting in the public domain, which differs slightly from the original. B also makes a reproduction of the Mona Lisa. A, who has copyrighted his derivative work, sues B for infringement. B's defense is that he was copying the original, not A's reproduction. But if the difference between the original and A's reproduction is slight, the difference between A's and B's reproductions will also be slight, so that if B had access to A's reproductions the trier of fact will be hard-pressed to decide whether B was copying A or copying the Mona Lisa itself." 698 F.2d at 303–304, 217 U.S.P.Q. at 1298.

[343] 698 F.2d at 305, 217 U.S.P.Q. at 1298.

[344] *See* § 4F[1][d].

[c] **Factual and Functional Works—Compilations—Maps—Forms.** The courts' oscillation between quantity of difference and quality of effort as the measure of originality is well illustrated in the cases on compilations.[345]

Further illustration of the tension between quantity and quality is found in cases on maps and business and legal forms.[346] Some early cases on maps adopted a "direct observation" rule under which a new map was not original for copyright purposes unless the cartographer did actual observations of physical features and did not simply synthesize and compile data from prior maps.[347] In *Hamilton,*[348] the Ninth Circuit rejected the "observation" rule as inconsistent with general principles of copyright law. KDB Enterprises produced two copyrighted maps of Ada County Idaho—one in 1970 and one in 1973. The 1973 map was primarily a synthesis of prior maps (including the 1970 map). KDB did add a few new features to the map based on direct observations by an employee. Hamilton precisely reproduced the 1973 map and was indicted. The court upheld the copyright as original even apart from the direct observations, which might have been characterized as trivial.[349]

The texts of legal and business forms and agreements are copyrightable subject matter, but the courts find a lack of originality when the creator of the form merely copies or varies in a minor way prior agreements. For example, in *Donald,*[350] plaintiff prepared a legal form for a security interest on behalf of repair service companies that extend credit to their customers. The form agreement reworded prototype agreements from books of standard legal forms. The plaintiff applied at most a minimum amount of original legal thought or analysis. Plaintiff sold a set of the forms to a repair service company. That company had the defendant print a new batch identical except for the plaintiff's copyright notice. The court found that the form failed to show "the minimum degree of creativity and originality necessary to support a valid copyright."[351]

---

[345] *See* § 4C[1][b].

[346] *See generally* P. Goldstein, Copyright §§ 2.14, 2.15.1 (1989).

[347] Amsterdam v. Triangle Publications, 93 F. Supp. 79 (E.D. Pa. 1950), *aff'd on opinion below,* 189 F.2d 104 (3d Cir. 1951).

[348] United States v. Hamilton, 583 F.2d 448, 200 U.S.P.Q. 14 (9th Cir. 1978).

[349] The court noted:

> "Expression in cartography is not so different from other artistic forms seeking to touch upon external realities that unique rules are needed to judge whether the authorship is original. Recording by direct observation is only one measure of a cartographer's skill and talent. . . .

> "Trivial elements of compilation and arrangement, of course, are not copyrightable since they fall below the threshold of originality. For example, it is well-settled that copyright of a map does not give the author an exclusive right to the coloring, symbols, and key used in delineating boundaries of and locations within territory depicted.

> ". . . [T]he elements of authorship embodied in a map consist not only of the depiction of a previously undiscovered landmark or the correction or improvement of scale or placement, but also in selection, design, and synthesis." 583 F.2d at 451–52.

[350] Donald v. Uarco Business Forms, 478 F.2d 764, 176 U.S.P.Q. 513 (8th Cir. 1973).

[351] 478 F.2d at 766.

Some forms cases rely on *Amsterdam,* the source of the "direct observation" rule for map copyrightability. *See also* Donald v. Zack Meyer's T.V. Sales and Service, 426 F.2d 1027 (5th Cir. 1970), *cert. denied,* 400 U.S. 992, 168 U.S.P.Q. 257 (1971) ("Donald has contributed

§ 4D   Acquisition—Formalities

Copyright protection arises automatically upon creation of a work.

Traditionally, United States copyright law imposed two formalities as requisites to copyright perfection: notice and registration. Notice on copies was essential to prevent loss of a work's copyright upon publication. Registration was necessary to file an infringement suit. The 1976 Copyright Act retained the traditional notice requirement but moderated the consequences of notice errors and omissions. The 1988 Berne Convention Implementation Act eliminated the mandatory notice requirement for all works publicly distributed after the Act and eliminated registration as a condition of suit "for infringement of copyright in Berne Convention works whose country of origin is not the United States."

[1]   Creation and Publication

Copyright subsists from a work's creation,[1] which occurs "when it is fixed in a copy or phonorecord for the first time."[2]

[a] **Publication under Pre-1976 Law.** Attachment of federal statutory copyright protection upon a work's creation is a major 1976 Act innovation. Under prior law, publication divided state common law copyright and federal statutory copyright.[3]

---

nothing more than the map maker in *Amsterdam*. While the 'Agreement' is not identical to any single existing form, the substance of each sentence can be found in an earlier form. Thus, like the map in *Amsterdam*, Donald's form is nothing more than a mosaic of the existing forms, with no original piece added. The Copyright Act was not designed to protect such negligible efforts. We reward creativity and originality with a copyright but we do not accord copyright protection to a mere copycat. As one noted authority has observed, 'to make the copyright turnstile revolve, the author should have to deposit more than a penny in the box.' B. Kaplan, An Unhurried View of Copyright 46 (1966). In our case not even the proverbial penny has been placed in the box. Indeed the box is virtually empty.").

Decisions such as *Donald*, which applies a comparable "independent research" rule to forms, may not reflect good law in view of later decisions such as *Hamilton*, discussed above, which reject the direct observation rule.

[1] 17 U.S.C. § 302(a).

[2] 17 U.S.C. § 101. Section 101 provides that "where a work is prepared over a period of time, the portion of it that has been fixed at any particular time constitutes the work as of that time, and where the work has been prepared in different versions, each version constitutes a separate work." For a discussion of what constitutes "fixation," see § 4C[.4].

[3] Some copyright law publication history: In old English common law, it was unclear whether an author or printer had legal protection against unauthorized printing or copying of a work. In 1710, Parliament enacted the Statute of Anne, which provided an exclusive right for printed works for a limited number of years (14 plus renewal for 14). In 1774, the House of Lords decided that an author had rights at common law that were potentially perpetual but that the Statute of Anne necessarily limited that right as to published works. Donaldson v. Beckett, 4 Burr. 2408 (1774). The Lords overruled, or at least limited, a prior common law court decision, Millar v. Taylor, 4 Burr. 2303, 98 Eng. Rep. 201 (Kings Bench 1769).

This pattern of potentially perpetual common law protection for unpublished works and limited statutory protection for published works was imported into United States law by the Supreme Court in Wheaton v. Peters, 33 U.S. 591, 8 L. Ed. 1055 (1834), but the Court took

Publication "divested" the author's common law rights against copying; it "invested" his federal copyright rights only if the published copies had a proper copyright notice.[4]

Publication vexed lawyers, courts, scholars, and students. A play's performance was not a publication,[5] but a painting's display was—if those displaying it took no steps to prevent viewer copying.[6] A "limited" publication, that is, a limited group, limited purpose distribution, was not a publication that divested common law rights.[7]

[b] **Publication under the 1976 Act.** Publication is no longer the critical dividing line between state common law and federal statutory protection but is still an important event for a number of reasons. For example, works created before 1978 are not protected by copyright if they fell into the public domain because of publication

---

a different view of what the common law had been prior to 1710. It read the common law as providing no right in published works: an author of a published work could only look to statutory protection, which in the United States was federal, and failure to comply with the statute's formal requirements caused loss of all rights.

The two divestiture theories lead to the same result in most cases, but the English theory would allow common law protection for works published but not within statutory copyright's scope; the Wheaton theory would deny such protection. Despite Wheaton, the Supreme Court held that state law could provide protection against unauthorized copying of published sound recordings, which were within the Constitutional definition of a writing but were not, until 1972, included within the statutory definition of copyrightable works. Goldstein v. California, 412 U.S. 546, 178 U.S.P.Q. 129 (1973), discussed at § 1D[3][a][ii].

[4] The 1909 Act permitted authors to register unpublished works, but provided little incentive to do so because registration started the 28 year copyright term.

[5] *E.g.,* Ferris v. Frohman, 223 U.S. 424 (1912). Early cases holding a performance not a publication involved dramatic and music performances to live audiences in which it was reasonable to assume that the audience could not or would not make copies and further circulate the work.

A historic application of this traditional rule is King v. Mister Maestro, Inc., 224 F. Supp. 101 (S.D.N.Y. 1963). Dr. Martin Luther King delivered his "I Have A Dream" speech to an audience of millions. The court held that the delivery was not a publication that would divest copyright for want of notice even though Dr. King must have known that his speech was being recorded, transcribed, and reproduced in a wide variety of ways.

[6] American Tobacco Co. v. Werckmeister, 207 U.S. 284 (1907) (dictum).

In Letter Edged in Black Press, Inc. v. Public Bldg. Comm. of Chicago, 320 F. Supp. 1303 (N.D. Ill. 1970), Picasso executed a maquette as a design of a monumental sculpture for the Chicago Civic Center in 1965. The Chicago Building Commission displayed the maquette for publicity purposes in 1966 and 1967. When unveiled in 1967, the actual sculpture contained a copyright notice. The Commission adopted a policy that anyone could photograph or copy the sculpture for private purposes but would need a license for commercial purposes. The court held public displays of the maquette without notice or effective restriction on photography to be a divesting publication.

[7] In a typical limited publication situation, an author distributes a limited number of copies to a limited group for a particular purpose. For example, a scholar or writer might distribute a manuscript to students or colleagues. In *King,* Dr. King circulated advance copies of his speech to the press. The court relied on the limited publication rule to hold that the circulation was not a divesting publication. One might ask: was King's distribution really limited? The court says the speech was "given to the press only," but the press would be expected to use the copies to publish the speech.

(Matthew Bender & Co., Inc.)

without adequate notice; whether the work suffered this fate depends on application of the concept of publication.[8]

Section 101 defines publication:

" 'Publication' is the distribution of copies or phonorecords of a work to the public by sale or other transfer of ownership, or by rental, lease, or lending. The offering to distribute copies or phonorecords to a group of persons for purposes of further distribution, public performance, or public display, constitutes publication. A public performance or display of a work does not of itself constitute publication."[9]

This retains the old rule that public performance is not a publication but rejects the rule that public display of an art work without restrictions against its reproduction is a publication.[10]

[2] Notice

United States copyright law's venerable requirement that a copyright notice, a "c" in a circle or the word "copyright" with the year of publication and the name of the author or copyright owner, was made optional by the Berne Convention Implementation Act.[11]

---

[8] *See* § 4E[1].

The Copyright Act relies on the publication concept in the following sections:

(1) Section 302(e): presumption that the author has been dead for at least fifty years, hence that the copyright has expired, "[a]fter a period of seventy-five years from the year of first publication of a work;"

(2) Section 401(a), (b)(2): notice required on publicly-distributed copies when the work is published, the notice including the year of "publication;"

(3) Section 407(a): deposit of copies within 3 months of publication;

(4) Section 409(8): statement as to year of first publication on registration application;

(5) Section 410(c): registration is prima facie evidence of validity if obtained within five years of "publication;"

(6) Section 405(a)(2): saving validity of copyright on works published without notice if registration is made within five years of publication;

(7) Section 406(b): errors in the date of publication given in notice of copyright;

(8) Section 412: distinguishing between published and unpublished works as to the availability of statutory damages and attorneys fees for acts of infringement occurring prior to registration;

(9) Section 203(a)(3): right of author to terminate transfers and licenses granted by author keyed to date of publication of work under grant;

(10) Section 104: distinguishing between published and unpublished works as to rights of foreign authors;

(11) Section 108(b): right of libraries and archives to copy "unpublished" works; and

(12) Section 110(9): limited right to perform a dramatic literary work "published" at least ten years before the date of the performance.

[9] 17 U.S.C. § 101.

[10] *See* H.R. Rep. No. 94–1476, 94th Cong., 2d Sess. 144 (1976).

[11] P.L. 100–568, 102 Stat. 2853 (Oct. 31, 1988).

Elimination of the mandatory notice requirement applies only to works first published on or after March 1, 1989. The notice requirement's ramifications will remain important for many years to determine whether works published before March 1, 1989 are copyrighted. Indeed, for older works, one must understand not only the 1976 Act notice requirement, which became effective January 1, 1978, but also the 1909 Act's stricter requirement, which governs works published before 1978.[12]

[a]   **Notice under Pre-1976 Law.** 1909 Act Section 10 required that notice be "affixed" to each copy of the work upon publication.[13] Early case law applied the notice requirement strictly. In *Louis Dejonge*,[14] a 1914 Supreme Court decision, the copyright owner sold the copyrighted work, a holly-mistletoe-spruce painting, as gift wrapping paper with twelve repetitions of the design per strip, placing one copyright notice at the edge of each strip. Justice Holmes found the copyright invalid for want of proper notice because the work is the painting, and notice must be "affixed" to each copy of it.

Later case law relaxed the notice requirement. For example, in *Peter Pan Fabrics*,[15] a fabric design copyright owner distributed cloth with the notice on the fabric's selvage, well knowing that buyers would remove or sew under the selvage.[16] The Second Circuit, per Judge Learned Hand, held that "at least in the case of a deliberate copyist . . . the absence of 'notice' is a defence that the copyist must prove, and that the burden is on him to show that 'notice' could have been embodied in the design without impairing its market value." The *Peter Pan* suggestion that the consequences of a defective notice should vary depending on whether the defendant is a "deliberate copyist" had little support in the 1909 Act or in the cases interpreting it. The prevailing rule was that notice was either effective or ineffective.

---

[12] *E.g.*, Data Cash Systems, Inc. v. JS&A Group, Inc., 628 F.2d 1038, 1042, 208 U.S.P.Q. 197 (7th Cir. 1980) ("whether a work entered the public domain prior to the effective date of the 1976 Act must be made according to the copyright law, common law and statutory, as it existed prior to the 1976 Act."); Simon v. Birraporetti's Restaurants Inc., 720 F. Supp. 85, 11 U.S.P.Q.2d 1372 (S.D. Tex. 1989).

[13] Sections 19 and 20 specified the notice's content and placement.

Section 21 provided some relief in cases of the "omission by accident or mistake of the prescribed notice from a particular copy or copies" but did not apply to a complete omission of notice from an entire edition. Data Cash Systems, Inc. v. JS&A Group, Inc., 628 F.2d 1038, 1043, 208 U.S.P.Q. 197 (7th Cir. 1980) ("section 21 does not prevent forfeiture where, as here, notice was omitted from all copies"); National Comics Publications v. Fawcett Publications, 191 F.2d 594, 601 (2d Cir. 1951). *See also* Wabash Publishing Co. v. Flanagan, 14 U.S.P.Q.2d 2037, 2043 (N.D. Ill. 1990) ("Under the 1909 Act, determining whether the number of published copies from which notice was omitted was sufficiently small as to constitute 'a particular copy or copies' turned on the relation of such number to the total number of copies published."); United Merchants & Mfgrs. Inc. v. Sarne Co., 278 F. Supp. 162, 165, 157 U.S.P.Q. 331 (S.D. N.Y. 1967) (no forfeiture when notice missing from between 42 and 500 yards out of 325,000 yards of fabric).

[14] Louis Dejonge & Co. v. Breuker & Kessler Co., 235 U.S. 33 (1914).

[15] Peter Pan Fabrics, Inc. v. Martin Weinger Corp., 274 F.2d 487 (2d Cir. 1960).

[16] Removal of copyright notice without the copyright owner's authority does not affect copyright validity. *See* 17 U.S.C. § 405(c).

[b] Notice under the 1976 Act. The 1976 Act retained the requirement that publicly distributed copies of a work published with the copyright owner's authority must have a copyright notice[17] but added provisions softening the consequences of notice errors or omissions.[18]

The 1976 Act's mandatory notice requirement applied to works published "in the United States *or elsewhere.*"[19] The United States copyright was forfeited if a work was published prior to March 1, 1989, the effective date of the Berne Convention Implementation Act, in another country without notice and compliance with the curative provisions on errors and omissions of notice.

The House Report on the 1976 Act listed four principal copyright notice functions: it (1) places "in the public domain a substantial body of published material that no one is interested in copyrighting"; (2) "informs the public as to whether a particular work is copyrighted"; (3) "identifies the copyright owner"; and (4) "shows the date of publication." It acknowledged the argument that the burdens and unfairness to copyright owners of the notice requirement outweighed the values of notice and that there was a "need to avoid the arbitrary and unjust forfeitures now resulting from unintentional or relatively unimportant omissions or errors in the copyright notice." The 1976 Act's approach was to retain the notice requirement but eliminate the 1909 Act's automatic forfeiture sanction.[20]

Under the 1976 Act, the notice must consist of (1) the symbol C in a circle, the word "Copyright," or the abbreviation "Copr.";[21] (2) the year of first publication;[22]

---

[17] 17 U.S.C. § 401. Section 401 applies to the distribution of "copies." Section 402 applies to publicly distributed "phonorecords." 17 U.S.C. § 402. A phonorecord is a material object in which sounds are fixed. *See* § 4C[4][b]. For phonorecords, the content of the notice is a "P" in a circle.

[18] 17 U.S.C. §§ 405–06.

[19] 17 U.S.C. § 401(a). *See* Hasbro Bradley, Inc. v. Sparkle Toys, Inc., 780 F.2d 189, 228 U.S.P.Q. 423 (2d Cir. 1985). *See also* H.R. Rep. No. 94–1476, 94th Cong., 2d Sess. 144 (1976):

> "The phrase 'or elsewhere,' which does not appear in the present law, makes the notice requirements applicable to copies or phonorecords distributed to the public anywhere in the world, regardless of where and when the work was first published. The values of notice are fully applicable to foreign editions of works copyrighted in the United States, especially with the increased flow of intellectual materials across national boundaries, and the gains in the use of notice on editions published abroad under the Universal Copyright Convention should not be wiped out."

[20] H.R. Rep. No. 94–1476, 94th Cong., 2d Sess. 143 (1976):

> "The fundamental principle underlying the notice provisions of the bill is that the copyright notice has real values which should be preserved, and that this should be done by inducing use of notice without causing outright forfeiture for errors or omissions. Subject to certain safeguards for innocent infringers, protection would not be lost by the complete omission of copyright notice from large numbers of copies or from a whole edition, if registration for the work is made before or within 5 years after publication. Errors in the name or date in the notice could be corrected without forfeiture of copyright."

[21] 17 U.S.C. § 401(b)(1). *See* Forry Inc. v. Neundorfer Inc., 837 F.2d 259, 5 U.S.P.Q.2d 1510, 1515 (6th Cir. 1988) (suggesting that "(c)," *i.e.*, a "c" in parentheses, may suffice to fulfill the notice requirement's "purpose of preventing innocent person from infringing the

and (3) the name of the copyright owner.[23] As to "position of notice," the notice "shall be affixed in such manner and location as to give reasonable notice of the claim of copyright."[24] The Act directs the Register of Copyright to adopt regulations on affixation and positions of notice.[25]

Despite the liberalizing approach of the 1976 Act, forfeiture of copyright for failure to comply with the notice requirement may still occur if the copyright owner does not meet the conditions of the provisions mitigating the consequences of omission of notice.

[i] *Omission of Notice.* Section 405(b) provided that omission of notice "from copies or phonorecords publicly distributed by authority of the copyright owner does not invalidate copyright in a work" if any one of three conditions is met.[26]

The first condition—(a)(1)—is that "the notice has been omitted from no more than a relatively small number of copies or phonorecords distributed to the public." Literally, this condition would apply when either (1) a large number of copies are distributed to the public and notice is omitted from a "relatively small number" of those copies or (2) only a "relatively small number" of copies are distributed to the public with notice omitted from all such copies.[27]

---

copyright"); Videotronics, Inc. v. Bend Electronics, 586 F. Supp. 478, 223 U.S.P.Q. 936 (D. Nev. 1984)(a "C" in a hexagon is sufficient).

[22] Section 401(b) states that "in the case of compilations or derivative works incorporating previously published material, the year date of first publication of the compilation or derivative work is sufficient." It also states that the year date may be omitted "where a pictorial, graphic, or sculptural work, with accompanying text matter, if any, is reproduced in or on greeting cards, postcards, stationery, jewelry, dolls, toys, or any useful articles."

[23] 17 U.S.C. § 401(b)(3). The notice may provide, in lieu of the name of the copyright owner, "an abbreviation by which the name can be recognized, or a generally known alternative designation of the owner."

[24] 17 U.S.C. § 401(c). *See* Forry Inc. v. Neundorfer Inc., 837 F.2d 259, 266, 5 U.S.P.Q.2d 1510, 1515 (6th Cir. 1988) (copyright notice for computer program embodied in a microprocessor placed on the underside of the chip such that it is between the chip and the circuit board; location adequate because "the only way to copy the program is to physically remove the chip from the board").

[25] 17 U.S.C. § 401(c). *See* 17 C.F.R. § 201.20. *See also* Videotronics, Inc. v. Bend Electronics, 586 F. Supp. 478, 223 U.S.P.Q. 936 (D. Nev. 1984).

[26] 17 U.S.C. § 405.

[27] *Compare* Original Appalachian Artworks, Inc. v. Toy Loft, Inc., 684 F.2d 821, 827, 215 U.S.P.Q. 745, 751 (11th Cir. 1982) ("only approximately 1% of . . . total sales [of 40,000] at the time of trial lacked the sewn-in copyright notice . . . [T]his percentage meets the 'relatively few' test . . . .") *with* Donald Frederick Evans & Associates v. Continental Homes, Inc., 785 F.2d 897, 910, 229 U.S.P.Q. 321, 330 (11th Cir. 1986) ("2500 copies . . . which totaled approximately 2.4 percent of the total number of copies, constitutes more than a relatively small number. Unlike the situation in *Original Appalachian Artworks* where the 1 percent had defective notices, the copies we are considering in the instant case had absolutely no indication of copyright affixed. Furthermore, 2,500 copies is a significant number in the absolute sense.").

See also Cooling Systems and Flexibles, Inc. v. Stuart Radiator, Inc., 777 F.2d 485, 489, 228 U.S.P.Q. 275, 279 (9th Cir. 1985) (20,000 out of 25,000 is more than a relatively small

In *Princess Fabrics*,[28] a fabric design copyright case, the Second Circuit held that the district court could properly find that notice was omitted from more than a relatively small number of copies when the defendant introduced one bolt of cloth without a notice and testified that he saw other bolts without notices in retail stores and the plaintiff offered no specific evidence of notice requirement compliance.

The second condition—(a)(2)—is that "registration for the work has been made before or is made within five years after the publication without notice, and a reasonable effort is made to add notice to all copies or phonorecords that are distributed to the public in the United States after the omission has been discovered."[29] This condition has two parts. The first, requiring registration within five years, is clear. The second, requiring a reasonable effort to add notice, is not. Must a copyright owner attempt to retrieve or place notice on copies in the hands of independent distributors and retailers—or even the public?[30] How much effort is "reasonable"?[31]

---

number); Videotronics, Inc. v. Bend Electronics, 586 F. Supp. 478, 482, 223 U.S.P.Q. 936, 938-39 (D. Nev. 1984) (computer program amusement game; notice appeared on screen "on a random and infrequent basis" and on pushing of reset button).

[28] Princess Fabrics, Inc. v. CHF, Inc., 922 F.2d 99, 17 U.S.P.Q.2d 1320 (2d Cir. 1990).

[29] 17 U.S.C. § 405(a)(2). Note that the obligation is only to add notice to copies distributed *in the United States. See* H.R. Rep. No. 94–1476, 94th Cong., 2d Sess. 147 (1976) ("it would be burdensome and impractical to require an American copyright owner to police the activities of foreign licensees in this situation.").

[30] *See, e.g.,* Princess Fabrics Inc. v. CHF Inc., 922 F.2d 99, 103 17 U.S.P.Q.2d 1320, 1323 (2d Cir. 1990) ("It has been widely held that the party seeking to cure the defect is required to make a reasonable effort to affix notice to copies in the possession of retail dealers as such copies are yet to be distributed to the public."); Forry, Inc. v. Neundorfer, Inc., 837 F.2d 259, 5 U.S.P.Q.2d 1510 (6th Cir. 1988); Lifshitz v. Walter Drake & Sons Inc., 806 F.2d 1426, 1433–34, 1 U.S.P.Q.2d 1254, 1259–60 (9th Cir. 1986) (copyright owner must make an effort to add notice to copies in the hands of a distributor, even though the distributor is an independent entity beyond the owner's control: "[T]he copyright holder need only make reasonable efforts to add notice to copies distributed to the public after discovery of the omission. . . . The addition of proper notice to copies held by foreign licensees, or to ones already widely disseminated among the public, would, in a high proportion of cases, prove extremely difficult if it were possible at all. . . . [W]hen Congress used the phrase 'distributed to the public' and then required only 'reasonable efforts' to effect a cure despite its strong interest in encouraging the use of proper copyright notice, it was contemplating a situation where offending copies were scattering among the public and difficult if not impossible to correct. In the situation before us, in contrast, the copies in question were not widely dispersed among the public, and locating them posed little, if any, burden. We hold, therefore, that they had not yet been 'distributed to the public' in the sense intended by section 405(a)(2). It is certainly possible that [the distributor], being an independent entity, would have declined to cooperate with [the copyright owner] in his efforts to add proper copyright notice to these copies. The statute, however, required only that [the owner] make reasonable efforts, not that he succeed."); M. Kramer Manufacturing Co. v. Andrews, 783 F.2d 421, 444, 228 U.S.P.Q. 705, 721 (4th Cir. 1986) ("The holder of copyright has no duty . . . to add a notice to copies that have already been distributed and therefore has no duty to send out replacement programs for games that have already been distributed to the public.").

[31] *See* Princess Fabrics Inc. v. CHF Inc., 922 F.2d 99, 103, 17 U.S.P.Q.2d 1320, 1323 (2d Cir. 1990) (rejecting copyright owner's argument that the district court erred by failing to give it time to make a reasonable cure effort when it discovered the defect six days before trial:

Can the condition ever apply when the copyright claimant has distributed all copies of the work prior to discovery of the omission?[32] The duty to add notice arises "after the omission has been discovered." Discovered by whom? Also, when is an omission "discovered" when a copyright owner distributes copies to the public, knowing that there is no copyright notice, but not knowing that there is any duty under United States copyright law to include such a notice?[33] Is the "discovery" when the

---

"efforts to cure should have commenced immediately" though the cure need not have been complete before trial); Lloyd v. Schlag, 884 F.2d 409, 11 U.S.P.Q.2d 1623 (9th Cir. 1989) (insufficient evidence of reasonable effort); Donald Frederick Evans & Associates v. Continental Homes, Inc., 785 F.2d 897, 911–12, 229 U.S.P.Q. 321, 330-31 (11th Cir. 1986); Shapiro & Son Bedspread Corp. v. Royal Mills Associates, 764 F.2d 69, 74, 226 U.S.P.Q. 340, 343 (2d Cir. 1985) (reversing summary judgment of invalidity of copyright on a design embedded in bed spreads; upon discovery of the defect in the notice on the bedspreads, the owner re-labelled its bedspread inventory but took no steps to add notice to bedspreads already shipped to retailers; a question of fact existed as to the reasonableness of the owner's efforts in view of its contentions that (1) the small inventory in retailers' hands would be sold before proper notices could be prepared and distributed, and (2) "the retailers would have to open the heat-sealed bags in which the bedspreads were contained and would not be able to re-seal those bags."); Videotronics, Inc. v. Bend Electronics, 586 F. Supp. 478, 223 U.S.P.Q. 936 (D. Nev. 1984) (no reasonable effort when computer program copyright owner added notice to new edition instead of correcting old one).

[32] *Compare* Eastern Publishing & Advertising Inc. v. Chesapeake Publishing & Advertising Inc., 831 F.2d 488, 491, 4 U.S.P.Q.2d 1637, 1639 (4th Cir. 1987) ("§ 405(a)(2) does not apply unless there is continuous production of identical products"; the plaintiff "claimed a copyright in two specific issues of its publication, each of which necessarily had not only a limited period of distribution but also a very limited lifespan in the hands of a consumer. Subsequent notice placed upon later, different issues . . . is ineffective to alert others that copyrights cover earlier issues.") *with* Werlin v. Reader's Digest Association, 528 F. Supp. 451, 461, 213 U.S.P.Q. 1041 (S.D.N.Y. 1981) ("Since no copies of [the copyright claimant's] work were distributed to the general public after the omission was discovered . . . the second prong of Section 405(a)(2) has . . . been satisfied.").

Cf. Canfield v. Ponchatoula Times, 759 F.2d 493, 499, 226 U.S.P.Q. 112, 116–117 (5th Cir. 1985) (the copyright claimant, a newspaper, designed and published an advertisement at the request of an advertiser; it omitted any notice; the accused infringer published the advertisement at the request of the advertiser; "What is considered a 'reasonable effort' . . . will vary from case to case. . . . [The copyright claimant's] failure to allege or prove it made any attempt to add notice prevents it from qualifying under (a)(2).").

[33] *See* Hasbro Bradley, Inc. v. Sparkle Toys, Inc., 780 F.2d 189, 228 U.S.P.Q. 423 (2d Cir. 1985).

In *Hasbro*, the original author, a Japanese company, sold 213,000 copies of the work (a toy) in Japan without a copyright notice. The author assigned the copyright to plaintiff, a United States company. The plaintiff had the author make new molds for the toy, which contained a copyright notice, and registered the claim of copyright.

Prior to *Hasbro*, some district courts interpreted the phrase "after the omission has been discovered" in Section 405(a)(2) as not applying to a "deliberate" omission because one cannot later "discover" an omission that was in fact deliberate. Beacon Looms, Inc. v. S. Lichtenberg & Co., 552 F. Supp. 1305, 220 U.S.P.Q. 960 (S.D.N.Y. 1982). Another district court disagreed. O'Neil Developments, Inc. v. Galen Kilburn, Inc., 524 F. Supp. 710, 216 U.S.P.Q. 1123 (N.D. Ga. 1981).

In *Hasbro*, the Second Circuit rejected the *Beacon Looms* analysis and adopted the second view as consistent with the language and legislative history of Section 405(a)(2).

copies are knowingly distributed without notice or when the copyright owner discovers legal mistake?

The third condition—(a)(3)—is that "the notice has been omitted in violation of an express requirement in writing that, as a condition of the copyright owner's authorization of the public distribution of copies or phonorecords, they bear the prescribed notice."[34]

Section 405(b) protects the rights of "innocent infringers" who rely on a copy of the work from which copyright notice has been omitted.[35]

[ii] *Errors in Notice.* Section 406 specifies the effect of errors in name and date in the notice when the work is published with the copyright owner's authority.[36]

"[T]he premise of the argument—namely, that a deliberate omission cannot be 'discovered'—is unsound. . . . [A]n assignee or licensee may effect cure under § 405(a)(2) on behalf of itself and its assignor or licensor. In such a situation . . . no violence is done to the statutory language by saying that the omission, though deliberate on the part of the assignor or licensor, was 'discovered' by the person later attempting to cure it. Similarly, a deliberate omission at a lower level of a corporate hierarchy might well be 'discovered,' in realistic terms, by someone at a higher level. . . .

" . . . [T]he legislative history . . . demonstrates that intentional as well as unintentional omissions were intended to be made curable. While there may be difficulties in determining what constitutes 'a reasonable effort to add notice to all copies . . . that are distributed to the public in the United States after the omission has been discovered' in cases where the omission was intentional and the person attempting to cure is the same person who omitted notice . . . these difficulties are by no means insuperable and constitute no sufficient reason for disregarding the declared legislative intent." 780 F.2d at 196, 228 U.S.P.Q. at 427–28.

[34] 17 U.S.C. § 405(a)(3). *See* Donald Frederick Evans & Associates v. Continental Homes, Inc., 785 F.2d 897, 229 U.S.P.Q. 321 (11th Cir. 1986) (exception not applicable when copyright owner was aware that his drawings would be published; as to a contractual provision requiring his written permission before such drawings could be copied, the owner did not enforce the contract provision); Fantastic Fakes, Inc. v. Pickwick International, Inc., 661 F.2d 479, 484 n.3, 212 U.S.P.Q. 727 (5th Cir. Unit B 1981) ("The logical inference from this requirement is that an implied condition, or even an express condition if not in writing, will not preserve a copyright against the effects of publication without notice or publication with inadequate notice.").

[35] 17 U.S.C. § 405(b).

[36] 17 U.S.C. § 406. An error in name does not affect the validity or ownership of the copyright. Section 406(a) provides "a complete defense" in cases of error in the name where a person begins an undertaking in good faith under a purported transfer from the person named. The defense applies only when the work is published by the copyright owner. Thus, it does not apply to cases in which the defendant obtained rights from a total interloper. That is, it applies only when X authorizes Y to make copies of X's copyrighted work but Y puts his own name in the notice. It does not apply when Y publicly distributes copies without X's permission.

If the year in the notice is *earlier* than the year of actual first publication, the only consequence is that any period from the year of first publication computed under Section 302 is to be computed from the year in the notice. If the year in the notice is "more than one year later than the year in which publication first occurred, the work is considered to have been published without notice and is governed by the provisions of section 405." *See* Lifshitz v. Walter Drake & Sons Inc., 806 F.2d 1426, 1 U.S.P.Q.2d 1254 (9th Cir. 1986).

[*iii*]   *United States Government Works.* Section 403 imposes a special notice requirement as to works "consisting preponderantly of one or more United States Government works."[37]

[*iv*]   *Collective Works.* Section 404 deals with notice on contributions to collective works, such as magazine and journal articles.

The Second Circuit's 1970 *Goodis* decision provides background on the problem to which Section 404 is directed.[38] Goodis, author of the novel "Dark Passage," granted rights to serialize the work in magazine form to Curtis. Curtis duly published the novel in eight installments in the *Saturday Evening Post.* Each magazine issue carried only a general copyright notice in Curtis' name. Later, the author's executor brought a copyright infringement action against United Artists concerning television right to the work. United Artists argued that the work was in the public domain, that is, its copyright was invalid, because it was published without a proper notice. The statute required notice in the name "of the copyright proprietor." Curtis did not own the copyright, only the right to serialize it on a one-time basis. This argument was supported by the old doctrine of indivisibility of copyright—the author or owner could not "assign" (*i.e.*, sell title) to less than all of the rights of copyright and for the full term. Any other grant was a mere license.

The Second Circuit held that a single notice is sufficient to preserve the rights of the actual author-owner.[39] As to the doctrine of indivisibility, the court noted that it developed primarily in the context of determining who had standing to sue for infringement. For example, suppose some pirate began reproducing the serial portions of the novel in the magazine. Could Curtis sue for infringement? No. The concern was that an accused infringer might face multiple or repetitious suits if ownership was split. That concern had little to do with the purposes of copyright notice.[40]

---

[37] United States Government works are not subject to copyright, see § 4C[1][f], but a compilation of such works or the addition to such works of editorial material may be copyrightable.

The notice prescribed by Section 403 must include "a statement identifying, either affirmatively or negatively, those portions of the copies or phonorecords embodying any work or works protected under this title." 17 U.S.C. § 403. Publishers of collections of United States Government works, such as judicial opinions or statutes and regulations, include statements such as "No claim of copyright is made for official U.S. or state government statutes, rules or regulations" or "Copyright is not claimed as to any part of the original work prepared by a United States government officer or employee as part of that person's official duties."

[38] Goodis v. United Artists Television, 425 F.2d 397, 165 U.S.P.Q. 3 (2d Cir. 1970).

[39] *Accord* Abend v. MCA Inc., 863 F.2d 1465, 9 U.S.P.Q.2d 1337 (9th Cir. 1988), *aff'd sub nom. on other grounds,* Stewart v. Abend, 110 S. Ct. 1750, 14 U.S.P.Q.2d 1614 (1990). *Cf.* Fantastic Fakes, Inc. v. Pickwick Int'l, Inc., 661 F.2d 479, 486, 212 U.S.P.Q. 727 (5th Cir. Unit B 1981) ("As to the [1909 Act's] requirement that notice include 'the name of the copyright proprietor,' courts have generally avoided technical forfeitures for failure to strictly comply with the provision, focusing instead on whether the purpose of the notice requirement was served despite the defect in the notice provided.").

[40] The 1976 Act abolished the indivisibility doctrine. A copyright's exclusive rights may be separately transferred. 17 U.S.C. § 201(d)(1). For example, a novel's author may separately assign hardcover book rights, paperback book rights, and motion picture rights. A nonexclusive license is not a copyright transfer. *See* 17 U.S.C. § 101.

The 1976 Copyright Act handles the problem of notice on collective works by providing in Section 404(a) that a separate contribution may bear its own notice but that a single notice applicable to the collective work is sufficient "regardless of the ownership of the copyright in the contributions and whether or not they have been previously published."[41] Section 404(b) provides that if a person named in the single notice is not the owner of the copyright in a separate contribution,[42] the case is treated as one of an error in name under Section 406(a). Copyright validity is not affected. Persons who received transfers or licenses from the named person are protected.

[c] **Notice under the 1988 Act.** The 1988 Berne Convention Implementation Act makes notice optional for copies publicly distributed by authority of the copyright owner after the effective date of the Act (March 1, 1989).[43] The Act retains an

---

[41] 17 U.S.C. § 404(a).

The statute excepts "advertisements inserted on behalf of persons other than the owner of copyright in the collective work." *See* Canfield v. Ponchatoula Times, 759 F.2d 493, 496, 226 U.S.P.Q. 112, 114 (5th Cir. 1985) ("[T]his exception was regarded as necessary because of the nature of advertisements which were regarded as a unique form of copyrightable material. Their uniqueness stems from the fact that advertisements are creations which are commonly published in more than one periodical and seldom display separate copyright notice. . . . Congress intended to adopt the presumption that advertisements, although copyrightable, are not generally copyrighted and often widely reprinted. Consequently, when an advertiser gives a publisher an advertisement which has been published previously in another publication and has no copyright notice affixed, it would be logical for the publisher to presume both that no copyright was claimed by the prior publisher and that reprinting of the advertisement verbatim would not infringe any right of the prior publisher.").

On what is an "advertisement," see Donald Frederick Evans & Associates v. Continental Homes, Inc., 785 F.2d 897, 908, 229 U.S.P.Q. 321, 328 (11th Cir. 1986) (architectural drawings appearing in a "Parade of Homes" supplement for newspapers constitute advertisements; however, a drawing and photograph appearing in "Professional Builder" magazine "was not an advertisement but rather was part of a feature article that constituted a separate contribution to the magazine").

[42] The Copyright Act states rules on collective work contribution ownership: copyright in a collective work and various contributions are "distinct," and a contribution's copyright vests initially in its author. Also, "[i]n the absence of an express transfer of the copyright or of any rights under it, the owner of copyright in the collective work is presumed to have acquired only the privilege of reproducing and distributing the contribution as part of that particular collective work, any revision of that collective work, and any later collective work in the same series." 17 U.S.C. § 201(c).

[43] Among the changes made by the Act are the following:

(1) Sections 401 and 402, the basic notice provisions: striking "shall be placed on all" and inserting "may be placed on;"

(2) Section 405, the provision on omission of notice: insert "With respect to copies and phonorecords publicly distributed by authority of the copyright owner before the effective date of the Berne Convention Implementation Act of 1988, the omission of the copyright notice described in . . . .";

(3) Section 406, the provision on error in name or date: insert "With respect to copies and phonorecords publicly distributed by authority of the copyright owner before the effective date of the Berne Convention Implementation Act of 1988, where . . . ."

incentive for placing notice by inserting a new Section 401(d) relating to the "defense based on innocent infringement in mitigation of actual or statutory damages."[44]

[3] Deposit and Registration

The Copyright Act imposes two related but distinct administrative submission requirements—deposit of copies, which is mandatory, and registration, which is optional.

[a] **Deposit of Copies.** The owner of copyright or of the exclusive right of publication of a work published in the United States, must, within three months of publication, deposit two complete copies of the best edition with the Copyright Office for the use or disposition of the Library of Congress.[45] The primary purpose of deposit

---

[44] Section 401(d) provides:

"If a notice of copyright in the form and position specified by this section appears on the published copy or copies to which a defendant in a copyright infringement suit had access, then no weight shall be given to such a defendant's interposition of a defense based on innocent infringement in mitigation of actual or statutory damages, except as provided in the last sentence of section 504(c)(2)."

Section 402(d) is an identical provision on phonorecord notice.

The House Report notes:

"To encourage use of notice, H.R. 4262 amends current law—sections 401(d) and 402(d)—to specify that in the case of defendants who have access to copies bearing proper notice of copyright, courts shall not give any weight to a claim of innocent infringement (that is, innocent intent) in mitigation of actual or statutory damages. While innocent intent does not constitute a defense to copyright liability, the courts have taken account of the relative innocence or guilt of the defendant in assessing both actual and statutory damages. As relates to statutory damages, the courts generally have exercised their discretion to award an amount between $250 and $10,000, using the relative innocence of the defendant as a major factor in setting the amount of the award. The intent of new sections 401(d) and 402(d) is to direct the courts not to consider the defendant's claim of innocence if the copyright owner has marked the copies properly with notice of copyright and the defendant has access to the marked copies.

"Newly amended sections 401(d) and 402(d) must be read together, however, in conjunction with the specific provisions for remission of all statutory damages in the last sentence of section 504(c)(2). In that situation, the court has no discretion. Current law provides that all statutory damages shall be remitted where certain employees of non-profit educational institutions, libraries, archives, or public broadcasting entities prove that they are innocent infringers. The proposed legislation makes no change to the existing scheme regarding this class of innocent infringers, even if the copies to which they have access bear notice of copyright. H.R. 4262 does change current law with respect to other classes of 'innocent infringers,' including those covered by the second sentence of section 504(c)(2), where the copies bear notice and the defendant had access to the marked copies."

H.R. Rep. 100–609, 100th Cong., 2d Sess. 45 (May 6, 1988).

[45] 17 U.S.C. § 407.

In Ladd v. Law & Technology Press, 762 F.2d 809, 226 U.S.P.Q. 774 (9th Cir. 1985), cert. denied, 475 U.S. 1045 (1986), the court rejected Fifth Amendment taking and First Amendment undue press burden challenges to the mandatory deposit law's constitutionality: "[T]he Copyright Clause grants copyright protection for the purpose of promoting the public interest in the arts and sciences. Conditioning copyrights on a contribution to the Library of Congress furthers this overall purpose." 762 F.2d at 814, 226 U.S.P.Q. at 778.

is to benefit the Library of Congress. Deposit is mandatory,[46] but noncompliance will not invalidate the copyright.[47] The 1988 Berne Convention Implementation Act left the deposit requirement unchanged.[48]

---

[46] The Register of Copyrights may demand deposit any time after publication in the United States. If no deposit is made within three months of demand, the defaulting persons are liable to fines of not more than $250 per work ($2500 in the case of willful or repeated failures to comply) plus the cost of obtaining a copy. 17 U.S.C. § 407(d).

[47] 17 U.S.C. § 407(a) ("Neither the deposit requirements of this subsection nor the acquisition provisions of subsection (e) are conditions of copyright protection.").

[48] See H.R. Rep. 100-609, 100th Cong., 2d Sess. 44-45 (May 6, 1988):

"The requirement of depositing a copy of the work in which copyright is claimed has been an integral part of the United States copyright systems for nearly 200 years. Since 1865 the Library of Congress has been the permanent beneficiary of copyright deposits, the copyright system therefore being one of the primary sources of acquisitions for the Library. Some of the collections were built almost exclusively through copyright deposits.

"Before the general revision of the law in 1978, deposit was tied to registration and both were mandatory. Under existing law, the Library receives deposits both through permissive registration and through mandatory deposit in the case of works published with notice of copyright in the United States.

"Since noncompliance with the mandatory deposit requirement does not result in forfeiture of any copyright protection, mandatory deposit is compatible with Berne. However, elimination of the copyright notice as a condition of copyright requires an amendment to section 407 of the Copyright Act. Under the proposed legislation, all original works of authorship published in the United States remain subject to mandatory deposit.

"Clearly, the mandatory deposit of all published works in which copyright is claimed advances the purposes of the Copyright Clause of the Constitution to promote the progress of science and the useful arts. The existing mandatory deposit requirement was recently held to pass constitutional muster. The elimination of copyright notice as a factor in subjecting works to mandatory deposit has no constitutional significance. It remains true that only those works published in the United States in which copyright is claimed are subject to mandatory deposit. The only change is that the law will no longer require affirmative marking of the copies as a condition of maintaining copyright. As in the past, all original works of authorship are under copyright from their creation, and authors and owners of copyright are required to deposit copies with the Library of Congress when their works are published in the United States.

"The public benefits of mandatory deposit are obvious. The entire society—including not only authors and copyright owners but students, academics, ordinary citizens, Members of Congress and their staffs—becomes the beneficiary of a strong and dynamic national library: a public institution that acquires, preserves and makes accessible to present and future generations the material expressions of our national cultural life and other cultures. The implementation of a deposit function cannot and should not be limited to 'printed publications', any more than our culture and communications can be confined to the printed page.

"Mandatory deposit is a very modest requirement and, once again, a very good bargain for the public. A maximum of two copies, and frequently only one copy, must be deposited for all of the United States. In view of the Committee, this condition is well within its authority under the Copyright Clause."

A deposit of copies must also be made if and when a copyright owner seeks to register. An applicant avoids double deposit by promptly applying for registration and having the deposit for registration serve to satisfy the deposit requirement.[49]

The Register of Copyright may exempt categories of material from deposit or provide for single copy deposit.[50] One exception is for "secure tests."[51] Prior to 1989, the Register also exempted "computer programs and automated databases, published in the United States only in the form of machine-readable copies." Effective October 16, 1989, the Register ended the exemption for "such machine-readable copies,"[52] but retained an exemption for "automated databases" available only on line in the United States but not including automated databases distributed only in the form of machine-readable copies.[53]

---

[49] The deposit-for-registration section, 17 U.S.C. § 408(b), provides: "Copies or phonorecords deposited for the Library of Congress under section 407 may be used to satisfy the deposit provisions of this section, if they are accompanied by the prescribed application and fee, and by any additional identifying material that the Register may, by regulation, require."

[50] 17 U.S.C. § 407(c). See 37 C.F.R. § 202.19.

[51] 37 C.F.R. § 202.19(c)(8). The Copyright Office makes special provision for deposits in connection with secure test registration. See § 4D[3][b].

[52] Library of Congress, Copyright Office, "Registration of Claims to Copyright; Mandatory Deposit of Machine-Readable Copies," 54 Fed. Reg. 42295 (Oct. 13, 1989).

The change's primary purpose was to build the Library of Congress' new "Machine-Readable Collections Reading Room," which consists of standard works available in machine-readable form, and IBM PC and Apple Macintosh format personal computer software. Even though the deposit requirement applied to machine-readable computer software generally, the Office indicated that "at present" it would not demand deposits of programs other than those in the IBM and Macintosh formats. It refused to expressly limit the regulations to such formats because such "would unduly hamper the Library's ability to acquire copies in the fast-changing environment of machine-readable works." The Office established policies for preventing the authorized copying of computer software by researchers using the Reading Room.

Insofar as computer software is concerned, the deposit for purposes of compliance with the deposit requirement (that is, a machine-readable copy) differs from the deposit for purposes of compliance with the registration requirement (preferably, source code, with trade secret material blocked out). The Office rejected suggestions for "harmonization" of the two deposit requirements.

"... The variation stems from the disparate purposes of deposit for registration and for enrichment of the Library's collections. The Examining Division is required to examine for copyrightable authorship. Machine-readable copies are generally unsuitable for this task.... The Examining Division requires human-readable deposits for examination, generally portions of source code. The Machine-Readable Collections Reading Room, on the other hand, can only utilize works in those machine-readable formats for which it has acquired hardware." 54 Fed. Reg. at 42298.

[53] 37 C.F.R. § 202.19(c)(5). The Office noted:

"The Library intends to secure through mandatory deposit machine-readable works which are publicly offered for sale or lease. In the case of 'hybrid' databases, the Library will seek deposit of the CD-ROM. Clearly, this is a work which is not 'only online.' The library will not demand deposit of the updates available online. However, once the updates are incorporated into a revised CD-ROM, the Library will seek deposit of the revised CD-ROM."

[b] **Registration.** The owner of a copyright or any exclusive right in a work may register his claim by filing an application and depositing copies with the Copyright Office.[54] Registration is a relatively simple process; the Office makes available forms for registration of different categories of works[55] and issues a certificate of registration if it determines that the deposit material is copyrightable subject matter.[56]

The 1909 Act, in effect until 1978, required that "after copyright has been secured by publication of the work with the notice of copyright . . . . , there shall be promptly deposited in the copyright office . . . two complete copies of the best edition thereof then published,"[57] provided that no action for infringement could be maintained until the provisions on deposit and registration were complied with, and provided that a copyright proprietor was liable to a fine for failure to make the required deposit.[58] In *Washington Publishing Co.,*[59] the Supreme Court held that "mere delay in making deposit of copies was not enough to cause forfeiture" of copyright that was otherwise properly secured by publication with notice. Plaintiff deposited and registered 14 months after publication.[60] The Court held the plaintiff could sue and recover even for infringements occurring prior to registration, rejecting defendant's argument that "although prompt deposit of copies is not prerequisite to copyright, no action can be maintained because of infringement prior in date to a tardy deposit."[61]

The 1976 Act continued the prior law making registration a prerequisite to filing an infringement suit and imposed no time period within which registration must be procured,[62] but provided procedural and remedial advantages for prompt registration.

---

[54] 17 U.S.C. § 408(a).

[55] Form TX covers "published or unpublished non-dramatic works," 37 C.F.R. § 202.3(b)(i). Other forms include (1) Form PA for works of the performing arts, such as musical, dramatic and choreographic works, motion pictures and other audiovisual works; (2) Form VA for works of the visual arts, such as photographs, prints and sculpture; and (3) Form SR for sounding recordings.

[56] 17 U.S.C. § 410.

[57] 17 U.S.C. § 13 (repealed).

[58] 17 U.S.C. § 14 (repealed).

[59] Washington Publishing Co. v. Pearson, 306 U.S. 30 (1939).

[60] *See also* Shapiro, Bernstein & Co. v. Jerry Vogel Music Co., Inc., 161 F.2d 406 (2d Cir. 1946), *cert. denied,* 331 U.S. 820 (1947) (27 year delay!).

[61] 306 U.S. at 35–36.
The Court believed the deposit and registration provisions of the 1909 Act "show clearly enough that deposit of copies is not required primarily in order to insure a complete, permanent collection of all copyrighted works open to the public. Deposited copies may be distributed or destroyed under the direction of the Librarian and this is incompatible with the notion that copies are now required in order that the subject matter of protected works may always be available for information and to prevent unconscious infringement." 306 U.S. at 38–39.

[62] 17 U.S.C. § 411. *See* M.G.B. Homes Inc. v. Ameron Homes, Inc., 903 F.2d 1486, 15 U.S.P.Q.2d 1282 (11th Cir. 1990). *But cf.* Pacific & Southern Co. v. Duncan, 744 F.2d 1490, 1499–1500, 224 U.S.P.Q. 131, 137 (11th Cir. 1984), *cert. denied,* 471 U.S. 1004 (1985) (injunction against threatened infringement of works to be created in future).
If the Register of Copyright refuses a copyright claimant's registration application, the claimant may file an infringement suit, giving notice to the Register, who may become a

The 1988 Berne Convention Implementation Act made registration not a prerequisite to suit for infringement of "Berne Convention works whose country of origin is not the United States."[63]

Copyright Office regulations make special provision for registration deposit of "secure tests" and "computer programs and databases embodied in machine readable copies," allowing copyright owners to obtain registration and maintain confidentiality in the test or trade secret rights in the structure of the computer program. For "secure tests,"[64] the copyright owner deposits one copy, which the Copyright Office returns "promptly after examination," retaining "sufficient portions, description, or the like . . . so as to constitute a sufficient archival record of the deposit."[65] For

---

party to the action with respect to the registrability issue. 17 U.S.C. § 411(a). Under the 1909 Act, the claimant could not sue until he obtained registration. Vacheron & Constanin-LeCoultre Watches, Inc. v. Benrus Watch Co., 260 F.2d 637 (2d Cir. 1958).

[63] P.L. 100–568, 102 Stat. 2853 (Oct. 31, 1988). The Act amended 17 U.S.C. § 411 by including the introductory phrase "Except for actions for infringement of copyright in Berne Convention works whose country of origin is not the United States." It defined "Berne Convention" work (see § 4D[4]) and "country of origin" of a Berne Convention work for purposes of 17 U.S.C. § 411 as follows:

"The 'country of origin' of a Berne Convention work, for purposes of section 411, is the United States if—

"(1) in the case of a published work, the work is first published—

"(A) in the United States;

"(B) simultaneously in the United States and another nation or nations adhering to the Berne Convention, whose law grants a term of copyright protection that is the same as or longer than the term provided in the United States;

"(C) simultaneously in the United States and a foreign nation that does not adhere to the Berne Convention; or

"(D) in a foreign nation that does not adhere to the Berne Convention, and all of the authors of the work are nationals, domiciliaries, or habitual residents of, or in the case of an audiovisual work legal entities with headquarters in, the United States;

"(2) in the case of an unpublished work, all the authors of the work are nationals, domiciliaries, or habitual residents of the United States, or, in the case of an unpublished audiovisual work, all the authors are legal entities with headquarters in the United States; or

"(3) in the case of a pictorial, graphic, or sculptural work incorporated in a building or structure, the building or structure is located in the United States.

For the purposes of section 411, the 'country of origin' of any other Berne Convention work is not the United States. 17 U.S.C. § 101.

[64] A secure test is: "a nonmarketed test administered under supervision at specified centers on specific dates, all copies of which are accounted for and either destroyed or returned to restricted locked storage following each administration. For these purposes a test is not marketed if copies are not sold but it is distributed and used in such a manner that ownership and control of copies remain with the test sponsor or publisher." 37 C.F.R. § 202.20(b)(4).

[65] 37 C.F.R. § 202.20(c)(vi). In National Conference of Bar Examiners v. Multistate Legal Studies, 692 F.2d 478, 216 U.S.P.Q. 279, 286 (7th Cir. 1982),, cert. denied sub nom. Multistate Legal Studios Inc. v. Ladd, 464 U.S. 814 (1983), the court upheld the secure test regulation: "whether the work is published or unpublished, the Copyright Act when viewed as a whole negates the notion that deposit requirements are for the purpose of delineating the scope of a copyright through public disclosure."

computer programs, the copyright owner may deposit "the first and last 25 pages or equivalent units of the source code" and block out material if the program contains trade secret material.[66]

[4] Authors and Works from Other Countries

Copyright Act Section 104 deals with copyright for other countries' authors' works and works published abroad.[67]

As to *unpublished* works, Section 104 provides, without reservation, that works within the statutory definition of copyrightable subject matter "while unpublished, are subject to protection under this title without regard to the nationality or domicile of the author."[68] Before the 1976 Act, common law copyright protected unpublished works without regard to national origin.[69] When Congress extended federal statutory copyright protection to unpublished works in the 1976 Act, it preserved this national origin neutrality rule.

As to *published* works, Section 104 provides that works receive protection if they fall in one of five categories.

1. Authors Who are Nationals and Domiciliaries of the United States or Treaty Nations

Section 104(b)(1) includes works of which "on the date of first publication, one or more of the authors is a national or domiciliary of the United States, or is a national, domiciliary, or sovereign authority of a foreign nation that is a party to a copyright treaty to which the United States is also a party, or is a stateless person, wherever that person may be domiciled."[70]

This category depends on the nationality or domicile of the author (or one of the authors in the case of joint works).[71]

---

[66] 37 C.F.R. § 202.20(c)(2)(vii). This rule on deposit of computer software and the like was revised effective May 1, 1989. If the registrant submits source code with portions blocked out to protect trade secrets, the blocked-out portions must be "proportionately less than the material remaining, and the deposit [must reveal] an appreciable amount of original computer code." 37 C.F.R. § 202.20(c)(2)(vii)(A)(2).

If the owner registers a program on the basis of "an object code deposit," the Copyright Office makes the registration "under its rule of doubt" and warns that "no determination has been made concerning the existence of copyrightable authorship." 37 C.F.R § 202.20(c)(2)(vii)(B).

If "an application to claim copyright in a computer program includes a specific claim in related screen displays," the deposit shall consist of a visual reproduction or a VHS format videotape. 37 C.F.R. § 202.20(c)(2)(vii)(C).

For a discussion of computer program copyrightability, see § 4C[2].

[67] The United States extended copyright to foreign authors in 1891. Act of Mar. 3, 1891, 26 Stat. 1106.

[68] 17 U.S.C. § 104(a).

[69] Palmer v. DeWitt, 47 N.Y. 532 (1872).

[70] 17 U.S.C. § 104(b)(1).

[71] Nationality presumably refers to formal citizenship. Domicile is a word of legal art that refers to the place where a person resides with an intent to remain indefinitely. *See* Restatement (Second) of Conflict of Laws §§ 15, 16, 18.

2. Publication in the United States or UCC Nations

Section 104(b)(2) includes works that are "first published in the United States or in a foreign nation that, on the date of first publication, is a party to the Universal Copyright Convention."[72]

3. United Nations and OAS Publications

Section 104(b)(3) includes works "first published by the United Nations or any of its specialized agencies, or by the Organization of American States."

4. Berne Convention Works

Section 104(b)(4) includes any "Berne Convention work."[73] The Berne Convention Implementation Act added this category effective March 1, 1989. Section 101 defines a "Berne Convention work."[74]

---

[72] 17 U.S.C. § 104(a)(2).

The 1952 Universal Copyright Convention supplemented the primary international treaty, the 1886 Berne Convention. It created a multi-national treaty to which the United States and other countries, mainly in the Americas, could adhere without abandoning the copyright notice requirement. The United States adhered to the U.C.C. in 1955 and joined the Berne Convention in 1989.

[73] 17 U.S.C. § 104(b)(4).

The "Berne Convention" is the conventional reference term for the Convention for the Protection of Literary and Artistic Works, signed at Berne, Switzerland, on September 9, 1886. Since 1886, the Convention has been revised seven times. Just prior to United States adherence, 77 nations had adhered to one or more of the versions, including every major state in Western and Eastern Europe, Canada, Japan, Brazil, India and Mexico.

For a discussion of the Berne Convention, see H.R. Rep. 100–609, 100th Cong., 2d Sess. 10–20 (May 6, 1988).

[74] "A work is a 'Berne Convention work' if—

"(1) in the case of an unpublished work, one or more of the authors is a national of a nation adhering to the Berne Convention, or in the case of a published work, one or more of the authors is a national of a nation adhering to the Berne Convention on the date of first publication;

"(2) the work was first published in a nation adhering to the Berne Convention, or was simultaneously first published in a nation adhering to the Berne Convention and in a foreign nation that does not adhere to the Berne Convention;

"(3) in the case of an audiovisual work—

"(A) if one or more of the authors is a legal entity, that author has its headquarters in a nation adhering to the Berne Convention; or

"(B) if one or more of the authors is an individual, that author is domiciled, or has his or her habitual residence in, a nation adhering to the Berne Convention; or

"(4) in the case of a pictorial, graphic, or sculptural work that is incorporated in a building or other structure, the building or structure is located in a nation adhering to the Berne Convention.

"For purposes of paragraph (1), an author who is domiciled in or has his or her habitual residence in, a nation adhering to the Berne Convention is considered to be a national of that nation. For purposes of paragraph (2), a work is considered to have been simultaneously published in two or more nations if its dates of publication are within 30 days of one another."

See § 4D[2][c].

5. Presidential Proclamation Works

Section 104(b)(5) includes works that come "within the scope of a Presidential proclamation."[75]

§ 4E Rights

Copyright consists of a set of statutorily defined exclusive rights of limited duration.[1]

[1] Duration

For works created on or after January 1, 1978, copyright subsists from creation and endures for a term consisting of the life of the author and fifty years after the author's death.[2] Special provisions govern joint works,[3] anonymous and pseudonymous works,[4] and works for hire.[5]

The life-plus-fifty term is among the 1976 Act's most significant changes. The 1909 Act conferred a 28 year initial term, which began on publication. The author or, if the author was not living, specified heirs,[6] could obtain a 28 year renewal term by

---

[75] 17 U.S.C. § 104(b)(5).

[1] There is no common law copyright in published works. See § 4B.

The United States adheres to several international treaties pertaining to copyright, including the Berne Convention. Under the United States Constitution, treaties are the "supreme Law of the Land," U.S. Const. art. VI, but, traditionally, the United States implements its international intellectual property treaty obligations by legislative enactment, and treaty obligations are not self-implementing. See D. Chisum, Patents § 14.02[3][a]. Congress explicitly followed this course with the 1988 Berne Convention Implementation Act.

> "(c) Effect of Berne Convention. No right or interest in a work eligible for protection under this title may be claimed by virtue of, or in reliance upon, the provisions of the Berne Convention, or the adherence of the United States thereto. Any rights in a work eligible for protection under this title that derive from this title, other Federal or State statutes, or the common law, shall not be expanded or reduced by virtue of, or in reliance upon, the provisions of the Berne Convention, or the adherence of the United States thereto." 17 U.S.C. § 104(c).

The Senate Report notes: "The courts are to resolve issues of the existence, scope or application of rights in works subject to copyright through the normal processes of statutory interpretation and the application of common law precedents, as appropriate, rather than by reference to the provisions of Berne or the fact of U.S. adherence to the Convention." S. Rep. No. 100–352, 100th Cong., 2d Sess. 41 (May 18, 1988).

[2] 17 U.S.C. § 302(a).

[3] 17 U.S.C. § 302(b) (life of the last surviving author plus fifty years).

[4] 17 U.S.C. § 302(c).

[5] 17 U.S.C. § 302(c) ("seventy-five years from the year of its first publication, or . . . one hundred years from the year of its creation, whichever expires first").

[6] These were: "the widow, widower, or children of the author, if the author be not living, or if such author, widow, widower, or children be not living, then the author's executors, or in the absence of a will, his next of kin." Under this provision, one could not know who would own the renewal rights until the renewal date arrived. The author could assign his renewal rights, but the assignee took nothing if the author did not survive to the renewal period and the renewal rights vested in a widow or child. See §§ 4G[4][a] and 4G[4][c][i].

filing an application during a one-year window period. The renewal provision spawned many problems and much litigation.[7] Eliminating the complexities of renewal was a major reason for adopting a unitary life-plus-fifty term.[8]

For works created before January 1, 1978, the 1976 Act distinguishes (1) works neither copyrighted nor in the public domain, and (2) subsisting copyrights obtained under the 1909 Act.[9] To the former, consisting of unpublished works that enjoyed potentially indefinite protection under common law copyright, Section 303 grants the normal term of Section 302 (life plus 50). To assure some term of protection to works the author of which died many years prior to 1978, Section 303 provides a minimum term of 25 years (to December 31, 2002), the minimum being extended another 25 years (to December 31, 2027) if the work is published on or before December 31, 2002. To the latter (subsisting copyrights), Section 304 retains the original 28 year term and lengthens the renewal term to 47 years. An author or his or her heirs must apply to renew copyrights that were in their first term on January 1, 1978.

The 1976 Act does not revive any works that fell into the public domain prior to its effective date.[10] Beginning in 1962, Congress began enacting legislation extending the duration of copyrights scheduled to expire after September 19, 1962 that would not so expire under the system of the proposed copyright revision legislation. These works gain the benefit of the 19-year extension of the renewal term (*i.e.,* the overall 75 year term), measured from the date copyright was secured.

---

[7] *See, e.g.,* Miller Music Corp. v. Charles N. Daniels, Inc., 362 U.S. 373 (1960); DeSylvia v. Ballentine, 351 U.S. 570 (1956) (whether "children" includes illegitimates depends on state law); Fred Fisher Music Co. v. M. Witmark & Sons, 318 U.S. 643 (1943) (author can by a specific written assignment convey his renewal rights, but such an assignment does not bind the stated heirs in case the author dies prior to the time for renewal).

See § 4G[4][a] and 4G[4][c][i].

[8] Other reasons were: (1) with increased life expectancies, authors see their works fall into the public domain during their lifetimes; (2) communications media growth lengthens many works' commercial life; (3) a short term discriminates against serious works whose value may not be recognized for many years; (4) an author's death is a definite event, unlike the vague "publication" concept, which measured the copyright terms under prior law; (5) a longer term compensates for the abolition of potentially indefinite common law protection of unpublished works under prior law; (6) the life-plus-fifty term means that all the works of an author fall into the public domain at the same time; and (7) adoption of the life-plus-fifty term brings U.S. law into conformity with the law of many countries and improves copyright relations with those countries, making possible adherence of the U.S. to the Berne Copyright Union. H.R. Rep. No. 94–1476, 94th Cong., 2d Sess. 134–35 (1976).

The first five reasons amount to the simple idea that more is better. Only the last two have merit apart from a subjective judgment that the 56 year period under prior law was too short.

The renewal provision benefited authors' heirs by providing a new term of copyright free of transfers granted by the author before the work's value was appreciated. The 1976 Act benefits authors and their heirs by providing a transfer termination right. It also prohibits any further transfer termination of rights until the right to termination vests. *See* § 4G[4][b].

[9] 17 U.S.C. §§ 303, 304.

[10] For this reason, the 1909 Act's publication and notice provisions remain important. *See* §§ 4D[1][a] and 4D[2][a].

(Matthew Bender & Co., Inc.)

[2] Exclusive Rights

Copyright law gives the author separate exclusive rights in a work. Copyright infringement is the unauthorized doing of an act covered by an exclusive right. Use of a work that does not implicate an exclusive right does not constitute infringement. For example, "No license is required by the Copyright Act . . . to sing a copyrighted lyric in the shower" because the Act confers no exclusive right to *private* performances.[11]

Exclusive rights fall into two groups: (1) copying rights (reproduction in copies, preparation of derivative works, and distribution of copies to the public); and (2) public performance and display rights.

A copyright owner may separately grant authority for different exclusive rights. For example, a musical or dramatic work copyright owner may sell copies without authorizing public performance.[12]

Statutory limitations moderate copyrights' exclusive rights.[13]

[3] Copying and Distribution Rights

Copyright confers exclusive rights to: (1) "reproduce the copyrighted work in copies or phonorecords"; (2) "prepare derivative works based upon the copyrighted work"; and (3) "distribute copies or phonorecords of the copyrighted work to the public by sale or other transfer of ownership, or by rental, lease, or lending."[14]

[a] **Reproduction and Distribution.** The reproduction and distribution rights are distinct. A person violates the reproduction right by copying a work without authority even if he does not sell it.[15] A person violates the distribution right by selling a work without authority even if he did not make the copy—or know that it was made without the copyright owner's authority.[16]

[b] **Derivative Work Preparation.** The exclusive derivative work preparation right overlaps the exclusive reproduction right. Early case law indicated that translations and dramatizations were not "copies" of a work.[17] In 1870, Congress closed that gap

---

[11] Twentieth Century Music Corp. v. Aiken, 422 U.S. 151 (1975).

[12] *See* § 4E[4].

[13] 17 U.S.C. §§ 107–112.

[14] 17 U.S.C. § 106(1)–(3).

[15] *See* H.R. Rep. No. 94–1476, 94th Cong., 2d Sess. 61 (1976). *Cf.* Chappell & Co., Inc. v. Costa, 45 F. Supp. 554, 556 (S.D.N.Y. 1942) (defendant printed the work; "The copying or printing of something which has been lawfully copyrighted has been judicially defined as an infringement of the copyright without any requirement that there be a sale or that profits be made from sale of the copies."). The absence of a sale affects damages. *See* § 4F[5][c].

The most important limitation on the reproduction right is the fair use doctrine. *See* § 4F[3].

[16] The major limitation on the distribution right is the first sale doctrine; one who purchases an authorized copy may use and resell that particular copy free of any restraint by the copyright owner. *See* § 4E[3][c].

[17] Stowe v. Thomas, 23 F. Cas. 201 (E.D. Pa. 1893) (unauthorized publication of a German translation of Stowe's "Uncle Tom's Cabin" is not a "printing" of "such book" within the meaning of the 1831 Copyright Act).

in authors' rights by conferring exclusive rights to dramatize and translate. The 1909 Act granted the exclusive right to make "other versions." The 1976 Act granted the same right, using the concept "derivative work."[18] Congress also expanded the statutory definition of a copy to include any object in which the work is fixed and "from which the work can be perceived . . . ."[19] The expanded definition makes most derivative works also a "copy" of the copyrighted work. An unfixed derivative work, such as an improvised performance, is not a copy,[20] but may be a performance within the copyright owner's exclusive rights.[21]

The question of how related a second work must be to a first work to be a derivative work of the latter[22] is worrisome because the exclusive derivative work preparation right, if carried too far, would give the copyright owner control over all uses of a work's ideas, contrary to fundamental copyright law policy.[23] The 1976 Act House Report notes: "to constitute a violation of [the exclusive right to prepare derivative works], the infringing work must incorporate a portion of the copyrighted work in some form; for example, a detailed commentary on a work or a programmatic musical composition inspired by a novel would not normally constitute infringements . . . ."[24]

A co-owner, for example, a joint author or a transferee of an interest in the copyright, may create or authorize the creation of a derivative work without permission of other co-owners.[25]

If an author prepares a derivative work, the derivative work is subject to copyright protection.[26]

---

[18] 17 U.S.C. § 106(2). The term "derivative work" is defined in Section 101. See § 4C[1][c]. See also § 4E[3][c][iii].

[19] 17 U.S.C. § 101.

[20] See H.R. Rep. No. 94–1476, 94th Cong., 2d Sess. 62 (1976) ("reproduction requires fixation in copies or phonorecords, whereas the preparation of a derivative work, such as a ballet, pantomime, or improvised performance, may be an infringement even though nothing is ever fixed in tangible form.").

[21] See 2 Nimmer on Copyright § 8.09[A] (1978).

[22] See § 4C[1][c].

[23] Cf. Litchfield v. Spielberg, 736 F.2d 1352, 1357, 222 U.S.P.Q. 965, 968 (9th Cir. 1984) ("The little available authority suggests that a work is not derivative unless it has been substantially copied from the prior work.").

[24] H.R. Rep. No. 94–1476, 94th Cong., 2d Sess. 62 (1976). See also G. Ricordi & Co. v. Mason, 201 F. 182 (S.D. N.Y. 1911), 201 F. 184 (S.D. N.Y. 1912), aff'd, 210 F. 277 (2d Cir. 1913) (one-half page synopsis of the plot of an opera is not an abridgment of the copyrighted opera). Cf. Addison-Wesley Publishing Co. v. Brown, 223 F. Supp. 219 (E.D.N.Y. 1963) (defendant's book giving solutions to the problems in plaintiff's copyrighted college physics texts constitutes an infringement).

The issue of what is a derivative work arises with computer programs. For example, a person may write a program that supplements another copyrighted program's operation. The supplemental program does not duplicate the copyrighted program and can only be used in conjunction with the original program. Is such a derivative work? Section 117 allows authorized program copy owners to make and authorize certain "adaptations." See § 4C[2][e].

[25] See § 4G[1].

[26] See § 4C[1][c].

[c] **First Sale Doctrine.** Copyright law, like patent law[27] and trademark law,[28] has a first sale doctrine, the theory of which is that a copyright owner's authorized sale of an item "exhausts" the exclusive intellectual property distribution right.[29] The purchaser may use or resell the item free of any charge of infringement.

The first sale doctrine does not apply to the separate exclusive rights of derivative work preparation, public performance, and public display.

Section 109, which codifies the copyright's first sale doctrine, contains exceptions for sound recording and computer software rentals[30] and for the public performance or display of videogames.[31]

[i] *Generally.* Early copyright acts contained no first sale provision. In *Bobbs Merrill Co.,*[32] a publisher, Bobbs Merrill, sold the book "The Castaway" to wholesalers with the following notice printed on each copy:

> "The price of this book at retail is $1 net. No dealer is licensed to sell it at a less price, and a sale at a less price will be treated as an infringement of the copyright.
>
> The Bobbs-Merrill Company."

Defendant Macy bought copies from the wholesalers and resold them for less than $1. Bobbs Merrill sued Macy for copyright infringement, relying solely on copyright and asserting no contract claim. The Supreme Court found no violation of the copyright owner's exclusive rights to multiply copies and vend.

> "[T]he copyright statutes, while protecting the owner of the copyright in his right to multiply and sell his production, do not create the right to impose, by notice . . . a limitation at which the book shall be sold at retail by future purchasers, with whom there is no privity of contract. This conclusion is reached in view of the language of the statute, read in the light of its main purpose to secure the right of multiplying copies of the work,—a right which is the special creation of the statute. True, the statute also secures, to make this right of multiplication effectual, the sole right to vend copies of the book . . . . The owner of the copyright in this case did sell copies of the book in quantities and at a price satisfactory to it. It has exercised the right to vend. What the complainant contends for embraces not only the right to sell the copies, but to qualify the title of a future purchaser by the reservation of the right to have the remedies of the statute against an infringer because of the printed notice of its purpose so to do unless the purchaser sells at a price fixed in the notice. To add to the right of exclusive sale the authority to control all future retail sales, by a notice that such sales must be made at a fixed sum,

---

[27] *See* § 2E[3].

[28] *See* § 5E[4].

[29] The symmetry between copyright's first sale doctrine and that of patent and trademark law is not perfect. Neither patent law nor trademark law contain the equivalent of copyright law's right to exclude others from making derivative works.

[30] 17 U.S.C. § 109(b). *See* § 4E[3][c][iv].

[31] 17 U.S.C. § 109(e). *See* § 4E[3][c][v].

[32] Bobbs Merrill Co. v. Straus, 210 U.S. 339 (1908).

would give a right not included in the terms of the statute, and, in our view, extend its operation, by construction, beyond its meaning, when interpreted with a view to ascertaining the legislative intent in its enactment."[33]

The 1976 Act's Section 109 codifies the first sale doctrine.

"(a) Notwithstanding the provisions of section 106(3), the owner of a particular copy or phonorecord lawfully made under this title, or any person authorized by such owner, is entitled, without the authority of the copyright owner, to sell or otherwise dispose of the possession of that copy or phonorecord.

. . .

"(d) The privileges prescribed by subsections (a) and (c) do not, unless authorized by the copyright owner, extend to any person who has acquired possession of the copy or phonorecord from the copyright owner, by rental, lease, loan or otherwise, without acquiring ownership of it."

The House Report approves *Bobbs-Merrill*: a copyright infringement remedy may not be used to enforce contractual restrictions on a copy's disposition after authorized sale, but "[t]his does not mean that conditions on future disposition of copies or phonorecords, imposed by a contract between their buyer and seller, would be unenforceable between the parties as a breach of contract, but it does mean that they could not be enforced by an action for infringement of copyright."[34]

[ii]   *Burden of Proof.* In civil copyright infringement cases, the accused infringer bears the initial burden of producing evidence that the copy in question was the subject of a first authorized sale.[35] In criminal copyright prosecutions, most courts hold that the government must prove the absence of a first sale.[36]

---

[33] 210 U.S. at 350-51.

[34] H.R. Rep. No. 94-1476, 94th Cong., 2d Sess. 79 (1976).

[35] *E.g.*, American International Pictures, Inc. v. Foreman, 576 F.2d 661, 663, 198 U.S.P.Q. 580, 581 (5th Cir. 1978).

In *American International Pictures*, motion picture copyright owners sued Foreman, a dealer who purchased and resold motion picture prints. The owners offered evidence at trial that none of the many prints made of motion pictures for distribution purposes was actually sold. Prints were sold to film salvage companies, lent to executives, and distributed to television broadcast stations, but a witness testified that these acts were tightly controlled. The owners did not specifically account for all authorized prints.

Foreman introduced evidence on salvage sales, VIP loans, and television distribution, but he did not attempt to show that his prints were acquired directly or indirectly from these sources.

Because neither party proved a title chain, the first sale burden of proof question became critical. The Fifth Circuit held that the district court erred in ruling for defendant Foreman because it incorrectly placed the burden of proving first sale nonoccurrence on the copyright owners.

[36] *E.g.*, United States v. Atherton, 561 F.2d 747, 195 U.S.P.Q. 615 (9th Cir. 1977); United States v. Wise, 550 F.2d 1180, 194 U.S.P.Q. 59 (9th Cir., *cert. denied*, 434 U.S. 929 (1977). *See also* United States v. Sachs, 801 F.2d 839, 842-43, 231 U.S.P.Q. 197, 199 (6th Cir. 1986) ("the government's burden encompasses proving that the copies were unauthorized copies, but does not necessarily extend to disproving 'every conceivable scenario in which appellant would be innocent of infringement.' . . . There are two acceptable methods of satisfying the

[iii]   *Preparation of Derivative Works—Public Performance and Display.* The first sale doctrine does not limit the distinct exclusive public performance right. For example, if a person buys an authentic copy of a play or a song, neither he nor a purchaser from him acquires the right to publicly perform the play or the song. A separate performance license from the author is necessary.[37]

Similarly, the first sale doctrine does not limit the distinct exclusive right of preparation of derivative works. A difficult issue encountered here and elsewhere in copyright law[38] is determining what quality and quantity of alteration of a copy makes it a derivative work. For example, in *C.M. Paula,*[39] plaintiff claimed infringement of its copyrights on "various pictorial art works imprinted on stationery and greeting cards." Defendant purchased the plaintiff's cards at retail and embedded the works on ceramic plaques. The court found no infringement of copyright, distinguishing *National Geographic,*[40] which held that rebinding of periodicals constituted infringement.

---

first sale doctrine. The first method entails tracing, step-by-step, every possible source of the particular copy of the work in question. This, in essence, requires the government to disprove the possibility that the tape came from any legitimate source. . . . The other recognized method of satisfying this doctrine is for the government to prove that the copy in question was made without authorization from another recording.").

Compare United States v. Goss, 803 F.2d 638, 644, 645, 231 U.S.P.Q. 730, 734, 735 (11th Cir. 1986) ("in a criminal copyright case involving unauthorized distribution of copies, section 109(a) is a defense. If a defendant presents any evidence that the copies were legally made and that he or she owned them, this is sufficient to create a jury issue with respect to the section 109(a) defense. When the defendant makes such a showing, the burden shifts to the government to demonstrate beyond a reasonable doubt that the pertinent copies were either not legally made or not owned by the defendant. . . . Even where the distributed copies are physically indistinguishable from the authorized copies, the government can rebut a section 109(a) defense by direct evidence that the copies were illegally made (e.g., clear admissions by defendant, or testimony by a third party who saw the copies being made without authorization) or circumstantial evidence to this effect (e.g., facts indicating that defendant or an upstream supplier purchased reproducing equipment which would enable them to make the copies without authorization.")

[37] *See, e.g.,* Columbia Pictures Industries, Inc. v. Aveco, Inc., 800 F.2d 59, 63–64, 230 U.S.P.Q. 869, 872 (3d Cir. 1986), discussed at § 4E[4][a] (lawful possession of video cassettes does not confer a right to use the cassettes for unauthorized public performances; "The first sale doctrine . . . prevents the copyright owner from controlling future transfers of a particular copy of a copyrighted work after he has transferred its 'material ownership' to another. . . . When a copyright owner parts with title to a particular copy of his copyrighted work, he thereby divests himself of his exclusive right to vend that particular copy. . . . The rights protected by copyright are divisible and the waiver of one does not necessarily waive any of the others. . . . In particular, the transfer of ownership in a particular copy of a work does not affect [the copyright owner's] Section 106(4) exclusive rights to do and to authorize public performances.").

Section 109(e) makes an exception for public performance and display of videogames. *See* § 4E[3][c][v].

[38] *See* § 4E[3][b].

[39] C. M. Paula Co. v. Logan, 355 F. Supp. 189, 177 U.S.P.Q. 559 (N.D. Tex. 1973).

[40] National Geographic Soc. v. Classified Geographic, 27 F. Supp. 655 (D. Mass. 1939).

"[P]laintiff [argues] that the making of the ceramic plaques [is] . . . an adaptation protected by the Copyright Act and that *National Geographic* . . . [is] controlling. There the defendant disassembled plaintiff's periodicals, reorganized them and sold them as new publications. The Court said that defendant's acts 'amounted to a "compilation" or an "adaption" [sic] or an "arrangement" of copyrighted works . . .' 27 F. Supp. at 660. This Court does not believe the process here in question results in a compilation, adaptation, or arrangement as those terms are contemplated by Section 7 of Copyright Act.

"While an individual is afforded the protection necessary to allow exploitation of other media . . . . the Court does not believe that the actions of defendant are such as would be proscribed either by the Act or under common law principles of unfair competition.

". . . *National Geographic* has apparently never been cited with approval for the point here advanced. Further, the holding has been questioned. Burke & Van Heusen, Inc. v. Arrow Drug, Inc., 233 F. Supp. 881, n.6 at 884 (E.D. Pa. 1964)."[41]

In *Mirage Editions*,[42] involving similar facts, the Ninth Circuit reached a contrary result. Plaintiff held copyrights on art works distributed as books or prints. Defendant purchased books and prints, glued prints on white ceramic tiles, covered each print with a plastic sheet, and sold the tiles. The court found that the defendant's acts fell within the 1976 Act's broad derivative work definition, which includes "any other form in which a work may be recast, transformed, or adapted."

"The language 'recast, transformed or adapted' seems to encompass other alternatives besides simple art reproduction. By removing the individual images from the book and placing them on the tiles, perhaps the appellant has not accomplished reproduction. We conclude, though, that appellant has certainly recast or transformed the individual images by incorporating them into its tile-preparing process.

"[U]nder the 'first sale' doctrine . . . appellant can purchase a copy of the [plaintiff's] book and subsequently alienate its ownership . . . . However, the right to transfer applies only to the particular copy of the book which appellant has purchased and nothing else. The mere sale of the book to the appellant without a specific transfer by the copyright holder of its exclusive right to prepare derivative works, does not transfer that right to appellant. The derivative works right, remains unimpaired and with the copyright proprietors . . . ."[43]

---

[41] 355 F. Supp. at 192, 193 n.6.

[42] Mirage Editions Inc. v. Albuquerque A.R.T. Co., 856 F.2d 1341, 8 U.S.P.Q.2d 1171 (9th Cir. 1988), *cert. denied*, 489 U.S. 1018 (1989).

[43] 856 F.2d at 1344, 8 U.S.P.Q.2d at 1172–73.

Compare Paramount Pictures Corp. v. Video Broadcasting Systems, Inc., 724 F. Supp. 808, 821, 12 U.S.P.Q.2d 1862, 1872 (D. Kan. 1989) (no derivative work preparation right violation when defendant added a commercial at the beginning of plaintiff's copyrighted motion picture videocassette):

[iv]   *Record and Software Rental.* In the Record Rental Amendment Act of 1984, Congress amended Section 109 to include a first sale doctrine exception for record and tape rental. Section 109(b)(1) provides:

> "Notwithstanding the provisions of subsection (a), unless authorized by owners of copyright in the sound recording and in the musical works embodied therein, the owner of a particular phonorecord may not, for purposes of direct or indirect commercial advantage, dispose of, or authorize the disposal of, the possession of that phonorecord by rental, lease, or lending, or by any other act or practice in the nature of rental, lease, or lending."[44]

The amendment targets "record rental stores," which rent records, tapes or compact discs and sell blank tapes, the evident intention being that customers will use recording equipment to make a copy. It makes unauthorized distribution by phonorecord rental an act of copyright infringement even though the renting party owns the copy.

In the Computer Software Rental Amendments Act of 1990,[45] Congress extended Section 109(b) to computer program rental.[46] The House Report comments:

> "The plaintiff has not presented any authority to support the conclusion that the mere addition of a commercial to the front of a videocassette recasts, transforms, or adapts the motion picture into what could represent an 'original work of authorship.'
>
> "The instant case does not resemble in any way the removing of a page from an artwork book and mounting it onto a tile as a separate piece of art for sale. . . . Nor can the court appreciate any comparison to the decision of *Midway Mfg. Co. v. Artic Intern., Inc.,* 704 F.2d 1009 (7th Cir.), *cert. denied,* 464 U.S. 823 (1983), where the court held that defendant's circuit board which speeded up the play of plaintiff's video game was a derivative work, because it was a 'substantially different product from the original game' in making the game more challenging and exciting. In both cases, the derivative work transformed, adapted or recast the original work into a new and different one. . . . While defendants' advertisement is an original work, the court does not recognize the addition of it to a videocassette in any way recasting, transforming or adapting the motion picture. The result is not a new version of the motion picture."

[44] 17 U.S.C. § 109(b)(1). The provision adds: "Nothing in the preceding sentence shall apply to the rental, lease, or lending of a phonorecord for nonprofit purposes by a nonprofit library or nonprofit education institution."

Clause (2) of subsection 109(b) provides that nothing in the subsection "shall affect any provision of the antitrust laws."

Clause (3) states that a person who distributes a phonorecord in violation of clause (1) is an infringer and is subject to the civil remedy provisions of the Copyright Act. Such a person is not liable for the criminal offense of willful copyright infringement.

[45] Pub. L. No. 101–650, 104 Stat. 5089 (1990).

[46] In House floor remarks, Representative Kastenmeier commented on "purchase leasebacks of hardware and software."

> "The question whether a transaction is a sale or a lease is typically one of State law. The computer industry uses a variety of license agreements, ranging from shrink wrap licenses for over-the-counter software to lengthy negotiated contracts for mainframe computers. Congress cannot draft legislation that addresses every such conceivable fact situation. We, however, should not disturb legitimate commercial activities that routinely involve a variety of products, one of which may include software. For example, most retail stores have return policies for purchases of products. Sometimes these policies include restocking

"Proposals to reform the first sale doctrine are neither easy nor without controversy. They occur in a shifting legal, technological and economic landscape.

"Frequently, calls to amend the first sale doctrine are made in response to a new technology developed for reproduction of copyrighted works. . . . [T]echnology has a habit of outstripping even the most flexible statutes. Copyright is, in large part, a response to new technology. Yet, technology has been both a boon and a bane to authors: a boon because it has fostered new methods of creation and distribution; a bane because it has also resulted in inexpensive, easy, and quick ways to reproduce copyrighted works, in many cases in private or semi-private environments that render detection all but impossible.

"In 1984, Congress was presented with evidence demonstrating that the nascent record rental business posed a genuine threat to the record industry. Copies of phonorecords were being rented at a fraction of their cost, in conjunction with advertisements exhorting customers to 'never buy another record.' Congress responded by prohibiting the rental of phonorecords for purposes of direct or indirect commercial advantage.

"Congress has now been presented with similar evidence by the computer software industry. Indeed, in some respects, the evidence is even more compelling in the case of software. The price disparity between the sale and rental prices is greater than the case with phonorecords: software selling for $495 has been rented for $35. And, unlike phonorecords, which are an entertainment product, software is typically a utilitarian product. Short term rental of software is, under most circumstances, inconsistent with the purposes for which software is intended. Rental of software will, most likely, encourage unauthorized copying, deprive copyright owners of a return on investment, and thereby discourage creation of new products."[47]

Recognizing that many products, including automobiles, contain microprocessors and stored computer programs that cannot be readily copied, and that rental of such products is a legitimate business, Congress provided:

"This subsection does not apply to—

"(i) a computer program which is embodied in a machine or product and which cannot be copied during the ordinary operation or use of the machine or product; or

"(ii) a computer program embodied in or used in conjunction with a limited purpose computer that is designed for playing video games and may be designed for other purposes."[48]

---

charges. Where software is purchased under such policies, there is not rental or lease. On the other hand, where a store offers to repurchase software for a substantial part of the purchase price and offers free blank diskettes for copying, questions may arise whether the activity involves indirect commercial advantage." Cong. Rec. 13315 (Oct. 27, 1990).

[47] H.R. Rep. No. 101–735, 101st Cong., 2d Sess. (1990).

[48] See H.R. Rep. No. 101–735, 101st Cong., 2d Sess. (1990) ("Automobiles, calculators, and other electronic consumer products contain computer programs, bu[t] these computer programs

[v] *Videogame Performances and Displays.* In the Computer Software Rental Amendments Act of 1990, Congress added Section 109(e) on public performance and display of electronic audiovisual games.[49]

In *Red Baron,*[50] the Fourth Circuit held that public arcade use of an authorized video game copy violated the game copyright owner's exclusive public performance right. Taito held the copyright in the videogame "Double Dragon" and conferred exclusive United States rights in the game to its wholly owned United States subsidiary, Taito America. An arcade video game unit consists of an electronic printed circuit board, a monitor, a cabinet, and a coin mechanism. Red Baron obtained Taito "Double Dragon" circuit boards through the "gray market," that is, it bought used circuit boards in Japan, imported them into the United States, and installed units with the boards in its arcades. Taito sued for copyright infringement. The Fourth Circuit found infringement. Red Baron publicly performed the video game in its arcades.

> "When a video game is activated by the insertion of a proper coin, the television monitor displays a series of images and the loudspeaker makes audible their accompanying sounds. . . . The exhibition of its images in sequence constitutes a 'performance' of an audiovisual work. Indeed, it is the sequential showing of its images that distinguishes the 'performance' of an audiovisual work from its 'display,' which is defined as a nonsequential showing of individual images. . . . True, the exact order of images will vary somewhat each time a video game is played depending on the skill of the player, but there will always be a *sequence* of images."[51]

That Red Baron used copies originally sold by the copyright owner did not excuse its unauthorized public performances: "[T]he first sale doctrine does not apply to the performance right" and "has no application to the rights of the owner of a copyright guaranteed by § 106, except the right of distribution."[52]

Responding to *Red Baron,* Congress in 1990 added a videogame performance and display exception to the first sale doctrine, which will be effective only for a trial five year period.[53] Section 109(e) provides:

> "Notwithstanding the provisions of sections 106(4) and 106(5), in the case of an electronic audiovisual game intended for use in coin-operated equipment, the owner of a particular copy of such a game lawfully made under this title, is entitled, without the authority of the copyright owner of the game, to publicly perform or display that game in coin-operated equipment, except that this subsection shall not apply to any work of authorship embodied in the

---

cannot now be copied by consumers during the ordinary operation of these products. The touchstone of the exemption is rental for the purpose of using the machine or products, and not rental in order to copy the computer program embodied in the machine or product.").

[49] Video games are copyrightable. *See* § 4C[2][b].

[50] Red Baron-Franklin Park Inc. v. Taito Corp., 883 F.2d 275, 11 U.S.P.Q.2d 1548 (4th Cir. 1989), *cert. denied,* 110 S. Ct. 869 (1990).

[51] 883 F.2d at 279, 11 U.S.P.Q.2d at 1551.

[52] 883 F.2d at 280–81, 11 U.S.P.Q.2d at 1552–53.

[53] Computer Software Rental Amendments Act of 1990, § 804(a), (c).

audiovisual game if the copyright owner of the electronic audiovisual game is not also the copyright owner of the work of authorship."[54]

The House Report illustrates the "except" clause: "before including a popular copyrighted song in an electronic audiovisual game, permission of the copyright owner (or his or her licensee) would be required to reproduce the song in the game and to publicly perform the song through operation of the game."[55]

[vi] *Importation—"Grey Market."* Section 602 provides: "Importation into the United States, without the authority of the owner of copyright under this title, of copies of the work that have been acquired outside the United States is an infringement of the exclusive right to distribute copies or phonorecords, actionable under Section 501 . . . . "[56] Section 501(a) provides that "Anyone who . . . imports copies or phonorecords into the United States in violation of section 602, is an infringer of the copyright."[57]

These provisions grant copyright owners remedies against importation of unauthorized copies of their works made abroad. Section 602(a) contains limited exemptions, for example, for certain copies imported as part of "personal baggage."[58]

Less clear is whether Sections 602(a) and 501(a) render unlawful importation of copies made or sold abroad by the copyright owner or his licensee. Section 602's legislative history indicates a Congressional intent to bar importation of copies made abroad by licensees and imported into the United States in violation of license restrictions.[59] The Copyright Act's provisions do not unequivocally confirm this

---

[54] 17 U.S.C. § 109(e). *See* H.R. Rep. 101–735, 101st Cong., 2d Sess. (1990):

"[S]ome of the most popular electronic audiovisual games are marketed only as so-called 'dedicated games': units consisting of a printed circuit board containing the game, plus a wooden cabinet containing a tv monitor, power supply, coin-acceptor mechanism, and many other parts. Dedicated games sell for approximately $2,500 compared with a cost of less than $1,000 for the printed circuit board alone.

"In order to rectify the anomaly in the Copyright Act that permits copyright owners of electronic audiovisual games designed for use in coin-operated equipment to sell printed circuit boards containing the games and then turn around and successfully sue to prevent use of the circuit boards for their intended purpose, the bill provides that the public performance right will not apply in the following very limited circumstance: where, in the case of electronic audiovisual games intended for use in coin-operated equipment, a lawfully made copy of such game has been purchased and is used in such equipment. . . .

"The Committee approaches proposed exceptions to the public performance right with great concern, since the right forms the backbone of the motion picture, musical, and theatrical industries. . . . The Committee is convinced, however, that this amendment is drafted in a way that carefully addresses the narrow issue presented in the *Red-Baron* decision."

[55] H.R. Rep. No. 101–735, 101st Cong., 2d Sess. (1990).

[56] 17 U.S.C. § 602(a).

[57] 17 U.S.C. § 501(a).

[58] 17 U.S.C. § 602(a)(2).

[59] H.R. Rep. No. 94–1476, 94th Cong., 2d Sess. 169 (1976) ("[s]ection 602 . . . deals with two separate situations: importation of 'piratical' articles (that is, copies or phonorecords made without any authorization of the copyright owner), and unauthorized importation of copies or phonorecords that were lawfully made.").

position: Section 602 references Section 501(a), which, in turn, references Section 106(a)'s exclusive rights listing, which, in turn, is limited by Section 109(a)'s first sale provision. Nevertheless, some district court decisions find infringement when licensee-produced copies are imported into the United States without authority.[60]

In *Sebastian International*,[61] the Third Circuit found no infringement when copies made by the copyright owner in the United States were exported and then imported back into the United States in violation of a license restriction. Plaintiff shipped "WET SHPRITZE FORTE" beauty supplies to 3-D Marketing Services, Edenvale, South Africa, which, despite its agreement to distribute the supplies only to South African professional hair styling salons, promptly shipped the supplies back to the United States. The supplies had copyrighted labels. The district court granted plaintiff's request for a preliminary injunction against distribution of the products with copyrighted labels. The appeals court reversed.

> "We do not confront a license agreement or copies produced in a foreign country under that agreement by someone other than the owner; instead, this case centers on actual copies of labels printed in this country by the copyright owner.

> "Under the first sale doctrine, when plaintiff made and then sold its copies, it relinquished all further rights 'to sell or otherwise dispose of possession of that copy.' Unquestionably that includes any right to claim infringement of the section 106(3) distributive rights for copies made and sold in the United States. With respect to future distribution of those copies in this country, clearly the copyright owner already has received its reward through the purchase price.

> "Nothing in the wording of section 109(a), its history or philosophy, suggests that the owner of copies who sells them abroad does not receive a 'reward for his work.' Nor does the language of section 602(a) intimate that a copyright owner who elects to sell copies abroad should receive 'a more adequate award' than those who sell domestically. That result would occur if the holder were to receive not only the purchase price, but a right to limit importation as well.

> ". . . [T]he place of sale is not the critical factor in determining whether section 602(a) governs. . . . [but] a first sale by the copyright owner extinguishes any right later to control importation of those copies.

> "Section 602(a) does not purport to create a right in addition to those conferred by section 106(3), but states that unauthorized importation is an infringement of 'the exclusive [106(3)] right to distribute copies.' Because that exclusive right is specifically limited by the first sale provisions of § 109(a), it necessarily follows that once transfer of ownership has cancelled the

---

[60] T.B. Harms Co. v. Jem Records, Inc., 655 F. Supp. 1575, 2 U.S.P.Q.2d 2025 (D. N.J. 1987); Columbia Broadcasting Sys. v. Scorpio Music Distrib., 569 F. Supp. 47 (E.D. Pa. 1983), *aff'd without opinion*, 738 F.2d 424 (3d Cir. 1984).

[61] Sebastian International, Inc. v. Consumer Contacts (Pty) Ltd., 847 F.2d 1093, 7 U.S.P.Q.2d 1077 (3d Cir. 1988).

distribution right to a copy, the right does not survive so as to be infringed by importation."[62]

[4] Performance Rights

The Copyright Act confers the exclusive right "to perform the copyrighted work publicly."[63]

[a] **"Public."** The Act broadly defines "perform" and "public." To "perform" a work "means to recite, render, play, dance, or act it, either directly or by means of any device or process or, in the case of a motion picture or other audiovisual work, to show its images in any sequence or to make the sounds accompanying it audible."[64] To perform a work "publicly" means:

"(1) to perform or display it at a place open to the public or at any place where a substantial number of persons outside of a normal circle of a family and its social acquaintances is gathered; or

"(2) to transmit or otherwise communicate a performance or display of the work to a place specified by clause (1) or to the public, by means of any device or process, whether the members of the public capable of receiving the performance or display receive it in the same place or in separate places and at the same time or at different times."[65]

---

[62] 847 F.2d at 1098–99, 7 U.S.P.Q.2d at 1081–82. *See also* Neutrogena Corp. v. United States, 7 U.S.P.Q.2d 1900, 1903 (D.S.C. 1988) (refusing to order U.S. Customs to hold reimported authentic goods; "the issue of the relationship between § 602 and § 109 . . . has yet to be conclusively resolved. . . . Under the facts of this case, especially the fact that the goods were manufactured in the United States and sold to the defendant by a third party, . . . the first sale defense may be applicable here").

[63] 17 U.S.C. § 106(4). The exclusive right applies only to "literary, musical, dramatic, and choreographic works, pantomimes, and motion pictures and other audiovisual works." This omits (1) pictorial, graphic, or sculptural works, which by their nature cannot be performed, but as to which the comparable right of public display applies, and (2) sound recordings. Congress omitted performance rights from the latter for policy reasons. *See* § 4C[1][e].

[64] 17 U.S.C. § 101.

[65] 17 U.S.C. § 101.

Clause (1)'s purpose is to cover performances at semiprivate places, such as clubs, lodges, factories, summer camps and schools. This alters prior court decisions.

"One of the principal purposes of the definition was to make clear that, contrary to the decision in *Metro-Goldwyn-Mayer Distribution Corp.* v. *Wyatt*, 21 C.O. Bull, 203 (D. Md. 1932), performances in 'semipublic' places such as clubs, lodges, factories, summer camps and schools are 'public performances' subject to copyright control. The term 'a family' in this context would include an individual living alone, so that a gathering confined to the individual's social acquaintances would normally be regarded as private. Routine meetings of businesses and governmental personnel would be excluded because they do not represent the gathering of a 'substantial number of persons.' "

H.R. Rep. No. 94–1476, 94th Cong., 2d Sess. 64 (1976). *See also* Fermata International Melodies Inc. v. Champions Golf Inc., 712 F. Supp. 1257, 1260, 11 U.S.P.Q.2d 1460, 1462 (S.D. Tex. 1989), *aff'd*, 915 F.2d 1567 (5th Cir. 1990) (unpublished) (that defendant is "a private club in the golfing business, . . . does not withdraw [it] from the statutory definition of 'public.'

In *Redd Horne*[66] and *Aveco*,[67] the Third Circuit applied the expansive statutory definition of "public" performance. Defendants provided private rooms or booths in which customers could view videocasettes of motion pictures rented from defendants. In *Redd Horne*, the videocassette players were in a central location; in *Aveco*, they were in the rooms under control of the customer:

> "The Copyright Act speaks of performances at a place open to the public. It does not require that the public place be actually crowded with people. A telephone booth, a taxi cab, and even a pay toilet are commonly regarded as 'open to the public,' even though they are usually occupied only by one party at a time. Our opinion in *Redd Horne* turned not on the precise whereabouts of the video cassette players, but on the nature of [the defendant's] stores. [In each case, the defendant] was willing to make a viewing room and video cassette available to any member of the public with inclination to avail himself of this service."[68]

In *Columbia Pictures Industries*,[69] the Ninth Circuit found that "a hotel did not violate the Copyright Act by renting videodiscs for viewing on hotel-provided video equipment in guests' rooms," reasoning that the hotel's acts fell within neither the "public place" clause nor the "transmit" clause[70] of the Section 101 definition of "To perform or display a work 'publicly'." As to the "public place clause," it distinguished *Aveco* and *Redd Horne*:

> "[The accused infringer's] operation differs from those in *Aveco* and *Redd Horne* because its 'nature' is the providing of living accommodations and general hotel services, which may incidentally include the rental of videodiscs to interested guests for viewing in guest rooms.

The legislative history is clear that a performance in a semipublic place, such as a club, constitutes a 'public' performance. Additionally, twenty-one members plus guests were present in the dining room of the club on the night of . . . the 'performance' in question. The court considers [this group] to be a 'substantial number of persons outside of a normal circle of a family.' ").

[66] Columbia Pictures Industries, Inc. v. Redd Horne, Inc., 749 F.2d 154, 224 U.S.P.Q. 641 (3d Cir. 1984).

[67] Columbia Pictures Industries, Inc. v. Aveco, Inc., 800 F.2d 59, 230 U.S.P.Q. 869 (3d Cir. 1986).

[68] 800 F.2d at 63, 230 U.S.P.Q. at 872.

[69] Columbia Pictures Industries, Inc. v. Professional Real Estate Investors, Inc., 866 F.2d 278, 9 U.S.P.Q.2d 1653 (9th Cir. 1989).

Compare Video Views, Inc. v. Studio 21, Ltd., 925 F.2d 1010, 17 U.S.P.Q.2d 1753 (7th Cir. 1991) (approving jury instruction: "To perform a work publicly means to perform or display it at a place open to the public. A work may be performed or displayed in a private setting, such as a booth, and still be a public performance if the booth itself is in a place open to the public. . . . We agree with the rationale of both *Redd Horne* and *Aveco*: the proper inquiry is directed to the nature of the place in which the private video booths are located, and whether it is a place where the public is openly invited. This is compatible with our view that the Copyright Act contemplates a broad interpretation of the concept of 'public performance.' . . . To the extent that *Professional Real Estate Investors* may be viewed to contradict the rule established by *Redd Horne* and *Aveco*, we decline to follow it.")

[70] *See* § 4E[4][c].

"While the hotel may indeed be 'open to the public,' a guest's hotel room, once rented, is not. . . . This conclusion is further supported by common experience. [The accused infringer's] guests do not view the videodiscs in hotel meeting rooms used for large gatherings. The movies are viewed exclusively in guest rooms, places where individuals enjoy a substantial degree of privacy, not unlike their own homes.

"Congress intended neither the number of persons at a performance nor the location of the performance to be determinative of the public character of a performance. Nevertheless, to the extent that a gathering of one's social acquaintances is normally regarded as private, we conclude that in-room videodisc movie showings do not occur at a 'place open to the public.' "[71]

As to the "transmit" clause, it rejected the copyright owner's argument that, even though the hotel did not "transmit" the work, it "otherwise communicated" it by providing guests videodiscs and machines.

"Although the term 'communicate' is undefined in the Copyright Act, and has countless meanings in common parlance, we are not persuaded that facilitation of the in-room performances means that [the hotel] 'otherwise communicates' under the transmit clause.

"A plain reading of the transmit clause indicates that its purpose is to prohibit transmissions and other forms of broadcasting from one place to another without the copyright owner's permission. . . . According to the rule of *ejusdem generis,* the term 'otherwise communicate' should be construed consistently with the term 'transmit.' . . . Consequently, the 'otherwise communicate' phrase must relate to a 'process whereby images or sounds are received beyond the place from which they are sent.' Section 101.

"This reading is reinforced by the rest of the transmit clause which refers to the use of transmission devices or processes and the reception by the public of the performance. Devices must refer to transmission or communication devices, such as, perhaps, wires, radio towers, communication satellites, and coaxial cable, while reception of the performance by the public describes acts, such as listening to a radio, or watching—a network, cable, or closed-circuit—television 'beyond the place' of origination."[72]

[b] Limitations—Nonprofit Performances. The 1976 Act includes all public performances of music, drama, and other works, except performances falling within one of a series of limitations.

The 1909 Act granted owners of *dramatic* works exclusive rights over all public performances but granted owners of *musical* works exclusive rights only over public performances "for profit." The reason for the distinction was that even a single, nonpublic performance diminishes the public's appetite for a play but that nonpublic performances do not similarly diminish the appetite for music.

In *Herbert,*[73] Justice Holmes, in a colorful opinion, held that performance of copyrighted musical compositions in a hotel dining room violated the copyright

---

[71] 866 F.2d at 281, 9 U.S.P.Q.2d at 1655.

[72] 866 F.2d at 281–82, 9 U.S.P.Q.2d at 1656.

[73] Herbert v. Shanely Co., 242 U.S. 591 (1917).

owner's public performance for profit exclusive right even though the hotel did not charge admission. The hotel's purpose in offering the performances was to make a profit.

> "The defendants' performances are not eleemosynary. They are part of a total for which the public pays, and the fact that the price of the whole is attributed to a particular item which those present are expected to order is not important. It is true that the music is not the sole object, but neither is the food, which probably could be got cheaper elsewhere. The object is a repast in surroundings that to people having limited powers of conversation, or disliking the rival noise, give a luxurious pleasure not to be had from eating a silent meal. If music did not pay, it would be given up. If it pays, it pays out of the public's pocket. Whether it pays or not, the purpose of employing it is profit, and that is enough."[74]

The 1976 Act abolished the general exclusion of nonprofit music performances and substituted a series of more specific limitations. Section 110 includes limitations on performances and displays in face-to-face teaching at nonprofit educational institutions,[75] performances during services at places of religious assembly,[76] and performances at retail record stores.[77] Section 110 includes other limitations that relate to transmissions of works.[78] No Section 110 limitation includes a privilege to make or distribute copies.

Section 110(4), which most closely approximates the prior general exemption for nonprofit performances of musical and nondramatic literary works,[79] follows *Herbert* by restricting the limitation to performances "without any purpose of direct or indirect commercial advantage."[80] It requires that there be no payment to performers, promoters or organizers. If these two conditions are met, the limitation applies absolutely if there is no direct or indirect admission charge. If there is an admission charge, further conditions apply: the net proceeds must be used for educational, religious and charitable purposes, and the copyright owner may cut off the limitation by serving a timely objection notice.[81]

---

[74] 242 U.S. at 594.

[75] 17 U.S.C. § 110(1). The classroom limitation covers "performance or display of a work by instructors or pupils in the course of face-to-face teaching activities of a nonprofit educational institution, in a classroom or similar place devoted to instruction. . . . " Not included are performances or displays of individual images of motion pictures or other audiovisual works "by means of a copy that was not lawfully made under this title" if "the person responsible for the performance knew or had reason to believe [the copy] was not lawfully made."

The House Report notes: "The clause covers all types of copyrighted works." H.R. Rep. No. 94–1476, 94th Cong., 2d Sess. 81 (1976).

[76] 17 U.S.C. § 110(3).

[77] 17 U.S.C. § 110(7).

[78] See § 4E[4][c].

[79] 17 U.S.C. § 110(4).

[80] See H.R. Rep. No. 94–1476, 94th Cong., 2d Sess. 85 (1976).

[81] The notice provision is an awkward compromise. On the one hand, a copyright owner by giving notice barely seven days in advance can upset an announced concert program. On

[c] **Transmissions—Broadcasting.** When the Congress enacted the 1909 Act, broadcasting was in a primitive state. Wireless sound and image transmission was unknown. The copyright statutes were not amended to take into account broadcasting until the 1976 Act; by which time the courts had largely settled the issues, applying the 1909 Act's "public performance" right.

Given *Herbert,* the profit element presented no serious difficulty: radio stations were profit enterprises even though they did not collect a fee from recipients. Was a broadcast "public," given that the audience was dispersed in private homes? The lower courts held it was:

> "While the fact that the radio was not developed at the time the Copyright Act . . . was enacted may raise some question as to whether it properly comes within the purview of the statute, it is not by that fact alone excluded from the statute. . . . [T]he statute may be applied to new situations not contemplated by Congress, if, fairly construed, such situations come within its intent and meaning. . . . While statutes should not be stretched to apply to new situations not fairly within their scope they should not be so narrowly construed as to permit their evasion because of changing habits due to new inventions and discoveries.

> "A performance . . . is no less public because the listeners are unable to communicate with one another, or are not assembled within an inclosure, or gathered together in some open stadium or park or other public place. Nor can a performance . . . be deemed private because each listener may enjoy it alone in the privacy of his home. Radio broadcasting is intended to, and in fact does, reach a very much larger number of the public at the moment of rendition than any other medium of performance. The artist is consciously addressing a great, though unseen and widely scattered, audience, and is therefore participating in a public performance." [82]

The 1976 Act's exclusive performance and display rights encompass all "transmissions," including, most importantly, radio and television broadcasting, by virtue of Section 101's definitions of "perform," [83] "publicly," [84] and "transmit." [85]

---

the other hand, the copyright owner may not be alerted to the concert's existence and hence not be able to give the notice. The notice must contain "reasons," but the statute does not indicate what reasons are acceptable.

A Copyright Office regulation defines the form, content, and manner of service of the notice. *See* 37 C.F.R. § 201.13.

[82] Jerome H. Remick & Co. v. American Automobile Accessories Co., 5 F.2d 411 (6th Cir. 1925). *See also* Twentieth Century Music Corp. v. Aiken, 422 U.S. 151, 158, 186 U.S.P.Q. 65 (1975) ("Although Congress did not revise the statutory language, copyright law was quick to adapt to prevent the exploitation of protected works through the new electronic technology. In short, it was soon established in the federal courts that the broadcast of a copyrighted musical composition by a commercial radio station was a public performance of that composition for profit—and thus an infringement of the copyright if not licensed.").

[83] 17 U.S.C. § 101: "To 'perform' a work means to recite, render, play, dance, or act it, either directly or by means of any device or process . . . ."

[84] *See* § 4E[4][a].

Section 110 excludes certain transmissions from the exclusive right of public performance.[86] Section 111 includes limitations relating to secondary transmissions, such as cable systems.[87]

The licensing of nondramatic performance rights in music is accomplished through performing rights organizations such as the American Society of Composers, Authors and Publishers (ASCAP).[88]

[d] *Public Reception—Sound Systems.* Public reception and retransmission of broadcasts and other transmissions of a copyrighted work are public performances or displays. In *Buck,*[89] a hotel installed a radio receiving set and piped sound into speakers in its public and private rooms. The set retransmitted a radio station's unlicensed broadcast of a copyrighted musical composition. The Supreme Court held that the hotel publicly performed the work, giving birth to the "multiple performances" doctrine—a single transmission results in several performances by different persons. A lower court extended *Buck* to a hotel that retransmitted a licensed broadcast into private rooms only; the system gave guests a choice of two channels.[90]

In *Aiken,*[91] the Supreme Court limited the *Buck* public reception doctrine. George Aiken had a radio with four speakers in his small restaurant and turned it on for the enjoyment of his customers. Relying on its two cable television cases,[92] the Court held that Aiken did not "perform" copyrighted works broadcasted by licensed radio stations and received through his radio-speaker system. It did not overrule *Buck* but reasoned that extension of *Buck* to the case before it "would result in a regime of copyright law that would be both wholly unenforceable and highly inequitable."

The Court's reliance on "practical unenforceability" is unconvincing; it is not just to deprive persons, including composers and other copyright owners, of rights merely because those rights are difficult to enforce.

The Court saw "two distinct reasons" for finding inequity in extension of *Buck* to Aiken. First, "a person in Aiken's position would have no sure way of protecting himself from liability for copyright infringement except by keeping his radio set turned off. For even if he secured a license from ASCAP, he would have no way of either foreseeing or controlling the broadcast of compositions whose copyright was held by someone else." Again, this proved too much. Every person publicly performing copyrighted musical compositions faces the same problem. Second, "to hold

---

[85] 17 U.S.C. § 101: "To 'transmit' a performance or display is to communicate it by any device or process whereby images or sounds are received beyond the place from which they are sent."

[86] Section 110(2) exempts certain instructional broadcasting. Sections 110(8) and (9) are companion exceptions for transmissions of dramatic and nondramatic literary works "specifically designed for and primarily directed to" deaf and blind persons.

[87] *See* 17 U.S.C. § 111(a). Retransmission by cable systems is discussed at § 4E[4][e].

[88] *See* § 4E[4][f].

[89] Buck v. Jewell-LaSalle Realty Co., 283 U.S. 191 (1931).

[90] Society of European Stage Authors & Composers, Inc. v. New York Hotel Statler Co., 19 F. Supp. 1 (S.D.N.Y. 1937).

[91] Twentieth Century Music Corp. v. Aiken, 422 U.S. 151, 186 U.S.P.Q. 65 (1975).

[92] *See* § 4E[4][e].

all in Aiken's position 'performed' these musical compositions would be to authorize the sale of an untold number of licenses for what is basically a single public rendition of a copyrighted work. The exaction of such multiple tribute would go far beyond what is required for the economic protection of copyright owners. . . . " The "multiple tribute" concept derives from the Supreme Court's two cable television cases.[93]

Aiken was decided just before enactment of the 1976 Act, Section 110(5) of which addresses the Aiken problem by exempting the following:

"[C]ommunication of a transmission embodying a performance or display of a work by the public reception of the transmission on a single receiving apparatus of a kind commonly used in private homes, unless—

(A) a direct charge is made to see or hear the transmission; or

(B) the transmission thus received is further transmitted to the public."

Legislative history approves Aiken's result as the outer limit of what public receptions are exempt from a copyright owner's public performance right.[94]

---

[93] See id.

Copyright owners obtain revenue from broadcasting by licensing broadcasters, the fee being a percentage of the broadcaster's advertising revenue. Advertisers pay according to the broadcaster's audience size. The bigger the audience, the greater the copyright holders take. Aiken's activity expands the size of the audience. Collecting a fee from him is in effect collecting twice. Or is it?

[94] The Conference Report indicated:

"[A] small commercial establishment of the type involved in Twentieth Century Music Corp v. Aiken, 422 U.S. 151 (1975), which merely augmented a home-type receiver and which was not of sufficient size to justify, as a practical matter, a subscription to a commercial background music service, would be exempt. However, where the public communication was by means of something other than a home-type receiving apparatus, or where the establishment actually makes a further transmission to the public, the exemption would not apply." H.R. Conference Report No. 94-1733, 94th Cong., 2d Sess. 75 (1976).

The House Reported indicated:

"Under the particular fact situation in the Aiken case, assuming a small commercial establishment and the use of a home receiver with four ordinary loudspeakers grouped within a relatively narrow circumference from the set, it is intended that the performances would be exempt under clause (5). However, the Committee consider this fact situation to represent the outer limit of the exemption, and believes that the line should be drawn at that point. Thus, the clause would exempt small commercial establishments whose proprietors merely bring onto their premises standard radio or television equipment and turn it on for their customers' enjoyment, but it would impose liability where the proprietor has a commercial 'sound system' installed or converts a standard home receiving apparatus (by agumenting [sic] it with sophisticated or extensive amplification equipment) into the equivalent of a commercial sound system. Factors to consider in particular cases would include the size, physical arrangement, and noise level of the areas within the establishment where the transmissions are made audible or visible, and the extent to which the receiving apparatus is altered or augmented for the purpose of improving the oral or visual quality of the performance for individual members of the public using those areas." H.R. Report No. 94-1476, 94th Cong., 2d Sess. 87 (1976).

Lower court decisions apply the Section 110(5) exemption. In *Sailor Music*,[95] the court held the exemption not applicable to the sound systems in defendant's clothing stores. Two stores had four and seven speakers recessed in the ceiling and 2,679 and 6,770 square feet respectively. The average size of all the stores was 3,500 square feet. The establishment in *Aiken*, intended by Congress to be the exemption's "outer limit," had only 620 square feet. Defendant's chain of stores was of sufficient size to justify commercial background music service subscription.

In *Springsteen*,[96] the court gave the exemption narrow scope. Defendant operated an indoor roller rink and an adjacent outdoor miniature golf ("Putt-Putt") course. The Putt-Putt course sound system consisted of a radio receiver wired to six speakers mounted on light poles interspersed over the course's 7,500 square foot area. The speakers were "unsophisticated," inferior in quality to those of many home systems. The course generated about $4000 per year in gross revenues. Relying on Section 110(5)'s legislative history, the court distinguished *Sailor Music*; the sound quality was poor, there was no sound augmentation, and the commercial establishment was not of the size to justify a commercial service subscription.

[e] **Cable Television—Secondary Transmissions.** A cable system consists of a central antenna to receive television and radio broadcast signals and cable to transmit the signals to subscribers. It may provide a subscriber with: (1) superior reception in areas where mountains or buildings block signals from local stations, or (2) signals from distant stations totally beyond the reach of an ordinary receiver.

For years, cable television was a thorn in copyright law's side. Relying on *Buck*,[97] owners of copyrighted works, such as motion pictures, contended that cable retransmission of a work broadcasted by television or radio station is a second public performance. The problem went to the Supreme Court twice; in each instance, it found that cable retransmission was not a "public performance" under the 1909 Copyright Act.[98] Cable transmission systems extended an audience's capacity to perceive a performance rather than a performer's capacity to project his performance. To allow copyright owners to extract one royalty from the original broadcaster and another from the cable television retransmitter would be unfair multiple tribute because copyright owners base royalties on estimated audience size.[99] The Court

---

[95] Sailor Music v. Gap Stores, Inc., 516 F. Supp. 923, 213 U.S.P.Q. 1089 (S.D.N.Y. 1981), *aff'd*, 668 F.2d 84 (7th Cir. 1981), *cert. denied*, 456 U.S. 945 (1982). *See also* Little Mole Music v. Mavar's Supermarket, 12 U.S.P.Q.2d 1209 (N.D. Ohio 1989); Broadcast Music, Inc. v. United States Shoe Corp., 211 U.S.P.Q. 43 (C.D. Cal. 1980), *aff'd*, 678 F.2d 861 (9th Cir. 1982).

[96] Springsteen v. Plaza Roller Dome, Inc., 602 F. Supp. 1113, 225 U.S.P.Q. 1008 (M.D.N.C. 1985).

[97] *See* § 4E[4][d].

[98] Teleprompter Corp. v. Columbia Broadcasting Systems, 415 U.S. 394, 181 U.S.P.Q. 65 (1974); Fortnightly Corp. v. United Artists Television, Inc., 392 U.S. 390, 158 U.S.P.Q. 1 (1968).

[99] *Fortnightly* involved a cable system that retransmitted *local* broadcasts of copyrighted television programs. *Teleprompter* involved a cable system that retransmitted distant signals. In *Teleprompter*, the Supreme Court entertained but rejected the argument that extracting a royalty for retransmission of distant programming did not constitute multiple tribute.

"It is contended that copyright holders will necessarily suffer a net loss from the dissemination of their copyrighted material if license-free use of 'distant' signal importation

confined *Buck* to its facts and urged Congress to resolve the difficult policy problems that cable television created.

In the 1976 Act, Congress opted to cover cable retransmissions but imposed a compulsory license that uses the amount of "distant non-network programming caused by a cable system" to compute the royalty fee and the royalty distribution to copyright claimants.[100] This approach responds to the multiple tribute concept. Advertisers on distant non-network programming are apt to be local businesses unlikely to pay higher rates because their messages are carried to distant markets.[101]

[f] Performance Rights Licensing. Making public performances subject to copyright created practical problems for both holders and users of copyrighted works, especially music. How can a composer monitor performances by thousands of concert halls, taverns, restaurants, broadcast stations and other establishments? How can an establishment owner, who wants to respect copyright and obtain performance licenses, contact composers of the numerous works that he may wish to use?

---

is permitted. It is said that importation of copyrighted material into a secondary market will result in a loss in the secondary market without increasing revenues from the extended primary market on a scale sufficient to compensate for that loss. The assumption is that local advertisers supporting 'first run' programs will be unlikely to pay significantly higher fees on the basis of additional viewers in a 'distant' market because such viewers will typically have no commercial interest in the goods and services sold by purely local advertisers. . . . At issue in this case is the limited question of whether CATV transmission of 'distant' signals constitutes a 'performance' under the [1909] Copyright Act. While securing compensation to the holders of copyrights was an essential purpose of that Act, freezing existing economic arrangements for doing so was not. It has been suggested that the best theoretical approach to the problem might be '[a] rule which called for compensation to copyright holders only for the actual advertising time "wasted" on local advertisers unwilling to pay for the increase in audience size brought about by the cable transmission.' Note, 87 Harv. L. Rev. 665, 675 n.32 (1974). But such a rule would entail extended factfinding and a legislative, rather than a judicial judgment." 415 U.S. at 413 n.15.

As noted below, Congress was persuaded of the validity of the distinction between retransmission of local and network broadcasting, on the one hand, and retransmission of distant nonnetwork broadcasting, on the other hand.

[100] 17 U.S.C. § 111(c)-(f).

[101] *See* Cablevision Systems Development Co. v. Motion Picture Association of America Inc., 836 F.2d 599, 603, 5 U.S.P.Q.2d 1400, 1403 (D.C. Cir.), *cert. denied,* 487 U.S. 1235 (1988) ("Because local retransmission does not carry the signal to households beyond those local advertisers would be willing to pay to reach, the advertising revenue base will be increased by any expansion of the scope of the dissemination due to the retransmission, and copyright owners will be able to negotiate with the broadcaster to receive appropriate compensation. By the same token, the retransmission of network signals, from whatever distance, causes no difficulty. Advertisers on national network television . . . expect to reach audiences nationwide and pay accordingly. . . . Distant non-network programming is altogether another matter. Local advertisers will not pay extra to reach viewers who cannot reasonably be expected to patronize their businesses, so the revenue base from which to compensate the owners understates the value of the use of the materials, and the copyright holders would, absent an adjustment mechanism, be undercompensated. . . . The Act therefore allows the copyright owners of *distant non-network programs* to receive a portion of the fee paid to the cable systems by subscribers.").

The following solution evolved: musical works copyright owners formed performing rights organizations that

(1)   issued licenses and collected fees from users;

(2)   monitored public performances of its members' works and took steps to bring copyright infringement suits against unlicensed public performances; and

(3)   distributed collected royalties to its members under an agreed formula.[102]

The two major United States performing rights societies are the American Society of Composers, Authors and Publishers ("ASCAP") and Broadcast Music, Inc. ("BMI").[103]

Two cases illustrate how these processes work and some of the problems they create.

In *Famous Music Corp.*,[104] the defendant, Bay State, used music at its race track. It directed its music contractor not to play "ASCAP music," a direction virtually impossible to comply with unless all popular music is avoided.[105] ASCAP investigators detected the playing of copyrighted works in the ASCAP inventory. Owners of these copyrighted works sued for copyright infringement. Bay State asserted, without success, two defenses. First, it contended that it was not responsible for the independent contractor's acts. The court rejected the defense and imposed vicarious liability.[106] Second, Bay State relied on an antitrust consent decree that requires ASCAP to keep a current list of all musical compositions in its repertory and to answer inquires as to whether a given work is in that repertory. (There are over three million works in ASCAP's inventory.) Defendant never made such a request. ASCAP indicated to

---

[102] Effective enforcement of performance rights of individual composers virtually necessitates the creation of something analogous to performing rights organizations. They are in a sense a natural monopoly. Should the function be performed by a government agency rather than by a private organization? In other countries, performing rights societies are often governmental or quasi-governmental in nature. In this country, the pattern has been to have private organizations and then to regulate them through antitrust suits and consent decrees to control the anticompetitive and monopolistic aspects of their practices. Some of the antitrust issues are discussed below in connection with the *Broadcast Music* case.

[103] The 1976 Copyright Act defined "performing rights society" in the jukebox compulsory licensing provision. 17 U.S.C. § 116(e)(3) ("A 'performing rights society' is an association or corporation that licenses the public performance of nondramatic musical works on behalf of the copyrights owners, such as the American Society of Composers, Authors and Publishers, Broadcast Music, Inc., and SESAC, Inc."). *See* Asociation de Compositores y Editores de Musica LatinoAmericana v. Copyright Royalty Tribunal, 835 F.2d 446, 5 U.S.P.Q.2d 1217 (2d Cir. 1987).

[104] Famous Music Corp. v. Bay State Harness Horse Racing, 554 F.2d 1213, 194 U.S.P.Q. 177 (1st Cir. 1977).

[105] Some persons exhibit hostility to paying fees to ASCAP for the use of music. They attack ASCAP as an abusive monopoly and have even succeeded in obtaining state legislation restricting ASCAP's practices. Behind such responses may be a reluctance to accept the concept of intellectual property rights or, possibly, regional bias and culture conflict—composers are concentrated in areas such as New York and Los Angeles, users more evenly spread across the United States.

[106] *See* § 4F[3][a][i](1).

the defendant that it would make its index available—or to sell one. The court held that was sufficient, even though, at any instant in time, ASCAP does not know the full extent of its repertory. Composer-members constantly create works that, under the terms of their ASCAP membership agreement, automatically fall into ASCAP's repertory. Members do not always comply with their duty to regularly report such "new births" to ASCAP.

In *Broadcast Music*, [107] the Supreme Court held that the standard ASCAP and BMI "blanket licenses" were not *per se* unlawful price fixing. The Court noted the blanket license gives broadcasters and networks unlimited use of all works in the ASCAP's and BMI's repertories for a fixed fee, typically, a percentage of advertising revenue. By virtue of an antitrust consent decree, the Court said, ASCAP and BMI must, in addition to the blanket licensee, offer per program and per time period licenses for a set fee, but these alternatives are still to the whole repertory, not individual works. If no fee is agreed on, the applicant may apply to a court to set a reasonable fee.[108]

ASCAP and BMI hold *nonexclusive* rights to grant licenses for nondramatic performances. Member composers and publishers may directly negotiate and issue licenses for individual works. Thus, in theory, a potential user of music has an alternative to the terms offered by ASCAP and BMI.

The ASCAP and BMI blanket licenses are convenient for composers and users. They relieve ASCAP and BMI of enforcement responsibility and expense. Music users may choose from the vast ASCAP and BMI repertories without concern about copyright infringement.

Columbia Broadcasting System ("CBS") asked ASCAP and BMI to quote a rate for network use of particular music compositions, that is, a per use per composition basis—in lieu of the standard blanket license.[109] Apparently, CBS felt that this would simplify its negotiations with producers from whom it obtained televisions series. After ASCAP and BMI refused to supply such quotes, CBS filed suit, alleging that the blanket license constituted unlawful price-fixing among ASCAP or BMI members (that is, among composers and publishers of music).[110]

---

[107] Broadcast Music, Inc. v. Columbia Broadcasting Sys., 441 U.S. 1, 201 U.S.P.Q. 497 (1979).

[108] *See* American Society of Composers, Authors and Publishers v. Showtime/The Movie Channel, Inc., 912 F.2d 563, 565, 16 U.S.P.Q.2d 1026, 1027 (2d Cir. 1990) (pay cable television service; "This appeal is the first to challenge a fee determination for a blanket license under the ASCAP consent decree.").

[109] An initial question of interest is whether ASCAP or BMI could feasibly provide what CBS was asking for. How would those organizations go about placing a price on particular compositions? They monitor compositions' use frequency and might base the price on that, but current usage is undoubtedly heavily influenced by the standard blanket license environment in which cost is, literally, no object in determining what music to "buy."

[110] There were ironies in CBS's antitrust suit. CBS, a giant, dominant firm in the entertainment industry, complained of anticompetitive practices by groups of creators, who were in effect CBS's suppliers. Also, CBS was instrumental in the foundation of BMI as a competitor to ASCAP. CBS disposed of its interest in BMI in 1959.

The Second Circuit held that the blanket license was price fixing by the ASCAP and BMI composer and publisher members; price fixing is *per se* illegal under the antitrust laws. The Supreme Court reversed and remanded for a rule of reason analysis.[111] Justice White in his majority opinion made the following points:

1. ASCAP has been subject to intense scrutiny in antitrust suits and, because of the consent decrees, is virtually a regulated utility.

2. Congress in the Copyright Act of 1976 used the blanket license in particular instances and was clearly aware of the existence of and need for performing rights organizations. ASCAP and BMI are mentioned by name in the Act.[112] The blanket license has long been a central feature of these organizations.

3. The *per se* theory could not be confined to dealings with networks, as to which it might make some sense to have more precise license negotiations. The theory would extend to licenses for all classes of potential licensees. Indeed, under the *per se* price-fixing theory, the quoting of per-use per-composition rates by ASCAP would also be illegal.

4. The blanket license achieves economies by eliminating the need for numerous individual transactions. Its purpose is not solely or primarily to eliminate competition among composers, who have other incentives to create popular works.

5. The ASCAP blanket license is a separate product from the individual copyright licenses potentially available from composers. ASCAP is simply quoting a price for its product, as any other producer has a right to do.

6. CBS has a realistic option of negotiating directly with copyright owners.

In his dissenting opinion, Justice Stevens argued for a different result under the rule of reason approach. The current system tends to favor established composers and reduces incentives to use less well known music.[113] Justice Stevens discussed

---

[111] On remand, the Second Circuit upheld the blanket licensing system. CBS, Inc. v. ASCAP, 620 F.2d 930, 205 U.S.P.Q. 880 (2d Cir. 1980). *See also* Buffalo Broadcasting Co. v. American Soc'y of Composers, Authors and Publishers, 744 F.2d 917, 223 U.S.P.Q. 478 (2d Cir. 1984), *cert. denied,* 469 U.S. 1211 (1985) (same result for blanket license for local television stations). *Compare* Broadcast Music, Inc. v. Hearst/ABC Viacom Entertainment Services, 746 F. Supp. 320, 16 U.S.P.Q.2d 1683 (S.D. N.Y. 1990) (denying motion to dismiss antitrust suit involving blanket license for cable program service).

[112] 17 U.S.C. § 116(e)(3).

[113] He noted:

"Because the cost to the user is unaffected by the amount used on any program or on all programs, the user has no incentive to economize by, for example, substituting what would otherwise be less expensive songs for established favorites or by reducing the quantity of music used on a program. The blanket license thereby tends to encourage the use of more music and also of a larger share of what is really more valuable music, than would be expected in a competitive system characterized by separate licenses. And since revenues are passed on to composers on a basis reflecting the character and frequency of the use of their music, the tendency is to increase the rewards of the established composers at the expense of those less well known. Perhaps the prospect is in any event unlikely, but the blanket license does not present a new songwriter with any opportunity to break into the market by offering his product for sale at an unusually low price." 441 U.S. at 32–33.

briefly the ASCAP and BMI function of determining how to distribute net licensing proceeds to composers and publishers.[114]

[5] Display Rights

The Copyright Act confers the exclusive right "to display the copyrighted work publicly."[115] Section 101 defines "display" of a work: "show a copy of it, either directly or by means of a film, slide, television image, or any other device or process or, in the case of a motion picture or other audiovisual work, to show individual images nonsequentially."[116]

Section 109(c) places an important limitation on the exclusive right of public display:

> "Notwithstanding the provisions of section 106(5), the owner of a particular copy lawfully made under this title, or any person authorized by such owner, is entitled, without the authority of the copyright owner, to display that copy publicly, either directly or by the projection of no more than one image at a time, to viewers present at the place where the copy is located."

The owner of a lawful copy of a work, such as a painting, a doll, or a puppet, may display that work directly to the public, without the permission of the owner of the

---

The soundness of Justice Steven's observation is subject to doubt. The blanket license creates financial neutrality, at least among composers who choose to join ASCAP or BMI, resulting in music being chosen solely on its merits and its relative popularity. Such neutrality may be more important than achieving greater economic efficiency.

[114] ASCAP's rules, altered by antitrust consent decrees, provide a complex formula for determining distributions to members. They are based on (1) the nature and extent of the use of compositions (which ASCAP determines by selective monitoring of broadcasts); (2) the nature of the compositions (e.g., classical (which gets a greater share), popular, etc.); and (3) other factors.

[115] 17 U.S.C. § 106(5). The exclusive right applies only to "literary, musical, dramatic, and choreographic works, pantomimes, and pictorial, graphic, or sculptural works, including the individual images of a motion picture or other audiovisual work." This omits sound recordings. Section 120 limits the public display right as to architectural works. 17 U.S.C. § 120.

The House Report discusses the Section 106(5) right of public display:

"Clause (5) of section 106 represents the first explicit statutory recognition in American copyright law of an exclusive right to show a copyrighted work, or an image of it, to the public. The existence or extent of this right under the present statute is uncertain and subject to challenge. . . .

"The corresponding definition of 'display' covers any showing of a 'copy' of the work, 'either directly or by means of a film, slide, television image, or any other device or process.' Since 'copies' are defined as including the material object 'in which the work is first fixed,' the right of public display applies to original works of art as well as reproductions of them. With respect to motion pictures and other audiovisual works, it is a 'display' (rather than a 'performance') to show their 'individual images nonsequentially.' In addition to the direct showings of a copy of a work, 'display' would include the projection of an image on a screen or other surface by any method, the transmission of an image by electronic or other means, and the showing of an image on a cathode ray tube, or similar viewing apparatus connected with any sort of information storage and retrieval system." H.R. Rep. No. 94–1476, 94th Cong., 2d Sess. 63–65 (1976).

[116] 17 U.S.C. § 101.

copyright on the work. The copyright owner's exclusive right of public performance is of value primarily only in relation to broadcasting or other transmissions of images of a work.[117]

[6] Moral Rights

Continental European countries traditionally protect authors' "moral rights," including integrity and attribution rights. Berne Convention Article 6*bis* recognizes moral rights:

---

[117] 17 U.S.C. § 109(c).

The House Report discusses Section 109(c), as follows:

"Section 109(b) [now (c)] adopts the general principle that the lawful owner of a copy of a work should be able to put his copy on public display without the consent of the copyright owner. As in cases arising under section 109(a), this does not mean that contractual restrictions on display between a buyer and seller would be unenforceable as a matter of contract law.

"The exclusive right of public display granted by section 106(5) would not apply where the owner of a copy wishes to show it directly to the public, as in a gallery or display case, or indirectly, as through an opaque projector. Where the copy itself is intended for projection, as in the case of a photographic slide, negative, or transparency, the public projection of a single image would be permitted as long as the viewers are 'present at the place where the copy is located.'

"On the other hand, section 109(b) [now (c)] takes account of the potentialities of the new communications media, notably television, cable and optical transmission devices, and information storage and retrieval devices, for replacing printed copies with visual images. First of all, the public display of an image of a copyrighted work would not be exempted from copyright control if the copy from which the image was derived were outside the presence of the viewers. In other words, the display of a visual image of a copyrighted work would be an infringement if the image were transmitted by any method (by closed or open circuit television, for example, or by a computer system) from one place to members of the public located elsewhere.

"Moreover, the exemption would extend only to public displays that are made either directly or by the projection of 'no more than one image at a time.' Thus, even where the copy and the viewers are located at the same place, the simultaneous projection of multiple images of the work would not be exempted. For example, where each person in a lecture hall is supplied with a separate viewing apparatus, the copyright owner's permission would generally be required in order to project an image of a work on each individual screen at the same time.

"The committee's intention is to preserve the traditional privilege of the owner of a copy to display it directly, but to place reasonable restrictions on the ability to display it indirectly in such a way that the copyright owner's market for reproduction and distribution of copies would be affected. Unless it constitutes a fair use under section 107, or unless one of the special provisions of section 110 or 111 is applicable, projection of more than one image at a time, or transmission of an image to the public over television or other communication channels, would be an infringement for the same reasons that reproduction in copies would be. The concept of 'the place where the copy is located' is generally intended to refer to a situation in which the viewers are present in the same physical surroundings as the copy, even though they cannot see the copy directly." H.R. Rep. No. 94–1476, 94th Cong., 2d Sess. 79–80 (1976).

"(1) Independently of the author's economic rights, and even after the transfer of the said rights, the author shall have the right to claim authorship of the work, and to object to any distortion, mutilation or other modification of, or any other derogatory action in relation to, the said work, which would be prejudicial to his honor or reputation. . . . "[118]

United States copyright law traditionally did not separately protect moral rights. Authors have exclusive copyright rights and may exercise them under contractual conditions that guarantee integrity and attribution, but if an author transfers copyright without such conditions, he loses this power. Copyright aside, authors have pressed various state and federal legal theories to protect moral rights. Several states enacted artist and author rights statutes.[119] In 1990, Congress enacted the Visual Artists Rights Act, providing limited attribution and integrity rights.

[a] **Moral Rights Cases.** Three cases illustrate the status of moral rights under federal and state law.

In *Gilliam*,[120] the Second Circuit recognized that an author's right to control preparation of derivative works could be so exercised as to prevent a work's mutilation. "Monty Python," a British writer and performer group's collective moniker, created scripts for 30 minute programs, "Monty Python's Flying Circus." Monty Python delivered the scripts to BBC television pursuant to a contract that granted Monty Python significant control over any changes in the script before recording, made no provision for post-recording alterations, and preserved its residual rights in the scripts. The contract allowed BBC to license television broadcasting of the recordings in "any overseas territory." A United States television network, ABC, obtained rights to Monty Python episodes from the BBC through an intermediary, Time-Life Films. ABC edited the 30 minute programs to accommodate commercial advertising and eliminate "offensive or obscene matter." Asserting that ABC mutilated

---

[118] Berne Convention for the Protection of Literary and Artistic Works (Paris Text, 1971).
[119] The House Report on the 1990 federal visual artists law lists the following 11 statutes:
"Cal. Civ. Code §§ 980–990; Conn. Gen. Stat. Ann. §§ 42–116s to 42–116t; Ill. Ann. Stat. ch. 121 1/2 ¶¶ 1401–1408; La. Rev. Stat. Ann. 51:2151–51:2156; Me. Rev. Stat. Ann. tit. 27 § 303; Mass. Gen. Laws Ann. ch. 231 §§ 85S; N.J. Stat. Ann. §§ 2A:24A–1 to 2A:24–8; N.M. Stat. Ann. §§ 56–11–1 to 56–11–3; N.Y. Arts & Cult. Aff. Law §§ 11.01–16.01; Pa. Stat. Ann. tit. 73 §§ 2101–2110; R.I. Gen. Laws §§ 5–62–2 to 5–62–6."
The federal act discussed below partially preempts these statutes. The House Report comments:

"While 11 States have enacted artists' rights laws, John Koegel, a practitioner who has represented various artistic interests, noted at the Subcommittee's hearings that those laws are a ' "patchwork" of rules which by itself vitiates somewhat the single, unified system of copyright. Artists, lawyers, courts, and even the owners of works deserve a single set of rules on this subject.'

"The Committee agrees, and notes that the 11 State statutes have operated successfully and that they 'have not engendered a blizzard of litigation, nor an outcry of opposition from groups who might be adversely affected by them.' " H.R. Rep. No. 101–514, 101st Cong., 2d Sess. (1990).
[120] Gilliam v. American Broadcasting Co., Inc., 538 F.2d 14, 192 U.S.P.Q. 1 (2d Cir. 1976).

its work,[121] Monty Python sued to enjoin broadcast of the programs. The court ruled for Monty Python, reasoning that the recordings were derivative works, based on the original scripts, which could not be lawfully used beyond the bounds of the original script copyright owner's permission.

"Since the copyright in the underlying script survives intact despite the incorporation of that work into a derivative work, one who uses the script, even with the permission of the proprietor of the derivative work, may infringe the underlying copyright. See Davis v. E. I. DuPont deNemours & Co., 240 F. Supp. 612 (S.D. N.Y. 1965) (defendants held to have infringed when they obtained permission to use a screenplay in preparing a television script but did not obtain permission of the author of the play upon which the screenplay was based).

"If the proprietor of the derivative work is licensed by the proprietor of the copyright in the underlying work to vend or distribute the derivative work to third parties, those parties will, of course, suffer no liability for their use of the underlying work consistent with the license to the proprietor of the derivative work. Obviously, it was just this type of arrangement that was contemplated in this instance. The scriptwriters' agreement between Monty Python and BBC specifically permitted the latter to license the transmission of the recordings made by BBC to distributors such as Time-Life for broadcast in overseas territories.

"One who obtains permission to use a copyrighted script in the production of a derivative work, however, may not exceed the specific purpose for which permission was granted. Most of the decisions that have reached this conclusion have dealt with the improper extension of the underlying work into media or time, i.e., duration of the license, not covered by the grant of permission to the derivative work proprietor. . . . Appellants herein do not claim that the broadcast by ABC violated media or time restrictions contained in the license of the script to BBC. Rather, they claim that revisions in the script, and ultimately in the program, could be made only after consultation with Monty Python, and that ABC's broadcast of a program edited after recording and without consultation with Monty Python exceeded the scope of any license that BBC was entitled to grant.

"The rationale for finding infringement when a licensee exceeds time or media restrictions on his license—the need to allow the proprietor of the underlying copyright to control the method in which his work is presented to the public—applies equally to the situation in which a licensee makes an unauthorized use of the underlying work by publishing it in a truncated version.

---

[121] The appeals court cited an example of the mutilation.

"In one skit, an upper class English family is engaged in a discussion of the tonal quality of certain words as 'woody' or 'tinny.' The father soon begins to suggest certain words with sexual connotations as either 'woody' or 'tinny,' whereupon the mother fetches a bucket of water and pours it over his head. The skit continues from this point. The ABC edit eliminates this middle sequence so that the father is comfortably dressed at one moment and, in the next moment, is shown in a soaked condition without any explanation for the change in his appearance." 538 F.2d at 25 n.12 (1976).

Whether intended to allow greater economic exploitation of the work, as in the media and time cases, or to ensure that the copyright proprietor retains a veto power over revisions desired for the derivative work, the ability of the copyright holder to control his work remains paramount in our copyright law. We find, therefore, that unauthorized editing of the underlying work, if proven, would constitute an infringement of the copyright in that work similar to any other use of a work that exceeded the license granted by the proprietor of the copyright.

"If the broadcast of an edited version of the Monty Python program infringed the group's copyright in the script, ABC may obtain no solace from the fact that editing was permitted in the agreements between BBC and Time-Life or Time-Life and ABC. BBC was not entitled to make unilateral changes in the script and was not specifically empowered to alter the recordings once made; Monty Python, moreover, had reserved to itself any rights not granted to BBC. Since a grantor may not convey greater rights than it owns, BBC's permission to allow Time-Life, and hence ABC, to edit appears to have been a nullity."[122]

In *Gilliam,* the majority also opined that Monty Python could use Lanham Act Section 43(a)[123] to vindicate its "moral rights," the theory being that ABC's broadcast of a mutilated version of its work identifying it as author was a false designation of origin.

"It also seems likely that appellants will succeed on the theory that, regardless of the right ABC had to broadcast an edited program, the cuts made constituted an actionable mutilation of Monty Python's work. This cause of action, which seeks redress for deformation of an artist's work, finds its roots in the continental concept of droit moral, or moral right, which may generally be summarized as including the right of the artist to have his work attributed to him in the form in which he created it.

"American copyright law, as presently written, does not recognize moral rights or provide a cause of action for their violation, since the law seeks to vindicate the economic, rather than the personal, rights of authors. Nevertheless, the economic incentive for artistic and intellectual creation that serves as the foundation for American copyright law, . . . cannot be reconciled with the inability of artists to obtain relief for mutilation or misrepresentation of their work to the public on which the artists are financially dependent. Thus courts have long granted relief for misrepresentation of an artist's work by relying on theories outside the statutory law of copyright, such as contract law, Granz v. Harris, 198 F.2d 585 (2d Cir. 1952) (substantial cutting of original work constitutes misrepresentation), or the tort of unfair competition, Prouty v. National Broadcasting Co., 26 F. Supp. 265 (D. Mass. 1939). . . . Although such decisions are clothed in terms of proprietary right in one's creation, they also properly vindicate the author's personal right to prevent the presentation

---

[122] 538 F.2d at 20–21.
[123] Section 43(a) is discussed at §§ 5C[2][c][iv] and 6E.

of his work to the public in a distorted form. See Gardella v. Log Cabin Products Co., 89 F.2d 891, 895–96 (2d Cir. 1937) . . . .

"Here, the appellants claim that the editing done for ABC mutilated the original work and that consequently the broadcast of those programs as the creation of Monty Python violated the Lanham Act § 43(a). . . . This statute, the federal counterpart to state unfair competition laws, has been invoked to prevent misrepresentations that may injure plaintiff's business or personal reputation, even where no registered trademark is concerned. See Mortellito v. Nina of California, 335 F. Supp. 1288, 1294 (S.D.N.Y. 1972). It is sufficient to violate the Act that a representation of a product, although technically true, creates a false impression of the product's origin. See Rich v. RCA Corp., 390 F. Supp. 530 (S.D.N.Y. 1975) (recent picture of plaintiff on cover of album containing songs recorded in distant past held to be a false representation that the songs were new); Geisel v. Poynter Products, Inc., 283 F. Supp. 261, 267 (S.D.N.Y. 1968).

"These cases cannot be distinguished from the situation in which a television network broadcasts a program properly designated as having been written and performed by a group, but which has been edited, without the writer's consent, into a form that departs substantially from the original work. 'To deform his work is to present him to the public as the creator of a work not his own, and thus makes him subject to criticism for work he has not done.' Roeder, *supra*, at 569. In such a case, it is the writer or performer, rather than the network, who suffers the consequences of the mutilation, for the public will have only the final product by which to evaluate the work. Thus, an allegation that a defendant has presented to the public a 'garbled,' Granz v. Harris, *supra* (Frank, J., concurring), distorted version of plaintiff's work seeks to redress the very rights sought to be protected by the Lanham Act . . . and should be recognized as stating a cause of action under that statute. See Autry v. Republic Productions, Inc., 213 F.2d 667 (9th Cir. 1954); Jaeger v. American Int'l Pictures, Inc., 330 F. Supp. 274 (S.D.N.Y. 1971), which suggest the violation of such a right if mutilation could be proven.

". . . [T]he edited version broadcast by ABC impaired the integrity of appellants' work and represented to the public as the product of appellants what was actually a mere caricature of their talents. We believe that a valid cause of action for such distortion exists and that therefore a preliminary injunction may issue to prevent repetition of the broadcast prior to final determination of the issues."[124]

The court commented on a concurring judge's opinion that an editing notice would avoid a Section 43(a) violation.

"Judge Gurfein's concurring opinion suggests that since the gravamen of a complaint under the Lanham Act is that the origin of goods has been falsely described, a legend disclaiming Monty Python's approval of the edited version would preclude violation of that Act. We are doubtful that a few words

---

[124] 538 F.2d at 23–25.

could erase the indelible impression that is made by a television broadcast, especially since the viewer has no means of comparing the truncated version with the complete work in order to determine for himself the talents of plaintiffs. . . . [A] disclaimer . . . would go unnoticed by viewers who tuned into the broadcast a few minutes after it began.

"We therefore conclude that Judge Gurfein's proposal that the district court could find some form of disclaimer would be sufficient might not provide appropriate relief."[125]

In *Weinstein*,[126] plaintiff and two university faculty colleagues wrote an article describing a clinical project. The two co-authors, under direction of a university administrator, reorganized and published the article, listing plaintiff as the third author. Plaintiff's complaint alleged that his reputation suffered because he was not listed as first author as had been agreed upon. His theory was that the two co-authors and university officials, acting under color of state law, "mutilated his work and stole the credit," thereby denying him his constitutional due process rights. The Seventh Circuit affirmed the district court's dismissal of the complaint. First, it found no copyright violation because the other two faculty members, as joint authors and co-owners of the copyright, had a right to revise the work.[127] Second, it rejected plaintiff's moral rights theory.

"Weinstein . . . [asserts] droit moral, the Continental principle that an author may prevent mutilation or misuse of his work. Copyright persists in 'derivative works', see 17 U.S.C. § 103, which gives authors control over changes and republications along the lines of droit moral, see WGN Continental Broadcasting Co. v. United Video, Inc., 693 F.2d 622, 625 (7th Cir. 1982); Gilliam v. American Broadcasting Cos., 538 F.2d 14 (2d Cir. 1976), but copyright does not prevent alterations by coauthors. So [plaintiff] must be claiming additional rights against [his co-author and the university] by virtue of state law. 'Property' is defined for purposes of the due process clause by principles of state law, see Bishop v. Wood, 426 U.S. 341, 344 (1976), and Weinstein does not contend that Illinois (or any other jurisdiction in the United States) recognizes droit moral as a general principle. Three states have enacted statutes extending rights similar to droit moral to works of art. . . . But no jurisdiction has created the sort of moral right Weinstein invokes, let alone created any moral right through judicial decision. A federal court is not about to foist so novel a principle on Illinois. There is no reason to suspect that the courts of Illinois are just about to adopt an approach that no American jurisdiction follows as a general matter."[128]

In *Wojnarowicz*,[129] the court applied New York's Artists' Authorship Rights Act[130] to grant an artist relief against mutilation of his work but dismissed state

---

[125] 538 F.2d at 25 n.13.

[126] Weinstein v. University of Illinois, 811 F.2d 1091 (7th Cir. 1987).

[127] *See* § 4G[1].

[128] 811 F.2d at 1095 n.3.

[129] Wojnarowicz v. American Family Ass'n, 745 F. Supp. 130, 17 U.S.P.Q.2d 1337 (S.D.N.Y. 1990).

[130] The Act provides in relevant part:

defamation and federal copyright and Lanham Act claims. Defendant, the National Federation For Decency, campaigns against federal government funding of "blasphemous" art. Plaintiff, multimedia artist David Wojnarowicz, through his work, seeks to expose the government's failure to deal effectively with the AIDS epidemic. His works include sexually explicit subject matter and frequently employ groupings of images. In 1990, a gallery, with federal funding through the National Endowment of the Arts (NEA), exhibited plaintiff's work and published a catalog reproducing sixty of them. Defendant distributed an anti-NEA art funding pamphlet, which reproduced 14 fragments of plaintiff's works.

The court found no copyright violation because defendant's reproduction of limited portions of plaintiff's works was fair use[131] and no Lanham Act Section 43(a) violation because defendant's acts were not commercial.[132] It found violation of the state artists' authorship rights law, rejecting defendant's argument that federal law preempted the state law under Copyright Act Section 301[133] or Constitutional Supremacy clause principles.[134] The Act "guards against alterations of reproductions

---

"1. [N]o person other than the artist or a person acting with the artist's consent shall knowingly display in a place accessible to the public or publish a work of fine art or limited edition multiple of not more than three hundred copies by that artist or a reproduction thereof in an altered, defaced, mutilated or modified form if the work is displayed, published or reproduced as being the work of the artist, or under circumstances which would reasonably be regarded as being the work of the artist, and damage to the artist's reputation is reasonably likely to result therefrom. . . .

"2. (b) The rights created by this subdivision shall exist in addition to any other rights and duties which may now or in the future be applicable.

"3. (e) The provisions of this section shall apply only to works of fine art or limited edition multiples of not more than three hundred copies knowingly displayed in a place accessible to the public, published or reproduced in this state.

"4. (a) An artist aggrieved under subdivision one or subdivision two of this section shall have a cause of action for legal and injunctive relief." New York's Artists' Authorship Rights Act, N.Y. Cultural Affairs Law, § 14.03 (McKinney's Supp. 1990).

[131] *See* § 4F[3].

[132] *Cf.* §§ 5E[3][b][ii](1) and 5F[1][d][ii].

[133] "Where the state law violation is predicated upon an act incorporating elements beyond mere copying, the action is qualitatively different and there is no preemption. . . . Although the rights to reproduce and to produce derivative work are protected by the Copyright Act, [the state artists' rights law] is indeed qualitatively different than federal copyright law in both its aim and its elements. The state Act endeavors to protect an artist's reputation from the attribution to him of altered, defaced, mutilated or modified works of art. . . . Moreover, a claim under this statute requires proof of elements not required to prove copyright infringement, namely (a) the artwork must be altered, defaced, mutilated or modified; (b) the altered, defaced, mutilated or modified artwork must be attributed to the artist, or displayed in such circumstances as to be reasonably understood to be his work; and (c) this attribution must be reasonably likely to damage the artist's reputation. . . . While both plaintiff's state law and copyright claims are based upon the same cropped reproductions contained in the AFA pamphlet, they are qualitatively different and hence there is no preemption." 745 F. Supp. at 135–36, 17 U.S.P.Q.2d at 1341.

[134] "Defendants offer the following two examples:

"A direct conflict exists where the artist transfers his artwork together with the copyright to such other person (Mr. X). Mr. X creates a derivative work by altering the artwork

as well as of the original works": "Sections 14.03(1) and 14.03(3)(b), read together, suggest that deliberate alterations (such as selective cropping), as distinguished from those that ordinarily result from the reproduction process (such as reduction in overall size or loss of detail), would constitute violations." "In fact, the mass mailing of an altered photographic reproduction is likely to reach a far greater audience and cause greater harm to the artist than the display of an altered original, which may reach only a limited audience. While this situation may not have been expressly contemplated by the drafters, the wording of the statute literally covers it, . . . and the spirit of the statute would be contravened by it."

> "[T]his Court rejects defendants' claim that the reproduction and publication of minor, unrepresentative segments of larger works, printed wholly without context, does not constitute an alteration, defacement, mutilation or modification of plaintiff's artworks. By excising and reproducing only small portions of plaintiff's work, defendants have largely reduced plaintiff's multi-imaged works of art to solely sexual images, devoid of any political and artistic context. Extracting fragmentary images from complex, multi-imaged collages clearly alters and modifies such work.

> . . .

> " . . . Defendants urge that plaintiff's reputation has not been diminished in the eyes of his peers or gallery directors, dealers and potential buyers who determine his livelihood but, to the contrary, the increased exposure and publicity has enhanced his reputation. However, the trial testimony of Philip Yenawine, an expert on contemporary art, employed by the Modern Museum of Art in New York, established that there is a reasonable likelihood that defendants' actions have jeopardized the monetary value of plaintiff's works and impaired plaintiff's professional and personal reputation.

> "Yenawine testified that because the details in the pamphlet imply that plaintiff's work consists primarily of explicit images of homosexual sex activity, plaintiff's name will be 'anathema' to museums. Museums unfamiliar with plaintiff's work, believing the pamphlet to be representative of his work, may fail to review his work, even though many of plaintiff's art works do not contain sexual images. Even museums familiar with plaintiff's work may be reluctant to show his work due to his perceived association with pornography."[135]

and places it on display to the public as the work of the artist, damaging his reputation. The artist's rights under section 14.03 have been violated, yet Mr. X's actions are expressly authorized under the Copyright Act.

"The same conflict occurs where the artist transfers his artwork to one person (Mr. Y) and the copyright to another (Mr. Z). Mr. Y may alter or modify the artwork and place it on display to the public as the work of the artist, damaging his reputation. Mr. Z may have no objection to this conduct. The artist, under the New York law, may restrain the conduct even though it is an exercise of a right expressly granted by the Copyright Act. See 17 U.S.C. § 106.

"Neither example supports defendants' position. The Court does not agree that the Copyright Act authorizes a copyright owner other than the creator to publish or display an altered work, attributing that altered work to the original creator, and defendants have cited no decisions to that effect." 745 F. Supp. at 136, 17 U.S.P.Q.2d at 1342.

[135] 745 F. Supp. at 138–39, 17 U.S.P.Q.2d at 1343–44.

The court granted an injunction, ordered defendant to distribute a corrective communication to the recipients of its pamphlet, and awarded $1 nominal damages.

[b] Berne Convention Implementation—The 1990 Visual Artists Rights Act. In 1988, the United States adhered to the Berne Convention, but Congress made no provision for authors' moral rights and indicated clearly that the Convention's rights were not self-executing in the United States and that Berne implementation had no impact, positive or negative, on the development of moral rights law.[136] In the Visual Artists Rights Act of 1990, Congress extended certain moral rights to a limited class of works.[137] The Act covers only single copy or limited edition visual or sculptural works and photographs "produced for exhibition purposes only."[138] It excludes "works for hire." Its rights apply to works created after its effective date and to works title to which has not been transferred before that date.[139] It preempts equivalent state legal and equitable rights.[140]

---

[136] Berne Convention Implementation Act of 1988, P.L. 100–568, § 2, 102 Stat. 2853 (Oct. 31, 1988). See H.R. Rep. 100–609, 100th Cong., 2d Sess. 32-40 (1988) (noting "The law relating to the rights of paternity and integrity is intended to be the same the day before, and the day after, adherence. Courts remain free to apply common law principles, to interpret statutory provisions, and to consider the experience of foreign countries to the same extent as they would be in the absence of United States adherence to Berne.")

[137] P.L. 101–650, 104 Stat. 5128, 5132 (Dec. 1, 1990).

[138] The Section 101 definition is:

"A 'work of visual art' is—

"(1) a painting, drawing, print, or sculpture, existing in a single copy, in a limited edition of 200 copies or fewer that are signed and consecutively numbered by the author, or, in the case of a sculpture, in multiple cast, carved, or fabricated sculptures of two hundred or fewer that are consecutively numbered by the author and bear the signature or other identifying mark of the author.

"(2) a still photographic image produced for exhibition purposes only, existing in a single copy that is signed by the author, or in a limited edition of 200 copes or fewer that are signed and consecutively numbered by the author.

"A work of visual art does not include—

"(A)(i) any poster, map, globe, chart, technical drawing, diagram, model, applied art, motion picture or other audiovisual work, book, magazine, newspaper, periodical, data base, electronic information service, electronic publication, or similar publication;

"(ii) any merchandising item or advertising, promotional, descriptive, covering, or packaging material or container;

"(iii) any portion or part of any item described in clause (i) or (ii);

"(B) any work made for hire; or

"(C) any work not subject to copyright protection under this title." 17 U.S.C. § 101.

[139] P.L. 101–650, 104 Stat. 5128, 5132.

[140] 17 U.S.C. § 301(f). See H.R. Rep. No. 101–514, 101st Cong., 2d Sess. (1990):

"Consistent with current law on preemption for economic rights, the new Federal law will not preempt State causes of action relating to works that are not covered by the law, such as audiovisual works, photographs produced for non-exhibition purposes, and works in which the copyright has been transferred before the effective date. Similarly, State artists' rights [laws] that grant rights not equivalent to those accorded under the

The Act confers on visual works authors rights of "attribution" and "integrity,"[141] which are independent of the Section 106 exclusive rights of copyright. The rights are nontransferable, but the author may expressly waive the rights in writing.[142]

An author's attribution right consists of the right to claim authorship of the work, to prevent use of his or her name on visual art works he or she did not create, and to prevent use of his or her name on a work "in the event of a distortion, mutilation, or other modification of the work which would be prejudicial to his or her honor [or] reputation."

An author's integrity right means:

(1) "any intentional distortion, mutilation, or other modification of that work which would be prejudicial to his or her honor or reputation, and any intentional distortion, mutilation, or modification of that work is a violation of that right,"[143] and

---

proposed law are not preempted, even when they relate to works covered by H.R. 2690. For example, the law will not preempt a cause of action for a misattribution of a reproduction of a work of visual art or for a violation of a right to a resale royalty. Further, State law causes of action such as those for misappropriation, unfair competition, breach of contract, and deceptive trade practices, are not currently preempted under section 301, and they will not be preempted under the proposed law.

"On the other hand, if a State attempts to grant an author the rights of attribution or integrity for works of visual art as defined in this Act, those laws will be preempted. For example, the new law will preempt a State law granting the right of integrity in paintings or sculpture, even if the State law is broader than Federal law, such as by providing a right of attribution or integrity with respect to covered works without regard to injury to the author's honor or reputation."

[141] 17 U.S.C. § 106A. *See also* H.R. Rep. No. 101–514, 101st Cong., 2d Sess. (1990) ("The rights of attribution and integrity are independent of the exclusive rights provided to owners of copyrights by 17 U.S.C. 106, and they in no way interfere with ordinary commerce in works of art by art dealers, auction houses, and others similarly situated.").

[142] 17 U.S.C. § 106A(e). Transfer of a copy of the work or of the copyright in the work is not a waiver. *See also* H.R. Rep. 101–514, 101st Cong., 2d Sess. (1990)("the bill's waiver provision permits the author to hold harmless specific activity that in the absence of a waiver would violate the law. However, a waiver applies only to the specific person to whom waiver is made. That person may not subsequently transfer the waiver to a third party. Any third parties must obtain waivers directly from the author. . . . The bill does not authorize blanket waivers.").

[143] 17 U.S.C. § 106A(a)(3)(A). The Act excludes from the definition of distortion, mutilation, and modification:

(1) "modification of a work of visual art which is a result of the passage of time or the inherent nature of the materials," 17 U.S.C. § 106A(c)(1);

(2) "modification . . . which is the result of conversion, or of the public presentation, including lighting and placement, of the work . . . unless the modification is caused by gross negligence," 17 U.S.C. § 106A(c)(2);

(3) "reproduction, depiction, portrayal, or other use of a work in, upon, or in connection with" certain listed items, such as posters, maps, books, motion pictures, magazines, and data bases, which are excluded from the Section 101 definition of a "work of visual art," 17 U.S.C. § 106A(c)(3).

(2) "any destruction of a work of recognized stature, and any intentional or grossly negligent destruction of that work is a violation of that right."[144]

For works incorporated into buildings, Section 113(d) limits the author's integrity rights.[145]

[7] Compulsory Licenses

A compulsory license is "[a] permission to use intellectual property, compelled by the government in order to accomplish some political or social objective."[146]

> "Compulsory licensing forces an intellectual property owner to allow others to use that property at a fee set by the government. The owner is not allowed to refuse to license or to negotiate voluntary license fees in a free market, but is compelled to license at a rate thought to be 'reasonable' by the government."[147]

United States intellectual property law rarely provides for compulsory license, but the 1976 Copyright Act contains five: (1) phonorecord recordings,[148] (2) cable television,[149] (3) jukeboxes,[150] (4) noncommercial broadcasting,[151] (5) satellite

As to the last, the House Report explains:

"[T]he bill protects original works in single copies and limited editions, and . . . does not protect reproductions, depictions, portrayals, and similar uses of works of visual art that are embodied in works such as audiovisual works, books and similar works that are excluded from protection by subparagraphs (A) and (B) of the definition of a work of visual art. Copyright owners and users are insulated from liability . . . under these circumstances. For example, a newspaper, book or magazine may include a photograph of a painting or a piece of sculpture. A motion picture may include a scene in an art gallery. The exclusion from the definition . . . would be of little or no value if these industries could be held liable under section 106A for the manner in which they depict, portray, reproduce, or otherwise make use of such a work. Moreover, because such actions do not affect the single or limited edition copy, imposing liability in these situations would not further the paramount goal of the legislation: to preserve and protect certain categories of original works of art." H.R. Rep. 101–514, 101st Cong., 2d Sess. (1990). Cf. Wojnarowicz v. American Family Ass'n, 745 F. Supp. 130, 17 U.S.P.Q.2d 1337 (S.D.N.Y. 1990), discussed supra (distorted reproduction in pamphlet violates New York artist's law).

[144] 17 U.S.C. § 106A(a)(3)(B).

[145] 17 U.S.C. § 113(d). See also H.R. Rep. 101–514, 101st Cong., 2d Sess. (1990) (noting that the provision is drawn from similar provisions in California's statute).

[146] J.T. McCarthy, McCarthy's Desk Encyclopedia of Intellectual Property 51-52 (1991).

[147] Id. at 52.

[148] 17 U.S.C. § 115.

[149] See § 4E[4][e].

[150] 17 U.S.C. §§ 116, 116A. See Broadcast Music, Inc. v. Xanthas, Inc., 855 F.2d 233, 8 U.S.P.Q.2d 1254 (5th Cir. 1988) ("a jukebox operator who wishes to play copyrighted music must, unless he has specific permission from the copyright owner, register his jukeboxes with the United States Copyright Office and pay an annual registration fee to the Copyright Office, which then forwards the fees to the principal performance-rights societies such as BMI. . . . The society then distributes the money pro rata to those of its members who created or owned the music. A jukebox operator who fails to register his jukeboxes and then

retransmission.[152] The Act establishes an independent agency, the Copyright Royalty Tribunal, with compulsory license rate-setting and fee collection and distribution responsibilities.[153]

Most significant is the phonorecord license, which limits nondramatic musical work copyright owner's Section 106 exclusive rights to reproduce and distribute "phonorecords." The license dates back to the 1909 Act and is carried forward in 1976 Act Section 115.[154] The owner need not grant recording rights, but once one person

---

performs copyrighted music infringes the copyright and is subject to penalties provided by the Copyright Act."); MCA, Inc. v. Parks, 796 F.2d 200, 230 U.S.P.Q. 463 (6th Cir. 1986) ("This appeal . . . asks the musical question whether it is as true in 1986 as it was in 1942 that 'we . . . just need a nickel to feed that jukebox Saturday night' ?"); Hulex Music v. Santy, 698 F. Supp. 1024, 7 U.S.P.Q.2d 1690 (D. N.H. 1988) ("the jukebox exemption applies only to establishments 'making no direct or indirect charge for admission.' ").

The 1988 Berne Convention Implementation Act, P.L. 100-568, 102 Stat. 2853 (1988), substituted a provision for negotiation and arbitration of "coin-operated phonorecord player" royalties.

[151] 17 U.S.C. § 118.

[152] 17 U.S.C. § 119.

[153] 17 U.S.C. § 801 *et seq.*

See Amusement and Music Operators Ass'n v. Copyright Royalty Tribunal, 676 F.2d 1144, 215 U.S.P.Q. 100 (7th Cir. 1982), *cert. denied*, 459 U.S. 907 (1982); Record Industry Association of America v. Copyright Royalty Tribunal, 659 F.2d 252, 662 F.2d 1, 212 U.S.P.Q. 69 (D.C. Cir. 1981).

[154] *See* Record Industry Association of America v. Copyright Royalty Tribunal, 659 F.2d 252, 662 F.2d 1, 212 U.S.P.Q. 69 (D.C. Cir. 1981):

> "The phonorecord compulsory licensing system dates back to 1909, when Congress first extended a composer's copyright protection to include the right to control manufacture of 'parts of instruments serving to reproduce mechanically the musical work.' . . . Industry representatives expressed a fear that this protection ran the risk of 'establishing a great music monopoly' because the Aeolian Company, a manufacturer of player-piano rolls, was acquiring exclusive contract rights from composers and publishers. . . . The music industry has undergone major transformations in the intervening years, but record producers have continued to argue that a danger of monopolization and discriminatory practices exists, and Congress has concluded that a compulsory licensing system is still warranted. . . .

> "Although the availability of the compulsory license under the 1909 Act has been very important to the structure of the recording industry, the statutory procedures for invoking the license have rarely been used. . . . The usual effect of the system is to make the statutory royalty rate a ceiling on the price copyright owners can charge for use of their songs under negotiated contracts: if the owner demands a higher price in voluntary negotiations, the manufacturer can turn to the statutory scheme, but if the owner is willing to accept less than the statutory rate, he is free to do so. . . . [N.7 The compulsory license applies only to the second and subsequent recordings of a musical work, after the copyright owner has authorized a first recording to be made. He is theoretically free to negotiate a higher price for the first recording. Also, the compulsory license and its royalty rate apply only to use of the musical work, not the other talents of the copyright owner; if the composer is also the performer, he is free to negotiate package prices for further recordings by himself of the same song, and the compulsory license only governs renditions of his song by others.] . . . Today, the vast

distributes a phonorecord of the work to the public in the United States with the owner's authority, any other person may obtain a compulsory license "if his or her primary purposes in making phonorecords is to distribute them to the public for private use." No license is available to someone who is unlawfully duplicating a sound recording.[155] To obtain the license, the person may file a notice[156] and pay periodic royalties.[157] The license includes "the privilege of making a musical arrangement" that does not "change the basic melody or fundamental character of the work"; the "necessary arrangement" is not subject to copyright protection as a derivative work except with the musical copyright owner's permission.[158]

§ 4F Infringement

To infringe an exclusive right of copyright, an accused work must (1) derive from the copyrighted work, directly or indirectly, and (2) be substantially similar in expression to the copyrighted work. A copyright owner may establish the first element by direct evidence of plagiarism (copying) or inference from the accused copier's access to the copyrighted work and substantial similarity between the two works. The second element—substantial similarity in expression—depends on average lay observer or listener response.

There are a number of defenses to a charge of copyright infringement. Foremost is fair use. Fair use of a copyrighted work, including copying, for purposes such as criticism, news reporting, teaching, or research, does not constitute infringement. Other defenses include copyright invalidity, inequitable conduct, and misuse.

[1] Derivation—Copying

To infringe, an accused work must derive from the copyrighted work. An independently created work does not infringe, no matter how similar to the copyrighted work. Indeed, a second *identical* but independently created work itself qualifies for copyright as a work of original authorship.[1]

---

majority of contracts for use of copyrighted musical works involve voluntary payment at precisely the statutory rate. . . . This was not the case earlier in the century, because the statutory rate was then high enough in terms of purchasing power to allow a greater range for individual bargaining. . . . The 1909 Act had set the royalty rate at two cents for each 'part' (e.g., disc) manufactured, and this rate remained unchanged until the passage of the 1976 Copyright Act, which increased the statutory rate to 2 3/4 cents per copy and provided for further adjustments by the Copyright Royalty Tribunal."

[155] For a discussion of copyright protection for sound recordings, see § 4C[1][e].

[156] 17 U.S.C. § 115(b).

[157] 17 U.S.C. § 115(c). Nonpayment leads to license termination. 17 U.S.C. § 115(c)(5). See Peer International Corp. v. Pausa Records, Inc., 909 F.2d 1332, 15 U.S.P.Q.2d 1530 (9th Cir. 1990).

[158] 17 U.S.C. § 115(a)(2). For a discussion of derivative work copyrightability, see § 4C[1][c].

[1] See § 4C[5][a].

The derivation requirement does not mean that copyright infringement must be knowing or willful.[2] Infringement may be entirely innocent, for example, as when a publisher or broadcaster reproduces or transmits in good faith an infringing copier's work.[3] For example, person A may obtain a manuscript from person B, believing the manuscript to be B's original creation when, in fact, it is a copy of person C's copyrighted work. If A copies the manuscript, A infringes C's copyright even though A acts without knowledge of B's copying or C's copyright.

[a] **Subconscious Copying.** Copying may be subconscious. Judge Learned Hand noted, "[o]nce it appears that another has in fact used the copyright as the source of his production, he has invaded the author's rights. It is no excuse that in so doing his memory has played him a trick."[4]

In *Bright Tunes Music*,[5] former Beatle George Harrison's song "My Sweet Lord" infringed plaintiff's copyrighted song "He's So Fine." After hearing the evidence on the alleged plagiarism, including an "extensive colloquy between the Court and Harrison covering forty pages in the transcript," Judge Owen concluded:

> "What happened? I conclude that the composer, in seeking musical materials to clothe his thoughts, was working with various possibilities. As he tried this possibility and that, there came to the surface of his mind a particular combination that pleased him as being one he felt would be appealing to a prospective listener; in other words, that this combination of sounds would work. Why? Because his subconscious knew it already had worked in a song his conscious mind did not remember. Having arrived at this pleasing combination of sounds, the recording was made, the lead sheet prepared for copyright and the song was an enormous success. Did Harrison deliberately use the music of He's So Fine? I do not believe he did so deliberately. Nevertheless, it is clear that My Sweet Lord is the very same song as He's So Fine with different words, and Harrison had access to He's So Fine. This is, under the law, infringement of copyright, and is no less so even though subconsciously accomplished."[6]

---

[2] Willfulness may impact the monetary remedy available to the copyright owner, *see* § 4F[5][d][i], but is not an element of an infringement case. *Cf.* Buck v. Jewell-LaSalle Realty Co., 283 U.S. 191, 198 (1931) ("Intention to infringe is not essential under the act.").

[3] *E.g.*, De Acosta v. Brown, 146 F.2d 408, 63 U.S.P.Q. 311 (2d Cir. 1944), *cert. denied*, 325 U.S. 862 (1945).

[4] Fred Fisher, Inc. v. Dillingham, 298 F. 145, 148 (S.D.N.Y. 1924). *See also* Sheldon v. Metro-Goldwyn Pictures Corp., 81 F.2d 49, 54, 28 U.S.P.Q. 330 (2d Cir. 1936), *cert. denied*, 298 U.S. 669 (1936) ("in concluding as we do that the defendants used the play pro tanto, we need not charge their witnesses with perjury. With so many sources before them they might quite honestly forget what they took; nobody knows the origin of his inventions; memory and fancy merge even in adults. Yet unconscious plagiarism is actionable quite as much as deliberate.").

[5] Bright Tunes Music Corp. v. Harrisongs Music, Ltd., 420 F. Supp. 177 (S.D.N.Y. 1976), *aff'd sub nom.*, ABKCO Music, Inc. v. Harrisongs Music, Ltd., 722 F.2d 988, 221 U.S.P.Q. 490 (2d Cir. 1983).

[6] 420 F. Supp. at 180.

On appeal in *Bright Tunes*, the Second Circuit rejected the argument that "it is unsound policy to permit a finding of copyright infringement on the basis of subconscious copying."

> "It is not new law in this circuit that when a defendant's work is copied from the plaintiff's, but the defendant in good faith has forgotten that the plaintiff's work was the source of his own, such 'innocent copying' can nevertheless constitute an infringement. . . . We do not find this stance in conflict with the rule permitting independent creation of copyrighted material. It is settled that '[i]ntention to infringe is not essential under the [Copyright] Act,' . . . Moreover, as a practical matter, the problems of proof inherent in a rule that would permit innocent intent as a defense to copyright infringement could substantially undermine the protections Congress intended to afford to copyright holders."[7]

[b] Burden of Proof: Inference of Copying. A copyright owner bears the initial burdens of evidence production and persuasion on the copying issue. An accused copyright infringer may admit copying in the sense of derivation. The admission is not necessarily equivalent to admission of copyright infringement because the copier may contend that he copied the copyright owner's ideas only, not copyrightable expression.

An accused infringer may vehemently deny plagiarism and contend that any similarity is coincidental. Requiring a copyright owner to produce direct evidence of derivation would unreasonably restrict the copyright owner's rights. A copyright owner may meet his burden of showing derivation by showing either (1) the person responsible for the accused work or copy had access to the copyrighted work and the accused work is substantially similar in expression to the protected work, or (2) the accused and protected works are "strikingly" similar in expression.[8]

[c] Access. Access means opportunity to perceive[9] and may consist of direct or indirect exposure to the copyrighted work.[10] It may be inferred from the

---

[7] 722 F.2d at 998–99, 221 U.S.P.Q. at 498.

[8] *E.g.*, Gaste v. Kaiserman, 863 F.2d 1061, 1066, 9 U.S.P.Q.2d 1300, 1305 (2d Cir. 1988) (upholding jury verdict of copying; "Because copiers are rarely caught red-handed, copying has traditionally been proven circumstantially by proof of access and substantial similarity."); Baxter v. MCA Inc., 812 F.2d 421, 424 n.2, 2 U.S.P.Q.2d 1059, 1061 n.2 (9th Cir. 1987) ("Proof of striking similarity is an alternative means of proving 'copying' where proof of access is absent.").

[9] M. Nimmer, Copyright § 13.02[A] (1978).

[10] *E.g.*, Gaste v. Kaiserman, 863 F.2d 1061, 9 U.S.P.Q.2d 1300, 1305 (2d Cir. 1988).

In *Gaste*, the Second Circuit upheld a judgment based on a jury verdict that Kaiserman's popular song "Feelings," which was composed in 1973 in Brazil, was a copy of Gaste's copyrighted song "Pour Toi," which was composed in 1953 in France as part of a motion picture score and had no great success. Gaste's theory was that Kaiserman gained access to his song through Lebendiger, the owner of Fermata, Kaiserman's publisher. Fermata had dealings with Gaste's publisher in the 1950's.

> "Although Gaste's theory of access relies on a somewhat attenuated chain of events extending over a long period of time and distance, we cannot say as a matter of law that the jury could not reasonably conclude that Kaiserman had access to the song through

copyrighted work's widespread dissemination[11] but "there must be evidence of a reasonable possibility of access. Access must be more than a bare possibility and may not be inferred through speculation or conjecture."[12]

In *Ferguson*,[13] the Fifth Circuit affirmed summary judgment against a music copyright owner because there was no genuine issue of material fact on copying. Plaintiff sent six copies of "Jeannie Michelle," composed in 1953 but never published or performed, to potential publishers Guy Lombardo, Mills Publishing Co., Dinah Shore, Broadcast Music Incorporated (BMI), Jerri Greene and Don Cherry, none of whom showed any interest and each of whom returned the copy. Plaintiff alleged that noted musician John William's composition, "A Time to Love," infringed her copyright. The defendant moved for summary judgment and submitted supporting affidavits by John Williams, stating he never heard of plaintiff or her song, and by music experts, opining that the only similarity between the two compositions was a recurring three note sequence found in the works of Bach. Plaintiff did not directly countervail the statements. The court held that plaintiff failed to establish such access as would permit an inference of copying. Williams did have some contacts with BMI, one of the six entities or persons to whom plaintiff sent a copy, but those contacts were not related to plaintiff or her composition.

> "Access has been defined to include an opportunity to view the copyrighted work.
>
> . . .
>
> "To find that Williams had access, we would have to assume that (1) although BMI professed no interest in plaintiff's composition and returned the original to her, it made and kept a copy which it later allowed Williams to

Lebendiger. Access through third parties connected to both a plaintiff and a defendant may be sufficient to prove a defendant's access to a plaintiff's work. . . . The lapse of time between the original publication of 'Pour Toi' and the alleged infringement and the distance between the locations of the two events may make copying less likely but not an unreasonable conclusion. Indeed, a copier may be more likely to plagiarize an obscure song from the distant past and a faraway land than a recent well-known hit." 863 F.2d at 1067, 9 U.S.P.Q.2d at 1305.

[11] *E.g.*, ABKCO Music, Inc. v. Harrisongs Music, Ltd., 722 F.2d 988, 998, 221 U.S.P.Q. 490, 497 (2d Cir. 1983) (access may be found from widespread dissemination of the copyrighted work); Cholvin v. B. & F. Music Co., 253 F.2d 102, 116 U.S.P.Q. 491 (7th Cir. 1958) (2000 professional copies of plaintiff's distributed; four recordings, totaling 200,000 records sold; several national broadcasts).

Compare Selle v. Gibb, 741 F.2d 896, 223 U.S.P.Q. 195 (7th Cir. 1984) (no wide dissemination when plaintiff played his song with his small band three times in Chicago and sent copies of the music to eleven music recording and publishing companies, eight of which returned the copies and three of which did not respond); Evans v. Wallace Berrie & Co., 681 F. Supp. 813, 816, 7 U.S.P.Q.2d 1659, 1661 (S.D. Fla. 1988) ("it can hardly be said that Plaintiff's work was 'widely disseminated' simply because publishers, some of whom are in Australia, received Plaintiff's work").

[12] Gaste v. Kaiserman, 863 F.2d 1061, 1066, 9 U.S.P.Q.2d 1300, 1304–05 (2d Cir. 1988).

[13] Ferguson v. National Broadcasting Co., Inc., 584 F.2d 111, 200 U.S.P.Q. 65 (5th Cir. 1978).

see, and (2) Williams was lying when he said he had never heard of the plaintiff's composition. Plaintiff has given us no reason to believe that either of these assumptions is true, and certainly they are not obviously compelling. Thus, a finding of access in this case would be based on speculation or conjecture, and this is impermissible. . . . To support a finding of access there must be a reasonable possibility of access—not a bare possibility. . . . "[14]

[d] **Substantial Similarity—Inferring Access from Striking Similarity.** The requirement of substantial similarity of expression does double duty. First, it is an evidentiary factor on derivation, providing a basis for inferring derivation rather than independent creation—either in combination with evidence of access, or alone when the similarity is "striking." Second, it is the test of infringement, not just an evidentiary factor, once derivation is established.

Similarity of the copyrighted and accused works may be so striking as to provide a basis for inferring derivation even absent any evidence of access.[15] In *Selle*,[16] involving alleged music plagiarism, the Seventh Circuit restricted the striking similarity rule, requiring that a copyright owner show a "reasonable possibility of access" in addition to strikingly similarity.

> "[N]o matter how great the similarity between the two works, it is not their similarity per se which establishes access; rather, their similarity tends to prove access in light of the nature of the works, the particular musical genre involved and other circumstantial evidence of access. In other words, striking similarity is just one piece of circumstantial evidence tending to show access and must not be considered in isolation; it must be considered together with other types of circumstantial evidence relating to access.

---

[14] 584 F.2d at 113.

[15] Arnstein v. Porter, 154 F.2d 464, 468-69 (2d Cir. 1946) (Judge Jerome Frank: "In some cases, the similarities between the plaintiff's and defendant's work are so extensive and striking as, without more, both to justify an inference of copying and to prove improper appropriation.").

Cf. Testa v. Janssen, 492 F. Supp. 198, 203, 208 U.S.P.Q. 213, 217 (W.D. Pa. 1980) ("The practical difference between 'substantial similarity,' that is, the degree of similarity necessary where proof of access is extant, and 'striking similarity,' lies in a plaintiff's method of proof. Expert testimony is not required to establish 'substantial similarity.' However, when a plaintiff seeks to dispense with direct proof of access and attempts to establish that two works are 'strikingly similar,' such testimony is required.").

[16] Selle v. Gibb, 741 F.2d 896, 223 U.S.P.Q. 195 (7th Cir. 1984).

In *Selle*, plaintiff, composer of "Let It End," alleged infringement by the Bee Gees' popular song "How Deep Is Your Love." Plaintiff's work was publicly performed three times in Chicago and never published. The accused infringer's evidence indicated that the Bee Gees composed their song while at a recording studio in the Chateau d'Herouville about 25 miles northwest of Paris.

At the trial before a jury, plaintiff presented the testimony of a music professor, who had never before compared two popular songs. The professor testified that, in his opinion, the two songs had such striking similarities that they could not have been written independent of each other. The defendants presented evidence as to the independent creative process followed in composing "How Deep Is Your Love." The jury rendered a verdict for the plaintiff. The district court granted defendants' motion for a judgment notwithstanding the verdict.

"As a threshold matter, therefore, . . . there must be at least some other evidence which would establish a reasonable possibility that the complaining work was *available* to the alleged infringer. . . . [T]wo works may be identical in every detail, but, if the alleged infringer created the accused work independently or both works were copied from a common source in the public domain, then there is no infringement. . . . [A]lthough it has frequently been written that striking similarity *alone* can establish access, the decided cases suggest that this circumstance would be most unusual."[17]

Applying this test, plaintiff failed to establish a reasonable possibility of access. The judgment was also supported by "a more traditional analysis of proof of access based only on the proof of 'striking similarity.' "[18]

In *Gaste*,[19] the Second Circuit applied a "less rigorous" test of access than the Seventh Circuit's *Selle* suggestion but, in approving a jury instruction that copying may be found if the two works are strikingly similar, it added a cautionary note:

"Appellants contend that undue reliance on striking similarity to show access precludes protection for the author who independently creates a similar work. However, the jury is only *permitted* to infer access from striking similarity; it need not do so. Though striking similarity alone can raise an inference of copying, that inference must be reasonable in light of all the evidence. A plaintiff has not proved striking similarity sufficient to sustain a finding of copying if the evidence as a whole does not preclude any reasonable possibility of independent creation."[20]

[2] Substantial Similarity

Substantial similarity, the central infringement standard, must lie in *expression* because copyright protects only the expression of ideas, not ideas themselves.[21]

---

[17] 741 F.2d at 904, 223 U.S.P.Q. at 198. *See also* Benson v. Coca-Cola Co., 795 F.2d 973, 230 U.S.P.Q. 592 (11th Cir. 1986).

[18] The court noted:

"The judicially formulated definition of 'striking similarity' states that 'plaintiffs must demonstrate that "such similarities are of a kind that can only be explained by copying, rather than by coincidence, independent creation, or prior common source." ' '

" . . . [T]he similarities should appear in a sufficiently unique or complex context as to make it unlikely that both pieces were copied from a prior common source . . . or that the defendant was able to compose the accused work as a matter of independent creation.

". . . [T]o bolster the expert's conclusion that independent creation was not possible, there should be some testimony or other evidence of the relative complexity or uniqueness of the two compositions." 741 F.2d at 904–05, 223 U.S.P.Q. at 200–01.

In a footnote, the court found "appropriate" plaintiff's attorney's suggestion that "the degree of similarity required to establish an inference of access [is] in an inverse ratio to the quantum of direct evidence adduced to establish access." 741 F.2d at 903, n.4, 223 U.S.P.Q. at 200, n.4.

[19] Gaste v. Kaiserman, 863 F.2d 1061, 9 U.S.P.Q.2d 1300 (2d Cir. 1988).

[20] 863 F.2d at 1068, 9 U.S.P.Q.2d at 1306.

[21] The centrality of substantial similarity in copyright infringement compares to that of likelihood of confusion in trademark infringement. *See* § 5F[1].

The copyright statutes provide no assistance in determining substantial similarity. Section 501 defines infringement as the violation of one of the exclusive rights of the copyright owner. The House Report discusses infringement standards only briefly:

"As under the present law, a copyrighted work would be infringed by reproducing it in whole or in any substantial part, and by duplicating it exactly *or by imitation or simulation*. Wide departures or variations from the copyrighted work would still be an infringement as long as the author's 'expression' rather than merely the author's 'ideas' are taken. An exception to this general principle, applicable to the reproduction of copyrighted sound recordings is specified in section 114."[22]

The prevailing substantial similarity test is "whether an average lay observer would recognize the alleged copy as having been appropriated from the copyrighted work."[23] The "key to the 'ordinary observer' test is . . . the similarities rather than the differences."[24] Determining substantial similarity "must . . . inevitably be ad hoc."[25] Some courts, such as the Ninth Circuit, further refine the test by distinguishing "extrinsic similarity" and "intrinsic" similarity.[26]

In a recent, thorough study, one commentator finds substantial similarity law woefully inadequate:

"The traditional approach to determining copyright infringement, and the modifications thus far attempted, are all seriously inadequate. Each relies in part on the concept of substantial similarity as determined by the ordinary observer. . . . [T]his concept cannot be used effectively to determine infringement because (1) it rejects the expert testimony and analysis necessary to determine if copying can be inferred; (2) it tends to blur the line between unprotected idea and protected expression; and (3) it does not define when similarity is substantial, *i.e.*, do we use audience confusion or some other

---

[22] H.R. Rep. No. 94–1476, 94th Cong., 2d Sess. 61 (1976) (Emphasis added.). Idea noncopyrightability is discussed at § 4C[1][d].

[23] Ideal Toy Corp. v. Fab-Lu Ltd., 360 F.2d 1021, 1022, 149 U.S.P.Q. 800 (2d Cir. 1966).

[24] Novelty Textile Mills Inc. v. Joan Fabrics Corp., 558 F.2d 1090, 1093 n.4, 195 U.S.P.Q. 1, n.4 (2d Cir. 1977) ("Only a slavish copy would have no differences and '[n]o one disputes that the copyright extends beyond a photographic reproduction of the design.' "); Sheldon v. Metro-Goldwyn Pictures Corp., 81 F.2d 49, 56, 28 U.S.P.Q. 330 (2d Cir.), *cert. denied*, 298 U.S. 669 (1936) (Judge Learned Hand: "it is enough that substantial parts were lifted; no plagiarist can excuse the wrong by showing how much of his work he did not pirate.").

[25] Peter Pan Fabrics, Inc. v. Martin Weiner Corp., 274 F.2d 487, 489, 124 U.S.P.Q. 154, 156 (2d Cir. 1960) (Judge Learned Hand). *See also* Educational Testing Services v. Katzman, 793 F.2d 533, 541–42, 230 U.S.P.Q. 156, 161–62 (3d Cir. 1986) (defendant's questions for standard test review course infringe copyright in standard test; "A finding of substantial similarity is an ad hoc determination. . . . [E]ven in the absence of closely similar language, courts have found copyright infringement on the basis of 'recognizable paraphrases'."); Couleur International Ltd. v. Opulent Fabrics Inc., 330 F. Supp. 152, 153, 169 U.S.P.Q. 294, 295-96 (S.D.N.Y. 1971) ("Good eyes and common sense may be as useful as deep study of . . . cases, which themselves are tied to highly particularized facts. . . . ").

[26] Sid & Marty Krofft Television Productions, Inc. v. McDonald's Corp., 562 F.2d 1157, 196 U.S.P.Q. 97 (9th Cir. 1977), discussed at § 4F[2][c].

measure tied to the value of the material being used? Despite years of trying to define and refine this concept of substantial similarity, it remains a confused, ambiguous, and unhelpful concept which enables courts to obscure the real reasons behind their decisions." [27]

[a] **Facets of Substantial Similarity.** Substantial similarity decisions display four facets.

[i] *Dissection.* The first facet is dissection: is it useful or appropriate to take two works apart and compare them element by element? Courts condemn dissection, focusing on overall similarities [28] —but on occasion rely expressly or implicitly on dissection as a way of organizing the inquiry into substantial similarity. [29] For example, some decisions allow dissection of the similarities between works (though not of the dissimilarities) to determine whether the similarities result from unprotectable expression, such as facts, "scenes a faire," or functional elements. [30]

---

[27] Cohen, *Masking Copyright Decisionmaking: The Meaninglessness of Substantial Similarity*, 20 U.C. Davis L. Rev. 719, 766–67 (1987).

[28] *E.g.*, Aliotti v. Dakin & Co., 831 F.2d 898, 901, 4 U.S.P.Q.2d 1869, 1871 (9th Cir. 1987) (defendant's stuffed dinosaurs infringe plaintiff's copyright; "Dissection of dissimilarities is inappropriate because it distracts a reasonable observer from a comparison of the total concept and feel of the works."); Hartman v. Hallmark Cards Inc., 833 F.2d 117, 120, 4 U.S.P.Q.2d 1864, 1866 (8th Cir. 1987) (defendant's "Rainbow Brite" character and products do not infringe plaintiff's copyright on "The Adventures of Rainbow Island" graphics and script; "The listing of similarities does not alone generate an issue of material fact precluding summary judgment."); Litchfield v. Spielberg, 736 F.2d 1352, 1356, 222 U.S.P.Q. 965, 967 (9th Cir. 1984), *cert. denied,* 470 U.S. 1052 (1985) (motion picture "E.T.—The Extra-Terrestrial" does not infringe the copyright of a musical play "Lokey from Maldemar"; "While we have relied on [copyright claimants'] lists of similarities in the past for 'illustrative purposes,' . . . they are inherently subjective and unreliable. We are particularly cautious where, as here, the list emphasizes random similarities scattered throughout the works."); Atari, Inc. v. North American Philips Consumer Electronics Corp., 672 F.2d 607, 618, 214 U.S.P.Q. 33, 42 (7th Cir. 1982), *cert. denied,* 459 U.S. 880 (1982) (copyright owner showed likelihood of success on issue whether "K.C. Munchkin" was substantially similar in expression to copyrighted video game "PAC-MAN"; "In comparing the two works, the district court focused on certain differences in detail and seemingly ignored (or at least failed to articulate) the more obvious similarities.").

[29] *E.g.*, Durham Industries, Inc. v. Tomy Corp., 630 F.2d 905, 913, 208 U.S.P.Q. 10 (2d Cir. 1980) ("As a matter of logic as well as law, the more numerous the differences between two works the less likely it is that they will create the same aesthetic impact so that one will appear to have been appropriated from the other.").

[30] *E.g.*, Data East USA, Inc. v. Epyx, Inc., 862 F.2d 204, 208, 9 U.S.P.Q.2d 1322, 1326 (9th Cir. 1988) ("To determine whether similarities result from unprotectable expression, analytic dissection of *similarities* may be performed. If this demonstrates that all similarities in expression arise from use of common ideas, then no substantial similarity can be found."); Olson v. National Broadcasting Co., Inc., 855 F.2d 1446, 1453, 8 U.S.P.Q.2d 1231, 1236 (9th Cir. 1988) ("Because those similarities that do exist arose from unprotectable scenes a faire, there exists no substantial similarity of protectable expression under the intrinsic test"); Concrete Machinery Co. v. Classic Lawn Ornaments, Inc., 843 F.2d 600, 608–09, 6 U.S.P.Q.2d 1357, 1363 (1st Cir. 1988) ("By dissecting the accused work and identifying those features which are protected in the copyrighted work, the court may be able to determine as a matter of law whether or not the former has copied protected aspects of the latter. The court can

[ii] Ordinary Observer. The second facet is the ordinary observer test: to what extent must we judge similarity from the viewpoint of the ordinary observer as opposed to that of the expert in the subject matter in question?[31] Court decisions endorse the use of the ordinary observer test,[32] but recognize exceptions and circumstances in which expert testimony is given sway.[33] Who constitutes the "ordinary

---

also determine, in at least a general way, those aspects of the work that are protected by the copyright and that should be considered in the subsequent comparative analysis under the ordinary observer test."); Aliotti v. Dakin & Co., 831 F.2d 898, 901, 4 U.S.P.Q. 1869, 1872 (9th Cir. 1987); Atari, Inc. v. North American Philips Consumer Electronics Corp., 672 F.2d 607, 614, 214 U.S.P.Q. 33 (7th Cir. 1982), *cert. denied,* 459 U.S. 880 (1982) ("While dissection is generally disfavored, the ordinary observer test, in application, must take into account that the copyright laws preclude appropriation of only those elements of the work that are protected by the copyright.").

Compare Hoehling v. Universal City Studios, Inc., 618 F.2d 972, 979-80, 205 U.S.P.Q. 681, 687 (2d Cir. 1980), *cert. denied,* 449 U.S. 841 (1980) ("We are aware . . . that in distinguishing between themes, facts, and scenes a faire on the one hand, and copyrightable expression on the other, courts may lose sight of the forest for the trees. By factoring out similarities based on non-copyrightable elements a court runs the risk of overlooking wholesale usurpation of a prior author's expression.").

For a discussion of the uncopyrightability of facts and "scenes a faire," see § 4C[1][f].

[31] Focus on the ordinary observer (the "audience" test) links the scope of copyright protection to the economic justification for copyright. As Professor Goldstein notes, "The test is a practical implementation of copyright law's traditional object: to secure to authors the exclusive market—audience—for their protected expression." 2 P. Goldstein, Copyright § 7.3.2 (1989).

The ordinary observer test is both overinclusive and underinclusive. On the one hand, an ordinary, that is, untrained, observer may find similarity because the accused work copies the "ideas" of the protected work or because both works borrow from the public domain. This may be avoided by allowing a preliminary "dissection" of the two works to determine whether the portions taken consist only of unprotectable elements. *See* § 4F[2][b]. On the other hand, an ordinary observer may see no similarity despite substantial taking of expression by the defendant because of clever disguising or changes in inconsequential matters. For example, simple changes in arrangement may cause the same musical composition to sound quite different.

[32] *E.g.,* Hartman v. Hallmark Cards Inc., 833 F.2d 117, 120, 4 U.S.P.Q.2d 1864, 1866 (8th Cir. 1987) ("response of the ordinary, reasonable person."); O'Neill v. Dell Publishing Co., Inc., 630 F.2d 685, 690, 208 U.S.P.Q. 705, 709 (1st Cir. 1980) (affirming summary judgment of lack of substantial similarity; "Nor can the testimony of an expert provide what is clearly lacking. Although we may not be qualified literary critics, we are fitted by training and experience to compare literary works and determine whether they evidence substantial similarity.").

[33] *E.g.,* Whelan Associates, Inc. v. Jaslow Dental Laboratory, Inc., 797 F.2d 1222, 1232–33, 230 U.S.P.Q. 481, 487–88 (3d Cir. 1986), *cert. denied,* 479 U.S. 1031 (1987) ("The ordinary observer test, which was developed in cases involving novels, plays, and paintings, and which does not permit expert testimony, is of doubtful value in cases involving computer programs on account of the program's complexity and unfamiliarity to most members of the public. . . . We . . . join the growing number of courts which do not apply the ordinary observer test in copyright cases involving exceptionally difficult materials, like computer programs, but instead adopt a single substantial similarity inquiry in which both law and expert testimony would be admissible.").

For a discussion of the scope of copyright protection for computer programs, see § 4C[2][d].

Under the Ninth Circuit "two-part" analysis, expert testimony is admissible on extrinsic similarity, that is, similarity of ideas but not on intrinsic similarity. *See* § 4F[2][c]. Expert

audience" depends upon the nature of the work.[34] Courts are cautious about accepting affidavits and surveys of actual observers,[35] and tend to rely on the perception of the judge (or jury, if the case is tried to a jury).

testimony is also admissible to determine such substantial similarity as will provide a basis for inferring derivation. *See* § 4F[1][d]. *See also* Walker v. Time Life Films, Inc., 784 F.2d 44, 228 U.S.P.Q. 510 (2d Cir. 1986), *cert. denied*, 476 U.S. 1159 (1986); Arnstein v. Porter, 154 F.2d 464, 468, 68 U.S.P.Q. 288 (2d Cir. 1946) ("[T]he trier of the facts must determine whether the similarities are sufficient to prove *copying*. On this issue, analysis (dissection) is relevant, and the testimony of experts may be received. . . . If copying is established, then only does there arise the second issue, that of *illicit copying* (unlawful appropriation). . . . On that issue . . . the test is the response of the ordinary lay hearer; accordingly, on that issue, 'dissection' and expert testimony are irrelevant.").

[34] *See, e.g.*, Data East USA, Inc. v. Epyx, Inc., 862 F.2d 204, 209–210 n.6, 9 U.S.P.Q.2d 1322, 1327 n.6 (9th Cir. 1988) (video game "World Karate Championship" does not infringe copyright on "Karate Champ" video game because "a discerning 17.5 year-old boy could not regard the works as substantially similar"; the district court found that "the average age of individuals purchasing 'Karate Champ' is 17.5 years, that the purchasers are predominantly male, and comprise a knowledgeable, critical, and discerning group"); Aliotti v. Dakin & Co., 831 F.2d 898, 902, 4 U.S.P.Q.2d 1869, 1872 (9th Cir. 1987) ("Because children are the intended market for the dolls, we must filter the intrinsic inquiry through the perception of children."); Warner Bros. Inc. v. American Broadcasting Co., 720 F.2d 231, 244, 222 U.S.P.Q. 101, 112 (2d Cir. 1983) (no substantial similarity between plaintiff's "Superman" character and defendant's "The Greatest American Hero"; "Perhaps if Hero were a children's series . . . we would have greater concern. . . . But when a work is presented to a general audience of evening television viewers, the possible misperception of some young viewers cannot prevent that audience from seeing a program that will readily be recognized by the 'average lay observer,' . . . as poking fun at, rather than copying a copyrighted work."); Atari, Inc. v. North American Philips Consumer Electronics Corp., 672 F.2d 607, 619, 214 U.S.P.Q. 33, 42–43 (7th Cir. 1982), *cert. denied*, 459 U.S. 880 (1982) ("Video games, unlike an artist's painting or even other audiovisual works, appeal to an audience that is fairly undiscriminating insofar as their concern about more subtle differences in artistic expression.").

[35] *E.g.*, Mihalek Corp. v. Michigan, 814 F.2d 290, 2 U.S.P.Q.2d 1161, 1163 (6th Cir. 1987), *cert. denied*, 484 U.S. 986 (1987) (affirming summary judgment of noninfringement despite copyright owner's submission of affidavits by "average lay observers" attesting to similarity: "In this case the works, materials, and expressions of [the copyright owner] as compared with those utilized [by the accused infringer] are crucial and determinative, not the opinions of lay observers, who have made no careful determinations of the entire concepts involved."); Warner Bros. Inc. v. American Broadcasting Co., 720 F.2d 231, 222 U.S.P.Q. 101 (2d Cir. 1983).

In *Warner*, the court noted:

"The 'substantial similarity' that supports an inference of copying sufficient to establish infringement of a copyright is not a concept familiar to the public at large. It is a term to be used in a courtroom to strike a delicate balance between the protection to which authors are entitled under an act of Congress and the freedom that exists for all others to create their works outside the area protected against infringement. We need not and do not decide whether survey evidence of the sort tendered in this case would be admissible to aid a jury in resolving a claim of substantial similarity that lies within the range of reasonable factual dispute. However, when a trial judge has correctly ruled that two works are not substantially similar as a matter of law, that conclusion is not to be altered by the availability of survey evidence indicating that some people applying some standard of their own were reminded by one work of the other. Courts have an important

In *Dawson*,[36] the Fourth Circuit modified the ordinary observer test to take account of the intended audience. The district court found no infringement of plaintiff's copyrighted arrangement of the spiritual song "Ezekiel Saw De Wheel," by defendant's arrangement of the same spiritual because, though expert testimony established similarities between the two works, "as an ordinary lay observer, with nothing before him other than the sheet music, he could not determine that the two works were substantially similar." The appeals court disagreed:

> "In light of the copyright law's purpose of protecting a creator's market, we think it sensible . . . that the ultimate comparison of the works at issue be oriented towards the works' intended audience.
>
> . . .
>
> "We suspect that courts have been slow to recognize explicitly the need for refining the ordinary observer test in such a way that it would adopt the perspective of the intended audience because, in most fact scenarios, the general lay public fairly represents the works' intended audience. As a result, 'a considerable degree of ambiguity exists in this area; courts have not always made it apparent whether they were using a member of a specific audience, or simply an average lay observer as their spectator.' . . . Fortunately, the advent of computer programming infringement actions has forced courts to recognize that sometimes the non-interested or uninformed lay observer simply lacks the necessary expertise to determine similarities or differences between products.
>
> . . .
>
> ". . . [O]nly a reckless indifference to common sense would lead a court to embrace a doctrine that requires a copyright case to turn on the opinion of someone who is ignorant of the relevant differences and similarities between two works. Instead, the judgment should be informed by people who are familiar with the media at issue.
>
> . . .
>
> "Under the foregoing logic, we state the law to be as follows. When conducting the second prong of the substantial similarity inquiry, a district court must consider the nature of the intended audience of the plaintiff's work. If, as will most often be the case, the lay public fairly represents the intended audience, the court should apply the lay observer formulation of the ordinary observer test. However, if the intended audience is more narrow in that it possesses specialized expertise, relevant to the purchasing decision, that lay people would lack, the court's inquiry should focus on whether a member of

---

responsibility in copyright cases to monitor the outer limits within which juries may determine reasonably disputed issues of fact. If a case lies beyond those limits, the contrary view of a properly drawn sample of the population, or even of a particular jury, cannot be permitted to enlarge (or diminish) the scope of statutory protection enjoyed by a copyright proprietor." 720 F.2d at 245, 222 U.S.P.Q. at 112.

[36] Dawson v. Hinsaw Music Inc., 905 F.2d 731, 15 U.S.P.Q.2d 1132 (4th Cir. 1990), *cert. denied*, 111 S. Ct. 511 (1990).

the intended audience would find the two works to be substantially similar. Such an inquiry may include, and no doubt in many cases will require, admission of testimony from members of the intended audience or, possibly, from those who possess expertise with reference to the tastes and perceptions of the intended audience."[37]

The court cautioned that "departure from the lay characterization is warranted only where the intended audience possesses 'specialized expertise.'" Distinguishing cases involving popular music,[38] it remanded the case for inquiry "whether the audience of [plaintiff's] work possessed specialized expertise that the lay public lacks and, therefore, whether the general, undifferentiated lay public fairly represents the intended audience of [his] arrangement. . . . It is quite possible that spiritual arrangements are purchased primarily by choral directors who possess specialized expertise relevant to their selection of one arrangement instead of another."[39]

[iii] *Public Domain and Third Party Works.* The third facet is public domain and third party works: to what extent is it relevant that there are works in the public domain similar to both the protected and accused works? Some decisions indicate that

---

[37] 905 F.2d at 734–36, 15 U.S.P.Q.2d at 1134–36.

[38] "It is true that the case with which we contend involves music and courts routinely, and properly, apply the ordinary lay observer test to music cases. *See, e.g., Baxter v. MCA*, 812 F.2d 421, 424 n.2 (9th Cir.1987) (rejecting, in *dictum*, in the context of recordings to be used as a popular movie soundtrack, the proposition that the mere fact that a case involves music requires departure from the lay observer test). . . . We suspect that the distinction may have implications for the determination of the intended audience of Dawson's work. It may be that a popular recording of a love ditty pitched at the broadest of audiences is marketed to the general public far more so than is a spiritual arrangement." 907 F.2d at 737, 15 U.S.P.Q.2d at 1137.

[39] 905 F.2d at 737, 15 U.S.P.Q.2d at 1137.

The court commented on plaintiff's failure to introduce sound recordings of the two works:

"Use of a recording is obviously appropriate where a plaintiff sells recordings for the public to buy. However, [plaintiff] . . . sells sheet music arrangements to those who may make a purchasing decision on the basis of the sheet music. Although the district court's heavy reliance upon Dawson's failure to present a recording of the arrangements made sense in light of its application of the ordinary lay observer test, the conclusion would not make sense if it were the case that the audience for Dawson's spiritual arrangement had specialized expertise relevant to its purchasing decision.

"Furthermore, it may be that recordings of performances of the arrangements would not only be irrelevant but could indeed hinder the relevant inquiry. It may be that the sound of the performance of an arrangement is a function of not only the arrangement itself, but of the choral director's interpretation of the arrangement. Thus, differences and similarities in the sound of performances of two arrangements may represent something other than differences and similarities in the arrangements themselves. In addition, comparison of two recordings of performances of the arrangements would fail to take account of the different interpretations to the arrangements that purchasers intended to inject, rendering such a comparison even more misleading. These problems, of course, are not presented when actual recordings are at issue and therefore further distinguish the problems posed by spiritual arrangements as compared to popular recordings." 905 F.2d at 737, 15 U.S.P.Q.2d at 1137.

the existence of such works is relevant only to reduce the basis for an inference that the accused work was derived from the protected work because of the similarity between the two.[40] Others give such works greater significance, excusing elements of similarity on the ground that they are public domain "ideas."[41]

[iv] *Originality.* The fourth facet is originality: does the scope of protection depend on the protected work's uniqueness or originality? Courts give broader protection to fanciful and highly original works than to works shaped by their factual or functional content,[42] but fail to articulate precisely the extent and rationale of the difference.

[b] **A Unitary Judgmental Approach: Judge Learned Hand and the "Levels of Abstraction" Test.** In *Nichols,*[43] the most influential substantial similarity decision,

---

[40] *E.g.,* Sheldon v. Metro-Goldwyn Pictures Corp., 81 F.2d 49, 54, 28 U.S.P.Q. 330 (2d Cir.), *cert. denied,* 298 U.S. 669 (1936) (Learned Hand: "If the copyrighted work is . . . original, the public demesne is important only on the issue of infringement; that is, so far as it may break the force of the inference to be drawn from likenesses between the work and the putative piracy. If the defendant has had access to other material which would have served him as well, his disclaimer becomes more plausible.").

[41] *Cf.* Eden Toys, Inc. v. Marshall Field & Co., 675 F.2d 498, 500, 216 U.S.P.Q. 560, 562 (2d Cir. 1982) (two stuffed toy snowmen: "For countless generations, children and the young at heart have built snowmen by rolling moist snow into balls and placing them one atop the other. Dark colored objects such as lumps of coal are then used to simulate facial features and buttons. Bearing in mind the traditional characteristics of all snowmen, we find no error in [the trial court conclusion on summary judgment] that any similarity between [the two snowmen] would appear to the ordinary observer to result solely from the fact that both are snowmen."); Franklin Mint Corp. v. National Wildlife Art Exchange, Inc., 575 F.2d 62, 197 U.S.P.Q. 721 (3d Cir. 1978), *cert. denied,* 439 U.S. 880 (1978) (two paintings of pairs of cardinals).

[42] The notion is a variant of the "merger" doctrine. *See* § 4C[1][d][iii]. *E.g.,* Atari, Inc. v. North American Philips Consumer Electronics Corp., 672 F.2d 607, 616–17, 214 U.S.P.Q. 33, 41 (7th Cir. 1982), *cert. denied,* 459 U.S. 880 (1982):

> "As [Herbert Rosenthal Jewelry Corp. v. Kalpakian, 446 F.2d 738, 170 U.S.P.Q. 557 (9th Cir. 1971), holding unprotectable a jeweled bee pin,] and other cases show, that a work is copyrighted says very little about the scope of its protection. But *Kalpakian* is nonetheless instructive in that it represents one end of a spectrum of protection. As a work embodies more in the way of particularized expression, it moves further away from the bee pin in *Kalpakian,* and receives broader copyright protection. At the opposite end of the spectrum lie the 'strongest' works in which fairly complex or fanciful artistic expressions predominate over relatively simplistic themes and which are almost entirely products of the author's creativity rather than concomitants of those themes."

See also Sid & Marty Krofft Television Productions, Inc. v. McDonald's Corp., 562 F.2d 1157, 196 U.S.P.Q. 97 (9th Cir. 1977) ("the scope of copyright protection increases with the extent expression differs from the idea."); Universal Athletic Sales Co. v. Salkeld, 511 F.2d 904, 908, 185 U.S.P.Q. 76 (3d Cir. 1975), *cert. denied,* 423 U.S. 863 (1975) ("between the extremes of conceded creativity and independent effort amounting to no more than the trivial, the test of appropriation necessarily varies.").

Fair use also depends on the copyrighted work's degree of fancifulness. *See* § 4F[3][b][ii].

[43] Nichols v. Universal Pictures Corp., 45 F.2d 119, 7 U.S.P.Q. 84 (2d Cir. 1930), *cert. denied,* 282 U.S. 902 (1931).

Judge Learned Hand characterized the task of determining the line between idea and expression as one of drawing a series of increasingly general patterns around the protected work and then selecting the appropriate pattern as the border between expression and idea. *Nichols* involved alleged plagiarism of dramatic works, but Judge Hand's analysis influenced subsequent decisions dealing with copying of other types of works, literary, musical, artistic, etc.[44]

In an often-quoted passage, Judge Hand commented:

> "It is of course essential to any protection of literary property . . . that the right cannot be limited literally to the text, else a plagiarist would escape by immaterial variations. That has never been the law, but, as soon as literal appropriation ceases to be the test, the whole matter is necessarily at large, so that . . . the decisions cannot help much in a new case. . . . When plays are concerned, the plagiarist may excise a separate scene. . . . or he may appropriate part of the dialogue. . . . Then the question is whether the part so taken is 'substantial', and therefore not a 'fair use' of the copyrighted work; it is the same question as arises in the case of any other copyrighted work. . . . But when the plagiarist does not take out a block in situ, but an abstract of the whole, decision is more troublesome. *Upon any work, and especially upon a play, a great number of patterns of increasing generality will fit equally well, as more and more of the incident is left out.* The last may perhaps be no more than the most general statement of what the play is about, and at times might consist only of its title; but *there is a point in this series of abstractions where they are no longer protected, since otherwise the playwright could prevent the use of his 'ideas', to which, apart from their expression, his property is never extended.* . . . Nobody has ever been able to fix that boundary, and nobody ever can."[45]

Judge Hand distinguishes "literal appropriation" of a part of the protected work from taking an "abstract of the whole." These two cases—literal copying of a fragment of a work, and nonliteral copying of the whole of a work—are the most difficult for

[44] *Cf.* Atari, Inc. v. North American Philips Consumer Electronics Corp., 672 F.2d 607, 214 U.S.P.Q. 33, 40 (7th Cir. 1982), *cert. denied,* 459 U.S. 880 (1982) ("This 'test' has proven useful in analyzing dramatic works, literary works, and motion pictures, where the recurring patterns can readily be abstracted into very general themes.").

As to whether there are or should be distinct standards for substantial similarity for different types of works, compare Sid & Marty Krofft Television Productions, Inc. v. McDonald's Corp., 562 F.2d 1157, 1168, 196 U.S.P.Q. 97 (9th Cir. 1977) ("There is no special standard of similarity required in the case of 'things.' ") with Whelan Associates, Inc. v. Jaslow Dental Laboratory, Inc., 797 F.2d 1222, 1233, 230 U.S.P.Q. 481, 488 (3d Cir. 1986), *cert. denied,* 479 U.S. 1031 (1987) (ordinary observer test should not apply to "exceptionally difficult materials, like [sic: such as] computer programs"). *See also* Shaw v. Lindheim, 908 F.2d 531, 15 U.S.P.Q.2d 1516 (9th Cir. 1990), discussed § 4F[2][c] (distinguishing literary and representational works); Dawson v. Hinsaw Music Inc., 905 F.2d 731, 15 U.S.P.Q.2d 1132 (4th Cir. 1990), *cert. denied,* 111 S. Ct. 511 (1990), discussed § 4F[2][a][ii] (modifying ordinary observer test to take account of specialized, intended audience).

[45] 45 F.2d at 121 (emphasis added).

determining substantial similarity of expression.[46] As to fragmented literal similarity,[47] Judge Hand equates infringement with fair use: one may take some of a copyrighted work but not too much; how much depends on the circumstances, including the purpose.[48] As to comprehensive nonliteral similarity, Judge Hand offers his famous "patterns" yardstick. One must compare the protected and accused works in a series of abstractions; if they become similar or identical only at a "high" level of abstractions, there is no substantial similarity of expression.[49]

Some courts and commentators treat Hand's patterns analysis as a test for drawing the line between substantial similarity of expression and mere similarity of ideas. But Judge Hand himself recognized that the test simply stated the problem to be analyzed without finally resolving it: *"Nobody has ever been able to fix that boundary, and nobody ever can."*[50]

---

[46] The other two of the four possibilities—comprehensive, literal similarity and fragmented, nonliteral similarity—are normally easy cases, the former constituting substantial similarity and the latter not constituting substantial similarity.

[47] *See* M. Nimmer & D. Nimmer, Copyrights § 13.03[A][2].

[48] *See* § 4F[3].
Later cases identify two tests for taking literal fragments. *E.g.,* Warner Bros. Inc. v. American Broadcasting Co., 720 F.2d 231, 242, 222 U.S.P.Q. 101, 110 (2d Cir. 1983) ("courts have invoked two distinct doctrines. First, a de minimus rule has been applied, allowing the literal copying of a small and usually insignificant portion of the plaintiff's work. . . . Second, under the 'fair use' doctrine, . . . courts have allowed the taking of words or phrases when adapted for use as commentary or parody . . . ").

[49] *E.g.,* Warner Bros. Inc. v. American Broadcasting Companies, 654 F.2d 204, 208, 211 U.S.P.Q. 97, 100 (2d Cir. 1981) ("in determining whether two such works are so substantially similar as to reveal an infringement of one by the other, courts must decide whether the similarities shared by the works are something more than mere generalized ideas or themes.").
See also Nash v. CBS, Inc., 899 F.2d 1537, 1540, 14 U.S.P.Q.2d 1755, 1757 (7th Cir. 1990):
  "Learned Hand, whose opinions still dominate this corner of the law, observed . . . that all depends on the level of abstraction at which the court conceives the interest protected by the copyright. If the court chooses a low level (say, only the words the first author employed), then a copier may take the plot, exposition, and all other original material, even though these may be the most important ingredients of the first author's contribution. As a practical matter this would mean that anyone could produce the work in a new medium without compensating the original author, despite the statute's grant to the author of the privilege to make 'derivative works'. If on the other hand the court should select a high level of abstraction, the first author may claim protection for whole genres of work ('the romantic novel' or, more modestly, any story involving doomed young lovers from warring clans, so that a copyright on *Romeo and Juliet* would cover *West Side Story* too). Even a less sweeping degree of abstraction creates a risk of giving copyright protection to 'the idea' although the statute protects only 'expression'."

[50] *See* Nash v. CBS, Inc., 899 F.2d 1537, 1539–41, 14 U.S.P.Q.2d 1755, 1758 (7th Cir. 1990):
  "Sometimes called the 'abstractions test', Hand's insight is not a 'test' at all. It is a clever way to pose the difficulties that require courts to avoid either extreme of the continuum of generality. It does little to help resolve a given case . . . Who is the 'ordinary' observer, and how does this person choose the level of generality? Ordinary observers, like reasonable men in torts, are fictitious characters of the law, reminders that judges must apply objective tests rather than examine their own perceptions. They do not answer the essential question: at what level of generality? After 200 years of wrestling with copy-

In *Nichols*, the infringement case involved the plaintiff's copyrighted play "Abie's Irish Rose" and the defendant's motion picture, "The Cohens and The Kellys." Both works involved an interfaith romance between children of a Jewish and an Irish Catholic family and complications arising from the objections of the respective fathers to their children marrying outside the family faith.

Judge Hand noted that "As respects plays, the controversy chiefly centers upon the characters and sequence of incident, these being the substance." He found insufficient similarity either as to "incident" (plot) or character.[51] As to plot:

> right questions, it is unlikely that courts will come up with the answer any time soon, if indeed there is 'an' answer, which we doubt.
>
> "Hand returned again and again to the opposing forces that make the formulation of a single approach so difficult. Intellectual (and artistic) progress is possible only if each author builds on the work of others. No one invents even a tiny fraction of the ideas that make up our cultural heritage. Once a work has been written and published, any rule requiring people to compensate the author slows progress in literature and art, making useful expressions 'too expensive', forcing authors to re-invent the wheel, and so on. Every work uses scraps of thought from thousands of predecessors, far too many to compensate even if the legal system were frictionless, which it isn't. Because any new work depends on others even if unconsciously, broad protection of intellectual property also creates a distinct possibility that the cost of litigation—old authors trying to get a 'piece of the action' from current successes—will prevent or penalize the production of new works, even though the claims be rebuffed. Authors as a group therefore might prefer limited protection for their writings—they gain in the ability to use others' works more than they lose in potential royalties. See William M. Landes & Richard A. Posner, An Economic Analysis of Copyright Law, 18 J. Legal Studies 325, 332–33, 349–59 (1989).
>
> "Yet to deny authors all reward for the value their labors contribute to the works of others also will lead to inefficiently little writing, just as surely as excessively broad rights will do. The prospect of reward is an important stimulus for thinking and writing, especially for persons such as Nash who are full-time authors. Before the first work is published, broad protection of intellectual property seems best; after it is published, narrow protection seems best. At each instant some new works are in progress, and every author is simultaneously a creator in part and a borrower in part. In these roles, the same person has different objectives. Yet only one rule can be in force. This single rule must achieve as much as possible of these inconsistent demands. Neither Congress nor the courts has the information that would allow it to determine which is best. Both institutions must muddle through, using not a fixed rule but a sense of the consequences of moving dramatically in either direction."

[51] For a later decision by Judge Hand finding infringement of a dramatic work, see Sheldon v. Metro-Goldwyn Pictures Corp., 81 F.2d 49, 28 U.S.P.Q. 330 (2d Cir. 1936), *cert. denied*, 298 U.S. 669 (1936).

In *Sheldon*, Judge Hand held that the play "Letty Lynton" infringed the copyrighted play, "Dishonored Lady" even though both works were based in part on an actual episode.

> "[A] play may be pirated without using the dialogue. . . . Speech is only a small part of a dramatist's means of expression; he draws on all the arts and compounds his play from words and gestures and scenery and costume and from the very looks of the actors themselves. Again and again a play may lapse into pantomime at its most poignant and significant moments; a nod, a movement of the hand, a pause, may tell the audience more than words could tell. To be sure, not all this is always copyrighted,

"The only matter common to the two is a quarrel between a Jewish and an Irish father, the marriage of their children, the birth of grandchildren and a reconciliation.

"If the defendant took so much from the plaintiff, it may well have been because her amazing success seemed to prove that this was a subject of enduring popularity. Even so, granting that the plaintiff's play was wholly original, and assuming that novelty is not essential to copyright, there is no monopoly in such a background. Though the plaintiff discovered the vein, she could not keep it to herself; so defined, the theme was too generalized an abstraction from what she wrote. It was only a part of her 'ideas.'"[52]

As to character:

"There are but four characters common to both plays, the lovers and the fathers. The lovers are so faintly indicated as to be no more than stage properties. They are loving and fertile; that is really all that can be said of them, and anyone else is quite within his rights if he puts loving and fertile lovers in a play of his own, wherever he gets the cue. The Plaintiff's Jew is quite unlike the defendant's. His obsession is his religion, on which depends such racial animosity as he has. He is affectionate, warm and patriarchal. None of these fit the defendant's Jew, who shows affection for his daughter only once, and who has none but the most superficial interest in his grandchild. He is tricky, ostentatious and vulgar, only by misfortune redeemed into honesty. Both are grotesque, extravagant and quarrelsome; both are fond of display; but these common qualities make up only a small part of their simple pictures. . . . The Irish fathers are even more unlike; the plaintiff's a mere symbol for religious fanaticism and patriarchal pride, scarcely a character at all. Neither quality appears in the defendant's, for while he goes to get his grandchild, it is rather out of a truculent determination not to be forbidden, than from pride in his progeny. For the rest he is only a grotesque hobblehoy, used for low comedy of the most conventional sort, which any one might borrow, if he chanced not to know the exemplar."[53]

[c] The Ninth Circuit's "Two Part" Test—Intrinsic and Extrinsic Similarity. Before the 1977 *Krofft* decision, the Ninth Circuit applied Judge Hand's *Nichols* unitary judgment approach. For example, in *Herbert Rosenthal Jewelry*,[54] Judge Browning wrote:

though there is not reason why it may not be, for those decisions do not forbid which hold that mere scenic tricks will not be protected. . . . The play is the sequence of the confluents of all these means, bound together in an inseparable unity; it may often be most effectively pirated by leaving out the speech, for which a substitute can be found, which keeps the whole dramatic meaning. That as it appears to us is exactly what the defendants have done here; the dramatic significance of the scenes we have recited is the same, almost to the letter." 81 F.2d at 55–56.

[52] 45 F.2d at 122.
[53] 45 F.2d at 122.
[54] Herbert Rosenthal Jewelry Corp. v. Kalpakian, 446 F.2d 738, 170 U.S.P.Q. 557 (9th Cir. 1971), discussed at § 4C[1][d][iii].

"The critical distinction between 'idea' and 'expression' is difficult to draw. As Judge Hand candidly wrote, 'Obviously, no principle can be stated as to when an imitator has gone beyond copying the "idea," and has borrowed its "expression." ' *Peter Pan Fabrics, Inc. v. Martin Weiner Corp.*, 274 F.2d 487, 489 (2d Cir. 1960). At least in close cases, one may suspect, the classification the court selects may simply state the result reached rather than the reason for it. In our view, the difference is really one of degree as Judge Hand suggested in his striking 'abstraction' formulation in Nichols v. Universal Pictures Corp., 45 F.2d 119, 121 (2d Cir. 1930). The guiding consideration in drawing the line is the preservation of the balance between competition and protection reflected in the patent and copyright laws."[55]

In *Krofft*,[56] the Ninth Circuit adopted a "two-part" test for substantial similarity that was based on an erroneous interpretation of the Second Circuit's *Arnstein* decision[57] and on a confusion between substantial similarity as an element of inferring derivation (that is, copying as opposed to independent creation) and substantial similarity as the ultimate infringement standard (that is, substantial similarity of expression as opposed to copying of mere ideas).[58]

At issue in *Krofft* was whether McDonald's "McDonaldland" characters, for example, Mayor McCheese, infringed Krofft's copyrighted "H.R. Pufnstuf" characters. The court affirmed a judgment based on a jury verdict of infringement. After citing with approval Judge Hand's "abstractions" test, the Court set forth the following "new dimension" to "the test for infringement."

"There must be ownership of the copyright and access to the copyrighted work. But there also must be substantial similarity not only of the general ideas but of the expressions of those ideas as well. Thus two steps in the analytic process are implied by the requirement of substantial similarity.

"The determination of whether there is substantial similarity in ideas may often be a simple one. [For example, a copyright could be obtained over a cheaply-manufactured plaster statue of a nude.] [T]he idea there embodied is a simple one—a plaster recreation of a nude human figure. A statue of a horse or a painting of a nude would not embody this idea and therefore could not infringe. The test for similarity of ideas is still a factual one, to be decided by the trier of fact.

"We shall call this the 'extrinsic test.' It is extrinsic because it depends not on the responses of the trier of fact, but on specific criteria which can be listed and analyzed. Such criteria include the type of artwork involved, the materials used, the subject matter, and the setting for the subject. Since it is an extrinsic test, analytic dissection and expert testimony are appropriate. Moreover, this question may often be decided as a matter of law.

---

[55] 446 F.2d at 742.

[56] Sid & Marty Krofft Television Productions, Inc. v. McDonald's Corp., 562 F.2d 1157, 196 U.S.P.Q. 97 (9th Cir. 1977).

[57] Arnstein v. Porter, 154 F.2d 464 (2d Cir. 1946), *cert. denied*, 330 U.S. 851 (1947).

[58] *See* § 4F[1].

"The determination of when there is substantial similarity between the forms of expression is necessarily more subtle and complex. . . . If there is substantial similarity in ideas, then the trier of fact must decide whether there is substantial similarity in the expressions of the ideas so as to constitute infringement.

"The test to be applied in determining whether there is substantial similarity in expressions shall be labeled an intrinsic one–depending on the response of the ordinary reasonable person. . . . Because this is an intrinsic test, analytic dissection and expert testimony are not appropriate.

"This same type of bifurcated test was announced in *Arnstein v. Porter*, 154 F.2d 464, 468–69 (2 Cir. 1946), *cert. denied*, 330 U.S. 851 (1947). The court there identified two separate elements essential to a plaintiff's suit for infringement: copying and unlawful appropriation. Under the *Arnstein* doctrine, the distinction is significant because of the different tests involved.

'[T]he trier of fact must determine whether the similarities are sufficient to prove copying. On this issue, analysis ("dissection") is relevant, and the testimony of experts may be received to aid the trier of facts. * * * If copying is established, then only does there arise the second issue, that of illicit copying (unlawful appropriation). On that issue . . . the test is the response of the ordinary lay hearer; accordingly, on that issue, "dissection" and expert testimony are irrelevant.' 154 F.2d at 468 (footnotes omitted).

"We believe that the court in *Arnstein* was alluding to the idea-expression dichotomy which we make explicit today. When the court in *Arnstein* refers to 'copying' which is not an infringement, it must be suggesting copying merely of the work's idea, which is not protected by the copyright. To constitute an infringement, the copying must reach the point of unlawful appropriation; or the copying of the protected expression itself. We analyze this distinction in terms both of the elements involved—idea and expression—and of the tests to be used—extrinsic and intrinsic—in an effort to clarify the issues involved." [59]

Krofft does not explain what independent function is performed by the extrinsic similarity test, that is, similarity of ideas. The second test is all that copyright law has ever demanded. If a work is substantially similar in expression to the copyrighted work, it infringes; if it is not, it does not. It is hard to imagine a work that would fail of infringement because it was substantially similar in expression (the intrinsic test) but not in ideas (the extrinsic test).[60]

---

[59] 562 F.2d at 1164–65.

[60] *Cf.* McCulloch v. Albert E. Price Inc., 823 F.2d 316, 319, 3 U.S.P.Q.2d 1502, 1505 (9th Cir. 1987) (affirming finding that defendant's decorative plate infringed plaintiff's copyrighted plate design). In *McCulloch*, the defendant contended that the district court found infringement only on the basis of the second, intrinsic test and erred by failing to make a finding as to similarity of ideas (the extrinsic test). The Ninth Circuit disagreed:

"Concluding that the plates are 'confusingly similar in appearance' is tantamount to finding substantial similarities in the objective details of the plates. Thus, although the district court did not expressly state that it was applying the two-part test, it is clear from the record that the court found a similarity of ideas and expression."

Krofft misunderstands *Arnstein*. The quoted *Arnstein* passage does refer to a first step of determining "copying" and does allow dissection and expert testimony, but this step related to the determination of copying (as opposed to independent derivation). Absent direct evidence of derivation or an admission by the accused infringer, copying may be inferred by proof of access and substantial similarity. The latter may be determined by dissection and expert testimony. By failing to distinguish the two—inference of copying through access and substantial similarity, and assessment of substantial similarity of expression as the direct test of infringement, *Krofft* promotes confusion, particularly in cases in which derivation is admitted or proved directly and the remaining issue is whether the accused work is substantially similar in expression to the copyrighted work (or only in ideas).

Ninth Circuit cases consistently cite and purport to apply the *Krofft* test but never adequately explain the significance of the extrinsic test of similarity of ideas.[61] For example, in *Narell*,[62] the court affirmed a summary judgment that defendant's romance novel "Illusions of Love" did not infringe plaintiff's social history "Our City: The Jews of San Francisco." It applied the "extrinsic test" as follows:

> "The extrinsic test determines whether the two works are substantially similar in general ideas and compares the individual features of the works to find specific similarities between the plot, theme, dialogue, mood, setting, pace, characters, and sequence of events. . . . The test focuses not on basic plot ideas, which are not protected by copyright, but on 'the actual concrete elements that make up the total sequence of events and the relationships between the major characters.
>
> . . .
>
> "Neither the mood, pace, nor sequence of the two works are alike. The comparative analytic dissection provided by the plaintiff's expert merely shows a common use of unprotected historical facts and ordinary phrases, not extrinsic similarity. . . . No reasonable juror could conclude that the extrinsic test is satisfied."[63]

An accused work that was substantially similar in expression but not in ideas should probably be considered an infringement unless the fair use defense applies. *See* MCA, Inc. v. Wilson, 677 F.2d 180, 211 U.S.P.Q. 577 (2d Cir. 1981), discussed at § 4F[3][d]. *MCA* found infringement by an off-color parody version of a copyrighted song. One might say that the "ideas" were apparently different but that the parody stole the copyrighted song's expression.

[61] *E.g.*, Litchfield v. Spielberg, 736 F.2d 1352, at 1356–57, 222 U.S.P.Q. 965 (9th Cir. 1984), *cert. denied*, 470 U.S. 1052 (1985) (motion picture "E.T.—The Extra-Terrestrial" does not infringe the copyright of a musical play "Lokey from Maldemar":

"Similarity of ideas may be shown by an extrinsic test which focuses on alleged similarities in the objective details of the works. . . . The extrinsic test requires a comparison of plot, theme, dialogue, mood, setting, pace and sequence. . . . Similarity of expression depends on a subjective, intrinsic test. "Whereas *E.T.* concentrates on the development of the characters and the relationship between a boy and an extraterrestrial, *Lokey* uses caricatures to develop its theme of mankind divided by fear and hate. No lay observer would recognize *E.T.* as a dramatization or picturization of *Lokey*.").

[62] Narell v. Freeman, 872 F.2d 907, 10 U.S.P.Q.2d 1596 (9th Cir. 1989).

[63] 872 F.2d at 912–13, 10 U.S.P.Q.2d at 1600.

It applied the "intrinsic test" as follows:

> "The intrinsic test is used to determine whether the forms of expression of the two works are substantially similar; it is subjective, depending on the response of an ordinary, reasonable reader. . . . To constitute infringement, the total concept and feel of the works must be substantially similar.
>
> . . .
>
> "The similarities between the two works are neither quantitatively nor qualitatively significant.
>
> "Because of the fundamental differences between the works and the insubstantial nature of the copied passages, no reasonable reader could conclude that the works are substantially similar."[64]

In *Shaw*,[65] a Ninth Circuit panel added a corollary to the two-part *Krofft* test, distinguishing literary from representational works. Plaintiff, author of the television script "The Equalizer," charged copyright infringement by defendant's television series, "The Equalizer."[66] The district court granted a noninfringement summary judgment; it found that there was a triable fact issue on extrinsic similarity of ideas, to wit, on "the objective characteristics of theme, plot, sequence of events, characters, dialogue, setting, mood, and pace" but "made a subjective determination under the intrinsic test that no reasonable juror could determine that the works had a substantially similar total concept and feel . . . "

The Ninth Circuit panel noted that cases applying the "extrinsic" test (similarity of ideas) to literary works had included such a "lengthy list of concrete elements" that "the extrinsic test as applied to books, scripts, plays, and motion pictures can no longer be seen as a test for mere similarity of ideas. . . . Because the criteria incorporated into the extrinsic test encompass all objective manifestations of creativity, the two tests are more sensibly described as objective and subjective analyses of expression, having strayed from *Krofft's* division between expression and ideas." This

---

[64] 872 F.2d at 913, 10 U.S.P.Q.2d at 1600–01.

[65] Shaw v. Lindheim, 919 F.2d 1353, 15 U.S.P.Q.2d 1516 (9th Cir. 1990).

[66] The Ninth Circuit ruled that "[t]he fact that the two works have identical titles . . . weighs in [the copyright owner's] favor."

> "In *Arnstein v. Porter*, 154 F.2d 464 (2d Cir.1946), the Second Circuit held that '[a] title cannot be copyrighted.' . . . This is true in the sense that titles, in and of themselves, cannot claim statutory copyright. . . . Nevertheless, '[i]f the copying of a title is not an act of copyright infringement, it may . . . have copyright significance as one factor in establishing whether the substance of plaintiff's work (not the title) has been copied.' . . . As the Seventh Circuit has stated, 'the title of a copyrighted work should be taken into account when the same title is applied to a work [allegedly] copied from it.' *Wihtol v. Wells*, 231 F.2d 550, 553 (7th Cir.1956); *see also Robert Stigwood Group, Ltd. v. Sperber*, 457 F.2d 50, 55 (2d Cir.1972) ('[T]he admitted desire of defendants to make reference to [the title "Jesus Christ Superstar"] in its advertisement provides further evidence that the performance is intended to come as close as possible to the original dramatic co-musical.'). Thus, we acknowledge and consider defendants' admitted copying of Shaw's title in determining whether there is substantial similarity of protected expression between the two works." 919 F.2d at 1362.

transformation affects summary judgment: "It is improper for a court to find . . . that there is no substantial similarity as a matter of law after a writer has satisfied the extrinsic test. To conclude otherwise would allow a court to base a grant of summary judgment on a purely subjective determination of similarity."[67] The panel reversed the summary judgment because the copyright owner "satisfied the extrinsic test for literary works and thus has presented a triable issue of fact regarding substantial similarity."[68]

---

[67] "The rule we announce today—that satisfaction of the extrinsic test creates a triable issue of fact in a copyright action involving a literary work—is in harmony with our prior decisions. [V]arious panels of this circuit have affirmed grants of summary judgment on the issue of substantial similarity between books, scripts, films, or plays, [but] none . . . rested on application of the intrinsic test alone. . . . By creating a discrete set of standards for determining the objective similarity of literary works, . . . this circuit . . . implicitly recognized the distinction between situations in which idea and expression merge in representational objects and those in which the idea is distinct from the written expression of a concept by a poet, a playwright, or a writer. . . . As a result, the scope of the copyright protection afforded such works is necessarily narrow. . . . In contrast, there is an infinite variety of novel or creative expression available to the author of a book, script, play, or motion picture based on a preexisting idea. Given the variety of possible expression and the objective criteria available under the extrinsic test to analyze a literary work's expression, as distinct from the ideas embodied in it, the intrinsic test cannot be the sole basis for a grant of summary judgment. Once a court has established that a triable question of objective similarity of expression exists, by analysis of each element of the extrinsic test, its inquiry should proceed no further. What remains is a subjective assessment of the 'concept and feel' of two works of literature—a task no more suitable for a judge than for a jury. This subjective assessment is not a legal conclusion; rather it involves the audience in an interactive process with the author of the work in question, and calls on us 'to transfer from our inward nature a human interest and a semblance of truth sufficient to procure for these shadows of imagination that willing suspension of disbelief for the moment, which constitutes poetic faith.' S.T. Coleridge, *Biographia Literaria*, ch. 14, *reprinted in 5 English Literature: The Romantic Period* (A. Reed ed. 1929). This interactive assessment is by nature an individualized one that will provoke a varied response in each juror, for what 'makes the unskillful laugh, cannot but make the judicious grieve.' W. Shakespeare, *Hamlet*, Act III, scene ii, ll. 27–28. . . .

"Where idea and expression merge, a court is well-suited to make the required determination of similarity on a motion for summary judgment. A comparison of literary works, on the other hand, generally requires the reader or viewer to engage in a two-step process. The first step involves the objective comparison of concrete similarities; the second employs the subjective process of comprehension, reasoning, and understanding. The imagery presented in a literary work may also engage the imagination of the audience and evoke an emotional response. Because each of us differs, to some degree, in our capability to reason, imagine, and react emotionally, subjective comparisons of literary works that are objectively similar in their expression of ideas must be left to the trier of fact.

"For these reasons, a showing of substantial similarity with reference to the eight objective components of expression in the extrinsic test applied to literary works creates a genuine issue for trial." 919 F.2d at 1360–61.

[68] *Compare* Pasillas v. McDonald's Corp., 927 F.2d 440, 442–43, 17 U.S.P.Q.2d 1874, 1876 (9th Cir. 1991) (plaintiff's "man in the moon" mask not infringed by defendant's "Mac Tonight" character; "*Shaw* differs from the present case in two critical respects. First, its holding is explicitly limited to literary works. In the *Shaw* panel's words, the rule it announced is 'that satisfaction of the extrinsic test creates a triable issue of fact in a copyright

Some decisions in other circuits adopt the Ninth Circuit's two part test of substantial similarity.[69]

[3] Fair Use

Fair use of a copyrighted work is not infringement. Now codified in the 1976 Copyright Act Section 107,[70] the fair use doctrine was well-established in pre-1976 case law.

> "The roots of what we now know as 'fair use' are firmly planted in the early English common law, where the defense was known as 'abridgment.' . . . From the earliest days of the doctrine, courts have recognized that when a second author uses another's protected expression in a creative and inventive way, the result may be the advancement of learning rather than the exploitation of the first writer.

> "Fair use made its debut in American law with Justice Story's opinion in *Folsom v. Marsh*, 9 F. Cas. 342 (C.C.D. Mass. 1841) (No. 4,901). *Folsom* involved a dispute over two biographical works about George Washington. The following passage is probably the most frequently cited one from Justice Story's discussion:

>> 'In short, we must often, in deciding questions of this sort, look to the nature of the objects of the selections made, the quantity and value of the materials used, and the degree in which the use may prejudice the sale, or diminish the profits, or supersede the objects, of the original work.'

---

action involving a literary work.'. . . Second, and more importantly, *Shaw* recognized and distinguished a line of cases involving works whose idea and expression are inseparable.").

[69] *E.g.*, Hartman v. Hallmark Cards Inc., 833 F.2d 117, 120, 4 U.S.P.Q.2d 1864, 1866 (8th Cir. 1987) ("Although expert opinion evidence is admissible in connection with the first step of the substantial similarity analysis to show similarity of ideas, analytical dissection and expert opinion are not called for under the second step in which substantial similarity of expression is measured by a different standard—the response of the ordinary, reasonable person."). *Cf.* Original Appalachian Artworks, Inc. v. Toy Loft, Inc., 684 F.2d 821, 829 n.11, 215 U.S.P.Q. 745, 752 n.11 (11th Cir. 1982) (describing *Krofft* as "an excellent discussion of the dichotomy between similar ideas and similar expression").

[70] Section 107 provides:

"Notwithstanding the provisions of section 106, the fair use of a copyrighted work, including such use by reproduction in copies or phonorecords or by any other means specified by that section, for purposes such as criticism, comment, news reporting, teaching (including multiple copies for classroom use), scholarship, or research, is not an infringement of copyright. In determining whether the use made of a work in any particular case is a fair use the factors to be considered shall include—

"(1) the purpose and character of the use, including whether such use is of a commercial nature or is for nonprofit educational purposes;

"(2) the nature of the copyrighted work;

"(3) the amount and substantiality of the portion used in relation to the copyrighted work as a whole; and

"(4) the effect of the use upon the potential market for or value of the copyrighted work." 17 U.S.C. § 107.

Section 106 is the enumeration of the exclusive rights of copyright.

"*Id.* at 348. He framed his analysis in terms of two extremes. At one extreme was the studied evasion, in which 'the whole substance of one work has been copied from another, with slight omissions and formal differences only . . . ' *Id.* at 344. At the other extreme was the use of verbatim portions of an earlier work to review or criticize. Justice Story wrote of this type of use:

> '[N]o one can doubt that a reviewer may fairly cite largely from the original work, if his design be really and truly to use the passages for the purposes of fair and reasonable criticism. On the other hand, it is as clear, that if he thus cites the most important parts of the work, with a view, not to criticize, but to supersede the use of the original work, and substitute the review for it, such a use will be deemed in law a piracy.' *Id.* at 344–45.

"As Justice Story observed, however, many uses would fall somewhere in between the two extremes. To evaluate cases falling in the gray area, he proposed an inquiry into the infringer's creative effort. In order to have a lawful abridgment, he said,

> '[t]here must be real, substantial condensation of the materials, and intellectual labor and judgment bestowed thereon; and not merely the facile use of the scissors; or extracts of the essential parts constituting the chief value of the original work.' *Id.* at 345."[71]

Results in fair use cases are difficult to predict and reconcile.[72] Producers of copyrighted works take a restrictive view of the doctrine; users take an expansive view.

Courts use "fair use" in two senses. In one, it means the absence of substantial similarity of expression, a taking of ideas only or of an insignificant amount of expression.[73] In another, more accurate sense, fair use means that unauthorized use of a substantial amount of the author's expression, which would otherwise infringe, is excused because of the circumstances, most particularly because of the user's *purpose.*

[a] **Supreme Court Decisions.** The lower federal courts developed the fair use defense as a policy-based limitation of copyright. Congress codified the defense as Section 107 of the 1976 Copyright Act. Despite the critical importance of fair use, it is the subject of only three Supreme Court decisions: *Sony,*[74] holding that the private viewers' videotaping of broadcasts of copyrighted audiovisual works for time-shifting (*i.e.,* delayed viewing) constitutes fair use; *Harper & Row,*[75] holding that the

---

[71] Maxtone-Graham v. Burtschaell, 803 F.2d 1253, 1259–60, 231 U.S.P.Q. 534, 538–39 (2d Cir. 1986), *cert. denied,* 481 U.S. 1059 (1987).

[72] This is evident from two recent Supreme Court fair use decisions, *Sony* and *Harper & Row. See* § 4F[3][a].

[73] *E.g.,* Nichols v. Universal Pictures Corp., 45 F.2d 119, 121, 7 U.S.P.Q. 84 (2d Cir. 1930), *cert. denied,* 282 U.S. 902 (1931) ("When plays are concerned, the plagiarist may excise a separate scene. . . . or he may appropriate part of the dialogue. . . . Then the question is whether the part so taken is 'substantial', and therefore not a 'fair use' of the copyrighted work; it is the same question as arises in the case of any other copyrighted work.").

[74] Sony Corp. of America v. Universal City Studios, Inc., 464 U.S. 417, 220 U.S.P.Q. 665 (1984).

[75] Harper & Row, Publishers, Inc. v. Nation Enterprises, 471 U.S. 539, 225 U.S.P.Q. 1073 (1985).

unauthorized preparation and publication of a short article summarizing, paraphrasing, and quoting portions of former President Gerald Ford's unpublished memoirs did not constitute fair use,[76] and *Stewart*,[77] holding that commercial distribution of a motion picture was not fair use of plaintiff's renewal copyright in the book forming the basis of the motion picture even though the infringers held derivative copyrights on the motion picture.

[*i*] *Sony Corporation v. Universal City Studios*. In 1976, Universal City Studios and Walt Disney Productions, motion picture copyright owners, sued Sony Corporation, manufacturer of "Betamax" video tape recording machines, Sony Corporation of America, Sony's United States distributor, four retailers who sold Sony's machines, Sony's advertising agency, and William Griffiths, an individual machine user. For convenience, plaintiffs-copyright owners will be referred to as "the Studios," and defendants will be referred to as "Sony."[78]

---

[76] Before 1984, the Supreme Court twice granted review of cases presenting important fair use issues, but, in each instance, affirmed by an equally-divided vote of the justices. Williams & Wilkins Co. v. United States, 487 F.2d 1345, 180 U.S.P.Q. 49 (1973), *aff'd by an equally divided Court*, 420 U.S. 376, 184 U.S.P.Q. 705 (1975) (photocopying of scientific journals by libraries); Benny v. Loew's Inc., 239 F.2d 532 (9th Cir. 1956), *aff'd sub nom.* Columbia Broadcasting System, Inc. v. Loew's Inc., 356 U.S. 43 (1958) (television skit as parody of copyrighted play/motion picture). These decisions are without precedential value, but the close division of the justices illustrates the difficulty of applying the fair use doctrine.

[77] Stewart v. Abend, 110 S. Ct. 1740, 14 U.S.P.Q.2d 161 (1990).

[78] The array of parties in the *Sony* litigation may have affected the Court's analysis of fair use and contributory infringement.

Plaintiffs, the studios, might have had greater success had they brought a class action suit. The two studios owned only a minor percentage of the copyrighted works broadcasted over commercial television. The Court commented that "this is not a class action on behalf of all copyright owners who license their works for television broadcast, and respondents have no right to invoke whatever rights other copyright holders may have to bring infringement actions based on Betamax copying of their works." 464 U.S. at 434. Numerous groups did submit *amicus curiae* briefs in *Sony*, including the Motion Picture Association of America and the Association of American Publishers, Inc., but the Court refused the Studios' "attempt to cast this action as comparable to a class action because of the positions taken by *amici* with copyright interests and then attempt to treat the statements made by *amici* as evidence." 464 U.S. at 434 n.16. Justice Blackmun in dissent argued that it was irrelevant that "no copyright owner other than the Studios has brought an infringement action. . . . Sony's liability does not turn on the fact that only two copyright owners thus far have brought suit. The amount of infringing use must be determined through consideration of the television market as a whole." 464 U.S. at 493 n.44. He admitted that the fashioning of a flexible, effective remedy "might require bringing other copyright owners into court through certification of a class or otherwise." 464 U.S. at 500 n.51.

The primary defendant, Sony, was charged with contributory infringement because it sold machines and did not, on plaintiffs' theory, itself commit direct infringement. This complicated the basic issue whether machine users' off-air taping was copyright infringement. Sony could and did escape liability by showing it was not guilty of contributory infringement because the machines it sold were useful for noninfringing as well as infringing purposes. Again, the plaintiffs may have had greater success had they brought the suit against selected machine users, especially those who were creating libraries of tapes. This would not have enabled the studios to ob-

The Studios' theory was that Sony's machine sales were contributory copyright infringement because purchasers used their machines primarily to make illegal tape copies of motion pictures that television stations broadcast over the public airwaves with the Studios' permission.

Sony's videotape recorders ("VTR")[79] consisted of three components: (1) a tuner, which receives broadcast signals, (2) a recorder, which records the signals on tape, and (3) an adapter, which converts the signals into a composite signal. The tuner enables the VTR to record a broadcast off one station while the television set connected to the VTR is tuned to another channel or is not in use. The VTR has (1) a timer, which allows the user to activate and deactivate the recorder at predetermined times (for example, to record for later viewing a program broadcast at an inconvenient time) and (2) fast-forward controls, which enable the user to pass over taped portions, such as the commercial advertisements recorded along with a motion picture.

Both the Studios and Sony introduced survey evidence on how consumers used VTR's, which showed that the machines' primary use was "time-shifting," "the practice of recording a program to view it once at a later time, and thereafter erasing it."[80] Some interviewees did accumulate permanent tape libraries.[81] There was no

---

tain sweeping injunctive and damages relief as would be available against the manufacturer Sony, but a successful action or series of actions against illegal taping would have established a principle and, perhaps, provided a basis for some sort of relief against video tape recorder manufacturers.

In *Sony*, an individual user, William Griffiths, was named as a defendant, but the studios did not seek relief against Griffiths. In a footnote, the Court refers to the fact that Griffiths was "a client of plaintiff's law firm." 464 U.S. at 424, n.3.

[79] The *Sony* majority and dissenting opinions use "video tape recorders" and "VTR." These types of machines became known in popular parlance as video *cassette* recorders or "VCR's."

[80] The surveys, taken in the late 1970's, formed the basis of the district court's findings of fact and were controlling even though the case did not reach the Supreme Court until the mid-1980's. Since the 1970's, video cassette recorder usage has spread dramatically. Further, today's machines are considerably more sophisticated than the Betamax machines involved in *Sony*. For example, they have more sophisticated "fast forward" functions, which make it easier to skip over commercials in a recording. Pre-recorded motion pictures are more readily available by rental or purchase than they were in the late 1970's. It is certainly conceivable that the Supreme Court, which split 5-4 in *Sony*, may have analyzed the fair use and contributory infringement issues differently if it had a more contemporary record. For one thing, the Studios' case that off-air taping was harming their potential markets would have been more substantial.

[81] The Court did not pass on whether "librarying," that is, making permanent copies of motion pictures was improper. Cf. Paramount Pictures Corp. v. Labus, 16 U.S.P.Q.2d 1142, 1146–47 (W.D. Wis. 1990):

> "[B]y August 31, 1986, defendant had begun to offer videocassettes for rent to guests at his resort and had listed the titles of the motion pictures in his videocassette collection in a notebook from which the guests could choose the tapes they wanted to borrow. Even if defendant originally accumulated his collection of videocassette as a personal hobby, by August 31, 1986, his taping of motion pictures from television served a commercial purpose. . . . [A]s a matter of law . . . this commercial purpose was sufficient to taint his activity and remove it from the realm of the fair use doctrine."

evidence of decreased television viewing by VTR owners. Sony's survey indicated that 7.3% of VTR use is to record sporting events. (Representatives of professional sports leagues testified that they did not object to the recording of their televised events for home use.)

After a lengthy trial, the district court denied the Studios' copyright infringement charge.[82] First, home VTR recording of copyrighted works broadcast free to the public at large did not constitute infringement.[83] Second, Sony would not be liable as a contributory infringer even if hometaping were an infringement because it merely sold a machine that was capable of a variety of uses, some of them infringing. Finally, the Studios' prayer for injunctive relief either preventing sale of Betamax machines or requiring that they be rendered incapable of recording copyrighted works off the air would be inappropriate even if Sony were otherwise liable as a contributory infringer because the injunction would cause harm to Sony and the public that outweighed that to the Studios.

The Ninth Circuit reversed, holding that, as a matter of law, home VTR use was not fair use because it was not a "productive use," and that Sony's VTR sales were contributory infringement because the primary purpose of VTR's is to copy television programming virtually all of which is copyrighted.[84] The court remanded for a determination of the appropriate relief, suggesting that a continuing royalty might be an acceptable remedy.

The Supreme Court reversed the Ninth Circuit by a 5 to 4 vote, finding no liability for copyright infringement, Justice Stevens writing the majority opinion, Justice Blackmun the dissent.

The Court resolved two major issues: (1) contributory infringement: under what circumstances would Sony, as a seller of a machine that is not covered by any copyright but that can be used to make unauthorized copies of copyrighted works, be liable

---

[82] Sony Corporation of America v. Universal City Studios, 480 F. Supp. 429 (C.D. Cal. 1979), rev'd, 659 F.2d 963, 211 U.S.P.Q. 761 (9th Cir. 1981), rev'd, 464 U.S. 417, 220 U.S.P.Q. 665 (1981).

[83] The district court relied heavily on the legislative history of the Sound Recording Act of 1971. See § 4C[1][f]. In Congress, sponsors of the legislation indicated that there was no intent to cover noncommercial, off-air audio taping. The House Report stated that "it is not the intention of the Committee to restrain the home recording, from broadcasts or from tapes or records, of recorded performances, where the home recording is for private use and with no purpose of reproducing or otherwise capitalizing commercially on it. This practice is common and unrestrained today." H.R. Rep. No. 92–487, at 7.

No similar statements appear in the legislative history of the 1976 Act, which made permanent the 1971 Act inclusion of sound recordings as copyrightable subject matter. Also, there are significant differences between audio works, which were the subject of the sound recording amendments, and audiovisual works such as motion pictures.

The Sony majority did not rely on the legislative history. In dissent, Justice Blackmun analyzed the issue and found in the 1976 Act "no implied exemption to cover the home taping of television programs, whether it be for a single copy, for private use, or for home use." 464 U.S. at 475.

[84] Sony Corporation of America v. Universal City Studios, 659 F.2d 963, 211 U.S.P.Q. 761 (9th Cir. 1981), rev'd, 464 U.S. 417, 220 U.S.P.Q. 665 (1981).

as a contributory infringer? and (2) fair use: did use of videotaping machines to make recordings of broadcasted copyrighted works constitute "fair use?" The Court concluded that Sony as maker and seller of a machine is a contributory infringer only if the machine is not capable of substantial noninfringing use, and the machines had at least two noninfringing uses: authorized time-shifting and unauthorized time-shifting, the latter being fair use.

(1) *Contributory Infringement—The Staple Article of Commerce Doctrine.* Nothing in the Copyright Act renders anyone liable for infringement committed by another, a contrast with the Patent Act, which has explicit provisions on inducement of infringement and contributory infringement by sale of nonstaple components.[85] Nonetheless, "[t]he absence of such express language in the copyright statute does not preclude the imposition of liability for copyright infringements on certain parties who have not themselves engaged in the infringing activity. For vicarious liability is imposed in virtually all areas of the law, and the concept of contributory infringement is merely a species of the broader problem of identifying the circumstances in which it is just to hold one individual accountable for the actions of another."[86]

Copyright law has a body of cases on vicarious liability,[87] but these cases do not support imposing liability on the seller of a machine that may be used to commit copyright infringement.[88] The vicarious liability doctrine is based on the defendant's continuing ability to control the behavior of performers who directly infringe. Sony, seller of such a machine, has no such control.

---

[85] 35 U.S.C. §§ 271(b), (c). *See* § 2E[2][c].

[86] 464 U.S. at 435.

[87] *See* P. Goldstein, Copyright § 6.3.
In a footnote, the Court contrasts the so-called "dance hall" cases, which find vicarious liability of owners of establishments such as cocktail lounges and racetracks that hire musicians to perform music, with the so-called "landlord-tenant" cases, which find no vicarious liability of landlords who simply lease premises to a direct infringer for a fixed rental and do not participate directly in any infringing activity. 464 U.S. at 437 n.18.

[88] The Court dismissed as a "gross generalization that cannot withstand scrutiny" the Studios' argument that *Kalem Co. v. Harper Brothers*, 222 U.S. 55 (1911), "stands for the proposition that supplying the 'means' to accomplish an infringing activity and encouraging that activity through advertisement are sufficient to establish liability for copyright infringement." 464 U.S. at 436. In *Kalem*, the Court, in an opinion by Justice Holmes, held that the producer of an unauthorized film dramatization of the copyrighted book "BEN HUR" was liable for his sale of the motion picture to jobbers, who in turn arranged for commercial exhibition of the film. (Note that the making of the film in *Kalem* was, apparently, an illegal copying of the plaintiff's work. Public performance of the film would be a separate infringing act, but the film could also, in theory, be used in a noninfringing manner, such as private screening.) As to *Kalem*, the Court in *Sony* stated:

> "The use for which the item sold in *Kalem* had been 'especially' made was, of course, to display the performance that had already been recorded upon it. . . . [T]he producer personally advertised the unauthorized public performances, dispelling any possible doubt as to the use of the film which he had authorized. . . . The producer in *Kalem* did not merely provide the 'means' to accomplish an infringing activity; the producer supplied the work itself, albeit in a new medium of expression." 464 U.S. at 436.

The "closest analogy is provided by the patent law cases to which it is appropriate to refer because of the historic kinship between patent law and copyright law."[89] Under patent law, "[t]he prohibition against contributory infringement is confined to the knowing sale of a component especially made for use in connection with a particular patent." Stated differently, "the sale of a 'staple article . . . suitable for substantial noninfringing use' is not contributory infringement."[90] This strict requirement is necessary in order not to allow a patentee (or copyright owner) "to extend his monopoly beyond the limits of his specific grant." A looser standard would "block the wheels of commerce." "The staple article of commerce doctrine must strike a balance between a copyright holder's legitimate demand for effective—not merely symbolic—protection of the statutory monopoly, and the rights of others freely to engage in substantially unrelated areas of commerce."[91]

Having reduced the question of Sony's contributory infringement liability to that of whether there are substantial or "commercially significant" noninfringing uses for the videotape recorders,[92] the Court found one potential use satisfied this standard: "private, noncommercial time-shifting in the home."

The Court discussed two types of time-shifting. As to *authorized* time-shifting, it relied on the district court's findings that many producers are willing to allow private time-shifting to continue because it may enlarge the total viewing audience.[93] It

---

[89] 464 U.S. at 439.

The Court found no similar kinship between copyright law and *trademark* law in view of the "fundamental differences" between them. Thus trademark law's narrow standard of intentional inducement stated in Inwood Laboratories, Inc. v. Ives Laboratories, Inc., 456 U.S. 844, 214 U.S.P.Q. 1 (1982), was not applicable. See § 5C[2][c][v](7).

[90] 464 U.S. at 440. The patent statute on contributory infringement, 35 U.S.C. § 271(c), is redundant in excluding (a) "staple" articles, (b) "especially made" for use in a patented combination, and (c) "not suitable for substantial noninfringing use." The three concepts, staple, especial making, and nonsuitability, restate the same idea in three ways.

[91] 464 U.S. at 441.

[92] In dissent, Justice Blackmun rejected the patent law standard of "no substantial noninfringing use" and advocated a "significant portion of use" test:

"[I]f a *significant* portion of the product's use is *noninfringing*, the manufacturers and sellers cannot be held contributorily liable for the product's infringing uses. . . . If virtually all of the product's use, however, is to infringe, contributory liability may be imposed; if no one would buy the product for noninfringing purposes alone, it is clear that the manufacturer is purposely profiting from the infringement, and that liability is appropriately imposed." 464 U.S. at 491.

Justice Blackmun conceded that "[t]he key question is not the amount of television programming that is copyrighted, but rather the amount of VTR usage that is infringing." He urged a remand for a determination of the fact issue of the proportion of VTR recording that is infringing. He listed instances of noninfringing uses as including recording works not protected by copyright, recording with the permission of the copyright owner, and recording that qualifies as fair use. Unlike the majority, Justice Blackmun regarded unauthorized time-shifting as an infringing use.

[93] Professional sports organization and religious broadcasting representatives testified that they had no objection to taping. The Court also noted the testimony of the station manager of a public broadcasting station as to the explicit consent it gave for the taping of some of

stressed that "[t]hird party conduct would be wholly irrelevant in an action for direct infringement" but that in an action for contributory infringement "the copyright holder may not prevail unless the relief that he seeks affects only his programs, or unless he speaks for virtually all copyright holders with an interest in the outcome."[94]

(2) *Unauthorized Time-Shifting as Fair Use.* The Court's discussion of "unauthorized time-shifting" is of great interest, being its inaugural voyage into copyright law's stormy fair use seas.

Noting that Section 107 "identifies various factors that enable a court to apply an equitable rule of reason analysis to particular claims of infringement," the Court of necessity gave little attention to two Section 107 factors—the second ("nature of the copyrighted work") and the third ("the amount . . . used"). These factors strongly pointed toward a finding of no fair use because the copyrighted works were dramatic works, motion pictures, normally given stronger protection than factual and functional works, and because the alleged copying was of the *entire* work.

The first factor is "the purpose and character of the use, including whether such use is of a commercial nature or is for nonprofit educational purposes." Copying for a commercial or profit-making purpose is "presumptively" unfair;[95] a "contrary presumption" applies to "noncommercial, nonprofit activity."

---

its programs and the testimony of Fred Rogers of "Mister Rogers Neighborhood," a program for children, to the effect that he approved of taping because it gave families more control over television viewing.

[94] 464 U.S. at 446.

In dissent, Justice Blackmun dismissed this analysis as "confus[ing] the question of liability with the difficulty of fashioning an appropriate remedy."

> "It may be that an injunction prohibiting the sale of VTR's would harm the interests of copyright holders who have no objection to others making copies of their programs. But such concerns should and would be taken into account in fashioning an appropriate remedy once liability has been found. Remedies may well be available that would not interfere with authorized time-shifting at all. . . . Sony may be able, for example, to build a VTR that enables broadcasters to scramble the signal of individual programs and 'jam' the unauthorized recording of them. Even were an appropriate remedy not available at this time, the Court should not misconstrue copyright holders' rights in a manner that prevents enforcement of them when, through development of better techniques, an appropriate remedy becomes available." 464 U.S. at 494.

It is difficult to quarrel with the last proposition; current practical difficulty in enforcing or protecting a right should not be a ground for defining the right out of existence.

[95] This statement is dictum in a sense because the use before the Court was a noncommercial one. Characterizing commercial uses as "presumptively" unfair is of doubtful utility in resolving fair use problems. First, it places too much emphasis on one of the four, nonexclusive Section 107 factors. Second, it fails to take into account that many uses are "mixed," in the sense that they are for one of the four Section 107 purposes, such as newsreporting or criticism, but also carried out in a for-profit manner or media, such as a publication. Third, it perpetuates the doctrinally-questionable concept that "harm" to a copyright owner is an independent requirement of infringement.

The limited utility of the presumptive unfairness notion became clear in *Harper & Row*, decided by the Supreme Court 16 months after *Sony*.

See § 4F[3][a][ii].

The Court linked the fourth factor—"the effect of the use upon the potential market for or value of the copyrighted work"—to the first one in the context of noncommercial uses. Because a use for a noncommercial purpose is presumptively fair (factor (1)), the burden is on the copyright owner to show that "some meaningful likelihood of future harm" to a potential market for the work will result from the use.

> "[A]lthough every commercial use of copyrighted material is presumptively an unfair exploitation of the monopoly privilege that belongs to the owner of the copyright, noncommercial uses are a different matter. A challenge to a noncommercial use of a copyrighted work requires proof either that the particular use is harmful, or that if it should become widespread, it would adversely affect the potential market for the copyrighted work. Actual present harm need not be shown; such a requirement would leave the copyright holder with no defense against predictable damage. Nor is it necessary to show with certainty that future harm will result. What is necessary is a showing by a preponderance of the evidence that *some* meaningful likelihood of future harm exists. If the intended use is for commercial gain, that likelihood may be presumed. But if it is for a noncommercial purpose, the likelihood must be demonstrated." [96]

The Studios failed to show "meaningful likelihood of future harm." The district court found unsupported the Studios' suggestions that time-shifting without librarying would (1) not be measured by rating services, which determine advertising revenue from an original telecast, (2) diminish the number of persons watching live telecast movies, (3) reduce demand for reruns, or (4) reduce theater or film rental exhibition of films. [97]

---

[96] 464 U.S. at 451.

[97] Justice Blackmun in dissent argued that "at least when the proposed use is an unproductive one, a copyright owner need prove only a *potential* for harm to the market for or the value of the copyrighted work." 464 U.S. at 482. He discounted the District Court's findings of no harm as based on "an incorrect substantive standard" and a misallocation of the burden of proof.

He stressed that the relevant harm, as stated in the market effect factor of Section 107(4), is that to a *potential* market.

> "[This] has two implications. First, an infringer cannot prevail merely by demonstrating that the copyright holder suffered no net harm from the infringer's action. . . . Rather, the infringer must demonstrate that he had not impaired the copyright holder's ability to demand compensation from (or to deny access to) any group who would otherwise be willing to pay to see or hear the copyrighted work. Second, the fact that a given market for a copyrighted work would not be available to the copyright holder were it not for the infringer's activities does not permit the infringer to exploit that market without compensating the copyright holder." 464 U.S. at 485.

Time-shifting was such a new potential market.

> "[T]he advent of the VTR technology created a potential market for their copyrighted programs. That market consists of those persons who find it impossible or inconvenient to watch the programs at the time they are broadcast, and who wish to watch them at other times. These persons are willing to pay for the privilege of watching copyrighted work at their convenience, as is evidenced by the fact that they are willing to pay for VTR's and tapes; undoubtedly, most also would be willing to pay some kind of royalty to copyright holders." 464 U.S. at 485.

Whether time-shifting was in fact a "noncommercial" use was the critical policy issue in *Sony*. The majority divided uses into commercial and noncommercial and adopted a narrow conception of what is "commercial," excluding personal consumption. The dissent, following the Ninth Circuit's approach, defined "noncommercial" uses as "productive" ones.[98] The dissent's position derives support from the undeniable fact that no court decision prior to *Sony* ever characterized as fair use the copying of more than *de minimis* amount of a copyrighted work for purposes of private enjoyment or consumption.

The confusion in *Sony* over purpose, commercial versus noncommercial use, presumptive unfairness, and productive versus consumptive uses, stems in part from ambiguities in Section 107. Section 107's first sentence is a nonexclusive listing of favored purposes—"criticism, comment, news reporting, teaching (including multiple copies for classroom use), scholarship, or research." The second sentence lists four factors to guide fair use determinations, the first factor being the "purpose" of the

---

[98] Justice Blackmun noted:

> "Each of [the uses enumerated in Section 107] reflects a common theme: each is a *productive* use, resulting in some added benefit to the public beyond that produced by the first author's work. The fair use doctrine, in other words, permits works to be used for 'socially laudable purposes.' . . . I am aware of no case in which the reproduction of a copyrighted work for the sole benefit of the user has been held to be fair use." 464 U.S. at 478–79.

He also stressed: "the fact that [the copyright owner] has licensed a single television performance is really irrelevant to the existence of his right to control its reproduction. Although a television broadcast may be free to the viewer, this fact is equally irrelevant; a book borrowed from the public library may not be copied any more freely than a book that is purchased." 464 U.S. at 480.

The majority responded to the "productive" use concept as follows:

> "It has been suggested that 'consumptive uses of copyrights by home VTR users are commercial even if the consumer does not sell the home-made tape because the consumer will not buy tapes separately sold by the copyrightholder.' . . . Furthermore, '[t]he error in excusing such theft as noncommercial,' we are told, 'can be seen by simple analogy: jewel theft is not converted into a noncommercial venality if stolen jewels are simply worn rather than sold.' . . . The premise and the analogy are indeed simple, but they add nothing to the argument. . . . Theft of a particular item of personal property of course may have commercial significance, for the thief deprives the owner of his right to sell that particular item to any individual. Timeshifting does not even remotely entail comparable consequences to the copyright owner. Moreover, the timeshifter no more steals the program by watching it once than does the live viewer, and the live viewer is no more likely to buy prerecorded videotapes than is the time-shifter." 464 U.S. at 450 n.33.

The majority's response is premised on a questionable distinction between tangible property and intangible intellectual property, such as copyright. The Copyright Act implicitly defines copyright in a work as an item of property. *See* 17 U.S.C. § 201 (defining "ownership" of copyright). The property interest in a copyright consists of rights to exclude certain uses, 17 U.S.C. § 106, and an unauthorized appropriation of such a use deprives the copyright owner of his right to "sell" that property interest every bit as much as the taking of tangible property such as jewelry. In a nonlegal sense, tangible and intellectual property are distinct in that one person's use of a copyrighted work does not effect another person's ability to use the work. But the law, for policy reasons, abolishes the distinction.

work. "Purpose" refers, in part, to the favored purposes listed in the first sentence. Confusion arises because of the first factor's second clause: "including whether such use is of a commercial nature or is for nonprofit educational purposes." "Commercial" and "nonprofit" introduce a new dimension of purpose. There is some but not a complete identity between "educational purposes" and "teaching" in the first paragraph. Properly interpreted, Section 107 does not create two complete and exhaustive categories—commercial versus noncommercial, the latter concept not being mentioned. Nor does Section 107 provide a basis for presumptions as to a required showing of harm or lack of harm from the use. Rather, commercial purpose is simply a disfavored purpose, and nonprofit educational use a favored purpose. Private use falls in neither category.

[ii]　*Harper & Row, Publishers, Inc. v. Nation Enterprises.* Former President Gerald Ford contracted with Harper & Row and Reader's Digest to publish his memoirs. Ford agreed to provide "significant hitherto unpublished material" concerning the Watergate crisis and Mr. Ford's pardon of former President Richard Nixon. He also agreed to "endeavor not to disseminate" in the media the "unique information not previously disclosed." Later, Harper & Row granted Time magazine the exclusive right to publish a 7500 word excerpt from the memoirs one week before shipment of the full length book. Time agreed to pay $12,500 in advance and an additional $12,500 at publication.

Several weeks before the Time article's scheduled release, an unidentified person secretly brought a copy of the Ford manuscript to Victor Navasky, editor of The Nation, a political commentary magazine. Navasky wrote a 2,250-word article consisting of quotes, paraphrases, and facts drawn from the manuscript.[99] It contained no independent commentary. Navasky returned the manuscript to its source. The article appeared on April 3, 1979. Time cancelled its plan to publish the excerpt and did not pay the remaining $12,500.

Harper & Row sued Nation, asserting copyright infringement and common law causes of action. The district court found copyright infringement.[100] Elements of the Ford memoirs were not copyrightable, including the basic facts and memoranda written by government employees,[101] but the totality of the facts, quoted conversations, and memoranda was a copyrightable work. Nation's article was not fair use because it was not news, containing no new facts, was published for profit, and took the "heart" of the soon-to-be published manuscript.

---

[99] The entire Navasky article is reproduced as an appendix to the opinion of the Supreme Court in *Harper & Row.* 471 U.S. at 570.

[100] Harper & Row Publishers, Inc. v. Nation Enterprises, 501 F. Supp. 848, 212 U.S.P.Q. 274 (S.D.N.Y. 1983), *aff'd in part, rev'd in part,* 723 F.2d 195, 220 U.S.P.Q. 321 (2d Cir. 1983), *rev'd,* 471 U.S. 539, 225 U.S.P.Q. 1073 (1985).

[101] Works created by employees of the United States are not subject to copyright. *See* § 4C[1][f].

The Second Circuit reversed, in a 2-1 decision.[102] The majority "stripped away" material copied by Nation that was not copyrightable to Ford and Harper & Row[103] and found approximately 300 of the copied words subject to copyright.[104] Applying the fourth Section 107 factors, the majority found fair use. The accused Nation article was news. Its publication did not adversely affect the market for the original. The publication did cause cancellation of the excerpt publication by Time, but that resulted from Nation's revelation of uncopyrightable facts, not its use of copyrightable expression. The majority stressed that it is not "the purpose of the Copyright Act to impede that harvest of knowledge so necessary to a democratic state."

The Supreme Court reversed the Second Circuit and found liability for copyright infringement by a 6-3 vote, Justice O'Connor writing the majority opinion, Justice Brennan writing the dissent.

The Court found no need to decide how much material copied by Nation was copyrightable.[105] Even accepting the Second Circuit majority's stripping of the

[102] Harper & Row Publishers, Inc. v. Nation Enterprises, 723 F.2d 195, 220 U.S.P.Q. 321 (2d Cir. 1983), rev'd, 471 U.S. 539, 225 U.S.P.Q. 1073 (1985).

[103] The majority ruled that memoranda and other public documents and quoted remarks of third parties were not copyrightable either because they were not original with Ford, originality being a fundamental requirement of copyright, or constituted works by United States government employees.

The majority's approach is questionable. First, when an author "quotes" the conversations of another, the quotation is rarely verbatim. Unless reproduced from an unedited transcript, a quotation of any length will reflect the author's original interpretation of the substance of what was said. Second, the collection and ordering of uncopyrightable elements constitutes an original, copyrightable work. See § 4C[1][b].

As noted below, the majority of the Supreme Court found it unnecessary to pass on the propriety of the Second Circuit majority's dissection approach because it found no fair use even if only the 300 words were considered.

[104] The following are examples of verbatim quotations.

"He was stretched out flat on his back. There were tubes in his nose and mouth and wires led from his arms, chest and legs to machines with orange lights that blinked on and off. His face was ashen, and I thought I had never seen anyone closer to death."

"A terribly proud man, he detested weakness in other people. I'd often heard him speak disparagingly of those whom he felt to be soft and expedient. (Curiously, he didn't feel that the press was weak. Reporters, he sensed, were adversaries. He knew they didn't like him, and he responded with reciprocal disdain.)" 723 F.2d at 211.

[105] The Court noted that "no author may copyright facts or ideas" but that "[c]reation of a nonfiction work, even a compilation of pure fact, entails originality," 471 U.S. at 547, but "[e]specially in the realm of factual narrative, the law is currently unsettled regarding the ways in which uncopyrightable elements combine with the author's original contributions to form protected expression." 471 U.S. at 548.

In dissent, Justice Brennan did address the "threshold copyrightability question" and agreed with the Second Circuit majority that Nation could be liable only if the 300 words of verbatim quotation constituted infringement. The balance of the material taken by Nation was not original or represented facts rather than expression. Under the originality requirement, "an author may not claim copyright in statements made by others and reported verbatim in the author's work." 471 U.S. at 581 n.3.

Justice Brennan noted that "infringement of copyright must be based on a substantial appropriation of literary form. . . . [T]he inquiry proceeds along two axes: how closely has

copyrightable material down to 300 words, the taking of those 300 words was not fair use.

(1) The Special Status of Unpublished Works. The Court began by noting that fair use has only limited application to unpublished works. Common law copyright, which, before enactment of the 1976 Copyright Act, defined the protection for unpublished works,[106] gave an author almost absolute control over use or publication of a work.

> "Perhaps because the fair use doctrine was predicated on the author's implied consent to 'reasonable and customary' use when he released his work for public consumption, fair use traditionally was not recognized as a defense to charges of copying from an author's as yet unpublished works. . . . This absolute rule, however, was tempered in practice by the equitable nature of the fair use doctrine. In a given case, factors such as implied consent through *de facto* publication on performance or dissemination of a work may tip the balance of equities in favor of prepublication use. . . . Publication of an author's expression before he has authorized its dissemination seriously infringes the author's right to decide when and whether it will be made public, a factor not present in fair use of published works."[107]

The 1976 Act did not alter the special solicitude for unpublished works. It extends copyright protection to unpublished works, includes the right of publication as one of the Section 106 exclusive rights of copyright, and makes all of the Section 106 exclusive rights subject to the Section 107 fair use provision.

> "Though the right of first publication, like the other rights enumerated in § 106, is expressly made subject to the fair use provision of § 107, fair use analysis must always be tailored to the individual case. . . . First publication is inherently different from other § 106 rights in that only one person can be the first publisher; . . . the commercial value of the right lies primarily in exclusivity."[108]

---

the second author tracked the first author's particular language and structure of presentation; and *how much* of the first author's language and structure has the second author appropriated." 471 U.S. at 582. As to "language," much of the information taken by Nation was in form of synopsis of lengthy discussions and not paraphrase: "A finding of infringement based on paraphrase generally requires far more close and substantial a tracking of the original language than occurred in this case." 471 U.S. at 586. As to "the structure of presentation," Nation did not present the information in the sequence in which Mr. Ford presented it. In a sense, Nation did "copy" Mr. Ford's selection of fact "because it reported only those facts Mr. Ford chose to select for presentation."

> "But this tracking of a historian's selection of facts generally should not supply the basis for a finding of infringement. . . . To hold otherwise would be to require a second author to duplicate the research of the first author so as to avoid reliance on the first author's judgment as to what facts are particularly pertinent." 471 U.S. at 587 n.12.

See § 4C[1][b].

[106] *See* § 4D[1][a].

[107] 471 U.S. at 550–51.

[108] 471 U.S. at 552–53.

The Court found support for its view in a paragraph in the Senate Committee report discussing fair use of photocopied materials in the classroom.[109]

The Court found unpersuasive Nation's argument that "fair use may be made of a soon-to-be published manuscript on the ground that the author has demonstrated he has no interest in nonpublication."

> "This argument assumes that the unpublished nature of copyrighted material is only relevant to letters or other confidential writings not intended for dissemination. It is true that common-law copyright was often enlisted in the service of personal privacy. . . . In its commercial guise, however, an author's right to choose when he will publish is not less deserving of protection. The period encompassing the work's initiation, its preparation, and its grooming for public dissemination is a crucial one for any literary endeavor. . . . The obvious benefit to author and public alike of assuring authors the leisure to develop their ideas free from fear of exploitation outweighs any short-term 'news value' to be gained from premature publication of the author's expression. . . . The author's control of first public distribution implicates not only his personal interest in creative control but his property interest in exploitation of prepublication rights, which are valuable in themselves and serve as a valuable adjunct to publicity and marketing. . . . Under ordinary circumstances, the author's right to control the first public appearance of his undisseminated expression will outweigh a claim of fair use."[110]

(2) *First Amendment Values—Matters of Public Interest.* The Court disagreed with the Second Circuit majority's view that First Amendment free speech and press values require a fair use defense of wider scope when the unpublished work concerns matters of high public interest. First, quoting the Second Circuit, the Court noted that copyright's idea and expression dichotomy "strike[s] a definitional balance between the First Amendment and the Copyright Act by permitting free communication

---

[109] The Report stated:

> "The applicability of the fair use doctrine to unpublished works is narrowly limited, since, although the work is unavailable, this is the result of a deliberate choice on the part of the copyright owner. Under ordinary circumstances, the copyright owner's 'right of first publication' would outweigh any needs of reproduction for classroom purposes." S. Rep. No. 94–473 (1975).

The Court found "unconvincing [Nation's] contention that the absence of the quoted passage from the House Reports indicates an intent to abandon the traditional distinction between fair use of published and unpublished works. . . . [T]he fair use discussion of photocopying of classroom materials was omitted from the final Report because educators and publishers in the interim had negotiated a set of guidelines that rendered the discussion obsolete." 471 U.S. at 554. See § 4F[3][e][ii].

The dissent took issue with the Court's reliance on the Senate Report.

"Given that the face of § 106 specifically allows for prepublication fair use, it would be unfaithful to the intent of Congress to draw from this circumscribed suggestion in the Senate Report a blanket presumption against any amount of prepublication fair use for any purpose and irrespective of the effect of that use on the copyright owner's privacy, editorial, or economic interests." 471 U.S. at 597.

[110] 471 U.S. at 554–55.

of facts while still protecting author's expression."[111] A special, enhanced fair use doctrine to preserve First Amendment values is unnecessary.[112] Second, an expansive fair use doctrine for works by public officials would leave "little incentive to create or profit in financing such memoirs, and the public would be denied an important source of significant historical information."

> "In our haste to disseminate news, it should not be forgotten that the Framers intended copyright itself to be the engine of free expression. By establishing a marketable right to the use of one's expression, copyright supplies the economic incentive to create and disseminate ideas."[113]

(3) *The Section 107 Factors.* The Court serially addressed the Section 107 factors.[114]

(aa) *Purpose of the Use.* The Court agreed that news reporting is a favored purpose and that the district court erred "in fixing on whether the information contained in the memoirs was actually new to the public."

"The fact that a publication was commercial as opposed to nonprofit is a separate factor that tends to weigh against a finding of fair use." Nation's argument that "the purpose of news reporting is not purely commercial" missed the point: "The crux of the profit/nonprofit distinction is not whether the sole motive of the use is monetary gain but whether the user stands to profit from exploitation of the copyrighted material without paying the customary price."[115]

In evaluating the purpose of the use, the Court took into account "Nation's stated purpose of scooping the forthcoming hardcover and Time abstracts."

---

[111] 471 U.S. at 556.

[112] The court noted:

> "In view of the First Amendment protections already embodied in the Copyright Act's distinction between copyrightable expression and uncopyrightable facts and ideas, and the latitude for scholarship and comment traditionally afforded by fair use, we see no warrant for expanding the doctrine of fair use to create what amounts to a public figure exception to copyright." 471 U.S. at 560.

[113] 471 U.S. at 558.

In dissent, Justice Brennan questioned the necessity of strong economic incentives for the production of historical works and memoirs.

> "[N]oneconomic incentives motivate much historical research and writing. For example, former public officials often have great incentive to 'tell their side of the story.' And much history is the product of academic scholarship. Perhaps most importantly, the urge to preserve the past is as old as humankind." 471 U.S. at 590, n.13.

[114] The Court stressed that "[t]he factors enumerated in the section are not meant to be exclusive." 471 U.S. at 560.

[115] 471 U.S. at 562.

The Court quoted the *Sony* statement that every commercial use of a work is presumptively unfair but did not rely on it in its analysis of the fairness of Nation's use.

In dissent, Justice Brennan commented: "[I]n light of the specific language of § 107, this presumption is not appropriately employed to negate the weight Congress explicitly gave to news reporting as a justification for limited use of another's expression." 471 U.S. at 592, n.16.

"The Nation's use had not merely the incidental effect but the *intended purpose* of supplanting the copyright holder's commercially valuable right of first publication. . . . The trial court found that the Nation knowingly exploited a purloined manuscript. . . . Unlike the typical claims of fair use, The Nation cannot offer up even the fiction of consent as justification."[116]

(*bb*) *Nature of the Copyrighted Work.* "The law generally recognizes a greater need to disseminate factual works than works of fiction or fantasy," but there are limits to the right to copy expression from fact works: one cannot use "the most expressive elements" of a fact work if such use "exceeds that necessary to disseminate the facts."[117]

The Court incorporated into this factor its previous discussion of the limited scope of fair use of unpublished works: "The fact that a work is unpublished is a critical element of its "nature.' "[118]

(*cc*) *Amount and Substantiality of the Portion Used.* The "amount" of the whole copyrighted work used by Nation was not quantitatively large, but the District Court's findings established that the portions taken were qualitatively substantial, constituting the "heart of the book."

The Court gave weight to the fact that a major part of the accused work consisted of copied material.

"As the statutory language indicates, a taking may not be excused merely because it is insubstantial with respect to the *infringing* work. . . . Conversely, the fact that a substantial portion of the infringing work was copied verbatim is evidence of the qualitative value of the copied material, both to the originator and to the plagiarist who seeks to profit from marketing someone else's copyrighted expression."[119]

---

[116] 471 U.S. at 562–63.

The dissent protested reliance on the alleged bad faith of Nation.

"No court has found that The Nation possessed the Ford manuscript illegally or in violation of any common-law interest of Harper & Row; all common-law causes of action have been abandoned or dismissed in this case. . . . Even if the manuscript had been 'purloined' by someone, nothing in this record imputes culpability to The Nation. On the basis of the record in this case, the most that can be said is that The Nation made use of the contents of the manuscript knowing the copyright owner would not sanction the use." 471 U.S. at 593.

[117] 471 U.S. at 563–64.

In dissent, Justice Brennan disagreed as to how much expression must be taken in order to effectively disseminate the facts. "The importance of the [Ford] work, after all, lies not only in revelation of previously unknown fact but also in revelation of the thoughts, ideas, motivations, and fears of two Presidents at a critical moment in our national history." 471 U.S. at 601.

[118] 471 U.S. at 564.

[119] 471 U.S. at 565.

In dissent, Justice Brennan interpreted the above-quoted paragraph as follows:

"As the statutory directive implies, it matters little whether the second author's use is 1- or 100-percent appropriated expression if the taking of that expression had no adverse effect

(dd) *Market Effect.* Market effect "is undoubtedly the f single most important element of fair use."[120] "Rarely will a case of copyright infringement present such clear-cut evidence of actual damage." The Court disagreed with the Second Circuit's conclusion that there was no proof of a causal connection between Nation's use of copyrighted expression and cancellation of the Time prepublication excerpts contract. Under the circumstances, the burden of proof on causation shifted to Nation, the accused infringer. "[O]nce a copyright holder establishes with reasonable probability the existence of a causal connection between the infringement and a loss of revenue, the burden properly shifts to the infringer to show that this damage would have occurred had there been no taking of copyrighted expression. This inquiry must take account not only of harm to the original but also of harm to the market for derivative works."[121]

[iii] *Stewart v. Abend.* In *Stewart,*[122] the Supreme Court addressed whether defendants' circa-1980 re-release of the 1954 motion picture, "Rear Window," which was based on an author's copyrighted story, "It Had to Be Murder," was infringement of the story's renewal copyright when the picture was originally made with the author's permission but the author died prior to renewal. The Court found that the defendants had no right to perform or distribute the motion picture without the story renewal copyright owner's permission.[123] The defendants argued that the fair use doctrine should be employed to "avoid [a] rigid applicatio[n] of the Copyright Act." The Court of Appeals rejected the fair use defense, and the Supreme Court agreed.

> "The motion picture neither falls into any of the categories enumerated in § 107 nor meets the four criteria set forth in § 107. '[E]very [unauthorized] commercial use of copyrighted material is presumptively an unfair exploitation of the monopoly privilege that belongs to the owner of the copyright.' *Sony Corp. of America v. Universal Studios, Inc., supra,* [464 U.S.], at 451. Petitioners received $12 million from the re-release of the motion picture during the renewal term. . . . Petitioners asserted before the Court of Appeals that

---

on the copyrighted work. . . . I presume, therefore, that the Court considered the role of the expression 'in the infringing work' only as indirect evidence of the qualitative value of the expression taken in this case." 471 U.S. at 599 n.23.

120 The Court cited economic analysis as supporting the importance of market effect.

"Economists . . . believe the fair use exception should come into play only in those situations in which the market fails or the price the copyright holder would ask is near zero. . . . As the facts here demonstrate, there is a fully functioning market that encourages the creation and dissemination of memoirs of public figures. In the economists' view, permitting 'fair use' to displace normal copyright channels disrupts the copyright market without a commensurate public benefit." 471 U.S. at 566, n.9.

121 471 U.S. at 567–68.

In dissent, Justice Brennan argued that this concept confused proof of liability with proof of damages. "Once infringement of a § 106 exclusive right has been shown, it is entirely appropriate to shift to the infringer the burden of showing that the infringement did not cause all the damages shown. But the *question* in this case is whether this particular use infringed any § 106 rights." 471 U.S. at 603, n.25.

122 Stewart v. Abend, 110 S. Ct. 1750, 14 U.S.P.Q.2d 1614 (1990).

123 *See* § 4E[3][b], 4E[3][c][iii].

their use was educational rather than commercial. The Court of Appeals found nothing in the record to support this assertion, nor do we.

"Applying the second factor, the Court of Appeals pointed out that '[a] use is less likely to be deemed fair when the copyrighted work is a creative product.' . . . In general, fair use is more likely to be found in factual works than in fictional works. . . . A motion picture based on a fictional short story obviously falls into the latter category.

"Examining the third factor, the Court of Appeals determined that the story was a substantial portion of the motion picture. . . . The motion picture expressly uses the story's unique setting, characters, plot, and sequence of events. Petitioners argue that the story comprised only 20% of the motion picture's story line, . . . but that does not mean that a substantial portion of the story was not used in the motion picture. '[A] taking may not be excused merely because it is insubstantial with respect to the *infringing* work.' *Harper & Row, supra,* [471 U.S.] at 565.

"The fourth factor is the 'most important, and indeed, central fair use factor.' . . . The record supports the Court of Appeals' conclusion that re-release of the film impinged on the ability to market new versions of the story. Common sense would yield the same conclusion. Thus, all four factors point to unfair use. 'This case presents a classic example of an unfair use: a commercial use of a fictional story that adversely affects the story owner's adaptation rights.' 863 F.2d, at 1482."[124]

[b] **The Section 107 Factors.** Section 107 lists four factors as among those that must be considered in determining whether a use is fair.

The factors are neither exclusive nor exhaustive.[125] Judge Oakes noted:

---

[124] 110 S. Ct. at 1768–69, 14 U.S.P.Q.2d at 1627–28.

[125] For decisions considering additional factors and equities, see Weissmann v. Freeman, 868 F.2d 1313, 1323, 10 U.S.P.Q.2d 1014, 1022 (2d Cir. 1989), *cert. denied,* 110 S. Ct. 219 (1989) ("Congress established these nonexclusive factors as a guide to courts considering fair use. Determining whether the doctrine applies requires that each case be individually examined. . . . Analysis begins not by elevating the statutory guides into inflexible rules, but with a review of the underlying equities."); Maxtone-Graham v. Burtschaell, 803 F.2d 1253, 1260-61, 231 U.S.P.Q. 534, 542 (2d Cir. 1986), *cert. denied,* 481 U.S. 1059 (1987) ("The factors listed in the statute are not intended to be exclusive. . . commission of errors in borrowing copyrighted material is a proper ingredient to consider in making the fair use determination" but "[o]nly where the distortions were so deliberate, and so misrepresentative of the original work that no reasonable person could find them to be the product of mere carelessness would we incline toward rejecting a fair use claim."); Iowa State University Research Foundation, Inc. v. American Broadcasting Companies, Inc., 621 F.2d 57, 62, 207 U.S.P.Q. 97, 101 (2d Cir. 1980) ("We cannot ignore the fact . . . that ABC copied [the work] while purporting to assess its value for possible purchase, or that the network repeatedly denied that it had ever used the film.").
Should the court consider factors such as (1) did the user know that the copyright owner would object to the use (because, for example, the owner denied the user's request for permission)? and (2) did the user include an attribution or citation as to the source of his or her material?

"The four factors which the fair use statute identifies as relevant to a determination of whether the doctrine applies . . . are equitable considerations to be assessed and weighed by the court; they are not simply hurdles over which an accused infringer may leap to safety from liability. Rather than a sequence of four rigid tests, the fair use analysis consists of a 'sensitive balancing of interests.' "[126]

[i] *The Purpose and Character of the Use, Including Whether Such Use is of a Commercial Nature or is for Nonprofit Educational Purposes.* A fundamental principle of fair use is that the permissibility of a use depends in part on its purpose. The same amount of copying may be fair if for a favored purpose but not fair if for a nonfavored purpose. Some of the favored purposes are listed in Section 107's first sentence.

The "including" clause distinguishes two purposes, "use . . . of a commercial nature," which is a disfavored purpose and "nonprofit educational purposes," which is a favored purpose.[127]

Court decisions on the significance of a use being "commercial" follow an erratic pattern. A good early example of unexcused purely commercial use is *Henry Holt.*[128]

In *Maxtone,* the court held that "Although bad faith by the user of copyrighted material suggests unfairness, [the user's] decision to publish despite [the copyright owner's] denial of permission does not deserve that characterization. . . . [The user] should not be penalized for erring on the side of safety." 803 F.2d at 1264, 231 U.S.P.Q. at 543. *Accord* Fisher v. Dees, 794 F.2d 432, 230 U.S.P.Q. 421, 424 (9th Cir. 1986) (parody of song is fair use; "Parodists will seldom get permission from those whose works are parodied. Self-esteem is seldom strong enough to permit the granting of permission even in exchange for a reasonable fee. . . . [T]o consider [the parodist] blameworthy because he asked permission would penalize him for this modest show of consideration. Even though such gestures are predictably futile, we refuse to discourage them.").

In *Weissmann,* the court relied, in part, on the defendant's inequitable behavior in neglecting to credit the plaintiff with authorship, "substituting his name as author in place of hers," and distributing copies of her work with a slightly modified title. Marcus v. Rowley, 695 F.2d 1171, 1176, n.8, 217 U.S.P.Q. 691, 695 n.8 (9th Cir. 1983) ("Attribution is, of course, but one factor. Moreover, acknowledgement of a source does not excuse infringement when the other factors listed in section 107 are present.").

[126] Financial Information, Inc. v. Moody's Investors Service, Inc., 751 F.2d 501, 224 U.S.P.Q. 632, 638 (2d Cir. 1984) (citing *Sony,* 464 U.S. at 454 n.40).

[127] As to the legislative history of the "including" clause, see H.R. Rep. No. 94–1476, 94th Cong., 2d Sess. 66 (1976):

"This amendment is not intended to be interpreted as any sort of not-for-profit limitation on educational uses of copyrighted works. It is an express recognition that, as under the present law, the commercial or non-profit character of an activity, while not conclusive with respect to fair use, can and should be weighed along with other factors in fair use decisions."

The reference to "educational use" is redundant to the inclusion of teaching, scholarship and research in Section 107's first sentence.

For a discussion of the "including" clause in connection with the *Sony* decision, see § 4F[3][a][i](2).

[128] Henry Holt & Co. v. Liggett & Myers Tobacco, 23 F. Supp. 302 (E.D. Pa. 1938). *See also* Supermarket of Homes, Inc. v. San Fernando Valley Bd. of Realtors, 786 F.2d 1400, 1409,

Plaintiff published a doctor's scientific book on the human voice, a small portion of which discussed the effect of smoking on the voice and found no apparent harm. Defendant, a tobacco company, reprinted the excerpt in an advertising pamphlet. Rejecting a fair use defense, the court stressed the commercial purpose. Quantitatively little of plaintiff's work was used; the purpose of the taking was what was critical.

That an author is paid for his or her efforts and that a publisher hopes to make a profit on a publication do not preclude fair use because "all publications presumably are operated for profit."[129] In *Rosemont Enterprises*,[130] defendant was about to publish an unauthorized biography of Howard Hughes, a figure who shrouded himself in secrecy. A company connected with Hughes bought the copyrights to a series of articles on Hughes published in 1954 in *Look* magazine and sought an injunction against publication, alleging that the book copied portions of the articles. In finding fair use, the court discounted the fact that the defendant's work was a popularized account and directed to commercial gain: "Whether an author or publisher reaps economic benefits from the sale of a biographical work, or whether its publication is motivated in part by a desire for commercial gain, or whether it is designed for the popular market, *i.e.*, the average citizen rather than the college professor, has no bearing on whether a public benefit may be derived from such a work."[131]

The issue of the commercial nature of the use arose in the Supreme Court's 1984 *Sony* and 1985 *Harper & Row* decisions.[132] In *Sony*, the Court noted that "every commercial use of copyrighted material is presumptively an unfair exploitation of the monopoly privilege that belongs to the owner of the copyright."[133] In *Harper & Row*,

---

230 U.S.P.Q. 316, 321 (9th Cir. 1986) (copying of real estate multiple listing book for commercial purposes is not fair use because the copying is for a use that parallels and is a substitute for the owner's commercial use).

Compare Consumers Union of United States v. General Signal Corp., 724 F.2d 1044, 1049, 221 U.S.P.Q. 400, 405 (2d Cir. 1983), *cert. denied*, 469 U.S. 823, 224 U.S.P.Q. 616 (1984) (manufacturer's inclusion of reference to Consumer Reports magazine approval of its product in advertisements is fair use; "copying of creative expression of a copyrighted work for the purpose of having that precise form of expression advance someone else's commercial interest— for example, using well-known copyrighted lines to attract attention to an advertisement" is less likely to constitute fair use than copying "excerpts from a copyrighted work for the purpose of having the content of the work advance his commercial interests").

[129] Rosemount Enterprises, Inc. v. Random House, Inc., 366 F.2d 303, 307, 150 U.S.P.Q. 715, 719 (2d Cir. 1966), *cert. denied*, 385 U.S. 1009, 152 U.S.P.Q. 844 (1967).

[130] *Id.*

[131] *Id.*

[132] *See* § 4F[3][a].

[133] Sony Corp. v. Universal City Studios, Inc., 464 U.S. 417, 448–49, 220 U.S.P.Q. 665, 680-82 (1984), discussed at § 4F[3][a]. The Court also noted that a "contrary presumption" applies to "noncommercial, nonprofit activity."

See also United Telephone Co. v. Johnson Publishing Co., 855 F.2d 604, 8 U.S.P.Q.2d 1058 (8th Cir. 1988) (taking new telephone listings in order to update directory sold for a profit is not fair use).

Compare Maxtone-Graham v. Burtschaell, 803 F.2d 1253, 1262, 231 U.S.P.Q. 534, 541 (2d Cir. 1986), *cert. denied*, 481 U.S. 1059 (1986) ("The commercial nature of a use is a matter

it noted that "The crux of the profit/nonprofit distinction is not whether the sole motive of the use is monetary gain but whether the user stands to profit from exploitation of the copyrighted material without paying the customary price."[134]

The *Sony* presumption is rebuttable, and other factors may establish fair use despite the use's commercial character.[135]

[ii] *The Nature of the Copyrighted Work.* Subsequent authors may rely more heavily on fact works, such as biographies, histories, and collections of interviews, than on works of fiction:[136] "The law generally recognizes a greater need to disseminate factual works than works of fiction or fantasy."[137] Paraphrase or even quotation of significant passages from "fact" works may constitute fair use.[138]

---

of degree, not an absolute, and we find that the educational elements [of the accused work] far outweigh [its] commercial aspects.") *with* Weissmann v. Freeman, 868 F.2d 1313, 1322, 10 U.S.P.Q.2d 1014, 1023 (2d Cir. 1989) (use by the defendant, a professor, in connection with review lectures was unfair even though the defendant only received a $250 honorarium; "Monetary gain is not the sole criterion. [Defendant] stood to gain recognition among his peers in the profession and authorship credit with his attempted use of [plaintiff's] article; he did so without paying the usual price that accompanies scientific research and writing, that is to say, by the sweat of his brow. Particularly in an academic setting, profit is ill-measured in dollars.").

[134] Harper & Row Publishers, Inc. v. Nation Enterprises, 471 U.S. 539, 562, 225 U.S.P.Q. 1073, 1081 (1985).

See also Iowa State University Research Foundation, Inc. v. American Broadcasting Companies, Inc., 621 F.2d 57, 61, 207 U.S.P.Q. 97 (2d Cir. 1980) ("The fair use doctrine is not a license for corporate theft, empowering a court to ignore a copyright whenever it determines the underlying work contains material of possible public importance.").

[135] *E.g.,* Narell v. Freeman, 872 F.2d 907, 914, 10 U.S.P.Q.2d 1596, 1601 (9th Cir. 1989) ("the first factor is only one of four factors"); Hustler Magazine Inc. v. Moral Majority Inc., 796 F.2d 1148, 1152, 230 U.S.P.Q. 646, 649 (9th Cir. 1986) ("Even assuming that the use had a purely commercial purpose, the presumption of unfairness can be rebutted by the characteristics of the use."), discussed at § 4F[3][c]; Fisher v. Dees, 794 F.2d 432, 437, 230 U.S.P.Q. 421, 425 (9th Cir. 1986) (parody of song is fair use; "the initial presumption need not be fatal to the defendant's cause. The defendant can rebut the presumption by convincing the court that the parody does not unfairly diminish the economic value of the original."); Triangle Publications, Inc. v. Knight-Ridder Newspapers, Inc., 626 F.2d 1171, 207 U.S.P.Q. 977 (5th Cir. 1980).

[136] *E.g.,* Rosemount Enterprises, Inc. v. Random House, Inc., 366 F.2d 303, 150 U.S.P.Q. 715 (2d Cir. 1966), *cert. denied,* 385 U.S. 1009, 152 U.S.P.Q. 844 (1967).

[137] Harper & Row Publishers, Inc. v. Nation Enterprises, 471 U.S. 539, 225 U.S.P.Q. 1073, 1082 (1985). *See also* Stewart v. Abend, 110 S. Ct. 1750, 1769, 14 U.S.P.Q.2d 1614, 1628 (1990) ("In general, fair use is more likely to be found in factual works than in fictional works."); Sony Corp. of America v. Universal City Studios, Inc., 464 U.S. 417, 455 n.4, 220 U.S.P.Q. 665, 683 n.40 (1984) ("Copying a news broadcast may have a stronger claim to fair use than copying a motion picture.").

[138] *E.g.,* Maxtone-Graham v. Burtschaell, 803 F.2d 1253, 1263–64, 231 U.S.P.Q. 534, 541 (2d Cir. 1986), *cert. denied,* 481 U.S. 1059 (1987) (defendant quoted and paraphrased passages from plaintiff's book of interviews of women discussing abortion and unwanted pregnancy experiences; the copying was fair use even though defendant (1) committed errors in borrowing copyrighted materials, and (2) took 4.3% of the words in plaintiff's work; defendant's work

In *Harper & Row*, the Court indicated that "[t]he fact that a work is unpublished is a critical element of its 'nature.' "[139]

[iii]   *The Amount and Substantiality of the Portion Used in Relation to the Copyrighted Work as a Whole.* "There are no absolute rules as to how much of a copyrighted work may be copied and still be considered a fair use."[140] Taking a small but qualitatively important portion of a copyrighted work may exceed fair use bounds.[141]

The Section 107 quantitative factor compares the portion used with the copyrighted work, not the portion used with the infringing work.[142] "As the statutory language indicates, a taking may not be excused merely because it is insubstantial with respect to the *infringing* work."[143]

---

was critical commentary; plaintiff's work was "essentially factual in nature"; "Like the biography, the interview is an invaluable source of material for social scientists and later use of verbatim quotations within reason is both foreseeable and desirable"; defendant did not take the "heart" of plaintiff's work, which had "no identifiable core"; "the two works served fundamentally different functions, by virtue both of their opposing viewpoints and disparate editorial formats.").

Compare Weissmann v. Freeman, 868 F.2d 1313, 1325, 10 U.S.P.Q.2d 1014, 1024 (2d Cir. 1989), *cert. denied*, 110 S. Ct. 219 (1989) ("while recognizing that fair use finds greater application in a factual scientific context, that recognition should not blind a court to the need to uphold those incentives necessary to creation of works such as [that in issue, an article on 'Hepatobiliary Imaging' used with a review course on nuclear medicine]"); Salinger v. Random House, Inc., 811 F.2d 90, 1 U.S.P.Q. 1673 (2d Cir. 1987), *cert. denied*, 484 U.S. 890 (1987), discussed at § 4F[3][g] (preliminary injunction against use of unpublished letters of J.D. Salinger in an unauthorized biography); Educational Testing Service v. Katzman, 793 F.2d 533, 543, 230 U.S.P.Q. 156 (3d Cir. 1986) (standardized test questions; "the unique nature of secure tests means that any use is destructive of [the copyright owner's] rights"); Financial Information, Inc. v. Moody's Investors Service, Inc., 751 F.2d 501, 509, 224 U.S.P.Q. 632, 638 (2d Cir. 1984) (plaintiff's work, a collection of bond redemption information, involved a minimum of editorial skill or judgment, but the defendant's use was similarly uncreative; "Given the equitable nature of the fair use analysis, we are somewhat unmoved by the pot here calling the kettle black.").

[139] Harper & Row Publishers, Inc. v. Nation Enterprises, 471 U.S. 539, 564, 225 U.S.P.Q. 1073, 1082 (1985). *See* § 4F[3][g].

[140] Maxtone-Graham v. Burtschaell, 803 F.2d 1253, 1263, 231 U.S.P.Q. 534, 541 (2d Cir. 1986), *cert. denied*, 481 U.S. 1059 (1987) ("In some instances, copying a work wholesale has been held to be fair use, . . . while in other cases taking only a tiny portion of the original work has been held unfair.").

[141] *E.g.*, Roy Export Co. Establishment of Vaduz, Liechtenstein, Black Inc. v. Columbia Broadcasting System, Inc., 503 F. Supp. 1137, 1145, 208 U.S.P.Q. 580, 586–587 (S.D.N.Y. 1980, *aff'd*, 672 F.2d 1095, 215 U.S.P.Q. 289 (2d Cir.), *cert. denied*, 459 U.S. 826 (1982) (55 seconds of one hour, 29 minute film).

[142] Sheldon v. Metro-Goldwyn Pictures Corp., 81 F.2d 49, 56, 28 U.S.P.Q. 330, 337 (2d Cir.), *cert. denied*, 298 U.S. 669 (1936) (Judge Learned Hand: "it is enough that substantial parts were lifted; no plagiarist can excuse the wrong by showing how much of his work he did not pirate.").

[143] Harper & Row Publishers, Inc. v. Nation Enterprises, 471 U.S. 539, 565, 225 U.S.P.Q. 1073, 1083 (1985).

In *Harper & Row*, the Supreme Court did indicate that the fact that the copied material was a major portion of the accused work tended to show that the portion taken was qualitatively

A component of larger work may be treated as a "whole work" for fair use purposes.[144]

[iv] *The Effect of the Use Upon the Potential Market for or Value of the Copyrighted Work.* In *Harper & Row*, the Supreme Court characterized market effect as "undoubtedly the single most important element of fair use."[145]

Market effect is supplanting demand for the work, including demand in other media.[146] The factor refers to the *"potential* market" effect.[147] "In determining

---

important. *See also* Salinger v. Random House, Inc., 811 F.2d 90, 93, 1 U.S.P.Q.2d 1673, 1678 (2d Cir. 1987), *cert. denied,* 484 U.S. 890 (1987) ("The copied passages, if not 'heart of the book' . . . are at least an important ingredient of the book as it now stands. To a large extent, they make the book worth reading.").

[144] Hustler Magazine Inc. v. Moral Majority Inc., 796 F.2d 1148, 230 U.S.P.Q. 646 (9th Cir. 1986) (parody advertisement in plaintiff's magazine is a whole work); Pacific & Southern Co., Inc. v. Duncan, 744 F.2d 1490, 1497, 224 U.S.P.Q. 131, 135 (11th Cir. 1985), *cert. denied,* 471 U.S. 1004 (1985) (story segment of news broadcast treated as whole work; "The Register of Copyrights issued a certificate of copyright for the . . . segment and for the entire broadcast. . . . "). *Compare* Triangle Publications, Inc. v. Knight-Ridder Newspapers, Inc., 626 F.2d 1171, 107 U.S.P.Q. 977 (5th Cir. 1980) (cover of magazine is not a whole work).

In *Hustler*, the Ninth Circuit discussed the matter as follows:

"[T]o determine whether the parody should be treated as an 'entire work,' we consider the relationship of the copied parody to the periodical as a whole. Unlike the cover of TV Guide in *Triangle Publications*, the inside pages of a magazine are not on public display. Moreover, the parody in this case, like the story in *Pacific and Southern Co.*, represents the 'essence' of Hustler Magazine. In addition, like the story in *Pacific and Southern Co.* and unlike the magazine cover in *Triangle Publications*, the parody is not an interwoven component of the magazine, but can stand totally alone. A creative work does not deserve less copyright protection just because it is part of a composite work." 796 F.2d at 1154–55, 230 U.S.P.Q. at 651.

[145] Harper & Row Publishers, Inc. v. Nation Enterprises, 471 U.S. 539, 225 U.S.P.Q. 1073 (1985).

[146] Harper & Row Publishers, Inc. v. Nation Enterprises, 471 U.S. 539, 568, 225 U.S.P.Q. 1073, 1084 (1985) ("[t]his inquiry must take account not only of harm to the original but also of harm to the market for derivative works."); Maxtone-Graham v. Burtschaell, 803 F.2d 1253, 1264, 231 U.S.P.Q. 534, 546 (2d Cir. 1986), *cert. denied,* 481 U.S. 1059 (1987) ("Harm to derivative works must be taken into account, . . . as must any effect on the value of adaptation and serialization rights."); D.C. Comics, Inc. v. Reel Fantasy, Inc., 696 F.2d 24, 28, 217 U.S.P.Q. 307, 310 (2d Cir. 1982) ("one of the benefits of ownership of copyrighted material is the right to license its use for a fee").

[147] *Compare* Salinger v. Random House, Inc., 811 F.2d 90, 99, 1 U.S.P.Q.2d 1673, 1678-79 (2d Cir. 1987), *cert. denied,* 484 U.S. 890 (1987) (preliminary injunction against use, primarily by paraphrasing, of unpublished letters of J.D. Salinger in an unauthorized biography; use is not fair even though Salinger had disavowed any intention to publish his letters: "First, the proper inquiry concerns 'the potential market' for the copyrighted work. . . . Second, Salinger has the right to change his mind. He is entitled to protect his *opportunity* to sell his letters, an opportunity estimated by his literary agent to have a current value in excess of $500,000. . . . To be sure, the book would not displace the market for the letters . . . Yet some impairment of the market seems likely. . . . For at least some appreciable number of persons, [the quotations and paraphrases] will convey the impression that they have read

whether the use has harmed the work's value or market, courts have focused on whether the infringing use: (1) 'tends to diminish or prejudice the potential sale of [the work],' . . . or (2) tends to interfere with the marketability of the work, . . . or (3) fulfills the demand for the original."[148] The factor does not pertain to diminished demand for a copyrighted work caused by the critical character of the accused work.[149]

Salinger's words, perhaps not quoted verbatim, but paraphrased so closely as to diminish interest in purchasing the originals.") *with* Maxtone-Graham v. Burtschaell, 803 F.2d 1253, 1264, 231 U.S.P.Q. 534, 542 (2d Cir. 1986), *cert. denied,* 481 U.S. 1059 (1987) (publication of defendant's book, a critique of literature on women's experiences with abortion, with quoted passages from plaintiff's copyrighted work, an out of-print collection of interviews with women who have had abortions, will not adversely effect the potential market for plaintiff's market; "[I]t is unthinkable that potential customers for a series of sympathetic interviews on abortion and adoption would withdraw their requests because a small portion of the work was used in an essay sharply critical of abortion . . . [T]he two works served fundamentally different functions, by virtue both of their opposing viewpoints and disparate editorial formats. Moreover, it is not beyond the realm of possibility that [defendant's] book might stimulate further interest in [plaintiff's book.] . . . [Plaintiff] is unable to point to a single piece of evidence portending future harm, and the fact that [plaintiff's book] was published a full decade before the appearance of [defendant's book] makes any such claim far too speculative to sustain upon mere allegation."); Hustler Magazine Inc. v. Moral Majority Inc., 796 F.2d 1148, 230 U.S.P.Q. 646 (9th Cir. 1986) (defendant Jerry Falwell, a fundamentalist minister with "The Moral Majority," copied and distributed a parody advertisement from plaintiff's "adult" magazine, "Hustler," to raise money to file a law suit against plaintiff: defendant did not sell the copies but rather used them to generate "moral outrage" among potential contributors, who, as followers of The Moral Majority, were unlikely to be readers of Hustler).

[148] Hustler Magazine Inc. v. Moral Majority Inc., 796 F.2d 1148, 1155-56, 230 U.S.P.Q. 646, 651 (9th Cir. 1986); S. Rep. No. 473, 94th Cong., 1st Sess. 65 (1975) ("With certain special exceptions . . . a use that supplants any part of the normal market for a copyrighted work would ordinarily be considered an infringement.").

See also Weissmann v. Freeman, 868 F.2d 1313, 1326, 10 U.S.P.Q.2d 1014, 1025 (2d Cir. 1989), *cert. denied,* 110 S. Ct. 219 (1989) (plaintiff, a professor, prepared an article on nuclear medicine, which was a revised and expanded version of papers previously jointly authored by plaintiff and defendant, also a professor, plaintiff's former mentor and a member of plaintiff's academic department; defendant's unconsented use of plaintiff's article in connection with a review course was not fair use, especially when defendant deleted plaintiff's name from the article; the district court erred in finding that defendant's use would not impair the marketability of papers from plaintiff's and defendant's department: "The district court's error on this fourth factor was in focusing on sales or dollars received, rather than upon the realities of promotion and tenure in an academic setting."); Financial Information, Inc. v. Moody's Investors Service, Inc., 751 F.2d 501, 510, 224 U.S.P.Q. 632, 639 (2d Cir. 1984) (plaintiff collects bond redemption information for large financial institutions; defendant used the information in its financial news reports; "the law does not require 'identity of products in nose-to-nose rival sales.' . . . [I]f [defendant] were unable merely to copy from the [plaintiff's work], [plaintiff] might be in a position to license that use for a fee.").

[149] *E.g.,* Fisher v. Dees, 794 F.2d 432, 438, 230 U.S.P.Q. 421, 425 (9th Cir. 1986) (parody of song is fair use; "[T]he economic effect of a parody with which we are concerned is not its potential to destroy or diminish the market for the original—any bad review can have that effect—but rather whether it *fulfills the demand* for the original. Biting criticism suppresses demand; copyright infringement usurps it.").

In *Sony*, the Court linked market effect factor to the purpose factor, noting that (1) if the intended use is for commercial gain, "harm" to the copyright owner may be presumed, but (2) if the intended use is for a noncommercial purpose, the copyright owner must show "by a preponderance of the evidence that *some* meaningful likelihood of future harm exists."[150]

[c] **News—Criticism—Response.** Section 107 lists "criticism," "comment," and "news reporting" as favored fair use purposes.[151] The majority and dissenting opinions in *Harper & Row* discuss news and the limits on the right to take excerpts and quotations from a former public official's unpublished manuscript.

The House Report mentions specialized newsletters as being particularly vulnerable to harm through unauthorized copying, even copying of small portions.[152] In *Wainwright*,[153] the Second Circuit rejected a fair use defense asserted by the *Wall Street Transcript*, a weekly financial newspaper, to justify its systematic abstracting of financial information gathered and distributed as research reports to 900 clients by H.C. Wainwright & Co., an institutional research and brokerage firm, as "research reports on particular companies."[154] The court conceded that "in considering the copyright

---

[150] 464 U.S. at 451. *See* § 4F[3][a][i](2).

[151] News reports of current events may be protected to a limited extent under the common law doctrine of misappropriation. *See* International News Service v. Associated Press, 248 U.S. 215 (1918), discussed at § 6F[1].

[152] H.R. Rep. No. 94–1476, 94th Cong., 2d Sess. 73–74 (1976):

"During the consideration of the revision bill in the 94th Congress it was proposed that independent newsletters, as distinguished from house organs and publicity or advertising publications, be given separate treatment. It is argued that newsletters are particularly vulnerable to mass photocopying, and that most newsletters have fairly modest circulations. Whether the copying of portions of a newsletter is an act of infringement or a fair use will necessarily turn on the facts of the individual case. However, as a general principle, it seems clear that the scope of the fair use doctrine should be considerably narrower in the case of newsletters than in that of either mass-circulation periodicals or scientific journals. The commercial nature of the user is a significant factor in such cases. Copying by a profit-making user of even a small portion of a newsletter may have a significant impact on the commercial market for the work."

[153] Wainwright Sec., Inc. v. Wall Street Transcript Corp., 558 F.2d 91 (2d Cir. 1977), *cert. denied*, 434 U.S. 1014 (1978).

[154] The court gave the following example of a typical abstract:

"W.D. Williams of H.C. Wainwright & Co. says in a Special Report (April 13 7 pp) on FMC CORP. (25) that 1976 prospects are strengthened by the magnitude of the increase in industrial and agricultural chemical earnings in last year's recessionary environment. And second, he says that likely to aid comparisons this year was the surprisingly limited extent to which the Fiber Division's losses shrank last year.

"His estimated earnings for 1976 is $3.76 per share compared with earnings of $3.24 per share in 1975.

"According to Williams, one of the most hopeful developments in recent years was the decision by management last year to attempt to negotiate sale of the Fiber Division. He says the company could wind up with possibly $100 million, plus a tax writeoff and a sizeable one-time charge against earnings. And, concerning the tanker situation, he writes that the company is now far enough along on the learning curve that additional costs overruns, if any, will be small, the major incremental financial cost to FMC will

protection due a report of news events or factual developments, it is important to differentiate between the substance of the information contained in the report, *i.e.*, the event itself, and 'the particular form or collocation of words in which the writer has communicated it.' " But the infringer "did not bother to distinguish between the events contained in the reports and the manner of expression used by Wainwright analysts."

> "Unlike traditional news coverage, . . . the Transcript did not provide independent analysis or research; it did not solicit comments on the same topics from other financial analysts; and it did not include any criticism, praise, or other reactions by industry officials or investors. Rather, the Transcript appropriated almost verbatim the most creative and original aspects of the reports, the financial analyses and prediction, which represent a substantial investment of time, money and labor."[155]

The court found unpersuasive the infringer's argument that other, established newspapers, such as the *Wall Street Journal*, publish as news accounts of Wainwright and other research reports. Such genuine news reports did not have the same market effect as the *Transcript*'s systematic abstracting.

> "The Wall Street Journal articles referred to by appellants, for example, were published a year apart. There apparently was no attempt to provide readers regularly with summaries of the Wainwright reports and there is no indication that the Wall Street Journal launched an advertising campaign portraying itself as a publisher of the same financial analyses available to large investors, but at a lower price. By contrast, the appellant's use of the Wainwright reports was blatantly self-serving, with the obvious intent, if not the effect, of fulfilling the demand for the original work. . . . This was not legitimate coverage of a news event; instead it was, and there is no other way to describe it, chiseling for personal profit."[156]

The House Report mentions, as an example of fair use, copying as part of a response to criticism: "When a copyrighted work contains unfair, inaccurate, or derogatory information concerning an individual or institution, the individual or institution may copy and reproduce such parts of the work as are necessary to permit understandable comment on the statements made in the work."[157]

In *Hustler Magazine*,[158] Hustler Magazine published a cartoon that was tasteless parody of television evangelist Jerry Falwell. Falwell and his organization reproduced and distributed the cartoon as part of an effort to finance a lawsuit against Hustler. Hustler sued for copyright infringement. The court found fair use because the purpose was response to criticism, even though two other Section 107 factors mitigated against fair use (the copyrighted work was "creative" in nature and the accused infringer

---

lie in the determination of what share of the present unreserved overrun is the company's responsibility." 558 F.2d at 94 n.1.

[155] 558 F.2d at 96.

[156] 558 F.2d at 96–97.

[157] H.R. Rep. No. 94–1476, 94th Cong., 2d Sess. 73 (1976).

[158] Hustler Magazine, Inc. v. Moral Majority, Inc., 796 F.2d 1148, 230 U.S.P.Q. 646 (9th Cir. 1986).

copied the whole work) and even though the court found the use presumptively unfair because Falwell used the parody for a profit-making purpose. It rejected Hustler's argument that "Falwell copied more than was necessary for his response." "[A]n individual in rebutting a copyrighted work containing derogatory information about himself may copy such parts of the work as are necessary to permit understandable comment. . . . [T]he public interest in allowing an individual to defend himself against such derogatory personal attacks serves to rebut the presumption of unfairness."[159]

[d]　**Parody.** Borrowing portions of a copyrighted work to create a parody or burlesque of that work may constitute fair use. The parodist may "take no more from the original than is necessary to accomplish reasonably its parodic purpose."[160] Most parody decisions are in the Ninth and Second Circuits, which encompass the entertainment centers of Hollywood and New York respectively.

In *Berlin*,[161] the Second Circuit formulated the "conjure up" test: a parodist can take enough expression to conjure up the original. It held "Mad Magazine" parodies that tracked the structure of copyrighted song lyrics—*e.g.*, "The last time I saw Maris" (the baseball player Roger Maris) for "The last time I saw Paris"—did not infringe.

The Ninth Circuit initially restricted the scope of parody as fair use. In *Benny*,[162] it indicated that a "parodized or burlesqued taking [was] to be treated no differently

---

[159] 796 F.2d at 1153, 230 U.S.P.Q. at 650.

[160] Fisher v. Dees, 794 F.2d 432, 439, 230 U.S.P.Q. 421, 427 (9th Cir. 1986).

[161] Berlin v. E.C. Publications, Inc., 329 F.2d 541, 141 U.S.P.Q. 1 (2d Cir. 1964), *cert. denied*, 379 U.S. 822, 143 U.S.P.Q. 464 (1964).

See also Elsmere Music, Inc. v. National Broadcasting Co., 482 F. Supp. 741, 206 U.S.P.Q. 913 (S.D.N.Y.), *aff'd per curiam*, 623 F.2d 252, 207 U.S.P.Q. 277 (2d Cir. 1980) (exonerating Saturday Night Live parody of the song "I Love New York" entitled "I Love Sodom").

Compare MCA, Inc. v. Wilson, 677 F.2d 180, 185, 211 U.S.P.Q. 577 (2d Cir. 1981) (no fair use parody defense for "Cunnilingus Champion of Company C," which closely tracked the music and meter of "Boogie Woogie Bugle Boy of Company B." At the time the composer wrote the offending work, he did not intend it to be a parody. "We are not prepared to hold that a commercial composer can plagiarize a competitor's copyrighted song, substitute dirty lyrics of his own, perform it for commercial gain, and then escape liability by calling the end result a parody or satire on the mores of society."); Tin Pan Apple Inc. v. Miller Brewing Co., 737 F. Supp. 826, 830, 832, 15 U.S.P.Q.2d 1412, 1415, 1417 (S.D. N.Y. 1990) (no fair use parody defense for defendant's beer commercial featuring rap group doing music in plaintiff Fat Boys' style: "a work, clearly copied from a protected work . . . must be a *valid* parody if it is to qualify even for consideration as an example of fair use under § 107. . . . The commercial's use is entirely for profit: to sell beer. Even if the concept of parody is impermissibly stretched to include this commercial, it does not qualify as fair use, since . . . the commercial in no manner 'builds upon the original,' nor does it contain elements 'contributing something new for humorous effect or commentary' ").

[162] Benny v. Loew's Inc., 239 F.2d 532, 112 U.S.P.Q. 11 (9th Cir. 1956), *aff'd by an equally divided Court*, 356 U.S. 43, 116 U.S.P.Q. 479 (1958).

from any other [copyright] appropriation."[163] Later, it retreated from *Benny* in view of criticism by commentators and other courts and of Congress' recognition of parody in the notes to the Copyright Act of 1976.[164] In *Air Pirates*,[165] it distinguished *Benny* as involving near-verbatim copying, which, as a threshold matter, is eliminated from the fair use defense. If the parody copying is not "near verbatim," the court should use the "conjure up" test to evaluate the substantiality of the taking.[166]

In *Fisher*,[167] the Ninth Circuit applied the first, fourth, and third fair use factors of Section 107 to hold that defendant's song, "When Sunny Sniffs Glue" did not infringe plaintiff's copyrighted song, "When Sunny Gets Blue." The defendant's song copied the first six of the copyrighted song's 38 bars, which was its recognizable theme. As to the first factor, purpose and character of the use, parody is a commercial use of the song, *Harper & Row* makes commercial uses presumptively unfair,[168] but the presumption is rebuttable, especially when the parody is more in the nature of editorial or social commentary. As to the fourth factor, effect on the potential market or value of the copyrighted work, the two works do not fulfill the same demand. Consequently, the parody has no cognizable economic effect on the original. The parody's critical impact must be excluded from consideration because "[c]opyright law is not designed to stifle critics." As to the third factor, amount and substantiality of the taking, the "conjure up" test applies. The test is not limited to the amount necessary to evoke *initial* recognition in the listener.

---

[163] Famous comedian Jack Benny produced a fifteen-minute burlesque of the copyrighted play and motion picture "Gas Light." The court rejected a fair use defense, focusing primarily on the quantity taken by the defendant Benny: "One cannot copy the substance of another's work without infringing his copyright. A burlesque presentation of such a copy is no defense to an action for infringement of copyright." 239 F.2d at 537.

[164] The House Report quotes the 1961 Report of the Register of Copyright, which lists as among "the sort of activities the courts might regard as fair use under the circumstances" "use in a parody of some of the content of the work parodied." H.R. Rep. No. 94–1476, 94th Cong., 2d Sess. 65 (1976).

[165] Walt Disney Productions v. Air Pirates, 581 F.2d 751, 199 U.S.P.Q. 769 (9th Cir. 1978), *cert. denied sub nom.* O'Neill v. Walt Disney Productions, 439 U.S. 1132 (1979).

[166] In *Air Pirates*, the defendants published a "counterculture" comic book in which characters that closely resembled Mickey Mouse, Minnie Mouse and Donald Duck engaged in various uncharacteristically unwholesome activities. The Ninth Circuit found infringement, rejecting a fair use/parody defense because the defendants took more of the copyrighted graphic depiction of the characters than "was necessary to recall or conjure up the original." As noted later in Fisher v. Dees, 794 F.2d 432, 439, 230 U.S.P.Q. 421, 426 (9th Cir. 1986), the *Air Pirates* decision "singled out three considerations that we thought important in determining whether a taking is excessive under the circumstances—the degree of public recognition of the original work, the ease of conjuring up the original work in the chosen medium, and the focus of the parody." The fame of the Disney characters, their graphic character, and the fact that "essence of this parody did not focus on how the characters looked, but rather parodied their personalities, their wholesomeness and their innocence" meant that very little taking was necessary to conjure up the original. *Air Pirates* also emphasized that a parodist is not necessarily privileged to make the "best" parody.

[167] Fisher v. Dees, 794 F.2d 432, 230 U.S.P.Q. 421 (9th Cir. 1986).

[168] *See* § 4F[3][a].

"The unavailability of viable alternatives is evident in the present case. Like a speech, a song is difficult to parody effectively without exact or near-exact copying. . . . This 'special need for accuracy,' provides some license for 'closer' parody. . . . To be sure, that license is not limitless: the parodist's desire to make the best parody must be 'balanced against the rights of the copyright owner in his original expressions.' . . . In view of the parody's medium, its purposes, and its brevity, it takes no more from the original than is necessary to accomplish reasonably its parodic purpose."[169]

The copied work must be, at least in part, the subject of the parody; there is no justification for using a work in an otherwise unlawful manner in order to parody or criticize other institutions, practices, or works.[170]

[e] **Copying for Teaching and Classroom Use.** Section 107 lists "teaching (including multiple copies for classroom use)" and "scholarship" as favored fair use purposes.[171]

[i] *Pre-1976 Case Law.* The case law on reproduction for education purposes prior to the 1976 Act was sparse although one notable decision did hold that reproduction of a whole work for such use was not fair use.[172]

---

[169] 794 F.2d at 439, 230 U.S.P.Q. at 426–27.

[170] *E.g.,* Fisher v. Dees, 794 F.2d 432, 436, 230 U.S.P.Q. 421, 424 (9th Cir. 1986)("a humorous or satiric work deserves protection under the fair-use doctrine only if the copied work is at least partly the target of the work in question. . . . Otherwise, there is no need to 'conjure up' the original in the audience's mind and no justification for borrowing from it").

Cf. MCA, Inc. v. Wilson, 677 F.2d 180, 185, 211 U.S.P.Q. 577 (2d Cir. 1981) ("[A] permissible parody need not be directed solely to the copyrighted song but may also reflect on life in general. However, if the copyrighted song is not at least in part an object of the parody, there is no need to conjure it up."); Acuff-Rose Music, Inc. v. Campbell, 754 F. Supp. 1150, 1154–55 (M.D. Tenn. 1991) (song "As Clean As They Wanna Be," by 2 Live Crew, "an anti-establishment rap group," is parody of the Roy Orbison song, "Oh Pretty Woman"; copyright owner's argument that 2 Live Crew's version was not a parody because it is about loneliness, unlike the Orbison original, which is "primarily about the physical attributes of women," is without merit; "The theme, content and style of the new version are different than the original. . . . Although the parody starts out with the same lyrics as the original, it quickly degenerates into a play on words, substituting predictable lyrics with shocking ones. . . . The physical attributes of the subject woman deviate from a pleasing image of femininity to bald-headed, hairy and generally repugnant. To complete the thematic twist, at the end of the parody the 'two-timin' woman turns out to be pregnant. . . . [2 Live Crew] is an anti-establishment rap group and this song derisively demonstrates how bland and banal the Orbison song seems to them . . . [It] employs a number of musical devices that exaggerate the original and help to create a comic effect. Plaintiff's argument that it would be prevented from releasing a parody of their work is meritless. In a world where copyright monopoly stretched to that great extent, parodies would be unlikely ever to be approved by the original author.").

[171] Library copying is discussed at § 4F[3][h].

[172] Wihtol v. Crow, 309 F.2d 777 (8th Cir. 1962). *See also* Encyclopaedia Britannica Educational Corp. v. Crooks, 447 F. Supp. 243, 197 U.S.P.Q. 280 (W.D.N.Y. 1978).

The facts and holding of *Wihtol* and *Encyclopaedia* are described in a later Ninth Circuit decision, Marcus v. Rowley, 695 F.2d 1171, 1176–77, 217 U.S.P.Q. 691 (9th Cir. 1983), as follows:

[ii]   *1976 Act Legislative History—Guidelines.* The question of reproduction for classroom use occupied a good portion of the legislative history of the 1976 Act. In addition to inserting the phrase "(including multiple copies for classroom use)" after "teaching" in Section 106, the House Report set forth two "agreements" reached by private groups concerning classroom copying of books and periodicals and of music.[173] The House-Senate Conference accepted these agreements "as part of their

(Text continued on page 4–206)

"Wihtol . . . involved alleged infringement by the defendant, a school teacher and church choir director, of a hymn entitled 'My God and I.' The defendant Crow incorporated plaintiff's original piano and solo voice composition into an arrangement for his choirs. He made forty-eight copies of his arrangement and had the piece performed on two occasions: once by the high school choir at the school chapel, and once in church on Sunday. The music was identified as 'arranged Nelson E. Crow,' but no reference was made to plaintiff as the original composer. The Eighth Circuit affirmed the trial court's finding that Crow had infringed plaintiff's copyright and in addressing the issue of whether Crow's copying constituted fair use, the court stated that '[w]hatever may be the breadth of the doctrine of "fair use", it is not conceivable to us that the copying of all, or substantially all, of a copyrighted song can be held to be a "fair use" merely because the infringer had no intent to infringe.' Id. at 780.

". . . Encyclopaedia Britannica Educational Corp. . . . also considered the issue of fair use in the educational context. . . . [T]hree corporations which produced educational motion picture films sued the Board of Cooperative Educational Services of Erie County ('BOCES') for videotaping several of plaintiffs' copyrighted films without permission. BOCES distributed the copied films to schools for delayed student viewing. Defendants' fair use defense was rejected on the ground that although defendants were involved in non-commercial copying to promote science and education, the taping of entire copyrighted films was too excessive for the fair use defense to apply."

[173] The pertinent portion of the House Report is set forth below:

"Intention as to classroom reproduction"

"Although the works and uses to which the doctrine of fair use is applicable are as broad as the copyright law itself, most of the discussion of section 107 has centered around questions of classroom reproduction, particularly photocopying. The arguments on the question are summarized at pp. 30-31 of this Committee's 1967 report (H.R. Rep. No. 83, 90th Cong., 1st Sess.), and have not changed materially in the intervening years.

"The Committee also adheres to its earlier conclusion, that 'a specific exemption freeing certain reproductions of copyrighted works for educational and scholarly purposes from copyright control is not justified.' At the same time the Committee recognizes as it did in 1967, that there is a 'need for greater certainty and protection for teachers.' In an effort to meet this need the Committee has not only adopted further amendments to section 107, but has also amended section 504(c) to provide innocent teachers and other non-profit users of copyrighted material with broad insulation against unwarranted liability for infringement. The latter amendments are discussed below in connection with Chapter 5 of the bill.

"In 1967 the Committee also sought to approach this problem by including in its report, a very thorough discussion of 'the considerations lying behind the four criteria listed in the amended section 107, in the context of typical classroom situations arising today.' This discussion appeared on pp. 32-35 of the 1967 report, and with some changes has been retained in the Senate report on S. 22 (S. Rep. No. 94-473, pp. 63-65). The committee has reviewed this discussion, and considers that it still has value as an analysis of various aspects of the problem.

(Text continued on page 4–206)

"At the Judiciary Subcommittee hearings in June 1975, Chairman Kastenmeier and other members urged the parties to meet together independently in an effort to achieve a meeting of the minds as to permissible educational uses of copyrighted material. The response to these suggestions was positive, and a number of meetings of three groups, dealing respectively with classroom reproduction of printed material, music, and audio-visual material, were held beginning in September 1975."

"In a joint letter to Chairman Kastenmeier, dated March 19, 1976, the representatives of the Ad Hoc Committee of Educational Institutions and Organizations on Copyright Law Revision, and of the Authors League of America, Inc., and the Association of American Publishers, Inc., stated :

'You may remember that in our letter of March 8, 1976 we told you that the negotiating teams representing authors and publishers and the Ad Hoc Group had reached tentative agreement on guidelines to insert in the Committee Report covering educational copying from books and periodicals under Section 107 of H.R. 2223 and S.22, and that as part of that tentative agreement, each side would accept the amendments to Sections 107 and 504 which were adopted by your Subcommittee on March 3, 1976.

'We are now happy to tell you that the agreement has been approved by the principals and we enclose a copy herewith. We had originally intended to translate the agreement into language suitable for inclusion in the legislative report dealing with Section 107, but we have since been advised by committee staff that this will not be necessary.

'As stated above, the agreement refers only to copying from books and periodicals, and is not intended to apply to musical or audiovisual works.'

. . .

"In a joint letter dated April 30, 1976, representatives of the Music Publisher's Association of the United States, Inc., the National Music Publishers' Association, Inc., the Music Teachers National Association, the Music Educators National Conference, the National Association of Schools of Music, and the Ad Hoc Committee on Copyright Law Revision, wrote to Chairman Kastenmeier as follows:

'During the hearings on H.R. 2223 in June 1975, you and several of your subcommittee members suggested that concerned groups should work together in developing guidelines which would be helpful to clarify Section 107 of the bill.

'Representatives of music educators and music publishers delayed their meetings until guidelines had been developed relative to books and periodicals. Shortly after that work was completed and those guidelines were forwarded to your subcommittee, representatives of the undersigned music organizations met together with representatives of the Ad Hoc Committee on Copyright Law Revision to draft guidelines relative to music.

'We are very pleased to inform you that the discussions thus have been fruitful on the guidelines which have been developed. Since private music teachers are an important factor in music education, due consideration has been given to the concerns of that group.

'We trust that this will be helpful in the report on the bill to clarify Fair Use as it applies to music.'

. . .

"The problem of off-the-air taping for nonprofit classroom use of copyrighted audiovisual works incorporated in radio and television broadcasts has proved to be difficult to resolve. The Committee believes that the fair use doctrine has some limited application in this area, but it appears that the development of detailed guidelines will require a more

understanding of fair use."[174]

The full text of the "Agreement on Guidelines for Classroom Copyright in Not-For-Profit Educational Institutions" is as follows:

"WITH RESPECT TO BOOKS AND PERIODICALS

"The purpose of the following guidelines is to state the minimum and not the maximum standards of educational fair use under Section 107 of H.R. 2223. The parties agree that the conditions determining the extent of permissible copying for educational purposes may change in the future; that certain types of copying permitted under these guidelines may not be permissible in the future; and conversely that in the future other types of copying not permitted under these guidelines may be permissible under revised guidelines.

"Moreover, the following statement of guidelines is not intended to limit the types of copying permitted under the standards of fair use under judicial decision and which are stated in Section 107 of the Copyright Revision Bill. There may be instances in which copying which does not fall within the guidelines stated below may nonetheless be permitted under the criteria of fair use.

---

thorough exploration than has so far been possible of the needs and problems of a number of different interests affected, and of the various legal problems presented. Nothing in section 107 or elsewhere in the bill is intended to change or prejudge the law on the point. On the other hand, the Committee is sensitive to the importance of the problem, and urges the representatives of the various interests, if possible under the leadership of the Register of Copyrights, to continue their discussions actively and in a constructive spirit. If it would be helpful to a solution, the Committee is receptive to undertaking further consideration of the problem in a future Congress.

"The Committee appreciates and commends the efforts and the cooperative and reasonable spirit of the parties who achieved the agreed guidelines on books and periodicals and on music. Representatives of the American Association of University Professors and of the Association of American Law Schools have written to the Committee strongly criticizing the guidelines, particularly with respect to multiple copying, as being too restrictive with respect to classroom situations at the university and graduate level. However, the Committee notes that the Ad Hoc group did include representatives of higher education, that the stated 'purpose of the . . . guidelines is to state the minimum and not the maximum standards of educational fair use' and that the agreement acknowledges 'there may be instances in which copying which does not fall within the guidelines . . . may nonetheless be permitted under the criteria of fair use.'

"The Committee believes the guidelines are a reasonable interpretation of the minimum standards of fair use. Teachers will know that copying within the guidelines is fair use. Thus, the guidelines serve the purpose of fulfilling the need for greater certainty and protection for teachers. The Committee expresses the hope that if there are areas where standards other than these guidelines may be appropriate, the parties will continue their efforts to provide additional specific guidelines in the same spirit of good will and give and take that has marked the discussion of this subject in recent months." H.R. Rep. No. 94–1476, 94th Cong., 2d Sess. 66–72 (1976).

[174] H.R. Conference Rep., No. 94–1733, 94th Cong., 2d Sess. (1976).

Guidelines

I. *Single Copying for Teachers*

A single copy may be made of any of the following by or for a teacher at his or her individual request for his or her scholarly research or use in teaching or preparation to teach a class:

A. A chapter from a book;

B. An article from a periodical or newspaper;

C. A short story, short essay or short poem, whether or not from a collective work;

D. A chart, graph, diagram, cartoon or picture from a book, periodical or newspaper;

II. *Multiple Copies for Classroom Use*

Multiple copies (not to exceed in any event more than one copy per pupil in a course) may be made by or for the teacher giving the course for classroom use or discussion; *provided that*:

A. The copying meets the tests of brevity and spontaneity as defined below; *and,*

B. Meets the cumulative effect test as defined below; *and,*

C. Each copy includes a notice of copyright.

Definitions

Brevity

(*i*) Poetry: (a) A complete poem if less than 250 words and if printed on not more than two pages or, (b) from a longer poem, an excerpt of not more than 250 words.

(*ii*) Prose: (a) Either a complete article, story, or essay of less than 2,500 words, or (b) an excerpt from any prose work of not more than 1,000 words or 10% of the work, whichever is less, but in any event a minimum of 500 words.

[Each of the numerical limits stated in 'i' and 'ii' above may be expanded to permit the completion of an unfinished line of a poem or of an unfinished prose paragraph.]

(*iii*) Illustration: One chart, graph, diagram, drawing, cartoon or picture per book or per periodical issue.

(*iv*) 'Special' works: Certain works in poetry, prose or in 'poetic prose' which often combine language with illustrations and which are intended sometimes for children and at other times for a more general audience fall short of 2,500 words in their entirety. Paragraph 'ii' above notwithstanding such 'special works' may not be reproduced in their entirety; however, an excerpt comprising not more than two of the published pages of such special work and containing not more than 10% of the words found in the text thereof, may not be reproduced.

Spontaneity

(*i*) The copying is at the instance and inspiration of the individual teacher, and *(ii)* The inspiration and decision to use the work and the moment of its use for maximum teaching effectiveness are so close in time that it would be unreasonable to expect a timely reply to a request for permission.

Cumulative Effect

(i) The copying of the material is for only one course in the school in which the copies are made.

(ii) Not more than one short poem, article, story, essay or two excerpts may be copied from the same author, nor more than three from the same collective work or periodical volume during one class term.

(iii) There shall not be more than nine instances of such multiple copying for one course during one class term.

[The limitations stated in 'ii' and 'iii' above shall not apply to current news periodicals and newspapers and current news sections of other periodicals.]

III. Prohibitions as to I and II above

Notwithstanding any of the above, the ollowing shall be prohibited:

(A) Copying shall not be used to create or replace or substitute for anthologies, compilations or collective works. Such replacement or substitution may occur whether copies of various works or excerpts therefrom are accumulated or reproduced and used separately.

(B) There shall be no copying of or from works intended to be 'consumable' in the course of study or of teaching. These include workbooks, exercises, standardized tests and test booklets and answer sheets and like consumable material.

(C) Copying shall not:

(a) substitute for the purchase of books, publisher's reprints, or periodicals;

(b) be directed by higher authority;

(c) be repeated with respect to the same item by the same teacher from term to term.

(D) No charge shall be made to the student beyond the actual cost of photocopying."

The text of the "agreement" relating to music is as follows:

"GUIDELINES FOR EDUCATIONAL USES OF MUSIC

"The purpose of the following guidelines is to state the minimum and not the maximum standards of educational fair use under Section 107 of HR 2223. The parties agree that the conditions determining the extent of permissible copying for educational purposes may change in the future; and conversely that in the future other types of copying not permitted under these guidelines may be permissible under revised guidelines.

"Moreover, the following statement of guidelines is not intended to limit the types of copying permitted under the standards of fair use under judicial decision and which are stated in Section 107 of the Copyright Revision Bill. There may be instances in which copying which does not fall within the guidelines stated below may nonetheless be permitted under the criteria of fair use.

A. *Permissible Uses*

1. Emergency copying to replace purchased copies which for any reason are not available for an imminent performance provided purchased replacement copies shall be substituted in due course.

2. (a) For academic purposes other than performance, single or multiple copies of excerpts of works may be made, provided that the excerpts do not comprise a part of the whole which would constitute a performable unit such as a selection, movement or aria, but in no case more than 10% of the whole work. The number of copies shall not exceed one copy per pupil.

(b) For academic purposes other than performance, a single copy of an entire performable unit (section, movement, aria, etc.) that is, (1) confirmed by the copyright proprietor to be out of print or (2) unavailable except in a larger work, may be made by or for a teacher solely for the purpose of his or her scholarly research or in preparation to teach a class.

3. Printed copies which have been purchased may be edited or simplified provided that the fundamental character of the work is not distorted or the lyrics, if any, altered or lyrics added if none exist.

4. A single copy of recordings of performances by students may be made for evaluation or rehearsal purposes and may be retained by the educational institution or individual teacher.

5. A single copy of a sound recording (such as a tape, disc or cassette) of copyrighted music may be made from sound recordings owned by an educational institution or an individual teacher for the purpose of constructing aural exercises or examinations and may be retained by the educational institution or individual teacher. (This pertains only to the copyright of the music itself and not to any copyright which may exist in the sound recording.)

B. *Prohibitions*

1. Copying to create or replace or substitute for anthologies, compilations or collective works.

2. Copying of or from works intended to be 'consumable' in the course of study or of teaching such as workbooks, exercises, standardized tests and answer sheets and like material.

3. Copying for the purpose of performance, except as in A(1) above.

4. Copying for the purpose of substituting for the purpose of music, except as in A(1) and A(2) above.

5. Copying without inclusion of the copyright notice which appears on the printed copy."[175]

[iii] *Court Decisions.* In *Marcus*,[176] the Ninth Circuit gave weight to the Congressionally-adopted guidelines, finding a teacher's reproduction of copyrighted

---

[175] H.R. Rep. No. 94–1476, 94th Cong., 2d Sess. 68–71 (1976).
[176] Marcus v. Rowley, 695 F.2d 1171, 217 U.S.P.Q. 691 (9th Cir. 1983).

materials not fair use. Plaintiff, a former public school teacher and an instructor of adult education classes, prepared a 35 page booklet entitled "Cake Decorating Made Easy." Defendant, a public school teacher, enrolled in plaintiff's class, bought a copy of the booklet, prepared a 24 page booklet on cake decorating, and used her booklet for classes in 1975, 1976, and 1977. Defendant admitted copying 11 pages of plaintiff's book; the pages consisted of "the supply list, icing recipes, three sheets dealing with color flow and mixing colors, four pages showing how to make and use a decorating bag, and two pages explaining how to make flowers and sugar molds." The court noted that defendant "did not give plaintiff credit for the eleven pages she copied, nor did she acknowledge plaintiff as the owner of a copyright with respect to those pages."[177]

The Ninth Circuit reversed the trial court's grant of summary judgment for defendant and denial of summary judgment for plaintiff. First, it applied the four Section 107 factors. The first factor, purpose and character of use, weighed in defendant's favor because the purpose of the copying was nonprofit education, but was diluted because the use was "for the same intrinsic purpose for which the copyright owner intended it to be used" and because the defendant's conduct in failing to seek permission and in failing to acknowledge plaintiff's copyright was inequitable.[178] The second factor, nature of the work, was of little assistance because plaintiff's work "involved both informational and creative aspects." The third factor, amount and substantiality of the portion used, favored the plaintiff/copyright owner. The case "presents a clear example of both substantial quantitative and qualitative copying" because "almost 50% of defendant's [work] was a verbatim copy of plaintiff's booklet and that 50% contained virtually all of the substance of defendant's book." The fourth factor, effect on the potential market for the copyrighted work, did not favor plaintiff because the district court found that defendant's copying had no effect on plaintiff's market. The factors as a whole weighed decisively in favor of the conclusion of no fair use.

In *Marcus*, the Ninth Circuit also considered the House Report agreement guidelines; "while they are not controlling on the court, they are instructive on the issue of fair use in the context of this case." Defendant's use passed the guidelines' "cumulative effect" test but failed brevity, spontaneity, and copyright notice inclusion tests. The taking exceeded the quantity limits, and plaintiff's work was arguably a "special work," that is, one combining language with illustrations, to which a special, restrictive brevity test applies. Defendant could not meet the spontaneity test because her use ran through three school years.

[f] **Scholarship and Research—History and Biography.** Section 107 of the 1976 Copyright Act lists "scholarship" and "research" as favored fair use purposes.

A long line of lower court decisions deal with fair use of historical, biographical and other works reflecting a substantial amount of research effort.[179] The cases

---

[177] 695 F.2d at 1173, 217 U.S.P.Q. at 693.

[178] The court noted: "Attribution is, of course, but one factor. Moreover, acknowledgement of a source does not excuse infringement when the other factors listed in section 107 are present." 695 F.2d at 1176, n.8, 217 U.S.P.Q. at 695, n.8.

[179] Special problems arise when a biographer or historian uses unpublished source materials, such as the subject's letters or writings. See § 4F[3][g].

yield no bright line test for how much a second author may rely on a first author's research.[180]

Three decisions dealing with biography illustrate the fine lines that the courts draw.

In *Toksvig*,[181] the plaintiff wrote a lengthy, serious biography of fairy tale writer Hans Christian Andersen, using original Danish sources. Defendant wrote a shorter, popular-style biography of Andersen, relying heavily on plaintiff's work and closely paraphrasing 24 passages. The court found infringement and rejected fair use, stressing that the defendant did no original research.

In *Rosemont Enterprises*,[182] the defendant prepared for publication an

---

[180] "Research," as such, is not copyrightable. *See* § 4C[1][b][i].

[181] Toksvig v. Bruce Publishing Co., 181 F.2d 664 (7th Cir. 1950).

Toksvig caused intercircuit copyright frictions. In Nash v. CBS, Inc., 899 F.2d 1537, 1541–42, 14 U.S.P.Q.2d 1755, 1759 (7th Cir. 1990), Judge Easterbrook commented:

> "Universal made a motion picture based on the premise that an idealistic crewman planted a bomb that destroyed the dirigible *Hindenburg* on May 6, 1937. The theory came straight from A.A. Hoehling's *Who Destroyed the Hindenburg?* (1962), a monograph based on exhaustive research. The motion picture added sub-plots and development, but the thesis and the evidence adduced in support of it could be traced to Hoehling. Nonetheless, the Second Circuit concluded that this did not infringe Hoehling's rights, because the book placed the facts (as opposed to Hoehling's exposition) in the public domain. *Hoehling v. Universal City Studios, Inc.*, 618 F.2d 972 (1980). . . . Cf. *Musto v. Meyer*, 434 F. Supp. 32 (S.D.N.Y.1977) (idea for The Seven Per Cent Solution derived from article in medical journal).
>
> "*Hoehling* suggested that '[t]o avoid a chilling effect on authors who contemplate tackling an historical issue or event, broad latitude must be granted to subsequent authors who make use of historical subject matter, including theories or plots'. . . . As our opinion in *Toksvig* shows, we are not willing to say that 'anything goes' as long as the first work is about history. *Toksvig* held that the author of a biography of Hans Christian Andersen infringed the copyright of the author of an earlier biography by using portions of Andersen's letters as well as some of the themes and structure. *Hoehling* rejected *Toksvig*, . . . concluding that '[k]nowledge is expanded . . . by granting new authors of historical works a relatively free hand to build upon the work of their predecessors.' . . . With respect for our colleagues of the east, we think this goes to the extreme of looking at incentives only *ex post*. The authors in *Hoehling* and *Toksvig* spent years tracking down leads. If all of their work, right down to their words, may be used without compensation, there will be too few original investigations, and facts will not be available on which to build.
>
> "In *Toksvig* the first author, who knew Danish, spent three years learning about Andersen's life; the second author, who knew no Danish, wrote her biography in less than a year by copying out of the first book scenes and letters that the original author discovered or translated. Reducing the return on such effort, by allowing unhindered use, would make the initial leg-work less attractive and so less frequent. Copyright law does not protect hard work (divorced from expression), and hard work is not an essential ingredient of copyrightable expression . . . ; to the extent *Toksvig* confuses work or ideas with expression, it has been justly criticized. . . . We need not revisit *Toksvig* on its own facts to know that it is a mistake to hitch up at either pole of the continuum between granting the first author a right to forbid all similar treatments of history and granting the second author a right to use anything he pleases of the first's work."

[182] Rosemont Enterprises, Inc. v. Random House, Inc., 366 F.2d 303, 150 U.S.P.Q. 715 (2d Cir. 1966), *cert. denied*, 385 U.S. 1009 (1967).

unauthorized biography of Howard Hughes. A Hughes company bought the copyrights to 1954 *Look* magazine articles on Hughes, which plaintiff used, and sought an injunction against publication of the biography. In finding fair use, the court discounted the fact that the defendant's work was a popularized account and directed to commercial gain.

In *Meeropol*,[183] plaintiffs were the children of Julius and Ethel Rosenberg, who were executed in June 1953 for conspiring to transmit atomic bomb information to the Soviet Union. Plaintiffs claimed ownership of copyright on letters the Rosenbergs wrote to each other while in prison, which were published in a volume entitled *Death House Letters*. Years later, the defendants wrote and published *The Implosion Conspiracy*, which reprinted verbatim portions of 30 Rosenberg letters. Plaintiffs sued for copyright infringement, defamation, and invasion of privacy. The trial court granted summary judgment against the copyright claim, finding fair use as a matter of law. The Second Circuit reversed because factual disputes concerning fair use factors made summary judgment improper.[184] It distinguished *Rosemont*: "*Rosemont* involved the use of copyrighted statements concerning the actions of a biographical subject, not as here the use of verbatim letters written by the subject. In addition, it appears that the fair use defense was upheld in *Rosemont* at least in part because the court found that the plaintiff there was acting in bad faith seeking to prevent the publication of a legitimate biography of Howard Hughes."[185]

[g] **Unpublished Works.** In *Harper & Row*, the Supreme Court indicated that "[t]he fact that a work is unpublished is a critical element of its 'nature,' "[186] which diminishes the likelihood that use of an unpublished manuscript will be excused as fair.

---

[183] Meeropol v. Nizer, 560 F.2d 1061, 195 U.S.P.Q. 273 (2d Cir. 1977), *cert. denied*, 434 U.S. 1013 (1978).

[184] The court noted:

"A key issue in fair use cases is whether the defendant's work tends to diminish or prejudice the potential sale of plaintiff's work. . . . The fact that the Rosenberg letters have been out of print for 20 years does not necessarily mean that they have no future market which can be injured. . . . The market for republication or for sale of motion picture rights might be affected by the infringing work.

. . .

"Defendants-appellees reprinted verbatim portions of 28 copyrighted letters, a total of 1957 words. Although these letters represent less than one percent *The Implosion Conspiracy*, the letters were prominently featured in promotional material for the book. The fact that the letters were quoted out of chronological order, many undated, without indication of elisions or other editorial modifications is relevant to a determination of the purpose for their use and the necessity for verbatim quotations for the sake of historical accuracy." 560 F.2d at 1070–71.

[185] 560 F.2d at 1069.

Arguably, the Rosenberg children as plaintiffs had motives comparable to those of the *Rosemont* plaintiffs, that is, they may have been using copyright more to suppress criticism of their deceased parents than to preserve the economic value of their right to publish the letters.

[186] Harper & Row Publishers, Inc. v. Nation Enterprises, 471 U.S. 539, 563, 225 U.S.P.Q. 1073, 1082 (1985).

Recent Second Circuit decisions grapple with the scope of fair use of unpublished works in unauthorized biographies. In *Salinger*,[187] the court directed the district court to enjoin a biographer's use of "Catcher in the Rye" author J.D. Salinger's unpublished letters, which were deposited in several university libraries. The biographer obtained access to the letters only after signing a form agreement restricting usage of the letters' contents.[188] In *Salinger*, the court noted:

> "Salinger's letters are unpublished, and they have not lost that attribute by their placement in libraries where access has been explicitly made subject to observance of at least the protections of copyright law. . . . [W]e encounter some ambiguity arising from the Supreme Court's observation that 'the *scope* of fair use is narrower with respect to unpublished works.' . . . This could mean either that the circumstances in which copying will be found to be fair use are fewer in number for unpublished works than for published works or that the amount of copyrighted material that may be copied as fair use is a lesser quantity for unpublished works than for published works. . . . [W]e think that the tenor of the Court's entire discussion of unpublished works conveys the idea that such works normally enjoy complete protection against copying any protected expression. Narrower 'scope' seems to refer to the diminished *likelihood* that copying will be fair use when the copyrighted material is unpublished."[189]

The court concluded: "Public awareness of the expressive content of the letters will have to await either Salinger's decision to publish or the expiration of his copyright."[190]

In *New Era*,[191] owners of copyright in Scientology founder L. Ron Hubbard's works sought to enjoin publication of a sharply critical biography that included passages quoted from Hubbard's published and unpublished works. The district court denied the request for a permanent injunction because of free speech concerns but left open the possibility of a damage recovery. It reluctantly agreed that *Harper* and *Salinger* mandated denial of fair use of some of the quoted passages from unpublished works, but suggested a Salinger-Hubbard distinction:

> "Many of the takings of Salinger's expression were for the purpose of enlivening that text with Salinger's expressive genius. . . . Hubbard's expression is taken primarily to show character flaws in a manner that cannot be accomplished without use of his words."[192]

---

[187] Salinger v. Random House, Inc., 811 F.2d 90, 1 U.S.P.Q.2d 1673 (2d Cir. 1987), *cert. denied*, 484 U.S. 890 (1987).

[188] "The Harvard form required permission 'to publish the contents of the manuscript or any excerpt therefrom.' The Princeton form obliged the signer 'not to copy, reproduce, circulate or publish' inspected manuscripts without permission." 811 F.2d at 93, 1 U.S.P.Q.2d at 1674.

[189] 811 F.2d at 97, 1 U.S.P.Q.2d at 1677.

[190] 811 F.2d at 100, 1 U.S.P.Q.2d at 1679.

[191] New Era Publications International v. Henry Holt & Co., 873 F.2d 576, 10 U.S.P.Q.2d 1561 (2d Cir. 1989), *reh'g denied*, 884 F.2d 659, 12 U.S.P.Q.2d 1121 (2d Cir. 1989), *cert. denied*, 110 S. Ct. 1168 (1990) (Miner, concurring, and Newman, dissenting).

[192] 873 F.2d at 582, 10 U.S.P.Q.2d at 1566.

In an opinion by Judge Miner, a Second Circuit panel affirmed denial of injunctive relief on a different ground—laches (undue delay). The panel rejected the district court's distinction:

> "The district court opinion adds a gloss to the second fair use factor—nature of the copyrighted work—that we think should be removed. While we made it clear in *Salinger* that unpublished works normally enjoy complete protection, the district court would parse this factor . . . with a distinction. . . . [T]he distinction is between the use of protected expression to 'enliven' text and the use of protected expression to communicate 'significant points' about the subject. We see no need for such an approach. Where use is made of materials of an 'unpublished nature,' the second fair use factor has yet to be applied in favor of an infringer. . . . "[193]

Panel member Judge Oakes filed a concurring opinion, indicating "the majority unnecessarily goes out of its way to take issue" with the district court opinion and "tends to cast in concrete" the *Salinger* decision.

In *New Era*, the Second Circuit denied a petition for rehearing *en banc*.[194] Judge Newman, with three other judges, disagreed with the panel decision's disapproval of the district court's distinction: "[T]he distinction between copying expression to enliven the copier's prose and doing so where necessary to report a fact accurately

---

[193] 873 F.2d at 583, 10 U.S.P.Q.2d at 1567.

Judge Miner also rejected the distinction as an element of the first factor (purpose of the use).

> "The tenor of the district court opinion is that special consideration should be afforded to Holt, to the extent that Hubbard's words are quoted to prove some traits of character either at odds with his public image or especially intriguing to the reader. The district court sees a significant distinction in purpose between the use of an author's words to display the distinctiveness of his writing style and the use of an author's words to make a point about his character, finding far greater justification in the latter than in the former. We find such a distinction unnecessary and unwarranted in applying the statutory fair use purpose factor. As long as a book can be classified as a work of criticism, scholarship or research, as can the book here, the factor cuts in favor of the book's publisher. . . . " 873 F.2d at 583, 10 U.S.P.Q.2d at 1567.

[194] The Second Circuit's unpublished works decisions caused a flurry of scholarly commentary by the judges. *See* New Era Publications International ApS v. Carol Publishing Co., 904 F.2d 152, 14 U.S.P.Q.2d 2030, 2032 (2d Cir. 1990), *cert. denied*, 111 S. Ct. 297 (1990) (Feinberg, J.):

> "Since the decisions in *Salinger* and *New Era*, there have been a number of articles on the subject of fair use. See, e.g., Weinreb, Fair's Fair: A Comment on the Fair Use Doctrine, 103 Harv. L. Rev. 1137 (1990). Indeed, several of the articles have been written by some of the judges involved in those decisions. See Oakes, Copyrights and Copyremedies: Unfair Use and Injunctions, to be published in a forth-coming edition of the Hofstra L. Rev.; Leval, Commentary: Toward a Fair Use Standard, 103 Harv. L. Rev. 1105 (1990); Miner, Exploiting Stolen Text: Fair Use or Foul Play?, 37 J. Copyright Soc'y 1 (1989); Newman, Not the End of History: The Second Circuit Struggles with Fair Use, 37 J. Copyright Soc'y 12 (1989). Some of these articles are highly critical of the state of the law with respect to the fair use doctrine and offer suggestions for improvement. But, our task is to apply as best we can the teachings of the governing precedents as we understand them."

and fairly has never been rejected even as to unpublished writings in any holding of the Supreme Court or of this Court."[195] Judge Miner concurred in the denial, arguing that the language in the panel opinion was "consistent with settled law": "I question whether judges, rather than literary critics, should decide whether literary material is used to enliven a text or demonstrate truth. It is far too easy for one author to use another's work on the pretext that it is copied for the latter purpose rather than the former."[196]

[h] **Photocopying—Library Copying.** The advent of low cost photocopying machines spawned unique problems for copyright law. Is copying of significant portions of works "for personal use" fair use? Can mechanisms for efficient enforcement of copyright against improper use of copy machines be devised? No clear, universally-accepted answers have emerged.

[i] *Library Photocopying—Williams & Wilkins.* In *Williams & Wilkins,*[197] the Court of Claims, in a questionable decision, held that massive, systematic photocopying by government research libraries was fair use. The Supreme Court granted the plaintiff's petition for certiorari but affirmed by an equally divided vote.[198] That the issue presented was a difficult one is confirmed by the fact that the 15 judges considering it (7 in the Court of Claims and 8 in the Supreme Court) split 8 to 7. Subsequent to *Williams,* Congress included in the 1976 Act a specific provision on library photocopying,[199] but it did not deal with the general problem of photocopying.

A medical journal publisher sued the United States, contending that the photocopying practices of the National Institute of Health (NIH) library and the National Library of Medicine infringed its journal article copyrights. The NIH employs over 4000 scientific researchers. The court described the NIH library's photocopying system as follows:

> "The library is open to the public, but is used mostly by NIH in-house research personnel. The library's budget for 1970 was $1.1 million; of this about $85,000 was for the purchase of journal materials.
>
> ". . . The library subscribes to two copies of . . . journals. . . . As a general rule, one copy stays in the library reading room and the other copy circulates . . . Demand by NIH research works for access to plaintiff's journals . . . is usually not met by in-house subscription copies. Consequently, . . . the library runs a photocopy service for the benefit of its research staff. On request, a researcher can obtain a photocopy of an article from . . . journals.

---

[195] 884 F.2d at 633, 12 U.S.P.Q.2d at 1124.

[196] 884 F.2d at 660, 12 U.S.P.Q.2d at 1122.

[197] Williams & Wilkins Co. v. United States, 487 F.2d 1345, 180 U.S.P.Q. 49 (Ct. Cl. 1973), *aff'd by an equally divided Court,* 420 U.S. 376, 184 U.S.P.Q. 705 (1975).

The permissibility of photocopying for classroom use arose in Wihtol v. Crow, 309 F.2d 777 (8th Cir. 1962), discussed at § 4F[3][e].

[198] If the Supreme Court affirms by an equally-divided vote, its decision has no precedential value. The Court of Claims decision remains as precedent at the intermediate appellate court level.

[199] 17 U.S.C. § 108.

. . . Usually, researchers request photocopies . . . to assist them in their on-going projects; sometimes photocopies are requested simply for background reading. . . . The photocopies are not returned to the library. . . .

"The library's policy is that, as a rule, only a single copy of a journal article will be made per request and each request is limited to about 40 to 50 pages, though exceptions may be . . . made in the case of long articles . . . Also, as a general rule, requests for photocopying are limited to only a single article from a journal issue. Exceptions to this rule are routinely made, so long as substantially less than an entire journal is photocopied, i.e., less than about half of the journal. Coworkers can, and frequently do, request single copies of the same article and such requests are honored."[200]

The system resulted in a substantial amount of copying: "In 1970, . . . the library filled 85,744 requests for photocopies of journal articles . . . , constituting about 930,000 pages. On the average, a journal article is 10 pages long, so that, in 1970, the library made about 93,000 photocopies of articles."

The National Library of Medicine ("NLM") is a "librarians' library." The court describes the NLM "interlibrary loan" program as follows:

"Upon request, NLM will loan to such institutions, for a limited time, books and other materials in its collection. In the case of journals the 'loans' usually take the form of photocopies of journal articles which are supplied by NLM free of charge and on a no-return basis. NLM's 'loan' policies are fashioned after the General Interlibrary Loan Code, which is a statement of self-imposed regulations to be followed by all libraries which cooperate in interlibrary loaning. . . . NLM, therefore, will provide only one photocopy of a particular article, per request, and will not photocopy on any given request an entire journal issue. Each photocopy reproduced by NLM contains a statement in the margin, 'This is a single photostatic copy made by the National Library of Medicine for purposes of study or research in lieu of lending the original.'

"In recent years NLM's stated policy has been not to fill requests for copies of articles from any of 104 journals which are included in a so-called 'widely-available list.' . . . A rejection on the basis of the 'widely-available list' is made only if the article requested was published during the preceding 5 years, but requests from Government libraries are not refused on the basis of the 'widely-available list.'

"Also, NLM's policy is not to honor an excessive number of requests from an individual or an institution. As a general rule, not more than 20 requests from an individual, or not more than 30 requests from an institution, within a month, will be honored. In 1968, NLM adopted the policy that no more than one article from a single journal issue, or three from a journal volume, would be copied. . . . Generally, requests for more than 50 pages of material will not be honored, though exceptions are sometimes made, particularly for Government institutions. Requests for more than one copy of a journal article are rejected, without exception.

---

[200] 487 F.2d at 1347–48.

(Matthew Bender & Co., Inc.)

"In 1968, a representative year, NLM received about 127,000 requests for interlibrary loans. Requests were received, for the most part, from other libraries or Government agencies. However, about 12 percent of the requests came from private or commercial organizations, particularly drug companies. . . . If the 'loan' was made by photocopy, the photocopy was given to the patron who was free to dispose of it as he wished. NLM made no effort to find out the ultimate use to which the photocopies were put; and there is no evidence that borrowing libraries kept the 'loan' photocopies in their permanent collections for use by other patrons."[201]

In a split 4-3 decision with three lengthy opinions, the Court of Claims held that, under the particular facts of the case, the library photocopying was fair use. In the opinion for the majority, Judge Davis took as "givens" certain "customary facts of copyright-life."

"Some forms of copying, at the very least of portions of a work, are universally deemed immune from liability, although the very words are reproduced in more than *de minimis* quantity. Furthermore, it is almost unanimously accepted that a scholar can make a handwritten copy of an entire copyrighted article for his own use, and in the era before photoduplication it was not uncommon (and not seriously questioned) that he could have his secretary make a typed copy for his personal use and files."[202]

Judge Davis then stated "summarily, in advance, three propositions we shall consider at greater length."

"First, plaintiff has not in our view shown, and there is inadequate reason to believe, that it is being or will be harmed substantially by these specific practices of NIH and NLM; second, we are convinced that medicine and medical research will be injured by holding these particular practices to be an infringement; and, third, since the problem of accommodating the interests of science with those of the publishers (and authors) calls fundamentally for legislative solution or guidance, which has not yet been given, we should not, during the period before congressional action is forthcoming, place such a risk of harm upon science and medicine."[203]

Judge Davis discusses eight elements. The eight, neither singly nor cumulatively, support the majority's controversial holding.

(1) *Nonprofit Status of the User Institutions.* "NIH and NLM were nonprofit institutions whose purpose in duplicating was to further scientific research."[204]

---

201 487 F.2d at 1348.

202 487 F.2d at 1350.

203 487 F.2d at 1354.

204 487 F.2d at 1354. The court noted:

"On both sides—library and requester—scientific progress, untainted by any commercial gain from the reproduction, is the hallmark of the whole enterprise of duplication. There has been no attempt to misappropriate the work of earlier scientific writers for forbidden ends, but rather an effort to gain easier access to the material for study and research. This is important because it is settled that, in general, the law gives copying for scientific purposes a wide scope." *Id.*

This proves little; virtually every major library is "nonprofit." Also, at least 12% of NLM's copying loans were to private organizations, including drug companies.

(2) Self-Imposed Limitations on Copying. "Both libraries have declared and enforced reasonably strict limitations which, to our mind, keep the duplication within appropriate confines."[205]

Rarely does the law give persons the right to establish unilaterally what constitutes reasonable conduct.

(3) Longstanding Practice of Library Photocopying. "[L]ibrary photocopying, though not of course to the extent of the modern development, has been going on ever since the 1909 Act was adopted."[206]

This element's weight is diluted by the court's admission that prior understandings as to the permissibility of copying predate the development of modern photocopying equipment, which makes massive copying feasible.

(4) Harm to Science. "There is no doubt in our minds that medical science would be seriously hurt if such library photocopying were stopped."[207]

---

[205] 487 F.2d at 1354. As to plaintiff's argument that the defendant's copying was large in absolute terms, the court responded:

> "The important factor is not the absolute amount, but the twin elements of (i) the existence and purpose of the system of limitations imposed and enforced, and (ii) the effectiveness of that system to confine the duplication for the personal use of scientific personnel who need the material for their work, with the minimum of potential abuse or harm to the copyright owner." 487 F.2d at 1355.

The court viewed the libraries' copying policies as equivalent to providing copying machines for the convenience of individual readers, a practice long followed by the Library of Congress.

[206] 487 F.2d at 1355. The court noted:

> "The fact that photocopying by libraries of entire articles was done with hardly any (and at most very minor) complaint, until about 10 or 15 years ago, goes a long way to show both that photoduplication cannot be designated as infringement per se, and that there was at least a time when photocopying, as then carried on, was 'fair use.' There have been, of course, considerable changes in the ease and extent of such reproduction, and these developments bear on 'fair use' as of today, but the libraries can properly stand on the proposition that they photocopied articles for many years, without significant protest, and that such copying was generally accepted until the proliferation of inexpensive and improved copying machines, less than two decades ago, led to the surge in such duplication. The question then becomes whether this marked increase in volume changes a use which was generally accepted as 'fair' into one which has now become 'unfair.' " 487 F.2d at 1356.

[207] 487 F.2d at 1356. The court noted:

> "We do not spend time and space demonstrating this proposition. It is admitted by plaintiff and conceded on all sides. . . . The supply of reprints and back numbers is wholly inadequate; the evidence shows the unlikelihood of obtaining such substitutes for photocopies from publishers of medical journals or authors of journal articles, especially for articles over three years old. . . . It is, moreover, wholly unrealistic to expect scientific personnel to subscribe regularly to large numbers of journals which would only occasionally contain articles of interest to them. Nor will libraries purchase extensive numbers of whole subscriptions to all medical journals on the chance that an indeterminate number

The court fails to pinpoint any harm to research other than making it marginally more expensive because of a license royalty obligation that a copyright owner might impose. Copyright always tends to reduce distribution and usage and increase the cost of the copyrighted work.

(5) *Absence of Harm to Copyright Owner.* "[W]e cannot mechanically . . . hold that the amount of photoduplication proved here 'must' lead to financial or economic harm. This is a matter of proof and plaintiff has not transformed its hypothetical assumption, by evidence, into a proven fact."[208]

The court applies a double standard on proof of "harm." It presumes scientific research would be harmed if the fair use claim is denied but dismisses as "speculative" that the copyright owner will suffer economic harm if the fair use claim is granted. Professor Nimmer charges that the court confuses "the issues of damages and liability": "It is often difficult for a plaintiff to prove actual damages against a given defendant. Far from this justifying a defense of fair use, failure to prove damages will in the usual case give rise to a minimum statutory damages liability."[209] Nimmer argues that the test should be whether plaintiff would be harmed if all potential defendants situated similarly to the actual defendant followed similar practices. The Supreme Court's discussion of "harm" in the *Sony* decision supports this view.[210]

(6) *Feasibility of a Licensing Scheme.* "Plaintiff's answer is that it is willing to license the libraries, on payment of a reasonable royalty, to continue photocopying as they have. Our difficulty with that response—in addition to the absence of proof that plaintiff has yet been hurt, and the twin doubts whether plaintiff has a viable license system and whether any satisfactory program can be created without legislation—is that the 1909 Act does not provide for compulsory licensing in this field."[211]

---

of articles in an indeterminate number of issues will be requested at indeterminate times. The result of a flat proscription on library photocopying would be, we feel sure, that medical and scientific personnel would simply do without, and have to do without, many of the articles they now desire, need, and use in their work." 487 F.2d at 1356–57.

[208] 487 F.2d at 1359. The court relied in part on testimony that plaintiff's publishing business was growing in sales and profitability.

"[Plaintiff's] argument . . . is that there 'must' be an effect because photocopies supplant the original articles, and if there were no photocopying those who now get the copies would necessarily buy the journals or issues. But this untested hypothesis, reminiscent of the abstract theorems beloved of the 'pure' classical economics of 70 or 80 years ago, is neither obvious nor self-proving. One need not enter the semantic debate over whether the photocopy supplants the original article itself or is merely in substitution for the library's loan of the original issue to recognize, as we have already pointed out, that there are other possibilities. If photocopying were forbidden, the researchers, instead of subscribing to more journals or trying to obtain or buy back-issues or reprints (usually unavailable), might expend extra time in note-taking or waiting their turn for the library's copies of the original issues—or they might very well cut down their reading and do without much of the information they now get through NLM's and NIH's copying system." 487 F.2d at 1358.

[209] Nimmer, Copyrights § 13.05[E][4][c].

[210] *See* § 4F[3][a].

[211] 487 F.2d at 1360.

A court cannot directly "order" licensing, but it can do so indirectly. A court of equity has traditional powers to shape remedies in the public interest—and specifically to refuse an injunction that would unduly harm the public interest. This in effect remits the plaintiff to a damage award, which could be based on a reasonable royalty. The court gives no reason why the self-interest of copyright owners and the free market system would not combine to make compensated copying possible and affordable.

(7) *The View of Congress.* The court cited a report of a committee of the House of Representatives, issued in the course of the revision of the 1909 Copyright, which stated that "Unauthorized library copying, like everything else, must be judged a fair use or an infringement on the basis of all the applicable criteria and the facts of the particular case." [212]

(8) *Practice in Other Countries.* The court cited the treatment of photocopying in the copyright laws of several other countries as "highly persuasive that the copying done here should be considered "fair use,' not an infringement."

Concluding that the above eight elements fused together show that the libraries' activities constituted fair use, the court emphasized "four interrelated aspects of our holding."

> "The first is that the conclusion that defendant's particular use of plaintiff's copyrighted material has been 'fair' rests upon all of the elements . . . , supra, and not upon any one, or any combination less than all. . . .

> "Connected with this point is the second one that our holding is restricted to the type and context of use by NIH and NLM, as shown by this record.

> "The third facet articulates the same general premise—our holding rests upon this record which fails to show a significant detriment to plaintiff but does demonstrate injury to medical and scientific research if photocopying of this kind is held unlawful.

. . .

> "Finally, but not at all least, we underline again the need for Congressional treatment of the problems of photocopying."

[ii] *Library Photocopying—Section 108.* In the 1976 Act, Congress did not include a specific provision dealing with photocopying in general. [213] It did include Section 108 on library and archival copying, [214] a highly detailed provision with layers of

---

[212] H.R. Rep. No. 83, 90th Cong., 1st Sess. 36 (1967).

[213] In 1974, Congress created a "National Commission on New Technological Uses of Copyrighted Works" (CONTU) to study, *inter alia,* "the reproduction and use of copyrighted works of authorship . . . by various forms of machine reproduction, not including reproduction by or at the request of instructors for use in face-to-face teaching." P.L. 93–573, 93d Cong. (1974). At the time of the enactment of the 1976 Act, CONTU had not finished its work. In its final report, issued July 31, 1978, CONTU did not recommend specific legislation relating to photocopying.

[214] 17 U.S.C. § 108.

The House Report sets forth the relationship between the general fair use provision, Section 107, and Section 108:

qualifications.[215]

(Text continued on page 4-223)

"The doctrine of fair use applies to library photocopying, and nothing contained in section 108 'in any way affects the right of fair use.' No provision of section 108 is intended to take away any rights existing under the fair use doctrine. To the contrary, section 108 authorizes certain photocopying practices which may not qualify as a fair use.

"The criteria of fair use are necessarily set forth in general terms. In the application of the criteria of fair use to specific photocopying practices of libraries, it is the intent of this legislation to provide an appropriate balancing of the rights of creators, and the needs of users." H.R. Rep. No. 94–1476, 94th Cong., 2d Sess. 74 (1976).

[215] The statute is as follows:

"17 U.S.C. § 108. Limitations on exclusive rights: Reproduction by Libraries and Archives

"(a) Notwithstanding the provisions of section 106, it is not an infringement of copyright for a library or archives, or any of its employees acting within the scope of their employment, to reproduce no more than one copy or phonorecord of a work, or to distribute such copy or phonorecord, under the conditions specified by this section, if-

(1) the reproduction or distribution is made without any purpose of direct or indirect commercial advantage;

(2) the collections of the library or archives are (i) open to the public, or (ii) available not only to researchers affiliated with the library or archives or with the institution of which it is a part, but also to other persons doing research in a specialized field; and

(3) the reproduction or distribution of the work includes a notice of copyright.

"(b) The rights of reproduction and distribution under this section apply to a copy or phonorecord of an unpublished work duplicated in facsimile form solely for purposes of preservation and security or for deposit for research use in another library or archives of the type described by clause (2) of subsection (a), if the copy or phonorecord reproduced is currently in the collections of the library or archives.

"(c) The right of reproduction under this section applies to a copy or phonorecord of a published work duplicated in facsimile form solely for the purpose of replacement of a copy or phonorecord that is damaged, deteriorating, lost, or stolen, if the library or archives has, after a reasonable effort, determined that an unused replacement cannot be obtained at a fair price.

"(d) The rights of reproduction and distribution under this section apply to a copy, made from the collection of a library or archives where the user makes his or her request or from that of another library or archives, of no more than one article or other contribution to a copyrighted collection or periodical issue, or to a copy or phonorecord of a small part of any other copyrighted work, if-

(1) the copy or phonorecord becomes the property of the user, and the library or archives has had no notice that the copy or phonorecord would be used for any purpose other than private study, scholarship, or research; and

(2) the library or archives displays prominently, at the place where orders are accepted, and includes on its order form, a warning of copyright in accordance with requirements that the Register of Copyrights shall prescribe by regulation.

"(e) The rights of reproduction and distribution under this section apply to the entire work, or to a substantial part of it, made from the collection of a library or archives where the user makes his or her request or from that of another library or archives, if the library or archives has first determined, on the basis of a reasonable investigation, that a copy or phonorecord of the copyrighted work cannot be obtained at a fair price, if-

(1) the copy or phonorecord becomes the property of the user, and the library or archives has had no notice that the copy or phonorecord would be used for any purpose other than private study, scholarship, or research; and

(Text continued on page 4–223)

(2) the library or archives displays prominently, at the place where orders are accepted, and includes on its order form, a warning of copyright in accordance with requirements that the Register of Copyrights shall prescribe by regulation.

"(f) Nothing in this section-

(1) shall be construed to impose liability for copyright infringement upon a library or archives or its employees for the unsupervised use of reproducing equipment located on its premises: Provided, That such equipment displays a notice that the making of a copy may be subject to the copyright law;

(2) excuses a person who uses such reproducing equipment or who requests a copy or phonorecord under subsection (d) from liability for copyright infringement for any such act, or for any later use of such copy or phonorecord, if it exceeds fair use as provided by section 107;

(3) shall be construed to limit the reproduction and distribution by lending of a limited number of copies and excerpts by a library or archives of an audiovisual news program, subject to clauses (1), (2), and (3) of subsection (a); or

(4) in any way affects the right of fair use as provided by section 107, or any contractual obligations assumed at any time by the library or archives when it obtained a copy or phonorecord of a work in its collections.

"(g) The rights of reproduction and distribution under this section extend to the isolated and unrelated reproduction or distribution of a single copy or phonorecord of the same material on separate occasions, but do not extend to cases where the library or archives, or its employee-

(1) is aware or has substantial reason to believe that it is engaging in the related or concerted reproduction or distribution of multiple copies or phonorecords of the same material, whether made on one occasion or over a period of time, and whether intended for aggregate use by one or more individuals or for separate use by the individual members of a group; or

(2) engages in the systematic reproduction or distribution of single or multiple copies or phonorecords of material described in subsection (d): Provided, That nothing in this clause prevents a library or archives from participating in interlibrary arrangements that do not have, as their purpose or effect, that the library or archives receiving such copies or phonorecords for distribution does so in such aggregate quantities as to substitute for a subscription to or purchase of such work.

"(h) The rights of reproduction and distribution under this section do not apply to a musical work, a pictorial, graphic or sculptural work, or a motion picture or other audiovisual work other than an audiovisual work dealing with news, except that no such limitation shall apply with respect to rights granted by subsections (b) and (c), or with respect to pictorial or graphic works published as illustrations, diagrams, or similar adjuncts to works of which copies are reproduced or distributed in accordance with subsections (d) and (e).

"(i) Five years from the effective date of this Act, and at five-year intervals thereafter, the Register of Copyrights, after consulting with representatives of authors, book and periodical publishers, and other owners of copyrighted materials, and with representatives of library users and librarians, shall submit to the Congress a report setting forth the extent to which this section has achieved the intended statutory balancing of the rights of creators, and the needs of users. The report should also describe any problems that may have arisen, and present legislative or other recommendations, if warranted."

[4] Other Defenses

[a] **Invalidity.** Copyright invalidity is a defense to an infringement charge. Compared to patents, copyright invalidity is less often raised or sustained, primarily because copyright law's originality standard is less onerous and complex than patent law's novelty and nonobviousness standards.

Section 410(c) establishes a validity presumption for registered copyrights.

> "In any judicial proceedings the certificate of registration made before or within five years after first publication of the work shall constitute prima facie evidence of the validity of the copyright and of the facts stated in the certificate. The evidentiary weight to be accorded the certificate of registration made thereafter shall be within the discretion of the court."[216]

The presumption shifts the evidentiary burden of proving invalidity to the accused infringer[217] but, unlike patent law's validity presumption,[218] carries little weight in enforcement suits because the Copyright Office does not conduct extensive examination of copyright claims; unlike the Patent and Trademark Office, which conducts a prior art search and makes an initial determination of novelty and unobviousness,[219] the Copyright Office does not independently assess originality.[220] Though it does determine whether proffered works are copyrightable subject matter, such matters are primarily questions of law.

In *Masquerade Novelty*,[221] in holding that plaintiff's "nose masks" were not uncopyrightable useful articles,[222] the court stressed that the presumption "is not an

---

[216] 17 U.S.C. § 410(c).

See also H. R. Rep. No. 94–1476, 94th Cong., 2d Sess. 157 (1976):

"The principle that a certificate represents prima facie evidence of copyright validity has been established in a long line of court decisions and is a sound one. It is true that, unlike a patent claim, a claim to copyright is not examined for basic validity before a certificate is issued. On the other hand, endowing a copyright claimant who has obtained a certificate with a rebuttable presumption of the validity of the copyright does not deprive the defendant in an infringement suit of any rights; it merely orders the burdens of proof. The plaintiff should not ordinarily be forced in the first instance to prove all of the multitude of facts that underlie the validity of the copyright unless the defendant, by effectively challenging them, shifts the burden of doing so to the plaintiff."

[217] *E.g.,* Hasbro Bradley, Inc. v. Sparkle Toys, Inc., 780 F.2d 189, 192, 228 U.S.P.Q. 423, 424 (2d Cir. 1985); Oboler v. Golden, 714 F.2d 211, 212, 220 U.S.P.Q. 166, 167 (2d Cir. 1983) ("Once [plaintiff] established the fact of copyright ownership and infringement, the burden of proof shifted to [defendant] to show invalidity or waiver of the copyright.").

[218] *See* § 2F[4][a][i].

[219] *See* § 2D[1].

[220] *Cf.* Midway Mfg. Co. v. Bandai-America, Inc., 546 F. Supp. 125, 143, 216 U.S.P.Q. 812, 824 (D. N.J. 1982) (rejecting argument that "17 U.S.C. § 410(a) requires the Copyright Office to conduct . . . an examination for, inter alia, originality").

[221] Masquerade Novelty, Inc. v. Unique Industries, Inc., 912 F.2d 663, 15 U.S.P.Q.2d 1881 (3d Cir. 1990).

[222] *See* § 4C[3][d].

insurmountable one," especially when "the only issue is the copyrightability of a particular article that . . . is incontestably original." [223]

> "The burden on the defendant to rebut the presumption varies depending on the issue bearing on the validity of the copyright. Where, for example, the issue is whether the copyrighted article is 'original,' the presumption will not be overcome unless the defendant offers proof that the plaintiff's product was copied from other works or similarly probative evidence as to originality. . . . Where, as is the case here, the issue is whether particular articles with certain undisputed characteristics are copyrightable, the defendant need not introduce evidence but instead must show that the Copyright Office erroneously applied the copyright laws in registering plaintiff's articles.
>
> . . . .
>
> "Absent an indication from the Copyright Office as to why it registered the nose masks, or the existence of a controlling administrative regulation or interpretation of 17 U.S.C. § 101, the only deference we can give to the Copyright Office's expertise in questions of copyright law . . . and the only meaning we can give to § 410(c) is to place the burden on [defendant] to show that the articles are not copyrightable." [224]

[b] Inequitable Conduct in Registration Procurement. Fraud or inequitable conduct in copyright registration procurement is a defense to an infringement charge. [225] "It has been consistently held that a plaintiff's knowing failure to advise the Copyright Office of facts that might have led to the rejection of a registration application constitutes grounds for holding the registration invalid and incapable of supporting

---

[223] 912 F.2d at 669, n.7, 15 U.S.P.Q.2d 1886 n.7.

See also Carol Barnhart, Inc. v. Economy Cover Corp., 773 F.2d 411, 414 (2d Cir.1985) ("While the expertise of the Copyright Office is in 'interpretation of the law and its application to the facts presented by the copyright application,' . . . it is permissible for the district court itself to consider how the copyright law applies to the articles under consideration."); Durham Industries, Inc. v. Tomy Corp., 630 F.2d 905, 908, 208 U.S.P.Q. 10, 13 (2d Cir. 1980) ("a certificate of registration creates no irrebuttable presumption of copyright validity").

Compare Norris Industries, Inc. v. International Telephone & Telegraph Corp., 696 F.2d 918, 922, 217 U.S.P.Q. 226, 229 (11th Cir. 1983) (in finding ornamental wire wheels not copyrightable, the district court properly "gave some deference to the expertise of the Register [of Copyright] in its decision" to refuse registration):

> "The expertise relied on is not technical expertise in the use of the article submitted for registration but expertise in the interpretation of the law and its application to the facts presented by the copyright application. The Copyright Office has been concerned with the distinction between copyrightable and uncopyrightable works of art since the Copyright Act of 1870 characterized copyrightable subject matter as works of fine arts. . . .
>
> "These determinations are routinely made by the Register and are unquestionably related to the substantive area of the agency's business. . . . This is not to say that the Court should simply accept the Register's decision without question. But our view of the uncontradicted evidence and the graphic description of the wheel cover reveals no abuse of administrative discretion by the Register."

[224] 912 F.2d at 668–69, n.7, 15 U.S.P.Q.2d at 1885–86, n.7.

[225] For a discussion of fraud and inequitable conduct in patent and trademark registration procurement, see §§ 2D[2] and 5F[2][b].

an infringement action."[226] The defense is less significant in copyright cases than in patent cases, primarily because Copyright Office examination is more limited than Patent and Trademark Office examination.[227]

A number of decisions involve alleged failure to disclose that the copyrighted work was derived from a prior work.[228] In *Russ Berrie,*[229] plaintiff registered copyright in its plush toy animal, "Gonga," a thumb-sucking stuffed gorilla. "Gonga" was a close copy of a pre-existing uncopyrighted work, a Japanese gorilla named "Gori-Gori." The copyright registration form requested the following information:

> "6. COMPILATION OR DERIVATIVE WORK: . . .
>
> "(PREEXISTING MATERIAL): (Identify any preexisting work or works that this work is based on or inccrporates) . . .
>
> "(MATERIAL ADDED TO THIS WORK): (Give a brief, general statement of the material that has been added to this work and in which copyright is claimed.)"

Plaintiff entered "not applicable" in Item 6. The district court found that the copyright owner's knowing failure to disclose the prior art origin of the work to the Copyright Office nullified the registration and rendered the copyright unenforceable.

> "Where as here the question of originality is a close one, a decision to grant or deny protection made in the first instance by the agency charged with administering the copyright laws would have been highly persuasive evidence of copyright validity. . . . The presumption of validity attaching to copyright registration is of course a function of judicial deference to the agency's expertise. Here, however, the Copyright Office had no opportunity to pass on plaintiff's claim accurately presented. The knowing failure to advise the Copyright Office of facts which might have occasioned a rejection of the application constitute reason for holding the registration invalid and thus incapable of supporting an infringement action . . . or denying enforcement on the ground of unclean hands. . . . "[230]

---

[226] Masquerade Novelty, Inc. v. Unique Industries, Inc., 912 F.2d 663, 667, 15 U.S.P.Q.2d 1881, 1884–85 (3d Cir. 1990).

[227] *See* § 4F[4][a].

[228] *E.g.,* Past Pluto Productions Corp. v. Dana, 627 F. Supp. 1435, 1440 n.5, 228 U.S.P.Q. 919, 922 n.5 (S.D. N.Y. 1986) ("the presumption of the validity of plaintiff's copyright is specifically endangered by Past Pluto's failure to alert the Copyright Office to the Crown of Liberty's relationship to a prior work, the Statue of Liberty. . . . When a copyright claimant fails to advise the Copyright Office of the existence of a prior work in the public domain, the Office is not afforded fair opportunity to pass upon the question of originality in relation to the prior work."); Knickerbocker Toy Co., Inc. v. Winterbrook Corp., 554 F. Supp. 1309, 1310, 216 U.S.P.Q. 621, 623 (D. N.H. 1982) (involving "the copyright status of two of America's most beloved and well-known dolls, Raggedy Ann and Raggedy Andy."); Vogue Ring Creations, Inc. v. Hardman, 410 F. Supp. 609 (D. R.I. 1976).

For a discussion of the originality requirement as applied to works based on prior works, see § 4C[5][b].

[229] Russ Berrie & Co. v. Jerry Elsner Co., 482 F. Supp. 980, 205 U.S.P.Q. 320 (S.D. N.Y. 1980).

[230] 482 F. Supp. at 988.

The court found the owner's omission intentional.[231] The owner knew of the pre-existing work and followed a conscious policy not to disclose to the Copyright Office such pre-existing works on which his designs were based. His assertion that he believed the gorilla to be a "wholly original design" was not credible given the minor character of the changes made in creating the copyrighted gorilla.

In *Whimsicality,*[232] the registrant misrepresented facts material to whether the works were useful articles not subject to copyright. Plaintiff marketed distinctive costumes. It submitted an application to register six of its creations: "Pumpkin," "Bee," "Penguin," "Spider," "Hippo Ballerina" and "Tyrannosaurus Rex," describing them as "soft sculptures" and submitting photographs of the costumes laid out on a flat surface. In plaintiff's commercial advertising, these "sculptures" were modelled by children. Plaintiff's attorney admitted that the Copyright Office would probably reject an application to register a "children's pumpkin costume" because apparel items are uncopyrightable unless they embody separate design elements.[233] The court held that the plaintiff's use of the term "soft sculpture" and its submission of the flat-form photographs constituted "fraud on the Copyright Office."

> "While the pictorial, graphic and sculptural aspects of useful articles may be copyrightable if they are separable from the article, physically or conceptually, . . . clothes are particularly unlikely to meet that test—the very decorative elements that stand out being intrinsic to the decorative function of the clothing. . . . In any event, the useful articles standing alone may never be registered. The registration must describe the separable elements. See Compendium

---

[231] *Compare* JBJ Fabrics, Inc. v. Brylane, Inc., 714 F. Supp. 107, 12 U.S.P.Q.2d 1839, 1840 (S.D. N.Y. 1989) ("Defendant contends that because the JBJ fabric design is based upon the Farkas painting, a painting that JBJ purchased without obtaining any formal writing assigning it a copyright in the underlying design, plaintiff is not the author of its design, and therefore its registration is invalid. . . . While it is true that plaintiff cannot hold a copyright in the Farkas design, it may nevertheless hold a copyright in a derivative work based on that design. . . . The fact that the design was not registered as a derivative work does not automatically invalidate plaintiff's registration. *See L. Batlin & Son, Inc. v. Snyder,* 536 F.2d 486, 490 n. 2 (2d Cir.1976) (*en banc*) (mere error in classification insufficient to invalidate registration). If, of course, plaintiff deliberately falsified its registration that registration would indeed be invalid. . . . However, whether plaintiff had the requisite scienter for a finding of fraud is a factual issue which cannot be resolved on this motion for summary judgment.").

[232] Whimsicality, Inc. v. Rubie's Costume Co., Inc., 891 F.2d 452, 13 U.S.P.Q.2d 1296 (2d Cir. 1989).

See also Kenbrooke Fabrics, Inc. v. Soho Fashions, Inc., 13 U.S.P.Q.2d 1472, 1477 (S.D. N.Y. 1989) (plaintiff obtained Copyright Office certification of transfer of copyright ownership by submitting certificate without factual basis: "At the very least, the certification submitted to the Copyright Office should have put on paper the entire 'situation' of which the document analyst in that office allegedly was 'well aware.' This 'failure to advise the Copyright Office of facts which might have occasioned a rejection of the application constitute[s] reason for holding the . . . [transfer of copyright] invalid and thus incapable of supporting an infringement action . . . or denying enforcement on the ground of unclean hands.' . . . [Plaintiff's] failure to turn square corners with the Copyright Office renders the transfer, if it did occur, unenforceable.").

[233] *See* § 4C[3][c].

II of Copyright Office Practices § 505.02 (1984). Appellant argues that although clothing may not be copyrightable, masquerade costumes are an exception to that general rule. In view of our disposition of this matter we need not address that contention.

"Whimsicality does not assert that it is ignorant of the prior case law as to the copyrightability of garments, or of the practices of the Copyright Office. It was aware, therefore, that an application for costumes as such would be rejected. The admission of Whimsicality's attorney before the district court proves as much. Anticipating rejection, Whimsicality had several options. It could have commenced an action for a declaratory judgment to compel the Copyright Office to change its classification of costumes as per se uncopyrightable. More practically, it could have acknowledged in its application that the articles in question were costumes, and have requested registration for only the features it claimed were separable.

"Instead Whimsicality chose to classify its creations as soft sculptures with no useful function as wearable articles. Unlike a useful article, a sculpture, soft or hard, is inherently copyrightable, assuming it is an original work. *Mazer v. Stein*, 347 U.S. 201, 213–14, 74 S. Ct. 460, 468–69, 98 L. Ed. 630 (1954). Unfortunately for Whimsicality here, the evidence demonstrates not only that the costumes were not soft sculpture, but that Whimsicality knew full well that no reasonable observer could believe that the costumes were soft sculpture.

". . . The word sculpture implies a relatively firm form representing a particular concept. The costumes in question have no such form. If hung from a hook or laid randomly on a flat surface, the particular animal or item depicted by the costume would be largely unidentifiable. The intended depiction is in fact recognizable only when the costume is worn by a person or is carefully laid out on a flat surface to reveal that depiction. We conclude therefore that these costumes do not constitute sculpture."[234]

As with inequitable conduct in the patent field, the courts require that a misrepresentation or omission be material and made with some degree of culpable intent. In

---

[234] 891 F.2d at 455–56, 13 U.S.P.Q.2d at 1299–1300. *Compare* Masquerade Novelty, Inc. v. Unique Industries, Inc., 912 F.2d 663, 15 U.S.P.Q.2d 1881 (3d Cir. 1990). In *Masquerade Novelty*, the court found no fraud in plaintiff's registration of its "nose masks."

"[T]he Copyright Office could reasonably be expected to know that an article explicitly described as a nose mask was meant to be worn.

"Thus, this case is unlike the recent case of *Whimsicality, Inc. v. Rubie's Costume Co.*, 891 F.2d 452 (2d Cir.1989), in which an applicant received copyright registration certificates for Halloween costumes by describing them as 'soft sculptures' and by omitting the word 'costume' totally from its application. The court held that this was calculated to hide the fact that the articles for which a copyright was sought were costumes, a category of articles that are not copyrightable because of their utility as clothing. In this case, however, the term 'nose mask' accurately characterized the articles for which copyright registration was sought by Masquerade." 912 F.2d at 668 n.6, 15 U.S.P.Q.2d 1885 n.60.

There is something ironic in the two case captions: "Whimsicality" found evil conduct but "Masquerade" found nothing hidden.

Eckes,[235] plaintiff published "Sport Americana Baseball Card Price Guide," a comprehensive listing of 1909-1979 baseball cards. In an infringement suit, defendant argued that the validity presumption was "overcome" because plaintiff failed to include on its copyright registration application form information on its prior 1976 and 1978 publications.[236] The court ruled against defendant's contention for two reasons. First, the registered work "represented a substantial change from the 1976 and 1978 publications." In effect, this reason was want of materiality—disclosure of the omitted information clearly would not have affected the Copyright Office's decision.[237] Second, the applicants' omissions "were inadvertent and innocent." Courts refuse to invalidate registered copyrights because of "innocent" or "inadvertent" misstatements or omissions[238] or because of positions taken in good faith and

---

[235] Eckes v. Card Prices Update, 736 F.2d 859, 861–62, 222 U.S.P.Q. 762, 763–64 (2d Cir. 1984).

[236] The Copyright Office's registration form TX, which is for nondramatic literary works, contains the following questions:

> "Has registration for this work, or for an earlier version of this work, already been made in the Copyright Office?"

> [If the work is a derivative work,] [i]dentify any preexisting work or works that this work is based on or incorporates" and "Give a brief, general statement of the material that has been added to this work and in which copyright is claimed."

[237] *E.g.,* New York Chinese TV Programs, Inc. v. U.E. Enterprises, Inc., 1989 Copr. L. Dec. P. 26,398, 1989 WL 22442 (S.D. N.Y. 1989) ("defendants have failed to show that the submission of this information would have resulted in rejection of IAVC's applications. Assuming, arguendo, that the Copyright Office would consider the edited version a 'derivative work,' IAVC would at worst be required to register both the edited and unedited versions."); Dynamic Solutions, Inc. v. Planning & Control, Inc., 646 F. Supp. 1329, 1341 (S.D.N.Y. 1986) ("Nor is there any reason to believe that the Copyright Office might have rejected the registrations had [applicants] given 1986 as the date of creation and publication."); Wales Industrial Inc. v. Hasbro Bradley, Inc., 612 F. Supp. 510, 515, 226 U.S.P.Q. 584, 587 (S.D. N.Y. 1985) ("Hasbro's error, if any, would not be jurisdictional but a technical misdescription: it should have identified Takara rather than itself as the 'copyright claimant' on the registration applications it submitted. Such error could be readily corrected by Hasbro's filing supplementary registrations with the Copyright Office. . . . Since there is no indication that the claimed error was committed knowingly, and since identification of the copyright claimant as Takara rather than Hasbro would not have occasioned rejection of the applications by the Copyright Office, the alleged error would not require dismissal of Hasbro's infringement claims."); Kenbrooke Fabrics, Inc. v. Holland Fabrics, Inc., 602 F. Supp. 151, 153, 225 U.S.P.Q. 153 (S.D. N.Y. 1984) ("An error in the registration regarding the date of first publication . . . does not invalidate the copyright . . . absent a showing of fraud").

[238] *E.g.,* Original Appalachian Artworks, Inc. v. Toy Loft, Inc., 684 F.2d 821, 828, 215 U.S.P.Q. 745, 751 (11th Cir. 1982) ("While these cases establish that omissions or misrepresentations in a copyright application can render the registration invalid, a common element among them has been intentional or purposeful concealment of relevant information. Where this element of 'scienter' is lacking, courts generally have upheld the copyright."); Tonka Corp. v. Tsaisun, Inc., 1987 Copr.L.Dec. P. 26,055, 1 U.S.P.Q.2d 1387, 1398 (D. Minn. 1986) ("Only the 'knowing failure' to advise the Copyright Office of facts which might have caused a rejection of the application constitutes reason for invalidating a copyright."); National Broadcasting Co., Inc. v. Sonneborn, 630 F. Supp. 524, 231 U.S.P.Q. 513 (D. Conn. 1985); Iris Arc v. S.S. Sarna, Inc., 621 F. Supp. 916, 919, 229 U.S.P.Q. 25, 28 (E.D. N.Y. 1985) ("The copyright law may be technical, but it is not so fragile that plaintiff's possible errors in its applications will destroy its copyright protection in these works.").

with a reasonable basis.[239]

The cases do not clearly indicate what consequences should flow from material misrepresentations or omissions in the registration. For example, can a registrant cure any alleged fraud or inequitable conduct by submitting further information to the Copyright Office? Should an "innocent" misrepresentation or omission, which does not invalidate the copyright, nevertheless eliminate the presumption of validity, shifting the burden of proof to the copyright owner?[240]

[c] **Misuse.** Anticompetitive practices in connection with the licensing of copyrighted works may violate the federal antitrust laws.[241] Also, by analogy to patent

---

[239] *E.g.*, Flag Fables, Inc. v. Jean Ann's Country Flags & Crafts, Inc., 753 F. Supp. 1007 (D. Mass. 1990).

See also Videotronics, Inc. v. Bend Electronics, 586 F. Supp. 478, 485, 487, 223 U.S.P.Q. 936, 941–42 (D. Nev. 1984). In *Videotronics*, plaintiff registered a computer program, "Keno Keypad," leaving blank the registration form space for "Date and Nation of First Publication," even though the program had been distributed in circuit board form. The court found no bad faith.

> "Plaintiff's counsel, Mr. McKenna, is not a copyright specialist and had no meaningful experience in that area of the law. He testified that he read some statutes pertaining to the issue of registration . . . and that he spoke with an attorney from San Francisco who sent him a completed registration form to use as a sample.
> * * *
> "We conclude that plaintiff has met its burden of showing that Mr. McKenna in good faith sought and received advice concerning the necessity of putting a publication date on the application form, and that he satisfied himself in his own mind that that information need not be supplied. He can be criticized for not learning more about copyright law so that he could have prepared the applications properly and so have avoided the problem with which we are now faced. He may well have been mistaken in concluding that the publication date need not have been supplied. However, his failure to obtain a correct and definitive opinion on the issue of whether a program could be considered published, means only that he may have been negligent; it does not mean that he acted with fraudulent intent. . . . In the absence of fraud, his mistake is not a basis for invalidating the registration."

[240] Masquerade Novelty, Inc. v. Unique Industries, Inc., 912 F.2d 663, 668 n.5, 15 U.S.P.Q.2d 1881, 1885 n.5 (3d Cir. 1990) ("It may be that the correct approach in situations where there has been a material, but inadvertent omission, is to deprive the plaintiff of the benefits of § 410(c) and to require him to establish the copyrightability of the articles he claims are being infringed.").

[241] *E.g.*, Broadcast Music, Inc. v. Columbia Broadcasting System, Inc., 441 U.S. 1, 19 (1979) (the copyright laws "confer no rights on copyright owners . . . to violate the antitrust laws. . . . "); United States v. Paramount Pictures, Inc., 334 U.S. 131, 143, 158 (1948) ("a copyright may no more be used than a patent to deter competition between rivals in the exploitation of their licenses"; finding "block booking" of copyrighted motion pictures, that is, refusal to license one copyright unless another copyright is accepted, violates the antitrust laws: "The copyright law, like the patent statutes, makes reward to the owner a secondary consideration. . . . It is said that reward to the author or artist serves to induce release to the public of the products of his creative genius. But the reward does not serve its public purpose if it is not related to the quality of the copyright. Where a high quality film greatly desired is licensed only if an inferior one is taken, the latter borrows quality from the former and strengthens its monopoly by drawing on the other. The practice tends to equalize rather than differentiate the reward for the individual copyrights.").

law's *Walker Process* doctrine, decisions recognize that enforcement of a fraudulently registered copyright may be actionable monopolization.[242]

Less clear is whether "misuse" is a defense to copyright infringement. The misuse doctrine derives from the equity concept of "unclean hands."[243] In patent law, improper extension of a patent, for example, through a tying arrangement, is misuse, which is a defense to patent infringement without regard to whether the extension violates the antitrust laws or to whether the defendant asserting misuse can show injury.[244]

A number of Court of Appeals decisions assume misuse is a defense to copyright infringement but find no improper activity under the circumstances of the case.[245]

---

[242] *E.g.,* Knickerbocker Toy Co., Inc. v. Winterbrook Corp., 554 F. Supp. 1309, 1321, 216 U.S.P.Q. 621, 631 (D.N.H. 1982) ("Fraudulent procurement of a copyright by means of knowing and willful misrepresentations to the Copyright Office may strip a copyright holder of its exemption from the antitrust laws. . . . *Cf.* Walker Process Equipment, Inc. v. Food Machinery & Chemical Corporation, 382 U.S. 172 (1965) [*Walker Process* concerns the antitrust consequences of the fraudulent procurement of a patent. The Court considers the holding of *Walker Process* fully applicable to this copyright case.] . . . An allegation of fraudulent procurement alone is not sufficient to establish a § 2 violation, however; other elements of the monopolization or attempted monopolization claim must be present.").

[243] *See* Chisum, Patents § 19.04.

[244] *See* § 2F[4][c].

[245] *See* United Telephone of Missouri v. Johnson Publishing Co., Inc., 855 F.2d 604, 611–12, 8 U.S.P.Q.2d 1058, 1064 (8th Cir. 1988):

"Although the misuse defense has been raised in several cases, Johnson has cited no case in which the misuse of a copyright has been held to constitute a successful defense to copyright infringement. The court, however, has found several cases in which courts have noted that the misuse of a copyright, in violation of the antitrust laws, may bar a plaintiff from recovering damages for copyright infringement."

"In *F.E.L. Publications, Ltd. v. Catholic Bishop,* 506 F. Supp. 1127 (N.D. Ill. 1981), *rev'd,* 214 U.S.P.Q. 409 (7th Cir.), *cert. denied,* 459 U.S. 859, 103 S. Ct. 131, 74 L. Ed. 2d 113 (1982), the plaintiff, a publisher of hymnals containing its copyrighted songs, sued the legal representative of the Roman Catholic diocese of Chicago for copyright infringement. The plaintiff alleged that various Chicago area parishes, which had refused to purchase its 'annual copying license,' persisted in infringing its copyrights by using its hymns. The district court denied plaintiff's claim, holding that the plaintiff's license, which required purchasers to pay for a license in plaintiff's entire collection of 1400 copyrighted songs regardless of how many songs are copied, was a 'per se' violation of the Sherman Act. . . . The court of appeals reversed, and held that the plaintiff's licensing agreement did not violate the Sherman Act. . . . The court's analysis, however, recognized or acknowledged that misuse of a copyright, in violation of the antitrust laws, may be asserted as a defense in copyright infringement cases.

"In *Edward B. Marks Music Corp. v. Colorado Magnetics, Inc.,* 357 F. Supp. 280 (W.D. Okla. 1973), *rev'd,* 497 F.2d 285 (10th Cir.1974), *cert. denied,* 419 U.S. 1120, 95 S. Ct. 801, 42 L. Ed. 2d 819 (1975), the plaintiff, a music publisher, seeking damages and injunctive relief, sued the defendants for infringing some of its copyrighted musical compositions. In defense, among other things, the defendants alleged that plaintiff was guilty of 'inequitable conduct, unclean hands and misuse of its musical compositions.' . . . The district court denied relief, holding that plaintiff had licensed its musical compositions

In *Lasercomb America,*[246] the Fourth Circuit recognized and applied copyright misuse. Plaintiff Lasercomb developed a program, "Interact," for computer assisted cardboard box die making. Defendants bought four copies of the program, circumvented protective devices on the software, and made three copies of the program for use on its machines. Later, they developed and marketed a similar program. Plaintiff sued for copyright infringement and fraud. Defendants asserted a misuse defense, based on restrictive clauses in plaintiff's standard software copyright license. The clauses prevented the licensee from developing or selling any "computer assisted die making software."[247] The court noted that there was little authority on copyright misuse but reasoned that the similarities between patent and copyright law compelled it to apply misuse to copyright.

> "The few courts considering the issue have split on whether the defense should be recognized, . . . and we have discovered only one case which has actually applied copyright misuse to bar an action for infringement. *M. Witmark & Sons v. Jensen,* 80 F. Supp. 843 (D. Minn. 1948), *appeal dismissed,* 177 F.2d 515 (8th Cir.1949).

> ". . . [S]ince copyright and patent law serve parallel public interests, a 'misuse' defense should apply to infringement actions brought to vindicate either right. . . . [T]he similarity of the policies underlying patent and copyright is great and historically has been consistently recognized. Both patent law and copyright law seek to increase the store of human knowledge and arts by rewarding inventors and authors with the exclusive rights to their works for a limited time.

'in violation of the Anti-Trust Laws,' and that plaintiff's conduct constituted 'an abuse and misuse of the [its] copyright monopoly rendering [its] copyright monopoly in the musical compositions in suit unenforceable against the Defendants.' *Id.* at 287, 288. The court of appeals reversed, stating in part, [a]ssuming *arguendo* that an antitrust violation is a defense in a copyright infringement action, the record made in the trial court simply does not support its findings and conclusions.' . . . *see also Supermarket of Homes, Inc. v. San Fernando Valley Bd. of Realtors,* 786 F.2d 1400, 1408 (9th Cir.1986) (alleged conduct did not constitute misuse of copyright).

"On the assumption that judicial authority teaches that the patent misuse doctrine may be applied or asserted as a defense to copyright infringement, the stipulated facts in this case do not support Johnson's contention that United Telephone 'misused' its copyright."

As to whether the immoral nature of the copyrighted work's subject matter is grounds for withholding relief against infringement, see § 4C[1][f].

[246] Lasercomb America, Inc. v. Reynolds, 911 F.2d 970, 15 U.S.P.Q.2d 1846 (4th Cir. 1990).
[247] The clauses provided:

"D. Licensee agrees during the term of this Agreement that it will not permit or suffer its directors, officers and employees, directly or indirectly, to write, develop, produce or sell computer assisted die making software.

"E. Licensee agrees during the term of this Agreement and for one (1) year after the termination of this Agreement, that it will not write, develop, produce or sell or assist others in the writing, developing, producing or selling [of] computer assisted die making software, directly or indirectly without Lasercomb's prior written consent. Any such activity undertaken without Lasercomb's written consent shall nullify any warranties or agreements of Lasercomb set forth herein." 911 F.2d at 973, 15 U.S.P.Q.2d at 1849.

At the same time, the granted monopoly power does not extend to property not covered by the patent or copyright."[248]

In determining that the restrictive clauses were misuse, the court found it unnecessary to decide whether they violated the antitrust laws.

"[W]hile it is true that the attempted use of a copyright to violate antitrust law probably would give rise to a misuse of copyright defense, the converse is not necessarily true—a misuse need not be a violation of antitrust law in order to comprise an equitable defense to an infringement action. The question is not whether the copyright is being used in a manner violative of antitrust law (such as whether the licensing agreement is 'reasonable'), but whether the copyright is being used in a manner violative of the public policy embodied in the grant of a copyright.

"Lasercomb undoubtedly has the right to protect against copying of the Interact code. Its standard licensing agreement, however, goes much further and essentially attempts to suppress any attempt by the licensee to independently implement the idea which Interact expresses. . . . Although one or another licensee might succeed in negotiating out the noncompete provisions, this does not negate the fact that Lasercomb is attempting to use its copyright in a manner adverse to the public policy embodied in copyright law, and that it has succeeded in doing so with at least one licensee."[249]

Other courts may follow *Lasercomb America* in recognizing misuse as a defense, equating copyright to patent law, but may not necessarily apply all patent law's rules as to what is misuse. In *Saturday Evening Post*,[250] the Post licensed Rumbleseat to manufacture porcelain dolls derived from illustrations done by the artist Norman Rockwell and published by Post. The license agreement contained a clause forbidding the licensee from contesting the copyright's validity and requiring arbitration of controversies arising out of the license. (In patent law, a licensee is not estopped from contesting the patent's validity.)[251] After cancellation of the license, Rumbleseat continued to sell dolls, causing Post to invoke arbitration. The arbitrators granted relief to Post. Post sought confirmation of the arbitration award. The Seventh Circuit addressed "whether a clause in a copyright licensing agreement forbidding the licensee to contest the validity of the copyright he has licensed is against public policy, as expressed in the Copyright Act or other possible sources of federal common law, and is therefore unenforceable."

"Suppose the Rockwell illustrations really were in the public domain and both the Post and Rumbleseat knew it, but, also knowing that both would be better off without competition, they agreed to give Rumbleseat an exclusive license with a no-contest clause, hoping that no other potential competitor would discover the invalidity of the copyrights and challenge (or defy) them. Somewhat analogous practices involving patents have been alleged. . . . The danger of this kind of

---

[248] 911 F.2d at 976, 15 U.S.P.Q.2d at 1852.

[249] 911 F.2d at 978, 15 U.S.P.Q.2d at 1853.

[250] Saturday Evening Post Co. v. Rumbleseat Press, Inc., 816 F.2d 1191, 2 U.S.P.Q.2d 1499 (7th Cir. 1987).

[251] *See* D. Chisum, Patents § 19.02[3].

cozy deal would be less if the law forbade the Post to enforce the no-contest clause, so that Rumbleseat, if it changed its mind about the advantages of mutual forbearance, could go into competition with the Post notwithstanding the license.

"We cannot call this danger nonexistent, although we suspect it is slight given . . . the unlikelihood that a copyright (especially one that by hypothesis is invalid!) would confer an economically significant monopoly, one that would raise the price of the monopolized good well above, and depress its output well below, the competitive level. The danger is not so great, however, as to justify a rule of federal common law outlawing no-contest clauses without evidence of any monopolistic danger or effect. Such a clause serves a useful purpose in most cases. Without it the licensee always has a club over the licensor's head: the threat that if there is a dispute the licensee will challenge the copyright's validity. The threat would discourage copyright licensing and might therefore retard rather than promote the diffusion of copyrighted works. Also, a no-contest clause might actually accelerate rather than retard challenges to invalid copyrights, by making the would-be licensee think hard about validity before rather than after he signed the licensing agreement. Rumbleseat had, in fact, used its expressed doubts of the validity of the Post's copyrights to obtain a lower royalty rate in the negotiations for the license.

"What is needed is a balancing of the pros and cons of the clause in each case. That balancing is best done under antitrust law. Section 1 of the Sherman Act, 15 U.S.C. § 1, forbids contracts that restrain trade. If Rumbleseat had wanted, it could have attacked the no-contest clause under that statute. It did not do so. We decline to create a federal common law rule that would jostle uncomfortably with the Sherman Act. Noting the convergence of patent-misuse principles with antitrust principles, we said in *USM Corp. v. SPS Technologies, Inc.*, 694 F.2d 505, 512 (7th Cir.1982): 'If misuse claims are not tested by conventional antitrust principles, by what principles shall they be tested? Our law is not rich in alternative concepts of monopolistic abuse; and it is rather late in the date to try to develop one without in the process subjecting the rights of patent holders to debilitating uncertainty.' This point applies with even greater force to copyright misuse, where the danger of monopoly is less. We hold that a no-contest clause in a copyright licensing agreement is valid unless shown to violate antitrust law.

"This holding is not barred by *Lear v. Adkins*, 395 U.S. 653, 89 S. Ct. 1902, 23 L. Ed. 2d 610 (1969), which held that federal law forbids a state court to hold that a patent licensee is, by virtue of having been licensed, estopped to challenge the patent's validity. Our case involves a negotiated clause rather than a doctrine that in effect reads a no-contest clause into every licensing agreement. The doctrine is apt to have a broader effect. . . . Furthermore, the logic of *Lear* does not extend to copyright licenses. The opinion is narrowly written. It emphasizes

'the important public interest in permitting full and free competition in the use of ideas which are in reality a part of the public domain. Licensees may often be the only individuals with enough economic incentive to challenge the patentability of an inventor's discovery. If they are muzzled, the public may continually be required to pay tribute to would-be monopolists without need or justification.'

". . . A patent empowers its owner to prevent anyone else from making or using his invention; a copyright just empowers its owner to prevent others from copying the particular verbal or pictorial or aural pattern in which he chooses to express himself. The economic power conferred is much smaller. There is no need for a rule that would automatically invalidate every no-contest clause. If a particular clause is used to confer monopoly power beyond the small amount that the copyright laws authorize, the clause can be attacked under section 1 of the Sherman Act as a contract in restraint of trade. Rumbleseat does not argue that the clause here restrained trade in that sense. The fact that we can find no antitrust case—or for that matter any other reported case—that deals with a no-contest clause in a copyright license is evidence that these clauses are not such a source of significant restraints on freedom to compete as might warrant a per se rule of illegality.

"A further point, already alluded to, is that the competitive interest in confining copyright and patent protection to valid copyrights and patents has to do with the originality, novelty, etc. of the work that is copyrighted or patented, rather than with the owner's identity. Only the last question is in issue here; the validity of the Post's copyrights, not the copyrightability of the Rockwell dolls, is in issue. Once it is decided that a work is copyrightable, the decision has been made that the additional cost per copy to the public is warranted by the encouragement that copyright protection gives to the creation of new and valuable works; whether or not the ownership of the copyright is contestable by a licensee is then a detail irrelevant to the competitive policies that underlie *Lear*.

"This overstates the case a little, because Rumbleseat argues among other things that the Post failed to register its copyrights properly. If that is right, maybe the Rockwell illustrations have fallen into the public domain. It seems more likely, though, that what happened . . . is that the Post failed to perfect copyright in its derivative works—the photographs, printed in the magazine, of Rockwell's illustrations. The Rockwell family, which owns the copyrights on the original illustrations, could still enjoin Rumbleseat's infringement. The argument that the family's copyrights fell into the public domain presumably relies on the old doctrine of indivisibility—a disfavored doctrine, however, and one rejected years ago for magazines.

"So probably the effect of the copyrights on the price and output of porcelain dolls would be about the same whether or not Rumbleseat succeeded in knocking out the Post's copyrights. At least this is a strong possibility. Unfortunately, because Rumbleseat failed to make the record before the arbitrators part of the record in this court, we have only the haziest idea of what was and was not in issue before the arbitrators; but doubts engendered by Rumbleseat's failures must be resolved against Rumbleseat. At all events the basic originality and hence copyrightability of the Rockwell drawings on which the design of the infringing dolls is ultimately based seem not to be in issue.

"So we have a narrow and a broad holding on no-contest clauses: they are valid in copyright licenses (broad); they are valid when no issue of copyrightability is presented (narrow). These, we emphasize, are both holdings, and therefore bind the district courts in this circuit. Of course a court of coequal or superior authority to this court might find one more persuasive than the other, and not being bound as a matter of authority to follow our decisions could decide to adopt just one."[252]

[d] Statute of Limitations—Laches and Estoppel. Copyright Act Section 507(b) imposes a three-year statute of limitations on civil copyright infringement actions.[253]

In applying the statute, courts use general equitable principles, such as tolling because of the infringer's fraudulent concealment.[254] In *Prather*,[255] the Fifth Circuit held that uniform federal standards, rather than state law standards, govern the copyright limitation statute's application and confirmed that "fraudulent concealment . . . of a cause of action by the defendant will toll the statute of limitations": "two elements are required before this equitable principle is applicable: the plaintiff must show both successful concealment of the cause of action and fraudulent means to achieve that concealment."[256] It held that "the mere fact that plaintiff was unable to procure a copy of the [accused] book is insufficient to show the successful concealment necessary to toll the statute of limitations": "This was merely ignorance of evidence, not ignorance of a potential claim. The appellant knew of the alleged

---

[252] 816 F.2d at 1199–1201, 2 U.S.P.Q.2d at 1506–07.

[253] 17 U.S.C. § 507(b): "No civil action shall be maintained under the provisions on this title unless it is commenced within three years after the claim accrued." *See, e.g.,* Hoste v. Radio Corp. of America, 654 F.2d 11, 212 U.S.P.Q. 153 (6th Cir. 1981). A similar three-year limitation applies to criminal copyright prosecutions. 17 U.S.C. § 507(a).

In Prather v. Neva Paperbacks, Inc., 446 F.2d 338, 170 U.S.P.Q. 378 (5th Cir. 1971), the court reviewed the copyright statute of limitation's history:

"Prior to 1957 there was no statute of limitations on civil suits relating to copyright infringement, and courts applied the law of the state in which the action was brought. This led to a wide divergence of time periods in which infringement suits could be brought in the various states and thus encouraged forum shopping. The Senate report on the bill which became the limitations statute leaves no doubt but that the purpose of the legislation incorporating the three year limitations period was to provide a uniform federal period of limitations applicable throughout the United States. . . . The report also makes it clear that the intent of the drafters was that the limitations period would affect the remedy only, not the substantive right, and that equitable considerations would therefore apply to suspend the running of the statute." 446 F.2d at 339-40.

[254] *See generally* Lampf, Pleva, Lipkind, Prupis & Petigrow v. Gilbertson, 111 S. Ct. 2773 (1991); Irwin v. Veterans Administration, 111 S. Ct. 453, 457 (1990) ("[t]ime requirements in law suits . . . are customarily subject to 'equitable tolling.' "); Hallstrom v. Tillamook County, 493 U.S. 20 (1989); Holmberg v. Armbrecht, 327 U.S. 392, 396-397 (1946); Bailey v. Glover, 21 Wall. 342, 348 (1874).

[255] Prather v. Neva Paperbacks, Inc., 446 F.2d 338, 170 U.S.P.Q. 378 (5th Cir. 1971).

[256] *See also* Wood v. Santa Barbara Chamber of Commerce, Inc., 705 F.2d 1515, 1521 (9th Cir. 1983) ("A fraudulent concealment defense requires a showing both that the defendant used fraudulent means to keep the plaintiff unaware of his cause of action, and also that the plaintiff was, in fact, ignorant of the existence of his cause of action.").

infringement, but did not have in his possession the precise minutiae of the plagiarism. The bells do not toll the limitations statute while one ferrets the facts." [257]

Some courts assume that running of the statute is tolled even absent fraudulent concealment if the copyright owner could not, in the exercise of reasonable care, have learned of the infringement. [258]

In common with all statutes of limitation, Section 507(b) presents difficult interpretation and application problems, such as determining when a claim accrues. For example, an infringer may improperly copy the copyright owner's work, reproduce multiple copies, and sell them over an extended period. There are at least three plausible positions on when the owner's claim "accrued": (1) treat the first infringing act as accrual; (2) treat the last infringing act as accrual; [259] and (3) treat each infringing act (reproduction and distribution) as a separate claim. [260]

---

[257] 446 F.2d at 341. *Compare* Taylor v. Meirick, 712 F.2d 1112, 219 U.S.P.Q. 420 (7th Cir. 1983) ("The fact that a publisher loses sales to a competitor is not in itself a clue to copyright infringement, since there is vigorous competition among copyrighted works. So we doubt that every time the sales of a publication dip, the publisher must, to preserve his right to sue for copyright infringement, examine all of his competitors' publications to make sure none is infringing any of his copyrights.").

[258] Taylor v. Meirick, 712 F.2d 1112, 1118, 219 U.S.P.Q. 420 (7th Cir. 1983) ("Although many cases state that mere ignorance of a cause of action does not toll the statute of limitations, in context these statements invariably mean only that the plaintiff has a duty of diligence: it is not enough that he did not discover he had a cause of action, if a reasonable man in his shoes would have. . . . The significance of fraudulent concealment . . . is that it frustrates even diligent inquiry. In a case such as this, where even if there had been no active concealment by the tortfeasor the injured party would have had no reason to suspect that he was the victim of a tort, there may be no duty of inquiry at all.").

Cf. Mount v. Book-of-the-Month Club, Inc., 555 F.2d 1108, 194 U.S.P.Q. 245 (2d Cir. 1977) ("plaintiff knew in or about January 1956 of the publication of McKibbin's pamphlet; he could tell if he had a potential infringement claim by comparing the two works and noting the similarities; if he thought actual access by McKibbin before January 1956 had to be proved, he could have found out through discovery whether and how McKibbin had seen the Mount book. That type of knowledge, available to plaintiff in 1956, was enough to start limitations running at that time, unless defendant successfully concealed the cause of action by fraudulent means.").

[259] *Cf.* United States v. Shabazz, 724 F.2d 1536 (11th Cir. 1984) (criminal prosecution, rejecting argument that "as the copying of copyrighted material occurred after three years [after] the date of copyright publication the indictment must be dismissed as not having been brought within the Statute of Limitations": "In copyright infringement actions, the period of limitation begins on the date of the last infringing act.").

[260] *See* Hoey v. Dexel Systems Corp., 716 F. Supp. 222, 223-24 (E.D. Va. 1989):

"Defendants argue that because plaintiff had knowledge of at least one of the alleged acts of infringement more than three years prior to the filing of the action, plaintiff should be barred from bringing suit for any of the acts of infringement. Plaintiff, on the other hand, requests the application of the 'rolling statute of limitations' theory. Under such a theory, so long as any allegedly infringing conduct occurs within the three years preceding the filing of the action, the plaintiff may reach back and sue for damages or other relief for all allegedly infringing acts. . . . It appears, however, that § 507(b) is clear on its face. It does not provide for a waiver of infringing acts within the limitation pe-

In *Taylor*,[261] the Seventh Circuit, in an opinion by Judge Posner, espoused the second ("last act") position.[262] In addition, it suggested that a publisher's infringing activity did not necessarily end when it ceased distributing the infringing articles: it was responsible for later sales by its dealers unless it took "reasonable steps . . . to get [the infringing articles] back before [they] were resold to consumers."[263] In

---

riod if earlier infringements were discovered and not sued upon, nor does it provide for any reach back if an act of infringement occurs within the statutory period. In a case of continuing copyright infringements an action may be brought for all acts which accrued within the three years preceding the filing of the suit. . . . Plaintiff, then, is entitled to proceed with this cause of action for any acts that accrued within the three year period preceding the filing of this action. . . . Acts accruing prior to that shall be dismissed." 716 F. Supp. at 223-24.

[261] Taylor v. Meirick, 712 F.2d 1112, 219 U.S.P.Q. 420 (7th Cir. 1983).

[262] "The next question is whether [the copyright owner] can complain about infringing sales that occurred more than three years before he sued. He invokes the supposed rule that only the last infringing act need be within the statutory period. . . . [T]here is no doubt of the rule's validity if it is regarded not as something peculiar to copyright law but as the application to that law of the general principle that the statute of limitations does not begin to run on a continuing wrong till the wrong is over and done with. . . .

"The principle strikes a balance between the plaintiff's interest in being spared having to bring successive suits, and the two distinct interests, . . . that statutes of limitations serve. One is evidentiary—to reduce the error rate in legal proceedings by barring litigation over claims relating to the distant past. The other is repose—to give people the assurance that after a fixed time they can go about their business without fear of having their liberty or property taken through the legal process. . . . When the final act of an unlawful course of conduct occurs within the statutory period, these purposes are adequately served, in balance with the plaintiff's interest in not having to bring successive suits, by requiring the plaintiff to sue within the statutory period but letting him reach back and get damages for the entire duration of the alleged violation. Some of the evidence, at least, will be fresh. And the defendant's uncertainty as to whether he will be sued at all will be confined to the statutory period. His uncertainty about the extent of his liability may be greater, but that is often true in litigation.

". . . The initial copying was not a separate and completed wrong but simply the first step in a course of wrongful conduct that continued till the last copy of the infringing map was sold by [defendant] or with his connivance." 712 F.2d 1119-20.

[263] *Id.*, at 1117.

Compare Mount v. Book-of-the-Month Club, Inc., 555 F.2d 1108, 194 U.S.P.Q. 245 (2d Cir. 1977) ("appellee's own infringement . . . ended completely in 1955-1956 and appellee cannot be held for what the Boston Museum has since done on its own responsibility. The principle is that of *Maloney v. Stone,* 171 F. Supp. 29 (D. Mass. 1959), in which Judge Wyzanski rejected an attempt to hold in damages a manufacturer of an allegedly infringing work more than the normal limitations period after it had turned over all copies of the infringing work to its customers who continued to market them. The court held that, more than the limitations period . . . prior to the bringing of the suit, the manufacturer 'ceased to infringe, if it ever did infringe, ceased to invade plaintiff's interest, if it ever had invaded plaintiff's interest, and discontinued all relations as agent of, associate of, or even as contractual party' with the customers. What the latter did with the manufacturer's products, 'they did on their own account and entirely on their own responsibility.' . . . The same is true here.").

Gaste,[264] a New York district court declined to follow *Taylor* because it was contrary to prevailing authority in the Second Circuit and elsewhere.[265]

A copyright owner's delay in filing suit may give rise to the equitable defenses of laches, estoppel, or acquiescence.[266] Laches may cause the court to limit or deny injunctive relief but will not necessarily deprive the owner of the right to monetary relief as provided by the Copyright Act.[267] Relatively short delay may operate to

---

[264] Gaste v. Kaiserman, 669 F. Supp. 583 (S.D. N.Y. 1987).

[265] "In Mount v. Book-of-the-Month Club, Inc., 555 F.2d 1108, 1111 (2d Cir. 1977), the Second Circuit addressed facts very similar to those involved here. The plaintiff, an author, had sued the Book-of-the-Month Club for its manufacture and sale of copies of an allegedly infringing book. All of the Book-of-the- Month Club's manufacture, promotion and sale of the book had taken place more than three years before the complaint was filed, except for a remainder sale of 116 copies. The Second Circuit held that the plaintiff was barred from recovering for anything but the remainder sale. . . . All other cases in this Circuit have followed this ruling unanimously. Plaintiffs in this case have asked me to disregard the relevant authority in this Circuit and to follow instead the ruling in *Taylor v. Meirick*, . . .

"In light of the overwhelming authority in the Second Circuit that plaintiff is entitled to recover damages which accrued no earlier than three years prior to the filing of the lawsuit, this Court will grant defendants' motion for partial summary judgment. Further, even if this were a question of first impression in this Circuit, this Court would employ the analysis and reasoning employed by the Second Circuit. To do otherwise, would render the words of the Copyright Act meaningless and eradicate the policy objectives of a statute of limitations period in copyright actions." 669 F. Supp. at 584.

See also Goldsmith v. Main Line Book Co., 14 U.S.P.Q.2d 1459 (S.D. N.Y. 1989) ("a victorious plaintiff may recover damages which accrued within the three-year period immediately preceding the filing of the lawsuit.").

[266] *E.g.*, Roulo v. Russ Berrie & Co., Inc., 886 F.2d 931, 12 U.S.P.Q.2d 1423 (7th Cir. 1989) (two year delay rarely sufficient to constitute laches); Hoste v. Radio Corp. of America, 654 F.2d 11, 212 U.S.P.Q. 153 (6th Cir. 1981) (summary judgment reversed: "A showing of prejudice is a requirement for application of the doctrine of laches. The district court apparently determined that prejudice to the defendants could be presumed from the inordinate delay in bringing this action. . . . Any presumption of injury to the defendants would merely shift the burden to the plaintiff to show absence of prejudice; it would not be a proper basis for summary judgment."); Russell v. Price, 612 F.2d 1123, 205 U.S.P.Q. 206 (9th Cir. 1979) ("Defendants at no time changed their film distribution activities in reliance on Janus' conduct. Defendants cite no case in which a false sense of security alone has been enough to bar an otherwise proper claim. . . . This is not a case where copyright holders speculated on the probable success of a costly but unauthorized exploitation of a work before asserting their rights in it.").

For a discussion of laches, estoppel, and acquiescence in patent, trade secret, and trademark cases, see §§ 2F[4][f], 3E[5][b], and 5F[2][e].

[267] *E.g.*, New Era Publications International v. Henry Holt & Co., 873 F.2d 576, 585, 10 U.S.P.Q.2d 1561 (2d Cir. 1989) ("a permanent injunction would result in the total destruction of the work since it is not economically feasible to reprint the book after deletion of the infringing material. . . . Such severe prejudice, coupled with the unconscionable delay already described, mandates denial of the injunction for laches and relegation of [plaintiff] to its damages remedy.").

bar a right to a *preliminary* injunction.[268] An infringer's fraud or bad faith conduct may bar him from relying on laches.[269]

[5] Remedies

A court may grant the following remedies for copyright infringement: preliminary and permanent injunctions;[270] impoundment and destruction of infringing articles;[271] monetary damages, including the copyright owner's actual damages plus the infringer's profits or statutory damages;[272] and costs and attorney fees.[273]

Willful copyright infringement for commercial gain may constitute a criminal offense.[274]

[a] Injunctions.

Copyright Act Section 502(a) provides that a court may "grant temporary and final injunctions on such terms as it may deem reasonable to prevent or restrain infringement of a copyright."[275]

[i] Preliminary Injunctions.

Courts apply general preliminary injunction standards to copyright cases.[276] Most courts require claimants to meet a four-prong test: (1) a substantial likelihood of success; (2) a substantial threat of irreparable injury; (3) the threatened injury to the claimant outweighs the injunction's harm to

---

268 *See* § 4F[5][a][i].

269 *Cf.* Stone v. Williams, 891 F.2d 401, 13 U.S.P.Q.2d 1166 (2d Cir. 1989) (defendants who used fraud to deprive plaintiff, daughter of a deceased country and western singer, of copyright renewal rights, cannot rely on laches defense; "To allow defendants to bar plaintiff from claiming her rights when the availability of the laches defense was obtained by them in such an unworthy manner would not only grant defendants a windfall in this suit to which they are not entitled, but would also encourage a party to deliberately mislead a court. Courts of equity exist to relieve a party from the defense of laches under such circumstances.").

270 17 U.S.C. § 502.

271 17 U.S.C. § 503.

272 17 U.S.C. § 504.

A court may increase statutory damages because of the infringer's willful infringement (see § 4F[5][d][i]), but otherwise punitive damages are not available for copyright infringement. Oboler v. Goldin, 714 F.2d 211, 213, 220 U.S.P.Q. 166, 167 (2d Cir. 1983); Cormack v. Sunshine Food Stores, Inc., 675 F. Supp. 374, 375, 4 U.S.P.Q.2d 1366, 1370 (E.D. Mich. 1987).

273 17 U.S.C. § 505.

274 17 U.S.C. § 506(a): "Any person who infringes a copyright willfully and for purposes of commercial advantage or private financial gain shall be punished as provided in section 2319 of title 18." The criminal code provision referred to, 18 U.S.C. Section 2319, provides for greater penalties for unauthorized reproduction and distribution of motion pictures, audiovisual works, and sound recordings.

See generally Dowling v. United States, 473 U.S. 207, 226 U.S.P.Q. 529 (1985); United States v. Cross, 816 F.2d 297, 2 U.S.P.Q.2d 1356 (7th Cir. 1987); United States v. Goss, 803 F.2d 638, 231 U.S.P.Q. 730 (11th Cir. 1986); United States v. Steerwell Leisure Corp., Inc., 598 F. Supp. 171, 224 U.S.P.Q. 1059 (W.D. N.Y. 1984).

275 17 U.S.C. § 502(a).

276 For a discussion of preliminary injunctions in patent and trade secret cases, see §§ 2F[5][a][i] and 3F[1][a].

the accused infringer; and (4) the injunction is not contrary to the public interest.[277] The first prong is the most important; copyright owners who show likely success of prevailing on the copyright infringement charge rarely fail to obtain injunctive relief.

Some courts modify the four-prong test. The Second Circuit requires a claimant to show irreparable harm and either (1) a likelihood of success on the merits or (2) sufficiently serious questions going to the merits to make them a fair ground for litigation and a balance of hardship "tipping decidedly" toward claimant.[278] The Ninth Circuit requires "either (1) a likelihood of success on the merits and the possibility of irreparable injury, or (2) the existence of serious questions going to the merits and the balance of hardships tipping in [claimant's] favor."[279]

(1) Success Likelihood. A claimant shows likely success by establishing a *prima facie* infringement case: copyright ownership and copying.[280] The accused infringer may raise any available defense to demonstrate that the claimant's copyright is not valid or infringed.

(2) Irreparable Injury. If the claimant shows likely success, most courts apply a rebuttable presumption of irreparable injury.[281] Copyright "protects the unique and somewhat intangible interest of creative expression. Unlike most property rights, the value of this interest is often fleeting."[282] Because fads come and go, a copyright's

---

[277] *E.g.,* Forry v. Neundorfer, Inc., 837 F.2d 259, 262, 5 U.S.P.Q.2d 1510, 1513 (6th Cir. 1988); Apple Barrel Productions, Inc. v. Beard, 730 F.2d 384, 386, 222 U.S.P.Q. 956, 957 (5th Cir. 1984); Dataphase Systems, Inc. v. CL Systems, Inc., 640 F.2d 109, 114 (8th Cir. 1981); E.F. Johnson Co. v. Uniden Corp. of America, 623 F. Supp. 1485, 1490-91, 228 U.S.P.Q. 891, 894-95 (D. Minn. 1985); Horn Abbot Ltd. v. Sarsaparilla Ltd., 601 F. Supp. 360, 364-65, 225 U.S.P.Q. 419, 421 (N.D. Ill. 1984).

[278] *E.g.,* Hasbro Bradley, Inc. v. Sparkle Toys, Inc., 780 F.2d 189, 192, 228 U.S.P.Q. 423, 424 (2d Cir. 1985).

[279] Apple Computer, Inc. v. Formula International, Inc., 725 F.2d 521, 523, 221 U.S.P.Q. 762, 763-64 (9th Cir. 1984).

[280] Educational Testing Series v. Katzman, 793 F.2d 533, 538, 230 U.S.P.Q. 156, 159 (3d Cir. 1986); Almo Music Corp. v. 77 East Adams, Inc., 647 F. Supp. 123, 124, 1 U.S.P.Q.2d 1159 (N.D. Ill. 1986).

[281] Concrete Machinery Co. v. Classic Lawn Ornaments, 843 F.2d 600, 6 U.S.P.Q.2d 1357 (1st Cir. 1988); Forry, Inc. v. Neundorfer, Inc., 837 F.2d 259, 267, 5 U.S.P.Q.2d 1510, 1516 (6th Cir. 1988); West Publishing Co. v. Mead Data Central, Inc., 799 F.2d 1219, 1228, 230 U.S.P.Q. 801, 806 (8th Cir. 1986), *cert. denied,* 479 U.S. 1070 (1987); Educational Testing Services v. Katzman, 793 F.2d 533, 543-44, 230 U.S.P.Q. 156, 163 (3d Cir. 1986); Hasbro Bradley, Inc. v. Sparkle Toys, Inc., 780 F.2d 189, 228 U.S.P.Q. 423 (2d Cir. 1985); Apple Computer, Inc. v. Formula International, Inc., 725 F.2d 521, 525, 221 U.S.P.Q. 762, 765 (9th Cir. 1984); Wainwright Securities, Inc. v. Wall Street Transcript Corp., 558 F.2d 91, 94 (2d Cir. 1977), *cert. denied,* 434 U.S. 1014 (1978).

But see Apple Barrel Productions, Inc. v. Beard, 730 F.2d 384, 390, 222 U.S.P.Q. 956, 960 (5th Cir. 1984) (Fifth Circuit has not yet expressed a view on a presumption's appropriateness).

[282] Concrete Machinery Co. v. Classic Lawn Ornaments, 843 F.2d 600, 611, 6 U.S.P.Q.2d 1357, 1365 (1st Cir. 1988).

commercial value may be lost before a trial can be held and permanent injunctive relief granted.[283]

The danger an accused infringer's marketing infringing articles poses to the copyright owner's competitive position pending trial justifies the presumption or, in the alternative, provides a basis for finding potential irreparable harm.[284] In *Houghton Mifflin*,[285] the court noted:

". . . [W]here two editions of a book of great popular interest are being actively promoted in competition with each other, it is obvious that much of the damage to a rightful owner of copyright, if any there be, will have been done by the time the action may be tried and final decree entered upon an accounting. Such owner needs protection now while the book is at the height of its sales, or else he may never be able to realize the fruits of ownership. Consequently it is settled in copyright cases that, if the plaintiff makes a *prima facie* showing of his right, a preliminary injunction should issue."[286]

In computer program copyright infringement cases,[287] courts suggest that the "considerable time and money" the copyright owner invests in developing the program justifies the irreparable harm presumption.[288]

Equitable considerations, such as the owner's unjustified delay in seeking a preliminary injunction, may rebut the presumption. In *Clark Equipment*,[289] plaintiff's three-year delay after seeking defendant's infringing article was grounds for denying a preliminary injunction. In *Forry*,[290] plaintiff knew of defendant's accused product for 22 months but was unable to obtain a copy until shortly before it filed the law suit. The court held the delay justified because Federal Rules of Civil Procedure Rule 11 required plaintiff to obtain and examine the infringing article before suing.[291]

---

[283] Atari v. North American Philips Consumer Electronics Corp., 672 F.2d 607, 620, 214 U.S.P.Q. 33 (2d Cir. 1982) (video games' short-lived market "further underscores" the need for a preliminary injunction). *See also* Apple Computer, Inc. v. Franklin Computer Corp., 714 F.2d 1240, 1254, 219 U.S.P.Q. 113, 125 (3d Cir. 1983), *cert. dismissed*, 464 U.S. 1033 (1984).

[284] E.F. Johnson Co. v. Uniden Corp. of America, 623 F. Supp. 1485, 1503, 228 U.S.P.Q. 891, 905 (D. Minn. 1985) (defendant's ongoing infringement jeopardized the plaintiff's "substantial investment" in its radios "as well as its competitive position in the marketplace"); O'Neill Developments, Inc. v. Galen Filburn, Inc., 524 F. Supp. 710, 715, 216 U.S.P.Q. 1123, 1127 (N.D. Ga. 1981) (defendant's continued use of infringing real estate brochures would irreparably harm plaintiff, a direct competitor in the office condominium market).

[285] Houghton Mifflin Co. v. Stackpole, Sons, Inc., 104 F.2d 306 (2d Cir. 1939).

[286] *Id.*, at 307.

[287] *See* § 4C[2].

[288] Apple Computer, Inc. v. Formula International, Inc., 725 F.2d 521, 525, 221 U.S.P.Q. 762, 765 (9th Cir. 1984). *See also* Apple Computer, Inc. v. Franklin Computer Corp., 714 F.2d 1240, 219 U.S.P.Q. 113 (3d Cir. 1983), *cert. dismissed*, 464 U.S. 1033 (1984).

[289] Clark Equipment Co. v. Harlan Corp., 539 F. Supp. 561, 570, 215 U.S.P.Q. 1150, 1156 (D. Kan. 1982).

[290] Forry v. Neundorfer, Inc., 837 F.2d 259, 5 U.S.P.Q.2d 1510 (6th Cir. 1988).

[291] *See also* Original Appalachian Artworks, Inc. v. Topps Chewing Gum, Inc., 642 F. Supp. 1031, 1040, 231 U.S.P.Q. 850, 857 (N.D. Ga. 1986) (no impermissible delay where defendant first sold infringing article in May 1985, plaintiff wrote a demand letter in October 1985 and sued in March 1986).

(3) *Harm Balancing.* A copyright owner who shows likely success will find it fairly easy to satisfy the balancing the parties' harms test some courts apply. For example, the First Circuit compares an owner's success likelihood with the injunction's potential harm to an accused infringer: a strong infringement case almost always outweighs the accused infringer's hardship, but the same hardship may outweigh a weak case.[292]

Defendants who show only that harm will befall their businesses if an injunction issues are rarely successful. Neither a defendant's profits lost from being unable to sell the infringing article pending trial,[293] nor a defendant's inability to fulfill contractual obligations to sell infringing articles and the resulting harm to his business reputation[294] are sufficient to tip the balance in his favor if the copyright owner demonstrates likely success.

Courts discount arguments that a preliminary injunction will have a "devastating effect" on a defendant's small business,[295] but may deny the injunction if it will completely bar him from competing. In *Apple Barrel Productions,*[296] plaintiff alleged that defendant's children's television show script infringed its copyright. To show irreparable injury, plaintiff argued that the television market could sustain only one program with the particular attributes of plaintiff's and defendant's scripts and that whoever aired second would be seen as the "copy cat" and fail. The court turned

---

[292] Concrete Machinery Co. v. Classic Lawn Ornaments, 843 F.2d 600, 612, 6 U.S.P.Q.2d 1357, 1366 (1st Cir. 1988). *See also* WPOW, Inc. v. MKLJ Enterprises, 584 F. Supp. 132, 138, 222 U.S.P.Q. 502, 507 (D.D.C. 1984).

[293] Concrete Machinery Co. v. Classic Lawn Ornaments, 843 F.2d 600, 612, 6 U.S.P.Q. 1357, 1366 (1st Cir. 1988) ("where the only hardship that the defendant will suffer is lost profits from an activity which has been shown likely to be infringing, such an argument in defense 'merits little equitable consideration' "); E.F. Johnson Co. v. Uniden Corp. of America, 623 F. Supp. 1485, 1503-04, 228 U.S.P.Q. 891, 905 (D. Minn. 1985) ("The only harm which defendant will suffer is lost profits on its infringing radios. This is not a weighty equitable consideration. A willful infringer which seeks to profit by copying from others' creative ideas should not be heard to complain that its interests will be disturbed by an injunction.").

[294] Recycled Paper Products, Inc. v. Pat Fashions Industries, Inc., 731 F. Supp. 624, 626-27, 15 U.S.P.Q.2d 1311, 1313 (S.D.N.Y. 1990).

[295] *E.g.,* Apple Computer, Inc. v. Franklin Computer Corp., 714 F.2d 1240, 219 U.S.P.Q. 113 (3d Cir. 1983), *cert. dismissed,* 464 U.S. 1033 (1984) ("If that were the correct standard, then a knowing infringer would be permitted to construct its business around infringement, a result we cannot condone . . . The size of the infringer should not be determinative of the copyright holder's ability to get prompt judicial redress.").

See also Horn Abbot Ltd. v. Sarsaparilla Ltd., 601 F. Supp. 360, 369-70, 225 U.S.P.Q. 419, 425 (N.D. Ill. 1984) (disregarding claim that temporary restraining order would put defendant, a willful infringer, out of business).

Cf. Apple Computer, Inc. v. Formula International, Inc., 725 F.2d 521, 526, 221 U.S.P.Q. 762, 765 (9th Cir. 1984) (rejecting defendant's argument that a preliminary injunction inhibited his entry into the market; he had sold only a few units before plaintiff sought the injunction). In *Formula International,* the court also noted that enjoining sale of the accused units did not work an undue hardship because they constituted only a small percentage of defendant's total sales.

[296] Apple Barrel Productions, Inc. v. R.D. Beard, 730 F.2d 384, 222 U.S.P.Q. 956 (5th Cir. 1984).

plaintiff's argument against it to find that a preliminary injunction would irreparably harm defendant.

> "If no injunction is ordered, at least each party is an equal competitor in the race to produce and market its show first. On the contrary, if an injunction *is* ordered, then defendants literally will be locked out of the television market until the conclusion of the trial on the results, with *no* opportunity to win the race to market their program first."[297]

If plaintiff only manages to demonstrate "serious questions going to the merits," the harms to a defendant referred to above may well tip the scales against a preliminary injunction.

(4) *Public Interest.* The public interest factor favors a copyright owner who demonstrates likely success: "public policy is rarely a genuine issue if the copyright owner has established a likelihood of success."[298]

In *E.F. Johnson,*[299] the defendant argued that enjoining his activities would reduce competition and thereby harm the public interest. The court retorted, "The public's interest . . . is in *fair* competition, and not the unlawful and unfair competition engaged in by the defendant."[300] There were other competitors in the market, and defendant was free to compete with non-infringing goods.[301]

[ii] *Permanent Injunctions.* "An injunction against the defendant will issue when a substantial likelihood of further infringement of plaintiffs' copyrights exists."[302] If a copyright owner establishes copyright infringement and "a threat of continuing infringement, he is *entitled* to an injunction."[303]

Likely future infringement may exist if an infringer has been the subject of a previous lawsuit[304] or willfully infringed up to trial.[305] A court may issue a permanent

---

[297] 730 F.2d at 390, 222 U.S.P.Q. at 960.

[298] Concrete Machinery Co. v. Classic Lawn Ornaments, 843 F.2d 600, 612, 6 U.S.P.Q.2d 1357, 1366 (1st Cir. 1988).

[299] E.F. Johnson Co. v. Uniden Corp. of America, 623 F. Supp. 1485, 228 U.S.P.Q. 891 (D. Minn. 1985).

[300] 623 F. Supp. at 1504.

[301] *See also* Horn Abbott Ltd. v. Sarsaparilla, Ltd., 601 F. Supp. 360, 369, 225 U.S.P.Q. 419, 425 (N.D. Ill. 1984) (restraining book's publication; "while the public might have an interest in access to the additional material in the book, this interest does not . . . outweigh the other interests noted above"); WPOW, Inc. v. MRLJ Enterprises, 584 F. Supp. 132, 138, 222 U.S.P.Q. 502, 507 (D.D.C. 1984) (public interest not injured when order enjoined defendant from using an infringing engineering report to support its Federal Communications Commission new broadcasting facility construction application).

[302] Milene Music, Inc. v. Gotauco, 551 F. Supp. 1288, 1295, 220 U.S.P.Q. 880, 886 (D.R.I. 1982).

[303] Walt Disney Co. v. Powell, 897 F.2d 565, 567, 14 U.S.P.Q.2d 1160, 1162 (D.C. Cir. 1990).

[304] Flyte Tyme Tunes v. Miszkiwicz, 715 F. Supp. 919, 921, 12 U.S.P.Q.2d 1073, 1075 (E.D. Wis. 1989).

[305] *E.g.,* Golden Torch Music Corp. v. Pier III Cafe, Inc., 684 F. Supp. 772, 774, 7 U.S.P.Q.2d 1583, 1585 (D. Conn. 1988); Rare Blue Music, Inc. v. Guttadauro, 616 F. Supp. 1528, 227 U.S.P.Q. 325 (D. Mass. 1985).

injunction against a willful infringer even though, at the time of trial, defendant had ceased his infringing activity.[306]

When a defendant has no infringement history and plaintiff shows no probability he is likely to resume infringing, the court will not issue a permanent injunction.[307]

The court may formulate an injunction as it deems appropriate. In *Walt Disney*,[308] the court held that if the defendant has "a history of infringement and a significant threat of future infringement remains, it is appropriate to permanently enjoin the future infringement of works owned by the plaintiff but not in suit." Disney sued defendant for selling shirts bearing unauthorized Mickey and Minnie Mouse likenesses.[309] The district court disregarded defendant's claim he had ceased selling infringing articles and therefore should not be permanently enjoined. The court found defendant had not truly reformed but merely reacted to being caught "red-handed." He faced two suits, one by Disney, another by the Hard Rock Cafe. The court of appeals upheld the injunction restraining defendant from violating any Walt Disney copyright, not just Minnie and Mickey Mouse.[310]

An injunction must meet Federal Rules of Civil Procedure Rule 65(d)'s specificity requirement and cannot be broader than necessary to restrain unlawful conduct. In *Educational Testing*,[311] the district court entered an order enjoining the defendant from "adapting . . . any other information" obtained from plaintiff's copyrighted tests. The court of appeals struck "adapting" and "any other information" because the words offered plaintiff protection broader than that copyright law affords. Defendant might be able to adapt ideas obtained from plaintiff's tests without violating plaintiff's copyright in the expression of those ideas.[312]

[b]   Copies Seizure. A court may impound infringing articles and the means of their reproduction while a copyright suit is pending and may order their destruction as part of a final judgment.

---

[306] Walt Disney Co. v. Powell, 897 F.2d 565, 568, 14 U.S.P.Q.2d 1160, 1162 (D.C. Cir. 1990); Milene Music, Inc. v. Gotauco, 551 F. Supp. 1288, 1295, 220 U.S.P.Q. 880, 886 (D.R.I. 1982).

[307] Dolori Fabrics, Inc. v. The Limited, Inc., 662 F. Supp. 1347, 1358, 3 U.S.P.Q.2d 1753, 1761 (S.D. N.Y. 1987).

[308] Walt Disney Co. v. Powell, 897 F.2d 565, 568, 14 U.S.P.Q.2d 1160, 1163 (D.C. Cir. 1990).

[309] For another Mickey Mouse case, see Walt Disney Productions v. Air Pirates, 581 F.2d 751, 199 U.S.P.Q. 769, (9th Cir. 1978), discussed at § 4C[1][d][vi] and 4F[3][d].

[310] In cases ASCAP and its members investigate and prosecute, some courts enjoin defendants from violating any of plaintiffs' copyrights, even though the lawsuit involved only a few copyright violations. *See, e.g.,* Brockman Music v. Mass. Bay Lines, Inc., 7 U.S.P.Q.2d 1089, 1091 (D. Mass. 1988); Billy Steinberg Music v. Cagney's Pub., 9 U.S.P.Q.2d 1749, 1751 (N.D. Ill. 1988). *But see* A&N Music Corp. v. Venezia, 733 F. Supp. 955, 958 (E.D. Pa. 1990) (inappropriate to enjoin defendant " 'from publicly performing all of ASCAP's members' copyrighted works' without evidence of infringement upon other works").

For a discussion of ASCAP and other performing rights organizations, see § 4E[4][f].

[311] Educational Testing Services v. Katzman, 793 F.2d 533, 230 U.S.P.Q. 156, 164 (3d Cir. 1986).

[312] 793 F.2d at 545, 230 U.S.P.Q. at 164.

For a discussion of the idea-expression distinction, see §§ 4C[1][d] and 4F[2][b].

[i] Impoundment. A district court has discretion to issue an order impounding infringing copies "on such terms as it may deem reasonable"[313] to "maintain the feasibility of eventual destruction of items found at trial to violate the copyright laws by safeguarding them during the pendency of the action."[314]

There are two impoundment procedures. First, a copyright owner may move for an order impounding the infringing articles, which 1976 Copyright Act Section 503(a) authorizes but does not set a standard for granting relief. A court does not usually grant these orders *ex parte.* Second, a copyright owner may seek a seizure writ under the Supreme Court's Rules of Practice,[315] which set forth specific procedures that permit a plaintiff to obtain a writ without notice to the defendant and without a showing of irreparable injury. Rule 3 requires plaintiff to file an affidavit with the clerk of the court setting forth the infringing articles' location and value and to post a bond. Only after seizure can the defendant seek relief from the court, demanding a higher bond or release of the articles after a showing that the goods are not infringing.[316]

The Rules of Practice predate the 1976 Act, and the question arises whether the Act repealed them.[317] In *WPOW*,[318] plaintiff sought a Rules of Procedure seizure writ or, in the alternative, a Section 503(a) impoundment order. The district court, without analysis, observed that the Rules predated the Act and were presumably inapplicable.[319] It held that plaintiff must meet Section 503(a) and preliminary injunction standards.

In *Warner Brothers*,[320] the Second Circuit distinguished *WPOW*[321] and noted with approval authorities that confirm that the Rules of Practice remain in force. Plaintiff obtained an *ex parte* order permitting plaintiff's private investigator to conduct the impoundment and to seize not only the infringing articles and their production means, but all documents relating to the infringing articles. The court held this order improper for many reasons, not least because plaintiff failed to follow the Rules of

---

[313] 17 U.S.C. § 503; Toro Co. v. R&R Products, Inc., 787 F.2d 1208, 1210 n.1, 229 U.S.P.Q. 282, 283 n.1 (8th Cir. 1986).

[314] Midway Manufacturing Company v. Omni Videogames, Inc., 668 F.2d 70, 72 (1st Cir. 1981).

[315] 17 U.S.C. fol. § 501.

[316] Rules of Practice, Rules 7-10.

[317] The House Report states:

> "The present Supreme Court rules with respect to seizure and impounding were issued even though there is no specific provision authorizing them in the copyright statute, and there appears to be no need for including a special provision on the point in the bill." H.R. Rep. No. 1476, 94th Cong., 2d Sess. 160 (1976).

[318] WPOW, Inc. v. MRLJ Enterprises, 584 F. Supp. 132, 222 U.S.P.Q. 502 (D.D.C. 1984).

[319] 554 F. Supp. at 135, 222 U.S.P.Q. at 504.

[320] Warner Brothers Inc. v. Dae Rim Trading, Inc., 877 F.2d 1120, 1124, 11 U.S.P.Q.2d 1272, 1275 (2d Cir. 1989).

[321] *WPOW* involved "a controverted motion and hearing for impoundment, not the expedited seizure to which Rules 4, 5, and 6 [of the Rules of Practice] are addressed." 877 F.2d at 1124, 11 U.S.P.Q.2d at 1275. This suggests that a plaintiff who simply proceeds under the Rules of Practice may avoid any substantive requirements the courts read into Section 503(a).

Practice. Alternatively, it noted that even if the 1976 Act repealed the Rules, plaintiff would still need to meet general preliminary injunction standards, including Federal Rules of Civil Procedure Rule 65. Rule 65 requires notice to the defendant unless the plaintiff can meet the requirements necessary to obtain an *ex parte* temporary restraining order.

[*ii*] *Destruction.* A court has discretion whether to order "destruction or other reasonable disposition" of the infringing articles and their production means.[322] The language "other articles by means of which such copies . . . may be reproduced" includes any machinery used in the duplication process.[323]

The House Report explains that, unlike the 1909 Act, which only mentioned destruction, 1976 Act Section 503(b) provides flexibility for the court to order something less than destruction, such as sale, to avoid "needless waste."[324] In *RSO Records,*[325] the court ordered plaintiffs to destroy the infringing articles but to sell machinery that could be used for non-infringing purposes, the net sale proceeds to be used to offset damage award.[326]

[c] **Compensatory Damages.** Plaintiff may recover "the actual damages suffered by him or her as a result of the infringement, and any profits of the infringer that are attributable to the infringement and are not taken into account in computing the actual damages."[327]

Under the 1909 Copyright Act, the courts did not agree on whether a copyright owner could recover the greater of damages and infringer profits or both.[328] If the court awarded plaintiff actual damages measured wholly or in part by defendant's profits and also the profits themselves, "double recovery" occurred.

The 1976 Act resolves the double recovery issue by expressly permitting actual damages and infringer profits as long as double recovery does not occur.

> "Damages are awarded to compensate the copyright owner for losses from the infringement, and profits are awarded to prevent the infringer from unfairly benefiting from a wrongful act. Where the defendant's profits are nothing more than a measure of the damages suffered by the copyright owner, it would be inappropriate to award damages and profits cumulatively, since in effect they amount to the same thing. However, in cases where the copyright owner has suffered damages not reflected in the infringer's profits, or where

---

[322] RSO Records, Inc. v. Peri, 596 F. Supp. 849, 863, 225 U.S.P.Q. 407, 417 (S.D. N.Y. 1984).

[323] 596 F. Supp. at 863, 225 U.S.P.Q. at 417-18.

[324] H.R. Rep. No. 1476, 94th Cong., 2d Sess. 160 (1976).

[325] RSO Records, Inc. v. Peri, 596 F. Supp. 849, 863, 225 U.S.P.Q. 407, 418 (S.D. N.Y. 1984).

[326] 596 F. Supp. at 863-64, 225 U.S.P.Q. at 418.

[327] 17 U.S.C. § 504(b).

[328] *See, e.g.,* Frank Music Corp. v. Metro-Goldwyn- Mayer, Inc., 772 F.2d 505, 512, 227 U.S.P.Q. 687, 690 (9th Cir. 1985) (plaintiff entitled to recover the greater of actual damages or defendant's profits); Miller v. Universal Studios, Inc., 650 F.2d 1365, 1376, 212 U.S.P.Q. 345 (5th Cir. 1981) (plaintiff allowed to recover both).

there have been profits attributable to the copyrighted work but not used as a measure of damages, subsection (b) authorizes the award of both."[329]

Multiple infringers are jointly and severally liable for the portion of the copyright owner's recovery representing actual damages[330] and statutory damages.[331] Each infringer is not jointly or severally liable for other infringers' profits.[332] "Exceptions to this general rule may be appropriate only where the infringement was not innocent or where the defendants engaged 'in a partnership, joint venture, or similar enterprise.' "[333]

[*i*] *Actual Damages.* Actual damages should reimburse the copyright owner for the "extent to which the market value of the copyrighted work at the time of the infringement has been injured or destroyed by the infringement."[334]

One common damage measure is the profits the copyright owner would have made but for the infringement. If the owner cannot show lost sales, he may recover the infringing use's fair market value, such as the copyright owner's established license fee or, under some court decisions, what a willing buyer would reasonably have been required to pay a willing seller for the right to engage in the infringing act.

(*1*) *Lost Sales.* A copyright owner may recover profits on sales he would have made but for the infringement.[335] If the infringing goods compete directly with the owner's goods and are similar in quality and price, plaintiff can usually show that he would have made every sale the infringer made. In *RSO,*[336] the court observed "It would be reasonable to assume that for every counterfeit copy of plaintiff's

---

[329] H.R. Rep. No. 1476, 94th Cong., 2d Sess. 161 (1976).

[330] Abeshouse v. Ultragraphics, Inc., 754 F.2d 467, 470 (2d Cir. 1985); Ford Motor Co. v. B & H Supply Inc., 646 F. Supp. 975 (D. Minn. 1986).

[331] Fitzgerald Publishing Co., Inc. v. Baylor Publishing Co., Inc., 807 F.2d 1110, 1116, 1 U.S.P.Q.2d 1261, 1265 (2d Cir. 1986); Lauratex Textile Corp. v. Allton Knitting Mills, 519 F. Supp. 730, 733, 215 U.S.P.Q. 521, 522-23 (S.D.N.Y. 1981).

Because willfulness and innocence are factors in determining statutory damages, see § 4F[5][d][i], problems arise when one infringer is more or less culpable than the other. In *Fitzgerald Publishing,* the district court rendered different awards against two defendants—one's infringement was "malicious," the other's merely willful. The court of appeals reversed on the grounds that when both defendants' infringement are willful, the copyright statute "does not distinguish between those who maliciously infringe another's copyright or those who simply act knowing that they are infringing upon the copyright." 807 F.2d at 1117, 1 U.S.P.Q.2d at 1267.

The court suggested that an infringer who proves innocent infringement under Section 504(c)(2), or shows he was not willful, "may escape the full measure of joint and several liability." *Id.*

[332] Abeshouse v. Ultragraphics, Inc., 754 F.2d 467, 472 (2d Cir. 1985).

[333] 754 F.2d at 472 (citing D. Nimmer & M. Nimmer, Nimmer on Copyrights § 13.04[c][3]).

[334] Fitzgerald Publishing Co., Inc. v. Baylor Publishing Co., Inc., 807 F.2d 1110, 1118, 1 U.S.P.Q.2d 1261, 1267 (2d Cir. 1986).

For a discussion of damages in patent cases, see § 2F[5][b].

[335] Fitzgerald Publishing Co., Inc. v. Baylor Publishing Co., Inc., 807 F.2d 1110, 1118, 1 U.S.P.Q.2d 1261, 1268 (2d Cir. 1986).

[336] RSO Records, Inc. v. Peri, 596 F. Supp. 849, 863, 225 U.S.P.Q. 407, 415 (S.D. N.Y. 1984).

copyrighted records and tapes sold by defendants plaintiffs lost a corresponding sale. Unlike the situation in *Stevens Linen* [discussed below] defendants' copies were presumably sold at retail for the same prices as plaintiffs'."

If the owner's and infringer's goods differ in quality, price, or intended use, fact-finders must "necessarily engage in some degree of speculation."[337] The owner must show that the infringer's acts caused the owner harm.[338]

A common issue is what effect the infringer's lower price should have.[339] Some decisions assume customer demand for the copyright owner's goods is inelastic, that is, not price-sensitive. In *Stevens Linen*,[340] the district court held that calculating what portion of defendant's sales plaintiff could have made was too speculative because defendant's infringing fabrics were cheaper than and inferior to plaintiff's. The court of appeals disagreed. One way to approximate lost sales would be to assume that plaintiff made defendant's sales because "customers of [of plaintiff] had a demand for this type of fabric and were shifting their purchasing to the cheaper infringing fabric and away from [plaintiff's fabric]."[341] Another way would be to use the difference between plaintiff's sales of the infringed fabric design and its average sales of its other fabric designs. In *Taylor*,[342] the court was unimpressed with defendant's argument that its infringing maps were so much lower in price than plaintiff's as to place them in a different market.

> ". . . [T]he price difference works in the wrong direction for [defendant]. . . . People who were buying [plaintiff's] maps for $10 would be delighted to be able to buy the same map for a fourth as much—though it would not be quite the same map; part of the difference in price reflects a difference in the quality of the materials used in making the maps."[343]

---

[337] Stevens Linen Associates, Inc. v. Mastercraft Corp., 656 F.2d 11, 14, 210 U.S.P.Q. 865 (2d Cir. 1981).

[338] A copyright owner must prove, not simply posit, a causal connection between infringement and loss. In Goldenberg v. Doe, 731 F. Supp. 1155 (E.D. N.Y. 1990), a comedian attempted to recover damages for poor showings at a live show in New York. His theory was that because defendant rented out infringing videocassettes customers did not attend his shows. The court found the theory too speculative; many reasons other than the infringement may have reduced plaintiff's audience.

[339] In most cases, defendant sells the infringing product at a lower price and argues that those sales would not have been made at plaintiff's higher price. If defendant charges more, a court will probably assume the plaintiff would make the sales at its lower price.

In Gund, Inc. v. Swank, Inc., 673 F. Supp. 1233, 5 U.S.P.Q. 1070 (S.D.N.Y. 1987), defendant sold, as part of an earring sales promotion, infringing stuffed lions of poorer quality but higher price than plaintiff's stuffed lions. The court, without discussion, calculated actual damages based on plaintiff's lost profits on all defendant's sales. A contrary result might have been reached if defendant could offer a reason why customers bought from him at a higher price. That reason may establish that the customers would purchase only from defendant, not from plaintiff.

[340] Stevens Linen Associates, Inc. v. Mastercraft Corp., 656 F.2d 11, 210 U.S.P.Q. 865 (2d Cir. 1981).

[341] 656 F.2d at 15.

[342] Taylor v. Meirck, 712 F.2d 1112, 219 U.S.P.Q. 420 (7th Cir. 1983).

[343] 712 F.2d at 1121, 219 U.S.P.Q. at 425.

In *Manufacturers Technologies*,[344] the court agreed with defendant's argument that some of its customers would not have purchased plaintiff's substantially more expensive computer program.

Nonprice factors may also affect what portion of defendant's sales plaintiff would have made. In *Manufacturers Technologies,* the court considered as tending to negate causation the competition plaintiff faced from other program vendors. On the other hand, it credited plaintiff's argument that it lost additional sales because its computer program's "new and fragile market" was damaged by "negative word of mouth" that arose because (1) defendant falsely advertised that their infringing program offered similar functionality for a much lower price, leading customers to believe plaintiff was "price gouging"; and (2) defendant's program worked poorly, causing potential customers to assume that the type of program was a bad investment.[345] Plaintiff's expert testified that "word of mouth" affected chances for additional sales, particularly in large companies with many divisions.

In *Regents of the University of Minnesota*,[346] the court considered factors similar to those in *Manufacturing Technologies* in determining how many customers plaintiff lost to defendant's infringements. It reduced plaintiff's suggested number by eliminating sales to customers who would not have purchased plaintiff's product because it was significantly more expensive than defendant's and sales to customers whose computers were incompatible with plaintiff's program.[347]

A court should require a defendant to disgorge his profits on any portion of defendant's infringing sales plaintiff would not have made. In *Manufacturers Technologies,* the court awarded plaintiff the defendant's profits on sales to "noncompeting" customers, for example those who would not have purchased plaintiff's program because the cost was prohibitive.[348]

A plaintiff who markets only through distributors should recover his profits on all sales an infringing distributor makes to retailers. In *Abeshouse*,[349] the defendant was the exclusive distributor of plaintiff's copyrighted posters. Fearing plaintiff would not be able to meet demand, defendant had obtained and sold 21,500 infringing copies. Plaintiff recovered both the profit it would have made on sales to the defendant of all the infringing posters and the profits defendant made on the retail sales.[350]

---

[344] Manufacturers Technologies, Inc. v. CAMS, Inc., 728 F. Supp. 75, 15 U.S.P.Q.2d 1623 (D. Conn. 1989).

[345] 728 F. Supp. at 81, 15 U.S.P.Q.2d at 1626.

[346] Regents of the University of Minnesota v. Applied Innovations, 685 F. Supp. 698, 5 U.S.P.Q.2d 1689 (D. Minn. 1987), aff'd, 876 F.2d 626, 637 (8th Cir. 1989).

[347] 685 F. Supp. at 711-12, 5 U.S.P.Q.2d at 1699.

[348] 728 F. Supp. at 84, 15 U.S.P.Q.2d at 1629.

[349] Abeshouse v. Ultragraphics, Inc., 754 F.2d 467 (2d Cir. 1985).

[350] The court rejected as speculative plaintiff's contention that the copied posters' inferior quality damaged his ability to sell posters to others. Plaintiff had entered into a license with another company without apparent difficulty. 754 F.2d at 471.

Actual damages for lost sales are net profits. For example, the court deducts overhead from the gross revenue plaintiff would have earned on the lost sales.[351] In *Taylor*, [352] the court responded to plaintiff's assertion that its gross sales revenue would have been all profit: "[T]he contention is sufficiently improbable to require him to come forward with substantiating evidence."[353]

The infringer's activity may cause the owner to lose sales of related products not covered by the copyright.[354] In *Sunset Lamp*,[355] the court held that defendant infringed plaintiff's copyright on a floor lamp with banana leaf ornamentation. Plaintiff argued that it should be permitted at trial to prove it lost sales on its entire line of lamps, not just those with the ornamentation.[356] Its damage theory required proof of three facts: the banana leaf floor lamp was a "door opener" into the major department store market; in that market, buyers typically purchased one company's entire product line; and defendant's sale of cheaper, infringing floor lamps disrupted plaintiff's ability to enter that market and sell its entire lamp product line. The court ruled that the Copyright Act does not bar an owner from relying on a "lost convoyed sales" theory if he can demonstrate by "credible evidence" that defendant's infringement caused the loss.[357]

(2)   *License Rate.* When the copyright owner has regularly licensed third parties to use the copyrighted work in a way comparable to the infringing use,[358] the license royalty rate sets fair market value.[359]

---

[351] Taylor v. Meirick, 712 F.2d 1112, 1121, 219 U.S.P.Q. 420, 425 (7th Cir. 1983); Manufacturers Technologies, Inc. v. CAMS, Inc., 728 F. Supp. 75, 83, 15 U.S.P.Q.2d 1623, 1628 (D. Conn. 1989).

[352] Taylor v. Meirick, 712 F.2d 1112, 219 U.S.P.Q. 420 (7th Cir. 1983).

[353] 712 F.2d at 1121, 219 U.S.P.Q. at 425.

[354] The lost convoyed sales theory is related to the theory discussed at § 4F[5][c][ii] that an owner should recover a defendant's profits on sales of noninfringing goods. If plaintiff can show that marketing the infringing goods enhanced defendant's sales of noninfringing goods, plaintiff may be able to recover at least a portion of defendant's profits on the noninfringing goods.

[355] Sunset Lamp Corp. v. Alsy Corp., 749 F. Supp. 520, 16 U.S.P.Q.2d 2051 (S.D.N.Y. 1990).

[356] Plaintiff also marketed a banana leaf *table* lamp but failed to include a copyright notice on the table lamps or to cure the omission. 749 F. Supp. at 521, 16 U.S.P.Q. at 2052.

[357] The court relied on Business Trends Analysts v. Freedonia Group, Inc., 887 F.2d 399, 12 U.S.P.Q.2d 1457 (2d Cir. 1989), discussed below (suggesting that plaintiff might recover defendant's profits on sales of goods other than the infringing goods).

For a discussion of recovery of lost profits for convoyed sales and collateral products in patent infringement cases, see § 2F[5][b].

The court warned that plaintiff might be assessed costs for failure to prove the necessary facts. 749 F. Supp. at 525. "Credible evidence" might include testimony from department store buyers that they decided not to buy plaintiff's lamps after deciding to buy defendant's infringing floor lamp.

[358] "Use" here is used in a generic sense to describe infringing acts such as unauthorized reproduction or public performance. Not all unauthorized uses of a copyrighted work constitute infringement. See § 4E[2].

[359] See, e.g., Kleier Advertising, Inc. v. Premier Pontiac, Inc., 921 F.2d 1036, 17 U.S.P.Q.2d 1200 (9th Cir. 1990); United Telephone Co. of Missouri v. Johnson Publishing Co., 671 F. Supp. 1514, 1524 (W.D. Mo. 1987), aff'd, 855 F.2d 604, 613 (8th Cir. 1988).

In *Kleier Advertising,*[360] the court found that defendant used plaintiff's copyrighted advertising material to promote his automobile dealership. The court awarded plaintiff both the license fee the defendant should have paid to use plaintiff's advertisements as actual damages and defendant's car sales profits attributable to the infringement. It rejected defendant's argument that the award allowed plaintiff to recover defendant's profits twice.

> "Because license fees represent saved acquisition costs and are distinct from the profits attributable to the infringements (although 'profits' should necessarily reflect the cost of the license defendants should have paid and now must pay), this court requires defendant . . . to pay Kleier a sum to include both the damages Kleier lost from licensing and also the profits Miller Chevrolet earned as a result of the infringement."[361]

The type and number of license transactions necessary to establish a royalty rate depends on the circumstances. In *Deltak,*[362] the plaintiff sought to recover damages measured by the list price it charged its customers. Noting that "while list price is evidence of fair market value, it is not conclusive," the court assigned defendant the burden of showing that the infringing use's fair market value was less than the list price.[363]

When the defendant does not use the copyrighted work to the full extent plaintiff's established license authorizes, the courts may or may not award the full license fee. In *Cream Records,*[364] the court awarded the full fee. Defendant used a short passage from plaintiff's copyrighted song in a beer advertisement. The district court found that the license market value was $80,000 and that 15% of that sum was the value of the portion used. The Ninth Circuit reversed, holding that the entire license fee measured actual damages because there was no evidence plaintiff would have accepted less for the right to use a portion of the song. Plaintiff presented evidence that another advertiser approached plaintiff for a license but withdrew after defendant's advertisement aired.[365] Contrariwise, in *Frank Music,*[366] the court refused the full fee. Defendant's show included five songs from plaintiff's copyrighted musical drama "Kismet."

For a discussion of established royalties in patent cases, see § 2F[5][b].

[360] Kleier Advertising Co., Inc. v. James Miller Chevrolet, Inc., 722 F. Supp. 1544, 14 U.S.P.Q.2d 1061 (N.D. Ill. 1989).

[361] 722 F. Supp. at 1546, 14 U.S.P.Q.2d at 1604.

In a separate case the same plaintiff brought against another infringing automobile dealership, the jury awarded the lost licensee fee but declined to award profits. Kleier Advertising, Inc. v. Premier Pontiac, Inc., 921 F.2d 1036, 1039-40, 17 U.S.P.Q.2d 1200, 1202 (10th Cir. 1990).

[362] Deltak, Inc. v. Advanced Systems, Inc., 767 F.2d 357, 226 U.S.P.Q. 919 (7th Cir. 1985).

[363] 767 F.2d at 364, 226 U.S.P.Q. 923-24.

[364] Cream Records, Inc. v. Jos. Schlitz Brewing Co., Inc., 754 F.2d 826, 225 U.S.P.Q. 896 (9th Cir. 1985).

[365] The court affirmed the district court's award of $5000 as defendant's profits attributable to the use. Defendant did not argue that an award of both license fee and profits constituted double recovery.

[366] Frank Music Corp. v. Metro-Goldwyn-Mayer, Inc., 772 F.2d 505, 227 U.S.P.Q. 687 (9th Cir. 1985), *cert. denied,* 110 S. Ct. 1321 (1990).

Plaintiff sought the royalties he would have earned from the musical's full production. The appeals court affirmed the district court's finding that plaintiff's theory was too speculative because it was based only on plaintiff's and his agent's testimony: "[I]t is not implausible to conclude . . . that a production presenting six minutes of music from *Kismet,* without telling any of the story of the play, would not significantly impair the prospects for presenting a full production of that play."[367] *Frank Music* distinguished *Cream Records*: there, plaintiff presented convincing evidence that defendant's infringing use depleted the song's market value.

(3) *Market Value—Value of Use.* Whether a copyright owner may recover damages based on a "market value" theory, absent evidence of lost sales or an established license rate, is a point of controversy.

In patent infringement suits, the governing statute provides a hypothetical "reasonable royalty" as a minimum. There is no comparable statutory direction for copyright suits. Unlike the patent statute, the copyright statute provides for an accounting of infringer profits and for statutory damages as an alternative to damages and profits. Statutory damages are not available if the copyright owner fails to register its copyright in a timely fashion.[368] Because of these differences, Professor Nimmer argued that a reasonable royalty or market value measure is not appropriate in copyright actions.[369]

Some decisions recognize a "value in use" theory, which resembles the patent law reasonable royalty theory. In *Sid & Marty Krofft Television,*[370] the Ninth Circuit assumed, without squarely holding, that copyright damages could be measured by "value in use."[371]

---

[367] 772 F.2d at 513, 227 U.S.P.Q. at 691.

[368] See § 4F[5][d][iii].

[369] D. Nimmer & M. Nimmer, Nimmer on Copyrights § 14.02[A].

[370] Sid & Marty Krofft Television v. McDonald's Corp., 562 F.2d 1157, 196 U.S.P.Q. 97 (9th Cir. 1977).

[371] *Sid & Marty Krofft Television* applied the 1909 Copyright Act. Defendants' "McDonaldland" television commercials infringed plaintiff's copyright on its "H. R. Pufnstuf" children's television show. See § 4F[2][c]. The jury awarded $50,000 damages.

The "value in use" issue arose in the following way. In a pre-trial order, plaintiffs and defendants agreed that the jury should consider damages but not infringer profits or statutory "in lieu" damages. The trial judge instructed the jury that a copyright plaintiff could recover "only such actual damages as he has proven to be attributable to the infringing use" and that "profits of defendants are not to be considered by you in determining plaintiffs' money damages claim hereunder." After the jury verdict, plaintiffs requested the trial judge to order an accounting of the defendants' profits. Defendants argued that the jury did in fact consider infringer profits because of Instruction 49, which read:

"If you find that defendants infringed plaintiffs' copyright, plaintiffs are entitled to all of the damages, if any suffered as a result of such infringement. In arriving at any such damages, *you may take into consideration* the reasonable value if any, of plaintiffs' work including the publication and republication rights therein, and *the value, if any, to defendants of the use of plaintiffs' works.*" (Emphasis added.)

The trial court agreed. The Ninth Circuit reversed. 562 F.2d at 1174, 196 U.S.P.Q. at 111.

The Ninth Circuit's discussion of "value in use" did not relate to whether the instruction was a proper statement of the law but only to whether the instruction could be interpreted

"The value of use . . . is defined as part of the reasonable value of plaintiff's work. It amounts to a determination of what a willing buyer would have been reasonably required to pay a willing seller for plaintiff's work. . . . An author might license the use of his copyright either for a lump sum based on the reasonable value of the work or for a royalty derived from the licensee's profits, or for a combination of both."[372]

In *Deltak*,[373] the Seventh Circuit adopted the *Krofft* "value in use" theory, distinguishing it from a reasonable royalty and infringer profits. Deltak sold data processing training materials, including a "Career Development Systems" (CDS) kit with a $5000 list price. The CDS kit included as one component a "Task List," a two-column pamphlet that listed data-processing tasks on the left hand and Deltak teaching materials available for that task on the right. Deltak's competitor, Advanced Systems (ASI), had consultants create a task list that had Deltak's task designations on the left and ASI's materials on the right. The rival task list enabled ASI salespeople and potential customers to select ASI materials to train programmers in Deltak specified tasks. It made about 50 copies and distributed 15 to Deltak customers. After Deltak sued ASI for copyright infringement, ASI retrieved the infringing documents. Deltak could not recover statutory damages or attorney fees because it had not timely registered its copyright. The trial court awarded Deltak no monetary relief.[374] First, it refused to award infringer profits. ASI made a substantial profit selling materials to the 15 customers, but "it would exceed the bounds of permissible speculation to base a damage award on the hypothesis that the infringing document boosted ASI's revenues." The appeals court questioned this analysis but did not reverse it because Deltak did not appeal the infringer profits portion of the judgment.[375]

Second, the trial court found no actual damages caused by the infringement. Deltak sought an award of its per-kit profit ($4925) times 50, the number of pamphlets ASI unlawfully reproduced. The appeals court reversed, holding that Deltak should recover the 15 distributed copies' "value of use" as marketing tools "based on saved acquisition cost." The court's reasoning is difficult to follow and sometimes

---

as submitting an infringer profits recovery theory to the jury. Citing patent cases, it held that considering "value in use," that is, potential profitability to the infringer, as a factor in assessing a reasonable royalty damage award is not the same as awarding the infringer's actual profits from infringement. *See* D. Chisum, Patents § 20.03[3][b][iv]. It did not address whether a reasonable royalty could be awarded in a copyright case over an infringer's objection.

[372] 562 F.2d at 1174.

[373] Deltak, Inc. v. Advanced Systems, Inc., 767 F.2d 357, 226 U.S.P.Q. 919 (7th Cir. 1985).

[374] *Deltak* involved a peculiar twist to district court and appeals courts relations. The trial judge was Judge Richard Posner, a Seventh Circuit judge, sitting by designation. The Seventh Circuit three judge panel, which reversed the judgment, included a senior district judge sitting by designation.

[375] "This analysis seemingly placed the burden of distinguishing profits due to the infringement from 'the elements of profit attributable to factors other than the copyrighted work,' . . . on the owner instead of on the infringer. See H.R. Rep. No. 1476, 94th Cong., 2d Sess. 161 . . . However, this questionable analysis is not before us because Deltak has, for reasons not clear to this court, elected not to appeal this portion of the district court's judgment." 767 F.2d at 360.

inconsistent,[376] which may be attributable in part to ASI's unexplained concessions on fact and law issues and in part to its reluctance to deny a copyright owner any monetary remedy for an infringement. *Deltak*'s "value in use" award makes sense only as infringer's profits or a hypothetical reasonable royalty that the infringer would have agreed to pay for its use. In a footnote, the court rejected ASI's "plausible argument" "that assessment of damages in terms of saved acquisition costs is equivalent to a reasonable royalty recovery, which it contends is not available in copyright cases."[377]

In *Business Trends Analysts*,[378] the Second Circuit disagreed with *Deltak*. Predicasts, Inc. produced and published marketing studies of particular industries. In 1984, it sold its inventory and goodwill to Business Trends (BT). BT sold a robotics industry study for $1500. Former employees of Predicast formed The Freedonia Group (TFG) and produced a robotics industry study, which the court later found to infringe BT's copyright. TFG initially priced its study at $1500, but, confronted with negligible sales, dropped its price to $150 to "expand [its] customer base by exposing as many prospective customers as possible to [its] work." It sold 37. The trial court found that BTA failed to establish that TFG's infringement caused it to lose sales but awarded "value in use" plus the infringer's profits. The value in use was the full list price ($1500), less the $150 actual price, times 37 ($49,950). The infringer's profits was its gross profits ($9,745) less expenses ($5666.65). The appeals court vacated the value in use award. It agreed that "market advantage or value of use" can be recovered as part of an infringer's profits: "Although we recognize that proving the value received from an infringing product used to enhance commercial reputation may be difficult, we are unpersuaded that the difficulty is so universal that an award for such gains may never be made as a matter of law."[379] But the evidence in the case did not support such an award: "Although some gain in market recognition was conceded by TFG's president, that gain cannot be attributed to the robotics study alone because other noninfringing studies were discounted as part of the same market strategy."[380]

---

[376] For example, at one point, the court pins the value in use theory on the copyright owner's presumptive loss of sales caused by infringer's decision to implement its marketing plan with infringing rather than purchased copies.

> "If ASI had cared to undertake its campaign in a legal manner, it could have purchased copies of the Deltak task list. Each of the copies ASI distributed had a value of use to it equal to the acquisition cost saved by infringement instead of purchase, which ASI was then free to put to other uses." 767 F.2d at 361.

But later, the court asserts that value in use is *not* based on a lost sales assumption.

> "We retain lingering doubts about whether, if ASI went hat in hand to Deltak to buy fifteen copies of the Task List, Deltak would have sold any to ASI. These doubts incline us to refrain from holding the district court's finding that Deltak did not lose any sales to ASI to be clearly erroneous. Application of the value of use measure of damages, however, even when based on saved acquisition cost, does not require us to hold this finding clearly erroneous, because it is based on actual savings, not on counterfactual lost sales." 767 F.2d at 363.

[377] *Id.*, at 362 at n.3.

[378] Business Trends Analysts, Inc. v. Freedonia Group, Inc., 887 F.2d 399, 12 U.S.P.Q.2d 1457 (2d Cir. 1989).

[379] *Id.*, at 404.

[380] *Id.*

The appeals court declined to adopt the *Deltak* "value in use" approach as an actual damage theory.

> "TFG no more priced the BTA study and then decided to copy than a purse-snatcher decides to forgo friendly negotiations. BTA did not, because of the infringement, lose sales that it would have made to TFG, and TFG did not save money that it would have paid to BTA for copies of the Predicasts study. Moreover, the market value of the infringed study seems an anomalous measure of the value of use in the amount of the saved acquisition cost because that market value is in large part based on the good will attributed to the copyright plaintiff's trademark. In both *Deltak* and the instant case, the last thing the infringers wanted to buy and to sell was the actual material produced by their competitors under their competitors' name.

> "We see no room for such a speculative and artificial measure of damages under Section 504(b). The language of the provision speaks of 'actual damages suffered by' the infringed party. That is hardly a reasonable description of the entirely hypothetical sales to TFG lost by BTA. Section 504(b) also authorizes damages for 'profits of the infringer.' True saved costs may well be counted as a gain in economic theory (although not by Deltak's market value test), but the statute had a more conventional view of profits in mind. It thus further states, 'In establishing the infringer's profits, the copyright owner is required to present proof only of the infringer's gross revenue. . . . ' This language clearly indicates that Congress means 'profits' in the lay sense of gross revenue less out-of-pocket costs, not the fictive purchase price that TFG hypothetically chose not to pay to BTA.

> ". . . *Deltak* is based on a perceived need to avoid 'the anomaly of affording plaintiffs a right without a remedy.' . . . It is surely true that where an infringer such as TFG sells the offending publication at a nominal price, and there is no evidence of lost sales of the infringed publication, a conventional profits test may seem inadequate. Nevertheless, we believe we must follow the statutory scheme. . . . Congress quite consciously limited the remedies available under Section 504(b). Although Section 504(b) may provide a conventional and narrow method of calculating damages and profits, the Copyright Act does not overlook the fact that this method, if the exclusive remedy, may lead to injustice and underenforcement of the copyright laws. Under Section 504(c), a copyright plaintiff may thus elect to recover statutory damages. The specific purpose of this section is to offer plaintiffs an alternative for use where Section 504(b) provides inadequate relief. The difficulty faced by BTA and the plaintiff in *Deltak* is that neither registered their copyright before the infringement and thus are not entitled to statutory damages."[381]

Cases involving architectural plans adopt market value damage measures. A plaintiff's copyright in architectural plans precludes others from copying the plans, not from creating their own plans and using them to construct a "substantially similar"

---

[381] *Id.,* at 405, 406.

building.[382] In *Robert R. Jones Associates*,[383] the court held that "where someone makes infringing copies of another's copyrighted architectural plans, the damages recoverable by the copyright owner include . . . use of the infringing copies." Plaintiff, who was in the house design and sale business, recovered the profits he would have made on defendant's sales of houses built using plaintiff's plans.[384] In *Aiken, Hazen, Hoffman, Miller, P.C.*,[385] plaintiff prepared plans for an apartment complex for defendant. Defendant, without plaintiff's permission, used the plan to build a second complex. Because there was no "ready market for architectural plans for apartment complexes," the court awarded the amount defendant paid for the first use as the second use's "fair market value."[386]

[ii] *Infringer Profits.* To establish the infringer's profits "the copyright owner is required to present proof of the infringer's gross revenue, and the infringer is required to prove his or her deductible expenses and the elements of profit attributable to factors other than the copyrighted work."[387]

(1) *Gross Revenue.* Gross revenue is the infringing sales quantity times the infringer's price. Plaintiff must make a reasonable gross revenue showing.[388] Defendant's records may make it difficult, as an evidentiary matter, to establish gross revenues attributable to the infringing activity. Establishing gross revenue is even more difficult when the infringer's activity is not direct sales, for example, when the infringer conducts an advertising campaign using infringing material.[389]

---

[382] A 1990 Copyright Act amendment, which has only limited prospectivity, extends copyright to architectural works, that is, buildings themselves, as well as architectural plans. *See* § 4C[3][f][ii].

[383] Robert R. Jones Associates, Inc. v. Nino Homes, 858 F.2d 274, 280, 8 U.S.P.Q.2d 1224, 1230 (6th Cir. 1988).

[384] Defendant's profit margin on the sales was much less than plaintiff's. The court did not permit plaintiff to recover defendant's profits because that would result in double recovery. 858 F.2d at 281, 8 U.S.P.Q.2d at 1231.

[385] Aitken, Hazen, Hoffman, Miller, P.C. v. Empire Construction Co., 542 F. Supp. 252, 218 U.S.P.Q. 409 (D. Neb. 1982).

[386] The court deducted the costs plaintiff would have incurred if defendant had paid plaintiff to revise its plans for the second apartment complex. 542 F. Supp. at 264, 218 U.S.P.Q. at 419. It permitted plaintiff to recover the profits defendants made from the second complex's construction and sale.

In May v. Watt, 822 F.2d 896, 3 U.S.P.Q.2d 1549 (9th Cir. 1987), plaintiff entered into a contract to provide defendant design services. Alleging defendant modified his design without his permission, plaintiff sued for breach of contract and copyright infringement. The jury awarded plaintiff contract damages equal to the amount due from the defendant under the contract and nothing for copyright infringement. The court held that plaintiff's right to actual damages for copyright infringement was satisfied by the contract amount. The court also held that the plaintiff had failed to show indirect profits possibly attributable to the enhanced value of the defendant's condominium complex because of plaintiff's association with the project.

[387] 17 U.S.C. § 504(b).

[388] *E.g.*, Taylor v. Meirick, 712 F.2d 1112, 1122, 219 U.S.P.Q. 420, 426 (7th Cir. 1983).

[389] For example, in Estate of Vane v. The Fair, Inc., 849 F.2d 186, 7 U.S.P.Q.2d 1479 (5th Cir. 1988), *cert. denied*, 488 U.S. 1008 (1989), plaintiff photographed defendant's merchandise.

(2) *Costs.* If the copyright owner proves gross revenues, an infringer must prove deductible expenses associated with the infringing articles' production,[390] which includes direct costs such as material and shipping.[391] An infringer cannot deduct general overhead such as rent, depreciation, or legal fees unless he demonstrates the expenses are linked with production costs.[392] If, for example, he rented additional warehouse space to store infringing products, the court will ordinarily allow deduction of the rental cost.

Courts suggest that they may bar a willful infringer from deducting overhead expenses.[393] Neither the 1909 nor the 1976 Act support such a rule.

(3) *Apportionment.* An infringer who adds value to the infringing product has the burden of apportioning profits to "factors other than the copyrighted work."[394]

Defendant provided the photographs, without plaintiff's permission, to an advertising agency, which used them to prepare commercials. Defendant's business records did not indicate the amount of sales of the merchandise shown in plaintiff's photographs. The court rejected as inadequate plaintiff's attempt to prove gross revenue on these clothing items by expert accounting testimony.

[390] Failure to prove expenses results in an award of gross revenues. National Broadcasting Co., Inc. v. Sonneborn, 630 F. Supp. 524, 541, 231 U.S.P.Q. 513, 524 (D. Conn. 1985); Williams v. Arndt, 626 F. Supp. 571, 582, 227 U.S.P.Q. 615, 622 (D. Mass. 1985).

[391] *See, e.g.,* Ford Motor Co. v. Auto Supply Co., Inc., 661 F.2d 1171, 1174 (8th Cir. 1981). In Sygma Photo News, Inc. v. High Society Magazine, 778 F.2d 89, 92, 228 U.S.P.Q. 580, 582 (2d Cir. 1985), defendant recovered costs associated with printing magazines that were never sold by showing that it was necessary to print twice as many magazines per issue as were actually sold to obtain proper distribution. Because the extra copies were destroyed, the court was persuaded that printing them was part of the magazines' selling costs.

[392] *E.g.,* Sygma Photo News, Inc. v. High Society Magazine, 778 F.2d 89, 93, 228 U.S.P.Q. 580, 583 (2d Cir. 1985); Frank Music Corp. v. Metro-Goldwyn-Mayer, Inc., 772 F.2d 505, 516, 227 U.S.P.Q. 687, 694 (9th Cir. 1985); Taylor v. Meirick, 712 F.2d 1112, 1121 (7th Cir. 1983) ("Costs that would be incurred anyway should not be subtracted, because by definition they cannot be avoided by curtailing the profit-making activity.").

In Aitken, Hazen, Hoffman, Miller, P.C. v. Empire Construction Co., 542 F. Supp. 252, 264, 218 U.S.P.Q. 409, 420 (D. Neb. 1982), the court permitted the defendant to deduct the following expenses without showing that they would not have been incurred if defendant had not engaged in the infringing activity: a percentage of overhead expenses for officers' salaries, other salaries, payroll taxes, auto and travel, rent, employee benefits, telephone, office supplies, general insurance, general taxes, utilities, professional services, and other operating expenses.

[393] *Cf.* Frank Music Corp. v. Metro-Goldwyn-Mayer, Inc., 772 F.2d 505, 515, 227 U.S.P.Q. 687, 693 (9th Cir. 1985), *cert. denied,* 110 S. Ct. 1321 (1990) (stating that overhead may be deducted "at least where the infringement was not willful, conscious, or deliberate").

In Manufacturers Technologies, Inc. v. Cams, Inc., 728 F. Supp. 75, 84, 15 U.S.P.Q.2d 1623, 1629 (D. Conn. 1989), the court refused to deduct taxes and overhead from defendant's gross revenues because the infringement was willful. In Harper House, Inc. v. Thomas Nelson, Inc., 4 U.S.P.Q.2d 1897, 1902 (C.D. Cal. 1987), *rev'd on other grounds,* 889 F.2d 197 (9th Cir. 1989), the defendant moved for a new trial on grounds that the jury was improperly instructed not to deduct overhead if they found the infringement willful. The court denied the motion because the defendant had not objected to the instruction at trial and because the challenged rule is supported in the case law.

[394] 17 U.S.C. § 504(b).

He is entitled to "an apportionment of profits to account for his independent contributions only when 'the evidence is sufficient to provide a fair basis of division so as to give the copyright proprietor all the profits that can be deemed to have resulted from the use of what belonged to him.' "[395] If the infringing portions of products " 'are so suffused and intertwined with non-infringing portions as to render [an apportionment] impossible' . . . no apportionment is appropriate."[396]

Inability to apportion infringing profits precisely is not grounds to deny apportionment completely. "Confronted with imprecision in the computation of expenses, the court should err on the side of guaranteeing the plaintiff a full recovery."[397]

It is difficult to predict how a court or jury will apportion profits. For example, in *Gaste*,[398] the defendant combined his lyrics and plaintiff's music to produce the popular song "Feelings." Defendant argued that his lyrics were responsible for 80 percent of the song's success. The court upheld the jury award to the opposite effect, stating that given the conflicting evidence, the jury's award was reasonable.[399] In *Sygma Photo News*,[400] defendant used a copyrighted picture of Raquel Welch on the cover of a special edition of its magazine. Apparently impressed by the picture, the district court awarded the plaintiff 75 percent of the edition's profits. The court of appeals reversed, observing that the district court failed to take into account the effect of the cover's inclusion of other famous female movie stars' pictures. "[I]n our view the highest percentage of sales and hence profits attributable to the cover photograph in this case which the district court could reasonably and correctly have awarded would be 50%."[401]

(4) *Indirect Profits.* Copyright owners argue that the infringer's activity contributed to profits in other business areas.

In *Frank Music*,[402] plaintiff sought a portion of defendant's hotel and gambling revenue on the grounds that defendant's infringing floor show drew customers to its

---

[395] Gaste v. Kaiserman, 863 F.2d 1061, 1069, 9 U.S.P.Q.2d 1300, 1307 (2d Cir. 1988) (quoting Sheldon v. Metro-Goldwyn Picture Corp., 309 U.S. 390 (1940)).

[396] Business Trends Analysts, Inc. v. Freedonia Group Inc., 887 F.2d 399, 407, 12 U.S.P.Q.2d 1457, 1463 (2d Cir. 1989). *See also* Roulo v. Russ Berrie & Co., Inc., 886 F.2d 931, 942, 12 U.S.P.Q.2d 1423, 1431 (7th Cir. 1989) (given that defendant appropriated the " 'total concept and feel' of [plaintiff's] cards, rather than a few distinct protected elements, the jury's failure to accept defendant's suggested apportionment is not against the weight of the evidence").

[397] Sygma Photo News, Inc. v. High Society Magazine, 778 F.2d 89, 95, 228 U.S.P.Q. 580, 584 (2d Cir. 1985).

[398] Gaste v. Kaiserman, 863 F.2d 1061, 9 U.S.P.Q.2d 1300 (2d Cir. 1988).

[399] Defendant's expert testified that there is no set rule in the industry but it is common for the lyricist and composer to split royalties evenly. On the other hand, he also testified that, depending on the lyricist's fame, the percentage could vary widely. Also, a successful French song used the same melody with different lyrics. The court noted that this could mean either that the melody was appealing or that the French lyrics were also successful. 863 F.2d at 1070, 9 U.S.P.Q.2d at 1308.

[400] Sygma Photo News, Inc. v. High Society Magazine, 778 F.2d 89, 228 U.S.P.Q. 580 (2d Cir. 1985).

[401] 778 F.2d at 96, 228 U.S.P.Q. at 585.

[402] Frank Music Corp. v. Metro-Goldwyn-Mayer, Inc., 772 F.2d 505, 512, 227 U.S.P.Q. 687, 695 (9th Cir. 1985).

hotel and casino. The court held that an owner may recover "indirect profits" under the 1909 Act if he shows the profits are attributable to the infringing activity. The defendant's annual shareholder report stated that its operations were "materially enhanced by the popularity of the hotel's entertainment."

In *Business Trends,*[403] the court agreed that an infringer's profits might include market advantage or enhanced commercial reputation but found insufficient evidence to support such an award in the case before it.

[iii] *Prejudgment Interest.* Whether a copyright owner may recover prejudgment interest is unsettled.[404] In *Kleier,*[405] the Tenth Circuit held that prejudgment interest should be awarded on lost profits and infringer profits awards to ensure the owner is fully compensated and prevent the infringer's unjust enrichment.[406] In *Robert R. Jones Assoc.,*[407] the Sixth Circuit came to the opposite conclusion that prejudgment interest is not available to copyright owners.

In *Frank Music,*[408] the Ninth Circuit held that prejudgment interest should be awarded under the 1909 Act even though it did not express provision for such interest. It also noted that Congress' continuing silence on prejudgment interest in the 1976 Act does not necessarily mean that Congress does not intend owner to recover interest.

[d] **Statutory Damages.** Section 504(c)(1) permits a copyright owner to elect, in lieu of actual damages, "an award of statutory damages for all infringements involved in the action, with respect to any one work, for which any one infringer is liable individually, or for which any two or more infringers are liable jointly and severally, in a sum of not less than $250 or more than $10,000 as the courts consider just."[409] A 1988 amendment raised the amounts to $500 and $20,000 for causes of action arising after March 1, 1989.[410] The owner may elect statutory damages even though actual damages are not proven or are difficult to prove.[411]

---

[403] Business Trends Analysts, Inc. v. Freedonia Group, Inc., 887 F.2d 399, 12 U.S.P.Q.2d 1457 (2d Cir. 1989), discussed at § 4F[5][c][i](3).

[404] For a discussion of prejudgment interest recovery in patent infringement cases, see § 2F[5][d].

[405] Kleier Advertising, Inc. v. Premier Pontiac, Inc., 921 F.2d 1036, 1041-42, 17 U.S.P.Q.2d 1200, 1203-04 (10th Cir. 1990).

In United States Naval Institute v. Charter Communications, Inc., 17 U.S.P.Q. 1063 (S.D.N.Y. 1990), a district court held prejudgment interest appropriate only on the owner's actual damages, not the infringer's ill-gotten gain.

[406] Should the same rationale apply to statutory damages awards? If Congress provided for statutory damages "in lieu" of actual damages because proof of actual damages in copyright cases is difficult to adduce, the purposes of Sections 504(b) and (c) are the same—to compensate the copyright owner—and the better rule would be to provide prejudgment interest on statutory damages.

[407] Robert R. Jones Assoc. v. Nino Homes, 858 F.2d 274, 282, 8 U.S.P.Q.2d 1224 (6th Cir. 1988).

[408] Frank Music Corp. v. Metro-Goldwyn-Mayer, Inc., 886 F.2d 1545, 1551-52, 12 U.S.P.Q.2d 1412, 1417 (9th Cir. 1989), *cert. denied,* 110 S. Ct. 1321 (1990).

[409] 17 U.S.C. § 504(c)(1).

[410] Berne Convention Implementation Act of 1988, P.L. 100-568, § 10.

[411] Warner Bros. Inc. v. Dae Rim Trading, Inc., 877 F.2d 1120, 1126, 11 U.S.P.Q.2d 1272, 1277 (2d Cir. 1989); Harris v. Emus Records Corp., 734 F.2d 1329, 1335, 222 U.S.P.Q. 466, 470 (9th Cir. 1984).

The copyright owner may elect statutory damages at any time prior to the entry of final judgment.[412]

The courts are divided over whether an owner who seeks only statutory damages is entitled to a jury trial on the issue of copyright infringement.[413]

"The court has wide discretion in determining the amount of statutory damages to be awarded, constrained only by the specific maxima and minima,"[414] and an appeals courts will overturn the trial court's award only for abuse of discretion.[415]

[i] *Factors—Willfulness and Innocence.* Courts consider a variety of factors in establishing a specific award. The factors fall into two categories: those focusing on the infringer's blameworthiness, and other considerations, such as the expenses saved, the infringer's profits, the owner's lost revenues, and the deterrent effect on other potential infringers.[416]

The infringer's revenues and savings and the copyright owner's lost revenues may be relatively unimportant.[417] In *RSO Records,*[418] the court noted that "Undoubtedly assessed statutory damages should bear some relation to actual damages suffered. Because statutory damages are often used in cases where actual damages cannot be precisely calculated, however, they cannot be expected to correspond exactly." It found $30,000 as a rough approximation of plaintiff's lost profits on one infringed record and awarded $50,000 per infringement because the defendant's acts were willful.

Section 504(c)(2) addresses willfulness and inadvertence.

---

[412] 17 U.S.C. § 504(c).
One court found that the owner may wait to elect until the court rules on whether his actual damages and profits would be larger than what the court would award as statutory damages. RSO Records, Inc. v. Peri, 596 F. Supp. 849, 864, 225 U.S.P.Q. 407, 417 (S.D. N.Y. 1984) (infringer did not object to the procedure).

[413] Video Views, Inc. v. Studio 21, Ltd., 925 F.2d 1010, 17 U.S.P.Q.2d 1753 (7th Cir. 1991) (owner entitled to a jury on infringement and willfulness issues); Raydiola Music v. Revelation Rob., Inc., 729 F. Supp. 369, 370-71, 14 U.S.P.Q.2d 1150, 1151 (D. Del. 1990) (collecting cases and finding the better view to be that the plaintiff is not entitled to a jury trial).

[414] Harris v. Emus Records Corp., 734 F.2d 1329, 1335, 222 U.S.P.Q. 466, 470 (9th Cir. 1984). *See also* Illinois Bell Telephone Co. v. Haines and Co., Inc., 905 F.2d 1081, 1089, 15 U.S.P.Q.2d 1353, 1358 (7th Cir. 1990).

[415] Peer International Corp. v. Pausa Records, Inc., 909 F.2d 1332, 1336, 15 U.S.P.Q.2d 1530, 1534 (9th Cir. 1990).

[416] Fitzgerald Publishing Co., Inc. v. Baylor Publishing Co., Inc., 807 F.2d 1110, 1117, 1 U.S.P.Q.2d 1261, 1266 (2d Cir. 1986). *See also* Milene Music Inc. v. Gotauco, 551 F. Supp. 1288, 1296, 220 U.S.P.Q. 880, 886 (D.R.I. 1982); Boz Scags Music v. KND Corp., 491 F. Supp. 908, 914, 208 U.S.P.Q. 307 (D. Conn. 1980) ("Among the factors to be considered in arriving at a determination of damages are the expenses saved and profits reaped by the defendants in connection with the infringements, the revenues lost by the plaintiffs as a result of the defendant's conduct, and the infringer's state of mind—whether willful, knowing, or merely innocent.").

[417] Milene Music Inc. v. Gotauco., 555 F. Supp. 1288, 1296, 220 U.S.P.Q. 880, 886 (D.R.I. 1982).

[418] RSO Records, Inc. v. Peri, 596 F. Supp. 849, 862, 225 U.S.P.Q. 407, 416 (S.D. N.Y. 1984).

"In a case where the copyright owner sustains the burden of proving, and the court finds that infringement was committed willfully, the court in its discretion may increase the award of statutory damages to a sum of not more than $50,000. In a case where the infringer sustains the burden of proving, and the court finds, that such infringer was not aware and had no reason to believe that his or her acts constituted an infringement of copyright, the court it [sic] its discretion may reduce the award of statutory damages to a sum of not less than $100."[419]

A 1988 amendment raised the amounts to $100,000 and $200 for causes of action arising after March 1, 1989.[420]

"Willful" means the infringer "knows his actions constitute an infringement; the actions need not be malicious."[421] "Something less" than defendant's actual knowledge that his activities infringe another's copyright may be sufficient for a finding of willfullness. In *Fitzgerald Publishing,*[422] the defendant publisher reprinted plaintiff's work, with minor modifications, with a copyright notice showing a co-defendant as copyright owner. The court found the publisher willfully infringed because, as an experienced publisher it should have known that its right to reprint plaintiff's work did not include the right to change the copyright notice.

Defendant's reckless disregard for whether he is violating plaintiff's copyright may show willfulness. In *Lauratex Textile,*[423] the defendant purchased fabric containing plaintiff's design and began producing his infringing fabric after plaintiff's fabric became successful. After starting production, the defendant first approached one of plaintiff's best customers. There was no proof defendant knew of plaintiff's copyright, but the court held that "at the very least, he acted with reckless disregard for the rights the plaintiff had in the design."[424] In *WOW & Flutter Music,*[425] a defendant who had previously been charged with infringement because of live performances argued that he did not know copyright extended to jukebox performances. The court held that the discovery and advice of counsel in connection with the earlier suit should have put defendant on notice that the copyright public performance right did include jukebox performances.

A copyright owner's repeated license offers may suffice to put defendant on notice that his actions constitute infringement.[426] Similarly, defendant's involvement in past

---

[419] 17 U.S.C. § 504(c)(2).

[420] Berne Convention Implementation Act of 1988, P.L. 100-568, § 10.

[421] Broadcast Music Inc. v. Xanthas Inc., 855 F.2d 233, 236, 8 U.S.P.Q.2d 1254, 1256 (5th Cir. 1988); Cable Home Communication v. Network Productions, 902 F.2d 829, 851, 15 U.S.P.Q.2d 1001, 1017 (11th Cir. 1990).

[422] Fitzgerald Publishing Co., Inc. v. Baylor Publishing Co., 807 F.2d 1110, 1115, 1 U.S.P.Q.2d 1261, 1265 (2d Cir. 1986).

[423] Lauratex Textile Corp. v. Allton Knitting Mills, 519 F. Supp. 730, 215 U.S.P.Q. 521 (S.D.N.Y. 1981).

[424] 519 F. Supp. at 733, 215 U.S.P.Q. at 523.

[425] WOW & Flutter Music v. Len's Tom Jones Tavern, Inc., 606 F. Supp. 554, 557, 226 U.S.P.Q. 795, 798 (W.D.N.Y. 1985).

[426] *See, e.g.,* International Korwin Corp. v. Kowalczyk, 855 F.2d 375, 380-81, 8 U.S.P.Q.2d 1050, 1054-55 (7th Cir. 1988) (ASCAP sent defendant eight letters in three years, which

infringement suits may justify treating refusal to take a license as willful infringement.[427]

A court may take a party's conduct during the litigation into account in setting statutory damages.[428]

To meet Section 504(c)(2)'s "innocence" standard, the infringer has the burden of proving he was unaware he was infringing and that his belief was reasonable.[429] The infringer's sophistication is an important factor. In *D.C. Comics*,[430] the court found that retail store owners who sold unauthorized "Batman" goods infringed innocently. The goods did not bear copyright notices, and the court noted that the store owners were recent immigrants who spoke little English and lacked the sophistication that would prompt them to inquire about possible copyright infringement. Plaintiff's licensing director testified that a layman would "probably not" be able to distinguish licensed from infringing goods based on their style or quality.[431]

In *Peer International Corp.*,[432] involving "a corporation engaged in the business of manufacturing and distributing copyrighted works," the court found the defendant corporation acted unreasonably when it ignored a letter from plaintiff terminating a license agreement and continued to use the plaintiff's copyrighted works.

[ii] *Multiple Infringement.* The 1909 Act permitted the court to award statutory damages for each infringement of each infringed work. The 1976 Act only permits "an award of statutory damages for all infringements involved in the action, with respect to any one work, for which any one infringer is liable individually, or for which any two or more infringers are liable jointly and severally."[433] All parts of a compilation or derivative work constitute one work.[434]

---

defendant ignored as a "nuisance"); Rare Blue Music, Inc. v. Guttadauro, 616 F. Supp. 1528, 1530-31, 227 U.S.P.Q. 325, 326 (D. Mass. 1985) (defendant ignored ASCAP's repeated attempts for seven years to convince him to obtain a license).

[427] Boz Scaggs Music v. KND Corp., 491 F. Supp. 908, 914-15, 208 U.S.P.Q. 307 (D. Conn. 1980).

[428] Warner Bros. Inc. v. Dae Rim Trading, Inc., 877 F.2d 1120, 1126, 11 U.S.P.Q.2d 1272, 1277 (2d Cir. 1989) (plaintiff's vexatious conduct in prosecution of lawsuit justified an award of only $100).

[429] Peer International Corp. v. Pausa Records, Inc., 909 F.2d 1332, 1336, 15 U.S.P.Q. 1530, 1533 (9th Cir. 1990).

[430] D.C. Comics, Inc. v. Mini Gift Shop, 912 F.2d 29, 15 U.S.P.Q.2d 1888 (2d Cir. 1990).

[431] *Compare* Paramount Pictures Corp. v. Labus, 16 U.S.P.Q.2d 1142, 1147 (W.D. Wis. 1990). In *Paramount Pictures,* defendant copied motion picture videocassettes and rented copies to his hotel guests for a fee. Citing the FBI warning at the beginning of each cassette, the court rejected defendant's argument that he had no reason to know his acts were infringing. Defendant's unsuccessful attempt to rely on the fair use defense demonstrated a "legal sophistication" that contradicted the "innocent infringer" argument.

[432] Peer International Corp. v. Pausa Records, Inc., 909 F.2d 1332, 1336, 15 U.S.P.Q.2d 1530, 1533 (9th Cir. 1990).

[433] 17 U.S.C. § 504(c)(1).

[434] 17 U.S.C. § 504(c).

"Both the text of the Copyright Act and its legislative history make clear that statutory damages are calculated according to the number of works infringed, not the number of infringements."[435] The House Report states:

> "A single infringer of a single work is liable for a single amount between $250 and $10,000, no matter how many acts of infringement are involved in the action and regardless of whether the acts were separate, isolated, or occurred in a related series. . . . Moreover, although the minimum and maximum amounts are to be multiplied where multiple 'works' are involved in the suit, the same is not true with respect to multiple copyrights, multiple owners, multiple exclusive rights, or multiple registrations. This point is especially important since, under a scheme of divisible copyright, it is possible to have the rights of a number of owners of separate 'copyrights' in a single 'work' infringed by one act of a defendant."[436]

Questions arise regarding what constitutes one work. The courts adopted a test that inquires whether separate works can "live their own copyright life."[437] If arguably separate works have "no separate economic value, whatever their artistic value, they must be considered part of [a] . . . 'work' for purposes of the copyright statute."[438]

In *Walt Disney*,[439] the court found that the defendant had only infringed two copyrights, one each in Mickey and Minnie Mouse, even though the plaintiff had registered copyrights depicting those characters in a variety of poses. In *RSO Records*,[440] the court found that the graphics for a recording and the recording itself were one "work" for statutory damages purposes. "Inasmuch as graphics simply complement the recording and have no separate economic value, whatever their artist [sic] value, they must be considered part of the musical 'work' for purposes of the copyright statute."[441]

In contrast, in *Cormack*,[442] the court found that plaintiff was entitled to separate statutory damage award for two copyrighted tests, one designed to detect honesty and the other workplace emotional status. Each test was "capable of living its 'own copyright life.' " They were designed to test different traits, had no questions in common, did not cross-reference each other, were independently scored, and had separate instruction sheets.

[iii] *Registration Requirement.* To recover statutory damages or attorney fees, Section 412 requires an owner to register his work within three months of first

---

[435] Walt Disney v. Powell, 897 F.2d 565, 569, 14 U.S.P.Q.2d 1160, 1163-64 (D.C. Cir. 1990).

[436] H.R. Rep. No. 1733, 94th Cong., 2d Sess. 162 (1976).

[437] Walt Disney Co. v. Powell, 897 F.2d 565, 569, 14 U.S.P.Q.2d 1160, 1164 (D.C. Cir. 1990).

[438] RSO Records, Inc. v. Peri, 596 F. Supp. 849, 862, 225 U.S.P.Q. 407, 416 (S.D. N.Y. 1984).

[439] Walt Disney Co. v. Powell, 897 F.2d 565, 569-70, 14 U.S.P.Q.2d 1160, 1164 (D.C. Cir. 1990).

[440] RSO Records, Inc. v. Peri, 569 F. Supp. 849, 862, 225 U.S.P.Q. 407, 416 (S.D.N.Y. 1984).

[441] 596 F. Supp. at 862, 225 U.S.P.Q. at 416.

[442] Cormack v. Sunshine Food Stores, Inc., 675 F. Supp. 374, 4 U.S.P.Q.2d 1366 (E.D. Mich. 1987).

publication or before the defendant's infringing activities began. This provision's purpose is to encourage registration.[443]

In most cases, Section 412's application is simple: an owner who failed to register is unable to elect statutory damages.[444] When the owner registers the copyright more than three months after publication and after the infringer commenced his activity, the owner may seek to avoid Section 412's effect by arguing that the infringer's acts after registration constitute separately actionable infringements. The general rule is that the owner may not recover statutory damages for continued post-registration activity.[445] Even when the infringer's acts take place intermittently over a lengthy time period, the acts are one continuous infringement if they are all of the same nature.

In *Mason*,[446] the infringer revised, copied, and distributed infringing maps in 1985, 1988, and 1989. The copyright owner registered in 1987. The court found the infringements continuous, rejecting the owner's argument that "[w]here a party has committed many widely separated, distinct acts of infringement commencing after registration of the copyrights, then statutory damages must be awarded if Plaintiff so elects." Section 412 eschewed the 1909 Act's multiple infringement doctrine.

[e] Attorney Fees and Costs. Section 505 grants the courts discretion to award full costs against "any party" except the United States and also to "award a reasonable attorney's fee to the prevailing party as part of the costs."[447] A prevailing copyright owner who failed to register his copyright within three months of the work's publication or before the infringement began cannot recover attorney fees.[448]

[i] *Costs.* The 1909 Copyright Act made a cost award to the prevailing party mandatory; the 1976 Act makes cost awards discretionary with the court. Typically, courts grant costs to the prevailing party without discussion—even when attorney fees are not awarded.[449]

[ii] *Attorney Fees.* The court can only award attorney fees to the "prevailing party." The prevailing party is "one who succeeds on a significant issue in the litigation that achieves some of the benefits the party sought in bringing suit."[450]

---

[443] Business Trends Analysts v. Freedonia Group, Inc., 887 F.2d 399, 406-07, 12 U.S.P.Q.2d 1457, 1463 (2d Cir. 1989).

[444] M.G.B. Homes, Inc. v. Ameron Homes, Inc., 903 F.2d 1486, 1493, 15 U.S.P.Q.2d 1282, 1288 (11th Cir. 1990).

[445] Mason v. Montgomery Data, Inc., 741 F. Supp. 1282, 1285, 16 U.S.P.Q.2d 1366, 1368 (S.D. Tex. 1990); Singh v. Famous Overseas, Inc., 680 F. Supp. 533, 536, 6 U.S.P.Q.2d 1969, 1971 (E.D. N.Y. 1988); Johnson v. University of Virginia, 606 F. Supp. 321, 325, 226 U.S.P.Q. 356, 358 (W.D. Va. 1985).

[446] Mason v. Montgomery Data, Inc., 741 F. Supp. 1282, 16 U.S.P.Q.2d 1366 (S.D. Tex. 1990).

[447] 17 U.S.C. § 505.

[448] 17 U.S.C. § 412(2); Aitken, Hazen, Hoffman, Miller, P.C. v. Empire Construction Co., 542 F. Supp. 252, 268, 218 U.S.P.Q. 409, 422 (D. Neb. 1982). See § 4G[4][c].

[449] E.g., Milene Music, Inc. v. Gotauco, 551 F. Supp. 1288, 1297, 220 U.S.P.Q. 880, 888 (D. R.I. 1982).

[450] Warner Brothers, Inc. v. Dae Rim Trading, Inc., 877 F.2d 1120, 1126, 11 U.S.P.Q.2d 1272, 1277 (2d Cir. 1989). See also Cable/Home Communication Corp. v. Network Productions, Inc., 902 F.2d 829, 853, 15 U.S.P.Q.2d 1001, 1019 (11th Cir. 1990).

A question of who is the prevailing party may arise when a copyright owner charges infringement of two copyrights and establishes infringement of only one. In *Warner Brothers*,[451] the district court awarded the accused infringer fees when the copyright owner withdrew one of its two infringement charges before trial and the owner obtained only a permanent injunction the infringer had agreed to long before trial. The Second Circuit reversed the award because neither parties' success was "sufficiently significant."

The statute gives courts discretion whether to award attorney fees. Courts disagree whether a finding that a party acted willfully or maliciously (if the infringer) or frivolously (if the copyright owner) is a prerequisite to a fee award. The Ninth Circuit requires a finding of "bad faith or frivolity";[452] the Eleventh Circuit requires only that the "party receiving the fee be the 'prevailing party' and that the fee be reasonable."[453] The Second Circuit distinguishes between prevailing copyright owners and infringers.[454] A prevailing infringer must show that the owner's claims were "objectively without arguable merit." The rationale is that public policy encourages copyright owners to bring "colorable" claims.

If an infringer acts willfully or deliberately, or if a copyright owner prosecutes a frivolous action, most courts will award fees.[455] Conversely, if an infringer acts innocently,[456] or the owner loses a difficult question of copyright law,[457] the court will probably not award fees.

Courts use a variety of factors to determine the amount of a reasonable award. In *Micromanipulator*,[458] the court listed the following factors, all of which must be considered:

---

[451] Warner Brothers, Inc. v. Dae Rim Trading, Inc., 677 F. Supp. 740, 6 U.S.P.Q.2d 1423 (S.D. N.Y. 1988), *rev'd,* 877 F.2d 1120, 1126, 11 U.S.P.Q.2d 1272, 1277 (2d Cir. 1989).

[452] Cooling Systems and Flexibles v. Stuart Radiator, 777 F.2d 485, 493, 228 U.S.P.Q. 275, 282 (9th Cir. 1985).

[453] Original Appalachian Artworks, Inc. v. Toy Loft, Inc., 684 F.2d 821, 832, 215 U.S.P.Q. 745, 755 (11th Cir. 1982).

See also Micromanipulator Co., Inc. v. Bough, 779 F.2d 255, 259, 228 U.S.P.Q. 443, 446 (5th Cir. 1985) ("Although attorney's fees are awarded in the trial court's discretion, they are the rule rather than the exception and should be awarded routinely.")

[454] Diamond v. Am-Law Publishing Corp., 745 F.2d 142, 148, 223 U.S.P.Q. 709, 713 (2d Cir. 1984).

[455] Cooling Systems and Flexibles v. Stuart Radiator, Inc., 777 F.2d 485, 493, 228 U.S.P.Q. 275, 282 (9th Cir. 1985) (frivolous prosecution justifies award against copyright owner); Taylor v. Meirick, 712 F.2d 1112, 1122, 219 U.S.P.Q. 420, 426 (7th Cir. 1983) (defendant's infringement is willful); Spectravest, Inc. v. Mervyn's, Inc., 673 F. Supp. 1486, 1493, 6 U.S.P.Q.2d 1135, 1140 (C.D. Cal. 1987).

[456] *E.g.,* Roulo v. Russ Berrie & Co., Inc., 886 F.2d 931, 12 U.S.P.Q.2d 1423 (7th Cir. 1989) (district court properly considered defendant's non-willfulness in determining not to award fees); Dolori Fabrics, Inc. v. Limited, Inc., 662 F. Supp. 1347, 1357-58, 3 U.S.P.Q.2d 1753, 1760 (S.D.N.Y. 1987) (attorney fees awarded against defendant who was a "deliberate infringer" but not against a co-defendant who was an "unintentional infringer").

[457] *E.g.,* Jartech, Inc. v. Clancy, 666 F.2d 403, 213 U.S.P.Q. 403 (9th Cir. 1982).

[458] Micromanipulator Co., Inc. v. Bough, 779 F.2d 255, 228 U.S.P.Q. 443 (5th Cir. 1985).

"(1) The time and labor required, (2) the novelty and difficulty of the questions, (3) the skill requisite to perform the legal service properly, (4) the preclusion of other employment by the attorney due to acceptance of the case, (5) the customary fee [for similar work in the community], (6) whether the fee is fixed or contingent, (7) time limitations imposed by the client or the circumstances, (8) the amount involved and the results obtained, (9) the experience, reputation, and ability of the attorneys, (10) the 'undesirability' of the case, (11) the nature and length of the professional relationship with the client, and (12) awards in similar cases."[459]

§ 4G   Ownership, Transfers and Terminations

Copyright "vests initially in the author or authors of the work"[1] and is a property item transferable by "any means of conveyance or by operation of law."[2] Transfers "other than by operation of law" are valid only if in writing.[3]

A work's "author" is the human who actually created it—with one important exception: A work-for-hire's author is the human creator's employer.[4]

---

[459] 779 F.2d at 259, 228 U.S.P.Q. at 446.

See also Oboler v. Goldin, 714 F.2d 211, 213, 220 U.S.P.Q. 166, 167 (2d Cir. 1983) ("courts consider the amount of work, the skill employed, damages at issue, and the result achieved"); Milene Music, Inc. v. Gotauco, 551 F. Supp. 1288, 1298, 220 U.S.P.Q. 880, 888 (D.R.I. 1982) (court must consider eight factors).

[1] 17 U.S.C. § 201(a).

[2] 17 U.S.C. § 201(d)(1).

[3] 17 U.S.C. § 204(a).

See Effects Associates Inc. v. Cohen, 908 F.2d 555, 15 U.S.P.Q.2d 1559 (9th Cir. 1990), *cert. denied sub nom.*, Danforth v. Cohen, 111 S. Ct. 1003 (1991) (rejecting "Movie-makers do lunch not contracts" argument; plaintiff made and delivered special effects movie footage to defendant, "a low-budget horror movie mogul," pursuant to an oral agreement; HELD: defendant did not obtain copyright ownership or an exclusive license, but plaintiff's handing over the film gave defendant an implied nonexclusive license to incorporate the footage into the intended movie ("The Stuff"). In *Effects Associates*, the court noted:

"The law couldn't be clearer:

. . .

"Common sense tells us that agreements should routinely be put in writing. This simple practice prevents misunderstanding by spelling out the terms of a deal in black and white, forces parties to clarify their thinking and consider problems that could potentially arise, and encourages them to take their promises seriously because it's harder to backtrack on a written contract than on an oral one. Copyright law dovetails nicely with common sense by requiring that a transfer of copyright ownership be in writing.

"Section 204's writing requirement is not unduly burdensome; it necessitates neither protracted negotiations nor substantial expense. The rule is really quite simple: If the copyright holder agrees to transfer ownership to another party that party must get the copyright holder to sign a piece of paper saying so. It doesn't have to be the Magna Charta; a one-line pro forma statement will do." 908 F.2d at 556–57, 15 U.S.P.Q.2d at 1560–61.

[4] 17 U.S.C. § 201(c). *See* § 4G[2].

Two or more persons are joint authors if they create "with the intention that their contributions be merged into inseparable or interdependent parts of a unitary whole."[5]

Licenses and assignments are vulnerable to abrogation or termination because of copyright law's transfer termination and renewal provisions.[6]

[1]   Distinguishing Works for Hire, Joint Works, Derivative Works, and Contributions to Collective Works

If more than one person (A and B) participates in a work's creation, it may be (1) a work for hire, (2) a joint work, (3) a derivative work, or (4) a separate work that is part of a collective work. The work's category affects copyright ownership, duration, and termination transfer rights.

A "work for hire" results if A and B are employer and employee and B creates the work in the course of her employment.[7] A, the employer, is the work's author for all copyright law purposes. A is deemed sole author by operation of law; A may or may not have participated in the actual creation of the work.[8] Copyright ownership initially vests in A, and B has no transfer termination rights. The work's copyright term is not dependent on the author's life.[9] A corporation or other legal entity may be a work-for-hire's author.

A "joint work" results if A and B make individual contributions of original expression, intending that they be merged into "inseparable or interdependent parts of a unitary whole."[10] A and B are co-owners of the copyright in the work. Each may authorize others to make copies, public performances, or derivative works. One author may assign, or be contractually obligated to assign, her ownership to the other. The work's copyright term is "the life of the last surviving author and fifty years after such last surviving author's death."[11] Each joint author has a right to terminate his or her transfers.

Two works, an "original work" and a "derivative work," result if A creates a work and B, with A's consent,[12] modifies A's work.[13] A and B remain sole authors and

---

[5] 17 U.S.C. §§ 101, 201(a). *See* § 4G[3].

[6] 17 U.S.C. §§ 203, 304(c). *See* § 4G[4].

[7] *See* § 4G[2].

[8] If a work is for hire, A is the author and that ends further inquiry. If it is not a work for hire, it may be necessary to determine whether A is a joint author with rights of co-ownership with B. *See* Community for Creative Non-Violence v. Reid, 490 U.S. 730, 10 U.S.P.Q.2d 1985 (1989), discussed at § 4G[2][b].

[9] 17 U.S.C. § 302(c) ("seventy-five years from the year of its first publication, or a term of seventy-five years from the year of its creation, whichever expires first").

[10] *See* § 4G[3].

[11] 17 U.S.C. § 302(b).

[12] If B does not obtain consent, copyright protection may be withheld because of the statutory direction that "protection for a work employing preexisting material in which copyright subsists does not extend to any part of the work in which such material has been used unlawfully." 17 U.S.C. § 103(a).

Consent to create a derivative work can be implied. *Cf.* JBJ Fabrics, Inc. v. Brylane, Inc., 714 F. Supp. 107, 110, 12 U.S.P.Q.2d 1839, 1841 (S.D. N.Y. 1989) ("the fact that plaintiff did not receive either a formal assignment of the right to make derivative works or an exclusive

owners of the copyrights—A of the original work and B of the derivative work. A's copyright gives A no right to make copies or to perform B's derivative work without B's permission.[14] B's copyright gives B no right to make further derivative works using A's original work without A's permission. Considerable complication arises if the derivative work falls into the public domain before the original work or the original work's author exercises his or her statutory right to terminate transfers.[15]

A and B may create separate works that are assembled into a collective work.[16] For example, A and B may write poems, which C compiles, with A and B's permission, into an anthology. A and B remain sole authors of separate works, with individual rights to terminate any subsequent transfer of copyright interests. No joint work of A and B results because there was no intention that the contributions be merged into an integral whole. Neither is a derivative work of the other because neither is based on the other. C's collective work may itself be copyrightable, but, absent a written transfer, A and B retain ownership of the copyright in their contributions and C, the creator of the collective work, only acquires the privilege of reproducing and distributing the contribution as part of the particular collective work.[17]

Complications arise when derivative works are based on joint works. A joint author, as co-owner of the joint work copyright, may create or authorize others to create derivative works without the other joint author's permission. The noncontributing joint author may infringe the derivative work copyright, for example, by making copies without authority. In *Weissmann*,[18] two scientists, Freeman and Weissmann, produced a series of articles on nuclear medicine. Later, Weissmann produced a paper ("P-1") derived from the prior jointly-authored papers but added new elements. Freeman made unauthorized copies of Weissmann's revised paper. In Weissmann's suit against Freeman, the district court found no copyright right infringement, reasoning that the entire series of works, including P-1, was a "single evolutionary joint work." The Second Circuit reversed.

---

license is not dispositive here. Section 103 . . . does no more than limit plaintiff's copyright protection to those aspects of its design which it has not unlawfully adopted, and, as the Second Circuit has held, unauthorized use is not equivalent to unlawful use. *See Eden Toys Inc. v. Florelee Undergarment Co.*, 697 F.2d 27, 34 n.6 (2d Cir. 1982). If the Farkas painting is not itself the subject of copyright, or if plaintiff did indeed have informal authorization from Farkas to use the painting in its fabric design, such as a non-exclusive license, then it is not using the painting unlawfully and may not face any limits on the scope of its copyright protection.").

If the original author assigns his copyright, the assignee may authorize the creation of derivative works. *See* Cortner v. Israel, 732 F.2d 267, 222 U.S.P.Q. 756 (2d Cir. 1984).

[13] *See* §§ 4C[1][c] and 4E[3][b][iii].

[14] This result obtains even when the original work is jointly authored by A and B. *See* Weissmann v. Freeman, 868 F.2d 1313, 1318, 10 U.S.P.Q.2d 1014, 1017–18 (2d Cir. 1989), *cert. denied*, 110 S. Ct. 219 (1989), discussed *infra*.

[15] *See* § 4G[4][c].

[16] *See* § 4C[1][b].

[17] 17 U.S.C. § 201(c).

[18] Weissmann v. Freeman, 868 F.2d 1313, 10 U.S.P.Q.2d 1014 (2d Cir. 1989), *cert. denied*, 110 S. Ct. 219 (1989).

"The finding was made based on the district court's mistaken view that joint authorship of the prior existing works automatically makes the two joint authors co-owners of the derivative work. Such a ruling stands copyright law on its head. It flies in the face of the Copyright Act which affords protection to each work at the moment of its creation.

"Of greater significance is that the trial court's view would convert all derivative works based upon jointly authored works into joint works, regardless of whether there had been any joint labor on the subsequent version. If such were the law, it would eviscerate the independent copyright protection that attaches to a derivative work that is wholly independent of the protection afforded the preexisting work."[19]

Weissmann's paper, P-1, was a derivative work because the added matter met the copyright originality standard; it was not a joint work because Freeman made no contribution to it, and Weissmann, as the sole contributor, did not intend that her work be merged into an integrated whole with the prior joint works. "Even though one co-author has the right to revise a joint work in order to create an individual derivative work, the other co-author acquires no property rights in the newly created work prepared without his involvement."[20]

In *Ashton-Tate Corp.*,[21] two computer programmers, Ross and Wigginton, agreed to collaborate in development of a spreadsheet program for the Apple Macintosh computer, Ross to work on the "engine," the computational component, Wigginton on the "user interface." Ross gave Wigginton a list of user commands. Later, the two disagreed on how to market the new program. Wigginton told Ross that he was going to work for Ashton-Tate, a major software publisher, and was taking the user interface portion of the new program with him. Ross completed the user interface and engine components and published the program as "MacCalc." Wigginton adapted his user interface to a new engine, which Ashton-Tate published as "Full Impact." Ross demanded that Ashton-Tate compensate him for his contribution to "Full Impact," and Ashton-Tate filed a declaratory judgment suit. The court held that Ross had no copyright interest in "Full Impact." Ross was not a joint author of the user interface because he did not contribute copyrightable expression. That "MacCalc" may be a Ross-Wigginton joint work and that "Full Impact" may be derived from it does not make Ross a joint author of "Full Impact."

"It is possible . . . to conceive of the entire MacCalc prototype as a joint work. Indeed, if Ross and Wigginton intended to create a joint work, and both contributed copyrightable material to the resulting work (the MacCalc prototype), then they may have both obtained an undivided interest in the entire work.

"In other words, Ross may have obtained a one-half ownership interest in the user interface and Wigginton may have obtained a one-half interest in the engine. We need not decide this issue now, however. Even assuming, arguendo, that Ross does have a one-half interest in the interface written by Wigginton,

---

[19] 868 F.2d at 1317, 10 U.S.P.Q.2d at 1017.

[20] 868 F.2d at 1318, 10 U.S.P.Q.2d at 1018.

[21] Ashton-Tate Corp. v. Ross, 916 F.2d 516, 16 U.S.P.Q.2d 1541 (9th Cir. 1990).

it does not follow that Ross is a joint author of the Full Impact program because its interface is derived from his and Wigginton's joint work. . . . Joint authorship in a prior work is insufficient to make one a joint author of a derivative work. . . . "[22]

Ross' remedy, if any, would be an accounting from Wigginton:

"While an author of a joint work does not acquire an authorship interest in derivative works that utilize part of the joint work, that author may be entitled to compensation for the use of the original joint work. The problem for Appellants in this appeal, however, is that such a claim for compensation is not a copyright claim. Furthermore, the claim would have to be against the alleged 'co-author' Wigginton, because he was the person who allegedly allowed Ashton-Tate to use the user interface portion of the joint work for use in Full Impact."[23]

[2] Works for Hire

Under copyright law's "work for hire" provisions, the employer is the author of works prepared by employees within the scope of their employment unless there is a written agreement to the contrary. The same is true of certain types of specially commissioned works.

A work for hire determination differs from a copyright transfer. With a transfer, the transferee acquires copyright ownership but does not become the author. With a work for hire, the employer becomes the author for all Copyright Act purposes,[24] and the human author has no transfer termination rights. Also, under Section 302(c), copyright duration for a work for hire is set at 75 years from publication or 100 years from creation, whichever comes first, rather than being based on the life of the real author. As the Supreme Court noted in *Community for Creative Non-Violence,*[25] "[t]he contours of the work for hire doctrine . . . carry profound significance for freelance creators—including artists, writers, photographers, designers,

---

[22] 916 F.2d at 522, 16 U.S.P.Q.2d at 1547.

[23] 916 F.2d at 523, 16 U.S.P.Q.2d at 1547.

[24] In Community for Creative Non-Violence v. Reid, 490 U.S. 730, 10 U.S.P.Q.2d 1985 (1989), the Supreme Court outlined the work-for-hire provisions of the 1976 Act and the importance of the determination of a work's status as a work for hire.

"The Copyright Act of 1976 provides that copyright ownership 'vests initially in the author or authors of the work.' 17 U.S.C. § 201(a). As a general rule, the author is the party who actually creates the work, that is, the person who translates an idea into a fixed, tangible expression entitled to copyright protection. § 102. The Act carves out an important exception, however, for 'works made for hire.' . . . If the work is for hire, 'the employer or other person for whom the work was prepared is considered the author' and owns the copyright, unless there is a written agreement to the contrary. § 201(b). Classifying a work as 'made for hire' determines not only the initial ownership of its copyright, but also the copyright's duration, § 302(c), and the owners' renewal rights, § 304(a), termination rights, § 203(a), and right to import certain goods bearing the copyright, § 601(b)(1)." 490 U.S. at 737, 10 U.S.P.Q.2d at 1989.

[25] Community for Creative Non-Violence v. Reid, 490 U.S. 730, 10 U.S.P.Q.2d 1985 (1989).

composers, and computer programmers—and for the publishing, advertising, music, and other industries which commission their works."[26]

The 1976 Act's work for hire provision differs from the prior copyright statute, the 1909 Act. Because the 1976 Act does not operate retroactively to alter ownership of works created prior to its effective date, January 1, 1978,[27] the interpretation of the 1909 Act is still important.

[a] **The 1909 Act.** Section 62 of the 1909 Act provided that "the word 'author' shall include an employer in the case of works made for hire"[28] but did not define "employer" or "works made for hire." The courts "concluded that the work for hire doctrine codified in § 62 referred only to works made by employees in the regular course of their employment. As for commissioned works, the courts generally presumed that the commissioned party had impliedly agreed to convey the copyright, along with the work itself, to the hiring party."[29]

Under the 1909 Act, a work by an employee or a person under commission was only presumptively a work for hire, a presumption a written or oral agreement or custom could defeat.[30]

---

[26] 490 U.S. at 737, 10 U.S.P.Q.2d at 1989.

[27] Real Estate Data, Inc. v. Sidwell Co., 809 F.2d 366, 1 U.S.P.Q.2d 1475 (7th Cir. 1987); Roth v. Pritikin, 710 F.2d 934, 939, 219 U.S.P.Q. 204, 208 (2d Cir. 1983), *cert. denied*, 464 U.S. 961, 220 U.S.P.Q. 385 (1983).

In *Roth*, Pritikin solicited Roth to write recipes in Pritikin's diet books. Roth and Pritikin made an oral agreement for a flat fee. Roth's contribution was completed by August 1977. After January 1, 1978, Roth sued, relying on the 1976 Act. The parties agreed that the oral contract was proper under the 1909 Act. The Second Circuit held that the 1909 Act, not the 1976 Act, applied. The court believed that "the Act's language, its legislative history, and generally applicable rules of statutory interpretation all mandate prospective application of the rules governing work for hire agreements." Section 103 of the 1976 Act does state that it applies to "all legal and equitable rights that are equivalent to any of the exclusive rights" of copyright. However, "Section 301 does not . . . purport to determine who holds a copyright for works created before January 1978. It merely clarifies the rights of individuals owning copyrights on that date, whomever they may be." Furthermore, retroactive application of the 1976 Act to work for hire questions would "raise a serious issue concerning the Act's constitutionality. . . . An interest in a copyright is a property right protected by the due process and just compensation clauses of the Constitution." 710 F.2d at 939, 219 U.S.P.Q. at 208.

[28] 17 U.S.C. § 26 (1976 ed.) (1909 Act).

[29] Community for Creative Non-Violence v. Reid, 490 U.S. 730, 744, 10 U.S.P.Q.2d 1985, 1992 (1989), discussed at § 4G[2][b].

For an interesting decision finding that works by a member of a religious order were not works for hire, see Schmid Brothers, Inc. v. W. Goebel Porzellanfabrik KG., 223 U.S.P.Q. 859 (E.D. N.Y. 1984).

[30] May v. Morganelli-Heumann & Associates, 618 F.2d 1363, 1368, 207 U.S.P.Q. 476, 481 (9th Cir. 1980) ("the doctrine is based on the presumed mutual intent of the parties, and does not operate as a matter of law"); Sargent v. American Greetings Corp., 588 F. Supp. 912, 921, 223 U.S.P.Q. 1327, 1334 (N.D. Ohio 1984) ("the presumption . . . operates only in the event it is not possible to ascertain the express or implied contractual intent of the parties").

In *Easter Seal*,[31] Judge Gee traced the evolution of the 1909 Act work for hire provision's application to works by independent contractors.

"The obvious question implicit in the statute was whether independent contractors could be statutory 'employees.' That question remained unanswered for a surprisingly long time.

"In the Second Circuit—the *de facto* Copyright Court of the United States— there was an early line of cases dealing with commissioned works by photographers. The court developed a presumption that the parties intended the buyer to hold the copyrights in the photographs. In *Yardley v. Houghton Mifflin Co.*, 108 F.2d 28 (2d Cir. 1939), *cert. denied*, 309 U.S. 686, 60 S. Ct. 891, 84 L. Ed. 1029 (1940), the court applied this presumption to a commissioned mural painted on a building. . . . These early cases presumed that the copyrights were *assigned* to the patron under the commission contract; there was nothing in them about 'work for hire.' *Yardley* itself was inconsistent with the 'works made for hire' clause of § 26. Under the 1909 Act, authors had rights different from assignees, including the right to renewal. If the *Yardley* court had deemed the mural a work 'made for hire,' the statutory employer (the patron) rather than the statutory employee (the artist) would have held the renewal rights as the statutory 'author.' Instead, the court explicitly assumed that the artist's executor rather than the patron had the right to renew the copyright in the mural. . . . As late as 1955, the 'presumed assignment' rule of *Yardley* was distinct from a more radical 'presumption' that the commissioning party was the surrogate author under the 'works made for hire' language of § 26. . . .

"In *Brattleboro Publishing Co. v. Winmill Publishing Corp.*, 369 F.2d 565 (2d Cir. 1966), the Second Circuit explicitly merged the *Yardley* rule into the 'work for hire' doctrine for the first time. Plaintiff newspaper sued defendant newspaper for using advertising copy that the plaintiff had prepared for merchants who later advertised in defendant's paper. The court recited a number of employer/employee cases and summarized them as creating the rule that the employer is the 'author' 'whenever an employee's work is produced at the instance and expense of his employer.' . . . Then came the critical twist: 'We see no sound reason why these same principles are not applicable when the parties bear the relationship of employer and independent contractor.' . . . The court held that there was no infringement because the merchants who paid for the ads were the 'authors' under the 'work for hire' doctrine. However, the court also discussed the unfairness to the newspaper's advertising customers of the contrary result, and Chief Judge Lumbard concurred solely on the

---

[31] Easter Seal Society for Crippled Children and Adults of Louisiana Inc. v. Playboy Enterprises, 815 F.2d 323, 2 U.S.P.Q.2d 1585 (5th Cir. 1987), *cert. denied*, 485 U.S. 981 (1988). Judge Gee notes that "this most delightful of casenames [is] seriously rivaled . . . only by *United States v. 11 1/4 Dozen Packages of Article Labeled in Part Mrs. Moffat's Shoo Fly Powders for Drunkenness*, 40 F. Supp. 208 (W.D.N.Y. 1941) . . . and *United States ex rel. Mayo v. Satan and his Staff*, 54 F.R.D. 282 (W.D. Pa. 1971)." 815 F.2d at 324 n.1, 2 U.S.P.Q.2d at 1586 n.1.

ground that 'probable intent' of the parties to a newspaper advertising contract was enough to sustain the judgment. . . . Thus, the relationship of the *Yardley* rule to the holding in *Brattleboro* was sufficiently ambiguous that the expansive language of the case could have been limited to its special facts.

"But *Brattleboro* was not so limited. In *Picture Music, Inc. v. Bourne, Inc.*, 457 F.2d 1213 (2d Cir.), *cert. denied*, 409 U.S. 997, 93 S. Ct. 320, 34 L. Ed. 2d 262 (1972), the Second Circuit confronted a copyright claim by the assignee of a paradigmatic independent contractor. The court affirmed the broad language of *Brattleboro* and the use of *Yardley* as a 'work for hire' case. Although there was little doubt after *Picture Music* that the 'presumption' of *Yardley* had been adopted without limitation in 'work for hire' doctrine so that whoever commissioned a work was presumed the statutory 'author,' the Second Circuit soon dispelled all doubt by announcing a pure 'instance and expense' test for 'works made for hire' in a case involving an independent contractor:

'[The "work for hire"] doctrine is applicable . . . when the employee's work is produced at the instance and expense of the employer, or, in other words, when the 'motivating factor in producing the work was the employer who induced the creation. . . .' *Siegel v. National Periodical Publications, Inc.*, 508 F.2d 909, 914 (2d Cir. 1974) . . .

"The final chapter of the expansion of the 'work for hire' doctrine under the regime of the 1909 Act was written in our Court. In *Murray v. Gelderman*, 566 F.2d 1307 (5th Cir. 1978), the author of a book written under contract argued that the book was not a 'work made for hire.' We responded with the now-familiar litany of the 'instance and expense' test:

'The crucial element in this ["employment"] determination appears to be whether the work was created at the employer's insistence [sic] and expense, or, in other words, whether the motivating factor in producing the work was the employer who induced its creation. *Siegel.* Another factor is whether the employer had the right to direct and supervise the manner in which the work was being performed. *Picture Music.* Actual exercise of that right is not controlling, and copyright is vested in the employer who has no intention of overseeing the detailed activity of any employee hired for the very purpose of producing the material. See *Yardley.*'

"The author contended, however, that the normal 'right to control' rules did not apply in her case because she had specifically contracted for complete control over the work and that she would have refused to take the job if the putative employer had demanded a right to control her efforts. Accepting this as true, our Court was unpersuaded:

'Allowing [author] Murray to [succeed on this argument] . . . would permit an employee to circumvent the works for hire doctrine simply by demanding creative freedom as a condition of employment. We decline Murray's invitation to adopt such a rule, where, as here, an employer has no intention of supervising the work of an employee hired specifically to produce certain material.'

"Thus at time of the adoption of the 1976 Act, the simple rule of *Yardley* for allocating the risk of uncertainty about whether the copyrights were assigned to the buyer had developed into an almost irrebuttable presumption that any person who paid another to create a copyrightable work was the statutory 'author' under the 'work for hire' doctrine. This presumption could not be avoided even by showing that the buyer had no actual right to control the manner of the production of the work, because the buyer was thought to maintain the 'right' to control simply by paying for the work and having the power to refuse to accept it. In other words, the class of persons who counted as 'employees' under the copyright statute was far greater than the class of regular or formal employees, and well beyond the somewhat extended class of employees—known as 'servants'—under agency law. *See, e.g.,* Restatement (Second) of Agency § 220(1) (1958) ('A servant is a person employed to perform services in the affairs of another and who with respect to the *physical conduct in the performance of the services* is subject to the other's control or right to control.') (emphasis added). Whenever one person bought authorship services from another, the seller was a copyright 'employee' and the buyer was a statutory 'author.' "[32]

[b]   The 1976 Act. Section 101 of the 1976 Act provides that a work is "for hire" under two sets of circumstances:

"(1) a work prepared by an employee within the scope of his or her employment; or

"(2) a work specially ordered or commissioned for use as a contribution to a collective work, as a part of a motion picture or other audiovisual work, as a translation, as a supplementary work, as a compilation, as an instructional text, as a test, as answer material for a test, or as an atlas, if the parties expressly agree in a written instrument signed by them that the work shall be considered a work made for hire."

Section 201(b) provides that, in the case of a work made for hire, the employer or other person for whom the work was prepared is considered the author and "unless the parties have expressly agreed otherwise in a written instrument signed by them, owns all of the rights comprised in the copyright."[33]

---

[32] 815 F.2d at 325–27, 2 U.S.P.Q.2d at 1586–88.

[33] As to the written agreement exception, see Baltimore Orioles, Inc. v. Major League Baseball Players Ass'n, 805 F.2d 663, 671–72, 231 U.S.P.Q. 673, 678 (7th Cir. 1986), *cert. denied,* 480 U.S. 941 (1987) ("The requirement that an agreement altering the presumption that an employer owns the copyright in a work made for hire represents a substantial change in the 'work made for hire' doctrine. Under prior law, 'such an agreement could be either *oral* or *implied.*' . . . § 201(b) requires that an agreement altering the statutory presumption be both *written* and *express.* In essence, this provision is a statute of frauds.").

In *Baltimore Orioles,* the court held that collective bargaining contracts between the Major League Baseball Clubs and Major League Baseball Players Association were not sufficiently express to alter the presumption that the players' performances before television cameras were works for hire, that is, by employees within the scope of their employment.

The "work made for hire" definition in Section 101 represents a "carefully balanced compromise."[34] Congress rejected proposals to strengthen the rights of employed authors. The provision on works prepared on special order or commission underwent extensive revision during the legislative process.

In *Community for Creative Non-Violence ("CCNV")*,[35] the Supreme Court held that "employee" and "within the scope of his or her employment" in the 1976 Act definition of work for hire refers to "a hired party in a conventional employment relationship" as determined by general agency law: "To determine whether a work is for hire under the Act, a court first should ascertain, using principles of general common law of agency, whether the work was prepared by an employee or an independent contractor. After making this determination, the court can apply the appropriate subsection of § 101."[36]

CCNV, an organization devoted to ending homelessness in America, and Mitch Snyder, a member and trustee, decided to participate in an annual Washington, D.C. Christmas pageant with a display dramatizing the plight of the homeless. The display was to be a modern Nativity scene with life-size figures of a homeless family huddled on a streetside steam grate. Snyder commissioned James Earl Reid to sculpt three human figures, and CCNV agreed to pay expenses up to $15,000. No agreement regarding copyright was made. After Reid made a sketch with standing and seated figures, he, at Snyder's suggestion, visited a family living in CCNV's shelter and also observed homeless people on the streets. Snyder pointed out that such people tended to recline on steam grates rather than sit or stand. In subsequent sketches, Reid used only reclining figures. CCNV members visited Reid and provided suggestions, such as that a shopping cart be included rather than suitcases or shopping bags. Reid completed a statue using a synthetic cast material in December 1985 and delivered it to CCNV. In January of 1986, CCNV returned the statue to Reid for repairs. Several weeks later, Snyder proposed to take the statue on a tour of several cities. Reid objected on the ground that the casting material was not strong enough and proposed that the work be cast in bronze. Snyder refused to spend the money required. After Reid refused to return the statue, both CCNV and Reid applied for copyright registration on the work. Snyder sued Reid for copyright infringement.

The district court determined that the statue was a work for hire and therefore that CCNV, the commissioning party, not Reid, the creator, owned the copyright. On appeal, the Court of Appeals for the District of Columbia reversed. It reasoned that the work did not fall within the "commissioned works" part of the Section 101 definition both because the work was not one of the types of works listed and because there was no written agreement that the work be treated as a work for hire. It reasoned that Reid was not an "employee" of CCNV, adopting an agency law definition of employment. The court of appeals remanded the case for a determination of whether CCNV was a joint author of the work because of the contributions it actually made to the creation of the work.

---

[34] H.R. Rep. No. 94–1476, 94th Cong., 2d Sess. 121 (1976).
[35] Community for Creative Non-Violence v. Reid, 490 U.S. 730, 10 U.S.P.Q.2d 1985 (1989).
[36] 490 U.S. at 750, 10 U.S.P.Q.2d at 1994.

The Supreme Court granted review because the courts of appeal were in conflict as to the proper test of employment. The Court affirmed the Court of Appeals' ruling that the work was not one for hire and that the case should be remanded for a determination as to possible joint authorship.[37]

The Court noted that four interpretations of the phrase "a work prepared by an employee within the scope of his or her employment" had emerged in the courts of appeal.

> "The first holds that a work is prepared by an employee whenever the hiring party retains the right to control the product. See *Peregrine v. Lauren Corp.*, 601 F. Supp. 828, 829 (Colo. 1985); *Clarkstown v. Reeder*, 566 F. Supp. 137, 142 (S.D.N.Y. 1983). Petitioners take this view. . . . A second, and closely related, view is that a work is prepared by an employee under § 101(1) when the hiring party has actually wielded control with respect to the creation of a particular work. This approach was formulated by the Court of Appeals for the Second Circuit, *Aldon Accessories Ltd. v. Spiegel, Inc.*, 738 F.2d 548, *cert. denied*, 469 U.S. 982 (1984), and adopted by the Fourth Circuit, *Brunswick Beacon, Inc. v. Schock-Hopchas Publishing Co.*, 810 F.2d 410 (1987), the Seventh Circuit, *Evans Newton, Inc. v. Chicago Systems Software*, 793 F.2d 889, *cert. denied*, 479 U.S. 949 (1986), and, at times, by petitioners. . . . A third view is that the term 'employee' within § 101(1) carries its common law agency law meaning. This view was endorsed by the Fifth Circuit in *Easter Seal Society for Crippled Children and Adults of Louisiana, Inc. v. Playboy Enterprises*, 815 F.2d 323 (1987), and by the Court of Appeals below. Finally, respondent and numerous *amici curiae* contend that the term 'employee' only refers to 'formal, salaried' employees. . . . The Court of Appeals for the Ninth Circuit recently adopted this view. See *Dumas v. Gommerman*, 865 F.2d 1093 (1989)."[38]

The first test, right to control, is unacceptable as contrary to the statutory language.

> "The exclusive focus of the right to control the product test on the relationship between the hiring party and the product clashes with the language of § 101(1), which focuses on the relationship between the hired and hiring parties. The right to control the product test also would distort the meaning of the ensuing subsection, § 101(2). Section 101 plainly creates two distinct ways in which a work can be deemed for hire: one for works prepared by employees, the other for those specially ordered or commissioned works which fall within one of the nine enumerated categories and are the subject of a written agreement. The right to control the product test ignores this dichotomy by transforming into a work for hire under § 101(1) any 'specially ordered or commissioned' work that is subject to the supervision and control of the hiring party. Because a party who hires a 'specially ordered or commissioned' work by definition has a right to specify the characteristics of the product

---

[37] The Court noted that "Neither CCNV nor Reid sought review of the Court of Appeals' remand order. We therefore have no occasion to pass judgment on applicability of the Act's joint authorship provisions to this case." 490 U.S. at 752 n.32, 10 U.S.P.Q.2d at 1996 n.32.
[38] 490 U.S. at 738–39, 10 U.S.P.Q.2d at 1989–90.

desired, at the time the commission is accepted, and frequently until it is completed, the right to control the product test would mean that many works that could satisfy § 101(2) would already have been deemed works for hire under § 101(1). Petitioners' interpretation is particularly hard to square with § 101(2)'s enumeration of the nine specific categories of specially ordered or commissioned works eligible to be works for hire, e.g., 'a contribution to a collective work,' 'a part of a motion picture,' and 'answer material for a test.' The unifying feature of these works is that they are usually prepared at the instance, direction, and risk of a publisher or producer. By their very nature, therefore, these types of works would be works by an employee under petitioners' right to control the product test." [39]

The second test, actual control, "fares only marginally better."

"Under this test, independent contractors who are so controlled and supervised in the creation of a particular work are deemed 'employees' under § 101(1). Thus work for hire status under § 101(1) depends on a hiring party's *actual* control, rather than *right* to control, of the product. . . . Under the actual control test, a work for hire could arise under § 101(2), but not under § 101(1), where a party commissions, but does not actually control, a product which falls into one of the nine enumerated categories. Nonetheless, we agree with the Fifth Circuit Court of Appeals that '[t]here is simply no way to milk the "actual control" test of *Aldon Accessories* from the language of the statute.' . . . Section 101 clearly delineates between works prepared by an employee and commissioned works. Sound though other distinctions might be as a matter of copyright policy, there is no statutory support for an additional dichotomy between commissioned works that are actually controlled and supervised by the hiring party and those that are not." [40]

The fourth test, only salaried, formal employment, fails to find support in the statutory language.

"While there is some support for such a definition in the legislative history, . . . the language of § 101(1) cannot support it. The Act does not say 'formal' or 'salaried' employee, but simply 'employee.' Moreover, the respondent and those *amici* who endorse a formal, salaried employee test do not agree upon the content of this test. Compare, e.g., Brief for Respondent 37 (hired party who is on payroll is an employee within § 101(1)) with Tr. of Oral Arg. 31 (hired party who receives a salary or commissions regularly is an employee within § 101(1)); and Brief for Volunteer Lawyers for the Arts Inc. et al. as *Amici Curiae* 4 (hired party who receives a salary *and* is treated as an employee for Social Security and tax purposes is an employee within § 101(1)). Even the one Court of Appeals to adopt what it termed a formal, salaried employee test in fact embraced an approach incorporating numerous factors drawn from the agency law definition of employee which we endorse. See *Dumas*, 865 F.2d, at 1104." [41]

[39] 490 U.S. at 741–42, 10 U.S.P.Q.2d at 1990–91.
[40] 490 U.S. at 742, 10 U.S.P.Q.2d at 1991.
[41] 490 U.S. at 743, n.8, 10 U.S.P.Q.2d at 1991 n.8.

The third test, common law agency, is preferable because it is consistent with both the general approach to the interpretation of federal statutes that refer to employment without giving a definition thereof and the legislative history of the 1976 Copyright Act. As to the general approach to the definition of employment:

> "In the past, when Congress has used the term 'employee' without defining it, we have concluded that Congress intended to describe the conventional master-servant relationship as understood by common law agency doctrine. . . . Nothing in the text of the work for hire provisions indicates that Congress used the words 'employee' and 'employment' to describe anything other than ' "the conventional relation of employer and employee." ' . . . On the contrary, Congress' intent to incorporate the agency law definition is suggested by § 101(1)'s use of the term, 'scope of employment,' a widely used term of art in agency law.

> "In past cases of statutory interpretation, when we have concluded that Congress intended terms such as 'employee,' 'employer,' and 'scope of employment' to be understood in light of agency law, we have relied on the general common law of agency, rather than on the law of any particular State, to give meaning to these terms. . . . This practice reflects the fact that 'federal statutes are generally intended to have uniform nationwide application.' . . . Establishment of a federal rule of agency, rather than reliance on state agency law, is particularly appropriate here given the Act's express objective of creating national uniform copyright law by broadly pre-empting state statutory and common-law copyright regulation."[42]

As to the legislative history of the 1976 Act, which was enacted "after two decades of negotiation by representatives of creators and copyright-using industries, supervised by the Copyright Office and, to a lesser extent, by Congress,"[43] the structure of the work for hire definition evolved from a 1965 compromise between competing interest groups.

> "The compromise retained as subsection (1) the language referring to 'a work prepared by an employee within the scope of his employment.' However, in exchange for concessions from publishers on provisions relating to the termination of transfer rights, the authors consented to a second subsection which classified . . . categories of commissioned works as works for hire if the parties expressly so agreed in writing. . . .

> . . .

> ". . . [T]he legislative history of the Act is significant for several reasons. First, the enactment of the 1965 compromise with only minor modifications demonstrates that Congress intended to provide two mutually exclusive ways for works to acquire work for hire status: one for employees and the other for independent contractors. Second, the legislative history underscores the clear import of the statutory language: only enumerated categories of commissioned works may be accorded work for hire status. The hiring party's right

---

[42] 490 U.S. at 739–40, 10 U.S.P.Q.2d at 1990.
[43] 490 U.S. at 743, 10 U.S.P.Q.2d at 1991.

to control the product simply is not determinative. . . . Indeed, importing a test based on a hiring party's right to control or actual control of a product would unravel the 'carefully worked out compromise aimed at balancing legitimate interests on both sides.'[44]

The Court was unpersuaded by CCNV's argument that "Congress, in enacting the Act, meant to incorporate a line of cases decided under the 1909 Act holding that an employment relationship exists sufficient to give the hiring party copyright ownership whenever that party has the right to control or supervise the artist's work."[45] Congressional silence cannot be used to support an interpretation contrary to the "text and structure of § 101." Furthermore, the work for hire provision of what became the 1976 Act was agreed upon in 1965 at a time when the courts had applied the 1909 Act exclusively to traditional employees. The first federal court decision extending the 1909 Act work for hire provision to a commissioned work was in 1966.[46]

Finally, the Court noted that adoption of petitioner's control test would "impede Congress' paramount goal in revising the 1976 Act of enhancing predictability and certainty of copyright ownership."

"In a 'copyright marketplace,' the parties negotiate with an expectation that one of them will own the copyright in the completed work. . . . With that expectation, the parties at the outset can settle on relevant contractual terms, such as the price for the work and the ownership of reproduction rights.

". . . Because [an actual control] test turns on whether the hiring party has closely monitored the production process, the parties would not know until late in the process, if not until the work is completed, whether a work will ultimately fall within § 101(1). Under petitioners' approach, therefore, parties would have to predict in advance whether the hiring party will sufficiently control a given work to make it the author. . . . This understanding of the work for hire provisions clearly thwarts Congress' goal of ensuring predictability through advance planning. Moreover, petitioners' interpretation 'leaves the door open for hiring parties, who have failed to get a full assignment of copyright rights from independent contractors falling outside the subdivision (2) guidelines, to unilaterally obtain work-made-for-hire rights years after the work has been completed as long as they directed or supervised the work, a standard that is hard not to meet when one is a hiring party.' Hamilton, Commissioned Works as Works Made for Hire Under the 1976 Copyright Act: Misinterpretation and Injustice, 135 U.Pa. L. Rev. 1281, 1304 (1987)."[47]

Turning to application of the common law agency test of employment, the Court described the relevant factors.

"In determining whether a hired party is an employee under the general common law of agency, we consider the hiring party's right to control the

---

[44] 490 U.S. at 746–48, 10 U.S.P.Q.2d at 1992–93.

[45] 490 U.S. at 748, 10 U.S.P.Q.2d at 1993.

[46] Brattleboro Publishing Co. v. Winmill Publishing Corp., 369 F.2d 565, 567–568, 151 U.S.P.Q. 666 (2d Cir. 1966).

[47] 490 U.S. at 749–750, 10 U.S.P.Q.2d at 1994.

manner and means by which the product is accomplished. Among the other factors relevant to this inquiry are the skill required; the source of the instrumentalities and tools; the location of the work; the duration of the relationship between the parties; whether the hiring party has the right to assign additional projects to the hired party; the extent of the hired party's discretion over when and how long to work; the method of payment; the hired party's role in hiring and paying assistants; whether the work is part of the regular business of the hiring party; whether the hiring party is in business; the provision of employee benefits; and the tax treatment of the hired party. See Restatement § 220(2) (setting forth a nonexhaustive list of factors relevant to determining whether a hired party is an employee). No one of these factors is determinative."[48]

Applying this test, the Court concluded that Reid was not an employee of CCNV but an independent contractor.

"True, CCNV members directed enough of Reid's work to ensure that he produced a sculpture that met their specifications. . . . But the extent of control the hiring party exercises over the details of the product is not dispositive. Indeed, all the other circumstances weigh heavily against finding an employment relationship. Reid is a sculptor, a skilled occupation. Reid supplied his own tools. He worked in his own studio in Baltimore, making daily supervision of his activities from Washington practically impossible. Reid was retained for less than two months, a relatively short period of time. During and after this time, CCNV had no right to assign additional projects to Reid. Apart from the deadline for completing the sculpture, Reid had absolute freedom to decide when and how long to work. CCNV paid Reid $15,000, a sum dependent on 'completion of a specific job, a method by which independent contractors are often compensated.' . . . Reid had total discretion in hiring and paying assistants. 'Creating sculptures was hardly "regular business" for CCNV.' . . . Indeed, CCNV is not a business at all. Finally, CCNV did not pay payroll or social security taxes, provide any employee benefits, or contribute to unemployment insurance or workers' compensation funds."[49]

[3] Joint Authorship.

A joint work results when two or more authors make contributions of original authorship "with the intention that their contributions be merged into inseparable or interdependent parts of a unitary whole."[50] For example, a joint work results when a composer and a lyricist write a song, an author and illustrator create a children's book, or two scholars produce a college textbook. The contributions of multiple authors "may be either 'inseparable' (as in the case of a novel or painting) or 'interdependent' (as in the case of a motion picture, opera, or the words and music of a song)."[51]

---

[48] 490 U.S. at 751, 10 U.S.P.Q.2d at 1995.

[49] 490 U.S. at 752, 10 U.S.P.Q.2d at 995.

[50] 17 U.S.C. § 101 (definition of "joint work").

[51] H.R. Rep. No. 94–1476, 94th Cong., 2d Sess. 120 (1976).

The authors of a joint work are co-owners of copyright in the work.[52] Each co-owner is "akin to a tenant in common. . . . [A] joint author cannot be held liable for copyright infringement to another joint owner . . .; compensation obtained from the unilateral exploitation of the joint work by one of the co-owners without the permission of the others is held in a 'constructive trust' for the mutual benefit of all co-owners and there is a duty to account therefor."[53] Each joint author may also use the joint work to create derivative works, such as revisions.[54]

[a] **The 1909 Act.** Early copyright statutes, including the 1909 Act, did not refer to multiple or joint authorship, but the courts acknowledged that more than one human author may contribute jointly to a single work and that the result was joint authorship with each author being a co-owner of the copyright in the work.[55]

---

[52] 17 U.S.C. § 201(a). Prior to the 1976 Act, the courts equated the rights of joint authors with the rights of tenants in common under traditional property concepts. *See, e.g.*, Picture Music, Inc. v. Bourne, Inc., 314 F. Supp. 640, 645, 167 U.S.P.Q. 348 (S.D.N.Y. 1970), *aff'd on other grounds*, 457 F.2d 1213, 173 U.S.P.Q. 449 (2d Cir.), *cert. denied*, 409 U.S. 997, 175 U.S.P.Q. 577 (1972) ("When two or more authors pursuing a common design together create a single work, they become joint owners of the work in undivided shares which are owned by each author.").

The 1976 Act specifies that joint authors are "co-owners." The legislative intent was to confirm existing law on the rights of co-ownership. *See* H.R. Rep. No. 94–1476, 94th Cong., 2d Sess. 121 (1976) ("There is also no need for a specific statutory provision concerning the rights and duties of the co-owners of a work; court-made law on this point is left undisturbed. Under the bill, as under the present law, co-owners of a copyright would be treated generally as tenants in common, with each co-owner having an independent right to use or license the use of a work, subject to a duty of accounting to the other co-owners for any profits.").

[53] Picture Music, Inc. v. Bourne, Inc., 314 F. Supp. 640, 167 U.S.P.Q. 348 (S.D.N.Y. 1970), *aff'd on other grounds*, 457 F.2d 1213, 173 U.S.P.Q. 449 (2d Cir.), *cert. denied*, 409 U.S. 997 (1972). *See also* Weissmann v. Freeman, 868 F.2d 1313, 1318, 10 U.S.P.Q.2d 1014, 1017–18 (2d Cir. 1989), *cert. denied*, 110 S. Ct. 219 (1989) ("In a joint work, each author 'automatically acquires an undivided ownership in the entire work', including any portion of it. . . . Thus, an action for infringement between joint owners will not lie because an individual cannot infringe his own copyright. The only duty joint owners have with respect to their joint work is to account for profits from its use.").

Cf. Oddo v. Ries, 743 F.2d 630, 633, 222 U.S.P.Q. 799, 801 (9th Cir. 1984) (account between partnership; "the duty to account does not derive from the copyright law's proscription of infringement. Rather, it comes from 'equitable doctrines relating to unjust enrichment and general principles of law governing the rights of co-owners.' ").

[54] Weissmann v. Freeman, 868 F.2d 1313, 1318, 10 U.S.P.Q.2d 1014, 1018 (2d Cir. 1989), *cert. denied*, 110 S. Ct. 219 (1989) ("one co-author has the right to revise a joint work in order to create an individual derivative work").

See § 4G[1].

[55] *See* Picture Music, Inc. v. Bourne, Inc., 314 F. Supp. 640, 645, 167 U.S.P.Q. 348 (S.D.N.Y. 1970), *aff'd on other grounds*, 457 F.2d 1213, 173 U.S.P.Q. 449 (2d Cir.), *cert. denied*, 409 U.S. 997 (1972) ("The doctrine of joint authorship is nowhere referred to in the basic federal copyright enactment, Title 17 U.S.C., which derives from the Copyright Act of March 4, 1909, 35 Stat. 1075. Rather, it is one of judicial creation which was imported wholesale from English Law by Judge Learned Hand. *See* Maurel v. Smith, 220 F. 195 (S.D.N.Y. 1915), *aff'd*, 271 F. 211 (2d Cir. 1921), citing Levy v. Rutley, L.R. 6 C.P. 523 (1871).").

When two or more persons collaborate to create a single work, the work is clearly joint. More difficult to classify is a work that results from a merger of parts created by two or more persons at different times and without collaboration. Two famous Second Circuit decisions, *Melancholy Baby* and *12th Street Rag*,[56] extended joint authorship status to musical compositions in which composer and lyricist worked separately and in which the contribution of one was completed before the other contributor was even selected.

Melancholy Baby[57] involved the following fact pattern. In 1911, Burnett wrote the music and Watson the lyrics of the song ("the 1911 version"). In 1912, with Burnett's consent, a publisher engaged Norton to write new lyrics, resulting in a second version, which became the commercial version ("the 1912 version"). In 1939, Burnett and Watson renewed the copyright on the 1911 version. Burnett also purported to renew the copyright on the 1912 version. Through later transfers, Shapiro held the rights of Burnett and Watson to the 1911 version and of Burnett to the 1912 version. Vogel held the rights of Norton, the second lyricist, to the 1912 version. The issue for the court was: who owned rights in the second song? That in turn depended on whether the 1912 work was a joint one or a separate one, perhaps a derivative work. Shapiro's theory was that there were separate works and that the copyright on Norton's lyrics expired for nonrenewal. Under that theory, Shapiro would have control over the music via the renewed copyright on the first version and free usage of Norton's lyrics. Vogel's theory was that the second version was a joint work. That would give it the benefit of a rule about renewal of joint works: renewal of a joint work by any joint author operates to the benefit of all of the joint authors. Vogel and Shapiro would then be co-owners.

In *Melancholy Baby*, the court held that Burnett and Norton were collaborators and joint authors of the second work: "The words and music of a song constitute a 'musical composition' in which the two contributions merge into a single work to be performed as a unit for the pleasure of the hearers; they are not a 'composite' work, like the articles in an encyclopedia, but are as little separable for purposes of the copyright as are the individual musical notes which constitute the melody."[58] The court relied on *Edward B. Marks Music*,[59] in which it found joint authorship when a lyricist wrote words to be set to music by some unknown composer and sold the words to another who then engaged a composer who wrote the music. *Edwards B. Marks* might be distinguished on the ground it involved a co-author A creating a contribution that A intended to be combined with a contribution by a second author, not yet identified, whereas *Melancholy Baby* involved a co-author A creating a joint work with another B and then A or an assignee of the rights to the work altering

---

[56] The labels "Melancholy Baby" and "12th Street Rag," after the name of the musical composition at issue in each case, are commonly used to distinguish the two cases, which, though dealing with independent controversies, bear the same case caption, Shapiro, Bernstein & Co. and Jerry Vogel Music Co.

[57] Shapiro, Bernstein & Co. v. Jerry Vogel Music Co., 161 F.2d 406 (2d Cir. 1946), *cert. denied*, 331 U.S. 820 (1947).

[58] 161 F.2d at 409.

[59] Edward B. Marks Music Corp. v. Jerry Vogel Music Co., 140 F.2d 266 (2d Cir. 1944).

the work by substituting the contribution of a third person C for that of B. But the court in *Melancholy Baby* viewed this as a distinction without a difference.[60]

12th Street Rag,[61] involved the following fact pattern. In 1914, Bowman composed and copyrighted the piece as an instrumental piano solo (version 1). In 1916, Bowman assigned his rights to Jenkins. In 1918, Jenkins had Sumner write lyrics (version 2). In 1919, Jenkins copyrighted version 2. In 1942, Bowman renewed the copyright in version 1 and assigned his rights to Shapiro. In 1947, Sumner renewed the copyright in version 2 and assigned his rights to Vogel. Vogel, the assignee of the lyricist, published the song with music and lyrics. The district court held that version 2 was a "composite" of Bowman's music and Sumner's lyrics and not a joint work and that Vogel, as assignee of Sumner's rights, could not publish the lyrics with the music without the permission of Shapiro, the owner of the rights in the music. The Second Circuit reversed, finding that version 2 was a joint work under an extension of the *Marks Music-Melancholy Baby* doctrine. The court admitted that "[i]n neither the *Marks* nor the *Shapiro* case . . . was the collaboration after the original author had assigned all his rights that he could assign." However, it believed that "the rule of these cases . . . should make the test the consent, by the one who holds the copyright on the product of the first author, at the time of the collaboration, to the collaboration by the second author."

> "[W]hen the assignee . . . procured the writing of the lyrics, [the assignee's] intent was that the lyrics and music be performed together as a single work, a song. That intent should govern. Since that intent was to merge the two contributions into a single work to be performed as a unit for the pleasure of the hearers we should consider the result 'joint' rather than 'composite.' The result reached in the district court would leave one of the authors of the 'new work' with but a barren right in the words of a worthless poem, never intended to be used alone. Such a result is not to be favored.' "[62]

---

[60] The court noted:

> "The applicability of the *Marks* case becomes clear if we approach the situation at bar step by step. Suppose, for example, that after Burnett had composed the music, expecting his wife to write the words, she had died or changed her mind about writing the lyrics, and Burnett had then gone to Bennett and asked him to find someone to write the words. We submit that no court would hold that the fact that when Burnett composed the music he expected his wife to write the words, would make the actual song any less a 'joint work' of Burnett and the lyricist found by Bennett. If that be true, it should make no difference that Burnett's original design to have his music combined with his wife's words was in fact realized." 161 F.2d at 410.

[61] Shapiro, Bernstein & Co. v. Jerry Vogel Music Co., 221 F.2d 569 (2d Cir. 1953), *on rehearing*, 223 F.2d 252 (2d Cir. 1955).

[62] 221 F.2d at 570.

There was a third alternative to the district court's "composite" work conclusion and the appeals court's joint work conclusion—the second version was a "derivative" work. This would give the assignee from the lyricist greater rights than if its copyright included only the bare lyrics (a separate part of the composite) but not rights equivalent to a joint owner.

The Second Circuit's *per curiam* opinion on petition for rehearing is interesting. The composer's assignee and lyricist's assignee were required to account reciprocally to each other— "not as an infringer but as a trustee"—for exploitation only of the joint work. The accounting

Because the parties were co-owners of the copyright in the joint work (version 2), each should account to the other for one-half of the royalties earned.

The *12th Street Rag* decision expanded *Melancholy Baby* to situations where the first author, such as a composer, had no intention at the time of creation that lyrics be added.

If accepted and applied widely, the *12th Street Rag* rule would substantially alter common understandings as to what constitutes a joint work and the rights of contributors to related works.[63] For example, does it make the author of a book a joint author of a motion picture based on the book? Not surprisingly, subsequent court decisions and legislation restrict or reject the *12th Street Rag* rule that a joint work can arise if an author or his or her assignee form, after creation of a work of authorship, an intent to merge the work with a contribution by another.

Three decisions concerning *12th Street Rag* are noteworthy. In *Picture Music,*[64] known as "Three Little Pigs" after the motion picture cartoon song at issue in the case, the District Court for the Southern District of New York held that the contribution of a subsequent person to the alteration of an existing copyrighted work must be "substantial" or "significant" before that person becomes a joint author of the altered work. This holding focused on the issue of the quality and quantity of a putative joint author's contribution, rather than the timing of the intention to merge contributions, which was the subject of the three decisions culminating with *12th Street Rag.*[65]

---

did not extend to the composer-assignee's exploitation of the instrumental music. 223 F.2d at 254.

If the song were treated as a sole derivative work, the following consequences would obtain (assuming the 1976 Act applies). The composer-assignee would have rights in the instrumental work but not the song after a renewal or termination of transfers of the copyright in the song. The lyricist-assignee would, most likely, have the right to continue to exploit the song as a derivative work even though it contains matter from the copyrighted song, but would not have the right to make further derivative works. *See* § 4G[4][c][iii].

[63] For a critique of *12th Street Rag*, see Cary, "Joint Ownership of Copyrights," in 1 Studies on Copyright 689, 696 (1963):

> "No longer does there seem to be required a preconcerted common design or any active collaboration. It is now sufficient if there be any 'fusion of effort' in the creation of a revision, adaptation or modification of any existing work. The authors of the original work are not required to have any knowledge of the modification, nor do they have to take part in it. Any action on the part of their transferees which utilizes the preexisting work in the creation of a new version thereof is sufficient to make the original creators joint authors with those who later revise their work. Not only does this extension of the joint author concept do violence to the renewal policy of the law, but it would appear to extend, for an indefinite period, the control of the original author over any subsequent revision of his work."

[64] Picture Music, Inc. v. Bourne, Inc., 314 F. Supp. 640, 167 U.S.P.Q. 348 (S.D.N.Y. 1970), *aff'd on other grounds*, 457 F.2d 1213, 173 U.S.P.Q. 449 (2d Cir.), *cert. denied*, 409 U.S. 997 (1972).

[65] Nevertheless, the district court's discussion of the line of cases on intent-to-merge is of interest.

> "Traditionally, joint authorship contemplated collaboration by the authors of the parts and a common purpose.

Two years later, in *Donna*,[66] which involved the illustrated children's book "Boy of the Masai," the same court distinguished *Three Little Pigs* and applied *12th Street Rag*, as at least an alternative holding.

> "However, in later cases the ingredient of collaboration was eliminated on a finding of a fusion of effort. In the Edward B. Marks case, . . . [t]he Court, per Learned Hand, J., found that the lyricist had intended the words to be set to music and that the composer was writing music to be used with those particular words, and found in the circumstances 'a joint laboring in furtherance of a common design.' . . . The Court observed that:
>
> > 'It makes no difference whether the authors work in concert, or even whether they know each other; it is enough that they mean their contributions to be complementary in the sense that they are to be embodied in a single work to be performed as such. 140 F.2d at 267.'
>
> "[In the] 'Melancholy Baby' case, . . . [t]he Court held the resultant composition a 'joint work' and the product of a 'joint authorship' notwithstanding that the composer of the music had originally intended his product to be joined with his wife's lyrics.
>
> "In the '12th Street Rag' case the element of common design was still further diluted, if not altogether eliminated." 314 F. Supp. at 645–46.

[66] Donna v. Dodd, Mead & Co., 374 F. Supp. 429, 183 U.S.P.Q. 166 (S.D.N.Y. 1974). In *Donna*, defendant took photographs that were incorporated in a children's book, "Boy of the Masai," to which plaintiff contributed the text. Later, defendant collaborated with another in the writing of three books, "Boy of Nepal," "Boy of Dahomey," and "Boy of Bolivia," which used substantially the same format as the original "Boy of the Masai." Plaintiff sued for copyright infringement, contending that the book was a "composite work" of plaintiff's text and defendant's photographs rather than a joint work. In dismissing plaintiff's infringement charge, Judge Lasker disagreed.

> "Although Larsen's photographs were not taken with Donna's text specifically in mind, it appears that they may have been intended from the start to become part of a joint work with text from another source. Donna's own affidavit states that she was informed by Larsen before she worked with him that he had already submitted the photographs to a publisher and been rejected. . . . If so, their subsequent collaboration would fall squarely within the *Marks—Melancholy Baby* rule. However, even if Larsen had no such intention when he took the photographs, Boy of the Masai is a joint work under the *12th Street Rag* approach, because once Larsen and Donna reached agreement on its creation it is evident that Larsen had the intention that his photographs be subsumed into their joint effort. At the very least, Donna's contribution, which came into being solely to complement Larsen's photographs, is jointly owned and can be licensed without her consent, subject only to a duty to account.
>
> "Donna concedes that, under the case law discussed above, 'Boy of the Masai would probably be considered a joint work'. . . . However, she argues that this approach was modified in *Picture Music, Inc. v. Bourne, Inc.* . . . While it is true that *Picture Music* points out that the *Marks—Melancholy Baby—12th Street Rag* approach has been criticized, there is no indication that the court intended to depart from it. Rather, it found that there was no collaboration whatever between the claimed joint authors, no intention conceived at any time by the original author to create a new work and no substantial contribution by any person other than the original author. . . . Moreover, the Second Circuit opinion in *Picture Music* does not consider the joint authorship question. Thus, the earlier cases stand as the law of this Circuit, and we decline plaintiff's invitation to depart from them." 374 F. Supp. at 430.

In *Gilliam*, [67] the Second Circuit itself expressed reservations about *12th Street Rag.* In *Gilliam*, the plaintiffs, a group of British writers and performers known as "Monty Python," provided scripts to the B.B.C. for a television series under an agreement that restricted B.B.C.'s right to make alterations. The agreement authorized B.B.C. to license transmission of recordings of the program in any overseas territory. A.B.C. acquired from B.B.C. rights to broadcast the programs in the United States. Plaintiffs filed suit to enjoin A.B.C. from broadcasting edited and abridged versions of the series. In defending against plaintiffs copyright claim, A.B.C. relied in part on the *12th Street Rag* case. The Second Circuit directed entry of a preliminary injunction.

> "ABC . . . argues that under the 'joint work' theory adopted in *Shapiro, Bernstein & Co. v. Jerry Vogel Music, Inc.*, 221 F.2d 569 (2d Cir. 1955), the script produced by Monty Python and the program recorded by BBC are symbiotic elements of a single production. Therefore, according to ABC, each contributor possesses an undivided ownership of all copyrightable elements in the final work and BBC could thus have licensed use of the script, including editing, written by appellants.

> "The joint work theory as extended in *Shapiro* has been criticized as inequitable unless 'at the time of creation by the first author, the second author's contribution [is envisaged] as an integrated part of a single work' and the first author intends that the final product be a joint work. See 1 M. Nimmer, Copyright §§ 67–73. Furthermore, this court appears to have receded from a broad application of the joint work doctrine where the contract which leads to a collaboration between authors indicates that one will retain a superior interest. See *Szekely v. Eagle Lion Films, Inc.*, 242 F.2d 266 (2nd Cir), cert. denied, 354 U.S. 922 (1957). In the present case, the screenwriter agreement between Monty Python and BBC provides that the group is to retain all rights in the script not granted in the agreement and that at some future point the group may license the scripts for use on television to parties other than BBC. These provisions suggest that the parties did not consider themselves joint authors of a single work." [68]

[b] The 1976 Act. Section 101 of the 1976 Act defines a joint work as "a work prepared by two or more authors with the intention that their contributions be merged into inseparable or interdependent parts of a unitary whole." [69]

[i] *Merged Contributions—The Intention Test.* The Section 101 definition of "joint work" might be interpreted as confirming *Melancholy Baby* 6ƒ's result, but it definitely excludes the *12th Street Rag* extension. [70] Under the definition, a work is a joint one if the authors collaborated with each other or the

---

[67] Gilliam v. American Broadcasting Companies, Inc., 538 F.2d 14, 192 U.S.P.Q. 1 (2d Cir. 1976).

[68] 538 F.2d at 22.

[69] 17 U.S.C. § 101.

[70] The House Report discusses joint works as follows:

> "Under the definition of section 101, a work is 'joint' if the authors collaborated with each other, or if each of the authors prepared his or her contribution with the knowledge and intention that it would be merged with the contributions of other authors

authors prepared their contributions with the intent that they be merged or combined into an integrated unit.[71] The intent to merge must be at the time of preparation, not later, as in *12th Street Rag*.[72]

In *Weissmann*,[73] the Second Circuit found no joint work when one person (Weissmann), who had jointly authored a series of articles and lectures with another person (Freeman), prepared a new, altered version of the prior works, distinguishing *Marks* and *Melancholy Baby*, and relying on *Gilliam*.[74] There was "no evidence

---

as 'inseparable or interdependent parts of a unitary whole.' The touchstone here is the intention, at the time the writing is done, that the parts be absorbed or combined into an integrated unit, although the parts themselves may be either 'inseparable' (as in the case of a novel or painting) or 'interdependent' (as in the case of a motion picture, opera, or the words and music of a song). The definition of 'joint work' is to be contrasted with the definition of 'collective work', also in section 101, in which the elements of merger and unity are lacking; there the key elements are assemblage or gathering of 'separate and independent works . . . into a collective whole.'

"The definition of 'joint works' has prompted some concern lest it be construed as converting the authors of previously written works, such as plays, novels, and music into coauthors of a motion picture in which their work is incorporated. It is true that a motion picture would normally be a joint rather than a collective work with respect to those authors who actually work on the film, although their usual status as employees for hire would keep the question of co-ownership from coming up. On the other hand, although a novelist, playwright, or songwriter may write a work with the hope or expectation that it will be used in a motion picture, this is clearly a case of separate or independent authorship rather than one where the basic intention behind the writing of the work was for motion picture use. In this case, the motion picture is a derivative work within the definition of that term, and section 103 makes plain that copyright in a derivative work is independent of, and does not enlarge the scope of rights in, any pre-existing material incorporated in it. There is thus no need to spell this conclusion out in the definition of 'joint work.'" H.R. Rep. No. 94–1476, 94th Cong., 2d Sess. 120–21 (1976).

[71] For a case finding an intent to merge resulting in a joint work, see Strauss v. Hearst Corp., 8 U.S.P.Q.2d 1832 (S.D.N.Y. 1988) (photograph for magazine article). *Compare* Grosset & Dunlap, Inc. v. Gulf & Western Corp., 534 F. Supp. 606, 609, 215 U.S.P.Q. 991, 993 (S.D.N.Y. 1982) (book's illustrator was not a joint author because the "stories could be enjoyed in full without the illustrations").

[72] *See* Eckert v. Hurley Chicago Company, Inc., 638 F. Supp. 699, 702, 230 U.S.P.Q. 612, 614 (N.D. Ill. 1986) ("The narrower and better view is that each author when making his or her contribution must intend it to constitute a part of a total work to which another shall make (or has already made) a contribution.").

[73] Weissmann v. Freeman, 868 F.2d 1313, 10 U.S.P.Q.2d 1014 (2d Cir. 1989), *cert. denied*, 110 S. Ct. 219 (1989). *See also* Kenbrooke Fabrics, Inc. v. Material Things, 223 U.S.P.Q. 1039 (S.D. N.Y. 1984) (Italian designer prepared a fabric design based on suggestions by U.S. company; a later variation on the design by the U.S. company is a separate derivative work and confers no rights to sue for infringement of the original Italian designer's copyrighted work).

[74] The court stated:

"In holding that the resulting song was a joint work, the critical fact [in *Marks*] was that both parties were equally aware that their individual authorship efforts would have to be combined in order to create the final integrated product—a commercially viable

that [the two] intended their joint product to be forever indivisible like the finite whole of the completed single song in *Marks*."[75]

[ii]   *Quality of Contributions—Suggestions and Directions.* A person's contribution of ideas and suggestions for a work created by another does not confer status as a joint author. Judge Grady noted, "While a co-author's contribution need not equal the other author's, at least when the authors are not immediately and obviously collaborating, the co-author's contribution must be 'significant' both in quality and quantity in order to permit an inference that the parties intended a joint work."[76]

One who contributes ideas, parameters or specifications for a work to be created by another is not a joint author because he or she does not make an original authorship contribution.[77] In *S.O.S. Inc.*,[78] the Ninth Circuit noted: "A person who

---

song. . . . From this, the rule has evolved that an author who intends to create a joint work must clearly demonstrate his or her intent in that regard. Although such an intent may, as in *Marks*, be inferred from the circumstances surrounding the creation of the work, in the absence of such a showing, the work is presumed to be the product of an individual author and is the sole property of its creator."

[75] 868 F.2d at 1319, 10 U.S.P.Q.2d at 1019.

[76] Eckert v. Hurley Chicago Co., Inc., 638 F. Supp. 699, 230 U.S.P.Q. 612, 615 (N.D. Ill. 1986). *Compare* Fishing Concepts, Inc. v. Ross, 226 U.S.P.Q. 692 (D. Minn. 1985).

As to whether a putative joint author's contribution must be sufficiently original to be "copyrightable standing alone," see Community for Creative Non-Violence v. Reid, 846 F.2d 1485, 6 U.S.P.Q.2d 1990, *aff'd, on other grounds and remanded*, 490 U.S. 730, 10 U.S.P.Q.2d 1985, 1989 (1989). The facts of *Community for Creative Non-Violence ("CCNV")* are discussed at § 4G[2]. In *CCNV*, the District of Columbia Circuit, in remanding the case for a determination of joint authorship, cited a portion of the Nimmer treatise that states "the standard of *de minimis* is not necessarily the same as the standard for copyrightability." M. Nimmer & D. Nimmer, Nimmer on Copyright § 6.07 (1988). Nimmer gives the following example: "Thus if authors A and B work in collaboration, but A's contribution is limited to plot ideas which standing alone would not be copyrightable, and B weaves the ideas into a completed literary expression, it would seem that A and B are joint authors of the resulting work."

Arguably, Nimmer's example is contrary to cases cited below finding no joint authorship with works such as architectural drawings and computer programs. See P. Goldstein, Copyright § 4.2.1.2 (1989). Professor Goldstein does note that "a collaborator who accompanies her ideas with original and expressive suggestions will be a joint author even though her contribution is smaller than the contributions of the other authors." *Id.*

See also Ashton-Tate Corp. v. Ross, 916 F.2d 516, 521, 16 U.S.P.Q.2d 1541, 1546 (9th Cir. 1990):

"Academic authorities split on what type of 'contribution' the copyright law requires for joint authorship purposes. . . . The district court adopted the view championed by Professor Goldstein. This court recently adopted the same position in *S.O.S. Inc. v. Payday Inc.*, 886 F.2d 1081, 1086–87 (9th Cir. 1989). . . . Even though this issue is not completely settled in the case law, our circuit holds that joint authorship requires each author to make an independently copyrightable contribution."

[77] *E.g.*, Eckert v. Hurley Chicago Co., Inc., 638 F. Supp. 699, 704, 230 U.S.P.Q. 612, 615 (N.D. Ill. 1986); Kenbrooke Fabrics, Inc. v. Material Things, 223 U.S.P.Q. 1039 (S.D.N.Y. 1984) (fabric design; commissioning party's "only contribution prior to creation of the fabric was the general request that [the artist] create a design incorporating a floral border and stripes,

merely describes to an author what the commissioned work should do or look like is not a joint author for purposes of the Copyright Act." For example, cases dealing with architectural drawings hold that a buyer or client who makes suggestions or submits sketches to an architect is not a joint author.[79] Similarly, cases dealing with computer programs hold that a person who supplies functional specifications or ideas to a programmer is not a joint author.[80]

---

a suggestion that gave rise to several variations on that theme"). *Compare* Mister B Textiles, Inc. v. Woodcrest Fabrics, Inc., 523 F. Supp. 21, 213 U.S.P.Q. 661 (S.D. N.Y. 1981) (fabric design; A and B are joint authors when A presented B with pictures of two garments from foreign magazines with instructions to combine and adapt them for the American market).

In *Eckert*, plaintiff Eckert sued for infringement of copyright on an 11 page sales brochure for water filters. Defendant asserted that its president Losos made such contributions to the work to make him a co-author, and, therefore, that it was a co-owner of the work and could not be guilty of copyright infringement. Defendant moved for summary judgment on the ground that the work was one of joint authorship. The court denied the motion against defendant because the contributions Eckert admitted receiving from Losos did not make the work a joint one.

> "Basically, the only contribution Losos made was a picture of the product, the water filter: he provided Eckert either a photograph or a drawing of a cross-section of the filter. Eckert also used the Hurley trademark and slogan, which HCI apparently owns. The brochure is eleven pages long. The first ten pages explain why someone should buy a water filter. The last page shows the particular water filter the author of the brochure wants the reader . . . to buy. The components of that product, that is, the picture, trademark and slogan, do not involve creative additions to the brochure itself. The creative and original aspect of the brochure lies in the arrangement of facts which encourage the reader to buy a water filter. Losos' admitted contribution involves merely the simple display of the filter which the reader is encouraged to buy. That display contribution is not an inseparable or interdependent part of the whole of the brochure." 638 F. Supp. at 704, 230 U.S.P.Q. at 615.

[78] S.O.S. Inc. v. Payday, Inc., 886 F.2d 1081, 12 U.S.P.Q.2d 1241 (9th Cir. 1989).

[79] Aitken, Hazen, Hoffman, Miller, P.C. v. Empire Construction Co., 542 F. Supp. 252, 218 U.S.P.Q. 409 (D. Neb. 1982); Meltzer v. Zoller, 520 F. Supp. 847, 216 U.S.P.Q. 776 (D.N.J. 1981). *Cf.* M.G.B. Homes, Inc. v. Ameron Homes, Inc., 903 F.2d 1486, 15 U.S.P.Q.2d 1282 (11th Cir. 1990).

[80] S.O.S. Inc. v. Payday, Inc., 886 F.2d 1081, 1087, 12 U.S.P.Q.2d 1241, 1245 (9th Cir. 1989) (putative "joint author," the client's employee, "did nothing more than describe the sort of programs [the client] wanted [the owner of the copyrighted program] to write. . . . To be an author, one must supply more than mere direction or ideas. . . . The supplier of an idea is no more an 'author' of a program than is the supplier of the disk on which the program is stored."); Whelan Associates v. Jaslow Dental Laboratory, Inc., 609 F. Supp. 1307, 225 U.S.P.Q. 156 (E.D. Pa. 1985), *aff'd*, 797 F.2d 1222, 230 U.S.P.Q. 481 (3d Cir. 1986), *cert. denied*, 479 U.S. 1031 (1987).

In *S.O.S.*, the Ninth Circuit approved as sound the district court's analysis in *Whelan*.

> "[In *Whelan*,] a dental laboratory owner commissioned software for use in his business, disclosed to the programmers the detailed operation of his business, dictated the functions to be performed by the computer, and even helped design the language and format of some of the screens that would appear on the computer's visual displays. The court nonetheless found that the programmer was the sole author of the software. The court's principal focus was on the creation of the source and object code. The

[4]　Renewals and Termination of Transfers

Both the 1909 and 1976 Copyright Acts allow authors or their heirs to reclaim ownership rights in their copyrights free of prior transfers and licenses. The 1909 Act split the term of copyright into an original 28-year original term and a 28-year renewal term. The renewal term vested in the author or in designated heirs if the author did not live to the renewal date. The renewal copyright was a "new estate" or property interest potentially free of encumbrances or transfers of interests in the original copyright. An author or a specified heir could contract to assign his or her renewal right. However, such a contract did not bind other potential heirs.

The 1976 Act provides a unitary term. After a specified number of years, the author or designated heirs may terminate transfers and licenses.

A difficult problem with both the 1909 Act renewal scheme and the 1976 Act transfer termination scheme is whether and under what conditions a derivative work based on an underlying work, such as a motion picture based on a novel, can continue to be utilized after renewal or termination of transfers of the copyright in the underlying work.

[a]　**Renewal Under the 1909 Act.** The 1909 Act set a 28 year original copyright term. Section 24 granted a right to renew for an additional 28 year term.[81] The renewal term's purpose was, in part, to protect authors and their heirs against unremunerative copyright transfers and licenses made before a work's value was recognized.[82] The renewal owner took a new property right that was independent of the encumbrances and transfers of the original property right.

---

owner's 'general assistance and contributions to the fund of knowledge of the author did not make [him] a creator of any original work, nor even the co-author. It is similar to an owner explaining to an architect the type and functions of a building the architect is to design for the owner. The architectural drawings are not co-authored by the owner, no matter how detailed the ideas and limitations expressed by the owner.' " 886 F.2d at 1086–87, 12 U.S.P.Q.2d at 1245.

[81] Section 24 also set the basic 28 year term. It provided that for certain works, including works for hire and posthumous works, the "proprietor" of the copyright could apply for a 28 year renewal and extension. For other types of works, Section 24 provided:

"[T]he author of such work, if still living or the widow, widower, or children of the author be not living, or if such author, widow or widower, or children be not living, then the author's executors, or in the absence of a will, his next of kin shall be entitled to a renewal and extension of the copyright in such work for a further term of twenty-eight years when application for such renewal and extension shall have been made to the copyright office and duly registered therein within one year prior to the expiration of the original term of copyright. . . . [I]n default of the registration of such application for renewal and extension, the copyright in any work shall determine at the expiration of twenty-eight years from first publication."

[82] See Fred Fisher Music Co. v. M. Witmark & Sons, 318 U.S. 643, 653 (1943) ("By providing for two copyright terms, each of relatively short duration, Congress enabled the author to sell his 'copyright' without losing his renewal interest. If the author's copyright extended over a single, longer term, his sale of the 'copyright' would terminate his entire interest. . . . [T]his is the basic consideration of policy underlying the renewal provision of the Copyright Act of 1909. . . . ").

Under Section 24, the renewal right vested in "the author . . . , if still living, or the widow, widower, or children of the author, if the author be not living, or if such author, widow, widower, or children be not living, then the author's executors, or in the absence of a will, his next of kin." Section 24 required the filing of an application for renewal "within one year prior to the expiration of the original term of copyright."

The renewal provisions spawned many problems and much litigation. In *Fred Fisher Music,*[83] the Supreme Court held that the author could by a specific written assignment convey his renewal rights, but the assignment would not bind the stated heirs if the author died prior to renewal time. In *DeSylva,*[84] the Court held that (1) when the author dies prior to renewal, a widow and any children take as a class, and (2) whether an illegitimate offspring constitutes one of the author's "children" depends on the law of a state rather than on a uniform federal copyright definition.[85] In *Miller Music,*[86] the Court held that an executor of an author's

---

[83] Fred Fisher Music Co. v. M. Witmark & Sons, 318 U.S. 643 (1943). The Court found nothing in the history or policy of the copyright renewal provisions that would alter an author's right to alienate his or her renewal rights. As to policy, it noted:

> "The policy of the copyright law, we are told, is to protect the author—if need be, from himself—and a construction under which the author is powerless to assign his renewal interest furthers this policy. We are asked to recognize that authors are congenitally irresponsible, that frequently they are so sorely pressed for funds that they are willing to sell their work for a mere pittance, and therefore assignments made by them should not be upheld.

> "It is not for courts to judge whether the interests of authors clearly lie upon one side of this question rather than the other. If an author cannot make an effective assignment of his renewal, it may be worthless to him when he is most in need. Nobody would pay an author for something he cannot sell. We cannot draw a principle of law from the familiar stories of garret-poverty of some men of literary genius. Even if we could do so, we cannot say that such men would regard with favor a rule of law preventing them from realizing on their assets when they are most in need of funds. Nor can we be unmindful of the fact that authors have themselves devised means of safeguarding their interests. We do not have such assured knowledge about authorship, and particularly about song writing, or the psychology of gifted writers and composers, as to justify us as judges in importing into Congressional legislation a denial to authors of the freedom to dispose of their property possessed by others. While authors may have habits making for intermittent want, they may have no less a spirit of independence which would resent treatment of them as wards under guardianship of the law." 318 U.S. at 656–57.

In the 1976 Act, Congress made the right to terminate transfers not subject to alienation. *See* § 4G[4][b].

[84] De Sylva v. Ballentine, 351 U.S. 570 (1956).

[85] The Court noted:

> "The scope of a federal right is, of course, a federal question, but that does not mean that its content is not to be determined by state, rather than federal law. . . . This is especially true where a statute deals with a familial relationship; there is no federal law of domestic relations, which is primarily a matter of state concern.

> "We think it proper, therefore, to draw on the ready-made body of state law to define the word 'children' in § 24. This does not mean that a State would be entitled to use

estate acquires the renewal right if neither the author nor his or her widow or widower or children survive to the renewal date—even though the author assigned his renewal right.[87]

[b]   The 1976 Act. The 1976 Act adopts a unitary copyright term, abolishing renewal.

the word 'children' in a way entirely strange to those familiar with its ordinary usage, but at least to the extent that there are permissible variations in the ordinary concept of 'children' we deem state law controlling.

"This raises two questions: first, to what State do we look, and second, given a particular State, what part of that State's law defines the relationship. The answer to the first question, in this case, is not difficult, since it appears from the record that the only State concerned is California . . . The second question, however, is less clear. An illegitimate child who is acknowledged by his father, by a writing signed in the presence of a witness, is entitled under § 255 of the California Probate Code to inherit his father's estate as well as his mother's. . . . Under California law the child is not legitimate for all purposes, however. . . .

"Considering the purposes of § 24 of the Copyright Act, we think it sufficient that the status of the child is that described by § 255 of the California Probate Code. The evident purpose of § 24 is to provide for the family of the author after his death. Since the author cannot assign his family's renewal rights, § 24 takes the form of a compulsory bequest of the copyright to the designated persons. This is really a question of the descent of property, and we think the controlling question under state law should be whether the child would be an heir of the author." 351 U.S. at 580–82.

In the 1976 Act, Congress rejected the state law approach to determining who constitutes a widow, child, etc. of the author. *See* § 4G[4][a].

[86] Miller Music Corp. v. Charles N. Daniels, Inc., 362 U.S. 373 (1960). The Court noted:

"What Congress has done by § 24 is to create contingent renewal rights. Congress has provided that, when the author dies before the renewal period arrives, special rules in derogation of the usual rules of succession are to apply for the benefit of three classes of people—(1) widows, widowers, and children; (2) executors, and (3) next of kin. We think we would redesign § 24 if we held that executors, named as one of the preferred classes, do not acquire the renewal rights, where there has been a prior assignment, though widows, widowers, and children or next of kin would acquire them.

"A purchaser of such an interest is deprived of nothing. Like all purchasers of contingent interests, he takes subject to the possibility that the contingency may not occur." 362 U.S. at 376, 378.

In Film Corp. v. Knowles, 261 U.S. 326 (1923), the Supreme Court held that the statute assured that an executor of an author's estate could renew the copyright even though the author did prior to the renewal period: "[I]f there is no widow or child the executor may exercise the power that the testator might have exercised if he had been alive. The executor represents the person of his testator, . . . and it is no novelty for him to be given rights that the testator could not have exercised while he lived." 261 U.S. at 329.

[87] *See also* Saroyan v. William Saroyan Foundation, 675 F. Supp. 843, 5 U.S.P.Q.2d 1532 (S.D. NY. 1987), *aff'd*, 862 F.2d 304 (2d Cir. 1988) (table) (author's surviving children have renewal rights to author's copyrighted works even though the author, by will, left certain property to his children, and the residue of his estate, including copyrights, to a charitable foundation).

For works in their first or renewal copyright terms on January 1, 1978, the Act retains the 1909 Act provision for renewals, including the requirement that an application for renewal be filed,[88] but lengthens the renewal term to 47 years, which, added to the original 28 year term, confers 75 years of copyright protection.[89]

The 1976 Act carries forward the policy of allowing authors or their heirs to avoid copyright transfers after a certain number of years by providing for "termination of transfers."

Section 203 establishes a right to terminate transfers or licenses, whether exclusive or nonexclusive, of a copyright or any right under a copyright executed by the author on or after January 1, 1978, other than by will.[90]

Section 304(c) establishes a right to terminate transfers and licenses executed by either the author or one of the designated beneficiaries before January 1, 1978 as to copyrights subsisting in either their first or their renewal terms on January 1, 1978.[91] The primary purpose of the Section 304(c) termination right is to assure that authors and their heirs benefit from the 19 year renewal term extension.

Neither termination of transfer provision applies to works for hire, that is, those in which the human author's employer is the author for copyright provisions.

The two termination provisions, Sections 203 and 304(c), set forth in detail the conditions and effect of terminations. The two provisions are similar, but there are important differences between them.[92]

---

[88] 17 U.S.C. § 304(a).

The House Committee noted:

"Subsection (a) of section 304 reenacts and preserves the renewal provision, now in section 24 of the statute, for all of the works presently in their first 28-year term. A great many of the present expectancies in these cases are the subject of existing contracts, and it would be unfair and immensely confusing to cut off or alter these interests." H.R. Rep. No. 94–1476, 94th Cong., 2d Sess. (1976).

[89] This is part of the "general approach" of the Act "to increase the present 56-year term to 75 years in the case of copyrights subsisting in both their first and their renewal terms." H.R. Rep. No. 94–1476, 94th Cong., 2d Sess. 139 (1976).

[90] 17 U.S.C. § 203.

[91] 17 U.S.C. § 304(c).

[92] For example, Section 203 applies only to *inter vivos* transfer or licenses executed by the author whereas Section 304(c) applies to transfers and licenses by the author and the designated class of beneficiaries (widows, children, etc.). The House Report explains the purpose of the distinction:

"Under section 203, an author's widow or widower and children are given rights of termination if the author is dead, but these rights apply only to grants by the author, and any effort by a widow, widower, or child to transfer contingent future interests under a termination would be ineffective. In contrast, under the present renewal provisions, any statutory beneficiary of the author can make a valid transfer or license of future renewal rights, which is completely binding if the author is dead and the person who executed the grant turns out to be the proper renewal claimant. Because of this, a great many contingent transfers of future renewal rights have been obtained from widows, widowers, children, and next of kin, and a substantial number of these will be binding. After the present 28-year renewal period has ended, a statutory beneficiary

[i] *Persons Entitled to Terminate.* Section 203 (post-1977 transfers) and Section 304(c) (pre-1978 transfers) vest the right of terminate in (1) the author, or (2) if the author be dead, the widow or widower and children or grandchildren. Both sections provide that termination "may be effected notwithstanding any agreement to the contrary, including an agreement to make a will or to make any future grant,"[93] thereby altering the *Fred Fisher Music* decision.[94] Section 101 gives a definition of "widow," "widower," and "children,"[95] thereby altering the *DeSylva* doctrine.[96]

The two major issues as to persons empowered to terminate a grant are (1) the class of beneficiaries in the case of joint works, and (2) whether less than unanimous consent of all those entitled to terminate should be required.

In resolving both issues, Section 203 adopts principles of majority rule and *per stirpes* representation to determine (1) the right to effect termination;[97] (2) the ownership of terminated rights;[98] and (3) the right to make further grants of reverted rights.[99]

who has signed a disadvantageous grant of this sort should have the opportunity to reclaim the extended term." H.R. Rep. No. 94–1476, 94th Cong., 2d Sess. 140–41 (1976).

For a critique of this distinction, see M. Nimmer & D. Nimmer, Nimmer on Copyright § 11.02[A][4][a] (1989).

Also, as noted below, Section 304(c) has different rules on who may effect a termination of transfers.

[93] 17 U.S.C. §§ 203(a)(5), 304(c)(5). The House Report states that "A provision of this sort is needed because of the unequal bargaining position of authors, resulting in part from the impossibility of determining a work's value until it has been exploited." H.R. Rep. No. 94–1476, 94th Cong., 2d Sess. 124 (1976).

[94] *See* § 4G[2][a]. The direct holding of *Fred Fisher Music*, that authors and their heirs may assign their personal renewal rights, presumably remains the law as to renewals under 17 U.S.C. § 304(a). Section 304(c) provides a right to terminate transfers as to the 1976 Act's 19 year extension of the 28 year renewal period. Thus, a transferee of an author's renewal right owns the right to renewal but the author (or widow, widower, children or grandchildren, etc.) may terminate 56 years after the copyright was originally secured, that is, 28 years into the renewal period.

[95] The relevant definitions in Section 101 state:

"A person's 'children' are that person's immediate offspring, whether legitimate or not, and any children legally adopted by that person."

"The author's 'widow' or 'widower' is the author's surviving spouse under the law of the author's domicile at the time of his or her death, whether or not the spouse has later remarried."

[96] *See* § 4G[4][a].

[97] Section 203(a)(1) and (2) state the majority and *per stirpes* rules for exercise of termination as to grants by more than one author of a joint work and to grants by an author when the author is dead.

[98] Section 203(b) provides that, upon the effective date of termination, "all rights" under the Copyright Act that were covered by the terminated grant revert to the persons owning the termination interests under Section 203(a)(1), (2).

[99] Section 203(b)(3) provides that a "further grant" of a right covered by a terminated grant is valid only if signed "by the same number and proportion of the owners . . . as are required to terminate the grant. . . ."

The House Report gives the following example of the majority rule, *per stirpes* principle:

> "Take, for example, a case where a dead author left a widow, two living children and three grandchildren by a third child who is dead. The widow will own half of the reverted interests, the two children will each own 16 2/3 percent, and the three grandchildren will each own a share of roughly 5 1/2 percent. But who can exercise the right of termination? Obviously, since she owns 50 percent, the widow is an essential party, but suppose neither of the two surviving children is willing to join her in the termination; is it enough that she gets one of the children of the dead child to join, or can the dead child's interest be exercised only by the action of a majority of his children? Consistent with the per stirpes principle, the interest of a dead child can be exercised only as a unit by majority action of his surviving children. Thus, even though the widow and one grandchild would own 55 1/2 percent, of the reverted copyright, they would have to be joined by another child or grandchild in order to effect a termination or a further transfer of reverted rights." [100]

The Report gives another example as to joint authors.

> "This principle also applies where, for example, two joint authors executed a grant and one of them is dead; in order to effect a termination, the living author must be joined by a per stirpes majority of the dead author's beneficiaries. The notice of termination may be signed by the specified owners of termination interests or by 'their duly authorized agents,' which would include the legally appointed guardians or committees of persons incompetent to sign because of age or mental disability." [101]

Section 304(c) (pre-1978 transfers) vests the rights in the same class of beneficiaries as Section 203 and adopts the *per stirpes* majority rule. However, because of differences between transfers and licenses made after the effective date of the 1976 Act (Section 203), and transfers and licenses made before that date as applied to the 19-year extended renewal term (Section 304(c)), Section 304(c) makes different provisions as to joint works, grants not executed by the author, and further grants. [102]

---

[100] H.R. Rep. No. 94–1476, 94th Cong., 2d Sess. 125–26 (1976).

[101] H.R. Rep. No. 94–1476, 94th Cong., 2d Sess. 126 (1976).

[102] The House Report gives the following summary of the most important distinctions between the termination rights under Section 203 and Section 304(c).

> "1. *Joint authorship.*—Under section 304, a grant of renewal rights executed by joint authors during the first term of copyright would be effective only as to those who were living at the time of renewal; where any of them are dead, their statutory beneficiaries are entitled to claim the renewal independently as a new estate. It would therefore be inappropriate to impose a requirement of majority action with respect to transfers executed by two or more joint authors.
>
> "2. *Grants not executed by author.*—Section 304(c) adopts the majority principle underlying the amendments of section 203 with respect to the termination rights of a dead author's widow or widower and children. There is much less reason, as a matter of policy, to apply this principle in the case of transfers and licenses of renewal rights executed under the present law by the author's widow, widower, children, executors, or next of kin,

[ii] *Time Period for Termination—Notice.* Under Sections 203 and 304(c), a termination "may be effected at any time during a period of five years" beginning on a specified date. For Section 203 terminations, the specified date is the end of 35 years from the date of publication or 40 years from the date of execution of the grant, whichever term ends earlier if the grant includes the right of publication; otherwise, the date is the end of 35 years from the date of execution of the grant.[103] For Section 304(c) terminations, the specified date is the end of 56 years from the date copyright was originally secured, or beginning on January 1, 1978, whichever is later.[104]

The appropriate owners effect termination by "serving an advance notice in writing."[105] The notice must (1) state the effective date of the termination, which must fall within the five-year period, and (2) comply in form, content, and manner of service with requirements prescribed by the Register of Copyrights.[106] The notice

---

and the practical arguments against doing so are conclusive. It is not clear how the shares of a class of renewal beneficiaries are to be divided under the existing law, and greater difficulties would be presented if any attempt were made to apply the majority principle to further beneficiaries in cases where one or more of the renewal beneficiaries are dead. Therefore, where the grant was executed by a person or persons other than the author, termination can be effected only by the unanimous action of the survivors of those who executed it.

"*3. Further grants.*—The reason against adopting a principle of majority action with respect to the right to terminate grants by joint authors and grants not executed by the author apply equally with respect to the right to make further grants under section 304(c). The requirement for majority action in clause (6)(C) is therefore confined to cases where the rights under a grant by the author have reverted to his or her widow or widower, or children, or both. Where the extended term reverts to joint authors or to a class of renewal beneficiaries who have joined in executing a grant, their rights would be governed by the general rules of tenancy in common; each coowner would have an independent right to sell his share, or to use or license the work subject to an accounting." H.R. Rep. No. 94–1476, 94th Cong., 2d Sess. 141 (1976).

See Bourne Co. v. MPL Communications Inc., 675 F. Supp. 859, 5 U.S.P.Q.2d 1951, 1952 (S.D. N.Y. 1987) (statutory successor of joint author may terminate to the extent of that author's share under 17 U.S.C. § 304(c)(1)).

For a critique of the distinction as to joint authors, see M. Nimmer & D. Nimmer, Nimmer on Copyright § 11.03[A][1] (1989).

[103] 17 U.S.C. § 203(a)(3). The alternative computation method for publications is "intended to cover cases where years elapse between the signing of a publication contract and the eventual publication of the work." H.R. Rep. No. 94–1476, 94th Cong., 2d Sess. 126 (1976).

[104] 17 U.S.C. § 304(c)(3). The latter date is effective only as to copyrights the renewal terms of which Congress specifically extended in anticipation of the enactment of the 1976 Act, which significantly lengthened the term of copyright beyond the 56 year term of the 1909 Act. As to these 56-plus-year-old copyrights, licenses and transfers became immediately subject to termination on the effective date of the 1976 Act (January 1, 1978). See H.R. Rep. No. 94–1476, 94th Cong., 2d Sess. 140 (1976).

[105] 17 U.S.C. §§ 203(a)(4), 304(c)(4).

[106] See 37 C.F.R. § 201.10.

Notable among the requirements of the Copyright Office regulation is that the notice contain a "brief statement reasonably identifying the grant to which the notice of termination applies."

"shall be served not less than two or more than ten years" before the effective date.[107] The notice must be served "upon the grantee or the grantee's successor in title"[108] and must be recorded in the Copyright Office.

---

37 U.S.C. § 201.10(b)(1)(iii). *See* Burroughs v. Metro-Goldwyn-Mayer, Inc., 683 F.2d 610, 621, 215 U.S.P.Q. 495, 504 (2d Cir. 1982) (statutory successors to author of the Tarzan books served a notice of termination listing 33 of the author's works, including "Tarzan of the Apes," but omitting five of the Tarzan books; "While we do not suggest that the omission of the five titles affected the efficacy of the notice to terminate the interest of [the grantee] in such titles as were listed, . . . it did leave [the grantee's] interest in those five books, all of which feature 'Tarzan,' intact.").

[107] The House Report gives, as examples, "two typical contract situations."

> "Case 1: Contract for theatrical production signed on September 2, 1987. Termination of grant can be made to take effect between September 2, 2022 (35 years from execution) and September 1, 2027 (end of 5 year termination period). Assuming that the author decides to terminate on September 1, 2022 (the earliest possible date) the advance notice must be filed between September 1, 2012 and September 1, 2020.

> "Case 2: Contract for book publication executed on April 10, 1980; book finally published on August 23, 1987. Since contract covers the right of publication, the 5-year termination period would begin on April 10, 2020 (40 years from execution) rather than April 10, 2015 (35 years from execution) or August 23, 2022 (35 years from publication). Assuming that the author decides to make the termination effective on January 1, 2024, the advance notice would have to be served between January 1, 2014, and January 1, 2022." H.R. Rep. No. 94–1476, 94th Cong., 2d Sess. 126 (1976).

[108] The disjunctive phrase leaves unclear whether service of the notice on the grantee is sufficient when the original grantee has made further grants or issued nonexclusive licenses to others. *See* Burroughs v. Metro-Goldwyn-Mayer, Inc., 683 F.2d 610, 632–34, 215 U.S.P.Q. 495, 513–16 (2d Cir. 1982) (Newman, concurring). Without question, the termination provisions apply to further grants and to nonexclusive licenses. Sections 203 and 304(c) refer to "exclusive or nonexclusive grant or a transfer or license." The question is whether such grantees and licensees must be served with notice.

In *Burroughs*, the author of the "Tarzan" books conveyed his literary property rights to a family-held corporation. That corporation in turn conveyed certain motion picture rights to MGM. Later, the author's statutory successors served a notice of termination listing 33 of the author's works. The majority held that the notice failed to list five other Tarzan works with the result that MGM retained certain rights to use the Tarzan character. Judge Newman disagreed with that conclusion but concurred in the result because he believed that the failure to serve notice on MGM vitiated any attempted termination of MGM's rights. Noting that "the statute provides few guides to its meaning," Judge Newman rejected the two extreme interpretations—notice only to the grantee or notice to all transferees and licensees.

> "Whatever the meaning of 'grantee' and 'successor in title' in the notice termination provision, it seems evident that their expression in the disjunctive was intended to cover various contingencies, not to afford those exercising termination rights a choice as to whom to serve. The statute is sensibly read to mean that notice is to be served (a) on the grantee, if the grantee has retained all rights originally conveyed, (b) on the transferee, if the grantee has conveyed all rights to a transferee, or (c) if only some rights have been conveyed, on the grantee or the transferee (or both) depending upon which rights are sought to be terminated." 683 F.2d at 634 n.8, 215 U.S.P.Q. at 514 n.8.

As to nonexclusive licensees, Judge Newman agreed that such were not "successors in title" within the meaning of the statute: "Interpreting 'successor in title' to include all assignees and

[*iii*] *Effect of Termination.* Under Section 203 (post-1977 transfers), "termination means that ownership of the rights covered by the terminated grant reverts to everyone who owns termination interests on the date the notice of termination was served, whether they joined in signing the notice or not."[109] Because the future rights vest on the date the notice of termination is served,[110] the heirs of a beneficiary who dies before the effective date will inherit his or her share.[111]

After a Section 203 termination, further grants or agreements as to the terminated rights may be made by the appropriate proportion of owners.[112] The further grant or agreement is effective as to all the owners, including those who did not join in signing it. Generally, the further grant "is valid only if it is made after the effective date of the termination."[113] However, an exception is made when the further grant is to "the original grantee or such grantee's successor in title."[114]

As noted above,[115] Section 304(c) contains different provisions for joint works, grants not executed by the author, and further grants.

---

exclusive licensees but to exclude non-exclusive licensees makes tolerable the notice burden upon those exercising termination rights." 683 F.2d at 634, 215 U.S.P.Q. at 515. However, he also agreed with MGM's argument that it should be treated as, in effect, a direct grantee from the author because the nominal original grantee was a corporation owned by the author's family: "[W]hen an author . . . has not in any realistic sense bargained away his rights by transferring them to his family corporation, non-exclusive licensees of that corporation should not bear the risk that their rights were terminated by service of notice solely upon the corporation." *Id.*

[109] H.R. Rep. No. 94–1476, 94th Cong., 2d Sess. 127 (1976).

[110] 17 U.S.C. § 203(b)(2).

[111] *See* Bourne Co. v. MPL Communications Inc., 675 F. Supp. 859, 862, 5 U.S.P.Q.2d 1951, 1953 (S.D. N.Y. 1987) ("Because [the author's statutory successor] died after the notice of termination was served, her rights under the terminated grant had vested and thus passed to her estate.").

[112] 17 U.S.C. § 203(b)(3).

[113] 17 U.S.C. § 203(b)(4). *Cf.* Bourne Co. v. MPL Communications Inc., 675 F. Supp. 859, 5 U.S.P.Q.2d 1951 (S.D. N.Y. 1987) (suggesting that an agreement may be negotiated prior to the effective date so long as it is not "made" prior to that date and that there is no statutory authority for declaring a termination of transfers invalid simply because it was done pursuant to an invalid agreement to make a further grant).

[114] 17 U.S.C. § 203(b)(4). The House Report refers to this exception as being "in the nature of a right of 'first refusal.'" H.R. Rep. No. 94-1476, 94th Cong., 2d Sess. 127 (1976). However, one court decision indicates that this characterization is not accurate. Bourne Co. v. MPL Communications Inc., 675 F. Supp. 859, 685–86, 5 U.S.P.Q.2d 1951, 1956 (S.D.N.Y. 1987):

> "The statute neither compels the terminating party to negotiate with the terminated grantee, nor forbids him from negotiating with anyone else. All it requires is that prior to the effective date of termination, the terminated grantee is the only person with whom the author or his successor can make an enforceable and effective agreement to transfer those rights. The provision does give the terminated grantee a preferred competitive position but '[i]f the author can afford to wait for competitive offers until after the effective date of termination, he can overcome any advantage the grantee or successor may seek to gain from the preferential position.' . . . If Congress intended to create a right of first refusal, it would have done so in clear language."

[115] *See* § 4G[4][b][i].

An important exception to termination for the continued utilization of derivative works is discussed below.

[c] Derivative Works—Renewal, Termination of Transfers, Expiration of Derivative Copyright Prior to Original Copyright. Difficult questions concerning the copyright term and the effect of renewals and terminations of transfers arise when a derivative work, such as a movie based on a novel,[116] is prepared under a grant of authority by the owner of the copyright in the original work. (For convenience, the work upon which a derivative work is based will be referred to as the "underlying" work.) These questions include:

(1) If the copyright on the underlying work was obtained under the 1909 Act and the copyright is renewed, can the owner of rights to the derivative work continue to utilize it without the permission of the owner of the renewal copyright?

(2) What rights does the owner of copyright on an underlying work have as to use of a derivative work when copyright on the latter expires before the former?

(3) What effect does a termination of transfer of the underlying work's copyright under the 1976 Act have upon utilization of the derivative work?

[i] Renewal. In Abend,[117] the Supreme Court resolved a conflict between the Second and Ninth Circuits over continued utilization of a derivative work after renewal of the original work's copyright. The Court held that when "[t]he author of a pre-existing work . . . assign[ed] to another the right to use it in a derivative work" and "agreed to assign the rights in his renewal copyright term to the owner of [the] derivative work, but died before the commencement of the renewal period," "the owner of the derivative work infringed the rights of the successor owner of the pre-existing work by continued distribution and publication of the derivative work during the renewal term of the pre-existing work."[118]

(1) The Second Circuit's Rohauer Decision. In *Rohauer,*[119] the Second Circuit recognized a right of continued utilization despite the basic theory that a renewal of copyright gives rise to a "new estate" or property interest that is free of transfers and licenses conferred by the owner of the original copyright. In 1925, Edith Maude Hull wrote, caused to be published, and obtained a copyright on a novel, "The Sons of the Sheik." The same year, Hull assigned to Moskowitz all motion picture rights in the novel. Hull agreed to renew the copyrights in the story and to assign to Moskowitz the motion picture rights for the renewal term. Pursuant to this agreement, in 1926, Moskowitz's assignee produced, released and copyrighted a successful motion picture, "The Son of the Shiek," starring Rudolph Valentino.

Hull died in 1943. In 1952, Hull's daughter renewed the copyright. In 1965, the daughter assigned the motion picture rights in the novel to Rohauer. In 1971, Killiam

---

[116] A good illustration of a chain of derivative works is in the "Madame Butterfly" case, G. Ricordi & Co. v. Paramount Pictures, Inc., 189 F.2d 469 (2d Cir. 1951), *cert. denied,* 342 U.S. 849 (1951), discussed at § 4C[1][c].

[117] Stewart v. Abend, 110 S. Ct. 1750, 14 U.S.P.Q.2d 1614 (1990).

[118] 110 S. Ct. at 1753, 14 U.S.P.Q.2d at 1615.

[119] Rohauer v. Killiam Shows, Inc., 551 F.2d 484, 192 U.S.P.Q. 545 (2d Cir. 1977), *cert. denied,* 431 U.S. 949 (1977).

produced a videotape using a print of the Shiek film and exhibited it on television. Rohauer and Hull sued Killiam and the television station, claiming that the motion picture broadcast infringed the renewal copyright on the novel. The district court held that upon expiration of the original term of the copyright on the novel and the daughter's renewal of the copyright, all the defendants' rights to authorize the motion picture's exhibition terminated.

The Second Circuit reversed in an opinion by Judge Henry Friendly. First, Judge Friendly found that the "force or validity" clause of Section 7 of the 1909 Copyright Act had no bearing on the problem.[120] Second, he found no prior Supreme Court or lower court decision directly ruling on the issue whether "the inability of an author to carry out his promise to effect a renewal of a copyright because of his death prior to the date for obtaining renewal terminates as a matter of copyright law the right of a holder of a derivative copyright to continue to publish a derivative work copyrighted before the author's death on which the copyright was thereafter renewed."[121]

Treating the issue as a novel one, Judge Friendly concluded that the "new estate" renewal theory did not mean that "the vesting of renewed copyright in the underlying work in a statutory successor deprives the proprietor of the derivative copyright of a right, stemming from the . . . 'consent' of the original proprietor of the underlying work, to use so much of the underlying copyrighted work as already has been embodied in the copyrighted derivative work, as a matter of copyright law." He relied on two considerations: policy and Congress' treatment in the 1976 Act of the analogous problem of the status of derivative works after a statutory termination of transfers.

As to policy, Judge Friendly found reasons for preserving the interests of a creator of an original derivative work, whose equities were greater than that of an assignee or licensee who merely published or distributed the work.[122]

---

[120] Section 7 provides, in pertinent part, that "other versions . . . of copyrighted works when produced with the consent of the proprietor of the copyright in such works . . . shall be regarded as new works subject to copyright under the provisions of this title; but the publication of any such new works shall not affect the force or validity of any subsisting copyright upon the matter employed or any part thereof. . . . "

The plaintiffs argued that the defendants' acts affected the "force" of the renewal copyright on the novel because they are contrary, inter alia, to a copyright owner's right to exclude others from unauthorized copying. The defendants argued that "sufficient 'force' is given to the renewal copyright on the novel if it is held to prevent any new or 'second generation' derivative works." 551 F.2d at 488.

Judge Friendly found that the legislative history of the 1909 Act confirmed the "force or validity" clause had no bearing on the problem of continued utilization of derivative works after renewal.

[121] A series of Supreme Court decisions on renewal "were concerned with the relative rights of persons claiming full assignment or ownership of the renewal term of an underlying copyright." 551 F.2d at 490. The Second's Circuit's "Madame Butterfly" decision, G. Ricordi & Co. v. Paramount Pictures, Inc., 189 F.2d 469 (2d Cir.), cert. denied, 342 U.S. 849 (1951), was distinguishable because the creator of the derivative work (an opera) did not obtain rights to the renewal term of the original work (a novel).

[122] Judge Friendly noted:

As to the 1976 Act, Judge Friendly cited the derivative works exception to Sections 203 and 304(c). He recognized that the exception did not directly control the relationship between derivative works and the renewal copyrights in original works[123] but accepted them as "evidence of a belief on the part of Congress of the need for special protection for derivative works."

(2) *The Ninth Circuit's* Abend *Decision.* In *Abend,*[124] the Ninth Circuit, in a 2-1 decision, disagreed with the Second Circuit's *Rohauer* decision and held that continued exploitation of a derivative work without the consent of the owner of the renewal copyright in the underlying work constituted copyright infringement. However, it also indicated that no injunction against utilization should be granted, the owner being limited to a monetary remedy.

In 1942, Cornell Woolrich wrote a short story, "It Had to be Murder," which was published in "Dime Detective Magazine." In 1945, Woolrich assigned motion picture rights to six stories, including "It Had to be Murder," to B.G. De Sylva Productions for $9,250. He agreed to renew the copyrights and to assign the same movie rights in the renewal to De Sylva. Alfred Hitchcock and others acquired the movie rights to the story. In 1954, Paramount produced and distributed Hitchcock's classic film "Rear Window," which was based on "It Had to be Murder." Woolrich died in 1968 without a surviving spouse or child. In 1969, his executor renewed the copyright. In 1972, the executor assigned the copyright to Sheldon Abend, a literary agent.

> "To such extent as it may be permissible to consider policy considerations, the equities lie preponderantly in favor of the proprietor of the derivative copyright. In contrast to the situation where an assignee or licensee has done nothing more than print, publicize and distribute a copyrighted story or novel, a person who with the consent of the author has created an opera or a motion picture film will often have made contributions literary, musical and economic, as great as or greater than the original author. . . . [T]he purchaser of derivative rights has no truly effective way to protect himself against the eventuality of the author's death before the renewal period since there is no way of telling who will be the surviving widow, children or next of kin or the executor until that date arrives. To be sure, this problem exists in equal degree with respect to assignments or licenses of underlying copyright, but in such cases there is not the countervailing consideration that large and independently copyrightable contributions will have been made by the transferee. As against this, the author can always protect his heirs by imposing a contractual limit upon the assignment. It is true that this might not be practicable from a business standpoint in cases where the assignment was made shortly before the expiration of the initial term, but those are the very cases where the inequity of terminating the transferee's rights with respect to so much of the underlying work as is embodied in the derivative work is the greatest." 551 F.2d at 493–94.

[123] "While it is true that this proviso was part of a package which extended the temporal rights of authors (but also of their assignees) and that the proviso thus does not deal with the precise situation here presented, we nevertheless regard it as evidence of a belief on the part of Congress of the need for special protection for derivative works. . . . We agree, of course, that provisions of the new Act cannot be read as varying clear provisions of the 1909 Act in cases to which the new Act does not apply." 551 F.2d at 494.

[124] Abend v. MCA, Inc., 863 F.2d 1465, 9 U.S.P.Q.2d 1337 (9th Cir. 1988), *aff'd and remanded sub nom.* Stewart v. Abend, 110 S. Ct. 175, 14 U.S.P.Q.2d 1614(1990).

Relying on the Second Circuit's *Rohauer* decision, the owners of the rights to the motion picture authorized Universal Pictures to re-release the film, which involved making new prints for theatrical exhibition, creating videocassettes, and publicly exhibiting the film in theaters, over cable TV, and through videodisc and videocassette rentals and sales. The re-release generated over $12 million. Abend sued for copyright infringement.

The Ninth Circuit reasoned that Rohauer was inconsistent with the rationale of the Supreme Court's 1960 Miller Music decision,[125] that its focus on "potential unfairness to makers of derivative works" overlooked important policies behind section 24 that favor the author,[126] and it improperly applied Congressional policy in the 1976 Act retroactively to the 1909 Act.[127]

---

[125] The court noted:

"In *Miller Music Corp. v. Charles N. Daniels, Inc.*, 362 U.S. 373, [125 U.S.P.Q. 147] (1960), the Supreme Court held that an assignment of full copyright renewal rights by the author *prior* to the time for renewal—i.e. within one year prior to the expiration of the original 28-year copyright term—*cannot* defeat the right of the author's statutory successor to the renewal copyright when the author dies before the time that the right for renewal has accrued.

"*Miller Music* provides ineluctable authority for Abend's position. Since Woolrich died before the renewal period arrived, his purported assignment of renewal rights is ineffective and irrelevant; the most defendants' predecessors could have acquired was an expectancy in the right to use the story that underlies the derivative work during the story's renewal period. The distinction *Rohauer* draws between cases where the author never agreed to assign renewal rights . . . and cases like ours, where the author's agreement is plainly unenforceable against his statutory successors, is meaningless." 863 F.2d at 1475, 9 U.S.P.Q.2d at 1344–45.

[126] The court noted:

"First, Congress sought to provide authors with a 'second chance' to reap the benefits of their work, particularly since authors must often negotiate from an unequal bargaining position.

"This concern is more compelling in the case before us. The infringement in *Rohauer* consisted of making one videotaped copy of a print of the film and broadcasting it over a public television station. This case, by contrast, involves a nationwide re-release of the film in theatres, in the video-cassette sales and rental markets, and on cable TV. Clearly, when Woolrich agreed to assign his renewal rights, he could not have foreseen the technological advances which have enabled the authors of the derivative work to expand tremendously their exploitation of the film.

"Second, by enacting section 24, Congress intended to provide protection to the author's family and so extended the renewal right to include the author's surviving family or heirs, should the author die during the original term of the copyright." 863 F.2d at 1477, 9 U.S.P.Q.2d at 1346–47.

[127] The court noted:

"[T]he 1976 Act included an exception for derivative works. The author's right to terminate prior grants or licenses for the 19-year extension period does not apply to existing derivative works for which the author had granted 28-year renewal rights. 17 U.S.C. § 304(c)(6)(A).

"*Rohauer* viewed this exception as evidence of Congress' intent to give 'special protection' to derivative works. . . . While Congress may, indeed, have intended section

The Ninth Circuit did recognize the equities of the derivative work owner in framing the proper remedy for infringement.

> "Our holding does not mean, however, that the equities of this case have no bearing on its outcome. We are mindful that this case presents compelling equitable considerations which should be taken into account by the district court in fashioning an appropriate remedy in the event defendants fail to establish any equitable defenses. Defendants invested substantial money, effort, and talent in creating the 'Rear Window' film. Clearly the tremendous success of that venture initially and upon re-release is attributable in significant measure to, inter alia, the outstanding performances of its stars—Grace Kelly and James Stewart—and the brilliant directing of Alfred Hitchcock.

> ". . . Professor Nimmer . . . states that 'where great public injury would be worked by an injunction, the courts might . . . award damages or a continuing royalty instead of an injunction in such special circumstances.'

> "We believe such special circumstances exist here. The 'Rear Window' film resulted from the collaborative efforts of many talented individuals other than Cornell Woolrich, the author of the underlying story. The success of the movie resulted in large part from factors completely unrelated to the underlying story, 'It Had To Be Murder.' It would cause a great injustice for the owners of the film if the court enjoined them from further exhibition of the movie. An injunction would also effectively foreclose defendants from enjoying legitimate profits derived from exploitation of the 'new matter' comprising the derivative work, which is given express copyright protection by section 7 of the 1909 Act. Since defendants could not possibly separate out the 'new matter' from the underlying work, their right to enjoy the renewal copyright in the derivative work would be rendered meaningless by the grant of an injunction. We also note that an injunction could cause public injury by denying the public the opportunity to view a classic film for many years to come.

> ". . . [T]he district court should award Abend actual damages and apportion profits between Abend and the defendants."[128]

(3) *The Supreme Court's* Abend *Decision.* The Supreme Court granted certiorari in *Abend*, and, in a 7-2 decision, affirmed the Ninth Circuit's decision and disapproved of *Rohauer*.[129] The renewal copyright owner's superior rights followed logically from *Miller Music*.

304(c)(6)(A) to provide additional protection in 1976, Congress' intent regarding the 1976 Act does not shed any light on the meaning of the 1909 Act. By its terms, section 304 only applies to the additional 19-year period. Abend persuasively argues that Rohauer thus does what Congress declined to do—apply the termination exception retroactively to the 28-year renewal period. When Congress enacted the 1976 Act, the prevailing view was that the owners of the renewal copyright in the underlying story could 'veto' the continued use of the derivative work. . . . We can reasonably presume that Congress knew of this prevailing view when it enacted the 1976 Act and chose not to alter the balance." 863 F.2d at 1478, 9 U.S.P.Q.2d at 1347.

[128] 863 F.2d at 1478–79, 9 U.S.P.Q.2d at 1348.

[129] 110 S. Ct. 1750, 14 U.S.P.Q.2d 1614 (1990). The Court did not review the Ninth Circuit's discussion of the appropriate remedy.

"An author holds a bundle of exclusive rights in the copyrighted work, among them the right to copy and the right to incorporate the work into derivative works. . . . By assigning the renewal copyright in the work without limitation, as in *Miller Music*, the author assigns all of these rights. After *Miller Music*, if the author dies before the commencement of the renewal period, the assignee holds nothing. If the assignee of all of the renewal rights holds nothing upon the death of the assignor before arrival of the renewal period, then, *a fortiori*, the assignee of a portion of the renewal rights, *e.g.*, the right to produce a derivative work, must also hold nothing. . . . Therefore, if the author dies before the renewal period, then the assignee may continue to use the original work only if the author's successor transfers the renewal rights to the assignee.[130]

Rohauer's reliance on the 1976 Act's derivative works exception as showing "an intent by Congress to prevent authors of pre-existing works from blocking distribution of derivative works" is unpersuasive.

"The process of compromise between competing special interests leading to the enactment of the 1976 Act undermines any such attempt to draw an overarching policy out of § 304(c)(6)(A), which only prevents termination with respect to works in their original or renewal copyright terms as of January 1, 1978, and only at the end of the renewal period. . . .

"In fact, if the 1976 Act's termination provisions provide any guidance at all in this case, they tilt against petitioners' theory. The plain language of the termination provision itself indicates that Congress assumed that the owner of the pre-existing work possessed the right to sue for infringement even after incorporation of the pre-existing work in the derivative work. . . .

"Congress would not have stated explicitly in § 304(c)(6)(A) that, at the end of the renewal term, the owner of the rights in the pre-existing work may not terminate use rights in existing derivative works unless Congress had assumed that the owner continued to hold the right to sue for infringement even after incorporation of the pre-existing work into the derivative work."[131]

Rohauer's policy-oriented approach is "problematic" because its rule "might make sense in some contexts" but "makes no sense in others."

"In the case of a condensed book, for example, the contribution by the derivative author may be little, while the contribution by the original author is great. Yet, under the *Rohauer* 'rule,' publication of the condensed book would not infringe the pre-existing work even though the derivative author has no license or valid grant of rights in the pre-existing work. See Brief for Committee for Literary Property Studies as *Amicus Curiae* 29-31; see also Brief for Songwriters Guild of America as *Amicus Curiae* 11-12 (policy reasons set forth in *Rohauer* make little sense when applied to musical compositions). Thus, even if the *Rohauer* 'rule' made sense in terms of policy in that case, it makes little sense when it is applied across the derivative works spectrum.

---

[130] 110 S. Ct. at 1760, 14 U.S.P.Q.2d at 1621.
[131] 110 S. Ct. at 1762–63, 14 U.S.P.Q.2d at 1623.

Indeed, in the view of the commentators, Rohauer did not announce a 'rule,' but rather an 'interest-balancing approach.' "[132]

Pointing to the renewal copyright owner's demand for 50% of the petitioner's gross proceeds in excess of advertising expenses, petitioner's argued that the Ninth Circuit's rule may undermine the Copyright Act's policy of encouraging dissemination of creative works. The argument is "better addressed by Congress than the courts."

"In any event, the complaint that the respondent's monetary request in this case is so high as to preclude agreement fails to acknowledge that an initially high asking price does not preclude bargaining. Presumably, respondent is asking for a share in the proceeds because he wants to profit from the distribution of the work, not because he seeks suppression of it.

"Moreover, although dissemination of creative works is a goal of the Copyright Act, the Copyright Act creates a balance between the artist's right to control the work during the term of the copyright protection and the public's need for access to creative works. The copyright term is limited so that the public will not be permanently deprived of the fruits of an artist's labors. . . . But nothing in the copyright statutes would prevent an author from hoarding all of his works during the term of the copyright. In fact, this Court has held that a copyright owner has the capacity arbitrarily to refuse to license one who seeks to exploit the work. See *Fox Film Corp. v. Doyal*, 286 U.S. 123, 127 (1932).

"The limited monopoly granted to the artist is intended to provide the necessary bargaining capital to garner a fair price for the value of the works passing into public use. . . ."[133]

The Court rejected the dissent's interpretation of Sections 3 and 7 of the 1909 Act as making derivative works independent of the original work.[134]

---

[132] 110 S. Ct. at 1763, 14 U.S.P.Q.2d at 1623–24.

[133] 110 S. Ct. at 1763, 14 U.S.P.Q.2d at 1624.

[134] Section 7 provides:

"Compilations or abridgments, adaptations, arrangements, dramatizations, translations, or other versions of works in the public domain or of copyrighted works when produced with the consent of the proprietor of the copyright in such works, or works republished with new matter, shall be regarded as new works subject to copyright under the provisions of this title; but the publication of any such new works shall not affect the force or validity of any subsisting copyright upon the matter employed or any part thereof, or be construed to imply an exclusive right to such use of the original works, or to secure or extend copyright in such original works." 17 U.S.C. § 7 (1976 ed.).

Section 3 provides:

"The copyright provided by this title shall protect all the copyrightable component parts of the work copyrighted, and all matter therein in which copyright is already subsisting, but without extending the duration or scope of such copyright." 17 U.S.C. § 3 (1976 ed.).

In dissent, Justice Stevens argued that Section 7 would be "surplusage" unless interpreted "to give the original author the power to sell the right to make a derivative work that upon creation and copyright would be completely independent of the original work."

"[U]nder the express language of § 3, one obtains a copyright on the entire work, but the parts previously copyrighted get copyright protection only according to the 'duration or scope' of the already existing copyright. Thus, if an author attempts to obtain copyright in a book derived from a short story, he can obtain copyright on the book for the full copyright term, but will receive protection of the story parts only for the duration and scope of the rights previously obtained. Correlatively, if an author attempts to copyright a novel, *e.g.*, about Cinderella, and the story elements are already in the public domain, the author holds a copyright in the novel, but may receive protection only for his original additions to the Cinderella story. . . .

"The plain language of the first clause of § 7 ensures that this scheme is carried out with respect to '[c]ompilations or abridgments, adaptations, arrangements, dramatizations, translations, or other versions of works in the public domain or of copyrighted works . . . or works republished with new matter,' *i.e.*, derivative works. The second clause of § 7 clarifies what might have been otherwise unclear—that the principle in § 3 of preservation of the duration or scope of the subsisting copyright applies to derivative works, and that neither the scope of the copyright in the matter employed nor the duration of the copyright in the original work is undermined by publication of the derivative work. . . .

"If one reads the plain language of § 7 and § 3 together, one must conclude that they were enacted in no small part to ensure that the copyright in the pre-existing work would not be abrogated by the derivative work. Section 7 requires consent by the author of the pre-existing work before the derivative work may be produced and both provisions explicitly require that the copyright in the 'subsisting work' will not be abrogated by incorporation of the work into another work." [135]

[ii]   *Expiration of Copyright on the Derivative Work.* A derivative work is created after the underlying work, but it is possible that the copyright on a derivative work will expire before that on the underlying work or that the derivative work will not be covered by copyright at all. Under the 1909 Act, this could occur because the copyright on the derivative work was not renewed or because the formalities and requirements of copyright, such as notice, were not complied with. Under the 1976 Act, the underlying work's author may live longer than the derivative work's author.

If the derivative work is not subject to copyright, then that work, including any "new matter" the derivative work's author contributed, falls into the public

---

"The Copyright Act of 1909 elsewhere accords protection to 'all the writings of an author,' § 4, including dramatic composition, § 5, and long before the Act of 1909, it was recognized that the additions and improvements to existing works of art were subject to copyright as original works of authorship. . . . Congress would hardly have needed to provide for the copyright of derivative works, including the detailed provisions on the limit of that copyright, if it intended only to accord protection to the improvements to an original work of authorship." 110 S. Ct. at 1772, 14 U.S.P.Q.2d at 1630–31.

[135] 110 S. Ct. at 1767, 14 U.S.P.Q.2d at 1626.

domain. However, because the derivative work also contains elements taken from the underlying work, the owner of the copyright on the underlying work may continue to exclude unauthorized use of the derivative work that falls within Section 106's exclusive rights.

The Ninth Circuit confirmed this principle in the *Russell* decision.[136] In 1913, George Bernard Shaw copyrighted his play "Pygmalion." The copyright was renewed in 1941. Shaw died in 1950. Originally scheduled to expire in 1969, Congress extended the copyright for 19 years to 1988. In 1938, under a license from Shaw, Gabriel Pascal produced a motion picture version of "Pygmalion." The motion picture constitutes a derivative work for copyright law purposes. The motion picture derivative work's copyright expired in 1966 when no renewal copyright was obtained.

In 1971, the owners of the Shaw play copyright granted an exclusive license to Janus Films to distribute the film. In 1972, Budget Films began renting copies of the film. The Shaw copyright owners sued for copyright infringement. The defendant Janus Films relied on a simple argument: "Because the film copyright on 'Pygmalion' has expired, that film is in the public domain, and, consequently, prints of that film may be used freely by anyone."

The Ninth Circuit reaffirmed "the well-established doctrine that a derivative copyright protects . . . only the new material contained in the derivative work, not the matter derived from the underlying work."

> "Thus, although the derivative work may enter the public domain, the matter contained therein which derives from a work still covered by statutory copyright is not dedicated to the public. . . . The established doctrine prevents unauthorized copying or other infringing . . . use of the underlying work or any part of that work contained in the derivative product so long as the underlying work itself remains copyrighted."[137]

[iii] *The "Derivative Work" Exception to Termination of Transfers under the 1976 Act.* The termination of transfer provisions in the 1976 Act contain an exception allowing continued utilization of a derivative work after termination of a grant, which provides:

> "A derivative work prepared under authority of the grant before its termination may continue to be utilized under the terms of the grant after its termination, but this privilege does not extend to the preparation after the termination of other derivative works based upon the copyright work by the terminated grant."

The House Report illustrates the distinction drawn in the exception: "[A] film made from a play could continue to be licensed for performance after the motion picture contract had been terminated but any remake rights covered by the contract would be cut off."

---

[136] Russell v. Price, 612 F.2d 1123, 205 U.S.P.Q. 20 (9th Cir. 1979), *cert. denied, sub nom.* Drebin v. Russell, 446 U.S. 952 (1980). *Accord* Filmvideo Releasing Corp. v. Hastings, 668 F.2d 91, 218 U.S.P.Q. 750 (2d Cir. 1981).

[137] 612 F.2d at 1128.

The derivative works exception causes interpretation problems. For example, the privilege of continued utilization applies only when the grantee prepares a "derivative work." Presumably, this includes only the alterations or modifications that involved original authorship and are separately copyrightable.[138]

Also, continued utilization is "under the terms of the grant." In *Mills Music,*[139] the Supreme Court considered the proper interpretation of this phrase as applied to multiple contractual arrangements in which an author grants rights to another who in turn makes a further grant of rights to third persons to create derivative works. *Mills* held that the derivative works exception's reference to utilization under the terms of the grant preserved the terms of the first grant as well as the second under which the derivative work is actually created.

Ted Snyder was one of three joint authors of the song "Who's Sorry Now" copyrighted in 1923. In 1932, Mills Music obtained ownership of the copyright. In 1940, Mills and Snyder entered into an agreement in which Snyder assigned his renewal rights in the copyright on the song in exchange for, inter alia, a royalty on sheet music and 50% of Mills' net royalties for recordings. In 1951, Mills obtained the renewal.

Mills issued, directly or through the Harry Fox Agency, over 400 licenses to record companies authorizing use of the song in specific phonograph records. The record companies, using "a variety of different artists and different musical arrangements," prepared recordings, that constitute copyrightable derivative works. Mills' licenses required the record companies to pay royalties to Mills. Fox acted as agent for Mills, collecting royalties, deducting its charges, and remitting the net receipts to Mills. Mills, pursuant to its contract with Snyder, remitted 50% of its income to Snyder. Snyder's widow and son succeed to his interest upon his death.

Section 304 of the 1976 Act altered the interests of Mills and the Snyders in three ways. First, it extended the term of the song's renewal copyright by 19 years so that the copyright expires in 1999 instead of 1980. Second, it gave Snyder's widow and son a right to terminate the grant to Mills of rights in the renewal copyright, the termination to be effective at any time during a 5-year period after January 1, 1978. Third, it provided that termination would cause all rights "covered by the terminated grant" to revert to the Snyders. However, the "all rights" reversion was subject to the derivative works exception.

On January 3, 1978, the Snyders promptly delivered a termination notice as to the song to Mills and notified Fox that all royalties on the derivative works should be remitted to them. Fox placed the royalties in escrow and began an interpleader action against Mills, the publishing company, and the Snyders, the statutory heirs. The district court ruled for the publisher Mills, reasoning that the derivative works

---

138 *See* Bourne Co. v. MPL Communications Inc., 675 F. Supp. 859, 864 n.8, 5 U.S.P.Q.2d 1951, 1955 n.8 (S.D. N.Y. 1987) (rejecting, in dictum, a party's argument that all sheet music arrangements of a song are derivative works, regardless of originality, because the statutory definition of a derivative work includes "arrangements;" "Neither the legislative history of the 1976 Act nor the policies underlying the copyright law support [such a] broad reading of the statute, especially since in the absence of such originality, the arrangements would not have been entitled to copyright protection in the first place.").

139 Mills Music, Inc. v. Snyder, 469 U.S. 153, 224 U.S.P.Q. 313 (1985).

exception does not distinguish between grantees who make or own derivative works and those who license others to do so. Accordingly, the various contracts in effect prior to termination governed the record companies' obligations after termination and those contracts provided for paying 50% of the royalties to the publisher and 50% to the heirs.

The Second Circuit reversed, ruling for the heirs, the Snyders, relying on on three propositions. First, the publisher relied on two separate grants, the 1940 grant from the author to the publisher, and the later grants by the publisher to record companies that authorized the preparation of the derivative works. The derivative works exception preserved only the second set of grants. Second, the termination provision was enacted for the benefit of authors. The derivative works exception was enacted to protect "utilizers." A publisher such as Mills is neither an author nor a "utilizer" and therefore not part of either benefited class. Third, the legislative history indicated that Congress did not contemplate the situation in which the authority to prepare derivative works came from two successive grants rather than a single grant directly from an author to a "utilizer." If it had done so, it would not have wanted "publishers and other noncreative middlemen to share in original derivative works royalties after termination."

In 5-4 decision, the Supreme Court reversed, ruling for the publisher Mills because it was "not persuaded that Congress intended to draw a distinction between authorizations to prepare derivative works that are based on a single direct grant and those that are based on successive grants. Rather, we believe the consequences of a termination that § 304 authorizes simply do not apply to derivative works that are protected by the Exception defined in § 304(c)(6)(A). The boundaries of that Exception are defined by reference to the scope of the privilege that had been authorized under the terminated grant and by reference to the time the derivative works were prepared. The derivative works involved in this case are unquestionably within those boundaries."[140]

The Court noted that the word "grant" is used three times in the exception. To give it a consistent meaning with the exception and throughout Section 304(c), "grant" must refer to an original grant by an author or his or her heirs. This is the grant the terms of which are preserved. The Court stressed that the termination provision caused ownership of the copyright to revert to the heirs but did not give them "any right to acquire any contractual rights that the Exception preserves."[141]

As to the Second Circuit's proposition that only "utilizers" are protected, the Court noted:

---

[140] 469 U.S. at 164, 224 U.S.P.Q. at 317.

[141] The Court stated:

"The Snyders' status as owner of the copyright gives them no right to collect royalties by virtue of the Exception from users of previously authorized derivative works. Stating the same point from the perspective of the licensees, it is clear that they have no direct contractual obligation to the new owner of the copyright. The licensees are merely contractually obligated to make payments of royalties under terms upon which they have agreed. The statutory transfer of ownership of the copyright cannot fairly be regarded as a statutory assignment of contractual rights." 469 U.S. at 167–68, 224 U.S.P.Q. at 319.

"The protection provided to those who utilize previously prepared derivative works is not . . . unlimited. The word 'utilized' as written in the Exception cannot be separated from its context and read in isolation. It is expressly confined by 'the terms of the grant.' The contractual obligation to pay royalties survives the termination and identifies the parties to whom the payment must be made. If the Exception is narrowly read to exclude Mills from its coverage, thus protecting only the class of "utilizers' as the Snyders wish, the crucial link between the record companies and the Snyders will be missing, and the record companies will have no contractual obligation to pay royalties to the Snyders. If the statute is read to preserve the total contractual relationship, which entitled Mills to make duly authorized derivative works, the record companies continue to be bound by the terms of their licenses, including any terms requiring them to continue to pay royalties to Mills."[142]

As to legislative history, the Court disagreed with the Second Circuit's proposition that Congress was not aware of multiparty licensing arrangements in the music publishing industry.[143] It disagreed that construing the exception to preserve multiple party contractual arrangements for the preparation of derivative works would be contrary to the purposes of the termination provision and its derivative works exception.[144] Justice White, joined by three other justices, dissented.

---

[142] 469 U.S. at 169, 224 U.S.P.Q. at 319.

[143] The Court noted:

"Rather than assuming that Congress was unaware of a common practice in one of the industries that the general revision of the copyright law, and the termination provisions, most significantly affected, we think it more probable that Congress saw no reason to draw a distinction between a direct grant by an author to a party that produces derivative works itself and a situation in which a middleman is given authority to make subsequent grants to such producers." 469 U.S. at 172, 224 U.S.P.Q. at 320–21.

[144] The Court noted:

"[T]he termination right was expressly intended to relieve authors of the consequences of ill-advised and unremunerative grants that had been made before the author had a fair opportunity to appreciate the true value of his work product.

"The Exception in § 304(c)(6)(A) was designed, however, to exclude a specific category of grants—even if they were manifestly unfair to the author—from that broad objective. . . . It is a matter of indifference—as far as the reason for giving protection to derivative works is concerned—whether the authority to prepare the work had been received in a direct license from an author, or in a series of licenses and sublicenses. The scope of the duly authorized grant and the time the derivative work was prepared are what the statute makes relevant because these are the factors that determine which of the statute's two countervailing purposes should control.

. . .

"The example most frequently discussed in the legislative history concerning the Exception involved the sale of a copyrighted story to a motion picture producer. The Court of Appeals explained the need for the Exception as the interest in protecting the large investment that is required to produce a motion picture, and recognized that record companies similarly must also make significant investment in compensating vocalists,

"[T]he underlying purpose of the Exception . . . is to protect the actual owners of derivative works, such as film producers, from having to renegotiate rights in underlying works, such as novels or plays on which the films were based. . . .

"To carry out this purpose of protecting derivative users, it is unnecessary to protect middlemen as well, and there is no indication that Congress intended to do so. The majority, however, unaccountably rejects the position that the Exception should be construed only so broadly as is necessary to effectuate this undisputed legislative intent. It also ignores the accepted principle of statutory construction that an ambiguous statute should be construed in light of the statutory purpose."[145]

---

musicians, arrangers, and recording engineers. . . . The court felt, however, that music publishers—as middlemen—were not similarity situated . . . As a matter of fact—or of judicial notice—we are in no position to evaluate the function that each music publisher actually performs in the marketing of each copyrighted song. . . . [W]e find no reason to differentiate between a book publisher's license to a motion-picture producer and a music publisher's license to a record company. Neither publisher is the author of the underlying work.

"Finally, respondents argue that the legislative history demonstrates that the Exception was designed to accomplish a well-identified purpose—to enable derivative works to continue to be accessible to the public after the exercise of an author's termination rights.

"The argument is unpersuasive. It explains why the Exception protects the utilizer of a derivative work from being required to pay an increased royalty to the author. It provides no support, however, for the proposition that Congress expected the author to be able to collect an increased royalty for the use of a derivative work." 469 U.S. at 172–77, 224 U.S.P.Q. at 321–23.

[145] 469 U.S. at 183–85, 224 U.S.P.Q. at 325–26.

CHAPTER 5

TRADEMARKS

---

§ 5A   Introduction

Trademark law establishes exclusive rights to use marks that distinguish one manufacturer, merchant or service provider's goods or services from those of others. A trademark is usually a word or group of words, but can consist of any device that serves to distinguish goods or services. Designs, color patterns, scents, packaging, even a good's nonfunctional design, are potential marks.

A merchant, manufacturer, or service provider acquires common law mark ownership by adopting and using the mark on goods and services. The mark must be distinctive of the goods or services. If a mark is the product's generic name, it cannot serve as a trademark. If it is descriptive (or deceptively misdescriptive) of a good's nature or geographic origin, it cannot serve as a trademark for the good unless it has acquired "secondary meaning," that is, through usage it becomes distinctive of origin. A mark must not be confusingly similar to marks or trade names others have previously adopted and not abandoned.

A common law mark owner may acquire important federal statutory benefits by registering the mark with the Patent and Trademark Office.

A trademark owner may prevent others from using the same or similar marks that create a likelihood of confusion, mistake or deception. Trademark law's essence is prevention of confusion as to the origin or sponsorship of goods or services. Trademark ownership confers no absolute monopoly on a word or symbol.

Trademarks have several commercial functions. First, they identify the goods or services to consumers. Second, they identify the source of the goods or services and may serve as a badge of their quality. A trademark does not guarantee that the product is of a certain or uniform quality level because the mark owner remains free to alter significantly the nature or quality of a product sold under the mark, and may transfer the rights to the mark to another as part of a sale of the business to which the mark pertains. Nevertheless, a trademark provides consumers a frame of reference regarding quality by informing them of a product manufacturer's identity. Finally, trademarks and service marks are advertising devices. Advertisers use trademarks prominently, attempting to develop consumer association with and good will toward the product being advertised.

Trademark law fosters these functions by balancing four interests. First is consumer interest in not being confused about the origin or sponsorship of goods or services. Confusingly similar marks may cause consumers to unwittingly purchase goods or services of different or inferior quality or reliability (or, at least, deprive them of free choice even when the goods or services are in fact of equal or superior quality). Second is trademark owner interest in preserving goodwill. The incentive to create goodwill by consistently providing uniform quality goods or services would be diminished if competitors could freely associate their goods or services with that goodwill through use of confusingly similar marks. Third is consumer and potential competitor interest in free competition and of actual or potential competitors in entering or expanding into markets for goods and services. Excessive trademark protection restricts market entry, limiting consumer choice and raising prices. Fourth is public interest in a fair and efficient legal system. Trademark law doctrines that are vague or subject to inconsistent application promote litigation, increase business costs, and tax judicial resources.

§ 5B   Historical Development

Competition is the foundation of the United States economic system. The competitive market structure's ideal is consumer benefit through lower prices and higher quality, more varied goods and services. In general, the more competitors in a given product or service market the better. The purpose of many legal doctrines and rules is to preserve and enhance competition, but the purpose of other doctrines and rules is to prevent unchecked competitive behavior from destroying the basic conditions necessary for competition itself or violating other public interests. Among these limiting doctrines and rules is the concept of unfair competition. "Unfair competition" is the umbrella term for the doctrines and rules that prohibit competition by deceptive, improper methods and provide remedies to one competitor who is or may be injured by another's activities.[1]

Because unfair competition law evolved primarily from court decisions rather than statutory enactments, it is referred to as "common law."[2] Unfair competition law developed when the Anglo-American legal system was divided into *law* courts, which held jury trials and awarded money damage judgments, and *equity* courts, which tried cases without juries and awarded specific, coercive relief, such as injunctions. Equity courts acted when a plaintiff's law court remedy was inadequate. Injured parties frequently brought unfair competition cases in equity because they could not show the precise extent of the money loss caused by the defendants' acts. The equity courts could directly halt the unfair practice. After the merger of law and equity in the United States,[3] equity's legacy remained in unfair competition law's substantive theories and defenses and its focus on fairness and a case-by-case, nondogmatic accommodation of trademark owner and competitor interests.[4]

Trademark law is one facet of unfair competition law. Courts recognized that a competitor who enters a market with a trademark confusingly similar to that of a market occupant competes unfairly.

In its early stages, trademark common law was narrowly focused. Only by adopting a distinctive mark, affixing it to goods, and selling the goods did a merchant or manufacturer secure trademark rights. Protection was geographically and competitively narrow. A trademark owner had no rights against another's later good faith use of the mark in separate geographic areas, and the later user could even acquire exclusive trademark rights in his own area. The owner had no rights against use of his mark on noncompeting goods or services. A first user could be denied relief in either case even though there was danger of confusion by consumers as to the origin of the second user's goods.

One reason for this narrow focus was trademark law's connection with the unfair competition law tort of palming off or passing off; that is, one person selling his goods as those of another. The tort of passing off rectified a specific wrong to and

---

[1] For a discussion of the ramifications of unfair competition law beyond the protection of marks, *see* § 6F.

[2] Today, statutes, such as Lanham Act Section 43(a), authorize judicial relief against unfair competition. *See* § 6E.

[3] Merger occurred in the federal court system with the adoption of the Federal Rules of Civil Procedure in 1938.

[4] *See, e.g.,* Soltex Polymer Corp. v. Fortex Industries, Inc., 832 F.2d 1325, 4 U.S.P.Q.2d 1785, 1788 (2d Cir. 1987), discussed at § 5F[3][d][iii] (a finding of a likelihood of confusion between two products bearing the same mark does not necessarily mandate an absolute injunction in favor of the trademark owner; "A basic principle of the law of equitable remedies . . . is that the relief granted should be no broader than necessary to cure the effects of the harm caused. . . . [W]e have rejected expressly an 'all-or-nothing' or *per se* rule mandating the use of an absolute injunction whenever likelihood of confusion is found. . . . This flexible approach also is in accord with the function of a court of equity.").

specific injury suffered by the plaintiff: a deceptive act causing a direct loss of sales to a competitor.

As the United States economy grew and goods were distributed nationwide, business people pressed for a federal trademark registration system to supplement local common law trademark protection. A federal system would enable competitors to use the same trademark throughout the country on an expanding range of goods without fear of conflicts with prior user rights and permit the United States to negotiate and implement treaties and conventions providing for trademark rights in the United States and abroad on an equal basis for U.S. citizens and foreign citizens and subjects.

The primary obstacle to enactment of a federal trademark system was the U.S. constitution: Article I's clause on the promotion of science and the useful arts allowed Congress to secure exclusive rights to inventors and authors in their respective discoveries and writings but did not encompass trademark owners. Article I did grant to Congress the power to regulate interstate and foreign commerce.

In 1870, Congress enacted a trademark registration statute, but in 1879 the Supreme Court declared the statute unconstitutional because a trademark was neither a copyrightable "writing" nor a patentable "discovery" in the constitutional sense.[5] The Court acknowledged that Congress could protect trademarks used in interstate and foreign commerce, but the 1870 law was not limited to interstate commerce. In all subsequent trademark legislation, Congress linked federal trademark registration to use of the mark in interstate commerce. In the mid-1900's, in civil rights and other cases not involving trademarks, the Supreme Court substantially expanded Congress's constitutional power to regulate interstate commerce.[6] As a result, the commerce limitation on Congress' power to provide trademark protection diminished.[7]

In 1881, Congress enacted legislation regulating trademarks in foreign commerce and with Indian tribes. Finally, in 1905, Congress passed a Trademark Act encompassing all interstate and foreign commerce. The 1905 Act was less than satisfactory as a source of federal trademark rights.[8] In 1947, Congress enacted the Lanham Act, which is still in force.[9] In 1988, Congress enacted a major Lanham Act revision, which, *inter alia*, allows persons to file trademark registration applications based on an "intent to use."[10]

§ 5C Protectability and Registrability

Trademark law distinguishes among (1) the right to *use* a mark, (2) the right to *exclude* others from using a mark, and (3) the right to *register* a mark.

---

[5] Trade-mark Cases 100 U.S. 82 (1879).

[6] *E.g.,* Heart of Atlanta Motel, Inc. v. United States, 379 U.S. 241 (1964).

[7] *In re* Silenus Wines, Inc., 557 F.2d 806, 194 U.S.P.Q. 261 (CCPA 1977).

[8] *See* J. T. McCarthy, Trademarks and Unfair Competition § 5.3 (2d ed. 1984).

[9] The Lanham Act is codified in Title 15 of the United States Code. In trademark cases, the Lanham Act is often cited by section number. The section does not correspond to the section number in Title 15. For example, Lanham Act Section 1 is 15 U.S.C. § 1051.

[10] *See* § 5D[2][b].

A merchant, manufacturer or service provider can use any word or mark on goods or services unless the use violates another's trademark rights or is otherwise contrary to law. One need not rely on trademark law to establish the *right to use* a word as a mark. Trademark law relates to the *right to exclude* others from using marks, that is, to establishing exclusive rights.

To acquire exclusive rights to use a mark, a merchant, manufacturer or service provider must meet protectability requirements.[1] Stated differently, in terms of property rights, a person acquires mark ownership by taking the steps trademark law prescribes—adoption and use of a distinctive mark. State common law is the initial source of mark protection.[2] Lanham Act Section 43(a) provides an additional and overlapping source of mark protection.[3] A person may have exclusive mark rights under both state and federal law without registering the mark.

---

[1] "Protectability" is an awkward word, but the courts use it to describe the conditions necessary to establish exclusive trademark rights. *See, e.g.,* Fuddruckers Inc. v. Doc's B.R. Others Inc., 826 F.2d 837, 842, 4 U.S.P.Q.2d 1026, 1030 (Fed. Cir. 1987). Awkward though it may be, it parallels other intellectual property law concepts, such as "patentability" and "copyrightability." *See* §§ 2C and 4C.

[2] With the advent of intent-to-use applications in 1988 (see § 5D[2][b]), a person may acquire inchoate federal law trademark property rights before acquiring state common law rights through actual use.

[3] Section 43(a) provides:

"(a) Any person who, on or in connection with any goods or services, or any container for goods, uses in commerce any word, term, name, symbol, or device, or any combination thereof, or any false designation of origin, false or misleading description of fact, or false or misleading representation of fact, which—

(1) is likely to cause confusion, or to cause mistake, or to deceive as to the affiliation, connection, or association of such person with another person, or as to the origin, sponsorship, or approval of his or her goods, services, or commercial activities by another person, or

(2) in commercial advertising or promotion, misrepresents the nature, characteristics, qualities, or geographic origin of his or her or another person's goods, services, or commercial activities,

shall be liable in a civil action by any person who believes that he or she is or is likely to be damaged by such act." 15 U.S.C. § 1125(a).

The 1988 Trademark Law Revision Act reworded Section 43(a) to the above form. Congress' intent was to codify existing law on Section 43(a) insofar as it provides remedies for infringement of unregistered trademarks and to extend Section 43(a) to disparagement. *See* § 6E[1]. The enormous body of pre-1988 Act Section 43(a) case law was grounded on the following language:

"(a) Any person who shall affix, apply, or annex, or use in connection with any goods or services, or any container or containers for goods, a false designation of origin, or any false description or representation, including words or other symbols tending falsely to describe or represent the same, and shall cause such goods or services to enter into commerce, and any person who shall with knowledge of the falsity of such designation of origin or description or representation cause or procure the same to be transported or used in commerce or deliver the same to any carrier to be transported or used, shall be liable to a civil action by any person doing business in the locality falsely indicated as that of origin or in the region in which said locality is situated, or by any person who believes that he is or is likely to be damaged by the use of any such false description or representation."

A merchant, manufacturer or service provider may obtain Lanham Act mark registration by complying with the Act's registrability requirements.[4] Registration is evidence (at least *prima facie* and under some conditions conclusive) of the registrant's exclusive right to use the mark.

Registrability requirements are substantially the same as protectability requirements. Lanham Act Section 2 on registrability incorporates established common law trademark protectability principles. Court decisions on registrability influence decisions on protectability and vice versa. This chapter treats registrability and protectability as a unitary concept.

There are four basic registrability requirements. First, a mark must fit in one of four categories of registrable marks: trademarks, service marks, collective marks and certification marks. Trade names and business names are not protectable under the Lanham Act though they are protectable under state unfair competition and business name laws.[5]

Second, a mark must be a "device" adopted and used to distinguish goods or services, which may include nonverbal as well as verbal symbols, packaging or the overall shape of a product, color, or even a smell. Policy considerations preclude registration or protection of some distinctive devices, such as those consisting of functional or immoral subject matter.

Third, a mark must be distinctive. Arbitrary and fanciful marks are distinctive *per se*. Descriptive or deceptively misdescriptive marks are presumptively nondistinctive, but the mark user may overcome the presumption by a showing that the mark has acquired secondary meaning, *i.e.*, has through use become distinctive of the goods or services. Suggestive marks are distinctive but enjoy only a narrow scope of protection. Generic terms are never protectable. Special conditions apply to personal name marks, words in foreign languages, and words that are, directly or after translation, descriptive or generic for the goods or services in other countries.

Fourth, a mark must not be confusingly similar to previously used or registered marks or trade names. Prior use ("senior right") disputes require consideration of both mark similarity and similarity between the goods or services upon which the marks are used and are resolved through application of the same likelihood of confusion standard that governs the question of mark infringement.[6] Generally, priority of use, under United States trademark law, rather than priority of filing or registration (as in many other countries) governs senior right.[7]

---

[4] States make comparable statutory provision for mark registration.

[5] *See, e.g.,* Galt House, Inc. v. Home Supply Co., 483 S.W.2d 107, 174 U.S.P.Q. 268 (Ky. Ct. App. 1972) (mere incorporation under a name without use thereof gives no right to enjoin subsequent use of that name for a hotel); Lawyers Title Ins. Co. v. Lawyers Title Ins. Corp., 109 F.2d 35, 43 U.S.P.Q. 166 (1939), *cert. denied,* 309 U.S. 684 (1940).

[6] *See* §5F[1].

[7] A junior user of a mark may acquire rights against a senior user of the mark through the incontestability provisions of the Lanham Act. *See* §§ 5E[1][c], 5E[2][e].

A 1988 Lanham Act amendment allows filing of intent-to-use application to establish constructive use priority. *See* § 5D[1][e].

[1] Mark Types

Traditional trademark law focused on marks for *goods*. The Lanham Act allows registration not only of goods trademarks but also *service* marks, *collective* marks and *certification* marks. It does not allow registration of trade or commercial names.

[a] **Trade Marks.** Lanham Act Section 2 states that "[n]o trademark by which the goods of the applicant may be distinguished from the goods of others shall be refused registration on the principal register on account of its nature, unless . . . " and recites exceptions to registration.[8] Section 45 defines "trademark" as including "any word, name, symbol, or device or any combination thereof" a manufacturer or merchant uses (or intends to use[9]) "to identify and distinguish his or her goods, including a unique product, from those manufactured or sold by others and to indicate the source of the goods, even if that source is unknown."[10]

"COKE" for soft drink beverages, "HUGGIES" for disposable diapers, "KO-DAK" for photographic film, and "EVER-READY" for batteries are examples of trademarks.

[b] **Service Marks.** Lanham Act Section 3 provides for registration of service marks "in the same manner and with the same effect as are trademarks."[11] Section 45 defines a "service mark" as "any word, name, symbol, or device or any combination thereof" that a person uses (or intends to use[12]) to "identify and distinguish the services of one person, including a unique service, from the services of others and to indicate the source of the services, even if that source is unknown."[13]

"MacDONALD's" for restaurant services and "HYATT" for hotel services are examples of service marks.

Courts define "service" expansively.[14] Typical services for which mark registrations may be obtained include transportation, communication, real estate marketing, restaurant, hotel, and entertainment services. Advertising and promotional services

---

[8] 15 U.S.C. § 1052.

[9] For a discussion of "intent to use" mark registration applications, see § 5D[2][b].

[10] 15 U.S.C. § 1127.

[11] 15 U.S.C. § 1053.

[12] For a discussion of "intent to use" mark registration applications, see § 5D[2][b].

[13] 15 U.S.C. § 1127.
The 1988 Trademark Amendments Act amended the "service mark" definition to reflect the new "intent to use" filing procedure. It did not change the meaning of "service." H.R. Rep. No. 100–1028, 100th Cong., 2d Sess. 15 (1988); S. Rep. No. 100–515, 100th Cong., 2d Sess. 44 (1988).

[14] American Int'l Reinsurance Co. v. Airco., 570 F.2d 941, 943, 197 U.S.P.Q. 69 (CCPA 1978), *cert. denied,* 439 U.S. 866, 200 U.S.P.Q. 64 (1978) ("While the [Lanham] Act defines the term 'service mark,' . . . . it does not define the broad term 'services.' Similarly, the legislative history of the Act addresses the term 'service mark' but sheds little light on what was intended to be meant by 'services.' . . . . It would appear self-evident that no attempt was made to define 'services' simply because of the plethora of services that the human mind is capable of conceiving. This, ipso facto, would suggest that the term be liberally construed.").

are included if the mark is used to identify those services and not merely the subject of the advertising.[15]

A service mark owner must use the mark to offer or render services to others because the Lanham Act's basic purpose is to protect the buying "public." Court decisions do not clearly define when a service rendered under a mark to a closed group becomes sufficiently "intermural" as to qualify for service mark protection.[16]

The services must be more than merely "ancillary" to the sale of goods or the rendering of another service.[17] The ancillary limitation prevents a manufacturer or

---

[15] See In re Advertising & Marketing Development Inc., 821 F.2d 614, 2 U.S.P.Q.2d 2010 (Fed. Cir. 1987) (the applicant, a provider of sales promotion services, created the mark "NOW GENERATION" as a campaign to advertise financial services; the applicant licensed the campaign to banks; the specimens submitted in support of the registration application showed that the applicant used the mark to advertise its promotional services; it was conceded that there would "not be any difficulty in distinguishing between the applicant's use of the mark for advertising services to banks and the banks' use of the same mark for financial services to individuals").

In A&M, the mark was put to two uses—to advertise A&M's promotional services and to advertise the banks' services. The latter was done under license by A&M. The registration sought by A&M was evidently only for the latter. Arguably, A&M could also have registered the latter as a service mark, claiming the benefit of the banks' use of the mark under the related company provisions of the Lanham Act. See § 5G[3].

[16] See In re Canadian Pacific Ltd., 754 F.2d 992, 996, 224 U.S.P.Q. 971, 974 (Fed. Cir. 1985) (a stock reinvestment plan offered solely to the corporation's own shareholders is not a service; "The Lanham Act does not afford this kind of intramural or internal protection."). See also USPTO, Trademark Manual of Examining Procedure § 1301.01.

Canadian Pacific distinguished Airco, which held that a mark used for a service of administering annuity plans for the corporation's employees, ex-employees, and their survivors was a "service" offered to "others." American Int'l Reinsurance Co. v. Airco, 570 F.2d 941, 944, 197 U.S.P.Q. 69 (CCPA 1978), cert. denied, 439 U.S. 866 (1978). Airco held it unimportant that the services were not the applicant's principal trade or business ("the Act makes no distinction between services on this basis"); that the services were merely "fringe benefits," an accessory to its own business ("the services in the present case . . . are totally separate from the sale of applicant's products"); and that the service recipients—employees—inevitably knew the benefits' source ("the fact that an employee may know that the services are provided by his employer does not preclude the mark from functioning to indicate origin. Moreover, the services are also performed for beneficiaries . . . whose knowledge of applicant, absent the mark in question, would be far from certain.").

The distinction between Canadian Pacific and Airco is refined, to say the least.

[17] See In re Dr Pepper Co., 836 F.2d 508, 5 U.S.P.Q.2d 1207 (Fed. Cir. 1987) (denying registration of "PEPPER MAN" for contest to promote the applicant's soft drink).

"[T]he rendering of a service which is normally 'expected or routine' in connection with the sale of one's own goods is not a registrable service whether denominated by the same or a different name from the trademark for its product. This interpretation is a refinement of the basic principle that the service for which registration is sought must be rendered to others. Merely advertising one's own goods, while, in a sense, an 'informational' service to others, was early held not to be a 'service' within the purview of sections 3 and 45. In re Tampax Inc., 91 U.S.P.Q. 215 (Dec. Comm'r Pat. 1951)." 836 F.2d at 509–10, 5 U.S.P.Q.2d at 1208.

merchant from "proliferat[ing] registrations by obtaining a trademark registration along with a whole raft of service mark registrations covering each and every 'service' which every other competitor also provides as an adjunct to the sale of goods."[18] There is a danger that a competitor may deliberately seek to block others from adopting desirable marks, but given the difficulty of determining whether a service is merely ancillary,[19] the game may not be worth the candle. Registration expenses may sufficiently deter unreasonable mark proliferation.

Whether a symbol is a mark used for services and eligible for Lanham Act registration or merely a nonregistrable business name is often a close call.[20]

[c] **Collective and Certification Marks—Appellations of Origin.** Lanham Act Section 4 provides for registration of "collective and certification marks, including indications of regional origin" "in the same manner and with the same effect as are trademarks."[21] Permitted registrants include "persons, and nations, states, municipalities, and the like exercising legitimate control over the use of the marks sought to be registered, even though not possessing an industrial or commercial establishment."[22] An entity otherwise entitled to protection will be denied same if the mark is used "so as to represent falsely that the owner or a user thereof makes or sells the goods or performs the services on or in connection with which such mark is used."[23]

[i] *Collective Marks.* Section 45 defines a "collective mark" as a "trademark or service mark" that members of a cooperative, an association or other collective group or organization use (or intend to use[24]) and "includes marks used to indicate

---

The court rejected the argument that the ancillary services exclusion would "preclude registration of marks for a vast array of activities currently recognized as services under the Act, such as those provided by retail department stores, mail order companies, and gasoline stations."

"[T]he key element . . . is that the activities being questioned here relate to promotion of [applicant's] *own goods.* Department stores and gasoline stations are service businesses and provide precisely the types of services intended to be brought under the Act. Indeed, advertising agency services as well as the service of conducting contests *for others* are within the Act."

Similarly, the argument that a department store would lose its right to service mark registration if it sold private label merchandise was "a straw man:" "There is no question but that one may acquire rights in a mark or marks both for goods and for services." 836 F.2d at 511, 5 U.S.P.Q.2d at 1209–10.

[18] J. T. McCarthy, Trademarks and Unfair Competition § 19.30 (2d ed. 1984).

[19] *Compare In re* Orion Research, Inc., 523 F.2d 1398, 187 U.S.P.Q. 485 (CCPA 1975) ("NO LEMON" for applicant's guarantee and repair services for its instruments cannot be registered; the circumstances' totality, including that Orion did not independently bill, promote or offer the "NO LEMON" guarantee, indicated that services were those typically provided in the sale of these goods) *with In re* Heavenly Creations, Inc., 168 U.S.P.Q. 317 (TTAB 1971) (instruction on hair piece styling is a separate service because it is not limited to hair pieces sold by the instructors).

[20] *See* § 5C[1][d].

[21] 15 U.S.C. § 1054.

[22] *Id.*

[23] *Id.*

[24] For a discussion of "intent to use" mark registration applications, see § 5D[2][b].

membership" in an organization.[25] The definition encompasses two types of marks: collective *membership* marks and collective *trademarks* or *service marks.* Collective membership marks are owned by a person or organization[26] and serve to indicate membership in that organization.[27] Collective trademarks and service marks are owned by an organization and serve to indicate that an organization member made or sold the goods or services.[28]

In *F.R. Lepage Bakery,*[29] the court held that transfer of ownership of a collective mark from a cooperative organization, which properly obtained original registration of the mark, to a company that uses the mark on goods, would require cancellation of the collective mark's registration. *"[U]sers of a collective mark* must be members of an 'organization,' rather than a maker or seller. . . . An individual person or corporation which is making and/or selling goods on which a trademark is being used is not, in that capacity, the owner of a *collective* mark and cannot register it as a collective mark."[30]

A collective mark owning organization may license nonmembers to use the mark "under its aegis and subject to proper control."[31] Courts struggle with the issue of

---

[25] 15 U.S.C. § 1127. The common law of trademarks did not recognize collective marks as such because the putative mark owner did not affix the mark to his own goods. *See* Huber Baking Co. v. Stroehmann Bros. Co., 252 F.2d 945, 116 U.S.P.Q. 348 (2d Cir. 1958), *cert. denied,* 358 U.S. 829 (1958).

[26] Apparently, the person or organization that owns the mark need not be a collective organization so long as the mark functions to indicate organization membership. *See In re* Stencel Aero Engineering Corp., 170 U.S.P.Q. 292 (PO TTAB 1971) (applicant, an aircraft escape equipment manufacturer, formed "The Grasshopper Club" composed of persons who had successfully used applicant's equipment; GRASSHOPPER CLUB is registrable as a collective membership mark).

[27] *See* Aloe Creme Laboratories, Inc. v. American Soc'y for Aesthetic Plastic Surgery, Inc., 192 U.S.P.Q. 170 (PTO TTAB 1976) ("Neither the collective nor its members uses the collective membership mark to identify and distinguish goods or services; rather, the sole function of such a mark is to indicate that the person displaying the mark is a member of the organized collective group. For example, if the collective group is a fraternal organization, members may display the mark by wearing pins or rings upon which the mark appears, by carrying membership cards bearing the mark, etc. . . . Of course, a collective group may itself be engaged in the marketing of its own goods or services under a particular mark, in which case the mark is not a collective mark but is rather a trademark for the collective's goods or a service mark for the collective's services.").

The marks in question must in fact be used to indicate membership rather than some other status, such as possession of a degree or satisfaction of a training course sponsored by the owner of the mark. *See In re* National Soc'y of Cardiopulmonary Technologists, Inc., 173 U.S.P.Q. 511 (PO TTAB 1972).

[28] *See* Aloe Creme Laboratories, Inc. v. American Soc'y for Aesthetic Plastic Surgery, Inc., 192 U.S.P.Q. 170 (PTO TTAB 1976) ("The 'collective' itself neither sells goods nor performs services under a collective trademark or collective service mark, but the collective may advertise or otherwise promote the goods or services sold or rendered by its members under the mark.").

[29] F.R. Lepage Bakery v. Rousch Bakery Products, 851 F.2d 351, 7 U.S.P.Q.2d 1395 (Fed. Cir. 1988), *modified,* 9 U.S.P.Q.2d 1335 (Fed. Cir. 1988)

[30] 851 F.2d at 353, 7 U.S.P.Q.2d at 1396.

[31] Professional Golfers Ass'n v. Bankers Life & Casualty, 514 F.2d 665, 668, 186 U.S.P.Q. 447 (5th Cir. 1975).

whether an organization may prevent unauthorized use of its mark or emblem on merchandise such as jewelry and clothing; courts have denied relief when there is no proof that members or others are confused as to the goods' origin and connection with the organization.[32]

[ii]   *Certification Marks.* Section 45 defines a "certification mark" as "any word, name, symbol, or device, or any combination thereof" that one or more persons other than the mark's owner uses (or intends to use[33]) "to certify regional or other origin, material, mode of manufacture, quality, accuracy or other characteristics of such person's goods or services or that the work or labor on the goods or services was performed by members of a union or other organization."[34]

(1)   *Certification Function.* As the definition indicates, certification marks certify or guarantee product or service characteristics.[35] From this purpose, certain principles of certification mark ownership follow. First, the mark owner may not offer products or services under the mark[36] because such activity would compromise the

---

[32] Supreme Assembly, Order of Rainbow for Girls v. J.H. Ray Jewelry Co., 676 F.2d 1079, 217 U.S.P.Q. 757 (5th Cir. 1982); International Order of Job's Daughter v. Lindeburg & Co., 633 F.2d 912, 208 U.S.P.Q. 718 (9th Cir. 1980), *cert. denied,* 452 U.S. 941 (1981). Compare University of Pittsburgh v. Champion Products, Inc., 686 F.2d 1040, 215 U.S.P.Q. 921 (3d Cir. 1982), *cert. denied,* 459 U.S. 1087 (1982); Boston Professional Hockey Assoc., Inc. v. Dallas Cap & Emblem Mfg., Inc., 510 F.2d 1004, 185 U.S.P.Q. 364 (5th Cir. 1975), *cert. denied,* 423 U.S. 868, 187 U.S.P.Q. 480 (1975). See § 5F[1][d][iii].

[33] For a discussion of "intent to use" mark registration applications, see § 5D[2][b].

[34] 15 U.S.C. § 1127. As to whether the common law protects marks certifying products' regional origin or other characteristics, see Black Hills Jewelry Mfg. Co. v. Gold Rush, Inc., 633 F.2d 746, 208 U.S.P.Q. 631 (8th Cir. 1980); Florida v. Real Juices, Inc., 330 F. Supp. 428, 171 U.S.P.Q. 66 (M.D. Fla. 1972).

[35] Certification marks's purpose is reinforced by Lanham Act Section 14's registration cancellation grounds, 15 U.S.C. § 1064(e): the "registrant (A) does not control, or is not able legitimately to exercise control over, the use of such mark, or (B) engages in the production or marketing of any goods or services to which the certification mark is applied, or (C) permits the use of the certification mark for purposes other than to certify, or (D) discriminately refuses to certify or to continue to certify the goods or services of any person who maintains the standards or conditions which such mark certifies. . . ."

See Midwest Plastic Fabricators, Inc. v. Underwriters Laboratories Inc., 906 F.2d 1568, 1571 (Fed. Cir. 1990) ("A certification mark registration may be cancelled if the mark is not used exclusively as a certification mark. 15 U.S.C. § 1064(e)(3). For example, if a certification mark's owner also allowed the mark to be used as a trademark, there would be a basis for cancellation of the registration. . . . ").

[36] *In re* Florida Citrus Comm'n, 160 U.S.P.Q. 495 (PTO TTAB 1968).

Florida Citrus Comm'n notes that the principle that a certification mark owner may not sell goods or services under the mark is imperfectly stated in the Lanham Act. Section 4, which applies to both collective and certification marks, states that protection shall be denied when the mark is "used so as to represent falsely that the owner or a user thereof makes or sells the goods or performs the services on or in connection with which such mark is used." 15 U.S.C. § 1054. Section 14(e)(2), which enumerates several grounds for cancellation of the registration of a certification mark upon petition by a person who is "damaged" by such registration, states that registration shall be cancelled if at any time the registrant "engages in the production or marketing or any goods or services to which the certification mark is applied."

owner's objectivity. Typically, owners of certification marks are government entities, suppliers of materials used to manufacture products, etc. Second, the owner may not discriminately refuse to allow use of the mark by a person whose products or services meet the certification standards.[37] Third, the owner must control the goods' or services' origin, nature or quality.[38]

In *Midwest Plastic Fabricators*,[39] the Federal Circuit held that the Trademark Trial and Appeal Board did not commit clear error in finding that registrant did not use its certification marks for purposes other than certification and did not fail to control its marks' use. Registrant Underwriters Laboratories (UL) promulgates product safety standards and certifies compliance with those standards. UL's registrations state that the marks are used by persons authorized by UL to certify that representative samplings of the goods conform to the safety standards or requirements established by UL. A manufacturer that wishes to use the UL marks must submit samples to UL for testing and evaluation. If the samples comply with UL standards, they are

---

The latter is an absolute bar; the former is a conditional one. In *Florida Citrus Comm'n*, the Board refused to allow the Commission to register a composite mark ("O.J. 'THE REAL THING' 'FROM FLORIDA' ") as a certification mark for orange juice because the Commission had already registered the same mark for its own services in promoting Florida orange juice. It adopted the absolute bar approach based on its perception of the purpose of a certification mark and the need to protect consumers: "It is not unreasonable to assume that purchasers familiar with the use of mark in connection with goods or services to certify quality, accuracy or other characteristics of such goods or services will, upon encountering the identical mark on or in association with other goods or services, mistakenly attribute to it the same certification function as that to which they have been previously exposed."

In a later decision, the Board admitted that "[t]here is . . . nothing in the definition of a certification mark and in particular, the proscription applied thereto, that serves to preclude a person from selling goods and services and also engaging in a certification program providing that the two activities are separate and distinct from one another and are identified by 'separate and distinct marks.' " *In re* Monsanto Co., 201 U.S.P.Q. 864 (PTO TTAB 1978) (registration of "WEAR-DATED" for apparel made from applicant's fibers and meeting certain quality standards denied in view of prior registrations of mark as a trademark). The Board cited as an example "the use of 'GOOD HOUSEKEEPING' and 'PARENTS MAGAZINE' as trademarks for publications and these same marks in different settings and with other wording denoting certification such as 'Approved by,' 'Tested by,' etc. for the goods or services of others that meet their prescribed standards."

[37] 15 U.S.C. § 1064(e)(4).

[38] Midwest Plastic Fabricators, Inc. v. Underwriters Laboratories Inc., 906 F.2d 1568, 1572, 15 U.S.P.Q. 2d 1359, (Fed. Cir. 1990) ("The purpose of requiring a certification mark registrant to control use of its mark is the same as for a trademark registrant: to protect the public from being misled. . . . In the case of a certification mark registrant, the risk of misleading the public may be even greater because a certification mark registration sets forth specific representations about the manufacture and characteristics of the goods to which the mark is applied. As the purpose of the control requirement is to protect the public, the requirement places an affirmative obligation on the certification mark owner to monitor the activities of those who use the mark.").

[39] Midwest Plastic Fabricators, Inc. v. Underwriters Laboratories Inc., 906 F.2d 1568, 15 U.S.P.Q. 2d 1359 (Fed. Cir. 1990).

eligible for UL listing with UL. Usually the manufacturer enters into a listing and follow-up service agreement with UL."[40]

UL "exercises authority over use of the UL certification marks as described above by employing some 500 inspectors who work out of over 200 inspection centers throughout the United States. In 1987, [UL's] inspectors conducted approximately 438,000 inspections in approximately 38,900 factories and over 9 billion UL labels were issued covering approximately 12,500 different products."[41]

Midwest manufactures polyvinyl chloride (PVC) fittings and elbows for use with PVC conduit which encases electrical wiring. The company entered into a listing and follow-up service agreement with UL. Midwest petitioned to cancel UL's certification marks on two grounds. First, it alleged that UL permits use of the marks for purposes other than certification, in violation of 15 U.S.C. § 1064(e)(3) (1982). Noting UL's president testified that application of UL's mark represents not UL's, but merely the manufacturer's declaration that the products meet UL standards, it argued that the failure of UL itself to certify that the products carrying the marks meet UL standards demonstrates that UL permits use of the marks for purposes other than certification. Second, it alleged UL fails to control the use of its marks. "Specifically, [it] alleged: (1) certain PVC elbows carrying the UL marks failed impact tests performed by its expert . . . and (2) certain conduit pipe manufactured by a competitor of Midwest, National Pipe Company (National), carried counterfeit UL marks."[42]

The court held that UL did not permit noncertification use simply because other persons applied the mark: "There is an important difference . . . between the mark's use and the user."

"That others test products and apply UL's certification marks simply is not probative that the marks are used for other than certification.

---

[40] The listing agreement "provides, inter alia, that the manufacturer order UL marks through [UL] from an authorized printer; that no UL mark shall be used on products not in compliance with [UL's] requirements; that the manufacturer agrees that it will ensure that the products bearing the UL mark are in compliance with [UL's] requirements; that a testing and inspection program will be maintained by the manufacturer to assure continued compliance . . . ; that access to [UL's] inspectors shall be allowed together with providing adequate facilities for the conducting of product testing and that any tests which indicate noncompliance with [UL's] requirements shall result in the manufacturer's being required to either correct the problem or remove the UL mark from the noncomplying products." 906 F.2d at 1569–70, 15 U.S.P.Q. 2d at 1360.
The follow-up service agreement "provides for a periodic inspection program whereby [UL's] inspectors will visit factories and plants in which listed products are produced. If an inspector finds a variation from [UL's] requirements, a variation notice is issued . . . [and] a manufacturer cannot ship products which are encompassed by the variation notice until the problem is resolved. The record shows that inspectors have discretion to allow products to be shipped with minor variations that do not affect the safety of the product. Inspectors are also authorized to remove the UL mark in appropriate situations." 906 F.2d at 1570, 15 U.S.P.Q. 2d at 1360.
[41] 906 F.2d at 1570, U.S.P.Q. 2d at 1360.
[42] 906 F.2d at 1570, 15 U.S.P.Q. 2d at 1361.

"The statute . . . does not require that . . . the registrant . . . itself must test the products. . . . It merely authorizes cancellation of a registration if the registrant allows use of the mark for purposes other than certification."

. . . .

". . . [B]oth registrations at issue here include a provision that the certification marks may be used by 'persons authorized by [UL]' to indicate that 'representative samplings' of the products conform to safety standards established by UL. . . . The registrations clearly state what the marks do and do not represent to the public. The registrations . . . do not require UL to represent that UL itself tests the items." [43]

It held that the statute requires the mark owner to control its mark's use but the statute "does not define 'control' or otherwise indicate the degree of control that it requires." A reasonableness rule governs control.

". . . [T]he statutory requirement cannot mean absolute control, because it would be impracticable, if not impossible, to satisfy. . . . The 'control' requirement of the statute means the mark owner must take reasonable steps, under all the circumstances of the case, to prevent the public from being misled." [44]

In rejecting the cancellation petition, the Trademark Trial and Appeal board properly found sufficient control. ". . . UL has 'a vast network of inspectors making hundreds of thousands of inspections of thousands of different products across the country' and . . . UL conducts comprehensive follow-up programs to ensure compliance with UL standards." [45] Petitioner relied on two types of evidence on control. First, it relied on the results of impact tests performed on certain conduit and elbows carrying the UL mark. The Board found the tests were not "shown to be reliable and [are] entitled to very little, if any, probative value." Second, it pointed to proven use of counterfeit UL marks on its competitor's products. "The Board concluded that this limited counterfeiting problem was not sufficient to cancel UL's registrations and that UL exercised control over subsequent use of its marks by this company. . . . " [46]

(2) *Geographic Origin.* Certification mark may indicate a product's geographic origin.[47] Geographic terms are normally not protectable as trademarks, but an exception is made for "indications of regional origin" registrable as certification marks.[48] A geographic term that becomes generic for a product cannot be protected, and its registration may be cancelled at any time.[49] Words such as "Champagne" for

---

[43] 906 F.2d at 1571, 15 U.S.P.Q. 2d at 1362.

[44] 906 F.2d at 1572, 15 U.S.P.Q. 2d at 1362.

[45] 906 F.2d at 1573, 15 U.S.P.Q. 2d at 1363.

[46] 906 F.2d at 1573, 15 U.S.P.Q. 2d at 1363.

[47] See § 5C[3][d].

[48] 15 U.S.C. § 1052(e)(2). See Community of Roquefort v. William Faehndrich, Inc., 303 F.2d 494 (2d Cir. 1962) ("ROQUEFORT" as a certification mark for sheep's milk blue-mold cheese made in the French community of Roquefort; the defendant infringed the mark by selling a similar type of cheese made in Hungary under the name "Roquefort").

[49] See Community of Roquefort v. William Faehndrich, Inc., 303 F.2d 494 (2d Cir. 1962) ("ROQUEFORT" not generic for sheep's milk blue-mold cheese).

sparkling white wine and "Swiss" for cheese are viewed as generic in the United States,[50] though not in other countries.

(3) *Distinguishing Licensed Marks, Certification Marks, and Collective Marks.* It is sometimes difficult to determine the status of a mark used by one or more persons under authòrity of another person who is not using the mark. The mark could, potentially, be (1) a collective trademark or service mark, that is, a mark owned by an association but used by its members on their goods or services, (2) a certification mark, or (3) a trademark or service marks used by licensees under the control of the licensor/owner of the mark in accordance with the "related company" provisions of the Lanham Act.[51] The difference between a certification mark and a licensed trademark or service mark lies in the mark owner's power to control use under quality standards.

> "The key in distinguishing between use of a trademark through related companies and use thereof as a certification mark is essentially the purpose and function that the mark performs in the marketplace, namely, whether it serves to indicate origin of goods or services or to convey a guarantee of quality. . . . [T]here is a basic difference in the concept of a mark which is used through related companies and a certification mark. This involves the right of a licensor to choose the licensees that use its mark as against the obligation of the owner of a certification mark to certify the goods or services of *any* person who meets and maintains the standards and conditions which such mark certifies."[52]

The difference between a certification mark and a collective trademark or service mark is "one of form."[53]

[d] **Trade and Business Names.** In common law trademark parlance, "trade name" meant a mark for goods that was inherently insufficiently distinctive to warrant

---

[50] *But cf.* G.H. Mumm & Cie (Société Vinicole de Champagne Successeurs of New York, Inc.) v. Desnoes & Geddes, Ltd., 917 F.2d 1292, 1293 n.1, 16 U.S.P.Q.2d 1635, 1636 n.1 (Fed. Cir. 1990) ("The term 'sparkling wine' includes champagne, but the term 'champagne,' although sometimes applied to sparkling wines in general, is more properly reserved for those sparkling wines produced in the Champagne region of France by the Champagne method. *See* H. Johnson, *The World Atlas of Wine* 106–09 (1977).").

[51] *See* § 5G[3].

[52] *In re* Monsanto, 201 U.S.P.Q. 864 (PTO TTAB 1978). *See also* National Trailways Bus System v. Trailway Van Lines, Inc., 155 U.S.P.Q. 507 (E.D.N.Y. 1965). In *National Trailways*, the court held that the plaintiff was guilty of fraud in registering "Trailways" as a service mark instead of as a collective mark. The plaintiff was merely an association of bus companies. The mark was used by the members, and the association did not control the nature and quality of the services offered under the mark.

[53] *See* J. T. McCarthy, Trademarks and Unfair Competition § 19:34 (2d ed. 1984) ("The only possible distinction is one of form. That is, as to a collective trade or service mark, the sellers are members of an organization with standards of admission, while as to a certification mark, sellers are not members of an organization, but their products are certified according to set standards."); Breitenfeld, *Collective Marks—Should They Be Abolished?*, 47 Trademark Rep. 1 (1957).

protection as a technical trademark but had become sufficiently distinctive through use to qualify for unfair competition protection.[54]

The Lanham Act changed this parlance. It included within the definition of potentially registrable marks designations that previously constituted "trade names" and excluded from registration "trade names" in the narrower sense of designations that identified a business and did not function as marks distinguishing specific goods or services. Originally, Lanham Act Section 45 defined a "trade name" as including "individual names and surnames, firm names and trade names used by manufacturers, industrialists, merchants, agriculturalists, and others to identify their businesses, vocations or occupations; the names or titles lawfully adopted and used by persons, firms, associations, corporations, companies, unions, and any manufacturing, industrial, commercial, agricultural, or other organizations engaged in trade or commerce and capable of suing and being sued in a court of law."[55] In 1988, Congress eliminated the redundant and excess verbiage, providing "The terms 'trade name' and 'commercial name' mean any name used by a person to identify his or her business or vocation."[56]

A trade or business name cannot be registered under the Lanham Act as such. The Lanham Act's purpose of providing uniform national protection to marks on goods or services offered in interstate and foreign commerce does not extend to trade names, which tend to have only local significance. Consequently, the protection of trade and business names is left primarily to state unfair competition law.

A trade or business name can be registered as a trademark if the name also functions as a trademark or service mark, *i.e.*, serves to identify and distinguish the goods or services of the business from those of others.[57]

A trade name can be the basis for refusing registration to a trademark or service mark. Refusal will occur if the mark so resembles a trade name previously used in the United States by another so as to cause confusion.[58]

---

[54] *See* Restatement of Torts §§ 715, 716 (1938).

[55] 15 U.S.C. § 1127 (amended by Pub. L.. 100-677, § 134(2)).

[56] 15 U.S.C. § 1127 (as amended by Pub. L.. 100-677, § 134(2)).

[57] *See In re* Unclaimed Salvage & Freight Co., 192 U.S.P.Q. 165 (TTAB 1976) (phrase "UNCLAIMED SALVAGE & FREIGHT CO." cannot be registered as a service mark because it functions as a business name rather than as a mark for goods or services: "[A] corporation or business trade designation may function as a trademark or service mark, or as a trade name, or as both, depending upon the manner in which the name or designation is used in any particular case. The distinction between trade name use and either trademark or service use is often a difficult one to make and often is nebulous in character. Obviously, the determination must be made on the basis of the use of the term on the specimens offered in support of trademark or service mark use and the commercial impact of such use upon purchasers and prospective customers as they encounter the goods and services bearing the designation in the appropriate marketplace environment.").

[58] 15 U.S.C. § 1052(d). *See* Sterling Drug, Inc. v. Sebring, 515 F.2d 1128, 185 U.S.P.Q. 649 (CCPA 1975) (registration of "ankh" symbol as trademark for hair products denied on basis of prior use of the symbol as a trade name by another).

See § 5C[4][c].

[2] Subject Matter

The Lanham Act indicates that a trademark, service, collective mark, or certification mark may consist of "any word, name, symbol, or device or any combination thereof."[59] This definition is broad because of the concepts "symbol" and "device." Any symbol or combination of symbols constitutes a trademark if it is actually used as a trademark—that is, to identify and distinguish goods.

Marks potentially eligible for registration and protection as trademarks or service marks may be verbal marks such as slogans, non-verbal marks such as numbers, colors, or smells, and in some instances, the product's packaging or design.

Two approaches to subject matter eligible for trademark protection are evident in the case law. One approach is to develop specific rules as to what does and does not constitute a proper mark. For example, a rule might be "A single color cannot function as a trademark." The other is to eschew rules and determine on the facts of each case whether the device or symbol serves as a trademark or service mark. Recent decisions tend to reject the rule-based approach in favor of the fact-based approach.[60] This may lead to fairer results in particular cases, but fairer results are achieved at the expense of greater uncertainty, making trademark right dispute resolution more difficult.

Lanham Act Section 2 excludes certain marks based on their content for policy reasons. Other Section 2 exclusions relate to the basic issues of distinctiveness (2(e) and (f)) and senior right (2(d)), which are discussed in later sections.[61]

---

[59] 15 U.S.C. § 1127.

[60] *Compare In re* Burgess Battery Co., 112 F.2d 820, 46 U.S.P.Q. 39 (CCPA 1940) (mere "dress," which gives a "distinctive external appearance to appellant's goods" does not distinctly point out the appellant's goods) *with In re* Swift & Co., 223 F.2d 950, 106 U.S.P.Q. 286 (CCPA 1955) ("if a distinctive trade-mark device or symbol is adopted and used primarily for the purpose of identifying and distinguishing a product, and it is capable of so doing, the mere fact that it renders the label to which it is applied more ornamental than it would otherwise be without that device thereon does not per se dictate a conclusion that it has no trade-mark function"). *See* P. Goldstein, Copyright, Patent, Trademark and Related State Doctrines 346 (2d ed. 1981) ("The evolution from *Burgess* to *Swift* reflects the modern trend in determining whether subject matter is registrable. *Burgess*, decided before passage of the Lanham Act, treated registration as question of law—whether certain forms or types of subject matter, such as trade dress, are registrable. *Swift*, decided fifteen years later, treated the question as one of fact—whether, regardless of its type or form, the subject matter is capable of indicating source.").

See also In re Owens-Corning Fiberglas Corp., 774 F.2d 1116, 1119-20, 227 U.S.P.Q. 417, 418 (Fed. Cir. 1985) ("Under the Lanham Act trademark registration became available to many types of previously excluded indicia. Change was gradual and evolutionary, as the Patent and Trademark Office and the courts were presented with new concepts. Registration has been granted, for example, for containers; product configurations; and packaging; for tabs having a particular location on a garment; slogans; sounds; ornamental labels; and goods which take the form of the mark itself.").

[61] *See* §§ 5C[3] and [4].

[a] **Words and Slogans.** Clearly, single words can and often do function as trademarks as can nicknames and other verbal symbols.[62] A slogan or word series may also be registered and protected if it functions to identify and distinguish the trademark owner's goods or services from those of others.[63] Even if not so registered, words and slogans may be protected by unfair competition principles.[64]

A slogan's length is relevant to its ability to act as a trademark. An increase in the total number of words in a phrase that is said to constitute an allegedly protectable or registrable mark has a tendency to transform the syntactical structure of the phrase into a form that makes it more difficult to understand when read casually and without careful study, thereby diminishing the uniqueness and distinctiveness of the phrase, which are essential to its function as a mark. Text of increasing length will have a proportionately higher likelihood of characterization as advertising copy, which may be protected only under the copyright laws.[65]

Slogans must meet the distinctiveness standard.[66] A slogan that is fanciful, arbitrary, or merely suggestive of the goods or services is protectable.[67] A slogan

---

[62] *E.g.*, Volkswagenwerk Aktiengesellschaft v. Church, 411 F.2d 350, 161 U.S.P.Q. 769 (9th Cir. 1969) ("VW").

[63] *E.g.*, *In re* E. Kahn's Sons Co. 343 F.2d 475 (CCPA 1965) ("THE WEINER THE WORLD AWAITED" constitutes a valid trademark); American Enka Corp. v. Marzall, 92 U.S.P.Q. 111 (D. D.C. 1952) ("THE FATE OF A FABRIC HANGS BY A THREAD").

Common slang expressions, though registrable, are given a narrow scope of protection. J.T. McCarthy, Trademarks and Unfair Competition § 7:5 (2d ed. 1984). *See* B & L Sales Associates v. H. Daroff & Sons, Inc., 421 F.2d 352, 165 U.S.P.Q. 353 (2nd Cir. 1970), *cert. denied*, 398 U.S. 952, 165 U.S.P.Q. 747 (1970) ("COME ON STRONG" for apparel is a common slang expression entitled to a narrow scope of protection; nevertheless, the registered mark is valid and infringed by the use of the same mark on similar products).

[64] *E.g.*, Chemical Corp. of America v. Anheuser-Busch, Inc., 306 F.2d 433, 134 U.S.P.Q. 524 (5th Cir. 1962) (defendant's use of "WHERE THERE'S LIFE . . . THERE'S BUGS" for an insecticide floor wax improperly impairs the property rights of plaintiff, a brewer, in "WHERE THERE'S LIFE . . . THERE'S BUD" because such use creates a likelihood of consumer confusion, and any association with bugs is anathema for potable items such as beer).

[65] *E.g.*, *In re* Sanda Hosiery Mills 154 U.S.P.Q. 631 (PO TTAB 1967) ("THE BABY BOOTIE SOCK THAT WILL NOT KICK OFF" held not to function as a mark because it is advertising copy rather than an identifying and distinguishing mark).

See also Smith v. M & B Sales & Manufacturing, 13 U.S.P.Q.2d 2002, 2010 (N.D. Cal. 1990) ("NEXT TIME YOU'RE CAUGHT IN A DOORWAY WITH YOUR ARMS FULL, THINK WIREHANDLER" not shown to function as a trademark):

"Although unregistered slogans can acquire trademark status, to do so they must be used in a manner calculated to project a single source of origin. . . .

". . . Because the slogan is twelve words long it is more likely to be advertising copy. . . . The slogan . . . is not emphasized or highlighted. It is not in larger or differently colored type-face. It simply does not stand out amongst all of the clutter. Rather, it is buried at the bottom of the page and in small print. For all of these reasons, it is very unlikely to function as a trademark." 13 U.S.P.Q.2d at 2010.

[66] *See* § 5C[3].

[67] *E.g.*, *In re* Kahn's Sons Co. 343 F.2d 475 (CCPA 1965) ("THE WEINER THE WORLD AWAITED" is arbitrary); *In re* Wilderness Group, Inc. 189 U.S.P.Q. 44 (TTAB 1975) ("LET YOUR HIPS SHOULDER THE LOAD" is merely suggestive rather than descriptive of hiking equipment).

that is descriptive of the goods or services will be registrable only on a showing of secondary meaning.[68] A generic phrase is not protectable.[69]

Slogans may contain words or phrases that are themselves registered or otherwise protectable trademarks. A slogan's registrability and protectability is determined independently of the protectability of the words within it.[70]

A slogan may be registered on the supplemental register if it is sufficiently distinctive to be capable of functioning to identify the registrant's goods or services.[71]

[b] Nonverbal Marks

[i] *Alphanumeric Symbols—Grade and Style Designations.* A trademark may consist of a number or alphanumeric symbol if the number or symbol is distinctive rather than descriptive.[72]

Manufacturers and merchants use words and alphanumeric symbols to designate a product's grade, style, or size. Whether grade, style or size designation constitutes a trademark depends on the circumstances surrounding its use. There are at least three possibilities.

First, if the symbol is used solely to designate a characteristic, it is not a protectable mark because it is used in a descriptive manner,[73] that is, the symbol distinguishes the characteristic rather than its origin, even though the symbol's meaning or substance is not inherently descriptive of the characteristic.[74]

---

[68] Roux Laboratories, Inc. v. Clairol, 427 F.2d 823, 166 U.S.P.Q. 34 (CCPA 1970) ("HAIR COLOR SO NATURAL ONLY HER HAIRDRESSER KNOWS FOR SURE" is descriptive of hair tinting preparations but is registrable because it has acquired secondary meaning). *See* § 5C[3][a][vii].

[69] *In re* Sun Oil Co., 426 F.2d 401, 165 U.S.P.Q. 718 (CCPA 1970) (Rich, concurring; "CUSTOM-BLENDED" generic for gasoline blended at the pump); *In re* McDonald's, 199 U.S.P.Q. 490 (PTO TTAB 1978) ("TWOALLBEEFPATTIESSPECIALSAUCELETTUCE-CHEESEPICKLESONIONSONASESAMESEEDBUN" not generic for restaurant services).

[70] *See* Carter-Wallace, Inc. v. Procter & Gamble Co. 434 F.2d 794, 167 U.S.P.Q. 713 (9th Cir. 1970) (slogan "USE 'ARRID' TO BE SURE" descriptive and possessed no secondary meaning prior to defendant's use of "Be Sure with SURE").

[71] *E.g., In re* Milk Foundation 170 U.S.P.Q. 50 (PO TTAB 1971) ("EVERY BODY NEEDS MILK" registerable on the supplemental register). *See* § 5D[2][e].

[72] *E.g.,* Standard Brands, Inc. v. Smilder, 151 F.2d 34, 66 U.S.P.Q. 337 (2d Cir. 1945) ("V-8" is arbitrary for vegetable juice—even though it is made from eight vegetables); *In re* Union Oil Co., 88 F.2d 492 (CCPA 1937) ("76" is descriptive or misdescriptive because it would be viewed as indicative of the chemical properties of the gasoline product); Southland Corp. v. Schubert, 297 F.Supp. 477, 160 U.S.P.Q. 375 (C.D.Cal 1968) ("7-ELEVEN" for convenience stores descriptive but protectable because of secondary meaning).

See generally Brezina, *Numerals as Trademarks,* 74 Trade-Mark Rep. 324 (1984).

[73] *E.g.,* Textron Inc. v. Omark Industries, Inc., 208 U.S.P.Q. 524 (PTO TTAB 1980) (numbers descriptive of pitch, gauge, and number of links of different size saw chains).

[74] *Cf.* Ideal Industries, Inc. v. Gardner Bender, Inc., 612 F.2d 1018, 1019-20, 204 U.S.P.Q. 177, 179-80 (7th Cir. 1979), *cert. denied,* 447 U.S. 924, 206 U.S.P.Q. 864 (1980) ("The 71B series are not 'arbitrary' marks in the trademark sense. Although the numbers were chosen arbitrarily in the sense that they do not refer directly to a characteristic of the connectors, the progression of numbers was adopted, and is currently used, to describe the relative sizes of

Second, if the symbol is inherently distinctive, *i.e.*, not descriptive of the characteristic in question, or, through use has acquired secondary meaning, and is used for dual purposes, that is, to designate the product's origin as well as its grade or style, it is a protectable mark.[75]

Finally, if a dual-purpose symbol, originally distinctive, becomes through use the generic name of the characteristic, it loses eligibility for trademark protection, as with any other generic term.[76]

If a symbol is a protectable mark owned by one competitor, other competitors may make "fair use" of the symbol—for example, to make product comparisons.[77]

[*ii*] *Color.* A trademark may consist of a color pattern if the pattern is distinctive rather than functional or merely ornamental.[78] A color may be a component of a

---

the connectors. Hence, they are merely descriptive, not arbitrary, terms . . . "); Digital Equipment Corp. v. C. Itoh and Co., Ltd., 229 U.S.P.Q. 598, 603 (D.N.J. 1985) (defendant adopted the designation "CIT-220+" for its computer terminal that emulated the plaintiff's "VT220"; "There are several marks similar to plaintiff's 'VT220' mark being used in the relevant market. The designation 'VT' stands for 'video terminal' and the numerals represent a model number; therefore, the mark is merely descriptive. Plaintiffs have failed to demonstrate either secondary meaning or likelihood of confusion with respect to this mark.").

[75] *E.g.*, Dayton Progress Corp. v. Lane Punch Corp., 917 F.2d 836, 16 U.S.P.Q.2d 1700 (4th Cir. 1990) (product designators for precision punchs using three letters, the first indicting the punch's grade or class, the second its function, and the third its tip's shape (*e.g.*, "VJB" or "MHX") are descriptive but acquired secondary meaning; plaintiff's competitors other than defendant used different designators); In re Clairol, 457 F.2d 509, 173 U.S.P.Q. 355 (CCPA 1972) ("SWEDISH CRYSTAL" for hair dying preparation is both a color designation and a trademark); Kiekhaefer Corp. v. Willys-Overland Motors, 236 F.2d 423, 111 U.S.P.Q. 105 (CCPA 1956) ("HURRICANE" for outboard motors is both a style designation and a trademark); In re Barry Wright Corp., 155 U.S.P.Q. 671 (PO TTAB 1967) ("8-480" is not descriptive of a computer with 48 storage registers and 480 or more memory steps even though it had been used in the past for a computer with 8 storage registers and 48 memory steps). *Compare* Bristol-Myers Co., 107 F. Supp. 800, 94 U.S.P.Q. 327 (S.D. N.Y. 1952) ("pH 3.5" is descriptive of the drug product's acidity).

[76] *E.g.*, K-S-H Plastics, Inc. v. Carolite, Inc., 408 F.2d 54, 59, 161 U.S.P.Q. 75, 78 (9th Cir. 1969), *cert. denied*, 396 U.S. 825, 163 U.S.P.Q. 704 (1969) (K-S-H's designations K-4, K-5, K-11, etc. for plastic lighting panels were not infringed by Carolite's use of C-4, C-5, C-11 etc. because the numbers had become "a short-hand industry expression for a given panel configuration.").

[77] *See* Ideal Industries, Inc. v. Gardner Bender, Inc., 612 F.2d 1018, 1027, 204 U.S.P.Q. 177 (7th Cir. 1979), *cert. denied*, 447 U.S. 924 (1980) (electrical connector number designations, which were initially descriptive of a series progression, became protectable marks based on evidence of secondary meaning; as to remedy, the defendant "should be allowed fairly to use the numbers on [its] labels, adjacent to the word 'size,' to inform buyers of the size of the connectors"). *See* § 5F2[d].

[78] *Compare* American Chicle Co. v. Topps Chewing Gum, Inc., 208 F.2d 560, 562 (2d Cir. 1953) (finding infringement of a distinctive design on a candy package that incorporated a specific color in a parallelogram-shaped element of the design to indicate the flavor of the candy within the package; Judge Learned Hand: "the defendant has not suggested even the most diaphanous reason for selecting for its peppermint box out of all possible permutations or color and design, just the plaintiff's— or at least almost the plaintiff's—combination, except for the

design trademark.[79] Use of a color so as to cause confusion as to goods' or services' source may be unfair competition,[80] but the traditional rule is that "A color, *per se*, is not capable of appropriation as a trademark."[81]

In *Owens-Corning Fiberglas,*[82] the Federal Circuit rejected the traditional *per se* rule, holding that a company could register the color pink as uniformly applied to fibrous glass residential insulation based on evidence that use of the color was not functional or necessary to compete in the industry and had acquired distinctiveness as an indicator of the insulation's source. The Lanham Act abolished *per se* exclusionary rules. The "color depletion" theory, which holds that "there are a limited number of colors in the palette, and that it is not wise policy to foster further limitation by permitting trademark registrants to deplete the reservoir . . . is not faulted for appropriate application, but following passage of the Lanham Act courts have declined to perpetuate its *per se* prohibition which is in conflict with the liberating purposes of the Act."

---

substitution of 'Topps' for 'Chiclets'.") *with* Campbell Soup Co. v. Armour & Co., 175 F.2d 795, 798-99, 81 U.S.P.Q. 430 (3d Cir. 1949), *cert. denied,* 338 U.S. 847 (1949) (denying trademark protection for the use of labels for food products that are half white and half red; "[c]olor is a perfectly satisfactory element of a trade-mark if it is used in combination with a design in the form, for example, of a picture or a geometrical figure. . . . The mere division of a label into two background colors, as in this case, is not, however, distinct or arbitrary. . . ."); Plastilite Corp. v. Kassnar Imports, 508 F.2d 824, 184 U.S.P.Q. 348 (CCPA 1975) (denying registration to combination of yellow and orange colors for fishing floats for lack of distinctiveness); *In re* Shaw, 184 U.S.P.Q. 253 (PO TTAB 1974) (denying registration for green suede book covers for lack of distinctiveness).

A pattern of contrasting colors, the actual colors being unspecified, may constitute a trademark. *E.g., In re* Data Packaging Corp., 453 F.2d 1300, 172 U.S.P.Q. 396 (CCPA 1972) (band on a computer tape reel of a color contrasting with that of the reel).

[79] *E.g., In re* Hehr Mfg. Co., 279 F.2d 526, 126 U.S.P.Q. 381 (CCPA 1960) (square red label for use on automobile trailer windows).

[80] *E.g.,* Yellow Cab Transit Co. v. Louisville Taxicab & Transfer Co., 147 F.2d 407, 64 U.S.P.Q. 348 (6th Cir. 1945) (yellow for taxicab services); Clifton Mfg. Co. v. Crawford- Austin Mfg. Co., 12 S.W.2d 1098 (Tex. Civ. App. 1929).

The courts will not prohibit a defendant from using a color that is functional—even in instances where the defendant committed acts of unfair competition by passing off its product as those of the plaintiff. William R. Warner & Co. v. Eli Lilly & Co., 265 U.S. 526 (1924) (brown color for chocolate-flavored quinine preparation).

[81] J. T. McCarthy, Trademarks and Unfair Competition § 7:16 (2d ed. 1984).

In an early decision, the Supreme Court noted: "Whether mere color can constitute a valid trade-mark may admit of doubt. Doubtless it may, if it be impressed in a particular design, as a circle, square, triangle, a cross or a star. But the authorities do not go farther than this." A. Leschen & Sons Rope Co. v. Broderick & Bascom Rope Co., 201 U.S. 166, 171 (1906).

Courts applied this dictum to deny the registrability of a color under the 1905 federal trademark statute. *In re* Security Engineering Co., Inc., 113 F.2d 494, 46 U.S.P.Q. 219 (CCPA 1940) (blue and aluminum color for oil well reamers); *In re* General Petroleum Corp. of California, 49 F.2d 966, 9 U.S.P.Q. 511 (CCPA 1931) (color violet for gasoline).

[82] *In re* Owens-Corning Fiberglas Corp., 774 F.2d 1116, 1120, 227 U.S.P.Q. 417, 419 (Fed. Cir. 1985).

Whether other courts will follow the Federal Circuit's approach in rejecting the *per se* rule on colors remains to be seen.[83] In *Nutrasweet*,[84] the Seventh Circuit disagreed with *Owens-Corning* and applied the old rule that color alone cannot function as a trademark. In 1982, plaintiff began selling its "Nutrasweet" sugar substitute "Equal" in individual *blue* packets, blue serving to distinguish competitors' *white* sugar packets. In 1958, defendant began selling a sugar substitute "Sweet 'N Low" in *pink* packets. In 1988, defendant introduced a new sugar substitute "Sweet One," which it placed in a packet that was blue but not the same shade of blue as plaintiff's "Equal" packets. In rejecting plaintiff's Lanham Act trade dress infringement claim, the court followed its 1950 *Life Savers* decision that "Color is not subject to trade-mark monopoly except in connection with some definite arbitrary symbol or design."[85] It gave four reasons for not following *Owens-Corning's* liberalizing color rule: (1) "Consistency and predictability of the law are compelling reasons for not lightly setting aside a settled principle of law"; (2) "[T]here is no need to change the law" because color is adequately protected when "used in connection with some symbol or design"; (3) "infringement actions could soon degenerate into questions of shade confusion"; and (4) protecting color "might create a barrier to otherwise lawful competition."[86]

Functionality and lack of distinctiveness are major obstacles to obtaining trademark rights in colors or color patterns, just as they are to obtaining rights in designs or three-dimensional configurations.[87] A color is functional if there is a competitive need to use the color.[88] An example of a functional color is one that is natural to or descriptive of the product.[89] In *Owens-Corning Fiberglas*, the color was not

---

[83] *See* First Brands Corp. v. Fred Meyer Inc., 809 F.2d 1378, 1382-83, 1 U.S.P.Q.2d 1779, 1781-82 (9th Cir. 1987) (denying a preliminary injunction against defendant's use of the color yellow on containers for private label anti-freeze that resembled in size, shape and color the plaintiff's containers; to grant relief to plaintiff based on its trade dress theory would in effect give it "a trademark on the color yellow as a background color for an ordinary-shaped container"; "*Owens-Corning* continues to apply the color depletion theory unless there is no competitive need for the color in a particular industry. The Federal Circuit merely declined to establish a *per se* prohibition against registering colors as trademarks. . . . Other than in extraordinary situations, such as that presented in *Owens-Corning*, the general rule remains that an element of distinctiveness of shape in combination with the color still exists before a trademark will be granted.").

[84] Nutra Sweet Co. v. The Stadt Corp., 917 F.2d 1024, 16 U.S.P.Q.2d 1959 (7th Cir. 1990).

[85] Life Savers v. Curtiss Candy Co., 182 F.2d 4, 9 (7th Cir. 1950).

[86] 917 F.2d at 1027-28, 16 U.S.P.Q.2d at 1962.

The court rejected plaintiff's urging that it "adopt a fact-driven standard which would require the trial court to scrutinize the tabletop sweetner market to determine the number of competitors and the likelihood of future competitors in that market to determine whether there is a competitive need for the color blue to remain available" because "[s]uch a standard would prove unworkable, for there is no way for a court to predict the likelihood of future competitors in a particular market." 917 F.2d at 1028, 16 U.S.P.Q.2d at 1962.

[87] *See* § 5C[2][c].

[88] Whether "functional" encompasses "aesthetic functionality" is discussed at § 5C[2][c][v](5).

[89] *E.g.*, Life Savers Corp. v. Curtiss Candy Co., 182 F.2d 4, 7 (7th Cir. 1950) (the trademark of the Life Savers Five Flavor wrapper (the background of the wrapper consisted of nine stripes of red, yellow, green, orange and purple) is not infringed by a Curtiss Candy wrapper (the

functional because the applicant was the only manufacturer who colored its insulation, there were few insulation producers, and there was no utilitarian reason to color the product, which was naturally light-yellow in color.

A color is usually perceived as mere ornamentation, rather than distinctive. In *Owens-Corning Fiberglas*, the court agreed that "[b]y their nature color marks carry a difficult burden in demonstrating distinctiveness and trademark character."[90] The applicant showed distinctiveness through evidence of an extensive advertising campaign stressing pink as a source indicator and consumer survey evidence showing 50% recognition of applicant as pink insulation's source.

The color designs of pharmaceutical products such as drug capsules present special problems.[91]

[iii] *Smells.* In *In re Clarke*,[92] the Trademark Trial and Appeal Board held that a smell could function as a trademark and be registered if distinctive. The applicant sought to register a smell, described as a "high impact, fresh, floral fragrance reminiscent of Plumeria blossoms" as a trademark for "sewing thread and embroidery yarn." She submitted a declaration indicating that, to her knowledge, she was the only one to offer scented embroidery yarn or thread and that she advertised the fact that she was the source of scented-yarn. She "made of record a complete sealed kit containing scented yarn and thread for making a scented skunk."[93]

The Examining Attorney rejected the application for two reasons: (1) lack of distinctiveness because a product's smell, like other ornamentation, is not the type of subject matter consumers perceive as origin indicators, and (2) de jure functionality because "there is a competitive need for free access to pleasant scents."[94] Later, the examiner withdrew the latter rejection. The Board reversed the former rejection because the evidence showed applicant's fragrance functioned as a trademark. It cautioned that "we are not here talking about the registrability of scents or fragrances of products which are noted for those features, such as perfumes, colognes or scented household products."[95]

[iv] *Designs.* A trademark may consist of a design that is distinctive rather than functional, descriptive, or merely ornamental.

The major obstacle to obtaining trademark rights in a design is lack of distinctiveness because of ornamentality. A distinctive design may be a trademark even though it is ornamental.[96] An attractive design is apt to be perceived by consumers as just

---

background of the wrapper included eleven red, orange, yellow and green stripes); "the color of the background is in fact descriptive and serves as a ready identification of the flavor of the candy in the package").

[90] 774 F.2d at 1127, 227 U.S.P.Q. at 424-25.

[91] *See* § 5C[2][c][5](7).

[92] *In re* Clarke, 17 U.S.P.Q.2d 1238 (PTO TTAB 1990).

[93] 17 U.S.P.Q.2d at 1239.

[94] *Id.* For a discussion of functionality, see § 5C[2][c][v].

[95] 17 U.S.P.Q.2d at 1239 n.4.

[96] *E.g., In re* Swift & Co., 223 F.2d 950, 954, 106 U.S.P.Q. 286 (CCPA 1955) ("if a distinctive trade-mark device or symbol is adopted and used primarily for the purpose of identifying and

that—attractive ornamentation—rather than as a product source indicator. The courts distinguish between designs that are inherently distinctive[97] and those that are not.[98] The former are analogous to arbitrary or fanciful word marks; the mark user need not show secondary meaning in order to establish a right to registration and protection.[99] The latter are analogous to descriptive word marks; the user must show secondary meaning.

A mark may consist of a design that is background to a word mark only if the background design creates a commercial impression separate from that of the word mark.[100]

A picture or drawing of a product will not usually constitute a trademark because consumers perceive it either as ornamental or descriptive of the product, rather than as distinctive of its origin. In *D.C. Comics*,[101] the CCPA refused to accept the

---

distinguishing a product, and it is capable of so doing, the mere fact that it renders the label to which it is applied more ornamental than it would otherwise be without that device thereon does not per se dictate a conclusion that it has no trade-mark function").

The doctrine of "aesthetic functionality" is discussed at § 5C[2][c][v](5).

[97] *E.g., In re* Penthouse International Limited, 565 F.2d 679, 195 U.S.P.Q. 698 (CCPA 1977) (stylized key logo for jewelry); *In re* Esso Standard Oil Co., 305 F.2d 495 (CCPA 1962) (red, white and blue "Esso" label with distinctive proportions and arrangement of elements for motor cleaner).

[98] *E.g., In re* Soccer Sport Supply Co., 507 F.2d 1400, 1402, 184 U.S.P.Q. 345 (CCPA 1975) (a design covering the surface of soccer balls is not inherently distinctive; "a design which is a mere refinement of a commonly-adopted and well-known form of ornamentation for a class of goods would presumably be viewed by the public as a dress or ornamentation for the goods. Especially would this be so when such design is applied repetitively to the entire surface of the goods."); *In re* David Crystal, Inc., 296 F.2d 771, 773, 132 U.S.P.Q. 1 (CCPA 1961) (colored bands on the calf portion of sock are not inherently distinctive; "[u]nless the design is of such nature that its distinctiveness is obvious, convincing evidence must be forthcoming to prove that in fact the purchasing public does recognize the design as a trademark which identifies the source of the goods.").

Simple geometric shapes, such as circles, stars, and squares, fall in this category of presumptive nondistinctiveness. *See* J. T. McCarthy, Trademarks and Unfair Competition § 7:12 (2d ed. 1984). *See also* Guess ? Inc. v. Nationwide Time Inc., 16 U.S.P.Q.2d 1804 (PTO TTAB 1990) (triangle design is not inherently distinctive).

[99] For a discussion of secondary meaning, *see* § 5C[3][a][vii].

[100] *E.g., In re* Schenectady Varnish Co., 280 F.2d 169, 126 U.S.P.Q. 395 (CCPA 1960) (design consisting of a cloud and a lightning flash creates a separate commercial impression apart from the word mark "Schenectady" that is superimposed on the central horizontal section of the flash). *Compare In re* Chemical Dynamics, Inc., 839 F.2d 1569, 1571, 5 U.S.P.Q.2d 1828 (Fed. Cir. 1988) (after registering both the word mark "7 Drops" and an overall design consisting of a watering can, medicine dropper and droplet falling from the dropper into the can, the applicant sought to register the dropper and droplet; HELD: the three background elements are "interrelated elements of a single unified design . . . [and create] a single commercial impression").

Whether a background design or a portion of a background design creates a separate impression involves "a very subjective judgment." J. T. McCarthy, Trademarks and Unfair Competition § 7:9 (2d ed. 1984).

[101] *In re* D.C. Comics, Inc., 689 F.2d 1042, 215 U.S.P.Q. 394, 397 (CCPA 1982).

See also Planters Nut & Chocolate Co. v. Crown Nut Co., 305 F.2d 916, 134 U.S.P.Q. 504 (CCPA 1962) (Planter's peanut man is more than a picture of the product (peanuts)).

broad proposition that "a picture of a product necessarily cannot function as a trademark for that product" and reversed the rejection of the appellant's application to register drawings of comic characters such as Superman as trademarks for toy dolls of those same characters.

Related to designs are marks consisting of a label's location. In 1960, the CCPA rejected any *per se* rule that a label location could not constitute a trademark.[102]

In 1936, Levi Strauss began using a pocket tab trademark on jeans. In 1938, it registered as a mark "a small marker or tab of textile material or the like, colored red" for overalls. Two Ninth Circuit decisions deal with the status of the Levi Strauss tab mark. In one suit ("*Blue Bell I* "), it upheld the district court finding that a tab on the right rear pocket of *pants* had acquired a strong secondary meaning in the pants market.[103] In a subsequent suit ("*Blue Bell II* "), decided *en banc*, it upheld the district court finding that the ubiquitous tab did not have comparable secondary meaning for *shirts* or garments generally.[104] It noted that "Secondary meaning in the pant tab does not necessarily inhere in the shirt tab since the pant tab was registered as a location specific mark. . . . We deal with different products (jeans v. shirts) and different markets; and the assumptions, perceptions and recognitions with which customers approach a purchase are different." It also affirmed the district court finding that Blue Bell's use of a tab on shirts did not create a likelihood of confusion with Levi Strauss' pants tab mark under the "related goods" doctrine.[105]

[c] **Packaging and Product Configurations—Functionality—Trade Dress.** A trademark may consist of a three dimensional design, such as the shape and ornamentation of product packaging, or even of the product itself, if the design is distinctive rather than functional.[106] State unfair competition law and Lanham Act Section 43(a) also provide protection against the creation of confusion by the simulation of a product or service's "trade dress."

---

[102] *In re Kotzin*, 276 F.2d 411, 125 U.S.P.Q. 347 (CCPA 1960) ("while granting that a 'location' per se cannot be a trademark, we do not see why a particular 'tag' . . . particularly located on particular goods, cannot indicate origin"). *Kotzin* affirmed the refusal to register the alleged tag mark because of the insufficiency of the evidence to show distinctiveness. Later decisions have allowed registration or granted protection to tag and location marks. *In re* G. Le Blanc Corp., 429 F.2d 989, 166 U.S.P.Q. 561 (CCPA 1970).

[103] *See* Levi Strauss & Co. v. Blue Bell, Inc., 200 U.S.P.Q. 434 (C.D.Cal 1978), *aff'd*, 632 F.2d 817, 208 U.S.P.Q. 713 (9th Cir. 1980) (tab located on the rear pocket of Levi Strauss pants functioned independently as a trademark despite the fact that the tab had the verbal mark "LEVI" emblazoned thereon); *In re* Levi Strauss & Co., 165 U.S.P.Q. 348 (PO TTAB 1970) (tab on hip pocket of jeans).

[104] Levi-Strauss & Co. v. Blue Bell, Inc., 778 F.2d 1352, 228 U.S.P.Q. 346 (9th Cir. 1985) (*en banc*).

[105] 778 F.2d at 1357, 228 U.S.P.Q. at 347-48.

See § 5E[3].

[106] The distinction between a product and its package is blurred in the case of products such as liquids and vapors that cannot be marketed without a container or a dispenser. *See, e.g., In re* Morton-Norwich Products, Inc., 671 F.2d 1332, 213 U.S.P.Q. 9 (CCPA 1982).

Functionality and lack of distinctiveness are the major obstacles to obtaining trademark rights in shapes and configurations. In covering nonfunctional, distinctive product configurations, trademark and unfair competition law overlaps copyright and design patent law.[107]

[i] *Product Simulation Under Common Law Unfair Competition Prior to 1964.* The common law of trademarks did not include packaging and product designs within the class of marks ownership of which could be acquired by mere adoption and use. Unfair competition law did afford protection against the copying of product designs that were nonfunctional and had through use acquired a "secondary meaning," that is, had become distinctive of the product's origin in consumers' minds. If a plaintiff established nonfunctionality and secondary meaning, he could obtain an injunction against a competitor using a product shape so similar to his own as to cause a likelihood of confusion.

In *Crescent Tool*,[108] a leading 1917 decision, plaintiff sold an adjustable wrench with a distinctive web and rib construction on the handle and a hole in the web end, which was then (and still is) commonly referred to as a "crescent wrench." Defendant sold a "substantially direct facsimile" of plaintiff's wrench with its own name on the wrench instead of "Crescent." The district court granted a temporary injunction against defendant's sales. The Second Circuit reversed because plaintiff failed to prove that the product's configuration had acquired secondary meaning—that is, that plaintiff's wrench "had come to indicate to the public any one maker as it source, or that the wrench had been sold in any part because of its source, as distinct from its utility or neat appearance." In his opinion, Judge Hand imposed a strict secondary meaning requirement:

> "It will not be enough only to show how pleasing they are, because all the features of beauty or utility which commend them to the public are by hypothesis already in the public domain. The defendant has as much right to copy the 'nonfunctional' features of the article as any others, so long as they have not become associated with the plaintiff as manufacturer or source. The critical question of fact at the outset always is whether the public is moved in any degree to buy the article because of its source and what are the features by which it distinguishes that source."[109]

He also put strict limits on the scope of relief that could be granted should a plaintiff establish secondary meaning but did not exclude the possibility that a court might order a change in a functional element if a case arose in which "no effective distinction was possible without change in functional elements."[110]

---

107 *See* §§ 4C[3] and 6B.

108 Crescent Tool Co. v. Kilborn & Bishop, 247 F. 299 (2d Cir. 1917).

109 247 F. at 300.

110 "[T]he court must require such changes in appearance as will effectively distinguish the defendant's wares with the least expense to him . . . The proper meaning of the phrase 'nonfunctional,' is only this: That in such cases the injunction is usually confined to nonessential elements, since these are usually enough to distinguish the goods, and are the least burdensome for the defendant to change. Whether changes in them are in all conceivable cases the limit of the plaintiff's right is a matter not before us. If a case should arise in which no effective distinction was possible without change in functional elements, it would demand consideration. . . . " 247 F. at 301.

The Restatement of Torts adopted these common law principles on unfair competition by product simulation.[111] The Restatement influenced the subsequent course of product simulation law even though these sections were omitted from the Second Restatement of Torts.[112]

[ii] *The Impact of Sears-Compco.* In *Sears* and *Compco*,[113] the Supreme Court held that state unfair competition law cannot prevent the copying of an article that is itself unprotected by federal patent or copyright law.

In both *Sears* and *Compco*, the plaintiff held a design patent on the configuration of a product (a pole lamp and a lighting reflector). The defendants sold a substantially identical product. The plaintiffs sued for infringement of the design patent and for unfair competition under Illinois state law. The lower federal courts held the design patents invalid but granted relief under state law based on a finding that the defendants' products had created a likelihood of confusion as to their source.

The lower court decisions were questionable applications of unfair competition law because they did not require the strict showing of secondary meaning that Judge Hand and the Restatement required. Rather, the lower courts relied primarily on an inherent likelihood of confusion stemming from exact copying. *Crescent Tool* clearly held that such was not a sufficient showing. Rather than simply reversing the lower federal courts' erroneous interpretation of state law,[114] the Supreme Court held that state law, as broadly interpreted so as to limit copying, was preempted by federal patent and copyright policy.

[111] Restatement Section 741 provided: "One who markets the goods, the physical appearance of which is a copy or imitation of the physical appearance of the goods of which another is the initial distributor, markets them with an unprivileged imitation" if "(b) the copied or imitated feature has acquired generally in the market a special significance identifying the other's goods, and (i) the copy or imitation is likely to cause prospective purchasers to regard his goods as those of the other, and (ii) the copied or imitated feature is nonfunctional, or, if it is functional, he does not take reasonable steps to inform prospective purchasers that the goods which he markets are not those of the other." The comment on clause (b) closely tracked Judge Hand's discussion of secondary meaning or "special significance." Section 742 defined functional. *See* § 5C[2][c][v].

[112] This section was "part of a group of sections on unfair competition and trade regulation which were not included in the Restatement (Second) of Torts because these fields were developing into independent bodies of law with diminishing reliance upon the traditional principles of tort law. 4 Restatement (Second) of Torts 1-2 (1979) (Introductory Note)." Keene Corp. v. Paraflex Industries, Inc., 653 F.2d 822, 211 U.S.P.Q. 201 (3d Cir. 1981).

Recently, the American Law Institute began work on a restatement of unfair competition law.

[113] Sears, Roebuck & Co. v. Stiffel Co., 376 U.S. 225, 140 U.S.P.Q. 524 (1964); Compco Corp. v. Day-Brite Lighting, Inc., 376 U.S. 234, 140 U.S.P.Q. 528 (1964).

For further discussion of *Sears-Compco*, see § 1D[3][a][i].

[114] This is what the Supreme Court had done 25 years before in a similar case in which a federal appeals court had granted broad relief against the copying of the shape of the plaintiff's shredded wheat cereal biscuit. Kellogg Co. v. National Biscuit Co., 305 U.S. 111 (1938).

The Court's approach in *Sears-Compco* is at odds with the usual principle that serious constitutional questions should be avoided if possible.

In *Sears*, the Court reasoned that "An unpatentable article, like an article on which the patent has expired, is in the public domain. . . . To allow a State by use of its law of unfair competition to prevent the copying of an article which represents too slight an advance to be patented would be to permit the State to block off from the public something which federal law has said belongs to the public." The Court did indicate that state law could provide certain protections in the interest of preventing confusion as to source so long as these protections did not extend to prohibitions against the copying of the article itself.

> "[M]ere inability of the public to tell two identical articles apart is not enough to support an injunction against copying or an award of damages for copying that which the federal patent laws permit to be copied. Doubtless a State may, in appropriate circumstances, require that goods, whether patented or unpatented, be labeled or that other precautionary steps be taken to prevent customers from being misled as to the source, just as it may protect businesses in the use of their trademarks, labels, or distinctive dress in the packaging of goods so as to prevent others, by imitating such markings, from misleading purchasers as to the source of the goods."[115]

In *Compco*, the Court commented on the competence of state law with regard to nonfunctional configurations that had acquired secondary meaning.

> "That an article copied from an unpatented article could be made in some other way, that the design is 'nonfunctional' and not essential to the use of either article, that the configuration of the article copied may have a 'secondary meaning' which identifies the maker to the trade, or that there may be 'confusion' among purchasers as to which article is which or as to who is the maker, may be relevant evidence in applying a State's law requiring such precautions as labeling; however, and regardless of the copier's motives, neither these facts nor any others can furnish a basis for imposing liability for or prohibiting the actual acts of copying and selling. . . . And of course a State cannot hold a copier accountable in damages for failure to label or otherwise to identify his goods unless his failure is in violation of valid state statutory or decisional law requiring the copier to label or take other precautions to prevent confusion of customers as to the source of the goods."[116]

Sears-Compco's reasoning and language, especially the above-quoted *Compco* passage, appeared to sound the death knell of product simulation unfair competition law. The tenor of the two cases was that state law could require labeling to prevent or cure confusion as to source but could not, even as a remedy for past acts of passing off or deception,[117] prevent exact copying of a product shape not protected by patent

---

[115] 376 U.S. at 232.

[116] 376 U.S. at 238-39.

[117] That the policy underpinnings relied upon by *Sears-Compco* would preclude injunctions against copying of a product even as a remedy for prior deceptive conduct, such as passing off, was underscored by Justice Harlan's concurring opinion. He indicated that he "would give the States more leeway in unfair competition 'copying' cases than the Court's opinions would allow. . . . If copying is found, other than by an inference arising from the mere act of copying, to have been undertaken with the dominant purpose and effect of palming off

or copyright. The Court only addressed the impact of federal patent policy on *state* law unfair competition remedies, but the rule that unpatented articles may be freely copied could easily extend to *federal* law, precluding protection of product configurations under Lanham Act Section 43(a), the broad federal remedy against unfair competition through false designations of origin.

The *Sears-Compco* blow to product simulation law proved not to be fatal.[118] The concept of providing protection against the creation of confusion by the copying of nonfunctional, source-indicating configurations did not die. Subsequent cases in the lower courts distinguished *Sears-Compco* on a variety of grounds. They allowed registration of distinctive product configurations as trademarks under the Lanham Act and extended the concept of trade "dress," which the Supreme Court in *Compco* indicated could be protected, to include nonfunctional product configuration and ornamentation as well as packaging.

Lower court emasculation of *Sears-Compco* received tacit Supreme Court support in *Inwood*,[119] a 1982 decision on contributory infringement.

[iii] *Registration of Packaging and Product Configuration Under the Lanham Act.* The Lanham Act expressly provides for the registration of distinctive packaging and of product configurations on the *supplemental* register. Section 23 includes in the definition of a registrable mark labels, packages, and configurations of goods that are "capable of distinguishing the applicant's goods or services."[120] The Act does not make similar provision for the registration of three dimensional marks on the *principal* register, but court decisions construe Section 45, which defines "trademark," as encompassing packaging and product ornamentations and configurations that are both nonfunctional and distinctive, either inherently or through the acquisition of a secondary meaning.

In *Mogen David*,[121] the CCPA held that a distinctive decanter bottle shape was eligible for registration as a mark on the Principal Register but affirmed denial of

---

one's goods as those of another or of confusing customers as to the source of such goods, I see no reason why the State may not impose reasonable restrictions on the future 'copying' itself." 376 U.S. at 239.

[118] For a discussion of the impact of *Sears* and *Compco* on the misappropriation doctrine, see § 6F.

[119] *See* § 5C[2][c][v](7). *But cf.* Bonito Boats Inc. v. Thunder Craft Boats Inc., 489 U.S. 141, 9 U.S.P.Q.2d 1847 (1989), discussed at § 1D[3][a][iv] (state "plug molding" law may not prevent copying of unpatented articles).

[120] 15 U.S.C. § 1091. For a discussion of the Supplemental Register, see § 5D[2][e].

[121] *In re* Mogen David Wine Corp., 328 F.2d 925, 140 U.S.P.Q. 575 (CCPA 1964) ("*Mogen David I* "); *In re* Mogen David Wine Corp., 372 F.2d 539, 152 U.S.P.Q. 593 (CCPA 1967) ("*Mogen David II* "). The PTO had previously held that a distinctively shaped bottle could be registered as a mark. *Ex parte* Haig & Haig, 118 U.S.P.Q. 229 (Ass't Comm'r Tm. 1958) (three-sided "Pinch" bottle for Scotch whiskey).

Mogen David I held that the Patent Office erred in rejecting the application to register the bottle shape on the sole ground that the shape was the subject of an expired design patent. On remand, the Office again rejected the application for insufficient proof of secondary meaning. *Mogen David II* affirmed but rebuffed the Office's argument that *Mogen David I* was contrary to *Sears-Compco*. In concurring, Judge Smith noted that *Sears-Compco* did not deal with the "boundaries between federal patent law and federal trademark law." 372 F.2d at 542.

registration for want of proof of secondary meaning. In *Honeywell*, [122] it held that an applicant could obtain registration of the configuration of a part of the product itself (a cover for a thermostat) if the configuration was nonfunctional and distinctive. The court dismissed *Sears-Compco* as "concerned with the conflict between a state's law of unfair competition and the federal law," not "registrability for federal trademark protection." [123]

The Lanham Act does not expressly exclude or even mention functional designs, but in *Deister Concentrator*, which pre-dated *Sears-Compco*, the CCPA, in an opinion by Judge Rich, held that a functional shape, even one that indicated source to the purchasing public, could not be registered because of overriding policy considerations. [124]

[iv] *Lanham Act Section 43(a) and Common Law Unfair Competition Nonfunctional Trade Dress and Design Protection.* Beginning with *Truck Equipment Services*, [125] a 1976 Eighth Circuit decision, the Courts of Appeals interpreted Lanham Act Section 43(a) as providing a federal unfair competition remedy that provided protection for "trade dress." "Trade dress" originally meant a product's packaging, but more recent decisions extend trade dress to include the configuration and ornamentation of the product itself. [126]

---

[122] *In re* Honeywell, 497 F.2d 1344, 181 U.S.P.Q. 821 (CCPA 1974), *cert. denied sub nom.* Dann v. Honeywell, 419 U.S. 1080, 184 U.S.P.Q. 129 (1974).

[123] 497 F.2d at 1345.

[124] *In re* Deister Concentrator Co., Inc., 289 F.2d 496, 501, 504, 129 U.S.P.Q. 314 (CCPA 1961) (coal cleaning table top working surface rhomboidal outline is not registrable because of functionality even though those in the trade recognized rhomboidal top tables as applicant's; "the socio-economic policy supported by the general law is the encouragement of competition by all fair means, and that encompasses the right to copy, very broadly interpreted, except where copying is lawfully prevented by a copyright or patent. . . . [G]overnment economic policy . . . must be determined by the legislature and the judiciary and cannot be left to depend wholly on the attitudes, reactions or beliefs of the purchasing public. Public acceptance of a functional feature as an indication of source is, therefore, not determinative of the right to register").

[125] Truck Equipment Service Co. v. Fruehauf Corp., 536 F.2d 1210, 191 U.S.P.Q. 79 (8th Cir. 1976), *cert. denied*, 429 U.S. 861, 191 U.S.P.Q. 588 (1976).

[126] Coach Leatherware Co., Inc. v. Anntaylor, Inc., 933 F.2d 162, 168, 18 USPQ2d 1907, 1912 (2d Cir. 1991) ("Section 43(a) extends protection to a product's 'trade dress'—the total image of a good as defined by its overall composition and design, including size, shape, color, texture, and graphics."); Rachel v. Banana Republic Inc., 831 F.2d 1503, 1506, 4 U.S.P.Q.2d 1877, 1879 (9th Cir. 1987) (" 'Trade dress' is the appearance of the product and may include features such as size, shape, color, color combinations, texture, or graphics."); John H. Harland Co. v. Clarke Checks, Inc., 711 F.2d 966, 980, 219 U.S.P.Q. 515, 528 (11th Cir. 1983) (" 'Trade dress' involves the total image of a product and may include features such as size, shape, color or color combinations, texture, graphics, or even particular sales techniques. . . . Most trade dress infringement actions involve the packaging or labeling of goods. . . . Recently, however, courts have recognized that the design of a product itself may constitute protectable trade dress under § 43(a) of the Lanham Act."); Ideal Toy Corp. v. Plawner Toy Manufacturing Corp., 685 F.2d 78, 80 n.2, 216 U.S.P.Q. 102, 104 n.2 (3d Cir. 1982) ("Although historically trade dress infringement consisted of copying a product's packaging, the parties and the district

In *Truck Equipment Services*, the court held that the defendant unfairly competed by copying the exterior design of the plaintiff's semi-trailer. The design was unique, nonfunctional, and had acquired a secondary meaning. It cited *Mogen David Wine* and dismissed *Compco's* language on nonfunctionality and secondary meaning as "dictum."

Other courts of appeal follow the Eighth Circuit in recognizing Section 43(a) as a source of trade dress protection though they waver in their articulation and application of the nonfunctionality,[127] distinctiveness, and likelihood of confusion standards.[128]

Many decisions recite generally that trade dress is protectable on a showing of secondary meaning.[129] Secondary meaning is generally not required under trademark

---

court used the term 'trade dress' in its more modern sense to refer to the appearance of the [product] itself as well as its packaging, and we will do the same.").

For a "trade dress" case that really involved the "dress" of a "trade," see Dallas Cowboys Cheerleaders, Inc. v. Pussycat Cinema, Ltd., 604 F.2d 200, 203 U.S.P.Q. 161 (2d Cir. 1979) (plaintiff's trade dress consisting of a cheerleader uniform was misappropriated by defendant's use of a strikingly similar uniform on a character in the pornographic movie "Debbie Does Dallas").

[127] The major dispute is over "aesthetic functionality." *See* § 5C[2][c][v](5).

[128] The general test for likelihood of confusion applies to trade dress and product configurations. *See* § 5F[1].

An issue of interest is whether clear labeling of the source of a product or service will obviate any claim for trade dress or product configuration infringement. *See* Fuddruckers Inc. v. Doc's B.R. Others Inc., 826 F.2d 837, 846 n.13, 4 U.S.P.Q.2d 1026, 1033 n.12 (9th Cir. 1987) ("Use of differing names or distinctive logos in connection with similar marks can reduce the likelihood of confusion but doesn't always do so."); Sno-Wizard Manufacturing, Inc. v. Eisemann Products Co., 791 F.2d 423, 429, 230 U.S.P.Q. 118, 122 (5th Cir. 1986) (configuration of "snowball" machine; "[T]he district court . . . noted that confusion was unlikely in that the 'origin of each machine is apparent from bold lettering appearing on each door.' . . . It is true that the labeling of a product will not always negate a likelihood of confusion."); Litton Sys., Inc. v. Whirlpool Corp., 728 F.2d 1423, 1446, 221 U.S.P.Q. 97, 112 (Fed. Cir. 1984) (district court committed clear error in finding a likelihood of confusion when both the plaintiff's and the defendant's products bore prominent labels indicating the manufacturer; "The legal effect of labeling a product with its manufacturer's name depends or may depend on both the prominence of the label and the type of product. There . . . are products whose consumer buyers would take little notice of a maker's name or disregard a name plainly evidence to the buyer's eye. . . . The district court made no findings . . . as to how a purchaser confronted with a correct brand or maker's name could still be confused or deceived."); John H. Harland Co. v. Clarke Checks, Inc., 711 F.2d 966, 981 n.24, 219 U.S.P.Q. 515, 528 n.24 (11th Cir. 1983) ("The presence of a manufacturer's name on a product is just one of many factors relevant to determining whether there is a likelihood of confusion."); Truck Equipment Service Co. v. Fruehauf Corp., 536 F.2d 1210, 191 U.S.P.Q. 79 (8th Cir. 1976), *cert. denied*, 429 U.S. 861, 191 U.S.P.Q. 588 (1976).

[129] *E.g.*, Coach Leatherware Co., Inc. v. Anntaylor, Inc., 933 F.2d 162, 168, 18 U.S.P.Q.2d 1907, 1912 (2d Cir. 1991) ("To prevail on a trade dress claim, the plaintiff must demonstrate that the product's appearance has acquired 'secondary meaning'—the consuming public immediately identifies the product with its maker—and that purchasers are likely to confuse the imitating goods with the originals. . . . The trade dress of a product attains

and unfair competition law if the mark or trade symbol in question is arbitrary or fanciful, that is, "inherently distinctive."[130] Secondary meaning should not be necessary if the trade dress is truly arbitrary and therefore inherently distinctive.[131] Most trade dress is ornamental and therefore not inherently distinctive.[132]

---

secondary meaning when the purchasing public 'associates' its design with a single producer or source rather than simply with the product itself. . . . The plaintiff is not required to establish that all consumers relate the product to its producer; it need only show that a substantial segment of the relevant consumer group makes this connection."); LeSportsac, Inc. v. K Mart Corp., 754 F.2d 71, 75, 225 U.S.P.Q. 654, 656 (2d Cir. 1985) ("The 'trade dress' of a product . . . may become an unregistered trademark eligible for protection under § 43(a) if it is nonfunctional and has acquired a secondary meaning in the marketplace by which it is identified with its producer of source.").

In *LeSportsac*, the court rejected the argument that survey evidence of secondary meaning must be introduced before a plaintiff may obtain a preliminary injunction: "The trade dress of a product has attained 'secondary meaning' when the purchasing public associates that dress with a single producer or source rather than just with the product itself. . . . While [plaintiff] might have presented additional evidence, it did offer proof of phenomenal sales success, substantial advertising expenditures, unsolicited media coverage, requests from third parties to license the use of its design, and [defendant's] deliberate attempt to imitate its trade dress." 754 F.2d at 78, 225 U.S.P.Q. at 659.

For a general discussion of secondary meaning, see § 5C[3][a][vii].

[130] See § 5C[3].

[131] Sicilia di R. Biebow & Co. v. Cox, 732 F.2d 417 (5th Cir. 1984) (citrus juice bottle's "tear-shape-on-a-pedestal" design is sufficiently distinctive to serve as an identifier of source; if the defendant were correct that the bottle simply resembled a lemon or lime, the design would be descriptive and a finding of secondary meaning would be required); Chevron Chemical Co. v. Voluntary Purchasing Groups, Inc., 659 F.2d 695, 702, 212 U.S.P.Q. 904 (5th Cir. 1981), *cert. denied*, 457 U.S. 1126 (1982) (secondary meaning proof is not necessary when a trade dress is "sufficiently distinctive of itself to identify the producer").

See also Brunswick Corp. v. Spinit Reel Co., 832 F.2d 513, 517 n.2, 4 U.S.P.Q.2d 1497, 1499 n.2 (10th Cir. 1987) ("While some circuits seem to require that the product have a secondary meaning, . . . other circuits have held that secondary meaning need not be shown if the trade dress itself is inherently distinctive."); Fuddruckers Inc. v. Doc's B.R. Others Inc., 826 F.2d 837, 843, 4 U.S.P.Q.2d 1026, 1030-31 (9th Cir. 1987) (argument that "a showing of secondary meaning should be unnecessary in connection with an inherently distinctive trade dress has some intuitive appeal. Secondary meaning is, after all, probative of whether claimed trade dress is distinctive, in the trade mark sense of signifying the source of a product or service to an appreciable portion of the purchasing public. . . . If . . . [plaintiff's] claimed trade dress is *inherently distinctive*, the further requirement of a showing of secondary meaning should be superfluous"; plaintiff "has not offered this court a definition of what 'inherently distinctive' in the trade mark sense might mean in the absence of secondary meaning.").

[132] See, e.g., Fuddruckers Inc. v. Doc's B.R. Others Inc., 826 F.2d 837, 844, 4 U.S.P.Q.2d 1026, 1031 (9th Cir. 1987) (plaintiff claims "trade dress protection for the impression created by a collection of common or functional elements of restaurant decor. Such an overall impression may receive protection, but it is simply not the sort of arbitrary or uncommon trade dress that might qualify as inherently distinctive."); Sno-Wizard Manufacturing, Inc. v. Eisemann Products Co., 791 F.2d 423, 426 n.2, 230 U.S.P.Q. 118, 119, n.2 (5th Cir. 1986) ("Unless a mark or dress is deemed 'inherently' or 'sufficiently' distinctive, . . . secondary meaning must be established.").

Applying the *Compco* dictum allowing state law to "protect businesses in the use of their trademarks, labels, or distinctive dress in the packaging of goods so as to prevent others, by imitating such markings, from misleading purchasers as to the source of the goods," court decisions recognize the protectability of trade dress under state common law principles,[133] equating the protection with that available under Section 43(a).[134]

[v] *Functionality—Aesthetic and Utilitarian.* The courts exclude functional designs from protection under any trademark or unfair competition theory. The policy basis for this exclusion is clear. To provide trademark or unfair competition protection for functional designs would undermine patent law's balancing of the interest in free competition and the interest in providing incentives to develop and disclose new technology.[135] Patent protection for an invention arises only upon compliance with both substantive and procedural requirements (such as the novelty requirement)[136] and endures only for a limited period of time. Trademark protection arises without any showing of novelty, distinctiveness being sufficient, and endures for as long as the mark is used and maintains that distinctiveness.[137]

(1) The Restatement Definition. The major problem with the functionality doctrine is how to define functionality.[138] The Restatement of Torts adopted the

---

[133] Time Mechanisms, Inc. v. Qonaar, 422 F. Supp. 905, 194 U.S.P.Q. 500 (D.N.J. 1976) (parking meter's "ice cream cone shaped top" protected as common law trademark). *Compare* Litton Sys., Inc. v. Whirlpool Corp., 728 F.2d 1423, 1448, 221 U.S.P.Q. 97, 113 (Fed. Cir. 1984) ("No Supreme Court case . . . limits the effect of the *Sears-Compco* doctrine with respect to factual situations similar to those at issue in the *Sears* and *Compco* cases. . . . [S]tate unfair competition law may not give relief 'against copying of a unpatented industrial design' "—even if the plaintiff can show secondary meaning and a likelihood of confusion).

[134] *E.g.,* Standard Terry Mills, Inc. v. Shen Manufacturing Co., 803 F.2d 778, 780 n.4, 231 U.S.P.Q. 555, 557 n.4 (3d Cir. 1986); American Greetings Corp. v. Dan-Dee Imports Inc., 807 F.2d 1136, 1141, 1 U.S.P.Q.2d 1001, 1004 (3d Cir. 1986) ("The federal law of unfair competition under § 43(a) is not significantly different from the New Jersey law of unfair competition.").

[135] *See, e.g.,* Keene Corp. v. Paraflex Industries, Inc., 653 F.2d 822, 824, 211 U.S.P.Q. 201 (3d Cir. 1981) ("One of the essential elements of the law of trademarks, even at common law where it was part of the law of unfair competition, was the principle that no legal protection would be available for products or features that were functional. . . . The purpose of the rule precluding trademark significance for functional features is to prevent the grant of a perpetual monopoly to features which cannot be patented. . . . If this area of the law were to be compartmentalized, one could ascribe to the patent laws protection of those utilitarian features which Congress has chosen to protect, and to the trademark law protection of fanciful or arbitrary features which have achieved recognition as indicia of origin. Products or features which have not qualified for patent protection but which are functional are in the public domain, and are fair game for imitation and copying. Our natural inclination to disapprove of such conduct must give way to the public policy favoring competition, even by slavish copying, of products not entitled to federal patent protection.").

[136] *See* § 2C[3].

[137] *See* § 5D[3].

[138] *See generally* Note, *The Problem of Functional Features: Trade Dress Infringement under Section 43(a) of the Lanham Act,* 82 Colum. L. Rev. 77 (1982).

following definition: "A feature of goods is functional . . . if it affects their purpose, action or performance, or the facility or economy of processing, handling or using them. . . . " Many court decisions cite and follow the Restatement definition.

(2)   *De Facto and De Jure Functionality.* In *Morton-Norwich*,[139] the CCPA held that the pistol-grip, contoured spray bottle for "Fantastik" cleaning fluid was not functional. Judge Rich distinguished *de facto* and *de jure* functionality.[140] Confusion in the law arises because the same word, functional, is used both in a lay, descriptive sense to mean that a feature has a function, and in a legal, conclusory sense to mean that a feature is so dictated by function that it cannot be registered or protected as a trademark. The design feature may be functional in the first sense (*de facto*) but not in the second sense (*de jure*) if numerous other designs can perform the same function with equal efficiency.

(3)   *Factors.* In *Morton-Norwich*, Judge Rich mentioned "a number of factors, both positive and negative, which aid in [the] determination" of *de jure* functionality.

> "Keeping in mind . . . that 'functionality' is determined in light of 'utility,' which is determined in light of 'superiority of design,' and rests upon the foundation 'essential to effective competition' . . . there exist a number of factors, both positive and negative, which aid in that determination. . . . [T]he existence of an expired utility patent which disclose[s] the *utilitarian advantage of the design* sought to be registered as a trademark [is] *evidence* that it [is] 'functional.' It may also be significant that the originator of the design touts its utilitarian advantages through advertising. Since the effect upon competition 'is really the crux of the matter,' it is, of course, significant that there are other alternatives available."[141]

The last mentioned factor—the availability of alternative designs that will perform the function in question equally well—is often the critical one in determining functionality because the availability of a large pool of alternative designs of equal efficiency, cost, etc. shows directly that the function of the device does not dictate the design.[142] The class of alternatives is products of the same general type.[143] The other

---

[139] *In re* Morton-Norwich, 671 F.2d 1332, 213 U.S.P.Q. 13 (CCPA 1982).

[140] *See also In re* Smith, 734 F.2d 1482, 1484, 222 U.S.P.Q. 1, 3 (Fed. Cir. 1984) ("In essence, de facto functionality means that the design of a product has a function, i.e., a bottle of any design holds fluid. De jure functionality, on the other hand, means that the product is in its particular shape because it works better in this shape. This distinction is useful because the configuration of a product is not necessarily lacking in trademark significance because of 'the mere *existence* of utility'; rather, it should depend on 'the *degree* of design utility.' . . . Evidence of distinctiveness is of no avail to counter a de jure functionality rejection.").

[141] 671 F.2d at 1340-41. *See also In re* Owens-Corning Fiberglas Corp., 774 F.2d 1116, 1121, 227 U.S.P.Q. 417, 419-20 (Fed. Cir. 1985) (*Morton-Norwich* "looked at the following factors to determine functionality: (1) whether a particular design yields a utilitarian advantage, (2) whether alternative designs are available in order to avoid hindering competition, and (3) whether the design achieves economies in manufacture or use.").

[142] *See, e.g.,* Brandir International Inc. v. Cascade Pacific Lumber Co., 834 F.2d 1142, 1148, 5 U.S.P.Q.2d 1089, 1094 (2d Cir. 1987) (the district court erred in granting summary judgment that bicycle rack design was functional because there are material fact issues on alternative bicycle rack constructions' nature, price and utility; "the true test of function-

two factors—advertising touting,[144] and utility patent coverage[145] —are in the nature

---

ality is not whether the feature in question performs a function, but whether the feature 'is dictated by the functions to be performed,' . . . as evidenced by available alternative constructions"); W.T. Rogers Co., Inc. v. Keene, 778 F.2d 334, 343, 228 U.S.P.Q. 145, 150 (7th Cir. 1985) (molded plastic stacking office tray hexagonal end panel; "[E]ven with the hexagon appropriated an infinity of geometrical patterns would remain open to competitors."; moreover, plaintiff only claimed a particular shaped hexagon); Ideal Toy Corp. v. Plawner Toy Manufacturing Corp., 685 F.2d 78, 216 U.S.P.Q. 102 (3d Cir. 1982) (cube puzzle trade dress consisting of six specific colors on cubes with a black grid background pattern is not functional because a wide variety of colors, shapes, and markings could have been used to differentiate puzzle's faces); In re World's Finest Chocolate, Inc., 474 F.2d 1012, 1014, 177 U.S.P.Q. 205, 206 (CCPA 1973) ("competitors can readily meet the demand for packaged candy bars by use of other packaging styles"); Time Mechanisms, Inc. v. Qonaar, 422 F. Supp. 905, 913 194 U.S.P.Q. 500, 506 (D.N.J. 1976) (parking meter "ice cream cone shaped top." "[M]eter mechanism can be contained by housings of many different configurations").

Compare Standard Terry Mills, Inc. v. Shen Manufacturing Co., 803 F.2d 778, 781, 231 U.S.P.Q. 555, 558 (3d Cir. 1986) (defendant could have made slight changes in its product without sacrificing workability, but failure to "make such miniscule changes did not render its design nonfunctional"); In re Bose, 772 F.2d 866, 227 U.S.P.Q. 1 (Fed. Cir. 1985) (five-sided speaker enclosure; because the pentagonal shape of the speaker sound matrix was functional, a pentagonal shape of the enclosure was also functional: "Logic dictates that the shape of a speaker enclosure which conforms to the shape of the sound matrix is an efficient and superior design as an enclosure and, thus, de jure functional, whether or not it contributes to the functionality of the sound system itself"); John H. Harland Co. v. Clarke Checks, Inc., 711 F.2d 966, 984 n.31, 219 U.S.P.Q. 515, 531 n.31 (11th Cir. 1983) (horizontal size of carry-around stub of plaintiff's check-book product was functional even though the defendant could have made it wider without affecting its utility or the production costs; there are functional limits on the size, and the limits would soon be reached if each competitor were required to widen its stub sufficiently to distinguish it from studs that had already been successfully marketed by its predecessors); Keene Corp. v. Paraflex Industries, Inc., 653 F.2d 822, 827, 211 U.S.P.Q. 201 (3d Cir. 1981) ("Because there are only a limited number of configurations or designs for a luminaire which are architecturally compatible with the type of structures on which they are placed, the selection of a luminaire design does not have the unlimited boundaries as does the selection of a wine bottle or ashtray design"); Schwinn Bicycle Co. v. Murray Ohio Mfg. Co., 339 F.2d 973, 980, 172 U.S.P.Q. 14, 19 (M.D. Tenn. 1971), aff'd, 470 F.2d 975, 176 U.S.P.Q. 161 (6th Cir. 1972) (bicycle rim surface design is not protectable because it softens the rough appearance resulting from welding sections together; the only other process used to achieve that effect is more complex and expensive).

[143] Brandir International Inc. v. Cascade Pacific Lumber Co., 834 F.2d 1142, 1148, 5 U.S.P.Q.2d 1089, 1095 (2d Cir. 1987) (functionality "should be viewed in terms of bicycle racks generally and not one-piece undulating bicycle racks specifically"); In re DC Comics, Inc., 689 F.2d 1042, 1045, 215 U.S.P.Q. 394, 397 (CCPA 1982) (depiction of Superman as mark for Superman doll; dolls generally, not Superman dolls, are the class by which functionality is determined; applicant "would not be in a position to impair competition in the sale of toy doll figures, nor could it deprive the public of access to imagery associated with toy dolls generally or 'super hero' or villain figures in particular").

[144] As to the effect of statements in advertising or other materials by touting the utility of the design features, American Greetings Corp. v. Dan-Dee Imports Inc., 807 F.2d 1136, 1142, 1 U.S.P.Q.2d 1001, 1005 (3d Cir. 1986) ("If the marketer of a product advertises the utilitarian advantages of a particular feature, this constitutes strong evidence of its functionality."); New

of admissions or evidence of the ultimate fact of nonfunctionality.

(4)   Trade Dress "As a Whole." The courts analyze trade dress "as a whole" in determining functionality.[146] A combination of functional and nonfunctional features may create a trade dress that is as a whole nonfunctional.[147] For example, in

---

England Butt Co. v. International Trade Commission, 756 F.2d 874, 225 U.S.P.Q. 260 (Fed. Cir. 1985); John H. Harland Co. v. Clarke Checks, Inc., 711 F.2d 966, 984 n.28, 219 U.S.P.Q. 515, 531 n.28 (11th Cir. 1983) (plaintiff's "own marketing materials indicate that the concept of an intermediate carry-around stub, designed to solve the portability problem associated with desk checkbooks, is functional").

[145] As to the effect of utility patent protection, see *In re* Bose Corp., 772 F.2d 866, 227 U.S.P.Q. 1 (Fed. Cir. 1985) (it is proper to look at statements in a utility patent as to the advantages of a five-sided speaker as evidence of the functionality of the shape sought to be registered as a trademark); Cable Electric Products, Inc. v. Genmark, Inc., 770 F.2d 1015, 1030, 226 U.S.P.Q. 881, 891 (Fed. Cir. 1985) ("the fact finder is to consider the appearance of the *products* in issue. Reference to utility patent claims that are, or have been asserted to read on either product, or to the appearance of the device depicted in figures included in the specification supporting such claims, must be done with caution. . . . Claims may be capable of reading on many devices of strikingly different configuration. Thus, even the fact that the claims read on two commercial devices in the marketplace is not support in itself for a finding that one is a copy of the other or confusingly similar thereto for section 43(a) purposes. A manufacturer may choose in its commercial embodiment of a patented device to less than faithfully replicate the exemplary depiction of a claimed embodiment shown in the figures of the patent.").

[146] *E.g.,* Fuddruckers Inc. v. Doc's B.R. Others Inc., 826 F.2d 837, 843 n.7, 4 U.S.P.Q.2d 1026, 1030 n.7 (9th Cir. 1987) ("our inquiry is not addressed to whether individual elements of the trade dress fall within the definition of functional, but to whether the whole collection of elements taken together are functional. Viewing the elements as a whole does not result in monopoly protection for necessary elements."); First Brands Corp. v. Fred Meyer Inc., 809 F.2d 1378, 1381, 1 U.S.P.Q.2d 1779, 1781 (9th Cir. 1987) ("In determining functionality, a product's trade dress must be analyzed as a whole"; but the combination of a standard, functional "F-style" container with a primary color (yellow) cannot be protectable trade dress for antifreeze because such protection would be the equivalent of protection for the color itself).

The "as a whole" test does not bar initial review of individual elements' functionality as part of the consideration of the whole design's functionality. *In re* Smith, 734 F.2d 1482, 1483, 222 U.S.P.Q. 1, 2 (Fed. Cir. 1984) (PTO established that overall design of pistol grip water nozzle was *prima facie* functional); *In re* Teledyne, 696 F.2d 968, 217 U.S.P.Q. 9 (Fed. Cir. 968 (Fed. Cir. 1982) (PTO properly rejected application to register the configuration of a showerhead spray nozzle with three groups of orifices; once PTO shows that the particular features of the design are functional, the burden shifts to the applicant to establish that the design as a whole is not de jure functional; evidence on matters such as whether there exist commercially feasible, alternative configurations is more readily available to the applicant than to the PTO).

[147] *E.g.,* American Greetings Corp. v. Dan-Dee Imports Inc., 807 F.2d 1136, 1144, 1 U.S.P.Q.2d 1001, 1006 (3d Cir. 1986) ("one may have a protectible interest in a combination of features or elements that includes one or more functional features"; a plaintiff "should not be required to show that the secondary meaning arises solely from non-functional features. . . . [W]here it is not feasible in practice to avoid the potential for confusion through the selection of alternative non-functional elements or the manner in which one combines imitated functional ones, the most that can be required is clear labeling disclosing the source or other reasonable steps to minimize the risk of confusion.").

LeSportsac,[148] the Second Circuit affirmed a preliminary injunction against the defendant's imitation of plaintiff's bags. It rejected the defendant's argument that plaintiff's design features, such as a hollow rectangular zipper pull, cotton carpet tape, and repeating logo, were functional: "[B]y breaking [plaintiff's] trade dress into its individual elements and then attacking certain of those elements as functional, [defendant] misconceives the scope of the appropriate inquiry. [Plaintiff] does not claim a trademark in all lightweight nylon bags using hollow zipper pulls or carpet tape trim. It claims as its mark the particular combination and arrangement of design elements that identify its bags and distinguish them from other bags."[149]

(5) *Aesthetic Functionality.* "Aesthetic functionality" originated with a Comment to the Restatement definition of functionality:

> "When goods are bought largely for their aesthetic value, their features may be functional because they definitely contribute to that value and thus aid the performance of an object for which the goods are intended. Thus, the shape of a bottle or other container may be functional though a different bottle or container may hold the goods equally well. A candy box in the shape of a heart may be functional, because of its significance as a gift to a beloved one, while a box of a different shape or the form in which a ribbon is tied around the box may not be functional. Or, a distinctive printing type face may be functional though the print from a different type may be read equally well. The determination of whether or not such features are functional depends upon the question of fact whether prohibition of imitation by others will deprive the others of something which will substantially hinder them in competition."[150]

In *Pagliero,*[151] the Ninth Circuit adopted aesthetic functionality. Plaintiff sold hotel china embellished with four distinctive designs. The defendant sold china that exactly copied the four designs. The court recognized that under *Crescent Tool* and the Restatement, "[i]mitation of the physical details and designs of a competitor's product may be actionable, if the particular features imitated are 'non-functional' and have acquired a secondary meaning." The court articulated an "importance to success" functionality test.

> "If the particular feature is an important ingredient in the commercial success of the product, the interest in free competition permits its imitation in the absence of a patent or copyright. On the other hand, where the feature or, more aptly, design, is a mere arbitrary embellishment, a form of dress for the goods primarily adopted for purposes of identification and individuality and, hence, unrelated to basic consumer demands in connection with the product, imitation may be forbidden where the requisite showing of secondary meaning is made."[152]

Applying this test, the court found the designs to be functional—even though the defendant could have developed alternative designs equally or even more aesthetically satisfying to customers:

---

[148] LeSportsac, Inc. v. K Mart Corp., 754 F.2d 71, 225 U.S.P.Q. 654 (2d Cir. 1985).
[149] 754 F.2d at 76, 225 U.S.P.Q. at 657.
[150] Restatement of Torts § 742 comment a (1938).
[151] Pagliero v. Wallace China Co., 198 F.2d 339, 95 U.S.P.Q. 45 (9th Cir. 1962).
[152] 198 F.2d at 343.

"The attractiveness and eye-appeal of the design sells the china. . . . [T]he possibility that an alternative product might be developed has never been considered a barrier to permitting imitation competition in other types of cases. The law encourages competition not only in creativeness but in economy of manufacture and distribution as well."[153]

Aesthetic functionality has had a stormy history since *Pagliero*. Professor McCarthy criticizes the concept on the ground that it inappropriately substitutes for consumer perception a court's perception of what is an important ingredient of a product's commercial success.[154] He notes that many cases would be decided the same way by application of the rule that a design does not operate as a trademark if consumers perceive it as mere ornamentation and not as an indication of source.[155] In *Keene*,[156] the Third Circuit criticized the "broad view" of aesthetic functionality for promoting ugliness in modern life: "The more appealing the design, the less protection it would receive. As our ambience becomes more mechanized and banal, it would be unfortunate were we to discourage use of a spark of originality that could transform an ordinary product into one of grace. The doctrine of aesthetic functionality need not be construed in such a manner for it to fulfill its important public policy function of protecting free competition."[157]

Decisions since *Pagliero* limit, refine or even reject outright "the important ingredient" test and the aesthetic functionality concept.[158] The Ninth Circuit itself no longer

(Text continued on page 5–46)

---

[153] 198 F.2d at 344.

[154] J. T. McCarthy, Trademarks and Unfair Competition § 7:26E (2d ed. 1984).

[155] *See* § 5C[2][b][iv].

[156] Keene Corp. v. Paraflex Industries, Inc., 653 F.2d 822, 211 U.S.P.Q. 201 (3d Cir. 1981).

[157] 653 F.2d at 825.

[158] *Federal Circuit (CCPA)*: *In re* DC Comics, Inc., 689 F.2d 1042, 1045, 215 U.S.P.Q. 394, 397 (CCPA 1982) (the "broad definition" of functionality in the ingredient of success test of *Pagliero* is "at odds with this court's precedent in this area").

Third Circuit: American Greetings Corp. v. Dan-Dee Imports Inc., 807 F.2d 1136, 1142, 1 U.S.P.Q.2d 1001, 1005 (3d Cir. 1986) ("a feature is not functional merely because it makes the product more attractive to consumers"; in *Keene*, "we rejected the concept of aesthetic functionality as interpreted by the . . . Ninth Circuit"); Keene Corp. v. Paraflex Industries, 653 F.2d 822, 211 U.S.P.Q. 201 (3d Cir. 1981) (shape of outdoor luminaire cannot be the subject of Section 43(a) protection when the evidence shows that the shape functioned to enhance its architectural compatibility). The Third Circuit took a narrow view of what is functional in drug capsule trade dress in Ciba-Geigy v. Bolar Pharmaceutical, 747 F.2d 844, 224 U.S.P.Q. 349 (1984), *cert. denied*, 471 U.S. 1137 (1985). *See* § 5C[2][c][v](7).

Fifth Circuit: Sno-Wizard Manufacturing, Inc. v. Eisemann Products Co., 791 F.2d 423, 230 U.S.P.Q. 118 (5th Cir. 1986) (*Sicilia* decision rejecting *Pagliero* aesthetic functionality test applies to product configurations as well as packaging; the ultimate inquiry is whether protection would hinder competition); Sicilia Di R. Biebow & Co. v. Cox, 732 F.2d 417, 422, 427-28 (5th Cir. 1984) (the expansive *Pagliero* "definition of functionality has often been criticized as overinclusive" because "[d]efining functionality as anything that is 'an important ingredient in the commercial success' of a product would almost always permit a second comer freely to copy the trade dress of a successful product that has accumulated goodwill. . . . To achieve the status of 'functional,' a design or feature must be superior or optimal in terms of engineering, economy of manufacture, or accommodation of utilitarian function or performance. . . . [A]n

(Text continued on page 5–46)

important component of functionality is whether appropriation of a design or feature will hinder competition").

Seventh Circuit: W.T. Rogers Co., Inc. v. Keene, 778 F.2d 334, 340-41, 228 U.S.P.Q. 145, 148-49 (7th Cir. 1985) ("It is doubtful that any simple rule could be devised to decide these cases. On the one hand, it would be unreasonable to deny trademark protection to a manufacturer who had the good fortune to have created a trade name, symbol, or design that became valued by the consuming public for its intrinsic pleasingness as well as for the information it conveyed about who had made the product, unless the feature in question had become generic, and therefore costly to engineer around; and we reject the contrary intimations in some cases from the Ninth Circuit, . . . as have most other courts. . . . But it would also be unreasonable to let a manufacturer use trademark law to prevent competitors from making pleasing substitutes for is own brand; yet that would be the effect of allowing him to appropriate the most pleasing way of configuring the product. . . . A feature can be functional not only because it helps the product achieve the objective for which the product would be valued by a person indifferent to matters of taste, charm, elegance, and beauty, but also because it makes the product more pleasing to people not indifferent to such things. But the fact that people like the feature does not by itself prevent the manufacturer from being able to use it as his trademark. He is prevented only if the feature is functional . . . that is, only if without it other producers of the product could not compete effectively."; instruction to jury on functionality contained three errors: (1) in defining "nonfunctional" as meaning that the primary purpose served by a design feature is to identify the manufacture—because it would exclude a design that two equally important purposes—to identify source and to please consumers; (2) in stating that a feature is functional when it serves to provide a reason for purchase unrelated to the source of product—because it would make a feature functional even though the nonsource-indicating reason was not the most important or even equally important reason; and (3) in stating that a feature cannot be considered nonfunctional if doing so would "limit the number of entrants into the market"—because limiting entrance may have no effect on competition if the market already contains many competitors).

Tenth Circuit: Brunswick Corp. v. Spinit Reel Co., 832 F.2d 513, 519, 4 U.S.P.Q.2d 1497, 1501 (10th Cir. 1987) (defendant violated Section 43(a) by copying plaintiff's closed face spincast fishing reel design, which had "a chrome, cone-shaped front cover, a 'stubby' back cover and a black and chrome finish"; rejecting *Pagliero* "important ingredient to success" test in favor of test focusing on competition; "[T]he question of whether the feature is functional should turn on whether 'the protection of the configuration would "hinder competition or impinge upon the rights of others to compete effectively in the sale of goods."' . . . Although this distinction may be subject to the same criticism as the 'important ingredient' test, that it is overbroad, we think it affords better protection to ensure that we do not discourage the 'use of a spark of originality which could transform an ordinary product into one of grace.' . . . Under our test, the claim may still be made that without a particular identifying design or feature a second-comer may be less effectively able to compete. If that feature must be slavishly copied in order to have an equally functional product, then the feature is not entitled to protection. . . . But if the feature enables the second-comer simply to market his product more effectively, it is entitled to protection.").

Eleventh Circuit: John H. Harland Co. v. Clarke Checks, Inc., 711 F.2d 966, 983 n.27, 219 U.S.P.Q. 515, 530 n.27 (11th Cir. 1983) (the following proffered jury instruction contained an incorrect definition of functionality: "When a feature of goods or of its wrappers or containers appeals to the consumer and affects his or her choice, that feature is functional. . . . [T]his definition is overly broad because many nonfunctional, arbitrary features of a product may appeal to the consumer and affect his or her choice.8).

fully endorses the *Pagliero* "important ingredient" test.[159] In *Vuitton*,[160] the Ninth Circuit upheld the validity of a registered design mark consisting of "LV" surrounded by three floral symbols in a mustard color contrasting with the dark brown, vinyl-impregnated canvas of registrant's luggage and handbags even though the design covered the entire surface of the products. *Pagliero* does not stand for the proposition that "any feature of a product which contributes to the consumer appeal and salability of the product is, as a matter of law, a functional element. . . . If the Vuitton mark increases consumer appeal only because of the quality associated with Vuitton goods, or because of the prestige associated with owning a genuine Vuitton product, then the design is serving the legitimate function of a trademark; it is identifying the source of the product, and thus should be protected." In *Vuitton*, the Ninth Circuit retreated (in effect though not expressly) from the apparent extension of *Pagliero* in *International Order of Job's Daughters*.[161]

Second Circuit decisions confirm that "aesthetic functionality" excludes from trade dress protection only ornamentation necessary to competition because of an absence of alternatives. In *Warner Bros.*,[162] it upheld Warner's Section 43(a) claim that toy cars marketed by Gay Toys and patterned after the "General Lee" automobile featured in Warner's television series "The Dukes of Hazard" tended to confuse purchasers as to their source or sponsorship. It rejected Gay Toy's argument that the design of the car was functional because it was "essential to enable children to play 'Dukes of Hazzard' with the cars."[163]

---

[159] First Brands Corp. v. Fred Meyer Inc., 809 F.2d 1378, 1382 n.3, 1 U.S.P.Q72d 1779, 1781 n.3 (9th Cir. 1987) ("In this circuit, the 'aesthetic' functionality test has been limited . . . if not rejected . . . in favor of the 'utilitarian' functionality test."); *Cf.* Rachel v. Banana Republic Inc., 831 F.2d 1503, 1506, 4 U.S.P.Q.2d 1877, 1880 (9th Cir. 1987) ("A product feature is functional if it is essential to the product's use or it affects the cost and quality of the product."); Vuitton et Fils S.A. v. J. Young Enterprises, Inc., 644 F.2d 769, 212 U.S.P.Q. 85 (9th Cir. 1981).

[160] Vuitton et Fils S.A. v. J. Young Enterprises, Inc., 644 F.2d 769, 212 U.S.P.Q. 85 (9th Cir. 1981).

[161] International Order of Job's Daughters v. Lindeburg & Co., 633 F.2d 912, 918, 208 U.S.P.Q. 718 (9th Cir. 1980), *cert. denied,* 452 U.S. 941 (1980). In *Job's Daughters*, plaintiff registered its name and emblem as collective marks. Defendant without authority reproduced the name and emblem on fraternal jewelry. Relying on *Pagliero*, the court found no infringement because "the name and emblem are functional aesthetic components of the jewelry, in that they are being merchandised on the basis of their intrinsic value, not as a designation of origin or sponsorship." Consumers desired the jewelry with the name and emblem in order to show their allegiance to the organization, not because they believed that the organization was the origin or sponsored the jewelry.

[162] Warner Bros., Inc. v. Gay Toys, Inc., 724 F.2d 327 (2d Cir. 1983).

[163] The court noted:

"While there has been some confusing language in the case law, particularly that linking what is functional to the commercially successful features of a product, . . . an examination of the roots and purposes of the functionality doctrine suggests coherent limits to its use. . . .

"The functionality defense . . . was developed to protect advances in functional design from being monopolized. . . . It is designed to encourage competition and the broadest dissemination of useful design features. . . .

In *LeSportsac*,[164] the Second Circuit noted criticism of the "important ingredient" test: "Trade dress associated with a product that has accumulated goodwill . . . will almost always be 'an important ingredient' in the 'salability' of the product." It also acknowledged "an obvious tension" between *Warner* and another decision rendered by different panel of judges at about the same time, *I.A. Fratelli Saporiti*,[165] which held that plaintiff cannot claim an unregistered trademark in its sofa design with interlocking back cushions because the design was an important ingredient in the salability of the sofa and therefore functional. The *LeSportsac* panel reasoned that *I.A. Fratelli Saporiti* was consistent in its actual holding with *Warner* because the sofa design was the subject of an expired design patent and constituted an improvement in the operation of goods that ought not be monopolized except under the patent laws. The panel cautioned that "we do not suggest that [the 'important ingredient' formulation] cannot be appropriately applied in certain circumstances."[166]

In *Wallace International Silversmiths*,[167] the Second Circuit endorsed "the view that, where an ornamental feature is claimed as a trademark and trademark

---

"Rather than representing an advance in the useful arts, the ['General Lee'] symbols [such as the Confederate flag emblem and numbers in tandem with the color orange] merely function to enable consumers, especially children, to identify a toy car with a particular television series. . . .

". . . [O]nly functions which represent development of useful features, and not functions which serve merely to identify, are considered in determining functionality. . . .

"What then of the consumer motivation language of the cases? . . . The 'consumer motivation' language may have some more specific application where there is a concern over the assertion of exclusive rights in the shape of useful objects, . . . or when the symbol in question generates a 'generalized linkage' to a particular source, but the symbol's primary significance remains its independent aesthetic or utilitarian appeal. . . .

"The ultimate test for secondary meaning . . . is simply whether the term, symbol or device identifies goods of 'a particular source,' in which case it is protectable. If it does not identify goods with a particular source, it is not protectable. . . . [T]he true inquiry is whether the primary function of a particular design is other than referential, leading to association in the public mind with no one or nothing, or, by virtue of its distinctiveness, it is designed to create an association with a single source. In making that inquiry, the actual motivation of purchasing consumers—whether they were motivated because of quality, source, feature, design, price, durability, prestige, or otherwise—is essentially irrelevant. . . . Different people, for example, buy Rolls Royce automobiles for different reasons including combinations of the above factors, but the distinctive overlapping 'R's' symbol is nevertheless surely protectable. Irrespective of customer's motivations in making a purchase, they recognize and associate the symbol with the auto manufacturer." 724 F.2d at 330-32, 333-34.

[164] LeSportsac, Inc. v. K Mart Corp., 754 F.2d 71, 77, 225 U.S.P.Q. 654, 658 (2d Cir. 1985).

[165] I.A. Fratelli Saporiti v. Charles Craig, Ltd., 725 F.2d 18, 222 U.S.P.Q. 754 (2d Cir. 1984).

[166] 754 F.2d at 77, 225 U.S.P.Q. at 658.

[167] Wallace International Silversmiths, Inc. v. Godinger Silver Art Co., 916 F.2d 76, 16 U.S.P.Q. 1555 (2d Cir. 1990).

See also Coach Leatherware Co., Inc. v. Anntaylor, Inc., 933 F.2d 162, 171, 18 U.S.P.Q.2d 1907, 1914 (2d Cir. 1991) ("Lanham Act protection does not extend to configurations of ornamental features which would significantly limit the range of competitive designs available.").

protection would significantly hinder competition by limiting the range of adequate alternative designs, the aesthetic functionality doctrine denies such protection. . . . This rule avoids the overbreadth of *Pagliero* by requiring a finding of foreclosure of alternatives while still ensuring that trademark protection does not exclude competitors from substantial markets."[168]

In *Wallace*, plaintiff marketed for many years its "GRANDE BAROQUE" line of silverware, the ornamentation of which was "ornate, massive and flowery [with] indented, flowery roots and scrolls and curls along the side of the shaft." Defendant began marketing a cheaper line, "20TH CENTURY BAROQUE," which was not identical to plaintiff's "GRANDE BAROQUE" but had similar scrolls, flowers, curls, etc. Plaintiff sued for trade dress infringement. The district court granted defendant summary judgment, finding the designs "aesthetically functional" and citing *Pagliero*. The appeals court affirmed. It reiterated *LeSportsac's* criticism of *Pagliero* but confirmed that "the doctrine of functionality applies to features of a product that are purely ornamental but that are essential to effective competition."

> "Our only hesitation in holding that the functionality doctrine applies is based on nomenclature. 'Functionality' seems to us to imply only utilitarian considerations and, as a legal doctrine, to be intended only to prevent competitors from obtaining trademark protection for design features that are necessary to the use or efficient production of the product. . . . Even when the doctrine is referred to as 'aesthetic' functionality, it still seems an apt description only of pleasing designs of utilitarian features. Nevertheless, there is no lack of language in caselaw endorsing use of the defense of aesthetic functionality where trademark protection for purely ornamental features would exclude competitors from a market."[169]

Applying this test, plaintiff cannot prevail because it "seeks protection, not for a precise expression of a decorative style, but for basic elements of a style that is part of the public domain . . . [and] important to competition in the silverware market."[170] A different result would follow if a plaintiff showed secondary meaning in a design and the defendant used an identical or "virtually identical design" because there would be alternative designs available to competitors.

The line between "aesthetic" and "utilitarian" functionality is difficult to draw if the product is one that customers value as much for its appearance as for what it will do.[171]

---

[168] 916 F.2d at 81, 16 U.S.P.Q.2d at 1559.

[169] 916 F.2d at 80-81, 16 U.S.P.Q.2d at 1558-59.

[170] 916 F.2d at 81, 16 U.S.P.Q.2d at 1559.

[171] For example, what is the "utilitarian" as opposed to "aesthetic" functionality of a "realistic" reproduction of a jungle animal? *See* Rachel v. Banana Republic Inc., 831 F.2d 1503, 4 U.S.P.Q.2d 1877, 1879 (9th Cir. 1987) (affirming directed verdict that designs of plaintiff's jungle animals were functional) or of "tummy graphics" (a symbol of a particular emotion) on stuffed teddy bears? *See* American Greetings Corp. v. Dan-Dee Imports Inc., 807 F.2d 1136, 1 U.S.P.Q.2d 1001 (3d Cir. 1986) (functional in view of plaintiff's own advertising that the function of the symbols is to help persons express their feelings).

See also Brunswick Corp. v. Spinit Reel Co., 832 F.2d 513, 519, 4 U.S.P.Q.2d 1497, 1501 (10th Cir. 1987) ("Because a function of certain products is aesthetic appeal, a feature intrinsic to the aesthetic appeal of those products may not be entitled to trademark protection. . . .

(6) Compatibility. An interesting variation of the aesthetic functionality enigma is aesthetic compatibility: can a second entrant justify copying the design and ornamentation of the first entrant in a way that may cause confusion as to origin on the ground that customers demand such compatibility and will not buy products that differ in design even if the different design, as an original matter, is equally pleasing?

In *W.T. Rogers*,[172] the plaintiff sold molded plastic stacking office trays with hexagonal end panels. Defendant copied the panel design. In defense to plaintiff's claim of trade dress infringement, the defendant argued that, because of consumer demand for "decor compatibility," a second manufacturer must be able to copy the design of another in order to compete effectively. Judge Posner noted that the "premise of the argument is that a stack of trays with differently shaped ends would be ugly, so that even if each shape were perfectly arbitrary in relation to any use made of an office tray, and therefore nonfunctional, whatever shape the first manufacturer adopted would establish a norm from which other manufacturers could not depart with any hope of competitive success." He questioned the compatibility argument's applicability to the case's facts,[173] but "the biggest objection to the point about decor compatibility . . . is that it is an open Sesame to trademark infringement."

> "Suppose Mr. Keene owned a complete set of Meissen china, and one of the plates broke. He might care more about replacing it with a plate that looked exactly like the plate than about who made the plate; but it would not follow that someone could make exact duplicates of Meissen china for sale to people who care more about aesthetic compatibility than about source. A design feature to be aesthetically functional must be pleasing in itself; it is not enough that a person who owns two items with that feature wants a matched pair. Otherwise we might be forced to admit that General Motors can duplicate the Rolls Royce, because a person who had one Rolls Royce might think a second Rolls would look good next to it in his garage."[174]

A similar issue arises as to *functional* compatibility, as, for example, when a competitor produces parts or supplies for use with the product of another.[175]

Although the determination of functional in this setting may be difficult, the decision should nevertheless rest on whether alternative appealing designs or presentations of the product can be developed.").

[172] W.T. Rogers Co., Inc. v. Keene, 778 F.2d 334, 228 U.S.P.Q. 145 (7th Cir. 1985).

[173] Judge Posner noted that plaintiff was not the first maker of stacking office trays, that trays were inexpensive enough that customers might be willing to replace an entire stack or office supply if someone came along with a more elegant design, that trays wear out, and that new offices constantly open. Plaintiff "was able to enter the market successfully with a tray shaped differently from the then dominant rectangular shape; why should other producers have greater difficulty?" 778 F.2d at 343, 228 U.S.P.Q. at 150.

[174] 778 F.2d at 344, 228 U.S.P.Q. at 150.

[175] See Sicilia di R. Biebow & Co. v. Cox, 732 F.2d 417, 428 (5th Cir. 1984) (tear-on-pedestal shaped bottle for citrus juice; "We particularly reject the suggestion that the doctrine of functionality insulates a second comer from liability for copying the first comer's design whenever the second comer can merely cite marketing reasons to justify the copying. For example, function did not require the [accused] Pompeii bottle to share the same dimensions as the [protected] Sicilia bottle, nor did merchandising or competitive considerations

By the weight of authority, functionality is a defense to be proved by the accused copier rather than an element of the Section 43(a) claimant's case in chief.[176]

(7) *Pharmaceutical Products—Capsules.* A series of cases deals with generic drug manufacturers' copying of the size, shape, and coloring of pharmaceutical products, such as drug capsules, sold under other drug manufacturers's trademarks.[177] One capsule case made its way up to the Supreme Court, but unfortunately, the Court focused on the narrow issue of the scope of review of a trial court's findings on contributory infringement and did not squarely address substantive trade dress protection standards.

In *Ives Laboratory*,[178] plaintiff developed, patented, and sold a drug under the registered trademark "Cyclospasmol." Plaintiff packaged the drug in 200 mg. pale blue capsules and 400 mg. red-and-blue capsules. After plaintiff's patent expired, defendant began selling a competing (generic) product in identically colored capsules. The plaintiff sought to enjoin defendant's use of the colors, relying on three grounds:

---

require [the defendants] to adopt Sicilita's pedestal base so that Pompeii bottles would fit into Sicilia trays or racks.").

Compare New England Butt Co. v. International Trade Commission, 756 F.2d 874, 879, 225 U.S.P.Q. 260, 263 (Fed. Cir. 1985) (Commission did not err in finding that an importer of maypole-type braiding machines was under a "competitive necessity to copy" the petitioner's machine design because the importer's customers "insisted that their respective machine's parts be interchangeable with those of [petitioner]."); John H. Harland Co. v. Clarke Checks, Inc., 711 F.2d 966, 984 n.31, 219 U.S.P.Q. 515, 531 n.31 (11th Cir. 1983) (trade dress of checkbook combining desk-style checkbook with intermediate carry-around stubs and accompanying carrying case; the carry-around stub's vertical size is an industry standard and therefore could not acquire secondary meaning; the stub's horizontal size is functional even though the defendant could vary it without affecting its utility or production costs; "check companies routinely fill reorders from consumers who initially had obtained their check products from a competitor. It would be very inefficient if each such reorder for desk-style checkbook checks with carry-around stubs had to include a new carry-around case, and possibly even a new desk-style checkbook, in order to accommodate the different-sized carry-around stubs.").

A comparable issue arises with copyright protection for computer software and other utility works. *See* § 4C[2][d][iv].

[176] Rachel v. Banana Republic Inc., 831 F.2d 1503, 1506, 4 U.S.P.Q.2d 1877, 1880 (9th Cir. 1987); Brunswick Corp. v. Spinit Reel Co., 832 F.2d 513, 520, 4 U.S.P.Q.2d 1497, 1501 (10th Cir. 1987); LeSportsac, Inc. v. K Mart Corp., 754 F.2d 71, 225 U.S.P.Q. 654 (2d Cir. 1985).

[177] *E.g.*, Ciba-Geigy Corp. v. Bolar Pharmaceutical Co., Inc., 747 F.2d 844, 224 U.S.P.Q. 349 (3d Cir. 1984), *cert. denied*, 471 U.S. 1137 (1985), discussed below. *Cf.* Ross-Whitney Corp. v. Smith Kline & French Labs., 207 F.2d 190, 99 U.S.P.Q. 1 (9th Cir. 1953) (orange, heart-shaped tablets protected). *Compare In re* American Home Products Corp., 226 U.S.P.Q. 327 (PTO TTAB 1985) (allowing registration of tri-colored analgesic table where the colors were nonfunctional) with *In re* Star Pharmaceuticals, Inc., 225 U.S.P.Q. 209 (PTO TTAB 1985) (denying registration of colored drug capsule for lack of distinctiveness).

See also First Brands Corp. v. Fred Meyer Inc., 809 F.2d 1378, 1383 n.4, 1 U.S.P.Q.2d 1779, 1781 n.4 (9th Cir. 1987) (distinguishing "pharmaceutical drug cases"; "background color is afforded stronger protection in drug cases because confusion of source or product can have disastrous consequences").

[178] Ives Laboratory, Inc. v. Darby Drug Co., 601 F.2d 631, 202 U.S.P.Q. 548 (2d Cir. 1979).

"(1) as contributory infringements in violation of the Lanham Act . . . in that the similarity encouraged retail druggists to use Ives' mark . . . in selling capsules not manufactured by it; (2) as a 'false designation of origin, or any false description or representation, including words or other symbols tending falsely to describe or represent' the goods sold by defendants in violation of § 43(a) of the Lanham Act . . . (3) as unfair competition under New York common and statutory law. . . . "[179] The Second Circuit affirmed the district court's denial of a preliminary injunction for want of sufficient evidence and as an exercise of discretion but did not view *Sears-Compco* as any "insurmountable barrier" to relief: "nothing in the *Sears* and *Compco* opinions suggests that the Court was aiming shafts at Congress, and it would be hard to argue that the time limitation on the power of Congress to protect 'writings and discoveries limits its power under the commerce clause to protect trademarks or other symbols of origin." There was "no basis in principle for saying that simply because the colored capsule is ingested the color cannot constitute 'trade dress.' "[180]

After trial in *Ives Laboratory*, the district court found insufficient evidence of "passing off" to establish a Section 32 claim. It dismissed the Section 43(a) trade dress claim on the ground that the drug capsule colors were functional.[181]

> "First, many elderly patients associate the appearance of their medication with its therapeutic effect. . . . Thus color is an important ingredient in the commercial success of the product. Second, some patients co-mingle their drugs in a single container and then rely on the appearance of the drug to follow their doctors' instructions. . . . Third, to some limited extent color is also useful to doctors and hospital emergency rooms in identifying overdoses of drugs."[182]

On appeal, the Second Circuit reversed,[183] finding contributory infringement under Lanham Act Section 32 in that defendants' "use of identically-colored, look-alike drug capsules assisted druggists in labeling generic cyclandelate as Ives' trademarked product cyclospasmol." It found no evidence supporting defendants' arguments concerning functionality.

The Supreme Court granted certiorari, reversed the Second Circuit's decision on contributory infringement as contrary to the "clearly erroneous" trial court fact finding appellate review standard, and remanded the Section 43(a) claim to the Second Circuit for review.[184] The Court's opinion primarily concerns the appellate review

---

[179] 601 F.2d at 635.

[180] 601 F.2d at 644.

[181] Ives Laboratories, Inc. v. Darby Drug Co., 488 F. Supp. 394, 206 U.S.P.Q. 238 (E.D. N.Y. 1980), *rev'd*, 638 F.2d 538, 209 U.S.P.Q. 449 (2d Cir. 1981), *rev'd and remanded sub nom.* Inwood Laboratories, Inc. v. Ives Laboratories, Inc., 456 U.S. 844, 214 U.S.P.Q. 1 (1982).
    [182] 488 F. Supp. at 399.

[183] Ives Laboratories, Inc. v. Darby Drug Co., 638 F.2d 538, 209 U.S.P.Q. 449 (2d Cir. 1981), *rev'd and remanded sub nom.* Inwood Laboratories, Inc. v. Ives Laboratories, Inc., 456 U.S. 844, 214 U.S.P.Q. 1 (1982).

[184] Inwood Laboratories, Inc. v. Ives Laboratories, Inc., 456 U.S. 844, 214 U.S.P.Q. 1 (1982). On remand, the Second Circuit affirmed the district court's findings on the absence of a Section 43(a) violation in an unpublished opinion. Ives Laboratories Inc. v. Darby Drug Co., Inc., 697 F.2d 291 (2d Cir. 1982).

standard, but some language suggests the Court's acceptance of the emerging view that Section § 43(a) prohibits copying nonfunctional design features that have acquired a secondary meaning but does not prohibit copying functional features. In a footnote, the Court defined functionality ("In general terms, a product feature is functional if it is essential to the use or purpose of the article or if it affects the cost or quality of the article") and secondary meaning ("To establish secondary meaning, a manufacturer must show that, in the minds of the public, the primary significance of a product feature or term is to identify the source of the product rather than the product itself"), citing *Kellogg* and *Sears*. The Second Circuit "was not entitled simply to disregard the District Court's finding of functionality."

> "When the doctrine of functionality is most directly related to the question of whether a defendant has violated § 43(a) of the Lanham Act . . . a finding of functionality may also be relevant to an action involving § 32. By establishing to the District Court's satisfaction that uniform capsule colors served a functional purpose, the petitioners offered a legitimate reason for producing an imitative product."[185]

In *Ciba-Geigy*,[186] a drug manufacturer had greater success in protecting capsule trade dress. Plaintiff patented hydrazaline hydrochloride/hydrochlorothiazide, an antihypertensive drug, and sold it in 25mg and 50mg capsules under the trademark "APRESAZIDE." After the patent expired, defendant introduced a generic equivalent and adopted plaintiff's capsules' size, shape and color. The Third Circuit held this copying was unprivileged imitation under both New Jersey unfair competition law and Section 43(a) of the Lanham Act because the dress of the capsules was nonfunctional, had acquired secondary meaning, and caused a likelihood of confusion as to origin. As to functionality, the district court found no medical or business reasons compelling adoption of the same capsule dress; another company successfully marketed the same drug using a different color. As to secondary meaning, the district court did not err in finding the capsules' dress distinctive of a single manufacturer given that (1) the plaintiff was the product's exclusive seller for more than five years; (2) "APRESAZIDE" is a registered trademark; (3) plaintiff extensively advertised the product; (4) defendant copied the product's trade dress exactly; and (5) defendant's purpose for copying was to increase its products' sales at plaintiff's expense.

[vi] *Architectural and Interior Designs—Restaurant Themes.* An architectural feature or even the overall design of a building's exterior or interior may serve to indicate the origin or goods or services.[187] As with other two- and three-dimensional

---

[185] 456 U.S. at 857.

[186] Ciba-Geigy Corp. v. Bolar Pharmaceutical Co., Inc., 747 F.2d 844, 224 U.S.P.Q. 349 (3d Cir. 1984), *cert. denied,* 471 U.S. 1137 (1985).

[187] For example, a golden arch rising next to a restaurant building indicates to a vast percentage of the population that the restaurant is part of the McDonald's fast food chain. Not surprisingly, McDonald's registered a building design with golden arches integrated therein. Reg. No. 764,837. *See* McDonald's Corp. v. Moore, 243 F. Supp. 255, 146 U.S.P.Q. 434 (S.D. Ala. 1965), *aff'd,* 363 F.2d 435, 150 U.S.P.Q. 488 (5th Cir. 1965). For a reproduction of the McDonald's trademark design, see J. T. McCarthy, Trademarks and Unfair Competition § 7:34 (2d ed. 1984).

For a discussion of copyright protection for architectural works, see § 4C[3][f].

design marks, the major obstacles to obtaining trademark rights are lack of distinctiveness and functionality.[188]

A number of decisions deal with attempts to protect a restaurant's total design and style.[189] In *Fuddruckers*,[190] the Ninth Circuit agreed that "a restaurant's decor, menu, layout and style of service may acquire the source-distinguishing aspects of protectable trade dress that their imitation is likely to cause consumer confusion." After failing to obtain a franchise from Fuddrucker's, a national chain of "upscale" hamburger restaurants, the defendants opened a restaurant ("Doc's B. R. Others") in the Phoenix, Arizona area. Shortly thereafter, Fuddrucker's also opened a restaurant in Phoenix. Fuddruckers sued, seeking to recover for Section 43(a) trade dress infringement. Fuddruckers appealed a judgment based on a jury verdict for Doc's, which found the absence of secondary meaning in the Phoenix area and of any likelihood of confusion. The nature of Fuddruckers's trade dress claim can be gleaned from the Ninth Circuit's description of the two restaurants:

---

[188] Two cases involved the Fotomat "hut" for drive-in photo finishing, which graced America's parking lots for many years. *Compare* Fotomat Corp. v. Photo Drive-Thru, Inc., 425 F. Supp. 693, 706, 193 U.S.P.Q. 343 (D.N.J. 1977) with Fotomat Corp. v. Cochran, 437 F. Supp. 1231, 194 U.S.P.Q. 128 (D. Kan. 1977). In *Photo Drive-Thru*, the New Jersey district court held that some elements of the Fotomat structure were functional "as an efficient drive-in retail outlet for photographic supplies." Other elements were non-functional. The non-functional elements were not infringed by the defendant's structure due to the absence of a likelihood of confusion; the defendant added "significant embellishments of a nonfunctional character which distinguish its design from that of Fotomat." In *Cochran*, the Kansas court held that the Fotomat hut roof structure was distinctive, the hut configuration was only incidentally functional and the Fotomat hut was infringed by a different defendant's hut, which had a roof structure similar to Fotomat's.

[189] *See* Prufrock, Ltd. v. Lasater, 781 F.2d 129, 134, 228 U.S.P.Q. 435, 438-39 (8th Cir. 1986) (aesthetic functionality doctrine precludes protection of so much of plaintiff's trade dress as relates to its "down home country cooking" concept; "Elements of the trade dress which do not relate to the concept or theme of the restaurant or which do not enhance consumer appeal for the food . . . may be capable of protection under the Lanham Act. . . . However, any element of a restaurant's trade dress that advances the concept cannot be protected because those elements are related to the consumer demand for the concept. . . . If a trade dress that creates a chosen theme or concept could be protected then others who wished to use the same concept would be severely limited in their ability to do so. Indeed, by protecting the trade dress that creates the concept, this court would be protecting the concept itself."); Shakey's, Inc. v. Covalt, 704 F.2d 426, 218 U.S.P.Q. 16 (9th Cir. 1983) (after terminating their franchise with the plaintiff, a national pizza chain, defendants continued to operate their restaurant under independent names; plaintiff's claim for infringement of its unregistered marks consisting of its slogan and menu names and for unfair competition failed because of insufficient evidence of likelihood of confusion); Warehouse Restaurant, Inc. v. Customs House Restaurant, Inc., 217 U.S.P.Q. 411 (N.D. Calif. 1982) (defendant's imitation of plaintiff's distinctive interior decor feature of dining booths encased in packing crates violates Section 43(a).

The problem posed in the restaurant decor unfair competition cases is analogous to that in "look and feel" computer software copyright cases. *See* § 4C[2][d][ii].

[190] Fuddruckers Inc. v. Doc's B.R. Others Inc., 826 F.2d 837, 841, 4 U.S.P.Q.2d 1026, 1028 (9th Cir. 1987).

"The heart of Fuddruckers' design concept is that its food preparation areas are visible to its customers. . . . Various food items are presented in glassed-in display cases. Another important facet of Fuddruckers' claimed trade dress is that various food items are kept in bulk in the main part of the establishment in both packaged and unpackaged forms . . .

"The most important non-food design elements at Fuddruckers are ubiquitous two-by-four white tiles found on the walls, the bar, and the counters. Fuddruckers also uses neon signs, many mirrors, brown and white checked flooring and tablecloths, brown director's chairs, and exterior yellow awnings.

"In addition to these visual items, Fuddruckers uses a number of devices that it considers part of its trade dress. Its bakery area is labeled 'Mother Fuddruckers.' It uses its ceiling music system to call patrons when their orders are ready. It offers a restaurant 'newspaper' to patrons at each table. Customers are allowed to buy bones for their dogs, with the proceeds going to animal shelters. There are several other less important design elements and devices that Fuddruckers also claims to be part of its trade dress.

. . . .

"Doc's has many interior features like those of Fuddruckers. . . . The major food preparation areas are exposed and look similar to Fuddruckers. The same shape and brand of ubiquitous white tile can be found around Doc's. Doc's also uses neon, mirrors, and director's chairs. Doc's has a newspaper like Fuddruckers, calls its bakery 'Mother Other's,' and sold dog bones for a time. A number of witnesses testified that they thought the restaurants looked very much alike and the photographs in evidence support this conclusion."[191]

The Ninth Circuit reversed the jury verdict finding against Fuddrucker's trade dress infringement claim because of error in the instructions. It noted that the evidence would not support a finding that the trade dress was inherently distinctive such as might dispense with the necessity of showing secondary meaning: "Fuddruckers claims trade dress protection for the impression created by a collection of common or functional elements of restaurant decor. Such an overall impression may receive protection, but it is simply not the sort of arbitrary or uncommon trade dress that might qualify as inherently distinctive."[192] It also refused to hold that "evidence of deliberate copying shifts the burden of proof on the issue of secondary meaning."[193]

[d] **Exclusions.** Lanham Act Section 2's first three subsections exclude certain marks from registration for policy reasons. These bars provide grounds not only for refusal to register a mark but also for a registration cancellation at any time. This contrasts with the Section 2(d) (likelihood of confusion with a mark or tradename previously registered or used) and Section 2(e) (descriptiveness) grounds, which provide a basis for cancellation only during the first five years after the mark's registration.

---

[191] 826 F.2d at 839-40, 4 U.S.P.Q.2d at 1027-28.
[192] 826 F.2d at 844, 4 U.S.P.Q.2d at 1031.
[193] 826 F.2d at 844, 4 U.S.P.Q.2d at 1032.

[i] *Immoral or Scandalous Matter.* Subsection 2(a) disqualifies any mark that "[c]onsists of or comprises immoral . . . scandalous matter."[194]

In *McGinley,*[195] the court held that a mark comprising "a photograph of a nude man and woman kissing and embracing in a manner appearing to expose the male genitalia," which the applicant sought to register for "Social Club" services, was "scandalous." The court applied the "ordinary and common meaning" of the term "scandalous," as reflected in dictionaries that were in existence on the Lanham Act's enactment date. A mark is scandalous if it is shocking to the sense of propriety, gives offense to the conscience or moral feelings or calls out for condemnation. The scandalous character of a mark is to be determined (1) "in the context of the market-place as applied to only the goods or services described in the application for registration"; and (2) "from the standpoint of not necessarily a majority, but a substantial composite of the general public."[196] Noting the "dearth of reported trademark decisions in which the term 'immoral' has been directly applied,"[197] the court did not determine whether the mark consisted of "immoral matter."

A mark is scandalous or immoral if it refers inappropriately to religion, especially if the mark is for goods that do not comport with religious tenets.[198]

---

[194] 15 U.S.C. § 1052(a).

As to who has standing to file an opposition or cancellation petition on the grounds of the mark's scandalous or immoral nature, see Bromberg v. Carmel Self Service, Inc., 198 U.S.P.Q. 176 (PTO TTAB 1978). In *Bromberg,* the applicant sought to register "ONLY A BREAST IN THE MOUTH IS BETTER THAN A LEG IN THE HAND" for restaurant services. The Board granted standing to petitioner, a woman, to oppose as an individual but denied standing to oppose on behalf of a class composed of women. Later, the mark was successfully opposed by the owner of the registered marks "PUT A LEG IN YOUR HAND" and "A LEG IN YOUR HAND WILL PUT A SMILE ON YOUR FACE." Golden Skillet Corp. v. Carmel Self Service, Inc. 201 U.S.P.Q. 790 (PTO TTAB 1979).

[195] *In re* McGinley, 660 F.2d 481, 211 U.S.P.Q. 668 (CCPA 1981). *See also* Greyhound Corp. v. Both Worlds, Inc., 6 U.S.P.Q.2d 1635 (TTAB 1988) (design mark depicting a defecating dog is immoral or scandalous mark; the applicant's argument that the mark is not scandalous because it is satirical commentary on the silliness of designer clothing labels loses force because many people who would not appreciate the satire would see the mark); *In re* Tinseltown, Inc., 212 U.S.P.Q. 863 (TTAB 1981) ("BULLSHIT" for accessories denied registration despite argument that mark was a satire on designer labelling of products); *In re* Runsdorf, 171 U.S.P.Q. 443 (PO TTAB 1971) ("BOOBY TRAP" for brassieres).

Compare In re Hershey 6 U.S.P.Q.2d 1470, 1471 (TTAB 1988), (mark "BIG PECKER BRAND" with "BRAND" disclaimed for T-shirts not scandalous or immoral; evidence cited by the examiner of public association of "pecker" with male genitalia, including slang dictionaries, and articles from publications such as Playboy, Medical Economics, Financial Times and Newsweek was insufficient to establish such an association; the "primary meaning" of "pecker"—a bird's beak—is not scandalous; the specimen submitted with the mark reinforced the primary definition by use of a bird head design).

[196] 660 F.2d at 485.

[197] 660 F.2d at 485 n.6.

[198] *E.g., In re* Riverbank Canning Co., 95 F.2d 327 (CCPA 1938) ("MADONNA" for wine is immoral). *Compare In re* Waughtel, 138 U.S.P.Q. 594 (TTAB 1963) ("AMISH" for cigars is not immoral or scandalous).

The United States Constitution's First Amendment, which prohibits government interference with freedom of expression, does not guarantee a right to register an immoral or scandalous mark even though the subject matter of the mark is not obscene under First Amendment standards.[199]

[ii] *Disparagement—False Connection.* Subsection 2(a) disqualifies any mark that "[c]onsists of or comprises . . . matter which may disparage or falsely suggest a connection with persons, living or dead, institutions, beliefs, or national symbols, or bring them into contempt or disrepute."[200] "Persons" includes corporations as well as natural persons.[201] "Institution" includes fraternal and professional organizations and universities.[202]

In *University of Notre Dame du Lac*,[203] the court held that an applicant's use of "Notre Dame" as a mark for cheese does not "falsely suggest a connection with . . . [the] institution" of the University of Notre Dame. It considered two ways the use might falsely suggest a connection with the university, one predicated on the university's prior use of "Notre Dame" on particular goods or services and one not so predicated. The court held that a finding that the applicant's mark did not create a likelihood of confusion within the meaning of Section 2(d) necessarily precluded any finding of false connection based on the university's prior use. Adoption of Section 2(d)'s confusion standard as the sole test for Section 2(a)'s false connection suggestion test would nullify the deliberate omission of Section 2(d) from the Section 14 unlimited cancellation grounds. Second, the use might create a false suggestion of a connection with the university as an institution not predicated on the university's prior use of "Notre Dame" on goods or services. Section 2(a) creates a bar only if the university could establish "a legally cognizable right with which [the] registration would conflict" other than the right to be free of confusion as to the source of goods or services. Section 2(a)'s drafters "sought . . . to embrace concepts of the right of privacy."[204]

> "Under concepts of the protection of one's 'identity,' in any of the forms which have so far been recognized, the initial and critical requirement is that the name (or an equivalent thereof) claimed to be appropriated by another must be unmistakenly associated with a particularly personality or 'persona.' . . . [T]o

---

[199] *In re* McKinley, 660 F.2d 481, 211 U.S.P.Q. 668 (CCPA 1981). *Cf.* Friedman v. Rogers, 490 U.S. 887 (1979), discussed at § 1D[4] (a state does not violate the First Amendment by prohibiting persons from doing business under a trademark or tradename).

[200] 15 U.S.C. § 1052(a).

As to what is a "national symbol," see National Aeronautics and Space Administration v. Bully Hill Vineyards Inc., 3 U.S.P.Q.2d 1671 (PTO TTAB 1987) ("SPACE SHUTTLE" *per se* not a national symbol).

[201] Morehouse Manufacturing Corp. v. J. Strickland & Co., 407 F.2d 881, 160 U.S.P.Q. 715 (CCPA 1969).

[202] *E.g.,* Gavel Club v. Toastmasters International, 127 U.S.P.Q. 88 (PTO TTAB 1960) (fraternal organization); Frederick Gash, Inc. v. Mayo Clinic, 461 F.2d 1395, 174 U.S.P.Q. 151 (CCPA 1972) (professional organization).

[203] University of Notre Dame du Lac v. J.C. Gourmet Good Imports Co., Inc., 703 F.2d 1372, 217 U.S.P.Q. 505 (Fed. Cir. 1983).

[204] 703 F.2d at 1376, 217 U.S.P.Q. at 509. For a discussion of publicity rights, see § 6G.

show an invasion of one's 'persona,' it is not sufficient to show merely prior identification with the name adopted by another. . . . The mark NOTRE DAME, as used by [the applicant], must point uniquely to the University."[205]

The applicant's mark did not meet this standard because "Notre Dame" is not solely associated with the University.[206]

A mark disparages a person or institution if (1) the public readily perceives the mark as referring to that person or institution, and (2) a reasonable person of ordinary sensibilities considers the mark offensive or objectionable.[207]

[iii] *Deceptive Matter.* Subsection (a) disqualifies any mark that "[c]onsists of or comprises . . . deceptive . . . matter."[208]

An important issue is how to differentiate among (1) "deceptive" matter, which subsection 2(a) *absolutely* bars from registration, (2) "deceptively misdescriptive" and "geographically . . . deceptively misdescriptive" matter, which subsection 2(e) only *conditionally* bars from registration,[209] and (3) matter that is misdescriptive but not deceptively so, which Section 2 *does not* bar from registration. Many cases

[205] 703 F.2d at 1367-77, 217 U.S.P.Q. at 509.

[206] *See also* National Aeronautics and Space Administration v. Bully Hill Vineyards Inc., 3 U.S.P.Q.2d 1671 (PTO TTAB 1987) ("SPACE SHUTTLE" for wines does not falsely suggest a connection with NASA; the mark is arbitrary for wine but generic for a reusable spacecraft, especially craft comprising an orbiter, two solid rocket boosters and an external tank; "where opposer's claimed mark is generic, it cannot point uniquely and unmistakably to any one entity"); U.S. Navy v. United States Manufacturing Co., 2 U.S.P.Q.2d 1254 (PTO TTAB 1987) ("USMC" for orthopedic braces does not falsely suggest a connection with the U.S. Marine Corps); Buffett v. Chi-Chi's, Inc., 226 U.S.P.Q. 428 (PTO TTAB 1985) ("MAR-GARITAVILLE" for restaurant services does not falsely suggest a connection with the opposer, a singer and composer of a song that describes opposer as "Wastin' away in Margaritaville").

Compare In re Cotter, 228 U.S.P.Q. 202 (PTO TTAB 1985) ("WESTPOINT" on firearms falsely suggests a connection with the United States Military Academy).

[207] *E.g.,* Greyhound Corp. v. Both Worlds, Inc., 6 U.S.P.Q..2d 1635 (TTAB 1988) (design mark depicting a defecating dog disparages opposer, a bus company, because the public would perceive the mark as opposer's familiar running dog in the act of defecating).

Compare In re In Over Our Heads Inc., 16 U.S.P.Q.2d 1653 (TTAB 1990). In *In Over Our Heads*, the Board held that "MOONIES" in a design did not comprise scandalous matter that disparages the Unification Church founded by the Reverend Sun Myung Moon. The two "O's" in Moonies were "caricatures of naked buttocks," and the mark was used on dolls "which drop their pants when a collapsible bulb is squeezed."

"[T]here are dictionary definitions . . . which show that the term 'Moonie(s)' refers, in one sense, to a member of the Unification Church. However, there are also dictionary listings of record showing that the term 'moon' means to expose one's buttocks. . . . We believe that applicant's mark MOONIES—with its naked buttocks design and spelled without emphasizing the letter 'm'—would, when used on a doll, most likely be perceived as indicating that the doll 'moons' and would not be perceived as referencing members of the Unification Church." 16 U.S.P.Q.2d at 1654.

[208] 15 U.S.C. § 1052(a).

[209] A user may register a deceptively misdescriptive mark by showing secondary meaning. 15 U.S.C. § 1052(f). *See* § 5C[3][a].

involving allegedly deceptive or deceptively misdescriptive marks involve geographic terms on goods or services that do not come from the geographic area described or suggested.

Subsection 2(e)'s conditional bar requires that the matter be not only misdescriptive but deceptively so. The matter must misdescribe the goods or services to an extent that someone is likely to believe the misrepresentation.[210]

Some cases suggest that the test for deceptiveness under Section 2(a), unlike that for deceptive misdescriptiveness under Section 2(e), depends upon the user's intent.[211] But commentators and later case authorities focus on the materiality of the misdescription to the purchase decision. Is the misrepresentation likely to affect the decision to purchase the goods? If so, it is "deceptive" rather than merely "deceptively misdescriptive?"[212] Materiality may be inferred from facts. For example, evidence that the

[210] E.g., In re Quady Winery Inc., 221 U.S.P.Q. 1213, 1214 (PTO TTAB 1984) ("First we must determine if the matter . . . misdescribes the goods. If so, then we must ask if it is also deceptive, that is, if anyone is likely to believe the misrepresentation. . . . ESSENSIA" is deceptively misdescriptive for domestic muscat wines because the word indicates a rare type of Hungarian Tokay wine; "The fact that there may be a relatively small number of prospective purchasers who are knowledgeable of the original essensia is not determinative. Even if the group would not be large, it is still the proper universe for our consideration". Knowledgeable buyers "would probably assume either that applicant's wine contains a small amount of essensia for flavoring . . . or . . . represents a domestic attempt to duplicate the foreign product. . . . Even less knowledgeable wine buyers are likely to believe the misrepresentation, since . . . reference works to which potential purchasers could refer note that essensia is a very desirable Hungarian wine.")

See also In re Woodward & Lothrop Inc., 4 U.S.P.Q.2d 1412 (PTO TTAB 1987) (design mark "CAMEO" for jewelry is misdescriptive because the dictionary definition of "cameo" is a two-layered stone and the applicant's jewelry contained no such cameo; the mark is deceptively misdescriptive despite applicant's argument that a reasonably informed consumer would determine that the jewelry was not cameo and that the test should not apply to a "class of 'ignorant' purchasers who do not know what cameos look like"; the jewelry might be sold by catalog or other advertising with an inadequate depiction).

Compare In re Automatic Radio Mfg. Co., 404 F.2d 1391, 160 U.S.P.Q. 233 (CCPA 1969) ("AUTOMATIC RADIO" on air conditioners and antennas not deceptively misdescriptive).

[211] E.g., In re Amerise, 160 U.S.P.Q. 687 (TTAB 1969) ("a mark consisting of or comprising a geographic term is not deceptive under Section 2(a) unless it involves a false assertion calculated, either planned, designed or implied to deceive the public as to the geographic origin of the goods bearing the mark. . . . [I]ntent can and has been inferred . . . where a geographical area or place is well known for the particular product as France for perfumes, Denmark for cheese, Switzerland for watches, and so forth").

[212] In re House of Windsor, Inc., 221 U.S.P.Q. 53 (TTAB 1983); Germain, Trademark Registration under Sections 2(a) and 2(e) of the Lanham Act: The Deception Decision, 44 Fordham L. Rev. 249 (1975); Leeds, Trademarks: The Rationale of Registrability, 26 Geo. Wash. L. Rev 653 (1958).

Cf. Gold Seal Co. v. Weeks, 129 F. Supp. 928, 105 U.S.P.Q. 407 (D.D.C. 1955), aff'd, 230 F.2d 832, 108 U.S.P.Q. 400 (D.C. Cir.), cert. denied, 352 U.S. 829, 111 U.S.P.Q. 467 (1956) ("GLASS WAX" for a metal and glass cleaner that contained no wax was deceptively misdescriptive but was not deceptive because the public would not likely be influenced to buy the product by a belief that it contained wax).

area named by the mark has, as one of its principal products, the applicant's goods supports an inference that the misrepresentation is material.[213]

[*iv*] *Government Insignia.* Subsection (b) disqualifies any mark that "[c]onsists of or comprises the flag or coat of arms or other insignia of the United States, or of any State or municipality, or of any foreign nation, or any simulation thereof."[214]

[*v*] *Names, Portraits and Signatures.* Subsection (c) disqualifies any mark that "[c]onsists of or comprises a name, portrait, or signature identifying a particular living individual except by his written consent, or the name, signature, or portrait of a deceased President of the United States during the life of his widow, if any, except by the written consent of the widow."[215]

The test of when a mark identifies a "particular" individual is "whether the particular individual bearing the name in question will be associated with the mark as used on the goods, either because that person is so well known that the public would reasonably assume the connection or because the individual is publicly connected with the business in which the mark is used."[216]

[3] Distinctiveness

A mark qualifies for registration and protection only if it is distinctive, that is, it distinguishes the mark user's goods or services from those of others.

The courts classify marks into four categories in terms of their relative distinctiveness.[217] In an ascending order of distinctiveness, and hence of relative protectability,

---

[213] *E.g., In re* House of Windsor, Inc., 221 U.S.P.Q. 53 (PTO TTAB 1983) ("BAHIA" for cigars is deceptive because cigars and tobacco are principal products of Brazil's Bahia province).

[214] *See* Vuitton et Fils S.A. v. J. Young Enterprises, Inc., 644 F.2d 769, 775, 212 U.S.P.Q. 85 (9th Cir. 1981) (a symbol resembling fleur-de-lis is not an insignia of France; "the fleur-de-lis is a traditional symbol of royalty rather than an 'insignia' of France . . . The term 'national insignia' . . . is restricted to the official symbols of a government. The reign of French royalty ended over a century ago. Furthermore, Vuitton's design was only in part inspired by the fleur-de-lis."); Liberty Mut. Ins. Co. v. Liberty Ins. Co., 185 F. Supp. 895, 127 U.S.P.Q. 312 (E.D. Ark. 1960) (representation of Statue of Liberty is not an "insignia of the United States"); U.S. Navy v. United States Manufacturing Co., 2 U.S.P.Q.2d 1254 (PTO TTAB 1987) ("USMC" is not a national symbol though it is the initials of the Marine Corps; "other insignia of the United States" includes "only insignia of the same general class as the flag or coats of arms of the United States.).

[215] 15 U.S.C. § 1052.

[216] Martin v. Carter Hawley Hale Stores, Inc., 206 U.S.P.Q. 931 (PTO TTAB 1979).

[217] For discussions of the four categories—and the difficulties encountered in placing particular marks into them, see 20th Century Wear, Inc. v. Sanmark-Stardust Inc., 747 F.2d 81, 87, 224 U.S.P.Q. 98, 101 (2d Cir. 1984) ("This determination . . . turns upon the particular context of the mark's use, the context of its time of use, and the context of its group of users. . . . Making such a determination—pigeonholing or labeling—has always been a slippery business, as Cardozo reminded us so many times."); Zatarains, Inc. v. Oak Grove Smokehouse, Inc., 698 F.2d 786, 790, 217 U.S.P.Q. 988, 993 (5th Cir. 1983) ("These categories, like the tones in a spectrum, tend to blur at the edges and merge together. The labels are more advisory than definitional, more like guidelines than pigeonholes."); Abercrombie & Fitch Co. v. Hunting World, Inc., 537 F.2d 4, 9, 189 U.S.P.Q. 759 (2d Cir. 1976) ("The lines of demarcation . . . are not always bright.").

the four categories are: (1) generic marks, which receive no protection, (2) descriptive marks, including surnames and geographically descriptive marks, which receive protection only upon a special showing of distinctiveness, to wit, that the mark has acquired "secondary meaning," (3) suggestive marks, which receive weak protection, and (4) arbitrary and fanciful marks, which receive strong protection.[218]

A mark's classification depends on the relationship between the mark and the goods or services upon which it is used. The same mark may be in one category as to one type of good but in another as to another type of good.[219]

A mark's distinctiveness may change due to shifts in usage.[220] A given mark may fit into one category for one user group but into another for another user group.[221]

In *Abercrombie & Fitch*,[222] Abercrombie & Fitch, a retail sporting goods store, sued Hunting World for infringement of its mark "Safari," which it registered for various classes of garments and sporting goods. The court held "Safari" was (1) generic as applied to some goods, such as broad flat-brimmed hats with a single, large band

---

[218] A fanciful term is one invented solely for use as a trademark, for example, "Exxon" for petroleum services. An arbitrary term is a common word used in an unfamiliar way, for example, "Apple" for computers. *See* Abercrombie & Fitch Co. v. Hunting World, Inc., 537 F.2d 4, 11 & n.12, 189 U.S.P.Q. 759 (2d Cir. 1976) ("fanciful or arbitrary terms enjoy all the rights accorded to suggestive terms as marks—without the need of debating whether the term is 'merely descriptive' and with ease of establishing infringement. . . . As terms of art, the distinctions between suggestive terms and fanciful or arbitrary terms may seem needlessly artificial. Of course, a common word may be used in a fanciful sense; indeed one might say that only a common word can be so used, since a coined word cannot first be put to a bizarre use. Nevertheless, the term 'fanciful,' as a classifying concept is usually applied to words invented solely for their use as trademarks. When the same legal consequences attach to a common word, i.e., when it is applied in an unfamiliar way, the use is called 'arbitrary.' ").

[219] *See* Abercrombie & Fitch Co. v. Hunting World, Inc., 537 F.2d 4 (2d Cir. 1976), discussed below.

[220] *E.g.*, Haughton Elevator Co. v. Seeberger, 85 U.S.P.Q. 80 (1950) ("elevator," originally fanciful or suggestive, became generic).
See also Thompson Medical Co., Inc. v. Pfizer, 753 F.2d 208, 213, 225 U.S.P.Q. 124, 128 (2d Cir. 1985) ("societal vicissitudes demand that the categories retain fluidity to accommodate a particular mark's evolving usage over time").

[221] *E.g.*, Bayer Co. v. United Drug Co., 272 F. 505 (S.D.N.Y. 1921) (coined word "Aspirin" is generic to the consuming public but not to chemists, druggists and physicians). *See also* Union National Bank of Texas, Laredo, Texas v. Union National Bank of Texas, Austin, Texas, 909 F.2d 839, 847, 16 U.S.P.Q.2d 1129, 1135 (5th Cir. 1990):
"The context in which a particular word or phrase is used is examined, not just with respect to how it is used with other words or the products or services to which it is applied, but also to the *audience* to which the relevant product or service is directed. . . . Thus, while for the general public the word 'roots' may only call to mind tuberous plant growths which extend below the surface of the earth, for *some* consumers it is apparently a generic term for vacuum pumps. *See* Dresser Indus., Inc. v. Heraeus Engelhard Vacuum, Inc., 267 F. Supp. 963, 969-70 (W.D.Pa.1967), *aff'd*, 395 F.2d 457 (3d Cir.), *cert. denied*, 393 U.S. 934, 89 S. Ct. 293, 21 L. Ed. 2d 270 (1968)."

[222] Abercrombie & Fitch Co. v. Hunting World, Inc., 537 F.2d 4, 189 U.S.P.Q. 759 (2d Cir. 1976).

and belted bush jackets, (2) merely descriptive or suggestive as applied to other goods, such as boots, and (3) suggestive or even arbitrary as to other goods, such as ice chests and tents.

[a] **Descriptiveness—Secondary Meaning.** Trademark law distinguishes marks that are "descriptive" of the nature, quality or intended use of the goods or services upon which they are used from marks that are merely "suggestive." Trademark protection is available for a descriptive term only with a showing that the term has acquired through usage a secondary meaning. On the other hand, trademark protection is available for a suggestive term without such a showing.

Policy reasons support conditionally excluding descriptive terms from trademark protection: every competitor should be entitled to use appropriate language to describe his or her goods or services.[223] It does not necessarily matter that there are alternative words to describe the product's characteristics or use.[224]

---

[223] 20th Century Wear, Inc. v. Sanmark-Stardust Inc., 747 F.2d 81, 89, 224 U.S.P.Q. 98, 103 (2d Cir. 1984) ("Descriptive terms deserve less protection than suggestive terms both because descriptive terms normally do not distinguish among similar products and because such terms 'should not be monopolized by a single use.' "); Scandia Down Corp. v. Euroquilt, Inc., 772 F.2d 1423, 1430, 227 U.S.P.Q. 138, 143 (7th Cir. 1985), *cert. denied,* 475 U.S. 1147, 229 U.S.P.Q. 560 (1986) ("There are but a limited number of words and images suitable fc.' use in describing a product, and sellers own neither the English language nor common depictions of goods. Descriptive items . . . are therefore not readily appropriable. . . . If descriptive words and pictures could be appropriated without evidence of a secondary meaning, sellers could snatch for themselves the riches of the language and make it more difficult for new entrants to identify their own products; consumers would be worse off."); *In re* DC Comics, Inc., 689 F.2d 1042, 1044, 215 U.S.P.Q. 394, 396 (CCPA 1982) ("Trademark law has traditionally imposed restrictions on the right to exclude others from using certain 'descriptive' symbols to ensure that the opportunity for all to associate such symbols with their common referents remains unencumbered.").

[224] *E.g.,* Thompson Medical Co., Inc. v. Pfizer, 753 F.2d 208, 217, 225 U.S.P.Q. 124, 131 (2d Cir. 1985) (as to claimant's pointing to the availability of alternative names to describe the product: "[T]his assertion misapprehends the relevant concern. The trademark law should not grant, in effect, a monopoly to the first mark that effectively and concisely describes a product's use or function. Were this exclusive appropriation to occur, future entrants would be required to adopt a 'less-descriptive' term, and engage in increased advertising to recoup the lost consumer appeal. Entry barriers would be created, discouraging entry and competition, particularly from small firms."); Zatarains, Inc. v. Oak Grove Smokehouse, Inc., 698 F.2d 786, 793, 217 U.S.P.Q. 988, 996 (5th Cir. 1983) ("the fact that a term is not the only or even the most common name for a product is not determinative, for there is no legal foundation that a product can be described in only one fashion").

See also Forum Corp. of North America v. Forum, Ltd., 903 F.2d 434, 444-45, 14 U.S.P.Q.2d 1950, 1958 (7th Cir. 1990) ("the word need not be necessary to the description of similar services. In *Liquid Controls,* we noted the fact that descriptive terms may be needed in order to describe 'services of a similar nature,' 802 F.2d at 936, in order to show why such words could not be removed from the public domain. We did not, either there or in any other case, find that a term must be necessary to describe similar products before it can be classified as descriptive. Such a rule would mean that any word which has a synonym is not descriptive, and that is clearly not the law in this circuit.").

The courts created the "suggestive" category in response to "the felt need to accord protection to marks that were neither exactly descriptive on the one hand nor truly fanciful on the other,"[225] a need that was particularly acute prior to the Lanham Act because the 1905 Act absolutely barred registration of descriptive marks—even those that had acquired secondary meaning.

The Lanham Act lumps misdescriptive terms together with descriptive ones, the theory being that one competitor cannot claim exclusive rights in a word that does not accurately describe his goods but might accurately describe a competitor's.

[i]   *The Imagination Test.* The descriptive-suggestive distinction is elusive. The courts frequently so state,[226] and the panoply of case results verifies their statements.[227]

---

[225] Abercrombie & Fitch Co. v. Hunting World, Inc., 537 F.2d 4, 10, 189 U.S.P.Q. 759 (2d Cir. 1976) ("Having created the category the courts have had great difficulty in defining it.").

[226] *E.g.,* Franklin Knitting Mills, Inc. v. Fashionit Sweater Mills, Inc., 297 F. 247, 248 (S.D.N.Y. 1923), *aff'd, per curiam,* 4 F.2d 1018 (2d Cir. 1925) (Judge Learned Hand: "It is quite impossible to get any rule out of the cases beyond this: That the validity of the mark ends when suggestion ends and description begins.").

See also Thompson Medical Co., Inc. v. Pfizer, 753 F.2d 208, 213, 225 U.S.P.Q. 124, 128 (2d Cir. 1985) ("[T]he judiciary is ill-equipped to distinguish between the descriptively suggestive and the suggestively descriptive mark."); Union Carbide Corp. v. Ever- Ready, Inc., 531 F.2d 366, 379, 380, 188 U.S.P.Q. 623 (7th Cir. 1976), *cert. denied,* 429 U.S. 830, 191 U.S.P.Q. 416 (1976) ("EVEREADY" is not descriptive of batteries because it "suggests the quality of long life, but no one in our society would be deceived into thinking that this type of battery would never wear out or that its shelf life was infinite. This court has not adopted a particular test for distinguishing between suggestive and descriptive marks. We disagree with the district court that it is a distinction without a difference, although it is often a difficult distinction to draw and is, undoubtedly, often made on an intuitive basis rather than as the result of a logical analysis susceptible of articulation.").

[227] Some examples:

Bursting thermometer design (connoting "hot"): descriptive for employee insurance plans. Murphy v. Provident Mutual Life Insurance Co. of Philadelphia, 923 F.2d 923, 927, 17 U.S.P.Q.2d 1299, 1303 (2d Cir. 1990) ("Marks that are laudatory and that describe the alleged qualities or characteristics of a product or service are descriptive marks.")

"Forum": descriptive of business employee training services. Forum Corp. of North America v. Forum, Ltd., 903 F.2d 434, 14 U.S.P.Q.2d 1950 (7th Cir. 1990).

"Papercutter": descriptive for folded paper ornaments. Papercutter, Inc. v. Fay's Drug Co., Inc., 900 F.2d 558, 14 U.S.P.Q.2d 1450 (2d Cir. 1990).

"FirsTier": descriptive of banking services (absent a disclaimer of the expression "first tier" apart from the mark as a whole). *In re* Omaha National Corp., 819 F.2d 1117, 2 U.S.P.Q.2d 1859 (Fed. Cir. 1987) (evidence showed that banks are ranked in "tiers").

"Beer Nuts": descriptive of salted nuts, Milwaukee Nut Co. v. Brewster Food Service, 277 F.2d 190 (CCPA 1960).

"Fashionknit": descriptive of sweaters. Franklin Knitting Mills, Inc. v. Fashionknit Sweater Mills, Inc., 297 F. 247 (S.D.N.Y. 1925), *aff'd,* 4 F.2d 1018 (2d Cir. 1925).

"KLB_6": only suggestive for kelp, lecithin, and vitamin B_6 pill. Nature's Bounty, Inc. v. Superx Drug Corp., 490 Supp. 50, 207 U.S.P.Q. 263 (E.D.N.Y.1980).

"Beef & Brew": descriptive of a restaurant. Beef & brew inc. v. Beef & Brew, Inc., 389 F. Supp. 179, 185 U.S.P.Q. 531 (D. Or. 1974).

Courts focus on "whether competitors would be likely to need the terms used in the trademark in describing their products."[228] A frequently evoked test is that of "imagination": "a term is suggestive if it requires imagination, thought and perception to reach a conclusion as to the nature of the goods. A term is descriptive if it forthwith conveys an immediate idea of the ingredients, qualities or characteristics of the goods."[229]

In *Security Center*,[230] the Fifth Circuit distilled from the case law "two overarching questions to be considered in determining whether a mark is descriptive or suggestive."

> "First, we must inquire how much imagination is required on the consumer's part in trying to cull some indication from the mark about the qualities, or ingredients of the product or service. . . . Second, we determine whether sellers of similar products are likely to use, or actually do use, the term in connection with their goods.

> . . . .

> "The imagination test might usefully be reversed by inquiring whether the first user has devised a term of some creativity or cleverness, as opposed to merely selecting a term that anyone might readily have chosen. . . . Creativity on the part of the mark's inventor is a correlative of imagination on the part of the consumer.

> ". . . We look into actual and likely use of a mark in order to determine whether its protection, i.e., its exclusion from the language freely available for commercial use, interferes with competition among providers of the same product or service. The more users there are of a term, the more its

---

Steer head design: only suggestive for a steak house restaurant. *In re* Big Wrangler Steak House, Inc., 230 U.S.P.Q. 634 (TTAB 1986) (a simple addition to the mark was sufficient to distinguish two steer head design marks due to the relatively weak protection afforded suggestive marks).

"Rapid Shave": only suggestive for shaving cream. Colgate-Palmolive Co. v. House for Men, Inc., 143 U.S.P.Q. 159 (TTAB 1964).

[228] Union Carbide Corp. v. Ever-Ready, Inc., 531 F.2d 366, 379, 188 U.S.P.Q. 623 (7th Cir. 1976), *cert. denied,* 429 U.S. 830, 191 U.S.P.Q. 416 (1976). *See also* Papercutter, Inc. v. Fay's Drug Co., Inc., 900 F.2d 558, 563, 14 U.S.P.Q.2d 1450, 1453 (2d Cir. 1990) ("Descriptive terms are distinguished from suggestive terms by evaluation of what prospective purchasers perceive in terms of an indication of source, as well as the potential impact on competitors of the appropriation of the term as a trademark by a particular seller.").

[229] Stix Products, Inc. v. United Merchants & Manufacturers Inc., 295 F. Supp. 479, 488 (S.D.N.Y. 1968).

See also Freedom Savings and Loan Association v. Way, 757 F.2d 1176, 1182 n.5, 226 U.S.P.Q. 123, 127 n.5 (11th Cir. 1985), *cert. denied,* 474 U.S. 845 (1985) ("Descriptive marks directly describe a characteristic or quality of the service, and can only be protected if they have acquired a 'secondary meaning.' . . . 'Vision Center,' when used to describe a place to purchase eyeglasses, would be a descriptive name. . . . Suggestive marks subtly connote something about the service so that a customer could use his or her imagination and determine the nature of the service. The term 'Penguin' would be suggestive of refrigerators.").

[230] Security Center, Ltd. v. First National Security Centers, 750 F.2d 1176, 1182 n.5, 225 U.S.P.Q. 373 (5th Cir. 1985).

protection in a given case would be commercially disruptive and unfair to competitors. Under our jurisprudence, the same holds true even for *likelihood* of use."[231]

[*ii*] *Nature, Purpose and Use.* A term may be descriptive because of its relation to the (1) the product or service's nature or quality,[232] (2) the nature or quality of its ingredients or properties,[233] or (3) the use to which the product or service is put.[234] In *20th Century Wear*,[235] the Second Circuit held "Cozy Warm ENERGY-SAVERS" descriptive of flannel pajamas and nightgowns. The term may have been suggestive in the early 1970's but became descriptive in the energy-conscious 1980's. It noted the precise subcategorization of descriptiveness in the Callman unfair competition treatise.[236]

"As one of the leading commentators reminds us, a term can be descriptive in two ways. It can literally describe the product, or it can describe the purpose

---

[231] 750 F.2d at 1299-1300, 225 U.S.P.Q. at 376-77.

[232] *In re* Omaha National Corp., 819 F.2d 1117, 1119, 2 U.S.P.Q.2d 1859, 1861 (Fed. Cir. 1987) ("FirstTier" is descriptive for banking services because the banking community uses "tiers" as words of art in classifying banks' size and quality; "appellant would limit merely descriptive rejections, as a matter of law, to terms which identify a characteristic or quality of an article or service . . . We cannot agree. The factual situations in which mere descriptiveness must be resolved are too varied to lend themselves to resolution under any rigid formula.").

[233] Forum Corp. of North America v. Forum, Ltd., 903 F.2d 434, 444, 14 U.S.P.Q.2d 1950, 1958 (7th Cir. 1990) ("it is not necessary that a descriptive term depict the service itself, but only that the term refer to a characteristic of the service"); *In re* Gyulay, 823 F.2d 1216, 1218, 3 U.S.P.Q.2d 1009, 1010 (Fed. Cir. 1987) (APPLE PIE descriptive of the scent of applicant's potpourri: "It is . . . sufficient that the term describes the scent, when potpourri is sold for and by its scent"); Zatarains, Inc. v. Oak Grove Smokehouse, Inc., 698 F.2d 786, 790, 217 U.S.P.Q. 988, 294 (5th Cir. 1983) (qualities or properties include "color, odor, function, dimensions, or ingredients"); *In re* Andes Candies, Inc., 478 F.2d 1264, 1267, 178 U.S.P.Q. 156, 157 (CCPA 1973) (flavor); Meehanite Metal Corp. v. International Nickel Co., 262 F.2d 806, 807, 120 U.S.P.Q. 293, 294 (CCPA 1959) ("word may be descriptive though it merely describes one of the qualities or properties of the goods").

[234] *E.g.*, Thompson Medical Co., Inc. v. Pfizer, 753 F.2d 208, 216 & n.15, 225 U.S.P.Q. 124, 131 & n.15 (2d Cir. 1985) ("SPORTSCREME" is descriptive for a topical analgesic designed to relieve muscle soreness associated with sports activities: "No exercise of the imagination is necessary for the public to understand that the product is a cream useful in connection with sports. Marks that describe the use to which a product is put are descriptive. . . . 'Sportscreme' does not, however, convey any thought (by way of description or suggestion) as to the significance of the product—i.e., whether it is useful to relieve dryness, itchiness, odor or pain. In this sense, the mark is inadequately descriptive."). *Compare* American Cyanamid Co. v. Campagna per la Farmacie in Italia S.P.A., 678 F. Supp. 1049, 1053, 6 U.S.P.Q.2d 1944, 1946 (S.D.N.Y. 1987), *aff'd*, 847 F.2d 53, 6 U.S.P.Q.2d 1948 (2d Cir. 1988) ("While MATERNA may suggest the market to which Cyanamid's product is aimed, the term does not describe vitamin tablets, and is therefore an arbitrary fanciful and strong mark.").

[235] 20th Century Wear, Inc. v. Sanmark-Stardust Inc., 747 F.2d 81, 224 U.S.P.Q. 98 (2d Cir. 1984), *cert. denied*, 470 U.S. 1052 (1985).

[236] 3 R. Callmann, The Law of Unfair Competition, Trademarks and Monopolies § 18.05 (L. Altman 4th ed. 1983).

or utility of the product. Under the first branch, 'if qualities, ingredients, effects or other features of the product are indicated naturally and in ordinary language, so that the consumer understands its significance without any exercise of the imagination, the words are descriptive'. . . . Under the second branch, Callmann distinguishes among three subcategories of marks that describe the product's purpose or utility: (1) marks describing the problem or condition that the trademarked product is designed to remedy or otherwise deal with; (2) marks that describe the use to which the product or service is put; and (3) marks that describe the effect that the product or service is supposed to produce after it is used. . . . He notes that courts generally hold that marks in the first two subcategories are descriptive, but that some courts have improperly tended to hold that marks in the third subcategory are not descriptive of goods or services."[237]

"Cozy Warm ENERGY-SAVERS" defied Callmann's subcategorization:

"It does describe the quality of warming that wearing the flannel pajamas or nightwear involves, and hence the effect of such wearing, since the use of flannel pajamas presumably permits one to turn down the heat somewhat lower at night. It also describes the problem or condition—energy waste—with which the product deals, however indirectly."[238]

[iii] *Average Customers.* The courts determined descriptiveness by reference to the "average" or "ordinary" customer or purchaser.[239] In *Omaha National*,[240] the court stressed that "[d]escriptiveness is not determined by its meaning only to the class of regular customers with the largest head count." "FirstTier" was descriptive of banking services even if only large corporate customers would recognize that banks were classified in "tiers." "In context, 'average' or 'ordinary' consumers simply refers to the class or classes of actual or prospective customers of the applicant's particular goods or services."

[iv] *Evidence.* A word or symbol's meaning depends on how humans use it to communicate. Any competent evidence of usage should be considered in determining descriptiveness.[241] In examining applications to register marks under the Lanham Act,

---

237 747 F.2d at 88, 224 U.S.P.Q. at 101.

238 747 F.2d at 88, 224 U.S.P.Q. at 102.

239 *In re* Abcor Development Corp., 588 F.2d 811, 814, 200 U.S.P.Q. 215 (CCPA 1978); *In re* Colonial Stores, Inc., 394 F.2d 549, 551, 157 U.S.P.Q. 382, 385 (CCPA 1968).

Cf. In re Gyulay, 820 F.2d 1216, 1217, 3 U.S.P.Q.2d 1009, 1010 (Fed. Cir. 1987) (the PTO did not err in basing a *prima facie* case of descriptiveness of "Apple Pie" for the scent of one variety of applicant's potpourri on statement in applicant's own *wholesale* catalog that the scents "simulate those unforgettable aromas. . . . [T]he trademark attribute of descriptiveness vel non is determined from the viewpoint of the purchaser," but "the burden of coming forward with evidence in support of applicant's argument was upon the applicant.").

240 *In re* Omaha National Corp., 819 F.2d 1117, 2 U.S.P.Q.2d 1859 (Fed. Cir. 1987).

241 *See, e.g., In re* Omaha National Corp., 819 F.2d 1117, 1119, 2 U.S.P.Q.2d 1859, 1860 (Fed. Cir. 1987) (applicant's attack on PTO examiner's use of excerpts from articles on banking in general and business publications using the term "tier" and "first tier" in determining the descriptiveness of "FirstTier" for banking services as "hearsay" is "meritless." "The articles were not used to support the truth of statements in the text but to illustrate common descriptive

PTO trademark attorneys use computer searches of newspapers and periodicals to assess the ways in which persons use words.[242]

In *Bed & Breakfast Registry*,[243] the Federal Circuit held that the P.T.O. did not err in finding that "BED & BREAKFAST REGISTRY" for "making lodging reservations for others in private homes" was merely descriptive despite the applicant's argument that "registry" means an official record and that it does not keep a "register" of lodgings for public use. A "NEXIS" computer search showed two newspaper articles describing bed and breakfast "registry" or "registries." "The descriptive use of the word 'registry' by others weighs against the applicant's argument that its own use is not descriptive of similar services." The court noted that "Whether a mark is merely descriptive is a question of fact, determined from the viewpoint of the relevant purchasing public. Evidence of the purchasing public's understanding of the term may be obtained from any competent source, such as dictionaries, newspapers, or surveys."[244] "[T]he public's understanding of the term may also change with time."

[v]   *Composite Marks—Misspellings.* Joining a descriptive word and a nondescriptive word, two descriptive words, or a descriptive word and a design may yield a mark that is, as a whole, nondescriptive.[245] In *Union-Carbide*,[246] the Seventh Circuit

---

use of the expression 'first tier.' As evidence of such descriptive usage of 'first tier' in connection with banking services, the articles are competent. . . . ").

[242] If an examiner cites excerpts from articles, the applicant is entitled to "place that fragment in context" by including more extensive excerpts. *In re* Bed & Breakfast Registry, 791 F.2d 157, 161, 229 U.S.P.Q. 818, 820 (Fed. Cir. 1986) ("Let it be clear that by citing only a portion of an article, that portion is not thereby insulated from the context from whence it came.").

[243] *In re* Bed & Breakfast Registry, 791 F.2d 157, 229 U.S.P.Q. 818 (Fed. Cir. 1986).

[244] As to the weight given to dictionary definitions, see Security Center, Ltd. v. First National Security Centers, 750 F.2d 1295, 1298 n.4, 225 U.S.P.Q. 373, 375 n.4 (5th Cir. 1985) ("Dictionaries lag behind linguistic realities . . . so the dictionary test may be of questionable validity in many instances."); Zatarains, Inc. v. Oak Grove Smokehouse, Inc., 698 F.2d 786, 792, 217 U.S.P.Q. 988, 995 (5th Cir. 1983) ("A suitable starting place is the dictionary, for '[t]he dictionary definition of the word is an appropriate and relevant indication of "the ordinary significance and meaning of words" to the public.' ").

Parties commonly submit surveys to establish or refute the existence of secondary meaning and a likelihood of confusion. *See* § 5C[3][a][vii], 5F[1][a][vii]. Surveys taken for these purposes are not necessarily probative of the distinctive issue of whether a mark is suggestive or descriptive. Zatarains, Inc. v. Oak Grove Smokehouse, Inc., 698 F.2d 786, 793 n.4, 217 U.S.P.Q. 988, 997 n4 (5th Cir. 1983).

[245] *E.g.,* Scandia Down Corp. v. Euroquilt, Inc., 772 F.2d 1423, 1431, 227 U.S.P.Q. 138, 143 (7th Cir. 1985), *cert. denied,* 475 U.S. 1147, 229 U.S.P.Q. 560 (1985) ("Down Shop" or "Shoppe" together with the outline of a goose for stores selling down-filled comforters; "The words and pictures surely are 'descriptive' if taken one at a time. But that is not the right way to take them. The eye sees the combination of words, typeface, and goose as a unit.").

Compare In re Bongrain International (American) Corp., *In re,* 894 F.2d 1316, 1317, 13 U.S.P.Q.2d 1727, 1728-29 (Fed. Cir. 1990) ("BABY BRIE" descriptive of soft ripened cheese; a 1961 French gastronomic reference text indicates that (i) "Brie" has been used for cheese since the 15th century, and (ii) "Brie" cheese is sold in various sizes; in the food industry, "baby" is often used to indicate size; a 1977 price list shows that "baby" was used specifically as a size indicator for cheese; as to the applicant's argument that it sells its small-size cheese in a package "somewhat larger than those of some other sellers" (10.6 oz. and 17.6 oz. v. 4.5

held that the district court, in finding the mark "EVEREADY" descriptive, erred: "In analyzing Carbide's mark, the district court noted the dictionary definitions of 'ever' and 'ready' and concluded: 'Thus, the combination of "ever" and "ready" means constantly prepared or available for service.' Dissecting marks often leads to error. Words which could not individually become a trademark may become one when taken together."

Misspelling or misjoining descriptive words will not necessarily make the work nondescriptive.[247]

[vi] *Federal Registration.* The Lanham Act ended the 1905 Act's absolute bar on the registration of descriptive terms. Section 2(e) excludes from registration a mark that "applied to the goods or the applicant is merely descriptive or deceptively misdescriptive of them."[248] Section 2(f) provides that nothing shall prevent registration of a mark "which has become distinctive of the applicant's goods in commerce."[249]

The Lanham Act does not use the terms "suggestive," "arbitrary," or "fanciful." The Act's cancellation and incontestability provisions use the phrase "generic."[250] The courts apply the classic four categories to determine the right to registration under Sections 2(e) and 2(f).[251] That is, Section 2(e) states the common law exception that bars trademark rights in descriptive terms or symbols, and Section 2(f) provides an exception to the exception that allows rights in a term or symbol that has "become distinctive" through use, that is, has acquired a "secondary meaning."

[vii] *Secondary Meaning.* A descriptive term becomes protectable as a trademark if it has shown to have acquired through usage a "secondary meaning." A term

---

oz.): "It would be intolerable sophistry if a seller . . . could escape the unregistrability of a merely descriptive mark by simply increasing the size of its package."); Pizzeria Uno Corp. v. Temple, 747 F.2d 1522, 1529-30, 224 U.S.P.Q. 185, 189 (4th Cir. 1984) ("Where the proposed mark consists of but two words, one of which is disclaimed, the word not disclaimed is generally regarded as the dominant or critical term in determining the distinctiveness or suggestiveness of the proposed mark.").

[246] Union Carbide Corp. v. Ever-Ready, Inc., 531 F.2d 366, 379, 188 U.S.P.Q. 623 (7th Cir.), *cert. denied,* 429 U.S. 830, 191 U.S.P.Q. 416 (1976).

[247] *E.g.,* Zatarains, Inc. v. Oak Grove Smokehouse, Inc., 698 F.2d 786, 792 n.3, 217 U.S.P.Q. 988, 995 n.3 (5th Cir. 1983) ("Fish-Fri": "Zatarain's use of the phonetic equivalents of the words 'fish fry'—that is, misspelling it—does not render the mark protectable."); *In re* New Orleans Wines, Ltd., 196 U.S.P.Q. 516 (TTAB 1977) ("BREADSPRED" is descriptive for jams).

[248] 15 U.S.C. § 1052(e).

[249] 15 U.S.C. § 1052(f).

[250] 15 U.S.C. § 1064 (cancellation at any time if the "mark becomes the generic name for the goods or services, or a portion thereof); 15 U.S.C. § 1065 ("no incontestable right shall be acquired in a mark which is the generic name for the goods or services or a portion thereof, for which it is registered").

Before the 1988 Trademark Revision Act, these provisions used the phrase "common descriptive name" of "an article or substance." The purpose of the change was to "reflect current usage of the term by the courts and in general language." Sen. Rep. No. 100-515, 100th Cong., 2d Sess. 34 (1988).

[251] *See In re* Merrill Lynch, Pierce, Fenner, and Smith, Inc., 828 F.2d 1567, 1569, 4 U.S.P.Q.2d 1141, 1142 (Fed. Cir. 1987) ("the distinctions are critical to the availability and the evidentiary requirements of registration").

acquires secondary meaning if it signifies to the purchasing public that the product comes from a single producer or source.[252] It is not necessary that the public be aware of the manufacturer's name: "It is sufficient if the public is aware that the product comes from a single, though anonymous source."[253] Factors relevant to the determination of secondary meaning include the amount and manner of advertising, the volume of sales, the length and manner of use, direct consumer testimony, and consumer surveys,[254] but the ultimate question "is not the *extent* of the promotional

---

[252] *E.g.,* Inwood Laboratories, Inc. v. Ives Laboratories, Inc., 456 U.S. 844, 851 n.11, 214 U.S.P.Q. 1, 4 n.11 (1982) ("To establish secondary meaning, a manufacturer must show that, in the minds of the public, the primary significance of a product feature or term is to identify the source of the product rather than the product itself."); Kellogg Co. v. National Biscuit Co., 305 U.S. 111, 118, 39 U.S.P.Q. 296, 299 (1938) ("Shredded Wheat" for cereal had not acquired secondary meaning; "The evidence shows only that due to the long period in which the plaintiff or its predecessor was the only manufacturer of the product, many people have come to associate the product, and as a consequence the name by which the product is generally known, with the plaintiff's factory at Niagara Falls. But to establish a trade name in the term 'shredded wheat' the plaintiff must show more than a subordinate meaning which applies to it. It must show that the primary significance of the term in the minds of the consuming public is not the product but the producer.").

See G. & C. Merriam Co. v. Saalfield, 198 F. 369, 373 (6th Cir. 1912):

> "[T]here can be no exclusive appropriation of geographical words or words of quality. This is because such words are, or may be, aptly descriptive, and one may properly use for his own product any descriptive words, because such words, are of public or common right. . . . [T]his . . . rule, literally applied in all cases, would encourage commercial fraud . . . hence came the 'secondary meaning' theory. [A] word . . . originally, and in that sense primarily, incapable of exclusive appropriation with reference to an article on the market, because geographically or otherwise descriptive, might nevertheless have been used so long and so exclusively by one producer with reference to his article that, in that trade and to that branch of the purchasing public, the word . . . had come to mean that the article was his product; in other words, had come to be, to them, his trademark. So it was said that the word had come to have a secondary meaning, although this phrase, 'secondary meaning,' seems not happily chosen, because, in this limited field this new meaning is primary rather than secondary. . . . "

[253] Union Carbide Corp. v. Ever-Ready, Inc., 531 F.2d 366, 380, 188 U.S.P.Q. 623 (7th Cir. 1976), *cert. denied,* 429 U.S. 830, 191 U.S.P.Q. 416 (1976).

See also Warner Bros., Inc. v. Gay Toys, Inc., 724 F.2d 327, 333-34 (2d Cir. 1983) ("The ultimate test for secondary meaning . . . is simply whether the term, symbol or device identifies goods of 'a particular source,' in which case it is protectable. . . . This is what 'secondary meaning' means; the true inquiry is whether the primary function of a particular design is other than referential, leading to association in the public mind with no one or nothing, or by virtue of its distinctiveness, it is designed to create an association with a single source. In making that inquiry, the actual motivation of purchasing consumers—whether they were motivated because of quality, source, feature, design, price, durability, prestige or otherwise—is essentially irrelevant.").

[254] *See* Yamaha International Corporation v. Hoshino Gakki Co., Ltd., 840 F.2d 1572, 1583, 6 U.S.P.Q.2d 1001, 1010 (Fed. Cir. 1988) (guitar peg head designs acquired secondary meaning; the evidence showed "8 years of continuous and exclusive use of the specific guitar head designs sought to be registered" and "substantial sales and promotion of the guitars"); Thompson Medical Co., Inc. v. Pfizer, 753 F.2d 208, 217, 225 U.S.P.Q. 124, 132 (2d Cir. 1985) ("In

efforts, but their *effectiveness* in altering the meaning of [the word] to the consuming public."[255]

(1) *Evidence.* A claimant seeking to establish secondary meaning must carefully marshall and present evidence showing consumer perception of the mark as indicating the source of the product or service.[256] For example, in *Soccer Sport Supply Co.,*[257]

---

determining whether a mark has acquired secondary meaning, we have examined: advertising expenditures, . . . consumer studies linking the name to a source, . . . sales success, . . . unsolicited media coverage of the product, . . . attempts to plagiarize the mark, . . . and length and exclusivity of the mark's use, . . . In assessing the existence of secondary meaning, no 'single factor is determinative,' . . . and every element need not be proved. Each case, therefore, must be resolved by reference to the relevant factual calculus.").

[255] Aloe Creme Laboratories, Inc. v. Milsan, Inc., 423 F.2d 845, 850 (5th Cir. 1970), *cert. denied,* 398 U.S. 928, 165 U.S.P.Q. 609 (1970).

See also Murphy v. Provident Mutual Life Insurance Co. of Philadelphia, 923 F.2d 923, 929, 17 U.S.P.Q.2d 1299, 1303 (2d Cir. 1990) ("Although we have suggested a number of factors that may be weighed in determining the existence of secondary meaning, . . . the existence of secondary meaning and likelihood of confusion are not to be determined by application of a rigid formula. . . . The crucial question is whether the public is moved to buy a product because of its source."); Mattel, Inc. v. Azrak-Hamway International, Inc., 724 F.2d 357, 361 n.2, 221 U.S.P.Q. 302, 305 n.2 (2d Cir. 1983) ("The fact that Mattel spent a great deal of money advertising its product, especially when coupled with commercial success, can also be a factor in determining whether the trademark has developed a secondary meaning. . . . However, proof of an expensive and successful advertising campaign in itself is of course not enough to prove secondary meaning.").

[256] *E.g.,* Papercutter, Inc. v. Fay's Drug Co., Inc., 900 F.2d 558, 564, 14 U.S.P.Q.2d 1450, 1454 (2d Cir. 1990) ("The existence of secondary meaning is a question of fact with the burden of proof on the party claiming exclusive rights in the designation. . . . This burden does not shift upon a decision of the Patent and Trademark Office to register the mark, absent evidence that the Office registered the mark upon finding that it had acquired secondary meaning. . . . 'Proof of secondary meaning entails vigorous evidentiary requirements,' . . . and may be established by either direct or circumstantial evidence, including survey evidence of a representative sample of consumers . . . Secondary meaning may also be inferred from evidence relating to the nature and extent of the public exposure achieved by the designation, including volume of sales, . . . length of time of use, . . . and advertising and other promotional efforts, with commercial success, rather than the amount of expenditures, being the likely measure."); American Television & Communications Corp. v. American Communications and Television Inc., 810 F.2d 1546, 1549, 1 U.S.P.Q.2d 2084, 2086 (11th Cir. 1987) ("A high degree of proof is necessary to establish secondary meaning for a descriptive term which suggests the basic nature of the product or service"); 20th Century Wear, Inc. v. Sanmark-Stardust Inc., 747 F.2d 81, 224 U.S.P.Q. 98 (2d Cir. 1984), *cert. denied,* 470 U.S. 1052 (1985) (claimant must satisfy a "heavy burden" of proof on secondary meaning); Ralston Purina Co. v. Thomas J. Lipton, Inc., 341 F. Supp. 129, 134, 173 U.S.P.Q. 820, 824 (S.D.N.Y. 1972) ("proof of secondary meaning entails vigorous evidentiary requirements").

[257] *In re* Soccer Sport Supply Co., 507 F.2d 1400, 184 U.S.P.Q. 345 (CCPA 1975).

See also Bank of Texas v. Commerce Southwest, Inc., 741 F.2d 785, 789, 223 U.S.P.Q. 1174, 1177 (5th Cir. 1984) (overturning jury verdict that "Bank of Texas" had acquired such secondary meaning in Dallas County so as to establish a property right protectable against defendant's use of "BancTexas"; as to the plaintiff's nine years of exclusive use, "length of time alone is [not] sufficient to establish secondary meaning"; two factors negated the significance of a

the applicant sought to register as a trademark a soccer ball surface pattern. The applicant attempted to establish secondary meaning by coaches and retailers' affidavits, advertisements, and a license agreement. The court held that the evidence did not show a nexus between the applicant's design and a single source. The advertising evidence failed "to disclose information from which the number of people exposed to the design could be estimated—such as circulation of the publications in which the advertisements appear, advertising expenditures, number of advertisements published, volume of sales of the soccer balls, and the like." Also, the advertisements showed the design coupled with word marks. The licensee agreement was not persuasive because it did not indicate the extent and manner of the license's use of the design. The affidavits could not be ignored simply because they were drafted by the applicant's attorney, but they failed to establish "association of the applicant's design with a single source by other than a small number of purchasers."

Courts state that survey evidence is the "most direct and persuasive way of establishing secondary meaning"[258] because "[the] chief inquiry is the attitude of the consumer toward the mark; does it denote to him a 'single thing coming from a single source?' "[259] Flaws in the surveyor's methodology dilute the survey evidence's persuasiveness.[260]

---

telephone survey of people in the area of the Bank of Texas that showed that 58.7% of the people questioned had heard of it: (1) "Most of the interviewees could not identify where the bank was located. . . . Knowledge of location is . . . helpful in determining whether an interviewee does in fact correctly associate a name with a service" and (2) the survey designer admitted that the results of the survey cannot be assumed to be representative of all of Dallas County).

[258] Security Center, Ltd. v. First National Security Centers, 750 F.2d 1295, 1300, 225 U.S.P.Q. 373, 377 (5th Cir. 1985). See also Mattel, Inc. v. Azrak-Hamway International, Inc., 724 F.2d 357, 361, 221 U.S.P.Q. 302, 304-05 (2d Cir. 1983) ("what has become a usual way to demonstrate either consumer confusion or secondary meaning, in a case where the existence of secondary meaning or consumer confusion is not otherwise obvious, is for the proponent to undertake some form of survey of consumer attitudes under actual market conditions. . . . Here for preliminary injunction purposes Mattel took no such survey, and it provided little other evidence demonstrating consumer confusion."). Compare Yamaha International Corp. v Hoshino Gakki Co. Ltd., 840 F.2d 1572, 1583, 6 U.S.P.Q.2d 1001, 1010 (Fed. Cir. 1988) ("absence of consumer surveys need not preclude a finding of acquired distinctiveness").

[259] Aloe Creme Laboratories, Inc. v. Milsan, Inc., 423 F.2d 845, 849, 165 U.S.P.Q. 37, 40 (5th Cir.), cert. denied, 398 U.S. 928 (1970).

Surveys are also used to show whether a term is generic and whether there is a likelihood of confusion. See §§ 5C[3][b][vi] and 5F[1][a][vii].

[260] Sno-Wizard Manufacturing, Inc. v. Eisemann Products Co., 791 F.2d 423, 427, 230 U.S.P.Q. 118, 120 (5th Cir. 1986) (no secondary meaning as to the configuration of a snowball machine despite survey results showing a high recognition of plaintiff as the source of the machine; the surveys were primarily of machine operators so that "the survey to a great extent can thus be interpreted to mean the operators of snowball machines can identify the type of machine they use each day"; also, "many of the interviews were conducted within full view of the Sno-Wizard machine and its identifying label.").

See J. T. McCarthy, Trademarks and Unfair Competition § 15.13D (2d ed. 1984) ("the questions to be asked in the survey must be carefully phrased so as to elicit honest and unprompted consumer reaction as to association between a given trade symbol and single source of the product.").

Claimants often rely on a second user's copying of a descriptive mark to establish secondary meaning. The courts accept intentional copying as evidence of secondary meaning,[261] but, in *Blau Plumbing*,[262] the Seventh Circuit held that the defendant's actual copying of plaintiff's trade dress did not fill the evidentiary void on secondary meaning.

> "The copying of a descriptive mark that has not acquired secondary meaning does not imply passing off, for by definition it describes the properties which the brand has in common with other brands. . . . Such copying informs rather than confuses consumers.

> "Granted, many cases do allow an inference of secondary meaning to be drawn from, or at least bolstered by, evidence that the defendant was deliberately trying to confuse consumers through an exact or nearly exact copying of his trade dress. . . . If the defendant thinks that the plaintiff's trade dress has acquired secondary meaning, so that he can confuse consumers by adopting the same or a confusingly similar trade dress for his own brand, this is some indication that it has acquired secondary meaning. The problem is that evidence of intent is often ambiguous. Maybe therefore a court should insist on other evidence of distinctiveness and not allow a trademark infringement case to get to a jury merely on proof that the defendant may have been trying to confuse consumers about whose brand they were buying; maybe that would be

---

[261] *E.g.*, Papercutter, Inc. v. Fay's Drug Co., Inc., 900 F.2d 558, 564, 14 U.S.P.Q.2d 1450, 1455 (2d Cir. 1990) ("Proof of intentional copying is often viewed as evidence of secondary meaning on the theory that the copying is motivated by a desire to benefit."); LeSportsac, Inc. v. K Mart Corp., 754 F.2d 71, 78, 225 U.S.P.Q. 654, 659 (2d Cir. 1985) (district court did not abuse its discretion in issuing a preliminary injunction, primarily relying on the defendant's intentional copying of the plaintiff's trade dress as the "most persuasive evidence" of secondary meaning); Transgro, Inc. v. Ajac Transmission Parts Corp., 768 F.2d 1001, 1016, 225 U.S.P.Q. 458, 464 (9th Cir. 1985), *cert. denied*, 474 U.S. 1059 (1986) ("Proof of exact copying, without any opposing proof, can be sufficient to establish secondary meaning."); Ciba-Geigy Corp. v. Bolar Pharmaceutical Co., Inc., 747 F.2d 844, 224 U.S.P.Q. 349, 354 (3d Cir. 1984), *cert. denied*, 471 U.S. 1137 (1985) (exact copying of trade dress of plaintiff's drug capsules); Ideal Toy Corp. v. Plawner Toy Manufacturing Corp., 685 F.2d 78, 82, 216 U.S.P.Q. 102, 106 (3d Cir. 1982) (extensive copying—counsel for defendant admitted that its product was a "knockoff"; "Although this admission of copying is itself persuasive evidence of secondary meaning, [plaintiff] offered other circumstantial evidence" of secondary meaning, including large advertising expenditures, a consumer survey showing that 40% of the respondents identified an imitation product as that of the plaintiff, and evidence that buyers of imitation products mistakenly returned them to plaintiff for repair).

[262] Blau Plumbing, Inc. v. S.O.S. Fix-It, Inc., 781 F.2d 604, 228 U.S.P.Q. 519 (7th Cir. 1986). *See also* Fuddruckers Inc. v. Doc's B.R. Others Inc., 826 F.2d 837, 844, 4 U.S.P.Q.2d 1026, 1031 (9th Cir. 1987) (jury finding that plaintiff's restaurant trade dress lacked secondary meaning: "evidence of deliberate copying is relevant to a determination of secondary meaning. . . . Indeed, in appropriate circumstances, deliberate copying may suffice to support an inference of secondary meaning. . . . The trial court's instruction permitted, but did not require, the jury to infer the existence of secondary meaning from a finding of intentional copying. [Plaintiff] would have us go further, and hold that evidence of deliberate copying shifts the burden of proof on the issue of secondary meaning. We decline to so hold. Competitors may intentionally copy product features for a variety of reasons.").

putting too much weight on evidence of intent. . . . Where as in this case the trade dress being copied is descriptive, copying is consistent with an inference that the copier wanted merely to inform consumers about the properties of his own product or service." [263]

(2) *Relation to Likelihood of Confusion.* Does the test for proof of secondary meaning differ, either analytically or in practical terms, from the test for likelihood of confusion in the context of a trademark infringement suit? Some decisions indicate that the tests are the same in practice,[264] but in *20th Century,*[265] the Second Circuit remanded a case in which the district court found that the mark was not descriptive and that there was a likelihood of confusion. The appeals court found that the mark was descriptive and remanded for a determination of whether the mark had acquired secondary meaning.

"We do not interpret the district court's finding with respect to the issue of likelihood of confusion as to source as including an implicit finding of secondary meaning. While confusion as to source is the fundamental inquiry in any infringement action, the elements that plaintiff must prove in a suit involving a suggestive term differ from those in a suit over a descriptive term. Proof of confusion as to source can be divided into two more specific showings: whether the public is unlikely to distinguish the source of the allegedly infringing product from that of the infringed product and whether the public makes the connection between the trademark and the plaintiff-source. The connection between the mark and source is assumed in the case of a suggestive or arbitrary term. Secondary

---

[263] 781 F.2d at 611, 228 U.S.P.Q. at 522-23.

[264] *E.g.,* Levi Strauss & Co. v. Blue Bell, Inc., 778 F.2d 1352, 1359, 228 U.S.P.Q. 346, 351 (9th Cir. 1985) ("The finding of no secondary meaning . . . would normally foreclose any possibility of likelihood of confusion . . . In order to establish customer confusion [the trademark claimant] must establish that use of the [accused] mark on [the goods of the accused infringer] is likely to cause a reasonably knowledgeable and prudent purchaser to believe that [the claimant] was the manufacturer of [those goods]. . . . A buyer cannot, however, be 'confused unless he is looking for a label he recognizes and picks up another in his confusion. Ergo, a buyer who does not recognize plaintiff's "mark" and does not distinguish it from any other, cannot be confused.' 1 J. McCarthy, [Trademarks and Unfair Competition] § 15:3 at p. 668 [(2d ed. 1984)].").

Cf. Interpace Corp. v. Lapp, Inc., 721 F.2d 460, 465 (3d Cir. 1983) (the district court erred in ruling that the plaintiff can demonstrate secondary meaning only by actually entering the defendant's market; "Though we did draw a formal distinction between likelihood of confusion and secondary meaning in [Scott Paper Co. v. Scott's Liquid Gold, Inc., 589 F.2d 1225 (3d Cir. 1978)], proof of one is proof of the other. Furthermore, we never in any way suggested that a plaintiff can prove secondary meaning only by entering the defendant's market.").

[265] 20th Century Wear, Inc. v. Sanmark-Stardust Inc., 747 F.2d 81, 224 U.S.P.Q. 98 (2d Cir. 1984), *cert. denied,* 470 U.S. 1052 (1985). *Cf.* Blau Plumbing, Inc. v. S.O.S. Fix-It, Inc., 781 F.2d 604, 610, 228 U.S.P.Q. 519, 522 (7th Cir. 1986) (a location box for Yellow Page advertising is descriptive and not shown to have acquired secondary meaning; "There may be some confusion from [defendant's] use of a similar location box, but confusion is endemic to consumer markets; and a court doesn't even reach the question of likelihood of confusion until persuaded that the putative mark is sufficiently distinctive to warrant prima facie protection as a trademark.").

meaning performs the role of establishing that connection here, in the case of a descriptive term."[266]

(3) *Presumption Based on Exclusive Use.* Lanham Act Section 2(f) allows an applicant to register an apparently descriptive mark if it has become distinctive. The applicant bears the burden of showing that an apparently descriptive term or symbol has acquired secondary meaning.[267] The second sentence aids applicants in meeting this burden by providing that the PTO may accept five years of exclusive use of the mark as prima facie evidence of distinctiveness,[268] but the section is permissive, and the PTO may find a mark not distinctive despite the existence of five or more years of exclusive use.[269]

(4) *"Secondary Meaning in the Making."* Several New York federal district court decisions approve a "secondary meaning in the making" theory under which a party who adopts and expends resources promoting a descriptive term or product trade dress that is not inherently distinctive[270] and has not yet developed secondary meaning may obtain relief against another who deliberately copies the term or dress.[271] Other

---

[266] 747 F.2d at 90 n.10, 224 U.S.P.Q. at 103. On remand, the district court found that the claimant failed to establish secondary meaning. 20th Century Wear, Inc. v. Sanmark- Stardust Inc., 815 F.2d 8, 2 U.S.P.Q.2d 1283 (2d Cir. 1987).

[267] See Yamaha International Corp. v. Hoshino Gakki Co. Ltd., 840 F.2d 1572, 1581, 6 U.S.P.Q.2d 1001, 1008 (Fed. Cir. 1988) ("the standard of proof in an opposition under section 2(f) has always been a preponderance of evidence, although logically that standard becomes more difficult to meet as the mark's descriptiveness increases").

[268] 15 U.S.C. § 1052(f): ". . . . The Commissioner may accept as prima facie evidence that the mark has become distinctive, as applied to the applicant's goods in commerce, proof of substantially exclusive and continuous use thereof as a mark by the applicant in commerce for the five years before the date on which the claim of distinctiveness is made."

[269] E.g., In re Smith, 734 F.2d 1482. 1485, 222 U.S.P.Q. 1, 3 (Fed. Cir. 1984) (product configuration found not to be distinctive despite eight years continuous and exclusive use).

[270] For a discussion whether secondary meaning is always a requisite to trade dress protection, see § 5C[2][c][iv].

[271] PAF S.r.l. v. Lisa Lighting Co., Ltd., 712 F. Supp. 394, 405, 12 U.S.P.Q.2d 1161, 1170 (S.D. N.Y. 1989) ("Without peradventure of doubt, defendants deliberately copied the Dove lamp; there is no evidence to the contrary. The Dove and Swan, even when viewed side by side, are virtually indistinguishable. . . . In trade dress cases, a product design may take longer than a wordmark to acquire secondary meaning . . . Nevertheless, even assuming arguendo that plaintiffs' trade dress has not yet acquired secondary meaning, where as here, it is demonstrated that a product is expanding in a new market, and where there is an intentional, deliberate attempt to capitalize on another's distinctive product, secondary meaning in the making is also entitled to protection. . . . However, the record establishes far more than secondary meaning in the making."); Jolly Good Industries, Inc. v. Elegra Inc., 690 F. Supp. 227, 9 U.S.P.Q.2d 1534 (S.D. N.Y. 1988) (trade dress; "With respect to the issue of intentional copying, the evidence was overwhelming. . . . No court in this circuit has explicitly rejected the theory of secondary meaning in the making, while the court of appeals has twice reviewed the theory without condemnation or criticism, especially where there exists strong evidence of intentional copying. . . . The theory of incipient secondary meaning has also been well-received by commentators . . . "); Elizabeth Taylor Cosmetics Co., Inc. v. Annick Goutal, S.A.R.L., 673 F. Supp. 1238 (S.D. N.Y. 1987); Metro Kane Imports, Ltd. v. Federated Department Stores Inc., 625 F. Supp. 313, 316, 228 U.S.P.Q. 761, 762-63 (S.D. N.Y. 1985),

courts reject secondary meaning in the making as inconsistent with trademark principles[272] or find it inapplicable to the facts before them.[273]

aff'd, 800 F.2d 1128 (2d Cir. 1986) (table) ("Metro Kane has asserted that a colorable Lanham Act claim may be based on the theory that, where secondary meaning is 'in the making' but not yet fully developed, a trademark or trade dress will be protected against intentional, deliberate attempts to capitalize on a distinctive product. While no previous case has apparently relied solely upon secondary meaning in the making to establish a Lanham Act violation, this court has demonstrated a nodding acquaintance with the concept. . . . There exists no controlling authority which holds that a Lanham Act claim based on secondary meaning in the making is without merit . . . "); Orion Pictures Co., Inc. v. Dell Publishing Co., 471 F. Supp. 392, 396, 202 U.S.P.Q. 819 (S.D. N.Y. 1979) ("there appears to be growing support for the proposition that a secondary meaning 'in the making' should be protected, at least to the extent of preventing intentional attempts, as by the defendant here, to capitalize on the efforts and goodwill of others."); National Lampoon, Inc. v. American Broadcasting Cos., Inc., 376 F. Supp. 733, 182 U.S.P.Q. 24 (S.D.N.Y. 1974), aff'd on other grounds, 497 F.2d 1343, 182 U.S.P.Q. 6 (2d Cir. 1974).

[272] Black & Decker Mfg. Co., v. Ever-Ready Appliance Mfg. Co., 684 F.2d 546, 550, 215 U.S.P.Q. 97, 100 (8th Cir. 1982) ("There is no secondary meaning established in this case—Black & Decker admits this. Nevertheless it urges us to adopt its theory of 'secondary meaning in the making,' under which the trade dress of the [product] would be deemed protectable by virtue of the substantial advertising outlay and marketing approach used by Black & Decker to promote the product. Such a theory focuses solely upon the intent and actions of the seller of the product to the exclusion of the consuming public; but the very essence of secondary meaning is the association in the mind of the public of particular aspects of trade dress with a particular product and producer. . . . We are directed to no case which actually applies Black & Decker's theory and we decline to adopt it."); A.J. Canfield Co. v. Concord Beverage Co., 629 F. Supp. 200, 211-12, 228 U.S.P.Q. 479, 487 (E.D.Pa.1985), aff'd on other grounds sub nom. A.J. Canfield Co. v. Honickman, 808 F.2d 291, 1 U.S.P.Q.2d 1364 (3d Cir.1986) (the theory " 'posits that a firm which is making efforts to create a secondary meaning but has not yet succeeded, should be protected as against a competitor who knowingly rushes in to market a product under a similar mark.' 1 McCarthy, [Trademarks and Unfair Competition] at § 15:21. . . . The cases upon which plaintiff grounds its argument however, are unpersuasive. In all of them the district court's endorsement of 'secondary meaning in the making' constituted dicta, given initial findings in each instance of secondary meaning. . . . Moreover, the mere notion of 'secondary meaning in the making' is inimical to the purpose of the doctrine of secondary meaning, which is to protect designations once they are indicative of a product's origin. See 1 McCarthy, supra § 15:21. Sanctioning the exclusive use of a designation even before it is associated with the origin of the product undercuts the premium placed by the Lanham Act on distinctiveness, and robs manufacturers of terms that may be necessary to market their products, thereby restricting competition.").

[273] G. Heileman Brewing Co., Inc. v. Anheuser-Busch, Inc., 873 F.2d 985, 998-99, 10 U.S.P.Q.2d 1801, 1812-13 (7th Cir. 1989) (descriptive term "LA" for low-alcohol beer; "Busch apparently concedes that the district court properly concluded that insufficient time had elapsed between April 1984, when Busch first used LA on beer labels distributed in retail markets, and several weeks later when Heileman commenced its use of LA. . . . Nevertheless, Busch now asserts that this court should apply the theory of 'secondary meaning in the making.' A few authorities espouse the view that secondary meaning in the making should be protected to prevent intentional attempts to capitalize on the efforts and goodwill of others. . . . Anheuser-Busch argues that Heileman and Miller sought to make LA the 'category generic' thereby sabotaging the development of secondary meaning and capitalizing on Busch's efforts to

In *Cicena*,[274] the Federal Circuit predicted that the Second Circuit, which reviews New York district court decisions, would not approve the theory.[275]

> "The doctrine of 'secondary meaning in the making' is generally credited to have begun with the case of *The National Lampoon, Inc. v. American Broadcasting Cos., Inc.*, 376 F. Supp. 733, 182 U.S.P.Q. 24 (S.D.N.Y.), *aff'd on other grounds*, 497 F.2d 1343, 182 U.S.P.Q. 6 (2d Cir.1974), in which the trial court cited the following passage from 3 Callman, *Unfair Competition, Trademarks and Monopolies* (3d ed. 1971) p. 356:
>
> > "A mark with secondary meaning in-the-making should also be protected, at least against those who appropriate it with knowledge or good reason to know of its potential in that regard, or with an intent to capitalize on its good-will. . . . 'Piracy should no more be tolerated in the earlier stages of development of good will than in the later.' " (citations omitted)

promote its new product. . . . [T]his court has never recognized the theory of secondary meaning in the making and we do not think this is an appropriate occasion for doing so. Here there was no evidence that Heileman and Miller used the LA label to capitalize intentionally on Busch's goodwill—assuming, for argument's sake, that goodwill can exist before secondary meaning has developed. To the contrary, the district court found that the plaintiffs used LA in good faith to describe a characteristic of their new low alcohol beer. . . . Moreover, if a doctrine of secondary meaning in the making were to be recognized, initials standing for a descriptive phrase would be an unlikely subject for its application. Rather than employing a doctrine of secondary meaning in the making, a more befitting doctrine here might recognize *primary* meaning, i.e., as a descriptive term, in the making. LA either means low alcohol or is a short step away from this meaning."); Scholastic, Inc. v. MacMillan, Inc., 650 F. Supp. 866, 872 n.3, 2 U.S.P.Q.2d 1191, 1195 n.3 (S.D. N.Y. 1987) ("Even assuming that such a claim may be maintained under the Lanham Act, which is an open question, . . . no such finding is warranted here. First, [plaintiff's] efforts to promote [its descriptive mark] have been minimal, and its current plans to use the name appear to be proceeding at a leisurely pace. Second, claims based on a secondary meaning 'in the making,' if they exist at all, may be employed only against 'intentional, deliberate attempts to capitalize on a distinctive product.' . . . The evidence in this case clearly indicates that [defendant] developed [its] name on its own and did not attempt to benefit from consumers' perceptions, if any, about [plaintiff's product]."); Loctite Corp. v. National Starch & Chemical Corp., 516 F. Supp. 190, 211 U.S.P.Q. 237 (S.D. N.Y. 1981) ("Super Glue" mark; "whether or not it is appropriate to protect a party who succeeds or seems likely to succeed in establishing secondary meaning by beginning that protection at some point before secondary meaning has actually been acquired, such protection would not be appropriate here. The facts in this case show that plaintiffs have not succeeded in establishing secondary meaning, and do not show signs of succeeding in the future. 'Super Glue' instead has functioned as a generic term or a descriptive term of widespread application without secondary meaning in favor of anyone.").

274 Cicena Ltd. v. Columbia Telecommunications Group, 900 F.2d 1546, 14 U.S.P.Q.2d 1401 (Fed. Cir. 1990).

275 For the Second Circuit's reaction to this prediction, see Murphy v. Provident Mutual Life Insurance Co. of Philadelphia, 923 F.2d 923, 939, 17 U.S.P.Q.2d 1299, 1304 (2d Cir. 1990) ("If this court ever decides to adopt the concept of secondary meaning in the making, a decision that the Federal Circuit believes we are unlikely to make, . . . this is not the case in which to do it" because the plaintiff had frequently changed his alleged mark).

"Later cases have refined the doctrine as follows:

'[A] Lanham Act claim may be based on the theory that, where secondary meaning is "in the making" but not yet fully developed, a trademark or trade dress will be protected against intentional, deliberate attempts to capitalize on a distinctive product.' "

Metro Kane Imports, Ltd. v. Federated Department Stores, Inc., 625 F. Supp. 313, 316, 228 U.S.P.Q. 761, 762 (S.D.N.Y.1985), *aff'd without opinion sub nom. Metro Kane Imports, Ltd. v. Brookstone Co.*, 800 F.2d 1128 (2d Cir.1986) . . . The purpose of the doctrine of secondary meaning in the making is to protect a plaintiff who has spent and is spending money and effort to create secondary meaning in a product, but has not yet succeeded, from others who try to profit from whatever goodwill the plaintiff has built up. *Id.*

"However, the doctrine of secondary meaning in the making is of questionable validity. . . . Furthermore, the discussions of the doctrine in the majority of the New York cases are dicta, since either secondary meaning was also found or the facts were insufficient to support even secondary meaning in the making. . . .

"The Second Circuit has had several opportunities to discuss the doctrine, but has not done so. . . . Therefore we are in the delicate position of deciding a question of first impression in the Second Circuit, trusting that it will agree. After considerable study of the matter, we are of the opinion that the Second Circuit, if faced with the question, would reject the doctrine of secondary meaning in the making. Our primary basis for reaching this conclusion rests in the language of § 43(a) which, in the area of trademark and trade dress law, protects only against 'false designation of origin.' . . . A trademark or trade dress which lacks secondary meaning, i.e., does not associate the product with a single source, by definition does not designate origin. . . . To allow a plaintiff to succeed on a theory of secondary meaning in the making would undermine the entire purpose of the secondary meaning requirement: to show that the public associates the product with a source rather than with the product itself.

"We quote with approval the following passage from an Eighth Circuit opinion:

'[Secondary meaning in the making] focuses solely upon the intent and actions of the seller of the product to the exclusion of the consuming public; but the very essence of secondary meaning is the association in the mind of the public of particular aspects of trade dress with a particular product and producer.'

Black & Decker, 684 F.2d at 550, 215 U.S.P.Q. at 100. . . . While the doctrine of secondary meaning in the making may serve an admirable goal—that of preventing the deliberate copier from capitalizing on the efforts of the first producer—such a goal is not encompassed by § 43(a) of the Lanham Act. . . . Instead, protection from such activity must be found in other more general unfair competition laws, such as New York state unfair competition law." [276]

---

[276] 900 F.2d at 1549-50, 14 U.S.P.Q.2d 1404-05.

[b] **Generic Terms.** A generic term is the name of the genus or class of which the individual product or service is a member.[277] It denotes the basic nature of the product or, perhaps, a prime or distinguishing ingredient of the product. A term can either (1) be generic at the time of its adoption, as when the ordinary meaning of the term is the name of the product, or (2) become generic, as when a term that was fanciful or arbitrary at the time of adoption becomes generic through usage.[278] If a term is generic for a particular product, then it cannot receive trademark protection. It is often stated that "proof of secondary meaning . . . cannot transform a generic term into a subject for trademark."[279] The rational for the absolute exclusion of generic terms from registrability or protectability is obvious: "To allow trademark protection for generic terms, i.e., names which describe the genus of goods being sold, even when these have become identified with a first user, would grant the owner of the mark a monopoly, since a competitor could not describe his goods as what they are."[280] The grant of exclusive rights in goods is solely the province of patent law. This rationale meshes with that excluding functional features from trade dress protection despite secondary meaning.[281]

[i] *The Primary Significance Test.* The generic-descriptive distinction is as allusive as the descriptive-suggestive.[282]

In *Bayer*,[283] a 1921 decision holding that "Aspirin," a fanciful term that the Bayer Company adopted for its pioneering new pharmaceutical product, had become

---

[277] Park 'N Fly v. Dollar Park and Fly, Inc., 469 U.S. 189, 194, 224 U.S.P.Q. 327, 329 (1985) ("Marks that constitute a common descriptive name are referred to as generic. A generic term is one that refers to the genus of which the particular product is a species.").

[278] Three classic cases are: King-Seely Thermos Co. v. Aladdin Industries, Inc., 321 F.2d 577, 138 U.S.P.Q. 349 (2d Cir. 1963) ("Thermos" for vacuum bottles); DuPont Cellophane Co. v. Waxed Products Co., 85 F.2d 75 (2d Cir. 1936), *cert. denied,* 299 U.S. 601 (1936) ("Cellophane" for clear wrapping paper); Bayer Co. v. United Drug Co., 272 F. 505 (S.D.N.Y. 1921) ("Aspirin" for acetyl salicylic acid).
The evolution from distinctive to generic may reverse. In 1896, the Supreme Court held that "SINGER" was the common name for a sewing machine. Singer Manufacturing Co. v. June Manufacturing Co., 163 U.S. 169 (1896). The term does not so clearly have that significance in late twentieth century usage.

[279] Abercrombie & Fitch Co. v. Hunting World, Inc., 537 F.2d 4, 9, 189 U.S.P.Q. 759 (2d Cir. 1976) ("no matter how much money and effort the user of a generic term has poured into promoting the sale of its merchandise and what success it has achieved in securing public identification, it cannot deprive competing manufacturers of the product of the right to call an article by its name").

[280] CES Publishing Corp. v. St. Regis Publications, Inc., 531 F.2d 11, 13, 188 U.S.P.Q. 612, 615 (2d Cir. 1975).

[281] A.J. Canfield Co. v. Honickman, 808 F.2d 291, 307, 1 U.S.P.Q.2d 1364, 1377 (3d Cir. 1986) ("Just as one producer may not use unfair competition law to prevent others from copying functional characteristics of its product, it may not use that law to prevent others from describing those characteristics in its products.").
See § 5C[2][c][v].

[282] *In re* Merrill Lynch, Pierce, Fenner, and Smith, Inc., 828 F.2d 1567, 1569, 4 U.S.P.Q.2d 1141, 1142 (Fed. Cir. 1987) ("Whether a term is classified as 'generic' or as 'merely descriptive' is not easy to discern when the term sits at the fuzzy boundary between these classifications.").

[283] Bayer Co. v. United Drug Co., 272 F. 505 (S.D.N.Y. 1921).

generic for acetyl salicylic acid, Judge Learned Hand provided the following, much-quoted test of genericness.

> "The single question, as I view it, in all these cases, is merely one of fact: What do these buyers understand by the word for whose use the parties are contending? If they understand by it only the kind of goods sold, then, I take it, it makes no difference whatever efforts the plaintiff has made to get them to understand more."[284]

In *Kellogg*,[285] the Supreme Court held that National Biscuit Co. could not claim exclusive trademark rights in the term "shredded wheat" for the familiar pillow-shaped breakfast cereal. National Biscuit was the sole source of shredded wheat for many years because it had utility and design patent protection on the product and on methods of producing it. The Court rejected National Biscuit's argument that "shredded wheat," though descriptive, had acquired secondary meaning.

> "The evidence shows only that due to the long period in which the plaintiff or its predecessor was the only manufacturer of the product, many people have come to associate the product, and as a consequence the name by which the product is generally known, with the plaintiff's factory at Niagara Falls. But to establish a trade name in the term 'shredded wheat' the plaintiff must show more than a subordinate meaning which applies to it. It must show that the primary significance of the term in the minds of the consuming public is not the product but the producer. This it has not done."[286]

The Court's "primary significance" language was, strictly speaking, a definition of secondary meaning rather than of the converse of genericness. Nevertheless, lower courts adopted the primary significance—product or producer?—test as applicable to genericness.[287]

Some decisions break the primary significance test down into two factual inquiries: "First, what is the genus of goods or services at issue? Second, is the term sought to be registered . . . understood by the relevant public primarily to refer to that genus of goods or services."[288]

[ii] *Lanham Act Registrability.* Lanham Act Section 2, which sets forth the subject matter exclusions from trademark registrability on the principal register, does

---

[284] 272 F. at 509.

[285] Kellogg Co. v. National Biscuit Co., 305 U.S. 111 (1938).

[286] 305 U.S. at 118.

[287] *See* Feathercombs, Inc. v. Solo Products Corp., 306 F.2d 251, 256 (2d Cir. 1962), *cert. denied,* 371 U.S. 910 (1962) ("When a mark loses [the] function [of being indicative of origin], and merely gives information as to the nature or class of an article, the holder of the mark suffers a total loss of rights in it. The mark then becomes non-distinctive, loses its secondary meaning, and becomes generic. *See Kellogg Co. v. National Biscuit Co.* . . . . *A mark is not generic merely because it has some significance to the public as an indication of the nature or class of an article. . . . In order to become generic the principal significance of the word must be its indication of the nature or class of an article, rather than an indication of its origin.*").

[288] H. Marvin Ginn Corp. v. International Ass'n of Fire Chiefs, 782 F.2d 987, 990, 228 U.S.P.Q. 528, 530 (Fed. Cir. 1986).

not mention generic terms. Section 14 provides for cancellation of a mark "at any time if the registered mark becomes the generic name for the goods or services, or a portion thereof."[289] The Act does not expressly prohibit the initial registration of a generic mark, but the courts construe it as implicitly barring such registration.[290] It would be pointless to register a mark that was immediately subject to cancellation.[291]

[iii] *Evidence of Generic Usage.* The primary significance test makes genericness a fact question.[292]

---

[289] 15 U.S.C. § 1064(c).

[290] *E.g., In re* G.D. Searle & Co., 360 F.2d 650, 149 U.S.P.Q. 619 (CCPA 1966) ("The Pill" cannot be registered for an oral contraceptive). *See also* Park 'N Fly v. Dollar Park and Fly, Inc., 469 U.S. 189, 194, 224 U.S.P.Q. 327, 329 (1985) ("Generic terms are not registrable, and a registered mark may be cancelled at any time on the grounds that it has become generic.").

[291] A generic term does not meet Section 2's preamble requirement that a trademark be one "by which the goods of the applicant may be distinguished from the goods of others." 15 U.S.C. § 1052.

[292] Some examples:

"MONTRACHET": not generic for particular type of goat cheese. *In re* Montrachet S.A., 878 F.2d 375, 11 U.S.P.Q.2d 1393 (Fed. Cir. 1989).

"SPACE SHUTTLE": generic for reusable spacecraft, especially such craft comprising an orbiter, two solid rocket boosters, and an external tank (resulting in denial of opposition to application to register "SPACE SHUTTLE" for wines). National Aeronautics and Space Administration v. Bully Hill Vineyards Inc., 3 U.S.P.Q.2d 1671 (PTO TTAB 1987).

"AIR SHUTTLE": generic for service consisting of hourly flights between cities with no reservations, etc. Eastern Air Lines, Inc. v. New York Air Lines, Inc., 559 F. Supp. 1270 (S.D.N.Y. 1983) (denying exclusive rights in "air shuttle" but granting relief against misleading advertising by the defendant regarding the extent to which its "shuttle" service was comparable to that of plaintiff).

"SEATS": not generic for ticket reservation services. *In re* Seats, 757 F.2d 274, 225 U.S.P.Q. 364 (Fed. Cir. 1985).

"TOLL HOUSE": generic for chocolate chip cookie type. Nestle Co., Inc. v. Chester's Market, Inc., 571 F. Supp. 763 (D. Conn. 1983).

"COKE": not generic for Coca-Cola brand cola drink. Coca-Cola Co. v. Koke Co. of America, 254 U.S. 143 (1920); Coca-Cola Co. v. Overland, Inc., 692 F.2d 1250, 216 U.S.P.Q. 579 (9th Cir. 1982). The COCA-COLA and COKE trademarks are probably the most famous and valuable trademarks. Their owner takes considerable pains to prevent them from becoming generic. In *Overland*, for example, it obtained an injunction preventing the defendant and its employees from substituting in response to a customer order for "Coca-Cola" or "Coke" any beverage other than that sold by the Coca-Cola Company unless they first give the customer oral notice of the substitution and obtain the customer's approval. The Ninth Circuit noted prior district court decisions holding that as a general rule signs and menu disclosures advising that a competitive brand was served were insufficient. It declined to hold that signs can never provide adequate notice of beverage substitutions but held that the signs in question were not sufficiently conspicuous to justify a departure from the general rule.

"TURBO-DIESEL": generic for engines having exhaust driven turbine superchargers. Cummins Engine Co. v. Continental Motors Corp., 359 F.2d 892, 149 U.S.P.Q. 559 (CCPA 1966).

"FIRE CHIEF": not generic for a magazine. H. Marvin Ginn Corp. v. Int'l Ass'n of Fire Chiefs, Inc., 789 F.2d 987, 228 U.S.P.Q. 528 (Fed. Cir. 1985).

Evidence of genericness may focus on the owner's use of the mark as well as on competitor, media, and public use.[293] Consumer use surveys play a major role in determinations of genericness as they do in other areas of trademark law.[294]

Dictionary definitions may dictate a conclusion that a mark is generic, especially when the applicant uses the mark consistently with the mark's dictionary sense. In *Gould Paper*,[295] the court rejected the applicant's attempt to register "SCREEN-WIPE" for a "pre-moistened, anti-static cloth for cleaning computer and television screens."

> "Gould's own submissions provided the most damaging evidence that its alleged mark is generic and would be perceived by the purchasing public as merely a common name for its goods rather than a mark identifying the good's source. On its own specimen supporting the application, Gould advises: 'a . . . wipe . . . for . . . screens.' . . . The compound immediately and unequivocally describes the purpose, function and nature of the goods. . . . "[296]

Occasional usage of a term in publications by persons other than the claimant does not dictate a finding of genericness— especially where the usage is improper or is accompanied by a reference to the claimant.[297] In *Books on Tape*,[298] the court held

---

[293] *See* National Aeronautics and Space Administration v. Bully Hill Vineyards Inc., 3 U.S.P.Q.2d 1671 (PTO TTAB 1987) ("SPACE SHUTTLE" held generic for reusable spacecraft, especially such craft comprising an orbiter, two solid rocket boosters and an external tank. Evidence on this point consisted of testimony of the public affairs officers connected with the SPACE SHUTTLE program, examination of NASA's program regarding use of its emblems, etc. by others, and use of the term within the aerospace industry, and by the United States government in promulgating rules, and the like, the media and the public.)

[294] A major part of the "MONOPOLY" trademark controversy focused on surveys. *See* § 5C[3][b][vi].

[295] *In re* Gould, 834 F.2d 1017, 5 U.S.P.Q.2d 1110 (Fed. Cir. 1987).

[296] 834 F.2d at 1019, 5 U.S.P.Q.2d at 1112.

[297] *E.g., In re* Merrill Lynch, Pierce, Fenner and Smith Inc., 828 F.2d 1567, 4 U.S.P.Q.2d 1141 (Fed. Cir. 1987). In *Merrill Lynch*, the Board rejected applicant's application to register "CASH MANAGEMENT ACCOUNT" as a service mark for "stock brokerage services, administration of money market fund services, and providing loans against securities services." It relied on use of the mark in publications as showing genericness. Three examples were:

> "Banks have also stated that brokerage firms, through cash management accounts, have held an unfair advantage over the banking industry. . . . "

> "Although it is a first step toward one-stop investment services, it differs from cash management accounts offered by Merrill Lynch and other brokerages. . . ."

> "The bank also offers customers an assert management account . . . that competes with the highly successful Cash Management Account pioneered by Merrill Lynch & Co." 828 F.2d at 1570, 4 U.S.P.Q.2d at 1143.

The court reversed, holding that the PTO failed to meet its burden to show that the proposed trademark was generic:

> "The burden of showing that a proposed mark is generic remains with the Patent and Trademark Office. . . . The mixture of usages unearthed by the NEXIS computerized retrieval services does not show, by clear evidence, that the financial community views and uses the term CASH MANAGEMENT ACCOUNT as a generic, common descriptive term for the brokerage services to which Merrill Lynch first applied the term. . . .

that PTO committed clear error in finding "BOOKS ON TAPE" generic for cassettes on which books are recorded: "While there have been some vernacular uses of 'books on tape' in newspaper articles, the great majority of those materials concern only petitioner and the fact that petitioner originated a new industry. Largely it appears to be that the media has misused or made a play on petitioner's name."[299]

[iv] *Combinations of Words.* The two-pronged genericness test applies to word combinations. In *Gould Paper*,[300] which denied registration to "SCREENWIPE," the Federal Circuit affirmed the PTO findings that "the separate words joined to form a compound have a meaning identical to the meaning common usage would ascribe to those words as a compound" and that "the common descriptive aspect of applicant's mark is not lost in the combined form."[301] A manufacturer's right to use terms that adequately describe his product precludes the registrability of a mark that "simply joined the two most pertinent and individually generic terms applicable to the product."[302]

[v] *Noun and Adjective.* The generic-descriptive distinction is not simply one between noun and adjective. In *Miller Brewing*,[303] the Seventh Circuit refused to uphold Miller's registered mark "Lite" for beer despite significant evidence of consumer brand identification.[304] "Lite" was descriptive of a product characteristic or

---

"[A] term that immediately and unequivocally describes the purpose and function of appellant's goods is a name for those goods, for '[t]hat is what *names* do. They tell you what the thing *is*.' The term CASH MANAGEMENT ACCOUNT was not shown to meet this standard." 828 F.2d at 1571, 4 U.S.P.Q.2d at 1143-44.

[298] *In re* Books on Tape, Inc., 836 F.2d 519, 520, 5 U.S.P.Q.2d 1301, 1302 (Fed. Cir. 1987).

[299] *See also In re* Montrachet S.A., 878 F.2d 375, 376, 11 U.S.P.Q.2d 1393, 1395 (Fed. Cir. 1989) ("MONTRACHET" is not a generic term for a particular type of goat cheese; examples of allegedly generic usage, including a recipe in a newspaper calling for the use of goat cheese, such as "Montrachet black ash goat cheese," a reference to a "Montrachet-style log" of cheese, and a listing of 92 "varieties" of goat cheese, one of which is "Montrachet," "are not inconsistent with the trademark status of MONTRACHET. . . . That a particular source makes a goat cheese with recognizable characteristics does not convert the designation of source to a common or generic name. . . . To the contrary, it is the trademark function to so identify a product that the consumer is assured of the quality and characteristics that it has come to associate with a particular source of that product.").

[300] *In re* Gould Paper, 834 F.2d 1017, 5 U.S.P.Q..2d 1110 (Fed. Cir. 1987).

[301] 834 F.2d at 1018, 5 U.S.P.Q.2d at 1112.

[302] 834 F.2d at 1019, 5 U.S.P.Q.2d at 1112.

[303] Miller Brewing Co. v. G. Heileman Brewing Co., 561 F.2d 75, 195 U.S.P.Q. 281 (7th Cir. 1977), *cert. denied,* 434 U.S. 1025, 196 U.S.P.Q. 592 (1978).

[304] Refusal to consider evidence on a term's primary significance has been criticized—at least as applied to situations in which the mark is denominative only of a central or distinctive characteristic of the product, rather than the product itself. *See In re* Seats, 757 F.2d 274, 225 U.S.P.Q. 364 (Fed. Cir. 1985).

See also Remington Products, Inc. v. North American Phillips Corp., 892 F.2d 1576, 13 U.S.P.Q.2d 1444 (Fed. Cir. 1990) ("TRAVEL CARE" is generic or descriptive as applied to travel irons and adapter plugs; there are degrees of descriptiveness, and in some cases it is difficult to distinguish a descriptive term, which may be a trademark if secondary meaning is shown, from a generic term, which cannot be a trademark).

ingredient, but "lite"—light—was so descriptive that the court equated it with a generic name for the product type.

[vi] *The Anti-Monopoly Controversy: The 1984 Lanham Act Amendment.* A major controversy over the proper test of genericness arose in connection with Parker Brother's mark "Monopoly" for the famous real estate trading game.[305] A small company sold "Anti-Monopoly," a game based on the original Parker Brothers version. When Parker Brothers objected, the Anti-Monopoly company sought a declaratory judgment that Parker Brother's mark, though registered since 1935, was invalid because it had become the game's name. Parker Brothers counterclaimed for infringement.

Initially, the district court found the trademark rights in "Monopoly" valid and granted declaratory and injunctive relief against infringement. It found that the relevant "genus" was all real estate trading board games. The word "Monopoly" was not the name of this product genus but rather of a particular game produced by a single company (Parker Brothers).

The Ninth Circuit reversed.[306] The "genericness doctrine" reflects consumer usage.

"A genus, in contrast to a species, is a product category including essentially interchangeable goods made by unique producers. To the extent the goods within the genus differ, their distinguishing characteristics are primarily source-particular, e.g., price, quality, and advertising jingle. When, in the consumers' minds, the characteristics which distinguish a particular product are no longer primarily source-particular, that product becomes its own genus, and its name becomes a generic name. . . .

"Once the genus-species distinction, or genericness doctrine is properly understood as reflecting consumer usage of a particular term, a court is prepared to ask the crucial question: whether consumers who ask for [a named game] are seeking the product of a particular producer (species), or are simply describing the product itself (genus)? Source identification is the only word function which trademark law is designed to protect. If the primary significance of the trademark

---

[305] Anti-Monopoly, Inc. v. General Mills Fun Group, 684 F.2d 1316, 216 U.S.P.Q. 588 (9th Cir. 1982), *cert. denied sub nom.* CPG Products Corp. v. Anti-Monopoly, Inc., 459 U.S. 1227 (1982).

For other cases involving game names, see Golomb v. Wadsworth, 592 F.2d 1184, 201 U.S.P.Q. 200 (CCPA 1979), *cert. denied,* 444 U.S.P.Q. 833, 203 U.S.P.Q. 651 (1979); Selchow & Righter Co. v. Western Printing & Lithographing Co., 47 F. Supp. 322, 326 (E.D. Wis. 1942), *aff'd,* 142 F.2d 707, 709 (7th Cir.), *cert. denied,* 323 U.S. 735 (1944) ("Parcheesi" generic to general public). *Cf.* Selchow v. Chaffee & Selchow Mfg. Co., 132 F. 996 (S.D.N.Y. 1904) *appeal dismissed,* 140 F. 989 (2d Cir. 1905) ("Parcheesi" signified the name of a game in India before its introduction into the United States).

See also In re Cooper, 254 F.2d 611, 614-17 (CCPA), *cert. denied,* 358 U.S. 840 (1958) (book title generic because it performs a product-denoting rather than a source-denoting function).

[306] Anti-Monopoly, Inc. v. General Mills Fun Group, 611 F.2d 296, 204 U.S.P.Q. 978 (9th Cir. 1979), *on remand,* 515 F. Supp. 448, 212 U.S.P.Q. 748 (N.D. Calif. 1981), *rev'd,* 684 F.2d 1316, 216 U.S.P.Q. 588 (9th Cir.), *cert. denied, sub nom.* CPG Products Corp. v. Anti-Monopoly, Inc., 459 U.S. 1227 (1982).

is to describe the type of product rather than the producer, the trademark has become a generic term and is no longer a valid trademark.

". . . [W]hen members of the consuming public use a game name to denote the game itself, and not its producer, the trademark is generic, and therefore, invalid." [307]

Applying its analysis of the genericness doctrine, the Ninth Circuit held that the district court erred by picking "the wrong genus—all board games involving real estate trading—for determining genericness, and thus obscured the basic issue: whether MONOPOLY primarily describes a product, or a producer."

"It may be that when a customer enters a game store and asks for MONOPOLY, he means: 'I would like Parker Brothers' version of a real estate trading game, because I like Parker Brothers' products. Thus, I am not interested in board games made by Anti-Monopoly or anyone other than Parker Brothers.' On the other hand, the consumer may mean: 'I want a "Monopoly" game. Don't bother showing me ANTI-MONOPOLY, or EASY MONEY, or backgammon. I am interested in playing the game of monopoly. *I don't much care who makes it.*'

". . . [T]he district court erred by first defining the genus, and then asking the 'primary significance' question about the wrong genus-species dichotomy. The proper mode of analysis is to decide but one question: whether the primary significance of a term is to denote product, or source. In making this determination, the correct genus-species distinction, that is, the correct genericness finding, follows automatically." [308]

The concept reflected in the emphasized phrase in the passage above—"I don't much care who makes it"—became significant on remand. The Antimonopoly company commissioned a survey of persons who (1) had purchased MONOPOLY recently, or (2) intended to purchase MONOPOLY in the near future. The Antimonopoly Survey asked four questions.

(1) Are you aware of "MONOPOLY," the business board game produced by Parker Brothers? [92% were so aware.]

(2) Have your purchased "MONOPOLY" within last couple of years? [Is it possible that you would buy "MONOPOLY" now or in the near future . . . ?] [62% gave an affirmative answer.]

(3) Why did you buy "MONOPOLY?" [82% mentioned some aspect of playing the game; 14% mentioned some educational aspect of the game; 7% mentioned the equipment; 1% mentioned the price; 34% gave other reasons (e.g. a gift for someone).]

(4) Which of these two statements best expresses your meaning when you ask [to purchase] MONOPOLY in a store:

(1) I would like Parker Brothers' "MONOPOLY" primarily because I like Parker Brothers' products. [32%]

---

[307] 611 F.2d at 303.
[308] 611 F.2d at 305-06.

(2) I want "MONOPOLY" game primarily because I am interested in playing "MONOPOLY." I don't much care who makes it. [65%]

The district court again found the MONOPOLY mark not generic. It agreed with Parker Brothers that the "motivation" survey missed the issue: "The dispositive issue . . . is not why consumers buy MONOPOLY sets, but rather, what is their understanding of the name MONOPOLY? Does it primarily denote product or producer? In a single producer case . . . it will not suffice to analyze source-related as opposed to source-irrelevant characteristics because most source related characteristics (e.g., price, style, durability, quality, etc.) are purely relative terms, implying a comparison with product substitutes, or near substitutes."[309]

The Ninth Circuit again reversed, holding that the district court's finding that MONOPOLY was not generic was clearly erroneous.

The court reviewed the "motivation" survey and three other consumer surveys.[310] Unlike the district court, it concluded that the motivation survey supported the

---

[309] 515 F. Supp. at 454.

[310] Parker Brokers' "brand-name" survey, based on a survey used in E.I. Du Pont de Nemours & Co. v. Yoshida International, Inc., 393 F. Supp. 502, 185 U.S.P.Q. 597 (E.D.N.Y. 1975), asked persons whether "Monopoly" is a brand-name, which was defined as follows: "By *brand* name, I mean a name like *Chevrolet*, which is made by *one* company; by common name, I mean 'automobile,' which is made by a number of different companies." The interviewee was then asked to identify as a brand name or common name eight product names. Three were common, three brand; one was Monopoly, and the last Thermos. 90% of the interviewees identified all the common (generic) names. 63% identified Monopoly as a brand name; 54% identified Thermos as a generic name. The Ninth Circuit held that this survey had "no relevance. . . . Under the survey definition, 'Monopoly' would have to be a 'brand name' because it is made by only one company. This tells us nothing at all about the *primary* meaning of "Monopoly' in the minds of consumers." 684 F.2d at 1323, 216 U.S.P.Q. at 594.

Anti-Monopoly's "Thermos" survey, based on a survey used in King-Seeley Thermos Co. v. Aladdin Industries, Inc., 207 F. Supp. 9 (D. Conn. 1962), aff'd, 321 F.2d 577, 138 U.S.P.Q. 349 (2d Cir. 1963), asked persons: "Are your familiar with business boards games of the kind in which players buy, sell, mortgage and trade city streets, utilities and railroads, build houses, collect rents and win by bankrupting all other players, or not?" [53% said yes] and if yes, "If you were going to buy this kind of game, what would you ask for, that is, what would you tell the sales clerk you wanted" [80% said "Monopoly"]. The Ninth Circuit held that the results of this survey constituted "compelling evidence of a proposition that is also dictated by common sense: an overwhelming proportion of those who are familiar with the game would ask for it by the name of 'Monopoly.'" 684 F.2d at 1323, 216 U.S.P.Q. 594.

Parker Brothers' "Tide Survey," offered as a *reductio ad absurdum*, inquired into persons' "motivation" for buying Tide by asking: "Would you buy Tide primarily because you like Procter and Gamble's products, or primarily because you like Tide detergent?" 68% indicated the latter. This arguably shows that many people simply do not understand the concept of a trademark sufficiently to respond correctly to the Motivation Survey because "Tide" is clearly a trademark indicating detergent from a particular source, not a type of detergent. The Ninth Circuit responded:

"There are various respects in which this survey was different from the motivation survey used by Anti-Monopoly, but we shall not suddenly attach great importance to technical considerations. We suspect that these results tend to show that the general public regards 'Tide' as the name of particular detergent, having particular qualities, rather than

conclusion that the primary significance of MONOPOLY is the product rather than source: "In our earlier opinion we made it clear that what was relevant was the sense in which a purchaser used the word 'Monopoly' when asking for the game by that name. The survey was a reasonable effort to find that out and was modelled closely on what we said in our opinion."[311]

Anti-Monopoly induced Congress to amend the Lanham Act to reject the "motivation" test of genericness. The 1984 Trademark Clarification Act[312] amended Sections 14(c) and 45 to protect marks for a "unique product or service," thereby eliminating the Ninth Circuit's genus-of-one view in favor of the traditional two-tiered inquiry. The "primary significance of the registered mark to the relevant public" must be considered in lieu of the "purchaser motivation" test. The Act's legislative history is replete with denunciations of the Ninth Circuit's motivation test as contrary to prior law and potentially destructive of valuable, distinctive trademarks and with declarations of an intent to restore the law of genericness to its pre-*Anti-Monopoly* state.

[vii] *Definition of a "Genus"—New and Unique Products.* The *Anti-Monopoly* controversy and attendant Lanham Act amendments did not resolve the problem of genericness with respect to new, unique products sold under a descriptive or suggestive name that can be viewed as either a new species of an existing product genus or a new genus. The "DIET CHOCOLATE FUDGE SODA" cases highlighted the lingering uncertainties.

> as one producer's brand name for the same detergent which is available from a variety of sources. . . . If the general public does think this, and if the test formulated in Anti-Monopoly I could be mechanically extended to the very different subject of detergents, then Procter and Gamble might have cause for alarm. . . . The motivation survey conducted by Anti-Monopoly, Inc. was in accordance with the views we expressed in Anti-Monopoly I. The results of the Tide Survey are of no relevance to this case." 684 F.2d at 1326, 216 U.S.P.Q. at 596.

For a discussions of the four surveys, see Zeisel, *The Surveys that Broke Monopoly*, 50 U. Chi. L. Rev. 896 (1983). Professor Zeisel criticizes the Ninth Circuit's reliance on the "Thermos" survey because the question assumes that there is a plurality of "games of a kind," when in reality there was only one. He criticizes its rejection of the "brand-name" survey, which provided "fairly direct evidence to the effect that a substantial majority of the population understands Monopoly to be a brand name." He notes that the "Ninth Circuit did not cope well" with the Tide survey, which showed that its legal test of genericness was flawed:

> "The traditional primacy test, measuring the proportion of customers who understand the name to mean the genus and not a species, a product category and not a brand, is clear and simple and can be translated into meaningful behavior, which in turn is directly related to the law's intent. It can be applied in all situations in which the genus consists of more than one member. The Ninth Circuit's primacy test, counting the proportion of persons who say they understand the name as primarily designating the product rather than the producer, is vague, and it is not at all certain that it can be translated with precision into any relevant behavior. Its juxtaposition to the old test, when there is more than one product in the genus, as was done by Parker Brothers' " 'Thermos' survey, reveals the inferiority of the Ninth Circuit's test."

[311] 684 F.2d at 1325, 216 U.S.P.Q. at 595.

[312] P.L. 98-620, 98 Stat. 3335 (Nov. 8, 1984).

Canfield, a Chicago bottler, sold "Canfield's Diet Chocolate Fudge Soda" since the 1970's. After a nationally syndicated columnist praised the product ("Heaven for Dieters: Two Calories Fudge Soda" . . .), Canfield's sales increased dramatically. Imitators appeared and sold competing products using the term "Diet Chocolate Fudge Soda" or "Chocolate Fudge Soda." Canfield brought a series of suits with mixed results. A key factual issue in the cases was whether "fudge" actually denotes a flavor or flavor variation of chocolate—and is therefore descriptive or generic for diet soda—or rather is indicative only of texture (thick candy made of sugar, butter, chocolate and cocoa, none of which are contained in diet soda)—and is therefore at most suggestive for diet soda.

In *A.J. Canfield*,[313] the Third Circuit provided an extended analysis of the genericness issue in the course of affirming the denial of a preliminary injunction. It noted that the primary significance test of genericness, that is, whether a term's primary significance in consumers' minds is the product or the producer, cannot be applied until the court determines the relevant product category or genus. Was the genus chocolate soda or chocolate *fudge* soda? The court offered the following test:

> "[W]hen a producer introduces a product that differs from an established product class in a significant, functional characteristic, and uses the common descriptive term of that characteristic as its name, that new product becomes its own genus, and the term denoting the genus becomes generic if there is no commonly used alternative that effectively communicates the same functional information."[314]

In *Canfield*, the Third Circuit noted that Congress' 1984 codification of the primary significance test confirmed that a trademark need not identify source directly (the "anonymous source rule") and that trademarks need not indicate source exclusively but may have a dual function, but that the test does not assist in product genus determination: "Although a term may primarily signify source if it primarily signifies a product emanating from a single, albeit anonymous, source, it does not primarily signify source if the product that emanates from a single source, *e.g.,* shredded wheat, constitutes its own product genus."[315]

It found unhelpful a "consumer understanding" test. In response to Canfield's survey, which asked respondents "what *kind* of drink chocolate fudge soda is or sounds like," few persons mentioned the term "fudge." According to Canfield, this indicated that "chocolate *fudge* soda" cannot be the kind of product or a product genus. The court disagreed. With a mark signifying goods produced by only one manufacturer, the survey "forces respondents to make a false dichotomy. Because consumers will never have had a reason to consider the question before, such a survey might not elicit real attitudes but merely answers developed on the spot that would be highly susceptible to the influences of survey phraseology."[316] The survey requests a legal conclusion but does not test the meaning of words to the public. A conscientious survey respondent might inquire as to what is meant by product name

---

[313] A.J. Canfield Co. v. Honickman, 808 F.2d 291, 1 U.S.P.Q.2d 1364 (3d Cir. 1986).
[314] 808 F.2d at 293, 1 U.S.P.Q.2d at 1365.
[315] 808 F.2d at 300-01, 1 U.S.P.Q.2d at 1372.
[316] 808 F.2d at 302, 1 U.S.P.Q.2d at 1373.

and brand name and how one distinguishes the two. The answer would be circular: "That question depends on the answers we obtain from you and other respondents."

It refused to endorse a "cross-elasticity of demand" test, which some commentators suggest can be borrowed from antitrust law to determine a product genus for trademark law purposes.[317]

Finding no satisfactory established test for differentiating product brand and product genus, the Third Circuit developed its test from basic principles of trademark law, focusing primarily on competitive need.[318] The genericness doctrine balances two different kinds of confusion so as to minimize confusion without allowing trademarks to serve as patent substitutes by preventing copying of the functional characteristics of a competitor's product.

"If only one manufacturer can use a designation for which there is no common alternative, buyers may be confused by their ignorance that other goods possess the characteristics they seek. If a particular designation is available to all, however, customers who believe that only one manufacturer makes a product with that name may be misled into buying the goods of others, at least in the short run, and may face disappointment because these alternatives differ in subtle characteristics from the brand they wished to buy. . . . The doctrine of genericness reflects the Congressional determination that the interest in preventing the second kind of confusion does not normally justify creating the first, in large part because producers may identify their goods through the use of terms that are not necessary to competitors.

"The genericness doctrine prevents trademarks from serving as the substitutes for patents, and protects the public right to copy any non-patented, functional characteristic of a competitor's product. . . . Trademark law seeks to provide a producer neither with a monopoly over a functional characteristic it has originated nor with a monopoly over a particularly effective marketing phrase. Instead the law grants a monopoly over a phrase only if and to the extent it is necessary to enable consumers to distinguish one producer's goods from others and even then only if the grant of such a monopoly will not substantially disadvantage competitors by preventing them from describing the nature of their goods. . . .

" . . . [T]o be consistent with the primary significance test, whether a product brand with a name used by one producer constitutes its own genus must turn on the extent to which the brand name communicates functional characteristics that differentiate the brand from the products of other producers. In making these

---

[317] The suggestion is that the greater the cross-elasticity of demand—that is, the public's willingness to substitute goods for each other as they vary in price—the more likely that the goods are of the same product genus. The Sixth Circuit noted that "no court . . . has truly attempted to apply this test," that the test "may be unfair to a manufacturer with strong brand loyalty, and that price is more important with some types of goods than others." Accordingly, it refused to endorse a cross-elasticity analysis absent "a method of applying it suited to the subtleties of the trademark context." 808 F.2d at 303, 1 U.S.P.Q.2d at 1374.

[318] This approach is the same as that many courts adopt in applying the functionality doctrine. See § 5C[2][c][v].

calculations, consumer understanding will determine the extent to which a term communicates functional characteristics and the significance of a term's role in doing so because of a dearth or abundance of alternative terms that effectively communicate the same functional information."[319]

Finally, it applied its test to the *Canfield* facts. It found that Canfield created demand for its product by emphasizing in its advertising the functional difference between soda tasting like chocolate fudge and a mere chocolate soda, an established product class. The term "chocolate fudge" is a common descriptive explanation of that functional difference. Flavors having unique characteristics, the court could "imagine no term other than 'chocolate fudge' that communicates the same functional information, namely, that this soda has the taste of chocolate fudge, a particular, full rich chocolate taste." As to Canfield's contention that "no diet soda can taste like chocolate fudge so that chocolate fudge soda cannot be the name of the product genus," the appeals court relied on the district court finding of fact that chocolate fudge did denote a taste.[320]

The Third Circuit's test for determining the genericness of terms used with new or altered products is analytically helpful, but one can seriously question its application of the test in *Canfield*, particularly with respect to the key findings that chocolate fudge is a common descriptive explanation of flavor (clearly it is not) and that no other term will adequately communicate the flavor difference between chocolate soda generally and chocolate "fudge" soda (clearly others will, such as "rich chocolate").

[c] **Surnames.** The common law of trademarks and the Lanham Act treat surnames in the same manner as marks descriptive of goods' nature or quality. Lanham Act Section 2(e) (3) conditionally excludes from registration a trademark that "consists of a mark which . . . (3) is primarily merely a surname." Trademark protection or registration is available for surnames only with a showing that the term has acquired through usage a secondary meaning.[321] When a first user does establish rights in a surname, a subsequent user may have a limited right to use in good faith his or her name in business provided he or she takes reasonable precautions to avoid customer confusion.

---

[319] 808 F.2d at 305, 1 U.S.P.Q.2d at 1375.

[320] The court noted that "[t]o the extent Canfield claims that its soda simply does not have the taste of chocolate fudge, . . . all such a fact would prove is that Canfield has misdescribed its product." 808 F.2d at 308, 1 U.S.P.Q.2d at 1378. Canfield would still not have the right to prevent others from advertising their soda as having that taste.

[321] For an early common law decision recognizing surname protectability on a showing of secondary meaning, see L. E. Waterman Co. v. Modern Pen Co., 235 U.S. 88 (1914), which affirmed an injunction requiring the defendant to use "ARTHUR A. WATERMAN & CO." instead of "A.A. WATERMAN & CO." and to include the disclaimer "not connected with L.E. Waterman." Said Justice Holmes: "whatever generality of expression there may have been in the earlier cases, it is now established that when the use of his own name upon his goods by a later competitor will and does lead the public to understand that those goods are the product of a concern already established and well known under that name, and when the profit of the confusion is known to, and, if that be material, is intended by, the later man, the law will require him to take reasonable precautions to prevent the mistake." 235 U.S. at 94.

Justice Holmes' *L.E. Waterman* opinion is foreshadowed by his *American Waltham* opinion on geographic terms, written for the Massachusetts Supreme Court. See § 5C[3][d].

The conditional surname registration and protection bar applies whether or not the word is in fact the name of a person associated with the mark user.[322] The bar has two possible purposes. One is the same as the exclusion of descriptive terms generally: confronted with a mark that is a surname on a product or service, the public may assume that the mark simply indicates that a person of that surname is the source of goods or services, not that it indicates a specific person (that is, that the mark indicates a single source). The other is that registration and protection of a surname will unjustifiably interfere with the right of other, similarly-named persons to enter business using their name. When a surname mark becomes distinctive (i.e. acquires secondary meaning), the first purpose no longer applies, and the second must be balanced with trademark law's purposes of preventing consumer confusion and protecting goodwill.[323]

[i] *Primary Significance.* Whether a word is "primarily merely a surname" depends on its primary significance to the public. In *Rivera Watch Corp.,*[324] the Board emphasized that a name's primary public significance rather than its rarity is controlling.

> "The terms 'primary' and 'secondary' have well understood meanings in trademark law. In construing 'primarily' in Section 2(e) . . . , we should . . . draw on that meaning. A trademark is a trademark only if it is used in trade. When it is used in trade it must have some impact upon the purchasing public, and it is that impact or impression which should be evaluated in determining whether or not the primary significance of a word when applied to a product is a surname significance. If it is, *and it is only that,* then it is primarily merely a surname. 'Reeves,' "Higgins' and 'Wayne' are thus primarily merely surnames. If the mark has well known meanings as a word in the language and the purchasing public, upon seeing it on the goods, may not attribute surname significance to it, it is not primarily merely a surname. 'King,' 'Cotton,' and 'Boatman' fall in this category.

> "There are some names which by their very nature have only a surname significance even though they are rare surnames. 'Seidenberg,' if rare, would be

---

[322] 815 Tonawanda Street Corp. v. Fay's Drug Co. Inc., 842 F.2d 643, 648, 6 U.S.P.Q.2d 1284, 1288 (2d Cir. 1988) ("FAY'S" is not entitled to federal protection absent evidence of secondary meaning; "For the purpose of trademark analysis, personal names—both surnames and first names—are generally regarded as descriptive terms which require proof of secondary meaning.").

[323] *See In re* Etablissements Darty et Fils, 759 F.2d 15, 225 U.S.P.Q. 652 (Fed. Cir. 1985) ("The statute in Section 2(e)(3) . . . reflects the common law that exclusive rights in a surname per se can not be established without evidence of long and exclusive use which changes its significance to the public from a surname of an individual to a mark for particular goods or services. The common law also recognizes that surnames are shared by more than one individual, each of whom may have an interest in using his surname in business, and by the requirement for evidence of distinctiveness, in effect, delays appropriation of exclusive rights in the name. . . . The statute, thus, provides a period of time, as under the common law, to accommodate the competing interests of others.").

[324] *Ex parte* Rivera Watch Corp., 106 U.S.P.Q. 145 (Comm'r Pat. 1955). The CCPA approved the *Rivera* test in *In re* Standard Elektrik Loreng Aktiengesellschaft, 371 F.2d 870, 152 U.S.P.Q. 563 (CCPA 1967).

in this class. And there are others which have no meaning—well known or otherwise—and are in fact surnames which do not, when applied to goods as trademarks, create the impression of being surnames.

". . . [T]he test to be applied . . . is not the rarity of the name, nor whether it is the applicant's name, nor whether it appears in one or more telephone directories, nor whether it is coupled with a baptismal name or initials. The test should be: What is its primary significance to the purchasing public?"

The Board found that "Rivera" as applied to watches was not primarily merely a surname. The applicant admitted that "Rivera" was a surname, but it was also a Spanish word meaning "small stream or rivulet": "the average member of the purchasing public" would not regard "Rivera" as a surname, even though it has no other meaning.[325]

In *Etablissements Darty et Fils*,[326] the Federal Circuit held that the TTAB did not err in ruling that the examiner established an unrebutted *prima facie* case that "DARTY" is primarily merely a surname. The word is the surname of a principal of the business and "is used in the company name in a manner which reveals its surname significance, at least to those with a modicum of familiarity with the French language." "Darty et Fils" translates as "Darty and Son." The word did not appear in dictionaries as a French or English word.

"The question of whether a word sought to be registered is primarily merely a surname within the meaning of the statute can be resolved only on a case by case basis. Even though a mark may have been adopted because it is the surname of one connected with the business, it may not be primarily merely a surname under the statute because it is also a word having ordinary language meaning. The language meaning is likely to be the primary meaning to the public. . . . On the other hand, where no common word meaning can be shown, a more difficult question must be answered concerning whether the mark presented for registration would be perceived as a surname or as an arbitrary term."[327]

[ii] *Names Combined with Descriptive Terms.* One must consider a mark in its entirety in determining whether it is "primarily merely a surname." In *Hutchinson Technology*,[328] the court found "HUTCHINSON TECHNOLOGY" not primarily

---

[325] The Board's decision reflects linguistic chauvinism. "Rivera" may be recognized as having primarily a surname significance by the Hispanic-speaking population in the United States.

[326] *In re* Etablissements Darty et Fils, 759 F.2d 15, 225 U.S.P.Q. 652 (Fed. Cir. 1985). *Compare In re* Kahan & Weisz, 508 F.2d at 832-33, 184 U.S.P.Q. at 421-22 (C.C.P.A. 1975) ("DUCHARME" for watches not primarily merely a surname); Fisher Radio Corp. v. Bird Electronic Corp., 162 U.S.P.Q. 265 (TTAB 1969) ("BIRD" not primarily merely a surname).

[327] 759 F.2d at 17, 225 U.S.P.Q. at 653.

[328] *In re* Hutchinson Technology Inc., 852 F.2d 552, 7 U.S.P.Q.2d 1490 (Fed. Cir. 1988). *Compare In re* I. Lewis Cigar Manufacturing Co., 205 F.2d 204, 98 U.S.P.Q. 265 (CCPA 1953) (addition of single initial "S" does not remove the mark "S. Seidenberg & Co" as a whole from the status of being primarily merely a surname); *In re* Pickett Hotel Co., 229 U.S.P.Q. 760 (TTAB 1986) ("PICKETT SUITE HOTEL"; addition of descriptive, perhaps even generic term, to surname does not alter primary significance of mark as a surname); *In re* Martinoni, 189 U.S.P.Q. 589 (TTAB 1975) ("MARTINONI LIQUORE"; addition of

merely a surname as applied to etched metal electronic components relating to computers. In rejecting appellant's application to register the mark, the Board erred, both in failing to consider the mark as a whole and in relying on the fact that "technology" was a commonly-used term for computer components.

[iii] *Right to Use Name—Transfer of Good Will of Business.* The courts adopt a flexible approach in balancing (1) the rights of a first user (or his or her successor in interest) of a family name that has acquired a secondary meaning and thus status as a protectable and registrable mark and (2) the rights of a second user who wishes in good faith to use his or her own true family name in a similar line of business. For example, they may permit a second user to use his or her name but only with an appropriate disclaimer.[329] They impose stronger restraints—even absolute prohibitions—when the use is in bad faith (as when a group adds a member to obtain the benefit of his or her name or changes its name to that of a famous competitor)[330] or when the second comer previously sold the business and associated goodwill to the trademark claimant.[331]

---

common descriptive name with no distinguishing capability does not alter surname quality of mark); *In re* Louis De Markus Corp., 136 U.S.P.Q. 677 (TTAB 1963) ("DUFFEY PROCESS"; "process" adds nothing to registrability of mark identifying a carbon dioxide producing apparatus).

Cf. In re Standard Elektrik Loreng Aktiengesellschaft, 371 F.2d 870, 152 U.S.P.Q. 563 (CCPA 1967) (PTO improperly dissected mark in determining that "SCHAUB-LORENZ" is primarily merely a surname).

[329] *But cf.* Basile, S.p.A. v. Basile, 899 F.2d 35, 14 U.S.P.Q.2d 1240 (D.C. Cir. 1989), discussed below.

[330] In Hat Corporation of America v. D.L. Davis Corp., 4 F. Supp. 613 (D. Conn. 1933), the court enjoined the defendant, who shared its profits with a William Dobbs for the apparent purpose of using his name, which was the same as the plaintiff, a well-known hat company, from using the name absolutely rather than with a "not connected with the original Dobbs" suffix: "[O]bviously, halfway limitations inadequate to prevent confusion, propagate litigation, devastating uncertainty in business, and a cynical reaction to the administration of law. Such results cannot be justified by a false tenderness for the rights of the individual. To be sure, he is entitled to protection in all proper use of his name, but not to a use which, though true to the few fully informed, is false to the many who are only partially informed." 4 F. Supp. at 622.

See also Société Vinicole de Champagne v. Mumm, 143 F.2d 240 (2d Cir. 1944); R.W. Rogers Co. v. William Rogers Mfg. Co., 70 F. 1017 (2d Cir. 1895).

[331] *See, e.g.,* Levitt Corp. v. Levitt, 593 F.2d 463, 201 U.S.P.Q. 513 (2d Cir. 1979):

"[S]everal persistent themes may be distilled from the judicial attempts to resolve conflicting interests in the use of trade names by imposing appropriate injunctive relief. If the infringing party has had some experience of his own in an industry, and wishes to establish a business under his own name, it is considered unfair to preclude him from using his name under all circumstances and for all times, although the first-comer has established a reputation and goodwill under the same appellation. . . .

"Where, as here, however, the infringing party has previously sold his business, including use of his name and its goodwill, to the plaintiff, sweeping injunctive relief is more tolerable.

"Goodwill is a valuable property right derived from a business's reputation for quality and service. . . . To protect the property interest of the purchaser, then, the courts will be especially alert to foreclose attempts by the seller to 'keep for himself the essential

Taylor Wine[332] is instructive.

"The conflict between a first comer who has given a secondary meaning (as well as trademark registration) to a family name, and a later comer who wishes to use his own true family name as a trademark in the same industry has been one of the more interesting issues in the law of trademark infringement. The problem is made more difficult when the second comer has his own background of experience in the particular industry, and is not simply a newcomer. See *John T. Lloyd Laboratories, Inc. v. Lloyd Brothers Pharmacists, Inc.*, 131 F.2d 703 (6th Cir. 1942).

"In the nineteenth and earlier twentieth centuries, both the state and federal courts tended to be highly solicitous of an individual's personal right to use his own name in trade. . . .

"With the passage of the Federal Trade-Mark Act of 1905, . . . and an increasing commercial reliance on marketing techniques to create name recognition and goodwill, the courts adopted a more flexible approach to the conflicting property interests involved in surname trademark infringement cases.

. . . .

"Since the field is one that does not lend itself to strict application of the rule of stare decisis because the fact patterns are so varied, we must try to identify the elements that have influenced decisions on the adequacy of the remedy.

"For example, the fact that an alleged infringer has previously sold his business with its goodwill to the plaintiff makes a sweeping injunction more tolerable. . . . So, too, if an individual enters a particular line of trade for no apparent reason other than to use a conveniently confusing surname to his advantage, the injunction is likely to be unlimited. See *Vick Medicine Co. v. Vick Chemical Co.*, 11 F.2d 33 (5th Cir. 1926). . . .

"If, however, the second comer owns the company himself and evinces a genuine interest in establishing an enterprise in which his own skill or knowledge can be made known to the public, that argues in favor of allowing him to use his own name in some restricted fashion. . . . As this court said in *Société Vinicole de Champagne v. Mumm*, 143 F.2d 240, 241 (2d Cir. 1944), to prohibit an individual from using his true family surname is to 'take away his identity: without it he cannot make known who he is to those who may wish to deal with him; and that is so grievous an injury that courts will avoid imposing it, if they possibly can.' . . .

---

thing he sold, and also keep the price he got for it,' Guth v. Guth Chocolate Co., . . . 224 F. at 934. And if the district court finds that the seller has attempted to arrogate to himself the trade reputation for which he received valuable consideration, broad remedies may be effected to restore to the plaintiff the value of his purchase." 593 F.2d at 468.

[332] Taylor Wine Co. v. Bully Hill Vineyards, Inc., 569 F.2d 731, 196 U.S.P.Q. 593 (2d Cir. 1978). *See also* David B. Findlay, Inc. v. Findlay, 18 N.Y.2d 12, 271 N.Y.S.2d 652, 218 N.E.2d 531 (1966), *cert. denied*, 385 U.S. 930 (1967) ("The so-called 'sacred right' theory that every man may employ his own name in his business is not unlimited"); John B. Stetson Co. v. Stephen L. Stetson Co., 128 F.2d 981 (2d Cir. 1942).

"When confusion is likely, however, there must obviously be some limitation on an individual's unrestricted use of his own name. Thus, a second comer may not use any name, mark or advertisement indicating that he is the successor of another corporation or that his goods are the products of that corporation. *Donnell v. Herring-Hall-Marvin Safe Co.*, 208 U.S. 267 (1908). Yet, he may retain a limited use of the family name even though goodwill has been conveyed to the plaintiff. *Marvin Safe Co. v. Hall's Safe Co.*, 208 U.S. 555, 558 (1908).

. . . .

"Speaking generally, when the defendant demonstrates a genuine desire to build a business under his own name, courts have been reluctant to proscribe all surname use whatever even though the defendant's conduct has been less than exemplary."[333]

In *Taylor*, the plaintiff, a major wine producer and distributor, was founded in about 1880 by Walter Taylor in New York's Finger Lakes region and is now well-known to the fruit-of-the-vine imbibing public. In the 1970s, Taylor's grandson, Walter S. Taylor, purchased the original family vineyard at Bully Hill and began marketing wines under the "Bully Hill" label. On the label, the words "Walter S. Taylor" and "Original" appeared in large print.

In the Taylor Wine Company's suit against Walter S. Taylor and his company, the district court granted an injunction that absolutely barred the defendants from using the word "Taylor" on their labels or advertising. On appeal, the Second Circuit agreed that the plaintiff's mark was protectable and that some relief was appropriate but found that the injunction was too broad. The defendant Taylor, a scholar of enology and sincerely interested in making and selling fine wines, should be able to show his personal connection with Bully Hill: "He may use his signature on a Bully Hill label or advertisement if he chooses, but only with appropriate disclaimer that he is not connected with, or a successor to, the Taylor Wine Company. He must also be restrained from using such words as 'Original' or 'Owner of the Taylor Family Estate.'" The court remanded the case to the district court to enter an appropriate order.[334]

In *Basile*,[335] the District of Columbia Circuit found a second comer's modifications of its surname mark inadequate to prevent confusion and protect the first user's rights. Plaintiff "Basile," an Italian design house, had an established United States market presence since 1972. Defendant Franchesco Basile made and sold watches in Italy since 1946 but did not enter the U.S. market until 1968, using a composite

---

[333] 569 F.2d at 734-35.

[334] The *Taylor* case's subsequent history is amusing. On remand, the district court formulated a detailed order. The Second Circuit modified the order. Taylor Wine Co. Inc. v. Bully Hill Vineyards Inc., 590 F.2d 701, 201 U.S.P.Q. 65 (2d Cir. 1978). The district court found the defendants guilty of contempt. Taylor Wine Co. Inc. v. Bully Hill Vineyards Inc., 208 U.S.P.Q. 80 (W.D. N.Y. 1980) (describing the defendants' "distaste for adherence to judicial directives." "It commenced marketing wines with printed labels containing references to Taylor highlighted in black ink . . . It also marked and masked the portraits on its wine labels so as to deride the injunction of this court." 208 U.S.P.Q. at 81.

[335] Basile, S.p.A. v. Basile, 899 F.2d 35, 14 U.S.P.Q.2d 1240 (D.C. Cir. 1989).

"Basile" mark with a double "B." The district court accepted as adequate to avoid confusion the defendant's proposed modifications, which involved changing the typestyle, enlarging the "double B" design to twice the size of the "Basile" name, adding the geographic designator "Venezia" to the mark, and including the following "affirmative" disclaimer (with no specification of typeface size): "BASILE watches emanate exclusively from Diffusione Basile de Francesco Basile & Co., S.A.S. in Venice, Italy. Diffusione Basile is devoted solely to the manufacture and sale of fine watches throughout the world." The appeals court disagreed.

"Common sense and experience make clear that under the district court's arrangement Francesco's watches will continue to be known as 'Basile watches.' . . .

"The spoken version of the marks will not differ even by prefix; the disclaimer itself even uses the protected name, and only that name. Neither the changed typestyle nor the enhanced 'double B' symbol can change this fact; we think it unlikely that watch buyers will ask for a 'double B watch' when the simple 'Basile watch' is at hand. . . . Nor do we think this confusion avoided by the inclusion of 'Venezia,' especially as Basile is also Italian, and we doubt many American buyers place it firmly or exclusively in Milan. . . .

. . . .

"Courts have rarely approved so mild a cure as that adopted by the district court here. They have routinely required second comers at a minimum to use full names, first as well as second in equal size. . . . The more recent trend is to forbid any use of the name as part of the proprietor's trademark, permitting use only in a subsidiary capacity, and again with the first name attached. . . . In either event, the junior user has almost uniformly been bound to display negative disclaimers. . . . So much for Francesco's plea that forcing him to include the full name 'Francesco Basile' on the watch would be an unreasonable or insupportable burden. . . .

". . . Francesco takes refuge in the precept that an individual has a 'right' to do business under his own name. If some confusion persists under the challenged regime, he seems to say, that is an acceptable price for protecting the privilege. A seller's right to use his family name might have carried the day against a risk of buyer confusion in an era when the role of personal and localized reputation gave the right a more exalted status. . . . But even quite old decisions have enjoined a second comer's use of his name where necessary to prevent confusion. . . .

"True, even recent decisions have invoked the right to use one's name, at least as an interest against which the senior user's are balanced. . . . But its weight has decidedly diminished. The courts are now consistent in imposing tighter restrictions on the second comer in the face of possible confusion. . . . ; any residual protection of the second comer's use of his own name seems amply explained by the more general principle that an equitable remedy should be no broader than necessary to correct the wrong. . . . Where the second comer had established no reputation under his own name, one court did not even purport to 'balance.' . . .

"This trend in the law unsurprisingly reflects trends in the marketplace. In a world of primarily local trade, the goodwill of an anchovy paste seller may well have depended on his individual reputation within the community. . . . Other than understandable pride and sense of identity, the modern businessman loses nothing by losing the name. A junior user's right to use his name thus must yield to the extent its exercise causes confusion with the senior user's mark. . . . Here Francesco Basile's interest in the use of his name is peculiarly weak. He has no reputation in the United States as a watchmaker. Even in Europe he had until recently marketed his wares under the tradenames 'BASMICH' and 'BM,' so we may infer that even his identity interests have been slight. (In fact we have been presented with the opinion of an Italian court which appears to prohibit Francesco from using his name in Italy. *Diffusione Basile di Francesco Basile & C. s.a.s. v. Basile S.p.A.*, Judgment No. 9877 (Civil Court of Milan Apr. 28, 1988) (unpublished opinion appended to Brief of Appellant).) . . . While finding no error in the district court's refusal to draw conclusions with respect to Francesco's intentions, . . . we think the only plausible motivation for his fight here is a wish to free-ride on Basile's goodwill, precisely what the law means to suppress. . . ."[336]

[d] **Geographic Marks.** The common law of trademarks and the Lanham Act treat marks that are primarily *geographically* descriptive of the goods in the same manner as marks that are descriptive of the goods' nature or quality.[337] Section 2(e)(2) conditionally excludes from registration a trademark that "consists of a mark which. . . . (2) when applied to the goods of the applicant is primarily geographically descriptive or deceptively misdescriptive of them. . . . "[338] Trademark protection or registration is available for marks that are primarily geographically descriptive only with a showing that the term has acquired secondary meaning through use.[339]

---

[336] 899 F.2d at 37-40, 14 U.S.P.Q.2d at 1242-43.

[337] *See* § 5C[3][a].

[338] 15 U.S.C. § 1052(e)(2). For an early common law decision, see Canal Co. v. Clarke, 80 U.S. (13 Wall.) 311 (1871).

[339] Common law decisions recognized the protectability of a geographic mark upon a showing of secondary meaning. In American Waltham Watch Co. v. United States Watch Co., 173 Mass. 85, 53 N.E. 141 (1899), Justice Holmes affirmed an injunction against a defendant's use of "Waltham" or "Waltham, Mass." on its watches' dials even though it in fact made the watches in Waltham. The plaintiff established that "Waltham," "by long use in connection with plaintiff's watches, has come to have a secondary meaning as a designation of the watches which the public has become accustomed to associate with the name." Opined Justice Holmes:

"It is desirable that the plaintiff should not lose custom by reason of the public mistaking another manufacturer for it. It is desirable that the defendant should be free to manufacture watches at Waltham, and to tell the world that it does so. The two desirata cannot both be had to their full extent, and we have to fix the boundaries as best we can. . . . It is true that a man cannot appropriate a geographical name; but neither can he a color, or any part of the English language, or even a proper name to the exclusion of others whose names are like his. . . . [T]he name of a person may become so associated with his goods that one of the same name coming into the business later will not be allowed to use even his own name without distinguishing his wares. . . . And so, we doubt not, may a geographical name acquire a similar association with a similar effect." 173 Mass. at 87, 53 N.E. at 142.

A term is primarily geographically descriptive or deceptively misdescriptive if it (1) has geographic significance, and (2) "would tend to be regarded by buyers as descriptive of the geographic location of origin of the goods or services."[340] The latter requirement calls for a goods/place association on the part of the average consuming public.

The common law and the Lanham Act lump geographically *mis*descriptive terms together with geographically descriptive ones, just as with other types of descriptive terms.[341] It does not matter whether the goods or services of the trademark claimant come from the area in question.

A geographic term that serves as an indication of regional origin may qualify for certification mark registration.[342]

[i]   *Geographic Significance.* In *Charles S. Loeb Pipes,*[343] the Board held "OLD DOMINION" primarily geographically descriptive of applicant's pipe tobacco because "OLD DOMINION" is understood to refer to Virginia. "Nicknames and even maps and geographical abbreviations used as trademarks, have, over the years, been treated under the common law and statutory interpretation in the same manner as ordinary geographical marks."[344]

[ii]   *Goods/Place Association.* A mark is primarily geographically descriptive or misdescriptive only if the public associates the goods with the referenced place.[345]

---

[340] McCarthy, Trademarks and Unfair Competition § 14:2 (2d ed. 1984).

[341] *See In re* Nantucket, Inc., 677 F.2d 95, 104, 213 U.S.P.Q. 889, 896-897 (CCPA 1982) (Nies concurring):

"It is simply illogical to say that CHICAGO is descriptive of shirts if the manufacturer is located in Chicago, but arbitrary, if he is not located there. The public is not aware of the actual locations of most businesses. The public is aware of trade practice and makes, or is presumed likely to make, a goods/place association in either instance. Nor is it any less objectionable to a Chicago merchant if the term is used by a non-local rather than another local merchant."

See also Singer Mfg. Co. v. Birginal-Bigsby Corp., 319 F.2d 273, 138 U.S.P.Q. 63 (CCPA 1963) ("AMERICAN BEAUTY" is primarily geographically deceptively misdescriptive when applied to sewing machines of Japanese origin).

[342] *See* § 5C[1][c].

[343] *In re* Charles S. Loeb Pipes, 190 U.S.P.Q. 238 (PTO TTAB 1976).

[344] 190 U.S.P.Q. 238. *See also In re* Canada Dry Ginger Ale, Inc., 32 U.S.P.Q. 49 (CCPA 1936) (map of Canada); Hart Schaffner & Marx v. Empire Manufacturing Co., 94 U.S.P.Q. 171 (CCPA 1952) ("DIXIE"); Chappell v. Goltsman, 91 U.S.P.Q. 30 (D. Ala. 1951) (" BAMA").

[345] Some examples of determinations of geographic significance and association follow.

"RODEO DRIVE": *not* geographically descriptive of perfumes even though Rodeo Drive is a Beverly Hills, California, center for shops selling expensive consumer items. *In re* Jacques Bernier, 894 F.2d 389, 13 U.S.P.Q.2d 1725 (Fed. Cir. 1990).

"WORLD": *not* geographically descriptive of carpets. World Carpets, Inc. v. Dick Littrell's New World Carpets, 438 F.2d 482, 486, 168 U.S.P.Q. 609 (5th Cir. 1971).

"LaTOURAINE": *not* geographically descriptive of coffee even though "Touraine" was an ancient French province. La Touraine Coffee Co. v. Lorraine Coffee Co., 157 F.2d 115 (2d Cir. 1946), *cert. denied,* 329 U.S. 771, (1946).

"ENGLISH LEATHER": *not* geographically descriptive of men's toiletries. Mem Co. v. The Hes Co., 149 U.S.P.Q. 8 (D. Cal. 1966).

It is quite possible that the same word may be excludably geographic when applied to one product or service but not when applied to another.[346]

In *Nantucket*,[347] the Board affirmed rejection of applicant's application to register "NANTUCKET" for men's shirts. Overruling prior board decisions to the contrary,[348] it held that it was not necessary to show public association of the goods with the place because such a requirement would import subjective determinations into the inquiry. It was sufficient that the term have a readily recognizable geographic meaning and no nongeographic significance.

The court reversed because there was no indication that the purchasing public would expect men's shirts to have their origin in Nantucket, a Massachusetts summer resort. The Board's simple test was contrary to the statute, which requires that a mark be geographically descriptive or deceptively misdescriptive "when applied to the goods." Also, if goods do not originate from the area denoted by the mark, the mark must not only be "misdescriptive" but "deceptively" so. "Before that statutory characterization may be properly applied, there must be a reasonable basis for believing that purchasers are likely to be deceived." Prior court decisions confirm that "geographically deceptive misdescriptiveness cannot be determined without considering whether the public associates the goods with the place which the mark names. If the goods do not come from the place named, and the public makes no goods-place association, the public is not deceived and the mark is accordingly not geographically deceptively misdescriptive."

In *Nantucket*, Judge Nies wrote an extensive concurring opinion, rejecting the position put forth by the applicant/appellant and supported by some prior board decisions that a mark could be geographically misdescriptive only if the geographic place in question is "noted for" products or services of the type in question:

"HYDE PARK": *not* geographically descriptive of men's suits. Hyde Park Clothes, Inc. v. Hyde Park Fashions, Inc., 93 U.S.P.Q. 250, 254 (S.D. N.Y. 1951), aff'd, 204 F.2d 223, 97 U.S.P.Q. 246 (2d Cir.), cert. denied, 346 U.S. 827, 99 U.S.P.Q. 491 (1953).

"DENVER WESTERNS": geographically descriptive for western-style shirts. In re Handler Fenton Westerns, Inc., 214 U.S.P.Q. 848 (PTO TTAB 1982).

"MONTE CARLO": geographically descriptive of watches. In re Datatime Corp., 203 U.S.P.Q. 878 (PTO TTAB 1979).

[346] *Compare* National Lead Co. v. Wolfe, 223 F.2d 195 (9th Cir. 1955), cert. denied, 350 U.S. 883 (1955) ("DUTCH BOY" not geographically deceptively misdescriptive of paints) *with* National Lead Co. v. Michigan Bulb Co., 120 U.S.P.Q. 115 (Comm'r 1959) ("DUTCH BOY" deceptively misdescriptive of flower bulbs not imported from Holland).

[347] *In re* Nantucket, Inc., 677 F.2d 95, 213 U.S.P.Q. 889 (CCPA 1982).

See also In re Jacques Bernier, 894 F.2d 389, 391, 13 U.S.P.Q.2d 1725, 1726 (Fed. Cir. 1990) ("[T]he word 'primarily' in section 2(e)(2) shows that 'the intent of the federal statute [is not] to refuse registration of a mark where the geographic meaning is minor, obscure, remote, or unconnected with the goods.' "); *In re* Loew's Theatres, Inc., 769 F.2d 764, 767, 226 U.S.P.Q. 865, 867 (Fed. Cir. 1985) ("the statute reflects the common law principle that a geographic term, used in a fictitious, arbitrary, or fanciful manner, is protectable like any other non-descriptive term. Usage in such a manner is not 'primarily' as a geographic designation.").

[348] *E.g., In re* Circus Ices, Inc., 158 U.S.P.Q. 64 (TTAB 1968) ("HAWAIIAN ICE" not geographically descriptive or misdescriptive of flavored ice products).

"Protection and registration of geographic names as marks embodies concepts comparable to those applicable to surnames as well as to terms which are descriptive of the nature or quality of goods or services. A geographic name might appropriately be viewed as a hybrid in this respect. Courts do not readily recognize trademark rights in such names or terms because of the legitimate interests of other merchants in truthfully being able to use them in connection with their own wares or services.

". . . [T]he first question is whether the name is primarily of geographic significance but . . . that does not end the matter.

"A geographic term may be used in a manner which is (1) inherently distinctive, which includes arbitrary and suggestive usage, (2) generic, (3) descriptive, (4) deceptively misdescriptive, or, (5) deceptive. . . . [S]uch a determination can only be made by consideration of the specific goods on which the name or term is used. In every case the issue which must be resolved is: What meaning, if any, does the term convey to the public with respect to the goods on which the name is used?

. . . .

"That a place is 'noted for' goods is only one circumstance under which a geographic name would be barred by § 2(e)(2). 'Noted for' and 'public association' thus, are not equivalent tests for determining public goods/place association."[349]

Judge Nies traced the treatment of geographic terms at common law[350] and under the Lanham Act.[351] She criticized prior decisions for failing to recognize that the bar

---

[349] 677 F.2d at 102.

[350] She noted:

"Basic to consideration of the registrability and protectability of any geographic term as a trademark is the routine commercial practice of merchants, whether they are growers, manufacturers, distributors, or local retailers, in placing the name of their location on their goods or using the name in their trade names. Because the public would be aware of common trade practice, the common law originally deemed all use of geographic names wholly informational and unprotectible. It was believed such names could not function and, in any event, should not be recognized as the identification of a single source. Thus, we must start with the concept that a geographic name of a place of business is a descriptive term when used on the goods of that business. There is a public goods/place association, in effect, presumed.

"However, as with other terms which are descriptive when first used, it came to be recognized that through substantially exclusive and extensive use, a merchant might develop a protectible goodwill in such a geographically descriptive name upon proof that the name ceased being informational to the public and came to indicate a source of goods." 677 F.2d at 102.

[351] She noted:

"Section 2(e) originally was drafted to preclude registration on the Principal Register of a term which has a 'geographic or descriptive meaning' when applied to the goods. The provision was restricted and divided and became (1) 'merely descriptive [of the goods],' or (2) 'primarily geographically descriptive.' The latter change was to exempt from § 2(e)(2)

to registrability and protectability of geographic terms is routed in competitive need. She also argued that "the defense of geographic descriptiveness, put forth by an alleged infringer, should be available only to one with a legitimate personal interest in use of the name."

[iii]   *Significance to Average U.S. Consumer.* In *Société*,[352] the court held that "VITTEL" and a bottle design for cosmetic products was not primarily geographically descriptive, emphasizing that a word's significance to "mill-run" purchasers rather than "well-travelled" sophisticates is controlling. The applicant's place of business was Vittel, France, a small town with some reputation as a watering place, spa, and resort, and containing producers of bottled water, salts, and pastilles.

> "[A] prima facie case of unregistrability cannot be made out simply by evidence showing that the mark sought to be registered is the name of a place known generally to the public; it is also necessary to show that the public would make a goods/place association, i.e., believe that the goods for which the mark is sought to be registered originate in that place. To hold such a belief, it is necessary, of course, that the purchasers perceive the mark as a place name and this is where the question of obscurity or remoteness comes to the fore.

> "In dealing with all of these questions of the public's response to word symbols, we are dealing with the supposed reactions of a segment of the American public, in this case the mill-run of cosmetics purchasers, not with the unusually well-travelled, the aficionados of European watering places, or with computer operators checking out the meaning of strange words on NEXIS."[353]

---

a mark, such as ALASKA for bananas. Next, § 2(e)(2) was changed to insert 'or misdescriptive' with the explanation . . .

. . . .

'. . . for example, in a case where New York was used in a place other than New York— "New York" was used in Boston as trade-mark. Now it might be descriptive if it were not used for New York, don't you see, but it would be misdescriptive and be equally objectionable.'

"It then appears that it was feared that this language might bar names and terms used in an arbitrary (or no more than suggestive) manner with respect to particular goods. Arguably any non-descriptive use, even if arbitrary, is, in a sense, misdescriptive. Accordingly, the word 'deceptively' was inserted before 'misdescriptive' in both § 2(e) (1) and § 2(e) (2), again, to avoid technical rejections of applications to register marks such as IVORY for soap, or ALASKA for bananas." 677 F.2d at 104.

[352] *In re* Société Generale des Eaux Minerales de Vittel S.A., 824 F.2d 957, 3 U.S.P.Q.2d 1450 (Fed. Cir. 1987). The court discussed with apparent approval two prior Board decisions. *In re* Bavaria St. Pauli Brauerie AG, 222 U.S.P.Q. 926 (PTO TTAB 1984) (JEVER not primarily geographic for beer even though the beer came from the small German town Jever); *In re* Brauerie: Aying Frank Inselkammer KG, 217 U.S.P.Q. 73 (PTO TTAB 1983) (AYINGER Bier not primarily geographic for beer even though the beer comes from the town Aying, a suburb of Munich, Germany).

[353] 824 F.2d at 959, 3 U.S.P.Q.2d at 1452.

The court stressed that "we are not concerned with the public in other countries."[354] It found no evidence that "the American cosmetic purchasing public is aware of the existence of Vittel, France, or with its production of mineral water."

[iv] *Registration Under Lanham Act—Prima Facie Case.* When an applicant seeks to register a mark, the PTO need only make a *prima facie* showing of a goods/place association. In *Loew's Theatres*,[355] the Federal Circuit affirmed the PTO's refusal to register "DURANGO" for chewing tobacco. Durango, Mexico, is not an obscure place name, and a reference work listed tobacco in a short list of the region's principal crops. No more could be expected of the PTO by way of proof because the PTO lacks means to conduct a marketing survey. Also, "it does not detract from the *prima facie* case made by the PTO that there are a few other uses of Durango as a geographic name, such as Durango, Colorado."

> "That there is more than one place bearing the name or that one place is better known than another is not dispositive. The issue is not the fame or exclusivity of the place name, but the likelihood that a particular place will be associated with particular goods. Thus, the mark DURANGO for skis might also be barred (without proof of secondary meaning) if it were shown that Durango, Colorado, is a ski resort."[356]

The court gave no significance to the fact that the applicant obtained a prior registration of the same word ("DURANGO") for a similar product (cigars): "Each application for registration of a mark for particular goods must be separately evaluated. Nothing in the statute provides a right *ipso facto* to register a mark for additional goods when items are added to a company's line or substituted for other goods covered by a registration."[357]

[e] **Foreign Words and Equivalents.** Questions arise as to the trademark status in the United States of words that are descriptive or generic in another country or in a language other than English. Two lines of legal authority are of interest. One is the "doctrine of foreign equivalents." Another is a line of cases dealing with terms (whether in English or another language) that are generic in other countries but not in the United States.

[i] *The Doctrine of Foreign Equivalents.* Under the doctrine of foreign equivalents, a word in a non-English language is "translated into English and then tested

---

[354] For a discussion of the treatment of foreign words and words descriptive or generic in other countries, see § 5C[3][e].

[355] *In re* Loew's Theatres, Inc., 769 F.2d 764, 226 U.S.P.Q. 865 (Fed. Cir. 1985). *Compare In re* Nantucket, Inc., 677 F.2d 95, 213 U.S.P.Q. 889, 898 (CCPA 1982) (Nies concurring; "That [a word] is considered 'primarily geographic' . . . does not make the term descriptive of the goods or make a prima facie case. . . . [I]t is incumbent on the PTO to put forth evidence that other businesses have or are likely to have legitimate interests in use of the geographic name claimed by the applicant. . . . The PTO frequently makes use of telephone directories in connection with proving surname significance. The same type of evidence could be made of record to show that businesses dealing in the same or related goods exist in the named area.").

[356] 769 F.2d at 768-69, 226 U.S.P.Q. at 868.

[357] 769 F.2d at 769, 226 U.S.P.Q. at 869.

for descriptiveness or genericness."[358] Under this doctrine, it would not seem to matter whether the "foreign equivalent" had ever been used in another country—generically, descriptively or otherwise. The doctrine of foreign equivalents also applies, to an extent, to the determination of likelihood of confusion between two marks.[359]

---

[358] McCarthy, Trademarks and Unfair Competition § 12:13.

See McKesson & Robbins, Inc. v. Charles H. Phillips Chemical Co., 53 F.2d 342, *modified*, 53 F.2d 1011 (2d Cir. 1931), *cert. denied*, 285 U.S. 552 (1932) (registration of LECHE-DE-MAGNESIA cancelled because it is generic as a literal translation into Spanish of the generic term MILK OF MAGNESIA for a pharmaceutical product); *In re* Northern Paper Mills, 64 F.2d 998, 999, 17 U.S.P.Q. 492 (CCPA 1933) (registration of GASA for toilet paper refused; the English equivalent of the Spanish word "gasa" was gauze, meaning a thin, slight, transparent fabric, which is at least descriptive of toilet paper; "a descriptive word, used in one of the modern languages of the principal nations of the word, cannot be properly registered as a trade mark. . . ."); *In re* Hag Aktiengesellschaft, 155 U.S.P.Q. 598 (PO TTAB 1967) (registration of the mark KABA for a coffee product refused because a word pronounced "kava" meant coffee in various Slavic languages); *In re* Zazzara, 156 U.S.P.Q. 348 (T.T.A.B. 1967) (registration of the mark PIZZE FRITTE for comestible fried dough refused; the Italian term "pizze fritte" translated to "fried dough" (plural) in English; "it is well established that no distinction can be made between English words and their foreign equivalents with respect to registrability").

A series of cases deal with a registrant's attempt to register the mark LA POSADA for lodging and restaurant services. In Spanish, "la posada" means "home, dwelling; lodging-house, inn, small hotel, lodging," and the applicant was in fact operating a hotel. *In re* Pan Tex. Hotel Corp., 178 U.S.P.Q. 445 (PO TTAB 1973) (registration on Principal Register refused); *In re* Pan Tex. Hotel Corp., 190 U.S.P.Q. 109 (PO TTAB 1973) (registration on Supplemental Register allowed because mark is capable of distinguishing the applicant's services from those of others; " 'La Posada' and its English equivalent 'the inn' create different commercial impressions. . . . "[B]ecause of the setting in which applicant uses 'La Posada', it is not likely that purchasers would stop and translate said notation into its English equivalent . . . ; while 'La Posada' may be literally translated as 'the inn', but it is clear from the Board's discussion in its prior decision of the various dictionary definitions thereof that such designation carries the added implication of a home or dwelling, and thus has a connotative flavor which is slightly different from that of the words 'the inn' . . . "); *In re* Central Soya, 220 U.S.P.Q. 914, 917-18 n.5 (PTO TTAB 1984) (POSADA for Mexican style prepared frozen enchiladas does not create likelihood of confusion with the mark LA POSADA for hotel services; the mark was different from LA POSADA because of the absence of the definite article "LA" and was for a class of products rather than for hotel services; the descriptive character of the two marks made confusion less likely—even though a majority of the public in the United States were not aware of the Spanish meaning of "la posada. . . . [T]he Board and the courts have recognized that, with respect to generic terms, no one can be granted the exclusive right to use the name of an article, either in our native tongue or its equivalent in any foreign language. . . . This is so despite the fact that the foreign term may not be commonly known to the general public. . . . By analogy, we do not believe that the registered mark should be considered any more arbitrary (confusion more likely) because some may not know its meaning.").

[359] McCarthy, Trademarks and Unfair Competition § 23:14. *See In re* Sarkli, Ltd., 721 F.2d 353, 220 U.S.P.Q. 111 (Fed. Cir. 1983) (no likelihood of confusion between the applicant's REPECHAGE mark and the prior registered mark SECOND CHANCE because, *inter alia*, the French and English terms are not exact synonyms and there is only a rough similarity in connotation). *Compare* Pizzeria Uno Corp. v. Temple, 224 U.S.P.Q. 185, 193 (4th Cir. 1984) (use of "Taco Uno" for a Mexican restaurant is confusingly similar to "Pizzeria Uno" for a pizza restaurant; "uno" as translated is suggestive, not descriptive).

Professor McCarthy states that, when the issue is the genericness or descriptiveness of a word in a foreign language, the "test is whether, to those American buyers familiar with the foreign language, the word would have a generic [or descriptive] connotation." [360] This view may not be fully supported by the cases. The case law refers to "American buyers familiar with the foreign language" for two purposes. One purpose is to exclude from the doctrine of foreign equivalents words from ancient or very obscure languages. The other purpose is to establish the proper translation of the foreign language word when, for example, there are several meanings or the word is misspelled or must be transliterated from another alphabet. The cases do *not* support the proposition that the foreign language speaking segment of the United States must recognize that the foreign language word is generic or descriptive—only that it be so once translated.

[ii] *Generic Terms in Other Countries.* There are two opposing lines of authority on whether a term that is generic in another country but not in the United States can be appropriated as a trademark in the United States.

A line of cases hold that a term that is a commonly-used, generic term for a type of product or service in another country cannot be appropriated as a trademark in the United States for that type of product or service—regardless of whether persons in this country would recognize or know of the generic usage. [361] The "absolute

---

[360] McCarthy, Trademarks and Unfair Competition §§ 11:14, 12:13 (citing *Hag Aktiengesellschaft, Zazzara, Pan Tex,* and *McKesson*).

[361] Dadirrian v. Yacubian, 72 F. 1010, 1014 (N.D. Ill. 1896) and 90 F. 812 (D. Mass. 1898), *aff'd,* 98 F. 872 (1st Cir. 1900) (liquid preparation under the mark MATZOON, a transliteration into English of the product's generic name in Armenia; "The ignorance of people in this country touching [Matzoon], its uses and its name, cannot be treated as property . . . "); Holland v. C. & A. Import Corp., 8 F. Supp. 259, 261, 22 U.S.P.Q. 249 (S.D.N.Y. 1934) (registration of mark EST EST EST for wine from the Montefiascone region of Italy is invalid because, in Italy, the wine from that region was known by the name "Est Est Est"—even though, literally translated, Est Est Est means "It is It is It is," which obviously was not descriptive or generic for wine in English or in the United States; "By the weight of authority, a word commonly used in other countries to identify a kind of product and there in the public domain as a descriptive or generic name may not be appropriated here as a trade-mark on that product, even though the person claiming the word was the one who introduced the product here and the word then had no significance to our people generally. The rule is a just one. Why should the first comer be given a monopoly of the word when he knew all along that he had no better right to it than any one else? If others who may bring the same product here later cannot sell it under its real name, fair competition would be greatly impeded."); Bart Schwartz International Textiles, Ltd. v. Federal Trade Commission, 289 F.2d 665 (CCPA 1961) (registration of the word "fiocco" for textile fabrics was fraudulently obtained because, at the time of the application and the filing of a supporting declaration, applicant knew that the term was used in Italy as descriptive of "spun rayon" and that others had been using the mark in that descriptive sense; "a descriptive word in a foreign language cannot be registered in the United States as a trademark for the described product."); Weiss Noodle Co. v. Golden Cracknel & Specialty Co., 290 F.2d 845, 847 (CCPA 1961) (ordering cancellation of the registered mark "Ha-Lush-Ka" for egg noodles and egg noodle products because, without the hyphenation, the word was "haluska," which means "noodles" in the Hungarian language. The registrant argued unsuccessfully that the term was merely descriptive and that it had acquired

bar" line of cases excludes generic words even when the word is in English or when a literal translation of the term into English does not yield a term that is generic or descriptive of the goods to consumers in the United States.

In *Selchow & Richter*,[362] plaintiff registered "Parcheesi" for a board game, which it had used continuously since 1869. The game originated in India where it was known by the word sounding very much like Parcheesi but correctly spelled as "Pachisi" (*i.e.*, with no r or e). In Hindu, the word "pachisi" literally means "twenty-five," but the term was used as the game's name. The defendant began selling the same game under the name "A Royal Game of India—Parcheesi—Popular Edition." A preliminary injunction was issued against such usage. The defendant then altered its game name to "Whitman's Pachisi, A Game of India." The court followed an earlier case,[363] in holding that the defendant had a right to use the correct Indian generic name "Pachisi" though it must take care to avoid fraud or palming off. The defendant avoided the possibility of such deception by adopting trade dress distinctively different from the plaintiff's game, using the altered phrase with "Whitman's" and the correct generic spelling.

In *Donald F. Duncan*,[364] the plaintiff, owner of a return top toy, sued for infringement of its registered trademark "Yo Yo." The court held that the mark was generic because the name and toy originated in the Philippines, where "Yo Yo" is the toy's name.

In *Le Sorbet*,[365] the Board upheld the refusal to register "LE SORBET" for "fruit ice" on the ground that it was generic. The applicant admitted that "sorbet" was used in English as the generic name of fruit ices but argued that the addition of the definite French article "Le" to what is understood as an English word made the mark registrable. The Board disagreed on several grounds. It noted that the entire phrase "Le sorbet" was unquestionably French and generic in that language for fruit ices. Citing *Weiss Noodle* and other cases, it noted that the "primary rationale for the . . . rule that generic terms in foreign languages are treated no differently under our law than are their English language equivalents concerns the maintenance of fair competition in the international movement of goods in commerce." The United States had officially protested against the registration in other countries of terms considered to be the generic names in English of products sold in the United States and sold or intended to be sold in export: "Obviously, to permit registration here of terms

---

secondary meaning in the United States. The court confirmed that a common descriptive name cannot be a trademark whatever the market situation: "no one can be granted the exclusive use of the name of an article, either in our native tongue or its equivalent in any foreign language.").

Unlike *Dadirrian*, and *Holland*, *Weiss Noodle* is a "foreign equivalents" case as well as foreign generic term case as the translation of the term yielded a term that was generic in English (*i.e.*, "noodles"). For a discussion of trademark laws' "universality" principle, see § 5E[5].

[362] Selchow & Richter Co. v. Western Printing & Lithographing Co., 142 F.2d 707 (7th Cir. 1944), *cert. denied*, 323 U.S. 735 (1944).

[363] Selchow v. Chafee & Selchow Mfg. Co., 132 F. 996 (S.D. N.Y. 1904).

[364] Donald F. Duncan, Inc. v. Royal Tops Mfg. Co., 343 F.2d 655, 144 U.S.P.Q. 617 (7th Cir. 1965).

[365] *In re* Le Sorbet, Inc., 228 U.S.P.Q. 27 (PTO TTAB 1985).

in a foreign language which are generic for products sold in a foreign country would be inconsistent with the rationale supporting these international protests."

The opposing line of cases holds that generic usage in other countries is not relevant. These "domestic significance" cases hold that the only test is what the relevant consuming public in the United States would understand the term to mean.[366] These cases do not cite or consider the "absolute bar" line of cases.

Some cases also suggest that a mark may be generic in one market but not in another.[367]

One possible way of reconciling the two lines of cases is to focus on whether there is available in the United States a readily available name for the product or service.[368]

---

[366] *E.g.*, Carcione v. The Greengrocer, Inc., 205 U.S.P.Q. 1075 (E.D. Calif. 1979) (GREEN-GROCER, admittedly generic in Great Britain, not generic in the United States; "Since we deal here with American trademark law, and thus American consumers, neither British usage nor the dictionary definition indicating such usage are determinative. . . . [E]vidence of usage in the United States is scattered, and may simply reflect instances of idiosyncratic usage in this country."); Seiko Sporting Goods USA, Inc. v. Kabushiki Kaisha Hattori Tokeiten, 545 F. Supp. 221, 226, 216 U.S.P.Q. 129, 134 (S.D.N.Y. 1982), aff'd, 697 F.2d 296 (2d Cir. 1982) (unpublished) (owner of registrations of "Seiko" for products such as watches, clocks, and electric shavers obtains injunctive relief against use by another of "Seiko" on tennis rackets; "[w]hile plaintiff has sought to show that Seiko is a generic term in Japan, it is not so recognized in this country.").

See also Anheuser-Busch Inc. v. Stroh Brewery Co., 750 F.2d 631, 642, 224 U.S.P.Q. 657, 665 (8th Cir. 1984) (the plaintiff sued for infringement of its alleged common law trademark "LA" for low-alcohol beer by the defendant's usage of "Schaefer LA" for a similar low-alcohol beer; the defendant relied, in part, on usage of the term "LA" in Australia; HELD: such usage is not pertinent; "Stroh argues that the 'bar call' for low alcohol beer in Australia has become 'Give me an L.A.' that the term LA is generic or descriptive there, and that a word that is generic or descriptive in a foreign country should be accorded the same status in the United States. The cases and treatise cited by Stroh in support of the latter proposition, however, deal with the question of whether words from modern languages should be treated as equivalent to their English translations (such as French 'café' for 'coffee'). A number of cases hold that a term may be generic in one country and suggestive in another.").

[367] Keebler Co. v. Rovira Biscuit Corp., 624 F.2d 366, 376, 207 U.S.P.Q. 465 (1st Cir. 1980) (finding of genericness in Puerto Rico market does not establish genericness in other United States markets); Abercrombie & Fitch Co. v. Hunting World, Inc., 537 F.2d 4, 189 U.S.P.Q. 759 (2d Cir. 1976).

[368] Some of the cases in the "absolute bar" line, such as *Dadirrian* ("Matzoon"), *Holland* ("Est Est Est"), *Donald F. Duncan, Inc.* ("Yo Yo" for return toy), and *Selchow* ("Parchisi" for board game) involved products for which, arguably, there was no available alternative. (Other cases in the line, such as *Bart Schwartz* ("fiocco" for spun rayon), *Weiss Noodle* ("Ha-Lush-Ka" for noodles), and *Le Sorbet* ("Le Sorbet" for fruit ices), involved terms for which there did seem to be such alternatives.) On the other hand, several of the cases in the "domestic significance" line involved words for which there were ready alternatives (*Seiko Sporting Goods*, "Seiko" v. various electrical products, tennis rackets, etc.; *Anheuser-Busch*, "LA" v. "low alcohol beer"). In one case (*Carcione*, "greengrocer"), there does not seem to be such a ready alternative (perhaps "fruit and vegetable stand").

[4] Prior Use

Lanham Act Section 2(d) provides that a mark may not be registered on the principal register if it "so resembles a mark registered in the Patent and Trademark Office, or a mark or trade name previously used in the United States by another and not abandoned, as to be likely, when applied to the goods of the applicant to cause confusion. . . . "[369] A disqualifying prior use may be of a trade name, that is, a symbol that has not been used in a manner that would entitle it to registration under the Lanham Act.

Section 2(d) prior use is a primary ground for rejecting applications to register trademarks and service marks. To determine a prior use bar, two issues must be resolved: which use is "prior?"[370] and will concurrent use of the two symbols create a likelihood of confusion?

[a] **Likelihood of Confusion Standard.** A critical issue in applying Section 2(d) is likelihood of confusion.[371] The same standard is essentially the same as that applied

---

[369] 15 U.S.C. § 1052(d).

[370] *See* § 5D[1][e].

[371] Some examples of determinations of likelihood of confusion:

"PECAN SHORTEES" for cookies is *not* confusingly similar to "PECAN SANDIES" for cookies. Keebler Co. v. Murray Bakery Products, 866 F.2d 1386, 9 U.S.P.Q.2d 1736 (Fed. Cir. 1989).

"B A D" for clothing is *not* confusingly similar to previously registered marks "B.V.D." and "BVD" for underwear and clothing despite the latter mark's fame. B.V.D. Licensing v. Body Action Design, 846 F.2d 727, 728, 6 U.S.P.Q.2d 1719, 1721 (Fed. Cir. 1988). The purchasing public will not read an "A" for "V" and "will react to [the mark "B A D"] as the common word "bad," not as a copy or simulation or suggestion of the well-known mark B.V.D."

"SUPERLOADER" for boat trailers is *not* confusingly similar to previously used marks "EZ LOADER" and "MINI LOADER" for trailers. EZ Loader Boat Trailers, Inc. v. Cox Trailers, Inc., 706 F.2d 1213, 217 U.S.P.Q. 986 (Fed. Cir. 1983). Though the goods are identical, the Board determined that there was no likelihood of confusion given the difference in marks. Appellant-opposer conceded that there was no "family of marks."

"THINKER TOYS" in a design for apparatus for computers *is* confusingly similar to the registered mark "TINKER TOYS" for games, toys and children's blocks. CBS Inc. v. Morrow, 708 F.2d 1579, 218 U.S.P.Q. 198 (Fed. Cir. 1983). Though "the mere fact that a mark is a caricature or pun based on a registered mark is insufficient to sustain an opposition," and though applicant does not currently make or sell computer games or programs, the description of goods in applicant's business practices may change over time. Applicant's current customers may be large and sophisticated, but opposer's registration does not restrict the nature of "games." Minor design elements do not obviate confusion as verbal portion is most likely source indicator, especially as applicant's products are listed in catalogs without design element. Opposer's agreement to allow third party to use "Thinker Toys" in a design for a local toy store is not conclusive as store was not seeking nationwide registration rights.

"GIANT HAMBURGERS" in a design for hamburgers, milk shakes and restaurant services *is* confusingly similar to registered marks "GIANT" and "Giant" in a design for grocery store services and private label food products. Giant Food, Inc. v. Nation's Foodservice, Inc., 710 F.2d 1565, 218 U.S.P.Q. 390 (Fed. Cir. 1983). Even though applicant is currently confined to California and registrant/opposer is in the Washington, D.C. area, applicant seeks a

to determine trademark infringement.[372] One difference is that the likelihood-of-confusion inquiry in determining a Section 2(d) rejection, opposition, or cancellation is upon the class of goods or services described in the application or registration for the mark in question whereas the inquiry in determining infringement is upon the actual goods or services upon which the two marks are used.[373] In *Canadian Imperial Bank*,[374] the court upheld a determination that the applicant's mark "COMM-CASH" for "banking services" so resembles the opposer's registered mark

---

geographically unrestricted registration, and it is not proper to limit consideration of confusion to areas currently occupied by parties. The registered mark is famous. Applicant's disclaimer of the words "Giant Hamburger" does not prevent confusion as consumers will not be aware of such a disclaimer. Marks are not to be dissected, but greater force should be given to the dominant verbal feature, especially when orders for the product are commonly taken orally. Third party usages of "Giant" include another origin indicator (*e.g.*, "Bob's Giant Burgers").

"GIANT OPEN AIR MARKETS" in a design for supermarket services, bread and other food items *is* confusingly similar to the registered marks "GIANT" and "Giant" with designs for grocery store services and private label food products. Rosso & Mastracco, Inc. v. Giant Food, Inc., 720 F.2d 1263, 219 U.S.P.Q. 1050 (Fed. Cir. 1983).

"BED & BREAKFAST REGISTRY" for "making lodging reservations for others in private homes" is *not* confusingly similar to the registered service mark "BED & BREAKFAST INTERNATIONAL" for "room booking agency services" as to create a likelihood of confusion. In re Bed & Breakfast Registry, 791 F.2d 157, 229 U.S.P.Q. 818 (Fed. Cir. 1986). "[M]arks must be considered in their entireties" and "common elements of the marks, even if descriptive, cannot be ignored," but "travellers acquainted with the term 'bed and breakfast' are more likely to rely on the non-common portion of each mark, *e.g.*, 'registry' vs. 'international', to distinguish among similar services." 791 F.2d at 159, 229 U.S.P.Q.2d at 819. The PTO's argument that consumers would tend to assume that applicant's mark is the "domestic counterpart" of the registrant's international service is but a "speculative assumption." The large number of variously named "bed and breakfast" services "weighs against the reasonableness of the assumption that two such services are related." Id.

"SPICE VALLEY" for tea *is* confusingly similar to "SPICE ISLANDS" for spices and teas. Specialty Brands, Inc. v. Coffee Bean Distributors, Inc., 748 F.2d 669, 223 U.S.P.Q. 1281 (Fed. Cir. 1984). The Board erred by relying solely on the so-called "sound, sight, and meaning" trilogy on confusion of marks and by failing to give due weight to the substantial fame of opposer's mark and products.

[372] *See* § 5F[1].

[373] *E.g.*, Octocom Systems, Inc. v. Houston Computer Services, Inc., 918 F.2d 937, 942, 16 U.S.P.Q.2d 1783, 1787 (Fed. Cir. 1990) (applicant's mark "OCTOCOM" for computer modems so resembled opposer's previously used and registered mark "OCTACOMM" for computer programs as to be likely to cause confusion; applicant argued the PTO erred by failing to consider its evidence showing no likelihood of confusion—for example, evidence its goods were expensive and sold to large institutions and sophisticated purchasers; "The issue in an opposition is the right of an applicant to register the mark depicted in the application for the goods identified therein. The authority is legion that the question of registrability of an applicant's mark must be decided on the basis of the identification of goods set forth in the application regardless of what the record may reveal as to the particular nature of an applicant's goods, the particular channels of trade or the class of purchasers to which sales of the goods are directed.").

[374] Canadian Imperial Bank of Commerce v. Wells Fargo Bank, 811 F.2d 1490, 1 U.S.P.Q. 2d 1813 (Fed. Cir. 1987).

"COMMUNICASH" for "banking services" as to create a likelihood of confusion. In determining likelihood of confusion, the Board did not err in focusing on the broad category of "banking services" even though both parties currently used their marks only for the highly specialized service of electronic cash management used by sophisticated and discerning customers, such as large corporations and banks. Likelihood of confusion must be determined on the basis of an analysis of the mark as applied to the goods or services recited in the applicant's application vis-á-vis the goods or services recited in the opposer's registration rather than on what the evidence shows the goods or services to be.

In *E. I. du Pont de Nemours & Co.*,[375] the court adopted a multi-factor approach to likelihood of confusion determinations in the prior use context. Emphasizing that "each case must be decided on its own facts" and that "[t]here is no litmus rule which can provide a ready guide to all cases," the court directed that "the following, when of record, must be considered:

"(1) The similarity or dissimilarity of the marks in their entireties as to appearance, sound, connotation and commercial impression.

"(2) The similarity or dissimilarity and nature of the goods or services as described in an application or registration or in connection with which a prior mark is in use.

"(3) The similarity or dissimilarity of established, likely-to-continue trade channels.

"(4) The conditions under which and buyers to whom sales are made, i.e., 'impulse' vs. careful, sophisticated purchasing.

"(5) The fame of the prior mark (sales, advertising, length of use).

"(6) The number and nature of similar marks in use on similar goods.

"(7) The nature and extent of any actual confusion.

"(8) The length of time during and conditions under which there has been concurrent use without evidence of actual confusion.

"(9) The variety of goods on which a mark is or is not used (house mark, 'family' mark, product mark).

"(10) The market interface between applicant and the owner of a prior mark:

(a) a mere 'consent' to register or use.

(b) agreement provisions designed to preclude confusion, i.e., limitations on continued use of the marks by each party.

(c) assignment of mark, application, registration and good will of the related business.

(d) laches and estoppel attributable to owner of prior mark and indicative of lack of confusion.

"(11) The extent to which applicant has a right to exclude others from use of its mark on its goods.

---

[375] *In re* E. I. du Pont de Nemours & Co., 476 F.2d 1357, 177 U.S.P.Q. 563 (CCPA 1973).

"(12) The extent of potential confusion, i.e., whether de minimis or substantial.

"(13) Any other established fact probative of the effect of use."[376]

As with infringement, the most difficult determination is when the goods or services for which registration is sought differ significantly from those sold under the previously used or registered mark or trade name.[377]

[b]   **Consent Agreements—Right to Use Versus Right to Register.** Persons using similar marks may agree on the terms and conditions under which both may use their marks. The senior user's consent to the junior user's use is not binding on the Patent and Trademark Office (PTO), which may deny registration of the junior mark in order to protect the public interest in freedom from confusion, but the PTO must give weight to the consent agreement because its terms may lessen the likelihood that confusion will result from simultaneous use.

---

[376] 476 F.2d at 1351.

[377] Some examples:

"VITTORIO RICCI" for handbags, scarves, neckties, blouses, sweaters, coats, jackets, pants, and retail store services in the areas of shoes, clothing and accessories *is* confusingly similar to "NINA RICCI," "SIGNORICCI," and "CAPRICCI" for perfumes, toiletries and cosmetic products, and clothing products despite a prior district court ruling allowing registration of applicant's "VITTORIO RICCI" for shoes and belts. Nina Ricci S.A.R.L. v. E.T.F. Enterprises Inc., 889 F.2d 1070, 12 U.S.P.Q.2d 1901 (Fed. Cir. 1989).

"DRC" for sheet metal fabric is *not* confusingly similar to registered mark "DRC" for back gauges for press brakers. Dynamics Research Corp. v. Langenau Mfg. Co., 704 F.2d 1575, 217 U.S.P.Q. 649 (Fed. Cir. 1983). Though the marks are identical, the goods are distinct and sold to large sophisticated customers. That two products are advertised in same trade magazine is not conclusive.

"ROPELOK" for safety fall protection equipment for attachment to workers operating at elevated heights, "said equipment comprising a lifeline engaging element actuated by a fall and a shock-absorber sold as a unit" *is* confusingly similar to the registered mark "ROPELOCK" registered on the supplemental register for "releasable locking buckles for ropes particularly for industrial purposes" as to create a likelihood of confusion. In re Research and Trading Corp., 793 F.2d 1276, 1278, 230 U.S.P.Q. 49, 50 (Fed. Cir. 1986). The two marks are nearly identical. The applicant's lifeline safety devices and the registrant's releasable locking buckles for ropes for industrial purposes are both "closely related safety equipment whose commercial purchasers would be likely to be confused as to source." "Sophistication of buyers and purchaser care are relevant considerations" but are not controlling. "That the relevant class of buyers may exercise care does not necessarily impose on that class the responsibility of distinguishing between similar trademarks for similar goods."

"NOTRE DAME" and design for cheese is *not* confusingly similar to common law mark "NOTRE DAME" for university. University of Notre Dame du Lac v. J.C. Gourmet Food Imports Co., Inc., 703 F.2d 1372, 217 U.S.P.Q. 505 (Fed. Cir. 1983). The University is not known for development or sponsorship of food products, and there is no evidence of intent by applicant to trade on University's goodwill.

Red stripe label for beer is *not* confusingly similar to a similar but not identical red stripe label for champagne. G.H. Mumm & Cie (Societe Vinicole de Champagne Successerurs of New York, Inc.) v. Desnoes & Geddes, Ltd., 917 F.2d 1292, 16 U.S.P.Q. 1635 (Fed. Cir. 1990) (noting, *inter alia*, that there are "substantial pricing differences" between champagne and beer).

In *E.I. du Pont de Nemours*,[378] du Pont applied in 1967 to register the mark "RALLY" for a combination wax and cleaning agent for use on automobiles. The PTO refused registration on the ground that the mark was confusingly similar to Horizon's mark "RALLY" for an all-purpose detergent, which was registered in 1959. While Du Pont's appeal was pending, du Pont purchased Horizon's mark "RALLY" for the automobile business, a 1968 application filed by Horizon to register "RALLY" for a combination polishing, glazing and cleaning agent for use on automobiles, and the good will of Horizon's automobile-related business. Because Horizon retained "RALLY" for all-purpose detergents, Horizon and du Pont entered into an agreement designed to avoid conflict. The agreement specified that du Pont's realm was the "automobile after-market" and Horizon's realm was the "commercial building or household market." The agreement set boundaries of use, permitting sale of products "incidentally usable" in the other party's market but prohibiting any promotion "as especially suited for use in such market." The PTO refused registration of the mark in the 1968 application, now owned by Du Pont: "[D]espite any agreement between the parties the public interest cannot be ignored, and when the goods are as closely related as those here involved, their sale under the identical mark 'RALLY' would be likely to result in confusion, mistake, or deception."[379]

In its appeal, du Pont argued that it had an unquestioned right to use the mark in its application and that the "right to register follows the right to use," especially when the right to use is exclusive. The CCPA welcomed the opportunity presented to it to clarify Section 2(d).[380] After listing factors that must be considered, the court concluded that the PTO erred in failing to give sufficient weight to the agreement, which was more than a mere consent to use because it allocated markets of exclusive use.[381] It criticized Du Pont's reliance on the equation of a right to use with

---

[378] *In re* E. I. du Pont de Nemours & Co., 476 F.2d 1357, 177 U.S.P.Q. 563 (CCPA 1973). *See also* Bongrain International (American) Corp. v Delice de France Inc., 1 U.S.P.Q.2d 1775, 1778-79 (Fed. Cir. 1987) (the Trademark Trial and Appeal Board (TTAB) erred in granting a summary judgement cancelling appellant's registration of the mark "LE PETIT DELICE DE FRANCE" for cheese and milk products in view of the opposer's prior use of the mark "DELICE DE FRANCE" in a design for bakery products; the parties had, prior to the TTAB decision, entered into a written agreement that there was no likelihood of confusion in the marketplace and that each could continue using its mark on its product; "[I]n trademark cases involving agreements reflecting parties' views on the likelihood of confusion in the marketplace, [the parties] are in a much better position to know the real life situation than bureaucrats or judges. . . . [S]uch agreements may, depending on the circumstances, carry great weight."; the likelihood of confusion standard of Section 2(d) of the Trademark Act should be construed in accordance with the policies and purposes of that Act, including the policy to "encourage the presence on the register of trademarks of as many as possible of the marks in actual use so that they are available for search purposes.").

[379] 476 F.2d at 1360.

[380] It noted that "concepts expressed in our prior opinions and inconsistent with what we say may be considered no longer viable in this court." 476 F.2d at 1360.

[381] "It has been said that agreement evidence may resolve 'doubt,' . . . but there are only two practical possibilities. Either there is no indication of likely confusion, in which case the registration promptly issues, or there is some indication that confusion may be likely. In the latter case, the question must remain open (*i.e.*, 'debatable') until any or all of the elements

a right to register [382] and the PTO's reliance on the "public interest." [383]

listed above have been reviewed and studied, the final decision being made on the basis of the entire record.

"In considering agreements, a naked 'consent' may carry little weight. Absent more, the consenter may continue or expand his use. The consent may be based on ignorance or misconception of the law. The facts may show, on the other hand, that consent could exist only in the absence of any real likelihood of confusion.

"The weight to be given more detailed agreements of the type presented here should be substantial. . . . [R]eputable businessmen-users of valuable trademarks have no interest in causing public confusion. The genius of the free competitive system is the paralleling of the interest of the entrepreneur and the consuming public so far as possible. Altruism aside, it is in his pecuniary interest, indeed a matter of economic survival, that the businessman obtain and retain customers, the very purpose and function of a trademark, and that he avoid and preclude confusion. Millions of advertising dollars are spent daily for that precise purpose. The history of trademark litigation and the substantial body of law to which it relates demonstrate the businessman's alertness in seeking to enjoin confusion. In so doing he guards both his pocketbook and the public interest.

"Thus when those most familiar with use in the marketplace and most interested in precluding confusion enter agreements designed to avoid it, the scales of evidence are clearly tilted. . . .

"The parties here agreed to restrict themselves in effect to the general purpose cleaning market (horizon) and the automobile market (DuPont). . . . The fact that the goods of one party 'could be used' in the field of the other is too conjectural and too widely applicable to form the sole basis of decision, particularly where, as here, the parties have agreed to avoid the promotion of such cross-use.

"The mere fact of diverse marketing emphasis alone may not in every case preclude confusion. Without more, it may well be that purchasers active in both markets and familiar with products sold under a particular mark could attribute to the same source closely related goods sold under the same mark. The agreements herein, however, considered as a whole and notwithstanding certain phrases subject to contrary interpretation, evidence that confusion will be unlikely. As we read them, the very purpose and aim of the present agreements is the avoidance of public confusion. Under provision 6 of the assignment the parties agreed 'to take any further actions and execute any further agreements needed to carry out the spirit and intent of this agreement.' . . . We cannot believe that horizon would have sold its automotive business, assigned its mark and entered into the agreement or that Du Pont would have accepted and paid for the assignment and entered into the agreement, if either thought for a moment that purchasers would seriously be confused as to source." 476 F.2d at 1362-63.

[382] "Decisional maxims like 'the right to register follows the right to use,' sometimes defended as 'reflecting the realities of the marketplace,' founder on their non-universality of application and the existence of Sec. 2(d). As attractive as that approach appears . . ., it is recognized as a goal and that the phrase 'as nearly as possible' must be read into it. Clearly, a right to use is not a right to confuse. The rights to use and register are not identical. . . . Many marks, including those described in Sec. 2(a), (b), and (c), merely descriptive terms and those on labels defective under other laws (Rule 2.69), might all be used but not registered.

"Although a naked right to use cannot always result in registration, the act does intend . . . that registration and use be coincident so far as possible. Post-Lanham Act opinions relating to Sec. 2(d) which maintain an iron curtain between the rights to use and register do not contribute to stability in the law. Treating those rights as totally divorced entities only perpetuates the 'arbitrary provisions' respecting confusion that the congress thought it was eliminating more than twenty-five years ago." 476 F.2d at 1364.

[383] "[W]hether offered in response to a right-to-use argument or against any of the evidentiary considerations listed above, citation of 'the public interest' as a basis for refusal of

[c]　**Trade Names.** Prior use of a confusingly similar mark, symbol, or logo is grounds for denial of registration of trademark rights even though that prior use was as a trade*name* rather than as a trade*mark*. Person A's tradename use of a symbol may bar person B's attempt to obtain trademark rights by adoption and use with goods or services even though person A's use would not be sufficient to obtain trademark rights that can be registered under the Lanham Act.[384]

For example, in *Sterling Drug*,[385] the applicant sought to register an ankh as a mark for hair conditioners and shampoos. Applicant's first use of the mark was in April 1966. A research institute, which developed products such as surgical scrubs and shampoos, successfully opposed registration by showing that it used an ankh on its building, stationary, etc. as early as 1950 and that use of the same symbol by the applicant would create a likelihood of confusion. The research institute did not use the ankh as a mark on shampoos or any other product. "Section 2(d) is not limited to use as a trademark or service mark; it refers broadly to 'a mark or trade name previously used in the United States by another.' If a mark such as the ankh has come to symbolize the business of an opposer, to be its identifying mark, its use by another may well lead the public to believe there is some connection, and confusion as to the origin or sponsorship of a product may well result."

In *Malcolm Nicol*,[386] the court confirmed that a Section 2(d) prior use bar to registration of a mark arises if the prior user shows proprietary rights in a trade name or trade identity symbol. The prior user need not show use of a term such as will establish trademark rights but must show sufficient usage to create an association of the term with the user's goods. Nicol registered the mark "BRITOL" for mineral oil. Witco sought to cancel Nicol's registration by showing prior use of the term "BRITOL" for mineral oil. Witco's evidence of prior use consisted of (a) product guides distributed to the public that identified Witco as a source of "BRITOL" mineral oil; and (b) the testimony of two long term Witco officers that they had personal knowledge of Witco selling mineral oil under the term BRITOL. The TTAB did not err in granting Witco's petition to cancel Nicol's registration based on its finding that

---

registration is a bootless cry. . . . After a likelihood of confusion is found (and the case thus decided) citation of the public interest is unnecessary.

"The Patent Office does have a guardianship role under Sec. 2(d). It lies not in a negative, nay-saying of refusal alone, but in the protection of a mark by registering it and then rejecting later improper attempts, of which the registrant is unaware, to register it or a similar mark. Refusal to register cannot prevent confusion. At most, it might discourage further use. Refusal can, under certain circumstances, encourage potential confusion. Absence of a registration of RALLY for auto cleansers in the present case may, for example, lead others to adopt and use that or a similar mark for auto cleansers. Granting a registration will not produce confusion. Use alone can do that and neither we nor the Patent Office can grant or deny a right to use.

"Presumably, everything the Patent Office and this court does is in the public interest. We find no place for 'the guardianship of the public interest' as support for refusals to register under Sec. 2(d)." 476 F.2d at 1364.

[384] *See* § 5D[1].

[385] *In re* Sterling Drug Co., Inc., 515 F.2d 1128, 185 U.S.P.Q.2d 649 (CCPA 1975).

[386] Malcolm Nicol & Co. Inc. v. Witco Corp., 881 F.2d 1063, 11 U.S.P.Q.2d 1638 (Fed. Cir. 1989).

"Witco used 'BRITOL' in a way that created in the minds of people the necessary association between 'BRITOL' and the Witco product."[387]

[d] **Opposition—Standing.** One who opposes registration of a mark because of an alleged prior use bar under Section 2(d) must show that the someone has proprietary rights in the prior mark or trade name,[388] but such rights need not reside in the opposer if the opposer otherwise has standing to bring the opposition.[389]

[e] **Concurrent Use.** Section 2(d) contains a major exception to the prior use bar that permits concurrent registration of marks that have been lawfully used in separate markets.[390]

[f] **Use by "Another"—Separate Legal Entities.** Prior registration or use of similar marks by a wholly-owned subsidiary of an applicant seeking registration of a mark does not *per se* support a refusal of registration under Lanham Act Section 2(d), which bars registration of marks that so resemble a mark registered or used "by *another*" as to cause confusion.

In *Wella*,[391] the court reversed the Board's refusal to register a German company's "WELLASTATE" mark for hair straightening products as confusingly similar

---

[387] 881 F.2d at 1065, 11 U.S.P.Q.2d at 1640.

[388] Towers v. Advent Software, Inc., 913 F.2d 942, 945, 16 U.S.P.Q.2d 1039, 1041 (Fed. Cir. 1990) ("[A] party opposing of a trademark due to a likelihood of confusion with his own unregistered term cannot prevail unless he shows that his term is distinctive of his goods, whether inherently or through the acquisition of secondary meaning or through 'whatever other type of use may have developed a trade identity.' "); Otto Roth & Co. v. Universal Foods Corp., 640 F.2d 1317, 209 U.S.P.Q. 40 (CCPA 1981).

In *Otto Roth*, applicant sought to register "Esprit Nouveau" for cheeses. Opposer showed prior use of "Brie Nouveau," which is similar at least in sound. However, opposer had already failed to obtain protection for its word because it was descriptive of a type of cheese. The court dismissed the opposition based on Section 2(d). Opposer could only assert the public rights against registration of descriptive terms under Section 2(e). Everyone seemed to concede that "Esprit Nouveau" was distinctive and not descriptive.

[389] Jewelers Vigilance Comm., Inc. v. Ullenberg Corp., 853 F.2d 888, 7 U.S.P.Q.2d 1628 (Fed. Cir. 1988). *See also* Jewelers Vigilance Comm., Inc. v. Ullenberg Corp., 823 F.2d 490, 2 U.S.P.Q.2d 2021 (Fed. Cir. 1987).

In *Jewelers Vigilance Comm.*, a diamond retailers' trade association ("JVC") opposed applicant's registration of a design mark with the words "FOREVER YOURS/DEBEERS DIA. LTD" on the ground that it would cause confusion with the name "DEBEERS" of a third party, DeBeers Consolidated Mines, the major world source of diamonds. JVC showed sound reasons for fearing damages to itself and its members from the applicant's use of a confusing mark. In upholding JVC's opposition to registration, the court distinguished *Otto Roth*: "Where an opposer asserts likelihood of confusion because of its prior use of what appears to be a merely descriptive term, as in *Otto Roth*, the opposer must show that such term has come to identify the opposer as the source of goods or services. . . . However, the *Otto Roth* references to an 'opposer' having such proprietary rights cannot simplistically be applied to the case *sub judice*. The substance of the holding of *Otto Roth* is that likelihood of confusion cannot be established unless the prior use on which the opposition is based is, in fact, a mark indicating source in another." 853 F.2d at 893.

[390] *See* § 5E.

[391] *In re* Wella A.G., 787 F.2d 1549, 229 U.S.P.Q. 274 (Fed Cir. 1986).

to various "WELLA" marks registered by the company's U.S. subsidiary without considering "the relationship between the related companies, the extent to which the controlling company supervises and manages the controlled company and its use of trademarks, and the public perception of the source of the goods to which the marks are applied." [392] "Where the applicant is a related company, the statute [Section 2(d)] requires a thorough inquiry into whether, considering all the circumstances, use of the mark by the applicant is likely to confuse the public about the source of the applicant's mark to the mark of the other company." [393] The question is: "is the public likely to believe that the source of that product is Wella U.S. rather than the German company or the Wella organization." [394] The court did not reach the appellant's contention that it was entitled to registration under the Lanham Act Section 5 "related companies" doctrine. [395]

§ 5D   Acquisition, Registration and Maintenance

A manufacturer or merchant establishes common law ownership of a distinctive mark by adopting it and using it on goods. Neither advertising nor a statement of intent to use a mark establishes trademark rights.

To obtain a federal registration, a person must file an application with the Patent and Trademark Office, which registers marks after examination to determine the mark's compliance with registrability requirements. Until the 1988 Trademark Revision Act, the Lanham Act followed the common law in requiring adoption and use to establish trademark ownership before a registration application could be filed. The use must also be in interstate or foreign commerce. The 1988 Act changed traditional trademark principles by authorizing application filings based on intent to use a mark. Mark use is necessary to obtain registration.

Trademark rights and registration continue indefinitely if the owner-registrant does not abandon the mark. Two years nonuse creates a presumption of mark

---

[392] 787 F.2d at 1551, 229 U.S.P.Q. at 275.

[393] 787 F.2d at 1552, 229 U.S.P.Q. at 276.

[394] *Id.* In a separate opinion, Judge Nies opined that the question of title ownership of the prior registrations by the U.S. subsidiary should be resolved in view of the parent corporation's assertion that it is "the *sole* owner of rights in the WELLA marks in U.S. commerce."

[395] For a discussion of Section 5 and the "related companies" doctrine, see § 5G[3].

The Board interpreted Section 5 to permit only the trademark owner to take advantage of the related companies exception. In the Board's view, a parent company that owns a first mark can register a second mark owned by it that is confusingly similar to the first mark even if a subsidiary company uses the marks. In this situation, the same legal entity owns both marks. Alternatively, the filing of an application for registration of a confusingly similar second mark by wholly owned subsidiary rather than the parent company itself would not qualify for the related company exception.

In an "additional views" opinion in *Wella*, Judge Nies distinguishes trademark owners from users in considering the scope of Section 5 of the Lanham Act. The trademark owner must be the applicant for trademark registration. Use by a related company can inure to the applicant or registrant. However, "[n]othing in section 5 confers a right to register on a non-owner." 787 F.2d at 1555, 229 U.S.P.Q. at 278.

abandonment. A Lanham Act registrant must file a use affidavit six years after registration and renew every ten years.

[1] Adoption and Use

A fundamental common law tenet is that trademark property rights arise from a manufacturer or merchant's actual adoption and use of a mark to distinguish his goods from those of others. Adoption and use creates mark ownership rights and confers a priority right against anyone who subsequently adopts and uses a similar mark.

[a] **Sufficient Use—The Token Use Doctrine.** Courts distinguished between a "sham" transaction, which would not suffice for priority or registration purposes, and a "token" transaction, which would, at least for registration purposes,[1] if followed by substantial commercial use.[2] In *Blue Bell,*[3] the court discussed common law use standards.

---

[1] *Cf.* Scholastic, Inc. v. Macmillan, Inc., 650 F. Supp. 866, 873, 2 USPQ2d 1191, 1196 (S.D. N.Y. 1987) ("Adoption and a single use of the mark may be sufficient to permit registration of the mark, but more is required if its owner seeks to use the mark to stifle the efforts of others.").

[2] If minimal use is *not* followed by substantial commercial use, the courts find insufficient trademark usage. *E.g.,* La Société Anonyme des Parfums Le Galion v. Patou, Inc., 495 F.2d 1265, 1271-72, 181 USPQ 545 (2d Cir. 1974) (Judge Friendly: "Adoption and a single use of the mark may be sufficient to entitle the user to register the mark . . . But more is required to sustain the mark against a charge of nonusage. . . . To prove bona fide usage, the proponent of the trademark must demonstrate that his use of the mark has been deliberate and continuous, not sporadic, casual or transitory. . . . "). In *La Société Anonyme des Parfums Le Galion,* Patou registered the mark "SNOB" in 1951 and used the registration to bar LeGalion, which sold "SNOB" perfume in numerous other countries, from using "SNOB" in the United States market. From 1950 to 1971, Patou sold only 89 bottles of perfume under the "SNOB" mark and made no serious effort to merchandise the product. It did not renew its federal registration but continued to assert common law rights against LeGalion. The court held that the "meager trickle of business" did not constitute "the kind of bona fide use intended to afford a basis for trademark protection."

> "[T]rademark rights have often been upheld in spite of modest sales programs . . . In those cases, however, the trademark usage, although limited, was part of an ongoing program to exploit the mark commercially. In numerous other cases, where no present intent has been found to market the trademarked product, minimal sales have been held insufficient to establish trademark rights. *See, e.g.,* LeBlume Import Co. v. Coty, 293 F. 344, 351 (2 Cir. 1923) (occasional sales so infrequent that 'it cannot be said that the producer of the goods had obtained a market for them here which entitled his trade-mark to protection'); Philip Morris, Inc. v. Imperial Tobacco Co., 251 F.Supp. 362 (E.D.Va.1965), *aff'd,* 401 F.2d 179 (4 Cir. 1968), *cert. denied,* 393 U.S. 1094, 89 S.Ct. 875, 21 L.Ed.2d 784 (1969) (shipments sporadic, casual and nominal in character). . . ." 495 F.2d at 1272.

Compare P.A.B. Produits et Appareils de Beauté v. Satinine Societa in Nome Collettivo di S.A. e. M. Usellini, 570 F.2d 328, 334 n.10, 196 U.S.P.Q. 801 (CCPA 1978) ("the realities of commercial life may compel manufacturers to make initial, and continuing, use on a small scale in order to obtain, and maintain, registrations.").

It is not clear whether these decisions rest on *failure to establish* trademark rights *or* on an *abandonment* of rights *for nonuse. See* Société de Developments et D'Innovations des Marches

"A trademark is a symbol (word, name, device or combination thereof) adopted and used by a merchant to identify his goods and distinguish them from articles produced by others. . . . Ownership of a mark requires a combination of both appropriation and use in trade. . . . Thus, neither conception of the mark nor advertising alone establishes trademark rights at common law. . . . Rather, ownership of a trademark accrues when goods bearing the mark are placed on the market.

"The exclusive right to a trademark belongs to one who first uses it in connection with specified goods. . . . Such use need not have gained wide public recognition, . . . and even a single use in trade may sustain trademark rights if followed by continuous commercial utilization. . . .

"Secret, undisclosed internal shipments are generally inadequate to support the denomination 'use.' " [4]

In *Blue Bell*, two manufacturers, Blue Bell and Farah, proceeded in good faith in the spring and summer of 1973 to create, adopt and use an identical mark "TIME OUT" for similar goods (men's clothing) to be sold in the same geographic market. The two sued and countersued in Federal court; jurisdiction was based on diversity of citizenship, and the parties agreed that Texas common law applied. Farah relied on a July 3 shipment of one pair of slacks to each of 12 sales managers with the "Time Out" mark attached as a tag. The court dismissed this transaction as merely an internal shipment, not a bona fide sale to customers.[5] A trademark is a badge of origin to consumers and others not connected with the corporation. Blue Bell relied on a July 5 shipment of several hundred items from its existing "Mr. Hicks" line with an additional "Time Out" tag attached. These were sales to customers not connected with the company. The court found this not a bona fide adoption and use: Blue Bell intended to create a new and different line to be sold under the mark. Its acts were an improper attempt to "reserve a mark" for future use. The court finally awarded priority to Farah based on commercial sales in September.

Mark use sufficiency commonly arises in determining whether the use supports a Lanham Act application to register the mark. Courts and the PTO tended to require

---

Agricoles et Aliminetaries-Sodima Union de Cooperatives Agricoles v. International Yogurt, 662 F. Supp. 839, 849, 3 U.S.P.Q. 2d 1641 (D. Ore. 1987) ("The liberal doctrine honoring token sales as sufficient use to register a mark does not extend to honoring mere token use to sustain the mark against a charge of non-use. . . . Although abandonment must always be proved by a preponderance of the evidence, some cases differentiate between those in which the registrant previously used the mark, and those in which it was not so used. . . . If the mark was previously used in a commercially significant way, the registrant may show plans to reintroduce the mark as evidence of intent to resume use, especially if the court determines that a residue of consumer goodwill toward the mark exists despite the erosion of time. . . . The cases are less generous when essentially no prior goodwill had been established. . . . ").

For a discussion of abandonment, see §5D[3][b].

[3] Blue Bell, Inc. v. Farah Mfg. Co., 508 F.2d 1260, 185 U.S.P.Q. 1 (5th Cir. 1975).

[4] 508 F.2d at 1264-65.

[5] *Cf.* Avakoff v. Southern Pacific Co., 765 F.2d 1097, 226 U.S.P.Q. 435 (Fed Cir 1985) (interstate shipment of trademark-bearing goods by manufacturer *to* trademark owner/ registration applicant does not qualify as "use in commerce" under §45 definition, despite related, but post-filing advertising campaign and sales of trademark-bearing goods).

less extensive use when the issue is Lanham Act registration eligibility rather than priority between two parties who have adopted and used the same mark. A "sham" transaction did not support an application,[6] but in *International Telephone & Telegraph*,[7] the court held that "[a]n initial commercial transaction is sufficient to

---

[6] In Blue Bell, Inc. v. Jaymar-Ruby, Inc., 497 F.2d 433, 182 U.S.P.Q. 65 (2d Cir. 1974), the court held that the plaintiff's registration application statement on use of its mark "Jeanie" (with an oversized "J") was false due to the use transaction's contrived nature.

"At the time of its application, plaintiff—on advice of counsel . . . submitted five tags bearing the pointed-J mark. The application stated: 'The trademark was first used October 26, 1961 and was first used in interstate commerce October 26, 1961 and is now in use in such commerce.' But internal memoranda make it clear that this 'use' consisted of a token shipment of goods worth a few dollars to a cooperating company which immediately returned them to the plaintiff. . . . Plaintiff's files further indicate that the sole purpose of this interstate exercise was to satisfy the trademark laws. . . .

". . . [A] number of decisions have held that a minimal amount of interstate commerce—either a sale or transportation—will suffice. . . . But while these decisions accept minimal use primarily intended to satisfy the trademark laws, none of them endorses sham transactions exclusively designed to do so. Rather we find a clear line of decisions holding that the use must be bona fide, with token transactions accepted only where there is an accompanying intent to engage in continuing commercial use in the future. . . . " 497 F.2d at 436.

The Lanham Act's genuine commercial use requirement was carried over from the prior 1905 federal trademark registration statute. *See* Phillips v. Hudnut, 263 F. 643, 644 (D.C. Cir. 1920) (holding that the following did not constitute sufficient use so as to confer priority over another person who had adopted and used the same mark: "[In the critical period, May 1914, Phillips] had no established place of business, but made some sample boxes of toilet powder, placed upon them the mark here involved, and then forwarded them from New York, through the house for which he was then working, to three dealers in goods of that character, one in Texas, one in Philadelphia, and one in New Orleans. The boxes were sent without previous request by the consignees, and the price paid for each was 5 cents, the usual sale price of such an article being about 50 cents. No other use of the mark was made by him until 1916.").

[7] International Telephone & Telegraph Corp. v. International Mobile Machines Corp., 800 F.2d 1118, 231 U.S.P.Q. 142 (Fed. Cir. 1986). The court deemed a single interstate shipment of a prototype telephone system sufficient to support an application to register the mark despite the facts that (1) the shipment was sent to a director-investor of the registering company; (2) the director-investor returned the system to the company; and (3) the product line actually shipped to the investor, an analog phone system, was dropped in favor of the development of a digital system. The director-investor was seriously interested in either adopting the phone to his business or becoming a franchiser for the system. The court noted that a transaction between the corporate-owner of a mark and a person who was an investor and a member of its board of directors is not *per se* a non-commercial transaction.

Compare Hydro-Dynamics Inc. v. George Putnam & Co., Inc., 811 F.2d 1470, 1474, 1 U.S.P.Q.2d 1772, 1774 (Fed. Cir. 1987) (shipment of the product with a mark affixed thereto to an independent distributor to obtain the distributor's opinion on and reaction to the mark does not constitute adoption and use of the mark sufficient to establish priority over another party who subsequently adopted the same mark; a single shipment in interstate commerce will suffice to support registration but only if the mark has already been adopted and used as a trademark. "Although a party may establish that a shipment in commerce was a bona fide commercial transaction by evidence of subsequent events, . . . the purpose of the shipment can not be changed retroactively.").

support the validity of a registration so long as the initial transaction is not a sham transaction and is followed by a continuing effort or intent to engage in commercial use."

The 1988 Trademark Revision Act abolished the "token use" doctrine as unnecessary in view of the newly-added intent-to-use application procedure. The Act amended the "use in commerce" definition to provide that use "means the bona fide use of a mark in the ordinary course of trade, and not made merely to reserve a right in a mark." [8]

---

[8] The legislative history of the new definition of "use in commerce" is of interest. The Senate Bill, S. 1883, defined "use in commerce" as "use of a mark in the ordinary course of trade, commensurate with the circumstances, and not made merely to reserve a right in a mark." The Committee Report indicated:

"The committee intends that the revised definition of 'use in commerce' be interpreted to mean commercial use which is typical in a particular industry. Additionally, the definition should be interpreted with flexibility so as to encompass various genuine, but less traditional, trademark uses, such as those made in test markets, infrequent sales of large or expensive items, or ongoing shipments of a new drug to clinical investigators by a company awaiting FDA approval, and to preserve ownership rights in a mark if, absent an intent to abandon, use of a mark is interrupted due to special circumstances." S. Rep. No. 100-515, 100th Cong., 2d Sess. 45 (1988).

The House Judiciary Committee reported a revised version of the Senate Bill, H.R. 5372, which added a requirement that the use be "bona fide." The House Report commented on the intent of this language:

"Obviously, what is real and legitimate will vary depending on the practices of the industry involved, and should be determined based on the standards of that particular industry. . . .

". . . [T]he Committee recognizes that the 'ordinary course of trade' varies from industry to industry. Thus, for example, it might be the ordinary course of trade for an industry that sells expensive or seasonal products to make infrequent sales. Similarly, a pharmaceutical company that markets a drug to treat a rare disease will make correspondingly few sales in the ordinary course of its trade; the company's shipment to clinical investigators during the Federal approval process will also be in its ordinary course of trade. The definition of 'use in commerce' is consistent with the Committee's intention to eliminate the practice of making a single shipment-'token use' solely for the purpose of reserving a mark."

On the Senate floor, Senator DeConcini commented on the House's change:

"The House amended these definitions to assure that the commercial sham of 'token use'—which becomes unnecessary under the intent-to-use application system we designed—would actually be eliminated. In doing so, however, Congress' intent that the revised definition still encompass genuine, but less traditional, trademark uses must be made clear. For example, such uses as clinical shipments of a new drug awaiting FFDA approval, test marketing, or infrequent sales of large or expensive or seasonal products, reflect legitimate trademark uses in the normal course of trade and are not to be excluded by the House language."

[b] Use on Different Goods—Mark Modifications—"Tacking"

[*i*]   *Modified Goods.* In *Ralston Purina*[9] and *International Diagnostic Technology*,[10] the Federal Circuit held that the bona fide initial use required to support an application to register a mark need not be on goods *identical* to those the user ultimately intends to sell with the mark. Use on goods later altered will suffice if the alteration does not change the goods' "inherent and identifiable character."[11] These decisions involved "token" uses, which will not suffice under the 1988 Trademark Revision Act, but the "inherent-identifiable character" test as to the nature of the goods upon which a mark is used can as easily be applied to the Act's "bona fide" use requirement.

---

[9] Ralston Purina Co. v. On-Cor Frozen Foods, Inc., 746 F.2d 801, 223 U.S.P.Q. 979 (Fed. Cir. 1984) (applicant used "ENCORE" on a cat food product and subsequently changed the product's formulation).

[10] International Diagnostic Technology, Inc. v. Miles Laboratories, Inc., 746 F.2d 798, 223 U.S.P.Q. 977 (Fed. Cir. 1984) (Miles first used a mark on several versions of reagent strip diagnostic products and later adopted an improved version of one of those products for commercial development under the mark).

Cf. Fast Chemical Products Corp. v. Pillsbury Co., 132 U.S.P.Q. 561, 562 (TTAB 1962) (trademark holder discontinued sale of a powder laundry detergent and substituted a liquid all-purpose cleaner; no abandonment requiring cancellation merely because of a mere change of formulae or primary use).

[11] In Société de Developments et D'Innovations des Marches Agricoles et Aliminetaries-Sodima Union de Cooperatives Agricoles v. International Yogurt, 662 F. Supp. 839, 3 USPQ2d 1641 (D. Ore. 1987), the court cancelled plaintiff's registration of the mark "YOCREME," finding that it "abandoned or warehoused" its mark "YOCREME" after engaging in a "token use" and obtaining registration for four broad good categories—a mousse, a plain custard-style refrigerated yogurt, a frozen yogurt, and a refrigerated soft cheese." Over a five year period, plaintiff tried the mark on a series of products, eventually settling on high fat yogurt.

"A product as eventually marketed need not be identical to that which was registered. . . . The test . . . is whether the goods bear the inherent and identifiable character of the product initially sold. . . . In this case, plaintiffs hoped that one of the four products for which the product was registered would be sufficiently similar to YOCREME as it was eventually marketed. I find that YOCREME does not have the inherent and identifiable characteristics of soft cheese. Nor is YOCREME, which is refrigerated but not frozen, sufficiently similar to frozen yogurt. Nor is the high-butterfat YOCREME, which is marketed as an extravagant dessert with exotic flavors, inherently identifiable from plain yogurt. It may be that YOCREME is inherently identifiable from plaintiffs' 1979 sale of chocolate mousse, although this is somewhat doubtful because mousse is a non-yogurt product. Herein lies plaintiffs' fatal flaw. The smorgasbord for which they registered YOCREME is strong evidence of their uncertainty. They did not know, except in a most general way, how they intended to use the trademark. An application based on initial use must reasonably target the specific product. . . . The scattershot approach smacks of improper 'warehousing.' Trademarks are intended to be the essence of competition, . . . not the means to hoard a good name." 662 F. Supp. at 851-53, 3 U.S.P.Q.2d at 1650-51.

[*ii*]   *Modified Marks.* A trademark owner may rely on prior use of a modified mark only if the current and prior marks create the "same commercial impression."[12] In *Ilco,*[13] Ilco petitioned to cancel Ideal Security's registration of "HOME PROTECTION CENTER" for lock display racks. The only question was use priority. In September 1965, Ideal Security began using "HOME PROTECTION *HARDWARE*"; in the latter part of 1966 or early 1967, it changed "Hardware" to "Center." In September 1966, Ilco also began using "HOME PROTECTION HARDWARE" and almost immediately switched from "Hardware" to "Center." The Board awarded Ideal priority in view of its clearly earlier use of "HOME PROTECTION HARDWARE," noting the parties regarded "Home Protection" as their marks' "distinguishing feature" and used the two terms interchangeably so that they "merged on into the other." The court held that this was error.

"The law permits a user who changes the form of its mark to retain the benefit of its use of the earlier form, without abandonment, if the new and old forms create the same, continuing commercial impression. We agree with the following

---

[12] If a mark owner alters the mark after Lanham Act registration, he may apply to amend the registration but only if "the amendment . . . does not alter materially the character of the mark." Lanham Act §7(e), 15 U.S.C. §1057(e). *See In re* Holland American Wafer Co., 737 F.2d 1015, 1019, 222 U.S.P.Q. 273, 276 (Fed. Cir. 1984) ("Amendment of a registration is allowed under the Lanham Act but not to extend the scope of protected rights or to change the nature of the mark. . . . No reexamination is made by the PTO to determine registrability over other marks. No opposition by third parties is sanctioned."); USPTO, Trademark Manual of Examining Procedure § 1607.02(a) ("The modified mark must contain . . . the essence of the original mark, and the new form must create the impression of being essentially the same mark. An example is found in marks which are words combined with surrounding design. If the word is the essence of the mark and the design is merely background . . . , not integrated into the mark in a necessary way, the removal or change of the design will not be a material alternation . . . [I]f a design is integrated into a mark and is a distinctive feature necessary for recognition of the mark, then a change in the design would materially alter the mark. When a mark is solely a picture or design, an alteration must be evaluated on the basis of whether the new form has the same meaning or creates a fundamentally different meaning which is contrary to the significance of the original mark, or by whether the form as altered would . . . likely . . . be recognized as the same mark. Marks which are entirely words can normally be varied as to their style of lettering, size, and other elements of form without resulting in a material alteration . . . A non-unique or descriptive word might be deleted if the essence of the mark in appearance or meaning is not changed thereby, but a unique word which is necessary to the significance of the mark may not be deleted.").

A registrant may make similar nonmaterial changes in applying for renewal. *Id.* ("if the revised mark is not materially different from the mark as registered, there is no substantive reason to deny renewal without an amendment. Accordingly, it is the practice of the office to allow renewal on the basis of a label which presents the mark in a somewhat different form from the form in which the mark is registered if the specimen does not show a material alteration of the mark as registered. . . . Thus, an amendment of the mark is not needed or required to obtain renewal in such cases and, more significantly, the filing of an amendment does not enhance a registrant's right to renew. Holland's proper course of action has been, and remains, the filing of an application to register its new mark.").

[13] Ilco Corp. v. Ideal Security Hardware Corp., 527 F.2d 1221, 188 U.S.P.Q. 485 (CCPA 1976).

statement of the Trademark Trial and Appeal Board in *Humble Oil & Refining Co. v. Sekisui Chemical Co.*, 165 USPQ 597, 603–604 (TTAB 1970):

> 'It is settled that a person may change the display of a mark at any time because whatever rights he may possess in the mark reside in the term itself rather than in any particular form or arrangement thereof. . . . The only requirement in these instances is that the mark be modified in such a fashion as to retain its trademark impact and symbolize a single and continuing commercial impression. That is, a change which does not alter its distinctive characteristics represents a continuity of trademark rights. Thus, where the distinctive character of the mark is not changed, the mark is, in effect, the same and the rights obtained by virtue of the earlier use of the prior form inure to the later form.' "[14]

Ideal Security could not rely on its prior use of the mark "HOME PROTECTION HARDWARE" because it created a different commercial impression than "HOME PROTECTION CENTER." The parties' interchangeable use "is not material because commercial impression is gauged by the impact on the public. . . . "[15] "Hardware" signifies the hardware itself; "center" signifies a unitary aggregation of related goods.

In *Van Dyne-Crotty*,[16] the court emphasized that "the standard of legal equivalence used in reviewing efforts to 'tack' the prior use of one mark onto that of another is higher than that used in evaluating two competing marks."[17]

> "The previously used mark must be the legal equivalent of the mark in question or indistinguishable therefrom, and the consumer should consider both as the same mark. . . . [F]or the purposes of 'tacking,' even if the two marks are confusingly similar, they still may not be legal equivalents. . . . Instead, the marks must create 'the same, continuing commercial impression,' . . . and the later mark should not materially differ from or alter the character of the mark attempted to be 'tacked.'
>
> . . .
>
> "Tacking is occasionally permitted where the two marks, though differing slightly in their literal meaning or grammatical presentation, nevertheless possess the same connotation in context. . . .
>
> ". . . [T]acking in general should be condoned only in 'rare instances.' . . . And it would be clearly contrary to well-established principles of trademark law

---

[14] 527 F.2d at 1224.

[15] 527 F.2d at 1224.

[16] Van Dyne-Crotty, Inc. v. Wear-Guard Corp., 926 F.2d 1156, 17 USPQ2d 1866 (Fed. Cir. 1991).

[17] *See* also Homeowners Group, Inc. v. Home Marketing Specialists, Inc., 931 F.2d 1100, 1106, 18 U.S.P.Q.2d 1587, 1591 (6th Cir. 1991) (plaintiff was first to use mark "HMS"; later plaintiff and defendant adopted marks consisting of "HMS" and a rooftop design; plaintiff's adoption of mere initials did not "convey ownership of marks consisting of those initials plus other designs. . . . [O]wnership of the mark HMS includes the right to exclude others from using a mark, such as Specialists' HMS-roof design mark, only if use of the subsequent mark will lead to a likelihood of confusion with the mark HMS.").

to sanction the tacking of a mark with a narrow commercial impression onto one with a broader commercial impression."[18]

[c] **Affixation.** The common law required that the merchant or manufacturer claiming trademark rights actually "affix" the mark to the goods.[19] The Lanham Act relaxed the strict affixation requirement by including in the definition of "use in commerce" placement "on the goods or their containers or the displays associated therewith or on the tags or labels affixed thereto."[20] The 1988 Trademark Revision Act further relaxed the affixation requirement by allowing "use on documents associated with the goods or their sale" "if the nature of the goods makes such placement impracticable."[21]

---

[18] 926 F.2d at 1159-60, 17 U.S.P.Q.2d at 1868-69.

Registrant and cancellation petitioner compete in the work clothes market. In 1986, registrant obtained registration of the mark "CLOTHES THAT WORK" (in block letters), claiming first use of July 1985. In 1987, petitioner petitioned to cancel registrant's mark, alleging that it had previously adopted in 1983 the marks "CLOTHING THAT WORKS," "CLOTHES THAT WORK HARD," and "CLOTHES THAT WORK OVERTIME." In 1988, registrant acquired the mark "CLOTHES THAT WORK. FOR THE WORK YOU DO" from Horace Small Manufacturing Co., a small uniform manufacturer, for $25,000, which had used the mark since the mid-1970s. Small made similar products (though in petite sizes) but targeted them to a different market than that occupied by registrant and petitioner. Registrant amended its pleadings and asserted that the registered ("CLOTHES THAT WORK") and acquired ("CLOTHES THAT WORK. FOR THE WORK YOU DO") marks are legal equivalents, entitling it to rely on the earlier Small use date. The TTAB granted cancellation, finding that petitioner's and registrant's marks were confusingly similar, that registrant's registered and acquired marks were not legal equivalents such as to allow registrant to "tack" its uses, and, therefore, petitioner was the prior user. The court affirmed, noting "[s]imply because a mark is a portion of an earlier mark" does not end analysis. Rather, the inquiry "must focus on both marks *in their entirety* to determine whether each conveys the same commercial impression." 926 F.2d at 1160, 17 U.S.P.Q.2d at 1869.

[19] *E.g.,* Western Stove Co. v. George D. Roper Corp., 82 F. Supp. 206, 80 U.S.P.Q. 393 (S.D. Calif. 1949) (defendant had priority when it was the first to actually affix the mark to its product even though the plaintiff was the first to use the mark in advertising).

[20] 15 U.S.C. §1127. *See In re* Castleton China, Inc., 156 U.S.P.Q. 691 (TTAB 1968) (use of "The Symphony Collection" in pamphlets advertising applicant's china dinnerware is not sufficient use on a display, etc.; "[A] 'display associated with the goods' is a conspicuous, eye catching assemblage of goods which leads to or induces sales of the merchandise so displayed. And, insofar as a mark is used in connection therewith, it must appear on the display itself in such a close physical association with the goods that a prospective purchaser viewing the display would immediately associate the mark with the goods. . . . Use of a designation in advertising does not constitute use as a trademark.").

Because a mark cannot be affixed to a service, the Lanham Act provided that a mark need only be "used or displayed in the sale or advertising of services." Lanham Act §45, 15 U.S.C. § 1127.

[21] The Senate Report explains that "strict affixation of a trademark is often impractical in the case of bulk goods." The amended definition "provides that use in commerce on or in connection with certain products, such as oil, chemicals and grain, can be established when the products are shipped in railroad cars, ships, aircraft, or other vehicles and the mark is used 'on documents associated with the goods or their sale.' " S. Rep. No. 100-515, 100th Cong., 2d Sess. 45 (1988).

[d] **Interstate and Foreign Commerce.** The Lanham Act, providing for federal registration and protection of trademarks, is an exercise of Congress' Article I power to regulate interstate and foreign commerce.[22] An application to register a mark must set forth either "the date of the applicant's first use of the mark in commerce" or a "bona fide intention . . . to use a trademark in commerce." Section 43(a)'s broad remedy against false designations of origin and false description relates to use in commerce.[23] The Act defines "commerce" as "all commerce which may lawfully be regulated by Congress."[24]

The United State Supreme Court's broad definition of the commerce that Congress may lawfully regulate, developed in non-trademark contexts,[25] applies to the Lanham Act. Regulatable commerce includes *intrastate* activity that "affects" interstate or foreign commerce. In *Gastown,*[26] the Court of Customs and Patent Appeals found sufficient interstate commerce use when the applicant sold automotive services to interstate travelers from its stations, all of which were within a single state. Some of the stations were on interstate highways. In *Silenus Wines,*[27] the court held that the *Gastown*'s reasoning extended to the use of trademarks on goods as well as services. Applicant imported wine from France and sold it under the "Stefmon" mark in Massachusetts only. The court focused only on the applicant's acts. (If the French shipper's acts were considered, it would be a clear case of transportation in commerce.) "[W]ere it not for the intrastate sales anticipated by the appellant-importer, the foreign commerce that occurred in this case would probably not have occurred." In *Larry Harmon Pictures,*[28] the court refused to adopt a per se rule excluding single location restaurants from interstate commerce.[29]

---

[22] *See* §5B.

[23] For a discussion of Section 43(a), see §§5C[2][c][iv] and 6E.

[24] Lanham Act §45, 15 U.S.C. §1127.

[25] *E.g.,* Heart of Atlanta Motel, Inc. v. United States, 379 U.S. 241 (1964) (1964 Civil Rights Act covers hotel operating in one state).

[26] *In re* Gastown, 326 F.2d 780, 140 U.S.P.Q. 216 (CCPA 1964).

[27] *In re* Silenus Wines, 557 F.2d 806, 194 U.S.P.Q. 261 (CCPA 1977).

[28] Larry Harmon Pictures Corp. v. Williams Restaurant Corp., 929 F.2d 662, 18 U.S.P.Q.2d 1292 (Fed. Cir. 1991).

[29] At issue was an application to register "BOZO'S" for restaurant services rendered at BOZO'S pit barbecue restaurant in Mason, Tennessee, since 1932. "Mason is about a 50 or 60 minute drive from Memphis, Tennessee, which is a large city and a major commercial center for the Mid-South region." BOZO'S is popular with Memphis residents, and it has been mentioned in publications in other states. In an affidavit, its owner estimated that 15% of its business is with out-of-state customers.

Opposer relied on *In re* Bookbinder's Restaurant, Inc., 240 F.2d 365, 112 USPQ 326 (CCPA 1957), for the proposition that a single-location restaurant, not situated on an interstate highway, does not render services in interstate commerce. Alternatively, it suggested a rule that such a restaurant must (1) be located on an interstate highway, (2) serve at least 50% of its meals to interstate travelers, or (3) regularly advertise in out-of-state media.

"The record here established that the BOZO'S mark has been used in connection with services rendered to customers traveling across state boundaries. It is not required that such services be rendered in more than one state to satisfy the use in commerce requirement. . . . [Opposer] does not dispute that there has been some use in commerce of Williams'

[e] Priority—Constructive Use—Equity and "Calendar Priority." If two rivals claim rights to the same mark or confusingly similar marks, the first to use the mark has priority.

If the second to use a mark on goods or services previously used the same symbol as a tradename, the prior tradename use is a Section 2(d) "prior use" bar to the claim of the first trademark users.[30] Some authority suggests that, in such a situation, the tradename user may "tack" its prior tradename use onto its subsequent trademark use to establish priority.[31]

The 1988 Trademark Revision Act authorizes filing applications to register trademarks based on an "intent to use" the mark on goods in commerce as well as on actual use.[32] No registration may issue until the applicant begins actual use of the mark. After registration, the application filing, whether based on actual use or on intent to use, becomes a nationwide "constructive use" of the mark for priority purposes.

> "Contingent on the registration of a mark on the principal register . . ., the filing of the application to register such mark shall constitute constructive use of the mark, conferring a right of priority, nationwide in effect, on or in connection with the goods or services specified in the registration against any other person except for a person whose mark has not been abandoned and who, prior to such filing—
>
> (1) has used the mark;
>
> (2) has filed an application to register the mark which is pending or has resulted in registration of the mark; or

---

mark. It contends only that the volume of such activity was less than Williams' affidavit would indicate. . . .

"We therefore reject [opposer's] argument that a certain increased threshold level of interstate activity is required before registration of the mark used by a single-location restaurant may be granted. The Lanham Act by its terms extends to all commerce which Congress may regulate. This court does not have the power to narrow or restrict the unambiguous language of the statute." 929 F.2d at 666, 18 U.S.P.Q.2d at 1295.

[30] *See* §5C[4].

[31] *See* Dynamet Technology, Inc. v. Dynamet, Inc., 593 F.2d 1007, 1010-11, 201 U.S.P.Q. 129 (CCPA 1979) ("In a trademark interference proceeding, the time period of a party's tradename use of a word may be tacked onto its first date of trademark use on goods in interstate commerce for the purpose of establishing priority of trademark use. . . . [N]o property rights in a trademark for goods arise except in connection with its use thereon by an existing business entity. Similarly, it would seem that there can be no property rights in a trade name except in connection with its use with a business entity that has engaged in *sufficient activities* to have acquired goodwill, because a trade name is representative of the goodwill of a business entity. . . . Accordingly, to establish its right to tack the time period of its tradename use of a word onto its first date of trademark use of the word on goods for the purpose of establishing priority of trademark use, a party must furnish evidence that, during the time period sought to be 'tacked,' it was a business entity and had engaged in sufficient activities to have acquired goodwill.").

[32] *See* §5D[2][b].

(Matthew Bender & Co., Inc.)

(3) has filed a foreign application to register the mark on the basis of which he or she has acquired a right of priority, and timely files an application under section 1126(d) [44(d)] to register the mark which is pending or has resulted in registration of the mark."[33]

The Senate Committee Report on the 1988 Act discusses this landmark new concept in United States trademark law.

"Constructive use will fix a registrant's nationwide priority rights in a mark from the filing of its application for registration, whether that applications is based on use or intent-to-use. This right of priority will have legal effect comparable to the earliest use of a mark at common law. . . .

"Provision for constructive use in the Lanham Act will accomplish three important objectives.

"First, it will extend to U.S. trademark owners a benefit which is presently available only to applicants applying to register their marks in the United States under Section 44 of the Act.

"Second, it will promote certainty in the acquisition of federal trademark rights. Without constructive use, the certainty envisioned by the intent-to-use application system would not be achieved; an intent-to-use applicant would be vulnerable to pirates and to anyone initiating use after it files its application. Constructive use will also resolve an important fact issue in current trademark law and thereby reduce the geographic fragmentation of trademark rights. Currently, an applicant who has made use of a mark in one area is at the mercy of another user who begins using the same or a similar mark in a remote area before the applicant obtains its registration and can claim the benefits of constructive notice. These situations result in practical problem for both of the users and consumers. The registrant is prohibited from expanding use of its mark nationally and is unable to benefit from the nationwide rights federal registration is design to provide. Similarly, the second user is prevented from expanding because it may be prohibited from using the mark in areas where it had no market presence at the time the first user obtains its registration. Finally, consumers who are exposed to the marks of both users may well be confused.

"Third, constructive use, by according conditional rights to those that publicly disclose their marks, will encourage the earlier filing of applications to register trademarks and will foster trademark searching by all parties before they adopt and invest in new marks."[34]

The Committee Report emphasized that the new constructive use concept was not intended to "replace equity." "As the courts have refused to make 'calendar

---

[33] 15 U.S.C. §1057(c). For a discussion of Section 44(d), see §5D[1][f][ii].

For a discussion of the constructive use provision's affect on multiple good faith users, see §5E[2][c].

[34] S. Rep. No. 100-515, 100th Cong., 2d Sess. 29-30 (1988).

priority' based on actual commercial use of a mark determinative of rights if doing so will cause inequity, they should not react differently with constructive use." [35]

The constructive use doctrine's benefits are contingent upon the applicant obtaining registration. The original Senate bill authorized an applicant relying upon constructive use to seek judicial relief prior to registration but provided that the court should not enter final judgment until actual use and registration occurred. The House deleted this provision because of practical and constitutional concerns. [36] In inter partes PTO proceedings, including opposition and cancellations, the Act does provide that "no final judgment shall be entered in favor of an applicant under section 1(b) before the mark is registered, if such applicant cannot prevail without establishing constructive use. . . . " [37]

[f] Priority Based On Registration or Use in Other Countries

[i] *Use in Other Countries.* United States trademark law generally follows a territoriality principle. [38] To obtain and maintain rights, one must use the mark in the

---

[35] *Id.* at 30.

An example of equitable refusal to adhere strictly to "calendar priority" is Manhattan Industries, Inc. v. Sweater Bee by Banff, Ltd., 627 F.2d 628, 207 U.S.P.Q. 89 (2d Cir. 1980), in which two parties, Sweater Bee and Don Sophisticates', raced to be first to adopt a famous mark "Kimberly" that a prior owner expressly abandoned. The court allowed both parties to use the mark with alterations.

"[I]n light of the significant shipments and investment by Sweater Bee, we do not believe that Don Sophisticates' slight priority in time justifies awarding to the appellees the exclusive, nationwide right to the 'Kimberly' mark. We have previously stated that the concept of priority in the law of trademarks is applied 'not in its calendar sense' but on the basis of 'the equities involved.' " Chandon Champagne Corp. v. San Marino Wine Corp., 355 F.2d 531, 534 (2d Cir. 1964). . . . Given the evenly balanced equities in this case, it would be inequitable to allow only the appellees to use the 'Kimberly' mark. Sweater Bee has proved 'that it entered the market sufficiently early to be equally entitled with [appellees] to the use of the ["Kimberly"] mark. In such case, to protect the public, each company [will] have to differentiate its product from that of the other company and perhaps also from the original ["Kimberly"] mark.' P. Daussa Corp. v. Sutton Cosmetics (P.R.) Inc., 462 F.2d 134, 136 (2d Cir. 1972)."

627 F.2d at 630-31.

[36] "The first concern was practical in nature, in that the filing system of the Federal Courts is incapable of routinely retaining in its files lawsuits that remain unresolved for up to four years. The second concern stems from the fact that the constitutional basis for the Federal trademark laws is use of the mark in commerce. Permitting a plaintiff to sue before use occurs thus raises serious questions about abuse of the judicial system, about whether Federal jurisdiction and a case or controversy exists, and about whether such a case is 'ripe.' " H.R. Rep. 100-1028, 100th Cong., 2d Sess. 4 (1988).

[37] Lanham Act §18, 15 U.S.C. §1068.

[38] *Cf.* Ingenohl v. Walter E. Olsen & Co., Inc., 273 U.S. 541 (1927). *See* §5E[5].

Ingenohl encapsulated some interesting history. Plaintiff started a cigar business with an appurtenant trademark in the Philippines, at that time a United States possession, and later opened a second factory in Hong Kong, a British colony. During World War I, the United States "Alien Property Custodian" seized plaintiff's property (plaintiff apparently being an "enemy alien") and sold it. A Hong Kong court ruled that plaintiff owned the Hong Kong

United States.[39] The United States belongs to the Paris Convention, which guarantees Convention member nationals national treatment rights and a six-month filing date priority right, but the Convention does not itself create trademarks rights in the United States.[40]

---

rights to the trademark and awarded plaintiff costs. Plaintiff sued in a Philippine court to execute on the Hong Kong court costs judgment. The Philippine Supreme Court rejected the suit, finding that the Hong Kong court committed clear error in not recognizing the Alien Property Custodian's transfer of the Hong Kong trademark. The United States Supreme Court reversed, relying on the trademark territoriality principle: "A trade-mark started elsewhere would depend for its protection in Hongkong upon the law prevailing in Hongkong and would confer no rights except by the consent of that law. . . . When then the judge who, in the absence of an appeal to the Privy Council, is the final exponent of that law, authoritatively declares that the assignment by the Custodian of the assets of the Manila firm cannot and will not be allowed to affect the rights of the party concerned in Hongkong, we do not see how it is possible for a foreign Court to pronounce his decision wrong." 273 U.S. at 544.

[39] E.g., Fuji Photo Film Co., Inc. v. Shinohara Shoji Kabushiki Kaisha, 754 F.2d 591, 599, 225 USPQ 540, 546 (5th Cir. 1985) ("The concept of territoriality is basic to trademark law; . . . trademark rights exist in each country solely according to that country's statutory scheme."); Le Blume Import Co. v. Coty, 293 F. 344, 350 (2d Cir. 1923) ("It is not essential that one who claims protection of his trade-mark should in all cases be able to show that he first used it. The prior use of a mark by another in some foreign country is not fatal, if the one claiming protection is able to show that he was first to use it in this country. . . . It may be true that a trader can protect his trade-mark in all the markets in which he sells without respect to territorial limits, but it is not true that one who has acquired a technical trade-mark and used it in a limited territory thereby acquires a prior right to its use in an entirely different territory."); Scholastic, Inc. v. Macmillan, inc., 650 F. Supp. 866, 873 n.6, 2 USPQ2d 1191, 1196 n.6 (S.D. N.Y. 1987) ("Scholastic's extensive use of the name 'Classroom' in Canada and Australia is, of course, of no relevance to its effort to create trademark rights in the United States."); Koppers Co., Inc. v. Krupp-Koppers GmbH, 517 F. Supp. 836, 852, 210 USPQ 711 (W.D. Pa. 1981) ("Prior use of a mark in other countries creates no right to common law protection."); Johnson & Johnson v. Diaz, 339 F. Supp. 60, 63-64, 172 USPQ 35 (C.D. Calif. 1971) ("Defendants lay great stress on the fact that their particular cologne water is explicitly imitative of a similar product formerly marketed in Cuba under the name Johnson and that defendants limit their sales to the submarket of Cuban immigrants and refugees residing in the United States. Plaintiff correctly argues, on the other hand, that prior use of a trademark in a foreign country does not entitle its owner to claim exclusive trademark rights in the United States against one who, in good faith, has adopted a like trademark of the same character prior to entry of the foreigner into the domestic market . . . Hence, the fact of prior use in Cuba of a trademark similar to defendants' is not, itself, a defense to this action. Similarly, the rights of one who has, in good faith, appropriated a trademark in a foreign country are not affected by the fact that such appropriation, if made in the United States, would have been an infringement of the trademark of a prior user. . . . Only as it may negate the likelihood of confusion does the fact of prior use in Cuba become material to this action.").

[40] Cf. Vanity Fair Mills, Inc. v. T. Eaton Co., 234 F.2d 633, 640-41 (2d Cir. 1956), cert. denied, 352 U.S. 871 (1956) ("The International Convention is essentially a compact between the various member countries to accord in their own countries to citizens of the other contracting parties trade-mark and other rights comparable to those accorded their own citizens by their domestic law. The underlying principle is that foreign nationals should be given the same treatment in each of the member countries as that country makes available to its own citizens. In addition, the Convention sought to create uniformity in certain respects by obligating

The good faith junior user doctrine allows a second user of mark previously used by another in the United States to obtain exclusive trademark rights in a geographic market remote from that of the first user if the second user adopts and uses the mark "in good faith." [41] In *Person's,* [42] the Federal Circuit held that "[k]nowledge of foreign use does not preclude good faith adoption and use in the United States." In 1977, Person's founder, Takaya Iwasaki, began using a stylized "PERSON'S" logo on clothing sold in Japan. In 1981, Christman, a U.S. citizen, visited a Person's store in Japan and purchased clothing items bearing the PERSON'S logo. Upon returning to the U.S., Christman consulted legal counsel and was advised that no one had established rights in the U.S. to the "PERSON'S" logo. In 1982, Christman began selling clothing with the "PERSON'S" logo. In April 1983, Christman filed an application to register the "PERSON'S" mark in the U.S. for wearing apparel. The registration issued in September 1984. In the 1982-1984 period, Person's became a known and respected force in the Japanese fashion industry. In 1985, it obtained registration of "PERSON'S" in the U.S. for luggage, clothing, and accessories. In 1985 and 1986, it secured a U.S. distributor and began advertising in the U.S.

Person's petitioned to cancel Christman's registration of "PERSON'S" for wearing apparel on the grounds of (a) likelihood of confusion based on Person's prior foreign use, (b) abandonment, and (c) unfair competition under the Paris Convention. The TTAB found that, at the time of Christman's U.S. adoption of "PERSON'S" in 1982: (a) the Japanese company's "PERSON'S" mark had acquired no notoriety in the U.S., and (b) Christman was not aware of Person's intention to enter the U.S. clothing and accessories market in the future. The Federal Circuit held that Christman's registration could not be cancelled. Christman was the prior user in United States commerce: "[F]oreign use has no effect on U.S. commerce and cannot form the basis for a holding that appellant has priority here. The concept of territoriality is basic to trademark law; trademark rights exist in each country solely according to that country's statutory scheme." [43] Christman's prior use in the United States was not

---

each member nation 'to assure to nationals of countries of the Union an effective protection against unfair competition.' . . . The Convention is not premised upon the idea that the trade-mark and related laws of each member nation shall be given extraterritorial application, but on exactly the converse principle that each nation's law shall have only territorial application. Thus a foreign national of a member nation using his trade-mark in commerce in the United States is accorded extensive protection here against infringement and other types of unfair competition by virtue of United States membership in the Convention. But that protection has its source in, and is subject to the limitations of, American law, not the law of the foreign national's own country. Likewise, the International Convention provides protection to a United States trade-mark owner such as plaintiff against unfair competition and trade-mark infringement in Canada— but only to the extent that Canadian law recognizes the treaty obligation as creating private rights or has made the Convention operative by implementing legislation.").

For a discussion of the Paris Convention's application to patent rights, see §2H[2].

[41] *See* §5E[2][b].

[42] Person's Co., Ltd. v. Christman, 900 F.2d 1565, 14 U.S.P.Q. 2d 1477 (Fed. Cir. 1990).

[43] 900 F.2d at 1568, 14 U.S.P.Q.2d at 1479. *Compare* CBS, Inc. v. Logical Games, 719 F.2d 1237, 221 U.S.P.Q. 498 (4th Cir. 1983) (trade dress infringement). In *CBS,* Logical purchased 3000 "Rubik's Cube" puzzles from its Hungarian manufacturer and imported them

so tainted with bad faith as to render his prior use insufficient to establish rights superior to those arising from Person's prior adoption in a foreign country.

"The concept of bad faith adoption applies to remote junior users seeking concurrent use registrations; in such cases, the likelihood of customer confusion in the remote area may be presumed from proof of the junior user's knowledge. In the present case, when Christman initiated use of the mark, Person's Co. had not yet entered U.S. commerce. . . .

". . . [A]n inference of bad faith requires something more than mere knowledge of prior use of a similar mark in a foreign country. . . . While adoption of a mark with knowledge of a prior actual user in U.S. commerce may give rise to cognizable equities as between the parties, no such equities may be based upon knowledge of a similar mark's existence or on a problematical intent to use such a similar mark in the future. . . .

" . . . While there is some case law supporting a finding of bad faith where (1) the foreign mark is famous here or (2) the use is a nominal one made solely to block the prior foreign user's planned expansion into the United States, . . . neither of these circumstances is present in this case."[44]

---

for sale into the United States. Later, the manufacturer granted CBS's predecessor, Ideal Toy, exclusive United States distribution rights. The court held that CBS, not Logical, held Section 43(a) "trade dress" rights because Logical's minimal use was insufficient to establish secondary meaning in the trade dress:

"While factual situations can be imagined in which extensive—especially reiterated—purchase abroad and marketing in the United States might operate to create in the American importer trade dress rights in the United States for a format employed elsewhere by the foreign manufacturer, in the present case the drawing of such an inference would be altogether unjustified. . . .

"To put things in perspective, we accept the assertion by Logical Games, Inc. that 'trade dress use in foreign countries does not create protectible trademark rights in the United States.' . . . Here, however, conceding that there were no American user rights in the Hungarian manufacturer or exporter, or in [the CBS], until exportation to and distribution in the United States by them had commenced, . . . nevertheless, although lacking the user rights, prior to actual distribution in the United States, the Hungarians did not lose the right to establish such rights. Such a loss of the rights would have occurred only if Logical Games, Inc. were to have taken sufficient steps to appropriate such rights. The importation of 3000 puzzles, employing a trade dress, for which Logical Games, Inc. could claim no originating responsibility, simply was insufficient to create the user rights claimed by Logical Games, Inc. Consequently, CBS, Inc., in whom reposed all interests of the Hungarian manufacturer and exporter had still the right to create, by importation to and distribution in the United States, an exclusive prior claim to the trade dress here at issue. CBS, Inc. did so through extensive use in the United States, and that provides the solution to the legal puzzle with which we have been challenged by the parties."

"Logical Games, Inc. saw a product complete in its preparation by the Hungarian manufacturer, who plainly possessed, and did nothing to surrender, the trade dress chosen for the puzzles. The right to the trade dress on items marketed in the United States did not arise in Logical Games, Inc., whose use was minimal, so regardless of when it came into existence it was Ideal Toy Corporation, not Logical Games, Inc. who established user rights in the United States." 719 F.2d at 1239-40, 221 U.S.P.Q. at 500-01.

[44] 900 F.2d at 1569-70, 14 U.S.P.Q.2d at 1480-81.

Some decisions grant non-United States owners relief against persons who deliberately copy and use famous marks and tradenames in the United States.[45] In *Vaudable,*[46] a New York court granted Paris' noted "Maxim's" restaurant an injunction barring defendant from opening a "Maxim's" in New York City. The defendant not only copied Maxim's name but "endeavored to create the illusion of identity" with it by using "Montmartre, a Parisian subdivision, as their corporate name,"[47] adopting a similar red and gold color decor, and replicating the distinctive script printing of "Maxim's." The court applied New York's expansive unfair competition law rather than trademark principles.

[ii] *Section 44 Priority and Registration Rights.* Lanham Act Section 44 implements the United States' Paris Convention obligation to confer a six-month "right of priority" to nationals of countries of the Paris Union who have applied for and obtain registration of their marks in their home countries.[48]

Section 44(d) provides a *priority right*: an application for registration of a mark filed by an eligible person[49] who has previously filed an application for registration of the same mark in an eligible country shall be accorded the "same force and effect" as would be accorded to the same application in the United States on the date on which the application was first filed in such foreign country.[50] Before the 1988 Trademark Revision Act, Section 44(d) imposed four provisions on this priority right. The second provision stated: "the application conforms as nearly as practicable to the requirements of this chapter, but use in commerce need not be alleged."[51] Section 44(e) provides a *basis for registration*: "A mark duly registered in the country of origin

---

[45] *Cf.* Davidoff Extension S.A. v. Davidoff International, Inc., 221 U.S.P.Q. 465, 467 (S.D. Fla. 1983) (noting that the "The Paris Convention is self-executing" and entitles the owner of a mark that is famous in other countries to protection against unfair competition).

[46] Vaudable v. Montmartre, Inc., 20 Misc. 2d 757, 193 N.Y.S.2d 332, 123 U.S.P.Q. 357 (N.Y. Sup. Ct. 1959).

[47] One can take scholarly notice of the fact that Maxim's is *not* in Montmartre.

[48] For a discussion of the comparable right of priority for patent applications see §2H[2].

[49] Under Section 44(b), an eligible person is "any person whose country of origin is a party to any convention or treaty relating to trade-marks, trade or commercial names, or repression or unfair competition, to which the United States is also a party, or extends reciprocal rights to nationals of the United States by law. . . . "

Nationals of most major countries are eligible entities because most such countries, including the United States, belong to the Paris Convention, which relates to industrial property rights, including trademarks and patents.

[50] Lanham Act §44(d), 15 U.S.C. §1126(d).

[51] 15 U.S.C. § 1126(d). The other three provisions are:

"(1) the application in the United States is filed within six months from the date on which the application was first filed in the foreign country;

"(3) the rights acquired by third parties before the date of the filing of the first application in the foreign country shall in no way be affected by a registration obtained on an application filed under this subsection;

"(4) nothing in this subsection shall entitle the owner of a registration granted under this section to sue for acts committed prior to the date on which his mark was registered in this country unless the registration is based on use in commerce."

of the foreign applicant may be registered on the principal register *if eligible*, otherwise on the supplemental register. . . . "[52]

The courts and the PTO had understandable difficulty in giving meaningful force to the Section 44(d) priority right. Section 44(d) assumes that a *filing date* is of significant substantive importance, which is true in most other countries but not in the United States in which trademark priority rights arise from use rather than filing. Only after a course of development did the courts and the PTO come to give Sections 44(d) and 44(e) their literal scope—that is, as recognizing eligible foreign nationals' right to file applications and obtain priority over use-based claimants without a showing of actual use, whether in the United States or elsewhere.[53]

---

[52] Lanham Act §44(e), 15 U.S.C. §1126(e) (Emphasis added.).

For a discussion of the difference between Section 44(d) and 44(e), and their relationship to the new Section 1(b) intent-to-use application procedure, see Patent and Trademark Office, Examination Guide 3-89: Implementation of the Trademark Act of 1988 and the Amended Rules of Practice in Trademark Cases C.3.:

"Section 44(d) only provides a basis for receiving a priority filing date but does not provide a basis for registration. . . . In most casts, the basic for registration will be the foreign registration which will issue from the foreign application relied upon for priority. . . .

". . . [T]he assertion of a different basis for registration more than six months after the filing of the foreign application, including reliance on a different foreign registration under Section 44(e), will result in the loss of the priority filing date under Section 44(d). . . . [T]he Office will change the filing date in the United States to the date on which the applicant perfects the new basis for registration by providing either a proper statement of dates of use in commerce, a proper assertion of an intent to use in commerce under Section 1(b) . . . or a certificate or certified copy of a foreign registration."

[53] The key decisions are SCM Corp. v. Langis Foods, Ltd., 539 F.2d 196, 190 U.S.P.Q. 288 (D.C. Cir. 1976) (known as the "Lemon Tree" decision after one of the marks at issue), and Crocker National Bank v. Canadian Imperial Bank of Commerce, 223 U.S.P.Q. 909 (PTO TTAB 1984).

In *Lemon Tree,* the court held that an applicant relying on a pre-use filing in another country for priority need not show use in the United States or anywhere as of the foreign filing date. Langis filed an application in Canada to register "Lemon Tree" on March 28, 1969, began using the mark in Canada on May 15, 1969, and applied for United States registration on September 19, 1969. SCM began using the mark in the United States on May 15, 1969 (the same day as Langis' first use). The court upheld Langis' right to registration. Langis was entitled to its foreign filing date as a "constructive use date." It relied on the express language of Section 44(d)(2), which provides that "use in commerce need not be alleged." The court did not reach the question whether a foreign applicant who had not used the mark anywhere could obtain United States registration. It did note that the "official policy of the Patent Office has shifted with some regularity" on the point.

In *Crocker National Bank,* the Board extended *Lemon Tree,* holding that an applicant properly relying on a foreign priority filing date need not (1) allege use (whether in the United States or elsewhere) or (2) provide specimens demonstrating such use. Canadian Imperial filed an application to register "COMMCASH" for banking services in Canada and, within the six month priority period, filed an application in the United States. It had not used the mark anywhere before the United States filing date. The Board held that Canadian Imperials' application was not "void ab initio" for failure to allege use or include specimens demonstrating use. In a lengthy opinion, Board Member Allen reviewed the "Lemon Tree" decision; prior Board decisions that restrictively interpreted Section 44(d); the history of Article 6 of the

Section 44(d) gives applicants who rely on prior foreign filings an advantage over domestic applicants. A major purpose of the Trademark Revision Act of 1988 was to reduce this discrimination by authorizing intent-to-use applications.

The 1988 Act imposes a bona fide intent to use requirement on Section 44 applicants. It altered the second condition in Section 44(d) by eliminating the phrase "but use in commerce need not be alleged" and substituting "including a statement that the applicant has a bona fide intention to use the mark in commerce."[54] It also added the following sentence to Section 44(e): "The application must state the applicant's bona fide intention to use the mark in commerce, but use in commerce shall not be required prior to registration."[55]

A Section 44 applicant who obtains registration without using the mark in the United States must either begin using it or show an excuse for nonuse sufficient to avoid abandonment.[56] In *Imperial Tobacco*,[57] on July 7, 1981, Imperial obtained United States registration of its mark "JPS" in a design based on its prior United Kingdom registration of the mark, in accordance with Lanham Act Section 44(e). It did not allege use of the mark in commerce in or with the United States. In November 1986, Philip Morris petitioned to cancel Imperial's registration on the ground that the registered mark was abandoned. Imperial made sales of approximately 50,000 "JPS" cigarettes after May 1987, "apparently to support the filing of a declaration of use under [Lanham Act Section 8, which dictates cancellation of a mark's registration unless the registrant files a declaration of use during the sixth year of registration]." Imperial submitted affidavits and evidence "purporting to show that it had no intention to abandon the mark because during [the 1981-1986] period it had been trying to open the United States market." The Federal Circuit affirmed summary judgment cancelling the registration because the undisputed facts showed a *prima facie* case of abandonment by nonuse of the mark from 1981 to 1987 and Imperial's proffered excuses were insufficient.[58]

The court noted that, before and after the 1988 Lanham Act amendments, Section 44 confers on foreign applicants a registration *procurement* advantage, not a registration *maintenance* advantage.

> "[S]ection 44(f) provided, and still provides, that a registration obtained under section 44(e) 'shall be independent of the registration in the country of origin and the duration, validity, or transfer in the United States of such registration shall be governed by the provisions of this chapter.' . . . Thus, after registration, a section 44(e) registrant is entitled only to the same national treatment as any other registrant.

Paris Convention, which Section 44 implements; the PTO rules of practice; practice under the 1905 federal trademark registration act; and the Lanham Act's legislative history.

[54] Lanham Act §44(d)(2), 15 U.S.C. § 1126(d)(2). *See* 37 CFR §2.21(a)(5)(iii).

[55] Lanham Act §44(e), 15 U.S.C. §1126(e). *See also* 37 CFR §2.21(a)(ii).

[56] A petition to cancel a registration for abandonment may be filed at any time. See §§5D[2][d][ii], 5D[3][a][iii], and 5D[3][b].

[57] Imperial Tobacco Limited v. Philip Morris, Inc., 899 F.2d 1575, 14 USPQ2d 1390 (Fed. Cir. 1990).

[58] For a discussion of excusing nonuse, see § 5D[3][b][i](3).

". . . [A] section 44(e) registration, like any other registration, may be cancelled on the ground of abandonment of the mark at any time."

. . .

". . . The statutory language is 'intent not to resume' use. Those words are appropriate for the usual situation in which a registered mark has been used at some time in this country. Where there is use, followed by a period of nonuse, the question is whether the registrant 'discontinued' use with an 'intent not to resume.' . . . [When registration is obtained without allegations of use of the mark in the United States,] [t]he statutory language 'discontinued' and 'intent not to resume,' . . . is inapt.

". . . [N]othing in the [Lanham Act] suggests that the registration of a never-used mark can be maintained indefinitely simply because the registrant does not have an affirmative intent to relinquish the mark. . . . A section 44(e) registrant is merely granted a dispensation from actual use prior to registration, but after registration, there is no dispensation of use requirements. If the registrant fails to make use of the registered mark for two years, the presumption of abandonment may be invoked against that registrant, as against any other."[59]

[2] Lanham Act Registration

The 1988 Trademark Revision Act and implementing PTO regulations substantially revised Lanham Act registration procedure.[60]

[a] Section 1(a) Use Applications. For a mark owner, that is, a person who has adopted and used a mark before applying for registration, registration entails the following steps:

(1) The owner files an application,[61] which includes:

---

[59] 899 F.2d at 1578-80, 1582, 14 USPQ2d at 1392-94, 1395.

[60] A useful resource is the PTO's "Examination Guide 3-89: Implementation of the Trademark Act of 1988 and the Amended Rules of Practice in Trademark Cases" (cited below as "PTO 1989 Guide"), which it published in the October 11, 1989, Official Gazette.

The 1988 Act's legislative history is massive. Three important documents are the House and Senate Committee Reports, H.R. Rep. No. 100-1028, 100th Cong., 2d Sess. (1988), and S. Rep. 100-515, 100th Cong., 2d Sess (1988), and the United States Trademark Association Trademark Review Commission Report. The last is a private organization's report, but its recommendations formed the basis for the Senate Bill that, with amendments and deletions, became the 1988 Act. See S. Rep. 100-515, 100th Cong., 2d Sess. 2- 3 (1988):

"[S. 1883], based on the results of extensive study conducted by the U.S. Trademark Association's Review Commission, was the product of more than 2 years of analysis, debate and consensus-building by trademark owners, attorneys and other private sector experts. . . . Throughout the process, input from the diverse public and private interests served by the Lanham Act was sought. Hundreds of trademark owners and practitioners, more than 50 organizations, Government officials in the United States and abroad, and eminent scholars in the fields of constitutional, commercial, trademarks and unfair competition law contributed to the project."

[61] Lanham Act §1(a), 15 U.S.C. §1051; 37 CFR §2.33.

(a) information on, *inter alia*:

(i) the applicant,[62]

(ii) the mark's adoption and use, including the first use and first use in commerce dates,[63]

(iii) "the particular goods or services on or in connection with which the mark is used,"[64]

(iv) the "class of goods or services according the official classification, if known to the applicant,"[65]

(v) Section 44 priority.[66]

(b) a drawing,[67]

---

[62] The applicant must be the mark's owner. *See* Huang v. Tzu Wei Chen Food Co. Ltd., 849 F.2d 1458, 7 U.S.P.Q.2d 1335 (Fed. Cir. 1988) (application void because the applicant did not own the mark on the date the application was filed, ownership having passed two days before to a newly-formed corporation pursuant to the terms of incorporation).

[63] *See* §5D[1].

[64] The identification should be "clear and concise." USPTO, Trademark Manual of Examining Procedure § 804.01. The PTO notes that "the applicant frequently likes to choose broad terms by which to identify the goods or services." "The appropriateness of any broad identification depends upon the facts in the particular case, but use of terms as broad as the circumstances justify is desirable." *Id.* at §804.02 (setting forth guidelines). The PTO has an "Acceptable Identification of Goods and Services Manual" for use by its trademark examining attorneys, which the United States Trademark Association reproduces and distributes.

The 1988 Trademark Revision Act increased the goods-services identification's importance because, after registration, the filing date becomes a "constructive use" conferring a priority right as to "the goods or services specified in the registration." Lanham Act §7(c), 15 U.S.C. §1057(c). *See* §5D[1][e].

For a discussion of amendments to the goods-services statement, see below.

[65] The PTO maintains a "classification of goods and services" for administrative convenience, such as searching, but classification does "not to limit or extend" applicant and registrant rights. Lanham Act §30, 15 U.S.C. § 1112. The PTO uses the international trademark classification, which the World Intellectual Property Organization establishes. Before September 1, 1973, the PTO used a unique United States classification.

An applicant may apply to register a mark for all the goods or services he uses (or intends to use) the mark on. The PTO multiplies fees if the applicant's goods or services "fall within a plurality of classes." *Id.* 37 CFR §2.86(b).

[66] For a discussion of priority based on application and registration in another country, see §5D[1][f].

[67] 37 CFR §2.51-.52. There are two types of drawings: (1) "typed drawings" consisting of "the mark typed in capital letters," which is suitable for an alphanumeric mark, 37 CFR §2.51(e), and (2) "special form" or "ink drawings" consisting of "a substantially exact representation of the mark as used," which is necessary for marks with script or design elements. The latter is "used to reproduce the mark in the Official Gazette and in the registration certificate." USPTO, Trademark Manual of Examining Procedure §807.

If the mark is "not capable of representation by a drawing," for example, a sound or a smell, see §5C[2][b][iii], the application must contain "an adequate description of the mark." 37 CFR §2.51(e).

(c) a filing fee,

(d) specimens showing the mark's use;[68] and

(e) an entitlement statement, that is, that the applicant believes he, she or it owns the mark sought to be registered, the mark is in use in commerce, and no other person "to the best of his knowledge and belief, has the right to use such mark in commerce either in the identical form thereof or in such near resemblance thereto as to be likely, when used on or in connection with the goods of such other person, to cause confusion, or to cause mistake, or to deceive."[69]

(2) The PTO, acting through its examining attorneys, examines the application to determine whether applicant is entitled to registration.[70]

(3) If the examiner finds that the applicant is not entitled to registration for any reason, for example, because the mark is descriptive[71] or confusingly similar to a previously registered mark,[72] he or she notifies the applicant, indicating "the reasons therefor" and "any formal requirements or objections."[73]

(4) The applicant must respond within six months to prevent application abandonment.[74] The response may be "with or without amendment and must include such proper action by the applicant as the nature of the action and the condition of the case may require."[75] The applicant may:

(a) amend the identification of goods or services "to clarify or limit the identification, but additions will not be permitted,"[76]

(b) substitute specimens but only if the applicant supports the substitution with an affidavit or declaration "verifying that [they] were in use in commerce at least as early as the filing date of the application,"[77]

(c) amend the description or drawing of the mark but "only if warranted by the specimens . . . as originally filed, or supported by additional specimens

---

[68] 37 CFR §2.56. The specimens may be "labels, tags, or containers bearing the mark." *Id.*
"An important function of specimens in a trademark application is . . . to enable the PTO to verify the statements made in the application regarding trademark use." *In re* Bose, 546 F.2d 893, 192 U.S.P.Q. 213 (CCPA 1976). Advertising material and instruction sheets are not acceptable for showing trademark use. USPTO, Trademark Manual of Examining Procedure §808.05.

[69] Lanham Act §1(a)(1)(A), 15 U.S.C. § 1051(a)(1)(A); 37 CFR §2.33(b)(1).
This application statement of lack of knowledge of prior uses leads to charges of fraud when it is shown that the applicant made the statement knowing of prior uses. *See* §5F[2].
An applicant knowing of other lawful uses may be able to file a concurrent use application. *See* §§5D[2][d][v] and 5E[2][d].

[70] Lanham Act §12, 15 U.S.C. §1062.

[71] *See* §5C[3][a].

[72] *See* §5C[4]. The examiner must make a *prima facie* case of unregistrability.

[73] 37 CFR §2.61.

[74] Lanham Act §12(b), 15 U.S.C. §1062(b); 37 CFR §2.65.

[75] 37 CFR §2.62.

[76] 37 CFR §2.71(b). For a discussion of goods-services amendments, see the PTO 1989 Guidelines at B.6.

[77] 37 CFR §2.59(a).

. . . and a supplemental affidavit or declaration . . . alleging that the mark shown in the amended drawing was in use prior to the filing date of the application,"[78] and not so as to "materially" alter the mark's character,[79]

(d) change the use date but not to a date later than the filing date and only if supported by an affidavit or declaration making "such showing as may be required,"[80]

(e) present evidence and make arguments in support of registrability.

(5) After a response, the examiner reconsiders the application. If examiner again refuses registration, the process of action and response may continue. If the examiner makes the refusal final, the applicant may appeal to the Trademark Trial and Appeal Board.[81] An applicant "dissatisfied" with the Board's decision may appeal to the courts.[82]

(6) If the examiner or Board determines the applicant is entitled to registration, the PTO published the mark in the Official Gazette.[83] Publication's purpose is to allow other persons to file opposition to the mark's registration.[84]

(7) "Unless registration is successfully opposed . . . a certificate of registration shall be issued, and notice of the registration shall be published in the Official Gazette . . . "[85]

[b]   Section 1(b) Intent-to-Use Applications. A person "who has a bona fide intention, under circumstances showing the good faith of such person, to use a trademark in commerce may apply to register the trademark. . . . "[86]

[i]   Legislative History. Authorizing intent-to-use applications was the most significant change in the 1988 Trademark Revision Act. Intent-to- use applications and the related constructive nationwide use concept are the most basic changes in United States trademark law since the 1946 Lanham Act introduced constructive notice and incontestability. Congress was moved to adopt the intent-to-use procedure because the existing use requirement "unfairly discriminates against U.S. citizens, as compared to foreign citizens, puts significant legal risks on the introduction of new products and services, and gives preference to certain industries over others, frequently disadvantaging small companies and individuals."[87]

Discrimination arose because foreign citizens and companies could exercise their Paris Convention and Section 44 right to establish priority without actually using the mark.[88] Other common law tradition countries, including the United Kingdom

---

[78] 37 CFR §2.72(b).

[79] 37 CFR §2.72(a).

[80] 37 CFR §2.71(d)(1), (2).

[81] 37 CFR §2.64.

[82] Lanham Act §21, 15 U.S.C. §1071.

[83] Lanham Act §12(a), 15 U.S.C. §1062(a).

[84] See §5D[2][d][i].

[85] Lanham Act §13(b), 15 U.S.C. §1063(b).

[86] Lanham Act §1(b), 15 U.S.C. §1051(b).

[87] S. Rep. 100-515, 100th Cong., 2d Sess. 5 (1988).

[88] See §5D[1][f][ii].

and Canada long ago decided "it is not in the interests of the business community to force businesspeople to use a mark before its protection could be assured."[89]

The use requirement creates "unnecessary legal uncertainty." "[A] U.S. business planning to introduce products or services in the marketplace" has "no assurance that after selecting and adopting a mark, and possibly making a sizable investment in packaging, advertising and marketing, it will not learn that its use of the mark infringes the rights another acquired through earlier use."[90]

To mitigate product introduction risk, the courts "sanctioned the practice of 'token' use,"[91] but "token use is not available to all businesses and industries."[92] Also, token use clogs the register with unused marks "making the clearance of new marks more difficult."[93]

Intent-to-use applications poses "potential for abuse" by persons seeking to tie up a "vast number of potential marks." "To minimize such risks, [the statute] requires the specified intent to be bona fide," which "focuses on an objective good-faith test to establish that the intent is genuine."[94]

[ii] *Requirements and Procedure.* A mark submitted for registration in an intent-to-use application must meet the Lanham Act's registrability requirements, such as distinctiveness. Because, by definition, the mark has not been used, the applicant cannot rely on secondary meaning evidence.[95]

Intent-to-use application requirements and registration procedures are the same as for use-based applications except for the following:

(1) The application must set forth a bona fide intent to use and goods and services upon which the applicant intends to use the mark rather than actual use on goods.

(2) After examination, publication, and resolution of any opposition, the PTO issues "a notice of allowance" rather than a certificate of registration[96] unless

---

[89] S. Rep. 100-515, 100th Cong., 2d Sess. 5 (1988).

[90] *Id.*

[91] *Id.* at 6. *See* §5D[1][a].

[92] *Id.* "For example, it is virtually impossible to make token use of a mark on a large or expensive product. . . . the same is true for service industries (that is, hotels, restaurants, and banks) prior to opening for business. Similarly, it is difficult for small business and individuals to avail themselves of token use because they frequently lack the resources or the knowledge to engage in the practice." *Id.*

[93] *Id.*

[94] *Id.*

[95] *See* PTO, Examination Guide 3-89: Implementation of the Trademark Act of 1988 and the Amended Rules of Practice in Trademark Cases 3.f: "An intent-to-use applicant may not assert that a nondistinctive designation has acquired distinctiveness . . . until the applicant has submitted an amendment to allege use or a statement of use. A claim of acquired distinctiveness, by definition, requires prior use. Section 2(f) is limited by its terms to 'a mark used by the applicant.').

[96] Lanham Act §13(b)(2), 15 U.S.C. §1063(b)(2).

the applicant has previously amended the application to make it a Section 1(a) use application.[97]

(3) Not later than six months after the notice of allowance date, the applicant must file a verified use statement with mark specimens and a fee or seek an extension. The use statement must confirm the fact, date and mode or manner of the mark's use in commerce on or in connection with the goods or services specified in the notice of allowance.[98]

(4) The PTO "shall extend, for one additional 6-month period, the time for filing the statement of use . . . upon written request of the applicant before the expiration of the 6-month period. . . . "[99] It may further extend the time for filing the use statement for periods aggregating not more than 24 months "upon a showing of good cause."[100] An intent-to-use applicant has, at a maximum, 36 months from the notice of allow to put the mark to use and file a statement to that effect with the PTO.

---

[97] A Section 1(b) intent-to-use applicant may "[a]t any time during examination . . . bring [his application] into conformity" with a use-based Section 1(a) application if he has "made use of the mark in commerce." Lanham Act §1(c), 15 U.S.C. §1051(c).

The PTO's rules create a "blackout" period—from approval for publication to notice of allowance—during which an applicant cannot make a conversion. An applicant may amend his Section 1(b) application to allege mark use in commerce "at any time between the filing of the application and the date the examiner approves the mark for publication or the date of expiration of the six-month response period after issuance of a final action." 37 CFR §2.76(a). After the latter date, the applicant must submit a statement of use after notice of allowance. *See also* 37 CFR §2.77 ("An application under section 1(b) . . . may not be amended during the period between the issuance of the notice of allowance . . . and the filing of a statement of use . . . except to delete specified goods or services.").

[98] Lanham Act §1(d)(1), 15 U.S.C. §1051(d)(1).

The use statement's specified goods or services "must conform to those goods or services identified in the notice of allowance." It may identify "goods or services to be deleted." 37 CFR §2.88(i).

[99] Lanham Act §1(d)(1), 15 U.S.C. §1051(d)(2).

[100] *Id.;* 37 CFR §2.89.

The statute directs that an applicant must support an extension request with "a verified statement by the applicant that the applicant has a continued bona fide intention to use the mark in commerce, specifying those goods or services identified in the notice of allowance on or in connection with which the applicant has a continued bona fide intention to use the mark in commerce."

It further directs the PTO to "issue regulations setting forth guidelines for determining what constitutes good cause. . . . " PTO Rule 89(d)(2) provides that a good cause showing must include:

"A statement of applicant's ongoing efforts to make use of the mark in commerce on or in connection with each of the goods or services specified in the verified statement of continued bona fide intention to use. . . . Those efforts may include, without limitation, product or service research or development, market research, manufacturing activities, promotional activities, steps to acquire distributors, steps to obtain required governmental approval, or other similar activities. In the alternative, a satisfactory explanation for the failure to make such efforts must be submitted." 37 CFR §2.89(d)(2).

(5) "Subject to examination and acceptance of the statement of use,"[101] the PTO issues a certificate of registration.[102]

To "prevent utilization of the intent-to-use system to traffic in marks,"[103] Section 10 provides that an intent-to-use application cannot be assigned prior to the verified statement of use "except to a successor to the business of the applicant, or portion thereof, to which the mark pertains, if that business is ongoing and existing."[104]

[iii]   *Bona Fide Intent to Use.* Standards for what constitutes a bona fide intent to use a mark will be shaped in the future on a case-by-case basis as challenges to an applicant's intent are raised in PTO inter partes proceedings and court proceedings.

The Senate Report on the 1988 Act contains the fullest discussion of bona fide intent to use.

> "Bona fide intent is measured by objective factors. A statement of intent to use a mark on specifically identified products in the future may be sufficient. An applicant may safely make this statement in its original application without having taken concrete steps to create and introduce a new product, provided that in fact it intends to use the mark.

> "However, other circumstances may cast doubt on the bona fide nature of the intent or even disprove it entirely. For example, an applicant may have filed numerous intent-to-use applications to register the same mark for many more new products than are contemplated, numerous intent-to-use applications for a variety of desirable trademarks intended to be used on single new product, numerous intent-to-use application to register marks consisting of or incorporating descriptive terms relating to a contemplated new product, numerous

---

[101] *See* 37 CFR §2.88(e), (f).
This "second examination" provision was controversial during Congressional consideration of the intent-to-use amendments. The Senate provided no second examination because it wished "that once the . . . [PTO] conditionally approved registration, the applicant would have the needed certainty to invest in actual use of the mark without fear that the PTO might reverse its earlier approval." Remarks of Senator DeConcini on the Senate Floor, Cong. Rec. S16973 (Oct. 20, 1988). The House of Representative insisted on the second examination "which permits the Office to raise issues of registrability that might not be evident until the applicant makes available specimens showing the mark as used and/or clarifying the nature of the goods or services involved." H.R. Rep. No. 100-1028, 100th Cong., 2d Sess. 9 (1988). In examining a statement of use, the examining attorney "must evaluate the specimens to confirm that [they] exhibit appropriate use." PTO 1989 Guide at A.9.f. Sensitive to the Senate's concern, the PTO follows a "clear error" rule in examining statement of use adequacy. It will "issue requirements or refusals concerning matters specifically related to the statement of use only" and "will not issue any requirements or refusals concerning matters which could have or should have been raised during initial examination, unless the failure to do so in initial examination constitutes a clear error." *Id.* at A.9.b. The clear error rule does not apply when the applicant *amends* a Section 1(b) intent-to- use application to convert it to a Section 1(a) use application. *Id.* at A.4.d.iii.
[102] Lanham Act §1(d)(1), 15 U.S.C. §1051(d)(1).
[103] S. Rep. 100-515, 100th Cong., 2d Sess. 25 (1988).
[104] Lanham Act §10, 15 U.S.C. §1060.

intent-to-use applications to replace applications which have lapsed because no timely declaration of use has been filed, an excessive number of intent-to-use applications to register marks which ultimately were not actually used, an excessive number of intent-to-use in relation to the number of products the applicant is likely to introduce under the applied-for marks during the pendency of the applications, or applications unreasonably lacking in specificity in describing the proposed goods."[105]

A specific "bona fide" use problem concerns multiple applications for different marks for the same intended product or service.

"An applicant's bona fide intention to use a mark must reflect an intention that is firm, though it may be contingent on the outcome of an event (that is, market research or product testing). Thus, an applicant, could, under certain circumstances, file more than one intent-to-use application covering the same goods and still have the requisite bona fide intention to use each mark. However, if a product has already been marketed under one mark and an applicant continues to main additional applications for marks intended for use on or in connection with the same product, without good cause, this may call into question the bona fide nature of the intent. . . .

"Because an applicant must declare its bona fide intention to use a mark with respect to every intent-to-use application it files, the committee rejected a statutory limit on the number of applications a given individual or company can file with respect to a planned new product or product line. Moreover, it determined that any such limitation would be difficult to monitor and enforce and could not be fairly applied to very conceivable business situation."[106]

[c] **Disclaimers.** The PTO may require a registration applicant "to disclaim an unregistrable component of a mark otherwise registrable."[107] An applicant "may voluntarily disclaim a component of a mark sought to be registered."[108] A disclaimer's purpose is "to make of record, if it might otherwise be misunderstood, that a significant element of a composite is not being exclusively appropriated by itself apart from the composite."[109] Typically, a disclaimer is appropriate as to descriptive or generic matter in a design mark, for example "Pizzeria" in "Pizzeria Uno."[110]

Contemporary disclaimer practice traces back to *Beckwith.*[111] The applicant sought to register under the 1905 federal trademark law a design mark for furnaces that included the phrase "Moistair Heating System." The Patent Office found the mark not descriptive as a whole but refused to register it unless the applicant "removed" the descriptive phrase. The Supreme Court reversed, holding there was no statutory

---

[105] S. Rep. 100-515, 100th Cong., 2d Sess. 23-24 (1988).

[106] *Id.* at 24-25.

[107] Lanham Act §6, 15 U.S.C. §1056.

[108] *Id.*

[109] USPTO, Trademark Manual of Examining Procedure §904.01(a).

[110] *See* Pizzeria Uno Corp. v. Temple, 747 F.2d 1522, 224 U.S.P.Q. 185 (4th Cir. 1984).

[111] Estate of P.D. Beckwith, Inc. v. Commissioner of Patents, 252 U.S. 538 (1920).

basis for the refusal but approving of the existing practice of requiring disclaimers even though there was no statutory basis for them.[112]

The Lanham Act Section 6, as amended in 1962, expressly authorizes disclaimers. The PTO's power to require a disclaimer is discretionary,[113] and its policy is that "a requirement to disclaim should not be made when the form or degree of integration of an element in the composite makes it obvious that no claim other than of the composite would be involved."[114]

A disclaimer usually pertains to descriptive matter in a composite multiple word mark or word-design mark,[115] but Section 6 refers generally to "unregistrable" matter. In *Franklin Press,*[116] the court allowed registration of a mark that contained as an element a reference to other's marks when the applicant claimed those marks and the circumstances suggested no likelihood of confusion.

A disclaimer highlights a composite mark's descriptive elements, which are less likely to form the basis of a likelihood of confusion conclusion, but it does not remove

---

[112] "While there is no specific provision for disclaimers in the trade-mark statute, the practice of using them is commended to our judgment by the statement of the Commissioner of Patents that, so far as known, no harm came to the public from the practice of distinguishing, without deleting, nonregistrable matter in the drawing of the mark as registered, when a statement, forming a part of the record, was required that the applicant was not making claim to an exclusive appropriation of such matter except in the precise relation and association in which it appeared in the drawing and description.

". . . [N]o one could be deceived as to the scope of such a mark, and . . . the registrant would be precluded by his disclaimer from setting up in the future any exclusive right to the disclaimed part of it. . . . [T]o require the deletion of descriptive words must result often in so changing the trade-mark sought to be registered from the form in which it had been used in actual trade that it would not be recognized as the same mark as that shown in the drawing which the statute requires to be filed with the application, or in the specimens produced as actually used, and therefore registration would lose much, if not all, of its value. . . .

". . . [A] disclaimer on the part of applicant that no claim is made to the use of the words 'Moistair Heating System' apart from the mark as shown in the drawing and as described, would preserve to all others the right to use these words in the future to truthfully describe a like property or result of another system, provided only that they be not used in a trade-mark which so nearly resembles that of the petitioner 'as to be likely to cause confusion in the mind of the public or to deceive purchasers' when applied 'to merchandise of the same descriptive properties.' . . .

". . . [The statute] would be fully complied with if registration of it were permitted with an appropriate declaration on the part of the applicant that no claim is made to the right to the exclusive use of the descriptive words, except in the setting and relation in which they appear in the drawing, description, and samples of the trade-mark filed with the application." 252 U.S. at 545-47.

[113] The 1962 amendment changed the Commissioner's disclaimer power from "shall" to "may."

[114] USPTO, Trademark Manual of Examining Procedure §904.01(a).

[115] *In re* Hercules Fasteners, Inc., 203 F.2d 753 (CCPA 1953).

[116] *In re* Franklin Press, Inc., 597 F.2d 270, 201 USPQ 662 (CCPA 1979) (composite word-design mark for printing services that included the disclaimed phrase "Employees Represented by ITU, IPPU & GCU, & GAIU"). Accord: Association of Co-Operative Members, Inc. v. Farmland Industries, Inc., 684 F.2d 1134, 1142, 216 USPQ 361 (5th Cir. 1982).

the disclaimed matter from the mark.[117] For example, in *National Data*,[118] the court affirmed rejection of the mark "THE CASH MANAGEMENT EXCHANGE" for financial services as confusingly similar to the registered mark "CASH MANAGE-MENT ACCOUNT" even though the applicant voluntarily disclaimed rights to "cash management." It reasoned that neither applicant's disclaimer nor the absence of a disclaimer in the prior registration altered the confusion analysis: "The technicality of a disclaimer in National's application to register its mark has no legal effect on the issue of likelihood of confusion. . . . The public is unaware of what words have been disclaimed during prosecution of the trademark application at the PTO. . . . It appears that National voluntarily disclaimed these words, as a tactical strategy, believing it would assist in avoiding a holding of likelihood of confusion with the cited mark. However, such action cannot affect the scope of protection to which *another's* mark is entitled."[119]

An applicant's disclaimer does not prejudice his or her common law trademark mark rights,[120] and the applicant can later register the disclaimed matter or the whole mark without disclaimer if it later acquires secondary meaning.[121]

---

[117] For a discussion of "dissection" of marks in determining likelihood of confusion, see § 5F[1][a][ii](2).

[118] *In re* National Data Corp., 753 F.2d 1056, 224 USPQ 749 (Fed. Cir. 1985).

[119] 753 F.2d at 1058, 224 U.S.P.Q. at 751.

See also Specialty Brands, Inc. v. Coffee Bean Distributors, Inc., 748 F.2d 669, 672, 223 U.S.P.Q. 1281, 1282 (Fed. Cir. 1984) (applicant's "SPICE VALLEY" is confusingly similar to opposer's mark "SPICE ISLANDS"; "[a]lthough the applicant disclaimed the word 'spice' apart from SPICE VALLEY as a whole, the marks are viewed in their entireties. . . . Indeed, opposer's registrations of SPICE ISLANDS for teas contain no disclaimer.").

[120] Section 6(b) provides that a disclaimer does not "prejudice or affect the applicant's or registrant's rights then existing or thereafter arising in the disclaimed matter." Lanham Act § 6(b), 15 U.S.C. §1056(b). *See* Official Airline Guides, Inc. v. Goss, 856 F.2d 85, 87, 8 U.S.P.Q.2d 1157, 1159 (9th Cir. 1988) (plaintiff registered "OAG Travel Planner," with "Travel Planner" disclaimed at the examiner's insistence; "OAG's disclaimer of the phrase 'Travel Planner' in its registration does not deprive it of any common law rights it may have in the disclaimed matter."); Association of Co-Operative Members, Inc. v. Farmland Industries, Inc., 684 F.2d 1134, 1142, 216 U.S.P.Q. 361, 367 (5th Cir. 1982), *cert. denied*, 460 U.S. 1038 (1983) ("while disclaimer may be required for registration, it cannot be a condition of common law rights in a trademark"); *In re* Franklin Press, Inc., 597 F.2d 270, 273, 201 USPQ 662 (CCPA 1979) ("common law rights in the composite mark as used in commerce will remain unaffected without regard to deletion or disclaimer of the phrase in question or to the procurement of a federal registration.").

[121] Section 6(b) provides that a disclaimer does not prejudice the registrant's "right of registration on another application if the disclaimed matter be or shall have become distinctive of his goods or services." Lanham Act §6(b), 15 U.S.C. §1056(b). *See In re* Hercules Fasteners, Inc., 203 F.2d 753, 756 (CCPA 1953) (noting that Section 6(b) changed "the disclaimer practice prior to the 1946 Act [that] if an applicant disclaimed certain subject matter as unregistrable he and his successors in interest were held estopped from later securing registration of such matter, even though the disclaimed portions subsequently became distinctive and protectable in the Federal courts as valid, common-law trade-marks.").

A registration procedure disclaimer must be distinguished from disclaimers courts require as part of injunctive relief to reduce the possibility of confusion from concurrent use of similar marks.[122]

[d] "Inter Partes" Proceedings. There are four PTO trademark "inter partes" proceedings, opposition, cancellations, interferences, and concurrent use proceedings, which the Trademark Trial and Appeal Board adjudicates. The Federal Rules of Civil Procedure govern the proceedings "except as otherwise provided, and wherever applicable and appropriate."[123]

[i] *Oppositions.* "Any person who believes that he would be damaged by the registration of a mark upon the principal register may . . . file an opposition . . . stating the grounds therefor, within thirty days after" the mark's publication.[124] The opposition "must set forth a short and plain statement showing why the opposer believes it would be damaged by the registration and state grounds for opposition."[125] The Board forwards an opposition notification to the applicant who must submit an answer admitting or denying the opposer's averments and setting forth defenses and counterclaims.[126]

Grounds for opposition are the same as those for registration denial under Lanham Act Section 2, including descriptiveness and confusing similarity to marks previously used by others.[127]

[ii] *Cancellations.* A person "who believes that he is or will be damaged by the registration of a mark on the principal register" may file a "petition to cancel a registration of a mark, stating the grounds relied upon."[128] Cancellation procedure is substantially the same as opposition procedure.[129]

For five years after registration, the grounds for cancellation are the same as for opposition—that is, the mark's registration can be cancelled for any ground that would

---

[122] For example, court use disclaimers when the second comer's name is the same as a first user's trademark. *See* §5C[3][c][iii]. *See also* § 5F[3][d][iii].

[123] 37 C.F.R. §2.116(a).

PTO rules provide for, *inter alia*, paper service, discovery, and motions. 37 C.F.R. §§2.119, .120, 127. The "trial" consists of successive "testimony periods" for the parties. *Id.* §2.121. Witnesses' testimony is taken by deposition. *Id.* §§2.123-.125. The parties file briefs, and the Board holds a "final hearing" and renders judgment. *Id.* §2.129.

[124] Lanham Act §13(a), 15 U.S.C. §1063(a).

The opposer must pay a fee. *See* 37 C.F.R. §2.101(d). A person may request a 30-day extension and further extensions "for good cause." Lanham Act §13(a), 15 U.S.C. §1063(a); 37 C.F.R. §2.102.

[125] 37 C.F.R. §2.104(a).

[126] 37 C.F.R. §2.105-.106.

A counterclaim is necessary to attack the validity of a registration pleaded in the opposition. 37 C.F.R. §2.106(b)(2).

[127] *See* §5C.

[128] Lanham Act §14, 15 U.S.C. §1064.

[129] *See* 37 C.F.R. §§2.111-.115.

under Section 2 justify denial of registration, including descriptiveness and confusing similarity to marks previously used by others.[130]

A person may seek cancellation "at any time" on the following grounds:

(1) the mark "becomes the generic name for the goods or services, or a portion thereof, for which it is registered";[131]

(2) the mark "has been abandoned";[132]

(3) the mark's "registration was obtained fraudulently";[133]

(4) the mark's registration was obtained contrary to Section 4's requirements for collective and certification marks;[134]

(5) the mark "is being used by, or with the permission of, the registrant so as to misrepresent the source of the goods or services on or in connection with which the mark is used";

(6) the mark's registration was obtained contrary to "subsection (a), (b), or (c) of section 2."[135]

Section 14's five-year limitation on cancellation grounds correlates with Lanham Act Section 15's incontestability provision. Section 14 protects the registrant's *registration*; the passage of five years makes a registration less vulnerable to attack by anyone who would otherwise have standing to oppose or cancel it.[136] Section 15, which has further procedural and substantive requirements, protects the registrant's right to *use* his mark from attack by other mark registrants or owners.

[*iii*] *Standing.* Sections 13 and 14 refer to the opposition or cancellation seeking party's perception of damage from the registration. This language creates a standing requirement.[137] Once a party establishes standing to oppose or seek cancellation,

---

[130] *E.g.,* International Order of Job's Daughters v. Lindeburg & Co., 727 F.2d 1087, 1091, 220 U.S.P.Q. 1017 (Fed. Cir. 1984) ("The legal issue in a cancellation proceeding is the right to register a mark. . . . For Principal Register registrations less than five years old . . . , cancellation may be based upon any ground which would have prevented registration initially.").

[131] Lanham Act § 14, 15 U.S.C. §1064. The 1988 Trademark Revision Act added the partial genericness language. As amended, Section 14 provides that "[i]f the registered mark becomes the generic name for less than all of the goods or services for which it is registered, a petition to cancel the registration for only those goods or services may be filed." 15 U.S.C. §1064(3).

For a discussion of generic marks, see §5C[3][b].

[132] For a discussion of abandonment, see §5D[3][b].

[133] For a discussion of "fraud" in trademark registration, see §5F[2][b].

[134] For a discussion of collective and certification marks, see §5C[1][c].

[135] For a discussion of these registration denial grounds, see §5C[2][d].

[136] *See* Wallpaper Mfrs., Ltd. v. Crown Wallcovering Corp., 680 F.2d 755, 761 n.6, 214 U.S.P.Q. 327, 332 n. 6 (CCPA 1982) (Section 14 imposes "in effect, a five year time limit barring certain attacks on a registration . . . . [T]his section is not dependent on the filing of a declaration under §15 which provides incontestable rights of use to a limited extent . . . ").

[137] The courts do not distinguish opposition and cancellations insofar as standing is concerned. Lipton Industries, Inc. v. Ralston Purina Co., 670 F.2d 1024, 213 U.S.P.Q. 185 (CCPA 1982).

he or she may pursue any available registration-precluding ground, including one not connected with the basis for standing.[138]

Court of Customs and Patent Appeals and Federal Circuit decisions attempted to eliminate prior confusion on the opposition-cancellation standing requirement.[139] The party must have a "real interest" in the proceeding and not be a mere "intermeddler" seeking to purify the federal trademark register.[140]

In *Lipton Industries*,[141] petitioner sought to cancel registrant's "FANCY FIX-IN'S" mark for cat food because of abandonment due to nonuse. Registrant registered the mark in 1969 but had made only two shipments by 1977; petitioner made a single shipment to enable it to file an application, which the PTO refused because of registrant's prior registration. The court found standing. First, it held that a petitioner's standing should not be determining by virtue of the allegations in its complaint.[142] Second, "[n]o absolute test can be laid down for what must be proved to establish standing as a petitioner in a cancellation proceeding or as an opposer in an opposition."[143]

> " 'A party has standing to oppose within the meaning of §13 if that party can demonstrate a real interest in the proceeding.'

---

[138] Jewelers Vigilance Committee, Inc. v. Ullenberg Corp., 823 F.2d 490, 493, 2 U.S.P.Q.2d 2021, 2023 (Fed. Cir. 1987) ("Once standing is established, the opposer is entitled to rely on any of the grounds set forth in section 2 of the Lanham Act which negate applicant's right to its subject registration."); Lipton Industries, Inc. v. Ralston Purina Co., 670 F.2d 1024, 1031, 213 U.S.P.Q. 185 (CCPA 1982) ("Standing having been established, petitioner is entitled to rely on any statutory ground which negates appellant's right to the subject registration and may invoke the general public interest in support of its claim.").

See also Imperial Tobacco Ltd. v. Philip Morris, Inc., 899 F.2d 1575, 1580, n.7, 14 U.S.P.Q.2d 1390, 1393 n.7 (Fed. Cir. 1990) (petition to cancel because of alleged abandonment; petitioner's allegations that it used a mark similar to the registered mark in other countries and that "some prospective U.S. purchasers . . . particularly travelers, would be likely to attribute [registrant's goods] to [petitioner] are sufficient, if proved, to establish standing"; "While likelihood of confusion could not be the basis for cancellation after five years, such allegations can afford standing.").

[139] *See* Selva & Sons, Inc. v. Nina Footwear, Inc., 705 F.2d 1316, 1325, 217 U.S.P.Q. 641 (Fed. Cir. 1983) ("Historically, there has been much confusion in the cases between standing and damage which recent decisions and opinions have, hopefully, been straightening out.").

[140] Would intermeddling in the public interest before the PTO be bad? The Patent Act allows *anyone* to request reexamination of a patent on payment of a fee, no showing of damage or standing being required. Standing to appeal to the courts involves other considerations, including the Article III "case or controversy" requirement.

[141] Lipton Industries, Inc. v. Ralston Purina Co., 670 F.2d 1024, 213 U.S.P.Q. 185 (CCPA 1982).

[142] "A party's pleading lays the foundation for standing. Thus, if it does not plead facts sufficient to show a personal interest in the outcome beyond that of the general public, the case may be dismissed for failure to state a claim. . . . However, it does not follow that the facts affording a party standing, which as pleaded are sufficient as a matter of law, do not have to be proved by that party. . . . The facts regarding standing . . . are part of a petitioner's case and must be affirmatively proved." 670 F.2d at 1028.

[143] 670 F.2d at 1028.

"The same general statement is applicable to cancellation proceedings. The purpose in requiring standing is to prevent litigation where there is no real controversy between the parties, where a plaintiff, petitioner or opposer, is no more than an intermeddler. Congress, however, has specified a broad class who must be deemed proper litigants.

"Thus, this court has found standing based on widely diverse interests:

"1. importation of petitioner's products deterred by a registration, Plastilite Corp. v. Kassnar Imports, 508 F.2d 824, 184 USPQ 348 (CCPA 1975).

"2. use of copyrighted appearance of doll, Knickerbocker Toy Co. v. Faultless Starch Co., 467 F.2d 501, 175 USPQ 417 (CCPA 1972).

"3. pecuniary interest of trade association, Tanners' Council of America, Inc. v. Gary Industries, Inc., 58 CCPA 1201, 440 F.2d 1404, 169 USPQ 608 (1971).

"4. prior registration but not priority in use, King Candy Co. v. Eunice King's Kitchen, Inc., 496 F.2d 1400, 182 USPQ 108 (CCPA 1974).

"5. protection of subsidiary's mark, Universal Oil Products Co. v. Rexall Drug & Chemical Co., [463 F.2d 1122, 174 USPQ 458 (CCPA 1972).

"6. descriptive use of term in registered mark, Golomb v. Wadsworth, 592 F.2d 1184, 201 USPQ 200 (CCPA); cert. denied, 444 U.S. 833, 100 S.Ct. 63, 62 L.Ed.2d 42 (1979).

"7. advertising emphasis of American origin, Singer Manufacturing Co. v. Birginal-Bigsby Corp., 50 CCPA 1380, 319 F.2d 273, 138 USPQ 63 (1963)."[144]

The court took into consideration that "no ex parte vehicle for removing 'dead' registrations from the register is provided in the statute except for the provisions of section 8 . . . requiring an affidavit or declaration of use to be filed during the sixth year of its term."[145]

"There is no procedure for the Commissioner of Patents and Trademarks to initiate action against defunct marks which appear in registrations. . . . [T]he public interest is served . . . in broadly interpreting the class of persons Congress intended to be allowed to institute cancellation proceedings."[146]

Under these standards, petitioner's standing allegations concerning its rejected application to register registrant's mark were sufficient.

"We regard the desire for a registration with its attendant statutory advantages as a legitimate commercial interest. To establish a reasonable basis for a belief that one is damaged by the registration sought to be cancelled, a petition may

---

[144] 670 F.2d at 1028-29.

Accord Star-Kist Foods, Inc. v. P.J. Rhodes & Co., 735 F.2d 346, 348-49, 222 U.S.P.Q. 674, 676 (9th Cir. 1984) ("Proof of actual damage is only relevant, not requisite, to establishing standing. . . . The petitioner, instead, must show a real and rational basis for his belief that he would be damaged by the registration sought to be cancelled, stemming from an actual commercial or pecuniary interest in his own mark.").

[145] For a discussion of Section 8 affidavits, see § 5D[3][a][i].

[146] 670 F.2d at 1029-30.

assert a likelihood of confusion which is not wholly without merit . . . or . . . a rejection of an application during prosecution.

". . . [T]o have standing in this case, it would be sufficient that appellee prove that it filed an application and that a rejection was made because of appellant's registration. . . . These facts do not provide a statutory ground for cancellation, . . . but no more is necessary for standing. Appellant could, of course, seek to attack the legitimacy of appellee's application or in some other way negate appellee's interest. . . . However, the legitimacy of the petitioner's activity from which its interest arises will be presumed in the absence of evidence to the contrary."[147]

In *International Order of Job's Daughters*,[148] in a prior infringement suit, the Ninth Circuit held that Job's Daughters' emblem did not function as a mark and therefore that Lindeburg did not violate their rights by selling emblem-bearing jewelry. Lindeburg petitioned to cancel Job's Daughters' registrations for jewelry and other products. The Federal Circuit held that Lindeburg had standing because it sold merchandise and should not be forced to rely on collateral estoppel to defend possible future Jobs' Daughter's infringement suits based on the registrations.

In *Jewelers Vigilance Committee*,[149] the court upheld a trade association's standing to oppose registration of applicant's mark as confusingly similar to a previously registered mark even though the association had no proprietary interest in the latter.[150] Applicant sought to register "FOREVER YOURS/DEBEERS DIA. LTD."

---

[147] 670 F.2d at 1029.

The court noted that the "statute would provide appellee standing as an interference party. 15 U.S.C. §1066 may in itself give standing in view of the virtual elimination of interferences by the PTO." *Id.*

[148] International Order of Job's Daughters v. Lindeburg & Co., 727 F.2d 1087, 1092, 220 USPQ 1017, 1020 (Fed. Cir. 1984) ("there is no requirement that damage be proved in order to establish standing or to prevail in a cancellation proceeding. . . . All the Lanham Act requires is that the cancellation petitioner plead and prove facts showing a 'real interest' in the proceeding in order to establish standing.").

[149] Jewelers Vigilance Committee, Inc. v. Ullenberg Corp., 823 F.2d 490, 2 U.S.P.Q.2d 2021 (Fed. Cir. 1987).

[150] "In the usual case where an opposition is brought under section 2(d), the opposer does have a proprietary interest in a mark, and standing is afforded through its assertion that it will incur some direct injury to its own established trade identity if an applicant's mark is registered. . . . In such cases, standing is closely related to the *grounds* (the merits) upon which the opposer relies in asserting that the applicant is not entitled to register his mark. That they are distinct inquiries is obscured. On the other hand, the distinctness of the inquiries is readily apparent where an opposition is based on the descriptiveness of the mark sought to be registered, *i.e.*, an opposition based on section 2(e). An opposer in such case need only assert an equal right to use the mark for the goods. Proprietary rights in the opposer are not required. . . . " 823 F.2d at 493, 2 U.S.P.Q.2d at 2024.

As to what constitutes "damage" to an opposer or cancellation petitioner who uses a mark allegedly confusingly similar to that of applicant (or registrant), see Rosso and Mastracco, Inc. v. Giant Food Inc., 720 F.2d 1263, 1265, 219 U.S.P.Q. 1050 (Fed. Cir. 1983) (affirming grant of opposition but disagreeing with Board's statement that " 'it is well established that even the owner of a weak mark is entitled to be protected from *damage* due to a likelihood

Opposer, a jewelers' trade association, alleged the applicant's mark was confusingly similar to DeBeers Consolidated Mines Ltd.'s famous "DEBEERS" mark for diamonds. Opposer's members purchase and market DEBEERS diamonds.

> "There is no question that a trade association, having a real interest in the outcome of the proceedings, may maintain an opposition without proprietary rights in a mark or without asserting that it has a right or has an interest in using the alleged mark sought to be registered by an applicant. . . . This is true irrespective of the grounds upon which the opposer relies in asserting the nonregistrability of applicant's mark.

> "In this case, JVC must have alleged an adverse affect on its own interests *or* those of its members which will result from the issuance of the registration to Ullenberg. JVC has met that requirement. As distributors of DeBeers' diamonds and users of that name to promote the sale of such goods, JVC's members have personal interests in continuing such use and in negating Ullenberg's assertion of exclusive rights in the mark DeBeers, which would be *prima facie* recognized by the grant of the registration which Ullenberg seeks. JVC as the watchdog for the industry has [an] interest . . . in preventing the imprimatur of registration from being given to one assertedly engaged in deception of the public. These allegations demonstrate a real interest in the outcome of the proceeding based on a likelihood of confusion with the DeBeers' trade name. Thus JVC is more than a meddlesome party."[151]

The court distinguished prior decisions holding that a party seeking to oppose or cancel another's mark registration on Section 2(d) prior use grounds must show that the mark he or she relies on is "proprietary," and not, for example, merely descriptive.[152] Those cases "dealt with the merits of an opposition, not standing."[153]

---

of confusion with another's use of the same or a confusingly similar mark.' (Emphasis ours.) There is no reason to assume that refusing registration to an applicant under [Lanham Act §2(d),] 15 U.S.C. §1052(d) will protect an opposer from 'damage' due to likelihood of confusion in the marketplace. . . . [L]ikelihood of confusion results only from the concurrent use of confusingly similar marks, not from their *registration*. . . . Nor was it necessary for the board to note that because it held confusion to be likely, 'registration to applicant would be damaging to opposer.' . . . Accuracy aside, the danger in making statements such as the board made is that it may be perceived that some form of 'damage' must be proved in order to prevail in an opposition or cancellation proceeding, and that is not the law. . . . The determinative issue, inquiry into which leads to one of only two possible results, is the right to register (or the right to maintain a registration). . . . Further, 'damage' from registration is mentioned in sections 13 and 14 of the Lanham Act, 15 U.S.C. §§1063 and 1064, only in connection with standing, and the similar language of those sections has been held to require only that the opposer or cancellation petitioner plead and prove facts showing a 'real interest' in the proceeding. . . . Actual damage from registration is relevant to that determination, of course, but it is not requisite. Absent actual damage from an existing registration, *e.g.*, Plastilite Corp. v. Kassnar Imports, 508 F.2d 824, 826, 184 USPQ 348, 350 (CCPA 1975) (destruction of goods by U.S. Customs), normally it is only after standing has been demonstrated that any potential damage from an existing registration may be apparent.").

[151] 823 F.2d at 493-94, 2 U.S.P.Q.2d at 2024.

[152] *See* Otto Roth & Co. v. Universal Foods Corp., 640 F.2d 1317, 209 U.S.P.Q. 40 (CCPA 1981), discussed at §5C[4][d].

[153] 823 F.2d at 494, 2 U.S.P.Q.2d at 2024.

[iv] *Interferences.* In "extraordinary circumstances," the PTO may declare an interference between an application and a previously registered mark or between two applications.[154] It will declare an interference only if a party would be "unduly prejudiced without an interference." "In ordinary circumstances, the unavailability of an opposition or cancellation proceeding to the party will be deemed to remove any undue prejudice."[155] In other words, an earlier mark user may ordinarily protect his interests by applying for registration or opposing or seeking cancellation of a later user's registration effort.[156]

[v] *Concurrent Use Proceedings.* A concurrent use proceeding arises when an applicant claims "concurrent use" rights, stating "exceptions to his claims of exclusive use."[157] Concurrent use rights arise most commonly when persons in good faith adopt and use the same or similar marks in different geographic markets.[158] Lanham Act Section 2 authorizes the PTO to issue concurrent registrations to persons who "have

---

[154] Lanham Act §16, 15 U.S.C. §1066.
See 37 C.F.R. §§2.91-.98.
[155] 37 C.F.R. §2.91
[156] *See* Lipton Industries, Inc. v. Ralston Purina Co., 670 F.2d 1024, 213 U.S.P.Q. 185 (CCPA 1982), discussed above (granting second user/applicant standing to seek cancellation of registrant's mark on the ground registrant abandoned its mark).
[157] Lanham Act §1(a), 15 U.S.C. §1051(a). *See* 37 CFR §2.99.
An application seeking concurrent registration may not be based on intent-to-use the mark. *Id.* §1(b). *See* S. Rep. 100-515, 100th Cong., 2d Sess. 26 (1988):

> "The underlying basis for concurrent use registrations is to provide a vehicle for giving statutory recognition to the rights of good faith common-law users who have established trademark rights in different geographic areas. However, under prevailing law, an intent-to-use applicant would not be in good faith if its mark was adopted with knowledge of the prior mark. Moreover, to permit an applicant who has not used the mark to assert concurrent use with another might result in businesses carving up the country in the absence of common law rights. This would defeat one of the principal purposes of the Lanham Act.
>
> "Nevertheless, an intent-to-use applicant who begins use before learning of a prior use by another will, like a use-based applicant be able to consent to a judgment sustaining an opposition filed by the prior user and request that concurrent use proceeding be instituted.
>
> "For example, A files an intent-to-use application to register a mark for restaurant services, unaware that for the past 20 years, in the State of Washington, B has been using an unregistered identical mark for a restaurant unknown outside Washington and Oregon. Several months after filing, A commences use in several States east of the Mississippi. A's unrestricted application is then published and opposed by B. B simultaneously files an unrestricted application. A would then consent to a judgment sustaining the opposition filed by B and would request that concurrent use proceeding be instituted.
>
> "In this scenario, even though A is an intent-to-use applicant (the character of its application being determined by the basis on which it is filed, not what occurred afterward), it would meet all the requirements for seeking concurrent use under the Lanham Act: (i) its use of the mark is 'lawful' since it commenced such use in good faith, (ii) it has 'become entitled' to use its mark prior to the filing date of B's application, and (iii) there has been 'continued use' by A and B."

[158] *See* §5E[2][d].

become entitled to use such marks as a result of their concurrent lawful use in commerce" if confusion is not likely to result from continued concurrent use.[159] It also authorizes concurrent registrations when "a court of competent jurisdiction has finally determined that more than one person is entitled to use the same or similar marks in commerce."[160] The PTO prescribes "conditions and limitations as to the mode or place of use."[161]

[e] **Supplemental Register.** The Lanham Act distinguishes the "Principal Register" and the "Supplemental Register." The "Supplemental Register" is a continuation of the register the 1920 Trademark Act established to enable United States trademark owners to pursue protection in other countries. The 1988 Trademark Revision Act eliminated the prior one-year lawful use requirement for filing an Supplement Register registration application.[162]

Marks that meet Section 2's distinctiveness requirements are eligible for registration on the Principal Register. Marks that do not met those requirements but "are capable of distinguishing the applicant's goods or services" are eligible for Supplemental Register registration. The Supplemental Register provision refers to several types of potential marks that are not explicitly mentioned in the Lanham Act's definition of a mark, including labels, configurations of goods, and slogans.[163]

There are few court decisions on what potential marks are and are not capable of distinguishing the applicant's goods or services. In *Simmons*,[164] applicant sought to register on the principal register a stitching pattern on the outer vertical face of mattresses as a trademark for its mattresses.[165] Applicant had through national advertising sought to cause the public to associate the stitches with its "Beautyrest Mattress." After the examiner indicated that the proposed mark did not "at this time . . . distinguish" applicant's goods, applicant amended its application to seek registration on the Supplemental Register. The examiner and Board rejected the application. The court reversed: "The test is not whether the mark, when registration is sought, is actually recognized by the average purchaser, or is distinctive of the applicant's goods in commerce, but whether it is capable of becoming so."[166] The asserted mark was not inherently functional or otherwise incapable of becoming distinctive.

In *Helena Rubinstein*,[167] the applicant sought to register on the Supplemental Register the marks "Pasteurized" and " 'Pasteurized' Face Cream Special" for face

---

[159] Lanham Act §2(d), 15 U.S.C. §1052(d).

[160] *Id.*

[161] *Id.*

[162] *See* S. Rep. 100-515, 100th Cong., 2d Sess. 36 (1988) ("Eliminating the 1-year use requirement will facilitate registration on the supplemental register and make it easier for U.S. trademark owners to obtain protection for their trademarks in certain foreign countries.").

[163] Despite this difference, case law confirms the eligibility for registration on the Principal Register of devices such as configurations of goods and slogans *if* they are sufficiently distinctive. *See* §§5C[2][a], 5C[2][c].

[164] *In re* Simmons Co., 278 F.2d 517 (CCPA 1960).

[165] For a discussion of the protectability of designs and trade dresses, see §§ 5C[2][b][iv] and 5C[2][c].

[166] 278 F.2d at 519.

[167] *In re* Helena Rubinstein, Inc., 410 F.2d 438, 161 U.S.P.Q. 606 (CCPA 1969).

cream, which applicant had used exclusively for 30 years. The PTO found that applicant's cream was "substantially pasteurized," in the dictionary sense. The court held that the word "pasteurized" was so "highly descriptive" as to be not capable of distinguishing applicant's goods from others. Judge Rich dissented as to the second "long form" mark, noting that it was capable of becoming distinctive even though three of its four words were descriptive.

In *Bush Brothers*,[168] the court held that "DELUXE" was capable of distinguishing the applicant's goods, canned pork and beans, even though it was a common laudatory term. Deluxe was not a recognized grade of canned pork and beans and did not signify anything other than a vaguely desirable characteristic.

An application for supplemental registration cannot be based on an "intent-to-use," is not published for opposition, but is subject to cancellation petitions.[169] Applicants commonly amend their applications to change from the Principal Register to Supplemental Register to avoid a descriptiveness rejection.[170] A disadvantage of accepting registration on the Supplemental Register is that it may create adverse inferences as to the mark's distinctiveness. Court decisions treat such registration as an admission that the mark is merely descriptive of its goods.[171] The Lanham Act provides that registration on the Supplemental Register "shall not preclude registration . . . on the principal register,"[172] which the registrant may seek on the ground that the mark, though originally descriptive, has acquired secondary meaning through use.[173] The 1988 Trademark Revision Act provides that "Registration of a mark on the supplemental register shall not constitute an admission that the mark has not acquired distinctiveness."[174] Professor McCarthy notes that "there is nothing in the amendment to preclude supplemental registration from being deemed an admission against interest that the term is not inherently distinctive."[175]

Supplemental registration does not confer the most important Lanham Act registration benefits:[176] constructive notice and use; *prima facie* evidence of validity,

---

[168] *In re* Bush Brothers & Co., 884 F.2d 569, 12 U.S.P.Q.2d 1058 (Fed. Cir. 1989).

[169] Lanham Act §§23-24, 15 U.S.C. §§1091-92; 37 CFR §2.82.

[170] 37 CFR §2.75(a).

[171] *E.g.,* Quaker State Oil Refining Corp. v. Quaker Oil Corp., 453 F.2d 1296, 1299, 172 U.S.P.Q. 361 (CCPA 1972) ("when appellant sought registration of Super Blend on the supplemental register, it admitted that the term was merely descriptive of its goods").

[172] Lanham Act §27, 15 U.S.C. §1095.

[173] *E.g., In re* Bush Brothers & Co., 884 F.2d 569, 570, 12 U.S.P.Q. 2d 1058, 1059 (Fed. Cir. 1989) ("If the mark later acquires distinctiveness through use in commerce, . . . the mark becomes eligible for registration on the Principal Register. . . . However, at the time of application for registration on the Supplemental Register the future is unknown, for it depends on such factors as the applicant's ensuing advertising and marketing efforts and their effect on the public.").

[174] Lanham Act §27, 15 U.S.C. §1095. *See* S. Rep. 100-515, 100th Cong., 2d Sess. 37 (1988) (noting that the amendment "codifies the court's holding in California Cooler v. Loretto Winery, Ltd., 774 F.2d 1451, 1454, 227 U.S.P.Q. 808, 810 (9th Cir. 1985), that the owner of a mark registered on the supplemental register is not precluded from establishing secondary meaning against an alleged infringer.").

[175] J. T. McCarthy, McCarthy's Desk Encyclopedia of Intellectual Property 324 (1991).

[176] Lanham Act §24, 15 U.S.C. §1092.

ownership, and exclusive use right; five-year limitation on cancellation grounds; incontestability; and customs importation exclusion.[177] It does confer federal court jurisdiction, which is relatively unimportant because owners of unregistered marks can use Lanham Act Section 43(a) to obtain access to the federal courts.

In *Clorox*,[178] the CCPA held that the PTO could use a mark registered on the Supplemental Register to reject an application on Section 2(d) likelihood of confusion grounds.[179] It held that the PTO properly rejected Clorox's application to register "ERASE" for a laundry soil and stain remover because it so resembled "STAIN ERASER," previously registered on the Supplemental Register for a stainer remover, as to create a likelihood of confusion, as proscribed by Lanham Act Section 2(d). Clorox argued that because marks registered on the Supplemental Register are presumptively descriptive, they should not serve as a basis for refusal to register under Section 2(d). The court disagreed: "Section 2(d)'s absence from the enumeration of statutory provisions made inapplicable to the Supplemental Register establishes unequivocally its applicability to 'registrations on the supplemental register.' "[180]

---

[177] *See In re* Bush Brothers & Co., 884 F.2d 569, 571 n.2, 12 USPQ2d 1058, 1059 n.2 (Fed. Cir. 1989) ("Registration on the Supplemental Register is not evidence of ownership, validity, or the exclusive right to use, and may not be used to stop importations; but *inter alia* enables the registrant to satisfy registration requirements under the trademark laws of foreign countries, enables the registrant to sue for infringement in federal court, and provides useful business information on a readily accessible, central register."); Clairol Inc. v. Gillette Co., 389 F.2d 264, 156 USPQ 593 (2d Cir. 1968).

[178] *In re* Clorox, 578 F.2d 305, 198 USPQ 337 (CCPA 1978). *See also In re* Research & Trading Corp., 793 F.2d 1276, 230 USPQ 49 (Fed. Cir. 1986).

Compare Towers v. Advent Software, Inc., 913 F.2d 942, 946 n.2, 16 USPQ2d 1039, 1042 n.2 (Fed. Cir. 1990) ("The result in *Clorox* has been characterized by Professor McCarthy as 'somewhat bizarre.' 1 J. McCarthy, *Trademarks and Unfair Competition* §19:8 at 888 (1984)" because "a term on the Supplemental Register is not, strictly speaking, a 'mark' because it is only 'capable' of becoming a mark upon the acquisition of secondary meaning. Thus, the holding in *Clorox* has the result that a 'non-mark' is used to prevent Principal registration of a 'real mark' to another party. As shown in *Clorox*, that result is supported by the plain terms of the statute. The result is also supported by the legislative history.").

[179] To be contrasted with *Clorox* are decisions holding that an opposer or cancellation petitioner may not establish Section 2(d) grounds by reference to his prior use of a descriptive term without secondary meaning. *See* §§ 5C[4][d], 5D[2][d][iii].

[180] The court cautioned:

"That the decision respecting likelihood of confusion is made in the PTO by comparing an applicant's mark and description of his goods with the registered marks on file in the PTO, and the goods described in the registrations of those marks, should not lead to the notion that the locus of potential confusion is in the files of the PTO. . . . The confusion sought to be prevented by the statute is not that of examiners, lawyers, board members, or judges. Confusion is likely, if at all, only in the marketplace, where marks are used. The public is both unaware of, and distinctly disinterested in, whether a mark is registered on either register. Registration is itself incapable of causing confusion. Under § 2(d), the PTO is not charged with a duty of permitting or denying a right to use any mark, or of protecting any registered mark against the mere registration of similar marks (unless use of the latter would be likely to lead to confusion)." 578 F.2d at 307-08.

"[M]arks registered on the Supplemental Register are required to be 'capable of distinguishing applicant's goods or services . . ..' 15 U.S.C. §1091. Further, appellant disregards the existence of varying degrees of descriptiveness. Appellant erroneously attributes to marks on the Supplemental Register, a degree of 'descriptiveness' equivalent to that of a generic or common descriptive word or term, and its argument that the merely descriptive nature of some marks on the Supplemental Register makes their use incapable of producing confusion is but another approach to the notion that marks on the Supplemental Register are not citable under §2(d). . . .

"The level of descriptiveness of a cited mark may influence the conclusion that confusion is likely or unlikely, . . . but that fact does not preclude citation under §2(d) of marks on the Supplemental Register."[181]

---

[181] 578 F.2d at 308–09.
Concurring, Chief Judge Markey offered "a view respecting the underlying rationale for the holding that the citation of marks 'registered' on either register is permissible in ex parte examination under §2(d)."
"Section 2(d) refers to marks 'registered' or 'previously used' and to likelihood of confusion. Because the confusion sought to be prevented by the Act is in the marketplace, where marks are used, the underlying basis for reference to marks 'registered' is necessarily the presumption that registered marks cited by an examiner under §2(d) are in use. For absent that presumption, confusion would be not only unlikely, but impossible. . . . Upon a proper showing that use of the registered mark cited by the examiner has been abandoned, without intent to resume, the presumption is destroyed and the registration may be cancelled. 15 U.S.C. §1064 (Principal Register); 15 U.S.C. §1092 (Supplemental Register). Because use of the mark is essential to a finding of likelihood of confusion, the presumption must be applied to 'registered' marks, cited by an examiner, including those on the Supplemental Register.
"No basis exists for a view that marks on the Principal Register are presumptively in use and marks on the Supplemental Register are not. Though one may own a supplemental registration, no one may own a merely descriptive mark itself. The presumption of use, however, is not derived from, nor dependent upon, the presumption of ownership of the mark. Extended and substantially exclusive use may, under 15 U.S.C. §1052(f), result in registration on the Principal Register and in the concomitant presumption of ownership under 15 U.S.C. §1057(b), but ownership of the mark is not a necessary element of the presumption that a mark registered on the Supplemental Register is in use. . . . In *inter partes* proceedings, evidence establishing earlier and continuing use of marks by third parties, and the effect of that use on the mind of the public, may take a variety of forms and may be adduced through testimony of witnesses. . . . In *inter partes* proceedings, therefore, the presumption that registered marks of third parties are in use is itself an insufficient basis on which to determine the issue presented. Accordingly, this court has repeatedly refused to permit the presumption to substitute for the proof required of the party offering third party registrations. . . .
"Third party registrations are often cited in an effort to prove that, because the marks appearing in those registrations are similar to the mark in use by an applicant, an opposer, or cancellation petitioner, the public has learned to distinguish among them and would not be confused by the addition to the marketplace of the mark sought to be registered or by continued use of the mark sought to be maintained on a register. . . . Whether the public has been so conditioned turns on whether it has been actually exposed to the similar third party marks in the marketplace, and on the extent and intensity of that expo-

[3] Registration and Rights Maintenance

A trademark owner maintains rights to registration and protection only for so long as he, or a person under his control, continues to use the mark.[182]

[a] Lanham Act Registration Duration. The Lanham Act's provisions seek to assure that only marks actually in use remain on the Principal and Supplemental Registers.

[i] Six-Year Continued Use Affidavits. The PTO cancels a mark registration unless the registrant files a continued use affidavit "within one year next preceding the expiration of . . . six years" following registration.[183] The continued use affidavit requirement reinforces United States trademark law's fundamental principle that mark rights depend on use, not registration. Court decisions and the PTO strictly enforce

---

sure. A registration does not inherently evidence that exposure, and the presumption that registered marks of third parties are in use does not clothe the cited registrations with that evidentiary effect.

"In *ex parte* refusals to register, yet another factor comes into play. The examiner does not have at hand the sources of evidence available to applicants and to the parties in an inter partes proceeding. The examiner must, therefore, be permitted to rely on the presumption that a registered mark he cites is currently being used. . . . Because of that presumption available to the examiner, a supplemental registration he cites becomes probative, and if not cancelled, persuasive evidence of a prior and continuing use of a mark which, if it so resembles an applicant's mark that confusion in the marketplace is likely, will sustain a refusal to register." 578 F.2d at 309-11.

Judge Miller disagreed with Judge Markey:

"Chief Judge Markey's specially concurring opinion regarding the underlying rational of presumed use of registered marks for purposes of *ex parte* examination under section 2(d) is not supported by the statute in the case of marks on the Supplemental Register. . . . [R]efusal to register under this part of section 2(d) is based on the existence of a registration in the PTO not on any presumption of use, and a primary purpose of such authority is to protect trademark registrants from 'misappropriation' of their marks. . . . Indeed, if a presumption of use were necessary to support an ex parte rejection under section 2(d), reversal of the board would be indicated in this appeal. Section 26 of the Act provides that ownership of a registration on the Supplemental Register is not given any of the presumptions of section 7(b) of the Act. These include 'ownership of the mark,' and ownership 'imparts *prima facie* evidence of use.' . . . Accordingly, the owner of a mark on the Supplemental Register would have to affirmatively prove use of that mark. . . . This contrasts with the presumption of continuing use of a mark by the owner of a registration on the Principal Register." 578 F.2d at 311-12.

[182] *Cf. In re* Clorox, 578 F.2d 305, 309 n.1, 198 U.S.P.Q. 337 (CCPA 1978) (Markey concurring: "what is subject to registration, and to maintenance on a register, are rights established, and maintained viable, by use, and only by use, of a mark."); Société de Developments et D'Innovations des Marches Agricoles et Aliminetaries-Sodima Union de Cooperatives Agricoles v. International Yogurt, 662 F. Supp. 839, 847, 3 U.S.P.Q.2d 1641, 1647 (D. Ore. 1987) ("An axiom of trademark law is: no trade, no trademark.").

[183] Lanham Act §8(a), 15 U.S.C. §1058(a); 37 C.F.R. §2.161.

the technical requirement that an affidavit or declaration be filed before the sixth year's expiration.[184]

The affidavit or declaration must, *inter alia*: (1) state that the registered mark is in use in commerce, (2) set forth "the goods or services recited in the registration on or in connection with which the mark is in use in commerce,"[185] and (3) attach a specimen showing the mark's current use. Alternatively, the registrant may show "that any nonuse is due to special circumstances which excuse such nonuse and is not due to any intention to abandon the mark."[186]

[*ii*]   *Term—Renewal.* The 1988 Trademark Revision Act lowered a Lanham Act mark registration's term from twenty to ten years.[187] A registrant may renew by filing an application "at any time within six months before" registration expiration or

---

[184] *In re* Mother Tucker's Food Experience (Canada) Inc., 925 F.2d 1402, 17 U.S.P.Q.2d 1795 (Fed. Cir. 1991) (registrant must explicitly aver use of the registered mark "in commerce"); *In re* Precious Diamonds, 635 F.2d 845, 847, 208 U.S.P.Q. 410 (CCPA 1980) (registrant was a corporation, Precious Diamonds, Inc.; the registrant's principal filed a timely Section 8 declaration signed "David K. Finkel, II dba Precious Diamonds Inc."; HELD: The PTO properly refused to accept the declaration or allow its abandonment after the Section 8 deadline had passed; "The failure of the registrant to file a declaration within the statutory period is not a 'minor technical defect.' Whereas the submission of a specimen label (as in *Morehouse* [quoted below]) is not a statutory requirement, the timely submission by the registrant of a declaration or affidavit is. Although we do not foreclose the possibility that, upon a sufficient showing, the term 'registrant' in the statute might be more broadly construed to overcome a technical defect while, at the same time, meeting the legislative purpose, appellant has failed to provide such a showing here.").

Compare Morehouse Manufacturing Corp. v. J. Strickland and Co., 407 F.2d 881, 887-88, 160 U.S.P.Q. 715 (CCPA 1969) ("the purpose of section 8 affidavits is to remove from the register automatically marks which are no longer in use. Failure of registrants to file affidavits results in removal of such deadwood. . . . The significant facts, therefore, are that an affidavit is filed and that a mark is actually still in use. Given the fact of continuing use, from which practically all of the user's substantive trademark rights derive, nothing is to be gained from and no public purpose is served by cancelling the registration of a technically good trademark because of a minor technical defect in an affidavit.").

[185] The 1988 Act added the requirement of setting forth goods or services. This change was one of several directed at reducing the amount of "deadwood," that is, unused marks, on the federal registers. H.R. Rep. No. 100-1028, 100th Cong., 2d Sess. 11 (1988) ("The amendments made by Section 10 and 11 will greatly reduce the amount of 'deadwood' on the Federal Trademark register. . . . [T]he problem of 'deadwood' is a serious one. Unused marks on the trademark register prevent others wishing to use those marks from doing so."); S. Rep. 100-515, 100th Cong., 2d Sess. 30 (1988).

[186] Lanham Act §8(a), 15 U.S.C. §1058(a)

[187] Lanham Act §9(a), 15 U.S.C. §1059(a). The amendment's purpose is the same as that for the Section 8(a) continuing use affidavit—reduction of "deadwood" on the registers.

The 1988 Act was effective November 16, 1989. Registrations issued on or after that date are for ten-year periods and subject to renewal for ten-year periods. Those issued before that date remain in force for 20 years but are thereafter subject to renewal for ten-year periods. 37 C.F.R. §2.181.

within three months after expiration upon payment of an additional fee.[188] An application filed *before* the renewal period is not sufficient even though it remains "pending" in the PTO at the beginning of that period.[189]

[*iii*] *Abandonment.* A Lanham Act registration may be cancelled at "any time if the registered mark . . . has been abandoned."[190]

[b] **Abandonment.** A mark owner who abandons a mark loses exclusive rights. Abandonment may occur by cessation of use with intent not to resume use or by failure to control the mark's use.[191]

---

[188] A renewal application must set forth "those goods or services recited in the registration or in connection with which the mark is still in use in commerce" and attach specimens "showing current use of the mark" or show "that any nonuse is due to special circumstances which excuse such nonuse and it is not due to any intention to abandon the mark." Lanham Act § 9(a), 15 U.S.C. §1059(a); 37 C.F.R. §2.183. *See* Torres v. Cantine Torresella S.r.l., 808 F.2d 46, 48, 1 U.S.P.Q.2d 1483 (Fed. Cir. 1986) ("An essential element of the application for renewal is the registrant's averment that the mark as registered is in current use for the goods covered by the registration or the reasons for the mark's nonuse. The purpose of this requirement, like that in section 8 of the Lanham Act, is 'to remove from the register automatically marks which are no longer in use.' ")

False or incomplete statements in renewal applications lead to charges of fraud. *E.g.* Torres v. Cantine Torresella S.r.l., 808 F.2d 46, 48, 1 U.S.P.Q.2d 1483, 1484 (Fed. Cir. 1986) ("Fraud in obtaining renewal of a registration amounts to fraud in obtaining a registration within the meaning of section 14(c) of the Lanham Act. . . . The obligation to refrain from knowingly making false, material statements applies with equal force to renewal applications."). *See* §5F[2][b].

[189] *In re* Holland American Wafer Co., 737 F.2d 1015, 1018, 222 U.S.P.Q. 273, 275 (Fed. Cir. 1984) ("A complete application must be submitted within a specific statutory time period. Timeliness set by statute is not a minor technical defect which can be waived by the Commissioner. . . . [T]he oath and evidence of use (*i.e.,* the *current* label) must pertain to the statutory renewal period. Appellant's 'pendency' theory wholly fails to take into account the substance of the application and totally ignores the regulations. A premature application simply does not contain the necessary averments and evidence of use during the critical period.").

[190] Lanham Act §14(3), 15 U.S.C. § 1064(3). *See* §5D[3][b].

Abandonment is also an exception to incontestability; Section 15 begins with the phrase "Except on a ground for which application to cancel may be filed at any time under paragraphs (3) and (5) . . . " Lanham Act §15, 15 U.S.C. §1065. For a discussion of incontestability, see §5E[1].

[191] *See, e.g.,* Defiance Button Machine Co. v. C & C Metal Products Corp., 759 F.2d 1053, 1059, 225 U.S.P.Q. 797, 800-01 (2d Cir. 1985), *cert. denied,* 474 U.S. 844 (1985) ("if the owner expressly abandons his mark, such as by cancelling it, or discontinues using it with the intent not to resume use, others are no longer restrained from using it since it ceases to be associated in the public's mind with the owner's goods or services. . . . The mark also ceases to be enforceable against others when it loses its significance as an indication of the origin of goods sold by and associated with the mark owner, such as when the owner makes the mark the subject of an unrestricted license or sale to others, . . . or the mark has become generic, . . . or the owner assigns the mark without the goodwill associated with it . . . Under such circumstances the mark is held to have been abandoned for the reason that there 'are no rights in a trademark apart from the business with which the mark has been associated' and the '[u]se of the mark by the assignee in connection with a different goodwill and different product would result in a fraud on the purchasing public who reasonably assume that the mark signifies the same thing, whether used by one person or another' . . . ").

Abandonment causes a loss of common law exclusive rights and of Lanham Act registration benefits. If the owner resumes using a mark after abandonment, he may or may not establish trademark rights, but he is not entitled to the benefit of his pre-abandonment priority date.[192]

A Lanham Act applicant or registrant may, intentionally or inadvertently, abandon an application or registration, but this does not necessarily mean that the applicant or registrant abandons common law rights in the mark or the right to reapply for Lanham Act registration.

[i] *Nonuse.* A trademark owner may expressly abandon a trademark.[193] More commonly, abandonment is "inferred from circumstances," especially from a substantial period of nonuse.[194]

"Nonuse" for abandonment purposes means a complete cessation of mark use in commercial transactions.[195] The 1988 Trademark Revision Act specifies that " 'Use'

---

[192] *E.g.,* Cerveceria Centroamericana, S.A. v. Cerveceria India, Inc., 892 F.2d 1021, 1027 n.1, 13 U.S.P.Q.2d 1307, 1312 n.7 (Fed. Cir. 1989) ("Once a trademark is abandoned, its registration may be cancelled even if the registrant resumes use."); Ambrit, Inc. v. Kraft, Inc., 812 F.2d 1531, 1551, 1 U.S.P.Q.2d 1161, 1177 (11th Cir. 1986), *cert. denied,* 481 U.S. 1041 (1987) ("Irrespective of whether a competitor has used the mark in question, a registered trademark, once abandoned, may be cancelled even after the holder resumes use of the mark."); Société de Developments et D'Innovations des Marches Agricoles et Aliminetaries-Sodima Union de Cooperatives Agricoles v. International Yogurt, 662 F. Supp. 839, 850, 3 USPQ2d 1641, 1649 (D. Ore. 1987) ("Once a mark is abandoned, subsequent use does not retroactively cure its past abandonment. . . . A court may cancel a mark because of abandonment even after the registrant has resumed use.").

[193] *E.g.,* Hiland Potato Chip Co. v. Culbro Snack Foods, Inc., 585 F. Supp. 17, 22, 221 U.S.P.Q. 142 (S.D. Iowa 1982), *aff'd,* 720 F.2d 981, 222 USPQ 790 (8th Cir. 1983) ("A public announcement of intention to discontinue the sale of a product may be a circumstance from which an intent not to resume may be inferred. . . . 'When a trademark has been abandoned, the effect is to leave the subject matter open to adoption for use as a mark by others. . . . It may be seized immediately and the person so doing acquires a right superior to the entire world.' . . . The November 10 communication from Kiefer was not equivocal. It stated that the Kitty Clover brand name 'will be eliminated' and it further stated: 'All items will be under the Hiland label.' All items in the enclosed price list were Hiland brand products. It is hard to imagine how a public declaration of discontinuance of a trademark could be more clear.").

See also Manhattan Industries, Inc. v. Sweater Bee by Banff, Ltd., 627 F.2d 628, 207 U.S.P.Q. 89 (2d Cir. 1980) (General Mills signed "Surrenders of Cancellation" to the mark "Kimberly" for women's clothing, apparently "for tax purposes," precipitating a "free-for-all" in which three parties attempted to be first to adopt and use the abandoned mark).

[194] *Cf.* Intrawest Financial Corp. v. Western National Bank of Denver, 610 F. Supp. 950, 958, 227 U.S.P.Q. 27, 33 (D. Colo. 1985) ("Objective evidence of intent not to resume use may outweigh subjective testimony to the contrary.")

[195] Person's Co., Ltd. v. Christman, 900 F.2d 1565, 1571, 14 U.S.P.Q.2d 1477, 1481 (Fed. Cir. 1990) ("Although sales by [the registrant] were often intermittent and the inventory . . . remained small, such circumstances do not necessarily imply abandonment. There is . . . no rule of law that the owner of a trademark must reach a particular level of success, measured either by the size of the market or by its own level of sales, to avoid abandoning a mark."); Citibank N.A. v. Citibanc Group, Inc., 724 F.2d 1540, 1545, 222 U.S.P.Q. 292, 296

of a mark means the bona fide use of that mark made in the ordinary course of trade, and not made merely to reserve a right in a mark."[196]

To avoid abandonment, a mark owner need not use or intend to use the mark throughout the United States market—use anywhere therein suffices.[197] Use outside the United States will not prevent abandonment.[198]

(1) *Intent.* Trademark law has always made mark owner *intent* a requirement for abandonment.[199] Early common law cases describe the intent as one to "abandon."[200] The Lanham Act requires only that the intent be "not to resume . . .

---

[196] Lanham Act §45, 15 U.S.C. §1127.

(11th Cir. 1984) ("Although the plaintiff admittedly used Citibank only sporadically before 1976, the use was fairly continuous and clearly sufficient to justify the district court's finding that plaintiff never intended to discontinue using the name.").

[196] Lanham Act §45, 15 U.S.C. §1127.

[197] For cases rejecting "regional abandonment" as to Lanham Act registrants, see United States Jaycees v. Philadelphia Jaycees, 639 F.2d 134, 209 U.S.P.Q. 457 (3d Cir. 1981) ("That the United States Jaycees has tolerated some of its disaffiliated or disobedient chapters in the use of its marks does not constitute non-use. Consistent and proper use of those marks elsewhere in the United States . . . defeats any claim of non-use."); Dawn Donut Co. v. Hart's Food Stores, Inc., 267 F.2d 358, 363 (2d Cir. 1959) (abandonment occurs only when registrant fails to use its mark anywhere in the United States); Cotton Ginny, Ltd. v Cotton Gin, Inc., 691 F. Supp. 1347, 10 U.S.P.Q.2d 1108 (S.D. Fla. 1988).

Common law rights extend only to the market in which the mark is actually used. *See* §5E[2][a].

[198] Imperial Tobacco Ltd. v. Philip Morris, Inc., 899 F.2d 1575, 1579-80, 14 U.S.P.Q.2d 1390, 1393 (Fed. Cir. 1990) ("The terms 'use' and 'nonuse' mean use and nonuse in the United States. . . . A foreign trademark may be known by reputation in this country and may even be protectable under concepts of unfair competition, but such mark is not entitled to either initial or continued *registration* where the *statutory requirements* for registration cannot be met."); Cerveceria Centroamericana, S.A. v. Cerveceria India, Inc., 892 F.2d 1021, 1024, 13 U.S.P.Q. 2d 1307, 1310 (Fed. Cir. 1989) (cancelling registration of "MEDALLA DE ORO" for beer because of abandonment; registrant shipped small quantities into the United States in 1971, 1972, 1975, and 1977; it did not import beer with the mark into the United States from 1977 to 1985; "In cases involving products made abroad, proof of non-use of the trademark may require both proof of no importations into the United States and no domestic sales," but the TTAB's implied finding that the petitioner proved no domestic sales between 1977 and 1986 was not clearly erroneous; because beer shipments to the United States in the 1970's were "of very small quantities," it was unlikely that MEDALLA DE ORO beer remained on sale in the United States after 1977).

See §5D[1][f][i].

[199] *E.g.*, Beech-Nut Co. v. Lorillard Co., 273 U.S. 629, 633 (1927); Saratoga Vichy Spring Co., Inc. v. Lehman, 491 F. Supp. 141, 155 (N.D. N.Y. 1979), *aff'd*, 625 F.2d 1037, 208 U.S.P.Q. 175 (2d Cir. 1980) ("It is ancient doctrine that evidence tending to establish abandonment may be overcome by a showing that there never was an intent to abandon a mark.").

[200] Baglin v. Cusenier Co., 221 U.S. 580, 597-98 (1911) ("There must be found an intent to abandon, or the property is not lost; and while, of course, as in other cases, intent may be inferred when the facts are shown, yet the facts must be adequate to support the finding."); Saxlehner v. Eisner & Mendelson Co., 179 U.S. 19, 31 (1900) ("To establish the defense of abandonment it is necessary to show not only acts indicating a practical abandonment, but an actual intent to abandon. Acts which unexplained would be sufficient to establish an abandonment may be answered by showing that there never was an intention to give up and relinquish the right claimed.").

use."[201] Recent cases confirm that a positive intent to abandon is not necessary for abandonment; a negative intent not to resume use suffices.

In *Exxon*,[202] the Fifth Circuit held that "limited arranged sales" of products under a mark as part of the trademark claimant's "trademark maintenance program" were insufficient uses to avoid *prima facie* abandonment.[203] Humble Oil and Refining Company was founded in 1917. Following a merger in 1959, Humble introduced new branding systems for its products and service stations, which involved use of the "ENCO" and "ESSO" marks in certain parts of the country in addition to "HUMBLE." In late 1972, after deciding that three marks confused customers, Humble's management adopted "EXXON" as its sole primary brand name and mark. It also adopted a "trademark maintenance program" to humbly protect the "HUMBLE" mark, which entailed making limited sales of packaged products with both "HUMBLE" and "EXXON" and forming three "name protection companies," which sold a limited quantity of fuel to selected customers.

In 1974, Pat Holloway formed "Humble Exploration Company," adopting the name "HUMBLE" because he believed that it was abandoned when Exxon changed its name. Exxon filed suit for trademark infringement. The district court held that limited use of a famous mark solely for protective purposes was use sufficient to preclude abandonment under the common law and the Lanham Act. Exxon withdrew its common law claims, focusing attention on the Lanham Act. The Fifth Circuit reversed, holding that the limited sales were not sufficient use because Exxon did not use "HUMBLE" as a mark, that is a source identifier,[204] remanding for a factual

---

[201] Lanham Act 45 §, 15 U.S.C. §1127. The Act is not consistent because the provisions on continuing use affidavits and renewals refers to nonuse being "due to special circumstances which excuse such nonuse" and not "any intention to *abandon* the mark." Lanham Act §§8(a), 9(a), 15 U.S.C. §§1058(a), 1059(a).

[202] Exxon Corp. v. Humble Exploration Co., 695 F.2d 96, 217 U.S.P.Q. 1200 (5th Cir. 1983).

[203] *See also* La Société Anonyme des Parfums LeGalion v. Jean Patou, Inc., 495 F.2d 1265, 181 U.S.P.Q. 545 (2d Cir. 1974) (token sales program not sufficient use to avoid abandonment); Procter and Gamble v. Johnson & Johnson, Inc., 485 F. Supp. 1185 (S.D.N.Y.1979), *aff'd without opinion*, 636 F.2d 1203 (2d Cir. 1980) ("minor brands program" not sufficient use).

[204] ". . . The limited sales of packaged products to targeted customers and the arranged sales of bulk products through the three shell corporations were not sufficient uses to avoid prima facie proof of abandonment under the statute. The HUMBLE trademark was not used to identify the source of the goods. The packaged products were Exxon products with HUMBLE used as a secondary name. Of course, 'the fact that a product bears more than one mark does not mean that each cannot be a valid trademark.' Old Dutch Foods, Inc. v. Dan Dee Pretzel & Potato Chip Co., 477 F.2d 150, 154 (6th Cir. 1973). For example, in *Old Dutch* the defendant had used concurrent marks, OLD DUTCH and DAN DEE, on all his products for over thirty years. Each mark must, however, be a bona fide mark. *See* Blue Bell, Inc. v. Farah Manufacturing Company, Inc., 508 F.2d 1260, 1267 (5th Cir. 1975). In this case, the mark HUMBLE was used only on isolated products or selected invoices sent to selected customers. No sales were made that depended upon the HUMBLE mark for identification of source. To the contrary, purchasers were informed that the selected shipments would bear the HUMBLE name or be accompanied by an HUMBLE invoice but were the desired Exxon products. That is, the HUMBLE mark did not with these sales play the role of a mark. . . . That casting, however, is central to the plot that the Lanham Act rests on the idea of registration of marks otherwise born of use rather than the creation of marks by the act of registration." 695 F.2d at 100-01, 217 U.S.P.Q. at 1203.

determination whether Exxon intended to resume use of the "HUMBLE" mark, noting the difference between an intent not to resume use and an intent to abandon,[205] holding that an abandonment sufficient to bar relief under a Lanham Act trademark infringement theory also bars relief under Lanham Act Section 43(a),[206] and leaving unresolved whether, under common law trademark principles, an intent not to resume use constituted an intent to abandon.[207]

Other courts follow *Exxon* in adopting an "intent not to resume use" abandonment standard.[208]

---

[205] "This court recognizes that the goodwill associated with the mark HUMBLE has immense value to Exxon. That fact, coupled with the efforts under the trademark maintenance program, could suggest Exxon's intent to resume use of the mark, . . . but the trial court did not make that finding. The court found that the trademark protection program evidenced 'an intent not to relinquish HUMBLE' and 'an intent not to abandon HUMBLE,' but it did not specifically address Exxon's intent to resume use as required by section 1127 the Lanham Act. . . . There is a difference between intent not to abandon or relinquish and intent to resume use in that an owner may not wish to abandon its mark but may have no intent to resume its use. In factual contexts where there is no issue of a hoarding of a mark, the language 'an intent to abandon or relinquish' may be used to express the Lanham Act requirement of an 'intent not to resume use.' For that reason, it is important that cases using the language of 'intent to abandon' be carefully laid into their factual molds. . . . In the context of a challenge strictly under the Lanham Act to an alleged warehousing program, as the facts of this case present, the application of the statutory language is critical. . . . [T]his court having found that the two types of uses under the trademark maintenance program were not sufficient uses to avoid *prima facie* proof of abandonment, the district court must specifically address Exxon's intent to resume use of the HUMBLE trademark. . . . An 'intent to resume' requires the trademark owner to have plans to resume commercial use of the mark. Stopping at an 'intent not to abandon' tolerates an owner's protecting a mark with neither commercial use nor plans to resume commercial use. Such a license is not permitted by the Lanham Act." 695 F.2d at 102-03, 217 U.S.P.Q. at 1204-05.

[206] "While §1125 [§43(a)] has a broader reach than § 1114, and claims under it can be maintained by plaintiffs who are not owners of a trademark, . . . when a claim is based on alleged ownership of a mark, the two sections must be applied in a parallel manner. Otherwise stated, the §1125 claim rises or falls on the issue of abandonment for the reason that the only basis for the trial court's holding that §1125 was violated was the use by appellant of the mark, a use not faulted if the mark has been abandoned. . . . It would be incongruous to hold that Exxon had abandoned the mark, discontinued the mark with no intent to resume use, and thus that appellant had a right to use that mark because of Exxon's abandonment, . . . and then to hold that appellant had engaged in false designation or representation of origin." 695 F.2d at 103-04, 217 U.S.P.Q. at 1206.

[207] "There have been few occasions that required a drawing of this distinction between an 'intent to abandon' and an 'intent not to resume use' because few cases have been bottomed solely on the Lanham Act. The legislative history of the Act suggests that the 'intent not to resume use' standard was adopted from the common law. . . . Common law cases preceding the adoption of the Act tended to use interchangeably the phrases an 'intent not to abandon' with an 'intent to resume.' . . . These cases did not, of course, address the situation of an alleged warehousing of marks." 695 F.2d at 103 n.7, 217 U.S.P.Q. at 1205 n.7.

[208] *E.g.,* Imperial Tobacco Ltd. v. Philip Morris, Inc., 899 F.2d 1575, 1580-81, 14 U.S.P.Q.2d 1390, 1394 (Fed. Cir. 1990) ("[I]n some post-Lanham Act opinions, 'intent not to resume' and 'intent to abandon' have been used interchangeably. However, . . . in the factual context of

In *Silverman*,[209] the Second Circuit, in holding that the owner of trademark rights in the "Amos and Andy" characters abandoned those rights by ceasing use because of civil rights concerns for 21 years even though it harbored a lingering desire to resume use should social conditions permit, concluded that "intent to resume use" means intent to resume use within the "reasonably foreseeable future."[210]

[ii] *Presumption.* The Lanham Act provides that "Nonuse for two consecutive years shall be *prima facie* evidence of abandonment."[211] The "presumption eliminates the challenger's burden to establish the intent element of abandonment as an initial

---

those cases, . . . the substitution of one phrase for the other made no difference. . . . Nothing in the statute entitles a registrant who has formerly used a mark to overcome a presumption of abandonment arising from subsequent nonuse by simply averring a subjective affirmative 'intent not to abandon.' "); Silverman v. CBS Inc., 870 F.2d 40, 46, 9 U.S.P.Q.2d 1778, 1782 (2d Cir. 1989), *cert. denied,* 492 U.S. 907 (1989) ("'[T]he statute requires proof of 'intent not to resume,' rather than 'intent to abandon.' The statute thus creates no state of mind element concerning the ultimate issue of abandonment. On the contrary, it avoids a subjective inquiry on this ultimate question by setting forth the circumstances under which a mark shall be 'deemed' to be abandoned. . . . Congress's choice of wording appears to have been deliberate. One early version of what became section 45 of the Lanham Act had provided that '[i]ntent to abandon may be inferred from the circumstances.' H.R. Rep. 4744, 76th Cong., 1st Sess. (1939) (emphasis added). However, shortly thereafter a new bill modified this phrase by substituting '[i]ntent not to resume' for '[i]ntent to *abandon*.' H.R. Rep. 6618, 76th Cong., 1st Sess. (1939). . . . [W]e agree with the Fifth Circuit that the phrases are better understood as having distinct meanings. . . . 'Abandonment' connotes permanent relinquishment. . . . "); Ambrit, Inc. v. Kraft, Inc., 812 F.2d 1531, 1550, 1 U.S.P.Q.2d 1161, 1177 (11th Cir. 1986) ("The proper inquiry is whether [the trademark claimant] intended to resume meaningful commercial use of the mark, not whether it intended to abandon the mark."); Hiland Potato Chip Co. v. Culbro Snack Foods, Inc., 720 F.2d 981, 222 U.S.P.Q. 790 (8th Cir. 1983) (trademark mark owner explicitly announced discontinuance of use of mark).

209 Silverman v. CBS Inc., 870 F.2d 40, 9 U.S.P.Q.2d 1778 (2d Cir. 1989).

210 "The statute provides that intent not to resume may be inferred from circumstances, and two consecutive years of non-use is *prima facie* abandonment. Time is thereby made relevant. Indeed, if the relevant intent were intent never to resume use, it would be virtually impossible to establish such intent circumstantially. Even after prolonged non-use, and without any concrete plans to resume use, a company could almost always assert truthfully that at some point, should conditions change, it would resume use of its mark. We do not think Congress contemplated such an unworkable standard. More likely, Congress wanted a mark to be deemed abandoned once use has been discontinued with an intent not to resume within the reasonably foreseeable future. This standard is sufficient to protect against the forfeiture of marks by proprietors who are temporarily unable to continue using them, while it also prevents warehousing of marks, which impedes commerce and competition. . . . [A] proprietor may not protect a mark if he discontinues using it for more than 20 years and has no plans to use or permit its use in the reasonably foreseeable future. A bare assertion of possible future use is not enough." 870 F.2d at 46- 47, 9 U.S.P.Q.2d at 1782-83.

211 Lanham Act §45, 15 U.S.C. §1127. Compare Intrawest Financial Corp. v. Western National Bank of Denver, 610 F. Supp. 950, 958, 227 U.S.P.Q. 27, 33 (D. Colo. 1985) ("abandonment may be inferred from the circumstances in cases where there has been a shorter period of discontinued use.").

part of its case."[212] In *Saratoga Vichy Spring*,[213] the Second Circuit held that the Lanham Act two-year *prima facie* provision merely creates a rebuttable presumption of abandonment, which disappears when rebutted by contrary evidence.[214]

---

[212] Imperial Tobacco Ltd. v. Philip Morris, Inc., 899 F.2d 1575, 1579, 14 U.S.P.Q.2d 1390, 1393 (Fed. Cir. 1990) ("At common law there was no similar presumption of abandonment of a mark simply from proof of nonuse. A challenger had to prove not only nonuse of the mark but also that the former user *intended to abandon* the mark. . . . [S]tatements from opinions under the common law of abandonment concerning the nature of the element of intent and who had the burden of proof cannot be applied indiscriminately to an abandonment case under the Lanham Act concerned with a party's entitlement to continued registration.").

[213] Saratoga Vichy Spring Co., Inc. v. Lehman, 625 F.2d 1037, 208 U.S.P.Q. 175 (2d Cir. 1980). *See also* Société de Developments et D'Innovations des Marches Agricoles et Alimineta-ries-Sodima Union de Cooperatives Agricoles v. International Yogurt, 662 F. Supp. 839, 3 U.S.P.Q.2d 1641 (D. Ore. 1987).

The Ninth Circuit, holding that a fish canner's trademark was not abandoned, cited *Saratoga Vichy* for the proposition that "nonuse for two consecutive years constitutes prima facie abandonment, but this is a presumption that may be rebutted by showing valid reasons for nonuse or by proving lack of intent to abandon." Star-Kist Foods, Inc. v. P.J. Rhodes & Co., 769 F.2d 1393, 1396, 227 U.S.P.Q. 44, 46 (9th Cir. 1985).

[214] The district court granted summary judgment that New York State did not abandon its mark "Saratoga Geyser" for Saratoga bottled water and therefore that its use preceded any date plaintiff could establish secondary meaning for its allegedly infringed mark "Saratoga Vichy." Saratoga Vichy Spring Co., Inc. v. Lehman, 491 F. Supp. 141 (N.D. N.Y. 1979), aff'd, 625 F.2d 1037, 208 U.S.P.Q. 175 (2d Cir. 1980). The undisputed facts were that, after an audit revealing substantial operating losses, the State legislature cut off funding for the bottling plant. The State ceased bottling in 1971; eight months later, it registered "Saratoga Geyser" with the New York Department of State. In 1978, it signed an agreement with a company to lease the bottling plant and begin bottling under its mark.

The appeals court affirmed.

"The statute . . . requires two elements for an abandonment non-use and intent not to resume use, and permits the first element, when established for a two-year period, to create a 'prima facie abandonment.' What the statute does not make clear is what 'prima facie' means in this context. It could mean that non-use for two years always creates an issue of fact for the trier, or it could mean that non-use for two years creates a presumption of abandonment that disappears when rebutted by contrary evidence. The matter is complicated by the fact that the second element of abandonment, intent, is a mental state and as such might be thought to be always inferable from an objective fact like non-use. In this case, plaintiff has shown non-use for more than two years. On the other hand, defendants have presented undisputed facts to rebut abandonment. New York's non-use was caused by the decision of the legislature to have the State withdraw from the mineral water business, and the State thereafter sought continuously to sell the business with its good will and trademark. These facts are completely inconsistent with an intent to abandon the mark. Indeed, Saratoga Vichy does not even allege an intent to abandon. Thus, whether the matter is appropriate for summary judgment depends on whether the period of non-use only creates a rebuttable presumption that disappears in the face of contrary evidence or permits the trier to infer intent to abandon, despite contrary evidence.

"We think 'prima facie abandonment' . . . means no more than a rebuttable presumption of abandonment. In the first place, abandonment, being a forfeiture of a property interest, should be strictly proved, . . . and the statutory aid to such proof should be narrowly construed. Moreover, though intent is always a subjective matter of inference

(3) *Excuses.* A trademark owner may excuse nonuse by showing that it is due to "special circumstances." [215] In *Defiance Button Machine*,[216] Defiance began selling metal buttons and metal button-making machines under its "DEFIANCE" trademark in 1886 and thrived until the mid-1970's when its fortunes took a turn for the worse. In 1980, its buttoned-down president, Frank Maner, attempted to sell the company as a going concern but was blocked by a 50% shareholder's conservative conservators. In 1982, Defiance defiantly announced it would terminate manufacturing but would supply items from inventory to its customers and hoped to keep its name and goodwill alive. A loan creditor caused Defiance's physical assets to be sold at auction. A competitor, C & C, purchased the assets. Maner approached several competitors, offering to sell Defiance's trademark and customer lists. In December 1982, competitor Handy handily offered to purchase the Defiance shareholders' stock and its stockholders' shares. Due to the conservators' opposition, which necessitated obtaining court approval, and pension fund problems, the sale was not consummated until May 19, 1984. Meanwhile, C & C incorporated a Defiance Button Machine Company in New Jersey, hired Defiance's general manager, and began using Defiance's established trade symbols. The original Defiance (New York) sued the interloping Defiance (New Jersey) for trademark infringement and other wrongs. The district court found that Defiance had abandoned its mark. The Second Circuit reversed: "[F]rom the time it ceased manufacturing activities until it became a wholly-owned subsidiary of Handy its conduct was at all times inconsistent with an intent to abandon its trademark or trade name." [217]

> "[A]n intent to abandon a mark will not be presumed from the owner's mere non-use of it for a period shorter than two years, as set forth in §1127(a), and the presumption of abandonment following from non-use for a longer period is rebuttable . . . Nor does a company's cessation of business automatically and immediately terminate its rights to a mark. . . . This rule recognizes that goodwill does not ordinarily disappear or completely lose its value overnight. Erosion from non-use is a gradual process. As long as the mark has significant remaining value and the owner intends to use it in connection with substantially the same business or service, the public is not deceived.

and thus rarely amenable to summary judgment, the cases that have found no intent to abandon suggest that objective facts can satisfactorily explain non-use to the point where an inference of intent to abandon is unwarranted. And if those facts are undisputed and strongly probative, summary judgment is appropriate. As the Supreme Court has observed, 'Acts which unexplained would be sufficient to establish an abandonment may be answered by showing that there never was an intention to give up and relinquish the right claimed.' Saxlehner v. Eisner & Mendelson Co., 179 U.S. 19, 31 . . . We agree with Judge Foley that the undisputed facts of this case justify summary judgment for defendants on the issue of abandonment . . . . " 625 F.2d at 1043-44.

[215] Imperial Tobacco Ltd. v. Philip Morris, Inc., 899 F.2d 1575, 1581, 14 U.S.P.Q.2d 1390, 1395 (Fed. Cir. 1990) ("Intent to resume use in abandonment cases has been equated with a showing of special circumstances which excuse a registrant's nonuse.").

[216] Defiance Button Machine Co. v. C & C Metal Products Corp., 759 F.2d 1053, 225 U.S.P.Q. 797 (2d Cir. 1985), *cert. denied,* 474 U.S. 844 (1985).

[217] 759 F.2d at 1061, 225 U.S.P.Q. at 802.

> "If neither the separation from tangible assets, by itself, nor the termination of a business, by itself, will necessarily and immediately vitiate a mark and its associated goodwill, we see no reason why, under appropriate circumstances, the combination of these two events must inevitably destroy instantaneously the owner's goodwill and strip the owner of any right to its mark. The policies and practices of prior abandonment cases are consistent with the preservation of the mark in this situation, so long as (a) the goodwill of the concern has not wholly dissipated, (b) the owner or its assignee retains the intent to produce or market within a reasonable time a product or service substantially the same in nature and quality as that with which the trademark has been associated, and (c) such resumption of operations occurs within a reasonable time under the circumstances."[218]

The court noted that "If the goodwill and mark had lost their value and significance as an indication of origin it is unlikely that C & C would have offered $10,000 for them . . . or tried to copy them overnight."[219]

Even a lengthy period of nonuse will not constitute abandonment if the circumstances validate the trademark owner's assertion of an intent to resume use when conditions permitted.[220] In *Sterling Brewers*,[221] the court found no abandonment despite nine years nonuse. F. W. Cook Company, Evansville, Indiana, sold "Cook's Goldblume" beer from around 1900 until 1955 when a strike forced the company to close its brewery. No beer was sold under the mark until 1964 when a purchaser acquired rights to the trademark registrations, advertising materials and labels, which had passed to its principal shareholder Hulman when the company dissolved in 1960. The brewery owners resisted selling the trademark apart from the physical assets. That the nine years of nonuse had not dissipated the goodwill surrounding the mark was demonstrated by the purchaser's willingness to pay a substantial sum for the marks and the purchaser's sales success upon reintroducing "Cook's Goldblume" beer.

> "The closing of the brewery was the result of a strike and not a voluntary act by Cook. The decision not to reopen, made but three months later when a strike settlement was not attained, was a qualified one, described by Cook's Vice-President as a decision not to reopen 'with the intent of operating it (the brewery) under its past methods' so far as labor contract negotiations were

---

[218] 759 F.2d at 1060, 225 U.S.P.Q. at 801-02.

[219] 759 F.2d at 1061, 225 U.S.P.Q. at 803.

[220] *E.g.,* Saratoga Vichy Spring Co., Inc. v. Lehman, 625 F.2d 1037, 1043-44, 208 U.S.P.Q. 175 (2d Cir. 1980) (no abandonment of state-owned mark despite seven years of non-use; the state legislature made the initial decision to cease use, and the state continuously sought to sell the mark along with the mineral water business to which it applied).

Compare E. Remy Martin & Co., S.A. v. Shaw-Ross International Imports, Inc., 756 F.2d 1525, 1532, 225 U.S.P.Q. 1131, 1136 (8th Cir. 1985) (*prima facie* case of abandonment when a wine importer discontinued use for six years due to "complications . . . and reorganization of his business"; importer let his federal registration expire in 1977 and took steps to re-register in 1981; "A businessman intending to resume commercial use of his mark would or should not allow such a long lapse to occur.").

[221] Sterling Brewers, Inc. v. Schenley Industries, Inc., 441 F.2d 675, 169 U.S.P.Q. 590 (CCPA 1971).

concerned. We do not think these actions in the early months of non-use of the mark demonstrate intent to abandon.

"The matter of whether the duration of the non-use and the attendant circumstances show legal intent not to resume use is more difficult. Nevertheless, we are satisfied that the facts of record negate the presumption of abandonment that arises from the non-use for more than two consecutive years. The continuous activity of Cook and Hulman directed to maintenance of the brewery during the period of non-use, coupled with the refusal to consider periodic efforts of appellant to negotiate purchase of the rights to the mark separately, demonstrates an intent to maintain conditions conducive to resumption of production under the mark on relatively short notice. There obviously was a continuing specific intent to preserve the capacity to transfer the right and ability to resume production of 'COOK'S GOLDBLUME' beer to a purchaser of the brewery assets." [222]

In *Imperial Tobacco*,[223] the court found the registrant's excuses for not using its JPS design mark for cigarettes in the United States for six years insufficient. Registrant indicated that it was engaged in development of a "marketing strategy," but the strategy related to marketing "incidental products," such as whisky, pens, watches, sunglasses, and food, under the mark. Concern with marketing incidental products does not excuse nonuse of the mark on the designated goods (cigarettes). It argued its nonuse was because of concern with potential legal problems with the cancellation petitioner, Philip Morris. The TTAB "recognized that suspension of actual use, or plans to use a mark pending resolution of litigation, may serve to justify nonuse. . . . " but reasonably inferred that "litigation fears . . . were attributable to [registrant's] desire to sell JPS cigarettes in a particular display, not because it could not use JPS as registered for cigarettes."

[ii] *Failure to Control—Loss of Trademark Significance—Naked Licensing and "In Gross" Transfers.* A mark owner's failure to control the mark's use may cause it to lose its trademark significance.

Unfortunately, the Lanham Act's abandonment definition confuses abandonment by failure to control with loss of protectability through genericness. It provides that a mark "shall be deemed to be 'abandoned'" when "any course of conduct of the owner, including acts of omission as well as commission, causes the mark to become the generic name for the goods or services on or in connection with which it is used or otherwise to lose its significance as a mark." [224] Despite this provision, the law is clear that a term that becomes *generic* through a language usage change is not protectable, even if a mark owner expended every effort to prevent the change. [225]

---

[222] 441 F.2d at 680.

[223] Imperial Tobacco Ltd. v. Philip Morris, Inc., 899 F.2d 1575, 14 U.S.P.Q.2d 1390 (Fed. Cir. 1990).

[224] Lanham Act §45, 15 U.S.C. §1127.

[225] For a discussion of generic terms, see §5C[3][b].

In the "Gay Olympics" case, the issue was raised (but not resolved) whether Congress could, consistently with the First Amendment, confer exclusive rights to a generic word. See §1D[4].

As the Act suggests, a mark may be deemed abandoned by loss of trademark significance even though it does not become generic.[226]

Fatal failure to control may consist of "naked licensing," that is, allowing others to use the mark without control over the nature and quality of goods or services offered under the mark. The Lanham Act's "related companies" provision permits trademarks licensing but only if there is adequate control.[227] Similarly, an "in gross" trademark transfer, that is, one not in connection with the sale of the goodwill of the business to which the trademark is appurtenant, is an abandonment.[228]

Courts do not equate failure to sue apparent infringing users with active consent or licensing others to use it: "evidence of a trademark owner's failure to prosecute infringers is relevant to a determination of the defense of abandonment only where such failure amounts to the mark's losing significance as an indication of source."[229] Similarly, trademark enforcement delay may constitute laches or estoppel

---

[226] The 1988 Trademark Revision Act changed the abandonment definition's second part designation from "(b)" to "(2)" and added the phrase "to become the generic name for the goods or services on or in connection with which it is used or otherwise" to the existing phrase "to lose its significance as a mark."

The Act's legislative history states that the change's purpose was "to clarify its meaning and to be consistent with other provisions of the Act" but not to alter the "current standard for nonuse abandonment, which requires intent and may be inferred from 2 consecutive years of nonuse." S. Rep. 100-515, 100th Cong., 2d Sess. 45 (1988). The amendment does nothing to clarify what is meant by "lose its significance as a mark" apart from genericness and licensing or assignment in gross, a question that has bothered courts in the past. See Defiance Button Machine Co. v. C & C Metal Products Corp., 759 F.2d 1053, 1061, 225 U.S.P.Q. 797, 802 (2d Cir. 1985), cert. denied, 474 U.S. 844 (1985), discussed above ("we question whether §1127(b) was intended by Congress to apply to conduct of the type existing here, in which the owner of the mark seeks to prevent its use by others and intends to keep the mark alive and to have it used in a resumed business; the statute was designed to preclude assertion of a right to enforce a mark that has become generic or has been licensed in gross or officially cancelled."); Wallpaper Manufacturers, Ltd. v. Crown Wallcovering Corp., 680 F.2d 755, 766 n.13, 214 U.S.P.Q. 327 (CCPA 1982) ("From the legislative history it is evident that abandonment under part (b) was principally intended to encompass acts of omission or commission by the registrant which resulted in the mark becoming a generic term. See e.g., Hearings on H.R. 102, H.R. 5461 and S. 895 before the Subcom. on Trademarks of the House Comm. on Patents, 77th Cong., 1st Sess. 104-115 (1941).").

[227] See §5G[3].

[228] See §5G[2].

[229] Sweetheart Plastics, Inc. v. Detroit Forming, Inc., 743 F.2d 1039, 1048, 223 U.S.P.Q. 1291, 1297 (4th Cir. 1984).

See United States Jaycees v. Philadelphia Jaycees, 639 F.2d 134, 139, 209 U.S.P.Q. 457 (3d Cir. 1981) ("Non-use means much more than failure to prosecute promptly trademark infringements. . . . "); National Lead Company v. Wolfe, 223 F.2d 195, 204 (9th Cir. 1955), cert. denied, 350 U.S. 883 (1955); Engineered Mechanical Services, Inc. v. Applied Mechanical Technology, Inc., 584 F. Supp. 1149, 1159, 223 U.S.P.Q. 324, 331 (M.D. La. 1984) ("There is some question as to whether a failure to prosecute other infringers constitutes a defense at all; the existence of other infringers seems irrelevant as to the defendants' wrongdoing."). See §5F[2][e].

restricting the trademark owner's remedies against one infringer without amounting to abandonment, which "results in a loss of rights as against the whole world."[230]

In *Wallpaper Manufacturers*,[231] registered "Crown" for wallpaper in 1956 and made extensive use of the mark thereafter. In 1975, CWC, an unrelated Canadian company which had used "Crown" extensively in marketing wallpaper in the United States since 1964, petitioned to cancel the mark, alleging abandonment. Many witnesses testified that they associated "Crown" with CWC, not WPML. The Board found that WPML had not abandoned the mark by nonuse but nevertheless ordered cancellation because registrant's failure to stop CWC's use caused "Crown" "to lose its significance as an indication of origin." The CCPA reversed. The association testimony was not pertinent: "Trademark rights are neither acquired nor lost on the basis of comparative popularity."[232]

> "If the board's premise is limited to circumstances where one party has allowed another to acquire an equitable right to use the mark in question, such circumstances do not create an abandonment of the mark or negate the first registrant's right to maintain its registration. Indeed, the registration of two marks which cause some confusion of the public has explicitly been recognized by this court. . . . The board's view that there is no trademark 'when a mark loses its capacity to point out uniquely the single source or origin of goods,' that is, unless one maintains exclusivity of rights, is, as argued by appellant, simply 'bad law.' Few longstanding trademarks could survive so rigid a standard. . . . The law cannot be and is not so divorced from commercial reality. Nor is the public interest served by declaring the mark publici juris, opening the way for greater confusion.

> "The most notable exception to a requirement of exclusive identification with a trademark is that provided in the statute itself. Under 15 U.S.C. §1064, likelihood of confusion of source ceases to be a ground for cancellation once a mark has been registered for five years. Thus, even one with an 'equal' right in a trademark based on priority may not attack the registration of another after five years on the grounds of likelihood of confusion of source. . . . The board's interpretation of abandonment, depending from its requirement that a trademark must not identify two sources, would negate the protection intended by the statute."[233]

The Board "failed to perceive the distinction between conduct of a trademark owner which results in a loss of right to enjoin a particular use because of an affirmative

---

[230] Sweetheart Plastics, Inc. v. Detroit Forming, Inc., 743 F.2d 1039, 1046, 223 U.S.P.Q. 1291, 1295 (4th Cir. 1984) ("While abandonment results in a loss of rights as against the whole world, laches or acquiescence is a personal defense which merely results in a loss of rights as against one defendant.").

[231] Wallpaper Manufacturers, Ltd. v. Crown Wallcovering Corp., 680 F.2d 755, 214 U.S.P.Q. 327 (CCPA 1982).

[232] 680 F.2d at 762. "[E]ven where there is reverse confusion of the public, that is, where the 'infringer' is better known as a source at the time of suit, another source with superior *de jure* rights may prevail regardless of what source or sources the public identifies with the mark." *Id.*

[233] 680 F.2d at 762-63.

defense available to that user and conduct which results in the loss of all rights of protection as a mark against use by anyone."[234] The court acknowledged that "distinctiveness can be lost by failing to take action against infringers."

> "If there are numerous products in the marketplace bearing the alleged mark, purchasers may learn to ignore the 'mark' as a source identification. When that occurs, the conduct of the former owner, by failing to police its mark, can be said to have caused the mark to lose its significance as a mark. . . . However, an owner is not required to act immediately against every possibly infringing use to avoid a holding of abandonment. . . . Such a requirement would unnecessarily clutter the courts. Some infringements are short-lived and will disappear without action by the trademark owner. In the case of a mark temporarily not in use or only used to a limited extent, a company may be hard pressed to extend its financial resources to fight an infringer when it has little or no current market under its mark. Frequently one cannot determine with any certainty that one has priority over another's use. To charge another with infringement under such circumstances can be disastrous. Other infringements may be characterized as 'creeping,' starting as a business name, and only become serious when later use is as a trademark. When that occurred here, WPML took effective action to stop the use of CROWN per se as a trademark. Assuming appellant accepted that CWC had some rights in CROWN as a trade name, . . . viewing CWC's use in the United States as an expansion of its longstanding Canadian operations, WPML may have considered that confusion could be avoided if both companies operated as they had and took reasonable precautions in their respective trademark vis-a-vis trade name usage. . . . The courts should not discourage such voluntary accommodations."[235]

§ 5E Rights

A common law trademark gives its owner the right to prevent others from using the same or a similar mark in any way that creates a likelihood of confusion.[1] The likelihood of confusion standard limits a trademark's exclusionary power. A trademark does not confer rights outside the markets in which it has been used or is known, or on products or services so unrelated to the mark owner's as to negate any possibility of confusion. It does not confer the right to prevent others' "collateral" mark use, for example, on repaired genuine goods or in comparative advertising.

---

[234] 680 F.2d at 765.

[235] 680 F.2d at 766.
Judge Markey dissented:
> "In this case, one who orders CROWN wallpaper cannot possibly be assured of getting or avoiding wallpaper of one expected quality. Hence CROWN has lost all trademark significance. That circumstance is due to WPML's acts of omission. 15 U.S.C. §1145(b). Its registration has in this case become an empty shell. Allowing registrants to retain registrations, while taking no action against years of adverse use of an identical mark on identical goods, demeans and degrades the register." 680 F.2d at 767.

[1] For a discussion of likelihood of confusion, see § 5F[1].

Lanham Act registration confers additional procedural and substantive rights:

(1) *prima facie* evidence of the registered mark's ownership and validity and of the mark owner's exclusive right to use it;[2]

(2) *conclusive* evidence of the registered mark's ownership and validity and of the mark owner's exclusive right to use it—subject to limited "defenses and defects"—if the registrants meet "incontestability" requirements,[3]

(3) nationwide constructive *notice* as of the registration date;

(4) nationwide constructive *use* as of the application filing date; and

(5) protection against importation of infringing goods.

[1] Incontestability

The Lanham Act's incontestability provision (Section 15) was an innovation:[4] after five years continuous use, a registrant can achieve "incontestable" status,[5] which eliminates other persons' ability to attack the registrant's right to use and to exclude others from using the mark because of descriptiveness or prior use.[6]

After this five year continuous use period[7] and compliance with specified conditions, subject to limited exceptions and provisions, Section 15 makes "incontestable"

---

[2] Brittingham v. Jenkins, 914 F.2d 447, 452, 16 U.S.P.Q.2d 1121, 1124 (4th Cir. 1990) ("a certificate of registration of a mark serves as *prima facie* evidence that the registrant owns the registered mark, has properly registered it under the Lanham Act, and is entitled to its exclusive use in commerce. 15 U.S.C. §1057(b). Thus, registration creates a presumption of the registrant's ownership of the mark, subject to any applicable legal or equitable defenses or defects. 15 U.S.C. §1115(a). This attribute of registration represents a change from the common law where the putative owner bears the burden of establishing ownership of the disputed mark in any trademark infringement action.").

[3] *See* § 5E[1].

[4] Park 'N Fly v. Dollar Park and Fly, Inc., 469 U.S. 189, 198, 224 U.S.P.Q. 327, 331 (1985) ("National protection of trademarks is desirable, Congress concluded, because trademarks foster competition and the maintenance of quality by securing to the producer the benefits of good reputation. . . . The incontestability provisions . . . provide a means for the registrant to quiet title in the ownership of his mark. . . . The opportunity to obtain incontestable status . . . encourages producers to cultivate the goodwill associated with a particular mark.").

[5] The Lanham Act makes makes only the "right to use" a registered mark "incontestable," but it is commonplace to refer to an incontestable mark or registration.

[6] For a discussion of descriptiveness and prior use, see §§ 5C[3][a] and 5C[4].

[7] The use necessary to comply with Section 15's "continuous use requirement" is stricter than the use necessary to avoid abandonment. *See* Brittingham v. Jenkins, 914 F.2d 447, 454, 16 U.S.P.Q.2d 1121 (4th Cir. 1990) ("a federally registered mark becomes incontestable only if the mark has been in continuous use for five consecutive years and several other requirements are satisfied. . . . In the present case, Brittingham did not use the THRASHER'S mark from 1978, when he closed his two Salisbury businesses, until 1980, when he opened his Baltimore store. At oral argument, Brittingham argued that there was no lapse in his use of the mark during this period because the mark was used in the name of a business which he helped to create, Thrasher's, Inc., because he had licensed the mark to the new corporation, because the corporation entered into a lease agreement with the owners of Baltimore's

a registrant's "right to use" the registered mark "in commerce for the goods or services on or in connection with which such registered mark has been in continuous use for five consecutive years subsequent to the date of such registration." Section 33(b) provides that the registration is "conclusive evidence" of mark validity and ownership and "of the registrant's exclusive right to use the mark in commerce" to the extent "the right to use the registered mark has become incontestable under section 15" and subject to listed "defenses or defects."

A "final decision adverse" to registrant's ownership or right to register the mark or "proceeding involving said rights pending" in the PTO or the courts precludes incontestability.

The registrant must file an affidavit within one year after the expiration of "any such five year period," that is, any post-registration five-year continuous use period.[8] Because Section 8 requires filing of a continued use affidavit during the sixth year,[9] registrants often kill two birds with one stone by filing a combination Section 8-Section 15 affidavit.[10]

[a] **Defensive and Offensive Use—*Park 'N Fly*.** In *Park 'N Fly*,[11] the Supreme Court held that descriptiveness is not a defense to an infringement charge based on a registered mark whose exclusive right of use is incontestable.

Park 'N Fly began using its mark "Park 'N Fly" in 1967 for a long-term parking lot near the St. Louis airport. Park 'N Fly opened facilities in five other cities and, in 1969, it applied to register a service mark consisting of an airplane logo and the words "Park 'N Fly." The PTO registered the mark in 1971; nearly six years later, Park 'N Fly filed a Section 15 affidavit.

Harborplace, and because advertising and news features heralded the opening of the new THRASHER'S store in Baltimore. Brittingham insists that these actions constituted an uninterrupted use of the THRASHER'S mark. We disagree. First, there was still a gap in time between the closing of the Salisbury stores and the founding of Thrasher's, Inc. Second, and more importantly, the five-year continuous use provision of 15 U.S.C. §1065 applies solely to the use of a mark in connection with the sale of goods and services, and not in relation to other business activities. . . . Thus, contrary to the claims made in his affidavit of use filed with the Patent and Trademark Office, Brittingham did not use the THRASHER'S mark continuously in connection with the sale of goods for the required five-year period following registration. Consequently, incontestability never attached to Brittingham's trademark registration. The Lanham Act contains no exceptions to the five-year continuous use requirement for incontestability . . . [Fn. 14 In contrast, excusable or justifiable non-continuous use, discontinued use, or temporary abandonment does not destroy per se a registrant's right to use a mark or claim ownership of the mark.]").

[8] Lanham Act §15(3), 15 U.S.C. §1065(3). The affidavit must, *inter alia*, "[r]ecite the goods or services stated in the registration on or in connection with which the mark has been in continuous use in commerce for a period of five years subsequent to the date of registration . . . and is still in use in commerce, specifying the nature of such commerce." 37 CFR §2.167(c).

[9] *See* §5D[3][a][i].

[10] *See* 37 CFR §2.168.

[11] Park 'N Fly v. Dollar Park and Fly, Inc., 469 U.S. 189, 224 U.S.P.Q. 327 (1985).

Dollar Park and Fly, Inc. ("Dollar") provided long-term parking services at the Portland, Oregon airport, where Park 'N Fly had no facility. Park 'N Fly sued Dollar for trademark infringement. Dollar defended on the ground that the mark was either generic or descriptive. The district court ruled for trademark owner Park 'N Fly, finding "Park 'N Fly" is not generic and "Dollar Park and Fly" is confusingly similar, and held that an incontestable mark cannot be challenged on descriptiveness grounds. The Ninth Circuit reversed, holding that incontestability provides a defense against mark registration cancellation but cannot be used offensively to enjoin another's use, and finding that Park 'N Fly's mark is in fact descriptive.[12]

Granting certiorari to resolve a Ninth Circuit-Seventh Circuit conflict,[13] the Supreme Court reversed the Ninth Circuit because the Lanham Act makes no distinction between incontestable mark "offensive" and "defensive" uses.[14] The Lanham Act distinguishes between a "merely descriptive" mark and one that is the "common descriptive name of an article or substance" (i.e., is generic). The latter but not the former is a defense or condition under Sections 15 and 33(b) to the conclusiveness of the registrant's exclusive right to use the mark after compliance with the incontestability requirements: "Mere descriptiveness is not recognized by either §15 or §33(b) as a basis for challenging an incontestable mark." Section 33(b)'s declaration that a registrant has an "exclusive right" to use the mark indicates that incontestable status may be used to enjoin infringement. Section 33(b) enumerates three defenses that clearly contemplate that trademark claimants can rely on incontestability in infringement actions.

The Court found nothing in the Lanham Act's legislative history to support a departure from the incontestability statutory provisions' plain language. It rejected respondent's argument that "the Lanham Act did not alter the substantive law of trademarks" and therefore cannot protect use of a mark that should not have been registered. The Act did alter existing law: the constructive notice and incontestability provisions are examples. Equally, it rejected the argument that the incontestable status of a descriptive mark might take from the public domain language that is merely descriptive. A similar argument was raised by opponents of the Lanham Act but necessarily rejected by Congress. The possibility of such an occurrence is mitigated

---

[12] Park 'N Fly v. Dollar Park and Fly, Inc., 718 F.2d 327 (9th Cir. 1983), rev'd, 469 U.S. 189, 224 U.S.P.Q. 327 (1985).

[13] Ever-Ready Inc. v. Union Carbide Corp., 531 F.2d 366, 188 U.S.P.Q. 623 (7th Cir.), cert. denied, 429 U.S. 830, 191 U.S.P.Q. 416 (1976).

There was an ironic twist to the Seventh Circuit-Ninth Circuit conflict. In Park 'N Fly, the Ninth Circuit relied on its prior decision, Tillamook County Creamery v. Tillamook Cheese & Dairy Assn., 345 F.2d 158, 163 (9th Cir. 1965), cert. denied, 382 U.S. 903 (1965), which relied in part on the Seventh Circuit decision, John Morrell & Co. v. Reliable Packing Co., 295 F.2d 314, 316 (7th Cir. 1961), which the Seventh Circuit overruled in Ever-Ready.

[14] Justice Stevens dissented: "The basic purposes of the Act, the unambiguous congressional command that no merely descriptive mark should be registered without prior proof that it acquired secondary meaning, and the broad power of judicial review granted by §37 combine to persuade me that the registrant of a merely descriptive mark should not be granted an injunction against infringement without ever proving that the mark acquired secondary meaning." 469 U.S. at 215, 224 U.S.P.Q. at 338.

by the PTO's ex parte examination procedure,[15] interested third parties' opportunities to oppose registration and to petition to cancel a descriptive mark during the five years after registration,[16] and the provision barring a generic mark from becoming incontestable.

[b] **Scope—Likelihood of Confusion.** There is confusion in the case law on Section 33(b)'s effect on the scope of the trademark owner's rights in terms of goods or services coverage and on infringement determination.

Section 33(b)'s conclusive evidence provision relates only to "the exclusive right to use the mark on or in connection with the goods or services" specified in the Section 15 affidavit or in a renewal affidavit "if the goods or services specified in the renewal are fewer in number." The 1988 Act added the phrase "Such conclusive evidence of the right to use the registered mark shall be subject to proof of infringement as defined in section 32." As the Senate Committee noted, this "makes clear that incontestability does not relieve the owner of an incontestable registration from the burden of proving likelihood of confusion."

The better view, confirmed by the 1988 amendment, is that incontestability pertains only to validity, except if the marks and goods or services are identical. For example, suppose registrant R's mark is M-1 for product P-1. If D uses M-1 for product P-1, it is an easy case: infringement by likelihood of confusion is clear and D cannot contest the R's mark's validity except on Section 33(b)'s limited grounds. But if D uses a similar but not identical mark M-2 for product P-1, or an identical mark M-1 for a different product P-2, registrant R must prove infringement.

One likelihood of confusion factor is the mark's "strength."[17] Some decisions suggest that incontestability conclusively dictates that the mark be considered not descriptive and therefore "strong," not "weak."[18] Following the better view that incontestability is validity preserving only, other decisions give no weight to incontestability.[19]

---

[15] *See* §5D[2][a].

[16] See §5D[2][d][ii].

[17] *See* § 5F[1][a][iii].

[18] *E.g.,* Dieter v. B & H Industries of Southwest Florida, Inc., 880 F.2d 322, 329, 11 U.S.P.Q.2d 1721, 1726 (11th Cir. 1989), *cert. denied,* 111 S. Ct. 369 (1990) ("incontestable status is a factor to be taken into consideration in likelihood of confusion analysis. Because Dieter's mark is incontestable, then it is presumed to be at least descriptive with secondary meaning, and therefore a relatively strong mark."). In *Dieter,* the court seemingly assumed that incontestability made the mark strong for purposes of determination likelihood of confusion under Lanham Act Section 43(a) and common law infringement claims as under the Lanham Act registered mark infringement claim.

[19] Munters Corp. v. Matsui America, Inc., 909 F.2d 250, 252, 15 U.S.P.Q.2d 1666 (7th Cir. 1990), *cert. denied,* 111 S. Ct. 591 (1990) ("strength of the mark is one of the factors in this Circuit for evaluating likelihood of confusion. . . . Some other circuits do not include this factor in their likelihood of confusion analysis. *See, e.g.,* Clamp Manufacturing Co., Inc. v. Enco Manufacturing Co., Inc., 870 F.2d 512, 517 (9th Cir. 1989) (strength of mark not among listed factors), *cert. denied,* — U.S. ——, 110 S. Ct. 202, 107 L.Ed.2d 155; Beer Nuts, Inc. v. Clover Club Foods Co., 805 F.2d 920, 925 (10th Cir.1986) (same). Munters has argued that since a strength of the mark analysis includes a discussion of whether the mark is merely descriptive,

[c] **Limitations, Defenses, and Defects.** Section 33(b)'s conclusive evidence provision strengthens the mark owner's exclusive use rights against descriptiveness or prior use validity attacks, but it states directly or incorporates by reference numerous exceptions.[20]

Section 33(b) lists eight "defenses and defects":

(1) fraudulent registration or incontestability procurement;[21]

(2) abandonment;[22]

(3) use to misrepresent the source of the goods or services;[23]

(4) fair use;[24]

---

the district court's discussion of the strength of Munters' mark disregarded the Supreme Court's holding in *Park 'N Fly* that an incontestable mark cannot be challenged on the grounds that it is merely descriptive. . . . This argument is unpersuasive. . . . The district court explicitly noted that [the accused infringer's] argument that Munters' mark was merely descriptive was not intended to demonstrate that [registrant's] mark was not protectible but rather was advanced solely to bolster Matsui's claim that there was no likelihood of confusion. . . . The Supreme Court's holding in *Park 'N Fly* does not address likelihood of confusion. In fact the Court specifically directed the district court to consider the likelihood of confusion argument on remand. . . . Therefore *Park 'N Fly* does not preclude consideration of a mark's strength for purposes of determining the likelihood of confusion."); Oreck Corp. v. U.S. Floor Systems, Inc., 803 F.2d 166, 171, 231 U.S.P.Q. 634 (5th Cir. 1986), *cert. denied*, 481 U.S. 1069 (1987) ("*Park 'N Fly* merely held, however, that an infringement action brought by the holder of an incontestable mark may not be defended on the ground that the mark is merely descriptive and therefore invalid. . . . U.S. Floor's argument was not that Oreck's mark was invalid, but that it was not infringed because there was no confusion. *Park 'N Fly* says nothing to preclude this argument. Incontestable status does not make a weak mark strong."); Source Services Corp. v. Source Telecomputing Corp., 635 F. Supp. 600, 610, 230 U.S.P.Q. 290, 295 (N.D. Ill. 1986) ("the conclusive presumption that the marks have secondary meaning established by the statutory incontestability of plaintiff's 'Source Edp' marks does not automatically transfer into a conclusive presumption of strength in a likelihood of confusion analysis.").

[20] The exceptions are numerous, but they are exclusive. *See, e.g.*, Opticians Association of America v. Independent Opticians of America, 920 F.2d 187, 193, 17 U.S.P.Q.2d 1117, 1121 (3d Cir. 1990) ("mischaracterization [of mark used as a certification mark as a collective mark] is not one of the enumerated Lanham Act defenses. Therefore, the mere fact that the marks served as certification, rather than collective marks, is insufficient to remove the incontestable status of [plaintiff's] marks.").

[21] *See* §5F[2][b].

[22] *See* §5D[3][b].

[23] Lanham §33(b)(3), 15 U.S.C. §1115(3): "That the registered mark is being used by or with the permission of the registrant or a person in privity with the registrant, so as to misrepresent the source of the goods or services on in connection with which the mark is used . . . ."

[24] Lanham §33(b)(4), 15 U.S.C. §1115(4): "That the use of the name, term, or device charged to be an infringement is a use, otherwise than as a mark, of the party's individual name of anyone in privity with such party, or of a term or device which is descriptive of and used fairly and in good faith only to describe the goods or services of such party, or their geographic origin . . . ." *See* §5F[2][d].

(5) prior use;[25]

(6) prior registration and use;

(7) antitrust violation; and

(8) equitable defenses.[26]

Section 33(b) also incorporates by reference Section 15's exceptions and limitations. Section 15 excludes from incontestability:

(1) generic terms; and

(2) another's "valid right acquired under" state law continuing from prior to the registration;[27]

Section 15 (and therefore Section 33(b)) incorporates Section 14(3) and (5)'s "any time" cancellation grounds. Section 14(3) includes Section 2(a), (b) and (c) prohibitions, generic terms, fraudulently registration procurement, and use to misrepresent goods and services. This complex scheme involves some duplication; for example, generic terms are explicitly excluded three times.

As Professor McCarthy emphasized, under Sections 33(a) and (b)'s literal language before a 1988 amendment, these "defenses" only eliminated the incontestability's conclusive effect.[28] They were not infringement or invalidity defenses but allowed a defendant to prove "any legal or equitable defense or defect . . . which might have been asserted if such mark had not been registered." Because the exceptions are, for the most part, the same as defenses and invalidity grounds recognized at common

---

[25] See §5E[2][c][ii].

[26] In *Park 'N Fly*, the Supreme Court left open the question whether incontestability cut of "equitable" defenses: "we need not address in this case whether traditional equitable defenses such as estoppel or laches are available in an action to enforce an incontestable mark." 469 U.S. at 203, 224 U.S.P.Q. at 332.

That equitable defenses may not be available was suggested by the wording difference between Section 33(a) and 33(b), as originally enacted. The former made registration "prima facie" evidence of validity, ownership and exclusive right but allowed opposing parties to prove "any legal or equitable defense or defect." The latter made registration "conclusive" evidence of exclusive right except "when one of the following defenses or defects is established" and did not include equitable defenses.

The 1988 Revision Act resolved the matter by providing "That equitable principles, including laches, estoppel, and acquiescence, are applicable." As to the effective date of this addition, see Brittingham v. Jenkins, 914 F.2d 447, 453 n.10, 16 U.S.P.Q.2d 1121, 1124 n.10 (4th Cir. 1990) ("This last exception was added by the Trademark Law Revision Act of 1988, Pub.L. 100-667, 102 Stat. 3938, and became effective on November 16, 1989. Although the 1988 law does not indicate whether this new exception is applicable to pending litigation, section 46(a) of the Act of July 5, 1946, 60 Stat. 427, provided that no trademark provision shall affect any suit, proceeding or appeal pending on the effective date of the provision except as specifically provided therein. . . . Accordingly, we conclude that the exception contained in section 1115(b)(8) does not apply to this controversy.").

[27] This provision is similar but not identical to Section 33(b)(5). See §5E[2][c][ii].

[28] J.T. McCarthy, Trademarks and Unfair Competition §§32.44, 32.45 (2d ed. 1984). Accord: GTE Corp. v. Williams, 904 F.2d 536, 14 U.S.P.Q.2d 1971 (10th Cir. 1990), *cert. denied*, 111 S. Ct. 557 (1990).

law and under Lanham Act Section 2, "most courts view proof of one of the § 33(b) elements as a defense on the merits, thus compressing the evidentiary two-step process into step."[29] He warns that the compression could lead to error if one of the Section 33(b) defenses is narrower or easier to prove than "the traditional scope of those defenses." He also notes that fraudulent registration procurement is a defense to a "count for infringement of the registered mark" but "should not be a defense on the merits of a count based on common law rights."

The 1988 Act added to Section 33(a) the phrase "any legal or equitable defense or defect, *including those set forth in subsection (b),*" dispelling any implication that "incontestable" marks[30] are subject to defenses different or in addition to those applicable to "contestable" marks.[31]

[2] Territorial Scope of Trademark Rights

At common law, a manufacturer or merchant's trademark rights geographically extended only to markets in which he sold the trademark-bearing goods. Notwithstanding the first use priority rule, a second user could obtain exclusive trademark rights by adopting and using in good faith in a remote market a mark similar or identical to a first user's.

The Lanham Act recognizes but limits multiple user rights. Its nationwide constructive use and notice provisions preclude anyone from adopting a mark in good faith after a first user files and obtains registration. A filing and registration freeze the geographic scope of any second user's rights. The Act's concurrent registration provisions allow multiple users to obtain registration benefits for their respective exclusive use territories.

[a] The Common Law Market Penetration Rule: *Hanover Star Milling* and *United Drug.*

In *Hanover Star Milling,*[32] and *United Drug,*[33] the Supreme Court confirmed that trademark rights extended only as far as the first user had extended his trade under the mark and that a good faith second user could acquire rights in a remote market area.

Hanover Star Milling involved rights to the trademark "Tea Rose," which three sellers independently adopted for flour. In 1872, Allen & Wheeler of Troy, Ohio,

---

[29] *Id.* at §32.44 C.

[30] Courts and commentators refer, for convenience, to "contestable" and "incontestable" marks. Literally, what becomes incontestable is neither a mark nor a registration but the registrant's right to use the mark in commerce on the specified goods or services.

[31] The Senate Report notes that the addition "codifies judicial decisions holding that the enumerated defenses or defects to an action for infringement of an incontestable registration, which are set forth in Section 33(b) of the Act, are equally applicable in actions for infringement of marks which are not incontestable." S. Rep. 100-515, 100th Cong., 2d Sess. 38 (1988).

The provision as amended is ambiguous. Does the last phrase "which might have been asserted if such mark had not been registered" restrict Section 33(b)? Or does it mean that a person may prove *either* a Section 33(b) defense *or* defect or any other defense or defect "which might have been asserted if such mark had not been registered"?

[32] Hanover Star Milling Co. v. Metcalf, 240 U.S. 403 (1916).

[33] United Drug Co. v. Rectanus Co., 248 U.S. 90 (1918).

adopted "Tea Rose" and used it continuously as a mark on sacks of flour sold only in Cincinnati, Ohio, except for isolated sales in Pittsburgh, Pennsylvania and Boston, Massachusetts. In 1885, Hanover, an Illinois corporation, adopted "Tea Rose" for flour. In 1904, it began advertising and selling Tea Rose flour in the whole of Alabama and in parts of Mississippi, Georgia, and Florida. In 1895, Steeleville of Illinois began selling flour under a "Tea Rose" mark in Illinois, Tennessee, Mississippi, Louisiana and Arkansas. Metcalf purchased Steeleville flour and sold it under the "Tea Rose" mark in Alabama.

This triple usage led to two federal court diversity of citizenship suits. Hanover sued Metcalf in Alabama, the district court granted a temporary injunction restraining Metcalf from selling Steeleville "Tea Rose" flour in Alabama, and the Fifth Circuit reversed, directing that the bill be dismissed. Allen & Wheeler sued Hanover in Illinois, the district court granted a temporary injunction without territorial restriction, and the Seventh Circuit reversed.

Reviewing the two cases, the Supreme Court noted that the two circuits had acted on differing fundamental trademark law principles. Because the parties had not registered their marks under the Federal Trademark Laws and relied on no special state rule or statute, the Court resolved the cases "according to common-law principles of general application." [34] It propounded a territorial trademark right theory.

> "The primary and proper function of a trade-mark is to identify the origin or ownership of the article to which it is affixed. Where a party has been in the habit of labeling his goods with a distinctive mark, so that purchasers recognize goods thus marked as being of his production, others are debarred from applying the same mark to goods of the same description, because to do so would in effect represent their goods to be of his production and would tend to deprive him of the profit he might make through the sale of the goods which the purchaser intended to buy. Courts afford redress or relief upon the ground that a party has a valuable interest in the good-will of his trade or business, and in the trade-marks adopted to maintain and extend it. The essence of the wrong consists in the sale of the goods of one manufacturer or vendor for those of another.

> . . .

> "Common-law trademarks, and the right to their exclusive use, are, of course to be classed among property rights . . . but only in the sense that a man's right to the continued enjoyment of his trade reputation and the goodwill that flows from it, free from unwarranted interference by others, is a property right. . . . [T]he right grows out of use, not mere adoption.

---

[34] *Hanover* preceded the landmark decision Erie Railroad v. Tompkins, 304 U.S. 64 (1938), which held that there "is no federal general common law" and that in diversity cases, the federal courts should follow the decision of the relevant state court interpreting the common law. In *Hanover*, Justice Holmes wrote a concurring opinion, arguing that Alabama common law governed the Hanover-Metcalf case. After *Erie*, state court autonomy on this issue became more apparent than real. State and federal courts regularly cite *Hanover* as the leading precedent on the trademark right territorial scope. Some decisions hold that the Lanham Act preempts any State rule giving junior users rights greater than *Hanover* confers. *E.g.*, Spartan Food Systems, Inc. v. H.F.S. Corp., 813 F.2d 1279, 2 U.S.P.Q.2d 1063 (4th Cir. 1987), *infra*.

. . .

". . . In the ordinary case of parties competing under the same mark in the same market, it is correct to say that prior appropriation settles the question. But where two parties independently are employing the same mark upon goods of the same class, but in separate markets wholly remote the one from the other, the question of prior appropriation is legally insufficient, unless, at least, it appear that the second adopter has selected the mark with some design inimical to the interests of the first user, such as to take the benefit of the reputation of his goods, to forestall the extension of his trade, or the like.

. . .

". . . Into whatever markets the use of a trade-mark has extended, or its meaning has become known, there will the manufacturer or trader whose trade is pirated by an infringing use be entitled to protection and redress. But this is not to say that the proprietor of a trade-mark, good in the markets where it has been employed, can monopolize markets that his trade has never reached, and where the mark signifies not his goods but those of another."[35]

The application of these principles carried the day both defensively and offensively for Hanover, the expansionist good faith second user. In the Illinois suit, the Seventh Circuit properly denied Allen & Wheeler, the first user, an injunction against Hanover's use of the mark. In the Alabama suit, the Fifth Circuit erroneously denied Hanover injunctive relief against Metcalf, the mark's third user and invader of territory Hanover had previously penetrated.[36]

The Supreme Court left open possible application of a natural expansion zone theory: "We are not dealing with a case where the junior appropriator of a trade-mark is occupying territory that would probably be reached by the prior user in the natural expansion of his trade, and need pass no judgment upon such a case."[37]

United Drug[38] involved rights to the trademark "Rex." In 1877, Ellen Regis of Massachusetts adopted and used the mark "Rex," derived from her surname, for a medicinal preparation, a "dyspepsia tablet." She later formed a partnership with her son and registered the mark under both Massachusetts law and under the 1881 federal registration statute. They successfully asserted their mark in litigation against United Drug Co. In 1911, United Drug purchased the firm with the trademark right and carried on their business through a chain of retail drug stores known as "Rexall stores." In 1883, Theodore Rectanus began using "rex" as a trade-mark for a "blood purifier" in the vicinity of Louisville, Kentucky. He later sold his business to the Rectanus company. In 1912, United Drug began shipping its "Rex" medicinal product into Kentucky. It filed suit seeking to enjoin Rectanus from using the "Rex" mark. The district court granted the injunction; the court of appeals reversed.

---

[35] 240 U.S. at 413-16.

[36] Metcalf was found to be guilty of actively palming off Steeleville "Tea Rose" flour as Hanover "Tea Rose" flour and thus of unfair competition apart from the question of trademark infringement.

[37] 240 U.S. at 420.

[38] United Drug Co. v. Rectanus Co. 248 U.S. 90 (1918).

Before the Supreme Court, United Drug pressed a "diligent territorial expansion" theory, to wit, that "whenever the first user of a trade-mark has been reasonably diligent in extending the territory of his trade, and as a result of such extension has in good faith come into competition with a later user of the same mark who in equal good faith has extended his trade locally before invasion of his field by the first user, so that finally it comes to pass that the rival traders are offering competitive merchandise in a common market under the same trade-mark, the later user should be enjoined at the suit of the prior adopter, even though the latter be the last to enter the competitive field and the former have already established a trade there." [39]

The Court, affirming the denial of injunctive relief, rejected the theory:

> "[T]he adoption of a trade-mark does not, at least in the absence of some valid legislation enacted for the purpose, project the right of protection in advance of the extension of the trade, or operate as a claim of territorial rights over areas into which it thereafter may be deemed desirable to extend the trade." [40]

The Massachusetts and federal registration statutes did not alter the parties' common law rights. They contained no "provision making registration equivalent to notice of rights claimed thereunder." [41]

[b] **Scope of Concurrent Common Law Rights.** The *Hanover Star Milling-United Drug* common law good faith remote market use rule requires determination of what constitutes good faith adoption, market remoteness, and sufficient market penetration.

[i] *Good Faith.* In *Hanover Star Milling*, the Supreme Court stated that a first user does not preclude another obtaining rights in a remote market "unless at least it appear that the second adopter has selected the mark with some design inimical to the interests of the first user, such as to take the benefit of the reputation of his goods, to forestall the extension of his trade . . . . " [42] It did not apply the exception or explain its purpose. [43]

The relevant time period for good faith is when the junior user adopts and uses the mark. [44] If the junior user begins use in good faith and then learns of the first

---

[39] 248 U.S. at 96-97.

[40] 248 U.S. at 97.

[41] 248 U.S. at 99.

[42] 240 U.S. at 415.

[43] Professor McCarthy questions the significance of junior user's knowledge because the critical question should be consumer perception and potential confusion in the market area. He concludes that "[p]roof of the junior user's knowledge could be viewed as establishing a presumption that the junior user must have intended to cause customer confusion and that such confusion (and hence lack of 'remoteness') did in fact occur." J.T. McCarthy, Trademarks and Unfair Competition §26:4 (2d ed. 1984).

[44] This rule applies to the Lanham Act's Section 33(b) prior use defense as well as to the common law. *See* Allied Telephone Co., Inc. v. Allied Telephone Systems Co., Inc., 565 F. Supp. 211, 217, 218 U.S.P.Q. 817, 821 (S.D. Ohio. 1982) ("The statute requires only that there has been *adoption* 'without knowledge of the registrant's prior use.' The statute does not require *continuous use* without knowledge.").

user's mark, he may expand his trade under the mark into "virgin" territory.[45] The senior user may "freeze" the junior user's territorial rights by obtaining a federal registration.[46]

Lower courts are not consistent on what constitutes "good faith" second user adoption. Some view mere knowledge of the first user's mark use as negating good faith.[47] In *Sweet Sixteen*[48] plaintiff began business in San Francisco in 1916 selling women's clothing under the name "Sweet Sixteen." It expanded to Los Angeles, Portland, and Seattle, and advertised in newspapers and nationally circulated trade journals that were distributed in Utah. Plaintiff also sold by mail order to customers in 12 to 15 states, including Utah. In 1923, it began planning to open a store in Utah, but defendant, with notice of plaintiff's mark in the form of a warning letter, opened a "Sweet 16" shop. The court granted plaintiff relief. *Hanover Star Milling* and *United Drug* recognized a subsequent user's rights in a discrete geographic market only if the use was begun in "good faith."

Others require some further evidence of intent to cause confusion or trade on the first user's good will. In *GTE*,[49] the Tenth Circuit adopted the latter view.

---

[45] *See* J.T. McCarthy, Trademarks and Unfair Competition §§26:3, 26:5 (2d ed. 1984) ("The critical date to test good faith is the date of the junior user's first use. . . . In the absence of federal registration, both parties have the right to expand into unoccupied territory and establish exclusive rights by being first in that territory.").

[46] *See* §5E[2][c][ii].

[47] *E.g.,* Fuddruckers, Inc. v. Doc's B.R. Others, Inc., 826 F.2d 837, 844, 4 U.S.P.Q.2d 1026, 1031 (9th Cir. 1987) ("'[Defendant] concedes that it was aware of [plaintiff's] operations, and familiar with its trade dress, so the good faith junior user line of cases does not apply here."). *Cf.* Fry v. Layne-Western Co., 282 F.2d 97, 104 (8th Cir. 1960) ("actual notice in a trade name situation would serve the same purpose as constructive notice in the trade-mark situation."); Johanna Farms, Inc. v. Citrus Bowl, Inc., 468 F. Supp. 866, 877, 199 U.S.P.Q. 16 (E.D. N.Y. 1978) ("if a junior's use of a mark in the face of constructive notice of the senior's use by virtue of the federal registration of the mark negates an inference of good faith. *See* Dawn Donut Co. [v. Hart's Food Stores, 267 F.2d 358, 362 (2d Cir. 1959)], then actual notice of another's claim to the mark must demand a similar conclusion . . . . ").

Compare Sweetarts v. Sunline, Inc., 380 F.2d 923, 154 U.S.P.Q. 459 (8th Cir. 1967), *on remand*, 299 F. Supp. 572, 162 U.S.P.Q. 179 (E.D. Mo. 1969), *aff'd in part, rev'd in part*, 436 F.2d 705, 168 U.S.P.Q. 483 (8th Cir. 1971) (defendant adopted mark "SweeTarts" for candy in good faith even though it knew of plaintiff's registration of "SweeTarts" for dried prunes; it had no knowledge that plaintiff used the mark for candy.)

One decision holds that knowledge of another's *intent* to use does not constitute knowledge and bad faith in the legal sense. Selfway, Inc. v. Travelers Petroleum, Inc., 579 F.2d 75, 198 U.S.P.Q. 271 (CCPA 1978) (the junior user disclosed an investment plan, which included the disputed mark, to potential investors, including the senior user; the senior user's knowledge of the junior's intent to use the mark did not justify awarding use priority to the junior user; the junior user's "disclosures were made neither in confidence nor in the course of a fiduciary relationship. . . . The law pertaining to registration of trademarks does not regulate all aspects of business morality. While adoption of a mark with knowledge of a prior actual *user* may give rise to cognizable equities as between the parties, . . . appellant has cited no authority warranting recognition of similar equities based on knowledge of another's Intent to use.").

[48] Sweet Sixteen Co. v. Sweet "16" Shop, Inc., 15 F.2d 920, 924 (8th Cir. 1926).

[49] GTE Corp. v. Williams, 904 F.2d 536, 14 U.S.P.Q.2d 1971 (10th Cir. 1990), *cert. denied*, 111 S. Ct. 557 (1990).

"While a subsequent user's adoption of a mark with knowledge of another's use can certainly support an inference of bad faith, . . . mere knowledge should not foreclose further inquiry. The ultimate focus is on whether the second user had the intent to benefit from the reputation or goodwill of the first user. . . .

"It may be that only in unusual cases will a defendant be found to have both knowledge of a senior user and good faith adoption of the allegedly infringing mark."[50]

Defendant adopted "General Telephone" for a mobile telephone and paging service in Utah's Wasatch Front area. The district court found that at the time defendant adopted General Telephone, he had heard of a company called " 'General Telephone and Electronics of California' in the context of its involvement in some litigation in California," that he "had no knowledge that GTE used or claimed to use 'General Telephone' as a trade or service mark, or that any other entity used or claimed to use that mark," and that Williams did not intend to benefit from GTE's reputation and goodwill. The Tenth Circuit held that defendant's good faith claim was "somewhat improbable," but it could not say that the district court finding of good faith was clearly erroneous under the Federal Rule of Civil Procedure 52(a) appellate review standard.[51]

[ii] *Remoteness.* In *Hanover Star Milling,* the Supreme Court referred to "separate markets wholly remote the one from the other."[52] In the late 19th and early 20th century, limited travel, transportation, and communication made markets for many goods and services local and remote. Ninety years later, the opposite is the case. With vastly increased human and commercial interaction in the United States, fewer markets can be considered "remote" in the *Hanover Star Milling* sense.

In *Travelodge,*[53] the district court noted that "[t]he traditional notions of limited market area pervading the earlier cases dealing with product trademarks are not persuasive in this day of modern communication and travel. Recent decisions involving restaurants and chain stores manifest this expanding concept of the market area for such establishments and the consequent reduced influence of the earlier cases." The expanding market area concept is particularly important for hotels and motels: "By definition, a motel draws its customers from an area other than the one of its location. In this area of expanding travel a motel's market is deemed nationwide."[54] In finding

---

[50] 904 F.2d at 541, 14 U.S.P.Q.2d at 1979.

[51] 904 F.2d at 541, 14 U.S.P.Q.2d at 1975.

[52] 240 U.S. at 415.

[53] Travelodge Corp. v. Siragusa, 228 F. Supp. 238, 141 U.S.P.Q. 719 (N.D. Ala. 1964), *aff'd,* 352 F.2d 516, 147 U.S.P.Q. 379 (5th Cir. 1965). *See also* Fuddruckers, Inc. v. Doc's B.R. Others, Inc., 826 F.2d 837, 844, 4 U.S.P.Q.2d 1026, 1031 (9th Cir. 1987) ("The rule has only limited applicability to services such as hotels or restaurants, because their customers are ambulatory and on the move back and forth across the nation.").

[54] 228 F. Supp. at 243.

Compare Matador Motor Inns, Inc. v. Matador Motel, Inc., 376 F. Supp. 385, 389, 182 U.S.P.Q. 460 (D.N.J. 1974) ("plaintiff . . . contends that the doctrine of innocent adoption is inapplicable in motel cases because of the mobility of actual and potential patrons in high-no local remote market, it noted that "prior to defendants' appropriation of plaintiff's mark, plaintiff was advertising its motels by listings in AAA and other auto club tour books and directories and was distributing postcards, stationery, matches, and other advertising material."[55]

In GTE,[56] the Tenth Circuit affirmed a district court finding of remoteness between plaintiff's subsidiaries' local telephone operations in various states other than Utah and defendant's operation of a mobile telephone and paging service in one area of Utah.

[iii]   Market Penetration. In determining what geographic areas parties have penetrated, the courts consider various factors including sales volume, sales growth patterns, number of customers, and advertising.[57]

In SweetTarts,[58] the senior user sold mail order candy, primarily to customers in three states. It made some sales in ten other states. The district court found that the sales were sufficient to constitute actual market penetration of eight of the states. The appeals court held that that finding was clearly erroneous.

> "Based on the figures available for the five fiscal years, 1962-1966, the plaintiff made its greatest market penetration in Idaho (population 667,191), . . . where its annual average sales amounted to approximately $1,285 over the five-year period. The plaintiff's sales in Idaho have been relatively stable over the years, but do not constitute effective market penetration in that state when analyzed

---

powered automobiles on a vast network of interstate highways. Although the mobility of the American public with respect to automobile travel is certainly open to question in these energy conscious times, the Court will deal with this contention. . . . The position taken is that the defense is only applicable in the area in which the prior continuous use is proved but that courts, when dealing with hotels, motels, and restaurants, have in effect read out that proviso because of travelling mobility and the wide geographical area from which establishments of this type draw their clientele. The Court need not concern itself with this aspect of the argument. All cases cited by plaintiff, and to some extent refuted by defendant, involved unfair competition and either of two situations: (1) where the owner of a registered trademark shows a likelihood of entry into the innocent prior user's market area, or (2) where the owner of a registered trademark actually enters into the market area of the innocent prior user.").

[55] 228 F. Supp. at 243.

[56] GTE Corp. v. Williams, 904 F.2d 536, 14 U.S.P.Q.2d 1971 (10th Cir. 1990).

[57] Market penetration questions arise in PTO concurrent use proceedings. See §5E[2][d][i].

[58] Sweetarts v. Sunline, Inc., 436 F.2d 705, 710, 168 U.S.P.Q. 483 (8th Cir. 1971) ("Minimal market penetration alone will not suffice to establish infringement of a common-law trademark. The market penetration must be 'significant enough to pose the real likelihood of confusion among the consumers in that area . . . . ' "); Sweetarts v. Sunline, Inc., 380 F.2d 923, 929, 154 U.S.P.Q. 459 (8th Cir. 1967) (prior user is not entitled to areas in which its sales were "so small, sporadic, and inconsequential that present or anticipated market penetration is de minimis."; the extent of the first user's market area is an issue of fact: "In determining this issue the trial court should weigh all the factors including plaintiff's dollar value of sales at the time defendants entered the market, number of customers compared to the population of the state, relative and potential growth of sales, and length of time since significant sales. Though the market penetration need not be large to entitle plaintiff to protection, . . . it must be significant enough to pose the real likelihood of confusion among the consumers in that area between the products of plaintiff and the products of defendants.").

under the four significant factors (volume, customers compared to population, potential growth of sales, time since significant sales) set forth in this court's prior opinion. . . . In the five most recent fiscal years, the plaintiff's sales in Idaho have ranged from a high of $1,876 in 1964 to a low of $1,005 in 1966. Such activity could hardly be characterized as reflecting a favorable growth potential for sales in that state and does not constitute a sales volume large enough to entitle the plaintiff to claim the entire state as its effective market area. The conclusion that Idaho does not fall within plaintiff's effective market area is further strengthened by a comparison of plaintiff's activity in that state with its business in Oregon, Washington and California. Sweetarts' total sales in Idaho from 1947 through 1963 amounted to $20,008. By comparison, the plaintiff sold $25,941 worth of candy in Washington in 1963 alone, and considerably more in the other two states that same year. Having considered the standards set forth in this court's prior opinion and other relevant factors, we conclude that the plaintiff's sales in Idaho are not significant enough to pose any real likelihood of confusion among consumers in that state.

"We reach a similar conclusion with regard to the other seven states involved on this appeal. . . . "[59]

In *Natural Footwear Ltd.,*[60] Roots, Inc. commenced business in Northern New Jersey in 1917. In 1950, it began applying "Roots" labels to its merchandise. It made catalog sales to out-of-state customers, such sales never exceeding 3% of its total sales. It advertised extensively in local New Jersey newspapers and only to a minor extent in regional and national media. In 1973, Natural began manufacturing and selling an "earth" shoe under the "ROOTS" mark. In 1974, it obtained federal registration of "ROOTS." Later, it expanded its product line to leather goods and wearing apparel and opened numerous "ROOTS" stores in the United States and abroad, directly or through franchisees, and advertised extensively in both local and national media.

In a trademark infringement suit, the district court found that Roots had penetrated the national market with its "ROOTS" mark and therefore granted a nationwide injunction forbidding Natural's use of "ROOTS."

The Fourth Circuit reversed. The district court erred by failing to assess Roots' market penetration on the basis of factors probative of such penetration.

"Although this court has not established a test for determining whether a party's reputation in a given state or region is sufficient to warrant injunctive relief for protection against the use of a confusingly similar mark in that area, two courts have developed tests that fully and accurately assess the extent of the mark's market penetration. [Sweetarts v. Sunline, Inc., 380 F.2d 923 (8th Cir.1967); Weiner King, Inc. v. Wiener King, Corp., 615 F.2d 512 (CCPA1980).] . . .

"[T]he following four factors should be considered to determine whether the market penetration of a trademark in an area is sufficient to warrant protection:

---

[59] 436 F.2d at 709.

[60] Natural Footwear Ltd. v. Hart, Schaffner & Mark, 760 F.2d 1383, 225 U.S.P.Q. 1104 (3d Cir. 1985), *cert. denied,* 474 U.S. 920 (1985).

(1) the volume of sales of the trademarked product; (2) the growth trends (both positive and negative) in the area; (3) the number of persons actually purchasing the product in relation to the potential number of customers; and (4) the amount of product advertising in the area." [61]

As to sales, the court must consider growth trends as well as sales volume: "A tripling in sales in a given area may be more properly attributable to new purchasing patterns for the same, very small group of buyers than to a marked increase in the products' market penetration." As to customers, "a proper evaluation of market penetration should normally include a comparison of the number of actual consumers of the trademarked product with the number of people in the market for the product, rather than with the full population of a given area." As to advertising, "[b]ecause advertising may be very important to the reputation of a product in a given area, . . . advertising should be recognized as an independent factor for determining market penetration." [62] Applying these factors, the senior user, Roots, had not achieved nationwide market penetration.

In *Wrist-Rocket Mfg.*,[63] the court relied heavily on the ratio of the parties' sales volume per population on a state-by-state basis to allocate territories between a senior user and a junior user-incontestable Lanham Act registrant. It cautioned: "We have found no simple dollar amount or population-to-sales ratio that will apply across the board to products of different types, uses and durability and that appeal to different segments of the population." [64]

[iv] *Natural Expansion Zone.* Some decisions endorse an expansive natural expansion zone doctrine.[65] Others restrict it to situations in which the first user

---

[61] 760 F.2d at 1398-99, 225 U.S.P.Q. at 1114.

[62] 760 F.2d at 1399, 225 U.S.P.Q. at 1115.

[63] Wrist-Rocket Mfg. Co. v. Saunders Archery Co., 578 F.2d 727, 198 U.S.P.Q. 257 (8th Cir. 1978).

[64] 578 F.2d at 732.

[65] *E.g.,* Tally-Ho, Inc. v. Coast Community College District, 889 F.2d 1018, 1023, 13 U.S.P.Q.2d 1133, 1136 (11th Cir. 1989) ("A senior user's rights also are geographically limited to only those territories in which it actually uses its mark or into which it might naturally expand (the zone of 'natural expansion'). For instance, if a senior user cannot prove that it directly competes in a geographic market with a junior user, it can still demonstrate that the junior user is operating in a market into which the senior user should be allowed to expand at a later time."); Food Fair Stores, Inc. v. Lakeland Grocery Corp., 301 F.2d 156, 162, 133 U.S.P.Q. 127, 132 (4th Cir. 1962), *cert. denied,* 371 U.S. 817 (1962) (first user of "Food Fair" began in 1953 and expanded into a national change; second user began use of "Food Fair" in parts of Virginia in 1953, prior to the first user's opening of stores in that area; "It has been generally recognized since the decisions of [*Hanover* and *United Drug*] that an established trade name is entitled to protection not only in the area in which it already renders service or sells goods but also in areas to which its trade may reasonably be expected to expand. . . . It is, therefore, necessary to determine whether at the time the defendant opened its store in Norfolk [Virginia] there was a reasonable prospect of the expansion of the plaintiff's business into that area. . . . The size and rate of expansion of the plaintiff's business at the time, the proximity and location of its existing stores including the Alexandria [Virginia] store operated under another name, the negotiation for a chain of stores in Newport News [Virginia] in 1955, the effort to buy out the defendant in 1956, and the actual opening of the plaintiff's store

established a reputation in the disputed area.[66]

In *Raxton*,[67] the First Circuit held that the doctrine does not apply when the first user failed to register its mark and the second party with no knowledge of the first use adopted a name "new to the area" that the first user claims as within its natural expansion zone.[68]

---

in 1958 give strong support to the testimony of the plaintiff that as early as 1949. . . . surveys of the area were made and expansion of the business into the area was not merely possible but probable."); Dawn Donut Company, Inc. v. Hart's Food Stores, Inc., 267 F.2d 358, 369 n.4 (2d Cir. 1959) ("Since the statutory standard for the invocation of injunctive relief is the likelihood of confusion, it is enough that expansion by the registrant into the defendant's market is likely in the normal course of its business. Even prior to the passage of the Lanham Act the courts held that the second user of a mark was not entitled to exclude the registered owner of the mark from using it in a territory which the latter would probably reach in the normal expansion of his business."); Koffler Stores v. Shoppers Drug Mart, 434 F. Supp. 697, 704, 193 U.S.P.Q. 165, 172 (E.D. Mich. 1976), aff'd, 559 F.2d 1219 (6th Cir. 1977) (table) (Detroit was a natural area of expansion for plaintiff, a Windsor, Ontario, Canada, company because it is on the Canadian-American border and because the area was "preconditioned through Plaintiff's advertising." "Protection under common law principles has been extended beyond the prior user's actual good will zone to the area of his natural or probable expansion"); Rainbow Shops v. Rainbow Specialty Shops, 176 Misc. 339, 27 N.Y.S.2d 390 (1941) (New York common law; "a prior trader is entitled to equitable protection in the exclusive right of his trade name not only within the immediate locality where his business has been previously conducted but also . . . within such territory as may reasonably be expected to constitute a likely field of normal expansion.").

[66] *E.g.*, Blue Ribbon Feed Co., Inc. v. Farmers Union Central Exchange, Inc., 731 F.2d 415, 222 U.S.P.Q. 785 (7th Cir. 1984) (Wisconsin law; no error in refusing to grant relief in "natural zone of expansion" when the trademark owner had operated a single store for 35 years: "[M]ere hope of expansion beyond its proven trade area is insufficient to support the protection sought"; in cases relied upon by the trademark owner, in which courts extended such protection, "the plaintiff undertook affirmative steps to enlarge his trade area. Those steps included negotiations for the purchase of a chain of stores in the affected area, . . . authorization of marketing surveys for the area, . . . and preconditioning the area through extensive advance advertising. . . . ").

Cf. Food Fair Stores, Inc. v. Food Fair, Inc., 83 F. Supp. 445, 452 (D. Mass. 1948), aff'd, 177 F.2d 177 (1st Cir. 1949) (applying Massachusetts statute; plaintiff "Food Fair" was a nationally-known chain of stores; defendant opened a "Food Fair" in Massachusetts when plaintiff had no store there but "after plaintiff had acquired a reputation in Massachusetts, had done business with wholesalers here, had acquired official permission for one of its subsidiaries to do business here and had negotiated for the acquisition of enterprises here. Before defendant opened its store plaintiff had something more than a mere hope of doing business in Massachusetts.")

If the mark is not inherently distinctive, the mark owner must show that it has acquired secondary meaning in the area in question. *See* §5E[2][b][vi].

[67] Raxton Corp. v. Anania Associates, Inc., 635 F.2d 924, 208 U.S.P.Q. 769 (1st Cir. 1980), *on remand*, 668 F.2d 662, 213 U.S.P.Q. 903 (1st Cir. 1982).

[68] *Compare* Puritan Furniture Corp. v. Comarc, Inc., 519 F. Supp. 56, 58 (D. N.H. 1981) ("the disputed trademark was known to consumers in the area of subsequent use prior to the subsequent user's adoption").

In May 1978, investors organized plaintiff ("Rax") to sell women's clothing and announced it would use the mark "Off the Rax" at a Norwood, Massachusetts, store soon to be opened. Various difficulties delayed the Norwood opening until August 1979, but Rax did open stores in New Jersey and Illinois in September 1978. By 1980, it had more than 20 stores.

In December 1978, other investors organized defendant ("Rack") to sell men's clothing and announced it would use the mark "Off the Rack" in a Brocton, Massachusetts, store. It began advertising its mark in January 1979. In February 1979, Rack obtained a Massachusetts state registration of "Off the Rack." In March 1979, Rax learned of Rack and sent it a letter objecting to use of "Off the Rack" as confusingly similar to "Off the Rax." Undaunted, Rack opened its store in April of 1979.

Rax sued Rack, alleging infringement of its common law trademark rights. The district court found Rax the prior user because of its use of the mark in Illinois but that it did not make actual use of its mark in Massachusetts until after Rack had opened its store in Brocton. Nevertheless, because Massachusetts was a "target area for expansion" for Rax, it held that Rax was entitled to protection in Massachusetts and granted Rax's request for an injunction and denied that of Rack.

The First Circuit reversed, finding no basis in either federal law or Massachusetts law for application of a natural expansion zone doctrine when the second user adopted its mark in good faith.[69] The doctrine's origin is in brief dictum in *Hanover Star Milling*.[70] Lower courts reiterated the natural expansion zone concept,[71] which the 1938 Restatement of Torts adopted.[72] Some later decisions questioned the

---

[69] On remand, the district court entered an injunction in Rack's favor barring Rax from using is mark in Massachusetts, where Rack was the prior user. On appeal, the First Circuit affirmed. It repulsed Rax's modified natural expansion zone theory—that Rax should have superior rights in Massachusetts regardless of priority of use because Massachusetts was its "origin, home base, nerve center and center of control. Although the situs of a company's headquarters may be relevant to showing bad faith or to showing that a reputation has been established among local consumers, it is far from conclusive. Indeed, it will usually be much less relevant than the proximity of the contested locality to the region in which actual use has been made." Raxton Corp. v. Anania Associates, Inc., 668 F.2d 622, 625, 213 U.S.P.Q. 903 (1st Cir. 1982).

[70] *Hanover* referred to markets in which the mark's "meaning has become known" and found no "need to pass judgment upon" a case "where the junior appropriator of a trade-mark is occupying territory that would probably be reached by the prior user in the natural expansion of his trade." 240 U.S. at 420.

Rectanus rejected a broad diligent territorial expansion theory. *See* §5E[2][a].

[71] *E.g.*, White Tower System, Inc. v. White Castle System of Eating Houses Corp., 90 F.2d 67 (6th Cir. 1937), *cert. denied*, 302 U.S. 720 (1937); Terminal Barber Shops v. Zoberg, 29 F.2d 807, 809 (2d Cir. 1928); Western Oil Refining Co. v. Jones, 28 F.2d 205 (6th Cir. 1928) (court chose to "pass" evidence of subsequent user's "intended deception" and instead placed holding on the ground of the "normal expansions of the business"); Sweet Sixteen Co. v. Sweet "16" Shop, 15 F.2d 920 (8th Cir. 1926).

[72] Restatement of Torts §732 ("The interest in a trade-mark or trade name is protected . . . with reference only to territory from which he receives or, with the probable expansion of his business, may reasonably expect to receive custom in the business in which he uses his trade-mark or trade name, and in territory in which a similar designation is used for the purpose of forestalling the expansion of his business.").

Restatement.[73] Others repeated the expansion zone theory,[74] but "in none of the cases cited by the parties before this court has a court applied the 'natural expansion' doctrine to bar a party from adopting a trademark in good faith merely on the ground that that user lay in the 'natural expansion path' of a prior appropriator from a remote area."[75]

"This absence is understandable. A 'natural expansion' doctrine that penalized innocent users of a trademark simply because they occupied what for them would be a largely undiscoverable path of some remote prior user's expansion strikes us as at once unworkable, unfair, and, in the light of statutory protection available today, unnecessary. Such a doctrine would have to weigh the remote prior user's intangible and unregistered interest in future expansion as more important than the subsequent user's actual and good faith use of its name. Besides involving the obvious practical difficulties of defining the 'natural expansion path' of a business, this doctrine would also allow trademark owners to 'monopolize markets that (their) trade ha[d] never reached.' . . .

"The unfairness of this doctrine vanishes if the hypothesis of an innocent subsequent user is dropped, or if it is shown that the disputed trademark is known to consumers in the area of subsequent use prior to the subsequent user's adoption. . . . In these cases it can be presumed unless demonstrated to the contrary that the subsequent user knowingly copied a mark. At the least, this suggests that the subsequent user should have been more careful to select a name free of prior rights and should be held to assume the risk of its negligence. At worst, this indicates a design to appropriate the good will of another."[76]

---

[73] See Katz Drug Co. v. Katz, 89 F. Supp. 528, 534-35 (E.D. Mo. 1950), aff'd, 118 F.2d 696 (8th Cir. 1951) ("A number of cases have been cited by plaintiff's counsel in support of the field of natural expansion theory. It is readily seen that these cases do not require the plaintiff to show competition or loss of trade in order to obtain injunctive relief; but it is also apparent that in these cases there was present a showing of one of the following facts: either (1) that the junior appropriator adopted the senior user's mark with a 'design inimical to the interests' of the latter, that is, adopted it in bad faith; or (2) that the senior user, at the time of the adoption of the mark by the junior user and in the territory in which the junior user employed the mark, had something variously denominated by different courts as 'secondary meaning', 'good-will' or 'reputation'. . . . The plaintiff argues only that in 1933 it would, in the natural expansion of its business enterprise, eventually have established a store in [the disputed area], and was at the time negotiating for the location of the store. I have found no case saying that alone is sufficient to entitle it to protection.").

See also Shoppers Fair of Arkansas, Inc. v. Sanders Co., 328 F.2d 496, 500-01 (8th Cir. 1964); Food Fair Stores, Inc. v. Lakeland Grocery Corp., 301 F.2d 156, 162-63 (4th Cir. 1962); beef & brew, inc. v. Beef & Brew, Inc., 389 F. Supp. 179, 185 U.S.P.Q. 531 (D.Ore.1974).

[74] E.g., Value House v. Phillip Mercantile Co., 523 F.2d 424, 431, 187 U.S.P.Q. 657 (10th Cir. 1975) ("Protection under common law principles has, nevertheless, been extended beyond the prior user's actual goodwill zone to the area of his natural or probable expansion.").

[75] 635 F.2d at 930.

[76] 635 F.2d at 930.

The Lanham Act eliminated the need for an expansive natural expansion zone doctrine.[77]

> "If a 'natural expansion' doctrine independent of a concern with the good faith of the subsequent user or the prior reputation of the mark in the contested territory ever had any place in federal law, we believe that this place could have existed only before federal statutes provided a procedure by which trademark owners could register their marks in an effort to gain preemptive protection beyond their area of actual trade. But the Lanham Act, which created the statutory tort at issue in this suit, also provides a comprehensive registration procedure establishing preemptive rights to the extent that Congress thought desirable. . . . The trademark owner who ignores this statutory mechanism, or whose claim to trademark rights depends on a timing difference so close that the delay in federal registration processing is fatal, cannot be heard to complain about its failure to preempt subsequent good faith users."[78]

In *Tally-Ho, Inc.,*[79] the Eleventh Circuit espoused a flexible approach to the doctrine: "[I]f the senior user has constantly expanded its business by the date of the junior user's adoption of the mark, and if distances are not great, it may be that the senior user is entitled to exclusive rights in a zone of natural expansion which includes the junior user's area, even though no actual sales have yet been made in that area by the senior user."

> "[T]here are few firm guidelines to define the senior user's imaginary zone of natural expansion. However, several criteria seem relevant:

> "(1) How great is the geographical distance from the senior user's actual location to a point on the perimeter of the zone of expansion?

> "(2) What is the nature of the business? Does it already have a large or small zone of actual market penetration or reputation?

> "(3) What is the history of the senior user's past expansion? Has it remained static for years, or has it continually expanded into new territories? Extrapolating prior expansion, how long would it take the senior user to reach the periphery of the expansion zone he claims?

> "(4) Would it require an unusual 'great leap forward' for the senior user to enter the zone, or is the zone so close to existing locations that expansion would be (or is) a logical, gradual, step of the same length as those previously made?

> In addition, the 'zone of territorial protection is determined by the nature of the [user's] business.' "[80]

---

[77] *See* § 5E[2][c].

[78] 635 F.2d at 930-31.

[79] Tally-Ho, Inc. v. Coast Community College District, 889 F.2d 1018, 13 U.S.P.Q.2d 1133 (11th Cir. 1989).

[80] 899 F.2d at 1028, 13 U.S.P.Q.2d at 1140-41. *See also* Spartan Food Systems, Inc. v. HFS Corp., 813 F.2d 1279, 1283, 2 U.S.P.Q.2d 1063, 1066 (4th Cir. 1987) (junior user not entitled to "zone of natural expansion" of a whole state, Virginia, when it operated only two restaurants in one part of state; there is "nothing to suggest it dominates contiguous areas"; and it had no specific plans to expand).

[v] *Relevance of State Boundaries.* In a concurring opinion in *Hanover Star Milling,* Justice Holmes suggested that state boundaries should be given weight in determining the scope of the respective rights of a first and second user.

Some court decisions follow or approve of the Holmes' integral state market theory.[81] Most confine junior users to the actual market penetration area without regard to state boundaries.[82] For example, in *Spartan Food Systems,*[83] one party,

---

[81] *E.g.,* Younker v. Nationwide Mutual Ins. Co., 175 Ohio 1, 191 N.E.2d 145, 150-51, 152, 137 U.S.P.Q. 901 (1963) (granting statewide protection to local insurance agency's tradename "Securance"; "One's interest in a trademark, service mark or trade name is entitled to legal protection in the territory from which he receives, or with the probable expansion of his business may reasonably expect to receive, custom in the business in which he uses his trademark, service mark or trade name. . . . The Court of Appeals found from the evidence that plaintiff uses the word, 'Securance,' in both daily and weekly newspapers circulating in Sandusky County and in advertisements on radio and television broadcasts originating in Sandusky, Lucas, Wood, Ottawa, Erie, Huron, Seneca and Hancock Counties. These broadcasts are transmitted to Sandusky County as well as other counties adjoining the county of transmission. The evidence in this case indicates that, although the bulk of plaintiff's business is conducted in Sandusky County, about 25 per cent thereof is conducted in Lucas County; that plaintiff sells insurance in 12 states other than Ohio; and that about 10 per cent of plaintiff's business is from outside the state of Ohio. Apparently plaintiff contemplates establishing an office in Arizona. Under the evidence it would appear that reasonable geographical limitations on the legal protection to which plaintiff is entitled would encompass the entire state in which it is operating, since there is a probable expansion of its business throughout the state."; TAFT, dissenting: "the extent of the right to a service mark depends upon the extent of the use or the probability of use in a territory for which the right to the mark is claimed. Here the plaintiff is a local insurance agency. The probability of plaintiff's use of the mark very far from Sandusky County would be very remote.").

Cf. Wrist-Rocket Mfg. Co. v. Saunders Archery Co., 578 F.2d 727, 732, 198 U.S.P.Q. 257 (8th Cir. 1978) (the senior user "contends that geographical market areas smaller than whole states should have been considered. He cites Safeway Stores, Inc. v. Safeway Quality Foods, Inc., 433 F.2d 99 (7th Cir. 1970); Burger King v. Hoots, 403 F.2d 904 (7th Cir. 1968); and Jerrico, Inc. v. Jerry's, Inc., 376 F. Supp. 1079 (S.D. Fla. 1974). Each case involved the rights of a common-law owner of a trademark used as the name of retail establishments which had geographically small areas of market power. By contrast, [the parties's] slingshots were sold . . . in interstate commerce to jobbers and retail chains which placed them on countless store shelves across the country. Because of the nature of the product and the channels of distribution utilized, it was proper for the District Court to use whole states as market areas."); Grocers Baking Co. v. Sigler, 132 F.2d 498, 502 (6th Cir. 1942) ("the appellant had built up a state-wide business in 'Honey-Krust' bread products long prior to appellee's use of the particular label. Good will may exist in a given territory where no business is done by the possessor of the good will. . . . The state has been held to be an appropriate division of trade territory. . . . Since positive and uncontradicted testimony establishes here the existence of a state-wide good will, the circumstance that appellee established his bread route a short while before appellant definitely entered [the area] is no defense to the application for injunction."); Noah's, Inc. v. Nark, Inc., 560 F. Supp. 1253, 222 U.S.P.Q. 697 (E.D.Mo. 1983), *aff'd,* 728 F.2d 410 (8th Cir. 1984) (plaintiff's single Des Moines restaurant enjoys a statewide reputation in Iowa; therefore, plaintiff has rights to the entire state or to expand within that state).

[82] *E.g.,* Food Fair Stores, Inc. v. Square Deal Market Co., Inc., 206 F.2d 482 (D.C. Cir. 1953), *cert. denied,* 346 U.S. 937 (1954) ("the secondary meaning of the words 'Food Fair'

Spartan, began using its mark "QUINCY'S" for restaurants in 1976. In 1984, it obtained a federal registration of its mark. The other party, H.F.S., began use of "QUINCY'S" for its restaurant in 1979 in northern Virginia suburbs of Washington, D.C. H.F.S. obtained a Virginia state registration of "QUINCY'S" in 1982. The district court rejected Spartan's argument that it was entitled to use its mark in all areas of Virginia except Northern Virginia and enjoined Spartan from using its mark anywhere in Virginia. The appeals court reversed: "Although *Hanover Milling* and *United Drug* were decided before passage of the Lanham Act, their common law exposition of trademark rights applies today. The common law rights are restricted to the locality where the mark is used and to the area of probable expansion." [84]

In applying the Lanham Act Section 33(b) "continuous use" area defense to incontestability, the courts reject the whole-state theory. [85]

[vi] *Secondary Meaning Marks.* A mark that is descriptive or primarily merely a surname receives trademark protection only if the manufacturer or merchant using

---

must be the same in the Maryland and Virginia counties adjacent to the District of Columbia as it is in the District itself, inasmuch as this meaning was established principally by means of advertising in Washington newspapers circulating generally throughout the area. . . . We therefore are not disposed to give state boundary lines the decisive significance which plaintiff would now attach to them.").

Cf. Natural Footwear Ltd. v. Hart, Schaffner & Mark, 760 F.2d 1383, 1399 n.34, 225 U.S.P.Q. 1104, 1114 n.34 (3d Cir. 1985), *cert. denied,* 474 U.S. 920 (1985) ("In the instant case, we consider Roots' market penetration on a state-by-state basis. We do not take this approach because we subscribe to Justice Holmes' theory of trademark appropriation announced in his concurring opinion in Hanover. . . . We have already rejected the Holmes' theory of the territorial scope of a trademark. . . . Our methodology in this case is also not reflective of our view that the area defined by state borders is most appropriate for evaluating the market penetration of the specific product. Thus, this case is unlike Wrist-Rocket Mfg. Co. v. Saunders Archery Co., 578 F.2d 727, 732 (8th Cir. 1978), in which the court concluded that state borders defined the market area for a special sling shot '[b]ecause of the nature of the product and the channels of distribution utilized.' We are, rather, compelled to consider Roots' market penetration within the states, because the only evidence presented at trial is categorized according to the state responsible for the sales. Under optimal conditions, we would scrutinize the product's market penetration on the basis of natural trading areas that may or may not be coextensive with a state's borders. In fact, for most products, including traditional wearing apparel and footwear, the relevant geographic market will comprise only a relatively small portion of a state (*e.g.,* the Pittsburgh area) or of several states (*e.g.,* the Delaware Valley area). Unfortunately the evidence precludes any opportunity to conduct this more meaningful market analysis.").

[83] Spartan Food Systems, Inc. v. HFS Corp., 813 F.2d 1279, 2 U.S.P.Q.2d 1063 (4th Cir. 1987).

[84] 813 F.2d at 1282, 2 U.S.P.Q.2d at 1065.

The court refused to follow the dictum in Armand's Subway, Inc. v. Doctor's Associates, Inc., 604 F.2d 849, 850-51 n.3 (4th Cir. 1979): "In delineating geographical areas for trademark use, whole States are the usual unit. . . . This may be a historical survival of the origin of trademark protection as part of the law of unfair competition. Perhaps individual areas less than statewide might be appropriate under certain circumstances. The sandwich shops in the instant case draw walk-in trade from a small surrounding area. The manufacture of brick is another local industry, where high transportation costs limit penetration of a wide market."

[85] *See* § 5E[2][c][ii].

it shows that it has acquired secondary meaning.[86] With such marks, some decisions modify the market penetration standard, requiring not only that the user advertise or make some use of the mark in the area but that mark has acquired secondary meaning there.

In *Shoppers Fair of Arkansas*,[87] plaintiff began opening "Shoppers Fair" discount department stores in various states. In 1961, defendant opened an "IGA Shoppers Fair" supermarket grocery store in Fort Smith, Arkansas. Defendant's president had never heard of plaintiff's stores and selected the name after a passer-by suggested that the pre-opening decorations looked "just like a fair." Plaintiff's stores did not advertise nationally. In 1961, its store closest to Fort Smith was in Tulsa Oklahoma, 138 miles away, which had been open less than nine months. Plaintiff had taken concrete steps to open a Fort Smith store. Some of the Tulsa Shoppers Fair's advertising did reach the Fort Smith area, but the trial court found that plaintiff's name "Shoppers Fair" had not achieved secondary meaning in Fort Smith. The Eighth Circuit affirmed denial of plaintiff's request for an injunction, stressing the defendant's good faith and the absence of secondary meaning in the local market.

Some decisions give the local secondary meaning corollary limited scope because of increased customer mobility and wider product distribution patterns. In *Fuddruckers*,[88] the Ninth Circuit held erroneous a jury instruction that plaintiff, a national restaurant chain, must show secondary meaning for its restaurant decor trade dress in the Phoenix, Arizona, area prior to the date defendant opened a restaurant with allegedly infringing trade dress in Phoenix.

> "The source of the geographical and time limitations the court included in its instructions is a line of cases defining rights in unregistered trademarks between geographically remote users who adopted similar marks in good faith and without knowledge of each other's use. . . . The rule that developed in those cases permits junior users to continue to use a mark adopted in good faith in the geographical area of the junior user's actual use. The rule has only limited applicability to services such as hotels or restaurants, because their customers 'are ambulatory and on the move back and forth across the nation.'
>
> . . .

---

[86] *See* §5C[3][a][vii].

[87] Shoppers Fair of Arkansas, Inc. v. Sanders Co., Inc., 328 F.2d 496, 140 U.S.P.Q. 496 (8th Cir. 1964). *See also* Katz Drug Co. v. Katz, 188 F.2d 696 (8th Cir. 1951) (plaintiff's surname mark "Katz" had acquired secondary meaning in the Kansas City, Missouri, area, but not in St. Louis, Missouri, where the defendant subsequently opened a "neighborhood drug store" under his surname "Katz.").

But cf. Travelodge Corp. v. Siragusa, 228 F.Supp. 238, 241, 141 U.S.P.Q. 719 (N.D. Ala. 1964), *aff'd*, 352 F.2d 516, 147 U.S.P.Q. 379 (5th Cir. 1965) (Section 33(b)(5) defense is not available when "defendants intentionally copied and adopted plaintiff's mark. . . . While the courts in some of the trademark cases lay emphasis upon the fact of an established secondary significance of plaintiff's mark in the area where defendant subsequently uses the mark, it will be noted, however, that in most, if not all, of those cases the junior user has unwittingly and unknowingly imitated plaintiff's mark. Where intentional appropriation is shown there is no requirement for the establishment of such secondary significance.").

[88] Fuddruckers, Inc. v. Doc's B.R. Others, Inc., 826 F.2d 837, 4 U.S.P.Q.2d 1026 (9th Cir. 1987).

> "[Defendant] concedes that it was aware of [plaintiff's] operations, and familiar with its trade dress, so the good faith junior user line of cases does not apply here. . . . [Plaintiff] is a national restaurant chain, and restaurant customers travel. . . . [It] should be permitted to show that its trade dress had acquired secondary meaning among some substantial portion of consumers nationally."[89]

[c] **Lanham Act Effect.** The Lanham Act's primary purpose was to create nation-wide trademark rights. Its provisions recognize but limit the *Hanover Star Milling-United Drug* common law good faith remote market use rule. The constructive notice and use provisions restrict junior user trademark rights acquisition. The registration and incontestability provisions limit the scope of existing local user rights.

[i] *Constructive Notice: Post-Registration Use.* Lanham Act registration is constructive notice of the registrant's rights.[90] A person cannot obtain concurrent rights in a mark otherwise confusingly similar to the registrant's mark by use beginning after the registration date.[91] Under the 1988 Trademark Revision Act,[92] registration

---

[89] 826 F.2d at 844, 4 U.S.P.Q.2d at 1031.

[90] "Registration of a mark on the principal register . . . shall be constructive notice of the registrant's claim of ownership thereof." Lanham Act §22, 15 U.S.C. §1072.

[91] If a registration is cancelled, it ceases, as of the cancellation date, to constitute constructive notice of the senior user-registrant's rights. *See* Action Temporary Services, Inc. v. Labor Force, Inc., 870 F.2d 1563, 1564, 10 U.S.P.Q.2d 1307, 1308 (Fed. Cir. 1989) ("[A] federal registration of a mark in force at the time of an applicant's adoption of the same or similar mark, which federal registration subsequently is canceled, does not prevent, as a matter of law, the applicant from being a 'lawful use[r]' of its mark, within the meaning of section 2(d) of the Lanham Act, subsequent to that cancellation.").

On July 1, 1975, the senior user (Labor) was granted federal registration of the mark "LABOR FORCE" for its service of supplying temporary help to others. On August 1, 1975, the junior user (Action) adopted the mark "LABOR FORCE" for its temporary help service. On July 1, 1981, the PTO cancelled the senior user's registration for failure to file a Section 8 continuing use affidavit. On July 21, 1982, senior user filed a new application to register the same mark for the same services. On February 2, 1984, junior user filed an application to register its mark. The PTO instituted a concurrent use proceeding. The TTAB determined that junior user was not a lawful concurrent user because, on the date of its adoption of the mark, senior user's registration was still effective and constituted constructive notice of its rights to junior user. The court reversed:

> "[A] canceled registration does not provide constructive notice of anything. . . . A canceled registration cannot prevent a party from being a 'lawful user' of a mark when that party's use is subsequent to the cancellation of the federal registration. . . . Whereas actual notice, once obtained by a party of another party's use of a mark, exists independent of the event giving rise to that notice, constructive notice, . . . exists, and lasts, only as long as the federal registration giving rise to that constructive notice remains in effect. . . . [I]n view of the existence of [the senior user's] federal registration, [the junior user's] use of its mark during the pendency of [senior user's] federal registration cannot be deemed 'lawful use.' Nevertheless, [the junior user's] use following the cancellation of [senior user's] federal registration was not subject to any former constructive notice effects of that registration." 870 F.2d at 1565, 10 U.S.P.Q.2d at 1309.

The court directed that, on remand, the TTAB should determine the relative rights of the parties, including the effects of the junior user's actual notice of the senior user's mark, "bearing

constitutes "constructive use" of the mark by the registrant as of the registration application *filing* date. A person cannot obtain rights by use beginning after the registrant's filing date.[93]

A court will enjoin further use by a person who began use in an area after the Lanham Act registrant's constructive notice or constructive use date only when the registrant penetrates the market so as to create a likelihood of confusion.[94]

> "After the Lanham Act, nationwide protection was extended to registered marks, regardless of the area in which the registrant actually used the mark, because . . . registration constituted constructive notice to competing users. . . . However, . . . the protection is only potential in areas where the registrant in fact does not do business. A competing user could use the mark there until the registrant extended its business to the area. Thereupon the registrant would be entitled to exclusive use of the mark and to injunctive relief against its continued use by prior users in that area."[95]

in mind . . . that '*mere knowledge of the existence of the prior user* should not, by itself, constitute bad faith.' 870 F.2d at 1566, 10 U.S.P.Q.2d at 1310.

[92] *See* §5D[2].

[93] The constructive use as of the filing date takes effect only if the applicant actually obtains registration. If the application is rejected or abandoned, there is no constructive use effect. *See* §5D[1][e].

[94] Dawn Donut Company, Inc. v. Hart's Food Stores, Inc., 267 F.2d 358, 369 n.4, 121 U.S.P.Q. 430 (2d Cir. 1959) ("Since the statutory standard for the invocation of injunctive relief is the likelihood of confusion, it is enough that expansion by the registrant into the defendant's market is likely in the normal course of its business.").

[95] Armand's Subway, Inc. v. Doctor's Associates, Inc., 604 F.2d 849, 850, 203 U.S.P.Q. 241 (4th Cir. 1979).

See also Comidas Exquisitos, Inc. v. O'Malley & McGee's Inc., 775 F.2d 260, 227 U.S.P.Q. 811 (8th Cir. 1985); Pizzo Uno Corp. v. Temple, 747 F.2d 1522, 1524, 224 U.S.P.Q. 185 (4th Cir. 1984) ("the absence of any actual competition between plaintiff and its possible franchisees on the one hand, and the defendant, on the other hand, in the geographical area where the defendant presently operates, compels the denial of injunctive relief in plaintiff's favor at this time. On that basis, we affirm the denial of relief to the plaintiff, without prejudice to plaintiff's right to renew its claims if it or one or more of its franchisees subsequently invades the same geographical area in which the defendant, using the challenged trademark, operates."); Holiday Inns of America, Inc. v. B & B Corp., 409 F.2d 614, 617-18, 161 U.S.P.Q. 385 (3d Cir. 1969) (no injunction against defendant's use of "Holiday Inn" for hotel in Virgin Islands when plaintiff, operator of a well-known national chain, had no hotel there; "With the development of today's mobile society, capable of many changes of domiciles, frequently utilizing as sources of retail services business establishments which are located hundreds, if not thousands, of miles from these domiciles, and generally relying on or being influenced by nationally-conducted advertising campaigns, there has been a corresponding diminution of older concepts that retail services are conducted in restricted or local marketing and trading areas. So instant is our communication and so efficient our transportation that it can be said that the American market place for most nationally advertised products is the entire United States. In most retail product situations, then, the question of competition within the same market or trading area is not, ordinarily, a point of much disputation. Where motel services are concerned, however, this is not an insignificant consideration. . . . We must protect that which is protectable, but, in so doing, we must limit the use of injunctive relief to situations where

In *Dawn Donut*,[96] the court held that the Lanham Act's constructive notice provision meant that no junior user could adopt a mark in a remote market in the United States in "good faith." Since 1922, Dawn Donut had continuously used "DAWN" as a trademark on bags of doughnut mix sold to local franchised bakers, licensing mix purchasing bakers to make and sell "DAWN" donuts. It federally registered its mark in 1927 and renewed the registration in 1947 after enactment of the Lanham Act, which introduced the constructive notice provision. In 1951, Starhart Bakeries began using "DAWN" as a mark for donuts and other baked products in a 45 mile radius around Rochester, New York, an area in which neither Dawn Donut nor its franchisees made sales. Dawn Donut sued Starhart Bakers for infringement of its federally-registered mark.

The court held that Dawn Donut was not entitled to an injunction against Starhart's current use of its mark in its geographic area. Because Dawn Donut had not expanded or planned to expand into that area, Starhart's use of its mark created no likelihood

it is necessary to prevent immediate and irreparable injury. The dramatic and drastic power of injunctive force may be unleashed only against conditions generating a presently existing actual threat; it may not be used simply to eliminate a possibility of a remote future injury, or a future invasion of rights, be those rights protected by statute or by the common law. An additional complication is our conclusion that the identity of the competing marks will certainly cause confusion if and when Holiday commences operations in the Virgin Islands. In the event of such expansion into this specific island territory, appellants, already the beneficiary of Holiday's concentrated national and international advertising campaign, would, through an unauthorized use of a statutorily-protected identical trade name, be likely to deceive or create confusion as to the source, origin, and type . . . of motel services being offered to the public. Nevertheless, Holiday had no right to immediate relief because it failed to present sufficient evidence of present debasement of its protected mark, and although it established a strong case of a future likelihood of confusion if and when the identical marks would begin to compete in the same market area for identical services, the geographic location of these islands militates against a finding that there is a use by the defendants of that type of competitive commerce envisioned by Congress."); American Foods, Inc. v. Golden Flake, Inc., 312 F.2d 619, 625, 136 U.S.P.Q. 286 (5th Cir. 1963) (the district court did not error in enjoining use of the defendant's infringing mark "in what was found to be the trade territory of plaintiff, Alabama, Florida, Mississippi, Tennessee, Georgia and that part of the State of Louisiana east of the Mississippi River" and denying relief "as to the remaining portions of the United States. Some ninety five per cent of the total business of plaintiff was done in Alabama with the remaining portion being done in the balance of the area included in the order. This was the situation after thirty eight years of doing business. There was no evidence presented that plaintiff might expand its business to other areas. Its advertising program covered no other area. . . . [T]he protection of the Act runs only to those areas where the trade-mark has gone on the goods through sale or advertisement, together with such additional areas as are warranted under the evidence for expansion.").

Compare Tisch Hotels, Inc. v. Americana Inn, Inc., 350 F.2d 609, 615 n.6, 146 U.S.P.Q. 566 (7th Cir. 1965) ("Federal court cases, whether based on trademark infringement, unfair competition, or state anti-dilution statutes, and involving hotels, motels or restaurants with the same or similar names have been practically unanimous in awarding injunctive relief to the prior user of the name who has established a national or widespread reputation for the name, even though the establishments are separated geographically and not in competition.").

[96] Dawn Donut Company, Inc. v. Hart's Food Stores, Inc., 267 F.2d 358, 121 U.S.P.Q. 430 (2d Cir. 1959).

of confusion,[97] but should Dawn Donut expand into the area in the future, it would have superior rights and could obtain injunctive relief. Starhart obtained no common law rights in its area because its use began after Dawn Donut's 1947 registration, which constituted nationwide constructive notice.[98]

The court rejected Starhart's "regional abandonment" argument, to wit, that Dawn Donut "abandoned" its rights in the defined area by failure to expand into it for over thirty years.[99] Abandonment under the Lanham Act means failure to use a mark anywhere in the United States, not failure to use a mark in particular areas.[100]

---

[97] The court noted:

"[B]ecause plaintiff and defendant use the mark in connection with retail sales in distinct and separate markets and because there is no present prospect that plaintiff will expand its use of the mark at the retail level into defendant's trading area, we conclude that there is no likelihood of public confusion arising from the concurrent use of the marks and therefore the issuance of an injunction is not warranted." 267 F.2d at 365.

[98] The court noted:

"But the Lanham Act, 15 U.S.C.A. 1072, provides that registration of a trademark on the principal register is constructive notice of the registrant's claim of ownership. Thus, by eliminating the defense of good faith and lack of knowledge, 1072 affords nationwide protection to registered marks, regardless of the areas in which the registrant actually uses the mark. . . .

"That such is the purpose of Congress is further evidenced by 15 U.S.C.A. 1115(a) and (b) which make the certificate of registration evidence of the registrant's 'exclusive right to use the . . . mark in commerce.' . . . 'Commerce' is defined in 15 U.S.C.A. 1127 to include all the commerce which may lawfully be regulated by Congress. These two provisions of the Lanham Act make it plain that the fact that the defendant employed the mark 'Dawn,' without actual knowledge of plaintiff's registration, at the retail level in a limited geographical area of New York state before the plaintiff used the mark in that market, does not entitle it either to exclude the plaintiff from using the mark in that area or to use the mark concurrently once the plaintiff licenses the mark or otherwise exploits it in connection with retail sales in the area." 267 F.2d at 362-63.

Accord: Old Dutch Foods, Inc. v. Dan Dee Pretzel & Potato Chip Co., 477 F.2d 150, 156, 177 U.S.P.Q. 496 (6th Cir. 1973) ("Contrary to the common law, a registrant of a valid trademark has rights in his mark even in areas in which he does not conduct business."); John R. Thompson Co. v. Holloway, 366 F.2d 108, 114, 150 U.S.P.Q. 728 (5th Cir. 1966) ("By eliminating the defense of good faith and lack of knowledge on the part of the junior user, sections 1072 and 1115 (giving the exclusive right to use the mark) afford a registrant nationwide protection for its registered marks, regardless of the geographic area in which the registrant actually uses his mark.").

[99] See §5D[3][b][i].

[100] " . . . . 15 U.S.C.A. §1127, which provides for abandonment in certain cases of non-use, . . . applies only when the registrant fails to use his mark, within the meaning of §1127, anywhere in the nation. Since the Lanham Act affords a registrant nationwide protection, a contrary holding would create an insoluble problem of measuring the geographical extent of the abandonment. Even prior to the passage of the Lanham Act, when trademark protection flowed from state law and therefore depended on use within the state, no case, as far as we have been able to ascertain, held that a trademark owner abandoned his rights within only part of a state because of his failure to use the mark in that part of the state." 267 F.2d at 363.

[ii]   *Freezing the Junior User's Market—Relation to State Common Law Rights.*
The Lanham Act preserves a junior user's common law remote area use rights even
after the senior user registers the mark,[101] but it freezes the scope of a junior
mark user's rights to the area in which he has used the mark continuously from a
date prior to registration.[102] State law may grant the junior user more limited
rights,[103] but the Lanham Act preempts any state law that expands junior rights

[101] Trademark claimants commonly use Lanham Act Section 43(a) to assert what are in
effect trademark infringement claims as to registered and unregistered marks. Courts apply the
common law and Lanham Act good faith remote user rule to Section 43(a) actions. *E.g.,*
GTE Corp. v. Williams, 904 F.2d 536, 542, 14 U.S.P.Q.2d 1971, 1976 (10th Cir. 1990), *cert.
denied,* 111 S. Ct. 557 (1990) ("We agree with Professor McCarthy . . . that when '§43(a) is
used as the basis for an alternative count along with a count for infringement of a registered
mark, a good faith remote use defense good against the registration should be good against
the §43(a) count as well.' "); Spartan Food Systems, Inc. v. H.F.S. Corp., 813 F.2d 1279, 2
U.S.P.Q.2d 1063 (4th Cir. 1987); Matador Motor Inns, Inc. v. Matador Motel, Inc., 376 F.
Supp. 385, 390, 182 U.S.P.Q. 460 (D.N.J. 1974) ("if innocent prior adoption in a particular
area has been proved as a defense to a service mark infringement action, then that innocent
prior adoption must also serve as a defense to a section 1125(a) action. . . . It would be
incongruous for this Court to find that defendant innocently adopted plaintiff's mark, thereby
giving defendant the right to use that mark in the area of continuous prior use, and then find
that defendant has engaged in a false designation or representation of origin.").

[102] A senior user's Lanham Act application *filing* date is "nationwide constructive use" after
registration issues, see §5415, but it does not operate to freeze the scope of a pre- filing date
junior user's rights.

The constructive use provision excepts any person "whose mark has not been abandoned
and who, prior to such filing—(1) has used the mark; (2) has filed an application to register
the mark which is pending or has resulted in registration of the mark; or (3) has filed a
foreign application to register the mark on the basis of which he or she has acquired a right
of priority, and timely files an application under section 44(d) to register the mark which is
pending or has resulted in registration of the mark." Lanham Act §7(c), 15 U.S.C. §1057(c).

See United States Trademark Association Review Commission Report (1987) ("The filing
of an intent-to-use or use-based application could not constitute nationwide constructive use
against anyone who used a mark before the filing date. According a filing date nationwide
constructive use is policy-justified as against a subsequent user who either knew of, or could
have searched, applicant's earlier trademark claim. A prior user, of course, cannot initially
know of a later-filed application. It would thus be inequitable to permit that application to
freeze the prior user's right to territorial expansion. Questions of priority and territorial rights
involving prior users should continue to be decided as under current law.").

[103] In Golden Door, Inc. v. Odisho, 646 F.2d 347, 208 U.S.P.Q. 638 (9th Cir. 1980), the
senior user began use in 1959 of "GOLDEN DOOR" for its health spa in Escondido, California.
It obtained federal registration of its mark in 1966. The junior user began good faith use in
1965 of "GOLDEN DOOR" for its hair salon in San Mateo County, California, approximately
500 miles from Escondido. The court held that the Lanham Act preserved the junior user's
use rights but that under California state law, the senior user could obtain an injunction against
such use. The court noted:

"Under California law, however, prior innocent use is no defense to claims for unfair
competition or tradename and trademark infringement. . . . [D]efendant contends that his
[federal Lanham Act] §1115(b) defense protects him from state as well as federal injunctive
relief. He relies principally on dicta from Mister Donut of America, Inc. v. Mr. Donut,

beyond the *Hanover Star-United Drug* common law good faith remote market use rule.

If the senior user registers and takes proper steps after five years to make his right to use incontestable, Section 33(b)(5) expressly limits the junior user's rights. It provides a defense to the registrant's conclusive exclusive right to use the mark only if "the mark whose use by a party is charged as an infringement was adopted without knowledge of the registrant's prior use and has been continuously used by such party or those in privity with him from a date prior to" the registration or constructive use (filing) date.[104]

In *Burger King*,[105] plaintiff Burger King of Florida, Inc. opened a "BURGER KING" restaurant in Florida in 1953 and steadily expanded thereafter. In July of

---

Inc., 418 F.2d 838, 844 (9th Cir. 1969), wherein the court said: 'What the effect of this California statutory provision might be if the Lanham Act had not been passed by Congress, we need not decide. The Lanham Act has pre-empted the field of trademark law and controls. It follows that the defense provided in Sec. 1115(b)(5) of the Act cannot be voided by state statute.'

"... In [Mariniello v. Shell Oil Co., 511 F.2d 853 (3rd Cir. 1975),] the 3rd Circuit said: 'Where conflict is alleged between federal and state law, the specific purpose of the federal act must be ascertained in order to assess any potential erosion of the federal plan by operation of the state law. The limited intent of Congress in enacting the Lanham Act is thus crucial to the discussion in the present case. Within the ambit of its intended operation, the Lanham Act expresses a Congressional design to legislate so that the public can buy with confidence, and the trademark holder will not be pirated. If state law would permit confusing or deceptive trademarks to operate, infringing on the guarantee of exclusive use to federal trademark holders, then the state law would, under the Supremacy Clause, be invalid. . . . ' 511 F.2d at 858.

"... [W]e agree with this preemption analysis of the Lanham Act and reject the *Mister Donut* dicta. Under this analysis §1115(b) cannot be said to preempt this plaintiff's rights under California law. By extending to federal registrants greater protection than is available under the Lanham Act, California law, like the Act, protects both the public from confusion about the services and products it is receiving and the public relations investment of plaintiff." 646 F.2d at 351-52.

[104] Lanham Act §33(b)(5), 15 U.S.C. §1115(b)(5). The date is the constructive use, that is, filing date, if the application for registration is filed on or after the 1988 Trademark Revision Act's effective date, which is November 16, 1989.

For registrations based on pre-November 16, 1989 filings, a junior user could establish rights by good faith adoption and use between the senior user's filing date and the registration. *See, e.g.,* Value House v. Phillips Mercantile Co., 523 F.2d 424, 430, 187 U.S.P.Q. 657 (10th Cir. 1975) (plaintiff's "contention is that since defendant would not have a concurrent right to use the mark for lack of use prior to first filing of plaintiff's application for registration under [Section 2(d)], he should likewise be denied such a defense under [Section 33(a)]. Plaintiff points to the delay between applications being filed and registration and the anomaly of the result if a prior use defense is recognized under §1115(a) when concurrent use rights could not be obtained because of prior filing by another user. The difficulty for plaintiff is that the statute is quite clear in making the availability of the defense turn on use prior to registration . . . , the defense being provided only for the area in which such continuous prior use is proved. . . . Regardless of any appeal of the policy arguments advanced, we can go no further than the plain terms of the statute.").

[105] Burger King of Florida, Inc. v. Hoots, 403 F.2d 904, 159 U.S.P.Q. 706 (7th Cir. 1968).

1961, it opened its first Illinois restaurant, in Skokie. On October 3, 1961, it obtained Lanham Act registration of its mark, and in 1966, its exclusive right to use its mark became incontestable.[106] In 1957, defendant opened a "BURGER KING" restaurant in Mattoon, Illinois. In 1959, it obtained an Illinois state registration of its mark. In 1962, with constructive notice of plaintiff's registered mark, it opened a second restaurant, in Charleston, Illinois. The parties sued each other for trademark infringement.

Rejecting the defendant's contention that it was entitled to all of Illinois because of its first use in that state, the court granted plaintiff relief against defendant's use of "BURGER KING" anywhere except in the Mattoon, Illinois, area in which it had actually used the mark before plaintiff's federal registration.[107] State registration could not expand the junior user's actual area.[108]

If the Lanham Act registrant's right to use was contestable, Section 33(b)(5) did not apply before the 1988 Trademark Revision Act amended it,[109] but the courts reached substantially the same result by applying the common law good faith remote use defense in conjunction with the Lanham Act's constructive notice provision.

In *Spartan Food Systems*,[110] Spartan had used "QUINCY'S" for restaurant services in interstate commerce since 1976, operating more than 200 restaurants in

[106] For a discussion of the Lanham Act's incontestability provisions, see § 5E[1].

[107] "Under 15 U.S.C. 1065 [§15] of the Act, plaintiffs, owners of the federally registered trade mark 'Burger King,' have the 'incontestable' right to use the mark in commerce, except to the extent that such use infringes what valid right the defendants have acquired by their continuous use of the same mark prior to plaintiffs' federal registration.

"Under 15 U.S.C. 1115(b) [§33(b)], the federal certificate of registration is 'conclusive evidence' of plaintiffs' 'exclusive right' to use the mark. This Section, however, also provides a defense to an exclusive right to use a trade mark: If a trade mark was adopted without knowledge of the federal registrant's prior use, and has been continuously used, then such use 'shall' constitute a defense to infringement, provided that this defense applies only for the area in which such continuous prior use is proved. Since the defendants have established that they had adopted the mark 'Burger King' without knowledge of plaintiffs' prior use and that they had continuously used the mark from a date prior to plaintiffs' federal registration of the mark, they are entitled to protection in the area which that use appropriated to them." 403 F.2d at 907.

[108] ". . . [W]hether or not Illinois intended to enlarge the common law with respect to a right of exclusivity in that state, the Illinois Act does not enlarge its right in the area where the federal mark has priority. . . . Congress expanded the common law, however, by granting an exclusive right in commerce to federal registrants in areas where there has been no offsetting use of the mark. Congress intended the Lanham Act to afford nation-wide protection to federally-registered marks, and that once the certificate has issued, no person can acquire any additional rights superior to those obtained by the federal registrant." 403 F.2d at 908.

See also Allied Telephone Co., Inc. v. Allied Telephone Systems Co., Inc., 565 F.Supp. 211, 217, 218 U.S.P.Q. 817, 821 (S.D. Ohio. 1982) ("Congress could easily have employed the term 'state' in lieu of the statutory term 'area,' but it did not. Instead, Congress used the more flexible term area and focused the inquiry on whether there had actually been continuous use in such area prior to the date of registration.").

[109] *See* §5E[1][c].

[110] Spartan Food Systems, Inc. v. H.F.S. Corp., 813 F.2d 1279, 2 U.S.P.Q.2d 1063 (4th Cir. 1987).

six Southern states. It registered its mark on August 21, 1984. H.F.S. had operated two "QUINCY" restaurants since September 1979 in Arlington and McLean, northern Virginia suburbs of Washington, D.C. In 1982, H.F.S. obtained a Virginia state registration for "QUINCY'S." In 1984, Spartan, knowing of H.F.S.'s use of QUIN-CY's opened three QUINCY'S restaurant in Newport News, Hampton, and Martinsville, Virginia. H.F.S. asserted entitlement to the exclusive use of "QUINCY's" throughout Virginia. The district court ruled for H.F.S., reasoning that because Spartan's federal registration was not incontestable, H.F.S. could assert its state registration as a defense to Spartan's Lanham Act claim to all of Virginia except northern Virginia. The Fourth Circuit reversed. It agreed that because Spartan's registration was not incontestable, Section 33(a), not 33(b), applied, and H.F.S. could rebut Spartan's *prima facie* exclusive right. H.F.S. offered no proof that Spartan's registration was invalid or defective. "Therefore, the scope of its defense under §33(a) and the geographical extent of the injunction it seeks under §43(a) are governed by common law as expounded by the Supreme Court [in *Hanover Star Milling* and *Metcalf*] . . ." which confines H.F.S.'s right to its area of actual penetration, northern Virginia. To the extent Virginia state law purports to expand common law trademark rights beyond the actual use area, it is preempted by the Lanham Act's constructive notice provision.[111]

The 1988 Trademark Revision Act amended Section 33(a) to say that an infringer may rely on Section 33(b) defenses and defects to rebut the registrant's *prima facie* exclusive right to use the mark, but these potential defenses are in addition to any legal or equitable defense "which might have been asserted if such mark had not been registered."

The Lanham Act confines a junior user to the area in which he used the mark continuously up to and after registration[112] In *Casual Corner Associates*,[113] the Ninth Circuit held that a junior user's use was not "continuing" when it ceased mark use for a one-year period. The court rejected the argument that "there is a continuing use within the meaning of the statute unless the owner has abandoned the mark."

> "To be a continuing use, the use must be maintained without interruption. . . . To equate continuing with a failure to abandon would shift the burden from the state-right claimant to the owner of a valid and incontestable trademark. Such a result would be inconsistent with the statute and with the protection afforded by the trademark laws."[114]

---

[111] 813 F.2d at 1282, 2 U.S.P.Q.2d at 1064-65. For a discussion of the "whole state" theory of common law junior user rights, see §5E[2][b][v].

[112] *E.g.*, Thrifty Rent-A-Car System, Inc. v. Thrift Cars, Inc., 831 F.2d 1177, 1182-83, 4 U.S.P.Q.2d 1709, 1713 (1st Cir. 1987) ("the scope of protection afforded by §1115(b)(5) is limited. . . . The policy behind the Lanham Act is very strong and the party challenging the federal registrant has the burden of showing a continued and actual market presence in order to qualify for the 'limited area' exception under the statute. . . . Under § 1115(b)(5), the junior user must show that it has made continuous use of the mark prior to the issuance of the senior user's registration and must further prove continued use up until trial. . . . Otherwise, the defense 'dries up' and the junior user cannot assert rights in the limited trade area.")

[113] Casual Corner Associates, Inc. v. Casual Stores of Nevada, Inc., 493 F.2d 709, 181 U.S.P.Q. 429 (9th Cir. 1974).

[114] 493 F.2d at 712.

Freezing and continuing use do not mean that the junior user can make no changes in his or her business. In *Safeway Stores, Inc.*,[115] the court held that a junior user's entitlement to use the senior user's registered mark "SAFEWAY" for grocery stores in the Indianapolis area should not be "limited to the conditions existing" on the registration date: "[I]t would be reasonable to expect a store owner to repair and improve his place of business, and it makes no difference whether such store be labeled market, super-market or corner grocery store."

[d] **Concurrent Lanham Act Registration.** The Lanham Act authorizes concurrent registrations of the same or similar marks when two or more persons "have become entitled to use such marks as a result of their concurrent lawful use in commerce."[116] Concurrent registration allows persons who establish trademark rights in remote market areas under the *Hanover Star-United Drug* rule to obtain Lanham Act registration benefits for those areas, including constructive notice and *prima facie* and conclusive exclusive rights.[117]

There are two routes to concurrent registration. First, the PTO may issue concurrent registrations if (1) the concurrent lawful uses began prior to "the earliest of the filing dates of the applications pending or of any registration"[118] and (2) it

---

[115] Safeway Stores, Inc. v. Safeway Quality Foods, Inc., 433 F.2d 99, 166 U.S.P.Q. 112 (7th Cir. 1970).

[116] Lanham Act §2(d), 15 U.S.C. §1052(d). The Lanham Act wins no awards for ease of comprehension. Concurrent registration authorization is stated as a proviso to Section 2(d)'s prior use registration bar. *See* § 5C[4][e]. Section 1(a), which states use-based registration application requirements, also contains a proviso directed to concurrent use:

> "Provided, That in the case of every application claiming concurrent use the applicant shall state exceptions to his claim of exclusive use, in which he shall specify, to the extent of his knowledge, any concurrent use by others, the goods on or in connection with which and the areas in which each concurrent use exists, the periods of each use, and the goods and area for which the applicant desires registration."

Lanham Act §1(a)(1)(A), 15 U.S.C. §1051(a)(1)(A). Concurrent use applications cannot be based on an "intent-to-use." *See* § 5D[1][b].

The Act has no section setting forth concurrent use proceeding procedure. *See* 37 CFR § 2.99. Section 17 provides that the Trademark Trial and Appeal Board determines registration rights in every case of "application to register as a lawful concurrent user." Lanham Act §17, 15 U.S.C. § 1067. Section 18 authorizes the action the PTO may take, which under a 1988 amendment, includes the power to "restrict or rectify" a registration, and directs the PTO "to determine and fix the conditions and limitations provided for" in Section 2(d). Lanham Act §18, 15 U.S.C. §1068. *See* § 5D[2][d][v].

[117] Concurrent use registration rights may arise when a trademark owner assigns his rights in discrete territories to different persons. See Houlihan v. Parliament Import Co., 921 F.2d 1258, 1261, 17 U.S.P.Q.2d 1208, 1211 (Fed. Cir. 1990) ("Nothing [in Lanham Act Section 2(d)'s concurrent use provision] precludes the Commissioner from issuing a concurrent registration merely because the prior owner of the mark assigned it for two contiguous domestic areas. . . . The criteria for granting concurrent use registration relate not to the prior ownership of the mark but to the likelihood of confusion resulting from such concurrent use.").

[118] The 1988 Trademark Revision Act added a consent exception to the filing date requirement: "Use prior to the filing date of any pending application or a registration shall not be required when the owner of such application or registration consents to the grant of a concurrent registration to the applicant." Lanham Act § 2(d), 15 U.S.C. §1052(d).

"determines that confusion, mistake, or deception is not likely to result from the continued use by more than one person of the same or similar marks under conditions and limitations as to the mode or place of use of the marks or the goods on or in connection with which such marks are used." Second, "[c]oncurrent registrations may also be issued by the Commissioner when a court of competent jurisdiction has finally determined that more than one person is entitled to use the same or similar marks in commerce."[119]

[i] *First User's Rights—Beatrice Foods.* The first major concurrent use proceeding court decision was *Beatrice Foods.*[120] The two parties began using the same mark for related products in discrete markets. They applied for Lanham Act registration in the reverse order of their use.

In 1953, Beatrice ("prior user") began use of "HOMESTEAD" for margarine. In 1956, Fairway ("prior applicant") began use of "HOMESTEAD" for diary products and baked goods and, in 1962, applied for Lanham Act registration. Prior user, Beatrice, filed an opposition. The two reached an agreement geographically dividing the nation; prior applicant received all or part of certain states,[121] which were deemed within its marketing area or area of probable expansion; prior user received the rest of the United States. To implement the agreement, prior applicant amended its registration application to restrict it to the agreed area, and prior user filed an application to register for the United States except for the area allocated to the prior applicant.

The Patent Office instituted a concurrent use proceeding between the parties. The Trademark Trial and Appeals Board ("TTAB") refused to follow the parties' agreement in two respects. First, it ruled that the prior user showed sufficient use of the mark only in 20 states and was therefore not entitled to registration covering all of the United States other than that allocated to the first applicant-second user. Second, it ruled that the first applicant-second user, Fairway, showed only an intent to expand, not sufficient use, in two areas allocated to it in the agreement, the Upper Peninsula of Michigan and the eastern portion of Montana. It relied in part on activity occurring after it filed its application. The Board stressed that (1) parties could not resolve by agreement a question that must be decided by the Patent Office and (2)

See H.R. Rep. No. 100-1028, 100th Cong., 2d Sess. 10 (1988) ("the amendment does not alter two important aspects of the law governing the issuance of concurrent use registrations. First, the Commissioner must still determine that confusion and deception are not likely to occur if the concurrent use registration is issued. Second, to prevent such confusion and deception, the Commissioner continues to be able to impose conditions relating to the mode and place of use of the marks.")

For a discussion of the impact of consent agreements on Section 2(d) bars, see § 5C[4][b]. *Beatrice Foods,* discussed below, emphasized that the parties' agreement as to areas of use should be given weight.

[119] Lanham Act §2(d), 15 U.S.C. §1052(d). *See* § 5E[2][d][iv].

[120] *In re* Beatrice Foods Co., 429 F.2d 466, 166 U.S.P.Q. 431 (CCPA 1970).

[121] Specifically, it received "the states of Wisconsin, Minnesota, Iowa, South Dakota, North Dakota, certain counties comprising the eastern portion of Montana, and that area of Michigan, called the Upper Peninsula, which is contiguous with the State of Wisconsin and separated from the rest of the state by the Straits of Mackinac. Prior user claimed the area comprising the remainder of the United States." 429 F.2d at 470.

user rights sufficient to warrant registration must be in existence at the time the party files its application.

On appeal, the court reversed the TTAB's decision not to allocate the "virgin territory." First, the Section 2(d) concurrent use registration provision implements the existing law on trademark use rights of first users and subsequent good faith users in discrete geographic markets.[122] Second, the Board's refusal to allocate the entire United States frustrates the Lanham Act's policy of reducing instances of concurrent use.[123] Third, "the starting point for any determination as to the extent to which the registrations are to be territorially restricted should be the conclusion that the prior user is *prima facie* entitled to a registration covering the entire United States."[124]

---

[122] ". . . [T]he proviso . . . [recognizes] that . . . occasions . . . arise where two or more persons will independently adopt the same or a similar trademark and use it under the same or similar circumstances, and . . . [provides] a mechanism . . . for an equitable resolution of the problems which such concurrent use creates. . . . [T]he statute . . . authorizes concurrent federal registrations. Much confusion can be avoided by recognizing that such registrations would not, in and of themselves, create any new right to use the trademark or to assert rights based on ownership of the trademark itself. Rights of trademark ownership, for example, the right to enjoin another from use of the mark, must be based upon actual use and can be enforced only in areas of existing business influence (i.e., current use or probability of expansion). . . . [T]he Lanham Act did not alter this aspect of the prior law." 429 F.2d at 472.

[123] " . . . [T]he constructive notice provision of . . . the Lanham Act . . . takes away from future users of the mark registered the defense of innocent appropriation. The owner of a federal registration now has the security of knowing that no one else may, henceforth legitimately adopt his trademark and create rights in another area of the country superior to his own. . . . [This provision] is, perhaps, the best example of the intent of Congress to provide for a thriving business environment by granting nationwide protection to expanding businesses. . . . [I]t would be illogical and inconsistent with the objectives of the Lanham Act, not to provide for nationwide coverage where there is more than one registration—provided there will be no public confusion created thereby. The constructive notice provision . . . was promulgated with the hope of cutting down on the number of instances of concurrent use and the uncertainty and confusion attached thereto. . . . Leaving territory open . . . would frustrate this policy and increase rather than reduce the possibility of confusion and litigation.

"The foregoing is not intended to imply that the Patent Office is required to issue registrations covering the whole of the United States in all circumstances. Certainly the applicant or applicants may always request territorially restricted registrations. . . . In addition, in carrying out the Commissioner's duty under the proviso of 2(d) of determining whether confusion, mistake or deception is likely to result from the continued concurrent use of a mark by two or more parties, it may be held that such likelihood will be prevented only when each party is granted a very limited territory with parts of the United States [g]ranted to no one." 429 F.2d at 372-73.

[124] "[A] prior user, who applies for a registration before registration is granted to another party, is entitled to a registration having nationwide effect no less than if there were no concurrent user having registrable rights. . . . His rights and, therefore, his registration, should be limited only to the extent that any other subsequent user, who can establish the existence of rights earlier than the prior user's application for registration, can also prove a likelihood of confusion, mistake or deception." 429 F.2d at 474.

In a footnote, the court suggested that, in some circumstances, a second user might be entitled to the virgin territory: "[W]here the prior user does not apply for a registration before registration is granted to another, there may be valid grounds, based on a policy of rewarding those who first seek federal registration, and a consideration of the rights created by the existing registration, for limiting his registration to the area of actual use and permitting the prior registrant to retain the nationwide protection of the act restricted only by the territory of the prior user."[125]

The court turned to the Board's allocation of territories. First, while the parties' territory allocation agreement is not binding, the Patent Office should give it weight in resolving a concurrent use registrations.[126] Second, in determining territory allocations, the Office is not restricted to the filing date.[127] Third, as to the second user's appeal of the Office's refusal to allocate the Upper Peninsula of Michigan and the eastern counties of Montana to it, it remanded the matter, offering a comment on the question as to "what circumstances, if any, short of actual use of the trademark, may create rights in a territory sufficient to warrant inclusion of that territory in a geographically restricted registration." It indicated that a party's area of "probable expansion" should be allocated to that party to implement the concurrent user statute's direction to avoid confusion.[128]

---

[125] 429 F.2d at 476 n.13.

[126] ". . . [W]e see no reason why agreements such as that worked out by the parties here should not be considered. Unquestionably, such stipulations are never binding on the board. Nevertheless, if it can be determined that they are in good faith, there can be no better assurance of the absence of any likelihood of confusion, mistake or deception than the parties' promises to avoid any activity which might lead to such likelihood.

"It is not to be inferred that the Patent Office should blindly adhere to any agreement or territorial stipulation made by the parties. Such arrangements should always be critically appraised. But the practical value of accepting agreements such as this, when made in good faith, should be apparent. We see no reason why they should not be given effect when it is plain that the statutory requirement of assuring the avoidance of confusion, mistake or deception is satisfied thereby. . . . Surely, the action taken by the board in this case, i.e., merely restricting the parties to areas of actual use, provides little, if any, more assurance." 429 F.2d at 474.

[127] "Nothing in the statute is apparent which requires that the filing date of an application for registration is the cut-off day for establishing rights by a showing of trademark use. The fact of trademark use in commerce, is . . . merely necessary to invoke the jurisdiction required to adjudicate the controversy. The extent of such use is important only in that it is necessary to consider in determining the rights to be granted each party. ". . . The extent to which concurrent registrations must be territorially restricted has an effect on the rights of both parties. In addition, there is the paramount interest of the public to be considered. . . . [I]t is both necessary and proper for the Patent Office to determine the 'conditions and limitations' with which the marks are to be registered 'on the basis of facts as they exist at the time when the issue of registrability is under consideration.' . . . In the present type of proceeding this would apparently mean up to the close of the testimony period. We have considered the possible problems which might result from such practice, but find they are outweighed by the interests involved." 429 F.2d at 475-76.

[128] ". . . [The second user-first applicant Fairway] asserted, on behalf of its rights to the contested areas, previous business activity, dominance of contiguous areas, a history of expansion, presently planned expansion into the two areas, and possible present penetration into

[ii]   *Concurrent Use Rights in Opposition and Cancellation Proceedings.* Section 2(d)'s concurrent use proviso permits junior applicants to obtain registrations recognizing their superior rights in defined areas. To provoke a concurrent use proceeding, a junior user must file a registration application, and Section 2(d) bars such applications if the junior user cannot allege use prior to the earliest of the parties' filing date,[129] even though good faith post-filing, pre-registration use could establish junior rights under the law before the 1988 Trademark Revision Act's introduction of the nationwide constructive use doctrine.

A series of CCPA decisions rebuffed junior users' attempts to restrict territorially senior users' registrations in opposition, cancellation, and interference proceedings. In *Hollowform*,[130] the court held that a post-filing date user could not oppose the

---

Montana by way of goods bought in the Dakotas. . . . The board [required] no less than actual use . . . . We think [that requirement was] wrong.

"The Commission[er] of Patents has the statutory responsibility to make sure that concurrent registrations are limited so as to prevent the likelihood of confusion, mistake or deception from occurring. Where a party has submitted evidence sufficient to prove a strong probability of future expansion of his trade into an area, that area would then become an area of likelihood of confusion if a registration covering it was granted to the other party. For example, many forms of evidence which would ordinarily be proffered to show a likelihood of expansion would be the same kind submitted to argue a likelihood of confusion if another party began use of the mark in that area. Thus, based on the premise that territorially restricted registrations must issue and, further, that said registrations combined will encompass the entire United States, if a likelihood of confusion is to be avoided, the territories of the parties must be limited in such a way as to exclude from each the area of probable expansion of the other party. Considering the Commissioner's indicated responsibility, which, of course, is based on a desire to protect the public, submission of evidence such as that submitted by Fairway in this case should be encouraged. And reiterating what was said earlier, any attempt, by the parties themselves, to solve the problem of public confusion, should be given serious consideration by the Patent Office." 429 F.2d at 475.

[129] As noted above, the 1988 allows concurrent registration by consent even though the junior user begins after filing, but the senior user may not give such consent.

[130] Hollowform, Inc. v. Aeh, 515 F.2d 1174, 185 U.S.P.Q. 790 (CCPA 1975).

On June 16, 1971, applicant filed an application to register "TOPKAT" for camping trailers and truck campers. Opposer filed an opposition, alleging it owned the trademark "TOP KAT" for truck campers in twelve western states. Opposer's use dates were after applicant's filing date. The court affirmed dismissal of the opposition: "[W]hatever common law rights opposer may have in its states of use are completely irrelevant here and that the fact that a subsequent user adopts a mark in good faith in a territory where the prior user's mark has not been known or used will not preclude registration of the prior user's mark. Since appellant's rights in the mark are not superior to appellee's right to registration, appellant cannot be legally 'damaged,' as that term has been construed, by the issuance of a registration to appellee." 515 F.2d at 1176.

Judge Miller dissented, arguing "[i]f an opposer shows facts which refute an applicant's claim that applicant is the owner of a trademark and that no one else has the right to use the mark in commerce, the Commissioner has clear authority to deny the application for an unrestricted registration. If such opposer shows that he is the owner and good faith user of the same trademark for the same goods in certain areas, the first-user applicant, upon being denied an unrestricted registration, can apply . . . for a registration with appropriate 'conditions and limitations,' . . . . " 515 F.2d at 1178.

senior user's application seeking a registration for the entire United States—even though the junior user might be entitled to lawful exclusive use in its own territory. In *American Security Bank*,[131] the court followed *Hollowform* in dismissing an opposition in which the opposer's use date predated the applicant's filing date: "this court, unless dealing with a concurrent use proceeding, approves the issuance of an unrestricted registration to an applicant having 'superior' rights in a mark acquired through prior use vis-a-vis an opposer, notwithstanding the opposer may have acquired some rights through subsequent innocent adoption and use."[132] In *Giant Food*,[133] the court followed *Hollowform* once again. *Giant Food* involved an interference[134] in which both Giant and Malone sought geographically unrestricted registrations of "GIANT FOOD" as a mark for supermarket services. Because junior applicant Giant's use (1936) predated that of senior applicant Malone (1966), Giant prevailed in the interference. Nevertheless, the Board denied registration to Giant on the basis of evidence that "GIANT FOOD" had been adopted in numerous states by third parties, indicating that Giant did not the exclusive right of use throughout the United States that an unrestricted registration would *prima facie* provide. The court reversed the denial because none of the uses predated Giant's.[135]

---

[131] American Security & Trust Co. v. American Security & Trust Co., 571 F.2d 564, 197 USPQ 65 (CCPA 1978).

[132] Who was first and second in *American Security* was complicated because the first user of one mark ("AMERICAN SECURITY") sought to register a variation on the mark ("AMERICAN SECURITY BANK") that had been first used by another in a separate geographic market. The court deemed the two marks legally equivalent because "Bank" was generic, both parties asserting trademark rights as to "banking services."

[133] Giant Food Inc. v. Malone & Hyde, Inc., 522 F.2d 1386, 187 USPQ 374 (CCPA 1975).

[134] For a discussion of trademark interferences, see § 5D[2][d][iv].

[135] "The fact that third-party rights are alleged, as distinguished from the rights of appellant in *Hollowform*, is not material to appellant's right to registration. In the absence of a showing that there is a *prior* third-party use, any common-law rights resulting from an innocent subsequent use are not superior to appellant's rights except in the particular state or states in which such subsequent use preceded appellant's use in such state or states. . . . Such common-law rights cannot be used as a basis for the denial of a nationwide registration to appellant except by way of a concurrent use proceeding. It has furthermore not been shown to our satisfaction that such third-party uses are *now*, or that they were at the time of appellant's February 1969 filing date, so extensive as to cast doubt on the trademark significance of appellant's mark. Appellant has made a sufficient showing that its mark is capable of distinguishing its services from the services of others in its market area. That market, embracing two states and the District of Columbia, is 'in commerce.' So far as the record reveals, appellant was the first to use the mark in commerce. No more is required by the statute. . . . .

"Third parties to these proceedings *may* have, in their specific areas of use, rights superior to those of appellant in those areas. Alternatively, they may have no rights at all, as would be the case if they had adopted their marks with knowledge of appellant's use in commerce. . . . Nor will our decision affect the rights, if any, of third parties to limit appellant's registration by means of the statutorily provided concurrent use proceedings instituted under §2(d) of the Lanham Act . . . .

"We cannot conceive that appellant, armed with its newly acquired registration, and the favorable presumptions appurtenant thereto by virtue of §7(b), will flail about the nation suing innocent subsequent users in their respective areas of use. . . .

In *Selfway, Inc.*,[136] the court held that the policy identified in *Beatrice* and applied in *Weiner King*[137] does not preclude a senior user from promptly obtaining cancellation of a junior user's improperly granted unrestricted registration. A mark's prior user filed a petition to cancel a subsequent user's unrestricted registration less than five months after it issued. The PTO granted cancellation. On appeal, the junior user argued that its registration "should have been ordered geographically restricted instead of cancelled in its entirety because petitioner's rights in the mark are, at best, those of a concurrent user; in other words, respondent, as prior registrant, should be entitled to retain national registration rights except for areas where petitioner actually used the mark prior to issuance of the registration." The court disagreed. First, Lanham Act Section 18's empowering of the Commissioner to "cancel or restrict" does not authorize a restriction in a cancellation proceeding; restriction pertains to concurrent use proceedings.[138] Second, *Beatrice* footnote policy

---

"One of the primary purposes of registration on the principal register under the Lanham Act is to establish a system of constructive notice whereby a first user of a mark may be enabled to pre-empt by registration all of the remaining virgin territory not yet occupied by subsequent users of the same or similar marks, although such area of first use may be in but a few states. . . . To restrict such first user to the two or three states in which such first use occurred would leave the remaining virgin territory open to wrongful exploitation by a subsequent user and would defeat one of the single most important purposes of the Act. . . . In the present case, for example, assuming that each of the uses cited by appellee occurred innocently in their particular areas prior to the entry into those areas of appellant, there would remain a virgin territory, so far as this record shows, of more than 30 states. The winner of the race for that territory, according to our system of federal registration, is the senior user at least in those instances where he is also the first to apply for a federal registration." 522 F.2d at 1394-96.

Judge Rich dissented, arguing that the evidence of subsequent third-party uses established that "GIANT FOOD" was not "capable, across the nation, of distinguishing appellant's services from the services of others. . . . The originally 'virgin territory' . . . has been deflowered and grown up to weeds; GIANT FOOD markets have sprung up all over the country." 522 F.2d at 1386, 1401.

136 Selfway, Inc. v. Travelers Petroleum, Inc., 579 F.2d 75, 198 U.S.P.Q. 271 (CCPA 1978).

137 *See* § 5E[2][d][i].

138 ". . . [W]e construe 'cancel' as necessarily meaning 'cancel entirely' and as not including 'partially cancel' since to do otherwise would reduce the express grant of the power to 'restrict' to the status of surplusage. . . . [T]he provision for cancellation proceedings in §14 speaks only of complete cancellation, and it is reasonable to presume that the power to cancel granted in §18 was intended to be exercised in a § 14 proceeding. Similarly, the only ways a registration can be 'restricted' are by placing limitations on the description of the goods, the channels of trade, or the areas of use. We find this functional definition of the term 'restrict' used in the §2(d) proviso . . . in reference to concurrent use proceedings, and it is reasonable to presume that the power to restrict granted in §18 was intended to be exercised in a §2(d) concurrent use proceeding.

"Moreover, to *logically* justify relief in the form of 'restriction' in any proceeding involving a registered mark, one must establish (1) that more than one person is entitled to use the mark and (2) that there would be no likelihood of confusion from the continued use of the mark under the conditions and limitations of the restriction. . . . If the party antagonistic to the registration is not entitled to use the mark, no relief, let alone restriction, would be in order. . . . If both parties are entitled to use the mark but confusion would be likely regardless

considerations favoring the first person to register do not apply to a timely petition to cancel.[139] Finally, citing its *Hollowform* decision,[140] the court noted that "the Lanham Act . . . provides for only one inter partes procedure *in the PTO* where such concurrent rights may be adjudicated, and that is the concurrent use proceeding."[141]

The 1988 Trademark Revision Act revised the PTO's Section 18 powers as follows:

> "In such proceedings [i.e. interference, opposition, and proceedings for concurrent use registration or for cancellation], the Commissioner may refuse to register the opposed mark, may cancel *the registration, in whole or in part, may modify the application or registration by limiting the goods or services specified therein, may otherwise restrict or rectify with respect to the register* [or restrict] the registration of a registered mark . . . "[142]

---

of adherence to restrictions in registrations thereof, the first sentence of §2(d) . . . mandates that the registrant, if the junior user, is not entitled to maintain *any* registration, restricted or otherwise. By necessary implication, the registrant, if the senior user, must be entitled to maintain his registration in unrestricted form (absent [a judicial] adjudication . . . " 579 F.2d at 80-81.

As to the possible impact of the 1988 Amendment to Section 18, see below.

[139] "Section 14 does more than provide for cancellation proceedings. It places particular time limitations on some of the various bases upon which cancellation will be granted (remembering that 'cancellation' connotes total removal), and in so doing, represents a congressional determination that in actions brought within the stated times, the rights created by the issued registrations are outweighed by the public interest in the removal of improvidently issued registrations. We cannot now say that the subsistence of appellant-respondent's registration for some lesser period of time clothes respondent with some greater rights. We conclude that the considerations noted in Beatrice Foods simply are not relevant in a situation where complete cancellation is still available under §14 and has been sought. To consider such rights and to allow restriction in lieu of cancellation, where available, would be to second guess the congressional determination that total cancellation should be available, based on §2(d) grounds, for five years after issuance of the registration." 579 F.2d at 82.

[140] Hollowform, Inc. v. Delma, AEH, 515 F.2d. 1174 (CCPA 1975).

[141] 579 F.2d at 82.

The court's emphasis on "in the PTO" refers to its footnote recognizing that the PTO may give effect to the results of litigation between the parties establishing their rights.

> "We do not here consider the situation, not presented by the facts of this case, where the respective rights of the parties to use the mark have been adjudicated by a court of competent jurisdiction. In such a situation, 'restriction' may well be available, in an appropriate proceeding, notwithstanding likelihood of confusion. See Holiday Inn v. Holiday Inns, Inc., 534 F.2d 312, 189 U.S.P.Q. 630 (Cust. & Pat.App.1976); Alfred Dunhill of London, Inc. v. Dunhill Tailored Clothes, Inc., 293 F.2d 685, 49 CCPA 730, 130 USPQ 412 (1961).

> "Such a prior adjudication clearly may be noticed in subsequent PTO proceedings involving the same parties, because the parties will be bound by the earlier result in their continuing relations. In this context, this court's consideration in *Dunhill* of the adjudicated concurrent rights of the parties in resolving the merits of an opposition proceeding is entirely consistent with our holding herein." 579 F.2d at 81 n.5.

For a discussion of concurrent use registrations based on judicial determinations, see § 5E[2][d][iv].

[142] Lanham Act §18, 15 U.S.C. §1068. [Emphasis added]

The Act's legislative history contains no suggestion that this language was intended to alter the *Selfway* interpretation of "restrict."[143]

[iii] *Allocating "Virgin" Territory: Senior Filing and Aggressive Junior Users.* *Beatrice Foods*[144] established a general presumption that the first user of a mark in the United States would be entitled to all the country except that occupied by good faith junior users, including unoccupied "virgin" territory, but the court suggested in a footnote that the Lanham Act's policy of providing nationwide mark protection might favor junior applicants who were the first to file and obtain registration of their marks. This policy could favor awarding a junior user nationwide registration covering the "virgin" territory beyond the senior and junior user actual use areas if the "equities" favored the junior user, for example, because junior user promptly registered and the senior user did not. Later decisions apply the suggestion and also indicate that a junior user who aggressively seeks to expand his market may obtain rights to the "virgin" territory.

Weiner King[145] involved the respective rights of two companies, Weiner King and WKNC, which used similar marks, "WEINER KING" and "WIENER KING" for hot dog restaurant services. In 1962, Weiner King began use in New Jersey of "Weiner King" as a mark for restaurant services featuring hot dogs. It continuously used the mark in Flemington and Beach Haven, New Jersey. In 1970, WKNC, without knowledge of Weiner King's activity, began using several "Wiener King" marks for a North Carolina restaurant, which also specialized in hot dogs. It expanded the number of its restaurants, both company-owned and franchised, and advertised extensively. By late 1975, it had more than 100 restaurants in 20 states.

In May 1972, WKNC obtained federal registration of its marks. In July 1972, it learned that Weiner King was using "WEINER KING" and a related design. In May of 1975, Weiner King petitioned the PTO to cancel WKNC's registrations and applied to register "WEINER KING," alleging a 1962 first use date. In June of 1975, Weiner King filed a New Jersey District Court civil action against WKNC. In June of 1975, the PTO declared a Weiner King-WKNC concurrent use proceeding. The PTO consolidated the cancellation and concurrent use proceeding.

Viewing the critical issue as the extent of the prior user Weiner King's trade territory, the New Jersey District Court enjoined WKNC's use of its mark within New Jersey and within 40 miles of Flemington. It also ordered cancellation of WKNC's marks and directed the PTO to determine the parties's rights in the concurrent use proceeding, which had been suspended pending resolution of the New Jersey action. On appeal, the Third Circuit restricted Weiner King to a 15 mile radius around Flemington. It vacated the district court's cancellation order, directing instead that the PTO decide both the cancellation and concurrent use issues.

---

[143] The amendment's purpose is to allow the TTAB to limit or otherwise modify the goods-services identification in an application or registration and to "determine trademark ownership rights where they are at variance with the register . . . . " S. Rep. 100-515, 100th Cong., 2d Sess. 35 (1988).

[144] *In re* Beatrice Foods Co., 429 F.2d 466, 166 U.S.P.Q. 431 (CCPA 1970).

[145] Weiner King, Inc. v. Wiener King Corp., 615 F.2d 512, 204 U.S.P.Q. 820 (CCPA 1980).

The PTO's Trademark Trial and Appeal Board ("TTAB") ruled for WKNC, reasoning that the senior user Weiner King was satisfied to remain a local New Jersey business whereas WKNC diligently pursued a national expansion plan. It was irrelevant that most of WKNC's expansion occurred after it learned of Weiner King's use of its marks in New Jersey. The Court of Customs and Patent Appeals affirmed. Under settled law, each party had a right to use its mark "in its own initial area of use." In dispute were "the registrable rights to the remainder of the United States." The case had "an added dimension of complexity for two reasons: the later adopter, WKNC, was the first to register, and 'even though an innocent adopter, WKNC underwent a large portion of its expansion after notice of the existence of Weiner King and its use of the WEINER KING mark in the Flemington, New Jersey, area.' "[146]

The court rejected Weiner King's argument that WKNC's expansion could not establish a right to register "in any of the areas it entered after notice."

> "The TTAB had the task of balancing the equities between a prior user who remained content to operate a small, locally-oriented business with no apparent desire to expand, and who, until recently, declined to seek the benefits of Lanham Act registration, and a subsequent user, whose expressed purpose has been, from its inception, to expand into a nationwide franchising operation, and who has fulfilled its purpose, taking advantage of Lanham Act registration in the process."[147]

If WKNC's expansion "was in bad faith it cannot support a right to registration for use in those areas," but "[t]he District Court found that this expansion was not an attempt to 'palm off' or trade on the reputation of Weiner King. 'Instead, they (sought) to gain from their own goodwill, founded upon the use of "Wiener King" throughout a large part of the United States.' " WKNC's knowledge of Weiner King's existence and use of the mark "is legally insufficient to support a finding of bad faith." The court cautioned "that such a determination must always be the product of the particular fact pattern involved in each case."

> "While an attempt to 'palm off,' or a motive to 'box in' a prior user by cutting into its probable area of expansion, each necessarily flowing from knowledge of the existence of the prior user, might be sufficient to support a finding of bad faith, mere knowledge of the existence of the prior user should not, by itself, constitute bad faith. . . . "[148]

As to "who gets what territory," *Beatrice Foods* held that "actual use in a territory was not necessary to establish rights in that territory, and that the inquiry should focus on the party's (1) previous business activity; (2) previous expansion or lack thereof; (3) dominance of contiguous areas; (4) presently-planned expansion; and, where applicable (5) possible market penetration by means of products brought in from other areas."[149] Factors 1, 2, 3 and 4 favored WKNC. Also, as stated in *Beatrice*,

---

[146] 615 F.2d at 522.

[147] *Id.*

[148] *Id.*

[149] 615 F.2d at 523, quoting *In re* Beatrice Foods Co., 429 F.2d 466, 475, 166 U.S.P.Q. 431, 437-38 (CCPA 1970).

"there is a policy of encouraging prompt registration of marks by rewarding those who first seek registration under the Lanham Act."[150] The Lanham Act Section 2(d) proviso "exhibits no bias in favor of the prior user" and directs that conditions be imposed to prevent confusion.

> "The TTAB found that 'it is an inescapable conclusion that, outside of Weiner King's little enclave, "WIENER KING" means WKNC's restaurants and to allow Weiner King to step out of its trading area, would cause confusion to the purchasing public.' . . . By finding that Weiner King's reputation zone is a circle with a 15-mile radius, the Third Circuit has made essentially the same finding. It is binding on the parties by stipulation. In light of this fact, the issuance to Weiner King of a concurrent registration which encompasses the entire United States except for the state of North Carolina would serve only to foster the very confusion which the act was meant to prevent. . . . "[151]

The court disclaimed reliance on Lanham Act Section 22's constructive notice provision: "[W]e do not believe that a mechanical approach which always defers to the first to register comprehends all of the factors which must be taken into account in order to come to a reasoned decision."[152]

In *Noah's, Inc.*,[153] the district court affirmed a PTO concurrent use proceeding determination that the senior user should receive a registration restricted to its market area and the junior user a registration nationwide (except for the senior user's territory and certain areas occupied by third parties). It did so even though both parties had only opened a single restaurant under the disputed mark.

> "The plaintiff has participated in little or no expansionist activities in any state other than Iowa. . . . At best, other than the use of the mark in the State of Iowa, the plaintiff's use of the trademark 'Noah's Ark' has been sporadic and transitional. However, the plaintiff has enjoyed statewide protection of his trademark since 1955. . . . In addition, plaintiff advertisements reach citizens throughout the State of Iowa and the restaurant is one of the better known

---

[150] 615 F.2d at 523, quoting *In re* Beatrice Foods Co., 429 F.2d at 474 n.13, 166 U.S.P.Q. at 436 n.13.

[151] 615 F.2d at 524.

[152] 615 F.2d at 525. "For instance, this approach would not reach the proper result in a case where the first registration was improvidently granted and should be cancelled. To rely on such a registration to restrict the expansion of a nonregistered prior user and then to cancel the registration would be an absurd result in a combined cancellation and concurrent use proceeding." 615 F.2d at 525 n.10.

[153] Noah's, Inc. v. Nark, Inc., 560 F.Supp. 1253, 1259, 222 U.S.P.Q. 697, 701 (E.D.Mo.1983), *aff'd*, 728 F.2d 410 (8th Cir. 1984) ("In addition to recognizing that a prior user's rights to a registration covering the United States, may be limited by a subsequent user's adoption of a service mark in another area of the country, the courts have further limited the rights of the prior user by recognizing that a senior party may abandon its right as a prior user to expand into a particular area or its right to enjoy nationwide protection of its mark. . . . Therefore, the senior user of a mark has the right to exclude others from its use, only so long as the initial appropriation and use are accompanied by an intention to continue exploiting the mark commercially, rather than by an abandonment of its use.").

Des Moines restaurants to Iowans who visit Des Moines for various reasons.
. . .

"... In order for the defendant, as the junior party, to obtain nation-wide protection of the mark . . . not only must the evidence establish that the plaintiff has abandoned its right to enjoy nationwide protection, it must also be demonstrated that the junior partner has 'substantial expansion activi-ties and a dynamic business save for the small area or enclave into which the senior party has boxed himself.' . . . [T]he defendant has made significant efforts to consummate franchises throughout the country and has been frustrated in its attempt largely if not almost completely by this litigation. . . . [T]he defendant has participated in previous attempts at expansion and has present plans for further expansion. . . . Therefore, equitable considerations require that the defendant receive a concurrent use registration for the trademark . . . for the entire United States with the exception of the State of Iowa; a twenty-mile radius around Mary Ellen Engel's restaurant in Cincinnati, Ohio; a twenty-mile radius around the 'Noah's Ark' restaurant considered to be in Raleigh, North Carolina; and a twenty-mile radius around the 'Noah's Ark Pub' in New York City, New York. In turn, the plaintiff is granted registrations on its application to register 'Noah's Ark' for restaurant services for the State of Iowa."[154]

The PTO may deny concurrent registration to a junior applicant who uses the mark beyond the area for which it seeks registration so as to create a likelihood of confusion. In *Gray*,[155] defendant DDB filed, on October 14, 1980, an application seeking registration for the entire United States of "DAFFY DAN'S" for retail clothing store services, alleging a 1961 first use date. Gray filed, on June 28, 1982, an ap-plication seeking registration for the entire United States except New Jersey, in which Gray acknowledged DDB's prior rights, of the same mark for clothing services, asserting a July, 1973 first use date. Gray began use of the mark in Ohio and later expanded into New Jersey. Gray admitted using his mark in New Jersey in connection with clothing distributorship services. The TTAB refused to grant Gray a concur-rent use registration because of this admission, reasoning that a likelihood of confusion could not be prevented on the conditions under which concurrent registration was sought. The court affirmed.[156] Unlike *Beatrice Foods*, the record showed that the

---

[154] 560 F. Supp. at 1259-60, 222 U.S.P.Q. at 702.

[155] Gray v. Daffy Dan's Bargaintown, 823 F.2d 522, 3 U.S.P.Q.2d 1306 (Fed. Cir. 1987).

[156] As to the junior user's argument that his initial use in good faith outside the senior party's use area established Section 2(d)'s "jurisdictional" requirement and his right to concurrent registration of some scope, the court responded:

"A valid application cannot be filed at all for registration of a mark without 'lawful use in commerce,' and, where a claim is made of concurrent rights, such use must begin prior to the filing date of any application by a conflicting claimant to the mark. In this sense, the requirement is 'jurisdictional.' . . . *Beatrice Foods* itself goes on to recognize that this 'jurisdictional' requirement is only one of the 'conditions precedent' which must be satisfied to establish 'entitlement' to a concurrent use registration: 'The touchstone, however, is the requirement that there be no likelihood of confusion, mistake or deception in the market place as to the source of the goods resulting from the continued concurrent

junior party's entry into the senior party's territory was continuing at the time of decision with no agreement between the parties that it would cease. *Weiner King* is distinguishable; "the court spoke of resolving issues in concurrent use proceedings in accordance with 'equitable principles' and the balancing of the competing interests of users of the mark. In that case, however, the question was whether the junior user could expand, with knowledge of a senior party's prior use, into an area in which the senior party did not use the mark."[157]

[*iv*] *Court Determination of Concurrent Right.* Section 2(d) states that "Concurrent registrations may also be issued by the Commissioner when a court of competent jurisdiction has finally determined that more than one person is entitled to use the same or similar marks in commerce." The word "also" indicates that concurrent registrations may issue even though Section 2(d)'s conditions are not met.[158]

---

use of the trademark. Only in satisfying this standard, can the Patent Office be sure that both the rights of the individual parties and those of the public are being protected.' " 823 F.2d at 526, 3 U.S.P.Q.2d at 1308.

As to the junior user's argument that the issue of likelihood of confusion in a concurrent use proceeding should be determined with respect to the geographic area which the current use applicant "claims" in its application, not on the basis of the parties actual territorial use of their marks, the court responded:

"[T]he exclusion of some geographic territory of use from a concurrent use application does not restrict the likelihood of confusion inquiry required by the statute. As this case illustrates, the mere statement by an applicant that a registration is not sought for a particular state or geographic area cannot be equated with a representation that the applicant does not and will not use its mark in the area. Here, there is no representation by Gray that he will limit the scope of geographic use of his mark or will take steps to prevent confusion of the public. What is attempted here is simply a manipulative use of the registration system to secure to Gray the advantages of registration with no undertaking whatsoever to protect the public from confusion. We see nothing in the statute, nor in the 'equities' to be resolved in a concurrent use proceeding, which requires the Commissioner to limit the likelihood of confusion inquiry to the area 'claimed' by a concurrent use applicant." 823 F.2d at 526, 3 U.S.P.Q.2d at 1309.

As to the second user's argument that "if his application is too broad with respect to the area he claims, the Commissioner (via the board) should not deny registration but must fix the conditions and limitations as to the place of use of the mark," the court responded: "While the Commissioner may resolve rights of expansion into areas in which neither party uses the mark, . . . the Commissioner has no authority to force a party to retreat from an area of actual use. That authority rests in the district courts." 823 F.2d at 527, 3 U.S.P.Q.2d at 1309.

[157] 823 F.2d at 526, 3 U.S.P.Q.2d at 1309.

[158] One appropriate situation might be when the second user begins use after the first user's filing date but before the first user's registration date. Section 2(d) bars a concurrent use proceeding in such a situation. *See* Hollowform, Inc. v. Delma Aeh, 515 F.2d 1174 (CCPA 1975), discussed at § 5E[2][d][ii]. Yet, for applications filed prior to the effective date of the 1988 Trademark Revision Act, which makes a trademark application filing a constructive nationwide use of the mark once a registration issues, the second user could obtain common law rights.

In *Old Dutch Foods*,[159] Old Dutch Foods began using "OLD DUTCH" for snack foods, including pretzels, in 1934 in Minnesota. It expanded to other states and obtained a Lanham Act registration in 1957. Dan Dee Pretzel began using "OLD DUTCH" for pretzels in Ohio in 1941, having previously used the mark for noodles, and expanded into six other states. It filed an application seeking concurrent registration for its area; the Patent Office stayed action on the application pending resolution of infringement litigation between the parties. In the infringement suit, the district court held that the Section 33(b)(5) exception preserved the junior user's right to use its mark but did not preclude use by the registrant. It denied concurrent registration because it found that the junior user had not actually used "OLD DUTCH" as a trademark. The Sixth Circuit reversed, questioning the district court's construction of Section 33(b)(5).[160] It held that the junior user did make trademark use of the mark and was entitled to concurrent registration[161] and rejected the view that only the Patent Office Commissioner could determine the "conditions and limitations" of concurrent registration.[162]

In *Holiday Inn*,[163] the court held that, once a court determines that parties are entitled to exclusive use in discrete geographic areas, the PTO should issue concurrent registrations without a fresh inquiry into the issue of likelihood of confusion.[164]

---

[159] Old Dutch Foods, Inc. v. Dan Dee Pretzel & Potato Chip Co., 477 F.2d 150, 177 U.S.P.Q. 496 (6th Cir. 1973).

[160] "It is difficult to reconcile a result that two merchants are selling similar goods with the same mark side by side on the retail shelves with the stated purpose of the Lanham Act; *i.e,* to protect the public by enabling the consumer to distinguish between competing goods and to protect the merchant who has invested time and money into presenting his specific product to the consumer." 477 F.2d at 1517 n.3.

[161] The court directed "the commissioner to issue concurrent registration to Dan Dee with these limitations: the registration shall reflect that the place of use of the mark 'Old Dutch' shall be limited to the states of Ohio, Pennsylvania, New York, West Virginia, Kentucky and Indiana, and the use restricted to the manner, means and packaged products previously employed by Dan Dee as set forth in detail in the opinion of the district court. The registration of the plaintiff shall reflect that the place of use of its mark includes the remainder of the United States." 477 F.2d at 157.

[162] *Compare* Safeway Stores, Inc. v. Safeway Quality Foods, Inc., 433 F.2d 99, 166 U.S.P.Q. 112 (7th Cir. 1970):

> "We agree with the District Court that more than one person is entitled to use the mark 'SAFEWAY' in commerce. Such registration can be ordered under 15 U.S.C. 1052(d). . . . However, we feel that the Commissioner should be the one to determine the place or places of use of the mark by defendants.
>
> . . ..
>
> ". . . [T]he District Court was without authority to prescribe the geographical limitations of the concurrent use. We order the District Court to certify to the Commissioner that it has been determined that defendants are entitled to concurrent registration of the mark 'SAFEWAY' and direct the Commissioner to issue such concurrent registration and to prescribe the conditions and limitations of such use in the light of the innocent use by defendants prior to [plaintiff's registration date]." 433 F.2d at 103-04.

[163] Holiday Inn v. Holiday Inns, Inc., 534 F.2d 312, 189 U.S.P.Q. 630 (CCPA 1976).

[164] The court disagreed with the national chain's argument that Section 2(d) uses "may" and is merely permissive, "allowing the Commissioner to register in the present situation only

Concurrent registration may issue to effect judicial decrees in situations not involving disparate geographic markets. For example, in *Alfred Dunhill of London, Inc.*,[165]
Alfred Dunhill established in a district court infringement suit that it was senior user
of the mark "DUNHILL" for various products. However, the court's injunction
indicated that the junior user was entitled to continue to use "DUNHILL TAILORS"
for clothing products under prescribed conditions because of the senior user's acquiescence in such use. The junior user then applied to register "DUNHILL TAILORS"
under the Lanham Act. The senior user filed an opposition. The court held that the
registration should issue but only under the judicially-established conditions.[166]

(Text continued on page 5–213)

'if he should determine that the touchstone requirement no likelihood of confusion has been
fulfilled.' "

> "The word 'may' is insufficient to condition the operation of the court determina-
> tion sentence of § 2(d) on a preliminary finding of no likelihood of confusion by the
> Commissioner pursuant to the first sentence of the proviso. There are other obvious
> reasons for using 'may.' The Trademark Act contains many conditions on registra-
> tion, other than no likelihood of confusion, which it is the Commissioner's duty to
> enforce. Courts may very well determine rights to use 'marks' which are not techni-
> cally trademarks, which fall into categories denied registration by the statute, which may
> be open to others than the parties to use, and in all cases every applicant to register
> must comply with all of the procedural requirements of the Patent and Trademark Office
> as set forth in statute and rules before the Commissioner is compelled to register.
> 'May' is a very appropriate word in view of these considerations. We also note its use
> in the first sentence of the §2(d) proviso where the requirement that the Commissioner
> find confusion, etc., to be 'not likely' is found." 534 F.2d at 318.

[165] Alfred Dunhill of London, Inc. v. Dunhill Tailored Clothes, Inc., 293 F.2d 685, 130
U.S.P.Q. 412 (CCPA 1961), *cert. denied,* 369 U.S. 864 (1962).

[166] "However one may choose to describe the situation in legal terms, the cardinal fact is
that applicant, by judicial decree, as against opposer, has the right to use DUNHILL TAILORS
. . .

"This right to continue to use DUNHILL TAILORS is the result of opposer's knowledge
and long acquiescence which gave rise to an equitable estoppel. It is not, however, an
unconditional right to use. It is indeed, explicitly restricted. . . .

"Though it has not been so designated, it is apparent that what we have before us, at least
with respect to right to use, is a court-approved concurrent use situation. Two corporations
which have each been using 'DUNHILL' for over a quarter century may, by judicial decree,
both legally use 'DUNHILL,' applicant being subject to certain restrictions imposed for the
protection of opposer, and opposer, correspondingly, restrained from interfering with applicant.
The Lanham Act, section 2(d), contemplates that where two parties have the legal right to use
'the same or similar marks' there may be corresponding concurrent registrations. But each
of the several provisions of that section providing for concurrent registrations contains reference to 'conditions and limitations as to the mode or place of use or the goods in connection with which such registrations may be granted which conditions any limitations shall
be prescribed in the grant of the concurrent registrations . . . ..' The 'conditions and limitations'
are such as would assure, if they were in fact restrictions on use, . . . that, in the words of
section 2(d), 'confusion or mistake or deceit of purchasers is not likely to result from the
continued use of' the marks concurrently registered. The second clause of the concurrent
registration proviso in section 2(d) reads:
'and concurrent registrations may be similarly granted by the Commissioner with such limitations and conditions when a court has finally determined that more than one person is entitled
to use the same or similar marks in commerce.'

[e] Junior User Incontestability. The Lanham Act's language is less than clear on the relative rights of senior users and junior user incontestable registrants. Section 2(d)'s concurrent use proviso and Section 15 do not refer to priority. Section 2(d) refers generally to "persons . . . entitled to use such marks as a result of their concurrent lawful use in commerce." Section 15's exception to a registrant's incontestable

"In the instant case the district court in New York made such a final determination. . . . But, apparently because applicant neither invoked the concurrent registration provision nor requested an order to register from the court (as it could have done under section 37), the board, by merely dismissing opposition, opened the way to registration of DUNHILL TAILORS without any of the 'conditions and limitations' in the grant which the statute contemplates in the case of concurrent registrations. It seems to us that such a registration would be contrary to the spirit, if not the letter, of the Lanham Act and would give a false picture of applicant's rights. Opposer would have good cause to complain of such a registration.

"Applicant argues its right to register on the broad principle that right to register should be conformed to the right to use, citing authorities for the proposition that this was one of the basic objectives of the Lanham Act . . . Applicant, however, does not appear to have made any effort to 'conform' the registration it seeks with the right to use which it actually possesses, as defined in the district court judgment, by incorporating in the registration the limitation and conditions to which its right to use is subject. Under the circumstances of this case, we feel that this is a necessary prerequisite to the granting of the registration. . . . .

"Opposer seems to regard it as an impossibility that two parties can own only register the same trademark. Not only is that a commonplace where there is a sufficient difference in goods, even as to identical marks, . . . but the concurrent registration provisions of section 2(d) contemplate it even in the case of the same or similar goods. In the instant case we have some difference in both goods and marks but nevertheless a close question requiring the inhibitions of the injunction to minimize confusion. . . . .

"Opposer attempts to show how it would be damaged by the granting of the registration in any event. The gist of the argument is that applicant would obtain the various advantages of registration which the Lanham Act affords, viz.: a finding and evidence of 'ownership,' the right to use the mark, to mark it with notice of registration, constructive notice and eventual incontestability. We see no reason why applicant should not enjoy these advantages with respect to the limited rights it already enjoys in the use of the mark under the judgment. Opposer has failed to show us how it would be any worse off as a result of registration than it is now under the terms of the judgment, provided the registration is restricted to conform to the judgment. Such a registration will do no more than aid applicant in the enforcement of substantive rights it already has.

"The next point of opposer is, in effect, that right to register does not necessarily follow right to use. Of course we agree. . . . Applicant admits the validity of this point but says in reply that section 19 of the Lanham Act provides that 'In all inter partes proceedings equitable principles of laches, estoppel, and acquiescence, where applicable may be considered and applied.' . . . We do not see where we have any occasion to apply equitable principles or section 19 in this case. The applicable equitable principles were all applied in the district court in New York where the facts to support their application were proved. . . .

"We are clearly of the view on the record before us that the applicable statutory law, which neither party has invoked but which we should nevertheless apply, . . . is that provision of section 2(d) which provides for concurrent registration 'when a court has finally determined that more than one person is entitled to use the same or similar marks in commerce.' " 292 F.2d at 690-93.

right to use a mark refers to another's "valid rights acquired under the law of any State or Territory by use . . . prior to the date of registration." On the other hand, Section 33(b)(5)'s exception to a registrant's *exclusive* right to use the mark on designated goods refers to a party's adoption "without knowledge of the registrant's *prior use*," which suggests either that the exception applies only when the registrant is a prior user or that a second user cannot achieve incontestable status. Neither alternative is satisfactory in policy terms.

Despite Section 33(b)(5)'s wording, court decisions recognize that a prior user loses his presumptive right to expand into "virgin" territory and to obtain nationwide registration when a subsequent user obtains registration and complies with the Lanham Act's incontestability requirements. When the junior user-registrant achieves incontestability, the senior user retains the right to use its mark only in its locally-occupied area. *Holiday Inn*[167] involved the well-known national hotel chain that began use of the Holiday Inn mark in 1952, obtained federal registration of the mark, and complied with the requirements for incontestability under Lanham Act Section 15. A local hotel had began use of the mark in 1949, in the area of Myrtle Beach, South Carolina. In trademark infringement litigation, the court enjoined the local motel from infringing the chain's mark but provided that the local hotel could continue to use "HOLIDAY INN" in Myrtle Beach.[168] The local hotel then filed an application to register "HOLIDAY INN" for its area, resulting in a concurrent use proceeding. The TTAB refused concurrent registration under Section 2(d) on the ground that confusion would result. The court reversed. Section 2(d) expressly provides for issuance of concurrent registration without a fresh determination of the likelihood of confusion: "Concurrent registrations may also be issued by the Commissioner when a court of competent jurisdiction has finally determined that more than one person is entitled to use the same or similar marks in commerce." In opposing concurrent registration, the national chain argued that its registration was "valid and incontestable." The court held the "valid state right" exception applicable.[169]

---

[167] Holiday Inn v. Holiday Inns, Inc., 534 F.2d 312, 189 U.S.P.Q. 630 (CCPA 1976).

[168] Holiday Inns, Inc. v. Holiday Inn, 364 F. Supp. 775, 177 U.S.P.Q. 640 (D.S.C. 1973), *aff'd*, 498 F.2d 1397, 182 U.S.P.Q. 129 (4th Cir. 1974) (unpublished).

[169] ". . . 'Incontestability' is provided for in §15 (15 U.S.C. §1065) of the Trademark Act. It says nothing about incontestability of registrations, . . . notwithstanding the popularity of the phrase. The only thing which ever becomes incontestable, whatever may be the significance of 'incontestability,' is 'the right of the registrant to use,' and even that is subject to numerous provisos. . . . Assuming that the Chain's right to use its marks as registered is incontestable under §15, that section contains an exception which covers Applicant's situation, as recognized by the Fourth Circuit courts. It must be remembered that Applicant is the prior user. The exception, which is immediately antecedent to the statement of incontestable right to use, reads:

> '. . . except to the extent, if any, to which the use of a mark registered on the principal register infringes a valid right acquired under the law of any State or Territory by use of a mark or trade name continuing from a date prior to the date of the publication under this Act of such registered mark. . . . '

"Under the law of South Carolina, Applicant acquired by use of HOLIDAY INN a right therein which would be infringed by the Chain's marks if the Chain used them in Myrtle Beach, and that right was acquired long before publication of the Chain's marks under the Act. Therefore, the Chain has no statutory incontestable rights under its registrations as against Applicant in Myrtle Beach." 534 F.2d at 319-20.

(Matthew Bender & Co., Inc.)

In the *Wrist-Rocket* decisions, Ellenburg invented a wrist-braced slingshot. He initially marketed the slingshot under the mark "HOWARD'S WRIST LOCKER SLINGSHOT." Saunders purchased Ellenburg's slingshots and resold them with a house trademark "WRIST ROCKET." In 1954, Ellenburg entered into a distributor-ship agreement with Saunders. Ellenburg granted Saunders the exclusive right to sell slingshots manufactured by Ellenburg but reserved the right to make direct sales to customers but not to dealers. Ellenburg and Saunders did not strictly follow the agreement. In 1964, Ellenburg applied for registration of "WRIST ROCKET" and obtained a registration on July 20, 1965. In 1971, Saunders terminated the distributorship. Ellenburg continued to manufacture and distribute "WRIST ROCKET" slingshots. Saunders continued to market similar slingshots under the "WRIST ROCKET" label. Ellenburg sued for infringement of its federally-registered mark; Saunders counterclaimed, contending that it owned the mark. The district court held that Saunders, the distributor, owned the mark.

On appeal ("Wrist-Rocket I"), a panel of the Eighth Circuit determined:[170]

(1) The "incontestable status" of Ellenburg's registration "does not confer upon the registrant rights not possessed at common law. It is not a sword. To prevail in the infringement action, Ellenburg had to establish his exclusive right to use the trademark independent of the registration."

(2) Saunders, the distributor, possessed the common law right to the mark because he was the first to distribute the product with that mark.

(3) The district court erred in cancelling Ellenburg's registration. "Saunders' common law right to use the trademark cannot destroy the incontestable status of Ellenburg's registration. . . . Incontestability is . . . a shield that protects the registrant from cancellation of his trademark by a prior user claiming superior rights." None of the exceptions to incontestability in Lanham Act 33(b), 15 U.S.C. § 1115(b), apply.

(4) False statements in Ellenburg's registration application did not vitiate the incontestable status of his registration because such statements were not made with the intent to defraud, such as to come within the fraud exception, 15 U.S.C. §1115(b).

(5) Because Saunders, the distributor, has common law rights and Ellenburg, the manufacturer, has statutory rights, both are entitled to use the "WRIST ROCKET" mark. "Saunders' common law right to use the mark extends to those market areas where he had established prior use before the publication of Ellenburg's registration. . . . If the parties disagree over the limits of Saunders' market, the same shall be determined by the District Court on remand."

(6) "This concurrent use of the mark, while equitable between the parties, does raise the real possibility of purchaser confusion as to the source of origin of the sling-shots bearing the 'Wrist Rocket' mark. . . . We believe this prospective confusion can be obviated, as a matter of law, by requiring each party to use the trademark only in conjunction with a prefix of equal prominence that identifies the source of origin."[171]

---

[170] Wrist-Rocket Manufacturing Co., Inc. v. Saunders Archery Co., 516 F.2d 846, 186 U.S.P.Q. 5 (8th Cir. 1975), *cert. denied,* 423 U.S. 870 (1975), *further appeal,* 578 F.2d 727, 198 U.S.P.Q. 257 (8th Cir. 1978).

[171] 516 F.2d at 853.

On remand, the district court decided that Saunder's common law rights extended to the entire United States. On further appeal (*"Wrist-Rocket II"*),[172] Saunders argued that the *Wrist-Rocket I* panel erred in holding that none of the Section 33(b) exceptions applied, citing the *Old Dutch Foods*[173] and *Burger King*[174] decisions. The court declined to reconsider the *Wrist-Rocket I* determination of the inapplicability of Section 33(b)(5). It did suggest that Section 33(b)(5) might not apply because, unlike *Old Dutch Foods* and *Burger King*, the "common law" claimant's right were prior rather than subsequent to that of the incontestability-benefitted registrant. Nevertheless, "[w]e can conceive of no reason to reach a different result in this case, where the common-law owner's use antedated the registrant's use. Therefore, geographically defined areas of exclusive use are required for each party in this situation to effectuate the will of Congress and meet the needs of business and the public." It went on to find that the district court erred in finding that Saunders had penetrated all 50 states prior to the registrant's publication date.[175]

[3] Product and Service Scope

Refecting its unfair competition law roots, trademark protection originally extended only to *competing* goods. Courts would not enjoin one person from using another's mark to sell goods the latter did not offer—even if the mark use confused customers as to the goods' origin. A series of Second Circuit cases expanded trademark protection to *related* goods. Under the *Polaroid* multiple factor approach, the relatedness of the trademark owner's and accused infringer's goods or services is one of several factors that determine the ultimate issue—whether the accused infringer creates a likelihood of confusion as to the goods' or services' origin or sponsorship.[176]

State antidilution statutes extend trademark protection farther—protecting against dilution of a famous mark's distinctive character even in the absence of competition or confusion.

[a] Second Circuit Dialectic: Thesis—Antithesis—Synthesis. In *Aunt Jemima Mills*,[177] Davis Milling Company of St. Joseph, Missouri adopted a trademark in 1899 consisting of "the words 'Aunt Jemima's,' accompanying the picture of a negress laughing" for "self-rising flour" (more specifically, pancake mix!). In 1906, it registered the mark with the United States Patent Office. In 1908, Rigney & Co. adopted and used precisely the same trademark for "certain syrups and sugar creams" (more specifically, pancake syrup!). On March 6, 1908, it filed an application to register the

---

[172] Wrist-Rocket Manufacturing Co., Inc. v. Saunders Archery Co., 578 F.2d 727, 198 U.S.P.Q. 257 (8th Cir. 1978).

[173] Old Dutch Foods, Inc. v. Dan Dee Pretzel & Potato Chip Co., 477 F.2d 150, 157 (6th Cir. 1973), discussed at § 5E[2][d][iv].

[174] Burger King of Florida, Inc. v. Hoots, 403 F.2d 904 (7th Cir. 1968).

[175] Before a 1982 Lanham Act Amendment, Sections 15 referred to use before the *publication* date and Section 33(b) referred to use before the *registration* date. In 1982, Congress change the former to conform to the latter.

[176] *See* § 5F[1][a][iv].

[177] Aunt Jemima Mills Co. v. Rigney & Co., 247 F. 407 (2d Cir. 1917), *cert. denied*, 245 U.S. 672 (1918).

mark. Noticing the application, Davis Milling wrote Rigney expressing interest in its products.[178] The Patent Office registered Rigney's mark in December 1908. In 1914, Davis Milling sold its business to Aunt Jemima Mills Company.

In 1915, Aunt Jemima Mills sued Rigney for trademark infringement. The district court denied relief on the ground that Rigney's conduct could not divert sales from Aunt Jemima Mills because "no one wanting syrup could possibly be made to take flour." The Second Circuit reversed. The case posed two difficult issues. First, did the Davis Milling letter constitute acquiescence in Rigney's use of the mark. Two of the three judges held it did not.[179] Second, did Aunt Jemima's trademark rights in

---

[178] The letter, undoubtedly trademark law's most famous, read:

"St. Joseph, Mo., March 14, 1908.

'Rigney & Co., Brooklyn, N.Y.— Gentlemen: We have your letter of the 5th. We are surprised to have you use the name "Aunt Jemima" for your syrup, but presume you can do so without violating any law in the matter. Mr. Jackson wrote us about this, but we did not know that you were going to do it right "hot off the pan" as one might say. We thought you were going to wait to hear from us. We note you say you have copyrighted "Aunt Jemima." Were you able to obtain a copyright of "Aunt Jemima" for maple syrup, or did you simply register it as a trade-mark? The sample which you sent us has been received, and it is as far as we can see, a very fine article. The looks of the Aunt Jemima Pancake Cream, as you call it, is not as good as the taste. The looks we think could be improved perhaps. Do you make this in a syrup as well as in the cream? Do you work the trade entirely through brokers, or do you handle it with salesmen working the retail trade? Would you be interest [sic] in taking on a pancake flour proposition along with your maple syrup and other lines? If so, we might have something of interest for you.

Yours truly,

The Davis Milling Co.,

Robert R. Clark."

Reprinted at 247 F. at 408.

Copyright Aunt Jemima for pancake syrup? This letter suggests that confusion about basic intellectual property concepts, for example, trademarks versus copyrights, was as common in the early 20th century as it is now.

[179] "The complainant was speaking of a matter of law, and said it 'presumed' that the defendants could do so without violating any law. But if, as matter of law, the defendants had no right to use the trade-mark, this expression of opinion by the complainant does not make the law other than it is, nor estop it from relying on the law as it really is. Bigelow on Estoppel, p. 634. Indeed, the complainant seems, in addition, to have been misled by the defendants as to the facts, because the letter goes on to say that the defendants had written they had copyrighted the trade-mark, and to ask whether they meant that they had registered it in the Patent Office. No reply to this letter was ever received. If the complainant had authorized the defendants to use the mark, or even had said it did not object to their doing so, mistake of law would not save it. When, however, it merely expressed a legal opinion, it did nothing to mislead the defendants, and they took the risk of acting on that opinion if it were erroneous." 247 F. at 408-09.

Judge Learned Hand dissented: "I find in the letter not only complete acquiescence, but in substance an invitation to co-operate with the defendant in the very infringement itself." He noted that on May 1, 1908, Davis Milling sent a retraction letter protesting Rigney's continuing use of the mark, but there was no adequate proof Rigney received the letter. 247 F. at 412.

(Matthew Bender & Co., Inc.)

a mark for flour extend to a noncompeting product, syrup? Writing for the majority, Judge Ward, relying on *Hanover Star Milling*, in the context of the territorial scope of trademark rights, noted that trademark rights did not extend to remote *geographic* markets "unless at least it appears that the second adopter has selected the mark with some design inimical to the interests of the first user, such as to take the benefit of the reputation of his goods, to forestall the extension of his trade, or the like."[180] Judge Ward viewed the *Hanover Star Milling* "inimical design" exception as grounds for expanding a trademark protection's product scope to "related" goods.

> "To use precisely the same mark . . . is . . . evidence of intention to make something out of it—either to get the benefit of the complainant's reputation or of its advertisement or to forestall the extension of its trade. There is no other conceivable reason why they should have appropriated this precise mark. . . .

> "It is said that even a technical trade-mark may be appropriated by any one in any market for goods not in competition with those of the prior user. . . . But we think that goods, though different, may be so related as to fall within the mischief which equity should prevent. Syrup and flour are both food products, and food products commonly used together. Obviously the public, or a large part of it, seeing this trade-mark on a syrup, would conclude that it was made by the complainant. Perhaps they might not do so, if it were used for flatirons. In this way the complainant's reputation is put in the hands of the defendants. It will enable them to get the benefit of the complainant's reputation and advertisement."[181]

In *Yale Electric*,[182] Judge Learned Hand, in a short but elegantly written opinion, described trademark law's progress. Yale Electric sought federal registration of the mark " 'Yale' in an ellipse, in turn surrounded by an irregular octagon" for "electric flash-light torches and their batteries." Yale & Towne, which owned the well-known mark "Yale" for locks, filed an opposition which the Patent Office sustained on the ground that "Yale" was an unregistrable surname.[183] The District of Columbia Court of Appeals affirmed on a different ground—that applicant's mark caused a likelihood of confusion between the two parties' wares. Persistent, Yale Electric sued the Commissioner to compel registration and joined Yale & Towne, which filed a counterclaim. The district court ruled for Yale & Towne and enjoined Yale Electric from using the mark upon "flash-lights or batteries" or "any article which is manufactured and consists in whole or in part of metal or other hard substance."

On appeal, Judge Hand noted ample evidence of confusion likelihood: "[T]he record contains many instances where the defendant's buyers did, or said that they should, suppose the plaintiff's flash-lights to be one of the defendant's products," leaving two legal issues: whether the defendant's goods had the "same descriptive properties" as plaintiff's, which the 1905 Trademark Act required for opposition on likelihood of

---

[180] 247 F.2d at 409.

[181] 247 F. at 409-410.

[182] Yale Electric Corp. v. Robertson, 26 F.2d 972 (2d Cir. 1928).

[183] For a discussion of surname registrability, see § 5C[3][c].

confusion grounds,[184] and, more important, "whether, in view of the fact that [defendant] makes no flash-lights or batteries, it may complain of the plaintiff's use of its name." On the latter:

> "The law of unfair trade comes down very nearly to this—as judges have repeated again and again—that one merchant shall not divert customers from another by representing what he sells as emanating from the second. This has been, and perhaps even more now is, the whole Law and the Prophets on the subject, though it assumes many guises. Therefore it was at first a debatable point whether a merchant's good will, indicated by his mark, could extend beyond such goods as he sold. How could he lose bargains which he had no means to fill? What harm did it do a chewing gum maker to have an ironmonger use his trade-mark? The law often ignores the nicer sensibilities.

> "However, it has of recent years been recognized that a merchant may have a sufficient economic interest in the use of his mark outside the field of his own exploitation to justify interposition by a court. His mark is his authentic seal; by it he vouches for the goods which bear it; it carries his name for good or ill. If another uses it, he borrows the owner's reputation, whose quality no longer lies within has own control. This is an injury, even though the borrower does not tarnish it, or divert any sales by its use; for a reputation, like a face, is the symbol of its possessor and creator, and another can use it only as a mask. And so it has come to be recognized that, unless the borrower's use is so foreign to the owner's as to insure against any identification of the two, it is unlawful. . . . Here we are dealing with a proper name, which, though it has been used quite generally, is shown to denote the defendant when applied to flash-lights. The disparity in quality between such wares and anything the plaintiff makes no longer counts, if that be true. The defendant need not permit another to attach to its good will the consequences of trade methods not its own."[185]

But Judge Hand also held that the injunction was "too broad."

> "Since the plaintiff has used the word upon nothing but flash-lights and batteries, and so far as appears does not mean to do more, the defendant needs no further protection. Besides, it does not inevitably follow that all metal objects, and all those made from any hard substance, should not bear the name 'Yale.' "[186]

---

[184] After finding that defendant could bar plaintiff's use of "Yale," Judge Hand circumvented the Trademark Act's "same descriptive properties" language:

> "It would plainly be a fatuity to decree the registration of a mark whose use another could at once prevent. The act cannot mean that, being drafted with an eye to the common law in such matters. . . . While we own that it does some violence to the language, it seems to us that the phrase should be taken as no more than a recognition that there may be enough disparity in character between the goods of the first and second users as to insure against confusion. That will indeed depend much upon trade conditions, but these are always the heart of the matter in this subject." 26 F.2d at 974.

[185] 26 F.2d at 973-74.

[186] 26 F.2d at 974.

In *L.E. Waterman*,[187] Judge Hand considered the impact of an accused infringer's intent and knowledge in adopting its mark on a related goods infringement determination. Plaintiff used "Waterman" for pens for 50 years but never made razor blades. Defendant adopted "Waterman" for razor blades and could provide "no excuse for pirating" plaintiff's mark. The district court granted a preliminary injunction. On appeal, Judge Hand first noted that the decision was correct "on the merits": *Aunt Jemima Mills* and *Yale Electric* established that "a trade-mark protects the owner against not only its use upon the articles to which he has applied it, but upon such other goods as might naturally be supposed to come from him."[188] When "the infringement is so wanton, there is no reason to look nicely at plaintiff's proofs in this regard."[189] Judge Hand then considered a jurisdictional problem caused by the 1905 federal trademark registration act's narrow focus. Because there was no diversity of citizenship, federal court jurisdiction over plaintiff's suit depended on its claim for infringement of its federal registration. Other circuits had held that a district court "has no jurisdiction over a cause based only upon registry of the mark, if the infringer uses it upon goods of another class than that for which it was registered in the Patent Office." Judge Hand viewed these decisions as "extremely questionable."

> "Registry does not create the cause of suit; it merely gives jurisdiction to the District Court, and certain procedural advantages. The theory on which the wrong has been extended to include the use of the mark on goods never made or sold by the owner, is that, though the infringer's user cannot at the moment take away his customers, it may indirectly do so by tarnishing his reputation, or it may prevent him from extending his trade to the goods on which the infringer is using the mark. That would seem as much a violation of the interest which the mark serves to protect, as though it was used upon the same kind of goods as the owner sells. That interest is that he shall be secure in the meaning of the mark to those who wish to deal with him. It is hard to see why the classes defined in the Patent Office have anything to do with that."[190]

He held it would not be necessary to dismiss the suit even if the circuit decisions were correct. The plaintiff's federal claim had enough substance to confer jurisdiction; the district court could then exercise pendent jurisdiction over the related common law claim.

In *S.C. Johnson & Son*,[191] Judge Hand assessed the 1946 Lanham Act's effect on the related goods problem. Beginning in 1886, plaintiff S.C. Johnson sold floor wax.

---

187 L.E. Waterman Co. v. Gordon, 72 F.2d 272 (2d Cir. 1934).

188 72 F.2d at 273. "There is indeed a limit; the goods on which the supposed infringer puts the mark may be too remote from any that the owner would be likely to make or sell. It would be hard, for example, for the seller of a steam shovel to find ground for complaint in the use of his trade-mark on a lipstick. But no such difficulty arises here; razor blades are sold very generally by others than razor blade makers, and might well be added to the repertory of a pen maker." *Id.*

189 72 F.2d at 273.

190 72 F.2d at 272-73.

191 S. C. Johnson & Son, Inc. v. Johnson, 116 F.2d 427 (2d Cir. 1940), *on motion to modify injunction*, 175 F.2d 176 (2d Cir. 1949), *cert. denied*, 338 U.S. 860 (1949).

Later, it introduced other preparations, including floor cleaners, varnishes, and polishes but never made a fabric cleaner. In 1915, it registered "Johnson's" as a trade mark for various products. In 1932, defendant adopted his surname "Johnson's" in large red letters on a yellow label as a mark for a fabric cleaner. S.C. Johnson sued. The district court found that defendant's use of Johnson confused plaintiff's customers and enjoined defendant from selling his product using "Johnson's." On appeal, Judge Hand was more cautious about expanding trademark rights to related goods than he had been in *Yale Electric* and *L.E. Waterman*.[192] The trademark owner's two "interests" in preventing use of his mark on noncompeting goods—reputation damage and future expansion—were contingent and did not justify granting a trademark owner a broad monopoly over a word. A likelihood of some consumer confusion did not justify giving a trademark owner a remedy if the confusion caused him no injury.[193] Judge Hand directed that defendant be subject only to a

---

[192] Judge Hand's heightened concern about monopoly paralleled the stricter judicial attitude toward patents that arose in the 1930s. *See* § 2B[4][c].

See also Standard Brands, Inc. v. Smidler, 151 F.2d 34, 41-42 (2d Cir. 1945) (FRANK, concurring: "Perhaps the course of the trade-name decisions has another explanation: The earlier, more generous, rulings seem to have occurred in that period when—deviating from their original attitude—the courts were silently minimizing the public interest in patents and were benignly disposed towards broad interpretations of grants of patent monopolies. Although the trade-name monopolies, unlike patents, were made by the judges without benefit of express legislative authority, . . . the courts' attitude towards patents, by a sort of intellectual osmosis, affected their rulings concerning trade symbols. When, more recently, the older, stricter, judicial views about patents re-emerged, . . . this strictness, in part at least, seems to have carried over into the trade-name decisions. . . . The public today is displaying a revived, lively interest in 'free enterprise.' That revived interest, one may hope, will not prevent a discriminating consideration of socially desirable monopolies or partial monopolies, an adequate cognizance of what, with increasing understanding, many modern economists call 'imperfect competition' or 'monopolistic competition.' Those who, oversimplifying economic problems, thoughtlessly urge the elimination of virtually all monopolies, not only disregard the unavoidable existence of monopolistic elements in almost all kinds of competition but dangerously invite a program which, by neglecting socially valuable aspects of some industrial integrations ('oligopolies') in some mass production industries, might tragically reduce our living standards.").

[193] "Since in such a situation the injured party has not lost any sales, the courts have based his right upon two other interests: first, his reputation with his customers; second, his possible wish to expand his business into the disputed market. The first of these is real enough, even when the newcomer has as yet done nothing to tarnish the reputation of the first user. Nobody willingly allows another to masquerade as himself; it is always troublesome, and generally impossible, to follow the business practices of such a competitor closely enough to be sure that they are not damaging, and the harm is frequently done before it can be prevented. Yet even as to this interest we should not forget that, so long as the newcomer has not in fact misconducted himself, the injury is prospective and contingent, and very different from taking away the first user's customers. The second interest is frequently less palpable. It is true that a merchant who has sold one kind of goods, sometimes finds himself driven to add other 'lines' in order to hold or develop his existing market; in such cases he has a legitimate present interest in preserving his identity in the ancillary market, which he cannot do, if others make his name equivocal there. But if the new goods have no such relation to the old, and if the first user's interest in maintaining the significance of his name when applied to the new goods is nothing more than the desire to post the new market as a possible preserve which he may later

limited injunction requiring it to use "Johnson's with 'cleaner' " as a single phrase together with "made by Johnson Products Company, Buffalo, N.Y." in "type equally large and conspicuous." The injunction could not prevent all confusion, but any stricter requirement would be too harsh on defendant, and plaintiff assumed some risk of confusion by adopting such a common surname as a mark.[194]

In 1948, plaintiff S.C. Johnson moved to modify the injunction, reasoning: "(1) that the label does not conform to the judgment; (2) that the original injunction did not give the plaintiff adequate relief or protect the public; (3) that the original defendant had taken in the four new partners; and (4) that the Lanham Act . . . had since been passed." Judge Hand affirmed the motion's denial, commenting that it "has not the slightest justification save for the enactment of the Lanham Act," which "did indeed put federal trade-mark law upon a new footing."[195]

As discussed in *L.E. Waterman*, the 1905 Act infringement section gave a registered mark owner a remedy against any who affixed the mark "to merchandise of substantially the same descriptive properties as those set forth in the registration." The Lanham Act used apparently broader language, prohibiting registered mark uses that are "likely to cause confusion or mistake or deceive purchasers as to the source of origin" of the goods on which the owner uses the mark. Judge Hand agreed that the Lanham Act created a uniform substantive federal trademark law, but "it does not follow that, in determining what [the law is], we are not to be guided by the existing common-law, especially in regard to issues as to which that law was well settled in 1946."[196] The Lanham Act remedy section was a "substantial change," but Judge Hand said Congress intended to follow, not extend, the court's interpretation of trademark and unfair competition common law principles. The 1905 Act's language

---

choose to exploit, it is hard to see any basis for its protection. The public may be deceived, but he has no claim to be its vicarious champion; his remedy must be limited to his injury and by hypothesis he has none. There is always the danger that we may be merely granting a monopoly, based upon the notion that by advertising one can obtain some 'property' in a name. We are nearly sure to go astray in any phase of the whole subject, as soon as we lose sight of the underlying principle that the wrong involved is diverting trade from the first deal with him. Unless therefore he can show that, in order to hold or develop his present business, he must preserve his identity in the disputed market, he cannot rely upon the second of the two interests at stake." 116 F.2d at 429.

194 ". . . [T]his will not surely advise the public that the defendant's cleaner is not made by the plaintiff; but it appears to us that the only alternatives are too drastic. That chosen by the district judge, while it did not entirely forbid the use of defendant's name, took from him a very natural idiom; it would have been appropriate enough, if he was competing, but not where the injury is so problematical as it is. The only other is to compel him to use the phrase, often prescribed in such cases, 'not connected with S. C. Johnson & Son Inc.' That is even more severe; it not only advertises the injured party, but directly suggests that the defendant has been found guilty of some unfair practice. When all is said, if a man allows the good will of his business to become identified with a surname so common as Johnson, it is fair to impose upon him some of the risk that another Johnson may wish to sell goods not very far afield; and he must show a substantial interest if he would seriously impair the second Johnson's privilege to use his own name in customary ways." 116 F.2d at 430.

195 175 F.2d at 178.

196 *Id.*

reflected the pre-*Aunt Jemima* law, which extended a trademark owner's rights to goods he did not sell only in limited situations. After 1905, common law decisions expanded trademark rights, which, in cases such as *L.E. Waterman*, raised questions whether the 1905 Act could extend as far as the common law. Congressional desire to make the federal law "coextensive with the law of unfair competition as it was in 1946" sufficiently explained the wording change. Further, "there is the strongest possible reason for not reading the language literally" because "to do so would frequently result in great hardship to others, and give to the first user of a mark a wholly unjustified power to preempt new markets."[197] Judge Hand conceded that a mere likelihood of confusion indeed might justify extending protection without regard to tarnishment or concrete expansion possibilities in "the case of fabricated marks which have no significance."

Judge Clark dissented. The majority "cut [the Lanham Act] so extensively heralded by sponsoring groups down to a size consistent with the court's conceptions of public policy."

> "While I regard these conceptions highly, I am troubled by the fact that the Act is rather clearly the expression of contrary views vigorously held by persons and groups who were able to exercise a persuasive influence in the halls of Congress during its long period of germination. That other interests, those of consumers, for example, may have been more imperfectly represented there does not seem to me to lessen our problem, for we must take the legislative process as we find it, not as we wish it might be."[198]

---

[197] "The 'Aunt Jemima Doctrine,' as we may for brevity call it, needs to be indeed carefully circumscribed. It recognizes two, but only two, interests on which the owner can stand: (1) the possibility that the trade practices of the second user may stain the owner's reputation in the minds of his customers; and (2) the possibility that at some time in the future he may wish to extend his business into that market which the second user has begun to exploit. These are legitimate interests and they are properly weighed against the second user's interests; but it is far from true that the mere fact of confusion between the two users should always and of itself tip the scales in favor of the first. In Emerson Electric Manufacturing Co. v. Emerson Radio & Phonograph Corporation [105 F.2d 908, 910 (2d Cir. 1939)] and Dwinell-Wright Company v. White House Milk Company, Inc., [132 F.2d 822 (2d Cir. 1943)] we tried to show how the power of a first user to establish such a premonitory lien upon a future market might lead to great injustice. . . . In deciding such 'interstitial' issues, which legislatures at times wisely leave to them, courts are obliged to take over their function *pro haec vice* and to decide which of the conflicting interests they think should prevail. The case at bar is an admirable example of how unfairly a literal enforcement of the language of the new act may operate. The plaintiff does not sell cleaning fluid; it makes waxes and other polishes, and the defendants cannot possibly turn away from it any customers who would buy these instead of cleaning fluids. When John W. Johnson began business in 1932 he did so under his own name—the customary and innocent identification of his goods with himself. . . . True, nobody likes to have his reputation subject to the hazards of another's conduct; but there is no suggestion that in fact the defendants have tarnished the plaintiff's name in the minds of those who may think they are buying its goods. Again, although the plaintiff may at some future time wish to make cleaning fluids, it does not now even intimate such a purpose." 175 F.2d 179-180.

[198] 175 F.2d at 180-81.

(Matthew Bender & Co., Inc.)

S.C. Johnson was during an era Professor McCarthy characterizes as "Judicial schizophrenia in [the] Second Circuit."[199] From about 1940 to about 1960, the circuit's judges divided into two camps:

[199] The following cases are representative of the many battles in the long war.

1. Standard Brands, Inc. v. Smidler, 151 F.2d 34, 42-43 (2d Cir. 1945) (owner of "V-8" for eight-vegetable juice granted injunction against use of "V-8" for vitamins; majority opinion by CHASE; FRANK, concurring: "With considerable doubt, I agree . . . that plaintiff has [a] monopoly" extending to vitamins; "In such cases, a plaintiff, who, by use, has pre-empted a name as the symbol of a certain product, asserts that no one else, including the defendant, may, without the plaintiff's consent, use that name as a symbol of another, different, product which the plaintiff has never sold. Obviously, purchasers of the second product are not fooled into believing that it is the same as the first product. The deception, if it exists, consists merely of the erroneous belief that both products come from a common source. No harm to purchasers (consumers) results from such an erroneous belief. The harm, if any, is to the plaintiff, and is said to be this: The defendant's product may be so 'inferior' as to create ill-will among consumers directed against the supposed common maker of both products, with the consequence that the good will of the plaintiff, as maker of the first product, will be impaired. Accepting that principle as the basis of plaintiff's suit, logically plaintiff should fail, absent proof that defendant's product is actually 'inferior,' i.e., so shoddy or substandard that such impairment of plaintiff's good will is a likely result. As plaintiff in the case at bar has offered no such proof, I am doubtful whether, on rational grounds, it is entitled to governmental protection of the widespread monopoly it claims.").

2. Triangle Publications, Inc. v. Rohrlich, 167 F.2d 969, 976- 80 (2d Cir. 1948) (owner of "Seventeen" mark for magazines granted injunction against use of "Miss Seventeen" for girdles; majority opinion by AUGUSTUS HAND; FRANK, dissenting: "I have questioned some adolescent girls and their mothers and sisters, persons I have chosen at random. I have been told uniformly by my questionees that no one could reasonably believe that any relation existed between plaintiff's magazine and defendants' girdles. . . . I think my colleagues misapply a correct doctrine: (a) It has been held that, in a case relating to competitive articles, where there is room for a reasonable belief that confusion of buyers might occur (i.e., where that fact on the face of things is within the realm of the plausible), then evidence that defendants knowingly selected plaintiff's trade-name, with the deliberate intention of benefiting by plaintiff's public exploitation of it, is enough to prove that confusion is likely. (b) But such rulings have never been made—in truth, they have been rejected—when, as here, the probability of confusion of source is so slight as to be virtually incredible. . . . [O]rdinarily, an intention, no matter how evil, to harm another is a damp squib if the means for effectuating it are completely wanting."; "Question has been raised as to whether the trade-name doctrine, by its creation of 'perpetual monopolies,' has not injured consumers, a question of peculiarly serious import in these days when living-costs are notoriously oppressive.").

3. Hyde Park Clothes, Inc. v. Hyde Park Fashions, Inc., 204 F.2d 223, 226-29 (2d Cir. 1953) (owner of "Hyde Park" for *men's* clothing denied injunction against use of "Hyde Park" for *women's* clothing; majority opinion by SWAN; CLARK, dissenting: "Plaintiff-appellant has had the misfortune—so it seems to me—to come before a panel of this court allergic to the doctrine historically associated with us because of its nurture by our most illustrious judges . . . of protecting trade names against competition which will create confusion as to the source of goods sold under such names. . . . For here we have the two competitors—the one with long established reputation, the other breaking in—manufacturing and selling in the same way in what seems to me the one industry, referred to in the opinion as 'the garment trade.' The connection seems to me much closer than, e.g., razor blades and fountain pens, L. E. Waterman Co. v. Gordon, 2 Cir., 72 F.2d 272, 273, or refrigerators and sewing ma-

> "Generally, Judges Learned Hand and Jerome Frank espoused the view that trademark protection should be sparingly, if at all applied to protect uses on noncompetitive goods. They feared creating a judge-made 'monopoly' in trademarks. Judges Clark and Augustus Hand generally favored application of the broad 'related goods' test of the old Aunt Jemima and Yale cases. Judges Swan and Chase sometimes went with the Learned Hand-Frank faction, sometimes to the Clark-Augustus Hand camp."[200]

Polaroid[201] concerned noncompeting goods and similar but not identical marks. Judge Friendly resolved the case on laches, but in dictum set forth a multiple factor likelihood of confusion approach.

> "The problem of determining how far a valid trademark shall be protected with respect to goods other than those to which its owner has applied it, has long been vexing and does not become easier of solution with the years . . . Where the products are different, the prior owner's chance of success is a function of many variables: the strength of his make, the degree of similarity between the two marks, the proximity of the products, the likelihood that the prior owner will bridge the gap, actual confusion, and the reciprocal of defendant's good faith in adopting its own mark, the quality of defendant's product, and the sophistication of the buyers. Even this extensive catalogue does not exhaust the possibilities—the court may have to take still other variables into account. American Law Institute, Restatement of Torts, 729, 730, 731."

The *Polaroid* multiple factors dictum became dominant—in the Second Circuit[202]

---

chines, Admiral Corp. v. Penco, Inc., supra, or other precedents therein cited. If we take the nine factors bearing on the issue of infringement and the 'limitation of protection with reference to kind of goods' so carefully formulated in 3 Restatement, Torts Sec 731, I suggest that practically everyone argues against limitation here. I shall not take space to go through them seriatim, but might stress such high lights as the general likelihood that the goods of one will be mistaken for those of the other, the extent to which the goods are marketed through the same channels, the relation in function between them, the degree of distinctiveness of the trade-mark or trade name, the length of time of use, etc. I rather deprecate the seizing on small distinctions in the goods—of a kind not quickly occurring to a shopping customer—to justify this form of competition. By making ever finer distinctions between products, we could easily do away with all possibility of protection to an established trade reputation.").

200 J. T. McCarthy, trademarks and unfair competition § 24:9 (2nd ed. 1984).

201 Polaroid Corp. v. Polarad Electronics Corp., 287 F.2d 492 (2d Cir. 1961), *cert. denied,* 368 U.S. 820 (1961).

202 *E.g.*, McGregor-Doniger Inc. v. Drizzle Inc., 599 F.2d 1126, 1139, 202 U.S.P.Q. 81 (2d Cir. 1979) (no likelihood of confusion between plaintiff's "DRIZZLER" golf jackets and defendant's "DRIZZLE" women's coats; "In trademark infringement cases involving noncompeting goods, it is rare that we are 'overwhelmed by the sudden blinding light of the justness of one party's cause.' . . . Most often our affirmances in such cases rest on the more modest conclusion that the trial judge was not wrong in reaching the result appealed from. . . . Although the two marks at issue are concededly quite similar, the court below found that the DRIZZLER mark is only moderately strong, that the competitive distance between the products is significant, that there was no intention to bridge the gap, that no actual confusion has occurred, and that Drizzle adopted its mark in good faith. . . . Because the goods are

and other circuits.[203]

---

concededly not competitive, McGregor's sales of DRIZZLER jackets cannot be expected to suffer. Where non-competitive goods are involved the trademark laws protect the senior user's interest in an untarnished reputation and his interest in being able to enter a related field at some future time. . . . Because consumer confusion as to source is unlikely, McGregor's reputation cannot be expected to be harmed. Because of the improbability that McGregor will enter the women's coat field under the DRIZZLER name, its right to expand into other fields has not been unduly restricted. Thus we see no injury to McGregor resulting from denial of the relief requested. On the other hand, if forced to give up its mark Drizzle could be expected to be harmed by loss of the goodwill that has been associated with the DRIZZLE name since 1969."); Mushroom Makers, Inc. v. R.G. Barry Corp., 580 F.2d 44, 199 U.S.P.Q. 65 (2d Cir. 1978), *cert. denied*, 439 U.S. 1116, 200 U.S.P.Q. 832 (1979) ("merely winning the race to the trademark office doorstep does not entitle a senior user to relief in equity. Rather, 'a senior user possesses but two legitimate interests which may properly call for injunctive relief against a use by a junior user on related goods, namely, that he may at some future date desire to expand his business into the related field in which the junior user is operating and that he, in any event, should be able to develop his present business free from the stain and tarnishment which may result from improper trade practices of the junior user.' "); Scarves by Vera, Inc. v. Todo Imports Ltd., Inc., 544 F.2d 1167, 1172-73, 192 U.S.P.Q. 289 (2d Cir. 1976) ("The trademark laws protect three interests which are present here: first, the senior user's interest in being able to enter a related field at some future time; second, his interest in protecting the good reputation associated with his mark from the possibility of being tarnished by inferior merchandise of the junior user; and third, the public's interest in not being misled by confusingly similar marks a factor which may weigh in the senior user's favor where the defendant has not developed the mark himself. We have heretofore protected the trademark owner's rights against use on related, non-competing products a result in accord with the realities of mass media salesmanship and the purchasing behavior of consumers. . . . Absent equities in the junior user's favor, he should be enjoined from using a similar trademark whenever the non-competitive products are sufficiently related that customers are likely to confuse the source of origin."); Chandon Champagne Corp. v. San Marino Wine Corp., 335 F.2d 531, 536, 142 U.S.P.Q. 239 (2d Cir. 1964) ("Although this court was the leader in granting relief to a trademark owner when there had been and was no likelihood of actual diversion [*i.e.* in cases involving non-competitive products], we have likewise emphasized that, in such cases, 'against these legitimate interests of the senior user are to be weighed the legitimate interests of the innocent second user' and that we must balance 'the conflicting interests both parties have in the unimpaired continuation of their trade mark use.' ").

[203] *E.g.*, Mutual of Omaha Insurance Co. v. Novak, 836 F.2d 397, 399, 5 U.S.P.Q.2d 1314, 1316 (8th Cir. 1987), *cert. denied*, 488 U.S. 933 (1988) ("confusion, not competition, is the touchstone of trademark infringement"); Fuji Photo Film Co., Inc. v. Shinohara Shoji Kabushiki Kaisha, 754 F.2d 591, 598, 225 U.S.P.Q. 540, 544 (5th Cir. 1985) ("Complementary products have been held particularly susceptible to confusion."); Interpace Corp. v. Lapp, Inc., 721 F.2d 460, 464 (3d Cir. 1983) ("The likelihood-of-expansion factor is pivotal in non-competing products cases such as this. One of the chief reasons for granting a trademark owner protection in a market not his own is to protect his right someday to enter that market. . . . To determine likelihood of confusion where the plaintiff and defendant deal in non-competing lines of goods or services, the court must look beyond the trademark to the nature of the products themselves, and to the context in which they are marketed and sold. The closer the relationship between the products, and the more similar their sales contexts, the greater the likelihood of confusion. . . . Once a trademark owner demonstrates likelihood of confusion, it is entitled to injunctive relief."); AMF Inc. v. Sleekcraft Boats, 599 F.2d 341, 354, 204

Triumph Hosiery Mills[204] sounded *Polaroid's* triumph as both a synthesis and extension of Judge Hand's "interest" test for related, noncompeting products. Plaintiff Triumph Hosiery Mills marketed women's stockings and tights under its "Triumph" mark. For many years, defendant's parent corporation had marketed women's foundation garments under the mark "Distinction by Triumph of Europe." Plaintiff sued when defendants began marketing in the United States. The district court initially denied relief, finding that because defendant's goods were of high quality and only slightly overlapped plaintiff's, "neither of the 'two legitimate interests' of a senior user—(1) possible expansion into the related field, and (2) stain and tarnishment to his reputation—would be infringed." Further, defendant was an " 'innocent' junior . . . user." The district court later granted relief based on new evidence that defendant's parent had marketed goods under its mark for many years but its corporate name was of more recent vintage and the Patent Office had rejected an application to register "Triumph of Europe" because it was merely a tradename, additional facts that stripped defendants of the "cloak of innocence." In any case, there was a likelihood of confusion between the parties' goods. The Second Circuit reversed.

> "Although, it must be confessed, it is difficult to reconcile all the decisions of this court dealing with this problem, we think the full Bench of the court would now accept the propositions set forth in the opinion in *Polaroid Corporation v. Polarad Electronics Corp.* . . .

> ". . . [T]his broadly stated summary includes the two conditions—(1) the prospect that the owner will want to extend his activities into the disputed area and (2) the hazard that the owner's reputation may be tarnished by the use by another—which Judge L. Hand in his opinion in *S. C. Johnson & Son v. Johnson* . . . thought should limit the extension of a trade-mark to cover related goods under the so-called 'Aunt Jemima' doctrine. . . . The *Polaroid* summary, recognizes that the reach of the trade-mark beyond its owner's present use depends upon factors which are variable and relative, none of which standing alone constitutes the sole criterion. In this, the *Polaroid* summary is not in conflict with the *Johnson* opinion. For in *Johnson*, Judge Hand strongly intimated that the two limiting conditions of the Aunt Jemima doctrine are in themselves not indispensable absolutes but rather relative variables."[205]

U.S.P.Q. 808 (9th Cir. 1979) ("Inasmuch as a trademark owner is afforded greater protection against competing goods, a 'strong possibility' that either party may expand his business to compete with the other will weigh in favor of finding that the present use is infringing."; there is a likelihood of confusion between plaintiff's "SLICKCRAFT" recreational boats and defendant's "SLEEKCRAFT" racing boats because, *inter alia*, both parties are expanding their model lines).

Cf. Homeowners Group, Inc. v. Home Marketing Specialists, Inc., 931 F.2d 1100, 1108, 18 U.S.P.Q.2d 1587, 1593-94, (6th Cir. 1991) ("Courts have recognized that there are basically three categories of cases: (1) direct competition of services, in which case confusion is likely if the marks are sufficiently similar; (2) services are somewhat related but not competitive, so that likelihood of confusion may or may not result depending on other factors; and (3) services are totally unrelated, in which case confusion is unlikely. . . . These categories are helpful in gauging how important relatedness may be in the ultimate likelihood of confusion determination.").

[204] Triumph Hosiery Mills, Inc. v. Triumph International Corp., 308 F.2d 196 (2d Cir. 1962).

[205] *Id.* at 198.

The court agreed that "it would not necessarily be fatal to the grant of an injunction that neither of the two 'Aunt Jemima' conditions existed,"[206] but the district court erred in finding that defendant's use of its mark was so lacking in "innocence" as to entitle plaintiff to relief.

> "An 'innocent' or a bona fide junior user . . . is one . . . whose use is not attributable to intent to obtain a free ride on the reputation of the owner of the trade-mark. Only one without such an intent is in position to contend that the resulting confusion as to the source of the goods, which is the statutory touchstone, will be too slight to bring the case above the rule of de minimis. . . . [T]he defendants' knowledge that the plaintiff was entitled to exclusive use of the Triumph trade-mark on hosiery, did not necessarily mean that they knew that notwithstanding their use of 'Triumph' abroad, the courts would exclude them from the use of their mark, 'Distinction by Triumph of Europe,' on their girdles, etc. From the bare fact that the Patent Office had refused the defendants' application for registration of 'Triumph of Europe,' it did not follow that the defendants could not have honestly believed that on a weighing of all the relative and variable pertinent factors a court of competent jurisdiction would not permit them to use the trade-mark 'Distinction by Triumph of Europe' on goods which they had long sold abroad under the Triumph trade name. Surely, error of an alleged infringer of a trade-mark, or indeed of a patent, in forecasting the decision of the ultimate arbiter, is not a species of bad faith which constitutes independent and substantive proof of infringement."[207]

Even if the district court were right that defendant was not an innocent junior user, this fact would not of itself justify the injunction. *Polaroid* "recognizes that no single factor may be taken as determinative."[208]

[b] Dilution. Many states have trademark "anti-dilution" statutes that extend mark protection beyond federal law's likelihood of confusion standard by providing that "[l]ikelihood of injury to business reputation or of dilution of the distinctive quality of a mark registered under this chapter, or a mark valid at common law, or a trade name valid at common law, shall be a ground for injunctive relief notwithstanding the absence of competition between the parties or the absence of confusion as to the source of goods or services."[209]

---

[206] *Id.* at 199.

[207] *Id.* at 199.

[208] *Id.* at 200.

[209] Cal. Bus. & Prof. Code § 14330. Massachusetts enacted the first anti-dilution statute in 1947. 15 Mass. Gen. L. ch. 110B § 12.

In addition to California and Massachusetts, other states with anti-dilution statutes include Alabama (Ala. St. § 8-12-17); Arkansas (Ark. St. § 4-71-113); Conn. Gen. St. Ann. § 35-11i(c); Delaware (6 Del. Code Ann. § 3313); Florida (Fla. Stat. § 495.151); Georgia (Ga. St. § 10-1-451); Idaho (Ida. St. 48-512); Illinois (Ill. Ann. Stat. ch. 140, § 22); Iowa (Iowa St. § 548.11); Louisiana (La. Rev. Stat. 51:223.1); Maine (Me. Rev. St. 10 § 1530); Missouri (Mo. Stat. 417.061); Nebraska (Neb. Rev. St. 87-122); New Hampshire (N.H. St. 350-A:12); New Mexico (N.M. St. § 57-3-10); New York (N.Y. Gen. Bus. § 368-d); Pennsylvania (54 Pa. Con.

"The concept of trademark dilution originated in England when a British court protected the trademark 'Kodak' from being used on bicycles. . . . Anti-dilution statutes have developed to fill a void left by the failure of trademark infringement law to curb the unauthorized use of marks where there is no likelihood of confusion between the original use and the infringing use. The law of trademark dilution aims to protect the distinctive quality of a trademark from deterioration caused by its use on dissimilar products. . . . The dilution injury 'is the gradual whittling away or dispersion of the identity and hold upon the public mind of the mark or name by its use on non-competing goods.' Schechter, The Rational Basis of Trademark Protection, 40 Harv.L.Rev. 813, 825 (1927). The overriding purpose of anti-dilution statutes is to prohibit a merchant of noncompetitive goods from selling its products by trading on the goodwill and reputation of another's mark."[210]

Stat. § 1124); Oregon (Ore. St. § 647.107); Rhode Island (R.I. St. § 6-2-12); and Tennessee (Tenn. St. § 47-25-512); Wash. Stat. 19.77.010.

The statutes use virtually the same language, most being based on the Model State Trademark Act. A major exception is the Washington State statute, enacted in 1989, and similar to the anti-dilution provision that Congress considered but rejected in 1988. See below. The Washington statute limits protection to "famous marks."

"The owner of a famous mark shall be entitled, subject to the principles of equity, to an injunction against another person's use in this state of a mark, commencing after the mark becomes famous, which causes dilution of the distinctive quality of the mark, and to obtain such other relief as is provided in this section. In determining whether a mark is famous and has distinctive quality, a court shall consider all relevant factors, including, but not limited to the following:

(1) Whether the mark is inherently distinctive or has become distinctive through substantially exclusive and continuous use;

(2) Whether the duration and extent of use of the mark are substantial;

(3) Whether the duration and extent of advertising and publicity of the mark are substantial;

(4) Whether the geographical extent of the trading area in which the mark is used is substantial;

(5) Whether the mark has substantial renown in its and in the other person's trading areas and channels of trade; and

(6) Whether substantial use of the same or similar marks is being made by third parties.

"The owner shall be entitled only to injunctive relief in an action brought under this section, unless the subsequent user willfully intended to trade on the registrant's reputation or to cause dilution of the owner's mark. If such willful intent is proven, the owner shall also be entitled to the remedies set forth in this chapter, subject to the discretion of the court and the principles of equity."

Wash. St. 19.77.160. It defines "dilution" as "the material reduction of the distinctive quality of a famous mark through use of a mark by another person, regardless of the presence or absence of (a) competition between the users of the mark, or (b) likelihood of confusion, mistake, or deception arising from that use. . . . " Wash. St. 19.77.010(4).

[210] L.L. Bean, Inc. v. Drake Publishers, Inc., 811 F.2d 26, 1 U.S.P.Q.2d 1753 (1st Cir. 1987), cert. denied, 483 U.S. 1013 (1987). See also Anti-Defamation League of B'Nai B'Rith v. Arab Anti-Defamation League, 72 Misc.2d 847, 340 N.Y.S.2d 532, 549 n.7, 177

In 1988, Congress considered but declined to add a federal anti-dilution provision to the Lanham Act.[211] Special federal legislation protects particular marks, such as the Olympic sports symbol, from unauthorized uses without regard to source confusion.[212]

Early court decisions approached dilution claims warily.[213] Courts, which generally respond only to claims based on concrete injury to a complainant, saw little harm to a trademark owner when there was no competitive injury or consumer confusion.

Allied Maintenance[214] inaugurated a new era of respect for anti-dilution statutes. Plaintiff, Allied Maintenance Corp., operated an office building cleaning and maintenance business in New York City since 1888. Defendant, Allied Mechanical Trades, Inc., began a heating, ventilating, and air-conditioning installation and repair business in the same city. Plaintiff sued in the New York courts. The court of appeals noted that prior federal court and state court decisions in New York and other states refused to apply the statute literally, reading into it "a requirement of some showing of confusion, fraud or deception."

> "Notwithstanding the absence of judicial enthusiasm for the anti-dilution statutes, we believe that section 368-d does extend the protection afforded trade-marks and trade names beyond that provided by actions for infringement and unfair competition. The evil which the Legislature sought to remedy was not public confusion caused by similar products or services sold by competitors, but a cancer-like growth of dissimilar products or services which feeds upon the business reputation of an established distinctive trade-mark or name. Thus, it would be of no significance under our statute that Tiffany's Movie Theatre is not a competitor of, nor likely to be confused with Tiffany's Jewelry.

U.S.P.Q. 650 (1972) ("The dilution theory originated in a 1924 German case involving the identical mark 'ODOL' in steel products and mouthwash and was introduced into American jurisprudence by Schechter, *The Rational Basis of Trademark Protection*, 40 Harv. L. Rev. 813, 831 (1927).").

[211] Acting on the United States Trademark Association Review Commission's recommendation, the Senate included a new Section 43(c) as part of the Trademark Revision Act. S. 1883, 100th Cong., 2d Sess. Section 43(c) would have protected "famous" and distinctive marks from uses that diluted their distinctive quality. Dilution meant "the material reduction of the distinctive quality of a famous mark." It listed five factors for determine a mark's fame. The House of Representatives deleted Section 43(c), noting that "Serious questions were raised about these provisions by persons concerned with the dissemination of First Amendment protected communications, and with advertising their goods and services to the public." H.R. Rep. No. 100-1028, 100th Cong., 2d Sess. (1988).

[212] *See* § 1D[4].

[213] *See* Anti-Defamation League of B'Nai B'Rith v. Arab Anti-Defamation League, 72 Misc.2d 847, 340 N.Y.S.2d 532, 542- 43, 177 U.S.P.Q. 650 (1972) ("The dilution approach has been recognized but 'sparingly applied' by the New York Courts. . . . The New York Courts cling to the talismanic standard of likelihood of confusion. . . . Perhaps these decisions may be attributed to the ambiguity as to the identification of the right of action in either 'dilution' or 'distinctive quality,' and to the absence of definition of the latter phrase with the risk that the statute may be read to grant a monopoly to the first user as a result of *stare decisis* effect of a judgment.").

[214] Allied Maintenance Corp. v. Allied Mechanical Trades, Inc., 42 N.Y.2d 538, 399 N.Y.S.2d 628, 369 N.E.2d 1162, 198 U.S.P.Q. 418 (1977).

. . . The harm that section 368-d is designed to prevent is the gradual whittling away of a firm's distinctive trade-mark or name. It is not difficult to imagine the possible effect which the proliferation of various noncompetitive businesses utilizing the name Tiffany's would have upon the public's association of the name Tiffany's solely with fine jewelry. The ultimate effect has been appropriately termed dilution.

"Although section 368-d does not require a showing of confusion or competition to obtain an injunction, it does require a '[l]ikelihood of injury to business reputation or of dilution of the *distinctive quality* of a mark or trade name.' (Emphasis added.) The statute prohibits any use of a name or mark likely to dilute the distinctive quality of a name in use. To merit protection, the plaintiff must possess a strong mark one which has a distinctive quality or has acquired a secondary meaning which is capable of dilution." [215]

Applying the dilution action's two elements, a distinctive mark and a likelihood of dilution, it held that "Allied Maintenance" was a weak mark not susceptible to dilution.[216] As a combination of common descriptive words, it was not "an inherently strong trade name susceptible to dilution" and had not acquired secondary meaning because many other businesses used "Allied" in their trade names.

Some decisions suggest that the anti-dilution statutes do not apply when the parties' goods or services compete or there is a likelihood of confusion,[217] but others view a dilution remedy as a supplement to trademark infringement claims based on the likelihood of findings of confusion.[218]

---

[215] 399 N.Y.S.2d at 632, 369 N.E.2d at 1165-66.

See also Sally Gee, Inc. v. Myra Hogan, Inc., 699 F.2d 621, 624-25, 217 U.S.P.Q. 658, 661 (2d Cir. 1983) ("Section 368-d's qualifying clause means exactly what its language denotes. Neither competition between the parties nor confusion about the source of products . . . appears to be necessary to state a cause of action for dilution. . . . The interest protected by § 368-d is not simply commercial goodwill, but the selling power that a distinctive mark or name with favorable associations has engendered for a product in the mind of the consuming public.").

[216] Dissenting, Judge Cooke argued that "The use of a name associated with a particular business by one in a closely related field is a dilution of a less well-known name and is of no less significance to the particular plaintiff than use of an extremely well-known trade name by a totally unrelated business." 399 N.Y.S.2d at 635, 369 N.E.2d at 1168.

[217] Edgewater Apartments Corp. v. Edgewater Beach Management Co., Inc., 12 Ill. App.3d 526, 299 N.E.2d 548, 554, 179 U.S.P.Q. 555 (1973) ("Where traditional remedies under theories of unfair competition are available, relief under the statute should not be granted. . . . In the instant case not only are the parties competitors with one another but there is . . . a likelihood of confusion between them.").

[218] *E.g.*, Markel v. Scovill Manufacturing Co., 471 F. Supp. 1244, 1253, 204 U.S.P.Q. 641 (W.D. N.Y. 1979), *aff'd*, 610 F.2d 807 (2d Cir. 1979) (unpublished) ("Not only have defendants shown that a likelihood of confusion will be caused by plaintiffs' use of the Markel name, there is a strong likelihood that they could satisfy the less stringent requirement of showing dilution, or a weakening of the identity and advertising value of their mark through Markel Heater's use of the Markel name."). *Cf.* Home Box Office v. Showtime/The Movie Channel, 665 F. Supp. 1079, 1087, 3 U.S.P.Q.2d 1806, 1811 (S.D. N.Y. 1987), *aff'd in part, vacated in part*, 832 F.2d 1311, 4 U.S.P.Q.2d 1789 (2d Cir. 1987) (no tarnishment or blurring when one competitor used another's mark in advertising slogans, such as "SHOWTIME & HBO. It's Not Either/Or

[i] *Distinctiveness*. A dilution claimant's mark must be distinctive,[219] as with trademark law's distinctiveness requirement,[220] but courts require that the mark be more distinctive than is minimally necessary for trademark protection.[221]

Anymore." "While State anti-dilution claims often appear as boilerplate in Lanham Act complaints, a claim for dilution differs markedly from a federal trademark claim and appears less well defined.").

[219] *E.g.*, Parenting Unlimited Inc. v. Columbia Pictures Television Inc., 743 F. Supp. 221, 16 U.S.P.Q.2d 1171 (S.D. N.Y. 1990) ("BABY TALK" for serious magazine not sufficiently distinctive to support preliminary injunction against defendant's use of "BABY TALK" for television "sitcom"); Wonder Labs, Inc. v. Procter & Gamble Co., 728 F. Supp. 1058, 14 U.S.P.Q.2d 1645 (S.D. N.Y. 1990) ("Dentists Choice" for tooth brushes is not sufficiently distinctive); Pullan v. Fulbright, 695 S.W.2d 830, 227 U.S.P.Q. 493 (Ark. Sup. Ct. 1985) (because "Shear Pleasure" is a descriptive term without secondary meaning, it is not a "trade name valid at common law" within meaning of Arkansas anti-dilution statute).

Cf. Bel Paese Sales Co., Inc. v. Macri, 99 App. Div.2d 740, 472 N.Y.S.2d 387 (1984) (overturning summary judgment that defendants' use of "Bel Paese" for their Italian-style delicatessen caused dilution of plaintiff's federally registered mark "Bel Paese" for "semi-soft Italian-style gourmet cheese" because there existed a disputed fact issue whether plaintiff's mark was sufficiently distinctive in view of defendants' affidavits that "bel paese" is a common Italian phrase meaning "beautiful place").

[220] *See, e.g.*, Sally Gee, Inc. v. Myra Hogan, Inc., 699 F.2d 621, 625, 217 U.S.P.Q. 658, 661-62 (2d Cir. 1983) ("Federal trademark infringement standards relating to strength of mark were not established with the concerns of the New York anti-dilution statute in mind."); P.F. Cosmetique, S.A. v. Minetonka Inc., 605 F.Supp. 662, 672, 226 U.S.P.Q. 86, 93 (S.D. N.Y. 1985) ("In essence, distinctiveness in the antidilution realm may be evaluated in much the same way as strength of the mark is evaluated in the area of likelihood of confusion. I concluded above that Klorane's trade dress is a weak mark for confusion purposes. That must therefore be at least as true for anti-dilution purposes, since there are numerous suggestions that only the strongest, most well-established marks are protected . . . against dilution.") *Cf.* Ringling Bros.-Barnum & Bailey Combined Shows, Inc. v. Celozzi- Ettelson Chevrolet, Inc., 855 F.2d 480, 483, 8 U.S.P.Q.2d 1072, 1075 (7th Cir. 1988) (finding it unnecessary to decide whether "distinctive" "means something different under the Anti-Dilution Act than it does under the Lanham Act"); Dolphin Homes Corp. Tocomoc Development Corp., 223 Ga. 455, 156 S.E.2d 45, 48, 155 U.S.P.Q. 543 (1967) ("we consider the terms 'distinctive quality' to mean that the trade name must be one of such originality as to be capable of exclusive appropriation, or one not capable of exclusive appropriation but which has acquired a secondary meaning").

For a discussion of distinctiveness, see §5C[3].

[221] *E.g.*, Hester Industries, Inc. v. Tyson Foods, Inc., 16 U.S.P.Q.2d 1275, 1278-79 (N.D. N.Y. 1990) ("in *Allied*, the majority indicated that the anti-dilution statute protects only extremely strong marks . . . perhaps not even all those that qualify as arbitrary or fanciful," but dilution is not limited to "famous" marks: "The renown of a senior mark is a factor a court should assess when evaluating the likelihood of dilution, not the strength of the mark."); Wedgwood Homes, Inc. v. Lund, 294 Ore. 493, 497-98, 659 P.2d 377, 379-80 (1982) ("We realize that the distinctiveness adequate to identify the origin of a product may be different from the distinctive quality deserving of protection from dilution. To this extent, the fact that a plaintiff may possess a distinctive tradename only begins our inquiry. The meaning of 'distinctive quality' must take shape within the confines of the interests sought to be protected by the antidilution statute. . . . The antidilution statutes . . . developed out of the growing recognition that trademarks now surpass the traditional identity role. . . . A mark may possess independent protectible value to the extent that it acquires advertising and selling power. . . .

In *Ringling Bros.-Barnum & Bailey Combined Shows,*[222] the court held that Ringling Bros. circus's trademark "The Greatest Show on Earth" was distinctive because of secondary meaning.

> "The fact that a mark is coined or invented may make distinctiveness easier to show, . . . but it is neither necessary nor sufficient to establish distinctiveness. . . . The length of time the mark has been used, the scope of advertising and promotions, the nature and extent of the business and the scope of the first user's reputation are also important factors that must be considered in determining the distinctiveness of a mark."[223]

In *Hyatt,*[224] the court found "Hyatt" distinctive for plaintiff's hotel services even though "Hyatt" is a personal name and many other businesses use it.

> "The fact that a mark is 'coined' or invented may make distinctiveness easier to show. . . . Other factors are also important, however, including the length of time the mark has been used, the scope of advertising and promotions, the nature and extent of the business, and the scope of the first user's reputation. . . .

> "In this case, Hyatt Hotels has been using its mark for some twenty-five years. It has been registered for thirteen years. Over the past several years, Hyatt Hotels has conducted an extensive advertising campaign designed to expand recognition of its trade name. That advertising in no way implies that 'Hyatt' is a particular person's name; rather 'Hyatt' is used as a trade name to indicate the source of the service. The hotel business is one in which travelers consider the name of a hotel to indicate its quality, cost, services, etc. Hyatt Hotels' reputation in its field is . . . excellent. Except for the appellee, the record shows no other national or regional business which uses the name 'Hyatt' to identify its services. In these circumstances, we have no difficulty in concluding that Hyatt Hotels' trade name 'Hyatt' is distinctive."[225]

In the context of dilution, the protectible quality of a mark has been defined as the mark's power to evoke images of the product, that is, its favorable associational value in the minds of consumers. This attribute may be developed in a variety of ways: long use, consistent superior quality instilling consumer satisfaction, extensive advertising. . . . In application the existence of the mark's distinctive quality must be proven by demonstrating what the mark signifies to the consuming public . . . If the mark has come to signify plaintiff's product in the minds of a significant portion of consumers and if the mark evokes favorable images of plaintiff or its product it possesses the distinctive quality of advertising value—consumer recognition, association and acceptance,—and will be entitled to protection from dilution.").

[222] Ringling Bros.-Barnum & Bailey Combined Shows, Inc. v. Celozzi-Ettelson Chevrolet, Inc., 855 F.2d 480, 8 U.S.P.Q.2d 1072 (7th Cir. 1988).

[223] 885 F.2d at 483, 8 U.S.P.Q.2d at 1075.

[224] Hyatt Corp. v. Hyatt Legal Services, 736 F.2d 1153, 222 U.S.P.Q. 669 (7th Cir. 1984), *cert. denied,* 469 U.S. 1019 (1984), *on remand,* 610 F. Supp. 381 (N.D. Ill. 1985).

[225] 736 F.2d at 1158, 222 U.S.P.Q. at 672. *See also* Cushman v. Mutton Hollow Land Development, Inc., 782 S.W.2d 150 (Mo. Ct. App. 1990) (plaintiffs, who used "Mutton Hollow" for a theme park for 17 years, are entitled to relief against defendant's use of "Mutton Hollow" for a recreational vehicle resort on property adjoining that of plaintiffs; though "Mutton Hollow" is geographically descriptive, it has acquired a secondary meaning and will be diluted by defendant's use).

In *Wedgwood*,[226] plaintiff Wedgwood, a house builder, promoted "the quality, styling and flair of [its] residential construction" in eastern Washington County. Defendant used "Wedgwood Downs" and "Wedgwood Place" for its "dormitory style housing" retirement complexes for the elderly in the same county. The Oregon Supreme Court held that "marks may become distinctive in three ways: by use of coined words, by use of arbitrary words, or by acquisition of secondary meaning." There is "no reason to assume that only coined marks posses advertising value." The statute extends to local as well as nationally renowned marks. "[I]t is not the manner by which distinctiveness is acquired nor the span of a mark's notoriety but rather the degree of advertising value the mark has gained which determines the [statute's] applicability."[227]

If a mark is inherently weak, for example because it is a commonplace word or symbol, but has acquired distinctiveness through its owner's extensive efforts, it may be particularly vulnerable to dilution.[228]

Most decisions hold that a mark need not be well known to the general public or throughout the United States to qualify for dilution protection,[229] but in *Mead Data Central*[230] the Second Circuit noted that "the fact that a mark has selling power in a limited geographical or commercial area does not endow it with a secondary meaning for the public generally." The mark in question, "LEXIS" for computerized legal research materials, was strong among attorneys and accountants but weak among the general public. This, together with other factors, meant that "LEXIS" was not diluted by Toyota's use of a different mark "LEXUS" for luxury automobiles.

> "The strength and distinctiveness of LEXIS is limited to the market for its services—attorneys and accountants. Outside that market, LEXIS has very little selling power. Because only one percent of the general population associates LEXIS with the attributes of Mead's service, it cannot be said that LEXIS identifies that service to the general public and distinguishes it from others. Moreover, the bulk of Mead's advertising budget is devoted to reaching attorneys through professional journals.
>
> . . . .
>
> "The possibility that someday LEXUS may become a famous mark in the mind of the general public has little relevance in the instant dilution analysis since it is quite apparent that the general public associates nothing with

---

[226] Wedgwood Homes, Inc. v. Lund, 294 Or. 493, 659 P.2d 377 (1982).

[227] 294 Or. at 500, 659 P.2d at 381.

[228] Dreyfus Fund Inc. v. Royal Bank of Canada, 525 F. Supp. 1108, 213 U.S.P.Q. 872 (S.D. N.Y. 1981) (through advertising, plaintiff transferred an inherently weak mark, a lion symbol, into a strong one, but the mark is vulnerable to dilution because it is based on a familiar subject; injunction limited to advertising that closely resembles plaintiff's lion use).

[229] *E.g.*, Dreyfus Fund Inc. v. Royal Bank of Canada, 525 F. Supp. 1108, 1125, 213 U.S.P.Q. 872 (S.D. N.Y. 1981) ("The statute should not be read to deprive marks from protection against dilution in limited areas of use, since otherwise it would afford protection only to the most notorious of all marks.").

[230] Mead Data Central, Inc. v. Toyota Motor Sales, U.S.A., Inc., 875 F.2d 1026, 10 U.S.P.Q.2d 1961 (2d Cir. 1989).

LEXIS. On the other hand, the recognized sophistication of attorneys, the principal users of the service, has substantial relevance. . . . Because of this knowledgeable sophistication, it is unlikely that, even in the market where Mead principally operates, there will be any significant amount of blurring between the LEXIS and LEXUS marks."[231]

[ii]   *Dilution Likelihood.* Court decisions acknowledge that dilution may consist of "blurring" or "tarnishing."[232] In *Sally Gee*,[233] plaintiff sold department store "ground floor" women's apparel and accessories under the "Sally Gee" mark.[234] Later, defendant began selling high price handmade "Sally Lee" women's apparel, the mark being the maker's name and her merchandise never being "relegated to a ground floor sales spot." The Second Circuit held there was no dilution.

"Dilution is not defined in §368-d and remains a somewhat nebulous concept in New York decisions. . . . Typically, dilution is characterized as a 'whittling down' of the identity or reputation of a tradename or mark. . . . A more helpful definition of dilution is provided by Callman: 'Dilution is an act which "threatens two separable but related components of advertising value. Junior uses may blur a mark's product identification or they may tarnish the affirmative associations a mark has come to convey." ' 3 R. Callman, The Law of Unfair Competition, Trademarks, and Monopolies §84.2 . . .

"Applying this definition to the present case, Sally Gee did not prove and could not have proven any tarnish to its products' reputation by Sally Lee's

---

[231] 875 F.2d at 1031-32, 10 U.S.P.Q.2d at 1965-66.

[232] Some decisions assume that anti-dilution law's tarnishment prong is based on the "likelihood of injury to business reputation" language in the statutes. *E.g.*, Hyatt Corp. v. Hyatt Legal Services, 736 F.2d 1153, 1157, n.2, 222 U.S.P.Q. 669, 671 n.2 (7th Cir. 1984), *cert. denied*, 469 U.S. 1019 (1984), *on remand*, 610 F. Supp. 381 (N.D. Ill. 1985) (relief granted on distinctiveness dilution theory, not on damage to reputation theory; "An injunction must also be granted if the prior user shows a likelihood of injury to reputation. The district court found that Hyatt Legal Services had conducted itself 'in a circumspect manner,' and there is no evidence to the contrary. We are unwilling to conclude that the mere possibility of a few malpractice claims against Hyatt Legal Services will result in harm to Hyatt Hotels' reputation.").

One decision suggests that "[a]n action for potential detraction from or tarnishment of the reputation associated with plaintiff's mark may be recognized in our statute as 'likelihood of injury to business reputation' or it may be encompassed within the meaning of dilution." Wedgwood Homes, Inc. v. Lund, 294 Or. 493, 501, 659 P.2d 377, 381-82 (1982).

[233] Sally Gee, Inc. v. Myra Hogan, Inc., 699 F.2d 621, 217 U.S.P.Q. 658 (2d Cir. 1983). *See also* L.L. Bean, Inc. v. Drake Publishers, Inc., 811 F.2d 26, 30, 1 U.S.P.Q.2d 1753, 1756 (1st Cir. 1987), *appeal dismissed, cert. denied*, 483 U.S. 1013 (1987) ("A trademark owner may obtain relief under an anti-dilution statute if his mark is distinctive and there is a likelihood of dilution due to (1) injury to the value of the mark caused by actual or potential confusion, (2) diminution in the uniqueness and individuality of the mark, or (3) injury resulting from use of the mark in a manner that tarnishes or appropriates the goodwill and reputation associated with plaintiff's mark.").

[234] In "the euphemistic language of the trade," ground floor merchandise "has a lower price point," but, alas, "[o]ccasionally, Sally Gee items have been displayed with higher priced merchandise on an upper floor." 699 F.2d at 622.

handmade, higher priced, and higher quality clothing. . . . Sally Gee also failed to prove that the product-evoking quality of its marks were likely to be weakened by use of the Sally Lee name. First, fanciful though its marks may be, Sally Gee must set forth some proof that its marks conjure up images of its clothing in the minds of the consuming public in order to establish associational qualities entitling it to protection from dilution. The record is barren of any proof that the use of the Sally Lee name is likely to blur Sally Gee's product identification, and none is readily inferable. Sophisticated retailers and discerning consumers of women's apparel are unlikely to have blurred vision causing them to see 'Sally Gee' upon viewing a Sally Lee label." [235]

(1) *Tarnishment.* Decisions find dilution when the accused diluter's use associates the claimant's distinctive mark with inferior products or services [236] or illegal or indelicate activity. [237] Courts reject tarnishment claims if the accused diluter's products or services are wholesome or of high quality. [238]

In *Community Federal Savings & Loan,* [239] the Eleventh Circuit upheld a bank's claim that its registered "cookie jar" and cookie jar design marks were diluted by

---

[235] 699 F.2d 625-26, 217 U.S.P.Q. at 662.

[236] *Compare* Wedgwood Homes, Inc. v. Lund, 294 Or. 493, 501, 659 P.2d 377, 382 (1982) (plaintiff made high quality residential construction; defendant made "dormitory" style retirement housing; "Although plaintiff attempted to show unfavorable associations cast upon its product's reputation by what plaintiff characterized as the inferior construction and design of defendant's buildings, the trial court found that such unfavorable associations were not proven.").

[237] *E.g.,* Eastman Kodak Co., v. Rakow, 739 F. Supp. 116, 118, 13 U.S.P.Q.2d 1631, 1633 (W.D. N.Y. 1989) (comedian's use of "Kodak" stage name would tarnish famous "Kodak" camera and film mark; "The defendant has admitted that his 'comedy act includes humor that relates to bodily functions and sex, and that [he] uses crude, off-color language repeatedly.' . . . In contrast, Kodak has adopted a corporate policy with respect to violence and sexual themes in programs with which it associates its advertising."); Coca-Cola Co. v. Alma-Leo U.S.A., Inc., 719 F.Supp. 725, 728, 12 U.S.P.Q.2d 1487, 1489 (N.D. Ill. 1989) (Illinois statute; granting temporary restraining order against defendant's sale of "Mad Scientist Magic Powder" bubble gum in a plastic container resembling the familiar Coca-Cola bottle; "the sale of Magic Powder will likely injure Coca-Cola's reputation. . . . The powder not only resembles cocaine but also has a texture remarkably similar to the drug."); Pillsbury Co. v. Milky Way Productions, Inc., 215 USPQ 124 (N.D. Ga. 1981) (Georgia statute; "Poppin' Fresh" and "Poppie Fresh" trade characters' owner entitled to injunction against *Screw* magazine's depiction of figures resembling those characters engaged in sexual activity); Coca-Cola Co. v. Gemini Rising, Inc., 346 F. Supp. 1183, 1189, 175 USPQ 56 (E.D. N.Y. 1972) (New York statute; granting preliminary injunction against sale of poster consisting of "an exact blown-up reproduction of plaintiff's familiar 'coca-cola' trademark and distinctive format except for the substitution of" "Enjoy Cocaine" for "Enjoy Coca Cola." "To associate such a noxious substance as cocaine with plaintiff's whole-some beverage as symbolized by its 'coca-cola' trademark and format would clearly have a tendency to impugn that product and injure plaintiff's business reputation. . . . ").

[238] *E.g.,* King Research, Inc. v. Shulton, Inc., 324 F. Supp. 631, 169 U.S.P.Q. 396 (S.D. N.Y. 1971), *aff'd,* 454 F.2d 66, 172 U.S.P.Q. 321 (2d Cir. 1972) (defendant's "Ship Shape" for men's hair spray does not dilute plaintiff's "Ship Shape" for comb and brush cleaners because defendant's product is held in high esteem among the purchasing public).

[239] Community Federal Savings & Loan Ass'n v. Orondorff, 678 F.2d 1034, 215 U.S.P.Q. 26 (11th Cir. 1982).

a topless go-go bar's "ANNIE'S COOKIE JAR—Adult Entertainment" mark on a billboard across from the bank and on "free drink cards, T'shirts, and matchbooks."

Decisions do not treat parody or humorous purpose as an independent defense to a dilution charge,[240] but First Amendment rights may preclude application of tarnishment claims to noncommercial parody.[241] In *L.L. Bean*,[242] "High Society" magazine published a sexually-explicit parody of L.L. Bean's catalog. L.L. Bean sued for trademark infringement and other alleged torts. The district court denied relief on the trademark infringement theory, finding no likelihood of confusion, but did grant relief on a state law trademark dilution theory. The First Circuit held that the constitutional (First Amendment) guarantees of freedom of speech and expression precluded any application of a dilution theory.[243] Distinguishing *Dallas Cowboys Cheerleaders*,[244] the First Circuit disagreed with the district court's dismissal of First Amendment concerns because of the trademark owner's property rights[245] and the availability

---

[240] *E.g.*, American Express Co. v. Vibra Approved Laboratories Corp., 10 U.S.P.Q.2d 2006, 2013-14 (S.D. N.Y. 1989) (New York statute; American Express entitled to injunction against use of its trademark slogan "DON'T LEAVE HOME WITHOUT IT" by defendant on an American Express card replica that opened to reveal a condom; "Dilution itself is an amorphous concept. . . . [D]efendant sought to capitalize on the recognizability of plaintiff's marks, to its own commercial advantage. . . . [D]efendants' condom card cannot be shrugged off as a mere bawdy jest, unreachable by any legal theory. American Express has a legitimate concern that its own products' reputation may be tarnished by defendants' conduct").

But cf. Tetley, Inc. v. Topps Chewing Gum, Inc., 556 F. Supp. 785, 794, 217 U.S.P.Q. 1128, 1135 (E.D.N.Y. 1983) ("the broad humor defendant employs serves to prevent the type of blurring which might result from a more subtle or insidious effort at humor at plaintiff's expense.").

[241] *See* § 5F[1][d][ii]. For a discussion of parody in copyright law, see §4F[3][d].

[242] L.L. Bean, Inc. v. Drake Publishers, Inc., 811 F.2d 26, 1 U.S.P.Q.2d 1753 (1st Cir. 1987), *appeal dismissed, cert. denied*, 483 U.S. 1013 (1987).

[243] "Parody is a humorous form of social commentary and literary criticism that dates back as far as Greek antiquity. . . . The Oxford English Dictionary defines parody as '[a] composition in which the characteristic turns of thought and phrase of an author are mimicked to appear ridiculous, especially by applying them to ludicrously inappropriate subjects.'. . . Since parody seeks to ridicule sacred verities and prevailing mores, it inevitably offends others . . .

". . . One need only open a magazine or turn on television to witness the pervasive influence of trademarks in advertising and commerce. Designer labels appear on goods ranging from handbags to chocolates to every possible form of clothing. Commercial advertising slogans, which can be registered as trademarks, have become part of national political campaigns. 'Thus, trademarks have become a natural target of satirists who seek to comment on this integral part of the national culture.' Dorsen, *Satiric Appropriation and the Law of Libel, Trademark and Copyright: Remedies Without Wrongs*, 65 B.U.L.Rev. 923, 939 (1986). . . .

"The ridicule conveyed by parody inevitably conflicts with one of the underlying purposes of the Maine anti-dilution statute, which is to protect against the tarnishment of the goodwill and reputation associated with a particular trademark." 811 F.2d at 28, 1 U.S.P.Q.2d at 1754.

[244] Dallas Cowboys Cheerleaders, Inc. v. Pussycat Cinema, Ltd., 604 F.2d 200 (2d Cir.1979).

[245] ". . . [W]e do not think the court fully assessed the nature of a trademark owner's property rights. A trademark is a form of intellectual property . . . The first amendment issues involved in this case cannot be disposed of by equating the rights of a trademark owner with the rights of an owner of real property: '[T]rademark is not property in the ordinary

to the parodist of alternative avenues of communication.[246] Dilution law's concern with "tarnishment" of a distinctive trademark cannot extend to noncommercial trademark parody.[247] The court distinguished prior cases finding trademark infringement or dilution cases in which defendants appropriated trademarks to promote dissimilar products or services[248] and found "no occasion to consider the constitutional limits

---

sense but only a word or symbol indicating the origin of a commercial product. The owner of the mark acquires the right to prevent the goods to which the mark is applied from being confused with those of others and to prevent his own trade from being diverted to competitors through their use of misleading marks.' . . . The limits on the scope of a trademark owner's property rights was considered recently in *Lucasfilm Ltd. v. High Frontier*. . . . In that case, the owners of the trademark 'Star Wars' alleged injury from public interest groups that used the term in commercial advertisements presenting their views on President Reagan's Strategic Defense Initiative. Judge Gesell stressed that the sweep of a trademark owner's rights extends only to injurious, unauthorized *commercial uses* of the mark by another. . . . Trademark rights do not entitle the owner to quash an unauthorized use of the mark by another who is communicating ideas or expressing points of view." 811 F.2d at 29, 1 U.S.P.Q.2d at 1755.

[246] "[W]e reject Bean's argument that enjoining the publication of appellant's parody does not violate the first amendment because 'there are innumerable alternative ways that Drake could have made a satiric statement concerning "sex in the outdoors" or "sex and camping gear" without using plaintiff's name and mark.' This argument fails to recognize that appellant is parodying L.L. Bean's catalog, not 'sex in the outdoors.' The central role which trademarks occupy in public discourse (a role eagerly encouraged by trademark owners), makes them a natural target of parodists. Trademark parodies, even when offensive, do convey a message. The message may be simply that business and product images need not always be taken too seriously; a trademark parody reminds us that we are free to laugh at the images and associations linked with the mark. The message also may be a simple form of entertainment conveyed by juxtaposing the irreverent representation of the trademark with the idealized image created by the mark's owner. . . . While such a message lacks explicit political content, that is no reason to afford it less protection under the first amendment. . . . Denying parodists the opportunity to poke fun at symbols and names which have become woven into the fabric of our daily life, would constitute a serious curtailment of a protected form of expression." 811 F.2d at 34, 1 U.S.P.Q.2d at 1759.

[247] The court noted: "Neither the strictures of the first amendment nor the history and theory of anti-dilution law permit a finding of tarnishment based solely on the presence of an unwholesome or negative context in which a trademark is used without authorization. Such a reading of the anti-dilution statute unhinges it from its origins in the marketplace. A trademark is tarnished when consumer capacity to associate it with the appropriate products or services has been diminished. The threat of tarnishment arises when the goodwill and reputation of a plaintiff's trademark is linked to products which are of shoddy quality or which conjure associations that clash with the associations generated by the owner's lawful use of the mark . . . ." 811 F.2d at 31, 1 U.S.P.Q.2d at 1756-57.

[248] "The law of trademark dilution has developed to combat an unauthorized and harmful appropriation of a trademark by another for the purpose of identifying, manufacturing, merchandising or promoting dissimilar products or services. The harm occurs when a trademark's identity and integrity—its capacity to command respect in the market—is undermined due to its inappropriate and unauthorized use by other market actors. When presented with such circumstances, courts have found that trademark owners have suffered harm despite the fact that redressing such harm entailed some residual impact on the rights of expression of commercial actors. See, *e.g., Dallas Cowboys Cheerleaders v. Pussycat Cinema, Ltd.*, 604 F.2d 200 (plaintiff's mark damaged by unauthorized use in content and promotion of a

which might be imposed on the application of anti-dilution statutes to unauthorized uses of trademarks on products whose principal purpose is to convey a message."[249]

(2) *Blurring.* Courts find "blurring" dilution in situations that do not involve tarnishing through unpleasant association.[250] Courts have not precisely defined

---

pornographic film); *Chemical Corp. of America v. Anheuser-Busch, Inc.*, 306 F.2d 433 (5th Cir.1962), *cert. denied*, 372 U.S. 965, 83 S.Ct. 1089, 10 L.Ed.2d 129 (1963) (floor wax and insecticide maker's slogan, "Where there's life, there's bugs," harmed strength of defendant's slogan, "Where there's life, there's Bud."); *Original Appalachian Artworks, Inc. v. Topps Chewing Gum*, 642 F.Supp. 1031 (N.D.Ga.1986) (merchandiser of "Garbage Pail Kids" stickers and products injured owner of Cabbage Patch Kids mark); *D.C. Comics, Inc. v. Unlimited Monkey Business*, 598 F.Supp. 110 (N.D.Ga.1984) (holder of Superman and Wonder Woman trademarks damaged by unauthorized use of marks by singing telegram franchisor); *General Electric Co. v. Alumpa Coal Co.*, 205 U.S.P.Q. (BNA) 1036 (D.Mass.1979) ("Genital Electric" monogram on underpants and T-shirts harmful to plaintiff's trademark); *Gucci Shops, Inc. v. R.H. Macy & Co.*, 446 F.Supp. 838 (S.D.N.Y.1977) (defendant's diaper bag labelled "Gucchi Goo" held to injure Gucci's mark); *Coca-Cola Co. v. Gemini Rising, Inc.*, 346 F.Supp. 1183 (E.D.N.Y.1972) (enjoining the merchandise of "Enjoy Cocaine" posters bearing logo similar to plaintiff's mark).

"While the cases cited above might appear at first glance to be factually analogous to the instant one, they are distinguishable for two reasons. First, they all involved unauthorized commercial uses of another's trademark. Second, none of those cases involved a defendant using a plaintiff's trademark as a vehicle for an editorial or artistic parody." 811 F.2d at 31-32, 1 U.S.P.Q.2d at 1757.

The court approved *Girl Scouts of U.S.A. v. Personality Posters Mfg. Co.*, 304 F.Supp. 1228 (S.D.N.Y.1969), which "reject[ed] plaintiff's claim of dilution caused by defendant's distribution of posters depicting a pregnant girl in a Girl Scout uniform along with a caption bearing the Girl Scout motto, 'Be Prepared'." It distinguished *Pillsbury Co. v. Milky Way Productions, Inc.*, 215 U.S.P.Q. 124 (N.D.Ga.1981), in which Pillsbury "obtained injunctive relief against *Screw* magazine, which had published pictures of facsimiles of Pillsbury's trade characters, 'Poppin Fresh' and 'Poppie Fresh,' engaged in sexual intercourse and fellatio."

"The pictorial also featured plaintiff's trademark and the refrain of its jingle, 'The Pillsbury Baking Song.' While the district court granted relief under Georgia's anti-dilution statute, 215 U.S.P.Q. at 135, it did so only after specifically declining to consider whether defendants' presentation constituted a parody. . . . The defendants in Pillsbury had tried to proffer parody as a defense to plaintiff's copyright infringement claim; they did not assert it as a defense to the dilution claim. *Pillsbury*, therefore, does not stand for the proposition that the publication of a parody properly may be enjoined under an anti-dilution statute, since the court never considered whether defendants had presented a parody, and defendants never asserted parody as a defense to the dilution claim." 811 F.2d at 33 n.5, 1 U.S.P.Q.2d at 1759 n.5.

[249] It did note that "[s]uch a situation undoubtedly would require a balancing of the harm suffered by the trademark owner against the benefit derived by the parodist and the public from the unauthorized use of a trademark on a product designed to convey a message." 811 F.2d at 32 n.4, 1 U.S.P.Q.2d at 1758 n.4.

[250] *E.g.*, *Ringling Bros.-Barnum & Bailey Combined Shows, Inc. v. Celozzi-Ettelson Chevrolet, Inc.*, 855 F.2d 480, 485, 8 U.S.P.Q.2d 1072, 1076 (7th Cir. 1988) (Illinois statute; Ringling Bros. circus's trademark "The Greatest Show on Earth" is diluted by defendant's slogan "The Greatest Used Car Show on Earth" for used car sales; defendant's use of the slogan "would blur the strong association the public now has between Ringling Bros.' mark");

"dilution" but require that there be a likelihood of mental association by reasonable buyers.[251]

Dreyfus Fund Inc. v. Royal Bank of Canada, 525 F. Supp. 1108, 1122- 24, 213 U.S.P.Q. 872 (S.D. N.Y. 1981) (plaintiff's several "lion" marks, including a "picture of a real lion", are diluted by bank's advertisements showing a lion in a variety of settings; "Harm from dilution is caused when a mark loses its advertising value, because its distinctiveness in the minds of consumers is undermined. Distinctiveness is valuable to the trademark owner because it identifies his product to consumers both effectively and positively. The Dreyfus lion, for example, is a potent symbol that identifies the Dreyfus companies in the minds of consumers with the service advertised, and that allegedly leads consumers to think positively about Dreyfus, because of the 'affirmative associations' consumers have both with lions (nobility, strength, leadership etc.) and with Dreyfus itself as a result of its perceived performance as a leader in money management. . . . The mark is diluted when consumers see lions that they initially associate with Dreyfus, but that they subsequently realize are being used to advertise some other product or enterprise. Any consumer so exposed will thereafter less readily identify realistic lions in financially oriented ads with Dreyfus. If still other financial products and enterprises are advertised with lions, the mark may entirely lose its value to Dreyfus as an identifying device, and to the extent the new uses of lions cause negative associations among consumers between similar lions and the products or enterprises they are used to advertise, the Dreyfus mark will lose its value as a device for evoking positive associations. In theory, one could argue that the Dreyfus marks could be diluted even by a use that creates no confusion whatever. But in reality, the Dreyfus marks' distinctiveness—whatever might be said of other marks—is limited to the area of financial management, and to lions of the type used in Dreyfus ads.- The MGM lion, for example, might dilute the Dreyfus mark, and vice versa. Yet the dilution that could be expected to flow from these coexisting uses is insubstantial, because of the absence of significant confusion; no protection would therefore seem proper for either user, under any theory of relief."); Wedgwood Homes, Inc. v. Lund, 294 Or. 493, 501, 659 P.2d 377, 382 (1982) (statute encompasses "dilution" in the sense of "a diminution in the uniqueness and individuality of the mark caused by another's use of the same or similar mark" that "does not depend on the relative quality of defendant's product or the undesirability of its association with plaintiff's product. . . . Where tradename owners have created a favorable association between their name and their product, they possess a valuable marketing tool. This aura of recognition enhances the value of plaintiff's name. Subsequent use of the name with a non-related product broadens the associations linking name and product in the minds of consumers of plaintiff's product and diminishes the specific association plaintiff seeks to foster."). Cf. Mortellito v. Nina of California, Inc., 335 F.Supp. 1288, 173 U.S.P.Q. 346 (S.D. N.Y. 1972).

Compare Parenting Unlimited Inc. v. Columbia Pictures Television Inc., 743 F. Supp. 221, 16 U.S.P.Q.2d 1171 (S.D. N.Y. 1990) ("Baby Talk" for serious magazine not diluted by defendant's use of "BABY TALK" for television "sitcom"; blurring is unlikely when plaintiff's mark circulates in only a limited market).

[251] Mead Data Central, Inc. v. Toyota Motor Sales, U.S.A., Inc., 875 F.2d 1026, 1031, 10 U.S.P.Q.2d 1961, 1965-66 (2d Cir. 1989) ("Very little attention has been given to date to the distinction between the confusion necessary for a claim of infringement and the blurring necessary for a claim of dilution. . . . Although the antidilution statute dispenses with the requirements of competition and confusion, it does not follow that every junior use of a similar mark will dilute the senior mark in the manner contemplated by the New York Legislature. . . . [T]here must be some mental association between plaintiff's and defendant's marks. '[I]f a reasonable buyer is not at all likely to link the two uses of the trademark in his or her own mind, even subtly or subliminally, then there can be no dilution. . . . [D]ilution theory presumes some kind of mental association in the reasonable buyer's mind between the two party's [sic]

In *Hyatt*,[252] the court found that defendant's use of "Hyatt" for legal services created a likelihood of dilution of plaintiff's famous "Hyatt" mark for hotels. .

> "Important factors in this determination are the similarity between the marks used by the parties, and the extent of the marketing effort by the second user. . . .

> "Hyatt Legal Services uses the same mark as Hyatt Hotels. It is not modified in any way to show that it is a personal name rather than a trademark, as would be the case if 'Joel Hyatt Legal Services' or 'Hyatt, Hyatt, Willis & Brooks' were used to identify the firm. . . . Hyatt Legal Services has extensively advertised in the past few years, spending millions of dollars. While it does not yet operate in every state or every major city, such a national operation is part of its expansion plans, and it presently has offices in nearly a third of the states."[253]

uses of the mark.' This mental association may be created where the plaintiff's mark is very famous and therefore has a distinctive quality for a significant percentage of the defendant's market. . . . However, if a mark circulates only in a limited market, it is unlikely to be associated generally with the mark for a dissimilar product circulating elsewhere.").

In *Mead Data Central*, Judge Sweet wrote a concurring opinion offering the following analytical framework.

> "Defining likelihood of dilution as 'tarnishing' is helpful because that principle can be applied in practice. . . . 'Blurring,' however, offers practitioners and courts only marginally more guidance than 'likelihood of dilution.'

> "There is much to be gained by defining a general concept like 'blurring' more specifically. As in this instance, confusion in the doctrine has created problems for trademark attorneys advising their clients about adopting trademarks, for potential litigants assessing their chances of pursuing or defending against dilution claims, and for courts attempting to apply the statute. . . . In the trademark infringement context, Judge Friendly defined a similarly broad standard—likelihood of confusion—by articulating a multi-factor balancing test that considers: 'the strength of [plaintiff's] mark, the degree of similarity between the two marks, the proximity of the products, the likelihood that the prior owner will bridge the gap, actual confusion, and the reciprocal of defendant's good faith in adopting its own mark, the quality of defendant's product, and the sophistication of the buyers.' . . . This test has provided practitioners and district courts a helpful framework for assessing likelihood of confusion. . . .

> "Like likelihood of confusion, blurring sufficient to constitute dilution requires a case-by-case factual inquiry. A review of the anti-dilution cases in this Circuit indicates that courts have articulated the following factors in considering the likelihood of dilution caused by blurring:

> 1) similarity of the marks

> 2) similarity of the products covered by the marks

> 3) sophistication of consumers

> 4) predatory intent

> 5) renown of the senior mark

> 6) renown of the junior mark."

875 F.2d at 1035, 10 U.S.P.Q.2d at 1968-69.

[252] Hyatt Corp. v. Hyatt Legal Services, 736 F.2d 1153, 222 U.S.P.Q. 669 (7th Cir. 1984), *cert. denied*, 469 U.S. 1019 (1984), *on remand*, 610 F. Supp. 381 (N.D. Ill. 1985).

[253] 736 F.2d at 1158. 222 U.S.P.Q. at 672.

(3) *Mark Similarity.* To support a dilution claim, the accused mark must be the same or substantially similar to the protected mark.[254]

In *Mead Data Central*,[255] the district court found that Toyota's proposed use of "LEXUS" for a luxury automobile would dilute Mead Data Central's established "LEXIS" mark for its computerized legal research service. The Second Circuit reversed, holding that the dilution statute requires that the accused and protected marks be substantially similar,[256] and that "in the field of commercial advertising which is the field subject to regulation, there is no substantial similarity between Mead's

---

[254] *E.g.*, Exxon v. Exxene Corp., 696 F.2d 544, 550, 217 U.S.P.Q. 215, 219 (7th Cir. 1982) (refusing to overturn jury finding that defendant's "EXXENE" mark for plastic, scratch resisting, anti-fogging sheets did not dilute plaintiff's "EXXON" mark for gasoline, motor oil, asphalt, plastic laminated sheets, fertilizer, insecticides, hosiery, yarn, and other products; "a threshold question, ordinarily one of fact, is whether two names are so similar that the distinctiveness of one—its singularity as an identifier of the product of a particular manufacturer—will be impaired by the other. It was within the jury's province to find that 'Exxon' and 'Exxene' neither look nor sound the same."); Holiday Inns, Inc. v. Holiday Out in America, 481 F.2d 445, 448, 450, 178 U.S.P.Q. 257 (5th Cir. 1973) (plaintiff's "HOLIDAY INN" mark for hotels not diluted by defendant's "HOLIDAY OUT" mark for campground services even though plaintiff had expanded into the outdoor market with its "Holiday Inn Trav-L-Park" franchised facilities and its expert, a noted lexicographer, testified that "the words 'in' and 'out' are intertwined in their meanings, so that one is normally defined with respect to the other. . . . Dilution is a concept most applicable where a subsequent user uses the trademark of a prior user for a product so dissimilar from the product of the prior user that there is no likelihood of confusion of the products or sources, but where the use of the trademark by the subsequent user will lessen the uniqueness of the prior user's mark with the possible future result that a strong mark may become a weak mark. It is not applicable in this situation, however, because it has been determined that the marks themselves are not confusing."); Alberto-Culver Co. v. Andrea Dumon, Inc., 466 F.2d 705, 709, 175 U.S.P.Q. 194 (7th Cir. 1972) (plaintiff's "FDS" design label mark for a feminine deodorant spray, "made especially for the external vaginal area," and defendant's label for a similar, competing product were not so similar as to create a likelihood of confusion; "Since plaintiff and defendant are competitors, there would be no need to rely on the dilution statute if there were a substantial similarity between the two labels or a 'likelihood' of confusion. Conversely, without such similarity or likelihood, there is no greater right to relief under that provision than on traditional infringement grounds.").

[255] Mead Data Central, Inc. v. Toyota Motor Sales, U.S.A., Inc., 875 F.2d 1026, 10 U.S.P.Q.2d 1961 (2d Cir. 1989).

[256] It noted that the dilution statute, literally applied, could be restricted to "the unauthorized use of the identical established mark," but "since the use of obvious simulations or markedly similar marks might have the same diluting effect as would an appropriation of the original mark, the concept of exact identity has been broadened to that of substantial similarity. Nevertheless, in keeping with the original intent of the statute, the similarity must be substantial before the doctrine of dilution may be applied."

". . . Indeed, some courts have gone so far as to hold that, although violation of an antidilution statute does not require confusion of product or source, the marks in question must be sufficiently similar that confusion may be created as between the marks themselves. . . . We need not go that far. We hold only that the marks must be 'very' or 'substantially' similar and that, absent such similarity, there can be no viable claim of dilution." 875 F.2d at 1029, 10 U.S.P.Q.2d at 1964.

mark and Toyota's."[257] "LEXUS" and "LEXIS" are visually distinct and would be pronounced differently by television and radio announcers.[258]

[iii] *Predatory Intent.* In *Sally Gee,*[259] the Second Circuit noted that "the absence of predatory intent by the junior user is a relevant factor in assessing a claim under the anti-dilution statute . . . since relief under the statute is of equitable origin."[260]

In *Mead Data Central,*[261] Toyota did a trademark search and obtained a trademark lawyer's opinion that its proposed mark "LEXUS" for a luxury car would not infringe the rights of the owner of the "LEXIS" mark for a computerized legal research service. The LEXIS owner objected to LEXUS, but Toyota refused to change its mark. The district court found that Toyota acted without predatory intent in adopting LEXUS but that "Toyota's refusal to acknowledge that its use of LEXUS might harm the LEXIS mark, deprived it of the argument that it acted in good faith." The Second Circuit held the latter finding erroneous: "[E]ven if the attorney's professional advice had been wrong, it does not follow that Toyota's reliance on that advice would have constituted bad faith."[262]

[iv] *Remedies.* Most anti-dilution statutes provide only for injunctive relief.[263] In *Ringling Bros.-Barnum & Bailey Combined Shows,*[264] the court suggested that

---

[257] 875 F.2d at 1030, 10 U.S.P.Q.2d at 1965.

[258] "Of course, anyone can pronounce 'lexis' and 'lexus' the same . . . But, properly, the distinction between unstressed I and unstressed U, or schwa, is a standard one in English; the distinction is there to be made in ordinary, reasonably careful speech. In addition, we do not believe that 'everyday spoken English' is the proper test to use in deciding the issue of similarity in the instant case. . . . 'The legitimate aim of the anti-dilution statute is to prohibit the unauthorized use of another's trademark in order to market incompatible products or services' . . . We take it as a given that television and radio announcers usually are more careful and precise in their diction than is the man on the street. Moreover, it is the rare television commercial that does not contain a visual reference to the mark and product, which in the instant case would be the LEXUS automobile." 875 F.2d at 1029-30, 10 U.S.P.Q.2d at 1964-65.

[259] Sally Gee, Inc. v. Myra Hogan, Inc., 699 F.2d 621, 217 U.S.P.Q. 658 (2d Cir. 1983). See also McDonald's Corp. v. McBagel's Inc., 649 F.Supp. 1268, 1281, 1 U.S.P.Q.2d 1761, 1771 (S.D. N.Y. 1986) ("a defendant has engaged in conduct with a predatory intent when he knowingly takes unfair advantage of the business values developed by plaintiff . . . .' ").

[260] 699 F.2d at 626, 217 U.S.P.Q. at 662.

[261] Mead Data Central, Inc. v. Toyota Motor Sales, U.S.A., Inc., 875 F.2d 1026, 10 U.S.P.Q.2d 1961 (2d Cir. 1989).

[262] 875 F.2d at 1028, 10 U.S.P.Q.2d at 1963.

[263] See Mastercard International, Inc. v. Arbel, 13 U.S.P.Q.2d 1958, 1966 (S.D. N.Y. 1989) ("The anti-dilution statutes of New York and California both expressly provide an injunction as the available remedy. No provision is made for monetary damages in either statute, and the Court has found no precedent to support an award of monetary damages for dilution."). The Washington statute is an exception in authorizing other remedies when "the subsequent user willfully intended to trade on the registrant's reputation or to cause dilution of the owner's mark." Wash. Rev Code §19.77.160.

[264] Ringling Bros.-Barnum & Bailey Combined Shows, Inc. v. Celozzi-Ettelson Chevrolet, Inc., 855 F.2d 480, 8 U.S.P.Q.2d 1072 (7th Cir. 1988).

"consideration of the factors generally required to obtain a preliminary injunction may not be necessary under the Illinois Anti-Dilution Act."

"The Act states that the 'court *shall* grant injunctions . . . if there exists a likelihood of . . . dilution of the distinctive quality of the mark.' . . . (emphasis added). The language of the statute suggests that the trial court's usual discretion is limited and that the only requirement is a finding of likelihood of dilution. . . . Since neither party presents this argument, our affirmance does not disturb the irreparable harm standard applied by the district court. . . . [T]he very nature of dilution, insidiously gnawing away at the value of a mark, makes the injury 'remarkably difficult to convert into damages.' . . . [B]y its nature, the injury caused by dilution will almost always be irreparable."[265]

As with injunctions against trademark infringement, those against dilution may be qualified.[266]

---

[265] 855 F.2d at 484-85, 8 U.S.P.Q.2d at 1076 & n.4. *See also* Hyatt Corp. v. Hyatt Legal Services, 736 F.2d 1153, 1158- 59, 222 U.S.P.Q. 669 (7th Cir. 1984), *cert. denied*, 469 U.S. 1019 (1984), *on remand*, 610 F. Supp. 381 (N.D. Ill. 1985) ("it is the very nature of dilution to gnaw away insidiously at the value of a mark. . . . Such an injury would be remarkably difficult to convert into damages. . . . We conclude that the difficulty Hyatt Hotels would encounter in proving damages incurred because of Hyatt Legal Services' dilution of its mark and the nature of the injury direct a finding of irreparable injury.").

[266] *Cf.* Hyatt Corp. v. Hyatt Legal Services, 736 F.2d 1153, 222 U.S.P.Q. 669 (7th Cir. 1984). In *Hyatt*, the court agreed that Hyatt Hotels was not entitled to an injunction barring defendant completely from using his name, Hyatt.

"The dilution of Hyatt Hotels' mark flows primarily from Hyatt Legal Services' use of the name 'Hyatt' without modification or any indication that it is a personal name, not a trade name. Hyatt Hotels' mark is also diluted because of the nationwide scope of Hyatt Legal Services' business. Hyatt Hotels has not requested that we enjoin Mr. Hyatt from further expanding his business, and we would not consider such an injunction appropriate in this case. Thus, protection of the 'Hyatt' mark must come by way of modification of Hyatt Legal Services' name. A name such as 'Joel Hyatt Legal Services' or some combination of the last names of the partners—the traditional means of identifying a law firm—would meet this concern. There may be other appropriate names which would not violate the Anti- Dilution statute. Rather than selecting the name ourselves, we believe the better practice would be to allow Hyatt Legal Services to select its new name. . . . If Hyatt Hotels believes the new name violates the Anti- Dilution Act or the Lanham Act, leave to amend its complaint should be freely granted." 736 F.2d at 1159-60, 672 U.S.P.Q. at 673.

The court had no sympathy for "Mr. Hyatt's claim that requiring a name change may force him to act unethically."

". . . Not to require a change would allow a violation of the Anti-Dilution Act to go unchecked. Mr. Hyatt and his partners must operate their law practice in compliance with both the Anti-Dilution Act and state ethics requirements. We believe that by allowing Mr. Hyatt and his partners to select their new name, the court can avoid the ethical questions which are not a proper matter for the district court to consider in the context of this case. We assume the name chosen will have no obvious ethical problems (i.e., 'The Best Law Firm in Town'); the ethical improprieties pointed out by Mr. Hyatt are much less clear, and might differ from state to state. In this case the district court cannot be required to investigate on its own, nor can Hyatt Hotels be

[4] Collateral Use

Trademark ownership does not confer the right to prohibit all uses of a mark. Anyone may use a mark to tell the truth about goods or services so long the use does not cause a likelihood of confusion as to their origin or sponsorship. For example, one who purchases genuine goods may resell them under the mark in their original condition or after repackaging or repair, and one may use a competitor's mark in comparative advertising and spare parts compatibility statements.[267]

[a] **Repackaged and Repaired Goods.** In *Prestonettes*,[268] plaintiff, a French citizen, owned the registered marks "Coty" and "L'Origan" for toilet powders and perfumes. Defendant purchased genuine "Coty" powder, subjected it to pressure, added a binder and sold the resulting product in a metal case. It also purchased genuine perfume in large bottles and resold it in smaller bottles. Plaintiff sought to enjoin defendant from using its mark. The district court allowed defendant to use the "Coty" mark but only with cautionary labels indicating that Prestonettes "not connected with Coty" independently compounded or rebottled the product. The court of appeals "considering the very delicate and volatile nature of the perfume, its easy deterioration, and the opportunities for adulteration, issued an absolute preliminary injunction against the use of the above marks except on the original packages as marked and sold by the plaintiff, thinking that the defendant could not put upon the plaintiff the burden of keeping a constant watch."

The Supreme Court reinstated the district court order in a short opinion by Justice Holmes. The court of appeals did not find that the defendant adulterated or deteriorated plaintiff's product but issued its decree on the assumption that "defendant handled the plaintiff's product without in any way injuring its qualities." In so decreeing, it went "too far." Plaintiff's trademark right in "Coty" gave it no right to prevent the defendant from "telling the truth" about its products' components[269]

---

charged with an investigation, of the propriety of the new name. That is the responsibility of Mr. Hyatt and his law partners." 736 F.2d at 1160, 222 U.S.P.Q. at 673 n.5.

[267] Sale of reverse-engineered, surplus, and reconditioned parts can lead to charges of "reverse palming off" and false designation of origin, as well as trademark infringement. *See, e.g.,* Williams v. Curtiss-Wright Corp., 691 F.2d 168, 217 U.S.P.Q. 108 (3d Cir. 1982).

[268] Prestonettes v. Coty, 264 U.S. 359 (1924).

[269] "The defendant of course by virtue of its ownership had a right to compound or change what it bought, to divide either the original or the modified product, and to sell it so divided. The plaintiff could not prevent or complain of its stating the nature of the component parts and the source from which they were derived if it did not use the trade-mark in doing so. For instance, the defendant could state that a certain percentage of its compound was made at a certain place in Paris, however well known as the plaintiff's factory that place might be. If the compound was worse than the constituent, it might be a misfortune to the plaintiff, but the plaintiff would have no cause of action, as the defendant was exercising the rights of ownership and only telling the truth. The existence of a trademark would have no bearing on the question. Then what new rights does the trade-mark confer? It does not confer a right to prohibit the use of the word or words. It is not a copyright. . . . A trade-mark only gives the right to prohibit the use of it so far as to protect the owner's good will against the sale of another's product as his. . . . When the mark is used in a way that does not deceive the public we see no such sanctity in the word as to prevent its being used to tell the truth.

nor from using plaintiff's mark "collaterally, not to indicate the goods, but to say that the trade-marked product is a constituent in the article now offered as new and changed."[270] Justice Holmes emphasized that the suit was one for trademark infringement, not unfair competition: "The question therefore is not how far the court would go in aid of a plaintiff who showed ground for suspecting the defendant of making a dishonest use of his opportunities, but is whether the plaintiff has the naked right alleged to prohibit the defendant from making even a collateral reference to the plaintiff's mark."[271]

In *Prestonettes*, Justice Holmes noted that the holding was *not* based on "a license implied from the special facts."[272] If the theory for allowing mark use on repackaged goods was implied license, the trademark owner presumably could negate any license by express declaration or contract. The *Prestonettes* non-trademark ("collateral") use theory made the owner's intent irrelevant.

In *Champion Spark Plug*,[273] the Supreme Court extended *Prestonettes* to repaired goods. Plaintiff manufactured and sold "Champion" sparkplugs. Defendant collected used Champion sparkplugs and reconditioned them for resale. Defendant retained the word "Champion," which plaintiff had imprinted on each plug. It sold the reconditioned plugs in boxes with the word "Champion," the plug's type designation, and the phrases "Perfect Process Spark Plugs Guaranteed Dependable" and "Perfect Process Renewed Spark Plugs." Defendant had engaged in unfair competition, apparently by inducing its customers to resell reconditioned sparkplugs to consumers who believed they were getting new ones.

The district court entered an injunction that required defendant to remove plaintiff's mark from the plugs by repainting them and to stamp the word "Repaired" in legible letters on them. It did allow defendant to include a legend on the plugs' carton stating they were "Used spark plugs originally made by Champion Spark Plug Company repaired and made fit for use up to 10,000 miles by Perfect Recondition Spark Plug

---

It is not taboo. . . . If the name Coty were allowed to be printed in different letters from the rest of the inscription dictated by the District Court a casual purchaser might look no further and might be deceived. But when it in no way stands out from the statements of facts that unquestionably the defendant has a right to communicate in some form, we see no reason why it should not be used collaterally, not to indicate the goods, but to say that the trade-marked product is a constituent in the article now offered as new and changed. As a general proposition there can be no doubt that the word might be so used. If a man bought a barrel of a certain flour, or a demijohn of Old Crow whisky, he certainly could sell the flour in smaller packages or in former days could have sold the whisky in bottles, and tell what it was, if he stated that he did the dividing up or the bottling. And this would not be because of a license implied from the special facts but on the general ground that we have stated. It seems to us that no new right can be evoked from the fact that the perfume or powder is delicate and likely to be spoiled, or from the omnipresent possibility of fraud. If the defendant's rebottling the plaintiff's perfume deteriorates it and the public is adequately informed who does the rebottling, the public, with or without the plaintiff's assistance, is likely to find it out. And so of the powder in its new form." 264 U.S. at 368-69.

270 *Id.*

271 *Id.*

272 *Id.*

273 Champion Spark Plug Co. v. Sanders, 331 U.S. 125 (1947).

Co." The court of appeals altered the injunction by eliminating the requirement that defendant removed the trademark and type designations from the plugs but requiring that the word "Repaired" be stamped on them.

The Supreme Court affirmed the court of appeal's refusal to require trademark removal from the reconditioned spark plugs. Defendant's right to retain the mark flowed from *Prestonette's* collateral use/tell-the-truth rationale.[274] The defendant's reconditioning process was not so extensive that it would be a "misnomer to call the article by its original name."[275] Unlike *Prestonettes,* the case involved unfair competition, but the Court could not "say that the conduct of [defendant] . . . or the nature of the article involved and the characteristics of the merchandising methods used to sell it, called for more stringent controls than those the Court of Appeals provided."[276]

Champion Spark Plug suggested that a purchaser's alteration of the trademark owner's goods could be so extensive as to result in a "new construction." In *Bulova Watch,*[277] defendant purchased through various dealers plaintiff's "BULOVA" watches, removed the works from their original cases, and placed them in "women's type, diamond-decorated wrist watches" with defendant's "Treasure Mates" mark together with the notation "17 J Bulova Movement." The recasing, if done properly, did not adversely affect the watch movement. Defendant's catalogs prominently featured the word "Bulova." Some purchasers of defendant's watches evidenced confusion as to their source by sending them to plaintiff for repair. The Seventh Circuit held that the recasing constituted a "new construction,"[278] resulting in trademark

---

[274] "We are dealing here with second-hand goods. The spark plugs, though used, are nevertheless Champion plugs and not those of another make. . . . There is evidence to support what one would suspect, that a used spark plug which has been repaired or reconditioned does not measure up to the specifications of a new one. But the same would be true of a second-hand Ford or Chevrolet car. And we would not suppose that one could be enjoined from selling a car whose valves had been reground and whose piston rings had been replaced unless he removed the name Ford or Chevrolet. . . . " 331 U.S. at 128-29.

[275] "The repair or reconditioning of the plugs does not give them a new design. It is no more than a restoration, so far as possible, of their original condition. The type marks attached by the manufacturer are determined by the use to which the plug is to be put. But the thread size and size of the cylinder hole into which the plug is fitted are not affected by the reconditioning. The heat range also has relevance to the type marks. And there is evidence that the reconditioned plugs are inferior so far as heat range and other qualities are concerned. But inferiority is expected in most second-hand articles. Indeed, they generally cost the customer less. That is the case here. Inferiority is immaterial so long as the article is clearly and distinctively sold as repaired or reconditioned rather than as new." 331 U.S. at 129-30.

As an example of a case in which reconditioning was so extensive that it would be a misnomer to continue to use an article's original mark, Justice Douglas cited Ingersoll v. Doyle, 247 F. 620 (D. Mass. 1917), in which the district court found that defendant's additions and alterations to plaintiff's watches made them "a new construction."

For a discussion of analogous "repair" and "reconstruction" doctrines in patent and copyright law, see §§ 2E[3] and 4E[3][b][iii].

[276] 331 U.S. at 131.

[277] Bulova Watch Co. v. Allerton Co., Inc., 328 F.2d 20, 140 U.S.P.Q. 440 (7th Cir. 1964).

[278] "The case of a wrist watch is a necessary and integral part of the complete product. The substitution of a different crown and case by defendants results in a different product.

infringement and unfair competition and ordered defendant to remove "Bulova" from its watch faces because the faces were too small to accommodate a suitable cautionary disclaimer.

[b] Surplus, Damaged and Rejected Goods. If the trademark owner disposes of surplus or damaged goods bearing his trademark, an immediate or subsequent purchaser may sell them without liability for trademark infringement or unfair competition.[279]

In *Independent News*,[280] a publisher sold comics to a distributor who sold them to a wholesaler who sold them to a retailer who returned comics not sold during the publisher's specified time period to the wholesaler. By agreement with the distributor, the wholesaler returned only the comics' covers and was obligated to "destroy . . . the remaining portions thereof so as to render them unsalable as publications."[281] Defendant purchased cover-removed comics from waste paper dealers and sold them on the open market. There was "no evidence that the defendant had any knowledge that any of the wastepaper dealers from whom he purchased were obligated to sell their coverless comics as wastepaper only."[282] The court held for the defendant, rejecting plaintiff's reliance on a number of legal theories, including trademark infringement. To distinguish *Prestonettes*, plaintiff argued "defendant's marketing of coverless comics, constitutes trademark infringement because the coverless comics are '. . . in a mutilated or adulterated state, . . . ' citing *R. B. Semler, Inc. v. Kirk*, D.C.E.D.Pa.1938, 27 F.Supp. 630 and *Bayer Co. v. Sumner Printing Co.*, D.C.N.D.Ohio 1934, 7 F.Supp. 740."

> ". . . [P]laintiffs state 'The theory of these cases is that the defendant may not utilize the plaintiffs' trademark to sell a product unless it is identical in every respect to the original product as marketed by plaintiffs. If it is adulterated or altered in any way, such sales infringe the plaintiffs' trademark rights. Such action damages the plaintiffs' good will and causes confusion and deception in the minds of the public.'
>
> "In *Semler* . . . , the court issued an injunction prohibiting defendant from rebottling Kreml hair tonic, holding that because of the peculiar nature of the product, and the disproportion of the ingredients caused by the rebottling

---

The watch is no longer a Bulova watch. It is a new and different 'watch' albeit one containing a 'movement' manufactured by Bulova. The case is not Bulova's and its fitting does not represent Bulova workmanship. . . . [C]hange in the original article may be such that the party making the change is without right to retain or use the manufacturer's trademark in connection with the resale of the changed product. . . . And, while the defendants are entitled to make a proper collateral reference to the source of the movement, without use of the trademark 'BULOVA' as such, any use of the trademark itself in connection with defendants' product must be in such a way that the public is not deceived." 328 F.2d at 23.

[279] One decision held that a provision in a damaged goods sale contract requiring removal of a trademark was enforceable against a subsequent purchaser of the goods as an "equitable servitude on a chattel." Nadell & Co., Inc. v. Grasso, 175 Cal. App.2d 420, 346 P.2d 505 (1959).

[280] Independent News Co., Inc. v. Williams, 293 F.2d 510 (3d Cir. 1961).

[281] 293 F.2d at 512.

[282] *Id.*

process, '. . . the resulting product is not Kreml but at best but a distortion of it.' In *Bayer*, the court rested the granting of the injunction prohibiting the defendant from repackaging aspirins on the firm ground that there was public deception . . .

"These decisions are not in point here. The defendant does not in any way change or alter the form, contents or appearance of the comics so as to come within the rationale of cases like *Semler* and *Bayer*. . . . Nor does the defendant do any act which respect to the trademarked article which causes public deception as is prohibited by the general doctrines of trademark infringement. . . . He merely resells the comics in the identical form in which he purchases them. . . . Any change of appearance or alteration of the comics is caused by plaintiffs. According to their own testimony, they require the wholesaler to remove the covers. They cannot now allege as the basis of an allegation of trademark infringement, the alterations that they themselves have caused."[283]

In *Alfred Dunhill*,[284] Dunhill received a shipment of tobacco that was damaged when a hole developed in the shipping container's roof, which allowed an undetermined amount of water to enter. In making a claim on its insurance carrier for water loss on 168 cases of tobacco, Dunhill could accept the insurer's estimate of partial loss, which was 25%, of insured value, or dispose of the product "by public sale" and collect the difference between the amount realized and the "sound market value." It agreed to the latter and shipped the goods to United Salvage Company, which sold them to Interstate Cigar, the bill of sale providing "Dunhill Tobacco—As Is—Salvage." Harris and Spielfogel, Dunhill's and Interstate's respective heavyweights, "conversed over the telephone," Harris demanding that Interstate label the goods as "salvage," Speilfogel rejecting the demand and offering to return the tobacco, Harris replying that "he didn't want the tobacco back." Interstate sold "quantities" of the tobacco to Miami Beach retailers, who, on some occasions, resold it "at unusually low prices" but without advising their customers of possible water damage. Finding Interstate violated Lanham Act Section 43(a) by falsely representing the tobacco's quality, the district court prohibited Interstate from selling the tobacco "without taking effective steps" to warn customers of possible water damage and allowed Dunhill to mark each tobacco tin in Interstate's possession with the legend "Subjected to Possible Water Damage." The Second Circuit reversed: "If Dunhill had wished to distinguish the salvaged tobacco from that sold through its normal channels of distribution, it should have done so while the allegedly damaged tobacco was still under its control and before it was released into the salvage markets. From the beginning Dunhill was in the best position to effect the relabeling. It would be unfair, under the circumstances, for one party in the chain of distribution to impose upon another further down the line an obligation to decrease the value of the goods."[285]

In *Monte Carlo Shirt*,[286] plaintiff contracted with defendant, a South Korean company, for purchase of 2400 dozen men's dress shirts manufactured to its

---

[283] 293 F.2d at 514-15.

[284] Alfred Dunhill Limited v. Interstate Cigar Co., Inc., 499 F.2d 232, 183 U.S.P.Q. 193 (2d Cir. 1974).

[285] 499 F.2d at 237-38.

[286] Monte Carlo Shirt, Inc. v. Daewoo International (America) Corp., 707 F.2d 1054, 219 U.S.P.Q. 594 (9th Cir. 1983).

specifications and bearing its label. Plaintiff rejected the shirts after defendant shipped them to the United States "because the documents necessary to clear the shipment arrived too late for Christmas sales." Defendant sold the shirts to discount retailers with plaintiff's labels intact. At trial, a jury awarded plaintiff damages for breach of contract and trademark infringement. The district court dismissed the trademark infringement theory, which was based on California law, and the Ninth Circuit affirmed because "no trademark infringement could be shown on these facts." Finding little authority on "the viability of a trademark claim for the unauthorized sale of a genuine product," [287] it reasoned that there could be no infringement because there was no confusion as to the good's origin. The defendant made the goods under plaintiff's supervision and control. [288]

> "[T]he injury that is remedied by the trademark cause of action is public confusion as to the source of the goods. . . .
>
> "No such confusion was possible in this case. The goods sold by Daewoo were not imitations of Monte Carlo shirts; they were the genuine product, planned and sponsored by Monte Carlo and produced for it on contract for future sale. The shirts were not altered or changed from the date of their manufacture to the date of their sale. . . . Their source was Monte Carlo; the absence of Monte Carlo's authorization of the discount retailers to sell does not alter this. Admittedly the law of trademark has extended well beyond its origin as a remedy for 'passing off,' but Monte Carlo has not demonstrated that it should reach as far as the facts of this case." [289]

---

[287] It noted that Ritz Cycle Car Co. v. Driggs-Seabury Ordnance Corp., 237 F. 125 (S.D.N.Y.1916), "an early common-law trademark case, did find an infringement when the manufacturer marketed goods rejected by the trademark owner," but *Ritz Cycle Car* "is not sufficient authority to overturn the cases requiring a likelihood of confusion." 707 F.2d at 1057 n.3, 219 U.S.P.Q. at n.3.

[288] The court rejected plaintiff's argument "that it could not determine the quality of the shirts manufactured by Daewoo without inspecting them on delivery and supervising their distribution."

> "Al Kaufler, Monte Carlo's president, testified to the many steps he took to ensure the quality of his product before contracting with Daewoo. Before placing his order, Kaufler visited Korea and thoroughly investigated Daewoo's production capabilities. He issued detailed instructions on the size specifications, measurements, and styling of the shirts—the very factors that he claimed established Monte Carlo's quality to the consuming public and distinguished its shirts from those of its competitors. Kaufler was also able to distinguish the quality of the various manufacturers working for Monte Carlo at this stage—before receipt of the goods. Once the shirts were produced, they were given the Monte Carlo logo, packed in polybags, and boxed. Kaufler testified that customers generally bought prepackaged shirts which they didn't try on until they went home. Monte Carlo's concerns about quality control are also suspect in light of its conceded willingness to have taken the shirts for spring delivery, and the absence of any complaint that it was injured by the quality of Daewoo's product." 707 F.2d at 1058 n.5, 219 U.S.P.Q. at 597 n.5.

[289] 707 F.2d at 1057-58, 219 U.S.P.Q. at 597-98.

See also Diamond Supply Co. v. Prudential Paper Products Co., Inc., 589 F. Supp. 470, 223 U.S.P.Q. 869 (S.D. N.Y. 1984). Compare Bill Blass, Ltd. v. SAZ Corp., 751 F.2d 152, 224 U.S.P.Q. 753 (3d Cir. 1984).

In *El Greco Leather Products*,[290] the Second Circuit distinguished *Monte Carlo Shirt* and held goods manufactured to the trademark owner's specifications were not "genuine" when they were shipped into the United States without the owner's contractually required inspection certificate. El Greco ordered 25,000 pairs of shoes bearing its "CANDIE'S" mark from Solemio, a Brazilian shoe factory. The order required that Sapatus, El Greco's agent in Brazil, issue a certificate of inspection declaring that the merchandise had been "approved for shipment in accordance with buyer's delivery and quality specifications." After El Greco cancelled the last two lots of its order, Solemio sold the shoes through an intermediary to Shoe World, which began selling them at a bargain price. El Greco sued Shoe World. The Second Circuit ruled for El Greco, the trademark owner. Even if the shoes met all the trademark owner's quality specifications, the unauthorized sale deprived it of the right of control.

> "One of the most valuable and important protections afforded by the Lanham Act is the right to control the quality of the goods manufactured and sold under the holder's trademark. . . . For this purpose the actual quality of the goods is irrelevant; it is the control of quality that a trademark holder is entitled to maintain. . . .

> "The holder of a trademark is entitled to require . . . that no merchandise be distributed without its first being inspected by the holder or its agent to insure quality. . . .

> . . .

> "The certificates of inspection required in this case were an integral part of appellant's effort at quality control. Earlier inspections by Sapatus of the shoes that eventually comprised lots A-E resulted in some shoes being rejected, and in changes in the procedures being followed in production. . . .

> "The district court concluded the shoes were 'genuine' because they had been manufactured pursuant to an order by El Greco, the undisputed holder of the CANDIE'S trademark, and because El Greco did not specifically instruct Solemio on how to dispose of the shoes once it cancelled the order.

> "This is an unjustifiably narrow view of the protection afforded trademark holders by the Lanham Act. The mere act of ordering a product to be labeled with a trademark does not deprive its holder of the right to control the product and the trademark. It is true that El Greco did not, at the time it cancelled the last two lots of its order, give instructions on how to dispose of the shoes that had already been manufactured and affixed with the CANDIE'S trademark. But we do not view such a step as necessary on the facts presented here.

> "Once it cancelled the order, El Greco was entitled to assume that Solemio would not dispose of the shoes without either removing the CANDIE'S trademark (as in the custom and practice in the industry), or affording El Greco an opportunity to inspect the goods and certify their quality prior to disposal, or, at the minimum, seeking instructions from El Greco on how to dispose

---

[290] El Greco Leather Products Co., Inc. v. Shoe World, Inc., 806 F.2d 392, 1 U.S.P.Q.2d 1016 (2d Cir. 1986), *cert. denied*, 484 U.S. 817 (1987), *on remand*, 726 F. Supp. 25, 14 U.S.P.Q.2d 1534 (E.D. N.Y. 1989).

of them. Since Solemio, at best, received no instructions from El Greco, this case is distinguishable from *Diamond Supply Co. v. Prudential Paper Products Co.*, 589 F.Supp. 470 (S.D. N.Y. 1984), wherein the trademark holder specifically instructed the manufacturer that he 'did not care' how the cancelled goods were disposed of. 589 F.Supp. at 474. No similar waiver here was given, or even sought.

. . .

" . . . Even though Shoe World was involved neither in the manufacture nor the affixing of the CANDIE'S trademark to the shoes, its sale of the shoes was sufficient 'use' for it to be liable for the results of such infringement and its claimed lack of knowledge of its supplier's infringement, even if true, provides no defense."[291]

[c] **Unauthorized Repair and Distribution.** Numerous decisions deal with "independent" service and repair businesses' right to refer to the manufacturer in whose product they specialize. In *Volkswagenwerk*,[292] the Ninth Circuit held that Church, who specialized in Volkswagen car repair, could refer to his business as "Independent Volkswagen Porsche Service." The district court's findings that his "extensive use of the word 'independent' sufficiently distinguished his business from those affiliated with" plaintiff, the Volkswagen manufacturer and that "the terms 'Volkswagen Service' and 'VW Service' did not belong exclusively to Volkswagen, but have 'come to mean in the mind of the public only that the advertiser services Volkswagen vehicles' " were not clearly erroneous.

"It is not disputed that Church may specialize in the repair of Volkswagen vehicles. He may also advertise to the effect that he does so, and in such advertising it would be difficult, if not impossible, for him to avoid altogether the use of the word 'Volkswagen' or its abbreviation 'VW,' which are the normal terms which, to the public at large, signify appellant's cars. . . . But these terms are not public property; they are registered trademarks. The goodwill inherent in them is Volkswagen's property. If another uses the marks in a manner which tends to deceive the public, Volkswagen is entitled to protection. . . . Although he may advertise to the public that he repairs appellant's cars, Church must not do so in a manner which is likely to suggest to his prospective customers that he is part of Volkswagen's organization of franchised dealers and repairmen. . . . The question of whether Church's business was adequately distinguished from appellant's is one of fact. Each case of this type must be decided on its own facts . . .

"In this case, on the basis of all of the facts and circumstances, we hold that the factual determinations of the District Court were not clearly erroneous. We cannot, therefore, overturn the decision that, in the light of the particular circumstances, Church's prominent use of the word 'Independent' whenever the terms 'Volkswagen' or 'VW' appeared in his advertising was sufficient to

---

[291] 806 F.2d at 395-96, 1 U.S.P.Q.2d at 1017-18.

[292] Volkswagenwerk Aktiengesellschaft v. Church, 411 F.2d 350, 161 U.S.P.Q. 769 (9th Cir. 1969), *opinion supplemented*, 413 F.2d 1126 (9th Cir. 1969).

distinguish his business to the eye of the customer 'exercising that care, caution and power of perception which the public may be expected to exercise in the matter which it has in mind.' . . . It was appropriate for the District Court to weigh all of the pertinent factors. The size, style and appearance of the advertising articles and displays were among these factors. Another was the fact that Church did not use Volkswagen's distinctive lettering style or color scheme, nor did he display the encircled 'VW' emblem. Under this view of the case, we need not reach the question whether the phrases 'Volkswagen Service' and 'VW Service' have become so identified in the public mind with appellant that their use by others constitutes unfair competition.

"Volkswagen further contends that the trial court erred in failing to enjoin Church's unlawful past practice of using 'Volkswagen' as part of his business name, although he had abandoned this usage at the time of trial. There is little or no evidence in the record casting doubt on Church's good faith abandonment of this infringement, or indicating that it will be resumed. . . . "[293]

Courts follow the *Prestonnettes* "tell the truth" theory in allowing independent distributors and retailers to resell trademark-bearing goods previously sold by or with the permission of the trademark owner—even if the resale is contrary to the owner's established distribution or franchise network.

In *Henry*,[294] Midwest bought from Chloride "unbranded batteries," that is, batteries that did not carry the manufacturer's name or warranty, and sold them with a label containing its own name and the notation "Batteries by Chloride." The district court ruled against Chloride on its trademark infringement claim, reasoning that Midwest's unauthorized use of Chloride's mark was "wrongful" and the public might believe Chloride sponsored Midwest's use but that the use was not infringement under the *Prestonnettes* "genuine" goods line of cases. The appeals court affirmed, holding that Midwest's label was truthful and constituted an adequate disclaimer of Chloride sponsorship.

"*Prestonettes* . . . deals with goods which are genuine and a mark which accurately describes those goods. Chloride argues that the restrictions placed by the Court on the use of the Coty mark mean that absent a similarly detailed disclaimer on the batteries, Midwest infringed defendant's mark. Although this argument is plausible, we think it goes too far. The disclaimer in *Prestonettes*, except for the statement that defendant was 'not connected with Coty,' dealt entirely with the fact that the product had been changed by defendant, and how that change was effected. . . . Other cases requiring disclaimers with the use of plaintiff's mark also involve products which have been altered in some way. . . .

"There is no suggestion here that the batteries were altered, . . . or that they were 'seconds' of inferior quality. . . . We think, therefore, that the principle of disclaimer was sufficiently served in this case. The label stated in

[293] 411 F.2d at 352.

[294] Henry v. Chloride, Inc., 809 F.2d 1334, 1 U.S.P.Q.2d 1610 (8th Cir. 1987).

large letters covering half the available space that the product was from
'MIDWEST BATTERIES.' Midwest's address was below its name in somewhat smaller letters, and in the lower right-hand corner, in still smaller letters, 'BATTERIES BY CHLORIDE.' While this would truthfully tell the
customer which company manufactured the battery, we think it unlikely that
a customer would assume that the concern which warranted the battery was
the one with the little letters tucked in the corner. This is not to say that
Midwest was entitled to replicate the Chloride label in toto and place it on
the unbranded battery. But had Chloride wished to prevent the use of its name
in any form on its unaltered, first-quality product, it could have contracted
for that very arrangement."[295]

Courts find trademark infringement or unfair competition if the reseller creates the
misleading impression that he is the trademark owner's authorized distributor or
franchisee or that the trademark owner is responsible for the reseller's alteration or
degradation of the goods or failure to provide service.[296]

---

[295] 809 F.2d at 1350, 1 U.S.P.Q.2d at 1622-23.

[296] *E.g.,* H.L. Hayden Co. of New York, Inc. v. Siemens Medical Systems, Inc., 879 F.2d
1005, 1023 (2d Cir. 1989) (defendant resold by catalog machines purchased from plaintiff's
dealers; "the unauthorized sale of a trademarked article does not, without more, constitute a
Lanham Act violation," but the district court properly prohibited "any representation by
[defendant] that [plaintiff's] warranty applies to [its] products purchased from [plaintiff]."); NEC
Electronics v. CAL Circuit Abco, 810 F.2d 1506, 1509, 1 U.S.P.Q.2d 2056, 2058 (9th Cir.
1987) ("Trademark law generally does not reach the sale of genuine goods bearing a true mark
even though such sale is without the mark owner's consent. . . . Once a trademark owner sells
his product, the buyer ordinarily may resell the product under the original mark without
incurring any trademark law liability. . . . The reason is that trademark law is designed to
prevent sellers from confusing or deceiving consumers about the origin or make of a product, which confusion ordinarily does not exist when a genuine article bearing a true mark is
sold."); Bandag, Inc. v. Al Bolser's Tire Stores, Inc., 750 F.2d 903, 910- 11, 223 U.S.P.Q. 982,
986-87 (Fed. Cir. 1984) (independent reseller created likelihood of confusion as to whether it
was plaintiff's franchisee; "An independent dealer may properly advertise that he sells merchandise associated by the public with a well-known trade or service mark so long as this does not
mislead customers into thinking that he is an authorized agent of, or directly connected with,
the owner of that mark. . . . In order to communicate accurate information about a product,
a right is implied to use any mark fairly associated with that product. . . . Although Bolser
was entitled to make known that it sold Bandag recaps, the Bandag mark, particularly in logo
form, was not public property. At the time of Bolser's alleged infringement, Bandag owned
four registrations for various forms and applications of its mark, . . . the use of which by then
had presumably become incontestable. . . . The goodwill inherent in the mark was the property
of Bandag. If Bolser's use of the mark occurred in such a manner as to deceive the public,
Bandag would be entitled to protection, . . . Although Bolser could advertise that it sold
Bandag recaps, it was obliged not to do so in a manner which would have been likely to suggest
to prospective customers that it was part of the Bandag organization of franchisees. . . .
The problem was primarily one of designing clear, truthful advertising copy and using
straightforward business practices.").

See also Stormor v. Johnson, 587 F. Supp. 275, 278, 223 U.S.P.Q. 665, 667 (W.D. Mich.
1984):

"[T]rademark infringement occurs when a defendant uses the plaintiff's trademark in a
manner that suggests that the defendant is affiliated with the plaintiff's company even

In *Clairol*,[297] Clairol sold "Miss Clairol" hair coloring "through two distinct channels of trade." It sold its "retail" product in individual packages with an instruction booklet to retail chains and wholesalers for sale to the general public for home use. It sold its "salon" product in six-pack cartons with a single instruction booklet through distributors only to beauty salons and schools, Clairol charging a substantially lower price for the salon product.[298] The retail product instruction booklet included a consumer warning statement that the ingredients might cause some individual skin irritation and that a preliminary test should be made first. It also contained detailed instructions directed to the "untrained consumer." The salon instruction sheet was shorter and stated that the product is for "Professional Use Only."

The defendants purchased Clairol's salon products and sold them at retail. The Sixth Circuit affirmed the district court's finding that such sales constituted unfair competition, rejecting the defendants' arguments that any injury to Clairol's goodwill resulted from its unlawful two-price structure and its refusal to put adequate instructions with the salon bottles. Their reliance on *Prestonettes* and *Champion Spark Plug* "misses the [trade?] mark."

> "The question is not simply whether defendants palmed off their own product as the plaintiff's and thereby deceived the public by appropriating plaintiff's name for their own product. Other practices may also constitute unfair competition under Michigan law. . . .

> though the defendant deals in the goods of the trademark owner. See Trail Chevrolet, Inc. v. General Motors Corp., 381 F.2d 353 (5th Cir.1967) (per curiam) (upholding a permanent injunction against defendant's use of the registered trademark Chevrolet in its advertising where the district court found that such use was likely to cause the public to believe that they were dealing with a business that was sponsored, supervised, endorsed or otherwise connected with the plaintiff); Volkswagenwerk Aktiengesellschaft v. Volks City, Inc., 348 F.2d 659 (3rd Cir. 1965) (upholding the district court's preliminary injunction enjoining defendant from using the Volkswagen trademark or any other name commonly associated with Volkswagen products where the trial court had found that defendant's advertisements were clearly intended to convey the impression of affiliation with plaintiff); Prompt Electrical Supply Co. v. Allen-Brady Co., 492 F.Supp. 344 (E.D.N.Y.1980) (holding that a former authorized distributor's use of the registrant's trademark after termination of the distributorship agreement constituted trademark infringement even though the distributor continued to deal in the trademarked products). . . .

> "It is equally well-settled that not every use of another's trademark without the owner's consent amounts to trademark infringement or unfair competition. . . .'.

> . . .

> "Although the Court agrees that unauthorized sale of a genuine trademarked product without more does not constitute trademark infringement, . . . the Court concludes that additional factors are involved here because defendants have used plaintiff's trademarks in a manner which is likely to cause the public to believe that defendants are part of Stormor's authorized sales network."

[297] Clairol, Inc. v. Boston Discount Center of Berkley, Inc., 608 F.2d 1114, 204 U.S.P.Q. 89 (6th Cir. 1979).

[298] From 1955 until 1974, after the filing of the law suit, the two product lines were of identical chemical formulation. In 1974, Clairol eliminated certain intermediates from the retail version.

". . . [T]he defendants' practice of selling the professional bottles of Miss Clairol to the consuming public for home use constituted unfair and unethical practice. . . . The practice is damaging both to the public and to Clairol and constitutes in the most general sense a deceit and thus a fraud upon the public.

. . .

" '. . . [T]he consumer who buys "Miss Clairol" in the naked bottle from defendant, although she may think she is purchasing the safe, effective product she associates with plaintiff, is not getting it. But the consumer will attribute any unsatisfactory performance from "Miss Clairol" to plaintiff, and not to defendant. Defendant thus uses plaintiff's goodwill to make sales, but acts in a manner which can only decrease plaintiff's goodwill, thus damaging an important property interest of plaintiff. . . . ' "[299]

[d] **Comparative Advertising and Labelling.** In *Smith*,[300] the Ninth Circuit applied the *Prestonettes* theory and trademark law policy considerations to hold that trademark use in comparative advertising does not constitute infringement. Defendant advertised its "Second Chance" perfume as a "duplicate" of plaintiff's "Chanel No. 5."[301] The court held that "one who has copied an unpatented product sold under a trademark may use the trademark in his advertising to identify the product he has copied," citing three prior cases that refused to enjoin comparative use of competitor's trademarks.[302] It linked a narrow conception of trademark protection's appropriate functions to free economic competition concerns.[303]

"The rule rests upon the traditionally accepted premise that the only legally relevant function of a trademark is to impart information as to the source or sponsorship of the product. . . . Appellees argue that protection should also

---

[299] 608 F.2d at 1120.

See also Adolph Coors Co. v. A. Genderson & Sons, Inc., 486 F. Supp. 131, 135, 209 U.S.P.Q. 103 (D. Colo. 1980) (Coors limited distribution of its unpasteurized beers to selected states and required distributors to maintain it under refrigeration and not to let it remain in retail stores more than 60 days from packaging; defendant purchased Coors beer in Colorado and distributed it in the Washington D.C. area without complying with Coor's distribution standards; HELD: defendant is guilty of trademark infringement and unfair competition; "The acts of defendant in this controversy pose a threat to the quality assurance function of trademarks.").

[300] Smith v. Chanel, Inc., 402 F.2d 562, 159 U.S.P.Q. 388 (9th Cir. 1968). *See also* SSP Agricultural Equipment, Inc. v. Orchard-Rite Ltd., 592 F.2d 1096, 202 U.S.P.Q. 1 (9th Cir. 1979).

[301] The court noted that if defendant's specific claims of equivalency are false, the plaintiff may have a Section 43(a) remedy for false advertising. On remand, the district court found that indeed defendant's equivalency assertion was false. *See* § 6E.

[302] Saxlehner v. Wagner, 216 U.S. 375 (1910); Société Comptoir de L'Industrie Cotonnière Etablissements Boussac v. Alexander's Dept. Stores, Inc., 299 F.2d 33, 132 U.S.P.Q. 475 (2d Cir. 1962); Viavi Co. v . Vimedia Co., 245 F. 289 (8th Cir. 1917).

[303] *Smith's* critical review of trademark goodwill lies at a pole opposite that of trademark dilution theory. *See* §5E[3][b].

be extended to the trademark's commercially more important function of embodying consumer good will created through extensive, skillful, and costly advertising. The courts, however, have generally confined legal protection to the trademark's source identification function for reasons grounded in the public policy favoring a free, competitive economy.

"Preservation of the trademark as a means of identifying the trademark owner's products, implemented both by the Lanham Act and the common law, serves an important public purpose. . . . It makes effective competition possible in a complex, impersonal marketplace by providing a means through which the consumer can identify products which please him and reward the producer with continued patronage. Without some such method of product identification, informed consumer choice, and hence meaningful competition in quality, could not exist. . . .

"On the other hand, it has been suggested that protection of trademark values other than source identification would create serious anti-competitive consequences with little compensating public benefit. . . .

"The object of much modern advertising is 'to impregnate the atmosphere of the market with the drawing power of a congenial symbol.' *Mishawaka Rubber & Woolen Mfg. Co. v. S. S. Kresge Co.*, 316 U.S. 203, 205 (1942), . . . rather than to communicate information as to quality or price. . . . To the extent that advertising of this type succeeds, it is suggested, the trademark is endowed with sales appeal independent of the quality or price of the product to which it is attached; economically irrational elements are introduced into consumer choices; and the trademark owner is insulated from the normal pressures of price and quality competition. In consequence the competitive system fails to perform its function of allocating available resources efficiently. . . .

"Moreover, the economically irrelevant appeal of highly publicized trademarks is thought to constitute a barrier to the entry of new competition into the market. 'The presence of irrational consumer allegiances may constitute an effective barrier to entry. Consumer allegiances built over the years with intensive advertising, trademarks, trade names, copyrights and so forth extend substantial protection to firms already in the market. In some markets this barrier to entry may be insuperable.' Papandreou, The Economic Effects of Trademarks, 44 Calif.L.Rev. 503, 508-09 (1956). . . . High barriers to entry tend, in turn, to produce 'high excess profits and monopolistic output restriction' and 'probably . . . high and possibly excessive costs of sales promotion.' J. Bain, Barriers to New Competition 203 (1955).

"A related consideration is also pertinent to the present case. Since appellees' perfume was unpatented, appellants had a right to copy it . . . But this public benefit might be lost if appellants could not tell potential purchasers that appellants' product was the equivalent of appellees' product. . . . The most effective way (and, where complex chemical compositions sold under trade names are involved, often the only practical way) in which this can be done is to identify the copied article by its trademark or trade name. To prohibit use of a competitor's trademark for the sole purpose of identifying the competitor's product would bar effective communication of claims of equivalence. . . . Assuming the equivalence of 'Second Chance' and 'Chanel No. 5,' the public interest would not be served by a rule of law which would preclude sellers of 'Second Chance' from advising consumers of the equivalence and thus effectively deprive consumers of knowledge that an identical product was being offered at one third the price.

. . .

"Against these considerations, two principal arguments are made for protection of trademark values other than source identification.

"The first . . . is that the creation of the other values inherent in the trademark require 'the expenditure of great effort, skill and ability,' and that the competitor should not be permitted 'to take a free ride' on the trademark owner's 'widespread goodwill and reputation.' . . .

"A large expenditure of money does not in itself create legally protectable rights. . . . Appellees are not entitled to monopolize the public's desire for the unpatented product, even though they themselves created that desire at great effort and expense. . . . As we have noted, the most effective way (and in some cases the only practical way) in which others may compete in satisfying the demand for the product is to produce it and tell the public they have done so, and if they could be barred from this effort appellees would have found a way to acquire a practical monopoly in the unpatented product to which they are not legally entitled.

"Disapproval of the copyist's opportunism may be an understandable first reaction, 'but this initial response to the problem has been curbed in deference to the greater public good.' . . . By taking his 'free ride,' the copyist, albeit unintentionally, serves an important public interest by offering comparable goods at lower prices. On the other hand, the trademark owner, perhaps equally without design, sacrifices public to personal interests by seeking immunity from the rigors of competition.

"Moreover, appellees' reputation is not directly at stake. Appellants' advertisement makes it clear that the product they offer is their own. If it proves to be inferior, they, not appellees, will bear the burden of consumer disapproval. . . .

"The second major argument for extended trademark protection is that even in the absence of confusion as to source, use of the trademark of another 'creates a serious threat to the uniqueness and distinctiveness' of the trademark, and 'if continued would create a risk of making a generic or descriptive term of the words' of which the trademark is composed. . . .

"The contention has little weight in the context of this case. Appellants do not use appellees' trademark as a generic term. They employ it only to describe appellees' product, not to identify their own. . . . The slight tendency to carry the mark into the common language which even this use may have is outweighed by the substantial value of such use in the maintenance of effective competition."[304]

In *G.D. Searle*,[305] the Second Circuit held that a competitor could make comparative use of a competitor's trademark on a product label as well as in advertising: "whether one is entitled to refer to a competitor's trademark depends not on where the reference appears but on whether the reference is truthful."[306]

[5] Parallel Importation—Gray-Market Goods

"A gray-market good is a foreign-manufactured good, bearing a valid United States trademark, that is imported without the consent of the U.S. trademark holder."[307]

---

[304] 402 F.2d at 566-69.

See also Société Comptoir de l'Industrie Cotonnière Etablissements Boussac v. Alexander's Department Stores, Inc., 299 F.2d 33, 36-37, 132 U.S.P.Q. 475 (2d Cir. 1962) (no preliminary injunction against defendant's extensive use of "Dior" and "Christian Dior" "to promote the sale of garments copied from original creations designed by the house of Dior"; "The registering of a proper noun as a trade-mark does not withdraw it from the language, nor reduce it to the exclusive possession of the registrant which may be jealously guarding against any and all use by others. Registration bestows upon the owner of the mark the limited right to protect his good will from possible harm by those uses of another as may engender a belief in the mind of the public that the product identified by the infringing mark is made or sponsored by the owner of the mark. . . . The Lanham Act does not prohibit a commercial rival's truthfully denominating his goods a copy of a design in the public domain, though he uses the name of the designer to do so. Indeed it is difficult to see any other means that might be employed to inform the consuming public of the true origin of the design. . . . Involved in the instant case is a conflict of values which necessarily arises in an economy characterized by competition and private property. The courts have come to recognize the true nature of the considerations often involved in efforts to extend protection of common law trade names so as to create a shield against competition. . . . The interest of the consumer here in competitive prices of garments using Dior designs without deception as to origin, is at least as great as the interest of plaintiffs in monopolizing the name.").

[305] G.D. Searle & Co. v. Hudson Pharmaceutical Corp., 715 F.2d 837, 220 U.S.P.Q. 496 (3d Cir. 1983).

[306] 715 F.2d at 842, 220 U.S.P.Q. at 501.

Searle sold a vegetable laxative—psyllium hydrophilic mucilloid—under the registered mark "METAMUCIL." The product is "highly profitable." Hudson sold the same vegetable laxative under the "REGACILIUM" mark and adopted a label that stated "Equivalent to META-MUCIL." The district court refused to prohibit Hudson from using Searle's mark provided "the defendant's container is changed such that 'METAMUCIL' appears in type no larger than the word 'Equivalent' and in green letters on the white background. Defendant shall place an TM next to the METAMUCIL mark and shall state adjacent to said mark the statement 'a product of G.D. Searle, not a Hudson product.'" The court later revised the statement to read: "METAMUCIL TM is made by G.D. Searle & CO. Searle does not make or license REGACILIUM TM." Both parties appealed. The appeals court affirmed. As to Hudson's appeal, the district court properly found a likelihood of confusion without the added statement. As to Searle's appeal, neither the Lanham Act nor case law support "Searle's contention that the law of trademarks distinguishes . . . between packages and advertisements." 715 F.2d at 841, 220 U.S.P.Q. at 500.

[307] K Mart Corp. v. Cartier, Inc., 486 U.S. 281, 6 U.S.P.Q.2d 1897 (1988). *See also* Olympus Corp. v. United States, 792 F.2d 315, 320, 230 U.S.P.Q. 123, 126 (2d Cir. 1986), *cert. de-*

Gray-market activity is also referred to as "parallel importation."[308]

The question whether gray-market goods may be imported into the United States and sold without infringing the United States trademark owner's rights is the subject of a complex history and continuing debate.

Opposing views on gray-market goods evoke competing trademark theories at the conceptual (universality, territoriality, and exhaustion)[309] and functional (source

---

nied, 486 U.S. 1042 (1988) ("The variations of the gray market are numerous. *See Vivitar*, 761 F.2d at 1570 n. 24 (U.S. and foreign trademark rights may be owned by the same entity, by related companies, or by wholly separate companies; imported goods may be identical to or different from the parallel import; the goods may be produced in the United States and different goods produced abroad; services and warranties may or may not be the same; foreign licensees may not be subject to U.S. control).").

[308] *See* Takamatsu, *Parallel Importation of Trademarked Goods: A Comparative Analysis*, 57 Wash. L. Rev. 433 (1982). *See also* Weil Ceramics and Glass, Inc. v. Dash, 878 F.2d 659, 662 n.1, 11 U.S.P.Q. 1001, 1003 n.1 (3d Cir. 1989), *cert. denied*, 110 S. Ct. 156 (1989) ("the term parallel import accurately describes the goods and is, perhaps, a better term [than 'gray-market'] because it is devoid of prejudicial suggestion.").

[309] *See* K Mart Corp. v. Cartier, Inc., 486 U.S. 281, 301, 308-09, 6 U.S.P.Q. 1897, 1906, 1909 (1988) (Brennan concurring in part and dissenting in part; "Under [the 'universality' theory of trademark law] trademarks do not confer on the owner property interests or monopoly power over intrabrand competition. Rather they merely protect the public from deception by indicating 'the origin of the goods they mark.' "; arguing that Congress' 1922 enactment of Tariff Act Section 526 did not reject the universality theory: "Congress typically would not sneak such a sweeping doctrinal change into a massive legislative overhaul on an unrelated topic (here tariff revision)."); Osawa & Co. v. B & H Photo, 589 F. Supp. 1163, 1171-72, 223 U.S.P.Q. 124, 130 (S.D. N.Y. 1984) (under the universality theory, "if a trademark was lawfully affixed to merchandise in one country, the merchandise would carry that mark lawfully wherever it went"; the territoriality theory "recognizes that a trademark has a separate legal existence under each country's laws, and that its proper lawful function is not necessarily to specify the origin or manufacture of a good (although it may incidentally do that), but rather to symbolize the domestic goodwill of the domestic markholder so that the consuming public may rely with an expectation of consistency on the domestic reputation earned for the mark by its owner, and the owner of the mark may be confident that his goodwill and reputation (the value of the mark) will not be injured through use of the mark by others in domestic commerce.").

Cf. Weil Ceramics and Glass, Inc. v. Dash, 878 F.2d 659, 677 n.5, 11 U.S.P.Q.2d 1001, 1016 n.5 (3d Cir. 1989), *cert. denied* 110 S. Ct. 156 (1989) (Becker, concurring; arguing that the common law and Paris Convention obligations, not *Katzel*, dictate the territoriality theory; "The doctrine of exhaustion developed as a corollary to the universality theory. Under this doctrine, once the markholder has sold an item, the subsequent sale of that item cannot serve as the basis for an infringement suit. The relevant issue . . . is whether the doctrine of exhaustion is meant to apply only within the borders of a sovereign or whether it applies universally, such that a sale in one country prevents an infringement suit in another. The latter position would make no sense in the context of the territoriality of trademarks. . . . If every time a foreign manufacturer placed its product on the market, the trademark rights were universally exhausted, then the territoriality theory . . . would lose most of its force and the right to control the trademark of an internationally available good in a given country would not be of much value. In fact, if the exhaustion theory were viable, that would mean that once a manufacturer sold the product to the domestic markholder, the product's trademark rights were exhausted

identification and quality guarantee) levels.[310]

and the domestic markholder could not assert his rights under the trademark laws. That makes no sense where trademark rights may rest in nonmanufacturers and the Lanham Act recognizes the validity of the assignment of trademarks. The more coherent way to view exhaustion in the context of the territoriality theory is to view it as applying individually to each markholder such that a markholder only exhausts its own trademark rights upon sale of the item, and not the trademark rights of other markholders in other countries.").

[310] See Original Appalachian Artworks, Inc. v. Granada Electronics, Inc., 816 F.2d 68, 2 U.S.P.Q.2d 1343 (2d Cir. 1987), cert. denied 484 U.S. 847 (1987) (parallel importation of "Cabbage Patch Kids" dolls made in Spain under license infringes rights of United States owner of "Cabbage Patch Kids" trademark because, inter alia, the license forbade export from Spain and the imported dolls carried Spanish rather than English language "birth certificate" papers and did not entitle purchasers the services, such as "adoption" certificates and a "birthday" card sent by the U.S. owner). In *Original Appalachian Artworks*, Judge Cardamone concurred:

"[T]o determine whether the importation of 'genuine' [goods] creates a likelihood of confusion as to their 'source', it is necessary to examine the functions and principles of trademark law.

"A. Trade Identity Theory

"Under the trade identity theory of trademark law, the only function of this body of law is to identify the ultimate source of the goods, i.e., the owner of the mark . . . Where . . . the domestic owner of the mark has licensed the use of its mark by a foreign manufacturer, this theory logically leads to the conclusion that there can be no confusion as to source. . . . Hence, it cannot serve as the rationale for granting a Lanham Act injunction.

"B. The Guarantee Function

"Many commentators however recognize that trademark law also serves to guarantee the quality of the trademarked product. . . . This is particularly apparent in the licensing context where the mark's owner licenses another to manufacture the product while retaining only the right to control quality. . . . Recognizing that sponsorship includes quality control—and viewing the territorial sales restrictions imposed by OAA as a means of quality control—it follows that Granada's importation of dolls with Spanish birth certificates, adoption papers and instructions into the United States may confuse the public as to whether OAA "sponsored" the importation of what the public perceives to be inferior dolls. This confusion is sufficient to constitute a violation of the Lanham Act. . . . "

"The necessity of providing a remedy against quality infringement by third-parties is particularly essential in a licensing arrangement because the Lanham Act imposes an affirmative duty upon the licensor to maintain quality control. . . .

"Even the guarantee function, . . . is not entirely free from doubt as a basis for issuing an injunction. It has been argued that the importation of genuine but inferior goods of a foreign licensee is the fault of the trademark owner 'in not exercising adequate supervision of the mark,' and that its failure 'should not be a justification for protecting it under the *trademark* laws for the situation it has created.' See Vandenburgh, *The Problem of Importation of Genuinely Marked Goods is Not a Trademark Problem*, 49 Trade Mark Rptr. 707, 716 (1959) (emphasis in original). See also Parfums Stern, Inc. v. United States Customs Service, 575 F.Supp. 416, 419 (S.D. Fla. 1983) (Criticizing mark owner for seeking federal trademark protection 'to insulate itself from what it placed in motion itself through its own foreign manufacturing and distribution sources.').

"This argument is not persuasive when, as in this case, it is not clear that OAA could not have prevented by contract the importation of these Cabbage Patch dolls by third-party distributors . . . As a practical matter OAA appears to have tried. Under its license Jesmar

In economic terms, the gray-market question turns largely on whether it is desirable to allow manufacturers to use trademark protection to enforce exclusive distribution schemes, adjust product quality to local tastes, and insulate their distributors from intrabrand competition. Manufacturers can always achieve that result by adopting a different trademark for each territorial market but are reluctant to do so for a variety of reasons. In a sense, manufacturers and distributors seeking protection against the gray-market want to have their cake and eat it too—enjoying a universal goodwill surrounding a single mark but cutting the universe into discrete pieces for protection purposes.

[a] **The Face-Powder Trilogy.** Three Supreme Court decisions, sometimes referred to as the "face-powder" trilogy because all three involved women's scented face powder imported from France,[311] launched modern United States parallel importation trademark law.

Most important is *Katzel*,[312] a short, enigmatic 1923 Supreme Court decision written by Justice Holmes.

In 1879, a French firm, A. Bourjois & Cie., and E. Wertheimer & Cie., began selling in the United States "Java" face powder, which it manufactured in France. In 1888, it registered "Java" in the United States Patent Office. In 1913, the French firm sold its United States business and goodwill to A. Bourjois & Co., Inc., a New York corporation.[313] A. Bourgois & Co. bought and imported in bulk the French firm's

---

agreed not to sell outside its Spanish-licensed territory, and further agreed to sell only to purchasers who also agreed not to sell outside that territory. Without any effective means of further controlling the distribution of its product, for example, by means of an equitable servitude on the dolls, OAA should not be held responsible for the dolls' importation. *See, e.g.,* . . . Z. Chafee, *The Music Goes Round and Round: Equitable Servitudes and Chattels*, 69 Harv.L.Rev. 1250, 1255-56 (1956) (only scarce authority on the validity of equitable servitudes on chattels)." 816 F.2d at 74-76, 2 U.S.P.Q.2d at 1348-49.

[311] *See* Lever Brothers Co. v. United States, 877 F.2d 101, 11 U.S.P.Q.2d 1117 (D.C. Cir. 1989).

[312] A. Bourjois & Co. v. Katzel, 260 U.S. 689 (1923).

[313] The district court, court of appeals, and Supreme Court opinions neither describe who owned the New York corporation's stock nor indicate the extent of the French firm's financial interest in it. The district court states:

"The plaintiff corporation was organized in 1913, and for a consideration, involving, inter alia, the obligation to pay $400,000, bought the entire business then and theretofore carried on by A. Bourjois & Cie., E. Wertheimer & Cie., Successeurs, in the United States, viz. the entire good will of said business in the United States, and any and all trademarks, trade-names, and trade-mark rights relating thereto in the United States, and also the sole and exclusive right to manufacture and sell in the United States any and all toilet preparations then or theretofore made by the French concern. This transfer of trade-marks included the transfer of the registered trade-mark 'Java,' the top and other labels of the boxes, and all of the trade-marks which the plaintiff has subsequently used were registered. Thus all of these trade-marks and labels are, so far as the United States is concerned, exclusively the property of the plaintiff. . . . [D]uring the time plaintiff has been in this business it has expended substantial sums of money for advertising, and . . . succeeded in creating a wide market in the United States for its products, and the boxes of face powder here under consideration are associated in the public mind with the plaintiff corporation." 274 F. at 857.

powder and packed and sold it in boxes. The boxes included a label stating: "Trade Marks Reg. U.S. Pat. Off. Made in France—packed in the U.S.A. By A. Bourgois & Co., Inc., of New York, Succ'rs in the U.S. to A. Bourjois & Cie. and E. Wertheimer & Cie."

Anna Katzel conducted "a retail pharmacy in New York City, and [sold] in New York, New Jersey, and other states the same genuine face powder manufactured by the French firm, imported by her in its original boxes, on which are printed its trademarks and labels."[314]

The district court granted A. Bourjois's preliminary injunction motion.[315] It treated as an important question of first impression "whether, because defendant's box is a genuine article made and sold by the French concern, it can be said to constitute an infringement of the trade-marks of plaintiff, when plaintiff is the exclusive owner of these trade-marks in the United States."[316] It assumed not only that defendant's trade-mark was genuine, in the sense that it was not spurious at the place of origin, and that no change had been made since it was sold but also that the French firm neither knew nor consented to Katzel's competition and that Katzel "relied upon what she regards as her legal rights."

The district court relied upon *Hanover Star Milling's* principle that trademark rights territorially extend only as far as the mark owner's market and goodwill.[317] The case was "obviously stronger" than *Hanover Star Milling* because "plaintiff has expended a large sum for the acquisition of the trade-mark title and rights and a large sum for the advertisement of its business."

> "Plaintiff had corralled the American market before defendant's boxes were brought into the American market. If, now, the original French boxes or packages can lawfully be permitted to compete with plaintiff's boxes or packages, it can be readily seen that plaintiff's business may be destroyed, and, in any event, impaired. The question, on its face, is one involving business interests in a large way. If an American business concern buys all of the rights, as in the case at bar, of a business established here by a foreign concern, and then the foreign concern is nevertheless at liberty to compete with the American concern, the result will be that the purchase of rights, under such circumstances, will give little or no protection; and the foreign concern, as well as the domestic concern, will be seriously injured in the long run, because American capital certainly will not be invested, and foreign concerns will find it difficult to sell the rights which they have developed in this country."[318]

The court distinguished *Fred Gretsch Mfg.*,[319] which interpreted the 1905 Federal Trademark Act's Section 27 as not authorizing United States Customs to ban

---

[314] 275 F. at 540. The Supreme Court characterized Katzel's practice in more mercenary terms: "The defendant, finding that the rate of exchange enabled her to do so at a profit, bought a large quantity of the same powder in France and is selling it here in the French boxes which closely resemble those used by the plaintiff. . . . " 260 U.S. at 691.

[315] A. Bourjois & Co. v. Katzel, 274 F. 856 (S.D. N.Y. 1920), rev'd, 275 F. 539 (2d Cir. 1921), rev'd, 260 U.S. 689 (1923).

[316] 274 F. at 858-59.

[317] See §5E[2][a].

[318] 274 F. at 859.

[319] Fred Gretsch Mfg. Co. v. Schoening, 238 F. 780 (2d Cir. 1916).

parallel-imported genuine goods, which the courts had, prior to the Act's passage, held not to constitute trademark infringement.[320] Section 27 was "in the nature of a customs regulations, to prevent the American public from being deceived by simulated name" and did "pass upon the question as to whether any given trade-mark was valid as matter of law as between contending parties."[321]

The Second Circuit reversed.[322] It assumed that "the plaintiff is entitled to the French firm's trade-marks . . . and that it would be a breach of the French firm's obligations to sell its face powder in this country"[323] but, relying on three prior decisions,[324] held that defendant had the right to sell goods under trademarks that

---

[320] Section 27 provided, *inter alia*, that "That no article of imported merchandise which shall . . . copy or simulate a trade-mark registered in accordance with the provisions of this act . . . shall be admitted to entry at any custom house of the United States; and, in order to aid the officers of the customs in enforcing this prohibition, any domestic manufacturer or trader . . . may require . . . a copy of the certificate of registration of his trade-mark . . . to be recorded . . . in the Department of the Treasury. . . . " Section 27 became Lanham Act Section 42. See §5E[5][b].

In *Fred Gretsch*, C. A. Mueller manufactured and sold violin strings under the "Eternelle" mark. Schoening, Mueller's "exclusive" United States agent registered the "Eternelle" mark and filed a Section 27 customs notice. Fred Gretsch bought Mueller "Eternelle" strings in Germany, but the New York port customs collector denied them entry. Gretsch obtained a preliminary injunction requiring Schoening to lift his Section 27 customs notice. The court noted that before passage of the 1905 Act, "it was the law of this circuit that it was not an infringement of a trade-mark to sell the genuine goods identified by the mark so marked." 238 F. at 781, citing Appollinaris Co. v. Scherer, 27 F. 18. Section 27 did not change this rule: "The act prohibits the entry of imported merchandise which shall 'copy or simulate' a trade-mark registered under it. The obvious purpose is to protect the public and to prevent any one from importing goods identified by their registered trade-mark which are not genuine." 238 F. at 782.

[321] "[I]f an article is genuine, . . . it may be imported into this country, and cannot be stopped at the door of the custom house; but whether or not the article may be marketed here under a particular trade-mark is a question to be determined in ascertaining the rights of parties, quite irrespective of section 27 of the Act of February 20, 1905. Section 27 concerns the action of the government, through its proper officials, in carrying out the safeguarding measures erected by the Congress. The case at bar concerns the rights of private parties, and those rights depend upon rules of law in respect of which section 27 is wholly irrelevant." 274 F. at 860.

[322] A. Bourjois & Co. v. Katzel, 275 F. 539 (2d Cir. 1921), *rev'd*, 260 U.S. 689 (1923).

[323] 275 F. at 540.

[324] Gretsch v. Schoening, 238 F. 780 (2d Cir. 1916); Russian Cement Co. v. Frauenhar, 133 F. 518 (2d Cir. 1904), *cert. denied* 196 U.S. 640 (1905); Apollinaris Co. v. Scherer, 27 F. 18 (C.C.N.Y. 1886). *Apollinaris* was directly on point.

"Saxlehner, owner of the Hunyadi Janos spring in Hungary, gave to the Apollinaris Company the exclusive right to sell the water under the trade-mark Hunyadi Janos' in Great Britain and the United States. The Apollinaris Company registered the name and the label as trade-marks in the United States Patent Office. Scherer applied to Saxlehner to sell him the water for importation into the United States, which Saxlehner refused to do, telling him of the Apollinaris Company's exclusive rights. Thereafter Scherer purchased the water from other parties in Germany, imported it into the United States, and sold it under the name Hunyadi Janos. . . . Judge Wallace said:

"truly indicate its origin." The court distinguished patent cases that found infringement of a United States patent owner's rights by importation of a patented product
that had been lawfully made abroad.[325]

> "The analogy between patents and trade-marks is not complete. A patent gives
> the patentee a monopoly to make, sell, and use and grant to others the right
> to make, sell, and use the subject patented in the United States for the term
> of the patent. Hence articles lawfully made, used, and sold in foreign coun-
> tries cannot be sold in this country if they infringe the patent. Trade-marks,
> on the other hand, are intended to show without any time limit the origin of
> the goods they mark, so that the owner and the public may be protected
> against the sale of one man's goods as the goods of another man. If the goods
> sold are the genuine goods covered by the trade-mark, the rights of the owner
> of the trade-mark are not infringed.[326]

Judge Hough dissented, noting that it "is not yet settled whether a trade-mark is to
be primarily regarded as protecting the trade-mark owner's business from a species of unfair competition, or protecting the public from imitations."[327] He argued
that the "genuine article has become an infringement because the business of dealing
in that article within the United States is the plaintiff's business."[328]

The Supreme Court granted certiorari and reinstated the district court's injunction.
Unlike the Second Circuit, it saw a resemblance between patent and trademark rights.

> "After the sale the French manufacturers could not have come to the
> United States and have used their old marks in competition with the plaintiff.
> That plainly follows from the statute authorizing assignments. . . . If for the
> purpose of evading the effect of the transfer it had arranged with the defendant
> that she should sell with the old label, we suppose that no one would doubt

---

> '. . . The complainant established an agency for the sale of the water in this country,
> but . . . is unable to maintain its own prices for the article because the defendant
> purchases the water in Germany from persons to whom it has been sold by Saxlehner,
> imports it, and sells it here at lower prices. . . .
>
> '. . . [T]he defendant is selling the genuine water, and therefore the trade-mark is not
> infringed. There is no exclusive right to the use of a name or symbol or emblematic device
> except to denote the authenticity of the article with which it has become identified
> by association. . . . '" 275 F. at 541.

Apollinaris suggested in dictum that the United States transferee would have a remedy against
the foreign transferor if the latter sold directly in the United States in violation of its
transfer or even if it cooperated with others who so sold.

> ". . . There would seem to be no doubt that the agreement between Saxlehner and the
> complainant was a valid one. . . . If Saxlehner were now endeavoring to compete with
> the complainant in the sale of the water in the ceded territory, his conduct would fur-
> nish a ground for equitable jurisdiction . . . It is equally clear that if the defendant were
> co-operating with Saxlehner collusively to violate the complainant's right to the exclusive
> sale of the water he also would be restrained. . . . " 27 F. at 20.

[325] *See* § 2E[2][b][ii].
[326] 275 F. at 543.
[327] *Id.*
[328] *Id.* at 544.

that the contrivance must fail. There is no such conspiracy here, but apart from the opening of a door to one, the vendors could not convey their goods free from the restriction to which the vendors were subject. Ownership of the goods does not carry the right to sell them with a specific mark. It does not necessarily carry the right to sell them at all in a given place. If the goods were patented in the United States a dealer who lawfully bought similar goods abroad from one who had a right to make and sell them there could not sell them in the United States. Boesch v. Graff, 133 U.S. 697 . . . The monopoly in that case is more extensive, but we see no sufficient reason for holding that the monopoly of a trade-mark, so far as it goes, is less complete. It deals with a delicate matter that may be of great value but that easily is destroyed, and therefore should be protected with corresponding care. It is said that the trade-mark here is that of the French house and truly indicates the origin of the goods. But that is not accurate. It is the trade-mark of the plaintiff only in the United States and indicates in law, and, it is found, by public understanding, that the goods come from the plaintiff although not made by it. It was sold and could only be sold with the good will of the business that the plaintiff bought. . . . It stakes the reputation of the plaintiff upon the character of the goods." [329]

The second face-powder trilogy decision, *Aldridge*,[330] was factually and legally tied to the first. A 1989 appeals court decision describes *Aldridge* as follows:

"Holmes' failure [in *Katzel*] to mention §27 of the 1905 Act at all, and his reliance in the last quoted sentence on the infeasibility of the French firm's both selling and retaining the US goodwill, leave the case's bearing on §27 uncertain. But the second case of the trilogy . . . forges a link to §27, albeit a vulnerable one. *Aldridge* appears to involve the same business transfer as lay at the root of *Katzel*. The Second Circuit described the US firm A. Bourjois & Co. as having acquired the 'exclusive right to manufacture and sell in the United States any and all toilet preparations now made by [Wertheimer & Cie.].' . . . The sale included the trademark 'Manon Lescaut,' used in selling a face-powder. As in *Katzel*, an unaffiliated importer bought Manon Lescaut face-powder from the French firm and resold it in the United States under that label. The only noticeable difference between the products' packaging was small print identifying the seller. (The ingredients of plaintiff's own Manon Lescaut powder, though chemically the same as the French version, were not always bought from the French firm.) The action was brought against the Collector of Customs, however, seeking to force him to exclude the third party's product. The Second Circuit certified two questions to the Supreme Court:

"(1) Is the sale in the United States of Wertheimer's Manon Lescaut powder an infringement of plaintiff's registered trade-marks?

"(2) Is the collector, by section 27 of the Trade-Mark Law, required to exclude from entry genuine Manon Lescaut powder so as aforesaid made in France?

---

[329] 260 U.S. at 691-92.

[330] A. Bourjois & Co. v. Aldridge, 263 U.S. 675 (1923).

> ". . . The government's three-page brief conceded that *Katzel* controlled. . . .
> The Court replied that '[t]he two questions certified by the Circuit Court of
> Appeals for Second Circuit are answered in the affirmative, upon the authority
> of Bourjois & Co. v. Katzel, . . . the defendant not objecting.' "[331]

Subsequent lower court decisions make light of *Aldridge*, especially in view of the
apparent absence of adversarial objection.[332]

The third decision is *Prestonettes*,[333] the leading decision on repackaged genuine
goods resales. *Prestonettes* can be distinguished from gray-market "genuine" goods
cases because it involved only "collateral" use of another's mark, not primary
trademark use, but it is significant to gray-market goods law because it dismissed
Katzel in a single sentence, suggesting the latter was confined to its special facts.

[b] The 1922 Trade Act, Customs Regulations, and COPIAT

[i] *Tariff Act Section 526.* After the Second Circuit's *Katzel* decision, but before its reversal by the Supreme Court, Congress responded to the parallel importation
problem by enacting 1922 Tariff Act Section 526, later incorporated into the 1930
Tariff Act.

> "[I]t shall be unlawful to import into the United States any merchandise of
> foreign manufacture if such merchandise, or the label, sign, print, package,
> wrapper, or receptacle, bears a trademark owned by a citizen of, or by a
> corporation or association created or organized within, the United States, and
> registered in the Patent and Trademark Office by a person domiciled in the
> United States, under the provisions of sections 81 to 109 of Title 15, and if
> a copy of the certificate of registration of such trademark is filed with the
> Secretary of the Treasury, in the manner provided in section 106 of said Title
> 15, unless written consent of the owner of such trademark is produced at the
> time of making entry."[334]

---

[331] Lever Brothers Co. v. United States, 877 F.2d 101, 106-07, 11 U.S.P.Q.2d 1117, 1121-22
(D.C. Cir. 1989).

[332] *E.g.,* Olympus Corp. v. United States, 792 F.2d 315, 321-22, 230 U.S.P.Q. 123, 128
(2d Cir. 1986), *cert. denied* 486 U.S. 1042 (1988) ("It is difficult to argue that *Aldridge*
can be distinguished on the basis that the domestic and foreign markholders there were
independent of each other because such an argument suggests that the words 'copy or simulate'
mean one thing when the companies are related and another when they are not. But the
interpretation of [Lanham Act § 42] urged by Olympus puts a great deal of strain on a one-
sentence per curiam opinion announcing a decision, to which the opposing party did not object,
based on the reasoning of the three-page opinion in *A. Bourjois & Co. v. Katzel,* . . . , a case
influenced by equities not present here. Absent the *Katzel* situation, [Lanham Act §42] applies
only to merchandise bearing counterfeit or spurious trademarks that 'copy or simulate' genuine trademarks. We are reassured in this conclusion by the fact that in *Prestonettes, Inc. v.
Coty,* . . . the Supreme Court suggested that *Katzel* had limited application to any but its own
special facts.").

[333] Prestonettes, Inc. v. Coty, 264 U.S. 359 (1924), discussed at §5E[4][a].

[334] 19 U.S.C. §1526(a). For a discussion of Section 526's legislative history, see K Mart Corp.
v. Cartier, Inc., 486 U.S. 281, 302-10, 6 U.S.P.Q.2d 1897, 1903-12 (1988) (Brennan concurring
in part and dissenting in part).

Section 526, in common with Lanham Act Section 42,[335] is a strong remedy in that a trademark owner may cause the Customs Service to halt offending articles at the border. Section 526 also provides the trademark owner a private remedy, enforceable by court action,[336] which can be used when the Customs Services fails or refuses to block imports.[337]

[ii] *Customs Regulations and COPIAT.* "The [Customs Service] regulations implementing §526 for the past 50 years have not applied the prohibition to all gray-market goods."[338] Regulation 133.21 prohibits imports of trademark-bearing articles without the U.S. trademark owner's consent[339] but states two exceptions relating to gray-market goods.[340] The "common control" exception, subparts (c)(1) and (2), applies when "[b]oth the foreign and the U.S. trademark or trade name are owned by the same person or business entity" or "the foreign and domestic trademark or trade name owners are parent and subsidiary companies or are otherwise subject to common ownership or control. . . . "[341] The "authorized use" exception, subpart

---

[335] See §5E[5][c].

[336] "Any person dealing in any such merchandise may be enjoined from dealing therein within the United States or may be required to export or destroy such merchandise or to remove or obliterate such trademark and shall be liable for the same damages and profits provided for wrongful use of a trademark, under the provisions of sections 81 to 109 of Title 15." 19 U.S.C. §1526(c).

[337] See Original Appalachian Artworks, Inc. v. Granada Electronics, Inc., 816 F.2d 68, 2 U.S.P.Q.2d 1343 (2d Cir. 1986), cert. denied 484 U.S. 847 (1987).

[338] K Mart Corp. v. Cartier, Inc., 486 U.S. 281, 288, 6 U.S.P.Q.2d 1897, 1900 (1988).

[339] Regulation 133.21 implements both Tariff Act Section 526 and Lanham Act Section 42. Section 133.21(a) implements Lanham Act Section 42:

"(a) Copying or simulating marks or names. Articles of foreign or domestic manufacture bearing a mark or name copying or simulating a recorded trademark or trade name shall be denied entry and are subject to forfeiture as prohibited importations. A 'copying or simulating' mark or name is an actual counterfeit of the recorded mark or name or is one which so resembles it as to be likely to cause the public to associate the copying or simulating mark with the recorded mark or name." 19 CFR §133.21(a).

Section 133.21(b) implements Tariff Act Section 526:

"(b) Identical trademark. Foreign-made articles bearing a trademark identical with one owned and recorded by a citizen of the United States or a corporation or association created or organized within the United States are subject to seizure and forfeiture as prohibited importations." 19 CFR § 133.21(b).

Unlike Section 526, Section 42 applies to articles "of foreign or domestic manufacture" and to marks owned by persons not United States citizens or corporations.

[340] 19 CFR §133.21(c).

[341] To implement the exception, Customs Rule 133.2(d) provides that a Customs trademark recording application must set forth "The identity of any parent or subsidiary company or other company under common ownership or control which uses the mark aboard."

". . . For this purpose:

"(1) 'Common ownership' means individual or aggregate ownership of more than 50 percent of the business entity; and

"(2) 'Common control' means effective control in policy and operations and is not necessarily synonymous with common ownership." 19 CFR §133.2(d).

(c)(3), applies when "[t]he articles of foreign manufacture bear a recorded trademark or trade name applied under authorization of the U.S. owner."[342]

In *K Mart*,[343] COPIAT, the Coalition to Preserve the Integrity of American Trademarks, an association of U.S. trademark owners, sued for a declaration that the Customs Service regulations were inconsistent with the statute.[344] The District of Columbia Circuit held the regulations invalid, disagreeing with the Federal Circuit's *Vivitar* decision.[345] The Supreme Court granted certiorari to resolve the circuit courts' split. In a complex voting pattern, a majority held the common control exception (subparts (c)(1) and (2)) valid; a different majority held the authorized use exception (subpart (c)(3)) invalid as contrary to Section 526's clear language. *K Mart's* major effect is that foreign manufacturers with United States distributing subsidiaries failed to gain the benefit of Customs Service gray-market import prohibition.

After *K Mart*, the Customs Service amended its regulations to eliminate subpart (c)(3).[346]

(1) Three Gray-Market Contexts. Announcing the Court's judgment, Justice Kennedy distinguished "three general contexts" in which gray-markets arise.

1. "Case 1": Independent United States Trademark Owner.

"The prototypical gray-market victim (case 1) is a domestic firm that purchases from an independent foreign firm the rights to register and use the latter's trademark as a U.S. trademark and to sell its foreign-manufactured products here."[347] In Case 1, the U.S. trademark owner's equities are strong.

> "Especially where the foreign firm has already registered the trademark in the United States or where the product has already earned a reputation for quality, the right to use that trademark can be very valuable. If the foreign manufacturer could import the trademarked goods and distribute them here, despite having sold the trademark to a domestic firm, the domestic firm would be forced into sharp intrabrand competition involving the very trademark it purchased. Similar intrabrand competition could arise if the foreign manufacturer markets its wares outside the United States, as is often the case, and

---

[342] 19 CFR §133.21(c).

[343] K Mart Corp. v. Cartier, Inc., 486 U.S. 281, 288, 6 U.S.P.Q.2d 1897, 1900-01 (1988).

[344] Cartier, Inc., a COPIAT member, joined as plaintiff. Two retailers, K Mart and 47th Street Photo intervened as defendants.

[345] Vivitar Corp. v. United States, 761 F.2d 1552, 225 U.S.P.Q. 990 (Fed. Cir. 1985), *cert. denied*, 486 U.S. 1042 (1988).

[346] Department of the Treasury, Customs Service, Gray Market Goods Final Rule, 55 Fed. Reg. 52040-01 (Nov. 9, 1990).

The Service noted that the Supreme Court held only that the authorized use exception was "not a permissible construction" of Section 526 and "did not rule on whether the regulation is consistent" with Lanham Act Section 42. Nonetheless, it eliminated the exception to "maintain its longstanding practice of interpreting both statutory provisions in tandem" and to accord United States trademark and trade name owners protection "from goods of foreign manufacture bearing recorded trademarks and trade names applied under authorization of the U.S. owner." *Id.*

[347] 486 U.S. at 286, 6 U.S.P.Q.2d at 1899.

a third party who purchases them abroad could legally import them. In either event, the parallel importation, if permitted to proceed, would create a gray market that could jeopardize the trademark holder's investment." [348]

Katzel was a Case 1 gray-market fact pattern. In *K Mart*, all the justices agreed that the Customs Service could reasonably interpret Section 526 as barring Case 1 gray-market goods imports.

2. "Case 2": Foreign and Domestic Affiliates.

The second gray-market context "is a situation in which a domestic firm registers the U.S. trademark for goods that are manufactured abroad by an affiliated manufacturer." [349] There are three variations.

a. "Case 2a": United States Trademark Owner Is Foreign Manufacturer's Subsidiary

"In its most common variation (case 2a), a foreign firm wishes to control distribution of its wares in this country by incorporating a subsidiary here. The subsidiary then registers under its own name (or the manufacturer assigns to the subsidiary's name) a U.S. trademark that is identical to its parent's foreign trademark. The parallel importation by a third party who buys the goods abroad (or conceivably even by the affiliated foreign manufacturer itself) creates a gray market." [350]

All the justices agreed that the Customs Service could reasonably interpret Section 526 as not prohibiting Case 2a gray-market goods imports. Section 526 requires that the United States trademark be "owned by" a United States citizen or corporation, and "[i]t may be reasonable for some purposes to say that a trademark nominally owned by a domestic subsidiary is 'owned by' its foreign parent corporation." [351] The dissenting justices believed that the Customs regulation's "common control" exception should nevertheless be held invalid because it was not limited to Case 2a.

b. "Case 2b": United States Trademark Owner Is Foreign Manufacturer's Parent

Case 2b occurs "when an American-based firm establishes abroad a manufacturing subsidiary corporation . . . to produce its U.S. trademarked goods, and then imports them for domestic distribution." [352] "If the trademark holder or its foreign subsidiary sells the trademarked goods abroad, the parallel importation of the goods competes on the gray market with the holder's domestic sales." [353]

c. "Case 2c": United States Trademark Owner Manufactures Abroad

Case 2c is similar to case 2b except that the American-based firm uses an "unincorporated manufacturing division" abroad.

3. "Case 3": Authorized Foreign User.

"In the third context (case 3), the domestic holder of a U.S. trademark authorizes an independent foreign manufacturer to use it."

---

[348] *Id.*
[349] *Id.*
[350] *Id.*
[351] 486 U.S. at 318, 6 U.S.P.Q.2d at 1913 (Scalia concurring in part and dissenting in part).
[352] 486 U.S. at 286-87, 6 U.S.P.Q.2d at 1899.
[353] 486 U.S. at 287, 6 U.S.P.Q.2d at 1900.

"Usually the holder sells to the foreign manufacturer an exclusive right to use the trademark in a particular foreign location, but conditions the right on the foreign manufacturer's promise not to import its trademarked goods into the United States. Once again, if the foreign manufacturer or a third party imports into the United States, the foreign-manufactured goods will compete on the gray market with the holder's domestic goods."[354]

(2) Common Control Exception. In upholding the "common control" exception, the majority applied the rules that "[i]f the statute is silent or ambiguous with respect to the specific issue addressed by the regulation, the question becomes whether the agency regulation is a permissible construction of the statute" and "[i]f the agency regulation is not in conflict with the plain language of the statute, a reviewing court must give deference to the agency's interpretation of the statute."[355]

Section 526 is ambiguous as to Case 2a (domestic subsidiary and foreign parent) because of the phrase "owned by." "This ambiguity arises from the inability to discern, from the statutory language, which of the two entities involved in case 2a can be said to 'own' the U.S. trademark if, as in some instances, the domestic subsidiary is wholly owned by its foreign parent."[356]

Section 526 is ambiguous as to Cases 2b and 2c because of the phrase "merchandise of foreign manufacture."

"This ambiguity parallels that of 'owned by,' which sustained case 2a, because it is possible to interpret 'merchandise of foreign manufacture' to mean (1) goods manufactured in a foreign country, (2) goods manufactured by a foreign company, or (3) goods manufactured in a foreign country by a foreign company. Given the imprecision in the statute, the agency is entitled to choose any reasonable definition and to interpret the statute to say that goods manufactured by a foreign subsidiary or division of a domestic company are not goods 'of foreign manufacture.' "[357]

In dissent, Justice Scalia argued that "merchandise of foreign manufacture" had a clear meaning.

"The phrase 'of foreign manufacture' is a common usage, well understood to mean 'manufactured abroad.' Hence, when statutes and regulations intend to describe the universe of manufactured goods, they do not refer to goods 'of foreign or citizen manufacture,' but to goods 'of foreign or domestic manufacture.' See, *e.g.*, 19 CFR §133.21(a) (1987). I know of no instance in which anyone, anywhere, has used the phrase with the meaning the majority suggests—and the majority provides no example."[358]

He suggested that "the majority's suggested interpretation is not merely unusual but inconceivable, since it would have the effect of eliminating §526(a)'s protection

---

[354] *Id.*
[355] 486 U.S. at 291-92, 6 U.S.P.Q.2d at 1902.
[356] 486 U.S. at 292, 6 U.S.P.Q.2d at 1902.
[357] 486 U.S. at 292-93, 6 U.S.P.Q.2d at 1902.
[358] 486 U.S. at 319, 6 U.S.P.Q.2d at 1913.

for some trademark holders in case 1—which contains what the Court describes as the 'prototypical' gray-market victims." [359]

> "Not uncommonly a foreign trademark owner licenses an American firm to use its trademark in the United States and also licenses one or more other American firms to use the trademark in other countries. In this situation, the firm with the U.S. license could not keep out gray-market imports manufactured abroad by the other American firms, since, under the majority's interpretation, the goods would not be 'of foreign manufacture.' Thus, to save the regulation, the majority proposes an interpretation that undermines even the core of the statute." [360]

(3) *Authorized Use Exception.* The majority struck down the "authorized use" exception as contrary to Section 526's clear meaning.

> "The ambiguous statutory phrases that we have already discussed, 'owned by' and 'merchandise of foreign manufacture,' are irrelevant to the proscription contained in subsection (3) of the regulation. This subsection of the regulation denies a domestic trademark holder the power to prohibit the importation of goods made by an independent foreign manufacturer where the domestic trademark holder has authorized the foreign manufacturer to use the trademark. Under no reasonable construction of the statutory language can goods made in a foreign country by an independent foreign manufacturer be removed from the purview of the statute." [361]

---

[359] *Id.*

[360] 486 U.S. at 320, 6 U.S.P.Q.2d at 1913.

To this argument, Justice Kennedy replied.

"[T]he regulation speaks to the hypothetical situation Justice SCALIA poses, and . . . the firm with the U.S. trademark could keep out 'gray-market imports manufactured abroad by the other American firms,' . . . because the regulation allows a company justifiably invoking the protection of the statute to bar the importation of goods of foreign or domestic manufacture. 19 CFR §133.21(a) (1987). In this instance, the domestic firm with the U.S. trademark could invoke the protection of the statute (case 1) and bar the importation of the other domestic firm's product manufactured abroad even though our interpretation of the phrase 'of foreign manufacture' would characterize these latter goods to be of domestic manufacture." 486 U.S. at 293 n.4, 6 U.S.P.Q.2d at 1902 n.4.

Justice Scalia found this reply "puzzling"—with some justification.

"[S]ubsection (a) of §133.21 has nothing to do with § 526(a), but rather implements §42 of the Lanham Trade-Mark Act . . . which prohibits importation of goods of foreign or domestic manufacture bearing not genuine trademarks identical to a U.S. trademark, but trademarks that 'copy or simulate' a recorded trademark. It is subsection (b) of §133.21 that implements §526(a), and which, consistent with that statute, only prohibits importation of [f]oreign-made [but not domestic-made] articles bearing a trademark identical with one owned' by a U.S. trademark holder." 486 U.S. at 319-20 n.1, 6 U.S.P.Q.2d at 1913-14 n.1.

For a discussion of Lanham Act Section 42, see § 5E[5][c].

[361] 486 U.S. at 293-94, 6 U.S.P.Q.2d at 1903.

Justice Brennan dissented from this holding, arguing that Section 526 should be narrowly confined to Case 1 situations. Congress could not have intended that it apply to situations in which a U.S. trademark owner licenses or assigns his rights in another country because in 1922 prevailing trademark law theory made licensing "philosophically impossible" and it was unclear whether "a trademark owner could authorize the use of its trademark in one geographic area by selling it along with business and goodwill, while retaining ownership of the trademark in another geographic area."[362]

> "Manifestly, the legislators who chose the term 'owned by' viewed trademark ownership differently than we view it today. Any prescient legislator who could have contemplated that a trademark owner might license the use of its trademark would almost certainly have concluded that such a transaction would divest the licensor not only of the benefit of §526's importation prohibition, but of *all* trademark protection; and anyone who gave thought to the possibility that a trademark holder might assign rights to use its trademark, along with business and goodwill, to an unrelated manufacturer in another territory had good reason to expect the same result. At the very least, it seems to me plain that Congress did not address case 3 any more clearly than it addressed case 2a, 2b, or 2c. To hold otherwise is to wrench statutory words out of their legislative and historical context and treat legislation as no more than a 'collection of English words' rather than 'a working instrument of government . . . ' "[363]

Justice Scalia disagreed with Justice Brennan's analysis. First, courts have no power to "decline to apply a statute to a situation that its language concededly covers, . . . on the ground that, if the enacting Congress had foreseen modern circumstances, it *would* have adopted such an exception, since otherwise the effect of the law would extend beyond its originally contemplated purpose."[364] Second, even if courts had that power, it should be exercised "only when (1) it is clear that the alleged changed circumstances were unknown to, and unenvisioned by, the enacting legislature, and (2) it is clear that they cause the challenged application of the statute to exceed its original purpose."[365] Section 526 meets neither condition because trademark assignments involving distinct markets were recognized in 1922, *Katzel* being "a textbook example of an assignment of the right to use a trademark in a distinct market."[366]

[c] Lanham Act Importation Ban—Trademark Infringement Principles. The Lanham Act contains two provisions that a registered mark owner may assert against gray-market goods importers and sellers separate and apart from Tariff Act Section 526, which the Supreme Court interpreted in *K Mart*. Section 42 provides that "no article of imported merchandise . . . which shall *copy or simulate* a [registered] trademark . . . shall be admitted to entry at any custom house of the United States."[367]

---

[362] 486 U.S. at 313, 6 U.S.P.Q.2d at 1911.
For a discussion of trademark licensing and assignment, see § 5G[2] and [3].
[363] 486 U.S. at 315, 6 U.S.P.Q.2d at 1911-12.
[364] 486 U.S. at 324, 6 U.S.P.Q.2d at 1915.
[365] 486 U.S. at 325, 6 U.S.P.Q.2d at 1916.
[366] 486 U.S. at 327, 6 U.S.P.Q.2d at 1916.
[367] Lanham Act §42, 15 U.S.C. §1124 (emphasis added).

Section 32, the general Lanham Act's general remedy section, provides registered mark owners a civil action right against any person who, without the owner's consent, uses a "reproduction, counterfeit, copy, or colorable imitation of a registered mark."[368] A mark owner may also assert common law trademark rights against gray-market goods.

Lower court decisions before *K Mart* did not follow a clear, consistent pattern but tended to find no trademark infringement or Section 42 violation[369] unless the U.S. trademark owner was wholly or partially independent of the foreign manufacturer[370] or the gray-market goods differed materially in quality, style, or warranty and service status from those the U.S. trademark owner sells.[371]

K Mart dealt only with the Tariff Act, but the Supreme Court's analysis has influenced lower court gray-market goods decisions. Two cases are illustrative.

Section 42 is based on the 1901 Act, Section 27. Lower courts interpreted Section 27 as not covering "genuine" goods. Fred Gretsch Mfg. Co. v. Schoening, 238 F. 780 (2d Cir. 1916). Whether the Supreme Court's *Aldridge* decision overturned this interpretation is subject to dispute. *See* §5E[5][a].

[368] Lanham Act §32(1)(a), 15 U.S.C. § 1114(1)(a).

[369] *E.g.,* NEC Electronics v. Cal Circuit ABCO, 810 F.2d 1506, 1509, 1511, 1 U.S.P.Q.2d 2056, 2058, 2059 (9th Cir. 1986), *cert. denied*, 484 U.S. 851 (1987) (distinguishing *Katzel*: "Parsing Justice Holmes's characteristically laconic opinion, we discern two rationales for the holding in *Katzel*. First, the American company that acquired the mark had made an arm's-length contract with the manufacturer . . . which was clearly intended to prohibit the manufacturer from selling its goods directly in this country. . . . The Court was not prepared to permit the manufacturer to 'evade' this restriction by selling to middlemen abroad for sale in the United States, thus to deprive the American mark owner of the entire benefit of its bargain. . . . Second, because the manufacturer had forgone all its rights to its trademark in this country, the American owner of that mark now had complete control over and responsibility for the quality of goods sold under that mark. . . . Both these rationales presuppose the American owner's real independence from the foreign manufacturer, and courts interpreting *Katzel* have repeatedly emphasized this factor. . . . If NEC-Japan chooses to sell abroad at lower prices than those it could obtain for the identical product here, that is its business. In doing so, however, it cannot look to United States trademark law to insulate the American market or to vitiate the effects of international trade. This country's trademark law does not offer NEC-Japan a vehicle for establishing a worldwide discriminatory pricing scheme simply through the expedient of setting up an American subsidiary with nominal title to its mark.").

Cf. Olympus Corp. v. United States, 792 F.2d 315, 230 U.S.P.Q. 123 (2d Cir. 1986), *cert. denied*, 486 U.S. 1042 (1988).

[370] *E.g.,* Premier Dental Products v. Darby Dental Supply Co., 794 F.2d 850, 858, 230 U.S.P.Q. 233, 239 (3d Cir.1986), *cert. denied*, 479 U.S. 950 (1986) ("where a trademark is owned and registered in this country by an exclusive distributor who is independent of the foreign manufacturer and who has separate goodwill in the product, the distributor is entitled under Section 526 to prevent the importation even of genuine merchandise obtained from the same foreign manufacturer.").

[371] *E.g.,* Original Appalachian Artworks, Inc. v. Granada Electronics, Inc., 816 F.2d 68, 2 U.S.P.Q.2d 1343 (2d Cir. 1987), *cert. denied*, 484 U.S. 847 (1987); Dial Corp. v. Encina Corp., 643 F. Supp. 951 (S.D. Fla. 1986).

Cf. Osawa & Co. v. B & H Photo, 589 F. Supp. 1163, 1171-74, 223 U.S.P.Q. 124, 130-34 (S.D. N.Y. 1984); Bell & Howell: Mamiya Co. v. Masel Supply Co., 548 F. Supp. 1063 (E.D. N.Y. 1982), *vacated and remanded*, 719 F.2d 42 (2nd Cir. 1983).

In *Weil Ceramics and Glass*,[372] the Third Circuit held that Section 42 did not apply to a Case 2(a) gray-market scenario, that is, the U.S. trademark owner is the foreign manufacturer's subsidiary.[373] Lladro S.A. makes porcelain in Spain, each piece bearing the "LLADRO" trademark and a flower logo. It grades the porcelain's quality, the top categories being "A" (highest) and "B." Its "grading . . . is highly confidential and its customers and purchasers throughout the world and in the United States are not made aware of this internal grading of quality."[374]

In 1966, Weil, a New York importer, became the exclusive United States Lladro porcelain distributor and obtained a U.S. registration of "Lladro." By a series of transactions, Weil and Lladro S.A. came to be owned by a common Spanish parent corporation. In 1982, Jalyn began purchasing genuine Lladro porcelain in Spain from Lladro S.A.'s distributors and importing it into the United States. Weil sued, alleging that Jalyn's sales constituted trademark infringement and a violation of Lanham Act Section 42 and Tariff Act Section 526. The district court granted relief, holding that *Katzel* established the "territoriality principle" that trademarks have separate legal existences in each country in which they are registered and finding that Weil had established independent goodwill in Lladro porcelain in the United States such that defendant's gray-market imports would create a likelihood of confusion.

The appeals court reversed. *K Mart* eliminated Weil's Section 526 claim. The facts resemble the Case 2a scenario, and there was no basis for limiting the "common control" exception to sham incorporations.

> "Although Weil is not a subsidiary that was incorporated by its parent, its affiliation with Lladro, S.A. enables it nonetheless to enjoy every benefit that inheres in the corporate relationship that the Supreme Court described in the case 2(a) scenario. More significantly, that relationship also provides the opportunity for the foreign manufacturer's control of the United States market—under the auspices of the trademark act—that §133.21 intended to preclude. Thus, although Weil was not a 'sham' incorporated by Lladro with the specific intent to benefit from the protections of the trademark act, its present relationship with Lladro nonetheless presents the potential for undesired monopoly of the domestic market and warrants application of § 133.21. Moreover, . . . the Court did not limit its holding in *K Mart* to the decision that §133.21 is a reasonable construction of §526 only so far as that regulation provides a 'presumption' of ownership in the trademark. We read §133.21 as providing an absolute exception from §526 for the import of parallel goods in the case 2a scenario and we read *K Mart* as upholding that construction."[375]

Turning to Weil's Lanham Act claims, the court rejected its argument that *Katzel* endorsed the territoriality theory that "recognizes the separate existence of a trademark

---

[372] Weil Ceramics and Glass, Inc. v. Dash, 878 F.2d 659, 11 U.S.P.Q.2d 1001 (3d Cir. 1989), *cert. denied*, 110 S. Ct. 156 (1989).

[373] Technically, the U.S. trademark owner and foreign manufacturer were "sibling" subsidiaries of a common foreign corporate parent.

[374] 878 F.2d at 682, 11 U.S.P.Q.2d at 1021.

[375] 878 F.2d at 666, 11 U.S.P.Q.2d at 1006-07.

in each territory in which it has been registered." [376] *Katzel* involved special circumstances: the U.S. trademark owner was completely independent of the foreign manufacturer, acquired the manufacturer's trademark rights in an arms-length transaction, obtained control over the product's quality, and had no control over the goods the manufacturer sold abroad. Weil was not in a comparable position and had "a panoply of options" to fight gray-market imports that "are unavailable to the independent purchaser of a foreign trademark." [377]

> "[E]ven if Weil loses some share of its United States market to Jalyn, it nonetheless benefits from the profits it received as part of the corporate entity from which Jalyn purchased the goods abroad. Moreover, if that corporate entity decides that the profit margin from the sale of the goods to Jalyn abroad is not as significant as would be the profit margin from a United States market in which Jalyn did not compete, it has an obvious self-help mechanism: it can cease the sale to Jalyn abroad and thereby eliminate effectively its United States competition with Weil. . . . We do not read the Lanham Act, however, to protect a foreign manufacturer—that either owns or is owned by a domestic trademark holder—from competition in the sale of its product in the United States by a domestic importer that it has supplied. Moreover, the LLA-DRO porcelain that Jalyn imports is *identical* to the porcelain that Weil distributes. . . . Weil has made no contention that, pursuant to its agreement with Lladro, S.A., Weil is entitled to, and does in fact, alter the quality of the porcelain that it distributes in the United States.

> ". . . [T]he Court's conclusion in *Katzel* does not represent the establishment of a broad 'territoriality theory' applicable to every instance in which a domestic company acquires the United States trademark for a foreign manufactured good. We read that decision as creating an exception to the general application of trademark law in order to protect adequately the interests of domestic trademark holders such as Bourjois." [378]

"Having concluded that *Katzel* did not create a broad territoriality principle that is applicable in every instance of parallel imports," the court could "more easily resolve the remainder" of Weil's argument. Sections 32 and 42, in using "copy," "simulate," "counterfeit," and "imitate," reflect "Congress' intent to provide a remedy only to the domestic trademark holder who is injured by the distribution of *like* goods,

---

[376] 878 F.2d at 666, 11 U.S.P.Q.2d at 1007.

[377] The firm and its foreign affiliate could "jointly decide in their mutual best interests that the manufacturer (1) should not import directly to any domestic purchaser other than its affiliate; (2) should, if legal, impose a restriction against resale (or against resale in the United States) as a condition on its sales abroad to potential parallel importers; or (3) should curtail sales abroad entirely. . . . [A]dditional self-help mechanisms available to the corporate entity in the case 2 circumstance include: sale of the products abroad at the *same* price as they are sold domestically, thereby assuring the same margin of profit; or distinguishing the goods sold abroad—either by producing or packaging or marking them differently, thereby assuring that the *trademark* will not be placed in domestic competition." 878 F.2d at 667-68 n.10, 11 U.S.P.Q.2d at 1008 n.10.

[378] 878 F.2d at 668-69, 11 U.S.P.Q.2d at 1008-09.

which bear facsimile marks, that result in confusion to consumers or detriment to the goodwill developed by the trademark holder in the trademarked goods."[379]

Judge Becker concurred, arguing that genuine goods importation may constitute trademark infringement by creating a likelihood of confusion but agreeing that Weil was not entitled to relief because its affiliate foreign manufacturer "engineered the possibility of a likelihood of confusion" by "sending into the stream of commerce identically marked goods of mixed quality."[380]

In *Lever Brothers*,[381] the District of Columbia Circuit considered a challenge to the Customs Service "common control" exception as applied to materially different gray-market goods. Affiliated corporations, Lever US and Lever UK, manufacture and sell "SHIELD" deodorant soap and "SUNLIGHT" liquid dishwashing detergent in the United States and the United Kingdom respectively. The US and UK versions are materially different in order to accommodate local preferences.[382] Third parties import UK "SHIELD" and "SUNLIGHT" into the United States without the Levers' consent. When the Customs Service refused to halt the importation, relying on the common control exception, Lever sued and moved for a preliminary injunction. The district court denied the motion.

The appeals court reached the "provisional" conclusion that the common control exception is contrary to Lanham Act Section 42 when applied to physically different goods.[383]

> "We think the natural, virtually inevitable reading of §42 is that it bars foreign goods bearing a trademark identical to a valid US trademark but physically different, regardless of the trademarks' genuine character abroad or affiliation between the producing firms. On its face the section appears to aim at deceit and consumer confusion; when identical trademarks have acquired

---

[379] 878 F.2d at 671, 11 U.S.P.Q.2d at 1011.

[380] 878 F.2d at 676, 11 U.S.P.Q.2d at 1015.

[381] Lever Brothers Co. v. United States, 877 F.2d 101, 11 U.S.P.Q.2d 1117 (D.C. Cir. 1989). *See also* Ferrero U.S.A., Inc. v. Ozak Trading, Inc., 753 F. Supp. 1240, 18 U.S.P.Q.2d 1052 (D. N.J. 1991), aff'd, 935 F.2d 1281 (3d Cir.1991) (unpublished) (sale of materially different gray-market goods violates Lanham Act and common law trademark rights).

[382] ". . . US Shield contains a higher concentration of coconut soap and fatty acids, and thus more readily generates lather. . . .The manufacturing choice evidently arises in part out of the British preference for baths, which permit time for lather to develop, as opposed to a US preference for showers. . . . Moreover, Britons interested in a soap's lathering properties turn to 'beauty and cosmetic' soaps rather than to deodorant soaps. . . . Further, US Shield contains an agent that inhibits growth of bacteria; Lever accounts for this difference in terms of some mix of 'differing consumer preferences, climatic conditions and regulatory standards.' . . . Finally, the two bars contain differing perfume formulas and colorants." 877 F.2d at 103, 11 U.S.P.Q.2d at 1118.

". . . UK Sunlight is designed for water with a higher mineral content than is generally found in the United States, and therefore does not perform as well as US Sunlight in the soft water typical of US metropolitan areas." *Id.*

[383] Because the parties had not briefed the legislative history and adminstratice practice in detail, the court did not make a final determination but remanded "to the district court so that the parties may join issue on those points." 877 F.2d at 111, 11 U.S.P.Q.2d at 1125.

different meanings in different countries, one who imports the foreign version to sell it under that trademark will (in the absence of some specially differentiating feature) cause the confusion Congress sought to avoid. The fact of affiliation between the producers in no way reduces the probability of that confusion; it is certainly not a constructive consent to the importation." [384]

The Supreme Court's face-powder trilogy reflects and enforces trademark territoriality. [385] More recent cases indicate "a readiness to find infringement" "[w]here the goods bearing a foreign trademark valid abroad are physically different from the US trademarked goods." [386]

The Customs Service offered policy arguments to support the common control exception. First, it suggested the affiliated group had self-help means for controlling undesirable gray-market imports and that "the dispute is better suited for resolution 'in the boardroom' than the court room." The court was unimpressed.

"Even if all the Lever affiliates were collapsed into a single corporate entity, its board could not single-handedly implement a decision to limit sales of UK Shield and UK Sunlight to the United Kingdom. So long as it uses third-party middlemen and retailers, it must launch those products into the stream of commerce, with the risk that some purchasers may seek to exploit the opportunity to ride on the US trademarks' value. Indeed, at some exchange rates an arbitrageur could buy Shield and Sunlight at retail from a completely vertically integrated Lever UK and profitably resell them here. We are not told how either the US markholder or the foreign affiliate is to prevent this without invoking governmental authority, either in the form of Customs Service action or trademark-based injunctions against the importer. Of course the 'boardroom' that evidently controls both Lever US and Lever UK could solve the problem by abandoning use of the Shield and Sunlight trademarks in the United Kingdom, or at least by abandoning their use for physically distinct products. But this solution is obviously costly. The Lever affiliates have succeeded in attaching to products designed for their respective markets ordinary words that have both a favorable 'spin' and a natural link to those products. Customs has offered us no shadow of a reason why it would serve any public interest implicit in §42 to compel Lever to abandon the resulting goodwill, or (looking ahead) to refrain in the first place from establishing such goodwill by use of identical words. The resources of English are finite and the quest for an apt word costly." [387]

---

[384] 877 F.2d at 111, 11 U.S.P.Q.2d at 1125.

[385] "We do not essay any grand resolution of the face-powder trilogy's legal message. None of the cases addresses the problem of affiliates generally, nor the special problem of affiliates using identical trademarks to sell products tailored for specific national conditions and tastes. On the other hand, the cases clearly view trademarks as having specific territorial scope, and are at least consistent with the view that §27 of the 1905 Act [which became Lanham Act Section 42] protects a domestic trademark holder from goods genuinely trademarked abroad but imported here by parties hoping to exploit consumer confusion between the domestic and foreign products." 877 F.2d at 108, 11 U.S.P.Q.2d at 1122.

[386] 877 F.2d at 109, 11 U.S.P.Q.2d at 1123.

[387] Id. at 1124.

Second, it suggested that "there is a consumer interest in access to lower-priced UK products."[388] Again, the court yawned.

> "[T]rademark law inherently denies consumers access to cheap goods sailing under false colors. Further, even if we were to accept Customs' dubious premise, it points to nothing supporting the idea that the mere fact of affiliation makes it more likely than in the general case that this potential consumer loss would exceed the gain from accurate signalling of quality by means of trademarks."[389]

Third, it suggested that its interpretation of Section 42 "is an administrative necessity" because the alternative would require Customs Service agents "to assess at the border the amount of consumer confusion and/or loss of goodwill likely to result from the importation of goods bearing genuine foreign trademarks." The court called strike three!

> "No one is suggesting that Customs assess the degree of consumer confusion or loss of goodwill, only that it distinguish between identical and non-identical goods. If Lever US's submissions here are correct, that would not be difficult in a case such as this. It is hard to see why Customs' arguments calls for more than allowing it room to choose inactivity in marginal cases."[390]

§ 5F Infringement

Trademark infringement is the unauthorized use of a mark that so resembles another person's valid trademark, service mark, collective mark, or certification mark as to create a likelihood of confusion.

> "The owner of the mark acquires the right to prevent his goods from being confused with those of others and to prevent his own trade from being diverted to competitors through their use of misleading marks. . . . To prevail on a statutory or common law trademark infringement claim a plaintiff must demonstrate an infringement of this limited property right. He must establish that the symbols in which this property right is asserted are valid, legally protectible trademarks; that they are owned by plaintiff; and that defendant's subsequent use of similar marks is likely to create confusion as to origin of the goods."[1]

For federally-registered marks, the Lanham Act gives a registrant a civil right of action against any person who uses, without the registrant's consent, a "reproduction, counterfeit, copy, or colorable imitation" of the mark to (a) sell, offer for sale, distribute, or advertise "any goods or services on or in connection with which such use is likely to cause confusion," or (b) reproduce the mark and apply it to "labels, signs, prints, packages, wrappers, receptacles or advertisements" intended for such

---

[388] *Id.*

[389] *Id.*

[390] *Id.*

[1] Pirone v. MacMillan, Inc., 894 F.2d 579, 581-82, 13 U.S.P.Q.2d 1799, 1800 (2d Cir. 1990).

sale, distribution, or advertising.[2] Persons other than sellers of infringing mark-bearing goods may be liable for either direct infringement[3] or inducement of infringement.[4]

There are a number of partial or complete defenses to a trademark infringement charge, including invalidity, fraud, antitrust violation, and fair use.[5]

Trademark infringement remedies include injunctions, damages, infringer profits, and other relief.[6]

[1] Likelihood of Confusion

"[T]he crucial issue in an action for trademark infringement or unfair competition is whether there is any likelihood that an appreciable number of ordinarily prudent purchasers are likely to be misled, or indeed simply confused, as to the source of the goods in question."[7]

The infringement standard based on likelihood of confusion derives from the basic purposes of trademark and unfair competition laws: prevention of consumer confusion and preservation of the mark owner's goodwill without undue impingement on competition .[8] The standard is essentially the same as that for denying trademark registration or protection based on prior use.[9]

Like copyright law's substantial similarity standard,[10] the standard of likelihood of confusion in trademark law requires that informed judgment be applied to

---

[2] Lanham Act § 32(1), 15 U.S.C. § 1114(1).

[3] Lanham Act Section 32 restricts the remedies available against nonsellers, such as printers and the news media. See § 6E[5].

[4] See Inwood Laboratories, Inc. v. Ives Laboratories, Inc., 456 U.S. 844, 853-54, 214 U.S.P.Q. 1 (1982) ("liability for trademark infringement can extend beyond those who actually mislabel goods with the mark of another. Even if a manufacturer does not directly control others in the chain of distribution, it can be held responsible for their infringing activities under certain circumstances. Thus, if a manufacturer or distributor intentionally induces another to infringe a trademark, or if it continues to supply its product to one whom it knows or has reason to know is engaging in trademark infringement, the manufacturer or distributor is contributorially responsible for any harm done as a result of the deceit."); David Berg and Co. v. Gatto International Trading Co., Inc., 884 F.2d 306, 311, 12 U.S.P.Q.2d 1116, 1120 (7th Cir. 1989) ("Because unfair competition and trademark infringement are tortious, the doctrine of joint tortfeasors does apply."); Sealy, Inc. v. Easy Living, Inc., 743 F.2d 1378, 224 U.S.P.Q. 364 (9th Cir. 1984).

For a discussion of contributory and inducing *patent* infringement, see § 2E[2][c].

[5] See § 5F[2].

[6] See § 5F[3].

A registered mark owner may secure Customs Service assistance in blocking infringing imports. See § 5E[5][c].

[7] Mushroom Makers, Inc. v. R.G. Barry Corp., 580 F.2d 44, 199 U.S.P.Q. 65 (2d Cir. 1978) (Friendly, J.).

The oft-quoted *Mushroom Makers* statement does not fully reflect contemporary trademark law, which protects against association and endorsement confusion as well as source confusion and extends the potentially confused persons class to persons other than "purchasers." See § 5F[1][d].

[8] See § 5A.

[9] See § 5C[4][a].

[10] See § 4F[2].

the facts of a particular case. Case precedent and precise rules are of limited value. In 1917, Judge Learned Hand, in holding that defendant's use of "Listogen" was likely to cause confusion when applied to a product rivaling plaintiff's established "Listerine" brand mouth wash, commented:

> "A discussion of the many cases in which similarities have, or have not, been thought infringements, serves no end; applications of the accepted principle no doubt vary, but no two cases are alike. One must trust one's own sense of the likelihood of confusion and the absence of any justification for the defendant's choice of name."[11]

[a] **The Factors Approach.** The 1938 Restatement of Torts set forth four factors for determining confusion likelihood:

> "(a) the degree of similarity between the designation and the trade-mark or tradename in
>
> (i) appearance;
>
> (ii) pronunciation of the words used;
>
> (iii) verbal translation of the pictures or designs involved;
>
> (iv) suggestion;
>
> "(b) the intent of the actor in adopting the designation;
>
> "(c) the relation in use and manner of marketing between the goods or services marketed by the actor and those marketed by the other.
>
> "(d) the degree of care likely to be exercised by purchasers."[12]

The Restatement set forth a separate list of nine factors for determining whether a trademark owner's rights extend to noncompeting goods.[13]

---

[11] Lambert Pharmacal Co. v. Bolton Chemical Corp., 219 F. 325, 328 (S.D. N.Y. 1915).

[12] Restatement of Torts § 729 (1938). The Comment to Section 729 cautioned: "This Section states factors generally important in determining the issue of confusing similarity. It is not an exclusive catalogue of factors which may be important in particular cases."

[13] Restatement of Torts § 731 (1938):

> "(a) the likelihood that the actor's goods, services or businesses will be mistaken for those of the other;
>
> "(b) the likelihood that the other may expand his business so as to compete with the actor;
>
> "(c) the extent to which the goods or services of the actor and those of the other have common purchasers or users;
>
> "(d) the extent to which the goods or services of the actor and those of the other are marketed through the same channels;
>
> "(e) the relation between the functions of the goods or services of the actor and those of the other;
>
> "(f) the degree of distinctiveness of the trade-mark or trade name;
>
> "(g) the degree of attention usually given to trade symbols in the purchase of goods or services of the actor and those of the other;
>
> "(h) the length of time during which the actor has used the designation;
>
> "(i) the intent of the actor in adopting and using the designation."

The Restatement's multiple factor approach applies to all infringement actions, whether based on a federally-registered mark,[14] state common law,[15] or the Lanham

[14] *E.g.*, Nutri/System Inc. v. Con-Stan Industries Inc., 809 F.2d 601, 1 U.S.P.Q.2d 1809 (9th Cir. 1987) (identical standards govern infringement of trademarks and service marks).

[15] State court decisions apply the confusion likelihood standard to statutory and common law trademark and trade name infringement and unfair competition actions. *E.g.*, California Western School of Law v. California Western University, 125 Cal. App. 3d 1002, 178 Cal. Rptr. 685 (1981); Draper Communications, Inc. v. Delaware Valley Broadcasters Limited Partnership, 505 A.2d 1283, 229 U.S.P.Q. 161 (Del. Ct. Chan. 1985); Tio Pepe, Inc. v. El Tio Pepe de Miami Restaurant, Inc., 523 So. 2d 1158, 1159-60 & n.6, 6 U.S.P.Q.2d 1228, 1229-30 & n.6 (Fla. Dist. Ct. App. 1988) ("Federal cases examining infringement claims under both the Lanham Act . . . and Florida's statutory law . . . and common law have formulated a list of factors which bear upon the issue of likelihood of confusion. These factors include: 1) the type of trademark; 2) the similarity of the two marks, 3) similarities of the products or service, 3) the similarities of retail outlets or purchasers; 4) the similarities of advertising media used; 5) the defendant's intent; and 6) evidence of actual confusion. . . . [I]nasmuch as the language contained in the Florida statute is so similar to its federal counterpart, the construction given the federal act should be examined as persuasive authority for interpreting the state act."); Carrington v. Sears, Roebuck & Co., 5 Hawaii App. 194, 683 P.2d 1220, 223 U.S.P.Q. 1338 (1984); Thompson v. Spring- Green Lawn Care Corp., 126 Ill. App. 3d 99, 466 N.E.2d 1004 (1984); Planned Parenthood Federation of America, Inc. v. Problem Pregnancy of Worcester, Inc., 398 Mass. 480, 498 N.E.2d 1044, 1049, 1 U.S.P.Q.2d 1465 (1986); Minneapple Co. v. Normandin, 338 N.W.2d 18 (Minn. Sup. Ct. 1983); Dynamic Sales Co. v. Dynamic Fastener Service, 803 S.W.2d 129, 132 (Mo. Ct. App. 1990) ("evidence of actual confusion is not required to prove a likelihood of confusion, . . . but where a mark is weak, evidence of actual confusion is important to prove 'that the public is likely to be confused as to the source or sponsorship of the defendant's services.' "); A.L.M.N., Inc. v. Rosoff, 104 Nev. 274, 757 P.2d 1319 (1988); Edison Electric Co., Inc. v. Edison Contracting Co.—Electrical Contractors, 203 N.J. Super. 50, 495 A.2d 905, 906, 227 U.S.P.Q. 229-30 (1985) ("The courts of this state have long entertained actions to enjoin unfair trade practices including infringement of trademarks and trade names. . . . However, no case has enjoined use of a trade name simply upon a showing that it was similar to the trade name of a prior user or that there was actual or potential confusion between the names. Rather, a finding of infringement invariably has been predicated on a comprehensive evaluation of a variety of factors, including the nature of the parties' trade names, the character of their businesses, the manner in which their products or services are marketed, the competitive relationship between the parties and the objective of the alleged infringer in adopting its trade name."); Cesare v. Work, 36 Ohio App. 3d 26, 520 N.E.2d 586, 590 (1987) ("where claims are made under Ohio common law and the deceptive trade practices statutes, courts are to apply essentially the same analysis as that applied in assessing unfair competition under the federal statutes. . . . We therefore look to federal law for guidance on those issues not clearly addressed by Ohio case law."); Willowbrook Home Health Care Agency, Inc. v. Willow Brook Retirement Center, 769 S.W.2d 862 (Tenn. Ct. App. 1988); Men of Measure Clothing, Inc. v. Men of Measure, Inc., 710 S.W.2d 43, 228 U.S.P.Q. 777 (Tenn. Ct. App. 1985); Ergon, Inc. v. Dean, 649 S.W.2d 772, 223 U.S.P.Q. 546 (Tex. Ct. App. 1983); Spheeris Sporting Goods, Inc. v. Spheeris on Capital, 157 Wis. 2d 298, 459 N.W.2d 581, 586 (1990) ("The criteria for determining whether names are confusingly similar varies. The decision is affected by the character of the goods or services, their use, the characteristics of the consumer group, and the manner of sale. . . . The circumstances surrounding the names' use are almost as important as the trade names themselves.").

Act's Section 43(a) false origin designation remedy,[16] which includes trade dress misappropriation claims.[17]

Courts expanded and refined the Restatement factors in two stages. First, they recognized an expanded list of factors as appropriate when the protected and accused marks are used on or with noncompeting goods or services. In *Polaroid*,[18] Judge Friendly, citing the Restatement, stated that "Where the products are different, the prior owner's chance of success is a function of many variables" and listed eight such variables:

"(1) the strength of his mark,

"(2) the degree of similarity between the two marks,

"(3) the proximity of the products,

"(4) the likelihood that the prior owner will bridge the gap,

"(5) actual confusion,

"(6) the reciprocal of defendant's good faith in adopting its own mark,

"(7) the quality of defendant's product,

"(8) the sophistication of the buyers."[19]

"Even this extensive catalogue does not exhaust the possibilities—the court may have to take still other variables into account."[20]

Second, after initially limiting the *Polaroid* factors to noncompeting goods cases,[21] a position suggested in part by the Restatement's two-list approach, the courts applied the factors to competing product or service cases.[22] In *Vitarroz*,[23] the senior user

---

[16] Accuride International Inc. v. Accuride Corp., 871 F.2d 1531, 10 U.S.P.Q.2d 1589 (9th Cir. 1989).

[17] *E.g.,* Century 21 Real Estate Corp. v. Sandlin, 846 F.2d 1175, 1178, 6 U.S.P.Q.2d 2034, 2036 (9th Cir. 1988) ("The 'ultimate test' for unfair competition is exactly the same as for trademark infringement: 'whether the public is likely to be deceived or confused by the similarity of the marks.' ").

[18] Polaroid Corp. v. Polarad Electronics Corp., 287 F.2d 492, 128 U.S.P.Q. 411 (2d Cir. 1961), *cert. denied,* 368 U.S. 820 (1961). *Polaroid* closed an era of impassioned debate among the Second Circuit's judges on the nature and role of trademark protection, especially as applied to noncompeting goods. *See* § 5E[3][a].

[19] 287 F.2d at 495, 128 U.S.P.Q. at 413.
The *Polaroid* list does not exactly conform to either of the *Restatement* lists.

[20] 287 F.2d at 495, 128 U.S.P.Q. at 413.

[21] *E.g.,* AMF, Inc. v. Sleekcraft Boats, 599 F.2d 341, 348, 204 U.S.P.Q. 808, 814 (9th Cir. 1979) ("When the goods produced by the alleged infringer compete for sales with those of the trademark owner, infringement usually will be found if the marks are sufficiently similar that confusion can be expected. When the goods are related, but not competitive, several other factors are added to the calculus. If the goods are totally unrelated, there can be no infringement because confusion is unlikely.").

[22] *E.g.,* Thompson Medical Co., Inc. v. Pfizer, 753 F.2d 208, 214, 225 U.S.P.Q. 124, 129 (2d Cir. 1985) ("Although the Polaroid balancing test was traditionally confined to products that were 'non-competing,' . . . 'non-competitive,' . . . or 'different,' . . . it now properly extends to competing products.").

[23] Vitarroz Corp. v. Borden, 644 F.2d 960, 209 U.S.P.Q. 969 (2d Cir. 1981).

of the mark "BRAVO'S" on crackers sued the junior user of "BRAVOS" on tortilla chips. Applying the *Polaroid* factors, the district court found no confusion likely because the mark was not strong, the senior user was unlikely to bridge the gap between the products, there was no evidence of actual confusion, the junior user adopted its mark in good faith, and the junior user's chips were of high quality. The senior user argued on appeal that "consideration of the *Polaroid* factors is proper only when the products do not compete" and that with competing goods the focus should be solely on mark similarity and product proximity. The Second Circuit found some support in prior case law for the senior user's "argument that a plaintiff must prevail when it shows virtually identical marks used for competing products."[24] Nevertheless, it agreed with the district court's comprehensive approach:

> "In no case . . . have we determined a senior user's right to injunctive relief solely on the basis of the similarity of the marks and the proximity of the products. . . .

> "Since the *Polaroid* decision, we have consistently considered all the *Polaroid* factors, including the junior user's good faith, despite the similarity of the marks and the close proximity of the products. . . . Indeed, rather than eschew consideration of any of the *Polaroid* factors, we have added to the original list, just as *Polaroid* anticipated.

> . . .

> "The plaintiff's per se rule based on the similarity of the marks and the competition between the products could be justified only if we could say with reasonable certainty that injury to the plaintiff is inevitable."[25]

Some decisions view all the factors as of equal importance[26] and others give more

---

[24] *Cf.* Homeowners Group, Inc. v. Home Marketing Specialists,, Inc., 931 F.2d 1100, 1107 n.4, 18 U.S.P.Q.2d 1587, 1592 (6th Cir. 1991) ("In some cases it may be unnecessary to undertake an extended analysis to infer confusion, *e.g.,* where there is no difference between the marks of directly competitive goods/services.").

[25] 644 F.2d at 966, 209 U.S.P.Q. at 974-75.

See also Levi Strauss & Co. v. Blue Bell, Inc., 778 F.2d 1352, 1359 n.8, 228 U.S.P.Q. 346, 351 n.8 (9th Cir. 1985) (en banc) ("The related goods test is not a separate test for establishing likelihood of confusion but incorporates the same factors which are applied in cases involving competitive goods with the addition of such factors as the 'proximity' of the goods and the likelihood of expansion of the product lines.").

[26] *E.g.,* Life Technologies Inc. v. Gibbco Scientific Inc., 826 F.2d 775, 776, 3 U.S.P.Q.2d 1795, 1796 (8th Cir. 1987) ("Each factor must be considered and excessive weight should not be given to any one factor to the exclusion of others. . . . The factors were meant to be weighed against each other, not individually viewed in a vacuum."); AmBRIT Inc. v. Kraft Inc., 812 F.2d 1531, 1538, 1 U.S.P.Q.2d 1161, 1166 (11th Cir. 1986) ("The issue of likelihood of confusion is not determined by merely analyzing whether a majority of the subsidiary factors indicates that such a likelihood exists. Rather, a court must evaluate the weight to be accorded the individual factors and then make its ultimate decision. The appropriate weight to be given to each of these factors varies with the circumstances of the case."); Thompson Medical Co., Inc. v. Pfizer Inc., 753 F.2d 208, 214, 225 U.S.P.Q. 124, 129 (2d Cir. 1985) ("The wisdom of the likelihood of confusion test lies in its recognition that each trademark infringement case presents its own unique set of facts. Indeed, the complexities attendant to

weight to one or more,[27] but the better view is that they are not a mandatory mode of analysis but "a useful guide through a difficult quagmire."[28] In *Wynn Oil,*[29] the court noted: "These factors are simply a guide to help determine whether confusion would be likely to result from simultaneous use of the two contested marks. They imply no mathematical precision, and a plaintiff need not show that all, or even most, of the factors listed are present in any particular case to be successful."

[*i*] *Circuit Variation.* The Second Circuit's *Polaroid* decision influenced the other circuits to adopt similar multiple factors tests for likelihood of confusion. The circuits vary as to the wording and number of factors.

The First Circuit identifies eight factors to be weighted in assessing likelihood of confusion:

"(1) similarity of the marks;

"(2) similarity of the goods;

"(3) relationship between the parties' channels of trade;

"(4) the relationship between the parties' advertising;

"(5) the classes of prospective purchasers;

"(6) evidence of actual confusion;

"(7) the defendant's intent in adopting the mark;

---

an accurate assessment of likelihood of confusion require that the entire panoply of elements constituting the relevant factual landscape be comprehensively examined. No single *Polaroid* factor is preeminent, nor can the presence or absence of one without analysis of the others, determine the outcome of an infringement suit.").

[27] *E.g.,* Ziebart International Corp. v. Aftermarket Associates, Inc., 802 F.2d 220, 226, 231 U.S.P.Q. 119, 124 (7th Cir. 1986) ("Of these seven factors, we have referred . . . to three of them—similarity of the marks, intent of the claimed infringer, and evidence of actual confusion—as 'the more important.' ").

Cf. Freixenet, S.A. v. Admiral Wine & Liquor Co., 731 F.2d 148, 151-52, 222 U.S.P.Q. 770, 773 (3d Cir. 1984) ("All these elements are helpful in arriving at a finding as to the likelihood of confusion. Nevertheless, it should not be necessary to consider all six when some are dispositive.").

[28] Lois Sportswear, U.S.A., Inc. v. Levi Strauss & Co., 799 F.2d 867, 872, 230 U.S.P.Q. 831, 834 (2d Cir. 1986).

See also Orient Express Trading Co. v. Federated Department Stores, Inc., 842 F.2d 650, 654, 6 U.S.P.Q.2d 1308 (2d Cir. 1988) (a district court need not "slavishly recite the litany of all eight *Polaroid* factors . . . [but] need only consider sufficient factors to reach the ultimate conclusion as to whether or not there is a likelihood of confusion."); McGraw-Edison Co. v. Walt Disney Productions, 787 F.2d 1163, 1168, 229 U.S.P.Q. 355, 359 (7th Cir. 1986) ("this court has reversed lower court decisions that have placed excessive importance on certain factors"); Marathon Mfg. Co. v. Enerlite Products Corp., 767 F.2d 214, 218, 226 U.S.P.Q. 836, 837 (5th Cir. 1985) ("None of these factors by itself is dispositive of the likelihood of confusion question, and different factors will weigh more heavily from case to case depending on the particular facts and circumstances involved.").

[29] Wynn Oil Co. v. Thomas, 839 F.2d 1183, 1186, 5 U.S.P.Q. 1944, 1946 (6th Cir. 1988).

"(8) the strength of the plaintiff's mark."[30]

It often considers the third, fourth, and fifth factors together because they are "interrelated."[31]

The Second Circuit consistently follows *Polaroid*'s eight factor test.[32] "[T]he *Polaroid* test is not a 'rigid formula' . . . where the party with the greatest number of factors weighing in its favor wins. Rather, it is a non-exhaustive catalogue of factors to be considered in determining likelihood of confusion."[33]

The Third Circuit applies a ten factor test:

"(1) the degree of similarity between the owner's mark and the alleged infringing mark;

"(2) the strength of owner's mark;

"(3) the price of the goods and other factors indicative of the care and attention expected of consumers when making a purchase;

"(4) the length of time the defendant has used the mark without evidence of actual confusion arising;

"(5) the intent of the defendant in adopting the mark;

"(6) the evidence of actual confusion;

"(7) whether the goods, though not competing, are marketed through the same channels of trade and advertised through the same media;

"(8) the extent to which the targets of the parties' sales efforts are the same;

"(9) the relationship of the goods in the minds of the public because of similarity of function; and

"(10) other factors suggesting that the consuming public might expect the prior owner to manufacture a product in the defendant's market."[34]

The Fourth Circuit applies a seven factor test:

---

[30] *E.g.*, Keds Corp. v. Renee International Trading Corp., 888 F.2d 215, 12 U.S.P.Q.2d 1808 (1st Cir. 1989).

See also Volkswagen Aktiengesellschaft v. Wheeler, 814 F.2d 812, 817, 2 U.S.P.Q.2d 1264, 1267 (1st Cir. 1987) ("No one factor is necessarily determinative, but each must be considered.").

[31] Boston Athletic Ass'n v. Sullivan, 867 F.2d 22, 30, 9 U.S.P.Q.2d 1690, 1697 (1st Cir. 1989) ("As in some of our previous cases, we treat these three factors simultaneously"); Volkswagenwerk AG v. Wheeler, 814 F.2d 812, 2 U.S.P.Q.2d 1264 (1st Cir. 1987).

[32] Polaroid Corp. v. Polarad Electronics Corp., 287 F.2d 492, 128 U.S.P.Q. 411 (2d Cir. 1961), *cert. denied*, 368 U.S. 820 (1961).

[33] Physicians Formula Cosmetics Inc. v. West Cabot Cosmetics Inc., 857 F.2d 80, 85, 8 U.S.P.Q.2d 1136, 1140 (2d Cir. 1988).

See also Hasbro, Inc. v. Lanard Toys, Ltd., 858 F.2d 70, 79, 8 U.S.P.Q.2d 1345, 1353 (2d Cir. 1988) ("The senior user's delay in asserting its trademark claim is an example of a factor which, when appropriate, may also be considered in addition to the enumerated *Polaroid* factors.").

[34] Scott Paper Co. v. Scott's Liquid Gold, 589 F.2d 1225, 1229, 220 U.S.P.Q. 421, 425 (3d Cir. 1978).

"(1) the strength or distinctiveness of the mark;

"(2) the similarity of the two marks;

"(3) the similarity of the goods/services the marks identify;

"(4) the similarity of the facilities the two parties use in their businesses;

"(5) the similarity of the advertising used by the two parties;

"(6) the defendant's intent;

"(7) actual confusion."[35]

The Fifth Circuit applies a seven factor test:

"(1) similarity of products;

"(2) identity of retail outlets and purchasers;

"(3) identity of advertising media;

"(4) type (i.e. strength) of trademark or trade dress;

"(5) defendant's intent;

"(6) similarity of design;

"(7) actual confusion."[36]

Also, "it is often appropriate to consider the degree of care exercised by purchasers."[37]

The Sixth Circuit applies an eight factor test:

"(1) strength of the plaintiff's mark;

"(2) relatedness of the goods;

"(3) similarity of the marks;

"(4) evidence of actual confusion;

"(5) marketing channels used;

"(6) likely degree of purchaser care;

---

[35] *E.g.,* Pizzeria Uno Corp. v. Temple, 747 F.2d 1522, 1527, 224 U.S.P.Q. 185, 187 (4th Cir. 1984).

The court has also identified a six-factor test:

"(1) the type of service [or trade] mark at issue;
"(2) the similarity of design and of the product offered;
"(3) the identity of the retail outlets and purchasers;
"(4) the identity of advertising media utilized;
"(5) defendant's intent; and
"(6) actual confusion."

Marcon, Ltd. v. Helena Rubenstein, 694 F.2d 953, 955, 217 U.S.P.Q. 310, 312 (4th Cir. 1982) (quoting with approval, Armand's Subway, Inc. v. Doctor's Associates, Inc., 202 U.S.P.Q. 305, 310 (E.D. Va. 1978), *rev'd on other grounds,* 604 F.2d 849, 203 U.S.P.Q. 241 (4th Cir. 1979).

[36] Sno-Wizard Manufacturing, Inc. v. Eisemann Products Co., 791 F.2d 423, 230 U.S.P.Q. 118 (5th Cir. 1986).

[37] 791 F.2d at 428, 230 U.S.P.Q. at 118.

"(7) defendant's intent in selecting the mark;

"(8) likelihood of expansion of the product lines."[38]

The Seventh Circuit applies a seven factor test:

"(1) the degree of similarity between the marks in appearance and suggestion;

"(2) the similarity of the products for which the name is used;

"(3) the area and manner of concurrent use;

"(4) the degree of care likely to be exercised by consumers;

"(5) the strength of the complaint's mark;

"(6) actual confusion; and

"(7) an intent on the part of the alleged infringer to palm off his products as those of another."[39]

The Eighth Circuit applies a six factor test:

"(1) the strength of the owner's mark;

"(2) the similarity between the owner's mark and the alleged infringer's mark;

"(3) the degree to which the products compete with each other;

"(4) the alleged infringer's intent to pass off its goods as those of the trademark owner (but intent is not an element of an infringement claim);

"(5) incidents of actual confusion;

"(6) whether the degree of purchaser care can eliminate any likelihood of confusion which would otherwise exist."[40]

---

[38] Frisch's Restaurants, Inc. v. Elby's Big Boy, 670 F.2d 642, 214 U.S.P.Q. 15 (6th Cir.), cert. denied, 459 U.S. 916 (1982).

See also Homeowners Group, Inc. v. Home Marketing Specialists,, Inc., 931 F.2d 1100, 1107, 18 U.S.P.Q.2d 1587, 1592 (6th Cir. 1991) ("These factors imply no mathematical precision, but are simply a guide to help determine whether confusion is likely. They are also interrelated in effect. Each case presents its own complex set of circumstances and not all of these factors may be particularly helpful in any given case. But a thorough and analytical treatment must nevertheless be attempted. . . . The ultimate question remains whether relevant consumers are likely to believe that the products or services offered by the parties are affiliated in some way.").

[39] Helene Curtis Industries, Inc. v. Church & Dwight Co., Inc., 560 F.2d 1325, 195 U.S.P.Q. 218 (7th Cir. 1977), cert. denied, 434 U.S. 1070 (1978). See also Roulo v. Russ Berrie & Co. Inc., 886 F.2d 931, 935, 12 U.S.P.Q.2d 1423, 1427 (7th Cir. 1989).

The Circuit has also articulated a six-factor test. Ziebart International Corp. v. Aftermarket Associates, Inc., 802 F.2d 220, 226, 231 U.S.P.Q. 119, 124 (7th Cir. 1986); Henri's Food Products Co., Inc. v. Kraft, Inc., 717 F.2d 352, 354, 220 U.S.P.Q. 386, 388 (7th Cir. 1983) ("In determining whether likelihood of confusion exists this Circuit considers such factors as distinctiveness of the trademark in issue, similarity of the marks, similarity of the products, similarity in the channels of distribution, identity of advertising media utilized, the intent of the alleged infringer, and evidence of actual confusion.").

[40] Squirtco v. Seven-Up Co., 628 F.2d 1086, 1091, 207 U.S.P.Q. 897, 900 (8th Cir. 1980).

Ninth Circuit panel decisions list five,[41] six,[42] and eight factors. In *Sleekcraft,*[43] the court listed the following:

"(1) strength of the mark;

"(2) proximity of the goods;

"(3) similarity of the marks;

"(4) evidence of actual confusion;

"(5) marketing channels used;

"(6) type of goods and the degree of care likely to be exercised by the purchaser;

"(7) defendant's intent in selecting the mark;

"(8) likelihood of expansion of the product lines."

In *Accuride International,*[44] the court noted that "There is no indication that the cases applying five or six factors were intended to undermine *Sleekcraft,* and eliminate consideration of the two or three *Sleekcraft* factors excluded in those cases."

In *Eclipse Associates,*[45] the court rejected the appellant's argument that the Ninth Circuit has used two distinct "likelihood of confusion" tests: one involving inexpensive impulse purchase-type goods (a 5-factor test), the other involving expensive goods purchased with a great deal of care by sophisticated consumers (an 8-factor test).

> "In fact, although the tests are described in slightly different terms, the content of the tests appears to have been applied interchangeably. . . .
>
>   . . .
>
> "The Ninth Circuit enumerated likelihood of confusion tests as helpful guidelines to the district court. These tests were not meant to be requirements or hoops that a district court need jump through to make the determination. Our court has never articulated specific factors that a district court must recite and apply, instead, we have identified a non- exclusive series of factors that are helpful in making the ultimate factual determination. . . .

---

[41] *E.g.,* Fuddruckers Inc. v. Doc's B.R. Others Inc., 826 F.2d 837, 845, 4 U.S.P.Q.2d 1026, 1032 (9th Cir. 1987) ("The factors are not weighted evenly."); Rodeo Collection Ltd. v. West Seventh, 812 F.2d 1215, 2 U.S.P.Q.2d 1204 (9th Cir. 1987); Nutri/System Inc. v. Con-Stan Industries Inc., 809 F.2d 601, 604, 1 U.S.P.Q.2d 1809, 1811 (9th Cir. 1987) ("In a series of cases, we developed a multi-factor analysis for determining the 'likelihood of confusion' between trademarks or service marks. These factors include: (1) strength of the mark; (2) similarity of the marks; (3) marketing channels and proximity of the goods or services; (4) good faith and intent; and (5) evidence of actual confusion.").

[42] *E.g.,* Clamp Manufacturing Co. Inc. v. Enco Manufacturing Co. Inc., 870 F.2d 512, 517, 10 U.S.P.Q.2d 1226, 1230 (9th Cir. 1989)("strength of [claimant's] mark; similarity of the marks; evidence of actual confusion; marketing channels used; type of goods and degree of care likely to be exercised by purchaser; and [accused infringer's] intent in selecting the marks.").

[43] AMF Inc. v. Sleekcraft Boats, 599 F.2d 341, 348–49, 204 U.S.P.Q. 808 (9th Cir. 1979).

[44] Accuride International Inc. v. Accuride Corp., 871 F.2d 1531, 1534, 10 U.S.P.Q.2d 1589, 1590 (9th Cir. 1989).

[45] Eclipse Associates Ltd. v. Data General Corp., 894 F.2d 1114, 13 U.S.P.Q.2d 1885 (9th Cir. 1990).

"The district court's primary task, in determining infringement of registered trademarks, is to make the factual determination whether the public is likely to be deceived or confused by the similarity of the marks as to source, relationship or sponsorship. . . . Regardless of what specific factors are discussed by the district court, we review the district court's ultimate factual finding under the clearly erroneous standard."[46]

The court affirmed the district court's finding that defendant's use of "Eclipse" for computer software and services made confusion likely in view of plaintiff's "ECLIPSE" mark for digital computers and hardware—even though the district court did not expressly list customer care or sophistication as a factor.

The Tenth Circuit follows the four primary factors stated by the Restatement of Torts.[47] In *Beer Nuts,*[48] the court noted: "Other courts have used some formulation of this same test. . . . The above list is not exhaustive and no one factor is determinative. The facts of a particular case may require consideration of other variables as well." It held that the district court erred in finding no likelihood of confusion based solely on a side-by-side comparison of the two products with the marks, "Beer Nuts" and "Brew Nuts." It also erred by equating likelihood of confusion with similarity: "Similarity must be considered along with the other factors set out in the Restatement to determine whether, under all the circumstances of the marketplace, confusion is likely."

The Eleventh Circuit applies a seven factor test:

"(1) the nature of the plaintiff's mark;

"(2) the similarity of the marks at issue;

"(3) the similarity of the products the marks represent;

"(4) the similarity of the parties' retail outlets and customers;

"(5) the nature of the parties' advertising;

"(6) the defendant's intent;

"(7) the extent of actual confusion.[49]

[ii]   *Mark Similarity.* The degree of the two marks' similarity is not the sole test for likely confusion[50] but is always an important factor.

---

[46] Id.

[47] Beer Nuts, Inc. v. Clover Club Foods Co., 711 F.2d 934, 221 U.S.P.Q. 209 (10th Cir. 1983). *See also* GTE Corp. v. Williams, 904 F.2d 536, 14 U.S.P.Q.2d 1971 (10th Cir. 1990). For a discussion of the Restatement, see § 5F[1].

[48] Beer Nuts, Inc. v. Clover Club Foods Co., 711 F.2d 934, 221 U.S.P.Q. 209 (10th Cir. 1983).

[49] *E.g.,* Wesco Manufacturing Inc. v. Tropical Attractions of Palm Beach Inc., 833 F.2d 1484, 1488 5 U.S.P.Q.2d 1190, 1193–94 (11th Cir. 1987).

See also Freedom Savings and Loan Association v. Way, 757 F.2d 1176, 1182, 226 U.S.P.Q. 123, 126 (11th Cir. 1985) ("Although these factors are not literally embodied in the statute, they direct the court's attention to the most pertinent facts.").

[50] *See, e.g.,* James Burrough Ltd. v. Sign of the Beefeater, Inc., 540 F.2d 266, 275, 192 U.S.P.Q. 555, 562 (7th Cir. 1976) (the issue is "not whether the public would confuse the

(1) *Sound, Sight and Meaning.* Following the Restatement,[51] the courts test mark similarity on three levels—sound, sight, and meaning. In *Beer Nuts,*[52] the Tenth Circuit discussed the Restatement mark similarity standard.

> "As set forth [in the Restatement], '[s]imilarity of the marks is tested on three levels: sight, sound, and meaning. . . . Each must be considered as [it] is encountered in the marketplace. Although similarity is measured by the marks as entities, similarities weigh more heavily than differences.' . . . 'It is not necessary for similarity to go only to the eye or the ear for there to be infringement. The use of a designation which causes confusion because it conveys the same idea, or stimulates the same mental reaction, or has the same meaning is enjoined on the same basis as where the similarity goes to the eye or the ear. Confusion of origin of goods may be caused alone by confusing similarity in the meaning of the designations employed. The whole background of the case must be considered.'

> "In evaluating similarity, '[i]t is axiomatic in trademark law that "side-by-side" comparison is not the test.' . . . The marks 'must be compared in the light of what occurs in the marketplace, not in the courtroom.' . . . 'A prospective purchaser does not ordinarily carry a sample or specimen of the article he knows well enough to call by its trade name, he necessarily depends upon the mental picture of that which symbolizes origin and ownership of the thing desired.' . . . Therefore, the court must determine whether the alleged infringing mark will be confusing to the public when singly presented."[53]

Similarity may reside in the two marks' pronunciation, especially when the goods or services in question are advertised or ordered orally.[54] In *G.D. Searle,*[55] the court

---

marks, but whether the viewer of an [allegedly infringing] mark would be likely to associate the product or service with which it is connected with the source or products or services with which an earlier mark is connected.").

[51] *See* § 5F[1].

[52] Beer Nuts, Inc. v. Clover Club Foods Co., 711 F.2d 934, 221 U.S.P.Q. 209 (10th Cir. 1983).

[53] 711 F.2d at 940-41, 221 U.S.P.Q. at 215-16.

[54] Restatement of Torts § 729 (1938) (Comment c.): "Similarity in pronunciation may exist despite difference in spelling or appearance. Or, such similarity may exist because the trade-mark or trade name is generally contracted by purchasers, so that, while in its full form it may differ from the designation in question, in its usual contracted form it may be similar."

See also AMF Inc. v. Sleekcraft Boats, 599 F.2d 341, 351, 204 U.S.P.Q. 808 (9th Cir. 1979) ("Sound is . . . important because reputation is often conveyed word-of-mouth."); Grotrian, Helfferich, Schulz, Th. Steinweg Nachf. v. Steinway & Sons, 523 F.2d 1331, 1340, 186 U.S.P.Q. 436 (2d Cir. 1975) ("Trademarks, like small children, are not only seen but heard. Similarity of sound also enters into the calculation of likelihood of confusion.").

[55] G.D. Searle & Co. v. Chas. Pfizer & Co., 265 F.2d 385, 121 U.S.P.Q. 74 (7th Cir. 1959), *cert. denied,* 361 U.S. 819 (1959); Beck & Co. v. Package Distributors of America, Inc., 198 U.S.P.Q. 573 (TTAB 1978) ("Ex Bier" is deceptively similar to "Beck's Beer." "While the marks . . . are distinctly different in significance and appearance, they are substantially similar in sound. In this regard, it has frequently been held that similarity in sound alone can lead to likelihood of confusion, particularly where the goods involved may be purchased by verbal order.").

held that "Bonamine" is confusing similar to "Dramamine:" "Slight differences in the sound of trademarks will not protect the infringer."

Similarity may reside in the verbal translation of a design mark (or in the pictorial representation of a verbal mark).[56] For example, in *Mobil Oil,*[57] the court found the defendant's word mark "PEGASUS" is similar to plaintiff's well-known "flying horse" symbol, which represents Pegasus, the winged horse of Greek mythology: "While we agree that words and their pictorial representations should not be equated as a matter of law, a district court may make such a determination as a factual matter."

Similarity may reside in the connotation or meaning of the two marks.[58] For example, in *Boston Athletic,*[59] the First Circuit held that defendant's three element logo—"MARATHON" with picture of runners and "Hopkinton-Boston"—is similar in meaning to plaintiff's mark "Boston Marathon" for the famous foot race from Hopkinton to Boston and for related apparel: "Meaning alone, without reference to appearance and sound, may be sufficiently close to constitute similarity."[60]

(2) Combination—Total Effect—Dissection. Trademarks often consist of combinations of words or of words and other symbols. The Restatement urges courts to assess marks' similarity on the basis of their total effect and to avoid dissecting marks for component-by-component comparison.[61] Often, two marks as a whole are dissimilar even though they contain similar or identical components. For example, in *Little Caesar Enterprises,*[62] the court found plaintiff's mark "LITTLE CAESAR'S" with a drawing of a toga-clad man eating a slice of pizza and defendant's

---

[56] Restatement of Torts § 729 (1938) (Comment d.): "When the trade-mark is a design or picture and the designation in question is a word, or vice versa, the similarity between the word and the verbal translation of the design or picture is to be considered. Thus a designation consisting of a picture of a camel might lead to confusion with the trademark-mark 'Camel' as readily as might the word 'Kamil.' "

[57] Mobil Oil Corporation v. Pegasus Petroleum Corp., 818 F.2d 254, 2 U.S.P.Q.2d 1677 (2d Cir. 1987).

[58] Restatement of Torts § 729 (1938) (Comment e.): "Some trade-marks may be remembered best by the suggestions they make to prospective purchasers. Similarity in suggestion as, for example, between 'Uneeda' and 'Uwanta,' is a factor to be considered."

See also Apple Computer, Inc. v. Formula International, Inc., 725 F.2d 521, 526, 221 U.S.P.Q. 762, 766 (9th Cir. 1984) ("PINEAPPLE" for computer kits is confusingly similar to "APPLE" for computers; "One of the possible effects of the use of the prefix may be to suggest that the computer kits are manufactured by licensees or subsidiaries of Apple.").

[59] Boston Athletic Ass'n v. Sullivan, 867 F.2d 22, 9 U.S.P.Q.2d 1690 (1st Cir. 1989).

[60] 867 F.2d at 29, 9 U.S.P.Q.2d at 1696.

[61] Restatement of Torts § 729 (1938) (Comment b.): "Similarity of appearance is determined on the basis of the total effect of the designation, rather than on a comparison of individual features. While individual features may be dissimilar, the total effect may be one of similarity. Or. the total effect may appear dissimilar despite similarities in individual features."

See also Mutual of Omaha Insurance Co. v. Novak, 836 F.2d 397, 399, 5 U.S.P.Q.2d 1314, 1316 (8th Cir. 1987) ("The similarity of appearance is to be determined by looking at the total effect of the designation, rather than by comparing individual features.").

[62] Little Caesar Enterprises Inc. v. Pizza Caesar Inc., 834 F.2d 568, 4 U.S.P.Q.2d 1942 (6th Cir. 1987).

mark "PIZZA CAESAR USA," sometimes accompanied by a drawing of a character in a horse-drawn chariot carrying a slice of pizza, even though both marks used "Caesar," did not make confusion likely.[63]

The general standard is the total effect, but some court decisions give less weight to some components,[64] for example, by eliminating common descriptive components to determine a mark's relative strength and the degree of similarity between it and another mark.[65] In *Henri's Food Products*,[66] the court found "YOGOWHIP" not similar to "MIRACLE WHIP" even though both marks were for similar goods: "[I]f one word or feature of a composite trademark is the salient portion of the mark, it may be given greater weight than the surrounding elements. . . . When one portion

---

[63] *See also* Pignons S.A. de Mecanique de Precision v. Polaroid Corp., 657 F.2d 482, 487, 212 U.S.P.Q. 246 (1st Cir. 1981) (plaintiff, which used the mark "Alpa" for cameras, charged defendant Polaroid was trademark infringement by use of "Polaroid SX-70 Land Camera Alpha 1."; HELD: the district court did not err in granting summary judgment that there was no likelihood of confusion; "in certain circumstances otherwise similar marks are not likely to be confused where used in conjunction with the clearly displayed name and/or logo of the manufacturer.").

[64] *E.g.*, American Cyanamid Corp. v. Connaught Laboratories, Inc., 800 F.2d 306, 309, 231 U.S.P.Q. 128, 130 (2d Cir. 1986) ("HibVAX" does not infringe HIB-IMUNE because suffix dissimilarity suffices to offset prefix identity).

[65] *Compare* Solventol Chemical Products v. Langfield, 134 F.2d 899, 903, 57 U.S.P.Q. 210, 214 (6th Cir. 1943), *cert. denied*, 320 U.S. 743, 59 U.S.P.Q. 495 (1943) (no likelihood of confusion between "SOLVENTOL" and "SOLVITE"; "solvent" and "sol" must be deleted as descriptive of the product; "The suffixes 'vite' and 'tol' distinguish one combination from the other and give an identifying character to the trade designation which makes it unlikely that one trade-mark could, with the exercise of ordinary care, be mistaken for or be confused with the other.") *with* Induct-O-Matic Corp. v. Inductotherm Corp., 747 F.2d 358, 363-64, 224 U.S.P.Q. 119, 122-23 (6th Cir. 1984) (likelihood of confusion between "INDUCTO" and "INDUCT-O-MATIC"; "The dominant common component in each mark . . . is 'induct.' . . . [T]his word has a known meaning, to lead, introduce or induce. . . . [T]his term is a suggestive one in that it suggests to the imaginative that each company is engaged in the electromagnetic induction field . . . [The letter] 'o' is a descriptive vowel common to 'IN-DUCTO' and 'INDUCT-O-MATIC' and must therefore be deleted . . . [O]nly the term 'matic' distinguishes the two marks. 'Matic' is clearly a descriptive phrase, and . . . indicates automation. As such, it also requires deletion. Accordingly, . . . there is no 'identifying character to the trade designations' . . . other than the suggestive term common to both, 'induct,' that makes it unlikely that one trademark will be mistaken for another.").

Cf. Banff Ltd. v. Federated Department Stores, 841 F.2d 486, 6 U.S.P.Q.2d 1187, 1191 (2d Cir. 1988) ("marks should be compared as composites for the purpose of determining the strength of the senior user's mark. The long-standing view that the nongeneric components of a mark must be compared in the context of the overall composite mark, . . . remains the rule in this Circuit."); John H. Harland Co. v. Clarke Checks, Inc., 711 F.2d 966, 976, 219 U.S.P.Q. 515, 524 (11th Cir. 1983) ("although the marks ultimately must be considered as a whole, the focus of the inquiry regarding appearance and sound is on the nongeneric portion"; there are "some similarities in the overall commercial impression" between plaintiff's "Memory Stub" mark and defendant's "Entry Stub" mark, both for desk-style check books; similarity enhanced by "the manner in which the marks are used.").

[66] Henri's Food Products Co. v. Kraft, Inc., 717 F.2d 352, 220 U.S.P.Q. 386 (7th Cir. 1983).

of a composite mark is a descriptive or generic word, that feature of the mark may be of less significance in designating a source of origin."

Two verbal marks may be dissimilar when used as part of a design logo or in connection with a party's name or other distinct indication of origin.[67] Similarity may nevertheless be found if the verbal marks are commonly used apart from the logo or name.[68]

(3)   *Mark Families.* In *J & J Snack Foods,*[69] the court found confusion likely between J & J's "McPretzel" mark for frozen soft pretzels and franchise giant McDonald's family of "Mc" marks, including "McDONUT," "McPizza," "McMuffin," "McCHICKEN," and "McRIB."[70]

> "A family of marks is a group of marks having a recognizable common characteristic, wherein the marks are composed and used in such a way that the public associates not only the individual marks, but the common characteristic of the family, with the trademark owner. Simply using a series of similar marks does not of itself establish the existence of a family. There must be a recognition among the purchasing public that the common characteristic is indicative of a common origin of the goods. For example, in *AMF, Inc. v. American Leisure Products, Inc.,* 474 F.2d 1403, 1406, 177 U.S.P.Q. 268, 270 (CCPA 1973) the court held that AMF had established a family of marks of 'fish' names for sailboats, based on advertising, use, and distinctiveness of the names. In *Motorola, Inc. v. Griffiths Electronics, Inc.,* 317 F.2d 397, 399, 137 U.S.P.Q. 551, 553, 50 C.C.P.A. 1518 (CCPA 1963) it was held that the use and advertisement of the marks GOLDEN VOICE, GOLDEN BEAM, GOLDEN VIEW, and

---

[67] *E.g.,* Ziebart International Corp. v. Aftermarket Associates, Inc., 802 F.2d 220, 226, 231 U.S.P.Q. 119, 124 (7th Cir. 1986) ("Prominent display of different names on the marks has been held to reduce the likelihood of confusion even where . . . the marks are otherwise similar."). *Cf.* Fuddruckers Inc. v. Doc's B.R. Others Inc., 826 F.2d 837, 846 n.13, 4 U.S.P.Q.2d 1026, 1033 n.13 (9th Cir. 1987) ("Use of differing names or distinctive logos in connection with similar marks can reduce the likelihood of confusion but doesn't always do so.").

Compare John H. Harland Co. v. Clarke Checks, Inc., 711 F.2d 966, 976 n.15, 219 U.S.P.Q. 515, 524 n.15 (11th Cir. 1983) ("The fact that the names of the parties appear in small print on the [goods] does not preclude a finding that there is a substantial similarity.").

[68] *E.g.,* Accuride International Inc. v. Accuride Corp., 871 F.2d 1531, 10 U.S.P.Q.2d 1589 (9th Cir. 1989) (district court erred in finding that the marks were not similar because of their differing stylized versions; the stylized versions do not appear in oral communications, newspaper typeface, etc.); AMF Inc. v. Sleekcraft Boats, 599 F.2d 341, 351, 204 U.S.P.Q. 808 (9th Cir. 1979) (SLEEKCRAFT is confusingly similar to SLICKCRAFT when both are used for boats; "the names appear dissimilar when viewed in conjunction with the logo, but the logo is often absent.").

[69] J & J Snack Foods Corp. v. McDonald's Corp., 932 F.2d 1460, 18 U.S.P.Q.2d 1889 (Fed. Cir. 1991).

[70] For more McCases, see Quality Inns International, Inc. v. McDonald's Corp., 695 F. Supp. 198, 8 U.S.P.Q.2d 1633 (D. Md. 1988) (defendant's "McSleep Inn" infringes; noting that "McDonald's created a language that it called McLanguage . . . "); McDonald's Corp. v. McBagel's Inc., 649 F. Supp. 1268, 1 U.S.P.Q.2d 1761 (S.D. N.Y. 1986) (Ken McShea's "McBagel's" bagels mcfringe McDonald's mcmark family; noting that "a news article about this very case was entitled 'McDonald's McMakes Trouble for McBagels.' ").

several other 'golden' marks, together with the primary mark MOTOROLA, established a pattern of use and recognition of a family of marks in which 'golden' is a dominant feature. In *International Diagnostics Technology, Inc. v. Miles Laboratories, Inc.*, 746 F.2d 798, 800, 223 U.S.P.Q. 977, 978 (Fed.Cir.1984) this court observed that millions of dollars in advertising contributed to recognition of the family of STIX marks.

"Recognition of the family is achieved when the pattern of usage of the common element is sufficient to be indicative of the origin of the family. It is thus necessary to consider the use, advertisement, and distinctiveness of the marks, including assessment of the contribution of the common feature to the recognition of the marks as of common origin. McDonald's showed extensive usage and promotion of various marks using the "Mc" formative, in association with the McDON-ALD'S mark, in advertising and at McDonald's restaurants. McDonald's showed that in 1987 it operated 7,600 outlets in the United States with sales of over $14 billion; that it engaged in extensive nationwide advertising, spending $405 million in 1987; that its current menu is diverse; and that two of its restaurants have sold pretzels."[71]

J & J argued that "a trademark owner must own trademark rights to the formative itself, . . . to establish rights to a family based on that formative," pointing out that "the 'Mc' mark, standing alone, is registered by McCormick & Company for use with species." The court disagreed.

"In *Colony Foods, Inc. v. Sagemark, Ltd.*, 735 F.2d 1336, 222 U.S.P.Q. 185 (Fed. Cir.1984), the court held that Colony Foods had not established a pattern of use sufficient to support public recognition of a family of restaurant marks incorporating the word 'hobo', although Colony Foods had more than one such mark. . . . While the court pointed out that Colony Foods did not have trademark rights in 'hobo' per se, the court did not hold that Colony Foods could not have a family of 'hobo' marks unless it did."[72]

---

[71] 932 F.2d at 1462-63, 18 U.S.P.Q.2d at 1891-92. Only 2? Out of 7600?

See also Spraying Systems Co. v. Delavan, Inc., 762 F. Supp. 772, 780 n.8, 19 U.S.P.Q.2d 1121, 1127 n.8 (N.D. Ill. 1991) ("It is still necessary to prove that the 'family' feature is arbitrary and distinctive, not just descriptive or highly suggestive or commonly used in the trade. . . ."); McDonald's Corp. v. McBagel's Inc., 649 F. Supp. 1268, 1272, 1 U.S.P.Q.2d 1761, 1763 (S.D. N.Y. 1986) ("The existence *vel non* of a family of marks is a question of fact based on the distinctiveness of the common formative component and other factors, including the extent of the family's use, advertising, promotion, and its inclusion in a number of registered and unregistered marks owned by a single party.").

[72] 932 F.2d at 1463, 18 U.S.P.Q.2d at 1892.

Compare Creamettee Co. v. Merlino, 299 F.2d 55 (9th Cir. 1962) (no confusion between defendant's "Majorette" macaroni products and plaintiff's "Creamette" or "ette" marks). In *Creamette*, the court questioned whether plaintiff "could ever, even by registering many marks ending in 'ette' or 'ettes' or 'et' and actively promoting all of them, acquire the exclusive use of the suffix for macaroni products."

"We find nothing in the Lanham Act, which speaks throughout in terms of 'a trademark' or 'a mark' . . . , and little in the authorities, to support Creamette's contentions. Here, it has made substantial use of only two of its many marks—'Creamettes' and 'Creamette'. To a much smaller extent, it has used 'Juniorettes', and to an even lesser

[iii]   *Mark Strength.* "Strong" marks get broader protection than "weak" ones.[73]

The Restatement of Torts recognized that some marks are more equal than others because their high degree of distinctiveness makes them "more effective in sales stimulation."[74] Ralph Lauren's polo symbol on shirts is a strong mark;[75] "Plus" for vitamins is a weak mark.[76]

In *Amstar,*[77] the court found senior user's "widely known" "DOMINO" for sugar and plaintiff's "DOMINO'S" for pizza did not make confusion likely, relying heavily on domino's relative weakness.

---

extent, 'Spagh-Ettes'. The actual use of the other marks is so minimal, and some of it so recent, as to make it clear that, at this stage, they cannot have achieved any significance whatever to the buying public. Nor does the registration of 'ettes' as a trade-mark strengthen Creamette's position. As a separate word, 'ettes' has an entirely different appearance and meaning from any of the registered words of which it is a part.

. . .

"Some cases squint at the possibility of acquiring rights in a 'family' of marks, but none has upheld such a claim under circumstances even remotely resembling those of this case. . . . The suffix 'ettes' (or 'et' or 'ette') is so widely used for a variety of products, and is capable of being used with such an infinite variety of wholly dissimilar words, that we doubt if it could ever be exclusively appropriated as the distinguishing feature of a 'family' of marks to be used on any line of goods." 299 F.2d at 58-59.

[73] This is analogous to the copyright and patent law concepts that more original works and pioneer inventions are entitled to a broader scope of protection. *See* §§ 2F[2][b][v] and 4F[2][a][iv].

[74] Restatement of Torts § 729 (1938) (Comment g.): "[W]hen the trade-mark is an important stimulant to the sale of the goods upon which it is affixed, less similarity may lead to confusion than when the trade-mark is not such a stimulant. Not all trade-marks are equally effective in sales stimulation. Some are effective because they are unique, as, for example, Kodak; others are less effective because common, as, for example, Simplex or Blue Ribbon. The greater the number of identical or more or less similar trade-marks already in use on different kinds of goods, the less the likelihood of confusion. . . . "

[75] *See* Polo Fashions Inc. v. Craftex Inc., 816 F.2d 145, 148, 2 U.S.P.Q.2d 1444, 1445 (4th Cir. 1987) ("The plaintiff's symbol, standing alone, is a strong mark of the identity of the source. . . . It has been widely use by plaintiff and . . . has not infrequently been imitated. The strength of the mark is the 'first and paramount factor' in assessing the likelihood of confusion. . . . Where, as here, one produces counterfeit goods in an apparent attempt to capitalize upon the popularity of, and demand for, another's product, there is a presumption of a likelihood of confusion.").

See also Mobil Oil Corporation v. Pegasus Petroleum Corp., 818 F.2d 254, 257, 2 U.S.P.Q.2d 1677, 1680 (2d Cir. 1987) ("The unparalleled strength of Mobil's [flying horse design] mark demands that it be given broad protection against infringers.").

[76] Plus Products v. Plus Discount Foods, Inc., 722 F.2d 999, 222 U.S.P.Q. 373 (2d Cir. 1983):
"The term PLUS is an everyday word that indicates something added, and when applied to goods, it merely implies additional quantity or quality. . . . [T]hird-party use of the word PLUS is extensive. Since 1970 Products has discovered over 130 different uses of marks that include the word PLUS, suggesting generic character.

". . . [T]he weaker the mark the less likely it is that consumers will view it as an indication of origin. . . . When a mark as weak as that of Products' PLUS—comprised of an undistinctive word and coexisting with extensive third-party usage—it is extremely unlikely that prudent consumers will confuse it with similar marks on non-competitive goods." 722 F.2d at 1005, 222 U.S.P.Q. at 378.

[77] Amstar Corp. v. Domino's Pizza, Inc., 615 F.2d 252, 205 U.S.P.Q. 969 (5th Cir. 1980).

" 'Domino,' . . . is . . . the surname of a good number of people, as a glance at a local telephone directory can verify. The word is a common English name for a game, a hooded costume, a type of mask, and a theory of political expansion. Thus, 'Domino' is not a coined word, is not purely fanciful, and while its application to sugar may be arbitrary, [Fn. 8: At one time, 'Domino' as applied to plaintiff's sugar was descriptive, not arbitrary. There is evidence that, near the turn of the century, plaintiff sold domino-shaped pieces of hard sugar in half bales.], it is still not to be accorded the same degree of protection given such coined and fanciful terms as 'Kodak' or 'Xerox.' *Armstrong Cork Co. v. World Carpets, Inc.*, 597 F.2d 496, 505 (5th Cir. 1979) (wide use of mark 'World' results in little likelihood of confusion); *Holiday Inns, Inc. v. Holiday Out in America*, 481 F.2d 445, 448 (5th Cir. 1973) (common word 'Holiday' is of weak trademark significance); *El Chico, Inc. v. El Chico Cafe*, 214 F.2d 721, 725 (5th Cir. 1954) (27 trademark registrations of 'El Chico,' along with fact it was the name of a Moorish king of Granada in 1482, and is the name of a Mexican town and a river in the Philippines, make the term a weak trade name deserving limited protection)."[78]

Courts consider two criteria in assessing mark strength. The first is the mark's placement in the traditional four category distinctiveness scale: arbitrary and fanciful marks, suggestive marks, descriptive marks, and generic marks.[79] Suggestive marks are weak; arbitrary and fanciful marks are strong. Descriptive marks are strong only if a showing of substantial secondary meaning is made. Applying the categorization criterion duplicates the protectability and registrability distinctiveness requirement.[80] A mark's categorization often has little relevance to its marketplace impact.[81]

---

[78] 615 F.2d at 260.

[79] *See* § 5C[3].

[80] Some decisions confuse the distinctiveness question and the question of a mark's strength in the marketplace to the point of conclusively presuming that a mark that has achieved incontestable status is strong. Wynn Oil Co. v. Thomas, 839 F.2d 1183, 1187, 5 U.S.P.Q.2d 1944, 1947 (6th Cir. 1988) (district court erred in finding that the mark in question was "merely a descriptive term" deserving "little, if any protection. " "Permitting [the accused infringer] to relitigate the original strength or weakness of the mark runs afoul of *Park 'N Fly's* requirement that courts give full effect to incontestable trademarks. . . . [O]nce a mark has been registered for five years, the mark must be considered strong and worthy of full protection.").

Compare M-F-G Corp. v. EMRA Corp., 817 F.2d 410, 411, 2 U.S.P.Q.2d 1538, 1539 (7th Cir. 1987) (plaintiff's right to use its mark "SUPERCUT" for shears had become incontestable under the Lanham Act and it sought relief against defendant's use of "SUPERCUTS" for haircutting salons; "Incontestability does not help; Supercut is incontestable only for shears.").

[81] *E.g.*, Homeowners Group, Inc. v. Home Marketing Specialists, Inc., 931 F.2d 1100, 1107, 18 U.S.P.Q.2d 1587, 1593 (6th Cir. 1991) (a mark "may indeed be arbitrary and hence inherently distinctive, yet have little customer recognition or 'strength' in the market, or perhaps have high recognition which is limited to a particular product or market segment."); Plus Products v. Plus Discount Foods, Inc., 722 F.2d 999, 222 U.S.P.Q. 373, 378 (2d Cir. 1983) ("To assess the strength of a mark, trademarks are generally categorized, in ascending degree of distinctiveness, as generic, descriptive, suggestive or arbitrary. Although this classification system is a helpful tool in conceptualizing this somewhat amorphous subject, it is not determinative, for the strength of a mark 'depends ultimately on its distinctiveness or its "origin-indicating" quality in the eyes of the purchasing public.' ").

The second criterion is relative marketplace distinctiveness as determined by factors such as third party similar mark usage and advertising and consumer recognition.[82]

Decisions vary as to the weight given to the two criteria.[83]

[iv]   *Similarity of the Goods or Services—Likelihood of "Bridging the Gap."* Historically, trademark rights expanded from protection only against use on competing goods to protection against uses on noncompeting goods that create a a likelihood

---

[82] *See, e.g.,* Boston Athletic Ass'n v. Sullivan, 867 F.2d 22, 32, 9 U.S.P.Q.2d 1690, 1698 (1st Cir. 1989) ("We have found the following factors useful in determining a trademark's relative strength: the length of time a mark has been used and the plaintiff's relative renown in its field . . . ; the strength of the mark in plaintiff's field of business, especially by looking at the number of similar registered marks . . . ; and the plaintiff's actions in promoting its mark."); Accuride International Inc. v. Accuride Corp., 871 F.2d 1531, 1536, 10 U.S.P.Q.2d 1589, 1593 (9th Cir. 1989) ("A descriptive or suggestive mark may be strengthened by such factors as extensive advertising, length of exclusive use, public recognition and uniqueness.").

Compare Homeowners Group, Inc. v. Home Marketing Specialists,, Inc., 931 F.2d 1100, 1108, 18 U.S.P.Q.2d 1587, 1593 (6th Cir. 1991) ("merely showing the existence of marks in the records of the Patent and Trademark Office will not materially affect the distinctiveness of another's mark which is actively used in commerce. In order to be accorded weight a defendant must show what actually happens in the marketplace."); McGraw-Edison Co. v. Walt Disney Productions, 787 F.2d 1163, 1171, 229 U.S.P.Q. 355, 361 (7th Cir. 1986) ("the third party registrations of trademarks similar to [plaintiff's mark] are material in determining the strength of the . . . mark only to the extent that the similar marks are promoted by their owners or recognized by the consuming public.").

[83] *See, e.g.,* Western Publishing Co., Inc. v. Rose Art Industries, Inc., 910 F.2d 57, 61, 15 U.S.P.Q.2d 1545, 1548 (2d Cir. 1990) ("Golden" for children's books and educational toys: "regardless of the . . . 'pigeonhole' into which the 'Golden' mark is placed, the origin-indicating quality of the mark is undercut by other parties' registration of over 2,000 trademarks incorporating the term 'Golden'—113 of which are registered in the toy, game and paper products fields."); Century 21 Real Estate Corp. v. Sandlin, 846 F.2d 1175, 1179, 6 U.S.P.Q.2d 2034, 2036 (9th Cir. 1988) ("'A "strong" mark is one which is used only in a "fictitious, arbitrary and fanciful manner," whereas a "weak" mark is a mark that is a meaningful word in common usage, or is merely a suggestive or descriptive trademark.' . . . Marks may be strengthened by extensive advertising length of time in business, public recognition, and uniqueness."); Charles of the Ritz Group Ltd. v. Quality King Distributors Inc., 832 F.2d 1317, 1321, 4 U.S.P.Q.2d 1778, 1781 (2d Cir. 1987) (strength of mark refers to "its tendency to identify the goods sold under the mark as emanating from a particular, although possibly anonymous, source."; "Opium" for perfume "is a strong mark both by definition and when placed in its market context."; the mark is arbitrary and the commercial success of the product reinforces its strength.); Nutri/System Inc. v. Con-Stan Industries Inc., 809 F.2d 601, 605, 1 U.S.P.Q.2d 1809, 1811 (9th Cir. 1987) ("Nutri" for dieting programs or health products is a weak mark; "In general, the more unique or arbitrary a mark, the more protection a court will afford it. . . . While consumer recognition of a mark may increase the amount of protection afforded it, . . . it does not mean the mark becomes arbitrary. . . . Advertising remains only one of many factors taken into account when classifying the strength of marks."); John H. Harland Co. v. Clarke Checks, Inc., 711 F.2d 966, 975, 219 U.S.P.Q. 515, 523 (11th Cir. 1983) (considering both extent of third party usage and classification of the mark; "while the fact that [the plaintiff's mark] and similar marks have not been used by other parties normally might indicate that [the plaintiff's mark] is strong, this indication is significantly weakened by the suggestive or possibly even descriptive nature of the . . . mark.").

of confusion.[84] Under current standards, courts treat goods-services similarity as one confusion likelihood factor.[85] There is a sliding scale—the more similar the goods, the less similar the marks must be, and vice versa.[86]

The courts consider goods-services relatedness in terms of function and use and the likelihood that the senior user may "bridge the gap" by introducing products or services similar or identical to those of the accused infringer.[87]

[v] *Channels of Trade and Advertising.* In assessing likelihood of confusion, the courts consider to what extent the trademark owner's and accused infringer's goods or services are distributed through the same trade channels and advertised in the same media.[88]

---

[84] *See* § 5E[3].

[85] *See e.g.,* Freedom Savings and Loan Association v. Way, 757 F.2d 1176, 1184, 226 U.S.P.Q. 123, 126 (11th Cir. 1985) ("real estate sales and real estate finance are highly complementary services").

Compare Life Technologies Inc. v. Gibbco Scientific Inc., 826 F.2d 775, 776, 3 U.S.P.Q.2d 1795, 1796 (8th Cir. 1987) ("The fact that two products are used together does not mean that they are in competition, especially where . . . the products perform different functions."); Pignons S.A. de Mecanique de Precision v. Polaroid Corp., 657 F.2d 482, 212 U.S.P.Q. 246 (1st Cir. 1981) (goods of plaintiff and defendant are cameras but differ in that plaintiff's is much more expensive and, unlike defendant's camera, is not a fixed lens "instant" camera); Amstar Corp. v. Domino's Pizza, Inc., 615 F.2d 252, 205 U.S.P.Q. 969, 977 (5th Cir. 1980) (little similarity between defendant's pizza and plaintiff's sugar), quoting California Fruit Growers Exchange v. Sunkist Baking Co., 166 F.2d 971, 973, 76 U.S.P.Q. 85, 86-87 (7th Cir. 1947) ("About the only things they have in common are that they are edible.").

[86] *See* Restatement of Torts § 729 (1938) (Comment g.): "When the goods on which the allegedly infringing designation is used are of the same kind as those upon which the trade-mark is used, less similarity may lead to confusion than when the goods are of a quite different kind, though not so different as to be beyond the zone in which the interest in the trade-mark is protected . . . Such is also the case when the two types of goods are related in their ultimate use."

See also AMF Inc. v. Sleekcraft Boats, 599 F.2d 341, 350, 204 U.S.P.Q. 808, 815 (9th Cir. 1979) (a diminished standard of similarity of marks ("SLICKCRAFT" v. "SLEEKCRAFT") applies when the goods of the parties are related though not competing (general recreation boats v. speed boats); "less similarity between the marks will suffice when the goods are complementary, . . . the products are sold to the same class of purchasers, . . . or the goods are similar in use and function.").

[87] *E.g.,* AMF Inc. v. Sleekcraft Boats, 599 F.2d 341, 354, 204 U.S.P.Q. 808 (9th Cir. 1979) ("Inasmuch as a trademark owner is afforded greater protection against competing goods, a 'strong possibility' that either party may expand his business to compete with the other will weigh in favor of finding that the present use is infringing."; likelihood of confusion between plaintiff's "SLICKCRAFT" recreational boats and defendant's "SLEEKCRAFT" racing boats because, *inter alia* both parties are expanding their model lines).

[88] *E.g.,* Accuride International Inc. v. Accuride Corp., 871 F.2d 1531, 1537, 10 U.S.P.Q.2d 1589, 1594 (9th Cir. 1989) ("The parties do not attend the same trade shows, and their products are not sold by the same retailers or displayed in adjacent areas."); Charles of the Ritz Group Ltd. v. Quality King Distributors Inc., 832 F.2d 1317, 4 U.S.P.Q.2d 1778, 1782 (2d Cir. 1987) (although plaintiff's "Opium" perfume is in displays and must be asked for by name and defendant's "Omni" perfume is on the counter, both are sold in the same stores;

In *American Cyanamid*,[89] the existence of a common channel of trade was important to a finding of likelihood of confusion. Plaintiff used "MATERNA" for vitamin and mineral preparations for pregnant women and new mothers available by prescription only; defendant used "MATERNITA" and "MATERNA" for cosmetics. The court noted that both products "are available in pharmacies and are marketed to the same class of consumers—high income pregnant women and new mothers."[90] In *Amstar*,[91] the disparity in advertising and classes of customers was a factor leading to a conclusion of no confusion between plaintiff's "DOMINO" for sugar, which was sold in grocery stores for home use, and defendant's "DOMINO'S" pizza.

> "Defendants' advertising program is geared to seek out and exploit a highly localized and rather specialized class of consumers. Defendants have not sought to undermine the good will established by plaintiff. In short, hardly anyone would confuse a 'Domino' sugar ad with a 'Domino's Pizza' sales pitch, nor would they likely believe the two advertisements emanated from the same source, considering the significant differences between the advertisements in message content and presentation."[92]

[iv] *Consumer Sophistication and Care—Cost.* Courts consider consumer sophistication and goods' or services' costs as factors in assessing likelihood of confusion.[93]

"Given this proximity, differences in methods of display do not eliminate 'the likelihood that customers may be confused as to the *source* of the products, rather than as to the products themselves.' ").

[89] American Cyanamid Co. v. Campagna per le Farmacie in Italia S.P.A., 847 F.2d 53, 6 U.S.P.Q.2d 1948 (2d Cir. 1988).

[90] *Compare* Life Technologies Inc. v. Gibbco Scientific Inc., 826 F.2d 775, 776, 3 U.S.P.Q.2d 1795, 1796 (8th Cir. 1987) ("GIBCO" for tissue culture media and "GIBBCO" hospital laboratory instruments; "Although they share many common customers, [the parties] supply different products to them and in all but the smallest laboratories these products are used in physically separate facilities.").

[91] Amstar Corp. v. Domino's Pizza, Inc., 615 F.2d 252, 205 U.S.P.Q. 969 (5th Cir. 1980), *cert. denied*, 449 U.S. 899 (1980).

[92] 615 F.2d at 262, 205 U.S.P.Q. at 978.

[93] Restatement of Torts § 729 (1938) (Comment g.): "If the goods are bought by purchasers who exercise considerable attention and inspect fairly closely, the likelihood of confusion is smaller than when the goods are bought by purchasers who make little or no inspection.").

See also Homeowners Group, Inc. v. Home Marketing Specialists,, Inc., 931 F.2d 1100, 1111, 18 U.S.P.Q.2d 1587, 1595-96 (6th Cir. 1991) ("Generally, in assessing the likelihood of confusion to the public, the standard used by the courts is the typical buyer exercising ordinary caution. However, when a buyer has expertise or is otherwise more sophisticated with respect to the purchase of the services at issue, a higher standard is proper. Similarly, when services are expensive or unusual, the buyer can be expected to exercise greater care in her purchases. When services are sold to such buyers, other things being equal, there is less likelihood of confusion."); Ford Motor Co. v. Summitt Motor Products, Inc., 930 F.2d 277, 293, 18 U.S.P.Q.2d 1417, 1431 (3d Cir. 1991) ("when a buyer class is mixed, the standard of care to be exercised by the reasonably prudent purchaser will be equal to that of the least sophisticated consumer in the class.").

In *Pignons,*[94] the court found confusion not likely, relying, in part, on the fact that plaintiff's cameras were high-quality, sophisticated equipment. The defendant's cameras were less expensive and more widely distributed. Connoisseurs of plaintiff's fine photographic hardware might, in a moment of weakness, while in a specialty camera store, purchase one of defendant's "convenient" instant cameras, but would not likely be confused about their acquisition's origin: "Courts have found less likelihood of confusion where goods are expensive and purchased after careful consideration. . . . Sophisticated consumers may be expected to exercise greater care."[95] Similarly, in *Fisher Stoves,*[96] the court noted: "In the case of a relatively high-priced single purchase article . . . 'there is hardly likelihood of confusion or palming off when the name of the manufacturer is clearly displayed.'"

The sophistication-expense factor is not conclusive; other factors may dictate a likelihood of confusion conclusion even though the customers are sophisticated, the goods or services expensive, or both;[97] similarly, other factors may dictate the opposite conclusion even though the customers are unsophisticated.[98]

[vii] *Actual Confusion—Surveys.* A court need not find actual consumer or user confusion to uphold a trademark infringement charge—only a "likelihood," something

---

[94] Pignons S.A. de Mecanique de Precision v. Polaroid Corp., 657 F.2d 482, 489, 212 U.S.P.Q. 246, 252 (1st Cir. 1981).

[95] *See also* Accuride International Inc. v. Accuride Corp., 871 F.2d 1531, 1537, 10 U.S.P.Q.2d 1589, 1594 (9th Cir. 1989) (90% of defendant's products are purchased by 15 salespeople; plaintiff's products are marketed by twenty technically-trained personnel; "the purchasers of the parties' goods are highly specialized professional purchasers who would be expected to exercise a high degree of care in making their purchase decisions.").

[96] Fisher Stoves, Inc. v. All Nighter Stove Works, Inc., 626 F.2d 193, 206 U.S.P.Q. 961 (1st Cir. 1980), quoting Bose Corp. v. Linear Design Labs, Inc., 467 F.2d 304, 310, 175 U.S.P.Q. 285, 389-90 (2d Cir. 1972).

See also Sno-Wizard Manufacturing, Inc. v. Eisemann Products Co., 791 F.2d 423, 429, 230 U.S.P.Q. 118, 122 (5th Cir. 1986) "the labeling of a product will not always negate a likelihood of confusion," but under the facts of the case, the label clearly distinguished defendant's goods from those of plaintiff).

[97] *E.g.,* Fuji Photo Film Co., Inc. v. Shinohara Shoji Kabushiki Kaisha, 754 F.2d 591, 595-96 225 U.S.P.Q. 540, 542 (5th Cir. 1985) ("expertise in the field of trademarks cannot be inferred from expertise in another area. . . . It is true that in most instances technicians would use the products of either party and they are a discriminating group of people but that does not eliminate the likelihood of purchaser confusion here. Being skilled in their own art does not necessarily preclude their mistaking one trademark for another when the marks are similar as those here in issue, and cover merchandise in the same general field."); Charles of the Ritz Group Ltd. v. Quality King Distributors Inc., 832 F.2d 1317, 1323, 4 U.S.P.Q.2d 1778, 1783 (2d Cir. 1987) ("While the sophistication of perfume buyers and the wide disparity in quality and price mitigate against any consumer confusion, the other factors overwhelmingly override these concerns."); Mobil Oil Corporation v. Pegasus Petroleum Corp., 818 F.2d 254, 259, 2 U.S.P.Q.2d 1677, 1682 (2d Cir. 1987) (likelihood of confusion despite sophistication of customers and scale of transactions (oil trading); "the probability that potential purchasers would be misled into an initial interest" may work "a sufficient trademark injury.").

[98] *E.g.,* Western Publishing Co., Inc. v. Rose Art Industries, Inc., 910 F.2d 57, 63, 15 U.S.P.Q.2d 1545, 1550 (2d Cir. 1990) (buyers are unsophisticated but "the complete lack of evidence of actual confusion militates against according this factor much weight.").

more than a "mere possibility," need be established,[99] but a substantial showing of actual confusion is, not surprisingly, strong evidence that confusion is likely.[100] If there is no evidence of actual confusion after the marks are used concurrently for a lengthy period, a court is likely to conclude that confusion is not likely.[101]

A trademark owner may establish actual confusion in two ways. The first way is through direct testimony of confused customers or evidence of misdirected communications, such as orders, complaint letters and warranty or repair work requests sent to the wrong party.[102] In *AmBRIT*,[103] the court relied on actual confusion evidence to support its conclusion of likelihood of confusion.

---

[99] *Cf.* WSM Inc. v. Hilton, 724 F.2d 1320, 1329, 221 U.S.P.Q.2d 410, 417 (8th Cir. 1984) ("Actual confusion is not essential to a finding of infringement; however, a mere possibility is not enough. There must be a substantial likelihood that the public will be confused.").

[100] *E.g.,* World Carpets, Inc. v. Dick Littrell's New World Carpets, 438 F.2d 482, 489, 168 U.S.P.Q. 609, 614 (5th Cir. 1971) ("there can be no more positive or substantial proof of the likelihood of confusion than proof of actual confusion. Moreover, reason tells us that while very little proof of actual confusion would be necessary to prove the likelihood of confusion, an almost overwhelming amount of proof would be necessary to refute such proof.").

[101] *E.g.,* Oreck Corp. v. U.S. Floor Systems, Inc., 803 F.2d 166, 174, 231 U.S.P.Q. 634, 639 (5th Cir. 1986), *cert. denied*, 481 U.S. 1069 (1987) ("In light of the concurrent use of the STEAMEX DELUXE 15 XL name and Oreck's XL mark for seventeen months, Oreck's inability to point to a single incident of actual confusion is highly significant."); Plus Products v. Plus Discount Foods, Inc., 722 F.2d 999, 1006, 222 U.S.P.Q. 373, 379 (2d Cir. 1983) ("While we recognize that it is difficult to establish actual confusion on the part of retail customers, . . . no evidence of confusion for over a three-year period, during which substantial sales occurred, is a strong indicator that the likelihood of confusion is minimal."); Amstar Corp. v. Domino's Pizza, Inc., 615 F.2d 252, 263, 205 U.S.P.Q. 969 (5th Cir. 1980), *cert. denied*, 449 U.S. 899 (1980) ("the fact that only three instances of actual confusion were found after nearly 15 years of extensive concurrent sales under the parties' respective marks raises a presumption against likelihood of confusion in the future.").

Compare Wynn Oil Co. v. Thomas, 839 F.2d 1183, 1188, 5 U.S.P.Q.2d 1944, 1948 (6th Cir. 1988) (lack of evidence of actual confusion is not a significant factor); Levi Strauss & Co. v. Blue Bell, Inc., 778 F.2d 1352, 1360 n.10, 228 U.S.P.Q. 346, 352 n.10 (9th Cir. 1985) (en banc) ("The absence of evidence of actual confusion need not give rise to an inference of no likelihood of confusion."); AMF Inc. v. Sleekcraft Boats, 599 F.2d 341, 204 U.S.P.Q. 808, 818 (9th Cir. 1979) ("Because of the difficulty in garnering such evidence, the failure to prove instances of actual confusion is not dispositive. . . . Consequently, this factor is weighed heavily only when there is evidence of past confusion or, perhaps, when the particular circumstances indicate such evidence should have been available.").

[102] *E.g.,* Boston Athletic Ass'n v. Sullivan, 867 F.2d 22, 31-32, 9 U.S.P.Q.2d 1690, 1696 (1st Cir. 1989) (defendant used on shirts a logo similar to that of plaintiff, sponsor of a famous race; one purchaser of defendant's shirts expressed surprise on learning they were not "official"; two other purchasers attempted to exchange defendant's shirts for those of the plaintiff; "While not as accurate as a survey might have been, . . . this evidence shows that some people were actually confused as to who sponsored defendants' shirts. This factor . . . weighs in favor of a likelihood of confusion."); International Kennel Club of Chicago v. Mighty Star Inc., 846 F.2d 1079, 6 U.S.P.Q.2d 1977 (7th Cir. 1988) (plaintiff received letters, phone calls, and inquiries as to defendant's product).

[103] AmBRIT Inc. v. Kraft Inc., 812 F.2d 1531, 1538, 1 U.S.P.Q.2d 1161, 1166 (11th Cir. 1986).

"Actual consumer confusion is the best evidence of likelihood of confusion. There is no absolute scale as to how many instances of actual confusion establish the existence of that factor. Rather, the court must evaluate the evidence of actual confusion in the light of the totality of the circumstances involved.

"In the instant case, [the trademark owner] presented four consumers who testified that they had been confused while making purchases in the market place. Each of the witnesses had notified [the trademark owner] of his or her confusion by letter or telephone. . . .

". . . With respect to the [infringer's] assertion that the reported instances of confusion are small given the high volume of sales, we note that it takes very little evidence to establish the existence of the actual confusion factor. Moreover, that there were only a few reported instances of actual confusion does not mean that only those individuals were actually confused. . . . It is likely that many consumers who were confused never realized they had been confused and that many of those who did realize they had been confused chose not to spend the time to register a complaint with a faceless corporation about the packaging of an item that retails for approximately $2.50 per six-pack."[104]

Actual confusion episodes are probative of likelihood of confusion only if they are relatively significant.[105] In *Scott Paper*,[106] the Third Circuit reversed a district court finding that confusion between "Scott" for plastic and paper household products and "Scott's Liquid Gold" for furniture polish was likely: "The evidence of actual

---

[104] 812 F.2d at 1543-44, 1 U.S.P.Q.2d at 1171-72.

[105] *See, e.g.,* Homeowners Group, Inc. v. Home Marketing Specialists,, Inc., 931 F.2d 1100, 1110, 18 U.S.P.Q.2d 1587, 1594 (6th Cir. 1991) ("Even though evidence of actual confusion is undoubtedly the best evidence of likelihood of confusion it does not follow that any type or quantum of such evidence is entitled to significant weight in the determination. Where the parties have been doing business in the same area for some time and where they have advertised extensively, isolated instances of actual confusion are not conclusive or entitled to great weight in the determination. . . . Indeed, the existence of only a handful of instances of actual confusion after a significant time or a significant degree of concurrent sales under the respective marks may even lead to an inference that no likelihood of confusion exists."); Accuride International Inc. v. Accuride Corp., 871 F.2d 1531, 1537, 10 U.S.P.Q.2d 1589, 1593 (9th Cir. 1989) (evidence of instances of misdirected deliveries and phone calls was "anecdotal and too weak to support a finding of actual confusion"); Clamp Manufacturing Co. Inc. v. Enco Manufacturing Co. Inc., 870 F.2d 512, 518, 10 U.S.P.Q.2d 1226, 1230 (9th Cir. 1989) (suggesting that "entrapment" efforts may not constitute evidence of actual confusion); Life Technologies Inc. v. Gibbco Scientific Inc., 826 F.2d 775, 777, 3 U.S.P.Q.2d 1795, 1797 (8th Cir. 1987) ("the instances of actual confusion were neither frequent nor serious"); Nutri/System Inc. v. Con-Stan Industries Inc., 809 F.2d 601, 606, 1 U.S.P.Q.2d 1809, 1813 (9th Cir. 1987) (district court "determined that, in light of both parties' high volume of business, the misdirection of several letters and checks proved insignificant."); Ziebart International Corp. v. Aftermarket Associates, Inc., 802 F.2d 220, 228, 231 U.S.P.Q. 119, 124 (7th Cir. 1986) ("a 'single misdirected communication' would not show actual confusion of the marks by the consuming public"); Pignons S.A. de Mecanique de Precision v. Polaroid Corp., 657 F.2d 482, 490, 212 U.S.P.Q. 246, 252 (1st Cir. 1981) ("[A] single misdirected communication is very weak evidence of consumer confusion.").

[106] Scott Paper Co. v. Scott's Liquid Gold, 589 F.2d 1225, 220 U.S.P.Q. 421 (3d Cir. 1978).

confusion . . . is insufficient. . . . The evidence relied on by the district court constituted merely nineteen misdirected letters received between 1972 and 1976 supported by depositions of some of the authors. However, during the same period [defendant] sold 50 million cans of its products." [107]

The second way to establish actual confusion is by survey. [108] In *Charles of the Ritz Group*, [109] the court upheld a finding that defendant's slogan comparing its "OMNI" perfume to plaintiff's "OPIUM" perfume made confusion likely. "[C]onsumers who had been randomly selected at a shopping mall were shown extremely brief glimpses of packages of fragrance products using a shadow-box"; 34% of a sample of 35 "misidentified a package of OMNI as one of OPIUM." [110] A survey may also establish that no confusion is likely. In *Levi Strauss*, [111] the Ninth Circuit rejected the trademark owner's argument that the district court erred by ignoring the multifactor test and relying on survey evidence and the testimony of retailers in finding no likelihood of confusion.

> "[C]ertain aspects of the multifactor test describe the circumstances to which a trier of fact would refer in making an educated *guess* as to what was going on in the minds of consumers in the absence of direct proof, such as survey evidence and testimony, as to how consumers were responding to the marks. Survey evidence and testimony may, however, outweigh whatever circumstantial evidence has been introduced. . . .
>
> "We recognize that survey evidence and retailer testimony are primarily relevant to the existence of actual confusion, which is but one facet of the multifactor test." [112]

Methodological flaws dilute a survey's impact. [113] In *Amstar*, [114] defects reduced

---

[107] *See also* Amstar Corp. v. Domino's Pizza, Inc., 615 F.2d 252, 263, 205 U.S.P.Q. 969 (5th Cir. 1980) ("Plaintiff's evidence of actual confusion amounted to two verbal inquiries as to whether 'Domino's Pizza' was related to 'Domino' sugar, and one misaddressed letter. . . . In view of the fact that both plaintiff's and defendants' sales currently run into the millions of dollars each year, these isolated instances of actual confusion are insufficient to sustain a finding of likelihood of confusion."). *Compare* Forum Corp. of North America v. Forum, Ltd., 903 F.2d 434, 443, 14 U.S.P.Q.2d 1950, 1957 (7th Cir. 1990) ("[D]e minimis evidence of confusion may be discounted. . . . Nevertheless, it does not seem reasonable to classify [plaintiff's evidence of phone calls from other persons confused about the identity of defendant] as de minimis, since it was not based on a full survey of customers. In other words, this is not a case in which we could conclude that there was a statistically insignificant percentage of confusion, since the actual percentage is unknown.").

[108] *E.g.*, Mutual of Omaha Insurance Co. v. Novak, 836 F.2d 397, 400, 5 U.S.P.Q.2d 1314, 1317 (8th Cir. 1987).

[109] Charles of the Ritz Group Ltd. v. Quality King Distributors Inc., 832 F.2d 1317, 4 U.S.P.Q.2d 1778 (2d Cir. 1987).

[110] 832 F.2d at 1322, 4 U.S.P.Q.2d at 1782.

[111] Levi Strauss & Co. v. Blue Bell, Inc., 778 F.2d 1352, 228 U.S.P.Q. 346 (9th Cir. 1985) (en banc).

[112] 778 F.2d at 1360, 228 U.S.P.Q. at 352.

[113] *E.g.*, Coherent, Inc. v. Coherent Technologies, Inc., 935 F.2d 1122, 1126, 19 U.S.P.Q.2d 1146 (10th Cir. 1991) ("surveys can be used to show actual confusion, but their evidentiary value depends on the relevance of the questions asked and the technical adequacy of the survey

the probative value of a survey that apparently showed a high confusion level between plaintiff's "DOMINO" sugar and defendant's "DOMINO'S" pizza.

"Plaintiff's survey was made by Dr. Russ Haley, Professor of Marketing at
the University of New Hampshire. It was conducted in ten cities among female
heads of households primarily responsible for making food purchases. Each
participant was shown, in her own home, a 'Domino's Pizza' box and was asked
if she believed the company that made the pizza made any other product. If
she answered yes, she was asked, 'What products other than pizza do you think
are made by the company that makes Domino's Pizza?' . . . Seventy-one percent of those asked the second question answered 'sugar.'

"While the possible confusion level shown by the Haley study is high, there
are several defects in the survey which significantly reduce its probative value.
First, one of the most important factors in assessing the validity of an opinion
poll is the adequacy of the 'survey universe,' that is, the persons interviewed
must adequately represent the opinions which are relevant to the litigation.
. . . The appropriate universe should include a fair sampling of those purchasers most likely to partake of the alleged infringer's goods or services. . . . Of
the ten cities in which the Haley survey was conducted, eight had no 'Domino's
Pizza' outlets, and the outlets in the remaining two had been open for less than
three months. Additionally, the persons interviewed consisted entirely of
women found at home during six daylight hours who identified themselves
as the member of the household primarily responsible for grocery buying. As
plaintiff's sugar is sold primarily in grocery stores, participants in the Haley
survey would have been repeatedly exposed to plaintiff's mark, but would have
had little, if any, exposure to defendants' mark. Furthermore, the survey
neglected completely defendants' primary customers young, single, male college
students. Thus, we do not believe that the proper universe was examined, and
the results of the survey must therefore be discounted. . . .

---

procedures, including how closely the survey mimics market conditions."); Universal City
Studios, Inc. v. Nintendo Co., Ltd., 746 F.2d 112, 118, 223 U.S.P.Q. 1000, 1004-05 (2d Cir.
1984) (where question in survey presented participant with the connection between Donkey
Kong and King Kong, it is leading); Penta Hotels Ltd. v. Penta Tours, 9 U.S.P.Q.2d 1081,
1105 (D. Conn. 1988) ("The party offering the survey bears the burden of establishing that
it complies in terms of methodology and survey techniques with professional research standards.").

In *Penta Hotels*, the court found no likelihood of confusion between plaintiff's mark "Penta
Hotels" and defendant's mark "Penta Tours" for travel services even though a survey of travel
agents in six cities indicated that about 26% felt there was some connection between plaintiff and defendant. The first four questions twice exposed the respondents to both parties' names.
The fifth asked whether the respondent felt "there is some connection between Penta Hotels and Penta Tours." The court noted: "Even an individual who before had never heard of
either company could easily 'feel' there was 'some' relationship between the two after having
been asked the previous questions." 9 U.S.P.Q.2d at 1105.

See generally Handbook of Recommended Procedures for the Trial of Protracted Cases, 25
F.R.D. 351, 425 (on surveys).

[114] Amstar Corp. v. Domino's Pizza, Inc., 615 F.2d 252, 205 U.S.P.Q. 969 (5th Cir. 1980),
cert. denied, 449 U.S. 899 (1980).

"Of additional concern, plaintiff's survey was a 'word association' test. Participants in the survey were confronted with the 'Domino's Pizza' mark, and more or less asked if it brought anything else to mind. We have previously held that such a procedure degenerates 'into a mere word-association test entitled to little weight.' Holiday Inns, Inc. v. Holiday Out in America, 481 F.2d 445, 448 (5th Cir. 1973). We do not believe the Haley survey presents any meaningful evidence of likelihood of confusion. . . . "[115]

What response percentage indicates that confusion is likely or unlikely? In *Henri's Food Products*,[116] the court held that "YOGOWHIP" and "MIRACLE WHIP" for salad dressing did not make consumer confusion likely: a survey indicated that only 7.6% of respondents believed that "YOGOWHIP" came from the same company as "MIRACLE WHIP."[117]

[viii] *Intent.* Intent is not a necessary element of trademark infringement,[118] but an accused infringer's intent to garner a senior user's goodwill is a factor tending to

---

[115] 615 F.2d at 263–64.

[116] Henri's Food Products Co., Inc. v. Kraft, Inc., 717 F.2d 352, 358, 220 U.S.P.Q. 386, 391 (7th Cir. 1983).

[117] The court noted that the trademark owner "pointed to no case in which a 7.6% figure constituted a likelihood of confusion."

"Kraft has pointed to no case in which a 7.6% figure constituted likelihood of confusion. *See James Burrough [v. Sign of Beefeater, Inc.*, 540 F.2d 266, 279 n.23 (7th Cir.1976)] (referring to a prior case showing 11%); *Union Carbide [Corp. v. Ever-Ready Inc.*, 531 F.2d 366, 386 (7th Cir.1976)] (referring to a prior case showing 11.4%); *McDonough [Power Equip., Inc. v. Weed Eater, Inc.*, 208 U.S.P.Q. 676, 685 (T.T.A.B. 1981),] at 685 (11%); *Jockey Internat'l, Inc. v. Burkard*, 185 U.S.P.Q. 201, 205 (S.D.Cal.1975) (11.4%). In *Grotrian, Helfferich, Schulz, Th. Steinweg Nachf v. Steinway & Sons*, 365 F. Supp. 707, 716 (S.D.N.Y.1973), *affirmed*, 523 F.2d 1331 (2d Cir.1975), the court held as strong evidence of likelihood of confusion a survey showing that 8.5% of the people interviewed confused the names Steinway and Grotrian-Steinweg, and 7.7% perceived a business connection between the two companies; it is not clear whether or not the figures were combined. In *James Burrough Ltd. v. Sign of Beefeater, Inc.* (Beefeater II), 572 F.2d 574, 578 (7th Cir.1978), this Court credited a survey showing that 10% of the respondents confronted with a Sign of the Beefeater restaurant sign mentioned that liquor came to mind; only 6% mentioned Beefeater specifically as a liquor that came to mind. . . . Again, it is not clear which figures the Court deemed sufficient to evidence likelihood of confusion. In contrast, Henri's points to *Wuv's Internat'l, Inc. v. Love's Enterprises, Inc.*, 208 U.S.P.Q. 736, 756 (D.Colo.1980), where the court found 9% to be a "questionable amount of confusion" and in combination with other factors found no infringement; and *S.S. Kresge Co. v. United Factory Outlet, Inc.*, 598 F.2d 694, 697 (1st Cir.1979), where the court found it unconvincing that 7.2% of the respondents believed that "The Mart" and "K-Mart" were owned by the same people, though the 7.2% figure was discredited because 5.7% of the respondents reached the same conclusion with respect to "The Mart" and "Kings Department Store." 717 F.2d at 358, 220 U.S.P.Q. at 391.

[118] *E.g.*, Fuji Photo Film Co., Inc. v. Shinohara Shoji Kabushiki Kaisha, 754 F.2d 591, 596, 225 U.S.P.Q. 540, 543 (5th Cir. 1985), *rehearing denied*, 761 F.2d 695 (5th Cir. 1985) (unpublished) ("Good faith is not a defense to trademark infringement. . . . The reason for this is clear: if potential purchasers are confused, no amount of good faith can make them less so. Bad faith, however, may, without more, prove infringement.").

show confusion likelihood because he, better than a court, can assess a similar mark's market impact.[119]

In *My-T Fine*,[120] plaintiff, who sold a distinctively-packaged chocolate pudding, sought to enjoin defendant's sale of a similarly packaged competing product.

> "The plaintiff has proved no more than that the boxes look a good deal alike, and that confusion may well arise; and were it not for the evidence of the defendants' intent to deceive and so to secure the plaintiff's customers, we should scarcely feel justified in interfering at this stage of the cause. We need not say whether that intent is always a necessary element in such causes of suit; probably it originally was in federal courts. . . . But when it appears, we think that it has an important procedural result; a late comer who deliberately copies the dress of his competitors already in the field, must at least prove that his effort has been futile. Prima facie the court will treat his opinion so disclosed as expert and will not assume that it was erroneous. . . . He may indeed succeed in showing that it was; that, however bad his purpose, it will fail in execution; if he does, he will win. . . . But such an intent raises a presumption that customers will be deceived.

> "In the case at bar, it seems to us fairly demonstrated that the defendants have copied the plaintiff's make-up as far as they dared. . . . At the very outset the directions were lifted bodily from the back of the plaintiff's box; and although the defendants were within their rights as to that, still the circumstance is relevant because it proves that the box had been before them when they designed their own make-up, and that it had been their point of departure. In addition they took solid green for the body, and put on a chevron; and while perhaps they did not choose a general combination of red and green, at least they adopted a red lettering. Whether or not they meant to get hold of the plaintiff's customers by that make-up, their next step was bolder, and put their intent beyond question; they added the red stripes at every edge; so that the real differences that remained were only the name and the color of

---

[119] *See* Restatement of Torts § 729 (1938) (Comment f.): "[O]ne may infringe another's trademark or trade name by adopting a confusingly similar designation whether he does so innocently or for the purpose of deceiving prospective purchasers. But his knowledge or purpose is an important factor in determining whether or not his designation is confusingly similar. If he adopts the designation in ignorance of the other's trade-mark or trade name, the similarity is determined on the basis of other factors. But if he adopts his designation with the intent of deriving benefit from the reputation of the trade-mark or trade name, his intent may be sufficient to justify the inference that there is confusing similarity. Since he was and is intimately concerned with the probable reaction in the market, his judgment manifested prior to the controversy, is highly persuasive. His denial that his conduct was likely to achieve the result intended by him will ordinarily carry little weight."

See also Charles of the Ritz Group Ltd. v. Quality King Distributors Inc., 832 F.2d 1317, 1322, 4 U.S.P.Q.2d 1778, 1782 (2d Cir. 1987) ("evidence of intentional copying raises a presumption that the second comer intended to create a confusing similarity"); Mobil Oil Corporation v. Pegasus Petroleum Corp., 818 F.2d 254, 258, 2 U.S.P.Q.2d 1677, 1680 (2d Cir. 1987) ("Intentional copying gives rise to a presumption of a likelihood of confusion.").

[120] My-T Fine Corp. v. Samuels, 69 F.2d 76 (2d Cir. 1934).

the chevron. As they had not the slightest original interest in the colors chosen and their distribution, they could only have meant to cause confusion, out of which they might profit by diverting the plaintiff's customers. This being the intent, the dissimilarities between the two do not in our judgment rebut the presumption."[121]

In *Little Caesar Enterprises*,[122] the Sixth Circuit likened "intent to appropriate another's property" to "an expression of opinion by an expert witness": "a defendant who purposely chooses a particular mark because it is similar to that of a [senior] user . . . saying, in effect, that he thinks there is at least a possibility that he can divert some business from the senior user—and the defendant ought to know at least as much about the likelihood of confusion as the trier of fact."[123]

Courts draw fine lines in assessing what constitutes intent that justifies an inference of confusion.[124] Because intent to offer a competing product is not improper,[125] the courts look for intent to cause confusion or at least to garner the trademark owner's goodwill.[126] Adopting a mark with knowledge of the trademark owner's mark does

---

[121] 69 F.2d at 77.

[122] Little Caesar Enterprises Inc. v. Pizza Caesar Inc., 834 F.2d 568, 572, 4 U.S.P.Q.2d 1942, 1945 (6th Cir. 1987) (finding that "In the case at bar there is no evidence that [the defendant] had actual knowledge of the existence of [plaintiff], much less that he had any larcenous intent.").

[123] 834 F.2d at 572, 4 U.S.P.Q.2d at 1945.

[124] *See, e.g.,* M-F-G Corp. v. EMRA Corp., 817 F.2d 410, 411, 2 U.S.P.Q.2d 1538, 1539 (7th Cir. 1987) (as to defendant's knowledge of plaintiff's mark "SUPERCUT" for shears before embarking on an expansion program of its "SUPERCUTS" haircutting salons: "But it is lawful to use a mark that does not infringe some other; intentional infringement creates problems, but intentional use of a mark that [the defendant] had every right to use is not itself a ground on which to draw an adverse inference. . . . Business are entitled to plan their conduct to take advantage of legal rights; this planning, actual or imputed, may not be used to diminish the rights with which the firm began.").

[125] *See* § 1D[3].

[126] *E.g.,* American Home Products Corp. v. Barr Laboratories, Inc., 834 F.2d 368, 371, 5 U.S.P.Q.2d 1073, 1076 (3d Cir. 1987) (product simulation case; no likelihood of confusion even though defendant deliberately copied the color of the capsule of plaintiff's dominant ADVIL brand of ibuprofen; "In an action for unlawful imitation of product appearance, evidence of defendant's intent does not relieve plaintiff of its burden of proving likelihood of confusion by a preponderance of the evidence. At most, defendant's intent is a factor tending to suggest likelihood of confusion. . . . [T]he [trial] court did not err in declining to infer likelihood of consumer confusion from a mere intent to imitate"; as to plaintiff's survey showing that almost one-fifth of the respondents "associated" defendant's capsule with ADVIL: "A response that one 'associates' a given product with the name of a competitive product may simply reflect the recognition that the two products are comparable and serve the same purpose."); Sno-Wizard Manufacturing, Inc. v. Eisemann Products Co., 791 F.2d 423, 230 U.S.P.Q. 118 (5th Cir. 1986) (decision to copy plaintiff's machine was dictated by defendant's desire to provide interchangeable parts).

Cf. Fuddruckers Inc. v. Doc's B.R. Others Inc., 826 F.2d 837, 846 n.11, 4 U.S.P.Q.2d 1026, 1033 n.11 (9th Cir. 1987) ("It may be that the shifting burden only applies when the evidence demonstrates that the defendant intended to exploit, rather than merely to copy.").

not constitute an intent to cause confusion if there are significant differences between the goods or the marks,[127] but intent to come "as close as the law will allow" may constitute "an intent to derive benefit from the other party's reputation" and be "probative on the likelihood of confusion issue," especially if the accused infringer "never sought an opinion from legal counsel."[128]

Court may find an intent to cause confusion or misappropriate goodwill when the accused infringer had a prior relationship with the trademark owner.[129] In *Century 21 Real Estate*,[130] a terminated "Century 21" franchisee chose a name with "Century" in it, "Century Investments & Realty," so that his old customers could find him: "This evidences wrongful intent."

Accused infringers may rebut intent evidence by showing their good faith in adopting the mark. For example, the accused infringer may have adopted a mark based on (1) a company founder or product originator's name,[131] (2) a mark used abroad, or (3) a mark used on other products.[132] The accused infringer may have conducted a search of prior marks and adopted the accused mark only after obtaining trademark counsel's advice.[133]

---

[127] *See, e.g.,* Carson v. Here's Johnny Portable Toilets, Inc., 698 F.2d 831, 834, 218 U.S.P.Q. 1, 3 (6th Cir. 1983) ("Here's Johnny," an introductory phrase associated with the famous entertainer, Johnny Carson, was used by defendant on portable toilets; "Although [the defendant] had intended to capitalize on the phrase popularized by Carson, the [trial] court concluded that [he] had not intended to deceive the public into believing that Carson was connected with the product."); Amstar Corp. v. Domino's Pizza, Inc., 615 F.2d 252, 263, 205 U.S.P.Q. 969, 978 (5th Cir. 1980) ("Bad faith in the adoption and use of a trademark normally involves the imitation of packaging material, use of identical code numbers, adopting of similar distribution methods or other efforts by a party to 'pass off' its product as that of another. . . . There is no evidence that defendants have ever attempted to 'pass off' their goods as those of plaintiff. Evidence introduced at trial established that the name 'Domino's Pizza' was adopted because Mr. Monaghan had been told he could no longer use the name 'Dominick's,' the new name sounded Italian, and it was quite close to the old name. Although Monaghan was aware of 'Domino' sugar at the time, he was unaware of any other pizzerias by that name. There is no evidence the name was adopted with any intent to confuse, mislead, or deceive the public.").

[128] AmBRIT Inc. v. Kraft Inc., 812 F.2d 1531, 1543, 1 U.S.P.Q.2d 1161, 1170 (11th Cir. 1986).

[129] *E.g.,* AmBRIT Inc. v. Kraft Inc., 812 F.2d 1531, 1543 n.61, 1 U.S.P.Q.2d 1161, 1171 n.61 (11th Cir. 1986) ("The parties' previous contractual or business relations" is "a subfactor relating to intent.").

[130] Century 21 Real Estate Corp. v. Sandlin, 846 F.2d 1175, 1180, 6 U.S.P.Q.2d 2034, 2037 (9th Cir. 1988).

[131] *E.g.,* Scott Paper Co. v. Scott's Liquid Gold, 589 F.2d 1225, 1230, 200 U.S.P.Q. 421 (3d Cir. 1978) (accused infringer's product was named "Scott's Liquid Gold" after its originator, Lee Scott; "This good faith explanation of the origin of the accused mark contrasts with the situation sometimes suggested in other cases.").

[132] Accuride International Inc. v. Accuride Corp., 871 F.2d 1531, 1536, 10 U.S.P.Q.2d 1589, 1594 (9th Cir. 1989) (defendant adopted as a tradename a mark that it had long used on goods).

[133] *E.g.,* Western Publishing Co., Inc. v. Rose Art Industries, Inc., 910 F.2d 57, 63, 15 U.S.P.Q.2d 1545, 1549 (2d Cir. 1990) (good faith finding based in part on attorney's trademark

The absence of intent or the presence of good faith is a neutral factor.[134]

[ix] *"Second Comer" Doctrine.* The so-called "second comer" doctrine traces to Judge Learned Hand's opinion in the "Listerine" case.[135]

> "In choosing an arbitrary trade-name, there was no reason whatever why they should have selected one which bore so much resemblance to the plaintiff's; and in such cases any possible doubt of the likelihood of damage should be resolved in favor of the plaintiff. Of course, the burden of proof always rests upon the moving party, but having shown the adoption of a similar trade name, arbitrary in character, I cannot see why speculation as to the chance that it will cause confusion should be at the expense of the man first in the field. He has the right to insist that others in making up their arbitrary names should so certainly keep away from his customers as to raise no question."[136]

---

search and advice as to mark's availability; bad faith not inferred from accused infringer's knowledge of owner's registration).

Compare Hasbro, Inc. v. Lanard Toys, Ltd., 858 F.2d 70, 78, 8 U.S.P.Q.2d 1345, 1352 (2d Cir. 1988) (defendant's decision to proceed with sales effort based on belief it was senior user did "not amount as a legal matter to bad faith" despite "the shortcomings of [its] narrow trademark search" and "some indication" that the plaintiff "might be a prior user."); John H. Harland Co. v. Clarke Checks, Inc., 711 F.2d 966, 977, 219 U.S.P.Q. 515, 525 (11th Cir. 1983) (rejecting the defendant's argument that "any possible inference of intent to trade on the reputation of [plaintiff's] mark by adopting a confusingly similar mark is necessarily negated by evidence that [defendant's] officials consulted trademark counsel before adopting [the accused mark]," including evidence the defendant rejected two other suggested marks because of counsel's advice: "Although the evidence of [defendant's] consultations with counsel can be read to suggest that [defendant] had no intent to adopt a mark which was confusingly similar to [plaintiff's] mark, the jury also might have inferred that [defendant] merely was attempting to come as close to [plaintiff's] mark as the law would allow."); American International Group, Inc. v. London American International Corporation Ltd., 664 F.2d 348, 353, 212 U.S.P.Q. 803 (2d Cir. 1981) (reversing summary judgment of no likelihood of confusion because, *inter alia*, there was a disputed fact issue as to the defendant's intent; as to the argument of defendant, an international company, that "it would be unreasonable to require a search of the trade name register in every country in which its subsidiaries conduct business": "it hardly seems onerous to conduct a search of the United States register when 'American' is part of the name and the company seeks to emphasize its United States business.").

[134] *E.g.,* Wynn Oil Co. v. Thomas, 839 F.2d 1183, 1189, 5 U.S.P.Q. 1944, 1948 (6th Cir. 1988) ("the defendant's good intentions do not in any way preclude a finding of likely confusion"; "While . . . we do consider intention to be relevant when a plaintiff shows that a defendant knowingly copied the contested trademark, we agree . . . that absent such a showing, intentions are irrelevant.").

Compare AMF Inc. v. Sleekcraft Boats, 599 F.2d 341, 354, 204 U.S.P.Q. 808 (9th Cir. 1979) ("Good faith is less probative of the likelihood of confusion, yet may be given considerable weight in fashioning a remedy.").

[135] Lambert Pharmacal Co. v. Bolton Chemical Corp., 219 F. 325 (S.D. N.Y. 1915).

[136] 219 F. at 326.

See also Forum Corp. of North America v. Forum, Ltd., 903 F.2d 434, 440, 14 U.S.P.Q.2d 1950, 1955 (7th Cir. 1990) ("Placing the responsibility for preventing confusion on appellant, who was the first user, is wrong. . . . It is the *second* user's responsibility to avoid confusion in its choice of a trademark, and that responsibility must include choosing a mark whose

Some years later, Judge Hand again commented on second users' equities:

> " 'Why [the defendant] should have chosen a mark that had long been employed by [plaintiff] and had become known to the trade instead of adopting some other means to identify [its] goods is hard to see unless there was a deliberate purpose to obtain some advantage from the trade which [plaintiff] had built up.' Indeed, it is generally true that, as soon as we see that a second comer in a mark has, for no reason that he can assign, plagiarized the 'make-up' of an earlier comer, we need no more. . . . [W]e feel bound to compel him to exercise his ingenuity in quarters further afield."[137]

In *Thompson Medical*,[138] the Second Circuit linked the second comer doctrine to two *Polaroid* factors—mark strength and intent:

> "A senior user in possession of a distinctive mark has a right not to have a second comer intentionally cause a likelihood of confusion between two marks in an attempt to exploit the reputation of the senior user's mark, since this would deprive the first user of control over its reputation and goodwill. . . .

> "This test has resisted doctrinal classification. Some courts have simply incorporated the second-comer doctrine into the *Polaroid* analysis. . . . But because the two elements necessary to trigger the second-comer doctrine—a strong mark and bad intent—are themselves included in the *Polaroid* analysis, the doctrine would appear to be a redundancy, unless it retains independent significance.

> "This seemingly superfluous approach may be an outgrowth of *Polaroid's* recent expansion into the realm of competing products. Prior to [that expansion], there did not exist a systematic mode of analysis capable of incorporating a second-comer's bad intent and the strength of the senior user's mark in trademark infringement cases involving competing products. As a result, the second-comer doctrine offered an avenue of relief for the senior user. But with *Polaroid's* expansive coverage, this is no longer the case. Consequently, courts that purport to apply the second-comer 'test' should recognize that they are merely emphasizing two of the *Polaroid* factors."

In *Thompson*, the appeals court found that second user Pfizer's "SportsGel" topical analgesic did not create a likelihood of confusion in view of first user Thompson's mark "Sportscreme." The district court erred in relying on the second comer doctrine:

> "[W]e have invoked [the second comer doctrine] only where there exists a highly distinctive mark of the senior user and proof of bad faith by the junior user. . . . Neither requisite element was found by the district judge. Indeed, his conclusion that 'the second-comer who knows about the name and package design and so

---

salient portion would not likely be confused with a first user's mark."); Volkswagen Aktiengesellschaft v. Wheeler, 814 F.2d 812, 817, 2 U.S.P.Q.2d 1264, 1268 (1st Cir. 1987) ("when one adopts a mark similar to one already in use, there is an affirmative duty to avoid any likelihood of confusion.").

[137] American Chicle Co. v. Topps Chewing Gum, Inc., 208 F.2d 560, 562-63 (2d Cir. 1953), quoting Miles Shoes Inc. v. R.H. Macy and Co., 199 F.2d 602, 603 (2d Cir. 1952).

[138] Thompson Medical Co., Inc. v. Pfizer, 753 F.2d 208, 225 U.S.P.Q. 124 (2d Cir. 1985).

forth of the first-comer has some obligation to name his product and design his packaging so as to avoid confusion,' would, if applied, confer exclusive trademark protection to the first user of a mark, regardless of the mark's distinctiveness. Such a result would be inimical to the purposes of trademark law."[139]

[b] **Question of Law or Fact; Appellate Review.** The circuit appeals courts suffer from actual, not merely likely, confusion on whether likelihood of confusion is a fact question, reviewable under the limited clearly erroneous appellate review standard,[140] or a legal question, freely reviewable on appeal.[141]

Pullman,[142] a civil rights case in which the Supreme Court held that discrimination was a fact question and refused to distinguish "subsidiary" and "ultimate" findings, created a trend to treat likelihood of confusion as one of fact.[143] For example, in

---

[139] 753 F.2d at 218, 225 U.S.P.Q. at 132-33.

[140] *E.g.*, Downtowner/Passport International Hotel Corp. v. Norlew Inc., 841 F.2d 214, 6 U.S.P.Q.2d 1646 (8th Cir. 1988); AmBRIT Inc. v. Kraft Inc., 812 F.2d 1531, 1 U.S.P.Q.2d 1161 (11th Cir. 1986); Amoco Oil Co. v. Rainbow Snow Inc., 809 F.2d 656, 662, 1 U.S.P.Q.2d 1403, 1407-08 (10th Cir. 1987) ("While the 'findings' may be more properly classified as conclusions derived from the fact finder's *evaluation* of the evidence and the surrounding circumstances, such a 'mixed bag' is . . . inevitable in the process of determining the likelihood of confusion under the criteria set forth in Restatement of Torts § 729 (1938). Determinations involving 'suggestion,' 'intent,' and 'the degree of care likely to be exercised by purchasers' require that the fact finder reach conclusions based on personal evaluation of evidence and reasonable inferences therefrom. On appeal, our task is to decide whether there is a reasonable basis for the trial court's findings and conclusions."); Keebler Co. v. Rovira Biscuit Corp., 624 F.2d 366, 377, 207 U.S.P.Q. 475 (1st Cir. 1980) ("although several courts have adopted the position that the nature of the determination of likelihood of confusion makes it a question of law, . . . we think the finding of the court in this case quite clearly called upon the court's 'experience with the mainsprings of human conduct' . . . , and therefore is reversible only if clearly erroneous."); American Int'l Group v. London American Int'l Corp., 664 F.2d 348, 212 U.S.P.Q. 803, 806 (2d Cir. 1981).

[141] *E.g.*, Carson v. Here's Johnny Portable Toilets, Inc., 698 F.2d 831, 833, 218 U.S.P.Q. 1, 3 (6th Cir. 1983) (the foundational factors are factual; the "weighing of these findings on the ultimate issue of the likelihood of confusion is a question of law.").

[142] Pullman-Standard v. Swint, 456 U.S. 273 (1982).

[143] *E.g.*, Forum Corp. of North America v. Forum, Ltd., 903 F.2d 434, 438, 14 U.S.P.Q.2d 1950, 1953 (7th Cir. 1990) ("We have stated a number of times that the trial court's ultimate conclusion on the likelihood of confusion is a finding of fact. . . . Other circuits have treated the final resolution of the confusion issue as legal. . . . We have considered the arguments in favor of treating the ultimate finding of confusion or no confusion as legal and rejected them. . . . However, we review the district court's statement of the law de novo for legal error and its conclusions for signs that the court's application of the law was infected with legal error, i.e., an erroneous general principle about the way the test should be applied."); Pirone v. MacMillan, Inc., 894 F.2d 579, 584, 13 U.S.P.Q.2d 1799, 1803 (2d Cir. 1990) ("Normally, the likelihood of confusion is a factual question, centering on the probable reactions of prospective purchasers of the parties' goods."); Keds Corp. v. Renee International Trading Corp., 888 F.2d 215, 222, 12 U.S.P.Q.2d 1808, 1813 (1st Cir. 1989) ("We review a district court's evaluation of evidence and finding of a likelihood of confusion based on a 'clearly erroneous' standard."); Dieter v. B & H Industries of Southwest Florida, Inc., 880 F.2d 322, 325 n.2, 11 U.S.P.Q. 1721, 1723 n.2 (11th Cir. 1989), *cert. denied*, 111 S. Ct. 369 (1990) ("Determination

Levi Strauss,[144] the Ninth Circuit, sitting en banc, indicated that likelihood of confusion is a mixed question of law and fact and that a district court's determination of that question is reviewable on appeal under the clearly erroneous standard.

> "Likelihood of confusion is the type of mixed question which fits within the categories suggested in [United States v. McConney, 728 F.2d 1195 (9th Cir.) (en banc)] as suited to clearly erroneous review—cases not implicating constitutional rights and those 'in which the applicable legal standard provides for a strictly factual test, such as state of mind.' *De novo* review of this issue would demand a significant diversion of appellate court resources to a task which more properly belongs to the district court judge. . . . Moreover, the limited precedential value of likelihood of confusion decisions, each of which stands upon its own facts, reduces the need for *de novo* review."[145]

Other decisions continue to treat the ultimate likelihood of confusion issue as one of law, freely reviewable on appeal.[146]

---

of 'likelihood of confusion' is a factual issue which is reviewed under the 'clearly erroneous' standard of Federal Rule of Civil Procedure 52(a).''); American Home Products Corp. v. Barr Laboratories, Inc., 834 F.2d 368, 370, 5 U.S.P.Q.2d 1073, 1075 (3d Cir. 1987) ("Some courts . . . have occasionally justified de novo review on the . . . ground that likelihood of confusion is a finding of 'ultimate' or inferred fact reviewable under a less deferential standard than findings of 'basic' or historical fact. . . . This position is no longer tenable in light of the Supreme Court's decision in *Pullman-Standard v. Swint*. . . . There the Court held that a district court's finding of discriminatory purpose may be reversed on appeal only if clearly erroneous, noting that '[rule 52(a)] does not divide facts into categories; in particular, it does not divide findings of fact into those that deal with "ultimate" and those that deal with "subsidiary" facts.' ''); Fuji Photo Film Co., Inc. v. Shinohara Shoji Kabushiki Kaisha, 754 F.2d 591, 595 n.4, 225 U.S.P.Q. 540, 542 n.4 (5th Cir. 1985), *rehearing denied*, 761 F.2d 695 (5th Cir. 1985) (unpublished) ("In this Circuit, a trial court's determination of likelihood of confusion is ordinarily a finding of fact, reviewable under the 'clearly erroneous' standard of Rule 52(a). . . . The 'clearly erroneous' rule does not apply, however, to determinations reached by application of an incorrect legal standard.''); Pizzeria Uno Corp. v. Temple, 747 F.2d 1522, 1526, 224 U.S.P.Q. 184, 187 (4th Cir. 1984) (the Supreme Court's *Pullman* decision makes "obsolete any distinction between 'subsidiary' and 'ultimate' findings in the application of the clearly erroneous rule and established the principle that all findings . . . were to be reviewed under the clearly erroneous rule. . . . But under this rule, a finding is clearly erroneous when there is no evidence in the record supportive of it and also, when, even though there is some evidence to support the finding, the reviewing court, on the review of the record, is left with a definite and firm conviction that a mistake has been made in the finding. . . . Nor will the clearly erroneous rule protect findings which have been made on the basis of the application of incorrect legal standards or made in disregard of applicable legal standards, such as burden of proof.'').

See also GTE Corp. v. Williams, 904 F.2d 536, 14 U.S.P.Q.2d 1971 (10th Cir. 1990); WSM Inc. v. Hilton, 724 F.2d 1320, 221 U.S.P.Q.2d 410 (8th Cir. 1984); Jellibeans, Inc. v. Skating Clubs of George, Inc., 716 F.2d 833, 222 U.S.P.Q. 10 (11th Cir. 1983).

[144] Levi Strauss & Co. v. Blue Bell, Inc., 778 F.2d 1352, 1355-56, 228 U.S.P.Q. 346, 348-49 (9th Cir. 1985).

[145] 778 F.2d at 1355-56, 228 U.S.P.Q. at 348.

[146] Homeowners Group, Inc. v. Home Marketing Specialists,, Inc., 931 F.2d 1100, 1107, 18 U.S.P.Q.2d 1587, 1592 (6th Cir. 1991) ("This Circuit considers the question of whether there is a likelihood of confusion a mixed question of fact and law. Factual findings must be

[c] **Reverse Confusion.** Trademark law focuses primarily on protecting against "forward" confusion—a false impression that a first user-trademark owner makes or endorses a second user's goods or services. In some instances, when the second user is larger or more famous than the first user, the focus is on "reverse" confusion—a false impression that the second user makes or endorses the first user-trademark owner's goods. Reverse confusion causes consumer confusion and may damage the first user's reputation by creating a false impression that it misappropriated the second user's good will.

In *Big O Tire Dealers*,[147] Big O Tire was a tire merchandising company that provided services to independent tire dealers. In 1973, Goodyear, a large tire manufacturer, began using "Bigfoot" as a trademark for snowmobile tracks. In February of 1974, Big O began using "Big Foot" as a trademark on tires. In July 1974, Goodyear decided to use "Bigfoot" in a nationwide advertising campaign to promote a new tire. In August of 1974, it learned of Big O's "Big Foot." Despite objections by Big O and its dealers, Goodyear launched a "Bigfoot" promotion in the Fall of 1974. In November of 1974, Big O sued Goodyear for trademark infringement. After a trial, a jury found for Big O, awarding $2,800,000 general compensatory damages and $16,800,000 punitive damages.

The Tenth Circuit affirmed the judgment on the verdict but reduced the damage awards to $678,302 (actual) and $4,069,812 (punitive). The trial judge's instruction permitted the jury to base liability on a likelihood of confusion. The plaintiff Big O did not claim that Goodyear intended to trade on Big O's goodwill or to palm off

---

made with respect to the likelihood of confusion factors set out above. However, the further determination of whether a given set of foundational facts establishes a likelihood of confusion is a legal conclusion."); Wynn Oil Co. v. Thomas, 839 F.2d 1183, 1186, 5 U.S.P.Q.2d 1944, 1946 (6th Cir. 1988) ("This Circuit considers the question of whether there is a likelihood of confusion a mixed question of fact and law. When reviewing a lower court's decision in these cases, we apply a clearly erroneous standard to findings of fact supporting the likelihood of confusion factors, but review *de novo* the legal question whether, given the foundational facts as found by the lower court, those facts constitute a 'likelihood of confusion.' "); Sweats Fashions v. Pannill Knitting Co., 833 F.2d 1560, 1565, 4 U.S.P.Q.2d 1793, 1797 (Fed. Cir. 1987) ("The uniform precedent of this court is that the issue of likelihood of confusion is one of law."); Life Technologies Inc. v. Gibbco Scientific Inc., 826 F.2d 775, 777, 3 U.S.P.Q.2d 1795, 1797 (8th Cir. 1987) ("While the district court's evaluation of each factor is subject to the clearly erroneous standard of review, the ultimate determination of the likelihood of confusion is a question of law which we review *de novo*."); Plus Products v. Plus Discount Foods, Inc., 722 F.2d 999, 1004-05, 222 U.S.P.Q. 373, 377 (2d Cir. 1983) ("the district court's determination of each of the Polaroid factors is a finding of fact to which the clearly erroneous standard is applicable. The court's use of those factors, though, and its determination of likelihood of confusion based on the balancing of or relative weight given to each of its findings is a legal conclusion which is reviewable by this court as a matter of law."); Carson v. Here's Johnny Portable Toilets, Inc., 698 F.2d 831, 833, 218 U.S.P.Q. 1, 3 (6th Cir. 1983) ("eight foundational factors are factual and subject to a clearly erroneous standard of review, while the weighing of these findings on the ultimate issue of the likelihood of confusion is a question of law.").

147 Big O Tire Dealers, Inc. v. Goodyear Tire & Rubber Co., 561 F.2d 1365, 195 U.S.P.Q. 417 (10th Cir. 1977).

its products as those Big O. Rather, Big O contended that Goodyear's use of "Bigfoot" created likely confusion as the source of Big O's goods.

> "[T]he usual trademark infringement case involves a claim by a plaintiff with a substantial investment in a well established trademark. The plaintiff would seek recovery for the loss of income resulting from a second user attempting to trade on the goodwill associated with that established mark by suggesting to the consuming public that his product comes from the same origin as the plaintiff's product. The instant case, however, involves reverse confusion wherein the infringer's use of plaintiff's mark results in confusion as to the origin of plaintiff's product."[148]

Relying on a Seventh Circuit decision holding that reverse confusion was not actionable under Indiana law,[149] Goodyear argued that second use of a trademark is not actionable if it merely creates a likelihood of confusion concerning the source of the first user's product.

The Tenth Circuit predicted that the Colorado courts would recognize reverse confusion because their decisions evidenced a "policy of protecting trade names and preventing public confusion" and "the tendency [of widening] the scope of that protection."

> "The district court very persuasively answered Goodyear's argument that liability for trademark infringement cannot be imposed without a showing that Goodyear intended to trade on the goodwill of Big O or to palm off Goodyear products as being those of Big O's when it said:
>
> > 'The logical consequence of accepting Goodyear's position would be the immunization from unfair competition liability of a company with a well established trade name and with the economic power to advertise extensively for a product name taken from a competitor. If the law is to limit recovery to passing off, anyone with adequate size and resources can adopt any trademark and develop a new meaning for that trademark as identification of the second user's products. The activities of Goodyear in this case are

---

[148] 561 F.2d at 1371.

[149] Westward Coach Manufacturing Co., Inc. v. Ford Motor Co., 388 F.2d 627, 633-34, 156 U.S.P.Q. 437 (7th Cir. 1968), *cert. denied*, 329 U.S. 927 (1968) ("Ford contends that under Indiana law and under federal law, if it is applicable, the second use of a trademark is not actionable if it merely creates a likelihood of confusion concerning the source of the first user's product. We are, therefore, called upon to decide whether, as a matter of Indiana law, the creation of such likelihood of confusion is actionable. As we have indicated, the Indiana cases have involved the adoption and use of a mark or name identical with, or similar to, the established trademark or tradename of a competitor. The Indiana appellate courts have not considered whether a second use creating the likelihood of confusion about the source of the first user's products is actionable. The tests of unfair competition and trademark infringement formulated by the Indiana courts . . . , do not embrace the latter type of confusion. Insofar as they appear to fix the boundaries of trademark infringement and unfair competition, they are mere dicta. Appellants apparently put forth a suggested doctrine of 'reverse confusion' concerning which we find no rational basis for support.").

unquestionably unfair competition through an improper use of a trademark and that must be actionable.' 408 F. Supp. at 1236."[150]

Other courts recognize reverse confusion as actionable harm to trademark rights in suits for infringement of state common law and federally-registered marks and for relief under Lanham Act Section 43(a).[151] In *Banff*,[152] the Second Circuit

---

[150] 561 F.2d at 1372.

See also Ameritech, Inc. v. American Information Technologies Corp., 811 F.2d 960, 1 U.S.P.Q.2d 1861 (6th Cir. 1987) (interpreting Ohio trademark law):

"Although trademark protection may have had its start in common law as an action in fraud, over the past one hundred fifty years it has come to focus also on protecting property interests in trademarks themselves. This shift is the result of the recognition of the purposes trademarks serve in the modern, impersonal economy. They act as a means of identifying a product as coming from or being associated with a particular, although anonymous, source, and inducing subsequent purchases by consumers. . . .

" . . . A reverse confusion claim differs from the stereotypical confusion of source or sponsorship claim. Rather than seeking to profit from the goodwill captured in the senior user's trademark, the junior user saturates the market with a similar trademark and overwhelms the senior user. The public comes to assume the senior user's products are really the junior user's or that the former has become somehow connected to the latter. The result is that the senior user loses the value of the trademark—its product identity, corporate identity, control over its goodwill and reputation, and ability to move into new markets.

. . .

"Not only is Ohio generous in protecting trademarks, but recognizing a reverse confusion claim is not a big step. Ohio has long protected trademark owners from confusion of source (i.e., 'palming off') and confusion of sponsorship. The same interests—protecting property interests in trademarks and preventing consumer confusion—are at stake in a reverse confusion case; the senior user's interests in the trademark can be suffocated by the junior user who takes the trademark as his own; and consumers can be confused that the senior user's products come from the junior user or that the senior has become associated with the junior." 811 F.2d at 964, 1 U.S.P.Q.2d at 1864.

[151] *E.g.*, Fuddruckers Inc. v. Doc's B.R. Others Inc., 826 F.2d 837, 845, 4 U.S.P.Q.2d 1026, 1032 (9th Cir. 1987) (actionable likelihood of confusion is not "limited to consumer belief that the infringer is being operated by the original user. The potential harm is equally great if the consumers believe that the infringer runs the original user."); Capital Films Corp. v. Charles Fries Productions, Inc., 628 F.2d 387, 393-94, 208 U.S.P.Q. 249 (5th Cir. 1980) (applying Texas law; "Reverse confusion has now become a recognized doctrine within the scope of unfair competition, and we see no reason why it should not be applied in this case unless the law of Texas—the forum of this case-would prevent its application."); Worthington Foods, Inc. v. Kellogg Co., 732 F. Supp. 1417, 1455, 14 U.S.P.Q.2d 1577, 1606 (S.D. Ohio 1990) (noting that the 1988 amendments make it clear that plaintiffs can assert a confusion of sponsorship or reverse confusion sponsorship theory under section 43(a). "In a reverse confusion of sponsorship suit, the plaintiff's action rests on the claim that the junior user of a mark is saturating the market with advertising bearing the mark, thereby causing consumer confusion. Specifically, consumers mistakenly believe that the senior user's products are the junior user's or that the senior user is somehow connected with the junior user. . . . The evil in this kind of confusion is that the 'senior user loses the value of the trademark—its product identity, corporate identity, control over its goodwill and reputation, and ability to move into new markets.' . . . Section 43(a) of the Lanham Act contemplates liability under the reverse confusion of sponsorship

subscribed to "reverse confusion." The senior user Banff used the mark "Bee Wear" for clothing. Bloomingdale's, the well-known department store, later used "B Wear" for clothing. The court held that both kinds of confusion, ordinary confusion and reverse confusion, were present and each was actionable under the Lanham Act.

"In the typical trademark infringement suit a senior user claims that a junior user is attempting to ride on the senior's coattails and to persuade consumers that the senior user is the source of the junior user's goods. On this appeal, we consider what the rule is when the junior user—because it is bigger and better known in the marketplace—is wrongly viewed as the source of the goods in question.

. . .

". . . Subsumed under the likelihood of confusion analysis, two types of potential confusion allegedly support a claim of infringement: ordinary confusion and reverse confusion. Under the Lanham Act confusion is ordinarily the misimpression that the senior user (Banff) is the source of the junior user's (Bloomingdale's) goods. Reverse confusion is the misimpression that the junior user is the source of the senior user's goods. . . .

"The principal marks in question, 'Bee Wear' and various typestyles of 'B Wear,' may create both types of confusion. Consumers who know of Banff's 'Bee Wear' may believe that Bloomingdale's . . . goods originate with Banff. . . . The Lanham Act protects against this kind of confusion in order to prevent Bloomingdale's from appropriating Banff's reputation, limiting Banff's expansion, or causing Banff a loss of patronage. . . . Other consumers initially aware of Bloomingdale's apparel may believe that Banff's 'Bee Wear' mark they later encounter originates with Bloomingdale's. These consumers may consider Banff an unauthorized infringer, and Bloomingdale's use of the mark may in that way injure Banff's reputation and impair its good will. . . . Thus, reverse confusion also inhibits fair competition and deprives Banff of its reputation and good will.

". . . The objectives of [the Lanham] Act—to protect an owner's interest in its trademark by keeping the public free from confusion as to the source of goods and ensuring fair competition—are as important in a case of reverse confusion as in typical trademark infringement. Were reverse confusion not a sufficient basis

theory. The statute encompasses the utilization of trademarks which causes confusion 'as to the affiliation, connection, or sponsorship' of goods. Since the statute is not limited by its plain language to situations where consumers believe the plaintiff sponsored the defendant's goods, the Court holds that this language imposes liability on defendants who create in consumers' minds the mistaken belief that the defendant sponsored the plaintiff's goods. In other words, the Court holds that claims of both confusion of sponsorship and reverse confusion of sponsorship are actionable under section 43(a) of the Lanham Act."); Mastercard International, Inc. v. Arbel Corp., 13 U.S.P.Q.2d 1958, 1963 (S.D N.Y. 1989) ("liability under the reverse confusion theory has been recognized in cases involving non-competitive products.").

Cf. Pignons S.A. de Mecanique de Precision v. Polaroid Corp., 657 F.2d 482, 492 n.4, 212 U.S.P.Q. 246, 254 n.4 (1st Cir. 1981) ("in either sort of infringement case, [ordinary trademark infringement or reverse confusion], likelihood of confusion must be established.").

192 Banff, Ltd. v. Federated Department Stores, Inc., 841 F.2d 486, 6 U.S.P.Q.2d 1187 (2d Cir. 1988).

to obtain Lanham Act protection, a larger company could with impunity infringe the senior mark of a smaller one. . . . Consequently, we hold that reverse confusion—perhaps the primary type of confusion involved in this case—is actionable under § 43(a) of the Lanham Act."[153]

In assessing reverse confusion, courts apply the multiple factors approach used in forward confusion cases. Some of the particular factors apply differently in reverse confusion cases. For example, in *Worthington Foods*,[154] the district court noted a difference in mark strength's role.

"The inherent nature of the plaintiff's mark is relevant since the more distinctive the mark, the more likely it is that a consumer, with a general recollection of the plaintiff's mark, will draw a connection between the two parties when seeing the defendant's mark. Yet the actual performance of the plaintiff's mark in the market place is relevant in a different way than it would be under the other theories.

"A plaintiff asserting this theory is not arguing that its mark is overwhelming or will be so well-known in the marketplace that the defendant's use of that mark causes consumers to believe it sponsored the defendant's goods. Instead, the plaintiff must show that the defendant's mark has captured greater consumer recognition than its own, that the defendant's mark is overwhelming or will overwhelm the plaintiff's mark. That is, the plaintiff is arguing that consumers are confused when they see the defendant's mark because they then associate the plaintiff's product with the defendant."[155]

[d] **Endorsement and Sponsorship Confusion.** At one time, the confusion the likelihood of which trademark law attempted to prevent was solely that of *purchasers* as to goods' origin. Today, "the test for likelihood of confusion . . . is broader, embracing confusion as to the association between the goods or sponsorship of the allegedly infringing goods."[156]

---

[153] 841 F.2d at 487, 490-91, 6 U.S.P.Q.2d at 1188, 1190-91.

[154] Worthington Foods, Inc. v. Kellogg Co., 732 F. Supp. 1417, 14 U.S.P.Q.2d 1577 (S.D. Ohio 1990).

[155] 732 F. Supp. at 1455, 14 U.S.P.Q.2d at 1607.

[156] Lindy Pen Co. v. Bic Pen Corp., 725 F.2d 1240, 226 U.S.P.Q. 17 (9th Cir. 1984).

See also Supreme Assembly, Order of Rainbow for Girls v. J.H. Ray Jewelry Co., 676 F.2d 1079, 1082 n. 3 (5th Cir. 1982) ("Prior to 1962, § 1114(1) provided that the use of the mark must be 'likely to cause confusion, or to cause mistake, or to deceive *purchasers as to the source or origin of such goods or services.*' (emphasis added). In 1962, it was amended to delete the underlined portion. Although this amendment 'clearly broadened the protection afforded by the statute,' it is equally clear that this amendment did not delete the confusion requirement entirely, and that a claimant must still prove a likelihood of confusion, mistake or deceit of 'typical' purchasers, or potential purchasers, as to the connection of the trademark owner with the infringing product."); Stop the Olympic Prison v. U.S. Olympic Committee, 489 F. Supp. 1112, 1121 (S.D. N.Y.1980) "[a]lthough 'confusion' in this context has traditionally meant confusion as to the source or origin of goods or services in connection with which a trademark is used, courts have come to accept confusion as to sponsorship, endorsement, or some other affiliation as satisfying the requirement."); Planned Parenthood Federation of America, Inc. v. Problem Pregnancy of Worcester, Inc., 398 Mass. 480, 498 N.E.2d 1044, 1049, 1

[i] *Confusion Off the Point of Sale.* Courts hold that likelihood of confusion includes possible confusion off the point of sale, such as luring potential purchasers before sale or misleading users after sale.[157]

In *Mastercrafters Clock & Radio Co.*,[158] Vacheron sold a distinctively designed "Atmos" (atmospheric) clock for $175. Mastercrafters sold a similar electric clock for $30, its intent being to "avail itself of an eye-catching design and . . . to cater to the price conscious purchaser who desires to own a copy of a luxury design clock regardless of mechanism or source." The district court denied Vacheron's trade dress infringement claim, noting that Mastercrafter's clock had an electric cord and no purchaser would assume that it was an atmospheric clock such as Vacheron sold. The Second Circuit reversed, noting, *inter alia*, that a purchaser would likely not be deceived as to the clock's source at the time of sale but visitors to his or her home might be.[159]

U.S.P.Q.2d 1465, 1469 (1986) ("Although the confusion referred to in unfair competition claims has generally meant confusion as to source or origin of goods or services, the trend has been to extend confusion to the factors of sponsorship or endorsement.").

[157] One decision suggests that *investor* confusion may suffice. Communications Satellite Corp. v. Comcet, Inc., 429 F.2d 1245, 1250 (4th Cir. 1970), *cert. denied*, 400 U.S. 942 (1970) ("A trade name symbolizes the reputation of a business. Consumers are interested in the quality and cost of the goods or services that it offers; suppliers are concerned with the prompt payment of bills and credit standing; investors, with financial stability, return and growth; labor, with rates of pay, fringe benefits and personnel policies; and the general public, with management's participation in public affairs. All of these factors, and more, make up 'the communication mosaic in which a business enterprise must fit' and which its trade name reflects. Infringement of a trade name is a tort touching all these factors."). *Compare* Perini Corp. v. Perini Construction, Inc., 915 F.2d 121, 128, 16 U.S.P.Q.2d 1289, 1294 (4th Cir. 1990) ("In order for a likelihood of confusion among the public, but not typical purchasers, to provide the basis for a trade name infringement action, it must be shown that public confusion will adversely affect the plaintiff's ability to control his reputation among its laborers, lenders, investors, or other group with whom the plaintiff interacts.").

[158] Mastercrafters Clock & Radio Co. v. Vacheron & Constantin-LeCoultre Watches, Inc., 221 F.2d 464 (2d Cir. 1955), *cert. denied*, 350 U.S. 832 (1955).

[159] ". . . [A]s the [trial] judge found, plaintiff copied the design of the Atmos clock because plaintiff intended to, and did, attract purchasers who wanted a 'luxury design' clock. This goes to show at least that some customers would buy plaintiff's cheaper clock for the purpose of acquiring the prestige gained by displaying what many visitors at the customers' homes would regard as a prestigious article. Plaintiff's wrong thus consisted of the fact that such a visitor would be likely to assume that the clock was an Atmos clock. Neither the electric cord attached to, nor the plaintiff's name on, its clock would be likely to come to the attention of such a visitor; the likelihood of such confusion suffices to render plaintiff's conduct actionable." 221 F.2d at 466.

See also Academy of Motion Picture Arts and Sciences v. Creative House Promotions, Inc., 944 F.2d 1446, 19 U.S.P.Q.2d 1491 (9th Cir. 1991) ("by considering only the initial purchasers . . . as the relevant market, the court overlooked the risk of post-sale confusion. Post-sale confusion occurs when consumers view a product outside the context in which it is originally distributed and confuse it with another, similar product."); Polo Fashions Inc. v. Craftex Inc., 816 F.2d 145, 148, 2 U.S.P.Q.2d 1444, 1446 (4th Cir. 1987) ("in the after sale context, one seeing the shirt being worn by its owner, would not see the label on the back of

In *Grotrian*,[160] Heinrich Steinweg began making pianos in Germany in 1835. In 1850, he emigrated to the United States with three sons, changed his name to "Steinway," and founded the now famous piano company. His oldest son, C.F. Theodor Steinweg, remained in Germany and founded Grotrian, to which he conveyed the right to use "C.F. Th. Steinweg Nachf." In 1969, Grotrian filed a suit seeking a declaratory judgment that its "Grotrian- Steinweg" mark did not conflict with Steinway's registered marks "Steinway" and "Steinway & Sons." The Second Circuit affirmed the district court's likelihood of confusion conclusion, rejecting Grotrian's argument that piano purchasers could not be confused given the nature and cost of pianos and the conditions under which they are purchased.

> "[I]n a trademark infringement action the kind of product, its cost and the conditions of purchase are important factors in considering whether the degree of care exercised by the purchaser can eliminate the likelihood of confusion which would otherwise exist. We decline to hold, however, that actual or potential confusion at the time of purchase necessarily must be demonstrated to establish trademark infringement under the circumstances of this case.

> "The issue here is not the possibility that a purchaser would buy a Grotrian-Steinweg thinking it was actually a Steinway or that Grotrian had some connection with Steinway and Sons. The harm to Steinway, rather, is the likelihood that a consumer, hearing the 'Grotrian-Steinweg' name and thinking it had some connection with 'Steinway', would consider it on that basis. The 'Grotrian-Steinweg' name therefore would attract potential customers based on the reputation built up by Steinway in this country for many years. The harm to Steinway in short is the likelihood . . . that potential piano purchasers will think that there is some connection between the Grotrian-Steinweg and Steinway pianos. . . . Such initial confusion works an injury to Steinway."[161]

In *Hon*,[162] in upholding a conviction for trafficking in wrist watches bearing prestige-brand counterfeit trademarks, the Second Circuit held that neither the Lanham Act nor the criminal trademark counterfeiting statute[163] were limited to purchaser confusion. Interpreting trademark law's confusion requirement "to include the non-purchasing public advances the important purpose underlying the trademark laws of protecting the trademark owner's investment in the quality of the mark

---

the neck. Seeing the polo player symbol, it is likely that the observer would identify the shirt with the plaintiff, and the plaintiff's reputation would suffer damage if the shirt appeared to be of poor quality."); Ferrari S.p.A. Esercizio Fabbriche Automobili e Corse v. McBurnie, 11 U.S.P.Q.2d 1843, 1847 (S.D. Calif. 1989) ("the universe of relevant consumers who might be confused includes those who would see the trademark or trade dress away from the point of purchase.").

Cf. Levi Strauss & Co. v. Blue Bell, Inc., 632 F.2d 817, 208 U.S.P.Q. 713 (9th Cir. 1980).

[160] Grotrian, Helfferich, Schulz, Th. Steinweg Nachf. v. Steinway & Sons, 523 F.2d 1331, 186 U.S.P.Q. 436 (2d Cir. 1975).

[161] 523 F.2d at 1342.

[162] United States v. Hon, 904 F.2d 803, 14 U.S.P.Q.2d 1959 (2d Cir. 1990), *cert. denied*, 111 S. Ct. 789 (1991).

[163] 18 U.S.C. § 2320.

and his product's reputation, one that is independent of the goal of preventing consumer deception."[164]

[ii] *Parody.* Cases commonly arise in which an accused infringer uses a trademark for parody or humor.[165] Trademark owners assert that even humorous use makes confusion likely under the general *Polaroid* factors approach or that the use is improper under state dilution statutes.[166]

Some decisions grant relief against parody trademark use, finding confusion likely,[167] but most deny relief, finding it unlikely.[168] In *Jordache Enterprises*,[169] the court applied the standard factors to find confusion not likely when a major blue jeans manufacturer's "JORDACHE" mark was challenged by an accused infringers' "LARDASHE" larger women's jeans mark.

> "Given the unlimited number of possible names and symbols that could serve as a trademark, it is understandable that a court generally presumes one who chooses a mark similar to an existing mark intends to confuse the public. However, where a party chooses a mark as a parody of an existing mark, the intent is not necessarily to confuse the public but rather to amuse. . . . "

---

[164] "At least as far back as *G.H. Mumm Champagne v. Eastern Wine Corp.*, 142 F.2d 499 (2d Cir.), *cert. denied*, 323 U.S. 715 (1944), a case where a cheap domestic champagne's label resembled that of the plaintiff's premium French import, we have recognized nonpurchaser confusion as relevant. In the words of Judge Learned Hand,

> 'as an evening wears on, the label, and only a very casual glance at the label, is quite enough to assure the host and his table that he remains as free-handed and careless of cost as when he began. At such stages of an entertainment nothing will be easier than for an unscrupulous restaurant keeper to substitute the domestic champagne.' " 904 F.2d at 807, 14 U.S.P.Q.2d at 1962.

[165] For a discussion of parody and copyright, *see* § 4F[3][d].

[166] *See* § 5E[3][b][ii](1).

[167] *E.g.*, Mutual of Omaha Insurance Co. v. Novak, 836 F.2d 397, 5 U.S.P.Q.2d 1314 (8th Cir. 1987).

[168] *E.g.*, Carson v. Here's Johnny Portable Toilets, Inc., 698 F.2d 831, 218 U.S.P.Q. 1 (6th Cir. 1983), *appeal after remand*, 810 F.2d 104, 1 U.S.P.Q.2d 2007 (6th Cir. 1987) (the famous entertainer, Johnny Carson, sought relief on various theories, including unfair competition, trademark infringement and publicity rights, against defendant's use of "HERE'S JOHNNY" for portable toilets; the phrase "Here's Johnny" has been consistently used to introduce Carson on his late night television program; HELD: no relief on trademark theory because of an absence of a likelihood of confusion; "The general concept underlying the likelihood of confusion is that the public believe that 'the mark's owner *sponsored or otherwise approved* the use of the trademark.' "); Tetley, Inc. v. Topps Chewing Gum, Inc., 556 F. Supp. 785, 790, 217 U.S.P.Q. 1128, 1131-32 (E.D. N.Y. 1983) ("The very broadness of the joke is a measure of the difference between Tetley's marks and Topp's sticker. While defendant has satirically adapted plaintiff's packaging colors and design and has substituted 'Petley' for the 'Tetley' mark printed on plaintiff's package, 'Orange Pekingese Fleas' for the 'Orange Pekoe and Pekoe Cut Black Tea' label printed on plaintiff's package, '40 Flea Bags' for the '48 Tea Bags' label printed on plaintiff's package, and 'Tiny Little Dog Fleas' for the 'The Tiny Little Tea Leaf Tea' mark printed on plaintiff's package, such broad satirical adaptation draws a heavy line between itself and the object of satire.").

[169] Jordache Enterprises, Inc. v. Hogg Wyld, Ltd., 828 F.2d 1482, 4 U.S.P.Q.2d 1216 (10th Cir. 1987).

"In one sense, a parody is an attempt 'to derive benefit from the reputation' of the owner of the mark, . . . if only because no parody could be made without the initial mark. The benefit to the one making the parody, however, arises from the humorous association, not from public confusion as to the source of the marks. A parody relies upon a difference from the original mark, presumably a humorous difference, in order to produce its desired effect. 'Now everything is funny as long as it is happening to somebody Else, but when it happens to you, why it seems to lose some of its Humor, and if it keeps on happening, why the entire laughter kinder Fades out of it.' W. Rogers, *Warning to Jokers: Lay Off the Prince*, in *The Illiterate Digest*, I-3 *The Writings of Will Rogers* 75 (1974). The same is true in trademark law. As McCarthy writes, "No one likes to be the butt of a joke, not even a trademark. But the requirement of trademark law is that a likely confusion of source, sponsorship or affiliation must be proven, which is not the same thing as a 'right' not to be made fun of." 2 J. McCarthy, *Trademarks and Unfair Competition* § 31:38 at 670 (2d ed. 1984).

"Of course, a parody of an existing trademark can cause a likelihood of confusion. For example, where two marks are confusingly similar, or where there is evidence of actual confusion, a likelihood of confusion can exist despite the intent to create a parody. Our single concern here, however, is whether an intent to parody an existing trademark supports an inference of a likelihood of confusion under the reasoning that one who chooses a mark similar to an existing mark intends to confuse the public. . . . We hold that it does not. An intent to parody is not an intent to confuse the public."[170]

Some decisions cite First Amendment free speech concerns in denying relief, especially when the accused infringer's use is not for commercial purposes.[171] In *Mutual of Omaha*,[172] the Eighth Circuit affirmed the district court's finding that defendant's "Mutant of Omaha" with an Indian head symbol on sweatshirts, mugs, etc. and an anti-nuclear weapons message is confusingly similar to plaintiff's "Mutual of Omaha" and Indian head symbol. A survey showed that, when exposed to defendant's shirt, about ten percent thought that plaintiff "goes along" with defendant's product: "Because manifestations of actual confusion serve as strong evidence of a likelihood of confusion, . . . and may, in fact, be the best such evidence, . . . this survey should be given substantial weight unless seriously flawed." The court distinguished prior cases finding no likelihood of confusion with "obvious parody": "Those cases either did not involve surveys demonstrating confusion or involved surveys of doubtful validity." It rejected the defendant's First Amendment free speech argument: "Mutual's trademarks are a form of property, . . . and Mutual's rights

---

[170] 828 F.2d at 1486, 4 U.S.P.Q.2d at 1220. *See also* Universal City Studies, Inc. v. T-Shirt Gallery, Ltd., 634 F. Supp. 1468, 230 U.S.P.Q. 23 (S.D. N.Y. 1986) ("A mere intent to parody, however, should not give rise to a presumption of likelihood of consumer confusion. Indeed, as discussed above, a successful parody should serve to dispel consumer confusion rather than create it.").

[171] *E.g.*, L.L. Bean, Inc. v. Drake Publishers, Inc., 811 F.2d 26, 1 U.S.P.Q.2d 1753 (1st Cir. 1987), discussed at § 5E[3][b][ii](1).

[172] Mutual of Omaha Insurance Co. v. Novak, 836 F.2d 397, 5 U.S.P.Q.2d 1314 (8th Cir. 1987), *cert. denied*, 488 U.S. 933 (1988).

therein need not 'yield to the exercise of First Amendment rights under circumstances where adequate alternative avenues of communication exist.' "[173] The Eighth Circuit distinguished the First Circuit's *L.L. Bean* decision: "*L.L. Bean* involved 'editorial or artistic' use of a mark 'solely for noncommercial purposes,' . . . and the holding did not encompass the likelihood of confusion issue." Judge Heaney dissented.[174]

In *Cliff's Notes Inc.*,[175] plaintiff published the well-known "Cliffs Notes" series of study guides, which contain condensed versions of literary works for use by college students. Defendant decided to publish "Spy Notes," double parodies in which contemporary novels are satirized in a format resembling plaintiff's "Cliffs Notes." Defendant admitted that it copied Cliffs Notes' prominent features, including the distinctive, yellow color, black diagonal stripes and black lettering. "Spy Notes" did have differences and prominently stated that it was "A Satire." The district court found confusion likely, based on the *Polaroid* test, and enjoined distribution of Spy Notes. The Second Circuit reversed, adopting a balancing approach[176] to trademark claims against works of artistic expression, including parody.[177]

---

[173] 836 F.2 at 402, 5 U.S.P.Q. at 1319, quoting Lloyd Corp. v. Tanner, 407 U.S. 551, 567 (1972).

[174] Judge Heaney noted:

"[T]he trial court's finding that there exists a likelihood of confusion is clearly erroneous. Moreover, the majority's holding sanctions a violation of Novak's first amendment rights. The T-shirts simply expressed a political message which irritated the officers of Mutual, who decided to swat this pesky fly buzzing around in their backyard with a sledge hammer (a federal court injunction). We should not be a party to this effort." 836 F.2d at 403, 5 U.S.P.Q.2d at 1320. As to the survey, he noted: "Neither T-shirts nor insurance were featured at the shopping malls where the interviews were conducted. No one was asked whether he or she was interested in buying a T-shirt or insurance." Scholarly opinion rejects both "the loose definition of property damage taken by the majority" and "the notion that product parodists must use 'adequate alternative avenues of communication.' " 836 F.2d at 405, 5 U.S.P.Q.2d at 1321.

[175] Cliff's Notes Inc. v. Bantam Doubleday Dell Publishing Group Inc., 886 F.2d 490, 12 U.S.P.Q.2d 1289 (2d Cir. 1989).

[176] The court took the balancing test from its recent decision, Rogers v. Grimaldi, 875 F.2d 994, 10 U.S.P.Q. 1825 (2d Cir. 1989), holding that Lanham Act Section 43(a)'s prohibition of false advertising "should be construed to apply to artistic works only where the public interest in avoiding consumer confusion outweighs the public interest in free expression." 875 F.2d at 999, 10 U.S.P.Q.2d at 1828. In *Rogers*, actress Ginger Rogers challenged the defendants' use of the title "Ginger and Fred" for a movie that was about two Italian cabaret performers who imitated Ginger Rogers and Fred Astaire, contending the film title created the false impression that she was the subject of the film or endorsed it. The court rejected the challenge.

[177] A balancing test was necessary because of a conflict in policies:

"[P]arody is a form of artistic expression, protected by the First Amendment. . . .

"At the same time, '[t]rademark protection is not lost simply because the allegedly infringing use in connection with a work of artistic expression.' . . .

"Conflict between these two policies is inevitable in the context of parody, because the keystone of parody is imitation. It is hard to imagine, for example, a successful parody of Time magazine that did not reproduce Time's trademarked red border. A parody must convey two simultaneous—and contradictory— messages: that it is the original, but also that it is *not* the original and is instead a parody. To the extent that it does only the former but not the latter, it is not only a poor parody but also vulnerable under trademark law, since the customer will be confused." 886 F.2d at 493-94, 12 U.S.P.Q.2d at 1291-92.

"[I]n any case where an expressive work is alleged to infringe a trademark, it is appropriate to weigh the public interest in free expression against the public interest in avoiding consumer confusion. . . . [T]he expressive element of parodies requires more protection than the labeling of ordinary commercial products.

". . . This approach takes into account the ultimate test in trademark law, namely, the likelihood of confusion ' as to the source of the goods in question ' . . . At the same time, a balancing approach allows greater latitude for works such as parodies, in which expression, and no commercial exploitation of another's trademark, is the primary intent, and in which there is a need to evoke the original work being parodied."[178]

A parody need not be an "obvious joke": "parody may be sophisticated as well as slapstick; a literary work is a parody if, taken as a whole, it pokes fun at its subject." Likelihood of confusion was not great because plaintiff's Cliffs Notes are not purchased on impulse and because Cliffs Notes are, with few exceptions, summaries of traditional "Great Books" while defendant's parodies are of contemporary works.

[iii]   *Decorative Mark Use—Merchandising Rights.* The parody cases are a part of a larger problem: can a notable trademark or trade identity symbol's owner control decorative uses of the mark—such as reproduction on clothing or accessories?

In *Bi-Rite Enterprises,*[179] the district court held that trademark and unfair competition law did not confer a categorical right to exclude the unlicensed use on buttons and other novelty items of the likenesses, logos, and names of recording artists. The mark owners must establish that "the particular use of a functional mark on the product involved will cause or was intended to cause consumer confusion as to source. In certain contexts, such as at concerts where the mark's owner performs, the public may, in fact, assume that the owner of the mark sponsored or even produced the goods—emblems, buttons or T-shirts—that bear its mark."[180]

---

[178] 886 F.2d at 494–95, 12 U.S.P.Q.2d at 1292–93.

[179] Bi-Rite Enterprises, Inc. v. Button Masters, 555 F. Supp. 1188, 217 U.S.P.Q. 910 (S.D. N.Y. 1983), *supplemental opinion,* 578 F. Supp. 59 (S.D. N.Y. 1983).

If the mark used for decoration is a personal identity symbol, the person may have a remedy under publicity right law. *See* § 6G.

[180] 555 F. Supp. at 1195, 217 U.S.P.Q. at 916.

The court noted that the recent "push to extend trademark protection to the use of established marks on collateral products is only the most recent manifestation of the effort (as old as the trademark law itself) to protect the full economic value of distinctive marks." However, intellectual property law and policy limit trademark owner's power to capture all the goodwill surrounding their marks.

"The cause is rooted in fairness and commercial good sense. People establish marks through effort and investment, and the value embodied in these marks should be protected against those who would steal or dilute it. The zeal to protect the full value of marks, and the feelings and economic interests that fuel it, however, cannot negate the fact that unfair competition law clearly requires confusion as to the source of goods before it will protect against the unauthorized use of a mark.

"Copyright and patent laws grant to the creators of original expression and ideas monopoly power over their use and sale. Congress sanctioned such monopoly power to reward and encourage originality and creativity in otherwise competitive markets. . . .

· In *Boston Athletic Ass'n*,[181] the court granted relief against defendant's unauthorized sale of shirts bearing plaintiff's "Boston Marathon" marks and discussed at length the difficulties encountered in applying trademark law's likelihood- of-confusion standard to "promotional goods" cases.

"In order to establish infringement in a promotional goods case, it has traditionally been the plaintiff's burden to show that prospective purchasers are in fact likely to be confused or misled into thinking that the defendant's product was produced, licensed, or otherwise sponsored by the plaintiff. *See, e.g., Supreme Assembly v. J.H. Ray Jewelry Co.*, 676 F.2d 1079, 1082 (5th Cir.1982); *International Order of Job's Daughters v. Lindeburg & Co.*, 633 F.2d 912, 919 (9th Cir.1980), *cert. denied*, 452 U.S. 941, 101 S. Ct. 3086, 69 L. Ed. 2d 956 (1981); *University of Pittsburgh v. Champion Products, Inc.*, 566 F. Supp. 711 (W.D. Pa. 1984); *NFL Football Properties, Inc. v. Wichita Falls Sportswear, Inc.*, 532 F. Supp. 651 (W.D. Wash. 1982).

. . . .

"There can be no doubt that the language and design on defendant's shirts intentionally calls attention to an event that has long been sponsored and supported by the BAA—an event that is, in fact, the subject of its registered mark. Defendants' shirts are clearly designed to take advantage of the Boston Marathon and to benefit from the good will associated with its promotion by plaintiffs. Defendants thus obtain a 'free ride' at plaintiffs' expense. . . .

". . . [P]laintiffs have to prove, of course, that the defendants are trading on plaintiffs' mark and good will. We do not think, however, that plaintiffs also have to prove that members of the public will actually conclude that defendants' product was *officially* sponsored by the Marathon's sponsor (whoever that sponsor may be). One difficulty with presenting such proof is that few people, other than legal specialists, could venture an informed opinion on whether someone using the logo of the sponsor of a sporting event is required to have the

---

Trademark laws do not share this purpose. They function instead to protect the individual reputation and good-will that parties build for their goods in the market. . . . This distinction made by Congress in its legislative scheme is not merely one of form, having no basis in policy or fairness. Although industry and investment are encouraged by protecting distinctive marks, they are also encouraged by a system that allows entrepreneurs to copy and exploit such marks in nonconfusing ways."

. . . .

"These principles do not as a matter of law preclude protection against the use of marks on emblems, buttons, or other novelty items. They require the owner to establish that the particular use of a functional mark on the product involved will cause or was intended to cause consumer confusion as to source. In certain contexts, such as at concerts where the mark's owner performs, the public may, in fact, assume that the owner of the mark sponsored or even produced the goods—emblems, buttons or T-shirts—that bear its mark. An evidentiary record that established such confusion, or created a presumption that the manufacturer sought to confuse consumers as to source, would supply a basis for protection. But plaintiffs have not even attempted to prove confusion in the sense required by the Act." 555 F. Supp. at 1194-95, 1196, 217 U.S.P.Q. at 914-15, 916.

[181] Boston Athletic Ass'n v. Sullivan, 867 F.2d 22, 9 U.S.P.Q.2d 1690 (1st Cir. 1989).

permission of the event's sponsor. Lacking such knowledge, the question of approval is pure guesswork. To ask a factfinder to determine whether the public would think that defendants' shirts were 'authorized' or 'official' shirts is to ask it to resolve a confusing in many contexts, virtually meaningless question. Asking a factfinder to make such a determination also raises a problem of circularity:

'If consumers think that most uses of a trademark require authorization, then in fact they will require authorization because the owner can enjoin consumer confusion caused by unpermitted uses or charge for licenses. And if owners can sue to stop unauthorized uses, then only authorized uses will be seen by consumers, creating or reinforcing the perception that authorization is necessary. This is a "chicken and the egg" conundrum.'

2 J.T. McCarthy, *Trademarks and Unfair Competition* s 24:3, at 170 (2d ed. 1984).

"The pertinent case law recognizes the difficulty of asking factfinders to decide whether particular uses are 'authorized'. The Fifth Circuit has held that a factual showing of confusion about source or sponsorship need not be made in order to enjoin a manufacturer of cloth emblems from the unlicensed sale of National Hockey League team emblems. The court held:

'The confusion or deceit requirement [of 15 U.S.C. § 1114] is met by the fact that the defendant duplicated the protected trademarks and sold them to the public knowing that the public would identify them as being the teams' trademarks. The certain knowledge of the buyer that the source and origin of the trademark symbols were in plaintiffs satisfies the requirement of the act.'

Boston Professional Hockey Ass'n, Inc. v. Dallas Cap & Emblem Mfg., Inc., 510 F.2d 1004, 1012 (5th Cir.) (emphasis added), *cert. denied*, 423 U.S. 868, 96 S. Ct. 132, 46 L. Ed. 2d 98 (1975). . . . More recently, the Eleventh Circuit affirmed an injunction against the sale of 'Battlin' Bulldog Beer,' with cans emblazoned with the University of Georgia's canine mascot, in part on the ground that ' "confusion" may relate to the public's knowledge that the trademark, which is "the triggering mechanism" for the sale of the products, originates with the plaintiff.' *University of Georgia Athletic Ass'n v. Laite*, 756 F.2d 1535, 1546 (11th Cir.1985) (citing Boston Professional Hockey Ass'n, 510 F.2d at 1012) (emphasis in original).

"Other examples of such increased concern with a mark holder's rights can be found in decisions by both the Second and Seventh Circuits to enjoin toy manufacturers from the unlicensed manufacture and sale of toy cars. *Warner Bros. v. Gay Toys, Inc.*, 658 F.2d 76 (2d Cir.1981), *decision on appeal after remand*, 724 F.2d 327 (2d Cir.1983); *Processed Plastic Co. v. Warner Communications, Inc.*, 675 F.2d 852 (7th Cir.1982). In each case plaintiff's evidence showed that children bought defendant's toy car (or prevailed on their parents to buy it for them) because they identified it with the 'General Lee' car on plaintiff's 'Dukes of Hazzard' television show. There was no probative evidence showing that the children or their parents were likely to believe that the television show's producers had authorized or licensed the toy. Nevertheless, the courts held that the evidence that purchasers recognized defendant's toy as plaintiff's 'General Lee' car was sufficient to provide the required 'likelihood of confusion.'

"In *Gay Toys*, the Second Circuit moved quickly from the evidence of the purchasers' recognition of the car as the 'General Lee' car to the inference that 'many of the consumers did confuse the "Dixie Racer" [defendant's toy car] with the "General Lee" and assumed that the car was sponsored by Warner Bros.' 658 F.2d at 79. As the district court noted on remand, the Second Circuit's opinion seemed to 'creat[e] a conclusive presumption that if children are reminded of the "General Lee" by seeing a facsimile thereof, they will assume distribution of the facsimile to have been "sponsored" by plaintiff.' *Warner Bros. v. Gay Toys, Inc.*, 553 F. Supp. 1018, 1021 (S.D.N.Y.), aff'd, 724 F.2d 327 (2d Cir.1983). . . .

"In the present case, we adopt a similar presumption. Given the undisputed facts that (1) defendants intentionally referred to the Boston Marathon on its shirts, and (2) purchasers were likely to buy the shirts precisely because of that reference, we think it fair to presume that purchasers are likely to be confused about the shirt's source or sponsorship. We presume that, at the least, a sufficient number of purchasers would be likely to assume—mistakenly—that defendants' shirts had some connection with the official sponsors of the Boston Marathon. In the absence of any evidence that effectively rebuts this presumption of a 'likelihood of confusion,' we hold that plaintiffs are entitled to enjoin the manufacture and sale of defendants' shirts."[182]

[2] Defenses

[a] **Invalidity.** If a person claims common law trademark infringement or relies upon Lanham Act Section 43(a)'s unfair competition remedy, he must establish the asserted mark's protectability.[183] Mark "validity" is a part of the plaintiff's prima facie case, not a defense.[184]

---

[182] 867 F.2d at 32-35, 9 U.S.P.Q.2d at 1698-1700.

[183] *See* § 5C.

[184] *E.g.*, Edison Brothers Stores, Inc. v. Cosmair, Inc., 651 F. Supp. 1547, 1563, 2 U.S.P.Q.2d 1013, 1025 (S.D. N.Y. 1987) ("federal registration of the mark constitutes prima facie evidence of its validity, and shifts to defendant the burden of persuasion on the validity issue.").

As to the burden of proof, see Pizzeria Uno Corp. v. Temple, 747 F.2d 1522, 1529 n.4, 224 U.S.P.Q. 185, 189 n.4 (4th Cir. 1984) ("This presumption may be overcome, according to early decisions, only by clear and convincing evidence, but under the modern rule the standard is by a preponderance of the evidence."); Vuitton et Fils S.A. v. J. Young Enterprises, Inc., 644 F.2d 769, 775-76, 210 U.S.P.Q. 351, 212 U.S.P.Q. 85 (9th Cir. 1981) ("registration . . . on the Principal Register . . . shifts the burden of proof from the plaintiff, who would have to establish his right to exclusive use in a common law infringement action, to the defendant, who must introduce sufficient evidence to rebut the presumption of plaintiff's right to such protected use. Until recently, the rule was that the presumption of validity of a registered trademark had to be overcome by clear and convincing evidence. See e. g., W. D. Byron & Sons, Inc. v. Stein Bros. Mfg. Co., 377 F.2d 1001 (C.C.P.A.1967); Aluminum Fabricating Co. v. Season-All Window Corp., 259 F.2d 314, 316 (2d Cir. 1958). The Court of Customs has since rejected this position and now requires only a preponderance of the evidence.").

If a person asserts infringement of a registered mark, Lanham Act Section 33(a) makes the registration "prima facie evidence of the validity of the registered mark and of the registration."[185] The accused infringer bears the burden of establishing invalidity.[186]

If a mark registrant complies with the Lanham Act's incontestability provision, Lanham Act Section 33(b) limits the invalidity grounds available to an accused infringer.[187]

[b] **Fraud.** Fraudulent procurement is grounds for cancelling a registration at any time[188] and is a preserved defense, that is, one available even when the registrant's exclusive right of use is incontestable.[189]

Professor McCarthy questions the propensity of accused trademark infringers to "expend so much time, effort and money in vigorously pursuing" fraud claims, noting that even when successful, the defense only strips the trademark owner of Lanham Act registration benefits.[190] The owner may still enforce common law trademark rights[191] and Lanham Act Section 43(a) unfair competition rights.[192] This view

---

[185] Lanham Act § 33(a), 15 U.S.C. § 1115(a). See Brittingham v. Jenkins, 914 F.2d 447, 452, 16 U.S.P.Q.2d 1121, 1124 (4th Cir. 1990) ("This attribute of registration represents a change from the common law where the putative owner bears the burden of establishing ownership of the disputed mark in any trademark infringement action.").

[186] E.g., GTE Corp. v. Williams, 904 F.2d 536, 538, 14 U.S.P.Q.2d 1971, 1972 (10th Cir. 1990) ("the Patent and Trademark Office's decision to register a mark without requiring proof of secondary meaning creates a rebuttable presumption that the mark is suggestive, arbitrary, or fanciful rather than merely descriptive.").

[187] Lanham Act § 33(b), 15 U.S.C. § 1115(b).

  See § 5E[1][c].

[188] Lanham Act § 14(c), 15 U.S.C. § 1064(3).

[189] Lanham Act § 33(b)(1), 15 U.S.C. § 1115(b)(1).

[190] 2 J.T. McCarthy, Trademarks and Unfair Competition § 31:21 (2d ed. 1984).

[191] E.g., Aveda Corp. v. Evita Marketing, Inc., 706 F. Supp. 1419, 1425, 12 U.S.P.Q.2d 1091, 1096 (D. Minn. 1989) ("even if a plaintiff's registration is shown to be fraudulently obtained, the plaintiff's common law rights in the mark may still support an injunction against an infringing defendant."); National Trailways Bus System v. Trailway Van Lines, Inc., 269 F. Supp. 352, 356-57, 155 U.S.P.Q. 507 (E.D. N.Y. 1965) ("Plaintiff's argument of incontestability under Section 33 of the Lanham Act (15 U.S.C. 1115) falls by express exception under subdivision (1) (where right is obtained fraudulently). . . . Plaintiff's first claim is dismissed and the registrations herein referred to will be cancelled by appropriate directions to the Commissioner in the judgment to be entered. . . . Plaintiff is thus denied the procedural advantages available a registrant under the Act. . . . Plaintiff's failure to establish a statutory right, however, does not affect its common law claim of unfair competition."). Professor McCarthy notes that "While it might be argued that fraud in obtaining a registration should constitute an unclean hands defense to common law rights, this argument has properly been rejected" as "inconsistent with the policy of trademark law and the equitable foundations of the unclean hands defense." 2 J.T. McCarthy, Trademarks and Unfair Competition § 31:21 (2d ed. 1984). In patent cases, courts do on occasion apply the uncleans hands defense to render unenforceable not only the patent directly tainted by inequitable conduct but also other related patents. See § 2D[2][f].

[192] See Orient Express Trading Co., Ltd., 842 F.2d 650, 654, 6 U.S.P.Q.2d 1308, 1311 (2d Cir. 1988).

may underestimate the increasing importance of Lanham Act registration benefits, especially constructive notice, constructive use, and incontestability. For example, accused infringers commonly charge fraudulent procurement because they cannot rely on descriptiveness or prior use when the registrant's right to exclusive use is incontestable.[193] With intent-to-use applications, early trademark priority rights are built on Lanham Act filing and registration, not common law use acquisition.[194]

Professor McCarthy also notes that "the standard of disclosure and hence of 'fraud' in the procurement of federal trademark registrations should be, and is, quite different from that in patent procurement."[195] Unlike patent procedure, trademark registration is not the sole source of the registrant's rights[196] and includes liberal provision for adversary opposition and cancellation.[197]

One alleging fraud must establish that a misrepresentation to the PTO was (1) material,[198] and (2) made with culpable intent.[199] Courts impose a "heavy burden

---

[193] See § 5E[1][a].

[194] See §§ 5D[1][e] and 5D[2][b].

[195] 2 J.T. McCarthy, Trademarks and Unfair Competition § 31:21-B(2) (2d ed. 1984).

[196] See Morehouse Manufacturing Corp. v. J. Strickland and Co., 407 F.2d 881, 888, 160 U.S.P.Q. 715 (CCPA 1969) ("There does not exist in trademark cases the fundamental reason for being on the alert to find fraud on the Patent Office which exists in patent cases. Every right a patentee has is given to him by the Patent Office. On the other hand, the acquisition of the right to exclude others from the use of a trademark results from the fact of use and the common law, independently of registration in the Patent Office. The happenstance that trademarks are registered in the Patent Office should not result in confusing the principles involved in dissimilar proceedings with respect to wholly dissimilar rights. It is in the public interest to maintain registrations of technically good trademarks on the register so long as they are still in use. The register then reflects commercial reality. Assertions of 'fraud' should be dealt with realistically, comprehending, as the board did, that trademark rights, unlike patent rights, continue notwithstanding cancellation of those additional rights which the Patent Office is empowered by statute to grant.").

[197] Aveda Corp. v. Evita Marketing, Inc., 706 F. Supp. 1419, 12 U.S.P.Q.2d 1091, 1096 (D. Minn. 1989) ("The courts and the trademark board both view charges of fraud in the registration of a trademark as a disfavored defense. . . . Trademarks are created by use, not registration. Federal registration creates valuable substantive and procedural rights, but the common law creates the underlying right to exclude. . . . Moreover, the trademark registration, contrary to patent procurement, is an adversary process. The stringent standards of disclosure applicable to patent applications are therefore not appropriate to applications for trademark registrations. . . . Thus, the law provides that a false statement in an application for trademark registration will justify cancellation of the registration only if the statement misrepresents a material fact and the statement was made with an intent to defraud."). See § 5D[2][d].

[198] E.g., Pony Express Courier Corporation of America v. Pony Express Delivery Corp. of America, 872 F.2d 317, 10 U.S.P.Q.2d 1475, 1477 (9th Cir. 1989) ("to prove fraud that would result in the cancellation of Baker's mark, there would have to be a material misrepresentation in the affidavit on the basis of which the mark was registered. The claim of a date of first use is not a material allegation as long as the first use in fact preceded the application date."); Orient Express Trading Co., Ltd., 842 F.2d 650, 6 U.S.P.Q.2d 1308, 1311 (2d Cir. 1988) ("the knowing misstatement must have been with respect to a material fact—one that would have affected the PTO's action on the applications."); Aveda Corp. v. Evita Marketing, Inc.,

of proof."[200]

[i] *Use Evidence—Specimens.* Fraud questions often focus on allegedly false or misleading use evidence, that is, statements and specimens on the mark's use, submitted with an original application, a Section 8 continued use affidavit,[201] a Section 15 incontestability affidavit,[202] or a renewal application.[203]

---

706 F. Supp. 1419, 12 U.S.P.Q.2d 1091, 1096 (D. Minn. 1989) ("a misstatement of the date of first use in an application for registration is not fraudulent as long as there has been some use of the mark prior to the filing date.").

But cf. Gear, Inc. v. L.A. Gear Co., 670 F. Supp. 508, 4 U.S.P.Q.2d 1192 (S.D.N.Y. 1987) (court may consider immaterial falsehood "in balancing the equities.").

[199] *E.g.,* Wrist-Rocket Manufacturing Co., Inc. v. Saunders Archery Co., 516 F.2d 846, 186 U.S.P.Q. 5 (8th Cir. 1975), *cert. denied,* 423 U.S. 870 (1975) (no fraud if false statement not made with intent to defraud); King Automotive, Inc. v. Speedy Muffler King, Inc., 667 F.2d 1008, 212 U.S.P.Q. 801 (CCPA 1981) (withholding of information "absent the requisite intent to mislead, does not qualify under the Lanham Act as fraud warranting cancellation."); Robert B. Vance & Associates, Inc. v. Baronet Corp., 487 F. Supp. 790, 205 U.S.P.Q. 24 (N.D. Ga. 1979) ("Defendant failed to prove that the Plaintiffs knew or believed that the representation was false. . . . Although the facts of this case reveal that Plaintiffs may have failed to use the necessary care in their dealings with the U.S. Patent Office, they do not support a finding of fraud."); Five Platters, Inc. v. Purdie, 419 F. Supp. 372, 384, 193 U.S.P.Q. 411 (D. Md. 1976) ("Statements of honest, but perhaps incorrect, belief or innocently inaccurate statements of fact are insufficient as are knowing misstatements which would have a de minimus effect on the validity of the service mark."); Schwinn Bicycle Co. v. Murrary Ohio Mfg. Co., 339 F. Supp. 973, 172 U.S.P.Q. 14 (M.D. Tenn. 1971), *aff'd on other grounds,* 470 F.2d 975, 176 U.S.P.Q. 161 (6th Cir. 1972) (corporate officer's false statement "can reasonably be construed to have resulted from inadvertence or ignorance of the applicable law of trademarks.").

[200] *E.g.,* Orient Express Trading Co., Ltd., 842 F.2d 650, 6 U.S.P.Q.2d 1308 (2d Cir. 1988) (clear and convincing evdience); W. D. Byron & Sons, Inc. v. Stein Bros. Mfg. Co., 377 F.2d 1001, 153 U.S.P.Q. 749 (CCPA 1967). *See also* Brittingham v. Jenkins, 914 F.2d 447, 453, 16 U.S.P.Q. 1121, 1125 (4th Cir. 1990) ("[T]he procurement of a trademark registration through the use of false or misleading statements does not constitute fraud within the meaning of 15 U.S.C. § 1115(b)(1) unless the statements were both material to the decision to grant the registration and made with a deliberate intent to defraud. Moreover, the alleged fraud must be established by clear and convincing evidence."); Beer Nuts, Inc. v. Clover Club Foods Co., 711 F.2d 934, 221 U.S.P.Q. 209 (10th Cir. 1983) ("Section 1064(c) . . . provides that an incontestable trademark may be cancelled if its registration was obtained fraudulently. A court should not lightly undertake cancellation on the basis of fraud, . . . and the burden of proving fraudulent procurement of a registration is heavy. . . . Any deliberate attempt to mislead the Patent Office must be established by clear and convincing evidence.").

Cf. King Automotive, Inc. v. Speedy Muffler King, Inc., 667 F.2d 1008, 212 U.S.P.Q. 801 (CCPA 1981) (in cancellation, fraud claim must be pleaded with particularity).

[201] *E.g.,* le Cordon Bleu, S.A. v. BPC Publishing Ltd., 451 F. Supp. 63, 72 n.14, 202 U.S.P.Q. 147 (S.D. N.Y. 1978) (registrant filed a Section 8 continued use affidavit that was known to be materially false). *See* § 5D[3][a][i].

[202] *E.g.,* Robi v. Five Platters, Inc., 918 F.2d 1439, 1444, 16 U.S.P.Q.2d 2015, 2019 (9th Cir. 1990) (any false statements made in an incontestability affidavit may jeopardize not only the incontestability claim, but also the underlying registration; "FPI President Jean Bennett submitted an incontestability affidavit to the United States Patent and Trademark Office stating that 'there has been no final decision adverse to Registrant's claim of ownership of said mark

In *Torres*,[204] the court found fraud in the registrant's submission of a registration renewal application that falsely alleged the mark was still in use on "wine, vermouth, and champagne," the mark in fact being only used on wine, and including a specimen label the registrant was not in fact using. The registered mark was "Torres" with a three tower design; the registrant had altered the design. The court affirmed a summary judgment of registration cancellation, rejecting the registrant's argument that the mark alteration was not a material change and that he did not believe the renewal application represented a fraud on the PTO.

"Fraud in procuring a trademark registration or renewal occurs when an applicant *knowingly* makes false, material representations of fact in connection with his application. . . . '[T]he obligation which the Lanham Act imposes on an applicant is that he will not make *knowingly* inaccurate or knowingly misleading statements in the verified declaration forming a part of the application for registration.' *Bart Schwartz International Textiles, Ltd. v. Federal Trade Commission*, 289 F.2d 665, 669, 129 U.S.P.Q. 258, 260 (CCPA 1961) (emphasis in original). The obligation to refrain from knowingly making false, material statements applies with equal force to renewal applications. . . .

". . . Clearly, under the circumstances, Torres knew or should have known that the mark as registered and the specimen submitted were not currently in use when he filed his renewal application.

". . . The problem of fraud arises because Torres submitted a label that he knew or should have known was not in use that contained a mark clearly different from the one in use. In addition, he submitted an affidavit stating the mark was in use on wine, vermouth, and champagne when he knew it was in use only on wine.

---

nor to its right to register the same or maintain it on the register.' Given the adverse 1974 Decision, which denied FPI's claim that it was the only entity entitled to use the name 'The Platters' and contained numerous findings adverse to FPI's ownership interest, the affidavit was . . . clearly false. . . . Moreover, given Bennett's admitted knowledge of that decision at the time she signed the affidavit, the district court did not err in concluding that the affidavit was not only false, but also fraudulent."); Duffy-Mott Co. v. Cumberland Packing Co., 424 F.2d 1095, 165 U.S.P.Q. 422 (CCPA 1970) (false goods statement in Rule 15 incontestability affidavit precludes opposer from relying on registration to oppose another's right to register; "If goods are named on which the mark has not been used continuously for 5 consecutive years, or is not currently in use, it amounts to an attempt to acquire a right as a result of a false statement. This can scarcely be characterized as mere carelessness or misunderstanding to be winked at as of no importance.").

Cf. Skippy, Inc. v. CPC International, Inc., 674 F.2d 209, 216 U.S.P.Q. 1061 (4th Cir. 1982) (false statement in Section 15 affidavit precludes incontestability; the applicable statutory no adverse decision requirement is not limited to the federal registration in support of which the Section 15 affidavit is filed and includes any adverse decisions from other attempts to register the same mark; "Unlike other statements required by § 1065, the requirement that party state there be no adverse decisions has no express time limitation.").

See § 5E[1].

[203] *See* § 5D[3][a][ii].

[204] Torres v. Cantine Torresella S.r.l., 808 F.2d 46, 1 U.S.P.Q.2d 1483 (Fed. Cir. 1986).

"If a registrant files a verified renewal application stating that his registered mark is currently in use in interstate commerce and that the label attached to the application shows the mark as currently used when, in fact, he knows or should know that he is not using the mark as registered and that the label attached to the registration is not currently in use, he has knowingly attempted to mislead the PTO. The decision whether the *current* usage is not materially different from the mark as registered *despite the change* must rest with the Board, not the trademark owner." [205]

[*ii*] *Entitlement Declaration.* Fraud questions also often focus on the registration application requirement that the applicant state that no other person "to the best of his knowledge and belief, has the right to use such mark in commerce either in the identical form thereof or in such near resemblance thereto as to be likely, when used on or in connection with the goods of such other person, to cause confusion, or to cause mistake, or to deceive." [206] The applicant may have information of other uses of similar marks from a trademark search or from another source.

Courts decline to impose on applicants a categorical duty to search for or investigate the circumstances of possible prior uses and refuse to find fraud unless the right to use statement was "knowingly false." [207]

In *Money Store,* [208] the Seventh Circuit held that the Lanham Act does not obligate "one seeking federal registration of a mark to investigate and report to the Patent

---

[205] 808 F.2d at 48, 1 U.S.P.Q.2d at 1484-85. *Compare* G. H. Mumm & Cie v. Desnoes & Geddes, Ltd., 917 F.2d 1292, 1296, 16 U.S.P.Q.2d 1635, 1638-39 (Fed. Cir. 1990) (no "inequitable conduct involving fraud and unclean hands" when registrant submitted partially completed labels in support of its renewal application; "The submitted specimens show a diagonal red stripe without any wording. The '907 registration is for a diagonal red stripe. The registration shows no wording. It is undisputed that, in use, the label directly affixed to the goods includes the words CORDON ROUGE superimposed on the stripe; however, the record shows multiple point of sale displays which present the '907 mark without any words superimposed on the stripe. . . . [W]e do not find Mumm's filing of partially completed labels as specimens to be appropriate or good practice. However, this inappropriate action does not go so far as to constitute inequitable conduct before the Patent and Trademark Office (Patent Office). As the Board found, had the words CORDON ROUGE appeared on the specimens submitted, such specimens would have been accepted.").

[206] Lanham Act § 1(a)(1)(A), 15 U.S.C. § 1051(a)(1)(A). *See* § 5D[2][a].

[207] *E.g.,* San Juan Products, Inc. v. San Juan Pools of Kansas, Inc., 849 F.2d 468, 7 U.S.P.Q.2d 1230 (10th Cir. 1988) (oath as to right to use mark not "knowingly false." "The 'oath' an applicant signs requires only that the declarant state 'to the best of his knowledge and belief no other person, firm, corporation, or association has the right to use said mark in commerce.' The statement questions the declarant's subjective, 'honestly held, good faith' belief. . . . 15 U.S.C. § 1051 and 37 C.F.R. § 2.33(b) 'require the statement of beliefs about exclusive rights, not their actual possession.' "); Allen Homes, Inc. v. Weersing, 510 F.2d 360, 184 U.S.P.Q. 705 (8th Cir. 1975), *cert. denied,* 421 U.S. 998, 95 S. Ct. 2395, 44 L. Ed. 2d 665 (1975) (knowledge and failure to disclose another's registration in another classification "does not demonstrate a clear intent to defraud."); King-Size, Inc. v. Frank's King Size Clothes, Inc., 547 F. Supp. 1138 (S.D. Tex. 1982).

[208] Money Store v. Harriscorp Finance, Inc., 689 F.2d 666, 216 U.S.P.Q. 11 (7th Cir. 1982).

Office regarding all other possible users of an identical or confusingly similar mark."[209]

"Nowhere does the Lanham Act specifically mandate a preapplication search by one who seeks federal registration of a mark. The language of section 17 does not explicitly place such a burden on a potential registrant. To imply the duty, either from that section or from the declaration of exclusive rights, . . . would appear inconsistent with the statutory scheme. First, implication of such a duty would be a disincentive for the first user of a mark in interstate commerce to seek federal registration. His rights to the mark would be equally protected if he remained idle until a junior user obtained federal registration. The prior user could seek cancellation of the registration on the grounds that the junior user, in failing to discover the prior use, perpetrated a fraud on the Patent Office. Such a result is obviously at odds with the Act's purpose of conditioning exclusive nationwide rights in a mark on federal registration.

"Second, creation of such a duty diminishes the importance of the role played by the Trademark Examiner and by those who might otherwise oppose registration of the mark following publication. . . . These sections are important because they encourage the disclosure of potentially confusing trademark usages before the marks have become established in the mind of the consuming public. Placing the burden of investigation on a junior user makes a senior user's early opposition to registration unnecessary. The senior user can even challenge the junior user's registration after five years because a fraudulently obtained mark is not protected by the incontestability provision, . . . Further, the senior user can recover any damage he might have suffered, . . . arguably including even his attorney's fees.

"The Act provides three opportunities for establishing potential confusion due to prior use of a similar mark for similar services: first, by the Trademark Examiner; second, by a prior user before the mark is registered; and third, by a prior user after the registration has issued. This three-tiered scrutiny encourages the disclosure of conflicting uses as early as possible and allocates a portion of the obligation to protect the rights of senior users to those persons or entities who claim such rights. Placing a burden of investigation on one seeking registration disturbs this scheme. The results are: (1) a disincentive for the first user of a mark in interstate commerce to seek federal registration; and (2) a greater possibility of customer confusion resulting from a scheme in which a senior user has no reason to ascertain and contest another's use of his mark at an early date. We believe that these results are inconsistent with the statutory scheme and with the purpose underlying the Lanham Act."[210]

In 1972, Modern Acceptance selected "Money Store" as a service mark for its lending and financial services business and authorized its advertising manager Costa to determine whether the mark could be registered. Costa had a trademark attorney conduct a search. The search showed no federal registrations or interstate uses of "Money Store" in connection with money-lending services but did disclose Kaufman's

---

[209] 689 F.2d at 670.
[210] 689 F.2d at 671-72.

pending application to register "Money Store" for advertising and public relations services and four state registrations: People Finance's (1959 Utah), Diversified Mountaineer (1966 Virginia and 1965 West Virginia), and Wilson Loan Plan (1963 Minnesota). The attorney advised Costa that "The Money Store" was eligible for federal registration but that the state registration holders might have superior rights in their local areas. Costa received a telephone call from Kaufman offering him a "Money Store" advertising package and indicating that an Indiana bank would soon begin using it. Costa declined the offer but sought his attorney's advice. The attorney indicated that Modern Acceptance should file an application because it had commenced interstate use before Kaufman's use on money lending services. Modern Acceptance subsequently filed an application with the statutorily required statement that "[n]o other persons . . . to the best of his knowledge or belief, has the right to use such mark in commerce either in the identical form thereof or in such near resemblance there as to be likely, when applied to the goods of such other person, to cause confusion." The PTO examiner found no conflict with Kaufman. The mark was published for opposition, but no one filed an opposition. The mark was registered on April 2, 1974.

Later, Modern Acceptance brought a trademark infringement suit against Harriscope, a junior user in the Chicago area. The trial court cancelled the registration for fraud. The appeals court reversed. First, the applicant, Modern Acceptance, did not have a duty to investigate further the uses by Peoples and Kaufman that the trademark search revealed. As to Kaufman, it was not "unreasonable for Modern Acceptance, upon the advice of counsel, to have believed that Kaufman's pending registration for advertising services gave Kaufman no prior rights in the mark for money-lending purposes." As to Peoples and the other prior state registrants, there was no indication that they were doing business outside their states: "[I]t is most likely that Modern Acceptance could not use its mark in Utah. We have found no authority, however, for the proposition that one cannot obtain federal registration of a mark that is registered and used in a single state." [211]

In *Rosso and Mastracco*, [212] the Federal Circuit noted that "a senior user *ordinarily* need not identify junior users in the oath" but "[o]n the other hand, the oath in an application for registration must be truthful.. . . [A] senior user would be making a false oath where he fails to acknowledge conflicting rights of a junior user which are clearly established, for example, by a court decree, by the terms of a settlement agreement, or by a registration." It emphasized that "the rights of a junior user must be clearly established and must be in an identical mark or one so similar as to be clearly likely to cause confusion."

[*iii*]   *Damage Claims*. Lanham Act Section 38 provides a damage remedy for anyone injured by another's use of a "false or fraudulent declaration or representation"

---

[211] 689 F.2d at 672.

[212] Rosso and Mastracco, Inc. v. Giant Food Inc., 720 F.2d 1263, 219 U.S.P.Q. 1050 (Fed. Cir. 1983). *Accord* Citibank, N.A. v. Citibanc Group, Inc., 724 F.2d 1540, 222 U.S.P.Q. 292 (11th Cir. 1984).

to procure a trademark registration.[213] Fraudulent registration procurement may also be grounds for an attorneys fee award.[214]

[c] *Antitrust Violations.* Mark use "to violate the antitrust laws of the United States" is a preserved defense, that is, one available even when the registrant's exclusive use right is incontestable.[215]

[d] *Fair Use.* Lanham Act Section 33(b)(4) makes "fair use" a preserved defense, that is, one available even when the registrant's exclusive use right is incontestable. The defense is:

> "That the use of the name, term, or device charged to be an infringement is a use, otherwise than as a mark, of the party's individual name in his own business, or of the individual name of anyone in privity with such party, or of a term or device which is descriptive of and used fairly and in good faith only to describe the goods or services of such party, or their geographic origin."[216]

The defense codifies common law principles: nonconfusing or collateral mark use does not constitute infringement.[217]

> "The defense is available only in actions involving descriptive terms and only when the term is used in its descriptive sense rather than its trademark sense. . . . In essence, the fair use defense prevents a trademark registrant from appropriating a descriptive term for its own use to the exclusion of others, who may be prevented thereby from accurately describing their own goods. . . . The holder of a protectable descriptive mark has no legal claim to an exclusive right in the primary, descriptive meaning of the term; consequently, anyone is

---

[213] Lanham Act § 38, 15 U.S.C. § 1120. *See* 2 J.T. McCarthy, Trademarks and Unfair Competition § 32:22 (2d ed. 1984).

[214] *E.g.,* Orient Express Trading Co., Ltd., 842 F.2d 650, 6 U.S.P.Q.2d 1308 (2d Cir. 1988).

[215] Lanham Act § 33(b)(7), 15 U.S.C. § 1115(b)(7). For a discussion of the relationship between trademarks and the antitrust laws, see 2 J.T. McCarthy, Trademarks and Unfair Competition § 31.23 *et seq.* (2d ed. 1984).

[216] Lanham Act § 33(b)(4), 15 U.S.C. § 1115(b)(4).

[217] *E.g.,* King-Size, Inc. v. Frank's King Size Clothes, Inc., 547 F. Supp. 1138, 1164 n.19, 216 U.S.P.Q. 426, 433 n.19 (S.D. Tex. 1982) ("Although . . . technically the fair use defense applies only in actions in which infringement of an incontestable mark is alleged, . . . the defense . . . is a restatement of the common law defense [and] is available in defense of a contestable mark"; defendants "used the term 'king size' not as a trademark, but in a descriptive manner as a means of conveying the nature of goods that defendants were selling: wearing apparel for large size men. . . . [D]efendants' fair use of 'king size' as a descriptive term serves to defeat plaintiffs' claim for trademark infringement, and for unfair competition. . . . ").

See also Soweco, Inc. v. Shell Oil Co., 617 F.2d 1178, 207 U.S.P.Q. 278 (5th Cir. 1980) ("It would make no sense to characterize defendant's use as 'fair' within the meaning of the Lanham Act for the purposes of a trademark infringement claim and at the same time characterize his use as 'unfair' for the purpose of a section 43(a) unfair competition claim under the same statute.").

free to use the term in its primary, descriptive sense so long as such use does not lead to customer confusion as to the source of the goods or services."[218]

In *Eli Lilly*,[219] the court held that Revlon's use of "lip repair cream" on its lip treatment cream product label did not impinge upon Eli Lilly's "LIP-FIX" trademark because there was no likelihood of confusion and, alternatively the use was a fair, nontrademark use. "Although Revlon has printed the words 'lip repair cream' in large letters, those words do not indicate the origin of the product. The identification function is served by the European Collagen Complex trademark and the Revlon name, even though these are in smaller print." Similarly, *Schmid Laboratories*,[220] the court held that defendant's use of "Ribbed" on its ribbed condom package label did not infringe plaintiff's "SENSI-RIBBED" condom trademark. Defendant's use was a descriptive, not a trademark use even though it capitalized "RIBBED" in letters larger than its "Trojan" brand name.[221]

---

[218] Zatarains, Inc. v. Oak Grove Smokehouse, Inc., 698 F.2d 786, 791, 217 U.S.P.Q. 988, 995 (5th Cir. 1983). *See also* Ringling Bros.-Barnum & Bailey Combined Shows, Inc. v. Celozzi-Ettlson Chevrolet, Inc., 855 F.2d 480, 8 U.S.P.Q.2d 1072 (7th Cir. 1988) (fair use defense requires that user act in good faith and that the use fairly describe the goods or services); Eli Lilly and Co. v. Revlon, Inc., 577 F. Supp. 477, 223 U.S.P.Q. 251 (S.D. N.Y. 1983) ("The defense recognizes that trademark rights should not be extended to prevent a party from describing his product to the public."); Clarke v. Dahlkemper, 468 F. Supp. 441, 204 U.S.P.Q. 505 (W.D. Pa. 1979) ("the presence of the elements of the § 1115(b)(4) defense can be readily determined by objective analysis of the packaging and affidavits supplied by the plaintiff and defendants, and that the case is accordingly susceptible to disposition by summary judgment in favor of the defendants.").

[219] Eli Lilly and Co. v. Revlon, Inc., 577 F. Supp. 477, 223 U.S.P.Q. 251 (S.D. N.Y. 1983). *See also* Jean Patou, Inc. v. Jacqueline Cochran, Inc., 201 F. Supp. 861, 865 (S.D. N.Y. 1962), *aff'd*, 312 F.2d 125, 136 U.S.P.Q. 236 (2d Cir. 1963) ("Joy" perfume trademark owner is not entitled to enjoin defendant's use of "Joy of Bathing" on its cosmetic bath product packages; "The use of a word such as 'joy' which is in the public domain is only unfair when a competitor uses it in its trade-mark or secondary sense. The competitor is free to use the word in its common or primary sense. The utmost that the plaintiff here may insist upon is that no one use its mark in an unfair way. . . . While it is desirable to protect a person who has built up a public association with certain products under his trade-mark from having his business taken by somebody else, it is also undesirable to block the channels of expression by giving protection to everyone who may go out and appropriate an ordinary descriptive word for his own business use. . . . The defendant's use of the word 'joy' in JOY OF BATHING falls on the side closer to its primary meaning, and hence does not invade any secondary meaning with which the plaintiff's use may have surrounded the word. It may be asked why the defendant chose this particular word to describe his product?There is nothing in the record to show that it was done to mislead the public into believing it is purchasing the product of the plaintiff. Rather, it is used to evoke a certain emotion on the part of the prospective purchaser. The use of the phrase JOY OF BATHING is designed to suggest the pleasure which will accompany the use of defendant's product in one's bath, and thus performs a descriptive function. To give the plaintiff the protection it seeks would be the first step in bestowing upon it a virtual monopoly of any phrase commencing with the word 'joy.' ").

[220] Schmid Laboratories v. Youngs Drug Products Corp., 482 F. Supp. 14, 206 U.S.P.Q. 468 (D. N.J. 1979).

[221] "A general examination of defendant's package reveals that 'RIBBED' is not used to 'identify and distinguish' defendant's condoms from those marketed by other companies. Visual

In *Venetianaire*,[222] the court rejected a fair use defense. Plaintiff's mark for mattress covers was "HYGIENT" displayed in white cross on a green oval. Defendant sold mattress covers with "HYGIENIC" in a similar design.

> "[T]he protection afforded trademarks by both the Lanham Act and the common law focuses on the use of words, not on their nature or meaning in the abstract. . . . [T]he defense which [defendant] asserts here can succeed only when the defendant's use of the term 'is a use, otherwise than as a trade or service mark' and the term is 'used fairly and in good faith only to describe' the goods sold. . . . Conceding that its use of 'Hygienic' in the manner shown by the proof here was likely to confuse its mattress covers with those of the plaintiff, defendant has not been able to establish that such use was nevertheless within the purview of the defense claimed. . . . Had the defendant chosen a different trademark and then used the word 'hygienic' in a sentence, or perhaps as the words 'Dust Tight . . . Water-proof . . . Allergy Free' . . . or 'anti-bacteria' appeared on its package, there would be no question of trademark infringement for there the word would appear to be 'used fairly and in good faith only to describe to users' a characteristic of the goods. But here the defendant obviously used the term 'as a symbol to attract public attention,' . . . That use of 'Hygienic' infringed the trademark owned by plaintiff, even though the word 'hygienic' was capable of descriptive, and therefore noninfringing, use. . . . [D]efendant, knowing of plaintiff's packaging, adopted a trademark and wrapper almost identical to plaintiff's. That fact eliminates any doubt that defendant was not entitled to claim fair use of a descriptive term as a defense to infringement of plaintiff's trademark."[223]

[e] Laches, Acquiescence, and Estoppel. Trademark law recognizes three related equitable defenses that may arise from the trademark owner's delay or misleading conduct in enforcing his rights: laches, acquiescence, and estoppel.[224] These defenses are distinct from abandonment, which extinguishes a trademark or service mark.[225]

---

attention is not focused on the mark, but on the brand name, 'TROJAN.' 'TROJAN' is printed in solid white lettering which noticeably contrasts with the varying shades of gold and brown in the background. On the other hand, 'RIBBED' is in pencil-lined gold lettering which blends in with the other color tones on the package.

"Additionally, whatever attention is drawn to 'RIBBED' serves only to inform the prospective purchaser what type of condom is contained within, not whose product it is. 'RIBBED' indicates one of this prophylactic's essential and distinguishing characteristics, that is, that it has a series of concentric ridges along its outer surface. . . . Unless attention is drawn to the particular word or term as being indicative of source of origin of that product, the term is not being used as a trademark."

[222] Venetianaire Corp. of America v. A & P. Import Co., 429 F.2d 1079, 167 U.S.P.Q. 481 (2d Cir. 1970).

[223] 429 F.2d at 1082-83.

[224] *See generally* 2 J.T. McCarthy, Trademarks and Unfair Competition § 31:1 *et seq.* (2d ed. 1984).

[225] *See* § 5D[3][b]. *See also* Elvis Presley Enterprises, Inc. v. Elvisly Yours, Inc. 936 F.2d 889, 893-94, 19 U.S.P.Q.2d 1377 (6th Cir. 1991) ("A plaintiff's failure to assert trademark rights against third parties is not relevant to the defenses of laches or acquiescence. . . . Further, [defendant] has never contended that [plaintiff] or its predecessors 'abandoned' the trademark . . .").

The 1988 Trademark Revision Act amended Lanham Act Section 33(b) to make clear that "equitable principles, including laches, estoppel, and acquiescence, are applicable" even when the mark's owner enjoys incontestability benefits.[226]

Unlike patent cases, which clearly and consistently distinguish laches from estoppel,[227] trademark cases exhibit a "good deal of confusion" as to terminology.[228] Properly speaking, "laches" consists of the trademark owner's unreasonable delay plus prejudice to the accused infringer. Laches will bar some remedies, such as an accounting for profits, but not necessarily others, such as an injunction. An "estoppel" arises when the owner represents, explicitly or by conduct, that he will not enforce his rights and the accused infringer relies on that representations.[229] A true estoppel usually bars all relief. Courts treat "acquiescence" as a laches-estoppel hybrid, involving either active consent or an extraordinarily lengthy period of inaction and often carrying consequences more serious than laches.[230]

---

[226] Lanham Act § 33(b), 15 U.S.C. § 1115(b)(8).

The Supreme Court's *Park 'N Fly* decision created doubt on the point by leaving open the question "whether traditional equitable defense such as estoppel or laches are available in an action to enforce an incontestable mark." Park 'N Fly, Inc. v. Dollar Park & Fly, Inc., 469 U.S. 189, 203 n.7 (1985), discussed at § 5E[1][a]. Some post-*Park 'N Fly* lower court decisions confirmed that the defenses were available. *E.g.*, Clamp Manufacturing Co., Inc. v. Enco Manufacturing Co., Inc., 870 F.2d 512, 515 10 U.S.P.Q.2d 1226, 1228 (9th Cir. 1989) ("We recognize estoppel by laches as a valid defense to an infringement action on behalf of an incontestable trademark."); Pyrodyne Corp. v. Pyrotronics, 847 F.2d 1398, 7 U.S.P.Q.2d 1082 (9th Cir. 1988).

[227] *See* § 2F[4][f].

[228] *See generally* 2 J.T. McCarthy, Trademarks and Unfair Competition § 31:1 *et seq.* (2d ed. 1984).

[229] *E.g.*, National Cable Television Ass'n, Inc. v. American Cinema Editors, Inc., 937 F.2d 1572, 19 U.S.P.Q.2d 1424 (Fed. Cir. 1991) (estoppel requires an affirmative act).

[230] *E.g.*, Elvis Presley Enterprises, Inc. v. Elvisly Yours, Inc. 936 F.2d 889, 19 U.S.P.Q.2d 1377 (6th Cir. 1991) ("Although sometimes used indiscriminately as if they were synonyms, 'laches' and 'acquiescence' are not the same. Laches is a negligent and unintentional failure to protect one's rights while acquiescence is intentional. Acquiescence requires 'a finding of conduct on the plaintiff's part that amounted to an assurance to the defendant, express or implied, that plaintiff would not assert his trademark rights against the defendant.'"); Coach House Restaurant, Inc. v. Coach and Six Restaurants, Inc., 934 F.2d 1551, 1558, 19 U.S.P.Q. 2d 1401 (11th Cir. 1991) ("The difference between acquiescence and laches is that laches denotes passive consent and acquiescence denotes active consent. . . . The distinction may be significant because in a general case a party who is guilty of active consent may be found less deserving of relief than a party guilty of mere passive consent. . . . The defense of acquiescence requires proof of three elements: (1) That petitioner actively represented that it would not assert a right or a claim; (2) that the delay between the active representation and assertion of the right or claim was not excusable; and (3) that the delay caused the registrant undue prejudice."); Tandy v. Malone & Hyde, Inc., 768 F.2d 362, 366, 226 U.S.P.Q. 703 (6th Cir. 1985), *rehearing denied*, 777 F.2d 1130, 1131, 228 U.S.P.Q. 621 (6th Cir. 1985) (acquiescence is "a doctrine related to laches relying on express or implied consent theories"); Piper Aircraft Corp. v. Wag-Aero, Inc. 741 F.2d 925, 223 U.S.P.Q. 202 (7th Cir. 1984) ("The doctrine of acquiescence is based on notions of reliance by the purported infringer.").

Complicating the laches, estoppel, and acquiescence defenses is the public interest, which may lead a court to grant injunctive relief to prevent consumer confusion despite the trademark owner's lack of diligence in pursuing his rights.[231]

[i] *Supreme Court Decisions.* The germinal Supreme Court case, *Menendez,*[232] indicated that mere delay may constitute laches so as to preclude the equitable monetary remedy of an accounting for profits but would not preclude an injunction against future trademark infringement unless the evidence established acquiescence or estoppel. Holt owned the mark "La Favorita" for flour. In 1868, a Holt partner, Ryder, withdrew from the Holt firm and began using "La Favorita." Holt did not sue Ryder until 1882. The district court refused an accounting but granted an injunction. The Supreme Court affirmed.[233]

> "The intentional use of another's trade-mark is a fraud; and when the excuse is that the owner permitted such use, that excuse is disposed of by affirmative action to put a stop to it. Persistence, then, in the use is not innocent, and the wrong is a continuing one, demanding restraint by judicial interposition when properly invoked. Mere delay or acquiescence cannot defeat the remedy by injunction in support of the legal right, unless it has been continued so long, and under such circumstances, as to defeat the right itself. . . . Acquiescence, to avail, must be such as to create a new right in the defendant. . . . .
>
> "So far as the act complained of is completed, acquiescence may defeat the remedy on the principle applicable when action is taken on the strength of encouragement to do it; but so far as the act is in progress, and lies in the future, the right to the intervention of equity is not generally lost by previous delay, in respect to which the elements of an estoppel could rarely arise. At the same time, as it is in the exercise of discretionary jurisdiction that the doctrine of reasonable diligence is applied, and those who seek equity must do it, a

---

[231] *See* Conagra, Inc. v. Singleton 743 F.2d 1508, 224 U.S.P.Q. 552 (11th Cir. 1984) ("a court determining whether the doctrine of laches estops the plaintiff from asserting its rights also must consider the public's interest in the trademark as a definite designation of a single source of the goods. Thus, although a defendant suffers some prejudice, the public interest in avoiding confusion might outweigh that prejudice."); Tustin Community Hospital, Inc. v. Santa Ana Community Hospital Ass'n, 89 Cal. App. 3d 889, 153 Cal. Rptr. 76 (1979) ("In the ordinary infringement case, the public interest is typically affected where, in spite of the plaintiff's delay, an injunction is nevertheless appropriate because the public would otherwise purchase the defendant's product believing it is the product of the plaintiff. . . . Of course, in a given case, the public may come to identify a name as describing the product of the defendant rather than the product of the plaintiff."). In many cases in which courts deny injunctive relief, the facts suggest that actual consumer deception is not a serious problem. In others, courts cavalierly concede that "[a] few consumers may be confused about the source of a product." E-Systems, Inc. v. Monitek, Inc, 720 F.2d 604, 607 222 U.S.P.Q. 115, 117 (9th Cir.1983)

[232] Menendez v. Holt, 128 U.S. 514 (1888).

[233] *See also* McLean v. Fleming, 96 U.S. 245, 253 (1877) ("Equity courts will not, in general, refuse an injunction on account of delay in seeking relief, where the proof of infringement is clear, even though the delay may be such as to preclude the party from any right to an account for past profits.").

court might hesitate as to the measure of relief, where the use by others for a long period, under assumed permission of the owner, had largely enhanced the reputation of a particular brand. But there is nothing here in the nature of an estoppel . . . There is no pretense of abandonment. That would require proof of non-user by the owner, or general surrender of the use to the public. . . . The evidence is positive that Holt & Co. continuously used the trade-mark, always asserted their exclusive right to it, and never admitted that of any other firm or person . . . It is idle to talk of acquiescence, in view of these facts. Delay in bringing suit there was, and such delay as to preclude recovery of damages for prior infringement; but there was neither conduct nor negligence which could be held to destroy the right to prevention of further injury." [234]

In *La Republicque Francaise*,[235] the Court found a long period of inaction constituted acquiescence barring injunctive relief.[236] In 1873, defendant began bottling and selling water from Saratoga Springs, New York, using "Vichy" on the label. In 1898, plaintiff sued, claiming trademark rights in "Vichy" for bottled water from Vichy, France. The Court noted that defendants' and other infringers' "open and notorious" activity for thirty years made it "impossible to suppose that the plaintiffs were not aware of these infringements upon their exclusive rights." "A clearer case of laches could hardly exist." [237] It found no bad faith or consumer deception that should preclude a laches defense.

"[C]onceding that the defense of laches would not be available in a case of actual fraud, or an attempt to foist upon the public the waters of the defendant as those of the original Vichy spring . . . we find but little evidence of such purpose in this record. The two waters not only differ in their ingredients and taste, but the French Vichy is a still, and the Saratoga Vichy, as well as the other American Vichies, an effervescing, water. There is no attempt made whatever by the defendant to simulate the label of the plaintiffs upon the body of the bottle. The word Vichy is never used by the defendant alone, but always in connection with Saratoga. The two labels not only differ wholly in their design and contents, but even in their language,— that of the plaintiffs being wholly in French." [238]

[ii] *Laches: Unreasonable Delay and Prejudice.* A laches defense consists of two elements: the trademark owner's unreasonable delay in suit and prejudice to the

---

[234] 128 U.S. at 523-525.

[235] La Republique Francaise v. Saratoga Vichy Spring Co., 191 U.S. 427 (1903).

[236] *Accord* Ancient Egyptian Arabic Order of Nobles of the Mastic Shrine v. Michaux, 279 U.S. 737, 748-49 (1939) ("the evidence demonstrates . . . not only that there was obvious and long-continued laches on the part of the [claimant], but also that the circumstances were such that its laches barred it from asserting an exclusive right, or seeking equitable relief. . . . ").

[237] Ironically, successors to Saratoga, the accused infringer who was victorious on laches, later lost a trademark action on account of laches. *See* Saratoga Vichy Spring Co., Inc. v. Lehman, 625 F.2d 1037, 208 U.S.P.Q. 175 (2d Cir. 1980).

[238] 191 U.S. at 439-440.

accused infringer.[239] Some decisions break the first element into two parts: delay and lack of a legally adequate excuse for the delay.[240]

> "The doctrine of laches . . . bars relief to those who delay the assertion of their claims for an unreasonable time. Laches is founded on the notion that equity aids the vigilant and not those who slumber on their rights. Several aims are served by requiring the reasonable diligence of plaintiffs in pursuing their legal rights. Plaintiffs are encouraged to file suits when courts are in the best position to resolve disputes. As claims become increasingly stale, pertinent evidence becomes lost; equitable boundaries blur as defendants invest capital and labor into their claimed property; and plaintiffs gain the unfair advantage of hindsight, while defendants suffer the disadvantage of an uncertain future outcome."[241]

---

[239] E.g., Brunswick Corp. v. Spinit Reel Co. 832 F.2d 513, 523, 4 U.S.P.Q.2d 1497 (10th Cir. 1987); University of Pittsburgh v. Champion Products, Inc., 686 F.2d 1040, 1044, 215 U.S.P.Q. 921, 924 n.14 (3d Cir. 1982), cert. denied, 459 U.S. 1087 (1982) ("It is hornbook law that laches consists of two essential elements: (1) inexcusable delay in instituting suit, and (2) prejudice resulting to the defendant from such delay. . . . Open and notorious use by the defendant is relevant to the plaintiff's knowledge and, thus, whether its delay is excusable. Evidence of the defendant's fraudulent intent goes to the question of whether 'prejudice' has been established as a matter of equity.").

[240] E.g., Brittingham v. Jenkins, 914 F.2d 447, 456, 16 U.S.P.Q.2d 1121, 1127 (4th Cir. 1990) ("While the operation of laches depends upon the particular facts and circumstances of each case, the following factors ordinarily should be considered: (1) whether the owner of the mark knew of the infringing use; (2) whether the owner's delay in challenging the infringement of the mark was inexcusable or unreasonable; and (3) whether the infringing user was unduly prejudiced by the owner's delay. . . . If these factors are satisfied, laches normally will bar a trademark owner's claim for damages against an infringer."); Ambrit, Inc. v. Kraft, Inc., 805 F.2d 974, 989 (11th Cir. 1986) ("To establish laches, a defendant must demonstrate: 1) a delay in asserting a right or a claim, 2) that the delay was not excusable, and 3) that there was undue prejudice to the party against whom the claim is asserted."); N.A.A.C.P. v. N.A.A.C.P. Legal Defense & Educational Fund, Inc. 753 F.2d 131, 137, 225 U.S.P.Q. 264, 268-69 (D.C. Cir. 1985) ("The essential elements of laches are well-defined by common law. There are three affirmative requirements: (1) a substantial delay by a plaintiff prior to filing suit; (2) a plaintiff's awareness that the disputed trademark was being infringed; and (3) a reliance interest resulting from the defendant's continued development of good-will during this period of delay."); Armco, Inc. v. Armco Burglar Alarm Co., Inc., 693 F.2d 1155, 1161, 217 U.S.P.Q. 145, 150 (5th Cir. 1982) ("The equitable defense of laches has three interrelated elements: (1) delay in asserting a right or claim; (2) that the delay was inexcusable; (3) that undue prejudice resulted from the delay. . . . The analysis of the defense is said to proceed on, 'LACHES = DELAY X PREJUDICE,' a factual calculation of the trial court.").

[241] N.A.A.C.P. v. N.A.A.C.P. Legal Defense & Educational Fund, Inc. 753 F.2d 131, 137, 225 U.S.P.Q. 264, 268-69 (D.C. Cir. 1985).

See also Piper Aircraft Corp. v. Wag-Aero, Inc. 741 F.2d 925, 939-40, 223 U.S.P.Q. 202, 212 (7th Cir. 1984) (Posner concurring: " 'Laches,' from the Old French lasche ("lax'), originally was just a shorthand expression for the equity maxim that one who seeks the help of a court of equity must not sleep on his rights. . . . The doctrine of laches in the law of intellectual property is descended from the original equity conception . . . that law being itself of equitable origin . . . but it has followed a separate path. Where once it barred just equitable relief, today it is a substantive defense and bars legal relief as well—indeed, sometimes legal but not equitable relief. . . . ").

In other words, "if you snooze, you lose."[242]

The delay period begins when the mark owner knew or should have known of the accused use.[243] In *Carter-Wallace*,[244] the Ninth Circuit noted that "no laches will be found where the defendant's interference with plaintiff's rights is minimal or inconsequential" or "where the defendant's encroachment is steady but slow."[245]

There is no precise yardstick for what delay is unreasonable delay or what constitutes prejudice.[246] Several decisions indicate that two years delay is unlikely to

---

[242] American International Group, Inc. v. American International Bank, 926 F.2d 829, 835, 17 U.S.P.Q.2d 1907, 1912 (9th Cir. 1991) (Kozinski, dissenting: "The fundamental premise of laches is that those who sleep on their rights surrender them. . . . ").

[243] *E.g.*, Armco, Inc. v. Armco Burglar Alarm Co., Inc., 693 F.2d 1155, 1161, 217 U.S.P.Q. 145, 150-51 (5th Cir. 1982) ("That time period begins when an owner of a mark first has knowledge of the accused use. We have not explicitly decided whether the dating of that beginning point is provided by inquiry into subjective knowledge or whether a mark owner ought to be charged with what it should have known. Other courts have adopted an objective standard."); Valmor Products Co. v. Standard Products Corp., 464 F.2d 200, 204,174 U.S.P.Q. 353 (1st Cir. 1972) (plaintiff cannot be charged with knowledge solely on the basis of defendant's registration where no claim was made that lack of knowledge was willful or negligent); Safeway Stores, Inc. v. Safeway Quality Foods, Inc., 433 F.2d 99, 103, 166 U.S.P.Q. 112 (7th Cir. 1970) been ("Plaintiff is chargeable with the information it might have received had due inquiry been made"); Chandon Champagne Corp. v. San Marino, 335 F.2d 531, 535, 142 U.S.P.Q. 239 (2d Cir. 1964) ("delay should be measured from the time plaintiff had 'ample opportunity' to discover defendant's infringement. . . . This precedent is persuasive. The objective standard of 'knew or should have known' is a logical implementation of the duty to police one's mark. Nor do we see a principled reason to read the law as distinguishing between inexcusable delay in obtaining knowledge of infringing activity and inexcusable delay after obtaining such knowledge.").

But cf. Georgia-Pacific Corp. v. Great Plains Bag Co., 614 F.2d 757, 759, 204 U.S.P.Q. 697 (CCPA 1980) ("To prove the defense of laches one must make a showing that the party, against which the defense is asserted, had actual knowledge of trademark use by the party claiming the defense or at least a showing that it would have been inconceivable that the party charged with laches would have been unaware of the use of the mark.").

[244] Carter-Wallace, Inc. v. Procter & Gamble Co., 434 F.2d 794, 803 n.4, 167 U.S.P.Q. 713 (9th Cir. 1970).

[245] *See also* E-Systems, Inc. v. Monitek, Inc, 720 F.2d 604, 607, 222 U.S.P.Q. 115, 117 (9th Cir. 1983) ("Had defendant's encroachment been minimal, or its growth slow and steady, there would be no laches.").

[246] *See* Tandy v. Malone & Hyde, Inc., 768 F.2d 362, 366, 226 U.S.P.Q. 703, 706 (6th Cir. 1985), *rehearing denied*, 777 F.2d 1130, 1131, 228 U.S.P.Q. 621 (6th Cir. 1985) ("A reasonable businessman should be afforded some latitude to assess both the impact of another's use of an allegedly infringing trademark as well as the wisdom of pursuing litigation on the issue."); Saratoga Vichy Spring Co., Inc. v. Lehman, 625 F.2d 1037, 1040, 1042, 208 U.S.P.Q. 175 (2d Cir. 1980) ("It is often said that 'mere delay' will not, by itself, bar a plaintiff's suit, but that there must be some element of estoppel, such as reliance by the defendant. . . . All this means, however, is that a balancing of equities is required, which would be the case with any principle of equity."; . . . When courts refuse to bar a suit on the basis of the plaintiff's 'mere delay,' they often do so because it would not be equitable to excuse a defendant who has been committing conscious fraud.").

constitute laches.[247] Some courts adopt as a guideline the state statute of limitations that would apply if the action were characterized as one at law for a single infringing act instead of one in equity to remedy a continuing wrong.[248] In *Tandy*,[249] the Sixth Circuit reversed a summary judgment that the trademark owner's 32-month delay in filing suit barred both injunctive and monetary relief. In 1979, Malone opened an "Auto Shack" store. By March 1982, it had 55 stores and had spent $1.5 millon promoting them. Tandy, which operates "Radio Shack" stores, learned of Malone's use in 1979. In March 1982, it notified Malone of its objections and filed suit in April 1982. A Tennessee statute provided a three-year limitations period for suits for tortious injury to property. After reviewing "the equitable doctrine of laches and the common law history of trademark litigation,"[250] the appeals court affirmed "the rule in the

---

[247] Ambrit, Inc. v. Kraft, Inc., 805 F.2d 974 (11th Cir. 1986); Piper Aircraft Corp. v. Wag-Aero, Inc. 741 F.2d 925, 933, 223 U.S.P.Q. 202, 207 (7th Cir. 1984) ("two years has rarely, if ever, been held to be a delay of sufficient length to establish laches.").

[248] E.g., University of Pittsburgh v. Champion Products, Inc., 686 F.2d 1040, 1045, 215 U.S.P.Q. 921, 925 (3d Cir. 1982) ("where the 'plaintiff sleeps on his rights for a period of time greater than the applicable statute of limitations,' the burden of proof shifts to the plaintiff to prove the absence of such prejudice to the defendant as would bar all relief."). *Compare* Clamp Manufacturing Co., Inc. v. Enco Manufacturing Co., Inc., 870 F.2d 512, 515 n.2 10 U.S.P.Q.2d 1226, 1229 n.2 (9th Cir. 1989) (unnecessary to decide "whether injury should be presumed if the delay in filing a trademark infringement suit exceeds the period of the analogous statute of limitations.").

Courts apply a similar presumption in patent cases, based not on a statute of limitations but on the Patent Act's six-year damage limitation.

[249] Tandy v. Malone & Hyde, Inc., 768 F.2d 362, 226 U.S.P.Q. 703 (6th Cir. 1985), *rehearing denied*, 777 F.2d 1130, 1131, 228 U.S.P.Q. 621 (6th Cir. 1985).

[250] "The substantive and remedial doctrines of trademark law draw upon legal principles developed both at law and in equity. Although trademark litigation began as early as the 1600's, the law of trademarks did not undergo significant development until the nineteenth century, when the increasing use of trademarks to symbolize and market products created the need for defining and protecting owners' rights. . . .

"Both equity and law courts decided trademark cases in England during the early stages of trademark development, but equitable principles seem to have . . . dominated that process because injunctive relief was generally considered the first and most effective step for courts to take in redressing a trademark infringement. . . . American courts also stressed equitable relief and principles in their responses to trademark disputes. . . . Thus, prior to statutory protection for trademarks, courts determined rights and liabilities primarily on the basis of equitable theory. They treated the damages portion of such suits as an equitable action in the nature of an accounting. Consistent with this history of trademark law, § 34 of the Lanham Act of 1946 allows for injunctive relief 'according to the principles of equity,' . . . and § 35 allows monetary relief 'subject to the principles of equity,' . . .

"Despite this pervasive equity background, the damages or accounting aspect of trademark infringement actions are considered legal actions for purposes of the jury trial clause of the Seventh Amendment. . . . [*Dairy Queen v. Wood*, 369 U.S. 469 (1962)] . . . Thus infringement actions are hybrids, a mixture of law and equity.

"The Lanham Act does not contain a statute of limitations. In determining when a plaintiff's suit should be barred under the Act, courts have consistently used principles of laches as developed by courts of equity. . . .

"Under equitable principles the statute of limitations applicable to analogous actions at law is used to create a 'presumption of laches.' This principle 'presumes' that an action is barred

trademark context that, if the analogous statute of limitation has not elapsed, there is a strong presumption that plaintiff's delay in bringing the suit for monetary relief is reasonable. Only rarely should laches bar a case before the analogous statute has run."[251]

"Several reasons underlie the use of the statutory period as the laches period. It enhances the stability and clarity of the law by applying neutral rules and principles in an evenhanded fashion rather than making the question purely discretionary. It also requires courts to make clear distinctions between threshold or special defenses or pleas in bar and the merits of the case. It enhances the rationality and objectivity of the process by preventing courts from short circuiting difficult issues on the merits by confusing or conflating the merits of an action with other defenses.

. . . .

"A strong presumption enhances objectivity and clear analysis in decision making. It clarifies and broadens the protection of the public from confusion and deception."[252]

In *Tandy*, the defendant filed "a strongly worded en banc petition criticizing the Court with a heavy hand for adopting 'with great fanfare,' according to the petition, the principle that the law presumes that in a suit in equity for trademark infringement the laches period will be the limitations period otherwise applicable to an analogous action at law, absent extraordinary circumstances." The court denied the petition: "Among the cases which actually meet and discuss the question of the effect of an analogous legal limitations period on laches, the Court finds no case which rejects the principle adopted. Counsel suggests no alternative principle other than leaving the cutoff period to the complete discretion of the trial court. For good reason, the law does not favor subjective judgments of this type incapable of review."[253]

---

if not brought within the period of the statute of limitations and is alive if brought within the period . . .

". . . [I]n the absence of unusual circumstances, a suit will not be barred before the analogous statute has run but will be barred after the statutory time has run.

"This principle has been applied in trademark cases. Layton Pure Food Co. v. Church & Dwight, 182 F. 35, 40 (8th Cir.1910) (except under 'unusual conditions extraordinary circumstances,' a federal court applying a limitation statute by analogy will not bar damages remedy in a trademark infringement action if the analogous statute of limitation would not bar the action).

. . . .

"Although early federal decisions faithfully followed the presumption, later decisions outside the trademark area have somewhat eroded the requirement that only 'extraordinary circumstances or unusual conditions' defeat the presumption favoring the statutory limitations period. . . . The presumption should remain strong and uneroded in trademark cases. They are not 'purely equitable' suits . . . They are mixed actions in law and equity." 769 F.2d at 364-65.

[251] *Id.* at 366.

[252] *Id.* at 365.

[253] 777 F.2d at 1130-31.

Attempts to settle a dispute through negotiations may excuse the mark owner's delay in filing suit.[254]

"For purposes of laches an assignee of a trademark can tack on the period during which the assignor used the mark, but only when the mark is assigned in conjunction with the sale of the goodwill of the business to which it is attached."[255]

The accused infringer's expenditure of substantial sums in entering a market does not necessarily constitute prejudice, particularly if it consistently asserts a legal right to do so in the face of notice of the owner's claim.[256]

---

[254] See N.A.A.C.P. v. N.A.A.C.P. Legal Defense & Educational Fund, Inc. 753 F.2d 131, n.59, 225 U.S.P.Q. 264, 269 n.59 (D.C. Cir. 1985) ("In some instances, courts excuse delay if there were on-going negotiations. . . . On the other hand, there are no court cases excusing twelve years of delay based purely on the motive, however well-meaning, of wishing to avoid the disadvantages of filing suit. Laches is not like the defenses of acquiescence or abandonment that may require evidence of an intent to abandon.").

Cf. Ambrit, Inc. v. Kraft, Inc., 805 F.2d 974 (11th Cir. 1986) (delay excusable because infringer was owner's Florida distributor; owner attempted, unsuccessfully, to resolve problem by persuading infringer to distribute more of its product; "This is not to say that a delay is excusable any time a party's immediate enforcement of its rights will cause it economic injury.").

[255] Tandy v. Malone & Hyde, Inc., 769, 706 F.2d 362, 367, 226 U.S.P.Q. 703, 706 (6th Cir. 1985), *rehearing denied*, 777 F.2d 1130, 1131, 228 U.S.P.Q. 621 (6th Cir. 1985) (citing PepsiCo, Inc. v. Grapette Co., 416 F.2d 285 (8th Cir.1969)).

[256] *E.g.*, Ambrit, Inc. v. Kraft, Inc., 805 F.2d 974, 990 (11th Cir. 1986) (development expenses do not constitute prejudice when infringer was "committed to the . . . product from the outset and believed it would prevail in any lawsuit"); Tandy v. Malone & Hyde, Inc., 777 F.2d 1130, 1131, 228 U.S.P.Q. at 621–22 (6th Cir. 1985) ("Equity does not normally favor the wealthy or those who can make large investments over those whose investments are small. The expenditure of large sums of money to appropriate another's trade name is no more justifiable in the eyes of the law than the expenditure of small sums to appropriate another's trade name. The law does not permit a court to refuse to reach the merits of a case by applying laches because a party is capable of spending large sums in the pursuit of the course of conduct that is alleged to constitute the wrong. In addition, if on the merits it should be determined that the defendant has appropriated plaintiff's trade name, defendant will not necessarily lose its investment as defendant suggests. A simple change of name is a possible remedy. Such a remedy should not produce any substantial waste of economic resources already invested by the defendant. Therefore, defendant's invested capital argument is not entitled to much weight."); Citibank, N.A. v. Citibanc Group, Inc., 724 F.2d 1540, 1546, 222 U.S.P.Q. 292, 297 (11th Cir. 1984) ("The test for determining laches is a flexible one: the court must examine both the amount of delay and the prejudice caused by that delay. In this case, plaintiff notified defendants of a possible infringement problem before defendants adopted Citibanc. Within a short period of time after plaintiff began widespread use of Citibank in 1976, defendants broadened their usage to Citibanc. During the entire period, defendants knew of plaintiff's objections but nevertheless proceeded to enlarge their use of the term. These actions were taken 'with the complete realization that the plaintiff disputed their use and did not intend to acquiesce in it.' . . . Defendants have not relied on the delay of plaintiffs in expanding their use of the mark; indeed, they have expanded their use while asserting their right to do so, in the face of plaintiff's constant complaints.").

Compare Saratoga Vichy Spring Co., Inc. v. Lehman, 625 F.2d 1037, 1042, 208 U.S.P.Q. 175 (2d Cir. 1980) ("It is sometimes said that the continued production and sale of an infringing product does not constitute reliance . . . But the defendant's entry into a new business in

An infringer's egregious bad faith conduct may preclude him from relying on the defense of laches,[257] but "a defendant's mere awareness of a plaintiff's claim to the same mark . . . [does not establish] the bad intent necessary to preclude the availability of the laches defense."[258]

[iii] *Damages—Bad Faith.* Laches clearly operates to bar a trademark owner from obtaining the equitable monetary remedy of an accounting for profits. Even absent laches, courts may deny an accounting if the infringer did not act in bad faith. Because of the 1938 merger of law and equity, courts treat laches as a defense to a "legal" compensatory damage remedy as well as to an equitable accounting remedy.[259]

[iv] *Injunctive Relief.* Whether laches should bar an injunction against further infringement is a question that has long plagued the courts. In *Menendez*,[260] the Supreme Court indicated that mere laches would not bar injunctive relief, but in later cases, it recognized that lengthy delay may constitute acquiescence justifying denial of an injunction.

Recent lower court decisions confirm that laches may bar injunctive relief.[261] Some apply a two-tier approach: mere unreasonable, prejudicial delay bars monetary relief

---

reliance on plaintiff's acquiescence in the validity of the trademark about to be licensed is a different matter.").

[257] Saxlehner v. Eisner & Mendelson Co., 179 U.S. 19 (1900) ("in cases of actual fraud, . . . the principle of laches has but an imperfect application, and delay even greater than that permitted by the statute of limitations is not fatal to plaintiff's claim. . . . Indeed, in a case of an active and continuing fraud like this, we should be satisfied with no evidence of laches that did not amount to proof of assent or acquiescence."); N.A.A.C.P. v. N.A.A.C.P. Legal Defense & Educational Fund, Inc. 753 F.2d 131, 225 U.S.P.Q. 264 (D.C. Cir. 1985) (listing as factor that "may negate the invocation of laches by excusing the delay . . . conscious fraud or bad faith by the defendant.").

[258] Conan Properties, Inc. v. Conans Pizza, Inc. 752 F.2d 145, 150, 225 U.S.P.Q. 379, 382 (5th Cir. 1985).

[259] E.g., Brittingham v. Jenkins, 914 F.2d 447, 456, 16 U.S.P.Q.2d 1121, 1127 (4th Cir. 1990) (denying prejudgment interest and limiting damages to those arising after entry of the district court's judgment because of owner's seven-year delay; "laches may be invoked as a defense against claims for damages in trademark infringement actions."); Skippy, Inc. v. CPC International, Inc., 674 F.2d 209, 212, 216 U.S.P.Q. 1061, 1063 (4th Cir. 1982) ("Laches is a defense to claims for damages for trademark infringement and unfair competition. . . . While the availability of laches as a defense to claims for injunctive relief may be limited when the defendant is guilty of bad faith infringement, . . . laches will bar a claim for damages for bad faith infringement.")

[260] Menendez v. Holt, 128 U.S. 514 (1888) discussed at § 5F [3][e][i].

[261] N.A.A.C.P. v. N.A.A.C.P. Legal Defense & Educational Fund, Inc. 753 F.2d 131, 225 U.S.P.Q. 264 (D.C. Cir. 1985); Prudential Ins. Co. of America v. Gibraltar Financial Corp. of California 694 F.2d 1150, 1152, 217 U.S.P.Q. 1097, 1098 (9th Cir. 1982) (rejecting argument that *Menendez* meant that "laches may preclude damages, but cannot bar injunctive relief."); Armco, Inc. v. Armco Burglar Alarm Co., Inc., 693 F.2d 1155, 1161, 217 U.S.P.Q. 145, 150 (5th Cir. 1982) ("laches may defeat claims for injunctive relief as well as claims for an accounting."); Saratoga Vichy Spring Co., Inc. v. Lehman, 625 F.2d 1037, 1041, 208 U.S.P.Q. 175 (2d Cir. 1980); Tustin Community Hospital, Inc. v. Santa Ana Community Hospital Ass'n, 89 Cal. App. 3d 889, 153 Cal. Rptr. 76 (1979) ("laches can be a defense to an injunction case based on unfair competition.").

for pre-suit conduct but not damages and injunctive relief for post-suit conduct, more egregious delay or affirmative acquiescence bars all relief.[262] In *James Burrough*,[263] the Seventh Circuit held that the plaintiff's delay barred an accounting for profits but did not constitute an estoppel that would preclude injunctive relief or post-suit filing damages and profits. Defendant's use of "Sign of the Beefeater" for its restaurants infringed plaintiff's "Beefeater" gin trademarks.

> "By reason of laches, a plaintiff in a trademark infringement action may lose the right to recover damages or wrongfully derived profits during the period prior to the filing of suit. Upon a showing of infringement, however, the plaintiff may still be entitled to injunctive relief, . . . and to damages and profits for the period subsequent to the filing of suit. Trademark infringement is a continuous wrong and, as such, gives rise to a claim for relief as long as the infringement persists. . . .

> "When considering a defense of estoppel in a case such as this one, a court must keep in mind the fact that a trademark infringement action involves not only the right of the trademark owner to control the reputation of his product, but also the right of the consuming public to be free of confusion. . . .

Cf. Hanover Star Milling Co. v. Metcalf, 240 U.S. 403, 419 (1916) ("As to laches and acquiescence it has been repeatedly held, in cases where defendants acted fraudulently or with knowledge of plaintiff's rights, that relief by injunction would be accorded although an accounting of profits should be denied.").

[262] *E.g.,* Tandy v. Malone & Hyde, Inc., 769 F.2d 362, 366 n.2 , 226 U.S.P.Q. 703, 706 n.2 (6th Cir. 1985), *rehearing denied*, 777 F.2d 1130, 1131, 228 U.S.P.Q. 621 (6th Cir. 1985) ("To deny injunctive relief in trademark litigation, however, some affirmative conduct in the nature of an estoppel . . . or conduct amounting to 'virtual abandonment.' "); Conan Properties, Inc. v. Conans Pizza, Inc. 752 F.2d 145, 151, 225 U.S.P.Q. 379, 383 (5th Cir. 1985) ("A finding of laches alone ordinarily will not bar the plaintiff's request for injunctive relief, although it typically will foreclose a demand for an accounting or damages. . . . This is because courts construe the plaintiff's unreasonable delay to imply consent to the defendant's conduct, which amounts to nothing more than a revocable license; the license is revoked once the plaintiff objects to the defendant's infringement. . . . In cases where the defendant actually relies upon the plaintiff's affirmative act, however, the fiction of implied consent is inapplicable and an injunction may not issue."); University of Pittsburgh v. Champion Products, Inc., 686 F.2d 1040, 1044-45, 215 U.S.P.Q. 921, 924-25 (3d Cir. 1982) ("In the trademark context, the concepts of 'mere delay' or 'laches without more,' although confusing as a matter of semantics, . . . are nonetheless relevant in two ways. . . . First, there is that narrow class of cases where the plaintiff's delay has been so outrageous, unreasonable and inexcusable as to constitute a virtual abandonment of its right. . . . Second, there is the much more common situation in which the plaintiff's less egregious delay will bar its claim for an accounting for past infringement but not for prospective injunctive relief."); Missouri Federation of the Blind v. National Federation of the Blind of Missouri, Inc., 505 S.W.2d 1, 181 U.S.P.Q. 583 (Mo. Ct. App. 1973); Air Reduction Co., 258 A.2d 302, 163 U.S.P.Q. 433 (Del. Ch. 1969).

Cf. Ameritech, Inc. v. American Information Technologies Corp. 811 F.2d 960, 963, 1 U.S.P.Q.2d 1861, 1864 (6th Cir. 1987) ("Laches will not bar injunctive relief where a defendant adopted the trade name with knowledge of a plaintiff's rights and objections.").

[263] James Burrough Ltd. v. Sign of the Beefeater, Inc., 572 F.2d 574. 197 U.S.P.Q. 277 (7th Cir. 1978).

"Under the uncontested facts of this case, it is clear that Distiller delayed instituting suit for infringement for an unreasonable period of time after becoming aware of the 'Sign of the Beefeater' restaurants. . . . For this reason, the equitable doctrine of laches precludes recovery by Distiller of damages or profits for the period prior to the filing of its suit. In fact, Distiller concedes as much. It is also clear, however, that Restaurant and its predecessors were aware of the potential risk involved in opening additional restaurants once this action was filed. We are therefore unable to find the requisites for application of the doctrine of estoppel."[264]

Some apply a multiple factors balancing test to determine the remedial effect of laches or acquiescence.[265]

"Where a person entitled to exclusive use of a trademark is guilty of unreasonable delay in asserting his rights against an infringer or junior user, or acquiesces in the latter's use, or evinces an intent to abandon his rights in the marks, a court of equity has the discretionary power, after weighing the respective interests of the parties, to deny injunctive relief or an accounting. . . . The denial of relief, however, is not determined by rules of thumb. The existence of laches or acquiescence, and whether it is sufficient to warrant such denial, depends upon a consideration of the circumstances of each particular case and a balancing of the interests and equities of the parties. Among the factors to be weighed in determining whether laches will bar relief are the strength and value of the trademark right asserted, . . . the plaintiff's diligence, or lack of it, in seeking to enforce the mark, . . . the harm that will result to the senior user if relief is denied, . . . whether the junior user is an innocent infringer who acted in good faith ignorance of the senior's rights, . . . the extent to which the senior and junior uses of the mark are competitive, . . . and the extent of harm or prejudice suffered by the junior user as a result of the senior's delay. . . . Where the owner of the trademark fails to take any action for many years to enforce a relatively weak trademark against a junior user who has proceeded innocently to use the same or similar mark on non-competing goods in which he has invested large sums, so that denial of relief would cause relatively little harm to the senior user in contrast to the serious prejudice that would result to the defendant, relief will be denied. As distinguished from laches, acquiescence constitutes a ground

---

[264] 572 F.2d at 578-79.

[265] *E.g.*, Tustin Community Hospital, Inc. v. Santa Ana Community Hospital Ass'n, 89 Cal. App. 3d 889, 153 Cal. Rptr. 76, 86-87 (1979) ("for the purpose of determining whether plaintiff has been guilty of inappropriate delay and, if so, whether it has so prejudiced defendants as to make it inequitable to grant injunctive relief, the trial court must weigh a number of factors. These will include the length of any such delay, excuses for delay, defendant's knowledge, in advance, that plaintiff was using its trade name, any actual fraud in defendants' conduct, plaintiff's acquiescence or consent, or the appearance thereof, the extent of competition between plaintiff and defendants, any prejudice to, or reliance by, defendants, possible changes in conditions during delay, the effect of delay upon the availability of evidence, alternative solutions, the effect of a granting of injunctive relief upon defendants, the effect of a denial upon plaintiff, and the impact of the parties' conduct, and of the ultimate judgment to be rendered, upon the public interest.").

for denial of relief only upon a finding of conduct on the plaintiff's part that amounted to an assurance to the defendant, express or implied, that the plaintiff would not assert his trademark rights against the defendant. . . . Although acquiescence may bar relief even where the plaintiff acts diligently, whether conduct amounts to acquiescence warranting denial of relief turns on an examination of all the surrounding circumstances, and requires a balancing of the equities." [266]

[v] *PTO Inter Partes Proceedings.* The equitable remedies of laches, estoppel, and acquiescence apply in PTO inter partes proceeding, such as cancellations and oppositions. [267]

In *National Cable Television,* [268] the Federal Circuit, resolving possibly conflicting prior precedent, held that laches runs against a party from knowledge of another's registration application, not knowledge of pre-application use:

"Logically, laches begins to run from the time action could be taken against the acquisition by another of a set of rights to which objection is later made. In an opposition or cancellation proceeding the objection is to the rights which flow from registration of the mark. . . . Moreover, an objection to registration does not legally equate with an objection to use, that is, a charge of infringement. . . . [O]ften it cannot be known immediately how a junior user will proceed to develop, display, or even change what it claims as its mark." [269]

[3] Remedies

The Lanham Act provides remedies for registered mark infringement and Section 43(a) false advertising and trademark or trade dress infringement, including temporary restraining orders, preliminary and permanent injunctions; [270] recall; [271] damages; [272]

---

[266] Carl Zeiss Stiftung v. V. E. B. Carl Zeiss, Jena, 293 F. Supp. 892, 917, 160 U.S.P.Q. 97 (S.D. N.Y. 1968), aff'd, 433 F.2d 686, 167 U.S.P.Q. 641 (2d Cir. 1970).

See also American International Group, Inc. v. American International Bank, 926 F.2d 829, 830-31, 17 U.S.P.Q.2d 1907 (9th Cir. 1991) ("a balancing test to be applied in examining the issue of laches which requires the district court to consider a variety of factors, including (1) the strength and value of the trademark rights asserted; (2) the senior user's diligence in enforcing the mark; (3) the harm to the senior user if relief is denied; (4) whether the junior user acted in good faith ignorance of the senior's rights; (5) the degree of competition between senior and junior users; and (6) the extent of harm suffered by the junior user because of the senior user's delay in asserting his rights."); E-Systems, Inc. v. Monitek, Inc, 720 F.2d 604, 222 U.S.P.Q. 115 (9th Cir.1983) (applying *Carl Zeiss* factors).

[267] Lanham Act § 19, 15 U.S.C. § 1069.

[268] National Cable Television Ass'n, Inc. v. American Cinema Editors, Inc., 937 F.2d 1572, 19 U.S.P.Q.2d 1424 (Fed. Cir. 1991).

[269] 937 F.2d at 1581, 19 U.S.P.Q. 2d at 1432.

See also Coach House Restaurant, Inc. v. Coach and Six Restaurants, Inc., 934 F.2d 1551, 19 U.S.P.Q. 1401 (11th Cir. 1991) (acquiescence in a particular use is not acquiescence in registration).

[270] Lanham Act § 34(a), 15 U.S.C. § 1116(a).

[271] Lanham Act § 34(a), 15 U.S.C. § 1116(a).

[272] Lanham Act § 35, 15 U.S.C. § 1117.

profits;[273] costs and attorneys fees;[274] seizure and impoundment;[275] and destruction.[276] These statutory remedies are not exclusive. The Lanham Act does not preempt state law. Trademark infringement and false advertising are forms of unfair competition for which common law and, in most states, statutory remedies are available.

The 1988 Trademark Law Revision Act eliminated one anomaly of potential remedies. Section 35's original language, strictly construed, extended the Act's remedies only to Section 32 *registered* mark infringement claims,[277] not to Section 43(a) unregistered marks infringement and false advertising claims.[278] Reluctantly, the Courts of Appeals held that Section 35 applied to Section 43(a) claims.[279] The Revision Act settled the issue, amending Sections 34(a), 35(a), and 36 to include Section 43(a) violations.

At least one statutory anomaly remains: Section 29 states that if a registrant fails to give notice via the circled "R" symbol, or equivalent words, "no profits and no damages shall be recovered under the provisions of this chapter unless the defendant had actual notice of the registration."[280] There is no similar provision restricting recovery for Section 43(a) unregistered mark infringement. This seemingly gives an unregistered mark owner greater potential remedies. Non-noticing registered mark owners can, presumably, use common law remedies to obtain damages or profits from infringers.

[a] Preliminary Injunction

[i] *Applicable Standards: Likelihood of Confusion.* Preliminary injunction standards vary from circuit to circuit. Two standards predominate. The first is:

> "[T]he moving party, must show either (1) combination of probable success on the merits and the possibility of irreparable harm, or (2) that serious questions are raised and the balance of hardships tips sharply in the moving party's favor."[281]

The Second Circuit varies this standard, requiring: "(a) irreparable harm and (b) either (1) likelihood of success on the merits or (2) sufficiently serious questions going to

---

[273] Lanham Act § 53, 15 U.S.C. § 1117.

[274] Lanham Act § 53, 15 U.S.C. § 1117.

[275] Lanham Act § 34(d), 15 U.S.C. § 1116(d).

[276] Lanham Act § 36, 15 U.S.C. § 1118.

[277] Lanham Act § 32, 15 U.S.C. § 1114.

[278] Lanham Act § 43(a), 15 U.S.C. § 1125(a).

[279] *See* NuPulse, Inc. v. Schlueter Co., 853 F.2d 545, 548, 7 U.S.P.Q.2d 1633, 1635 (7th Cir. 1988) (holding that Section 35 applied to Section 43(a) cases and citing opinions of the Courts of Appeals for the 2d, 6th, 8th, 9th, 10th, and 11th Circuits in support). *But see* Standard Terry Mills, Inc. v. Shen Manufacturing Co., 803 F.2d 778, 782, 231 U.S.P.Q. 555, 559 (3d Cir. 1986) (expressing doubt whether Section 35 should apply, but not deciding issue).

[280] Lanham Act § 29, 15 U.S.C. § 1111.

[281] Rodeo Collection, Ltd. v. West Seventh, 812 F.2d 1215, 1217, 2 U.S.P.Q.2d 1204, 1205 (9th Cir. 1987).

See also Miss World (UK), Ltd. v. Mrs. America Pageants, Inc., 856 F.2d 1445, 1448, 8 U.S.P.Q.2d 1237, 1239 (9th Cir. 1988).

the merits to make them fair ground for litigation and a balance of hardships tipping decidedly toward the party requesting preliminary relief."[282] The Sixth and Eighth Circuits use the standard as an alternative.[283]

The second and more prevalent standard adds public interest consideration and hardship balancing to irreparable harm and probability of success on the merits.[284] Invariably, the two most important factors are irreparable harm and likelihood of success on the merits. Because courts presume irreparable harm from trademark infringement, the two collapse into the one issue—likelihood of confusion: "a showing of likelihood of [consumer] confusion establishes both a likelihood of success on the merits and irreparable harm."[285]

Two further considerations may modify that standard. The first lowers the threshold requirements: "Where confusion from the use of [a] trademark could result in physical harm to the consuming public the court may as a matter of policy grant relief on lesser proof of confusion."[286] The second raises the required showing: movant's delay

---

[282] Hasbro, Inc. v. Lanard Toys, Ltd., 858 F.2d 70, 73, 8 U.S.P.Q.2d 1345, 1347 (2d Cir. 1988) (quoting Jackson Dairy, Inc. v. H.P. Hood & Sons, Inc., 596 F.2d 70, 72 (2d Cir. 1979) (per curiam)).

[283] The Sixth Circuit's stated factors involve balancing public interest considerations and third party harm with irreparable harm and "[w]hether the movant has shown a strong or substantial likelihood or probability of success on the merits," Frisch's Restaurant, Inc. v. Shoney's Inc., 759 F.2d 1261, 1263, 225 U.S.P.Q. 1169 (6th Cir. 1985), but closer inspection shows a standard more like that of the Second Circuit. See 759 F.2d at 1270, 225 U.S.P.Q. at 1175 (court could enter preliminary injunction on showing of serious questions going to the merits and irreparable harm decidedly outweighing potential harm to defendant). See also Holmsten Ice Rinks, Inc. v. Burley's Rink Supply, Inc., 14 U.S.P.Q.2d 1492, 1493 (D. Minn. 1990).

[284] See, e.g., Keds Corp. v. Renee International Trading Corp., 888 F.2d 215, 220, 12 U.S.P.Q.2d 1808, 1811 (1st Cir. 1989); American Greetings Corp. v. Dan-Dee Imports, Inc., 807 F.2d 1136, 1140, 1 U.S.P.Q.2d 1001, 1003 (3d Cir. 1986); Schwinn Bicycle Co. v. Ross Bicycles, Inc., 870 F.2d 1176, 1181, 10 U.S.P.Q.2d 1001, 1005 (7th Cir. 1989); Mutual of Omaha Insurance Co. v. Novak, 775 F.2d 247, 248, 227 U.S.P.Q. 801, 802 (8th Cir. 1985); Amoco Oil Co. v. Rainbow Snow, Inc., 809 F.2d 656, 661, 1 U.S.P.Q.2d 1403, 1408-09 (10th Cir. 1987); Swatch Watch, S.A. v. Taxor, Inc., 785 F.2d 956, 958-59, 229 U.S.P.Q. 391, 392-93 (11th Cir. 1986), Nabisco Brands, Inc. v. Conusa Corp., 722 F. Supp. 1287, 1290, 11 U.S.P.Q.2d 1788, 1790 (M.D.N.C.), aff'd, 892 F.2d 74, 14 U.S.P.Q.2d 1324 (4th Cir. 1989) (unpublished).

[285] Hasbro, Inc. v. Lanard Toys, Ltd., 858 F.2d 70, 73, 8 U.S.P.Q.2d 1345, 1347 (2d Cir. 1988). Accord: Keds Corp. v. Renee International Trading Corp., 888 F.2d 215, 220, 12 U.S.P.Q.2d 1808, 1811 (1st Cir. 1989); Home Box Office, Inc. v. Showtime/The Movie Channel Inc., 832 F.2d 1311, 1314, 4 U.S.P.Q.2d 1789, 1791 (2d Cir. 1987); General Mills, Inc. v. Kellogg Co., 824 F.2d 622, 625 (8th Cir. 1987); Vaughan Manufacturing Co. v. Brikam International, Inc., 814 F.2d 346, 351, 1 U.S.P.Q.2d 2067, 2071 (7th Cir. 1987); Nabisco Brands, Inc. v. Conusa Corp., 722 F. Supp. 1287, 1290, 11 U.S.P.Q.2d 1788, 1790-91 (M.D.N.C.), aff'd, 892 F.2d 74, 14 U.S.P.Q.2d 1324 (4th Cir. 1989) (unpublished); Chemlawn Services Corp. v. GNC Pumps, Inc., 690 F. Supp. 1560, 1569 (S.D. Tex), aff'd, 856 F.2d 202 (Fed. Cir. 1988) (unpublished).

[286] Playskool, Inc. v. Product Development Group, Inc., 699 F. Supp. 1056, 1060-61, 9 U.S.P.Q.2d 1712, 1715-1716 (E.D.N.Y. 1988) (citing Syntex Laboratories, Inc. v. Norwich Pharmacal Co., 437 F.2d 566, 569, 169 U.S.P.Q. 1, 2-3 (2d Cir. 1971)).

may, absent justifying circumstances, result in denial of a preliminary injunction.[287]

[ii]   *Movant's Delay as an Additional Factor.* The justification for considering the moving party's delay varies depending on the circuit's preliminary injunction standard.

In circuits where hardship balancing is mandatory, delay is part of the equities against movant, especially when the delay results in defendant making additional commitments. " '[D]elay is only one among several factors to be considered; these cases do not support a general rule that irreparable injury cannot exist if the plaintiff delays in filing its motion for a preliminary injunction.' "[288]

In the Second Circuit, where hardship balancing is not mandatory, delay's impact is greater. In *Citibank*,[289] the Court of Appeals held that unjustified delay in moving against an infringer, coupled with prejudice to defendant, neutralizes the usual irreparable harm presumption.[290]

Citibank's rationale is not satisfactory because it equates irreparable harm with harm requiring immediate, emergency treatment. It faults the trademark owner for not giving the irreparable harm the highest priority without regard to whether the infringement is the trademark owner's most important business concern. *Citibank* is more a principle of equity between the movant and the judge than equity between the parties: the true rationale may be judicial exasperation with a party who waited several months to bring its preliminary injunction motion and then expects the court to act quicker than the movant.

Comic Strip,[291] a district court decision exemplifying the awkwardness of the Second Circuit's reasoning on delay, can be interpreted on one level as espousing the extreme position of denying a preliminary injunction solely on the basis of a three month delay, notwithstanding the court's determination that a preliminary injunction would otherwise be warranted. Closer examination shows *sub silentio* equity balancing in a circuit where balancing is a permissible and mandatory factor only if the movant shows merely "sufficiently serious questions going to the merits," rather than a full "likelihood of success on the merits."[292] *Comic Strip* used *Citibank* to hold that "[t]he plaintiffs' dilatory prosecution of its rights somewhat vitiates the notion of irreparable harm,"[293] but in the last paragraph indicated a different motivation for denying a preliminary injunction:

---

[287] Delay may also be a factor in fashioning a preliminary injunction's scope. *E.g.*, Harlequin Enterprises Ltd. v. Gulf & Western Corp., 644 F.2d 946, 950, 210 U.S.P.Q. 1, 3 (2d Cir. 1981) (delay in seeking preliminary relief meant that defendant could sell off existing stock).

[288] Vaughan Manufacturing Co. v. Brikam International, Inc., 814 F.2d 346, 351, 1 U.S.P.Q.2d 2067, 2071 (7th Cir. 1987) (upholding preliminary injunction notwithstanding delay of about nine months from knowledge of infringement to commencement of action) (quoting Ideal Industries, Inc. v. Gardner Bender, Inc., 612 F.2d 1018, 1025, 204 U.S.P.Q. 177, 185 (7th Cir. 1979), *cert. denied*, 447 U.S. 924 (1980)).

[289] Citibank, N.A. v. Citytrust, 756 F.2d 273, 225 U.S.P.Q. 708 (2d Cir. 1985).

[290] 756 F.2d at 276. *See* GTE Corp. v. Williams, 731 F.2d 676, 678-79, 222 U.S.P.Q. 803, 804-05 (10th Cir. 1984).

[291] *See* The Comic Strip, Inc. v. Fox Television Stations, Inc., 710 F. Supp. 976, 10 U.S.P.Q.2d 1608 (S.D.N.Y. 1989).

[292] 710 F. Supp. at 977.

[293] *Id.* at 981.

"Although we believe that the plaintiffs are likely to succeed on the merits, they do not appear to be in jeopardy of irreparable harm during the pendency of the litigation. Indeed, favorable publicity from television may accrue to their benefit. *The defendant, on the other hand, stands to suffer great loss if the preliminary injunction is granted* and it is forced to discontinue or alter its existing television programming."[294]

Cases allowing only innocent infringers to use delay demonstrate the factor's equitable nature. In *Chandon Champagne*,[295] the Court of Appeals stressed the need for the senior user of a mark to move promptly because "the owner's delay in asserting his rights may lead the defendant to build up innocently an important reliance on the publicity of his mark, so that its loss would cost dearly."[296]

Courts are not consistent on whether the delay clock begins only when the trademark owner gains actual knowledge of the infringing activity or when he should have known. The Second Circuit, generally harsh on delay, uses the actual knowledge standard in most decisions,[297] but district court decisions explicitly, and *Citibank* implicitly, apply a "should have known" standard through their credibility determinations, expressing doubt about delayed actual knowledge assertions, especially those made by large, sophisticated corporations.[298]

---

[294] *Id.* (emphasis added).

[295] Chandon Champagne Corp. v. San Marino Wine Corp., 335 F.2d 531, 142 U.S.P.Q. 239 (2d Cir. 1964) (emphasis added).

[296] 335 F.2d at 535 (*quoted in* Inc. Publishing Corp. v. Manhattan Magazine, Inc., 616 F. Supp. 370, 397, 227 U.S.P.Q. 257, 277 (S.D.N.Y. 1985), *aff'd*, 788 F.2d 3 (2d Cir. 1986) (unpublished). *Accord*: Ventura Travelware Inc. v. A to Z Luggage Co., 1 U.S.P.Q.2d 1552, 1553 (E.D.N.Y. 1986) (where there is sufficient evidence of deliberate copying, delay will not negate finding of irreparable harm).

[297] *See* Majorica, S.A. v. R.H. Macy & Co., 762 F.2d 7, 8, 226 U.S.P.Q. 624, 624 (2d Cir. 1985) ("It is undisputed that Majorica *was aware* of the conduct complained of for several years prior to its motion for a preliminary injunction." (emphasis added)); Citibank, N.A. v. Citytrust, 756 F.2d 273, 276, 225 U.S.P.Q. 708, 711 (2d Cir. 1985) ("Citibank did not seek the injunction until September 14—more than ten weeks after it *learned directly* of Citytrust's plans, and more than nine months after it *received notice* through the press that Citytrust intended to open a Long Island branch." (emphasis added)). *Cf.* Saratoga Vichy Spring Co. v. Lehman, 625 F.2d 1037, 1040, 208 U.S.P.Q. 175, 177 (2d Cir. 1980) (" 'Defendant's proof in its laches defense must show that plaintiff *had knowledge* of defendant's use of its marks, that plaintiff inexcusably delayed in taking action with respect thereto, and that defendant will be prejudiced by permitting plaintiff inequitably to assert its rights at this time.' " (emphasis added), quoting Cuban Cigar Brands, N.V. v. Upmann International, Inc., 457 F. Supp. 1090, 1096, 199 U.S.P.Q. 193, 198 (S.D.N.Y. 1978), *aff'd mem.*, 607 F.2d 995 (2d Cir. 1979)).

[298] *See, e.g.*, Citibank, N.A. v. Citytrust, 756 F.2d 273, 277, 225 U.S.P.Q. 708, 711 (2d Cir. 1985) ("It strains one's credulity to argue that a major financial institution such as Citibank, with all its resources and information sources, could not establish before mid-September 1984 that a potential competitor had opened a branch more than ten weeks earlier near the heart of Citibank territory."); Warner Lambert Co. v. McCrory's Corp., 718 F. Supp. 389, 395, 12 U.S.P.Q.2d 1884, 1888 (D.N.J. 1989) (expressing doubt that industry leader would not know that own customer and major retailer was selling infringing product and because of plaintiff's "practice of sending personnel to conduct field checks of retail stores"); Calvin

Post-*Citibank* Second Circuit cases show that delay alone is not determinative. In *Horgan*,[299] a copyright decision, the court phrased a *Citibank* argument as follows: "[A]ppellees claim that when a copyright holder has *definitive advance knowledge* of a planned infringement, yet fails to take legal action, and *the defendant changes its position to its detriment*, preliminary injunction relief may be denied."[300]

In *Church of Scientology*,[301] it emphasized that factors other than mere delay led to the reversal of the preliminary injunction. *Citibank* "did not create an exception to our traditional rule that a finding of irreparable harm follows from a trademark plaintiff's showing of infringing use and likelihood of confusion. *Citibank* essentially stands for the proposition that absent a likelihood of confusion between two banks operating for years in the same market with the similar names of 'Citytrust' and 'Citicorp', and because of plaintiff's substantial delay in seeking an injunction, irreparable harm did not follow."

Other courts measure delay not necessarily from actual notice of the infringing conduct, but " 'from the date that defendant's acts first significantly impacted on plaintiff's goodwill and business reputation.' "[302] Courts distinguish minor encroachment, not worthy of action, and significant escalation.[303]

Settlement encouragement policy dictates that time spent in settlement talks not count against the movant in considering any assertion of delay.[304] Similarly, time

Klein Co. v. Farah Manufacturing Co., 229 U.S.P.Q. 795, 801 (S.D.N.Y. 1985); Mego Corp. v. Mattel, Inc., 203 U.S.P.Q. 377, 383 (S.D.N.Y. 1978) ("[E]ven if plaintiff did not know by late spring that Battlestar Galactica was the title of the television series they should have known this and could have know this.").

[299] Horgan v. MacMillan, Inc., 789 F.2d 157, 229 U.S.P.Q. 684 (2d Cir. 1986).

[300] 789 F.2d at 164, 225 U.S.P.Q. at 689 (emphasis added).

[301] Church of Scientology International v. Elmira Mission of the Church of Scientology, 794 F.2d 38, 42, 230 U.S.P.Q. 325, 328 (2d Cir. 1986).

For a survey and discussion of cases on the impact of delay in preliminary injunction motions and of the mitigating factors, see Raskopf & Edelman, *Delay in Filing Preliminary Injunction Motions: How Long Is Too Long?*, 80 Trademark L. Rep. 36 (1990).

[302] Nabisco Brands, Inc. v. Conusa Corp., 722 F. Supp. 1287, 1292, 11 U.S.P.Q.2d 1788, 1792 (M.D.N.C.), *aff'd*, 892 F.2d 74, 14 U.S.P.Q.2d 1324 (4th Cir. 1989) (unpublished) (quoting 2 J. McCarthy, Trademarks § 31:6, at 570; entering preliminary injunction and recall order notwithstanding delay from late 1987 to March 1989 in filing suit where delay up to October 1988 was result of plaintiff's perception that defendant's infringing sales had sharply declined).

[303] *See, e.g.*, Parrot Jungle, Inc. v. Parrot Jungle, Inc., 512 F. Supp. 266, 270, 213 U.S.P.Q. 49, 52-53 (S.D.N.Y. 1981) ("A modest encroachment is one thing, a sudden proposed national exploitation of plaintiff's name is quite another, and plaintiff's failure to challenge the former will not entirely disable plaintiffs [sic] from preventing the latter."); Calamari Fisheries, Inc. v. The Village Catch, Inc., 698 F. Supp. 994, 1014, 8 U.S.P.Q.2d 1953, 1969 (D. Mass. 1988) (excusing delay until opening of third restaurant near plaintiff's location and expansion of advertising increased incidents of actual confusion); Floralife, Inc. v. Floraline International, Inc., 633 F. Supp. 108, 113 (N.D. Ill. 1985) (delay measured from expansion of retail store to telemarketing activity).

[304] *See, e.g.*, Central Benefits Mutual Insurance Co. v. Blue Cross and Blue Shield Association, 711 F. Supp. 1423, 1434, 11 U.S.P.Q.2d 1103, 1112 (S.D. Ohio 1989); Girls Clubs of America, Inc. v. Boys Clubs of America, Inc., 683 F. Supp. 50, 54, 6 U.S.P.Q.2d 2049, 2052 (S.D.N.Y.),

spent in good faith litigation preparation, such as in conducting a consumer survey, should not count.[305]

[iii] *Temporary Restraining Orders.* Temporary restraining order applications are preliminary injunction motions escalated in exigency to *ex parte* proceedings that raise a host of procedural issues.

In the garden variety temporary restraining order application on notice to the defendant, the sole issue added to the preliminary injunction motion is whether the plaintiff can show the possibility that irreparable harm will occur between the time of the application and the date when the preliminary injunction motion may be heard.[306] Obvious examples would be if introduction or escalation of the infringing product or false advertising were immediately imminent. One step up in the level of aggression and difficulty is obtaining a temporary restraining order without giving notice to the defendant. *Vuitton et Fils*[307] explicitly affirmed the availability of *ex parte* temporary restraining orders to trademark owners.

Courts frown on requests for restraining orders without even telephoned notice but will grant them if the trademark owner "sufficiently demonstrates the reason that notice 'should not be required,' " and that notice itself will "serve only to render fruitless further prosecution of the action."[308] The typical case is one in which the defendant's business is sufficiently mobile and the merits of any defense sufficiently dubious that the defendant is more likely to hide or flee than stand and defend.

The final step up in aggression is *ex parte* seizure. The 1984 Trademark Counterfeiting Act gives specific statutory authority and sets statutory standards for a procedure some courts had already developed for granting *ex parte* seizure orders for counterfeit mark bearing goods and often for infringements not rising to the level of counterfeits when the defendant also engaged in counterfeiting.[309]

---

aff'd, 859 F.2d 148 (2d Cir. 1988) (unpublished); Iris Arc v. S.S. Sarna, Inc., 621 F. Supp. 916, 229 U.S.P.Q. 25 (E.D.N.Y. 1985); Earth Technology Corp. v. Environmental Research & Technology, Inc., 222 U.S.P.Q. 585, 587 (C.D. Cal. 1983); Clark, Inc. v. Resnick, 219 U.S.P.Q. 619, 624-25 (D.R.I. 1982).

[305] *See* Warner Lambert Co. v. McCrory's Corp., 718 F. Supp. 389, 395, 12 U.S.P.Q.2d 1884, 1888 (D.N.J. 1989).

[306] 11 C. Wright & A. Miller, Federal Practice and Procedure § 2951, at 498 (1973).

[307] *In re* Vuitton et Fils, S.A., 606 F.2d 1, 204 U.S.P.Q. 1 (2d Cir. 1979).

[308] 606 F.2d at 4-5. Fed. R. Civ. P. 65 (b) states that a temporary restraining order granted without notice must expire by its terms in ten days and may be granted "only if (1) it clearly appears from specific facts shown by affidavit or by the verified complaint that immediate and irreparable injury, loss, or damage will result to the applicant before the adverse party or that party's attorney can be heard in opposition, and (2) the applicant's attorney certifies to the court in writing the efforts, if any, which have been made to give the notice and the reasons supporting the claim that notice should not be required."

[309] Lanham Act § 34(d), 15 U.S.C. § 1116(d). Cases preceding the amendment in which *ex parte* seizure order were granted include Polo Fashions, Inc. v. Magic Trimmings, Inc. 603 F. Supp. 13, 15-16 (S.D. Fla. 1984); Lacoste Alligator, S.A. v. Bluestein's Men's Wear, 569 F. Supp. 491, 493, 219 U.S.P.Q. 1001, 1002 (D. S.C. 1983); Billy Joel v. Various John Does, 499 F. Supp. 7912 (E.D. Wis. 1980).

Literally, the Counterfeiting Act's procedure applies only to an action against a *counterfeit* of a *registered* mark,[310] but it does not prohibit *ex parte* seizure orders for lesser forms of trademark infringement or repeal prior case law that made those remedies available in instances short of counterfeiting. A reasonable assumption is that *ex parte* seizures of infringing but non-counterfeit articles will continue but that courts will require compliance with the new strict procedural requirements. In *General Electric*,[311] the court upheld seizure of goods bearing a counterfeit of an unregistered mark in connection with the seizure of goods using a counterfeit mark.

[*iv*] *Seizure and Impoundment.* The 1984 Trademark Counterfeiting Act sets out explicit requirements for *ex parte* seizure orders; the order must be based on an affidavit or verified complaint establishing:

(a) an order on notice is not adequate to protect the rights of the trademark owner set forth in Section 1114,

(b) the applicant has not publicized the requested seizure,

(c) the applicant is likely to succeed in proving counterfeiting by the defendant,

(d) an immediate and irreparable harm will occur without the *ex parte* seizure,

(e) the matter to be seized will be located at the place identified in the application,

(f) the harm to the applicant from denying the order outweighs the harm to the legitimate interests of the person against whom seizure would be ordered, and

(g) if the applicant is required to give notice, the person against whom seizure would be ordered, or those acting in concert, would destroy, move, hide, or otherwise make the counterfeit matter inaccessible to the court.[312]

The requirements explicitly apply only to counterfeit seizures of registered marks, but the standards presumably apply with equal or greater force to infringements short of counterfeiting or counterfeiting of an unregistered mark.

The Trademark Counterfeiting Act establishes statutory remedies for wrongful seizure:

"A person who suffers damage by reason of a wrongful seizure under this subsection has a cause of action against the applicant for the order under which such seizure was made, and shall be entitled to recover such relief as may be appropriate, including damages for lost profits, cost of materials, loss of good will, and punitive damages in instances where the seizure was sought in bad faith, and unless the court finds extenuating circumstances, to recover a reasonable attorney's fee."[313]

---

[310] A counterfeit mark is "a counterfeit of a mark that is registered on the principal register . . . for such goods or services sold, offered for sale, or distributed and that is in such use . . . ," Lanham Act § 34(d)(1)(B), 15 U.S.C. § 1116(d)(1)(B). "Counterfeit" is "a spurious mark which is identical with, or substantially indistinguishable from, a registered mark." Lanham Act § 45, 15 U.S.C. § 1127.

[311] General Electric Co. v. Speicher, 877 F.2d 531, 11 U.S.P.Q.2d 1125 (7th Cir. 1989).

[312] Lanham Act § 34(d)(1)-(4), 15 U.S.C. § 1116(d)(1)-(4).

[313] *Id.*

[b] Permanent Injunction. An injunction is the most common Lanham Act remedy because of the nature of the proscribed wrongs—trademark and trade dress infringement and false advertising are presumed to cause irreparable harm[314] —and the difficulty of proving damages and profits.[315]

Central to trademark infringement liability, and therefore to permanent injunction entitlement, is likelihood of confusion; actual confusion need not be found.[316]

A court may deny injunctive relief if the infringer ceases the challenged activity and there is no likelihood of repetition or continuing hazard to the public from the infringing activity.[317] Denial is permissive: "Regardless of whether the unfair conduct has stopped and is not likely to recur, the trial court still has the discretion to grant or deny an injunction against such conduct."[318]

[c] Recall. Recall resembles the affirmative injunction common in civil rights cases: the person enjoined is commanded to do something affirmative to undo the harm from a violation rather than simply refrain from the violation in the future, which is the classic negative injunction.

Recall, whether in a final or preliminary injunction, is reserved for egregious behavior, such as willful infringement[319] or consumer confusion with public danger potential. Public danger may arise with pharmaceuticals,[320] personal hygiene products,[321] and products directed toward children.[322]

---

[314] *See, e.g.,* Rodeo Collection, Ltd. v. West Seventh, 812 F.2d 1215, 1220, 2 U.S.P.Q.2d 1204, 1208 (9th Cir. 1987); Amoco Oil Co. v. Rainbow Snow, Inc., 809 F.2d 656, 663, 1 U.S.P.Q.2d 1403, 1409 (10th Cir. 1987); Processed Plastic Co. v. Warner Communications, Inc., 675 F.2d 852, 858, 216 U.S.P.Q. 1072, 1076 (7th Cir. 1982).

[315] What one court noted with respect to false advertising would also apply to trademark infringement: "The thin body of case law on actual damages for successful false-advertising claims reflects the fact that litigants, who best understand their real losses, almost always settle these cases once a court has given its view of the merits." Alpo Petfoods, Inc. v. Ralston Purina Co., 913 F.2d 958, 969 n.12, 16 U.S.P.Q.2d 1081, 1090 n.12 (D.C. Cir. 1990).

[316] *See, e.g.,* Boston Athletic Association v. Sullivan, 867 F.2d 22, 28, 9 U.S.P.Q.2d 1690, 1695 (1st Cir. 1989); Hasbro, Inc. v. Lanard Toys, Ltd., 858 F.2d 70, 73, 8 U.S.P.Q.2d 1345, 1349-1350 (2d Cir. 1988).

[317] Burndy Corp v. Teledyne Industries, Inc., 748 F.2d 767, 774, 224 U.S.P.Q. 106, 111 (2d Cir. 1984).

[318] Brunswick Corp. v. Spinit Reel Co., 832 F.2d 513, 525, 4 U.S.P.Q.2d 1497, 1506 (10th Cir. 1987).

[319] Perfect Fit Industries, Inc. v. Acme Quilting Co., 646 F.2d 800, 210 U.S.P.Q. 175 (2d Cir. 1981), *cert. denied,* 459 U.S. 832 (1982). *But see* Shen Manufacturing Co. v. Suncrest Mills, Inc., 673 F. Supp. 1199, 1201, 4 U.S.P.Q.2d 1438, 1439 (S.D.N.Y. 1987) (retailer ordered to recall and destroy all infringing articles in stock notwithstanding absence of bad faith infringement).

[320] Upjohn Co. v. Riahom Corp., 641 F. Supp. 1209, 1226, 1 U.S.P.Q.2d 1433, 1444 (D. Del. 1986).

[321] C.B. Fleet Co. v. Complete Packaging Corp., 739 F. Supp. 393, 399 (N.D. Ill. 1990) (recall of feminine hygiene product manufactured by trademark owner's authorized manufacturer that failed its quality tests and there was evidence of contamination).

[322] Nabisco Brands, Inc. v. Conusa Corp., 722 F. Supp. 1287, 1294, 11 U.S.P.Q.2d 1788, 1793 (M.D.N.C.), *aff'd,* 892 F.2d 74, 14 U.S.P.Q.2d 1324 (4th Cir. 1989) (unpublished) (order-

[d] Form. A trademark anti-infringement injunction must follow Federal Rules of Civil Procedure Rule 65's form and specificity standards. There are some principles peculiar to trademarks. The injunction may make affirmative commands, such as infringing product recall and destruction.[323] Equitable considerations, such as prejudicial delay, may persuade the court to allow a phase-out rather than an immediate halt to infringing conduct. Finally, the line between permissible and impermissible conduct may shift once a person has infringed.

[i] *Equitable Factors Such as Delay.* Delay in seeking a preliminary injunction against an innocent infringer may be considered as a factor mitigating against the harshness of an immediately effective injunction. For example, one court used delay as a consideration favoring permitting an innocent infringer to sell off its existing inventory.[324]

[ii] *Staying Away from the Vague Line Between Permissible and Impermissible Conduct.* Drawing the line between infringing and noninfringing conduct in the first instance is often difficult,[325] but, once a party has infringed, it must stay far away from the line: "[A] party who has once infringed a trademark may be required to suffer a position less advantageous than that of an innocent party."[326]

[iii] *Use of Disclaimers.* Whether to order a disclaimer rather than an absolute prohibition often arises when the defendant uses a competitor's mark in comparative advertising[327] or adopts a personal name similar to someone else's trademark.[328] It also arises when the infringement is innocent and the likelihood of confusion small.[329]

Whether disclaimers are truly effective percolated in trademark law literature and became prominent in three Second Circuit cases decided the same day.[330]

---

ing recall of hard roll candy); Playskool, Inc. v. Product Development Group, Inc., 699 F. Supp. 1056, 1063, 9 U.S.P.Q.2d 1712, 1718 (E.D.N.Y. 1988) (recall ordered in addition to preliminary injunction in a false advertising case "[b]ecause the misleading language on defendant's packaging creates a potential safety hazard for children.").

[323] *See* § 5F[3][c].

[324] *See* Harlequin Enterprises Ltd. v. Gulf & Western Corp., 644 F.2d 946, 950, 210 U.S.P.Q. 1, 3 (2d Cir. 1981).

[325] *See* § 5F[1].

[326] Oral-B Laboratories, Inc. v. Mi-Lor Corp., 810 F.2d 20, 24, 1 U.S.P.Q.2d 1867, 1870 (2d Cir. 1987); Conan Properties, Inc. v. Conans Pizza, Inc., 752 F.2d 145, 154, 225 U.S.P.Q. 379, 385 (5th Cir. 1985); Chevron Chemical Co. v. Voluntary Purchasing Groups, Inc., 659 F.2d 695, 705, 212 U.S.P.Q. 904, 913 (5th Cir. 1981), *cert. denied*, 457 F.2d 1126 (1982).

[327] *See, e.g.,* Charles of the Ritz Group Ltd. v. Quality King Distributors, Inc., 832 F.2d 1317, 4 U.S.P.Q.2d 1778 (2d Cir. 1987); Home Box Office, Inc. v. Showtime/The Movie Channel Inc., 832 F.2d 1311, 4 U.S.P.Q.2d 1789 (2d Cir. 1987).

[328] Joseph Scott Co. v. Scott Swimming Pools, Inc., 764 F.2d 62, 69, 226 U.S.P.Q. 496, 502 (2d Cir. 1985); Sardi's Restaurant Corp. v. Sardie, 755 F.2d 719, 725-26, 226 U.S.P.Q. 23, 27 (9th Cir. 1985).

[329] Soltex Polymer Corp. v. Fortex Industries, Inc., 832 F.2d 1325, 4 U.S.P.Q.2d 1785 (2d Cir. 1987).

[330] Soltex Polymer Corp. v. Fortex Industries, Inc., 832 F.2d 1325, 4 U.S.P.Q.2d 1785 (2d Cir. 1987); Charles of the Ritz Group Ltd. v. Quality King Distributors, Inc., 832 F.2d 1317,

Soltex involved the innocently infringing use of a similar mark, rather than the explicit use of a competitor's mark for comparative purposes. The district court required only a "not connected with" disclaimer.[331] In affirming, the appeals court noted doubts expressed concerning "the effectiveness of disclaimers in trademark infringement cases involving a substantial likelihood of confusion"[332] but emphasized flexibility, citing basic equity principles: "the relief granted should be no broader than necessary to cure the effects of the harm caused";[333] and " '[t]he essence of equity jurisdiction has been the power . . . to mould each decree to the necessities of the particular case[;] [f]lexibility rather than rigidity has distinguished it.' "[334] Factors favoring a district court's decision to order a disclaimer rather than an injunction to cure the wrong include (1) the defendant's good faith and use of the mark only in conjunction with its own stylized logo, (2) its legitimate interest in using the mark as part of a family of long-used marks, and (3) a finding that the potential confusion was "minimal or moderate."[335]

The absence of such factors and the fact that the defendants were using a competitor's exact mark in a confusing attempt at comparative advertising led the Second Circuit to affirm a district court's determination that a disclaimer was not adequate to prevent potential confusion in *Charles of the Ritz* and to reverse a determination that a disclaimer was sufficient in *Home Box Office*. A defendant requesting judicial sanction for a disclaimer bore a "heavy burden . . . to come forward with evidence sufficient to demonstrate that any proposed [disclaimer] materials would significantly reduce the likelihood of confusion."[336] The form that this evidence must take was left open.[337]

---

4 U.S.P.Q.2d 1778 (2d Cir. 1987); Home Box Office, Inc. v. Showtime/The Movie Channel Inc., 832 F.2d 1311, 4 U.S.P.Q.2d 1789 (2d Cir. 1987).

[331] 832 F.2d at 1328, 4 U.S.P.Q.2d at 1787.

[332] 832 F.2d at 1330.

[333] *Id.* at 1329 (citing Swann v. Charlotte-Mecklenberg Board of Education, 402 U.S. 1, 16 (1971)).

[334] *Id.* at 1329 (quoting Hecht Co. v. Bowles, 321 U.S. 321, 329 (1944)).

[335] *Id.* at 1330.

[336] *Id.* at 1316. The Court of Appeals noted "that there is a body of academic literature that questions the effectiveness of disclaimers in preventing consumer confusion as to the source of a product." *Id.* at 1315 (citing Jacoby & Raskoff, Disclaimers as a Remedy for Trademark Infringement Litigation: More Trouble Than They Are Worth?, 76 Trademark Rep. 35 (1986); Radin, Disclaimers as a Remedy for Trademark Infringement: Inadequacies and Alternatives, 76 Trademark Rep. 59 (1986); 2 H. Nims, Unfair Competition and Trademarks § § 366f, 379a (4th ed. 1947)). Other cases have discouraged the use of disclaimers. *See, e.g.,* International Kennel Club v. Mighty Star, Inc., 846 F.2d 1079, 1093, 6 U.S.P.Q.2d 1977, 1988-89 (7th Cir. 1988) ("Especially where the infringement in issue is a verbatim copying of the plaintiff's name, we are convinced that the plaintiff's reputation and goodwill should not be rendered forever dependent on the effectiveness of fineprint disclaimers often ignored by consumers.").

[337] Dissenting in *Charles of the Ritz*, Judge Altimari expressed concern that the opinion would be understood "to require empirical [presumably survey] evidence of the effectiveness of a proposed disclaimer in alleviating consumer confusion." 832 F.2d at 1325, 4 U.S.P.Q. 2d at 1784.

[e] Damages

[i] *Standard for Entitlement to Damages.* Likelihood of confusion is the test for liability and injunctive relief, but proof of actual confusion is required for recovery of damages.[338] Actual consumer confusion would ordinarily be established through direct evidence or use of consumer surveys or market research, but there is a rebuttable presumption of it if "a defendant has intentionally set out to deceive the public."[339]

The Lanham Act is not consistent on punitive damages. On the one hand, it provides "[i]n assessing damages the court may enter judgment, according to the circumstances of the case, for any sum above the amount found as actual damages, not exceeding three times such amount."[340] In awarding defendant's profits, the court may enter judgment for any sum above or below the amount of actual profits, "as the court shall find to be just, according to the circumstances of the case."[341] In counterfeiting cases, the court must triple plaintiff's actual damages or defendant's profits "unless the court finds extenuating circumstances."[342] On the other hand, it states that any sum above the amount of actual damages or profits "shall constitute compensation and not a penalty." From that statement, most courts have concluded that the Lanham Act does not permit punitive damages.[343] What remains unexplained is how an award of triple the plaintiff's actual damages can be "compensation and not a penalty."

---

[338] Trademark cases include: Web Printing Controls Co. v. Oxy-Dry Corp., 906 F.2d 1202, 15 U.S.P.Q.2d 1562, 1564-65 (7th Cir. 1990); Brunswick Corp. v. Spinit Reel Co., 832 F.2d 513, 525, 4 U.S.P.Q.2d 1497, 1506 (10th Cir. 1987) ("Actual consumer confusion may be shown by direct evidence, a diversion of sales or direct testimony from the public, or by circumstantial evidence such as consumer surveys."); PPX Enterprises Inc. v. Audiofidelity Enterprises, Inc. 818 F.2d 266, 267, 2 U.S.P.Q.2d 1672, 1676 (2d Cir. 1987); Ramada Inns, Inc. v. Gadsden Motel Co., 804 F.2d 1562, 1564, 1 U.S.P.Q.2d 1011, 1013 (11th Cir. 1986) ("[A] trademark infringement award must be based on proof of actual damages and . . . some evidence of harm arising from the violation must exist.").

False advertising cases include: Resource Developers, Inc. v. The Statue of Liberty-Ellis Island Foundation, Inc., 926 F.2d 134, 17 U.S.P.Q.2d 1842 (2d Cir. 1991); Harper House, Inc. v. Thomas Nelson, Inc., 889 F.2d 197, 210 (9th Cir. 1989).

[339] Resource Developers Inc. v. The Statue of Liberty-Ellis Island Foundation Inc., 926 F.2d 134, 140, 17 U.S.P.Q.2d 1842, 1845 (2d Cir. 1991); U-Haul International, Inc. v. Jartran, Inc., 601 F. Supp. 1140, 1149, 225 U.S.P.Q. 306, 312 (D. Ariz. 1984), *aff'd in pertinent part and modified and reversed in part on other grounds,* 793 F.2d 1034, 1040-41, 230 U.S.P.Q. 343 (9th Cir. 1986); Ambrit, Inc. v. Kraft, Inc., 812 F.2d 1531, 1542 (11th Cir. 1986).

See also PPX Enterprises, Inc. v. Audiofidelity Enterprises, 818 F.2d 266, 272, 2 U.S.P.Q.2d 1672, 1677 (2d Cir. 1987) ("Given the egregious nature of Audiofidelity's actions, we see no need to require appellant to provide consumer surveys or reaction tests in order to prove entitlement to damages.").

[340] Lanham Act § 35(a), 15 U.S.C. § 1117(a).

[341] *Id.*

[342] Lanham Act § 35(b), 15 U.S.C. § 1117(b).

[343] *See, e.g.,* Getty Petroleum Corp. v. Bartco Petroleum Corp., 858 F.2d 103, 8 U.S.P.Q.2d 1336, 1344 (2d Cir. 1988), *cert. denied,* 490 U.S. 1006 (1989); Metric & Multistandard Components Corp. v. Metric's, Inc., 635 F.2d 710, 209 U.S.P.Q. 97 (8th Cir. 1980). *But see* Gorenstein Enterprises, Inc. v. Quality Care-USA, Inc. 874 F.2d 431, 435-36, 10 U.S.P.Q.2d 1762, 1764 (7th Cir. 1989).

Moreover, because trademark infringement is a tort, and most states allow punitive damages for egregious conduct in tort cases, the Lanham Act's punitive damage prohibition can be avoided by pleading a state common law trademark infringement claim.

[ii] *Standard for Assessing Damages.* "When determining damages in an unfair trade practices case, the courts distinguish between the amount of proof needed to show 'that some damages were the certain result of the wrong' and the amount of proof needed to ascertain the exact amount of damages. The plaintiff is held to a lower burden of proof in ascertaining the exact amount of damages because, '[t]he most elementary conceptions of justice and public policy require that the wrongdoer shall bear the risk of the uncertainty which hiʳ own wrong has created.' . . . However, the plaintiff may not recover if he fails to prove that the defendant's actions caused the claimed harm."[344]

Actual damages recoverable under section 35(a) include:

— profits lost by the plaintiff on sales actually diverted . . . ;

— profits lost by the plaintiff on sales made at prices reduced as a demonstrated result of the false advertising [or infringement] . . . ;

— the costs of any completed advertising that actually and reasonably responds to the defendant's offending [conduct] . . . ; and

— quantifiable harm to the plaintiff's good will, to the extent that completed corrective advertising has not repaired that harm. . . .[345]

To show lost sales, it is not necessary to show decreases in actual sales; "unrealized growth potential" may be compensated.[346]

Damages have also been awarded in trademark infringement cases for reputational harm[347] and as a reasonable royalty for trademark use.[348] A reasonable royalty is

---

[344] Otis Clapp & Son, Inc. v. Filmore Vitamin Co., 754 F.2d 738, 745, 225 U.S.P.Q. 387, 392 (7th Cir. 1985). *See also* Harper House, Inc. v. Thomas Nelson, Inc., 889 F.2d 197, 209, 12 U.S.P.Q.2d 1779, 1789 (9th Cir. 1989). Burndy Corp v. Teledyne Industries, Inc., 748 F.2d 767, 771, 224 U.S.P.Q. 106, 109 (2d Cir. 1984) ("Although a court may engage in some degree of speculation in computing the *amount* of such damages, particularly when the inability to compute them is attributable to the defendant's wrongdoing, [citation omitted] causation must first be established [citation omitteJ]."); Alpo Petfoods, Inc. v. Ralston Purina Co., 913 F.2d 958, 969, 16 U.S.P.Q.2d 1081, 1090 (D.C. Cir. 1990) ("When assessing these actual damages, the district court may taken into account the difficulty of proving an exact amount of damages from false advertising, as well as the maxim that ' "the wrongdoer shall bear the risk of the uncertainty which his own wrong has created." ' ").

[345] Alpo Petfoods, Inc. v. Ralston Purina Co., 913 F.2d 958, 969, 16 U.S.P.Q.2d 1081, 1089-90 (D.C. Cir. 1990). *See also* Century Distilling Co. v. Continental Distilling Corp., 86 F. Supp. 503, 506 (E.D. Pa. 1949); Ford Motor Co. v. B & H Supply, Inc., 646 F. Supp. 975, 991, 998, 1 U.S.P.Q.2d 1094, 1105 (D. Minn. 1986); Koelemay, *Monetary Relief for Trademark Infringement Under the Lanham Act*, 72 Trademark Rep. 458, 505-07 (1982).

[346] Otis Clapp & Son, Inc. v. Filmore Vitamin Co., 754 F.2d 738, 745-46, 225 U.S.P.Q. 387, 392-93 (7th Cir. 1985).

[347] A damage award may not be based solely on reputational harm. Playboy Enterprises, Inc. v. P. K. Sorren Export Co., 546 F. Supp. 987, 998, 218 U.S.P.Q. 795, 803 (S.D. Fla. 1982).

[348] An award of a reasonable royalty may be appropriate when the trademark owner has

appropriate only in specific situations, such as when the infringer is a former licensee.

Notwithstanding the Ninth Circuit's spectacular $40 million damages award in *U-Haul*,[349] significant damage awards remain primarily theoretical possibilities (for the plaintiff) and threats (to the defendant). In *Alpo*, the district court's $10.4 million award based on a doubling of the amount spent on the deceptive advertising, which also approximated the net profits earned on the product during the period of the deceptive advertising, was vacated and remanded for re-calculation, with the appeals courts noting some reservations about *U-Haul's* damage award standard.[350] The Ninth Circuit itself stated that the *U-Haul* standard was a crude surrogate measure of damage to plaintiff's good will that may be limited to "cases of 'palming off' or *direct* comparative advertising."[351]

As noted in the *Alpo* opinion's review of the available remedies: "The thin body of case law on actual damages for successful false-advertising claims reflects the fact that litigants, who best understand their real losses, almost always settle these cases once a court have given its view of the merits."[352]

[f] Profits

[i] Profits Disgorgement Entitlement Standard. The cases are not consistent on profits award standards. Some require an element of bad faith, such as deliberateness or willfulness.[353] The District of Columbia Circuit further refined that standard to mean "willful, targeted wrongdoing."[354] "Targeted" refers to action directed at a

---

in fact licensed or offered to license the mark in the past. *See, e.g.,* Howard Johnson Co. v. Khimani, 892 F.2d 1512, 1519-20, 13 U.S.P.Q.2d 1808, 1814 (11th Cir. 1990); Bandag, Inc. v. Al Bolser's Tire Stores, Inc., 750 F.2d 903, 920, 223 U.S.P.Q. 982, 994 (Fed. Cir. 1984); Boston Professional Hockey Association v. Dallas Cap & Emblem Manufacturing, Inc., 597 F.2d 71, 202 U.S.P.Q. 536 (5th Cir. 1979); Holiday Inns, Inc. v. Airport Holiday Corp., 493 F. Supp. 1025, 212 U.S.P.Q. 208 (N.D. Tex. 1980), *aff'd on other grounds*, 683 F.2d 931, 216 U.S.P.Q. 568 (5th Cir. 1982). Otherwise, the award would be too speculative. Sands, Taylor & Wood v. The Quaker Oats Co., 18 U.S.P.Q.2d 1457, 1476 (N.D. Ill. 1990).

For a discussion of reasonable royalty awards in patent and copyright cases, see §§ 2F[5][b] and 4F[5][c].

[349] U-Haul International, Inc. v. Jartran, Inc., 793 F.2d 1034, 230 U.S.P.Q. 343 (9th Cir. 1986).

[350] Alpo Petfoods, Inc. v. Ralston Purina Co., 913 F.2d 958, 967-70 & 968 n.9, 16 U.S.P.Q.2d 1081, 1088-89 & 1088 n.9 (D.C. Cir. 1990), *vacating in pertinent part and remanding*, 720 F. Supp. 194, 215 (D.D.C. 1989).

[351] Harper House, Inc. v. Thomas Nelson, Inc., 889 F.2d 197, 209, 12 U.S.P.Q.2d 1779, 1789 (9th Cir. 1989) (emphasis in original).

[352] Alpo Petfoods, Inc. v. Ralston Purina Co., 913 F.2d 958, 969 n.12, 16 U.S.P.Q.2d 1081, 1090 n.12 (D.C. Cir. 1990).

[353] Alpo Petfoods, Inc. v. Ralston Purina Co., 913 F.2d 958, 968, 16 U.S.P.Q.2d 1081, 1089 (D.C. Cir. 1990) ("an award based on a defendant's profits requires proof that the defendant acted willfully and in bad faith"); Frisch's Restaurant, Inc. v. Elby's Big Boy, 849 F.2d 1012, 1015 (6th Cir. 1988).

[354] Alpo Petfoods, Inc. v. Ralston Purina Co., 913 F.2d 958, 961, 16 U.S.P.Q.2d 1081, 1082 (D.C. Cir. 1990).

specific competitor: "In the broader false-advertising context, as in the trademark infringement context, 'willfulness' and 'bad faith' require a connection between a defendant's awareness of its competitors and its actions at those competitors' expense."[355]

Most decisions follow a more flexible approach: "there is no express requirement that the parties be in direct competition or that the infringer willfully infringe . . . to justify an award of profits. [citation omitted] Profits are awarded under different rationales including unjust enrichment, deterrence, and compensation."[356]

> "[T]he decision as to whether a defendant will be ordered to account for profits under § 1117 rests in the broad discretion of the district court guided by principles of equity. [citation omitted] Normally an accounting will be ordered only if the 'defendant is unjustly enriched, if the plaintiff sustained damages from the infringement, or if an accounting is necessary to deter a willful infringer from doing so again.' "[357]

Some cases ignore the difference between damage and profits awards and simply assume virtually automatic entitlement to the infringer's profits.[358]

[ii] *Standard for Calculating Profits.* The statute employs a burden-shifting device that requires the plaintiff to prove only defendant's sales revenues, the defendant having to prove any deductions to arrive at actual profits.[359] Courts allow considerable leeway, even on plaintiff's initial burden to show gross revenues, when the infringer's lack of records or poor recordkeeping prevents a more exact determination.[360]

---

[355] *Id.* at 966, 16 U.S.P.Q.2d at 1087.

[356] Roulov v. Russ Berrie & Co., 886 F.2d 931, 941, 12 U.S.P.Q.

[357] Burndy Corp. v. Teledyne Industries, Inc., 748 F.2d 767, 772, 224 U.S.P.Q. 106, 110 (2d Cir. 1984) (quoting W.E. Bassett Co. v. Revlon, Inc., 435 F.2d 656, 664, 168 U.S.P.Q. 1, 7 (2d Cir. 1970)); Burger King Corp. v. Mason, 855 F.2d 779, 781, 8 U.S.P.Q.2d 1263, 1264 (11th Cir. 1988) (profits award neither depends on a finding of defendant's bad faith nor is precluded when a defendant has acted in good faith, but is intended "to further the congressional purpose by making infringement unprofitable, and is justified because it deprives the defendant of unjust enrichment and provides a deterrent to similar activity in the future."). Cf. Playboy Enterprises, Inc. v. Baccarat Clothing Co., 692 F.2d 1272, 1274, 216 U.S.P.Q. 1083, 1085 (9th Cir. 1982) (profits award may be necessary to prevent unjust enrichment).

[358] *See, e.g.,* Wesco Manufacturing, Inc. v. Tropical Attractions of Palm Beach, Inc., 833 F.2d 1484, 1487-88, 5 U.S.P.Q.2d 1190, 1193 (11th Cir. 1987) (assuming entitlement to defendant's profits and remanding for a determination of the amount, notwithstanding the affirmance of a denial of attorneys fees); Tonka Corp. v. Tonk-A-Phone, Inc., 805 F.2d 793, 794, 231 U.S.P.Q. 872, 873 (8th Cir. 1986) ("Under the Lanham Act, a plaintiff may recover as damages for trademark infringement . . . the defendant's profits. . . . ").

[359] The plaintiff need only prove the amount of defendant's sales revenues attributable to the infringement, and defendant "must prove all elements of cost or deduction claimed." Lanham Act § 35(a), 15 U.S.C. § 1117(a).

[360] Wesco Manufacturing, Inc. v. Tropical Attractions of Palm Beach, Inc., 833 F.2d 1484, 1488, 5 U.S.P.Q.2d 1190, 1193 (11th Cir. 1987); Louis Vuitton S.A. v. Spencer Handbags Corp., 765 F.2d 966, 973, 227 U.S.P.Q. 377, 381 (2d Cir. 1985); Reebok International Ltd. v. Pak, 17 U.S.P.Q.2d 1333, 1334 (S.D. N.Y. 1990).

One major issue in calculating profits is whether the plaintiff is entitled to profits from sales of the entire product or whether defendant is allowed to introduce proof that a certain percentage of the profits are due to non-infringing factors in the product. There are few cases on the issue. Some hold that defendant is entitled to prove that profits should be allocated between infringing and non-infringing elements and therefore that a certain portion of the profits from the product are not attributable to an infringing use of the mark.[361]

Another issue is whether the defendant may deduct overhead (fixed) expenses or only variable costs. In *Roulo*,[362] the Seventh Circuit adopted a bright line rule: "Fixed costs are not deducted from the profits calculation." In *Maltina*,[363] the Fifth Circuit left open the possibility of deducting overhead expenses, but only if the defendant proves that sales of the infringing product "actually increased its overhead expenses." It adopted a rule of thumb that "a proportionate share of overhead is not deductible when the sales of an infringing product constitute only a small percentage [6% in this case] of total sales."[364]

The Second Circuit adopts a generally permissive approach to overhead deduction,[365] but imposes on defendant rigorous proof standards for each overhead element to be deducted: "Although [defendant] need not prove its overhead expenses and their relationship to the production of the . . . goods in 'minute detail,' . . . it still must carry its burden of demonstrating a sufficient nexus between each expense claimed and the sale of the unlawful goods."[366] Defendant sustained its burden as to deduction of "sales commission, returns, samples and markdowns, shipping costs, interest on

---

[361] Roulo v. Russ Berrie & Co., 886 F.2d 931, 941, 12 U.S.P.Q.2d 1423, 1431 (7th Cir. 1989), *cert. denied*, 493 U.S. 1075 (1990); Wolfe v. National Lead Co., 272 F.2d 867, 872 (9th Cir. 1959), *cert. denied*, 362 U.S. 950 (1960); Century Distilling Co. v. Continental Distilling Corp., 205 F.2d 140, 148 (3d Cir.), *cert. denied*, 346 U.S. 900 (1953). *But see* Truck Equipment Service Co. v. Fruehauf Corp., 536 F.2d 1210, 1222, 191 U.S.P.Q. 79, 90 (8th Cir.), *cert. denied*, 429 U.S. 861 (1976) (defendant not allowed to submit proof that only certain percentage of profits attributable to infringing use of plaintiff's mark).

In Sands, Taylor & Wood v. The Quaker Oats Co., 18 U.S.P.Q.2d 1457, 1474 (N.D. Ill. 1990), the court awarded plaintiff 10% of defendants' pre-tax profits on the infringing product.

[362] Roulo v. Russ Berrie & Co., 886 F.2d 931, 941, 12 U.S.P.Q.2d 1423, 1431 (7th Cir. 1989), *cert. denied*, 110 S. Ct. 1124 (1990).

The Fourth Circuit has hinted that in the proper context it might disallow any overhead deduction. Polo Fashions, Inc. v. Craftex, Inc., 816 F.2d 145, 149, 2 U.S.P.Q.2d 1444, 1446 (4th Cir. 1987).

[363] Maltina Corp. v. Cawy Bottling Co., 613 F.2d 582, 586, 205 U.S.P.Q. 489, 492 (5th Cir. 1980).

[364] 613 F.2d at 586, 205 U.S.P.Q. 489. *Accord* Clamp Manufacturing Co. v. Enco Manufacturing Co., 5 U.S.P.Q.2d 1643, 1648 (C.D. Cal. 1987), *aff'd*, 870 F.2d 512, 10 U.S.P.Q.2d 1226 (9th Cir. 1989), *cert. denied*, 110 S. Ct. 202 (1989).

[365] *See* W.E. Bassett Co. v. Revlon, Inc., 435 F.2d 656, 665, 168 U.S.P.Q. 1, 8 (2d Cir. 1970) ("Subject to a determination of the reasonableness of the claimed deductions, Revlon should be able to deduct from its net sales its overhead, most of its operating expenses, and the federal income taxes on the [infringing] items.").

[366] Manhattan Industries, Inc. v. Sweater Bee By Banff, Ltd., 885 F.2d 1, 7–8, 12 U.S.P.Q.2d 1368, 1374 (2d Cir. 1989), *cert. denied*, 110 S. Ct. 1477 (1990).

money borrowed from its corporate parent, and taxes" but offered insufficient proof of its overhead expenses. The court held that the defendant could not approximate overhead allocable to unlawful sales by simply using the percentage of overhead to total sales without some demonstration that more reliable data specific to the unlawful sales are not available.[367]

In *Wolfe*,[368] the Ninth Circuit held that income taxes paid on infringing sales, attorneys fees for the infringement litigation, and compensation to the business' principals are not proper deductions, but otherwise permitted deduction of overhead expenses according to a ratio of infringing product sales to overall sales.

In certain situations, for example, when an infringer dumps merchandise "at cost" once the trademark owner takes action, the court may award the trademark owner the defendant's gross revenues,[369] the rationale being that "the purpose of Section 1117 is to 'take all the economic incentive out of trademark infringement.' "[370]

[g] **Destruction of Infringing Articles.** The Lanham Act authorizes orders to destroy all depictions of the trademark itself. "[T]he court may order that all labels, signs, prints, packages, wrappers, receptacles, and advertisements . . . bearing the [mark] . . . or . . . colorable imitation thereof . . . shall be delivered up and destroyed."[371]

Courts readily order destruction of advertising, labels, and packaging.[372] Similarly, they will order destruction of the goods themselves if the goods and the infringing

---

[367] 885 F.2d at 8. *Cf.* Warner Bros., Inc. v. Gay Toys, Inc., 598 F. Supp. 424, 431, 223 U.S.P.Q. 503, 505 (S.D.N.Y. 1984) (" ' "Overhead" which does not assist in the production of the infringement should not be credited to the infringer; that which does, should be; it is a question of fact in all cases.' ") (quoting Sheldon v. Metro-Goldwyn Pictures Corp., 106 F.2d 45, 54, 42 U.S.P.Q. 540 (2d Cir. 1939)).

[368] Wolfe v. National Lead Co., 272 F.2d 867, 871-72 (9th Cir. 1959), *cert. denied*, 362 U.S. 950 (1960).

[369] Polo Fashions, Inc. v. Dick Bruhn, Inc., 793 F.2d 1132, 1134-35, 230 U.S.P.Q. 538, 541 (9th Cir. 1986).

[370] 793 F.2d at 1135 (quoting Playboy Enterprises, Inc. v. Baccarat Clothing Co., 692 F.2d 1272, 1275, 216 U.S.P.Q. 1083, 1085 (9th Cir. 1982)).

[371] Lanham Act § 36, 15 U.S.C. § 1118.

[372] *See, e.g.,* R.J. Toomey Co. v. Toomey, 683 F. Supp. 873, 880, 7 U.S.P.Q.2d 1623, 1628 (D. Mass. 1988); Marker International v. deBruler, 635 F. Supp. 986, 1004 (D. Utah 1986), *aff'd*, 844 F.2d 763, 6 U.S.P.Q.2d 1575 (10th Cir. 1988); Chassis Master Corp. v. Borrego, 610 F. Supp. 473, 479, 225 U.S.P.Q. 1240, 1244 (S.D.Fla. 1985); Emerson Electric Co. v. Emerson Quiet Kool Corp., 577 F. Supp. 668, 681, 221 U.S.P.Q. 782, 792 (E.D.Mo. 1983); Toys "R" Us, Inc. v. Games-R-Us, No. 83-4542, slip. op. at 1-2 (N.D. Ill. 1983) (packages, wrappers, labels, etc. to be destroyed, but not toys which may or may not have a manufacturer's trademark already affixed); Schroeder v Lotito, 577 F. Supp. 708, 725, 221 U.S.P.Q. 812, 827 (D.R.I. 1983), *aff'd*, 747 F.2d 801, 224 U.S.P.Q. 97 (1st Cir. 1984); Amana Society v. Gemeinde Brau, Inc., 417 F. Supp. 310, 311 (N.D. Iowa 1976), *aff'd*, 557 F.2d 638, 195 U.S.P.Q. 145 (8th Cir. 1977), *cert. denied*, 434 U.S. 967 (1977) (advertisements and beer cans with infringing mark to be destroyed, but presumably not beer in the cans); Nat'l Dairy Products Corp. v. Willever, 139 U.S.P.Q. 443, 449 [last pg] (E.D.Mich. 1963) (containers, but not contents, bearing trademark were to be destroyed).

trademark are inseparable, for example, the offending trademark is woven into a cloth good or indelibly imprinted on the good.[373] Less settled is whether the court may order product destruction if the packaging alone bears the offending mark and the product could be repackaged and sold in a non-infringing manner. Some decisions assume without much discussion that this authority exists.[374]

In *Fendi S.A.S. Di Paola Fendi E Sorelle*,[375] Judge Sand held that Lanham Act Sections 34 and 36, as amended by the 1984 Trademark Counterfeiting Act, authorize goods destruction. Amended Section 34(d) provides "for the seizure of goods and counterfeit marks." Amended Section 36 requires a party seeking destruction of goods seized pursuant to Section 34(d) to give the United States Attorney notice, so that the prosecutor could guard against destruction of evidence to be used in a criminal proceeding. The Criminal Code was amended to grant "prosecutors in criminal prosecutions for trademark counterfeiting the right to seek destruction of the goods themselves."[376] Finding the statutes ambiguous, Judge Sand found congressional intent to allow destruction of goods in civil cases in the 1984 Act's legislative history, which states that the criminal statute " 'gives the court the same options it has in ordering destructions under 15 U.S.C. 1118.' "[377]

[h] Prejudgment Interest. Lanham Act Section 35(a) makes no reference to prejudgment interest. Courts have determined that prejudgment interest may be awarded as a matter of inherent judicial power but disagree on when an award is appropriate. The Seventh Circuit held that "prejudgment interest should be presumptively available to victims of federal law violations" as a matter of federal common law.[378]

---

[373] *See* Shen Manufacturing Co. v. Suncrest Mills, Inc., 673 F. Supp. 1199, 1207, 4 U.S.P.Q.2d 1438, 1444 (S.D.N.Y. 1987) (ordering destruction of dishcloths in which the infringing trademark was woven in); Nike Inc. v. Leslie, 2 U.S.P.Q.2d 1232, 1233 (M.D. Fla. 1987) (destruction of socks bearing counterfeit mark in addition to packaging, advertising, and other materials); Moore Business Forms, Inc. v. Seidenburg, 619 F. Supp. 1173, 1185, 229 U.S.P.Q. 821, 827-28 (W.D. La. 1985) (infringing goods included stationery and business forms with the infringing trademark part of them); Gucci Shops, Inc. v. Dreyfoos & Associates, Inc., 222 U.S.P.Q. 302, 305 (S.D. Fla. 1983) (handbags and watches with infringing mark intrinsic to the products).

[374] *See* Worthington Foods, Inc. v. Kellogg Co., 732 F. Supp. 1417, 1462 n.100, 14 U.S.P.Q.2d 1577, 1613 n.100 (S.D. Ohio 1990) (noting the possibility of recalling and repackaging cereal, but noting in dictum that plaintiff may, if it ultimately prevailed, "be able to secure the destruction of the cereal [and not just the packaging] in the long run"); General Motors Corp. v. Gibson Chemical & Oil Corp., 627 F. Supp. 678, 680, 229 U.S.P.Q. 349, 350 (E.D.N.Y. 1986); Ford Motor Co. v. B & H Supply, Inc., 646 F. Supp. 975, 991, 997, 1 U.S.P.Q.2d 1094, 1104 (D. Minn. 1986); Playboy Enterprises Inc. v. P. K. Sorren Export Co., 546 F. Supp. 987, 997, 218 U.S.P.Q. 795, 802 (S.D.Fla. 1982) (ordering destruction of infringing labels and delivery of shirts with infringing design, presumably for destruction).

[375] Fendi S.A.S. Di Paola Fendi E Sorelle v. Cosmetic World, Ltd., 642 F. Supp. 1143, 1146-47, 1 U.S.P.Q.2d 1508, 1510 (S.D.N.Y. 1986).

[376] 642 F. Supp. at 1146.

[377] *Id.* at 1147 (quoting The Joint Explanatory Statement of Both Houses of Congress, 130 Cong. Record H. 12,076, 12,077 (Oct. 10, 1984)).

[378] Gorenstein Enterprises, Inc. v. Quality Care-USA Inc., 874 F.2d 431, 436, 10 U.S.P.Q.2d 1762, 1765 (7th Cir. 1989).

The Second Circuit held that prejudgment interest "is normally reserved for 'exceptional' cases."[379]

[i] *Costs and Attorneys Fees.* Section 35(a) authorizes attorneys fees awards to the prevailing party in an "exceptional case,"[380] which has been interpreted to mean one "involving willful or bad-faith conduct."[381]

Except when counterfeiting is proven, the language is permissive rather than mandatory; a court has discretion to deny a request for counsel fees even if it determines that the case is exceptional.[382] Courts interpret "exceptional" to mean that the plaintiff or defendant "prosecuted or defended an action in bad faith."[383] If the plaintiff prevails, "exceptional" means that the unlawful conduct was deliberate or willful.[384] If the defendant prevails, "exceptional" means the action was brought in bad faith or, as one district judge put it, "[t]here is a substantial overtone in this case to warrant an inference that this suit was initiated as a competitive ploy."[385]

One appellate case defines "exceptional" more expansively. In *Noxell*,[386] the District of Columbia Circuit awarded attorneys fees to a defendant who had the case dismissed for improper venue, noting: "Congress did not intend rigidly to limit recovery of fees by a defendant to the rare case in which a court finds that the plaintiff

---

[379] American Honda Motor Co. v. Two Wheel Corp., 918 F.2d 1060, 1064, 16 U.S.P.Q.2d 1956, 1959 (2d Cir. 1990).

[380] Lanham Act § 35(a), 15 U.S.C. § 1117(a). Congress enacted the attorney fee provision in 1975. Previously, the Supreme Court had held that the Lanham Act did not permit such awards. Fleischmann Distilling Corp. v. Maier Brewing Corp., 386 U.S. 714, 153 U.S.P.Q. 432 (1967).

[381] Alpo Petfoods, Inc. v. Ralston Purina Co., 913 F.2d 958, 961, 16 U.S.P.Q.2d 1081, 1083 (D.C. Cir. 1990); Tambrands, Inc. v. Warner-Lambert Co., 673 F. Supp. 1190, 1198 (S.D.N.Y. 1987); see Transgo, Inc. v. Ajac Transmission Parts Corp., 768 F.2d 1001, 1026, 227 U.S.P.Q. 598, 612 (9th Cir. 1985) (attorneys fee award appropriate where conduct "constituted extraordinary, malicious, wanton, and oppressive conduct"); International Olympic Committee v. San Francisco Arts & Athletics, 781 F.2d 733, 738, 228 U.S.P.Q. 585, 588 (9th Cir. 1986), aff'd, 483 U.S. 522 (1987); Jellibeans, Inc. v. Skating Clubs of Georgia, Inc., 716 F.2d 833, 846-47, 222 U.S.P.Q. 10, 22 (11th Cir. 1983).

[382] An award of attorneys fees to the trademark owner is mandatory if counterfeiting is proven, "unless the court finds extenuating circumstances." Lanham Act § 35(a), 15 U.S.C. § 1117(b).

[383] Motown Productions, Inc. v. Cacomm, Inc. 849 F.2d 781, 786, 7 U.S.P.Q.2d 1320, 1324 (2d Cir. 1988).

[384] Shroeder v. Lotito, 747 F.2d 801, 224 U.S.P.Q. 97 (1st Cir. 1984); Banff, Ltd. v. Federated Department Stores, Inc., 841 F.2d 486, 493, 6 U.S.P.Q.2d 1187, 1193 (2d Cir. 1988); Hindu Incense v. Meadows, 692 F.2d 1048, 1051-52, 216 U.S.P.Q. 853, 856 (6th Cir. 1982); Roulo v. Russ Berrie & Co., 886 F.2d 931, 942, 12 U.S.P.Q.2d 1423, 1431 (7th Cir. 1989).

[385] Mennen Co. v. Gillette Co., 565 F. Supp. 648, 657, 220 U.S.P.Q. 354, 360 (S.D.N.Y. 1983), aff'd, 742 F.2d 1437 (2d Cir. 1984) (unpublished). Accord Universal City Studios Inc. v. Nintendo Co., 797 F.2d 70, 230 U.S.P.Q. 409 (2d Cir.), cert. denied, 479 U.S. 987 (1986); Fuddruckers, Inc. v. Doc's B.R. Others, Inc., 623 F. Supp. 21, 22, 227 U.S.P.Q. 408, 408 (D. Ariz. 1985), rev'd on other grounds, 826 F.2d 837, 4 U.S.P.Q.2d 1026 (9th Cir. 1987) (infringement case determined to be groundless and brought as competitive ploy).

[386] Noxell Corp. v. Firehouse No. 1 Bar-B-Que Restaurant, 771 F.2d 521, 526, 227 U.S.P.Q. 115, 118-119 (D.C. Cir. 1985).

'acted in bad faith, vexatiously, wantonly, or for oppressive reasons.' . . . Something less than 'bad faith,' we believe, suffices to mark a case as 'exceptional.' 'Exceptional' is most reasonably read to mean what the word is generally understood to indicate—uncommon, not run-of-the-mine." [387]

The court protested that it did not use a "bad faith" standard, but, in fact, it did because it predicated its affirmance of attorneys fees on a standard similar to Rule 11: The plaintiff had brought its trademark case about as far away from the defendant's place of business as possible, and its argument for proper venue was squarely contradicted by Supreme Court precedent. [388]

Subsequently, a different panel of the same court of appeals did not even mention *Noxell* and defined "exceptional cases" in the context of § 35(a) as "cases involving willful or bad-faith conduct," and reversed an award of attorneys fees where the district court had not made that finding. [389]

The Sixth Circuit, after extensive discussion of *Noxell*, determined that it need not decide the issue. In *WSM*,[390] the district court had initially "expressly found that the defendants' conduct was not 'malicious, fraudulent, deliberate or willful' " but had, in a later opinion, awarded attorneys fees for conduct occurring after the point where the untenability of the defendant's case was obvious. It held that "[t]he continuation of the litigation beyond the point where the outcome was certain, particularly in view of WSM's offer of settlement, makes this case an exceptional one justifying an award of attorney fees from that time forward." The appeals court reversed, holding that the defendant was justified in continuing to litigate and therefore it was an abuse of discretion to allow attorneys fees even if the *Noxell* standard applied. [391]

That a party "seeks counsel's advice in a timely manner, makes adequate disclosure to counsel, receives counsel's opinion and then acts on it," weighs against a finding of bad faith, but "taking counsel's advice does not *ipso facto* and in all circumstances shield the actor from the consequences of his act." [392] Courts have held that a party

---

[387] *Id.*

[388] 771 F.2d at 527.

[389] Alpo Petfoods, Inc. v. Ralston Purina Co., 913 F.2d 958, 961, 971, 16 U.S.P.Q.2d 1081, 1091 (D.C. Cir. 1990) (citing Reader's Digest Ass'n v. Conservative Digest, Inc., 821 F.2d 800, 808, 3 U.S.P.Q.2d 1276, 1282-83 (D.C. Cir. 1987)).

[390] WSM, Inc. v. Wheeler, 223 U.S.P.Q. 1062, 1064 (M.D. Tenn. 1984), *rev'd*, 810 F.2d 113 (6th Cir. 1987). *See also* Walt Disney Productions v. Jeffries, 212 U.S.P.Q. 670, 672 (N.D. Ill. 1981) (fees awarded from point after three depositions "at which it can be said without doubt that the defendant knew her use of the mark was likely to cause confusion.").

[391] Neither court discussed the availability of 28 U.S.C. Section 1927 to cover the problem of counsel continuing a case beyond the point of reasonability. The provision allows a court to assess attorneys fees on any lawyer who "multiplies the proceedings in any case unreasonably and vexatiously."

[392] Cuisinarts, Inc. v. Robot-Coupe International Corp., 580 F. Supp. 634, 638, 222 U.S.P.Q. 318, 321 (S.D.N.Y. 1984). Accord Takecare Corp. v. Takecare of Oklahoma, Inc., 889 F.2d 955, 957, 12 U.S.P.Q.2d 2015, 2017 (10th Cir. 1989) ("under certain circumstances, a party's reasonable reliance on the advice of counsel may defuse otherwise wilful conduct.").

relying on advice of counsel must waive any attorney-client privilege relating to the advice and fully disclose counsel's opinion and its bases.[393]

If there are multiple claims, the fee award may be allocated according to which claims the party prevailed on and whether those claims were Lanham Act claims. Thus, where a party prevailed on some but not all claims, the fee award may be reduced by the amount allocated to work on the claims on which the party did not prevail. If some claims on which a party prevailed are premised on statutes or common law theories for which there is no statutory grant of attorneys fees, a court may, depending on the degree of relatedness among the claims, deny counsel fees on the non-Lanham Act claims.[394] If the Lanham Act and non-Lanham Act claims, or the prevailing and non-prevailing claims, involved a " 'common core of facts or [were] based on related legal theories,' " the court may award fees for the whole case.[395]

The courts of appeals have split as to whether the "exceptional case" standard applies to the entire case or whether it may be split into the trial and appellate stages. Some courts have held that if the underlying violation is willful, the plaintiff may be awarded fees for the entire case including the appeal, even if the appeal is not pursued in bad faith. In *Gorenstein*, the court held:

> "If a plaintiff wins a suit and is entitled by statute to a reasonable attorney's fee, the entitlement extends to the fee he reasonably incurs in defending the award of that fee. . . . Stated differently, the appeal of a litigant whose

---

[393] Takecare Corp. v. Takecare of Oklahoma, Inc., 889 F.2d 955, 957-58, 12 U.S.P.Q.2d 2015, 2017. *See* Cuisinarts, Inc. v. Robot-Coupe International Corp., 580 F. Supp. 634, 638, 222 U.S.P.Q. at 318, 321 (S.D. N.Y. 1984).

[394] *See* Gorenstein Enterprises Inc. v. Quality Care-USA Inc., 874 F.2d 431, 437, 10 U.S.P.Q.2d 1762, 1765-66 (7th Cir. 1989) (judge should have awarded attorneys' fees under § 1117 only for trademark infringement portion of the action, and not for breach of contract claim for unpaid royalties); Elnicky Enterprises, Inc. v. Spotlight Presents, Inc., 213 U.S.P.Q. 855, 864 (S.D.N.Y. 1981) (awarding fees for time spent on Lanham Act claim, but not on state law claims for breach of contract and misuse of trade secrets). In Transgo, Inc. v. Ajac Transmission Parts Corp., 768 F.2d 1001, 227 U.S.P.Q. 598 (9th Cir. 1985), *cert. denied*, 474 U.S. 1059 (1986), the Court of Appeals quoted Hensley v. Eckerhart, 461 U.S. 424, 440 (1983):

> "Where the plaintiff has failed to prevail on a claim that is distinct in all respects from his successful claims, the hours spent on the unsuccessful claim should be excluded in considering the amount of a reasonable fee. Where a lawsuit consists of related claims, a plaintiff who has won substantial relief should not have his attorney's fee reduced simply because the district court did not adopt each contention raised. But where the plaintiff achieved only limited success, the district court should award only that amount of fees that is reasonable in relation to the results obtained."

[395] Celebrity Service International Inc. v. Celebrity World Inc., 9 U.S.P.Q.2d 1673, 1687-88 (S.D.N.Y. 1988) (quoting Hensley v. Eckerhart, 461 U.S. 424, 435 (1983)). *See* Post Office v. Portec, Inc., 913 F.2d 802, 812-13, 15 U.S.P.Q.2d 1865 (10th Cir. 1990) (affirming district court's award of attorneys fees for entire case because "plaintiff's claims were so tightly bound together that the majority of the work on the Lanham Act claim would also have been necessary for the other claims," and reduction of total fees by twenty percent because "some of the non-Lanham Act claims involved separate issues.").

position in the district court was correctly adjudged frivolous is frivolous per se."[396]

Other courts have held that if the appeal is not in bad faith, then attorneys fees should not be awarded for the appeal.[397] In determining the amount of the award, courts rely on general attorneys fee award standards.[398]

§ 5G Ownership and Transfer

[1] Initial Ownership

Ownership vests in the person or entity who first adopts and uses a mark to distinguish his, her or its goods or services.[1] Most often, the mark owner is the manufacturer (or, in the case of service marks, the service provider), but the Lanham Act, which defines "trademark" in terms of ability to distinguish goods "manufactured *or sold*,"[2] confirms the common law rule that a merchant or distributor can be a trademark owner.[3]

---

[396] Gorenstein Enterprises Inc. v. Quality Care-USA Inc., 874 F.2d 431, 438, 10 U.S.P.Q.2d 1762, 1766 (7th Cir. 1989).

[397] San Juan Products Inc. v. San Juan Pools of Kansas Inc., 849 F.2d 468, 476, 7 U.S.P.Q.2d 1230, 1237 (10th Cir. 1988) (ruling based on court's inherent equitable powers rather than Lanham Act).

[398] *See, e.g.,* Transgo, Inc. v. Ajac Transmission Parts Corp., 768 F.2d 1001, 1027, 227 U.S.P.Q. 598, 611 (9th Cir. 1985), *cert. denied,* 474 U.S. 1059 (1986); Selchow & Righter, Inc. v. Decipher, Inc. 228 U.S.P.Q. 374, 376 (E.D. Va. 1985).

[1] *See* J.T. McCarthy, Trademarks and Unfair Competition § 16:13 (2d ed. 1984) ("Trademark ownership inures to the legal entity who is in fact using the mark as a symbol of origin.").

[2] Lanham Act § 45, 15 U.S.C. § 1127 (Emphasis added).

[3] *E.g.,* Menendez v. Holt, 128 U.S. 514, 520 (1888) ("The fact that Holt & Co. were not the actual manufacturers of the flour upon which they had for years placed the brand in question does not deprive them of the right to be protected in the use of that brand as a trademark. They used the words 'La Favorita' to designate flour selected by them, in the exercise of their best judgment, as equal to a certain standard. The brand did not indicate by whom the flour was manufactured, but it did indicate the origin of its selection and classification. It was equivalent to the signature of Holt & Co. to a certificate that the flour was the genuine article which had been determined by them to possess a certain degree of excellence."); Premier Dental Products Co. v. Darby Dental Supply Co., Inc. 794 F.2d 850, 853, 230 U.S.P.Q. 233, 235 (3d Cir. 1986), *cert. denied,* 479 U.S.. 950 (1946) ("[A] distributor may own the trademark in goods it does not manufacture."); Power Test Petroleum Distributors, Inc. v. Calcu Gas, Inc., 754 F.2d 91, 225 U.S.P.Q. 368 (2d Cir. 1985); E.F. Prichard Co. v. Consumers Brewing Co., 136 F.2d 512, 519 (6th Cir. 1943), *cert. denied,* 321 U.S. 763 (1944) ("It is the law that one need not himself manufacture goods to acquire a valid trade-mark, even though the name of the real manufacturer is used as a part of the device. . . . It is sufficient, as regards . . . the claim of ownership in the trade-mark, that the goods are manufactured for the claimant, or that they pass through his hands in the course of trade and that he gives to them the benefits of his name and business style. . . . And it is not important that a party does not himself manufacture the articles which he sells, and upon which he places his trade-mark. It is sufficient that the goods are manufactured for him and that he owns or controls the goods which he offers for sale, and upon which he places a trade-mark or Trade-name."); Victor Tool & Machine Corp. v. Sun Control Awnings, Inc., 299 F. Supp. 868, 874, 162 U.S.P.Q. 389 (E.D. Mich. 1968), *aff'd,* 411 F.2d 792, 162 U.S.P.Q. 387 (6th Cir. 1969).

A recurring trademark law problem is determining mark ownership in a manufacturer-distributor relationship. If the manufacturer acquired mark ownership through adoption and use in the market before establishing the relationship, the distributor, whether exclusive or nonexclusive, cannot acquire ownership rights except through a valid assignment.[4] Ownership rights are less clear when the manufacturer and distributor jointly introduce a product or service and its distinguishing mark to a market and fail to make explicit provision for mark ownership.[5] Courts apply a

---

[4] *E.g.*, E.F. Prichard Co. v. Consumers Brewing Co., 136 F.2d 512, 519 (6th Cir. 1943) ("A manufacturer of a certain commodity, by agreeing to allow the purchaser thereof the use of its trade name for a certain period, did not lose the exclusive right to the name after the expiration of the term . . . and one may introduce his trade-mark and create a demand for his variety of goods in a new territory, by licenses."); United States Ozone Co. v. United States Ozone Co. of America, 62 F.2d 881 (7th Cir. 1932); Omag Optik und Mechanik A.G. v. Weinstein, 85 F. Supp. 631, 637 (S.D. N.Y. 1949) ("In the absence of inequitable conduct on the part of the manufacturer, a distributor who employs the mark of his principal, does not acquire a proprietary interest in the mark that will serve to extinguish the rights of the manufacturer.").

In *Omag Optik*, the court rejected the defendant's reliance on three cases in which "distributors were accorded rights in marks originally belonging to the manufacturer."

"[In *Overhamm v. Westall*, 271 App.Div. 492, 66 N.Y.S.2d 371 (1946), and *George B. Graff Co. v. H. C. Cook Co.*, 1924, 55 App.D.C. 136, 2 F.2d 938 (1924)], the distributor had expended considerable time and money in exploiting the mark, and the court found that the same had, in fact, become associated with the distributor, rather than with the manufacturer, and that, in the circumstances, it would be inequitable to grant an exclusive right to the manufacturer. This inequity was based on more than the fact that the parties stood in the relation of manufacturer and distributor. In the *Overhamm* case, the manufacturer unreasonably deprived the distributor of the right to use a second associated mark. In the *Graff* case the manufacturer had the right to insist that its name appear along with the mark, and that the distributor's name should not appear. Instead, the manufacturer permitted the distributor's name to appear, while the manufacturer's did not.

"These cases do not dispute the general rule, above referred to, but rely on the fact that there was some particular inequity in the manufacturer's conduct. . . .

". . . [In *Roma Wine Co. v. Roma Wine & Liquor Co., Inc.*, 80 U.S.P.Q. 69 (D. Del. 1948)] the distributor employed the mark in question on goods purchased from third parties, apparently in violation of the obligations owed to the manufacturer with whom it had established a fiduciary relationship, and yet the distributor was protected. Nevertheless, upon the existing facts, the distributor was held to be protected, within certain limitations, in its use of the mark. The theory was that an estoppel had arisen against the manufacturer. The estoppel was based on two grounds. In the first place, the manufacturer consented, after some dispute, to the distributor's registration of its corporate name, which included the mark 'Roma.' Secondly, while the court found that there was no credible evidence that the manufacturer knew that the distributor was selling wine purchased from third parties, under the manufacturer's mark, the court held that 'it is clear from the weight of the credible evidence that plaintiff (the manufacturer) knew defendant had built up a very substantial wine and whiskey business independently of any goods that it purchased from plaintiff, which plaintiff should have thoroughly investigated from the trade mark aspect, and plaintiff might have obtained relief by appropriate court proceedings several years ago. . . . " 85 F. Supp. at 637-38.

[5] *E.g.*, E.F. Prichard Co. v. Consumers Brewing Co., 136 F.2d 512 (6th Cir. 1943), *cert. denied*, 321 U.S. 763 (1944) (beer: distributor, not brewer, owns mark); Atlas Beverage Co.

multiple factors analysis to determine whether the mark symbolizes manufacturer or merchant good will.

> "Absent an agreement between the parties, the Court must look to various factors in determining which party has a superior right to the ownership of the disputed mark. Aside from federal registration, such factors include: (1) which party invented and first affixed the mark onto the product; (2) which party's name appeared with the trademark; (3) which party maintained the quality and uniformity of the product; and (4) with which party did the public identify the product and make complaints. . . . [N]o single factor is determinative. . . . "[6]

In *Wrist-Rocket Manufacturing,*[7] the court found the distributor, not the manufacturer, owned the mark when the distributor selected the mark and used it with his house mark without mentioning the manufacturer, and suggested product changes. Whether the parties' business relationship was properly characterizable as that of manufacturer and exclusive distributor or "merely a buy-sell arrangement" was relevant but not conclusive:

> "This is not then a case where a distributor appropriates to its own use an existing trademark of the manufacturer. The issue here is who, as between the manufacturer and distributor, has ownership of a trademark created after the formation of the business relationship. In this context, the relationship of the parties is clearly relevant, but the underlying and dispositive question remains: which party has priority of appropriation and use of the trademark in connection with his business."[8]

---

v. Minneapolis Brewing Co., 113 F.2d 672 (8th Cir. 1940) (beer: brewer, not distributor, owns mark); Distillers Brands, Inc. v. American Distilling Co., 26 F. Supp. 988, 989 (S.D. N.Y. 1938) (whiskey: distributor, not bottler, owns mark: "The bottles bore the mark 'King's Pride', followed by the words 'Bottled for King Distributing Company', and carried no mention of the plaintiff. The mark itself, 'King's Pride', is internal evidence that it was the mark of the King Company, and the collocation of the mark with the name of the King Company on the labels makes unmistakable the fact that it was the mark of the King Company. So far as consumers were concerned, the distillers and the bottler were anonymous. The King's Pride whiskey had only the sponsorship of the King Company as distributor. Where a trademark indicates a distributor of merchandise rather than the maker, it is the distributor who acquires the trade-mark rights. For the public associates the goods so marked with the distributor and knows not the identity of its maker.").

[6] Spectrum Marketing, Inc. v. Omega Nutrition U.S.A. Inc., 756 F. Supp. 435, 438-39, 18 U.S.P.Q.2d 1371, 1376 (N.D. Calif. 1991).

[7] Wrist-Rocket Manufacturing Co., Inc. v. Saunders Archery Co., 379 F. Supp. 902 (D. Neb. 1974), aff'd, in part, rev'd, in part, & remanded, 516 F.2d 846, 186 U.S.P.Q. 5 (8th Cir. 1975), cert. denied, 423 U.S. 870, 187 U.S.P.Q. 413 (1975), appeal after remand, 578 F.2d 727, 198 U.S.P.Q. 257 (9th Cir. 1978).

[8] 516 F.2d at 850.

In *Wrist-Rocket*, the mark ownership question was complicated by the fact that the manufacturer obtained a Lanham Act registration of the mark and complied with the Act's incontestability provision, which made its exclusive right to use the mark conclusive except as those areas the manufacturer, as common law owner, had penetrated as of the registrant's publication date. See § 5E[2][e].

Manufacturer-distributor trademark ownership conflicts frequently arise in the importation context. Trademark law's territoriality concept complicates the already difficult ownership determination.[9] Because a manufacturer's prior use abroad does not establish United States trademark rights,[10] the U.S. distributor may have a plausible claim to having created the United States good will surrounding the mark. "As between a foreign manufacturer and an exclusive United States distributor, courts have held that the foreign manufacturer is presumed to be the owner of the mark absent some other agreement. . . . An exclusive distributor may rebut that presumption in the absence of a written agreement by showing that the goods are manufactured for it, that it controls their production or that the goods pass through its hands in the course of trade and that it gives the goods the benefits of its reputation, name or business style."[11]

---

[9] *See* § 5E[2].

[10] *See* § 5D[1][f][i].

[11] *E.g.,* Ilapak Research & Development S.A. v. Record Spa, 762 F. Supp. 1318, 1323, 19 U.S.P.Q.2d 1617, 1621 (N.D. Ill. 1991) (Illapak, the distributor, failed to rebut presumption that Record, the manufacturer, owned the mark: "the fact that Ilapak sold and serviced the machines did not necessarily mean that customers associated Ilapak with the marks. Rather, Record placed its name in closest proximity to the marks, and the court finds that a reasonable customer would have associated Record, rather than Ilapak (whose name appeared in an entirely different part of the machine, well separated from the marks), with those marks. Another avenue open to Ilapak is to demonstrate that it, rather than Record, exercised control over the quality of the machines . . . , but again, this argument must fail. Record built the 'core' machine, which it modified to meet a particular customer's specifications. . . . Ilapak and Record's relationship was such that Ilapak knew what information Record required in order to build a machine to meet a particular customer's needs. Ilapak provided that information and Record built the machine. Ilapak did not have its own, independent specifications with which it required Record to comply. . . . Ilapak found the customers, and conveyed their individual needs to Record but, just as a person who buys a car from a particular dealership (even one who promises to service and repair the car forever) knows that it is purchasing a Ford or a Chevy—not an Al Piemonte. The Record 'core' is the critical, constant in all the machines, and the customers knew it.").

Compare Spectrum Marketing, Inc. v. Omega Nutrition U.S.A. Inc., 756 F. Supp. 435, 18 U.S.P.Q.2d 1371 (N.D. Calif. 1991) (U.S. distributor owns the mark because, *inter alia*, it conceived and first applied it) *with* Energy Jet, Inc. v. Forex Corp., 589 F. Supp. 1110, 1116, 223 U.S.P.Q. 643, 647 (E.D. Mich. 1984) (foreign manufacturer owns the mark even though the U.S. distributor conceived it because, *inter alia*, the manufacturer was the first to use it and the products clearly identified the manufacturer as their source: "The mere conception of a trademark does not give rise to ownership rights.").

See also CBS, Inc. v. Logical Games, 719 F.2d 1237, 1239, 221 U.S.P.Q. 498, 500 (4th Cir. 1983) (company that purchased and imported a limited quantity of foreign manufacturer's product does not acquire rights in the product's trade dress when it had no contract relation with manufacturer: "While factual situations can be imagined in which extensive—especially reiterated—purchase abroad and marketing in the United States might operate to create in the American importer trade dress rights in the United States for a format employed elsewhere by the foreign manufacturer, in the present case the drawing of such an inference would be altogether unjustified.").

United States law governs trademark ownership and transfer questions even when an ownership dispute is between citizens or companies residing in another country.[12]

[2] Assignment

A trademark or service mark owner may only assign a mark together with business goodwill.[13] He need not transfer his entire business—only that portion to which the mark pertains.[14]

[12] See Berni v. International Gourmet Restaurants of America, Inc., 838 F.2d 642, 5 U.S.P.Q.2d 1723 (2d Cir. 1988) (involving ownership of mark designed by Italian restauranteur Alfredo DiLelio, who invented "Fettucini Alfredo").

[13] E.g., Premier Dental Products Co. v. Darby Dental Supply Co., 794 F.2d 850, 853, 230 U.S.P.Q. 233, 235 (3d Cir. 1986), cert. denied, 479 U.S. 950 (1986) ("Because a trademark is symbolic, it may be transferred or assigned only to represent the transfer of goodwill connected with a particular business, and cannot be transferred separately from the goodwill of the business. . . . "); Visa, U.S.A., Inc. v. Birmingham Trust National Bank, 696 F.2d 1371, 1375, 216 U.S.P.Q. 649, 651 (Fed. Cir. 1982), cert. denied sub nom. South Trust Bank of Alabama, Birmingham v. Visa U.S.A., Inc., 464 U.S. 826, 220 U.S.P.Q. 385 (1983) ("Unlike patents or copyrights, trademarks are not separate property rights. They are integral and inseparable elements of the goodwill of the business or services to which they pertain. 'Since goodwill is inseparable from the business with which it is associated' . . . , when one speaks of the transfer of goodwill that accompanies a mark, one necessarily means the transfer of the portion of the business or service with which the mark is associated."); Mister Donut of America, Inc. v. Mr. Donut, Inc., 418 F.2d 838, 842, 164 U.S.P.Q. 67 (9th Cir. 1969) ("The law is well settled that there are no rights in a trademark alone and that no rights can be transferred apart from the business with which the mark has been associated. Such was the common law rule and is now made a part of the Lanham Act."); Avon Shoe Co., Inc. v. David Crystal, Inc., 171 F. Supp. 293, 300 (S.D. N.Y. 1959), aff'd, 279 F.2d 607, cert. denied, 364 U.S. 909 ("Trade-marks, unlike patents or copyrights, cannot be freely bought or sold.").

Compare Mulhens & Kropff, Inc. v. Ferd. Muelhens, Inc., 43 F.2d 937, 940 (2d Cir. 1930), cert. denied, 282 U.S. 881 (1930) (Judge Learned Hand dissenting: "The transfer of a trade-mark along with a business is lawful, though it is somewhat doubtful whether customers who have come to rely upon the mark as the warrant for a certain standard of excellence, or commercial integrity, or the like, are in such cases really getting what they suppose. Under modern conditions, however, where the personnel of a business is so shifting, this consideration has not been controlling; it is assumed that the successor will maintain those qualities which the mark has come to identify. At any rate the practice has been long recognized and the public probably reckons with it.").

[14] E.g., Ph. Schneider Brewing Co. v. Century Distilling Co., 107 F.2d 699, 703 (10th Cir. 1939) ("where the mark only identifies a portion of the goods sold by a particular trader who is not the manufacturer thereof, the mark may be assigned, along with the good will associated with the goods which the mark identifies, to a person who will continue to sell the same goods, without a transfer of the remainder of the business or the physical plant of the assignor."); Texaco, Inc. v. Kane County Oil, Inc., 96 Ill. App. 2d 383, 238 N.E.2d 622, 624, 159 U.S.P.Q. 766 (1968) ("While it is true that a trade name may not be transferred apart from the business to which it is related . . . , it is equally well recognized that business entities may in fact operate distinct and separable businesses and transfer such a distinct and separable portion of the entity, together with the good will, trade names and trade marks connected therewith. . . . Such an assignment is not an assignment in gross.").

"The necessity to assign more than the naked mark was premised upon the primary object of the trademark 'to indicate by its meaning or association the origin of the article to which it is affixed.' . . .

"As pointed out in the Restatement (Second) of Torts, 756, comment a at 136 (Tent. Draft No. 8, 1963):

'A trademark or tradename is not itself an independent object of property, nor is the right to use such mark or name. The designation is only a means of identifying particular goods, services, or a business associated with a particular commercial source, whether known or anonymous. . . . Goodwill is property, and since it is transferable the symbol of the property is transferable along with it.'

"Strict adherence to this rule has been vigorously criticized as impractical and legalistic. . . . According to these commentators, the continuum of the rule fails to comprehend the modern image of the trade-mark to the consuming public. Strict application of the rule undoubtedly fails to recognize the function of the trade-mark as representing as well (1) a guaranty of the product and (2) the inherent advertising value of the mark itself."[15]

A naked or "in gross" assignment cannot transfer trademark rights, which means the assignee's trademark rights are effective only as of its own use date, which may be too late if another claimant began use after the assignor but before the assignee.[16]

Cf. E. Leitz, Inc. v. Watson, 152 F. Supp. 631 (D.D.C. 1957), *aff'd*, 254 F.2d 777 (D.C. Cir. 1958) ("a trademark is a property right which may validly be sold with the business to which it is appurtenant . . . , sold for use in one segment of a business, even though it be not yet established (*Coca-Cola Bottling Co. v. Coca-Cola Co.*, D.C., 269 F. 796), assigned for a term of years with an exclusive agency in a particular geographical location (*Scandinavia Belting Co. v. Asbestos & Rubber Works*, 2 Cir., 257 F. 937, 954), or sold by a foreign manufacturer [to] any vendor together with his business and goodwill in the United States . . . ").

An owner may assign rights in restricted geographic areas if no consumer confusion is likely to result. *E.g.*, Houlihan v. Parliament Import Co., 921 F.2d 1258, 17 U.S.P.Q.2d 1208 (Fed. Cir. 1990). *Cf.* Maola Ice Cream Co. of North Carolina, Inc. v. Maola Milk & Ice Cream Co., 238 N.C. 317, 77 S.E.2d 910 (1953). For a discussion of concurrent use rights, see § 5E[2][d].

[15] Pepsico, Inc. v. Grapette Co., 416 F.2d 285, 287, 163 U.S.P.Q. 193 (8th Cir. 1969). *See also* Visa, U.S.A., Inc. v. Birmingham Trust National Bank, 696 F.2d 1371, 1375, 216 U.S.P.Q. 649, 652 (Fed. Cir. 1982), *cert. denied sub nom.* South Trust Bank of Alabama, Birmingham v. Visa U.S.A., Inc., 464 U.S. 826, 220 U.S.P.Q. 385 (1983) ("The rationale for the prohibition against a naked assignment of the mark without the accompanying goodwill stems from the nature of trademarks themselves. They identify the source of the goods and services offered. A key objective of the law of trademarks is protection of the consumer against being misled or confused as to the source of the goods or services he acquires. The rule against assignment of a mark in gross thus reflects 'the need, if consumers are not to be misled from established associations with the mark, that it continue to be associated with the same or similar products after the assignment.' ").

Cf. United Drug Co. v. Theodore Rectanus Co., 248 U.S. 90, 97 (1918) ("There is no such thing as property in a trade-mark except as a right appurtenant to an established business or trade in connection with which the mark is employed.").

[16] *E.g.*, Visa, U.S.A., Inc. v. Birmingham Trust National Bank, 696 F.2d 1371, 216 U.S.P.Q. 649 (Fed. Cir. 1982), *cert. denied sub nom.* South Trust Bank of Alabama, Birmingham v. Visa U.S.A., Inc., 464 U.S. 826, 220 U.S.P.Q. 385 (1983).

An invalid assignment does not, as such, cause mark or registration abandonment, but abandonment will occur if, as is commonly the case, the assignor ceases using the mark.[17]

Courts early recognized that a trademark can be transferred with business goodwill. In *Kidd,*[18] the Supreme Court held that a common law trademark could be assigned along with a transfer of the physical facilities used to produce the goods upon which the mark was used. In 1849, Pike adopted "S.N. Pike's Magnolia Whiskey" for liquor he made at a distillery in Cincinnati, Ohio. In 1868, Pike's firm sold the real property and all apparatus in his distillery to another whiskey firm for $125,000. Pike stated in a separate instrument that he extended to the purchaser "the use of all his brands formerly used by him in his Cincinnati house." The Court confirmed the assignment's validity.

> "[T]he primary object of a trade-mark is to indicate by its meaning or association the origin of the article to which it is affixed. As distinct property, separate from the article created by the original producer or manufacturer, it may not be the subject of sale. But when the trade-mark is affixed to articles manufactured at a particular establishment and acquires a special reputation in connection with the place of manufacture, and that establishment is transferred either by contract or operation of law to others, the right to the use of the trade-mark may be lawfully transferred with it. Its subsequent use by the person to whom the establishment is transferred is considered as only

---

Assignment validity also arises when an assignee seeks to assert the assignor's status as a good faith junior user, Money Store v. Harriscorp Finance, Inc., 689 F.2d 666, 216 U.S.P.Q. 11 (7th Cir. 1982), or to rely on the assignor's potential laches defense arising from the trademarks owner's failure to take action against the assignor for a lengthy time period. *E.g.,* Tandy Corp. v. Malone & Hyde, Inc., 769 F.2d 362, 226 U.S.P.Q. 703 (6th Cir. 1985), *cert. denied,* 476 U.S. 1158 (1986); Pepsico, Inc. v. Grapette Co., 416 F.2d 285, 163 U.S.P.Q. 193 (8th Cir. 1969).

[17] Li'l' Red Barn, Inc. v. Red Barn Sys., Inc., 322 F. Supp. 98, 107, 167 U.S.P.Q. 741 (N.D. Ind. 1970), *aff'd per curiam,* 174 U.S.P.Q. 193 (7th Cir. 1972) ("Defendant contends that assignment in gross constitutes abandonment per se; but in every case cited in support of that proposition, the assignor stopped using his mark after attempting to assign it and had no intention of resuming. In other words, the statutory elements of abandonment were present."). *Cf.* Hy-Cross Hatchery, Inc. v. Osborne, 303 F.2d 947, 949, 133 U.S.P.Q. 687 (CCPA 1962) ("Nothing quoted tends to show that an invalid assignment is, *ipso facto,* an abandonment of a mark.").

But see Defiance Button Machine Co. v. C & C Metal Products Corp., 759 F.2d 1053, 1059, 225 U.S.P.Q. 797 (2d Cir. 1985), *cert. denied,* 474 U.S. 844 (1985) (dictum: "The mark . . . ceases to be enforceable against others when it loses its significance as an indication of the origin of goods sold by and associated with the mark owner, such as when . . . the owner assigns the mark without the goodwill associated with it . . . Under such circumstances the mark is held to have been abandoned for the reason that there 'are no rights in a trademark apart from the business with which the mark has been associated' and the '[u]se of the mark by the assignee in connection with a different goodwill and different product would result in a fraud on the purchasing public who reasonably assume that the mark signifies the same thing, whether used by one person or another . . . ' ").

[18] Kidd v. Johnson, 100 U.S. (10 Otto) 617 (1879).

indicating that the goods to which it is affixed are manufactured at the same place and are of the same character as those to which the mark was attached by its original designer." [19]

Lanham Act Section 10 codified the common law rule.

"A registered mark or a mark for which application to register has been filed shall be assignable with the goodwill of the business in which the mark is used, or with that part of the goodwill of the business connected with the use of and symbolized by the mark. . . . In any assignment authorized by this section it shall not be necessary to include the goodwill of the business connected with the use of and symbolized by any other mark used in the business or by the name or style under which the business is conducted." [20]

The trend of decisions applying the goodwill transfer requirement and "in gross" assignment prohibition is away from "stereotyped formalties" and toward interpretation in view of its purpose—consumer confusion prevention. [21] A trademark assignor need not transfer physical assets or specific intangibles, such as customer lists and production specifications, to convey good will. [22] Trademark transfers among related

---

[19] 100 U.S. (10 Otto) at 620.

[20] Lanham Act § 10, 15 U.S.C. § 1060. See Avon Shoe Co., Inc. v. David Crystal, Inc., 171 F. Supp. 293, 301 (S.D. N.Y. 1959), aff'd, 279 F.2d 607, cert. denied, 364 U.S. 909 ("Since good will is inseparable from the business with which it is associated, this requirement of the transfer of good will restates the common-law rule that a trademark can only be transfered with the business or part of the business which it symbolizes. Without the transfer of some business with which the mark has been used, the assignment is a void assignment in gross and conveys no title to the assignee.").

The 1988 Trademark Revision Act restricts intent-to-use application assignments. See § 5D[2][b].

[21] Syntex Laboratories, Inc. v. Norwich Pharmacal Co., 315 F. Supp. 45, 54, 166 U.S.P.Q. 312 (S.D. N.Y. 1970), aff'd, 437 F.2d 566, 169 U.S.P.Q. 1 (2d Cir. 1971) ("The various technical rules connected with the assignment of trademarks to which defendant appeals were not evolved for the purpose of invalidating all trademark assignments which do not satisfy a stereotyped set of formalities. Their central purpose is protection against consumer confusion, . . . and it is in light of that goal that they are to be interpreted and applied.").

[22] E.g., Defiance Button Machine Co. v. C & C Metal Products Corp., 759 F.2d 1053, 1059, 225 U.S.P.Q. 797, 801 (2d Cir. 1985), cert. denied, 474 U.S. 844 (1985) ("a trademark may be validly transferred without the simultaneous transfer of any tangible assets, as long as the recipient continues to produce goods of the same quality and nature previously associated with the mark."); Money Store v. Harriscorp Finance, Inc., 689 F.2d 666, 676, 216 U.S.P.Q. 11, 20 (7th Cir. 1982) ("it is not necessary to the continuing validity of the mark that tangible assets of the assignor pass to the assignee"); Visa, U.S.A., Inc. v. Birmingham Trust National Bank, 696 F.2d 1371, 1375, 216 U.S.P.Q. 649, 652 (Fed. Cir. 1982), cert. denied sub nom. South Trust Bank of Alabama, Birmingham v. Visa U.S.A., Inc., 464 U.S. 826, 220 U.S.P.Q. 385 (1983) ("A valid transfer of a mark . . . does not require the transfer of any physical or tangible assets. All that is necessary is the transfer of the goodwill to which the mark pertains."); Glamorene Products Corp. v. Procter & Gamble Co., 538 F.2d 894, 895-96, 190 U.S.P.Q. 543 (CCPA 1976) ("transfer of tangible assets (inventory, labels, customer lists, formulas, etc.) is not necessary to an effective trademark assignment."): Sterling Brewers, Inc. v. Schenley Industries, Inc., 441 F.2d 675, 680, 169 U.S.P.Q. 590 (CCPA 1971) (brewery's physical assets and goodwill, including trademarks, sold to different purchasers; "The agreement to sell the rights to the trademarks having originated on the same day as the agreement to part

corporate entities or as part of corporate reorganizations do not violate the "in gross" assignment prohibition if there is management continuity and the assignee maintains the assignor's quality standards.[23] Similarly, trademark rights may be

---

with the physical assets, we think that the sale of the latter is not an indication of abandonment of the former. As to the sales being to different parties, we see no reason why tangible assets must necessarily be included in the assignment of a trademark with the good will of the business associated with it . . . [T]he trademarks still symbolized substantial good will and had not already become abandoned. By the assignment to [purchaser], [seller] relinquished the right to market 'COOK'S GOLDBLUME' beer, and [purchaser] promptly began the exercise of that right. [Purchaser] did not acquire a list of [seller's] customers, but as a former competitor, it knew who the customers were. Similarly, the fact that no written formula [for production of seller's beer] was available is not critical, it being apparent that [purchaser] was able to provide a satisfactory duplication of the qualities of the . . . product from information that was available.").

Cf. J.C. Hall Co. v. Hallmark Cards, Inc., 340 F.2d 960, 963, 144 U.S.P.Q. 435 (CCPA 1965) ("It is a matter of no significant import with reference to its impingement upon the validity of the assignment and the rights accruing to [the assignee] thereunder that the assignment was accomplished through an intermediary or that no tangible assets were transferred thereunder nor that the assignor held the mark only one day prior to assigning same to [the assignee].")

For judicial definitions of goodwill, see Premier Dental Products Co. v. Darby Dental Supply Co., Inc. 794 F.2d 850, 853 n.3, 230 U.S.P.Q. 233, 235 n.3 (3d Cir. 1986) (" 'Goodwill' is the advantage obtained from use of a trademark. This includes public confidence in the quality of the product and in the warranties made on behalf of the product, and the 'name recognition' of the product by the public that differentiates that product from others."); Sands, Taylor & Wood v. Quaker Oats Co., 18 U.S.P.Q.2d 1457, 1465 (N.D. Ill. 1990) ("Good will is an intangible asset, defined as 'the favorable consideration shown by the purchasing public to goods known to emanate from a particular source.' . . . Good will is the advantage obtained from use of a trademark. It includes public confidence in the quality of the product and the name recognition of the product by the public that differentiates that product from others.").

[23] E.g., J. Atkins Holdings Ltd. v. English Discounts, Inc., 729 F. Supp. 945, 950, 951 n.5, 14 U.S.P.Q.2d 1301, 1304, 1305 n.5 (S.D. N.Y. 1990) ("where there is 'continuity of management,' so that the assignee will continue to provide the same quality of service, a transfer without good-will is not subject to invalidation. . . . The assignment of trademarks among related corporate entities is not uncommon."). But cf. In re Wella A.G., 787 F.2d 1549, 229 U.S.P.Q. 274 (Fed Cir. 1986), discussed at § 5C[4][f].

Cf. Browne-Vintners Co., Inc. v. National Distillers and Chemical Corp., 151 F. Supp. 595, 602 (S.D. N.Y. 1957) (Mumm's champagne; "In 1948 the French Société assigned the trade-marks to the New York Société which then assigned them to Browne-Vintners, the exclusive distributor of the French Société's champagne. Browne-Vintners thereafter assigned them back to the New York Société in whose name they were thereupon registered. The New York Société then issued to Browne-Vintners a new exclusive license to import and sell the champagne. By the terms of the assignments the New York Société, which concededly does not itself sell or advertise the champagne, was given authority and responsibility to determine the quality of the champagne to be imported, the advertising of it by Browne-Vintners and the disposition of complaints. It was also charged with responsibility to protect the marks. It is not clear just why it was thought necessary to make all of these assignments. . . . This, however, need not be explored since all that is here material is the effect of the assignments on the validity of the marks. National contends the effect was to invalidate the trade- marks by separating them from the good will of the French Société's business. The contention is rejected. The New York Société is the wholly-owned and completely controlled subsidiary of

assigned between manufacturers and distributors.[24]

A formal goodwill transfer recital in the assignment documents is not controlling.[25]

Trademark transfers for strategic or defensive purposes are commonplace despite the prohibition of "naked" trademark assignments. For example, a company introducing an important new product line under a mark may purchase rights to the same or a similar mark in use by another on a related product to avoid a conflict and to establish an earlier use date.

In *Glamorene Products,*[26] Cowles Chemical Company registered "BOUNCE" for dry cleaning detergent in 1966. It assigned the mark to Stauffer. In May 1971, Procter & Gamble (P&G) began using "BOUNCE" for a fabric softener. In October 1971, Stauffer assigned its "BOUNCE" detergent mark to P&G. The agreement formally recited that Stauffer assigned "the goodwill of the business symbolized by said trademark" to P&G, but Stauffer conveyed no tangible assets, customer lists, or formulas and disposed of its own inventory after the assignment. P&G used the mark on its own dry cleaning detergent, upon which it "had been actively working . . . since 1968." P&G likely purchased the mark to protect its mark in the fast-growing fabric softener market, not because of its interest in the dry cleaning detergents, but the court found no assignment in gross.

---

the French Société. The same officers conduct both corporations. Indeed the former appears to be, for all practical purposes, merely an American office or department of the latter. It is, in any event, a related company under Sec. 45 of the Lanham Act. . . . And under Sec. 5 of that Act either Société may register the marks and either may use them without affecting their validity or the validity of the registrations, provided the public is not deceived thereby. Since 1920 the marks have never been applied to nor have they signified any champagne other than that produced by the French Société. There has not been and there is not any deception of the public. Browne-Vintners as the exclusive distributor of the champagne has a monopoly of its sale in the United States and thus a sufficient interest of its own in the marks to entitle it to register them in its name. . . . The 'related' Sociétés and their exclusive distributor are united in a common enterprise to produce, import and sell the champagne; to exploit and enhance the good will of the business; and to protect the marks. The good will has not been separated from the marks, they have not been invalidated and they certainly have not been abandoned. All three plaintiffs have valid interests in the marks entitling them to maintain this action.")

[24] *E.g.,* Premier Dental Products Co. v. Darby Dental Supply Co., Inc. 794 F.2d 850, 856, 230 U.S.P.Q. 233, 237 (3d Cir. 1986), *cert. denied,* 479 U.S. 950 (1986) ("if an exclusive distributor is known as the exclusive domestic source and as the one who stands behind the product in this country, it may own and enforce the trademark" even though the product's foreign manufacturer put conditions on the assignment and the distributor did not exercise day-to-day control over product quality).

[25] *E.g.,* Money Store v. Harriscorp Finance, Inc., 689 F.2d 666, 675, 216 U.S.P.Q. 11, 20 (7th Cir. 1982) ("although the assignment stated that the mark was assigned 'together with the good will of the business symbolized by the mark,' such a recitation is not necessarily dispositive").

[26] Glamorene Products Corp. v. Procter & Gamble Co., 538 F.2d 894, 190 U.S.P.Q. 543 (CCPA 1976).

In *Money Store,* [27] the court rejected plaintiff's claim "that the assignment is ineffective because it was a sham transaction, initiated by [assignee] for the sole purpose of obtaining superior rights to the mark in [a geographic] area":

> "Presumably, [assignee] sought the assignment because it knew of the plaintiff's prior rights in the mark. [It] did in fact know of the plaintiff's pending registration and it would be naive to conclude that that knowledge was completely irrelevant to its decision to seek an assignment from [the assignor]. It is also true, however, that so long as [the assignor] retained any rights in the mark, that institution was itself an impediment to the [the assignee's] usage of the mark. Obtaining the assignment from [the assignor] is consistent with the [assignee's] documented belief that the plaintiff could not successfully assert nationwide rights in the mark, and therefore another institution was free to use the mark in the [geographic area] . . . We do not believe that an assignment motivated at least in part by sound business judgment should be set aside as a sham transaction." [28]

[a] **The Business Cessation Cases.** Some decisions hold that a mark use right transfer from one user to another is valid even though the transferor convey no tangible or intangible assets but merely cedes to the transferee the right to offer similar goods and services under the mark.

In *Hy-Cross Hatchery,* [29] Osborne registered the mark "Hy-Cross" for "Live Poultry for Breeding Purposes and Eggs for Hatching" in 1950. Osborne used the mark to sell chickens. In 1955, Osborne executed and recorded in the Patent Office an assignment to Welp of his "trademark and the registration thereof" "together with that part of the good will of the business connected with the use of and symbolized by the mark." [30] Appellant petitioned to cancel the "Hy-Cross" registration on abandonment grounds, citing cases condemning "in gross" assignments and noting that the assignor Osborne did not convey any chickens, eggs, or chicken breeding formula to Welp. The Patent Office Board found no abandonment based on the facts that the assignor Osborne used the mark at the time of the assignment and ceased use after the assignment and that the assignee Welp began use after the assignment. The appeal court affirmed.

> "Unlike the cases relied on, Osborne . . . was using the mark at the time he executed the assignment of it. He had a valid registration which he also assigned. With these two legal properties he also assigned, in the very words of the statute, 'that part of the goodwill of the business connected with the use of and symbolized by the mark . . . .' He was selling chicks which his advertising of record shows were '(designated as No. 111 HY-CROSS (Trade Mark) AMERICAN WHITES.' As part of his assignment, by assigning the goodwill, he gave up the right to sell 'HY-CROSS' chicks. This had been a part of his 'business.' By the assignment Welp, the assignee, acquired that right.

---

[27] Money Store v. Harriscorp Finance, Inc., 689 F.2d 666, 216 U.S.P.Q. 11 (7th Cir. 1982), discussed below.

[28] 689 F.2d at 678, 216 U.S.P.Q. at 22.

[29] Hy-Cross Hatchery, Inc. v. Osborne, 303 F.2d 947, 133 U.S.P.Q. 687 (CCPA 1962).

[30] 303 F.2d at 948-49.

The record shows that he began selling 'Hy-Cross Hatching Eggs' and chicks designated as 'HY-CROSS 501,' 'HY-CROSS 610,' and 'HY-CROSS 656.' . . . We do not see what legal difference it would have made if a crate of eggs had been included in the assignment, or a flock of chickens destined to be eaten. As for the argument that the transfer should have been held illegal because Osborne sold one kind of chick and Welp sold another under the mark, whereby the public would be deceived, we think the record does not support this. The type of chick appears to have been otherwise indicated than by the trademark, as by the numbers above quoted as well as by name. Osborne, moreover, was not under any obligation to the public not to change the breed of chicks he sold under the mark from time to time."[31]

In *Pepsico,*[32] Judge (later Justice) Blackmun in a concurring opinion suggested that *Hy-Cross* was either limited to special facts or an aberration.

"*Hy-Cross* is a peculiar case factually in that, among other aspects, live baby chicks were the product of both assignor and assignee. The court did place some reliance on what it seemed to regard as a genuine transfer of goodwill, . . . and, accordingly, saw little legal significance in the absence of an assignment of tangible chicks themselves. . . . But if . . . the *Hy-Cross* holding has greater import than its peculiar facts suggest for me, then I would regard it as aberrational to settled authority. I prefer to stay with the usual rule, long established I thought, that a trademark may not validly be assigned in gross. And product difference is only an aspect of this traditional rule."[33]

Judge Blackmun's cautionary comment did not deter the Seventh Circuit from later following *Hy-Cross*. In *Money Store,*[34] Harriscope selected in 1972 "The Money Store" as its preferred mark for money-lending services facilities it planned to open in the Chicago area. A trademark search revealed that Modern Acceptance had applied to register the same mark for money lending services. Harriscope learned that United Bank had used "The Money Store" in Chicago since August, 1972 without knowledge of Modern Acceptance's use or registration application. United Bank planned to discontinue use, but, before it did so, Harriscope took an assignment, which recited that "for good and valuable consideration, the receipt of which is hereby acknowledged . . . [the mark is assigned] together with the goodwill of the business symbolized by the mark."[35] Harriscope did not acquire customer lists, receivables, accounts or tangible assets and paid one dollar. When Modern Acceptance sued Harriscope for trademark infringement, Harriscope asserted it was a good faith junior user in the Chicago area, based on its assignor's use date.[36] Modern Acceptance argued that the assignment was invalid because it conveyed no goodwill. The Seventh Circuit followed

[31] 303 F.2d at 950.

See also Syntex Laboratories, Inc. v. Norwich Pharmacal Co., 315 F. Supp. 45, 166 U.S.P.Q. 312 (S.D. N.Y. 1970), aff'd, 437 F.2d 566, 169 U.S.P.Q. 1 (1971).

[32] Pepsico, Inc. v. Grapette Co., 416 F.2d 285, 163 U.S.P.Q. 193 (8th Cir. 1969).

[33] 416 F.2d at 290.

[34] Money Store v. Harriscorp Finance, Inc., 689 F.2d 666, 216 U.S.P.Q. 11 (7th Cir. 1982).

[35] 689 F.2d at 670, 230 U.S.P.Q. at 15.

[36] For a discussion of good faith junior user's rights, see § 5E[2][b].

Hy-Cross and disagreed that Justice Blackmun's *Pepsico* concurring opinion undermined *Hy-Cross*'s persuasiveness.

> "It is admittedly difficult to determine when a transfer of goodwill has occurred. This is particularly so in the case of a service mark. . . .

> . . .

> ". . . The circumstances in this case are also 'peculiar' in that United and Harriscorp offered the identical service. A customer who was drawn first to United and later to Harriscorp because of the 'MONEY STORE' mark would not be misled as to the nature of the services offered. United's use of the mark in advertising, including highly visible billboards, strongly suggests that the mark carried with it a degree of goodwill. What United gave up in assigning the mark was the right to attract customers through use of the mark. The fact that one cannot say with certainty how many customers might have gone to a Harriscorp office, rather than a United office, because they recognized the mark does not compel the conclusion that no goodwill passed with the assignment.

> "The cases cited by both sides of this controversy are consistent with the underlying purpose of why a transfer of goodwill is required in order for an assignment of a mark to be effective. The cases all seek to protect customers from deception and confusion. In the case of a service mark, such confusion would result if an assignee offered a service different from that offered by the assignor of the mark."[37]

[b] Assignor License Back. In *Visa, U.S.A.,*[38] the Federal Circuit held that a license-back to the assignor allowing it to continue to use the mark as before the assignment is not fatal to an assignment's validity if the license meets trademark law requirements, including licensor quality control.[39] Alpha Beta, an Arizona and California grocery store chain, began using "Check-O.K." in 1970 to identify a customer personal check acceptance card program. It issued cards to more than 1.5 million customers. In 1976, Visa entered the check guaranty card business on a nationwide basis under the "Check-O.K." mark. Visa discovered Alpha Beta's prior use, and they reached an agreement under which Alpha Beta transferred its mark "together with the goodwill of the business symbolized by the mark" to Visa for $10,000, and Visa granted Alpha Beta a "nonexclusive, nontransferable license to use the mark in connection with check approval services for Alpha Beta's customers."[40] Alpha Beta agreed that "the nature and quality of all services rendered in connection with the Mark shall conform to standards set by . . . [Visa]."[41] After the agreement, in

---

[37] 689 F.2d at 676, 678, 216 U.S.P.Q. at 20, 21. *See also* Main Street Outfitters, Inc. v. Federated Department Stores, Inc., 730 F. Supp. 289, 13 U.S.P.Q.2d 1332 (D. Minn. 1989).

[38] Visa, U.S.A., Inc. v. Birmingham Trust National Bank, 696 F.2d 1371, 216 U.S.P.Q. 649 (Fed. Cir. 1982), *cert. denied sub nom.* South Trust Bank of Alabama, Birmingham v. Visa U.S.A., Inc., 464 U.S. 826, 220 U.S.P.Q. 385 (1983).

[39] See § 5G[3].

[40] 696 F.2d at 1373, 216 U.S.P.Q. at 650.

[41] 696 F.2d at 1374, 216 U.S.P.Q. at 651.

November, 1976, Visa established its own "Check-O.K." check guaranty program, and Alpha Beta continued its "Check-O.K." in its Arizona stores.

In May 1976, Birmington Trust began using "Check-O.K." When Visa and Birmington Trust each sought to register the mark, the question of use priority arose. Visa claimed the benefit of Alpha Beta's first use. Birmington Trust contended that the Alpha Beta-Visa assignment was an invalid "in gross" transfer. The appeals court ruled for Visa. First, Alpha Beta's and Visa's services were not substantially different. Both provided means by which card holders could make purchases by check upon showing the card. Unlike Alpha Beta, Visa provided the service to independent merchants, but the goodwill attached to the mark was among customers, not stores.

> "The Visa and Alpha Beta programs were not identical. But the transfer of goodwill requires only that the services be sufficiently similar to prevent consumers of the service offered under the mark from being 'misled from established associations with the mark.' Where, as here, the basic service offered by the assignor is offered by the assignee, albeit in a significantly expanded way, there is no reason to presume that consumers will not be properly protected."[42]

Second, the license back giving the assignor the right to continue using the mark did not vitiate the otherwise valid assignment.

> "A license back of an assigned mark to enable the assignor-licensee to continue to conduct the same business or provide the same services under the mark is not a novelty. A number of courts, without discussion, tacitly have upheld the practice. *E.g.*, Geo. A. Hormel & Co. v. Hereford Heaven Brands, 341 F.2d 158, 52 Cust. & Pat. App. 1012, 144 U.S.P.Q. 493 (1965) (continued use by assignor-licensee does not affect assignee-licensor's claim to priority in opposition to registration); Raufast S.A. v. Kicker's Pizzazz, 208 U.S.P.Q. 699 (E.D.N.Y.1980) (license back to assignor did not mislead consumers); Andrew Jergens Co. v. Woodbury, Inc., 273 F. 952 (C.D.Del.1921), *aff'd* 279 F. 1016 (3d Cir.1922); but see Greenlon, Inc. of Cincinnati v. Greenlawn, Inc., 542 F. Supp. 890 (S.D.Ohio 1982) (assignment invalid when assignor continued to operate own business using mark concurrently with geographically remote use by assignee). Indeed, a leading trademark treatise, after stating that '[a]n assignment is valid even though it may reserve certain rights of use of the mark in the assignor,' suggests that '[u]sually such a situation should be handled by an assignment of the mark and good will, followed by license back to the assignor of the mark.' " J. McCarthy, Trademarks and Unfair Competition, § 18.1(E) at 608 (1973).

> . . .

> "A license back is valid if it satisfies the conditions of validity for trademark licenses generally. The principal requirement, and the only one here critical, is that 'the licensing agreement provides for adequate control by the licensor over the quality of goods or services produced under the mark by a licensee.

---

[42] 696 F.2d at 1376, 216 U.S.P.Q. at 652.

. . . The purpose of such a requirement is to protect the public from being misled.' "[43]

The Visa-Alpha Beta license gave Visa quality control over the services rendered under the mark.[44]

[c] Substantial Similarity Between the Assignor's and Assignee's Products or Services. Courts will uphold a trademark assignment only if the products or services sold under the mark are "essentially the same before and after the transfer."[45]

Pepsico[46] invalidated an assignment when the assignee's beverage differed in flavor from the assignor's. Pepsi bottled beverages under various "Pepsi" marks for many years. In 1985, Grapette, a national bottler-distributor, developed a new "pepper type bottle beverage" syrup formula. Searching for a name, it found Fox's 1926 "Peppy" trademark registration. Fox used the "Peppy" mark on bottles of cola syrup. In 1965, Grapette bought from Fox, then in a Chapter 11 bankruptcy proceeding, Fox's "Peppy" trademark for $7500. The purchase agreement recited that Fox assigned its "good-will," but Grapette acquired no inventory, customers lists, formulas, or tangible assets. Fox continued to sell its cola syrup under the "Fox Brand" mark and agreed to act as distributors of Grapette's "Peppy" beverages. When Grapette began distributing "Peppy" beverages, Pepsi sued for trademark infringement. Grapette asserted a laches defense, relying on Fox's long period of use, which Pepsi had not challenged. Pepsico argued that the Fox-Grapette transfer was invalid as a trademark assignment "in gross." The court agreed, finding no need to decide "whether the strict common law rule must apply or whether the approach, as suggested by *Hy-Cross*, should prevail."[47] The assignment was ineffective for another reason:

---

[43] 696 F.2d at 1376–77, 216 U.S.P.Q. at 653.

Contra: Greenlon, Inc. of Cincinnati v. Greenlawn, Inc., 542 F. Supp. 890, 895, 217 U.S.P.Q. 790, 794 (S.D. Ohio 1982) (assignment with royalty-free license back to assignor to continue to use the mark in those areas in which the assignor was doing business, the assignor's standards to be approved but its existing standards being expressly approved, is an invalid in gross assignment: "Although no tangible assets must be transferred to the assignee to validate the assignment of a mark, some part of the business, [in the cases relied upon by the assignee] the relinquishment of the right to do business under the mark in favor of the assignee, must be transferred in order that the Lanham Act requirement of a transfer of goodwill with the mark be met. . . . In the instant case, defendant received no part of his assignor's business, the assignor having retained his business and all tangible and intangible assets appurtenant thereto, including the right to do business under the mark and all the goodwill he had built up associated with the mark.").

[44] *See also* Syntex Laboratories, Inc. v. Norwich Pharmacal Co., 315 F. Supp. 45, 56, 166 U.S.P.Q. 312 (S.D. N.Y. 1970), *order aff'd*, 437 F.2d 566, 169 U.S.P.Q. 1 (2d Cir. 1971) ("reliance upon the integrity of a licensee is sufficient to fulfill the control requirement where a history of trouble-free manufacture provides a basis for such reliance. . . . [T]he purpose of the control requirement is to avoid the danger that the public may be deceived as to the quality of a product sold under a recognized name.").

[45] Bambu Sales, Inc. v. Sultana Crackers, Inc., 683 F. Supp. 899, 906, 7 U.S.P.Q.2d 1177, 1183 (E.D. N.Y. 1988).

[46] Pepsico, Inc. v. Grapette Co., 416 F.2d 285, 163 U.S.P.Q. 193 (8th Cir. 1969).

[47] *Id.* at 288.

the assignee did not use the transferred mark on a product "having substantially the same characteristics."

"Inherent in the rules involving the assignment of a trademark is the recognition of protection against consumer deception. Basic to this concept is the proposition that any assignment of a trademark and its goodwill (with or without tangibles or intangibles assigned) requires the mark itself be used by the assignee on a product having substantially the same characteristics. *See e.g., Independent Baking Powder Co. v. Boorman*, 175 F. 448 (C.C. D.N.J. 1910) (alum baking powder is distinctive from phosphate baking powder); *Atlas Beverage Co. v. Minneapolis Brewing Co.*, 113 F.2d 672 (8 Cir. 1940) (whiskey is a different product than beer); *H. H. Scott, Inc. v. Annapolis Electroacoustic Corp.*, 195 F. Supp. 208 (D.Md. 1961) (audio reproduction equipment is distinctive from hi-fidelity consoles). . . .

"Historically, this requirement is founded in the early case of Filkins v. Blackman, 9 Fed.Cas. 50 (No. 4786) (C.C. D.Conn. 1876), wherein the court observed:

'If the assignee should make a different article, he would not derive, by purchase from Jonas Blackman, a right which a court of equity would enforce, to use the name which the inventor had given to his own article, because such a use of the name would deceive the public. The right to the use of a trade-mark cannot be so enjoyed by an assignee that he shall have the right to affix the mark to goods differing in character or species from the article to which it was originally attached.'

. . .

"Where a transferred trademark is to be used on a new and different product, any goodwill which the mark itself might represent cannot legally be assigned. . . . To hold otherwise would be to condone public deceit. The consumer might buy a product thinking it to be of one quality or having certain characteristics and could find it only too late to be another. To say that this would be remedied by the public soon losing faith in the product fails to give the consumer the protection it initially deserves."

. . .

". . . Grapette's intended use of the mark is one to simply describe its new pepper beverage. . . . The evidence is clear that Grapette did not intend to adopt or exploit any 'goodwill' from the name 'Peppy' and Fox's long association and use of it with a cola syrup. When one considers that Grapette did not acquire any of the assets of Fox, did not acquire any formula or process by which the Fox syrup was made, . . . and then changed the type of beverage altogether, the assignment on its face must be considered void. It seems fundamental that either the defendant did not acquire any 'goodwill' as required by law or if it did, assuming as defendant argues the mark itself possesses 'goodwill,' by use of the mark on a totally different product, Grapette intended to deceive the public. Either ground is untenable to the validity of the assignment." [48]

In *Bambu Sales,* [49] the assignee applied the "Bambu" cigarette paper mark to paper that was thinner and therefore more difficult to roll than the assignee's paper. The court rejected the argument that the quality difference invalidated the assignment, applying Callman's distinction between fungible and unique goods:[50] "a substantial change in the goods sold under a mark may so alter the nature of the good will symbolized that use of the mark is tantamount to a fraud on consumers and the original right to the mark is abandoned or lost . . . ," but "where the product or service is essentially the same before and after the transfer, variations in type or quality will not invalidate the assignment." [51]

Mulhens & Kropff is an interesting case on assignee product quality maintenance.[52] The Muelhens began making eau de cologne in Cologne, Germany in 1792. Their "4711" cologne, made according to a carefully guarded secret formula, became world famous.[53] In 1878, Kropff entered into a partnership with a Muelhens family member

---

[48] *Id.* at 288-290. The court rejected Grapette's argument that its new product was substantially the same as Fox's old "Peppy" because it fell within the same trademark registration classification.

> "[T]he classes set up under the federal statutes to simplify registration, are not controlling. . . . Thus, the fact that defendant's 'Peppy,' and Fox's 'Peppy' are registered in Class 45 (soft drinks and carbonated waters, and nonalcoholic maltless beverage and syrup respectively) cannot mean that these products are within the 'same class' in determining the validity of the assignment to defendant Grapette." *Id.* at 289.

[49] Bambu Sales, Inc. v. Sultana Crackers, Inc., 683 F. Supp. 899, 7 U.S.P.Q.2d 1177 (E.D. N.Y. 1988).

[50] "[O]ne commentator draws a distinction based on the nature of the trademarked goods. 3 R. Callmann, *The Law of Unfair Competition Trademarks and Monopolies,* § 19.40 at 176-187. If the goods are unique (for example, made under a patent or secret formula, or by an enterprise of established tradition such as the porcelain manufacturers of Limoges or Copenhagen), 'the provenance of the article is a value in and of itself. . . . [T]he public wants only the "genuine" article.' Under such circumstances, assignment of the mark without the business it symbolizes creates a high likelihood of consumer deception. . . . With respect to fungibles, however, goods that are 'familiar to all and can be produced by many under varying trademarks,' '[t]he public is no longer concerned with . . . the origin of the article. The article itself is what the buyer wants and will continue to buy so long as it satisfies consumer demand, and until another article, better advertised or more effective, replaces it.' . . . Thus, . . . a trademark relating to fungible goods should be more freely alienable; the owner may relinquish the use of a trademark and, without more, transfer his rights thereunder to an assignee. The latter may then use the trademark as he pleases, but on similar goods only. He may legitimately exploit the reputation of the trademark, as did his predecessor, and if his product does not satisfy the public, that will be reflected in his business success. He must decide whether he will preserve or risk the goodwill of the old mark. But if he applies the trademark to dissimilar goods, he then adopts a 'different' trademark." 683 F. Supp. at 907-08, 7 U.S.P.Q.2d at 1183.

[51] 683 F. Supp. at 906, 907, 7 U.S.P.Q.2d at 1182, 1183.

[52] Mulhens & Kropff, Inc. v. Ferd. Muelhens, Inc., 43 F.2d 937 (2d Cir. 1930), *cert. denied,* 282 U.S. 881 (1930).

[53] Their business was at 4711 Glockengasse.

to distribute Muelhens products in the United States. Muelhens granted "Mulhens & Kropff" a license to use and register its marks in the United States, reserving the right to take over the business and have all recipes returned if the partnership dissolved. During World War I, the U.S. Alien Property Custodian seized Muelhens interest in the partnership, including the "4711" trademark, and sold it to Kropff, who had dissolved the partnership. Plaintiff bought Kropff's interests. After the War, the Muelhens firm formed defendant to distribute its products in the United States. Plaintiff sued for trademark infringement. The district court found that the wartime transfer gave plaintiff ownership of the 4711 mark but that Kropff did not know the 4711 secret formula and that he and plaintiff sold 4711 cologne products differing from the Muelhens original, thereby deceiving customers. It enjoined defendant from using "4711" provided plaintiff "purge" its fault by applying for ten years a label disclaimer ("Not manufactured in accordance with the original secret recipe in use since 1792 and before 1917"). The Second Circuit reversed in a split decision. The majority saw a conflict between the mark's two meanings: (1) origin in the house of Muelhens; and (2) manufacture under a secret recipe:

> "Plaintiff has succeeded to Muelhens' business in this country, which would entitle plaintiff to use the mark in its first meaning. It has not succeeded to Muelhens' ownership of the recipe, and therefore may not truthfully use the second meaning. The defendant, on the other hand, if allowed to use the mark, will truthfully represent the quality of its article, but will misrepresent that it is continuing Muelhens' former American business . . . On the one hand, it is said that to allow one who does not know the recipe to seize the good will dependent on marketing the product of the secret formula runs counter to the admitted principle that good will cannot be assigned in gross; on the other, that, since Muelhens would have had the privilege of somewhat changing the formula and still applying to the modified product the old mark, his successor in business should have the same privilege, and the right to prevent Muelhens' user." [54]

The majority decided that "assignment of the recipe is essential to give the assignee the exclusive right of a mark which denotes a product manufactured thereunder." [55] "The law affords trade-mark protection to a merchant in order that prospective customers may not be lured away by one who counterfeits his goods. Those who insist upon the genuine 4711 eau de cologne are not prospective customers of the plaintiff, for he cannot supply it. On the whole we think the plaintiff should not be protected in the use of a mark which he can himself use only deceptively." [56]

Judge Hand dissented.

> "[T]he Custodian by seizing Muhlens's rights became vested with the business, which included his chattels, choses in action and his good will . . . [T]his authorized the plaintiff to use the marks in selling any goods on which it had come to mean no more than the accustomed source, Muhlens or Muhlens's successor . . .

---

[54] 43F.2d at 939.
[55] Id..
[56] Id..

". . . [S]o far as applied to cologne, made under the recipe, the mark meant more. It had for so long been associated with declarations that the cologne was made under the recipe, that two meanings had coalesced; these were, (1) 'emanating from the old source,' (2) 'made under the old recipe.' The plaintiff could truthfully say the first; it could not say the second; in fact it said both. But when the defendant came into the market and sold cologne made under the recipe but by Muhlens, it made the same representations, and the first was untrue, while the second was true. I say that the first was untrue, because the cologne did not come from the old source, which was the American branch. . . . I agree that the right here becomes very thin, since in fact Muhlens was always the real source; and the essences were made by him in Germany and sent over to be made up here. Customers presumably cared nothing about the place where the cologne was made up, and much about the essence. Still, it was Muhlens's rights that were sold, including all but the recipe. It can make no difference where he made the essences. We must hold the marks to have been transferred unless we are to say that no separate branch can be sold without the whole business. The case stands otherwise as to the use of proper names.

"Therefore, the plaintiff's path still seems to me clear except for the fact that it has been deceiving its customers . . . [I]t is possible to purge the user of the deceit, certainly if that be done long enough before bill filed to make certain that its effect has passed. . . . The argument of the District Court seems to me unanswerable, that as Muhlens could have changed his recipe, his successor may, if he declares so plainly enough to avoid deception. The first of the two meanings would then alone survive; the plaintiff having made it clear that the cologne was not of the old kind, the mark would stand merely for its origin, just as in the case of any of its other products.

"However, the plaintiff did not do this; it had a change of heart only when the suit was brought, and that was too late. . . . The District Court thought that only ten years would be enough under the circumstances, and I see no reason to think that less will do . . . But until the mark has been so purged, the plaintiff ought not to be able to protect it; and for this reason the decree should be modified."[57]

[d] **Security Assignments—Bankruptcy Transfers.** "An assignee for benefit of creditors or trustee in bankruptcy succeeds to *all* assets, both tangible and intangible, and for this reason can validly assign trademark rights with appurtenant goodwill and assets to a subsequent purchaser for value."[58]

---

[57] *Id.* at 940.
[58] Haymaker Sports, Inc. v. Turian, 581 F.2d 257, 262, 198 U.S.P.Q. 610 (CCPA 1978). *See also* Dirigold Corp. v. Dirigold Metals Corp., 125 F.2d 446, 453 (6th Cir. 1942) ("in a voluntary sale of a business as an entirety, trademarks and trade names, which have been lawfully established and identified with such business, will pass to one who purchases as a whole the physical assets or elements of the business, even though not specifically mentioned in the conveyance. . . . The law make[s] no distinction between voluntary and involuntary sales, and where the trademark involved is not in law a personal one and the transfer is made by operation of law through bankruptcy or a general assignment for the benefit of creditors, the

In *Haymaker Sports,*[59] the court held that an assignment to two "escrowees" to secure a debt was a naked assignment justifying the mark registration's cancellation even though the assignment formally recited that it included goodwill. A debtor and two creditors entered into an agreement on June 13, 1963 providing that the debtor's marks were assigned as collateral security for payment. The escrowees recorded the assignment in the Patent and Trademark Office on March 26, 1964. A week later, the escrowees and assignor reached a new agreement, which stipulated that the mark was assigned as collateral security for payment. The court noted that the escrowees "never played an active role in the business . . . , never used the mark themselves, and never acquired any tangible assets or goodwill." It distinguished trademark security assignment cases in which no default occurred and the assignment term was not recorded in the PTO.[60] Even if the assignment were valid, the implied license back to the debtor to use the mark "would have been nothing more than a mere naked license."[61]

Judge Baldwin dissented.[62]

---

courts have held that, although not specifically mentioned in the proceedings, the trademarks or trade names lawfully identified with the business pass to one who purchases the business substantially as a whole."); Woodward v. White Satin Mills Corp., 42 F.2d 987 (8th Cir. 1929) (corporation, not its founding shareholder, owned trademark, which passed on bankruptcy trustee's sale of corporation's business and goodwill).

[59] Haymaker Sports, Inc. v. Turian, 581 F.2d 257, 198 U.S.P.Q. 610 (CCPA 1978).

Compare Li'l' Red Barn, Inc. v. Red Barn Sys., Inc., 322 F. Supp. 98, 107, 167 U.S.P.Q. 741 (N.D. Ind. 1970), *aff'd per curiam,* 174 U.S.P.Q. 193 (7th Cir. 1972) ("a mere agreement for the future assignment of a trademark is not an assignment of either the mark itself or the good will attached to it.").

[60] *E.g.,* Li'l' Red Barn, Inc. v. Red Barn System, Inc., 322 F. Supp. 98, 167 U.S.P.Q. 741 (N.D. Ind. 1970), *aff'd per curiam,* 174 U.S.P.Q. 193 (7th Cir. 1972).

[61] 581 F.2d at 261.

[62] "I certainly disapprove of any assignment which enables the assignee to mislead and defraud the public by associating a trademark with a substantially different business, product or goodwill. . . . But . . . all of the important circumstances surrounding an assignment must be considered before it is determined to be 'in gross' in order to avoid an erroneous finding of invalidity because of a mere failure to comply with stereotyped formalities. . . . The record before us is replete with evidence that the parties intended the first agreement and the assignment to constitute an assignment of the mark to the escrowees and a simultaneous license for Avon. . . .

"While generally the mere provision that an assignment of a trademark also conveys the goodwill associated with the mark is insufficient to constitute a valid assignment, . . . the actions of the parties . . . resulted in a valid assignment with a license back to Avon. Avon was both assignor and licensee of the marks and since Avon was to continue its use of the mark there was no need to transfer equipment, inventory or facilities to the escrowees. The end result of the transactions was that any purchaser of HAYMAKERS shoes received precisely what was bargained for, i. e., shoes manufactured and sold by Avon.

"The majority finds the hiatus between the recording of the assignment on March 26, 1964 and the execution of the second agreement on April 7, 1964 as somehow significantly altering the relationship between Avon and the escrowees. Initially, I note that the recording provision in the statute is merely a device for providing constructive notice to potential bona fide purchasers. . . . Next, there is no evidence on the record that the escrowees terminated Avon's

In *Marshak*,[63] Rick managed and promoted musical groups under the trade-name "Vito and the Salutations" and sued a competing group for infringement. An unsatisfied judgment creditor obtained a levy of execution and sale of Rick's tradename. The Second Circuit set aside the sale.

"Although no case has been found precisely such as this in which a Federal Court has confronted the issue of whether a trade name by itself can be subjected to a forced sale, courts have held that registered trade names or marks may not be validly assigned in gross. A sale of a trade name or mark divorced from its goodwill is characterized as an 'assignment in gross.'

"A trade name or mark is merely a symbol of goodwill; it has no independent significance apart from the goodwill it symbolizes. . . . [A] trademark cannot be sold or assigned apart from the goodwill it symbolizes, Lanham Act, § 10 . . . Use of the mark by the assignee in connection with a different goodwill and different product would result in a fraud on the purchasing public who reasonably assume that the mark signifies the same thing, whether used by one person or another. . . .

"In a case which touches the issue present herein, Ward-Chandler Bldg. Co. v. Caldwell, 8 Cal. App. 2d 375, 47 P.2d 758, 760 (1935), a judgment creditor attempted to force the sale of a trademark and goodwill of the debtor's beauty parlor. The attempt was turned aside. The Court there held that a judgment creditor could not force the sale of the trademark and goodwill of the debtor's beauty parlor. "The reason for this is that if the bare right of user could be transferred the name or mark would no longer serve to point out and protect the business with which it has become identified, or to secure the public against deception, but would tend to give a different business the benefit of the reputation established by the business to which the name had previously been applied." Id. 47 P.2d at 760. . . . Cf. Haymaker Sports, Inc. v. Turian, 581 F.2d 257 (C.C.P.A. 1978) (trademark cannot be given as collateral in security agreements).

---

license and, thus, the status quo was maintained. Also, the second agreement reaffirmed the license agreement in the provision controlling disposition of the mark should Avon cease business operations, and this further emphasizes that these events did not affect Avon's right to use the marks.

"When a trademark is licensed, the general rule is that the licensor must exercise control over the quality of the goods which the licensee sells in connection with the mark. . . . Courts have, however, approved of certain licensing arrangements wherein the licensor relied upon the licensee to maintain the quality of the goods. . . . I find the instant situation to be such an exception. Avon had continually used the marks for over twenty years and had established considerable goodwill in the marks. The assignment to the escrowees was temporary and was only to continue until such time as Avon paid off the debt. Also, Avon intended to reacquire the mark and, therefore, it possessed an obvious interest in maintaining its reputation of quality. These factors, when considered with Avon's long time experience in the shoe manufacturing business and the lack of any showing of a deterioration in the quality of the shoes, demonstrate that Avon was in the best position to control quality and that it was clearly reasonable for the escrowees to rely thereon." 581 F.2d at 263-64.

[63] Marshak v. "Doc" Green, 746 F.2d 927, 223 U.S.P.Q. 1099 (2d Cir. 1984).

. . .

"Exceptions do exist. The courts have upheld such assignments if they find that the assignee is producing a product or performing a service substantially similar to that of the assignor and that the consumers would not be deceived or harmed. . . . Courts have also upheld such assignments if there is a continuity of management. . . .

"There was no evidence that this case fits into either of the above exceptions. Entertainment services are unique to the performers. Moreover, there is neither continuity of management nor quality and style of music. If another group advertised themselves as VITO AND THE SALUTATIONS, the public could be confused into thinking that they were about to watch the group identified by the registered trade name."[64]

The issue of *where* to file a creditor security interest in a trademark is a difficult one, especially because a trademark owner may have ownership rights under both federal statutory law and state common law.[65]

---

[64] 746 F.2d at 929-30, 223 U.S.P.Q. at 1099-1100.

Compare Marshak v. Green, 505 F. Supp. 1054, 1058, 212 U.S.P.Q. 493 (S.D. N.Y. 1981). In *Marshak*, the "Drifters," a music group including Green, Hobbs, Thomas and others, performed and recorded popular music in the 1950s and 1960s. After a 1966 to 1970 hiatus, Green, Hobbs, and Thomas resumed performing and recording as the "Drifters." In 1971, Marshak became the Drifters' manager. In 1976, Green, Hobbs, and Thomas filed an application to register "Drifters" as a service mark for "entertainment services namely a singing group" and assigned the application to Marshak, who promised to continue as their manager and to "be vigilant in stopping others from using 'The Drifters' name.' " The registration issued in 1978. In 1979, Green broke away, formed a new group with Rick as his new manager, and began using "Drifters." Marshak sued for trademark infringement. The court rejected Green and Rick's argument that the assignment was invalid for failure to pass good will: "Not only did the instrument itself provide for the transfer of goodwill, but also the use of the mark that is, the singing in The Drifters style by Thomas, Hobbs and Green remained unchanged in the public eye."

[65] *Cf. In re* Roman Cleanser Co., 225 U.S.P.Q. 140, 142, 43 B.R. 940, 944 (Bankr. E.D. Mich., S.D. 1984), aff'd, 802 F.2d 207 (6th Cir.1986) ("Trademark cases distinguish between security interests and assignments. *E.g.*, Li'l' Red Barn, Inc. v. Red Barn System, Inc., 322 F. Supp. 98 (N.D. Ind. 1970), aff'd per curiam, 174 U.S.P.Q. 193 (7th Cir. 1972). An 'assignment' of a trademark is an absolute transfer of the entire right, title and interest to the trademark. 'In order for a transfer of rights in a trademark to constitute a sale or assignment, thereby vesting title to the trademark in a party, the transfer must be absolute and must relate to the entire rights in the trademark.' Acme Valve & Fitting Company v. Wayne, 386 F. Supp. 1162, 1165 (S.D. Tex. 1974). The grant of a security interest is not such a transfer. It is merely what the term suggests—a device to secure an indebtedness. It is a mere agreement to assign in the event of a default by the debtor. '[T]he rule is well established that a mere agreement for the future assignment of a trademark is not an assignment of either the mark itself or the good will attached to it.' Li'l' Red Barn at 107; accord, SMI Industries Canada Ltd. v. Caelter Industries, Inc., 586 F. Supp. 808 (N.D. N.Y. 1984). Since a security interest in a trademark is not equivalent to an assignment, the filing of a security interest is not covered by the Lanham Act. Accordingly, the manner of perfecting a security interest in trademarks is governed by Article 9 and not by the Lanham Act.").

[3] Licensing

A trademark or service mark owner may license others to apply the mark only if the owner controls the nature and quality of the goods or services licensees produce and sell under the mark.[66] Trademark licensing is a critical component of a huge worldwide industry—product and service franchising.[67]

[a] Historical Development—Lanham Act "Related Company" Provision. Early common law decisions viewed licensing as fundamentally inconsistent with a trademark's origin-indicating function.[68] An example is *Everett O. Fisk & Co.,*[69] in which

---

[66] Trademark licensing, properly understood, involves the trademark owner authorizing others to apply the mark to goods or services. There is no licensing in this sense—or any duty to exercise quality control—when a trademark owner allows others to purchase and resell the owner's trademark-bearing products. *See, e.g.,* Heaton Distributing Co. v. Union Tank Car Co., 387 F.2d 477, 485, 156 U.S.P.Q. 299 (8th Cir. 1967) ("The generally accepted meaning of 'uncontrolled licensing' is where a trademark owner has licensed someone else to make or manufacture its products and then fails to control the quality of the products made by the licensee, thus permitting a deception of the public.").

[67] *Cf.* Power Test Petroleum Distributors, Inc. v. Calcu Gas, Inc., 754 F.2d 91, 225 U.S.P.Q. 368, 372 n.8 (2d Cir. 1985) ("Franchising . . . is often a sophisticated form of trademark licensing. Although a trademark or trade name is usually included in a franchise system, a franchise system can go well beyond being merely a trademark license.").

See also Siegel v. Chicken Delight, Inc., 448 F.2d 43, 48-49, 171 U.S.P.Q. 269 (9th Cir. 1971), *cert. denied,* 405 U.S. 955 (1972):

> "The historical conception of a trade-mark as a strict emblem of source of the product to which it attaches has largely been abandoned. The burgeoning business of franchising has made trade-mark licensing a widespread commercial practice and has resulted in the development of a new rationale for trade-marks as representations of product quality. . . . This is particularly true in the case of a franchise system set up not to distribute the trade-marked goods of the franchisor, but . . . to conduct a certain business under a common trade-mark or trade name. . . . Under such a type of franchise, the trade-mark simply reflects the goodwill and quality standards of the enterprise which it identifies."

[68] *E.g.,* American Broadcasting Co. v. Wahl Co., 121 F.2d 412, 413 (2d Cir. 1941) ("A trade-mark is intended to identify the goods of the owner and to safeguard his good will. The designation if employed by a person other than one whose business it serves to identify would be misleading. . . . A license of a trade-mark that has never been connected with the business of the licensee is objectionable for the same reason as an assignment of a trade-mark in gross and transfers no rights."); MacMahan Pharmacal Co. v. Denver Chemical Mfg. Co., 113 F. 468, 474-75 (8th Cir. 1901) ("A trade-mark cannot be assigned, or its use licensed, except as incidental to a transfer of the business or property in connection with which it has been used. An assignment or license without such a transfer is totally inconsistent with the theory upon which the value of a trade-mark depends and its appropriation by an individual is permitted. The essential value of a trade-mark is that it identifies to the trade the merchandise upon which it appears as of a certain origin, or as the property of a certain person.")

Cf. Reddy Kilowatt, Inc. v. Mid-Carolina Electric Cooperative, Inc., 240 F.2d 282, 289 (4th Cir. 1957) (stating that "A trademark cannot be licensed by the mere granting of permission to use it—in fact, it has no legal existence apart from its function to indicate the origin of goods or services and hence it cannot be transferred apart from the business itself . . . ").

[69] Everett O. Fisk & Co. v. Fisk Teachers' Agency, Inc., 3 F.2d 7 (8th Cir. 1924).

the court struck down a mark used in what is today a familiar form of franchising. The plaintiff established a teacher referral agency in Boston. Later, it licensed others to conduct similar businesses in other cities under specified conditions using its trade-name "Fisk Teacher's Agency" in exchange for a percent of cash receipts. Plaintiff was "a liberal advertiser" of his chain of agencies. The Denver agency owner refused to pay the prescribed fee, and plaintiff sued for trade name infringement. The court held that the plaintiff abandoned its mark.

> "The plaintiff was not the proprietor of these local offices, and the managers of them were not the agents of the plaintiff. They were owned and managed by those having them in charge, who alone were responsible for their conduct, except for the contractual obligations to the plaintiff. The plaintiff did not undertake to sell its business, or a part thereof, when it entered into these contracts for the conduct of these local offices, if it could be said that it might sell the right to conduct them. . . . The plaintiff's attempted license of the right to use its trade-name was ineffective, because a trade-name cannot be assigned, except as an incident to the sale of the business and good will in connection with which it has been used. . . . The evidence shows that the use of the plaintiff's trade-name by the many local offices, under the sanction of contracts made by the plaintiff assuming to license the use of the trade-name, has caused the name to lose its distinctiveness as the trade-name of the plaintiff. The service rendered to teachers and officers of schools has for many years represented generally to such persons and to the public, not the efforts, the experience, or the responsibility of the plaintiff, but of the persons conducting these local offices. . . . The question of abandonment of a trade name or mark is a question of intent . . . , and abandonment is not necessarily to be inferred from mere failure to prosecute infringement . . . , but may be inferred from disuse, lapse of time, and other circumstances evidencing the intention to discontinue its distinctiveness. . . . The intention of the plaintiff has been plainly manifested by the formal contracts and its acquiescence in the performance of these contracts, whereby, for a monetary consideration, it has for a long time allowed its trade-name to represent to the public the business of other. After thus misleading the public, it is not in position to ask the aid of a court of equity to protect the reputation of that name as an indication of the plaintiff's services."[70]

Later decisions held that a trademark could be licensed to others provided the licensor exercised quality control over the licensee's mark-bearing goods. An example is *E. I. du Pont de Nemours*[71] in which the court refused to cancel Celanese Corporation's "Celanese" dyestuff mark registration even though Celanese granted another company a nonexclusive license to use "Celanese" on dyestuffs. The dyestuffs were to meet the licensor's quality standards, and the licensor had the right to test the dyestuffs before they were offered for sale. The court noted: "It is well

---

[70] 3 F.2d at 8-9.

[71] E. I. du Pont de Nemours & Co. v. Celanese Corporation of America, 167 F.2d 484 (CCPA 1948).

settled that the owner of a trade-mark may license its use to another and others so long as such agreements are not merely naked license agreements."[72]

The Lanham Act "carries forward the view . . . that controlled licensing does not work an abandonment of the licensor's registration, while a system of naked licensing does."[73] The Act does not expressly refer to "licensing," but its "related company" provisions enable controlled authorized use. Section 5 provides that "Where a . . . mark . . . is or may be used legitimately by related companies, such use shall inure to the benefit of the registrant or application . . . and . . . shall not affect the validity of such mark or of its registration."[74] Section 45 defines a "related company" as "any person whose use of a mark is controlled by the owner of the mark with respect to the nature and quality of the goods or services on or in connection with which the mark is used."[75]

[b] **Quality Control.** To preserve a licensed mark's validity,[76] the licensor must exercise a reasonable degree of supervision and control over licensees.[77] The necessary

---

[72] 167 F.2d at 489.

[73] Dawn Donut Co., Inc. v. Hart's Food Stores, Inc., 267 F.2d 358, 363 (2d Cir. 1959).

[74] Lanham Act § 5, 15 U.S.C. § 1055.

[75] Lanham Act § 45, 15 U.S.C. § 1127.

[76] Courts usually hold that a mark is unenforceable and abandoned when its owner engages in "naked" licensing. The failure to control destroys the mark's distinctiveness and source-designating function.

In one decision, involving an unusual fact pattern, the court held that the first user's failure to control a licensee's use for a period of time only resulted in abandonment of its rights in the areas in which licensor had failed to use its mark. Sheila's Shine Products, Inc. v. Sheila Shine, Inc., 486 F.2d 114, 179 U.S.P.Q. 577 (5th Cir. 1973). This holding runs contrary to the general rule that there can be no "regional abandonment." See § 5D[3][b].

[77] E.g., General Motors Corp. v. Gibson Chemical & Oil Corp., 786 F.2d 105, 110, 229 U.S.P.Q. 352, 355 (2d Cir. 1986) ("Although a naked or uncontrolled license may provide the basis for an inference of abandonment of a trademark, . . . a controlled licensing program will not. . . . The critical question in determining whether a licensing program is controlled sufficiently by the licensor to protect his mark is whether the licensees' operations are policed adequately to guarantee the quality of the products sold under the mark."); Transgo, Inc. v. Ajac Transmission Parts Corp., 768 F.2d 1001, 1017, 225 U.S.P.Q. 458, 465 (9th Cir. 1985), cert. denied, 474 U.S. 1059 (1986) ("A trade name licensor must maintain control over the quality of the finished product or service to guarantee to the public that the goods or services are of the same, pre-license quality."); Kentucky Fried Chicken Corp. v. Diversified Packaging Corp., 549 F.2d 368, 387, 193 U.S.P.Q. 649 (5th Cir. 1977) ("Courts have long imposed upon trademark licensors a duty to oversee the quality of licensees' products. . . . The rationale for this requirement is that marks are treated by purchasers as an indication that the trademark owner is associated with the product. Customers rely upon the owner's reputation when they select the trademarked goods. If a trademark owner allows licensees to depart from its quality standards, the public will be misled, and the trademark will cease to have utility as an informational device. A trademark owner who allows this to occur loses its right to use the mark."); Dawn Donut, Inc. v. Hart's Food Stores, Inc., 267 F.2d 358, 367 (2d Cir. 1959) ("Without the requirement of control, the right of a trademark owner to license his mark separately from the business in connection with which it has been used would create the danger that products bearing the same trademark might be of diverse qualities. . . . If the licensor is not compelled to take some reasonable steps to prevent misuses of his trademark in the hands

control is for trademark preservation purposes and does not, as such, make the licensee the licensor's agent.[78]

Courts espouse the control requirement but do not enforce it strictly and only rarely invalidate marks for want of licensor control.[79] In *Dawn Donut,*[80] Dawn Donut sold donut mix and licensed bakers to sell donuts with its "Dawn" trademark. It had written contracts providing product preparation and quality standards with only some of its baker-licensees and even these did not establish an inspection system. The appeals court noted "[t]he absence . . . of an express contract right to inspect and supervise a licensee's operations does not mean that the plaintiff's method of licensing failed to comply with the requirements of the Lanham Act. Plaintiff may in fact have exercised control in spite of the absence of any express grant by licensees of the right

---

of others the public will be deprived of its most effective protection against misleading uses of a trademark. The public is hardly in a position to uncover deceptive uses of a trademark before they occur and will be at best slow to detect them after they happen. Thus, unless the licensor exercises supervision and control over the operations of its licensees the risk that the public will be unwittingly deceived will be increased and this is precisely what the Act is in part designed to prevent. . . . Clearly the only effective way to protect the public where a trademark is used by licensees is to place on the licensor the affirmative duty of policing in a reasonable manner the activities of his licensees.").

[78] *E.g.,* Oberlin v. Marlin American Corp., 596 F.2d 1322, 1327 (7th Cir. 1979) ("The Lanham Act requires supervision of trademark licensees at the expense of abandonment of the trademark. The licensor must control the operations of its licensees to ensure that the trademark is not used to deceive the public as to the quality of the goods or services bearing the name. . . . The purpose of the Lanham Act, however, is to ensure the integrity of registered trademarks, not to create a federal law of agency. Furthermore, the scope of the duty of supervision associated with a registered trademark is commensurate with this narrow purpose. The duty does not give a licensor control over the day-to-day operations of a licensee beyond that necessary to ensure uniform quality of the product or service in question. It does not automatically saddle the licensor with the responsibilities under state law of a principal for his agent.").

[79] *E.g.,* United States Jaycees v. Philadelphia Jaycees, 639 F.2d 134, 140, 209 U.S.P.Q. 457 (3d Cir. 1980) ("the proponent of a claim of insufficient control must meet a high burden of proof. The purpose of the control requirement is the protection of the public. If a licensor does not maintain control of his licensees in their use of the license, the public may be damaged by products that, despite their trademark, do not have the normal quality of such goods. 'The amount of control required varies with the circumstances.' "); Kentucky Fried Chicken Corp. v. Diversified Packaging Corp., 549 F.2d 368, 387, 193 U.S.P.Q. 649 (5th Cir. 1977) ("Retention of a trademark requires only minimal quality control, for in this context we do not sit to assess the quality of products sold on the open market. We must determine whether Kentucky Fried has abandoned quality control; the consuming public must be the judge of whether the quality control efforts have been ineffectual."); Edwin K. Williams & Co., Inc. v. Edwin K. Williams & Co.-East, 542 F.2d 1053, 1059 (9th Cir. 1976), *cert. denied,* 433 U.S. 908 (1977) ("Because a finding of insufficient control essentially works a forfeiture, a person who asserts insufficient control must meet a high burden of proof."); Turner v. H M H Publishing Co., Inc., 380 F.2d 224, 154 U.S.P.Q. 330 (5th Cir. 1967); Carl Zeiss Siftung v. V.E.B. Carl Zeiss, Jena, 293 F. Supp. 892, 917, 160 U.S.P.Q. 97 (S.D. N.Y. 1968), *modified on other grounds,* 433 F.2d 686 (2d Cir. 1970), *cert. denied,* 403 U.S. 905 (1971).

[80] Dawn Donut Co., Inc. v. Hart's Food Stores, Inc., 267 F.2d 358 (2d Cir. 1959).

to inspect and supervise."[81] The only evidence of actual control consisted of testimony by two of Dawn Donut's sales representatives that they regularly visited customers and had " 'in many instances' an opportunity to inspect [their] operations." Nevertheless, the appeals court majority held the trial court's fact finding that there was a reasonable degree of supervision and control was not clearly erroneous. Judge Lumbard dissented: "I do not believe that we can fairly determine on this record whether plaintiff subjected its licensees to periodic and thorough inspections by trained personnel or whether its policing consisted only of chance, cursory examinations of licensees' operations by technically untrained salesmen. The latter system of inspection hardly constitutes a sufficient program of supervision to satisfy the requirements of the Act."[82] He did note that the licensor's lack of control over its licensee's use of the mark at the *retail* level should lead only to a limited registration cancellation, which would confirm its rights to use the mark on sales of mixes to bakers at the *wholesale* level.

Courts find sufficient control even absent actual control or an express contractual right of control when the licensor has sufficient prior experience with an individual licensee to justify relying on the licensee to maintain quality standards.[83] An example is *Taco Cabana International*,[84] in which the court upheld a jury verdict finding

---

[81] 267 F.2d at 368. *See also* Embedded Moments, Inc. v. International Silver Co., 648 F. Supp. 187 (E.D. N.Y. 1986) ("[T]he licenses [need not] contain a written provision for control; actual control by the licensor is sufficient.").

[82] 267 F.2d at 369.

[83] *E.g.*, Transgo, Inc. v. Ajac Transmission Parts Corp., 768 F.2d 1001, 1017-18, 225 U.S.P.Q. 458, 465-66 (9th Cir. 1985), *cert. denied*, 474 U.S. 1059 (1986) (based on ten year association, licensor had respect for licensee's ability and expertise and justified reliance on licensee "to maintain high standards by performing his own quality control"; the licensor's confidence was "backed by the fact [it] never received any complaints from the field about parts produced by [the licensee] . . . 'The purpose of the Lanham Act . . . is to ensure the integrity of registered trademarks, not to create a federal law of agency.' The scope of a licensor's duty of supervision of a licensee who has been granted use of a trademark must be commensurate with this limited goal."); Stock Pot Restaurant, Inc. v. Stockpot, Inc., 737 F.2d 1576, 222 U.S.P.Q. 665 (Fed. Cir. 1984) (no abandonment when owner leased it to an associate who operated the restaurant for one year: the owner lived in the building and consulted with the associate); Land O' Lakes Creameries, Inc. v. Oconomowoc Canning Co., 330 F.2d 667, 670, 141 U.S.P.Q. 281 (7th Cir. 1964) (trademark owner granted its distributor Jones an oral license to use its mark on goods the distributor produced; "The district judge found that [the owner's] reliance on Jones' control over the quality of products should be deemed sufficient supervision to protect the quality of the goods bearing the trade-mark and, therefore, met the requirements of 15 U.S.C.A. 1064(e). In light of the fact that [the owner's] name appeared on the label used by Jones and that during the forty years of the license agreement there were no complaints about the quality of the goods, we think the finding that the arrangement with Jones was more than a naked license not effecting an abandonment of the mark was not erroneous."); Edwin K. Williams & Co., Inc. v. Edwin K. Williams & Co.-East, 542 F.2d 1053, 191 U.S.P.Q. 563 (9th Cir. 1976); Embedded Moments, Inc. v. International Silver Co., 648 F. Supp. 187 (E.D. N.Y. 1986); Syntex Laboratories, Inc. v. Norwich Pharmacal Co., 315 F. Supp. 45, 46, 166 U.S.P.Q. 312 (S.D. N.Y. 1970), *aff'd*, 437 F.2d 566 (2d Cir. 1971) ("reliance upon the integrity of a licensee is sufficient to fulfill the control requirement where a history of trouble-free manufacture provides a basis for such reliance.").

[84] Taco Cabana International, Inc. v. Two Pesos, Inc., 932 F.2d 1113, 19 U.S.P.Q.2d 1253 (5th Cir. 1991).

sufficient control when restaurant chain co-owners, who were brothers, divided restaurants, one becoming "Taco Cabana," the other "TaCasita," with each retaining right to use the restaurants' trade dress.

> "An owner may license its trademark or trade dress and retain proprietary rights if the owner maintains adequate control over the quality of goods and services that the licensee sells with the mark or dress. . . . [Defendant] argues that the cross-license creates two separate sources of good will and thus cannot indicate a single origin. This argument ignores the emergence of the 'quality theory,' which broadens the older source theory 'to include not only manufacturing source but also the source of the standards of quality of goods bearing the mark' or dress. . . . So long as customers entering a Taco Cabana or a TaCasita can expect a consistent level of quality, the trade dress retains its 'utility as an informational device.' "[85]

The court refused to require evidence of "bilateral quality monitoring": "the law requires consistent quality, not equivalent policing."

> "The purpose of the quality-control requirement is to prevent the public deception that would ensue from variant quality standards under the same mark or dress. Where the particular circumstances of the licensing arrangement persuade us that the public will not be deceived, we need not elevate form over substance and require the same policing rigor appropriate to more formal licensing and franchising transactions. Where the license parties have engaged in a close working relationship, and may justifiably rely on each parties' intimacy with standards and procedures to ensure consistent quality, and no actual decline in quality standards is demonstrated, we would depart from the purpose of the law to find an abandonment simply for want of all the inspection and control formalities. . . .

> "The history of the . . . brothers' relationship warrants this relaxation of formalities. Prior to the licensing agreement at issue, the Stehling brothers operated Taco Cabana together for approximately eight years. Taco Cabana and TaCasita do not use significantly different procedures or products, and the brothers may be expected to draw on their mutual experience to maintain the requisite quality consistency. They cannot protect their trade dress if they operate their separate restaurants in ignorance of each other's operations, but they need not maintain the careful policing appropriate to more formal license arrangements."[86]

> The control requirement applies to the licensing of characters as trademarks.[87]

---

[85] *Id.* at 1121.

[86] *Id.* at 1121-22.

[87] Universal City Studios, Inc. v. Nintendo Co., Ltd., 578 F. Supp. 911, 922, 221 U.S.P.Q. 991, 999 (S.D. N.Y. 1983), *aff'd on other grounds,* 746 F.2d 112, 223 U.S.P.Q. 1000 (2d Cir.1984) (KING KONG trademark rights transfer was, patently, a "gross" license or assignment: "Because a trademark is not a right in gross, it cannot be transferred except by means of a supervised license or in connection with an ongoing business or some aspect of that business. . . . This rule is no less valid where the trademark is in a character name.").

CHAPTER 6

OTHER INTELLECTUAL PROPERTY RIGHTS

SYNOPSIS

(Matthew Bender & Co., Inc.)

§ 6A   Introduction

The four major areas of intellectual property protection—utility patents, trade secrets, copyrights and trademarks—dominate United States intellectual property law, but there are other important rights involving particular situations or subject matter. Three are federal statutory creations: design patents,[1] plant patents and plant variety protection,[2] and semiconductor chip protection.[3] Two are state common law or statutory creations: misappropriation,[4] idea submission, and publicity rights.[5] One, false advertising,[6] is a blend of state unfair competition law and a federal statute, Lanham Act Section 43(a). With the exception of the design patent statute, these special protection systems are twentieth century innovations, relatively young compared to the patent, trade secret, copyright and trademark systems.[7]

These systems are worth study not only for their direct applications, but also for the lessons they provide on how intellectual property law can effectively accomplish its major task: providing adequate incentives to create, disclose, and market valuable new works, inventions, products and information without unduly dampening economic competition or discouraging creation of improvements on prior creations.

When technology and society make available new means of creating and efficiently reproducing technology and information, the question arises: should the incentive-competition balance be achieved by applying or expanding the established general systems or should a special ("*sui generis*") scheme be adopted? The existing special systems' successes and failures provide guidance.

§ 6B   Design Protection

United States law provides three methods for protecting industrial designs against unauthorized copying: (1) design patents, (2) copyright, and (3) trade dress protection under trademark and unfair competition principles. Each method is subject to significant limitations.

A design patent may cover a manufactured article's ornamental design, but to qualify for a patent, the design must meet novelty and nonobviousness standards, and the design inventor must promptly apply for protection by filing an application with the Patent and Trademark Office (PTO).

Copyright is available for "applied art" but not "industrial design"; a useful article's design qualifies for copyright only if it "incorporates pictorial, graphic, or sculptural features that can be identified separately from, and are capable of existing independently of, the utilitarian aspects of the article."[1] The separate identification-independent existence test excludes attractive ornamental designs that are integral parts of manufactured products.

---

[1] See § 6B.

[2] See § 6C.

[3] See § 6D.

[4] See § 6F.

[5] See § 6G.

[6] See § 6E.

[7] The United States' first patent and copyright statutes were enacted in 1790. See §§ 2B, and 4B. Common law trademark and trade secret protection grew in the 19th century though statutory coverage did not become significant until this century. See §§ 3B, and 5B.

[1] 17 U.S.C. § 101.

Trade dress protection is available for nonfunctional features if they distinguish the goods' origin. Its effectiveness is limited by the need to show nonfunctionality, distinctiveness, and a likelihood of confusion between the protected and accused designs.

Many other countries have a specially tailored design registration law. For more than 20 years, design protection proponents have urged the United States Congress to adopt a similar law. Because of the current high level of concern about intellectual property protection and its international trade ramifications, there is a good chance the United States will, at long last, join its major trading partners in stimulating more attractive product design by enacting a design registration law separate from the patent system.

Copyright and trade dress protection for three-dimensional articles is discussed in other sections.[2] This section covers design patent law.[3]

[1] Historical Development

In 1842, Congress, at the Commissioner of Patents's request, enacted a design patent law to fill a gap between copyright protection for authors and patent protection for inventors in the mechanical arts.[4]

In *Gorham,* [5] which involved patents on spoon and fork handle designs, the Supreme Court reviewed the statute's purpose.

> "The [act was] plainly intended to give encouragement to the decorative arts. . . . The law manifestly contemplated that giving certain new and original appearances to a manufactured article may enhance its salable value, may enlarge the demand for it, and may be meritorious service to the public. . . . The appearance may be the result of peculiarity of configuration, or of ornament alone, or of both conjointly. . . . "[6]

It adopted an ordinary observer-purchaser test for design patent infringement:

> "[I]f, in the eye of an ordinary observer, giving such attention as a purchaser usually gives, two designs are substantially the same, if the resemblance is such as to deceive such an observer, inducing him to purchase one supposing it to be the other, the first one patented is infringed by the other."[7]

This test is a hybrid of copyright law's ordinary observer test[8] and trademark law's likelihood of confusion test.[9]

---

[2] *See* §§ 4C[3] and 5C[2][c].

[3] *See generally* D. Chisum, Patents § 1.04.

[4] Act of August 29, 1842, ch. 263, § 2, 5 Stat. 543.

[5] Gorham Mfg. v. White, 81 U.S. (14 Wall.) 511 (1871).

[6] 81 U.S. (14 Wall.) at 524–25.

[7] 81 U.S. (14 Wall.) at 528.

[8] *See* § 4F[2].

[9] *See* § 5F.

[2] Protection Requirements

To be patentable, a design must be of an "article of manufacture" and meet the ornamentality, nonfunctionality, novelty and nonobviousness requirements.

The design patent statute provides that the "provisions of [the] title relating to patents for inventions shall apply to patents for designs, except as otherwise provided."[10]

[a] **Article of Manufacture.** A patentable design may consist of a manufactured article's configuration, surface ornamentation or a configuration-ornamentation combination. In *Zahn*,[11] the court held that a part of an article, such as a drill bit shank, could be the subject of a design patent. In *Hruby*,[12] the court, relying on the dictionary definition that "a manufacture is anything made 'by the hands of man' from raw materials, whether literally by hand or by machinery or by art," held that a fountain water-pattern was an article of manufacture design, reversing the Patent Office's view that the claimed design was a mere "fleeting product of nozzle arrangements."

[b] **Ornamentality.** A patentable design must be "ornamental," but the design patent statute does not authorize the PTO or the courts to impose a subjective, qualitative ornamentality standard. In *Koehring*,[13] the court reversed rejection of a patent application for a concrete mixer design: "[T]he beauty and ornamentation requisite in design patents is not confined to such as may be found in the 'aesthetic or fine arts.'" Congress intended to encourage "elimination of much of unsightly repulsiveness that characterizes many machines and mechanical devices which have a tendency to depress rather than excite the esthetic sense."[14]

Courts have found insufficient ornamentality in designs of articles that are hidden in their intended use,[15] but in *Webb*,[16] the court held that the PTO erred in rejecting an application claiming the ornamental design of a grooved femoral hip stem prosthesis. An article's design is statutory subject matter if, at some point in its life, its appearance is a matter of concern: "Many commercial items, such as colorful and representational vitamin tablets, or caskets, have designs clearly intended to be noticed during the process [of sale] and equally clearly intended to be completely hidden from view in the final use."[17]

---

[10] 35 U.S.C. § 171. This means that utility patent law's substantive standards, such as the nonobviousness requirement, apply to design inventions. *See* § 6B[2][e].

The design patent statute expressly varies certain requirements. The Section 119 priority right, see § 2H[2][b], and Section 102(d) bar provision, see § 2C[5][b][vii], are six months rather than a year. A design patent's term is 14 rather than 17 years. 35 U.S.C. § 173.

Patent law's specification disclosure requirements necessarily vary in the case of design inventions. *See* § 6B[3].

[11] *In re* Zahn, 617 F.2d 261, 204 U.S.P.Q. 988 (CCPA 1980).

[12] *In re* Hruby, 373 F.2d 997, 153 U.S.P.Q. 61 (CCPA 1967).

[13] *In re* Koehring, 37 F.2d 421, 4 U.S.P.Q. 169 (CCPA 1930).

[14] 37 F.2d at 422–23.

[15] *E.g., In re* Cornwall, 230 F.2d 457, 109 U.S.P.Q. 57 (CCPA 1956); *In re* Stevens, 173 F.2d 1015, 81 U.S.P.Q. 362 (CCPA 1949).

[16] *In re* Webb, 916 F.2d 1553, 16 U.S.P.Q.2d 1433 (Fed. Cir. 1990).

[17] 916 F.2d at 1558, 16 U.S.P.Q.2d at 1436.

[c] Nonfunctionality. An inventor cannot obtain a design patent for a design that is "primarily functional rather than ornamental."[18]

> "However, a distinction exits between the functionality of an article or features thereof and the functionality of the particular design of such article or features thereof that perform a function. Were that not true, it would not be possible to obtain a design patent on a utilitarian article of manufacture. . . . "[19]

In *Avia,*[20] the court held that design patents claiming athletic shoes' outer soles and uppers were not invalid for functionality.

[d] Novelty—Statutory Bars. Patent law's novelty[21] and statutory bar[22] requirements apply to design patents. In *Yardley,*[23] the court held that caricature or other artistic treatment of a natural object may render it patentable.

[e] Nonobviousness. Patent law's fundamental requirement that the claimed invention be not obvious in view of the prior art[24] applies to design inventions.[25] Whether a design would have been obvious at the invention date is assessed by reference to the "designer of ordinary capability who designs articles of the type presented in the application."[26]

[3] Application and Examination

To obtain a design patent, an inventor must file an application disclosing the design with the PTO, which examines the application and issues a patent if it determines that the claimed design meets patentability requirements.

Patent applications for designs are considerably simpler than those for utility inventions. A utility patent application requires a detailed written description.[27] For

---

[18] Power Controls Corp. v. Hybrinetics, Inc., 806 F.2d 234, 231 U.S.P.Q. 774 (Fed. Cir. 1986); *In re* Carletti, 328 F.2d 1020, 140 U.S.P.Q. 653 (CCPA 1964).

[19] Avia Group International, Inc. v. L.A. Gear California, Inc., 853 F.2d 1557, 1563, 7 U.S.P.Q.2d 1548, 1553 (Fed. Cir. 1988).

[20] Avia Group International, Inc. v. L.A. Gear California, Inc., 853 F.2d 1557, 7 U.S.P.Q.2d 1548 (Fed. Cir. 1988).

[21] *See* § 2C[3].

A prior art *identical* design anticipates (that is, negates novelty of) a claimed design even if it is of an article for a different use. *In re* Glavas, 230 F.2d 447, 450, 109 U.S.P.Q. 50 (CCPA 1956).

[22] *See* § 2C[5][b][ii]. The "experimental use" exception to the public use and on sale bars has limited application to design inventions. *In re* Mann, 861 F.2d 1581, 8 U.S.P.Q.2d 2030 (Fed. Cir. 1988).

[23] *E.g., In re* Yardley, 493 F.2d 1389, 181 U.S.P.Q. 331 (CCPA 1974).

[24] *See* § 2C[4].

[25] Smith v. Whitman, 148 U.S. 674 (1893); Litton Sys., Inc. v. Whirlpool Corp., 728 F.2d 1423, 1443, 221 U.S.P.Q. 97, 109 (Fed. Cir. 1984).

See also In re Sung Nam Cho, 813 F.2d 378 F.2d, 1 U.S.P.Q.2d 1662 (Fed. Cir. 1987); Pacific Furniture Mfg. Co. v. Preview Furniture Corp., 800 F.2d 1111, 231 U.S.P.Q. 67 (Fed. Cir. 1986).

[26] *In re* Nalbandian, 661 F.2d 1214, 211 U.S.P.Q. 782 (CCPA 1981). *Compare* Petersen Mfg. Co. v. Central Purchasing Inc., 740 F.2d 1541, 222 U.S.P.Q. 562 (Fed. Cir. 1984).

[27] *See* § 2D[3].

designs, patent law's disclosure and claiming requirements are fulfilled primarily by the drawings, which illustrate the design.[28] Design patent applications contain a single claim to the ornamental design of the article "as shown" in the drawings.[29] In *Rubenfield*,[30] the court held that a design applicant could illustrate more than one embodiment of a design but could not include more than one claim.[31]

[4] Exclusive Rights—Infringement—Remedies

The utility patent statute's provisions on exclusive rights, infringement and remedies apply to design patents.[32] Section 289 provides an additional remedy that allows a design patentee to recover the infringer's illicit profits.[33] Section 289 includes unauthorized exposing for sale as an infringing act.

Does one infringe a design patent by applying the design to an article of manufacture differing from that disclosed in the patent? No court decision addresses the precise question.[34] Because design patents are for the ornamental design of an "article of manufacture" as illustrated in the patent drawings, it is likely that courts will not give them broad product coverage. In *Avia*,[35] the court found infringement when the patentee's designs were on tennis player's shoes and the infringer's designs were on children's shoes. It stressed that the "products of the parties need not be directly

---

[28] *Cf.* Racing Strollers Inc. v. TRI Industries Inc., 878 F.2d 1418, 1420, 11 U.S.P.Q.2d 1300, 1301 (Fed. Cir. 1989) ("In the case of an 'ornamental design for an article of manufacture,' . . . the 'best mode' requirement of the first paragraph of § 112 is not applicable, as a design has only one 'mode' and it can be described only by illustrations showing what it looks like (though some added description in words may be useful to explain the illustrations).").

[29] Dobson v. Dornan, 118 U.S. 10 (1886); Dobson v. Harford Carpet Co., 114 U.S. 439 (1885); In re Mann, 861 F.2d 1581, 1582, 8 U.S.P.Q.2d 2030, 2031 (Fed. Cir. 1988) ("The claim [of a design patent application] . . . is limited to what is shown in the application drawings.").

[30] *In re* Rubenfield, 270 F.2d 391, 123 U.S.P.Q. 210 (CCPA 1959), *cert. denied*, 362 U.S. 903 (1960).

[31] The applicant illustrated his floor waxer design in two forms of "generally similar but specifically different appearance" and sought three claims—one each to the two forms and one to the generic design. The court affirmed the Patent Office's rejection of the three claims as violating Rule 153, which prohibits more than one claim.

> "[I]t is the appearance of a design as a whole which is controlling in determining questions of patentability and infringement. . . . [N]o useful purpose could be served by the inclusion of more than one claim in a design application or patent." 270 F.2d 395–96.

[32] Section 171 directs that Title 35's provision on patents for inventions apply to designs "except as otherwise provided." 35 U.S.C. § 171.

For a discussion of utility patent exclusive rights, infringement, and remedies, see §§ 2E and 2F[5].

[33] 35 U.S.C. § 289. *See* Trans-World Mfg. Corp. v. Al Nyman & Sons, Inc., 750 F.2d 1552, 224 U.S.P.Q. 259 (Fed. Cir. 1984).

Section 289 is a vestige of an older era of patent remedies. *See* D. Chisum, Patents § 20.03[5].

[34] *See* Symons, The Law of Patents for Designs 70–71 (1914) (no court decisions found; "is a design for a lamp shade infringed by the use of the same design for a door knob?").

[35] Avia Group International, Inc. v. L.A. Gear California, Inc., 853 F.2d 1557, 7 U.S.P.Q.2d 1548 (Fed. Cir. 1988).

competitive; indeed an infringer is liable even when the patent owner puts out no product."[36]

The *Gorham* ordinary purchaser test governs design patent infringement determinations.

> "While . . . infringement can be found for designs that are not identical to the patented design, such designs must be equivalent in their ornamental, not functional, aspects. . . . The accused devices must meet the *Gorham* test of similarity of ornamental appearance such that an ordinary observer would be likely to purchase one thinking it was the other."[37]

The court determines the similarity "as though the ordinary observer is seeing the patented design for the first time."[38] A side-by-side comparison showing differences does not necessarily establish nonsimilarity.[39]

Courts sometimes state the comparison as between the patentee's and the accused infringer's products, but, properly speaking, the accused product must be compared with the patent drawings.[40] An accused device will not escape infringement by adding distinguishing features, such as color, that are not in the patented design's drawings.[41]

---

[36] 853 F.2d at 1565, 7 U.S.P.Q.2d at 1555.

[37] Lee v. Dayton-Hudson Corp., 838 F.2d 1186, 1190, 5 U.S.P.Q.2d 1625, 1628 (Fed. Cir. 1988). *See also* Litton Sys., Inc. v. Whirlpool Corp., 728 F.2d 1423, 1444, 221 U.S.P.Q. 97, 110 (Fed. Cir. 1984) (design patent on microwave oven; "Where . . . a field is crowded with many references relating to the design of the same type of appliance, we must construe the range of equivalents very narrowly.").

[38] D. Chisum, Patents § 1.04[4]. *See* Sanson Hosiery Mills, Inc. v. Warren Knitting Mills, Inc., 202 F.2d 395, 96 U.S.P.Q. 247 (3d Cir. 1953).

[39] Sanson Hosiery Mills v. S.H. Kress & Co., 109 F. Supp. 383, 384, 95 U.S.P.Q. 142 (M.D. N.C. 1952) ("Actual comparison for minute inspection is not a fair test. The imitation may be on display when the patented article is not present. In such a situation, one seeking a stocking with a picture frame border would readily accept the imitation. . . . A design patent protects the general design, the pictured effect on the mind from a general view, rather than details revealed by a minute test."). *See also* Ashley v. Weeks-Numan Co., 220 F. 899, 902 (2d Cir. 1915) ("It is not a proper test to place the two inkstands side by side, to determine whether or not there are certain differences."). *Compare* FMC Corp. v. Hennessy Industries, Inc., 836 F.2d 521, 527, 5 U.S.P.Q.2d 1272, 1277 (Fed. Cir. 1987) ("[I]nfringement requires appropriation of the novelty in the patented device. . . . [D]ifferences between patented and accused designs are not irrelevant. Courts should take into account similarities *and* differences. . . .").

[40] *Cf.* Lee v. Dayton-Hudson Corp., 838 F.2d 1186, 1189, 5 U.S.P.Q.2d 1625, 1627 (Fed. Cir. 1988) (the district court did not err in comparing the accused devices with a model of the patented device, rather than solely with the drawing in the patent: "When no significant distinction in design has been shown between the patent drawing and its physical embodiment, it is not error for the court to view them both, and to compare the embodiment of the patented design with the accused devices.").

[41] *E.g.,* Ashley v. Weeks-Numan Co., 220 F. 899 (2d Cir. 1915); FMC Corp. v. Hennessy Industries, 650 F. Supp. 688, 702, 2 U.S.P.Q.2d 1479, 1490 (N.D. Ill. 1986), *aff'd*, 836 F.2d 521, 5 U.S.P.Q.2d 1272 (Fed. Cir. 1988) ("color and designations are not part of the patented design and must be ignored. On the other hand, it is not enough to say that to the casual observer the two devices look rather similar. In the first place, the hypothetical observer is

The infringement test is not the same as the trademark law likelihood of confusion test.[42]

Design patent infringement "requires appropriation of the novelty in the patented device."[43] In *Winner International*,[44] the Federal Circuit affirmed a district court's grant of summary judgment of noninfringement of a design patent covering an automobile steering lock. It rejected the patentee's argument that the district court "erred in not considering the overall configuration and appearance of the patented design as a 'point of novelty' ":

> "To consider the overall appearance of a design without regard to prior art would eviscerate the purpose of the 'point of novelty' approach, which is to focus on those aspects of a design which render the design different from prior art designs."[45]

The magistrate "properly focussed on those aspects of the . . . patented design which distinguish it from the prior art, and found the differences between the patented design and the [accused design] to be so numerous and substantial that a reasonable jury could not find infringement."[46]

§ 6C   Plant Protection

United States law provides three potential sources of statutory protection[1] for plant-related inventions: (1) the Plant Patent Act;[2] (2) the Plant Variety Protection Act (PVPA);[3] and (3) the general utility patent statute.[4]

---

neither a casual passerby nor an expert, but rather is an ordinary purchaser. . . . Further, what that ordinary purchaser is observing is a design in which detail dictated solely by function is ignored and in which similarity to the accused device arises from the novelty which distinguishes the patented device from the prior art.").

[42] *E.g.,* Unette Corp. v. Unit Pack Co., Inc., 785 F.2d 1026, 228 U.S.P.Q. 933 (Fed. Cir. 1986) (likelihood of confusion as to the source of the goods is not a necessary or appropriate factor for determining design patent infringement; a design patent owner need not have manufactured or sold a product in order to have a remedy against infringement; a determination that the shape of the alleged infringing product is not visible to the consumer at the time of sale and therefore that the consumer is unlikely to be confused is inapposite).

[43] FMC Corp. v. Hennessy Industries, Inc., 836 F.2d 521, 5 U.S.P.Q.2d 1272 (Fed. Cir. 1987). *See also* Avia Group International, Inc. v. L.A. Gear California, Inc., 853 F.2d 1557, 1565, 7 U.S.P.Q.2d 1548, 1554 (Fed. Cir. 1988) ("In addition to overall similarity of designs, 'the accused device must appropriate the novelty in the patented device which distinguishes it from the prior art.' ").

[44] Winner International Corp. v. Wolo Manufacturing Corp., 905 F.2d 375, 15 U.S.P.Q.2d 1076 (Fed. Cir. 1990).

[45] 905 F.2d at 376, 15 U.S.P.Q.2d at 1077.

[46] 905 F.2d at 376, 15 U.S.P.Q.2d at 1077.

[1] Common law theories, such as trade secret law, see chapter 3, contract law, and unfair competition law, see § 6F, may also protect against unauthorized misappropriation of plant technology.

[2] 35 U.S.C. § 161–164.

[3] 7 U.S.C. § 2321 *et seq.*

[4] 35 U.S.C. § 101. For a discussion of utility patent law, see chapter 2.

[1] Plant Patent Act

In 1930, Congress provided for patents on asexually reproduced distinct and new plant varieties, such as flowering plants and fruit trees.[5] The purpose was to "afford agriculture, so far as practicable, the same opportunity to participate in the benefits of the patent system as has been given industry."[6] Without intellectual property protection, a plant breeder would have "no adequate financial incentive to enter upon his work"[7] because those who purchased his new varieties could use asexual reproduction techniques, such as budding and grafting, to multiply copies of the variety.

[a] Requirements. Section 161 provides:

"Whoever invents or discovers and asexually reproduces any distinct and new variety of plant, including cultivated sports, mutants, hybrids, and newly found seedlings, other than a tuber propagated plant or a plant found in an uncultivated state, may obtain a patent therefor, subject to the conditions and requirements of this title."[8]

To be eligible for plant patent protection, subject matter must meet several requirements. First, it must be a "plant."[9] In *Arzberger*,[10] the court held that a bacterium species cultured from Louisiana cane field soil was not a "plant" because the statute contemplated only plants in the ordinary common sense meaning.

Second, the inventor must asexually reproduce the new variety, that is, by "means other than from seeds, such as by the rooting of cuttings, by layering, budding, grafting, inarching, etc."[11] Asexual reproduction is necessary to preserve the unique genetic structure of a hybrid, mutant or sport: "For example, without asexual reproduction, there would have been but one true McIntosh or Greening apple tree."[12]

Third, the subject matter must be a "distinct and new variety." It must "have characteristics clearly distinguishable from those of existing varieties." A distinguishing characteristic may be disease immunity, flower color, flavor or productivity.

Fourth, the plant must be new and not subject to a Section 102(b) statutory bar.[13] Using or selling a plant variety in the United States more than one year prior to the application date bars a patent unless the experimental use doctrine excuses the use or sale.[14] A prior art publication illustrating the plant variety will not necessarily

---

[5] *See generally* D. Chisum, Patents § 1.05.

[6] S. Rep. No. 315, 71st Cong., 2d Sess. (1930).

[7] *Id.*

[8] 35 U.S.C. § 161.

[9] The patent claim is to "the plant shown and described" in the inventor's specification, 35 U.S.C. § 162.

[10] *In re* Arzberger, 112 F.2d 834, 46 U.S.P.Q. 32 (CCPA 1940).

[11] U.S. Patent & Trademark Office, Manual of Patent Examining Procedure § 1601 (3d ed. rev. 1977).

Asexual reproduction is analogous to reduction to practice of an invention. *See* D. Chisum, Patents § 1.05[1][b][ii].

[12] S. Rep. No. 314, 71st Cong., 2d Sess. (1930).

[13] For a discussion of prior art and statutory bars, see § 2C[5].

[14] *See* Bourne v. Jones, 114 F. Supp. 413, 419–20, 98 U.S.P.Q. 206 (S.D. Fla. 1951), *aff'd*, 207 F.2d 173, 98 U.S.P.Q. 205 (5th Cir. 1953), *cert. denied*, 346 U.S. 987 (1953).

constitute an anticipation because the publication may not be sufficient to enable a person of ordinary skill in the art to reproduce the plant.[15]

Fifth, the plant must meet patent law's nonobviousness requirement. The Plant Patent Act does not mention the nonobviousness requirement but does state that "the provisions of this title relating to patents for inventions shall apply to patents for plants, except as otherwise provided." In *Yoder Bros.,*[16] the Fifth Circuit applied a modified version of the *Graham* nonobviousness analysis to determine the patentability of several chrysanthemum varieties.

[b] **Application and Examination.** To obtain a patent, a plant developer must file an application with the PTO, which examines the application and issues a patent if patentability conditions are met.[17]

As with designs,[18] the drawings rather than a written description fulfill patent law's disclosure and claiming requirements.[19] Done in color, the drawings must be "artistically and competently executed" and "disclose all the distinctive characteristics of the plant capable of visual representation."[20]

---

[15] *In re* Le Grice, 301 F.2d 929, 938, 133 U.S.P.Q. 365 (CCPA 1962) (full color photograph of the new rose variety more than one year before the patent application filing date is not a bar: "While man can and does assist nature by the cross-pollination of selected parent plants, the actual creation of the new plant, because of the almost infinite number of possible combinations between the genes and chromosomes, is not presently subject to a controlled reproduction by act of man.").

In *Le Grice,* the court noted that Congress altered the patent specification enabling disclosure requirement for plants, 35 U.S.C. § 162, see § 6C[1][b], but made no similar alteration of the anticipatory effect of publications.

[16] Yoder Bros., Inc. v. California-Florida Plant Corp., 537 F.2d 1347, 193 U.S.P.Q. 264 (5th Cir. 1976), *cert. denied,* 429 U.S. 1094 (1977).

Yoder upheld seven patents on chrysanthemums. Five were on plants developed from parent plant "sports." The defendant offered evidence that sports of a similar type recurred on the parent plant. The trial court excluded the evidence, and the Fifth Circuit affirmed, noting "the only possible probative value of the sport recurrence evidence would be to show that a sport of that particular size, shape, color, or other trait is predictable from a given variety of parent plant." Congress did not intend that sport recurrence predictability would preclude patentability: "the purpose of the . . . Act would be frustrated by a requirement that only those rare, never-before-seen, if not genetically impossible sports or mutations would be patentable." This broad reading of the Act did not offend the constitutional patent requirement of innovation because patents on recurring sports did not deprive the public of existing knowledge: "An infinite number of a certain sized sport could appear on a plant, but until someone recognized its uniqueness and difference and found that the traits could be preserved by asexual reproduction in commercial quantities, no patentable plant would exist." 537 F.2d at 1382.

[17] For a discussion of the patenting process, see § 2D[1].

[18] *See* § 6B.

[19] 35 U.S.C. § 162: "The claim in the specification shall be in formal terms to the plant shown and described."

[20] 37 C.F.R. § 1.165.

Section 162 relaxed the enabling disclosure requirement: "No plant patent shall be declared invalid for noncompliance with Section 112 of this title if the description is as complete as is reasonably possible."[21]

[c] **Exclusive Rights—Infringement.** A plant patent confers "the right to exclude others from asexually reproducing the plant or selling or using the plant so reproduced."[22]

Comparable to a utility patent's three rights to exclude—making, using, and selling—a plant patent confers the right to exclude others from asexually reproducing, sale of an asexually reproduced plant, and use of an asexually reproduced plant.[23]

In patent law generally, "independent development" is not a defense, and one who without authority makes, uses or sells a product or process covered by another's patent infringes even if he did not directly or indirectly copy the patent's disclosures.[24] This may not be true of plant patent infringement: "It is quite possible that infringement of a plant patent would occur only if stock obtained from one of the patented plants is used, given the extreme unlikelihood that any other plant could actually infringe."[25] Infringement can still be innocent because "[a] direct infringer need not have knowledge of the patent or the source of the plant which is asexually reproduced, sold, or used."[26]

Because a plant patent covers the entire plant, one cannot commit direct infringement by using or selling fruit or flowers from an infringing plant.[27]

---

[21] 35 U.S.C. § 162.

In Diamond v. Chakrabarty, 447 U.S. 303, 311, 206 U.S.P.Q. 193 (1980), the Supreme Court noted that easing the written description requirement was a major reason Congress passed the Plant Patent Act: "Because new plants may differ from old only in color or perfume, differentiation by written description was often impossible."

The Court's description of the problem of describing new plant varieties is not fully accurate. The difficulty is not so much describing the new variety's characteristics as providing sufficient information to enable practitioners to reproduce the variety without direct access to the patentee's actual plant stock. Court decisions recognize that the plant inventor must "clearly and precisely describ[e] those characteristics which define the new variety." In re Greer, 484 F.2d 488, 491, 179 U.S.P.Q. 301 (CCPA 1973).

[22] 35 U.S.C. § 163.

[23] See Yoder Bros., Inc. v. California-Florida Plant Corp., 537 F.2d 1347, 1380, 193 U.S.P.Q. 264 (5th Cir. 1976), cert. denied, 429 U.S. 1094 (1977) (sale of immature cuttings infringes; "the act of asexual reproduction was complete at the time the cutting was taken . . . [C]ommission of one of those acts would constitute infringement.").

[24] See § 2F[3][b].

[25] Yoder Bros., Inc. v. California-Florida Plant Corp., 537 F.2d 1347, 1380, 193 U.S.P.Q. 264 (5th Cir. 1976). See D. Chisum, Patents § 1.05[1][d].

[26] D. Chisum, Patents § 1.05[1][d]. See also Kim Bros. v. Hagler, 167 F. Supp. 665, 668, 120 U.S.P.Q. 210 (S.D. Cal. 1958), aff'd, 276 F.2d 259, 125 U.S.P.Q. 44 (9th Cir. 1960).

[27] See Hayman, Botanical Plant Patent Law, 11 Cleveland-Marshall L. Rev. 430, 433 (1962).

Under some circumstances, sale of plant parts, fruit or flowers constitutes contributory infringement. See Armstrong Nurseries, Inc. v. Smith, 170 F. Supp. 519, 120 U.S.P.Q. 220 (E.D. Tex. 1958). For there to be contributory infringement, there must be an act of direct infringement, which may not occur if the whole plant is propagated outside the United States.

[2] Plant Variety Protection Act

In 1970, Congress enacted the Plant Variety Protection Act (PVPA), recognizing plant breeders' ability to produce seeds expressing stable genetic characteristics. It authorized patent-like protection to *sexually* reproduced plants in the form of plant variety protection certificates, which the Secretary of Agriculture, rather than the Patent and Trademark Office, issues. The PVPA's purpose is "to encourage the development of novel varieties of sexually reproduced plants and to make them available to the public, providing protection available to those who breed, develop, or discover them, and thereby promoting progress in agriculture." [28]

[a] **Requirements.** The PVPA covers seed-bearing plants but excludes fungi, bacteria,[29] and first generation hybrids.[30]

To be eligible for PVPA certification, the subject matter must be a "novel variety." The novelty requirement includes statutorily defined distinctiveness, uniformity, and stability criteria.[31] Patent law's nonobviousness requirement does not apply.[32]

---

[28] Pub. L. 91–577 (preamble).

See also Diamond v. Chakrabarty, 447 U.S. 303, 313, 206 U.S.P.Q. 193 (1980) ("sexually reproduced plants were not included under the 1930 Act because new varieties could not be reproduced true-to-type through seedlings. . . . By 1970, however, it was generally recognized that true-to-type reproduction was possible and that plant patent protection was therefore appropriate."); Public Varieties of Mississippi Inc. v. Sun Valley Seed Co. Inc., 734 F. Supp. 250, 14 U.S.P.Q.2d 2055 (N.D. Miss. 1990).

[29] Because both the Plant Patent Act and the PVPA exclude new bacteria, isolated from nature or genetically-altered, the utility patent statute is the only statutory protection source. *See* Diamond v. Chakrabarty, 447 U.S. 303, 206 U.S.P.Q. 193 (1980), discussed at § 2C[1][d].

[30] First generation hybrids are ineligible because they are inherently genetically unstable and are incapable of reproducing themselves with uniform characteristics.

[31] 7 U.S.C. § 2401(a). *See In re* John Walker, 40 Agric. Dec. 1017 (1981) (novelty requirement met if variety differs from known varieties by even a single distinct, uniform, and stable characteristic).

[32] In so doing, the PVPA considerably simplifies the protectability issue. A novelty-only standard for intellectual property eligibility is balanced by the relatively narrow scope of protection.

Is the PVPA's elimination of a nonobviousness-type standard constitutional? In the copyright and patent arenas, the Supreme Court indicates that there is a constitutional floor of innovation and creativity. Feist Publications v. Rural Telephone Service Co., 111 S. Ct. 1282, 18 U.S.P.Q.2d 1275 (1991); Graham v. John Deere Co., 383 U.S. 1, 148 U.S.P.Q. 459 (1966).

It may be pertinent that in enacting the PVPA, Congress evoked not only its Article I Patent-Copyright Clause powers but also its Article I power to regulate interstate and foreign commerce. *See* 7 U.S.C. § 2581:

> "It is the intent of Congress to provide the indicated protection for new varieties by exercise of any constitutional power needed for that end, so as to afford adequate encouragement for research, and for marketing when appropriate, to yield for the public the benefits of new varieties. Constitutional clauses 3 and 8 of article I, section 8 are both relied upon."

Other countries' nationals are eligible for plant variety certification protection only if a treaty applies[33] or reciprocity conditions are met.[34]

The PVPA contains statutory bar provisions similar to the utility patent statute. For example, certification is barred if, "more than one year before the effective filing date of the application therefor," the variety was "a public variety in this country."[35] It also includes a "first-to-breed" priority principle analogous to the patent system's first-to-invent principle.[36]

[b] **Application and Examination.** The new plant variety "owner"[37] may file an application for certification with the Department of Agriculture's Plant Variety Protection Office (PVPO) setting forth (1) the variety's name or temporary designation, (2) a description setting forth novelty, (3) the genealogy and breeding procedure if known, (4) a declaration that "a viable sample of basic seed necessary for propagation of the variety" will be deposited with a public repository and replenished periodically,[38] and (5) a statement of the basis of applicant's ownership.[39] The PVPO examines certification applications in a fashion comparable to PTO examination and issues a certificate if it determines that the variety meets statutory requirements.[40]

[c] **Exclusive Rights—Infringement.** The PVPA specifically defines a certificate owner's exclusive rights in the protected new variety and what constitutes infringement. Section 2483 confers rights to exclude others from selling, offering for sale, reproducing, importing, exporting, and using to produce hybrid or different varieties.[41] Section 2541 lists eight infringing acts.[42]

---

[33] The United States is a party to the International Union for the Protection of New Varieties of Plants (UPOV).

[34] 7 U.S.C. § 2403.

Patent protection is openly available to other countries' nationals.

[35] 7 U.S.C. § 2402(a)(1). The Act contains an analog of the experimental use exception. See § 2F[4][d]. It provides that a public variety does not include "use for the purpose of testing, or sale or use as individual plants not known to be sexually reproducible . . ." 7 U.S.C. § 2401[i].

[36] See 7 U.S.C. § 2401(d) (defining "date of determination" as "the date when there has been at least tentative determination that the variety has been sexually reproduced with recognized characteristics, whether or not the novelty of those characteristics has been determined"); § 2401(f) (defining "sexually reproduced"); § 2402 (priority and protectability based, in part, on "date of determination"); § 2502 (procedure for "priority contest").

For a discussion of the first-to-invent rule and patent interferences, see § 2D[5].

[37] "The owner is the breeder of the variety, but by statute a principal is considered to be the breeder where the relevant actions are by an agent on the principal's behalf." D. Chisum, Patents, § 1.05[2][c]. See 7 U.S.C. § 2401(e).

For employer-employee ownership rules with patents and copyrights, see §§ 2G[1] and 4G[2].

[38] The certificate may expire if the owner fails to comply with the replenishment requirement. 7 U.S.C. § 2483(c).

For a discussion of biological material deposits for utility patent purposes, see § 2D[3][a][vi].

[39] 7 U.S.C. §§ 2421, 2422.

[40] 7 U.S.C. § 2441.

[41] 7 U.S.C. § 2483.

[42] 7 U.S.C. § 2541.

The protection term expires 18 years after the certificate's issue date, but may be shortened if the certificate does not issue within three years from filing and the delay is attributable to the applicant.[43] Unlike patent owners, variety owners may recover for infringements occurring before the certificate issues but after distribution of the variety with notice.[44]

Section 2534 grants farmers a limited right to save and sell seeds.[45] Section 2544 provides a research exemption: "The use and reproduction of a protected variety for plant breeding or other bona fide research shall not constitute an infringement. . . ."[46]

The PVPA's infringement remedies are substantially the same as those for patent infringement.[47]

[3] Utility Patents for Plants

The PTO now recognizes that plant matter falls within the utility patent statute's subject matter definitions and that a new plant may receive a utility patent even though it is also eligible for protection under the plant patent or plant variety protection statutes.

In *Chakrabarty*,[48] the Supreme Court held that genetically-altered microorganisms, which are living organisms but fall outside the two plant statutes' coverage, were Section 101 patentable subject matter as "compositions of matter" or "manufactures." It rejected the PTO's argument that Congress intended the Plant Patent Act and the Plant Variety Protection Act to be the exclusive means for protecting living subject matter.

> "Prior to 1930, two factors were thought to remove plants from patent protection. The first was the belief that plants, even those artificially bred, were products of nature for purposes of the patent law . . . . The second . . . was the fact that plants were thought not amenable to the 'written description' requirement of the patent law.
>
> "In enacting the Plant Patent Act, Congress addressed both of these concerns. It explained at length its belief that the work of the plant breeder 'in aid of nature' was patentable invention . . . . And it relaxed the written description requirement in favor of 'a description . . . as complete as is reasonably possible.' . . . No Committee or Member of Congress, however, expressed the broader view . . . that the terms 'manufacture' or 'composition of matter' exclude living things. The sole support for that position . . . is found in the conclusionary statement of Secretary of Agriculture Hyde . . . that 'the patent laws . . . at the

---

[43] 7 U.S.C. § 2483(b).

[44] 7 U.S.C. §§ 2541, 2567. By using the notice, the owner obtains protection for more than 18 years. The owner must apply for a certificate within one year of public distribution. 7 U.S.C. § 2402(a)(1).

[45] 7 U.S.C. § 2543.

[46] 7 U.S.C. § 2544.

[47] 7 U.S.C. §§ 2561–2569. *See* § 2F[5].

[48] Diamond v. Chakrabarty, 447 U.S. 303, 206 U.S.P.Q. 193 (1980), discussed at § 2C[1][d].

present time are understood to cover only inventions or discoveries in the field of inanimate nature.' . . . Secretary Hyde's opinion, however, is not entitled to controlling weight. His views were solicited on the administration of the new law and not on the scope of patentable subject matter—an area beyond his competence. Moreover, there is language in the House and Senate Committee reports suggesting that to the extent Congress considered the matter it found the Secretary's dichotomy unpersuasive. The reports observe:

> 'There is a clear and logical distinction *between the discovery of a new variety of plant and of certain inanimate things,* such, for example, as a new and useful natural mineral. The mineral is created wholly by nature unassisted by man . . . . On the other hand, a plant discovery resulting from cultivation is unique, isolated, and is not repeated by nature, nor can it be reproduced by nature unaided by man . . .' . . . . (emphasis added).

"Congress thus recognized that the relevant distinction was not between living and inanimate things, but between products of nature, whether living or not, and human-made inventions. . . .

"Nor does the passage of the 1970 . . . Act support the Government's position. . . . As the Court of Customs and Patent Appeals suggested, [the exclusion of bacteria from plant variety protection] may simply reflect congressional agreement with the result reached by that court in deciding *In re* Arzberger, 112 F.2d 834 (1940), which held that bacteria were not plants for the purposes of the 1930 Act. Or it may reflect the fact that prior to 1970 the Patent Office had issued patents for bacteria under § 101. [Footnote 9: In 1873, the Patent Office granted Louis Pasteur a patent on 'yeast, free from organic germs or disease, as an article of manufacture.' And in 1967 and 1968, immediately prior to the passage of the Plant Variety Protection Act, that office granted two patents which . . . state claims for living micro-organisms . . .] "[49]

In *Hibberd*,[50] the PTO's Board of Patent Appeals and Interferences extended *Chakrabarty* to hold that plants, plant seeds, and plant tissue cultures constituted Section 101 patentable subject matter. The applicants developed technology for plants producing corn with increased tryptophan, which has greater nutritional value than ordinary corn. The applicants presented claims specifying the corresponding tryptophan content, including claims to: (1) maize seed, (2) a maize plant, (3) a maize tissue culture, (4) a hybrid seed, (5) a hybrid plant, (6) a method for producing a maize plant, and (7) a method for producing hybrid seed. The examiner rejected the maize seed, plant, and tissue culture claims on the ground that subject matter potentially protectable under either PVPA or the Plant Patent Act (PPA) was not eligible for Section 101 patent protection under the general ("utility") patent statute, 35 U.S.C. Section 101.[51] The examiner therefore rejected the first three types of claims

---

[49] 447 U.S.at 311–314.

[50] *Ex parte* Hibberd, 227 U.S.P.Q. 443 (PTO Bd. Pat. App. & Int'f 1985).

[51] The examiner also argued that Section 101 protection for plants would violate the International Union for the Protection of New Plant Varieties (UPOV) Article 2. The Board held that UPOV was an unratified executive agreement that could not override conflicting statutory law.

on the ground that the maize seed (1) claims and maize plant (2) claims were for subject matter protectable under the PVPA and the maize tissue culture (3) claims were for subject matter protectable under the PPA. The examiner allowed the hybrid seed, hybrid plant, and method claims because the two plant acts did not cover that subject matter.

The Board reversed the examiner's rejections (though it did enter a new ground for rejection based on deficiencies in the evidence as to the adequacy of a deposit of seeds made by the applicants with a public depository in order to comply with the enablement requirement). *Chakrabarty* confirmed that man-made life forms constituted patentable subject matter under Section 101 but did not deal with subject matter covered by the plant-specific statutes. The critical issue is one of statutory construction: did enactment of the plant-specific statutes in 1930 and 1970 narrow Section 101's scope? The statutes' legislative histories revealed no Congressional intent to narrow the plant statutes. The Board noted that "repeals by implication are not favored" and that "when there are two acts on the same subject, . . . the rule is to give effect to both unless there is such a 'positive repugnancy' or 'irreconcilable conflict' that the statutes cannot co-exist."[52]

The examiner noted five areas in which protection under the plant-specific statutes differs from that under the general patent statute:

"(1) the PVPA contains both research (experimental use) and farmer's crop exemptions, while Section 101 does not explicitly contain such exemptions;

"(2) the PVPA spells out infringement in great detail and includes a compulsory licensing provision, while no such congressional guidance exists under Section 101 protection;

"(3) the PVPA limits protection to a single variety, whereas the opportunity for greater and broader exclusionary rights exists under Section 101 protection;

"(4) under 35 U.S.C. 162 (PPA), the applicant is limited to one claim in formal terms to the plant described, whereas there is no such limitation on coverage under Section 101; and

"(5) under 35 U.S.C. 163 (PPA), the plant patent conveys the right to exclude others from asexually reproducing the plant, or selling or using the plant so produced."[53]

---

[52] 227 U.S.P.Q. at 445.

[53] 227 U.S.P.Q. at 446. There are other differences among the general patent statute, Plant Patent Act and Plant Variety Protection Act. For example, the nonobviousness standard applies to the two patent acts but not to the PVPA. The PVPA's protection term is 18 years from the issue date (as opposed to 17 years for patents) and can actually be shortened if there is undue delay in prosecution. Maintenance fees are due on utility patents but not plant patents. Under the PVPA (but not under the patent statutes), one may obtain protection before issue. Ownership rights may vary because the PVPA, unlike the patent acts, gives a principal intellectual property rights in his agent's creations. The patent statutes offer protection to inventors regardless of nationality; the PVPA is open to non-United States breeders only on a reciprocity basis.

The Board noted that these differences established only that the plant-specific statutes and the general patent statute differed in scope, not that there is any "irreconcilable conflict or positive repugnancy." "There is ample precedent that the availability of one form of statutory protection does not preclude (or irreconcilably conflict with) the availability of protection under another form." [54]

Hibberd does not address the problem of election—that is, whether one must elect one form of protection or may seek several forms of protection concurrently. If a person seeks both a utility patent and a plant patent for similar subject matter, the problem would presumably be handled by applying the double patenting doctrine, as is done with utility and design patents. [55] Multiple protection will be allowed provided the two patents do not claim identical subject matter and provided a terminal disclaimer is entered if the claimed subject matter of one patent would be obvious in view of the claimed subject matter of the other patent. If a person seeks both a utility patent and PVPA protection, the problem is more difficult. Is the appropriate analogy that between design patent protection and copyright [56] (where nothing equivalent to a terminal disclaimer is required)—or between multiple patents?

[4] Protection Source Choice Factors

In choosing among utility, plant, and PVPA protection for plant-related inventions, the utility patent option has several advantages. First, in a utility patent, the inventor may claim multiple plant parts, including plant genomes coding for nonplant proteins, cells and cell cultures, and plant tissue. The PVPA allows similar protection, but a plant patent covers only an entire plant.

Second, a utility patent may cover multiple varieties or an entire species or even genus if the applicant can show disclosure support sufficient to satisfy the enablement requirement.

Third, like a PVPA certification but unlike a plant patent, a utility patent protects against sexual as well as asexual reproduction.

Fourth, like a plant patent, a utility patent is not subject to the PVPA's specific farmers' surplus seed sale exemption.

The plant patent option eases the enabling disclosure requirement. The PVPA requires a seed stock deposit. Depending on the circumstances, an inventor may have to make a similar deposit to obtain a utility patent. Biological material

---

[54] 227 U.S.P.Q. at 446. The Board cited *In re* Yardley, 493 F.2d 1389, 181 U.S.P.Q. 331 (CCPA 1974). More fundamental is the Supreme Court's decision in Mazer v. Stein, 347 U.S. 201, 100 U.S.P.Q. 325 (1954), discussed at § 4C[3][a]. In *Mazer*, the Court rejected the argument that a design's eligibility for protection under the design patent statute precluded protection under copyright. The Court reasoned that the requirements for and scope of protection under design patent law and copyright law differed and that protection under copyright would not simply subvert limitations on design patent protection, such as the novelty requirement. *Yardley* addressed a separate issue—whether by electing to seek one form of protection a person surrenders the right to seek the other form.

[55] *See* § 2D[3][a][iv].

[56] *See In re* Yardley, 493 F.2d 1389, 181 U.S.P.Q. 331 (CCPA 1974).

deposits are expensive and may cause surrender of otherwise valuable proprietary advantages.

The PVPA certification option has the advantage that the nonobviousness patentability requirement need not be met.

§ 6D Semiconductor Chip Protection

[1] Introduction

The 1984 Semiconductor Chip Protection Act (SCPA)[1] established a special form of intellectual property protection for "masks" used to create semiconductor chips' electronic circuitry.[2] Semiconductors are used in computers and many other products, such as televisions, telephones, medical equipment, industrial control systems, machine tools, microwave ovens, and automobiles.

Congress enacted the SCPA because of concern that existing law did not adequately protect United States companies' huge investment in chip development and manufacture.[3] A single chip costing up to $100 million to develop could be copied for a fraction of that cost. Congress feared patent law did not adequately protect this investment because chip layouts, though time-consuming and costly to produce, usually lacked patentable novelty and nonobviousness over the prior art.[4] Copyright law was inadequate because it traditionally did not cover utilitarian items such as semiconductor chips, and any protection was limited to copying the chips' drawings, not the final chip product.[5]

Congress considered but rejected amending the Copyright Act to cover semiconductor chips[6] for two reasons: to maintain copyright law's "integrity"[7] and to avoid

---

[1] 17 U.S.C. § 901–914.

[2] The SCPA covers all mask works "first commercially exploited or . . . registered under this chapter, or both, on or after" its enactment date (November 8, 1984). 17 U.S.C. § 913(c). It also has limited retroactive application, covering chips exploited on or after July 1, 1983, provided the owner registered his protection claim before July 1, 1985, and subject to the right of others to import and distribute chips made before the enactment date on payment of a reasonable royalty. 17 U.S.C. § 913(d).

[3] H.R. Rep. No. 781, 98th Cong., 2d Sess. 2 (1984) [hereinafter "House Report"].

[4] *See* § 2C[4].

[5] House Report at 3–4, 8.

For discussions of the copyrightability of useful articles, depiction of useful articles, and computer programs, see §§ 4C[2] and [3].

[6] The Senate favored a copyright approach but acceded to the House of Representative's insistence on a *sui generis* approach.

[7] "[T]he formidable philosophical, constitutional, legal and technical problems associated with any attempt to place protection for mask works for semiconductor chip designs under the copyright law could be avoided entirely by creating a *sui generis* form of protection. . . . This new form of legal protection would avoid the possible distortion of the copyright law and would establish a more appropriate and efficacious form of protection for mask works. Rather than risk confusion and uncertainty in, and distortion of, existing copyright law as a result of attempting to modify fundamental copyright principles to suit the unusual nature of chip design, . . . a new body of statutory and decisional law should be developed." House Report at 10.

automatic extension of United States protection to foreign nationals' mask works under international copyright law's national treatment principle.[8] Instead, it created a new form of legal protection that borrows many copyright law concepts but also includes patent concepts and new concepts. The SCPA's purpose is "to protect semiconductor chip products in such a manner as to reward creativity, encourage innovation, research and investment in the semiconductor industry, prevent piracy, while at the same time protecting the public."[9]

The SCPA has an extensive legislative history that offers guidance on its interpretation, but there is only one court decision applying it.[10] Many issues remain unclear.

[2] Protection Requirements
[a] Definitions. The SCPA protects "mask works" "fixed" in a "semiconductor chip product."

It defines a "mask work" as:

"a series of related images, however fixed or encoded—

(A) having or representing the predetermined, three-dimensional pattern of metallic, insulating, or semiconductor material present or removed from the layers of a semiconductor chip product; and

(B) in which series the relation of the images to one another is that each image has the pattern of the surface of one form of the semiconductor chip product[.]"[11]

It defines a "semiconductor chip product" as:

"(A) having two or more layers of metallic, insulating, or semiconductor material, deposited or otherwise placed on, or etched away or otherwise removed from, a piece of semiconductor material in accordance with a predetermined pattern; and

(B) intended to perform electronic circuitry functions."[12]

A mask work is "fixed" in a semiconductor product when "its embodiment in the product is sufficiently permanent or stable to permit the mask work to be perceived or reproduced from the product for a period of more than transitory duration."[13]

The House Report explains that masks are the stencils used to etch an electronic circuit on a semiconductor chip.[14] A mask work is "the layout determination and

---

[8] "If the United States enacts copyright legislation to protect mask works, we would be required to give equivalent protection under the UCC [Universal Copyright Convention]; arguably we could stand thereafter alone in the obligation to protect works first published in UCC countries or created by UCC nationals. The United States could be required to protect, for example, the mask works of Japan, West Germany, and the Soviet Union, and receive no protection in return." House Report at 7.

[9] House Report at 1.

[10] Brooktree Corp. v. Advanced Micro Devices, Inc., 757 F. Supp. 1101 (S.D. Cal. 1990); Brooktree Corp. v. Advanced Micro Devices, Inc., 705 F. Supp. 491, 495 (S.D. Cal. 1988).

[11] 17 U.S.C. § 901(a)(2).

[12] 17 U.S.C. § 901(a)(1).

[13] 17 U.S.C. § 901(a)(3).

[14] House Report at 12–13.

the sum total of the individual masks, set upon each other, used to fabricate the entire chip."[15]

It emphasizes that the SCPA "is drafted flexibly so as not to freeze into place existing technologies," and is intended to cover new semiconductor manufacturing technologies.[16] Because the mask work definition covers a series of related images "however fixed or encoded," commentators suggest the definition is broad enough to cover the layout of the electronic circuit itself, and thus protects against circuit design copying by techniques that do not use masks to create the circuit design.[17]

[b] **Originality.** A mask work is not eligible for protection if it is not "original," or "consists of designs that are staple, commonplace, or familiar in the semiconductor industry, or variations of such designs, combined in a way that, considered as a whole, is not original."[18]

The SCPA's legislative history indicates that its originality standard is lower than patent law's nonobviousness requirement,[19] but the mask work must display "some minimum of creativity" to qualify for protection.[20] One commentator states that this creativity requirement is higher than the copyright law's *de minimis* originality standard.[21] The legislative history offers little specific guidance,[22] and no court has interpreted the standard.

[c] **Owner Nationality.** The SCPA encourages other countries to adopt similar legislation. A mask work qualifies for protection only if one of four alternative conditions is met. The first two alternatives are that the work is (1) first commercially exploited in the United States, or (2) owned by a national or domiciliary of the United States, a stateless person, or a national or domiciliary of a country that has signed a treaty protecting mask works to which the United States is a party.[23]

These alternatives currently have limited significance for non-United States mask work owners who ordinarily first exploit a mask work outside the United

---

[15] House Report at 13–14.

[16] House Report at 14.

[17] McManis, *International Protection for Semiconductor Chip Designs and the Standard of Judicial Review of Presidential Proclamations Issued Pursuant to the Semiconductor Chip Protection Act of 1984*, 22 Geo. Wash. J. Int'l L. & Econ. 331, 338 (1988); Note, *Semiconductor Protection: Foreign Response to a U.S. Initiative*, 25 Colum. J. Transnat'l L. 345, 360–61 (1987).

[18] 17 U.S.C. § 902(b).

[19] House Report at 19–20.

[20] House Report at 19.

[21] R. Stern, Semiconductor Chip Protection § 5.3(A)(1) (1986).

[22] A draft version of the SCPA defined an "original" mask work as "the independent creation of an author who did not copy it," adopting "the essence of the customary copyright law concept of originality and appl[ying] it to mask works, to the extent it is appropriate and feasible to do so." *See* House Report at 17.

[23] The SCPA defines an owner as the work's creator or the creator's legal representative or assignee except that a work created in the course of a person's employment is owned by the employer or the employer's assignee. 17 U.S.C. § 901(a)(6).

For a discussion of ownership of other intellectual property rights arising from employment, see §§ 2G[1] (patents), 3D[6] (trade secrets), 4G[2] (copyright), and 6C[2][b] (plant variety protection).

States.[24] The United States is not a party to the only treaty to date expressly relating to semiconductor chips, to which forty countries agreed in 1989.[25]

A third alternative is that a mask work may qualify for protection if the owner is a national of a country covered by a Presidential proclamation finding that the nation protects mask works of United States owners (a) on substantially the same basis as mask works of its own nationals; or (b) on substantially the same basis as the SCPA.[26] One might interpret the test's first part to mean that a country offering little or no protection to mask works could obtain a Presidential proclamation if it made the "protection" equally available to its nationals and United States nationals. This interpretation is not consistent with the SCPA's purpose, and United States government practice to date makes clear that it does not so interpret the statute.[27]

Finally, the SCPA authorizes the Secretary of Commerce to extend protection on an interim basis to countries making good faith progress towards entering a semiconductor protection treaty to which the United States is a party or adopting legislation complying with the SCPA's reciprocity requirements, provided that that country's nationals are not engaged in infringing activities and that the extension promotes the SCPA's purposes.[28]

A number of countries have adopted legislation similar to the SCPA, and the United States has extended interim protection to nineteen countries.[29] The United States has withheld full reciprocal protection because of concern about whether those countries offer substantially equivalent protection.[30] Congress extended Section 914's transitional authority twice, in 1988 and 1991.

---

[24] For the definition of commercial exploitation, see § 6D[3].

[25] Treaty on Intellectual Property in Respect of Integrated Circuits, World Intellectual Property Organization Doc. IPIC/DC 46 (adopted May 26, 1989).

The United States objected to this treaty because (1) it provides for broad compulsory licensing; (2) it does not adequately deal with importation and distribution of products containing infringing chips; (3) innocent infringers are not required to pay a reasonable royalty after receiving notice of protection; (4) protection is limited to eight rather than ten years; and (5) the dispute resolution procedure is too politicized as it involves the WIPO assembly. See U.S., Japan Refuse to Sign WIPO Treaty on Protection of Semiconductor Chips, 38 Pat. Trademark & Copyright J. (BNA) No. 933, at 123–24 (June 1, 1989).

[26] 17 U.S.C. § 902(a)(1)(C), (2).

[27] See, e.g., Erstling, The Semiconductor Chip Protection Act and Its Impact on the International Protection of Chip Designs, 15 Rutgers Comp. & Tech. L. J. 303, 312–13 (1989).

[28] 17 U.S.C. § 914(a).

[29] These are: Australia, Austria, Belgium, Canada, Denmark, Finland, France, Germany, Greece, Ireland, Italy, Japan, Luxembourg, the Netherlands, Portugal, Spain, Sweden, Switzerland, and the United Kingdom.

For a description of chip protection legislation in some of these countries, see Erstling, The Semiconductor Chip Protection Act and Its Impact on the International Protection of Chip Designs, 15 Rutgers Comp. & Tech. L. J. 303, 322–39 (1989); Note, Semiconductor Protection: Foreign Responses to a U.S. Initiative, 25 Colum. J. Transnat'l L. 357–71 (1987).

[30] Erstling, The Semiconductor Chip Protection Act and Its Impact on the International Protection of Chip Designs, 15 Rutgers Comp. & Tech. L. J. 303, 315, 319–20 (1989).

[3] Registration

A mask work owner must register the work with the Register of Copyrights (the Copyright Office) within two years of first commercially exploiting the work anywhere in the world.[31] The SCPA defines "commercially exploit" as "to distribute to the public for commercial purposes a semiconductor chip product embodying the mask work; except that such term includes an offer to sell or transfer a semiconductor chip product only when the offer is in writing and occurs after the mask work is fixed in the semiconductor chip product."[32] If the owner fails to register the work during this two-year grace period, protection terminates.[33]

The SCPA registration form is a simple one-page document that requests information about the work's title, the owner's name, address, and nationality, the date and nation of first commercial exploitation, and the method of acquisition of ownership. It provides two lines to describe "the new, original contribution in this mask work." The owner must also deposit certain identifying material with the Copyright Office.

If the Register approves the registration application, the owner receives a registration certificate, effective from the date the Register received the application.[34] The certificate is *prima facie* evidence of the facts stated in the certificate.[35] If the Register refuses registration or fails to act within four months, the owner may seek judicial review.[36]

Mask work registration procedure is similar to copyright in that the Office only examines the application information and conducts no prior art search.[37] As a result, the Register grants almost all registration requests.[38]

[4] Exclusive Rights—Infringement

[a] **Rights Granted.** The SCPA grants a protected mask owner:

---

[31] 17 U.S.C. § 908(a).

[32] 17 U.S.C. § 901(a)(5).

For a discussion of patent law's "on sale" and "public use" concepts, see § 2C[5][b].

[33] The owner receives protection during the two-year grace period even without timely registration.

[34] 17 U.S.C. § 908(e).

[35] 17 U.S.C. § 908(f).

For a discussion of the patent, trademark, and copyright validity presumptions, see §§ 2F[4][a][i], 4F[4][a] and 5F[2][a].

[36] 17 U.S.C. § 908(g).

[37] For a discussion of copyright registration and patent examination, see §§ 2D[1]and 4D[3][b].

[38] Copyright Office statistics indicate that, as of January 1, 1991, there were 6546 registrations and only 306 refusals. The reasons for refusal were as follows: Commercially exploited before 7/1/83: 33; Deposit incomplete on 7/1/85 deadline: 60; De minimis: 56; Not a semiconductor chip product: 55; Embodied in another claim: 4; Claim in circuit board: 17; Over two years since first commercial exploitation: 83.

The first two grounds pertain to the SCPA's transition provisions.

"[T]he exclusive rights to do and to authorize any of the following:

(1) reproduce the mask work by optical, electronic, or any other means;

(2) to import or distribute a semiconductor chip product in which the mask work is embodied; and

(3) to induce or knowingly to cause another person to do any of the acts described in paragraph (1) and (2)."[39]

These rights begin upon registration or commercial exploitation anywhere in the world, whichever occurs first, and end ten years after protection begins.[40] As noted above, protection terminates if the mask work is not registered within two years of commercial exploitation.

To "reproduce" a mask work or to "embody" a mask work in a chip means to copy the work. Two copyright-like concepts are implicit in the SCPA's structure if not explicit from its language. First, an infringing mask or chip must be substantially similar, though not identical,[41] to the protected mask work.[42] The SCPA's reverse engineering limitation[43] and its legislative history[44] recognize that a functionally equivalent but different design will not infringe.[45] The House Report indicates that the substantial similarity principles of copyright law as applied to fact and functional works[46] should provide guidance.

"Legal concepts used to establish infringement in copyright law—substantial similarity, ideas versus expression, and merger of idea and expression when

---

[39] 17 U.S.C. § 905.

[40] 17 U.S.C. § 904(a), (b). The protection term is actually slightly longer than 10 years because registrations run "to the end of the calendar year in which they would otherwise expire." 17 U.S.C. 904(c).

[41] The House Report recognizes that substantial similarity, not identity, is sufficient.

"Complete reproduction of a mask work is not required in order to constitute an infringement of the owner's exclusive right of reproduction. Unless a valid defense is presented, a judge or jury could find an infringement if the mask work embodied in the 'copied' semiconductor chip is substantially similar to the registered mask work. If this was otherwise, an infringer could immunize himself by adding a mistake to a mask work copied in its entirety. Difficult fact finding responsibilities are commonly assigned to Federal judges and juries in our justice system, and the Committee is confident that these individuals will successfully implement the judicial components of this Act." House Report at 20.

If the accused infringer establishes "reverse engineering," the infringement standard narrows to whether the the accused work is "original." See § 6D[2][b].

[42] For a discussion of substantial similarity of expression in copyright law, see § 4F[2].

[43] See § 6D[4][b][i].

[44] "If the mask work embodied in the alleged infringing chip is not substantially similar to the registered work, there could be no infringement. The second manufacturer is simply engaged in privileged, and socially valuable, free competition from which the public benefits." House Report at 26.

[45] See Brooktree Corp. v. Advanced Micro Devices, Inc., 705 F. Supp. 491, 495 (S.D. Cal. 1988), discussed at § 6D[4][b][i].

[46] See § 4F[2][a].

function dictates form—are all carried forward, insofar as applicable, to the new law for mask works. . . .

. . .

"While . . . the courts may usefully consider the copyright law precedents concerning substantial similarity, . . . [they] should have sufficient flexibility to develop a new body of law specifically applicable to semiconductor chip infringement. Moreover, the concept of 'substantial similarity' varies depending upon the nature of the work. Cases concerning fictional or imaginative works are not necessarily relevant to semiconductor chip infringement. . . . [T]he line of cases regarding infringement of fact-based works, compilations, and directories provides precedents more applicable to semiconductor chips."[47]

Second, an independently-produced chip design will not infringe a mask work right even though the second design is in fact substantially similar to the first protected work.[48] If the second chip's creator had no access to the protected design, directly or indirectly, there can be no infringement. The point may be academic because of the extreme improbability that a design meeting the SCPA's originality standard, which excludes standard industry designs, would be independently created by more than one person or company.

The House Report notes that special substantial similarity problems may arise with "cells," discrete functional portions of chips.[49] In *Brooktree*,[50] the alleged infringement related to two cells repeated many times that comprised about 30% of the total chip area. The mask work owner argued that the two cells comprised 80% of the chip's transistors and were "the heart and soul of the chip." Denying a preliminary injunction motion, the district court noted that the SCPA protects against both literal copying and "the misappropriation of a material portion of a mask work." At trial, the jury found infringement. The court refused to overturn the verdict, noting that a mask work owner "need not prove that every single layer, circuit and cell of the [accused] chip is similar to [the owner's] mask work."[51]

[b] **Limitations.** The SCPA provides four express limitations on exclusive rights: (1) reverse engineering; (2) the first sale doctrine; (3) innocent infringement; and (4) ideas, procedures, and principles.

[*i*] *Reverse Engineering.* It is not an infringement to reproduce a mask work for "teaching, analyzing, or evaluating the concepts or techniques embodied in the

---

[47] House Report at 26.

[48] For a discussion of copyright law's concept of independent creation, see § 4C[5][a]. In this respect, the Copyright Act and the SCPA different from patent law. *See* § 2F[3][b].

[49] "Mask works sometimes contain substantial areas of (so-called 'cells') whose layouts involve creativity and are commercially valuable. 51 [51 *For example,* the layout for a counter of an oscillator may be contained in a mask work along with many other 'cells' or other parts that together comprise the entire semiconductor chip product. Such a cell may be usable in other chips, and may be the subject of a 'cell library license.'] In appropriate fact settings, the misappropriation of such a cell—assuming it meets the originality standards of this chapter—could be the basis for an infringement action . . ." House Report at 26–27.

[50] Brooktree Corp. v. Advanced Micro Devices, Inc., 705 F. Supp. 491, 495 (S.D. Cal. 1988).

[51] 757 F. Supp. at 1095.

mask work or the circuitry, logic flow, or organization of components used in the mask work."[52] It is also not an infringement to incorporate the results of such analysis in another original mask work.[53]

The "reverse engineering"[54] exception endorses the existing industry practice of photographing and analyzing an existing chip to create chips with the same external specifications—"form, fit, and function" compatibility.[55] Congress found that this practice promotes fair competition and often provides a needed second source for chips.[56] The limitation permits reverse engineering, even when substantial parts of the first chip design are incorporated into the second design, provided the second design is itself original and not merely a copy of the first design.[57]

The House Report asserts that the reverse engineering limitation should not be difficult to apply, emphasizing that legitimate reverse engineering can be distinguished from mere piracy by the enormous "paper trail" of computer simulations, time records, and other documents showing the effort involved in analyzing the chip.[58]

Brooktree,[59] the one reported SCPA decision, shows that the reverse engineering limitation may not be as easy to apply as the House Report suggests. Brooktree developed chips that convert digital graphics image information to analog information at high frequencies for display on very high resolution computer video screens. It claimed that its chip captured a "niche market" previously dominated by Advanced Micro Devices (AMD), a much larger company, and that AMD in response copied its chips. Brooktree sued AMD for both mask work and patent infringement. AMD

---

[52] 17 U.S.C. § 906(a)(1).

[53] 17 U.S.C. § 906(b).

[54] The phrase "reverse engineering" does not appear in the statute but is in its title ("Limitation on exclusive rights: reverse engineering; first sale."). 17 U.S.C. § 906.

For a discussion of "reverse engineering" in trade secrets and copyright law, see §§ 3E[3] and 4C[2][d][iv].

[55] House Report at 21–22.

[56] House Report at 22.

[57] "It is the intent of the Committee to permit . . . the 'unauthorized' creation of a second mask work whose layout, in substantial part, is similar to the layout of the protected mask work—if the second mask work was the product of substantial study and analysis, and not the mere result of plagiarism accomplished without such study or analysis." House Report at 22.

See also "Explanatory Memorandum on Semiconductor Chip Protection Act of 1984—Senate Amendment to H.R. 6163, Title III, as Considered by the House of Representatives," 130 Cong. Rec. E4432 (daily ed. Oct. 10, 1984):

> "The end product of the reverse engineering process is not an infringement, and itself qualifies for protection under this Act, if it is an original mask work, as contrasted with a substantial copy. If the resulting semiconductor chip product is not substantially identical to the original, and its design involved significant toil and investment so that it is not a mere plagiarism, it does not infringe the original chip, even if the layout of the two chips is, in part, similar."

[58] "The Committee intends that the courts, in interpreting section 906(a), should place great weight on objective documentary evidence of this type." House Report at 21.

[59] Brooktree Corp. v. Advanced Micro Devices, Inc., 705 F. Supp. 491 (S.D. Cal. 1988).

argued that functional requirements dictated its design.[60] It also relied on a paper trail to show it spent more time and money than Brooktree. Brooktree responded that AMD's paper trail did not establish reverse engineering because it related mostly to work done before AMD was allegedly shown a copy of Brooktree's design.

The district court denied Brooktree's request for a preliminary injunction, finding that it failed to show a strong likelihood of overcoming AMD's reverse engineering defense, but at trial the jury rejected the defense and awarded $25 million in damages for mask work and patent infringement. AMD moved for judgment notwithstanding the verdict, arguing that as a matter of law (1) AMD produced its chip through reverse engineering and therefore did not infringe unless its chip was "substantially identical" to Brooktree's, and (2) AMD's design was not substantially identical. The district court denied AMD's motion, finding that a reasonable jury could reject the reverse engineering defense based on its evaluation of the conflicting evidence on whether AMD's analysis "was of the type contemplated by the Chip Act" and "whether the mask works were 'original.' " The court found it unnecessary "to reach AMD's further argument as to the test for infringement once a finding of 'reverse engineering' has been made."[61]

[ii] *First Sale.* The SCPA contains a first sale doctrine analogous to that of copyright and patent law.[62] An owner of "a particular semiconductor chip product" that is made by (1) the mask work owner, or (2) "any person authorized by the mask work owner" may "import, distribute or otherwise dispose of or use, but not reproduce, that particular semiconductor chip product" without the mask work owner's authority.[63]

---

[60] To rebut the functionality contention, Brooktree offered "two alternative designs developed by two separate individuals with limited knowledge of Brooktree's own layout." In its opinion denying Brooktree's preliminary injunction motion, the court discounted the alternative designs' significance.

> "[R]ather than prove that there are a wide variety of potential layouts, these two new layouts, at best, merely confuse the issue, and, at worst, confirm AMD's position that functionally there is little room for diversity.

> "The two new designs do not utilize the same donut and pyramid shapes that Brooktree refers to in describing its own layout, but they do have the same basic clusters of components as the original designs. Also, the two new layouts were admittedly developed in a matter of hours. It is possible that if these designs had undergone testing to determine whether they would perform in the desired manner, they would have been modified and eventually appear more similar to the original layouts." 705 F. Supp. at 495.

[61] 705 F. Supp. 1093. Brooktree argued, and the court apparently agreed, that there was sufficient evidence that AMD's design was not original because key portions of the design differed only in trivial respects from Brooktree's design. Brooktree's Opposition to AMD's Motion for Judgment Notwithstanding the Verdict, filed November 2, 1990, at 6–9.

[62] 17 U.S.C. § 906(b).

For a discussion of first sale in patent and copyright law, see §§ 2E[3] and 4E[3][c].

[63] 17 U.S.C. § 906(b).

> "As in the case of copyrighted products, the owner of a mask work has no right to try to exercise 'remote control' over the pricing or other business conduct of its

The first sale limitation's language confirms that it does not apply to reproduction; one purchasing a product lawfully embodying a mask work has no right to copy it except as the owner authorizes or the reverse engineering exception permits.

The SCPA first sale provision's language resolves the parallel importation (grey market) problem that plagues other intellectual property areas.[64] One who purchases abroad a chip made by the mask work owner's licensee may import the chip into the United States even if the mask owner attempts by contract to establish exclusive territories.

[iii] *Innocent Infringement.* The SCPA limits the liability of an "innocent purchaser," defined as "a person who purchases a semiconductor chip product in good faith and without having notice of protection with respect to the semiconductor chip product."[65] The innocent purchaser limitation protects not only persons directly purchasing chips but also those who purchase for resale items such as computers, televisions, and automobiles, that contain infringing chips.

An innocent purchaser has no liability for chips he resells before receiving notice of protection and is liable only for a reasonable royalty for products he resells after that date.[66] The innocent purchaser limitation extends to "any person who directly or indirectly purchases an infringing semiconductor chip product from an innocent purchaser."[67]

The innocent purchaser limitation applies only to products purchased before the purchaser receives notice of protection.[68] Once a company receives notice of protection, it can no longer be an innocent purchaser and will be liable in full for all products purchased after that date. The SCPA defines "notice of protection" as "having actual knowledge that, or reasonable grounds to believe that, a mask work is protected under this chapter."[69] Placing a mask work notice on products embodying the mask work is "prima facie evidence of notice of protection."[70] An infringing product, of course, is unlikely to bear a notice, and one who purchases it may never have seen a product legitimately embodying the mask work. A purchaser may be able to overcome the prima facie evidence of notice of protection by showing that it never saw the marked products and did not otherwise have reason to believe that the mask work was protected.

---

semiconductor chip customers, once the semiconductor chips have passed into their hands. Except where the Congress expressly orders otherwise, the exhaustion of any rights by the first authorized sale is a basic tenet of our intellectual property law. . . . Accordingly, the Act specifies that purchasers of semiconductor chips have the right to use and resell them freely (whether as chips or incorporated into other products which contain chips)." House Report at 23.

[64] *See* § 4E[3][b][vi].
[65] 17 U.S.C. § 901(a)(7).
[66] 17 U.S.C. § 907(a).
[67] 17 U.S.C. § 907(c).
[68] 17 U.S.C. § 907(d).
[69] 17 U.S.C. § 901(a)(8).
[70] 17 U.S.C. § 909(a).

The innocent purchaser limitation, like that on first sale, relates only to distribution and not to reproduction. An innocent purchaser who improperly reproduces a protected mask is subject to full liability even if the purchaser had no notice of protection.

[iv] *Ideas, Procedures, and Principles.* Mask work protection does not extend to "any idea, procedure, process, system, method of operation, concept, principle, or discovery, regardless of the form in which it is described, explained, illustrated or embodied in [the] work."[71] This limitation overlaps the reverse engineering defense. A mask work's ideas are not protected, and it is lawful to extract them by reverse engineering and incorporate them into an original mask work.

The idea limitation is also related to the SCPA's originality requirement.[72] A mask work is not eligible for protection if it consists merely of ideas and procedures, for example, reproduction of commonplace industry designs.

[c] **Infringement Actions.** The SCPA provides that "[e]xcept as otherwise provided in this chapter, any person who violates any of the exclusive rights of the owner of a mask work under this chapter, by conduct in or affecting commerce, shall be liable as an infringer of such rights."[73]

A mask work owner or his exclusive licensee may bring a federal court civil action or seek International Trade Commission relief against infringement.[74] As with the Copyright Act,[75] an owner may sue only if the Copyright Office has issued a registration certificate,[76] or, if the Office refuses registration, by serving notice of the action on the Register of Copyrights.[77]

The SCPA imposes a statute of limitations; an infringement action is barred "unless commenced within three years after the claim accrues."[78]

A person accused of infringement may assert as defenses the four SCPA limitations to the extent they apply. He may also assert other defenses similar to those of copyright and patent law. For example, he may argue that the registration is invalid because the mask work fails to meet the SCPA's protection requirements.[79]

---

[71] 17 U.S.C. § 902(c).

[72] *See* § 6D[2][b].

[73] 17 U.S.C. § 910(a).
The reference to "conduct in or affecting commerce" reflects the Congressional decision to base the SCPA on its constitutional authority to regulate commerce, as well as on its authority to protect the rights of patent and copyright holders. *See generally* Burchfiel, *The Constitutional Intellectual Property Power: Progress of Useful Arts and the Legal Protection of Semiconductor Technology,* 28 Santa Clara L. Rev. 473 (1988).
Congress made a similar decision with respect to the 1970 Plant Variety Protection Act. *See* § 6C[2][a].

[74] 17 U.S.C. § 910(b), (c).

[75] *See* § 4D[3][b].

[76] 17 U.S.C. § 910(b)(1).

[77] 17 U.S.C. § 910(b)(2). The Register may join the action but is not required to do so.

[78] 17 U.S.C. § 911(d).

[79] *See* § 6D[2]. As noted above, the registration is prima facie evidence that the registrant has met the SCPA's requirements. For a discussion of copyright law's validity presumption, see § 4F[4][a].

One commentator suggests that the courts will likely recognize patent and copyright defenses such as inequitable conduct in procurement and misuse.[80]

[d] Remedies

[i] *Injunctive Relief.* The SCPA authorizes federal courts to grant "temporary restraining orders, preliminary injunctions, and permanent injunctions on such terms as the court may deem reasonable to prevent or restrain infringement. . . . "[81] Ancillary to a preliminary injunction or temporary restraining order, the court may impound allegedly infringing semiconductor chip products, masks, and drawings.[82] It may order infringing products destroyed as part of a final judgment.[83]

The SCPA's general language suggests that usual preliminary injunction standards should apply.[84] In *Brooktree*,[85] the district court found that the mask owner failed to demonstrate a strong likelihood of success on the merits in light of the accused infringer's evidence that it engaged in legitimate reverse engineering or to demonstrate that a preliminary injunction was necessary to prevent irreparable harm that could not be compensated by monetary damages. The court rejected the mask owner's attempt to invoke the copyright law principle that infringement creates a presumption of irreparable harm, finding that the owner had not shown infringement. Applying an alternate preliminary injunction standard, it found that the owner raised serious question on the merits but failed to show that the balance of hardships tipped sharply in its favor.

[ii] *Damages—Attorney Fees.* The court "shall award [the mask work owner] actual damages suffered . . . as a result of the infringement" and "the infringer's profits that are attributable to the infringement and are not taken into account in computing the award of actual damages."[86] Alternatively, the owner may elect to recover statutory damages of up to $250,000 for "all infringements involved in the action, with respect to any one mask work for which any one infringer is liable individually, or for which any two or more infringers are liable jointly and severally."[87]

In *Brooktree*,[88] the jury awarded $25 million in damages for mask work and patent infringement. The district court held that prejudgment interest could be awarded only

---

[80] R. Stern, Semiconductor Chip Protection § 5.4 (1986).

See §§ 2F[4][b], 2F[4][c], 4F[4][b] and 4F[4][c].

[81] 17 U.S.C. § 911(a).

[82] 17 U.S.C. § 911(e)(1).

[83] 17 U.S.C. § 911(e)(2).

[84] For a discussion of preliminary injunction standards in patent infringement suits, see § 2F[5][a][i].

[85] Brooktree Corp. v. Advanced Micro Devices, Inc., 705 F. Supp. 491 (S.D. Cal. 1988).

[86] 17 U.S.C. § 911(b).

In establishing profits, the owner need only show the infringer's gross revenues, and "the infringer is required to prove his or her deductible expenses and the elements of profit attributable to factors other than the mask work." *Id.*

For a discussion of damages for patent, copyright, trademark infringement, see §§ 2F[5][b], 4F[5][c] and 5F[3][e].

[87] 17 U.S.C. § 911(c).

[88] Brooktree Corp. v. Advanced Micro Devices, Inc., 757 F. Supp. 1101 (S.D. Cal. 1990).

on the damage award's patent portion [89] and directed the mask owner to submit "data that clearly shows the allocation of damages between the patent and mask work claims." [90] The owner submitted a declaration segregating the damages.

In *Brooktree*, the infringer challenged the jury's award on the ground that it included losses incurred before the infringing chips appeared on the market. The owner countered by arguing that "it first lowered its prices in response to [the infringer's] aggressive marketing and pre-selling of its products." [91] The district court denied the infringer's new trial motion, noting that "the jury's determination finds support in the evidence presented." [92]

The SCPA grants a court discretion to "allow the recovery of full costs, including reasonable attorneys' fees, to the prevailing party." [93] The House Report states that this section is similar to Copyright Act Section 505. [94] In *Brooktree*, the prevailing mask work owner argued that attorney fees should generally be awarded to a prevailing owner, relying on copyright decisions. [95] The district court agreed that a SCPA attorney fee award "should be the rule rather than the exception" but declined to award fees because the suit involved complex and novel issues.

[*iii*]   *International Trade Commission Remedies.* As an alternative or addition to bringing a federal court infringement suit, a protected mask work owner may petition the International Trade Commission (ITC) to preclude importation of infringing products. ITC relief is available only if the petitioner's case meets ITC statutory requirements, including that there be imported products and the mask work relates to a domestic (United States) industry. [96] The ITC cannot award damages, but ITC actions offer mask work owners substantial advantages over district court infringement suits. An important advantage is that statutory deadlines require the ITC to render a decision promptly. ITC's rapid actions pressure accused infringers to settle on terms favorable to an intellectual property owner.

[5]   **The SCPA's Future**

Congress enacted the SCPA because in the early 1980's the semiconductor industry saw a substantial need for a new intellectual property form to protect chip design investments from inappropriate copying. Yet in an era of intellectual property litigiousness in the United States, there have been few SCPA infringements suit filings, and only one case litigated through trial.

---

[89] "[G]iven that the Chip Act itself is silent as to the award of prejudgment interest, this court should not imply an additional remedy without some indication in the statute or the legislative history." 757 F. Supp. at 1099.

For a discussion of prejudgment interest in patent and copyright cases, see §§ 2F[5][d], 4F.

[90] 757 F. Supp. at 1100.

[91] 757 F. Supp. at 1095.

[92] *Id.*

[93] 17 U.S.C. § 911(f).

[94] House Report at 28.

[95] *E.g.,* McCullough v. Albert E. Price, Inc., 823 F.2d 316, 322–23 (9th Cir. 1987).

[96] *See* § 2E[2][b][ii].

Marketing, economic, and technological changes since the early 1980's may account for the dearth of SCPA cases.[97] One of the fastest growing markets is for semi-custom chips, which are not economically attractive copying targets. Today, there are many different processes for using masks to create chips, many of which have trade secret or patent protection, and which must be used to reproduce particular chips. Computer-assisted chip mask design dramatically reduced the time for designing masks (from years to months or weeks, even days) and for reverse engineering chips to produce functionally equivalent chips.

The SCPA's future may depend on how the courts interpret the reverse engineering limitation. If they interpret it broadly to authorize everything but piracy or close copying, the SCPA will probably have minimal significance. If they interpret it narrowly, the SCPA may enjoy rejuvenation.

§ 6E   Section 43(a) False Advertising

[1]   Historical Development

Before the Lanham Act's passage in 1943, any false and misleading advertising claim was brought as a common law unfair competition or trade disparagement claim and was generally restricted to situations where defendant had "passed-off" its goods as those of the plaintiff.[1] In *American Washboard*,[2] the leading case articulating this limiting view, the sole manufacturer of aluminum washboards sought relief against a manufacturer who falsely advertised that its washboards were made from aluminum. In rejecting the claim, the court stated that "it is only where . . . deception induces the public to buy the goods as those of complainant that a private right of action arises."[3]

Later decisions expanded the common law false advertising unfair competition remedy in certain respects,[4] but *American Washboard* continued to limit false

---

[97] *See* Laurie, *The First Year's Experience under the Chip Protection Act or "Where Are the Pirates Now That We Need Them?"*, Computer Lawyer, February 1986, at 11, 20–21; Comment, *Five Years Without Infringement Litigation Under the Semiconductor Chip Protection Act: Unmasking the Spectre of Chip Piracy in an Era of Diverse and Incompatible Process Technologies*, 1990 Wis. L. Rev. 241.

[1] *See, e.g.,* Johnson & Johnson v. Carter-Wallace, Inc. 631 F.2d 186, 189, 208 U.S.P.Q. 169, 171–72 (2d Cir. 1980).
For a discussion of "passing off" and the origins of trademark and unfair competition law, see § 5B.

[2] American Washboard Co. v. Saginaw Manufacturing, 103 F. 281 (6th Cir. 1900).

[3] 103 F. at 284–85.

[4] In Ely-Norris Safe Co. v. Mosler Safe Co., 7 F.2d 603 (2d Cir. 1925), *rev'd,* 273 U.S. 132 (1927), Judge Learned Hand held that a plaintiff company could sue a defendant who falsely described his goods as having the same qualities as plaintiff's when plaintiff had a monopoly on the goods, thereby making it more certain that defendant's falsity caused plaintiff to lose customers. The Supreme Court granted certiorari to reconcile the conflict between *Eli-Norris Safe* and *American Washboard,* 268 U.S. 684 (1925), but instead reversed on a different ground.
See also American Philatelic Society v. Claibourne, 3 Cal. 2d 689, 46 P.2d 135 (1935); Motor Improvements, Inc. v. A.C. Spark Plug Co., 80 F.2d 385 (6th Cir. 1936), *cert. denied,* 298 U.S. 671 (1936).

advertising claims for more than fifty years.[5]

Commentators heralded Lanham Act Section 43(a) as a significant revision of the *American Washboard* doctrine,[6] but courts and practitioners were slow to recognize the breadth of Section 43(a)'s condemnation of "any false description or representation, including words or other symbols tending falsely to describe or represent . . . goods or services."[7] Ten years after its enactment, Judge Clark caustically noted "there is indication here and elsewhere that the bar has not yet realized the potential impact of this statutory provision."[8]

Modern Section 43(a) false advertising liability law began with *L'Aiglon Apparel.*[9] Plaintiff accused defendant of using a likeness of plaintiff's dress in advertisements for defendant's cheaper dress. The district court dismissed plaintiff's Section 43(a) claim because defendant used its own name and thus had not "passed-off" its goods as those of plaintiff. The allegedly false representation that defendant's cheaper dress looked like plaintiff's dress did not state a Section 43(a) claim. The appeals court reversed.

> "It seems to us that Congress has defined a statutory civil wrong of false representation of goods in commerce and has given a broad class of suitors injured or likely to be injured by such wrong the right to relief in the federal courts. This statutory tort is defined in language which differentiates it in some particulars from similar wrongs which have developed and have become defined in the judge made law of unfair competition."[10]

Over the subsequent decades, and particularly in the 1970s and 1980s, false advertising claims proliferated and encompassed new and different factual

---

[5] See California Apparel Creators v. Wieder of California, Inc., 162 F.2d 893, 74 U.S.P.Q. 221 (2d Cir. 1947), *cert. denied,* 332 U.S. 816, 75 U.S.P.Q. 365 (1947) (no relief for false advertising can be granted absent a showing of actual diversion of trade).

[6] *See, e.g.,* Robert, The New Trade-Mark Manual 186–88 (1947); Callmann, *The New Trade-Mark Act of July 5, 1946,* 46 Col. L. Rev. 929, 931 (1946).

[7] Lanham Act § 43(a), 15 U.S.C. § 1125(a).

[8] Maternally Yours, Inc. v. Your Maternity Shop, Inc., 234 F.2d 538, 546, 110 U.S.P.Q. 462, 468 (2d Cir. 1956) (Clark, J., concurring).

[9] L'Aiglon Apparel, Inc. v. Lana Lobell, Inc.,214 F.2d 649, 102 U.S.P.Q. 94 (3d Cir. 1954).

In an early Lanham Act case, the Ninth Circuit held that Section 44(b), 15 U.S.C. § 1126(b), embodied Congress' intent to create a new federal law of false advertising and other aspects of unfair competition, Pagliero v. Wallace China Co., 198 F.2d 339, 343, 95 U.S.P.Q. 45, 48 (9th Cir. 1952), but it later joined the majority of courts in holding that Section 43(a) is the proper location of such intent. Toho Co., Ltd. v. Sears, Roebuck & Co., 645 F.2d 788, 792, n.4, 210 U.S.P.Q. 547, 551 n.4 (9th Cir. 1981). *Cf.* Wallace International Silversmiths, Inc. v. Godinger Silver Art Co., Inc., 916 F.2d 76, 16 U.S.P.Q.2d 1555 (2d Cir. 1990).

[10] 214 F.2d at 651. The Third Circuit thereby aligned itself with the view that § 43(a) signified a new federal tort that was not limited to the common-law elements of pre-Lanham Act unfair competition claims. See S.C. Johnson & Son, Inc. v. Johnson, 175 F.2d 176, 178, 81 U.S.P.Q. 509, 511 (2d Cir. 1949) (Clark, J., dissenting), *cert. denied,* 338 U.S. 860, 83 U.S.P.Q. 543 (1949); Dad's Root Beer Co. v. Doc's Beverages, Inc., 193 F.2d 77, 80, 91 U.S.P.Q. 306, 309 (2d Cir. 1951).

situations,[11] but the *American Washboard* doctrine limiting false advertising claims to "passing-off" situations retained some force even as late as 1988.[12]

The Trademark Law Revision Act of 1988 (the "Revision Act")[13] precludes any argument that false advertising claims under Section 43(a) are limited to "passing off" situations by codifying the non-passing-off cases' primary substantive theories.[14]

The Revision Act forbids advertisements that falsely represent the nature, characteristics, or qualities of the advertiser's or another's goods or services.[15] It clarified the availability of certain remedies for false advertising claims[16] and confirmed that the statute includes pure disparagement claims in which a competitor's product is falsely described but no false claims are made about the defendants' product. The Act also confirms that the statute encompasses false claims that do not address an inherent quality or characteristic of the advertised product.[17] Left unresolved,

---

[11] *See, e.g.,* McNeilab Inc. v. American Home Products, Inc., 848 F.2d 34, 37, 6 U.S.P.Q.2d 2007, 2009 (2d Cir. 1988) (advertisements that deceive only a "not insubstantial fraction" of viewers); Allen v. National Video, Inc., 610 F. Supp. 612, 625, 226 U.S.P.Q. 483, 490-491 (S.D.N.Y. 1985) (misleading use of celebrity likeness); Gucci Shops, Inc. v. R.H. Macy & Co., 446 F. Supp. 838, 840 n. 4 (S.D.N.Y. 1977) (parody as actionable false and misleading statement); Zandelin v. Maxwell Bentley Mfg. Co., 197 F. Supp. 608, 612, 131 U.S.P.Q. 69, 71–72 (S.D.N.Y. 1961) (use of retouched photographs of competitor's product).

[12] *See, e.g.,* Clamp-All Corp. v. Cast Iron Soil Pipe Institute, 851 F.2d 478, 491, 7 U.S.P.Q.2d 1429, 1437–38 (1st Cir. 1988), *cert. denied,* 488 U.S. 1007 (1989) (relying on Sampson Crane Co. v. Union National Sales Inc., 87 F. Supp. 218, 83 U.S.P.Q. 507 (D. Mass. 1949), *aff'd,* 180 F.2d 896, 96 U.S.P.Q. 454 (1st Cir. 1950), to hold that Section 43(a) is limited to passing-off situations); Coca-Cola Co. v. Proctor & Gamble Co., 642 F. Supp. 936, 939 (S.D. Ohio 1986) (not citing *American Washboard,* but stating "Section 43(a) . . . applies only to merchandising practices equivalent to the misuse of trademarks and palming off of one's goods for another's"), *rev'd,* 822 F.2d 28, 31, 3 U.S.P.Q.2d 1364 (6th Cir. 1987) (Section 43(a) encompasses claims of false advertising as well as claims of passing off one's goods as those of another).

[13] Pub. L.. No. 100–667, 102 Stat. 3935 (1988); 15 U.S.C. § 1051–1127 (1989).

For a discussion of the 1988 Revision Act, see § 5D[2].

[14] The courts divide on whether the Revision Act applies retroactively. *Compare* Alpo Petfoods, Inc. v. Ralston Purina Co., 913 F.2d 958, 963–64 n.6, 16 U.S.P.Q.2d 1081, 1084–85 n.6 (D.C. Cir. 1990) (not retroactive) *with* U.S. Healthcare, Inc. v. Blue Cross of Greater Philadelphia, 898 F.2d 914, 922 n.9, 14 U.S.P.Q.2d 1257, 1261 n.9 (3d Cir. 1990), *cert. denied,* 111 S. Ct. 58 (1990) (retroactive).

[15] Lanham Act § 43(a)(1) and (2), 15 U.S.C. § 1125(a)(1) and (2).

[16] Lanham Act § 35, 15 U.S.C. § 1117. *See* § 5F[3].

[17] Lanham Act § 35, 15 U.S.C. § 1125(a)(2). Some courts had previously held that "[f]alse advertising or representations made by a defendant about a plaintiff's product are not covered by section 43(a)." Bernard Food Industries, Inc. v. Dietene Co., 415 F.2d 1279, 1283, 163 U.S.P.Q. 264, 266–67 (7th Cir. 1969), *cert. denied,* 397 U.S. 912, 164 U.S.P.Q. 481 (1970). *See also* Fur Information and Fashion Council, Inc. v. E.F. Timme & Son, Inc., 501 F.2d 1048, 1051, 183 U.S.P.Q. 129, 131 (2d Cir. 1974), *cert. denied,* 419 U.S. 1022, 183 U.S.P.Q. 641 (1974) (§ 43(a) "was intended to apply only to misrepresentations relating to the inherent qualities of defendant's own goods"); SSP Agricultural Equipment, Inc. v. Orchard-Rite Ltd., 592 F.2d 1096, 1103 n.6, 202 U.S.P.Q. 1, 7 n.6 (9th Cir. 1979); American Rockwool, Inc. v. Owens-Corning Fiberglas Corp., 640 F. Supp. 1411, 1440 (E.D.N.C. 1986).

however, was the controversy over whether consumers have standing to sue.[18]

[2] Overview

The Revision Act explicitly split Section 43(a) into two parts.[19] The first part pertains to false origin and provides a cause of action for infringement of unregistered trademarks and trade dress.[20] The second part forbids any "false or misleading description of fact, or false or misleading representation of fact, which . . . (2) in commercial advertising or promotion, misrepresents the nature, characteristics, qualities, or geographic origin of his or her or another person's goods, services, or commercial activities."

Advertising may be explicitly or implicitly false, and it may make a false claim or one that is merely unsubstantiated. Different burdens and types of proof may be required according to how the advertising is classified.

In addition to falsity, a plaintiff must prove that the challenged representations are "actually or likely deceptive, material in their effects on buying decisions, connected with interstate commerce, and actually or likely injurious to the plaintiff."[21] Intent to deceive is not a necessary element,[22] but proof of intent to deceive may be relevant to interpreting an advertisement and, specifically, whether a false claim was effectively communicated.[23]

Generally speaking, Section 43(a) does not impose a duty to disclose any particular facts in an advertisement. One version of the bill that became the 1988

---

[18] See § 6E[4][b].

[19] Section 43(a) provides:

"(a) Any person who, on or in connection with any goods or services, or any container for goods, uses in commerce any word, term, name, symbol, or device, or any combination thereof, or any false designation of origin, false or misleading description of fact, or false or misleading representation of fact, which—

(1) is likely to cause confusion, or to cause mistake, or to deceive as to the affiliation, connection, or association of such person with another person, or as to the origin, sponsorship, or approval of his or her goods, services, or commercial activities by another person, or

(2) in commercial advertising or promotion, misrepresents the nature, characteristics, qualities, or geographic origin of his or her or another person's goods, services, or commercial activities,

shall be liable in a civil action by any person who believes that he or she is or is likely to be damaged by such act." Lanham Act § 43(a), 15 U.S.C. § 1125(a).

[20] For a discussion of trade dress infringement, see § 5C[2][c][iv].

[21] Alpo Petfoods, Inc. v. Ralston Purina Co., 913 F.2d 958, 964, 16 U.S.P.Q.2d 1081, 1085 (D.C. Cir. 1990); U.S. Healthcare, Inc. v. Blue Cross of Greater Philadelphia, 898 F.2d 914, 922–23, 14 U.S.P.Q.2d 1257, 1262 (3d Cir. 1990), cert. denied, 111 S. Ct. 58 (1990).

[22] Johnson & Johnson v. Carter-Wallace, Inc., 631 F.2d 186, 189, 208 U.S.P.Q. 169, 172 (2d Cir. 1980).

[23] Alpo Petfoods, Inc. v. Ralston Purina Co., 720 F. Supp. 194, 211, 12 U.S.P.Q.2d 1178, 1192 (D.D.C. 1989), aff'd in part, rev'd in part, 913 F.2d 958, 16 U.S.P.Q.2d 1081 (D.C. Cir. 1990); McNeilab, Inc. v. American Home Products Corp., 501 F. Supp. 517, 530, 207 U.S.P.Q. 573, 584 (S.D.N.Y. 1980).

Revision Act would have added such a duty by making omissions of material information actionable in some circumstances, but the Senate Judiciary Committee deleted the addition because of "concerns that [such a provision] could be misread to require that all facts material to consumer's decision to purchase a product or service be contained in each advertisement."[24] The Committee feared making advertisements like a securities prospectus and decided to leave to the courts the task of deciding to what extent Section 43(a) may reach failures to disclose material information.[25]

"[I]t cannot be said that as conceived or enacted [Section 43(a)] was designed to make all failures to disclose actionable,"[26] but neither can it be said that courts have been indifferent to omissions of material facts when an advertising statement tends to be deceptive cithout critical disclosures.[27]

[3] Falsity

When an advertising statement "is literally or explicitly false, the court may grant relief without reference to the advertisement's impact on the buying public. . . . When the challenged advertisement is implicitly rather than explicitly false, its tendency to violate the Lanham Act by misleading, confusing or deceiving should be tested by public reaction."[28]

[a] **Explicit (Literal) Falsity.** The test of literal truth or falsity is not taken to a literal extreme. The court may engage in some degree of interpretation, as indicated in an appellate court's admonition that courts must avoid the " 'tyranny of literalness' " by applying the "principle that text must yield to context."[29]

---

[24] S. Rep. No. 100–515, 100th Cong., 2d Sess. 41 (1988).

[25] *Id.*

[26] Universal City Studios v. Sony Corp. of America, 429 F. Supp. 407, 410, 200 U.S.P.Q. 142, 145 (C.D. Calif. 1977).

[27] *See* Alpo Petfoods, Inc. v. Ralston Purina Co., 720 F. Supp. 194, 212, 12 U.S.P.Q.2d 1178, 1192 (D.D.C. 1989), *aff'd in part, rev'd in part,* 913 F.2d 958, 16 U.S.P.Q.2d 1081 (D.C. Cir. 1990) (Section 43(a) created cause of action against statement that are "untrue due to a failure to disclose information"); U-Haul International, Inc. v. Jartran, Inc., 601 F. Supp. 1140, 1147, 225 U.S.P.Q. 306, 309–10 (D. Ariz. 1984), *aff'd in relevant part,* 793 F.2d 1034, 230 U.S.P.Q. 343 (9th Cir. 1986) (failure to reveal that advertised prices did not include drop-off charges or were "special prices"); Tyco Industries, Inc. v. Lego Systems, Inc., 5 U.S.P.Q.2d 1023 (D.N.J. 1987), *aff'd,* 853 F.2d 921 (3d Cir. 1988), (unpublished), *cert. denied,* 488 U.S. 955 (1988); Performance Industries Inc. v. Koos Inc., 18 U.S.P.Q. 1767, 1771 (E.D. Pa. 1990) (statement that product is more "economical" held deceptive in context of representation as to coverage of product without disclosure of price difference).

One decision, Tambrands, Inc. v. Warner-Lambert Co., 673 F. Supp. 1190, 1193–94 (S.D.N.Y. 1987), may be interpreted to hold that the statement that a pregnancy test kit would give results "in as fast as 10 minutes" was false because of its failure to disclose that it was only a positive result that would come as fast as 10 minutes and that a negative result could not be confirmed until 30 minutes had passed.

[28] Coca-Cola Co. v. Tropicana Products, Inc., 690 F.2d 312, 317, 216 U.S.P.Q. 272, 275–76 (2d Cir. 1982).

[29] Avis Rent A Car System, Inc. Hertz Corp., 782 F.2d 381, 385, 228 U.S.P.Q. 849, 852 (2d Cir. 1986) (quoting United States v. Witkovich, 353 U.S. 194, 199 (1957)). In *Avis,* the

[b] Implicit Falsity

[i] *Evidence.* If an advertisement is not literally false, the plaintiff usually must introduce a survey showing that the relevant potential consumers give it a meaning that is false.[30] Courts caution that their "reaction is at best not determinative and at worst irrelevant. *The question in such cases is—'what does the person to whom the advertisement is addressed find to be the message?'* "[31] Such cautionary statements do not completely deter judges from coming to their own conclusions about an ambiguous statement's meaning. In the analgesic war between the manufacturers of "ADVIL" and "TYLENOL," the district court found that a literally true advertising claim gave a false impression even though it found both parties' survey results on the advertisement's meaning unreliable.[32] In a comparative razor blade advertising case, the district court determined that a claim that the Wilkinson Sword razor blade's lubricating strip is "six times smoother" than Gillette's was implicitly a claim about the shave's overall smoothness, not just about the strip itself. The court also used a combination of dictionary definitions and judicial notice of recent news events to construe a statement that Gillette's strips "melt down" as implying a dangerous condition.[33] One court noted that "although [its] own reaction to the advertisement is not determinative, it is obliged to judge for itself whether the evidence of record establishes that consumers are likely to be misled or confused."[34]

Surveys are not the only evidence that courts will look to in interpreting advertising language. Following the maxim that one may presume that a person communicated what was intended, courts look to evidence of the advertiser's intent. "[P]roof that the advertiser intended to communicate a false or misleading claim is evidence that that claim was communicated."[35] An intent to mislead may be found in the

---

court fondly quoted Judge Learned Hand's warning that " '[t]here is no surer way to misread any document than to read it literally.' " *Id.* (quoting Guiseppi v. Walling, 144 F.2d 608, 624 (2d Cir. 1944) (concurring opinion), *aff'd sub. nom.* Gemsco, Inc. v. Walling, 324 U.S. 244 (1945)).

[30] *E.g.,* Avis Rent A Car System, Inc. v. Hertz Corp., 782 F.2d 381, 385, 228 U.S.P.Q. 849, 852 (2d Cir. 1986); American Home Products Corp. v. Johnson & Johnson, 577 F.2d 160, 165, 198 U.S.P.Q. 132 (2d Cir. 1978).

[31] *Id.* at 165-66 (emphasis added) (quoting American Brands, Inc. v. R.J. Reynolds Tobacco Co., 413 F. Supp. 1352, 1356–57 (S.D.N.Y. 1976).

[32] American Home Products Corp. v. Johnson & Johnson, 654 F. Supp. 568, 583 (S.D.N.Y. 1987).

[33] Gillette Co. v. Wilkinson Sword, Inc., 89 Civ. 3586 (KMW) (S.D.N.Y. July 6, 1989), 1989 WL 82453, at 2, 4.

See also Tambrands, Inc. v. Warner-Lambert Co., 673 F. Supp. 1190, 1194 (S.D.N.Y. 1987) (advertisements held "facially false" because of what "they state by necessary implication"); Playskool, Inc. v. Product Development Group, Inc., 699 F. Supp. 1056, 1060, 9 U.S.P.Q.2d 1712, 1715 (E.D.N.Y. 1988) (false implicit safety claim).

[34] Upjohn Co. v. American Home Products Corp., 598 F. Supp. 550, 557, 225 U.S.P.Q. 109, 114 (S.D.N.Y. 1984). *See also* Playskool, Inc. v. Product Development Group, Inc., 699 F. Supp. 1056, 1059, 9 U.S.P.Q.2d 1712, 1714 (E.D. N.Y. 1988); McNeilab, Inc. v. American Home Products Corp., 501 F. Supp. 517, 525, 207 U.S.P.Q. 573, 580 (S.D.N.Y. 1980).

[35] McNeilab, Inc. v. American Home Products Corp., 501 F. Supp. 517, 530, 207 U.S.P.Q. 573, 584 (S.D.N.Y. 1980).

defendant's advertising strategy, as evidenced by its internal documents, its advertising agency's documents, and testimony concerning instructions to and intentions of the advertising's creators.[36]

Use of the dictionary as an interpretive tool has a checkered history. On the one hand is Judge Learned Hand's admonition in the context of statutory interpretation that "it is one of the surest indexes of a mature and developed jurisprudence not to make a fortress out of the dictionary."[37] On the other hand, one does not have to search far for instances where courts have relied on dictionary definitions to resolve disputes over an advertisement's meaning.[38]

In industries regulated by governmental agencies, the court may also use relevant regulations establishing standards for advertising statements or defining key words to interpret potentially ambiguous advertising statements.[39]

[ii] *The "Not Insubstantial Number of Potential Consumers" Confusion Test.* An advertisement is implicitly false if a "not insubstantial" number of potential consumers "receive a false or misleading impression from it."[40] The critical issues are what constitutes a "not insubstantial" number and how is that number proven.

The parties and courts discuss the "not insubstantial number" issue in terms of comparative percentages that surveys show,[41] but it is risky to draw conclusions from

---

[36] *See, e.g.*, Alpo Petfoods, Inc. v. Ralston Purina Co., 720 F. Supp. 194, 211, 12 U.S.P.Q.2d 1178, 1192 (D.D.C. 1989), *aff'd in part, rev'd in part*, 913 F.2d 958, 16 U.S.P.Q.2d 1081 (D.C. Cir. 1990); Eastern Air Lines, Inc. v. New York Air Lines, Inc., 559 F. Supp. 1270, 1279-80, 218 U.S.P.Q. 71, 79 (S.D.N.Y. 1983).

[37] Cabell v. Markham, 148 F.2d 737, 739 (2d Cir.), *aff'd*, 326 U.S. 404 (1945) (quoted in Avis Rent A Car System, Inc. Hertz Corp., 782 F.2d 381, 385, 228 U.S.P.Q. 849, 852 (2d Cir. 1986)).

[38] *E.g.*, Home Box Office v. Showtime/The Movie Channel, 665 F. Supp. 1079, 1084, 3 U.S.P.Q.2d 1806, 1809 (S.D.N.Y. 1987), *aff'd in part, vacated in part*, 832 F.2d 1311, 4 U.S.P.Q.2d 1789 (2d Cir. 1989); Thompson Medical Co., Inc., v. Ciba-Geigy Corp., 643 F. Supp. 1190, 1199–200 (S.D.N.Y. 1986); Toro Co. v. Textron, Inc., 499 F. Supp. 241, 252 (D. Del. 1980).

[39] Grove Fresh Distributors, Inc. v. Flavor Fresh Foods, Inc., 720 F. Supp. 714, 716 (N.D. Ill. 1989) (plaintiff may rely on an FDA regulation defining orange juice to support contention as to meaning of "100% orange juice from concentrate").

[40] McNeilab v. American Home Products, 501 F. Supp. 517, 528, 207 U.S.P.Q. 573, 582 (S.D.N.Y. 1980); R.J. Reynolds Tobacco Co. v. Loew's Theatres, Inc., 511 F. Supp. 867, 210 U.S.P.Q. 291 (S.D.N.Y. 1980) (over 25% of potential customers is "not insubstantial number of consumers.").

Cf. Coca-Cola Co. v. Tropicana Products, Inc., 690 F.2d 312, 216 U.S.P.Q. 272 (2d Cir. 1982) (evidence that a small number of potential consumers were clearly deceived is sufficient to meet the irreparable injury requirement for preliminary injunctive relief).

[41] The percentages of survey respondents perceiving a false message vary considerably. *See, e.g.*, Stiffel Co. v. Westwood Lighting Group, 658 F. Supp. 1103, 1114 (D.N.J. 1987) (surveys showing that "between 16% and 40% of the trade buyers" and "between 22% and 57% of the consuming public" would be misled were "not insubstantial"); R.J. Reynolds Tobacco Co. v. Loew's Theatres, Inc., 511 F. Supp. 867, 876, 210 U.S.P.Q. 291, 298 (S.D.N.Y. 1980) (perception of false message by 23% to 33% of those surveyed).

specific survey percentages.[42] First, as one district judge noted: "Conclusions about consumer deception in other comparable cases tend to be so fact-specific to those cases that they are of little aid in the case at bar."[43]

Second, the survey results noted in many cases, which indicate that X% of respondents answered a survey question indicating perception of a false message, are not theoretically sound. Survey experts point out that answers to survey questions may show "noise"—responses that reflect guessing or being influenced by the form of the question and that the noise should be eliminated to obtain a true estimate of the level of perception.[44] The problem is coming up with a sound estimate of the noise. One attempt to do so by constructing a control survey was thrown out because of flaws in the control survey.[45] In one trademark case, the court accepted an estimate of a five to six percent noise level in measuring consumer confusion; the estimate was based on a control survey that showed that five to six percent of the respondents made objectively wrong choices among options that did not require subjective assessment.[46]

[c] **Puffery.** Advertising "puffery"—variously described as opinionated, general, vague, or highly subjective statements—is not actionable. Case examples include statements that a collection agency entails "lower costs and superiority" over attorneys,[47] and that a product "represents the current state of the art, a definite advance over" its competition.[48] Courts dismiss as puffery claims using superlatives or

---

[42] For a discussion of surveys in trademark cases, see §§ 5C[3][a][vii](1), 5C[3][b][vi] and 5F[1][a][vii].

[43] Stiffel Co. v. Westwood Lighting Group, 658 F. Supp. 1103, 1114 n.5 (D.N.J. 1987).

[44] Recognition of the theory that "noise" should be taken into account may be found in American Home Products Corp. v. Johnson & Johnson, 654 F. Supp. 568, 581 (S.D.N.Y. 1987). The court ultimately discounted the survey entirely as unreliable and therefore did not resolve the issue of how to deal with the concept of noise. Similarly inconclusive is the court's mention of the noise factor in American Olean Tile Co. v. American Marazzi Tile Inc., 9 U.S.P.Q.2d 1145, 1149 (E.D. Pa. 1988).

[45] Weight Watchers International, Inc. v. Stouffer Corp., 744 F. Supp. 1259, 1274–76 (S.D.N.Y. 1990). In Quality Inns International, Inc. v. McDonald's Corp., 695 F. Supp. 198, 219, 8 U.S.P.Q.2d 1633, 1649 (D. Md. 1988), the court noted that both survey experts estimated that noise would not rise above "a few percentage points," but mentioned no methodology for the estimates.

[46] Clairol, Inc. v. Cosmair, Inc. 592 F. Supp. 811, 817, 224 U.S.P.Q. 229, 233–34 (S.D.N.Y. 1984).

[47] Cook, Perkiss & Liehe, Inc. v. Northern California Collection Service, Inc., 911 F.2d 242, 246, 15 U.S.P.Q.2d 1894, 1898 (9th Cir. 1990). *But see* Performance Industries Inc. v. Koos Inc., 18 U.S.P.Q.2d 1767, 1771 (E.D. Pa. 1990) (statement that product is more "economical" than competitor because one pound of it goes twice as far is not puffery when the product is eight times more expensive at retail).

[48] McNeilab, Inc. v. American Home Products Corp., 675 F. Supp. 819, 823, 6 U.S.P.Q.2d 2001, 2004 (S.D.N.Y. 1987), aff'd, 848 F.2d 34, 6 U.S.P.Q.2d 2007 (2d Cir. 1988). *See also* Gillette Co. v. Wilkinson Sword, Inc., 89 Civ. 3586 (KMW) (S.D.N.Y. July 6, 1989), 1989 WL 82453 (that razor was "major breakthrough" is at worst puffery).

general assertions of superiority,[49] but a superiority claim is not mere puffery if it purports to rest on test results that are not substantiated.[50]

Courts excuse puffery because it is "an expression of opinion and not a representation of fact,"[51] vague and general rather than specific, and not by its nature something on which a reasonable consumer relies.[52]

[d] **False Substantiation Claims.** It is generally considered well settled that an advertising claim does not violate the Lanham Act simply because the proponent of the claim cannot substantiate its truth. The plaintiff bears the burden of proving falsity.[53] Only if the advertisement itself refers to or relies on substantiation, or if it is shown that the consuming public perceives the advertisement as substantiated would the absence of reliable substantiation make the advertisement false or misleading. "A product claim is false under the Lanham Act if the representation cites tests or other authority that does not substantiate the claim made; that is if the false substantiation is part of the representation."[54] Substantiation developed after the claim was made is irrelevant.[55]

---

[49] Transgo, Inc. v. Ajac Transmission Parts Corp., 768 F.2d 1001, 1029, 227 U.S.P.Q. 598, 614 (9th Cir. 1985), *cert. denied,* 474 U.S. 1059 (1986); Radio Today, Inc. v. Westwood One, Inc., 684 F. Supp. 68, 74 (S.D.N.Y. 1988) (statement of comparability or superiority is puffing; statement as to who was the creative force behind radio program is not); Main Street Publishers, Inc. v. Landmark Communications, Inc. 701 F. Supp. 1289 (N.D. Miss. 1988).

[50] Stiffel Co. v. Westwood Lighting Group, 658 F. Supp. 1103, 1115 (D.N.J. 1987).

[51] Radio Today, Inc. v. Westwood One, Inc., 684 F. Supp. 68, 74 (S.D.N.Y. 1988); *see also* Manufacturing Research Corp. v. Greenlee Tool Co., 693 F.2d 1037, 1040 (11th Cir. 1982).

[52] Cook, Perkiss & Liehe, Inc. v. Northern California Collection Service, Inc., 911 F.2d at 246, 15 U.S.P.Q.2d at 1897; U.S. Healthcare, Inc. v. Blue Cross of Greater Philadelphia, 898 F.2d 914, 922, 14 U.S.P.Q.2d 1257, 1262 (3d Cir.), *cert. denied,* 111 S. Ct. 58 (1990). Bose Corp. v. Linear Design Labs, Inc. 467 F.2d 304, 310–11, 172 U.S.P.Q. 385, 390-91 (2d Cir. 1972), illustrates the distinction between nonactionable general product superiority statements, characterized as puffery, and actionable specific product performance statements.

[53] U.S. Healthcare, Inc. v. Blue Cross of Greater Philadelphia, 898 F.2d 914, 922, 14 U.S.P.Q.2d 1257 (3d Cir. 1990), *cert. denied,* 111 S. Ct. 58 (1990); Sandoz Pharmaceuticals Corp. v. Richardson-Vicks, Inc., 902 F.2d 222, 229 (3d Cir. 1990); Procter & Gamble Co. v. Cheseborough-Pond's, Inc., 747 F.2d 114, 119, 224 U.S.P.Q. 344, 348 (2d Cir. 1984).

[54] Alpo Petfoods, Inc. v. Ralston Purina Co., 720 F. Supp. 194, 213, 12 U.S.P.Q.2d 1178, 1194 (D.D.C. 1989), *aff'd in part, rev'd in part on other grounds,* 913 F.2d 958, 16 U.S.P.Q.2d 1081 (D.C. Cir. 1990). *See also* Sandoz Pharmaceuticals Corp. v. Richardson-Vicks, Inc., 902 F.2d 222, 229 (3d Cir. 1990) ("a plaintiff must produce consumer surveys or some surrogate therefor to prove whether consumers expect an advertising claim to be substantiated and whether they expect the level of substantiation to be greater than that which the defendant has performed"); Procter & Gamble Co. v. Cheseborough-Pond's, Inc., 747 F.2d 114, 119, 224 U.S.P.Q. 344, 348 (2d Cir. 1984).

[55] Alpo Petfoods, Inc. v. Ralston Purina Co., 720 F. Supp. 194, 205 n.12, 12 U.S.P.Q.2d 1178, 1187–88 n.12 (D.D.C. 1989), *aff'd in pertinent part, rev'd in part,* 913 F.2d 958, 16 U.S.P.Q.2d 1081 (D.C. Cir. 1990); Sandoz Pharmaceuticals Corp. v. Richardson-Vicks, Inc., 902 F.2d 222, 229 (3d Cir. 1990); Hobart Corp. v. Welbilt Corp., 89 Civ. 1726, 1989 U.S. Dist. LEXIS 14447 (N.D. Ohio 1989).

The general distinction between the usual false advertising claim and a false substantiation claim is shown in *Gillette*, [56] where three advertising representations were at issue: (1) that Wilkinson's "Ultra Glide" razor provided a shave "six times smoother" than that of Gillette's "Atra Plus" blade, (2) that "in a recent test, men preferred Ultra Glide to Gillette," and (3) "recent consumer testing indicated that 8 out of 10 Atra/Atra Plus consumers would definitely or probably buy Ultra Glide." The court found representation (2) adequately substantiated but enjoined representation (3) because the defendant admitted it had no substantiation. It found that representation (1) was not a substantiation claim and did not enjoin it even though substantiation was inadequate because the plaintiff failed to prove it false. [57]

To prove lack of substantiation, the plaintiff bears the burden to show "that the tests referred to by [the defendant] were not sufficiently reliable to permit one to conclude with reasonable certainty that they established the proposition for which they were cited. The fact-finder's judgment should consider all relevant circumstances, including the state of the testing art, the existence and feasibility of superior procedures, the objectivity and skill of the persons conducting the tests, the accuracy of their reports, and the results of other pertinent tests." [58]

In *McNeil*, [59] the Second Circuit appeared to question the above distinction. The advertisment at issue proclaimed that " 'in doctor supervised clinical studies . . . [AF] Excedrin was shown to provide greater headache relief' than ES Tylenol." There was also a consumer advertisement that did not refer to clinical studies or otherwise claim substantiation. In the district court, the case was tried as one of false substantiation. Plaintiff did not create its own clinical studies but produced expert witnesses who refuted the defendant's studies and reinterpreted part of the data from one study to show that there was "no significant statistical difference between AF Excedrin and ES Tylenol in relieving headache pain." [60] The district court ruled that reanalysis of the data "satisfied [McNeil's] burden of proving the falsity of Bristol-Myers' superiority claim." [61] The appellate court affirmed that finding and noted "even if the tests were not directly referred to in connection with Bristol-Myers' superiority claim, McNeil still could have relied on and analyzed data generated by Bristol-Myers as scientific proof that the challenged advertisement was false." [62] That note was not unusual, but the court arguably went further. In rejecting Bristol-Myers' argument that McNeil could prevail only by conducting its own studies, it stated:

---

[56] Gillette Co. v. Wilkinson Sword, Inc., 89 Civ. 3586 (KMW), 1989 WL 82453 (S.D. N.Y. 1989).

[57] *Id.* at 1–3.

[58] Procter & Gamble Co. v. Cheseborough-Pond's, Inc., 747 F.2d 114, 119, 224 U.S.P.Q. 344 (2d Cir. 1984). *See also* Upjohn Co. v. Riahom Corp. 641 F. Supp. 1209, 1224, 1 U.S.P.Q.2d 1433, 1443 (D. Del. 1986); Ciba-Geigy Corp. v. Thompson Medical Co., 672 F. Supp. 679, 686 (S.D.N.Y. 1985).

[59] McNeil-P.C.C., Inc. v. Bristol-Myers Squibb Co., 938 F.2d 1544, 19 U.S.P.Q.2d 1525 (2d Cir. 1991).

[60] 938 F.2d at 1548.

[61] 938 F.2d at 1548.

[62] 938 F.2d at 1549.

> "Bristol-Myers' claim was part of a comprehensive advertising campaign
> directly comparing the efficacy of AF Excedrin and ES Tylenol. As Bristol-
> Myers' initial trade advertising made plain, the 'works better' claim was bot-
> tomed on the results of the AF Excedrin studies. *McNeil could therefore meet
> its burden of proof by demonstrating that these studies did not establish that
> AF Excedrin provided superior pain relief.*"[63]

The emphasized sentence leaves tantalizingly open the possibility that a plaintiff could,
in certain circumstances, prove a false advertising claim by showing that it was not
substantiated even when the advertisement itself did not purport to rely on substantiation.

That the appeals court did not intend to make new law is suggested by its citation
of *Procter & Gamble*. Therefore, the statement may well be ignored or disowned in
future cases. It could also be limited to either of two exceptional situations present in *McNeil*: cases involving pharmaceuticals, which generally implicate heightened
public safety concerns; or situations where at least one part of a comprehensive
advertising campaign does in fact rely on faulty substantiation. On the other
hand, the statement could be developed to hold advertisers to a higher standard than
previously required.

[4]　Standing

[a]　**Injury.** Section 43(a) authorizes actions by anyone "who believes that he is
or is likely to be damaged" by the allegedly false advertising.[64]

If an advertisement falsely represents the defendants' own product but makes no
direct reference to any competitor's product, courts require a plaintiff to show actual
injury and causation and disallow claims based purely on speculative damage.[65] "The
injury . . . accrues equally to all competitors; none is more likely to suffer from the
offending [advertisement] than any other."[66] A plaintiff must prove a reasonable basis
for believing it is likely to be damaged as a result of the false advertising.[67] A
reasonable basis is more than a "mere subjective belief," but the plaintiff need not
establish a specific quantity of damage: "What matters is whether a commercial party
has a 'reasonable interest to be protected' against the alleged false advertising."[68]

---

[63] 938 F.2d at 1549 (emphasis added).

[64] Lanham Act § 43(a), 15 U.S.C. § 1125(a).

[65] Coca-Cola Co. v. Tropicana Products, Inc., 690 F.2d 312, 316, 216 U.S.P.Q. 272 (2d Cir.
1982); Johnson & Johnson v. Carter-Wallace, Inc. 631 F.2d 186, 189–90, 208 U.S.P.Q. 169,
172–73 (2d Cir. 1980).

[66] McNeilab, Inc. v. American Home Products Corp., 848 F.2d 34, 38, 6 U.S.P.Q.2d 2007,
2010 (2d Cir. 1988).

[67] Johnson & Johnson v. Carter-Wallace, Inc., 631 F.2d 186, 190, 208 U.S.P.Q. 169, 173
(2d Cir. 1980).

[68] National Association of Pharmaceutical Manufacturers, Inc. v. Ayerst Laboratories, 850
F.2d 904, 914, 7 U.S.P.Q.2d 1530, 1538 (2d Cir. 1988) (quoting PPX Enters. v. Audiofidelity,
Inc., 746 F.2d 120, 125, 224 U.S.P.Q. 340, 343 (2d Cir. 1984)).

In Hertz Corp. v. Avis, Inc., 725 F. Supp. 170 (S.D.N.Y. 1989), the court held that an
advertisement in a trade publication that falsely claimed one car rental company paid commissions to travel agents faster did not meet Section 43(a) requirements because there was no

Courts presume injury if the advertisement makes a false comparison between the advertiser's and the plaintiff's products.[69]

[b] **Consumers.** Courts divide over whether consumers have standing to bring Section 43(a) false advertising claims. In *Colligan*,[70] the Second Circuit held that consumers do not have standing. The Ninth and Third Circuits rejected that interpretation as without statutory basis.[71] During deliberations on the 1988 Revision Act, the House Judiciary Committee recommended that Congress resolve this split in favor of according consumers such standing, but Congress did not adopt the recommendation.[72]

Even if consumers have standing, such claims are unlikely to be brought because of the small amount of individual damage unless they can be pursued as class actions. Recent cases hold that consumer false advertising claims cannot proceed as class actions because individualized proof of exposure to and reliance on the false advertisement would be necessary.[73]

[5] **Responsible Parties**

Section 43(a) false advertising claims are most frequently brought against the the falsely advertised product's manufacturer or marketer. Claims may also be brought against any person or entity allegedly responsible for the false advertising. Advertising agencies are frequently joined as co-defendants.[74] One case held that a

---

proof that the advertising ever reached the consuming public. This rationale unduly restricts the nature of the "reasonable interest" protected against false claims by Section 43(a). The decision was vacated and dismissed after the case was settled. Hertz v. Avis, 732 F. Supp. 26 (S.D.N.Y. 1990).

[69] McNeilab, Inc. v. American Home Products Corp., 848 F.2d 34, 38, 6 U.S.P.Q.2d 2007, 2010 (2d Cir. 1988); U-Haul Int'l v. Jartran, Inc., 793 F.2d 1034, 1040-41, 230 U.S.P.Q. 343, 348 (9th Cir. 1986) (deliberately false comparative advertising gives rise to a rebuttable presumption of injury).

[70] Colligan v. Activities Club of New York, Ltd., 442 F.2d 686, 170 U.S.P.Q. 113 (2d Cir. 1971), *cert. denied*, 404 U.S. 1004, 172 U.S.P.Q. 97 (1971).

[71] Thorn v. Reliance Van Company, Inc., 736 F.2d 929, 932 n.5, 222 U.S.P.Q. 775, 778 n.5 (3d Cir. 1984); Smith v. Montoro, 648 F.2d 602, 608, 211 U.S.P.Q. 775, 781–82 (9th Cir. 1981).

[72] H.R. Report 100–1028, 100th Cong., 2d Sess. 33 ("any person, *including a consumer,* who believes that he is or is likely to be damaged by the use of any such false description or representation" could bring suit).

[73] Strain v. Nutri/System, Inc., No. 90–2772, 1990 WL 209325 (E.D. Pa. 1990); Rosenstein v. CPC International, No. 90–4970, 1991 WL 1783 (E.D. Pa. 1991).

The above cases also presented RICO claims, an increasing phenomenon in false advertising litigation. *But see* Savastano v. Thompson Medical Co., 640 F. Supp. 1081 (S.D.N.Y. 1986); R.R. Brittingham v. Mobil Corp., No. 90–3998, 1990 WL 275819 (E.D. Pa. 1990) (dismissing RICO claims in false advertising cases).

[74] *See, e.g.,* Maybelline Co. v. Noxell Corp. and SSC&B: Lintas Worldwide, 813 F.2d 901, 2 U.S.P.Q.2d 1126 (8th Cir. 1987); Tambrands, Inc. v. Warner-Lambert Co., 673 F. Supp. 1190 (S.D.N.Y. 1987).

non-profit research firm whose work formed the basis of a false comparative advertisement could be held liable.[75]

The Revision Act added a provision protecting publishers and broadcasters from liability unless the plaintiff proves actual malice.[76]

[6] Use of Another's Trademark in Advertising

Using another's trademark in advertising does not violate the Lanham Act as long as the advertisement does not create a likelihood that the public will be confused as to the source, sponsorship, or approval of the product advertised and the comparative statement itself is not false or misleading.[77] "The free flow of information regarding the substitutability of products is valuable to individual consumers and to society collectively, and by providing it a supplier engages in fair competition based on those aspects—for example, price—in which the products differ."[78]

Use of a non-competitor's mark in advertising, for example, quoting a review or evaluation, may give rise to a false sponsorship claim.[79] In *Consumers Union,*[80] a magazine that evaluates products tried to prevent its name from being used in an advertisement for a product that it had generally praised. The court rejected as a factual matter Consumers Union's claim that the advertisement misleadingly conveyed that it sponsored or endorsed the product but held the claim to be theoretically sound: "In addition to prohibiting false representations, Section 43(a) of the Lanham Act also proscribes advertisements which are not technically false, but which lead to a mistaken public belief that 'the mark's owner sponsored or otherwise approved the use.' "[81]

---

[75] Grant Airmass Corp. v. Gaymar Industries, Inc., 645 F. Supp. 1507 (S.D.N.Y. 1986). The Revision Act's amendment of Section 43(a) to explicitly refer to "promotional activities" may increase the likelihood that defendants other than advertising agencies and manufacturers will face false advertising claims.

[76] Lanham Act § 32, 15 U.S.C. § 1114 (as amended).

[77] *E.g.,* Home Box Office, Inc. v. Showtime/The Movie Channel Inc., 832 F.2d 1311, 4 U.S.P.Q.2d 1789 (2d Cir. 1987); Calvin Klein Cosmetics Corp. v. Parfums de Coeur, Ltd., 824 F.2d 665, 668, 3 U.S.P.Q.2d 1498, 1500-1501 (8th Cir. 1987); G.D. Searle & Co. v. Hudson Pharmaceutical Corp., 715 F.2d 837, 841, 220 U.S.P.Q. 496, 500 (3d Cir. 1983); SSP Agricultural Equipment, Inc. v. Orchard-Rite, Ltd., 592 F.2d 1096, 1103, 202 U.S.P.Q. 1, 6-7 (9th Cir. 1979); Weight Watchers International, Inc. v. Stouffer Corp., 744 F. Supp. 1259, 1269 (S.D.N.Y. 1990); Playskool, Inc. v. Product Development Group, Inc., 699 F. Supp. 1056, 1060–61, 9 U.S.P.Q.2d 1712, 1715–16 (E.D.N.Y. 1988).

[78] American Home Products Corp. v. Barr Laboratories Inc., 656 F. Supp. 1058, 1068, 3 U.S.P.Q.2d 1194, 1202 (D. N.J.), *aff'd,* 834 F.2d 368, 5 U.S.P.Q.2d 1073 (3d Cir. 1987). Accord Weight Watchers International, Inc. v. Stouffer Corp., 744 F. Supp. 1259, 1269, 1277 (S.D. N.Y. 1990).

[79] *See* § 5F[1][d].

[80] Consumers Union of United States, Inc. v. General Signal Corp., 724 F.2d 1044, 221 U.S.P.Q. 400 (2d Cir. 1983), *cert. denied,* 469 U.S. 823, 224 U.S.P.Q. 616 (1984).

[81] 724 F.2d at 1052 (quoting Dallas Cowboys Cheerleaders, Inc. v. Pussycat Cinema, Ltd. 604 F.2d 200, 205, 203 U.S.P.Q. 161, 164 (2d Cir. 1979)).

(Matthew Bender & Co., Inc.)

More frequently litigated are false comparison claims, where a competitor contends that its own product is a "copy of" or is "like" the better known product.[82]

[7] Celebrity Identity

Unauthorized advertising use of a celebrity's likeness may violate state statutory or common law publicity rights.[83] It may also violate Lanham Act Section 43(a) if it falsely implies that the celebrity endorses the advertised product.[84] When an advertisement uses a celebrity "lookalike" instead of an actual photograph or other likeness, the plaintiff must show that the public is likely to confuse the lookalike with the genuine commodity.

[8] Moral Rights

Moral rights, such as the paternity (attribution) right and the integrity right, are generally analyzed as an adjunct to copyright.[85] Section 43(a) has enjoyed some limited success in recognizing a right equivalent to the paternity moral right. Courts apply it to forbid false authorship attributions, such as listing someone as an author who did not in fact contribute to the work,[86] or omitting someone who did.[87] A court found a Lanham Act violation in a misrepresentation of the nature of an artist's contribution and substituting one actor's name for another in film credits and advertising.[88]

---

[82] Calvin Klein Cosmetics Corp. v. Parfums de Coeur, Ltd., 824 F.2d 665, 668, 3 U.S.P.Q.2d 1498, 1500–1501 (8th Cir. 1987) ("If you like OBSESSION you'll love CONFESS"); Charles of the Ritz Group Ltd. v. Quality King Distributors, Inc., 832 F.2d 1317, 1318, 4 U.S.P.Q.2d 1778, 1779 (2d Cir. 1987) ("If you like OPIUM, you'll love OMNI"); Saxony Products, Inc. v. Guerlain, Inc., 513 F.2d 716, 722, 185 U.S.P.Q. 474, 478 (9th Cir. 1975) ("Fragrance S is 'LIKE' or 'similar' to SHALIMAR"); Sherrell Perfumers, Inc. v. Revlon, Inc., 483 F. Supp. 188, 205 U.S.P.Q. 250 (S.D.N.Y. 1980); Chanel, Inc. v. Smith, 178 U.S.P.Q. 630 (N.D. Cal. 1973).

[83] See § 6G.

[84] E.g., Allen v. National Video, Inc., 610 F. Supp. 612 (S.D.N.Y. 1985) (use of actor who resembled Woody Allen to advertise video rental club violates § 43(a)); Jackson v. MPI Home Video, 694 F. Supp. 483, 8 U.S.P.Q.2d 1572 (N.D. Ill. 1988) (Use of photograph of well known politician on video cassette box falsely implied endorsement of the product and therefore violated § 43(a)).

[85] See §§ 1D[3][c][ii](5) and 4E[6].

[86] Dodd v. Fort Smith Special School District No. 100, 666 F. Supp. 1278, 1284–85, 4 U.S.P.Q.2d 1395, 1400 (W.D. Ark. 1987).

[87] Lamothe v. Atlantic Recording Corp., 847 F.2d 1403, 1407–08, 7 U.S.P.Q.2d 1249, 1252–53 (9th Cir. 1988) (attribution of "authorship to less than all of the joint authors of the musical compositions" violates Section 43(a)).

[88] PPX Enterprises, Inc. v. Audiofidelity Enterprises, Inc., 818 F.2d 266, 268, 272, 2 U.S.P.Q.2d 1072, 1676 (2d Cir. 1987) (marketing of record albums "purporting to contain feature performances by Jimi Hendrix, but which either did not contain Hendrix performances at all or contained performances in which Hendrix was merely a background performer or undifferentiated session player" is false advertising); Smith v. Montoro, 648 F.2d 602, 211 U.S.P.Q. 775 (9th Cir. 1981).

Section 43(a) cannot prevent a work's distortion or destruction, but it can regulate what is said about a work and may provide a limited right to disavow a work if it is changed without the author's permission.[89]

§ 6F   Unfair Competition—Misappropriation

The law regards competition, even competition calculated to eliminate competitors, as lawful and in the public interest.[1] Early unfair competition law focused narrowly on two "unfair" competitive methods: deception as to the origin or nature of goods and use of breaches of confidence and improper means to obtain competitively useful information. The former, known as the "passing off" or "palming off" tort, is the foundation of modern trademark law.[2] The latter is the foundation of modern trade secret law.[3]

The deception branch of unfair competition law expanded to encompass a competitor's remedy for a rival's false advertising and labeling, that is, a defendant's misrepresentations as to the nature or qualities of his own goods that tended to divert plaintiff's sales.[4]

The Supreme Court's 1918 *INS* decision[5] provoked debate on whether unfair competition law could go beyond deception to encompass "misappropriation," that is, a second competitor's unauthorized taking of publicly disclosed information that a first competitor invests time and effort to create when the taking diminishes or eliminates the first competitor's incentive to continue to create the information.

Since *INS*, the misappropriation doctrine has had uncertain status. After *Erie* decreed that there is no general federal common law,[6] the misappropriation

---

[89] Gilliam v. American Broadcasting Companies, 538 F.2d 14, 23–24, 192 U.S.P.Q. 1, 8 (2d Cir. 1976), discussed at § 4E[6]. See Jaeger v. American International Pictures, Inc., 330 F. Supp. 274, 278, 169 U.S.P.Q. 658, 670 (S.D.N.Y. 1971) ("It is at least arguable that there is a [Lanham Act Section 43(a)] claim . . . in the charge that defendant represents to the public that what the plaintiff had nothing to do with is the plaintiff's product. . . . ").

But cf. Paramount Pictures Corp. v. Video Broadcasting Systems, Inc., 724 F. Supp. 808, 819 (D. Kan. 1989) (grafting unauthorized commercials onto a videotape so that they overlapped and therefore erased advertisements of the manufacturer of the videotape did not mutilate the motion picture and therefore did not violate the Lanham Act).

[1] *E.g.*, Tuttle v. Buck, 107 Minn. 145, 150, 119 N.W. 946, 948 (1909) ("To divert to one's self the customers of a business rival by the offer of goods at lower prices is in general a legitimate mode of serving one's own interest, and justifiable as fair competition;" recognizing as an exception that "when a man starts an opposition place of business, not for the sake of profit to himself, but regardless of loss to himself, and for the sole purpose of driving his competitor out of business, and with the intention of himself retiring upon the accomplishment of his malevolent purpose, he is guilty of a wanton wrong and an actionable tort.").

[2] *See* Chapter 5.

[3] *See* Chapter 3.

[4] For a discussion of false advertising law, see § 6E.

[5] International News Service v. Associated Press, 248 U.S. 215 (1918).

[6] Erie R.R. v. Tompkins, 304 U.S. 64 (1938).

doctrine's existence and scope became a question of state law. Decisions in some states, particularly New York, relied on the *INS* misappropriation doctrine to provide relief when no other theory adequately supported relief against improper copying. Other decisions restricted *INS* to its specific facts[7] or held federal patent and copyright policy preempted the doctrine.[8] More recent decisions do not reject the doctrine entirely but confine it to situations in which the alleged misappropriator's use of information is in direct competition with the producer's primary use of the information and there is a clear threat that unchecked misappropriation will diminish the producer's incentive to produce the information.[9]

[1] The *INS* Decision

INS[10] involved a clash between competing news gathering services, the Associated Press (AP) and the International News Service (INS), over news reporting in the European theater during the First World War. AP, a collective of 950 daily newspapers that shared its news gathering costs, the member newspapers agreeing not to permit pre-publication disclosure of AP stories, sought an injunction restraining INS from pirating AP news.

AP complained of three practices. First, INS allegedly bribed employees of AP member newspapers to furnish news to INS's clients. Second, it allegedly induced AP members to violate AP by-laws and permit INS to obtain AP news. The district court's injunction restraining these practices was not a point of controversy.

The point of controversy was INS's third practice: "copying news from bulletin boards and from early editions of [AP member] newspapers and selling this, either bodily or after rewriting it, to defendant's customers." Following this practice, INS's customer newspaper could report the news almost as soon as AP members. Its west coast newspapers could report stories simultaneously or earlier than their AP competitors because of the three-hour time difference from the east to the west coast of the United States.

AP did not rely on copyright infringement. Whether or not AP copyrighted its stories as literary works, it could not obtain copyright protection for the news described in its stories; news consists of facts and ideas, and copyright law protects only the *expression* of facts and ideas.[11] Rather, AP relied on unfair competition law principles. It sought, and the appeals court awarded, a preliminary injunction

---

[7] Cheney Brothers v. Doris Silk Corp., 35 F.2d 279 (2d Cir. 1929), *cert. denied*, 281 U.S. 728 (1930).

[8] *E.g.*, Columbia Broadcasting Sys., Inc. v. DeCosta, 377 F.2d 315 (1st Cir. 1967), *cert. denied*, 389 U.S. 1007 (1967). *See* §§ 1D[3][c] and 4C[1][d][vi].

[9] *Compare* Standard & Poor's Corp. v. Commodity Exchange, Inc., 683 F.2d 704, 216 U.S.P.Q. 841 (2d Cir. 1982); Board of Trade v. Dow Jones & Co., 98 Ill. 2d 109, 456 N.E.2d 84 (1983) *with* United States Golf Association v. St. Andrews Systems, Data-Max, Inc., 749 F.2d 1028, 224 U.S.P.Q. 646 (3d Cir. 1984); National Football League v. Governor of the State of Delaware, 435 F. Supp. 1372, 195 U.S.P.Q. 801 (D. Del. 1977).

[10] International News Service v. Associated Press, 248 U.S. 215 (1918).

[11] *See* §§ 4C[1][d] and 4F[2].

"against any bodily taking of the words or substance of complainant's news until its commercial value as news had passed away."[12]

On certiorari, the Supreme Court affirmed; Justices Holmes and Brandeis wrote separate dissenting opinions.

[a] **Majority Opinion.** The Court majority opinion addresses three questions in AP's argument:

> "(1) Whether there is any property in news; (2) Whether, if there be property in news collected for the purpose of being published, it survives the instant of its publication in the first newspaper to which it is communicated by the news-gatherer; and (3) whether defendant's admitted course of conduct in appropriating for commercial use matter taken from bulletins or early editions of Associated Press publications constitutes unfair competition in trade."[13]

The need to resolve news' status as "property" arose from the historic equity requirements that an injunction only issue in aid of property rights. The Court clearly did not wish to say that AP or anyone else had an absolute property right in disclosed news. Improvising, it regarded news as "quasi property." Between either party and the public, disclosed news could not be property; between the parties as competitors, the news was "stock in trade, to be gathered at the cost of enterprise, organization, skill, labor, and money, and to be distributed and sold to those who will pay money for it, as for any other merchandise."[14] This satisfied equity because "[t]he rule that a court of equity concerns itself only in the protection of property rights treats any civil right of a pecuniary nature as a property right . . . and the right to acquire property by honest labor or the conduct of a lawful business is as much entitled to protection as the right to guard property already acquired. . . . It is this right that furnishes the basis of the jurisdiction in the ordinary case of unfair competition."[15]

Property aside, the key question was one of "unfair competition in business." Characterizing the facts, the Court put forth a harvest sowing and reaping metaphor.

> "[*Defendant*] is taking material that has been acquired by complainant as the result of organization and the expenditure of labor, skill, and money, and which is salable by complainant for money, and . . . in appropriating it and selling it as its own *is endeavoring to reap where it has not sown, and . . . is appropriating to itself the harvest of those who have sown.* Stripped of all disguises, the process amounts to an unauthorized interference with the normal operation of complainant's legitimate business precisely at the point where the profit is to be reaped, in order to divert a material portion of the profit from those who have earned it to those who have not; with special advantage to defendant in the competition because of the fact that it is not burdened with any part of the expense of gathering the news. The transaction speaks for itself

---

[12] 248 U.S. at 232.
[13] 248 U.S. at 232.
[14] 248 U.S. at 236.
[15] 248 U.S. at 236–37.

and a court of equity ought not to hesitate long in characterizing it as unfair competition in business."[16]

The Court faced the hurdle of unfair competition's traditional requirement that there be deception, typically a defendant's "attempt . . . to palm off its goods as those of the complainant." Agreeing palming off was the most familiar unfair competition activity, the Court refused to confine equitable relief to "that class of cases."

> "In the present case the fraud upon complainant's rights is more direct and obvious. Regarding news matter as the mere material from which these two competing parties are endeavoring to make money, and treating it, therefore, as quasi property for the purposes of their business because they are both selling it as such, defendant's conduct differs from the ordinary case of unfair competition in trade principally in this that, instead of selling its own goods as those of complainant, *it substitutes misappropriation in the place of misrepresentation*, and sells complainant's goods as its own."[17]

The Court found elements of false representation in INS's practices—its publication of AP-derived news stories without crediting the source was a misrepresentation to readers that "the news transmitted is the result of [INS's] own investigation in the field"—but these elements "although accentuating the wrong, are not the essence of it. It is something more than the advantage of celebrity of which complainant is being deprived."[18]

INS raised an "unclean hands" defense, arguing that AP engaged in equally culpable news piracy. AP reporters used INS stories as " 'tips' to be investigated, and if verified by independent investigation the news thus gathered is sold."[19] AP admitted the practice and had no objection to INS employing it. The Court noted its inclination "to think a distinction may be drawn between the utilization of tips and the bodily appropriation of news matter, either in its original form or after rewriting and without independent investigation and verification. . . . "[20]

INS also objected to the injunction's vagueness, but the Court concluded that "if [the injunction] be indefinite, it is no more so than the criticism" and declined to revise it, leaving the matter open for consideration at trial on the merits.[21]

---

[16] 248 U.S. at 239–40 (Emphasis added.)

[17] 248 U.S. at 242 (Emphasis added.)

[18] 248 U.S. at 242.

[19] 248 U.S. at 243.

[20] 248 U.S. at 243.

[21] "Perhaps it would be better that the terms of the injunction be made specific, and so framed as to confine the restraint to an extent consistent with the reasonable protection of complainant's newspapers, each in its own area and for a specified time after its publication, against the competitive use of pirated news by defendant's customers. But the case presents practical difficulties; and we have not the materials, either in the way of a definite suggestion of amendment, or in the way of proofs, upon which to frame a specific injunction; hence, while not expressing approval of the form adopted by the District Court, we decline to modify it at this preliminary stage of the case, and will leave that court to deal with the matter upon appropriate application made to it for the purpose." 248 U.S. at 245–46.

[b] The Holmes Dissent. Justice Holmes argued that AP's only sound ground of complaint was against INS's false implied representation that it was the source of news stories it in fact derived from AP.

Holmes rejected the concept of property in publicly disclosed facts—even though effort and expenses must be expended to create them.

> "When an uncopyrighted combination of words is published there is no general right to forbid other people repeating them—in other words there is no property in the combination or in the thoughts or facts that the words express. Property, a creation of law, does not arise from value, although exchangeable—a matter of fact. Many exchangeable values may be destroyed intentionally without compensation. Property depends upon exclusion by law from interference, and a person is not excluded from using any combination of words merely because some one has used it before, even if it took labor and genius to make it." [22]

He reasoned that "[i]f a given person is to be prohibited from making the use of words that his neighbors are free to make[,] some other ground must be found." A possible ground is "unfair trade" (*i.e.*, unfair competition), but unfair competition consists only of misrepresentation. The ordinary case is palming off, that is, "a representation by device, appearance, or other indirection that the defendant's goods come from the plaintiff," but "the same evil may follow from the opposite falsehood—from saying whether in words or by implication that the plaintiff's product is the defendant's." INS' conduct constituted a case of implied false advertising, misrepresenting the source of its news stories.

> "Fresh news is got only by enterprise and expense. To produce such news as it is produced by the defendant represents by implication that it has been acquired by the defendant's enterprise and at its expense. When it comes from one of the great news collecting agencies like the Associated Press, the source generally is indicated, plainly importing that credit; and that such a representation is implied may be inferred with some confidence from the unwillingness of the defendant to give the credit and tell the truth. If the plaintiff produces the news at the same time that the defendant does, the defendant's presentation impliedly denies to the plaintiff the credit of collecting the facts and assumes that credit to the defendant. If the plaintiff is later in Western cities it naturally will be supposed to have obtained its information from the defendant. The falsehood is a little more subtle, the injury, a little more indirect, than in ordinary cases of unfair trade, but I think that the principle that condemns the one condemns the other." [23]

Holmes' analysis lead to the conclusion that AP was only entitled to limited injunctive relief, requiring INS to acknowledge the source of its news stories.

---

[22] 248 U.S. at 246.

[23] 248 U.S. at 247.

[c] **The Brandeis Dissent.** Justice Brandeis also dissented. Unlike Holmes, he would grant no relief because he found no merit in either the property[24] or the implied misrepresentation theories.[25] Thoroughly reviewing common law case authorities plaintiff AP relied upon, he found no basis for restraining competition not involving "fraud or force or the doing of acts otherwise prohibited by law."[26] The relief AP sought would entail "the making of a new rule in analogy to an existing one" for policy reasons. The judge-made common law can grow, adapt to new conditions, and provide relief against injustices, but the unfair practices that technological change such as the telegraph enabled INS to carry on were too complex and called for legislative, not judicial, solutions.[27]

---

[24] "[T]he fact that a product of the mind has cost its producer money and labor, and has a value for which others are willing to pay, is not sufficient to ensure to it this legal attribute of property. The general rule of law is, that the noblest of human productions—knowledge, truths ascertained, conceptions, and ideas—became, after voluntary communication to others, free as the air to common use. Upon these incorporeal productions the attribute of property is continued after such communication only in certain classes of cases where public policy has seemed to demand it. These exceptions are confined to productions which, in some degree, involve creation, invention, or discovery. But by no means all such are endowed with this attribute of property. The creations which are recognized as property by the common law are literary, dramatic, musical, and other artistic creations; and these have also protection under the copyright statutes. The inventions and discoveries upon which this attribute of property is conferred only by statute, are the few comprised within the patent law. There are also many other cases in which courts interfere to prevent curtailment of plaintiff's enjoyment of incorporeal productions; and in which the right to relief is often called a property right, but is such only in a special sense. In those cases, the plaintiff has no absolute right to the protection of his production; he has merely the qualified right to be protected as against the defendant's acts, because of the special relation in which the latter stands or the wrongful method or means employed in acquiring the knowledge or the manner in which it is used. Protection of this character is afforded where the suit is based upon breach of contract or of trust or upon unfair competition. The knowledge for which protection is sought in the case at bar is not of a kind upon which the law has heretofore conferred the attributes of property; nor is the manner of its acquisition or use nor the purpose to which it is applied, such as has heretofore been recognized as entitling a plaintiff to relief." 248 U.S. at 250–51.

[25] "[N]o representation can properly be implied from omission to mention the source of information except that the International News Service is transmitting news which it believes to be credible." 248 U.S. at 261.

[26] 248 U.S. at 258.

[27] "The unwritten law possesses capacity for growth; and has often satisfied new demands for justice by invoking analogies or by expanding a rule or principle. This process has been in the main wisely applied and should not be discontinued. Where the problem is relatively simple, as it is apt to be when private interests only are involved, it generally proves adequate. But with the increasing complexity of society, the public interest tends to become omnipresent; and the problems presented by new demands for justice cease to be simple. Then the creation or recognition by courts of a new private right may work serious injury to the general public, unless the boundaries of the right are definitely established and wisely guarded. In order to reconcile the new private right with the public interest, it may be necessary to prescribe limitations and rules for its enjoyment; and also to provide administrative machinery for enforcing the rules. It is largely for this reason that, in the effort to meet the many new demands for justice incident to a rapidly changing civilization, resort to legislation has latterly been had with increasing frequency." 248 U.S. at 262–63.

"Courts are ill-equipped to make the investigations which should precede a determination of the limitations which should be set upon any property right in news or of the circumstances under which news gathered by a private agency should be deemed affected with a public interest. Courts would be powerless to prescribe the detailed regulations essential to full enjoyment of the rights conferred or to introduce the machinery required for enforcement of such regulations. Considerations such as these should lead us to decline to establish a new rule of law in the effort to redress a newly disclosed wrong, although the propriety of some remedy appears to be clear." [28]

[2] From *INS* to *Sears-Compco*

"The language of the I.N.S. opinion is very broad, and courts have struggled over the years to define the limits of the doctrine." [29]

Some courts applied the misappropriation doctrine to fact patterns resembling *INS*.[30] The Second Circuit gave the misappropriation doctrine narrow scope. In *Cheney Brothers*,[31] the plaintiff, a manufacturer of "silks," put out new patterns each season. Only a few "catch the public fancy" and then only for a short period, often only a single season. Because of the short product life, plaintiff did not seek design patents, and many of its designs would not have met patentability standards. The

---

[28] 248 U.S. at 267.

[29] United States Golf Association v. St. Andrews Systems, Data-Max, Inc., 749 F.2d 1028, 224 U.S.P.Q. 646 (3d Cir. 1984).

[30] *E.g.*, Associated Press v. KVOS, Inc., 80 F.2d 575 (9th Cir.1935), *rev'd on other grounds*, 299 U.S. 269 (1936) (radio broadcast of news taken from A.P. newspaper).

For a news misappropriation case predating *INS*, see National Telegraph News Co. v. Western Union Telegraph Co., 119 F. 294 (7th Cir.1902) (a rival company's rebroadcasts of Western Union's stock price quotations over its own telegraph network constituted misappropriation).

[31] Cheney Brothers v. Doris Silk Corp., 35 F.2d 279 (2d Cir. 1929), *cert. denied*, 281 U.S. 728 (1930).

See also Hartford Charga-Plate Associates v. Youth Centre-Cinderella Stores, Inc., 215 F.2d 668, 670 (2d Cir. 1954) (no misappropriation when defendants' stores used for billing and credit checking purposes credit cards plaintiff association issued to its member firms' customers; "there is no claim of misrepresentation of plaintiff's goods or of palming-off defendant's goods as plaintiff's. There is no claim of appropriation of any concepts or ideas of plaintiff or of confusion of goods; nor does plaintiff contend that plateholders were under contract as to use of the plates, or seek relief on the ground of inducement of breach of contract. No infringement of a patent is claimed. . . . The contention has to be, therefore, that defendant has wrongfully appropriated something of value from plaintiff and is taking a 'free ride' as against competitors. . . . [P]laintiff's belated attempt to preserve ownership and restriction upon the use of the plates shows no differentiation of practical substance or significance in this setting from the situation of admitted sale or gift of the plates. . . . Defendant was not in competition in selling either a credit system or its paraphernalia or credit information."); RCA Manufacturing Co. v. Whiteman, 114 F.2d 86 (2d Cir. 1940), *cert. denied*, 311 U.S. 712 (1940) (rebroadcast of recordings); Millinery Creators' Guild, Inc. v. Federal Trade Commission, 109 F.2d 175 (2d Cir. 1940), *aff'd*, 312 U.S. 469 (1941) (design of high-priced hats).

Compare Capitol Records, Inc. v. Mercury Records Corp., 221 F.2d 657 (2d Cir.1955) (subsequent New York state court decision undermined *RCA*).

Copyright Office viewed clothing designs as uncopyrightable subject matter. For these reasons, "plaintiff, which is put to much ingenuity and expense in fabricating them, finds itself without protection of any sort for its pains." Defendant "copied one of the popular designs in the season beginning in October, 1928, and undercut the plaintiff's price." For the Second Circuit, Judge Learned Hand found no common law basis for relief even though plaintiff sought protection only for a short period.

> "The plaintiff asks for protection only during the season, and needs no more, for the designs are all ephemeral. It seeks in this way to disguise the extent of the proposed innovation, and to persuade us that, if we interfere only a little, the solecism, if there be one, may be pardonable. But the reasoning which would justify any interposition at all demands that it cover the whole extent of the injury. A man whose designs come to harvest in two years, or in five, has prima facie as good right to protection as one who deals only in annuals. Nor could we consistently stop at designs; processes, machines, and secrets have an equal claim. The upshot must be that, whenever any one has contrived any of these, others may be forbidden to copy it. That is not the law. In the absence of some recognized right at common law, or under the statutes—and the plaintiff claims neither—a man's property is limited to the chattels which embody his invention. Others may imitate these at their pleasure.[32]

Plaintiff relied upon *INS*. Judge Hand saw and was troubled by the two cases' close similarity, but he dispatched the Supreme Court's decision as inherently limited to its facts and not creating a "general doctrine."

> "While it is of course true that law ordinarily speaks in general terms, there are cases where the occasion is at once the justification for, and the limit of, what is decided. This appears to us such an instance; we think that no more was covered than situations substantially similar to those then at bar. The difficulties of understanding it otherwise are insuperable. We are to suppose that the court meant to create a sort of common-law patent or copyright for reasons of justice. Either would flagrantly conflict with the scheme which Congress has for more than a century devised to cover the subject-matter.

> "Qua patent, we should at least have to decide, as tabula rasa, whether the design or machine was new and required invention; further, we must ignore the Patent Office whose action has always been a condition upon the creation of this kind of property. Qua copyright, although it would be simpler to decide upon the merits, we should equally be obliged to dispense with the conditions imposed upon the creation of the right. Nor, if we went so far, should we know whether the property so recognized should be limited to the periods prescribed in the statutes, or should extend as long as the author's grievance. It appears to us incredible that the Supreme Court should have had in mind any such consequences. To exclude others from the enjoyment of a chattel is one thing; to prevent any imitation of it, to set up a monopoly in the plan of its structure, gives the author a power over his fellows vastly greater, a power which the Constitution allows only Congress to create."[33]

---

[32] 35 F.2d at 279–80.
[33] 35 F.2d at 280.

Other federal and state courts also rejected misappropriation arguments.[34] In *Broadcasting & Television*,[35] plaintiffs were television stations in one locality (Salt Lake City, Utah) that sold rights to carry their broadcast signal to a local station in Twin Falls, Idaho, a city too distant from Salt Lake City for receipt of signals by ordinary television receivers. Defendant was a cable television system that picked up plaintiffs' signals by antenna and provided television service to home subscribers for a fee.[36] Plaintiff sought relief against defendant relying on the *INS* misappropriation doctrine. In denying relief, the district court noted *INS's* uncertain status:

> "Those courts which have followed and applied the doctrine . . . have done so in identical fact situations . . . or in cases where there was manifest unjust enrichment, for example, where rights in private enterprises or events for which the investor had granted exclusive TV or Radio licenses were involved—unique situations in which the primary purpose of an investor to charge the public for the privilege of watching an event, would be frustrated or defeated through exhibition by others than itself or its exclusive licensee."[37]

Federal legislation partially regulated interstate television and radio transmission, and a "cautious approach to recognition of novel rights protectible upon the theory of unfair competition is especially wise when the unjust practice complained of occurs in a field over which the Congress has already assumed a control sufficient to enable it, if it so chooses, to regulate the practice one way or another in the public interest."[38] There were "basic differences" between *INS* and the instant case. Plaintiff and defendant were not in the identical businesses, and defendant's practice did not interfere with plaintiff's primary business "at the point at which profit is to be made" from plaintiff's efforts, to wit, sale of advertising to program sponsors.

[3] New York Law

New York state courts tend to apply the misappropriation doctrine expansively.

In *Metropolitan Opera*,[39] the New York courts granted the Metropolitan Opera Association ("Met") and Columbia Records, its authorized recording company, an injunction restraining the defendant from recording and distributing phonorecords of the Met's opera performances, which American Broadcasting Company broadcast with the Met's permission. Defendant's records were cheaper, and, according to plaintiffs, inferior in quality to plaintiffs' authorized records. The case's facts suggested implied misrepresentation on the source of defendant's recordings and direct competition between plaintiff Columbia Records and defendant, but the court refused to limit its holding to cases of palming off or directive competitive injury.

---

[34] *E.g.*, Addressograph-Multigraph Corp. v. American Expansion Bolt & Manufacturing Co., 124 F.2d 706 (7th Cir.1941), *cert. denied*, 316 U.S. 682 (1942) (applying Illinois law); Triangle Publications v. New England Newspaper Publishing Co., 46 F. Supp. 198 (D. Mass.1942) (applying Massachusetts law).

[35] Broadcasting & Television v. Idaho Microwave, Inc., 196 F. Supp. 315 (D. Idaho 1961).

[36] For a discussion of cable television's copyright status, see § 4E[4][e].

[37] 196 F. Supp. at 323.

[38] *Id.*

[39] Metropolitan Opera Ass'n v. Wagner-Nichols Recorder Corp., 199 Misc. 786, 101 N.Y.S.2d 483 (1950), *aff'd*, 279 A.D. 632, 107 N.Y.S.2d 795 (1951).

"[T]his branch of law originated in the conscience, justice and equity of common-law judges. It developed within the framework of a society dedicated to freest competition, to deal with business malpractices offensive to the ethics of that society. . . . [T]he legal concept of unfair competition has evolved as a broad and flexible doctrine with a capacity for further growth to meet changing conditions. There is no complete list of the activities which constitute unfair competition. . . .

. . .

"With the passage of those simple and halcyon days when the chief business malpractice was 'palming off' and with the development of more complex business relationships and, unfortunately, malpractices, many courts, including the courts of this state, extended the doctrine of unfair competition beyond the cases of 'palming off.' The extension resulted in the granting of relief in cases where there was no fraud on the public, but only a misappropriation for the commercial advantage of one person of a benefit or 'property right' belonging to another.

. . .

"The modern view as to the law of unfair competition does not rest solely on the ground of direct competitive injury, but on the broader principle that property rights of commercial value are to be and will be protected from any form of unfair invasion or infringement and from any form of commercial immorality, and a court of equity will penetrate and restrain every guise resorted to by the wrongdoer. The courts have thus recognized that in the complex pattern of modern business relationships, persons in theoretically noncompetitive fields may, by unethical business practices, inflict as severe and reprehensible injuries upon others as can direct competitors. That defendants' piratical conduct and practices have injured and will continue to injure plaintiffs admits of no serious challenge, and possible money damages furnishes no adequate remedy."[40]

The court also noted that (1) the authorized broadcasts did not cause plaintiffs' common law property rights to be forfeited because, under common law copyright,[41] a performance did not constitute a publication, and (2) the plaintiff stated a sufficient alternative tort cause of action—unjustifiable interference with plaintiffs' contractual rights.

In *Leonard Storch Enterprises*,[42] a federal district court held that a complaint alleging that the defendant "photographically reproduces the essential portions of [plaintiff's] film fonts, and thereby bypasses much of the cost in creating the original fonts" "states a cause under New York law."

"Many other New York cases have found a cause of action for misappropriation of a property right created by labor, skill and expenditure. *Bond*

---

[40] 101 N.Y.S.2d at 488–89, 492.

[41] *See* § 4D[1].

[42] Leonard Storch Enterprises, Inc. v. Mergenthaler Linotype Co., 202 U.S.P.Q. 623 (E.D. N.Y. 1979).

Buyer v. Dealers Digest Publishing Co., 25 A.D.2d 158, 267 N.Y.S.2d 944 (1966); *New York World's Fair 1964-1965 Corp. v. Colour Picture Publishers, Inc.*, 21 A.D.2d 896, 251 N.Y.S.2d 885 (1964); *Madison Sq. Garden Corp. v. Universal Pictures Co.*, 255 A.D. 459, 7 N.Y.S.2d 845 (1938); *Columbia Broadcasting System Inc. v. Documentaries Unlimited, Inc.*, 42 Misc. 2d 723, 248 N.Y.S.2d 809 (1964); *Capitol Records, Inc. v. Greatest Records, Inc.*, 43 Misc. 2d 878, 252 N.Y.S.2d 553 (1964); *Frank M. Shaw, Inc. v. C.H. Cleworth & Associates, Inc.*, 110 U.S.P.Q. 394 (Sup. Ct., N.Y. Co. 1956); *National Exhibition Co. v. Fass*, 143 N.Y.S.2d 767 (Sup. Ct., N.Y. Co. 1955); *Mutual Broadcasting Sys., Inc. v. Muzak Corp.*, 177 Misc. 489, 30 N.Y.S.2d 419 (1941).

"But what greatly complicates any understanding of New York law is the fact that the New York Court of Appeals case whose facts are most similar to those of the present case, appears to have gone the other way. *Hebrew Publishing Co. v. Scharfstein*, 288 N.Y. 374, 43 N.E.2d 449 (1942). In this case defendant, bookseller, reproduced a publisher's religious text by means of photo offset plates. There was no finding of palming off, interference with business, or the existence of a copyright which could be infringed. The only possible ground for recovery was the unfair competition of misappropriating plaintiff's text. The expense saved by making offset plates, without more, was deemed an insufficient reason for requiring a permanent injunction. But the *Scharfstein* case, may well turn on the fact that the plaintiff itself had created the books upon which it based its equitable claim by photo offsetting prior text already in the public domain. The labor, skill and expenditure which characterized the similar New York cases in which recovery was granted, were not present in *Scharfstein*."[43]

---

[43] *See also* Roy Export Co. Establishment of Vaduz, Liechtenstein, v. Columbia Broadcasting Sys., Inc., 672 F.2d 1095, 1105, 215 U.S.P.Q. 289, 297 (2d Cir. 1982), *cert. denied*, 459 U.S. 826 (1982) (defendant's unauthorized broadcast of a compilation of Charlie Chaplin's films after his death constitutes misappropriation under New York law because it diminishes the marketability of plaintiff's film "The Gentleman Tramp," an authorized Chaplin retrospective film; "With the subsequent decline of general federal common law, the doctrine was developed by the states, New York in particular; there it has flourished in a variety of factual settings, . . . despite some early efforts by this Court to limit the doctrine to the narrow circumstances of the INS case, ... An unfair competition claim involving misappropriation usually concerns the taking and use of the plaintiff's property to compete against the plaintiff's own use of the same property. . . . By contrast, in this case the Compilation was taken and used to compete unfairly against a different property, 'The Gentleman Tramp.' Despite the unusual facts, we are satisfied that the plaintiffs have established an unfair competition tort under New York law. New York courts have noted the 'incalculable variety' of illegal practices falling within the unfair competition rubric, . . . calling it a 'broad and flexible doctrine' that depends 'more upon the facts set forth . . . than in most causes of action,'. . . . It has been broadly described as encompassing 'any form of commercial immorality,' . . . or simply as 'endeavoring to reap where [one] has not sown'. . . . ").

[4] *Sears-Compco* and Federal Preemption

In *Sears*[44] and *Compco*,[45] the United States Supreme Court held that federal patent and copyright policy preempted state unfair competition law insofar as it would bar copying of publicly distributed products not covered by a valid patent or copyright. The decisions dealt a blow to the misappropriation doctrine,[46] but it was not fatal.

> "The Court held that the decision by Congress to exclude certain types of intellectual property from protection under the patent and copyright laws was a policy decision that the societal interest in free access to those ideas outweighed the need to provide incentives for their production, and that state law doctrines which protected such intellectual property were preempted by that policy decision. Subsequent decisions of the Supreme Court have made clear, however, that the misappropriation doctrine has not been completely eviscerated. See *Kewanee Oil Co. v. Bicron Corp.*, 416 U.S. 470, 94 S. Ct. 1879, 40 L. Ed. 2d 315 (1974); *Goldstein v. California*, 412 U.S. 546, 93 S. Ct. 2303, 37 L. Ed. 2d 163 (1973). . . . The Court has not rejected the *Sears-Compco* doctrine, nor has it clearly defined where the power of the states to protect interests in intellectual property ends, and where the realm of federal preemption begins."[47]

In *Bonito Boats*,[48] the Supreme Court reconfirmed that federal policy restricts state law anti-copying remedies as applied to subject matter potentially eligible for patent or copyright protection.

Misappropriation's status arose during Congressional consideration of the 1976 Copyright Act's Section 301, which preempts state common law and statutory rights that meet two tests: (1) the right is "equivalent to any of the exclusive rights within the general scope of copyright . . . in works of authorship that are fixed in a tangible medium of expression," and (2) "come within the subject matter of copyright. . . ."[49] Section 301(b)(3) saves state rights and remedies "with respect to . . . (3) activities violating legal or equitable rights that are not equivalent to any of the exclusive

---

[44] Sears, Roebuck & Co. v. Stiffel Co., 376 U.S. 225 (1964).
For a discussion of *Sears* and *Compco*, see §§ 1D[3][a][i] and 5C[2][c][ii].
[45] Compco Corp. v. Day-Brite Lighting, Inc., 376 U.S. 234 (1964).
[46] *E.g.*, Columbia Broadcasting Sys., Inc. v. DeCosta, 377 F.2d 315, 318–19, 153 U.S.P.Q. 649 (1st Cir. 1967), *cert. denied*, 389 U.S. 1007 (1967) (no unfair competition for poaching of plaintiff's publicly disclosed character; "the leading case affording a remedy for mere copying, *International News Serv. v. Associated Press* . . . is no longer authoritative for [at] least two reasons: . . . it was decided as a matter of general federal law before the decision in *Erie R. R. v. Tompkins* . . . ; and, as it prohibited the copying of published written matter that had not been copyrighted (indeed, as news it could not be copyrighted) . . . it has clearly been overruled by the Supreme Court's recent decisions in *Sears* . . . and *Compco* . . .").
[47] United States Golf Association v. St. Andrews Systems, Data-Max, Inc., 749 F.2d 1028, 224 U.S.P.Q. 646, 652–53 (3d Cir. 1984).
[48] Bonito Boats, Inc. v. Thunder Craft Boats, Inc., 489 U.S. 141, 9 U.S.P.Q.2d 1847 (1989).
[49] 17 U.S.C. § 301(a).
For a discussion of Section 301, see § 1D[3][c].

rights within the general scope of copyright as specified by section 106. . . . "[50] The bill that became the 1976 Act, as it went to the House floor, had a clause at the end of Section 301(b)(3) listing saved state-created rights: "including rights against misappropriation not equivalent to any of such exclusive rights, breaches of contract, breaches of trust, trespass, conversion, invasion of privacy, defamation, and deceptive trade practices such as passing off and false representation." The Justice Department objected to the approving reference to misappropriation. On the House floor, Congressman Seiberling amended Section 301(b) to delete the entire "including" clause.

The House floor remarks of Seiberling and other Congressmen leave the purpose of the amendment unclear as it relates to preemption of misappropriation. Seiberling stated:

> "[M]y amendment is intended to save the 'Federal preemption' of State law section . . . from being inadvertently nullified because of the inclusion of certain examples in the exemptions from preemption. . . . The amendment is strongly supported by the Justice Department, which believes that it would be a serious mistake to cite as an exemption from preemption the doctrine of 'misappropriation.' The doctrine was created by the Supreme Court in 1922 [sic : 1918], and it has generally been ignored by the Supreme Court itself and the lower courts ever since. Inclusion of a reference to the misappropriation doctrine in this bill, however, could easily be construed by the courts as authorizing Sates to pass misappropriation laws. We should not approve such enabling legislation, because a misappropriation law could be so broad as to render the preemption section meaningless."[51]

That statement suggested that federal preemption of misappropriation, at least in its expanded forms, was intended. But Seiberling's response to a question by Congressman Railsback suggested the opposite intention.

> "Mr. RAILSBACK. . . . [T]he gentleman in no way is attempting to change the existing state of the law . . . in certain States that have recognized the right of recovery relating to 'misappropriation'; is that correct?
>
> "Mr. SEIBERLING. That is correct. All I am trying to do is prevent the citing of them as examples in the statute. We are, in effect, adopting a rather amorphous body of State law and codifying it, in effect. Rather I am trying to have this bill leave the State law alone and make it clear we are merely dealing with copyright laws. . . . "

Congressman Kastenmeier then compounded the confusion by stating: "the amendment . . . is consistent with the position of the Justice Department."

Given the Congressmen's oscillation, Section 301(b)'s legislative history sheds little light on preemption of Section 301(b).

Applying Section 301's text straightforwardly suggests that it will not preempt some misappropriation claims, to wit, those that relate to subject matter that does not constitute copyrightable subject matter, works of authorship fixed in a tangible

---

[50] 17 U.S.C. § 301(b).

[51] 122 Cong. Rec. H10,910 (September 22, 1976).

medium of expression. Even as to copyrightable subject matter, there is a strong argument that misappropriation is not a remedy equivalent to an exclusive right of copyright when it is strictly confined to its core heritage—the taking of information that constitutes the producer's "product" for purposes of directly competing in the producer's primary market under circumstances that will eliminate or substantially reduce the producer's incentive to continue producing the information. If a producer stretches misappropriation to suppress simple competition through imitation of its products, then the case for preemption strengthens.[52]

[5] Contemporary Applications

[a] **Sound Recording Piracy.** Courts evoked the misappropriation doctrine to suppress unauthorized reproduction of pre-1972 sound recordings, which federal copyright law does not cover.[53] In *Columbia Broadcasting Sys.*,[54] a New Jersey court noted: "In the setting of contemporary business practices, there is a critical, albeit fine, line separating commercial parroting from pirating. A dichotomy exists between the copying, simulation or imitation of the design of a product, or even an idea inherent in a product, on the one hand, and, on the other, the actual use of the product itself."

> "Permissible imitation entails the imitator bringing to bear its own efforts and resources in producing its own product, although it endeavors to simulate or ape the product of another. . . . Thus, tolerable copying of a product in this sense might be presented here, for example, if defendants had analyzed the recorded performances of CBS and then hired the same or comparable artists and musicians to perform the identical musical composition, in a like manner, and under the same conditions as achieved by CBS and recorded by it on a particular record or tape.

> . . .

> "What is involved in this case is the direct taking by defendants of the artistic and highly creative work of plaintiff—the recorded performance of a specially arranged musical composition. Defendants have thus appropriated the unique product of CBS by rerecording its original records. The commercial injury ensues because defendants have accomplished this at a minimal cost and then sold their 'original' duplicates for a substantial profit. The actionable unfairness of this practice inheres in a combination of factors—the substantial investment of time, labor, money and creative resources in the product by plaintiff, the utilization of the actual product by defendant, the misappropriation or use of the appropriated product by defendant in competition with plaintiff, and commercial damage to plaintiff."[55]

---

[52] *E.g.*, Schuchart & Associates, Professional Engineers, Inc. v. Solo Serve Corp., 540 F. Supp. 928, 217 U.S.P.Q. 1227 (W.D. Tex. 1982) (claim for misappropriation of architectural plans preempted under Section 301). *See* § 1D[3][c][ii](1).

[53] *See* § 4C[1][e].

[54] Columbia Broadcasting Sys., Inc. v. Melody Recordings, Inc., 134 N.J. Super. 368, 341 A.2d 348, 187 U.S.P.Q. 113 (1975).

[55] 341 A.2d at 353–54.

[b] Event Results, Indices, and Formulae. Courts deal with misappropriation arguments directed to unauthorized commercial use of event results, indices, and formulae. Like the news in *INS*, the copied subject matter is information that does not fit easily within either patent or copyright statutory subject matter.

In *National Football League,*[56] the NFL sought to restrain Delaware from basing a lottery on NFL game results. The NFL invested time and "vast sums of money" in developing and promoting its teams' games. Delaware picked NFL games because of their popularity. Relying on these facts and *INS,* the NFL asserted misappropriation. The district court rejected the assertion though it had "no doubt about the continuing vitality of the INS case and the doctrine of misappropriation which it spawned." Delaware used only the NFL's publicly disclosed schedule and game scores.

> "I do not believe the INS case or any other case suggests use of information that another has voluntarily made available to the public at large is an actionable 'misappropriation.'
>
> "Plaintiffs insist, however, that defendants are using more than the schedules and scores to generate revenue for the State. They define their 'product' as being the total 'end result' of their labors, including the public interest which has been generated.
>
> . . .
>
> "We live in an age of economic and social interdependence. The NFL undoubtedly would not be in the position it is today if college football and the fan interest that it generated had not preceded the NFL's organization. To that degree it has benefited from the labor of others. The same, of course, can be said for the mass media networks which the labor of others have developed.
>
> ". . . It is true that Delaware is thus making profits it would not make but for the existence of the NFL, but I find this difficult to distinguish from the multitude of charter bus companies who generate profit from servicing those of plaintiffs' fans who want to go to the stadium or, indeed, the sidewalk popcorn salesman who services the crowd as it surges towards the gate.
>
> "While courts have recognized that one has a right to one's own harvest, this proposition has not been construed to preclude others from profiting from demands for collateral services generated by the success of one's business venture."[57]

Alternatively, the NFL argued that Delaware was misappropriating not only its schedule and game scores but its "good will" and "reputation." The district court was not persuaded.

> "To the extent they relate to a claim that defendants' activities have damaged, as opposed to appropriated, plaintiff's good will and reputation, I believe one must look to other lines of authority to determine defendants' culpability.

---

[56] National Football League v. Governor of the State of Delaware, 435 F. Supp. 1372, 195 U.S.P.Q. 803 (D. Del. 1977).
[57] 435 F. Supp. at 1377–1378.

> "In the event a differing analysis is determined to be appropriate in the course of appellate review, I should add that the plaintiffs have not demonstrated that the existence of gambling on its games, per se, has or will damage its good will or reputation for integrity." [58]

Two cases apply misappropriation to bar unauthorized use of stock market indices to create publicly traded futures contracts. The contracts enable investors with diversified stock portfolios to "hedge" against "systematic" stock market risks. In *Standard & Poor's*,[59] the Commodity Exchange (Comex) sought a license from Standard & Poor's to use the "Standard & Poor's 500 Index," a weighted common stock price compilation. Comex and S&P failed to agree. Later, S&P did contract with Chicago Mercantile Exchange ("CME"), which began trading a 500 Stock index futures contract. S&P sued Comex, relying on a plethora of legal theories, including trademark infringement, Lanham Act Section 43(a) false origin designation, common law trademark infringement, trademark dilution, common law unfair competition and misappropriation, business relations interference, and copyright infringement. The district court granted a temporary restraining order. The Second Circuit affirmed, finding that "the broad preliminary injunction is adequately supported by S&P's misappropriation claim against Comex." Under the governing preliminary injunction standard,[60] it did not decide whether S&P's misappropriation claim was valid; it was sufficient that "the record indicates the presence of sufficiently serious questions going to the merits of S&P's misappropriation claim to make them fair grounds for litigation, a balance of hardships tipping decidedly in S&P's favor, and irreparable harm to S&P and the public."

On the misappropriation issue, Judge Pierce's opinion for the court's three judge panel noted that "the focus of *International News Service* is upon the defendant's use of plaintiff's salable product."[61] Judge Newman, joined by the third panel judge, took a different position.

---

[58] 435 F. Supp. at 1378.

[59] Standard & Poor's Corp. v. Commodity Exchange, Inc., 683 F.2d 704, 216 U.S.P.Q. 841 (2d Cir. 1982).

[60] For a discussion of preliminary injunctions in patent, trade secrets, copyright, and trademark cases, see §§ 2F[5][a][i], 3F[1][a], 4F[5][a][i] and 5F[3][a].

[61] The judge noted:

> "[T]here is little question that S&P expends a significant amount of money, labor and expertise in calculating the 500 Index—an index respected for its accuracy. . . .

> "S&P disseminates the S&P 500 Index to some entities, such as newspapers, free of charge; others receive the data by purchasing S&P's various publications which S&P promotes through advertising. In 1981, S&P's sales revenues for its lead publication, Outlook, exceeded $5 million. In addition, pursuant to a contractual arrangement with S&P, General Telephone & Electronics sells a minute-to-minute calculation of the Standard & Poor's 500 Index. Thus, the Standard & Poor's 500 Index appears to be a salable product.

> "While S&P has traditionally been in the business of disseminating financial information, it now has a significant interest in the futures contracts business by virtue of its licensing agreement with CME. Pursuant to that arrangement, S&P receives a fixed annual fee from CME plus a royalty based upon the number of S&P 500 futures contracts traded on the CME. Therefore, S&P and Comex are, at least to this extent, in competition."

"When Standard & Poor's enters the business of publishing an index of selected stock issues, there can be little doubt that another company endeavoring to publish the same index would face liability for misappropriation no matter how it merchandised its product and would face liability for trademark infringement if its merchandising created a risk of confusion between its product and that of Standard & Poor's. However, when Standard & Poor's makes its stock index known to the public, different, novel, and, in my judgment, close questions are presented when another company enters a business other than the publishing of stock indices—here, the marketing of futures contracts—and in its business uses the Standard & Poor's index as a reference point-here, the settlement price for the contracts. And the issues remain different, novel, and close notwithstanding the fact that Standard & Poor's itself has elected to contract with another entity for the marketing of futures contracts based on the Standard & Poor's stock index. The issues in this case include the issue of whether Standard & Poor's has the type of interest in its index that is capable of being protected by license against the unlicensed use by Comex in marketing a futures contract using the Standard & Poor's index as a settlement price."[62]

In *Board of Trade*,[63] which involved a fact pattern substantially the same as *Standard & Poor's*, the plaintiff Chicago Board of Trade sought a declaration that it could offer a commodity futures contract using defendant's "Dow Jones Industrial Average." Plaintiff initially developed its own stock average, but regulatory authorities required that stock market average commodity contracts be based on well-known averages. Dow Jones declined the Board's request for a royalty-bearing license. The Illinois Supreme Court held that the Board's proposal to use defendant's Average without its permission would constitute misappropriation. The court refused to confine misappropriation to cases in which the copier directly competes in the producer's primary market. Recognizing proprietary rights not only protects the producer's investment but creates incentives for the would-be misappropriator to invest in creating new and possibly improved alternatives for achieving the same function.[64]

"Competing with the policy that protection should be afforded one who expends labor and money to develop products is the concept that freedom to imitate and duplicate is vital to our free market economy.

". . . From S&P's standpoint, Comex' proposed use is no different than INS' condemned conduct in *International News Service*: Comex is taking S&P's Index, on which S&P expends substantial money, labor and expertise, and is planning to use it as an integral part of a commercial venture which competes directly with CME's S&P 500 futures contract, in which S&P has a significant financial stake." 683 F.2d at 710–11, 216 U.S.P.Q. 845.

[62] 683 F.2d at 712, 216 U.S.P.Q. at 846.

[63] Board of Trade of the City of Chicago v. Dow Jones & Co., 98 Ill. 2d 109, 74 Ill. Dec. 582, 456 N.E.2d 84 (1983).

[64] For a critique of the Illinois court's competitor incentive rationale, see United States Golf Association v. St. Andrews Systems, Data-Max, Inc., 749 F.2d 1028, 224 U.S.P.Q. 646 (3d Cir. 1984), discussed below.

. . .

"In balancing the factors that should determine which of the competing concepts should prevail, it appears unlikely that an adverse decision will cause defendant to cease to produce its averages or that the revenue it currently receives for the distribution of those averages will be materially affected. Defendant correctly asserts that it will lose its right to prospective licensing revenues in the event that in the future it elects to have its name associated with stock index futures contracts, but reliance upon the existence of a property right based upon the ability to license the product to prospective markets which were not originally contemplated by the creator of the product is somewhat 'circular.'

"Alternatively, holding that plaintiff's use of defendant's indexes in the manner proposed is a misappropriation may stimulate the creation of new indexes perhaps better suited to the purpose of 'hedging' against the 'systematic' risk present in the stock market.

"Whether protection against appropriation is necessary to foster creativity depends in part upon the expectations of that sector of the business community which deals with the particular intangible. If the creator of an intangible product expects to be able to control the licensing or distribution of the intangible in order to profit from his effort, and similarly those who would purchase the product expect and are willing to pay for the use of the intangible, a better argument can be made in favor of granting protection.

"To hold that defendant has a proprietary interest in its indexes and averages which vests it with the exclusive right to license their use for trading in stock index futures contracts would not preclude plaintiff and others from marketing stock index futures contracts. The extent of defendant's monopoly would be limited, for . . . there are an infinite number of stock market indexes which could be devised.

". . . [T]he possibility of any detriment to the public which might result from our holding that defendant's indexes and averages may not be used without its consent in the manner proposed by plaintiff are outweighed by the resultant encouragement to develop new indexes specifically designed for the purpose of hedging against the 'systematic' risk present in the stock market." [65]

In *United States Golf Association*,[66] plaintiff U.S.G.A., the United States amateur golf governing body, sought to bar defendant Data-Max from using the U.S.G.A. handicapping system, which included a mathematical formula, in a computer program. There were two aspects to Data-Max's business. First, it sold or leased computers to U.S.G.A.-member golf clubs, which used the computer to calculate handicaps. U.S.G.A. did not object to this aspect. Second, Data-Max marketed a subscription telephone handicap service that enables a golfer to call in a new score and

---

[65] 456 N.E.2d at 89.

[66] United States Golf Association v. St. Andrews Systems, Data-Max, Inc., 749 F.2d 1028, 224 U.S.P.Q. 646 (3d Cir. 1984).

immediately receive an updated handicap, and a computer that enabled a golfer to directly enter a new score and receive an updated handicap. U.S.G.A. objected to this aspect. Relying on the misappropriation doctrine, it argued that "it has invested time, effort, and money in the creation of the formula, and therefore is entitled to protection against Data-Max's using the formula as the basis of its own products and services." Data-Max responded by arguing that "any use of the misappropriation doctrine to effect the monopolization of an arithmetic formula" is preempted by the exclusion of such formulas from the federal patent statutes.[67]

Applying New Jersey law, the Third Circuit held that misappropriation could apply only if the claimant and the alleged misappropriator were direct competitors.

> "The doctrine has been applied to a variety of situations in which the courts have sensed that one party was dealing 'unfairly' with another, but which were not covered by the three established statutory systems protecting intellectual property: copyright, patent, and trademark/deception as to origin. . . . Application of the misappropriation doctrine requires courts to contend with the basic problem of the law of intellectual property: balancing the rights of the creator of ideas or information to exploit them for commercial gain against the public's right to free access to those ideas. Concomitantly, the dilemma posed by the doctrine can best be viewed as an attempt to provide the necessary incentives to the creators of intellectual property without unnecessarily restricting the public's free access to information."[68]

The court saw similarities between the stock indices cases and the case before it. The formulae "serve useful functions—in the stock market cases, the index is designed to track the general movement of the stock market; in this case, the formula is designed to indicate a golfer's level of competence." They are not unique to their function in that there are many potential alternatives, but the formulae "are generally accepted by the public as reliable means of performing their respective functions." The particular formulae's primary value lies not in "their inherent value in performing the underlying functions, but rather in the fact that they enable the public to discuss the underlying matters (i.e., the direction of the stock market or the ability of golfers) by means of a common set of terms."

Despite the similarities, the court declined to follow the stock indices cases, emphasizing the "basic policies that underlie the doctrine and its limits." Critical was the presence of direct competition with the producer's primary use of the information and a clear threat that unchecked misappropriation would diminish the producer's incentive to produce the information. "Indirect competition," that is, "use of information in competition with the creator outside of its primary market, falls outside the scope of the misappropriation doctrine, since the public interest in free access outweighs the public interest in providing an additional incentive to the creator or gatherer of information." Data-Max's competition was indirect in this sense.[69]

---

[67] For a discussion of the patentability of algorithms, see § 2C[1][f].

[68] 749 F.2d at 1034–35, 224 U.S.P.Q. at 651–52.

[69] "The U.S.G.A. is not in the business of selling handicaps to golfers, but is primarily interested in the promotion of the game of golf, and in its own position as the governing body of amateur golf. The handicap formula was developed to further these two goals. A

The court found that neither of the stock indices cases "makes a persuasive argument for dispensing with the 'direct competition' requirement." In *Board of Trade*, the Illinois court relied on the incentive an injunction against misappropriating the producer's index would provide to copiers to create new indices. The *INS* doctrine's traditional inquiry into the *producer's* incentive to create is one a court can manage; further inquiry into *competitors'* incentives is too speculative, especially because some of the potential competitors are not before the court.

The court considered a "possible justification for dispensing with the direct competition requirement in this case, which was also present in Dow Jones and Standard & Poor's." The justification would be that the information "is so closely associated with the creator" and "has so little intrinsic value" because of the availability of alternatives that "the use of the information by the competitors is really an attempt to trade on the 'good will' of the creator." The court found the possible justification insufficient. The handicap formula lacks "intrinsic value," but it has great extrinsic value because of its function as an "industry standard for the golfing public." With stock market indices, competitors face practical difficulties but not an inherently insurmountable obstacle in creating rival indices. With a golfing handicap formula, the public demands a single, uniform system that will enable comparisons.

> "Because the U.S.G.A. formula is the equivalent of an 'industry standard' for the golfing public, preventing other handicap providers from using it would effectively give the U.S.G.A. a national monopoly on the golf handicapping business. . . . Where such a monopoly is unnecessary to protect the basic incentive for the production of the idea or information involved, we do not believe that the creator's interest in its idea or information justifies such an extensive restraint on competition."[70]

§ 6G Publicity Rights

[1] Introduction

Publicity rights give a person control over commercial use of his or her identity. Like trade secret law,[1] publicity rights are governed by state, not federal law

---

member of a golf club who obtains his handicap through his club does not pay for that service, and the U.S.G.A. is not directly affected by the number of official handicaps the clubs calculate each year or by the number of golfers who obtain handicaps. Data-Max, on the other hand, is in the business of providing 'instant handicaps' to golfers, either by selling or leasing its computers to golf clubs, or by providing handicaps directly to golfers who cannot obtain 'instant handicaps' through their clubs. The U.S.G.A. does not object to the sale or lease of Data-Max's computers, and does not attempt to provide the direct services which Data-Max provides to golfers. Thus, it is inconceivable that Data-Max's business will interfere with the U.S.G.A.'s incentive to maintain or update the handicap formula." 749 F.2d at 1038, 224 U.S.P.Q. at 654.

[70] 749 F.2d at 1040–41, 224 U.S.P.Q. at 656.

[1] *See* Chapter 3.

and vary from state to state. Some states have publicity statutes;[2] in others, courts recognize a common law publicity right.[3] More than half have yet to recognize publicity rights. Publicity rights protect personal identity features, including name, voice, signature, appearance or likeness,[4] and personality.[5]

Courts and scholars have articulated several policy bases for granting individuals control over the commercial exploitation of their identities. Under one theory, human identity is a self-evident property right.[6] Under another theory, talented individuals should have an economic incentive to undertake socially beneficial activities that require entering the public scene.[7] Some say publicity rights are necessary to prevent fraudulent or misleading business practices.[8]

Unfair competition law and common law copyright protection can overlap publicity rights. For a publicity right claim to arise, the plaintiff need not show likelihood of confusion, only that his identity was used without his authority. If an unauthorized use of a celebrity name is likely to confuse consumers as to the endorsement of goods or services, a claim may arise under both publicity rights and unfair competition law.[9]

---

[2] Cal. Civ. Code §§ 990, 3344 (West Supp. 1991); Fla. Stat. Ann. § 540.08 (West 1988); Ky. Rev. Stat. Ann. § 391.170 (Michie/Bobbs-Merrill 1984); Mass. General Laws Ann. ch. 214 § 3A (West 1989); Neb. Rev. Stat. § 20–202 (1987); Nev. Rev. Stat. Ann. § 598.980–.982 (Michie Supp. 1989); N.Y. Civ. Rights Law § 51 (McKinney Supp. 1991); Okla. Stat. Ann. tit. 21, §§ 839.1– 839.3 (West 1983); R.I. Gen. Law § 9-1-28 (1985); Tenn. Code Ann. §§ 47–25–1101–1108 (1988); Tex. Prop. Code Ann. § 26 (Vernon 1991) (protecting rights of deceased persons); Va. Code Ann. §§ 8.01–40 (1984), 18.2–216.1 (1988); Wis. Stat. Ann. § 895.50 (West 1974).

In California, Florida, Wisconsin and Texas, publicity rights have also been recognized in common law.

[3] Cher v. Forum International Ltd., 692 F.2d 634, 217 U.S.P.Q. 407 (9th Cir. 1982), *cert. denied*, 462 U.S. 1120 (1983) (applying California law); Bi-Rite Enterprises Inc. v. Bruce Miner Co., 757 F.2d 440, 225 U.S.P.Q. 793 (1st Cir. 1985) (applying Connecticut law); Martin Luther King, Jr. Center for Social Change v. American Heritage Products, Inc., 250 Ga. 135, 296 S.E.2d 697, 216 U.S.P.Q. 711 (1982); Fergerstrom v. Hawaiian Ocean View Estates, Inc., 50 Hawaii 374, 441 P.2d 141 (1968); Stone v. Creative Communications, Inc., 216 U.S.P.Q. 261 (N.D. Ill. 1981); Carson v. Here's Johnny Portable Toilets, Inc., 698 F.2d 831, 218 U.S.P.Q. 1 (6th Cir. 1983) (applying Missouri law); Uhlaender v. Harris, 153 Mo. App. 652, 134 S.W. 1076 (1911); Palmer v. Schonhorn Enterprises, Inc., 96 N.J. Super. 72, 232 A.2d 458 (1967); Zacchini v. Scripps-Howard Broadcasting Co., 47 Ohio St. 2d 224, 351 N.E.2d 454 (1976), *rev'd on other grounds*, 433 U.S. 562, 205 U.S.P.Q. 741 (1977); Hogan v. A.S. Barnes & Co., 114 U.S.P.Q. 314 (Pa. Tr. Ct. 1957) (applying Pennsylvania law).

[4] Cal. Civ. Code §§ 990(a), 3344(a) (West Supp. 1991).

[5] Neb. Rev. Stat. § 20–202 (1987).

[6] *See* Pavesich v. New England Life Insurance Co., 122 Ga. 190, 50 S.E. 68, 79 (1905); J. T. McCarthy, The Rights of Publicity and Privacy § 2.1[A] at 2–1 (1987).

[7] Zacchini v. Scripps-Howard Broadcasting Co., 433 U.S. 562, 205 U.S.P.Q. 741 (1977); J. T. McCarthy, The Rights of Publicity and Privacy § 2.2 at 2–9 (1987).

[8] *E.g.*, Felcher & Rubin, *Privacy, Publicity, and the Portrayal of Real People by the Media*, 88 Yale L. J. 1566, 1600 (1979).

[9] Allen v. Men's World Outlet, Inc., 679 F. Supp. 360, 5 U.S.P.Q.2d 1850 (S.D.N.Y. 1988); P. Goldstein, Copyright § 15.17 at 603 (1989).

If the unauthorized use constitutes a "false description or representation," a Lanham Act Section 43(a) claim may arise. 15 U.S.C. § 1125(a); J. T. McCarthy, The Rights of Publicity and Privacy § 6.16[B] at 6–88 (1987).

Similarly, unauthorized copying of a live performance closely linked with a performer's identity could infringe the performer's common law copyright and publicity right.[10] Here, too, the claims are separate and distinct; they simply arise out of the same factual nexus.[11]

Publicity rights have stimulated scholarly comment and, as discussed below, the right developed in response to this comment.[12]

[2] Historical Development

The roots of publicity rights lie in the law of privacy. Both ancient Jewish and Roman law recognized an individual's right to be left alone,[13] but the English common law did not. Samuel Warren and Louis Brandeis' germinal 1890 Harvard Law Review article introduced the concept of the right of privacy to the United States. Warren and Brandeis argued that the law should "protect the privacy of private life. . . . [T]he matters of which the publication should be repressed may be described as those which concern the private life, habits, acts and relations of an individual."[14]

In *Roberson*,[15] the New York Court of Appeals specifically rejected the Warren-Brandeis article in a case involving unauthorized use of a young woman's photograph in flour advertisements. The court noted the "so-called 'right of privacy' has not as yet found an abiding place in our jurisprudence. . . . "[16] In response to *Roberson*,

---

If the celebrity's name is a registered trademark or service mark, unauthorized use may also be trademark infringement. Under Lanham Act Section 2(c), 15 U.S.C. § 1052(c), a person can prevent another from registering a mark comprising his or her name, portrait, or signature. *See* § 5C[2][d][v].

[10] *See* Zacchini v. Scripps-Howard Broadcasting Co., 47 Ohio St. 2d 224, 351 N.E.2d 454 (1976), *rev'd on other grounds*, 433 U.S. 562, 205 U.S.P.Q. 741 (1977).

If the performance is fixed in a tangible medium of expression,such as a film, then the publicity rights may be preempted by federal copyright law. *See* § 6G[4][c][ii].

For a discussion of the fixation requirement, see § 4C[4].

[11] Commentators suggest that because copyright and publicity right subject matter are different—"expression" as opposed to "identity"—there is no overlap between the two, and cases suggesting such overlap are mislabelling the legal theories involved. *See* J. T. McCarthy, The Rights of Publicity and Privacy § 8.13[D] at 8–94 (1987); M.Nimmer & D. Nimmer, Nimmer on Copyright § 1.01[B] n.49.1 (1990).

Under this argument, the best known publicity right case, Zacchini v. Scripps-Howard Broadcasting Co., 433 U.S. 562, 205 U.S.P.Q. 741 (1977), involving the news broadcast of a 15 second human cannotball act, is *not* a publicity right case at all, but a mislabelled common law copyright or misappropriation case. It is conceivable, however, that a performer's identity might become inextricably linked with a character or style that rises to the level of "expression." *See* M. Nimmer & D. Nimmer, Nimmer on Copyright §§ 2.12, 2.13 (1990). Thus, copyright and publicity right can overlap in certain instances, and if the character or style is fixed in a tangible medium of expression (see § 4C[4]), copyright law may preempt the publicity right. *See* §§ 1D[3][c][ii](4) and 6G[4][c][ii].

[12] The authoritative contemporary work is J.T. McCarthy, The Rights of Publicity and Privacy (1987).

[13] Hofstader & Horowitz, The Right to Privacy 9 (1964).

[14] Warren & Brandeis, *The Right to Privacy*, 4 Harv. L. Rev. 193, 195 (1890).

[15] Roberson v. Rochester Folding Box Co., 171 N.Y. 538, 64 N.E. 442 (1902).

[16] 64 N.E. at 447.

in 1903 New York's legislature enacted a statute making use of a person's name or picture for advertising purposes without consent a tort and a misdemeanor.[17] Following *Roberson*, the New York courts have yet to recognize a common law privacy or publicity right.

In *Pavesich*,[18] the Georgia Supreme Court recognized the Warren-Brandeis common law right of privacy in a case involving unauthorized use of a photograph and a false testimonial in a life insurance advertisement.

In the ensuing years other courts divided. Those courts following *Pavesich* viewed violation of the right of privacy as a personal tort in which the injury was the damage "to an individual's self respect in being made a public spectacle."[19] Accordingly, courts awarded damages only for mental anguish. Some courts refused to find injury when an advertiser used a celebrity's name or photograph without authority, reasoning that because celebrities seek publicity, they cannot be harmed by additional, albeit unauthorized, publicity.[20]

In *Haelan Laboratories*,[21] Judge Jerome Frank overturned the limited mental anguish view and identified a property right in a person's identity, calling it "the right of publicity." The following year, Melville Nimmer wrote an influential article highlighting the deficiencies of traditional privacy and trademark laws in protecting the commercial interest of individuals in their identities.[22] The publicity right received additional legitimacy in 1960 when William Prosser included as the fourth of his four privacy torts: "Appropriation, for the defendant's advantage, of the plaintiff's name or likeness."[23]

During the 1960s and 1970s, courts and legislatures recognized publicity rights, either on their own or as part of a broader privacy right. Publicity rights became firmly entrenched in American jurisprudence with *Zacchini*,[24] the only Supreme Court case involving the publicity right. *Zacchini* did not involve the typical situation of unauthorized use of a name or likeness in advertising, but a television news broadcast of Zacchini's 15-second "human cannonball" act.[25] Zacchini sued the television station for broadcasting the performance without his authority. The issue before the Court was whether the First Amendment immunized the station. The Court held that

---

[17] This statute, as amended, is now codified at N.Y. Civ. Rights Law § 51 (McKinney Supp. 1991).

[18] Pavesich v. New England Life Insurance Co., 122 Ga. 190, 50 S.E. 68 (1905).

[19] Bloustein, *Privacy as an Aspect of Human Dignity: An Answer to Dean Prosser*, 39 N.Y.U. L. Rev. 962, 981 (1964).

[20] *E.g.*, O'Brien v. Pabst Sales Co., 124 F.2d 167 (5th Cir. 1941), *cert. denied*, 315 U.S. 823 (1942).

[21] Haelan Laboratories, Inc. v. Topps Chewing Gum, Inc., 202 F.2d 866 (2d Cir.), *cert. denied*, 346 U.S. 816 (1953).

[22] Nimmer, *The Right of Publicity*, 19 Law & Contemporary Problems 203 (1954).

[23] Prosser, *Privacy*, 48 Calif. L. Rev. 383, 389 (1960). The second torts restatement included the four Prosser privacy torts. Restatement (Second) of Torts §§ 652A–652I (1977).

[24] Zacchini v. Scripps-Howard Broadcasting Co., 433 U.S. 562, 205 U.S.P.Q. 741 (1977).

[25] As noted in § 6G[1], *Zacchini* arguably is not a publicity right case, but a common law copyright case.

the First Amendment did not permit the station to broadcast the entire act and, in dictum, recognized the publicity right's virtues.[26]

[3] Rights

Publicity rights grant an individual exclusive control over commercial use of his or her identity.[27] Publicity right subject matter includes elements that identify a person, such as name, likeness, voice, performing style, and signature. In a given case, an identity element's protectability turns on whether the element in fact identifies the individual.[28]

[a] **Names.** A person's first name,[29] family name, stage name, and nickname[30] are protectable. Because many persons have the same name, a plaintiff must show

---

[26] The Court distinguished "false light" privacy claims from other privacy claims, including claims of "a performer, a person with a name having commercial value, or . . . to a 'right of publicity.' "

> "The differences between these two torts are important. First, the State's interests in providing a cause of action in each instance are different. 'The interest protected' in permitting recovery for placing the plaintiff in a false light 'is clearly that of reputation, with the same overtones of mental distress as in defamation.' . . . By contrast, the State's interest in permitting a 'right of publicity' is in protecting the proprietary interest of the individual in his act in part to encourage such entertainment. . . . [T]he State's interest is closely analogous to the goals of patent and copyright law, focusing on the right of the individual to reap the reward of his endeavors and having little to do with protecting feelings or reputation. Second, the two torts differ in the degree to which they intrude on dissemination of information to the public. In 'false light' cases the only way to protect the interests involved is to attempt to minimize publication of the damaging matter, while in 'right of publicity' cases the only question is who gets to do the publishing. An entertainer such as petitioner usually has no objection to the widespread publication of his act as long as he gets the commercial benefit of such publication. Indeed, in the present case petitioner did not seek to enjoin the broadcast of his act; he simply sought compensation for the broadcast in the form of damages." 433 U.S. at 573–74.

[27] Some decisions hold that only "celebrities" have publicity rights. *E.g.*, Delan by Delan v. CBS, Inc., 91 App. Div.2d 255, 262, 458 N.Y.S.2d 608, 615 (1983).

The majority of courts recognize non-celebrities' publicity rights. J. T. McCarthy, The Rights of Publicity and Privacy § 4.3[C] (1987). To date, neither courts nor legislatures have recognized a publicity right in animals, corporations or institutions. *Id.* §§ 4.7, 4.8. Several decisions extend publicity right protection to music groups. *E.g.*, Bi-Rite Enterprises, Inc. v. Button Master, 555 F. Supp. 1188, 217 U.S.P.Q. 910 (S.D.N.Y. 1983). Institutions, such as universities and companies, use trademark, unfair competition, and dilution principles to attempt to suppress unauthorized use of their names and symbols. *See* § 5F[1][d][iii].

[28] The number of people who identify plaintiff from the use has no bearing on whether the use identifies the plaintiff: "the question is whether the figure is recognizable, not the number of people who recognized it." Negri v. Schering Corp., 333 F. Supp. 101, 104 (S.D.N.Y. 1971). The number of people that could identify plaintiff does influence the amount of damages awarded. *Id.*; P. Goldstein, Copyright § 15.20.1.1 (1989).

[29] *E.g.*, Cher v. Forum International Ltd., 692 F.2d 634, 217 U.S.P.Q. 407 (9th Cir. 1982), *cert. denied*, 462 U.S. 1120 (1983).

[30] *E.g.*, Hirsch v. S.C. Johnson & Sons, Inc., 90 Wis. 2d 379, 280 N.W.2d 129 (1979). Some courts have found that the New York statute protects only names, not nicknames. *E.g.*, Geisel v. Poynter Prods., Inc., 295 F. Supp. 331, 355–56, 158 U.S.P.Q. 450 (S.D.N.Y. 1968) (penname "Dr. Seuss").

more than that the defendant used his name. Rather, plaintiff must show from the use's context that he was identifiable. For example, one court held that a fictional policeman, "T.J. Hooker," did not refer to T.J. Hooker, a woodcarver,[31] but another found that defendant's "Crazylegs" women's moisturizing shaving gel identified football star Elroy "Crazylegs" Hirsch.[32]

In *Carson*,[33] the court held that defendant's use of the "Here's Johnny!" slogan together with the phrase "The World's Foremost Commodian" to market its portable toilets, identified entertainer Johnny Carson.[34]

---

[31] T.J. Hooker v. Columbia Pictures Indus., Inc., 551 F. Supp. 1060 (N.D. Ill. 1982).

[32] Hirsch v. S.C. Johnson & Sons, Inc., 90 Wis. 2d 379, 280 N.W.2d 129, 205 U.S.P.Q. 920 (1979).

[33] Carson v. Here's Johnny Portable Toilets, Inc., 698 F.2d 831, 218 U.S.P.Q. 1 (6th Cir. 1983).

[34] In *Carson*, the majority noted:

"The right of publicity, as we have stated, is that a celebrity has a protected pecuniary interest in the commercial exploitation of his identity. If the celebrity's identity is commercially exploited, there has been an invasion of his right whether or not his 'name or likeness' is used. Carson's identity may be exploited even if his name, John W. Carson, or his picture is not used.

. . .

"In this case, Earl Braxton, president and owner of Here's Johnny Portable Toilets, Inc., admitted that he knew that the phrase 'Here's Johnny' had been used for years to introduce Carson.

. . .

". . . [A] celebrity's identity may be appropriated in various ways. It is our view that, under the existing authorities, a celebrity's legal right of publicity is invaded whenever his identity is intentionally appropriated for commercial purposes.

". . . Certainly appellant Carson's achievement has made him a celebrity which means that his identity has a pecuniary value which the right of publicity should vindicate. Vindication of the right will tend to encourage achievement in Carson's chosen field. Vindication of the right will also tend to prevent unjust enrichment by persons such as appellee who seek commercially to exploit the identity of celebrities without their consent. "The dissent also suggests that recognition of the right of publicity here would somehow run afoul of federal monopoly policies and first amendment proscriptions. If, as the dissent seems to concede, such policies and proscriptions are not violated by the vindication of the right of publicity where the celebrity's 'name, likeness, achievements, identifying characteristics or actual performances' have been appropriated for commercial purposes, we cannot see why the policies and proscriptions would be violated where, as here, the celebrity's identity has admittedly been appropriated for commercial exploitation by the use of the phrase 'Here's Johnny Portable Toilets.' " 698 F.2d at 835–37

Judge Cornelia Kennedy dissented in an extensive opinion reviewing the policies and parameters of the law of publicity rights.

"While I agree that an individual's identity may be impermissibly exploited, I do not believe that the common law right of publicity may be extended beyond an individual's name, likeness, achievements, identifying characteristics or actual performances, to include phrases or other things which are merely associated with the individual, as is the phrase 'Here's Johnny.' The majority's extension of the right of publicity to include phrases or other things which are merely associated with the individual permits a popular entertainer

Disguising a name—for example, using "Charlie Aplin" instead of "Charlie Chaplin"—will not shield a defendant if the plaintiff is still identifiable from the name's disguised use.[35]

[b] **Likeness.** A person's likeness—facial and other physical features—are protected from unauthorized use, whether by photograph,[36] drawing,[37] or celebrity lookalike.[38] Identifiability is less of a problem with photographs than with names because facial and physical features are more distinctive than names,[39] but it can be an issue with drawings[40] and photographs that do not include plaintiff's face.[41]

[c] **Roles.** A role with which an actor is closely identified can be the subject of a publicity right. Courts have protected the Marx Brothers persona,[42] Charlie Chaplin's "Little Tramp,"[43] and Laurel and Hardy[44] from unauthorized use. The difficult issue is whether the role identifies the actor. In *Lugosi*,[45] for example, a divided California Supreme Court concluded that an imitation of actor Bela Lugosi's portrayal of Count Dracula did not identify Lugosi.

[d] **Voice—Style—Associated Objects.** In the past, courts did not protect vocal styles,[46] but in *Midler*[47] the Ninth Circuit found unlawful an imitation of performer Bette Midler's distinctive voice in an automobile advertisement. Some statutes also grant an individual a publicity right in his or her voice, but these statutes

---

or public figure, by associating himself or herself with a common phrase, to remove those words from the public domain." 698 F.2d at 837.
She noted that "society's interests in free enterprise and free expression must be balanced against the interests of an individual seeking protection in the right of publicity where the right is being expanded beyond established limits." 698 F.2d at 839.

[35] Chaplin v. Amador, 93 Cal. App. 358, 269 P. 544 (1928).

[36] Grant v. Esquire, Inc., 367 F. Supp. 876 (S.D.N.Y. 1973) (photograph of actor Cary Grant).

[37] Ali v. Playgirl, Inc., 447 F. Supp. 723, 206 U.S.P.Q. 1021 (S.D.N.Y. 1978) (drawing of boxer Muhammad Ali).

[38] Onassis v. Christian Dior—New York, Inc., 122 Misc. 2d 603, 472 N.Y.S.2d 254 (1984), aff'd *without opinion*, 110 App. Div.2d 1095, 488 N.Y.S.2d 943 (1985).

[39] P. Goldstein, Copyright § 15.20.1.1 (1989).

[40] Ali v. Playgirl, Inc., 447 F. Supp. 723, 206 U.S.P.Q. 1021 (S.D.N.Y. 1978). In Nurmi v. Peterson, 10 U.S.P.Q.2d 1775, 1777–78 (C.D. Cal. 1989), the court interpreted the term "likeness" in California's publicity right statute to refer to an actual depiction of an individual, not just general resemblance.

[41] Cohen v. Herbal Concepts, Inc., 100 App. Div.2d 175, 473 N.Y.S.2d 426, aff'd, 63 N.Y.2d 379, 482 N.Y.S.2d 457, 472 N.E.2d 307 (1984) (photograph of nude back).

[42] Groucho Marx Prod., Inc. v. Day & Night Co., 523 F. Supp. 485, 491, 212 U.S.P.Q. 926 (S.D.N.Y. 1981), rev'd *on other grounds*, 689 F.2d 317, 216 U.S.P.Q. 553 (2d Cir. 1982).

[43] Chaplin v. Amador, 93 Cal. App. 358, 269 P. 544 (1928).

[44] Price v. Hal Roach Studios, Inc., 400 F. Supp. 836 (S.D.N.Y. 1975).

[45] Lugosi v. Universal Pictures, 25 Cal. 3d 813, 603 P.2d 425, 160 Cal. Rptr. 323, 205 U.S.P.Q. 1090 (1979).

[46] Lahr v. Adell Chemical Co., 300 F.2d 256, 132 U.S.P.Q. 662 (1st Cir. 1962); Sinatra v. Goodyear Tire & Rubber Co., 435 F.2d 711, 168 U.S.P.Q. 12 (9th Cir. 1970), *cert. denied*, 402 U.S. 906, 169 U.S.P.Q. 321 (1971).

[47] Midler v. Ford Motor Co., 849 F.2d 460, 7 U.S.P.Q.2d 1398 (9th Cir. 1988).

have been interpreted to prevent unauthorized use of the actual voice, not imitations.[48] Courts have also extended the publicity right to objects identified with particular individuals. In *Motschenbacher*,[49] for example, the Ninth Circuit found that a distinctively painted car identified a race car driver.

[4] Infringement

Publicity right infringement consists of defendant making commercial use of some element of plaintiff's identity without authorization in such a way that plaintiff is identifiable from defendant's use.[50]

[a] **Intent.** Courts typically have not included intent to identify plaintiff as a necessary element of a *prima facie* publicity right infringement case.[51] The California statute does require that defendant "knowingly" make use of plaintiff's identity for an infringement to occur.[52] Even where intent is not an element of a *prima facie* case, it can be probative of the fact that plaintiff is identifiable from the use.[53]

Proof of intent may also support an exemplary damage award.[54]

[b] **Speech and Press Freedom.** In *Zacchini*,[55] the Supreme Court held that the United States Constitution's First Amendment, which protects speech and press freedom, was no defense to a suit to recover damages for the unauthorized television news broadcast of a performer's entire 15-second "human cannonball" act. The court reasoned that "[t]he broadcast of a film of petitioner's entire act poses a substantial threat to the economic value of that performance," and that "the Constitution does not prevent Ohio from . . . deciding to protect the entertainer's incentive in order to encourage the production of this type of work."[56]

The First Amendment does protect some unauthorized uses of personal identity from law suits alleging publicity right infringement. For example, news reports that use an individual's name or likeness have been held to be privileged under the First

---

[48] 849 F.2d at 463.

[49] Motschenbacher v. R.J. Reynolds Tobacco Co., 498 F.2d 821, 827 (9th Cir. 1974).

[50] J. T. McCarthy, The Rights of Publicity and Privacy § 3.1[B] (1987)

[51] *E.g.*, Flake v. Greensboro News Co., 212 N.C. 780, 792–93, 195 S.E. 55, 61 (1938); Welch v. Mr. Christmas, Inc., 57 N.Y.2d 143, 144, 454 N.Y.S.2d 971, 972, 440 N.E.2d 1317 (1982). In Davis v. High Society Magazine, Inc., 90 A.D. 374, 383, 457 N.Y.S.2d 308, 316 (1982), the court required a showing of intent.

[52] Cal. Civ. Code § 3344 (West Supp. 1991). The use need not be knowing to violate a publicity right relating to a deceased person. Cal. Civ. Code § 990 (West Supp. 1988).

[53] As Professor McCarthy explains,

> "This proceeds upon the presumption that when a person intends a result, that result is presumed to have taken place. If it is proven that defendant knew of plaintiff and made a commercial use from which it knew reader[s] or viewers would identify plaintiff, then identification should be presumed, with the burden shifting to defendant to try to prove that its customers did not in fact identify plaintiff."

J.T. McCarthy, The Rights of Publicity and Privacy § 3.6[D][2] (1987) (footnotes omitted).

[54] *See, e.g.*, Big Seven Music Corp. v. Lennon, 554 F.2d 504, 513 (2d Cir. 1977).

[55] Zacchini v. Scripps-Howard Broadcasting Co., 433 U.S. 562, 578, 205 U.S.P.Q. 741 (1977).

[56] 433 U.S. at 575–77

Amendment or state constitutional equivalents.[57] The statutory publicity right definitions in several states put news reporting and similar uses, such as biographies, out of the right's reach by applying the right only to unconsented uses "for advertising purposes or for the purposes of trade,"[58] or by excluding uses "in connection with any news, public affairs, or sports broadcast or account, or any political campaign. . . . "[59]

[c] Other Defenses

[i] *Fair Use.* In some publicity right cases, defendants have invoked copyright law's "fair use" defense.[60] Courts acknowledge that it could be successful in an appropriate case, such as a parody or satire, but that in the instant cases the "defendants have gone beyond merely building on the original to the point of duplicating as faithfully as possible the [original] performances."[61]

[ii] *Copyright Preemption.* Copyright Act Section 301[62] preempts state law publicity rights if a work is fixed in a tangible medium of expression, the work is copyrightable subject matter, and the rights state law grants in the work are equivalent to rights the Copyright Act grants. Because name and likeness—the publicity right's core subject matter—are, in copyright terminology, "ideas" rather than "expressions," they typically are not copyrightable subject matter, and publicity rights in them are not preempted. A photographer's copyright in an individual's photograph does not preempt the individual's state law publicity right to prevent the photographer from using his or her likeness, as captured in the photograph, for commercial purposes.[63]

If a performer's identity becomes inextricably linked with a character or style that rises to the level of expression protectable under copyright law, the performer's publicity rights in that character may be preempted.[64] In *Baltimore Orioles,*[65] the

---

[57] *See, e.g.,*Ann-Margret v. High Society Magazine, Inc., 498 F. Supp. 401, 406–97, 208 U.S.P.Q. 428 (S.D.N.Y. 1980) (publication of photographs of actress in celebrity skin care article did not violate her publicity right). *See also* P. Goldstein, Copyright § 15.20.2.1 at n.27 (1989) and cases cited therein.

[58] N.Y. Civ. Rights Law §§ 50, 51 (McKinney Supp. 1991). *See* Gautier v. Pro-Football, Inc., 304 N.Y. 354, 359, 107 N.E.2d 485, 488 (1952) (news-related uses are not "for purposes of trade" under the statute).

[59] Cal. Civ. Code § 3344(d) (West Supp. 1991). *See also* Neb. Rev. Stat. § 20–202(1) (1987); Tenn. Code Ann. § 47–25–1107(a) (1988).

[60] Groucho Marx Productions, Inc. v. Night and Day Co., Inc., 523 F. Supp. 485, 493, 212 U.S.P.Q. 926 (S.D.N.Y. 1981) (rejecting "fair use" defense), *rev'd on other grounds,* 689 F.2d 317, 216 U.S.P.Q. 553 (2d Cir. 1982); Estate of Presley v. Russen, 513 F. Supp. 1339, 1359–60, 211 U.S.P.Q. 415 (D.N.J. 1981) (rejecting "fair use" and First Amendment free speech defenses).

[61] Groucho Marx Productions, Inc. v. Night and Day Co., Inc., 523 F. Supp. 485, 493, 212 U.S.P.Q. 926 (S.D.N.Y. 1981), *rev'd on other grounds,* 689 F.2d 317, 216 U.S.P.Q. 553 (2d Cir. 1982).

[62] 17 U.S.C. § 301 (1988).

[63] P. Goldstein, Copyright §§ 15.22.1.1–15.22.1.2 (1989). By the same token, the individual cannot copy the photograph without the photographer's authority.

[64] *See* D. Nimmer & M. Nimmer, Nimmer on Copyright §§ 2.12, 2.13 (1990); P. Goldstein, Copyright 15.22.1.2 (1989).

Seventh Circuit held that professional baseball players' publicity rights in their on-field performances were preempted by the copyrighted broadcast of their performances.

[*iii*] *Antitrust.* Publicity right licensing programs have faced antitrust challenges. The courts and the Federal Trade Commission have held that baseball players' exclusive contracts licensing their identities in connection with baseball cards and chewing gum violated neither Sherman Act Section 1 or Section 2[66] nor Federal Trade Commission Act Section 5.[67]

[*iv*] *Statute of Limitations.* In many states, courts apply the relatively short (often one- or two-year) libel and invasion of privacy statute of limitations periods to publicity right cases;[68] elsewhere, courts apply the longer "property" torts statute of limitations.[69] For statute of limitations purposes, the cause of action accrues upon the infringing "publication." Under the rule most states follow,[70] any "one edition of a book or newspaper, or any radio or television broadcast, exhibition of a motion picture or similar aggregate communication" constitutes a "publication."[71]

[5] Remedies

The standard publicity right infringement remedy is an injunction. Money damages for personal identity infringement are typically inadequate and difficult to measure.[72] One advantage of an injunction in this context is that it can be carefully tailored to prohibit the illegal conduct at issue without prohibiting conduct that is either protected speech or within a consent or license.[73] A preliminary injunction

---

[65] Baltimore Orioles v. Major League Baseball Players Association, 805 F.2d 663, 231 U.S.P.Q. 673 (7th Cir. 1986), *cert. denied,* 480 U.S. 941 (1987). Professor Goldstein criticizes this holding on the ground that it overlooked the distinction between the person depicted— here, the on-field performance—and the depiction—the broadcast: "the court erred in its evident assumption that the broadcast's fixation constituted fixation of the players' [individual] performances." P. Goldstein, Copyright § 15.22.1.1 (1989).

[66] Fleer Corp. v. Topps Chewing Gum, Inc., 658 F.2d 139 (3d Cir. 1981), *cert. denied,* 455 U.S. 1019 (1982); Topps Chewing Gum, Inc. v. Fleer Corp., 799 F.2d 851 (2d Cir. 1986); Topps Chewing Gum, Inc. v. Major League Baseball Players Ass'n, 641 F. Supp. 1179 (S.D.N.Y. 1986).

[67] *In re* Topps Chewing Gum, Inc., 67 F.T.C. 744 (1965).

[68] *See, e.g.,* Lugosi v. Universal Pictures, Inc., 25 Cal. 3d 813, 854, 603 P.2d 425, 160 Cal. Rptr. 323, 349, 205 U.S.P.Q. 1090 (1979); Neb. Rev. Stat. § 20–211 (1987).

[69] Canessa v. J.I. Kislak, Inc., 97 N.J. Super. 327, 332-353, 235 A.2d 62, 65-76 (1967) (applying New Jersey's six-year statute).

[70] *See* Keeton v. Hustler Magazine, Inc., 465 U.S. 770, 777 n.8 (1984); J.T. McCarthy, The Rights of Publicity and Privacy §§ 11.5, 11.11 (1987).

[71] Uniform Single Publication Act § 1, 14 Uniform Laws Annotated 351 (1980) (in effect in Arizona, California, Idaho, Illinois, New Mexico, North Dakota and Pennsylvania). Only one damages action can be maintained per publication. *Id.*; Restatement (Second) of Torts § 577A(3) (1977).

[72] *See* Ali v. Playgirl, Inc., 447 F. Supp. 723, 729, 206 U.S.P.Q. 1021 (S.D.N.Y. 1978); J.T. McCarthy, The Rights of Publicity and Privacy § 11.6A at 11–24. (1987)

[73] *See, e.g.,*Commonwealth v. Wiseman, 356 Mass. 251, 262, 249 N.E.2d 610, 618 (1969), *cert. denied,* 398 U.S. 960 (1970) (to balance mental institution inmates' privacy rights against a documentary filmmaker's free speech rights, court enjoined showings to general public but

can issue in publicity right cases, but a request for one may trigger the rule against prior restraints.[74] Courts have the power to issue extraterritorial or nationwide injunctions,[75] but they may decline to do so in cases in which the conduct may not violate other states' laws.[76]

In addition to an injunction, courts may award damages for publicity right violations. Damages can be for emotional distress, most often granted for noncelebrities,[77] or for commercial loss.

Courts use a reasonable royalty or market value test to measure commercial loss. Courts look to amounts comparable persons receive for comparable uses,[78] or, if possible, to amounts plaintiff received for similar authorized use of his or her identity.[79] Damages can also be awarded to compensate for injury to professional standing or future income.[80] Some states allow plaintiff to recover the infringer's profits.[81]

Finally, most states allow plaintiff to recover punitive or exemplary damages for publicity right violations. Plaintiff must show the defendant acted with culpable intent, but the exact state of mind necessary varies from state to state.[82]

[6] Ownership and Transfer

In most states, publicity rights are descendible property interests that can be exploited for a limited time period after the person's death.

Because publicity rights originated from traditional, personal privacy rights that protected dignity and reputation, some courts held that the right could not be asserted

---

allowed showings to qualified professionals); Leavy v. Cooney, 214 Cal. App. 2d 496, 504, 29 Cal. Rptr. 580, 585 (1963) (because plaintiff consented to television showing of film, injunction granted only against theater showings).

[74] See, e.g., Organization for a Better Austin v. Keefe, 402 U.S. 415, 419 (1971).

[75] See, e.g., Carson v. Here's Johnny Portable Toilets, Inc., 810 F.2d 104, 105, 1 U.S.P.Q.2d 2007 (6th Cir. 1987); Ali v. Playgirl, Inc., 447 F. Supp. 723, 731, n.10, 206 U.S.P.Q. 1021 (S.D.N.Y. 1978).

[76] See, e.g., Rosemont Enterprises v. Urban Systems, Inc., 42 App. Div.2d 544, 345 N.Y.S.2d 17 (1973).

[77] J.T. McCarthy, The Rights of Publicity and Privacy § 11.7[A] at 11–35 (1987).

[78] See, e.g., National Bank of Commerce v. Shaklee Corp., 503 F. Supp. 533, 546–47, 207 U.S.P.Q. 1005 (W.D. Tex. 1980).

[79] See, e.g., Clark v. Celeb Publishing, Inc., 530 F. Supp. 979, 983 (S.D.N.Y. 1981).

[80] See, e.g., Hirsch v. S.C. Johnson & Son, Inc., 90 Wis. 2d 379, 400, 280 N.W.2d 129, 138, 205 U.S.P.Q. 920 (1979).

[81] See, e.g., Tenn. Code Ann. § 47–25–1106(d) (1988); Wis. Stat. Ann. § 895.50(1)(b) (West 1974).

Under California's statute, plaintiff need only prove defendant's total revenues; the defendant then has the burden of showing its deductible expenses. Cal. Civ. Code §§ 990(a), 3344(a) (West Supp. 1991).

[82] Compare N.Y. Civ. Rights Law § 51 (McKinney Supp. 1991) ("knowingly used") with Hogan v. A.S. Barnes & Co., Inc., 114 U.S.P.Q. 314, 322 (Pa. Tr. Ct. 1957) ("malicious, wanton, reckless or oppressive" conduct).

by relatives or after a person's death.[83] Other courts recognized post-mortem publicity rights, following principles of unfair competition protection,[84] but limited recognition to cases where the person exploited the publicity during his or her lifetime[85] or transferred the publicity rights in connection with a transfer of other assets.[86]

Academic commentators criticized the survival limitations on publicity rights,[87] and courts[88] and statutory enactments[89] in many states reject them. The statutes generally provide that the right survives the individual's death for a limited number of years.[90] Currently, the only states recognizing publicity rights that continue to reject a post-mortem right are New York,[91] Ohio,[92] Nebraska,[93] and Wisconsin.[94]

---

[83] Lugosi v. Universal Pictures, Inc., 25 Cal. 3d 813, 603 P.2d 425, 160 Cal. Rptr. 323, 205 U.S.P.Q. 1090 (1979) (no post-mortem publicity right); Memphis Devel. Foundation v. Factors Etc. Inc., 616 F.2d 956, 205 U.S.P.Q. 784 (6th Cir. 1980), cert. denied, 449 U.S. 953 (1980); Maritote v. Desilu Productions, Inc., 345 F.2d 418, 420 (7th Cir. 1965), cert. denied, 382 U.S. 883 (1965); J.T. McCarthy, The Rights of Publicity and Privacy § 9.1 (1987).

[84] P. Goldstein, Copyright § 15.19 at 607–08 (1989).

[85] Factors Etc., Inc. v. Pro Arts, Inc., 444 F. Supp. 288, 290 (S.D.N.Y. 1977), aff'd, 579 F.2d 215, 222 & n.11 (2d Cir. 1978), cert. denied, 440 U.S. 908 (1979); Hicks v. Casablanca Records, 464 F. Supp. 426, 204 U.S.P.Q. 126 (S.D.N.Y. 1978); Lerman v. Chuckleberry Publishing, Inc., 521 F. Supp. 228, 232 (S.D.N.Y. 1981), rev'd sub nom. Lerman v. Flynt Dist. Co., Inc., 745 F.2d 123, 134 (2d Cir. 1984), cert. denied, 471 U.S. 1054 (1985).

[86] Hanna Mfg. Co., v. Hillerich & Bradsby Co., 78 F.2d 763, 766–67 (5th Cir. 1935), cert. denied, 296 U.S. 645 (1935).

[87] See Felcher & Rubin, The Descendibility of the Right of Publicity: Is There Commercial Life After Death?, 89 Yale L. J. 1125 (1980); Sims, Right of Publicity: Survivability Reconsidered, 49 Fordham L. Rev. 453 (1981); Hoffman, The Right of Publicity: Heirs' Right, Advertisers' Windfall, or Courts' Nightmare, 31 DePaul L. Rev. 1 (1981); Kwall, Is Independence Day Dawning for the Right of Publicity?, 17 U.C. Davis L. Rev. 191 (1983); Comment, Inheritability of the Right of Publicity upon the Death of the Famous, 33 Vand. L. Rev. 1251 (1980); Comment, An Assessment of the Commercial Exploitation Requirement as a Limit on the Right of Publicity, 96 Harv. L. Rev. 1703 (1983); Comment, Descendibility of the Right of Publicity, 1983 So. Ill. U.L.J. 547 (1986). See also J. T. McCarthy, The Rights of Publicity and Privacy §§ 9.2[C], 9.3[B][2] (1987).

[88] Martin Luther King, Jr. Center for Social Change, Inc. v. American Heritage Products, Inc., 250 Ga. 135, 145–146, 296 S.E.2d 697, 705, 216 U.S.P.Q. 711 (1982), upon response to certified question, 694 F.2d 674 (11th Cir. 1983); Estate of Presley v. Russen, 513 F. Supp. 1339, 211 U.S.P.Q. 415 (D. N.J. 1981).

[89] Cal Civ. Code § 990(b) (West Supp. 1991) (overruling Lugosi decision); Fla. Stat. Ann. § 540.08(4) (West 1988); Ky. Rev. Stat. Ann. § 391.170 (Michie/Bobbs-Merrill 1984); Nev. Rev. Stat.Ann. § 598.982 (Michie Supp. 1989); Okla. Stat. Ann. tit. 12, § 1448 (West 1991); Tenn. Code Ann. § 47–25–1103(b) (1988); Tex. Prop. Code Ann. §§ 26.005–26.010 (Vernon 1991); Va. Code Ann. § 8.01.40 (1984).

[90] California, Kentucky, Nevada and Texas provide 50 years, Florida 40, Oklahoma 100, Tennessee 10 and Virginia 20.

[91] Stephano v. News Group Publications, Inc., 64 N.Y.2d 174, 182–183, 474 N.E.2d 580, 584, 485 N.Y.S.2d 220, 224 (1984) (rejecting common law right of publicity as separate from statutory privacy rights); Antonetty v. Cuomo, 131 Misc. 2d 1041, 502 N.Y.S.2d 902, 906 (1986), aff'd without opinion, 125 App. Div.2d 1010, 509 N.Y.S.2d 443 (1986), app. denied, 70 N.Y.2d 602, 512 N.E.2d 551, 518 N.Y.S.2d 551 (1987) (no post-mortem right); Smith v.

Publicity rights may be assigned[95] or licensed.[96]

§ 6H Idea Submission

"[I]deas are as free as the air."[1] Or are they?[2] In some situations, the law obligates one person to compensate another for an idea. Typically, an individual submits an idea to a company expecting compensation if the idea is used. The company uses the idea but does not pay the submitter. The submitter sues, alleging that his or idea was improperly used.

Idea submission law encompasses four interrelated theories: property, express contract, implied contract; and unjust enrichment/quasi-contract. Courts do not always carefully distinguish the theories and may use elements commonly associated with one theory to grant or deny recovery under a different theory, and many cases decided under one theory contain facts that would support recovery under another theory as well.[3] Shifting theories may alter the applicable statute of limitations or the

---

Long Island Jewish-Hillside Med. Center, 118 App. Div.2d 553, 554, 499 N.Y.S.2d 167, 168 (1986) (same).

[92] Reeves v. United Artists, 572 F. Supp. 1231, 222 U.S.P.Q. 541 (N.D. Ohio 1983), aff'd, 765 F.2d 79 (6th Cir. 1985).

[93] Neb. Rev. Stat. § 20–207, –.208 (1987) (no post-mortem publicity right).

[94] Heinz v. Frank Lloyd Wright Foundation, 229 U.S.P.Q. 201, 206 (W.D. WIs. 1986) (construing statutory right as limited to living persons but not considering common law rights).

[95] Haelan Laboratories, Inc. v. Topps Chewing Gum, Inc., 202 F.2d 866, 868 (2d Cir. 1953), cert. denied, 346 U.S. 816 (1953); Bi-Rite Enterprises v. Button Master, 555 F. Supp. 1188, 1200, 217 U.S.P.Q. 910 (S.D.N.Y. 1983); Acme Circus Operating Co. v. Kuperstock, 711 F.2d 1538, 221 U.S.P.Q. 420 (11th Cir. 1983); Fleer v. Topps Chewing Gum, Inc., 658 F.2d 139, 148 (3d Cir. 1981), cert. denied, 455 U.S. 1019 (1982); Estate of Presley v. Russen, 513 F. Supp. 1339, 1346–49, 211 U.S.P.Q. 415 (D.N.J. 1981); Factors Etc., Inc. v. Pro Arts, Inc., 579 F.2d 215, 221 (2d Cir. 1978), cert. denied, 480 U.S. 908 (1979).

Unlike trademarks, a person may assign publicity rights "in gross," that is, without also transferring a business. See J. T. McCarthy, The Rights of Publicity and Privacy § 10.14 (1987).

[96] Douglass v. Hustler Magazine, Inc., 769 F.2d 1128, 1138 (7th Cir. 1985), cert. denied, 475 U.S. 1094 (1986). See generally J. T. McCarthy, The Rights of Publicity and Privacy § 10.4 et seq. (1987).

[1] Desny v. Wilder, 46 Cal. 2d 715, 731, 299 P.2d 257, 265 (1965).

[2] See Desny v. Wilder, 46 Cal. 2d 715, 731, 299 P.2d 257, 265 (1965) ("there can be circumstances when neither air nor ideas may be acquired without cost. The diver who goes deep in the sea, even as the pilot who ascends high in the troposphere, knows full well that for life itself he, or someone on his behalf, must arrange for air (or its respiration essential element, oxygen) to be specially provided at the time and place of need. The theatrical producer likewise may be dependent for his business life on the procurement of ideas from other persons as well as the dressing up and portrayal of his self-conceptions; he may not find his own sufficient for survival.").

[3] Nimmer adds a fifth theory: confidential relationships. 3 D. Nimmer & M. Nimmer, Nimmer on Copyright § 16.02. Epstein properly considers confidential relationships to be a subset of implied contracts. M. Epstein, Modern Intellectual Property § 7 (1989).

measure of damage recovery.[4] Courts often treat an idea's status as property as a prerequisite to recovery under other theories.[5]

Idea submission law is based on state law, typically common (nonstatutory) law and is closely related to trade secret[6] and misappropriation law.[7] In common with those two areas, questions arise whether state intellectual property protection conflicts with federal policy or is preempted by Copyright Act Section 301.[8] State law may protect confidential relationships and enforce express and implied contracts, which are the foundations of most of idea submission law.[9] Federal preemption becomes a serious problem only if state law prohibits copying, without more, of publicly-disclosed ideas and products.

Until 1978, state law could protect unpublished copyrightable works of authorship. After 1978, federal copyright is the sole source of copyright protection for unpublished works.[10] Courts clearly distinguish submitted "ideas" from "literary properties" and other expressions of ideas that are the subject of copyright.[11] In idea submission situations, the submitter's potential copyright remedies are frequently ineffective even when the submission includes "expression" because the defendant uses only the idea, not the submitter's expression.[12]

---

[4] *E.g.,* Vantage Point, Inc. v. Parker Bros., Inc., 529 F. Supp. 1204, 1216, 213 U.S.P.Q. 782 (E.D. N.Y. 1981), *aff'd,* 697 F.2d 301 (2d Cir. 1982) (table).

[5] *E.g.,* Downey v. General Foods Corp., 31 N.Y.2d 56, 334 N.Y.S.2d 874, 877, 286 N.E.2d 257, 259 (1972) ("when one submits an idea to another, no promise to pay for its use may be implied, and no asserted agreement enforced, if the elements of novelty and originality are absent, since the property right in an idea is based upon these two elements.").

[6] *See* § Chapter 3.

[7] *See* § 6F.

[8] *See* §§ 1D[3][a] and 1D[3][c][i].

[9] *See* Aronson v. Quick Point Pencil Co., 440 U.S. 257, 201 U.S. 1 (1979), discussed at § 1D[3][b][iii].

See also Smith v. Weinstein, 578 F. Supp. 1247 (S.D. N.Y. 1984), *aff'd,* 738 F.2d 419 (2d Cir. 1984) (table) ("A party may by contract agree to pay for ideas, even though such ideas could not be protected by copyright law. Rights under such an agreement are qualitatively different from copyright claims, and their recognition creates no monopoly in the ideas involved. Similarly, plaintiff's breach of confidence claim is nonequivalent to the rights one can acquire under copyright law; rather it rests on an obligation not to disclose to third parties ideas revealed in confidence, which obligation is judicially imposed only upon a party that accepts the relationship, and thus results in no monopoly. In short, these claims, narrowly read, focus on the relationship between individual parties and make actionable breaches of agreements between parties, or breaches of the trust they place in each other because of the nature of their relationship.").

[10] *See* §§ 1D[3][c] and 4D[1].

[11] *E.g.,* International News Service v. Associated Press, 248 U.S. (1918), discussed at § 6F; Desny v. Wilder, 46 Cal. 2d 715, 299 P.2d 257 (1965).

[12] *E.g.,* Landsberg v. Scrabble Crossword Game Players, Inc., 736 F.2d 485, 221 U.S.P.Q. 1140 (9th Cir. 1986), *cert. denied,* 469 U.S. 1037 (1986); Werlin v. Reader's Digest Ass'n, 528 F. Supp. 451, 213 U.S.P.Q. 1041 (S.D. N.Y. 1981).

[1] **Property Theory**

The property theory focuses on the idea's nature, unlike the other three theories, which focus on the parties' relationship. The majority of jurisdictions recognize a "property" right in ideas.[13] A handful do not.[14] In discussing idea submissions, court use "property" loosely, recognizing it is more a legal conclusion than a factual description.[15]

Most courts applying a property theory agree the idea must be (1) novel and original, and (2) concrete.[16] Once an idea is recognized as property, the submitter must show that it was used without his or her authority.[17]

[a] **Novelty and Originality.** To be legally protectible property, an idea must be novel and original. Ideas that are commonly used, well-known, or variations of old familiar themes do not quality.[18]

Examples of ideas found to be novel include (1) a magazine article on a Down's Syndrome afflicted girl's bat mitzvah,[19] (2) a radio show that would select student talent by holding auditions in a high school assembly format;[20] (3) an elaborate contest among sales staff to boost sales,[21] and (4) using tapes for sales training and indoctrination.[22]

---

[13] *E.g.,* Educational Sales Program, Inc. v. Dreyfus Corp., 65 Misc. 2d 412, 317 N.Y.S.2d 840, 843, 169 U.S.P.Q. 117 (Sup. Ct. 1970); Peunte v. President and Fellows of Harvard College, 248 F.2d 799, 802 (1st Cir. 1957), *cert. denied,* 356 U.S. 947 (1958); Wilson v. Barton & Ludwiz, Inc., 163 Ga. 721, 296 S.E.2d 74, 220 U.S.P.Q. 375 (1982); Davies v. Carnation Co., 352 F.2d 393, 147 U.S.P.Q. 350 (9th Cir. 1965); Boop v. Ford Motor Co., 278 F.2d 197, 199 (7th Cir. 1960).

[14] *See, e.g.,* Whitfield v. Lear, 751 F.2d 90, 224 U.S.P.Q. 540 (2d Cir. 1984) (refusing property theory recovery because California does not recognize property in ideas but granting implied contract recovery); Weitzenkorn v. Lesser, 40 Cal. 2d 778, 256 P.2d 947 (1953); B & M Die Co. v. Ford Motor Co., 167 Mich. App. 176, 421 N.W.2d 620, 623 (1988).

Some courts refrain from using the property label but apply property theory's three-requisite analysis—novelty and originality, concreteness, and unauthorized use.

[15] *See* Desny v. Wilder, 46 Cal. 2d 715, 731, 299 P.2d 257, 265 (1965) ("An idea is usually not regarded as property, because all sentient beings may conceive and evolve ideas throughout the gamut of their powers of cerebration and because our concept of property implies something which may be owned and possessed to the exclusion of all other persons.")

[16] Novelty and concreteness are also requisites for recovery under express, implied, and quasi-contract theories.

[17] This is akin to a conversion claim, but courts do not label it as such.

[18] As with trade secret law, see § 3C[1][c][vi], idea submission law's novelty standard should not be as strict as patent law's novelty and nonobviousness requirements. *But cf.* Tate v. Scanlan International, Inc., 403 N.W.2d 666, 671 (Minn. Ct. App. 1987) (applying by "analogy" patent law novelty concepts: "A novel idea is an original idea, something that is not already known or in use. . . . The novelty essential to a protected property right cannot arise solely from the fact that something already known and in use is put to a new use.")

[19] Werlin v. Reader's Digest Ass'n, 528 F. Supp. 451, 213 U.S.P.Q. 1041 (S.D. N.Y. 1981).

[20] Hamilton National Bank v. Belt, 210 F.2d 706 (D.C. Cir. 1953).

[21] Bergman v. Electrolux, 558 F. Supp. 1351 (1987) (plaintiff presented enough evidence to raise a question of fact as to novelty).

[22] Educational Sales Programs, Inc. v. Dreyfuss Corp., 65 Misc. 2d 412, 317 N.Y.S.2d 840, 844, 169 U.S.P.Q. 117 (1970).

Examples of ideas found to be not novel include (1) takeover a food service company and sell part of its operations,[23] (2) a video make-over program,[24] (3) a greeting card character with a halo and wings called "Little Angel Food Cake,"[25] and (4) a business should raise its product's price.[26]

Murray[27] is a good example of a case in which a court denied recovery for want of novelty. Plaintiff claimed that the "Cosby Show" producers improperly took her television sitcom idea, which called for a show centered on a wholesome, intact, non-stereotypical Black American family. The court found the idea lacked novelty because (1) twenty years earlier, Bill Cosby publicly espoused the idea, and (2) the idea represented an "adaptation of existing knowledge" using "known ingredients": when "an idea consists in essence of nothing more than a variation on a basic theme, novelty cannot be found."[28] It acknowledged that "even novel and original ideas to a greater or lesser extent combine elements that are themselves not novel. Originality does not exist in a vacuum."[29]

[b] **Concreteness.** To be classified as property, a novel and original idea must be concrete, not abstract. In assessing an idea's concreteness, courts examine its development and require a degree of maturity. An idea must be embodied in a "tangible" form.[30] An idea that requires "extensive investigation, research and planning" before implementation does not qualify.[31] One court held that the idea "must be ready for immediate use without embellishment."[32] In contrast, a California court held that a partially developed idea that gave insight into a final product was sufficiently concrete.[33]

---

[23] Orderline Wholesale Distributors Inc. v. Gibbons, Green, van Amerongen Ltd., 675 F. Supp. 122 (S.D. N.Y. 1987).

[24] Ring v. Estee Lauder, Inc., 702 F. Supp. 76, 78, 10 U.S.P.Q.2d 1172 (S.D. N.Y. 1988), aff'd, 874 F.2d 109, 10 U.S.P.Q.2d 1796 (2d Cir. 1984) ("New York law is abundantly clear that a plaintiff is not entitled to relief under any theory for theft of an idea, absent proof that the idea was novel or original.").

[25] Pittman v. American Greeting Corp., 619 F. Supp. 939 (W.D. Ky. 1985).

[26] Soule v. Bon Ami Co., 201 A.D. 794, 195 N.Y.S. 574 (1922), aff'd, 235 N.Y. 609, 139 N.E. 754 (1923).

[27] Murray v. National Broadcasting Co., 844 F.2d 988, 993, 6 U.S.P.Q.2d 1618 (2d Cir. 1988), cert. denied, 488 U.S. 955 (1988).

[28] 844 F.2d at 993. The court noted:

"[I]ideas that reflect 'genuine novelty and invention' are fully protected against unauthorized use. . . . But those ideas that are not novel 'are in the public domain and may freely be used by anyone with impunity.' . . . Since such non-novel ideas are not protectible as property, they cannot be stolen. In assessing whether an idea is in the public domain, the central issue is the uniqueness of the creation."

See also Tate v. Scanlan International Inc., 403 N.W.2d 666, 671 (Minn. Ct. App. 1987).

[29] 844 F.2d at 993.

[30] E.g., O'Brien v. RKO Radio Pictures Inc., 68 F. Supp. 13, 14 (S.D. N.Y. 1946).

[31] Tate v. Scanlan Int'l Inc., 403 N.W.2d 666, 672 (Minn. Ct. App. 1987).

[32] Smith v. Recrion Corp., 91 Nev. 666, 541 P.2d 663, 665, 191 U.S.P.Q. 397 (1975).

[33] Fink v. Goodson-Todman Ent. Ltd., 9 Cal. App. 3d 996, 88 Cal. Rptr. 679, 169 U.S.P.Q. 106 (1970).

In *Hamilton*,[34] the court found plaintiff's plan for a weekly radio program sufficiently concrete. It called for a weekly radio show, using local high school talent, to be "presented and recorded as a student assembly, retaining the atmosphere of a school by referring to the show as a class, to the acts as assignment, and the actions as recitations." The shows would have minimal conversation and no commercial breaks, only a brief sponsorship acknowledgement at the show's beginning and end. The court concluded that these details, "when added to the basic general idea which alone would be abstract, gave sufficient concreteness."[35]

In *Smith*,[36] the court set forth a more demanding concreteness standard. Plaintiff presented defendant a proposal, illustrated with a detailed brochure, to construct and operate a recreational vehicle park in connection with defendant's luxury hotel. Defendant rejected the proposal but, two years later, opened a hotel with an RV park. The court denied plaintiff's claim for compensation because it found the brochure lacked concreteness. To be concrete, the idea must be capable of "immediate use without embellishment." To develop plaintiff's idea sufficiently so that it was "ripe for implementation required extensive investigation and planning."[37] The court did not discuss what details the brochure contained or what else plaintiff should have included so as to make the idea ready for "immediate use."

Two cases concerning advertising ideas illustrate how concreteness standards vary. In *Liggett*,[38] the court found sufficiently concrete plaintiff's suggested advertisement in which two men, either in working clothes or hunting gear, converse, one offers the other a cigarette, the other responds: "No thanks, I smoke Chesterfields." Defendant ran advertisements that depicted two men on a golf course and a man and a woman, in each instant the offeree responding: "I'll stick to Chesterfields." The court concluded that even though defendants used different settings, plaintiff's slogan, by itself, was sufficiently concrete to merit protection. In *Baily*,[39] the court found not sufficiently concrete plaintiff's suggested advertising slogan "Neighborly Haberle." Can these two cases be reconciled? One could argue that the difference in result is justified because the plaintiff in *Liggett* offered more than a slogan, an entire sketch, whereas the plaintiff in *Baily* offered only a slogan. One could respond that this argument is not persuasive because in *Liggett* the defendant did not use plaintiff's backgrounds, only his slogan, and the court found the slogan alone sufficiently concrete.

---

[34] Hamilton Nat'l Bank v. Belt, 210 F.2d 706 (D.C. Cir. 1953).

[35] 210 F.2d at 709. *Hamilton's* detailed concreteness analysis has guided subsequent court decisions on radio and television program ideas.

[36] Smith v. Recrion Corp., 91 Nev. 666, 541 P.2d 663, 191 U.S.P.Q. 397 (1975).

[37] 91 Nev. at 669, 541 P.2d at 665. Nimmer criticizes the "immediate use" concreteness definition:

> "If we think of an idea as a conception . . . a preliminary plan, then surely to speak of an idea developed to the point where it is ready for use presents a contraction in terms since if an idea is so developed that it ceases to be merely an idea. Indeed, it might well be argued that these courts which truly adhere to the doctrine that only concrete ideas may be protected in fact protect no idea at all." 3 D. Nimmer & M. Nimmer, Nimmer on Copyright § 16.08[A].

[38] Liggett & Meyers Tobacco Co. v. Meyer, 101 Ind. App. 420, 194 N.E. 206 (1935).

[39] Baily v. Haberle Congress Brewing Co., 193 Misc. 723, 85 N.Y.S.2d 51 (1941).

In assessing concreteness, the form in which the idea is presented is not crucial. Courts have found that concrete ideas can be submitted in a variety of forms: an oral presentation of a radio program idea;[40] a letter describing an idea for a new detergent combining two other products;[41] or a drawing and a non-workable mock-up.[42]

In assessing concreteness, courts consider custom and industry practice regarding idea submissions.[43]

[c] **Unauthorized Use.** Some decisions explicitly require the plaintiff to demonstrate that defendant used plaintiff's idea without authority.[44] An idea submitter can prove use by showing (1) the alleged user's access to the submitted idea, and (2) a substantial similarity between the submitted idea and defendant's product.[45]

To avoid liability for using an idea substantially similar to a submitted idea, the recipient may try to show that the idea was otherwise known or available to it or that its internal procedures were such that it could not have used the submitted idea.[46] A court is apt to reject a nonuse argument if the defendant was exposed to plaintiff's idea and defendant's product or practice is substantially similar to the concrete submitted idea.

[2] Express Contracts

A company or individual may expressly agree to compensate submitter for an idea, whether it is used or not. In general, courts enforce express idea submission contracts,[47] but there are limiting circumstances.

---

[40] Hamilton National Bank v. Belt, 210 F.2d 706, 709 (D.C. Cir. 1953).

[41] Galanis v. Procter & Gamble Corp., 153 F. Supp. 34, 38 (S.D. N.Y. 1957).

[42] Dewey v. American Stair Glide Corp., 557 S.W.2d 643, 646–47, 200 U.S.P.Q. 632 (Mo. Ct. App. 1977).

[43] Tate v. Scanlan Int'l, 403 N.W.2d 666, 672 (Minn. Ct. App. 1987)("Oral presentations and demonstrations of ideas and written proposals of ideas have been held to be sufficiently developed to be 'usable,' and thus satisfy the concreteness requirement. . . . The undisputed testimony . . . was that 'concrete' in the field of medical marketing meant that the concept was very well defined, with reasonable access to all parts necessary to develop it. He also testified that in this field a working model of an idea was rarely presented."); Hamilton Nat'l Bank v. Belt, 210 F.2d 706, 709 (D.C. Cir. 1953).

[44] See, e.g., McGhan v. Ebersol, 608 F. Supp. 277, 286 (S.D. N.Y. 1985).

[45] Fleming v. Ronson Corp., 107 N.J. Super. 221, 258 A.2d 153, 157, 164 U.S.P.Q. 369 (N.J. Sup. Law. Div. 1969), aff'd, 114 N.J. Super. 221, 275 A.2d 759 (App. Div. 1917).

This proof rule resembles that for copyright infringement. See § 4F[1].

[46] For example, the recipient may show that it always returns unsolicited ideas unopened or that the person who opens and returns unsolicited ideas is screened from others who might use the idea. See Downey v. General Foods Corp., 31 N.Y.2d 56, 334 N.Y.S.2d 874, 286 N.E.2d 257 (1972).

[47] The California Supreme Court suggested that an express promise to pay is enforceable even if made after the idea submission. Desny v. Wilder, 46 Cal. 2d 715, 731, 299 P.2d 257, 265 (1965) ("where an idea has been conveyed with the expectation by the purveyor that compensation will be paid if the idea is used, there is no reason why the producer who has been the beneficiary of the conveyance of such an idea, and who finds it valuable and is profiting by it, may not then for the first time, although he is not at that time under any legal obligation so to do, promise to pay a reasonable compensation for that idea that is, for the past service of furnishing it to him and thus create a valid obligation.").

[a] **Novelty and Concreteness.** Courts split on whether an idea must be novel and concrete before an express contract for its submission will be enforced. Some hold that if parties expressly contract for the disclosure of an idea, lack of novelty or concreteness will not vitiate the obligation.[48] Others disagree.[49]

In *Masline,*[50] the court denied recovery. Plaintiff, a railroad employee, informed defendant, a railroad, that he had "information of value" and if defendant used it, it would earn at least $100,000. The parties entered into an express oral agreement that if defendant used the idea, plaintiff would receive five percent of the revenue derived from his idea. Plaintiff disclosed his idea: selling advertising space in and on the railroad's stations, depots, cars, fences, and the like. The railroad had not sold advertising space before, immediately began to do so, earning a large amount of money from advertising, but refused to pay plaintiff. The court found plaintiff's idea was not novel or original. Because the idea was common knowledge, plaintiff had no property right in it. Defendant's promise to pay was unenforceable because of lack of consideration.[51]

[b] **Standard Release Forms.** Companies often require all idea submitters to sign a standard release form with language disclaiming or limiting liability for using the idea. Courts will not enforce such release forms unless they are completely unambiguous. Some courts impose a reasonableness requirement even if the defendant's exculpatory language is unambiguous. Courts adopt a wide range of approaches to release forms.[52]

In *Downy,*[53] the court implied a reasonableness standard in interpreting defendant's exculpatory release form, which read: "the use, if any, to be made of this suggestion by . . . [defendant] and the compensation to be paid therefore, if any, if . . . [defendant] uses it, are matters solely in . . . [defendant's] discretion." The court found that defendant had sole discretion whether to use the idea but must pay a reasonable amount if it decided to use it. It would be unreasonable and unfair to give defendant complete discretion to determine compensation.

---

[48] *See, e.g.,* Vantage Point, Inc. v. Parker Bros., Inc., 529 F. Supp. 1204, 1216, 213 U.S.P.Q. 782 (E.D. N.Y. 1981), *aff'd,* 697 F.2d 301 (2d Cir. 1982) (table); Donahue v. Ziv Television Programs, Inc., 245 Cal. App. 2d 593, 54 Cal. Rptr. 130, 134, 151 U.S.P.Q. 657 (1966).

[49] *See, e.g.,* Tate v. Scanlan International Inc., 403 N.W.2d 666, 671 (Minn. Ct. App. 1987); Bergman v. Electrolux Corp., 558 F. Supp. 1351, 1353 (D. Nev. 1983).

[50] Masline v. New York, New Haven and Hartford R.R., 95 Conn. 702, 112 A. 639 (1921).

[51] Many criticize *Masline.* E.g., 3 D. Nimmer & M. Nimmer, Nimmer on Copyright § 16.04 ("The . . . decision [is] unsound, since it seems to ignore the fact that defendant promised to pay for the idea without conditioning such promise upon plaintiff producing an idea which would be regarded as property' "); Havighurst, *The Right to Compensation for an Idea,* 49 N.W.U. L. Rev. 295 (1954); Stanley v. Columbia Broadcasting Sys., 35 Cal. 2d 653, 674, 221 P.2d 73, 85 (1950) (Traynor J., dissenting).

[52] *See* Welles v. Columbia Broadcasting Sys., 308 F.2d 810 (9th Cir. 1962); Burten v. Milton Bradley Co., 592 F. Supp. 1021, 224 U.S.P.Q. 391 (D. R.I. 1984), *rev'd,* 763 F.2d 461 (1985) (applying Massachusetts law).

[53] Downy v. General Foods Corp., 37 App. Div.2d 250, 323 N.Y.S.2d 578, 171 U.S.P.Q. 421 (1971), *rev'd on other grounds,* 31 N.Y.2d 56, 286 N.E.2d 257, 175 U.S.P.Q. 374 (1972).

In *Davis*,[54] the court applied the following release clause literally to allow defendant to avoid contractual liability: "We shall be glad to examine your idea for a new food product, but only with the understanding that the use to be made of it by us, and the compensation, *if any,* are matters resting solely in our discretion." (Emphasis added.)

In *Burten*,[55] the court denied defendant's claim that its release form barred plaintiff's recovery. Plaintiffs alleged they revealed their computerized board game idea to defendant in confidence and that defendant breached the confidence by marketing the idea without compensating plaintiffs. To avoid liability, defendant argued that plaintiffs signed a release form that precluded recovery on the theory of confidential relationship. The form stated that plaintiff's submission "does not create . . . any relationship" between the parties. The court found this to be unlike the unambiguous release form language that courts had upheld as negating a confidential relationship.[56] "[A]bsent such clear language . . . a jury could reasonably read relationship as it is used in the [defendant's] form to embrace only those ties and obligations established by consensual understanding or course of dealing and not those legal constructs which may be triggered by unanticipated, covert, and devious misuse."[57]

[3]　Implied Contracts

In an implied contract, the parties' agreement is expressed through their conduct rather than through their words.[58] In deciding whether the parties's conduct involving idea submission created an implied compensation contract, courts consider a number of factors: was the idea solicited or unsolicited? did defendant have an opportunity to prevent disclosure? was the submission in confidence? how did the parties interact?[59]

---

[54] Davis v. General Foods Corp., 21 F. Supp. 445 (S.D. N.Y. 1937). *See also* Lueddecke v. Chevrolet Motor Co., 70 F.2d 345 (8th Cir. 1934); Thomas v. R.J. Reynolds Tobacco Co., 350 Pa. 262, 38 Atl. 61 (1944).

[55] Burten v. Milton Bradley Co., 763 F.2d 461, 226 U.S.P.Q. 605 (1st Cir. 1985).

[56] *See, e.g.,* Crown Industries v. Kawneer, 335 F. Supp. 749, 754, 171 U.S.P.Q. 401 (N.D. Ill. 1971) (the form read: "No confidential relationship is to be created by such submission"); Kearns v. Ford Motor Co., 203 U.S.P.Q. 884, 886 (E.D. Mich. 1978) (the form read: "Ford Motor Company cannot receive suggestions in confidence.").

[57] *See also* Gordon v. Vincent Youmans Inc., 358 F.2d 261, 148 U.S.P.Q. 93 (2d Cir. 1965) (suggesting "the broad language of a release form was mere boilerplate"); Houser v. Snap-On Tools Corp., 202 F. Supp. 181 (D. Md. 1962) (signing parties did not waive all rights by signing release; doubtful whether such a document "would give a manufacturer the right to expropriate a disclosure without remuneration, where the course of dealings between the parties indicates . . . that the disclosing party was seeking remuneration for the use of his creation.").

[58] *See* 3 D. Nimmer & M. Nimmer, Nimmer on Copyright § 16.05.

[59] *Cf.* Faris v. Enberg, 97 Cal. App. 3d 309, 318, 158 Cal. Rptr. 704, 709 (1979) ("no contract may be implied where an idea has been disclosed not to gain compensation for that idea but for the sole purpose of inducing the defendant to enter a future business relationship.").

[a] Unsolicited Submissions

[i] *Involuntarily Received.* Courts generally do not find an implied contract when the defendant receives an idea without solicitation and without warning[60] and deny compensation even if the plaintiff submits a truly valuable idea expecting compensation and the defendant, aware of plaintiff's expectation, uses the idea.[61] In *Desny,*[62] the California Supreme Court noted: "The idea man who blurts out his idea without having first made his bargain has no one but himself to blame for the loss of his bargaining power even if the idea has been conveyed with some hope of entering into a contract."

Courts will imply a contract if the circumstances justify the implication. In *Landsberg,*[63] the court suggested that after plaintiff initially submitted an unsolicited idea that defendant had rejected, defendant's request for a second copy of plaintiff's manuscript may create an implied-in-fact contract. In several cases, industry practice or custom led to a finding of implied contract. If defendant usually pays for unsolicited ideas of the kind the plaintiff submitted, this may be sufficient to create an implied contract.[64]

[ii] *Failure to Reject After Notice.* If a defendant receives advance notice of an unsolicited submission and fails to reject it before disclosure, the defendant's conduct may be sufficient to create an implied contract to compensate the submitter for use of his idea. In California, if the recipient knows the submitter expects compensation and the idea is used, inaction in failing to reject before disclosure can lead to implication of a promise to pay.[65]

---

[60] *E.g.,* Aliotti v. R. Dakin & Co., 831 F.2d 898, 903, 4 U.S.P.Q.2d 1869 (9th Cir. 1987).

[61] 3 D. Nimmer & M. Nimmer, Nimmer on Copyright § 16.32.

See also Smith v. Recrion Corp., 91 Nev. 666, 541 P.2d 663, 191 U.S.P.Q. 397 (1975); Bowen v. Yankee Network, 46 F. Supp. 62 (D. Mass. 1942); O'Brien v. RKO Radio Pictures, 68 F. Supp. 13 (S.D. N.Y. 1946); Larkin v. Pennsylvania R. Co., 125 Misc. 238, 210 N.Y.S. 375 (1925), *aff'd*, 216 A.D. 832, 215 N.Y.S. 875 (1925); Davies v. Carnation Co., 352 F.2d 393, 147 U.S.P.Q. 350 (9th Cir. 1965); Thompson v. California Brewing Co., 150 Cal. App. 2d 69, 310 P.2d 436 (1957); Official Airlines Schedule Infornation Service v. Eastern Airlines, 333 F.2d 672, 141 U.S.P.Q. 546 (5th Cir. 1964); Landsberg v. Scrabble Crossword Game Players, Inc., 802 F.2d 1193, 1196 (9th Cir. 1986).

[62] Desny v. Wilder, 46 Cal. 2d 715, 731, 299 P.2d 257, 265 (1956).

[63] Landsberg v. Scramble Crossword Game Players, Inc., 736 F.2d 485, 221 U.S.P.Q. 1140 (9th Cir. 1984), *cert. denied,* 469 U.S. 1037 (1984). On remand, the district court found for plaintiff but on a different theory. Plaintiff's second disclosure was confidential, and this created an implied contract. The appeals court affirmed. Landsberg v. Scrabble Crossword Game Players, Inc., 802 F.2d 1193, 1196, 231 U.S.P.Q. 658 (9th Cir. 1986).

[64] Karlan v. Columbia Broadcasting System, Inc., 40 Cal. 2d 799, 256 P.2d 962 (1953); Vantage Point Inc. v. Parker Bros., Inc., 529 F. Supp. 1204, 213 U.S.P.Q. 782 (E.D. N.Y. 1981), *aff'd sub nom.* Vantage Point, Inc. v. Milton Bradley Co., 697 F.2d 301 (2d Cir. 1982); McGhan v. Ebersol, 608 F. Supp. 277, 285 (S.D. N.Y. 1985).

[65] Donahue v. Ziv Television Prog. Inc., 245 Cal. App. 2d 593, 54 Cal. Rptr. 130, 151 U.S.P.Q. 657 (1966). *See also* Smith v. Weinstein, 578 F. Supp. 1247 (S.D. N.Y. 1984), *aff'd,* 738 F.2d 419 (2d Cir. 1984) (table).

"[T]he idea purveyor cannot prevail in an action to recover compensation for an abstract idea unless (a) before or after disclosure he has obtained an express promise to pay, or (b) the circumstances preceding and attending disclosure, together with the conduct of the offeree acting with knowledge of the circumstances, show a promise of the type usually referred to as 'implied' or 'implied-in-fact.' . . . That is, if the idea purveyor has clearly conditioned his offer to convey the idea upon an obligation to pay for it if it is used by the offeree and the offeree, knowing the condition before he knows the idea, voluntarily accepts its disclosure (necessarily on the specified basis) and finds it valuable and uses it, the law will either apply the objective test . . . and hold that the parties have made an express (sometimes called implied-in-fact) contract, or under those circumstances, as some writers view it, the law itself, to prevent fraud and unjust enrichment, will imply a promise to compensate."[66]

In *Whitfield*,[67] the Second Circuit, applying California law, reversed a lower court decision granting defendant summary judgment. The court observed that in the television industry, studios not seeking unsolicited submissions explicitly say so and return unsolicited submissions without opening them. The defendant received plaintiff's mailgram announcing that a script would arrive, opened the script, and reviewed it. By such conduct, the defendant implicitly agreed to pay for use.[68]

[b] **Solicited Submissions.** If a person requests that another reveal an idea, most courts consider the solicitation sufficient to imply a promise to pay for the idea if used. In *Moore*,[69] defendant solicited plaintiff's submission, but specified that there was an understanding that there was "no obligation on [defendant's] part." Plaintiff responded that he understood "that there is no obligation on [defendant's] part." The court interpreted the language to mean that defendant had no obligation to use plaintiff's idea or to compensate plaintiff for the mere submission. Defendant had a legal obligation to pay plaintiff if the idea was used.

[c] **Confidential Submission.** A confidential relationship arises when defendant, by an implied agreement, agrees to review plaintiff's idea in confidence.[70] Courts assess the parties' conduct in determining whether there was a confidential relationship. They generally treat a confidential relationship as an implied contract not to reveal the

---

[66] Desny v. Wilder, 46 Cal. 2d 715, 731, 299 P.2d 257, 270 (1956).

[67] Whitfield v. Lear, 751 F.2d 90, 224 U.S.P.Q. 540 (2d Cir. 1984).

[68] Nimmer argues for limiting the failure-to-reject contract implication theory.

"Suppose a man is wandering through Central Park, looking for a bench to rest. At this point, a woman emerges and states 'I expect to be paid for what I'm about to disclose unless you tell me not to speak.' The man says nothing. The woman goes on to say 'There is an unoccupied bench beyond the hedge.' Now, if the man uses the bench, is he obligated to pay the woman?" 3 D. Nimmer & M. Nimmer, Nimmer on Copyright § 16.03.

[69] Moore v. Ford Motor, 43 F.2d 685 (2d Cir. 1930).

[70] Desny v. Wilder, 46 Cal. 2d 715, 299 P.2d 257 (1956). Confidential reception is a significant concept in trade secret law. *See* § 3D[7][a].

idea.[71] If defendant, by using the idea, discloses it to others, defendant has breached the contract.[72]

[d] Other Considerations. In determining whether to imply an agreement, courts consider any evidence bearing on the parties' interaction.[73] They consider the parties' expectations[74] and whether the parties entered into negotiations regarding payment.[75]

Industry practice and custom is always important. If most businesses in an industry compensate idea submitters, a court is more likely to find an implied contract.[76]

[e] Novelty and Concreteness. Most courts require that an idea be novel and concrete before they will find an implied contract to pay for its use.[77]

---

[71] *See also* Aliotti v. R. Dakin & Co., 831 F.2d 898, 4 U.S.P.Q.2d 1869 (9th Cir. 1987) ("To prevail on their claim for breach of confidence, appellants must show that: (1) they conveyed confidential and novel information; (2) Dakin had knowledge that the information was being disclosed in confidence; (3) there was an understanding between Dakin and appellants that the confidence be maintained; and (4) there was disclosure or use in violation of the understanding. . . . Constructive notice of confidentiality is not sufficient.")

[72] Gilbert v. General Motors Corp., 32 F. Supp. 502 (W.D. N.Y. 1940); Heckenkamp v. Ziv Television Programs Inc., 157 Cal. App. 2d 293, 321 P.2d 137 (1958); Carneval v. William Morris Agency, Inc., 124 N.Y.S.2d 319 (1953), *aff'd*, 284 A.D. 1041, 137 N.Y.S.2d 612 (1954); Sloan v. Mud Products Inc., 114 F. Supp. 916 (N.D. Okla. 1953); Official Airlines Schedule Information Service, Inc. v. Eastern Airlines, 333 F.2d 672, 141 U.S.P.Q. 546 (5th Cir. 1964).

[73] Courts apply to idea submission cases general contract law principles on implying contracts. *See* Faris v. Enberg, 97 Cal. App. 3d 309, 318, 158 Cal. Rptr. 704, 709, 211 U.S.P.Q. 277 (1979) (California law: "for an implied contract, one must show: that he or she prepared the work, that he or she disclosed the work to the offeree for sale; under all the circumstances attending the disclosure it can be concluded that the offeree voluntarily accepted the disclosure knowing the conditions on which it was tendered (*i.e.* the offeree must have the opportunity to reject the attempted disclosure if the conditions are unacceptable).")

[74] Liggett & Meyer Tobacco Co. v. Meyer, 101 Ind. App. 420, 194 N.E. 206 (1939).

[75] Landsberg v. Scrabble Crossword Game Players Inc., 736 F.2d 485, 489, 221 U.S.P.Q. 1140 (9th Cir. 1984), *cert. denied,* 469 U.S. 1037 (1984); Smith v. Weinstein, 578 F. Supp. 1297, 1305, 222 U.S.P.Q. 381 (S.D. N.Y. 1984), *aff'd,* 738 F.2d 414 (2d Cir. 1984); Annisgard v. Bray, 11 Mass. App. 726, 419 N.E.2d 315, 318 (1981).

[76] Vantage Point v. Parker Bros., 529 F. Supp. 1204, 213 U.S.P.Q. 782 (E.D. N.Y. 1981), *aff'd,* 697 F.2d 330 (2d Cir. 1982); McGhan v. Ebersol, 608 F. Supp. 277, 285 (S.D. N.Y. 1985); Whitfield v. Lear, 751 F.2d 90 (2d Cir. 1984).

[77] *See, e.g.,* Murray v. National Broadcasting Co., 844 F.2d 988, 6 U.S.P.Q. 1618 (2d Cir. 1988), *cert. denied,* 488 U.S. 955 (1988); Marcus Advertising Inc. v. M.M. Fisher Assoc. Inc., 444 F.2d 1061, 1064, 170 U.S.P.Q. 244 (7th Cir. 1971); Stevens v. Continental Can Co., 308 F.2d 100, 104 (6th Cir. 1962), *cert. denied,* 374 U.S. 810 (1963); Tate v. Scanlan International Inc., 403 N.W.2d 666, 675 (Minn. Ct. App. 1987); Fleming v. Ronson Corp., 107 N.J. Super. 311, 258 A.2d 153, 157, 164 U.S.P.Q. 369 *aff'd,* 11 N.J. Super. 221, 275 A.2d 759 (N.J. Super. Ct. App. Law Div. 1969); Downey v. General Foods Corp., 31 N.Y.2d 56, 334 N.Y.S.2d 874, 877, 286 N.E.2d 257, 175 U.S.P.Q. 374 (1972); Surplus Equip. Inc. v. Xerox Corp., 120 A.D. 582, 502 N.Y.S.2d 491, 492 (1986), *appeal denied,* 68 N.Y.2d 606, 506 N.Y.S.2d 1031, 498 N.E.2d 151 (1986).

[4] Unjust Enrichment—Quasi-Contract

Of the four idea submission recovery theories, unjust enrichment and quasi-contract is the least used. "Quasi-contracts, unlike true contracts, are not based on the apparent intent of the parties. . . . They are obligations created by law for reasons of justice."[78] The theory is an equitable one.

The courts apply an unjust enrichment theory when it believes one party should not be allowed to receive an unfair advantage or benefit over another party even if there is no express or implied contract. To recover under quasi-contract, plaintiff need not prove that the parties intended to agree on compensation, that the disclosure was made in confidence, or that a special relationship existed. The plaintiff must simply convince the court that the idea recipient was enriched by the idea and not compensating the idea submitter would be unfair.[79]

With its simple requirements for recovery, one might expect quasi-contract to be a catch-all that courts would use to grant recovery when other theories fail. In fact, many courts discuss it; few apply it.[80]

---

[78] Weitzenkorn v. Lesser, 40 Cal. 2d 778, 794, 256 P.2d 947, 959 (1953).

[79] *See* Vantage Point, Inc. v. Parker Bros., Inc., 529 F. Supp. 1204, 1216-17, 213 U.S.P.Q. 782 (E.D. N.Y. 1981), *aff'd*, 697 F.2d 301 (2d Cir. 1982) (table):

"Beyond the threshold requirements that the idea be 'novel' and 'concrete,' . . . inquiry has focused on the circumstances under which the plaintiff's ideas became known to the defendant. . . . Absent an express agreement, the conduct of the parties may indicate that use of the idea is governed by an agreement implied-in-fact. . . . And there is support for the proposition that such an implied agreement may be based upon industry custom or usage regarding submission and use of ideas. . . .

"Even where the facts may not support an actual contractual relationship, the circumstances of the disclosure remain critical. Despite contrary intimations in earlier decisions, . . . it is now accepted that recovery may be had wholly apart from contract where there has been undue advantage through unfair conduct-a breach of confidence [or] reprehensible means of obtaining the valuable property rights of another without compensation.' . . . The restitutionary theories of unjust enrichment . . . received more explicit expression in *Puente v. President & Fellows of Harvard College*, 248 F.2d 799, 802 (1st Cir. 1957):

'An idea, as distinguished from the copyrighted contents of a book or a patented device or process, is accorded no protection in the law unless it is acquired and used under such circumstances that the law will imply a contractual or fiduciary relationship between the parties.' . . .

"To sustain recovery in quasi-contractual restitution it is unnecessary that the disclosure have been made in confidence, or that the parties be in a confidential relationship. . . . On the other hand, the mere voluntary act of submitting an idea to one with whom the plaintiff has had no prior dealings will not make the disclosure one in confidence, even if stated to be so."

[80] One decision relying solely on quasi-contract is Werlin v. Reader's Digest Association, Inc., 528 F. Supp. 451, 465, 213 U.S.P.Q. 1041 (S.D. N.Y. 1981) ("In certain cases, however, the courts have held that, even if the plaintiff has no property right in an idea, and even though no express or implied-in-fact contract for the sale or use of such an idea has been established, the defendant may, in appropriate circumstances, nevertheless be found liable to the plaintiff in quasi contract on a theory of unjust enrichment. . . . A 'quasi' or 'implied-in-law' contract is, of course, not a contract or an agreement at all, but an obligation imposed by law to avoid

[5] Damages

Damage measures that courts have actually used or discussed include the reasonable value of an ad slogan;[81] the actual value of the benefit to defendant, not the market value of a magazine article;[82] actual value to defendant to a radio program;[83] fair value for the use of a television program based on defendant's typical royalty and percentage of profits;[84] expectation damages;[85] and the full profits by defendant plus attorney's fees and prejudgment interest.[86] In *Tate*,[87] the court, in an implied contract context, applied patent law reasonable royalty standards to affirm a jury verdict awarding a 30% royalty in view of defendant's high 60% profit on sale of product.[88] One court affirmed a punitive damage award based on California law.[89]

---

unjust enrichment. . . . Where the defendant has benefitted from its use of an idea generated by the plaintiff, a court will allow recovery in quasi contract if the circumstances make it inequitable for the defendant to profit from the use of plaintiff's idea or material.").

[81] Healy v. R.H. Macy & Co., 277 N.Y. 681, 14 N.E.2d 388 (1938) (property theory); Matarese v. Moore-McCormack Lines Inc., 158 F.2d 631 (2d Cir. 1946) (quasi-contract).

[82] Werlin v. Reader's Digest Ass'n, 528 F. Supp. 451, 213 U.S.P.Q. 1041 (S.D. N.Y. 1981) (quasi-contract).

[83] Stanley v. Columbia Broadcasting System, Inc., 35 Cal. 2d 653, 221 P.2d 73 (1950).

[84] Donahue v. UA Corp., 2 Cal. App. 3d 794, 83 Cal. Rptr. 131 (1969) (implied contract).

[85] Elfenbein v. Luckenbach Terminals Inc., 111 N.J. L. 67, 166 A. 91 (1933) (express contract).

[86] Landsberg v. Scrabble Crossword Game Players, Inc., 802 F.2d 1193, 1196 (9th Cir. 1986) (implied contract).

[87] Tate v. Scanlan International, Inc., 403 N.W.2d 666 (Minn. Ct. App. 1987).

[88] For a discussion of damages in patent and copyright cases, see §§ 2F[5] and 4F[5].

[89] Landsberg v. Scrabble Crossword Game Players, Inc., 802 F.2d 1193, 1196 (9th Cir. 1986) (implied contract; applying California's *Seaman's* doctrine that "a party to a contract may incur tort remedies when, in addition to breaching the contract, it seeks to shield itself from liability by denying, in bad faith and without probable cause, that the contract exists.").

INDEX

[References are to sections.]

A

ABANDONMENT
Patents; abandonment of invention . . . . .
2C[5][b][vi]; 2D[5][g]
Trademarks (See TRADEMARKS, subhead:
Abandonment of mark)

ACQUISITION
Copyright (See COPYRIGHT)

ADVERTISING
Comparative use of trademark . . 5E[4][d];
5F[3][d][iii]
Use of another's trademark in advertising
. . . 6E[6]

**AMERICAN SOCIETY OF COMPOSERS,
AUTHORS AND PUBLISHERS ("AS-
CAP")**
Performance rights licensing . . . 4E[4][f]

ANTI-DILUTION STATUTES
Trademarks . . . 5E[3][b]

ANTITRUST LAW
Copyright infringement . . . 4F[4][c]
Publicity rights . . . 6G[4][c][iii]
Trademark infringement . . . 5F[2][c]

ARBITRATION
Patents; interference procedure . . . .
2D[5][h][v]

ARCHITECTURAL WORKS
1990 Architectural Works Copyright Protection Act . . . 4C[3][f], [ii]
Pre-1991 law . . . 4C[3][f][i]

ARTISTIC WORKS
Artists' moral rights
Copyright act preemption . . . .
1D[3][c][ii](5)
Visual Artists Rights Act . . . 4E[6][b]
Three-dimensional works (See COPYRIGHT,
subhead: Three-dimensional works)

ASCAP (See AMERICAN SOCIETY OF
COMPOSERS, AUTHORS AND PUB-
LISHERS ("ASCAP"))

ASSIGNMENT OF OWNERSHIP
Patents; assignment contracts . . . 2G[1]
Trademarks (See TRADEMARK OWNER-
SHIP, subhead: Transfer of)

ASSIGNMENT OF OWNERSHIP—Cont.
Trade secret law; employment agreements
. . . 3D[6][b][i], [ii]

ATTORNEYS' FEES
Copyright infringement; remedies . . . . . .
4F[5][e], [i], [ii]
Patent infringement; remedies . . . 2F[5][e]
Trademark infringement; remedies . . . . .
5F[3][i]
Trade secret law; remedies . . . 3F[3]

AUTHORS
Copyright ownership (See AUTHORSHIP)
Moral rights of (See COPYRIGHT, subhead:
Authors' moral rights)
Works by authors from other countries . . .
4D[4]

AUTHORSHIP
Collective work . . . 4G[1]
Definition of author . . . 4G
Derivative work . . . 4G[1]
Joint authorship
Co-author's contribution, quality of
. . . 4G[3][b][ii]
Definition; Section 101 . . 4G[3][b], [i]
Derivative works based on joint works
. . . 4G[1]
Generally . . . 4G[1]; 4G[1], [3]
Intention test . . . 4G[3][b][i]
Melancholy Baby . . . 4G[3][a]
Merged contributions . . . 4G[3][b][i]
Musical compositions; court decisions
. . . 4G[3][a]
1909 Act . . . 4G[3][a]
Suggestions and directions, contribution
of . . . 4G[3][b][ii]
12th Street Rag . . . 4G[3][a]
Melancholy Baby; joint authorship . . . . .
4G[3][a]
Original and derivative work . . . 4G[1]
12th Street Rag; joint authorship . . . . . .
4G[3][a]
Works for hire . . . 4G[1], [2]

B

**BERNE CONVENTION IMPLEMENTA-
TION ACT OF 1988**
Copyright notice requirement . . 1B[3]; 4D,
[2][c]

[References are to sections.]

[References are to sections.]

[References are to sections.]

[References are to sections.]

[References are to sections.]

[References are to sections.]

[References are to sections.]

[References are to sections.]

[References are to sections.]

D

DAMAGES
Copyright infringement (See COPYRIGHT INFRINGEMENT, subheads: Compensatory damages; Statutory damages)
Idea submission infringement . . . 6H[5]
Patent infringement . . . 2F[5][b], [c]
Publicity rights infringement . . . 6G[5]
Semiconductor chip protection infringement . . . 6D[4][d][ii]
Trademark infringement (See TRADEMARK INFRINGEMENT)
Trade secret law (See TRADE SECRET LAW)

DATA COMPILATIONS (See COPYRIGHT)

DERIVATIVE WORKS (See COPYRIGHT)

DESIGN PATENT INFRINGEMENT
Generally . . . 6B[4]
Gorham decision . . . 6B[4]
Novelty, appropriation of . . . 6B[4]
Ordinary purchaser test . . . 6B[4]
Remedies . . . 6B[4]

DESIGN PATENTS
Application . . . 6B[3]
Article of manufacture, defined . . 6B[2][a]
Double patenting, design-utility . . . .
   2D[4][a][iv]
Exclusive rights . . . 6B[4]
Historical development . . . 6B[1]
Infringement (See DESIGN PATENT INFRINGEMENT)
Ordinary observer test . . . 6B[1], [4]
Patentable subject matter . . . 2C[1]
Requirements
   Article of manufacture . . . 6B[2][a]
   Generally . . . 6B
   Nonfunctionality . . . 6B[2][c]
   Nonobviousness . . . 6B[2][e]
   Novelty-statutory bars . . . 6B[2][d]
   Ornamentality . . . 6B[2][b]

DESIGN PROTECTION (GENERALLY)
Copyright requirements . . . 6B
Design patents (See DESIGN PATENTS)
Internationally . . . 6B
Trade dress requirements . . . 6B

DISCLOSURE
Patents (See PATENT APPLICATIONS)
Trade secrets (See TRADE SECRET LAW, subhead: Disclosure issues)

DISTRIBUTION RIGHTS (See COPYRIGHT, subheads: Copying and distribution rights; Reproduction and distribution rights)

DOCTRINE OF EQUIVALENTS
"All elements" rule . . . 2F[2][b][iii]
Comparison standard of equivalency . . . .
   2F[2][b][iii]
Corning Glass decision . . . 2F[2][b][iii]
Generally . . . 2B[2]; 2F[2][b]
Graver Tank decision . . . 2F[2][b][i]
"Heart of the invention" . . . 2F[2][b][iv]
Later developed equivalents . . 2F[2][b][vi]
Limitations, relative importance of . . . . .
   2F[2][b][iv]
Means-plus-function limitations . . 2F[1][d]
Patented improvements, equivalency of . .
   2F[2][b][vi]
Pennwalt decision . . . 2F[2][b][iii]
Pioneer patents . . . 2F[2][b][v]
Prior art, limiting effect of . . 2F[2][b][viii]
Prosecution history estoppel, effect of . . . .
   2F[2][c][iii]
Range of equivalents . . . 2F[2][b][v]
Reverse equivalents . . . 2F[2][b][vii]
Tri-partite test . . . 2F[2][b][ii]

DRUG PRICE COMPETITION AND PATENT TERM RESTORATION ACT
Enactment of . . . 2B[6]

E

EMPLOYER/EMPLOYEE RELATIONSHIPS
Patents; employee inventions . . . 2G[1]
Trade secrets (See TRADE SECRET LAW, subhead: Employment relationship)

EXCLUSIVE RIGHTS
Copyright . . . 4E[2]
Design patents . . . 6B[4]
Patents . . . 2E[2], [3]
Plant protection . . . 6C[1][c], [2][c]
Semiconductor chip protection
   Generally . . . 6D[4][a]
   Limitations . . . 6D[4][b][i] *et. seq.*
Trade secret law . . . 3C[2]

EXCLUSIVE USE OF TRADEMARKS
Evidence of secondary meaning . . . .
   5C[3][a][vii](3)
"Olympic," USOC's exclusive use of . . . .
   1D[4]

[References are to sections.]

F

FAIR USE DEFENSE

[References are to sections.]

[References are to sections.]

[References are to sections.]

M

[References are to sections.]

[References are to sections.]

[References are to sections.]

[References are to sections.]

[References are to sections.]

[References are to sections.]

[References are to sections.]

[References are to sections.]

[References are to sections.]

[References are to sections.]

[References are to sections.]

[References are to sections.]

[References are to sections.]

[References are to sections.]

[References are to sections.]

[References are to sections.]

[References are to sections.]

[References are to sections.]